NW14923 ML-CEN/51 £40.00

KT-472-495

THE LIBRARY
NEWMAN COLLEGE
BARTLEY GREEN
BIRMINGHAM

NW14923 ML-CEN/51 £40.00

N 0111590 1

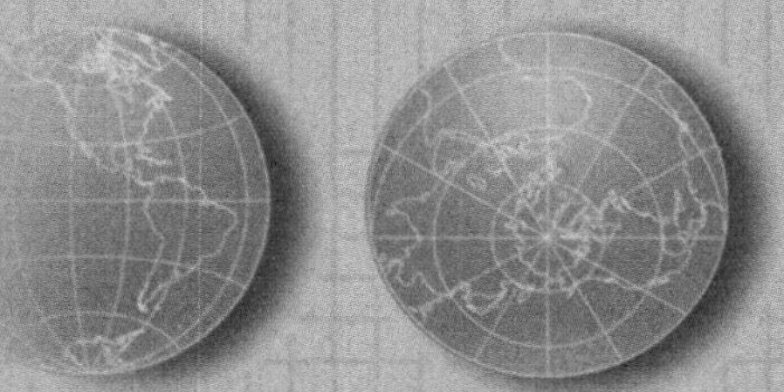

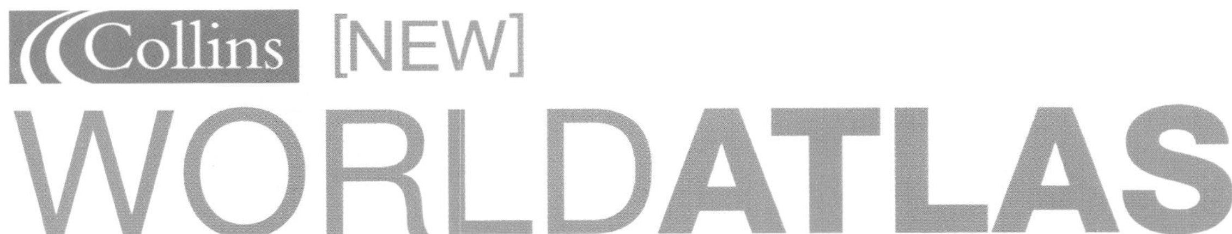

Collins [NEW] WORLDATLAS

COLLINS NEW WORLD ATLAS

Collins

An imprint of HarperCollins*Publishers*
77-85 Fulham Palace Road
London
W6 8JB

First Published 2001

Copyright © HarperCollins*Publishers* 2001
Maps © Bartholomew Ltd 2001

Collins® is a registered trademark of HarperCollins*Publishers* Ltd

All rights reserved. No part of this publication may be reproduced,
stored in a retrieval system, or transmitted, in any form or by any means,
electronic, mechanical, photocopying, recording or otherwise without the
prior written permission of the publisher and copyright owners.

The contents of this edition of the Collins New World Atlas are believed
correct at the time of printing. Nevertheless the publisher can accept
no responsibility for errors or omissions, changes in the detail given,
or for any expense or loss thereby caused.

Printed in Italy

British Library Cataloguing in Publication Data.
A catalogue record for this book is available from the British Library.

ISBN 0 00 448936 5

MH10306 Imp 001

The maps in this product are also available for purchase in digital format
from Bartholomew Mapping Solutions. For details and information visit
http://www.bartholomewmaps.com
or contact
Bartholomew Mapping Solutions
Tel: +44 (0) 141 306 3162
Fax: +44 (0) 141 306 3104
e-mail: bartholomew@harpercollins.co.uk

www.**fire**and**water**.com
Visit the book lover's website

Collins [NEW]

NEWMAN COLLEGE
BARTLEY GREEN
DI...
C... R 912
BA... 01115901
AUTHOR COL

WORLDATLAS

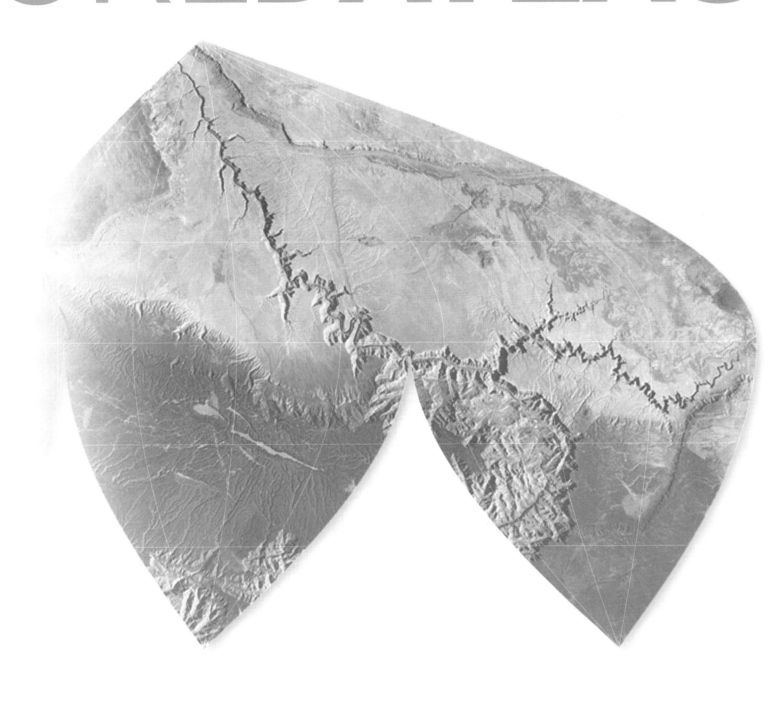

CONTENTS

The atlas is arranged into a world thematic section and continental sections as defined in the contents list below. Full details of the contents of each section can be found on the introductory spread within the section. As indicated on the contents list, each section is distinctively colour-coded to allow easy identification.

The continental sections contain detailed, comprehensive reference maps of the continent, which are preceded by introductory pages consisting of a mixture of statistical and thematic maps, geographical statistics, and photographs and images illustrating specific themes. Each map and thematic spread contains a 'connections' box, which indicates links to other pages in the atlas containing related information.

title	pages
world	**6–7**
[physical features]	8–9
[countries]	10–11
[land images]	12–13
[earthquakes and volcanoes]	14–15
[climate and weather]	16–17
[land cover]	18–19
[changes]	20–21
[population]	22–23
[cities]	24–25
[communications]	26–27
europe	**28–29**
[landscapes]	30–31
[countries]	32–33
[countries/issues]	34–35
[environments]	36–37
[reference maps]	38–59
asia	**60–61**
[landscapes]	62–63
[countries]	64–65
[countries/issues]	66–67
[changes]	68–69
[threats]	70–71
[reference maps]	72–109
africa	**110–111**
[landscapes]	112–113
[countries]	114–115
[countries/issues]	116–117
[locations]	118–119
[reference maps]	120–133

title	pages
oceania	**134–135**
[landscapes]	136–137
[countries]	138–139
[threats]	140–141
[features]	142–143
[reference maps]	144–153
northamerica	**154–155**
[landscapes]	156–157
[countries]	158–159
[threats]	160–161
[environments]	162–163
[reference maps]	164–187
southamerica	**188–189**
[landscapes]	190–191
[countries]	192–193
[contrasts]	194–195
[impacts]	196–197
[reference maps]	198–207
oceans and poles	**208–209**
oceans [features]	210–211
antarctica [features]	212–213
the arctic [features]	214–215
oceans and poles [reference maps]	216–224
index	**225–335**
acknowledgements	336

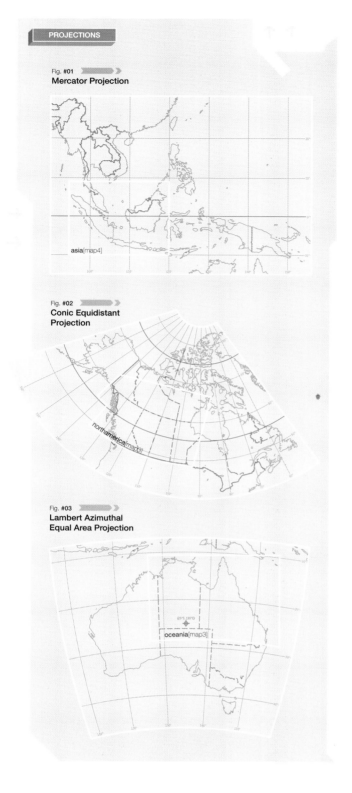

PROJECTIONS

Fig. #01
Mercator Projection

asia[map4]

Fig. #02
Conic Equidistant Projection

northamerica[map1]

Fig. #03
Lambert Azimuthal Equal Area Projection

oceania[map3]

REFERENCE MAPS

Symbols and generalization

Maps show information by using signs, or symbols, which are designed to reflect the features on the Earth which they represent. Symbols can be in the form of points, lines, or areas and variations in the size, shape and colour of the symbols allow a great range of information to be shown. The symbols used on the reference maps are explained opposite.

Not all features on the ground can be shown, nor can all characteristics of a feature be depicted. Much detail has to be generalized to be clearly shown on the maps, the degree of generalization being determined largely by the scale of the map. As map scale decreases, fewer features can be shown, and their depiction becomes less detailed. The most common generalization techniques are selection and simplification. Selection is the inclusion of some features and the omission of others of less importance. Smaller scale maps can show fewer features than larger scales, and therefore only the more important features are selected. Simplification is the process of smoothing lines, combining areas, or slightly displacing symbols to add clarity. Smaller scale maps require more simplification. These techniques are carried out in such a way that the overall character of the area mapped is retained.

Scale

The amount of detail shown on a map is determined by its scale – the relationship between the size of an area shown on the map and the actual size of the area on the ground. Larger scales show more detail, smaller scales require more generalization and show less. The scale can be used to measure the distance between two points and to calculate comparative areas.

Scales used for the reference maps range from 1:3M (large scale) to 1:48M (small scale). Insets are used to show areas of the world of particular interest or which cannot be included in the page layouts in their true position. The scale used is indicated in the margin of each map.

Map projections

The 'projection' of the three-dimensional globe onto a two-dimensional map is always a problem for cartographers. All map projections introduce distortions to either shape, area or distances. Projections for the maps in this atlas have been specifically selected to minimize these distortions. The diagrams above illustrate three types of projection used. The red lines represent the 'centres' of the projections where there is no distortion and scale is correct.

Each reference map is cut to the shape of the graticule (the lines of latitude and longitude), which is determined by the projection used. This gives each map a unique shape, suggesting its position on the globe, as illustrated by the examples on the diagrams.

Geographical names

There is no single standard way of spelling names or of converting them from one alphabet, or symbol set, to another. Instead, conventional ways of spelling have evolved, and the results often differ significantly from the original name in the local language. Familiar examples in English include Munich (München in German), Florence (Firenze in Italian) and Moscow (Moskva from Russian). A further complication is that in many countries different languages are in use in different regions.

These factors, and any changes in official languages, have to be taken into account when creating maps. The policy in this atlas is generally to use local name forms which are officially recognized by the governments of the countries concerned. This is a basic principle laid down by the Permanent Committee on Geographical Names (PCGN) – the body responsible for determining official UK government policy on place names around the world. PCGN rules are also applied to the conversion of non-roman alphabet names, for example in the Russian Federation, into the roman alphabet used in English.

However, English conventional name forms are used for the most well-known places for which such a form is in common use. In these cases, the local form is included in brackets on the map and appears as a cross-reference in the index. Other alternative names, such as well-known historical names or those in other languages, may also be included in brackets. All country names and those for international physical features appear in their English forms.

Boundaries

The status of nations and their boundaries, and the names associated with them, are shown in this atlas as they are in reality at the time of going to press, as far as can be ascertained. All recent changes of the status of nations and their boundaries have been taken into account. Where international boundaries are the subject of dispute, the aim is to take a strictly neutral viewpoint and every reasonable attempt is made to show where an active territorial dispute exists. Generally, prominence is given to the situation as it exists on the ground (the de facto situation). The depiction on the maps of boundaries and their current status varies accordingly.

International boundaries are shown on all the reference maps, and those of a large enough scale also include internal administrative boundaries of selected countries. The delineation of international boundaries in the sea is often a very contentious issue, and in many cases an official alignment is not defined. Boundaries in the sea are generally only shown where they are required to clarify the ownership of specific islands or island groups.

Indexing

All names appearing on the reference maps are included in the index and can be easily found from the information included in the index entry. Details of all alternative name forms are included in the index entries and as cross-references. Gazetteer entries, with important geographical information, are included for selected places and features. Full details of index policies and content can be found in the Introduction to the Index on page 225.

SETTLEMENTS

Population	National Capital	Administrative Capital	Other City or Town
over 5 million	BEIJING ✦	Tianjin ◉	New York ◉
1 million to 5 million	KĀBUL ✦	Sydney ◉	Kaohsiung ◉
500 000 to 1 million	BANGUI ✦	Trujillo ◎	Jeddah ◎
100 000 to 500 000	WELLINGTON ✿	Mansa ◎	Apucarana ⊙
50 000 to 100 000	PORT OF SPAIN ✿	Potenza ○	Arecibo ⊙
10 000 to 50 000	MALABO ✿	Chinhoyi ○	Ceres ○
1 000 to 10 000	VALLETTA ✿	Ati ○	Venta ○
under 1000		Chhukha ○	Shapki ○

Built-up area

BOUNDARIES

- ▪▪▪▪▪ International boundary
- ▪▮▪▮▪ Disputed international boundary or alignment unconfirmed
- ▬▬▬▬ Administrative boundary
- ••••• Ceasefire line

MISCELLANEOUS

- --------- National park
- ———— Reserve or Regional park
- ✿ Site of specific interest
- ▭▭▭▭ Wall

LAND AND SEA FEATURES

- Desert
- ⌄ Oasis
- Lava field
- 1234 △ Volcano height in metres
- Marsh
- Ice cap / Glacier
- Escarpment
- Coral reef
- 1234 Pass height in metres

LAKES AND RIVERS

- Lake
- Impermanent lake
- Salt lake or lagoon
- Impermanent salt lake
- Dry salt lake or salt pan
- 123 Lake height surface height above sea level, in metres
- ——— River
- - - - - Impermanent river or watercourse
- ‖ Waterfall
- — Dam
- | Barrage

RELIEF

Contour intervals and layer colours

Continents	Oceans and Poles
>6000m	>6000m
5000-6000m	5000-6000m
4000-5000m	4000-5000m
3000-4000m	3000-4000m
2000-3000m	2000-3000m
1500-2000m	1000-2000m
1000-1500m	500-1000m
500-1000m	200-500m
200-500m	0-200m
100-200m	<0m
0-100m	
<0m	0-200m
	200-2000m
0-50m	2000-3000m
50-100m	3000-4000m
100-200m	4000-5000m
200-500m	5000-6000m
500-1000m	6000-7000m
1000-2000m	>7000m
2000-3000m	
3000-4000m	
4000-5000m	
5000-6000m	
>6000m	

1234 △ Summit height in metres ·123 Spot height height in metres 123 Ocean deep height in metres

TRANSPORT

- ▭▭▭◦ ----- Motorway (tunnel; under construction)
- ———◦ - - - - Main road (tunnel; under construction)
- ———◦ - - - - Secondary road (tunnel; under construction)
- .... Track
- ▬▬▮▬ - - - - Main railway (tunnel; under construction)
- ———▮— - - - - Secondary railway (tunnel; under construction)
- ———▮— - - - - Other railway (tunnel; under construction)
- ——————— Canal
- ✈ Main airport
- ✈ Regional airport

SATELLITE IMAGERY

MAIN SATELLITES/SENSORS

satellite/sensor name	launch dates	owner	aims and applications	wavelengths	resolution of imagery	web address
Landsat 4, 5, 7	July 1972-April 1999	National Aeronautics and Space Administration (NASA), USA	The first satellite to be designed specifically for observing the Earth's surface. Originally set up to produce images of use for agriculture and geology. Today is of use for numerous environmental and scientific applications.	Visible, near-infrared, short-wave and thermal infrared wavelength bands.	15m in the panchromatic band (only on Landsat 7), 30m in the six visible, near and short-wave infrared bands and 60m in the thermal infrared band.	geo.arc.nasa.gov ls7pm3.gsfc.nasa.gov
SPOT 1, 2, 3, 4 (Satellite Pour l'Observation de la Terre)	February 1986-March 1998	Centre National d'Etudes Spatiales (CNES) and Spot Image, France	Particularly useful for monitoring land use, water resources research, coastal studies and cartography.	Visible and near infrared.	Panchromatic 10m. Multispectral 20m.	www.cnes.fr www.spotimage.fr
Space Shuttle	Regular launches from 1981	NASA, USA	Each shuttle mission has separate aims. Astronauts take photographs with high specification hand held cameras. The Shuttle Radar Topography Mission (SRTM) in 2000 obtained the most complete near-global high-resolution database of the earth's topography.	Visible with hand held cameras. Radar on SRTM Mission.	SRTM: 30m for US and 90m for rest of the world.	science.ksc.nasa.gov/shuttle/countdown www.jpl.nasa.gov/srtm
IKONOS	September 1999	Space Imaging	First commercial high-resolution satellite. Useful for a variety of applications mainly Cartography, Defence, Urban Planning, Agriculture, Forestry and Insurance.	Visible and near infrared.	Panchromatic 1m. Multispectral 4m.	www.spaceimaging.com

ADDITIONAL IMAGERY

satellite/sensor name	web address
ASTER	asterweb.jpl.nasa.gov www.nasda.go.jp
SeaWiFS	seawifs.gsfc.nasa.gov
Radarsat	www.rsi.ca
MODIS	modis.gsfc.nasa.gov
TOPEX/Poseidon	topex-www.jpl.nasa.gov
ERS-1 (European Space Agency) Earth Resources Satellite	earthnet.esrin.esa.it

PHOTOGRAPHS AND IMAGES

The thematic pages of the atlas contain a wide variety of photographs and images. These are a mixture of 3-D perspective views, terrestrial and aerial photographs and satellite imagery. All are used to illustrate specific themes and to give an indication of the variety of imagery, and different means of visualizing the Earth, available today. The main types of imagery used in the atlas are described in the table above.

Satellite imagery, and the related science of satellite remote sensing – the acquisition, processing and interpretation of images captured by satellites – is a particularly valuable tool in observing and monitoring the Earth. Satellite sensors can capture electromagnetic radiation in a variety of wavelengths, including those visible to the eye (colours), infrared wavelengths and microwave and radio radiation as detected by radar sensors. The data received by the sensors can be processed in different ways to allow detailed interpretation of the landscape and environmental conditions. Panchromatic images represent a single wavelength in values of grey (black and white) while multispectral sensors can combine several wavelengths in a single image. Imagery also varies in the amount of detail it can show. The ability to distinguish visual detail, and the size of the smallest feature which can be detected, is known as the image's resolution, and is usually expressed in metres.

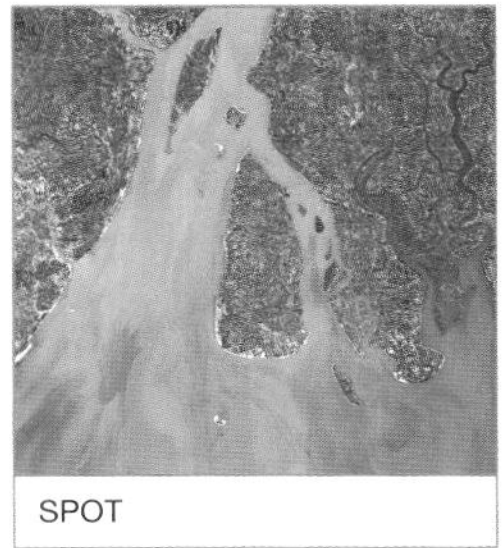
SPOT

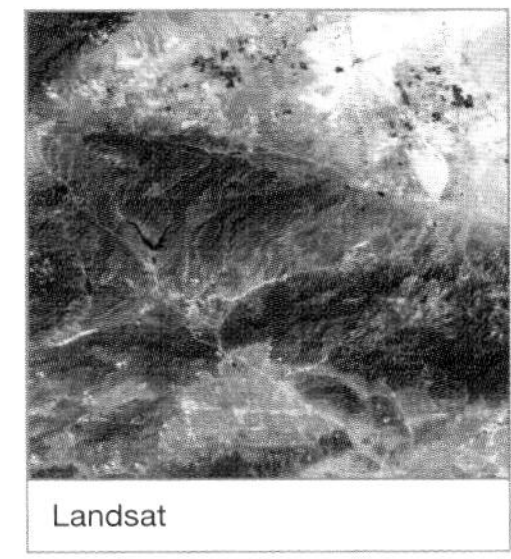
Landsat

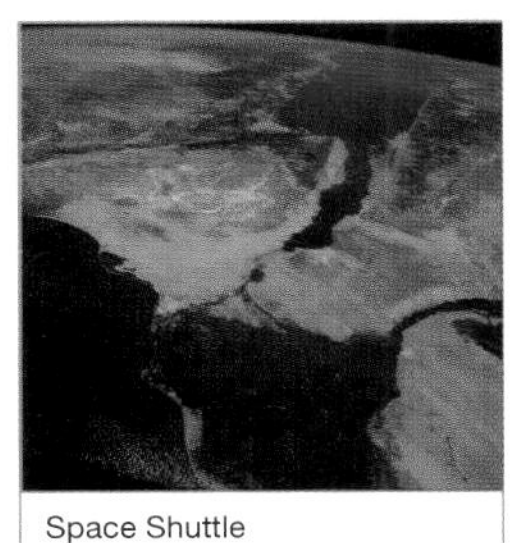
Space Shuttle

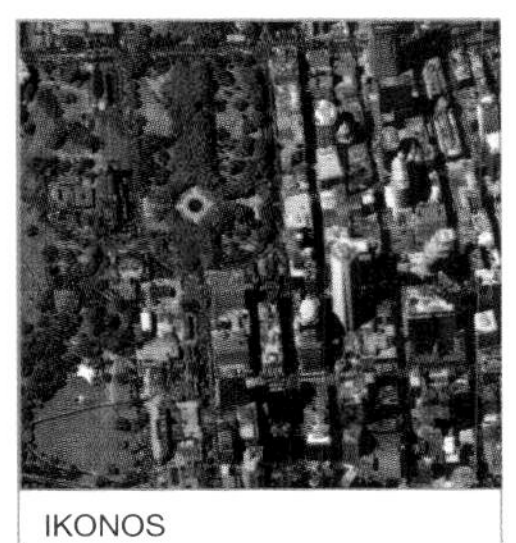
IKONOS

Omsk, *Russian Federation*

world

[contents]

1   Nile Delta and Sinai Peninsula, *Africa/Asia*

Several distinct physical features can be seen in this oblique Shuttle photograph which looks southeast from above the Mediterranean Sea over northeast Africa and southwest Asia. The dark, triangular area at the bottom of the photograph is the Nile delta. The Sinai peninsula in the centre of the image is flanked by the two elongated water bodies of the Gulf of Aqaba on the left, and the Gulf of Suez on the right. These gulfs merge to form the Red Sea. The Dead Sea is also visible on the left edge of the image.

Satellite/Sensor : Space Shuttle

2   Himalayas, *Asia*

The Himalayan mountain chain forms a major physical barrier across Jammu and Kashmir, northern India, Nepal and Bhutan and contains the world's highest mountains. This Space Shuttle photograph looks west along the mountains. The low plains on the left contain three major rivers, the Ganges, Indus and Brahmaputra. To the right of the permanently snow-capped mountains is the Plateau of Tibet, a vast barren area over 4 000 m above sea level.

Satellite/Sensor : Space Shuttle

Fig. #01
World physical features

>6000m
5000-6000m
4000-5000m
3000-4000m
2000-3000m
1000-2000m
500-1000m
200-500m
0-200m
<0m

0-200m
200-2000m
2000-3000m
3000-4000m
4000-5000m
5000-6000m
6000-7000m
>7000m

NORTH AMERICA

Coast Ranges   Rocky Mountains   Great Plains   Lake Michigan   Lake Huron   Lake Erie   Chesapeake Bay   Appalachian Mountains   Long Island   Cape Cod   Nova Scotia

SOUTH AMERICA

Andes   Selvas   Mato Grosso   Bahia de São Marcos   Ponta do Calcanhar

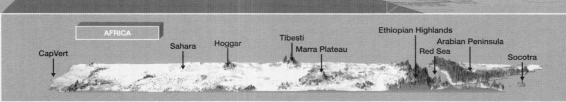

AFRICA

CapVert   Sahara   Hoggar   Tibesti   Marra Plateau   Ethiopian Highlands   Red Sea   Arabian Peninsula   Socotra

HIGHEST MOUNTAINS

	m	ft	location	map
Mt Everest	8 848	29 028	China/Nepal	97 E4
K2	8 611	28 251	China/Jammu and Kashmir	96 C2
Kangchenjunga	8 586	28 169	India/Nepal	97 F4
Lhotse	8 516	27 939	China/Nepal	97 E3
Makalu	8 463	27 765	China/Nepal	97 E3
Cho Oyu	8 201	26 906	China/Nepal	97 E3
Dhaulagiri	8 167	26 794	Nepal	97 D3
Manaslu	8 163	26 781	Nepal	97 E3
Nanga Parbat	8 126	26 660	Jammu and Kashmir	96 B2
Annapurna I	8 091	26 545	Nepal	97 D3

LONGEST RIVERS

	km	miles	continent	map
Nile	6 695	4 160	Africa	121 F2
Amazon	6 516	4 049	South America	202 B1
Yangtze	6 380	3 964	Asia	87 G2
Mississipi-Missouri	5 969	3 709	North America	179 E7
Ob'-Irtysh	5 568	3 459	Asia	38 G3-39 I5
Yenisey-Angara-Selenga	5 550	3 448	Asia	39 I2-K4
Yellow	5 464	3 395	Asia	85 H4
Congo	4 667	2 900	Africa	127 B6
Rio de la Plata - Parana	4 500	2 796	South America	204 F4
Irtysh	4 440	2 759	Asia	38 G3

LARGEST ISLANDS

	sq km	sq miles	location	map
Greenland	2 175 600	840 004	North America	165 O3
New Guinea	808 510	312 167	Oceania	73 J8
Borneo	745 561	287 863	Asia	77 F2
Madagascar	587 040	226 657	Africa	131 J3
Baffin Island	507 451	195 927	North America	165 L2
Sumatra	473 606	182 860	Asia	76 C3
Honshu	227 414	87 805	Asia	91 F6
Great Britain	218 476	84 354	Europe	47 J9
Victoria Island	217 291	83 897	North America	165 H2
Ellesmere Island	196 236	75 767	North America	165 K2

LARGEST LAKES

	sq km	sq miles	continent	map
Caspian Sea	371 000	143 243	Asia / Europe	102 B4
Lake Superior	82 100	31 698	North America	172 D3
Lake Victoria	68 800	26 563	Africa	128 B5
Lake Huron	59 600	23 011	North America	173 I6
Lake Michigan	57 800	22 316	North America	172 E7
Aral Sea	33 640	12 988	Asia	102 D3
Lake Tanganyika	32 900	12 702	Africa	129 A6
Great Bear Lake	31 328	12 095	North America	166 F1
Lake Baikal	30 500	11 776	Asia	39 K4
Lake Nyasa	30 044	11 600	Africa	129 B7

EARTH'S DIMENSIONS

Equatorial diameter	12 756.274 km (7 926.381 miles)
Polar diameter	12 713.505 km (7 899.806 miles)
Mass	5.974 X 10^9 tonnes
Total area	509 450 000 sq km/196 672 000 sq miles
Land area	149 450 000 sq km/57 688 000 sq miles
Water area	360 000 000 sq km/138 984 000 sq miles
Volume	1 083 207 X 10^6 cubic km/259 875 X 10^6 cubic miles

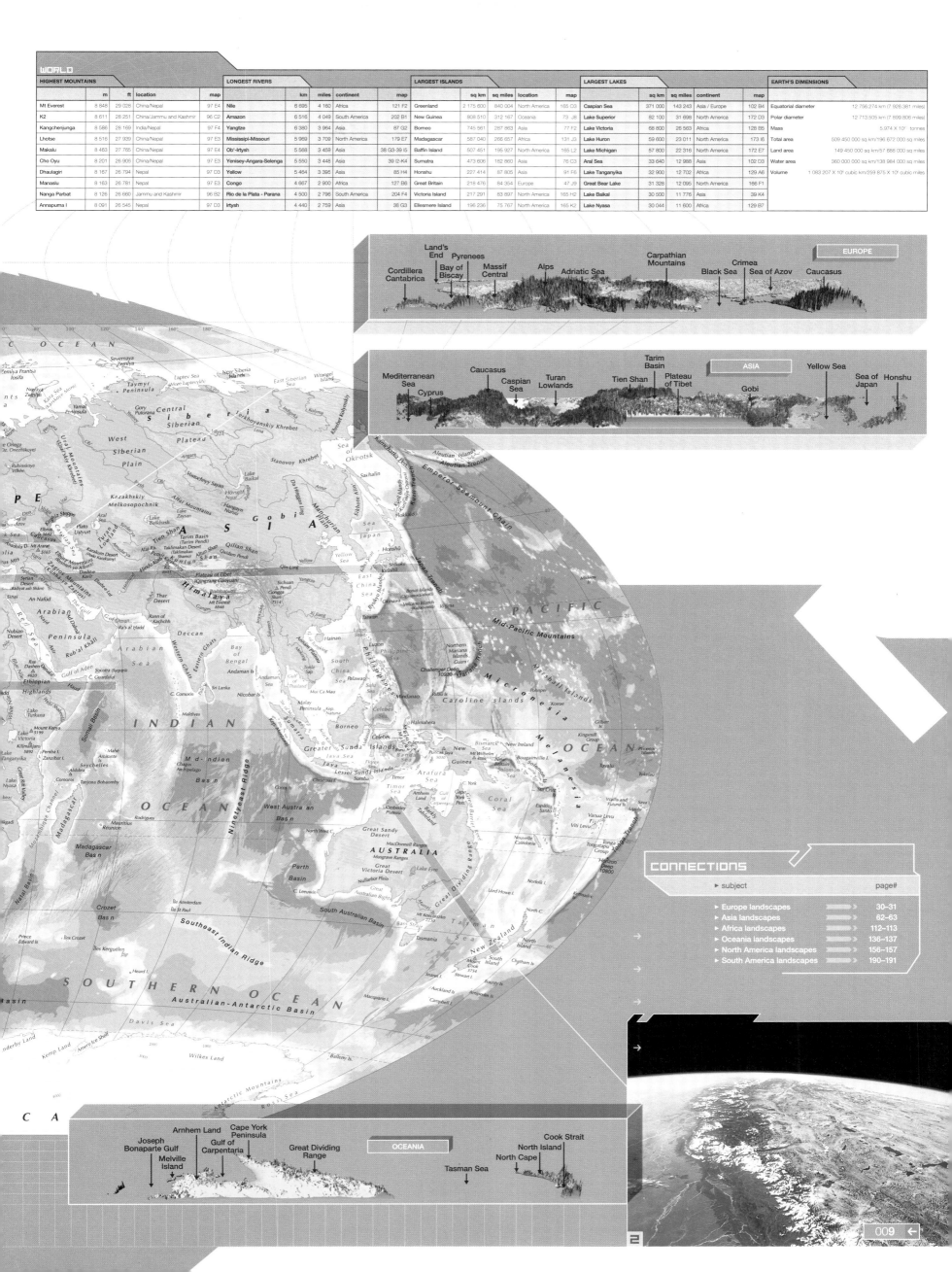

EUROPE

Cordillera Cantabrica · Land's End · Bay of Biscay · Pyrenees · Massif Central · Alps · Adriatic Sea · Carpathian Mountains · Black Sea · Crimea · Sea of Azov · Caucasus

ASIA

Mediterranean Sea · Cyprus · Caucasus · Caspian Sea · Turan Lowlands · Tien Shan · Tarim Basin · Plateau of Tibet · Gobi · Yellow Sea · Sea of Japan · Honshu

OCEANIA

Joseph Bonaparte Gulf · Melville Island · Arnhem Land · Gulf of Carpentaria · Cape York Peninsula · Great Dividing Range · Tasman Sea · Cook Strait · North Cape · North Island

CONNECTIONS

subject	page#
► Europe landscapes	30–31
► Asia landscapes	62–63
► Africa landscapes	112–113
► Oceania landscapes	136–137
► North America landscapes	156–157
► South America landscapes	190–191

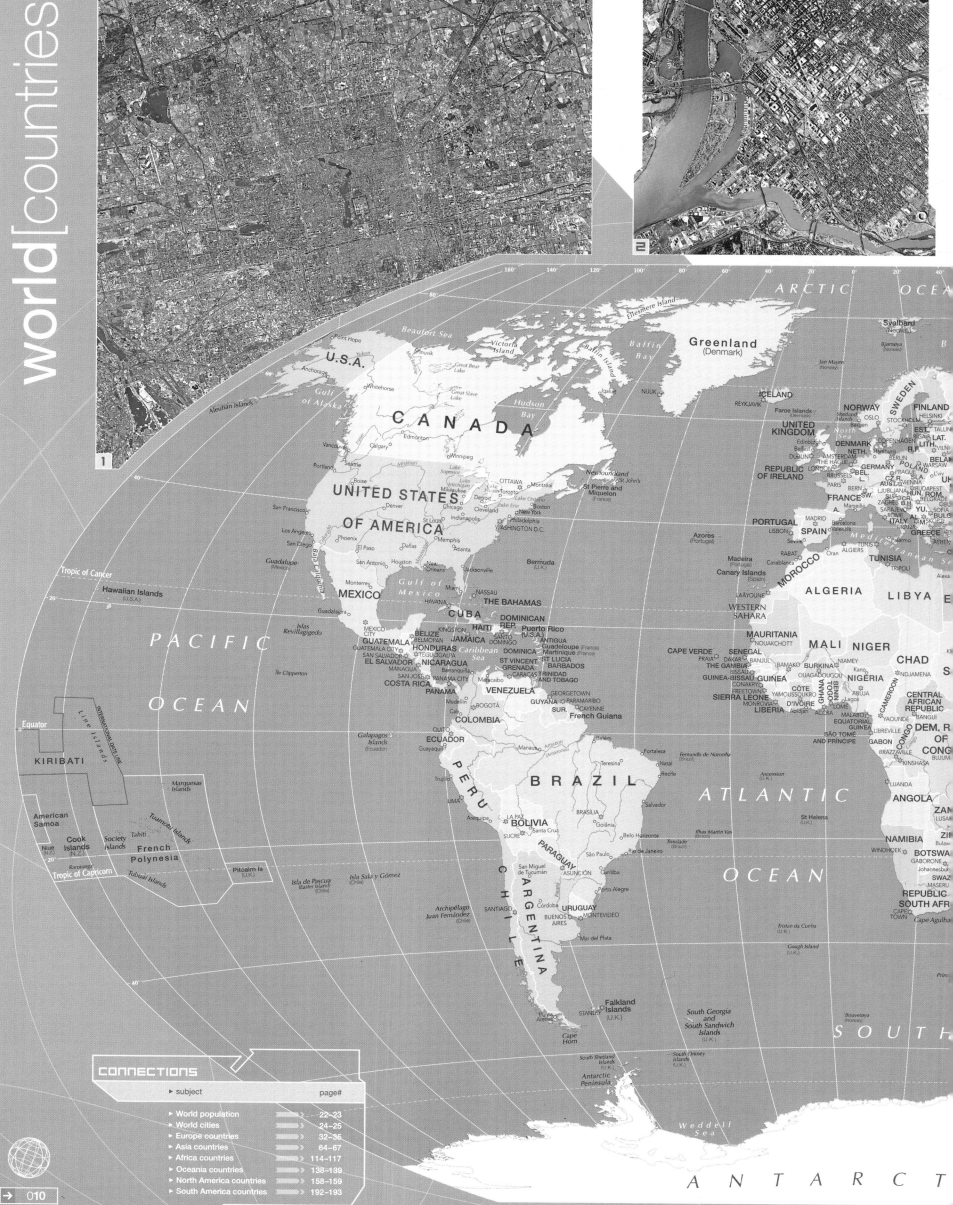

ARCTIC **OCEA**

Ellesmere Island

Svalbard
(Norway)

Point Hope
Beaufort Sea
Victoria
Island
Baffin
Bay
Greenland
(Denmark)
Jan Mayen
(Norway)
Bjørnøya
(Norway)
B

U.S.A.
Inuvik
Baffin Island
ICELAND
Faroe Islands
NORWAY
SWEDEN
FINLAND

Anchorage
Great Bear
Lake
NUUK
REYKJAVÍK
Shetland
Islands
Bergen
OSLO
STOCKHOLM
HELSINKI
EST. TALLINN
RIGA LAT.

Whitehorse
Great Slave
Lake
Hudson
Bay
UNITED
KINGDOM
Edinburgh
DENMARK
COPENHAGEN
R.F.
LITH. VILNI

Aleutian Islands
C A N A D A
Iqaluit
Belfast
DUBLIN
AMSTERDAM
THE HAGUE
BERLIN
POLAND
WARSAW
BELA

Vancouver
Calgary
Edmonton
Winnipeg
Lake
Superior
OTTAWA
Newfoundland
St John's
REPUBLIC
OF IRELAND
LONDON
BRUSSELS
BEL.
GERMANY
PRAGUE
C.Z.R.
SLA.
L'viv

Portland
Seattle
Boise
UNITED STATES
Milwaukee
Lake
Michigan
Detroit
Toronto
Lake Ontario
St Pierre and
Miquelon
(France)
PARIS
BERN
SW.
LJUBLJANA
VIENNA
BUDAPEST
HUN.
ROM.

San Francisco
Denver
Chicago
Cleveland
New York
Boston
FRANCE
Marseille
ZAGREB
SARAJEVO
CRO.
YU.
SOFIA
BULG.

Los Angeles
OF AMERICA
Indianapolis
WASHINGTON D.C.
Philadelphia
PORTUGAL
MADRID
Barcelona
ITALY
ROME
TIRANA
GREECE
ATHENS

San Diego
Phoenix
El Paso
St Louis
Memphis
Atlanta
LISBON
SPAIN
Valencia
Seville
Med
TUNIS

Dallas
San Antonio
Houston
New
Orleans
Jacksonville
Bermuda
(U.K.)
RABAT
Casablanca
Oran
ALGIERS
TUNISIA
TRIPOLI

Baja California
Monterrey
Gulf of
Mexico
Miami
NASSAU
Azores
(Portugal)
Madeira
(Portugal)
Canary Islands
(Spain)
MOROCCO
Alexa

Tropic of Cancer
Guadalupe
(Mexico)
HAVANA
THE BAHAMAS
LAAYOUNE
WESTERN
SAHARA
ALGERIA
LIBYA
E

Hawaiian Islands
(U.S.A.)
Guadalajara
MEXICO
CUBA
DOMINICAN
REP.
Puerto Rico
(U.S.A.)
MAURITANIA
MALI
NIGER
CHAD

Islas
Revillagigedo
MEXICO
CITY
BELIZE
BELMOPAN
HAITI
JAMAICA
KINGSTON
SANTO
DOMINGO
ANTIGUA
Guadeloupe (France)
Martinique (France)
NOUAKCHOTT
CAPE VERDE
PRAIA
SENEGAL
DAKAR
BANJUL
BAMAKO
BURKINA
NIAMEY
Kano
NDJAMENA
Sa

Île Clipperton
GUATEMALA
GUATEMALA CITY
HONDURAS
TEGUCIGALPA
DOMINICA
BARBADOS
THE GAMBIA
BISSAU
OUAGADOUGOU
NIGERIA

PACIFIC
SAN SALVADOR
EL SALVADOR
NICARAGUA
ST VINCENT
GRENADA
ST LUCIA
GUINEA-BISSAU
CONAKRY
GUINEA
YAMOUSSOUKRO
FREETOWN
ABUJA
CAMEROON
CENTRAL
AFRICAN
REPUBLIC

MANAGUA
SAN JOSÉ
PANAMA CITY
CARACAS
TRINIDAD
AND TOBAGO
SIERRA LEONE
MONROVIA
D'IVOIRE
Abidjan
ACCRA
LOMÉ
YAOUNDÉ
BANGUI

OCEAN
COSTA RICA
PANAMA
Maracaibo
GEORGETOWN
PARAMARIBO
LIBERIA
GHANA
TOGO
MALABO
LIBREVILLE
DEM. R
OF
CONG

VENEZUELA
GUYANA
SUR.
CAYENNE
French Guiana
EQUATORIAL
GUINEA
GABON
BRAZZAVILLE
KINSHASA

COLOMBIA
BOGOTÁ
SÃO TOMÉ
AND PRÍNCIPE
BUJUM

Cali
Galapagos
Islands
(Ecuador)
ECUADOR
QUITO
LUANDA
Equator
Guayaquil
Manaus
Amazon
Belém
Fortaleza
Ascension
(U.K.)
ATLANTIC
ANGOLA

KIRIBATI
Line Islands
PERU
Trujillo
Natal
Recife
ZAM
LUSA

Marquesas
Islands
LIMA
BRAZIL
Teresina
Fernando de Noronha
(Brazil)

American
Samoa
Arequipa
BRASÍLIA
Salvador
St Helena
(U.K.)
NAMIBIA
ZI

Niue
(N.Z.)
Cook
Islands (N.Z.)
Society
Islands
Tahiti
Tuamotu Islands
French
Polynesia
LA PAZ
BOLIVIA
Santa Cruz
Goiânia
Belo Horizonte
Ilhas Martin Vaz
WINDHOEK
BOTSWA
GABORONE

Rarotonga
SUCRE
Rio de Janeiro
Trindade
(Brazil)
Johannesburg
SWAZ

Tropic of Capricorn
Tubuai Islands
Pitcairn Is
(U.K.)
Isla de Pascua
(Easter Island)
(Chile)
Isla Sala y Gómez
(Chile)
PARAGUAY
São Paulo
Curitiba
Porto Alegre
MASERU
REPUBLIC
OF
SOUTH AFR

San Miguel
de Tucumán
ASUNCIÓN
CAPE
TOWN
Cape Agulhas

Archipélago
Juan Fernández
(Chile)
SANTIAGO
Córdoba
URUGUAY
MONTEVIDEO
Tristan da Cunha
(U.K.)
OCEAN

CHILE
ARGENTINA
BUENOS
AIRES
Gough Island
(U.K.)

Mar del Plata

Bouvetøya
(Norway)
S O U T H

Falkland
Islands
(U.K.)
STANLEY
South Georgia
and
South Sandwich
Islands
(U.K.)

Punta
Arenas
Cape
Horn

South Shetland
Islands
(U.K.)
South Orkney
Islands
(U.K.)
Prince

Antarctic
Peninsula
Weddell
Sea

A N T A R C T

1

2

CONNECTIONS

▶ subject	page#
▶ World population	22–23
▶ World cities	24–25
▶ Europe countries	32–35
▶ Asia countries	64–67
▶ Africa countries	114–117
▶ Oceania countries	138–139
▶ North America countries	158–159
▶ South America countries	192–193

1 Beijing, China

This infrared SPOT satellite image of Beijing shows the extent of the capital city of China spreading out from the Forbidden City and Tiananmen Square, just to the right of the lake in the centre. The central city has a very marked grid-iron street pattern, with very densely packed low-rise buildings. On the outskirts, areas of intensive cultivation are represented in shades of red.

Satellite/Sensor : SPOT

2 Washington, D.C., *United States of America*

The capital of the United States, Washington, D.C., is shown in this infrared aerial photograph. The city is situated on the confluence of the Potomac and Anacostia rivers, seen here to the left and bottom of the photograph respectively. It has become a leading political, educational and research centre. The Pentagon, home of the US Department of Defense is at the far left of the photograph and The Mall, the Capitol, the White House and Union Station can all be seen in the centre.

3 La Paz, *Bolivia*

This infrared satellite image shows the highest capital in the world, La Paz, which lies at a height of over 3 500 metres above sea level. It is located at the edge of the Altiplano between two mountain belts within the Andes mountains. The mountains seen at the top of the image have year-round snow cover. The grey-blue area to the right of centre is the urban area of La Paz, with the city's airport clearly visible to the west.

Satellite/Sensor : SPOT

4 Mauritania/Senegal, *Africa*

The Senegal river creates a natural border between the northeast African countries of Mauritania and Senegal. The top of this infrared satellite image shows the southern edge of the Sahara desert in Mauritania. The semi-desert southern fringe of the Sahara, the Sahel, stretches east from Mauritania to Chad. The orange-red colour in the bottom half of the image represents mixed scrub and bush savanna vegetation of Senegal.

Satellite/Sensor : SPOT

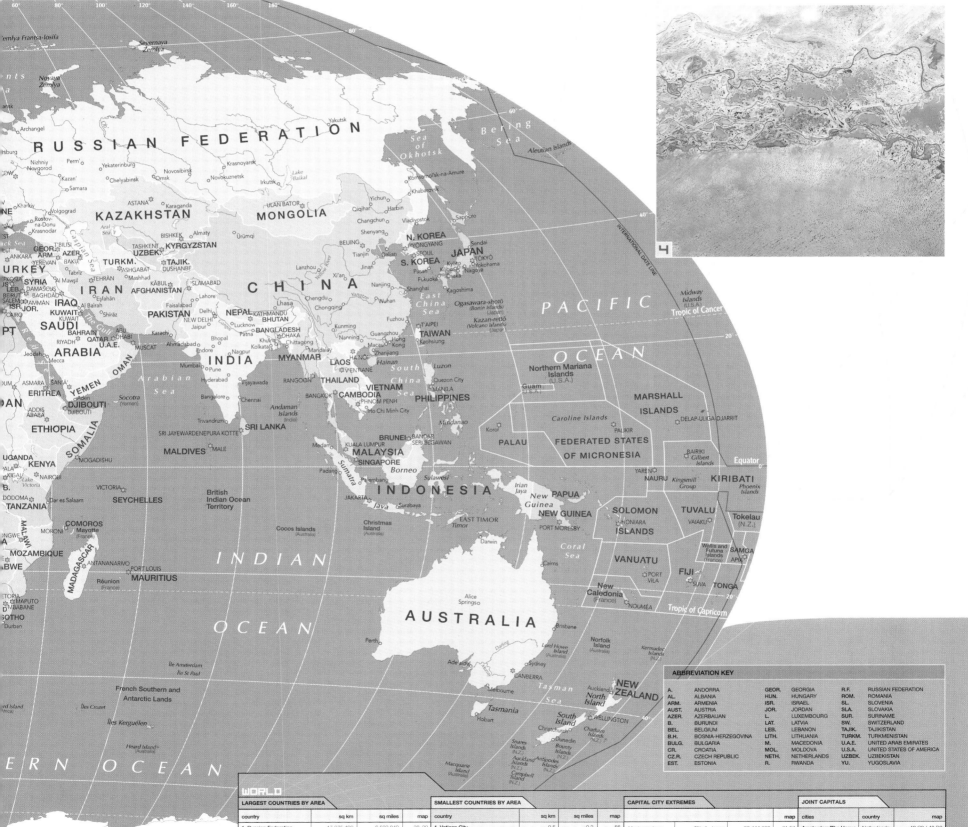

ABBREVIATION KEY

A.	ANDORRA	GEOR.	GEORGIA	R.F.	RUSSIAN FEDERATION
AL.	ALBANIA	HUN.	HUNGARY	ROM.	ROMANIA
ARM.	ARMENIA	ISR.	ISRAEL	SL.	SLOVENIA
AUST.	AUSTRIA	JOR.	JORDAN	SLA.	SLOVAKIA
AZER.	AZERBAIJAN	L.	LUXEMBOURG	SUR.	SURINAME
B.	BURUNDI	LAT.	LATVIA	SW.	SWITZERLAND
BEL.	BELGIUM	LEB.	LEBANON	TAJIK.	TAJIKISTAN
B.H.	BOSNIA-HERZEGOVINA	LITH.	LITHUANIA	TURKM.	TURKMENISTAN
BULG.	BULGARIA	M.	MACEDONIA	U.A.E.	UNITED ARAB EMIRATES
CR.	CROATIA	MOL.	MOLDOVA	U.S.A.	UNITED STATES OF AMERICA
CZ.R.	CZECH REPUBLIC	NETH.	NETHERLANDS	UZBEK.	UZBEKISTAN
EST.	ESTONIA	R.	RWANDA	YU.	YUGOSLAVIA

WORLD

LARGEST COUNTRIES BY AREA

country	sq km	sq miles	map
1. Russian Federation	17 075 400	6 592 849	38–39
2. Canada	9 970 610	3 849 674	164–165
3. United States of America	9 809 378	3 787 422	170–171
4. China	9 584 492	3 700 593	80–81
5. Brazil	8 547 379	3 300 161	202–203
6. Australia	7 682 395	2 966 189	144–145
7. India	3 065 027	1 183 414	92–93
8. Argentina	2 766 889	1 068 302	204–205
9. Kazakhstan	2 717 300	1 049 155	102–103
10. Sudan	2 505 813	967 500	120–121

SMALLEST COUNTRIES BY AREA

country	sq km	sq miles	map
1. Vatican City	0.5	0.2	56
2. Monaco	2	1	51
3. Nauru	21	8	145
4. Tuvalu	25	10	145
5. San Marino	61	24	56
6. Liechtenstein	160	62	51
7. St Kitts and Nevis	261	101	187
8. Maldives	298	115	93
9. Grenada	378	146	187
10. St Vincent and the Grenadines	389	150	187

CAPITAL CITY EXTREMES

				map
Most populous	Tōkyō, Japan	26 444 000		91 F7
Least populous	Yaren, Nauru	600		145 F2
Highest	La Paz, Bolivia	3 636m / 11 910ft		200 C4
Lowest	Mariana, Bahrain and Male, Maldives	0.9m / 3ft		100 B5 / 93 D10
Furthest north	Nuuk, Greenland	64° 11'N		165 N3
Furthest south	Wellington, New Zealand	41° 18'S		152 I9
Furthest east	Funafuti, Tuvalu	179° 13'E		145 G2
Furthest west	Nuku'alofa, Tonga	175° 12'W		145 H4

JOINT CAPITALS

cities	country	map
Amsterdam/The Hague	Netherlands	48 C3 / 48 B3
La Paz/Sucre	Bolivia	200 C4 / 200 D4
Pretoria/Cape Town	South Africa	133 M2 / 132 C10

1 Orinoco River, *South America*

The Orinoco river flows from right to left in this Shuttle photograph which looks towards the southeast. The upper section of the image shows the dense forests of the western edge of the Guiana Highlands. The main tributary joining the Orinoco is the Meta river with the town of Puerto Páez at the confluence. The Orinoco and the Meta form part of the boundary between Colombia and Venezuela.

Satellite/Sensor : Space Shuttle

2 Zaskar Mountains, *Asia*

The brackish waters of Tso Morari lake, surrounded by the Zaskar Mountains, can be seen at the left hand edge of this Shuttle photograph. North is to the right of the image. The mountains form one of the ranges at the western end of the Himalayas in the disputed area of Jammu and Kashmir. The lake is more than 4 000 m above sea level, the surrounding mountains rise to over 6 000 m.

Satellite/Sensor : Space Shuttle

3 Altiplano, *South America*

The Altiplano is a high plateau which stretches from western Bolivia to southern Peru. It has an average height of over 3 600 m and is bordered to the west and east by two main ridges of the Andes mountains. This Shuttle photograph shows part of Lake Coipasa. Unusually, the water level is high. The lake is normally a dry lakebed for the majority of the year. The photograph shows individual volcanoes which are common in this region.

Satellite/Sensor : Space Shuttle

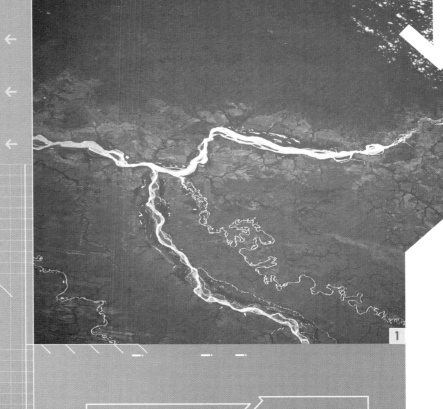

1

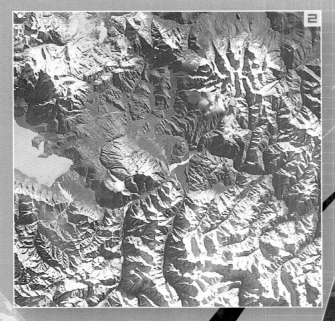

2

CONNECTIONS

► subject		page#
► Types of imagery		4-5
► World physical features		8-9
► Volcanoes		14-15
► Land cover types		18-19
► Coral reefs		140-141

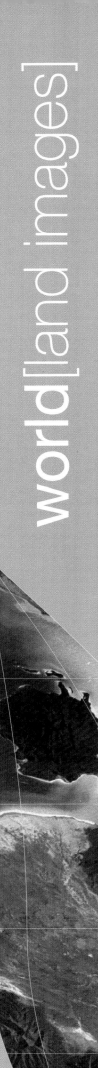

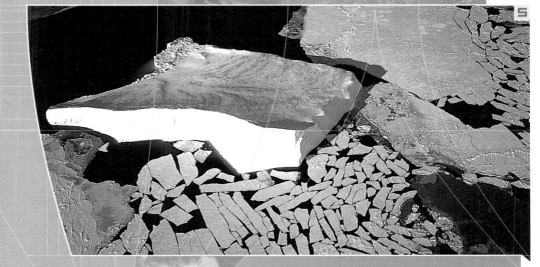

4

3

5

4 French Polynesia, *Oceania*

This view of Bora-Bora, an island group within the Society Islands of French Polynesia in the southern Pacific Ocean, is typical of this area which consists of many scattered groups of islands. The main island, just visible at the top of the photograph, lies in a large lagoon surrounded by numerous coral reefs and small islands.

5 Greenland, *North America*

Icebergs are usually formed either by sections breaking off glaciers which flow into the sea, or from the breaking up of ice-sheets as temperatures start to rise in spring. This one, off the northwest coast of Greenland in the Arctic Ocean, is surrounded by flat sections of broken up sea ice.

6 Namib Desert, *Africa*

This satellite image of the west coast of Africa clearly shows the natural barrier formed by the Kuiseb river at the northern edge of the Namib Desert in Namibia. To the north of the river are the Khomas Highlands which are rich in minerals, including uranium, to the south are the extensive dunes within the desert. The town of Walvis Bay is at the mouth of the river with the area's capital of Swakopmund just to the north.

Satellite/Sensor : Landsat

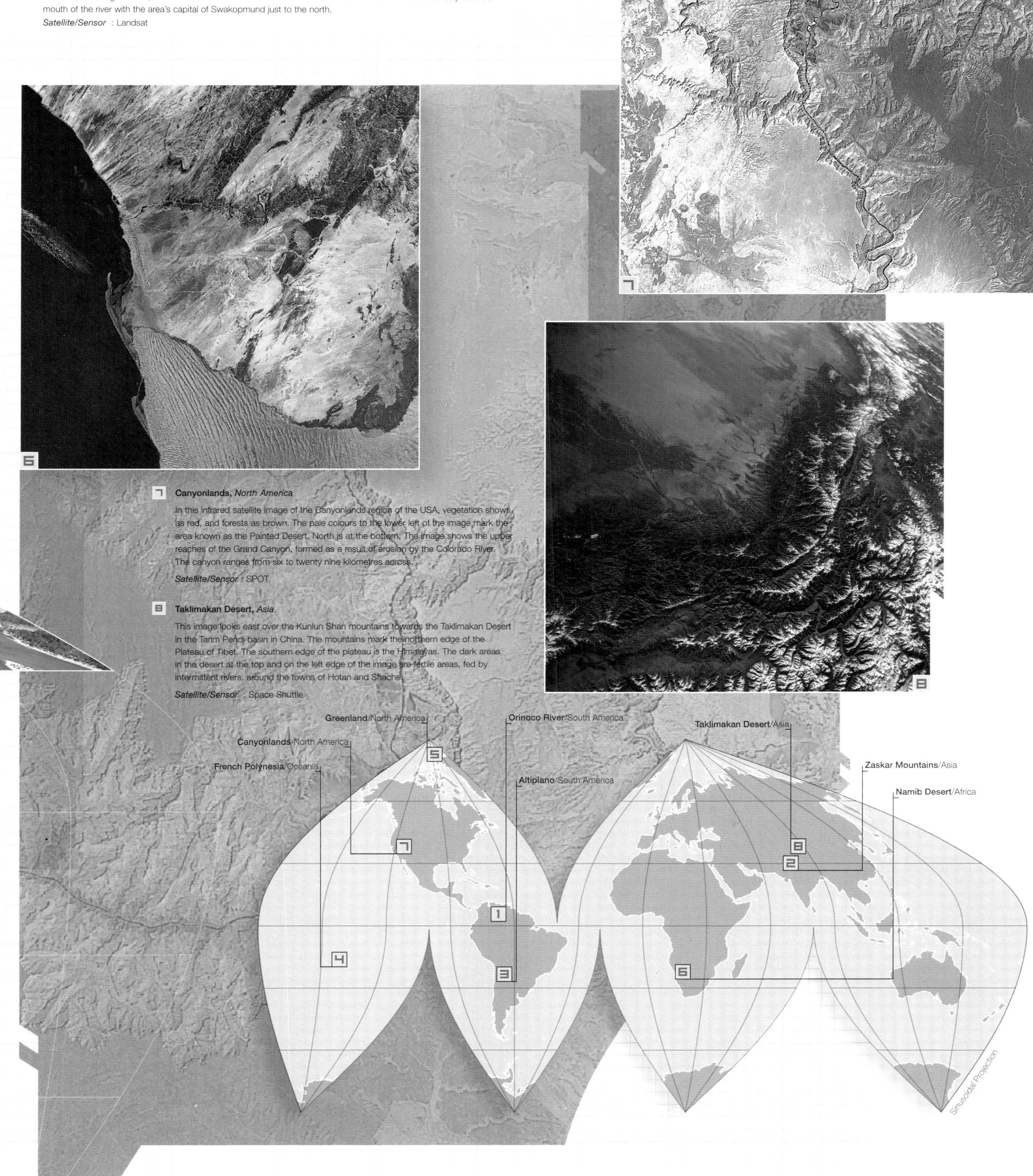

7 Canyonlands, *North America*

In this infrared satellite image of the Canyonlands region of the USA, vegetation shows as red, and forests as brown. The pale colours to the lower left of the image mark the area known as the Painted Desert. North is at the bottom. The image shows the upper reaches of the Grand Canyon, formed as a result of erosion by the Colorado River. The canyon ranges from six to twenty nine kilometres across.

Satellite/Sensor : SPOT

8 Taklimakan Desert, *Asia*

This image looks east over the Kunlun Shan mountains towards the Taklimakan Desert in the Tarim Pendi basin in China. The mountains mark the northern edge of the Plateau of Tibet. The southern edge of the plateau is the Himalayas. The dark areas in the desert at the top and on the left edge of the image are fertile areas, fed by intermittent rivers, around the towns of Hotan and Shache.

Satellite/Sensor : Space Shuttle

Greenland/North America · Orinoco River/South America · Taklimakan Desert/Asia · Canyonlands/North America · Altiplano/South America · Zaskar Mountains/Asia · French Polynesia/Oceania · Namib Desert/Africa

Sinusoidal Projection

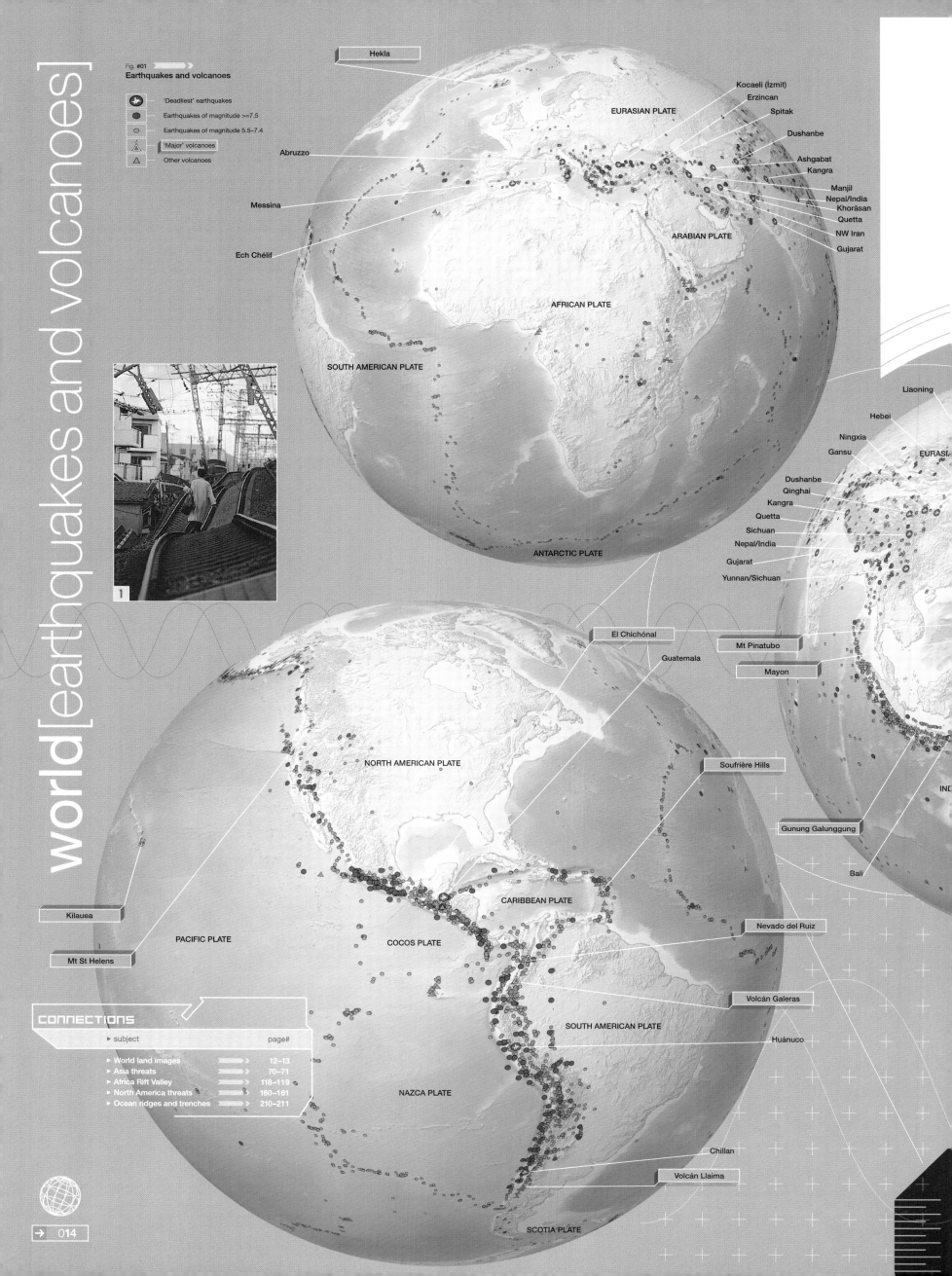

Fig. #01
Earthquakes and volcanoes

⊕ 'Deadliest' earthquakes
● Earthquakes of magnitude >=7.5
○ Earthquakes of magnitude 5.5–7.4
▲ 'Major' volcanoes
△ Other volcanoes

Hekla

EURASIAN PLATE

Kocaeli (İzmit)
Erzincan
Spitak
Dushanbe
Ashgabat
Kangra
Abruzzo
Manjil
Nepal/India
Messina
Khorāsan
Quetta
NW Iran
ARABIAN PLATE
Gujarat

Ech Chélif

AFRICAN PLATE

SOUTH AMERICAN PLATE

ANTARCTIC PLATE

Liaoning
Hebei
Ningxia
Gansu
EURASIA

Dushanbe
Qinghai
Kangra
Quetta
Sichuan
Nepal/India
Gujarat
Yunnan/Sichuan

El Chichónal
Guatemala
Mt Pinatubo
Mayon

NORTH AMERICAN PLATE

IND

Soufrière Hills

Gunung Galunggung

Bali

Kilauea

PACIFIC PLATE

Mt St Helens

CARIBBEAN PLATE

COCOS PLATE

Nevado del Ruiz

Volcán Galeras

SOUTH AMERICAN PLATE

Huánuco

NAZCA PLATE

Chillan

Volcán Llaima

SCOTIA PLATE

CONNECTIONS

► subject   page#

► World land images   12–13
► Asia threats   70–71
► Africa Rift Valley   118–119
► North America threats   160–161
► Ocean ridges and trenches 210–211

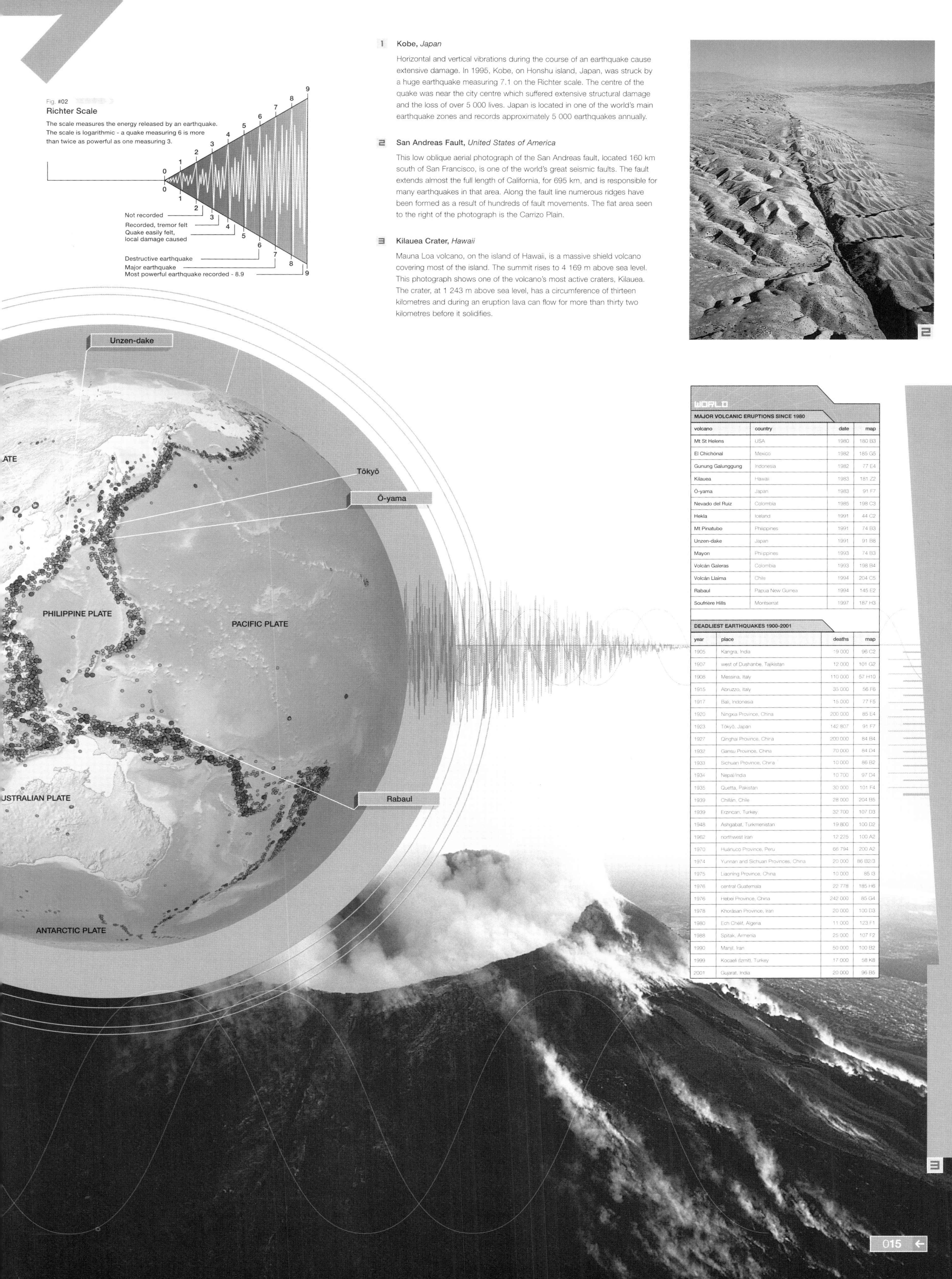

Fig. #02
Richter Scale

The scale measures the energy released by an earthquake.
The scale is logarithmic - a quake measuring 6 is more
than twice as powerful as one measuring 3.

Not recorded
Recorded, tremor felt
Quake easily felt,
local damage caused

Destructive earthquake
Major earthquake
Most powerful earthquake recorded - 8.9

1 **Kobe,** *Japan*

Horizontal and vertical vibrations during the course of an earthquake cause
extensive damage. In 1995, Kobe, on Honshu island, Japan, was struck by
a huge earthquake measuring 7.1 on the Richter scale. The centre of the
quake was near the city centre which suffered extensive structural damage
and the loss of over 5 000 lives. Japan is located in one of the world's main
earthquake zones and records approximately 5 000 earthquakes annually.

2 **San Andreas Fault,** *United States of America*

This low oblique aerial photograph of the San Andreas fault, located 160 km
south of San Francisco, is one of the world's great seismic faults. The fault
extends almost the full length of California, for 695 km, and is responsible for
many earthquakes in that area. Along the fault line numerous ridges have
been formed as a result of hundreds of fault movements. The flat area seen
to the right of the photograph is the Carrizo Plain.

3 **Kilauea Crater,** *Hawaii*

Mauna Loa volcano, on the island of Hawaii, is a massive shield volcano
covering most of the island. The summit rises to 4 169 m above sea level.
This photograph shows one of the volcano's most active craters, Kilauea.
The crater, at 1 243 m above sea level, has a circumference of thirteen
kilometres and during an eruption lava can flow for more than thirty two
kilometres before it solidifies.

Unzen-dake
Tōkyō
Ō-yama
Rabaul

PHILIPPINE PLATE
PACIFIC PLATE
AUSTRALIAN PLATE
ANTARCTIC PLATE

WORLD

MAJOR VOLCANIC ERUPTIONS SINCE 1980

volcano	country	date	map
Mt St Helens	USA	1980	180 B3
El Chichónal	Mexico	1982	185 G5
Gunung Galunggung	Indonesia	1982	77 E4
Kilauea	Hawaii	1983	181 Z2
Ō-yama	Japan	1983	91 F7
Nevado del Ruiz	Colombia	1985	198 C3
Hekla	Iceland	1991	44 C2
Mt Pinatubo	Philippines	1991	74 B3
Unzen-dake	Japan	1991	91 B8
Mayon	Philippines	1993	74 B3
Volcán Galeras	Colombia	1993	198 B4
Volcán Llaima	Chile	1994	204 C5
Rabaul	Papua New Guinea	1994	145 E2
Soufrière Hills	Montserrat	1997	187 H3

DEADLIEST EARTHQUAKES 1900-2001

year	place	deaths	map
1905	Kangra, India	19 000	96 C2
1907	west of Dushanbe, Tajikistan	12 000	101 G2
1908	Messina, Italy	110 000	57 H10
1915	Abruzzo, Italy	35 000	56 F6
1917	Bali, Indonesia	15 000	77 F5
1920	Ningxia Province, China	200 000	85 E4
1923	Tōkyō, Japan	142 807	91 F7
1927	Qinghai Province, China	200 000	84 B4
1932	Gansu Province, China	70 000	84 D4
1933	Sichuan Province, China	10 000	86 B2
1934	Nepal/India	10 700	97 D4
1935	Quetta, Pakistan	30 000	101 F4
1939	Chillan, Chile	28 000	204 B5
1939	Erzincan, Turkey	32 700	107 D3
1948	Ashgabat, Turkmenistan	19 800	100 D2
1962	northwest Iran	12 225	100 A2
1970	Huánuco Province, Peru	66 794	200 A2
1974	Yunnan and Sichuan Provinces, China	20 000	86 B2/3
1975	Liaoning Province, China	10 000	85 I3
1976	central Guatemala	22 778	185 H6
1976	Hebei Province, China	242 000	85 G4
1978	Khorāsān Province, Iran	20 000	100 D3
1980	Ech Chélif, Algeria	11 000	123 F1
1988	Spitak, Armenia	25 000	107 F2
1990	Manjil, Iran	50 000	100 B2
1999	Kocaeli (Izmit), Turkey	17 000	58 K8
2001	Gujarat, India	20 000	96 B5

world[climate and weather]

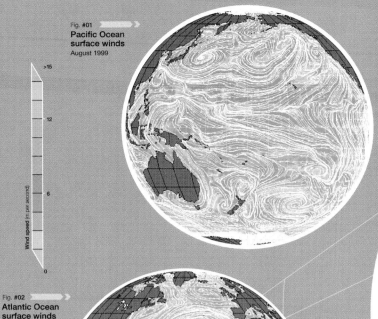

Fig. #01
Pacific Ocean surface winds
August 1999

Fig. #02
Atlantic Ocean surface winds
August 1999

Fig. #03
Indian Ocean surface winds
August 1999

Fig. #04
Satellite Image of Earth

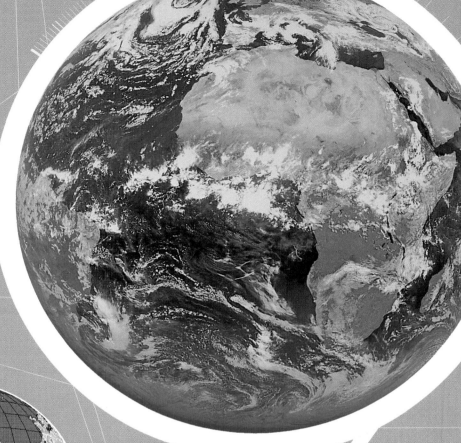

Fig. #01–#03 Ocean surface winds

Winds play a major role in every aspect of weather on Earth. They affect the exchanges of heat, moisture and greenhouse gases between Earth's atmosphere and the oceans. These images were taken on 1 August 1999 from the QuikSCAT satellite carrying a radar instrument called a scatterometer which can record surface wind speeds in the oceans. In the image of the Pacific Ocean yellow spirals representing typhoon Olga can be seen moving around South Korea and the East China Sea. Intense winter storms can also be seen around Antarctica in all three images.

Satellite/Sensor : QuikSCAT/SeaWinds

Fig. #10–#11 Climate change in the future

Future climate change will depend to a large extent on the effect human activities have on the chemical composition of the atmosphere. As greenhouse gases and aerosol emissions increase the atmospheric temperatures rise. The map of predicted temperature in the 2050s shows that average annual temperatures may rise by as much as 5°C in some areas if current emission rates continue. The map of precipitation change shows some areas are likely to experience a significant increase in precipitation of over 3 mm per day, while others will experience a decrease. Such changes are likely to have significant impacts on sea level which could rise by as much as 50 cm in the next century. The changes would also have implications for water resources, food production and health.

Fig. #04 Satellite image of Earth

Images such as this from the Meteosat satellite provide valuable meteorological information on a global scale. Dense clouds appear white, thinner cloud cover as pink . A swirling frontal weather system is clearly seen in the Atlantic Ocean to the west of Europe.

Satellite/Sensor : Meteosat

Fig. #05
Major climatic regions and sub-types

Köppen classification system

A   Rainy climate with no winter: coolest month above 18°C (64.4°F).
B   Dry climates; limits are defined by formulae based on rainfall effectiveness: BS Steppe or semi-arid climate. BW Desert or arid climate.
*C Rainy climates with mild winters: coolest month above 0°C (32°F), but below 18°C (64.4°F); warmest month above 10°C (50°F).
*D Rainy climates with severe winters: coldest month below 0°C (32°F); warmest month above 10°C (50°F).
E   Polar climates with no warm season: warmest month below 10°C (50°F). ET Tundra climate: warmest month below 10°C (50°F) but above 0°C (32°F). EF Perpetual frost: all months below 0°C (32°F).
a   Warmest month above 22°C (71.6°F).
b   Warmest month below 22°C (71.6°F).
c   Less than four months over 10°C (50°F).
d   As 'c', but with severe cold: coldest month below -38°C (-36.4°F).
f   Constantly moist rainfall throughout the year.
*h Warmer dry: all months above 0°C (32°F).
*k Cooler dry: at least one month below 0°C (32°F).
m   Monsoon rain: short dry season, but is compensated by heavy rains during rest of the year.
n   Frequent fog.
s   Dry season in summer.
w   Dry season in winter.

* Modification of Köppen definition

Polar
EF Ice cap
ET Tundra

Cooler humid
Dc Dd Subarctic
Db Continental cool summer
Da Continental warm summer

Warmer humid
Cb Cc Temperate
Ca Humid subtropical
Cs Mediterranean

Dry
BS Steppe
BW Desert

Tropical humid
Aw As Savanna
Af Am Rain forest

CONNECTIONS

► subject	page#
► Asia threats	70–71
► Africa issues	116–117
► North America threats	160–161
► South America impacts	196–197
► Antarctica features	212–213
► Arctic features	214–215

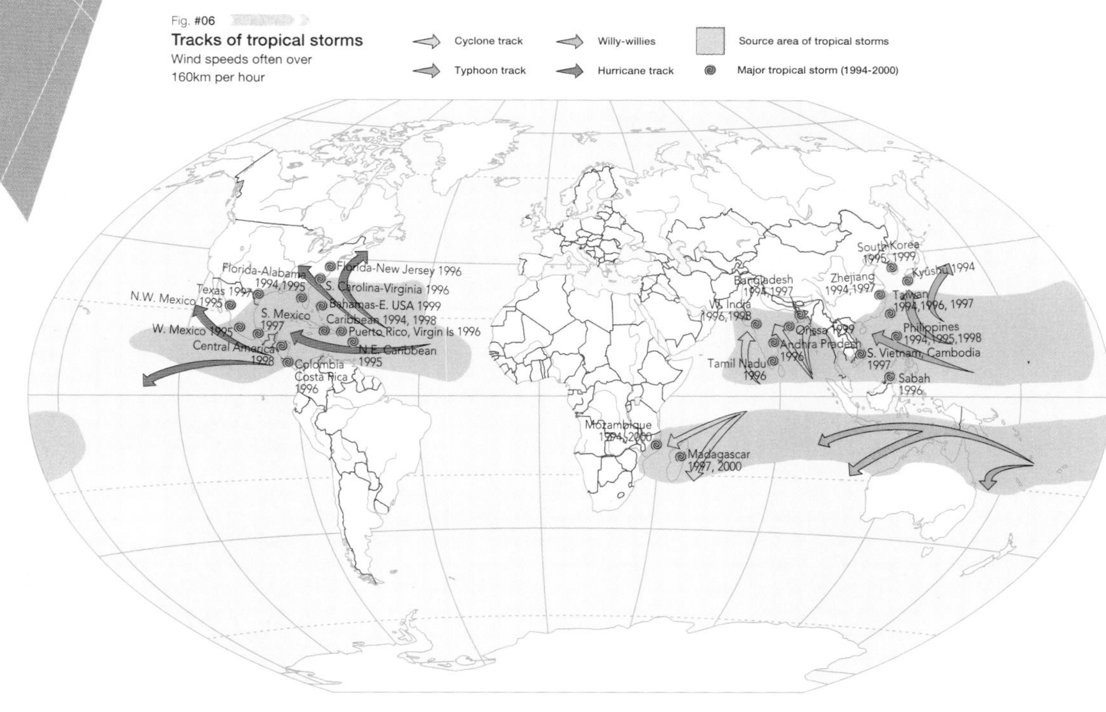

Fig. #06
Tracks of tropical storms
Wind speeds often over 160km per hour

Cyclone track → Willy-willies
Typhoon track → Hurricane track
Source area of tropical storms
● Major tropical storm (1994-2000)

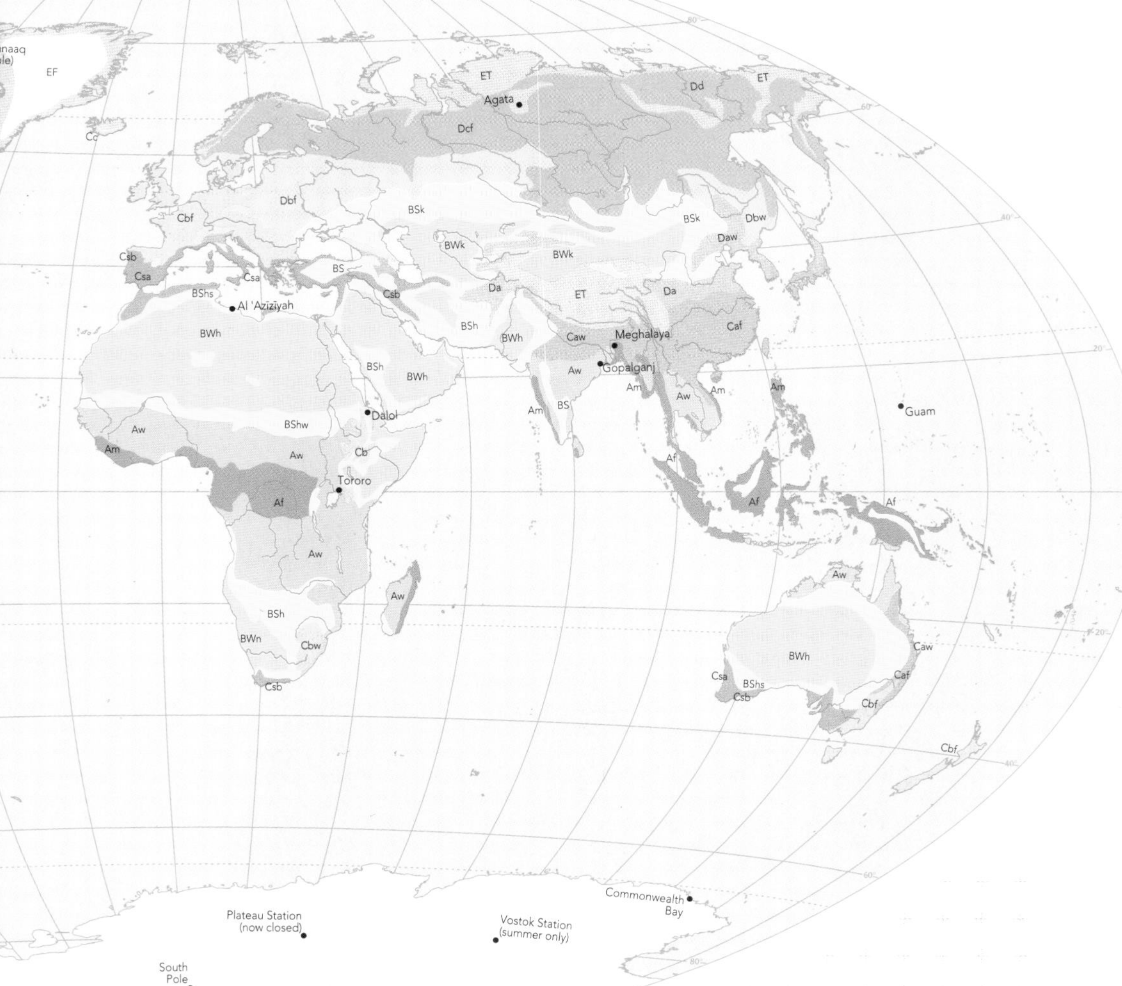

Fig. #07
Actual surface temperature
January

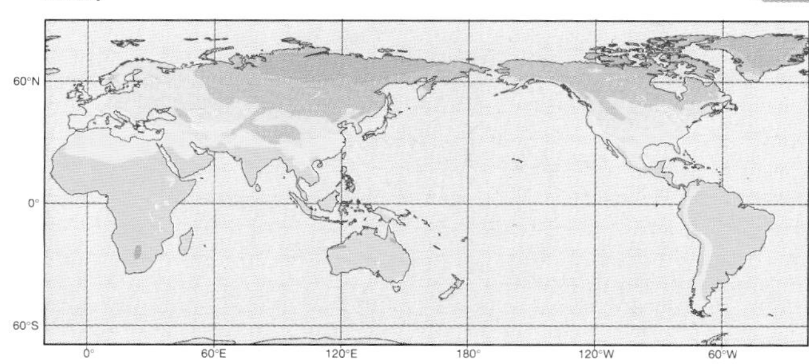

Fig. #08
Actual surface temperature
July

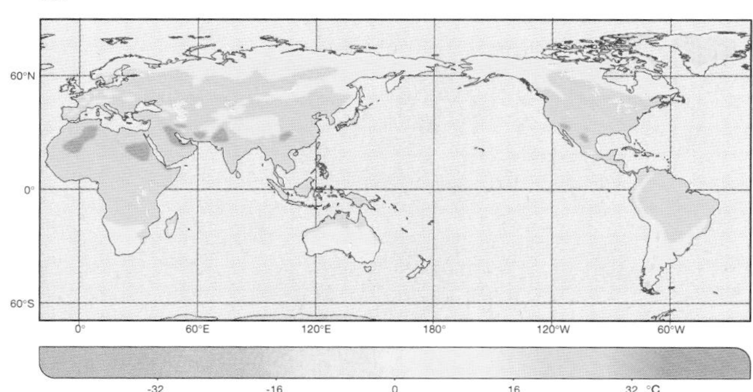

-32   -16   0   16   32 °C

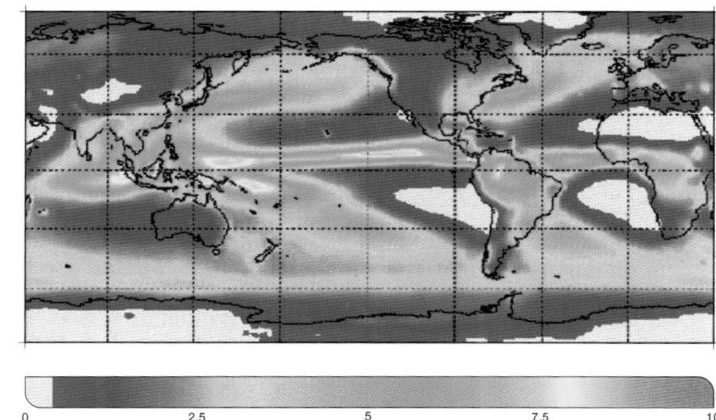

Fig. #09
Average annual precipitation

0   2.5   5   7.5   10
Precipitation (mm per day)

WORLD
WEATHER EXTREMES

Highest shade temperature	57.8°C/136°F Al 'Azīzīyah, Libya (13th September 1922)
Hottest place — Annual mean	34.4°C/93.9°F Dalol, Ethiopia
Driest place — Annual mean	0.1 mm/0.004 inches Atacama Desert, Chile
Most sunshine — Annual mean	90% Yuma, Arizona, USA (over 4 000 hours)
Least sunshine	Nil for 182 days each year, South Pole
Lowest screen temperature	-89.2°C/-128.6°F Vostok Station, Antarctica (21st July 1983)
Coldest place — Annual mean	-56.6°C/-69.9°F Plateau Station, Antarctica
Wettest place — Annual mean	11 873 mm/467.4 inches Meghalaya, India
Most rainy days	Up to 350 per year Mount Waialeale, Hawaii, USA
Windiest place	322 km per hour/200 miles per hour in gales, Commonwealth Bay, Antarctica
Highest surface wind speed	
High altitude	372 km per hour/231 miles per hour Mount Washington, New Hampshire, USA (12th April 1934)
Low altitude	333 km per hour/207 miles per hour Qaanaaq (Thule), Greenland (8th March 1972)
Tornado	512 km per hour/318 miles per hour Oklahoma City, Oklahoma, USA (3rd May 1999)
Greatest snowfall	31 102 mm/1 224.5 inches Mount Rainier, Washington, USA (19th February 1971—18th February 1972)
Heaviest hailstones	1 kg/2.21 lb Gopalganj, Bangladesh (14th April 1986)
Thunder-days Average	251 days per year Tororo, Uganda
Highest barometric pressure	1 083.8 mb Agata, Siberia, Russian Federation (31st December 1968)
Lowest barometric pressure	870 mb 483 km/300 miles west of Guam, Pacific Ocean (12th October 1979)

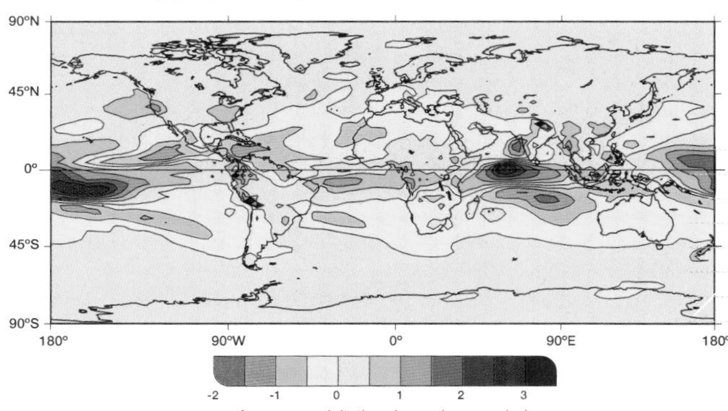

Fig. #10 - #11
Climate changes in the future

#10 Precipitation in 2050s
Predicted average precipitation change

-2 -1 0 1 2 3
Average precipitation change (mm per day)

#11 Temperature in 2050s
Predicted annual mean temperature change

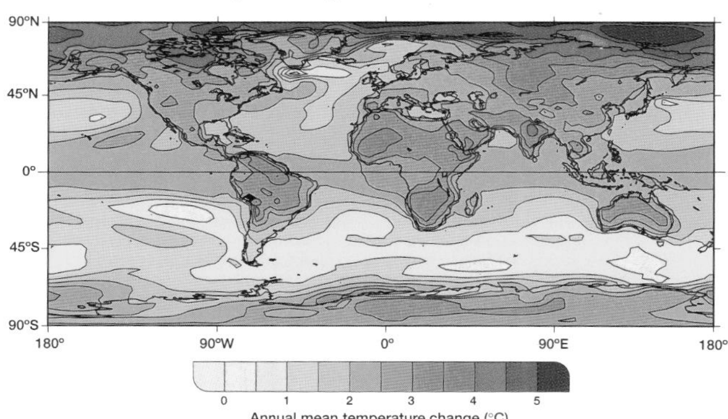

0 1 2 3 4 5
Annual mean temperature change (°C)

1 Wetland

Wetland areas make up less than 1 per cent of world land cover. This aerial photograph of the Okavango Delta in Botswana shows an unusual environment. Set in the centre of southern Africa, the Okavango river drains into this low lying area, not into the sea. The extent of the wetland varies with the amount of rainfall in the catchment area. The high water table allows for a wide diversity of vegetation to grow in an area surrounded by grassland.

2 Crops/Mosaic

Fertile land which is cultivated by man often produces geometric patterns. The infrared satellite image shows part of the Everglades swamp in Florida, USA, east of Lake Okeechobee. Bare fields appear as dark pink and planted fields as green. The pattern continues into the urban areas depicted in blue. Regular field systems such as these enable mechanized agriculture and crop diversification. The dark mottled area to the top right of the image is an undeveloped part of the Everglades.

Satellite/Sensor : Landsat

3 Urban

Representing approximately 0.2 per cent of total world land cover, the urban environment is probably the farthest removed from the Earth's original, natural land cover. This aerial view of Manhattan in New York, USA, shows the 'grid iron' street pattern typical of many modern cities. Major natural features, such as the Hudson River in this image, interrupt this regular plan. Parkland areas, such as that appearing at the top left of the image, are manufactured rather than natural.

4 Grass/Savanna

This view of Ngorongoro, Tanzania is typical of tropical savanna grasslands. Over 25 per cent of Africa's land cover falls within this category. Large areas of tropical grasslands also occur in South America and northern Australia, with temperate grasslands in North America (prairie) and Asia (steppe). Seasonal rainfall provides a regular cycle of lush, tall grass interspersed by scattered trees and shrubs. The savanna areas of east Africa support large numbers of wild animals.

5 Forest/Woodland

The type of woodland coverage in this photograph is tropical rainforest or jungle. This accounts for over 40 per cent of land cover in South America. Dense coverage includes tall hardwood trees which provide a high canopy over smaller trees and shrubs capable of surviving with little direct sunlight. Natural forest or woodland areas such as the Amazon are under continuous threat from the external pressures of agriculture, mineral exploration or urbanization.

6 Barren

The Hoggar region of Algeria is part of the 30 per cent of barren land in Africa, the most extensive land cover type on the continent. This area is a plateau of bare rock lying at a height of over 2 000 m above sea level. It is surrounded by the sandy desert of the Sahara. Rainfall is negligible and the extreme temperatures result in little, or no vegetation and wildlife.

7 Shrubland

Shrubland areas, shown here around Ayers Rock in central Australia, develop on the fringes of desert regions. Sporadic rainfall and less severe temperatures than in the deserts, are enough for hardy plants and shrubs to grow in the thin soil. Moving away from the desert areas, as conditions become less harsh, the vegetation changes and the range of plants increases.

8 Snow/Ice

The continent of Antarctica is almost completely covered by snow and ice. In the northern hemisphere, Spitsbergen, shown here, is one of a large group of islands within the Arctic Circle which is also permanently covered. There is no vegetation on land and any wildlife must survive on food caught in the sea. Although inhospitable areas at the polar extremes see little human interaction, they are affected by global increases in temperature. Resultant melting of glaciers and icecaps threatens a rise in sea level.

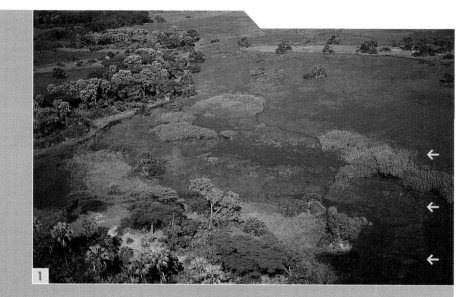

CONNECTIONS

► subject	page#
► Changes to land cover	20–21
► World cities	24–25
► North America environments	162–163
► South America contrasts	194–195
► Arctic regions	210–211

Fig. #01
Continental land cover composition

Legend: Urban, Wetland, Snow/Ice, Barren, Grass/Savanna, Shrubland, Crops/Mosaic, Forest/Woodland

(bar chart: South America, North America, Eurasia, Australia, Antarctica, Africa — Land cover composition (per cent), 0–100)

Fig. #02
Global land cover composition

0.2% 0.9% 11.4% 12.6% 14.0% 14.2% 19.2% 27.5%

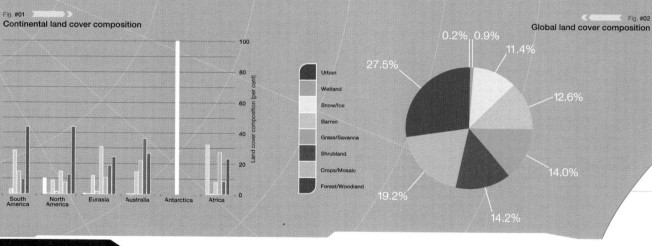

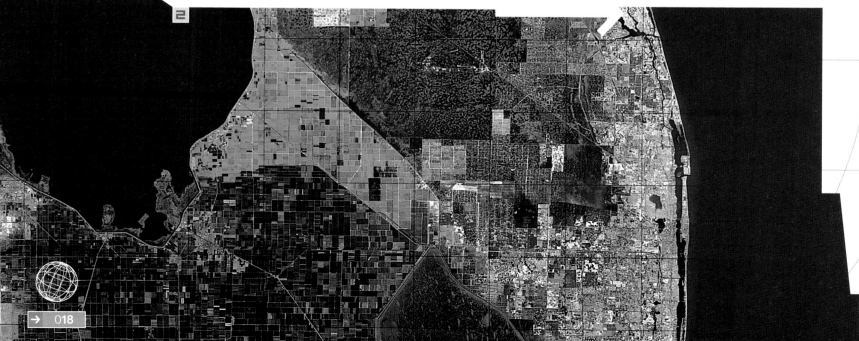

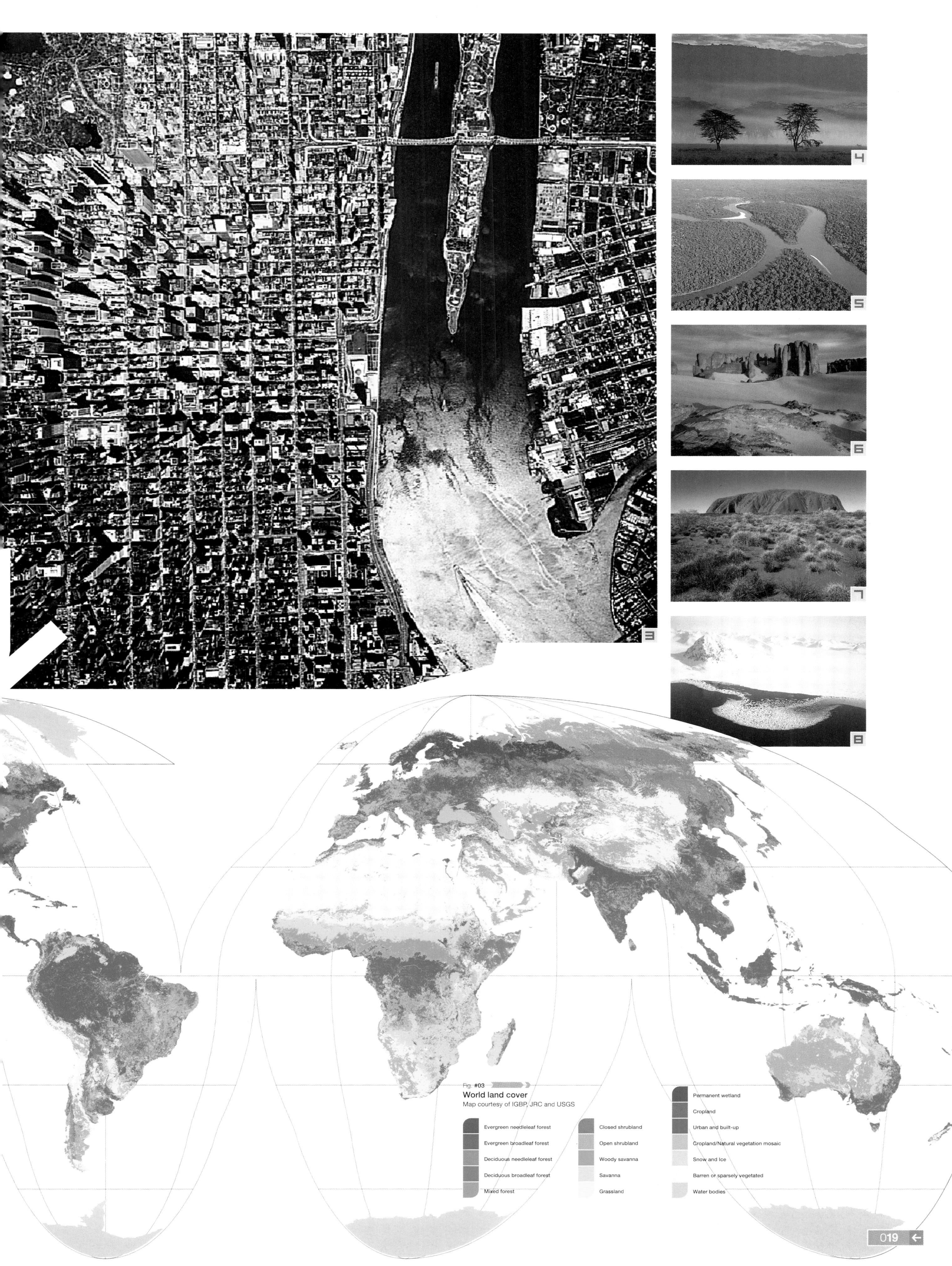

Fig. #03

World land cover
Map courtesy of IGBP, JRC and USGS

Evergreen needleleaf forest

Evergreen broadleaf forest

Deciduous needleleaf forest

Deciduous broadleaf forest

Mixed forest

Closed shrubland

Open shrubland

Woody savanna

Savanna

Grassland

Permanent wetland

Cropland

Urban and built-up

Cropland/Natural vegetation mosaic

Snow and Ice

Barren or sparsely vegetated

Water bodies

2 Changing Land Use

The changes in land use between Alberta, Canada (top) and Montana, USA (bottom) can be seen on this infrared satellite image. The straight international boundary runs diagonally from centre left to upper right. Intense cultivation on the US side has created regular field patterns, whereas on the Canadian side plantations of forest and thick mountain vegetation cover extensive areas.

Satellite/Sensor : Landsat

3 Deforestation

This aerial photograph shows the dramatic effect the clearcut logging method of deforestation can have on a landscape. The change in appearance and the effects on the immediate environment can be dramatic. It shows part of the northwest US state of Washington, which has large areas of thick forest, particularly on the western slopes of the Cascade mountain range. More than half of the state is forested and lumber and lumber-related products form the basis of much of the state's economic activity.

1 Changing River Courses

This aerial infrared photograph shows a small section of the Mississippi river near Lake Providence in Louisiana state. The pattern of old loops and bends identifies old courses of the river, showing changes which have occurred over many years. Some loops have become isolated 'oxbow' lakes as shown on the west bank of the river in the left of the image. At the bottom right one former loop of the river can be identified within the cultivated area.

4 Urban Growth

These Landsat images illustrate how such imagery can be used to monitor environmental change. They show the rapid urban growth which has taken place in and around Shenzhen, China, between 1988 (left) and 1996 (right). This city has benefited greatly from its location adjacent to Hong Kong. One of the most obvious changes is the development along the coastline, where huge off-shore structures and large areas of reclaimed land can be seen in the 1996 image. Much of the vegetation (red) in the left image has been cleared and replaced by urban development, leaving only scattered patches of the original vegetation.

Satellite/Sensor : Landsat

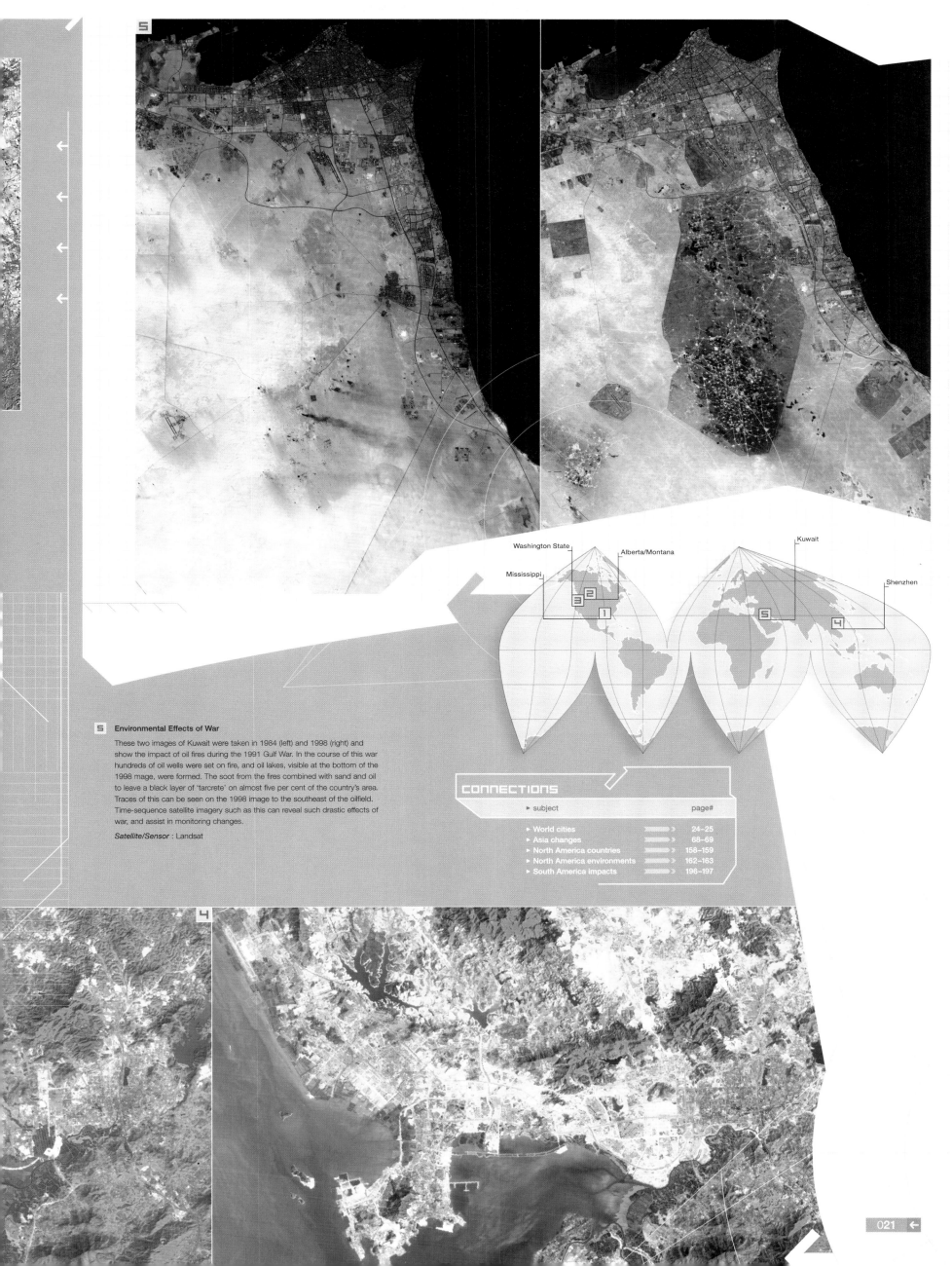

5 Environmental Effects of War

These two images of Kuwait were taken in 1984 (left) and 1998 (right) and show the impact of oil fires during the 1991 Gulf War. In the course of this war hundreds of oil wells were set on fire, and oil lakes, visible at the bottom of the 1998 image, were formed. The soot from the fires combined with sand and oil to leave a black layer of 'tarcrete' on almost five per cent of the country's area. Traces of this can be seen on the 1998 image to the southeast of the oilfield. Time-sequence satellite imagery such as this can reveal such drastic effects of war, and assist in monitoring changes.

Satellite/Sensor : Landsat

Washington State
Alberta/Montana
Mississippi
Kuwait
Shenzhen

CONNECTIONS

► subject		page#
► World cities		24–25
► Asia changes		68–69
► North America countries		158–159
► North America environments		162–163
► South America impacts		196–197

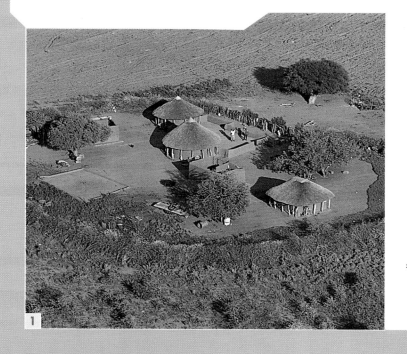

1

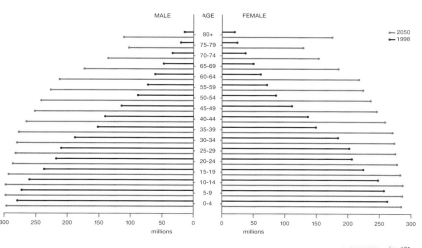

MALE | AGE | FEMALE

| 80+ |
| 75-79 |
| 70-74 |
| 65-69 |
| 60-64 |
| 55-59 |
| 50-54 |
| 45-49 |
| 40-44 |
| 35-39 |
| 30-34 |
| 25-29 |
| 20-24 |
| 15-19 |
| 10-14 |
| 5-9 |
| 0-4 |

300 250 200 150 100 50 0 | 0 50 100 150 200 250 300
millions | millions

— 2050
— 1998

Fig. #01
Age pyramid
Less developed countries

---

1 **Village Settlement,** *Botswana*

The Kalahari Desert stretches across the southwest and central part of Botswana and into Namibia and South Africa. This photograph shows a small village settlement in this very isolated and sparsely populated region. Such villages are usually temporary with the area's people living nomadic lives, moving on to new locations when food sources run low. Although surface water is practically non-existent in the desert, underlying groundwater supports deep-rooted shrubs and trees.

2 **Tokyo,** *Japan*

A small section of Tokyo, the world's largest city and the capital of Japan, is shown in this aerial photograph mosaic. The contrasting pattern of high-rise development and densely packed low-rise buildings is typical of many major Asian cities. While displaying all the characteristics of a modern city, it has retained much of its cultural and historical identity. It is renowned for its excellent transport systems and is the centre of government, industry, commerce and education in Japan.

CONNECTIONS

► subject | page#

► World countries | 10–11
► World cities | 24–25
► Chinese migration | 66–67
► Ethnic groups in the Balkans | 34–35
► Arctic peoples | 214–215

Fig. #03
World population growth by continent
1750-2050

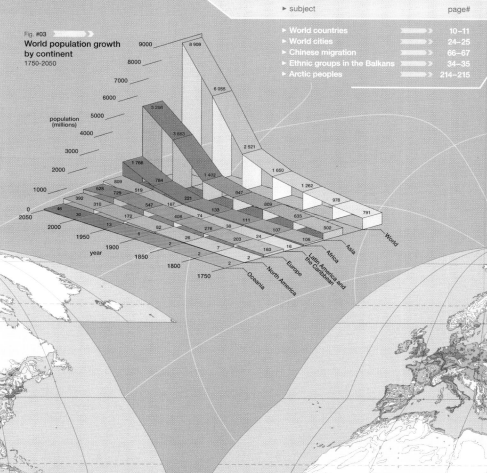

Fig. #04
World population distribution

inhabitants per sq mile	inhabitants per sq km
over 500	over 200
250 – 500	100 – 200
100 – 250	40 – 100
50 – 100	20 – 40
25 – 50	10 – 20
5 – 25	4 – 10
1 – 5	2 – 4
0 – 1	0 – 2
uninhabited	uninhabited

Arctic circle

Equator

Tropic of Capricorn

Antarctic Circle

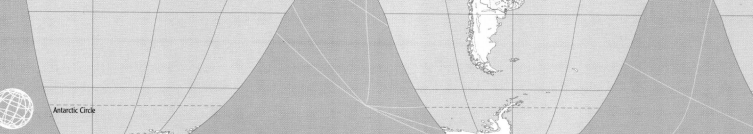

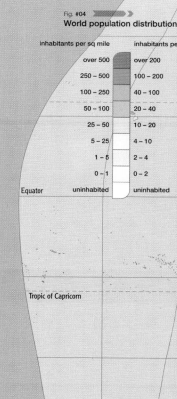

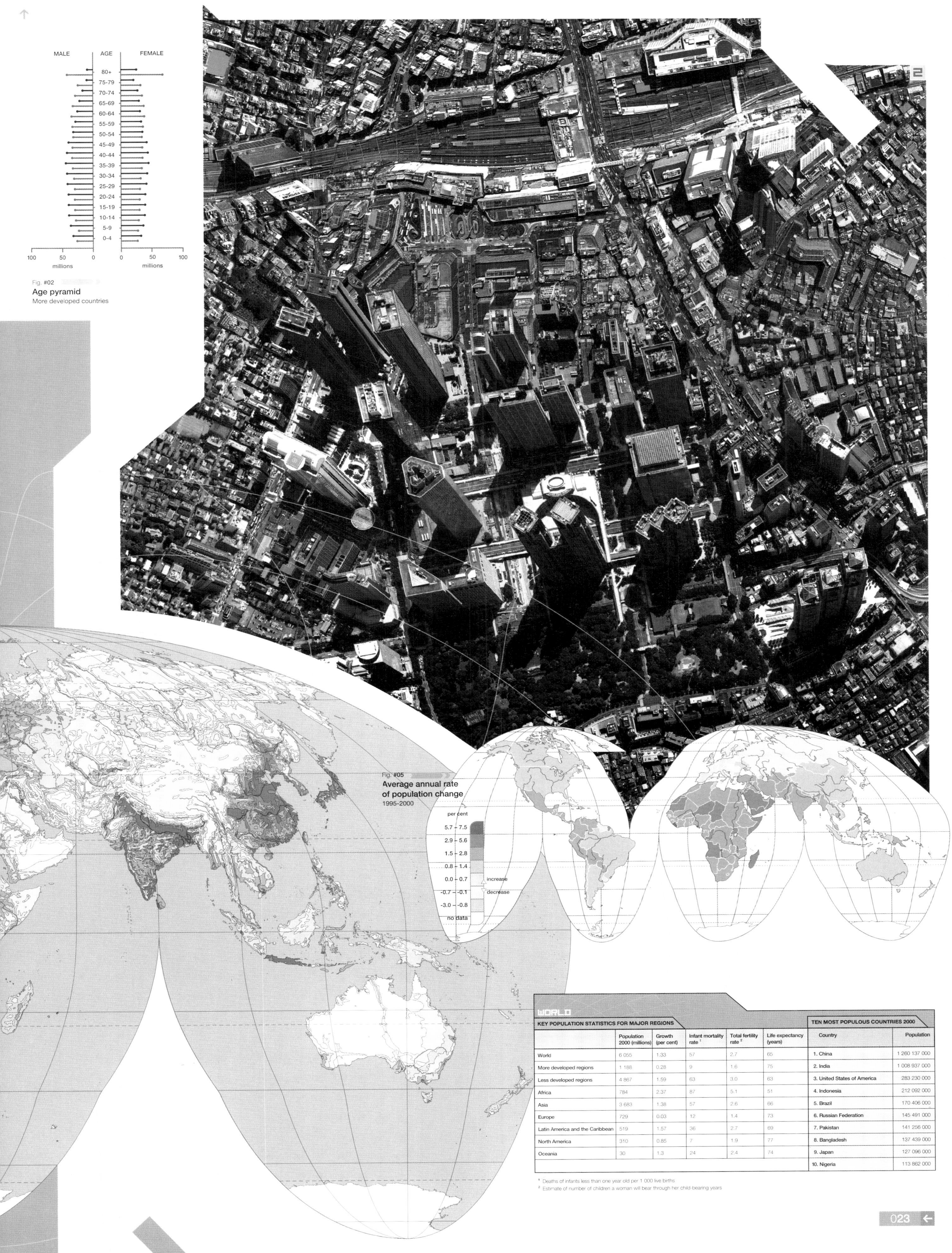

MALE | AGE | FEMALE

80+
75-79
70-74
65-69
60-64
55-59
50-54
45-49
40-44
35-39
30-34
25-29
20-24
15-19
10-14
5-9
0-4

100   50   0   0   50   100
millions   millions

Fig. #02
Age pyramid
More developed countries

Fig. #05
Average annual rate of population change
1995-2000

per cent

5.7 – 7.5
2.9 – 5.6
1.5 – 2.8
0.8 – 1.4
0.0 – 0.7   increase
-0.7 – -0.1   decrease
-3.0 – -0.8
no data

WORLD

KEY POPULATION STATISTICS FOR MAJOR REGIONS

	Population 2000 (millions)	Growth (per cent)	Infant mortality rate [1]	Total fertility rate [2]	Life expectancy (years)
World	6 055	1.33	57	2.7	65
More developed regions	1 188	0.28	9	1.6	75
Less developed regions	4 867	1.59	63	3.0	63
Africa	784	2.37	87	5.1	51
Asia	3 683	1.38	57	2.6	66
Europe	729	0.03	12	1.4	73
Latin America and the Caribbean	519	1.57	36	2.7	69
North America	310	0.85	7	1.9	77
Oceania	30	1.3	24	2.4	74

TEN MOST POPULOUS COUNTRIES 2000

Country	Population
1. China	1 260 137 000
2. India	1 008 937 000
3. United States of America	283 230 000
4. Indonesia	212 092 000
5. Brazil	170 406 000
6. Russian Federation	145 491 000
7. Pakistan	141 256 000
8. Bangladesh	137 439 000
9. Japan	127 096 000
10. Nigeria	113 862 000

[1] Deaths of infants less than one year old per 1 000 live births
[2] Estimate of number of children a woman will bear through her child-bearing years

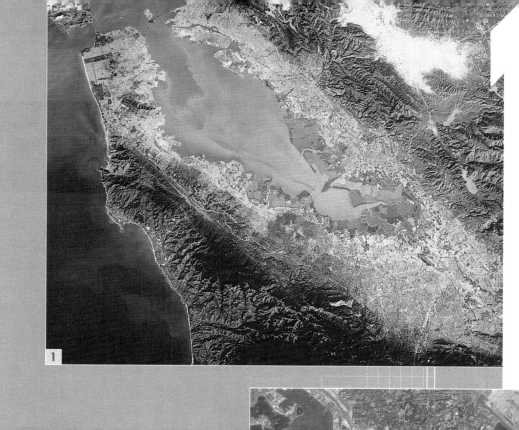

1 San Francisco, *United States of America*

The city of San Francisco is situated on the peninsula which lies to the western side of San Francisco Bay. The Golden Gate, upper left, bridges the entrance to the bay and three other bridges are visible in the image. San Francisco has frequently suffered extensive damage from earthquakes and the two lakes south of the city mark the line of the San Andreas fault. The southern end of the bay is surrounded by a green patchwork of salt beds.

Satellite/Sensor : Landsat

2 Hong Kong, *China*

A British colony until 1997, Hong Kong is now a Special Administrative Region of China. This high resolution satellite image is centred on Hong Kong Harbour, with the Kowloon Peninsula to the north (top) and Hong Kong Island to the south. Much of the coastline shown is reclaimed land, including the old Kai Tak airport, seen in the top right of the image. This airport has been closed since the completion of the new Hong Kong International airport 25 kilometres west of the harbour.

Satellite/Sensor : IKONOS

3 Cairo, *Egypt*

This oblique aerial photograph looks north across the suburbs of southwest Cairo. There has been a major expansion of the city and its suburbs over the last fifty years and the city now has a population of over 10 million. The urban expansion brings the city up against the important historical site of the Giza Pyramids. The Pyramid of Khufu and the Great Sphinx can be seen at the left of the photograph.

4 Tokyo, *Japan*

This false-colour infrared image of Tokyo shows the northwest edge of Tokyo Bay. It shows just a small part of the vast expanse of Tokyo, the world's largest city with over 26 million inhabitants. The amount of land reclamation in the bay is obvious, and the reclaimed land includes Tokyo International (Haneda) Airport, at the bottom of the image. Vegetation shows as red, making the grounds of the Imperial Palace clearly visible in the top left.

Satellite/Sensor : Terra/ASTER

CONNECTIONS

▶ subject	page#
▶ World countries	10–11
▶ World land cover	18–19
▶ Urban growth	20–21
▶ World population	22–23
▶ Oceania capitals	138–139

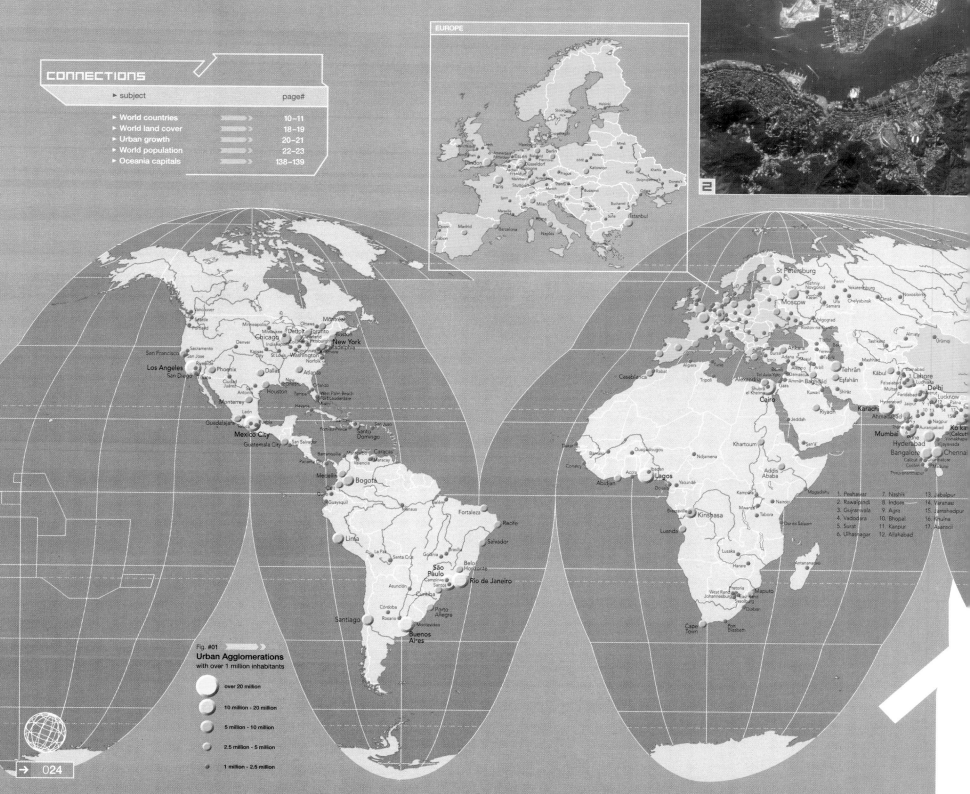

Fig. #01
Urban Agglomerations
with over 1 million inhabitants

- over 20 million
- 10 million - 20 million
- 5 million - 10 million
- 2.5 million - 5 million
- 1 million - 2.5 million

1. Peshawar
2. Rawalpindi
3. Gujranwala
4. Vadodara
5. Surat
6. Ulhasnagar
7. Nashik
8. Indore
9. Agra
10. Bhopal
11. Kanpur
12. Allahabad
13. Jabalpur
14. Varanasi
15. Jamshedpur
16. Khulna
17. Asansol

Fig. #02
10 Million Cities
Dates at which cities attained 10 million population
1950-2015

Fig. #03
World Top 10 Cities
1900-2015

Legend (Fig. #03):
- London
- New York
- Berlin
- Chicago
- Wuhan
- Tokyo
- Philadelphia
- St Petersburg
- Paris
- Moscow
- Shanghai
- Osaka
- Buenos Aires
- Essen
- Kolkata (Calcutta)
- Beijing
- Los Angeles
- Mexico City
- São Paulo
- Mumbai (Bombay)
- Lagos
- Dhaka
- Karachi
- Jakarta

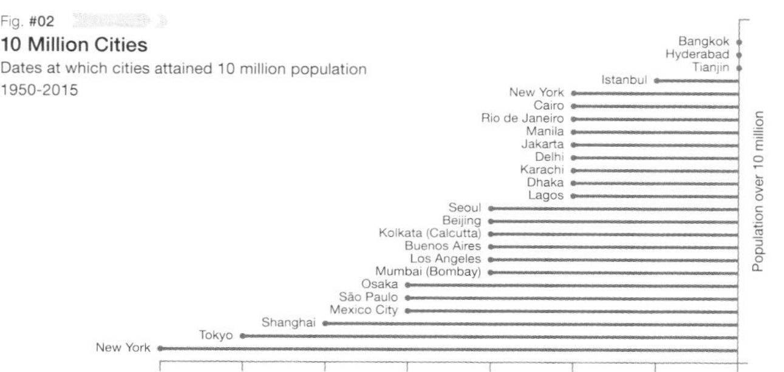

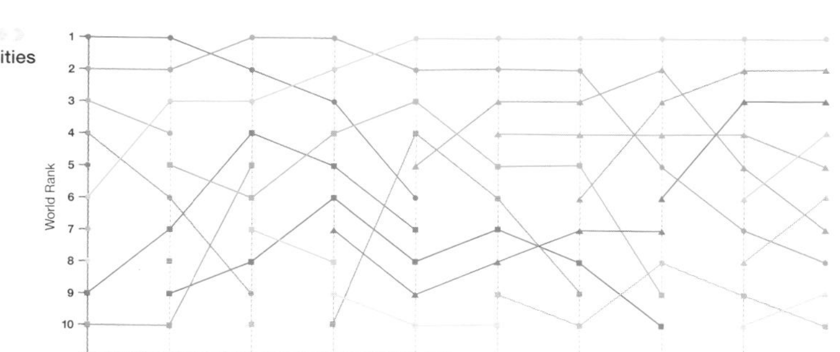

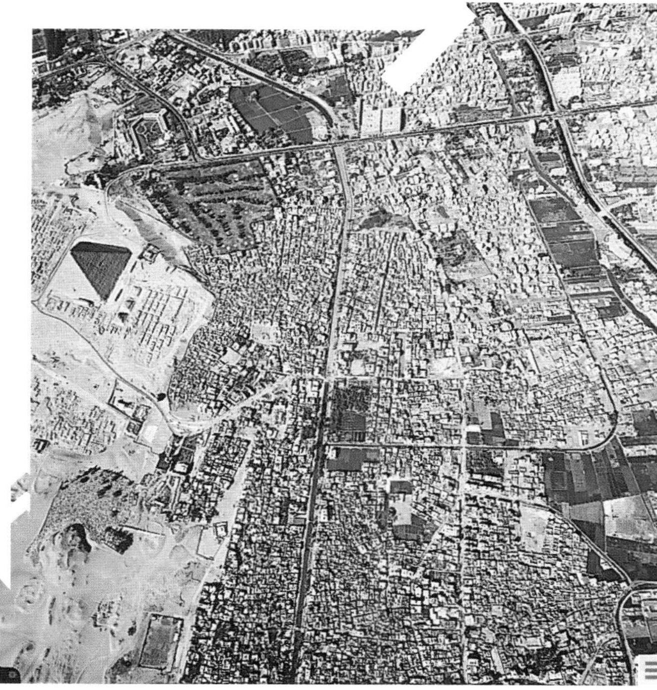

WORLD

THE WORLD'S LARGEST CITIES 2000

city	country	population
Tōkyō	Japan	26 444 000
Mexico City	Mexico	18 131 000
Mumbai (Bombay)	India	18 066 000
São Paulo	Brazil	17 755 000
New York	United States of America	16 640 000
Lagos	Nigeria	13 427 000
Los Angeles	United States of America	13 140 000
Kolkata (Calcutta)	India	12 918 000
Shanghai	China	12 887 000
Buenos Aires	Argentina	12 560 000
Dhaka	Bangladesh	12 317 000
Karachi	Pakistan	11 794 000
Delhi	India	11 695 000
Jakarta	Indonesia	11 018 000
Ōsaka	Japan	11 013 000
Manila	Philippines	10 870 000
Beijing	China	10 839 000
Rio de Janeiro	Brazil	10 582 000
Cairo	Egypt	10 552 000
Seoul	South Korea	9 888 000

CHINA AND JAPAN

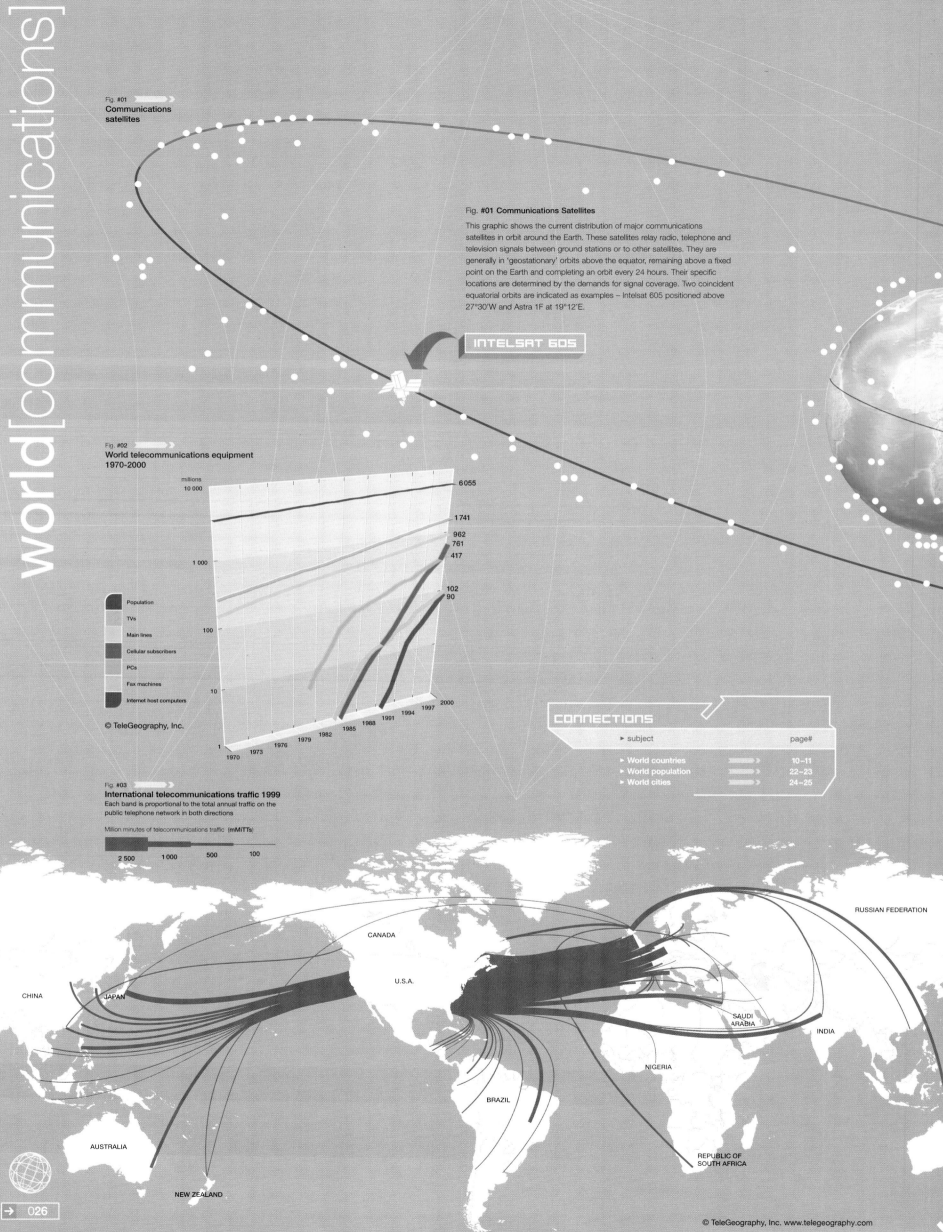

Fig. #01
Communications satellites

Fig. #01 Communications Satellites

This graphic shows the current distribution of major communications satellites in orbit around the Earth. These satellites relay radio, telephone and television signals between ground stations or to other satellites. They are generally in 'geostationary' orbits above the equator, remaining above a fixed point on the Earth and completing an orbit every 24 hours. Their specific locations are determined by the demands for signal coverage. Two coincident equatorial orbits are indicated as examples – Intelsat 605 positioned above 27°30'W and Astra 1F at 19°12'E.

INTELSAT 605

Fig. #02
World telecommunications equipment 1970-2000

millions
10 000

6 055
1 741
962
761
417
102
90

1 000

- Population
- TVs
- Main lines
- Cellular subscribers
- PCs
- Fax machines
- Internet host computers

100

10

© TeleGeography, Inc.

1
1970 1973 1976 1979 1982 1985 1988 1991 1994 1997 2000

CONNECTIONS

► subject		page#
► World countries		10–11
► World population		22–23
► World cities		24–25

Fig. #03
International telecommunications traffic 1999
Each band is proportional to the total annual traffic on the public telephone network in both directions

Million minutes of telecommunications traffic (mMiTTs)

2 500   1 000   500   100

RUSSIAN FEDERATION

CANADA

CHINA

JAPAN

U.S.A.

SAUDI ARABIA

INDIA

NIGERIA

BRAZIL

AUSTRALIA

REPUBLIC OF SOUTH AFRICA

NEW ZEALAND

© TeleGeography, Inc. www.telegeography.com

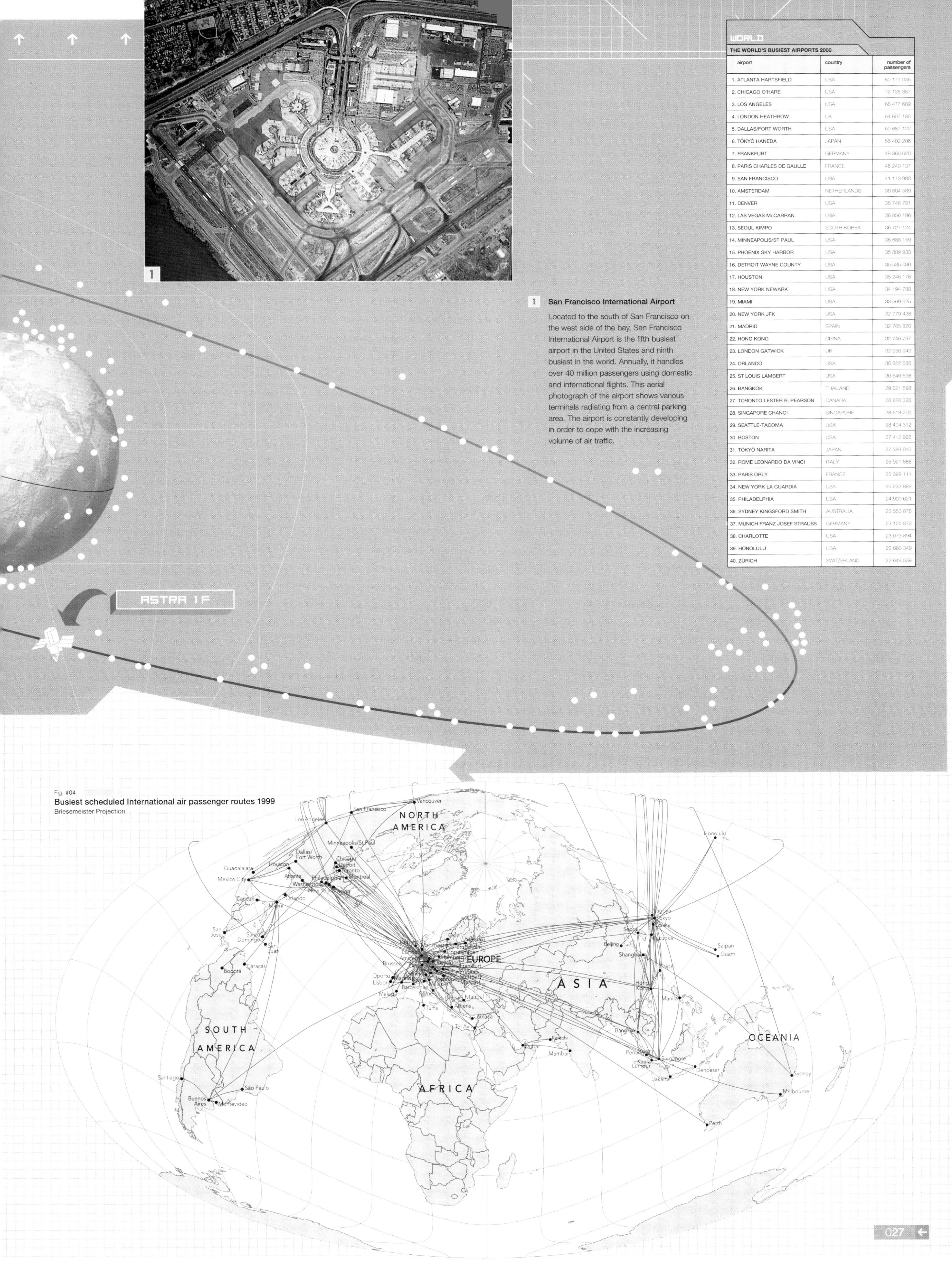

airport	country	number of passengers
1. ATLANTA HARTSFIELD	USA	80 171 036
2. CHICAGO O'HARE	USA	72 135 887
3. LOS ANGELES	USA	68 477 689
4. LONDON HEATHROW	UK	64 607 185
5. DALLAS/FORT WORTH	USA	60 687 122
6. TŌKYŌ HANEDA	JAPAN	56 402 206
7. FRANKFURT	GERMANY	49 360 620
8. PARIS CHARLES DE GAULLE	FRANCE	48 240 137
9. SAN FRANCISCO	USA	41 173 983
10. AMSTERDAM	NETHERLANDS	39 604 589
11. DENVER	USA	38 748 781
12. LAS VEGAS McCARRAN	USA	36 856 186
13. SEOUL KIMPO	SOUTH KOREA	36 727 124
14. MINNEAPOLIS/ST PAUL	USA	36 688 159
15. PHOENIX SKY HARBOR	USA	35 889 933
16. DETROIT WAYNE COUNTY	USA	35 535 080
17. HOUSTON	USA	35 246 176
18. NEW YORK NEWARK	USA	34 194 788
19. MIAMI	USA	33 569 625
20. NEW YORK JFK	USA	32 779 428
21. MADRID	SPAIN	32 765 820
22. HONG KONG	CHINA	32 746 737
23. LONDON GATWICK	UK	32 056 942
24. ORLANDO	USA	30 822 580
25. ST LOUIS LAMBERT	USA	30 546 698
26. BANGKOK	THAILAND	29 621 898
27. TORONTO LESTER B. PEARSON	CANADA	28 820 326
28. SINGAPORE CHANGI	SINGAPORE	28 618 200
29. SEATTLE-TACOMA	USA	28 404 312
30. BOSTON	USA	27 412 926
31. TŌKYŌ NARITA	JAPAN	27 389 915
32. ROME LEONARDO DA VINCI	ITALY	25 921 886
33. PARIS ORLY	FRANCE	25 399 111
34. NEW YORK LA GUARDIA	USA	25 233 889
35. PHILADELPHIA	USA	24 900 621
36. SYDNEY KINGSFORD SMITH	AUSTRALIA	23 553 878
37. MUNICH FRANZ JOSEF STRAUSS	GERMANY	23 125 872
38. CHARLOTTE	USA	23 073 894
39. HONOLULU	USA	22 660 349
40. ZÜRICH	SWITZERLAND	22 649 539

1 San Francisco International Airport

Located to the south of San Francisco on the west side of the bay, San Francisco International Airport is the fifth busiest airport in the United States and ninth busiest in the world. Annually, it handles over 40 million passengers using domestic and international flights. This aerial photograph of the airport shows various terminals radiating from a central parking area. The airport is constantly developing in order to cope with the increasing volume of air traffic.

ASTRA 1F

Fig. #04
Busiest scheduled International air passenger routes 1999
Briesemeister Projection

Alps, *France*

europe

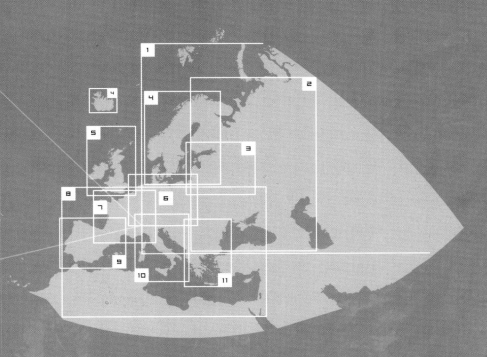

[contents]

		page#
europe [landscapes]		30–31
europe [countries]		32–33
europe [countries/issues]		34–35
europe [environments]		36–37

	map coverage	scale	page#
europe [map 1]	RUSSIAN FEDERATION	1:18 000 000	38-39
europe [map 2]	RUSSIAN FEDERATION West	1:7 500 000	40–41
europe [map 3]	ESTONIA, LATVIA, LITHUANIA and the MOSCOW REGION	1:3 000 000	42–43
europe [map 4]	ICELAND, NORWAY, SWEDEN, FINLAND and DENMARK	1:4 500 000	44–45
europe [map 5]	UNITED KINGDOM and REPUBLIC OF IRELAND	1:3 000 000	46–47
europe [map 6]	EUROPE North Central	1:3 000 000	48–49
europe [map 7]	FRANCE and SWITZERLAND	1:3 000 000	50–51
europe [map 8]	EUROPE South and the MEDITERRANEAN	1:9 000 000	52–53
europe [map 9]	SPAIN and PORTUGAL	1:3 000 000	54–55
europe [map 10]	ITALY, SLOVENIA, CROATIA and BOSNIA-HERZEGOVINA	1:3 000 000	56–57
europe [map 11]	EUROPE Southeast	1:3 000 000	58–59

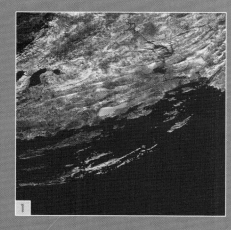

Dalmatia, *Croatia*

The Dalmatian coast of Croatia joins the Adriatic Sea in a series of mountainous limestone ridges running parallel to the coast. The mountains continue into the sea leaving strings of long, thin fragmented islands. The Krka river, to the right of this image, is one of a very few rivers which cross this remote region. The soil is thin and patchy but such a coastline provides many sheltered harbours. The large lake which appears green has a high salt content which has seeped through from the sea.

Satellite/Sensor : Space Shuttle

Europe, the world's second smallest continent, is located on the western tip of the vast Eurasian land-mass. The curve of mountain ranges, which includes the Alps, the Pyrenees and the Carpathians divides the north of the continent from the south. The highest peak in Europe, Mt Elbrus (5 642 m) lies in the Caucasus, the mountain range between the Black Sea and the Caspian Sea. North of these mountains, the rolling plains of Ukraine and European Russia extend to the Ural Mountains which, together with the Caucasus and the Bosporus in Turkey, form the physical boundary between Europe and Asia.

The Mediterranean Sea, in the south, is a large inland sea which is enclosed by mainland Europe to the north and west, Africa to the south, and Asia to the east. The Strait of Gibraltar connects the Mediterranean to the Atlantic Ocean on the west and in the southeast the Suez canal is the seaway to the Red Sea.

Largest island

Great Britain
218 476 sq km / 84 354 sq miles
Map reference 47 J7

CONNECTIONS

▸ subject		page#
▸ Types of imagery	⟩⟩⟩	4–5
▸ World physical features	⟩⟩⟩	8–9
▸ Arctic land cover	⟩⟩⟩	18–19
▸ European states and territories	⟩⟩⟩	32–33
▸ Reference maps of Europe	⟩⟩⟩	38–59

Spitsbergen

Norwegian Sea

Scandinavia

Gul
Botl

North Sea

Elbe River

Rhine River

Great Britain

Ireland

Seine River

English Channel

Faroe Islands

Loire River

Massif Central

Bay of Biscay

Pyrenees

Balear

Atlantic Ocean

Iberian Peninsula

Tagus River

Strait of Gibraltar

Alps, *Europe*

The snow-capped crescent-shaped Alps, seen here in early spring, separate Italy from the rest of central Europe. The valley in the lower centre of the image is that of the Po river and also visible are Lake Garda, right of centre, and Lake Geneva left of the snow covered area. The Alps are the source of several major European rivers including the Danube, Rhine and Rhone. The highest peak in the mountain range, Mont Blanc 4 804 m, is located on the France/Italy border, centre left on the image.

Satellite/Sensor : MODIS

Volga Delta, *Russian Federation*

The Volga river flows south into the Caspian Sea, over 3 600 km from its source, making it Europe's longest river. In this high oblique shuttle photograph the river delta, viewed from the north, fans out into the landlocked Caspian Sea. The city of Astrakhan is situated at the head of the delta on the west bank of the river. The silt from the delta provides a rich environment for flora and fauna.

Satellite/Sensor : Space Shuttle

Barents Sea

Novaya Zemlya

Lappland

Ural Mountains

Lake Ladoga

Baltic Sea

North European Plain

Vistula River

Don River

Volga River

Dnieper River

Elbrus

Caspian Sea

Carpathian Mountains

Crimea

Caucasus

Danube River

Black Sea

Alps

Bosporus

Po River

Dalmatia

Adriatic Sea

Apennines

Corsica

Sardinia

Sicily

Crete

Mediterranean Sea

Islands

Highest point

Elbrus
Russian Federation
5 642 m / 18 510 feet
Map reference 107 E2

Longest river

Volga
3 688 km / 2 291 miles
Drainage basin
1 380 000 sq km / 533 000 sq miles
Map reference 41 I7

Largest lake

Caspian Sea
371 000sq km / 143 243 sq miles
Map reference 102 B4

EUROPE

HIGHEST MOUNTAINS	m	ft	location	map
Elbrus	5 642	18 510	Russian Federation	107 E2
Gora Dykh-Tau	5 204	17 073	Russian Federation	41 G8
Shkhara	5 201	17 063	Georgia/Russian Federation	41 G8
Kazbek	5 047	16 558	Georgia/Russian Federation	107 F2
Mont Blanc	4 808	15 774	France/Italy	51 M7
Durfourspitze	4 634	15 203	Italy/Switzerland	51 N7

LARGEST ISLANDS	sq km	sq miles	map
Great Britain	218 476	84 354	47 J9
Iceland	102 820	39 699	44 inset
Novaya Zemlya	90 650	35 000	38 T2
Ireland	83 045	32 064	47 D11
Spitzbergen	37 814	14 600	38 B2
Sicily	25 426	9 817	57 F1

LONGEST RIVERS	km	miles	map
Volga	3 688	2 291	41 I7
Danube	2 850	1 770	58 K3
Dnieper	2 285	1 419	41 E7
Kama	2 028	1 260	40 J4
Don	1 931	1 199	41 F7
Pechora	1 802	1 119	38 F3

LAKES	sq km	sq miles	map
Caspian Sea	371 000	143 243	102 B4
Lake Ladoga	18 390	7 100	40 D3
Lake Onega	9 600	3 706	40 E3
Vanern	5 585	2 156	45 C4
Rybinskoye Vodokhranilishche	5 180	2 000	43 T3

LAND AREA		map
Most northerly point	Ostrov Rudol'fa, Russian Federation	38 F1
Most southerly point	Gavdos, Crete, Greece	59 F14
Most westerly point	Bjargtangar, Iceland	44 A2
Most easterly point	Mys Flissingskiy, Russian Federation	39 G2
Total land area: 9 908 599 sq km / 3 825 731 sq miles		

EUROPE
COUNTRIES

		area sq km	area sq miles	population	capital	languages	religions	currency	map
ALBANIA		28 748	11 100	3 134 000	Tirana (Tiranë)	Albanian, Greek	Sunni Muslim, Albanian Orthodox, Roman Catholic	Lek	58–59
ANDORRA		465	180	86 000	Andorra la Vella	Spanish, Catalan, French	Roman Catholic	French franc, Spanish peseta	55
AUSTRIA		83 855	32 377	8 080 000	Vienna (Wien)	German, Croatian, Turkish	Roman Catholic, Protestant	Schilling, Euro	48–49
BELARUS		207 600	80 155	10 187 000	Minsk	Belorussian, Russian	Belorussian Orthodox, Roman Catholic	Rouble	42–43
BELGIUM		30 520	11 784	10 249 000	Brussels (Bruxelles)	Dutch (Flemish), French (Walloon), German	Roman Catholic, Protestant	Franc, Euro	51
BOSNIA–HERZEGOVINA		51 130	19 741	3 977 000	Sarajevo	Bosnian, Serbian, Croatian	Sunni Muslim, Serbian Orthodox, Roman Catholic, Protestant	Marka	56
BULGARIA		110 994	42 855	7 949 000	Sofia (Sofiya)	Bulgarian, Turkish, Romany, Macedonian	Bulgarian Orthodox, Sunni Muslim	Lev	58
CROATIA		56 538	21 829	4 654 000	Zagreb	Croatian, Serbian	Roman Catholic, Serbian Orthodox, Sunni Muslim	Kuna	56
CZECH REPUBLIC		78 864	30 450	10 272 000	Prague (Praha)	Czech, Moravian, Slovak	Roman Catholic, Protestant	Koruna	49
DENMARK		43 075	16 631	5 320 000	Copenhagen (København)	Danish	Protestant	Krone	45
ESTONIA		45 200	17 452	1 393 000	Tallinn	Estonian, Russian	Protestant, Estonian and Russian Orthodox	Kroon	42
FINLAND		338 145	130 559	5 172 000	Helsinki (Helsingfors)	Finnish, Swedish	Protestant, Greek Orthodox	Markka, Euro	44–45
FRANCE		543 965	210 026	59 238 000	Paris	French, Arabic	Roman Catholic, Protestant, Sunni Muslim	Franc, Euro	50–51
GERMANY		357 028	137 849	82 017 000	Berlin	German, Turkish	Protestant, Roman Catholic	Mark, Euro	48–49
GREECE		131 957	50 949	10 610 000	Athens (Athina)	Greek	Greek Orthodox, Sunni Muslim	Drachma	58–59
HUNGARY		93 030	35 919	9 968 000	Budapest	Hungarian	Roman Catholic, Protestant	Forint	49
ICELAND		102 820	39 699	279 000	Reykjavik	Icelandic	Protestant	Króna	44
IRELAND, REPUBLIC OF		70 282	27 136	3 803 000	Dublin (Baile Átha Cliath)	English, Irish	Roman Catholic, Protestant	Punt, Euro	46–47
ITALY		301 245	116 311	57 530 000	Rome (Roma)	Italian	Roman Catholic	Lira, Euro	56–57
LATVIA		63 700	24 595	2 421 000	Riga	Latvian, Russian	Protestant, Roman Catholic, Russian Orthodox	Lat	42
LIECHTENSTEIN		160	62	33 000	Vaduz	German	Roman Catholic, Protestant	Swiss franc	51
LITHUANIA		65 200	25 174	3 696 000	Vilnius	Lithuanian, Russian, Polish	Roman Catholic, Protestant, Russian Orthodox	Litas	42
LUXEMBOURG		2 586	998	437 000	Luxembourg	Letzeburgish, German, French	Roman Catholic	Franc, Euro	51
MACEDONIA (F.Y.R.O.M.)		25 713	9 928	2 034 000	Skopje	Macedonian, Albanian, Turkish	Macedonian Orthodox, Sunni Muslim	Denar	58
MALTA		316	122	390 000	Valletta	Maltese, English	Roman Catholic	Lira	57
MOLDOVA		33 700	13 012	4 295 000	Chişinău (Kishinev)	Romanian, Ukrainian, Gagauz, Russian	Romanian Orthodox, Russian Orthodox	Leu	41
MONACO		2	1	33 000	Monaco-Ville	French, Monegasque, Italian	Roman Catholic	French franc	51
NETHERLANDS		41 526	16 033	15 864 000	Amsterdam/The Hague	Dutch, Frisian	Roman Catholic, Protestant, Sunni Muslim	Guilder, Euro	48
NORWAY		323 878	125 050	4 469 000	Oslo	Norwegian	Protestant, Roman Catholic	Krone	44–45

CONNECTIONS

▶ subject	page#
▶ World countries	10–11
▶ Europe landscapes	30–31
▶ Europe issues	34–35
▶ Reference maps of Europe	38–59
▶ Atlantic Ocean	216–217

1   **Rock of Gibraltar**, *Gibraltar, Europe*

The narrow passage of water, appearing as a horizontal band of blue across the centre of this photograph is the 13 km wide Strait of Gibraltar which connects the Atlantic Ocean to the Mediterranean Sea. The strait forms a physical boundary between the continents of Europe and Africa. The photograph shows the 426 m high Rock of Gibraltar, viewed from Ceuta, a small Spanish enclave in Morocco, on the northern coast of Africa.

2   **Bosporus**, *Turkey, Europe/Asia*

The continents of Europe and Asia are physically separated by a narrow strait of water, the Bosporus, in Turkey. The strait, which at its narrowest point is less than 1 km wide, is 31 km long and connects the Sea of Marmara in the north to the Black Sea in the south. It is straddled by the city of Istanbul. The strait and the city are clearly shown in this SPOT satellite image. Istanbul airport is located near the coast toward the lower left of the image.

Satellite/Sensor : SPOT

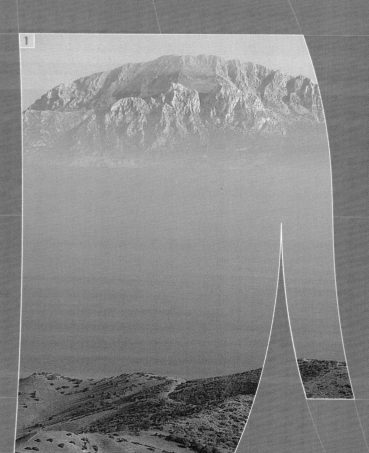

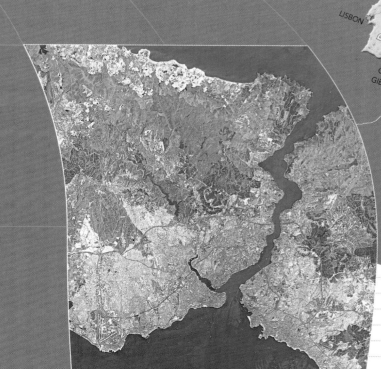

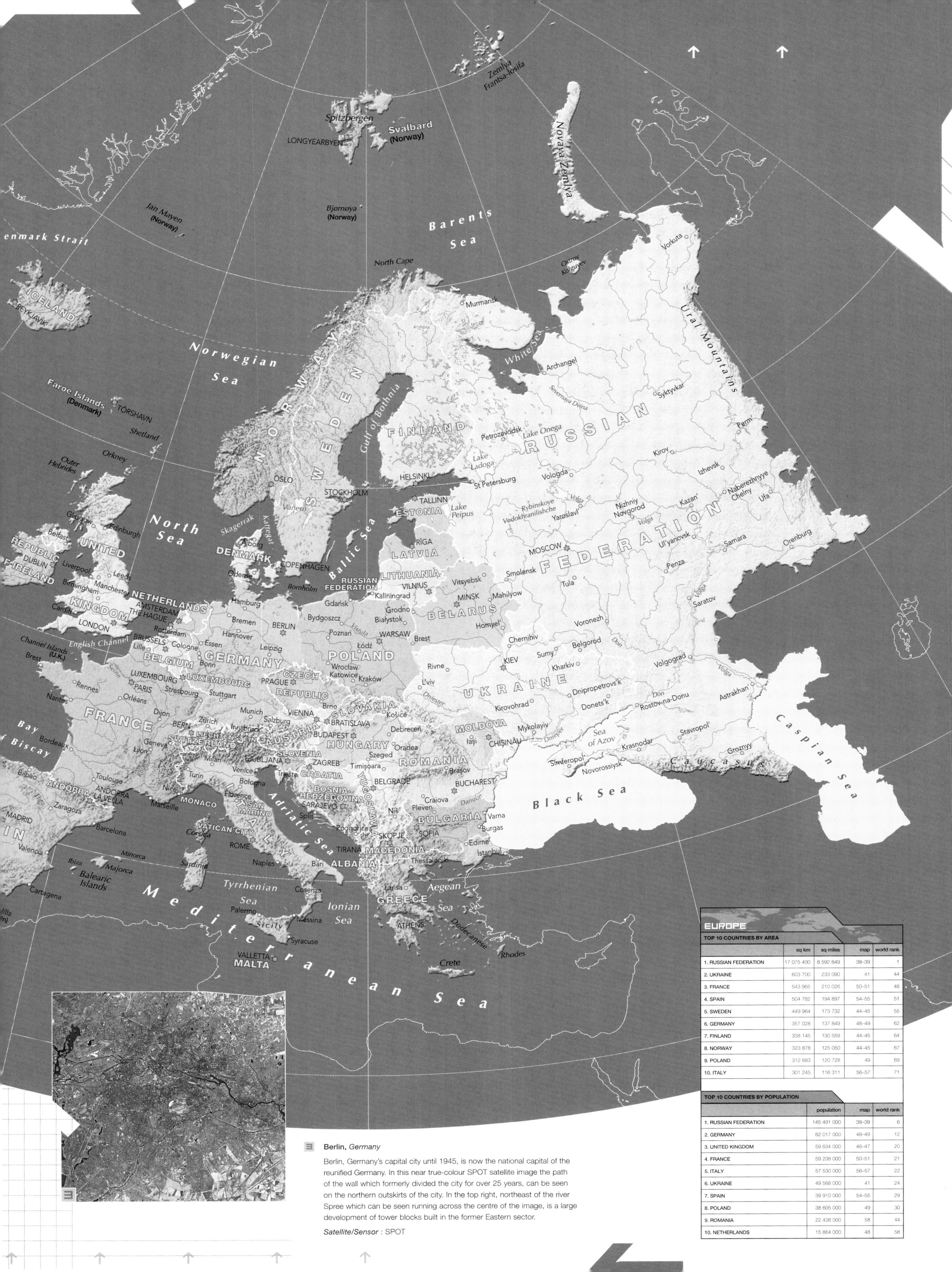

Berlin, Germany

Berlin, Germany's capital city until 1945, is now the national capital of the reunified Germany. In this near true-colour SPOT satellite image the path of the wall which formerly divided the city for over 25 years, can be seen on the northern outskirts of the city. In the top right, northeast of the river Spree which can be seen running across the centre of the image, is a large development of tower blocks built in the former Eastern sector.

Satellite/Sensor : SPOT

EUROPE

TOP 10 COUNTRIES BY AREA

	sq km	sq miles	map	world rank
1. RUSSIAN FEDERATION	17 075 400	6 592 849	38–39	1
2. UKRAINE	603 700	233 090	41	44
3. FRANCE	543 965	210 026	50–51	48
4. SPAIN	504 782	194 897	54–55	51
5. SWEDEN	449 964	173 732	44–45	55
6. GERMANY	357 028	137 849	48–49	62
7. FINLAND	338 145	130 559	44–45	64
8. NORWAY	323 878	125 050	44–45	67
9. POLAND	312 683	120 728	49	69
10. ITALY	301 245	116 311	56–57	71

TOP 10 COUNTRIES BY POPULATION

	population	map	world rank
1. RUSSIAN FEDERATION	145 491 000	38–39	6
2. GERMANY	82 017 000	48–49	12
3. UNITED KINGDOM	59 634 000	46–47	20
4. FRANCE	59 238 000	50–51	21
5. ITALY	57 530 000	56–57	22
6. UKRAINE	49 568 000	41	24
7. SPAIN	39 910 000	54–55	29
8. POLAND	38 605 000	49	30
9. ROMANIA	22 438 000	58	44
10. NETHERLANDS	15 864 000	48	58

EUROPE
COUNTRIES

		area sq km	area sq miles	population	capital	languages	religions	currency	map
POLAND		312 683	120 728	38 605 000	Warsaw (Warszawa)	Polish, German	Roman Catholic, Polish Orthodox	Złoty	49
PORTUGAL		88 940	34 340	10 016 000	Lisbon (Lisboa)	Portuguese	Roman Catholic, Protestant	Escudo, Euro	54
ROMANIA		237 500	91 699	22 438 000	Bucharest (Bucureşti)	Romanian, Hungarian	Romanian Orthodox, Protestant, Roman Catholic	Leu	58
RUSSIAN FEDERATION		17 075 400	6 592 849	145 491 000	Moscow (Moskva)	Russian, Tatar, Ukrainian, local languages	Russian Orthodox, Sunni Muslim, Protestant	Rouble	38–39
SAN MARINO		61	24	27 000	San Marino	Italian	Roman Catholic	Italian lira	56
SLOVAKIA		49 035	18 933	5 399 000	Bratislava	Slovak, Hungarian, Czech	Roman Catholic, Protestant, Orthodox	Koruna	49
SLOVENIA		20 251	7 819	1 988 000	Ljubljana	Slovene, Croatian, Serbian	Roman Catholic, Protestant	Tólar	56
SPAIN		504 782	194 897	39 910 000	Madrid	Castilian, Catalan, Galician, Basque	Roman Catholic	Peseta, Euro	54–55
SWEDEN		449 964	173 732	8 842 000	Stockholm	Swedish	Protestant, Roman Catholic	Krona	44–45
SWITZERLAND		41 293	15 943	7 170 000	Bern (Berne)	German, French, Italian, Romansch	Roman Catholic, Protestant	Franc	51
UKRAINE		603 700	233 090	49 568 000	Kiev (Kyïv)	Ukrainian, Russian	Ukrainian Orthodox, Ukrainian Catholic, Roman Catholic	Hryvnia	41
UNITED KINGDOM		244 082	94 241	59 634 000	London	English, Welsh, Gaelic	Protestant, Roman Catholic, Muslim	Pound	46–47
VATICAN CITY		0.5	0.2	480	Vatican City	Italian	Roman Catholic	Italian lira	56
YUGOSLAVIA		102 173	39 449	10 552 000	Belgrade (Beograd)	Serbian, Albanian, Hungarian	Serbian Orthodox, Montenegrin Orthodox, Sunni Muslim	Dinar	58

DEPENDENT TERRITORIES

		territorial status	area sq km	area sq miles	population	capital	languages	religions	currency	map
Azores (Arquipélago dos Açores)		Autonomous Region of Portugal	2 300	888	243 600	Ponta Delgada	Portuguese	Roman Catholic, Protestant	Port. Escudo	216
Faroe Islands		Self-governing Danish Territory	1 399	540	46 000	Tóshavn (Thorshavn)	Faroese, Danish	Protestant	Danish krone	46
Gibraltar		United Kingdom Overseas Territory	7	3	27 000	Gibraltar	English, Spanish	Roman Catholic, Protestant, Sunni Muslim	Pound	54
Guernsey		United Kingdom Crown Dependency	78	30	64 555	St Peter Port	English, French	Protestant, Roman Catholic	Pound	50
Isle of Man		United Kingdom Crown Dependency	572	221	77 000	Douglas	English	Protestant, Roman Catholic	Pound	47
Jersey		United Kingdom Crown Dependency	116	45	89 136	St Helier	English, French	Protestant, Roman Catholic	Pound	50

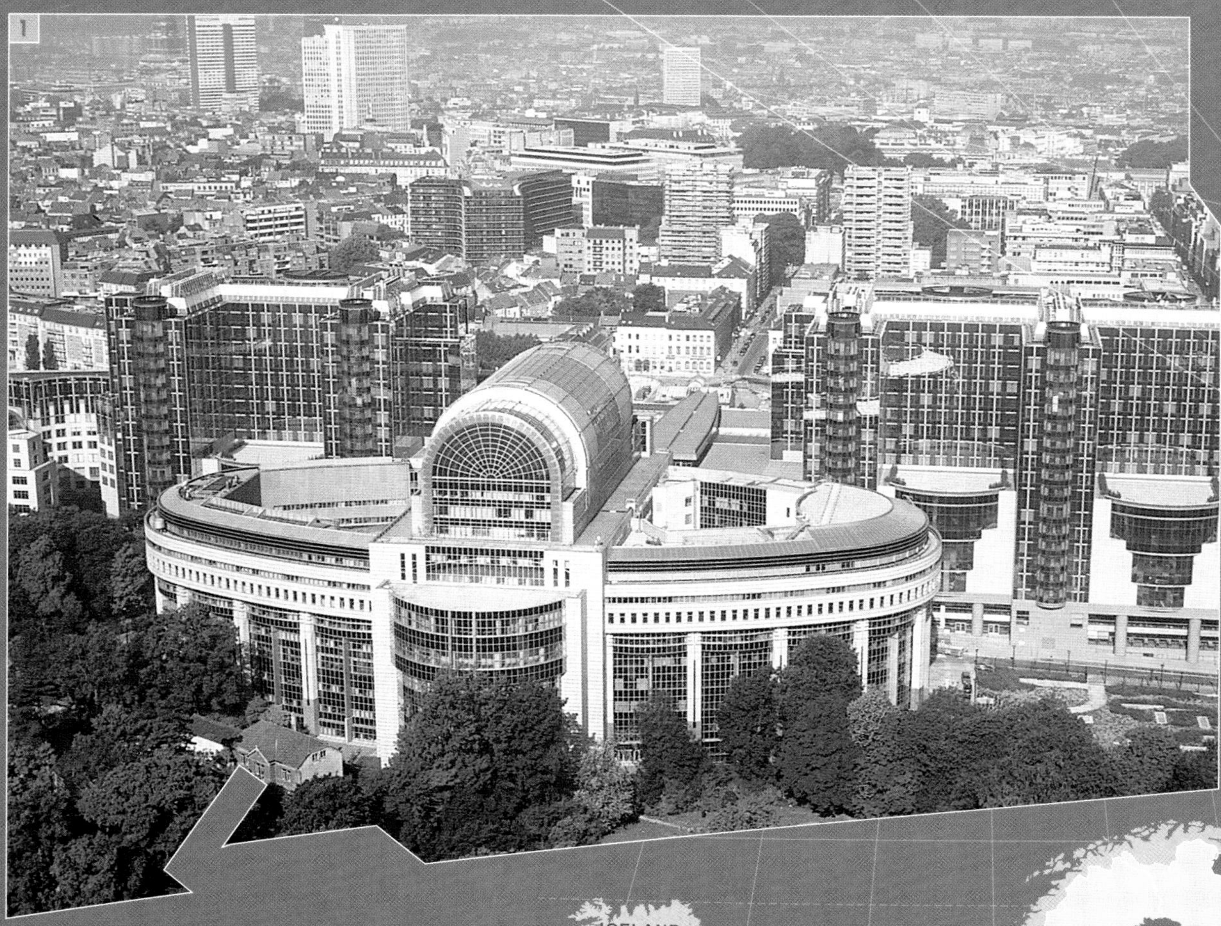

1 The European Union

The European Union (EU) is a union of fifteen independent European states. It was founded as the European Economic Commission by the Treaty of Rome in 1957. Its purpose is to enhance political, economic and social cooperation. As shown on the map, the EU has grown from six to fifteen members and thirteen new applicants are currently negotiating for membership. The headquarters of the EU, in the Belgian capital Brussels, is the curved glass roofed building, known as the Hémicycle Européen, shown in the photograph.

Fig. #01
The European Union

- Founder members (1957)
- Joined in 1973
- Joined in 1981
- Joined in 1986
- Joined in 1995
- Current applicant
- Non-member

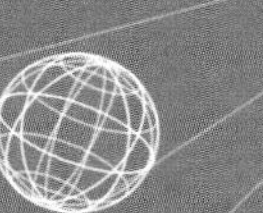

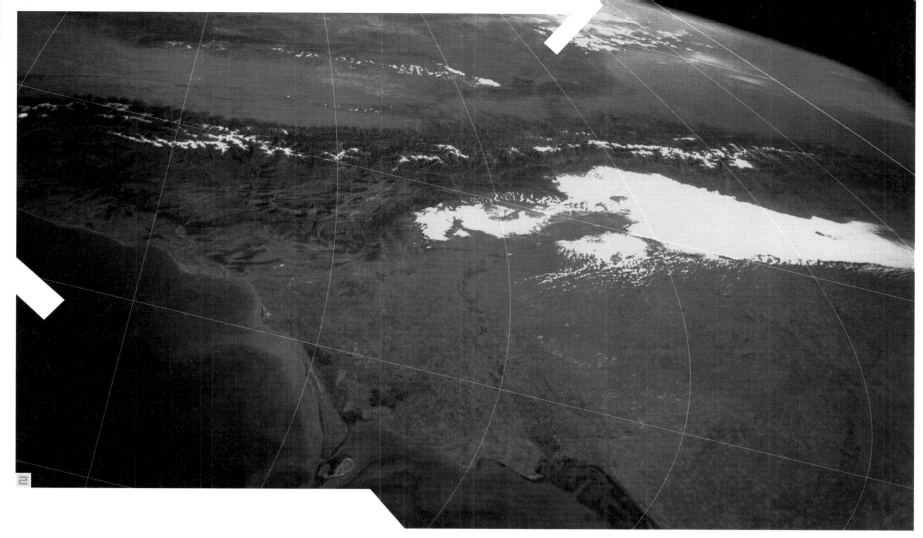

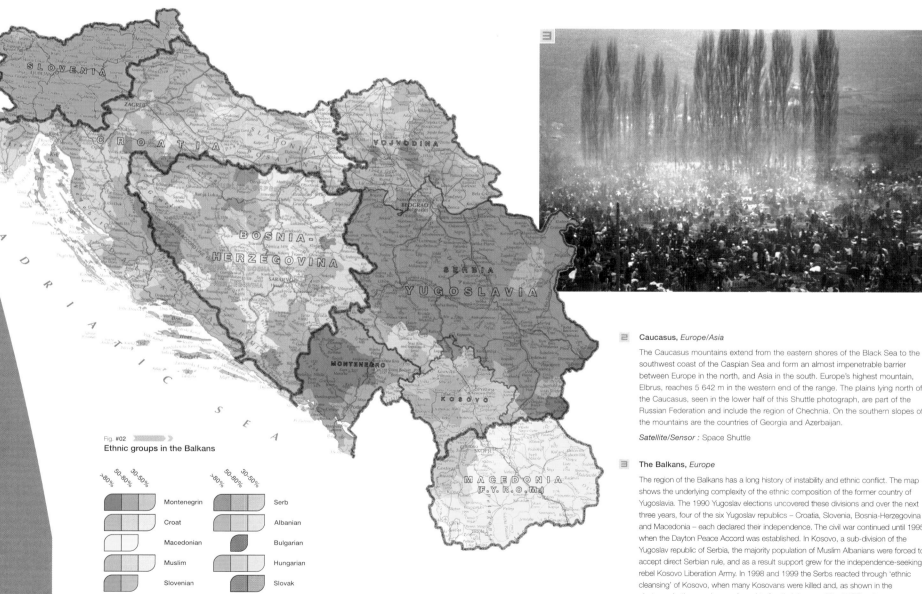

Fig. #02
Ethnic groups in the Balkans

>80%	50-80%	30-50%		>80%	50-80%	30-50%	
			Montenegrin				Serb
			Croat				Albanian
			Macedonian				Bulgarian
			Muslim				Hungarian
			Slovenian				Slovak

2   **Caucasus,** *Europe/Asia*

The Caucasus mountains extend from the eastern shores of the Black Sea to the southwest coast of the Caspian Sea and form an almost impenetrable barrier between Europe in the north, and Asia in the south. Europe's highest mountain, Elbrus, reaches 5 642 m in the western end of the range. The plains lying north of the Caucasus, seen in the lower half of this Shuttle photograph, are part of the Russian Federation and include the region of Chechnia. On the southern slopes of the mountains are the countries of Georgia and Azerbaijan.

Satellite/Sensor : Space Shuttle

3   **The Balkans,** *Europe*

The region of the Balkans has a long history of instability and ethnic conflict. The map shows the underlying complexity of the ethnic composition of the former country of Yugoslavia. The 1990 Yugoslav elections uncovered these divisions and over the next three years, four of the six Yugoslav republics – Croatia, Slovenia, Bosnia-Herzegovina and Macedonia – each declared their independence. The civil war continued until 1995 when the Dayton Peace Accord was established. In Kosovo, a sub-division of the Yugoslav republic of Serbia, the majority population of Muslim Albanians were forced to accept direct Serbian rule, and as a result support grew for the independence-seeking rebel Kosovo Liberation Army. In 1998 and 1999 the Serbs reacted through 'ethnic cleansing' of Kosovo, when many Kosovans were killed and, as shown in the photograph, thousands were forced to flee their homes. After NATO action, an agreement for Serb withdrawal was reached in June 1999.

⌐ CONNECTIONS

► subject	page#
► World physical features	8–9
► World countries	10–11
► Europe landscapes	30–31
► Europe countries	32–33
► Reference maps of Europe	38–59

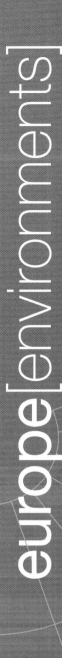

① Lakelands, *Finland*

This aerial photograph, taken to the east of Kuopio, shows an environment typical of the lakeland areas of central Finland. The country is mostly lowland, with many lakes, marshes, and low hills. The vast forested interior plateau includes approximately 60 000 lakes, many of which are linked by short rivers, or canals to form commercial waterways.

② Volcanic Environment, *Iceland*

The steam rising from the mountain side in this photograph is a result of volcanic activity. Iceland is a country with nearly 200 volcanoes, many of them still active. These create, and have created, great lava fields and rough mountainous terrain. Perhaps the most notable volcano is Hekla which rises to 1 491 m and had a major eruption in 1991. Hot springs and geysers are also common, and their geothermal energy is commonly used for domestic heating.

③ Mediterranean Island, *Europe*

This satellite image of the French island of Corsica in the Mediterranean Sea shows a mountainous island with some flat areas in the form of lagoons and marshes on the eastern coast. The highest point of the island is Monte Cinto, 2 706 m, which is towards the north of the pale, mountainous area.

Satellite/sensor : SPOT

④ Agricultural Region, *Italy*

The numerous rectangles in this satellite image are a patchwork of fields found in the Fucino plain, to the east of Avezzano, Italy. This area was formerly a lake which was drained in the mid-nineteenth century and now provides over 160 square kilometres of fertile farmland. Today the area is intensely cultivated with a variety of crops being grown, including cereals, potatoes, sugar beet, grapes and fruit.

Satellite/Sensor : Landsat

⑤ Planned Village, *The Netherlands*

This aerial photograph shows the village of Bourtange located in the extreme south-east of Groningen province in the Netherlands, less than 2 km from the German border. The star-shaped fortress dates back to the late sixteenth century. The old core of the village was restored in 1967 and has since been protected as a national monument.

⑥ Mountainous Coastline, *United Kingdom*

This satellite image of the west coast of Scotland clearly shows the effect of the last ice age on this landscape. Retreating glaciers left long, deep valleys, high mountains and a very rugged, indented coastline. The barren mountains are clearly identified as the white areas of bare rock. Water appears as darker areas with Loch Maree being the largest loch in the centre of the image.

Satellite/Sensor : Landsat

⑦ Urban Environment, *United Kingdom*

This aerial photograph shows part of the centre of London, the capital city of the United Kingdom. Westminster, the seat of the British government, is located on the left bank of the River Thames at the bottom of the photograph. Other notable features are Buckingham Palace (bottom left), St James's Park, Waterloo Station (bottom right) and the London Eye observation wheel in its flat construction position over the river, prior to its final erection and completion.

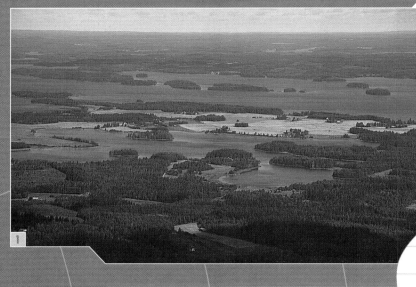

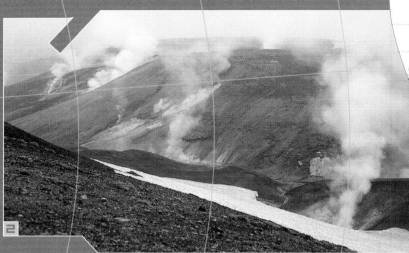

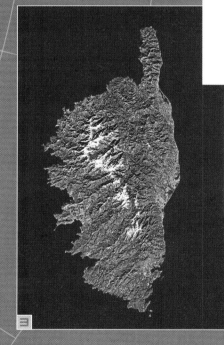

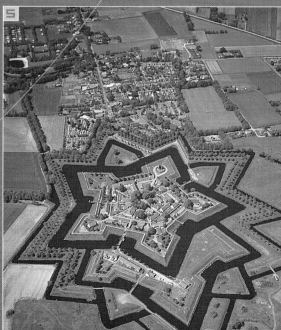

CONNECTIONS

► subject	page#
► World land cover types	18–19
► World cities	24–25
► Europe landscapes	30–31
► Reference maps of Europe	38–59
► North America environments	162–163

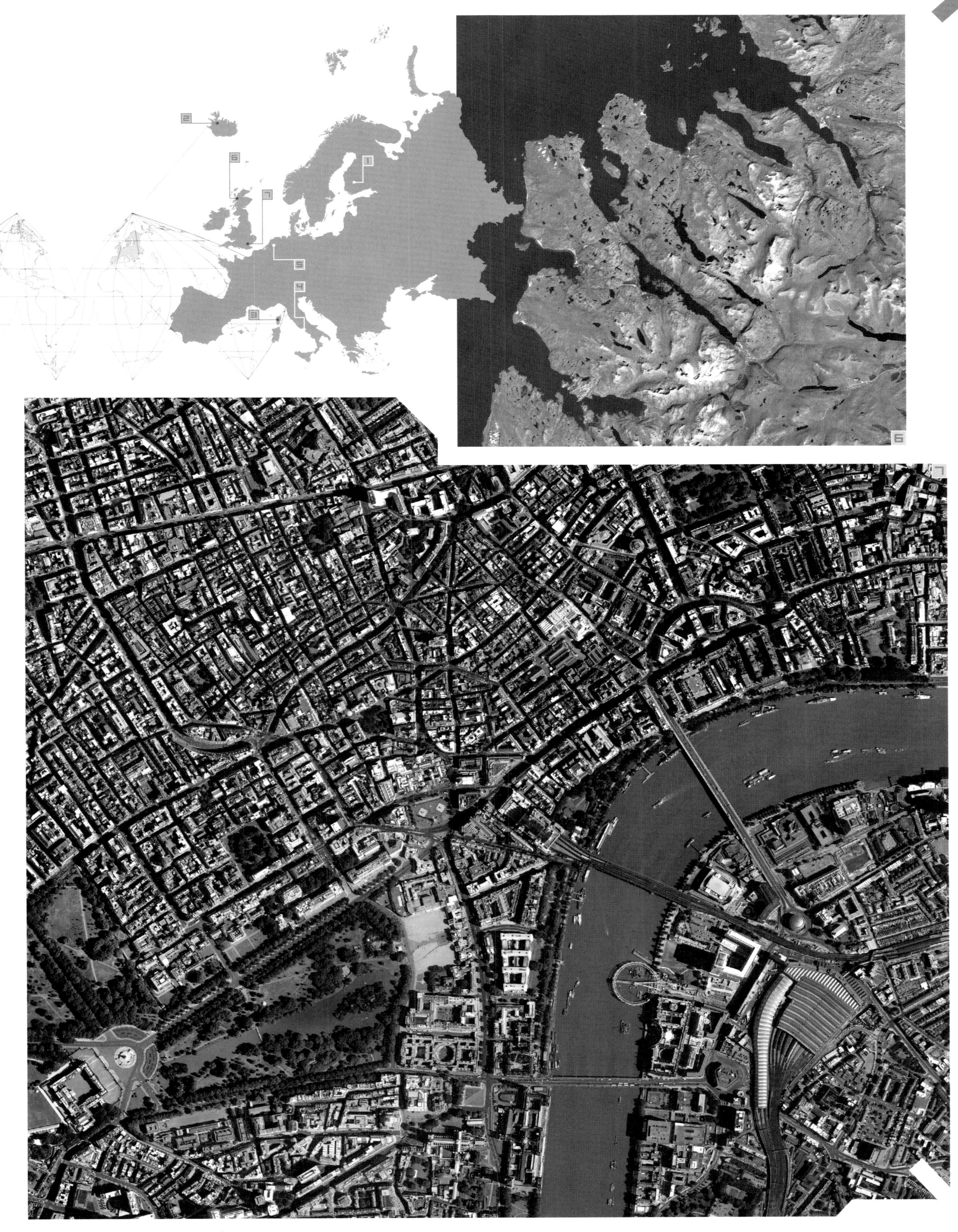

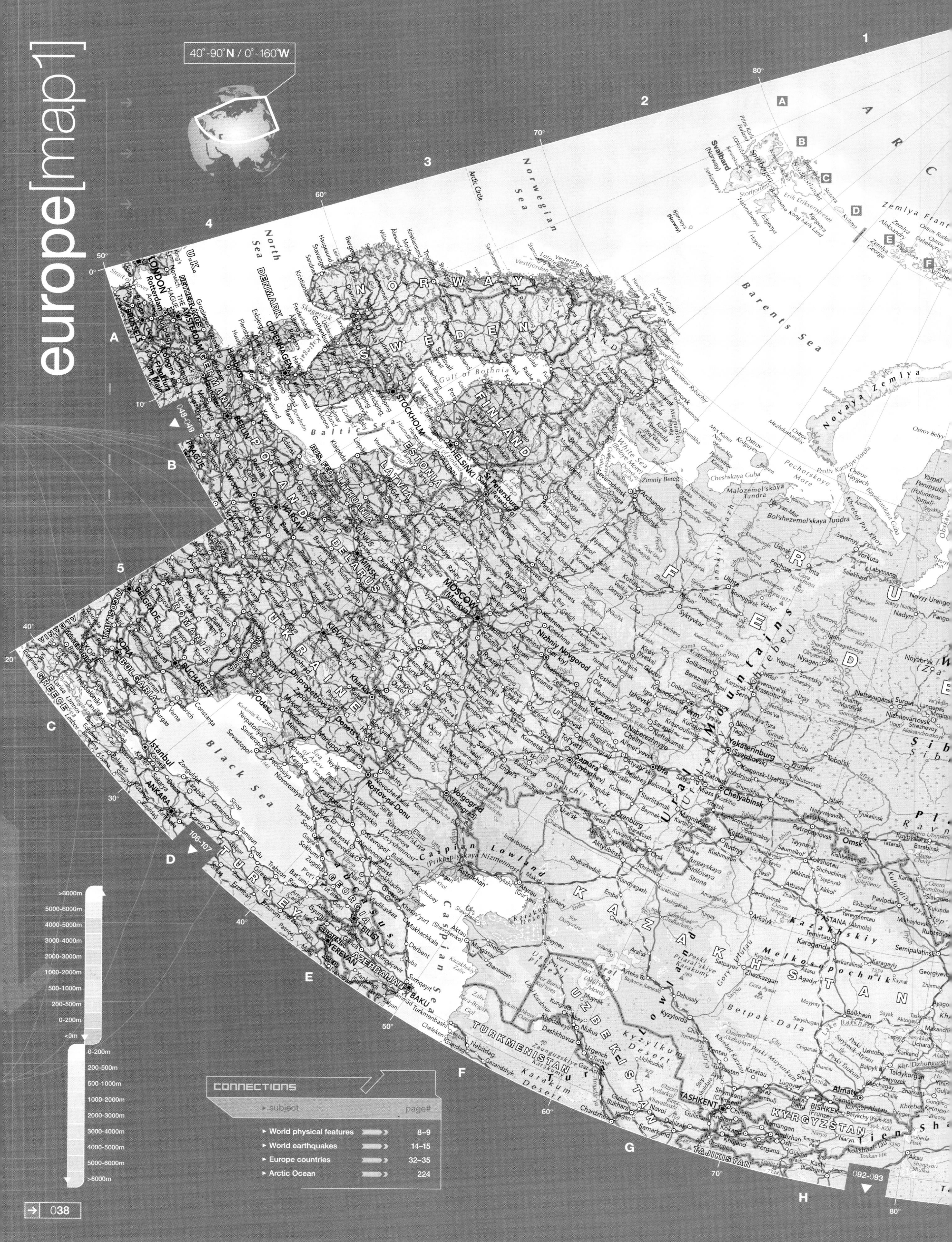
europe[map1]
40°-90°N / 0°-160°W
>6000m
5000-6000m
4000-5000m
3000-4000m
2000-3000m
1000-2000m
500-1000m
200-500m
0-200m
<0m
0-200m
200-500m
500-1000m
1000-2000m
2000-3000m
3000-4000m
4000-5000m
5000-6000m
>6000m
048-049
106-107
092-093
Norwegian Sea
North Sea
Barents Sea
Baltic Sea
Gulf of Bothnia
White Sea
Black Sea
Caspian Sea
Caspian Lowland
Novaya Zemlya
Zemlya Frantsa
Svalbard (Norway)
U.K.
NETHERLANDS
DENMARK
GERMANY
NORWAY
SWEDEN
FINLAND
ESTONIA
LATVIA
LITHUANIA
POLAND
BELARUS
UKRAINE
MOLDOVA
ROMANIA
BULGARIA
YUGOSLAVIA
ALBANIA
GREECE
TURKEY
GEORGIA
ARMENIA
AZERBAIJAN
KAZAKHSTAN
UZBEKISTAN
TURKMENISTAN
KYRGYZSTAN
TAJIKISTAN
Ural Mountains
LONDON
AMSTERDAM
BRUSSELS
COPENHAGEN
BERLIN
PRAGUE
STOCKHOLM
HELSINKI
WARSAW
MINSK
MOSCOW (Moskva)
KIEV
BELGRADE
SOFIA
BUCHAREST
İstanbul
ANKARA
TBILISI
YEREVAN
BAKU
ASTANA (Akmola)
TASHKENT
BISHKEK
Almaty
St Petersburg
Volgograd
Yekaterinburg
Omsk

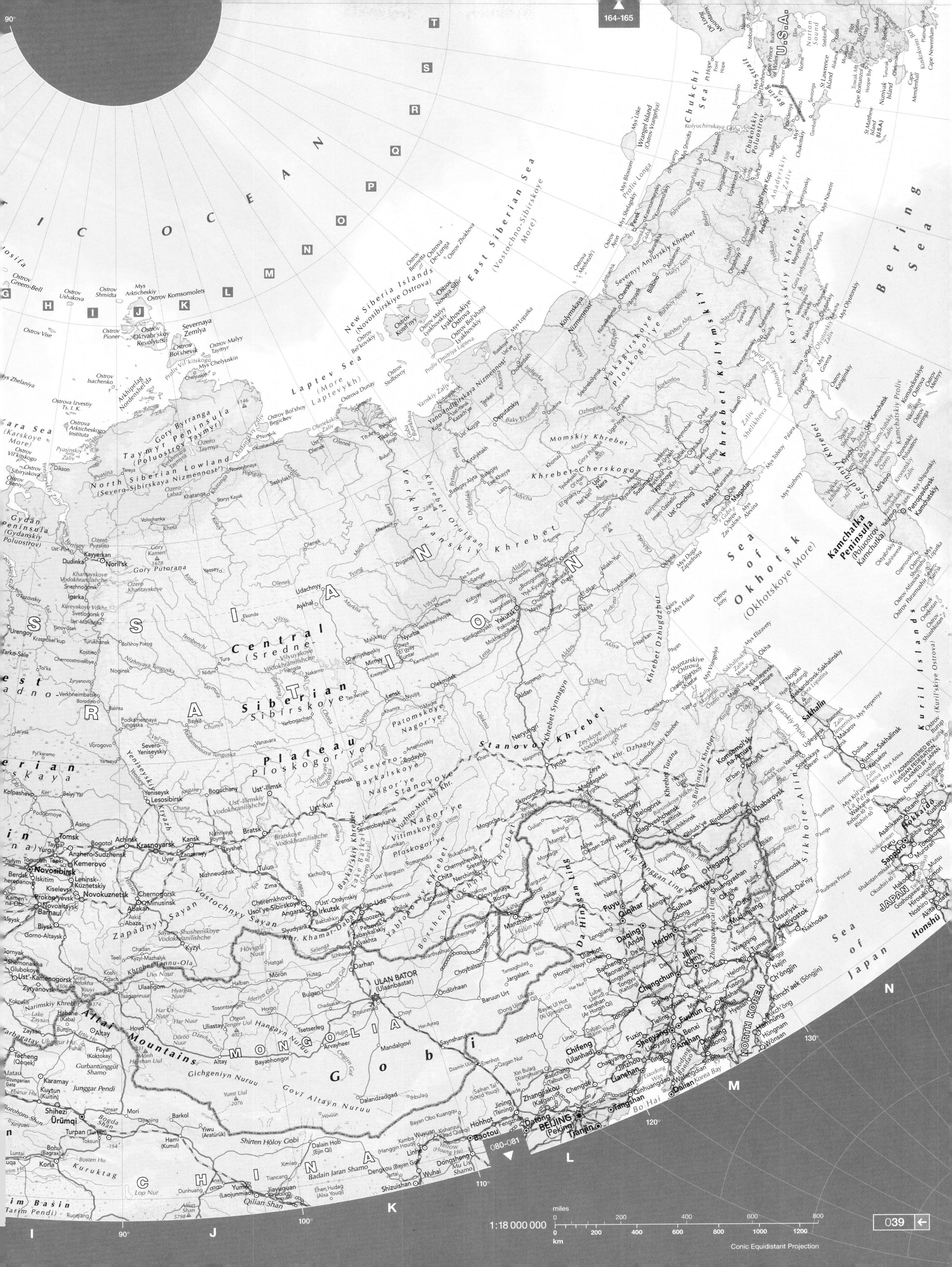

164-165
ARCTIC OCEAN
East Siberian Sea
(Vostochno-Sibirskoye More)
Laptev Sea
(More Laptevykh)
New Siberia Islands
(Novosibirskiye Ostrova)
Severnaya Zemlya
Kara Sea
(Karskoye More)
Chukchi Sea
Wrangel Island
(Ostrov Vrangelya)
Bering Strait
Bering Sea
U.S.A.
Norton Sound
St Lawrence Island
Anadyrskiy Zaliv
Chukotskiy Poluostrov
Koryakskiy Khrebet
Khrebet Kolymskiy
Kolymskaya Nizmennost'
Yukagirskoye Ploskogor'ye
Momskiy Khrebet
Khrebet Cherskogo
Verkhoyanskiy Khrebet
Taymyr Peninsula
(Poluostrov Taymyr)
Gory Byrranga
North Siberian Lowland
(Severo-Sibirskaya Nizmennost')
Gydan Peninsula
(Gydanskiy Poluostrov)
Gory Putorana
Central Siberian Plateau
(Sredne-Sibirskoye Ploskogor'ye)
RUSSIAN FEDERATION
Kamchatka Peninsula
(Poluostrov Kamchatka)
Sea of Okhotsk
(Okhotskoye More)
Kuril Islands
(Kuril'skiye Ostrova)
Sakhalin
Stanovoy Khrebet
Magadan
Yakutsk
Noril'sk
Petropavlovsk-Kamchatskiy
Khabarovsk
Vladivostok
Irkutsk
Lake Baykal
Novosibirsk
Krasnoyarsk
Barnaul
Novokuznetsk
Kemerovo
Tomsk
Bratsk
Chita
Ulan-Ude
Altai Mountains
Zapadnyy Sayan
Vostochnyy Sayan
MONGOLIA
ULAN BATOR
(Ulaanbaatar)
Gobi
CHINA
BEIJING
(Peking)
Tianjin
Harbin
Shenyang
Dalian
Qiqihar
Changchun
Ürümqi
Da Hinggan Ling
Bo Hai
Korea Bay
NORTH KOREA
Sea of Japan
JAPAN
Hokkaidō
Sapporo
Honshū
Tarim Basin
(Tarim Pendi)
Junggar Pendi
Lop Nur
080-081
1:18 000 000
miles
0 200 400 600 800
0 200 400 600 800 1000 1200
km
Conic Equidistant Projection

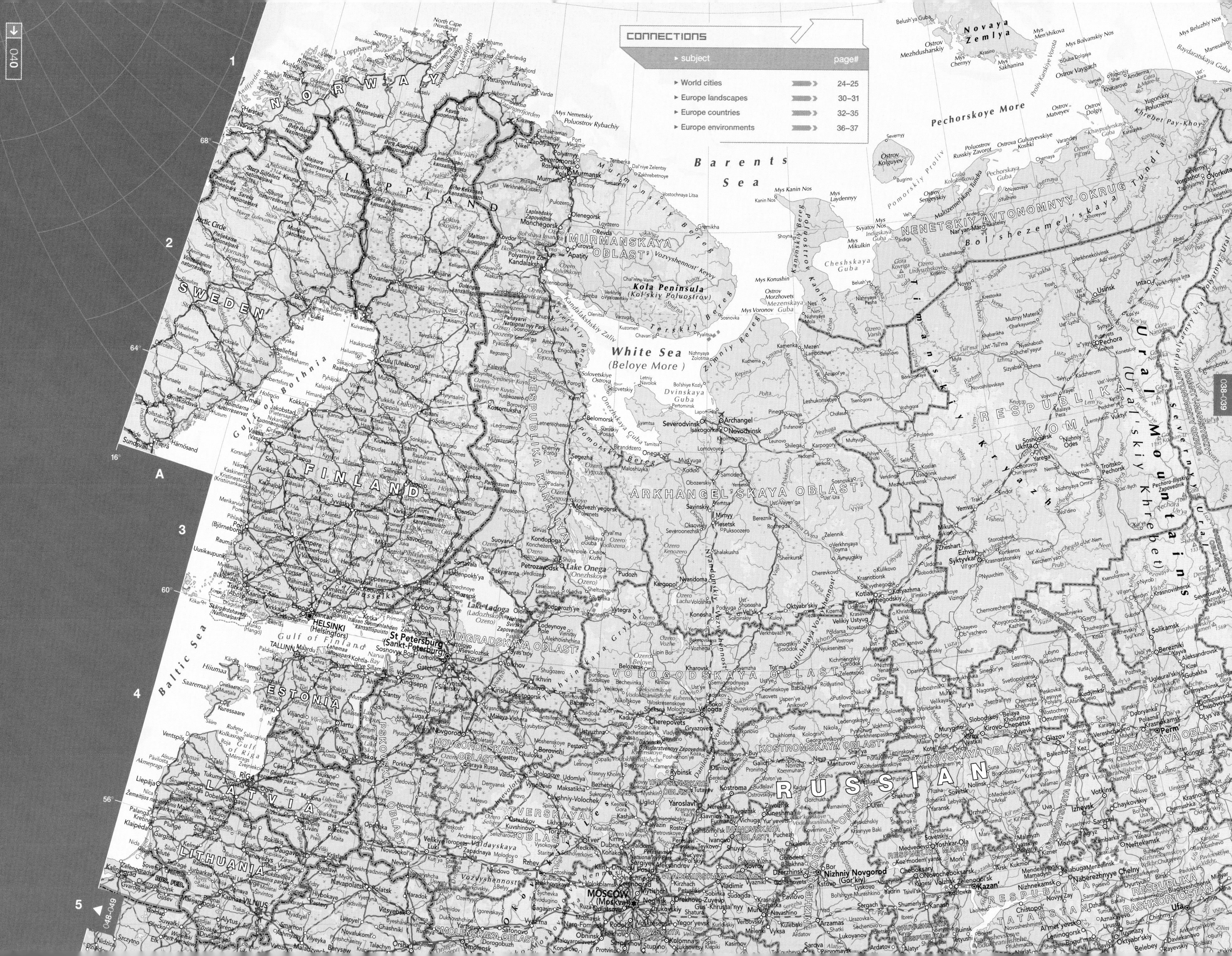

Ural Mountains
(Ural'skiy Khrebet)

Barents Sea

Novaya Zemlya

Pechorskoye More

White Sea
(Beloye More)

Kola Peninsula
(Kol'skiy Poluostrov)

RESPUBLIKA KOMI

NENETSKIY AVTONOMNYY OKRUG

ARKHANGEL'SKAYA OBLAST'

MURMANSKAYA OBLAST'

RESPUBLIKA KARELIYA

VOLOGODSKAYA OBLAST'

RUSSIAN

Lake Ladoga
(Ladozhskoye)

Lake Onega
(Onezhskoye Ozero)

NORWAY

SWEDEN

FINLAND

ESTONIA

LATVIA

LITHUANIA

Baltic Sea

Gulf of Finland

Gulf of Bothnia

Gulf of Riga

HELSINKI
(Helsingfors)

St Petersburg
(Sankt-Peterburg)

TALLINN

RIGA

VILNIUS

MOSCOW
(Moskva)

Nizhniy Novgorod
(Gor'kiy)

LENINGRADSKAYA OBLAST'

NOVGORODSKAYA OBLAST'

PSKOVSKAYA OBLAST'

TVERSKAYA OBLAST'

KOSTROMSKAYA OBLAST'

KIROVSKAYA OBLAST'

PERMSKAY OBLAST'

NIZHEGORODSKAYA OBLAST'

RESPUBLIKA BASHKORTOSTAN

RESPUBLIKA TATARSTAN

Arctic Circle

048-049

europe[map2]

41°71'N / 20°54'E

1:7 500 000

Conic Equidistant Projection

Administrative divisions in Russian Federation numbered on the map:

1. RESPUBLIKA ADYGEYA (G7)
2. CHECHENSKAYA RESPUBLIKA (CHECHNIA) (H8)
3. RESPUBLIKA INGUSHETIYA (INGUSHETIA) (H8)
4. KABARDINO-BALKARSKAYA RESPUBLIKA (G8)
5. KARACHAYEVO-CHERKESSKAYA RESPUBLIKA (G8)
6. RESPUBLIKA SEVERNAYA OSETIYA-ALANIYA (NORTH OSSETIA) (H8)

miles
km

0   100   200   300
0   100   200   300   400   500

>6000m
5000-6000m
4000-5000m
3000-4000m
2000-3000m
1000-2000m
500-1000m
200-500m
0-200m
<0m
0-200m
200-500m
500-1000m
1000-2000m
2000-3000m
3000-4000m
4000-5000m
5000-6000m
>6000m

europe[map3]

52°-61°N / 20°-40°E

>6000m
5000-6000m
4000-5000m
3000-4000m
2000-3000m
1500-2000m
1000-1500m
500-1000m
200-500m
100-200m
0-100m
<0m

0-50m
50-100m
100-200m
200-500m
500-1000m
1000-2000m
2000-3000m
3000-4000m
4000-5000m
5000-6000m
>6000m

048-049

1 : 3 000 000

miles
0   25   50   75   100   125

km
0   25   50   75   100   125   150   175   200

Conic Equidistant Projection

Map labels:

Gulf of Bothnia
Åland Islands
FINLAND
VARSINAIS-SUOMI
LÄNSI-SUOMI
HELSINKI (Helsingfors)
Gulf of Finland
Baltic Sea
TALLINN
ESTONIA
Hiiumaa
Saaremaa
Gulf of Riga
Lake Peipus
LATVIA
RIGA
Jūrmala
Liepāja
Vidzemes Centrālā Augstiene
Augstiene
Klaipėda
LITHUANIA
KALININGRADSKAYA OBLAST
RUSSIAN FEDERATION
Kaliningrad
VILNIUS
KAUNAS
MINSK
MINSKAYA VOBLASTS
HRODZYENSKAYA VOBLASTS
BRESTSKAYA VOBLASTS
BELA
Nizina
POLEZIERZE MAZURSKIE
POLAND
Nizina Mazowiecka
WARSAW (Warszawa)
Gulf of Gdańsk
Nizina Mazowiecka

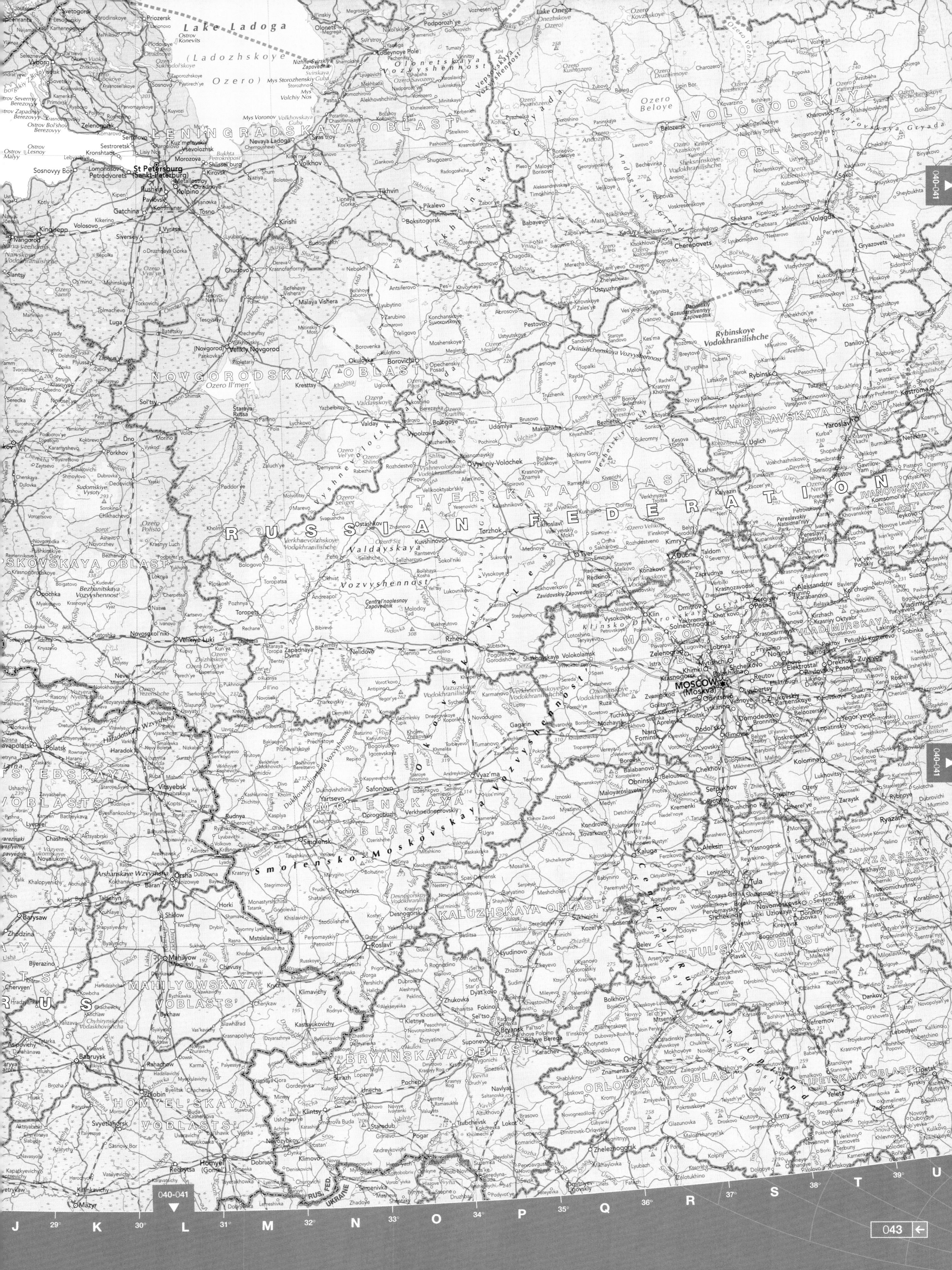

Lake Ladoga
(Ladozhskoye Ozero)
Lake Onega
LENINGRADSKAYA OBLAST'
VOLOGODSKAYA OBLAST'
NOVGORODSKAYA OBLAST'
YAROSLAVSKAYA OBLAST'
TVERSKAYA OBLAST'
IVANOVSKAYA OBLAST'
PSKOVSKAYA OBLAST'
MOSKOVSKAYA OBLAST'
VLADIMIRSKAYA OBLAST'
RUSSIAN FEDERATION
SMOLENSKAYA OBLAST'
RYAZANSKAYA OBLAST'
KALUZHSKAYA OBLAST'
TUL'SKAYA OBLAST'
BRYANSKAYA OBLAST'
ORLOVSKAYA OBLAST'
LIPETSKAYA OBLAST'
VITSYEBSKAYA VOBLASTS'
MAHILYOWSKAYA VOBLASTS'
HOMYEL'SKAYA VOBLASTS'
St Petersburg (Sankt-Peterburg)
MOSCOW (Moskva)
Rybinskoye Vodokhranilishche
Valdayskaya Vozvyshennost'
Smolensko-Moskovskaya Vozvyshennost'
Vologda
Cherepovets
Yaroslavl'
Kostroma
Tver'
Velikiy Novgorod
Pskov
Smolensk
Kaluga
Tula
Ryazan'
Bryansk
Orel
Vitsyebsk
Mahilyow (Mogilev)
Homyel' (Gomel')
UKRAINE
040-041
J
29°
K
30°
L
31°
M
32°
N
33°
O
34°
P
35°
Q
36°
R
37°
S
38°
T
39°
U

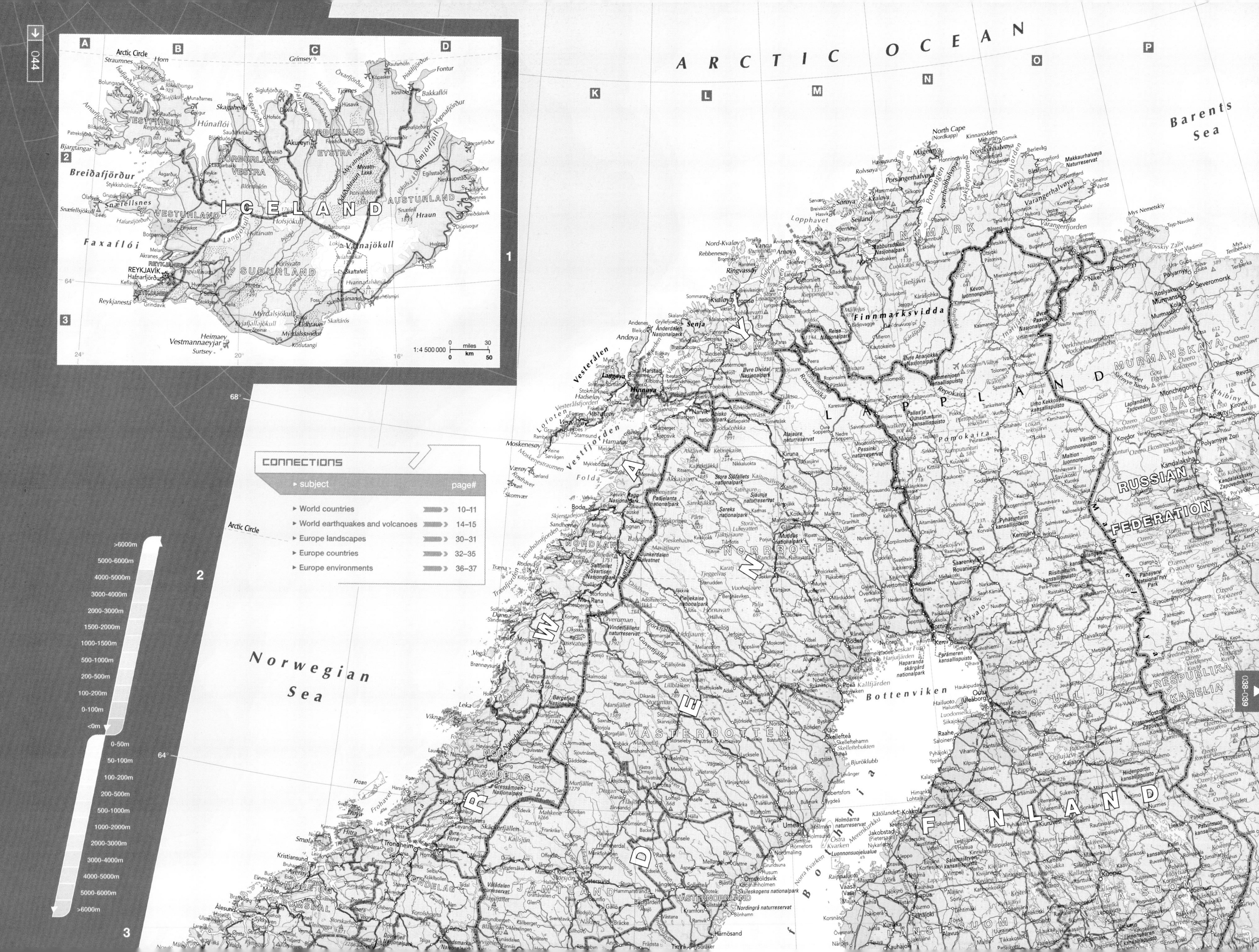

europe[map4]

54°-72°N / 4°-28°E

1:4 500 000

Conic Equidistant Projection

miles

km

50 100 150 200

100 150 200 250 300

048-049

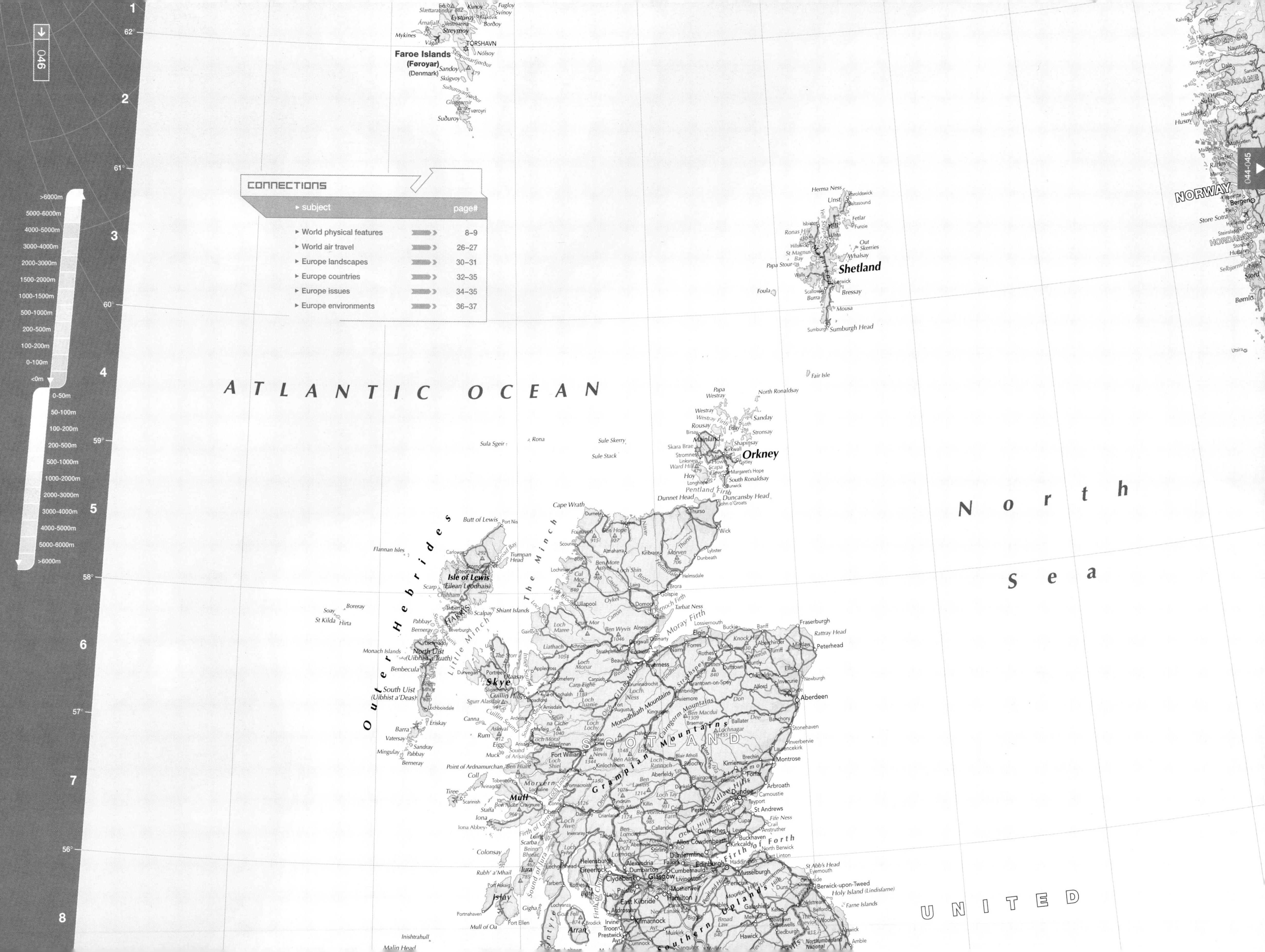
CONNECTIONS
subject
page#
World physical features 8–9
World air travel 26–27
Europe landscapes 30–31
Europe countries 32–35
Europe issues 34–35
Europe environments 36–37
ATLANTIC OCEAN
North Sea
UNITED
NORWAY
SCOTLAND
Faroe Islands
(Føroyar)
(Denmark)
TÓRSHAVN
Mykines
Sandoy
Skúgvoy
Suðuroy
Shetland
Herma Ness
Unst
Fetlar
Whalsay
Out Skerries
Papa Stour
Foula
Bressay
Mousa
Sumburgh Head
Fair Isle
Orkney
North Ronaldsay
Papa Westray
Westray
Sanday
Stronsay
Rousay
Shapinsay
Mainland
Hoy
South Ronaldsay
Pentland Firth
Dunnet Head
Duncansby Head
John o'Groats
Thurso
Wick
Cape Wrath
Sula Sgeir
Rona
Sule Skerry
Sule Stack
Butt of Lewis
Flannan Isles
Isle of Lewis
(Eilean Leodhais)
HARRIS
Shiant Islands
Outer Hebrides
The Minch
Little Minch
St Kilda
Hirta
Boreray
Soay
Monach Islands
North Uist
(Uibhist a Tuath)
Benbecula
South Uist
(Uibhist a'Deas)
Barra
Vatersay
Mingulay
Pabbay
Berneray
Skye
Cuillin Hills
Canna
Rum
Eigg
Muck
Coll
Tiree
Mull
Iona
Staffa
Colonsay
Jura
Islay
Gigha
Arran
Ullapool
Inverness
Moray Firth
Elgin
Fraserburgh
Peterhead
Aberdeen
Stonehaven
Montrose
Arbroath
Dundee
St Andrews
Perth
Stirling
Fort William
Oban
Monadhliath Mountains
Cairngorm Mountains
Grampian Mountains
Firth of Forth
Edinburgh
Glasgow
Greenock
Paisley
Motherwell
Hamilton
East Kilbride
Kilmarnock
Irvine
Troon
Prestwick
Ayr
Southern Uplands
Hawick
Galashiels
Berwick-upon-Tweed
Holy Island (Lindisfarne)
Farne Islands
St Abb's Head
Malin Head
Inishtrahull
Mull of Oa
Bergen
Stord
Bømlo
Utsira
044-045

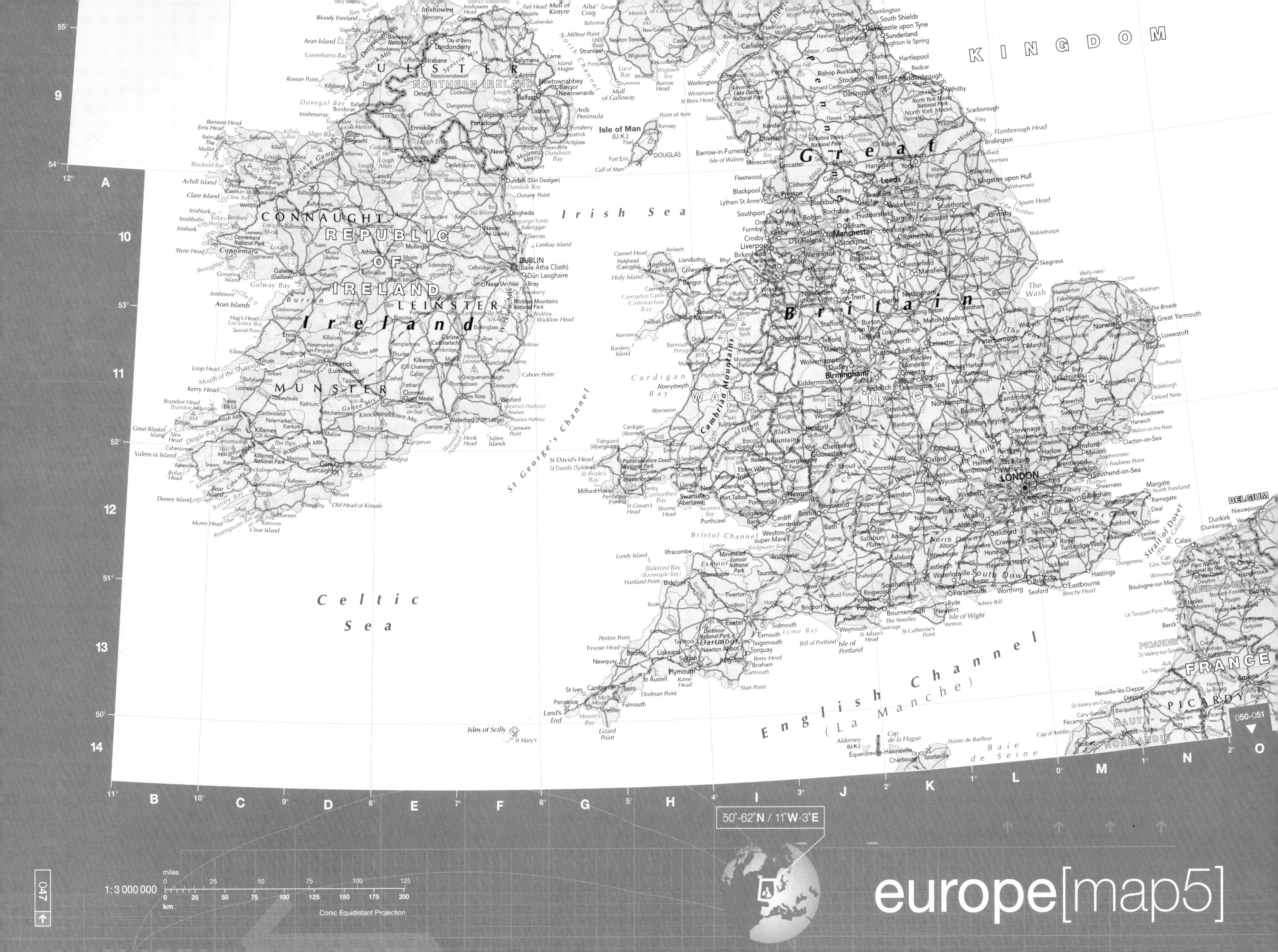

UNITED KINGDOM

Great Britain

Pennines

REPUBLIC OF IRELAND

CONNAUGHT

MUNSTER

LEINSTER

ULSTER

NORTHERN IRELAND

WALES

Cambrian Mountains

ENGLAND

LONDON

DUBLIN (Baile Átha Cliath)

FRANCE

PICARDIE

HAUTE-NORMANDIE

BELGIUM

Isle of Man (U.K.)

DOUGLAS

Irish Sea

North Channel

St George's Channel

Celtic Sea

Bristol Channel

English Channel (La Manche)

Cardigan Bay

Galway Bay

Baie de Seine

Conic Equidistant Projection

miles

km

050-051

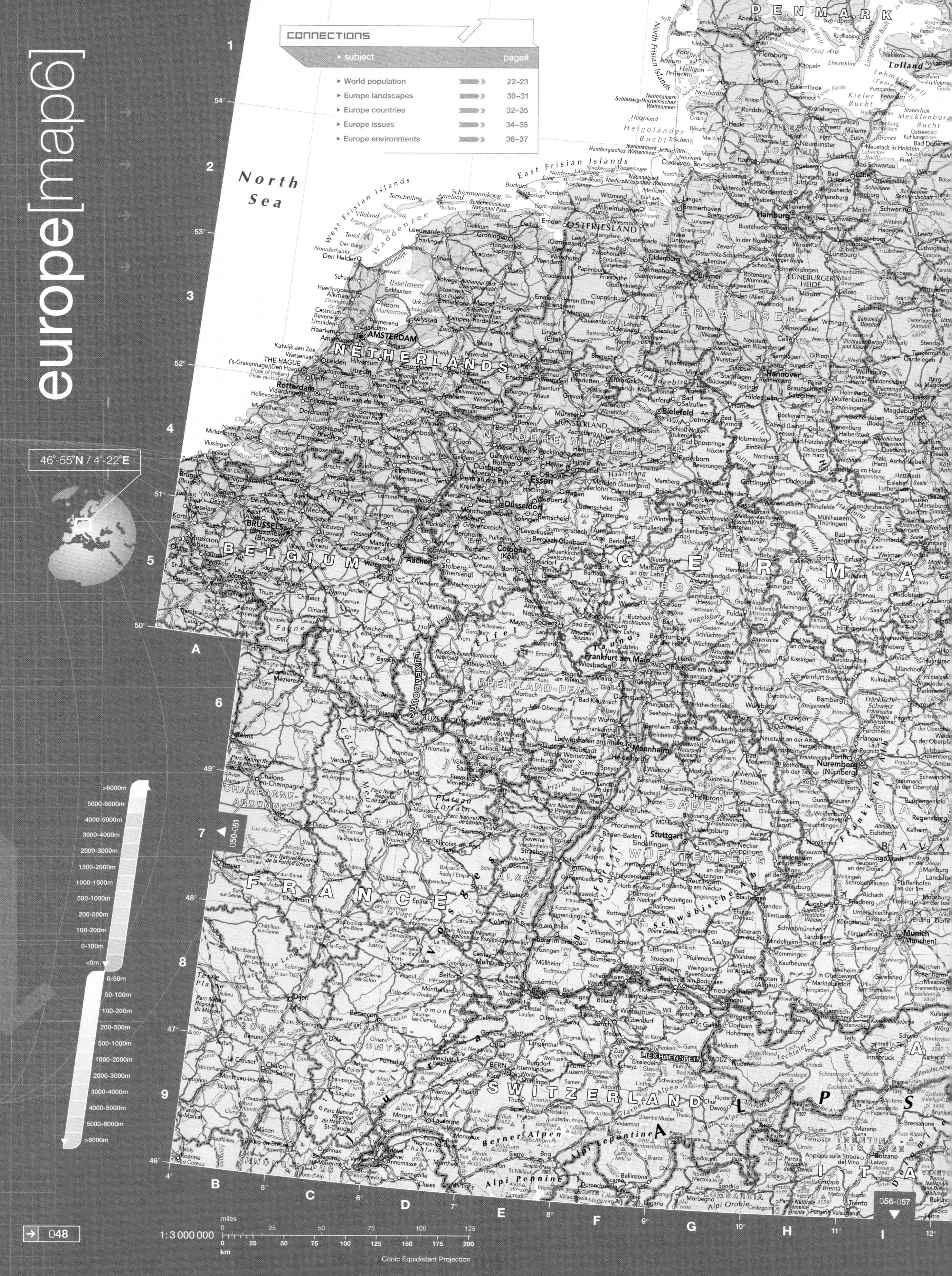

46°-55°N / 4°-22°E

North Sea

>6000m
5000–6000m
4000–5000m
3000–4000m
2000–3000m
1500–2000m
1000–1500m
500–1000m
200–500m
100–200m
0–100m
<0m

0–50m
50–100m
100–200m
200–500m
500–1000m
1000–2000m
2000–3000m
3000–4000m
4000–5000m
5000–6000m
>6000m

DENMARK

NETHERLANDS

BELGIUM

LUXEMBOURG

FRANCE

GERMANY

SWITZERLAND

ALPS

ITALIA

LIECHTENSTEIN

1:3 000 000

miles
0   25   50   75   100   125

km
0   25   50   75   100   125   150   175   200

Conic Equidistant Projection

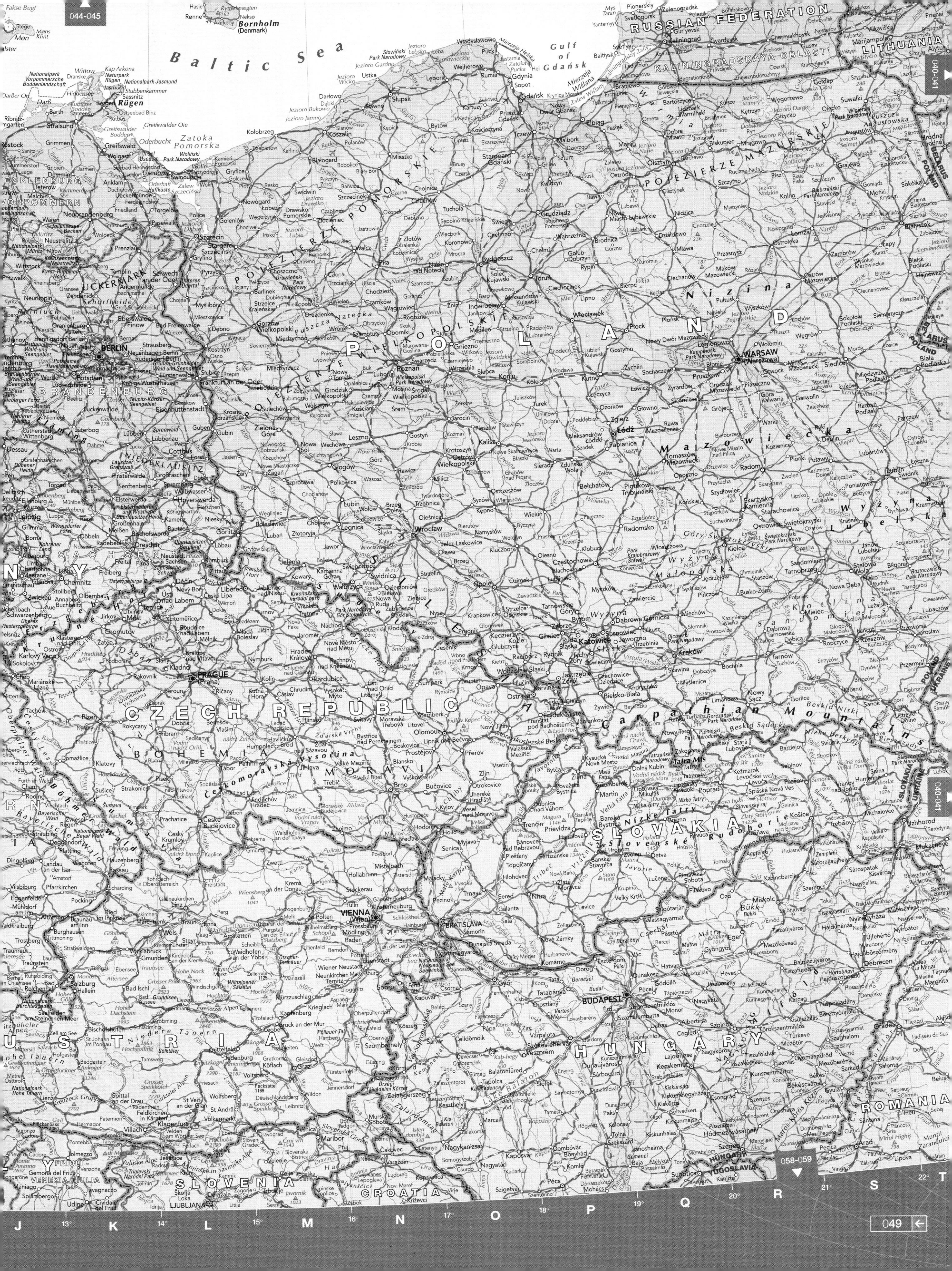
044-045
Baltic Sea
Gulf of Gdańsk
Bornholm (Denmark)
RUSSIAN FEDERATION
KALININGRADSKAYA OBLAST'
LITHUANIA
040-041
BELARUS
POLAND
P O L A N D
WARSAW (Warszawa)
BERLIN
PRAGUE (Praha)
CZECH REPUBLIC
BOHEMIA
MORAVIA
SLOVAKIA
BRATISLAVA
VIENNA (Wien)
BUDAPEST
HUNGARY
ROMANIA
UKRAINE
SLOVENIA
LJUBLJANA
CROATIA
YUGOSLAVIA
Carpathian Mountains
Tatra Mts
POJEZIERZE POMORSKIE
POJEZIERZE MAZURSKIE
Mazowiecka
Nizina
Wyżyna Lubelska
Kotlina Sandomierska
SACHSEN
BRANDENBURG
NIEDERLAUSITZ
UCKERMARK
VORPOMMERN
Rügen
Zatoka Pomorska
Balaton
Alföld
058-059
13° 14° 15° 16° 17° 18° 19° 20° 21° 22°
J K L M N O P Q R S T

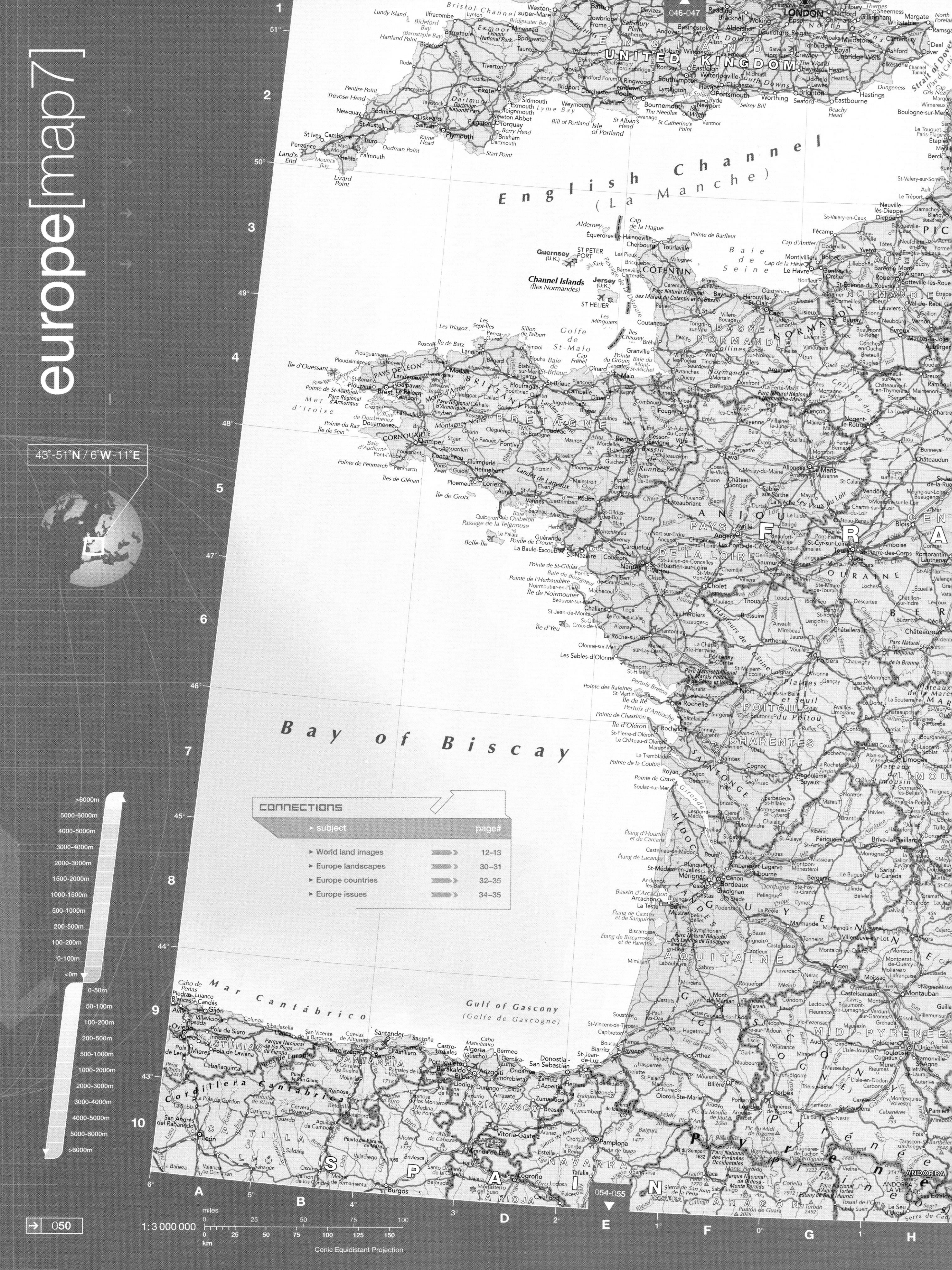

europe[map7]
43°-51°N / 6°W-11°E
046-047
054-055
English Channel
(La Manche)
Bay of Biscay
Mar Cantábrico
Gulf of Gascony
(Golfe de Gascogne)
Bristol Channel
UNITED KINGDOM
ENGLAND
FRANCE
SPAIN
ANDORRA
Channel Islands
(Îles Normandes)
Guernsey
(U.K.)
Jersey
(U.K.)
BRITTANY
BRETAGNE
BASSE NORMANDIE
HAUTE NORMANDIE
PAYS DE LA LOIRE
ANJOU
TOURAINE
POITOU-CHARENTES
AQUITAINE
GASCOGNE
MIDI-PYRÉNÉES
Pyrénées
ASTURIAS
CANTABRIA
PAÍS VASCO
NAVARRA
CASTILLA Y LEÓN
LA RIOJA
ARAGÓN
Cordillera Cantábrica
LONDON
Plymouth
Southampton
Brighton
Cherbourg
Caen
Le Havre
Rouen
Rennes
Brest
Nantes
Le Mans
Tours
Angers
Poitiers
La Rochelle
Limoges
Bordeaux
Toulouse
Bilbao
Santander
Pamplona
Donostia - San Sebastián
Vitoria-Gasteiz
Burgos
León
Logroño
CONNECTIONS
subject
page#
World land images 12–13
Europe landscapes 30–31
Europe countries 32–35
Europe issues 34–35
>6000m
5000-6000m
4000-5000m
3000-4000m
2000-3000m
1500-2000m
1000-1500m
500-1000m
200-500m
100-200m
0-100m
<0m
0-50m
50-100m
100-200m
200-500m
500-1000m
1000-2000m
2000-3000m
3000-4000m
4000-5000m
5000-6000m
>6000m
1:3 000 000
miles
0 25 50 75 100
km
0 25 50 75 100 125 150
Conic Equidistant Projection

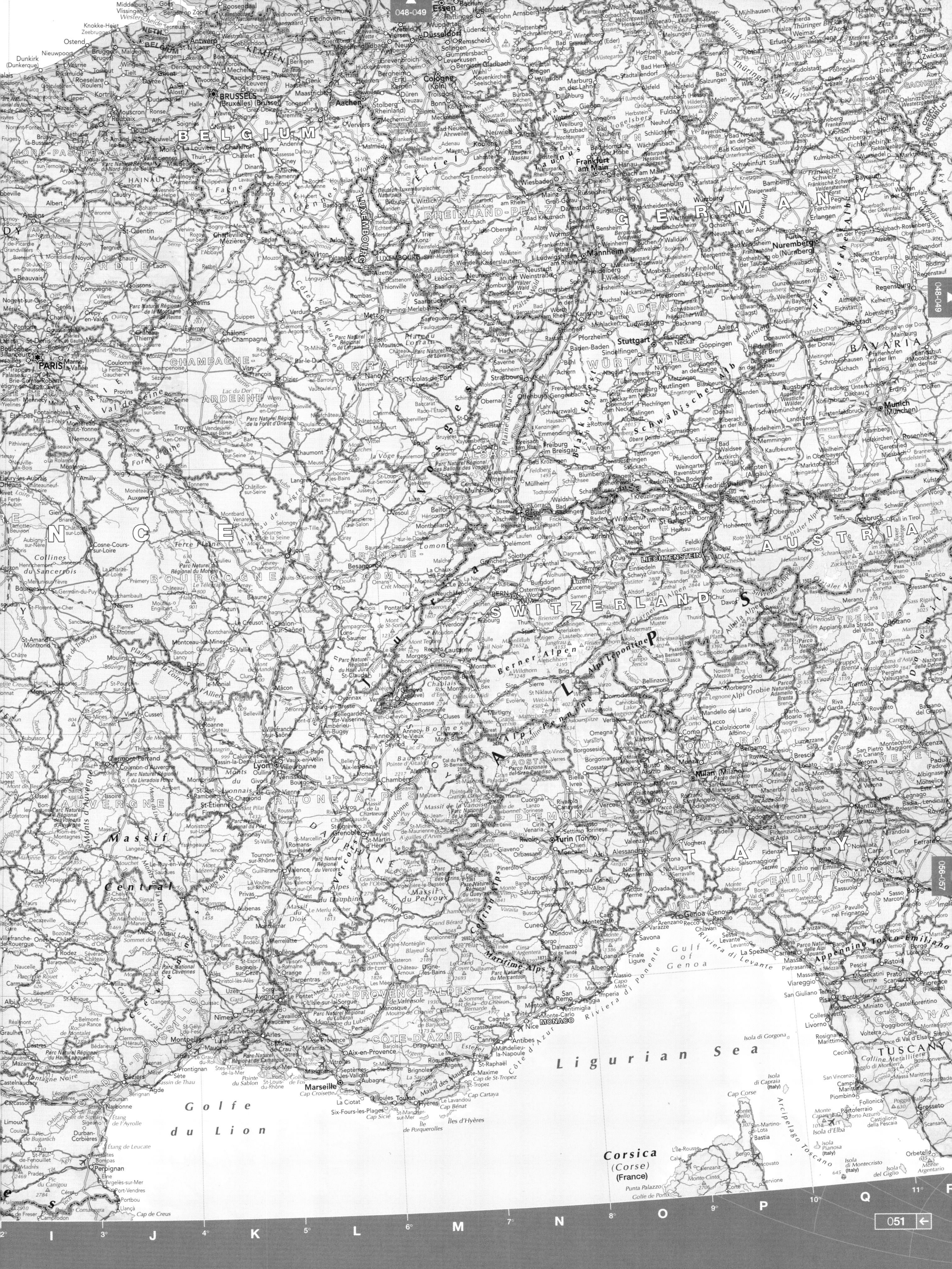

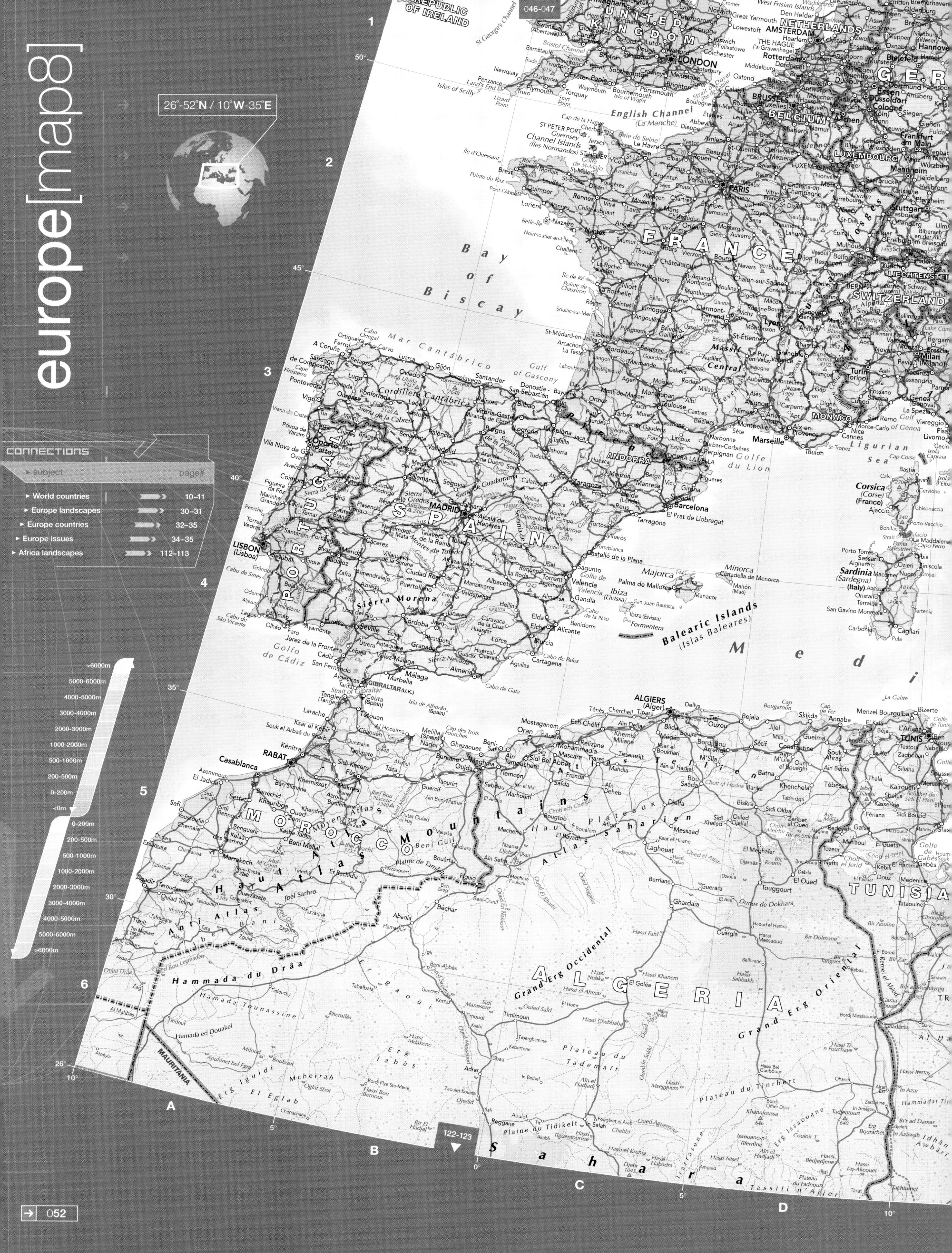

europe[map8]
26°-52°N / 10°W-35°E
CONNECTIONS
subject page#
World countries 10–11
Europe landscapes 30–31
Europe countries 32–35
Europe issues 34–35
Africa landscapes 112–113
>6000m
5000-6000m
4000-5000m
3000-4000m
2000-3000m
1000-2000m
500-1000m
200-500m
0-200m
<0m
0-200m
200-500m
500-1000m
1000-2000m
2000-3000m
3000-4000m
4000-5000m
5000-6000m
>6000m
046-047
122-123
REPUBLIC OF IRELAND
UNITED KINGDOM
LONDON
NETHERLANDS
AMSTERDAM
BRUSSEL (Bruxelles)
BELGIUM
LUXEMBOURG
GER
English Channel (La Manche)
Channel Islands (Îles Normandes)
PARIS
FRANCE
Massif Central
SWITZERLAND
LIECHTENSTEIN
Bay of Biscay
Mar Cantábrico
Gulf of Gascony
Cordillera Cantábrica
PORTUGAL
LISBON (Lisboa)
SPAIN
MADRID
Sierra Morena
ANDORRA
MONACO
Golfe du Lion
Ligurian Sea
Corsica (Corse) (France)
Sardinia (Sardegna) (Italy)
Balearic Islands (Islas Baleares)
Majorca
Minorca
Ibiza (Eivissa)
Golfo de Cádiz
GIBRALTAR (U.K.)
Strait of Gibraltar
Medi
ALGIERS (Alger)
TUNIS
RABAT
Casablanca
MOROCCO
Haut Atlas
Anti Atlas
Atlas Mountains
Atlas Tellien
Hauts Plateaux
Atlas Saharien
TUNISIA
ALGERIA
Grand Erg Occidental
Grand Erg Oriental
Hammada du Drâa
Plateau du Tademaït
Plateau du Tinrhert
MAURITANIA
Sahara
50°
45°
40°
35°
30°
26°
10°
5°
0°
5°
10°
1
2
3
4
5
6
A
B
C
D

BELARUS

POLAND

GERMANY

BERLIN

WARSAW
(Warszawa)

CZECH REPUBLIC

PRAGUE
(Praha)

SLOVAKIA

RUSSIAN FEDERATION

Kharkiv

KIEV

UKRAINE

Dnipropetrovs'k

Donets'k

VIENNA
(Wien)

BRATISLAVA

AUSTRIA

BUDAPEST

HUNGARY

MOLDOVA

CHIŞINĂU

Odesa

Rostov-na-Donu

Sea
of Azov

Crimea

SLOVENIA

LJUBLJANA

ZAGREB

CROATIA

ROMANIA

BUCHAREST
(Bucureşti)

Danube

Constanţa

Black Sea

BOSNIA-
HERZEGOVINA

SARAJEVO

YUGOSLAVIA

BELGRADE
(Beograd)

BULGARIA

Sevastopol

Yalta

SAN MARINO

Balkan Mountains
(Stara Planina)

SOFIA
(Sofiya)

Varna

Burgas

Samsun

Sinop

ROME
(Roma)

VATICAN CITY

ALBANIA

SKOPJE

MACEDONIA

TIRANA
(Tiranë)

Thessaloniki

Istanbul

Kocaeli

ANKARA

Anadolu Dağları

Naples (Napoli)

ITALY

Sea of Marmara
(Marmara Denizi)

Bursa

TURKEY

Tyrrhenian
Sea

GREECE

Aegean
Sea

Lesbos

İzmir
Smyrna

Taurus Mountains
(Toros Dağları)

Adana

Aleppo

Corfu
(Kerkyra)

ATHENS
(Athína)

Chios

Palermo

Sicily
(Sicilia)

Ionian
Sea

Cephalonia
(Kefallonia)

Zakynthos
(Zante)

Cyclades
(Kyklades)

Dodecanese
(Dodekanisos)

Rhodes
(Rodos)

Antalya
Körfezi

NICOSIA

CYPRUS

SYRIA

LEBANON

BEIRUT

Catania

Mirtoö
Pelagos

Krytiko Pelagos

Crete
(Kriti)

Iraklion
(Irakleio)

Karpathos

DAMASCUS

MALTA

VALLETTA

ISRAEL

Tel Aviv-Yafo

JERUSALEM

AMMAN

GAZA

JORDAN

Mediterranean Sea

TRIPOLI
(Ṭarābulus)

Benghazi

Darnah

Tubruq

Alexandria
(El Iskandariya)

Port Said
(Bûr Saîd)

CAIRO
(El Qâhira)

Gulf of Sirte
(Khalīj Surt)

CYRENAICA

Qattara
Depression

Libyan
Plateau

SINAI

Gebel et Tih

Suez

LIBYA

EGYPT

Great Sand Sea

Western Desert
(Sahara el
Gharbîya)

Eastern Desert
(Sahara el
Sharqîya)

Red
Sea

Libyan
Desert

As Sarīr

1:9 000 000

miles

km

Conic Equidistant Projection

E   F   G   H   I

15°   20°   25°   30°

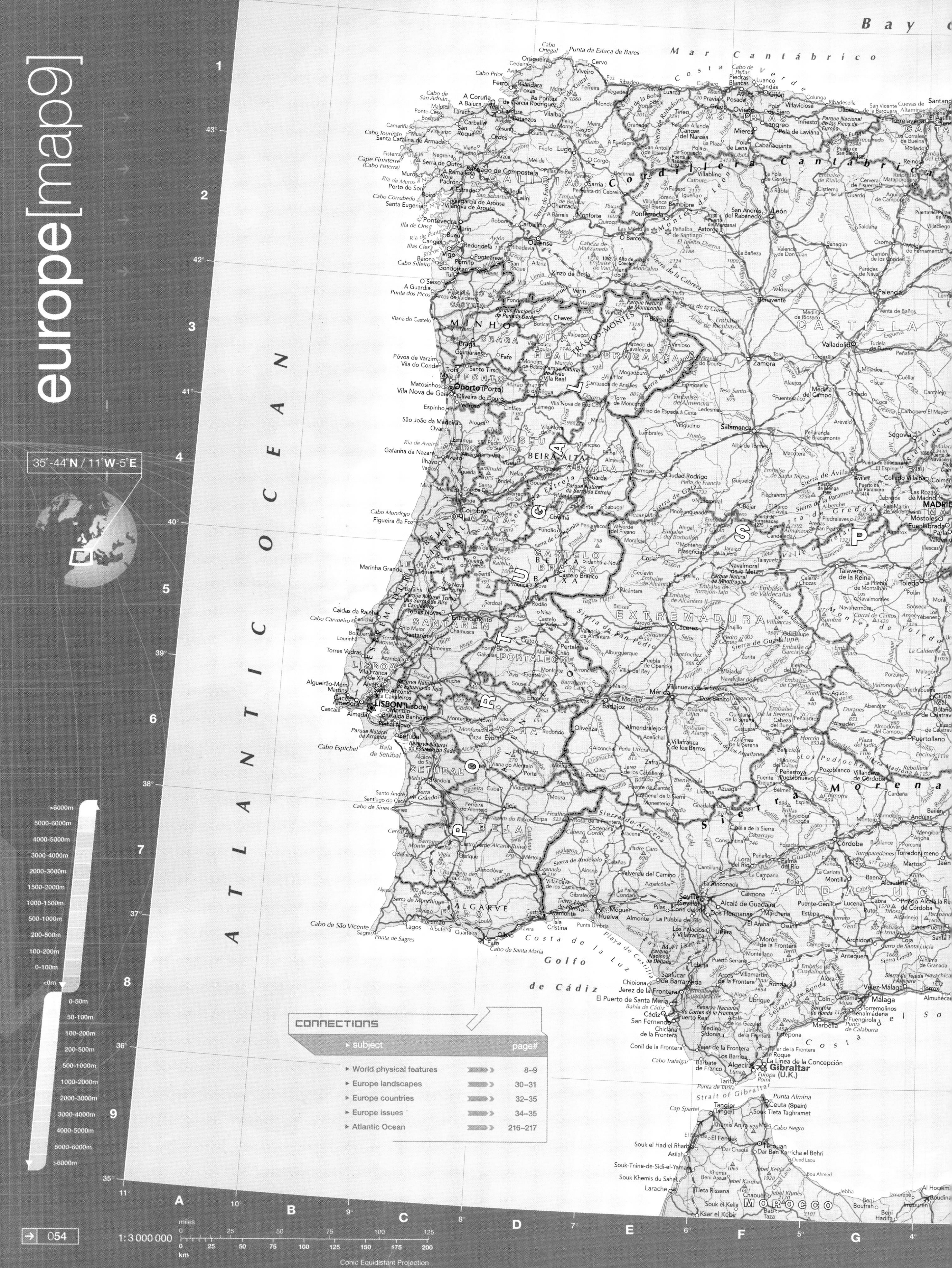

35°-44°N / 11°W-5°E

1:3 000 000

miles
0   25   50   75   100   125

km
0 25 50 75 100 125 150 175 200

Conic Equidistant Projection

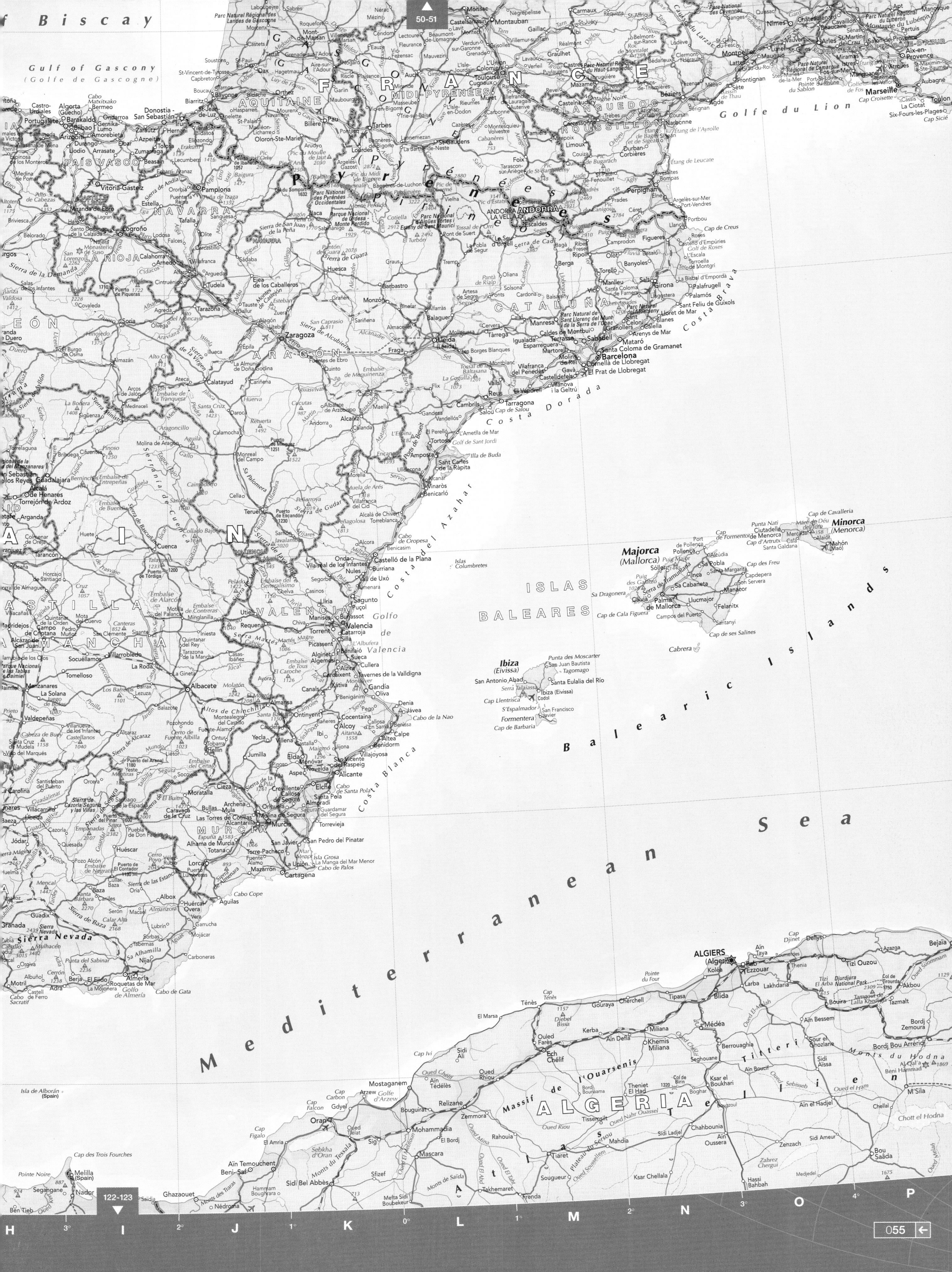
50-51
Bay of Biscay
Gulf of Gascony
(Golfe de Gascogne)
FRANCE
AQUITAINE
MIDI-PYRÉNÉES
LANGUEDOC-ROUSSILLON
PROVENCE-ALPES-CÔTE-D'AZUR
Golfe du Lion
Marseille
Toulouse
Montpellier
Perpignan
Pyrénées
ANDORRA
ANDORRA LA VELLA
PAÍS VASCO
NAVARRA
LA RIOJA
ARAGÓN
CATALUÑA
Costa Brava
Costa Dorada
Costa del Azahar
Costa Blanca
SPAIN
CASTILLA-LA MANCHA
VALENCIA
MURCIA
Barcelona
Zaragoza
Pamplona
Vitoria-Gasteiz
Donostia - San Sebastián
Bilbao
Logroño
Lleida (Lérida)
Tarragona
Teruel
Cuenca
Guadalajara
Valencia
Golfo de Valencia
Castelló de la Plana
Albacete
Alicante
Murcia
Cartagena
Almería
Granada
Sierra Nevada
Majorca (Mallorca)
Minorca (Menorca)
Ibiza (Eivissa)
Formentera
Cabrera
ISLAS BALEARES
Balearic Islands
Palma de Mallorca
Mediterranean Sea
ALGIERS (Alger)
ALGERIA
Oran
Mostaganem
Blida
Médéa
Chlef
Tizi Ouzou
Bejaïa
Massif de l'Ouarsenis
Atlas Tellien
Isla de Alborán (Spain)
Melilla (Spain)
Nador
122-123
H I J K L M N O P
055

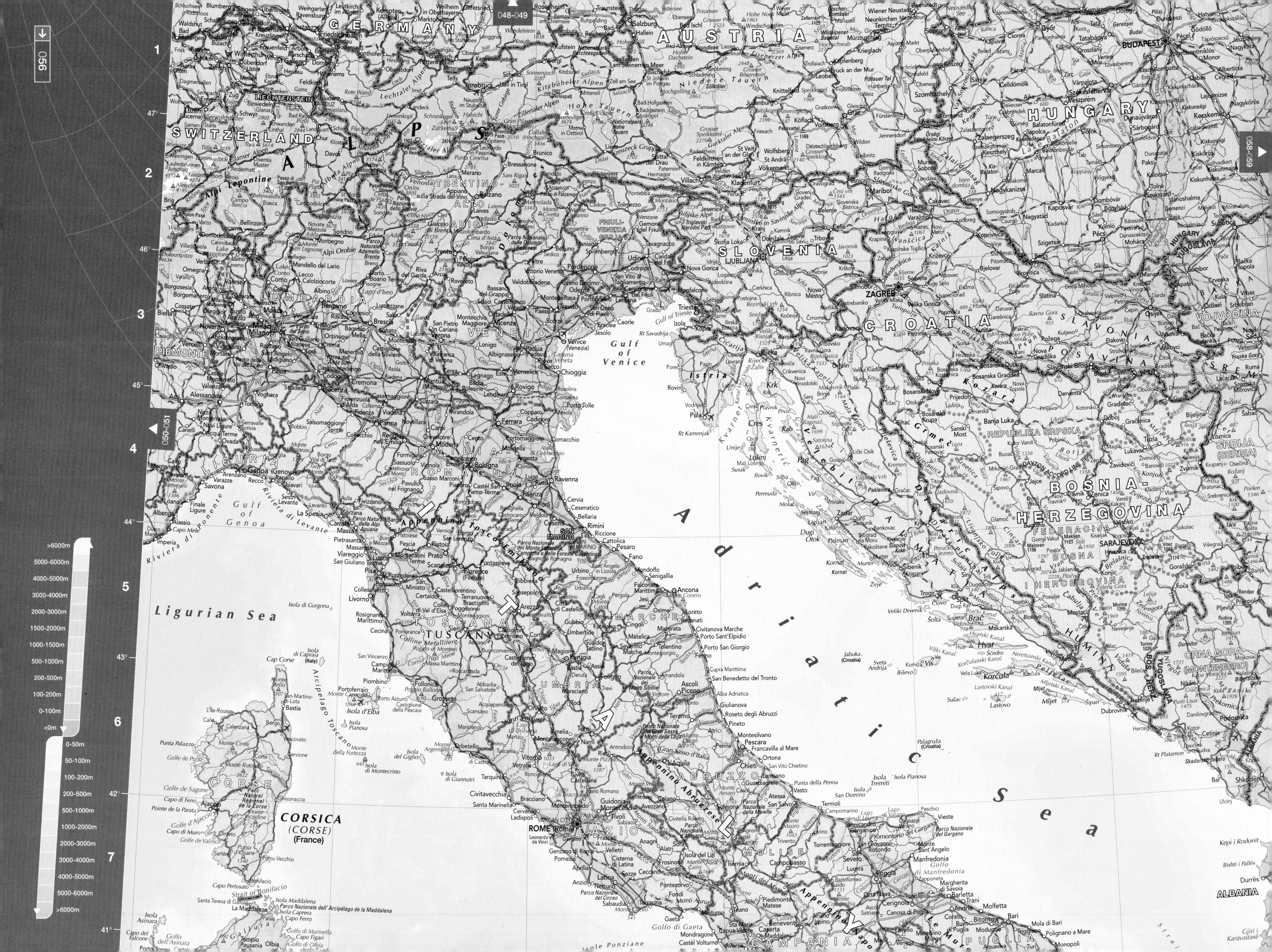

GERMANY
AUSTRIA
SWITZERLAND
LIECHTENSTEIN
HUNGARY
SLOVENIA
CROATIA
BOSNIA-HERZEGOVINA
ALBANIA
ALPS
CORSICA (CORSE) (France)
Adriatic Sea
Ligurian Sea
Gulf of Venice
Gulf of Genoa
>6000m
5000-6000m
4000-5000m
3000-4000m
2000-3000m
1500-2000m
1000-1500m
500-1000m
200-500m
100-200m
0-100m
<0m
0-50m
50-100m
100-200m
200-500m
500-1000m
1000-2000m
2000-3000m
3000-4000m
4000-5000m
5000-6000m
>6000m
048-049
058-059
050-051

europe[map10]

35°48'N / 8°19'E

1:3 000 000

Conic Equidistant Projection

CONNECTIONS	
► subject	page#
► World physical features	8–9
► World cities	24–25
► Europe landscapes	30–31
► Europe countries	32–35
► Europe issues	34–35
► Europe environments	36–37

Tyrrhenian Sea

Ionian Sea

Mediterranean Sea

Sicilian Channel

SARDINIA (SARDEGNA) (Italy)

SICILY (SICILIA)

CALABRIA

BASILICATA

Isole Lipari

Isole Pelagie (Italy)

TUNISIA

ALGERIA

MALTA — VALLETTA

Palermo

Catania

Syracuse (Siracusa)

Messina

Trapani

Marsala

Cagliari

Sassari

Taranto

Golfo di Taranto

Brindisi

Lecce

TUNIS

Golfe de Tunis

Golfe de Hammamet

Sousse

Kairouan

Bizerte

122–123

057

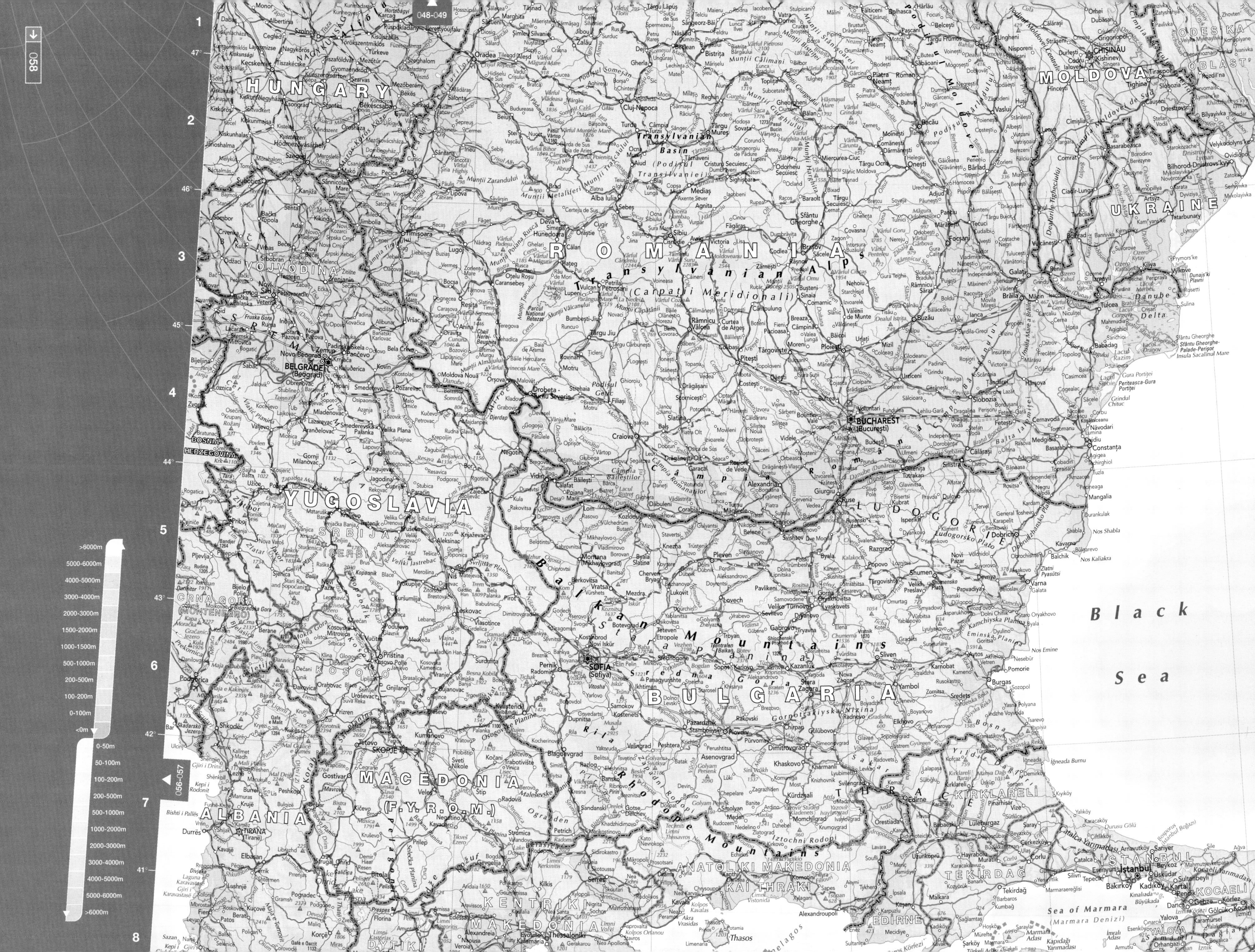
HUNGARY
ROMANIA
MOLDOVA
UKRAINE
BULGARIA
YUGOSLAVIA
ALBANIA
MACEDONIA (F.Y.R.O.M.)
Black Sea
Sea of Marmara
BUCHAREST (București)
SOFIA (Sofiya)
BELGRADE (Beograd)
SKOPJE
TIRANA (Tiranë)
CHIŞINĂU (Kishinev)
İstanbul
Transylvanian Alps (Carpații Meridionali)
Transylvanian Basin (Podișul Transilvaniei)
Balkan Mountains (Stara Planina)
Rhodope Mountains
Danube Delta
048-049
056-057
>6000m
5000-6000m
4000-5000m
3000-4000m
2000-3000m
1500-2000m
1000-1500m
500-1000m
200-500m
100-200m
0-100m
<0m
0-50m
50-100m
100-200m
200-500m
500-1000m
1000-2000m
2000-3000m
3000-4000m
4000-5000m
5000-6000m
>6000m

europe[map11]

35°-47°N / 19°-29°E

CONNECTIONS

subject	page#
▲ Europe landscapes	30–31
▲ Europe countries	32–33
▲ Europe issues	34–35
▲ Mediterranean Sea	52–53

1:3 000 000

miles
km
Conic Equidistant Projection

A e g e a n   S e a

Mediterranean Sea

Ionian Sea

GREECE

TURKEY

PELOPONNISOS

Crete (Kríti)

Rhodes (Ródos)

Cyclades (Kykládes)

Dodecanese (Dodekánisos)

Lesbos (Lésvos)

ATHENS (Athína)

Pindus Mountains

Gulf of Corinth

ATHENS · Piraeus · Smyrna (Izmir) · Bursa · Corfu (Kérkyra) · Cephalonia (Kefallonía) · Zakynthos (Zante) · Evvoia · Límnos · Chíos · Sámos · Náxos · Páros · Mýkonos · Tínos · Andros · Thíra (Santoríni) · Kos · Kárpathos

A   K   D   E   N   I   Z

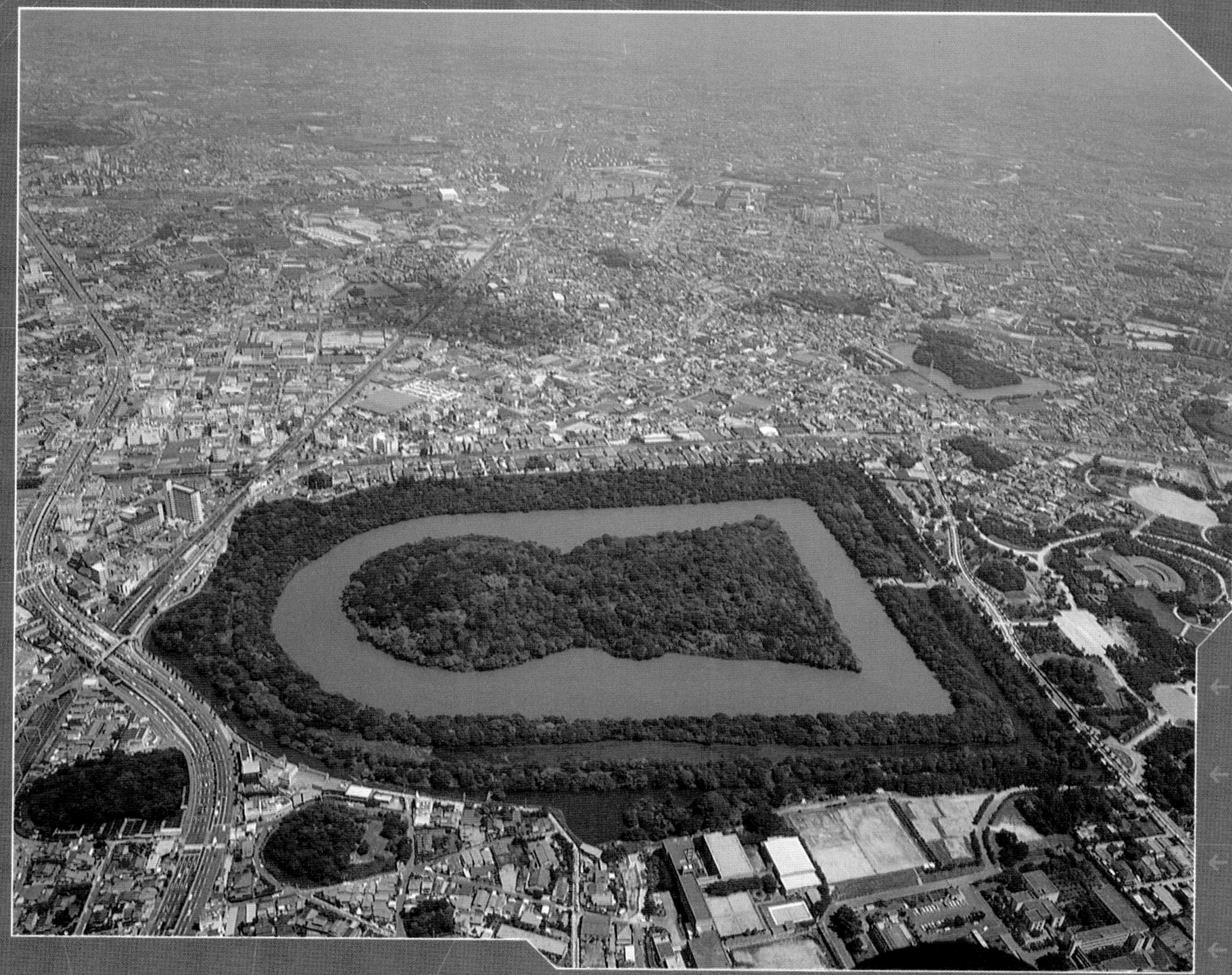

Osaka, *Japan*

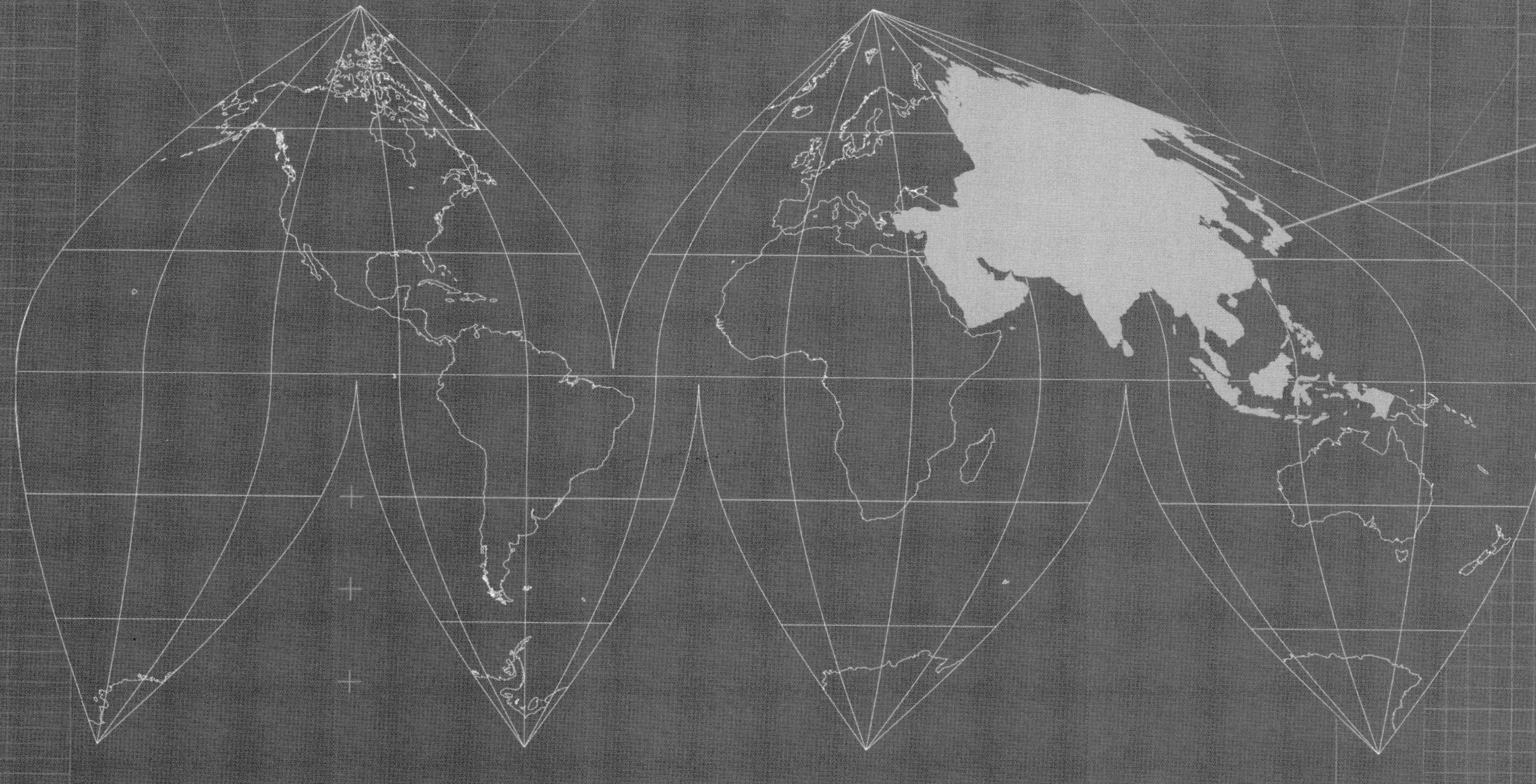

asia

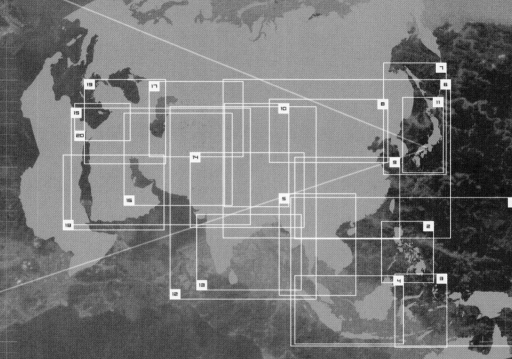

[contents]

		page#
asia [landscapes]		62–63
asia [countries]		64–65
asia [countries/issues]		66–67
asia [changes]		68–69
asia [threats]		70–71

	map coverage	scale	page#
asia [map 1]	ASIA Southeast	1:13 000 000	72–73
asia [map 2]	PHILIPPINES	1:6 000 000	74
asia [map 3]	INDONESIA Central	1:6 000 000	75
asia [map 4]	INDONESIA West, MALAYSIA and SINGAPORE	1:6 000 000	76–77
asia [map 5]	MYANMAR, THAILAND, LAOS and VIETNAM	1:6 000 000	78–79
asia [map 6]	ASIA East	1:13 000 000	80–81
asia [map 7]	ASIA Northeast	1:6 000 000	82–83
asia [map 8]	CHINA North and MONGOLIA	1:6 000 000	84–85
asia [map 9]	CHINA South	1:6 000 000	86–87
asia [map 10]	CHINA West	1:6 000 000	88–89
asia [map 11]	JAPAN	1:4 000 000	90–91
asia [map 12]	ASIA Central and South	1:12 000 000	92–93
asia [map 13]	INDIA South and SRI LANKA	1:6 000 000	94–95
asia [map 14]	INDIA North, BANGLADESH and NEPAL	1:6 000 000	96–97
asia [map 15]	ASIA Southwest	1:11 000 000	98–99
asia [map 16]	IRAN, AFGHANISTAN and PAKISTAN	1:6 000 000	100–101
asia [map 17]	KAZAKHSTAN, UZBEKISTAN and KYRGYZSTAN	1:6 000 000	102–103
asia [map 18]	SAUDI ARABIA and THE GULF STATES	1:6 000 000	104–105
asia [map 19]	TURKEY, IRAQ, and TRANS-CAUCASIAN REPUBLICS	1:6 000 000	106–107
asia [map 20]	MIDDLE EAST	1:3 000 000	108–109

asia[landscapes]

Largest drainage basin
Ob'-Irtysh
2 990 000 sq km / 1 154 000 sq miles
Map reference 38 G3-39 I5

Largest lake
Caspian Sea
371 000 sq km / 143 243 sq miles
Map reference 102 B4

Highest point
Mt Everest
China/Nepal
8 848 m / 29 028 ft
Map reference 97 E4

Longest river
Yangtze
6 380 km / 3 964 miles
Map reference 87 G2

Largest island
Borneo
745 561 sq km /287 863 sq miles
Map reference 77 F2

Black Sea
Mediterranean Sea
Caucasus
Kirghiz Steppe
Ural Mountains
Ob' River
Yenisey River
West Siberian Plain
Siberia
Irtysh River
Caspian Sea
Euphrates River
Elburz Mountains
Aral Sea
Tigris River
Zagros Mountains
Arabian Peninsula
The Gulf
Lake Balkhash
Central Siberian Plateau
Hindu Kush
Tien Shan
Tarim Pendi
Altai Mountains
Lake Baikal
Indus River
Mount Everest
Ganges River
Gobi
Yellow River
Arabian Sea
Yangtze River
Bay of Bengal
Sri Lanka
Irrawaddy River
Eas
Indian Ocean
Gulf of Thailand
Malay Peninsula
South China Sea
Ryuky
Mekong River
Sumatra
Philippines
Borneo
Java
Java Sea
Celebes
Palau
Timor
New Guinea

CONNECTIONS

▸ subject	page#
▸ World physical features	10–11
▸ Asian states and territories	64–65
▸ Water issues	66–67
▸ Tropical storms in Asia	70–71
▸ Reference maps of Asia	72–109

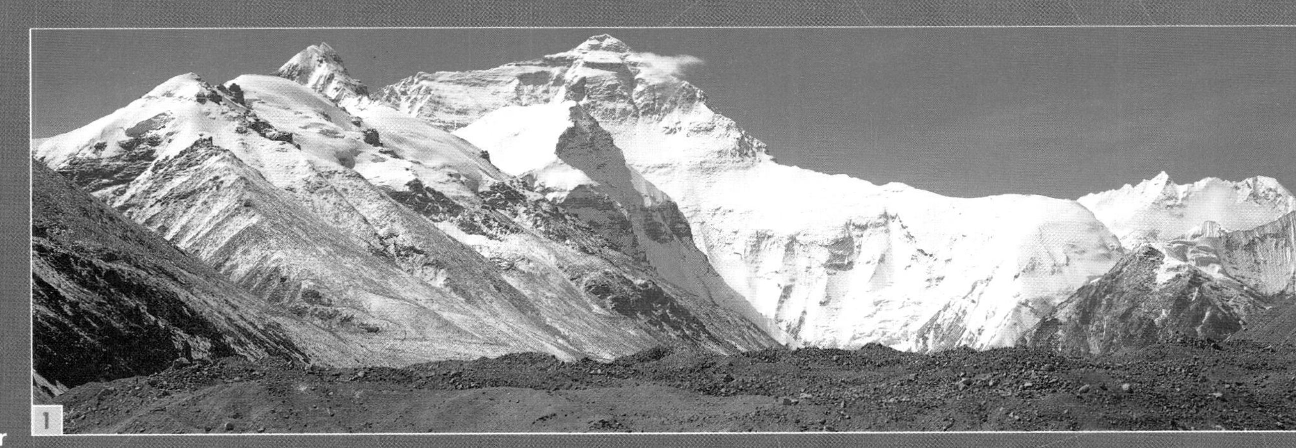

1

Arctic Ocean

Lena River

Argun River

Heilong Jiang River

Sea of Okhotsk

Kamchatka Peninsula

Sea of Japan

China ~~ea~~

Honshu

~~slands~~

Pacific Ocean

Northern Mariana Islands

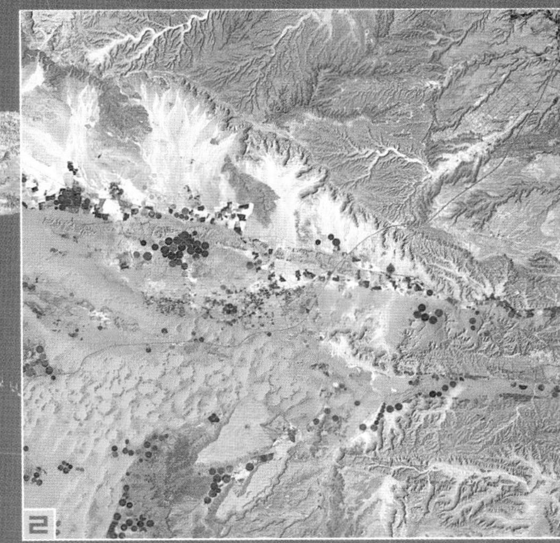

2

Asia is the world's largest continent and its huge range of physical features is evident in this perspective view from the southeast. These include in southwest Asia the Arabian Peninsula, in southern Asia the Indian subcontinent, in southeast Asia the vast Indonesian archipelago, in central Asia the Plateau of Tibet and the Gobi desert and in east Asia the volcanic islands of Japan and the Kamchatka Peninsula.

North to south, the continent extends over 76 degrees of latitude from the Arctic Ocean in the north to the southern tip of Indonesia in the south. The Ural Mountains and the Caucasus in the west form the boundary with Europe. Asia's most impressive mountain range is the Himalaya, which contains the world's highest peaks. The continent is drained by some of the world's longest rivers and the Caspian Sea is the world's largest lake or inland sea.

1 Himalayas, *China/Nepal*

This view of the Himalayas shows Mount Everest, at 8 848 m the world's highest mountain. The photograph looks south from the Plateau of Tibet, with its typical barren landscape in the foreground. The plateau lies at a height of over 4 000 m. The Himalayas mark the southern limit of the plateau and stretch for over 2 000 km, forming the northern limit of the Indian sub-continent.

2 Arabian Desert, *Saudi Arabia*

The arid desert areas to the southwest of Riyadh, Saudi Arabia are shown in this infrared satellite image. Sand shows as yellow and bare rock as grey. Extensive drainage patterns belie the fact that this area only receives 100 mm of rain each year. These are dry river beds for most of the year. The red dots are circular fields with centre-pivot irrigation systems. Water is fed through large revolving sprinklers.

Satellite/Sensor : SPOT

3 Ganges Delta, *India*

This infrared satellite image shows the Hugli river in the western part of the Ganges delta, flowing into the Bay of Bengal. Vegetation shows as red in the image and the pale blue areas depict water full of sediment. The strong red indicates areas of mangrove swamp. The delta is a huge area, over 300 km across. The fertile soil is intensively farmed but the area is often flooded, particularly as a result of tropical cyclones.

Satellite/Sensor : SPOT

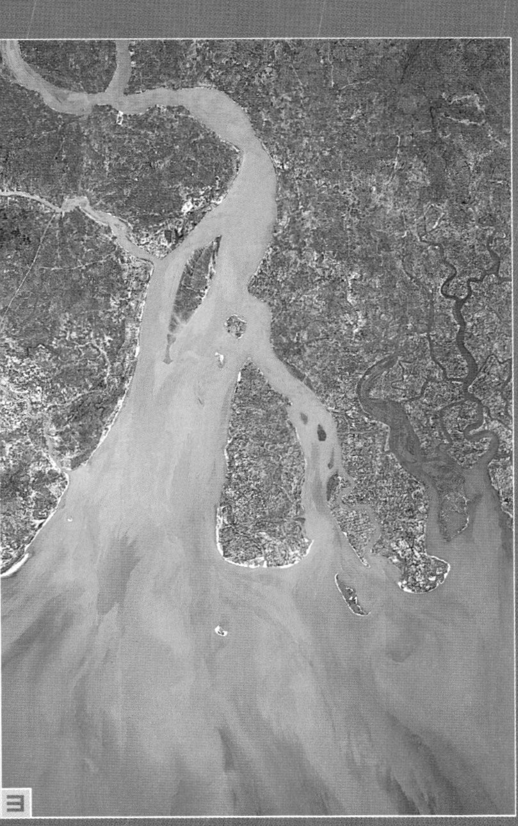

3

ASIA

HIGHEST MOUNTAINS

	m	ft	location	map
Mt Everest	8 848	29 028	China/Nepal	97 E4
K2	8 611	28 251	China/Jammu and Kashmir	96 C2
Kangchenjunga	8 586	28 169	India/Nepal	97 F4
Lhotse	8 516	27 939	China/Nepal	97 E3
Makalu	8 463	27 765	China/Nepal	97 E4
Cho Oyu	8 201	26 906	China/Nepal	97 E3
Dhaulagiri	8 167	26 794	Nepal	97 D3
Manaslu	8 163	26 781	Nepal	97 E3
Nanga Parbat	8 126	26 660	Jammu and Kashmir	96 B2
Annapurna 1	8 091	26 545	Nepal	97 D3

LARGEST ISLANDS

	sq km	sq miles	map
Borneo	745 561	287 863	77 F2
Sumatra	473 606	182 860	76 C3
Honshu	227 414	87 805	91 F6
Celebes	189 216	73 057	75 B3
Java	132 188	51 038	77 E4
Luzon	104 690	40 421	76 B2
Mindanao	94 630	36 537	74 C5
Hokkaido	78 073	30 144	90 H3
Sakhalin	76 400	29 498	82 F2
Sri Lanka	65 610	25 332	94 D5
Kyushu	36 554	14 114	91 B8
Taiwan	35 873	13 851	87 G4

LONGEST RIVERS

	km	miles	map
Yangtze	6 380	3 964	87 G2
Ob'-Irtysh	5 568	3 459	38 G3 – 39 I5
Yenisey-Angara -Selenga	5 550	3 448	39 I2 –K4
Yellow	5 464	3 395	85 H4
Irtysh	4 440	2 759	38 G3
Mekong	4 425	2 749	79 D6
Heilong Jiang -'Argun'	4 416	2 744	81 M3
Lena-Kirenga	4 400	2 734	39 M2 – K4
Yenisey	4 090	2 541	39 I2
Ob'	3 701	2 300	38 H3

LAKES

	sq km	sq miles	map
Caspian Sea	371 000	143 243	102 B4
Aral Sea	33 640	12 988	102 D3
Lake Baikal	30 500	11 776	39 K4
Lake Balkhash	17 400	6 718	103 H3
Ysyk-Kol	6 200	2 393	103 I4

LAND AREA

		map
Most northerly point	Mys Arkticheskiy, Russian Federation	39 J1
Most southerly point	Pamana, Indonesia	75 B5
Most westerly point	Bozcaada, Turkey	59 H9
Most easterly point	Mys Dezhneva, Russian Federation	39 T3

Total land area: 45 036 492 sq km / 17 388 686 sq miles

asia[countries]

		area sq km	area sq miles	population	capital	languages	religions	currency	map
AFGHANISTAN		652 225	251 825	21 765 000	Kābul	Dari, Pushtu, Uzbek, Turkmen	Sunni Muslim, Shi'a Muslim	Afghani	101
ARMENIA		29 800	11 506	3 787 000	Yerevan (Erevan)	Armenian, Azeri	Armenian Orthodox	Dram	107
AZERBAIJAN		86 600	33 436	8 041 000	Baku	Azeri, Armenian, Russian, Lezgian	Shi'a Muslim, Sunni Muslim, Russian and Armenian Orthodox	Manat	107
BAHRAIN		691	267	640 000	Manama (Al Manāmah)	Arabic, English	Shi'a Muslim, Sunni Muslim, Christian	Dinar	105
BANGLADESH		143 998	55 598	137 439 000	Dhaka (Dacca)	Bengali, English	Sunni Muslim, Hindu	Taka	97
BHUTAN		46 620	18 000	2 085 000	Thimphu	Dzongkha, Nepali, Assamese	Buddhist, Hindu	Ngultrum	97
BRUNEI		5 765	2 226	328 000	Bandar Seri Begawan	Malay, English, Chinese	Sunni Muslim, Buddhist, Christian	Dollar	77
CAMBODIA		181 000	69 884	13 104 000	Phnom Penh	Khmer, Vietnamese	Buddhist, Roman Catholic, Sunni Muslim	Riel	79
CHINA		9 584 492	3 700 593	1 260 137 000	Beijing (Peking)	Mandarin, Wu, Cantonese, Hsiang, regional languages	Confucian, Taoist, Buddhist, Christian, Sunni Muslim	Yuan	80–81
CYPRUS		9 251	3 572	784 000	Nicosia (Lefkosia)	Greek, Turkish, English	Greek Orthodox, Sunni Muslim	Pound	108
GEORGIA		69 700	26 911	5 262 000	T'bilisi	Georgian, Russian, Armenian, Azeri, Ossetian, Abkhaz	Georgian Orthodox, Russian Orthodox, Sunni Muslim	Lari	107
INDIA		3 065 027	1 183 414	1 008 937 000	New Delhi	Hindi, English, many regional languages	Hindu, Sunni Muslim, Shi'a Muslim, Sikh, Christian	Rupee	92–93
INDONESIA		1 919 445	741 102	212 092 000	Jakarta	Indonesian, local languages	Sunni Muslim, Protestant, Roman Catholic, Hindu, Buddhist	Rupiah	72–73
IRAN		1 648 000	636 296	70 330 000	Tehrān	Farsi, Azeri, Kurdish, regional languages	Shi'a Muslim, Sunni Muslim	Rial	100–101
IRAQ		438 317	169 235	22 946 000	Baghdād	Arabic, Kurdish, Turkmen	Shi'a Muslim, Sunni Muslim, Christian	Dinar	107
ISRAEL		20 770	8 019	6 040 000	Jerusalem (Yerushalayim) (El Quds)	Hebrew, Arabic	Jewish, Sunni Muslim, Christian, Druze	Shekel	108
JAPAN		377 727	145 841	127 096 000	Tōkyō	Japanese	Shintoist, Buddhist, Christian	Yen	90–91
JORDAN		89 206	34 443	4 913 000	'Ammān	Arabic	Sunni Muslim, Christian	Dinar	108–109
KAZAKHSTAN		2 717 300	1 049 155	16 172 000	Astana (Akmola)	Kazakh, Russian, Ukranian, German, Uzbek, Tatar	Sunni Muslim, Russian Orthodox, Protestant	Tenge	102–103
KUWAIT		17 818	6 880	1 914 000	Kuwait (Al Kuwayt)	Arabic	Sunni Muslim, Shi'a Muslim, Christian, Hindu	Dinar	107
KYRGYZSTAN		198 500	76 641	4 921 000	Bishkek (Frunze)	Kyrgyz, Russian, Uzbek	Sunni Muslim, Russian Orthodox	Som	103
LAOS		236 800	91 429	5 279 000	Vientiane (Viangchan)	Lao, local languages	Buddhist, traditional beliefs	Kip	78–79
LEBANON		10 452	4 036	3 496 000	Beirut (Beyrouth)	Arabic, Armenian, French	Shi'a Muslim, Sunni Muslim, Christian	Pound	108–109
MALAYSIA		332 965	128 559	22 218 000	Kuala Lumpur	Malay, English, Chinese, Tamil, local languages	Sunni Muslim, Buddhist, Hindu, Christian, traditional beliefs	Ringgit	76–77
MALDIVES		298	115	291 000	Male	Divehi (Maldivian)	Sunni Muslim	Rufiyaa	93
MONGOLIA		1 565 000	604 250	2 533 000	Ulan Bator (Ulaanbaatar)	Khalka (Mongolian), Kazakh, local languages	Buddhist, Sunni Muslim	Tugrik	84–85
MYANMAR		676 577	261 228	47 749 000	Rangoon (Yangôn)	Burmese, Shan, Karen, local languages	Buddhist, Christian, Sunni Muslim	Kyat	78–79
NEPAL		147 181	56 827	23 043 000	Kathmandu	Nepali, Maithili, Bhojpuri, English, local languages	Hindu, Buddhist, Sunni Muslim	Rupee	96–97
NORTH KOREA		120 538	46 540	22 268 000	P'yŏngyang	Korean	Traditional beliefs, Chondoist, Buddhist	Won	82–83
OMAN		309 500	119 499	2 538 000	Muscat (Masqat)	Arabic, Baluchi, Indian languages	Ibadhi Muslim, Sunni Muslim	Rial	105

1   Middle East Boundaries

International boundaries are often visible from space because of differences in land use. In this Shuttle photograph the borders between Egypt, Gaza and Israel can be clearly identified. Grazing is the predominant agricultural activity in this part of Egypt, to the bottom of the image, and in Gaza in the centre, and has removed much of the vegetation. In contrast, Israel, to the east of the boundary, appears darker and more cultivated because of irrigation from the Jordan river.

Satellite/Sensor : Space Shuttle

2   Egypt/Gaza Border, *Middle East*

Borders between countries frequently follow the alignment of natural physical features, such as rivers, mountains or lake shores. Some borders, however, are demarcated only by man-made features, such as this fence at Rafah on the boundary between Egypt and Gaza. Gaza is a small semi-autonomous region on the southeast shore of the Mediterranean Sea. It is home to about 1 million Palestinian Arabs and was formerly under complete Israeli control.

3   The Great Wall, *China*

The Great Wall of China was built in various stages and forms over a period of 1 000 years from the third century BC. It is one of China's most distinctive and spectacular features. The wall is visible in this aerial photograph as a light coloured line running across the hills from lower right to upper left. Stretching a total length of over 2 400 km from the coast east of Beijing, to the Gobi desert in Gansu province, the wall was first built to protect China from the Mongols and nomadic peoples to the north of the country.

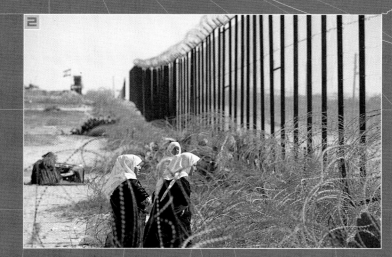

CONNECTIONS

► subject	page#
► World physical features	8–9
► World countries	10–11
► Asia landscapes	62–63
► Asia issues	66–67
► Reference maps of Asia	72–109

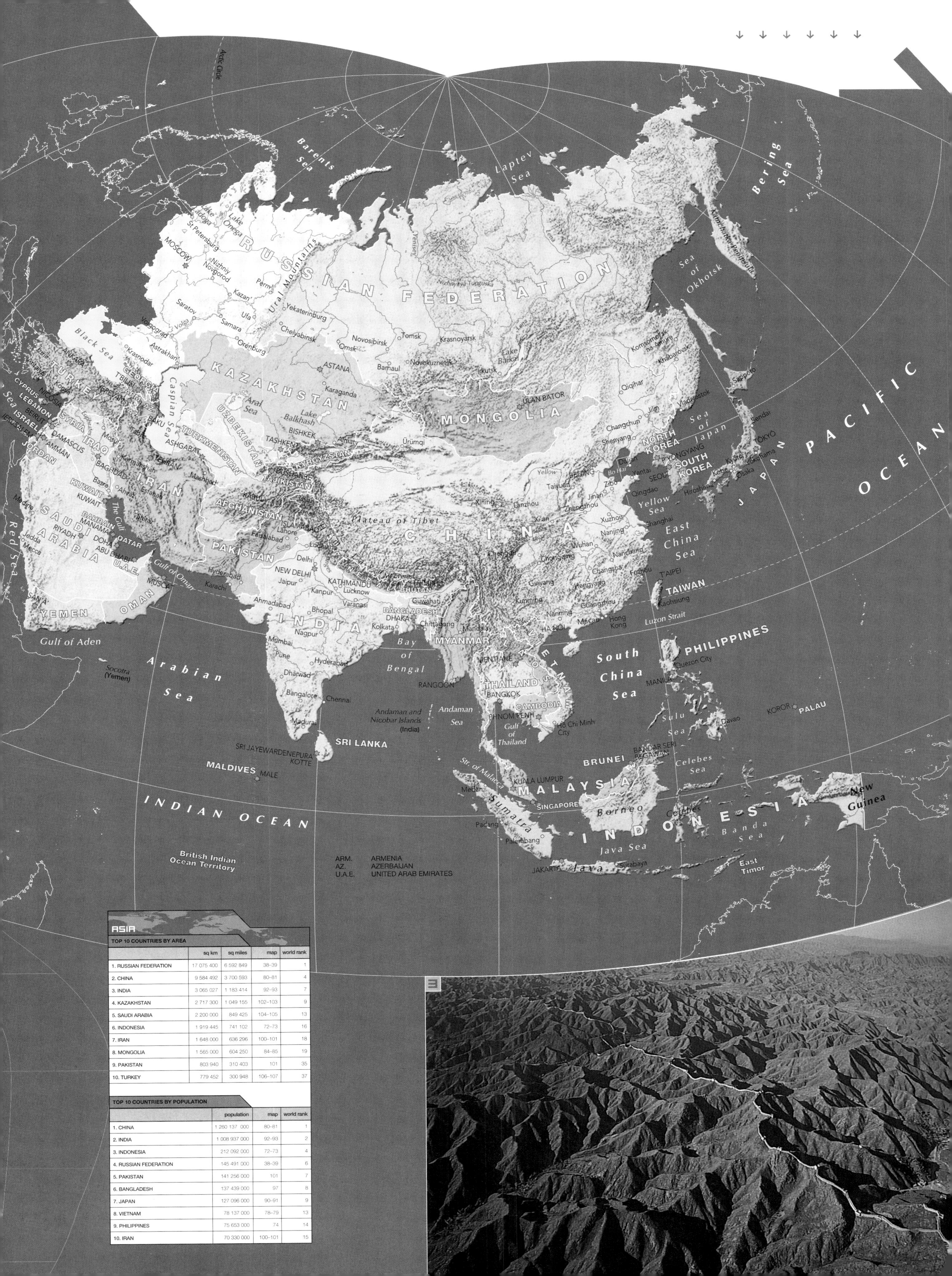

ARM. ARMENIA
AZ.   AZERBAIJAN
U.A.E. UNITED ARAB EMIRATES

ASIA

TOP 10 COUNTRIES BY AREA

	sq km	sq miles	map	world rank
1. RUSSIAN FEDERATION	17 075 400	6 592 849	38–39	1
2. CHINA	9 584 492	3 700 593	80–81	4
3. INDIA	3 065 027	1 183 414	92–93	7
4. KAZAKHSTAN	2 717 300	1 049 155	102–103	9
5. SAUDI ARABIA	2 200 000	849 425	104–105	13
6. INDONESIA	1 919 445	741 102	72–73	16
7. IRAN	1 648 000	636 296	100–101	18
8. MONGOLIA	1 565 000	604 250	84–85	19
9. PAKISTAN	803 940	310 403	101	35
10. TURKEY	779 452	300 948	106–107	37

TOP 10 COUNTRIES BY POPULATION

	population	map	world rank
1. CHINA	1 260 137 000	80–81	1
2. INDIA	1 008 937 000	92–93	2
3. INDONESIA	212 092 000	72–73	4
4. RUSSIAN FEDERATION	145 491 000	38–39	6
5. PAKISTAN	141 256 000	101	7
6. BANGLADESH	137 439 000	97	8
7. JAPAN	127 096 000	90–91	9
8. VIETNAM	78 137 000	78–79	13
9. PHILIPPINES	75 653 000	74	14
10. IRAN	70 330 000	100–101	15

ASIA
COUNTRIES

		area sq km	area sq miles	population	capital	languages	religions	currency	map
PAKISTAN		803 940	310 403	141 256 000	Islamabad	Urdu, Punjabi, Sindhi, Pushtu, English	Sunni Muslim, Shi'a Muslim, Christian, Hindu	Rupee	101
PALAU		497	192	19 000	Koror	Palauan, English	Roman Catholic, Protestant, traditional beliefs	US dollar	73
PHILIPPINES		300 000	115 831	75 653 000	Manila	English, Pilipino, Cebuano, local languages	Roman Catholic, Protestant, Sunni Muslim, Aglipayan	Peso	74
QATAR		11 437	4 416	565 000	Doha (Ad Dawhah)	Arabic	Sunni Muslim	Riyal	105
RUSSIAN FEDERATION		17 075 400	6 592 849	145 491 000	Moscow (Moskva)	Russian, Tatar, Ukrainian, local languages	Russian Orthodox, Sunni Muslim, Protestant	Rouble	38–39
SAUDI ARABIA		2 200 000	849 425	20 346 000	Riyadh (Ar Riyāḍ)	Arabic	Sunni Muslim, Shi'a Muslim	Riyal	104–105
SINGAPORE		639	247	4 018 000	Singapore	Chinese, English, Malay, Tamil	Buddhist, Taoist, Sunni Muslim, Christian, Hindu	Dollar	76
SOUTH KOREA		99 274	38 330	46 740 000	Seoul (Sŏul)	Korean	Buddhist, Protestant, Roman Catholic	Won	83
SRI LANKA		65 610	25 332	18 924 000	Sri Jayewardenepura Kotte	Sinhalese, Tamil, English	Buddhist, Hindu, Sunni Muslim, Roman Catholic	Rupee	94
SYRIA		185 180	71 498	16 189 000	Damascus (Dimashq)	Arabic, Kurdish, Armenian	Sunni Muslim, Shi'a Muslim, Christian	Pound	108–109
TAIWAN		36 179	13 969	22 300 000	T'aipei	Mandarin, Min, Hakka, local languages	Buddhist, Taoist, Confucian, Christian	Dollar	87
TAJIKISTAN		143 100	55 251	6 087 000	Dushanbe	Tajik, Uzbek, Russian	Sunni Muslim	Rouble	101
THAILAND		513 115	198 115	62 806 000	Bangkok (Krung Thep)	Thai, Lao, Chinese, Malay, Mon–Khmer languages	Buddhist, Sunni Muslim	Baht	78–79
TURKEY		779 452	300 948	66 668 000	Ankara	Turkish, Kurdish	Sunni Muslim, Shi'a Muslim	Lira	106–107
TURKMENISTAN		488 100	188 456	4 737 000	Ashgabat (Ashkhabad)	Turkmen, Uzbek, Russian	Sunni Muslim, Russian Orthodox	Manat	102–103
UNITED ARAB EMIRATES		83 600	32 278	2 606 000	Abu Dhabi (Abū Ẓabī)	Arabic, English	Sunni Muslim, Shi'a Muslim	Dirham	105
UZBEKISTAN		447 400	172 742	24 881 000	Tashkent	Uzbek, Russian, Tajik, Kazakh	Sunni Muslim, Russian Orthodox	Sum	102–103
VIETNAM		329 565	127 246	78 137 000	Ha Nôi	Vietnamese, Thai, Khmer, Chinese, local languages	Buddhist, Taoist, Roman Catholic, Cao Dai, Hoa Hao	Dong	78–79
YEMEN		527 968	203 850	18 349 000	Şan'ā'	Arabic	Sunni Muslim, Shi'a Muslim	Rial	104–105

DEPENDENT AND DISPUTED TERRITORIES

		territorial status	area sq km	area sq miles	population	capital	languages	religions	currency	map
British Indian Ocean Territory		United Kingdom Overseas Territory	60	23	uninhabited					219
Christmas Island		Australian External Territory	135	52	2 195	The Settlement	English	Buddhist, Sunni Muslim, Protestant, Roman Catholic	Australian dollar	72
Cocos Islands (Keeling Islands)		Australian External Territory	14	5	637	West Island	English	Sunni Muslim, Christian	Australian dollar	218
East Timor		under UN Transitional Administration	14 874	5 743	737 000	Dili	Portuguese, Tetun, English	Roman Catholic		75
French Southern and Antarctic Lands		French Overseas Territory	439 580	169 723	uninhabited					219
Gaza		semi-autonomous region	363	140	3 191 000*	Gaza	Arabic	Sunni Muslim, Shi'a Muslim	Israeli shekel	108
Heard and McDonald Islands		Australian External Territory	412	159	uninhabited					219
Jammu and Kashmir		Disputed territory (India/Pakistan)	222 236	85 806	13 000 000					96–97
West Bank		Disputed territory	5 860	2 263			Arabic, Hebrew	Sunni Muslim, Jewish, Shi'a Muslim, Christian		108

*includes occupied West Bank

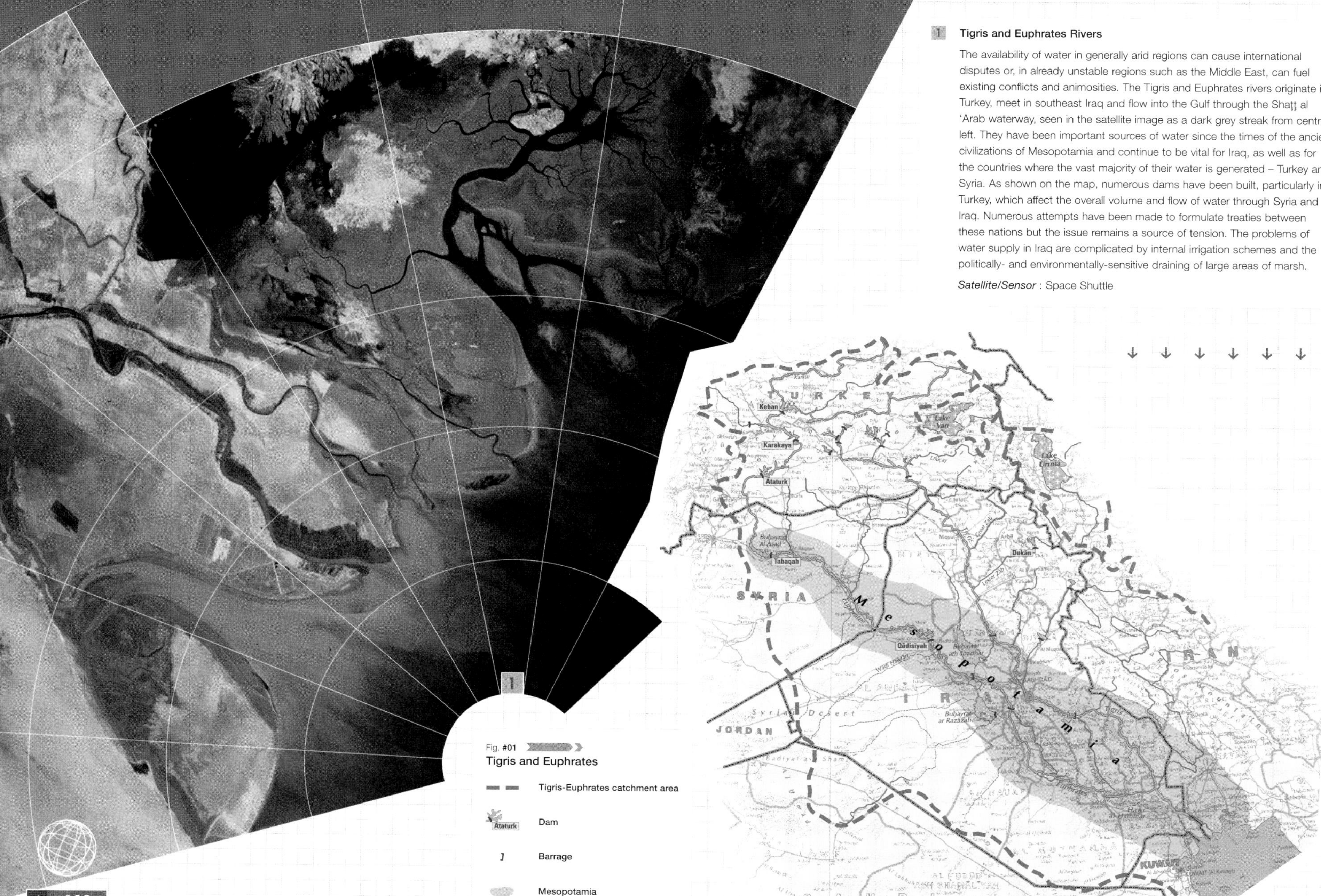

1 Tigris and Euphrates Rivers

The availability of water in generally arid regions can cause international disputes or, in already unstable regions such as the Middle East, can fuel existing conflicts and animosities. The Tigris and Euphrates rivers originate in Turkey, meet in southeast Iraq and flow into the Gulf through the Shaṭṭ al 'Arab waterway, seen in the satellite image as a dark grey streak from centre left. They have been important sources of water since the times of the ancient civilizations of Mesopotamia and continue to be vital for Iraq, as well as for the countries where the vast majority of their water is generated – Turkey and Syria. As shown on the map, numerous dams have been built, particularly in Turkey, which affect the overall volume and flow of water through Syria and Iraq. Numerous attempts have been made to formulate treaties between these nations but the issue remains a source of tension. The problems of water supply in Iraq are complicated by internal irrigation schemes and the politically- and environmentally-sensitive draining of large areas of marsh.

Satellite/Sensor : Space Shuttle

Fig. #01
Tigris and Euphrates

--- Tigris-Euphrates catchment area

Dam

] Barrage

Mesopotamia

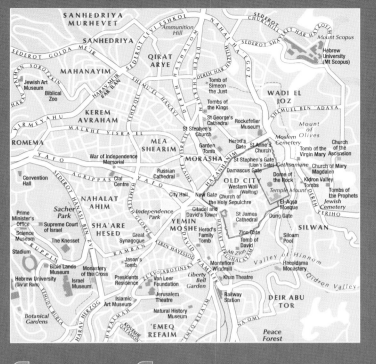

General place of interest
Place of worship

Transport location
Academic/municipal building

Fig. #02
Jerusalem

Jerusalem

The city of Jerusalem is a holy city for Jews, Muslims and Christians alike, and remains a focus of the ongoing conflicts between Israelis and Palestinians. This aerial photograph shows the Old City outlined by the city walls, the full outline of which is shown on the map. The Old City is divided into the Jewish, Muslim, Christian and Armenian quarters. The Muslim quarter, seen on the right of this photograph, is the busiest and most densely populated area. Just left of centre is the distinctive golden-roofed Dome of the Rock and to the left of this the El-Aqsa Mosque.

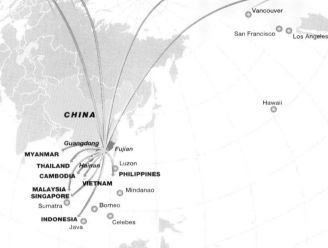

Fig. #03
Chinese migration

Main regions of Chinese emigration

Main destination countries

Principal overseas communities

CONNECTIONS

► subject		page#
► World countries		10–11
► Asia landscapes		62–63
► Asia countries		64–65
► Reference maps of Asia		72–109

Chinese migration

There has been a pattern of population migration from China since the early nineteenth century. This has resulted in a large overseas Chinese population, or *diaspora*, today estimated at over 30 million. Historically, the most common reasons for this population movement have been economic hardship, famine and political instability. As can be seen from the map, the majority of migrants settle in southeast Asia, mainly in Indonesia, Thailand, Malaysia and Singapore. In some countries this can create tensions between ethnic groups. Over eighty per cent of the Chinese overseas population lives in Asia, with most of them living in Chinese communities within the major cities. Europe and North America have also been important destinations, where the immigrants have again created distinctive communities in large cities, such as Chinatown in San Francisco, part of which is shown in the photograph.

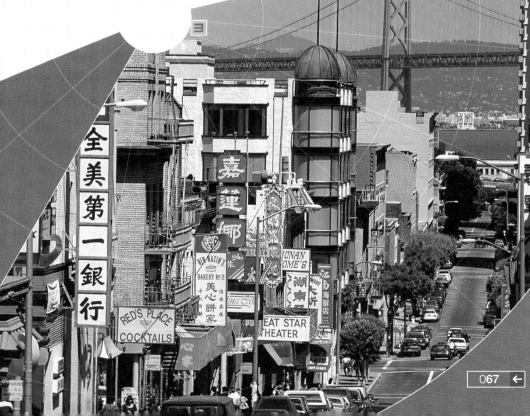

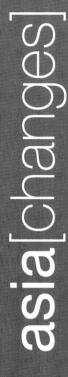

asia[changes]

CONNECTIONS

► subject	page#
► Types of imagery	4–5
► World changes	20–21
► Asia landscapes	62–63
► Asia issues	66–67
► Reference maps of Asia	72–109

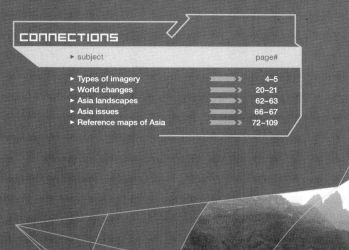

1 **Three Gorges Dam Project,** *China*

The Three Gorges Dam Project on the Yangtze river is the world's largest hydroelectric project. The term refers to a 190 km stretch of the Yangtze river where it flows through the precipitous Quitang, Wu and Xiling gorges, as shown on the satellite image and map. The photograph at the top shows part of the project area before construction began in 1997. The centre photograph shows part of the construction work and gives some idea of the effect it will have on the landscape. When complete, the dam will be over two kilometres wide and will create a 620 km long reservoir which will engulf over 400 sq km of farmland, thirteen cities, hundreds of villages, and archaeological sites. While the project, due for completion in 2009, will improve flood management, generate electricity and transfer water to dry areas further north, it raises many social and environmental issues, including the resettlement of between 1–2 million people, the potential accumulation of pollutants and the destruction of precious natural habitats.

Satellite/Sensor : Landsat (bottom)

Fig. #01 ▶▶▶▶
Three Gorges Dam project

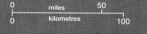

0 — miles — 50
0 — kilometres — 100

- Area to be inundated
- Area affected by Three Gorges Dam project
- Three Gorges Dam
- Gorge
- Inundated town
- Provincial boundary

SHAANXI

HUBEI

SICHUAN

Wuxi
Xingshan
Xiang Xi
Daning He
Kaixian
Wushan
Zigui
Fengjie
Badong *Xiling Gorge*
Quitang Gorge *Wu Gorge*
Sandouping
Gezhouba Dam
Yunyang
Yichang
Wanxian
Yangtze
Zhongxian

Fengdu
Shizhu
Changshou
Dong He
Fuling
Jialing Jiang
Jiangbei
CHONGQING
Chongqing
Mudong
Wu Jiang
Ba Xian
Wulong

GUIZHOU

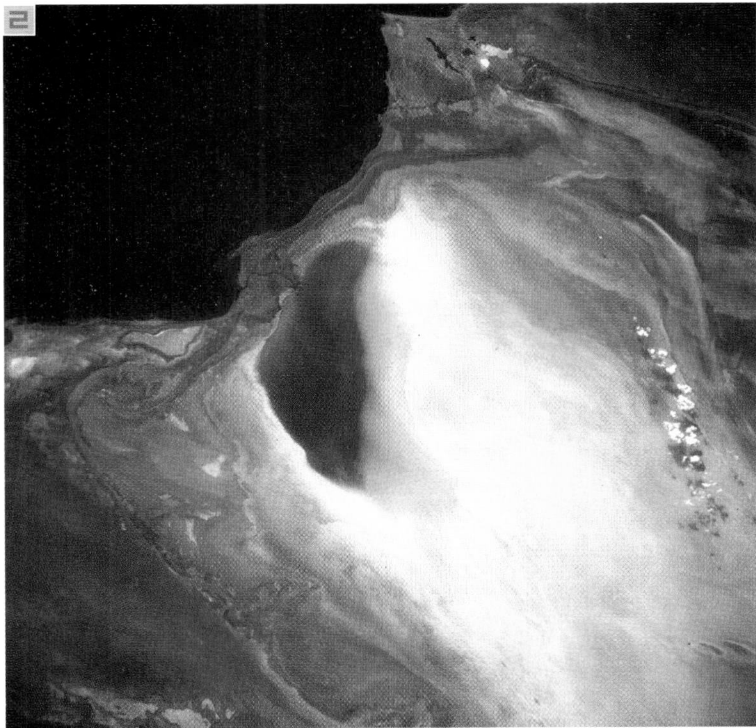

Lake Level Variations

A natural evaporation basin, the Kara-Bogaz-Gol is located in a semi-arid region of Turkmenistan on the eastern shore of the Caspian Sea. In these northwest-looking oblique Shuttle photographs the difference in water level, due to both evaporation and variation in the flow of water from the Caspian Sea into the basin, is striking. The 1985 image (top) shows water in only a small section near the western end. In contrast to this, the 1995 image (bottom) shows the water level to be high in the whole basin. The level of the Caspian Sea is normally approximately three metres above that of the basin, and water flows from one to the other through a dyke built in the late 1970s. However, low rainfall in the region can result in exceptionally low water levels in the Caspian Sea, which dramatically affect the amount of water flowing into the basin.

Satellite/Sensor : Space Shuttle

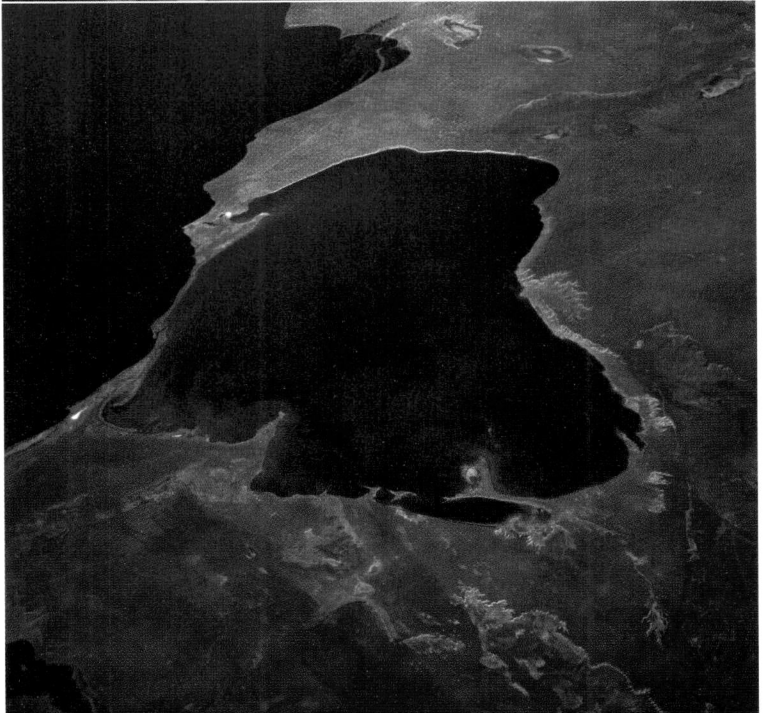

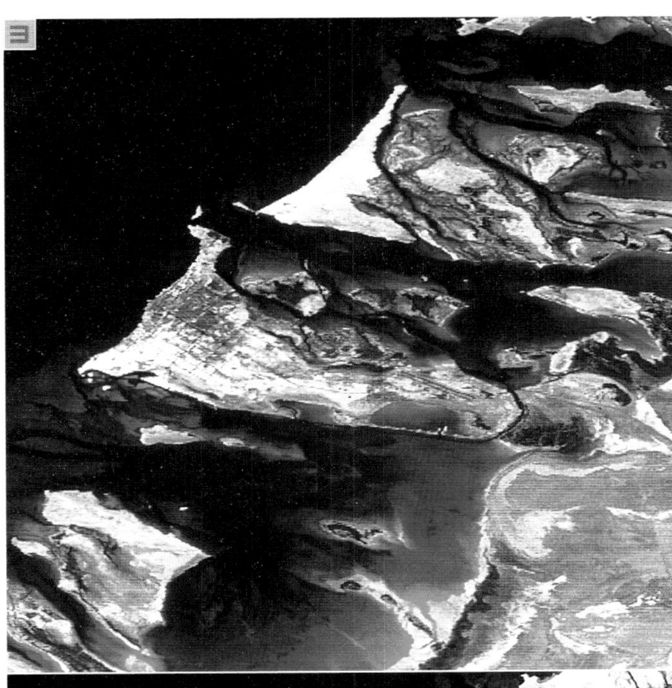

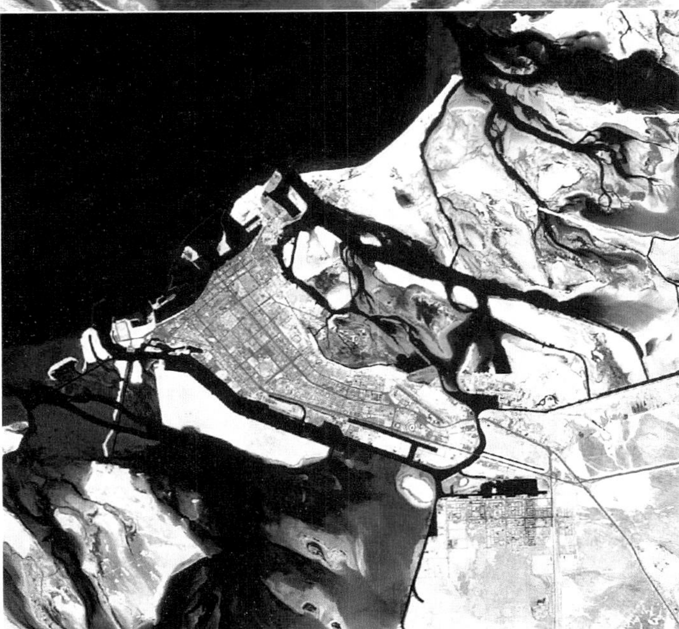

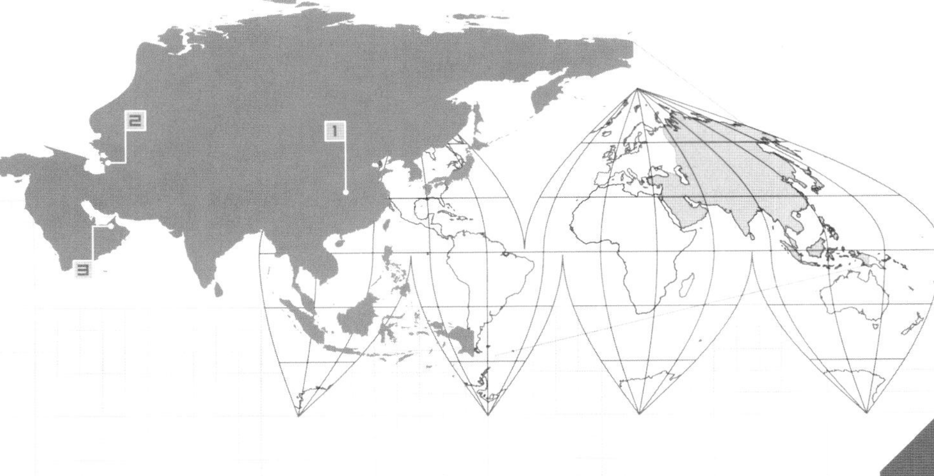

Urban Development and Land Reclamation

These satellite images show the development of the capital of the United Arab Emirates, Abu Dhabi. In the 1950s the town was little more than a small fishing village, but this changed after the discovery of offshore oil in the early 1960s. The changes, particularly to the extent of the city and to the coastline, in the period between the image at the top (1972) and the one below (1989), are dramatic. A national development program was implemented to help improve the city's harbour and to construct buildings, roads, and an international airport.

Satellite/Sensor : Landsat

asia[threats]

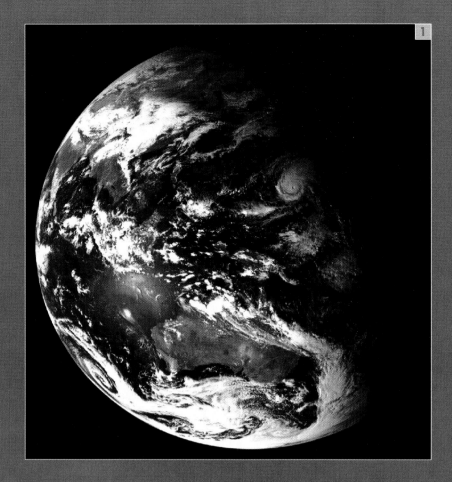

CONNECTIONS

▸ subject	page#
▸ World earthquakes and volcanoes	14–15
▸ World tropical storms	16–17
▸ Mozambique floods	116–117
▸ North America threats	160–161

1 Tropical Storms

Tropical storms are among the most powerful and destructive weather systems on Earth. Worldwide between eighty and one hundred develop over tropical oceans each year. The northwest Pacific area experiences an average of thirty one typhoons annually and most of these occur between July and October. If they reach land they can cause extensive damage to property or loss of life as a result of high winds and heavy rain. This image gives an idea of the overall size of a typhoon as it moves westwards across the Pacific Ocean towards the island of Guam. Wind speeds in this typhoon reached over 370 km per hour.

Satellite/Sensor : GOES

2 Tropical Cyclone Hudah, *Southwest Indian Ocean*

Tropical cyclone Hudah was one of the most powerful storms ever seen in the Indian Ocean and was typical of the storms which frequently occur in the Pacific and Indian Oceans and which threaten the coasts of Asia and Africa. At the end of March 2000 the storm began a fairly straight westerly track across the entire south Indian Ocean, as shown on the map, struck Madagascar as an intense tropical cyclone, weakened, then regained intensity in the Mozambique Channel before making a final landfall in Mozambique on 9 April. This image was taken just before the cyclone hit the coast of Madagascar where wind gusts reached over 296 km per hour causing the destruction of 90% of the city of Antalaha.

Satellite/Sensor : MODIS

3 Bangladesh Cyclone Damage

Bangladesh, lying at the northern edge of the Bay of Bengal often experiences extreme climatic conditions which can wreak havoc. Cyclones regularly occur in the Bay of Bengal often having devastating effects on the flat coastal regions as shown in this photograph. In 1991 the country was hit by a massive cyclone which killed more than 140 000 people.

4 Klyuchevskaya Volcano, *Russian Federation*

Klyuchevskaya is the highest mountain in eastern Russian Federation and one of the most active volcanoes on the Kamchatka Peninsula. This view shows the major eruption of 1994 when the eruption cloud reached 18 300 m above sea level and the winds carried ash as far as 1 030 km to the southeast. The Kamchatka Peninsula is a sparsely populated area and the volcano's threat to human life is not serious. However, it lies on a major airline route and volcanic eruptions frequently cause aircraft to divert around the region.

Satellite/Sensor : Space Shuttle

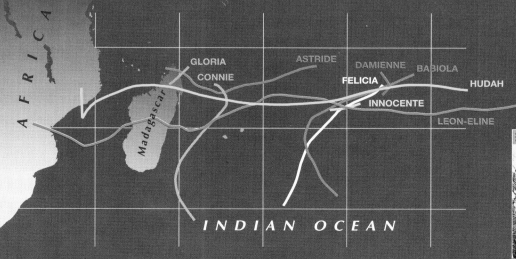

Fig. #01
Tracks of tropical cyclones in the southwest Indian Ocean 2000

AFRICA

GLORIA
CONNIE
ASTRIDE
DAMIENNE
BABIOLA
FELICIA
HUDAH
INNOCENTE
LEON-ELINE

Madagascar

INDIAN OCEAN

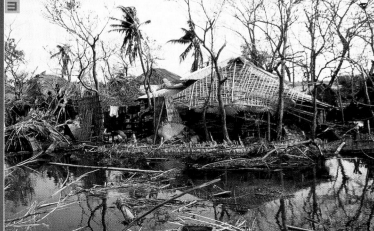

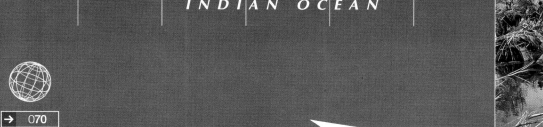

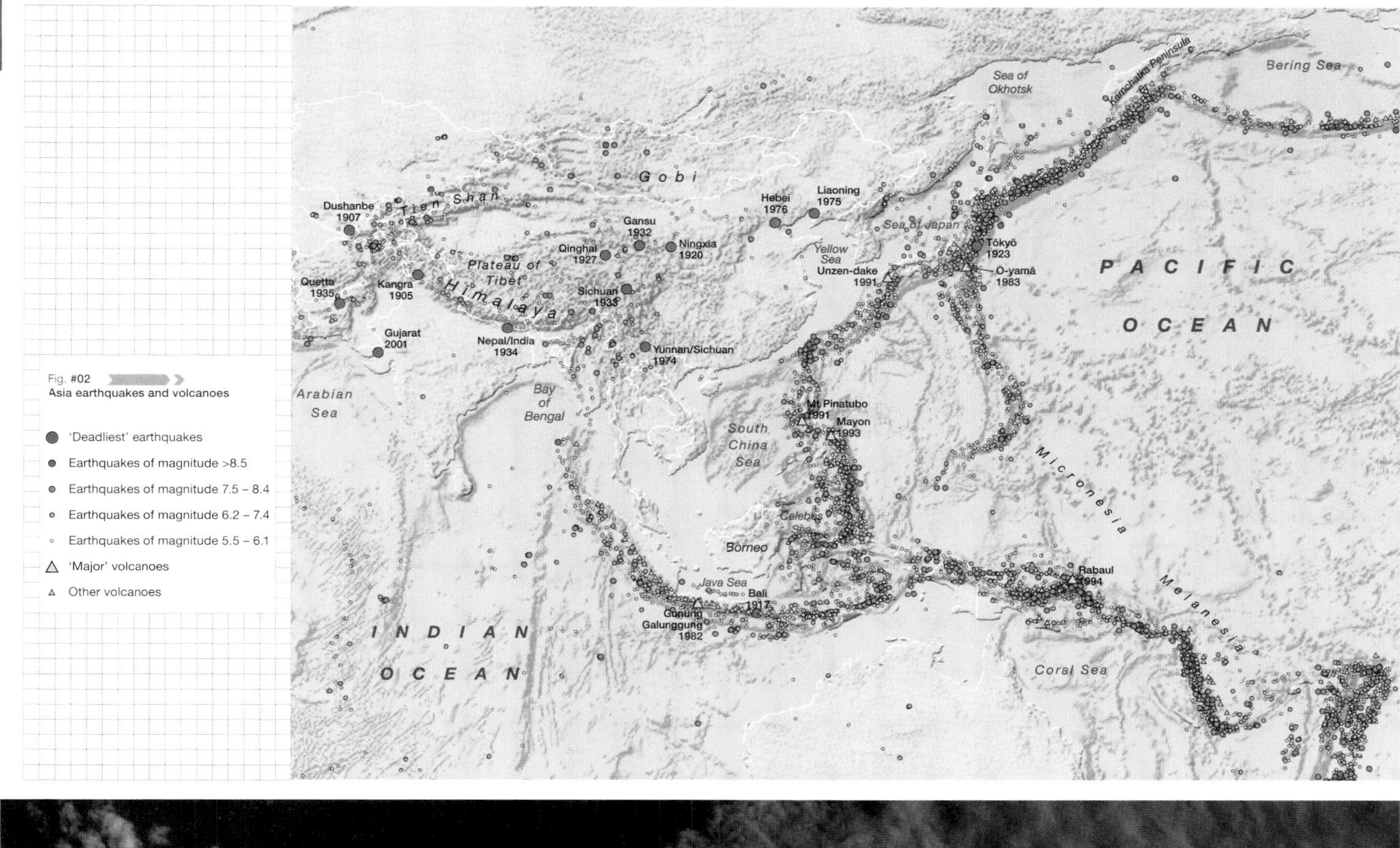

Fig. #02
Asia earthquakes and volcanoes

- ● 'Deadliest' earthquakes
- ● Earthquakes of magnitude >8.5
- ● Earthquakes of magnitude 7.5 – 8.4
- ○ Earthquakes of magnitude 6.2 – 7.4
- ○ Earthquakes of magnitude 5.5 – 6.1
- △ 'Major' volcanoes
- △ Other volcanoes

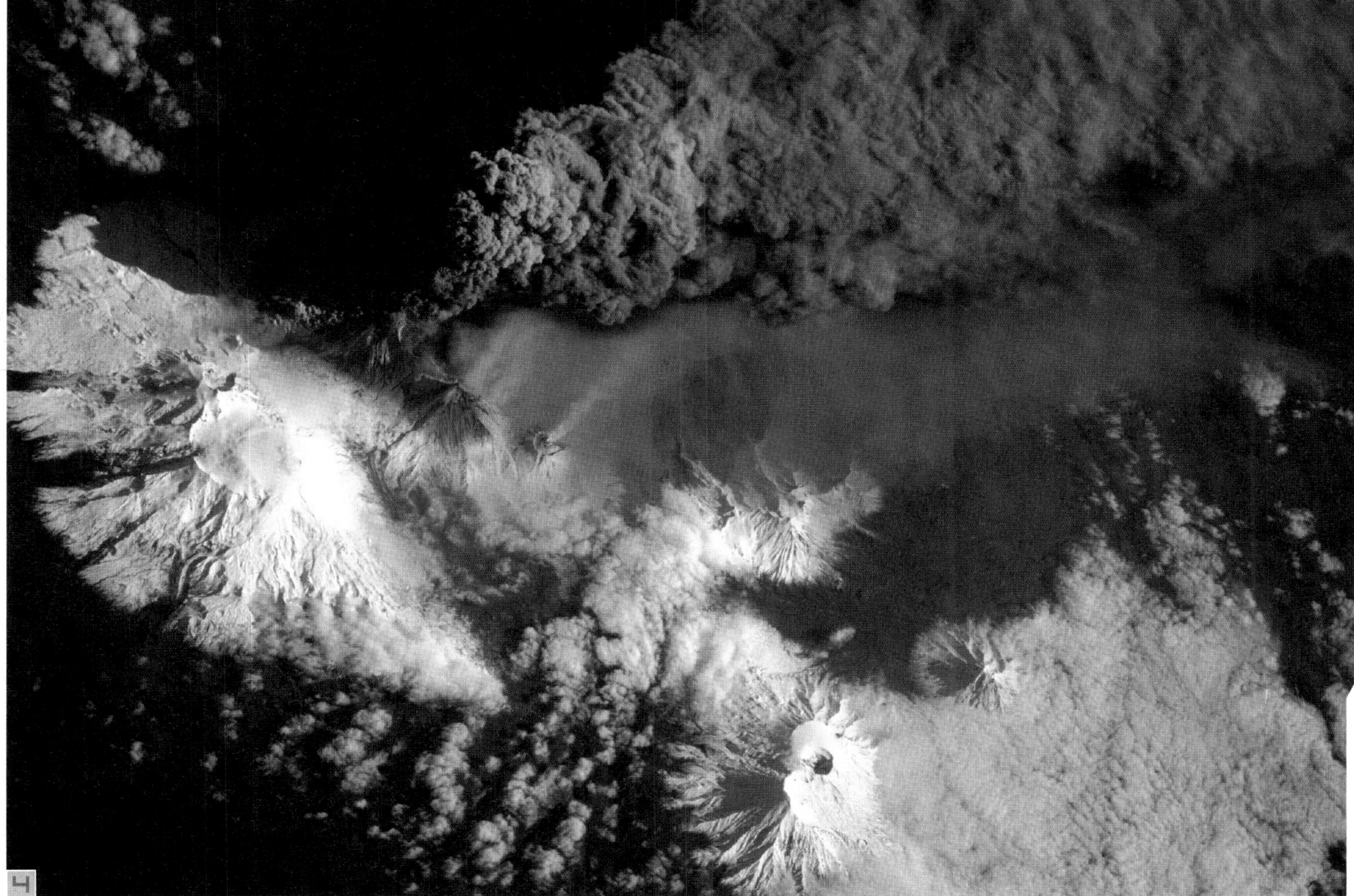

5 **Kamchatka Peninsula,** *Russian Federation*

The Kamchatka Peninsula in the eastern Russian Federation is a volcanic landscape
between the Sea of Okhotsk and the Bering Sea. This near-horizontal perspective view
shows the western side of the peninsula with the Sea of Okhotsk in the foreground.
Inland from the coast, vegetated floodplains and low hills rise towards the snow-capped
volcanoes of the Sredinnyy Khrebet mountain range which forms the spine of the
peninsula. The image was generated using topographic data from the Shuttle Radar
Topography Mission and a Landsat 7 satellite image.

Satellite/Sensor : SRTM/Landsat

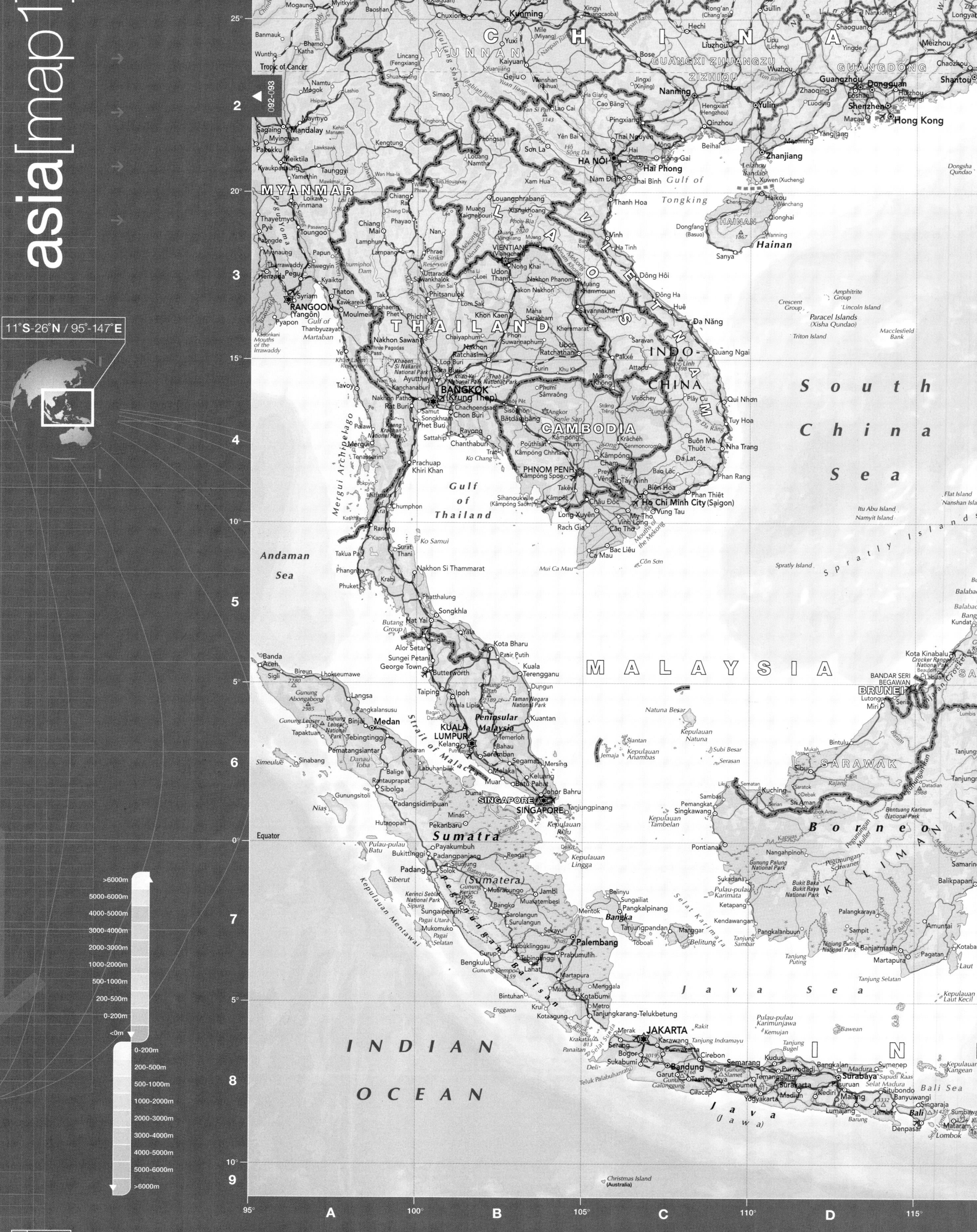

asia[map1]

11°S-26°N / 95°-147°E

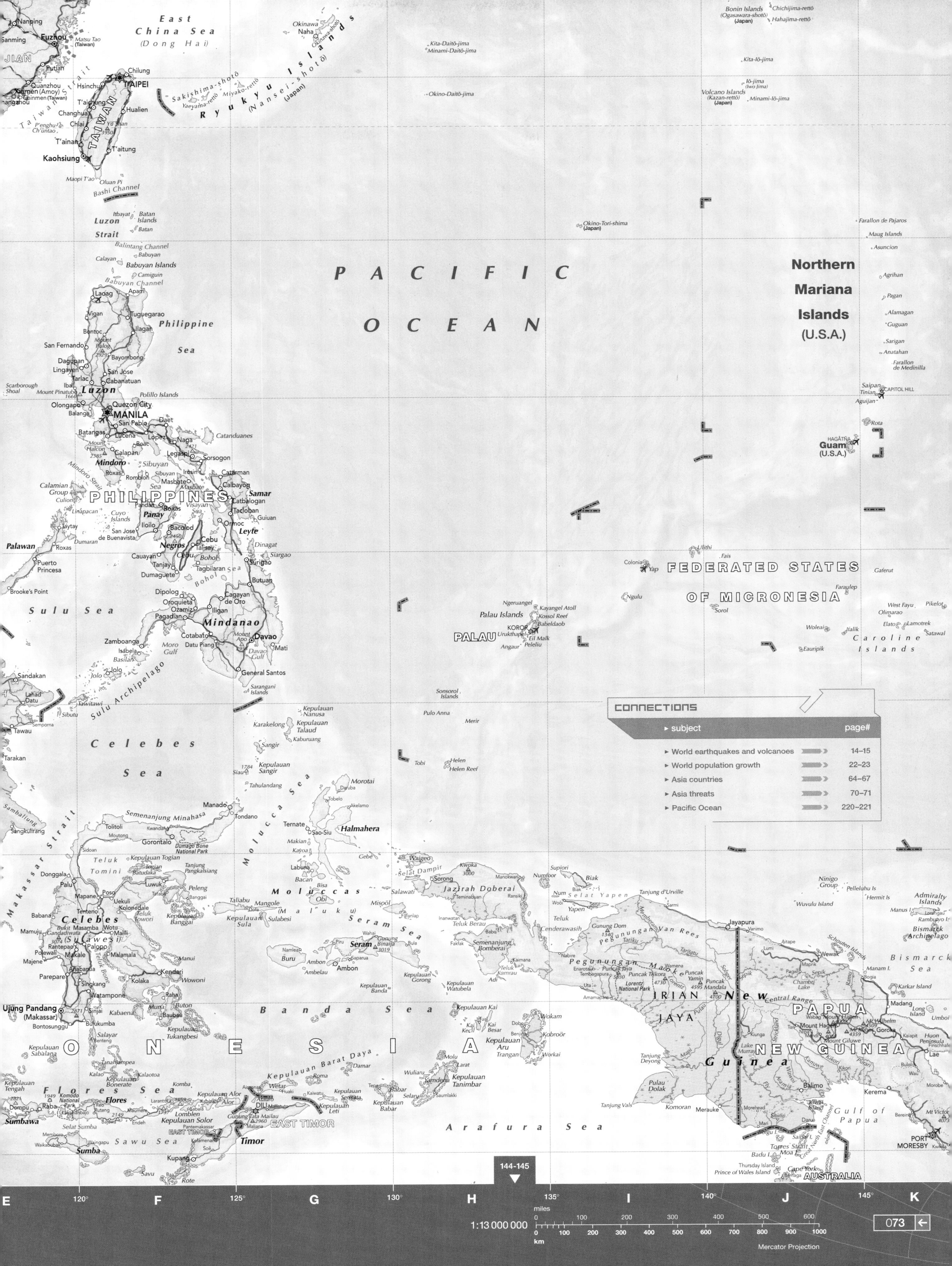

Nanping
Fuzhou
Sanming
JIAN
Quanzhou
Xiamen (Amoy)
Putian
hangzhou

**East
China
Sea
(Dong Hai)**

Matsu Tao (Taiwan)
Chilung
Hsinchu
Chai
T'aichung
Changhua
Hualien

TAIPEI
TAIWAN
Ya Shan

Penghu
Ch'üntao
T'ainan
T'aitung

Kaohsiung

Maopi T'ao
Oluan Pi
Bashi Channel

Okinawa Naha
Okinawa-shotō

Sakishima-shotō
Miyako-rettō
Yaeyama-rettō (Japan)

**Ryukyu Islands
(Nansei-shotō) (Japan)**

Kita-Daitō-jima
Minami-Daitō-jima

Okino-Daitō-jima

Okino-Tori-shima
(Japan)

Bonin Islands Chichijima-rettō
(Ogasawara-shotō) Hahajima-rettō
(Japan) (Japan)

Kita-Iō-jima

Iō-jima (Iwo Jima)
**Volcano Islands
(Kazan-rettō)
(Japan)** Minami-Iō-jima

Farallon de Pajaros

Maug Islands

Asuncion

PACIFIC

OCEAN

**Northern
Mariana
Islands
(U.S.A.)**

Agrihan

Pagan

Alamagan
Guguan

Sarigan
Anatahan

Farallon
de Medinilla

Saipan
Tinian
Aguijan
CAPITOL HILL

Rota

HAGÅTÑA
**Guam
(U.S.A.)**

Luzon
Itbayat
Batan Islands
Babuyan
Batan
Strait

Balintang Channel
Calayan
Babuyan
Camiguin
Babuyan Channel
Laoag
Aparri
Vigan
Tuguegarao
Ilagan
Bontoc
Mount Iñulog
Bayombong
San Fernando
Dagupan
Lingayen
San Jose
Tarlac
Ibat
Cabanatuan
Mount Pinatubo 1600?
Luzon
Quezon City
Olongapo
MANILA
Balanga
San Pablo
Batangas
Lucena
Mount
Halcon
Boac
Naga
2471
Calapan
Mindoro
Roxas
Legaspi
Sibuyan
Catanduanes
Romblon
Irosin
Sorsogon
Philippine
Sea
Catarman
Masbate
Samar
Calbayog
Catbalogan
Tacloban
Guiuan

Scarborough
Shoal

Okino-Tori-shima

Calamian
Group
Culion
Cuyo
Islands
Linapacan
PHILIPPINES
Pandan
Roxas
Panay
Iloilo
Bacolod
Leyte
Ormoc
Cebu
San Jose
de Buenavista
Taytay
Dumaran
Negros
Cebu
Talisay
Bohol
Dumaguete
Tagbilaran
Bohol Sea
Dinagat
Siargao
Surigao

Palawan
Puerto
Princesa
Butuan
Dipolog
Oroquieta
Ozamiz
Cagayan
de Oro
Iligan
Pagadian
Mindanao
Cotabato
Zamboanga
Datu Piang
Mount
Apo
Davao
Isabela
Basilan
Davao
Gulf
Mati

Sulu Sea
General Santos
Sarangani
Islands

Colonia
Yap
Ulithi
Fais

FEDERATED STATES

OF MICRONESIA

Gaferut

Faraulep

West Fayu
Olimarao
Pikelot

Woleai
Ifalik
Elato
Lamotrek
Satawal
**C a r o l i n e
I s l a n d s**

Ngeruangel
Kayangel Atoll
Kossol Reef
Palau Islands
KOROR
Urukthapel
Babeldaob
Eil Malk
PALAU
Peleliu
Angaur

Ngulu

Ngeruangel

Sorol

Eauripik

Brooke's Point

Sandakan
Lahad
Datu
Tawau
Sulu
Archipelago
Jolo
Jolo
Tawitawi
Semporna
Sibutu

Sonsorol
Islands

Pulo Anna
Merir

Helen
Helen Reef

Tobi

Kepulauan
Nanusa
Karakelong
Kepulauan
Talaud
Sangir
Kaburuang

Celebes

Sea
1784
Kepulauan
Sangir
Siau

Tahulandang

Manado
Tondano

**Molucca
Sea**

Morotai

Tobelo
Akelamo

Tarakan

Sangkulirang

Donggala
Palu
Mapane
Poso
Uekuli
Tentena
Celebes
Luwuk
(Sulawesi)
Kolonedale

Toli-Toli
Moutong
Gorontalo

Semenanjung Minahasa

Kwandang
Dumaga Bone
National Park

Sao-Siu
Makian
Kayoa
Ternate
Halmahera

Daruba

CONNECTIONS

► subject   page#

► World earthquakes and volcanoes   14–15
► World population growth   22–23
► Asia countries   64–67
► Asia threats   70–71
► Pacific Ocean   220–221

Sidoan
Teluk
Tomini
Kepulauan
Togian
Batudaka
Tanjung
Pangkalsiang

Moluccas
Taliabu
(Maluku)
Mangole
Kepulauan
Sula
Sulabesi
Gebe
Waigeo
Selat Dampir
Obi
Misool
Salawati
Sorong
Jazirah Doberai
Manokwari
Ransiki
Biak
Supiori
Numfoor

Mamuju
Majene
Polewali
Makale
Parepare
Pinrang
Sidrap
Sinjai
Kendari
Kolaka
Peleng
Banggai
Kepulauan
Banggai
Namlea
Buru
Piru
Seram
Binaia
3019
Bula
Seram Sea
Wahai
Gunung
Kaimana
Fakfak
Semenanjung
Bomberai
Teluk
Berau
Inanwatan
Teluk
Kamrau
Pegunungan
Enarotali
Puncak Jaya
Tembagapura
4730
Puncak Trikora
4750
Wamena
Nabire
Gunung Dom
1340
Pegunungan Van Rees
Sarmi
Num
Yapen
Selat Yapen
Woo
Tanjung d'Urville
Jayapura
Yanimo

Ujung Pandang
(Makassar)
Bontosunggu
2871

Watampone
Raha
Buton
Baubau

Banda Sea

Singkang
Kabaena
Muna

Bulukumba

Kepulauan
Sabalana
Kepulauan
Tukangbesi

Kalao
Salayar
Benteng

O   **N**   **E**   **S**   **I**   **A**

Ambon
Ambon
Ambelau
Kepulauan
Gorong
Kepulauan
Watubela
Adi
Kaimana
Irian
Lorentz
National Park
Enarotali
Tembagapura
Timika
Jaya
Puncak
Yamin
4595
Puncak
Mandala
4700
Amamapare

Kepulauan
Banda
Kepulauan
Aru
Trangan

Wokam
Kobroör
Workai

Central Range
New
Mount Hagen
4359
PAPUA
Mount Wilhelm
4509
Goroka
Mendi
NEW GUINEA
Mount Giluwe
4368
Guinea

Kepulauan
Sabalana
1949
Flores Sea
Komodo
Gandadiwata
3074
Rantepao
Palopo
Malamala
Wowoni

Kepulauan
Bonerate

Wuliaru
Larat
Kepulauan
Tanimbar
Saumlakki
Selaru
Molu
Kepulauan
Kai
Kai
Besar
Dobo
Benjina
Kai
Kecil

Tanjung
Deyong
Pulau
Dolak
Komoran
Merauke
Morehead
Digul
Lake
Murray
Balimo
Gulf of
Papua
Kerema

Kepulauan
Tengah
Dompu
Raba
Sumbawa
Rantepao
2149
Endeh
Flores
Maumere
Larantuka
Kepulauan
Solor
Pantemakassar
EAST TIMOR
DILI
Gunung Tata Mailau
2960
EAST TIMOR
Timor
Kupang

Arafura Sea

Tanjung Vals
Mari
Daru
Kiwai
North East
Torres
Strait
Badu I.
Moa
Thursday Island
Prince of Wales Island
Cape York
Bamaga
AUSTRALIA
PORT
MORESBY
Mt Victor

Waingapu
Sumba
Savu

Sawu Sea
Rote

E   120°   F   125°   G   130°   H   135°   I   140°   J   145°   K

miles
0   100   200   300   400   500   600

1:13 000 000

0 100 200 300 400 500 600 700 800 900 1000
km

Mercator Projection

5°-21°N / 117°-128°E

CONNECTIONS

PHILIPPINES

Luzon Strait

Philippine Sea

South China Sea

Sulu Sea

Celebes Sea

Luzon

Mindoro

Palawan

Panay

Negros

Cebu

Bohol

Leyte

Samar

Mindanao

MANILA

MALAYSIA

SABAH

INDONESIA

>6000m
5000-6000m
4000-5000m
3000-4000m
2000-3000m
1000-2000m
500-1000m
200-500m
0-200m
<0m
0-200m
200-500m
500-1000m
1000-2000m
2000-3000m
3000-4000m
4000-5000m
5000-6000m
>6000m

076-077

075

1:6 000 000

miles 0 50 100 150 200 250

km 0 50 100 150 200 250 300 350 400

Mercator Projection

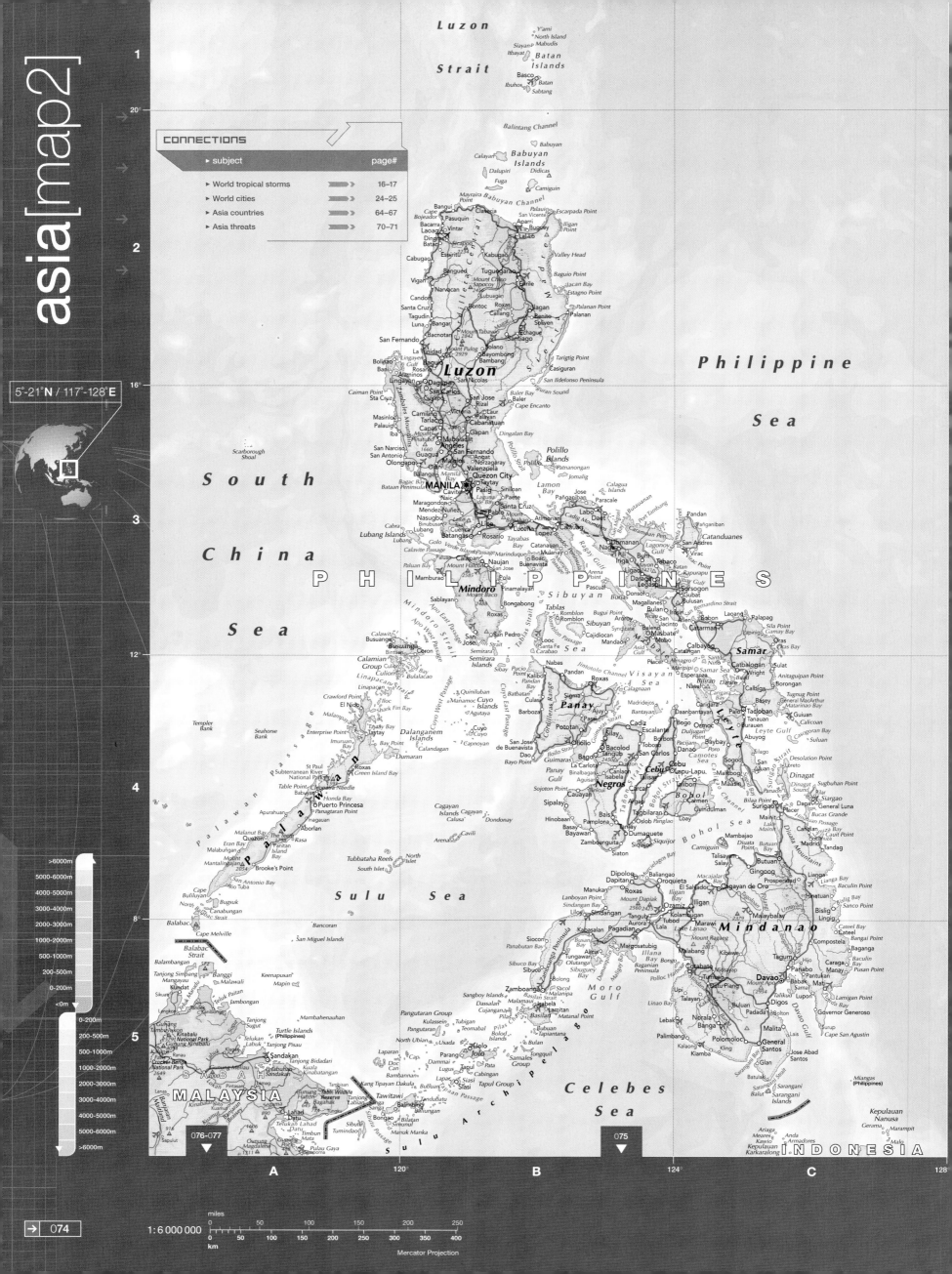

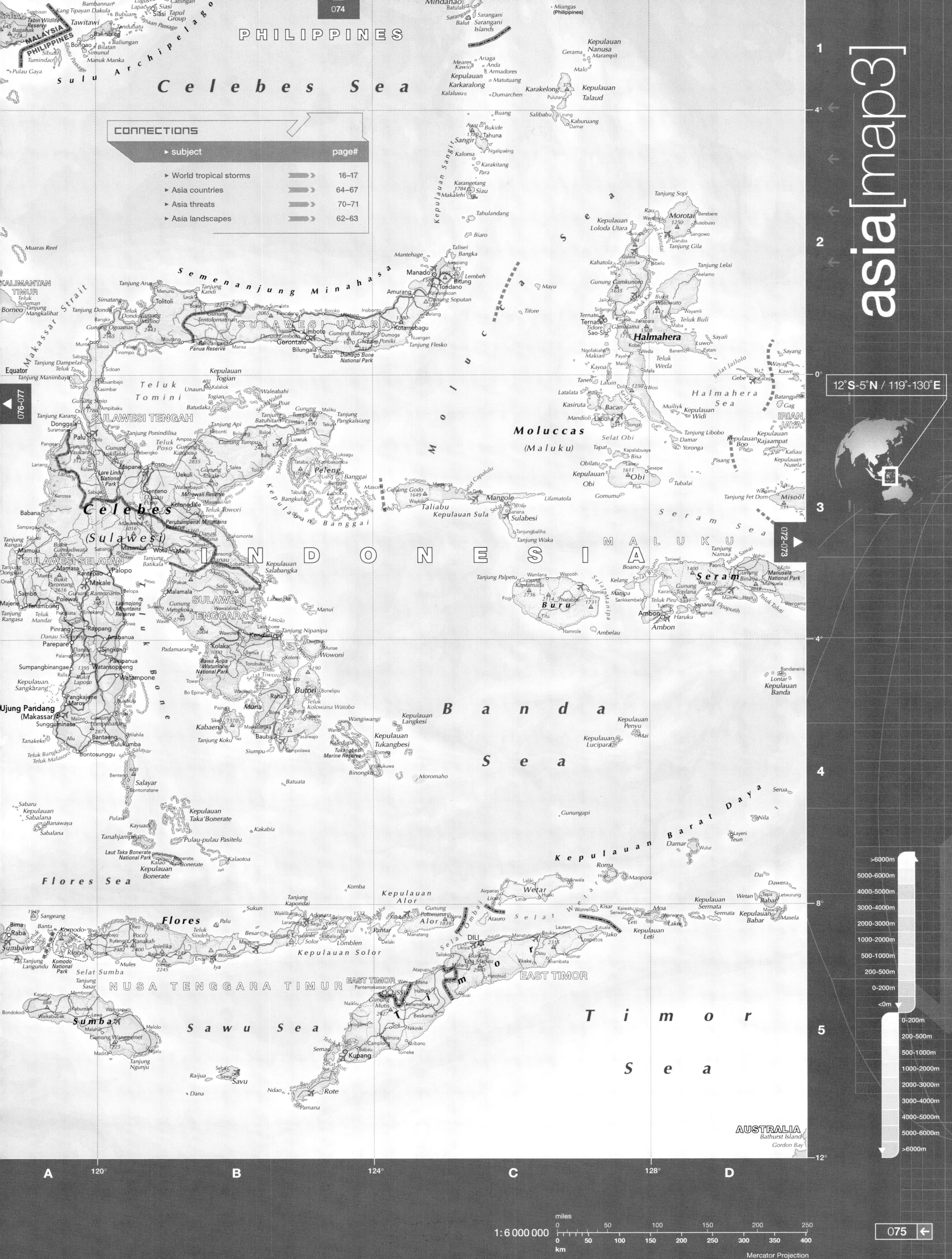
asia[map3]
12°S-5°N / 119°-130°E
CONNECTIONS
subject page#
World tropical storms 16–17
Asia countries 64–67
Asia threats 70–71
Asia landscapes 62–63
074
076-077
072-073
PHILIPPINES
Celebes Sea
Sulu Archipelago
MALAYSIA
Mindanao
Kepulauan Talaud
Kepulauan Sangir
Semenanjung Minahasa
SULAWESI UTARA
Manado
Gorontalo
Makassar Strait
KALIMANTAN TIMUR
Borneo
Equator
Teluk Tomini
SULAWESI TENGAH
Palu
Celebes (Sulawesi)
SULAWESI SELATAN
SULAWESI TENGGARA
Kendari
Teluk Bone
Ujung Pandang (Makassar)
Pare Pare
INDONESIA
Molucca Sea
Moluccas (Maluku)
MALUKU
Halmahera
Halmahera Sea
Morotai
Ternate
Kepulauan Sula
Kepulauan Banggai
Peleng
Obi
Seram Sea
Seram
Buru
Ambon
IRIAN JAYA
Misoöl
Banda Sea
Buton
Kepulauan Tukangbesi
Kepulauan Barat Daya
Wetar
Flores Sea
Flores
Sumbawa
Selat Sumba
NUSA TENGGARA TIMUR
EAST TIMOR
DILI
Timor
Kupang
Rote
Savu
Sumba
Sawu Sea
Timor Sea
AUSTRALIA
Bathurst Island
>6000m
5000-6000m
4000-5000m
3000-4000m
2000-3000m
1000-2000m
500-1000m
200-500m
0-200m
<0m
A B C D
120° 124° 128°
1:6 000 000
miles
km
Mercator Projection

asia[map4]

8°N-10°S / 95°-120°E

078-079

THAILAND

MALAYSIA

Peninsular Malaysia

SINGAPORE

Strait of Malacca

Sumatra

INDIAN OCEAN

Kepulauan Mentawai

Selat Mentawai

Pegunungan Barisan

SINGAPORE

MALAYSIA

Strait of Singapore

1 : 360 000

miles 0 3

km 0 5

Elevation
>6000m
5000-6000m
4000-5000m
3000-4000m
2000-3000m
1000-2000m
500-1000m
200-500m
0-200m
<0m

Depth
0-200m
200-500m
500-1000m
1000-2000m
2000-3000m
3000-4000m
4000-5000m
5000-6000m
>6000m

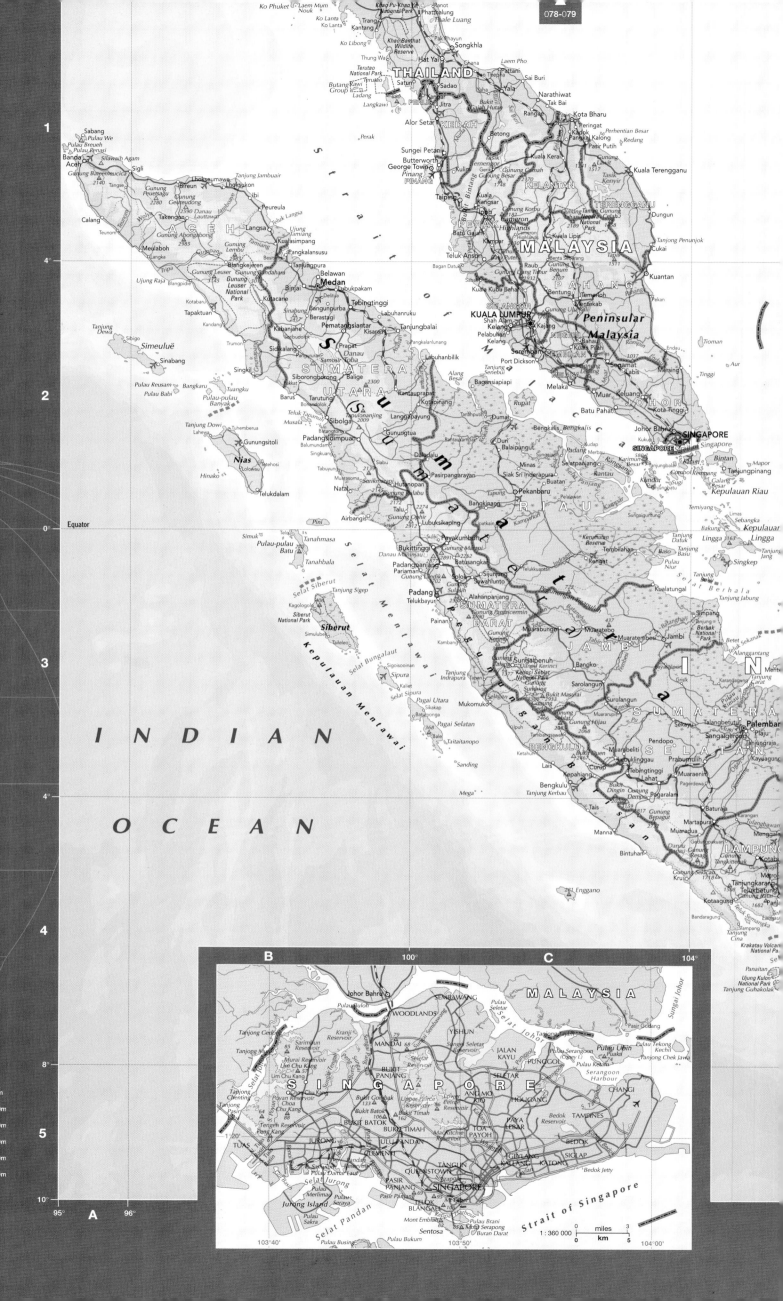

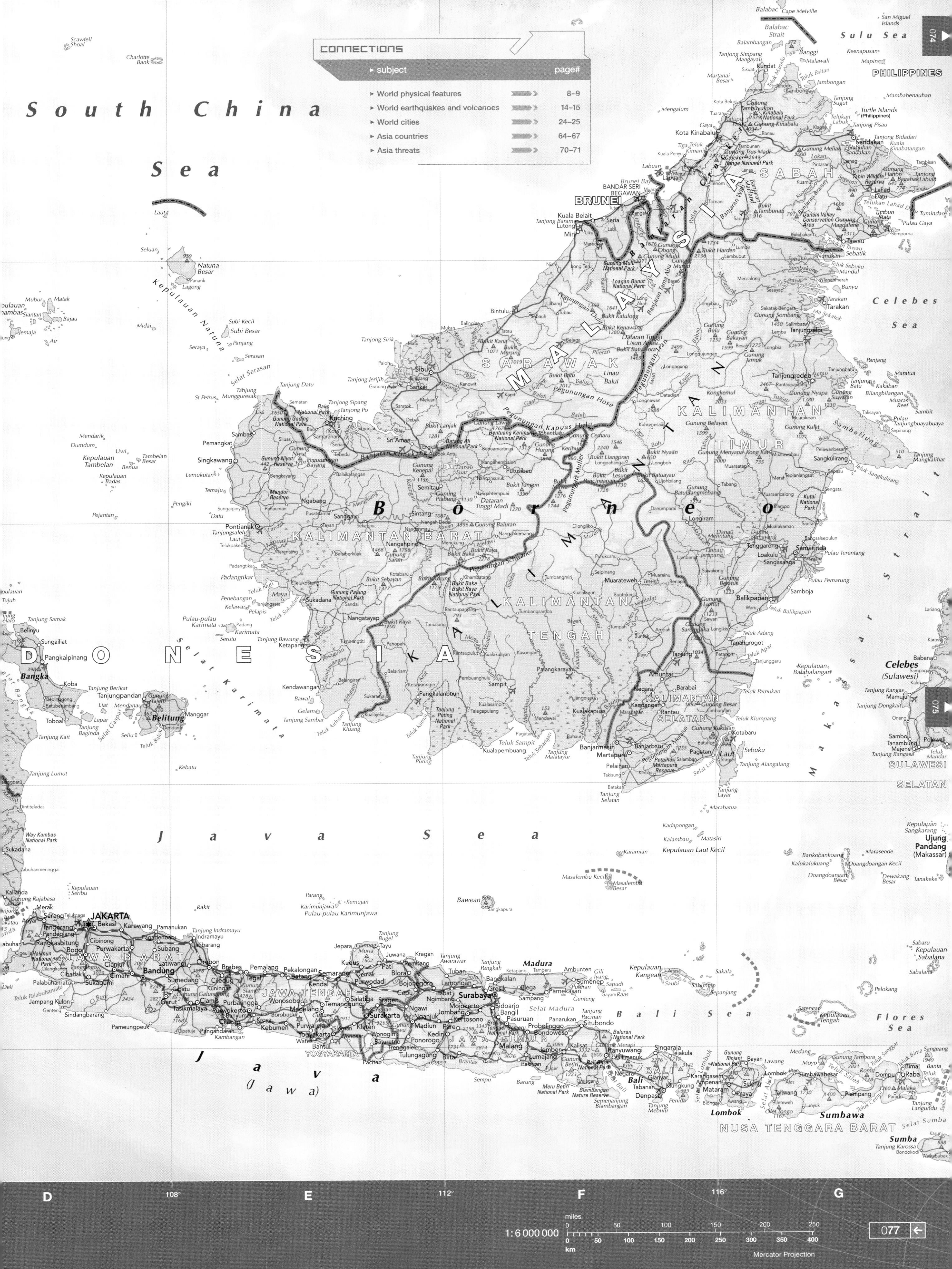

CONNECTIONS
subject page#
World physical features 8–9
World earthquakes and volcanoes 14–15
World cities 24–25
Asia countries 64–67
Asia threats 70–71
South China Sea
Sulu Sea
PHILIPPINES
Celebes Sea
Java Sea
Bali Sea
Flores Sea
Makassar Strait
Borneo
MALAYSIA
SABAH
SARAWAK
BRUNEI
BANDAR SERI BEGAWAN
INDONESIA
KALIMANTAN TIMUR
KALIMANTAN BARAT
KALIMANTAN TENGAH
KALIMANTAN SELATAN
Celebes (Sulawesi)
SULAWESI SELATAN
Ujung Pandang (Makassar)
Kota Kinabalu
Sandakan
Tawau
Kuching
Sibu
Bintulu
Pontianak
Balikpapan
Samarinda
Banjarmasin
Palangkaraya
Kepulauan Natuna
Natuna Besar
Bangka
Belitung
Pangkalpinang
Java (Jawa)
JAKARTA
Bandung
JAWA BARAT
JAWA TENGAH
JAWA TIMUR
YOGYAKARTA
Semarang
Surabaya
Malang
Madura
Bali
Denpasar
Lombok
Mataram
Sumbawa
Sumba
NUSA TENGGARA BARAT
D
E
F
G
108°
112°
116°
1:6 000 000
miles 0 50 100 150 200 250
km 0 50 100 150 200 250 300 350 400
Mercator Projection
074
075

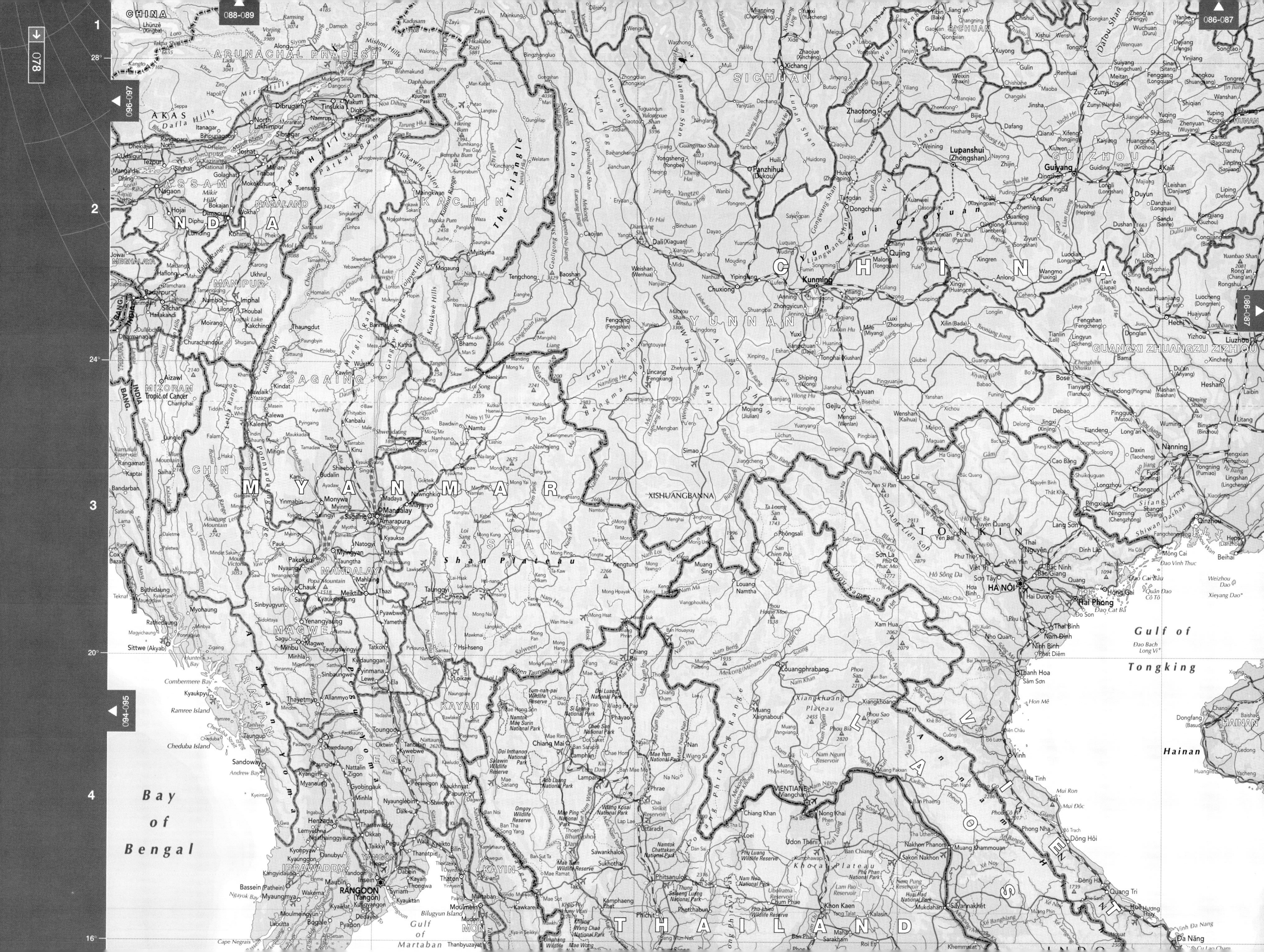
CHINA
INDIA
MYANMAR
THAILAND
LAOS
VIETNAM
YUNNAN
SICHUAN
GUIZHOU
GUANGXI ZHUANGZU ZIZHIQU
HAINAN
ARUNACHAL PRADESH
ASSAM
NAGALAND
MANIPUR
MIZORAM
MEGHALAYA
TRIPURA
BANG.
KACHIN
SAGAING
CHIN
MANDALAY
MAGWE
SHAN
KAYAH
KAYIN
PEGU
ARAKAN
IRRAWADDY
YANGON
MON
TONKIN
XISHUANGBANNA
Shan Plateau
Khorat Plateau
Xiangkhoang Plateau
The Triangle
Yun Gui Gaoyuan
Bay of Bengal
Gulf of Martaban
Gulf of Tongking
Hainan
Kunming
Guiyang
Nanning
HA NOI
Hai Phong
RANGOON (Yangon)
Mandalay
VIENTIANE (Viangchan)
Chiang Mai
Louangphrabang
Tropic of Cancer
28°
24°
20°
16°
1
2
3
4
078
088-089
086-087
096-097
094-095

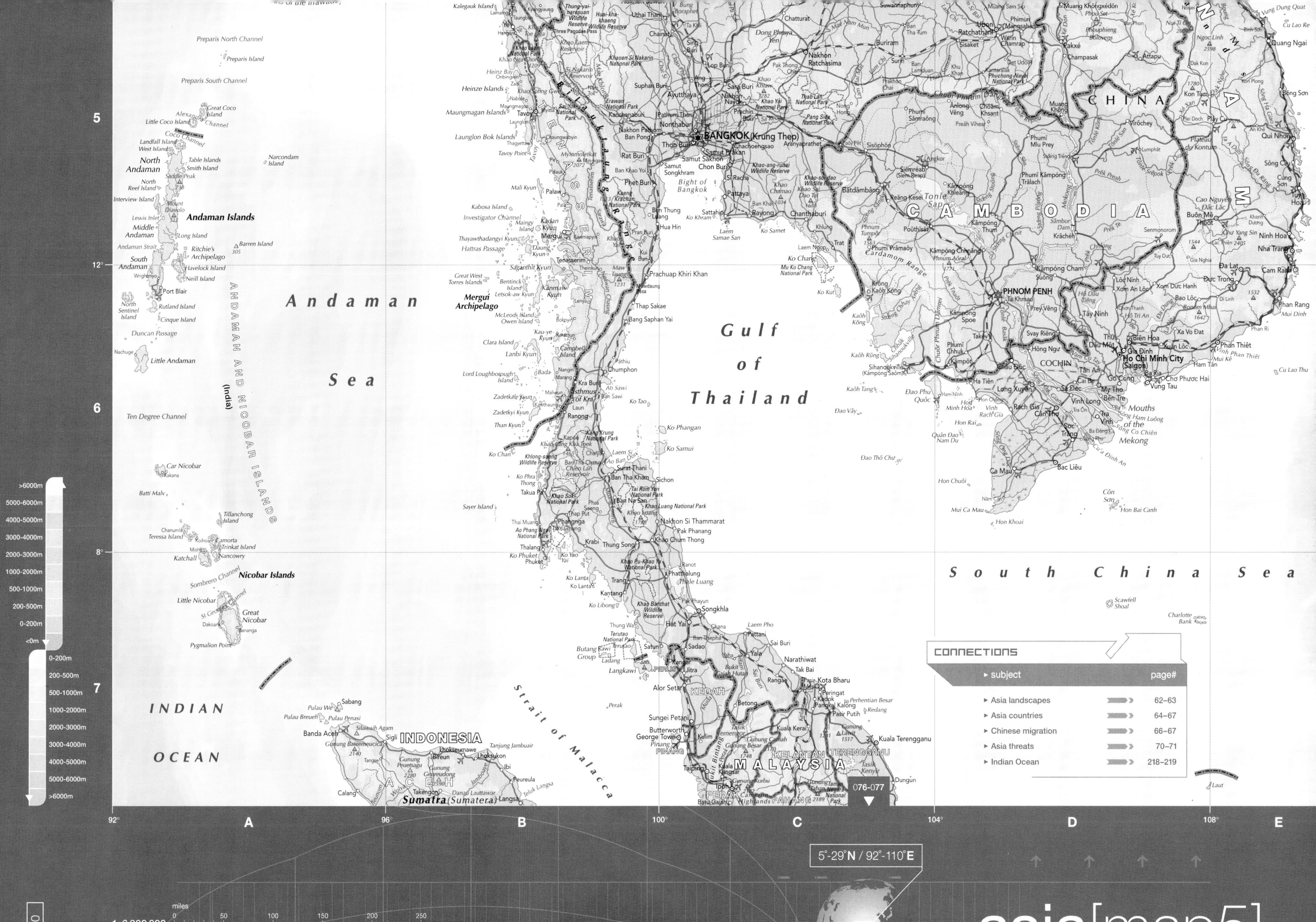

5°-29'N / 92°-110'E

1:6 000 000

Mercator Projection

CONNECTIONS

▶ subject	page/#
▲ Asia landscapes	62–63
▲ Asia countries	64–67
▲ Chinese migration	66–67
▲ Asia threats	70–71
▼ Indian Ocean	218–219

076–077

Elevation legend:

0–200m
200–500m
500–1000m
1000–2000m
2000–3000m
3000–4000m
4000–5000m
5000–6000m
>6000m

<dm

>6000m
5000–6000m
4000–5000m
3000–4000m
2000–3000m
1000–2000m
500–1000m
200–500m
0–200m

Major labels:

CHINA

C A M B O D I A

PHNOM PENH

BANGKOK (Krung Thep)

V I E T N A M

COCHIN

South China Sea

Gulf of Thailand

Bight of Bangkok

Andaman Sea

INDIAN OCEAN

Strait of Malacca

MALAYSIA

KELANTAN

KEDAH

PERAK

TERENGGANU

INDONESIA

Sumatra (Sumatera)

ACEH

Banda Aceh

ANDAMAN AND NICOBAR ISLANDS (India)

Andaman Islands

North Andaman

Middle Andaman

South Andaman

Nicobar Islands

Great Nicobar

Little Nicobar

Car Nicobar

Port Blair

Ten Degree Channel

Mergui Archipelago

T E N A S S E R I M

Bilauktaung Range

George Town Penang

Butterworth

Kota Bharu

Kuala Terengganu

Nha Trang

Ho Chi Minh City (Saigon)

Vung Tau

Mouths of the Mekong

A B C D E

1 2 5 6 7 8

scale: km / miles
50 100 150 200 250
100 150 200 250 300 350 400

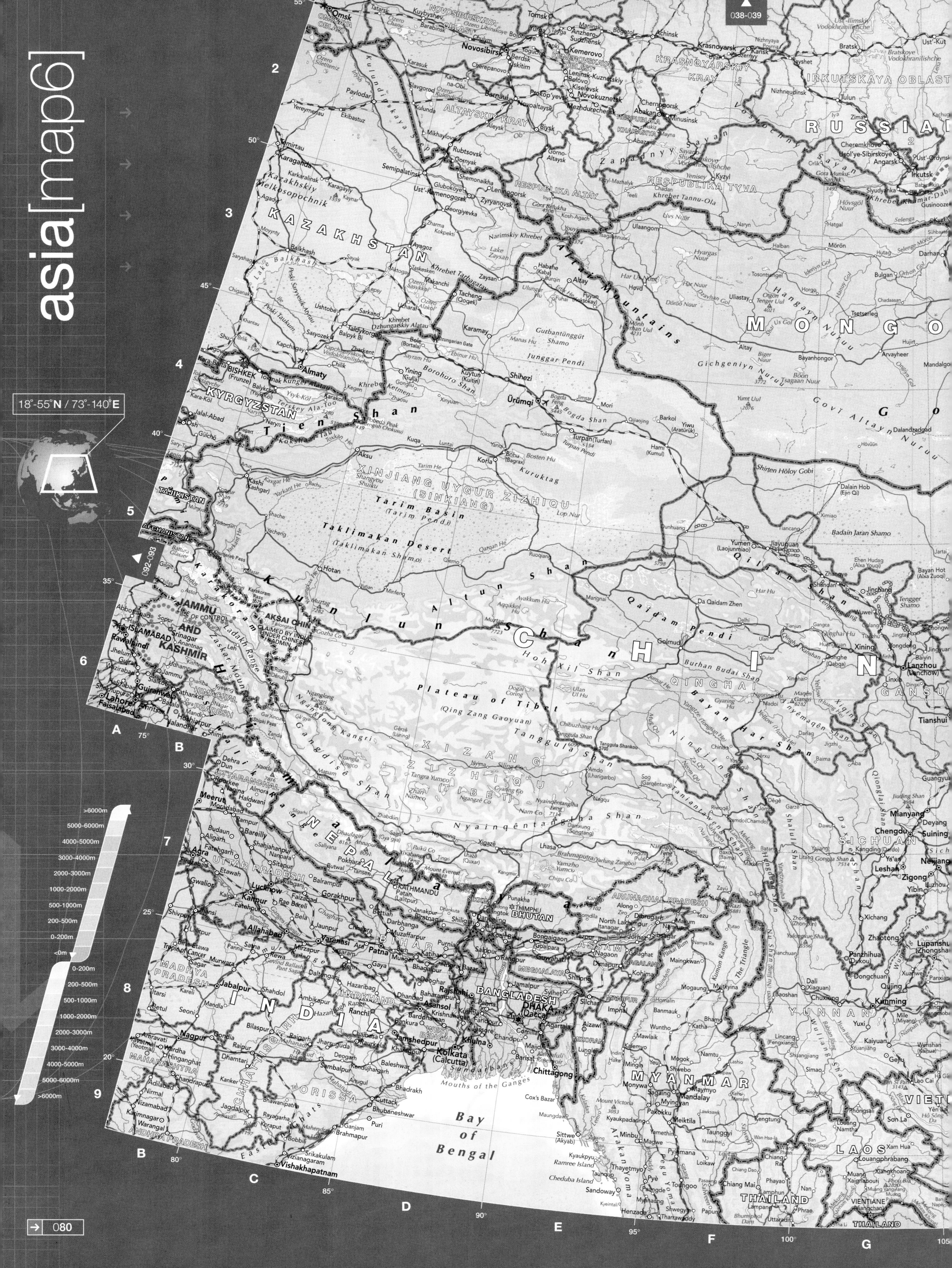
asia[map6]
18°-55°N / 73°-140°E
038-039
092-093
>6000m
5000-6000m
4000-5000m
3000-4000m
2000-3000m
1000-2000m
500-1000m
200-500m
0-200m
<0m
0-200m
200-500m
500-1000m
1000-2000m
2000-3000m
3000-4000m
4000-5000m
5000-6000m
>6000m
RUSSIA
KAZAKHSTAN
KYRGYZSTAN
TAJIKISTAN
AFGHANISTAN
MONGOLIA
CHINA
INDIA
NEPAL
BHUTAN
BANGLADESH
MYANMAR
LAOS
THAILAND
VIETNAM
JAMMU AND KASHMIR
AKSAI CHIN
XINJIANG UYGUR ZIZHIQU (SINKIANG)
XIZANG ZIZHIQU (TIBET)
QINGHAI
GANSU
SICHUAN
YUNNAN
UTTAR PRADESH
MADHYA PRADESH
BIHAR
JHARKHAND
WEST BENGAL
ORISSA
ASSAM
ARUNACHAL PRADESH
MEGHALAYA
ALTAYSKIY KRAY
KRASNOYARSKIY KRAY
IRKUTSKAYA OBLAST
RESPUBLIKA ALTAY
RESPUBLIKA TYVA
Tarim Basin (Tarim Pendi)
Taklimakan Desert (Taklimakan Shamo)
Plateau of Tibet (Qing Zang Gaoyuan)
Tien Shan
Kunlun Shan
Altun Shan
Qilian Shan
Karakoram
Altay Mountains
Gurbantünggüt Shamo
Junggar Pendi
Qaidam Pendi
Badain Jaran Shamo
Lake Balkhash
Bay of Bengal
Mouths of the Ganges
Omsk
Novosibirsk
Barnaul
Tomsk
Krasnoyarsk
Irkutsk
Almaty
BISHKEK (Frunze)
ISLAMABAD
Lahore
Ürümqi
Kashi (Kashgar)
Hotan
Lhasa
KATHMANDU
THIMPHU
DHAKA (Dacca)
Kolkata (Calcutta)
Patna
Lucknow
Kanpur
Agra
Nagpur
Chittagong
Mandalay
Kunming
Chengdu
Lanzhou
Xining
Golmud
Chiang Mai
VIENTIANE
Vishakhapatnam
A
B
C
D
E
F
G
2
3
4
5
6
7
8
9
75°
80°
85°
90°
95°
100°
105°
20°
25°
30°
35°
40°
45°
50°
55°

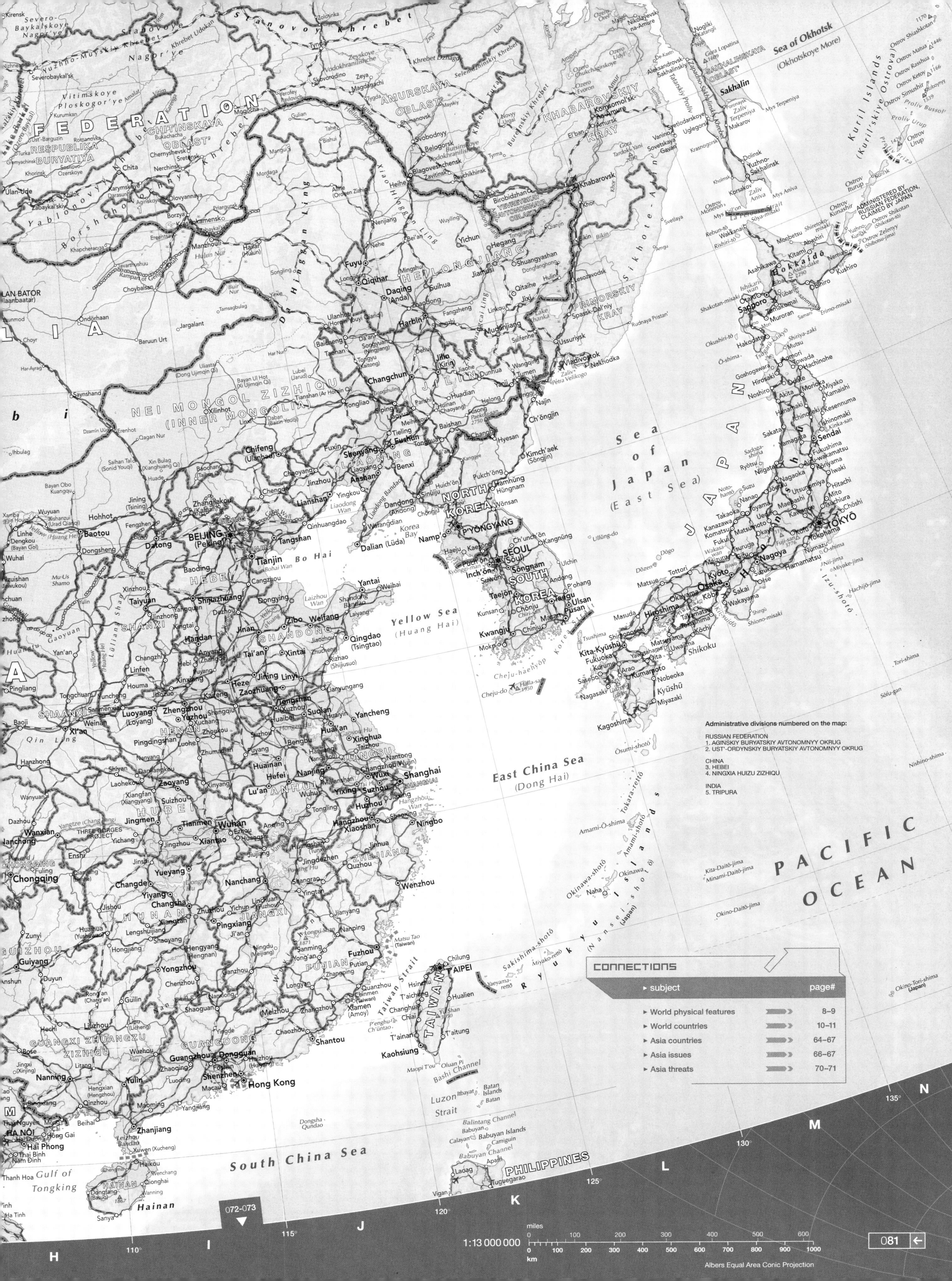

Sea of Okhotsk
(Okhotskoye More)
Sakhalin
Kuril Islands
(Kuril'skiye Ostrova)
ADMINISTERED BY RUSSIAN FEDERATION, CLAIMED BY JAPAN
FEDERATION
CHITINSKAYA OBLAST'
RESPUBLIKA BURYATIYA
AMURSKAYA OBLAST'
KHABAROVSKIY KRAY
SAKHALINSKAYA OBLAST'
YEVREYSKAYA AVTONOMNAYA OBLAST'
PRIMORSKIY KRAY
Stanovoy Khrebet
Vitimskoye Ploskogor'ye
Yablonovyy Khrebet
Sikhote-Alin'
Da Hinggan Ling
HEILONGJIANG
JILIN
LIAONING
NEI MONGOL ZIZHIQU (INNER MONGOLIA)
HEBEI
SHANXI
SHANDONG
SHAANXI
HENAN
JIANGSU
ANHUI
HUBEI
ZHEJIANG
HUNAN
JIANGXI
FUJIAN
GUIZHOU
CHONGQING
GUANGXI ZHUANGZU ZIZHIQU
GUANGDONG
HAINAN
TAIWAN
NORTH KOREA
SOUTH KOREA
JAPAN
Hokkaidō
Honshū
Shikoku
Kyūshū
PHILIPPINES
ULAN BATOR (Ulaanbaatar)
BEIJING (Peking)
P'YONGYANG
SEOUL (Sŏul)
TŌKYŌ
TAIPEI
HA NOI
Harbin
Changchun
Shenyang
Dalian (Lüda)
Tianjin
Shanghai
Nanjing
Wuhan
Chongqing
Guangzhou
Hong Kong
Macau
Shenzhen
Vladivostok
Khabarovsk
Sapporo
Sendai
Nagoya
Ōsaka
Kyōto
Hiroshima
Kita-Kyūshū
Fukuoka
Pusan
Inch'ŏn
Kaohsiung
Sea of Japan (East Sea)
Bo Hai
Korea Bay
Yellow Sea (Huang Hai)
East China Sea (Dong Hai)
PACIFIC OCEAN
South China Sea
Gulf of Tongking
Taiwan Strait
Luzon Strait
Bashi Channel
Ryukyu Islands (Nansei-shotō)
Izu-shotō
Hainan
Administrative divisions numbered on the map:
RUSSIAN FEDERATION
1. AGINSKIY BURYATSKIY AVTONOMNYY OKRUG
2. UST'-ORDYNSKIY BURYATSKIY AVTONOMNYY OKRUG
CHINA
3. HEBEI
4. NINGXIA HUIZU ZIZHIQU
INDIA
5. TRIPURA
CONNECTIONS
subject page#
World physical features 8–9
World countries 10–11
Asia countries 64–67
Asia issues 66–67
Asia threats 70–71
072-073
H
I
J
K
L
M
N
110°
115°
120°
125°
130°
135°
1:13 000 000
miles 0 100 200 300 400 500 600
km 0 100 200 300 400 500 600 700 800 900 1000
Albers Equal Area Conic Projection

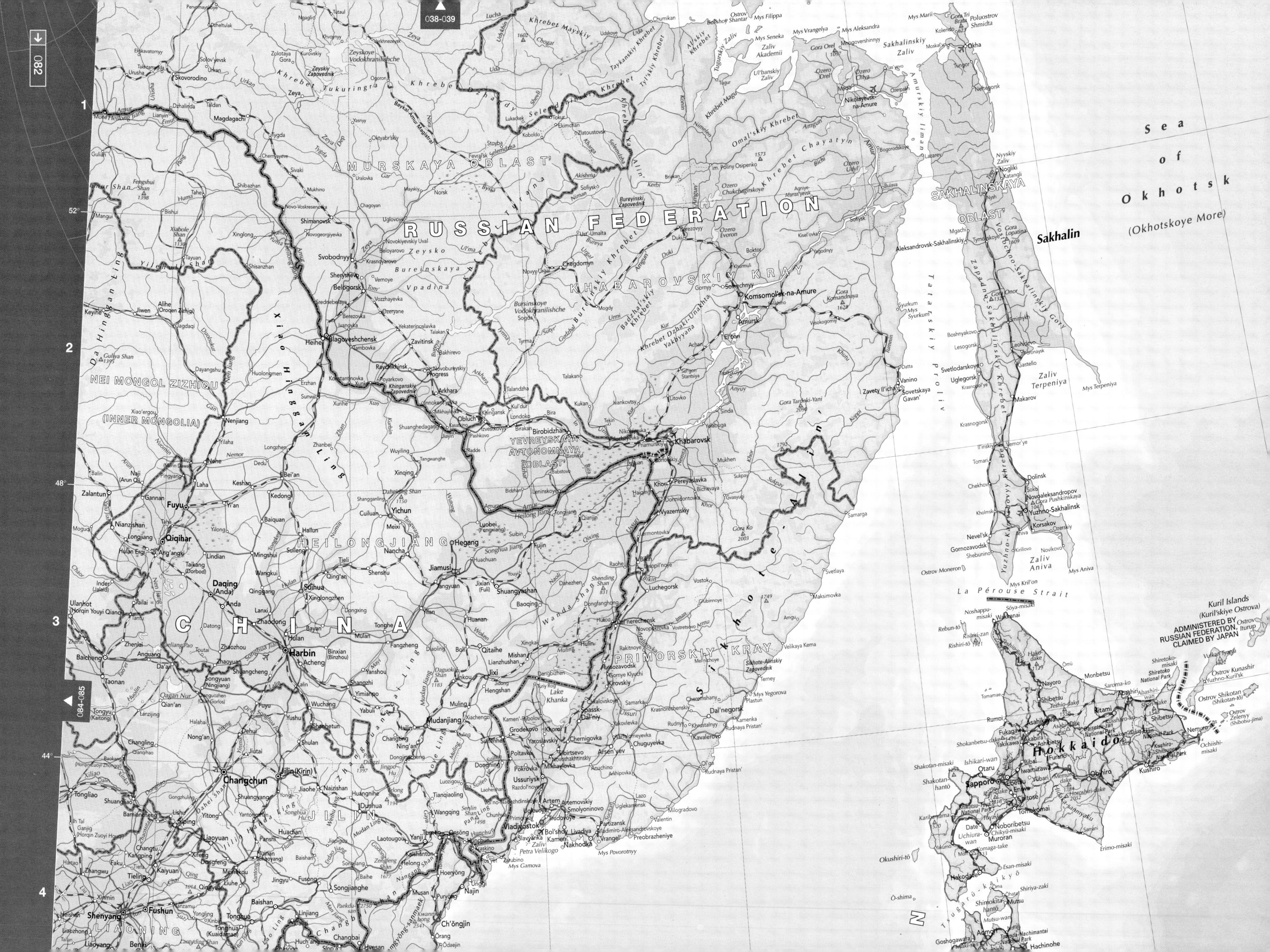

Sea of Okhotsk
(Okhotskoye More)
Sakhalin
SAKHALINSKAYA OBLAST'
Tatarskiy Proliv
La Pérouse Strait
Zaliv Terpeniya
Zaliv Aniva
Hokkaidō
Kuril Islands
(Kuril'skiye Ostrova)
ADMINISTERED BY RUSSIAN FEDERATION, CLAIMED BY JAPAN
RUSSIAN FEDERATION
AMURSKAYA OBLAST'
KHABAROVSKIY KRAY
PRIMORSKIY KRAY
YEVREYSKAYA AVTONOMNAYA OBLAST'
CHINA
HEILONGJIANG
JILIN
LIAONING
NEI MONGOL ZIZHIQU
(INNER MONGOLIA)
Xiao Hinggan Ling
Da Hinggan Ling
Khabarovsk
Komsomol'sk-na-Amure
Blagoveshchensk
Vladivostok
Harbin
Changchun
Shenyang
Qiqihar
Daqing
Jilin (Kirin)
Sapporo
Lake Khanka
1
2
3
4
52°
48°
44°
038-039
084-085

29°-55°N / 122°-148°E

CONNECTIONS

▸ subject	page#
▴ World population	22–23
▴ World cities	24–25
▴ Asia landscapes	62–63
▴ Asia countries	64–67
▴ Pacific Ocean	220–221

1:6 000 000
Conic Equidistant Projection

miles
km

>6000m
5000-6000m
4000-5000m
3000-4000m
2000-3000m
1000-2000m
500-1000m
200-500m
0-200m
<0m
0-200m
200-500m
500-1000m
1000-2000m
2000-3000m
3000-4000m
4000-5000m
5000-6000m
>6000m

Seas and Oceans

Sea of Japan (East Sea)

Yellow Sea (Huang Hai)

Korea Bay

East China Sea (Dong Hai)

PACIFIC OCEAN

NORTH KOREA

PYŎNGYANG
Namp'o
Hamhŭng
Sinŭiju
Kimch'aek (Sŏngjin)
Kilchu
Hyesan
Musan

SOUTH KOREA

SEOUL (Sŏul)
Inch'ŏn
Suwŏn
Taejŏn
Taegu
Kwangju
Pusan
Ulsan
Masan
Chinhae
Chŏnju
P'ohang
Cheju
Cheju-do

JAPAN

TOKYO
Sendai
Niigata
Nagoya
Kyoto
Osaka
Kobe
Hiroshima
Nagasaki
Kumamoto
Kagoshima
Fukuoka
Kita-Kyūshū
Matsuyama
Kōchi

HONSHŪ
SHIKOKU
KYŪSHŪ

Izu-shotō
Tanega-shima
Yaku-shima
Ōsumi-shotō

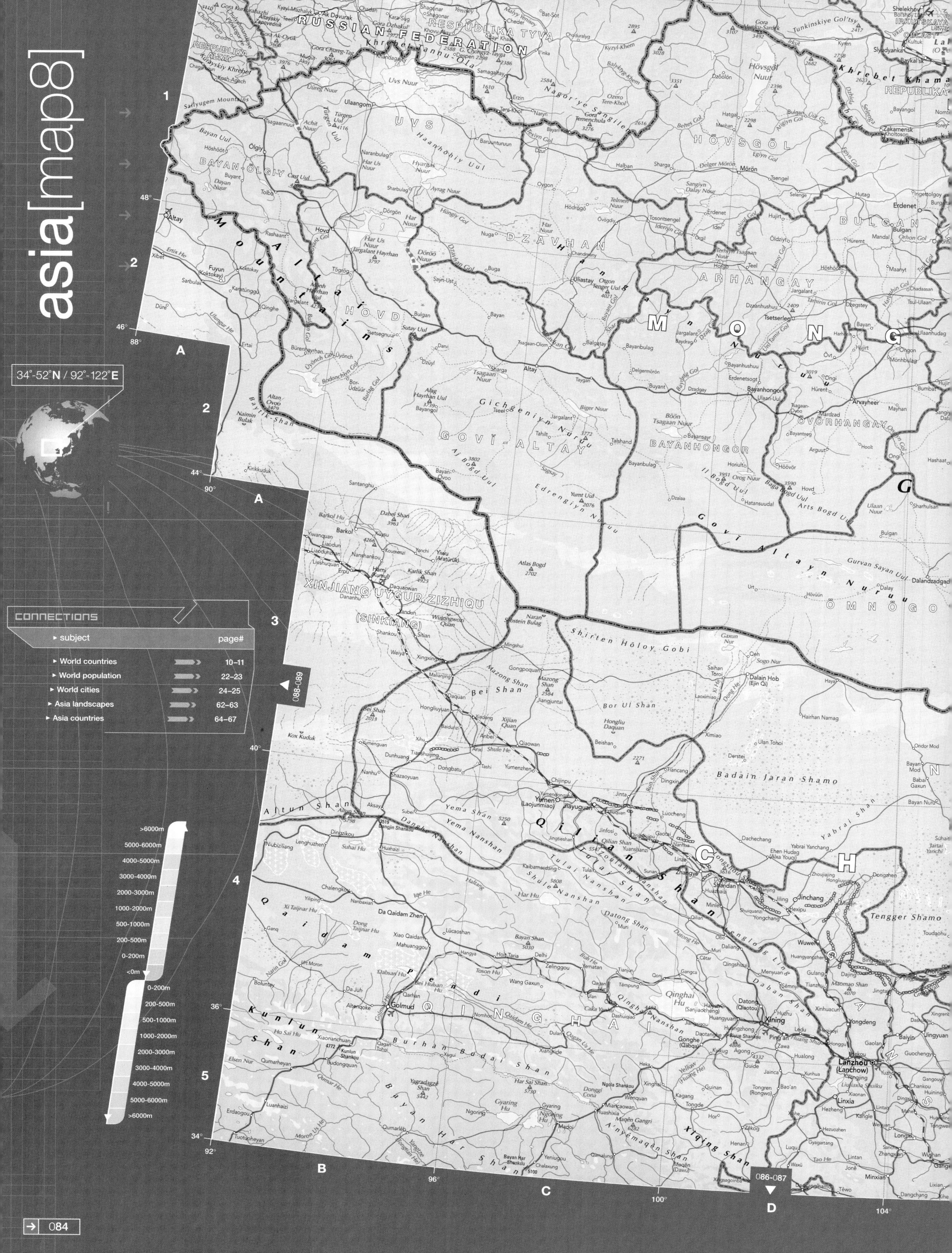

asia[map8]

34°-52°**N** / 92°-122°**E**

>6000m
5000-6000m
4000-5000m
3000-4000m
2000-3000m
1000-2000m
500-1000m
200-500m
0-200m
<0m

0-200m
200-500m
500-1000m
1000-2000m
2000-3000m
3000-4000m
4000-5000m
5000-6000m
>6000m

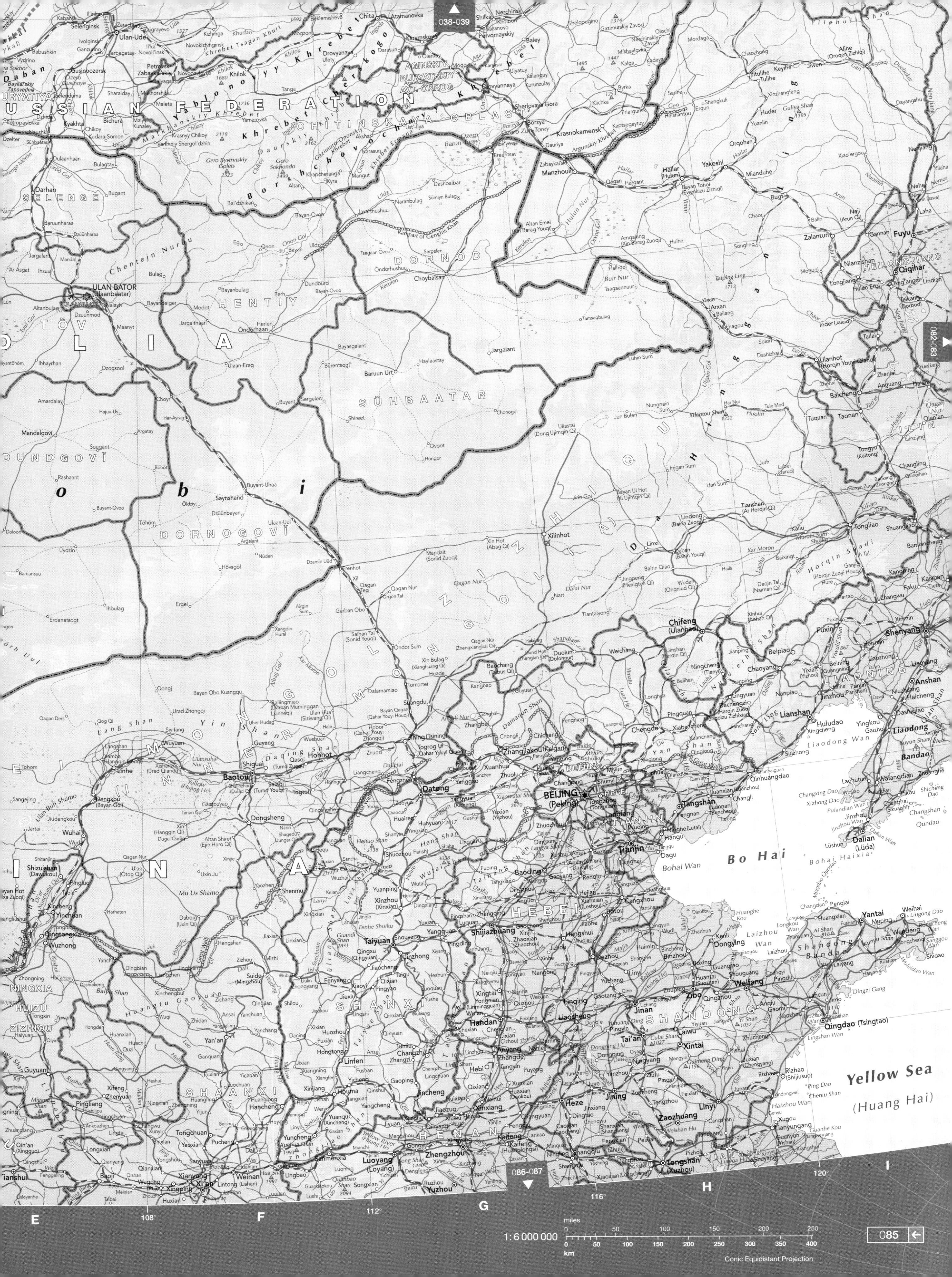
038-039
RUSSIAN FEDERATION
CHITINSKAYA OBLAST
AGINSKIY BURYATSKIY AVT. OKRUG
Ulan-Ude
Chita
Krasnokamensk
Manzhouli
Hailar
Yakeshi
Qiqihar
HEILONGJIANG
ULAN BATOR (Ulaanbaatar)
SELENGE
HENTIY
DORNOD
TÖV
SÜHBAATAR
DUNDGOVĬ
DORNOGOVĬ
Gobi
Choybalsan
Baruun Urt
Xilinhot
Tongliao
Ulanhot
Chifeng
JILIN
LIAONING
Shenyang
Anshan
Dalian (Lüda)
Liaodong Wan
Bo Hai
Bohai Wan
BEIJING (Peking)
TIANJIN
Tianjin
HEBEI
Shijiazhuang
Zhangjiakou
Datong
Hohhot
Baotou
Taiyuan
SHANXI
SHAANXI
Xi'an
Zhengzhou
Luoyang
HENAN
Jinan
SHANDONG
Qingdao (Tsingtao)
Yantai
Weifang
Zibo
Tangshan
Qinhuangdao
Yellow Sea (Huang Hai)
Yin Shan
Great Wall
NEI MONGOL ZIZHIQU
NINGXIA HUIZU ZIZHIQU
086-087
082-083
E
F
G
H
I
108°
112°
116°
120°
1: 6 000 000
miles 0 50 100 150 200 250
km 0 50 100 150 200 250 300 350 400
Conic Equidistant Projection

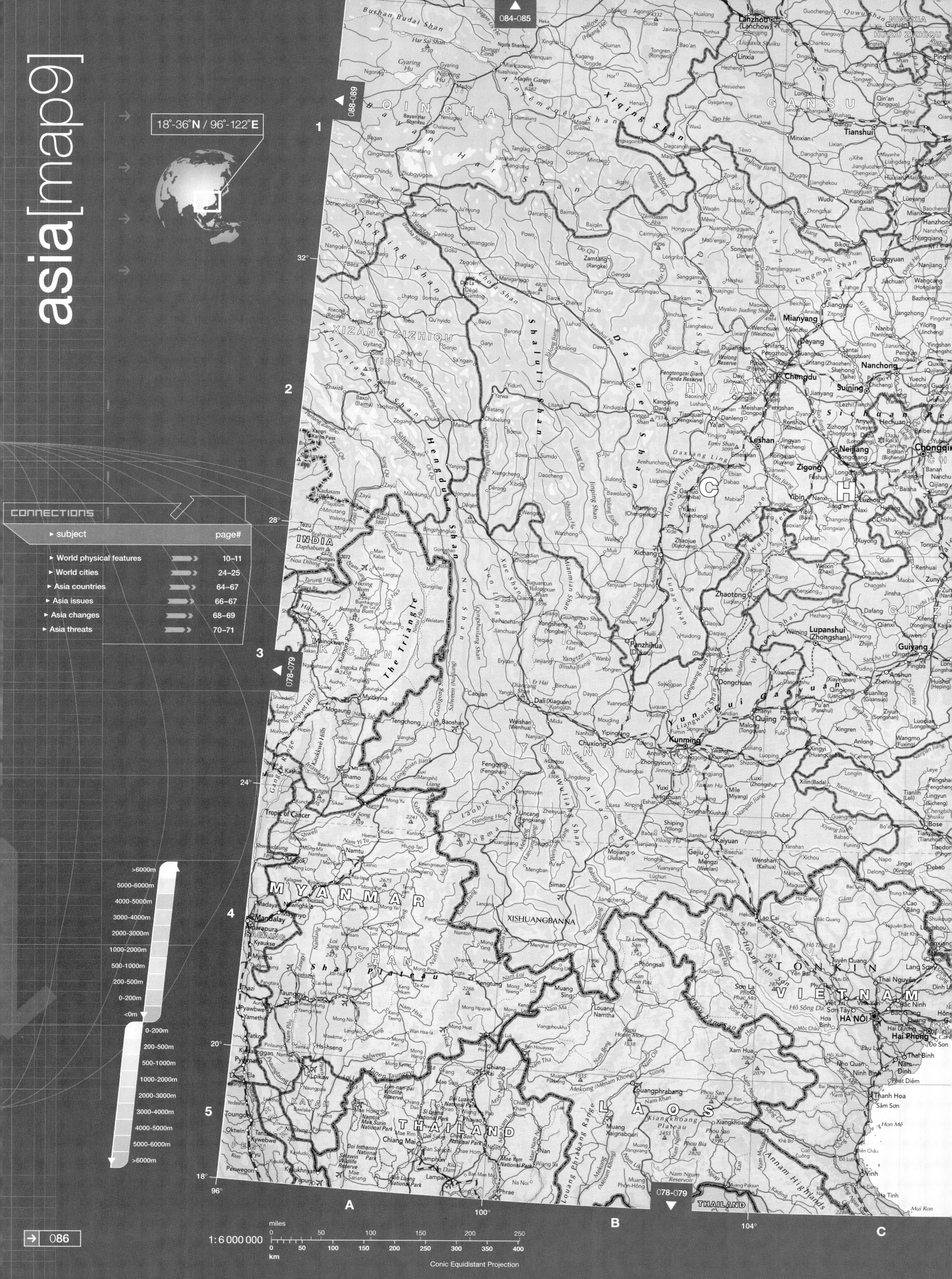
asia[map9]
18°-36°N / 96°-122°E
CONNECTIONS
subject page#
World physical features 10–11
World cities 24–25
Asia countries 64–67
Asia issues 66–67
Asia changes 68–69
Asia threats 70–71
>6000m
5000-6000m
4000-5000m
3000-4000m
2000-3000m
1000-2000m
500-1000m
200-500m
0-200m
<0m
0-200m
200-500m
500-1000m
1000-2000m
2000-3000m
3000-4000m
4000-5000m
5000-6000m
>6000m
084-085
088-089
078-079
078-079
QINGHAI
GANSU
SICHUAN
YUNNAN
XIZANG ZIZHIQU (TIBET)
INDIA
KACHIN
MYANMAR
SHAN
THAILAND
LAOS
VIETNAM
TONKIN
KAYAH
XISHUANGBANNA
Chengdu
Chongqing
Kunming
Lanzhou (Lanchow)
Mandalay
HÀ NỘI
Hai Phong
Chiang Mai
Tropic of Cancer
1:6 000 000
miles
km
Conic Equidistant Projection
086

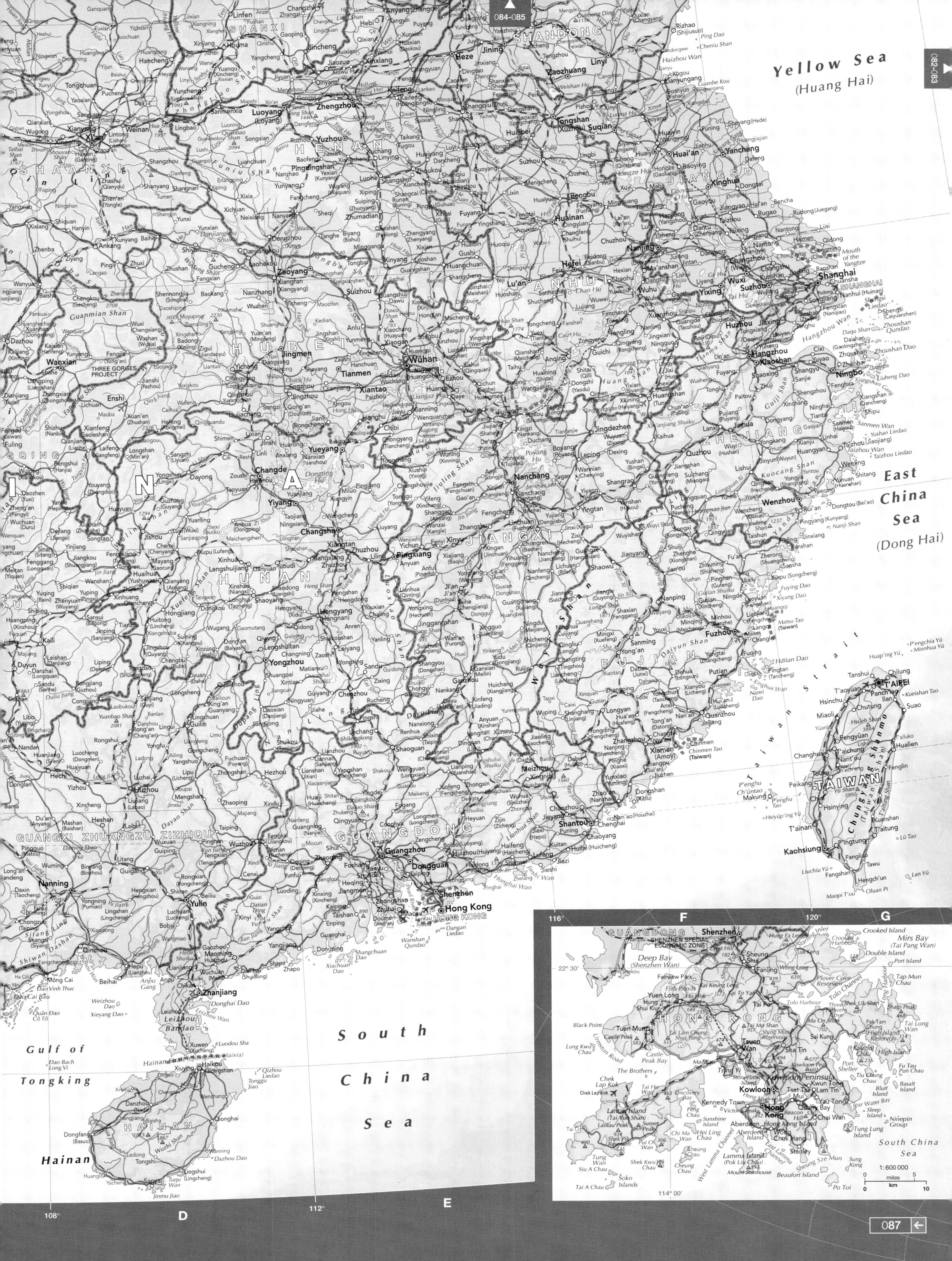

Yellow Sea
(Huang Hai)

East
China
Sea
(Dong Hai)

South

China

Sea

Gulf of

Tongking

SHANXI

SHANDONG

HENAN

JIANGSU

ANHUI

HUBEI

SHAANXI

CHINA

HUNAN

JIANGXI

ZHEJIANG

FUJIAN

GUIZHOU

GUANGXI ZHUANGZU ZIZHIQU

GUANGDONG

HAINAN

TAIWAN

Taiwan Strait

Nanning

Zhanjiang

Haikou

Hong Kong

Guangzhou

Shenzhen

Shantou

Xiamen (Amoy) (Taiwan)

Fuzhou

T'AIPEI

Kaohsiung

Nanchang

Changsha

Wuhan

Xi'an

Zhengzhou

Luoyang (Loyang)

Shanghai

Nanjing

Hangzhou

Ningbo

Wenzhou

Hefei

HONG KONG

1:600 000

SHENZHEN SPECIAL
ECONOMIC ZONE

GUANGDONG

Deep Bay
(Shenzhen Wan)

Mirs Bay
(Tai Pang Wan)

Shenzhen

Hong Kong

Kowloon

South China
Sea

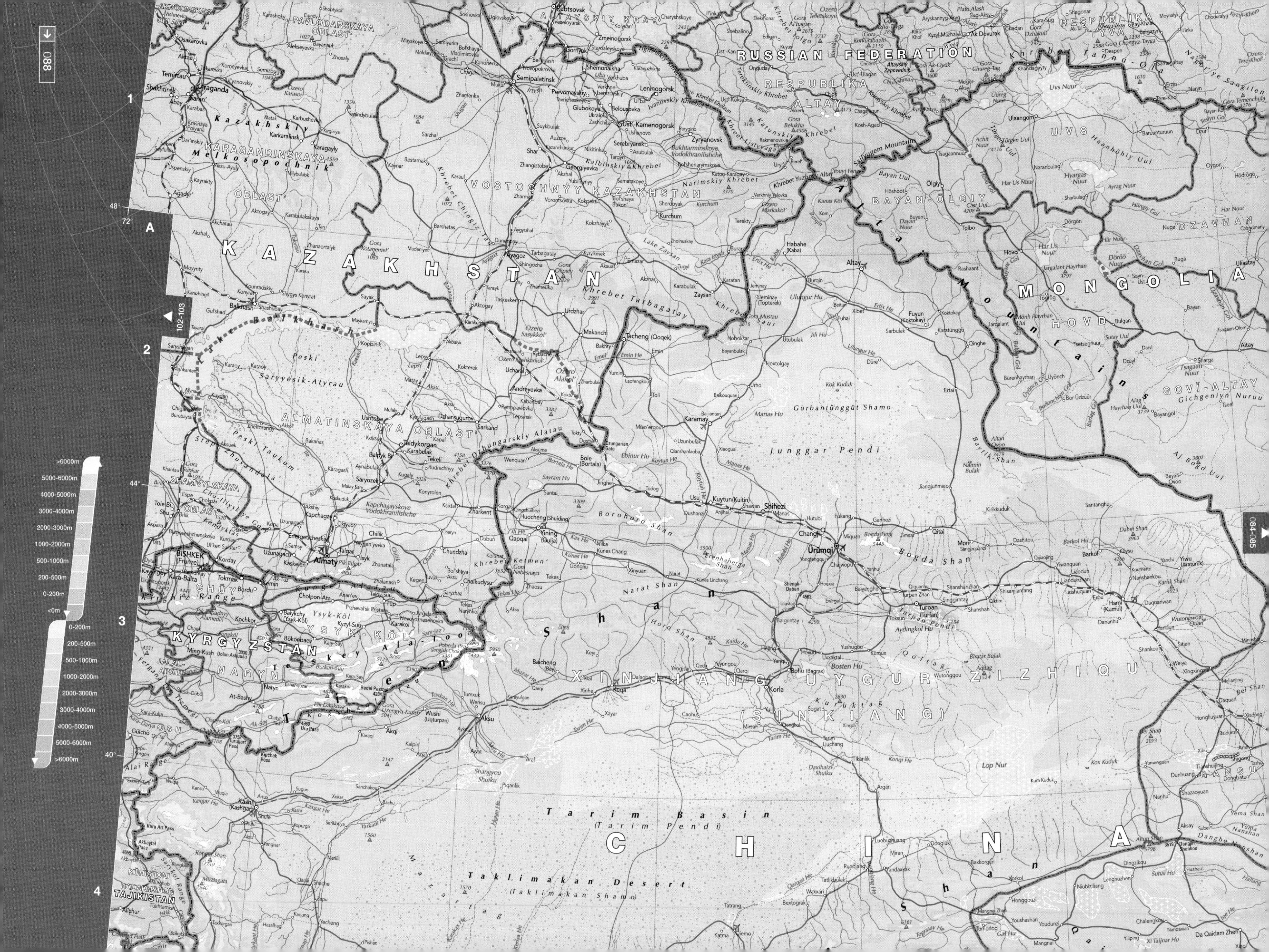
RUSSIAN FEDERATION
KAZAKHSTAN
MONGOLIA
CHINA
KYRGYZSTAN
TAJIKISTAN
RESPUBLIKA ALTAY
RESPUBLIKA TYVA
ALTAYSKIY KRAY
VOSTOCHNYY KAZAKHSTAN
ALMATINSKAYA OBLAST'
KARAGANDINSKAYA OBLAST'
PAVLODARSKAYA OBLAST'
ZHAMBYLSKAYA OBLAST'
XINJIANG UYGUR ZIZHIQU (SINKIANG)
GANSU
BAYAN-ÖLGIY
HOVD
UVS
GOVĬ-ALTAY
DZAVHAN
Altai Mountains
Tarim Basin (Tarim Pendi)
Taklimakan Desert (Taklimakan Shamo)
Junggar Pendi
Gurbantünggüt Shamo
Turpan Pendi
Lake Zaysan
Lake Balkhash
Peski Saryyesik-Atyrau
Peski Taukum
Ysyk-Köl
Lop Nur
Almaty
Bishkek (Frunze)
Ürümqi
Semipalatinsk
Karaganda
Kashi (Kashgar)
Aksu
Korla
Turpan (Turfan)
Hami (Kumul)
Karamay
Shihezi
Yining (Gulja)
Altay
Hovd
Ölgiy
Ulaangom
Naryn
Taldykorgan
Ust'-Kamenogorsk
Tacheng (Qoqek)
Ruoqiang
Khrebet Tarbagatay
Dzhungarskiy Alatau
Borohoro Shan
Bogda Shan
Narat Shan
Altun Shan
Alai Range
Sarykol Range
Kirghiz Range
Kazakhskiy Melkosopochnik
Khrebet Chingiz-Tau
Kuruktag
Qoltag
Mazartag
A
1
2
3
4
48°
72°
44°
40°
084-085
102-103
088
>6000m
5000-6000m
4000-5000m
3000-4000m
2000-3000m
1000-2000m
500-1000m
200-500m
0-200m
<0m

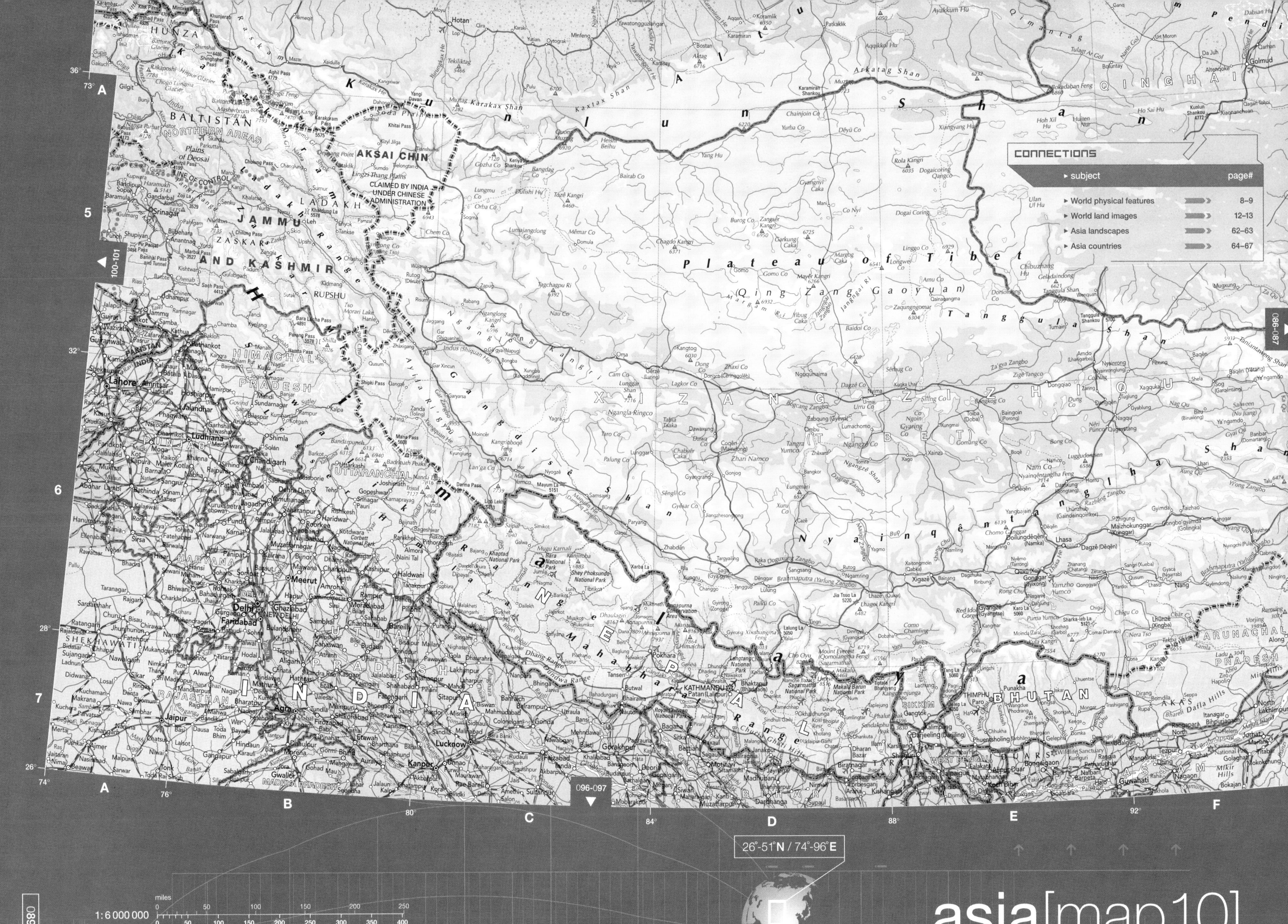

086-087

096-097

100-101

CONNECTIONS

subject	page#
▲ World physical features	8-9
▲ World land images	12-13
▲ Asia landscapes	62-63
▲ Asia countries	64-67

26°-51'N / 74°-96°E

1:6 000 000

Conic Equidistant Projection

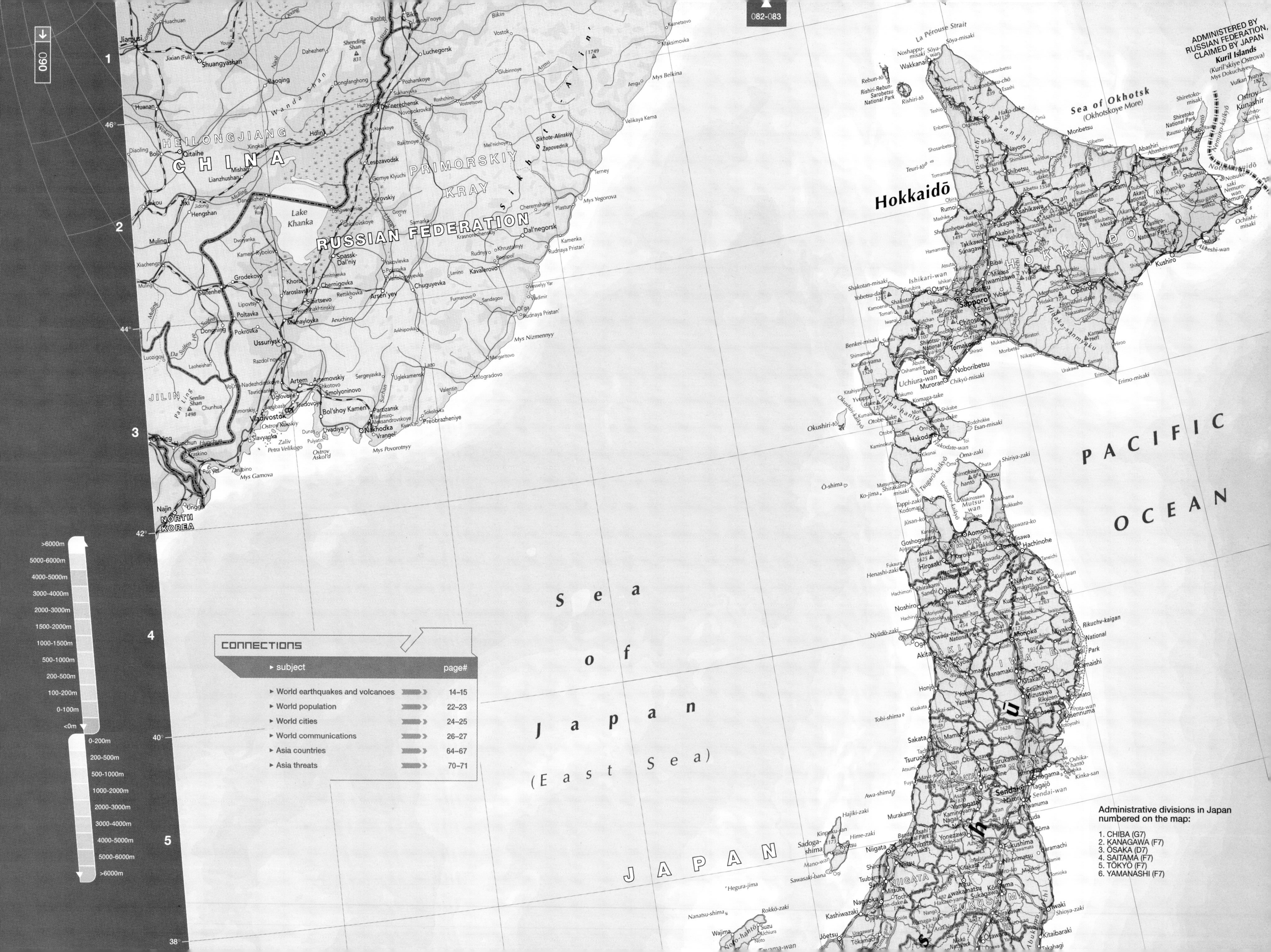

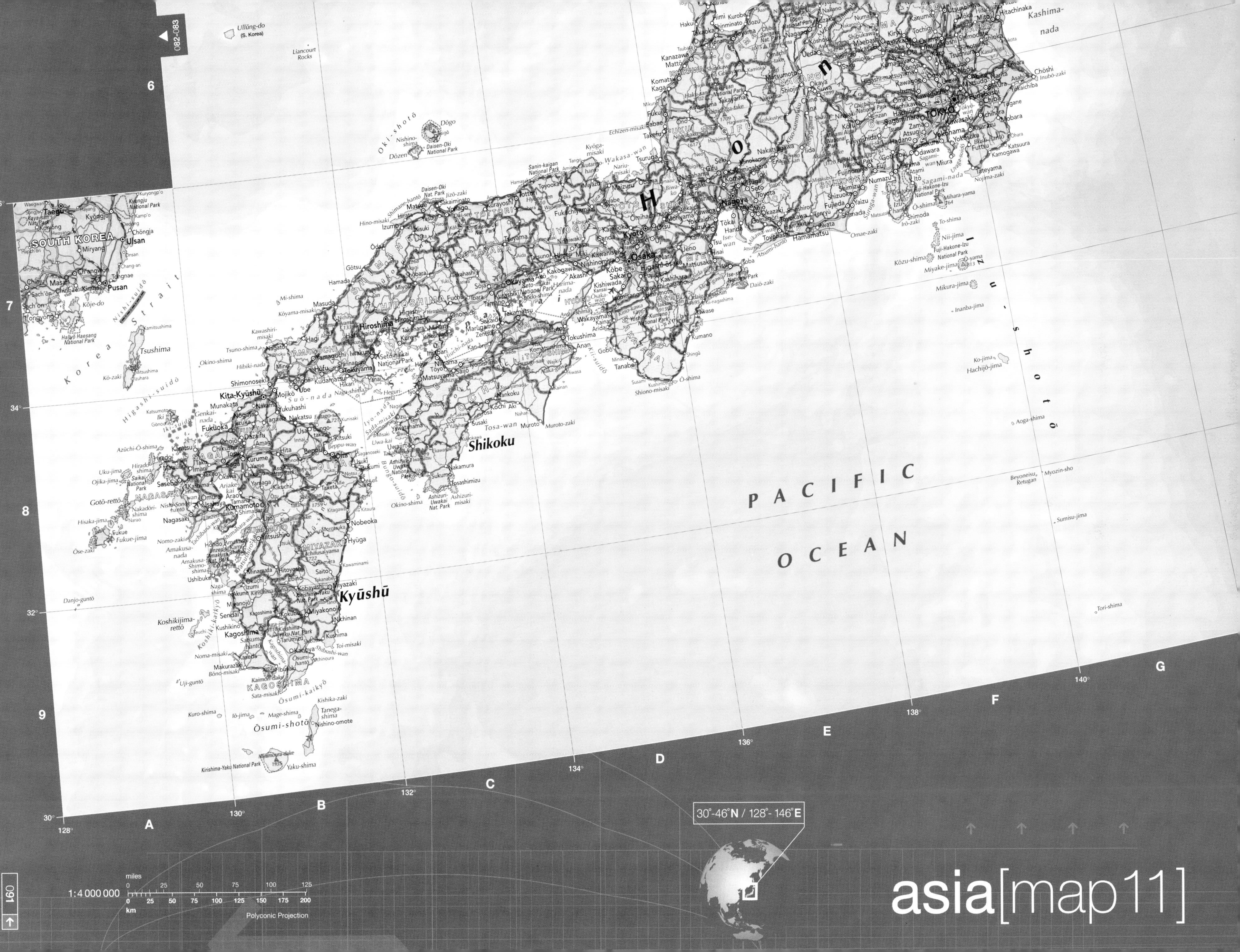

asia[map11]
30°-46°N / 128°-146°E
1:4 000 000
miles 0 25 50 75 100 125
km 0 25 50 75 100 125 150 175 200
Polyconic Projection
082-083
PACIFIC OCEAN
Honshū
Shikoku
Kyūshū
SOUTH KOREA
Korea Strait
Tsushima
Izu-shotō
Oki-shotō
TOKYO
Ōsaka
Kyōto
Nagoya
Kōbe
Hiroshima
Kita-Kyūshū
Fukuoka
Kumamoto
Kagoshima
Nagasaki
Pusan
Taegu
Ulsan
Shimonoseki
Okayama
Matsuyama
Kōchi
Tokushima
Wakayama
Shizuoka
Hamamatsu
Yokohama
Kawasaki
Chiba
Kanazawa
Sendai
Miyazaki
Ōita
Ōsumi-shotō
Gotō-rettō
Danjo-guntō
Suō-nada
Tosa-wan
Ullŭng-do (S. Korea)
Liancourt Rocks
Kashima-nada
Hachijō-jima
Tori-shima
Sumisu-jima
Tanega-shima
Yaku-shima
Kirishima-Yaku National Park
A B C D E F G
6 7 8 9
128° 130° 132° 134° 136° 138° 140°
30° 32° 34° 36°

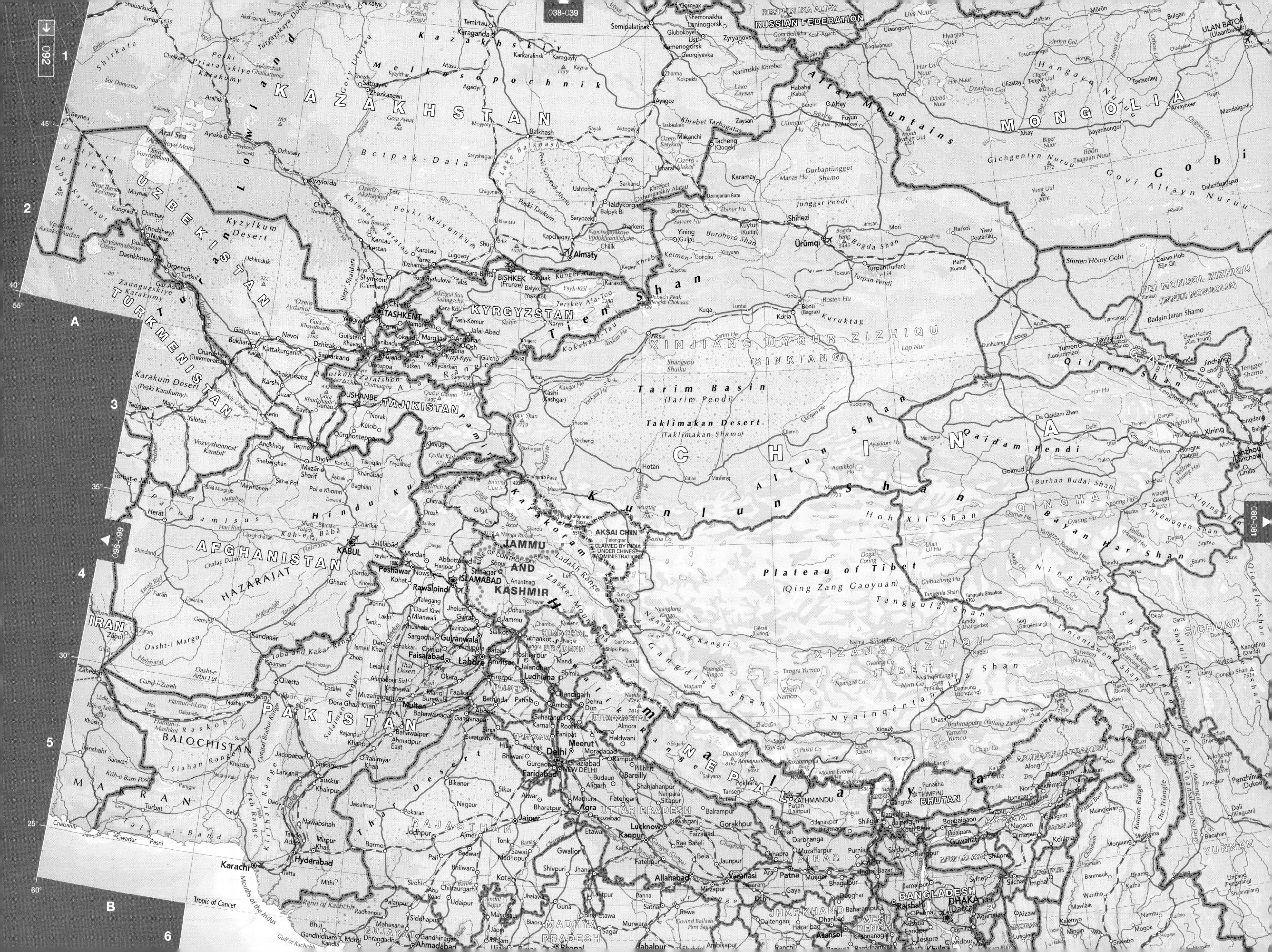

KAZAKHSTAN
UZBEKISTAN
TURKMENISTAN
KYRGYZSTAN
TAJIKISTAN
AFGHANISTAN
PAKISTAN
IRAN
NEPAL
BHUTAN
BANGLADESH
MONGOLIA
RUSSIAN FEDERATION
CHINA
XINJIANG UYGUR ZIZHIQU
(SINKIANG)
XIZANG ZIZHIQU
(TIBET)
QINGHAI
GANSU
SICHUAN
YUNNAN
NEI MONGOL ZIZHIQU
(INNER MONGOLIA)
JAMMU
AND
KASHMIR
AKSAI CHIN
CLAIMED BY INDIA UNDER CHINESE ADMINISTRATION
Tarim Basin
(Tarim Pendi)
Taklimakan Desert
(Taklimakan Shamo)
Plateau of Tibet
(Qing Zang Gaoyuan)
Kunlun Shan
Altun Shan
Tien Shan
Hindu Kush
Karakoram Range
Altai Mountains
Gobi
Qaidam Pendi
Kyzylkum Desert
Karakum Desert
(Peski Karakumy)
Thar Desert
Aral Sea
TASHKENT
BISHKEK
DUSHANBE
KABUL
ISLAMABAD
NEW DELHI
KATHMANDU
THIMPHU
DHAKA
ULAN BATOR
Almaty
Ürümqi
Karachi
Lahore
Delhi
Tropic of Cancer
Mouths of the Indus
038-039
080-081
098-099
A
B
1
2
3
4
5
6

asia[map12]

CONNECTIONS

▶ subject	page#
▲ World physical features	8–9
▲ World land images	12–13
▲ World population	22–23
▲ World cities	24–25
▲ Asia landscapes	62–63
▲ Asia countries	64–67
▲ Asia threats	70–71

1°S–50°N / 60°–97°E

Administrative divisions in India numbered on the map:

1. DADRA AND NAGAR HAVELI (D6)
2. DAMAN AND DIU (D6)
3. TRIPURA (H6)

1:12 000 000

Albers Equal Area Conic Projection

miles
km

INDIAN OCEAN

Bay of Bengal

Arabian Sea

Andaman Sea

MYANMAR

THAILAND

INDONESIA

Sumatra

ANDAMAN AND NICOBAR ISLANDS (India)

Andaman Islands

Nicobar Islands

LAKSHADWEEP (India)

Laccadive Islands

MALDIVES

MALE

SRI LANKA

SRI JAYEWARDENEPURA KOTTE

Colombo

INDIA

MAHARASHTRA

ANDHRA PRADESH

KARNATAKA

TAMIL NADU

KERALA

GOA

ORISSA

CHHATTISGARH

Mumbai (Bombay)

Hyderabad

Bangalore

Chennai (Madras)

Kolkata (Calcutta)

RANGOON (Yangon)

Cape Comorin

Coromandel Coast

Malabar Coast

Western Ghats

Eastern Ghats

Deccan

>6000m
5000–6000m
4000–5000m
3000–4000m
2000–3000m
1000–2000m
500–1000m
200–500m
0–200m
<0m

0–200m
200–500m
500–1000m
1000–2000m
2000–3000m
3000–4000m
4000–5000m
5000–6000m
>6000m

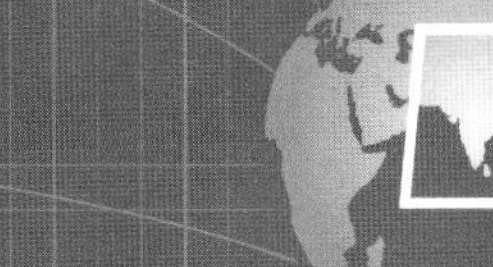

asia[map13]

5°–22°N / 70°–96°E

Arabian Sea

A r a b i a n

S e a

GUJARAT

MADHYA   PRADESH

CHHAT

MAHARASHTRA

I N D I A

D E C C A N

KARNATAKA

ANDHRA   PRADESH

GOA

TAMIL   NADU

KERALA

Mumbai (Bombay)
Pune
Surat
Vadodara (Baroda)
Indore
Nashik
Aurangabad
Nagpur
Hyderabad
Secunderabad
Vijayawada
Bangalore
Chennai (Madras)
Pondicherry (Puducherry)
Mangalore
Calicut (Kozhikode)
Coimbatore
Cochin (Kochi)
Madurai
Trivandrum (Thiruvananthapuram)
Cape Comorin

Laccadive Islands
Amindivi Islands
LAKSHADWEEP (India)
Cannanore Islands

Sesostris Bank
Bassas de Pedro Padua Bank
Cherbaniani Reef
Byramgore Reef

Nine Degree Channel
Eight Degree Channel
Minicoy

MALDIVES

SRI LANKA
Colombo
SRI JAYEWARDENEPURA KOTTE
Jaffna
Kandy

Gulf of Mannar
Palk Strait
Palk Bay

Coromandel Coast
Gulf of Khambhat

Elevation legend

>6000m
5000–6000m
4000–5000m
3000–4000m
2000–3000m
1000–2000m
500–1000m
200–500m
0–200m
<0m

0–200m
200–500m
500–1000m
1000–2000m
2000–3000m
3000–4000m
4000–5000m
5000–6000m
>6000m

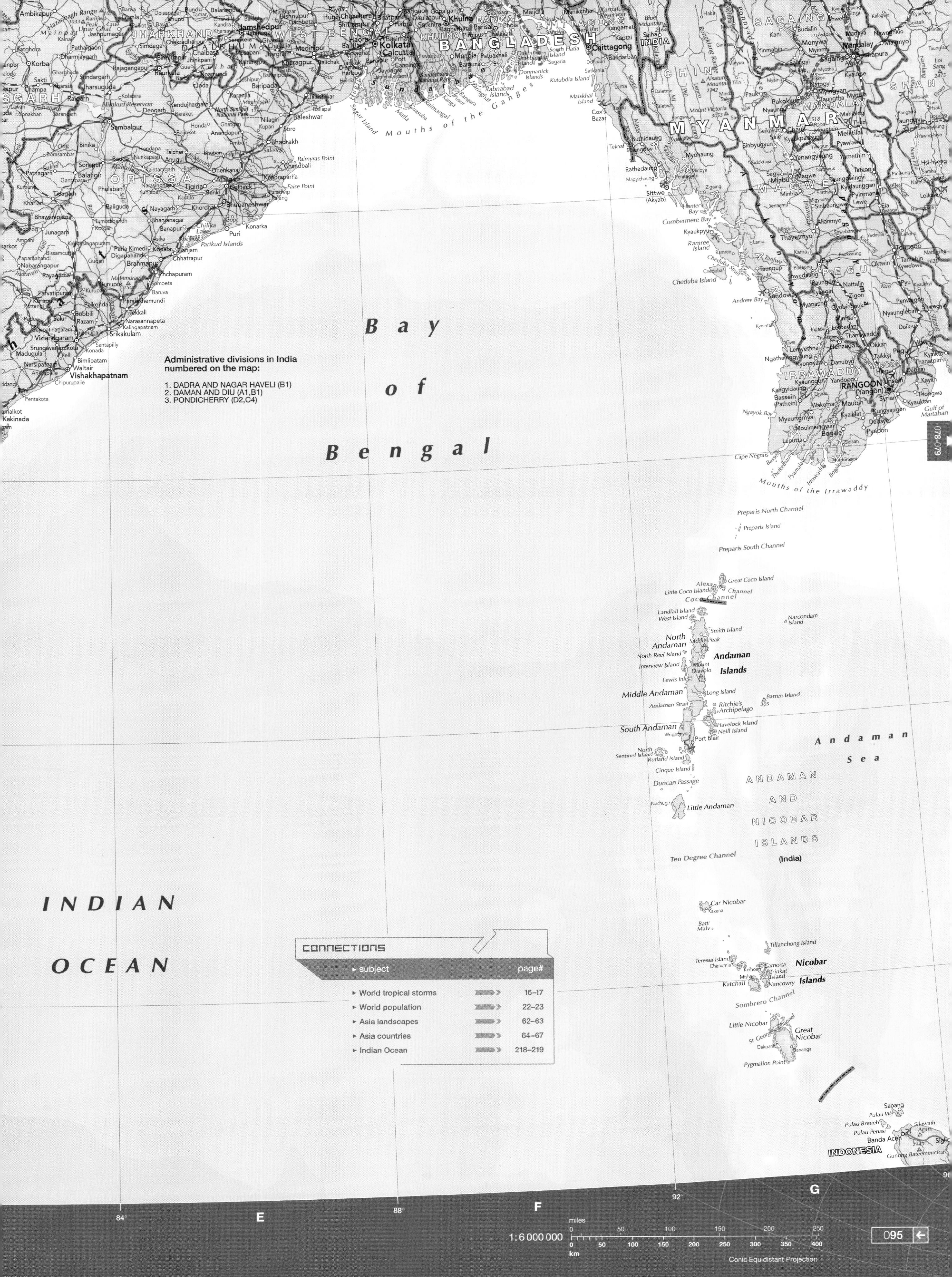

CONNECTIONS

▸ subject	page#
▸ World tropical storms	16–17
▸ World population	22–23
▸ Asia landscapes	62–63
▸ Asia countries	64–67
▸ Indian Ocean	218–219

asia[map14]

20°-38°N / 68°-96°E

100-101

>6000m
5000-6000m
4000-5000m
3000-4000m
2000-3000m
1000-2000m
500-1000m
200-500m
0-200m
<0m

0-200m
200-500m
500-1000m
1000-2000m
2000-3000m
3000-4000m
4000-5000m
5000-6000m
>6000m

Administrative divisions in India
numbered on the map:

1. DADRA AND NAGAR HAVELI (B5)
2. DAMAN AND DIU (A5,B5)

Tropic of Cancer

Arabian Sea

Gulf of Khambhat

AFGHANISTAN

PAKISTAN

TAJIKISTAN

Taklimakan

AKSAI CHIN
CLAIMED BY INDIA
UNDER CHINESE
ADMINISTRATION

JAMMU AND KASHMIR

I N D I A

RAJASTHAN

GUJARAT

MADHYA PRADESH

UTTAR

New Delhi

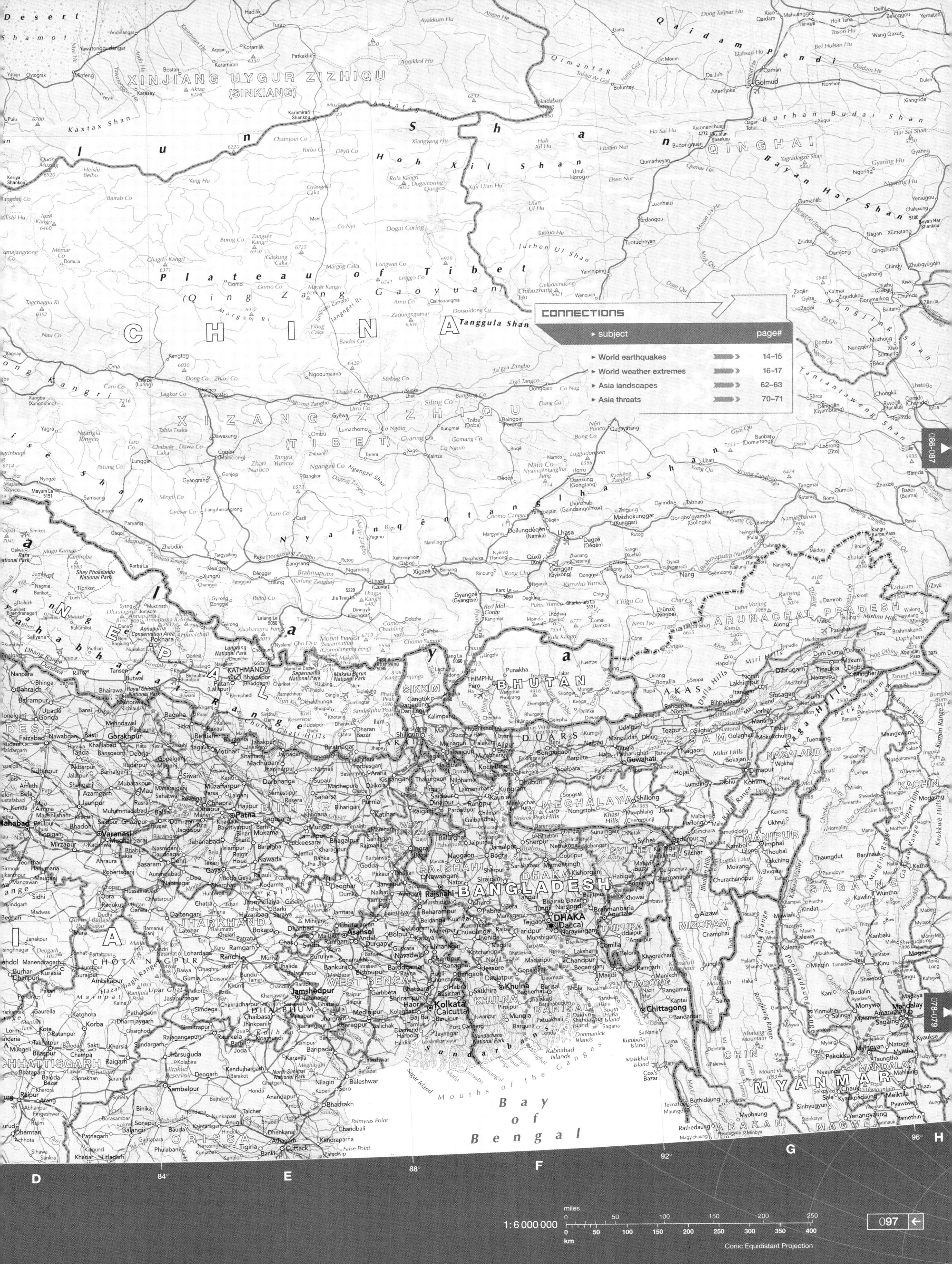

13°-42°N / 30°-80°E

040-041

052-053

120-121

128-129

Elevation scale:
>6000m
5000-6000m
4000-5000m
3000-4000m
2000-3000m
1000-2000m
500-1000m
200-500m
0-200m
<0m

0-200m
200-500m
500-1000m
1000-2000m
2000-3000m
3000-4000m
4000-5000m
5000-6000m
>6000m

Black Sea

Mediterranean Sea

RUSSIAN FEDERATION
GEORGIA
ARMENIA
AZERBAIJAN
TURKEY
CYPRUS
SYRIA
LEBANON
ISRAEL
JORDAN
IRAQ
KUWAIT
SAUDI ARABIA
EGYPT
SUDAN
ERITREA
ETHIOPIA
YEMEN
QATAR

ANKARA
YEREVAN
BAKU
T'BILISI
TEHRĀN
BAGHDĀD
DAMASCUS (Dimashq)
BEIRUT
JERUSALEM
'AMMĀN
GAZA
CAIRO (El Qāhira)
KHARTOUM
ASMARA
ŞAN'Ā'
KUWAIT (Al Kuwayt)
RIYADH (Ar Riyād)
NICOSIA (Lefkoşa)
Tel Aviv-Yafo

Red Sea
Gulf of Aden
Caspian Sea
Gulf of Suez
Gulf of Aqaba

An Nafūd
Rub' al Khali
Ad Dahnā'
Nubian Desert
Eastern Desert
Syrian Desert
Tropic of Cancer

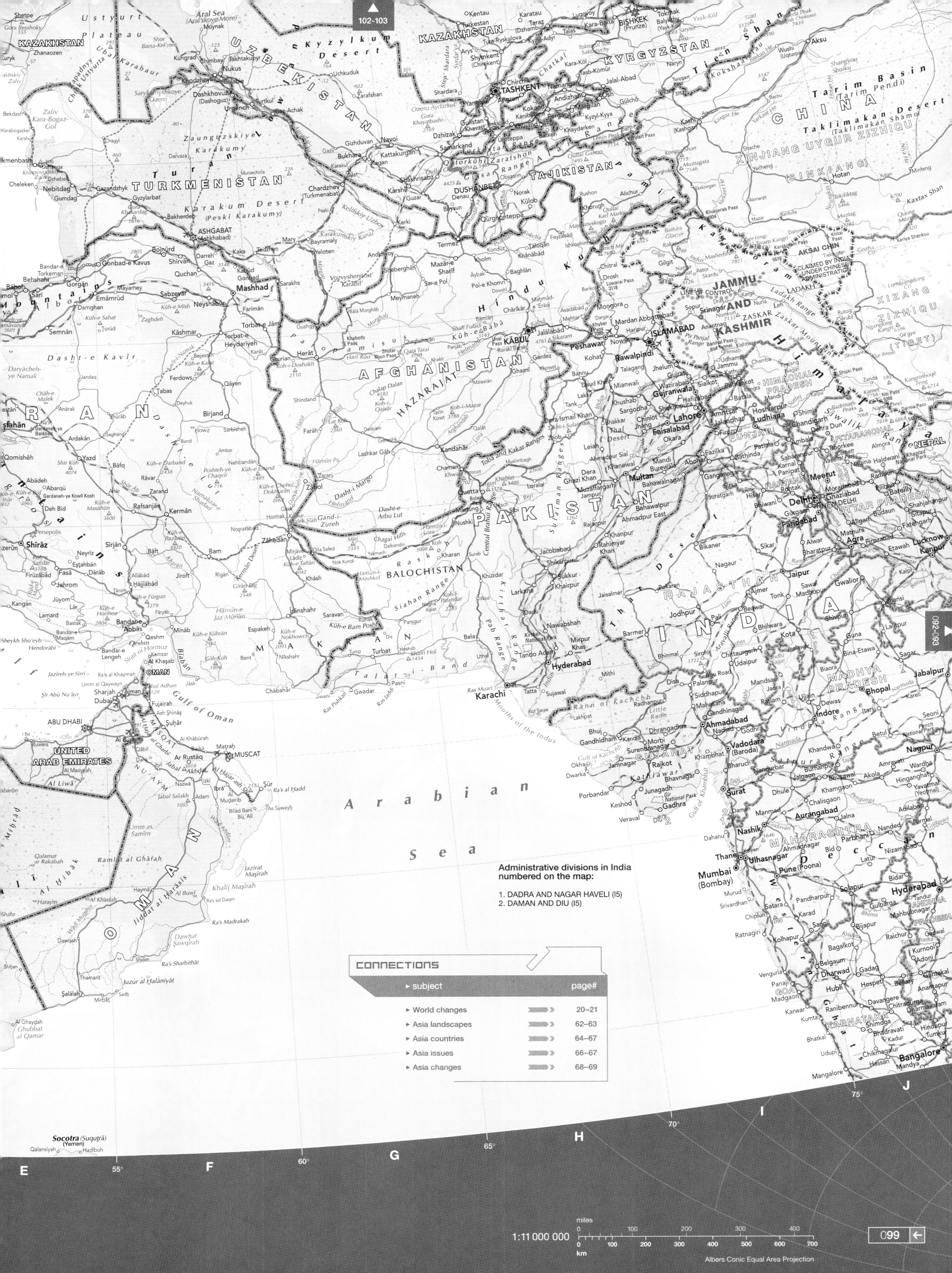

Administrative divisions in India
numbered on the map:

1. DADRA AND NAGAR HAVELI (I5)
2. DAMAN AND DIU (I5)

CONNECTIONS

► subject	page#
► World changes	➤➤➤ 20–21
► Asia landscapes	➤➤➤ 62–63
► Asia countries	➤➤➤ 64–67
► Asia issues	➤➤➤ 66–67
► Asia changes	➤➤➤ 68–69

1:11 000 000

miles
0   100   200   300   400

km
0   100   200   300   400   500   600   700

Albers Conic Equal Area Projection

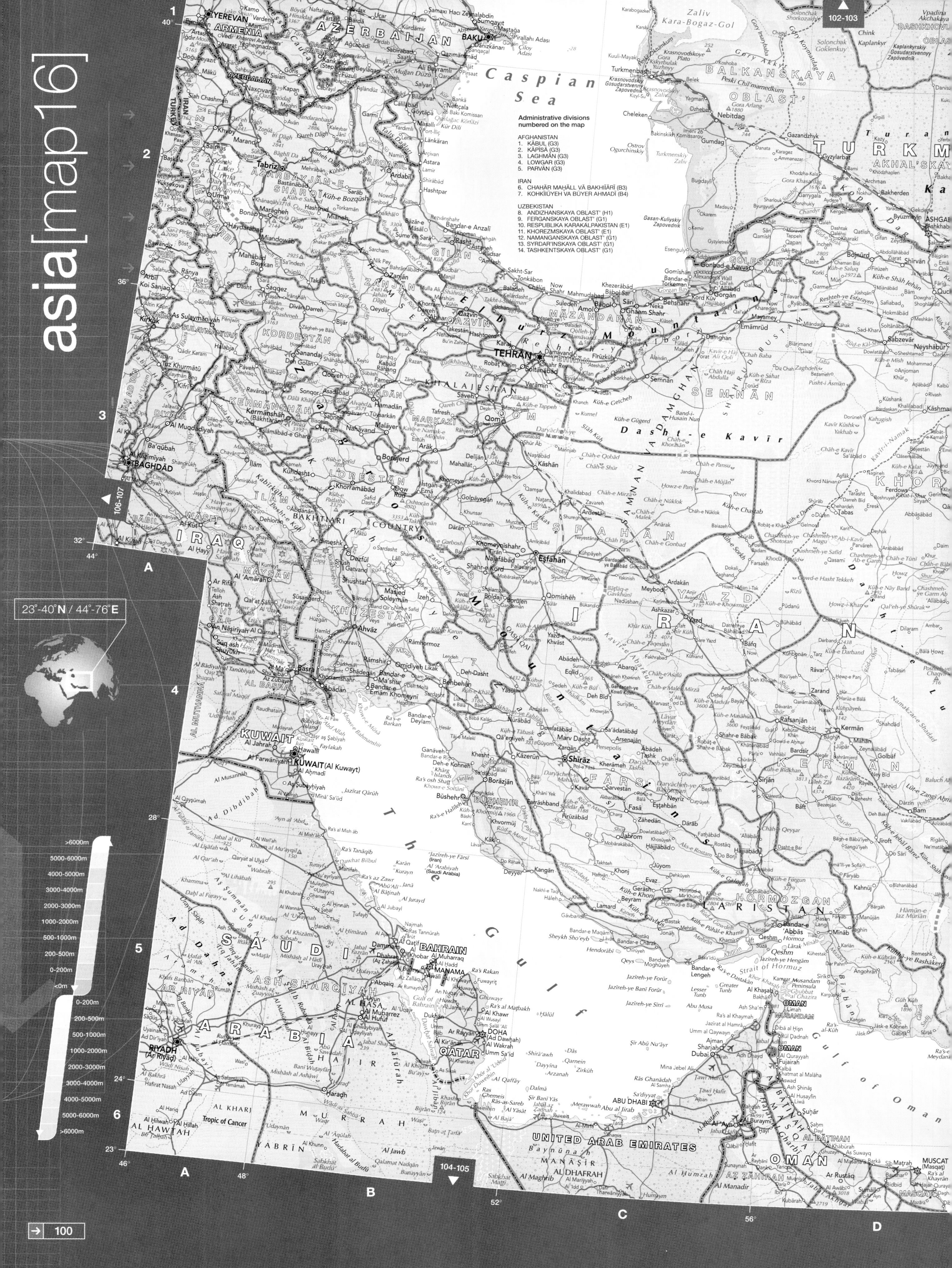

asia[map16]

23°-40°N / 44°-76°E

Caspian Sea

Administrative divisions numbered on the map

AFGHANISTAN
1. KĀBUL (G3)
2. KĀPĪSĀ (G3)
3. LAGHMĀN (G3)
4. LOWGAR (G3)
5. PARVĀN (G3)

IRAN
6. CHAHĀR MAHĀLL VÄ BAKHTIĀRĪ (B3)
7. KOHKĪLŪYEH VA BŪYER AHMADĪ (B4)

UZBEKISTAN
8. ANDIZHANSKAYA OBLAST' (H1)
9. FERGANSKAYA OBLAST' (G1)
10. RESPUBLIKA KARAKALPAKSTAN (E1)
11. KHOREZMSKAYA OBLAST' (E1)
12. NAMANGANSKAYA OBLAST' (G1)
13. SYRDAR'INSKAYA OBLAST' (G1)
14. TASHKENTSKAYA OBLAST' (G1)

YEREVAN
ARMENIA
AZERBAIJAN
BAKU
TURKMENISTAN

TEHRĀN
IRAN
IRAQ
BAGHDĀD

KUWAIT
KUWAIT (Al Kuwayt)

BAHRAIN
MANAMA
QATAR
DOHA (Ad Dawhah)

SAUDI ARABIA
RIYADH (Ar Riyāḍ)

ABU DHABI
UNITED ARAB EMIRATES
OMAN
MUSCAT (Masqaṭ)

The Gulf
Gulf of Oman
Strait of Hormuz
Tropic of Cancer

106-107

>6000m
5000-6000m
4000-5000m
3000-4000m
2000-3000m
1000-2000m
500-1000m
200-500m
0-200m
<0m

0-200m
200-500m
500-1000m
1000-2000m
2000-3000m
3000-4000m
4000-5000m
5000-6000m
>6000m

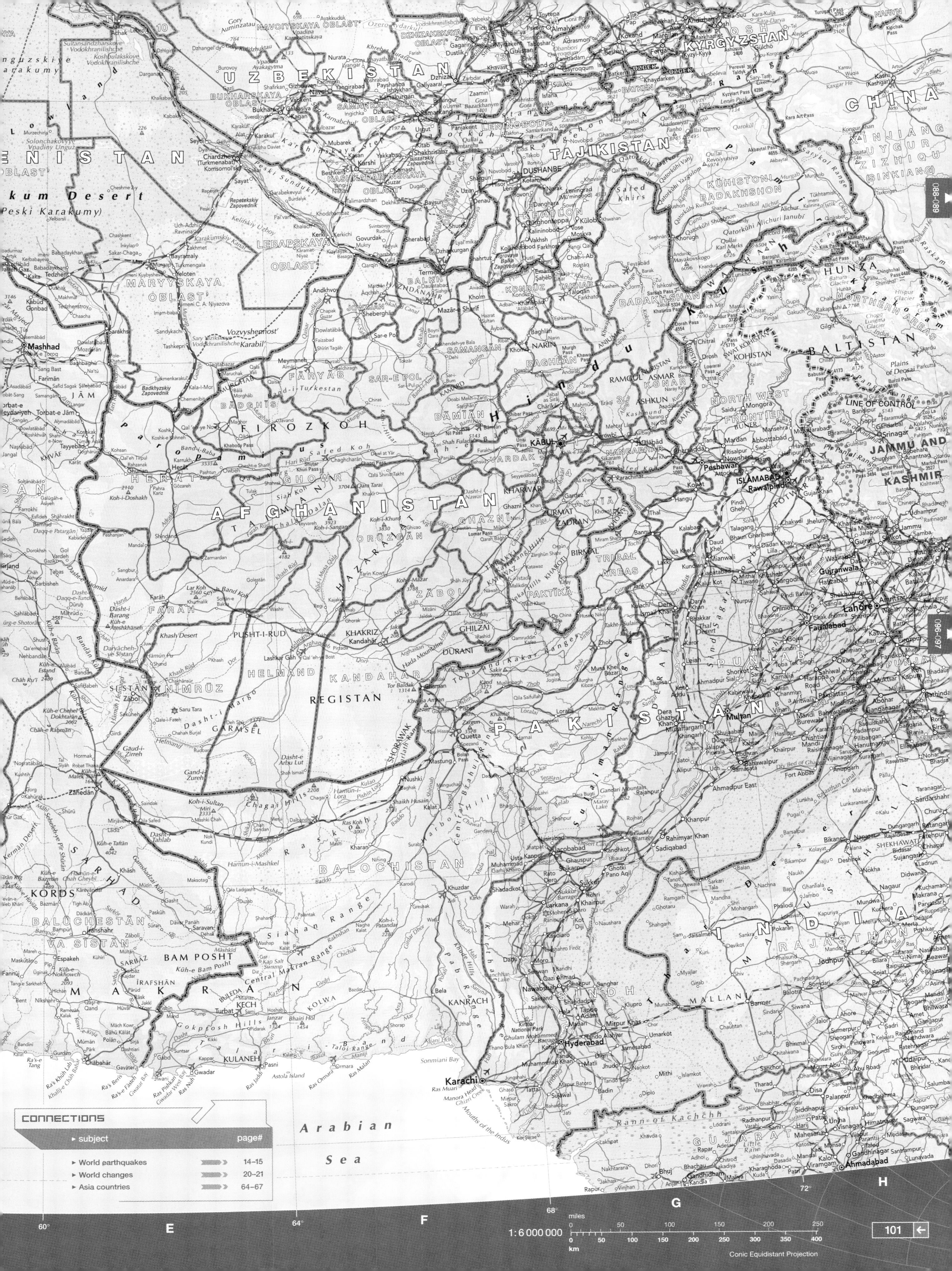

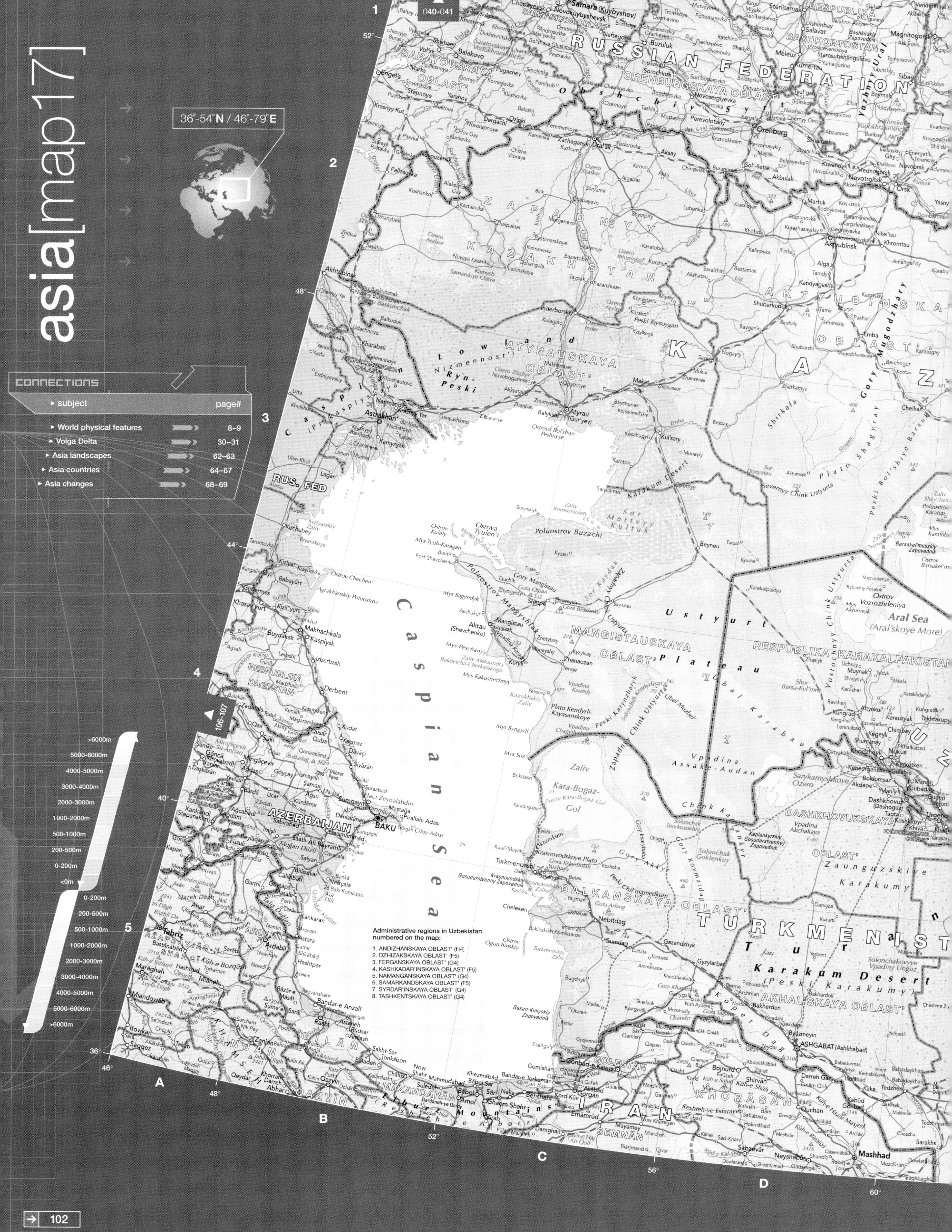

asia[map17]

36°-54°N / 46°-79°E

Administrative regions in Uzbekistan numbered on the map:

1. ANDIZHANSKAYA OBLAST' (H4)
2. DZHIZAKSKAYA OBLAST' (F5)
3. FERGANSKAYA OBLAST' (G4)
4. KASHKADAR'INSKAYA OBLAST' (F5)
5. NAMANGANSKAYA OBLAST' (G4)
6. SAMARKANDSKAYA OBLAST' (F5)
7. SYRDAR'INSKAYA OBLAST' (G4)
8. TASHKENTSKAYA OBLAST' (G4)

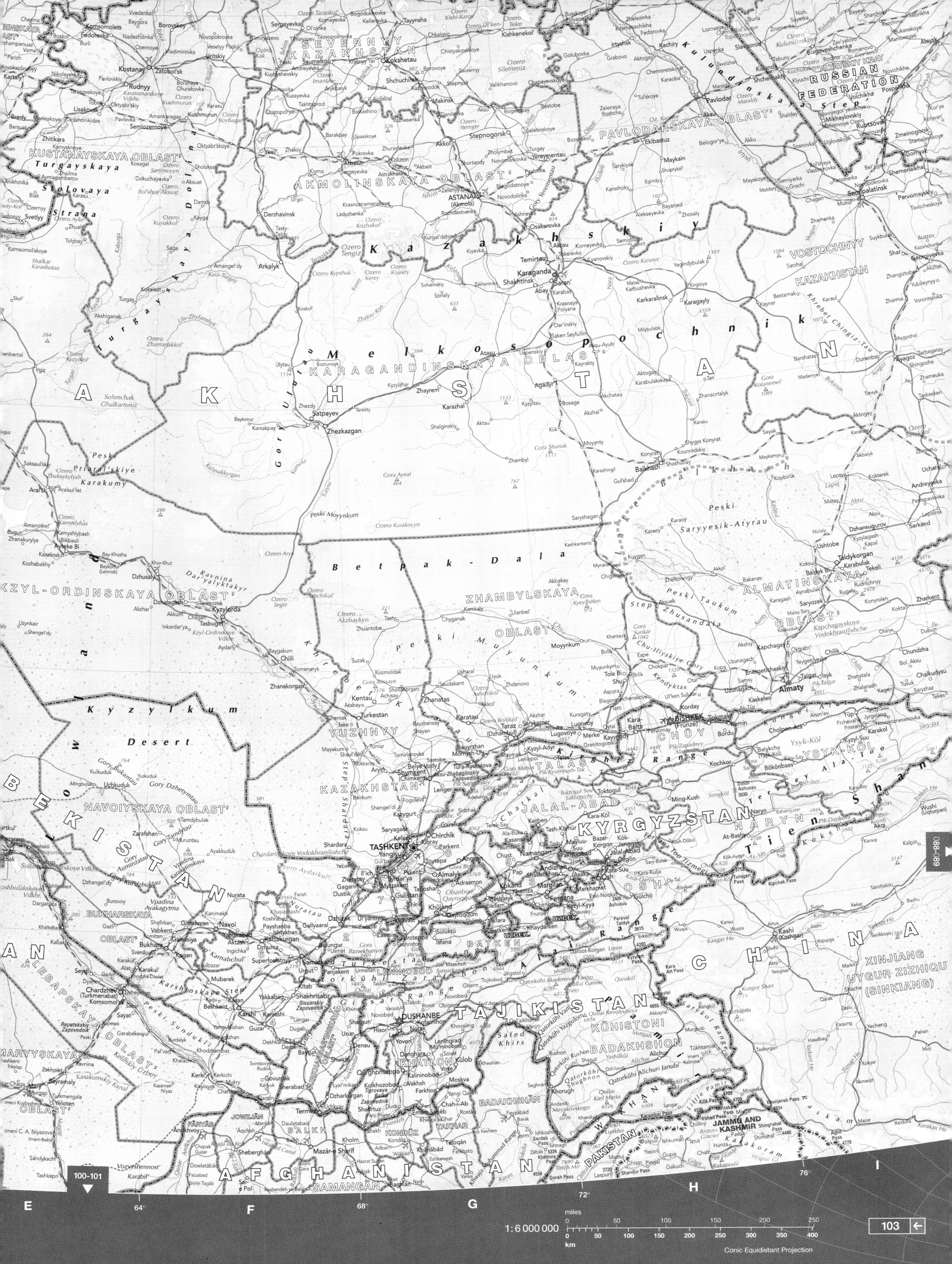

KAZAKHSTAN
RUSSIAN FEDERATION
KYRGYZSTAN
TAJIKISTAN
AFGHANISTAN
CHINA
UZBEKISTAN
PAKISTAN
JAMMU AND KASHMIR
XINJIANG UYGUR ZIZHIQU (SINKIANG)
SEVERNYY KAZAKHSTAN
KUSTANAYSKAYA OBLAST'
AKMOLINSKAYA OBLAST'
PAVLODARSKAYA OBLAST'
VOSTOCHNYY KAZAKHSTAN
ALTAYSKIY KRAY
KARAGANDINSKAYA OBLAST'
ZHAMBYLSKAYA OBLAST'
ALMATINSKAYA OBLAST'
KZYL-ORDINSKAYA OBLAST'
YUZHNYY KAZAKHSTAN
NAVOIYSKAYA OBLAST'
BUKHARSKAYA OBLAST'
LEBAPSKAYA OBLAST'
MARYYSKAYA OBLAST'
JALAL-ABAD
TALAS
CHÜY
YSYK-KÖL
NARYN
OSH
BATKEN
LENINOBOD
KHATLON
KŬHISTONI BADAKHSHON
BADAKHSHAN
TAKHAR
KONDŪZ
BALKH
JOWZJĀN
FĀRYĀB
SAMANGAN
Kazakhskiy Melkosopochnik
Betpak-Dala
Kyzylkum Desert
Turanskaya Nizmennost'
Peski Moyynkum
Peski Muyunkum
Peski Saryyesik-Atyrau
Peski Taukum
Turgayskaya Dolina
Turgayskaya Stolovaya Strana
Kulundinskaya Step
Khrebet Karatau
Kirgizskiy Khrebet
Tien Shan
Turkestan Range
Zarafshon Range
Gissar Range
Alay Range
Pamir
Karakoram
Wakhan
Ozero Balkhash
Ozero Tengiz
Ysyk-Köl
Kapchagayskoye Vodokhranilishche
ASTANA (Akmola)
Karaganda
Pavlodar
Semipalatinsk
Kostanay
Kokshetau
Zhezkazgan
Balkhash
Almaty
BISHKEK (Frunze)
TASHKENT
DUSHANBE
Kyzylorda
Shymkent (Chimkent)
Taraz (Dzhambul)
Samarkand
Bukhara
Navoi
Namangan
Andizhan
Fergana
Osh
Khŭjand
Termez
Mazār-e Sharīf
Kashi (Kashgar)
Chardzhev (Turkmenabat)
Rubtsovsk
Taldykorgan
E
F
G
H
I
64°
68°
72°
76°
100-101
89-089
1:6 000 000
miles
0 50 100 150 200 250
0 50 100 150 200 250 300 350 400
km
Conic Equidistant Projection

108-109

120-121

128-129

EGYPT

JORDAN

SUDAN

ETHIOPIA

ERITREA

SAUDI ARABIA

Gulf of Aqaba

Gulf of Suez

RED SEA

Nubian Desert

Baiyuda Desert

Tropic of Cancer

HALAIB TRIANGLE
UNDER SUDANESE
ADMINISTRATION

Port Sudan (Bûr Sudan)

Jeddah (Jiddah)

Mecca (Makkah)

Medina (Al Madinah)

Al Tā'if

An Nafūd

JABAL SHAMMAR

AL QASIM

KHARTOUM

KASSALA

GEDAREF

EL GEZIRA

SENNAR

BLUE NILE

NILE

ASMARA

Massawa

Dahlak Archipelago

Dahlak Marine National Park

Suakin Archipelago

Farasan Islands

SAN'Ā'

Hodeidah (Al Ḥudaydah)

Ta'izz

DJIBOUTI

TIGRAY

AMHARA

GONDER

Lake Tana

JIZAN

ASIR

BISHAH

AL BAHAH

MAKKAH

AL MADINAH

TABUK

Hurghada

Quseir

Marsa Alam

ASWAN

QENA

EL BAHR EL AHMAR

JANÛB SINÂ'

SINAI

Yanbu' al Bahr

Rābigh

Al Qunfidhah

Abha

Khamis Mushayt

Najrān

Elevation scale:
>6000m
5000-6000m
4000-5000m
3000-4000m
2000-3000m
1000-2000m
500-1000m
200-500m
0-200m
<0m

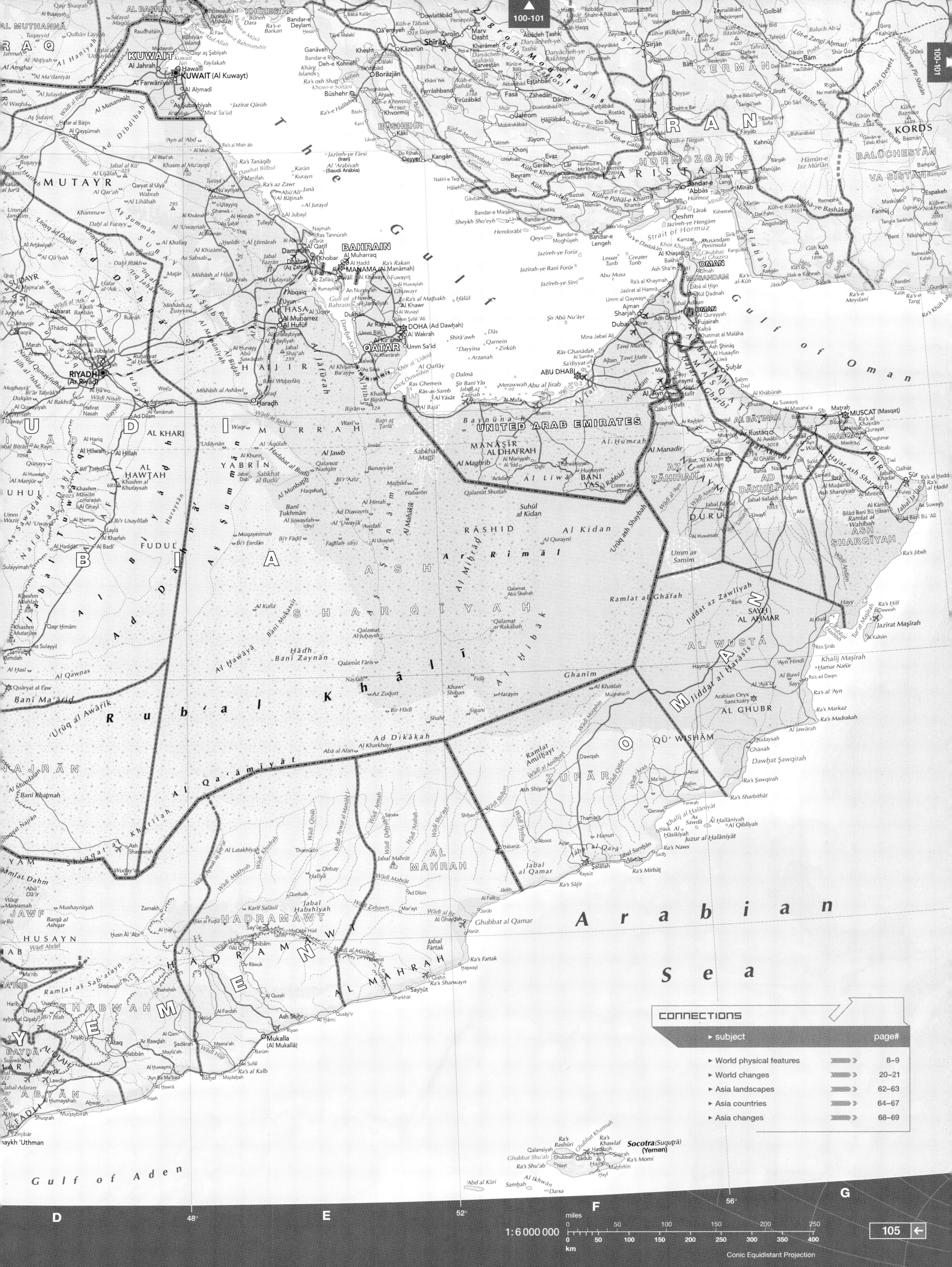

► subject		page#
► World physical features		8–9
► World changes		20–21
► Asia landscapes		62–63
► Asia countries		64–67
► Asia changes		68–69

1:6 000 000

miles
0 50 100 150 200 250

km
0 50 100 150 200 250 300 350 400

Conic Equidistant Projection

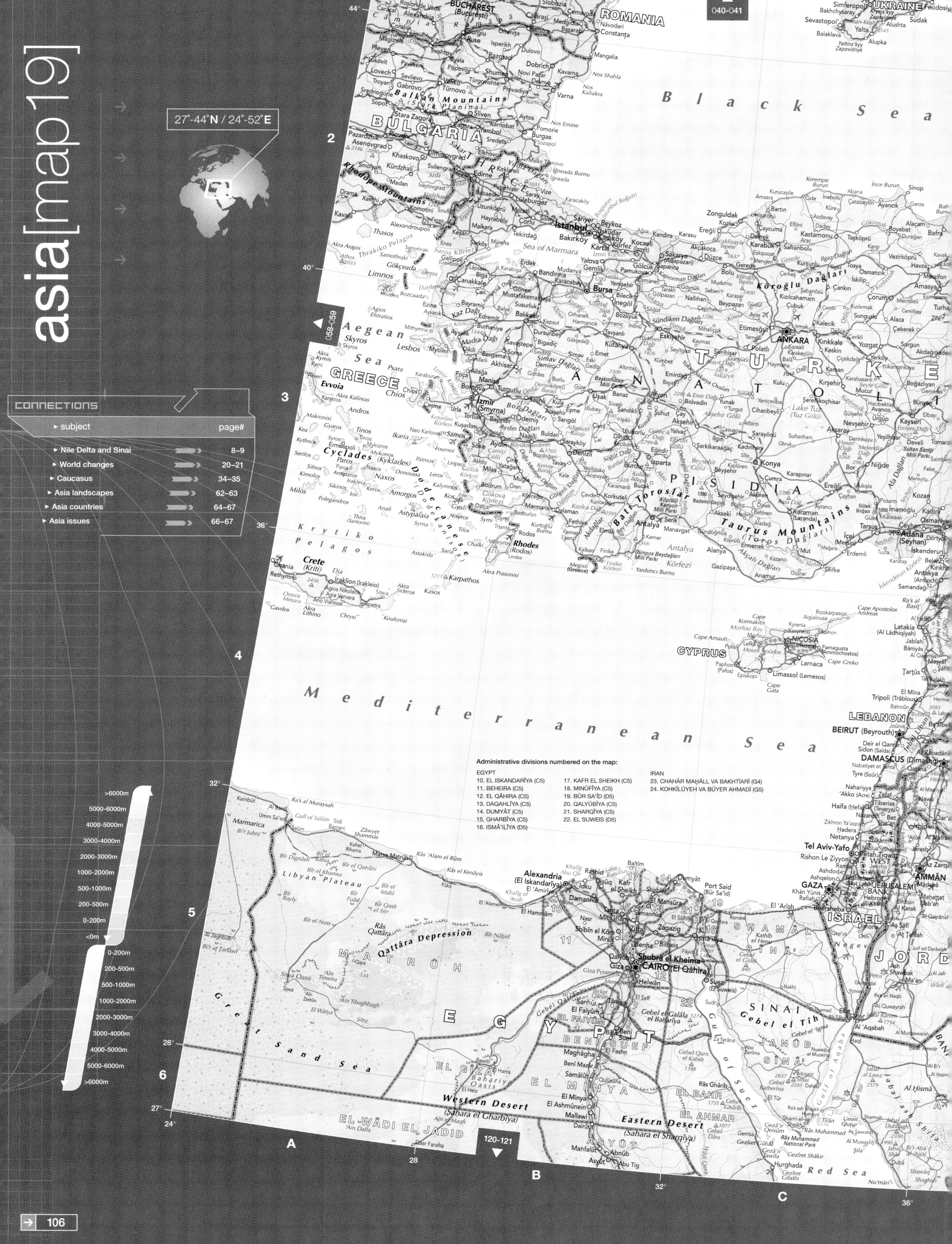

asia[map19]

27°-44°N / 24°-52°E

040-041

058-059

CONNECTIONS

>6000m
5000-6000m
4000-5000m
3000-4000m
2000-3000m
1000-2000m
500-1000m
200-500m
0-200m
<0m

0-200m
200-500m
500-1000m
1000-2000m
2000-3000m
3000-4000m
4000-5000m
5000-6000m
>6000m

Administrative divisions numbered on the map:

EGYPT
10. EL ISKANDARÏYA (C5)
11. BEHEIRA (C5)
12. EL QÂHIRA (C5)
13. DAQAHLÏYA (C5)
14. DUMYÂT (C5)
15. GHARBÏYA (C5)
16. ISMÂ'ILÏYA (D5)
17. KAFR EL SHEIKH (C5)
18. MINÛFÏYA (C5)
19. BÛR SA'ÏD (D5)
20. QALYÛBÏYA (C5)
21. SHARQÏYA (C5)
22. EL SUWEIS (D5)

IRAN
23. CHAHÂR MAHÂLL VA BAKHTÏARÏ (G4)
24. KOHKÏLÛYEH VA BÛYER AHMADÏ (G5)

120-121

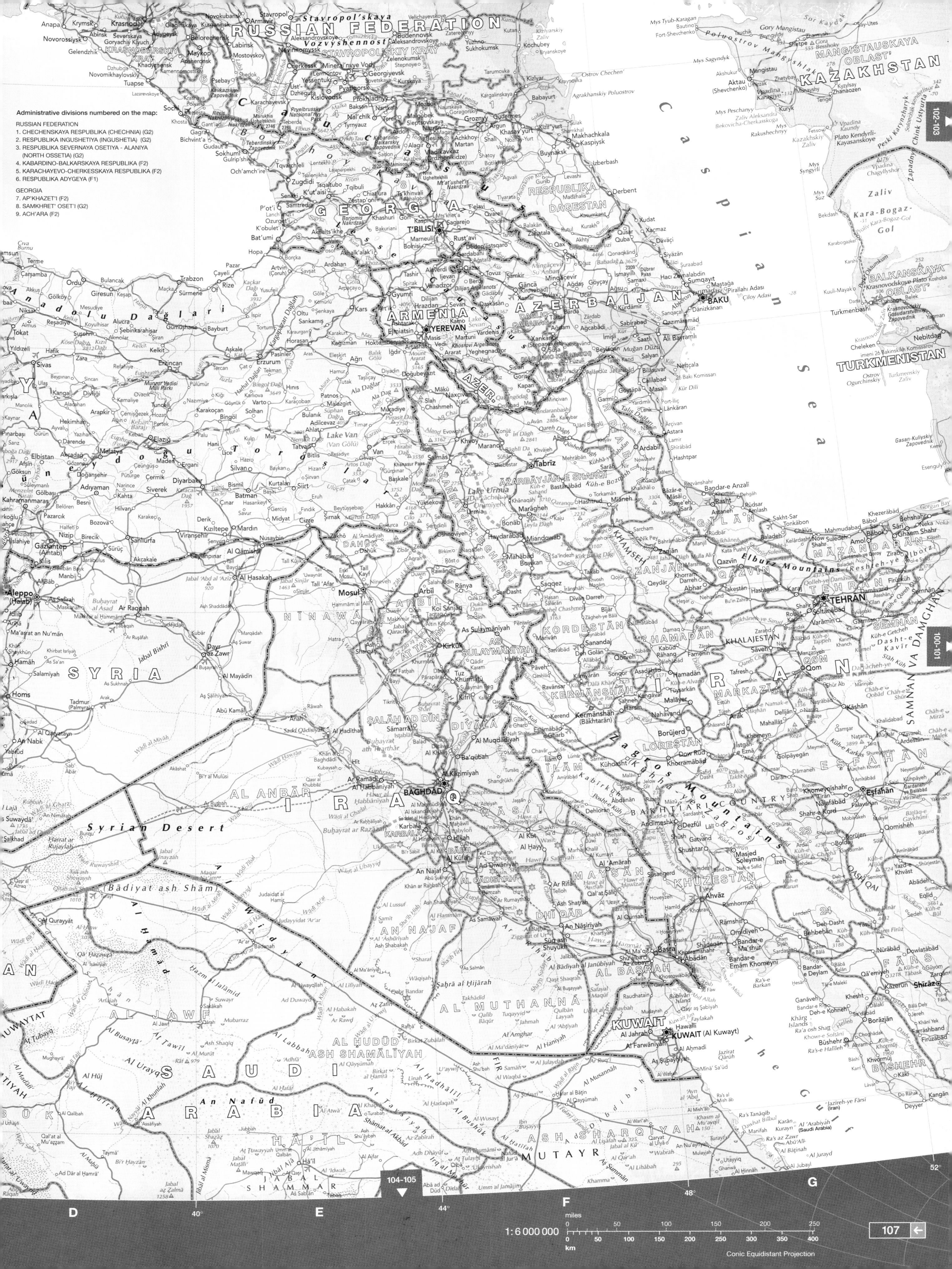
Administrative divisions numbered on the map:
RUSSIAN FEDERATION
1. CHECHENSKAYA RESPUBLIKA (CHECHNIA) (G2)
2. RESPUBLIKA INGUSHETIYA (INGUSHETIA) (G2)
3. RESPUBLIKA SEVERNAYA OSETIYA - ALANIYA (NORTH OSSETIA) (G2)
4. KABARDINO-BALKARSKAYA RESPUBLIKA (F2)
5. KARACHAYEVO-CHERKESSKAYA RESPUBLIKA (F1)
6. RESPUBLIKA ADYGEYA (F1)
GEORGIA
7. AP'KHAZET'I (F2)
8. SAMKHRET' OSET'I (G2)
9. ACH'ARA (F2)
RUSSIAN FEDERATION
STAVROPOL'SKIY KRAY
KRASNODARSKIY KRAY
GEORGIA
T'BILISI
ARMENIA
YEREVAN
AZERBAIJAN
BAKU
AZER.
RESPUBLIKA DAGESTAN
KAZAKHSTAN
MANGISTAUSKAYA OBLAST'
TURKMENISTAN
BALKANSKAYA OBLAST'
Caspian Sea
I R A N
TEHRAN
I R A Q
BAGHDAD
S Y R I A
SAUDI ARABIA
KUWAIT
KUWAIT (Al Kuwayt)
The Gulf
Syrian Desert
Lake Van
Lake Urmia
Elburz Mountains
Zagros Mountains
Aleppo (Halab)
Mosul
Tabrīz
Eşfahān
Shīrāz
Basra
Ābādān
Ahvāz
Kermānshāh (Bākhtarān)
Hamadān
Qom
Rasht
Sochi
Tuapse
Novorossiysk
Groznyy
Vladikavkaz
Erzurum
Trabzon
Diyarbakır
Sanliurfa
104-105
102-103
100-101
D
E
F
G
40°
44°
48°
52°
1:6 000 000
miles
0 50 100 150 200 250
km
0 50 100 150 200 250 300 350 400
Conic Equidistant Projection

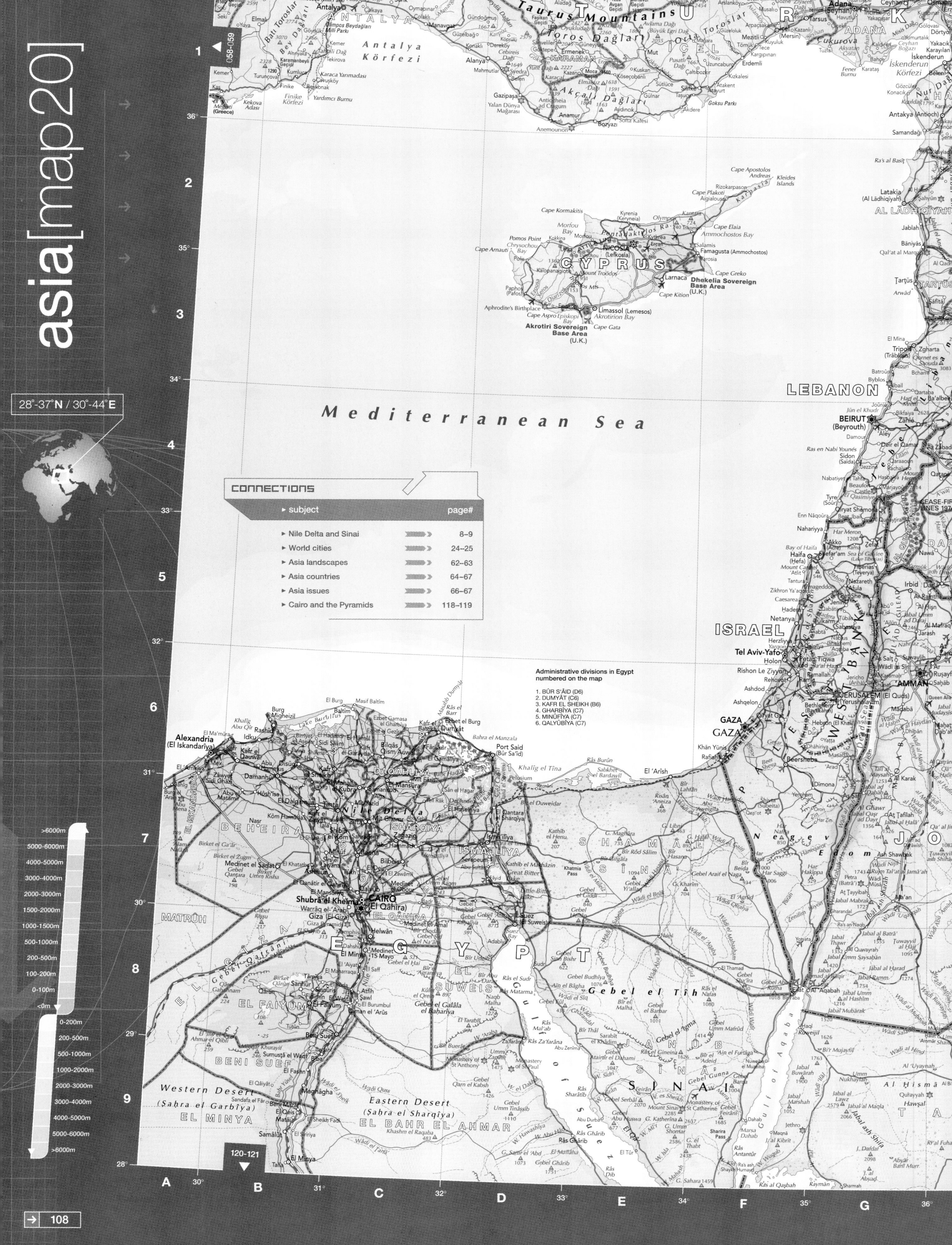

CONNECTIONS

Administrative divisions in Egypt numbered on the map

1. BŪR S'ĀID (D6)
2. DUMYĀT (C6)
3. KAFR EL SHEIKH (B6)
4. GHARBĪYA (C7)
5. MINŪFĪYA (C7)
6. QALYŪBĪYA (C7)

Mediterranean Sea

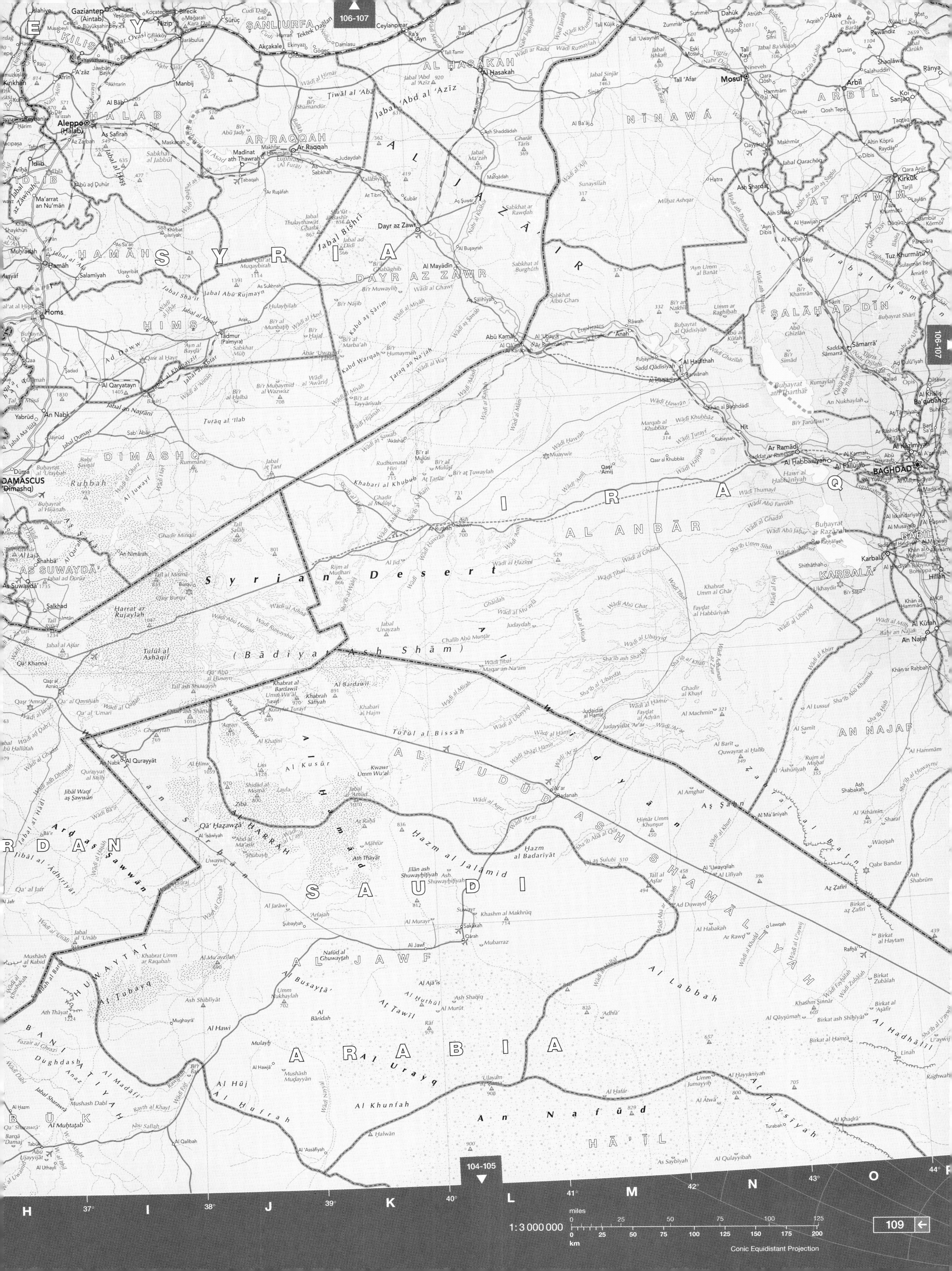

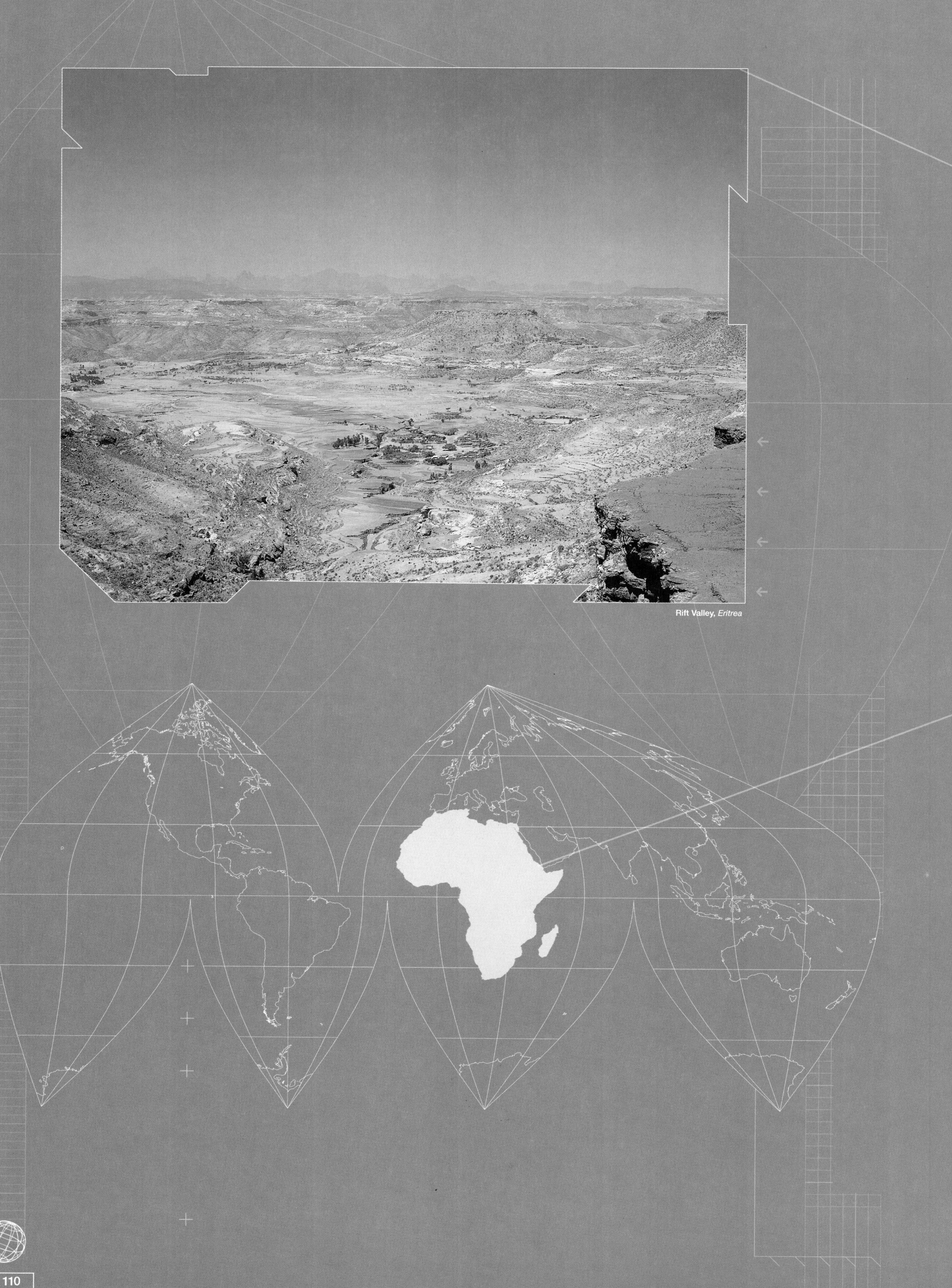

Rift Valley, *Eritrea*

africa

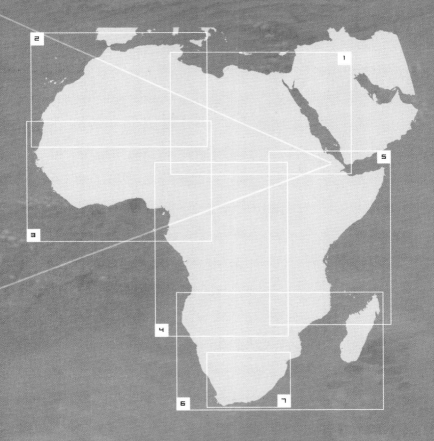

[contents]

			page#
africa [landscapes]			112–113
africa [countries]			114–115
africa [countries/issues]			116–117
africa [locations]			118–119

	map coverage	scale	page#
africa [map 1]	AFRICA Northeast	1:8 000 000	120–121
africa [map 2]	AFRICA Northwest	1:8 000 000	122–123
africa [map 3]	AFRICA West	1:8 000 000	124–125
africa [map 4]	AFRICA West Central	1:8 000 000	126–127
africa [map 5]	AFRICA East Central	1:8 000 000	128–129
africa [map 6]	AFRICA South	1:8 000 000	130–131
africa [map 7]	REPUBLIC OF SOUTH AFRICA	1:3 500 000	132–133

africa[landscapes]

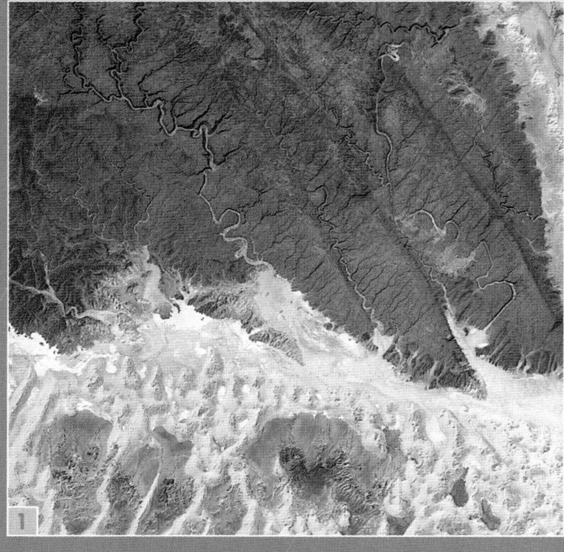

Africa, viewed here from above the southern Indian Ocean, is dominated by several striking physical features. The Sahara desert extends over most of the north and in the east the geological feature, known as the Great Rift Valley, extends from the valley of the river Jordan in Southwest Asia to Mozambique. The valley contains a string of major lakes including Lake Turkana, Lake Tanganyika and Lake Nyasa.

The river basin of the Congo, in central Africa draining into the Atlantic Ocean, is the second largest river basin in the world. The land south of the equator is higher than in the north and forms a massive plateau dissected by several large rivers which flow east to the Indian Ocean or west to the Atlantic. The most distinctive feature in the south is the Drakensberg, a range of mountains which run southwest to northeast through Lesotho and South Africa. The large island separated from Africa by the Mozambique Channel is Madagascar, the fourth largest island in the world.

1 Sahara Desert, *Algeria*

The Sahara desert crosses the continent of Africa from the Atlantic Ocean to the Red Sea. Within this vast area there is a great variety in topography with heights from 30 m below sea level to mountains over 3 300 m. This satellite image of east central Algeria shows the sand dunes stopping at the higher ground of the dark base rock. Although rain is scarce, dry river beds can be seen cutting through the rock.

Satellite/Sensor : SPOT

2 Congo River, *Democratic Republic of Congo*

This satellite image shows broken clouds above a heavily braided Congo river in Congo. The river is over 4 600 km long and has many long tributaries which result in a drainage basin of approximately 3 700 000 sq km. In this tropical area the river acts as a highway between communities where roads do not exist. The river flows into the Atlantic Ocean, forming the boundary between Angola and the Democratic Republic of Congo.

Satellite/Sensor : Space Shuttle

3 Atlas Mountains, *Morocco*

The Atlas Mountains of Morocco in northwest Africa form a major boundary between the Sahara desert and the fertile coastal plain. They are a composite of several ranges created from extensive fault movements and earthquakes, resulting in distinct rock layers and folds, as seen in this image. The dark areas are sandy beds of a seasonal river system.

Satellite/Sensor : SIR-C/X-SAR

Canary Islands

Atlas Mountains

Cape Verde Islands

Sahara

Lake Volta

Benue River

Niger River

Gulf of Guinea

Bioco

São Tome

Atlantic Ocean

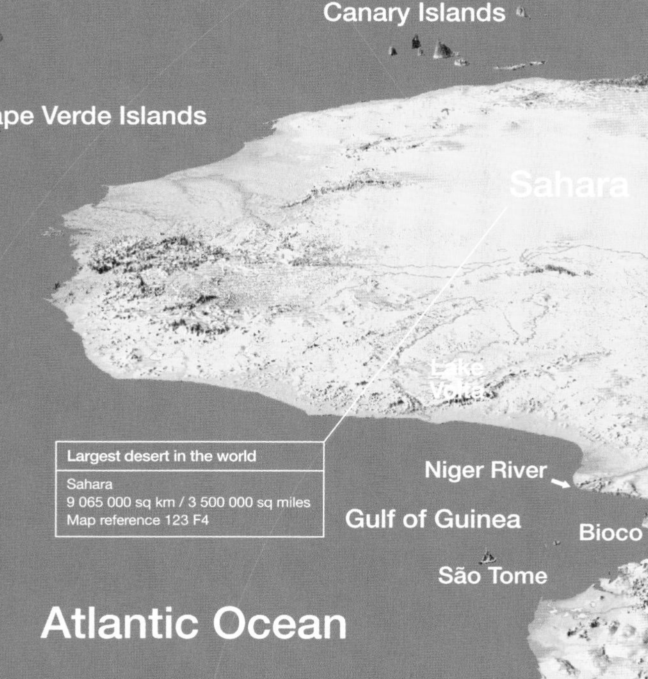

Largest desert in the world
Sahara
9 065 000 sq km / 3 500 000 sq miles
Map reference 123 F4

Congo River

Largest drainage basin
Congo Basin
3 700 000 sq km / 1 429 000 sq miles
Map reference 126 C5

Bié Plateau

Victoria Falls

Namib Desert

Okavango Delta

Kalahari Desert

Orange River

Great Karoo

Cape of Good Hope

Drakensberg

Limpop

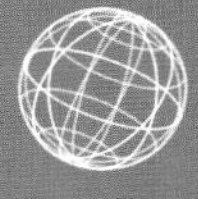

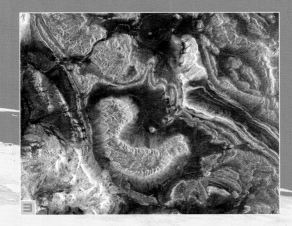

Mediterranean Sea

Hoggar

Tibesti

Lake Chad

Qattara Depression

Lake Nasser

Nile River

Sinai

Red Sea

Arabian Peninsula

Ubangi River

Congo Basin

Blue Nile River

White Nile River

Sudd

Lake Tana

Ethiopian Highlands

Lake Assal

Gulf of Aden

Lake Turkana

Lake Tanganyika

Great Rift Valley

Kilimanjaro

Webi Shabeelle River

Aldabra Islands

Comoro Islands

Zambezi River

Mozambique Channel

Indian Ocean

Madagascar

River

Longest river
Nile
6 695 km / 4 160 miles
Map reference 121 F2

Lowest point
Lake Assal
Djibouti
-152 m / -500 ft
Map reference 128 D2

Highest point
Kilimanjaro
Tanzania
5 892 m / 19 331 ft
Map reference 128 C5

Largest lake
Lake Victoria
68 800 sq km / 26 563 sq miles
Map reference 128 B5

CONNECTIONS

► subject	page#
► World physical features	10–11
► Land cover types	18–19
► Water issues	116–117
► African states and territories	114–115
► Rift Valley perspective	118–119
► Reference maps of Africa	120–133

AFRICA

HIGHEST MOUNTAINS

	m	ft	location	map
Kilimanjaro	5 892	19 331	Tanzania	128 C5
Mt Kenya	5 199	17 057	Kenya	128 C5
Margherita Peak	5 110	16 765	Democratic Republic of Congo/Uganda	126 F4
Meru	4 565	14 977	Tanzania	128 C5
Ras Dashen	4 533	14 872	Ethiopia	128 C1
Mt Karisimbi	4 510	14 796	Rwanda	126F5

LARGEST ISLANDS

	sq km	sq miles	map
Madagascar	587 040	226 657	131 J3

LONGEST RIVERS

	km	miles	map
Nile	6 695	4 160	121 F2
Congo	4 667	2 900	127 B6
Niger	4 184	2 599	122 F5
Zambezi	2 736	1 700	131 H2
Webi Shabeelle	2 490	1 547	128 D5
Ubangi	2 250	1 398	126 C5

LAKES

	sq km	sq miles	map
Lake Victoria	68 800	26 563	128 B5
Lake Tanganyika	32 900	12 702	129 A6
Lake Nyasa	30 044	11 600	129 B7
Lake Chad	10 000-26 000	3 861-10 039	125 I3
Lake Volta	8 485	3 276	124 F5
Lake Turkana	6 475	2 500	128 C4

LAND AREA

		map
Most northerly point	La Galite, Tunisia	123 H1
Most southerly point	Cape Agulhas, South Africa	130 C7
Most westerly point	Santo Antao, Cape Verde	122 inset
Most easterly point	Raas Xaafuun, Somalia	128 F2
Total 30 343 578 sq km / 11 715 721 sq miles		

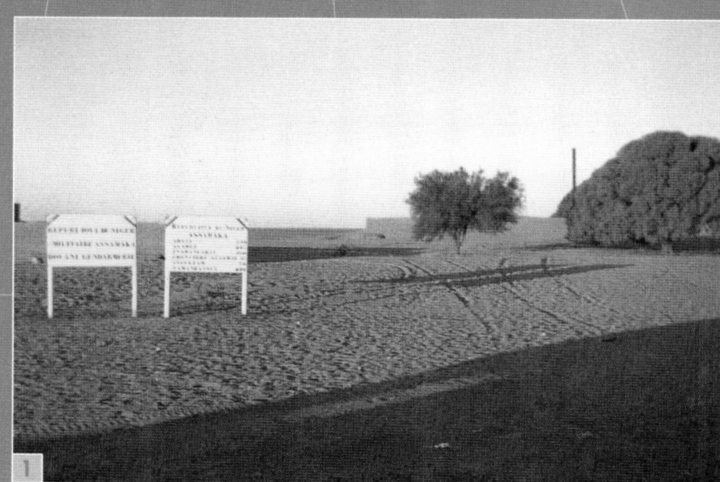

Border Post, *Algeria/Niger*

The border between Algeria and Niger lies in the centre of the Sahel region of Africa. Both countries have largely geometric borders in the relatively featureless landscape which offers no obvious physical boundaries. As a result simple indicators of the presence of a border, such as the marker shown in this photograph taken south of the actual boundary line, are the only features which advise of the passage from one country to the other.

Refugee Camp, *Tanzania*

Much internal migration in Africa has been instigated by war, ethnic conflict, economic disparities and famine. In 1994 over 2 million Rwandans fled to the neighbouring countries of Tanzania and the Democratic Republic of Congo to escape tribal war between Hutus and Tutsis. This photograph shows a refugee camp in Tanzania just across the border from Rwanda and gives an indication of the difficult conditions in such centres. Tanzania is currently one of East Africa's most important host countries with a refugee population of nearly half a million.

AFRICA
COUNTRIES

	area sq km	area sq miles	population	capital	languages	religions	currency	map
ALGERIA	2 381 741	919 595	30 291 000	Algiers (Alger)	Arabic, French, Berber	Sunni Muslim	Dinar	122–123
ANGOLA	1 246 700	481 354	13 134 000	Luanda	Portuguese, Bantu, local languages	Roman Catholic, Protestant, traditional beliefs	Kwanza	127
BENIN	112 620	43 483	6 272 000	Porto-Novo	French, Fon, Yoruba, Adja, local languages	Traditional beliefs, Roman Catholic, Sunni Muslim	CFA franc	125
BOTSWANA	581 370	224 468	1 541 000	Gaborone	English, Setswana, Shona, local languages	Traditional beliefs, Protestant, Roman Catholic	Pula	130–131
BURKINA	274 200	105 869	11 535 000	Ouagadougou	French, Moore (Mossi), Fulani, local languages	Sunni Muslim, traditional beliefs, Roman Catholic	CFA franc	124–125
BURUNDI	27 835	10 747	6 356 000	Bujumbura	Kirundi (Hutu, Tutsi), French	Roman Catholic, traditional beliefs, Protestant	Franc	126
CAMEROON	475 442	183 569	14 876 000	Yaoundé	French, English, Fang, Bamileke, local languages	Roman Catholic, traditional beliefs, Sunni Muslim, Protestant	CFA franc	126
CAPE VERDE	4 033	1 557	427 000	Praia	Portuguese, creole	Roman Catholic, Protestant	Escudo	124
CENTRAL AFRICAN REPUBLIC	622 436	240 324	3 717 000	Bangui	French, Sango, Banda, Baya, local languages	Protestant, Roman Catholic, traditional beliefs, Sunni Muslim	CFA franc	126
CHAD	1 284 000	495 755	7 885 000	Ndjamena	Arabic, French, Sara, local languages	Sunni Muslim, Roman Catholic, Protestant, traditional beliefs	CFA franc	120
COMOROS	1 862	719	706 000	Moroni	Comorian, French, Arabic	Sunni Muslim, Roman Catholic	Franc	129
CONGO	342 000	132 047	3 018 000	Brazzaville	French, Kongo, Monokutuba, local languages	Roman Catholic, Protestant, traditional beliefs, Sunni Muslim	CFA franc	126–127
CONGO, DEMOCRATIC REPUBLIC OF	2 345 410	905 568	50 948 000	Kinshasa	French, Lingala, Swahili, Kongo, local languages	Christian, Sunni Muslim	Franc	126–127
CÔTE D'IVOIRE	322 463	124 504	16 013 000	Yamoussoukro	French, creole, Akan, local languages	Sunni Muslim, Roman Catholic, traditional beliefs, Protestant	CFA franc	124
DJIBOUTI	23 200	8 958	632 000	Djibouti	Somali, Afar, French, Arabic	Sunni Muslim, Christian	Franc	128
EGYPT	1 000 250	386 199	67 884 000	Cairo (El Qâhira)	Arabic	Sunni Muslim, Coptic Christian	Pound	120–121
EQUATORIAL GUINEA	28 051	10 831	457 000	Malabo	Spanish, French, Fang	Roman Catholic, traditional beliefs	CFA franc	125
ERITREA	117 400	45 328	3 659 000	Asmara	Tigrinya, Tigre	Sunni Muslim, Coptic Christian	Nakfa	121
ETHIOPIA	1 133 880	437 794	62 908 000	Addis Ababa (Adīs Ābeba)	Oromo, Amharic, Tigrinya, local languages	Ethiopian Orthodox, Sunni Muslim, traditional beliefs	Birr	128
GABON	267 667	103 347	1 230 000	Libreville	French, Fang, local languages	Roman Catholic, Protestant, traditional beliefs	CFA franc	126
THE GAMBIA	11 295	4 361	1 303 000	Banjul	English, Malinke, Fulani, Wolof	Sunni Muslim, Protestant	Dalasi	124
GHANA	238 537	92 100	19 306 000	Accra	English, Hausa, Akan, local languages	Christian, Sunni Muslim, traditional beliefs	Cedi	124–125
GUINEA	245 857	94 926	8 154 000	Conakry	French, Fulani, Malinke, local languages	Sunni Muslim, traditional beliefs, Christian	Franc	124
GUINEA–BISSAU	36 125	13 948	1 199 000	Bissau	Portuguese, crioulo, local languages	Traditional beliefs, Sunni Muslim, Christian	CFA franc	124
KENYA	582 646	224 961	30 669 000	Nairobi	Swahili, English, local languages	Christian, traditional beliefs	Shilling	128–129
LESOTHO	30 355	11 720	2 035 000	Maseru	Sesotho, English, Zulu	Christian, traditional beliefs	Loti	133
LIBERIA	111 369	43 000	2 913 000	Monrovia	English, creole, local languages	Traditional beliefs, Christian, Sunni Muslim	Dollar	124
LIBYA	1 759 540	679 362	5 290 000	Tripoli (Tarābulus)	Arabic, Berber	Sunni Muslim	Dinar	120
MADAGASCAR	587 041	226 658	15 970 000	Antananarivo	Malagasy, French	Traditional beliefs, Christian, Sunni Muslim	Franc	131
MALAWI	118 484	45 747	11 308 000	Lilongwe	Chichewa, English, local languages	Christian, traditional beliefs, Sunni Muslim	Kwacha	129
MALI	1 240 140	478 821	11 351 000	Bamako	French, Bambara, local languages	Sunni Muslim, traditional beliefs, Christian	CFA franc	124–125
MAURITANIA	1 030 700	397 955	2 665 000	Nouakchott	Arabic, French, local languages	Sunni Muslim	Ouguiya	122
MAURITIUS	2 040	788	1 161 000	Port Louis	English, creole, Hindi, Bhojpuri, French	Hindu, Roman Catholic, Sunni Muslim	Rupee	218
MOROCCO	446 550	172 414	29 878 000	Rabat	Arabic, Berber, French	Sunni Muslim	Dirham	122–123
MOZAMBIQUE	799 380	308 642	18 292 000	Maputo	Portuguese, Makua, Tsonga, local languages	Traditional beliefs, Roman Catholic, Sunni Muslim	Metical	131
NAMIBIA	824 292	318 261	1 757 000	Windhoek	English, Afrikaans, German, Ovambo, local languages	Protestant, Roman Catholic	Dollar	130
NIGER	1 267 000	489 191	10 832 000	Niamey	French, Hausa, Fulani, local languages	Sunni Muslim, traditional beliefs	CFA franc	125
NIGERIA	923 768	356 669	113 862 000	Abuja	English, Hausa, Yoruba, Ibo, Fulani, local languages	Sunni Muslim, Christian, traditional beliefs	Naira	125
RWANDA	26 338	10 169	7 609 000	Kigali	Kinyarwanda, French, English	Roman Catholic, traditional beliefs, Protestant	Franc	126
SÃO TOMÉ AND PRÍNCIPE	964	372	138 000	São Tomé	Portuguese, creole	Roman Catholic, Protestant	Dobra	125
SENEGAL	196 720	75 954	9 421 000	Dakar	French, Wolof, Fulani, local languages	Sunni Muslim, Roman Catholic, traditional beliefs	CFA franc	124
SEYCHELLES	455	176	80 000	Victoria	English, French, creole	Roman Catholic, Protestant	Rupee	218
SIERRA LEONE	71 740	27 699	4 405 000	Freetown	English, creole, Mende, Temne, local languages	Sunni Muslim, traditional beliefs	Leone	124
SOMALIA	637 657	246 201	8 778 000	Mogadishu (Muqdisho)	Somali, Arabic	Sunni Muslim	Shilling	128
SOUTH AFRICA, REPUBLIC OF	1 219 090	470 693	43 309 000	Pretoria/Cape Town	Afrikaans, English, nine official local languages	Protestant, Roman Catholic, Sunni Muslim, Hindu	Rand	130–131
SUDAN	2 505 813	967 500	31 095 000	Khartoum	Arabic, Dinka, Nubian, Beja, Nuer, local languages	Sunni Muslim, traditional beliefs, Christian	Dinar	120–121
SWAZILAND	17 364	6 704	925 000	Mbabane	Swazi, English	Christian, traditional beliefs	Lilangeni	133
TANZANIA	945 087	364 900	35 119 000	Dodoma	Swahili, English, Nyamwezi, local languages	Shi'a Muslim, Sunni Muslim, traditional beliefs, Christian	Shilling	128–129
TOGO	56 785	21 925	4 527 000	Lomé	French, Ewe, Kabre, local languages	Traditional beliefs, Christian, Sunni Muslim	CFA franc	125
TUNISIA	164 150	63 379	9 459 000	Tunis	Arabic, French	Sunni Muslim	Dinar	123
UGANDA	241 038	93 065	23 300 000	Kampala	English, Swahili, Luganda, local languages	Roman Catholic, Protestant, Sunni Muslim, traditional beliefs	Shilling	128
ZAMBIA	752 614	290 586	10 421 000	Lusaka	English, Bemba, Nyanja, Tonga, local languages	Christian, traditional beliefs	Kwacha	127
ZIMBABWE	390 759	150 873	12 627 000	Harare	English, Shona, Ndebele	Christian, traditional beliefs	Dollar	131

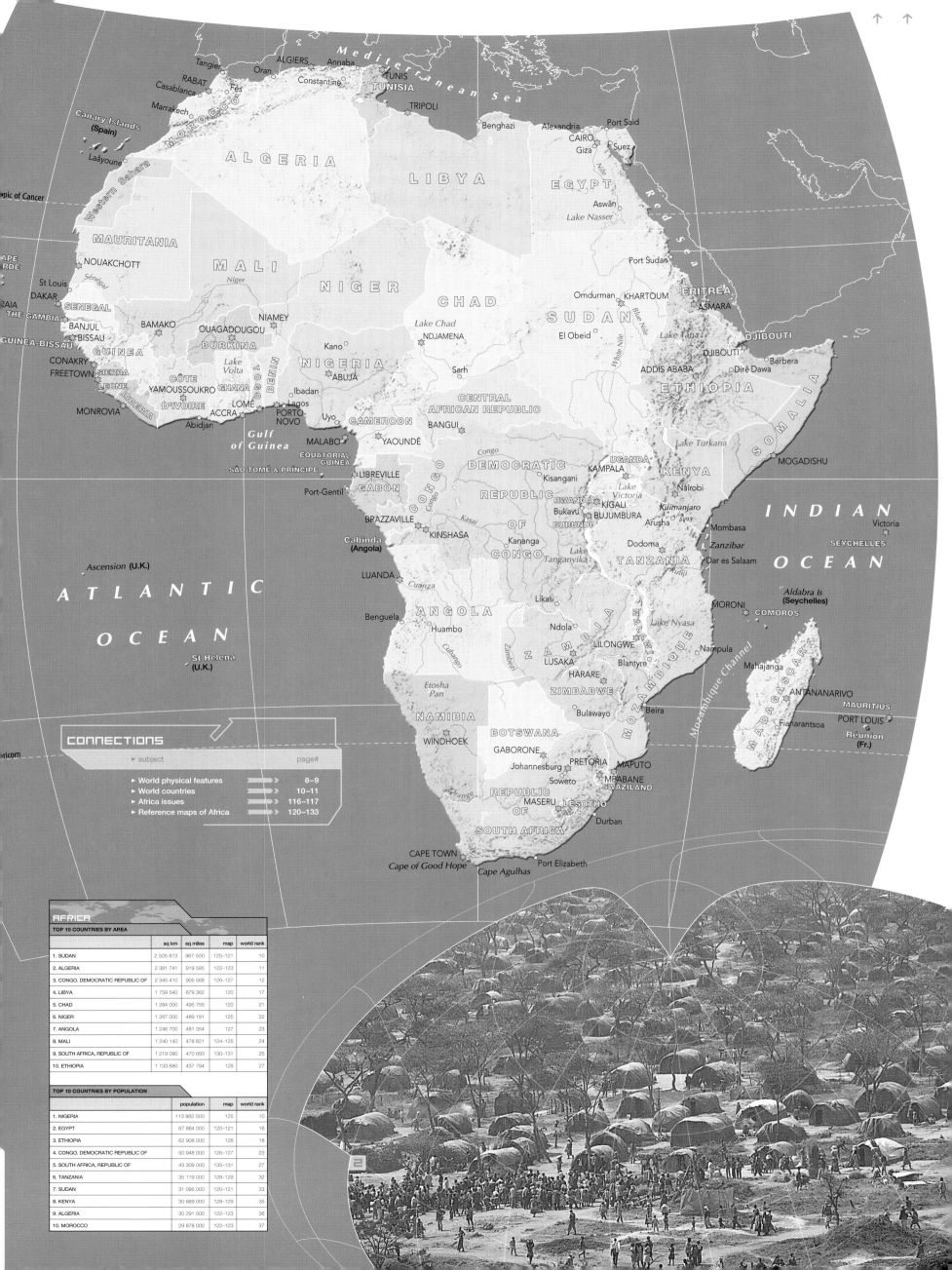

CONNECTIONS

► subject	page#
► World physical features	8–9
► World countries	10–11
► Africa issues	116–117
► Reference maps of Africa	120–133

AFRICA

TOP 10 COUNTRIES BY AREA

	sq km	sq miles	map	world rank
1. SUDAN	2 505 813	967 500	120–121	10
2. ALGERIA	2 381 741	919 595	122–123	11
3. CONGO, DEMOCRATIC REPUBLIC OF	2 345 410	905 568	126–127	12
4. LIBYA	1 759 540	679 362	120	17
5. CHAD	1 284 000	495 755	120	21
6. NIGER	1 267 000	489 191	125	22
7. ANGOLA	1 246 700	481 354	127	23
8. MALI	1 240 140	478 821	124–125	24
9. SOUTH AFRICA, REPUBLIC OF	1 219 090	470 693	130–131	25
10. ETHIOPIA	1 133 880	437 794	128	27

TOP 10 COUNTRIES BY POPULATION

	population	map	world rank
1. NIGERIA	113 862 000	125	10
2. EGYPT	67 884 000	120–121	16
3. ETHIOPIA	62 908 000	128	18
4. CONGO, DEMOCRATIC REPUBLIC OF	50 948 000	126–127	23
5. SOUTH AFRICA, REPUBLIC OF	43 309 000	130–131	27
6. TANZANIA	35 119 000	128–129	32
7. SUDAN	31 095 000	120–121	33
8. KENYA	30 669 000	128–129	35
9. ALGERIA	30 291 000	122–123	36
10. MOROCCO	29 878 000	122–123	37

CONNECTIONS

▸ subject	page#
▸ World physical features	8–9
▸ World countries	10–11
▸ World land cover types	18–19
▸ Africa countries	114–115
▸ Reference maps of Africa	120–133
▸ South America impacts	196–197

DEPENDENT AND DISPUTED TERRITORIES

		territorial status	area sq km	area sq miles	population	capital	languages	religions	currency	map
Canary Islands (Islas Canarias)		Autonomous Community of Spain	7 447	2 875	1 606 522	Santa Cruz de Tenerife, Las Palmas	Spanish	Roman Catholic	Peseta	122
Ceuta		Spanish Territory	19	7	68 796	Ceuta	Spanish, Arabic	Roman Catholic, Muslim	Peseta	122
Madeira		Autonomous Region of Portugal	779	301	259 000	Funchal	Portuguese	Roman Catholic, Protestant	Port. escudo	122
Mayotte		French Territorial Collectivity	373	144	144 944	Dzaoudzi	French, Mahorian	Sunni Muslim, Christian	French franc	129
Melilla		Spanish Territory	13	5	59 576	Melilla	Spanish, Arabic	Roman Catholic, Muslim	Peseta	123
Réunion		French Overseas Department	2 551	985	721 000	St-Denis	French, creole	Roman Catholic	French franc	218
St Helena and Dependencies		United Kingdom Overseas Territory	121	47	6 000	Jamestown	English	Protestant, Roman Catholic	Pound sterling	216
Western Sahara		Disputed territory (Morocco)	266 000	102 703	252 000	Laâyoune	Arabic	Sunni Muslim	Moroccan dirham	122

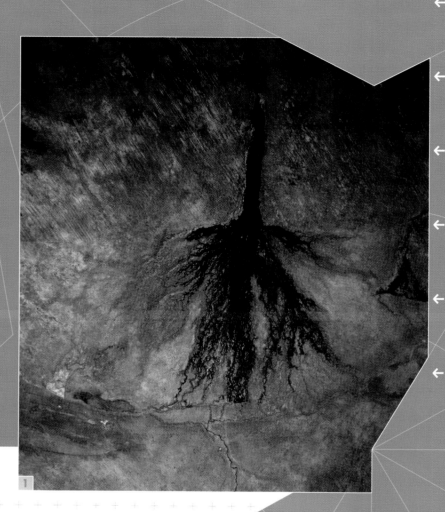

1 Okavango Delta, *Botswana*

This Shuttle photograph shows the world's largest inland delta, the Okavango Delta in Botswana. The Okavango river originates in southeast Angola and ends in this spectacular and unique alluvial plain covering 10 000 square kilometres. The river is fed by rains from October to March which produce rich seasonal vegetation and support great numbers of wildlife. Scientists have identified this to be one of the most ecologically sensitive areas on Earth.

Satellite/Sensor : Space Shuttle

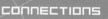

2 Nile Valley, *Egypt*

The Nile river winds through Egypt in this satellite image, ending in the distinctive triangular delta on the Mediterranean coast. The dark blue water and green vegetation of the irrigated valley and delta provide a striking contrast to the surrounding desert. Thick layers of silt carried downstream for thousands of years provide the delta with the most fertile soil in Africa. The Suez Canal is also visible on the image, providing a link between the Mediterranean Sea at the top of the image and the Gulf of Suez and the Red Sea to the right.

Satellite/Sensor : MODIS

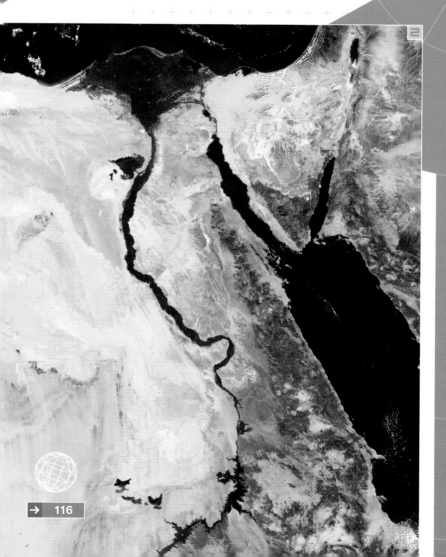

3 Flooded Village, *Kenya*

This village near Garsen was flooded when the Tana river burst its banks. An increase in extreme weather patterns occurred throughout the world in 1998. Some cases were blamed on the periodic warming of Pacific Ocean waters known as El Niño. In east Africa the regular problems of drought were replaced by excessive rainfall which led to the destruction of crops and the threat of famine. This village felt the affect of Kenya's annual rainfall increasing by over 1000mm in 1998.

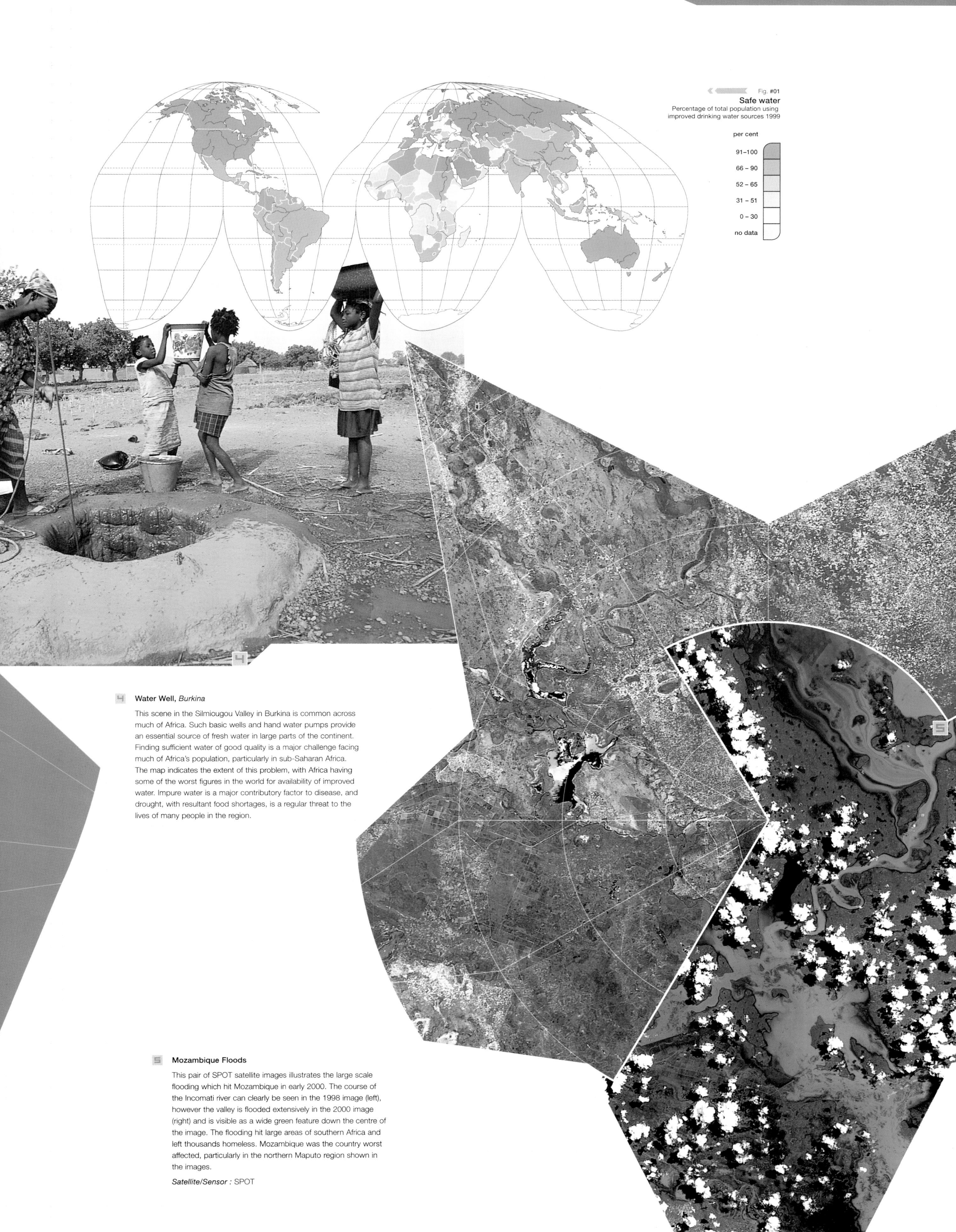

Fig. #01
Safe water
Percentage of total population using
improved drinking water sources 1999

per cent

91–100
66 – 90
52 – 65
31 – 51
0 – 30
no data

4   Water Well, *Burkina*

This scene in the Silmiougou Valley in Burkina is common across
much of Africa. Such basic wells and hand water pumps provide
an essential source of fresh water in large parts of the continent.
Finding sufficient water of good quality is a major challenge facing
much of Africa's population, particularly in sub-Saharan Africa.
The map indicates the extent of this problem, with Africa having
some of the worst figures in the world for availability of improved
water. Impure water is a major contributory factor to disease, and
drought, with resultant food shortages, is a regular threat to the
lives of many people in the region.

5   Mozambique Floods

This pair of SPOT satellite images illustrates the large scale
flooding which hit Mozambique in early 2000. The course of
the Incomati river can clearly be seen in the 1998 image (left),
however the valley is flooded extensively in the 2000 image
(right) and is visible as a wide green feature down the centre of
the image. The flooding hit large areas of southern Africa and
left thousands homeless. Mozambique was the country worst
affected, particularly in the northern Maputo region shown in
the images.

Satellite/Sensor : SPOT

africa[locations]

1 Cape Town, *Republic of South Africa*

Cape Town is the legislative capital of South Africa, the capital city of Western Cape Province and is located 40 km from the Cape of Good Hope. This view from Table Mountain shows the full extent of the city spreading out to the waterfront area on the shores of Table Bay.

2 Cairo, *Egypt*

The largest city in Africa and capital of Egypt, Cairo is situated on the right bank of the river Nile. The main built-up area appears grey in this image. The famous pyramids and the suburb of Giza are visible to the lower left where the city meets the desert. Cairo airport can be seen at the upper right. Agricultural areas, achieved by extensive irrigation, show as deep red around the city.

Satellite/Sensor : SPOT

3 The Great Rift Valley, *Africa*

The Great Rift Valley is a huge, linear depression which marks a series of geological faults resulting from tectonic activity. The section of the valley shown in this 3-D perspective view extends from Lake Nyasa in the south to the Red Sea coast in the north. The valley splits into two branches north of Lake Nyasa and then combines again through the Ethiopian Highlands. The western branch is very prominent in the image and contains several lakes, including Lake Tanganyika. The eastern branch passes to the west of Kilimanjaro, the highest mountain to the right of the image, and contains Lake Turkana on the northern border of Kenya.

4 Victoria Falls, *Zambia/Zimbabwe*

The Victoria Falls are located in the Zambezi river on the Zambia/Zimbabwe border near the town of Livingstone. The river is over 1.7 km wide at the point where the falls drop 108 m over a precipice into a narrow chasm. The volume of water in the falls varies with the seasons. Land on the Zimbabwe side of the falls is preserved as a national park.

5 Sahara Desert, *Africa*

This photograph was taken in the eastern Sahara in Libya and illustrates sharp contrasts in the landscape. At the top are huge sand dunes which have been shaped by the wind. The area in the middle view has been planted with trees, to prevent the movement of sand and soil, and the irrigated area in the near view is typical of a fertile oasis, where the land has been worked to produce crops and to support livestock.

6 The Pyramids, *Egypt*

The suburbs of Giza, shown on the left of this satellite image, spread out from the city of Cairo to an arid plateau on which stand the famous Great Pyramids. The largest, shown at the bottom centre of the image, is the Great Pyramid of Cheops. To the left of this are three small pyramids collectively known as the Pyramids of Queens. Above them is the Great Sphinx. The pyramid at the centre right of the image is Chephren and the small one at the top right is Mycerinus.

Satellite/Sensor : IKONOS

1

2

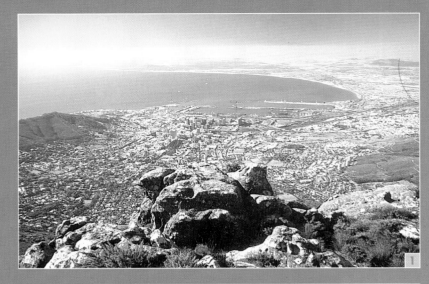

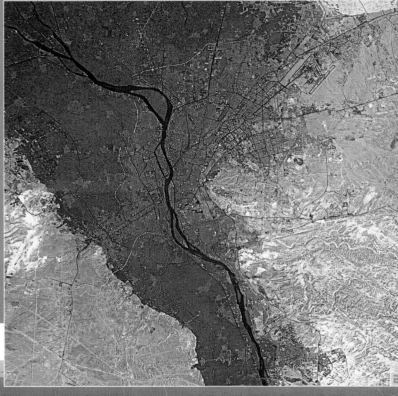

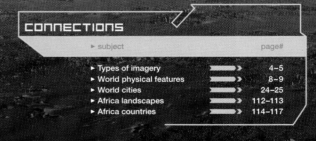

CONNECTIONS

subject	page#
Types of imagery	4–5
World physical features	8–9
World cities	24–25
Africa landscapes	112–113
Africa countries	114–117

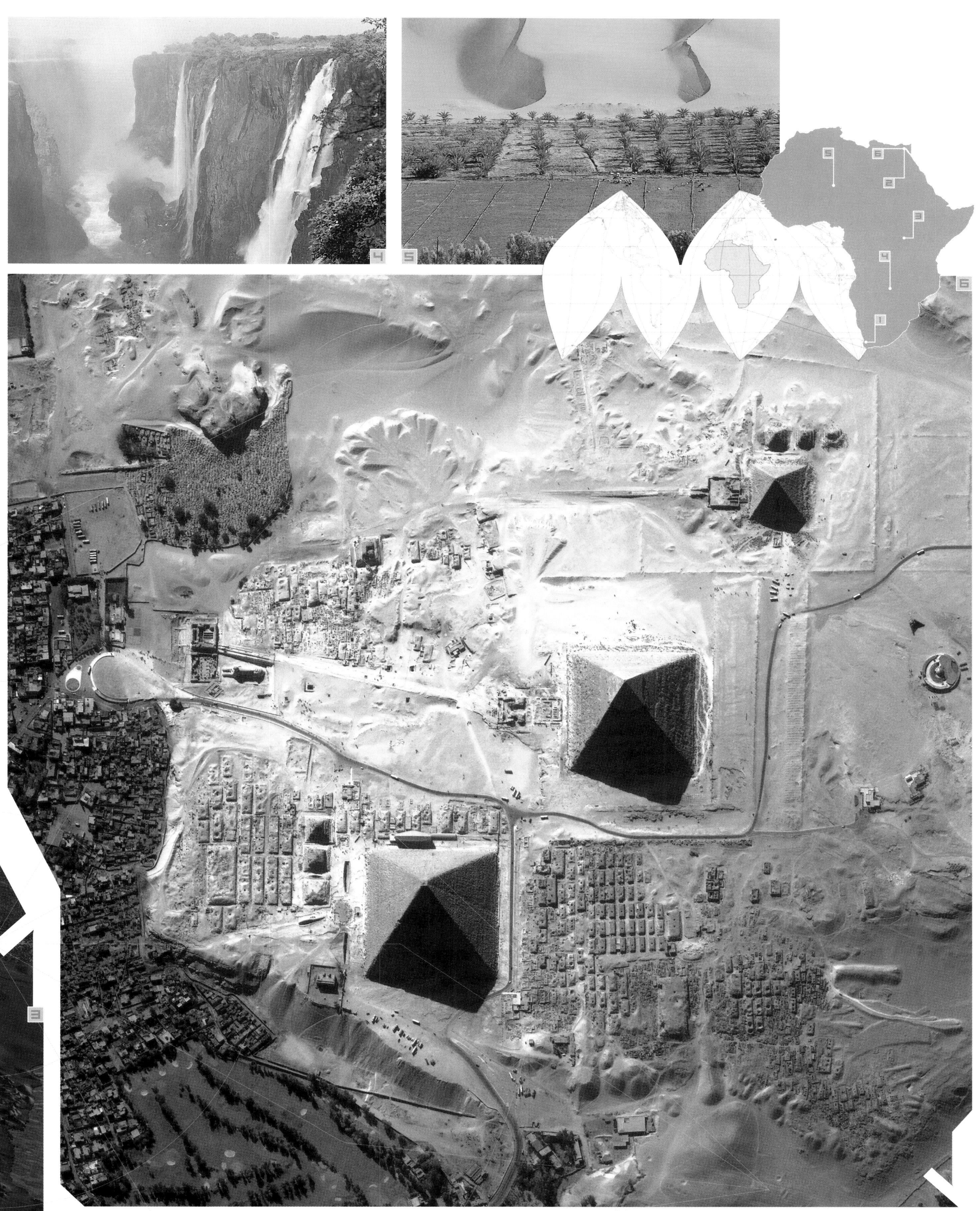

Elevation scale:
>6000m
5000-6000m
4000-5000m
3000-4000m
2000-3000m
1000-2000m
500-1000m
200-500m
0-200m
<0m

0-200m
200-500m
500-1000m
1000-2000m
2000-3000m
3000-4000m
4000-5000m
5000-6000m
>6000m

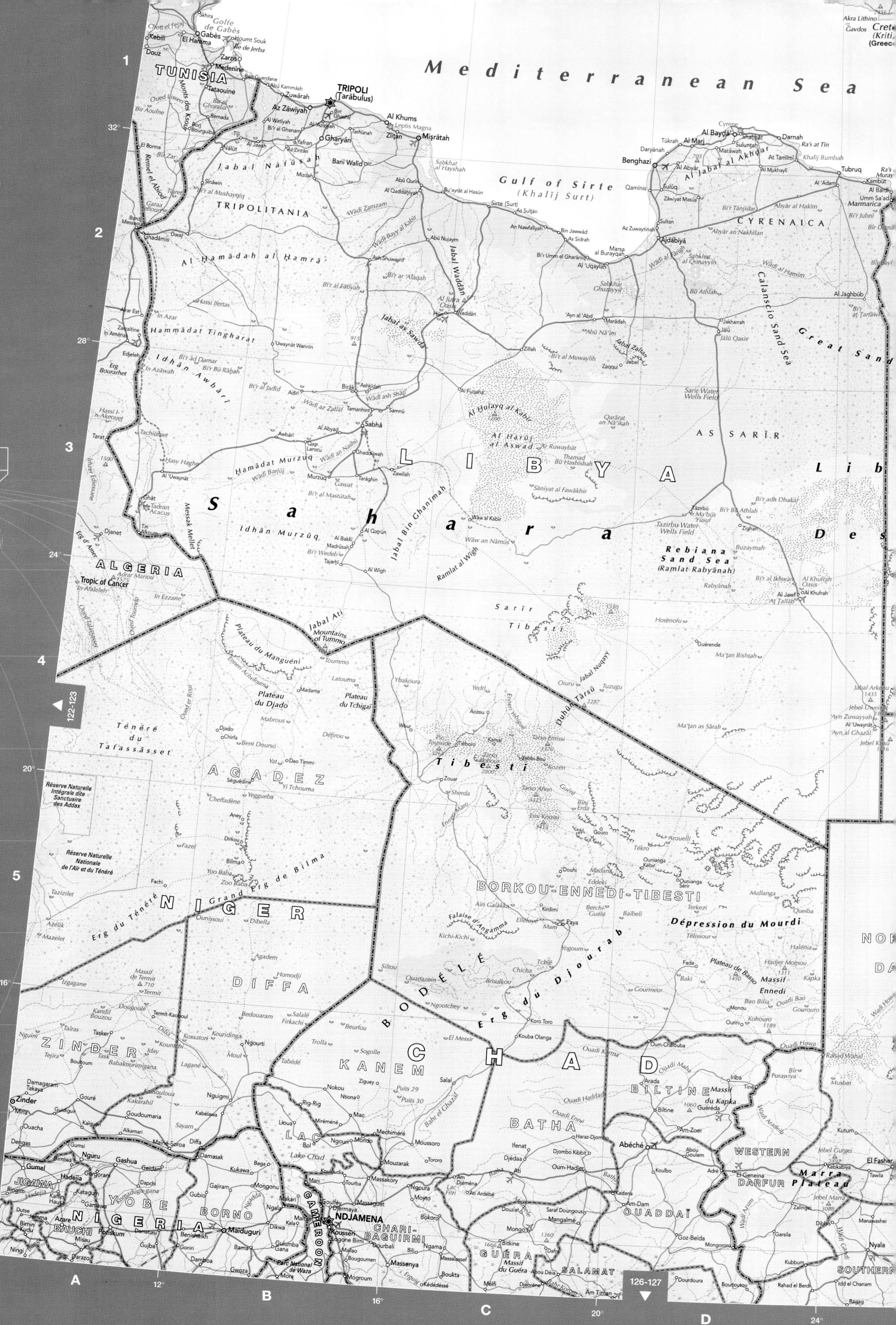

Mediterranean Sea

Gulf of Sirte
(Khalīj Surt)

TUNISIA

TRIPOLI
(Ṭarābulus)

TRIPOLITANIA

CYRENAICA

LIBYA

Libyan Desert

ALGERIA

Sahara

Tropic of Cancer

NIGER

Réserve Naturelle Intégrale dite Sanctuaire des Addax
Réserve Naturelle Nationale de l'Aïr et du Ténéré

Ténéré du Tafassâsset

AGADEZ

DIFFA

ZINDER

Erg du Ténéré

Tibesti

BORKOU-ENNEDI-TIBESTI

Dépression du Mourdi

Erg du Djourab

BODÉLÉ

KANEM

CHAD

BATHA

LAC

BILTINE

Massif du Kapka

WESTERN DARFUR

OUADDAÏ

GUÉRA

CHARI-BAGUIRMI

SALAMAT

Lake Chad

NDJAMENA

CAMEROON

NIGERIA

YOBE

BORNO

JIGAWA

BAUCHI

Zinder

Benghazi

Al Jabal al Akhḍar

Ajdabiyā

AS SARĪR

Great Sand Sea

Rebiana Sand Sea
(Ramlat Rabyānah)

Marra Plateau

Massif Ennedi

122-123

126-127

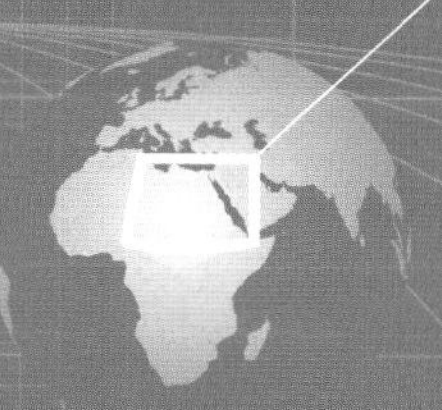

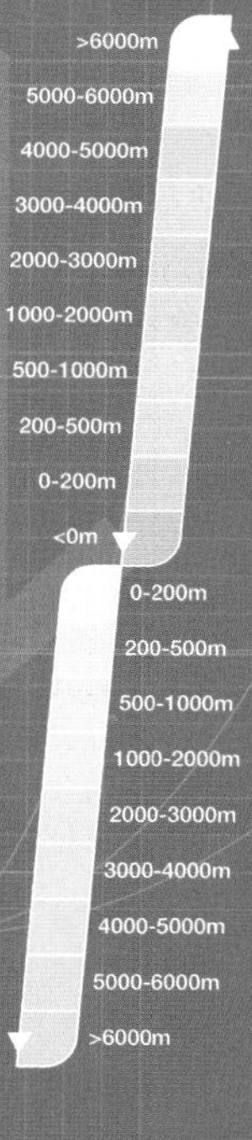

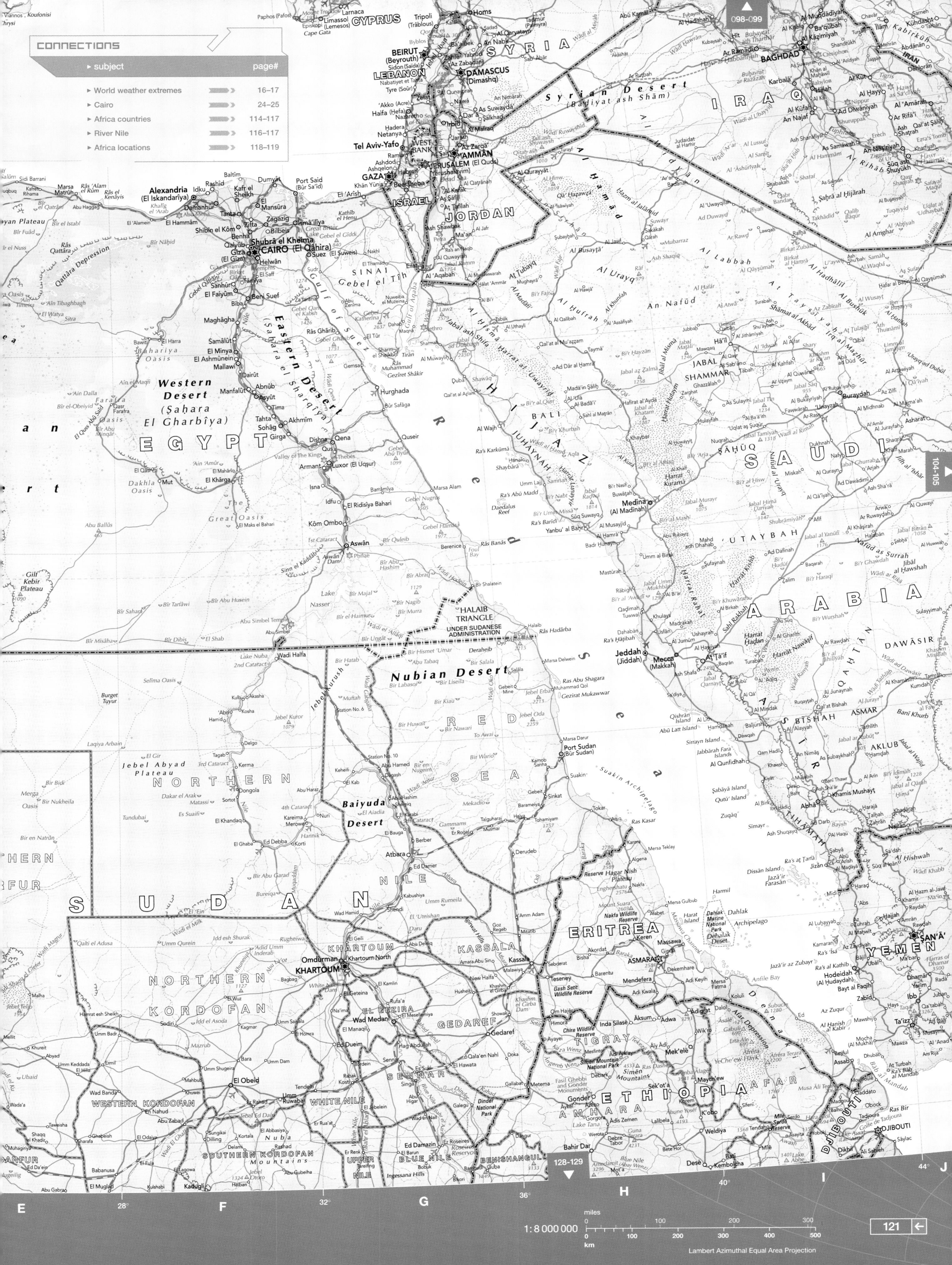

CONNECTIONS
subject
page#
World weather extremes 16–17
Cairo 24–25
Africa countries 114–117
River Nile 116–117
Africa locations 118–119
098–099
104–105
128–129
CYPRUS
LEBANON
SYRIA
ISRAEL
JORDAN
IRAQ
EGYPT
SAUDI ARABIA
SUDAN
ERITREA
ETHIOPIA
YEMEN
DJIBOUTI
Syrian Desert (Bādiyat ash Shām)
Western Desert (Şaḩara El Gharbîya)
Eastern Desert (Şaḩara el Sharqîya)
Nubian Desert
Red Sea
HALAIB TRIANGLE
UNDER SUDANESE ADMINISTRATION
BEIRUT (Beyrouth)
DAMASCUS (Dimashq)
JERUSALEM (El Quds) (Yerushalayim)
AMMAN
BAGHDAD
Alexandria (El Iskandarîya)
CAIRO (El Qâhira)
Medina (Al Madīnah)
Jeddah (Jiddah)
Mecca (Makkah)
Port Sudan (Bûr Sudan)
KHARTOUM
ASMARA
ŞAN'Ā'
DJIBOUTI
1:8 000 000
miles
km
Lambert Azimuthal Equal Area Projection
121

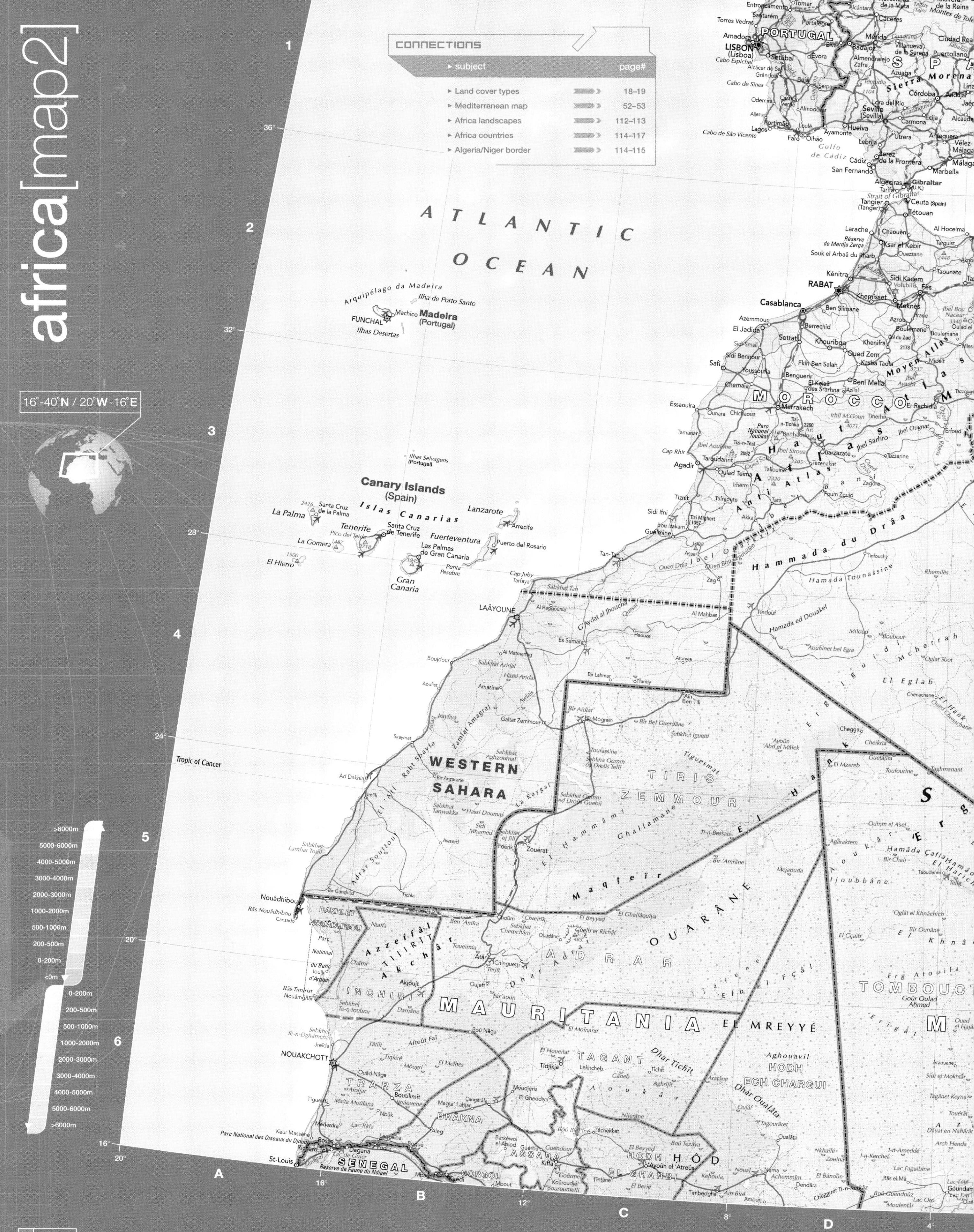

16°-40°**N** / 20°**W**-16°**E**

1 2 3 4 5 6

A T L A N T I C   O C E A N

Arquipélago da Madeira
Ilha de Porto Santo
Machico **Madeira**
FUNCHAL (Portugal)
Ilhas Desertas

Ilhas Selvagens
(Portugal)

Canary Islands
(Spain)
Islas Canarias
La Palma Santa Cruz de la Palma 2426
Lanzarote
Tenerife Arrecife
Santa Cruz de Tenerife
La Gomera Fuerteventura
El Hierro 1500 Las Palmas de Gran Canaria Puerto del Rosario
Gran Canaria
Punta Pesebre
Cap Juby
Tarfaya

LAÂYOUNE
Al Haggounia
Boujdour Es Semara
Sabkhat Aridal
Hassi Arjila
Aousfist Amasine
Asviin
WESTERN
Traifiya
Ad Dakhla
Imilli
SAHARA
El Alti Rabt Sbayta
Skaymat
Sabkhet Tanwakka
Hassi Doumas
Sidi Nhamed
Awserd

Tropic of Cancer

Nouâdhibou
Râs Nouâdhibou Bir Gandouz
Cansado
DAKHLET
NOUÂDHIBOU
Chami
AZZEFFÂL
TIJIRÎT
AKCHÂR
INCHIRI
Râs Timiris Nouâmghâr
Sebkhet te-n-loubrar
TRARZA
Sebkhet Te-n-Dghâmcha
Jreida
NOUAKCHOTT
Tiguent
BRAKNA
Keur Massène
Parc National des Oiseaux du Djoudj
St-Louis
Rosso Dagana
Richard Toll
SENEGAL
Réserve de Faune du Ndiael

MAURITANIA
Atâr Chinguetti
Terjit
ADRAR
Oujeft Far'aoun
Akjoujt
Aftoût Fai
Târît Tidjikja
Moudjeria
TAGANT
Lekhcheb Tichît
Ganeb
Aleg Magta' Lahjar
GORGOL
ASSABA Kiffa
Kaédi Mbout
HODH EL GHARBI

MOROCCO
RABAT
Casablanca
El Jadida Berrechid
Azemmour
Settat Khouribga
Safi Khenifra
Sidi Bennour Beni Mellal
Youssoufia Azilal
Chemaia Kelaâ des Srarna
Essaouira
Marrakech
Agadir
Taroudannt
Tiznit
Sidi Ifni Tata
Guelmine
Tan-Tan
Tarfaya
Haut Atlas
Anti Atlas
Moyen Atlas
Oued Drâa
Hammada du Drâa
Hamada Tounassine
Tindouf
Al Mahbas
Hamada ed Douakel
TIRIS ZEMMOUR
Zouérat
Fdérik
Bir Mogreïn
EL HANK
OUARÂNE
EL MREYYÉ
HODH ECH CHARGUI
Tombouctou

PORTUGAL
LISBON (Lisboa)
Setúbal
Évora
Cabo Espichel
Cabo de Sines
Cabo de São Vicente
Faro Olhão
Golfo de Cádiz
Cádiz
San Fernando
Algeciras Gibraltar
Tarifa Ceuta (Spain)
Strait of Gibraltar
Tangier (Tanger)
Tétouan
Al Hoceima
Larache
Ksar el Kebir
Souk el Arbaâ du Rharb
Kénitra Fès
Meknès
SPAIN
Seville (Sevilla)
Córdoba
Sierra Morena
Málaga
MADRID

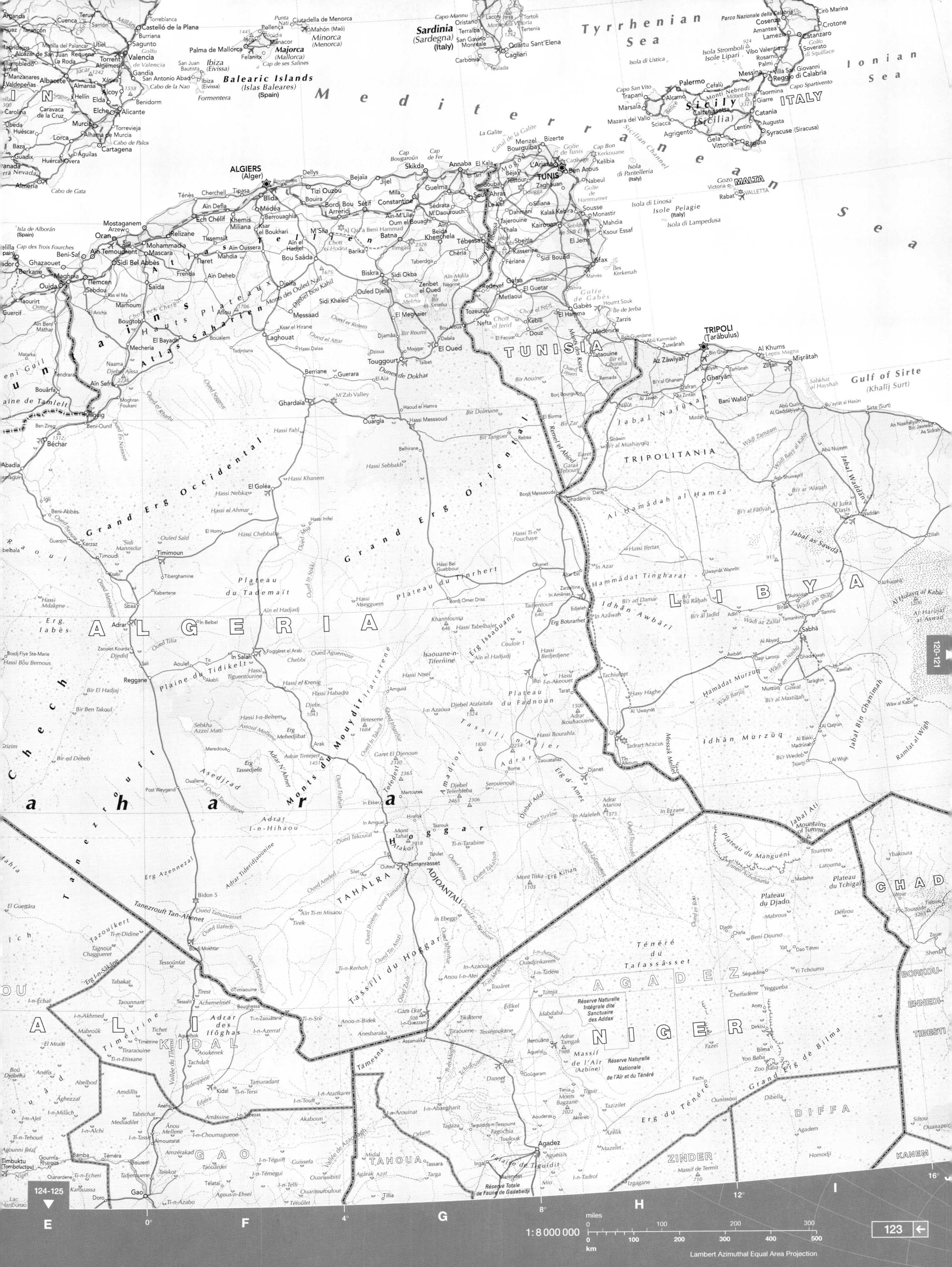

2°S-22°N / 18°W-16°E

Elevation scale:
- >6000m
- 5000-6000m
- 4000-5000m
- 3000-4000m
- 2000-3000m
- 1000-2000m
- 500-1000m
- 200-500m
- 0-200m
- <0m

1:8 000 000

Ilhas do Cabo Verde

CAPE VERDE

ATLANTIC OCEAN

WESTERN SAHARA

MAURITANIA

SENEGAL

THE GAMBIA

GUINEA-BISSAU

GUINEA

SIERRA LEONE

LIBERIA

CÔTE D'IVOIRE

SAHEL

Capital cities: NOUAKCHOTT, DAKAR, BANJUL, BISSAU, CONAKRY, FREETOWN, MONROVIA, BAMAKO, YAMOUSSOUKRO, PRAIA

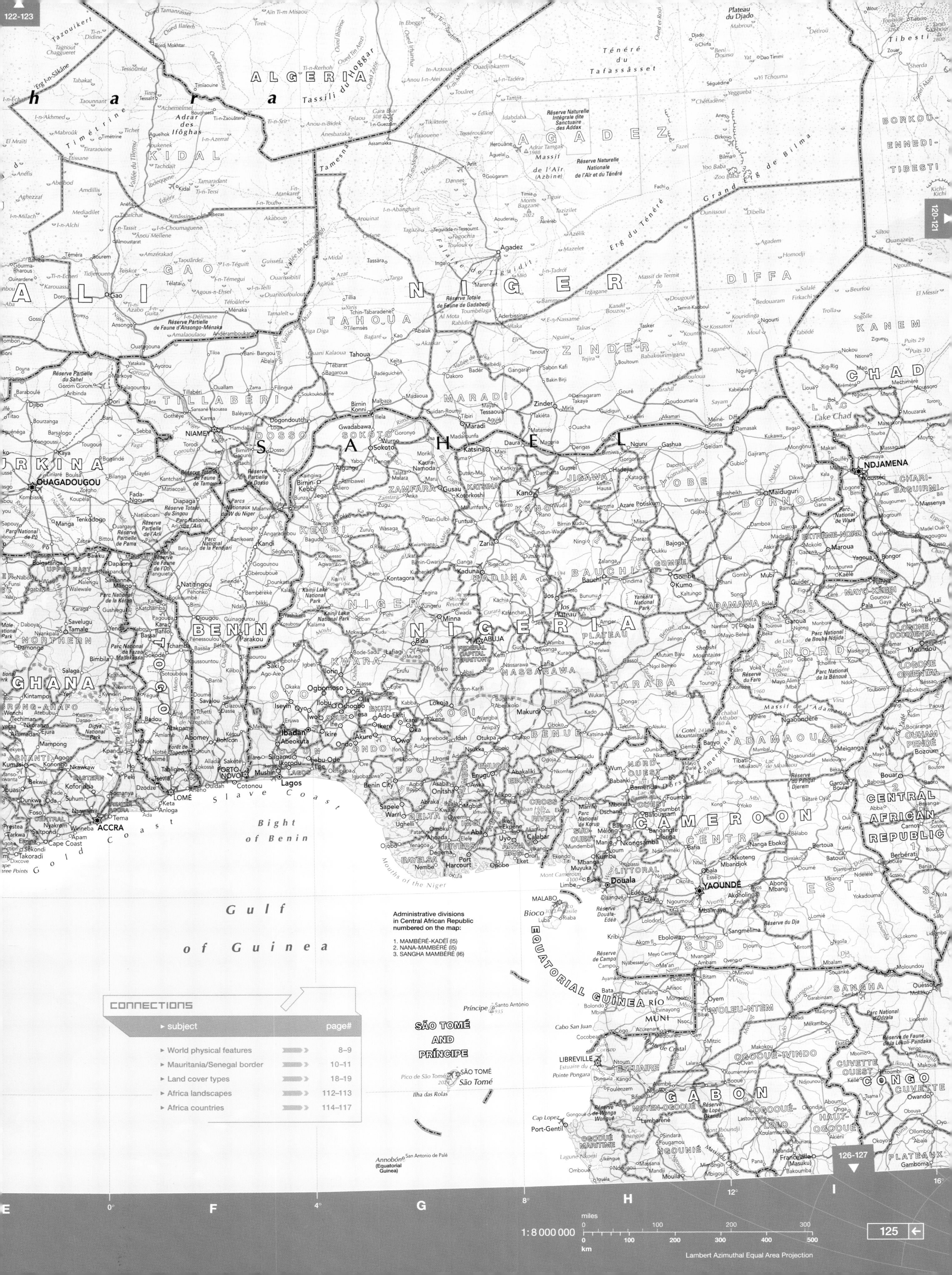

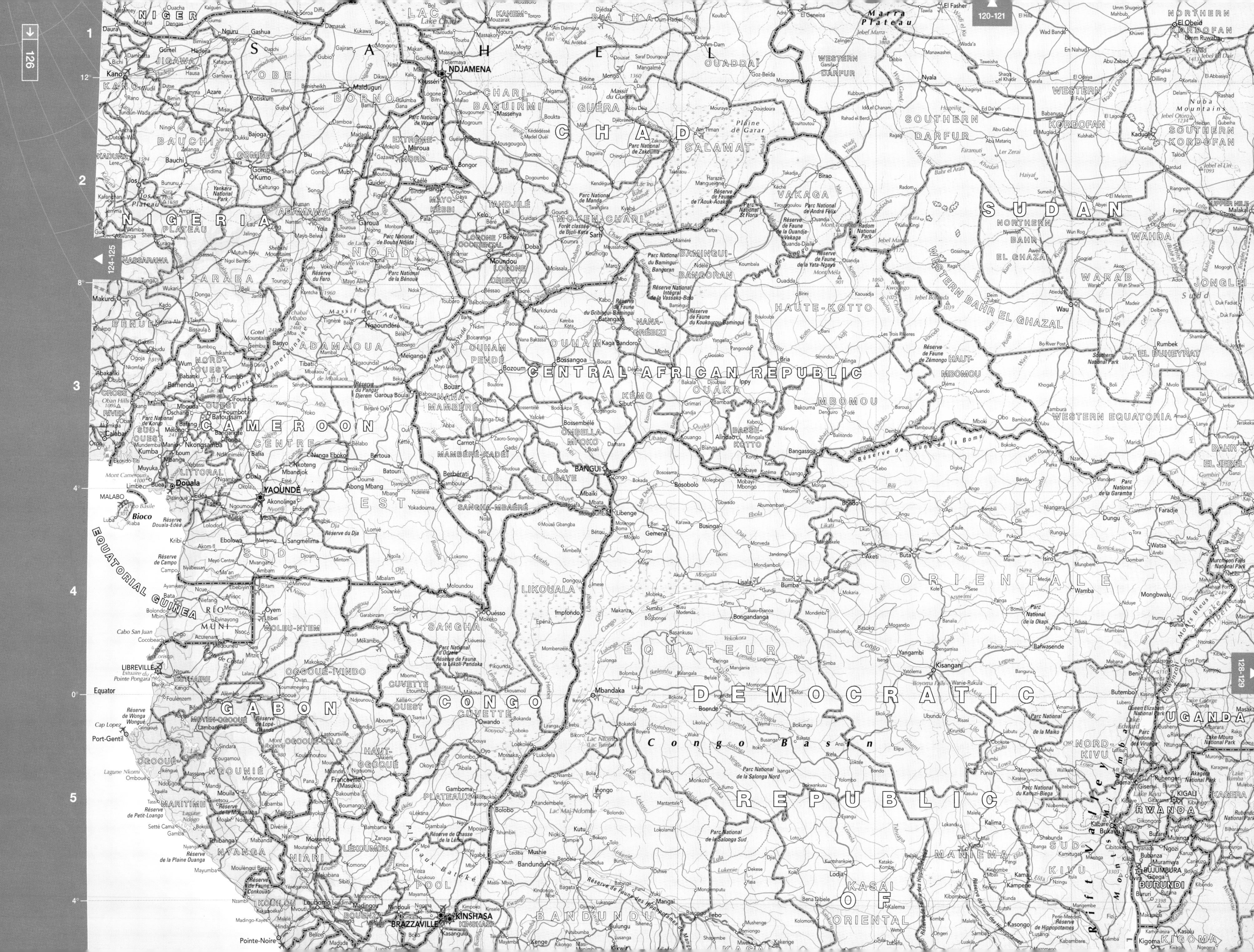
SUDAN
CHAD
NIGERIA
CAMEROON
CENTRAL AFRICAN REPUBLIC
DEMOCRATIC REPUBLIC OF CONGO
CONGO
GABON
EQUATORIAL GUINEA
UGANDA
RWANDA
BURUNDI
NIGER
NDJAMENA
BANGUI
YAOUNDÉ
LIBREVILLE
MALABO
KINSHASA
BRAZZAVILLE
KIGALI
BUJUMBURA
Kano
Maiduguri
Douala
Kisangani
Mbandaka
Pointe-Noire
Port-Gentil
Equator
Congo Basin
120-121
128-129
124-125

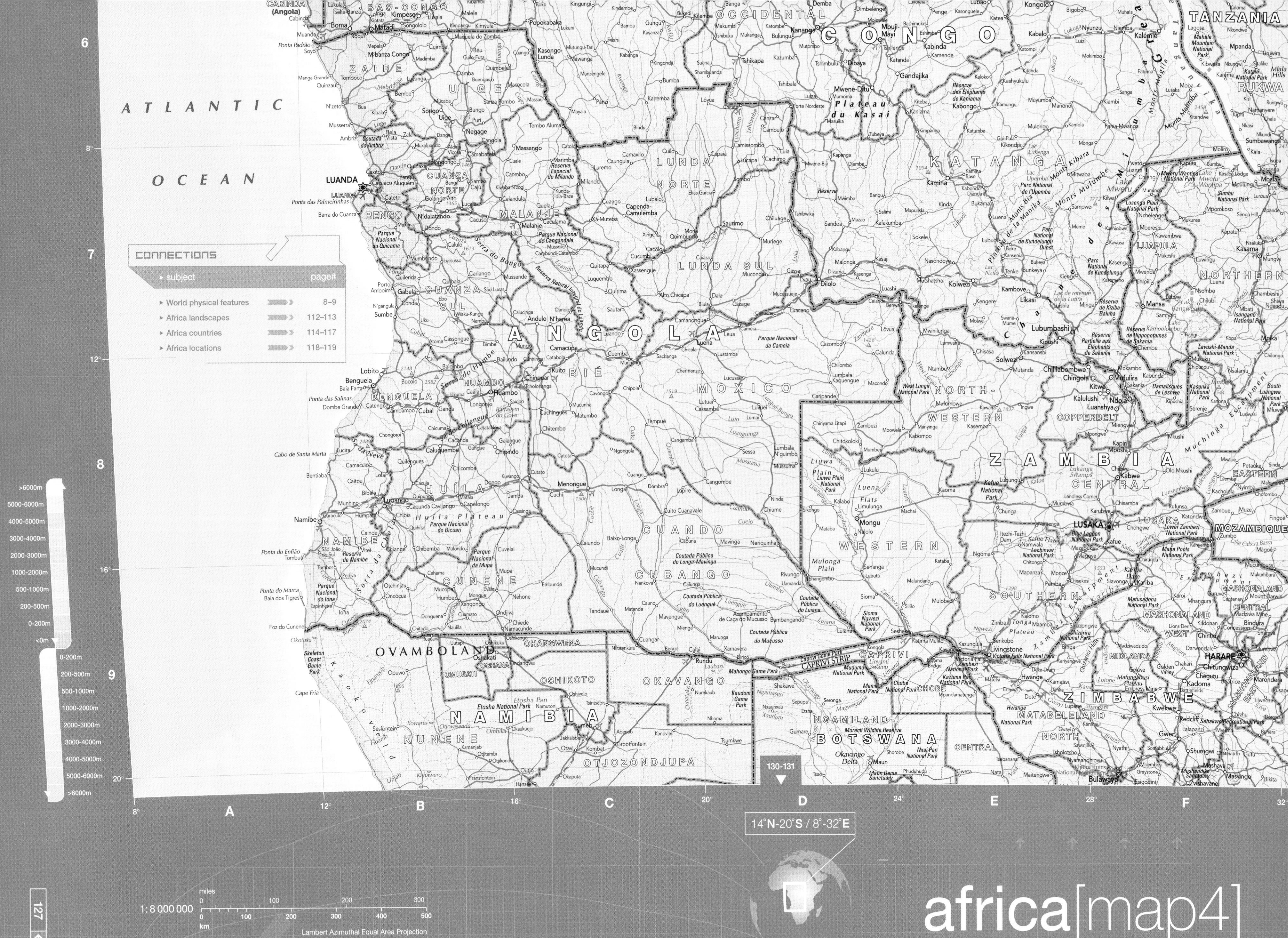

14°N-20°S / 8°-32°E

130–131

CONNECTIONS

↑ subject	page#
▲ World physical features	8–9
▲ Africa landscapes	112–113
▲ Africa countries	114–117
▲ Africa locations	118–119

1:8 000 000

Lambert Azimuthal Equal Area Projection

miles

km

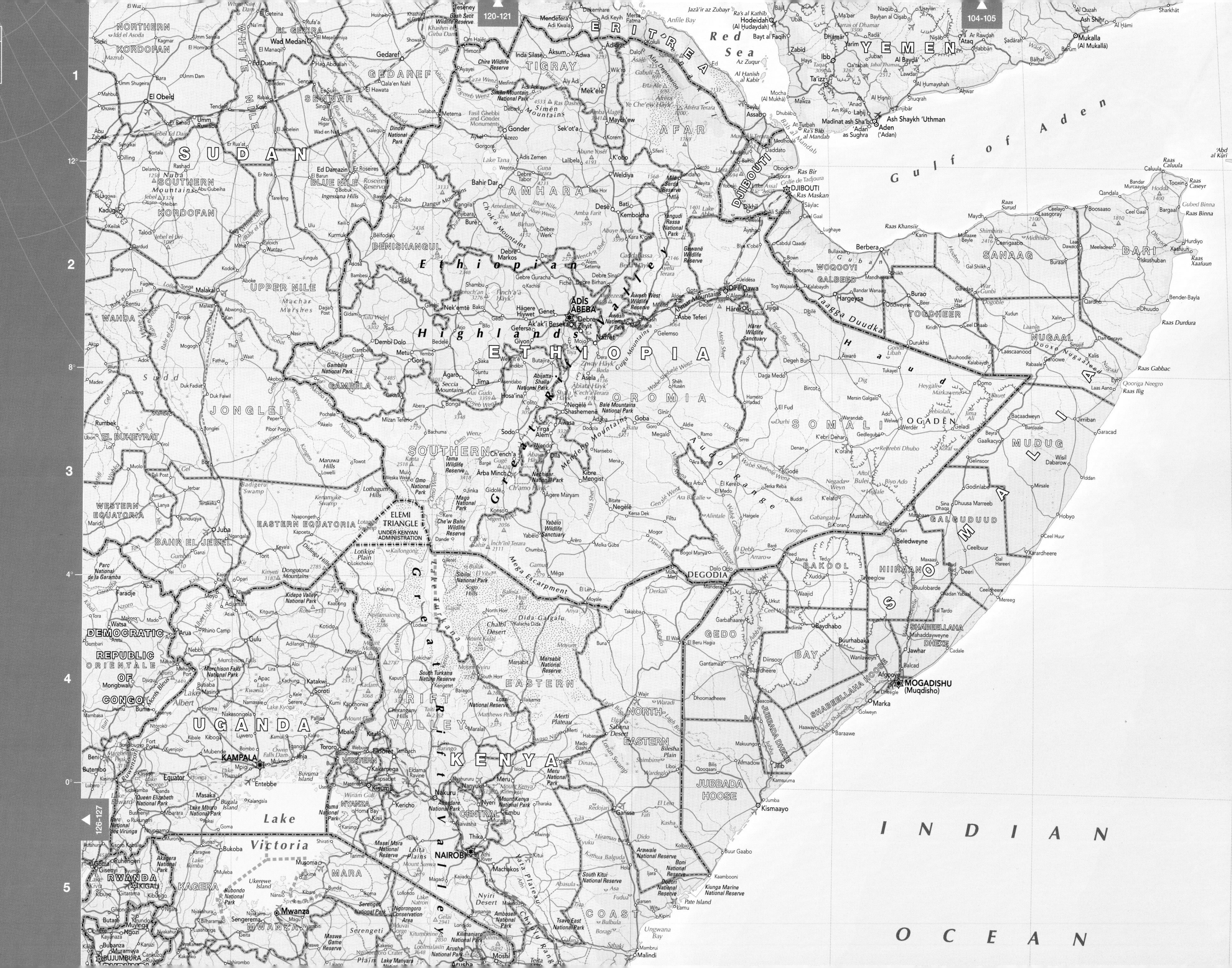

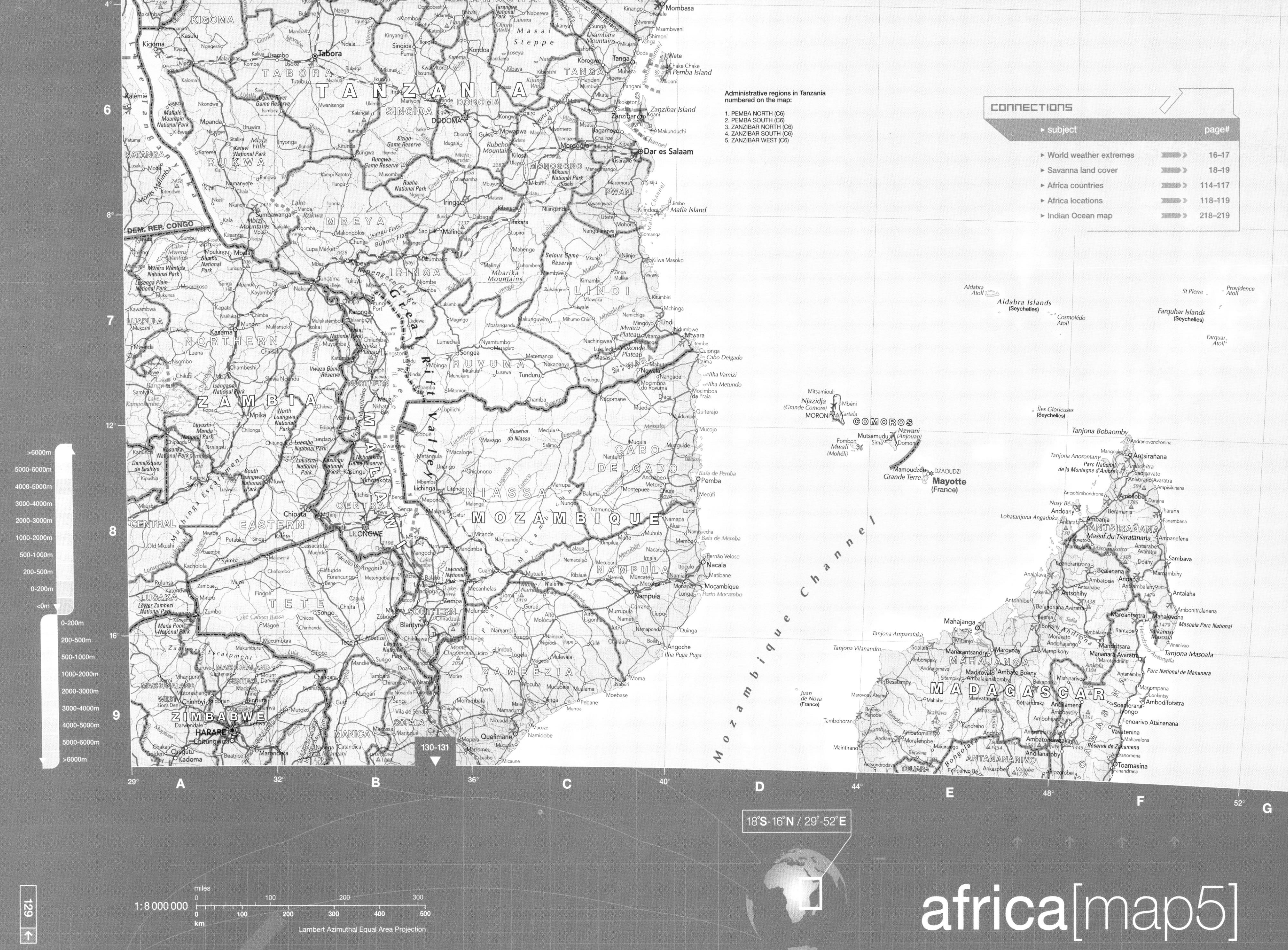

africa[map5]

18°S-16'N / 29°-52°E

1:8 000 000

Lambert Azimuthal Equal Area Projection

miles
km   0   100   200   300   400   500

>6000m
5000-6000m
4000-5000m
3000-4000m
2000-3000m
1000-2000m
500-1000m
200-500m
0-200m
<0m

0-200m
200-500m
500-1000m
1000-2000m
2000-3000m
3000-4000m
4000-5000m
5000-6000m
>6000m

CONNECTIONS

▶ subject	page#
▲ World weather extremes	16–17
▲ Savanna land cover	18–19
▲ Africa countries	114–117
▲ Africa locations	118–119
▲ Indian Ocean map	218–219

Administrative regions in Tanzania
numbered on the map:

1. PEMBA NORTH (C6)
2. PEMBA SOUTH (C6)
3. ZANZIBAR NORTH (C6)
4. ZANZIBAR SOUTH (C6)
5. ZANZIBAR WEST (C6)

MADAGASCAR

MOZAMBIQUE

TANZANIA

ZAMBIA

MALAWI

ZIMBABWE

COMOROS

Mayotte
(France)

Mozambique Channel

Great Rift Valley

Lake Malawi (Lake Nyasa)

Lake Tanganyika

DEM. REP. CONGO

Dar es Salaam

Mombasa

HARARE

LILONGWE

DODOMA

Aldabra Islands
(Seychelles)

Farquhar Islands
(Seychelles)

130·131

130-131

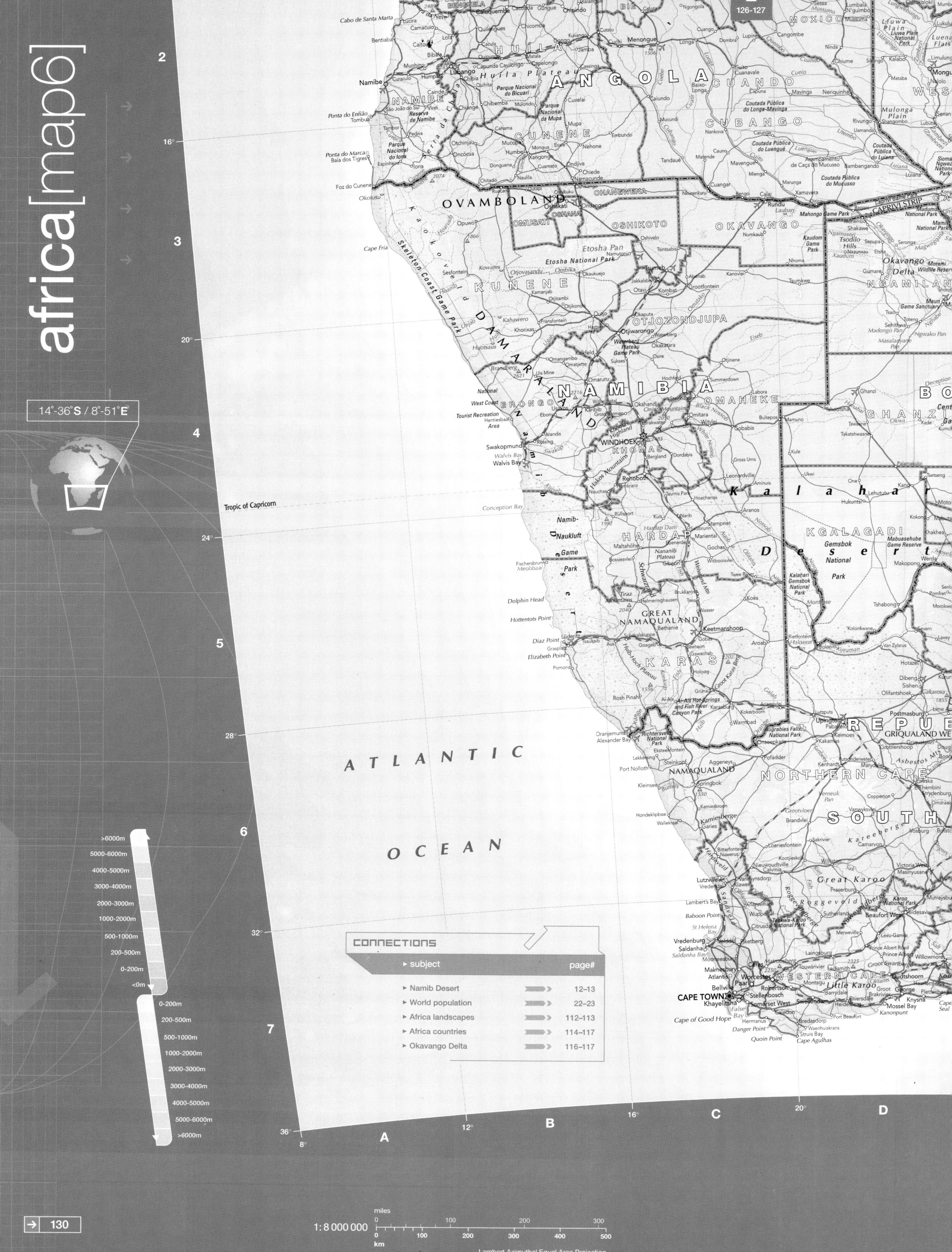

africa[map6]

14°–36°S / 8°–51°E

1 : 8 000 000

Lambert Azimuthal Equal Area Projection

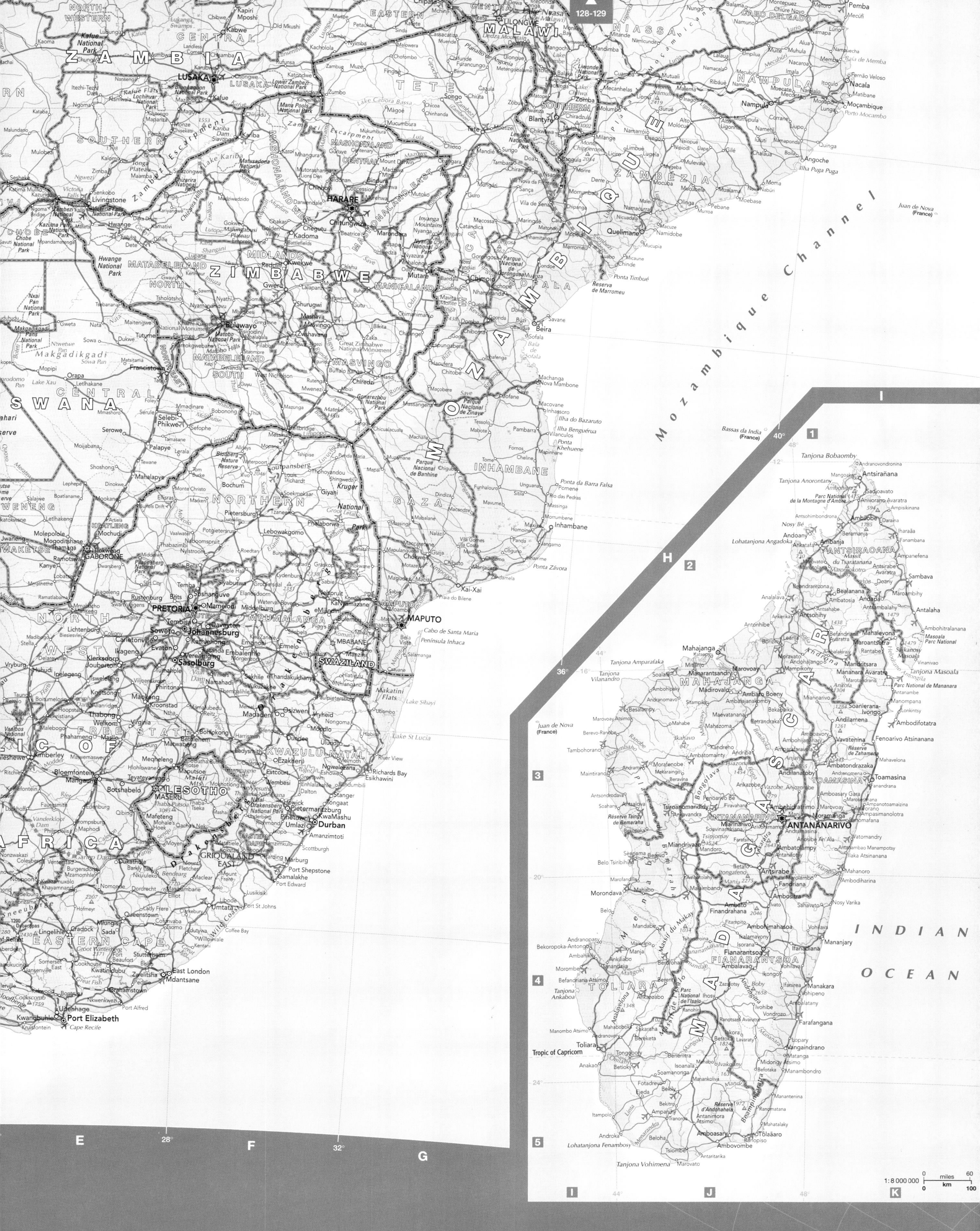

1:8 000 000

miles 60
km 100

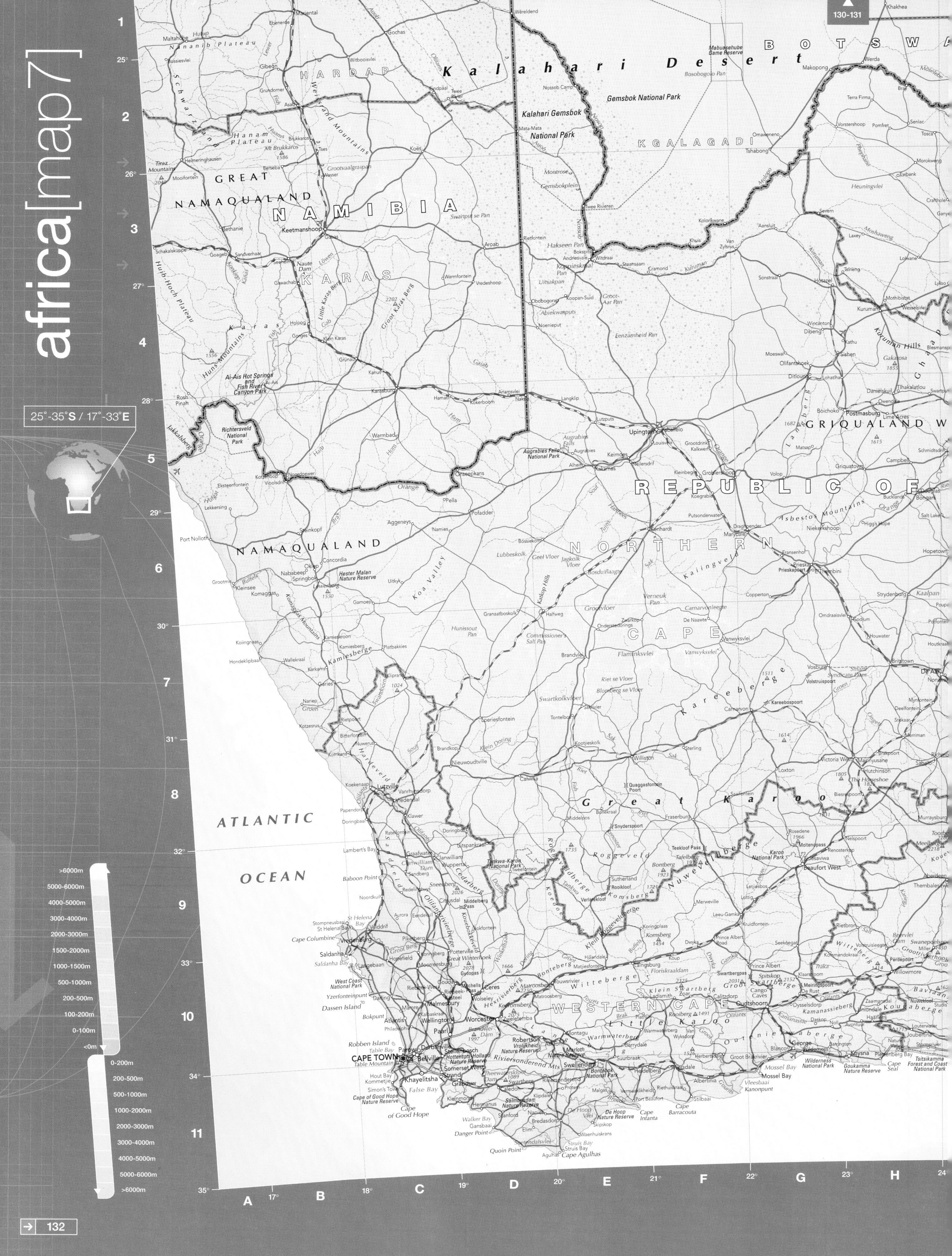

africa [map 7]
25°-35°S / 17°-33°E
130-131
132
NAMIBIA
BOTSWANA
REPUBLIC OF
NORTHERN CAPE
WESTERN CAPE
Kalahari Desert
KGALAGADI
HARDAP
KARAS
GREAT NAMAQUALAND
NAMAQUALAND
GRIQUALAND W
Great Karoo
Little Karoo
ATLANTIC OCEAN
Gemsbok National Park
Kalahari Gemsbok National Park
Richtersveld National Park
Ai-Ais Hot Springs and Fish River Canyon Park
Augrabies Falls National Park
Hester Malan Nature Reserve
Tankwa-Karoo National Park
Karoo National Park
West Coast National Park
Cape of Good Hope Nature Reserve
De Hoop Nature Reserve
Bontebok National Park
Wilderness National Park
Tsitsikamma Forest and Coastal National Park
Keetmanshoop
Upington
Springbok
Port Nolloth
Calvinia
Beaufort West
Fraserburg
Sutherland
Worcester
Paarl
Stellenbosch
CAPE TOWN
Bellville
Khayelitsha
Saldanha
Vredenburg
Swellendam
Oudtshoorn
George
Mossel Bay
Knysna
Cape Agulhas
Cape of Good Hope
Robben Island
Table Bay
False Bay
St Helena Bay
Saldanha Bay
Mossel Bay
>6000m
5000-6000m
4000-5000m
3000-4000m
2000-3000m
1500-2000m
1000-1500m
500-1000m
200-500m
100-200m
0-100m
<0m
0-200m
200-500m
500-1000m
1000-2000m
2000-3000m
3000-4000m
4000-5000m
5000-6000m
>6000m
A B C D E F G H
17° 18° 19° 20° 21° 22° 23° 24°
25° 26° 27° 28° 29° 30° 31° 32° 33° 34° 35°

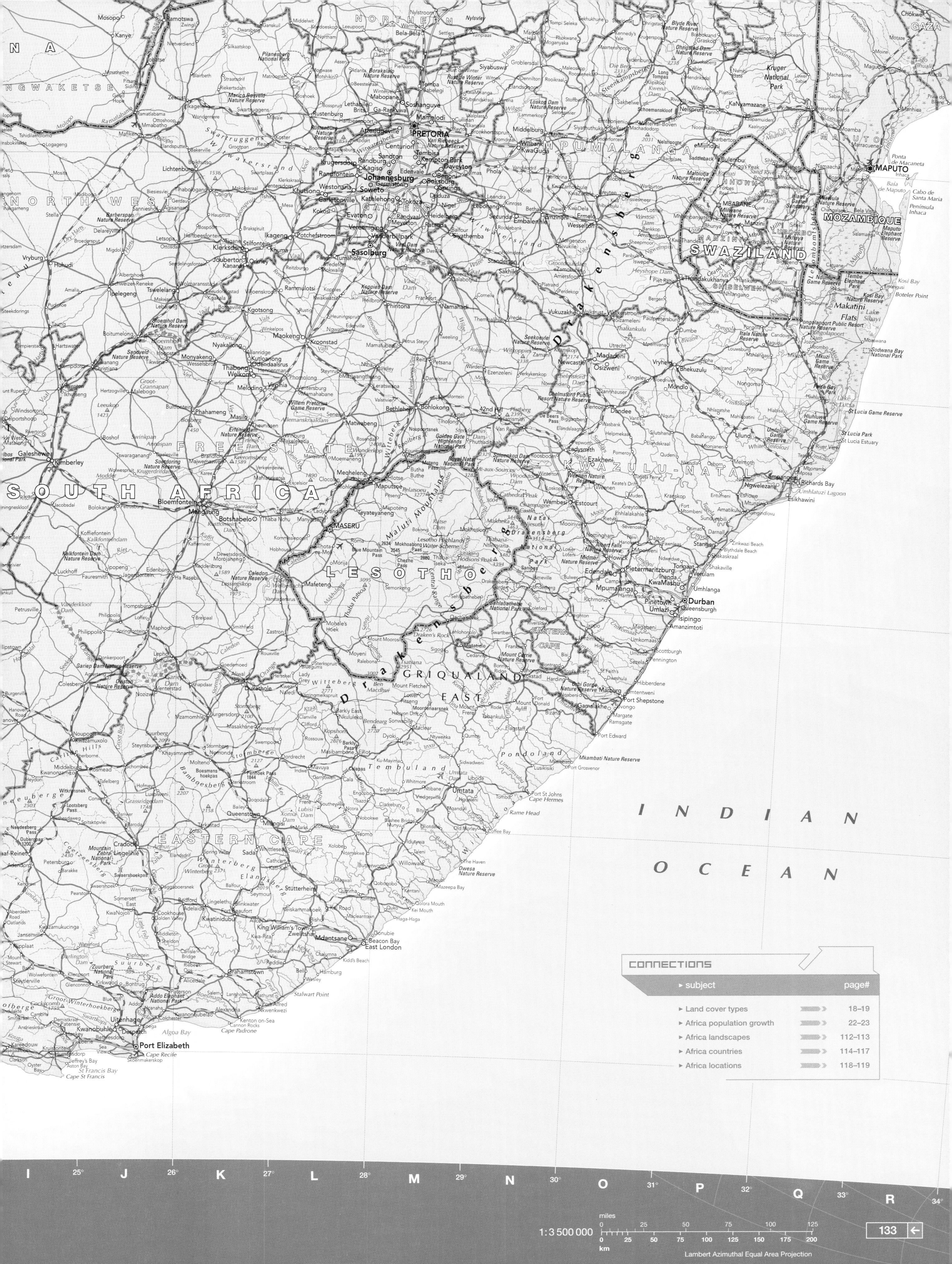

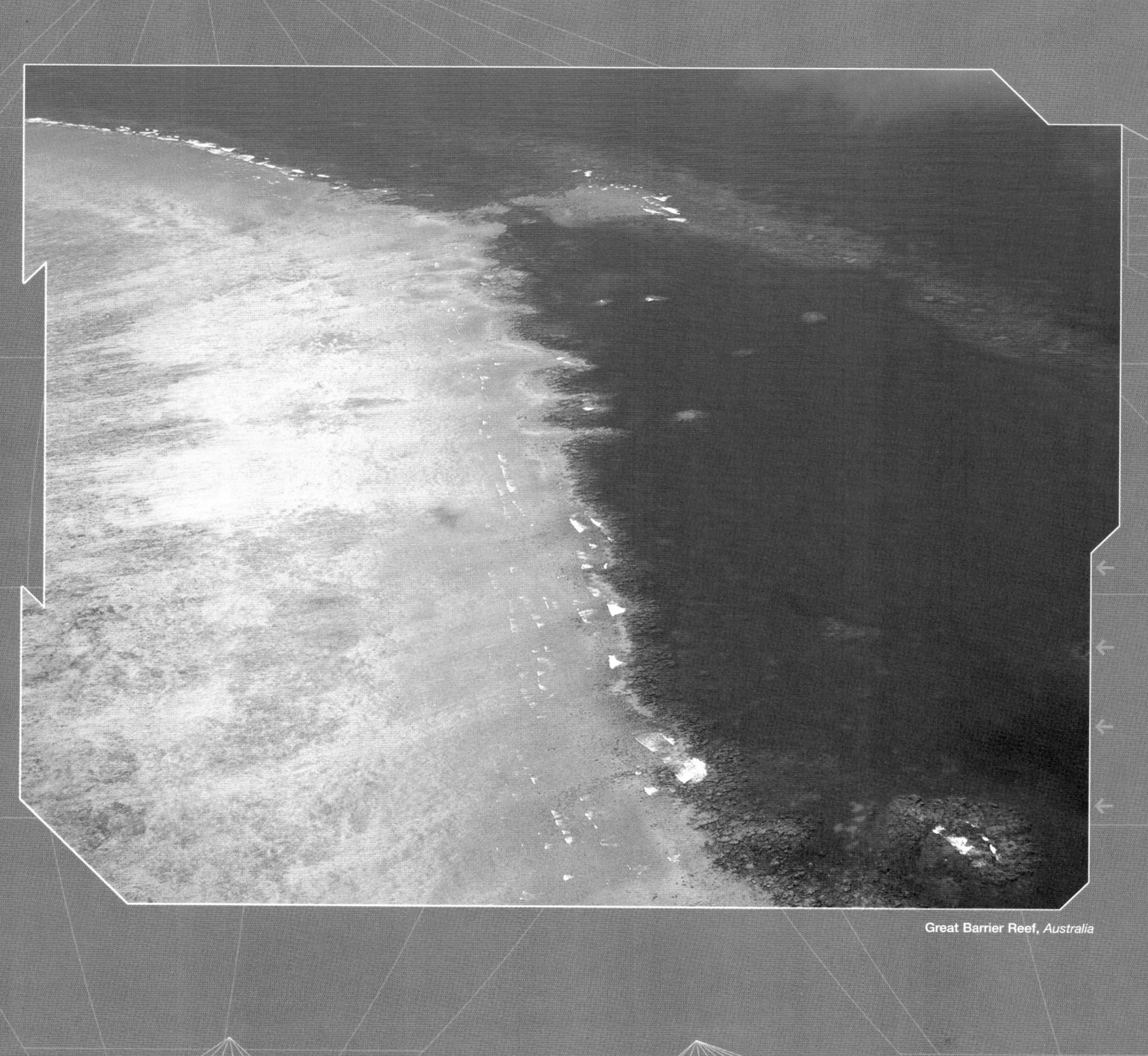

Great Barrier Reef, *Australia*

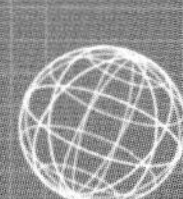

oceania

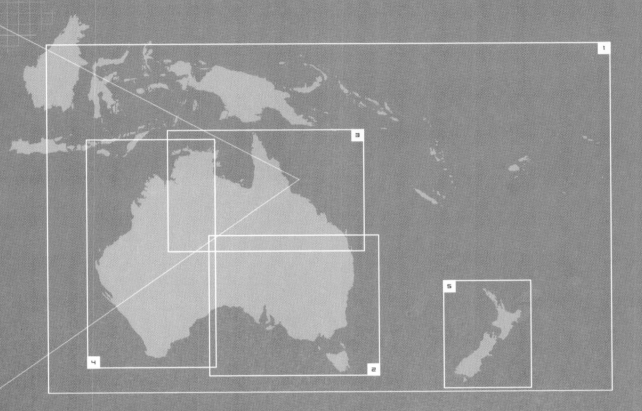

[contents]

	page#
oceania [landscapes]	136–137
oceania [countries]	138–139
oceania [threats]	140–141
oceania [features]	142–143

	map coverage	scale	page#
oceania [map 1]	AUSTRALIA and PACIFIC Southwest	1:18 000 000	144–145
oceania [map 2]	AUSTRALIA Southeast	1:6 000 000	146–147
oceania [map 3]	AUSTRALIA Northeast	1:6 000 000	148–149
oceania [map 4]	AUSTRALIA West	1:6 000 000	150–151
oceania [map 5]	NEW ZEALAND	1:3 250 000	152–153

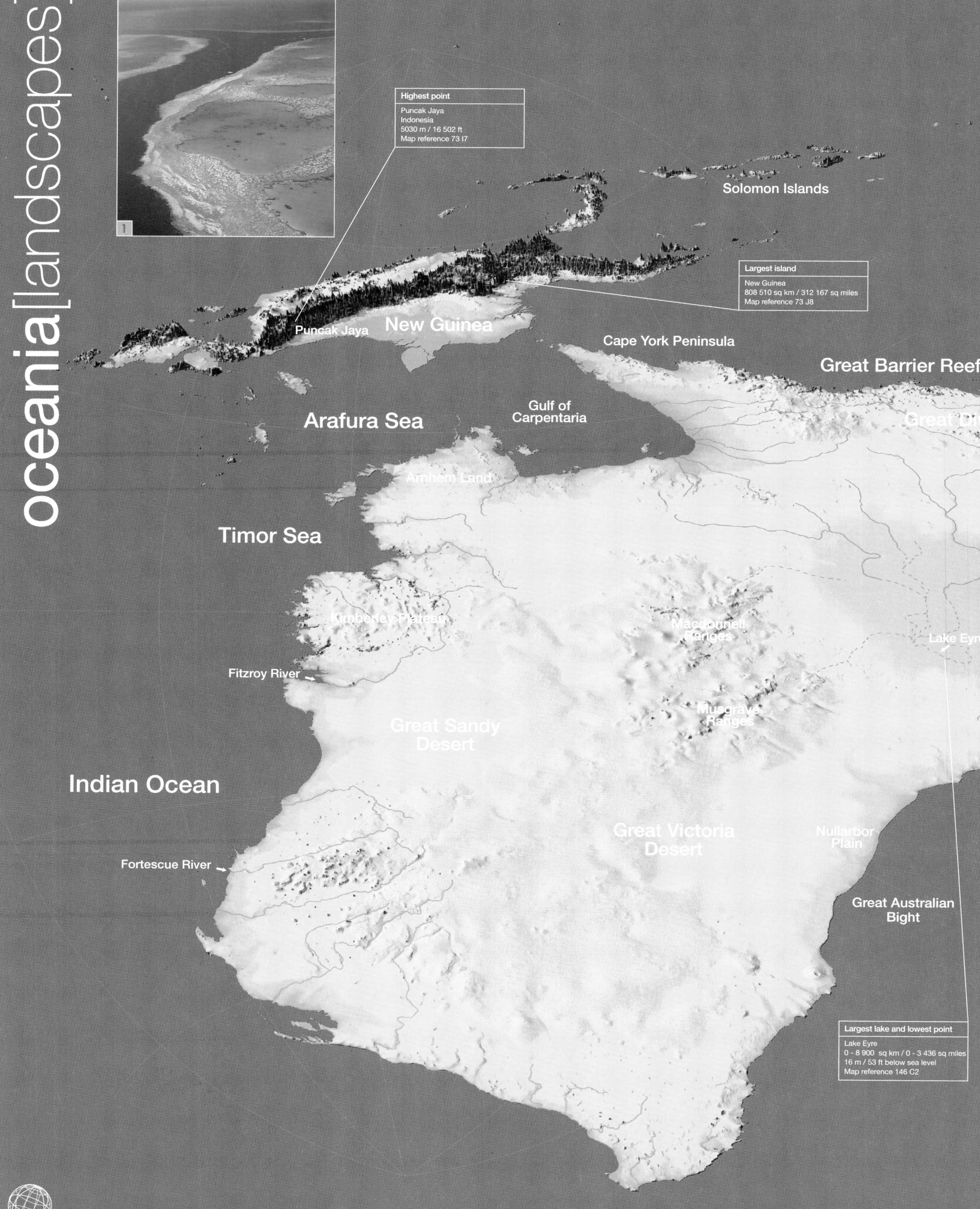

Highest point

Puncak Jaya
Indonesia
5030 m / 16 502 ft
Map reference 73 I7

Solomon Islands

Largest island

New Guinea
808 510 sq km / 312 167 sq miles
Map reference 73 J8

Puncak Jaya

New Guinea

Cape York Peninsula

Great Barrier Reef

Arafura Sea

Gulf of
Carpentaria

Great Div

Arnhem Land

Timor Sea

Kimberley Plateau

Macdonnell
Ranges

Lake Eyre

Fitzroy River

Great Sandy
Desert

Musgrave
Ranges

Indian Ocean

Great Victoria
Desert

Nullarbor
Plain

Fortescue River

Great Australian
Bight

Largest lake and lowest point

Lake Eyre
0 - 8 900 sq km / 0 - 3 436 sq miles
16 m / 53 ft below sea level
Map reference 146 C2

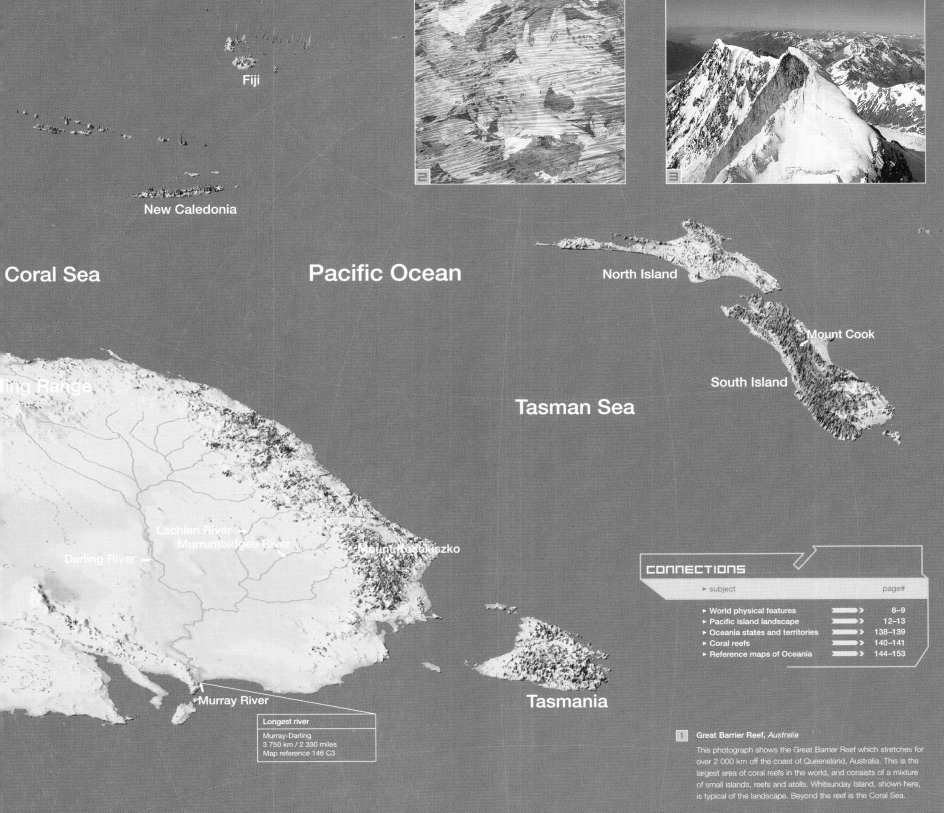

Fiji

New Caledonia

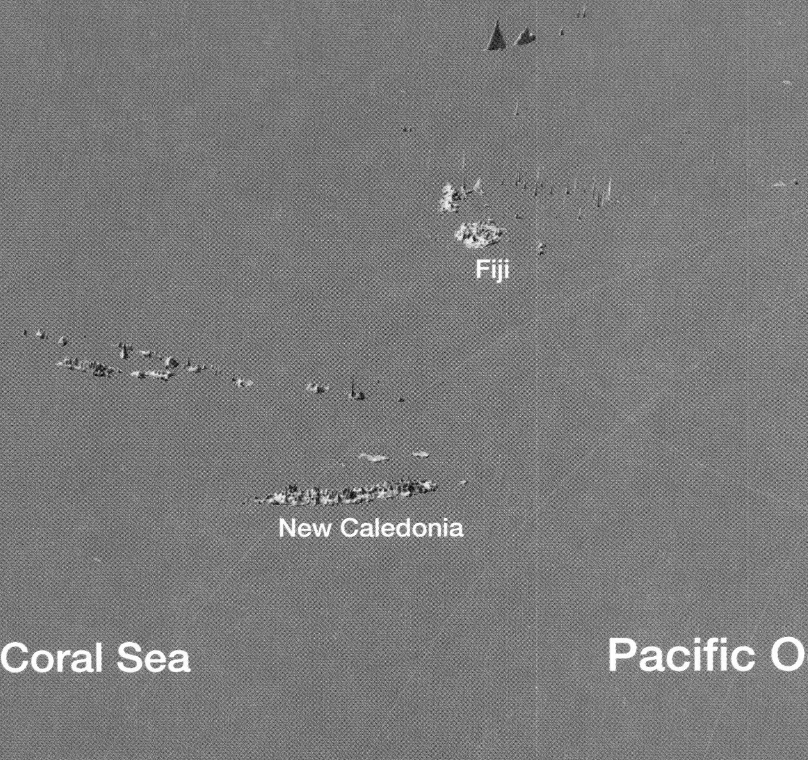

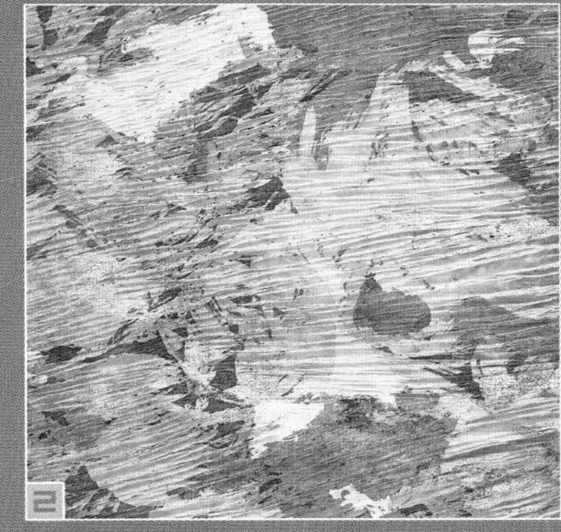

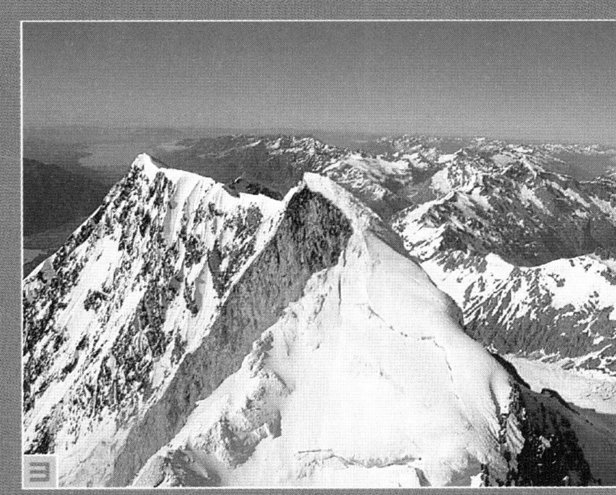

Coral Sea

Pacific Ocean

North Island

...ling Range

Tasman Sea

Mount Cook

South Island

Lachlan River →
Murrumbidgee River

Darling River →

Mount Kosciuszko

Murray River

Tasmania

Longest river
Murray-Darling
3 750 km / 2 330 miles
Map reference 146 C3

CONNECTIONS

› subject   page#

› World physical features   8–9
› Pacific island landscape   12–13
› Oceania states and territories   138–139
› Coral reefs   140–141
› Reference maps of Oceania   144–153

1 Great Barrier Reef, *Australia*

This photograph shows the Great Barrier Reef which stretches for over 2 000 km off the coast of Queensland, Australia. This is the largest area of coral reefs in the world, and consists of a mixture of small islands, reefs and atolls. Whitsunday Island, shown here, is typical of the landscape. Beyond the reef is the Coral Sea.

2 Gibson Desert, *Australia*

The Gibson Desert in Western Australia has distinctive long, thin dune-like ridges which are covered with resilient desert grasses. The different coloured patches are due to a combination of seasonal new growth and fire damage. The dark areas on this image indicate the most recent summer fire outbreaks. The darkness fades as new growth appears.

Satellite/Sensor : SPOT

3 Mount Cook, *New Zealand*

Mount Cook on South Island, New Zealand is the highest peak in the country at 3 754 m. This photograph looks southeast towards Lake Pukaki, close to the horizon on the left. The peak is part of the Southern Alps mountain range and the National Park surrounding Mount Cook is designated a World Heritage area. The bare rock face below the summit resulted from a major avalanche in 1991 which reduced the height of the mountain by 20 m.

The continent of Oceania comprises Australia, the islands of New Zealand, New Guinea and numerous small islands and island groups in the Pacific Ocean, including Micronesia, Melanesia and Polynesia. The main landmass of Australia is largely desert, with many salt lakes and a low artesian basin in the east central area. The mountains of the Great Dividing Range run parallel to the east coast and are the source of the main river system, the Murray-Darling. The Great Barrier Reef, which stretches off the coast of Queensland, Australia, is the world's largest deposit of coral.

New Guinea is a mountainous island, most of which is covered with tropical forest. New Zealand has a great variety of landscape types, from tropical environments in the north of North Island to sub-Antarctic conditions in the south of South Island. North Island has extensive volcanic areas and South Island is mountainous, being dominated by the Southern Alps range.

OCEANIA

HIGHEST MOUNTAINS

	m	ft	location	map
Puncak Jaya	5 030	16 502	Indonesia	73 I7
Puncak Trikora	4 730	15 518	Indonesia	73 I7
Puncak Mandala	4 700	15 420	Indonesia	73 J7
Puncak Yamin	4 595	15 075	Indonesia	73 J7
Mt Wilhelm	4 509	14 793	Papua New Guinea	73 J8
Mt Kubor	4 359	14 301	Papua New Guinea	73 J8

LARGEST ISLANDS

	sq km	sq miles	map
New Guinea	808 510	312 167	73 J8
South Island, New Zealand	151 215	58 384	153 F11
North Island, New Zealand	115 777	44 702	152 J6
Tasmania	67 800	26 178	147 E5

LONGEST RIVERS

	km	miles	map
Murray-Darling	3 750	2 330	146 C3
Darling	2 739	1 702	146 D3
Murray	2 589	1 608	146 C3
Murrumbidgee	1 690	1 050	147 E3
Lachlan	1 480	919	147 D3
Macquarie	950	590	147 E2

LAKES

	sq km	sq miles	map
Lake Eyre	0-8 900	0-3 436	146 C2
Lake Torrens	0-5 780	0-2 232	146 C2

LAND AREA

		map
Most northerly point	Eastern Island, North Pacific Ocean	220 H4
Most southerly point	Macquarie Island, South Pacific Ocean	220 F9
Most westerly point	Cape Inscription, Australia	151 A5
Most easterly point	Île Clipperton, North Pacific Ocean	221 L5
Total land area: 8 844 516 sq km / 3 414 887 sq miles (includes New Guinea and Pacific island nations)		

OCEANIA

COUNTRIES

		area sq km	area sq miles	population	capital	languages	religions	currency	map
AUSTRALIA		7 682 395	2 966 189	19 138 000	Canberra	English, Italian, Greek	Protestant, Roman Catholic, Orthodox	Dollar	144–145
FIJI		18 330	7 077	814 000	Suva	English, Fijian, Hindi	Christian, Hindu, Sunni Muslim	Dollar	145
KIRIBATI		717	277	83 000	Bairiki	Gilbertese, English	Roman Catholic, Protestant	Australian dollar	145
MARSHALL ISLANDS		181	70	51 000	Delap-Uliga-Djarrit	English, Marshallese	Protestant, Roman Catholic	US dollar	220
MICRONESIA, FEDERATED STATES OF		701	271	123 000	Palikir	English, Chuukese, Pohnpeian, local languages	Roman Catholic, Protestant	US dollar	220
NAURU		21	8	12 000	Yaren	Nauruan, English	Protestant, Roman Catholic	Australian dollar	145
NEW ZEALAND		270 534	104 454	3 778 000	Wellington	English, Maori	Protestant, Roman Catholic	Dollar	152–153
PAPUA NEW GUINEA		462 840	178 704	4 809 000	Port Moresby	English, Tok Pisin (creole), local languages	Protestant, Roman Catholic, traditional beliefs	Kina	144–145
SAMOA		2 831	1 093	159 000	Apia	Samoan, English	Protestant, Roman Catholic	Tala	145
SOLOMON ISLANDS		28 370	10 954	447 000	Honiara	English, creole, local languages	Protestant, Roman Catholic	Dollar	145
TONGA		748	289	99 000	Nuku'alofa	Tongan, English	Protestant, Roman Catholic	Pa'anga	145
TUVALU		25	10	11 000	Vaiaku	Tuvaluan, English	Protestant	Dollar	145
VANUATU		12 190	4 707	197 000	Port Vila	English, Bislama (creole), French	Protestant, Roman Catholic, traditional beliefs	Vatu	145

DEPENDENT TERRITORIES

		territorial status	area sq km	area sq miles	population	capital	languages	religions	currency	map
American Samoa		United States Unincorporated Territory	197	76	68 000	Fagatoga	Samoan, English	Protestant, Roman Catholic	US dollar	145
Ashmore and Cartier Islands		Australian External Territory	5	2	uninhabited					150
Baker Island		United States Unincorporated Territory	1	0.4	uninhabited					145
Cook Islands		Self-governing New Zealand Territory	293	113	20 000	Avarua	English, Maori	Protestant, Roman Catholic	Dollar	221
Coral Sea Islands Territory		Australian External Territory	22	8	uninhabited					145
French Polynesia		French Overseas Territory	3 265	1 261	233 000	Papeete	French, Tahitian, Polynesian languages	Protestant, Roman Catholic	Pacific franc	221
Guam		United States Unincorporated Territory	541	209	155 000	Agana	Chamorro, English, Tapalog	Roman Catholic	US dollar	73
Howland Island		United States Unincorporated Territory	2	1	uninhabited					145
Jarvis Island		United States Unincorporated Territory	5	2	uninhabited					221
Johnston Atoll		United States Unincorporated Territory	3	1	uninhabited					221
Kingman Reef		United States Unincorporated Territory	1	0.4	uninhabited					221
Midway Islands		United States Unincorporated Territory	6	2	uninhabited					220
New Caledonia		French Overseas Territory	19 058	7 358	215 000	Nouméa	French, local	Roman Catholic, Protestant, Sunni Muslim	Pacific franc	145
Niue		Self-governing New Zealand Overseas Territory	258	100	2 000	Alofi	English, Polynesian	Christian	NZ dollar	145
Norfolk Island		Australian External Territory	35	14	2 000	Kingston	English	Protestant, Roman Catholic	Australian Dollar	145
Northern Mariana Islands		United States Commonwealth	477	184	73 000	Capitol Hill	English, Chamorro, local languages	Roman Catholic	US dollar	73
Palmyra Atoll		United States Unincorporated Territory	12	5	uninhabited					221
Pitcairn Islands		United Kingdom Overseas Territory	45	17	68	Adamstown	English	Protestant	NZ dollar	221
Tokelau		New Zealand Overseas Territory	10	4	1 000		English, Tokelauan	Christian	NZ dollar	145
Wake Island		United States Unincorporated Territory	7	3	uninhabited					220
Wallis and Futuna Islands		French Overseas Territory	274	106	14 000	Mata'utu	French, Wallisian, Futunian	Roman Catholic	Pacific franc	145

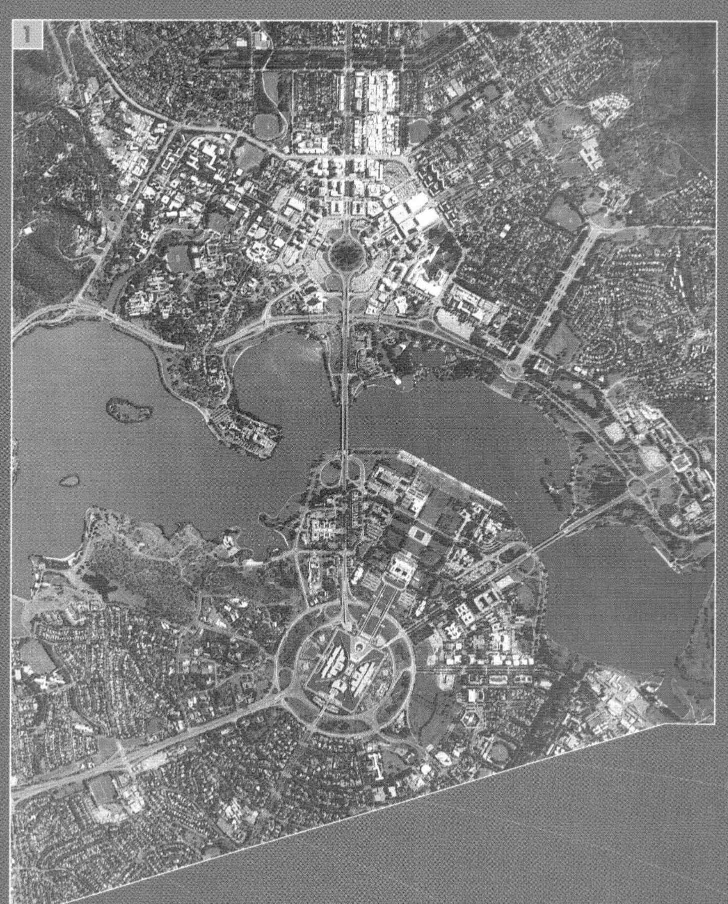

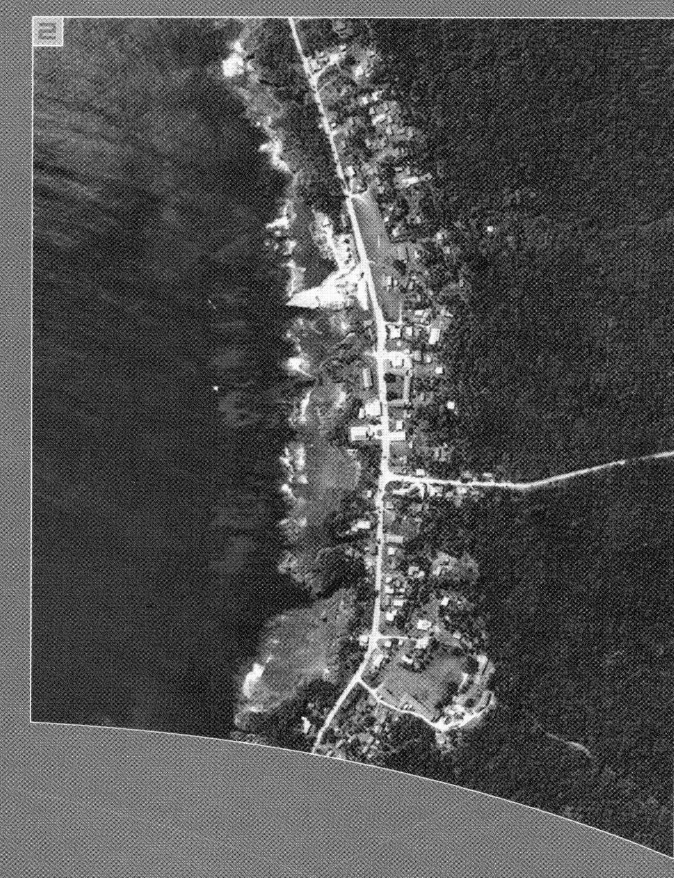

Equator

Timor Sea

Barrow I.

North West Cape

Tropic of Capricorn

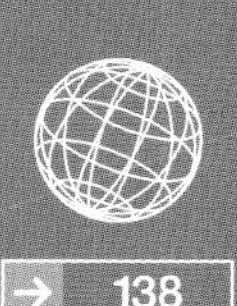

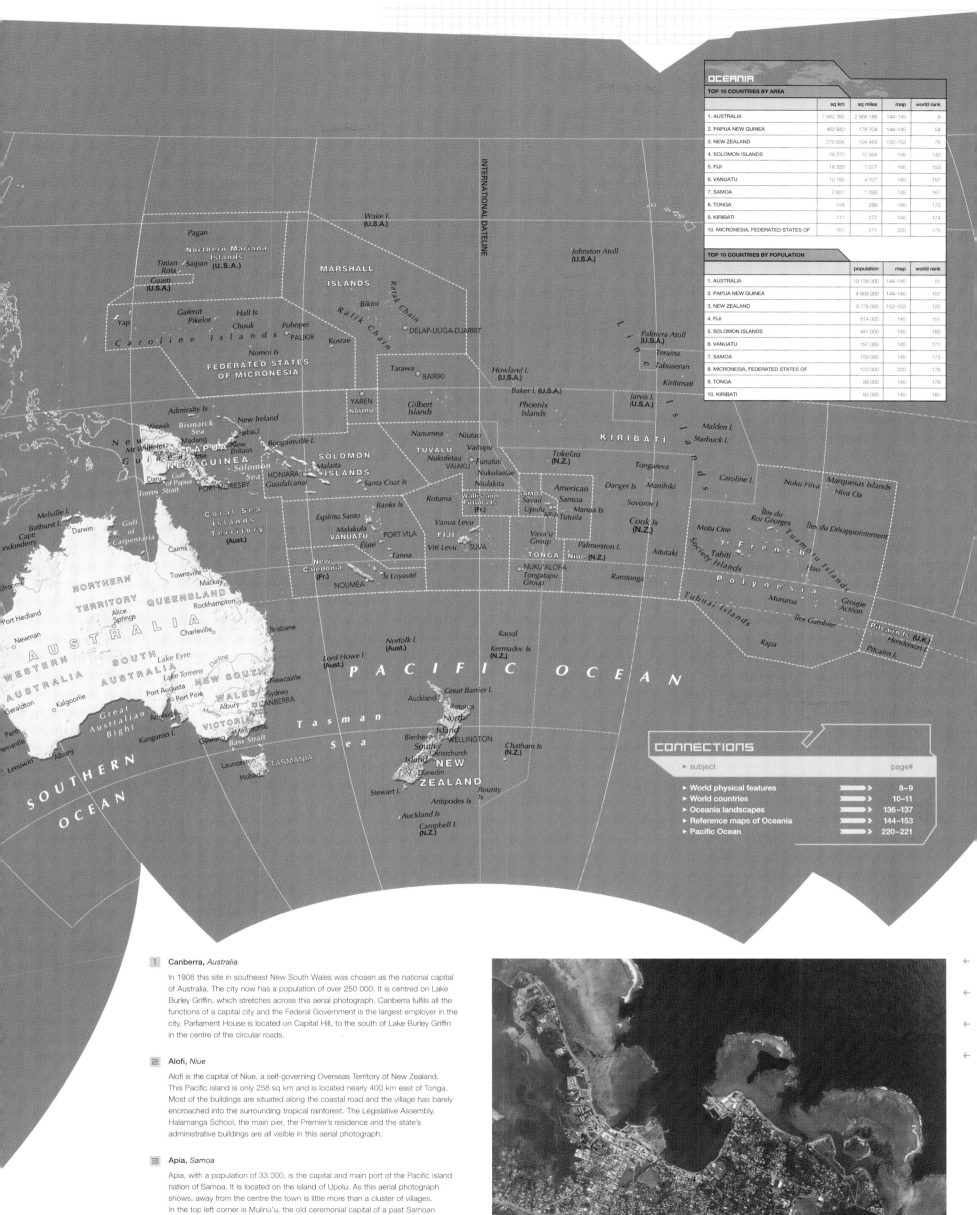

OCEANIA

TOP 10 COUNTRIES BY AREA

	sq km	sq miles	map	world rank
1. AUSTRALIA	7 682 395	2 966 189	144–145	6
2. PAPUA NEW GUINEA	462 840	178 704	144–145	54
3. NEW ZEALAND	270 534	104 454	152–153	75
4. SOLOMON ISLANDS	28 370	10 954	145	142
5. FIJI	18 330	7 077	145	153
6. VANUATU	12 190	4 707	145	157
7. SAMOA	2 831	1 093	145	167
8. TONGA	748	289	145	173
9. KIRIBATI	717	277	145	174
10. MICRONESIA, FEDERATED STATES OF	701	271	220	175

TOP 10 COUNTRIES BY POPULATION

	population	map	world rank
1. AUSTRALIA	19 138 000	144–145	51
2. PAPUA NEW GUINEA	4 809 000	144–145	107
3. NEW ZEALAND	3 778 000	152–153	120
4. FIJI	814 000	145	151
5. SOLOMON ISLANDS	447 000	145	160
6. VANUATU	197 000	145	171
7. SAMOA	159 000	145	173
8. MICRONESIA, FEDERATED STATES OF	123 000	220	176
9. TONGA	99 000	145	178
10. KIRIBATI	83 000	145	181

CONNECTIONS

▶ subject — page#

▶ World physical features — 8–9
▶ World countries — 10–11
▶ Oceania landscapes — 136–137
▶ Reference maps of Oceania — 144–153
▶ Pacific Ocean — 220–221

1 Canberra, *Australia*

In 1908 this site in southeast New South Wales was chosen as the national capital of Australia. The city now has a population of over 250 000. It is centred on Lake Burley Griffin, which stretches across this aerial photograph. Canberra fulfils all the functions of a capital city and the Federal Government is the largest employer in the city. Parliament House is located on Capital Hill, to the south of Lake Burley Griffin in the centre of the circular roads.

2 Alofi, *Niue*

Alofi is the capital of Niue, a self-governing Overseas Territory of New Zealand. This Pacific island is only 258 sq km and is located nearly 400 km east of Tonga. Most of the buildings are situated along the coastal road and the village has barely encroached into the surrounding tropical rainforest. The Legislative Assembly, Halamanga School, the main pier, the Premier's residence and the state's administrative buildings are all visible in this aerial photograph.

3 Apia, *Samoa*

Apia, with a population of 33 000, is the capital and main port of the Pacific island nation of Samoa. It is located on the island of Upolu. As this aerial photograph shows, away from the centre the town is little more than a cluster of villages. In the top left corner is Mulinu'u, the old ceremonial capital of a past Samoan government. In the centre, the Vasigano river flows into the harbour and then into the Pacific Ocean through the surrounding reef.

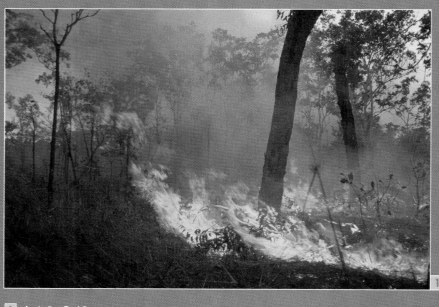

1 Australian Bushfires

Bushfires are an annual threat in the arid and savanna regions of Australia. Although fire can be of great benefit environmentally and ecologically, if it is not managed and controlled effectively it can have dramatic effects and can directly threaten settlements. In 1994 the suburbs of Sydney were affected by bushfires which destroyed 4 000 sq km of bush and grassland and in northern Australia over 300 000 sq km are affected each year. Satellite imagery, such as this image of a fire in northern Queensland, is an important tool in monitoring and managing bushfires. Imagery can be used to detect and map areas at risk, to map fire occurrences and to monitor post-fire recovery of the environment.

Satellite/Sensor : Apollo 7

CONNECTIONS

► subject	page#
► World land cover types	18–19
► World climate and weather	16–17
► Oceania landscapes	136–137
► Oceania features	142–143
► Pacific Ocean	220–221

Fig. #01
Australia salinity hazard

Cropland or pasture
Cropland

Irrigated areas

◯ >100 000ha

◯ 50 000 - 100 000ha

◦ 20 000 - 50 000ha

· 10 000 - 20 000ha

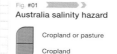

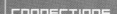

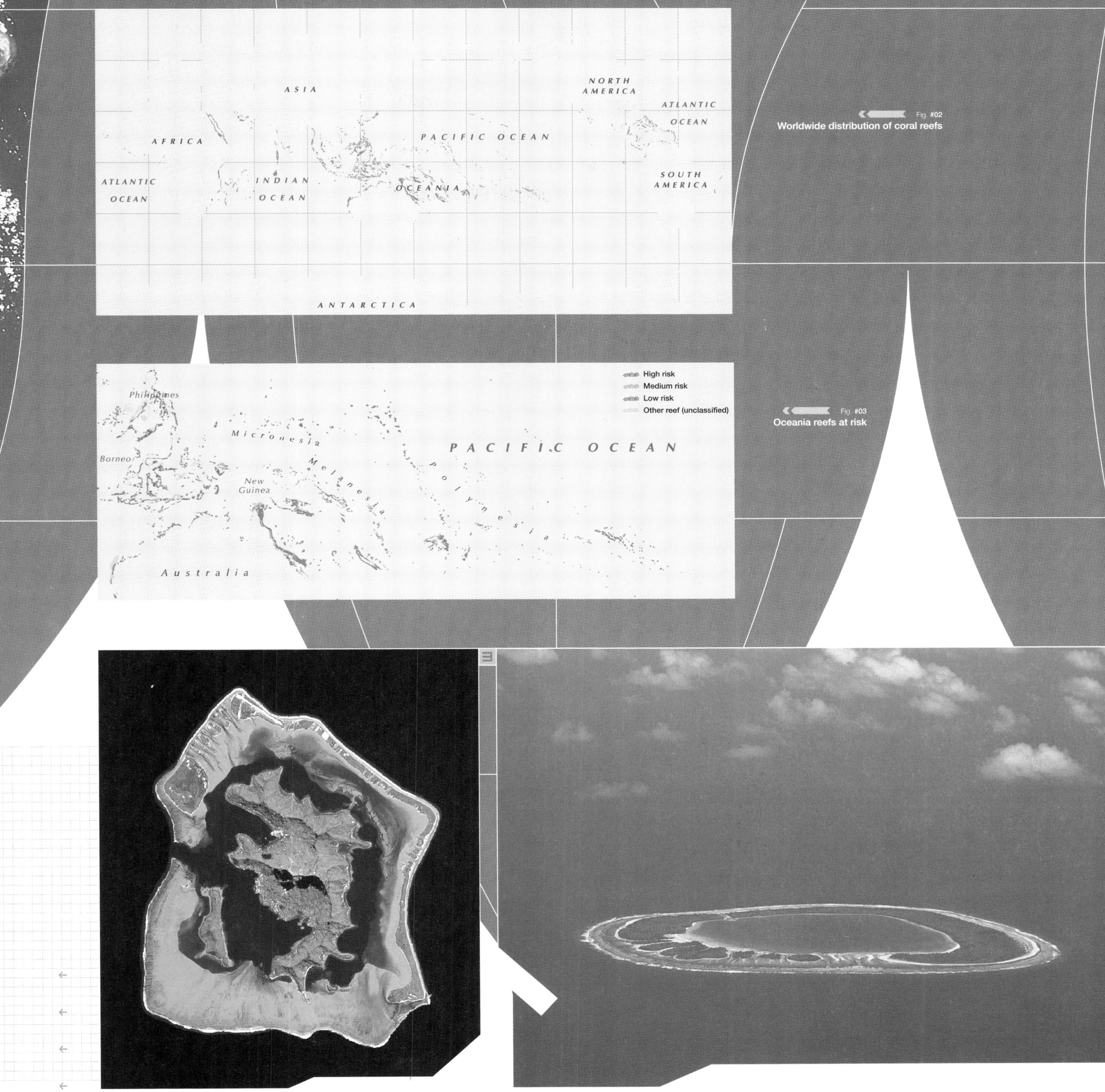

<← Fig. #02
Worldwide distribution of coral reefs

High risk
Medium risk
Low risk
Other reef (unclassified)

<← Fig. #03
Oceania reefs at risk

⊟ Salinity

Australia is a dry continent. Over millions of years, salt carried onshore from the sea by winds and deposited by rain has accumulated in the soils. This salt becomes a problem when native vegetation is cleared, allowing excess water to percolate through the soil. This raises groundwater levels, bringing the salt to the surface and leaching salt into streams and rivers. Irrigation schemes add more water, making the problem worse. Salt kills crops and pastureland, damages roads and buildings, impairs water quality for both irrigation and human consumption and reduces biodiversity. The photograph shows an area badly affected by salinity near Kellerberrin, Western Australia. Approximately 5.7 million hectares of Australia's farmland is currently affected by salinity and it is predicted that, unless effective solutions are implemented, 17 million hectares of land and 20 000 km of streams could be salinized by 2050. The map shows areas where salt stored in the landscape is being mobilised by surplus water, creating the risk of salinity.

☰ Coral Reefs

Although coral reefs make up only less than a quarter of 1 per cent of the Earth's marine environment, they are vitally important habitats, being home to over 25 per cent of all known marine fish species. They are also important sources of food and tourist income, and they provide physical protection for vulnerable coastlines. Reefs are widely distributed around the world (Fig. #02) with major concentrations in the Caribbean Sea, the Indian Ocean, southeast Asia and the Pacific Ocean.

Reefs are fragile environments, and many are under threat from coastal development, pollution and overexploitation of marine resources. The degree of risk varies, with the reefs of southeast Asia under the greatest threat. Over 25 per cent of the world's reefs are judged to be at high risk. In the Pacific Ocean over 40 per cent of reefs are at risk (Fig. #03). The beauty and fragility of these environments are suggested in the images above. The aerial photograph (right) shows the coral island of Mataiva and the SPOT satellite image (left) shows the island and reefs of Bora-Bora. Both are in the Pacific territory of French Polynesia.

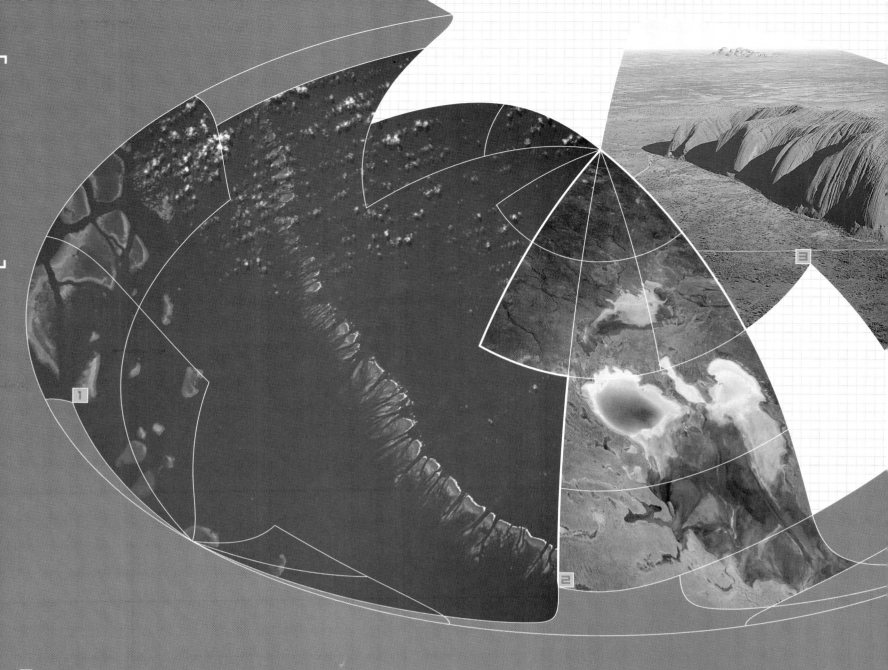

1 Great Barrier Reef, *Queensland, Australia*

This Shuttle photograph of the northern end of the Great Barrier Reef shows two separate reef zones. The line of unbroken coral reefs, at the bottom right of the image contrasts to the randomly spaced reefs in the shallow waters off the coast of the Cape York Peninsula, at the left hand edge. The image captures only a tiny fraction of the whole reef which extends over 2 000 km along the northeast coast of Queensland.

Satellite/Sensor : Space Shuttle

2 Lake Eyre, *South Australia, Australia*

Lake Eyre, situated in one of the driest regions in South Australia, is the largest salt lake in Australia. The lake actually comprises two lakes, Lake Eyre North and the much smaller Lake Eyre South. Salt has been washed into the lake from underlying marine sediments and when dry, which is its usual state, the lake bed is a glistening sheet of white salt. In this photograph, the lake, viewed from the north, is in the process of drying out after being at a higher level.

Satellite/Sensor : Space Shuttle

3 Uluru (Ayers Rock), *Northern Territory, Australia*

Uluru (Ayers Rock), is a large single rock outcrop which rises 350 m above the vast plain of central Australia. This aerial photograph, looking west, shows how the steep, almost vertical walls of the rock rise from the flat surrounding land. The rock is composed of a collection of vertically bedded strata. In the far distance of the photograph, a similar rock formation, the Olgas, can be seen.

4 Banks Peninsula, *New Zealand*

The only recognizable volcanic feature on South Island, New Zealand is Banks Peninsula. It has been extensively eroded over the years yet it still possess the circular shape and radial drainage pattern typical of many volcanoes. The peninsula has been formed by two overlapping volcanic centres which are separated by a large harbour, Akaroa Harbour. In this aerial photograph, the peninsula is viewed from the east and at the top the Canterbury Plains are just visible.

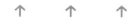

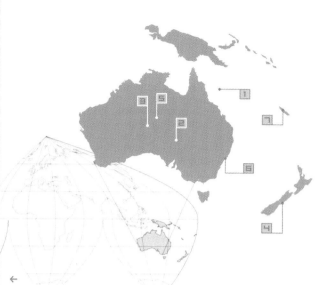

5 **Palm Valley,** *Northern Territory, Australia*

The dark brown and blue area of this radar image, is a broad valley located in the arid landscape of central Australia, approximately 50 km south west of Alice Springs. Palm Valley, the oval shaped feature at the top left of the image, contains many rare species of palms. The mountains of the Macdonnell Ranges are seen as curving bands of folded sedimentary outcrops. In the top right of the image, the river Finke cuts across the mountain ridge and continues in a deep canyon to the lower centre of the image.

Satellite/Sensor : Space Shuttle/SIR-C/X-SAR

6 **Sydney,** *Australia*

Sydney, the largest city in Australia and capital of New South Wales state, has one of the world's finest natural harbours. It is Australia's chief port, and its main cultural and industrial centre. This satellite image of the city, in which north is at the bottom, was captured by the IKONOS satellite in late 1999. The image highlights the renowned Sydney Opera house, located on Bennelong Point. Also clearly visible are the Royal Botanical Gardens and west of these the main urban area of the city centre.

Satellite/Sensor : IKONOS

7 **New Caledonia and Vanuatu,** *Pacific Ocean*

The long narrow island of New Caledonia lies in the southern Pacific Ocean approximately 1 500 km east of Queensland, Australia. The territory comprises one large island and several smaller ones. This SeaWiFS satellite image clearly shows the extensive reef formations which extend far out into the ocean. The island has a landscape of rugged mountains with little flat land. Almost obscured by clouds, at the top right of this image, is a group of islands which collectively make up the small republic of Vanuatu.

Satellite/Sensor : OrbView2/SeaWiFS

CONNECTIONS

► subject	page#
► Uluru (Ayers Rock)	18–19
► Oceania landscapes	136–137
► Oceania countries	138–139
► Coral reefs	140–141
► Southwest Pacific Ocean	144–145
► Pacific Ocean	220–221

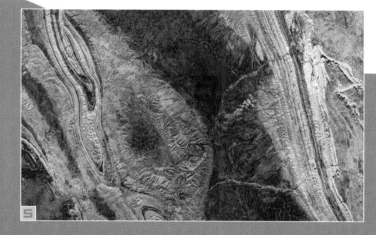

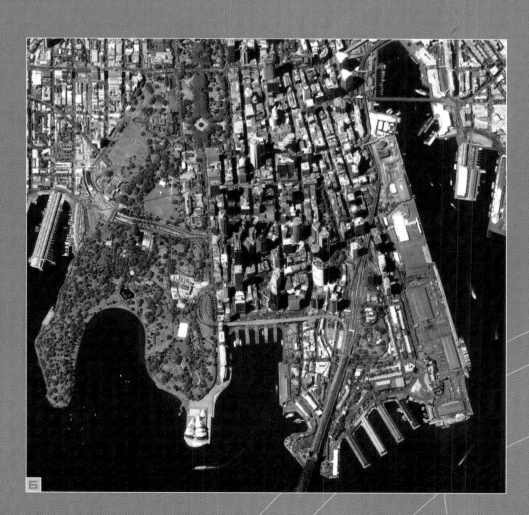

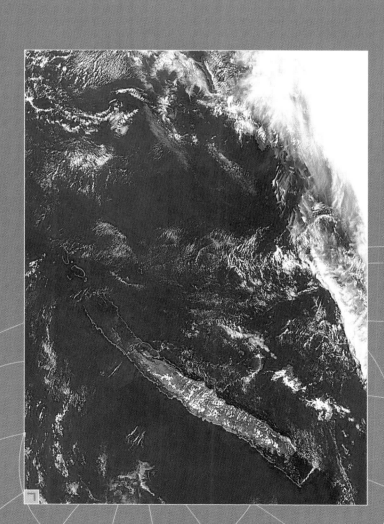

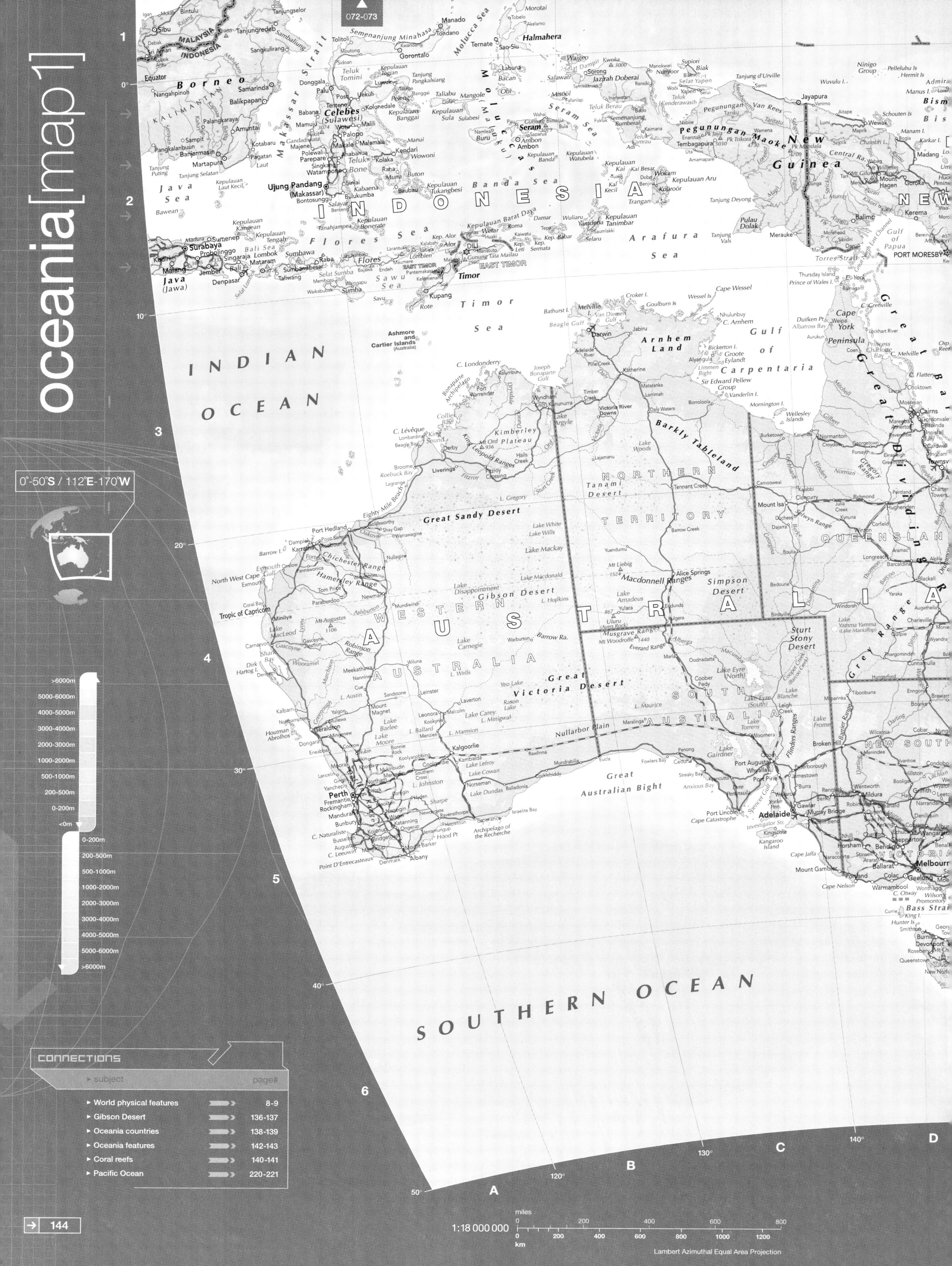

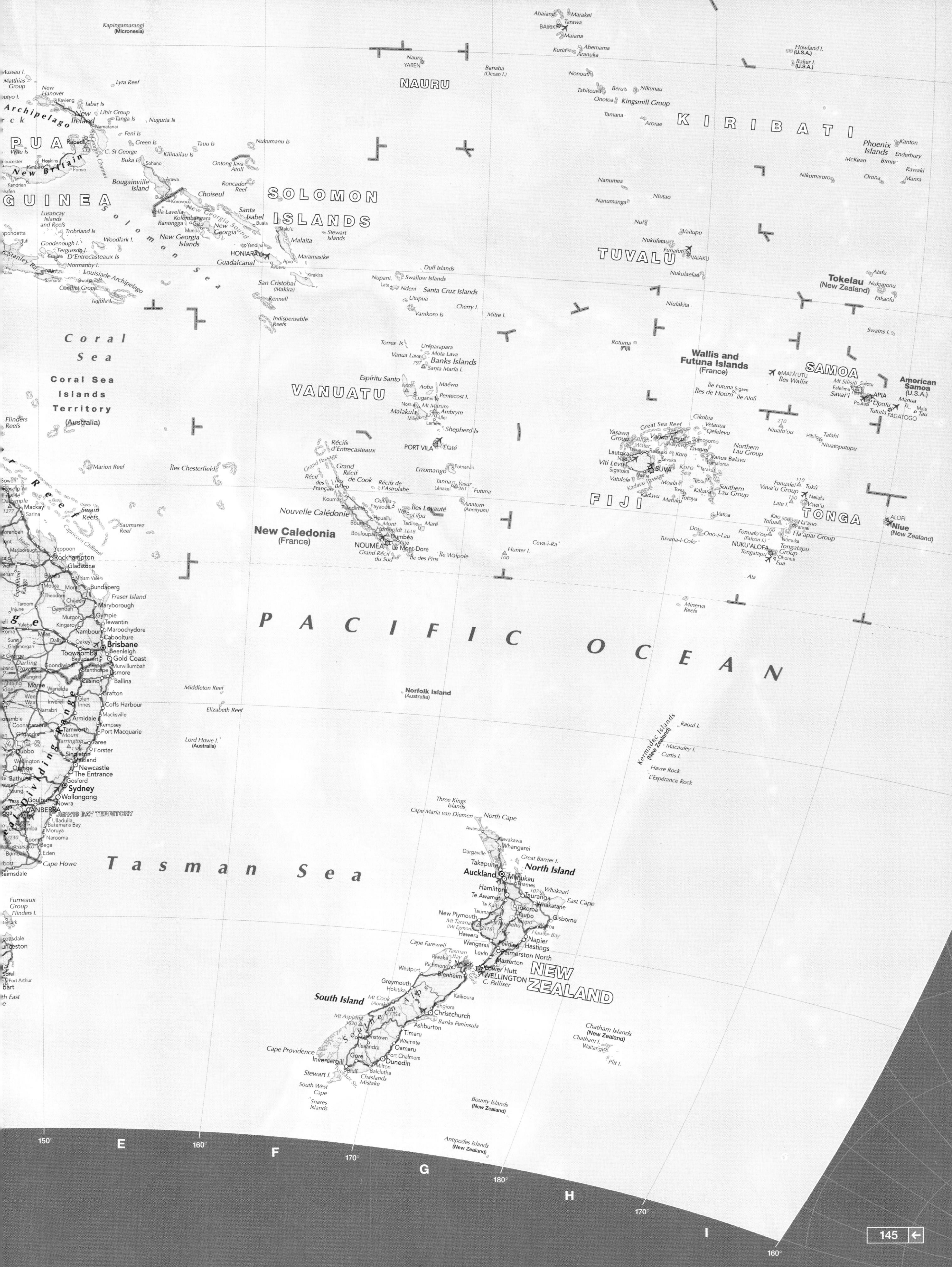

Kapingamarangi (Micronesia)
Abaiang
Marakei
Tarawa
BAIRIKI
Maiana
Abemama
Kuria
Aranuka
Howland I. (U.S.A.)
Baker I. (U.S.A.)
Nauru
YAREN
NAURU
Banaba (Ocean I.)
Nonouti
Tabiteuea
Beru
Nikunau
Onotoa
Kingsmill Group
Tamana
Arorae
KIRIBATI
Phoenix Islands
Kanton
Enderbury
McKean
Birnie
Rawaki
Nikumaroro
Orona
Manra
Mussau I.
Matthias Group
New Hanover
Kavieng
Lyra Reef
Tabar Is
Lihir Group
Tanga Is
Archipelago
New Ireland
Namatanai
Nuguria Is
Feni Is
Green Is
PUA
Rabaul
C. St George
Buka I.
Tauu Is
Nukumanu Is
Kilinailau Is
New Britain
Sohano
Ontong Java Atoll
Bougainville Island
Roncador Reef
Arawa
SOLOMON ISLANDS
GUINEA
Choiseul
Solomon Sea
Lusancay Islands and Reefs
Vella Lavella
Kolombangara
Ranongga
New Georgia Sound
Santa Isabel
Buala
Trobriand Is
Munda
New Georgia
New Georgia Islands
Malu'u
Malaita
Stewart Islands
Woodlark I.
Goodenough I.
Fergusson I.
D'Entrecasteaux Is
HONIARA
Guadalcanal
Maramasike
Auki
Apio
Normanby I.
Alotau
Louisiade Archipelago
Samarai
Conflict Group
Tagula I.
Kirakira
San Cristobal (Makira)
Rennell
Duff Islands
Nupani
Swallow Islands
Lata
Nendeni
Santa Cruz Islands
Utupua
Vanikoro Is
Cherry I.
Mitre I.
Indispensable Reefs
Coral Sea
Coral Sea Islands Territory (Australia)
Flinders Reefs
Nanumea
Nanumanga
Niutao
Nui
Vaitupu
Nukufetau
Funafuti
VAIAKU
TUVALU
Nukulaelae
Niulakita
Tokelau (New Zealand)
Atafu
Nukunonu
Fakaofo
Swains I.
Rotuma (Fiji)
Torres Is
Uréparapara
Vanua Lava
Mota Lava
Banks Islands
Santa María I.
Espíritu Santo
VANUATU
Maéwo
Aoba
Pentecost I.
Luganville
Malakula
Mt Marum
Ambrym
Lamen
Shepherd Is
PORT VILA
Éfaté
Récifs d'Entrecasteaux
Grand Passage
Grand Récif de Cook
Récif des Français
Îles Bélep
Récifs de l'Astrolabe
Erromango
Potnarvin
Tanna
Yasur
Lénakel
Futuna
Anatom (Aneityum)
Nouvelle Calédonie
Koumac
Ouvéa
Fayaoué
Poindimié
Îles Loyauté
Wé
Lifou
Houailu
Mont
Tadine
Maré
Bourail
Humboldt
New Caledonia (France)
Bouloupari
NOUMÉA
Dumbéa
Le Mont-Dore
Grand Récif du Sud
Île des Pins
Île Walpole
Hunter I.
Ceva-i-Ra
Wallis and Futuna Islands (France)
MATĀ'UTU
Îles Wallis
Île Futuna
Sigave
Îles de Hoorn
Île Alofi
SAMOA
Mt Silisili
Safotu
Falelima
Savai'i
APIA
Upolu
Poutasi
American Samoa (U.S.A.)
Manua Is.
Maia
Tau
Tutuila
FAGATOGO
Niuafo'ou
Hihifo
Tafahi
Niuatoputapu
Cikobia
Great Sea Reef
Vetauua
Qelelevu
Yasawa Group
Vanua Levu
Somosomo
Taveuni
Northern Lau Group
Lautoka
Nadi
Viti Levu
Rakiraki
Levuka
Koro
Koro Sea
Vanua Balavu
Sigatoka
Vatulele
SUVA
Kadavu Passage
Tubou
Moala
Totoya
Matuku
Kabara
Southern Lau Group
Kadavu
FIJI
Vatoa
Fonualei
Tokū
Vava'u Group
Neiafu
Vava'u
Late I.
Kao
Tofua
Ha'ano
Pangai
Ha'apai Group
Nomuka
TONGA
ALOFI
Niue (New Zealand)
Ono-i-Lau
Doi
Fonuafo'ou (Falcon I.)
Tuvana-i-Colo
NUKU'ALOFA
Tongatapu
Tongatapu Group
'Ohonua
'Eua
Ata
Minerva Reefs
Bowen
Proserpine
Whitsunday
Mackay
Sarina
Swain Reefs
Saumarez Reef
Marion Reef
Îles Chesterfield
Capricorn Channel
Yeppoon
Rockhampton
Gladstone
Bundaberg
Fraser Island
Maryborough
Gympie
Tewantin
Maroochydore
Caboolture
Brisbane
Beenleigh
Gold Coast
Toowoomba
Murwillumbah
Lismore
Ballina
Casino
Grafton
Coffs Harbour
Glen Innes
Inverell
Narrabri
Armidale
Macksville
Kempsey
Port Macquarie
Tamworth
Taree
Forster
Singleton
Maitland
Newcastle
The Entrance
Gosford
Sydney
Wollongong
Nowra
Goulburn
CANBERRA
JERVIS BAY TERRITORY
Ulladulla
Batemans Bay
Moruya
Narooma
Bega
Eden
Cape Howe
Dubbo
Orange
Bathurst
Great Dividing Range
Middleton Reef
Elizabeth Reef
Lord Howe I. (Australia)
Norfolk Island (Australia)
PACIFIC OCEAN
Kermadec Islands (New Zealand)
Raoul I.
Macauley I.
Curtis I.
Havre Rock
L'Espérance Rock
Three Kings Islands
Cape Maria van Diemen
North Cape
Kawakawa
Whangarei
Dargaville
Great Barrier I.
Takapuna
Auckland
Manukau
North Island
Thames
Hamilton
Te Awamutu
Tauranga
Whakaari
Whakatane
East Cape
Rotorua
Taupo
New Plymouth
Mt Taranaki (Mt Egmont)
Gisborne
Hawera
Wanganui
Hawke Bay
Napier
Hastings
Feilding
Palmerston North
Levin
Masterton
Cape Farewell
Tasman Bay
Westport
Nelson
Blenheim
Lower Hutt
WELLINGTON
C. Palliser
NEW ZEALAND
Greymouth
Hokitika
Kaikoura
South Island
Mt Cook (Aoraki)
Southern Alps
Rangiora
Christchurch
Banks Peninsula
Mt Aspiring
Ashburton
Timaru
Waimate
Oamaru
Queenstown
Alexandra
Port Chalmers
Dunedin
Cape Providence
Invercargill
Gore
Milton
Balclutha
Bluff
Chaslands Mistake
Stewart I.
Foveaux Str.
South West Cape
Snares Islands
Tasman Sea
Chatham Islands (New Zealand)
Chatham I.
Waitangi
Pitt I.
Bounty Islands (New Zealand)
Antipodes Islands (New Zealand)
Furneaux Group
Flinders I.
Launceston
Port Arthur
150°
160°
170°
180°
170°
160°
E
F
G
H
I

oceania[map2]

28°-44°S / 128°-158°E

148-149

150-151

Anangu Pitjantjatjara Aboriginal Lands

Everard Range

Great Victoria Desert Conservation Park

WESTERN AUSTRALIA

Great Victoria Desert

Great Victoria Desert Nature Reserve

Maralinga-Tjarutja Aboriginal Lands

Woomera Prohibited Area

Tallaringa Conservation Park

SOUTH AUSTRALIA

Nullarbor Plain

Nullarbor Regional Reserve

Nullarbor National Park

Yellabina Regional Reserve

Simpson Desert Regional Reserve

Witjira National Park

Sturt Stony Desert

Innamincka Regional Reserve

Lake Eyre (North)

Lake Eyre National Park

Lake Eyre (South)

Strzelecki Regional Reserve

Lake Torrens

Lake Torrens National Park

Lake Gairdner

Lake Gairdner National Park

Flinders Ranges

Flinders Ranges National Park

Gawler Ranges

Great Australian Bight

Eyre Peninsula

Spencer Gulf

Yorke Peninsula

Gulf St Vincent

Adelaide

Port Augusta

Port Pirie

Port Lincoln

Whyalla

Ceduna

Coober Pedy

Broken Hill

Kangaroo Island

Investigator Strait

Lake Alexandrina

Coorong National Park

Mount Gambier

Portland

SOUTHERN OCEAN

1

2

3

4

5

A

B

C

28°

32°

36°

40°

44°

128°

132°

136°

140°

>6000m

5000-6000m

4000-5000m

3000-4000m

2000-3000m

1000-2000m

500-1000m

200-500m

0-200m

<0m

0-200m

200-500m

500-1000m

1000-2000m

2000-3000m

3000-4000m

4000-5000m

5000-6000m

>6000m

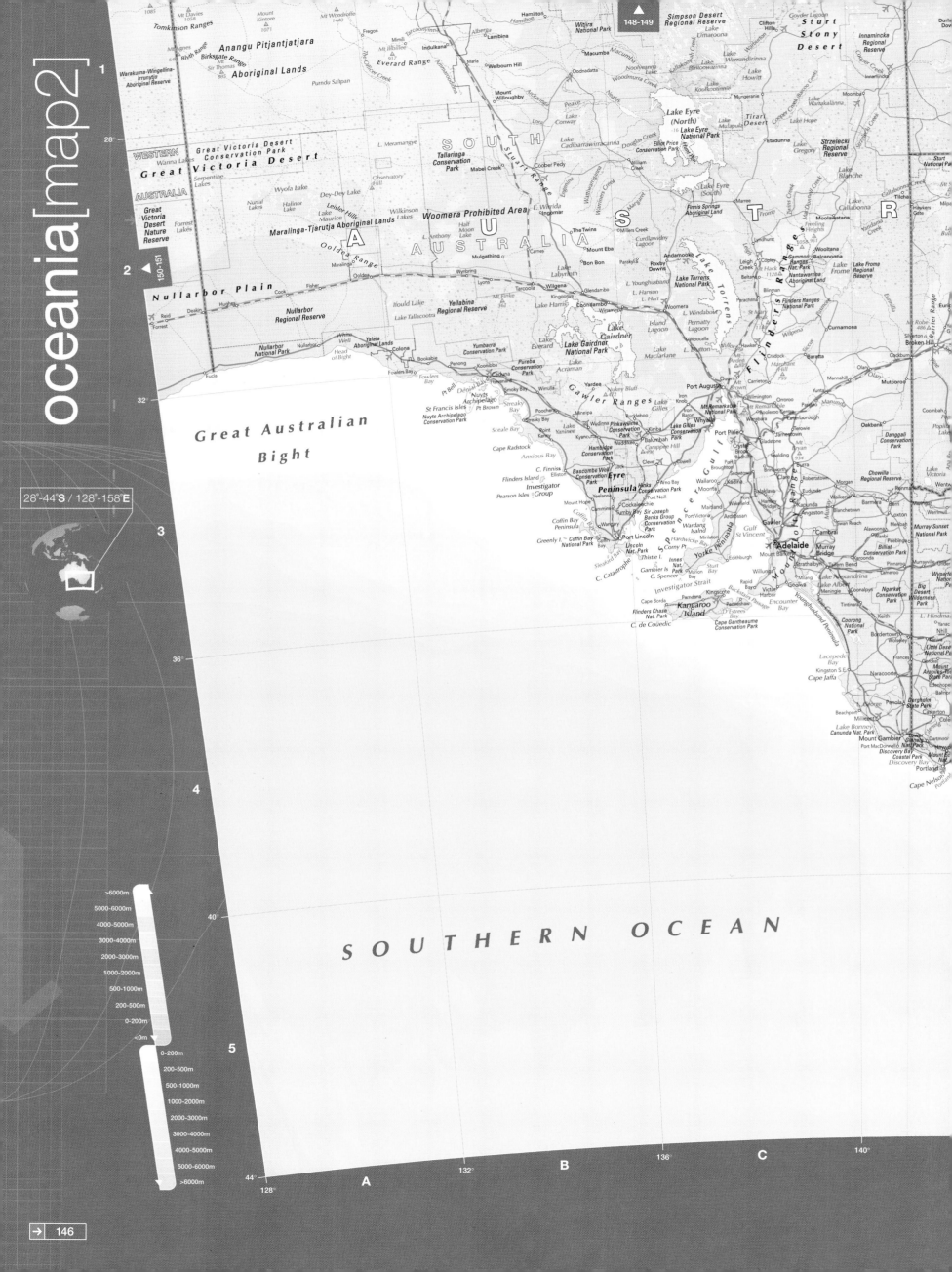

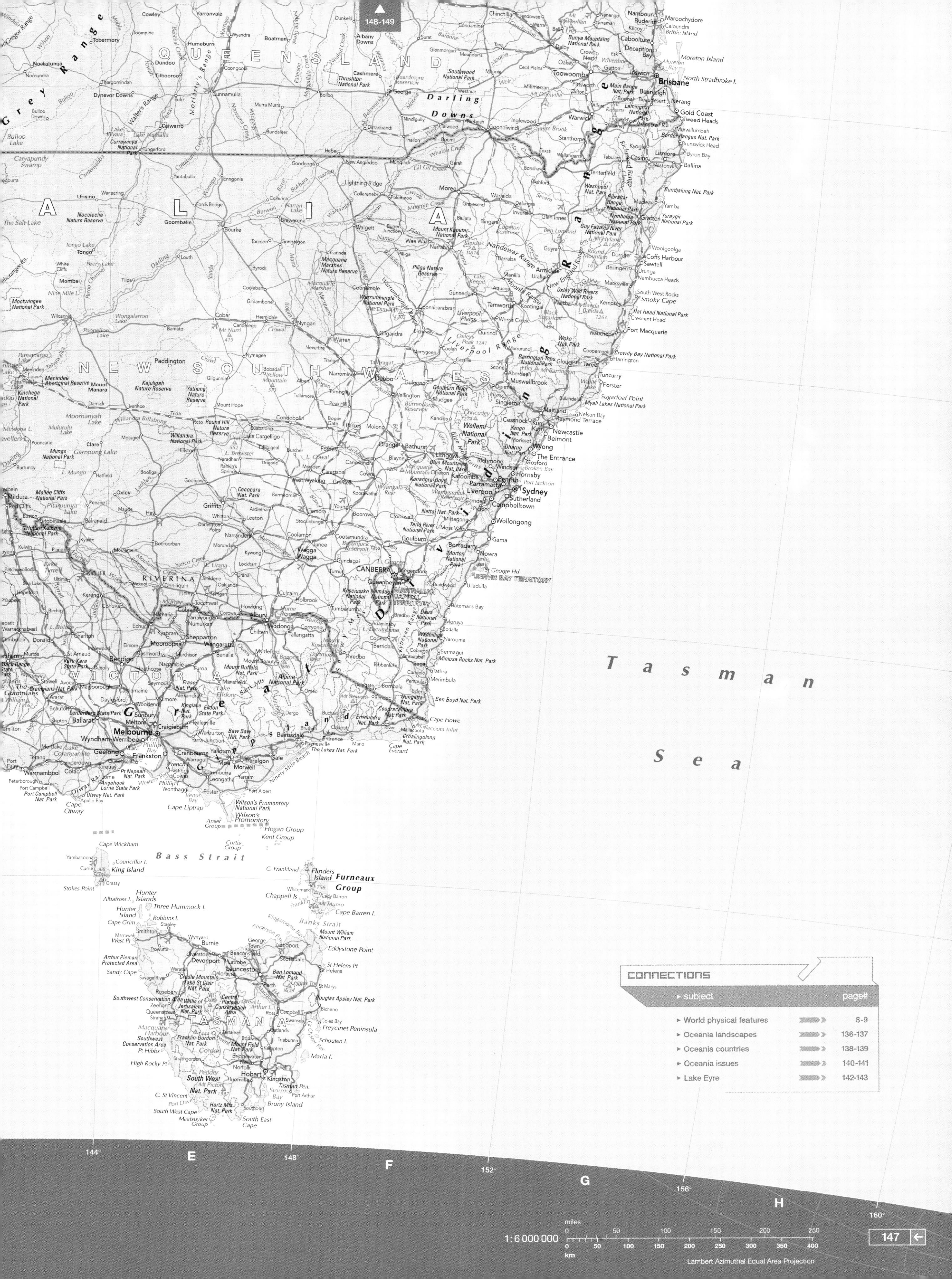

CONNECTIONS

1 : 6 000 000

Lambert Azimuthal Equal Area Projection

11°-28°S / 128°-154°E

150-151

146-147

Elevation scale:
>6000m
5000-6000m
4000-5000m
3000-4000m
2000-3000m
1000-2000m
500-1000m
200-500m
0-200m
<0m

0-200m
200-500m
500-1000m
1000-2000m
2000-3000m
3000-4000m
4000-5000m
5000-6000m
>6000m

1:6 000 000

miles
0 50 100 150 200 250

km
0 50 100 150 200 250 300 350 400

Lambert Azimuthal Equal Area Projection

Grid references: 1, 2, 3, 4, 5 (rows); A, B, C (columns)
Latitude: 12°, 16°, 20°, 24°, 28°
Longitude: 128°, 132°, 136°

Timor Sea

Gulf of Carpentaria

Selected labels:

Bathurst Island, Melville Island, Van Diemen Gulf, Beagle Gulf, Darwin, Palmerston, Cobourg Pen., Croker I., C. Croker, C. Van Diemen, Tiwi Aboriginal Land, Dundas Strait, Clarence Strait, Goulburn Islands, Elcho I., Cape Wessel, Wessel Islands, The English Company's Is, Cape Wilberforce, Nhulunbuy, Gove Pen., Cape Arnhem, Port Bradshaw, Caledon Bay, C. Grey, C. Shield, Blue Mud Bay, Groote Eylandt, Groote Eylandt Aboriginal Land, C. Beatrice, Numbulwar, Edward I., Port Roper, Limmen Bight, Sir Edward Pellew Group, Vanderlin I., Wellesley Islands Aboriginal Reserve, Mornington I.

Arnhem Land, Arnhem Land Aboriginal Land, Kakadu National Park, Kakadu Aboriginal Land, Jabiru, Bulman Gorge, Bulman, Mainoru, Roper Bar, Roper Bar Aboriginal Land, Mataranka, Larrimah, Daly Waters, Dunmarra, Newcastle Creek, Beetaloo, Elliot, Renner Springs, Banka Banka, Tennant Creek, Helen Springs, Brunette Downs, Barkly Tableland, Connells Lagoon Conservation Reserve, Lawn Hill National Park, Corella Lake, Lake Sylvester, Soudan, Camooweal, Camooweal Caves National Park, Mount Isa, Lake Nash, Lake Julius

Timor Sea, Joseph Bonaparte Gulf, Hyland Bay, Wadeye, Pearce Pt, Port Keats Aboriginal Land, Daly River, Port Keats Aboriginal Land, Pine Creek, Katherine, Flora, Kathleen Falls, Gregory National Park, Victoria River, Timber Creek, Victoria River Downs, Wyndham, Kununurra, Lake Argyle, Ord River Dam, Purnululu National Park, Kalkarindji, Daguragu Aboriginal Land, Lajamanu, Hooker Creek Aboriginal Land, Balgo Aboriginal Reserve, Lake White, Lake Mackay, Lake Mackay Aboriginal Land, Central Australia Aboriginal Reserve, Lake Hazlett, Lake Wills, Lake Dennis, Tanami Downs Aboriginal Land, Western Desert Aboriginal Land

NORTHERN TERRITORY, Tanami Desert, Central Desert Aboriginal Land, Karlantijpa North Aboriginal Land, Karlantijpa South Aboriginal Land, Warumungu Aboriginal Land, Anurrete Aboriginal Land, Davenport Ranges, Murray Downs, Hatches Creek, Barrow Creek, Stirling, Ti Tree, Woola Downs, Aileron, Napperby, Yuendumu, Yuendumu Aboriginal Land, Mount Denison, Mount Gardiner, Reynolds Range, Hann Range, Harts Range, Jervois Range, Atnetye Aboriginal Land, Marshall, Lucy Creek, Tobermorey, Argadargada, Austral Downs, Urandangi, Dajarra

AUSTRALIA, Lake Mackay, Lake Macdonald, Kintore, Mt Leisler, Haasts Bluff Aboriginal Land, Papunya, Mt Zeil 1510, Mt Liebig, Ehrenberg Ra., MacDonnell Ranges, West MacDonnell Nat. Park, Alice Springs, Hermannsburg, James Ranges, Finke Gorge Nat. Park, Watarrka Nat. Park, Kings Canyon, Lake Amadeus, Petermann Aboriginal Land, Katiti Aboriginal Land, Mt Olga, Uluru (Ayers Rock), Yulara, Uluru National Park, Mt Conner, Tropic of Capricorn

Petermann Ranges, Olia Chain, Musgrave Ranges, Mann Ranges, Tomkinson Ranges, Mt Woodroffe, Anangu Pitjantjatjara Aboriginal Lands, Everard Range, Central Australia Aboriginal Reserve, Warakurna-Wingellina-Irrunytju Aboriginal Reserve, Giles Meteorological Station, Bloods Range, Lake Neale, Lake Hopkins, Lake Anec

SOUTH AUSTRALIA, Kulgera, Victory Downs, Mulga Park, Black Hill Range, Finke Aboriginal Land, Umbeara, Finke, Horseshoe Bend, Eridunda, Maryvale, Santa Teresa, Titjikala, Atitjere, Simpson Desert, Simpson Desert Regional Reserve, Simpson Desert Conservation Park, Witjira National Park, Oodnadatta, Marryat, Indulkana, Welbourn Hill, Coober Pedy

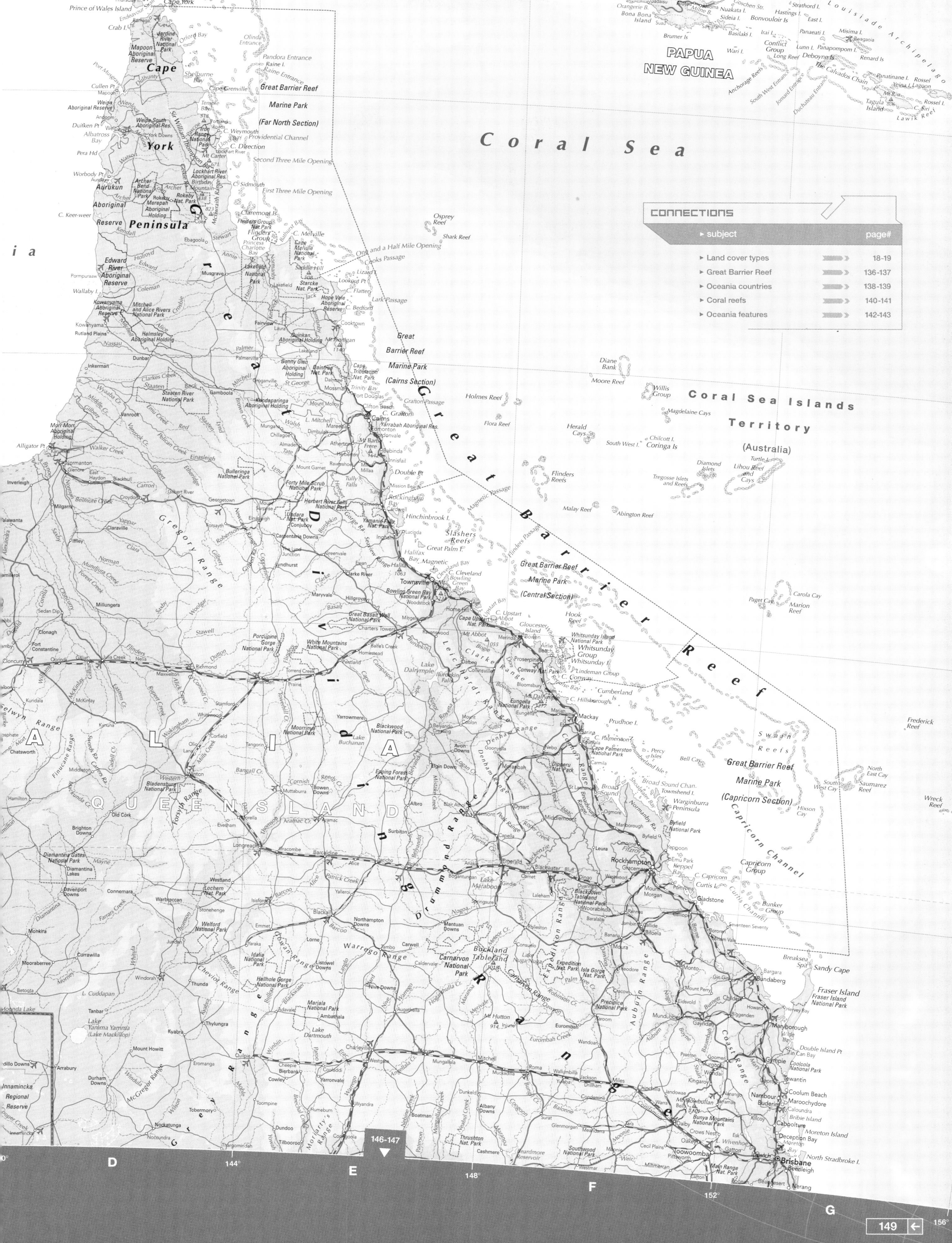

CONNECTIONS
subject
page#
Land cover types 18-19
Great Barrier Reef 136-137
Oceania countries 138-139
Coral reefs 140-141
Oceania features 142-143
Coral Sea
Coral Sea Islands Territory (Australia)
PAPUA NEW GUINEA
Louisiade Archipelago
Great Barrier Reef Marine Park (Far North Section)
Great Barrier Reef Marine Park (Cairns Section)
Great Barrier Reef Marine Park (Central Section)
Great Barrier Reef Marine Park (Capricorn Section)
Great Barrier Reef
Great Dividing Range
Cape York Peninsula
QUEENSLAND
Gregory Range
Grey Range
Warrego Range
Carnarvon National Park
Capricorn Channel
Swain Reefs
Whitsunday Group
Fraser Island
Cape York
Thursday I.
Prince of Wales Island
Weipa
Cooktown
Cairns
Townsville
Charters Towers
Mackay
Rockhampton
Gladstone
Bundaberg
Maryborough
Gympie
Nambour
Toowoomba
Brisbane
Emerald
Longreach
Barcaldine
Charleville
Roma
Hughenden
Winton
Cloncurry
Normanton
Karumba
Quilpie
Dalby
Kingaroy
Caboolture
Redcliffe
Beaudesert
Diane Bank
Moore Reef
Willis Group
Holmes Reef
Flora Reef
Herald Cays
Coringa Is
Lihou Reef and Cays
Flinders Reefs
Osprey Reef
Shark Reef
Marion Reef
Frederick Reef
Saumarez Reef
Wreck Reef
Hinchinbrook I.
Bowling Green Bay
Moreton Island
North Stradbroke I.
Sandy Cape
146-147
144°
148°
152°
156°
D
E
F
G

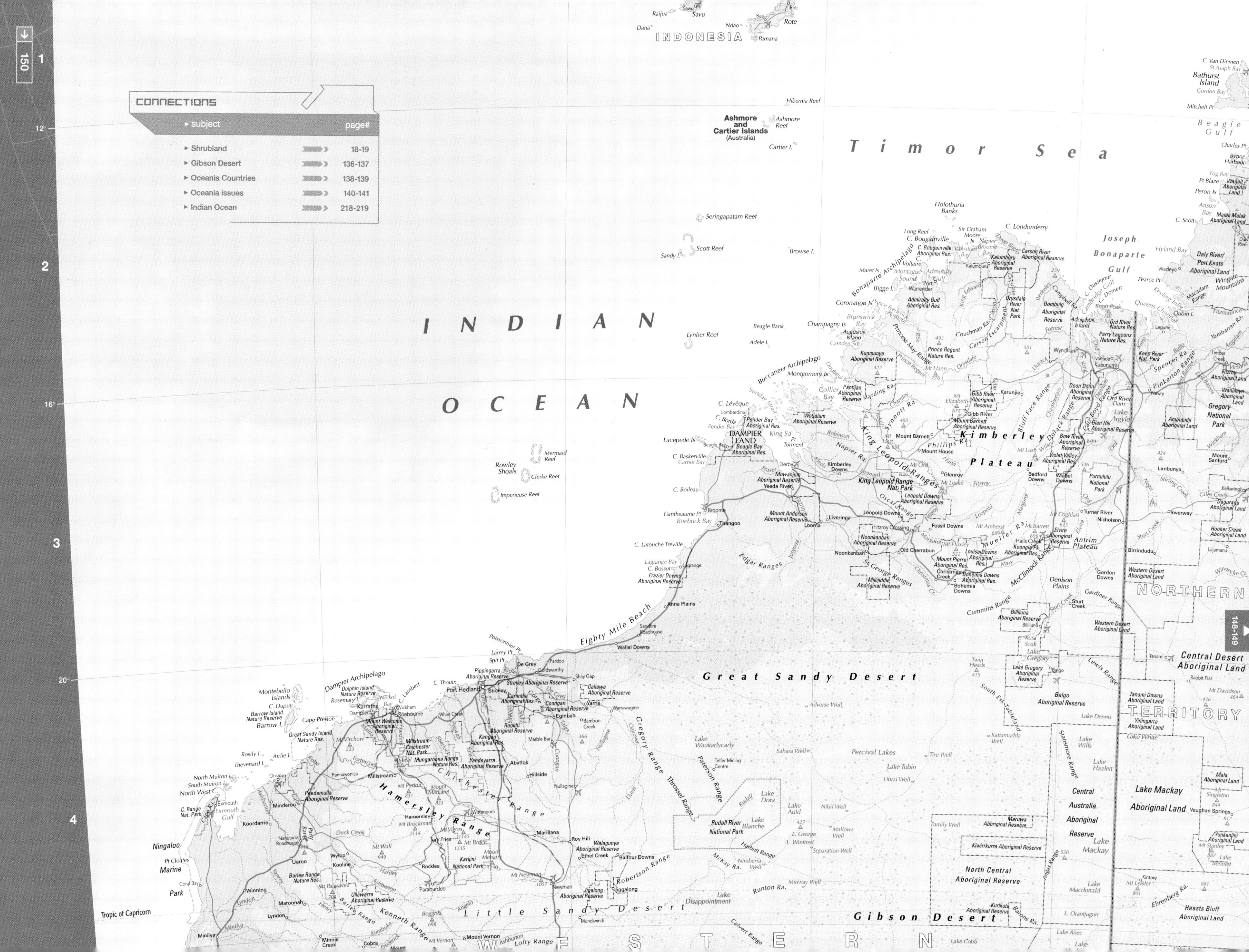
CONNECTIONS
subject page#
Shrubland 18-19
Gibson Desert 136-137
Oceania Countries 138-139
Oceania issues 140-141
Indian Ocean 218-219
INDIAN OCEAN
Timor Sea
INDONESIA
Ashmore and Cartier Islands (Australia)
Joseph Bonaparte Gulf
Beagle Gulf
Bathurst Island
Rowley Shoals
Mermaid Reef
Clerke Reef
Imperieuse Reef
Scott Reef
Seringapatam Reef
Browse I.
Holothuria Banks
Buccaneer Archipelago
Bonaparte Archipelago
Dampier Archipelago
DAMPIER LAND
Kimberley Plateau
King Leopold Ranges
Eighty Mile Beach
Great Sandy Desert
Little Sandy Desert
Gibson Desert
Hamersley Range
Chichester Range
Kenneth Range
Lake Mackay
Central Australia Aboriginal Reserve
North Central Aboriginal Reserve
Central Desert Aboriginal Land
NORTHERN TERRITORY
WESTERN
Port Hedland
Broome
Derby
Wyndham
Kununurra
Karratha
Roebourne
Newman
Marble Bar
Halls Creek
Fitzroy Crossing
Ningaloo Marine Park
Tropic of Capricorn
148-149
1
2
3
4
12°
16°
20°

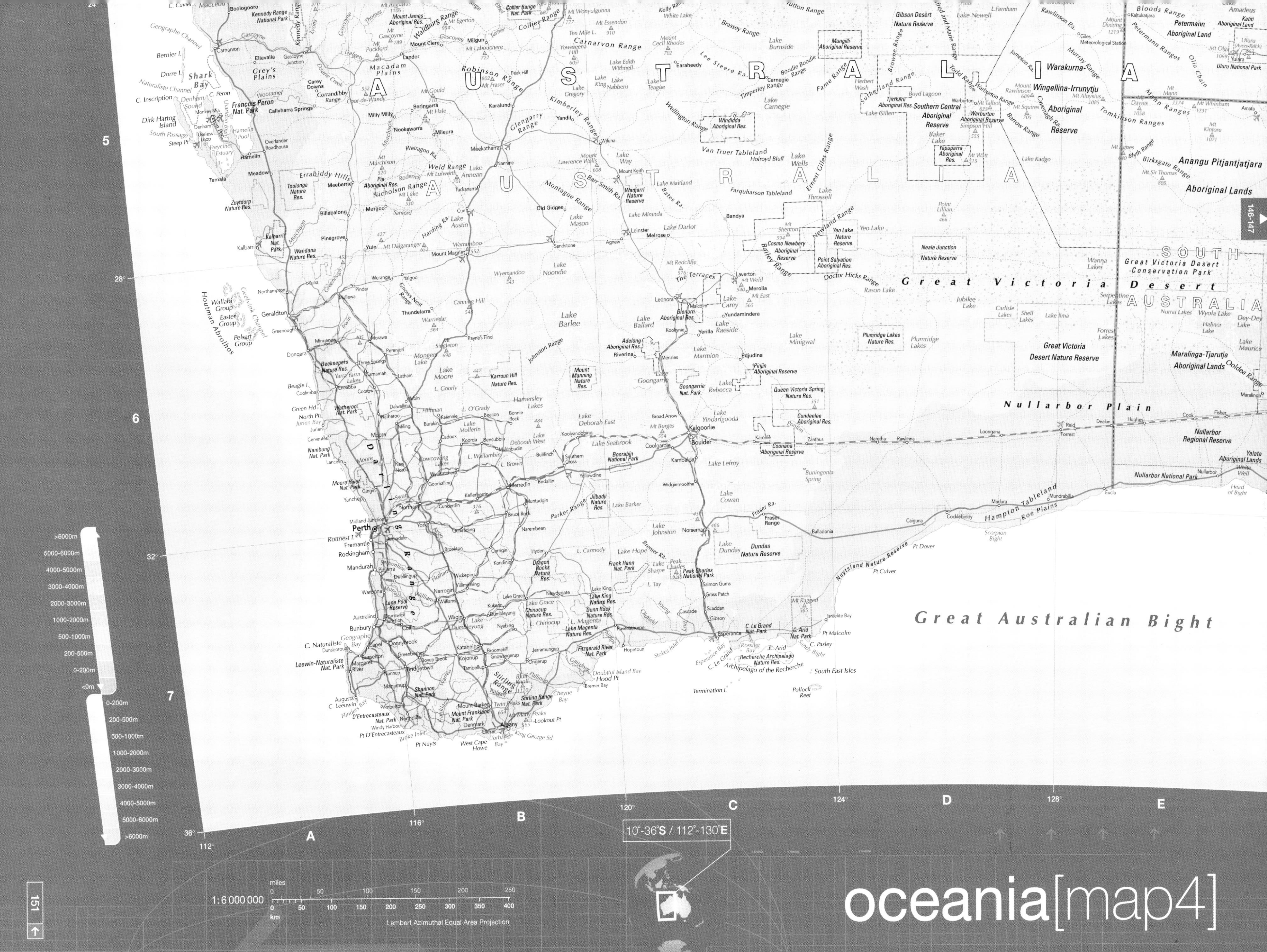

oceania[map4]
10°-36°S / 112°-130°E
1:6 000 000
miles
km
Lambert Azimuthal Equal Area Projection
146-147
AUSTRALIA
WESTERN AUSTRALIA
SOUTH AUSTRALIA
Great Victoria Desert
Nullarbor Plain
Great Australian Bight
Darling Range
Perth
Fremantle
Rottnest I.
Rockingham
Mandurah
Bunbury
Busselton
Albany
Esperance
Geraldton
Kalgoorlie
Boulder
Coolgardie
Norseman
Carnarvon
Shark Bay
Houtman Abrolhos
Geographe Bay
C. Naturaliste
C. Leeuwin
Stirling Range
Hampton Tableland
Roe Plains
Eucla
Nullarbor National Park
Nullarbor Regional Reserve
Great Victoria Desert Nature Reserve
Great Victoria Desert Conservation Park
Maralinga-Tjarutja Aboriginal Lands
Anangu Pitjantjatjara Aboriginal Lands
Gibson Desert Nature Reserve
Queen Victoria Spring Nature Res.
Dundas Nature Reserve
Recherche Archipelago Nature Res.
Archipelago of the Recherche
Lake Barlee
Lake Moore
Lake Carnegie
Lake Wells
Lake Dundas
Lake Cowan
Robinson Range
Carnarvon Range
Kimberley Range
Weld Range
Van Truer Tableland
Farquharson Tableland
Nuytsland Nature Reserve
Leeuwin-Naturaliste Nat. Park
Kennedy Range National Park
Francois Peron Nat. Park
Kalbarri Nat. Park
>6000m
5000-6000m
4000-5000m
3000-4000m
2000-3000m
1000-2000m
500-1000m
200-500m
0-200m
<0m

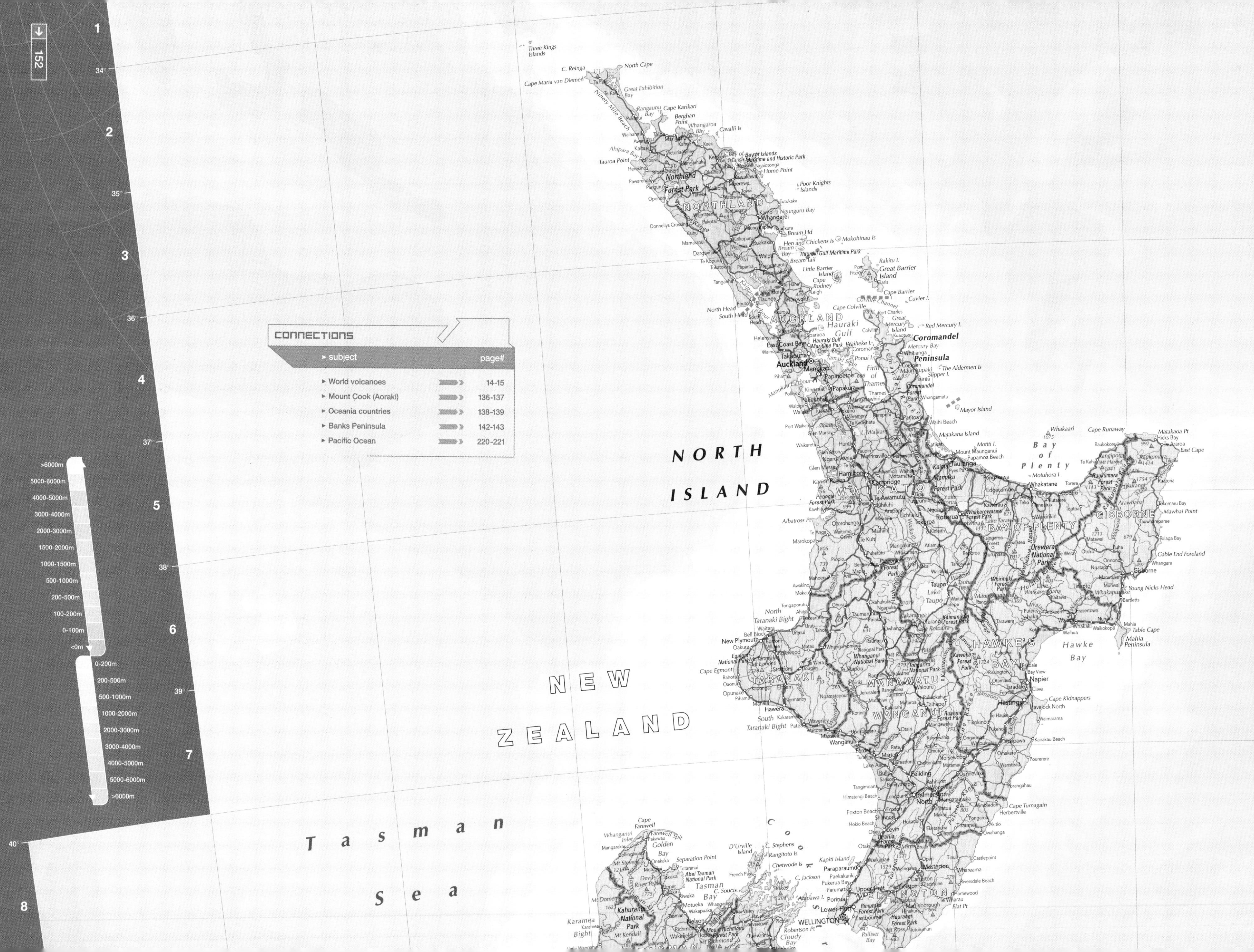

NORTH
ISLAND

NEW
ZEALAND

Tasman
Sea

CONNECTIONS

▸ subject	page#
▲ World volcanoes	14-15
▲ Mount Cook (Aoraki)	136-137
▲ Oceania countries	138-139
▲ Banks Peninsula	142-143
▲ Pacific Ocean	220-221

>6000m
5000-6000m
4000-5000m
3000-4000m
2000-3000m
1500-2000m
1000-1500m
500-1000m
200-500m
100-200m
0-100m
<0m

0-200m
200-500m
500-1000m
1000-2000m
2000-3000m
3000-4000m
4000-5000m
5000-6000m
>6000m

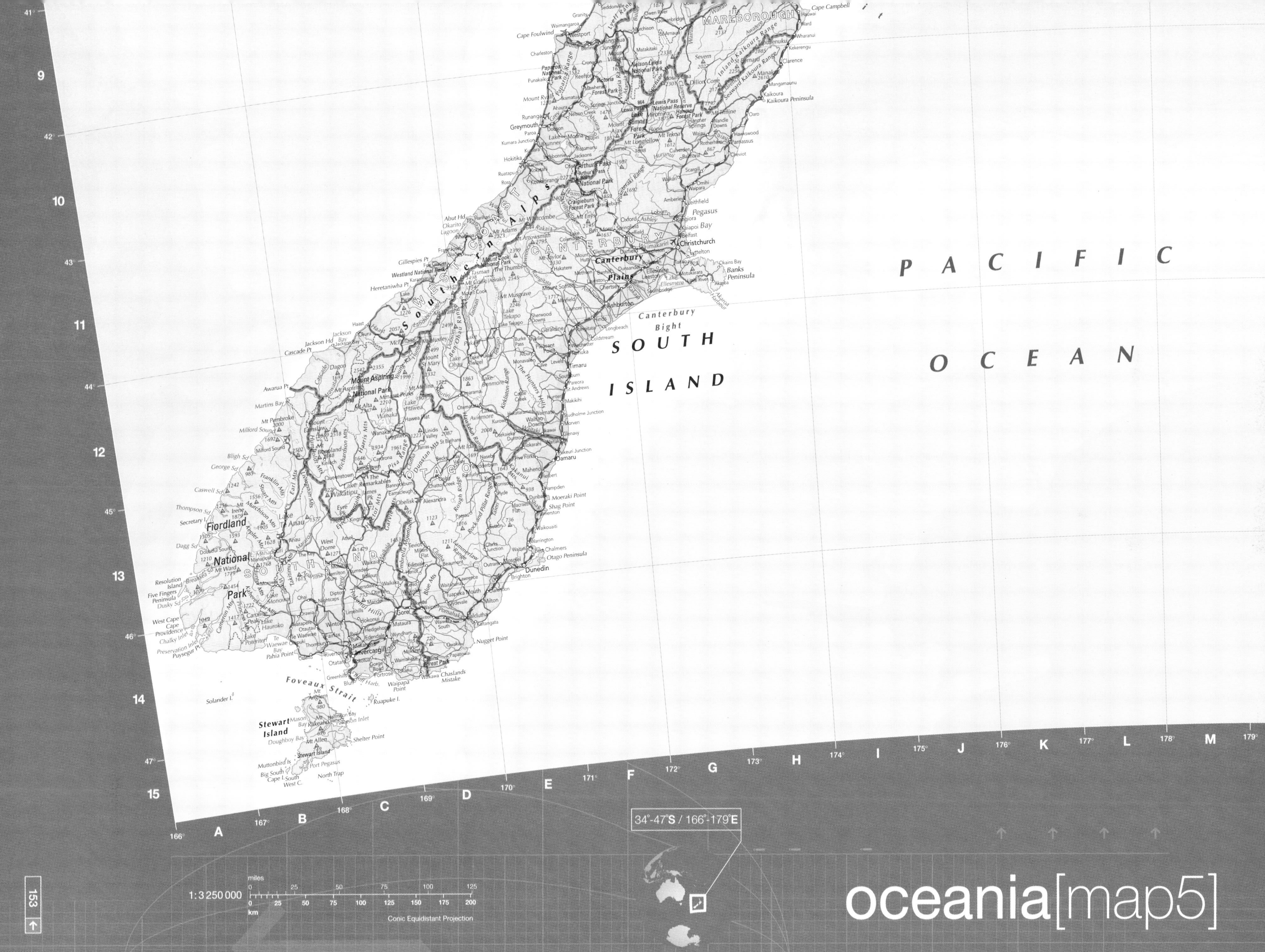

PACIFIC

OCEAN

SOUTH ISLAND

Canterbury Bight

Canterbury Plains

MARLBOROUGH

SOUTHLAND

Fiordland National Park

Mount Aspiring National Park

Foveaux Strait

Stewart Island

Christchurch

Dunedin

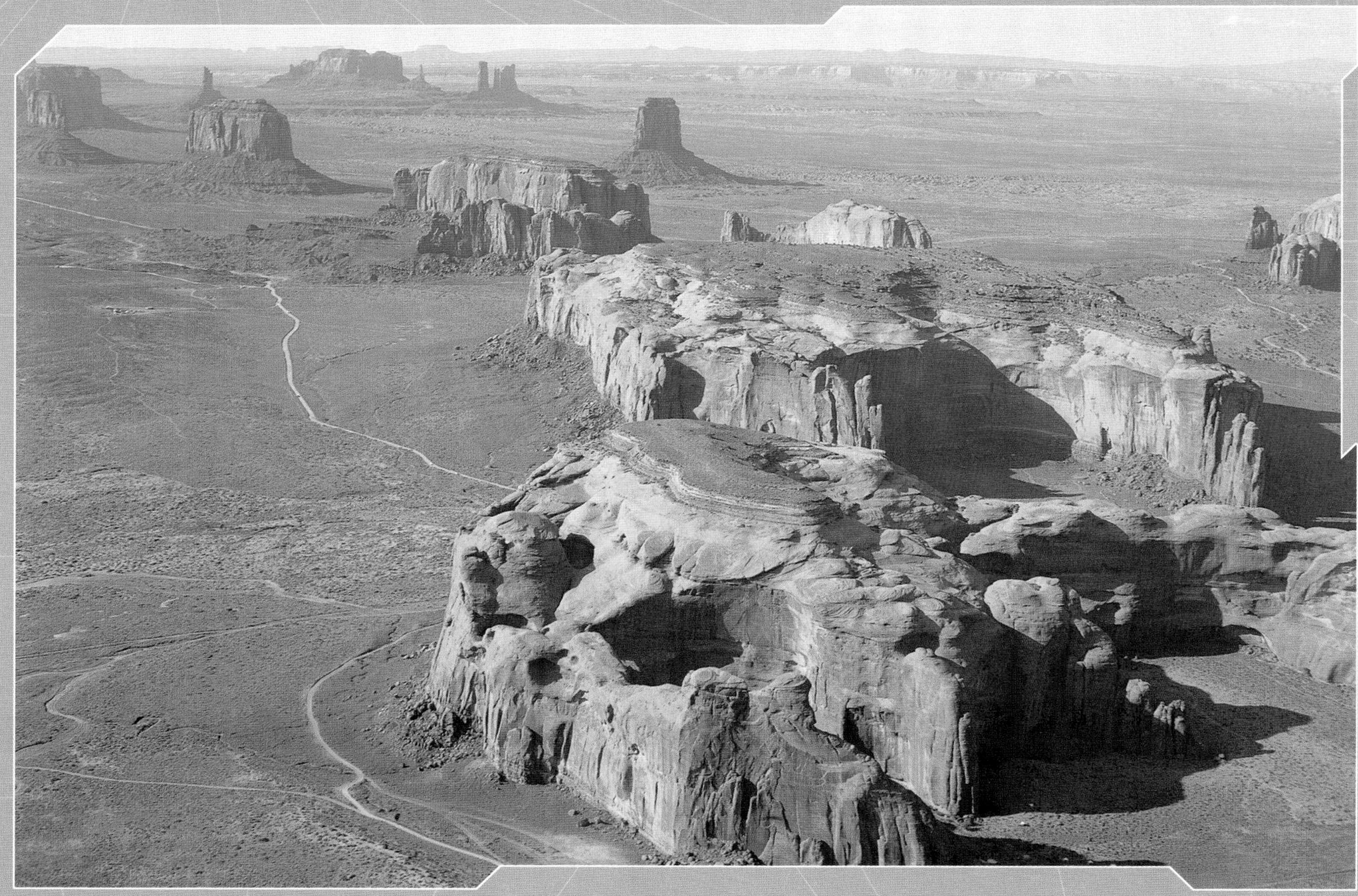

Monument Valley, *Arizona, USA*

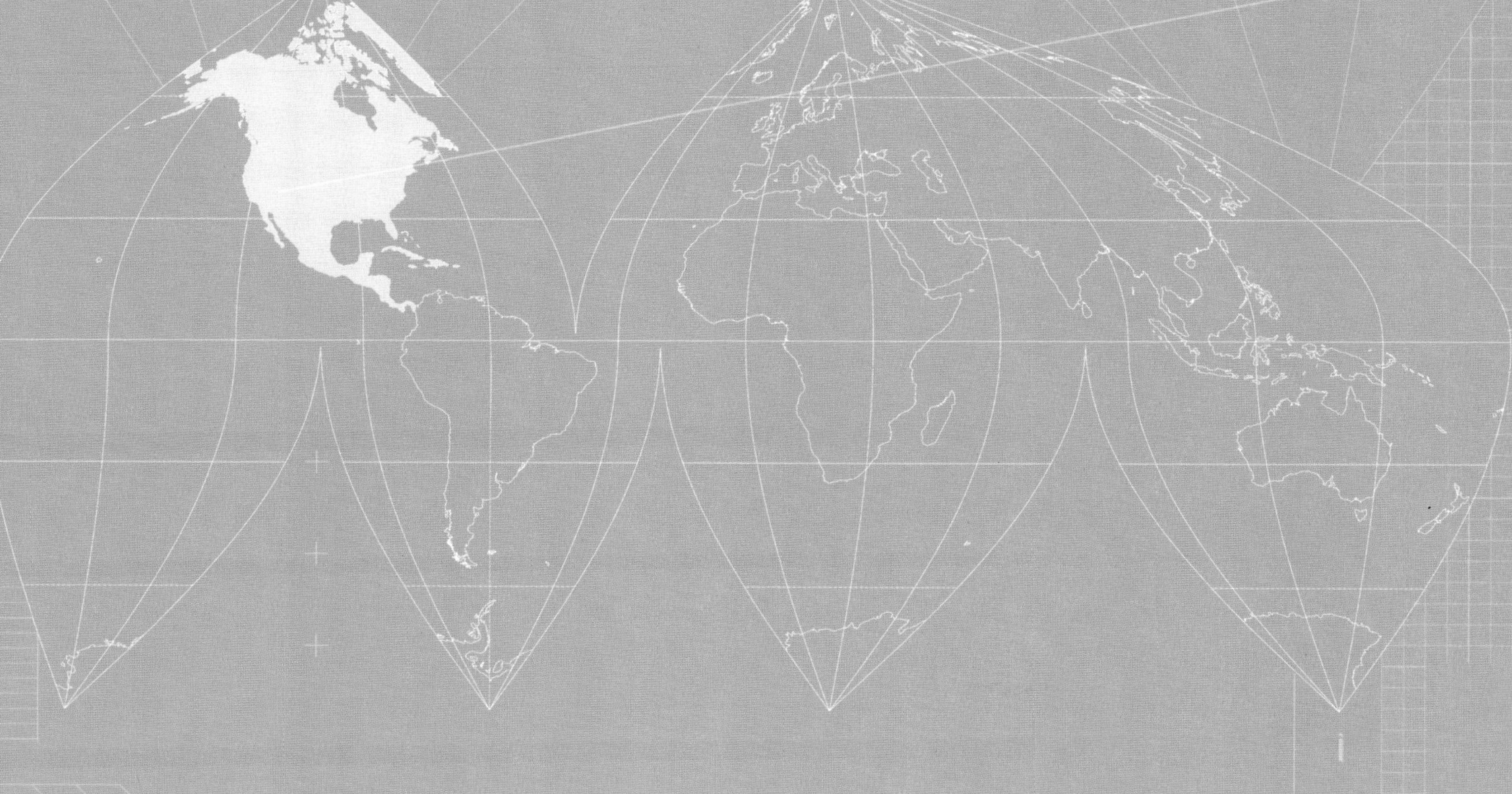

northamerica

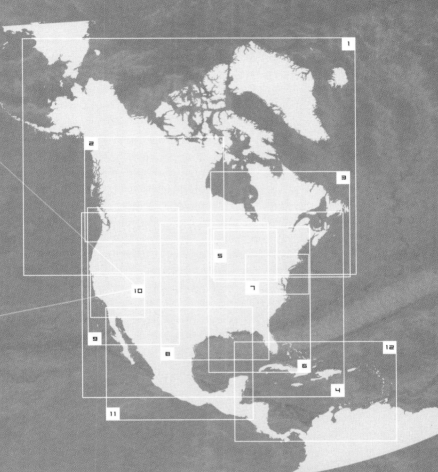

[contents]

	page#
northamerica [landscapes]	156–157
northamerica [countries]	158–159
northamerica [threats]	160–161
northamerica [environments]	162–163

	map coverage	scale	page#
northamerica [map 1]	CANADA	1:15 000 000	164–165
northamerica [map 2]	CANADA West	1:6 500 000	166–167
northamerica [map 3]	CANADA Central and East	1:6 500 000	168–169
northamerica [map 4]	UNITED STATES OF AMERICA	1:12 000 000	170–171
northamerica [map 5]	THE GREAT LAKES	1:3 000 000	172–173
northamerica [map 6]	UNITED STATES OF AMERICA East	1:6 500 000	174–175
northamerica [map 7]	UNITED STATES OF AMERICA Northeast	1:3 000 000	176–177
northamerica [map 8]	UNITED STATES OF AMERICA Central	1:6 500 000	178–179
northamerica [map 9]	UNITED STATES OF AMERICA West	1:6 500 000	180–181
northamerica [map 10]	UNITED STATES OF AMERICA Southwest	1:3 000 000	182–183
northamerica [map 11]	MEXICO	1:7 000 000	184–185
northamerica [map 12]	CENTRAL AMERICA and the CARIBBEAN	1:7 000 000	186–187

Arctic Ocean

Mount McKinley

Mackenzie River

Victoria Island

Great Bear Lake

Gulf of Alaska

Great Slave Lake

Highest point

Mt McKinley
United States of America
6 194 m / 20 321 ft
Map reference 164 D3

Coast Mountains

Peace River

Pacific Ocean

Lake Winnipeg

Rocky Mountains

Snake River

North America is the largest continent in the western hemisphere. This view illustrates how the west coast is dominated by the Rocky Mountains which stretch from Alaska in the north through Canada, USA, Mexico and Central America. The Great Plains stretch gradually east of the Rockies, and extend from the Arctic Ocean to the Gulf of Mexico. The Appalachian Mountains dominate the east of the USA, with lowlands skirting the east coast of the continent and the Gulf of Mexico.

Great Basin

Platte River

Major water bodies are the Great Lakes, and Great Slave Lake and Great Bear Lake in the Arctic regions of Canada. In the northeast, Hudson Bay is a huge inland sea connected to the Atlantic Ocean by the Hudson Strait. The large purple feature at the centre top of the image is the high, snow-covered plateau in Greenland. The Caribbean Sea contains numerous islands, stretching from the Bahamas to the north coast of South America. In the south the Isthmus of Panama forms the link between Central and South America.

Grand Canyon

Death Valley

Great Plains

Lowest point

Death Valley
86 m / 282 ft below sea level
Map reference 181 C5

Colorado River

Baja California

Gulf of California

Sierra Madre Occidental

Grand Canyon, Arizona, *USA*

The Grand Canyon in northern Arizona, USA, is the largest canyon in the world and one of the most famous World Heritage Sites. It has been established as a National Park since 1919. This aerial view shows how the canyon has been carved out by the Colorado river, exposing many layers of sedimentary rock. The canyon reaches depths of over 1.5 km and there are many peaks and smaller canyons within the main gorge.

Mackenzie River Delta, *Canada*

This photograph looks west across the delta of the Mackenzie river towards the Richardson Mountains in the Northwest Territories of Canada. The isolated village of Alavik is located inside the tight bend in the river. The severe climate means that the river is only navigable here between June and October. The Mackenzie, including the Peace and Finlay rivers to the east of the Great Slave Lake, is the second longest river system in North America.

Appalachian Mountains, *USA*

This photograph from the Space Shuttle shows the heavily wooded ridges of the Appalachian Mountains in southwest Virginia. This narrow range, which is only approximately 160 km wide, forms the principal mountains in the eastern United States and runs parallel to the Atlantic coast. In the area shown in this image, some peaks exceed 1 200 m in height. The valleys between the mountain ridges have rich agricultural soils

Satellite/Sensor: Space Shuttle

CONNECTIONS

▸ subject	page#
▸ World physical features	8–9
▸ World land images	12–13
▸ North American countries	158–159
▸ USA protected areas	162–163
▸ Reference maps of North America	164–187

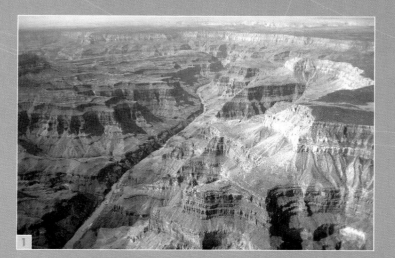

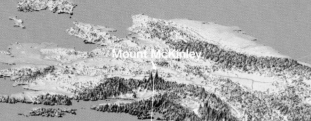

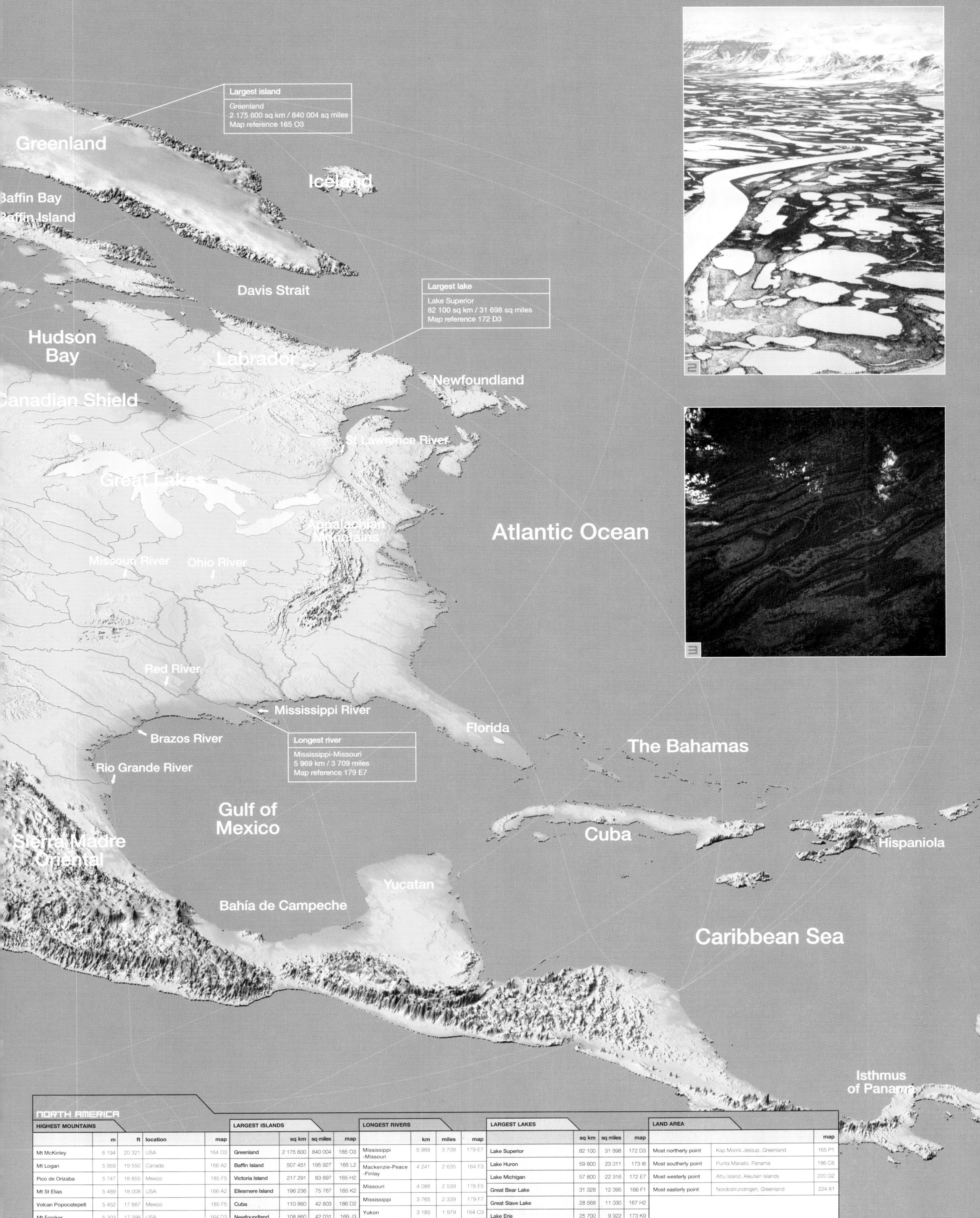

Greenland

Iceland

Baffin Bay

Baffin Island

Davis Strait

Hudson
Bay

Labrador

Newfoundland

Canadian Shield

St Lawrence River

Great Lakes

Appalachian
Mountains

Missouri River

Ohio River

Atlantic Ocean

Red River

Mississippi River

Brazos River

Florida

The Bahamas

Rio Grande River

Gulf of
Mexico

Cuba

Hispaniola

Yucatan

Sierra Madre
Oriental

Bahía de Campeche

Caribbean Sea

Isthmus
of Panama

Largest island

Greenland
2 175 600 sq km / 840 004 sq miles
Map reference 165 O3

Largest lake

Lake Superior
82 100 sq km / 31 698 sq miles
Map reference 172 D3

Longest river

Mississippi-Missouri
5 969 km / 3 709 miles
Map reference 179 E7

NORTH AMERICA

HIGHEST MOUNTAINS

	m	ft	location	map
Mt McKinley	6 194	20 321	USA	164 D3
Mt Logan	5 959	19 550	Canada	166 A2
Pico de Orizaba	5 747	18 855	Mexico	185 F5
Mt St Elias	5 489	18 008	USA	166 A2
Volcan Popocatepetl	5 452	17 887	Mexico	185 F5
Mt Foraker	5 303	17 398	USA	164 D3

LARGEST ISLANDS

	sq km	sq miles	map
Greenland	2 175 600	840 004	165 O3
Baffin Island	507 451	195 927	165 L2
Victoria Island	217 291	83 897	165 H2
Ellesmere Island	196 236	75 767	165 K2
Cuba	110 860	42 803	186 D2
Newfoundland	108 860	42 031	169 J3
Hispaniola	76 192	29 418	187 F3

LONGEST RIVERS

	km	miles	map
Mississippi-Missouri	5 969	3 709	179 E7
Mackenzie-Peace-Finlay	4 241	2 635	164 F3
Missouri	4 086	2 539	178 E5
Mississippi	3 765	2 339	179 E7
Yukon	3 185	1 979	164 C3
Rio Grande	3 057	1 899	171 E8

LARGEST LAKES

	sq km	sq miles	map
Lake Superior	82 100	31 698	172 D3
Lake Huron	59 600	23 011	173 I6
Lake Michigan	57 800	22 316	172 E7
Great Bear Lake	31 328	12 095	166 F1
Great Slave Lake	28 568	11 030	167 H2
Lake Erie	25 700	9 922	173 K9
Lake Winnipeg	24 387	9 415	167 L4
Lake Ontario	18 960	7 320	173 N7

LAND AREA

		map
Most northerly point	Kap Morris Jessup, Greenland	165 P1
Most southerly point	Punta Mariato, Panama	186 C6
Most westerly point	Attu Island, Aleutian Islands	220 G2
Most easterly point	Nordostrundingen, Greenland	224 X1

Total land area: 24 680 331 sq km / 9 529 129 sq miles

NORTH AMERICA
COUNTRIES

		area sq km	area sq miles	population	capital	languages	religions	currency	map
ANTIGUA AND BARBUDA		442	171	65 000	St John's	English, creole	Protestant, Roman Catholic	E. Carib. dollar	187
THE BAHAMAS		13 939	5 382	304 000	Nassau	English, creole	Protestant, Roman Catholic	Dollar	186–187
BARBADOS		430	166	267 000	Bridgetown	English, creole	Protestant, Roman Catholic	Dollar	187
BELIZE		22 965	8 867	226 000	Belmopan	English, Spanish, Mayan, creole	Roman Catholic, Protestant	Dollar	185
CANADA		9 970 610	3 849 674	30 757 000	Ottawa	English, French	Roman Catholic, Protestant, Eastern Orthodox, Jewish	Dollar	164–165
COSTA RICA		51 100	19 730	4 024 000	San José	Spanish	Roman Catholic, Protestant	Colón	186
CUBA		110 860	42 803	11 199 000	Havana (La Habana)	Spanish	Roman Catholic, Protestant	Peso	186–187
DOMINICA		750	290	71 000	Roseau	English, creole	Roman Catholic, Protestant	E. Carib. dollar	187
DOMINICAN REPUBLIC		48 442	18 704	8 373 000	Santo Domingo	Spanish, creole	Roman Catholic, Protestant	Peso	187
EL SALVADOR		21 041	8 124	6 278 000	San Salvador	Spanish	Roman Catholic, Protestant	Colón	185
GRENADA		378	146	94 000	St George's	English, creole	Roman Catholic, Protestant	E. Carib. dollar	187
GUATEMALA		108 890	42 043	11 385 000	Guatemala City	Spanish, Mayan languages	Roman Catholic, Protestant	Quetzal	185
HAITI		27 750	10 714	8 142 000	Port-au-Prince	French, creole	Roman Catholic, Protestant, Voodoo	Gourde	186
HONDURAS		112 088	43 277	6 417 000	Tegucigalpa	Spanish, Amerindian languages	Roman Catholic, Protestant	Lempira	186
JAMAICA		10 991	4 244	2 576 000	Kingston	English, creole	Protestant, Roman Catholic	Dollar	186
MEXICO		1 972 545	761 604	98 872 000	Mexico City	Spanish, Amerindian languages	Roman Catholic, Protestant	Peso	184–185
NICARAGUA		130 000	50 193	5 071 000	Managua	Spanish, Amerindian languages	Roman Catholic, Protestant	Córdoba	186
PANAMA		77 082	29 762	2 856 000	Panama City	Spanish, English, Amerindian languages	Roman Catholic, Protestant, Sunni Muslim	Balboa	186
ST KITTS AND NEVIS		261	101	38 000	Basseterre	English, creole	Protestant, Roman Catholic	E. Carib. dollar	187
ST LUCIA		616	238	148 000	Castries	English, creole	Roman Catholic, Protestant	E. Carib. dollar	187
ST VINCENT AND THE GRENADINES		389	150	112 000	Kingstown	English, creole	Protestant, Roman Catholic	E. Carib. dollar	187
TRINIDAD AND TOBAGO		5 130	1 981	1 294 000	Port of Spain	English, creole, Hindi	Roman Catholic, Hindu, Protestant, Sunni Muslim	Dollar	187
UNITED STATES OF AMERICA		9 809 378	3 787 422	283 230 000	Washington	English, Spanish	Protestant, Roman Catholic, Sunni Muslim, Jewish	Dollar	170–171

DEPENDENT TERRITORIES

		territorial status	area sq km	area sq miles	population	capital	languages	religions	currency	map
Anguilla		United Kingdom Overseas Territory	155	60	11 000	The Valley	English	Protestant, Roman Catholic	E. Carib. Dollar	187
Aruba		Self-governing Netherlands Territory	193	75	101 000	Oranjestad	Papiamento, Dutch, English	Roman Catholic, Protestant	Florin	187
Bermuda		United Kingdom Overseas Territory	54	21	63 000	Hamilton	English	Protestant, Roman Catholic	Dollar	171
Cayman Islands		United Kingdom Overseas Territory	259	100	38 000	George Town	English	Protestant, Roman Catholic	Dollar	186
Clipperton, Île		French Overseas Territory	7	3	uninhabited					221
Greenland		Self-governing Danish Territory	2 175 600	840 004	56 000	Nuuk (Godthåb)	Greenlandic, Danish	Protestant	Danish krone	165
Guadeloupe		French Overseas Department	1 780	687	428 000	Basse-Terre	French, creole	Roman Catholic	French franc	187
Martinique		French Overseas Department	1 079	417	383 000	Fort-de-France	French, creole	Roman Catholic, traditional beliefs	French franc	187
Montserrat		United Kingdom Overseas Territory	100	39	4 000	Plymouth	English	Protestant, Roman Catholic	E. Carib. Dollar	187
Navassa Island		United States Unincorporated Territory	5	2	uninhabited					186
Netherlands Antilles		Self-governing Netherlands Territory	800	309	215 000	Willemstad	Dutch, Papiamento, English	Roman Catholic, Protestant	NA guilder	187
Puerto Rico		United States Commonwealth	9 104	3 515	3 915 000	San Juan	Spanish, English	Roman Catholic, Protestant	US dollar	187
St Pierre and Miquelon		French Territorial Collectivity	242	93	7 000	St-Pierre	French	Roman Catholic	French franc	169
Turks and Caicos Islands		United Kingdom Overseas Territory	430	166	17 000	Grand Turk	English	Protestant	US dollar	187
Virgin Islands (U.K.)		United Kingdom Overseas Territory	153	59	24 000	Road Town	English	Protestant, Roman Catholic	US dollar	187
Virgin Islands (U.S.A.)		United States Unincorporated Territory	352	136	121 000	Charlotte Amalie	English, Spanish	Protestant, Roman Catholic	US dollar	187

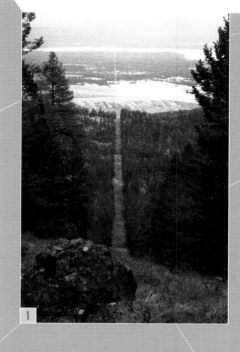

1

Tropic of Cancer

Hawaiian Islands (U.S.A.)

Honolulu

HAWAII

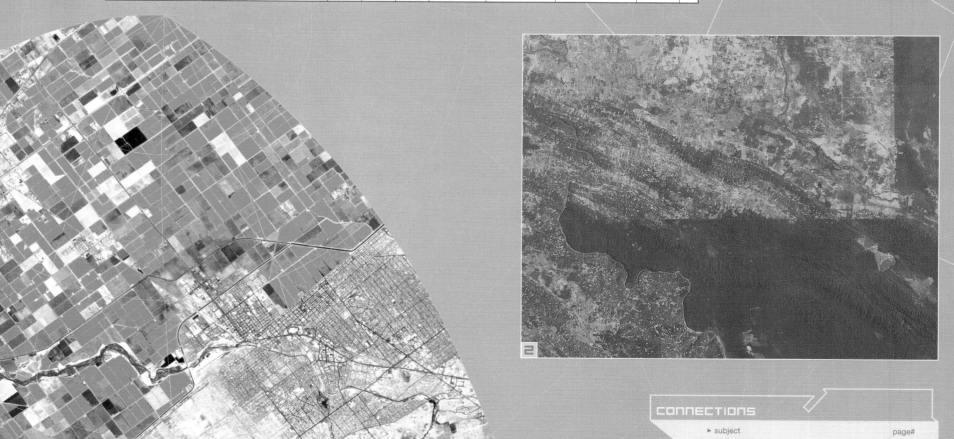

2

CONNECTIONS

► subject	page#
► World physical features	8–9
► World countries	10–11
► North America landscapes	156–157
► North America environments	162–163
► Reference maps of North America	164–187

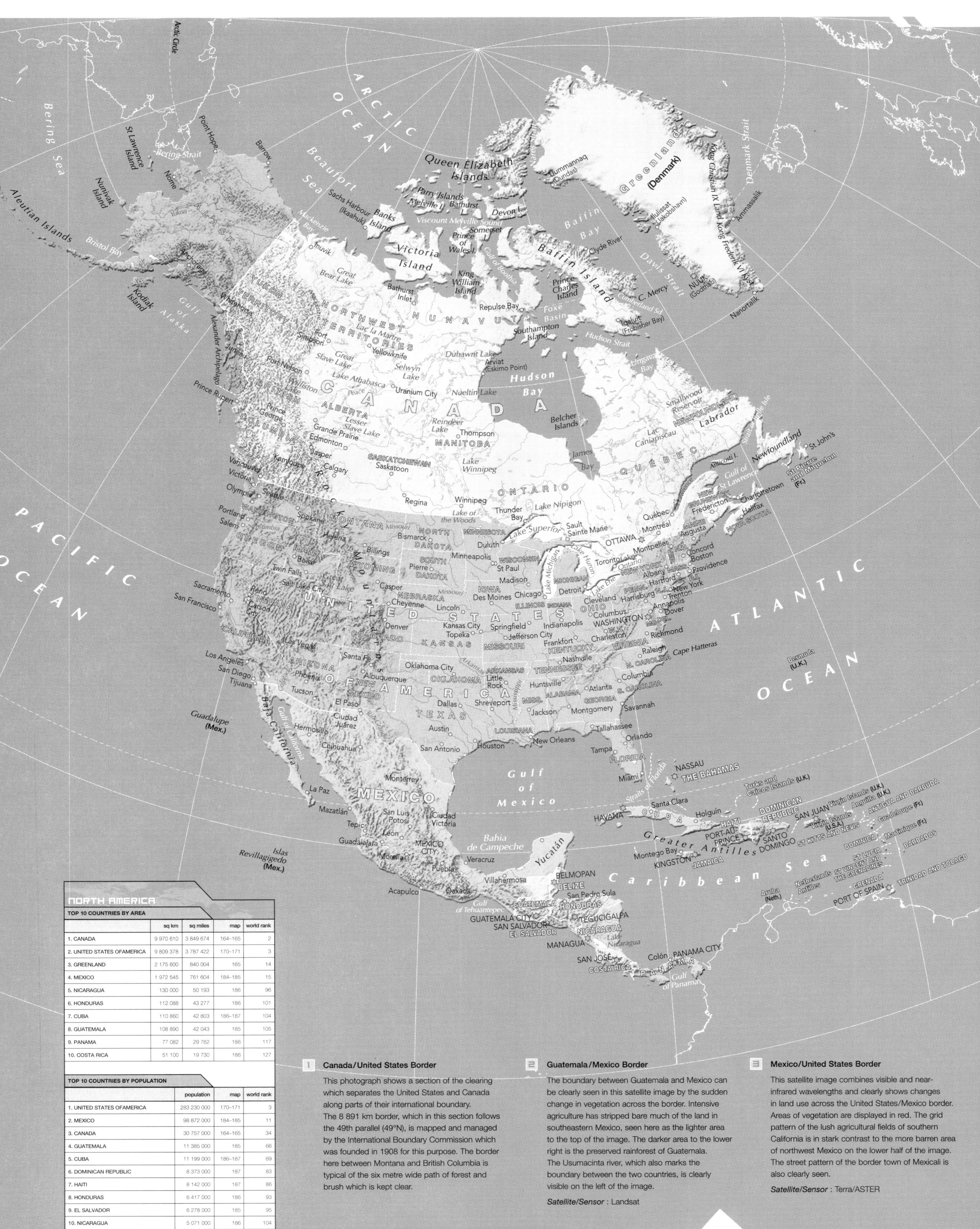

NORTH AMERICA

TOP 10 COUNTRIES BY AREA

	sq km	sq miles	map	world rank
1. CANADA	9 970 610	3 849 674	164–165	2
2. UNITED STATES OF AMERICA	9 809 378	3 787 422	170–171	3
3. GREENLAND	2 175 600	840 004	165	14
4. MEXICO	1 972 545	761 604	184–185	15
5. NICARAGUA	130 000	50 193	186	96
6. HONDURAS	112 088	43 277	186	101
7. CUBA	110 860	42 803	186–187	104
8. GUATEMALA	108 890	42 043	185	105
9. PANAMA	77 082	29 762	186	117
10. COSTA RICA	51 100	19 730	186	127

TOP 10 COUNTRIES BY POPULATION

	population	map	world rank
1. UNITED STATES OF AMERICA	283 230 000	170–171	3
2. MEXICO	98 872 000	184–185	11
3. CANADA	30 757 000	164–165	34
4. GUATEMALA	11 385 000	185	66
5. CUBA	11 199 000	186–187	69
6. DOMINICAN REPUBLIC	8 373 000	187	83
7. HAITI	8 142 000	187	86
8. HONDURAS	6 417 000	186	93
9. EL SALVADOR	6 278 000	185	95
10. NICARAGUA	5 071 000	186	104

1 Canada/United States Border

This photograph shows a section of the clearing which separates the United States and Canada along parts of their international boundary.

The 8 891 km border, which in this section follows the 49th parallel (49°N), is mapped and managed by the International Boundary Commission which was founded in 1908 for this purpose. The border here between Montana and British Columbia is typical of the six metre wide path of forest and brush which is kept clear.

2 Guatemala/Mexico Border

The boundary between Guatemala and Mexico can be clearly seen in this satellite image by the sudden change in vegetation across the border. Intensive agriculture has stripped bare much of the land in southeastern Mexico, seen here as the lighter area to the top of the image. The darker area to the lower right is the preserved rainforest of Guatemala. The Usumacinta river, which also marks the boundary between the two countries, is clearly visible on the left of the image.

Satellite/Sensor : Landsat

3 Mexico/United States Border

This satellite image combines visible and near-infrared wavelengths and clearly shows changes in land use across the United States/Mexico border. Areas of vegetation are displayed in red. The grid pattern of the lush agricultural fields of southern California is in stark contrast to the more barren area of northwest Mexico on the lower half of the image. The street pattern of the border town of Mexicali is also clearly seen.

Satellite/Sensor : Terra/ASTER

1 San Andreas Fault, *California, USA*

The San Andreas fault is a large break in the Earth's crust between the North American and Pacific plates. It runs for over 950 km from northwest California to the Gulf of California. Movement between the two plates causes earthquakes which present a serious threat to this part of the United States. The fault runs diagonally across this satellite image from left to right, with the supplementary Garlock fault stretching to the top of the image. The proximity of the faults to Los Angeles, the large grey area at the bottom of the image, is obvious.

Satellite/Sensor : Landsat

2 Mount St Helens, *Washington, USA*

After lying dormant since 1857, Mount St Helens in the Cascade mountain range in Washington state, USA erupted violently in May 1980. The eruption was one of the largest volcanic events in North American history and caused the loss of sixty lives. The explosion reduced the height of the mountain by 390 m and flattened trees and killed wildlife over an area of twenty five kilometres radius. The result was the new horseshoe-shaped crater seen in this aerial photograph.

3 Popocatépetl, *Mexico*

This false-colour satellite image shows the Mexican volcano Popocatépetl four days after its eruption in December 2000. The eruption sent molten rock high into the air and over 50 000 people were evacuated from the surrounding area. The bright green spot in the crater indicates that its temperature is still very high. The volcano lies only seventy kilometres southeast of Mexico City, and its name, which is the Aztec word for 'smoking mountain' is suggestive of the threat it presents.

Satellite/Sensor : SPOT

4 Atlantic Hurricanes

Tropical storms have different names in different parts of the world – typhoons in the northwest Pacific Ocean, cyclones in the Indian Ocean region and hurricanes in the Atlantic Ocean and east Pacific. The effects of their strong winds and heavy rain can be devastating.

The Atlantic hurricane season lasts from June to November, with the majority of storms occurring between August and October. The storms present a threat to the islands of the Caribbean and Bermuda and to the east coast of the United States of America. In both 1999 and 2000 there were eight tropical storms which reached hurricane force, as shown on the map Fig. #01. The most severe of these was Hurricane Floyd which developed during early September 1999. It achieved maximum sustained wind speeds of 249 km per hour and made landfall near Cape Fear, North Carolina, USA. Although wind speeds had dropped to around 166 km per hour, it had a devastating effect and fifty seven deaths were directly attributed to the hurricane, making it the deadliest US hurricane since 1972. The computer-generated images show Floyd just off the Florida coast and the inset image indicates wind directions and rainfall levels (yellow-orange over 10mm per hour) at the centre of the hurricane.

CONNECTIONS

► subject	page#
► World earthquakes and volcanoes	14–15
► World climate and weather	16–17
► Asia threats	70–71
► North America landscapes	156–157
► North America environments	162–163

Fig. #01 ▶▶▶▶ ▶ ▶
Atlantic hurricane tracks
1999-2000

Hurricane Strength
1999 ▷▷▷ ▬▬▬▬▬▬▷
2000 ▷▷▷ ▬▬▬▬▬▬▷

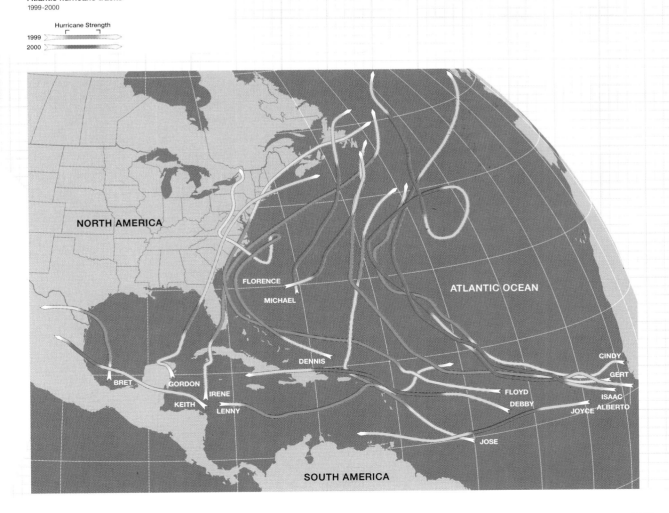

NORTH AMERICA

ATLANTIC OCEAN

FLORENCE
MICHAEL

DENNIS

BRET
GORDON
KEITH   IRENE
LENNY

FLOYD
DEBBY

CINDY
GERT
ISAAC
JOYCE   ALBERTO

JOSE

SOUTH AMERICA

1 **Suburbia, California,** *USA*

A new housing development west of Stockton, California is shown in this vertical aerial photograph. Water-front properties are in great demand in this area and each house on the finger-like promontories has its own berth, with access via canals to the California Delta waterways of the Sacramento and San Joaquin rivers. Development is continuing on the empty plots at the lower right of the photograph.

2 **Island Environment, Hawaii,** *USA*

This image shows a perspective view of Honolulu and surrounding area on the Hawaiian island of Oahu. The three-dimensional effect is a result of using height data collected during the Shuttle Radar Topography Mission (SRTM) of the Space Shuttle Endeavour. This height data has been combined with a Landsat 7 satellite image which has been draped over the surface of the elevation model. Honolulu, Pearl Harbour, the Koolau mountain range and offshore reef patterns are all visible on the image.

Satellite/Sensor : Space Shuttle and Landsat

3 **Great Plains, Montana,** *USA*

A wheat farm on the Great Plains of Montana is shown in this aerial photograph. The high grasses of the Great Plains once sustained large herds of buffalo and the cattle and sheep of large ranches. Today the environment is dominated by large farms using modern extensive farming techniques.

4 **Arctic Coastline,** *Greenland*

This Space Shuttle photograph gives a northeast view of the south-southeast tip of Greenland. This is a typical scene of the glaciated coastline which surrounds the world's largest island. The dark elongated fingers are inlets, or fjords, which stretch from the North Atlantic Ocean towards the interior. Large white areas to the top of the image mark the start of the permanent ice cap which stretches north across the island to the Arctic Ocean.

Satellite/Sensor : Space Shuttle

5 **Protected Environment, Yellowstone National Park,** *USA*

The Lower Falls in the Grand Canyon of the Yellowstone River are one of many spectacular features in Yellowstone National Park, Wyoming. The park mainly lies within a volcanically active basin in the Rocky Mountains. It became the world's first national park in 1872 with the purpose of preserving this area of great natural beauty. As well as many geysers, hot springs, lakes and waterfalls the park has a rich variety of flora and fauna.

6 **Irrigation, Wyoming,** *USA*

This aerial photograph shows fields watered by centre-pivot irrigation next to the Bighorn river in northern Wyoming. This method of irrigation has created circular patterns in the landscape. Each circle is fed from a rotating structure of up to 300 m in length. The flow is carefully controlled so that the whole area is supplied with an equal amount of water. The system makes it possible to grow crops in otherwise infertile parts of the state.

CONNECTIONS

► subject	page#
► Land cover types	18–19
► World land use patterns	20–21
► Europe environments	36–37
► North America landscapes	156–157
► Reference maps of North America	164–187
► Arctic features	214–215

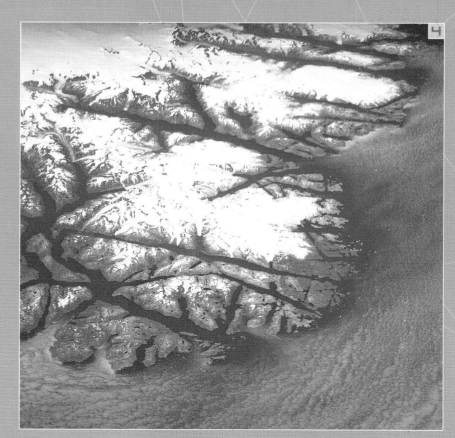

Fig. #01
Land protected by the US Federal Government
Kobuk Valley N.P.
Gates of the Arctic N.P.
ALASKA
Denali N.P.
Wrangell-St Elias N.P.
Katmai N.P.
Kenai Fjords N.P.
Glacier Bay N.P.
Kauai
Oahu
Maui
Haleakala N.P.
Hawaiian Islands
Hawaii
Hawaii Volcanoes N.P.
Olympic N.P.
North Cascades N.P.
Colville I.R.
Mount Rainier N.P.
Yakima I.R.
Glacier N.P.
Blackfeet I.R.
Flathead I.R.
Fort Peck I.R.
Crater Lake N.P.
Yellowstone N.P.
Grand Teton N.P.
Northern Cheyenne I.R.
Crow I.R.
Wind River I.R.
Standing Rock I.R.
Cheyenne River I.R.
Badlands N.P.
Pine Ridge I.R.
Rosebud I.R.
Lake Traverse I.R.
Voyageurs N.P.
Isle Royale N.P.
Uintah & Ouray I.R.
Rocky Mountain N.P.
Yosemite N.P.
Kings Canyon N.P.
Sequoia N.P.
Death Valley N.P.
Capitol Reef N.P.
Canyonlands N.P.
Bryce Canyon N.P.
Navajo I.R.
Mojave N.P.
Grand Canyon N.P.
Hopi I.R.
Channel Is. N.P.
Joshua Tree N.P.
Fort Apache I.R.
San Carlos I.R.
Organ Pipe Cactus N.P.
White Sands Nat. Mon.
Osage I.R.
Shenandoah N.P.
Great Smoky Mts N.P.
Big Bend N.P.
Everglades N.P.
National forest
National grassland
National wildlife refuge
National park
Indian reservation
Bureau of Land Management land
Military reservation
National wild and scenic river
1
2
3
4
5
6
5
6

northamerica[map1]

40°-85°N / 10°-180°W

CONNECTIONS

RUSSIAN FEDERATION

Arctic Circle

Chukchi Sea

Bering Strait

Seward Peninsula

Aleutian Islands

Fox Islands

Bristol Bay

ALASKA

Alaska Peninsula

Aleutian Range

Alaska Range

Brooks Range

Philip Smith Mountains

Kuskokwim Mountains

Beaufort Sea

ARCTIC OCEAN

Gulf of Alaska

YUKON TERRITORY

NORTHWEST TERRITORIES

Great Bear Lake

Great Slave Lake

Yellowknife

BRITISH COLUMBIA

Mackenzie Mountains

Cassiar Mountains

Coast Mountains

ROCKY Mountains

ALBERTA

SASKATCHEWAN

Edmonton

Calgary

Vancouver Island

Vancouver

PACIFIC OCEAN

Queen Charlotte Islands

WASHINGTON

Seattle

Portland

OREGON

IDAHO

NEVADA

CALIFORNIA

MONTANA

WYOMING

UTAH

COLORADO

UNITED STATES

Elevation scale:
>6000m
5000-6000m
4000-5000m
3000-4000m
2000-3000m
1000-2000m
500-1000m
200-500m
0-200m
<0m

0-200m
200-500m
500-1000m
1000-2000m
2000-3000m
3000-4000m
4000-5000m
5000-6000m
>6000m

1:15 000 000

miles
0 200 400 600

0 200 400 600 800 1000
km

Lambert Conformal Conic Projection

Greenland
(Kalaallit Nunaat)
(Denmark)
Greenland Sea
Denmark Strait
ICELAND
REYKJAVÍK
Arctic Circle
Lincoln Sea
Baffin Bay
Davis Strait
Labrador Sea
Hudson Bay
James Bay
Hudson Strait
Foxe Basin
Ungava Bay
Gulf of St Lawrence
Cabot Strait
ATLANTIC OCEAN
Queen Elizabeth Islands
Ellesmere Island
Axel Heiberg Island
Devon Island
Baffin Island
Victoria Island
Parry Islands
Southampton Island
Péninsule d'Ungava
Labrador
NEWFOUNDLAND
Newfoundland
NUNAVUT
TERRITORIES
MANITOBA
ONTARIO
QUÉBEC
NEW BRUNSWICK
NOVA SCOTIA
PRINCE EDWARD ISLAND
CANADA
UNITED STATES OF AMERICA
NORTH DAKOTA
SOUTH DAKOTA
NEBRASKA
MINNESOTA
IOWA
WISCONSIN
MICHIGAN
ILLINOIS
INDIANA
OHIO
PENNSYLVANIA
NEW YORK
MAINE
VERMONT
Lake Superior
Lake Michigan
Lake Huron
Lake Erie
Lake Winnipeg
North Magnetic Pole (2000)
North Geomagnetic Pole (2000)
NUUK (Godthåb)
OTTAWA
Montréal
Québec
Toronto
Winnipeg
Detroit
Chicago
Boston
New York
Halifax
St John's
Administrative divisions in the U.S.A. numbered on the map:
1. CONNECTICUT
2. MASSACHUSETTS
3. NEW HAMPSHIRE
4. RHODE ISLAND
170-171

48°-65°N / 92°-142°W

CONNECTIONS

Elevation scale:
>6000m
5000-6000m
4000-5000m
3000-4000m
2000-3000m
1000-2000m
500-1000m
200-500m
0-200m
<0m
0-200m
200-500m
500-1000m
1000-2000m
2000-3000m
3000-4000m
4000-5000m
5000-6000m
>6000m

PACIFIC OCEAN

YUKON TERRITORY

NORTHWEST TERRITORIES

BRITISH COLUMBIA

ALASKA U.S.A.

WASHINGTON

Coast Mountains

Mackenzie Mountains

Selwyn Mountains

Pelly Mountains

Cassiar Mountains

Skeena Mountains

Omineca Mountains

Cariboo Mountains

Columbia Mountains

Fraser Plateau

Stikine Plateau

Liard Plateau

Alexander Archipelago

Queen Charlotte Islands

Vancouver Island

Whitehorse
Prince George
Prince Rupert
Kitimat
Terrace
Smithers
Williams Lake
Kamloops
Vancouver
Victoria
Dawson Creek
Fort Nelson
Fort St John
Quesnel
Kelowna

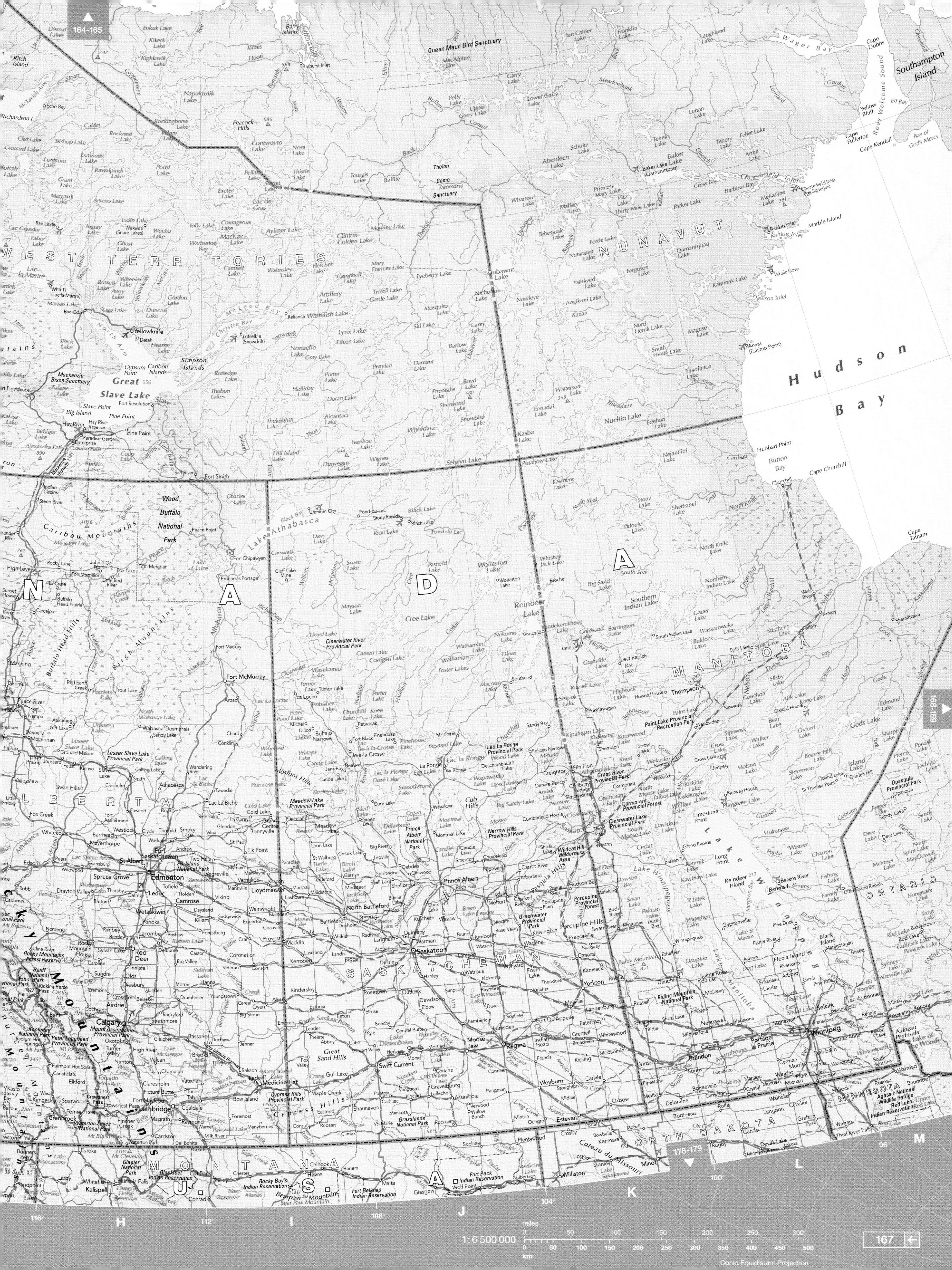

40°-57°N / 52°-95°W

166-167

174-175

174-175

Elevation legend:

>6000m
5000-6000m
4000-5000m
3000-4000m
2000-3000m
1000-2000m
500-1000m
200-500m
0-200m
<0m

0-200m
200-500m
500-1000m
1000-2000m
2000-3000m
3000-4000m
4000-5000m
5000-6000m
>6000m

CONNECTIONS

subject	page#
World physical features	8–9
World land cover types	18–19
World air travel	26–27
North America landscapes	156–157
North America countries	158–159

17°-50°N / 67°-125°W

164-165

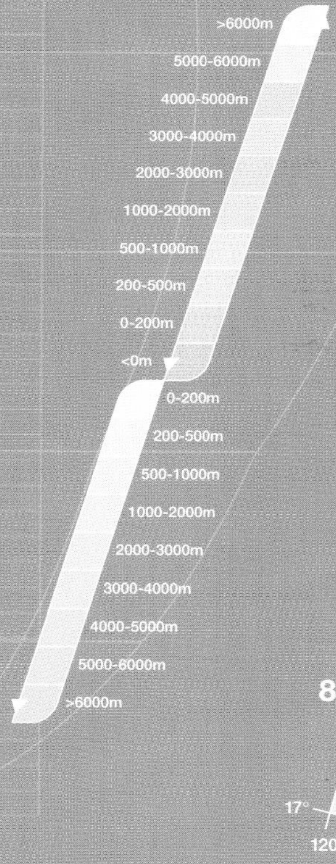

>6000m
5000-6000m
4000-5000m
3000-4000m
2000-3000m
1000-2000m
500-1000m
200-500m
0-200m
<0m
0m
0-200m
200-500m
500-1000m
1000-2000m
2000-3000m
3000-4000m
4000-5000m
5000-6000m
>6000m

miles
0   100   200   300   400   500
1:12 000 000
0 100 200 300 400 500 600 700 800
km

Lambert Conformal Conic Projection

PACIFIC OCEAN

Tropic of Cancer

CANADA

MANITOBA

NORTH DAKOTA

MINNESOTA

WISCONSIN

UNITED STATES

IOWA

NEBRASKA

ILLINOIS

INDIANA

OHIO

MISSOURI

KANSAS

AMERICA

OKLAHOMA

ARKANSAS

TENNESSEE

KENTUCKY

MISSISSIPPI

ALABAMA

GEORGIA

LOUISIANA

TEXAS

FLORIDA

QUEBEC

ONTARIO

Lake Superior

Lake Michigan

Lake Huron

Lake Ontario

Lake Erie

NEW YORK

PENNSYLVANIA

WEST VIRGINIA

VIRGINIA

NORTH CAROLINA

SOUTH CAROLINA

MARYLAND

DELAWARE

NEW JERSEY

VERMONT

NEW HAMPSHIRE

MAINE

MASSACHUSETTS

NEW BRUNSWICK

NOVA SCOTIA

PRINCE EDWARD ISLAND

Newfoundland

Gulf of St Lawrence

Gulf of Maine

Minneapolis
St Paul
Milwaukee
Chicago
Detroit
Cleveland
Cincinnati
Indianapolis
Columbus
Pittsburgh
Kansas City
St Louis
Washington
Baltimore
Philadelphia
New York
Boston
OTTAWA
Montréal
Toronto
Norfolk
Atlanta
Memphis
Nashville
Charlotte
Dallas
Houston
Austin
New Orleans
Jacksonville
Orlando
Tampa
West Palm Beach
Fort Lauderdale
Miami

ATLANTIC

OCEAN

Bermuda
(U.K.)
HAMILTON

Gulf of Mexico

THE BAHAMAS

NASSAU

Turks and
Caicos Islands
(U.K.)
GRAND TURK
(Cockburn Town)

West Indies

Straits of Florida

Great Bahama Bank

HAVANA
(La Habana)

CUBA

Cayman Islands
(U.K.)

Caribbean Sea

Greater Antilles

JAMAICA

KINGSTON

Hispaniola

HAITI
PORT-AU-PRINCE

DOMINICAN
REPUBLIC

SANTO
DOMINGO

Lesser Antilles

YUCATÁN

Bahía de Campeche

GUATEMALA

BELIZE
BELMOPAN

41°-49°**N** / 76°-93°**W**

>6000m
5000-6000m
4000-5000m
3000-4000m
2000-3000m
1500-2000m
1000-1500m
500-1000m
200-500m
100-200m
0-100m
<0m

0-50m
50-100m
100-200m
200-500m
500-1000m
1000-2000m
2000-3000m
3000-4000m
4000-5000m
5000-6000m
>6000m

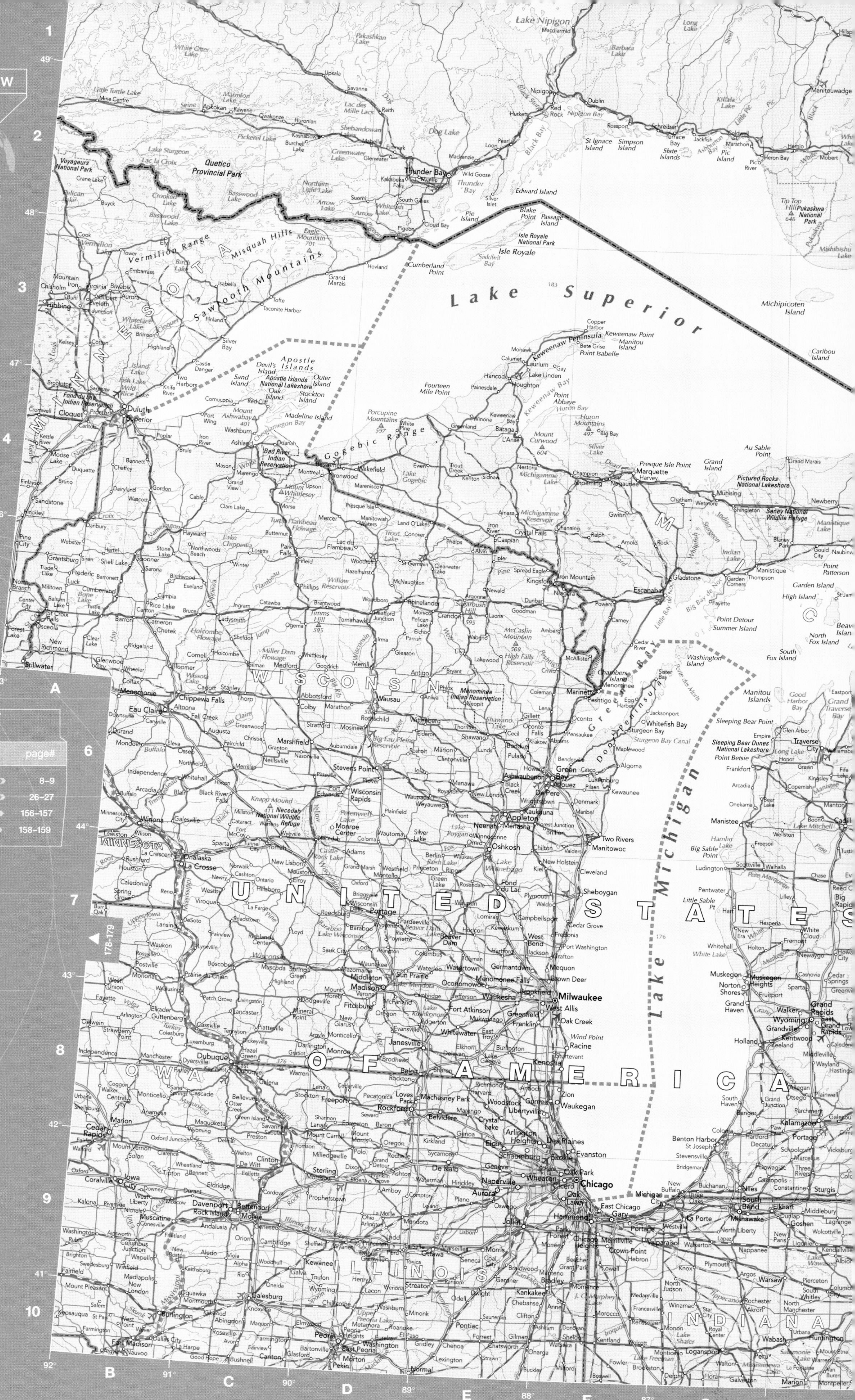

Lake Superior

Lake Michigan

MINNESOTA

WISCONSIN

UNITED STATES OF AMERICA

IOWA

ILLINOIS

INDIANA

MICHIGAN

Thunder Bay

Quetico Provincial Park

Voyageurs National Park

Duluth
Superior
Eau Claire
La Crosse
Madison
Milwaukee
Chicago
Rockford
Cedar Rapids
Iowa City
Davenport
Rock Island
Dubuque
Green Bay
Appleton
Oshkosh
Manitowoc
Sheboygan
Marquette
Escanaba
Peoria
Muskegon
Grand Rapids
Evanston
Waukegan

178-179

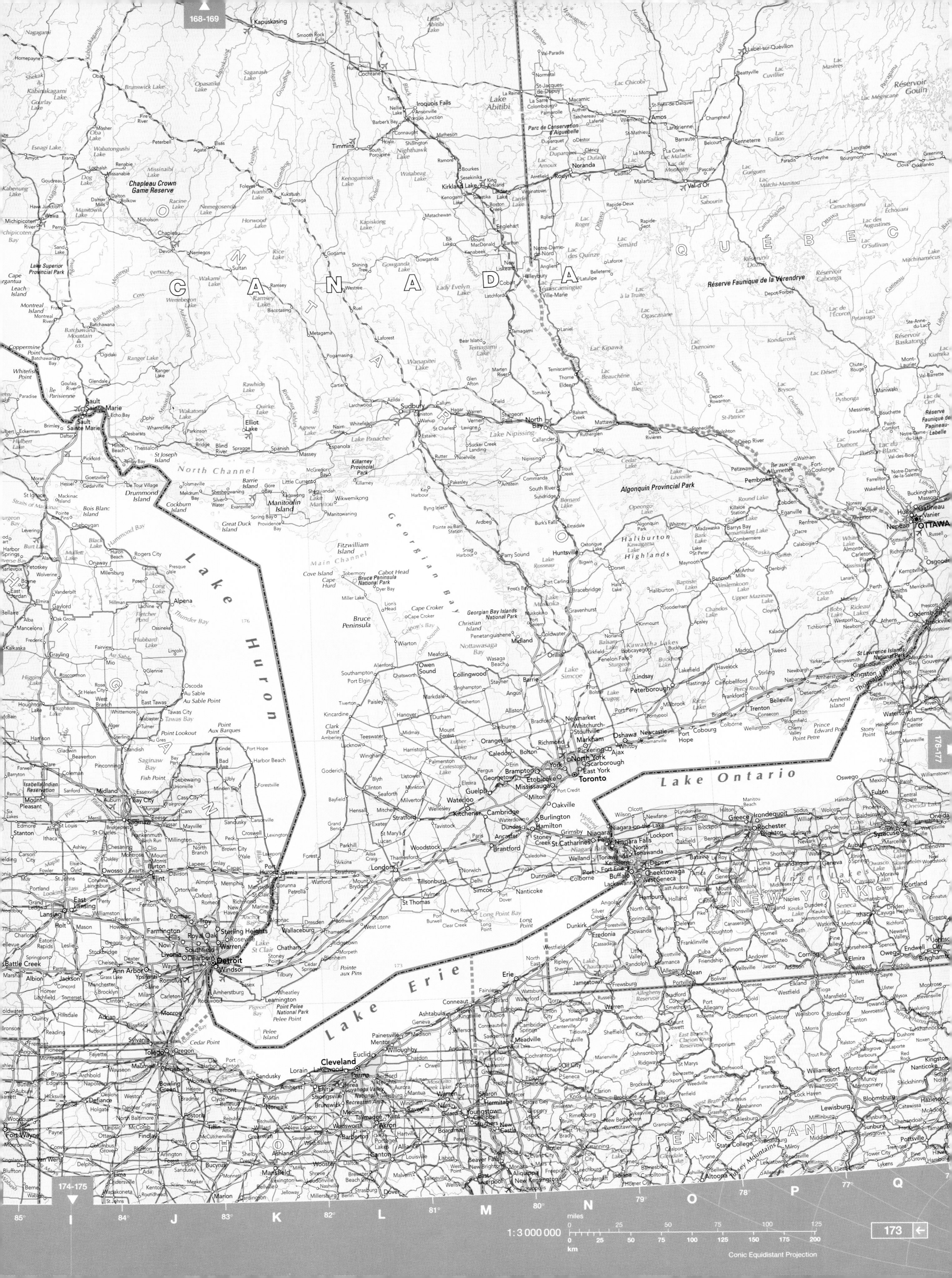

1:3 000 000

miles
0   25   50   75   100   125

km
0   25   50   75   100   125   150   175   200

Conic Equidistant Projection

Administrative divisions in the U.S.A.
numbered on map:

1. CONNECTICUT
2. MASSACHUSETTS
3. RHODE ISLAND
4. DELAWARE

22°-48'N / 92°-70'W

1:6 500 000

Lambert Conformal Conic Projection

CONNECTIONS

▶ subject	page#
▶ World land cover types	18–19
▶ World cities	24–25
▶ North America landscapes	156–157
▶ North America countries	158–159
▶ North America threats	160–161
▶ Atlantic Ocean	216–217

A T L A N T I C

O C E A N

Gulf

of

Mexico

THE
BAHAMAS

CUBA

HAVANA
(La Habana)

F L O R I D A

G E O R G I A

A L A B A M A

MISSISSIPPI

LOUISIANA

SOUTH CAROLINA

New Orleans

Atlanta

Miami

Fort Lauderdale

West Palm Beach

Orlando

Tampa

St Petersburg

Jacksonville

Montgomery

Tropic of Cancer

Straits of Florida

Great Bahama Bank

Little Bahama Bank

Andros

NASSAU

Grand Bahama

Freeport

Eleuthera

Cat Island

San Salvador

Long Island

Crooked Island

Acklins Island

Mayaguana

>6000m
5000–6000m
4000–5000m
3000–4000m
2000–3000m
1000–2000m
500–1000m
200–500m
0–200m
0m
0–200m
200–500m
500–1000m
1000–2000m
2000–3000m
3000–4000m
4000–5000m
5000–6000m
>6000m

miles
km

186–187 ▶

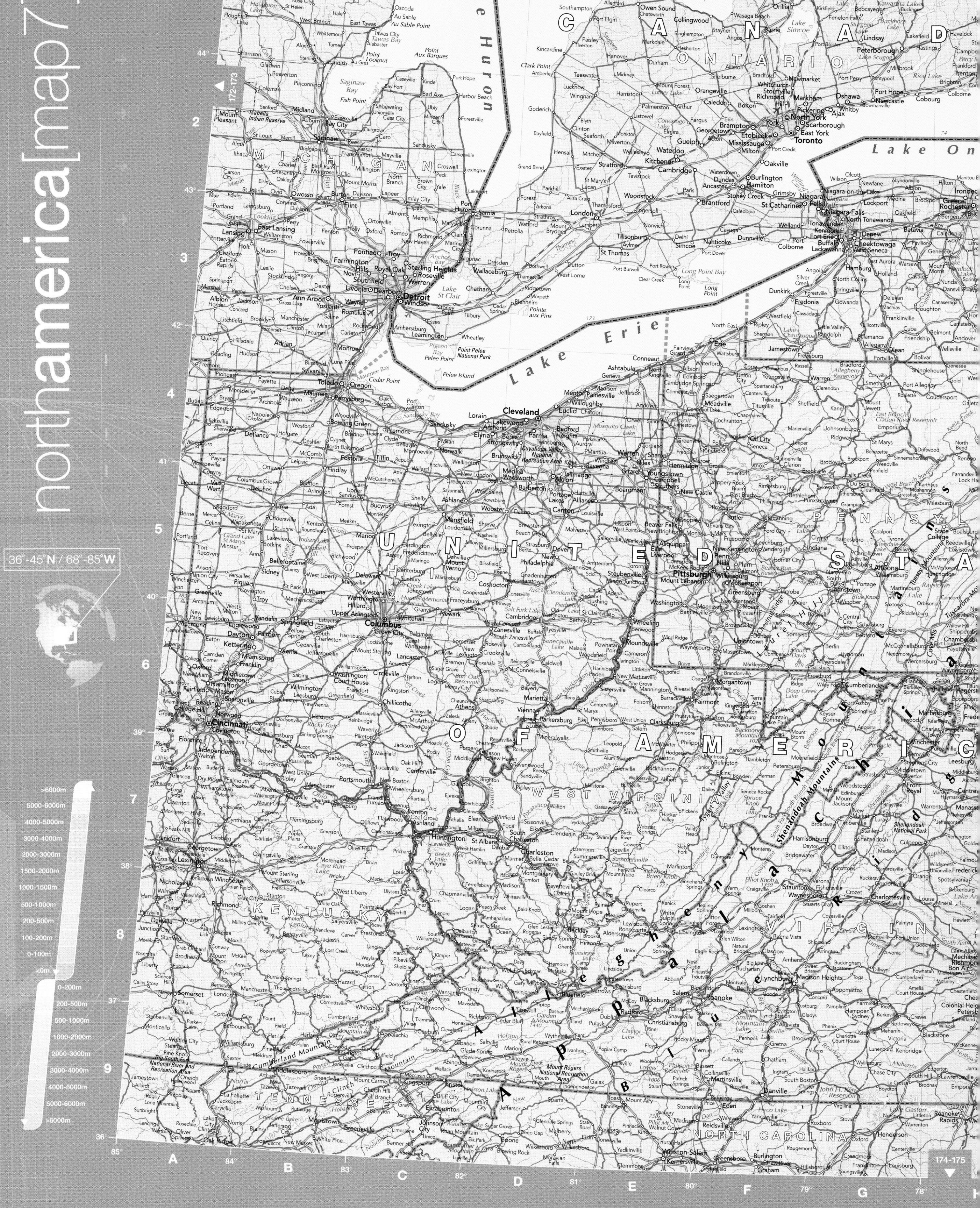

northamerica[map7

36°-45'N / 68°-85'W

>6000m
5000-6000m
4000-5000m
3000-4000m
2000-3000m
1500-2000m
1000-1500m
500-1000m
200-500m
100-200m
0-100m
<0m

0-200m
200-500m
500-1000m
1000-2000m
2000-3000m
3000-4000m
4000-5000m
5000-6000m
>6000m

172-173

174-175

CONNECTIONS

► subject	page#
► World countries	10–11
► World land cover types	18–19
► World cities	24–25
► North America landscapes	156–157
► North America countries	158–159

1:3 000 000

Lambert Conformal Conic Projection

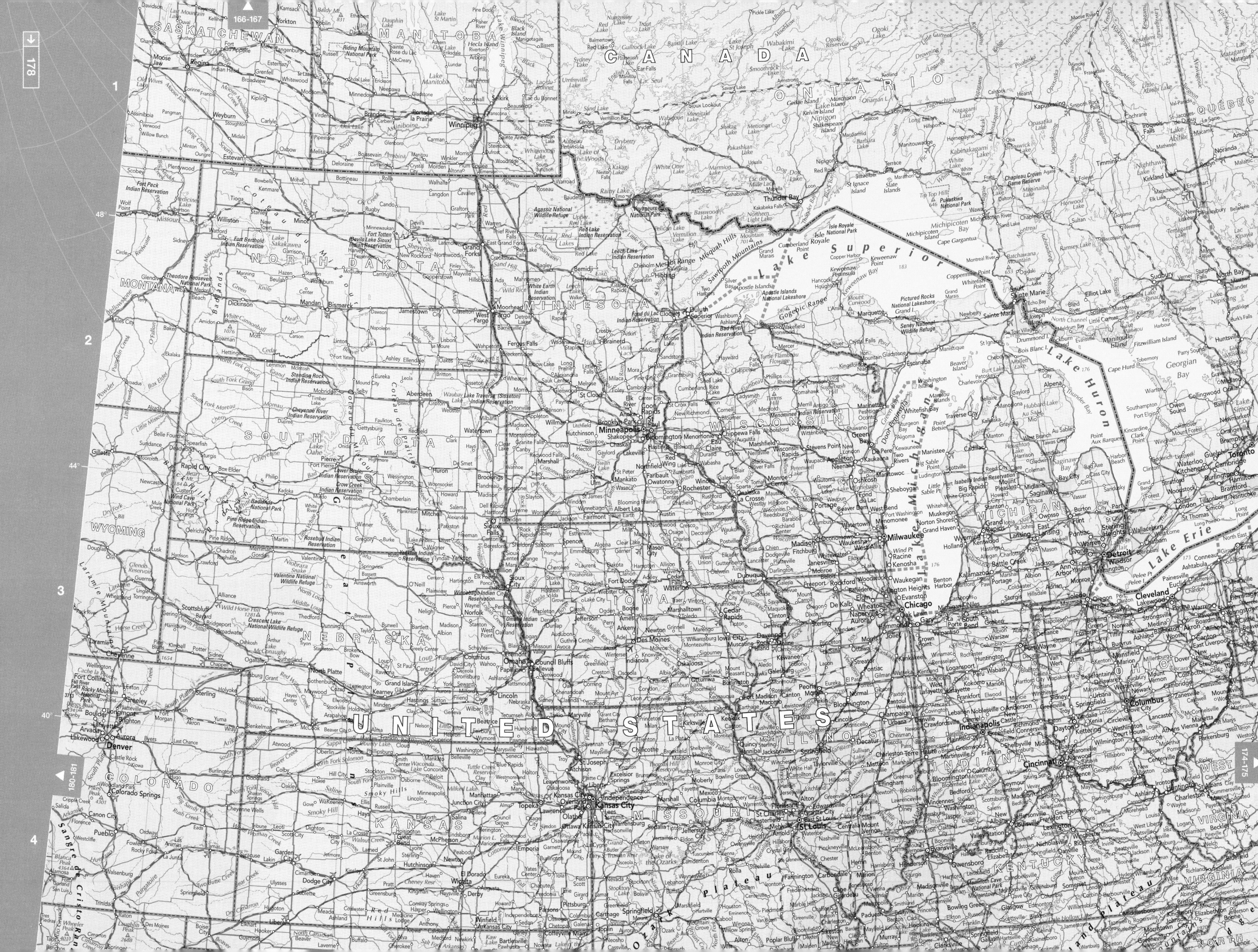

180-181

CONNECTIONS

► subject   page#

► World physical features   8–9
► World changes   20–21
► North America countries   158–159
► North America environments   162–163

A B C D E F G

5 6 7

1:6 500 000   Lambert Conformal Conic Projection

25°52'N / 82°–104°W

Gulf of Mexico

Sierra Madre Oriental

M E X I C O

COAHUILA

TAMAULIPAS

NUEVO LEÓN

T E X A S

Edwards Plateau

Stockton Plateau

L O U I S I A N A

M I S S I S S I P P I

A L A B A M A

G E O R G I A

F L O R I D A

T E N N E S S E E

A R K A N S A S

O K L A H O M A

N E W   M E X I C O

Ouachita Mountains

Boston Mountains

Wichita Mountains

Houston

Dallas

San Antonio

Austin

New Orleans

Atlanta

Memphis

Montgomery

Monterrey

Gulf Coastal Plain

miles   0   50   100   150   200   250
km   0   100 200 300 400 500

8000m
6000m
5000m
4000m
3000m
2000m
1000m
500m
200m
0

0–200m
200–500m
500–1000m
1000–2000m
2000–3000m
3000–4000m
4000–5000m
5000–6000m
6000–8000m
>8000m

179

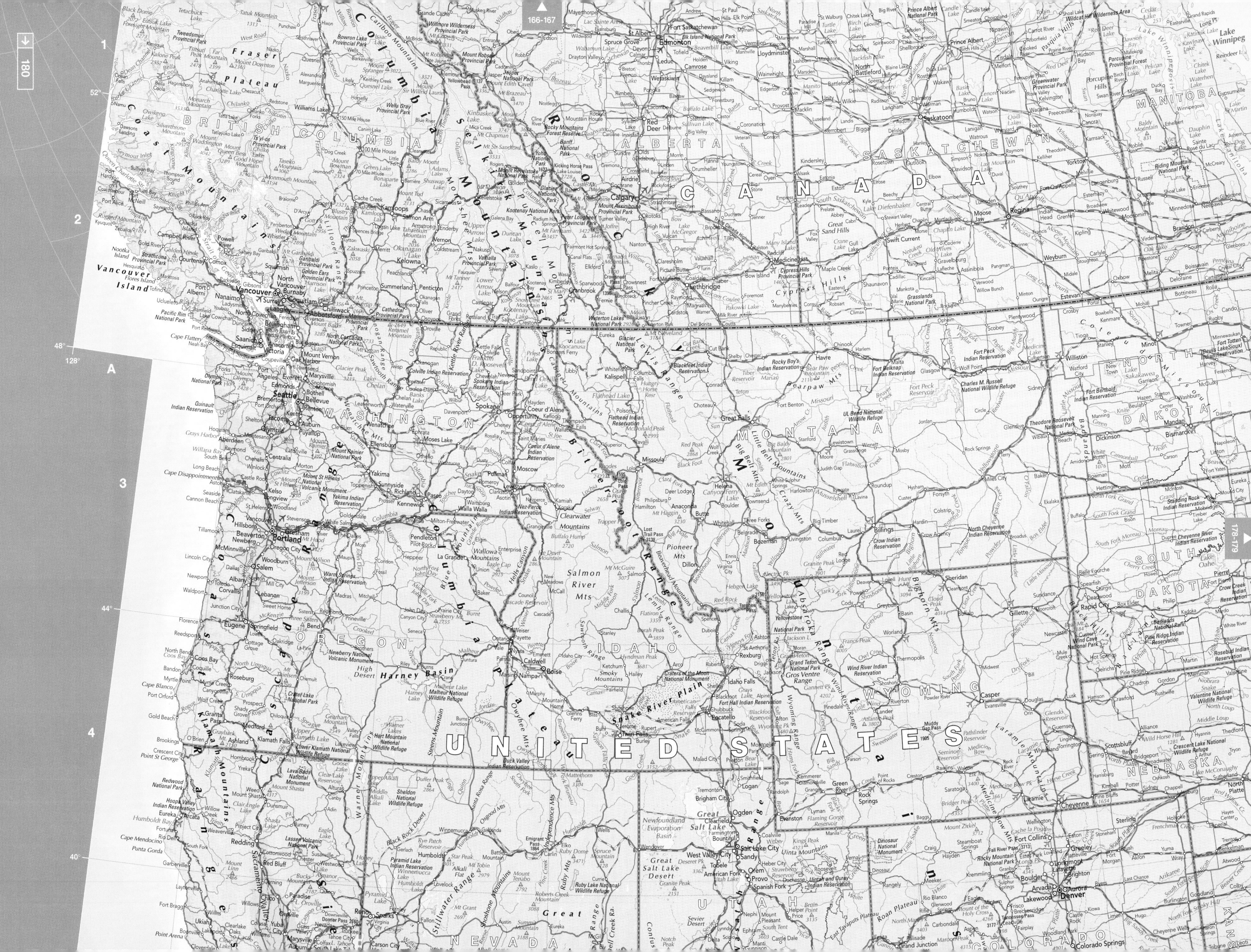

27°-53°N / 103°-126°W

184–185 ▼

CONNECTIONS

▶ subject   page#

▲ World land images   12–13
▲ World earthquakes   14–15
▲ North America countries   158–159
▲ North America threats   160–161
▲ North America environments   162–163

1:6 500 000
Lambert Conformal Conic Projection

north**america**[map10]

32°-40°**N** / 109°-124°**W**

180-181

PACIFIC OCEAN

Elevation
>6000m
5000-6000m
4000-5000m
3000-4000m
2000-3000m
1500-2000m
1000-1500m
500-1000m
200-500m
100-200m
0-100m
<0m
0-200m
200-500m
500-1000m
1000-2000m
2000-3000m
3000-4000m
4000-5000m
5000-6000m
>6000m

CONNECTIONS

subject	page#
World earthquakes	14–15
World cities	24–25
North America landscapes	156–157
North America countries	158–159
North America threats	160–161
North America environments	162–163

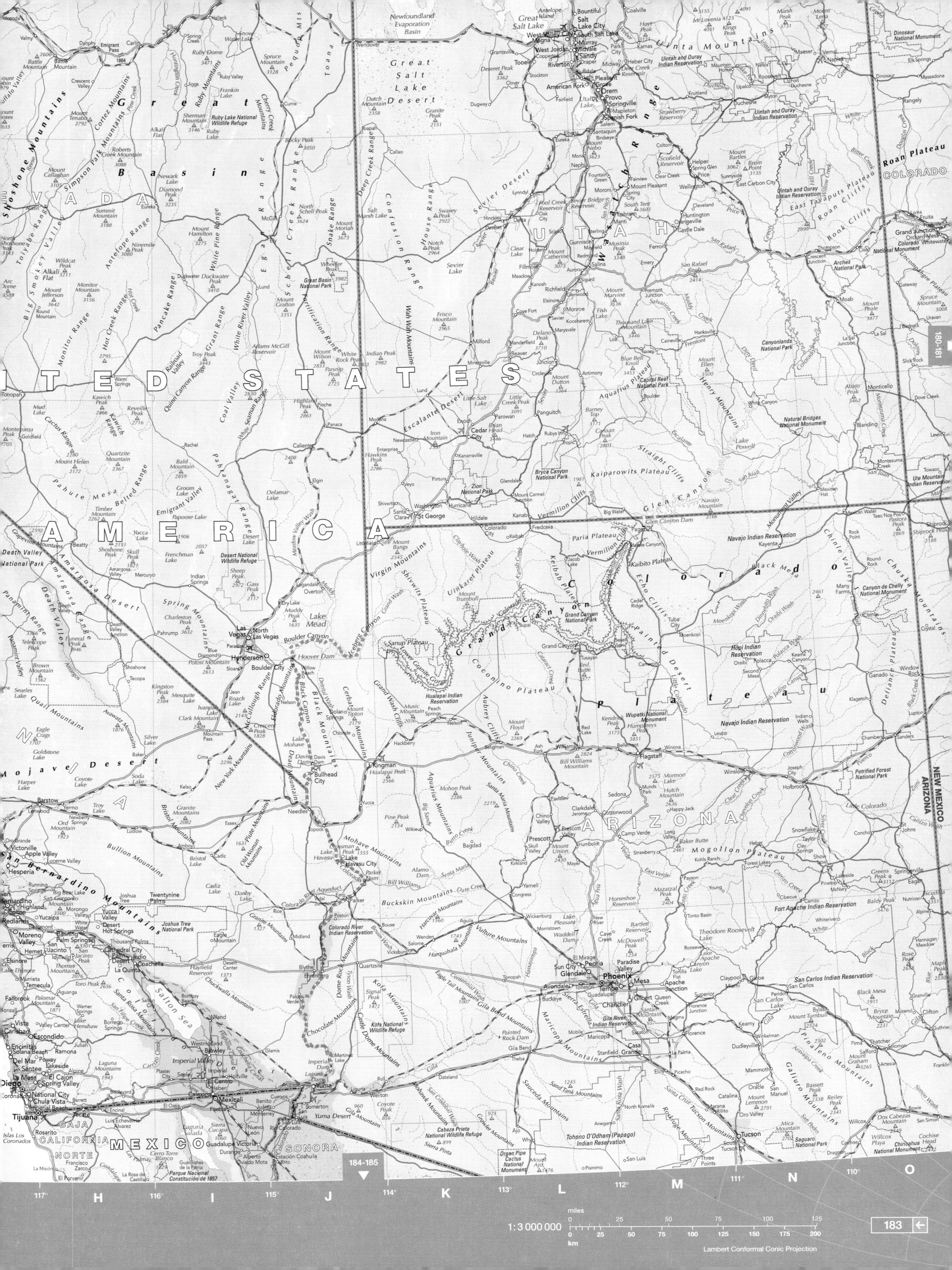

CONNECTIONS

subject	page#
World countries	10–11
World volcanoes	14–15
World cities	24–25
North America countries	158–159
North America threats	160–161
Pacific Ocean	220–221

Administrative divisions in Mexico
numbered on the map:

1. AGUASCALIENTES
2. DISTRITO FEDERAL
3. MORELOS
4. TLAXCALA

Gulf

of

Mexico

Bahía
de Campeche

UNITED STATES OF AMERICA

T E X A S

Edwards

Plateau

LOUISIANA

MISSISSIPPI

ALABAMA

FLORIDA

COAHUILA

NUEVO
LEÓN

TAMAULIPAS

ZACATECAS

SAN LUIS
POTOSÍ

MÉXICO

GUANAJUATO

QUERÉTARO

HIDALGO

VERACRUZ

MICHOACÁN

GUERRERO

Sierra

Madre

del

Sur

OAXACA

PUEBLA

YUCATÁN

QUINTANA
ROO

CAMPECHE

TABASCO

CHIAPAS

BELIZE

GUATEMALA

HONDURAS

EL
SALVADOR

Gulf of

Tehuantepec

Gulf of
Honduras

MEXICO CITY

GUATEMALA CITY

SAN SALVADOR

New Orleans

Houston

San Antonio

Austin

Dallas

Fort Worth

Monterrey

Corpus Christi

Laredo

Tampico

Veracruz

Puebla

Acapulco

Oaxaca

Mérida

Cancún

Campeche

Chetumal

Villahermosa

Tuxtla
Gutiérrez

BELMOPAN

E   F   G   H
100°   96°   92°   88°

185 ←

1:7 000 000

miles
0   100   200

km
0   100   200   300   400

Lambert Conformal Conic Projection

186-187

174-175
184-185

6°-26°N / 60°-89°W

Elevation scale
>6000m
5000-6000m
4000-5000m
3000-4000m
2000-3000m
1000-2000m
500-1000m
200-500m
0-200m
<0m

0-200m
200-500m
500-1000m
1000-2000m
2000-3000m
3000-4000m
4000-5000m
5000-6000m
>6000m

1 : 7 000 000

miles
0 50 100 150 200 250 300
km
0 50 100 150 200 250 300 350 400 450 500

Lambert Conformal Conic Projection

Gulf of Mexico

U.S.A. — FLORIDA — West Palm Beach, Fort Lauderdale, Hollywood, Miami, Miami Beach, Homestead, Florida Keys, Key West, Dry Tortugas, Ten Thousand Islands, Everglades National Park, Big Cypress National Preserve, Naples, Cape Coral, Fort Myers, North Port, Port Charlotte

THE BAHAMAS — NASSAU, Grand Bahama, Freeport City, Great Abaco, Little Abaco, Andros, Eleuthera, Great Exuma

Straits of Florida

CUBA — HAVANA (La Habana), Guanabacoa, Marianao, Matanzas, Cárdenas, Santa Clara, Cienfuegos, Sancti Spíritus, Ciego de Ávila, Camagüey, Las Tunas, Holguín, Bayamo, Manzanillo, Santiago de Cuba, Nuevitas, Puerto Padre, Gibara
Isla de la Juventud, Península de Zapata, Archipiélago de Sabana, Archipiélago de Camagüey, Golfo de Guacanayabo, Sierra Maestra, Bay of Pigs, Cayo Largo

Tropic of Cancer

Cayman Islands (U.K.) — GEORGE TOWN, Grand Cayman, Cayman Brac, Little Cayman

JAMAICA — KINGSTON, Spanish Town, Montego Bay, May Pen, Savanna-la-Mar, Portland Point, Morant Point

Yucatan Channel

MEXICO — YUCATÁN, QUINTANA ROO, Cancún, Cozumel, Isla de Cozumel, Mérida, Tulum, Chetumal, Playa del Carmen, Valladolid, Río Lagartos, Cabo Catoche, Isla Mujeres, Reserva de la Biosfera Sian Ka'an, Bahía de la Ascensión, Banco Chinchorro

Yucatán Peninsula

BELIZE — BELMOPAN, Belize, Dangriga, Orange Walk, San Pedro, Punta Gorda, Turneffe Islands, Lighthouse Reef, Glover Reef, Ambergris Cay

Gulf of Honduras — Islas de la Bahía, Utila, Roatán, Guanaja, Puerto Barrios, Puerto Cortés

HONDURAS — TEGUCIGALPA, San Pedro Sula, La Ceiba, El Progreso, Choloma, Comayagua, Danlí, Juticalpa, Olanchito, Trujillo, Puerto Lempira, Mosquitia, Reserva Biósfera del Río Plátano, Parque Nacional Patuca

EL SALVADOR — SAN SALVADOR, Santa Ana, San Miguel, Sonsonate, San Francisco Gotera, Usulután, La Unión

NICARAGUA — MANAGUA, León, Chinandega, Masaya, Granada, Matagalpa, Estelí, Jinotega, Juigalpa, Bluefields, Puerto Cabezas, Lake Nicaragua, Costa de Mosquitos, Laguna de Perlas, Isla de Ometepe, Corn Islands (Islas del Maíz)

COSTA RICA — SAN JOSÉ, Cartago, Liberia, Puntarenas, Limón, Alajuela, Heredia, Nicoya, Península de Nicoya, Golfo de Nicoya, Parque Nacional Tortuguero, Parque Nacional Corcovado, Volcán Irazú, Volcán Arenal

PANAMA — PANAMA CITY, Colón, David, Santiago, Chitré, Las Tablas, Aguadulce, San Miguelito, La Chorrera, Lago Gatún, Archipiélago de San Blas, Golfo de Panamá, Golfo de los Mosquitos, Gulf of Panama, Península de Azuero

Caribbean Sea

Isla de Providencia (Colombia), Isla de San Andrés (Colombia), Cayos de Albuquerque (Colombia), Roncador Cay (Colombia), Serranilla Bank, Serrana Bank, Quita Sueño Bank, Rosalind Bank, Thunder Knoll, Pedro Bank, Banco Gorda, Swan Islands (Honduras)

CO... (COLOMBIA) — Medellín, Cartagena, Turbo, Chocó

ATLANTIC OCEAN

West Indies

Leeward Islands

Turks and Caicos Islands (U.K.)

Hispaniola

HAITI
PORT-AU-PRINCE
Santiago
DOMINICAN REPUBLIC
SANTO DOMINGO

Puerto Rico (U.S.A.)
SAN JUAN
Virgin Is (U.K.)
Virgin Is (U.S.A.)

Anguilla (U.K.)
THE VALLEY
Saint Martin (Fr.)
St-Barthélemy (Fr.)
St Maarten (Neth.)
Barbuda
Codrington
ANTIGUA AND BARBUDA
ST JOHN'S
Antigua
ST KITTS AND NEVIS
BASSETERRE
Montserrat
PLYMOUTH (U.K.)

Guadeloupe (France)
BASSE-TERRE
Îles des Saintes
Marie-Galante

Aves (Venezuela)

ROSEAU
DOMINICA

FORT-DE-FRANCE
Martinique (France)

CASTRIES
ST LUCIA

St Vincent Passage

St Vincent
KINGSTOWN
ST VINCENT AND THE GRENADINES
The Grenadines
Mustique
Canouan
Carriacou

BARBADOS
BRIDGETOWN

Antilles

Greater Antilles

Caribbean Sea

GRENADA
ST GEORGE'S

Lesser Antilles

Aruba (Neth.)
ORANJESTAD
Curaçao
WILLEMSTAD
Netherlands Antilles
Bonaire

Isla Blanquilla
Islas Las Aves
Islas Los Roques
Isla Orchila
Los Testigos

Isla de Margarita
NUEVA ESPARTA
La Asunción

Península de Paria
Golfo de Paria

TRINIDAD AND TOBAGO
Tobago
PORT OF SPAIN
Trinidad

Golfo de Venezuela

COLOMBIA
Santa Marta
Riohacha
GUAJIRA
Maicao
Maracaibo
ZULIA
Lake Maracaibo
FALCÓN
CARACAS
DISTRITO FEDERAL
Valencia
Maracay
MIRANDA
Barcelona
ANZOÁTEGUI
SUCRE
Cumaná
MONAGAS
Maturín
DELTA AMACURO

VENEZUELA

Ciudad Guayana
Ciudad Bolívar
BOLÍVAR

Orinoco

GUYANA

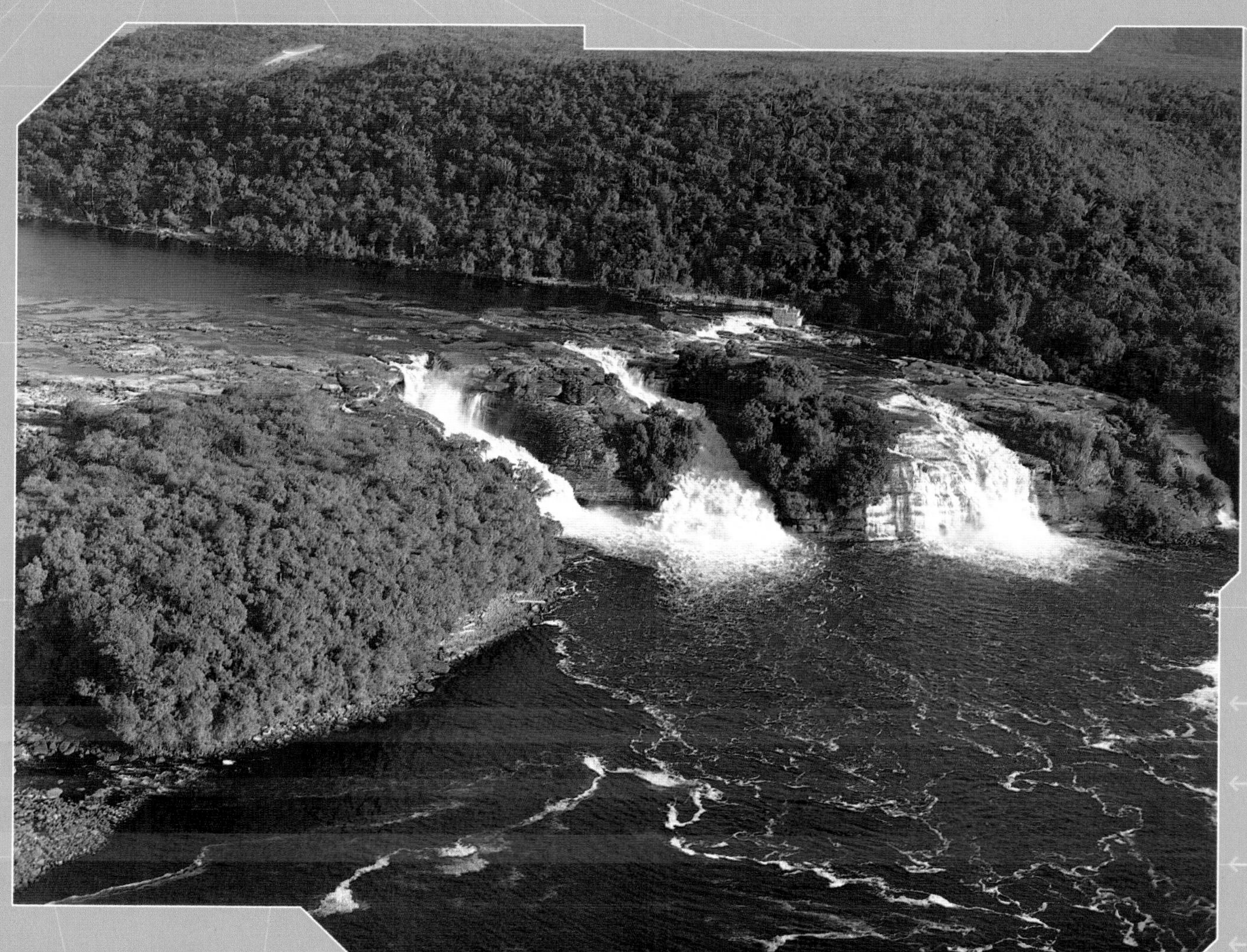

Canaima National Park, *Venezuela*

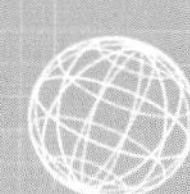

southamerica

[contents]

	page#
southamerica [landscapes]	190–191
southamerica [countries]	192–193
southamerica [contrasts]	194–195
southamerica [impacts]	196–197

	map coverage	scale	page#
southamerica [map 1]	SOUTH AMERICA North	1:8 000 000	198–199
southamerica [map 2]	SOUTH AMERICA Central	1:8 000 000	200–201
southamerica [map 3]	SOUTH AMERICA East	1:8 000 000	202–203
southamerica [map 4]	SOUTH AMERICA South	1:8 000 000	204–205
southamerica [map 5]	BRAZIL Southeast	1:3 300 000	206–207

Gulf of
Mexico

Caribbean Sea

Lake
Maracaibo

Orinoco
River

Llanos

Guiana Highlands

Negro River

Japurá River

Amazon

Largest drainage basin

Amazon
7 050 000 sq km / 2 722 000 sq miles
Map reference 199 F5

Galapagos Islands

Purus River

Selvas

Madeira River

Lake
Titicaca

Largest lake

Lake Titicaca
Bolivia/Peru
8 340 sq km / 3 220 sq miles
Map reference 200 C3

Altiplano

Atacama Desert

Pacific Ocean

Andes

Salado River

Parana River

Highest point

Cerro Aconcagua
Argentina
6 960 m / 22 834 ft
Map reference 204 C4

Cerro Aconcagua

Pampas

Colorado River

Negro River

Peninsula
Valdés

Patagonia

Lowest point

Peninsula Valdés
Argentina
40 m / 131 ft below sea level
Map reference 205 E6

Largest island

Isla Grande de Tierra del Fuego
Argentina/Chile
47 000 sq km / 18 147 sq miles
Map reference 205 C9

Falkland Islands

Tierra del Fuego

Cape Horn

CONNECTIONS

▶ subject   page#

▶ World physical features ══════▷ 8–9
▶ World land images ══════▷ 12–13
▶ South American states and territories ══════▷ 192–193
▶ Physical contrasts ══════▷ 194–195
▶ Reference maps of South America ══════▷ 198–207

← Orinoco River Delta
Angel Falls

Longest river

Amazon
6 516 km / 4 049 miles
Map reference 202 B1

Mouths of the Amazon

Basin

Amazon River

Tocantins River

Sao Francisco River

Mato Grosso

Chaco

Brazilian Highlands

Uruguay River

Atlantic Ocean

Rio de la Plata

The spectacular Andes mountains dominate the western side of South America, bordering the Pacific for the entire length of the landmass. They stretch from Tierra del Fuego in the south, to Panama in the north. This huge mountain system has many volcanoes, is the source of many of the continent's large rivers, including the Amazon and Orinoco, and surrounds the Atacama Desert, the driest place on earth. The Altiplano is a high plateau within the Andes between the main west and east mountain ranges. Other upland areas include the Brazilian Highlands in the northeast and Patagonia, where the land rises steadily from the Atlantic coast to the Andes.

The Amazon Basin is a large lowland area, lying just south of the equator, through which the Amazon river and its many tributaries flow towards the huge delta on the Atlantic coast. The region contains vast areas of tropical rain forest. Huge, sparsely populated plains known as Llanos in the north and Pampas in the south provide further contrasts in the landscapes of the continent.

1 Amazon River, *Brazil*

The grey area on this satellite image is the isolated city of Manaus in northern Brazil. It sits at the confluence of the Amazon and Negro rivers. The Amazon, flowing from west to east, originates in the Andes mountains in Peru and carries a thick solution of silt and sand giving it a brown colour. The Negro river flows over hard base rock giving little sediment so the water is clearer, appearing dark in this image. The waters do not combine immediately but flow side by side for some distance before merging.

Satellite/Sensor : Terra, MISR

2 Pampas, *Argentina*

The Pampas grassland plains of Argentina stretch from the foothills of the Andes mountains to the east coast.
This photograph shows the Pampas in Neuquen Province. Eastern areas tend to be better irrigated but the whole area supports a major livestock industry.

3 Lake Viedma, *Argentina*

Lake Viedma in the centre of this image. Lake Argentino to the left, and Lake San Martin to the right are situated in southern Argentina. This image looks southwest and shows the lakes being fed by meltwater from the glaciers of the Andes Mountains. Lake Viedma is over 300 m above sea level. Waters from it flow into Lake Argentino then into the Santa Cruz river, across the Patagonia plateau to the Atlantic Ocean. The snow-capped ridge behind the lakes forms the boundary between Argentina and Chile.

Satellite/Sensor : Space Shuttle

SOUTH AMERICA

HIGHEST MOUNTAINS

	m	ft	location	map
Cerro Aconcagua	6 960	22 834	Argentina	204 C4
Nevado Ojos del Salado	6 908	22 664	Argentina/Chile	204 C2
Cerro Bonete	6 872	22 546	Argentina	204 C2
Cerro Pissis	6 858	22 500	Argentina	204 C2
Cerro Tupungato	6 800	22 309	Argentina/Chile	204 C4
Cerro Meredario	6 770	22 211	Argentina	204 B3

LARGEST ISLANDS

	sq km	sq miles	map
Isla Grande de Tierra del Fuego	47 000	18 147	205 C9
Isla de Chiloe	8 394	3 240	205 B6
East Falkland	6 760	2 610	205 F8
West Falkland	5 413	2 090	205 E8

LONGEST RIVERS

	km	miles	map
Amazon	6 516	4 049	202 B1
Rio de la Plata-Parana	4 500	2 796	204 F4
Purus	3 218	1 999	199 F5
Madeira	3 200	1 988	199 G5
Sao Francisco	2 900	1 802	202 E4
Tocantins	2 750	1 708	202 B2

LAKES

	km	miles	map		sq km	sq miles	map
Lake Titicaca					8 340	3 220	200 C3

LAND AREA

		map
Most northerly point	Punta Gallinas, Colombia	198 D1
Most southerly point	Cape Horn, Chile	205 D9
Most westerly point	Galapagos Islands, Ecuador	216 H6
Most easterly point	Ilhas Martin Vas, Atlantic Ocean	216 M7
Total land area: 17 815 420 sq km / 6 878 572 sq miles		

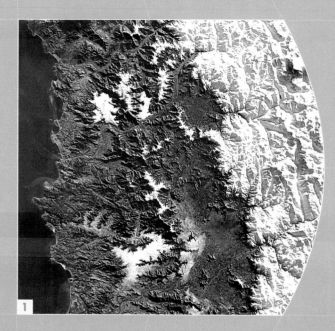

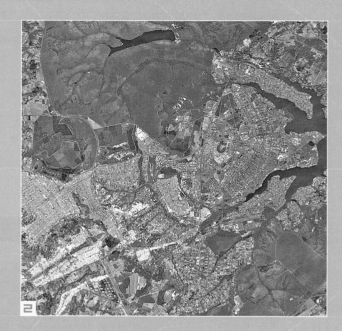

CONNECTIONS

subject	page#
World physical features	8–9
World countries	10–11
South America landscapes	190–191
South America contrasts	194–195
Reference maps of South America	198–207

SOUTH AMERICA

COUNTRIES

	area sq km	area sq miles	population	capital	languages	religions	currency	map
ARGENTINA	2 766 889	1 068 302	37 032 000	Buenos Aires	Spanish, Italian, Amerindian languages	Roman Catholic, Protestant	Peso	204–205
BOLIVIA	1 098 581	424 164	8 329 000	La Paz/Sucre	Spanish, Quechua, Aymara	Roman Catholic, Protestant, Bahaî	Boliviano	200–201
BRAZIL	8 547 379	3 300 161	170 406 000	Brasília	Portuguese	Roman Catholic, Protestant	Real	202–203
CHILE	756 945	292 258	15 211 000	Santiago	Spanish, Amerindian languages	Roman Catholic, Protestant	Peso	204–205
COLOMBIA	1 141 748	440 831	42 105 000	Bogotá	Spanish, Amerindian languages	Roman Catholic, Protestant	Peso	198
ECUADOR	272 045	105 037	12 646 000	Quito	Spanish, Quechua, other Amerindian languages	Roman Catholic	Sucre	198
GUYANA	214 969	83 000	761 000	Georgetown	English, creole, Amerindian languages	Protestant, Hindu, Roman Catholic, Sunni Muslim	Dollar	199
PARAGUAY	406 752	157 048	5 496 000	Asunción	Spanish, Guaraní	Roman Catholic, Protestant	Guaraní	201
PERU	1 285 216	496 225	25 662 000	Lima	Spanish, Quechua, Aymara	Roman Catholic, Protestant	Sol	200
SURINAME	163 820	63 251	417 000	Paramaribo	Dutch, Surinamese, English, Hindi	Hindu, Roman Catholic, Protestant, Sunni Muslim	Guilder	199
URUGUAY	176 215	68 037	3 337 000	Montevideo	Spanish	Roman Catholic, Protestant, Jewish	Peso	204
VENEZUELA	912 050	352 144	24 170 000	Caracas	Spanish, Amerindian languages	Roman Catholic, Protestant	Bolívar	198–199

DEPENDENT TERRITORIES

	territorial status	sq km	sq miles	population	capital	languages	religions	currency	map
Falkland Islands	United Kingdom Overseas Territory	12 170	4 699	2 000	Stanley	English	Protestant, Roman Catholic	Pound	205
French Guiana	French Overseas Department	90 000	34 749	165 000	Cayenne	French, creole	Roman Catholic	French franc	199
South Georgia and South Sandwich Islands	United Kingdom Overseas Territory	4 066	1 570	uninhabited					217

1 **Santiago,** ***Chile***

In this Landsat satellite image, Santiago, capital city and main industrial centre of Chile, can be seen to the left of the snow-capped Andes mountains which form a natural boundary between Chile and its easterly neighbour, Argentina. The city, which has suffered many earthquakes and floods, was established as Chile's capital when the country became independent in 1818.

Satellite/Sensor : Landsat

2 **Brasília,** ***Brazil***

Construction of Brasília as the administrative and political centre of Brazil began in 1956 and four years later it replaced Rio de Janeiro as the capital city of Brazil, South America's largest country. It is located on the Paraná, a headstream of the Tocantins river. In this infrared satellite image the city is in the centre, where buildings appear as light blue-grey. Lakes to the north and east of the city are blue-black, and vegetation along the small tributaries shows as red.

Satellite/Sensor : SPOT

3 **Lake Titicaca,** ***Bolivia/Peru***

Lake Titicaca, located in a depression within the high plains (Altiplano) of South America, is the largest freshwater lake on the continent. The international boundary between Bolivia and Peru passes through the lake. In this oblique Shuttle photograph, the Andes mountains can be seen in the top right and bottom left. Persistent drought in the area has caused water levels to drop and expose the bottom of the lake, shown as white patches on the lake shore.

Satellite/Sensor : Space Shuttle

Caribbean Sea

ATLANTIC OCEAN

PACIFIC OCEAN

ATLANTIC OCEAN

Barranquilla
Cartagena
Golfo del Darién
Gulf of Panama
Monteria
San Cristóbal
Medellín
Tunja
Ibagué
BOGOTÁ
COLOMBIA
Cali
Neiva
Pasto
QUITO
Manta
ECUADOR
Guayaquil
Cuenca
Golfo de Guayaquil
Iquitos
Chiclayo
Trujillo
PERU
Pucallpa
Huancayo
Cusco
LIMA
Ica
Juliaca
Arequipa
Arica
Iquique
Antofagasta

Isla de Coco
Isla de Malpelo (Colombia)
Galapagos Islands (Ecuador)

BARRANQUILLA
CARACAS
Barquisimeto
Maracay
Cumaná
Orinoco
Ciudad Bolívar
VENEZUELA
Puerto Ayacucho
GEORGETOWN
PARAMARIBO
CAYENNE
GUYANA
SURINAME
French Guiana (Fr.)
Boa Vista
Orinoco
Branco
Negro
Santarém
Amazon
Belém
São Luís
Parnaíba
Fortaleza
Teresina
Natal
João Pessoa
Floresta
Recife
Maceió
Aracaju
Salvador

Putumayo
Japurá
Tonantins
Manaus
Amazon
Carauari
Yavari
Juruá
Purus
Madeira
Tapajós
Xingu
Iriri
Marabá
Araguaia
Tocantins
BRAZIL
Cruzeiro do Sul
Porto Velho
Rio Branco
Juàzeiro
São Francisco
Marañón

Trinidad
Guaporé
Mamoré
Cuiabá
BRASÍLIA
Goiânia
Patos de Minas
Teófilo Otôni
Uberaba
Belo Horizonte
LA PAZ
BOLIVIA
Cochabamba
SUCRE
Santa Cruz
Potosí
Tarija
PARAGUAY
Paraguai
Campo Grande
Araçatuba
Pedro Juan Caballero
Campinas
Vitória
Ilha da Trindade (Brazil)
Ilhas Martin Vas (Brazil)

San Salvador de Jujuy
Teuco
ASUNCIÓN
Paraná
Maringá
Iguaçu
São Paulo
Rio de Janeiro
Curitiba
San Miguel de Tucumán
Posadas
Catamarca
Corrientes
Florianópolis
La Rioja
Salado
Santa Maria
Porto Alegre
Santa Fé
Concordia
Paraná
San Juan
Córdoba
Cerro Aconcagua
Mendoza
Rosario
Rio Grande
Valparaíso
Salado
URUGUAY
BUENOS AIRES
SANTIAGO
MONTEVIDEO
Río de la Plata
Concepción
Santa Rosa
Bahía Blanca
Mar del Plata
Colorado
Neuquén
Negro
Viedma
Golfo San Matías

Tropic of Capricorn
Islas de los Desventurados (Chile)
Archipiélago Juan Fernández (Chile)

Isla de Chiloé
Archipiélago de los Chonos
Golfo de San Jorge
Comodoro Rivadavia
Trelew

Bahía Grande
STANLEY
Falkland Islands (U.K.)
Puerto Natales
Punta Arenas
Isla Grande de Tierra del Fuego
Ushuaia
Cape Horn

South Georgia and South Sandwich Islands (U.K.)

Antarctic Circle

SOUTH AMERICA

TOP 10 COUNTRIES BY AREA

	sq km	sq miles	map	world rank
1. BRAZIL	8 547 379	3 300 161	202–203	5
2. ARGENTINA	2 766 889	1 068 302	204–205	8
3. PERU	1 285 216	496 225	200	20
4. COLOMBIA	1 141 748	440 831	198	26
5. BOLIVIA	1 098 581	424 164	200–201	28
6. VENEZUELA	912 050	352 144	198–199	33
7. CHILE	756 945	292 258	204–205	38
8. PARAGUAY	406 752	157 048	201	59
9. ECUADOR	272 045	105 037	198	74
10. GUYANA	214 969	83 000	199	83

TOP 10 COUNTRIES BY POPULATION

	population	map	world rank
1. BRAZIL	170 406 000	202–203	5
2. COLOMBIA	42 105 000	198	28
3. ARGENTINA	37 032 000	204–205	31
4. PERU	25 662 000	200	38
5. VENEZUELA	24 170 000	198–199	40
6. CHILE	15 211 000	204–205	59
7. ECUADOR	12 646 000	198	63
8. BOLIVIA	8 329 000	200–201	84
9. PARAGUAY	5 496 000	201	97
10. URUGUAY	3 337 000	204	125

1 La Paz, *Bolivia*

The Bolivian city of La Paz is the highest capital city in the world. It lies just southeast of Lake Titicaca, in a valley between the Cordillera Oriental and the Andes, sheltered from the severe winds and weather of the Altiplano. It has a population of over 1 million. The city was established by the Spanish conquistadors in the mid 1500's.

2 Farmland, *Ecuador*

On the western slopes of the Andes, erosion of the high volcanic peaks has created rich soils for farming, as seen here in Ecuador. The scattered farms are worked by indigenous Indian people who gather to sell, buy and barter at local weekly markets. Over 30 per cent of Ecuador's population is employed in agriculture and agricultural products account for almost half of the country's exports.

3 Glacier, *Patagonia*

Glaciers such as this, in the region of Patagonia, which straddles the Chile/Argentina border, are a great influence on the landscape. The surface of the glacier is deeply scarred by crevasses and patterns of debris within the ice indicate its current flow. Braided streams carry fine sediment away from the glacier.

Satellite/Sensor : Terra/ASTER

4 Galapagos Islands, *Ecuador*

This satellite image shows part of the Galapagos Islands, a group of islands created by volcanic activity. The craters of volcanoes on the main island of Isla Isabela and on Isla Fernandina to the west, can be clearly seen. Vegetation, which appears red, is limited as the landscape is dominated by lava flows. The Galapagos Islands are a group of isolated islands lying over 1 000 km west of the coast of Ecuador. They are renowned for their rich and unique wildlife.

Satellite/Sensor : SPOT

5 Andes Mountains

The Andes mountain range forms a formidable barrier down the whole length of the western side of the South American continent. This is clearly seen in this dramatic visualization created from digital terrain data. The western edge of the Andes descends steeply towards the Pacific Ocean with very little coastal lowland. Likewise to the east, the transition from high ground to low, flatter areas is also sudden, emphasizing the barrier of the mountains. To the south, the lowland areas form the grassy plains of the Pampas and to the north, the Amazon basin.

CONNECTIONS

► subject		page#
► La Paz	⇒	10–11
► World weather extremes	⇒	16–17
► Land cover types	⇒	18–19
► World's largest cities	⇒	24–25
► South America landscapes	⇒	190–191
► South America countries	⇒	192–193
► South America impacts	⇒	196–197

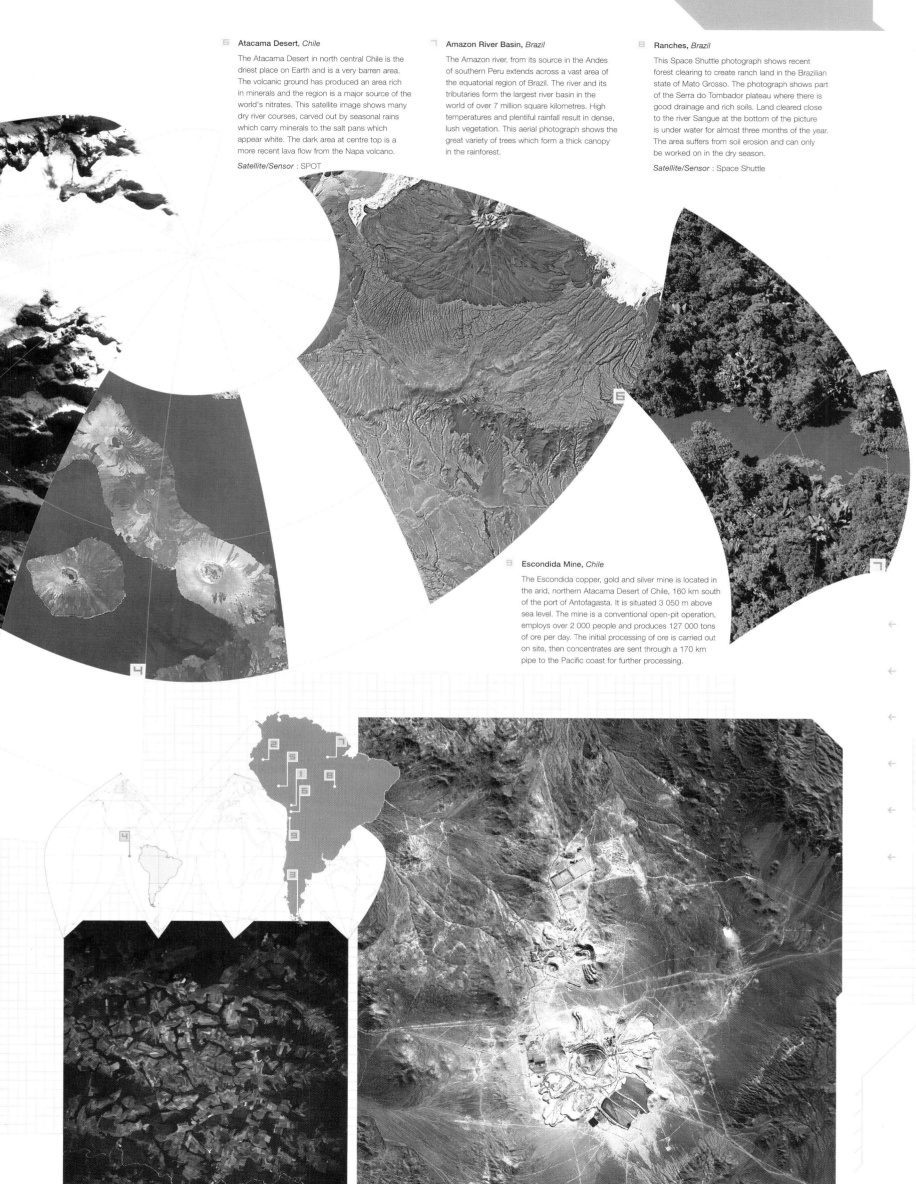

Atacama Desert, *Chile*

The Atacama Desert in north central Chile is the driest place on Earth and is a very barren area. The volcanic ground has produced an area rich in minerals and the region is a major source of the world's nitrates. This satellite image shows many dry river courses, carved out by seasonal rains which carry minerals to the salt pans which appear white. The dark area at centre top is a more recent lava flow from the Napa volcano.

Satellite/Sensor : SPOT

Amazon River Basin, *Brazil*

The Amazon river, from its source in the Andes of southern Peru extends across a vast area of the equatorial region of Brazil. The river and its tributaries form the largest river basin in the world of over 7 million square kilometres. High temperatures and plentiful rainfall result in dense, lush vegetation. This aerial photograph shows the great variety of trees which form a thick canopy in the rainforest.

Ranches, *Brazil*

This Space Shuttle photograph shows recent forest clearing to create ranch land in the Brazilian state of Mato Grosso. The photograph shows part of the Serra do Tombador plateau where there is good drainage and rich soils. Land cleared close to the river Sangue at the bottom of the picture is under water for almost three months of the year. The area suffers from soil erosion and can only be worked on in the dry season.

Satellite/Sensor : Space Shuttle

Escondida Mine, *Chile*

The Escondida copper, gold and silver mine is located in the arid, northern Atacama Desert of Chile, 160 km south of the port of Antofagasta. It is situated 3 050 m above sea level. The mine is a conventional open-pit operation, employs over 2 000 people and produces 127 000 tons of ore per day. The initial processing of ore is carried out on site, then concentrates are sent through a 170 km pipe to the Pacific coast for further processing.

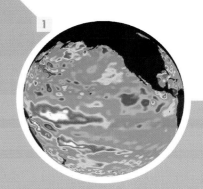
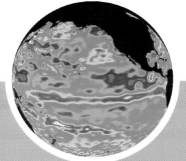
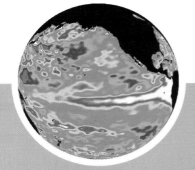
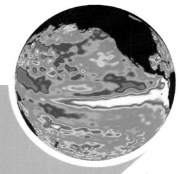

1 El Niño, South America

Periodically, atmospheric pressure becomes abnormally low in the middle of the Pacific Ocean and abnormally high over northern Australia. This results in the prevailing easterly winds weakening and changing direction. As a result, water off the west coast of South America becomes warmer by 4°–5°C. This phenomenon, known as El Niño, can have a dramatic effect on the world's climate, including higher rainfall in east Africa, and much lower rainfall and higher temperatures than normal in Australia.

The satellite images of the Earth show the development of El Niño during 1997. The red/white areas represent El Niño moving eastwards across the Pacific Ocean. The impacts of this on South America were drier conditions along the north coast, higher temperatures on the east and more rain in the northwest and southeast. The area most severely affected was the northwest coast. High river levels and flash floods were frequent and mudslides destroyed villages. Over 30 000 homes were lost in Peru during the course of the 1997–1998 El Niño event.

Satellite/Sensor : TOPEX/Poseidon

2 Mining, South America

The mineral distribution map of South America (Fig. #01) shows the great concentration of copper mining along the Andes mountain range. Large quantities of bauxite, the main ore for the production of aluminium, are mined in those areas with a tropical humid climate in the north of the continent. Symbol sizes on the map are proportional to mineral production as a percentage of world production, the largest representing over five per cent. While mining contributes enormously to the overall economy of South America, it also depletes natural resources and damages the environment. The photograph of the Bon Futuro tin mine in the Rondônia region of Brazil (number 7 on the map) shows how landscapes can be scarred by mining activities. Additional impacts can be the displacement of communities and the pollution of rivers and lakes.

Fig. #01
South America minerals

Metallic minerals

- Iron **Fe**
- Copper **Cu**
- Gold **Au**
- Aluminium **Al**
- Manganese **Mn**
- Lead **Pb**, Zinc **Zn**, Silver **Ag**
- Tin **Sn**, Antimony **Sb**
- Nickel **Ni**, Molybdenum **Mo**, Niobium **Nb**, Chromium **Cr**, Tungsten **W**

Industrial (non metallic) minerals

- Phosphate **P**, Borates **B**,
- Fluorspar **F**
- Diamonds **Diam.**

Symbol sizes reflect level of production from less than 1% to over 5% of world production.

Argentina
1 Aguilar, **Pb, Zn, Ag**
2 Bajo de la Alumbrera, **Cu, Mo, Au**
3 El Pachon, **Cu, Mo, Au**
4 Northern Provinces, **B**

Bolivia
5 Potosí, Oruro, **Sn, Sb, Pb, Zn, Ag, W**

Brazil
6 Trombetas, **Al**
7 Rondônia, **Sn**
8 Carajás, **Fe**
9 Igarapé Azul, Carajás, **Mn**
10 Caraíba, **Cu**
11 Campo Formoso, **Cr**
12 Cana Brava, **Cr**
13 Niquelândia, **Ni**
14 Morro do Niquel, **Ni**
15 Tocantins, **Ni**
16 Urucum, **Mn, Fe**
17 Vazante, **Pb, Zn**
18 Boquira, **Pb, Zn**
19 Jequitinhonha, **Diam.**
20 Araxá, **Nb, P**
21 Morro Velho, **Au**
22 Iron Quadrilateral, **Fe**
23 Morro da Fumaça, **F**
24 Roraima, **Diam.**

Chile
25 Chuquicamata, **Abra, Cu, Mo**
26 Escondida, El Salvador, **Cu, Mo, Au**
27 Disputada, Andina, Pelambres, **Cu, Mo**
28 El Teniente, **Cu, Mo**
29 Cerro Colorado, Quebrada Blanca, **Cu, Mo**
30 La Candelaria, **Cu, Mo, Au**
31 Atacama, **Fe**

Colombia
32 Titiribi, **Au**
33 Cerro Matoso, **Ni**

Ecuador
34 Portovelo, **Au**

Guyana
35 Guyana, **Al**
36 Omai, **Au**

Peru
37 Northern Peru, **Pb, Zn, Ag, Cu, Mo**
38 Cerro de Pasco, central Peru, **Pb, Zn, Ag, Cu, Mo**
39 Cuajone, Toquepala, **Cu, Mo**
40 Tintaya, **Cu, Mo**
41 Cerro Verde, **Cu, Mo**
42 Marcona, **Fe**
43 Yanacocha, **Au**

Suriname
44 Suriname, **Al**

Venezuela
45 Cedeno, **Al**
46 Cerro Bolivar, San Isidro, **Fe**
47 Cristinas, **Au, Cu**

Deforestation, *Bolivia*

The two Landsat satellite images below were produced fifteen years apart. The upper image shows an area of tropical rainforest near the Bolivian city of Santa Cruz in 1984. The Piray river is the dark blue line in the bottom left of the image. Forest and natural vegetation appears as green, bare ground as red. The lower image, dated 1998, demonstrates the impact of deforestation in the region. Huge areas of the forest east of the river have been completely cleared for agriculture, in a similar way to that shown in the aerial photograph. Destruction of the rainforest is a major environmental issue and interrupting the forest canopy in this way causes humidity to drop rapidly and huge areas of forest become vulnerable to fire.

Satellite/Sensor : Landsat

CONNECTIONS

► subject	page#
► World climate and weather	16–17
► World land cover types	18–19
► World changes	20–21
► South America landscapes	190–191
► South America countries	192–193
► South America contrasts	194–195

8°S-14°N / 51°-82°W

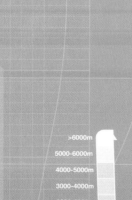

>6000m
5000-6000m
4000-5000m
3000-4000m
2000-3000m
1000-2000m
500-1000m
200-500m
0-200m
<0m

0-200m
200-500m
500-1000m
1000-2000m
2000-3000m
3000-4000m
4000-5000m
5000-6000m
>6000m

Administrative regions numbered on the map:

COLOMBIA
1. QUINDO (C3)
2. RISARALDA (C3)
3. SANTAFÉ DE BOGOTÁ (C3)

ECUADOR
4. BOLÍVAR (B5)
5. CHIMBORAZO (B5)
6. TUNGURAHUA (B5)
7. ZAMORA-CHINCHIPE (B5)

186-187

Martinique (France)
St Lucia Channel
CASTRIES Gros Islet
SOUFRIÈRE ST LUCIA
Micoud
Vieux Fort

St Vincent Passage

St Vincent
Soufrière 1234
ST VINCENT Soufrière
AND KINGSTOWN
THE GRENADINES
Bequia
Canouan Mustique
The Grenadines
Hillsborough Carriacou
Ronde
ST GEORGE'S Grenville
GRENADA

Speightstown
BRIDGETOWN BARBADOS
Six Cross Roads

Plymouth Charlotteville
Scarborough
Tobago
Canaan
Galera
PORT Point
OF SPAIN
Trinidad
TRINIDAD
AND
TOBAGO
San
Fernando
Claro

Sea

Antilles

Bonaire
Kralendijk
Islas
Las Aves
Islas
Los Roques   Isla Orchila
Isla Blanquilla
Isla La Tortuga
Los
Isla La Asunción
Margarita

NUEVA ESPARTA
Porlamar
Isla Cubagua Río
La Asunción
Isla de Margarita
Isla Coche Caribe
Península de Paria
Parque Nacional Carúpano Güiria
Mochima Cumaná
Península de Araya
Gulf
of Paria

Maiquetía
DISTRITO
FEDERAL
CARACAS Petare
Los Teques
MIRANDA
El Pao
Ortiz San Juan
de los Morros
GUÁRICO

A T L A N T I C

O C E A N

VENEZUELA

BOLÍVAR

Guiana

GEORGETOWN
New Amsterdam

GUYANA

PARAMARIBO

SURINAME

CAYENNE

French
Guiana

AMAPÁ

AMAZONAS

RORAIMA

Boa Vista

BRAZIL

B R A Z I L

PARÁ

Manaus

200-201

202-203

E   64°   F   60°   G   56°   H   52°   I

miles
0   100   200   300

1 : 8 000 000

km
0   100   200   300   400   500

Lambert Azimuthal Equal Area Projection

6°-28°S / 48°-80°W

PACIFIC

OCEAN

Tropic of Capricorn

CONNECTIONS

>6000m
5000-6000m
4000-5000m
3000-4000m
2000-3000m
1000-2000m
500-1000m
200-500m
0-200m
<0m

0-200m
200-500m
500-1000m
1000-2000m
2000-3000m
3000-4000m
4000-5000m
5000-6000m
>6000m

198-199
202-203
204-205
BRAZIL
PARÁ
TOCANTINS
MATO GROSSO
MATO GROSSO DO SUL
GOIÁS
DISTRITO FEDERAL
BRASÍLIA
MINAS GERAIS
SÃO PAULO
PARANÁ
SANTA CATARINA
RONDÔNIA
PARAGUAY
ASUNCIÓN
ARGENTINA
FORMOSA
CHACO
SANTIAGO DEL ESTERO
MISIONES
SANTA CRUZ
CHUQUISACA
ATLANTIC OCEAN
Serra do Cachimbo
Serra dos Parecis
Serra do Roncador
Planalto do Mato Grosso
Pantanal Matogrossense
Chaco Boreal
Gran Chaco
Parque Indígena do Xingu
Ilha do Bananal
Goiânia
Campo Grande
Cuiabá
Corumbá
Santa Cruz
Curitiba
São Paulo
Campinas
Santos
Florianópolis
Foz do Iguaçu
Posadas
Corrientes
Resistencia
Concepción
Pedro Juan Caballero
Uberlândia
Londrina
Maringá
64°
60°
56°
52°
48°
E
F
G
H
I
1: 8 000 000
miles
0
100
200
300
km
0
100
200
300
400
500
Lambert Azimuthal Equal Area Projection

202
198-199
1
2
3
4
5
Equator
0°
4°
8°
12°
16°
ATLANTIC
OCEAN
Mouths of the Amazon
Atol das Rocas
BRAZIL
AMAPÁ
PARÁ
MARANHÃO
CEARÁ
PIAUÍ
RIO GRANDE DO NORTE
PARAÍBA
PERNAMBUCO
ALAGOAS
SERGIPE
BAHIA
TOCANTINS
GOIÁS
MATO GROSSO
DISTRITO FEDERAL
BRASÍLIA
Macapá
Belém
São Luís
Teresina
Fortaleza (Ceará)
Natal
João Pessoa
Recife (Pernambuco)
Maceió
Aracaju
Salvador (Bahia)
Palmas
Goiânia
Santarém
Marabá
Imperatriz
Ilha de Marajó
Serra do Tiracambu
Serra dos Carajás
Serra do Cachimbo
Serra do Roncador
Serra Geral de Goiás
Chapada Diamantina
Serra da Ibiapaba
LITIGATED AREA
Planalto do Mato Grosso

south america [map3]
0°-31°S / 32°-56°W
1:8 000 000
miles 0 100 200 300
km 0 100 200 300 400 500
Lambert Azimuthal Equal Area Projection
CONNECTIONS
subject page#
World countries 10–11
World population distribution 22–23
World cities 24–25
South America countries 192–193
Atlantic Ocean 216–217
ATLANTIC
OCEAN
MINAS GERAIS
SÃO PAULO
PARANÁ
SANTA CATARINA
RIO GRANDE DO SUL
MATO GROSSO DO SUL
RIO DE JANEIRO
ESPÍRITO SANTO
PARAGUAY
ARGENTINA
MISIONES
Planalto do Brasil
Serra da Mantiqueira
Tropic of Capricorn
Belo Horizonte
São Paulo
Rio de Janeiro
Curitiba
Porto Alegre
Florianópolis
Campinas
Santos
Vitória
>6000m
5000-6000m
4000-5000m
3000-4000m
2000-3000m
1000-2000m
500-1000m
200-500m
0-200m
<0m
200-201
204-205

200-201
202-203
204
Tropic of Capricorn
PARAGUAY
BRAZIL
URUGUAY
ARGENTINA
PACIFIC OCEAN
Atacama Desert
ASUNCIÓN
MONTEVIDEO
BUENOS AIRES
SANTIAGO
Río de la Plata
Sierras de Córdoba
PARANÁ
SANTA CATARINA
RIO GRANDE DO SUL
MISIONES
CORRIENTES
ENTRE RÍOS
SANTA FE
CHACO
FORMOSA
SANTIAGO DEL ESTERO
CÓRDOBA
SAN LUIS
MENDOZA
SAN JUAN
LA RIOJA
CATAMARCA
TUCUMÁN
SALTA
LA PAMPA
RÍO NEGRO
NEUQUÉN
BUENOS AIRES
ANTOFAGASTA
ATACAMA
COQUIMBO
VALPARAÍSO
MAULE
BÍO-BÍO
LA ARAUCANÍA
Córdoba
Rosario
Mendoza
Valparaíso
Concepción
Porto Alegre
Mar del Plata
Bahía Blanca

southamerica[map4]

CONNECTIONS

subject	page#
World cities	24–25
South America landscapes	190–191
South America countries	192–193
South America contrasts	194–195
Antarctica	222–223

15°-24°S / 38°-53°W

202-203

Elevation legend:

- >6000m
- 5000-6000m
- 4000-5000m
- 3000-4000m
- 2000-3000m
- 1500-2000m
- 1000-1500m
- 500-1000m
- 200-500m
- 100-200m
- 0-100m
- <0m

- 0-200m
- 200-500m
- 500-1000m
- 1000-2000m
- 2000-3000m
- 3000-4000m
- 4000-5000m
- 5000-6000m
- >6000m

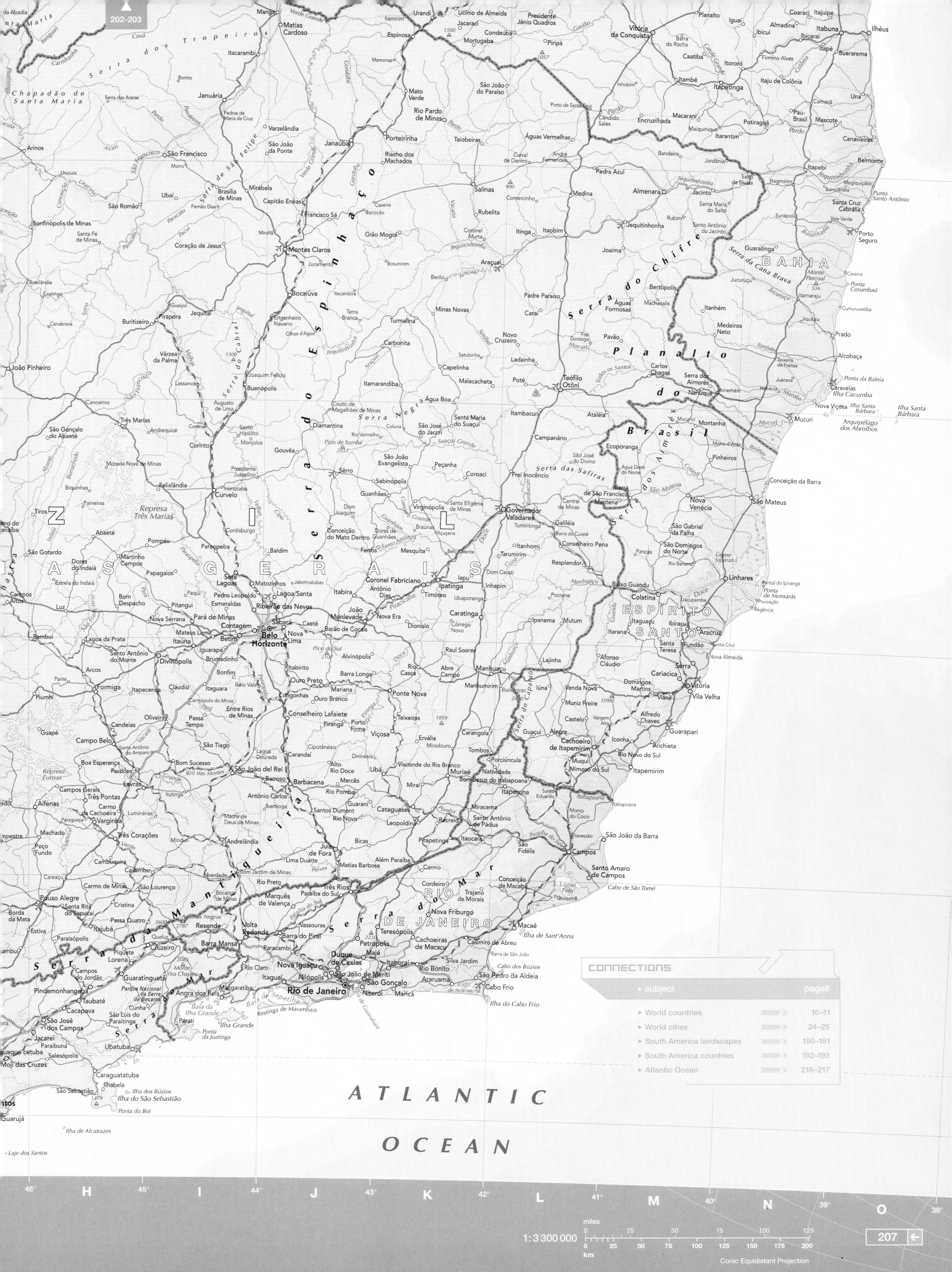

1:3 300 000

Conic Equidistant Projection

Paradise Bay, *Antarctica*

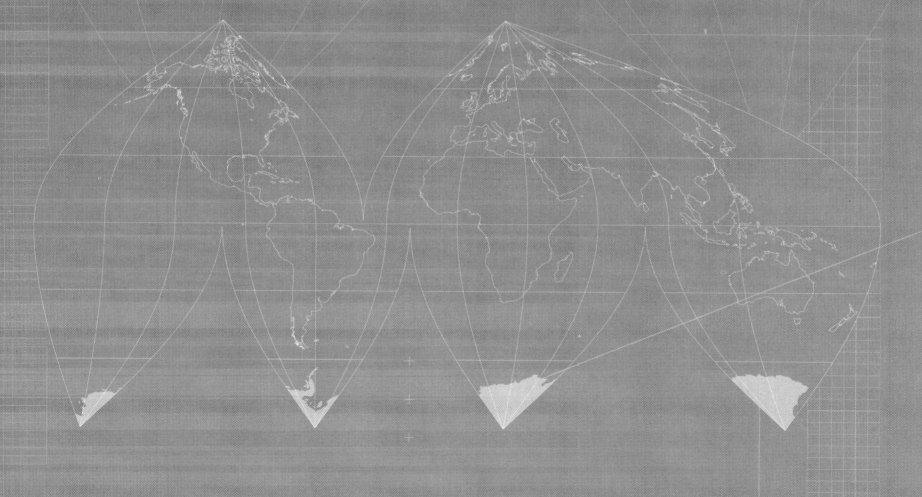

oceansandpoles

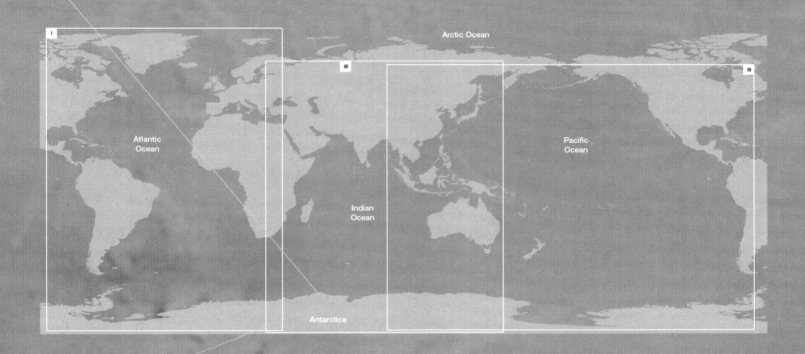

[contents]

		page#
oceans [features]		210–211
antarctica [features]		212–213
the**arctic** [features]		214–215

	map coverage	scale	page#
oceans [map1]	ATLANTIC OCEAN	1:40 000 000	216–217
oceans [map 2]	INDIAN OCEAN	1:40 000 000	218–219
oceans [map 3]	PACIFIC OCEAN	1:45 000 000	220–221
antarctica [map 1]	ANTARCTICA	1:18 000 000	222–223
the**arctic** [map 1]	ARCTIC OCEAN	1:24 000 000	224

1

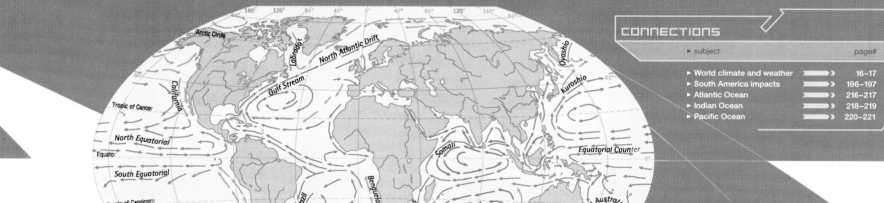

CONNECTIONS

► subject		page#
► World climate and weather	➤	16–17
► South America impacts	➤	196–197
► Atlantic Ocean	➤	216–217
► Indian Ocean	➤	218–219
► Pacific Ocean	➤	220–221

Fig. #01
Ocean surface currents

→ Warm current
→ Cold current
→ Seasonal drift during northern winter

Fig. #02
Sea surface height

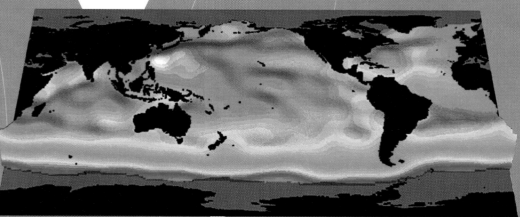

Fig. #01–#02 Sea surface currents and height

Most of the Earth's incoming solar radiation is absorbed by the surface waters of the oceans. The resultant warming is greatest around the equator and ocean surface currents, as shown on the map above (Fig. #01), redistribute the heat around the globe. They are influenced by winds, by density gradients caused by variations in temperature and salinity, and by the Earth's rotation which tends to deflect currents to the right in the northern hemisphere and to the left in the southern hemisphere. The circulation of ocean currents is a major influence on the world's climate. Sea surface circulation is reflected in variations in sea surface height (Fig. #02) which can vary greatly across currents. Currents flow along the slopes and are strongest where the slopes are steepest.

Satellite/Sensor : TOPEX/POSEIDON

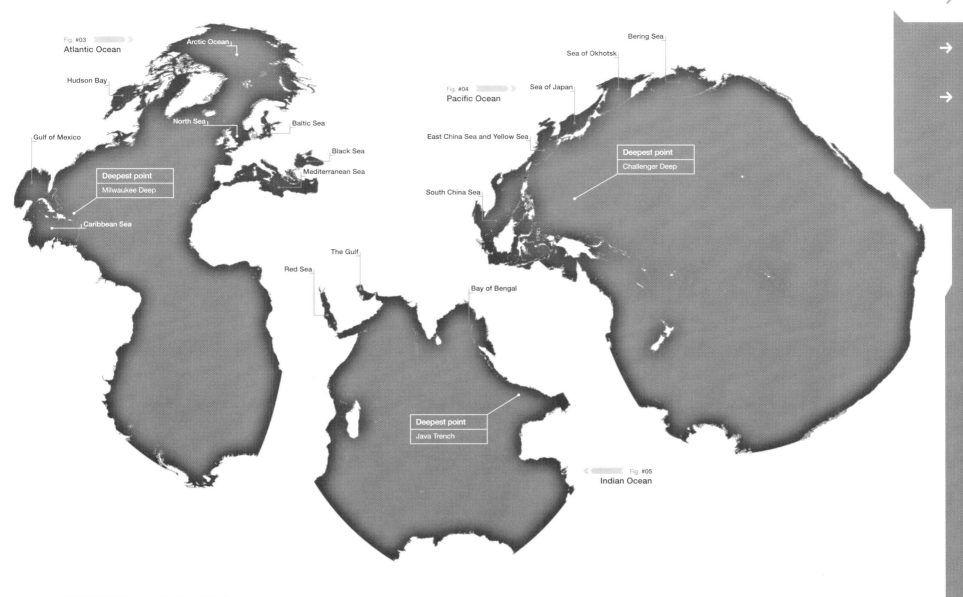

Fig. #03 Atlantic Ocean

Arctic Ocean

Hudson Bay

North Sea

Baltic Sea

Gulf of Mexico

Black Sea

Mediterranean Sea

Deepest point
Milwaukee Deep

Caribbean Sea

Bering Sea

Sea of Okhotsk

Fig. #04 Pacific Ocean

Sea of Japan

East China Sea and Yellow Sea

Deepest point
Challenger Deep

South China Sea

The Gulf

Red Sea

Bay of Bengal

Deepest point
Java Trench

Fig. #05 Indian Ocean

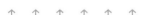

OCEANS

ATLANTIC OCEAN	area sq km	area sq miles	maximum depth metres	maximum depth feet	INDIAN OCEAN	area sq km	area sq miles	maximum depth metres	maximum depth feet	PACIFIC OCEAN	area sq km	area sq miles	maximum depth metres	maximum depth feet
Atlantic Ocean	86 557 000	33 420 000	8 605	28 231	Indian Ocean	73 427 000	28 350 000	7 125	23 376	Pacific Ocean	166 241 000	64 186 000	10 920	35 826
Arctic Ocean	9 485 000	3 662 000	5 450	17 880	Bay of Bengal	2 172 000	839 000	4 500	14 763	South China Sea	2 590 000	1 000 000	5 514	18 090
Caribbean Sea	2 512 000	970 000	7 680	25 196	Red Sea	453 000	175 000	3 040	9 973	Bering Sea	2 261 000	873 000	4 150	13 615
Mediterranean Sea	2 510 000	969 000	5 121	16 800	The Gulf	238 000	92 000	73	239	Sea of Okhotsk (Okhotskoye More)	1 392 000	537 000	3 363	11 033
Gulf of Mexico	1 544 000	596 000	3 504	11 495						East China Sea (Dong Hai) and Yellow Sea (Huang Hai)	1 202 000	464 000	2 717	8 913
Hudson Bay	1 233 000	476 000	259	849						Sea of Japan (East Sea)	1 013 000	391 000	3 743	12 280
North Sea	575 000	222 000	661	2 168										
Black Sea	508 000	196 000	2 245	7 365										
Baltic Sea	382 000	147 000	460	1 509										

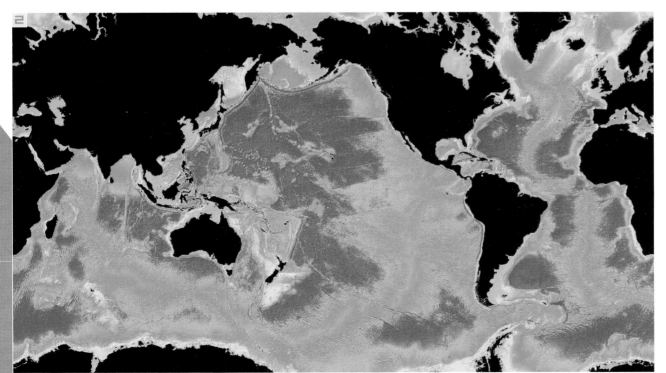

1 Perspective View, Pacific Ocean

This 3-D perspective view shows the sea trenches, ridges and basins of the western side of the Pacific Ocean. The image has been generated using sea depth values and extends from Australia and Melanesia at the bottom to Japan and the Kamchatka Peninsula at the top. Severe variations in depth of the sea bed are clearly seen. Deep trenches are shown by the darker areas. The New Hebrides, South Solomon and New Britain Trenches are visible at the bottom of the image and the Mariana Trench, the world's deepest, in the upper centre.

2 Global Seafloor Topography

This image has been produced from a combination of shipboard depth soundings and gravity data derived from satellite altimetry from the ERS-1 and Geosat satellites. The range of colours represents different depths of the ocean – from orange and yellow on the shallow continental shelves to dark blues in the deepest ocean trenches. The heavily fractured mid-ocean ridges (ranging from green to yellow) are particularly prominent.

ANTARCTICA

HIGHEST MOUNTAINS

	m	ft
Vinson Massif	4 897	16 066
Mt Tyree	4 852	15 918
Mt Kirkpatrick	4 528	14 855
Mt Markham	4 351	14 275
Mt Jackson	4 190	13 747
Mt Sidley	4 181	13 717

AREA

	sq km	sq miles
Total land area (excluding ice shelves)	12 093 000	4 669 292
Ice shelves	1 559 000	601 954
Exposed rock	49 000	18 920

HEIGHTS

	m	ft
Lowest bedrock elevation (Bentley Subglacial Trench)	-2 496	-8 189
Maximum ice thickness (Astrolabe Subglacial Basin)	4 776	15 669
Mean ice thickness (including ice shelves)	1 859	6 099

VOLUME

	cubic km	cubic miles
Ice sheet (including ice shelves)	25 400 000	10 160 000

CLIMATE

	°C	°F
Lowest screen temperature (Vostok Station, 21st July 1983)	-89.2	-128.6
Coldest place – Annual mean (Plateau Station)	-56.6	-69.9

1 Ozone Depletion

Since the 1970s, measurements have shown a thinning of the protective ozone layer in the Earth's atmosphere and the appearance of an ozone 'hole' over Antarctica. A major cause of this appears to be emissions of CFCs chlorofluorocarbons (CFCs) and halon gasses. This image from the Total Ozone Mapping Spectrometer (TOMS) sensor shows the ozone hole (blue) at its maximum extent of 11 million square miles in 2000. The unit of measurement for Ozone is the Dobson Unit (DU) with 300 being an average figure. In the image, yellow and orange represent high levels of 300–340DU, and dark blue low levels of 100–200 DU.

Satellite/Sensor : TOMS

2 Sea Ice Concentration

These images have been derived from data collected by the Special Sensor Microwave Imager (SSM/I) carried on US Department of Defense meteorological satellites. The colours represent ice concentration, ranging from the purple and red areas with a concentration of over 80 per cent, through to the green and yellow areas with concentrations between 20 and 40 per cent. The top image shows the ice at its lowest 2000 level in February, towards the end of the Antarctic summer. Ice builds up through the winter and by September (bottom), the ice is at its most extensive. In places the sea is frozen to a distance of over 1 000 km from the land.

Satellite/Sensor : SSM/I

3 Larsen Ice Shelf

This satellite image shows the edge of the Larsen Ice Shelf on the eastern side of the Antarctic Peninsula, and icebergs which have split, or 'calved' from the shelf. Ice shelves, which account for about 2 per cent of all Antarctic ice, typically undergo cycles of advance and retreat over many decades. Warmer surface temperatures over just a few months can cause an ice shelf to splinter and may prime it for a major collapse. This process can be expected to become more widespread if global, and particularly Antarctic summer, temperatures increase.

Satellite/Sensor : Landsat

4 Ice Sheet Thickness

Antarctica is covered by a permanent ice sheet that is in places more that 4 500 m thick. This map shows the thickness of ice, with the orange/red areas representing ice over 3 000 m thick. The thinnest ice is around the coast and on the high mountains, represented by the blue areas. The cross-section shows the ice cap (pale blue) in relation to the bedrock of Antarctica. This clearly shows that the thickest ice occurs above the deep glacial trenches, where the bedrock lies well below sea level.

5 Radar Image of Antarctica

This image of the whole of Antarctica is derived from data gathered by the Canadian RADARSAT satellite. In the image, light and dark areas represent relative measurements of radar reflectivity. Areas of finely powdered snow and smooth ice with few imperfections tend not to scatter radar waves projected against it, hence they appear dark. Irregular surfaces such as old, pitted ice, rock slides, and crevasses scatter the radar beam, giving a strong radar signal and thus appearing bright. Images such as this are valuable tools in the study of ice flow and stability on the continent.

Satellite/Sensor : RADARSAT

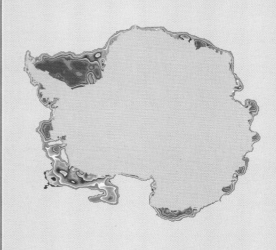

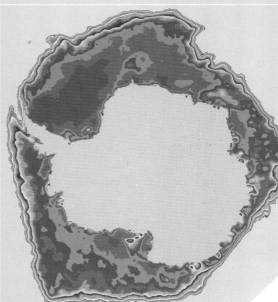

Fig. #01

Cross section of West Antarctica

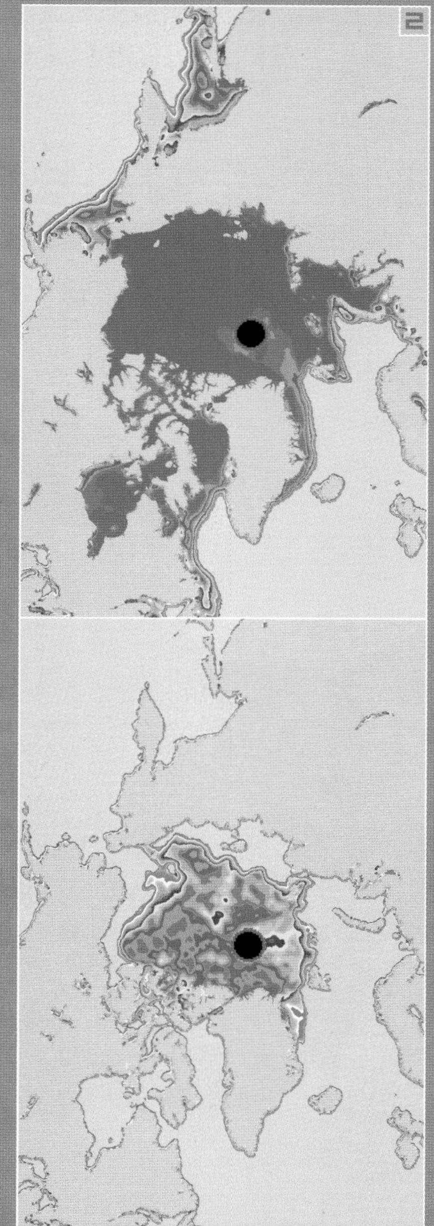

1 Tundra Landscape

Lakes and meandering rivers in a tundra landscape are shown in this photograph, taken in the short Arctic summer. Tundra is a cold-climate landscape type characterized by very low winter temperatures and short, cool summers. It is found in the region between 60°N and the Arctic ice cap and also at high altitudes beyond the climatic limits of tree growth. Tundra vegetation consists of dwarf shrubs, low herbaceous plants, lichens and mosses, on a permanently frozen subsoil.

2 Sea Ice Concentration

Although much of the Arctic Ocean is constantly frozen, there are wide variations in the amount of sea ice throughout the year, as shown by these images from the Special Sensor Microwave Imager (SSM/I). The purple areas show almost completely frozen sea (over ninety six per cent concentration) which extends as far south as Hudson Bay, Canada in February (top). By the end of the summer most of this ice has melted, as seen in the September image (bottom). The remaining sea ice at this time is thinner and more fragmented, even near the North Pole. Pink and brown areas represent concentrations of between sixty and eighty per cent.

Satellite/Sensor : SSM/I

Fig. #01 ▶▶▶▶▶▶ ▶
Peoples of the Arctic

The Arctic regions of Alaska, northern Canada, Greenland, and northern Scandinavia and Russian Federation contain the homelands of a diverse range of indigenous peoples. The main groups are shown on this map. These native peoples have subsisted for thousands of years on the resources of land and sea, as hunters, fishermen and reindeer herders. More recently, conflicts have arisen with governments eager to exploit the rich natural resources of the Arctic. There have also been moves towards greater autonomy for such groups. Most notably, in 1992 the Tungavik Federation of Nunavut and the government of Canada signed an agreement which addressed Inuit land claims and harvesting rights and established the new territory of Nunavut.

ALEUT
DENE TANANA
INUVIALUIT KOYUKON YUPIK
INUPIAQ
CHUKCHI
YUKAGHIR
YAKUT
DOLGAN
CANADIAN INUIT
Arctic Ocean
NENETS
KHANTY
CREE
LABRADOR INUIT
GREENLAND INUIT
SAAMI
Arctic Circle
Atlantic Ocean

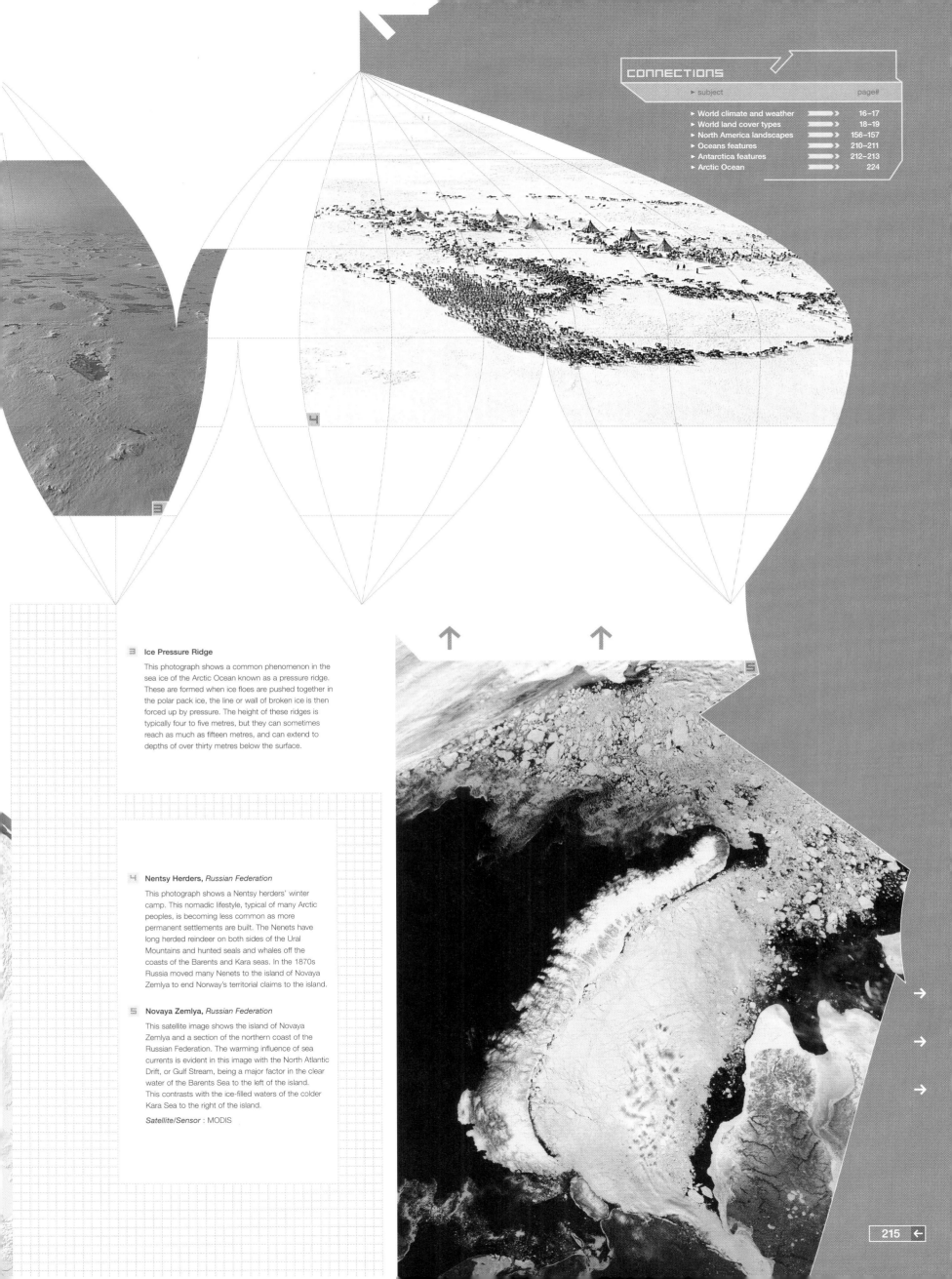

CONNECTIONS

► subject	page#
► World climate and weather	16–17
► World land cover types	18–19
► North America landscapes	156–157
► Oceans features	210–211
► Antarctica features	212–213
► Arctic Ocean	224

☰ Ice Pressure Ridge

This photograph shows a common phenomenon in the sea ice of the Arctic Ocean known as a pressure ridge. These are formed when ice floes are pushed together in the polar pack ice, the line or wall of broken ice is then forced up by pressure. The height of these ridges is typically four to five metres, but they can sometimes reach as much as fifteen metres, and can extend to depths of over thirty metres below the surface.

☷ Nentsy Herders, *Russian Federation*

This photograph shows a Nentsy herders' winter camp. This nomadic lifestyle, typical of many Arctic peoples, is becoming less common as more permanent settlements are built. The Nenets have long herded reindeer on both sides of the Ural Mountains and hunted seals and whales off the coasts of the Barents and Kara seas. In the 1870s Russia moved many Nenets to the island of Novaya Zemlya to end Norway's territorial claims to the island.

☶ Novaya Zemlya, *Russian Federation*

This satellite image shows the island of Novaya Zemlya and a section of the northern coast of the Russian Federation. The warming influence of sea currents is evident in this image with the North Atlantic Drift, or Gulf Stream, being a major factor in the clear water of the Barents Sea to the left of the island. This contrasts with the ice-filled waters of the colder Kara Sea to the right of the island.

Satellite/Sensor : MODIS

ATLANTIC OCEAN
PACIFIC OCEAN
Mid-Atlantic Ridge
CANADA
UNITED STATES OF AMERICA
MEXICO
Greenland (Denmark)
ICELAND
BRAZIL
PERU
BOLIVIA
COLOMBIA
VENEZUELA
GUYANA
ECUADOR
CUBA
SPAIN
PORTUGAL
FRANCE
ITALY
MOROCCO
ALGERIA
LIBYA
MALI
NIGER
CHAD
MAURITANIA
NIGERIA
ANGOLA
SWEDEN
POLAND
UKRAINE
RUSSIAN FEDERATION
Sahara
Caribbean Sea
Gulf of Mexico
Sargasso Sea
Hudson Bay
Labrador Sea
Norwegian Sea
North Sea
Gulf of Guinea
Guinea Basin
Cape Verde Basin
Guiana Basin
Hatteras Abyssal Plain
Nares Abyssal Plain
New England Seamounts
Bermuda Rise
Northwest Atlantic Mid-Ocean Channel
Reykjanes Ridge
Iceland Basin
Porcupine Abyssal Plain
Biscay Abyssal Plain
Monaco Basin
Cape Verde Plateau
Sierra Leone Basin
Ceara Abyssal Plain
Demerara Abyssal Plain
Pernambuco Abyssal Plain
Equator
Tropic of Cancer

oceans[map 1]

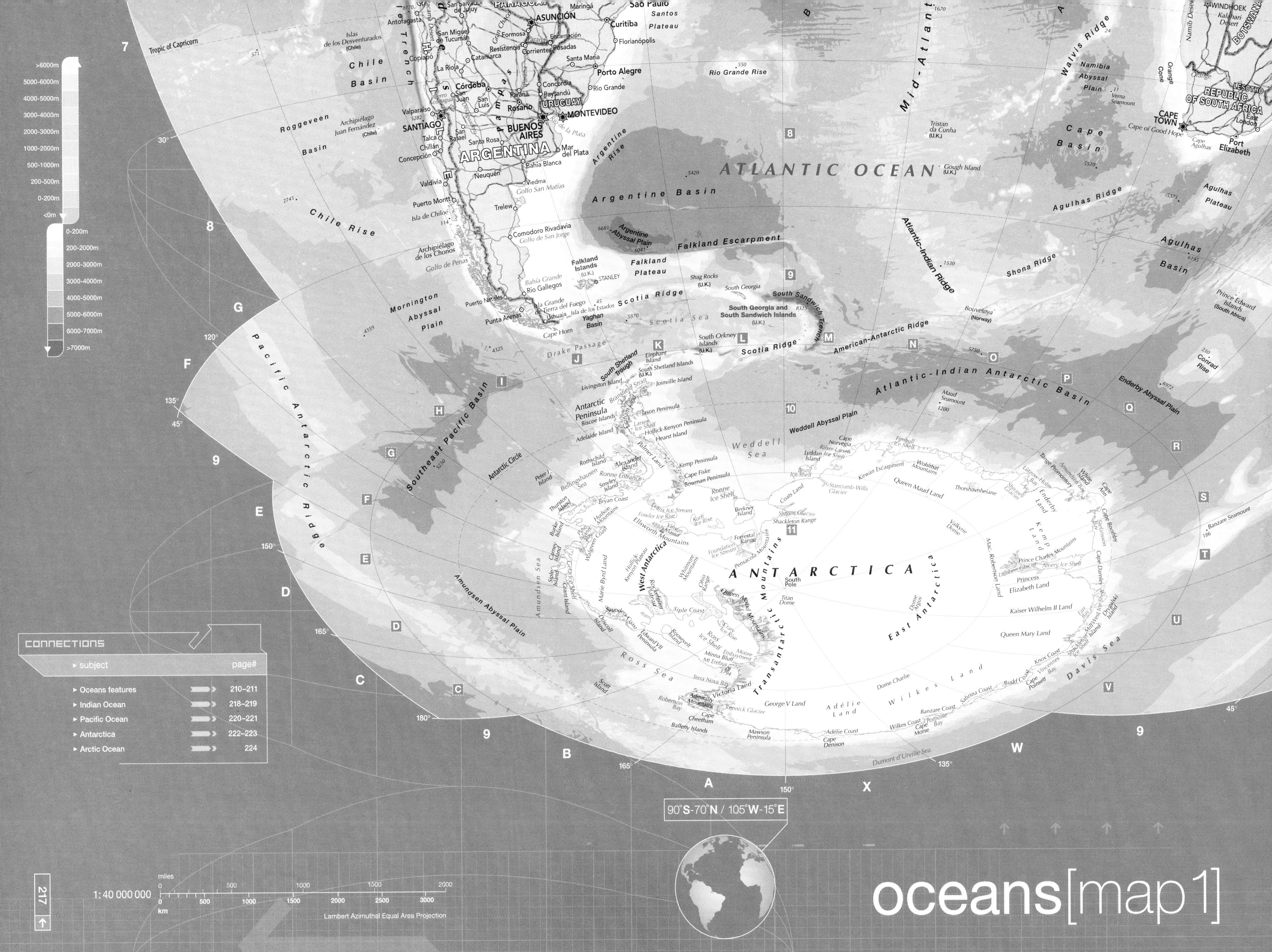

CONNECTIONS	
subject	page#
Oceans features	210–211
Indian Ocean	218–219
Pacific Ocean	220–221
Antarctica	222–223
Arctic Ocean	224

1:40 000 000

Lambert Azimuthal Equal Area Projection

→ 218

RUSSIAN FEDERATION
West Siberian Plain
KAZAKHSTAN
MONGOLIA
Gobi
CHINA
Plateau of Tibet
Himalaya
INDIA
PAKISTAN
AFGHANISTAN
IRAN
IRAQ
SAUDI ARABIA
YEMEN
OMAN
EGYPT
LIBYA
CHAD
SUDAN
ETHIOPIA
SOMALIA
KENYA
TANZANIA
DEMOCRATIC REPUBLIC OF CONGO
ANGOLA
ZAMBIA
MOZAMBIQUE
MADAGASCAR
TURKEY
UKRAINE
JAPAN
MYANMAR
THAILAND
MALAYSIA
INDONESIA
PHILIPPINES
AUSTRALIA
INDIAN OCEAN
Arabian Sea
Bay of Bengal
South China Sea
Caspian Sea
Black Sea
Mediterranean Sea
Sea of Okhotsk
Sea of Japan
Arabian Basin
Somali Basin
Mascarene Basin
Madagascar Basin
Mid-Indian Basin
West Australian Basin
Cocos Basin
Carlsberg Ridge
Chagos-Laccadive Ridge
Mid-Indian Ridge
Ninetyeast Ridge
Java Trench (Sunda Trench)
Kyushu - Palau Ridge
South Honshu Ridge
MOSCOW
BEIJING
TŌKYŌ
SEOUL
TEHRĀN
CAIRO
BAGHDAD
RIYADH
KĀBUL
ISLAMABAD
DHAKA
BANGKOK
JAKARTA
MANILA
NAIROBI
ADDIS ABABA
KHARTOUM
MOGADISHU
ANKARA

90°S-60°N / 0°-135°E

1:40 000 000

Lambert Azimuthal Equal Area Projection

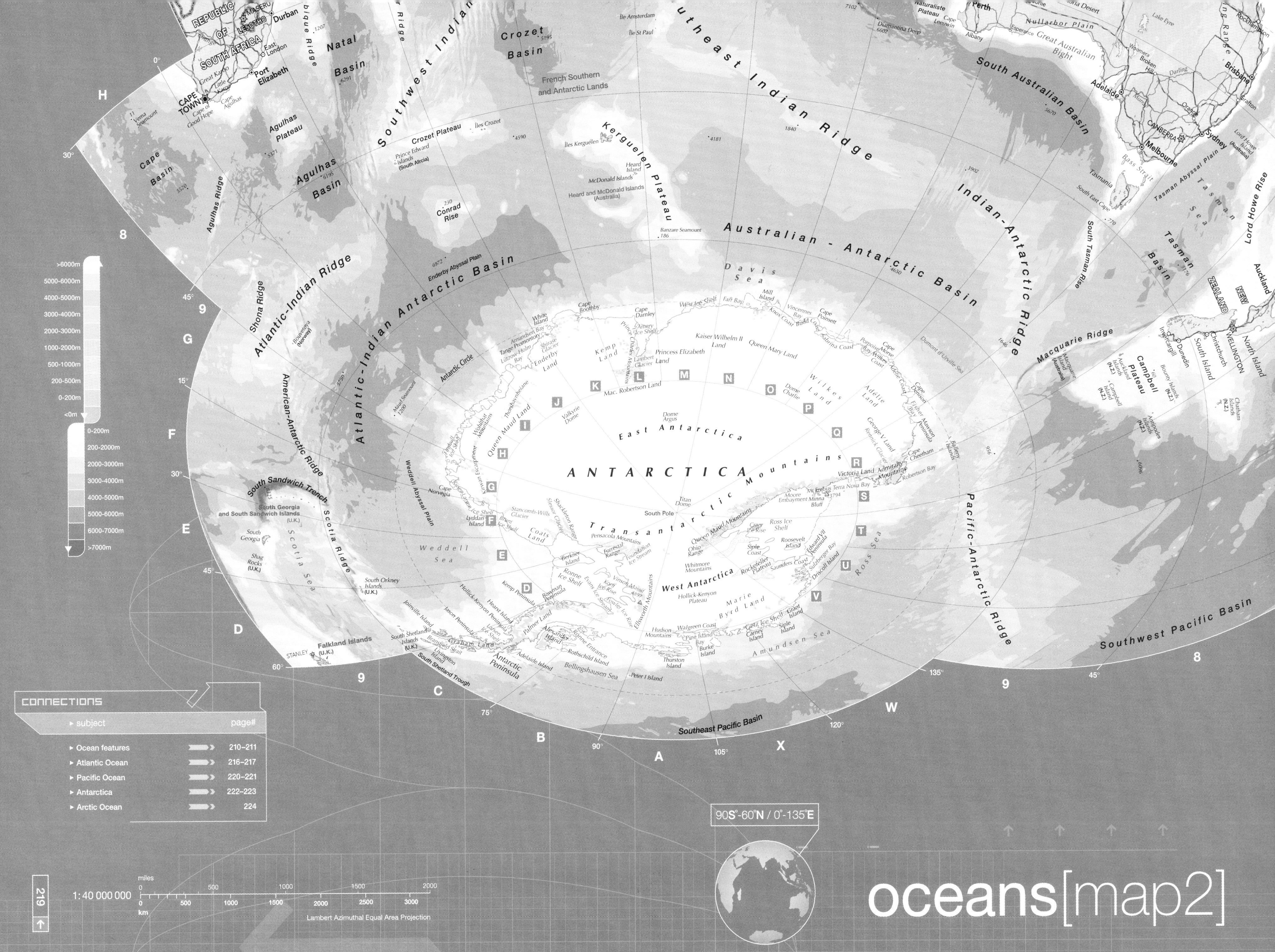

CONNECTIONS

► subject | page/ref
- ► Ocean features | 210–211
- ► Atlantic Ocean | 216–217
- ► Pacific Ocean | 220–221
- ► Antarctica | 222–223
- ► Arctic Ocean | 224

miles
0   500   1000   1500   2000

km
0   500   1000   1500   2000   2500   3000

Depth scale (m)
>6000m · 5000–6000m · 4000–5000m · 3000–4000m · 2000–3000m · 1000–2000m · 500–1000m · 200–500m · 0–200m
200–0m

ANTARCTICA

East Antarctica

West Antarctica

South Pole

Transantarctic Mountains

Ross Sea

Ross Ice Shelf

Weddell Sea

Weddell Abyssal Plain

Ronne Ice Shelf

Filchner Ice Shelf

Amundsen Sea

Bellingshausen Sea

Antarctic Peninsula

Scotia Sea

Scotia Ridge

South Sandwich Trench

American-Antarctic Ridge

Atlantic-Indian Antarctic Basin

Atlantic-Indian Ridge

Southwest Indian Ridge

Southeast Indian Ridge

Indian-Antarctic Ridge

Pacific-Antarctic Ridge

Australian–Antarctic Basin

Kerguelen Plateau

Crozet Basin

Agulhas Basin

Agulhas Plateau

Natal Basin

Cape Basin

South Australian Basin

Southwest Pacific Basin

Southeast Pacific Basin

Tasman Basin

Tasman Sea

Campbell Plateau

South Tasman Rise

Macquarie Ridge

Davis Sea

Ross Sea

Weddell Abyssal Plain

Enderby Abyssal Plain

Conrad Rise

Crozet Plateau

Shona Ridge

REPUBLIC OF SOUTH AFRICA

CAPE TOWN

Durban

East London

Port Elizabeth

NEW ZEALAND

North Island

South Island

WELLINGTON

Auckland

Christchurch

Dunedin

Invercargill

AUSTRALIA

CANBERRA

Sydney

Melbourne

Adelaide

Perth

Brisbane

Tasmania

Bass Strait

Chatham Islands (N.Z.)

Campbell Island (Australia)

Falkland Islands (U.K.)

STANLEY

South Georgia (U.K.)

Lord Howe Rise

Kerguelen (Iles Kerguelen)

Heard and McDonald Islands (Australia)

French Southern and Antarctic Lands

oceans[map3]
90°S-60°N / 90°E-60°W
CONNECTIONS
subject
page#
Ocean features 210–211
Atlantic Ocean 216–217
Indian Ocean 218–219
Antarctica 222–223
Arctic Ocean 224
1: 45 000 000
miles
km
Lambert Azimuthal Equal Area Projection
>6000m
5000-6000m
4000-5000m
3000-4000m
2000-3000m
1000-2000m
500-1000m
200-500m
0-200m
<0m
0-200m
200-2000m
2000-3000m
3000-4000m
4000-5000m
5000-6000m
6000-7000m
>7000m
Northwest Pacific Basin
Emperor Seamount Chain
Mapmakers Seamounts
Mid - Pacific Mountains
Philippine Basin
West Mariana Basin
East Mariana Basin
Magellan Seamounts
MARSHALL ISLANDS
FEDERATED STATES OF MICRONESIA
East Caroline Basin
West Caroline Basin
Central Pacific Basin
Melanesian Basin
NAURU
SOLOMON ISLANDS
PAPUA NEW GUINEA
TUVALU
VANUATU
FIJI
TONGA
Coral Sea Basin
North Australian Basin
West Australian Basin
Exmouth Plateau
AUSTRALIA
Great Sandy Desert
Great Victoria Desert
Perth Basin
South Australian Basin
Tasman Basin
South Fiji Basin
NEW ZEALAND
Campbell Plateau
Indian - Antarctic Ridge
Southeast Indian Ridge
Australian - Antarctic Basin
INDONESIA
MALAYSIA
PHILIPPINES
SINGAPORE
THAILAND
VIETNAM
CAMBODIA
LAOS
MYANMAR
CHINA
MONGOLIA
JAPAN
Cocos Basin
Java Trench (Sunda Trench)
Investigator Ridge
Broken Plateau
Naturaliste Plateau
INDIAN OCEAN
Tasman Sea
Coral Sea
Arafura Sea
Java Sea
South China Sea

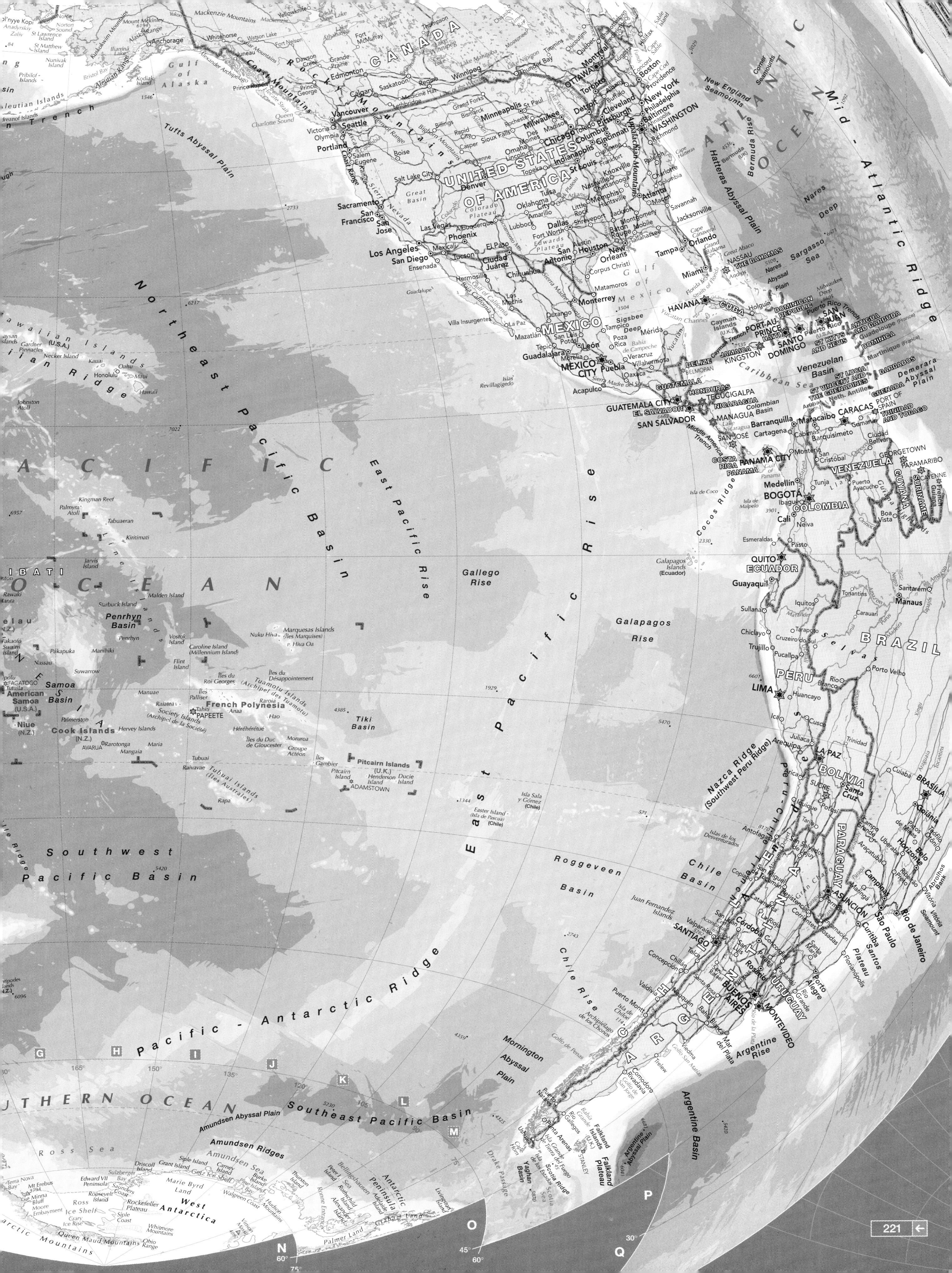

antarctica[map1]

50°-90°**S** / 0°-180°-0°

ARGENTINE CLAIM
BRITISH ANTARCTIC TERRITORY

Grid references
U · T · S · R · Q · P · O · N
V · U · T · S · R · Q
1 · 2 · 3

Seas, oceans and undersea features
Scotia Sea
Scotia Ridge
Weddell Sea
Weddell Abyssal (Plain)
Drake Passage
Yaghan Basin
South Shetland Trough
Bransfield Strait
SOUTHERN OCEAN
Southeast Pacific Basin
Pacific-Antarctic Ridge
Pacific Ocean
Bellingshausen Sea
Amundsen Sea
Amundsen Ridges
Amundsen Abyssal Plain
Ronne Ice Shelf
Filchner Ice Shelf
ROSS (Sea)
Antarctic Circle

Territorial claims
ARGENTINE CLAIM
CHILEAN CLAIM
BRITISH ANTARCTIC TERRITORY

Land features
ARGENTINA
CHILE
Tierra del Fuego
Isla Grande
Antarctic Peninsula
Palmer Land
George VI Sound
Ellsworth Land
West Antarctica
Ellsworth Mountains
Sentinel Range
Heritage Range
Hollick-Kenyon Plateau
Marie Byrd Land
Ford Range
Rupert Coast

Stations and places
STANLEY
Falkland Islands (U.K.)
Río Gallegos
Río Grande
Punta Arenas
Puerto Natales
Orcadas (Arg.)
South Orkney (U.K.)
Coronation Island
Laurie Island
Esperanza (Argentina)
Marambio (Argentina)
Palmer (U.S.A.)
Vernadsky (Ukraine)
San Martín (Argentina)
Rothera (U.K.)
Belgrano II (Argentina)
Halley (U.K.)
Elephant Island
King George Island
South Shetland Islands
Livingston Island
Smith Island
Adelaide Island
Peter I Island
Thurston Island
Thwaites Glacier Tongue

Elevation scale (land)
>6000m
5000-6000m
4000-5000m
3000-4000m
2000-3000m
1000-2000m
500-1000m
200-500m
0-200m
<0m

Elevation scale (sea)
0-200m
200-2000m
2000-3000m
3000-4000m
4000-5000m
5000-6000m
6000-7000m
>7000m

CONNECTIONS

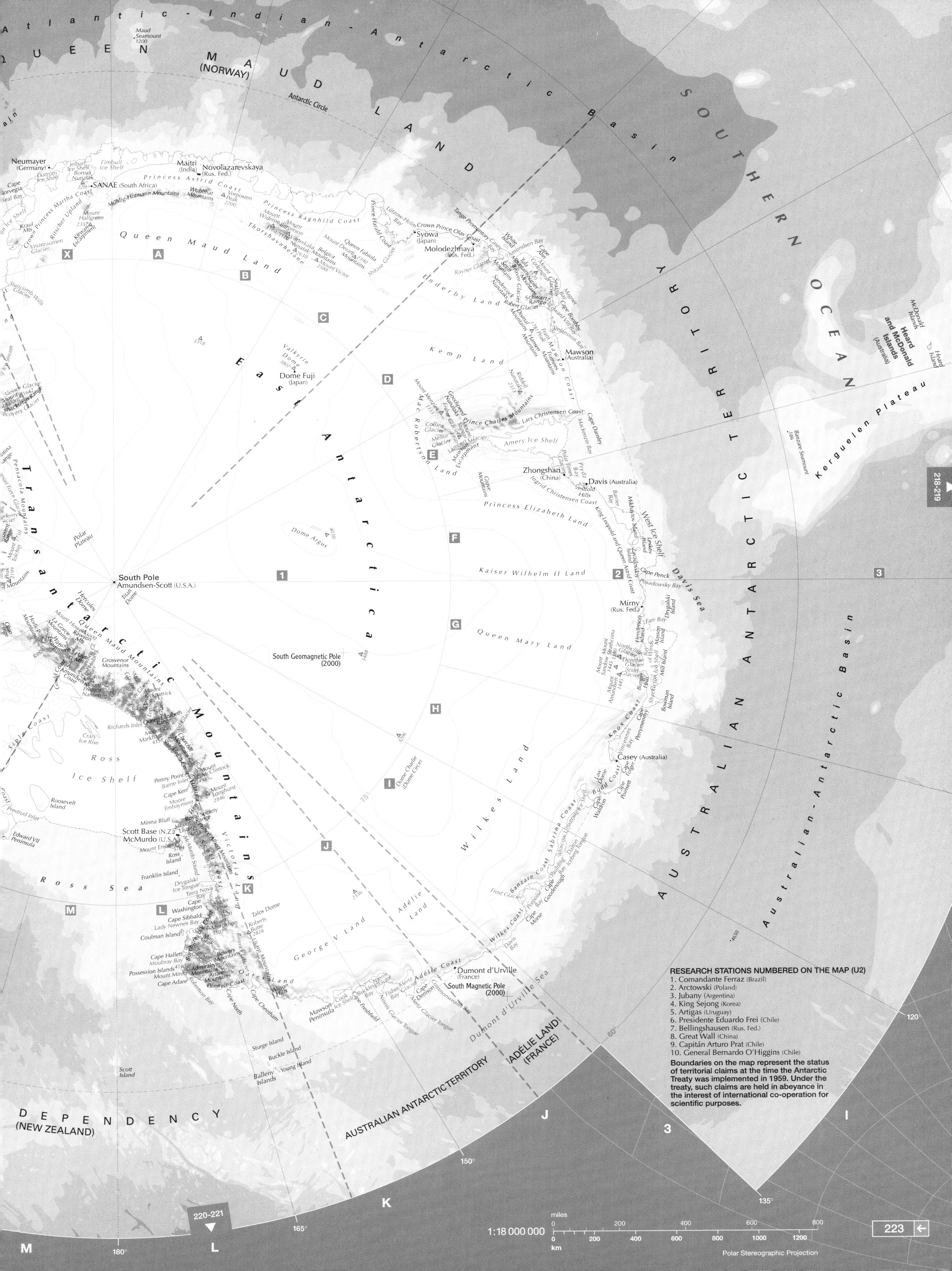
Atlantic-Indian-Antarctic Basin
QUEEN MAUD LAND
(NORWAY)
Antarctic Circle
SOUTHERN OCEAN
AUSTRALIAN ANTARCTIC TERRITORY
Australian-Antarctic Basin
Kerguelen Plateau
Heard and McDonald Islands (Australia)
McDonald Islands
Heard Island
Banzare Seamount
Maud Seamount 1200
Neumayer (Germany)
Maitri (India)
Novolazarevskaya (Rus. Fed.)
SANAE (South Africa)
Princess Astrid Coast
Princess Martha Coast
Mühlig-Hofmann Mountains
Wohlthat Mountains
Princess Ragnhild Coast
Prince Harald Coast
Crown Prince Olav Coast
Syowa (Japan)
Molodezhnaya (Rus. Fed.)
Queen Maud Land
Belgica Mountains
Enderby Land
Kemp Land
Mawson (Australia)
Valkyrie Dome 3807
Dome Fuji (Japan)
East Antarctica
Prince Charles Mountains
Lars Christensen Coast
Amery Ice Shelf
Mac Robertson Land
Cape Darnley
Zhongshan (China)
Davis (Australia)
Ingrid Christensen Coast
Princess Elizabeth Land
West Ice Shelf
Dome Argus
Polar Plateau
South Pole
Amundsen-Scott (U.S.A.)
Kaiser Wilhelm II Land
Davis Sea
Mirny (Rus. Fed.)
Queen Mary Land
South Geomagnetic Pole (2000)
Transantarctic Mountains
Queen Maud Mountains
Ross Ice Shelf
Roosevelt Island
Edward VII Peninsula
Siple Coast
Scott Base (N.Z.)
McMurdo (U.S.A.)
Ross Island
Ross Sea
Franklin Island
Victoria Land
Knox Coast
Casey (Australia)
Budd Coast
Wilkes Land
Sabrina Coast
Banzare Coast
Adélie Land
George V Land
Dome Charlie (Dome Circe)
Talos Dome
Cape Adare
Oates Land
Dumont d'Urville (France)
South Magnetic Pole (2000)
Adélie Coast
Dumont d'Urville Sea
Mawson Peninsula
Balleny Islands
Scott Island
DEPENDENCY
(NEW ZEALAND)
AUSTRALIAN ANTARCTIC TERRITORY
ADÉLIE LAND (FRANCE)
RESEARCH STATIONS NUMBERED ON THE MAP (U2)
1. Comandante Ferraz (Brazil)
2. Arctowski (Poland)
3. Jubany (Argentina)
4. King Sejong (Korea)
5. Artigas (Uruguay)
6. Presidente Eduardo Frei (Chile)
7. Bellingshausen (Rus. Fed.)
8. Great Wall (China)
9. Capitán Arturo Prat (Chile)
10. General Bernardo O'Higgins (Chile)
Boundaries on the map represent the status of territorial claims at the time the Antarctic Treaty was implemented in 1959. Under the treaty, such claims are held in abeyance in the interest of international co-operation for scientific purposes.
1:18 000 000
miles 0 200 400 600 800
km 0 200 400 600 800 1000 1200
Polar Stereographic Projection
218-219
220-221
180° 165° 150° 135° 120°

thearctic[map1]

60°-90°N / 0°-180°-0°

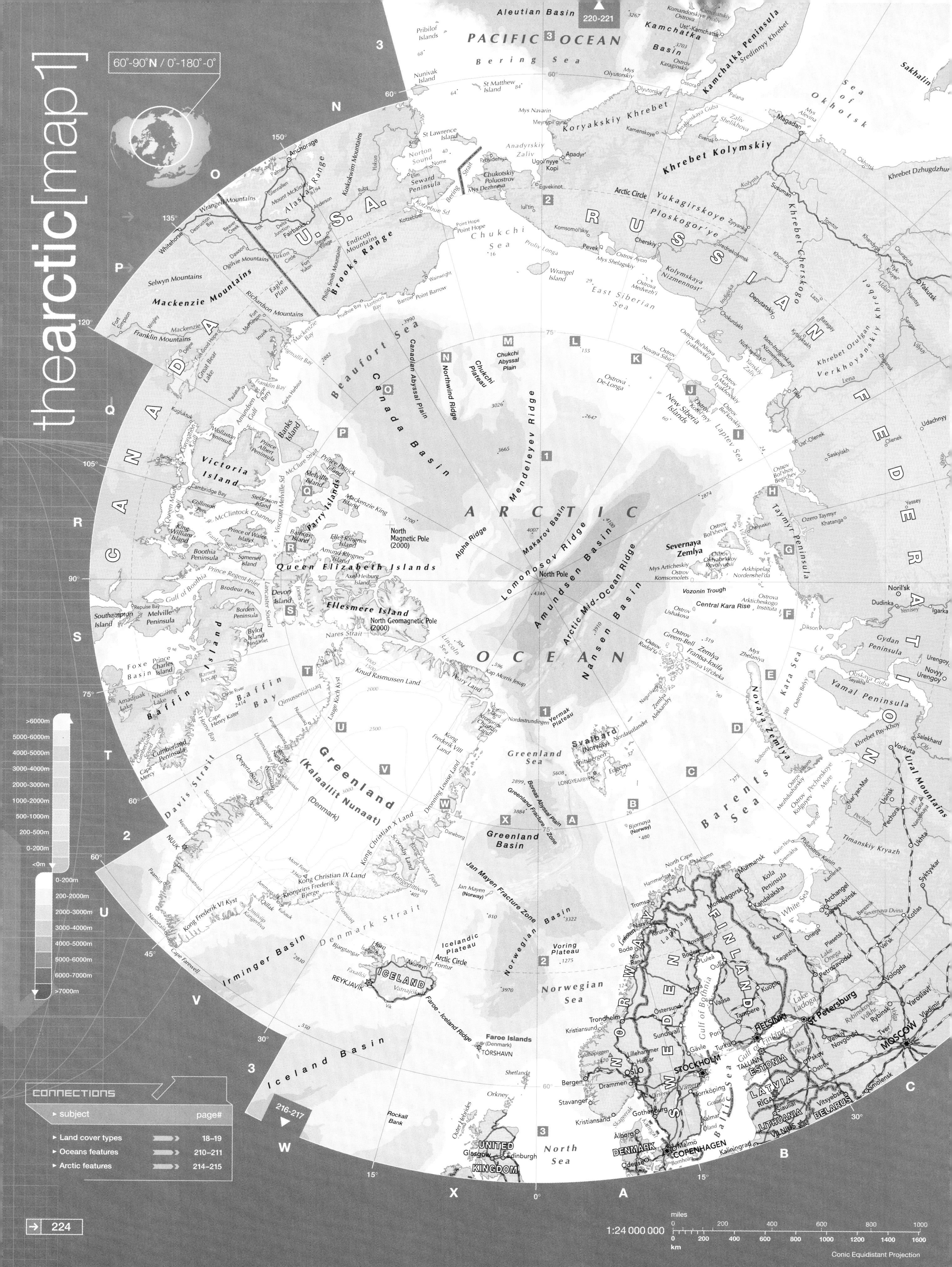

CONNECTIONS

▸ subject	page#
▸ Land cover types	18–19
▸ Oceans features	210–211
▸ Arctic features	214–215

INTRODUCTION TO THE INDEX

The index includes all names shown on the reference maps in the atlas. Each entry includes the country or geographical area in which the feature is located, a page number and an alphanumeric reference. Additional entry details and aspects of the index are explained below.

Referencing

Names are referenced by page number and by grid reference. The grid reference relates to the alphanumeric values which appear in the margin of each map. These reflect the graticule on the map – the letter relates to longitude divisions, the number to latitude divisions.

Names are generally referenced to the largest scale map page on which they appear. For large geographical features, including countries, the reference is to the largest scale map on which the feature appears in its entirety, or on which the majority of it appears.

Rivers are referenced to their lowest downstream point – either their mouth or their confluence with another river. The river name will generally be positioned as close to this point as possible.

Alternative names

Alternative names appear as cross-references and refer the user to the index entry for the form of the name used on the map. Details of alternative names and their types also appear within the main entry. The different types of name form included are: alternative forms or spellings currently in common use; English conventional name forms normally used in English-language contexts; historical and former names; and long and short name forms.

For rivers with multiple names – for example those which flow through several countries – all alternative name forms are included within the main index entries, with details of the countries in which each form applies.

Administrative qualifiers

Administrative divisions are included in an entry to differentiate duplicate names – entries of exactly the same name and feature type within the one country – where these division names are shown on the maps. In such cases, duplicate names are alphabetized in the order of the administrative division names.

Additional qualifiers are included for names within selected geographical areas, to indicate more clearly their location.

Descriptors

Entries, other than those for towns and cities, include a descriptor indicating the type of geographical feature. Descriptors are not included where the type of feature is implicit in the name itself, unless there is a town or city of exactly the same name.

Insets

Where relevant, the index clearly indicates [inset] if a feature appears on an inset map.

Name forms and alphabetical order

Name forms are as they appear on the maps, with additional alternative forms included as cross-references. Names appear in full in the index, although they may appear in abbreviated form on the maps.

The Icelandic characters Þ and þ are transliterated and alphabetized as 'Th' and 'th'. The German character ß is alphabetized as 'ss'. Names beginning with Mac or Mc are alphabetized exactly as they appear. The terms Saint, Sainte, etc, are abbreviated to St, Ste, etc, but alphabetized as if in the full form.

Name form policies are explained in the Introduction to the Atlas (pp 4–5).

Numerical entries

Entries beginning with numerals appear at the beginning of the index, in numerical order. Elsewhere, numerals are alphabetized before 'a'.

Permuted terms

Names beginning with generic, geographical terms are permuted – the descriptive term is placed after, and the index alphabetized by, the main part of the name. For example, Mount Everest is indexed as Everest, Mount; Lake Superior as Superior, Lake. This policy is applied to all languages. Permuting has not been applied to names of towns, cities or administrative divisions beginning with such geographical terms. These remain in their full form, for example, Lake Isabella, USA.

Gazetteer entries and connections

Selected entries have been extended to include gazetteer-style information. Important geographical facts which relate specifically to the entry are included within the entry in coloured type.

Entries for features which also appear on, or which have a topical link to, the thematic pages of the atlas include a connection to those pages indicated by the symbol ➠.

Tables

Several tables, ranking geographical features by size, are included within the main index listing. Where possible these have been placed directly below the index entry for the feature ranked 1 in the table.

ABBREVIATIONS

admin. dist.	administrative district	imp. l.	impermanent lake	pref.	prefecture
admin. div.	administrative division	IN	Indiana	prov.	province
admin. reg.	administrative region	Indon.	Indonesia	pt	point
Afgh.	Afghanistan	Kazakh.	Kazakhstan	Qld	Queensland
AK	Alaska	KS	Kansas	Que.	Québec
AL	Alabama	KY	Kentucky	r.	river
Alg.	Algeria	Kyrg.	Kyrgyzstan	r. mouth	river mouth
AR	Arkansas	l.	lake	r. source	river source
Arg.	Argentina	LA	Louisiana	reg.	region
aut. comm.	autonomous community	lag.	lagoon	res.	reserve
aut. div.	autonomous division	Lith.	Lithuania	resr	reservoir
aut. reg.	autonomous region	Lux.	Luxembourg	RI	Rhode Island
aut. rep.	autonomous republic	MA	Massachusetts	Rus. Fed.	Russian Federation
AZ	Arizona	Madag.	Madagascar	S.	South
Azer.	Azerbaijan	Man.	Manitoba	S.A.	South Australia
b.	bay	MD	Maryland	salt l.	salt lake
B.C.	British Columbia	ME	Maine	Sask.	Saskatchewan
Bangl.	Bangladesh	Mex.	Mexico	SC	South Carolina
Bol.	Bolivia	MI	Michigan	SD	South Dakota
Bos.-Herz.	Bosnia-Herzegovina	MN	Minnesota	sea chan.	sea channel
Bulg.	Bulgaria	MO	Missouri	Sing.	Singapore
c.	cape	Moz.	Mozambique	Switz.	Switzerland
CA	California	MS	Mississippi	Tajik.	Tajikistan
Cent. Afr. Rep.	Central African Republic	MT	Montana	Tanz.	Tanzania
CO	Colorado	mt.	mountain	Tas.	Tasmania
Col.	Colombia	mt s	mountains	terr.	territory
CT	Connecticut	N.	North	Thai.	Thailand
Czech Rep.	Czech Republic	N.B.	New Brunswick	TN	Tennessee
DC	District of Columbia	N.S.	Nova Scotia	Trin. and Tob.	Trinidad and Tobago
DE	Delaware	N.S.W.	New South Wales	Turkm.	Turkmenistan
Dem. Rep. Congo	Democratic Republic of Congo	N.T.	Northern Territory	TX	Texas
depr.	depression	N.W.T.	Northwest Territories	U.A.E.	United Arab Emirates
des.	desert	N.Z.	New Zealand	U.K.	United Kingdom
Dom. Rep.	Dominican Republic	nat. park	national park	U.S.A.	United States of America
E.	East, Eastern	nature res.	nature reserve	Ukr.	Ukraine
Equat. Guinea	Equatorial Guinea	NC	North Carolina	union terr.	union territory
esc.	escarpment	ND	North Dakota	UT	Utah
est.	estuary	NE	Nebraska	Uzbek.	Uzbekistan
Eth.	Ethiopia	Neth.	Netherlands	VA	Virginia
Fin.	Finland	NH	New Hampshire	Venez.	Venezuela
FL	Florida	NJ	New Jersey	Vic.	Victoria
for.	forest	NM	New Mexico	vol.	volcano
Fr. Guiana	French Guiana	NV	Nevada	vol. crater	volcanic crater
g.	gulf	NY	New York	VT	Vermont
GA	Georgia	OH	Ohio	W.	West, Western
Guat.	Guatemala	OK	Oklahoma	W.A.	Western Australia
H.K.	Hong Kong	OR	Oregon	WA	Washington
HI	Hawaii	P.E.I.	Prince Edward Island	WI	Wisconsin
Hond.	Honduras	P.N.G.	Papua New Guinea	WV	West Virginia
i.	island	PA	Pennsylvania	WY	Wyoming
IA	Iowa	pen.	peninsula	Y.T.	Yukon Territory
ID	Idaho	plat.	plateau	Yugo.	Yugoslavia
IL	Illinois	Port.	Portugal		

index

1st Cataract rapids Egypt 121 G3
2nd Cataract rapids Sudan 121 F4
3rd Cataract rapids Sudan 121 F5
4th Cataract rapids Sudan 121 G5
5th Cataract rapids Sudan 121 G5
9 de Julio Arg. 204 E4
long form Nueve de Julio
15th of May City Egypt see Medinet 15 Mayo
25 de Mayo Buenos Aires Arg. 204 E4
long form Veinticinco de Mayo
25 de Mayo La Pampa Arg. 204 D5
long form Veinticinco de Mayo
25 de Mayo Mendoza Arg. 204 C4
long form Veinticinco de Mayo
26 Bakı Komissarı Azer. 107 G3
also known as imeni 26 Bakinskikh Komissarov; formerly known as Neftechala; long form İyirmi Altı Bakı Komissarı
42nd Hill S. Africa 133 N5
70 Mile House Canada 166 F5
100 Mile House Canada 166 F5
150 Mile House Canada 166 F4

A

Aabenraa Denmark see Åbenrå
Aachen Germany 48 D5
formerly known as Aix-la-Chapelle; historically known as Aquae Grani or Aquisgranum
Aadan Yabaal Somalia 128 E4
Aalborg Denmark see Ålborg
Aalen Germany 48 H7
Aalesund Norway see Ålesund
Aaley Lebanon see 'Âley
Aalst Belgium 51 K2
also spelt Alost
Aanaar Fin. see Inari
Äänekoski Fin. 44 N3
Aansluit S. Africa 132 G3
Aarau Switz. 51 O5
Aarberg Switz. 51 N5
Aareavaara Sweden 44 M2
Aarhus Denmark see Århus
Aarlen Belgium see Arlon
Aarschot Belgium 51 K2
Aasiaat Greenland 165 N3
also known as Egedesminde
Aath Belgium see Ath
Aavasaksa Fin. 44 M2
Aba China 86 B1
also known as Ngawa
Aba Dem. Rep. Congo 126 F4
Aba Nigeria 125 G5
Abā ad Dūd Saudi Arabia 104 D2
Abā al Afan oasis Saudi Arabia 105 E4
Abā al Qūr, Sha'īb watercourse Saudi Arabia 109 M6
Abā ar Ruwāth, Wādī watercourse Saudi Arabia 109 N7
Abacaxis r. Brazil 199 G6
Ābādān Iran 100 B4
English form Abadan
Abadan Iran see Ābādān
Abādān, Jazīrah i. Iran/Iraq 105 E1
Ābādeh Iran 100 C4
Ābādeh Ṭashk Iran 100 C4
Abadia dos Dourados Brazil 206 F5
Abadiânia Brazil 206 E3
Abadla Alg. 123 E3
Abádszalók Hungary 49 R8
Abaeté Brazil 207 H6
Abaeté r. Brazil 207 H5
Abaetetuba Brazil 202 B2
Abagnar Qi China see Xilinhot
Abag Qi China see Xin Hot
Abaí Para. 201 G6
Abaiang atoll Kiribati 145 G1
also spelt Apaiang; formerly known as Apia
A Baiuca Spain 54 C1
Abaji Nigeria 125 G4
Abajo Peak U.S.A. 183 O4
Abakaliki Nigeria 125 H5
Abakan Rus. Fed. 80 E2
formerly known as Ust'-Abakanskoye
Abala Congo 126 B5
Abala Niger 125 F3
Abalak Niger 125 G3
Abalyanka r. Belarus 43 L7
Abana Turkey 106 C2
Abancay Peru 200 B3
Abanga r. Gabon 126 A5
Abapó Bol. 201 E4
Abariringa i. Kiribati see Kanton
Abarqū Iran 100 C4
A Barrela Spain 54 D2
Abarshahr Iran see Neyshābūr
Ābār 'Uwayrid Ṭahtānī well Syria 109 K3
Abashiri Japan 90 I2
Abashiri-wan b. Japan 90 I2
Abasolo Mex. 185 F3
Abasula waterhole Kenya 128 C5
Abau P.N.G. 145 D3
Abava r. Latvia 42 C4
Abay Kazakh. 103 H2
also known as Churubay Nura; formerly known as Abay Bazar
Abay Kazakh. see Karaul
Abaya, Lake Eth. 128 C3
also known as Ābaya Hāyk'; formerly known as Margherita, Lake
Ābaya Hāyk' l. Eth. see Abaya, Lake
Abay Bazar Kazakh. see Abay
Ābay Wenz r. Eth./Sudan 128 C2 see Blue Nile
Abaza Rus. Fed. 80 E2
Abba Cent. Afr. Rep. 126 B3
Abbadia San Salvatore Italy 56 D6
Abbāsābād Iran 100 D3
Abbasanta Sardegna Italy 57 A8
Abbatis Villa France see Abbeville
Abbaye, Point U.S.A. 172 E4
Abbe, Lake Djibouti/Eth. 128 D2
Abbeville France 51 H2
historically known as Abbatis Villa
Abbeville GA U.S.A. 175 D6
Abbeville LA U.S.A. 179 D6
Abbeville SC U.S.A. 175 D5
Abbey Canada 167 I5
Abbeyfeale Rep. of Ireland 47 C11
Abbiategrasso Italy 56 A3
Abborrträsk Sweden 44 L2
Abbot, Mount Australia 149 E4
Abbot Bay Australia 149 E3
Abbotsford Canada 166 F5
Abbotsford U.S.A. 172 C6
Abbott NM U.S.A. 181 F5
Abbott VA U.S.A. 176 E8
Abbott WV U.S.A. 176 E7
Abbottabad Pak. 101 H3
Abbott Ice Shelf Antarctica 222 R2
Abchuha Belarus 43 K7
Abd, Oued el watercourse Alg. 55 L9
'Abd al 'Azīz, Jabal hill Syria 109 L1
'Abd al 'Azīz, Jabal plat. Syria 109 K1
'Abd al Kūrī i. Yemen 105 F5
'Abd Allah, Khawr sea chan. Iraq/Kuwait 107 G5
Abd al Ma'asīr well Saudi Arabia 109 J7
Ābdānān Iran 100 A3
Abdollāhābād Iran 100 D2
Abdulino Rus. Fed. 41 J5
Abéché Chad 120 D6
also known as Abeshr
Abejukolo Nigeria 125 G5
Abelbod well Mali 125 E2
Abellinum Italy see Avellino
Abel Tasman National Park N.Z. 152 H8
Abemama atoll Kiribati 145 G1
also spelt Apamama
Abenab Namibia 130 C3
Abengourou Côte d'Ivoire 124 E5
Abenójar Spain 54 G6
Åbenrå Denmark 45 J5
also spelt Aabenraa
Abensberg Germany 48 I7
Abeokuta Nigeria 125 F5
Abera Eth. 128 B3
Aberaeron U.K. 47 H11
Aberchirder U.K. 46 J6
Abercorn Zambia see Mbala
Abercrombie r. Australia 147 F3
Aberdare U.K. 47 I12
Aberdare National Park Kenya 128 C5
Aberdaron U.K. 47 H11
Aberdaugleddau U.K. see Milford Haven
Aberdeen Australia 147 F3
Aberdeen Hong Kong China 87 [inset]
also known as Heung Kong Tsai
Aberdeen S. Africa 132 I9
Aberdeen U.K. 46 J6
historically known as Devana
Aberdeen MD U.S.A. 177 I6
Aberdeen MS U.S.A. 175 B5
Aberdeen OH U.S.A. 176 B7
Aberdeen SD U.S.A. 178 C2
Aberdeen WA U.S.A. 180 B3
Aberdeen Island Hong Kong China 87 [inset]
also known as Ap Lei Chau
Aberdeen Lake Canada 167 L1
Aberdeen Road S. Africa 133 I9
Aberfeldy U.K. 46 I7
Aberfoyle U.K. 46 H7
Abergavenny U.K. 47 I12
also known as Y Fenni; historically known as Gobannium
Ābergelē Eth. 104 B5
Abergwaun U.K. see Fishguard
Aberhonddu U.K. see Brecon
Abermaw U.K. see Barmouth
Abernathy U.S.A. 179 B5
Abertawe U.K. see Swansea
Aberteifi U.K. see Cardigan
Aberystwyth U.K. 47 H11
Abeshr Chad see Abéché
Abez' Rus. Fed. 40 L2
Abhā Saudi Arabia 104 C4
Abhā, Jabal hill Saudi Arabia 104 C2
Abhanpur India 97 D5
Abhar Iran 100 B2
Abhar Rūd r. Iran 100 B3
Abia state Nigeria 125 G5
Abiad, Bahr el r. Sudan/Uganda 128 B2 see White Nile
Ābīata Hāyk' l. Eth. 128 C3
Ab-i-Bazuft r. Iran 100 B4
Abibe, Serranía de mts Col. 198 B2

▶Abidjan Côte d'Ivoire 124 D5
Former capital of Côte d'Ivoire.

Abiekwasputs salt pan S. Africa 132 E4
Ab-i-Istada l. Afgh. 101 G3
Abijatta-Shalla National Park Eth. 128 C3
also known as Rift Valley Lakes National Park
Ab-i-Kavīr salt flat Iran 100 D3
Abiko Japan 91 G7
Abilene KS U.S.A. 178 C4
Abilene TX U.S.A. 179 C5
Abingdon U.K. 47 K12
Abingdon IL U.S.A. 172 C10
Abingdon VA U.S.A. 176 C9
Abington U.S.A. 177 O3
Abington Reef Australia 149 F3
Abinsk Rus. Fed. 41 F7
Ab-i-Panja r. Afgh./Tajik. see Pyandzh
Ab-i-Safed r. Afgh. 101 F2
Abiseo, Parque Nacional nat. park Peru 200 A1
Abisko nationalpark nat. park Sweden 44 L1
Abitibi r. Canada 168 D3
Abitibi, Lake Canada 168 D3
Āb Naft r. Iraq 107 F4
also known as Naft
Abnūb Egypt 121 F3
Åbo Fin. see Turku
Abohar India 96 B3
Aboisso Côte d'Ivoire 124 E5
Aboke Sudan 128 B2
Abomey Benin 125 F5
Abongabong, Gunung mt. Indon. 76 B1
Abong Mbang Cameroon 125 I6
Aboot Oman 105 F4
Aborlan Phil. 74 A4
Abou Déia Chad 126 C2
Abou Goulem Chad 120 D6
Aboumi Gabon 126 B5
Abqaiq Saudi Arabia 105 E2
also known as Buqayq
Abra, Lago del l. Arg. 204 E6
Abrād, Wādī watercourse Yemen 105 D5
Abraham's Bay Bahamas 187 E2
Abraka Nigeria 125 G5
Abrams U.S.A. 172 E6
Abra Pampa Arg. 200 D5
Abre Campo Brazil 207 K7
Abreojos, Punta pt Mex. 184 B3
'Abri Sudan 121 F4
Abrolhos, Arquipélago dos is Brazil 207 O5
Abrosovo Rus. Fed. 43 Q3
Abrud Romania 58 E2
Abruka i. Estonia 42 D3
Abruzzi admin. reg. Italy see Abruzzo
Abruzzo admin. reg. Italy 56 F6
also spelt Abruzzi
Abruzzo, Parco Nazionale d' nat. park Italy 56 F7
'Abs Yemen 104 C4
Absalom, Mount Antarctica 223 W1
Absaroka Range mts U.S.A. 180 E3
Absecon U.S.A. 177 K6
Abşeron Yarımadası pen. Azer. 107 G2
also known as Apsheronskiy Poluostrov
Absterna, Vozyera l. Belarus 42 I6
Abtar, Jabal al hills Syria 109 I3
Abū ad Duhūr Syria 109 I2
Abū al Ḥusayn, Qā' imp. l. Jordan 109 J5
Abū 'Alī i. Saudi Arabia 105 E2
Abu al Jirab i. U.A.E. 105 F2
Abū al Kūfah waterhole Iraq 109 N3
Abū 'Āmūd, Wādī watercourse Jordan 108 H7
Abū 'Arīsh Saudi Arabia 104 C4
Abu 'Aweigîla well Egypt 108 F7
Abu Ballûs hill Egypt 121 E3
Abū Dā'ir des. Yemen 105 D4
Abu Deleiq Sudan 121 G6

▶Abu Dhabi U.A.E. 105 F2
Capital of the United Arab Emirates. Also spelt Abū Ẓabī.
asia [changes] ⟶ 68–69

Abū Ḍibā' waterhole Saudi Arabia 104 B3
Abu Durba Egypt 108 E9
Abu el Matâmir Egypt 108 B7
Abufari Brazil 199 F6
Abū Farrūkh, Wādī watercourse Iraq 109 O4
Abu Gabra Sudan 126 E2
Abu Gamel Sudan 104 B5
Abū Ghar, Wādī watercourse Iraq 109 M5
Abū Ghizlān waterhole Iraq 109 O3
Abū Ghurayb Iraq 109 P4
Abu Gubeiha Sudan 128 A2
Abu Ḥâd, Wâdi watercourse Egypt 108 E9
Abū Ḥafnah, Wādī watercourse Jordan 109 J5
Abu Haggag Egypt 121 E2
Abū Ḥallūfah, Jabal hill Jordan 109 H6
Abu Hamed Sudan 121 G5
Abu Hammâd Egypt 108 C7
Abu Haraz Sudan 121 G5
Abu Hashim Sudan 121 G5
Abu Higar Sudan 121 G6
Abu Hummus Egypt 108 B6
Abu Huswa, Gebel hill Egypt 108 E9

▶Abuja Nigeria 125 G4
Capital of Nigeria.

Abū Jaḥaf, Wādī watercourse Iraq 109 O5
Abū Kamāl Syria 109 L3
Abū Kammāsh Libya 120 A1
Abu Kebîr Egypt 108 C7
Abû Khamsât, Sha'îb watercourse Iraq 109 O6
Abukuma-kōchi plat. Japan 90 G6
Abu La'ot watercourse Sudan 121 F6
Abū Latt Island Saudi Arabia 104 C4
Abū Madd, Ra's hd Saudi Arabia 104 B2
Abu Matariq Sudan 126 E2
Abu Mena tourist site Egypt 121 F2
Abū Mīnā tourist site Egypt 108 A7
Abumombazi Dem. Rep. Congo 126 D4
Abu Musa i. The Gulf 105 F2
also known as Abū Mūsá, Jazīreh-ye
Abū Mūsá, Jazīreh-ye i. The Gulf see Abu Musa
Abunã r. Bol. 200 D2
Abunã Brazil 200 D2
Abunai Brazil 199 E5
Abū Nā'im well Libya 120 C2
Ābune Yosēf mt. Eth. 128 C1
Abū Nujaym Libya 120 B2
Abū Qīr, Khalīg b. Egypt 108 B6
Abū Qurīn Libya 120 B2
Abū Rāqah well Saudi Arabia 104 B2
Aburo mt. Dem. Rep. Congo 126 F4
Abu Road India 96 B4
also known as Kharari
Abū Rubayq Saudi Arabia 104 B3
Abū Rujmayn, Jabal mts Syria 109 J3
Abu Rûtha, Gebel mt. Egypt 108 F8
Abu Sallah watercourse Saudi Arabia 109 I9
Abū Sawādah well Saudi Arabia 105 E2
Abu Shagara, Ras pt Sudan 121 H4
Abu Simbel Egypt 121 F4
Abu Simbel Temple tourist site Egypt 121 F4
Abū Şukhayr Iraq 107 F5
Abu Sultân Egypt 108 D7
Abuta Japan 90 G3
Abu Tabaq well Sudan 121 G4
Abū Tarfa, Wâdi watercourse Egypt 108 E8
Abut Head N.Z. 153 E11
Abu Tig Egypt 106 B6
Abû Tiyûr, Gebel mt. Egypt 121 G3
Abū Ujayyijāt well Saudi Arabia 109 H9
Abuye Meda mt. Eth. 128 C2
Abuyog Phil. 74 C4
Abu Zabad Sudan 121 F6
Abū Ẓabī U.A.E. see Abu Dhabi
Abu Zenîma Egypt 121 G2
Abwong Sudan 128 B2
Åby Sweden 45 L4
Abyad Sudan 121 E6
Abyaḍ, Jabal al hill Saudi Arabia 108 G9
Abyaḍ, Jabal al mts Syria 109 I3
Abyān governorate Yemen 105 D5
Abyār al Hakīm well Libya 120 D2
Abyār an Nakhīlan well Libya 120 D2
Abyār Banī Murr well Saudi Arabia 108 G9
Abydos Australia 150 B4
Abyei Sudan 126 F2
Åbyn Sweden 44 M2
Abyssinia country Africa see Ethiopia
Abzakovo Rus. Fed. 102 D1
Abzanovo Rus. Fed. 102 D2
Acacias Col. 198 C4
Academician Vernadskiy research station Antarctica see Vernadsky
Academy Bay Rus. Fed. see Akademii, Zaliv
Academy Glacier Antarctica 223 T1
Acadia prov. Canada see Nova Scotia
Acadia National Park U.S.A. 177 Q1
Açailândia Brazil 202 C3
Acajutiba Brazil 202 E4
Acajutla El Salvador 185 H6
Acala Mex. 185 G5
Acamarachi mt. Chile see Pili, Cerro
Acambaro Mex. 185 E4
Acampamento de Caça do Mucusso Angola 127 D9
Acancéh Mex. 185 H4
Acandí Col. 198 B2
Acaponeta Mex. 184 D4
Acapulco Mex. 185 F5
long form Acapulco de Juárez
Acapulco de Juárez Mex. see Acapulco
Acará Brazil 202 B2
Acará r. Brazil 202 B2
Acará Mirí r. Brazil 202 B2
Acaraú Brazil 202 D2
Acaraú r. Brazil 202 D2
Acaray, Represa de resr Para. 201 G6
Acari Brazil 202 E3
Acari r. Brazil 207 H2
Acari Peru 200 B3
Acari r. Peru 200 B3
Acari, Serra hills Brazil/Guyana 199 G4
Acarigua Venez. 198 D2
Acatlan Mex. 185 F5
Acatzingo Mex. 185 F5
Acay, Nevado de mt. Arg. 200 D6
Acayucán Mex. 185 G5
Accho Israel see 'Akko
Accomac U.S.A. 177 J8
also spelt Accomack
Accomack U.S.A. see Accomac

▶Accra Ghana 125 E5
Capital of Ghana.

Aceguá Brazil 204 G3
Aceh admin. dist. Indon. 76 B1
formerly spelt Acheh or Atjeh; historically known as Achin
Aceuchal Spain 54 E6
Achacachi Bol. 200 C4
Achaguas Venez. 199 D3
Achalpur India 96 C5
formerly known as Dadra or Elichpur
Achampet India 94 C2
Achan Rus. Fed. 82 E2
formerly known as Bolon'
Achanta India 94 D2
Achayvayam Rus. Fed. 39 R3
Acheh admin. dist. Indon. see Aceh
Achemelmel well Mali 123 F5
Achemmîm well Mauritania 124 D2
Acheng China 82 B3
Achern Germany 48 F7
Achhota India 94 D1
Achikulak Rus. Fed. 107 F1
Achill Island Rep. of Ireland 47 B10
Achim Germany 48 G2
Achin admin. dist. Indon. see Aceh
Achinsk Rus. Fed. 80 E1
Achisay Kazakh. 103 G4
also spelt Ashchysay
Achit Rus. Fed. 40 K4
Achit Nuur l. Mongolia 84 A1
Achkhoy-Martan Rus. Fed. 107 F2
formerly known as Novoselskoye
Achlades, Akra pt Greece 59 G12
Achnasheen U.K. 46 G6
Achosa-Rudnya Belarus 43 M9
Aci Castello Sicilia Italy 57 H11
Aci Catena Sicilia Italy 57 H11
Acıgöl l. Turkey 106 B3
Acıpayam Turkey 106 B3
Acireale Sicilia Italy 57 H11
Ackerman U.S.A. 175 B5
Ackley U.S.A. 174 A3
Acklins Island Bahamas 187 E2
Acobamba Huancavelica Peru 200 B3
Acobamba Junín Peru 200 B2
Acomayo Cusco Peru 200 C3
Acomayo Huánuco Peru 200 A2

▶Aconcagua, Cerro mt. Arg. 204 C4
Highest mountain in South America.
southamerica [landscapes] ⟶ 190–191

Acopiara Brazil 202 E3
Acora Peru 200 C3
A Coruña Spain 54 C1
English form Corunna; also spelt La Coruña
Acostambo Peru 200 B3
Acoyapa Nicaragua 186 B5
Acquapendente Italy 56 D6
Acqui Terme Italy 56 A4
historically known as Aquae Statiellae
Acra U.S.A. 177 K3
Acragas Sicilia Italy see Agrigento
Acraman, Lake salt flat Australia 146 B3
Acre r. Brazil 200 D2
formerly known as Aquiry
Acre state Brazil 200 C2
Acre Israel see 'Akko
Acreúna Brazil 206 C4
Acri Italy 57 I9
Ács Hungary 49 P8
Actaeon Group is Fr. Polynesia see Actéon, Groupe
Actéon, Groupe is Fr. Polynesia 221 I7
English form Actaeon Group
Acton Canada 173 M7
Acton U.S.A. 182 F7
Actopán Mex. 185 F4
Açuã r. Brazil 201 D1
Açuçena Brazil 207 K6
Acunum Acusio France see Montélimar
Acurenam Equat. Guinea 125 H6
Açurizal Brazil 201 F3
Ada Ghana 125 F5
Ada MN U.S.A. 178 C2
Ada OH U.S.A. 176 B5
Ada OK U.S.A. 179 C5
Ada Vojvodina, Srbija Yugo. 58 B3
Ādaba Eth. 128 C3
Adabazar Turkey see Sakarya
Adabiya Egypt 108 D8
Adaf, Djebel mts Alg. 123 H5
Adaja r. Spain 54 G3
Adak Sweden 44 L2
Adalia Turkey see Antalya
Adam Oman 105 G3
Adam, Mount hill Falkland Is 205 F8
Adamantina Brazil 206 B8
Adamaoua prov. Cameroon 125 I5
Adamas Greece 59 F12
also spelt Adhámas
Adamawa state Nigeria 125 H4
Adamclisi Romania 58 I4
Adamello mt. Italy 56 C2
Adamello-Brenta, Parco Naturale nature res. Italy 56 C2
Adaminaby Australia 147 F4
Adamovka Rus. Fed. 102 D2
Adams KY U.S.A. 176 C7
Adams MA U.S.A. 177 L3
Adams NY U.S.A. 177 I2
Adams WI U.S.A. 172 D7
Adams, Cape Antarctica 222 T2
Adams, Mount N.Z. 153 E11
Adam's Bridge sea feature India/Sri Lanka 94 C4
Adams Center U.S.A. 177 I2
Adams Lake Canada 166 G5
Adams McGill Reservoir U.S.A. 183 I3
Adams Mountain U.S.A. 166 D4
Adam's Peak Sri Lanka 94 D5
also known as Samanala or Sri Pada
Adams Peak U.S.A. 182 D2

▶Adamstown Pitcairn Is 221 J7
Capital of the Pitcairn Islands.

Adamstown U.S.A. 177 I5
'Adan Yemen see Aden
Adana Turkey 106 C3
also known as Seyhan; historically known as Ataniya
Adana prov. Turkey 108 G1
Adana Yemen see Aden
'Adan as Sughra Yemen 104 D5
English form Little Aden
Adang, Teluk b. Indon. 77 G3
Adani Nigeria 125 G5
Adapazari Turkey see Sakarya
Adaran, Jabal mt. Yemen 105 D5
Adare Rep. of Ireland 47 D11
Adare, Cape Antarctica 223 L2
Adarmo, Khawr watercourse Sudan 104 A3
Adatara-san vol. Japan 90 G6
Adavale Australia 149 E5
Adaži Latvia 42 F4
Adban Afgh. 101 G2
Adda r. Italy 56 B3
Ad Dabbah Sudan see Ed Debba
Ad Dafīnah Saudi Arabia 104 C3
Ad Daghghārah Iraq 107 F4
Ad Dahnā' des. Saudi Arabia 105 D3
also spelt Dahana
Ad Dakhilīyah admin. reg. Oman 105 G3
Ad Dakhla W. Sahara 122 B5
also spelt Dakhla; formerly known as Villa Cisneros
Ad Dālī' Yemen 104 D5
Ad Damir Sudan see Ed Damer
Ad Dammām Saudi Arabia see Dammam
Addanki India 94 C3
Ad Dār al Ḥamrā' Saudi Arabia 104 B2
Ad Darb Saudi Arabia 104 C4
Adda Sud, Parco dell' park Italy 56 B3
Addatigala India 94 D2
Ad Dawādimī Saudi Arabia 104 D2
Ad Dawḥah Qatar see Doha
Ad Dawr plain Syria 109 I3
Addax, Réserve Naturelle Intégrale dite Sanctuaire des nature res. Niger 125 H2
Ad Dibdibah plain Saudi Arabia 105 D2
Ad Dibīn Yemen 105 E4
Ad Dikākah des. Saudi Arabia 105 E4
Ad Dilam Saudi Arabia 105 D3
Ad Dir'īyah Saudi Arabia 105 D2

▶Addis Ababa Eth. 128 C2
Capital of Ethiopia. Also spelt Ādīs Ābeba.

Addison U.S.A. 177 H3
Ad Dīwānīyah Iraq 107 F5
also spelt Diwaniyah
Ad Dīwānīyah governorate Iraq see Al Qādisīyah
Addo S. Africa 133 J10
Addo Elephant National Park S. Africa 133 J10
Addoo Atoll Maldives see Addu Atoll
Addu Atoll Maldives 93 D11
also known as Seenu Atoll; also spelt Addoo Atoll
Ad Dulū'īyah Iraq 109 P3
Ad Duwayd well Saudi Arabia 107 E5
Ad Duwayhirah Saudi Arabia 104 D2
Ad Duwaym Sudan see Ed Dueim
Ad Duwayris well Saudi Arabia 105 E3
Adel GA U.S.A. 175 D6
Adel IA U.S.A. 178 D3

▶Adelaide Australia 146 C3
State capital of South Australia.

Adelaide Bahamas 175 E7
Adelaide S. Africa 133 K9
Adelaide Island Antarctica 222 T2
Adelaide River Australia 148 A2
Adelebsen Germany 48 G4
Adele Island Australia 150 C2
Adelfoi i. Greece 59 H12
Adélie Coast Antarctica 223 J2
Adélie Coast reg. Antarctica see Adélie Land
Adélie Land reg. Antarctica 223 J2
also known as Adélie Coast or Terre Adélie
Adelong Aboriginal Reserve Australia 151 C6
Adelsheim Germany 48 G6
Adelunga Uzbek. 103 G4
Aden Yemen 104 D5
also spelt 'Adan; historically known as Adana
Aden, Gulf of Somalia/Yemen 128 E2
Adena U.S.A. 176 E5
Adenau Germany 48 D5
Adendorp S. Africa 133 I9
Aderbissinat Niger 125 G3
Adernò Sicilia Italy see Adrano
Adesar India 96 A5
Adhaman az Zaur, Wādī watercourse Iraq 109 N5
Adhámas Greece see Adamas
Adhan, Jabal mt. U.A.E. 105 G2
Adhanah, Wādī watercourse Yemen 104 D5
Adh Dhayd U.A.E. 105 F2
Adh Dhāfir well Saudi Arabia 104 D2
'Adhfā' well Saudi Arabia 107 E5
'Ādhirīyāt, Jibāl al mts Jordan 109 H7
Adhoi India 96 A5
Adi i. Indon. 73 H7
Ādī Ārk'ay Eth. 128 C1
Adícora Venez. 198 D2
Ādī Da'iro Eth. 104 B5
'Adid Umm Inderab well Sudan 121 F6
Adige r. Italy 56 E3
Adigey Autonomous Oblast aut. rep. Rus. Fed. see Adygeya, Respublika
Ādīgrat Eth. 128 C1
Adıgüzel Barajı resr Turkey 106 B3
Adi Keyih Eritrea 121 H6
Adi Kwala Eritrea 121 H6
Adilabad India 94 C2
Adilanga Uganda 128 B4
Adilcevaz Turkey 107 E3
Adin U.S.A. 180 B4
Adīrī Libya 120 B3
Adirondack Mountains U.S.A. 177 K1
Ādīs Ābeba Eth. see Addis Ababa
Ādīs Zemen Eth. 128 C1
Adi Ugri Eritrea see Mendefera
Adıyaman Turkey 107 D3
Adjoantali reg. Alg. 123 G5
Adjud Romania 58 I2
Adjumani Uganda 128 A4
Adlavik Islands Canada 169 J2
Admiralty Gulf Australia 150 D2
Admiralty Gulf Aboriginal Reserve Australia 150 D2
Admiralty Inlet Canada 165 K2
Admiralty Island Canada 165 I3
Admiralty Island U.S.A. 164 F4
Admiralty Island National Monument - Kootznoowoo Wilderness nat. park U.S.A. 164 F4
Admiralty Islands P.N.G. 73 K7
Admiralty Mountains Antarctica 223 L2
Ādo Eth. 128 E3
Ado-Ekiti Nigeria 125 G5
Adok Sudan 128 A2
Adolfo Gonzáles Chaves Arg. 204 E5
Adolfsström Sweden 44 L2
Adolphus Island Australia 150 E2
Adonara i. Indon. 75 B5
also spelt Adunara
Adoni India 94 C3
Adour r. France 50 E9
Adra India 97 E5
Adra Spain 55 H8
Adra r. Spain 55 I8
Adramyttium Turkey see Edremit
Adramyttium, Gulf of Turkey see Edremit Körfezi
Adrano Sicilia Italy 57 G11
also spelt Aderno; historically known as Hadranum
Adrar Alg. 123 E4
Adrar mts Alg. 123 G4
Adrar hills Mali see Ifôghas, Adrar des
Adrar admin. reg. Mauritania 122 C5
Adraskand r. Afgh. 101 E3
Adrasmon Tajik. 101 G1
Adré Chad 120 D6
Adrian MI U.S.A. 173 I9
Adrian TX U.S.A. 179 B5
Adrianople Turkey see Edirne
Adrianopolis Turkey see Edirne
Adriatic Sea Europe 56 F4
Adua Eth. see Ādwa
Adunara i. Indon. see Adonara
Adur India 94 C4
Adusa Dem. Rep. Congo 126 F4
Adutiškis Lith. 42 H6
Aduwa Eth. see Ādwa
Adverse Well Australia 150 C4
Ādwa Eth. 128 C1
also spelt Aduwa; formerly spelt Adua
Adwufia Ghana 124 E5
Adycha r. Rus. Fed. 39 N3
Adygeya aut. rep. Rus. Fed. see Adygeya, Respublika
Adygeya, Respublika aut. rep. Rus. Fed. 41 F7
formerly known as Adigey Autonomous Oblast or Adygeyskaya Avtonomnaya Oblast'; short form Adygeya
Adygeysk Rus. Fed. 41 F7
formerly known as Teuchezhsk
Adygeyskaya Avtonomnaya Oblast' aut. rep. Rus. Fed. see Adygeya, Respublika
Adyk Rus. Fed. 41 H7
formerly known as Yuzhnyy
Adzhiyan Turkm. 102 C5
Adzopé Côte d'Ivoire 124 E5
Adz'va r. Rus. Fed. 40 L2
Adz'vavom Rus. Fed. 40 K2
Aegean Sea Greece/Turkey 59 F10
Aegina i. Greece see Aigina
Aegna i. Estonia 42 F2
Aegviidu Estonia 42 G2
Aegyptus country Africa see Egypt
Aela Jordan see Al 'Aqabah
Aelana Jordan see Al 'Aqabah
Aelia Capitolina Israel/West Bank see Jerusalem
Aelōnlaplap atoll Marshall Is see Ailinglapalap
Aenus Turkey see Enez
Ærø i. Denmark 48 H1
Aerzen Germany 48 G3
Aesernia Italy see Isernia
A Estrada Spain 54 C2
Äetsä Fin. 45 M3
Afabet Eritrea 121 H5
Afal watercourse Saudi Arabia see 'Ifāl, Wādī
Afanas'yevo Rus. Fed. 40 J4
Afándou Greece see Afantou
Afantou Greece 59 J12
also spelt Afándou

Afar admin. reg. Eth. 128 D1
Afar Oman 105 G3
Afar Depression Eritrea/Eth. 121 I6
Āfdem Eth. 128 D2
Afféri Côte d'Ivoire 124 E5
Affreville Alg. see Khemis Miliana
Afghānestān country Asia see Afghanistan
▶Afghanistan country Asia 101 E3 spelt Afghānestān in Dari and Pushtu asia [countries] 64–67
Afgooye Somalia 128 E4
'Afif Saudi Arabia 104 C3
Afikpo Nigeria 125 G5
Afim'ino Rus. Fed. 43 P4
Afiun Karahissar Turkey see Afyon
Åfjord Norway 44 J3
Aflou Alg. 123 F2
Afmadow Somalia 128 D4
Afognak Island U.S.A. 164 D4
Afojjar well Mauritania 124 B2
A Fonsagrada Spain 54 D1 also known as Fonsagrada
Afonso Cláudio Brazil 207 L7
Afragola Italy 56 G8
Afrânio Brazil 202 D4
Āfrēra Terara vol. Eth. 128 D1
Āfrēra YeChe'ew Hāyk' l. Eth. 128 D1
Africa Nova country Africa see Tunisia
'Afrīn Syria 109 H1
'Afrīn, Nahr r. Syria/Turkey 109 H1
Afşar Barajı resr Turkey 59 J10
Afşin Turkey 107 D3 also known as Efsus
Afsluitdijk barrage Neth. 48 C3
Aftol well Eth. 128 E3
Afton NY U.S.A. 177 J3
Afton WY U.S.A. 180 E4
Aftoût Faï depr. Mauritania 124 B2
Afuá Brazil 202 B2
'Afula Israel 108 G5
Afyon Turkey 106 B3 also known as Afyonkarahisar; historically known as Afiun Karahissar
Afyonkarahisar Turkey see Afyon
Aga Egypt 108 C7
Aga r. Rus. Fed. 85 G1
Aga-Buryat Autonomous Okrug admin. div. Rus. Fed. see Aginskiy Buryatskiy Avtonomnyy Okrug
Agadem well Niger 125 I2
Agadès Niger see Agadez
Agadez Niger 125 G2 also spelt Agadès
Agadez dept Niger 125 H2
Agadir Morocco 122 C3
Agadyr' Kazakh. 103 H2 also spelt Aqadyr
Agaie Nigeria 125 G4
Agalega Islands Mauritius 218 K6
Agalta nat. park Hond. 186 B4
Agana Guam see Hagåtña
Agapovka Rus. Fed. 102 D1
Agar India 96 C5
Agârak well Niger 125 G2
Agâraktem well Mali 122 D5
Ägaro Eth. 128 C3
Agartala India 97 F5
Agashi India 94 B2
Agassiz National Wildlife Refuge nature res. U.S.A. 178 D1
Agate Canada 168 D3
Agathe France see Agde
Agathonisi i. Greece 59 H11
Agatti i. India 94 B4
Agawa r. Canada 173 I3
Agbor Bojiboji Nigeria 125 G5
Agboville Côte d'Ivoire 124 D5
Ağcabädi Azer. 107 F2 also spelt Agdzhabedi
Ağdam Azer. 107 F3
Ağdaş Azer. 107 F2 also spelt Agdash
Agdash Azer. see Ağdaş
Agde France 51 J9 historically known as Agathe
Agdzhabedi Azer. see Ağcabädi
Agedabia Libya see Ajdābiyā
Agen France 50 G8 historically known as Aginnum
Agenebode Nigeria 125 G5
Ägere Maryam Eth. 128 C3
Ageyevo Rus. Fed. 43 R7
Aggeneys S. Africa 132 C6
Aggershus county Norway see Akershus
Aggteleki nat. park Hungary 49 R7
Agharri, Sha'īb al watercourse Iraq 109 L4
Aghezzaf well Mali 122 E5 also spelt Arezzaf
Aghil Pass China/Jammu and Kashmir 89 B4
Aghireşu Romania 58 E2
Aghouâvil des. Mauritania 124 D2
Aghrîjît well Mauritania 124 C2
Aghzoumal, Sabkhat salt pan W. Sahara 122 B4
Agia Greece 59 D9 also spelt Ayiá
Agiabampo Mex. 184 C3
Agia Eirinis, Akra pt Greece 59 G9
Agia Marina Greece 59 H11
Agiasos Greece 59 H9 also spelt Ayiásos
Agia Vervara Greece 59 G13
Agigea Romania 58 J4
Aghiol Romania 58 J3
Agiguan i. N. Mariana Is see Aguijan
Ağın Turkey 107 D3
Aginskiy Buryatskiy Avtonomnyy Okrug admin. div. Rus. Fed. 85 G1 English form Aga-Buryat Autonomous Okrug
Aginskoye Rus. Fed. 85 G1
Aginnum France see Agen
Agioi Apostoloi Greece 59 E10
Agioi Dimitrios Greece 59 E11 also spelt Áyios Dhimítrios
Agios Dimitrios, Akra pt Greece 59 F11 also spelt Áyios Dhimítrios, Ákra
Agios Efstratios Greece 59 F9
Agios Efstratios i. Greece 59 G9 also spelt Áyios Evstrátios
Agios Fokas, Akra pt Greece 59 H9
Agios Georgios i. Greece 59 E11 also spelt Áyios Yeóryios
Agios Ioannis, Akra pt Greece 59 G13
Agios Kirykos Greece 59 H11
Agios Konstantinos Greece 59 D10
Agios Nikolaos Greece 59 G13 also spelt Áyios Nikólaos
Agios Paraskevi Greece 59 H9
Agios Petros Greece 59 D11
Agiou Orous, Kolpos b. Greece 59 E8
Agirwat Hills Sudan 121 G5
Agisanang S. Africa 133 J4
Agly r. France 51 J10
Agnantero Greece 59 C9
Agnes, Mount hill Australia 146 A1
Agnew Australia 151 C6
Agnew Lake Canada 173 L4
Agnibilékrou Côte d'Ivoire 124 E5
Agnita Romania 58 F3
Agniye-Afanas'yevsk Rus. Fed. 82 E2
Agno r. Italy 56 D3
Agnone Italy 56 G7
Ago-Are Nigeria 125 F4
Agogo Ghana 125 E5
Agona Junction Ghana 125 E5
Agong China 84 D4
Agounni Jefal well Mali 124 E2
Agoura U.S.A. 182 F7
Agous-n-Ehsel well Mali 125 F2 also known as Ehcel
Agout r. France 51 H9
Agra India 96 C4
Agrakhanskiy Poluostrov pen. Rus. Fed. 102 A4
Agram Croatia see Zagreb
Agreda Spain 55 J3
Agri r. Italy 57 I8
Ağrı Turkey 107 E3 also known as Karaköse
Agria Gramvousa i. Greece 59 E13
Ağrı Dağı mt. Turkey see Ararat, Mount
Agrigan i. N. Mariana Is see Agrihan
Agrigento Sicilia Italy 57 F11 formerly known as Girgenti; historically known as Acragas or Agrigentum
Agrigentum Sicilia Italy see Agrigento
Agrihan i. N. Mariana Is 73 K3 also spelt Agrigan; formerly spelt Grigan
Agrii r. Romania 58 E1
Agrinio Greece 59 C10
Agropoli Italy 57 G8
Agryz Rus. Fed. 40 J4
Ågskaret Norway 44 K2
Ağstafa Azer. 107 F2
Ağsu Azer. 107 G2 also spelt Akhsu
Agtertang S. Africa 133 J7
Agua Blanca Arg. 204 D5
Água Boa Brazil 207 K4
Agua Brava, Laguna lag. Mex. 184 D4
Agua Clara Bol. 200 D3
Água Clara Brazil 206 A7
Aguaclara Col. 198 C3
Aguada Mex. 185 H5
Aguadilla Puerto Rico 187 G3
Aguado Cecilio Arg. 204 D6
Agua Doce do Norte Brazil 207 L5
Aguados, Serra dos mts Brazil 206 D9
Agua Dulce Bol. 200 D3
Aguadulce Panama 186 C5
Agua Escondida Arg. 204 C5
Agua Fria r. U.S.A. 183 L8
Aguanaval r. Mex. 185 E3
Aguanga U.S.A. 183 H8
Aguanqueterique Hond. 186 B4
Aguanus r. Canada 169 I3
Aguapeí Brazil 201 F4
Aguapeí r. Mato Grosso do Sul Brazil 206 B8 also known as Feio
Aguapeí r. Brazil 201 F3
Aguapeí, Serra hills Brazil 201 F4
Agua Prieta Mex. 184 C2
Aguaragüe, Cordillera de mts Bol. 201 E5
Aguaray Arg. 201 E5
A Guardia Spain 54 C3 also spelt La Guardia
Aguaro-Guariquito, Parque Nacional nat. park Venez. 199 E2
Aguaruto Mex. 184 D3
Aguas r. Spain 55 J7
Águas Belas Brazil 202 E4
Aguascalientes Mex. 185 E4
Aguascalientes state Mex. 185 E4
Águas Formosas Brazil 203 D6
Águas Vermelhas Brazil 207 L2
Aguasvivas r. Spain 55 K3
Água Verde r. Brazil 201 F3
Água Vermelha, Represa resr Brazil 206 C6
Aguaytia Peru 200 B2
Agudo Spain 54 G6
Agudos Brazil 206 E9
Águeda Port. 54 C4
Águeda r. Port./Spain 54 E3
Aguelal Niger 125 H2
Aguelhok Mali 125 F2
Aguemour, Oued watercourse Alg. 123 F4
Aguessis well Niger 123 H6
Aguié Niger 125 G3
Aguijan i. N. Mariana Is 73 K4 also spelt Agiguan
Aguila mt. Spain 55 J4
Aguila U.S.A. 183 K8
Aguilar de Campóo Spain 54 G2
Águilas Spain 55 J7
Aguililla Mex. 185 E5
Aguisan Phil. 74 B4
Āgula'i Eth. 104 B5
Agulhas S. Africa 132 E11
▶Agulhas, Cape S. Africa 132 E11 Most southerly point of Africa.
Agulhas Negras mt. Brazil 203 C7
Aguntum Italy see San Candido
Agusan r. Phil. 74 C4
Agutaya i. Phil. 74 B4
Ağva Turkey 106 B2
Agvali Rus. Fed. 102 A4
Agwarra Nigeria 125 G4
Agwei r. Sudan 128 B3
Ahaggar plat. Alg. see Hoggar
Ahakeye Aboriginal Land res. Australia 148 B4
Ahar Iran 100 A2
Ahaura N.Z. 153 F10
Ahaura r. N.Z. 153 F10
Ahaus Germany 48 E3
Ahigal Spain 54 E4
Ahillo mt. Spain 54 G7
Ahimanawa Range mts N.Z. 152 K6
Ahioma P.N.G. 149 F1
Ahipara N.Z. 152 H3
Ahipara Bay N.Z. 152 H3
Ahiri India 94 D2
Ahititi N.Z. 152 I6
Ahja r. Estonia 42 I3
Ahklun Mountains U.S.A. 164 C4
Ahlat Turkey 107 E3
Ahlen Germany 48 E4
Ahmadabad India 96 B5 formerly spelt Ahmedabad
Ahmadābād Iran 101 E3
Aḥmad al Bāqir, Jabal mt. Jordan 108 G8
Ahmadnagar India 94 B2 formerly spelt Ahmednagar
Ahmadpur India 94 C2 also known as Rajura
Ahmadpur East Pak. 101 G4
Ahmadpur Sial Pak. 101 G4
Ahmar Mountains Eth. 128 D2
Ahmedabad India see Ahmadabad
Ahmednagar India see Ahmadnagar
Ahmetli Turkey 59 I10
Ahoada Nigeria 125 G5
Ahome Mex. 184 C3
Ahore India 96 B4
Ahoskie U.S.A. 177 I9
Ahram Iran 100 B4
Ahrāmāt el Jīzah tourist site Egypt see Giza Pyramids
Ahraura India 97 D4
Ahrensburg Germany 48 H2
Ähtäri Fin. 40 C3
Ahtme Estonia 42 I2
Āhū Iran 100 B4
Ahuacatlán Mex. 184 D4
Ahuachapán El Salvador 185 H6
Ahualulco Jalisco Mex. 184 E4
Ahualulco San Luis Potosí Mex. 185 E4
Ahun France 51 I6
Ahunapalu Estonia 42 I3
Ahuriri r. N.Z. 153 E12
Ahvāz Iran 100 B4 also spelt Ahwāz
Ahvenanmaa is Fin. see Åland Islands
Ahwa India 94 B1
Aḥwar Yemen 105 D5
Ahwāz Iran see Ahvāz
Ai r. China 83 B4
Ai-Ais Namibia 130 C5
Ai-Ais Hot Springs and Fish River Canyon Park nature res. Namibia 130 C5
Aibag Gol r. China 85 F3
Aibetsu Japan 90 H3
Aichach Germany 48 I7
Aichi pref. Japan 91 E7
Aid U.S.A. 176 C7
Aida Japan 91 D7
Aidin Turkm. 102 C5
Aigiali Greece 59 G12 also spelt Aiyiáli
Aigialousa Cyprus 108 F2 also known as Yialousa
Aigina Greece 59 E11
Aigina i. Greece 59 E11 English form Aegina; also spelt Aíyina
Aiginio Greece 58 D8 also known as Aiyínion
Aigio Greece 59 D10 also known as Aiyion
Aigle Switz. 51 M6
Aigle de Chambeyron mt. France 51 M8
Aigoual, Mont mt. France 51 J8
Aiguá Uruguay 204 G4
Aiguebelle, Parc de Conservation d' nature res. Canada 173 O2
Aigües Tortes i Estany de St Maurici, Parque Nacional d' nat. park Spain 55 L2
Aiguille de Scolette mt. France/Italy 51 M7
Aiguilles d'Arves mts France 51 M7
Aiguille Verte mt. France 51 M7
Aigurande France 50 H6
Aihua China see Yunxian
Aihui China see Heihe
Aija Peru 200 A2
Aijal India see Aizawl
Aiken U.S.A. 175 D5
Ailao Shan mts China 86 B3
Aileron Australia 148 B4
Aileu East Timor 75 C5
Ailigandi Panama 186 D5
Ailing China 87 D3
Ailinglabelab atoll Marshall Is see Ailinglapalap
Ailinglapalap atoll Marshall Is 220 F6 also spelt Aelōnlaplap or Ailinglabelab; formerly known as Lambert
Ailly-sur-Noye France 51 I3
Ailsa Craig Canada 173 L7
Ailsa Craig i. U.K. 47 G8
Aimogasta Arg. 204 D3
Aimorés, Serra dos hills Brazil 203 D6
Ain r. France 51 L7
'Aîn 'Amûr spring Egypt 121 F3
Ainaži Latvia 42 F4
Aïn Beïda Alg. 123 G2 formerly known as Daoud
Aïn Beni Mathar Morocco 123 E2
'Aîn Ben Tili Mauritania 122 C4
Aïn Bessem Alg. 55 O8
Aïn Biré well Mauritania 124 C2
Aïn Boucif Alg. 55 O9
'Aîn Dalla spring Egypt 121 E3
Aïn Defla Alg. 123 F1 formerly known as Duperré
Aïn Deheb Alg. 123 F2
Aïn Draham Tunisia 57 A12
Aïn el Bâgha well Egypt 108 E8
'Aîn el Furtâga well Egypt 108 F8
Aïn el Hadjadj well Alg. 123 F3
'Aîn el Hadjadj well Alg. 123 G4
Aïn el Hadjel Alg. 123 F2
'Aîn el Maqfi spring Egypt 121 F3
Aïn Galakka spring Chad 120 C5
Aïn Mdila well Alg. 123 G2
Aïn-M'Lila Alg. 123 G1
Ainos nat. park Greece 59 B10
Aïn Oussera Alg. 123 F2
Aïn Salah Alg. see In Salah
Aïn Sefra Alg. 123 E2
Ainslie, Lake Canada 169 I4
Ainsworth IA U.S.A. 172 B9
Ainsworth NE U.S.A. 178 C3
Aintab Turkey see Gaziantep
Aïn Taya Alg. 55 O8
Aïn Tédélès Alg. 55 L9
Aïn Temouchent Alg. 123 E2
'Aîn Tibaghbagh spring Egypt 121 E2
'Aîn Timeira spring Egypt 121 E2
Aïn Ti-m Misaou well Alg. 123 F5
'Aîn Zeitûn Egypt 106 A5
Aipe Col. 198 C4
Aiquile Bol. 200 D4
Air i. Indon. 77 D2 also known as Raibu
Airão Brazil 199 F5
Airbangis Indon. 76 B2
Airdrie Canada 167 H5
Aire r. France 51 K3
Aire-sur-l'Adour France 50 F9
Air Force Island Canada 165 L3
Airgin Sum China 85 F3
Airhitam r. Indon. 77 E3
Airhitam, Teluk b. Indon. 77 E3
Airlie Beach Australia 149 F4
Airlie Island Australia 150 A4
Airolo Switz. 51 O6
Airpanas Indon. 75 C4
Air Ronge Canada 167 J4
Airvault France 50 F6
Aisatung Mountain Myanmar 78 A3
Aisch r. Germany 48 I6
Aisén admin. reg. Chile 205 B7
Aishalton Guyana 199 G4
Ai Shan hill China 85 I4
Aishihik Canada 166 B2
Aishihik Lake Canada 166 B2
Aisimi Greece see Aisymi
Aisne r. France 51 I3
Aïssa, Djebel mt. Alg. 123 E2
Aisymi Greece 58 G7 also spelt Aisími
Aitamännikkö Fin. 44 N2
Aitana mt. Spain 55 K6
Aitape P.N.G. 73 J7 also spelt Eitape
Aït Benhaddou tourist site Morocco 122 D3
Aitkin U.S.A. 174 A2
Aitoliko Greece 59 C10
Aitova Rus. Fed. 41 J5
Aiud Romania 58 E2 also known as Nagyenyed
Aivadzh Tajik. 101 G2 also spelt Ayvadzh
Aiviekste r. Latvia 42 G5
Aix France see Aix-en-Provence
Aix r. France 51 K7
Aix-en-Othe France 51 J4
Aix-en-Provence France 51 L9 historically known as Aquae Sextiae; short form Aix
Aixe-sur-Vienne France 50 H7
Aix-la-Chapelle Germany see Aachen
Aix-les-Bains France 51 L7 historically known as Aquae Gratianae
Āiy Ādi Eth. 128 C1
Aiyiáli Greece see Aigiali
Aíyina i. Greece see Aigina
Aiyínion Greece see Aiginio
Aiyion Greece see Aigio
Aizawl India 97 G5 formerly spelt Aijal
Aizenay France 50 E6
Aizkraukle Latvia 42 G5 formerly known as Stučka or Stuchka or imeni Petra Stuchki
Aizpute Latvia 42 C5
Aizu-wakamatsu Japan 90 F6
Ajā, Jibāl mts Saudi Arabia 104 C2
Ajaccio Corse France 52 D3
Ajaccio, Golfe d' b. Corse France 56 A7
Ajaigarh India 96 D4
Ajajú r. Col. 198 C4
Ajalpán Mex. 185 F5
Ajanta India 94 B1
Ajanta Range hills India see Sahyadriparvat Range
Ajasse Nigeria 125 G4
Ajax Canada 173 N7
Ajax, Mount N.Z. 153 G10
Ajayameru India see Ajmer
Ajban U.A.E. 105 F2
Aj Bogd Uul mts Mongolia 84 B2
Ajdābiyā Libya 120 D2 formerly spelt Agedabia
Ajdovščina Slovenia 56 F3
a-Jiddét des. Oman see Ḥarāsīs, Jiddat al
Ajigasawa Japan 90 G4
'Ajīj, Wādī al watercourse Iraq 109 M2
Ajimganj India 97 F4
Ajka Hungary 49 O8
'Ajlūn Jordan 108 G5
Ajman U.A.E. 105 F2
Ajmer India 96 B4 formerly known as Ajayameru or Ajmer-Merwara
Ajmer-Merwara India see Ajmer
Ajo U.S.A. 183 L9
Ajo, Mount U.S.A. 183 L9
Ajra India 94 B2
Ajuy Phil. 74 B4
Akāashat Iraq 107 D4
Akabira Japan 90 H3
Akabli Alg. 123 F4
Akaboun well Mali 125 F2
Akademii, Zaliv b. Rus. Fed. 82 E1 English form Academy Bay
Akademii Nauk, Khrebet mt. Tajik. see Akademiyai Fanho, Qatorkŭhi
Akademiyai Fanho, Qatorkŭhi mt. Tajik. 101 G2 also known as Akademii Nauk, Khrebet
Akagera National Park Rwanda 126 F5 also known as Kagera, Parc National de la or L'Akagera, Parc National de
Akagi Japan 91 C7
Akaishi-dake mt. Japan 91 F7
Āk'ak'ī Beseka Eth. 128 C2
Akalkot India 94 C2
Akama, Akra c. Cyprus see Arnauti, Cape
Akamagaseki Japan see Shimonoseki
Akamkpa Nigeria 125 H5
Akan Japan 90 I3
Akan-ko l. Japan 90 H3
Akan National Park Japan 90 I3
Akarkar well Niger 125 G3
Akarnanika mts Greece 59 B10
Akaroa N.Z. 153 G11
Akaroa Harbour N.Z. 153 G11
Akas reg. India 97 G4
'Akāsh, Wādī watercourse Iraq 109 L3
Akasha Sudan 121 F4
'Akāshāt Iraq 109 K4
Akashi Japan 91 D7
Äkäsjokisuu Fin. 44 M2
Akbakay Kazakh. 103 H3
Akbalyk Kazakh. 103 I3 also spelt Aqbalyq
Akbarābād Iran 100 C4
Akbarpur Uttar Pradesh India 96 D4
Akbarpur Uttar Pradesh India 97 D4
Akbasty Kazakh. 102 E3
Akbaytal Tajik. 101 H2 also known as Rabatakbaytal or Rabotoqbaytal
Akbaytal Pass Tajik. 101 H2
Akbeit Kazakh. 103 G2 also spelt Aqbeyit
Akbou Alg. 55 P8
Akbulak Rus. Fed. 102 C2
Akçadağ Turkey 107 D3
Akçakale Turkey 107 D3
Akçakertikbeli Geçidi pass Turkey 59 J9
Akçakoca Turkey 106 B2
Akçalı Dağları mt. Turkey 106 C3
Akçalı Dağları mts Turkey 108 D1
Akçaova Turkey 59 I11
Akçay r. Turkey 59 J11
Akchakaya, Vpadina depr. Turkm. 102 D4
Akchâr reg. Mauritania 124 B2
Akchatau Kazakh. 103 H3 also known as Aqshatau
Akchi Kazakh. see Akshiy
Akdağ mt. Turkey 59 J9
Akdağlar mts Turkey 106 B3
Akdağmadeni Turkey 106 C3
Akdepe Turkm. 102 D4 formerly known as Leninsk
Akdere Turkey 108 E1
Ak Dovurak Rus. Fed. 84 A1
Akelamo Indon. 75 D2
Akele Guzai prov. Eritrea 104 B5
Akelo Sudan 128 B3
Åkersberga Sweden 45 L4
Akershus county Norway 45 J3 formerly spelt Aggershus
Åkerstrømmen Norway 45 J3
Akespe Kazakh. 103 E3
Aketi Dem. Rep. Congo 126 D4
Akgyr Erezi hills Turkm. see Akkyr, Gory
Akhalgori Georgia 107 F2 formerly known as Leningori
Akhalk'alak'i Georgia 107 E2
Akhal Oblast admin. div. Turkm. see Akhal'skaya Oblast'
Akhal'skaya Oblast' admin. div. Turkm. 102 D5 English form Akhal Oblast; formerly known as Ashkhabadskaya Oblast'
Akhalts'ikhe Georgia 107 E2
Akhḍar, Al Jabal al mts Libya 120 D2
Akhḍar, Jabal mts Oman 105 G3
Akhḍar, Wādī al watercourse Saudi Arabia 109 H9
Akheloy Bulg. 58 I6
Akhisar Turkey 106 A3 historically known as Thyatira
Akhmīm Egypt 121 F3 also spelt Ekhmîm; historically known as Chemmis or Panoplis
Akhnoor Jammu and Kashmir 96 B2
Akhsu Azer. see Ağsu
Akhta Armenia see Hrazdan
Akhtarīn Syria 109 I1
Akhtubinsk Rus. Fed. 102 A2
Akhty Rus. Fed. 102 A4
Akhtyrka Ukr. see Okhtyrka
Aki Japan 91 C8
Akiéni Gabon 126 B5
Akimiski Island Canada 168 D2
Akıncılar Turkey see Selçuk
Akıncılar Turkey 107 D2
Åkirkeby Denmark 45 K5
Akishma r. Rus. Fed. 82 D1
Akita Japan 90 G5
Akita pref. Japan 90 G5
Akitio N.Z. 152 K8
Akjoujt Mauritania 124 B2
Akka Morocco 122 C3
Akkajaure l. Sweden 44 L2
Akkala Uzbek. 102 D4 also spelt Oqqal'a
Akkem Rus. Fed. 88 D1
Akkerman Ukr. see Bilhorod-Dnistrovs'kyy
Akkermanovka Rus. Fed. 102 D2
Akkeshi Japan 90 I3
Akkeshi-wan b. Japan 90 I3
'Akko Israel 108 G5 historically known as Accho or Acre or St-Jean-d'Acre or Ptolemais
Akkol' Akmolinskaya Oblast' Kazakh. 103 G1 also spelt Aqköl; formerly known as Alekseyevka
Akkol' Almatinskaya Oblast' Kazakh. 103 H3
Akkol' Atyrauskaya Oblast' Kazakh. 41 I7 also spelt Akkul' or Aqköl
Akkol' Zhambylskaya Oblast' Kazakh. 103 G4
Akköy Turkey 106 A3
Akköy Turkey 59 K11
Akku Kazakh. 103 I2 formerly known as Lebyazh'ye
Akkul' Kazakh. see Akkol'
Akkum Kazakh. 103 F3
Akkuş Turkey 107 D2
Akkyr, Gory hills Turkm. 102 C4 also known as Akgyr Erezi
Akkystau Kazakh. 102 B3 also known as Aqqystaū
Aklavik Canada 164 F3
Aklera India 96 C4
Aklub reg. Saudi Arabia 104 D4
Ak-Mechet Kazakh. see Kyzylorda
Akmena r. Lith. 42 D6
Akmenė Lith. 42 D5
Akmeņrags pt Latvia 42 C5
Akmeqit China 88 B4
Akmola Kazakh. see Astana
Akmola Oblast admin. div. Kazakh. see Akmolinskaya Oblast'
Akmolinsk Kazakh. see Astana
Akmolinskaya Oblast' admin. div. Kazakh. 103 G2 English form Aqmola Oblast; also known as Aqmola Oblysy; formerly known as Akmola Oblast or Tselinogradskaya Oblast'
Akniste Latvia 42 G5
Aknoul Morocco 122 E2
Akō Japan 91 D7
Akobo Sudan 128 B3
Akobo Wenz r. Eth./Sudan 128 B3
Akodia India 96 C5
Akola Maharashtra India 94 B2
Akola Maharashtra India 94 C1
Akom II Cameroon 125 H6
Akonolinga Cameroon 125 I6
Akop Sudan 126 F2
Akordat Eritrea 121 H6
Akören Turkey 106 C3
Akot India 96 C5
Akouménaye Fr. Guiana 199 H4
Akoupé Côte d'Ivoire 124 E5
Ak-Oyuk, Gora mt. Rus. Fed. 84 A1
Akpatok Island Canada 165 M3
Akqi China 88 B3
Akraifnio Greece 59 E10
Akranes Iceland 44 [inset] B2
Akrathos, Akra pt Greece 59 F8
Åkrē Iraq 109 O1
Akréréb Niger 125 H2
Akritas, Akra pt Greece 59 C12
Akron CO U.S.A. 178 B3
Akron IN U.S.A. 172 G9
Akron OH U.S.A. 176 D4
Akrotiri Bay Cyprus 108 E3 also known as Akrotirion Bay or Akrotiriou, Kolpos
Akrotirion Bay Cyprus see Akrotiri Bay
Akrotiriou, Kolpos b. Cyprus see Akrotiri Bay
Akrotiri Sovereign Base Area military base Cyprus 108 D3
▶Aksai Chin terr. Asia 89 B5 Disputed territory (China/India). Also known as Aqsayqin Hit.
Aksakal Turkey 59 J8
Aksakovo Bulg. 58 I5
Aksakovo Rus. Fed. 40 J5
Aksaray Turkey 106 C3
Aksarka Rus. Fed. 38 G3
Aksay China 84 B4 also known as Hongliuwan
Aksay Kazakh. 102 C2 also spelt Aqsay; formerly known as Kazakhstan
Ak-Say r. Kyrg. 103 H4
Aksay Rus. Fed. 41 F7
Akşehir Turkey 106 B3 historically known as Philomelium
Akşehir Gölü l. Turkey 106 B3
Akseki Turkey 106 B3
Aksenovo Rus. Fed. 41 J5
Aks-e Rostam r. Iran 100 C4
Aksha Rus. Fed. 85 G1
Akshatau Kazakh. 102 C2
Akshiganak Kazakh. 103 E2
Akshiy Kazakh. 103 I4 also spelt Aqshi; formerly spelt Akchi
Akshukur Kazakh. 102 B4 also spelt Aqshuqyr
Aksu Xinjiang China 88 C3
Aksu Xinjiang China 88 C3
Aksu Almatinskaya Oblast' Kazakh. 103 I3 also spelt Aqsū
Aksu Pavlodarskaya Oblast' Kazakh. 103 I1 also spelt Aqsū; formerly known as Ermak or Yermak
Aksu Severnyy Kazakhstan Kazakh. 103 G1 also spelt Aqsū
Aksu Zapadnyy Kazakhstan Kazakh. 102 C2 also spelt Aqsū
Aksu r. Kazakh. 103 I3
Aksu r. Tajik. see Oksu
Aksu Turkey 108 B1
Aksu r. Turkey 107 B3
Aksuat Kustanayskaya Oblast' Kazakh. 103 F2
Aksuat Vostochnyy Kazakhstan Kazakh. 88 C2 also spelt Aqsūat
Aksuat, Ozero salt l. Kazakh. see Bol'shoy Aksuat, Ozero
Aksu-Ayuly Kazakh. 103 H2 also spelt Aqsū-Ayuly
Aksuek Kazakh. 103 H3
Aksu He r. China 88 C3
Āksum Eth. 128 C1 historically known as Axum
Aksüme China 88 C2
Aksu-Zhabaglinskiy Zapovednik nature res. Kazakh. 103 G4
Aktag mt. China 89 D4
Ak-Tal Rus. Fed. 88 F1
Aktash Uzbek. 103 F5 also spelt Oqtosh
Aktau Karagandinskaya Oblast' Kazakh. 103 G3
Aktau Karagandinskaya Oblast' Kazakh. 103 H2
Aktau Mangistauskaya Oblast' Kazakh. 102 B4 also spelt Aqtaū; formerly known as Shevchenko
Aktepe Turkey 109 H1
Akto China 88 B4
Aktogay Karagandinskaya Oblast' Kazakh. 103 H2 also spelt Aqtoghay
Aktogay Pavlodarskaya Oblast' Kazakh. 103 H1 also spelt Aqtoghay; formerly known as Krasnokutsk or Krasnokutskoye
Aktogay Vostochnyy Kazakhstan Kazakh. 103 I3
Aktsyabrskaya Belarus 43 L6 also spelt Oktyabr'skaya
Aktsyabrski Belarus 43 J9 also spelt Oktyabr'skiy; formerly known as Karpilovka
Aktsyabrski Belarus 43 K7 also spelt Oktyabr'skiy
Aktumsyk Kazakh. 102 D3
Aktumsyk, Mys pt Uzbek. 102 D3
Ak-Tüz Kyrg. 103 H4 also spelt Aktyuz
Aktyubinsk Kazakh. 102 D2 also known as Aqtöbe
Aktyubinskaya Oblast' admin. div. Kazakh. 102 D2 English form Aktyubinsk Oblast; also known as Aqtöbe Oblysy
Aktyubinsk Oblast admin. div. Kazakh. see Aktyubinskaya Oblast'
Aktyuz Kyrg. see Ak-Tüz
Akujärvi Fin. 44 N1
Akula Dem. Rep. Congo 126 D4
Akulichi Rus. Fed. 43 O8
Akulivik Canada 165 L3
Akumadan Ghana 125 E5
Akune Japan 91 B8
Akur mt. Uganda 128 B4
Akure Nigeria 125 G5
Akureyri Iceland 44 [inset] C2
Akuroa N.Z. 152 I4
Akwa Ibom state Nigeria 125 G5
Akwanga Nigeria 125 H4
Akyab Myanmar see Sittwe
Ak"yar Rus. Fed. 102 D2
Akyatan Gölü salt l. Turkey 108 G1
Akzhal Karagandinskaya Oblast' Kazakh. 103 H3
Akzhal Vostochnyy Kazakhstan Kazakh. 103 J2 also spelt Aqzhal
Akzhar Kzyl-Ordinskaya Oblast' Kazakh. 103 F3
Akzhar Vostochnyy Kazakhstan Kazakh. 88 C2 also spelt Aqzhar
Akzhar Zhambylskaya Oblast' Kazakh. 103 G4
Akzhaykyn, Ozero salt l. Kazakh. 103 F3 also known as Aqzhayqyn Köli
Ål Norway 45 J3
Ala r. Belarus 43 K9
Ala Italy 56 D3
'Alā, Jabal al hills Syria 109 H2
Alabama r. U.S.A. 175 C6
Alabama state U.S.A. 175 C5
Alabaster AL U.S.A. 175 C5
Alabaster MI U.S.A. 173 J6
Al 'Abṭīyah well Iraq 107 F5
Ala-Buka Kyrg. 103 G4
Al Abyaḍ Libya 120 B3
Al Abyār Libya 120 D2
Alaca Turkey 106 C2 also known as Huseyinabat
Alacahan Turkey 107 D3
Alaçam Turkey 106 C2
Alaçam Dağları mts Turkey 59 J9
Alacant Spain see Alicante
Alaçatı Turkey 59 H10
Alacrán, Arrecife reef Mex. 185 H4
Aladag mt. Bulg. 58 G7
Aladağ Turkey 106 C3 also known as Bademli
Ala Dag mt. Turkey 107 E3
Ala Dağlar mts Turkey 107 E3
Ala Dağlar mts Turkey 106 C3
Al 'Adam Libya 120 D2
Alaejos Spain 54 F3
Al Aflāj reg. Saudi Arabia 105 D3
Alagadiço Brazil 199 F4
Alagapuram India 94 C4
Alag Hayrhan Uul mt. Mongolia 84 B2
Alagir Rus. Fed. 41 H8
Alagoas state Brazil 202 E4
Alagoinhas Brazil 202 E5
Alagón Spain 55 J3
Alagón r. Spain 54 E5
Alah r. Phil. 74 C5
Alahanpanjang Indon. 76 C3
Alahärmä Fin. 44 M3
Al Aḥmadī Kuwait 107 G5
Alaid, Ostrov i. Rus. Fed. see Atlasova, Ostrov
Alaior Spain 55 P5
Alai Range mts Asia 99 I2 also known as Alay Kyrka Toosu or Alayskiy Khrebet or Oloy, Qatorkŭhi
Ālaivān Iran 100 C3
Al Aja'is hills Saudi Arabia 109 K8
Al 'Ajā'iz well Oman 105 G4
Al Ajām Saudi Arabia 105 E2
Alajärvi Fin. 44 M3
Alajaure naturreservat nature res. Sweden 44 M1
Al Ajfar Saudi Arabia 104 C2
Alajõgi r. Estonia 42 I2
Alajuela Costa Rica 186 B5
Alakanuk U.S.A. 164 C3
Alaknanda r. India 96 C3
Alakol', Ozero salt l. Kazakh. 88 C2
Ala Kul salt l. Kazakh. see Alakol', Ozero
Alakurtti Rus. Fed. 44 O2
Al 'Alamayn Egypt see El 'Alamein
Alalaú r. Brazil 199 F5
Al 'Alayyah Saudi Arabia 104 C4
Alama Somalia 128 D3
Al 'Amādīyah Iraq 107 E3
Alamagan i. N. Mariana Is 73 K3 also spelt Alamaguan
Alamaguan i. N. Mariana Is see Alamagan
Al'Amār Saudi Arabia 104 C2
Al 'Amārah Iraq 107 F5
'Alāmarvdasht watercourse Iran 100 C4
Ālamat'ā Eth. 104 B5
'Alam el Rûm, Râs pt Egypt 121 E2
Al Amghar waterhole Iraq 107 F5
Al Amghar waterhole Saudi Arabia 109 N7
Alamicamba Nicaragua 186 B4
Alaminos Phil. 74 A2
Alamito Creek r. U.S.A. 181 F7
Al Amlah Saudi Arabia 104 C3
'Alam Nafâza hill Egypt 108 A7
Alamo U.S.A. 174 B5
Alamo Dam U.S.A. 183 K7
Alamogordo U.S.A. 181 F6
Alamo Heights U.S.A. 179 C6
Álamos Sonora Mex. 184 C2
Álamos Sonora Mex. 184 C3
Álamos r. Mex. 185 E3
Álamos, Sierra mts Mex. 184 C3
Alamosa U.S.A. 181 F5
Alamosa Creek r. U.S.A. 181 F6
Álamos de Peña Mex. 184 D2
Alampur India 94 C3
Al 'Anad Yemen 104 D5
Alanäs Sweden 44 K2
Al Anbār governorate Iraq 107 E4
Åland is Fin. see Åland Islands
Aland r. Germany 48 I2
Aland India 94 C2
Aland r. Iran 107 F3
Åland Islands Fin. 45 L3 also known as Ahvenanmaa; short form Åland
Ålands Hav sea chan. Fin./Sweden 45 L4
Alandur India 94 D3
Alangalang, Tanjung pt Indon. 77 G3
Alang Besar i. Indon. 76 C2
Alange, Embalse de resr Spain 54 E6
Alanggantang i. Indon. 76 D3
Alanson U.S.A. 173 I5
Alanya Turkey 106 C3 historically known as Coracesium
'Alā' od Dīn Iran 100 C4
Alapaha r. U.S.A. 175 D6
Alapakam India 94 C4
Alaplı Turkey 41 D8
Alappuzha India see Alleppey
Alapur India 96 C4
Al 'Aqabah Jordan 108 G8 also spelt 'Aqaba; historically known as Aela or Aelana
Al 'Aqīq Saudi Arabia 104 C3
Al 'Aqūlah well Saudi Arabia 105 E3
Al 'Arabīyah i. Saudi Arabia 107 G6
Al 'Arabīyah as Sa'ūdīyah country Asia see Saudi Arabia
Alarcón, Embalse de resr Spain 55 I5
Al 'Arīḍah Saudi Arabia 104 C4
Al Arīn Saudi Arabia 104 C4
Al Arṭāwīyah Saudi Arabia 105 D2
Alas Indon. 77 G5
Alas, Selat sea chan. Indon. 77 G5

index

A

Alaşehir Turkey 106 B3
historically known as Philadelphia
Alash r. Rus. Fed. 88 E1
Alash, Plato plat. Rus. Fed. 88 E1
Alashiya country Asia see Cyprus
Al 'Āshūrīyah well Iraq 107 E5
Alaska state U.S.A. 164 E3
Alaska, Gulf of U.S.A. 164 E4
Alaska Highway Canada/U.S.A. 166 A2
Alaska Peninsula U.S.A. 164 C4
Alaska Range mts U.S.A. 164 E3
Al 'Assāfīyah Saudi Arabia 104 B1
Alassio Italy 56 A4
Älät Azer. 107 G3
Alat Uzbek. 103 E5
also spelt Olot
Alataw Shankou pass China/Kazakh. see Dzungarian Gate
Al 'Athāmīn hill Iraq 109 O7
Alatri Italy 56 F7
historically known as Aletrium
Al Atwā' well Saudi Arabia 104 C1
Alatyr' Rus. Fed. 40 H5
Alatyr' r. Rus. Fed. 40 H5
Alauksts l. Latvia 42 G4
Alausí Ecuador 198 B5
Alaverdi Armenia 107 F2
Alavieska Fin. 44 N2
Ala-Vuokki Fin. 44 O2
Alavus Fin. 44 M3
Alawa Aboriginal Land res. Australia 148 B2
Al Awābī Oman 105 G3
Al 'Awdah Saudi Arabia 105 D2
Alawoona Australia 146 D3
Al Awshazīyah Saudi Arabia 104 C2
Alaykel' Kyrg. see Alaykuu
Alaykuu Kyrg. 103 H4
also known as Këk-Art or Kögart or Kök-Art; formerly known as Alaykel'
Alay Kyrka Toosu mts Asia see Alai Range
Al 'Ayn Oman 105 G3
Al 'Ayn Saudi Arabia 104 B2
Al 'Ayn U.A.E. 105 F2
Alayskiy Khrebet mts Asia see Alai Range
Al A'ẓamīyah Iraq 109 P4
Alazani r. Azer./Georgia 107 F2
Alazeya r. Rus. Fed. 39 P2
Al 'Azīzīyah Iraq 107 F4

Al 'Azīzīyah Libya 120 B1
Highest recorded shade temperature in the world.
world [climate and weather] ➡ 16–17

Alba Italy 51 O8
Alba U.S.A. 173 I6
Alba Adriatica Italy 56 F6
Al Ba'ā'ith Saudi Arabia 104 C2
Al Ba'āj Iraq 109 M1
Al Bāb Syria 109 I1
Albacete Spain 55 J5
Al Badā'i' Saudi Arabia 104 B2
Alba de Tormes Spain 54 F4
Al Badī' Saudi Arabia 105 D3
Al Bādiyah al Janūbīyah hill Iraq 107 F5
Ålbæk Denmark 45 J4
Ålbæk Bugt b. Denmark 45 J4
Al'bagan, Gora mt. Rus. Fed. 88 D1
Al Bāḩah prov. Saudi Arabia 104 C3
Al Bahrayn country Asia see Bahrain
Alba Iulia Romania 58 E2
also known as Gyulafehérvár; formerly known as Karlsburg; historically known as Apulum
Al Bajā' well U.A.E. 105 E2
Al Ba'jah Saudi Arabia 104 C2
Al Bakhrā well Saudi Arabia 105 D2
Al Bakkī Libya 120 B3
Albalate de Arzobispo Spain 55 K3
Albanel, Lac l. Canada 169 F3
Albania country Europe 58 A7
known as Republika e Shqipërisë in Albanian
europe [countries] ➡ 32–35
Albano Brazil 199 G5
Albany Australia 151 B7
Albany r. Canada 168 D2
Albany Jamaica 186 D3
Albany GA U.S.A. 175 C6
Albany MO U.S.A. 178 D3

Albany NY U.S.A. 177 L3
State capital of New York. Historically known as Fort Orange.

Albany OH U.S.A. 176 C6
Albany OR U.S.A. 180 B3
Albany TX U.S.A. 179 C5
Albany Downs Australia 147 F1
Albardão do João Maria coastal area Brazil 204 G4
Al Bardawīl depr. Saudi Arabia 109 K6
Al Bardī Libya 120 E2
Al Bāridah hills Saudi Arabia 109 K8
Al Barīt waterhole Iraq 109 N6
Al Barrah Saudi Arabia 105 D2
Al Başrah Iraq see Basra
Al Başrah governorate Iraq 107 F5
Al Baṭha' marsh Iraq 107 F5
Al Bāṭinah admin. reg. Oman 105 G3
Al Bāṭinah reg. Oman 105 G2
Al Bāṭinah i. Saudi Arabia 105 E2
Albatross Bay Australia 149 D2
Albatross Island Australia 147 E5
Albatross Point N.Z. 152 I6
Al Bayḑā' Libya 120 D1
also spelt Beida
Al Bayḑā' Yemen 105 D5
Al Bayḑā' governorate Yemen 105 D5
Albay Gulf Phil. 74 B3
Albemarle U.S.A. 174 D5
Albemarle Sound sea chan. U.S.A. 174 E5
Albenga Italy 56 A4
Alberche r. Spain 54 G5
Alberdi Para. 201 F6
Alberga watercourse Australia 146 B1
Albergaria-a-Velha Port. 54 C4
Albergian, Monte mt. Italy 51 M7
Albert Australia 147 E3
Albert r. Australia 148 C3
Albert France 51 I3
Albert, Lake Australia 146 C3
Albert, Lake Dem. Rep. Congo/Uganda 128 A4
formerly known as Mobutu, Lake or Mobutu Sese Seko, Lake
Albert, Parc National nat. park Dem. Rep. Congo see Virunga, Parc National des
Alberta prov. Canada 167 H4
Albert Falls Nature Reserve S. Africa 133 O6
Albertinia S. Africa 132 F11
Albertirsa Hungary 49 Q8
Albert Kanaal canal Belgium 51 L2
Albert Lea U.S.A. 174 A3
Albert Nile r. Sudan/Uganda 126 G4
Alberto de Agostini, Parque Nacional nat. park Chile 205 C9
Alberton Canada 169 H4
Alberto Oviedo Mota Mex. 183 I9
Albertshoek S. Africa 133 J4
Albert Town Bahamas 187 E2
Albertville Dem. Rep. Congo see Kalémié
Albertville France 51 M7
Albertville U.S.A. 174 C5
Albeşti Romania 58 I2
Albi France 51 I9
Albia U.S.A. 174 A3
Al Bi'ār Saudi Arabia 104 B3
Al Bīḑah des. Saudi Arabia 105 E2
Albignasego Italy 56 D3
Albina Suriname 199 H3
Albino Italy 56 B3
Albion CA U.S.A. 182 A2
Albion IN U.S.A. 174 C3
Albion MI U.S.A. 173 I8
Albion NE U.S.A. 178 C3
Albion NY U.S.A. 176 G2
Albion PA U.S.A. 176 E4
Al Bi'r Saudi Arabia 104 B1
also known as Bi'r Ibn Hirmās
Al Birk Saudi Arabia 104 C4
Al Birkah Saudi Arabia 104 C3
Al Biyāḑh reg. Saudi Arabia 105 D3
Alborán, Isla de i. Spain 55 H9
Ålborg Denmark 45 J4
also spelt Aalborg
Ålborg Bugt b. Denmark 45 J4
Alborz, Reshteh-ye mts Iran see Elburz Mountains
Albota Romania 58 F4
Albox Spain 55 I7
Albro Australia 149 E4
Albstadt Germany 48 G7
Al Budayyi Bahrain 105 E2
Albufeira Port. 54 C7
Ālbū Ghars, Sabkhat salt l. Iraq 109 M3
Al Bukayrīyah Saudi Arabia 104 C2
Albula Alpen mts Switz. 51 P6
Albuñol Spain 55 H8
Albuquerque U.S.A. 181 F6
Albuquerque, Cayos de is Caribbean Sea 186 C4
Al Buraymī Oman 105 F2
Alburg U.S.A. 177 L1
Alburno, Monte mt. Italy 57 H8
Alburquerque Spain 54 E5
Albury Australia 147 E4
Albury N.Z. 153 E12
Al Buşayrah Syria 109 L2
also spelt Buseire
Al Busayṭā' plain Saudi Arabia 107 D5
Al Buşayyah Iraq 107 F5
Al Bushūk well Saudi Arabia 104 D1
Al Buṭayn plain Saudi Arabia 105 D2
Al Buwī well Oman 105 G4
Alca Peru 200 B3
Alcácer do Sal Port. 54 C6
Alcáçovas r. Port. 54 C6
Alcalá de Chivert Spain 55 L4
Alcalá de Guadaira Spain 54 F7
Alcalá de Henares Spain 55 H4
Alcalá de los Gazules Spain 54 F8
Alcalá la Real Spain 54 H7
Alcalde, Punta pt Chile 204 C3
Alcamo Sicilia Italy 57 E11
Alcanadre r. Spain 55 L3
Alcanar Spain 55 L4
Alcañiz Spain 55 K3
Alcântara Brazil 202 C2
Alcántara Spain 54 E5
Alcántara, Embalse de resr Spain 54 E5
Alcántara II, Embalse de resr Spain 54 E5
Alcantara Lake Canada 167 I2
Alcantarilla Spain 55 J7
Alcaraz Spain 55 I6
Alcaraz, Sierra de mts Spain 55 I6
Alcaria Ruiva hill Port. 54 D7
Alcarrache r. Port./Spain 54 D6
Alcatrazes, Ilha de i. Brazil 207 H11
Alcaudete Spain 54 G7
Alcázar de San Juan Spain 55 H5
Alcazarquivir Morocco see Ksar el Kebir
Alchevs'k Ukr. 41 F6
formerly known as Kommunarsk or Voroshilovsk
Alcira Arg. 204 D4
Alcira Spain see Alzira
Alcobaça Brazil 203 E6
Alconchel Spain 54 D6
Alcora Spain 55 K4
Alcorneo r. Port./Spain 54 E5
Alcorta Arg. 204 E4
Alcoy Spain 55 K6
Alcubierre, Sierra de mts Spain 55 K3
Alcúdia Spain 55 O5
Aldabra Atoll Seychelles 129 E7
Aldabra Islands Seychelles 129 E7
Aldama Chihuahua Mex. 184 D2
Aldama Tamaulipas Mex. 185 F4
Aldan Rus. Fed. 39 M4
Aldan r. Rus. Fed. 39 M3
Aldeburgh U.K. 47 N11
Aldeia Velha Brazil 202 B4
Aldeia Viçosa Angola 127 B7
Alder Creek U.S.A. 177 J2
Alderney i. Channel Is 50 D3
also known as Aurigny
Alder Peak U.S.A. 182 C6
Aldershot U.K. 47 L12
Alderson U.S.A. 176 E8
Al Dhafrah reg. U.A.E. 105 F3
Aldie Eth. 128 D3
Aledo U.S.A. 174 B3
Aleg Mauritania 124 B2
Alegre Brazil 203 D7
Alegrete Brazil 203 A9
Alegros Mountain U.S.A. 181 E6
Alejandro Korn Arg. 204 F4
Alekhovshchina Rus. Fed. 43 O1
Aleksandra, Mys hd Rus. Fed. 82 E1
Aleksandra Bekovicha-Cherkassogo, Zaliv b. Kazakh. 102 B4
Aleksandriya Ukr. see Oleksandriya
Aleksandropol Armenia see Gyumri
Aleksandrov Rus. Fed. 43 T5
Aleksandrovac Srbija Yugo. 58 C5
Aleksandrov Gay Rus. Fed. 102 B2
Aleksandrovka Rus. Fed. 41 J5
Aleksandrovo Bulg. 58 G6
Aleksandrovo Bulg. 58 F5
Aleksandrovsk Rus. Fed. 40 K4
formerly known as Aleksandrovskiy
Aleksandrovsk Ukr. see Zaporizhzhya
Aleksandrovskaya Rus. Fed. 43 R2
Aleksandrovskiy Rus. Fed. see Aleksandrovsk
Aleksandrovskoye Stavropol'skiy Kray Rus. Fed. 41 G7
Aleksandrovskoye Stavropol'skiy Kray Rus. Fed. 41 H7
Aleksandrovskoye Tomskaya Oblast' Rus. Fed. 38 H3
Aleksandrovsk-Sakhalinskiy Rus. Fed. 82 F2
Aleksandrów Kujawski Poland 49 P3
Aleksandrów Łódzki Poland 49 Q4
Aleksandry, Zemlya i. Rus. Fed. 38 E1
English form Alexandra Land
Alekseyevka Kazakh. see Akkol'
Alekseyevka Kazakh. 103 H2
Alekseyevka Kazakh. see Terekty
Alekseyevka Belgorodskaya Oblast' Rus. Fed. 41 F6
Alekseyevka Belgorodskaya Oblast' Rus. Fed. 41 F6
Alekseyevka Bryanskaya Oblast' Rus. Fed. 43 N8
Alekseyevskaya Rus. Fed. 41 G6
Aleksin Rus. Fed. 43 S7
Aleksinac Srbija Yugo. 58 C5
Aleksino-Shatur Rus. Fed. 43 U6
Alèmbé Gabon 126 A5
'Alem Ketema Eth. 128 C2
'Alem Maya Eth. 128 D2
Além Paraíba Brazil 203 D7
Ålen Norway 44 J3
Alençon France 50 G4
Alenquer Brazil 199 H5
Alentejo reg. Port. 54 C6
Alenuihaha Channel U.S.A. 181 [inset] Z1
Alep Syria see Aleppo
Alépé Côte d'Ivoire 124 E5
Aleppo Syria 109 I1
also known as Ḩalab or Yamkhad; also spelt Alep; historically known as Beroea
Aler r. India 94 C2
Alert Canada 165 M1
Alerta Peru 200 C2
Alert Bay Canada 166 E5
Alès France 51 K8
Aleşd Romania 58 D1
Aleshki Ukr. see Tsyurupyns'k
Aleshnya Rus. Fed. 43 O8
Aleşkirt Turkey see Eleşkirt
Alessandria Italy 56 A4
Alessio Albania see Lezhë
Ålesund Norway 44 I3
also spelt Aalesund
Aletrium Italy see Alatri
Aletschhorn mt. Switz. 51 N6
Aleutian Islands U.S.A. 220 G2
Aleutian Range mts U.S.A. 164 D4
Alevina, Mys c. Rus. Fed. 39 P4
Alevişik Turkey see Samandağı
Alexander, Cape Antarctica 222 T2
Alexander, Mount hill Australia 148 C2
Alexander Archipelago is U.S.A. 164 F4
Alexander Bay S. Africa 130 C6
Alexander City U.S.A. 175 C5
Alexander Island Antarctica 222 T2
Alexandra Australia 147 E4
Alexandra r. Australia 149 C3
Alexandra N.Z. 153 D13
Alexandra, Cape S. Georgia 205 [inset]
Alexandra Channel India 95 G3
Alexandra Falls Canada 167 G2
Alexandra Land i. Rus. Fed. see Aleksandry, Zemlya
Alexandreia Greece 58 D8
Alexandretta Turkey see İskenderun
Alexandria Afgh. see Ghaznī
Alexandria B.C. Canada 166 F4
Alexandria Ont. Canada 169 F4

Alexandria Egypt 121 F2
4th most populous city in Africa. Also known as Al Iskandarīyah; also spelt El Iskandarîya.
world [cities] ➡ 24–25

Alexandria Romania 58 G5
Alexandria S. Africa 133 K10
Alexandria Turkm. see Mary
Alexandria U.K. 46 H8
Alexandria KY U.S.A. 176 A7
Alexandria LA U.S.A. 179 D6
Alexandria MN U.S.A. 178 D2
Alexandria SD U.S.A. 178 C3
Alexandria VA U.S.A. 177 H7
Alexandria Arachoton Afgh. see Kandahār
Alexandria Areion Afgh. see Herāt
Alexandria Bay U.S.A. 177 J1
Alexandria Prophthasia Afgh. see Farāh
Alexandrina, Lake Australia 146 C3
Alexandroupoli Greece 58 G8
Alexânia Brazil 206 E3
Alexis r. Canada 169 J2
'Āley Lebanon 108 G4
also spelt Aaley
Aley r. Rus. Fed. 103 J1
Aleyak Iran 100 D2
Aleysk Rus. Fed. 103 J1
Al Fallūjah Iraq 109 O4
Alfambra r. Spain 55 J4
Al Fardah Yemen 105 E5
Alfaro Spain 55 J2
Alfarràs Spain 55 L3
Al Farūq reg. Saudi Arabia 105 E2
Al Farwānīyah Kuwait 107 F5
Al Fas Morocco see Fès
Alfatar Bulg. 58 I5
Al Fatḩah Iraq 107 E4
Al Fatk Yemen 105 F4
Al Fāw Iraq 107 G5
Al Fayyūm Egypt see El Faiyûm
Al Fāzih Yemen 104 C5
Alfeios r. Greece 59 C11
also spelt Alfíos
Alfeld (Leine) Germany 48 G4
Alfenas Brazil 203 C7
Alfíos r. Greece see Alfeios
Alföld plain Hungary 49 R9
Alford U.K. 46 J6
Alfred U.S.A. 177 O2
Alfred and Marie Range hills Australia 151 D5
Alfred M. Terrazas Mex. 185 F4
Alfredo Chaves Brazil 207 M7
Alfredton N.Z. 152 J8
Alfta Sweden 45 L3
Al Fujayrah U.A.E. see Fujairah
Al Fuqahā' Libya 120 C3
Al Furāt r. Iraq/Syria see Euphrates
Alga Kazakh. 102 D2
also spelt Algha
Algabas Kazakh. 102 C2
Algar Spain 54 F8
Ålgård Norway 45 I4
Algarinejo Spain 54 G7
Algarrobal Chile 204 C3
Algarrobo del Aguilla Arg. 204 D5
Algarve reg. Port. 54 C7
Algasovo Rus. Fed. 41 G5
Algeciras Spain 54 F8
Algemesí Spain 55 K5
Algena Eritrea 121 H5
Alger Alg. see Algiers
Alger U.S.A. 173 I6

Algeria country Africa 123 E4
2nd largest country in Africa.
africa [countries] ➡ 114–117

Algha Kazakh. see Alga
Al Ghāfāt Oman 105 G3
Al Ghardaqah Egypt see Hurghada
Al Gharīth Saudi Arabia 104 C3
Al Ghāṭ Saudi Arabia 105 D2
Al Ghawr plain Jordan/West Bank 108 G7
also spelt El Ghor
Al Ghayḑah Yemen 105 F4
Al Ghayl Saudi Arabia 105 D3
Alghero Sardegna Italy 57 A8
Al Ghubr reg. Oman 105 G4
Al Ghuwayr well Qatar 105 E2
Al Ghwaybiyah Saudi Arabia 105 E2

Algiers Alg. 123 F1
Capital of Algeria. Also known as Al Jaza'ir or Argel or El Djezair; also spelt Alger; historically known as Icosium.

Alginet Spain 55 K5
Algoa Bay S. Africa 133 J10
Algodón r. Peru 198 D5
Algodor r. Spain 54 H5
Algoma U.S.A. 172 F6
Algona U.S.A. 178 D3
Algonac U.S.A. 173 K8
Algonquin Park Canada 168 E4
Algonquin Provincial Park Canada 173 O5
Algorta (Guecho) Spain 55 I1
Algōsh Iraq 109 O1
Al 'grûd Egypt 108 D7
Älgsjö Sweden 44 L2
Algueirao Moz. see Hacufera
Algueirão-Mem Martins Port. 54 B6
Al Habakah well Saudi Arabia 107 E5
Al Ḩabbānīyah Iraq 107 E4
Al Ḩadaqah well Saudi Arabia 104 D1
Al Ḩadbah reg. Saudi Arabia 104 C3
Al Ḩadd Bahrain 105 E2
Al Ḩaddār Saudi Arabia 105 D3
Al Ḩadhālīl plat. Saudi Arabia 107 E5
Al Ḩadīthah Iraq 107 E4
Al Ḩaḑr Iraq see Hatra
Al Ḩafār well Saudi Arabia 104 C1
Al Ḩaffah Syria 108 H2
Al Ḩaggounia W. Sahara 122 B4
Al Ḩā'ir Saudi Arabia 105 D2
Al Ḩajar Oman 105 G3
Al Ḩajar al Gharbī mts Oman 105 G2
Al Ḩajar ash Sharqī mts Oman 105 G3
Al Ḩajr Yemen 105 D4
Al Ḩallānīyah i. Oman 105 G4
Alhama r. Spain 55 J2
Al Ḩamād plain Asia 98 B3
Al Ḩamādah al Ḩamrā' plat. Libya 120 A2
Alhama de Granada Spain 54 H7
Alhama de Murcia Spain 55 J7
Al Ḩamar Saudi Arabia 105 D3
Al Ḩāmi Yemen 105 E5
Alhamilla, Sierra hills Spain 55 I8
Al Hammām well Iraq 107 E5
Al Ḩamrā' Saudi Arabia 104 B3
Al Ḩanākīyah Saudi Arabia 104 C2
Al Ḩanīsh al Kabīr i. Yemen 104 C5
Al Ḩaniyah esc. Iraq 107 F5
Al Ḩaqlānīyah Iraq 109 N3
Al Ḩaqū Saudi Arabia 104 C4
Al Ḩariq Saudi Arabia 105 D3
Al Ḩarrah reg. Saudi Arabia 109 J7
Al Ḩarūj al Aswad hills Libya 120 C3
Al Hasa reg. Saudi Arabia 105 E2
Al Ḩasakah Syria 109 L1
Al Ḩasakah governorate Syria 109 L1
Al Ḩasāni i. Saudi Arabia 104 B2
Al Ḩāshimīyah Iraq 107 F4
Al Ḩasī well Saudi Arabia 105 D3
Al Ḩāsikīyah i. Oman 105 F4
Al Ḩaşwah Iraq 109 P5
Al Ḩatīfah plain Saudi Arabia 105 D2
Al Ḩawāyā des. Saudi Arabia 105 E3
Al Hawi salt pan Saudi Arabia 109 J8
Al Ḩawījah Iraq 109 O2
Al Ḩawīyah Saudi Arabia 104 C3
Al Ḩawjā' Saudi Arabia 109 J9
Al Ḩawrā Yemen 105 D5
Al Ḩawṭah reg. Saudi Arabia 105 D3
Al Ḩayy Iraq 107 F4
Al Ḩayyānīyah waterhole Saudi Arabia 109 N9
Al Ḩazm Saudi Arabia 104 B1
Al Ḩazm al-Jawf Yemen 104 D4
Alheit S. Africa 132 E5
Al Ḩibāk des. Saudi Arabia 105 F4
Al Ḩillah Iraq see Hillah
Al Ḩillah governorate Iraq see Bābil
Al Ḩillah Saudi Arabia 105 D3
Al Ḩilwah Saudi Arabia 105 D3
Al Ḩimārah well Saudi Arabia 105 E2
Al Hindīyah Iraq 107 F4
Al Ḩinnāh Saudi Arabia 105 E2
Al Ḩinw mt. Saudi Arabia 107 D5
Al Hirrah well Saudi Arabia 105 E3
Al Ḩishwah hills Yemen 104 D4
Al Ḩismā plain Saudi Arabia 104 A1
Al Ḩişn Jordan 108 G5
also spelt Husn
Al Ḩişn Yemen 105 D5
Al Hoceima Morocco 122 E2
formerly known as Villa Sanjurjo
Alhuampa Arg. 204 E2
Al Ḩudaydah Yemen see Hodeidah
Al Ḩudaydah governorate Yemen 104 C5
Al Ḩudūd ash Shamālīyah prov. Saudi Arabia 104 C1
Al Ḩufayrah well Saudi Arabia 105 E2
Al Ḩufrah reg. Saudi Arabia 104 B1
Al Hufūf Saudi Arabia 105 E2
also spelt Hofūf
Al Hūj hills Saudi Arabia 104 B1
Al Ḩulayq al Kabīr hills Libya 120 C3
Al Ḩumayshah Yemen 105 D5
Al Ḩumrah reg. U.A.E. 105 F3
Al Ḩunayy Saudi Arabia 105 E2
Al Husayfīn Oman 105 G2
Al Ḩuthūl hill Saudi Arabia 109 K8
Al Huwatsah Oman 105 G3
Al Huwaylah Qatar 105 E2
Al Ḩuwaymi Yemen 105 D5
Al Ḩuwayyiṭ Saudi Arabia 104 C2
Al Ḩuwayz Syria 109 H2
Al Huwwah Saudi Arabia 105 D3
Ali China 89 B5
also known as Shiquanhe
'Alīābād Afgh. 101 G2
'Alīābād Golestān Iran 100 C2
'Alīābād Hormozgan Iran 100 C4
'Alīābād Khorāsan Iran 100 D3
'Alīābād Khorāsan Iran 101 E4
'Alīābād Kordestān Iran 100 A3
'Alīābād Qom Iran 100 B3
Alīābād, Kūh-e mt. Iran 100 B3
Aliağa Turkey 106 A3
Aliakmonas r. Greece 59 D8
Aliakmonas, Limni l. Greece 59 C8
Aliambata East Timor 75 C5
Aliartos Greece 59 E10
Alibag India 94 B2
Äli Bayramlı Azer. 107 G3
Alibey Adası i. Turkey 59 H9
Alibunar Vojvodina, Srbija Yugo. 58 B3
Alicante Spain 55 K6
also spelt Alacant
Alice Australia 149 E4
Alice r. Australia 149 D2
Alice watercourse Australia 149 E5
Alice S. Africa 133 K9
Alice U.S.A. 179 C7
Alice, Punta pt Italy 57 J9
Alice Arm Canada 166 D4
Alicedale S. Africa 133 K10
Alice Springs Australia 148 B4
Alice Town Bahamas 186 D1
Aliceville U.S.A. 175 B5
Alichur Tajik. 101 H2
Alichur r. Tajik. 101 H2
Alichuri Janubí, Qatorkŭhi mts Tajik. 101 H2
also known as Yuzhno-Alichurskiy, Khrebet
Alicia Phil. 74 B5
Alick Creek r. Australia 149 D4
Alicoto Fr. Guiana 199 H4
Alicudi, Isola i. Isole Lipari Italy 57 G10
Al 'Idd U.A.E. 105 F3
Al 'Idwah well Saudi Arabia 104 C2
Aliero Nigeria 125 G3
Alife Italy 56 G7
Aligarh India 96 C4
Alīgūdarz Iran 100 B3
Alihe China 85 I1
also known as Oroqen Zizhiqi
Alījūq, Kūh-e mt. Iran 100 B4
'Alī Kheyl Afgh. 101 G3
Al Ikhwān is Yemen 105 F5
English form The Brothers
Alima r. Congo 126 C5
Al Imām Iraq 109 P5
Al Imārāt al 'Arabīyah at Muttaḩidah country Asia see United Arab Emirates
Alimia i. Greece 59 I12
Alindao Cent. Afr. Rep. 126 D3
Alinghar r. Afgh. 101 G3
Alingsås Sweden 45 K4
Alintale well Eth. 128 D3
Aliova r. Turkey 106 B3
Alipur India 94 C1
Alipur Pak. 101 G4
Alipur Duar India 97 F4
Aliquippa U.S.A. 176 E5
Alirajpur India 96 B5
Ali Sabieh Djibouti 128 D2
Al 'Īsāwīyah Saudi Arabia 107 D5
Al Iskandarīyah Egypt see Alexandria
Al Iskandarīyah Iraq 107 F4
Aliskerovo Rus. Fed. 39 Q3
Al Ismā'īlīyah Egypt see Ismâ'ilîya
Aliste r. Spain 54 E3
Alitåive mt. Sweden 44 L2
Al Ittihab Yemen see Madīnat ash Sha'b
Aliveri Greece 59 F10
Aliwal North S. Africa 133 K7
Alix Canada 167 H4
Aliyaha r. Ukr. 58 K3
Al Jafr Jordan 109 H7
Al Jāfūrah des. Saudi Arabia 105 E2
Al Jaghbūb Libya 120 E2
Al Jahrah Kuwait 107 F5
Al Jamalīyah Qatar 105 E2
Al Jarāwī well Saudi Arabia 109 J7
Al Jarf mts Saudi Arabia 104 B2
Al Jawārah well Oman 105 G4
Al Jawb reg. Saudi Arabia 105 E3
Al Jawf Libya 120 D3
Al Jawf Al Jawf Saudi Arabia 107 D5
also spelt Al Jauf
Al Jawf prov. Saudi Arabia 104 B1
Al Jawf governorate Yemen 105 D4
Al Jawlān hills Syria see Golan
Al Jawsh Libya 120 A1
Al Jaza'ir Alg. see Algiers
Al Jazā'ir reg. Iraq/Syria 109 K1
Alj Beyk Iran 100 C2
Aljezur Port. 54 C7
Al Jībān reg. Saudi Arabia 105 E2
Al Jid well Iraq 109 K5
Al Jilh esc. Saudi Arabia 104 D2
Al Jisr Iraq 109 P4
Al Jithāmīyah Saudi Arabia 104 C2
Al Jīzah Egypt see Giza
Al Ju'ayfirah Saudi Arabia 104 C4
Al Jubayl Saudi Arabia 105 E2
Al Jubayl hills Saudi Arabia 105 D2
Al Jubaylah Saudi Arabia 105 D2
Aljucén r. Spain 54 E6
Al Jufra Oasis Libya 120 B2
Al Julaydah well Saudi Arabia 105 D1
Al Jumūm Saudi Arabia 104 B3
Al Junaynah Saudi Arabia 104 C3
Al Jurayd i. Saudi Arabia 105 E2
Al Jurayfah Saudi Arabia 105 D2
Al Jurayr well Saudi Arabia 104 C3
Al Jurdhāwīyah Saudi Arabia 104 C2
Al Juwayf depr. Syria 109 I4
Al Juwayfah well Saudi Arabia 105 E3
Al Kahfah Saudi Arabia 104 C2
Al Kalbān Oman 105 G3
Alkali Flat salt flat NV U.S.A. 182 G1
Alkali Flat salt flat NV U.S.A. 183 G3
Alkaliya r. Ukr. 58 L3
Alkamari Niger 125 H3
Al Kāmil Oman 105 G3
Al Karābilah Iraq 109 M3
Al Karak Jordan 108 G6
also spelt Karak
Al Karāmah Jordan 108 G6
Al Karmah Iraq 109 O4
Al Kāẓimīyah Iraq 107 F4
also known as Kādhimain
Al Khābūrah Oman 105 G3
Al Khaḑrā' well Saudi Arabia 104 C1
Al Khafaq well Saudi Arabia 105 D2
Al Khafqān salt pan Saudi Arabia 104 C3
Al Khalf Saudi Arabia 104 C2
Al Khalīf Oman 105 G3
Al Khalīl West Bank see Hebron
Al Khāliş Iraq 107 F4
Al Khamāsīn Saudi Arabia 104 D3
Al Kharfah Saudi Arabia 105 D3
Al Khārijah Egypt see El Khârga
Al Kharj reg. Saudi Arabia 105 D3
Al Kharkhayr oasis Saudi Arabia 105 E4
Al Kharrārah Qatar 105 E2
Al Khaşab Oman 105 G2
Al Khasfah well Oman 105 F4
Al Khāşirah Saudi Arabia 104 C3
Al-Khatam reg. U.A.E. 105 F2
Al Khaṭīnī vol. Saudi Arabia 109 J6
Al Khawkhah Yemen 104 C5
Al Khawr Qatar 105 E2
Al Khawtamah i. Yemen 104 C5
Al Khīşah well Saudi Arabia 105 E2
Al Khizāmī well Saudi Arabia 105 E2
Al Khobar Saudi Arabia 105 E2
Al Khubrah Saudi Arabia 105 E2
Al Khuff reg. Saudi Arabia 104 D2
Al Khufrah Libya 120 D3
Al Khufrah Oasis Libya 120 D3
Al Khums Libya 120 B1
also spelt Homs
Al Khunfah sand area Saudi Arabia 104 B1
Al Khunn Saudi Arabia 105 E3
Al Khuwayr Qatar 105 E2
Al Kidan well Saudi Arabia 105 F3
Al Kifl Iraq 107 F4
Al Kir'ānah Qatar 105 E2
Alkmaar Neth. 48 B3
Al Kūfah Iraq 107 F4
Al Kufla well Saudi Arabia 105 E3
Al Kumayt Iraq 107 F4
Al Kurá lava field Saudi Arabia 104 B2
Al Kusūr hills Saudi Arabia 109 J6
Al Kūt Iraq 107 F4
also known as Kut-al-Imara
Al Kuwayt country Asia see Kuwait
Al Kuwayt Kuwait see Kuwait
Al Labbah plain Saudi Arabia 107 E5
Allada Benin 125 F5
Al Lādhiqīyah Syria see Latakia
Al Lādhiqīyah governorate Syria 108 G2
Allagadda India 94 C3
Allahabad India 97 D4
Al Lajā lava field Syria 109 H5
Allakh-Yun' Rus. Fed. 39 N3
Allanmyo Myanmar 78 A4
Allanridge S. Africa 133 K4
Allapalli India 94 D2
'Allâqi, Wâdi el watercourse Egypt 121 G4
Allardt U.S.A. 176 A9
Allardville Canada 169 H4
Allariz Spain 54 D2
Al Latakhīyah well Yemen 105 E4
Alldays S. Africa 131 F4
Allegan U.S.A. 172 H8
Allegany U.S.A. 176 G3
Allegheny r. U.S.A. 176 F5
Allegheny Mountains U.S.A. 176 C9
Allegheny Reservoir U.S.A. 176 G4
Allemanskraaldam resr S. Africa 133 L5
Allen Phil. 74 C3
Allen, Lough l. Rep. of Ireland 47 D9
Allen, Mount hill N.Z. 153 B15
Allen, Mount U.S.A. 166 A2
Allendale U.S.A. 175 D5
Allende Coahuila Mex. 185 E2
Allende Nuevo León Mex. 185 E3
Allendorf (Lumda) Germany 51 O2
Allenford Canada 173 L6
Allenstein Poland see Olsztyn
Allensville OH U.S.A. 176 C6
Allensville PA U.S.A. 176 H5
Allentown U.S.A. 177 J5
Alleppey India 94 C4
also known as Alappuzha
Aller r. Germany 48 G3
Allianc Suriname 199 H3
Alliance NE U.S.A. 178 B3
Alliance OH U.S.A. 176 D5
Al Lībīyah country Africa see Libya
Allier r. France 51 J6
Al Līfīyah well Iraq 107 E5
Alligator Point Australia 149 D3
Al Lihābah well Saudi Arabia 105 D2
Allikher India 94 C2
Allinge-Sandvig Denmark 45 K5
Al Lişāfah well Saudi Arabia 105 D2
Al Lisān pen. Jordan 108 G6
Allison U.S.A. 174 A3
Alliston Canada 173 N6
Al Līth Saudi Arabia 104 C3
Al Liwā' oasis U.A.E. 105 F3
Alloa U.K. 46 I7
Allonnes Pays de la Loire France 50 G5
Allonnes Pays de la Loire France 50 G5
Allora Australia 147 G2
Allouez U.S.A. 172 E6
Allschwil Switz. 51 N5
Allu Indon. 75 A4
Al Luḩayyah Yemen 104 C5
Allumettes, Île aux i. Canada 173 P5
Allur India 94 D3
Alluru Kottapatnam India 94 D3
Al Lussuf well Iraq 107 E5
Alma Canada 169 G3
formerly known as St-Joseph-d'Alma
Alma KS U.S.A. 178 C4
Alma MI U.S.A. 173 I7
Alma NE U.S.A. 178 C3
Al Ma'ānīyah Iraq 107 E5
Alma-Ata Kazakh. see Almaty
Alma-Ata Oblast admin. div. Kazakh. see Almatinskaya Oblast'
Almacelles Spain 55 L3
Al Machmin waterhole Iraq 109 N6
Almada Port. 54 B6
Al Madāfi' plat. Saudi Arabia 104 B1
Al Madā'in Iraq 109 P4
Al Ma'danīyāt well Iraq 107 F5
Al Maḑāyā Saudi Arabia 104 C4
Almaden Australia 149 E3
Almadén Spain 54 G6
Almadina Brazil 207 N1
Al Madīnah Iraq 100 A4
Al Madīnah Saudi Arabia see Medina
Al Madīnah prov. Saudi Arabia 104 B2
Al Mafraq Jordan 108 H5
also spelt Mafraq
Al Maghrib reg. U.A.E. 105 F3
Almagro i. Phil. 74 C4
Al Mahākīk reg. Saudi Arabia 105 E3
Al Maḩāwīl Iraq 109 P5
Al Mahbas W. Sahara 122 C4
Al Mahḑam Saudi Arabia 104 C3
Al Maḩiā depr. Saudi Arabia 104 B2
Al Maḩmūdīyah Iraq 107 F4
Al Mahrah governorate Yemen 105 E4
Al Mahrah reg. Yemen 105 E5
Al Maḩwīt Yemen 104 C5
Al Maḩwīt governorate Yemen 104 C5
Al Majma'ah Saudi Arabia 105 D2
Almăjului, Munţii mts Romania 58 D4
Al Malsūnīyah reg. Saudi Arabia 105 E2
Almalyk Uzbek. 103 G4
also spelt Olmaliq
Al Manadir reg. Oman 105 F3
Al Manāmah Bahrain see Manama
Al Manjūr well Saudi Arabia 105 D3
Almanor, Lake U.S.A. 182 C1
Almansa Spain 55 J6
Al Manşūrah Egypt see El Mansûra
Almanzor mt. Spain 54 F4
Almanzora r. Spain 55 J7
Al Ma'qil Iraq 107 F5
Almār Afgh. 101 F3
Almar r. Spain 54 F4
Al Mariyyah U.A.E. 105 F3
Al Marj Libya 120 D1
also known as Barce
Almaş r. Romania 58 E1
Almas, Rio das r. Brazil 206 D1
Al Masana'a Oman 105 G3
Almatinskaya Oblast' admin. div. Kazakh. 103 I3
English form Almaty Oblast; also known as Almaty Oblysy; formerly known as Alma-Ata Oblast
Al Matmarfag W. Sahara 122 B4

Almaty Kazakh. 103 I4
Former capital of Kazakhstan. English form Alma-Ata; formerly known as Vernyy.

Almaty Oblast admin. div. Kazakh. see Almatinskaya Oblast'
Almaty Oblysy admin. div. Kazakh. see Almatinskaya Oblast'
Al Mawşil Iraq see Mosul
Al Mayādīn Syria 109 L2
Almazán Spain 55 I3
Almeida Port. 54 E4
Almeirim Brazil 199 H5
Almeirim Port. 54 C5
Almelo Neth. 48 D3
Almenara Brazil 202 D6
Almenara Spain 55 K5
Almenara, Sierra de hills Spain 55 J7
Almendra, Embalse de resr Spain 54 E3
Almendralejo Spain 54 E6
Almere Neth. 48 C3
Almería Spain 55 I8
Almería, Golfo de b. Spain 55 I8
Almetievsk Rus. Fed. see Al'met'yevsk
Al'met'yevsk Rus. Fed. 40 J5
also spelt Almetievsk
Älmhult Sweden 45 K4
Al Midhnab Saudi Arabia 104 D2
Al Miḩrāḑ reg. Saudi Arabia 105 F3
Almina, Punta pt Spain 54 F9
Al Mindak Saudi Arabia 104 C3
Al Mintirib Oman 105 G3
Almirantazgo, Seno del sea chan. Chile 205 C9
Almirante Panama 186 C5
Al-Mirfa U.A.E. 105 F2
Almirós Greece see Almyros
Al Mish'āb Saudi Arabia 105 E1
Al Mismīyah Syria 109 H4
Almodôvar Port. 54 C7
Almodóvar del Campo Spain 54 G6
Almoloya Mex. 185 E5
Almont U.S.A. 173 J8
Almonte Canada 173 Q5
Almonte Spain 54 E7
Almonte r. Spain 54 E5

Almora India 96 C3
Almoradí Spain 55 K6
Almorox Spain 54 G4
Al Mota well Niger 125 G3
Almoustarat Mali 125 F2
Al Mu'ayzīlah hill Saudi Arabia 109 J8
Al Mubarrez Saudi Arabia 105 E2
Al Muḍairib Oman 105 G3
Al Mudawwarah Jordan 108 H8
Al Muharraq Bahrain 105 E2
Al Muḥtaṭab depr. Saudi Arabia 109 H9
Al Mukallā Yemen see Mukalla
Al Mukhā Yemen see Mocha
Al Mukhaylī Libya 120 D1
Al Munbaṭiḥ des. Saudi Arabia 105 E3
Al Mundafan pass Saudi Arabia 105 D4
Almuñécar Spain 54 H8
historically known as Sexi
Al Muqdādīyah Iraq 107 F4
Al Murayr well Saudi Arabia 109 K7
Al Mūrītānīyah country Africa see Mauritania
Al Murūt well Saudi Arabia 107 D5
Almus Turkey 107 D2
also known as Tozanlı
Al Musannāh ridge Saudi Arabia 105 D1
Al Musayjīd Saudi Arabia 104 B2
Al Musayyib Iraq 109 P5
Al Muthanná governorate Iraq 107 F5
Al Muwayh Saudi Arabia 104 C3
Al Muwayliḥ Saudi Arabia 104 A2
Almyropotamos Greece 59 F10
Almyros Greece 59 D9
also spelt Almirós
Almyrou, Ormos b. Greece 59 F13
Alness U.K. 46 H6
Alnwick U.K. 46 K8

▶ Alofi Niue 145 I3
Capital of Niue.
oceania [countries] ➡ 138–139

Alofi, Île i. Wallis and Futuna Is 145 H3
Aloi Uganda 128 B4
Aloja Latvia 42 F4
Alol' Rus. Fed. 43 K5
Alolya r. Rus. Fed. 43 J5
Along India 97 G3
Alonnisos i. Greece 59 E9
Alonso r. Brazil 206 B11
Alor i. Indon. 75 C5
Alor, Kepulauan is Indon. 75 C5
Alor, Selat sea chan. Indon. 75 B5
Álora Spain 54 G8
Alor Setar Malaysia 76 C1
also spelt Alur Setar; formerly spelt Alor Star
Alor Star Malaysia see Alor Setar
Alosno Spain 54 D7
Alost Belgium see Aalst
Alot India 96 B5
Alota Bol. 200 D5
Alotau P.N.G. 149 F1
Aloysius, Mount Australia 151 E5
Alpachiri Arg. 204 E5
Alpagut Turkey 59 J9
Alpaugh U.S.A. 182 E6
Alpena U.S.A. 173 J5
Alpercatas, Serra das hills Brazil 202 C3
Alpha Australia 149 E4
Alpha S. Africa 133 P4
Alpha U.S.A. 172 C9
Alpi Apuane, Parco Naturale delle nature res. Italy 56 C4
Alpine AZ U.S.A. 183 O8
Alpine CA U.S.A. 183 H9
Alpine NY U.S.A. 177 I3
Alpine TX U.S.A. 179 B6
Alpine WY U.S.A. 180 E4
Alpine National Park Australia 147 E4
Alpinópolis Brazil 206 G7
▶ Alps mts Europe 51 M7
europe [landscapes] ➡ 30–31
Al Qā' Saudi Arabia 104 C3
Al Qa'āmīyāt reg. Saudi Arabia 105 D4
Al Qaddāḥīyah Libya 120 B2
Al Qādisīyah governorate Iraq 107 F5
formerly known as Ad Dīwānīyah
Al Qadmūs Syria 108 H2
Al Qaffāy i. U.A.E. 105 F2
Al Qafrah Yemen 105 D5
Al Qāhirah Egypt see Cairo
Al Qaḥmah Saudi Arabia 104 C4
Al Qā'im Iraq 109 L3
Al Qā'īyah Saudi Arabia 104 C2
Al Qā'īyah well Saudi Arabia 105 D2
Al Qal'a Beni Hammad tourist site Alg. 123 G2
Al Qalībah Saudi Arabia 104 B1
Al Qāmishlī Syria 107 E3
Al Qar'ah well Saudi Arabia 105 D2
Al Qar'ah lava field Syria 109 H5
Al Qarn Yemen 105 D5
Al Qaryatayn Syria 109 I3
Al Qaṣīm prov. Saudi Arabia 104 C2
Al Qaṣr Saudi Arabia 104 C2
Al Qaṭīf Saudi Arabia 105 E2
Al Qaṭn Yemen 105 E5
Al Qaṭrānah Jordan 108 H6
Al Qaṭrūn Libya 120 B3
Al Qawnas reg. Saudi Arabia 105 D3
Al Qayṣūmah Saudi Arabia 105 D1
Al Qāyṣūmah well Saudi Arabia 107 E5
Al Qiblīyah i. Oman 105 G4
Al Qulayyibah waterhole Saudi Arabia 109 N9
Al Qumur country Africa see Comoros
Al Qunayṭirah Syria 108 G4
Al Qunayṭirah governorate Syria 108 G4
Al Qunfidhah Saudi Arabia 104 C4
Al Qurayn Saudi Arabia 104 C2
Al Quraynī oasis Saudi Arabia 105 F3
Al Qurayyah Saudi Arabia 104 C2
Al Qurayyah U.A.E. 105 G2
Al Qurayyāt Saudi Arabia 107 D5
Al Qurnah Iraq 107 F5
Al Quwārah Saudi Arabia 104 C2
Al Quwayi' Saudi Arabia 105 D3
Al Quwayīyah Saudi Arabia 105 D2
Al Quwayrah Jordan 108 G8
Al Quzah Yemen 105 E5
Al Rabbād reg. U.A.E. 105 F3
Alrar Est Alg. 123 H3
Alroy Downs Australia 148 C3
Alsace admin. reg. France 51 N4
Alsace, Plaine d' valley France 51 N5
Al Samha U.A.E. 100 C5
Al Samīt well Iraq 107 E5
Alsask Canada 167 I5
Alsek r. U.S.A. 164 F4
Alsfeld Germany 48 G5
Al'skiy Khrebet mt. Rus. Fed. 82 E1
Alston U.K. 47 J9
Alstonville Australia 147 G2
Alsuku Nigeria 125 H5
Alsunga Latvia 42 C5
Alsviķi Latvia 42 H4
Alta Norway 44 M1
Alta, Mount N.Z. 153 C12
Altadena U.S.A. 182 F7
Altaelva r. Norway 44 M1
Altafjorden sea chan. Norway 44 M1
Alta Floresta Brazil 201 F2
Alta Gracia Arg. 204 D3
Alta Gracia Nicaragua 186 B5
Altai Mountains Asia 88 D1
also known as Altayskiy Khrebet
Altamaha r. U.S.A. 175 D6
Altamira Amazonas Brazil 199 E4
Altamira Pará Brazil 199 H5
Altamira Chile 204 C2
Altamira Col. 198 C4
Altamira Costa Rica 186 B5
Altamíra Mex. 185 F4
Altamira, Cuevas de tourist site Spain 54 G1
Altamira, Sierra de mts Spain 54 F5
Altamonte Springs City U.S.A. 175 D6
Altamura Italy 57 I8
Altan Rus. Fed. 85 F1
Altanbulag Mongolia 85 E2
Altan Emel China 85 H1
also known as Xin Barag Youqi
Altan Ovoo mt. China/Mongolia 84 A2
Altan Shiret China 85 F4
also known as Ejin Horo Qi; also spelt Altan Xiret
Altan Xiret China see Altan Shiret
Alta Paraiso de Goiás Brazil 202 C5
Altapirire Venez. 199 E2
Altar Mex. 184 C2
Altar r. Mex. 181 E7
Altar, Desierto de des. Mex. 184 B1
Altata Mex. 184 D3
Altavista U.S.A. 176 F8
Altay China 84 A2
Altay Mongolia 84 C2
Altay, Respublika aut. rep. Rus. Fed. 84 A1
English form Altay Republic; formerly known as Gorno-Altayskaya Avtonomnaya Oblast' or Gornyy Altay
Altay Kray admin. div. Rus. Fed. see Altayskiy Kray
Altay Republic aut. rep. Rus. Fed. see Altay, Respublika
Altayskiy Khrebet mts Asia see Altai Mountains
Altayskiy Kray admin. div. Rus. Fed. 88 C1
English form Altay Kray
Altayskiy Zapovednik nature res. Rus. Fed. 84 A1
Altdorf Switz. 51 O6
Altea Spain 55 K6
Alteidet Norway 44 M1
Altenburg Germany 49 J5
Altenkirchen (Westerwald) Germany 48 E5
Altenqoke China 84 B4
Alter do Chão Brazil 199 H5
Alter do Chão Port. 54 D5
Altevatnet l. Norway 44 L1
Altin Köprü Iraq 107 F4
Altınoluk Turkey 59 H9
Altinópolis Brazil 206 F8
Altınova Turkey 59 H9
Altınözü Turkey 108 H1
Altıntaş Turkey 106 B3
Altınyaka Turkey 108 B1
Altiplano plain Bol. 200 C4
Altmühltal park Germany 48 I7
Altnaharra U.K. 46 H5
Alto U.S.A. 172 H8
Alto Araguaia Brazil 203 A6
Alto Cedro Cuba 186 E2
Alto Chicapa Angola 127 C7
Alto Cruz mt. Spain 55 I3
Alto Cuchumatanes mts Guat. 185 H6
Alto de Cabezas mt. Spain 55 H2
Alto de Covelo pass Spain 54 D2
Alto del Moncayo mt. Spain 55 J3
Alto de Pencoso hills Arg. 204 D4
Alto do Trevim mt. Port. 54 C4
Alto Garças Brazil 202 A6
Alto Ligonha Moz. 131 H2
Alto Madidi, Parque Nacional nat. park Bol. 200 C3
Alto Molócuè Moz. 131 H2
Alton U.K. 47 L12
Alton IL U.S.A. 174 B4
Alton KY U.S.A. 176 A7
Alton MO U.S.A. 174 B4
Alton NH U.S.A. 177 N2
Altona B.C. Canada 166 F3
Altona Man. Canada 167 L5
Alto Nevado mt. Chile 205 B7
Altoona PA U.S.A. 176 G5
Altoona WI U.S.A. 172 B6
Alto Pacajá r. Brazil 202 B2
Alto Parnaíba Brazil 202 C4
Alto Purús r. Peru 200 C2
Alto Rio Doce Brazil 207 J8
Alto Río Senguerr Arg. 205 C7
Altos Brazil 202 D3
Altos de Chacaya Chile 200 C4
Altos de Chinchilla mts Spain 55 J6
Alto Sucuriú Brazil 206 A6
Altotero mt. Spain 55 H2
Altotonga Mex. 185 F5
Altötting Germany 49 J7
Alto Uruguai Brazil 203 A8
Altukhovo Rus. Fed. 43 P9
Altun Ha tourist site Belize 185 H5
Altun Shan mt. China 84 B4
Altun Shan mts China 84 B4
also known as Astin Tag
Alturas U.S.A. 180 B4
Altus U.S.A. 179 C5
Altynkul' Uzbek. 102 D4
also spelt Oltinkŭl
Altyn-Topkan Tajik. see Oltintopkan
Alu Estonia 42 F2
Alua Moz. 131 H2
Al 'Ubaydī Iraq 109 M3
Al Ubaylah Saudi Arabia 105 E3
Alucra Turkey 107 D2
Al 'Uḍaylīyah Saudi Arabia 105 E2
Al Udayn Yemen 104 C5
Alūksne Latvia 42 I4
Alūksnes l. Latvia 42 I4
Al 'Ulā Saudi Arabia 104 B2
Al'ulah reg. Yemen 105 D5
Alūm Iran 100 B3
Alum Bridge U.S.A. 176 E6
Alum Creek Lake U.S.A. 176 C5
Alunda Sweden 45 L3
Aluniș Romania 58 F2
Alupka Ukr. 106 C1
Al 'Uqaylah Libya 120 C2
Al 'Uqaylah Saudi Arabia see An Nabk
Al 'Uqayr Saudi Arabia 105 E2
Al Uqṣur Egypt see Luxor
Alur India 94 C3
Al Urayq des. Saudi Arabia 107 D5
Al 'Urdun country Asia see Jordan
Alur Setar Malaysia see Alor Setar
Alushta Ukr. 41 E7
Al Uthaylī Saudi Arabia 104 B1
Aluva India see Alwaye
Al 'Uwayjā' well Saudi Arabia 105 D3
Al 'Uwayjā' well Saudi Arabia 105 E3
Al 'Uwaynah well Saudi Arabia 105 E2
Al 'Uwaynāt Libya 120 E4
Al 'Uwaynāt Libya 120 A3
Al 'Uwaynidhiyah i. Saudi Arabia 104 B2
Al 'Uwayqīlah Saudi Arabia 107 E5
Al Uyainah Saudi Arabia 105 D2
Al 'Uyaynah well Saudi Arabia 108 H9
Al 'Uẓaym Saudi Arabia 104 C2
Al 'Uzayr Iraq 107 F5
Alva r. Port. 54 C4
Alva U.S.A. 178 C4
Alvand, Kūh-e mt. Iran 100 B3
Alvão, Parque Natural do nature res. Port. 54 D3
Alvarado Mex. 185 G5
Alvarado U.S.A. 179 C5
Alvarães Brazil 199 E5
Álvares Machado Brazil 206 B9
Älvdalen Sweden 45 K3
Älvdalen valley Sweden 45 K3
Alvedro airport Spain 54 C1
Alverca Port. 54 B6
Alvesta Sweden 45 K4
Alvin TX U.S.A. 179 D6
Alvin WI U.S.A. 172 E5
Alvinópolis Brazil 207 J7
Älvkarleby Sweden 45 L3
Älvsbyn Sweden 44 M2
Al Wafrah Kuwait 107 F5
also spelt Wafra
Al Wajh Saudi Arabia 104 B2
Al Wakrah Qatar 105 E2
Al Wannān Saudi Arabia 105 E2
Al Waqbá well Saudi Arabia 105 D1
Alwar India 96 C4
Al Warī'ah Saudi Arabia 105 D2
Al Watīyah Libya 120 A1
Alwaye India 94 C4
also known as Aluva
Al Widyān plat. Iraq/Saudi Arabia 107 E4
Al Wīgh Libya 120 B3
Al Wīgh, Ramlat des. Libya 120 C3
Al Wusayl Qatar 105 E2
Al Wusayṭ well Saudi Arabia 104 D1
Al Wusţá admin. reg. Oman 105 G3
Alxa Youqi China see Ehen Hudag
Alxa Zuoqi China see Bayan Hot
Al Yamāmah Saudi Arabia 105 D2
Alyangula Australia 148 C2
Al Yāsāt i. U.A.E. 105 E2
Alyawarra Aboriginal Land res. Australia 148 B4
Alytus Lith. 42 F7
Al Yūsufīyah Iraq 109 P4
Alzada U.S.A. 178 A2
Alzey Germany 48 F6
Alzira Spain 55 K5
also spelt Alcira
Amacayacu, Parque Nacional nat. park Col. 198 D5
Åmådalen Sweden 45 K3
Amadeus, Lake salt flat Australia 148 A5
Amadi Sudan 128 A3
Amadjuak Lake Canada 165 L3
Amadora Port. 54 B6
Amadror plain Alg. 123 G4
Amaga Col. 198 C3
Amagi Japan 91 B8
Amahai Indon. 75 D3
Amakusa-Kami-shima i. Japan 91 B8
Amakusa-nada b. Japan 91 A8
Amakusa-Shimo-shima i. Japan 91 B8
Amal Oman 105 F4
Åmål Sweden 45 K4
Amalaoulaou well Mali 125 F3
Amalapuram India 94 D2
Amalat r. Rus. Fed. 81 J2
Amalia S. Africa 133 J4
Amaliada Greece 59 C11
Amalner India 96 B5
Amamapare Indon. 73 I7
Amambaí Brazil 201 G5
Amambaí, Serra de hills Brazil/Para. 201 G5
Amami-Ō-shima i. Japan 81 L7
Amami-shotō is Japan 81 L7
Amamula Dem. Rep. Congo 126 E5
Amån r. Sweden 45 K3
Amanã, Lago l. Brazil 199 E5
Amanbidji Aboriginal Land res. Australia 148 A3
Amanda U.S.A. 176 C6
Amandola Italy 56 F6
Amangel'dy Aktyubinskaya Oblast' Kazakh. 102 D2
also spelt Amankeldi
Amangel'dy Kustanayskaya Oblast' Kazakh. 103 F2
also spelt Amankeldi
Amankaragay Kazakh. 103 F1
also spelt Amanqaraghay
Amankeldi Kazakh. see Amangel'dy
Amankeldi Kazakh. see Amangel'dy
Amanotkel' Kazakh. 103 E3
Amanqaraghay Kazakh. see Amankaragay
Amantea Italy 57 I9
Amanzimtoti S. Africa 133 O7
Amapa Brazil 200 C2
Amapá state Brazil 199 I4
Amapala Hond. 186 B4
Amapari r. Brazil 199 I4
Amara Abu Sin Sudan 121 G6
Amaradia r. Romania 58 E4
Amaral Ferrador Brazil 203 A9
Amarante Brazil 202 D3
Amarante do Maranhão Brazil 202 C3
Amarapura Myanmar 78 B3
Amaravati r. India 94 C4
Amardalay Mongolia 85 E2
Amargosa Brazil 202 E5
Amargosa watercourse U.S.A. 181 C5
Amargosa Desert U.S.A. 183 H5
Amargosa Range mts U.S.A. 183 H5
Amargosa Valley U.S.A. 183 H5
Amargura Island Tonga see Fonualei
Amarillo U.S.A. 179 B5
Amarkantak India 97 D5
Amaro, Monte mt. Italy 56 G6
Amarpur India 97 F5
Amarwara India 96 C5
Amasa U.S.A. 172 E4
Amasia Turkey see Amasya
Amasine W. Sahara 122 B4
Amasra Turkey 106 C2
Amâssine well Mali 125 F2
Amasya Turkey 106 C2
historically known as Amasia
Amata Australia 151 E5
Amataurá Brazil 199 D5
Amatenango Mex. 185 G5
Amatikulu S. Africa 133 P6
Amatique, Bahía de b. Guat. 185 H6
Amatlán de Cañas Mex. 184 D4

▶ Amazon r. S. America 202 B1
Longest river in South America and 2nd in the world. Also spelt Amazonas.
southamerica [landscapes] ➡ 190–191
southamerica [contrasts] ➡ 194–195

Amazon, Mouths of the Brazil 202 B1
Amazon, Source of the Peru 200 C3
Amazonas state Brazil 199 E6
Amazonas dept Col. 198 D5
Amazonas dept Peru 198 B6
Amazonas r. S. America see Amazon
Amazonas state Venez. 199 E4
Amazónia, Parque Nacional nat. park Brazil 199 G6
Āmba Ālagē mt. Eth. 128 C1
Ambad India 94 B2
Amba Farit mt. Eth. 128 C2
Ambahikily Madag. 131 [inset] I4
Ambajogai India 94 C2
also spelt Ambejogai
Ambala India 96 C3
Ambalajanakomby Madag. 131 [inset] J3
Ambalakirajy Madag. 131 [inset] K2
Ambalangoda Sri Lanka 94 D5
Ambalatany Madag. 131 [inset] J4
Ambalavao Madag. 131 [inset] J4
Ambam Cameroon 125 H6
Ambanja Madag. 131 [inset] K2
Ambar Iran 100 D4
Ambarchik Rus. Fed. 39 Q3
Ambarès-et-Lagarve France 50 F8
Ambargasta, Salinas de salt pan Arg. 204 D3
Ambarnyy Rus. Fed. 40 E2
Ambasa India 97 F5
Ambasamudram India 94 C4
Ambathala Australia 149 E5
Ambato Ecuador 198 B5
Ambato, Sierra mts Arg. 204 D3
Ambato Boeny Madag. 131 [inset] J3
Ambato Finandrahana Madag. 131 [inset] J4
Ambatolahy Madag. 131 [inset] J4
Ambatolampy Madag. 131 [inset] J3
Ambatomainty Madag. 131 [inset] J3
Ambatondrazaka Madag. 131 [inset] K3
Ambatosia Madag. 131 [inset] K2
Ambazac France 50 H7
Ambejogai India see Ambajogai
Ambelau i. Indon. 75 C3
Ambelón Greece see Ampelonas
Amberg Germany 48 I6
Amberg U.S.A. 172 F5
Ambergris Cay i. Belize 185 I5
Ambergris Cays is Turks and Caicos Is 187 F2
Ambérieu-en-Bugey France 51 L7
Amberley Canada 173 L6
Amberley N.Z. 153 G11
Ambert France 51 J7
Ambgaon India 94 D1
Ambianum France see Amiens
Ambidédi Mali 124 C3
Ambika r. India 94 B1
Ambikapur India 97 D5
Ambilobe Madag. 131 [inset] K2
Ambition, Mount Canada 166 D3
Amble U.K. 46 K8
Ambleside U.K. 47 J9
Amblève r. Belgium 51 L2
Ambo India 97 E5
Ambo Peru 200 A2
Amboasary Madag. 131 [inset] J5
Amboasary Gara Madag. 131 [inset] K3
Amboavory Madag. 131 [inset] K3
Ambodifotatra Madag. 131 [inset] K3
Ambodiharina Madag. 131 [inset] K4
Ambohidratrimo Madag. 131 [inset] J3
Ambohijanahary Madag. 131 [inset] K3
Ambohimahasoa Madag. 131 [inset] J4
Ambohipaky Madag. 131 [inset] J3
Ambohitra mt. Madag. 131 [inset] K2
Ambohitralanana Madag. 131 [inset] K2
Amboina Indon. see Ambon
Amboise France 50 G5
Ambon Indon. 75 D3
formerly known as Amboina
Ambon i. Indon. 75 C3
Amboró, Parque Nacional nat. park Bol. 201 D4
Amboseli National Park Kenya 128 C5
Ambositra Madag. 131 [inset] J4
Ambovombe Madag. 131 [inset] J5
Amboy CA U.S.A. 183 I7
Amboy IL U.S.A. 172 D9
Ambre, Cap d' c. Madag. see Bobaomby, Tanjona
Ambrim i. Vanuatu see Ambrym
Ambriz Angola 127 B6
Ambriz, Coutada do nature res. Angola 127 B6
Ambrizete Angola see N'zeto
Ambrosio Brazil 198 D5
Ambrym i. Vanuatu 145 F3
also spelt Ambrim
Ambunten Indon. 77 F4
Ambur India 94 C3
Åmdals Verk Norway 45 J4
Am-Dam Chad 120 D6
Amded, Oued watercourse Alg. 123 F5
Amderma Rus. Fed. 40 L1
Amdillis well Mali 125 E2
Am Djéména Chad 120 C6
Amdo China 89 E5
also known as Lharigarbo
Amealco Mex. 185 E4
Ameca Mex. 184 D4
Amecameca Mex. 185 F5
Amedamit mt. Eth. 128 C2
Ameghino Arg. 204 E4
Ameland i. Neth. 48 C2
Amelia Italy 56 E6
Amelia Court House U.S.A. 176 H8
Amellu India 96 D4
Amendolara Italy 57 I9
Amenia U.S.A. 177 L4
American, North Fork r. U.S.A. 182 C3
Americana Brazil 206 F9
American Falls U.S.A. 180 D4
American Falls Reservoir U.S.A. 180 D4
American Fork U.S.A. 183 M1

▶ American Samoa terr. S. Pacific Ocean 145 I3
United States Unincorporated Territory. Formerly known as Eastern Samoa.
oceania [countries] ➡ 138–139

Americus U.S.A. 175 C5
Ameringkogel mt. Austria 49 L8
Amersfoort Neth. 48 C3
Amersfoort S. Africa 133 N4
Amery Canada 167 M3
Amery Ice Shelf Antarctica 223 E2
Ames U.S.A. 174 A3
Amesbury U.S.A. 177 O3
Amet India 96 B4
Amethi India 97 D4
Amfilochia Greece 59 C10
Amfissa Greece 59 D10
Amga Rus. Fed. 39 N3
Amgalang China 85 H1
also known as Xin Barag Zuoqi
Amgu Rus. Fed. 82 E3
Amguema Rus. Fed. 39 S3
Amguid Alg. 123 G4
Amgun' r. Rus. Fed. 82 E1
Amhara admin. reg. Eth. 128 C2
Amherst Canada 169 H4
Amherst MA U.S.A. 177 M3
Amherst OH U.S.A. 176 C4
Amherst VA U.S.A. 176 F8
Amherst, Mount hill Australia 150 D3
Amherstburg Canada 173 J8
Amherstdale U.S.A. 176 D8
Amherst Island Canada 173 Q6
Amherstview Canada 173 Q6
Amida Turkey see Diyarbakır
Amidon U.S.A. 178 B2
Amiens France 51 I3
historically known as Ambianum or Samarobriva
'Amīj, Wādī watercourse Iraq 107 E4
Amik Ovası marsh Turkey 107 D3
Amilḥayt, Wādī al r. Oman 105 F4
Amilly France 51 I5
'Amīnābād Iran 100 C4
Amíndhaion Greece see Amyntaio
Amindivi i. India see Amini
Amindivi Islands India 94 B4
Amini i. India 94 B4
also known as Amindivi
Amino Japan 91 D7
Aminuis Namibia 130 C4
Amioun Lebanon 108 G3
Amipshahr India 96 C3
Amīrābād Eşfahān Iran 100 B3
Amīrābād Īlām Iran 100 A3
Amirabad Iran see Fūlād Maīalleh
Amirante Islands Seychelles 218 K6
Āmirlī Iraq 109 P3
Amisk Lake Canada 167 K4
Amistad, Represa de resr Mex./U.S.A. see Amistad Reservoir
Amistad Reservoir Mex./U.S.A. 185 E2
also known as Amistad, Represa de
Amisus Turkey see Samsun
Amite U.S.A. 175 B6
Amite Creek r. U.S.A. 175 B6
Amla India 96 C5
also known as Sarni
Amlaḥ, Jabal al hill Saudi Arabia 104 C4
Amlamé Togo 125 F5
Amlash Iran 100 B2
Amlekhganj Nepal 97 E4
Åmli Norway 45 J4
Amlwch U.K. 47 H10
'Amm Adam Sudan 121 H5
Amman Jordan see 'Ammān

▶ 'Ammān Jordan 108 G6
Capital of Jordan. English form Amman; historically known as Philadelphia or Rabbath Ammon.

Ammanazar Turkm. 102 C5
Ämmänsaari Fin. 44 O2
'Ammār reg. Yemen 105 D5
'Ammār, Tall hill Syria 109 H5
Ammarnäs Sweden 44 L2
Ammaroodinna watercourse Australia 146 B1
Ammassalik Greenland 165 P3
also known as Tasiilaq; also spelt Angmagssalik
Ammer r. Germany 48 I8
Ammerån r. Sweden 44 L3
Ammersee l. Germany 48 I8
Ammochostos Cyprus see Famagusta
Ammochostos Bay Cyprus 108 F2
also known as Famagusta Bay
Am Nābiyah Yemen 104 C5
Amne Machin Range mts China see A'nyêmaqên Shan
Amnok-kang r. China/N. Korea see Yalu Jiang
Amod India 96 B5
Amo Jiang r. China 86 B4
Amol Iran 100 C2
Amolar Brazil 201 F4
Amoliani i. Greece 59 E8
Amontada Brazil 202 E2
Amor mt. Spain 54 G5
Amorebieta Spain 55 I1
Amores r. Arg. 204 F3
Amorgos i. Greece 59 G12
Amorinópolis Brazil 206 B3
Amory U.S.A. 175 B5
Amos Canada 168 E3
Åmot Buskerud Norway 45 J4
Åmot Telemark Norway 45 I4
also known as Ytre Vinje
Amotape, Cerros de mts Peru 198 A6
Åmotfors Sweden 45 K4
Amourj Mauritania 124 D2
Amoy China see Xiamen
Ampah Indon. 77 F3
Ampanefena Madag. 131 [inset] K2
Ampani India 95 D2
Ampanihy Madag. 131 [inset] J5
Ampanotoamaizina Madag. 131 [inset] K3
Amparafaka, Tanjona pt Madag. 131 [inset] J2
Amparafaravola Madag. 131 [inset] K3
Amparai Sri Lanka 94 D5
Amparo Brazil 206 G9
Ampasimanolotra Madag. 131 [inset] K3
formerly known as Vohibinany
Ampelonas Greece 59 D9
also known as Ambelón
Ampenan Indon. 77 G5
Amper r. Germany 48 I7
Amper Nigeria 125 H4
Amphitrite Group is Paracel Is 72 D3
Ampibaku Indon. 75 B3
Ampisikinana Madag. 131 [inset] K2
formerly spelt Ampitsikinana
Ampitsikinana Madag. see Ampisikinana
Ampoa Indon. 75 B3
Amposta Spain 55 L4
Amqui Canada 169 H3
Amrabad India 94 C2
'Amrah, Jabal hill Saudi Arabia 104 C2
Amrān Yemen 104 C5
Amraoti India see Amravati
Amravati India 94 C1
formerly spelt Amraoti
Amreli India 96 A5
Am Rijā' Yemen 121 J6
Amritsar India 96 B3
Amroha India 96 C3
Amrum i. Germany 48 F1
Åmsele Sweden 44 L2
Amstelveen Neth. 48 B3

▶ Amsterdam Neth. 48 B3
Official capital of the Netherlands.
world [countries] ➡ 10–11

Amsterdam S. Africa 133 O3
Amsterdam NY U.S.A. 177 K3
Amsterdam OH U.S.A. 176 E5
Amsterdam, Île i. Indian Ocean 219 M8
English form Amsterdam Island
Amsterdam Island Indian Ocean see Amsterdam, Île
Amstetten Austria 49 L7
Am Timan Chad 126 D2
Amú r. Col. 198 C4
Amu Co l. China 89 E5
'Amūd, Jabal al mt. Saudi Arabia 109 K7
Amudar'ya r. Asia 99 F1
English form Amu Darya; also known as Dar"yoi Amu; also spelt Amudaryo, Amyderya; historically known as Oxus
Amu Darya r. Asia see Amudar'ya
Amudaryo r. Asia see Amudar'ya
Amund Ringnes Island Canada 165 J2
Amundsen, Mount Antarctica 223 G2
Amundsen Bay Antarctica 223 D2
Amundsen Coast Antarctica 223 O1
Amundsen Glacier Antarctica 223 N1
Amundsen Gulf Canada 164 G2
Amundsen-Scott research station Antarctica 223 A1
Amundsen Sea Antarctica 222 Q2
Amuntai Indon. 77 F3
Amur r. Rus. Fed. 82 F1
also known as Heilong Jiang
'Amur, Wadi watercourse Sudan 121 G5
Amurang Indon. 75 C2
Amur Oblast admin. div. Rus. Fed. see Amurskaya Oblast'
Amursk Rus. Fed. 82 E2
formerly known as Padali
Amurskaya Oblast' admin. div. Rus. Fed. 82 C1
English form Amur Oblast
Amurskiy Rus. Fed. 102 D1
Amurskiy liman strait Rus. Fed. 82 F1
Amurzet Rus. Fed. 82 C3
Amvrakikos Kolpos b. Greece 59 B10
Amyderya r. Asia see Amudar'ya
Amyntaio Greece 58 C8
also known as Amíndhaion
Amyot Canada 173 I2
Amzacea Romania 58 J5
Amzérakad well Mali 125 F2
Am-Zoer Chad 120 D6
Ana r. Turkey 58 I7
Anaa atoll Fr. Polynesia 221 I7
Anabanua Indon. 75 B3
Anabar r. Rus. Fed. 39 L2
Ana Branch r. Australia 146 D3
Anabtā West Bank 108 G5
Anacapa Islands U.S.A. 182 E7
Anaco Venez. 199 E2
Anaconda U.S.A. 180 D3
Anacortes U.S.A. 180 B2
Anadarko U.S.A. 179 C5
Anadolu Dağları mts Turkey 107 D2
Anadyr' Rus. Fed. 39 R3
Anadyr' r. Rus. Fed. 39 R3
Anadyr, Gulf of Rus. Fed. see Anadyrskiy Zaliv
Anadyrskiy Zaliv b. Rus. Fed. 39 S3
English form Anadyr, Gulf of
Anafi Greece 59 G12
Anafi i. Greece 59 G12
Anagé Brazil 202 D5
Anagni Italy 56 F7
historically known as Anagnia
Anagnia Italy see Anagni
'Ānah Iraq 107 E4
Anaheim U.S.A. 182 G8
Anahim Lake Canada 166 E4
Anáhuac Nuevo León Mex. 185 E3
Anáhuac Veracruz Mex. 185 F4
Anahuac U.S.A. 179 D6
Anaimalai Hills India 94 C4
Anai Mudi Peak India 94 C4
Anaiteum i. Vanuatu see Anatom
Anajás Brazil 202 B2
Anajás, Ilha i. Brazil 202 B2
Anajatuba Brazil 202 C2
Anakao Madag. 131 [inset] I4
Anakapalle India 95 D2
Anakie Australia 149 E4
Analalava Madag. 131 [inset] J2
Analavelona mts Madag. 131 [inset] I4
Anamã Brazil 199 F5
Ana María, Golfo de b. Cuba 186 D2
Anambas, Kepulauan is Indon. 77 D2
Anambra state Nigeria 125 G5
Anamosa U.S.A. 174 B3
Anamu r. Brazil 199 G4
Anamur Turkey 106 C3
Anan Japan 91 D8
Anand India 96 B5
Anandapur India 97 E5
Anandpur India 96 C3
Anandpur r. India 97 E5
Ananes i. Greece 59 F12
Anan'ev Kyrg. 103 I4
also known as Anan'yevo
Anangu Pitjantjatjara Aboriginal Lands res. Australia 146 A1
Anantapur India 94 C3
Anantnag Jammu and Kashmir 96 B2
also known as Islamabad
Anant Peth India 96 C4
Ananyev Ukr. see Anan'yiv
Anan'yevo Kyrg. see Anan'ev
Anan'yiv Ukr. 41 D7
also spelt Ananyev
Anapa Rus. Fed. 41 F7
Anápolis Brazil 206 E3
Anapú r. Brazil 199 I5
Anár Fin. see Inari
Anār Iran 100 C4
Anārak Iran 100 C3
Anarbar r. Iran 100 B3
Anardara Afgh. 101 E3
Anare Mountains Antarctica 223 L2
Añasco Puerto Rico 187 G3
Ånäset Sweden 44 M2
Anatahan i. N. Mariana Is 73 K3
formerly spelt Anatajan
Anatajan i. N. Mariana Is see Anatahan
Anatolia reg. Turkey 106 B3
Anatoliki Makedonia kai Thraki admin. reg. Greece 58 G7
Anatom i. Vanuatu 145 F4
also known as Anetchom, Île or Aneytioum, Île or Kéamu; also spelt Aneityum or Anaiteum
Añatuya Arg. 204 E3
Anatye Aboriginal Land res. Australia 148 C4
Anauá r. Brazil 199 F4
Anaurilândia Brazil 206 A9
Anavilhanas, Arquipélago das is Brazil 199 F5
Anaypazari Turkey see Gülnar
Anaz mts Saudi Arabia 109 H9
Anbei China 84 C3
Anbyon N. Korea 83 B5
Ancares, Serra dos mts Spain 54 D2
Ancash dept Peru 200 A2
Ancaster Canada 173 N7
Ancasti, Sierra mts Arg. 204 D3
Ancenis France 50 E5
Anchán Arg. 205 D6
Anchang China see Anxian
Anchau Nigeria 125 H4
Anchieta Brazil 207 M7
Anchodaya Bol. 200 C3
Anchorage U.S.A. 164 E3
Anchorage Island atoll Cook Is see Suwarrow
Anchorage Reefs P.N.G. 149 F1
Anchor Bay U.S.A. 173 K8
Anchuthengu India see Anjengo
Anci China see Langfang
Ančia r. Lith. 42 D6
Anclitas, Cayo i. Cuba 186 D2
An Cóbh Rep. of Ireland see Cóbh
Ancón Peru 200 A2
Ancona Italy 56 F5
Ancuabe Moz. 129 C8
Ancud Chile 205 B6
Ancud, Golfo de g. Chile 205 B6
Ancyra Turkey see Ankara
Anda China see Daqing
Anda China 82 B3
Anda i. Indon. 75 C1
Andacollo Chile 204 C3
Andahuaylas Peru 200 B3
Andal India 97 E5
also spelt Ondal
Andalgalá Arg. 204 D2
Åndalsnes Norway 44 I3
Andalucía aut. comm. Spain 54 G7
English form Andalusia
Andalusia S. Africa see Jan Kempdorp
Andalusia aut. comm. Spain see Andalucía
Andalusia AL U.S.A. 175 C6
Andalusia IL U.S.A. 172 C9
Andām, Wādī r. Oman 105 G3
Andaman and Nicobar Islands union terr. Andaman & Nicobar Is India 95 G4
Andaman and Nicobar Islands union terr. India 93 H9
Andaman Islands India 95 G3
Andaman Sea Indian Ocean 79 A6
Andaman Strait India 95 G3
also known as Middle Strait
Andamooka Australia 146 C2
Andapa Madag. 131 [inset] K2
Andarāb Afgh. 101 G3
also known as Banow
Andarob Tajik. 101 G2
also spelt Anderob
Andeba Ye Midir Zerf Chaf pt Eritrea 104 C5
Andeg Rus. Fed. 40 J2
Andegavum France see Angers
Andelle r. France 50 H3
Andenes Norway 44 L1
Andenne Belgium 51 L2
Andéramboukane Mali 125 F3
Ånderdalen Nasjonalpark nat. park Norway 44 L1
Andermatt Switz. 51 O6
Andernos-les-Bains France 50 E8
Anderob Tajik. see Andarob
Anderson r. Canada 164 G3
Anderson AK U.S.A. 164 E3
Anderson CA U.S.A. 182 B1
Anderson IN U.S.A. 174 C3
Anderson MO U.S.A. 178 D4
Anderson SC U.S.A. 174 D5
Anderson Bay Australia 147 E5
Anderson Reservoir U.S.A. 182 C4
Andes Col. 198 C3
▶ Andes mts S. America 200 A2
southamerica [contrasts] ➡ 194–195
Andévalo, Sierra de hills Spain 54 D7
Andfjorden sea chan. Norway 44 L1
Andhíparos i. Greece see Antiparos
Andhra Pradesh state India 94 C2
Andía, Sierra de mts Spain 55 J2
Andijon Uzbek. see Andizhan

index A

Andijon Wiloyati admin. div. Uzbek. see Andizhanskaya Oblast'
Andikíra Greece see Antikyra
Andikithira i. Greece see Antikythira
Andilamena Madag. 131 [inset] K3
Andilanatoby Madag. 131 [inset] K3
Andīmeshk Iran 100 B3
Andímilos i. Greece see Antimilos
Andípaxoi i. Greece see Antipaxoi
Andípsara i. Greece see Antipsara
Andirá Brazil 206 C10
Andir He r. China 89 C4
Andırın Turkey 107 D3
Andirlangar China 89 C4
Andiyskoye Koysu r. Rus. Fed. 102 A4
Andiyur India 94 C4
Andizhan Uzbek. 103 H4
also spelt Andijon
Andizhan Oblast admin. div. Uzbek. see Andizhanskaya Oblast'
Andizhanskaya Oblast' admin. div. Uzbek. 103 H4
English form Andizhan Oblast; also known as Andijon Wiloyati
Andkhui r. Afgh. 101 F2
Andkhvoy Afgh. 101 F2
Andoany Madag. 131 [inset] K2
formerly known as Hell-Ville
Andoas Peru 198 B5
Andoas Nuevo Ecuador 198 B5
Andoga r. Rus. Fed. 43 S2
Andogskaya Gryada hills Rus. Fed. 43 S2
Andohahela, Réserve d' nature res. Madag. 131 [inset] J5
Andohajango Madag. 131 [inset] K2
Andol India 94 C2
Andola India 94 C2
Andong China see Dandong
Andong S. Korea 83 C5
Andongwei Shandong China 85 H5
Andoom Australia 149 D2
▶Andorra country Europe 55 M2
europe [countries] ➡ 32–35
Andorra Spain 55 K4

▶Andorra la Vella Andorra 55 M2
Capital of Andorra. Also spelt Andorra la Vieja.

Andorra la Vieja Andorra see Andorra la Vella
Andover U.K. 47 K12
Andover MA U.S.A. 177 N3
Andover NH U.S.A. 177 N2
Andover NY U.S.A. 176 H3
Andover OH U.S.A. 176 E4
Andøya i. Norway 44 K1
Andozero, Ozero l. Rus. Fed. 43 S2
Andradas Brazil 206 G9
Andrade U.S.A. 183 J9
Andradina Brazil 206 B7
Andramasina Madag. 131 [inset] J3
Andramy Madag. 131 [inset] J3
Andranomavo Madag. 131 [inset] J3
Andranomena Madag. 131 [inset] K3
Andranopasy Madag. 131 [inset] I4
Andranovondronina Madag. 131 [inset] K2
Andranovory Madag. 131 [inset] J4
Andreanof Islands U.S.A. 221 G2
Andreapol' Rus. Fed. 43 N5
André Félix, Parc National de nat. park Cent. Afr. Rep. 126 D2
André Fernandes Brazil 207 L2
Andrelândia Brazil 203 C7
Andrequicé Brazil 207 I5
Andrew Canada 167 H4
Andrew Bay Myanmar 78 A4
Andrews SC U.S.A. 175 E5
Andrews TX U.S.A. 179 B5
Andreyevka Almatinskaya Oblast' Kazakh. 103 J3
Andreyevka Severnyy Kazakhstan Kazakh. 103 F1
Andreyevka Rus. Fed. 102 B1
Andreyevskoye Rus. Fed. see Dneprovskoye
Andreykovichi Rus. Fed. 43 O9
Andreykovo Rus. Fed. 43 P6
Andria Italy 56 I7
Andriba Madag. 131 [inset] J3
Andrieskraal S. Africa 133 I10
Andriesvale S. Africa 132 E3
Andringitra mts Madag. 131 [inset] J4
Androka Madag. 131 [inset] J5
Androna reg. Madag. 131 [inset] K2
Androniki Rus. Fed. 43 U4
Andropov Rus. Fed. see Rybinsk
Andros i. Bahamas 186 D1
Andros Greece 59 F11
Andros i. Greece 59 F11
Androscoggin r. U.S.A. 177 P2
Androsovka Rus. Fed. 102 B1
Andros Town Bahamas 186 D1
Andrott i. India 94 B4
Andrushevka Ukr. see Andrushivka
Andrushivka Ukr. 41 D6
also spelt Andrushevka
Andrychów Poland 49 Q6
Andselv Norway 44 L1
Andsnes Norway 44 M1
Andújar Spain 54 G6
Andulo Angola 127 C7
Anec, Lake salt flat Australia 150 E4
Anecón Grande mt. Arg. 205 C6
Aneen-Kio terr. N. Pacific Ocean see Wake Atoll
Anéfis Mali 125 F2
Anéfis well Mali 125 E2
Anegada i. Virgin Is (U.K.) 187 G3
Anegada, Bahía b. Arg. 204 E6
Anegada Passage Virgin Is (U.K.) 187 H3
Anegam U.S.A. 183 L9
Aného Togo 125 F5
Aneityum i. Vanuatu see Anatom
'Aneiza, Jabal hill Iraq see 'Unayzah, Jabal
Anekal India 94 C3
Añelo Arg. 204 C5
Anemourion tourist site Turkey 108 D1
Anesbaraka well Alg. 123 G6
Anet France 50 H4
Anetchom, Île i. Vanuatu see Anatom
Aneto mt. Spain 55 L2
Aney Niger 125 I2
Aneytioum, Île i. Vanuatu see Anatom
Anfile Bay Eritrea 121 I6
Anfu China 87 E3
also known as Pingdu
Angadippuram India 94 C4
Angadoka, Lohatanjona hd Madag. 131 [inset] J2
Angahook Lorne State Park nature res. Australia 147 D4
Angalarri r. Australia 148 A2
Angamma, Falaise d' esc. Chad 120 C5
Angamos, Isla i. Chile 205 B8
Angamos, Punta pt Chile 200 C5
Ang'angxi China 85 I2

▶Angara r. Rus. Fed. 84 E1
Part of the Yenisey-Angara-Selenga, 3rd longest river in Asia. English form Upper Tunguska; also known as Verkhnyaya Tunguska.
asia [landscapes] ➡ 62–63

Angaradébou Benin 125 F4
Angarapa Aboriginal Land res. Australia 148 B4
Angarsk Rus. Fed. 80 G2
Angas Downs Australia 148 B5
Angas Range hills Australia 150 E4
Angaston Australia 146 C3
Angat Phil. 74 B3
Angatuba Brazil 206 E10
Angaur i. Palau 73 H5
also spelt Ngeaur or Niaur
Ånge Sweden 44 K3
Ángel, Salto del waterfall Venez. see Angel Falls
Ángel de la Guarda, Isla i. Mex. 184 B2
Angeles Phil. 74 B3

▶Angel Falls Venez. 199 F3
Highest waterfall in the world. Also known as Ángel, Salto del.

Ängelholm Sweden 45 K4
Angelina r. U.S.A. 179 D6
Angellala Creek r. Australia 149 E5
Angelo r. Australia 150 B4
Angels Camp U.S.A. 182 D3
Ångereb Eth. 104 B5
Ångereb Wenz r. Eth. 128 C1
Ångermanälven r. Sweden 44 L3
Angermünde Germany 49 L2
Angers France 50 F5
historically known as Andegavum or Juliomagus
Anggana Indon. 77 G3
Angical Brazil 202 C4
Angicos Brazil 202 E3
Angikuni Lake Canada 167 L2
Angiola U.S.A. 182 E6
Angkor tourist site Cambodia 79 C5
Anglem, Mount hill N.Z. 153 B14
also known as Hananui
Anglesey i. U.K. 47 H10
also known as Ynys Môn
Angleton U.S.A. 179 D6
Angliers Canada 173 N3
Anglin r. France 50 G6
Anglo-Egyptian Sudan country Africa see Sudan
Angmagssalik Greenland see Ammassalik
Ang Mo Kio Sing. 76 [inset]
Ango Dem. Rep. Congo 126 E3
Angoche Moz. 131 H3
formerly known as António Enes
Angohrān Iran 100 D5
Angol Chile 204 B5
▶Angola country Africa 127 C7
formerly known as Portuguese West Africa
africa [countries] ➡ 114–117
Angola IN U.S.A. 174 C3
Angola NY U.S.A. 176 F3
Angonia, Planalto de plat. Moz. 131 G2
Angoon U.S.A. 164 F4
Angora Turkey see Ankara
Angostura Mex. 184 C3
Angoulême France 50 G7
historically known as Iculisma
Angra dos Reis Brazil 207 I10
Angren Uzbek. 103 G4
Ångsö naturreservat nature res. Sweden 45 L4
Ang Thong Thai. 79 C5
Angu Dem. Rep. Congo 126 E4
Angualasto Arg. 204 C3
Anguang China 85 I2

▶Anguilla terr. West Indies 187 H3
United Kingdom Overseas Territory.
oceania [countries] ➡ 138–139

Anguilla Cays is Bahamas 186 D2
Anguille, Cape Canada 169 J4
Anguli Nur l. China 85 G3
Anguo China 85 G4
Angurugu Australia 148 C2
Angus Canada 173 N6
Angustura Brazil 201 E2
Angwin U.S.A. 182 B3
Anhanguera Brazil 206 E5
Anholt i. Denmark 45 J4
Anhua China 87 D2
also known as Dongping
Anhui prov. China 87 F1
English form Anhwei
Anhumas Brazil 202 A6
Anhwei prov. China see Anhui
Aniak U.S.A. 164 D3
Aniakchak National Monument and Preserve nat. park U.S.A. 164 D4
Anicuns Brazil 206 D3
Anidhros i. Greece see Anydro
Anié Togo 125 F5
Anie, Pic d' mt. France 50 F10
Aniene r. Italy 56 E7
Anikhovka Rus. Fed. 103 E2
Anikovo Rus. Fed. 40 G4
Animas r. U.S.A. 181 E5
Anina Romania 58 C3
Anishino Rus. Fed. 43 S7
Añisoc Equat. Guinea 125 H6
Anitaguipan Point Phil. 74 C4
Anıtlı Turkey 108 D1
Aniva Rus. Fed. 82 F3
Aniva, Mys c. Rus. Fed. 82 F3
Aniva, Zaliv b. Rus. Fed. 82 F3
Anivorano Madag. 131 [inset] K3
Anivorano Avaratra Madag. 131 [inset] K2
Anjad India 96 B5
Anjafy mt. Madag. 131 [inset] J3
Anjalankoski Fin. 45 N3
Anjangaon India 96 C5
Anjar India 96 A5
Anjengo India 94 C4
also known as Anchuthengu
Anji China 87 F2
also known as Dipu
Anji India 94 C1
Anjiang China see Qianyang
Anjihai China 88 D2
Anjir Avand Iran 100 C3
Anjō Japan 91 E7
Anjoman Iran 100 D3
Anjou reg. France 50 F5
Anjou, Val d' valley France 50 F5
Anjouan i. Comoros see Nzwani
Anjozorobe Madag. 131 [inset] J3
Anjŭ N. Korea 83 B5
Anjuman reg. Afgh. 101 G3
Anka Nigeria 125 G3
Ankaboa, Tanjona pt Madag. 131 [inset] I4
formerly known as St-Vincent, Cap
Ankang China 87 D1

▶Ankara Turkey 106 C3
Capital of Turkey. Historically known as Ancyra or Angora.

Ankaratra mts Madag. 131 [inset] J3
Ankarsrum Sweden 45 L4
Ankatafa Madag. 131 [inset] K2
Ankavandra Madag. 131 [inset] J3
Ankazoabo Madag. 131 [inset] J4
Ankazobe Madag. 131 [inset] J3
Ankeny U.S.A. 174 A3
Ankerika Madag. 131 [inset] J2
An Khê Vietnam 79 E5
formerly known as An Tuc
Ankiliabo Madag. 131 [inset] I4
Anklam Germany 49 K2
Ankleshwar India 96 B5
formerly spelt Anklesvar
Anklesvar India see Ankleshwar
Ankofa mt. Madag. 131 [inset] K3
Ankogel mt. Austria 49 K8
Ankola India 94 B3
Ankouzhen China 85 E5
An'kovo Rus. Fed. 43 U5
Ankpa Nigeria 125 G5
Anling China see Yanling
Anloga Ghana 125 F5
Anlong China 86 C3
Ânlong Vêng Cambodia 79 D5
Anlu China 87 E2
Anmoore U.S.A. 176 E6
An Muileann gCearr Rep. of Ireland see Mullingar
Anmyŏn-do i. S. Korea 83 B5
Ann, Cape Antarctica 223 D2
Ann, Cape U.S.A. 177 O3
Anna Rus. Fed. 41 G6
Anna U.S.A. 176 A5
Anna, Lake U.S.A. 176 H7
Annaba Alg. 123 G1
formerly known as Bône; historically known as Bona or Hippo Regius
Annaberg-Buchholtz Germany 49 K5
An Nabk Saudi Arabia 109 I6
also known as Al 'Uqaylah
An Nabk Syria 109 H3
An Nafūd des. Saudi Arabia 104 C1
Annai Guyana 199 G4
An Nā'ikah, Qarārat depr. Libya 120 C3
An Najaf Iraq 107 F5
An Najaf governorate Iraq 107 E5
An Najaf, Baḥr l. Iraq 109 P6
Annalee r. Rep. of Ireland 47 E9
Annam reg. Vietnam 78 D4
Annam Highlands mts Laos/Vietnam 78 D4
Annan U.K. 47 I9
Annan r. U.K. 47 I9
'Annān, Wādī al watercourse Syria 109 J3
Annandale U.S.A. 177 H7
Anna Plains Australia 150 C3

▶Annapolis U.S.A. 177 I7
State capital of Maryland. Historically known as Anne Arundel Town or Providence.

Annapolis Royal Canada 169 H4
Annapurna Conservation Area nature res. Nepal 97 E3

▶Annapurna I mt. Nepal 97 D3
10th highest mountain in the world and in Asia.
world [physical features] ➡ 8–9

Annapurna II mt. Nepal 97 E3
Ann Arbor U.S.A. 173 J8
Anna Regina Guyana 199 G3
An Nás Rep. of Ireland see Naas
An Nashū, Wādī watercourse Libya 120 B3
An Nāṣirīyah Iraq 107 F5
Annaspan imp. l. S. Africa 133 J5
An Nawfalīyah Libya 120 C2
Annean, Lake salt flat Australia 151 B5
Anne Arundel Town U.S.A. see Annapolis
Annecy France 51 M7
Annecy, Lac d' l. France 51 M7
Annecy-le-Vieux France 51 M7
Anne Marie Lake Canada 169 I2
Annemasse France 51 M6
Annette Island U.S.A. 166 D4
Annie r. Australia 149 D2
Annikvere Estonia 42 H2
An Nimārah Syria 109 I5
An Nimāş Saudi Arabia 104 C4
Anning China 86 B3
formerly known as Lianran
Anning He r. China 86 B3
Annino Rus. Fed. 43 Q3
Anniston U.S.A. 175 C5
Annobón i. Equat. Guinea 125 G7
formerly known as Pagalu
Annonay France 51 K7
Annotto Bay Jamaica 186 D3
An Nu'ayrīyah Saudi Arabia 105 E2
An Nukhayb waterhole Iraq 109 P4
An Nu'mānīyah Iraq 107 F4
An Nuqay'ah Qatar 105 E2
An Nuṣayrīyah, Jabal mts Syria 108 H2
Annville U.S.A. 176 B8
Anogeia Greece 59 F13
also spelt Anóyia
Anoka U.S.A. 174 A2
Anori Brazil 199 F5
Anorontany, Tanjona hd Madag. 131 [inset] I2
Anosibe An'Ala Madag. 131 [inset] K3
Anou I-n-Atei well Alg. 123 G5
Anou Mellene well Mali 125 F2
Anou-n-Bidek well Alg. 123 G6
Ano Viannos Greece 59 G13
Anóyia Greece see Anogeia
Anpu China 87 D4
Anpu Gang b. China 87 D4
Anqing China 87 F2
Anqiu China 85 H4
Anren China 87 E3
Ansai China 85 F4
also known as Zhenwudong
Anse-à-Galets Haiti 187 E3
Anse-à-Pitre Haiti 187 F3
Anse-à-Veau Haiti 187 E3
Anseba Shet watercourse Eritrea 104 B4
Anse d'Hainault Haiti 187 E3
Anser Group is Australia 147 E4
Anserma Col. 198 C3
Anshan China 85 I3
Anshun China 86 C3
Anshunchang China 86 B2
Ansina Uruguay 204 G3
An Sirhān, Wādī watercourse Saudi Arabia 107 D5
Ansjö Sweden 44 L3
Anson U.S.A. 179 C5
Anson Bay Australia 148 A2
Ansongo Mali 125 F3
Ansongo-Ménaka, Réserve Partielle de Faune d' nature res. Mali 125 F3
Ansonia U.S.A. 176 A5
Ansonville Canada 173 M2
Ansted U.S.A. 176 D7
Anstruther U.K. 46 J7
Ansu China see Xushui
Anta India 96 C4
Anta Peru 200 B3
Antabamba Peru 200 B3
Antakya Turkey 106 D3
also known as Hatay; historically known as Antioch or Antiochia
Antalaha Madag. 131 [inset] K2
Antalya Turkey 106 B3
also spelt Adalia; historically known as Attalea or Attalia
Antalya prov. Turkey 108 B1
Antalya Körfezi g. Turkey 106 B3
Antanambao Manampotsy Madag. 131 [inset] K3
Antanambe Madag. 131 [inset] K3

▶Antananarivo Madag. 131 [inset] J3
Capital of Madagascar. Formerly spelt Tananarive; short form Tana.

Antananarivo prov. Madag. 131 [inset] J3
Antanifotsy Madag. 131 [inset] J3
Antanimora Atsimo Madag. 131 [inset] J5
Antantûr, Râs pt Egypt 108 F9
An tAonach Rep. of Ireland see Nenagh

▶Antarctica 222
Most southerly and coldest continent, and the continent with the highest average elevation.
world [land cover] ➡ 18–19
antarctica [features] ➡ 212–213

Antarctic Peninsula Antarctica 222 T2
Antaritarika Madag. 131 [inset] J5
Antelope Island U.S.A. 183 L1
Antelope Range mts U.S.A. 183 H2
Antequera Spain 54 G7
Anthony KS U.S.A. 178 C4
Anthony NM U.S.A. 181 F6
Anthony, Lake salt flat Australia 146 B2
Anthony Lagoon Australia 148 B3
Anti Atlas mts Morocco 122 C3
also known as Petit Atlas
Antibes France 51 N9
Anticosti, Île d' i. Canada 169 I3
English form Anticosti Island
Anticosti Island Canada see Anticosti, Île d'
Antifer, Cap d' c. France 50 G3
Antigo U.S.A. 172 D5
Antigonish Canada 169 I4
Antigua i. Antigua and Barbuda 187 H3
Antigua Guat. 185 H6
long form Antigua Guatemala
Antigua country West Indies see Antigua and Barbuda
▶Antigua and Barbuda country West Indies 187 H3
short form Antigua
northamerica [countries] ➡ 158–159
Antigua Guatemala Guat. see Antigua
Antiguo-Morelos Mex. 185 F4
Antikyra Greece 59 D10
also spelt Andikíra
Antikythira i. Greece 59 E13
also spelt Andikithira
Antikythiro, Steno sea chan. Greece 59 E13
Anti Lebanon mts Lebanon/Syria see Sharqī, Jabal ash
Antilla Arg. 204 D2
Antilla Cuba 186 E2
Antimilos i. Greece 59 F12
also spelt Andímilos
Antimony U.S.A. 183 M3
An tInbhear Mór Rep. of Ireland see Arklow
Antioch Turkey see Antakya
Antioch CA U.S.A. 182 C3
Antioch IL U.S.A. 172 E8
Antiocheia ad Cragum tourist site Turkey 108 D1
Antiochia Turkey see Antakya
Antioquia Col. 198 C3
Antioquia dept Col. 198 C3
Antiparos i. Greece 59 G11
also spelt Andhíparos
Antipaxoi i. Greece 59 B9
also spelt Andípaxoi
Antipino Rus. Fed. 43 O6
Antipodes Islands N.Z. 145 G6
Antipsara i. Greece 59 G10
also spelt Andípsara
Antitilos i. Greece 59 I12
Antium Italy see Anzio
Antlers U.S.A. 179 D5
An t-Ob U.K. see Leverburgh
Antofagasta Chile 200 C5
Antofagasta admin. reg. Chile 200 C5
Antofagasta de la Sierra Arg. 204 D2
Antonibe Madag. 131 [inset] J2
Antônio Carlos Brazil 207 J8
Antonio de Biedma Arg. 205 D7
Antônio Dias Brazil 207 K6
Antônio Enes Moz. see Angoche
Antônio Lemos Brazil 202 B2
Antón Recio Cuba 186 C2
Antopal' Belarus 42 F9
Antrim U.K. 47 F9
Antrim Hills U.K. 47 F8
Antrim Plateau Australia 150 E3
Antrodoco Italy 56 F6
Antropovo Rus. Fed. 40 G4
Antsahabe Madag. 131 [inset] K2
Antsalova Madag. 131 [inset] J3
Antsambalahy Madag. 131 [inset] K2
Antseranana Madag. see Antsirañana
Antsiferovo Rus. Fed. 43 O3
Antsirabe Madag. 131 [inset] J3
Antsirabe Avaratra Madag. 131 [inset] K2
Antsirañana Madag. 131 [inset] K2
formerly known as Diégo Suarez; formerly spelt Antseranana
Antsirañana prov. Madag. 131 [inset] K2
Antsla Estonia 42 H4
Antsohihy Madag. 131 [inset] J2
Antsohimbondrona Madag. 131 [inset] K2
formerly known as Port St-Louis
Antsondrodava Madag. 131 [inset] J3
Anttis Sweden 44 M2
Anttola Fin. 45 N3
Antu China see Songjiang
An Tuc Vietnam see An Khê
Antuco Chile 204 C5
Antuco, Volcán vol. Chile 204 C5
Antufash, Jazīrat i. Yemen 104 C5
English form Antufush Island
Antufush Island Yemen see Antufash, Jazīrat
Antwerp Belgium 51 K1
also known as Anvers; also spelt Antwerpen
Antwerp U.S.A. 177 J1
Antwerpen Belgium see Antwerp
An Uaimh Rep. of Ireland see Navan
Anuc, Lac l. Canada 169 F1
Anuchino Rus. Fed. 82 D4
Anueque, Sierra mts Arg. 205 C6
Anugul India 95 E1
Anupgarh India 96 B3
Anuradhapura Sri Lanka 94 D4
Anurrete Aboriginal Land res. Australia 148 B4
Anvers Belgium see Antwerp
Anvers Island Antarctica 222 T2
Anvil Range mts Canada 166 C2
Anxi Fujian China 87 F3
also known as Fengcheng
Anxi Gansu China 84 B3
also known as Yuanquan
Anxian China 86 C2
also known as Anchang
Anxiang China 87 E2
Anxin China 85 G4
also known as Xin'an
Anxious Bay Australia 146 B3
Anxur Italy see Terracina
Anyang China see Du'an
Anyang China 85 G4
also known as Zhangde
Anyang S. Korea 83 B5
Anyar Indon. 77 D4
Anydro i. Greece 59 G12
also known as Ánidhros
A'nyêmaqên Shan mts China 86 A1
English form Amne Machin Range
Anyi China 87 E2
also known as Longjin
Anykščiai Lith. 42 G6
Anyuan Jiangxi China 87 E3
also known as Xinshan
Anyuan Jiangxi China 87 E3
Anyue China 86 C2
also known as Yueyang
Anyuy r. Rus. Fed. 82 E2
Anyuysk Rus. Fed. 39 Q3
Anzac Alta Canada 167 I3
Anzac B.C. Canada 166 F4
Anze China 85 G4
Anzhero-Sudzhensk Rus. Fed. 80 D1
Anzi Dem. Rep. Congo 126 D5
Anzio Italy 56 E7
historically known as Antium
Anzoátegui state Venez. 199 E2
Aoba i. Vanuatu 145 F3
also known as Omba; also spelt Oba
Aob Luang National Park Thai. 78 B4
Aoga-shima i. Japan 91 F8
Aohan Qi China see Xinhui
Aomen China see Macau
Aomori Japan 90 G4
Aomori pref. Japan 90 G4
Aono-yama hill Japan 91 B7
Aoos r. Greece 59 B8
Ao Phang Nga National Park Thai. 79 B6
Aoraki N.Z. see Mount Cook
Aoraki mt. N.Z. see Cook, Mount
Aôral, Phnum mt. Cambodia 79 D5
Aorangi mt. N.Z. see Cook, Mount
Aorere r. N.Z. 152 G8
Aosta Italy 51 N7
Aotearoa country Oceania see New Zealand
Aouderas Niger 125 H2
Aoufist W. Sahara 122 B4
Aouhinet bel Egra well Alg. 122 D4
Aouk, Bahr r. Cent. Afr. Rep./Chad 126 C2
Aoukalé r. Cent. Afr. Rep./Chad 126 D2
Aoukâr reg. Mali/Mauritania 122 D5
Aoukenek well Mali 125 F2
Aoulef Alg. 123 F4
Aoulime, Jbel mt. Morocco 122 C3
Aourou Mali 124 C3
Aoxi China see Le'an
Aoya Japan 91 D7
Aoyang China see Shanggao
Aozou Chad 120 C4
Apa r. Brazil 201 F5
Apac Uganda 128 B4
Apache U.S.A. 179 C5
Apache, Lake U.S.A. 183 M8
Apache Junction U.S.A. 183 M8
Apagado, Volcán vol. Bol. 200 D5
Apahida Romania 58 E2
Apaiaí r. Brazil 206 E10
Apaiang atoll Kiribati see Abaiang
Apalachee Bay U.S.A. 175 C6
Apalachicola U.S.A. 175 C6
Apalachicola r. U.S.A. 175 C6
Apalachicola Bay U.S.A. 175 C6
Apam Ghana 125 E5
Apamama atoll Kiribati see Abemama
Apamea Turkey see Dinar
Apan Mex. 185 F5
Apaporis r. Col. 198 D5
Apar, Teluk b. Indon. 77 G3
Aparecida do Rio Doce Brazil 206 B5
Aparecida do Tabuado Brazil 206 B7
Aparima N.Z. see Riverton
Aparima r. N.Z. 153 C14
Aparri Phil. 74 B2
Aparurén Venez. 199 F3
Apas, Sierra hills Arg. 205 D6
Apaščia r. Lith. 42 F5
Apatin Vojvodina, Srbija Yugo. 56 K3
Apatity Rus. Fed. 44 P2
Apatou Fr. Guiana 199 H3
Apatzingán Mex. 185 E5
Ape Latvia 42 H4
Apediá r. Brazil 201 E2
Apeldoorn Neth. 48 C3
Apennines mts Italy 53 D3
also known as Appennino
Apere r. Bol. 200 D3
Apex Mountain Canada 166 B2
Aphrodite's Birthplace tourist site Cyprus 108 D3
also known as Petra tou Romiou
Api Dem. Rep. Congo 126 E4
Api mt. Nepal 96 D3
Api, Tanjung pt Indon. 75 B3
Apia Col. 198 C3
Apia atoll Kiribati see Abaiang

▶Apia Samoa 145 H3
Capital of Samoa.
oceania [countries] ➡ 138–139

Apiacas, Serra dos hills Brazil 201 F2
Apiaí Brazil 203 B8
Apiaú, Serra do mts Brazil 199 F4
Apio Solomon Is 145 F2
Apipilulco Mex. 185 F5
Apishapa r. U.S.A. 178 B4
Apiti N.Z. 152 J7
Apizaco Mex. 185 F5
Apizolaya Mex. 179 B7
Aplao Peru 200 B4
Ap Lei Chau i. Hong Kong China see Aberdeen Island
Apo, Mount vol. Phil. 74 C5
Apodi Brazil 202 E3
Apodi, Chapada do hills Brazil 202 E3
Apo East Passage Phil. 74 B3
Apoera Suriname 199 G3
Apolda Germany 48 I4
Apollinopolis Magna Egypt see Idfu
Apollo Bay Australia 147 D4
Apollonia Bulg. see Sozopol
Apollonia Greece 59 F12
Apolo Bol. 200 C3
Apopka U.S.A. 175 D6
Aporé Brazil 206 C6
Aporé r. Brazil 206 B6
Apostle Islands U.S.A. 172 C4
Apostle Islands National Lakeshore nature res. U.S.A. 172 C3
Apostolens Tommelfinger mt. Greenland 165 O3
Apóstoles Arg. 204 G2
Apostolos Andreas, Cape Cyprus 108 F2
also known as Zafer Burnu
Apoteri Guyana 199 G3
Apo West Passage Phil. 74 B3
Appalachia U.S.A. 176 C9
▶Appalachian Mountains U.S.A. 176 B9
northamerica [landscapes] ➡ 156–157
Appalla i. Fiji see Kabara
Appennino mts Italy see Apennines
Appennino Abruzzese mts Italy 56 F6
Appennino Lucano mts Italy 57 H8
Appennino Napoletano mts Italy 56 H7
Appennino Tosco-Emiliano mts Italy 56 C5
Appiano sulla Strada del Vino Italy 56 D2
Applecross U.K. 46 G6
Appleton MN U.S.A. 178 C2
Appleton WI U.S.A. 172 E6
Apple Valley U.S.A. 183 G7
Appomattox U.S.A. 176 G8
Aprelevka Rus. Fed. 43 S6
Aprilia Italy 56 E7
Apsheronsk Rus. Fed. 41 F7
formerly known as Apsheronskaya
Apsheronskaya Rus. Fed. see Apsheronsk
Apsheronskiy Poluostrov pen. Azer. see Abşeron Yarımadası
Apsley Canada 173 O6
Apsley Strait Australia 148 A1
Apt France 51 L9
Apucarana Brazil 206 B10
Apucarana, Serra da hills Brazil 206 B10
Apulum Romania see Alba Iulia
Apurahuan Phil. 74 A4
Apure r. Venez. 198 E3
Apure state Venez. 198 D3
Apurímac dept Peru 200 B3
Apurimac r. Peru 200 B3
Apurito Venez. 198 D3
Aq"a Georgia see Sokhumi
'Aqaba Jordan see Al 'Aqabah
Aqaba, Gulf of Asia 104 A1
'Aqaba, Wâdi el watercourse Egypt 108 E7
Aqadyr Kazakh. see Agadyr'
Aqal China 88 B3
Aqbalyq Kazakh. see Akbalyk
Aqbeyit Kazakh. see Akbeit
Āqchah Afgh. 101 F2
Aq Chai r. Iran 107 F3
Āqdā Iran 100 C3
Aqdoghmish r. Iran 100 A2
Aqiq Sudan 121 H5
Aqiq, Khalīg b. Sudan 104 B4
Aqiq, Wādī al watercourse Saudi Arabia 104 C2
Aqitag mt. China 88 E3
Aqkōl Kazakh. see Akkol'
Aqkōl Kazakh. see Akkol'
Aqla well Saudi Arabia 104 B2
Aqmola Kazakh. see Astana
Aqmola Oblast admin. div. Kazakh. see Akmolinskaya Oblast'
Aqmola Oblysy admin. div. Kazakh. see Akmolinskaya Oblast'
Āq Qal'eh Iran 100 C2
formerly known as Pahlavī Dezh
Aqqan China 89 D4
formerly known as Atqan
Aqqikkol Hu salt l. China 89 E4
Aqqystaū Kazakh. see Akkystau
Aqra', Wādī al watercourse Saudi Arabia 109 L7
'Aqraba West Bank 108 G5
'Aqrah Iraq 107 E3
'Aqran hill Saudi Arabia 109 J6
Aqsay Kazakh. see Aksay
Aqsayqin Hit terr. Asia see Aksai Chin
Aqshataū Kazakh. see Akchatau
Aqshī Kazakh. see Akshiy
Aqshuqyr Kazakh. see Akshukur
Aqsū Kazakh. see Aksu
Aqsū Kazakh. see Aksu
Aqsū Kazakh. see Aksu
Aqsūat Kazakh. see Aksuat
Aqsū-Ayuly Kazakh. see Aksu-Ayuly
Aqtaū Kazakh. see Aktau
Aqtōbe Kazakh. see Aktyubinsk
Aqtōbe Oblysy admin. div. Kazakh. see Aktyubinskaya Oblast'
Aqtoghay Kazakh. see Aktogay
Aqtoghay Kazakh. see Aktogay
Aquae Grani Germany see Aachen
Aquae Gratianae France see Aix-les-Bains
Aquae Sextiae France see Aix-en-Provence
Aquae Statiellae Italy see Acqui Terme
Aquarius Mountains U.S.A. 183 K7
Aquarius Plateau U.S.A. 183 M4
Aquaviva delle Fonti Italy 56 I8
Aquidabánmi r. Para. 201 F5
Aquidauana Brazil 201 G5
Aquidauana r. Brazil 201 F4
Aquila Mex. 184 E5
Aquiles Mex. 184 D2
Aquin Haiti 187 E3
Aquincum Hungary see Budapest
Aquiry r. Brazil see Acre
Aquisgranum Germany see Aachen
Aquitaine admin. reg. France 50 F8
Aqzhal Kazakh. see Akzhal
Aqzhar Kazakh. see Akzhar
Aqzhayqyn Kōli salt l. Kazakh. see Akzhaykyn, Ozero
Ara India 97 E4
formerly spelt Arrah
Ara r. Spain 55 L2
Āra Ārba Eth. 128 D3
Arab U.S.A. 174 C5
Arab, Bahr el watercourse Sudan 126 F2
'Arab, Khalîg el b. Egypt 121 F2
'Araba, Wâdi el watercourse Egypt 108 D8
'Arābābād Iran 100 D3
Ara Bacalle well Eth. 128 D3
'Arabah, Wādī r. Yemen 105 E4
'Arabah, Wādī al watercourse Israel/Jordan 108 G8
also known as Ha 'Arava
Arabelo Venez. 199 E3
Arabian Gulf Asia see The Gulf
Arabian Oryx Sanctuary tourist site Saudi Arabia 105 G4
Arabian Sea Indian Ocean 99 H6
Ara Bonel Eth. 128 D3
Arabopó Venez. 199 F3
Araç Turkey 106 C2
Araça r. Brazil 199 F5
Aracaju Brazil 202 E4
Aracanguy, Montes de hills Para. 201 G6
Aracar, Volcán vol. Arg. 200 D6
Aracati Brazil 202 E3
Aracatu Brazil 202 D5
Araçatuba Brazil 206 C8
Aracena Spain 54 E7
Aracena, Isla i. Chile 205 C9
Aracena, Sierra de hills Spain 54 D7
Arachthos r. Greece 59 C9
also spelt Arakhthos
Aračinovo Macedonia 58 C6
Aracoiaba Brazil 202 E3
Aracruz Brazil 203 D6
Araçuaí Brazil 203 D6
Araçuaí r. Brazil 203 D6
'Arad Israel 108 G6
Arad Romania 58 C2
Arada Chad 120 D6
'Arādah U.A.E. 105 F3
Arādān Iran 100 C3
Aradeib, Wadi watercourse Sudan 120 D6
Arafura Sea Australia/Indon. 144 C2
Aragarças Brazil 206 A2
Aragón aut. comm. Spain 55 K3
Aragón r. Spain 55 J2
Aragoncillo mt. Spain 55 I4
Aragua state Venez. 199 E2
Araguacema Brazil 202 B4
Araguaçu Brazil 202 B5
Aragua de Barcelona Venez. 199 E2
Aragua de Maturín Venez. 199 F2
Araguaia r. Brazil 206 A3
Araguaia, Parque Nacional de nat. park Brazil 202 B4
Araguaiana Brazil 206 B2
Araguaína Brazil 202 B3
Araguana Brazil 202 B3
Araguao, Boca r. mouth Venez. 199 F2
Araguapiche, Punta pt Venez. 199 F2
Araguari Brazil 206 E5
Araguari r. Amapá Brazil 199 I4
Araguari r. Minas Gerais Brazil 206 E5
Araguatins Brazil 202 B3
Aragvi r. Georgia 107 F2
'Arāh, Ra's pt Yemen 104 C5

'Ārah, Wādī r. Oman 105 F4
Arai Japan 90 F6
Araif el Naga, Gebel hill Egypt 108 F7
Araiosos Brazil 202 D2
Arak Alg. 123 F4
Arāk Iran 100 B3
formerly known as Sultanabad
Arak Syria 109 J3
Arakai-yama mt. Japan 90 F6
Arakaka Guyana 199 F3
Arakan state Myanmar 78 A3
also known as Rakhaing or Rakhine or Yagaing
Arakan Yoma mts Myanmar 78 A3
Arakhthos r. Greece see Arachthos
Arakkonam India 94 C3
formerly spelt Arkonam
Aral China 88 C3
Aral Kazakh. see Aral'sk
Aral Tajik. see Vose

▶Aral Sea salt l. Kazakh./Uzbek. 102 D3
2nd largest lake in Asia and 6th in the world. Also known as Aral Tengizi or Orol Dengizi.
asia [landscapes] ➡ 62–63

Aral'sk Kazakh. 103 E3
also known as Aral
Aralsor, Ozero l. Kazakh. 102 B2
Aralsor, Ozero salt l. Kazakh. 102 C2
Aralsul'fat Kazakh. 103 E3
Aral Tengizi salt l. Kazakh./Uzbek. see Aral Sea
Aramac Australia 149 E4
Aramac Creek watercourse Australia 149 E4
Aramah plat. Saudi Arabia 105 D2
A Ramallosa Spain 54 C2
Aramberri Mex. 185 F3
Arame Brazil 202 C3
Aramia r. P.N.G. 73 J8
Aran r. India 94 C2
Arancibia Arg. 204 C3
Aranda de Duero Spain 55 H3
Arandelovac Srbija Yugo. 58 B4
Arandis Namibia 130 B4
Arang India 97 D5
Arani India 94 C3
Aran Island Rep. of Ireland 47 D9
Aran Islands Rep. of Ireland 47 C10
Aranjuez Spain 55 H4
Aranos Namibia 130 C5
Aransas Pass U.S.A. 179 C7
Arantangi India 94 C4
Arantes r. Brazil 206 C6
Aranuka atoll Kiribati 145 G1
formerly known as Henderville
Aranyaprathet Thai. 79 C5
Arao Japan 91 B8
Araouane Mali 124 E2
Arapaho U.S.A. 179 C5
Arapahoe U.S.A. 178 C3
Arapari Brazil 199 H5
Arapawa Island N.Z. 152 I9
Arapicos Ecuador 198 B5
Arapiraca Brazil 202 E4
Arapis, Akra pt Greece 59 F8
Arapkir Turkey 107 D3
Arapongas Brazil 206 B10
Arapoti Brazil 206 D11
Arapsun Turkey see Gülşehir
Araquá Brazil 206 A7
Arapuni N.Z. 152 J6
'Ar'ar Saudi Arabia 107 E5
'Ar'ar, Wādī watercourse Iraq/Saudi Arabia 107 E5
Arara r. Brazil 199 F5
Araracuara Col. 198 C5
Araracuara, Cerros de hills Col. 198 C5
Araranguá Brazil 203 B9
Araraquara Brazil 206 E8
Araras Amazonas Brazil 200 C2
Araras Pará Brazil 199 H6
Ararás Brazil 200 D2
Araras São Paulo Brazil 206 F9
Araras, Açude resr Brazil 202 D3
Araras, Serra das hills Brazil 203 A6
Araras, Serra das mts Brazil 203 A8
Ararat Armenia 107 F3
Ararat Australia 147 D4
Ararat, Mount Turkey 107 F3
also known as Ağrı Dağı
Arari Brazil 202 C2
Araria India 97 E4
Araripe Brazil 202 D3
Araripe, Chapada do hills Brazil 202 D3
Araripina Brazil 202 D3
Araruama Brazil 207 K9
Araruama, Lago de lag. Brazil 207 K9
Aras Turkey 107 E3
also known as Velibaba
Aras r. Turkey see Araz
Ar Asgat Mongolia 85 E1
Araṭâne well Mauritania 124 C2
Arataú r. Brazil 202 B2
Aratürük China see Yiwu
Arauá r. Brazil 199 F6
Arauá r. Brazil 199 F6
Arauã r. Brazil 200 D2
Arauca Col. 198 D3
Arauca dept Col. 198 D3
Arauca r. Venez. 198 E3
Arauco Chile 204 B5
Arauco, Golfo de b. Chile 204 B5
Arauquita Col. 198 D3
Araure Venez. 198 D2
Aravaipa Creek watercourse U.S.A. 183 N9
Aravalli Range mts India 96 B4
Aravete Estonia 42 G2
Araviana r. Spain 55 I3
Aravissos Greece 58 D8
Arawa P.N.G. 145 E2
Arawale National Reserve nature res. Kenya 128 D5
Arawata r. N.Z. 153 C12
formerly spelt Arawhata
Arawhana mt. N.Z. 152 L6
Arawhata r. N.Z. see Arawata
Araxá Brazil 206 G6
Araxos, Akra pt Greece 59 C10
Araya, Península de pen. Venez. 199 E2
Arayıt Dağı mt. Turkey 106 B3
Araz r. Azer. 107 G2
also spelt Aras
Arba r. Spain 55 J3
Arbailu Iraq see Arbīl
Arba Minch Eth. 128 C3
Arbela Iraq see Arbīl
Arbīl Iraq 107 F3
also known as Hawlēr; also spelt Irbil; historically known as Arbailu or Arbela
Arbīl governorate Iraq 107 E4
Arboga Sweden 45 K4
Arbois France 51 L6
Arboletes Col. 198 B2
Arbon Switz. 51 P5
Arborfield Canada 167 K4
Arborg Canada 167 L5
Arbrå Sweden 45 L3
Arbroath U.K. 46 J7
Arbuckle U.S.A. 182 B2
Arbu Lut, Dasht-e des. Afgh. 101 E4
Arc r. France 51 M7
Arcachon France 50 E8
Arcachon, Bassin d' inlet France 50 E8
Arcadia FL U.S.A. 175 D7
Arcadia LA U.S.A. 179 D5
Arcadia MI U.S.A. 172 G6
Arcadia WI U.S.A. 172 B6
Arcalod, Pointe d' mt. France 51 M7
Arcanum U.S.A. 176 A6
Arcas, Cayos is Mex. 185 H4
Arcata U.S.A. 180 A4
Arc Dome mt. U.S.A. 183 G3
Arcelia Mex. 185 E5
Archangel Rus. Fed. 40 G2
also known as Arkhangel'sk; historically known as Novyj Cholmogory or Novyy Kholmogory
Archangel Oblast admin. div. Rus. Fed. see Arkhangel'skaya Oblast'
Archangelos Greece 59 J12
Archar r. Bulg. 58 D5
Archbold U.S.A. 176 A4
Archena Spain 55 J6
Archer r. Australia 149 D2
Archer Bend National Park Australia 149 D2
Archer City U.S.A. 179 C5
Arches National Park U.S.A. 183 O3
Arch Henda well Mali 124 E2
Archidona Spain 54 G7
Archie Creek r. Australia 148 C3
Archman Turkm. 102 D5
Arci, Monte hill Sardegna Italy 57 A9
Arcipélago de la Maddalena, Parco Nazionale dell' nat. park Sardegna Italy 56 B7
Ärçivan Azer. 107 G3
Arckaringa watercourse Australia 146 B2
Arco Italy 56 C3
Arco U.S.A. 180 D4
Arcola U.S.A. 176 H7
Arconce r. France 51 J6
Arcos Brazil 207 H7
Arcos de Jalón Spain 55 I3
Arcos de la Frontera Spain 54 F8
Arcos de Valdevez Port. 54 C3
Arcot India 94 C3
Arcoverde Brazil 202 E4
Arctic Bay Canada 165 K2
Arctic Institute Islands Rus. Fed. see Arkticheskogo Instituta, Ostrova
▶Arctic Ocean 224 O1
arctic [features] ➡ 214–215
Arctic Red r. Canada 166 C1
Arctic Red River Canada see Tsiigehtchic
Arctowski research station Antarctica 222 U2
long form Henryk Arctowski
Arda r. Bulg. 58 H7
also known as Ardas
Ardabīl Iran 100 B2
Ardabīl prov. Iran 100 A2
Ardahan Turkey 107 E2
Ardakān Iran 101 D2
Ardakān Fārs Iran 100 C4
Ardakān Yazd Iran 100 C3
Ardal Iran 100 B4
Årdal Norway 45 I3
Årdalstangen Norway 45 I3
Ardas r. Greece 58 H7
Arḍ aş Şawwān plain Jordan 109 I7
Ardatov Nizhegorodskaya Oblast' Rus. Fed. 40 G5
Ardatov Respublika Mordoviya Rus. Fed. 40 H5
Ardbeg Canada 173 M5
Ardèche r. France 51 K8
Ardee Rep. of Ireland 47 F10
Arden, Mount hill Australia 146 C3
Ardennes plat. Belgium 51 K3
also known as L'Ardenne, Plateau de
Ardentes France 50 H6
Arden Town U.S.A. 182 C3
Ardestān Iran 100 C3
Ardglass U.K. 47 G9
Ardila r. Port. 54 D6
Ardino Bulg. 58 G7
Ardkeen N.Z. 152 L6
Ardlethan Australia 147 E3
Ardmore U.S.A. 179 C5
Ardnamurchan, Point of U.K. 46 F7
Ardon Rus. Fed. 107 F2
Ardrossan Australia 146 C3
Ardrossan U.K. 46 H8
Ards Peninsula U.K. 47 G9
Ardvasar U.K. 46 G6
Åre Sweden 44 K3
Areado Brazil 207 G8
Arebi Dem. Rep. Congo 126 F4
Arecibo Puerto Rico 187 G3
Arefino Rus. Fed. 43 U3
Arefu Romania 58 F3
Areguá Para. 201 F6
Areia Branca Brazil 202 E3
Arekhawsk Belarus 43 L7
also spelt Orekhovsk; formerly known as Orekhi-Vydritsa
Arel Belgium see Arlon
Arelas France see Arles
Arelate France see Arles
Arena reef Phil. 74 B4
Arena, Point U.S.A. 182 A3
Arena de la Ventana, Punta pt Mex. 184 C3
Arenal, Campo del plain Arg. 204 D2
Arenal, Puerto del pass Spain 55 I6
Arenal, Volcán vol. Costa Rica 186 B5
Arena Point Phil. 74 B3
Arenápolis Brazil 201 F3
Arenas, Punta de pt Arg. 205 C9
Arenas de San Pedro Spain 54 F4
Arendal Norway 45 J4
Arendsee (Altmark) Germany 48 I3
Arenys de Mar Spain 55 N3
Arenzano Italy 56 A4
Areopoli Greece 59 D12
Areponapuchi Mex. 181 F8
Arequipa Peru 200 C4
Arequipa dept Peru 200 B3
Arere Brazil 199 H5
Ārēro Eth. 128 C3
Aresa r. Belarus 42 J9
Arévalo Spain 54 G3
Areza Eritrea 104 B5
Arezzaf well Mali see Aghezzaf
Arezzo Italy 56 D5
historically known as Arretium
'Arfajah well Saudi Arabia 107 D5
Arfara Greece 59 D11
Arga r. Spain 55 J2
Argadargada Australia 148 C4
Argalant Mongolia 85 F2
Argalasti Greece 59 E9
Argan China 88 E3
Arganda Spain 55 H4
Arganil Port. 54 C4
Argao Phil. 74 B4
Argatay Mongolia 85 E2
Argel Alg. see Algiers
Argelès-Gazost France 50 F9
Argelès-sur-Mer France 51 J10
Argens r. France 51 M9
Argenta Italy 56 D4
Argentan France 50 F4
Argentario, Monte hill Italy 56 D6
Argentat France 51 H7
Argentera, Cima dell' mt. Italy 51 N8

▶Argentina country S. America 204 C4
2nd largest country in South America and 8th in the world. 3rd most populous country in South America. Long form Argentine Republic.
world [countries] ➡ 10–11
southamerica [countries] ➡ 192–193

Argentina Range mts Antarctica 223 V1
Argentine Republic country S. America see Argentina
Argentino, Lago l. Arg. 205 B8
Argenton r. France 50 F5
Argentoratum France see Strasbourg
Argentre France 50 F4
Argeş r. Romania 58 H4
Argeşel r. Romania 58 F4
Arghandab r. Afgh. 101 F4
Arghastan r. Afgh. 101 F4
Argolikos Kolpos b. Greece 59 D11
Argonne U.S.A. 172 E5
Argos Greece 59 D11
Argos U.S.A. 172 G9
Argos Orestiko Greece 59 C8
Argostoli Greece 59 B10
Arguedas Spain 55 J2
Argun' r. China/Rus. Fed. 85 H1
also known as Ergun He
Argun r. Georgia/Rus. Fed. 107 F2
Argun Rus. Fed. 107 F2
Argungu Nigeria 125 G3
Argunskiy Khrebet mts Rus. Fed. 85 H1
Argus Range mts U.S.A. 182 G6
Arguut Mongolia 84 D2
Argyle Canada 169 H5
Argyle IA U.S.A. 172 B10
Argyle WI U.S.A. 172 D8
Argyle, Lake Australia 150 E3
Argyrokastron Albania see Gjirokastër
Arḥab reg. Yemen 104 D5
Arhangay prov. Mongolia 84 D2
Ar Horqin Qi China see Tianshan
Århus Denmark 45 J4
also spelt Aarhus
Aria N.Z. 152 I6
Ariaga i. Indon. 75 C1
Ariake-kai b. Japan 91 B8
Ariamsvlei Namibia 130 C6
Ariano Irpino Italy 56 H7
Arias Arg. 204 E4
Ari Atoll Maldives 93 D10
Ariaú Brazil 199 G5
Aribí r. Venez. 199 F2
Aribinda Burkina 125 E3
Arica Chile 200 C4
Arica Col. 198 D5
Aricagua Venez. 198 D2
Arid, Cape Australia 151 C7
Arida Japan 91 D7
Aridaia Greece 58 D8
Aridal, Sabkhat salt pan W. Sahara 122 B4
Arid Island N.Z. see Rakitu Island
Ariège r. France 50 H9
Arieş r. Romania 58 E2
Arieşul Mic r. Romania 58 E2
Arigíyn Gol r. Mongolia 84 D1
Arīḩā Syria 109 H2
Arihā West Bank see Jericho
Arikaree r. U.S.A. 178 B3
Arilje Srbija Yugo. 58 B5
Arimã Brazil 199 F6
Ariminum Italy see Rimini
Arimu Mine Guyana 199 G3
'Arīn, Wādī al watercourse Saudi Arabia 104 C4
Arinagour U.K. 46 F7
Arinos Mato Grosso Brazil 201 G3
Arinos Minas Gerais Brazil 202 C5
Arinos r. Brazil 201 F2
Ario de Rosáles Mex. 185 E5
Ariogala Lith. 42 E6
Ariporo r. Col. 198 D3
Aripuanã Brazil 201 F2
Aripuanã r. Brazil 199 F6
Ariquemes Brazil 201 E2
Ariranhá r. Brazil 203 A6
Arisaig U.K. 46 G7
Arisaig, Sound of sea chan. U.K. 46 G7
Arisaru Falls Guyana 199 G3
'Arīsh, Wādī el watercourse Egypt 108 E6
Arismendi Venez. 198 D2
Aristazabal Island Canada 166 D4
Aristizábal, Cabo c. Arg. 205 D7
Aristóbulo del Valle Arg. 201 G6
Aritwala Pak. 101 H4
Arivonimamo Madag. 131 [inset] J3
Arixang China see Wenquan
Ariya waterhole Kenya 128 C4
Ariyalur India 94 C4
Arizaro, Salar de salt flat Arg. 200 D6
Arizgoiti Spain 55 I1
Arizona Arg. 204 D4
Arizona state U.S.A. 183 M7
Arizpe Mex. 184 C2
'Arjah Saudi Arabia 104 D2
Årjäng Sweden 45 K4
Arjasa Indon. 77 F4
'Arjāwī, Wādī al watercourse Iraq 109 O5
Arjeplog Sweden 44 L2
Ārjo Eth. 128 C2
Arjona Col. 198 C2
Arjona Spain 54 G7
Arjuni India 96 D5
Arkadak Rus. Fed. 41 G6
Arkadelphia U.S.A. 179 D5
Arkagala Rus. Fed. 39 O3
Arkalgud India 94 C3
Arkalochori Greece 59 G13
Arkalyk Kazakh. 103 F2
also spelt Arqalyq
Arkansas r. U.S.A. 179 E5
Arkansas state U.S.A. 174 A5
Arkansas City AR U.S.A. 175 B5
Arkansas City KS U.S.A. 178 C4
Arkata r. Bulg. 58 D6
Arkatag Shan mts China 89 E4
Arkell, Mount Canada 166 C2
Arkenu, Jabal mt. Libya 120 E4
Arkhangel'sk Rus. Fed. see Archangel
Arkhangel'skaya Oblast' admin. div. Rus. Fed. 40 G3
English form Archangel Oblast
Arkhangel'skoye Respublika Bashkortostan Rus. Fed. 40 K5
Arkhangel'skoye Tul'skaya Oblast' Rus. Fed. 43 S8
Arkhara Rus. Fed. 82 C2
Arkhara r. Rus. Fed. 82 C2
Arkhipovka Rus. Fed. 82 D4
Arkhipovka Rus. Fed. 43 M7
Árki i. Greece see Arkoi
Arklow Rep. of Ireland 47 F11
also known as An tInbhear Mór
Arkoi i. Greece 59 H11
also known as Árki
Arkona Canada 173 L7
Arkona, Kap c. Germany 49 K1
Arkonam India see Arakkonam
Arkosund Sweden 45 L4

▶Arkticheskiy, Mys is Rus. Fed. 39 J1
Most northerly point of Asia.

Arkticheskogo Instituta, Ostrova is Rus. Fed. 39 I2
English form Arctic Institute Islands
Arkul' Rus. Fed. 40 I4
Ärla Sweden 45 L4
Arlanc France 51 J7
Arlang, Gora mt. Turkm. 102 C5
Arlanza r. Spain 55 G2
Arlanzón r. Spain 54 G2
Arles France 51 K9
historically known as Arelas or Arelate
Arli Burkina 125 F4
Arlington IA U.S.A. 172 B8
Arlington IL U.S.A. 172 D9
Arlington NY U.S.A. 177 L4
Arlington OH U.S.A. 176 B5
Arlington OR U.S.A. 180 B3
Arlington VA U.S.A. 177 H7
Arlington WI U.S.A. 172 D7
Arlington Heights U.S.A. 174 B3
Arlit Niger 125 G2
Arlon Belgium 51 L3
also known as Arel; also spelt Aarlen
Arltunga Australia 148 B4
Arlyeya Belarus 43 K6
Arm r. Canada 167 J5
Armadale Australia 151 A7
Armadores i. Indon. 75 C1
Armageddon tourist site Israel see Tel Megiddo
Armagh U.K. 47 F9
Armah, Wādī r. Yemen 105 E4
Armançon r. France 51 J5
Armando Bermudez nat. park Dom. Rep. 187 F3
Armant Egypt 121 G3
historically known as Hermonthis
Armathia i. Greece 59 H13
Armavir Rus. Fed. 41 G7
▶Armenia country Asia 107 F2
known as Haikakan in Armenian; formerly known as Armyanskaya S.S.R.; historically known as Urartu
asia [countries] ➡ 64–67
Armenia Col. 198 C3
Armenistis, Akra pt Greece 59 I12
Armenki Rus. Fed. 43 V4
Armenopolis Romania see Gherla
Armeria Mex. 184 E5
Armi, Capo dell' c. Italy 57 H11
Armidale Australia 147 F2
Armit Lake Canada 167 N1
Armona U.S.A. 182 E5
Armori India 94 D1
Armorique, Parc Régional d' park France 50 C4
Armour U.S.A. 178 C3
Armstrong Arg. 204 E4
Armstrong r. Australia 148 A3
Armstrong B.C. Canada 166 G5
Armstrong Ont. Canada 168 B3
Armstrong, Mount Canada 166 C2
Armstrong Island Cook Is see Rarotonga
Armu r. Rus. Fed. 82 E3
Armur India 94 C2
Armutçuk Dağı mts Turkey 106 A3
Armutlu Turkey 58 J8
Armutova Turkey see Gömeç
Armyans'k Ukr. 41 E7
Armyanskaya S.S.R. country Asia see Armenia
Arnå r. Denmark 48 F1
Arna Greece 59 D12
Árnafjall hill Faroe Is 46 E1
Arnage France 50 G5
Arnaia Greece 58 E8
Arnaoutis, Cape Cyprus see Arnauti, Cape
Arnarfjörður inlet Iceland 44 [inset] A2
Arnaud r. Canada 169 G1
Arnauti, Cape Cyprus 108 D2
also known as Akama, Akra; also spelt Arnaoutis, Cape
Arnavutköy Turkey 58 J7
Arnay-le-Duc France 51 K5
Arnedo Spain 55 I2
Arneiroz Brazil 202 D3
Årnemark Sweden 44 M2
Arnes Norway 45 J3
Arnett U.S.A. 179 C4
Arnhem Neth. 48 C4
Arnhem, Cape Australia 148 C2
Arnhem Land reg. Australia 148 B2
Arnhem Land Aboriginal Land res. Australia 148 B2
Arnionys 1 Lith. 42 G6
Arnisdale U.K. 46 G6
Arnissa Greece 58 C8
Arno r. Italy 56 C5
Arno Bay Australia 146 C3
Arnoia r. Spain 54 C2
also spelt Arnoya
Arnold MD U.S.A. 177 I6
Arnold MI U.S.A. 172 F4
Arnold MO U.S.A. 174 B4
Arnold's Cove Canada 169 K4
Arnoldstein Austria 49 K9
Arnon r. France 51 I5
Arnon r. Jordan see Mawjib, Wādī al
Arnoux, Lac l. Canada 173 N2
Arnøya i. Norway 44 M1
Arnoya r. Spain see Arnoia
Arnprior Canada 168 E4
Arnsberg Germany 48 F4
Arnstadt Germany 48 H5
Arnstein Canada 173 N5
Arnstorf Germany 49 J7
Arntfield Canada 173 N2
Aro r. Venez. 199 E3
Aroab Namibia 130 C5
Aroania mt. Greece 59 D11
Aroeira Brazil 203 A7
Aroland Canada 168 C3
Arolsen Germany 48 G4
Aroma Sudan 104 B5
Aromas U.S.A. 182 C5
Aron r. France 51 J6
Aron India 96 C4
Arona Italy 56 A3
Arorae i. Kiribati 145 G2
also spelt Arore; formerly known as Hurd Island
Arore i. Kiribati see Arorae
Aroroy Phil. 74 B3
Aros r. Mex. 184 C2
Arosa, Ría de est. Spain see Arousa, Ría de
Arossi i. Solomon Is see San Cristobal
Arouca Port. 54 C4
Arouelli well Chad 120 D5
Arousa, Ría de est. Spain 54 B2
also spelt Arosa, Ría de
Arpa r. Armenia/Turkey 107 E2
Arpaçay Turkey 107 E2
Arpaçsakarlar Turkey 108 F1
Arpajon-sur-Cère France 51 I8
Arqalyq Kazakh. see Arkalyk
Arquata del Tronto Italy 56 F6
Arquipélago dos Açores terr. N. Atlantic Ocean see Azores
Arra r. Pak. 101 F5
Arrábida, Parque Natural da nature res. Port. 54 C6
Arrabury Australia 149 D5
Arrah Côte d'Ivoire 124 E5
Arrah India see Ara
Ar Raḩá hill Saudi Arabia 109 K7
Ar Raḩḩālīyah Iraq 107 E4
Ar Rāhidah Yemen 104 D5
Arraias r. Brazil 202 A4
Arraias, Serra de hills Brazil 202 C5
Arraiolos Port. 54 D6
Ar Ramādī Iraq 107 E4
Ar Ramthā Jordan 108 H5
Arran i. U.K. 46 G8
Ar Raqqah Syria 109 K2
also spelt Raqqa; historically known as Nicephorium
Ar Raqqah governorate Syria 109 J1
Arraro well Eth. 128 D3
Arras France 51 I2
historically known as Nemetocenna
Ar Ra's al Abyaḍ pt Saudi Arabia 104 B3
Arrasate Spain 55 I1
also known as Mondragón
Ar Rashidiyah Iraq 109 P4
Ar-Rass Saudi Arabia 104 C2
Arrats r. France 50 G8
Ar Rawḍ well Saudi Arabia 107 E5
Ar Rawḍah Saudi Arabia 104 C3
Ar Rawḍah Yemen 105 D5
Ar Rāwuk Yemen 105 E5
Ar Rayḥānī Oman 105 F3
Ar Rayn Saudi Arabia 105 D3
Ar Rayyān Qatar 105 E2
Arrecifal Col. 198 D4
Arrecife Canary Is 122 B3
Arrecifes Arg. 204 E4
Arrée, Monts d' hills France 50 B4
Arretium Italy see Arezzo
Arriagá Mex. 185 G5
Arriaga Mex. 185 E4
Arribeños Arg. 204 E4
Ar Rifā'ī Iraq 107 F5
Ar Riḥāb salt flat Iraq 107 F5
Ar Rimāl des. Saudi Arabia 105 F3
Arrington U.S.A. 176 G8
Ar Riyāḍ Saudi Arabia see Riyadh
Ar Riyāḍ prov. Saudi Arabia 104 D2
Arroio Grande Brazil 204 G4
Arronches Port. 54 D5
Arros r. France 50 F9
Arroux r. France 51 J6
Arrow r. Canada 172 D2
Arrow, Lough l. Rep. of Ireland 47 D9
Arrow Creek r. U.S.A. 180 E3
Arrow Lake Canada 172 C2
Arrowsmith, Mount N.Z. 153 E11
Arrowtown N.Z. 153 C12
Arroyo de la Luz Spain 54 E5
Arroyo Grande U.S.A. 182 D6
Arroyo Seco Mex. 185 F4
Ar Rubay'iyah Saudi Arabia 104 D2
Arruda Brazil 201 F3
Ar Rumādīyat Saudi Arabia 104 C2
Ar Rumaythā Bahrain 105 E2
Ar Rumaythah Iraq 107 F5
Ar Rummānah Iraq 109 M3
Ar Ruq'ī well Saudi Arabia 105 D1
Ar Ruṣāfah Syria 109 J2
Ar Ruṣayfah Jordan 108 H5
Ar Rustāq Oman 105 G3
Ar Ruṭbah Iraq 107 E4
Ar Ruwaybāt well Libya 120 C3
Ar Ruwayḍah Saudi Arabia 104 D3
Arruwurra Aboriginal Land res. Australia 148 C4
Års Denmark 45 J4
Ars Iran 100 A2
Arsaköy Turkey 59 K12
Ärsarybaba Erezi hills Turkm. see Irsarybaba, Gory
Arsenajān Iran 100 C4
Arseno Lake Canada 167 H1
Arsen'yev Rus. Fed. 82 D3
Arsen'yevo Rus. Fed. 43 R8
Arshanskaye Wzvyshsha hills Belarus 43 K7
Arsikere India 94 C3
Arsk Rus. Fed. 40 I4
Arslanköy Turkey 108 F1
Arta Greece 59 B9
Artashat Armenia 107 F3
formerly known as Kamarlu
Arteaga Coahuila Mex. 185 E3
Arteaga Michoacán Mex. 185 E5
Artem Rus. Fed. 82 D4
Artemisa Cuba 186 C2
Artemivs'k Ukr. 41 F6
also spelt Artemovsk; formerly known as Bakhmut
Artemovsk Ukr. see Artemivs'k
Artemovskiy Rus. Fed. 39 L4
Artemovskiy Rus. Fed. 82 D4
Artenay France 51 H4
Artesa de Segre Spain 55 M3
Artesia AZ U.S.A. 183 O9
Artesia NM U.S.A. 181 F6
Arthur Canada 173 M7
Arthur NE U.S.A. 178 B3
Arthur TN U.S.A. 176 B9
Arthur, Lake S. Africa 133 J9
Arthur, Lake U.S.A. 176 E5
Arthur Lake Australia 147 E5
Arthur Pieman Protected Area nature res. Australia 147 E5
Arthur's Pass N.Z. 153 F10
Arthur's Pass National Park N.Z. 153 F10
Arthur's Town Bahamas 186 E1
Artigas research station Antarctica 222 U2
Artigas Uruguay 204 F3
Art'ik Armenia 107 E2
Artillery Lake Canada 167 I2
Artisia Botswana 131 E5
Artjärvi Fin. 42 H1
Artos Dağı mt. Turkey 107 E3
Artova Turkey 107 D2
Artrutx, Cap d' c. Spain 55 O5
Artsakh aut. reg. Azer. see Dağlıq Qarabağ
Arts Bogd Uul mts Mongolia 84 D2
Artsiz Ukr. see Artsyz
Artsyz Ukr. 41 D7
also spelt Artsiz
Artur de Paiva Angola see Kuvango
Artux China 88 B4
Artvin Turkey 107 E2
also known as Çoruh
Artyk Turkm. 102 D5
Aru Dem. Rep. Congo 126 F4
Aru, Kepulauan is Indon. 73 H8
Arua Uganda 128 A4
Aruajá Brazil 199 E6
Aruanã Brazil 206 B1

▶Aruba terr. West Indies 198 D1
Self-governing Netherlands Territory.
oceania [countries] ➡ 138–139

Arudy France 50 F9
Arumã Brazil 199 F6
Arun r. China 85 J2
Arun r. Nepal 97 E4
Arunachal Pradesh state India 97 G4
formerly known as North-East Frontier Agency
Arun Qi China see Naji
Aruppukkottai India 94 C4
Arus, Tanjung pt Indon. 75 B2
Arusha Tanz. 128 C5
Arusha admin. reg. Tanz. 129 C5
Arusha National Park Tanz. 128 C5
Arut r. Indon. 77 E3
Aruti Brazil 199 E5
Aruwimi r. Dem. Rep. Congo 126 D4
Arvada U.S.A. 180 F5
Arvayheer Mongolia 84 D2
Arvi India 94 C1
Arviat Canada 167 M2
formerly known as Eskimo Point
Arvidsjaur Sweden 44 L2
Arvika Sweden 45 K4
Årviksand Norway 44 M1
Arvin U.S.A. 182 F6
Arvonia U.S.A. 176 G8
Arwā' Saudi Arabia 104 D3
Arwād i. Syria 108 G3
Arwala Indon. 75 C4
Arxan China 85 H2
Aryanah Tunisia see L'Ariana
Arykbalyk Kazakh. 103 G1
also spelt Aryqbayq
Aryqbayq Kazakh. see Arykbalyk
Arys' Kazakh. 103 G4
Arys' r. Kazakh. 103 G4
Arys, Ozero salt l. Kazakh. 103 F3
Aryskannyg-Aryg Rus. Fed. 88 E1
Arzamas Rus. Fed. 40 G5
Arzanah i. U.A.E. 105 F2
Arzew Alg. 123 E2
Arzew, Golfe d' g. Alg. 55 K9
Arzgir Rus. Fed. 41 H7
Arzila Morocco see Asilah
Arzúa Spain 54 C2
Arzubikha Rus. Fed. 43 V1
Aš Czech Rep. 49 J5
Asa waterhole Kenya 128 C5
Åsa Sweden 45 K4
Asab Namibia 130 C5
Asaba Nigeria 125 G5
Asad, Buḩayrat al resr Syria 109 J1
Asadābād Afgh. 101 G3
Asadābād Hamadān Iran 100 B3
Asadābād Khorāsan Iran 101 D3
Asagny, Parc National d' nat. park Côte d'Ivoire 124 D5
Asahan r. Indon. 76 B2
Asahi Chiba Japan 91 G7
Asahi Toyama Japan 91 E6
Asahi-dake mt. Japan 90 F5
Asahi-dake vol. Japan 90 H3
Asahi-gawa r. Japan 91 C7
Asahikawa Japan 90 H3
Asaka Uzbek. 103 H4
also spelt Assake; formerly known as Leninsk
Āsalē l. Eth. 128 D1
Asālem Iran 100 B2
Asama-yama vol. Japan 91 F6
Asankranguaa Ghana 124 E5
Asan-man b. S. Korea 83 B5
Asansol India 97 E5
Asanwenso Ghana 124 E5
Āsayita Eth. 128 D2
Asbestos Hill Canada see Purtuniq
Asbestos Mountains S. Africa 132 G6
Āsbe Teferi Eth. 128 D2
Asbury Park U.S.A. 177 K5
Ascalon Israel see Ashqelon
Ascea Italy 57 H8
Ascensión Bol. 201 E3
Ascensión Chihuahua Mex. 184 D2
Ascensión Nuevo León Mex. 185 F3
Ascension atoll Micronesia see Pohnpei

▶Ascension i. S. Atlantic Ocean 216 N6
Dependency of St Helena.

Aschaffenburg Germany 48 G6
Ascheberg Germany 48 E4
Aschersleben Germany 48 I4
Asciano Italy 56 D5
Ascoli Piceno Italy 56 F6
historically known as Asculum or Asculum Picenum
Ascoli Satriano Italy 56 H7
historically known as Ausculum or Ausculum Apulum
Ascotán Chile 200 C5
Ascotán, Salar de salt flat Chile 200 C5
Asculum Italy see Ascoli Piceno
Asculum Picenum Italy see Ascoli Piceno
Ascutney U.S.A. 177 M2
Åse Norway 44 K1
Āseb Eritrea see Assab
Asedjrad plat. Alg. 123 F4
Āsela Eth. 128 C3
Åsele Sweden 44 L2
Āsendabo Eth. 128 C3
Asenovgrad Bulg. 58 F6
Åseral Norway 45 I4
Aseri Estonia 42 H2
Asfāk Iran 100 D3
Aşfar, Jabal al mt. Jordan 109 H5
Aşfar, Tall al hill Saudi Arabia 109 M7
Aşfar, Tall al hill Syria 109 H4
Ásgarður Iceland 44 [inset] B2
Asha Rus. Fed. 40 K5
Ashanti admin. reg. Ghana 125 E5
Asharat Saudi Arabia 105 D2
Ashbourne U.K. 47 K10
Ashburn U.S.A. 175 D6
Ashburton watercourse Australia 150 A4
Ashburton N.Z. 153 F11
Ashburton r. N.Z. 153 F12
also known as Hakatere
Ashburton Bay Canada 172 G2
Ashburton Range hills Australia 148 B3
Ashchikol', Ozero salt l. Kazakh. 103 F3
Ashchikol', Ozero salt l. Kazakh. 103 G4
Ashchysay Kazakh. see Achisay
Ashcroft Canada 166 F5
Ashdod Israel 108 F6
historically known as Azotus
Ashdown U.S.A. 179 D5
Asheboro U.S.A. 174 E5
Ashern Canada 167 L5
Asheville U.S.A. 174 D5
Ashevo Rus. Fed. 43 K4
Asheweig r. Canada 168 C2
Ashford Australia 147 F2
Ashford U.K. 47 M12
Ash Fork U.S.A. 183 L6

▶Ashgabat Turkm. 102 D5
Capital of Turkmenistan. Formerly spelt Ashkhabad; historically known as Poltoratsk.

Ashhurst N.Z. 152 J8
Ashibetsu Japan 90 H3
Ashikaga Japan 91 F6
Ashington U.K. 47 K8
Ashiro Japan 90 G4
Ashizuri-misaki pt Japan 91 C8
Ashizuri-Uwakai National Park Japan 83 D6
Ashkazar Iran 100 C4
Ashkelon Israel see Ashqelon
Ashkhabad Turkm. see Ashgabat
Ashkhabadskaya Oblast' admin. div. Turkm. see Akhal'skaya Oblast'
Ashkīdah Libya 120 B3
Ashkum U.S.A. 172 F10
Ashkun reg. Afgh. 101 G3
Ashland AL U.S.A. 175 C5
Ashland KS U.S.A. 178 C4
Ashland KY U.S.A. 176 C7
Ashland ME U.S.A. 174 H2
Ashland NE U.S.A. 178 C3
Ashland NH U.S.A. 177 N2
Ashland OH U.S.A. 176 C5
Ashland OR U.S.A. 180 B4
Ashland VA U.S.A. 176 H8
Ashland WI U.S.A. 172 C4
Ashland City U.S.A. 174 C4
Ashley r. N.Z. 153 G11
also known as Rakahuri
Ashley IN U.S.A. 173 H9
Ashley MI U.S.A. 173 I7
Ashley ND U.S.A. 178 C2
Ashley OH U.S.A. 176 C5

▶Ashmore and Cartier Islands terr. Australia 144 B3
Australian External Territory.
oceania [countries] ➡ 138–139

Ashmore Reef Australia 150 C2
Ashmûn Egypt 108 B7
Ashmyanskaye Wzvyshsha hills Belarus 42 G7
Ashmyany Belarus 42 G7
also spelt Oshmyany
Ashmyany Belarus 42 H7
Ashoknagar India 96 C4
Ashoro Japan 90 H3
Ashqelon Israel 108 F6
also spelt Ashkelon; historically known as Ascalon
Ash Sha'ār Saudi Arabia 104 C4
Ash Shabakah Iraq 107 E5
Ash Shabrūm waterhole Saudi Arabia 109 O7
Ash Shaddādah Syria 109 L1
Ash Shafa Saudi Arabia 104 C3
Ash Shakk Iraq 109 O2
Ash Sham Syria see Damascus
Ash Sha'm U.A.E. 105 G2
Ash Shanāfīyah Iraq 107 F5
also spelt Shināfīyah
Ash Shaqīq well Saudi Arabia 107 E5
Ash Sha'rā' Saudi Arabia 104 D2
Ash Sharawrah Saudi Arabia 105 D4
Ash Shāriqah U.A.E. see Sharjah
Ash Sharqāṭ Iraq 107 E4
also spelt Sharqāt; historically known as Ashur
Ash Sharqīyah admin. reg. Oman 105 G3
Ash Sharqīyah reg. Oman 105 G3

index

AB

Ash Sharqīyah prov. Saudi Arabia 105 E3
Ash Shaṭrah Iraq 107 F5
Ash Shawbak Jordan 108 G7
also spelt Shaubak
Ash Shawr hill Iraq 109 L4
Ash Shaykh 'Uthman Yemen 104 D5
English form Sheikh Othman
Ash Shiblīyāt hill Saudi Arabia 109 I8
Ash Shiḥr Yemen 105 E5
Ash Shināṣ Oman 105 G2
Ash Shiṣar well Oman 105 F4
Ash Shu'aybah Saudi Arabia 104 C2
Ash Shu'bah Saudi Arabia 104 D1
Ash Shubaykīyah Saudi Arabia 104 C2
Ash Shumlūl Saudi Arabia 105 D2
Ash Shuqayq Saudi Arabia 104 C4
Ash Shurayf Saudi Arabia see Khaybar
Ash Shuwayhiṭīyah waterhole Saudi Arabia 109 L7
Ash Shuwayrif Libya 120 B2
Ashta Madhya Pradesh India 96 C5
Ashta Maharashtra India 94 B2
Ashtabula U.S.A. 176 E4
Ashtarak Armenia 107 F2
Ashti Maharashtra India 94 B2
Ashti Maharashtra India 94 C2
Ashti Maharashtra India 96 C5
Ashton S. Africa 132 E10
Ashton ID U.S.A. 180 E3
Ashton IL U.S.A. 172 D9
Ashuanipi r. Canada 169 H2
Ashuanipi Lake Canada 169 H2
Ashuapmushuan r. Canada 174 F1
formerly known as Chamouchouane
Ashuapmushuan, Réserve Faunique nature res. Canada 169 F3
Ashur Iraq see Ash Sharqāṭ
Ashusuu pass Kyrg. 103 H4
also known as Chiyirchik, Pereval
Ashville AL U.S.A. 175 C5
Ashville ME U.S.A. 177 Q1
Ashville PA U.S.A. 176 G5
Ashwabay, Mount hill U.S.A. 172 C4
Ashwaubenon U.S.A. 172 E6
'Āṣī r. Lebanon/Syria see Orontes
'Āṣī, Nahr al r. Asia see Orontes
Asid Gulf Phil. 74 B3
Asientos Mex. 185 E4
Asifabad India 94 C2
Asika India 95 E2
Asikkala Fin. 45 N3
Asilah Morocco 54 E9
formerly spelt Arzila
Asillo Peru 200 C3
Asimi Greece 59 G13
Asinara, Golfo dell' b. Sardegna Italy 56 A8
Asinara, Isola i. Sardegna Italy 56 A7
Asind India 96 B4
Asino Rus. Fed. 39 I4
Asintorf Belarus 43 L7
Asipovichy Belarus 43 J8
also spelt Osipovichi
'Asīr prov. Saudi Arabia 104 C3
'Asīr reg. Saudi Arabia 104 C4
Asisium Italy see Assisi
Askainen Fin. 42 C1
Askale Turkey 107 E3
Askarovo Rus. Fed. 102 D1
Asker Norway 45 J4
Askersund Sweden 45 K4
Askim Norway 45 J4
Askino Rus. Fed. 40 K4
Askio mt. Greece 59 C8
Askira Nigeria 125 I4
Askival hill U.K. 46 F7
Askiz Rus. Fed. 80 E2
Askola Fin. 45 N3
Askol'd, Ostrov i. Rus. Fed. 90 C3
Askot India 96 D3
Askvoll Norway 45 I3
Aslam, Wādī watercourse Saudi Arabia 104 D3
Aslāndūz Iran 100 A2
Aslanköy r. Turkey 108 F1
Aslik r. Belarus 43 K8
Asólközpont Hungary see Mórahalom
Asmar Afgh. 96 A2
Asmar reg. Afgh. 101 G3
Asmar reg. Saudi Arabia 104 C4

▶Asmara Eritrea 121 H6
Capital of Eritrea. Also spelt Āsmera.

Āsmera Eritrea see Asmara
Åsnen l. Sweden 45 K4
As Neves Spain 54 C2
also spelt Nieves
Asoenangka Brazil 199 G4
Aso-Kuju National Park Japan 91 B8
Asola Italy 56 C3
Asopos r. Greece 59 D11
Asopos r. Greece 59 E10
Āsosa Eth. 128 B2
Asoteriba, Jebel mt. Sudan 121 H4
Asotin U.S.A. 180 C3
Aspang-Markt Austria 49 N8
Aspara Kazakh. 103 H4
Asparukhovo Bulg. 58 I6
Aspås Sweden 44 K3
Aspe Spain 55 K6
Åspea Sweden 44 L3
Aspen U.S.A. 180 F5
Aspermont U.S.A. 179 B5

Aspiring, Mount N.Z. 153 C12
also known as Tititea
As Pontes de García Rodríguez Spain 54 D1
also spelt Puentes de García Rodríguez
Aspro, Cape Cyprus 108 D3
also known as Aspron, Cape
Asprokavos, Akra pt Greece 59 B9
Aspromonte, Parco Nazionale dell' nat. park Italy 57 H10
Aspron, Cape Cyprus see Aspro, Cape
Asprovalta Greece 58 E8
Aspur India 96 B5
Asquith Canada 167 J4
Assa Morocco 122 C3
As Sa'an Syria 109 I2
Assab Eritrea 121 I6
also spelt Āseb
Assaba admin. reg. Mauritania 124 C2
Aš Sab'ān Saudi Arabia 104 C2
As Sabkhah Syria 109 K2
As Sabsab well Saudi Arabia 105 E2
Assabu Japan 90 G4
Aş Şafā lava field Syria 109 H4
Aş Şafāqis Tunisia see Sfax
Aş Şāfī Jordan 108 G6
also spelt Safi
As Safirah Syria 109 I1
Aş Şaḥāf Saudi Arabia 105 E2
Aş Şahīf Yemen 104 C5
Aş Şaḥn hills Iraq/Saudi Arabia 109 N7
Assake Uzbek. see Asaka
Assake-Audan, Vpadina depr. Uzbek. 102 D4
'Assal, Lac l. Djibouti see Assal, Lake

▶Assal, Lake Djibouti 128 D2
Lowest point in Africa. Also known as 'Assal, Lac.
africa [landscapes] 112–113

As Salamīyah Saudi Arabia 105 D2
Aş Şālihīyah Syria 109 L3
also known as Dura Europos
As Salmān Iraq 107 F5
As Salṭ Jordan 108 G5
also spelt Salt
Assam state India 97 F4
Assamakka Niger 125 G2
As Samāwah Iraq 107 F5
Aş Şanām reg. Saudi Arabia 105 E3
Assaq watercourse W. Sahara 122 B4
As Sarir reg. Libya 120 D3
Assateague Island National Seashore nature res. U.S.A. 177 J8
As Sawādah reg. Saudi Arabia 105 D3
As Sawdā i. Oman 105 F4
Aş Şawrah Saudi Arabia 104 A2
As Saybīyah waterhole Saudi Arabia 109 M9
Assegaaibos S. Africa 133 I10
Assemini Sardegna Italy 57 B9
Assen Neth. 48 D2
Assen S. Africa 133 L2
Assens Denmark 45 J5
Assesse Belgium 51 L2
As Sidrah Libya 120 C2
Assigny, Lac l. Canada 169 H2
As Sikak Saudi Arabia 105 E2
Assiniboia Canada 167 J5
Assiniboine r. Canada 167 L5
Assiniboine, Mount Canada 167 H5
Assinica, Lac l. Canada 168 F3
Assis Brazil 206 C9
Assisi Italy 56 E5
historically known as Asisium
Assomada Cape Verde 124 [inset]
Assouf Mellene watercourse Alg. 123 F4
Aş Şubayḥīyah Kuwait 107 F5
As Subaykhah Saudi Arabia 104 C4
As Sufāl Yemen 105 E5
Aş Şufayrī well Saudi Arabia 105 D1
As Sukhnah Syria 109 J3
As Sulaymānīyah Iraq 107 F4
As Sulaymānīyah governorate Iraq 107 F4
As Sulaymī Saudi Arabia 104 C2
As Sulayyil Saudi Arabia 105 D3
Aş Şulb reg. Saudi Arabia 105 E2
Aş Şulṭān Libya 120 C2
Aş Şummān plat. Saudi Arabia 105 D2
Aş Şummān plat. Saudi Arabia 105 E3
As Sūq Saudi Arabia 104 C3
As Sūrīyah country Asia see Syria
Aş Şuwar Syria 109 L2
As Suwaydā' Syria 109 H5
As Suwaydā' governorate Syria 109 H5
As Suwayḥ Oman 105 G3
As Suwayq Oman 105 G3
Aş Şuwayrah Iraq 107 F4
As Suwayriqīyah Saudi Arabia 104 C3
As Suways Egypt see Suez
As Suwwādīyah Yemen 105 D5
Asta r. Norway 45 J3
Asta, Cima d' mt. Italy 56 D2
Astacus Turkey see Kocaeli
Astaffort France 50 G8
Astakida i. Greece 59 H13
Astakos Greece 59 C10
Astalu Island Pak. see Astola Island

▶Astana Kazakh. 103 G2
Capital of Kazakhstan. Formerly known as Akmola or Aqmola or Akmolinsk or Tselinograd.

Astaneh Iran 100 B2
Astara Azer. 107 G3
Åsteby Sweden 45 K3
Asterabad Iran see Gorgān
Asti Italy 56 A4
Astica Arg. 204 D3
Astillero Peru 200 C3
Astin Tag mts China see Altun Shan
Astipálaia i. Greece see Astypalaia
Astola Island Pak. 101 E5
also spelt Astalu Island
Aston Bay S. Africa 133 I11
Astor Jammu and Kashmir 96 B2
Astor r. Pak. 101 H3
Astorga Brazil 206 B10
Astorga Spain 54 E2
historically known as Asturica Augusta
Astoria U.S.A. 180 B3
Astra Arg. 205 D7
Astrabad Iran see Gorgān
Astrakhan' Kazakh. see Astrakhanka
Astrakhan' Rus. Fed. 102 B3
Astrakhan' Bazar Azer. see Cälilabad
Astrakhanka Kazakh. 103 G2
also known as Astrakhan'
Astrakhan Oblast admin. div. Rus. Fed. see Astrakhanskaya Oblast'
Astrakhanskaya Oblast' admin. div. Rus. Fed. 102 A3
English form Astrakhan Oblast
Astravyets Belarus 42 G7
Astrida Rwanda see Butare
Astrolabe, Récifs de l' reef New Caledonia 145 F3
Astros Greece 59 D11
Astryna Belarus 42 F8
Astsyer r. Belarus 43 M8
Asturias aut. comm. Spain 54 E1
Asturica Augusta Spain see Astorga
Astypalaia Greece 59 H12
Astypalaia i. Greece 59 H12
also known as Astipálaia; formerly known as Stampalia
Asubulak Kazakh. 88 C1
also spelt Asūbulaq
Asūbulaq Kazakh. see Asubulak
Asunción Bol. 200 D2
Asunción r. Mex. 181 D7
Asuncion i. N. Mariana Is 73 K3

▶Asunción Para. 201 F6
Capital of Paraguay.

Asunción Mita Guat. 185 H6
Asvyeya Belarus 42 J5
Asvyeyskaye, Vozyera l. Belarus 42 J5
Aswa r. Uganda 128 A4
Aswad Oman 105 G2
Aswad, Ar Ra's al pt Saudi Arabia 104 B3
Aswad, Wādī watercourse Oman 105 F3
Aswān Egypt 121 G3
Aswān governorate Egypt 104 A2
Aswān Dam Egypt 121 G3
Asyūṭ Egypt 121 F3
historically known as Lycopolis
Asyūṭ governorate Egypt 106 B6
Ata i. Tonga 145 H4
formerly known as Sola
Atabapo r. Col./Venez. 199 E3
Atabay Kazakh. 103 G4
Atacama admin. reg. Chile 204 C2
Atacama, Desierto de des. Chile see Atacama Desert
Atacama, Salar de salt flat Chile 200 C5

▶Atacama Desert Chile 204 C2
Driest place in the world. Also known as Atacama, Desierto de.
world [climate and weather] 16–17
southamerica [contrasts] 194–195

Atacames Ecuador 198 B4
Ataco Col. 198 C4
Atafaitafa, Djebel mt. Alg. 123 G4
Atafu atoll Tokelau 145 H2
formerly known as Duke of York
Atairtīr el Dahami, Gebel mt. Egypt 108 E9
Atakent Turkey 108 F1
Atakor mts Alg. 123 G5
Atakpamé Togo 125 F5
Atalaia Brazil 202 F4
Atalaia hill Port. 54 C6
Atalaia do Norte Brazil 198 D6
Atalaya Panama 186 C5
Atalaya Madre de Dios Peru 200 C3
Atalaya Ucayali Peru 200 B2
Ataléia Brazil 203 D6
Atamanovka Rus. Fed. 85 G1
Atami Japan 91 F7
Atamisqui Arg. 204 E3
Atammik Greenland 165 N3
Ataniya Turkey see Adana
Atapupu Indon. 75 C5
'Atāqa, Gebel hill Egypt 108 D8
Atâr Mauritania 122 B5
Ataran r. Myanmar 78 B4
Atascadero U.S.A. 182 D6
Atascosa watercourse U.S.A. 179 C6
Atasu Kazakh. 103 G2
Atatan He r. China 88 E4
Atatürk Milli Parkı nat. park Turkey 59 J12
Atauro i. East Timor 75 C5
formerly known as Kambing, Pulau
Atáviros mt. Greece see Attavyros
Atayurt Turkey 108 E1
Atbara Sudan 121 G5
Atbara r. Sudan 121 G5
Atbasar Kazakh. 103 G2
At-Bashy Kyrg. 103 H4
Atchafalaya Bay U.S.A. 175 B6
Atchison U.S.A. 178 D4
Atebubu Ghana 125 E5
Ateca Spain 55 J3
Aten Bol. 200 C3
Atenguillo Mex. 184 D4
Ateransk Kazakh. see Atyrau
Aterno r. Italy 56 F6
Āteshān Iran 100 C3
Āteshkhāneh, Kūh-e hill Afgh. 101 E3
Atessa Italy 56 G6
Atfīh Egypt 108 C8
Ath Belgium 51 J2
also spelt Aath
Athabasca Canada 167 H4
Athabasca r. Canada 167 I3
Athabasca, Lake Canada 167 I3
Athagarh India 95 E1
Athalia U.S.A. 176 C7
Athapapuskow Lake Canada 167 K4
Athboy Rep. of Ireland 47 F10
Athenae Greece see Athens
Athenry Rep. of Ireland 47 D10
Athens Canada 173 R6

▶Athens Greece 59 E11
Capital of Greece. Also known as Athínai; also spelt Athína; historically known as Athenae.

Athens AL U.S.A. 174 C5
Athens GA U.S.A. 175 D5
Athens NY U.S.A. 177 L3
Athens OH U.S.A. 176 C6
Athens TN U.S.A. 174 C5
Athens TX U.S.A. 179 D5
Atherton Australia 149 E3
Athi r. Kenya 128 C5
Athina Greece see Athens
Athínai Greece see Athens
Athi River Kenya 128 C5
Athlone Rep. of Ireland 47 E10
also known as Baile Átha Luain
Athnā', Wādī al watercourse Jordan 109 J5
Athni India 94 B2
Athol N.Z. 153 C13
Athol U.S.A. 177 M3
Athos mt. Greece 59 F8
Ath Tharthār, Wādī r. Iraq 107 E4
Ath Thāyat hills Saudi Arabia 109 K7
Ath Thāyat mt. Saudi Arabia 109 H8
Ath Thumāmī well Saudi Arabia 105 D2
Athy Rep. of Ireland 47 F11
Ati Chad 120 C6
Ati, Jabal mts Libya 120 B4
Atiabad Iran 100 D3
Atiak Uganda 128 B4
Atiamuri N.Z. 152 K6
Ati Ardébé Chad 120 C6
Atibaia Brazil 206 G10
Atico Peru 200 B4
Atiedo Sudan 126 E3
Atikameg Canada 167 H4
Atikameg r. Canada 168 D2
Atik Lake Canada 167 M4
Atikokan Canada 168 B3
Atikonak Lake Canada 169 H2
Atimonan Phil. 74 B3
Atima Italy 56 F7
Atirampattinam India 94 C4
Atitlán Guat. 185 H6
Atitlán, Parque Nacional nat. park Guat. 185 H6
Atjeh admin. dist. Indon. see Aceh
'Atk, Wādī al watercourse Saudi Arabia 105 D2
Atka Rus. Fed. 39 P3
Atkarsk Rus. Fed. 41 H6
Atkri Indon. 75 D3
Atlacomulco Mex. 185 F5
Atlanta S. Africa 133 L2

▶Atlanta GA U.S.A. 175 C5
State capital of Georgia.

Atlanta TX U.S.A. 179 D5
Atlanti Turkey 106 C3
Atlantic IA U.S.A. 178 D3
Atlantic ME U.S.A. 177 Q1
Atlantic City U.S.A. 177 K6
Atlántico dept Col. 198 C2

▶Atlantic Ocean 216 K3
2nd largest ocean in the world.
oceans [features] 210–211

Atlantic Peak U.S.A. 180 E4
Atlantis S. Africa 132 C10
Atlas Bogd mt. Mongolia 84 C3
Atlas Méditerranéen mts Alg. see Atlas Tellien

▶Atlas Mountains Africa 122 D3
africa [landscapes] 112–113

Atlasova, Ostrov i. Rus. Fed. 39 P4
formerly known as Alaid, Ostrov
Atlas Saharien mts Alg. 123 F2
English form Saharan Atlas
Atlas Tellien mts Alg. 123 F2
also known as Atlas Méditerranéen or Tell Atlas
Atlin Canada 166 C3
Atlin Lake Canada 166 C3
Atlin Provincial Park Canada 166 C3
'Atlit Israel 108 F5
Atlixco Mex. 185 F5
Atmakur Andhra Pradesh India 94 C3
Atmakur Andhra Pradesh India 94 C3
Atmore U.S.A. 175 C6
Atna Norway 45 J3
Atner India 96 C5
Atnetye Aboriginal Land res. Australia 148 C4
Atnur India 94 C2
Atō Japan 91 B7
Atocha Bol. 200 D5
Atoka U.S.A. 179 C5
Atome Angola 127 B7
Atonyia W. Sahara 122 C4
Atotonilco el Alto Mex. 185 E4
Atouat mt. Laos 78 D4
Atoyac de Álvarez Mex. 185 E5
Atpadi India 94 B2
Atqan China see Aqqan
Atqasuk U.S.A. 164 D2
Atrai r. India 97 F4
Atrak, Rūd-e r. Iran/Turkm. see Atrek
Ātran r. Sweden 45 K4
Atranh India 96 C4
Atrato r. Col. 198 B2
Atrek r. Iran/Turkm. 100 C2
also known as Atrak, Rūd-e or Etrek
Atri Italy 56 F6
Atropatene country Asia see Azerbaijan
Atrūsh Iraq 109 O1
Atsiki Greece 59 G9
Atsion U.S.A. 177 K6
Atsugi Japan 91 F7
Atsumi Aichi Japan 91 E7
Atsumi Yamagata Japan 90 F5
Atsumi-hantō pen. Japan 91 E7
Atsuta Japan 90 G3
Aṭ Ṭaff reg. U.A.E. 105 F2
Aṭ Ṭafīlah Jordan 108 G7
also spelt Tafila
Aṭ Ṭā'if Saudi Arabia 104 C3
Aṭ Ṭājī Iraq 109 P4
Attalea Turkey see Antalya
Attalia Turkey see Antalya
Attalla U.S.A. 175 C5
Aṭ Ṭallāb oasis Libya 120 D3
At Ta'mīm governorate Iraq 107 E4
At Tamīmī Libya 120 D1
Attapu Laos 79 D5
also spelt Attopeu
Attar, Oued el watercourse Alg. 123 G2
Aṭ Ṭarfāt waterhole Iraq 109 L4
Aṭ Ṭarmīyah Iraq 109 P4
Attavyros mt. Greece 59 I12
also spelt Atáviros
Attawapiskat Canada 168 D2
Attawapiskat r. Canada 168 D2
Attawapiskat Lake Canada 168 C2
Aṭ Ṭawīl mts Saudi Arabia 107 D5
At Taysīyah plat. Saudi Arabia 104 C1
Aṭ Ṭayyibah Jordan 108 G7
Attendorn Germany 48 E4
Attersee l. Austria 49 K8
At Tibnī Syria 109 K2
Attica IN U.S.A. 174 C3
Attica NY U.S.A. 176 G3
Attica OH U.S.A. 176 C4
Attikamagen Lake Canada 169 H2
Attiki admin. reg. Greece 59 E11
At Tīn, Ra's pt Libya 120 D1
Attingal India 94 C4
Attleboro U.S.A. 177 N4
Attock City Pak. 101 H3
Attopeu Laos see Attapu
Attu Greenland 165 N3
Aṭ Ṭubayq reg. Saudi Arabia 107 D5

▶Attu Island U.S.A. 220 F2
Most westerly point of North America.

Aṭ Ṭulayḥī well Saudi Arabia 104 D2
Attunga Australia 147 F2
At Tūnisīyah country Africa see Tunisia
Attur Tamil Nadu India 94 C4
Attur Tamil Nadu India 94 C4
At Turbah Yemen 104 C5
At Turbah Yemen 104 D5
Aṭ Ṭuwayyah well Saudi Arabia 104 C2
Atūd Yemen 105 E5
Atuel r. Arg. 204 D5
Åtvidaberg Sweden 45 K4
Atwari Bangl. 97 F4
Atwater U.S.A. 182 D4
Atwood U.S.A. 178 B4
Atyrau Kazakh. 102 B3
formerly known as Ateransk or Gur'yev
Atyrau Oblast admin. div. Kazakh. see Atyrauskaya Oblast'
Atyraū Oblysy admin. div. Kazakh. see Atyrauskaya Oblast'
Atyrauskaya Oblast' admin. div. Kazakh. 102 B3
English form Atyrau Oblast; also known as Atyraū Oblysy; formerly known as Gur'yevskaya Oblast'
Atzinging Lake Canada 167 L2
Auati-Paraná r. Brazil 199 E5
Aubagne France 51 L9
Aube r. France 51 J4
Aubenas France 51 K8
Aubergenville France 50 H4
Aubigny-sur-Nère France 51 I5
Aubin France 51 I8
Aubinadong r. Canada 168 D4
Aubonne Switz. 51 M6
Auboué France 51 L3
Aubrey Cliffs mts U.S.A. 183 L6
Aubry Lake Canada 164 G3
Auburn r. Australia 149 F5
Auburn AL U.S.A. 175 C5
Auburn CA U.S.A. 182 C3
Auburn IL U.S.A. 174 B4
Auburn IN U.S.A. 174 C3
Auburn MA U.S.A. 177 N3
Auburn ME U.S.A. 177 O1
Auburn MI U.S.A. 173 I7
Auburn NE U.S.A. 178 D3
Auburn NY U.S.A. 177 I3
Auburn WA U.S.A. 180 B3
Auburndale U.S.A. 172 C6
Auburn Range hills Australia 149 F5
Aubusson France 51 I7
Auca Mahuida, Sierra de mt. Arg. 204 C5
Auce Latvia 42 D5
Auch France 50 G9
historically known as Augusta Auscorum or Elimberrum
Auche Myanmar 78 B2
Auchi Nigeria 125 G5

▶Auckland N.Z. 152 I4
5th most populous city in Oceania.
world [cities] 24–25

Auckland admin. reg. N.Z. 152 I4
Auckland Islands N.Z. 220 F9
Aude r. France 51 J9
Auden Canada 168 C3
Audenarde Belgium see Oudenaarde
Audierne, Baie d' b. France 50 B5
Audincourt France 51 M5
Audo Range mts Eth. 128 D3
Audru Estonia 42 F3
Audruicq France 51 I2
Audubon U.S.A. 178 D3
Aue Germany 49 J5
Aue r. Germany 48 G3
Auerbach in der Oberpfalz Germany 48 I6
Auersberg mt. Germany 51 S2
Augathella Australia 149 E5
Augrabies S. Africa 132 E5
Augrabies Falls S. Africa 132 E5
Augrabies Falls National Park S. Africa 132 E5
Au Gres U.S.A. 173 J6
Augsburg Germany 48 H7
historically known as Augusta Vindelicorum
Augsburg-Westliche Wälder park Germany 48 H7
Augšligatne Latvia 42 G4
Augšzemes Augstiene hills Latvia 42 H5
Augusta Australia 151 A7
Augusta Sicilia Italy 57 H11
Augusta AR U.S.A. 174 B5
Augusta GA U.S.A. 175 D5
Augusta KS U.S.A. 178 C4
Augusta KY U.S.A. 176 A7

▶Augusta ME U.S.A. 177 P1
State capital of Maine.

Augusta WI U.S.A. 172 B6
Augusta WV U.S.A. 176 G6
Augusta, Golfo di b. Sicilia Italy 57 H11
Augusta Auscorum France see Auch
Augusta Taurinorum Italy see Turin
Augusta Treverorum Germany see Trier
Augusta Victoria Chile 200 C6
Augusta Vindelicorum Germany see Augsburg
Augustin Cadazzi Col. 198 C2
Augustine Island U.S.A. 164 D4
Augustines, Lac des l. Canada 173 R3
Augusto Cardosa Moz. see Metangula
Augusto de Lima Brazil 207 I5
Augustodunum France see Autun
Augusto Severo Brazil 202 E3
Augustów Poland 49 T2
Augustowski, Kanał canal Poland 49 U2
Augustus, Mount Australia 151 B5
Augustus Island Australia 150 D2
Aukan Island Eritrea 104 C5
Aukštaitijos nacionalinis parkas nat. park Lith. 42 H6
Aukštelkai Lith. 42 E6
Aukštelkė Lith. 42 E6
Auktsjaur Sweden 44 L2
Aulavik National Park Canada 165 H2
Auld, Lake salt flat Australia 150 C4
Auliye Ata Kazakh. see Taraz
Aulla Italy 56 B4
Aulneau Peninsula Canada 167 M5
Aulnoye-Aymeries France 51 J2
Aulon Albania see Vlorë
Ault France 50 H3
Aumale France 50 H3
Aumance r. France 51 I6
Auminzatau, Gory hills Uzbek. 103 E4
also known as Owminzatow Toghi
Auna Nigeria 125 G4
Aungban Myanmar 78 B3
Auning Denmark 45 J4
Auob watercourse Namibia/S. Africa 132 E3
Aupaluk Canada 169 G1
formerly known as Hopes Advance Bay
Aur i. Malaysia 76 D2
Aura Fin. 45 M3
Aurad India 94 C2
Auraiya India 96 C4
Aurajoki r. Fin. 42 D1
Aurangabad Bihar India 97 E4
Aurangabad Maharashtra India 94 B2
Auray France 50 D5
Aure Norway 44 J3
Aurich Germany 48 E2
Auriflama Brazil 206 C7
Aurigny i. Channel Is see Alderney
Aurilândia Brazil 206 C3
Aurillac France 51 I8
Aurino r. Italy 56 D2
Auron r. France 51 I5
Auronzo di Cadore Italy 56 E2
Aurora Phil. 74 B5
Aurora S. Africa 132 C9
Aurora CO U.S.A. 180 F5
Aurora IL U.S.A. 174 B3
Aurora IN U.S.A. 176 A6
Aurora MN U.S.A. 172 A3
Aurora MO U.S.A. 178 D4
Aurora NE U.S.A. 178 C3
Aurora OH U.S.A. 176 D4
Aurora UT U.S.A. 183 M3
Aurora Island Vanuatu see Maéwo
Aurukun Australia 149 D2
Aurukun Aboriginal Reserve Australia 149 D2
Auronci, Monti mts Italy 56 F7
Aus Namibia 130 C5
Ausa India 94 C2
Au Sable U.S.A. 173 J6
Au Sable r. U.S.A. 173 J6
Ausable r. U.S.A. 177 L1
Ausable Forks U.S.A. 177 L1
Au Sable Point MI U.S.A. 172 G4
Au Sable Point MI U.S.A. 173 J6
Auschwitz Poland see Oświęcim
Ausculum Italy see Ascoli Satriano
Ausculum Apulum Italy see Ascoli Satriano
Austafjord Norway 44 J2
Aust-Agder county Norway 45 J4
Austari-Jökulsá r. Iceland 44 [inset] C2
Austertana Norway 44 O1
Austin MN U.S.A. 174 A3
Austin NV U.S.A. 183 G2

▶Austin TX U.S.A. 179 C6
State capital of Texas.

Austin, Lake salt flat Australia 151 B5
Austral Downs Australia 148 C4
Australes, Îles is Fr. Polynesia see Tubuai Islands

▶Australia country Oceania 144 A4
Largest country in Oceania and 6th in the world. Most populous country in Oceania. Historically known as New Holland.
world [countries] 10–11
oceania [countries] 138–139

Australian-Antarctic Basin sea feature Indian Ocean 219 N9
Australian Antarctic Territory Antarctica 223 J2
Australian Capital Territory admin. div. Australia 147 F3
Australind Australia 151 A7
▶Austria country Europe 49 J8
known as Österreich in German
europe [countries] 32–35
Austrumkursas Augstiene hills Latvia 42 D5

Austurland constituency Iceland 44 [inset] D2
Austvågøy i. Norway 44 K1
Autazes Brazil 199 G5
Auterive France 50 H9
Autesiodorum France see Auxerre
Authie r. France 51 H2
Authier Canada 173 O2
Autlán Mex. 184 D5
Autti Fin. 44 N2
Autun France 51 K6
historically known as Augustodunum
Auvergne admin. reg. France 51 J7
Auvergne, Monts d' mts France 51 I7
Auvézère r. France 50 G7
Auxerre France 51 J5
historically known as Autesiodorum
Auxonne France 51 L5
Auyan Tepuí plat. Venez. 199 F3
Auyuittuq National Park Reserve Canada 165 M3
Auzoue r. France 50 G8
Auzzov Kazakh. 103 J2
Ava Myanmar 78 A3
Ava MO U.S.A. 178 D4
Ava NY U.S.A. 177 J2
Avaí Brazil 206 D9
Availles-Limouzine France 50 G6
Avallon France 51 J5
Avalon U.S.A. 182 F8
Avalon Peninsula Canada 169 K4
Avalon Wilderness nature res. Canada 169 K4
Avān Iran 100 A2
Avanashi India 94 C4
Avanganna mt. Guyana 199 G3
Avanigadda India 94 D2
Avanos Turkey 106 C3
Avarau atoll Cook Is see Palmerston
Avaré Brazil 206 E10
Avaricum France see Bourges
Avarskoye Koysu r. Rus. Fed. 102 A4

▶Avarua Cook Is 221 H7
Capital of the Cook Islands, on Rarotonga island.

Avaträsk Sweden 44 L2
Avawatz Mountains U.S.A. 183 H6
Ave r. Port. 54 C3
Aveiro Brazil 199 H5
Aveiro Port. 54 C4
Aveiro admin. dist. Port. 54 C4
Aveiro, Ria de est. Port. 54 C4
Āvej Iran 100 B3
Avellaneda Arg. 204 F3
Avellino Italy 56 G8
historically known as Abellinum
Avenal U.S.A. 182 D5
Avenio France see Avignon
Averøya i. Norway 44 I3
Aversa Italy 56 G8
Aves i. West Indies 187 H4
Aves is West Indies see Las Aves, Islas
Avesnes-sur-Helpe France 51 J2
Avesta Sweden 45 L3
Aveyron r. France 51 H8
▶Avezzano Italy 56 F6
europe [environments] 36–37
Avgan Geçidi pass Turkey 108 E1
Avgo i. Kythira Greece 59 E12
Avgo i. Greece 59 G13
Aviá Terai Arg. 204 E2
Aviemore U.K. 46 I6
Aviemore, Lake N.Z. 153 E12
Avigliano Italy 57 H8
Avignon France 51 K9
historically known as Avenio
Ávila Spain 54 G4
Ávila, Sierra de mts Spain 54 F4
Avilés Spain 54 F1
Aviño Spain 54 C1
Avinurme Estonia 42 H3
Avión mt. Spain 54 C2
Avis Port. 54 D5
Avisio r. Italy 56 D2
Avize France 51 K4
Avlama Dağı mt. Turkey 108 E1
Avlemonas Greece 59 E12
Avlida Greece 59 E10
Avlona Albania see Vlorë
Avlum Denmark 45 J4
Avnyugskiy Rus. Fed. 40 H3
Avoca Australia 147 D4
Avoca r. Australia 147 D3
Avoca S. Africa 133 P2
Avoca IA U.S.A. 178 D3
Avoca NY U.S.A. 176 H3
Avola Sicilia Italy 57 H12
Avon r. Australia 151 B6
Avon r. England U.K. 47 J11
Avon r. England U.K. 47 J12
Avon r. England U.K. 47 K13
Avon IL U.S.A. 172 C10
Avon NY U.S.A. 176 H3
Avondale U.S.A. 183 L8
Avon Downs Australia 149 E4
Avonmore r. Rep. of Ireland 47 F11
Avon Park U.S.A. 175 D7
Avontuur S. Africa 132 H10
Avoti Latvia 42 F5
Avram Iancu Romania 58 C2
Avranches France 50 E4
Avre r. France 51 I3
Avrig Romania 58 F3
Avrillé France 50 F5
Avsuyu Turkey 109 H1
Avuavu Solomon Is 145 F2
Avveel Fin. see Ivalo
Avvil Fin. see Ivalo
A'waj r. Syria 108 G4
Awaji-shima i. Japan 91 D7
Awakeri N.Z. 152 K6
Awakino N.Z. 152 I6
Awālī Bahrain 105 E2
Awang Indon. 77 G5
Awanui N.Z. 152 H3
Awarawar, Tanjung pt Indon. 77 F4
Āwarē Eth. 128 E2
'Awārid, Wādī al watercourse Syria 109 K3
Awarua Point N.Z. 153 C12
Āwasa Eth. 128 C3
Āwash Eth. 128 D2
Āwash r. Eth. 128 D2
Awa-shima i. Japan 90 F5
Āwash National Park Eth. 128 C2
Āwash West Wildlife Reserve nature res. Eth. 128 C2
Awat China 88 C3
Āwatā Shet' r. Eth. 128 C3
Awatere r. N.Z. 153 I9
Awbārī Libya 120 B3
Awd reg. Yemen 104 D5
'Awdah well Saudi Arabia 105 E3
'Awdah, Hawr al imp. l. Iraq 107 F5
Aw Dheegle Somalia 128 E4
Awdiinle Somalia 128 D4
Awe, Loch l. U.K. 46 G7
Aweil Sudan 126 E2
Awgu Nigeria 125 G5
Awka Nigeria 125 G5
Awlitis watercourse W. Sahara 122 B4
Awry Lake Canada 167 H2
Awserd W. Sahara 122 B5
Awu vol. Indon. 75 C2
Axe r. U.K. 47 I13
Axel Heiberg Glacier Antarctica 223 N1
Axel Heiberg Island Canada 165 J2
Axente Sever Romania 58 F2
Axim Ghana 125 E5
Axinim Brazil 199 G6

Axioma Brazil **199** E6
Axios r. Greece **58** D8
Axmars naturreservat *nature res.* Sweden **45** L3
Axum Eth. *see* **Āksum**
Ay Kazakh. **103** J3
Ayabe Japan **91** D7
Ayachi, Jbel *mt.* Morocco **122** D2
Ayacucho Arg. **204** F5
Ayacucho Peru **200** B3
Ayacucho *dept* Peru **200** B3
Ayadaw Myanmar **78** A3
Ayagoz Kazakh. **103** J3
also spelt Ayaköz; *formerly spelt* Ayaguz
Ayagoz *watercourse* Kazakh. **103** J3
Ayaguz Kazakh. *see* **Ayagoz**
Ayakagytma, Vpadina *depr.* Uzbek. **103** F4
Ayakkuduk Uzbek. **103** F4
also spelt Oyoqquduq
Ayakkum Hu *salt l.* China **89** E4
Ayaköz Kazakh. *see* **Ayagoz**
Ayamé Côte d'Ivoire **124** E5
Ayamiken Equat. Guinea **125** H6
Ayamonte Spain **54** D7
Ayan Rus. Fed. **39** N4
Ayancık Turkey **106** C2
Ayang N. Korea **83** B5
Ayangba Nigeria **125** G5
Ayanka Rus. Fed. **39** Q3
Ayapel, Serranía de *mts* Col. **198** C3
Ayaş Turkey **106** C2
Ayaviri Peru **200** C3
Ayayei Eth. **128** C1
Āybak Afgh. **101** G2
Aydabul Kazakh. **103** G1
Aydar *r.* Ukr. **41** F6
Aydarkul', Ozero *l.* Uzbek. **103** F4
Aydarly Kazakh. **103** F3
'Aydim, Wādī *r.* Oman **105** F4
Aydın Turkey **106** A3
Aydın *prov.* Turkey **59** J11
Aydıncık Turkey **108** E1
also known as Gilindire
Aydın Dağları *mts* Turkey **106** A3
Aydingkol Hu *marsh* China **88** E3
Ayeat, Gora *hill* Kazakh. **103** G3
Ayedo *mt.* Spain **55** I2
Āyelu Terara *vol.* Eth. **128** D2
Ayem Gabon **126** A5
Ayer U.S.A. **177** N3
Ayers Rock *hill* Australia *see* **Uluru**
Ayeyarwady *r.* Myanmar *see* **Irrawaddy**
Aygyrzhal Kazakh. **103** J2
Ayiá Greece *see* **Agia**
Ayiásos Greece *see* **Agiasos**
Ayila Ri'gyü *mts* China **89** B5
Áyios Dhimítrios Greece *see* **Agios Dimitrios**
Áyios Dhimítrios, Ákra *pt* Greece *see* **Agios Dimitrios, Akra**
Áyios Evstrátios *i.* Greece *see* **Agios Efstratios**
Áyios Nikólaos Greece *see* **Agios Nikolaos**
Áyios Yeóryios *i.* Greece *see* **Agios Georgios**
Ayke, Ozero *l.* Kazakh. **103** E2
Āykel Eth. **128** C1
Aykhal Rus. Fed. **39** L3
Aykino Rus. Fed. **40** I3
Aykol China **88** C3
Aylesbury U.K. **47** L12
Aylett U.S.A. **177** H8
Ayllón, Sierra de *mts* Spain **55** H3
Aylmer Canada **173** M2
Aylmer Lake Canada **167** I1
Aymagambetov Kazakh. **103** E2
'Ayn, Ra's al *c.* Oman **105** G4
'Ayn, Wādī al *watercourse* Oman **105** F3
Ayna Peru **200** B3
Aynabulak Kazakh. **103** I3
'Ayn al 'Abd Libya **120** C2
'Ayn al 'Abd *well* Saudi Arabia **105** E1
'Ayn al Bayḍā' *well* Syria **109** I3
'Ayn al Ghazāl *spring* Libya **120** E4
'Ayn al Mazr'ah *well* Saudi Arabia **104** B2
'Ayn Ba Ma'bad Yemen **105** D5
'Ayn Dibis Iraq **109** O2
'Ayn Hindī *oasis* Oman **105** G4
Aynī Tajik. **101** G2
'Aynīn *well* Saudi Arabia **104** C3
'Ayn Sifnī Iraq **109** O1
'Ayn Umm al Banāt *waterhole* Iraq **109** N3
'Ayn Zuwayyah *spring* Libya **120** E4
Ayon, Ostrov *i.* Rus. Fed. **39** Q3
Ayoquezco Mex. **185** F5
Ayora Spain **55** J5
Ayorou Niger **125** F3
Ayos Cameroon **125** I6
'Ayoûn 'Abd el Mâlek *well* Mauritania **122** D4
'Ayoûn el 'Atroûs Mauritania **124** C2
Ayr Australia **149** E3
Ayr U.K. **46** H8
Ayr *r.* U.K. **46** H8
Ayrag Nuur *salt l.* Mongolia **84** B1
Ayrancı Turkey **106** C3
Ayrancılar Turkey **59** I10
Ayre, Point of Isle of Man **47** H9
Aysarinskoye Kazakh. *see* **Zaozernyy**
Aysary Kazakh. *see* **Zaozernyy**
Āysha Eth. **128** D2
Ayteke Bi Kazakh. **103** E3
formerly known as Novokazalinsk *or* Zhangaqazaly
Aytos Bulg. **58** I6
Aytoska Reka *r.* Bulg. **58** I6
Aytré France **50** E6
Ayun Oman **105** F4
Ayutthia Thai. *see* **Ayutthaya**
Ayutla *Guerrero* Mex. **185** F5
Ayutla *Jalisco* Mex. **184** D4
Ayutthaya Thai. **79** C5
also known as Krungkao; *also spelt* Ayuthia; *long form* Phra Nakhon Si Ayutthaya
Ayvacık Turkey **106** A3
Ayvadzh Tajik. *see* **Aivadzh**
Ayvalı Turkey **107** D3
Ayvalık Turkey **106** A3
Aywat al Manāhīl, Wādī *r.* Yemen **105** E4
Aywat aş Şay'ar, Wādī *r.* Yemen **105** E4
Azacualpa Hond. **186** B4
Azak Rus. Fed. *see* **Azov**
Azambuja Port. **54** C5
Azamgarh India **97** D4
Azangaro Peru **200** C3
Azanja *Srbija* Yugo. **58** B4
Azaouâd *reg.* Mali **124** E2
Azaouagh, Vallée de *watercourse* Mali/Niger **125** F2
Azapa Chile **200** C4
Azar *watercourse* Niger **125** G2
Azaran Iran *see* **Hashtrud**
Azärbayjan *country* Asia *see* **Azerbaijan**
Āzarbāyjān-e Gharbī *prov.* Iran **100** A2
Āzarbāyjān-e Sharqī *prov.* Iran **100** A2
Azare Nigeria **125** H4
Azarychy Belarus **43** K9
Azatskoye, Ozero *l.* Rus. Fed. **43** S2
A'zāz Syria **109** I1
Azazga Alg. **55** P8
Azbine *mts* Niger *see* **L'Aïr, Massif de**
Azdavay Turkey **106** C2
Azélik *well* Niger **125** H2
Azemmour Morocco **122** C2
▶**Azerbaijan** *country* Asia **107** F2
spelt Azärbaycan *in Azeri; formerly known as* Azerbaydzhanskaya S.S.R.; *historically known as* Atropatene
asia [countries] ▶▶ 64–67
Azerbaydzhanskaya S.S.R. *country* Asia *see* **Azerbaijan**
Azergues *r.* France **51** K7
Āzezo Eth. **128** C1
Azhu-Tayga, Gora *mt.* Rus. Fed. **88** E1
Azilal Morocco **122** D2
Azilda Canada **173** L4
Azingo Gabon **126** A5
'Azīzābād Iran **100** D4
Azizbekov Armenia *see* **Vayk'**
Aziziye Turkey *see* **Pınarbaşı**
Azlam, Wādī *watercourse* Saudi Arabia **104** A2
Aznakayevo Rus. Fed. **40** J5
Aznalcóllar Spain **54** E7
Azogues Ecuador **198** B5
Azopol'ye Rus. Fed. **40** H2

▶**Azores** *terr.* N. Atlantic Ocean **216** M3
Autonomous Region of Portugal. Long form Arquipélago dos Açores.
europe [countries] ▶▶ 32–35

Azotus Israel *see* **Ashdod**
Azov Rus. Fed. **41** F7
historically known as Azak
Azov, Sea of Rus. Fed./Ukr. **41** F7
also known as Azovs'ke More *or* Azovskoye More
Azovo-Sivashskiy Zapovidnyk *nature res.* Ukr. **41** E7
Azovs'ke More *sea* Rus. Fed./Ukr. *see* **Azov, Sea of**
Azovskoye More *sea* Rus. Fed./Ukr. *see* **Azov, Sea of**
Azpeitia Spain **55** I1
Azraq, Bahr el *r.* Eth./Sudan **104** A5 *see* **Blue Nile**
Azrou Morocco **122** D2
Azrou, Oued *watercourse* Alg. **123** G5
Aztec U.S.A. **181** E5
Azua Dom. Rep. **187** F3
Azuaga Spain **54** F6
Azuay *prov.* Ecuador **198** B5
Azúcar *r.* Chile **204** C2
Azuchi-Ō-shima *i.* Japan **91** A8
Azuer *r.* Spain **55** H5
Azuero, Península de *pen.* Panama **186** C6
Azufre, Cerro del *mt.* Chile **204** C2
Azul Arg. **204** F5
Azul *r.* Mex. **185** H5
also known as Blue Creek
Azul, Cordillera *mts* Peru **200** B2
Azul, Serra *hills* Brazil **201** G3
Azum, Wadi *watercourse* Sudan **120** D6
Azuma-san *vol.* Japan **90** G6
Azurduy Bol. **201** D5
Azyory Belarus **42** F8
'Azza Gaza *see* **Gaza**
Az Zabadānī Syria **108** H4
Az Zabīrah *well* Saudi Arabia **104** C2
Az Zafīrī *reg.* Iraq **107** E5
Az Zāhirah *admin. reg.* Oman **105** G3
Az Zahrān Saudi Arabia *see* **Dhahran**
Az Zallāf, Wādī *watercourse* Libya **120** B3
Az Zallāq Bahrain **105** E2
Azzano Decimo Italy **56** E3
Az Zaqāzīq Egypt *see* **Zagazig**
Az Zarbah Syria **109** H1
Az Zarqā' Jordan **108** H5
also spelt Zarqā'
Az Zāwiyah Libya **120** B1
Az Zaydīyah Yemen **104** C5
Azzeffāl *hills* Mauritania/W. Sahara **122** B5
Azzel Matti, Sebkha *salt pan* Alg. **123** F4
Az Zilfī Saudi Arabia **104** D2
Az Zintān Libya **120** B2
Az Zubayr Iraq **107** F5
Az Zuhrah Yemen **104** C5
Az Zuqur *i.* Yemen **104** C5
English form Az Zuqur Island
Az Zuqurt *oasis* Saudi Arabia **105** E4
Az Zuwaytīnah Libya **120** D2

↓ B

Baa Indon. **75** B5
Baai *r.* Indon. **77** G2
Ba'albek Lebanon **108** H3
Ba'al Hazor *mt.* West Bank **108** G6
Baardheere Somalia **128** D4
formerly spelt Bardera
Bab India **96** C4
Baba *mt.* Bulg. **58** E6
Bābā, Kūh-e *mts* Afgh. **101** G3
Baba Burnu *pt* Turkey **59** H9
Babaçulândia Brazil **202** C3
Babadağ *mt.* Azer. **107** G2
Babadag Romania **58** J4
Babadağ Turkey **59** J11
Baba Dağ *mt.* Turkey **59** K12
Babadagului, Podişul *plat.* Romania **58** J4
Babadaykhan *Akhal'skaya Oblast'* Turkm. **102** E5
formerly known as Kirovsk
Babadaykhan *Akhal'skaya Oblast'* Turkm. **102** E5
formerly known as Kommuna
Babadurmaz Turkm. **102** D5
Babaeski Turkey **106** A2
Babahoyo Ecuador **198** B5
Babai *r.* Nepal **97** D3
Babai Gaxun China **84** E3
Babak Phil. **74** C5
Bābā Kalān Iran **100** B4
Babakourimigana *well* Niger **125** H3
Bāb al Mandab *strait* Africa/Asia **121** I6
Bab al Mandab, Cape Yemen *see* **Bāb al Mandab, Ra's**
Bāb al Mandab, Ra's *c.* Yemen **104** C5
English form Bab al Mandab, Cape
Babana Indon. **75** A3
Babanango S. Africa **133** P5
Babanki Cameroon **125** H5
Babanusa Sudan **126** E2
Babao China *see* **Qilian**
Babao China **86** C4
Babar *i.* Indon. **75** D4
Babar, Kepulauan *is* Indon. **75** D4
Babat Indon. **77** F4
Babati Tanz. **129** B6
Babau Indon. **75** B5
Babayevo Rus. Fed. **43** Q2
Babayurt Rus. Fed. **102** A4
Babeldaob *i.* Palau **73** H5
also spelt Babelthuap
Babelegi S. Africa **133** M2
Babelthuap *i.* Palau *see* **Babeldaob**
Băbeni Romania **58** F4
Baberu India **96** D4
Bab Ezzouar Alg. **55** O8
Babi, Pulau *i.* Indon. **76** B2
Babia Góra *mt.* Poland **49** Q6
Babian Jiang *r.* China **86** B4
Bābil Egypt **108** C7
Bābil *governorate* Iraq **107** F4
formerly known as Al Ḥillah
Babile Eth. **128** D2
Babimost Poland **49** M3
Babinavichy Belarus **43** L7
Babinda Australia **149** E3
Babine *r.* Canada **166** E4
Babine Lake Canada **166** E4
Babine Range *mts* Canada **166** E4
Babinga Dem. Rep. Congo **126** C5
Babītes ezers *l.* Latvia **42** E5
Babo Indon. **73** H7
Bābol Iran **100** C2
Bābol Sar Iran **100** C2
Baboná *r.* Brazil **199** E6
Babongo Cameroon **125** I5
Baboon Point S. Africa **132** C9
Baboua Cent. Afr. Rep. **126** B3
Babruysk Belarus **43** K8
also spelt Bobruysk
Babstovo Rus. Fed. **82** D2
Babtai Lith. **42** E6
Bab Taza Morocco **54** F9
Babu China *see* **Hezhou**
Babuna Planina *mts* Macedonia **58** C7
Babusar Pass Pak. **101** H3
Babushkin Rus. Fed. **85** E1
formerly known as Mysovsk
Babušnica *Srbija* Yugo. **58** D5
Babuyan Phil. **74** A4
Babuyan *i.* Phil. **74** B2
Babuyan Channel Phil. **74** B2
Babuyan Islands Phil. **74** B2
Babylon *tourist site* Iraq **107** F4
Babynino Rus. Fed. **43** Q7
Bač *Vojvodina, Srbija* Yugo. **58** A3
Bacaadweyn Somalia **128** E3
Bacaba *r.* Brazil **198** D5
Bacabáchi Mex. **184** C3
Bacabal *Maranhão* Brazil **202** C3
Bacabal *Pará* Brazil **199** G6
Bacajá *r.* Brazil **199** I5
Bacakliyayla Tepesi *mt.* Turkey **106** B2
Bacalar Mex. **185** H5
Bacalar Chico, Boca *sea chan.* Mex. **185** I5
Bacan *i.* Indon. **75** C3
Bacanora Mex. **184** C2
Bacarra Phil. **74** B2
Bacău Romania **58** H2
Baccarat France **51** M4
Baccaro Point Canada **169** H5
Bacchiglione *r.* Italy **56** E3
Băc Giang Vietnam **78** D3
Bachaquero Venez. **198** D2
Bacheykava Belarus **43** K6
Bach Ice Shelf Antarctica **222** T2
Bachiniva Mex. **181** F7
Bach Long Vi, Đao *i.* Vietnam **78** D3
Bachu China **88** B4
formerly known as Maralbashi *or* Maralwexi
Bachuma Eth. **128** B3
Back *r.* Australia **149** D3
Back *r.* Canada **167** M1
Bačka *reg.* Hungary/Yugo. **58** A2
Bačka Palanka *Vojvodina, Srbija* Yugo. **58** A3
Bačka Topola *Vojvodina, Srbija* Yugo. **58** A3
Backbone Mountain U.S.A. **176** F6
Backbone Ranges *mts* Canada **166** D2
Backe Sweden **44** L3
Bäckefors Sweden **45** K4
Bäckhammar Sweden **45** K4
Bački Petrovac *Vojvodina, Srbija* Yugo. **58** A3
Backnang Germany **48** G7
Bačko Gradište *Vojvodina, Srbija* Yugo. **58** B3
Backstairs Passage Australia **146** C3
Bac Lac Vietnam **78** D3
Bac Liêu Vietnam **79** D6
Băc Ninh Vietnam **78** D3
Bacnotan Phil. **74** B2
Baco, Mount Phil. **74** B3
Bacoachi Mex. **184** C2
Bacoachi *watercourse* Mex. **181** E7
Bacobampo Mex. **184** C3
Bacolod Phil. **74** B4
Bắc Quang Vietnam **78** D3
Bacqueville-en-Caux France **50** G3
Bácsalmás Hungary **49** Q9
Bactra Afgh. *see* **Balkh**
Bacubirito Mex. **184** D3
Baculin Bay Phil. **74** C5
Baculin Point Phil. **74** C4
Bacuri Brazil **202** C2
Bad *r.* U.S.A. **178** B2
Bada China *see* **Xilin**
Bada *mt.* Eth. **128** C3
Bada *i.* Myanmar **79** B6
Badagara India **94** B4
Badain Jaran Shamo *des.* China **84** D3
Badajós *Amazonas* Brazil **199** F5
Badajós *Pará* Brazil **202** C2
Badajós, Lago *l.* Brazil **199** F5
Badajoz Spain **54** E6
Badakhshān *prov.* Afgh. **101** G2
Badakhshan *aut. rep.* Tajik. *see* **Kŭhistoni Badakhshon**
Badakhshoni Kŭhī *aut. rep.* Tajik. *see* **Kŭhistoni Badakhshon**
Badami India **94** B3
Badanah Saudi Arabia **107** E5
Badaojiang China *see* **Baishan**
Badarinath *mts* India *see* **Badrinath Peaks**
Badarīyāt, Ḥazm al *plat.* Saudi Arabia **109** L7
Badarpur India **97** G4
Badas, Kepulauan *is* Indon. **77** D2
Bad Aussee Austria **49** K8
Bad Axe U.S.A. **173** K7
Bad Bergzabern Germany **48** E6
Bad Berka Germany **48** I5
Bad Berleburg Germany **48** F4
Bad Bevensen Germany **48** H2
Baddeck Canada **169** I4
Badderen Norway **44** M1
Baddo *r.* Pak. **101** F4
Bad Doberan Germany **48** I1
Badéguichéri Niger **125** G3
Bademli Turkey *see* **Aladağ**
Bademli Geçidi *pass* Turkey **106** B3
Bad Ems Germany **48** E5
Baden Austria **49** N7
Baden Switz. **51** O5
Baden-Baden Germany **48** F7
Baden-Württemberg *land* Germany **48** F7
Badér Niger **125** G3
Badgastein Austria **49** K8
Badger Canada **169** K3
Bādghīs *prov.* Afgh. **101** E3
Bad Harzburg Germany **48** H4
Bad Hersfeld Germany **48** G5
Bad Hofgastein Austria **49** K8
Bad Homburg vor der Höhe Germany **48** F5
Badi *r.* Guinea **124** B4
Badia Polesine Italy **56** D3
Badigeru Swamp Sudan **128** B3
Badin Pak. **101** G5
Badinko, Réserve du *nature res.* Mali **124** C3
Badiraguato Mex. **184** D3
Bad Ischl Austria **49** K8
Bādiyat ash Shām *des.* Asia *see* **Syrian Desert**
Badje-Sohppar Sweden *see* **Övre Soppero**
Badkhyzskiy Zapovednik *nature res.* Turkm. **101** E3
Bad Kissingen Germany **48** H5
Bad Königsdorff Poland *see* **Jastrzębie-Zdrój**
Bad Kreuznach Germany **48** E6
Bad Krozingen Germany **48** E8
Badlands *reg. ND* U.S.A. **178** B2
Badlands *reg. SD* U.S.A. **178** B3
Badlands National Park U.S.A. **178** B3
Bad Langensalza Germany **48** H4
Bad Lauterberg im Harz Germany **48** H4
Bad Liebenwerda Germany **49** K4
Bad Lippspringe Germany **48** F4
Bad Mergentheim Germany **48** G6
Bad Nauheim Germany **48** F5
Badnawar India **96** B5
Bad Neuenahr-Ahrweiler Germany **48** E5
Bad Neustadt an der Saale Germany **48** H5
Bad Oldesloe Germany **48** H2
Badong China **87** D2
also known as Xinling
Ba Đông Vietnam **79** D6
Badou Togo **125** F5
Badplaas S. Africa **133** O2
Bad Pyrmont Germany **48** G4
Bad Ragaz Switz. **51** P5
Badr City Egypt **108** C7
Bad Reichenhall Germany **49** J8
Badr Ḥunayn Saudi Arabia **104** B3
Badrinath Peaks India **96** C3
also known as Badarinath *or* Chaukhamba
Bad River Indian Reservation *res.* U.S.A. **172** C4
Bad Säckingen Germany **48** E8
Bad Salzuflen Germany **48** F3
Bad Salzungen Germany **48** H5
Bad Schwartau Germany **48** H2
Bad Segeberg Germany **48** H2
Badu China **87** F3
Badu Island Australia **73** J9
Badulla Sri Lanka **94** D5
Badvel India **94** C3
Bad Waldsee Germany **48** G8
Bad Windsheim Germany **48** H6
Badzhal'skiy Khrebet *mts* Rus. Fed. **82** D2
Bad Zwischenahn Germany **48** F2
Bae Colwyn U.K. *see* **Colwyn Bay**
Bæir Iceland **44** [inset] B2
Baena Spain **54** G7
Baeza Ecuador **198** B5
Baeza Spain **55** H7
Bafang Cameroon **125** H5
Bafatá Guinea-Bissau **124** B3
Baffa Pak. **101** H3
Baffin Bay *sea* Canada/Greenland **165** M2

▶**Baffin Island** Canada **165** L2
2nd largest island in North America and 5th in the world.
northamerica [landscapes] ▶▶ 156–157

Bafia Cameroon **125** H5
Bafilo Togo **125** F4
Bafing *r.* Guinea/Mali **124** C3
Bafing, Réserve du *nature res.* Mali **124** C3
Bafing Makana Mali **124** C3
Bafoulabé Mali **124** C3
Bafoussam Cameroon **125** H5
Bāfq Iran **100** C4
Bafra Turkey **106** C2
Bafra Burnu *pt* Turkey **106** C2
Bāft Iran **100** D4
Bafwasende Dem. Rep. Congo **126** E4
Baga Nigeria **125** I3
Bagà Spain **55** M2
Baga Bogd Uul *mts* Mongolia **84** D2
Bagac Bay Phil. **74** B3
Bagaha India **97** E4
Bagahak *hill Sabah* Malaysia **77** G1
Bagalkot India **94** B2
Bagamoyo Tanz. **129** C6
Bagan China **86** A1
Bagan Datoh Malaysia *see* **Bagan Datuk**
Bagan Datuk Malaysia **76** C2
formerly known as Bagan Datoh
Baganga Phil. **74** C5
Bagani Namibia **130** D3
Baganian Peninsula Phil. **74** B5
Bagansiapiapi Indon. **76** C2
Bagar *watercourse* Kazakh. **88** C1
Bağarası Turkey **59** I11
Bagaré *well* Niger **125** G3
Bagaroua Niger **125** G3
Bagata Dem. Rep. Congo **126** C5
Bagazán Peru **198** C6
Bagdad Sudan **121** F6
Bagdad U.S.A. **183** K7
Bagé Brazil **204** G3
Bagepalli India **94** C3
Bagerhat Bangl. *see* **Bagherhat**
Bages et de Sigean, Étang de *lag.* France **51** I9
Bageshwar India **96** C3
Bagevadi India **94** C2
Baggå Sweden **45** K4
Baggs U.S.A. **180** F4
Bagh India **96** B5
Baghak Pak. **101** F4
Baghbaghū Iran **101** E2

▶**Baghdād** Iraq **107** F4
Capital of Iraq. English form Baghdad.

Baghdad Iraq *see* **Baghdād**
Bāgh-e Bābū'īyeh Iran **100** D4
Bagherhat Bangl. **97** F5
also spelt Bagerhat
Bagheria *Sicilia* Italy **57** F10
Bāghīn Iran **100** D4
Baghlān Afgh. **101** G2
Baghlān *prov.* Afgh. **101** G3
Baghlī Da *hill* Iran **100** A2
Baginda, Tanjung *pt* Indon. **77** D3
Bağırsak Deresi *r.* Syria/Turkey *see* **Sājūr, Nahr**
Bagley U.S.A. **178** D2
Baglung Nepal **97** D3
Bagn Norway **45** J3
Bagnara Calabra Italy **57** H10
Bagnères-de-Bigorre France **50** G9
Bagnères-de-Luchon France **50** G10
Bagno di Romagna Italy **56** D5
Bagnolo Mella Italy **56** C3
Bagnols-sur-Cèze France **51** K8
Bagnuiti *r.* Nepal **97** E4
Bago Myanmar *see* **Pegu**
Bago *admin. div.* Myanmar *see* **Pegu**
Bago Phil. **74** B4
Bagoé *r.* Côte d'Ivoire/Mali **124** D3
Bagong China *see* **Sansui**
Bagrationovsk Rus. Fed. **42** B7
historically known as Eylau *or* Preussisch-Eylau
Bagrax China *see* **Bohu**
Bagrax Hu *l.* China *see* **Bosten Hu**
Bagre Brazil **202** B2
Bagua Peru **198** B6
Bagudo Nigeria **125** G4
Baguio Phil. **74** B2
Baguio Point Phil. **74** B2
Bağyurdu Turkey **59** I10
Bagzane, Monts *mts* Niger **125** H2
Bahadurganj Nepal **89** C7
Bahadurgarh India **96** C3
Bahāmabād Iran *see* **Rafsanjān**
▶**Bahamas** *country* West Indies **186** D1
northamerica [countries] ▶▶ 158–159
Baharampur India **97** F4
formerly spelt Berhampur
Bahardipur Pak. **101** G5
Bahariya Oasis Egypt **121** F3
Bahau *r.* Indon. **77** G2
Bahau Malaysia **76** C2
Bahaur Indon. **77** F3
Bahawalnagar Pak. **101** H4
Bahawalpur Pak. **101** G4
Bahçe *Adana* Turkey **108** G1
Bahçe *Osmaniye* Turkey **107** D3
Ba He *r.* China **86** C2
Bäherden Turkm. *see* **Bakherden**
Baheri India **96** C3
Bahi Tanz. **129** B6
Bahia Brazil *see* **Salvador**
Bahia *state* Brazil **202** D5
Bahía Asunción Mex. **181** D8
Bahía Blanca Arg. **204** E5
Bahía Bustamante Arg. **205** D7
Bahía Kino Mex. **184** C2
Bahía Laura Arg. **205** D8
Bahía Negra Para. **201** F5
Bahía San Blas Arg. **204** E6
Bahía Tortugas Mex. **184** B3
Bahig Egypt **108** A7
Bahir Dar Eth. **128** C2
Bahlā Oman **105** G3
Bahlui *r.* Romania **58** I1
Bahmanshīr, Khowr-e *r.* Iran **100** B4
Bahomonte Indon. **75** B3
Bahr Saudi Arabia **104** C4
Bahraich India **97** D4
▶**Bahrain** *country* Asia **105** E2
spelt Al Baḥrayn *in Arabic*
asia [countries] ▶▶ 64–67
Bahrain, Gulf of Asia **105** E2
Bahrāmābād Iran **100** B2
Bahrāmjerd Iran **100** D4
Bahr el Jebel *state* Sudan **128** A3
Bahror India **96** C4
Bahuaja-Sonene, Parque Nacional *nat. park* Peru **200** C3
Bāhū Kālāt Iran **101** E5
Bahushewsk Belarus **43** L7
Baia Romania **58** H1
Baia Romania **58** J4
Baia de Aramă Romania **58** D4
Baia de Arieş Romania **58** E2
Baía dos Tigres Angola **127** A9
Baía Farta Angola **127** B8
Baia Mare Romania **53** G2
Baião Brazil **202** B2
Baiazeh Iran **100** C3
Baibeli *well* Chad **120** D5
Baibokoum Chad **126** B3
Baicheng China *see* **Xiping**
Baicheng *Jilin* China **85** I2
Baicheng *Xinjiang* China **88** C3
also known as Bay
Băicoi Romania **58** G3
Baidoa Somalia *see* **Baydhabo**
Baidoi Co *l.* China **89** D5
Baidu China **87** F3
Baidunzi China **84** B3
Baie-aux-Feuilles Canada *see* **Tasiujaq**
Baie-Comeau Canada **169** G3
Baie de Henne Haiti **187** E3
Baie-du-Poste Canada *see* **Mistissini**
Baie-Johan-Beetz Canada **169** I3
Baie-St-Paul Canada **169** G4
Baie-Trinite Canada **169** H3
Baie Verte Canada **169** J3
Baigou *r.* China **85** H4
Baiguan China *see* **Shangyu**
Baiguo China **87** E2
Baigura *mt.* Spain **55** J2
Baihanchang China **86** A3
Baihar India **96** D5
Baihe *Jilin* China **82** C4
formerly known as Erdaobaihe
Baihe *Shaanxi* China **87** D1
Bai He *r.* China **87** E1
Baiji Iraq *see* **Bayjī**
Baijiantan China **88** D2
Baijnath *Himachal Pradesh* India **96** C2
Baijnath *Uttaranchal* India **96** C3

▶**Baikal, Lake** Rus. Fed. **81** H2
Deepest lake in the world and in Asia. 3rd largest lake in Asia and 9th in the world. Also known as Baykal, Ozero.
world [physical features] ▶▶ 8–9

Baikanthpur India **97** D4
Baikouquan China **88** D2
Baikunthpur India **97** D5
Bailang China **85** I2
Bailanhe Shuiku *resr* China **87** E2
Baile Átha Cliath Rep. of Ireland *see* **Dublin**
Baile Átha Luain Rep. of Ireland *see* **Athlone**
Băile Govora Romania **58** F3
Băile Herculane Romania **58** D4
Bailén Spain **54** H6
Băile Olăneşti Romania **58** F3
Băileşti Romania **58** E4
Băileştilor, Câmpia *plain* Romania **58** E4
Băile Tuşnad Romania **58** G2
Bailey S. Africa **133** K8
Bailey Ice Stream Antarctica **223** W1
Bailey Range *hills* Australia **151** C6
Baileyton U.S.A. **176** C9
Bailicun China **87** D3
Bailingmiao China **85** F3
also known as Darhan Muminggan Lianheqi
Baillie *r.* Canada **167** J1
Bailong Jiang *r.* China **86** C1
Bailundo Angola **127** B8
formerly known as Teixeira da Silva
Baima China **86** B1
also known as Sêraitang
Baima China *see* **Baxoi**
Bainang China **89** E6
also known as Norkyung
Bainbridge *GA* U.S.A. **175** C6
Bainbridge *NY* U.S.A. **177** J3
Bainbridge *OH* U.S.A. **176** B6
Bain-de-Bretagne France **50** E5
Bainduru India **94** B3
Bainet Haiti **187** E3
Baingoin China **89** E6
also known as Porong
Baini China *see* **Yuqing**
Baiona Spain **54** C2
also spelt Bayona
Baiqên China **86** B1
Baiquan China **82** B3
Bā'ir Jordan **109** H7
Bā'ir, Wādī *watercourse* Jordan/Saudi Arabia **109** I6
Bairab Co *l.* China **89** C5
Bairagnia India **97** E4
Baird U.S.A. **179** C5
Baird, Mount Canada **166** C1
Baird Mountains U.S.A. **164** D3

▶**Bairiki** Kiribati **145** G1
Capital of Kiribati, on Tarawa atoll.

Bairin Qiao China **85** H3
formerly known as Balinqiao
Bairin Youqi China *see* **Daban**
Bairin Zuoqi China *see* **Lindong**
Bairkum Kazakh. **103** G4
also spelt Bayyrqum
Bairnsdale Australia **147** E4
Bais France **50** F4
Bais Phil. **74** B4
Baïse *r.* France **50** G8
Baisha *Chongqing* China **86** C2
Baisha *Hainan* China **87** D5
also known as Yacha
Baisha *Jiangxi* China **87** E3
Baisha *Sichuan* China **87** D2
Baishan China *see* **Mashan**
Baishan *Jilin* China **82** B4
formerly known as Badaojiang *or* Hunjiang
Baishan *Jilin* China **82** B4
Baishi Shuiku *resr* China **85** I3
Baishui China **85** F5
Baishui Jiang *r.* China **86** C1
Baišogala Lith. **42** E6
Baitadi Nepal **96** D3
Baitang China **86** A1
Bai Thuong Vietnam **78** D4
Baitle *r.* China **85** H3
Baixa da Banheira Port. **54** B6
Baixi China *see* **Yibin**
Baixiang China **85** G4
Baixingt China **85** I3
Baixo Guandu Brazil **207** M6
Baixo-Longa Angola **127** C8
Baiyang Dian *resr* China **85** H4
Baiyanghe China **88** E3
Baiyashi China *see* **Dong'an**
Baiyin China **84** E4
Baiyü China **86** A2
also known as Jianshe
Baiyuda Desert Sudan **121** G5
Baiyu Shan *mts* China **85** E4
Baja Hungary **49** P9
Baja, Punta *pt* Mex. **184** B2
Baja California *pen.* Mex. **184** B2
English form Lower California
Baja California Norte *state* Mex. **184** B2
Baja California Sur *state* Mex. **184** B3
Bajan Mex. **185** E3
Bajang Nepal **96** D3
Bajau *i.* Indon. **77** D2
Bajaur *reg.* Pak. **101** G3
Bajawa Indon. **75** B5
Baj Baj India **97** F5
Bājgīrān Iran **100** D2
Bājil Yemen **104** C5
Bajina Bašta *Srbija* Yugo. **58** A5
Bajitpur Bangl. **97** F4
Bajmok *Vojvodina, Srbija* Yugo. **58** A3
Bajna India **96** B5
Bajo Baudó Col. **198** B3
Bajo Boquete Panama **186** C5
Bajo Caracoles Arg. **205** C7
Bajoga Nigeria **125** H4
Bajo Grande Arg. **205** C7
Bajo Hondo Arg. **204** D3
Bajrakot India **97** E5
Bajram Curri Albania **58** B6
Baka, Bukit *mt.* Indon. **77** F3
Bakaba Chad **126** C3
Bakala Cent. Afr. Rep. **126** D3
Bakaly Rus. Fed. **40** J5
Bakanas Kazakh. **103** I3
Bakanas *watercourse* Kazakh. **103** I3
Bakau Gambia **124** A3
Bakayan, Gunung *mt.* Indon. **77** G2
Bakel Senegal **124** B3
Baker *CA* U.S.A. **183** H6
Baker *LA* U.S.A. **175** B6
Baker *MT* U.S.A. **180** F3
Baker *OR* U.S.A. **180** C3
Baker *WV* U.S.A. **176** G6
Baker, Mount *vol.* U.S.A. **180** B2
Baker Butte *mt.* U.S.A. **183** M7

▶**Baker Island** N. Pacific Ocean **145** H1
United States Unincorporated Territory.
oceania [countries] ▶▶ 138–139

Baker Island U.S.A. **166** C4
Baker Lake *salt flat* Australia **151** D5
Baker Lake Canada **167** M1
also known as Qamanittuaq
Baker Lake *l.* Canada **167** M1
Baker's Dozen Islands Canada **168** E1
Bakersfield U.S.A. **182** F6
Bakerville S. Africa **133** K2
Bakhā Oman **105** G2
Bakharden Turkm. *see* **Bakherden**
Bakhardok Turkm. **102** D5
also spelt Bokurdak
Bākharz *mts* Iran **101** E3
Bakhchisaray Ukr. *see* **Bakhchysaray**
Bakhchysaray Ukr. **41** E7
also spelt Bakhchisaray
Bakherden Turkm. **102** D5
also spelt Bäherden; *formerly spelt* Bakharden
Bakhirevo Rus. Fed. **82** C2
Bakhmach Ukr. **41** E6
Bakhmut Ukr. *see* **Artemivs'k**
Bakhmutovo Rus. Fed. **43** P5
Bakhta Rus. Fed. **39** I3
Bākhtarān Iran *see* **Kermānshāh**
Bākhtarān *prov.* Iran *see* **Kermānshāh**
Bakhtegan, Daryācheh-ye *l.* Iran **100** C4
Bakhtiari Country *reg.* Iran **100** B3
Bakhtiyarpur India **97** E4
Bakhty Kazakh. **88** C2
also spelt Baqty
Bakhuis Gebergte *mts* Suriname **199** G3
Bakı Azer. *see* **Baku**
Baki *well* Chad **120** D5
Bakin Birji Niger **125** H3
Bakır *r.* Turkey **59** I10
Bakırköy Turkey **106** B2
Bakkaflói *b.* Iceland **44** [inset] D2
Baklan Turkey **59** K11
Baklanka Rus. Fed. **43** V3
Baklanovo Rus. Fed. **43** M6
Bakloh India **96** B2
Bako Côte d'Ivoire **124** D4
Bako Eth. **128** C2
Bako National Park *Sarawak* Malaysia **77** E2
Bakool *admin. reg.* Somalia **128** D4
Bakota Dem. Rep. Congo **126** D5
Bakouma Cent. Afr. Rep. **126** D3
Bakoumba Gabon **126** B5
Bakoy *r.* Mali **124** C3
Baksan Rus. Fed. **41** G8
Baktalórántháza Hungary **49** T8

▶**Baku** Azer. **107** G2
Capital of Azerbaijan. Also spelt Bakı or Bakı.

Bakung *i.* Indon. **76** D2
Bakuny Belarus **42** F9
Bakuriani Georgia **107** E2
Bakutis Coast Antarctica **222** P2
Baky Azer. *see* **Baku**
Baky Uyandino *r.* Rus. Fed. **39** O3
Bala Turkey **106** C3
Bala U.K. **47** I11
also known as Y Bala
Bala, Cerros de *mts* Bol. **200** C3
Balabac *i.* Phil. **74** A5
Balabac Strait Malaysia/Phil. **77** G1
Balābād, Gardaneh-ye *pass* Iran **100** C3
Balabalangan, Kepulauan *atolls* Indon. **77** G3
Balabanovo Rus. Fed. **43** R6
Bălăceanu Romania **58** I3
Bălăciţa Romania **58** E4
Balad Iraq **107** F4
Bālā Deh Iran **100** B4
Baladeh *Māzandarān* Iran **100** B2
Baladeh *Māzandarān* Iran **100** B2
Balaghat India **96** D5
Balaghat Range *hills* India **94** B2
Balaguer Spain **55** L3
Bālā Ḥowz Iran **100** D4
Balaiberkuak Indon. **77** E3
Balaikarangan Indon. **77** E2
Balaipungut Indon. **76** C2
Balairiam Indon. **77** E3
Balaïtous *mt.* France **50** F10
Balaka Malawi **129** B8
Balakān Azer. **107** F2
Balakhna Rus. Fed. **40** G4
Balakirevo Rus. Fed. **43** T5
Balaklava Australia **146** C3
Balaklava Ukr. **41** E7
Balakleya Ukr. *see* **Balakliya**
Balakliya Ukr. **41** F6
also spelt Balakleya
Balakovo Rus. Fed. **102** A1
Balama Moz. **131** H2
Balambangan *i. Sabah* Malaysia **77** G1
Bālā Morghāb Afgh. **101** E3
Balan India **96** A4
Bălan Romania **58** G2
Balancán Mex. **185** H5
Balanda Rus. Fed. *see* **Kalininsk**
Balan Dağı *hill* Turkey **59** J12
Balanga Phil. **74** B3
Balangala Dem. Rep. Congo **126** C4
Balangir India **95** D1
Balangoda Sri Lanka **94** D5
Balapur India **94** C1
Balarampur India **97** E5
Balase *r.* Indon. **75** B3
Bălăşeşti Romania **58** I2
Balashi Rus. Fed. **102** B2
Balashikha Rus. Fed. **43** S6
Balashov Rus. Fed. **41** G6
Balasinor India **96** B5
Balassagyarmat Hungary **49** Q7
Balaton *l.* Hungary *see* **Balaton, Lake**

index

B

Balaton, Lake Hungary 49 O9 also known as Balaton
Balatonboglár Hungary 49 O9
Balatonfüred Hungary 49 O9
Balatonlelle Hungary 49 O9
Balauring Indon. 75 B5
Balazote Spain 55 I6
Balbieriškis Lith. 42 E7
Balbina Brazil 199 G5
Balbina, Represa de resr Brazil 199 G5
Balbriggan Rep. of Ireland 47 F10
Balcad Somalia 128 E4
Balcanoona Australia 146 C2
Balcarce Arg. 204 F5
Balchik Bulg. 58 J5
Balclutha N.Z. 153 D14
Baldim Brazil 207 J6
Bald Knob AR U.S.A. 174 B5
Bald Knob WV U.S.A. 176 D8
Bald Mountain U.S.A. 183 I4
Baldock Lake Canada 167 L3
Baldwin U.S.A. 175 D6
Baldwinsville U.S.A. 177 I2
Baldwinville U.S.A. 177 M3
Baldy Mount Canada 166 G5
Baldy Mountain hill Canada 167 K5
Baldy Peak U.S.A. 183 O8
Bal'dzhikan Rus. Fed. 85 F1
Bale Indon. 76 C3
Bâle Switz. see Basel
Baléa Mali 124 C3
Baleares, Islas is Spain see Balearic Islands
Baleares Insulae is Spain see Balearic Islands
Balearic Islands is Spain 55 M5 also known as Baleares, Islas or Balears, Illes; historically known as Baleares Insulae
Balears, Illes is Spain see Balearic Islands
Baleh r. Sarawak Malaysia 77 F2
Baleia, Ponta da pt Brazil 203 E6
Baleines, Pointe des pt France 50 E6
Bale Mountains National Park Eth. 128 C3
Băleni Romania 58 G4
Baleno Phil. 74 B3
Baler Phil. 74 B3
Baler Bay Phil. 74 B3
Balesa well Kenya 128 C4
Baleshwar India 97 E5
Balestrand Norway 45 I3
Baley Rus. Fed. 85 H1
Baléyara Niger 125 F3
Balezino Rus. Fed. 40 J4
Balfate Hond. 186 B4
Balfe's Creek Australia 149 E4
Balfour Canada 167 G5
Balfour N.Z. 153 C13
Balfour E. Cape S. Africa 133 K9
Balfour Mpumalanga S. Africa 133 M3
Balfour Downs Australia 150 C4
Balgatay Mongolia 84 C2 formerly known as Shilüüstey
Balgazyn Rus. Fed. 88 F1
Balgo Australia 150 D4
Balgo Aboriginal Reserve Australia 150 E4
Balguda well Kenya 128 C5
Balguntay China 88 D3
Bālḩaf Yemen 105 E5
Balho Djibouti 128 D1
Bali India 96 B4
Bali i. Indon. 77 F5
Bali prov. Indon. 77 F5
Bali reg. Saudi Arabia 104 B2
Bali, Selat sea chan. Indon. 77 F5
Baliangao Phil. 74 B4
Baliapal India 97 E5
Bali Barat National Park Indon. 77 F5
Balichak India 97 E5
Balige Indon. 76 B2
Baliguda India 95 D1
Balihan China 85 H3
Balıkesir Turkey 106 A3
Balıkesir prov. Turkey 59 J9
Balık Gölü l. Turkey 107 E3
Balīkh r. Syria/Turkey 109 K2
Balıkliçeşme Turkey 59 I8
Balikpapan Indon. 77 G3
Balikpapan, Teluk b. Indon. 77 G3
Bălilești Romania 58 F3
Balimbing Phil. 74 A5
Balimila Reservoir India 94 D2
Balimo P.N.G. 73 J8
Balin China 85 I1
Balingen Germany 48 F7
Balingian Sarawak Malaysia 77 F2
Balingian r. Sarawak Malaysia 77 F2
Baliqiao China see Bairin Qiao
Balintang Channel Phil. 74 B2
Bali Sea Indon. 77 F4
Balitondo Cent. Afr. Rep. 126 D3
Baliungan i. Phil. 74 B5
Baljurshi Saudi Arabia 104 C4
▶Balkan Mountains Bulg./Yugo. 58 D5 also known as Stara Planina europe [issues] ⇒ 34–35
Balkan Oblast admin. div. Turkm. see Balkanskaya Oblast'
Balkanskaya Oblast' admin. div. Turkm. 102 C4 English form Balkan Oblast; formerly known as Krasnovodskaya Oblast'
Balkashino Kazakh. 103 G1
Balkh Afgh. 101 F2 historically known as Bactra or Zariaspa
Balkh prov. Afgh. 101 F2
Balkhab r. Afgh. 101 F2
Balkhash Kazakh. 103 H3 also spelt Balqash
▶Balkhash, Lake Kazakh. 103 H3 4th largest lake in Asia. Also known as Balkhash, Ozero or Balqash Köli. asia [landscapes] ⇒ 62–63
Balkhash, Ozero l. Kazakh. see Balkhash, Lake
Balkonda India 94 C2
Balkuduk Kazakh. 102 A3
Balla Bangl. 97 F4
Balla Balla Zimbabwe see Mbalabala
Ballachulish U.K. 46 G7
Balladonia Australia 151 C7
Ballaghaderreen Rep. of Ireland 47 D10
Ballangen Norway 44 L1
Ballantrae U.K. 47 H8
Ballarat Australia 147 D4
Ballard, Lake salt flat Australia 151 C6
Ballarpur India 94 C2
Ballater U.K. 46 I6
Ballé Mali 124 C3
Ballena, Punta pt Chile 204 C2
Ballenero, Canal sea chan. Chile 205 C9
Balleny Islands Antarctica 223 K2
Ballia India 97 E4
Ballina Australia 147 G2
Ballina Rep. of Ireland 47 C9 also spelt Béal an Átha
Ballinasloe Rep. of Ireland 47 D10 also spelt Béal Átha na Sluaighe
Ballineen Rep. of Ireland 47 D12
Ballinger U.S.A. 179 C6
Ballinrobe Rep. of Ireland 47 C10
Ballons des Vosges, Parc Naturel Régional des nature res. France 51 M5
Ballsh Albania 58 A8
Ballston Spa U.S.A. 177 L2
Bally U.S.A. 177 J5
Ballybunnion Rep. of Ireland 47 C11
Ballycastle Rep. of Ireland 47 C9
Ballycastle U.K. 47 F8
Ballyhaunis Rep. of Ireland 47 D10
Ballymena U.K. 47 F9
Ballymoney U.K. 47 F8
Ballyshannon Rep. of Ireland 47 D9
Balmaceda Aisén Chile 205 C7
Balmaceda Antofagasta Chile 200 C6
Balmaseda Spain 55 H1 also spelt Valmaseda
Balmazújváros Hungary 49 S8
Balmer India see Barmer
Balmertown Canada 167 M5
Balmoral Australia 146 D4
Balmoral N.Z. 153 G10
Balnearia Arg. 204 E3
Baloa Indon. 75 B3
Balochistan prov. Pak. 101 F4
Balochistan reg. Pak. 92 B5 formerly spelt Baluchistan
Balod India 94 D1
Baloda India 97 D5
Baloda Bazar India 97 D5
Balok, Teluk b. Indon. 77 D3
Balombo Angola 127 B8 formerly known as Norton de Matos
Balonne r. Australia 147 F2
Balotra India 96 B4
Balpahari Reservoir India 97 E4
Balpyk Bi Kazakh. 103 I3 formerly known as Kirov or Kirovskiy
Balqash Kazakh. see Balkhash
Balqash Köli l. Kazakh. see Balkhash, Lake
Balrampur India 97 D4
Balranald Australia 147 D3
Balş Romania 58 F4
Balsam Creek Canada 173 N4
Balsam Lake l. Canada 173 O6
Balsam Lake U.S.A. 172 A5
Balsapuerto Peru 198 B6
Balsareny Spain 55 M3
Balsas Brazil 202 C3
Balsas Mex. 185 F5
Balsas r. Mex. 185 E5
Balsas, Rio das r. Brazil 202 C3
Bal'shavik Belarus 43 L9
Bålsta Sweden 45 L4
Balta Ukr. 41 D7
Baltasi Rus. Fed. 40 I4
Baltasound U.K. 46 L3
Baltay Rus. Fed. 102 A1
Bălţi Moldova 41 C7 formerly spelt Bel'ts' or Bel'tsy
Baltic Sea g. Europe 45 L5
Baltîm Egypt 121 F2
Baltimore Rep. of Ireland 47 C12
Baltimore MD U.S.A. 177 I6
Baltimore OH U.S.A. 176 C6
Baltinava Latvia 42 I5
Baltinglass Rep. of Ireland 47 F11
Baltistan reg. Jammu and Kashmir 96 B2
Baltiysk Rus. Fed. 42 A7 historically known as Pillau
Baltoji Vokė Lith. 42 G7
Baltoro Glacier Jammu and Kashmir 96 C2
Baluarte Brazil 202 D4
Baluch Ab well Iran 100 D4
Balūchestān va Sīstān prov. Iran 101 E5
Baluchistan reg. Pak. see Balochistan
Balui r. Sarawak Malaysia 77 F2
Balumath India 97 E5
Balumbah Australia 146 C3
Balumundam Indon. 76 B2
Balupe r. Latvia 42 H5
Baluran, Gunung mt. Indon. 77 F3
Baluran National Park Indon. 77 F4
Balurghat India 97 F4
Balut i. Phil. 74 C5
Balvatnet l. Norway 44 K2
Balvi Latvia 42 I4
Balya Turkey 106 A3
Balyaga Rus. Fed. 85 F1
Balykchy Kyrg. 103 I4 formerly known as Issyk-Kul' or Ysyk-Köl or Rybach'ye
Balykshi Kazakh. 102 B3 also spelt Balyqshy
Balyktyg-Khem r. Rus. Fed. 84 C1
Balyqshy Kazakh. see Balykshi
Balzar Ecuador 198 B5
Bam Iran 100 D4
Bām Iran 100 D2
Bama China 87 C3
Bama Nigeria 125 I4
Bamaga Australia 149 D1
Bamaji Lake Canada 168 B3
▶Bamako Mali 124 D3 Capital of Mali.
Bamba r. Cent. Afr. Rep. 126 C3
Bamba Dem. Rep. Congo 127 C6
Bamba Mali 125 E2
Bambama Congo 126 B5
Bambang Phil. 74 B2
Bambangando Angola 127 D9
Bambannan i. Phil. 74 B5
Bambari Cent. Afr. Rep. 126 D3
Bamberg Germany 48 H6
Bamberg U.S.A. 175 D5
Bambesi Eth. 128 B2
Bambey Senegal 124 A3
Bambili Dem. Rep. Congo 126 E4
Bambio Cent. Afr. Rep. 126 C4
Bamboesberg mts S. Africa 133 K8
Bamboi Ghana 125 E4
Bamboo Creek Australia 150 C4
Bambou well Mali 125 E2
Bambouk reg. Mali 124 C3
Bambouti Cent. Afr. Rep. 126 E3
Bambudi Eth. 128 B2
Bambuí Brazil 203 C7
Bamda China 86 A2
Bāmdezh Iran 100 B4
Bamenda Cameroon 125 H5
Bamendjing, Lac de l. Cameroon 125 H5
Bamfield Canada 166 E5
Bami Turkm. 102 D5 also spelt Bamy
Bāmīān Afgh. 101 F3
Bāmīān prov. Afgh. 101 F3
Bamiancheng China 85 J3
Bamiantong China see Muling
Bamingui Cent. Afr. Rep. 126 D3
Bamingui r. Cent. Afr. Rep. 126 C2
Bamingui-Bangoran pref. Cent. Afr. Rep. 126 D2
Bamingui-Bangoran, Parc National du nat. park Cent. Afr. Rep. 126 C2
Bamiyan r. Afgh. 101 G3
Bammo well Niger 125 H3
Bamoa Mex. 184 C3
Bamor India 96 C4
Bam Posht reg. Iran 101 E5
Bam Posht, Kūh-e mts Iran 101 E5
Bampūr Iran 101 E5
Bampūr watercourse Iran 101 D5
Bamrūd Iran 101 E3
Bamy Turkm. see Bami
Bamyili Australia 148 B2 also known as Barunga
Ban Burkina 124 E3
Bana, Wādī watercourse Yemen 105 D5
Banaba i. Kiribati 145 F2 also known as Ocean Island; also spelt Paanopa
Banabuiu, Açude resr Brazil 202 E3
Bañados del Atuel marsh Arg. 204 D5
Bañados del Izozog swamp Bol. 201 E4
Bañados de Otuquis marsh Bol. 201 F4
Banahao, Mount vol. Phil. 74 B3
Banalia Dem. Rep. Congo 126 E4
Banamba Mali 124 D3
Banan China 86 C2 formerly known as Baxian
Banana Australia 149 F5
Bananal, Ilha do i. Brazil 202 B4
Bananga India 95 G5
Banankoro Guinea 124 C4
Banapur India 95 E2
Banarlı Turkey 58 I7
Banas r. India 96 C4
Banās, Râs pt Egypt 121 G4
Banatski Karlovac Vojvodina, Srbija Yugo. 58 C3
Banawaya i. Indon. 75 A4
Banaz Turkey 106 B3
Banaz r. Turkey 59 K10
Ban Ban Laos 78 C4
Banbar China 89 F6 also known as Domartang
Banbridge U.K. 47 F9
Ban Bua Yai Thai. 79 C5
Banbury U.K. 47 K11
Banca Romania 58 I2
Banc d'Arguin, Parc National du nat. park Mauritania 122 A5
Ban Chiang tourist site Thai. 78 C4
Banchory U.K. 46 J6
Bancoran i. Phil. 74 A5
Bancroft Canada 168 E4
Bancroft Zambia see Chililabombwe
Band Iran 100 D3
Banda Dem. Rep. Congo 126 E3
Banda Madhya Pradesh India 96 C4
Banda Uttar Pradesh India 96 D4
Banda, Kepulauan is Indon. 75 D4
Banda Aceh Indon. 76 A1 formerly known as Kutaraja
Banda Banda, Mount Australia 147 G2
Bandahara, Gunung mt. Indon. 76 B2
Bandai-Asahi National Park Japan 90 F6
Bandama r. Côte d'Ivoire 124 D5
Bandama Blanc r. Côte d'Ivoire 124 D4
Bandān Iran 101 E4
Bandaneira Indon. 75 D4
Bandān Kūh mts Iran 101 E4
Bandar India see Machilipatnam
Bandar Abbas Iran see Bandar-e 'Abbās
Bandaragung Indon. 76 D4
Bandarban Bangl. 97 G5
Bandar-e 'Abbās Iran 100 D5 English form Bandar Abbas; historically known as Gombroon
Bandar-e Anzalī Iran 100 B2 formerly known as Bandar-e Pahlavī
Bandar-e Chārak Iran 100 C5
Bandar-e Deylam Iran 100 B4
Bandar-e Emām Khomeynī Iran 100 B4 formerly known as Bandar-e Shāhpūr
Bandar-e Lengeh Iran 100 C5
Bandar-e Maqām Iran 100 C5
Bandar-e Ma'shur Iran 100 B4
Bandar-e Moghūyeh Iran 100 C5
Bandar-e Pahlavī Iran see Bandar-e Anzalī
Bandar-e Rīg Iran 100 B4
Bandar-e Shāh Iran see Bandar-e Torkeman
Bandar-e Shāhpūr Iran see Bandar-e Emām Khomeynī
Bandar-e Torkeman Iran 100 C2 formerly known as Bandar-e Shāh
Bandar Lampung Indon. see Tanjungkarang-Telukbetung
Bandar Murcaayo Somalia 128 F2
Bandarpunch mt. India 96 C3
▶Bandar Seri Begawan Brunei 77 F1 Capital of Brunei. Formerly known as Brunei.
Bandar Wanaag Somalia 128 E2
Banda Sea Indon. 75 D4
Bandeira Brazil 207 M2
Bandeirante Brazil 202 B5
Bandeirantes Brazil 206 C10
Bandeiras, Pico de mt. Brazil 203 D7
Bandera Arg. 204 E3
Bandera U.S.A. 179 C6
Banderas Mex. 184 D2
Banderas, Bahía de b. Mex. 184 D4
Bandhi Pak. 101 G5
Bandhogarh India 96 D5
Bandi r. India 96 B4
Bandia r. India 94 D2
Bandiagara Mali 124 E3
Bandiagara, Falaise de esc. Mali 124 E3
Band-i-Amir r. Afgh. 101 F2
Band-i-Baba mts Afgh. 101 E3
Band-i-Husain Nun mts Iran 100 C3
Bandikui India 96 C4
Bandīnī Iran 101 D5
Bandipur Jammu and Kashmir 96 B2
Bandipur Nepal 97 E4
Bandipur National Park India 94 C4
Bandırma Turkey 106 A2
Band-i-Turkestan mts Afgh. 101 E3
Bandjarmasin Indon. see Banjarmasin
Bandjer pass Yugo. 58 A5
Bandon Rep. of Ireland 47 D12
Bandon r. Rep. of Ireland 47 D12
Ban Don Thai. see Surat Thani
Bandon U.S.A. 180 A4
Ban Don, Ao b. Thai. 79 B6
Band Qīr Iran 100 B4
Bandra India 94 B2
Bandua Moz. 131 G3
Bandula Moz. 131 G3
Bandundu Dem. Rep. Congo 126 C5 formerly known as Banningville
Bandundu prov. Dem. Rep. Congo 126 C6
Bandung Indon. 77 D4
Bandya Australia 151 C6
Băneasa Romania 58 I4
Băneasa Romania 58 H4
Bāneh Iran 100 A3
Banemo Indon. 75 D2
Banera India 96 B4
Bañeres Spain 55 K6
Banes Cuba 186 E2
Banff Canada 167 H5
Banff U.K. 46 J6
Banff National Park Canada 167 G5
Banfora Burkina 124 D4
Bang Cent. Afr. Rep. 126 B3
Banga Angola 127 B7
Banga Dem. Rep. Congo 127 D6
Banga Phil. 74 C5
Banga r. Phil. 74 C5
Bangai Point Phil. 74 C5
Bangall Creek watercourse Australia 149 E4
Bangalore India 94 C3
Banganapalle India 94 C3
Banganga r. India 96 C4
Bangangté Cameroon 125 H5
Bangaon India 97 F5
Bangar Brunei 77 F1
Bangar Phil. 74 B2
Bangara r. Bangl. 97 F5
Bangarapet India 94 C3
Bangassou Cent. Afr. Rep. 126 D3
Bangdag Co salt l. China 89 C5
Bangfai, Xé r. Laos 78 D4
Banggai Indon. 75 B3
Banggai i. Indon. 75 B3
Banggai, Kepulauan is Indon. 75 B3
Banggi i. Sabah Malaysia 77 G1
Banghāzī Libya see Benghazi
Banghiang, Xé r. Laos 78 D4
Bangil Indon. 77 F4
Bangka i. Indon. 75 C2
Bangka i. Indon. 77 D3
Bangka, Selat sea chan. Indon. 77 D3
Bangkala, Teluk b. Indon. 75 A4
Bangkalan Indon. 77 F4
Bangkaru i. Indon. 76 B2
Bangkinang Indon. 76 C2
Bangkir Indon. 75 B2
Bangko Indon. 76 C3
Bangkog Co salt l. China 89 E6
▶Bangkok Thai. 79 C5 Capital of Thailand. Also known as Krung Thep.
Bangkok, Bight of b. Thai. 79 C5
Bangkor China 89 D6
Bangkulu i. Indon. 75 B3
Bangla state India see West Bengal
▶Bangladesh country Asia 97 F4 8th most populous country in the world. Formerly known as East Bengal or East Pakistan. world [population] ⇒ 22–23 asia [countries] ⇒ 64–67
Bangma Shan mts China 86 A4
Bang Mun Nak Thai. 78 C4
Bångnäs Sweden 44 K2
Bangolo Côte d'Ivoire 124 D5
Bangong Co salt l. China/Jammu and Kashmir 89 B5 also spelt Pangong Tso
Bangor Gwynedd, Wales U.K. 47 H10
Bangor Northern Ireland U.K. 47 G9
Bangor ME U.S.A. 177 Q1
Bangor MI U.S.A. 172 G8
Bangor PA U.S.A. 177 J5
Bangriposi India 97 E5
Bangs, Mount U.S.A. 183 K5
Bangsalsepulun Indon. 77 G3
Bang Saphan Yai Thai. 79 B6
Bangsund Norway 44 J2
Bangu Dem. Rep. Congo 127 D7
Bangued Phil. 74 B2
▶Bangui Cent. Afr. Rep. 126 C3 Capital of Central African Republic.
Bangui Phil. 74 B2
Bangula Malawi 129 B9
Bangunpurba Indon. 76 B2
Banguru Dem. Rep. Congo 126 E4
Bangweulu, Lake Zambia 127 F7
Banhā Egypt see Benha
Banhine, Parque Nacional de nat. park Moz. 131 G4
Ban Houayxay Laos 78 C3 also spelt Ban Houei Sai
Ban Houei Sai Laos see Ban Houayxay
Bani Burkina 125 E3
Bani Cent. Afr. Rep. 126 D3
Baní Dom. Rep. 187 F3
Bani r. Mali 124 D3
Bani Phil. 74 A2
Bani, Jbel ridge Morocco 122 C3
Bania Cent. Afr. Rep. 126 C3
Banī Atiyah reg. Saudi Arabia 106 D5
Bani-Bangou Niger 125 F3
Banifing r. Mali 124 D3
Banifing r. Mali 124 D3
Banī Forūr, Jazīreh-ye i. Iran 100 C5
Banihal Pass and Tunnel Jammu and Kashmir 96 B2
Banī Khatmah reg. Saudi Arabia 105 D4
Banī Khurb hills Saudi Arabia 104 D4
Banikoara Benin 125 F4
Banī Ma'āriḍ des. Saudi Arabia 105 D4
Banī Mukassir des. Saudi Arabia 105 E3
Banī Sa'd Iraq 109 P4
Banister r. U.S.A. 176 G9
Banī Suwayf Egypt see Beni Suef
Banite Bulg. 58 G7
Banī Thawr Saudi Arabia 104 C4
Banitsa Bulg. 58 E7
Banī Ṭukhmān reg. Saudi Arabia 105 E3
Banī Walīd Libya 120 B2
Banī Wuṭayfān well Saudi Arabia 105 E2
Bāniyās Syria 108 G2 historically known as Caesarea Philippi or Paneas
Bani Yas reg. U.A.E. 105 F3
Banja Srbija Yugo. 58 A5
Banja Luka Bos.-Herz. 56 J4
Banjar India 96 C3
Banjarbaru Indon. 77 F3
Banjarmasin Indon. 77 F3 formerly spelt Bandjarmasin
▶Banjul Gambia 124 A3 Capital of The Gambia. Formerly known as Bathurst.
Bankā Azer. 100 B2
Banka India 97 E4
Banka Banka Australia 148 B3
Bankapur India 94 B3
Bankass Mali 124 E3
Ban Khai Thai. 79 C5
Ban Khao Yoi Thai. 79 B5
Banki India 95 E1
Bankim Cameroon 125 H5
Bankkop S. Africa 133 O3
Banko, Massif de mt. Guinea 124 C4
Bankobankoang i. Indon. 77 G4
Bankol India 94 B2
Bankon Guinea 124 C4
Banks Island B.C. Canada 166 D4
Banks Island N.W.T. Canada 164 G2
Banks Islands Vanuatu 145 F3
Banks Lake U.S.A. 180 C3
▶Banks Peninsula N.Z. 153 H11 oceania [features] ⇒ 142–143
Banks Strait Australia 147 F5
Bankura India 97 E5
Bankya Bulg. 58 E6
Bankya Bulg. 58 D6
Ban Lamduan Thai. 79 C5
Banlan China 87 D3
Banloc Romania 58 C3
Ban Mae Mo Thai. 78 B4
Banmauk Myanmar 78 A2
Bann r. U.K. 47 F8
Ban Napè Laos 78 D4
Ban Na San Thai. 79 B6
Banner Hill U.S.A. 176 C9
Bannerman Town Bahamas 186 D1
Bannertown U.S.A. 176 E9
Banning U.S.A. 183 H8
Banningville Dem. Rep. Congo see Bandundu
Bannivka Ukr. 58 J3
Bannockburn N.Z. 153 D13
Ban Noi Myanmar 78 B4
Bannu Pak. 101 G3 formerly known as Edwardesabad
Bañolas Spain see Banyoles
Baños Ecuador 198 B5
Baños de Puritama Chile 200 C5
Bánovce nad Bebravou Slovakia 49 P7
Banovići Bos.-Herz. 56 K4
Banow Afgh. see Andarāb
Ban Phaeng Thai. 78 D4
Ban Phai Thai. 78 C4
Ban Phon Laos 79 D5
Banphot Phisai Thai. 78 B5
Ban Pong Thai. 79 B5
Banqiao China 86 C3
Bansang Gambia 124 B3
Ban Saraphi Thai. 78 B4
Ban Sawi Thai. 79 B6
Bansgaon India 97 D4
Bansi Rajasthan India 96 B4
Bansi Uttar Pradesh India 96 C4
Bansi Uttar Pradesh India 97 D4
Banská Bystrica Slovakia 49 Q7
Banská Štiavnica Slovakia 49 P7
Bansko Bulg. 58 E7
Banslol r. India 97 E4
Ban Sut Ta Thai. 78 B4
Banswada India 94 C2
Banswara India 96 B5
Banta i. Indon. 77 G4
Bantaeng Indon. 75 A4
Bantayan i. Phil. 74 B4
Bantè Benin 125 F4
Ban Tha Chang Thai. 79 B6
Ban Tha Kham Thai. 79 B6
Ban Tha Song Yang Thai. 78 B4
Banthat mts Cambodia see Cardamom Range
Ban Tha Tako Thai. 79 C5
Ban Tha Tum Thai. 79 C5
Ban Thepha Thai. 79 C7
Ban Thung Luang Thai. 79 B5
Bantry Rep. of Ireland 47 C12
Bantry Bay Rep. of Ireland 47 C12
Bantul Indon. 77 E4
Bantva India 96 A5
Bantval India 94 B3
Banyak, Pulau-pulau is Indon. 76 B2
Banyo Cameroon 125 H5
Banyoles Spain 55 N2 also spelt Bañolas
Banyuasin r. Indon. 76 D3
Banyumas Indon. 77 E4
Banyuwangi Indon. 77 F5
Banzare Coast Antarctica 223 I2
Banzart Tunisia see Bizerte
Banzyville Dem. Rep. Congo see Mobayi-Mbongo
Bao, Embalse del resr Spain see Vao, Embalse de
Bao, Ouadi watercourse Chad 120 D5
Bao'an China see Shenzhen
Bao'an China 84 D5
Bao'an China see Zhidan
Bao Bilia well Chad 120 D5
Baochang China 85 G3 also known as Taibus Qi
Baocheng China 86 C1
Baodi China 85 H4
Baoding China 85 G4
Baofeng China 87 E1
Baoji Shaanxi China 86 C1
Baoji Shaanxi China 87 C1 also known as Guozhen
Baokang Hubei China 87 D2
Baokang Nei Mongol China 85 I2 also known as Horqin Zuoyi Zhongqi
Bao Lôc Vietnam 79 D6
Baoqing China 82 D3
Baoro Cent. Afr. Rep. 126 B3
Baoshan Shanghai China 87 G2
Baoshan Yunnan China 86 A3
Baotou China 85 F3
Baoulé r. Mali 124 C3
Baoulé r. Mali 124 D3
Baoxing China 86 B2
Baoxiu China 86 B4
Baoying China 87 F1
Baoyou China see Ledong
Bap India 96 B4
Bapatla India 94 D3
Bapaume France 51 I2
Baptiste Lake Canada 173 O5
Bapu China see Meigu
Baqar, Bahr el canal Egypt 108 D6
Baqarah Saudi Arabia 104 C3
Baqên Xizang China 89 F5 also known as Dartang
Baqên Xizang China 89 F6 also known as Yêtatang
Baqiu China see Xiajiang
Baqrān Saudi Arabia 104 C3
Baqty Kazakh. see Bakhty
Ba'qūbah Iraq 107 F4
Bar Crna Gora Yugo. 58 A6
Bara Nigeria 125 H4
Bara Sudan 121 F6
Bara well Sudan 126 E2
Baraawe Somalia 128 E4
Barabai Indon. 77 F3
Bara Banki India 96 D4
Barabanovo Rus. Fed. 43 T7
Barabash Rus. Fed. 90 B3
Barabhum India 97 E5
Barabinsk Rus. Fed. 80 B1
Baraboo U.S.A. 172 D7
Baraboo r. U.S.A. 172 D7
Barabouté Burkina 125 E3
Baraboy r. Ukr. 58 L2
Baracaldo Spain see Barakaldo
Baracoa Cuba 187 E2
Baradá, Nahr r. Syria 108 H4
Baradero Arg. 204 F4
Baradine r. Australia 147 F2
Baraga U.S.A. 172 E4
Bărăganului, Câmpia plain Romania 58 I4
Baragoi Kenya 128 C4
Baragua Venez. 198 D2
Baragua, Sierra de mts Venez. 198 D2
Barahanuddin Bangl. 97 F5
Barahona Dom. Rep. 187 F3
Barail Range mts India 97 G4
Bara Issa r. Mali 124 E2
Barajevo Srbija Yugo. 58 B4
Barak Afgh. 101 G2
Barak r. India 97 G4
Baraka watercourse Eritrea/Sudan 121 H5
Barakaldo Spain 55 I1 also spelt Baracaldo
Baraki Barak Afgh. 101 G3
Barakke S. Africa 133 I9
Barakot India 97 E5
Barakovo Rus. Fed. 43 U7
Barakpay Kazakh. 103 F1 also spelt Baraqbay
Baralaba Australia 149 F5
Bara Lacha Pass India 96 C2
Baram r. Sarawak Malaysia 77 F1
Baram, Tanjong pt Sarawak Malaysia 77 F1
Baramanni Guyana 199 G3
Baramati India 94 B2
Barambah r. Australia 149 F5
Barameiya Sudan 121 H5
Baramula Jammu and Kashmir 96 B2
Baran' Belarus 43 L7
Baran India 96 C4
Baran r. Pak. 101 G5
Bārān, Kūh-e mts Iran 101 E3
Baranavichy Belarus 42 H8 also spelt Baranovichi; formerly spelt Baranowicze
Barang, Dasht-i des. Afgh. 101 E3
Baranikha Rus. Fed. 39 Q3
Baranivka Ukr. 41 C6
Baranoa Col. 187 E5
Baranof Island U.S.A. 164 F4
Baranovichi Belarus see Baranavichy
Baranowicze Belarus see Baranavichy
Barão de Cocais Brazil 207 J6
Barão de Grajaú Brazil 202 D3
Barão de Melgaço Brazil 201 G4
Barão de Melgaço Brazil 201 E2
Baraolt Romania 58 G2
Baraqbay Kazakh. see Barakpay
Baraqueville France 51 I8
Bararati r. Brazil 201 F1
Bārat, Chiyā-e hill Iraq 109 P1
Barat Daya, Kepulauan is Indon. 75 C4
Baratta Australia 146 C3
Barauaná, Serra mts Brazil 199 F4
Baraut India 96 C3
Baraya Col. 198 C4
Barbacena Minas Gerais Brazil 203 D7
Barbacena Pará Brazil 199 H5
▶Barbados country West Indies 187 I4 northamerica [countries] ⇒ 158–159
Barbar, Gebel el mt. Egypt 108 E8
Barbara Lake Canada 168 C3
Barbaria, Cap de c. Spain 55 M6
Barbaros Turkey 58 I8
Barbastro Spain 55 L2
Barbate de Franco Spain 54 F8
Bārbele Latvia 42 F5
Barber's Bay Canada 173 M2
Barberspan Nature Reserve S. Africa 133 J3
Barberton S. Africa 133 P2
Barberton U.S.A. 176 D4
Barbezieux-St-Hilaire France 50 F7
Barbigha India 97 E4
Barbil India 97 E5
Barbosa Col. 198 C3
Barbour Bay Canada 167 M2
Barbours U.S.A. 177 I4
Barbourville U.S.A. 176 B9
Barboza Phil. 74 B4
Barbuda i. Antigua and Barbuda 187 H3
Bârca Romania 58 E5
Barcaldine Australia 149 E4
Barcău r. Romania 58 C1
Barce Libya see Al Marj
Barcellona Pozzo di Gotto Sicilia Italy 57 H10
Barcelona Spain 55 N3 historically known as Barcino
Barcelona Venez. 199 E2
Barcelonnette France 51 M8
Barcelos Brazil 199 F5
Barcin Poland 49 O3
Barcino Spain see Barcelona
Barclay de Tolly atoll Fr. Polynesia see Raroia
Barclayville Liberia 124 C5
Barcoo watercourse Australia 149 D5
Barcoo Creek watercourse Australia see Cooper Creek
Barcoo National Park Australia see Welford National Park
Barcs Hungary 56 J3
Barczewo Poland 49 R2
Bärdä Azer. 107 F2
Barda Rus. Fed. 40 J4
Bardaale Somalia 128 E3
Bárðarbunga mt. Iceland 44 [inset] C2
Bardas Blancas Arg. 204 C4
Bardaskan Iran 100 D3
Bardawil, Khabrat al salt pan Saudi Arabia 109 J6
Bardawil, Sabkhet el lag. Egypt 108 E6
Barddhaman India 97 E5 formerly spelt Burdwan
Bardejov Slovakia 49 S6
Bardera Somalia see Baardheere
Bardsey Island U.K. 47 H11
Bard Shah Iran 100 B3
Bardsīr Iran 100 D4
Barðsneshorn pt Iceland 165 R3
Bardstown U.S.A. 174 C4
Barduli Italy see Barletta
Bardwell U.S.A. 174 B4
Barē Eth. 128 D3
Bareilly India 96 C3
Bareli India 96 C5
Barengapara India 97 F4
Barentin France 50 G3
Barenton France 50 F4
Barentsburg Svalbard 38 B2
Barents Island Svalbard see Barentsøya
Barentsøya i. Svalbard 38 C2 English form Barents Island
Barents Sea Arctic Ocean 38 E2
Barentu Eritrea 121 H6
Bareo Sarawak Malaysia 77 F2
Barfleur, Pointe de pt France 50 E3
Barga China 89 C6
Barga Italy 56 C4
Bargaal Somalia 128 F2
Bārgāh Iran 100 D5
Bargara Australia 149 G5
Bargē Eth. 128 C3
Barge Italy 51 N8
Bargi India 96 C5
Bargiri Turkey see Muradiye
Bargteheide Germany 48 H2
Barguna Bangl. 97 F5
Bargur India 94 C4
Barh India 97 E4
Barhaj India 97 D4
Barhalganj India 97 D4
Bar Harbor U.S.A. 177 Q1
Barharwa India 97 E4
Bari Dem. Rep. Congo 126 C4
Bari India 96 C4
Bari Italy 56 I7 historically known as Barium
Bari admin. reg. Somalia 128 F2
Ba Ria Vietnam 79 D6
Barīdī, Ra's hd Saudi Arabia 104 B2
Bari Doab lowland Pak. 101 H4
Barik Oman 105 G3
Barika Alg. 123 G2
Barikot Afgh. 101 G3
Barikot Nepal 97 D3
Barīm i. Yemen 104 C5 English form Perim Island
Barima r. Guyana 199 G2
Barima r. Venez. 187 H5
Barinas Venez. 198 D2
Barinas state Venez. 198 D2
Baringa Dem. Rep. Congo 126 D4
Baringo, Lake Kenya 128 C4
Baripada India 97 E5
Bariri Brazil 206 E9
Bari Sadri India 96 B4
Barisal Bangl. 97 F5
Barisal admin. div. Bangl. 97 F5
Barisan, Pegunungan mts Indon. 76 C3
Barito r. Indon. 77 F3
Baritu, Parque Nacional nat. park Arg. 201 D5
Barium Italy see Bari

Barjaude, Montagne de mt. France 51 M9
Barjols France 51 M9
Barjora India 97 E5
Barjūj, Wādī watercourse Libya 120 B3
Barka prov. Eritrea 104 B4
Barkā Oman 105 G3
Barkam China 86 B2
Barkan, Ra's-e pt Iran 100 B4
Barkava Latvia 42 H5
Barker, Lake salt flat Australia 151 C6
Barkerville Canada 166 F4
Barkéwol el Abiod Mauritania 124 B2
Barkhan Pak. 101 G4
Barki Saraiya India 97 E4
Bark Lake Canada 173 P5
Barkley, Lake U.S.A. 174 C4
Barkley Sound inlet Canada 166 E5
Barkly East S. Africa 133 L7
Barkly Pass S. Africa 133 L8
Barkly Tableland reg. Australia 148 B3
Barkly West S. Africa 133 I5
Barkol China 84 B3
Barkol Hu salt l. China 84 B3
Barkot India 96 C3
Bârlad Romania 58 I2 formerly spelt Bîrlad
Bârladului, Podişul plat. Romania 58 I2
Barlag Gol watercourse Mongolia 84 B2
Bar-le-Duc France 51 L4
Barlee, Lake salt flat Australia 151 B6
Barlee Range hills Australia 150 A4
Barlee Range Nature Reserve Australia 150 A4
Barletta Italy 56 I7 historically known as Barduli
Barlinek Poland 49 M3
Barlow Canada 166 B2
Barlow Lake Canada 167 K2
Barmedman Australia 147 E3
Barmen-Elberfeld Germany see Wuppertal
Barmer India 96 A4 also spelt Balmer
Barmera Australia 146 D3
Barm Fīrūz, Kūh-e mt. Iran 107 G5
Barmouth U.K. 47 H11 also known as Abermaw
Barmstedt Germany 48 G2
Barnagar India 96 B5
Barnala India 96 B3
Barnard, Mount Canada/U.S.A. 166 B3
Barnard Castle U.K. 47 K9
Barnato Australia 147 E2
Barnaul Rus. Fed. 80 C2
Barnegat U.S.A. 177 K6
Barnegat Bay U.S.A. 177 K6
Barne Inlet Antarctica 223 K1
Barnesboro U.S.A. 176 G5
Barnes Icecap Canada 165 L2
Barnesville GA U.S.A. 175 D5
Barnesville MN U.S.A. 178 C2
Barnet U.S.A. 177 M1
Barneveld Neth. 48 C3
Barneville-Carteret France 50 E3
Barney Top mt. U.S.A. 183 M4
Barnhart U.S.A. 179 B6
Barnjarn Aboriginal Land res. Australia 148 B2
Bârnova, Dealul hill Romania 58 I1
Barnsdall U.S.A. 178 C4
Barnsley U.K. 47 K10
Barnstable U.S.A. 177 O4
Barnstaple U.K. 47 H12
Barnstaple Bay U.K. see Bideford Bay
Barnwell U.S.A. 175 D5
Baro Nigeria 125 G4
Baroda India see Vadodara
Baroda India 96 C4
Baroda S. Africa 133 J8
Baroe S. Africa 133 I10
Baroghil Pass Afgh. 101 H2
Barong China 86 A2
Baron'ki Belarus 43 N8
Barons Range hills Australia 150 D5
Baroua Cent. Afr. Rep. 126 E3
Baro Wenz r. Eth. 128 B2
Barowka Belarus 42 I6
Barpeta India 97 F4
Bar Pla Soi Thai. see Chon Buri
Barqa, Gebel mt. Egypt 108 F9
Barqā al Ashqar reg. Yemen 105 D4
Barqā 'Damaj well Saudi Arabia 109 H9
Barques, Point Aux U.S.A. 173 K6
Barquisimeto Venez. 198 D2
Barr, Râs el pt Egypt 108 C6
Barra Brazil 202 D4
Barra i. U.K. 46 E7 also spelt Barraigh
Barraba Australia 147 F2
Barra Bonita Brazil 206 E9
Barra Bonita, Represa resr Brazil 206 E9
Barracão do Barreto Brazil 201 F2
Barrackville U.S.A. 176 E6
Barracouta, Cape S. Africa 132 F11
Barra da Estiva Brazil 202 D5
Barra de Navidad Mex. 184 D5
Barra de Santos inlet Brazil 206 G11
Barra de São Francisco Brazil 207 M5
Barra de São João Brazil 207 L9
Barra do Bugres Brazil 201 F3
Barra do Corda Brazil 202 C3
Barra do Cuanza Angola 127 B7
Barra do Cuieté Brazil 207 L6
Barra do Garças Brazil 206 A2
Barrado Mendes Brazil 202 D4
Barra do Piraí Brazil 207 J9
Barra do Rocha Brazil 207 M1
Barra do São Manuel Brazil 201 F1
Barra do Una Brazil 206 F11
Barra Falsa, Ponta da pt Moz. 131 G4
Barraigh i. U.K. see Barra
Barra Kruta Hond. 186 C4
Barra Longa Brazil 207 J7
Barra Mansa Brazil 207 I9
Barrāmīya Egypt 121 G3
Barranca Peru 200 A2
Barranca Venez. 198 C2
Barrancabermeja Col. 198 C3
Barranca del Cobre, Parque Natural nature res. Mex. 184 D3
Barrancas r. Arg. 204 C5
Barrancas Barinas Venez. 198 D2
Barrancas Monagas Venez. 199 F2
Barranco de Loba Col. 198 C2
Barranquilla Atlántico Col. 198 C2
Barranquilla Guaviare Col. 198 C4
Barranquita Peru 198 B6
Barras Brazil 202 D3
Barraute Canada 173 P2
Barrax Spain 55 I5
Barre MA U.S.A. 177 M3
Barre VT U.S.A. 177 M1
Barreal Arg. 204 C3
Barre des Ecrins mt. France 51 M8
Barreiras Brazil 202 C5
Barreirinha Brazil 199 G5
Barreirinhas Brazil 202 D2
Barreiro r. Brazil 206 A2
Barreiro do Nascimento Brazil 202 B4
Barreiros Brazil 202 F4
Barren Island India 95 G3
Barren Island Kiribati see Starbuck Island
Barren Islands U.S.A. 164 D4
Barretos Brazil 206 E7
Barrett U.S.A. 183 H9
Barrett, Mount hill Australia 150 D3
Barrhead Canada 167 H4
Barrhill N.Z. 153 F11
Barri i. Saudi Arabia 104 C4
Barrie Canada 168 E4
Barrie Island Canada 173 K5
Barrier, Cape N.Z. 152 J4
Barrier Bay Antarctica 223 F2
Barrière Canada 166 F5
Barrier Range hills Australia 146 D2
Barrier Reef Belize 185 I5
Barrington Canada 169 H5
Barrington S. Africa 132 G10
Barrington, Mount Australia 147 F3
Barrington Lake Canada 167 K3
Barrington Tops National Park Australia 147 F3
Barro Alto Brazil 206 E2
Barrocão Brazil 207 J3
Barrolândia Brazil 207 N3
Barron U.S.A. 172 B5
Barronett U.S.A. 172 B5
Barroso Brazil 207 J8
Barrow Arg. 204 E5
Barrow r. Rep. of Ireland 47 F11
Barrow U.S.A. 164 D2
Barrow, Point U.S.A. 164 D2
Barrow Creek Australia 148 B4
Barrow-in-Furness U.K. 47 I9
Barrow Island Australia 150 A4
Barrow Island Nature Reserve Australia 150 A4
Barrow Range hills Australia 151 D5
Barrow Strait Canada 165 J2
Barr Smith Range hills Australia 151 C5
Barry U.K. 47 I12
Barrydale S. Africa 132 E10
Barry Islands Canada 167 I1
Barry Mountains Australia 147 E4
Barrys Bay Canada 168 E4
Barryton U.S.A. 173 H7
Barryville N.Z. 152 J6
Barryville U.S.A. 177 K4
Barsakel'mes, Ostrov i. Kazakh. 102 D3
Barsakel'messkiy Zapovednik nature res. Kazakh. 102 E3
Barsalogo Burkina 125 E3
Barsalpur India 96 B3
Barshatas Kazakh. 103 I2 formerly known as Chubartau
Barshi India see Barsi
Barsi India 94 B2 formerly spelt Barshi
Barstow U.S.A. 183 G7
Barstyčiai Lith. 42 C5
Barsuki Rus. Fed. 43 S7
Barsur India 94 D2
Bar-sur-Aube France 51 K4
Bar-sur-Seine France 51 K4
Bārta Latvia 42 C5
Bārta r. Latvia 42 C5
Bartang r. Tajik. 101 G2
Barth Germany 49 J1
Bartholomew, Bayou r. U.S.A. 175 A5
Bartica Guyana 199 G3
Bartın Turkey 106 C2
Bartle Frere, Mount Australia 149 E3
Bartles U.S.A. 176 C7
Bartles, Mount U.S.A. 183 N2
Bartlesville U.S.A. 178 C4
Bartlett NE U.S.A. 178 C3
Bartlett NH U.S.A. 177 N1
Bartlett Lake Canada 167 G2
Bartlett Reservoir U.S.A. 183 M8
Bartletts N.Z. 152 L6
Barton U.S.A. 177 M1
Bartonville U.S.A. 172 D10
Bartoszyce Poland 49 R1
Bartow U.S.A. 175 D7
Bartuva r. Lith. 42 C5
Barú, Isla de i. Col. 198 C2
Baruipur India 97 F5
Barūm Yemen 105 E5
Barumun r. Indon. 76 C2
Barung i. Indon. 77 F5
Barunga Australia see Bamyili
Barun-Torey, Ozero l. Rus. Fed. 85 G1
Barus Indon. 76 B2
Baruunharaa Mongolia 85 E1
Baruunsuu Mongolia 85 E3
Baruunturuun Mongolia 84 B1
Baruun Urt Mongolia 85 G2
Baruva India 95 E2
Barwa India 97 E5
Barwah India 96 C5
Barwala Gujarat India 96 A5
Barwala Haryana India 96 B3
Barwānah Iraq 109 N3
Barwani India 96 B5
Barwa Sagar India 96 C4
Barwice Poland 49 N2
Barwon r. Australia 147 E2
Baryatino Rus. Fed. 43 P7
Barybino Rus. Fed. 43 S6
Barycz r. Poland 49 N4
Barygaza India see Bharuch
Barysaw Belarus 43 J7 also spelt Borisov
Barysh Rus. Fed. 41 H5
Basaga Turkm. 101 F2 formerly spelt Bossaga
Bāsa'īdū Iran 100 C5
Basail Arg. 204 F2
Basăk, Tônlé r. Cambodia 79 D6
Basalt r. Australia 149 E3
Basalt Island Hong Kong China 87 [inset] also known as Fo Shek Chau
Basanga Dem. Rep. Congo 127 E6
Basankusu Dem. Rep. Congo 126 C4
Basantpur India 97 E4
Basarabeasca Moldova 58 J2 formerly known as Romanovka; formerly spelt Bessarabka
Basarabi Romania 58 J4
Basargechar Armenia see Vardenis
Basavilbaso Arg. 204 F4
Basay Phil. 74 B4
Basco Phil. 74 B1
Bascombe Well Conservation Park nature res. Australia 146 B3
Bas-Congo prov. Dem. Rep. Congo 127 B6 formerly known as Bas-Zaïre
Bascuñán, Cabo c. Chile 204 C3
Bascuñana, Sierra de mts Spain 55 I4
Basedow Range hills Australia 148 B5
Basel Switz. 51 N5 English form Basle; also spelt Bâle
Basel-Mulhouse airport France 51 N5
Basentello r. Italy 56 I8
Basento r. Italy 57 I8
Basey Phil. 74 C4
Bashākerd, Kūhhā-ye mts Iran 100 D5
Bashan China see Chongren
Bashanta Rus. Fed. see Gorodovikovsk
Bashaw Canada 167 H4
Bashee r. S. Africa 133 M9
Bashee Bridge S. Africa 133 M8
Bashgul r. Afgh. 101 G3
Bāshī Iran 100 B4
Bashi Channel Taiwan 73 F2
Bashimuke Dem. Rep. Congo 127 E6
Ba'shīqah, Jabal mt. Iraq 109 O1
Bashkaus r. Rus. Fed. 88 D1
Bashkiria aut. rep. Rus. Fed. see Bashkortostan, Respublika
Bashkirskaya A.S.S.R. aut. rep. Rus. Fed. see Bashkortostan, Respublika
Bashkirskiy Zapovednik nature res. Rus. Fed. 102 D1
Bashkortostan, Respublika aut. rep. Rus. Fed. 102 D1 formerly known as Bashkiria or Bashkirskaya A.S.S.R.
Bashmakovo Rus. Fed. 41 G5
Bāsht Iran 100 B4
Bashtanka Ukr. 41 E7
Bashtīn, Ra's pt Yemen 105 F5
Basi India 96 C4
Basia India 97 E5
Basilaki Island P.N.G. 149 F1
Basilan i. Phil. 74 B5
Basilan Strait Phil. 74 B5
Basildon U.K. 47 M12
Basile U.S.A. 179 D6
Basile, Pico mt. Equat. Guinea 125 H6
Basilicata admin. reg. Italy 57 H8
Basin U.S.A. 180 E3
Basingstoke U.K. 47 K12
Basin Lake Canada 167 J4
Bāsīra r. Iraq 107 F4
Basirhat India 97 F5
Basīţ, Ra's al pt Syria 108 G2
Baskakovka Rus. Fed. 43 P7
Başkale Turkey 107 F3
Baskatong, Réservoir Canada 168 F4
Baskerville, Cape Australia 150 C3
Başkomutan Milli Parkı nat. park Turkey 106 B3
Baskunchak, Ozero l. Rus. Fed. 102 A2
Basle Switz. see Basel
Basmat India 94 C2
Baso i. Indon. 76 C3
Basoda India 96 C5
Basoko Dem. Rep. Congo 126 D4
Basongo Dem. Rep. Congo 126 D6
Basotu Tanz. 129 B6
Basque Country aut. comm. Spain see País Vasco
Basra Iraq 107 F5 also spelt Al Başrah
Bassano Canada 167 H5
Bassano del Grappa Italy 56 D3
Bassar Togo 125 F4
Bassas da India reef Indian Ocean 131 H4
Bassas de Pedro Padua Bank sea feature India 94 B3 also known as Munyal-Par
Bassawa Côte d'Ivoire 124 D4
Bassein Myanmar 78 A4 also spelt Puthein; formerly spelt Pathein
Bassein r. Myanmar 78 A4
Basse-Kotto pref. Cent. Afr. Rep. 126 D3
Basse-Normandie admin. reg. France 50 F4
Basse Santa Su Gambia 124 B3

▶Basse-Terre Guadeloupe 187 H3
Capital of Guadeloupe.

Basse-Terre i. Guadeloupe 187 H3

▶Basseterre St Kitts and Nevis 187 H3
Capital of St Kitts and Nevis.

Bassett NE U.S.A. 178 C3
Bassett VA U.S.A. 176 F9
Bassett Peak U.S.A. 183 N9
Bassikounou Mauritania 124 D3
Bassila Benin 125 F4
Basso, Plateau de Chad 120 D5
Bass Strait Australia 147 E4
Basswood Lake Canada 168 B3
Basswood Lake U.S.A. 172 B2
Båstad Sweden 45 K4
Bastak Iran 100 C5
Bastānābād Iran 100 A2
Basti India 97 D4
Bastia Corse France 51 P10
Bastia Italy 56 E5
Bastian U.S.A. 176 D8
Bastogne Belgium 51 L2
Bastos Brazil 206 C8
Bastrop LA U.S.A. 175 B5
Bastrop TX U.S.A. 179 C6
Bastuträsk Sweden 44 M2
Basu, Tanjung pt Indon. 76 C3
Basul r. Pak. 101 F5
Basuo China see Dongfang
Basutoland country Africa see Lesotho
Basya r. Belarus 43 M8
Bas-Zaïre prov. Dem. Rep. Congo see Bas-Congo
Bat mt. Croatia 56 I5
Bat, Al-Khutm and Al-Ayn tourist site Oman 105 G3
Bata Equat. Guinea 125 H6
Bataan Peninsula Phil. 74 B3
Batabanó, Golfo de b. Cuba 186 C2
Batac Phil. 74 B2
Batagay Rus. Fed. 39 N3
Batagay-Alyta Rus. Fed. 39 N3
Bataguassu Brazil 206 A8
Batak Bulg. 58 F7
Batakan Indon. 77 F4
Batala India 96 B3
Batalha Brazil 202 D3 formerly known as Belo Monte
Batalha Port. 54 C5
Batam i. Indon. 76 D2
Batama Dem. Rep. Congo 126 E4
Batamay Rus. Fed. 39 M3
Batamshinskiy Kazakh. 102 D2 also known as Batamshy
Batamshy Kazakh. see Batamshinskiy
Batan i. Phil. 74 B1
Batan i. Phil. 74 C3
Batang China 86 A2 also known as Xiaqiong
Batang Indon. 77 E4
Batangafo Cent. Afr. Rep. 126 C3
Batang Ali National Park Sarawak Malaysia 77 F2
Batangas Phil. 74 B3
Batanghari r. Indon. 76 D3
Batangpele i. Indon. 75 D3
Batangtoru Indon. 76 B2
Batan Islands Phil. 74 B1
Bátaszék Hungary 49 P9
Batatais Brazil 206 F7
Batavia Indon. see Jakarta
Batavia NY U.S.A. 176 G3
Batavia OH U.S.A. 176 A6
Bataysk Rus. Fed. 41 F7
Batbatan i. Phil. 74 B4
Batchawana Canada 173 I3
Batchawana r. Canada 173 I4
Batchawana Bay Canada 173 I4
Batchawana Mountain hill Canada 168 C4
Batchelor Australia 148 A2
Bătdâmbâng Cambodia 79 C5 also spelt Battambang
Bateemeucica, Gunung mt. Indon. 76 A1
Batéké, Plateaux Congo 126 B5
Batemans Bay Australia 147 F3
Båteng Norway 44 N1
Batesburg U.S.A. 175 D5
Bates Range hills Australia 151 C5
Batesville AR U.S.A. 174 B5
Batesville MS U.S.A. 174 B5
Batetskiy Rus. Fed. 43 L3
Bath N.B. Canada 169 H4
Bath Ont. Canada 173 Q6
Bath U.K. 47 J12
Bath ME U.S.A. 177 P2
Bath NY U.S.A. 177 H3
Bath PA U.S.A. 177 J5
Batha pref. Chad 120 C6
Batha watercourse Chad 120 C6
Bathinda India 96 B3 also spelt Bhatinda
Bathurst Australia 147 F3
Bathurst Canada 169 H4
Bathurst Gambia see Banjul
Bathurst S. Africa 133 K10
Bathurst, Cape Canada 164 G2
Bathurst Bay Australia 149 E2
Bathurst Inlet Canada 167 I1
Bathurst Inlet inlet Canada 167 I1
Bathurst Island Australia 148 A1
Bathurst Island Canada 165 J2
Batī Eth. 128 D2
Batia Benin 125 F4
Batié Burkina 124 E4
Batikala, Tanjung pt Indon. 75 B3
Batı Menteşe Dağları mts Turkey 59 I11
Bāţin, Wādī al watercourse Asia 105 D1
Batista, Serra da hills Brazil 202 D4
Batı Toroslar mts Turkey 106 B3
Batken Kyrg. 103 G5
Batken admin. div. Kyrg. 103 G5
Bāţlāq-e Gavkhūnī marsh Iran 100 C3
Batman Turkey 107 E3
Batna Alg. 123 G2
Baţn aţ Ţarfā' depr. Saudi Arabia 105 E3
Batočina Srbija Yugo. 58 C4
Batok, Bukit Sing. 76 [inset]
Batok, Bukit hill Sing. 76 [inset]

▶Baton Rouge U.S.A. 175 B6
State capital of Louisiana.

Batopilas Mex. 184 D3
Batote Jammu and Kashmir 96 B2
Batouri Cameroon 125 I5
Batrā' tourist site Jordan see Petra
Batrā, Jabal mt. Saudi Arabia 104 B2
Batrā', Jabal al mt. Jordan 108 G8
Ba Tri Vietnam 79 D6
Batroûn Lebanon 108 G3
Båtsfjord Norway 44 O1
Bat-Sot Rus. Fed. 84 B1
Battambang Cambodia see Bătdâmbâng
Batti India 96 B3
Batticaloa Sri Lanka 94 D5
Batti Malv i. India 95 G4
Battipaglia Italy 57 G8
Battle r. Canada 167 I4
Battle Creek r. Australia 148 A2
Battle Creek r. Canada/U.S.A. 167 I5
Battle Creek U.S.A. 173 H8
Battlefields Zimbabwe 131 F3
Battleford Canada 167 I4
Battle Mountain U.S.A. 183 H1
Battle Mountain mt. U.S.A. 183 G1
Battura Glacier Jammu and Kashmir 96 B1
Batu mt. Eth. 128 C3
Batu, Bukit mt. Sarawak Malaysia 77 F2
Batu, Pulau-pulau is Indon. 76 B3
Batu, Tanjung pt Indon. 77 G2
Batuata i. Indon. 75 B4
Batuayau, Bukit mt. Indon. 77 F2
Batubetumbang Indon. 77 D3
Batu Bora, Bukit mt. Sarawak Malaysia 77 F2
Batudaka i. Indon. 75 B3
Batu Gajah Malaysia 76 C1
Batuhitam, Tanjung pt Indon. 75 B3
Batui Indon. 75 B3
Batulaki Phil. 74 C5
Batulicin Indon. 77 G3
Batulilangmebang, Gunung mt. Indon. 77 F2
Batum Georgia see Bat'umi
Bat'umi Georgia 107 E2 English form Batum
Batumonga Indon. 76 C3
Batu Pahat Malaysia 76 C2
Batu Puteh, Gunung mt. Malaysia 76 C1
Baturaja Indon. 76 D4
Baturetno Indon. 77 E5
Baturino Rus. Fed. 43 N6
Batusangkar Indon. 76 C3
Batyrevo Rus. Fed. 40 H5
Batys Qazaqstan Oblysy admin. div. Kazakh. see Zapadnyy Kazakhstan
Batz, Île de i. France 50 B4
Bau r. Brazil 201 G1
Bau Sarawak Malaysia 77 E2
Baubau Indon. 75 B4
Baucau East Timor see Baukau
Bauchi Nigeria 125 H4
Bauchi state Nigeria 125 H4
Bauda India 95 E1
Baudette U.S.A. 178 D1
Baudo, Serrania de mts Col. 198 B3
Baudouinville Dem. Rep. Congo see Moba
Bauet well Eth. 128 E3
Baugé France 50 F5
Bauges mts France 51 M7
Baukau East Timor 75 C5 also known as Baucau
Bauld, Cape Canada 169 K3
Baumann Fiord inlet Canada 165 K2
Baume-les-Dames France 51 M5
Baunei Sardegna Italy 57 B8
Bauru Brazil 206 D9
Baús Brazil 206 A5
Baushar Oman 105 G3
Bauska Latvia 42 F5
Bautino Kazakh. 102 B3
Bautzen Germany 49 L4
Bauyrzhan Momysh-Uly Kazakh. 103 G4 formerly known as Burnoye
Bavaria land Germany see Bayern
Bavaria reg. Germany 48 I7 also known as Bayern
Bavda India 94 B2
Båven l. Sweden 45 L4
Baviaanskloofberge mts S. Africa 132 H10
Bavispe Mex. 184 C2
Bavispe r. Mex. 184 C2
Bavla India 96 B5
Bavleny Rus. Fed. 43 U5
Bavly Rus. Fed. 40 J5
Baw Myanmar 78 A3
Bawal India 96 C3
Bawal i. Indon. 77 E3
Bawan Indon. 77 F3
Bawang, Tanjung pt Indon. 77 E3
Baw Baw National Park Australia 147 E4
Bawdwin Myanmar 78 B3
Bawean i. Indon. 77 F4
Bawiti Egypt 121 F2
Bawku Ghana 125 E4
Bawlake Myanmar 78 B4
Bawolung China 86 B2
Baxi China 86 B1
Baxian China see Banan
Baxian China see Bazhou
Baxkorgan China 88 E4
Baxley U.S.A. 175 D6
Baxoi China 86 A2 also known as Baima
Bay China see Baicheng
Bay admin. reg. Somalia 128 D4
Bay, Laguna de lag. Phil. 74 B3
Bay, Réserve de nature res. Mali 124 E3
Baya r. Côte d'Ivoire 124 E5
Bayad Alg. 57 A13
Bayamo Cuba 186 D2
Bayamón Puerto Rico 187 G3
Bayan China 82 B3
Bayan China see Hualong
Bayan Indon. 77 G5
Bayan Arhangay Mongolia 84 D2
Bayan Govĭ-Altay Mongolia 84 B2
Bayan Hentiy Mongolia 85 F1
Bayana India 96 C4
Bayanaul Kazakh. 103 H2
Bayanbulag Bayanhongor Mongolia 84 C2
Bayanbulag Bayanhongor Mongolia 84 C2
Bayanbulag Hentiy Mongolia 85 F2
Bayanbulak China 88 D2
Bayandelger Mongolia 85 F2
Bayang, Pegunungan mts Indon. 77 E2
Bayanga-Didi Cent. Afr. Rep. 126 B3
Bayan Gol China see Dengkou
Bayangol Mongolia 84 B2
Bayangol Rus. Fed. 84 D1
Bayan Har Shan mts China 84 B5
Bayan Har Shankou pass China 86 A1
Bayanhongor Mongolia 84 D2
Bayanhongor prov. Mongolia 84 C2
Bayan Hot China 85 E4 also known as Alxa Zuoqi
Bayanhushuu Mongolia 84 D2
Bayan-Kol Respublika Tyva Rus. Fed. 84 B1
Bayan-Kol Rus. Fed. 88 G1
Bayan Mod China 84 E3
Bayan Nuru China 84 E3 also known as Xar Burd
Bayano, Lago l. Panama 186 D5
Bayan Obo Kuangqu China 85 F3
Bayan-Ölgiy prov. Mongolia 84 A1
Bayan-Ovoo Govĭ-Altay Mongolia 84 B2
Bayan-Ovoo Hentiy Mongolia 85 F1
Bayan-Ovoo Hentiy Mongolia 85 G2
Bayan Qagan China 85 G3 also known as Qahar Youyi Houqi
Bayansayr Mongolia 84 C2
Bayan Shan mt. China 84 C4
Bayanteeg Mongolia 84 D2
Bayan Tohoi China 85 H1 also known as Ewenkizu Zizhiqi
Bayantöhöm Mongolia 85 E2
Bayan Ul Hot China 85 H2 also known as Xi Ujimqin Qi
Bayan Uul mts Mongolia 84 A1
Bayard NE U.S.A. 178 B3
Bayard WV U.S.A. 176 F6
Bayasgalant Mongolia 85 G2
Bayat Turkey 106 B3
Bayawan Phil. 74 B4
Bayāz Iran 100 C4
Baybay Phil. 74 C4
Bay Bulls Canada 169 K4
Bayburt Turkey 107 E2
Baychunas Kazakh. 102 C3 also spelt Bayshonas
Bay City MI U.S.A. 173 J7
Bay City TX U.S.A. 179 C6
Baydā, Jabal al hill Saudi Arabia 104 B2
Baydaratskaya Guba Rus. Fed. 40 M1
Baydhabo Somalia 128 D4 formerly known as Baidoa
Baydrag Mongolia 84 C2
Baydrag Gol r. Mongolia 84 C2
Bay du Nord Wilderness nature res. Canada 169 K3
Baydzhansay Kazakh. see Bayzhansay
Bayelsa state Nigeria 125 G5
Bayerische Rhön park Germany 48 G5
Bayerischer Wald mts Germany 49 J6
Bayerischer Wald nat. park Germany 49 J6
Bayern land Germany 51 R3 English form Bavaria
Bayern reg. Germany see Bavaria
Bayer Wald, Nationalpark nat. park Germany 49 K7
Bayeux France 50 F3
Bayeva Belarus 43 M7
Bayevo Rus. Fed. 103 J1
Bayfield Canada 173 L7
Baygakum Kazakh. 103 F3
Bayganin Kazakh. 102 C2 formerly known as Karaulkel'dy
Baygora Kazakh. 103 E1
Bayḩān al Qişab Yemen 105 D5
Bayındır Turkey 106 A3
Bay Islands is Hond. see La Bahía, Islas de
Bayizhen China 89 F6
Bayjī Iraq 107 E4 also spelt Baiji
Baykadam Kazakh. see Saudakent
Baykal, Ozero l. Rus. Fed. see Baikal, Lake
Baykal-Amur Magistral Rus. Fed. 82 C1
Baykal Range mts Rus. Fed. see Baykal'skiy Khrebet
Baykal'sk Rus. Fed. 84 E1
Baykal'skiy Khrebet mts Rus. Fed. 81 H2 English form Baykal Range
Baykal'skiy Zapovednik nature res. Rus. Fed. 85 E1
Baykan Turkey 107 E3
Bay-Khaak Rus. Fed. 84 B1
Bay-Khozha Kazakh. 103 E3
Baykibashevo Rus. Fed. 40 K5
Baykit Rus. Fed. 39 J3
Baykonur Karagandinskaya Oblast' Kazakh. 103 F3
Baykonur Kzyl-Ordinskaya Oblast' Kazakh. 103 E3 also spelt Baykonyr or Bayqongyr; formerly known as Leninsk or Toretam or Tyuratam
Baykonyr Kazakh. see Baykonur
Bayley Point Aboriginal Reserve Australia 148 C3
Baymak Rus. Fed. 102 D1
Bay Minette U.S.A. 175 C6
Baynūna'h reg. U.A.E. 105 F3
Bay of Islands Maritime and Historic Park nature res. N.Z. 152 I3
Bay of Plenty admin. reg. N.Z. 152 K5
Bayombong Phil. 74 B2
Bayona Spain see Baiona
Bayonne France 50 E9 historically known as Lapurdum
Bayo Point Phil. 74 B4
Bayóvar Peru 198 A6
Bay Point Phil. 74 A4
Bay Port U.S.A. 173 J7
Bayqadam Kazakh. see Saudakent
Bayqongyr Kazakh. see Baykonur
Bayramaly Turkm. 103 E5
Bayramiç Turkey 106 A3
Bayreuth Germany 48 I6
Bayrūt Lebanon see Beirut
Bay St Louis U.S.A. 175 B6
Baysh watercourse Saudi Arabia 104 C4
Bayshonas Kazakh. see Baychunas
Bay Springs U.S.A. 175 B6
Baysun Uzbek. 103 F5 also spelt Boysun
Baysuntau, Gory mts Uzbek. 103 F5
Bayt al Faqīh Yemen 104 C5
Baytik Shan mts China 84 A2
Bayt Lahm West Bank see Bethlehem
Baytown U.S.A. 179 D6
Bayu Indon. 75 B3
Bayunglincir Indon. 76 C3
Bay View N.Z. 152 K7
Bayy al Kabīr, Wādī watercourse Libya 120 B2
Bayyrqum Kazakh. see Bairkum
Bayzhansay Kazakh. 103 G4 also spelt Baydzhansay
Baza Spain 55 I7
Baza, Sierra de mts Spain 55 I7
Bazarchulan Kazakh. 102 B2 formerly spelt Bazarshulan
Bazardyuzi, Gora mt. Azer./Rus. Fed. 107 F2
Bāzār-e Māsāl Iran 100 B2
Bazarkhanym, Gora mt. Uzbek. 103 G5
Bazar-Korgon Kyrg. 103 H4 also spelt Bazar Kurgan
Bazar Kurgan Kyrg. see Bazar-Korgon
Bazarnyy Karabulak Rus. Fed. 41 H5
Bazarnyy Syzgan Rus. Fed. 41 H5
Bazarshulan Kazakh. see Bazarchulan
Bazartobe Kazakh. 102 B2
Bazaruto, Ilha do i. Moz. 131 G4
Bazas France 50 F8
Bazdar Pak. 101 F5
Bazhong China 86 C2
Bazhou China 85 H4 formerly known as Baxian
Bazin r. Canada 169 F4
Baziwehn Liberia 124 C4
Bazmān Iran 101 E5
Bazmān, Kūh-e mt. Iran 101 E4
Bcharre Lebanon 108 H3
Be r. Vietnam 79 D6
Bé, Nossi i. Madag. see Bé, Nosy
Bé, Nosy i. Madag. 131 [inset] K2 formerly spelt Bé, Nossi
Beach U.S.A. 178 B2
Beachburg Canada 173 Q5
Beach City U.S.A. 176 D5
Beach Haven U.S.A. 177 K6
Beachport Australia 146 D4
Beachy Head U.K. 47 M13
Beacon Australia 151 B6
Beacon U.S.A. 177 L4
Beacon Bay S. Africa 133 L9
Beaconsfield Australia 147 E5
Beagle, Canal sea chan. Arg. 205 C9
Beagle Bank reef Australia 150 C2
Beagle Bay Australia 150 C3
Beagle Bay Aboriginal Reserve Australia 150 C3
Beagle Gulf Australia 148 A2
Beagle Island Australia 151 A6
Bealanana Madag. 131 [inset] K2
Béal an Átha Rep. of Ireland see Ballina
Béal Átha na Sluaighe Rep. of Ireland see Ballinasloe
Beampingaratra mts Madag. 131 [inset] J5
Beandrarezona Madag. 131 [inset] K2
Bear r. U.S.A. 180 D4
Bearalváhki Norway see Berlevåg
Bear Creek Canada 166 B1
Bear Creek r. U.S.A. 178 B4
Beardmore Glacier Antarctica 223 L1
Beardmore Reservoir Australia 147 F1
Beardstown U.S.A. 174 B3
Bear Island i. Arctic Ocean see Bjørnøya
Bear Island Canada 173 M4
Bear Island i. Canada 168 D2
Bear Island i. Rep. of Ireland 47 C12
Bear Lake l. Canada 167 L4
Bear Lake U.S.A. 172 G6
Bear Lake l. U.S.A. 180 E4
Bearma r. India 96 C4
Bear Mountain U.S.A. 178 B3
Bearnaraigh i. U.K. see Berneray
Bear Paw Mountain U.S.A. 180 E2
Bearpaw Mountains U.S.A. 180 E2
Bear Peninsula Antarctica 222 Q2
Bearskin Lake Canada 168 B2
Beas r. India 96 B3
Beasain Spain 55 I1
Beata, Cabo c. Dom. Rep. 187 F3
Beata, Isla i. Dom. Rep. 187 F3
Beatrice U.S.A. 178 C3
Beatrice Zimbabwe 131 F3
Beatrice, Cape Australia 148 C2
Beatton r. Canada 166 F3
Beatty U.S.A. 183 H5
Beattyville Canada 168 E3
Beattyville U.S.A. 176 B8
Beaucaire France 51 K9
Beauchêne, Lac l. Canada 173 O4
Beauchene Island Falkland Is 205 F9
Beaudesert Australia 147 G1
Beaufort Australia 147 D4
Beaufort Sabah Malaysia 77 F1
Beaufort NC U.S.A. 174 E5
Beaufort SC U.S.A. 175 D5
Beaufort Castle tourist site Lebanon 108 G4
Beaufort-en-Vallée France 50 F5
Beaufort Island Hong Kong China 87 [inset] also known as Lo Chau
Beaufort Sea Canada/U.S.A. 164 G2
Beaufort West S. Africa 132 G9
Beaugency France 50 H5
Beaulieu-sur-Dordogne France 50 H8
Beauly U.K. 46 H6
Beauly r. U.K. 46 H6
Beaumont Belgium 51 K2
Beaumont N.Z. 153 D13
Beaumont CA U.S.A. 183 H8
Beaumont MS U.S.A. 175 B6
Beaumont TX U.S.A. 179 D6
Beaumont-de-Lomagne France 50 G9
Beaumont-le-Roger France 50 G3
Beaune France 51 K5
Beaune-La Rolande France 51 I4
Beauraing Belgium 51 K2
Beauséjour Canada 167 L5
Beauvais France 51 I3
Beauval Canada 167 J4
Beauvoir-sur-Mer France 50 D6
Beaver r. Alta/Sask. Canada 167 J4
Beaver r. Ont. Canada 168 C2
Beaver r. Y.T. Canada 166 C2
Beaver r. Y.T. Canada 166 E3
Beaver OK U.S.A. 178 B4
Beaver UT U.S.A. 183 L3
Beaver r. OK U.S.A. 178 B4
Beaver r. UT U.S.A. 183 L2
Beaver City U.S.A. 178 C3
Beaver Creek Canada 166 A2
Beaver Creek r. MO U.S.A. 178 D4
Beaver Creek r. MT U.S.A. 180 F2
Beaver Creek r. ND U.S.A. 178 B2
Beaver Creek r. NE U.S.A. 178 C3
Beaver Dam KY U.S.A. 174 C4
Beaver Dam WI U.S.A. 172 E7
Beaver Dam Lake U.S.A. 172 E7
Beaver Falls U.S.A. 176 E5
Beaver Glacier Antarctica 223 D2
Beaverhead r. U.S.A. 180 D3
Beaverhead Mountains U.S.A. 180 D3
Beaverhill Lake Canada 167 H4
Beaver Hill Lake Canada 167 M4
Beaver Island U.S.A. 172 H5
Beaverlodge Canada 166 G4
Beaver Run Reservoir U.S.A. 176 F5
Beaverton MI U.S.A. 173 I7
Beaverton OR U.S.A. 180 B3
Beawar India 96 B4
Beazley Arg. 204 D4
Bebedero, Salina del salt pan Arg. 204 D4
Bébédjia Chad 126 C2
Bebedouro Brazil 206 E7
Beberibe Brazil 202 E3
Bebra Germany 48 G5
Bêca China 86 A2
Beccles U.K. 47 N11
Bečej Vojvodina, Srbija Yugo. 58 B3 also known as Óbecse
Becerreá Spain 54 D2
Becerrero hill Spain 54 G7
Becerro, Cayos is Hond. 186 C4
Béchar Alg. 123 E3 formerly known as Colomb-Béchar
Becharof Lake U.S.A. 164 D4
Bechevinka Rus. Fed. 43 S2
Bechuanaland country Africa see Botswana
Beçin Turkey 59 I11
Becker, Mount Antarctica 222 T1
Beckley U.S.A. 176 D8
Becks N.Z. 153 D12
Becky Peak U.S.A. 183 J2
Beclean Romania 58 F1
Bečva r. Czech Rep. 49 O6
Beda Hāyk' l. Eth. 128 D2
Bédarieux France 51 J9
Bedeau Alg. see Ras el Ma
Bedel', Pereval pass China/Kyrg. see Bedel Pass
Bedelē Eth. 128 C2
Bedel Pass China/Kyrg. 88 B3 also known as Bedel', Pereval
Bedford Canada 169 I4
Bedford S. Africa 133 K9
Bedford U.K. 47 L11
Bedford IA U.S.A. 178 D3
Bedford IN U.S.A. 174 C4
Bedford KY U.S.A. 174 C4
Bedford NY U.S.A. 177 L4
Bedford PA U.S.A. 176 G5
Bedford VA U.S.A. 176 F8
Bedford, Cape Australia 149 E2
Bedford Downs Australia 150 D3
Bedford Heights U.S.A. 176 D4
Bedi India 96 A5
Bedingong Indon. 77 D3
Bednja r. Croatia 56 I2
Bednodem'yanovsk Rus. Fed. 41 G5

index

B

Bedok Sing. 76 [inset]
Bedok, Sungai r. Sing. 76 [inset]
Bedok Jetty Sing. 76 [inset]
Bedok Reservoir Sing. 76 [inset]
Bedouaram *well* Niger 125 I3
Bedourie Australia 148 C5
Bedrock U.S.A. 183 P3
Bedum Neth. 48 D2
Beechal Creek *watercourse* Australia 147 E1
Beecher U.S.A. 172 F9
Beech Fork Lake U.S.A. 176 C7
Beechy Canada 167 J5
Beekeepers Nature Reserve Australia 151 A6
Beelitz Germany 49 J3
Beenleigh Australia 147 G1
Beer Somalia 128 E2
Beersheba Israel 108 F6
also spelt Be'ér Sheva'
Be'ér Sheva' Israel *see* Beersheba
Beer Sheva *watercourse* Israel 108 F6
Beervlei Dam S. Africa 132 H10
Beeskow Germany 49 L3
Beestekraal S. Africa 133 L2
Beetaloo Australia 148 B3
Beethoven Peninsula Antarctica 222 T2
Beeville U.S.A. 179 C6
Befale Dem. Rep. Congo 126 D4
Befandriana Atsimo Madag. 131 [inset] I4
Befandriana Avaratra Madag. 131 [inset] K2
Befori Dem. Rep. Congo 126 D4
Befotaka Madag. 131 [inset] J4
Bega Australia 147 F4
Bega *r.* Romania 58 C3
Begamganj Bangl. 97 F5
Bégard France 50 C4
Begari *r.* Pak. 101 G4
Begicheva, Ostrov *i.* Rus. Fed. *see* Bol'shoy Begichev, Ostrov
Begovat Uzbek. *see* Bekabad
Begun India 96 B4
Begusarai India 97 E4
Béhague, Pointe *pt* Fr. Guiana 199 I3
Behbehān Iran 100 B4
Beheira *governorate* Egypt 108 B7
Behm Canal *sea chan.* U.S.A. 166 D4
Behrendt Mountains Antarctica 222 T2
Behshahr Iran 100 C2
Behsūd Afgh. 101 F3
Bei'an China 82 B2
Bei'ao China *see* Dongtou
Beiba China 86 C1
Beibei China 86 C2
Beichuan China 86 C2
also known as Qushan
Beida Libya *see* Al Bayḍā'
Beigang Taiwan *see* Peikang
Beihai China 87 D4
historically known as Pakhoi
Bei Hulsan Hu *salt l.* China 84 B4
Bei Jiang *r.* China 87 E4

▶Beijing China 85 H4
Capital of China. Formerly known as Peking; historically known as Khanbalik.
world [countries] ▶ 10–11
world [cities] ▶ 24–25

Beijing *municipality* China 85 H3
Beilen Neth. 48 D3
Beiliu China 87 D4
Béinamar Chad 126 B2
Beining China 85 I3
also known as Guangning; *formerly known as* Beizhen
Beinn Bhreac *hill* U.K. 46 G7
Beinn Mhòr *hill* U.K. 46 E6
Beinn na Faoghla *i.* U.K. *see* Benbecula
Beipiao China 85 I3
Beira Moz. 131 G3
Beira *prov.* Moz. *see* Sofala
Beira Alta *reg.* Port. 54 D4
Beira Baixa *reg.* Port. 54 D5
Beira Litoral *reg.* Port. 54 C4
Beiru *r.* China 87 E1

▶Beirut Lebanon 108 G4
Capital of Lebanon. Also spelt Bayrūt or Beyrouth; historically known as Berytus.

Beiseker Canada 167 H5
Beishan China 84 C3
Bei Shan *mt.* China 84 B3
Bei Shan *mts* China 84 B3
formerly spelt Pei Shan
Beitbridge Zimbabwe 131 F4
Beit Jālā West Bank 108 G6
Beitun China 88 D2
Beiuş Romania 58 D2
Beizhen China *see* Beining
Beja Brazil 202 B2
Beja Port. 54 D6
Beja *admin. dist.* Port. 54 C7
Béja Tunisia 123 H1
Bejaïa Alg. 123 G1
formerly known as Bougie; *historically known as* Saldae
Béjar Spain 54 F4
Bejestān Iran 100 D3
Beji *r.* Pak. 101 G4
Béjucos Mex. 185 E5
Béka *Adamaoua* Cameroon 125 I5
Béka *Est* Cameroon 125 I5
Béka *Nord* Cameroon 125 I4
Bekabad Uzbek. 92 C2
also spelt Bekobod; *formerly spelt* Begovat
Bekapaika Madag. 131 [inset] J3
Bekasi Indon. 77 D4
Bekdash Turkm. 102 C4
Beke Dem. Rep. Congo 127 E7
Békés Hungary 49 S9
Békéscsaba Hungary 49 S9
Beketovskaya Rus. Fed. 43 U1
Bekilli Turkey 59 K10
Bekily Madag. 131 [inset] J5
Bekitro Madag. 131 [inset] J5
Bekkai Japan 90 I3
Beklemishevo Rus. Fed. 85 G1
Bekobod Uzbek. *see* Bekabad
Bekopaka Madag. 131 [inset] J3
Bekoropoka-Antongo Madag. 131 [inset] I4
Bekovo Rus. Fed. 41 G5
Bekwai Ghana 125 E5
Bekyem Ghana 125 E5
Bela *Bihar* India 97 E4
Bela *Uttar Pradesh* India 97 D4
Bela Pak. 101 F5
Belab *r.* Pak. 101 G4
Bela-Bela S. Africa 133 M1
Bélabo Cameroon 125 I5
Bela Crkva *Vojvodina, Srbija* Yugo. 58 C4
Belaga *Sarawak* Malaysia 77 F2
Bel'agash Kazakh. 103 J2
Bel Air U.S.A. 177 I6
Belalcázar Spain 54 F6
Belang Indon. 75 C2
Belangiran Indon. 77 E3
Bela Palanka *Srbija* Yugo. 58 D5
Bělá pod Bezdězem Czech Rep. 49 L5
Belapur India 94 B2
▶Belarus *country* Europe 42 H8
formerly known as Belorussia *or* Belorusskaya S.S.R. *or* Byelorussia *or* White Russia
europe [countries] ▶ 32–35
Belasica *mts* Bulg./Macedonia 58 D7
also known as Kerkini Oros; *also spelt* Belasitsa
Belasitsa *mts* Bulg./Macedonia *see* Belasica
Belau *country* N. Pacific Ocean *see* Palau
Bela Vista Angola 127 B6
Bela Vista *Amazonas* Brazil 199 E4
Bela Vista *Mato Grosso do Sul* Brazil 201 F5
Bela Vista Moz. 131 G5
Bela Vista de Goiás Brazil 206 E3
Belawan Indon. 76 B2
Belaya *r.* Rus. Fed. 39 R3
Belaya Glina Rus. Fed. 41 G7
Belaya Kalitva Rus. Fed. 41 G6
Belaya Kholunitsa Rus. Fed. 40 I4
Belayan *r.* Indon. 77 G3
Belayan, Gunung *mt.* Indon. 77 F2
Belaya Rechka Rus. Fed. 43 U5
Belaya Tserkva Ukr. *see* Bila Tserkva
Bełbėdji Niger 125 G3
Belcești Romania 58 I1
Bełchatów Poland 49 Q4
Belcher U.S.A. 176 C8
Belcher Islands Canada 168 E1
Belchiragh Afgh. 101 F3
Belcourt Canada 173 P2
Beldanga India 97 F5
Belden U.S.A. 182 C1
Beldibi Turkey 59 J12
Belding U.S.A. 173 H7
Beleapani *reef* India *see* Cherbaniani Reef
Belebey Rus. Fed. 40 J5
Beled Hungary 49 O8
Beledweyne Somalia 128 E3
Belek Turkm. 102 C5
Bélèl Cameroon 125 I5
Belel Nigeria 125 I4
Belém Brazil 202 B2
Belén Arg. 204 D2
Belén Para. 201 F5
Belen *Antalya* Turkey 108 D1
Belen *Hatay* Turkey 106 D3
Belen U.S.A. 181 F6
Belén, Cuchilla de *hills* Uruguay 204 F3
Belene Bulg. 58 G5
Bélep, Îles *is* New Caledonia 145 F3
Belesar, Embalse de *resr* Spain 54 D2
Belev Rus. Fed. 43 R8
Belevi Turkey 59 I10
Belfast N.Z. 153 G11
Belfast S. Africa 133 O2

▶Belfast U.K. 47 G9
Capital of Northern Ireland.

Belfast U.S.A. 177 P1
Bēlfodiyo Eth. 128 B2
Belford U.K. 46 K8
Belfort France 51 M5
Belgaum India 94 B3
Belgian Congo *country* Africa *see* Congo, Democratic Republic of
Belgicafjella *mts* Antarctica *see* Belgica Mountains
Belgica Mountains Antarctica 223 C2
also known as Belgicafjella
België *country* Europe *see* Belgium
Belgique *country* Europe *see* Belgium
▶Belgium *country* Europe 51 K2
known as België *in Dutch (Flemish) or* Belgique *in French; historically known as* Spanish Netherlands
europe [countries] ▶ 32–35
Belgorod Rus. Fed. 41 F6
Belgorod-Dnestrovskyy Ukr. *see* Bilhorod-Dnistrovs'kyy
Belgorod Oblast *admin. div.* Rus. Fed. *see* Belgorodskaya Oblast'
Belgorodskaya Oblast' *admin. div.* Rus. Fed. 41 F6
English form Belgorod Oblast
Belgrade *ME* U.S.A. 177 P1
Belgrade *MT* U.S.A. 180 E3

▶Belgrade *Srbija* Yugo. 58 B4
Capital of Yugoslavia. Also spelt Beograd; historically known as Singidunum.

Belgrano II *research station* Antarctica 222 V1
long form General Belgrano II
Belhirane Alg. 123 G3
Béli Guinea-Bissau 124 B4
Beli Nigeria 125 H5
Belice *r. Sicilia* Italy 57 E11
Beli Drim *r.* Yugo. 58 B6
Beliliou *i.* Palau *see* Peleliu
Beli Lom *r.* Bulg. 58 H5
Beli Manastir Croatia 56 K3
Belin-Béliet France 50 F8
Belington U.S.A. 176 F6
Belingwe Zimbabwe *see* Mberengwa
Belinskiy Rus. Fed. 41 G5
Belint Romania 58 C3
Belinyu Indon. 77 D3
Beli Timok *r.* Yugo. 58 D4
Belitsa Bulg. 58 E7
Belitung *i.* Indon. 77 E3
also spelt Billiton
Belize Angola 126 B6

▶Belize Belize 185 H5
Former capital of Belize.

▶Belize *country* Central America 185 H5
formerly known as British Honduras
northamerica [countries] ▶ 158–159

Bélizon Fr. Guiana 199 H3
Beljak Austria *see* Villach
Beljanica *mt.* Yugo. 58 C4
Belkina, Mys *pt* Rus. Fed. 90 E2
Bel'kovskiy, Ostrov *i.* Rus. Fed. 39 N2
Bell Australia 149 F5
Bell *r.* Australia 147 F3
Bell *r.* Canada 168 E3
Bell S. Africa 133 L10
Bell, Point Australia 146 B3
Bella Bella Canada 166 D4
Bellac France 50 H6
Bella Coola Canada 166 E4
Bella Coola *r.* Canada 166 E4
Bellagio Italy 56 B3
Bellaire *MI* U.S.A. 173 H6
Bellaire *TX* U.S.A. 179 D6
Bellaria Italy 56 E4
Bellary India 94 C3
Bellata Australia 147 F2
Bella Unión Uruguay 204 F3
Bella Vista *Corrientes* Arg. 204 F3
Bella Vista *Santa Cruz* Arg. 205 C8
Bella Vista Bol. 201 E3
Bella Vista Para. 201 F5
Bellavista Peru 198 C5
Bella Vista U.S.A. 182 B1
Bella Vista, Salar de *salt flat* Chile 200 C5
Bell Block N.Z. 152 I7
Bell Cay *reef* Australia 149 F4
Belle U.S.A. 176 D7
Belle-Anse Haiti 187 E3
formerly known as Saltrou
Belledonne *mts* France 51 L7
Bellefontaine U.S.A. 176 B5
Belle Fourche U.S.A. 178 B2
Belle Fourche *r.* U.S.A. 178 B2
Bellegarde-sur-Valserine France 51 L6
Belle Glade U.S.A. 175 D7
Belle-Île *i.* France 50 C5
Belle Isle *i.* Canada 169 K3
Belle Isle, Strait of Canada 169 J3
Bellemont U.S.A. 183 M6
Belleterre Canada 168 E4
Belleville Canada 168 E4
Belleville France 51 K6
Belleville U.S.A. 178 C4
Bellevue *IA* U.S.A. 174 B3
Bellevue *MI* U.S.A. 173 H8
Bellevue *NE* U.S.A. 178 D3
Bellevue *OH* U.S.A. 176 C4
Bellevue *WA* U.S.A. 180 B3
Belley France 51 L7
Bellin Canada *see* Kangirsuk
Bellingen Australia 147 G2
Bellingham U.K. 47 J8
Bellingham U.S.A. 180 B2
Bellingshausen *research station* Antarctica 222 U2
Bellingshausen Sea Antarctica 222 S2
Bellinzona Switz. 51 P6
Bell Island Canada 169 K3
Bello Col. 198 C3
Bellows Falls U.S.A. 177 M2
Bellpat Pak. 101 G4
Belluno Italy 56 E2
Belluru India 94 C3
Bell Ville Arg. 204 E4
Bellville S. Africa 132 C10
Bellville *OH* U.S.A. 176 C5
Bellville *TX* U.S.A. 179 C6
Bellwood U.S.A. 176 G5
Belly *r.* Canada 167 H5
Bélmez Spain 54 F6
Belmont Australia 147 F3
Belmont S. Africa 133 I6
Belmont *NH* U.S.A. 177 N2
Belmont *NY* U.S.A. 176 G3
Belmonte Brazil 202 E5
Belmonte Port. 54 D4
Belmont-sur-Rance France 51 I9

▶Belmopan Belize 185 H5
Capital of Belize.

Belmore Creek *r.* Australia 149 D3
Belmullet Rep. of Ireland 47 C9
Belo Madag. 131 [inset] J4
Beloe More Rus. Fed. *see* Beloye More
Beloe More *sea* Rus. Fed. *see* White Sea
Beloevo Rus. Fed. *see* Beloyevo
Belogorsk Rus. Fed. 82 C2
formerly known as Kuybyshevka-Vostochnaya
Belogorsk Ukr. *see* Bilohirs'k
Belogor'ye Kazakh. 103 I2
Belogradchik Bulg. 58 D5
Beloha Madag. 131 [inset] J5
Belo Horizonte *Amazonas* Brazil 199 E5
Belo Horizonte *Minas Gerais* Brazil 203 D6
Beloit *KS* U.S.A. 178 C4
Beloit *WI* U.S.A. 172 D8
Belo Jardim Brazil 202 E4
Belo Monte Brazil 199 I5
Belo Monte Brazil *see* Batalha
Belomorsk Rus. Fed. 40 E2
Belonia India 97 F5
Beloomut Rus. Fed. 43 U7
Belo Oriente Brazil 207 K6
Belozersk Belarus *see* Byelaazyorsk
Beloozerskiy Rus. Fed. 43 T6
Belopa Indon. 75 B3
Belorechensk Rus. Fed. 41 F7
formerly known as Belorechenskaya
Belorechenskaya Rus. Fed. *see* Belorechensk
Belören *Adıyaman* Turkey 107 D3
Belören *Konya* Turkey 106 C3
also known as Sarıoğlan
Beloretsk Rus. Fed. 38 F4
Belorussia *country* Europe *see* Belarus
Belorusskaya S.S.R. *country* Europe *see* Belarus
Beloslav Bulg. 58 I5
Belostok Poland *see* Białystok
Belot, Lac *l.* Canada 166 E1
Belotintsi Bulg. 58 D5
Belo Tsiribihina Madag. 131 [inset] J3
Belousovka Kazakh. 88 C1
Belousovo Rus. Fed. 43 R6
Belo Vale Brazil 207 I7
Belovo Bulg. 58 F6
Belovo Rus. Fed. 80 D2
Beloyarovo Rus. Fed. 82 C2
Beloye Rus. Fed. 43 U3
Beloye, Ozero *l.* Rus. Fed. 43 S1
Beloye More Rus. Fed. 44 P2
also spelt Beloe More
Beloye More *sea* Rus. Fed. *see* White Sea
Beloyevo Rus. Fed. 40 J4
also spelt Beloevo
Belozerka Rus. Fed. 102 C1
Belozersk Rus. Fed. 43 S1
Belpre U.S.A. 176 D6
Beltana Australia 146 C2
Belted Range *mts* U.S.A. 183 H4
Belterra Brazil 199 H5
Beltes Gol *r.* Mongolia 84 C1
Belton *MO* U.S.A. 178 D4
Belton *TX* U.S.A. 179 C6
Bel'ts' Moldova *see* Bălţi
Bel'tsy Moldova *see* Bălţi
Belukha, Gora *mt.* Kazakh./Rus. Fed. 88 D1
Belur India 94 B3
Belush'ya Guba Rus. Fed. 40 J1
Belush'ye Rus. Fed. 40 H2
Beluzhiy Nos, Mys *c.* Rus. Fed. 40 M1
Belva U.S.A. 176 D7
Belvès France 50 H8
Belvidere *IL* U.S.A. 174 B3
Belvidere *NJ* U.S.A. 177 J5
Belyando *r.* Australia 149 E4
Belyando Crossing Australia 149 E4
Belyayevka Rus. Fed. 102 D2
Belyayevka Ukr. *see* Bilyayivka
Belyayevo Rus. Fed. 43 M6
Belye Vody Kazakh. 103 G4
Belyuen Australia 148 A2
Belyy Rus. Fed. 43 N6
Belyy, Ostrov *i.* Rus. Fed. 38 H2
Belyye Berega Rus. Fed. 43 P8
Belyye Stolby Rus. Fed. 43 S6
Belyy Gorodok Rus. Fed. 43 S5
Belyy Yar Rus. Fed. 39 I4
Belzig Germany 49 J3
Belzoni U.S.A. 175 B5
Bełżyce Poland 49 T4
Bemaraha, Plateau du Madag. 131 [inset] J3
Bembe Angola 127 B6
Bembèrèkè Benin 125 F4
Bembibre Spain 54 E2
Bemidji U.S.A. 178 D2
Béna Burkina 124 D3
Bena Dibele Dem. Rep. Congo 126 D6
Benagin Indon. 77 F3
Ben Alder *mt.* U.K. 46 H7
Benalla Australia 147 E4
Benalmádena Spain 54 G8
Ben 'Amîra *well* Mauritania 122 B5
Benares India *see* Varanasi
Ben Arous Tunisia 123 H1
Bénat, Cap *c.* France 51 M9
Benavente Spain 54 F2
Benavides Bol. 200 D3
Benbecula *i.* U.K. 46 E6
also known as Beinn na Faoghla
Ben Boyd National Park Australia 147 F4
Benbury *hill* Rep. of Ireland 47 C10
Bencha China 87 G1
Bencheng China *see* Luannan
Bencubbin Australia 151 B6
Bend U.S.A. 180 B3
Bendearg *mt.* S. Africa 133 L8
Bendela Dem. Rep. Congo 126 C5
Bender Moldova *see* Tighina
Bender-Bayla Somalia 128 F2
Benderville U.S.A. 172 F6
Bendery Moldova *see* Tighina
Bendigo Australia 147 E4
Bendoc Australia 147 F4
Bēne Latvia 42 E5
Bene Moz. 131 G2
Benedict, Mount *hill* Canada 169 J2
Beneditinos Brazil 202 D3
Benedito Leite Brazil 202 C3
Bénéna Mali 124 D3
Benenitra Madag. 131 [inset] J4
Benešov Czech Rep. 49 L6
Benevento Italy 56 G7
historically known as Beneventum
Beneventum Italy *see* Benevento
Benezette U.S.A. 176 G4
Benfeld France 51 N4
Beng *r.* China 85 H5
Beng, Nam *r.* Laos 78 C4
Benga Malawi 129 B8
Bengal, Bay of *sea* Indian Ocean 95 F2
Bengamisa Dem. Rep. Congo 126 E4
Bengbis Cameroon 125 I6
Bengbu China 87 F1
Benghazi Libya 120 D1
also spelt Banghāzī; *historically known as* Berenice
Benghisa Point Malta 57 G13
also known as Il-Ponta ta' Benghajsa
Bengkalis Indon. 76 C2
Bengkalis *i.* Indon. 76 C2
Bengkayang Indon. 77 E2
Bengkulu Indon. 76 C3
Bengkulu *prov.* Indon. 76 C3
Bengo Angola 127 C9
Bengo *prov.* Angola 127 B7
Bengtsfors Sweden 45 K4
Benguela Angola 127 B8
Benguela *prov.* Angola 127 B8
Ben Guerdane Tunisia 123 H2
Benguerir Morocco 122 D2
Benguérua, Ilha *i.* Moz. 131 G4
Benha Egypt 121 F2
also spelt Banhā
Ben Hiant *hill* U.K. 46 F7
Ben Hope *hill* U.K. 46 F5
Beni *dept* Bol. 200 D3
Beni *r.* Bol. 200 D2
Beni Dem. Rep. Congo 126 F4
Beni Nepal 97 D3
Beni-Abbès Alg. 123 E3
Beni Boufrah Morocco 54 G9
Benicarló Spain 55 L4
Benicasim Spain 55 L4
Benicia U.S.A. 182 B3
Benidorm Spain 55 K6
Beni Dourso *well* Niger 125 I1
Benifaió Spain 55 K5
also spelt Benifayo
Benifayo Spain *see* Benifaió
Benigánim Spain 55 K6
Beni Guil *reg.* Morocco 123 E2
Beni Hadifa Morocco 54 G9
Benî Mazâr Egypt 106 B5
Beni Mellal Morocco 122 D2
▶Benin *country* Africa 125 F4
formerly known as Dahomey
africa [countries] ▶ 114–117
Benin *r.* Nigeria 125 G5
Benin, Bight of *g.* Africa 125 F5
formerly known as Biafra, Bight of
Benin City Nigeria 125 G5
Beni-Ounif Alg. 123 E3
Beni-Saf Alg. 123 E2
Benishangul *admin. reg.* Eth. 128 B2
Benisheikh Nigeria 125 I4
Benissa Spain 55 L6
Beni Suef Egypt 121 F2
also spelt Banī Suwayf
Beni Suef *governorate* Egypt 108 A9
Benithora *r.* India 94 C2
Benito *r.* Equat. Guinea *see* Mbini
Benito, Islas *is* Mex. 184 B2
Benito Juárez Arg. 204 F5
Benito Juárez Mex. 185 J9
Benito Soliven Phil. 74 B2
Benjamim Constant Brazil 198 D6
Benjamin U.S.A. 179 C5
Benjamín, Isla *i.* Chile 205 B7
Benjamin Hill Mex. 184 C2
Benjamín Zorrillo Arg. 204 D5
Benjina Indon. 73 H8
Benkei-misaki *pt* Japan 90 G3
Benkelman U.S.A. 178 B3
Benken Switz. 51 P5
Benkovac Croatia 56 H4
Benkovski Bulg. 58 I5
Ben Lawers *mt.* U.K. 46 H7
Ben Lomond *mt.* Australia 147 F2
Ben Lomond *hill* U.K. 46 H7
Ben Lomond U.S.A. 182 B4
Ben Lomond National Park Australia 147 E5
Ben Macdhui *mt.* Lesotho 133 L7
Ben Macdui *mt.* U.K. 46 I6
Ben Mahidi Alg. 57 A12
Benmara Australia 148 C3
Ben More *mt.* N.Z. 153 F11
Ben More *hill* U.K. 46 F7
Ben More *mt.* U.K. 46 H7
Benmore, Lake N.Z. 153 E12
Ben More Assynt *hill* U.K. 46 H5
Bennett Canada 166 C3
Bennett *IA* U.S.A. 172 C9
Bennett *WI* U.S.A. 172 B4
Bennett, Lake *salt flat* Australia 148 A4
Bennetta, Ostrov *i.* Rus. Fed. 39 O2
English form Bennett Island
Bennett Island Rus. Fed. *see* Bennetta, Ostrov
Bennett Lake Canada 166 C3
Bennettsville U.S.A. 174 E5
Ben Nevis *mt.* U.K. 46 G7
Benneydale N.Z. 152 J6
Bennington *NH* U.S.A. 177 N2
Bennington *VT* U.S.A. 177 L3
Ben Ohau Range *mts* N.Z. 153 D12
Benoi Basin *dock* Sing. 76 [inset]
Benoni S. Africa 133 M3
Bénoué *r.* Cameroon 125 I4
Bénoy Chad 126 C2
Ben Rinnes *hill* U.K. 46 I6
Bensheim Germany 48 F6
Ben Slimane Morocco 122 D2
formerly known as Boulhaut
Benson *AZ* U.S.A. 181 E7
Benson *MN* U.S.A. 178 D2
Bensonville Liberia 124 C5
Bens Run U.S.A. 176 D6
Bent Iran 101 D5
Benta Seberang Malaysia 76 C1
Benteng Indon. 75 B4
Bentiaba Angola 127 B8
formerly known as São Nicolau
Ben Tieb Morocco 55 H9
Bentinck Island Australia 148 C3
Bentinck Island Myanmar 79 B6
Bentiu Sudan 126 F2
Bent Jbail Lebanon 108 G4
Bentley Canada 167 H4
Bentleyville U.S.A. 176 E5
Bento Gomes *r.* Brazil 201 F4
Benton *AR* U.S.A. 179 D5
Benton *CA* U.S.A. 182 F4
Benton *IL* U.S.A. 174 B4
Benton *KY* U.S.A. 174 B4
Benton *LA* U.S.A. 179 D5
Benton *MO* U.S.A. 174 B4
Benton *TN* U.S.A. 174 C5
Bentong Malaysia *see* Bentung
Benton Harbor U.S.A. 172 G8
Bentonville U.S.A. 179 D4
Bên Tre Vietnam 79 D6
formerly known as Truc Giang
Bentsy Rus. Fed. 43 M5
Bentuang Karimun National Park Indon. 77 F2
Bentung Malaysia 76 C2
also spelt Bentong
Benua Indon. 75 B4
Benua *i.* Indon. 77 D2
Benuamartinus Indon. 77 F2
Benue *r.* Nigeria 125 G5
Benue *state* Nigeria 125 H5
Benum, Gunung *mt.* Malaysia 76 C2
Ben Vorlich *hill* U.K. 46 H7
Benwa Zambia 127 E7
Benwee Head Rep. of Ireland 47 C9
Benwood U.S.A. 176 E5
Ben Wyvis *mt.* U.K. 46 H6
Benxi China 82 A4
Ben Zireg Alg. 123 E3
Beograd *Srbija* Yugo. *see* Belgrade
Beohari India 97 D4
Béoumi Côte d'Ivoire 124 D5
Bepagut, Gunung *mt.* Indon. 76 C4
Bepian Jiang *r.* China 86 C3
Beppu Japan 91 B8
Beppu-wan *b.* Japan 91 B8
Bequia *i.* St Vincent 187 H4
Bequimão Brazil 202 C2
Bera Bangl. 97 F4
Berach *r.* India 96 B4
Beramanja Madag. 131 [inset] K2
Berane *Crna Gora* Yugo. 58 A6
formerly known as Ivangrad
Bérard, Lac *l.* Canada 169 G1
Berasia India 96 C5
Berastagi Indon. 76 B2
Berat Albania 58 A8
Beratus, Gunung *mt.* Indon. 77 G3
Berau *r.* Indon. 77 G2
Berau, Teluk *b.* Indon. 73 H7
Beravina Madag. 131 [inset] J3
Berbak National Park Indon. 76 D3
Berber Sudan 121 G5
Berbera Somalia 128 E2
Berbérati Cent. Afr. Rep. 126 B3
Berbice S. Africa 133 P4
Bercel Hungary 49 Q8
Berceto Italy 56 B4
Berchi-Guélé *well* Chad 120 C5
Berchogur Kazakh. 102 D2
also spelt Birshoghyr
Berchtesgaden, Nationalpark *nat. park* Germany 49 J8
Berck France 50 H2
Berd Armenia 107 F2
Berdichev Ukr. *see* Berdychiv
Berdigestyakh Rus. Fed. 39 M3
Berdsk Rus. Fed. 80 C2
Berdyans'k Ukr. 41 F7
formerly known as Osipenko
Berdychiv Ukr. 41 D6
also spelt Berdichev
Béré Chad 126 C2
Berea *KY* U.S.A. 176 A8
Berea *OH* U.S.A. 176 D4
Berebere Indon. 75 D2
Bereg Rus. Fed. 43 S1
Beregdaróc Hungary 49 T7
Beregovo Ukr. *see* Berehove
Berehove Ukr. 49 T7
also spelt Beregovo
Bereina P.N.G. 73 K8
Bereketa Madag. 131 [inset] J4
Berekum Ghana 124 E5
Berel' Kazakh. 88 D1
Beremend Hungary 56 K3
Berendeyevo Rus. Fed. 43 U5
Berenguela Bol. 200 C4
Berenice Egypt 121 G4
Berenice Libya *see* Benghazi
Berens *r.* Canada 167 L4
Berens Island Canada 167 L4
Berens River Canada 167 L4
Berenty Madag. 131 [inset] J4
Beresford Canada 169 H4
Beresford U.S.A. 178 C3
Berești Romania 58 I2
Berettyó *r.* Hungary 49 S8
Berettyóújfalu Hungary 49 S8
Berevo Madag. 131 [inset] J3
Berevo-Ranobe Madag. 131 [inset] J3
Bereza Belarus *see* Byaroza
Berezayka Rus. Fed. 43 O4
Berezeni Romania 58 J2
Berezino Belarus *see* Byerazino
Berezino Belarus *see* Byerazino
Berezivka Ukr. 41 D7
also spelt Berezovka
Berezne Ukr. 41 C6
Bereznik Rus. Fed. 40 G3
formerly known as Semyonovskoye
Berezniki Rus. Fed. 40 K4
Berezov Rus. Fed. *see* Berezovo
Berezovaya *r.* Rus. Fed. 40 K3
Berezovka Belarus *see* Byarozawka
Berezovka *Amurskaya Oblast'* Rus. Fed. 82 B2
Berezovka *Orenburgskaya Oblast'* Rus. Fed. 102 D1
Berezovka *Permskaya Oblast'* Rus. Fed. 40 K4
Berezovka Ukr. *see* Berezivka
Berezovo Rus. Fed. 38 G3
formerly known as Berezov
Berezovyy Rus. Fed. 82 D2
Berezyne Ukr. 58 K2
Berga Spain 55 M2
Bergama Turkey 106 A3
Bergamo Italy 56 B3
historically known as Bergomum
Bergantes *r.* Spain 55 K4
Bergby Sweden 45 L3
Bergen *Mecklenburg-Vorpommern* Germany 49 K1
Bergen *Niedersachsen* Germany 48 G3
Bergen Norway 45 I3
Bergen S. Africa 133 O4
Bergen U.S.A. 176 H2
Bergen op Zoom Neth. 48 B4
Bergerac France 50 G8
Bergerson, Mount Antarctica 223 B2
Berghan Point N.Z. 152 H2
Bergheim (Erft) Germany 48 D5
Bergisch Gladbach Germany 48 E5
Bergland Namibia 130 C4
Bergnäs Sweden 44 L2
Bergnäsviken Sweden 44 L2
Bergomum Italy *see* Bergamo
Bergsjö Sweden 45 L3
Bergstraße-Odenwald *park* Germany 48 G6
Bergsviken Sweden 44 M2
Bergues France 51 I2
Bergville S. Africa 133 N5
Berh Mongolia 85 F2
Berhala, Selat *sea chan.* Indon. 76 C3
Berhampur India *see* Baharampur
Berheci *r.* Romania 58 I2
Berikat, Tanjung *pt* Indon. 77 D3
Berilo Brazil 207 K3
Beringa, Ostrov *i.* Rus. Fed. 220 F2
Beringarra Australia 151 B5
Beringen Belgium 51 L1
Bering Land Bridge National Preserve *nature res.* U.S.A. 164 C3
Beringovskiy Rus. Fed. 39 R3
formerly known as Ugolnyy
Bering Sea N. Pacific Ocean 39 R4
Bering Strait Rus. Fed./U.S.A. 164 C3
Berîs, Ra's *pt* Iran 101 E5
Berislav Ukr. *see* Beryslav
Berja Spain 55 I8
Berkåk Norway 44 J3
Berkane Morocco 123 E2
Berkel *r.* Neth. 48 D3
Berkeley *r.* Australia 150 D2
Berkeley U.S.A. 182 B4
Berkeley Springs U.S.A. 176 G6
Berkner Island Antarctica 222 U1
Berkovitsa Bulg. 58 E5
Berkshire Hills U.S.A. 177 L3
Berland *r.* Canada 166 G4
Berlevåg Norway 44 O1
also known as Bearalváhki

▶Berlin Germany 49 K3
Capital of Germany.
europe [countries] ▶ 32–33

Berlin *MD* U.S.A. 177 J7
Berlin *NH* U.S.A. 177 N1
Berlin *NJ* U.S.A. 177 K6
Berlin *OH* U.S.A. 176 D5
Berlin *PA* U.S.A. 176 G6
Berlin *WI* U.S.A. 172 E7
Berlin, Mount Antarctica 222 O1
Berlins N.Z. 153 F9
Berliște Romania 58 C4
Bermagui Australia 147 F4
Berme Turkm. 102 D5
Bermeja, Punta *pt* Arg. 204 E6
Bermejillo Mex. 184 E3
Bermejo *r.* Arg. 204 D4
Bermejo *r.* Arg./Bol. 201 F6
Bermejo Bol. 201 D5
Bermeo Spain 55 I1

▶Bermuda *terr.* N. Atlantic Ocean 216 J3
United Kingdom Overseas Territory.
oceania [countries] ▶ 138–139

▶Bern Switz. 51 N6
Capital of Switzerland. Also spelt Berne.

Bernalda Italy 57 I8
Bernalillo U.S.A. 181 F6
Bernardino de Campos Brazil 206 D10
Bernard Lake Canada 173 N5
Bernardo O'Higgins, Parque Nacional *nat. park* Chile 205 B8
Bernau Germany 49 K3
Bernau am Chiemsee Germany 49 J8
Bernay France 50 G3
Bernburg (Saale) Germany 48 I4
Berndorf Austria 49 N8
Berne Switz. *see* Bern
Berne U.S.A. 176 A5
Berner Alpen *mts* Switz. 51 N6
English form Bernese Alps
Berneray *i. Western Isles, Scotland* U.K. 46 E6
also known as Bhearnaraigh, Eilean
Berneray *i. Western Isles, Scotland* U.K. 46 E7
also spelt Bearnaraigh
Bernese Alps *mts* Switz. *see* Berner Alpen
Bernesga *r.* Spain 54 F2
Bernier Bay Canada 165 K2
Bernier Island Australia 151 A5
Bernina Pass Switz. 51 Q6
Berninches *mt.* Spain 55 I4
Bernkastel-Kues Germany 48 E6
Bernstadt U.S.A. 176 A8
Beroea Greece *see* Veroia
Beroea Syria *see* Aleppo
Beroroha Madag. 131 [inset] J4
Beroun Czech Rep. 49 L6
Berounka *r.* Czech Rep. 49 L6
Berovina Madag. *see* Beravina
Berovo Macedonia 58 D7
Berre, Étang de *lag.* France 51 L9
Berrechid Morocco 122 D2
Berri Australia 146 D3
Berriane Alg. 123 F2
Berridale Australia 147 F4
Berrigan Australia 147 E3
Berrouaghia Alg. 123 F1
Berry *reg.* France 50 H6
Berry Creek *r.* Canada 167 I5
Berryessa, Lake U.S.A. 182 B3
Berry Head U.K. 47 I13
Berry Islands Bahamas 186 D1
Berryville *AR* U.S.A. 179 D4
Berryville *VA* U.S.A. 176 H6
Berseba Namibia 132 B3
Bersenbrück Germany 48 E3
Bersuat Rus. Fed. 103 E1
Berté, Lac *l.* Canada 169 G3
Bertinho Brazil 202 B2
Bertolinia Brazil 202 D3
Bertópolis Brazil 207 M4
Bertoua Cameroon 125 I5
Bertraghboy Bay Rep. of Ireland 47 C10
Beru *atoll* Kiribati 145 G2
also spelt Peru; *formerly known as* Francis
Beruni Uzbek. 102 E4
formerly known as Shabbaz; *formerly spelt* Biruni
Beruri Brazil 199 F5
Beruwala Sri Lanka 94 C5
Berveni Romania 49 T8
Berwick-upon-Tweed U.K. 46 J8
Beryslav Ukr. 41 E7
also spelt Berislav
Berytus Lebanon *see* Beirut
Berzasca Romania 58 C4
Bērzaune Latvia 42 H5
Bērzpils Latvia 42 I5
Bès *r.* France 51 J8
Besah Indon. 77 G2
Besalampy Madag. 131 [inset] J3
Besalú Spain 55 N2
Besançon France 51 M5
historically known as Vesontio
Besar *i.* Indon. 75 B5
Besar, Gunung *mt.* Indon. 77 F3
Besar, Gunung *mt.* Malaysia 76 C1
Besbay Kazakh. 102 C3
Besbre *r.* France 51 J6
Besed' *r.* Rus. Fed. 43 M9
Beshariq Uzbek. *see* Besharyk
Besharyk Uzbek. 103 G4
also spelt Beshariq; *formerly known as* Kirovo

Beshir Turkm. 103 F5
Beshkent Uzbek. 103 F5
Beshneh Iran 100 C4
Besh-Ter, Gora mt. Kyrg./Uzbek. 103 G4
also known as Besh-Ter Toosu or Beshtor Toghi
Besh-Ter Toosu mt. Kyrg./Uzbek. see Besh-Ter, Gora
Beshtor Toghi mt. Kyrg./Uzbek. see Besh-Ter, Gora
Besikama Indon. 75 C5
Beşiri Turkey 107 E3
Besitang Indon. 76 B1
Beskid Niski hills Poland 49 S6
Beskid Sądecki mts Poland 49 R6
Beskra Alg. see Biskra
Beslan Rus. Fed. 41 H8
Beslet mt. Bulg. 58 F7
Besna Kobila mt. Yugo. 58 D6
Besnard Lake Canada 167 J4
Besni Turkey 107 D3
Besor watercourse Israel 108 F6
Beşparmak Dağları mts Cyprus see Pentadaktylos Range
Béssao Chad 126 B3
Bessarabka Moldova see Basarabeasca
Bessaye, Gora mt. Kazakh. 103 G4
Bessemer AL U.S.A. 175 C5
Bessemer MI U.S.A. 172 C4
Besshoky, Gora hill Kazakh. 102 C3
Bessines-sur-Gartempe France 50 H6
Bessonovka Rus. Fed. 41 H5
Bessou, Mont de hill France 51 I7
Bestamak Aktyubinskaya Oblast' Kazakh. 102 C2
Bestamak Vostochnyy Kazakhstan Kazakh. 103 I2
Bestobe Kazakh. 103 H1
Beswick Australia 148 B2
Beswick Aboriginal Land res. Australia 148 B2
Betafo Madag. 131 [inset] J3
Betanzos Bol. 200 D4
Betanzos Spain 54 C1
Bétaré Oya Cameroon 125 I5
Bete Grise U.S.A. 172 F3
Bete Hor Eth. 128 C2
Bétérou Benin 125 F4
Betet i. Indon. 76 D3
Beth, Oued r. Morocco 122 D2
Bethal S. Africa 133 N3
Bethanie Namibia 130 C5
Bethany MO U.S.A. 178 D3
Bethany OK U.S.A. 179 C5
Bethari Nepal 97 D4
Bethel AK U.S.A. 164 C3
Bethel ME U.S.A. 177 O1
Bethel OH U.S.A. 176 A7
Bethesda MD U.S.A. 177 H6
Bethesda OH U.S.A. 176 D5
Bethesdaweg S. Africa 133 I8
Bethlehem S. Africa 133 M5
Bethlehem U.S.A. 177 J5
Bethlehem West Bank 108 G6
also spelt Bayt Lahm or Bet Lehem
Bethlesdorp S. Africa 133 J10
Bethulie S. Africa 133 J7
Béthune France 51 I2
Betijoque Venez. 198 D2
Betim Brazil 207 I6
Betioky Madag. 131 [inset] J4
Betiri, Gunung mt. Indon. 77 F5
Bet Lehem West Bank see Bethlehem
Betlitsa Rus. Fed. 43 O7
Betma India 96 B5
Betong Thai. 79 C7
Betoota Australia 149 D5
Bétou Congo 126 C4
Betpak-Dala plain Kazakh. 103 G3
Betrandraka Madag. 131 [inset] J3
Betroka Madag. 131 [inset] J4
Bet She'an Israel 108 G5
Betsiamites Canada 169 G3
Betsiamites r. Canada 169 G3
Betsiboka r. Madag. 131 [inset] J2
Betsie, Point U.S.A. 172 G6
Betsy Bay Bahamas 187 E2
Betsy Lake U.S.A. 173 H4
Bettendorf U.S.A. 172 C9
Bettiah India 97 E4
Betul India 96 C5
Betwa r. India 96 C4
Betws-y-coed U.K. 47 I10
Betygala Lith. 42 E6
Béu Angola 127 B6
Beulah U.S.A. 178 B2
Beurfou well Chad 120 B6
Beuthen Poland see Bytom
Beuvron r. France 50 H5
Beverley U.K. 47 L10
Beverly MA U.S.A. 177 O3
Beverly OH U.S.A. 176 D6
Beverly Hills U.S.A. 182 F7
Beverungen Germany 48 G4
Beverwijk Neth. 48 B3
Bex Switz. 51 N6
Bextograk China 88 D4
Beyağaç Turkey 59 J11
Beyazköy Turkey 58 I7
Beyce Turkey see Orhaneli
Beydağ Turkey 59 J10
Bey Dağları mts Turkey 106 B3
Beykonak Turkey 108 B1
Beykoz Turkey 106 B2
Beyla Guinea 124 C4
Beylagan Azer. see Beyläqan
Beyläqan Azer. 107 F3
also spelt Beylagan; formerly known as Zhdanovsk
Beylul Eritrea 121 I6
Beyneu Kazakh. 102 C3
Beyoneisu Retugan i. Japan 91 F9
Beypazarı Turkey 106 B2
Beypınarı Turkey 107 D3
Beypore India 94 B4
Beyra Somalia 128 E3
Beyram Iran 100 C5
Beyrouth Lebanon see Beirut
Beyşehir Turkey 106 B3
Beyşehir Gölü l. Turkey 106 B3
Beytüşşebap Turkey 107 E3
also known as Elki
Bezameh Iran 100 D3
Bezbozhnik Rus. Fed. 40 I4
Bezdan Vojvodina, Srbija Yugo. 56 K3
Bezenjān Iran 100 D4
Bezhanitskaya Vozvyshennost' hills Rus. Fed. 43 K5
Bezhanitsy Rus. Fed. 43 K5
Bezhanovo Bulg. 58 F5
Bezhetsk Rus. Fed. 43 R4
Bezhetskiy Verkh reg. Rus. Fed. 43 R4
Béziers France 51 J9
Bezmein Turkm. see Byuzmeyin
Bezwada India see Vijayawada
Bhabhar India 96 A4
Bhabra India 96 B5
Bhabua India 97 D4
Bhachau India 96 A5
Bhadar r. India 96 A5
Bhadarwah Jammu and Kashmir 96 B2
Bhadaur India 101 H4
Bhadgaon Nepal see Bhaktapur
Bhadohi India 97 D4
Bhadra India 96 B3
Bhadrachalam India 94 D2
Bhadrachalam Road Station India see Kottagudem
Bhadrakh India 97 E5
Bhadra Reservoir India 94 B3
Bhadravati India 94 B3
Bhag Pak. 101 F4
Bhagalpur India 97 E4
Bhagirathi r. India 97 F5
Bhainsa India 94 C2
Bhainsdehi India 96 C5
Bhairab Bazar Bangl. 97 F4
Bhairawa Nepal 97 D4
also known as Siddharthanagar; also spelt Bhairawaha
Bhairawaha Nepal see Bhairawa
Bhairi Hol mt. Pak. 101 F5
Bhakkar Pak. 101 G4
Bhaktapur Nepal 97 E4
also known as Bhadgaon
Bhalki India 94 C2
Bhalwal Pak. 101 H3
Bhamgarh India 96 C5
Bhamo Myanmar 78 B2
Bhandara India 96 C5
Bhander India 96 C4
Bhanjanagar India 95 E2
Bhanpura India 96 B4
Bhanrer Range hills India 96 C5
Bharat country Asia see India
Bharatpur India 96 C4
Bharatpur Nepal 97 E4
Bhareli r. India 97 G4
Bhari r. Pak. 101 F5
Bharthana India 96 C4
Bharuch India 96 B5
formerly known as Broach; historically known as Barygaza or Bhrigukaccha
Bhatapara India 97 D5
Bhatghar Lake India 94 B2
Bhatiapara Ghat Bangl. 97 F5
Bhatinda India see Bathinda
Bhatkal India 94 B3
Bhatnair India see Hanumangarh
Bhatpara India 97 F5
Bhaun Gharibwal Pak. 101 H3
Bhavani India 94 C4
Bhavani r. India 94 C4
Bhavani Sagar l. India 94 C4
Bhavnagar India 96 B5
Bhawana Pak. 101 H4
Bhawanipatna India 95 D2
Bhearnaraigh, Eilean i. U.K. see Berneray
Bheemavaram India see Bhimavaram
Bhekuzulu S. Africa 133 O4
Bhera Pak. 101 H3
Bheri r. Nepal 97 D3
Bhilai India 96 D5
Bhildi India 96 B4
Bhilwara India 96 B4
Bhima r. India 94 C2
Bhimavaram India 94 D2
formerly spelt Bheemavaram
Bhimbar Pak. 101 H3
Bhimnagar India 97 E4
Bhimphedi Nepal 97 E4
Bhind India 96 C4
Bhindar India 96 B4
Bhinga India 97 D4
Bhingar India 94 B2
Bhinmal India 96 B4
Bhiwandi India 94 B2
Bhiwani India 96 C3
Bhogat India 96 A5
Bhojpur Nepal 97 E4
Bhokardan India 94 B1
Bhola Bangl. 97 F5
Bhongaon India 96 C4
Bhongir India 94 C2
Bhongweni S. Africa 133 N7
Bhopal India 96 C5
Bhopalpatnam India 94 D2
Bhor India 94 B2
Bhrigukaccha India see Bharuch
Bhuban India 95 E1
Bhubaneshwar India 95 E1
formerly spelt Bhubaneswar
Bhubaneswar India see Bhubaneshwar
Bhuban Hills India 97 G4
Bhuj India 96 A5
Bhumiphol Dam Thai. 78 B4
Bhunya Swaziland 133 P3
Bhurgaon Bhutan 97 F4
Bhusawal India 96 B5
▶Bhutan country Asia 97 F4
known as Druk-Yul in Dzongkha
asia [countries] ▶▶ 64–67
Bhuttewala India 96 A4
Bhuvanagiri India 94 C4
Biá r. Brazil 199 E5
Bia, Monts mts Dem. Rep. Congo 127 E7
Bia, Phou mt. Laos 78 C4
Biābān mts Iran 100 D5
Biafra, Bight of g. Africa see Benin, Bight of
Biak Irian Jaya Indon. 73 I7
Biak Sulawesi Tengah Indon. 75 B3
Biak i. Indon. 73 I7
Biała r. Poland 49 R5
Biała Piska Poland 49 T2
Biała Podlaska Poland 49 U3
Białobrzegi Poland 49 R4
Białogard Poland 49 M2
Białowieski Park Narodowy nat. park Poland 42 E9
Biały Bór Poland 49 N2
Białystok Poland 49 U2
formerly spelt Belostok
Biancavilla Sicilia Italy 57 G11
Bianco Italy 57 I10
Bianco, Monte mt. France/Italy see Blanc, Mont
Bianga Cent. Afr. Rep. 126 D3
Biankouma Côte d'Ivoire 124 D5
Bianouan Côte d'Ivoire 124 E5
Bianzhuang China see Cangshan
Biaora India 96 C5
Bī'ār Ghabāghib well Syria 109 K2
Biārjmand Iran 100 C2
Biaro i. Indon. 75 C2
Biarritz France 50 E9
Bi'ār Tabrāk well Saudi Arabia 105 D2
Biasca Switz. 51 O6
Biba Egypt 121 F2
Bibai Japan 90 G3
Bibala Angola 127 B8
formerly known as Vila Arriaga
Bibas Gabon 126 A4
Bibbenluke Australia 147 F4
Bibbiena Italy 56 D5
Biberach an der Riß Germany 48 G7
Bibiani Ghana 124 E5
Bibirevo Rus. Fed. 43 N5
Bibiyana r. Bangl. 97 F4
Biblos Lebanon see Jbail
Bicas Brazil 207 J8
Bicaz Romania 58 H2
Bicheng China see Bishan
Bicheno Australia 147 F5
Bichevaya Rus. Fed. 82 D3
Bichi Nigeria 125 H3
Bichi r. Rus. Fed. 82 E1
Bicholim India 94 B3
Bichraltar Nepal 97 E4
Bichura Rus. Fed. 85 E1
Bichvint'a Georgia 107 E2
also known as Pitsunda
Bickerton Island Australia 148 C2
Bicuari, Parque Nacional do nat. park Angola 127 B8
Bid India 94 B2
also spelt Bir
Bida Nigeria 125 G4
Bidache France 50 E9
Bidadari, Tanjong pt Sabah Malaysia 77 G1
Bidar India 94 C2
Bidasar India 96 B4
Bidbid Oman 105 G3
Biddeford U.S.A. 177 O2
Bideford U.K. 47 H12
Bideford Bay U.K. 47 H12
also known as Barnstaple Bay
Bidente r. Italy 56 E4
Bidjovagge Norway 44 M1
Bidkhan, Kūh-e mt. Iran 100 D4
Bidokht Iran 100 D3
Bidon 5 tourist site Alg. 123 F5
Bidzhan Rus. Fed. 82 C3
Bidzhar r. Rus. Fed. 82 D3
Bié Angola see Kuito
Bié prov. Angola 127 C8
Biebrza r. Poland 49 T2
Biebrzański Park Narodowy nat. park Poland 49 T2
Biedenkopf Germany 48 F5
Biel Switz. 51 N5
also known as Bienne
Bielawa Poland 49 N5
Bielefeld Germany 48 F3
Bielitz Poland see Bielsko-Biała
Biella Italy 56 A3
Bielsko-Biała Poland 49 Q6
historically known as Bielitz
Bielsk Podlaski Poland 49 U3
Bielstein hill Germany 51 P1
Bienenbüttel Germany 48 H2
Biên Hoa Vietnam 79 D6
Bienne r. France 51 L6
Bienne Switz. see Biel
Bienvenida hill Spain 54 E6
Bienvenue Fr. Guiana 199 H4
Bienville, Lac l. Canada 169 F2
Bierbank Australia 149 E5
Bierutów Poland 49 O4
Biesiesvlei S. Africa 133 J3
Biesiespoort S. Africa 132 H8
Bieszczady mts Poland 49 T6
Bieszczadzki Park Narodowy nat. park Poland 49 T6
Bièvre Belgium 51 L3
Biferno r. Italy 56 H7
Bifoun Gabon 126 A5
Bifröst Iceland 44 [inset] B2
Bifuka Japan 90 H2
Big r. U.S.A. 182 A2
Biga Turkey 106 A2
Biga r. Turkey 59 I8
Bigadiç Turkey 106 B3
Biganos France 50 F8
Biga Yarımadası pen. Turkey 59 H9
Big Baldy Mountain U.S.A. 180 E3
Big Bay U.S.A. 172 F4
Big Bay de Noc U.S.A. 172 F5
Big Bear Lake U.S.A. 183 H7
Big Belt Mountains U.S.A. 180 E3
Big Bend Swaziland 133 P3
Big Bend National Park U.S.A. 179 B6
Big Black r. U.S.A. 175 B5
Big Blue r. U.S.A. 178 C4
Big Canyon watercourse U.S.A. 179 B6
Big Cypress National Preserve nature res. U.S.A. 175 D7
Big Desert Wilderness Park nature res. Australia 146 D3
Big Eau Pleine Reservoir U.S.A. 172 D6
Biger Nuur salt l. Mongolia 84 C2
Big Fork r. U.S.A. 174 A1
Biggar Canada 167 J4
Biggar U.K. 46 I8
Biggar, Lac l. Canada 168 F3
Biggarsberg S. Africa 133 N5
Bigge Island Australia 150 D2
Biggenden Australia 149 G5
Bigger, Mount Canada 166 B3
Biggleswade U.K. 47 L11
Biggs U.S.A. 182 C2
Big Hole r. U.S.A. 180 D3
Bighorn r. U.S.A. 180 F3
Bighorn Mountains U.S.A. 180 F3
Bigil'dino Rus. Fed. 43 U8
Big Island i. Nunavut Canada 165 L3
Big Island i. N.W.T. Canada 167 G2
Big Island U.S.A. 176 F8
Big Kalzas Lake Canada 166 C2
Big Lake U.S.A. 179 B6
Big Lake l. U.S.A. 174 H2
Big Muddy Creek r. U.S.A. 180 F2
Bignona Senegal 124 A3
Bigobo Dem. Rep. Congo 127 E6
Big Otter r. U.S.A. 176 F8
Big Pine U.S.A. 182 F4
Big Pine Peak U.S.A. 182 E7
Big Rapids U.S.A. 172 H7
Big Rib r. U.S.A. 172 D6
Big River Canada 167 J4
Big Sable Point U.S.A. 172 G6
Big Salmon Canada 166 C2
Big Salmon r. Canada 166 C2
Big Sand Lake Canada 167 L3
Big Sandy r. U.S.A. 180 E4
Big Sandy watercourse U.S.A. 183 K7
Big Sandy Creek r. U.S.A. 178 B4
Big Sandy Lake Canada 167 J4
Big Sioux r. U.S.A. 178 C3
Big Smokey Valley U.S.A. 183 G3
Big South Cape Island N.Z. 153 B15
Big South Fork National River and Recreation Area park U.S.A. 176 A9
Big Spring U.S.A. 179 B5
Big Stone Canada 167 I5
Big Sur U.S.A. 182 C5
Big Thicket National Preserve nature res. U.S.A. 179 D6
Big Timber U.S.A. 180 E3
Big Trout Lake Canada 168 B2
Big Trout Lake l. Canada 168 B2
Big Valley Canada 167 H4
Big Water U.S.A. 183 M4
Bigwin Canada 173 N5
Bihać Bos.-Herz. 56 H4
Bihar state India 97 E4
Bihariganj India 97 E4
Bihar Sharif India 97 E4
Bihor, Vârful mt. Romania 58 D2
Bihoro Japan 90 I3
Bihpuriagaon India 97 G4
Bijagós, Arquipélago dos is Guinea-Bissau 124 A4
Bijainagar India 96 B4
Bijaipur India 96 C4
Bijapur India 94 B2
Bijar Iran 100 A3
Bijarpur India 94 D2
Bijawar India 96 C4
Bijbehara Jammu and Kashmir 96 B2
Bijeljina Bos.-Herz. 56 L4
Bijelolasica mt. Croatia 56 H3
Bijelo Polje Crna Gora Yugo. 58 A5
Bijie China 86 C3
Bijni India 97 F4
Bijnor India 96 C3
Bijolia India 96 B4
Bijrān well Saudi Arabia 105 E2
Bijrān, Khashm hill Saudi Arabia 105 E2
Bikampur India 96 B4
Bikaner India 96 B3
Bikbauli Kazakh. 103 E3
Bikfaiya Lebanon 108 G4
Bikin Rus. Fed. 82 D3
Bikin r. Rus. Fed. 82 D3
Bikini atoll Marshall Is 220 F5
Bikita Zimbabwe 131 F4
Bikori Sudan 128 B2
Bikoro Dem. Rep. Congo 126 C5
Bikou China 86 C1
Bikramganj India 97 E4
Bilaa Point Phil. 74 C4
Bilād Banī Bū 'Alī Oman 105 G3
Bilād Banī Bū Ḥasan Oman 105 G3
Bilād Ghāmid reg. Saudi Arabia 104 C3
Bilād Zahran reg. Saudi Arabia 104 C3
Bilanga Burkina 125 E3
Bilangbilangan i. Indon. 77 G2
Bilara India 96 B4
Bilari India 96 C3
Bilaspur Chhattisgarh India 97 D5
Bilaspur Himachal Pradesh India 96 C3
Biläsuvar Azer. 107 G3
formerly known as Pushkino
Bilatan i. Phil. 74 B5
Bila Tserkva Ukr. 41 D6
also spelt Belaya Tserkva
Bilauktaung Range mts Myanmar/Thai. 79 B5
Bilbao Spain 55 I1
also spelt Bilbo
Bilbeis Egypt 121 F2
Bilbo Spain see Bilbao
Bilbor Romania 58 G1
Bildudalur Iceland 44 [inset] B2
Bileća Bos.-Herz. 56 K6
Bilecik Turkey 106 B2
Biled Romania 58 B3
Bilesha Plain Kenya 128 D4
Biłgoraj Poland 49 T5
Bilharamulo Tanz. 128 A5
Bilhaur India 96 D4
Bilhorod-Dnistrovs'kyy Ukr. 41 D7
also spelt Belgorod-Dnestrovskyy; formerly known as Akkerman; historically known as Cetatea Albă or Tyras
Bili Chad 126 C2
Bili r. Dem. Rep. Congo 126 D3
Bilibino Rus. Fed. 39 Q3
Bilibiza Moz. 129 D8
Bilikol' l. Kazakh. see Biylikol', Ozero
Bilin Myanmar 78 B4
Bilin r. Phil. 74 C4
Bilisht Albania 58 B8
Bilis Qooqaani Somalia 128 D4
Biliu r. China 85 I4
Bill U.S.A. 180 F4
Billabalong Australia 151 A5
Billabong Creek r. Australia see Moulamein Creek
Billdal Sweden 45 J4
Billère France 50 F9
Billiat Conservation Park nature res. Australia 146 D3
Billiluna Australia 150 D3
Billiluna Aboriginal Reserve Australia 150 D3
Billings U.S.A. 180 E3
Billiton i. Indon. see Belitung
Bill of Portland hd U.K. 47 J13
also known as Portland Bill
Billund airport Denmark 45 J5
Bill Williams r. U.S.A. 183 J7
Bill Williams Mountain U.S.A. 183 L6
Bilma Niger 125 I2
Bilo Eth. 128 C2
Biloela Australia 149 F5
Bilohirs'k Ukr. 41 E7
also spelt Belogorsk; formerly known as Karasubazar
Bilohir"ya Ukr. 41 C6
Biloku Guyana 199 G4
Biloli India 94 C2
Bilolutsk Ukr. 41 F6
Bilovods'k Ukr. 41 F6
Biloxi U.S.A. 175 B6
Bilpa Morea Claypan salt flat Australia 148 C5
Bilqās Qism Auwal Egypt 108 C6
Bilshausen Germany 48 H4
Bilsi India 96 C3
Biltine Chad 120 D6
Biltine pref. Chad 120 D6
Bilugyun Island Myanmar 78 B4
Bilungala Indon. 75 B2
Bilwascarma Nicaragua 186 C4
Bilyayivka Ukr. 41 D7
also spelt Belyayevka
Bima r. Dem. Rep. Congo 126 E4
Bima Indon. 77 G5
Bima, Teluk b. Indon. 77 G5
Bimbe Angola 127 B7
Bimbila Ghana 125 F4
Bimini Islands Bahamas 186 D1
Bimlipatam India 95 D2
Bina-Etawa India 96 C4
Binaija, Gunung mt. Indon. 75 D3
Binalbagan Phil. 74 B4
Binālūd, Kūh-e mts Iran 100 D2
Binatang Sarawak Malaysia 77 E2
Binboğa Dağı mt. Turkey 107 D3
Bincheng China 85 H4
formerly known as Binxian
Binchuan China 86 B3
also known as Niujing
Binder Chad 126 B2
Bindki India 96 D4
Bindu Dem. Rep. Congo 127 C6
Bindura Zimbabwe 131 F3
Binefar Spain 55 L3
Binga Zimbabwe 131 E3
Binga, Monte mt. Moz. 131 G3
Bingara Australia 147 F2
Bingaram i. India 94 B4
Bing Bong Australia 148 C2
Bingcaowan China 84 D4
Bingen am Rhein Germany 48 E6
Bingham U.S.A. 174 G2
Binghamton U.S.A. 177 J3
Bin Ghanīmah, Jabal hills Libya 120 B3
Bin Ghashir Libya 120 B1
Bingmei China see Congjiang
Bingöl Turkey 107 E3
also known as Çapakçur
Bingol Dağı mt. Turkey 107 E3
Bingxi China see Yushan
Bingzhongluo China 86 A2
Binh Son Vietnam 79 E5
Binicuil Phil. 74 B4
Bini Erda well Chad 120 C4
Binika India 97 D5
Binjai Indon. 76 B2
Bin Jawwād Libya 120 C2
Binna, Raas pt Somalia 128 F2
Binnaway Australia 147 F2
Binongko i. Indon. 75 C4
Binpur India 97 E5
Bintan i. Indon. 76 D2
Bintang, Bukit mts Malaysia 76 C1
Bintuan Phil. 74 B3
Bintuhan Indon. 76 C4
Bintulu Sarawak Malaysia 77 F2
Binubusan Phil. 74 B3
Binxian Heilong. China 82 B3
also known as Binzhou
Binxian Shaanxi China 87 D1
Binxian China see Bincheng
Binyang China 87 D4
also known as Binzhou
Bin-Yauri Nigeria 125 G4
Binzhou China see Binyang
Binzhou China see Binxian
Binzhou China 85 H4
Biobío admin. reg. Chile 204 B5
Biobío r. Chile 204 B5
Bioco i. Equat. Guinea 125 H6
also spelt Bioko; formerly known as Fernando Póo or Macias Nguema
Biograd na Moru Croatia 56 H5
Biogradska Gora nat. park Yugo. 58 A6
Bioko i. Equat. Guinea see Bioco
Biokovo park Croatia 56 J5
Biquinhas Brazil 207 H5
Bir India see Bid
Bir, Ras pt Djibouti 128 D2
Bira Rus. Fed. 82 D2
Bira r. Rus. Fed. 82 D2
Bi'r Abā al 'Ajjāj well Saudi Arabia 104 B2
Bi'r Abraq well Egypt 121 G4
Bîr Abu Darag well Egypt 108 D8
Bîr Abu Garad well Sudan 121 F5
Bîr Abu Hashim well Egypt 121 G4
Bîr Abu Husein well Egypt 121 F4
Bi'r Abū Jady oasis Syria 109 J1
Bîr Abu Minqâr well Egypt 121 E3
Bi'r ad Damar well Libya 120 A3
Bi'r adh Dhakar well Libya 120 D3
Bir Aïdiat well Mauritania 122 C4
Birāk Libya 120 B3
Birakan Rus. Fed. 82 C2
Bi'r al Amīr well Saudi Arabia 104 B2
Bi'r al Aṭbaq well Saudi Arabia 104 B2
Bi'r al 'Awādī well Saudi Arabia 104 B3
Bi'r al Fātiyah well Libya 120 B2
Bi'r al Ghanam Libya 120 B1
Bi'r al Halbā well Syria 109 J3
Bi'r al Ḥisw well Saudi Arabia 104 C2
Bi'r al Ikhwān well Libya 120 D3
Bi'r al Jadīd well Libya 120 B3
Bi'r al Jāhilīyah well Saudi Arabia 104 C3
Bi'r al Marba'ah well Syria 109 K3
Bi'r al Mashī well Saudi Arabia 104 B2
Bi'r al Mastūtah well Saudi Arabia 104 B3
Bi'r al Mūlūsī Iraq 107 E4
Bi'r al Mulūsī waterhole Iraq 109 L4
Bi'r al Munbaṭih well Syria 109 J3
Bi'r al Mushayqiq well Libya 120 A2
Bi'r al Muwaylih well Libya 120 C2
Bi'r al Qurr well Saudi Arabia 104 B2
Bir 'Amrāne well Mauritania 122 C5
Birandozero Rus. Fed. 40 F3
Bi'r an Nakhīlī waterhole Iraq 109 N3
Bir Anzarane W. Sahara 122 B5
Birao Cent. Afr. Rep. 126 D2
Bir Aouine well Tunisia 123 H2
Bi'r ar 'Alaqah well Libya 120 B2
Bi'r 'Arja well Saudi Arabia 104 C2
Bi'r as Sakhā well Saudi Arabia 104 C3
Biratar Bulak spring China 88 E3
Biratnagar Nepal 97 E4
also known as Morang
Biratori Japan 90 H3
Bi'r at Tarfāwī well Libya 120 E2
Bi'r at Tayyārīyah well Syria 109 K3
Bi'r at Tuwayīah waterhole Iraq 109 L4
Bi'r 'Azīz well Saudi Arabia 105 E3
Bi'raz Zurq well Saudi Arabia 104 C4
Bi'r Başīrī well Syria 109 I3
Bi'r Baydā well Saudi Arabia 104 B2
Bîr Bayly well Egypt 120 E2
Bîr Beiḍa well Egypt 108 F7
Bîr Bel Guerdâne well Mauritania 122 C4
Bir Ben Takoul well Alg. 123 E4
Bir Bidi well Sudan 121 E5
Bi'r Bū Athlah well Libya 120 D3
Bi'r Budayy well Saudi Arabia 104 B2
Bîr Buerât well Egypt 108 D8
Bi'r Bū Rāḥah well Libya 120 A3
Bi'r Buraym well Saudi Arabia 104 C3
Birch r. Canada 167 H3
Bir Chali well Mali 122 D5
Birch Hills Canada 167 J4
Birchip Australia 147 D3
Birch Lake N.W.T. Canada 167 G2
Birch Lake Sask. Canada 167 I4
Birch Lake U.S.A. 172 B3
Birch Mountains Canada 167 H3
Birch River Canada 167 K4
Birch River U.S.A. 176 E7
Birch Run U.S.A. 173 J7
Birchwood U.S.A. 172 B5
Bircot Eth. 128 D3
Bir Di Sudan 126 F3
Bîr Dibis well Egypt 121 F4
Bîr Dignâsh well Egypt 120 E2
Bird Island N. Mariana Is see Farallon de Medinilla
Bir Dolmane well Alg. 123 H3
Birdsboro U.S.A. 177 J5
Birdseye U.S.A. 183 M2
Birdsville Australia 148 C5
Birdum r. Australia 148 B2
Birecik Turkey 107 D3
Bir ed Deheb well Alg. 123 E4
Bîr el 'Adeid well Egypt 108 F9
Bîr el 'Agramîya well Egypt 108 C8
Bîr el Duweidar well Egypt 108 D7
Bir el Fakama well Sudan 104 A4
Bir el Ghoralia well Tunisia 123 H2
Bir El Hadjaj well Alg. 123 E4
Bîr el Haimur well Egypt 121 G4
Bîr el Istabl well Egypt 121 E2
Bîr el Khamsa well Egypt 106 A5
Bîr el Malha well Egypt 108 E8
Bîr el Nuss well Egypt 121 E2
Bîr el-Obeiyid well Egypt 121 E3
Bîr el Qatrâni well Egypt 121 E2
Bîr el Râbia well Egypt 106 A5
Birendranagar Nepal see Surkhet
Bir en Natrûn well Sudan 121 E5
Bir en Nugeim well Sudan 121 G5
Bir es Smeha well Alg. 123 G2
Bireun Indon. 76 B1
Bi'r Fāḍil well Saudi Arabia 105 E3
Bi'r Fajr well Saudi Arabia 104 B1
Bir Fanoidig well Sudan 104 A4
Bi'r Fardān well Saudi Arabia 105 E3
Bîr Fuâd well Egypt 121 E2
Bir Furawiya well Sudan 120 D6
Bir Gandouz W. Sahara 122 A5
Bi'r Ghawdah well Saudi Arabia 104 D3
Bîr Gifgâfa well Egypt 108 E7
Bîr Gindali well Egypt 108 C8
Bir Hādī oasis Saudi Arabia 105 E4
Bi'r Ḥajal well Syria 109 K3
Birhan mt. Eth. 128 C2
Bi'r Haraqī well Saudi Arabia 104 C3
Bîr Hasana well Egypt 108 E7
Bir Hatab well Sudan 121 G4
Bi'r Ḥaymir well Saudi Arabia 104 B2
Bi'r Ḥayzān well Saudi Arabia 104 B2
Bir Hismet 'Umar well Sudan 121 G4
Bi'r Ḥudūf well Saudi Arabia 104 C3
Bi'r Ḥumaymah well Syria 109 K3
Bir Huwait well Sudan 121 G4
Bi'r Ḥuwaymidah well Saudi Arabia 104 C2
Bi'r Ibn Ghunayn well Saudi Arabia 104 B2
Bi'r Ibn Hirmās Saudi Arabia see Al Bi'r
Bi'r Ibn Sarrār well Saudi Arabia 104 C4
Bi'r Īdīmah well Saudi Arabia 104 D4
Birigüi Brazil 206 C8
Birin, Col de pass Alg. 55 N9
Birini Cent. Afr. Rep. 126 D3
Bīrjand Iran 101 D3
Bi'r Jaydah well Saudi Arabia 104 B2
Bi'r Jifah well Yemen 105 D5
Bi'r Jubnī well Libya 120 E2
Bi'r Jugjug well Saudi Arabia 104 C3
Birkat Abū Salīm waterhole Saudi Arabia 104 C2
Birkat al 'Aṣāfīr waterhole Saudi Arabia 109 O8
Birkat al Ḥamrā well Saudi Arabia 104 C1
Birkat al Haytam waterhole Saudi Arabia 109 O8
Birkat ash Shīḥīyāt waterhole Saudi Arabia 109 O8
Birkat aẓ Ẓafīrī waterhole Saudi Arabia 109 O8
Birkat Zubālah waterhole Saudi Arabia 107 E5
Birkeland Norway 45 J4
Birkenhead U.K. 47 I10
Birket Qârûn l. Egypt 121 F2
Bi'r Khamrān waterhole Iraq 109 O3
Bi'r Khurbah well Saudi Arabia 104 B2
Bi'r Khuwārah well Saudi Arabia 104 C3
Bir Kiau well Sudan 121 G4
Bīrkim Iraq 107 F3
Birkirkara Malta 57 G13
Birksgate Range hills Australia 146 A1
Bir Labasoi well Sudan 121 G4
Bîrlad Romania see Bârlad
Bîr Lahfân well Egypt 108 E6
Bir Lahmar W. Sahara 122 C4
Birlik Kazakh. 103 H3
formerly spelt Brlik
Birlik Kazakh. see Brlik
Bir Likeit el Fauqani well Sudan 104 A3
Bir Liseila well Sudan 121 G4
Bîr Majal well Egypt 121 G4
Birmal reg. Afgh. 101 G3
Bi'r Malīyah well Saudi Arabia 104 C3
Birmingham U.K. 47 K11
Birmingham U.S.A. 175 C5
Bîr Misâha well Egypt 121 E4
Birmitrapur India 97 E5
Bîr Mogreïn Mauritania 122 C4
formerly known as Fort Trinquet
Bi'r Muḥaymid al Wazwaz well Syria 109 J3
Bi'r Mujayfil well Saudi Arabia 108 G8
Bîr Murra well Egypt 121 G4
Bi'r Muwayliḥ well Syria 109 K3
Bi'r Nabt well Saudi Arabia 104 B2
Bîr Nagib well Egypt 121 G4
Bîr Nâḥid oasis Egypt 121 F2
Bi'r Najib well Syria 109 K3
Bi'r Nasīf Saudi Arabia 104 B2
Bir Nawari well Sudan 121 G4
Birni Benin 125 F4
Birnie i. Kiribati 145 H2
Birnin-Gaouré Niger 125 F3
Birnin-Gwari Nigeria 125 G4
Birnin-Kebbi Nigeria 125 G3
Birnin Konni Niger 125 G3
Birnin Kudu Nigeria 125 H4
Birniwa Nigeria 125 H3
Bir Nukheila well Sudan 121 E5
Birobidzhan Rus. Fed. 82 D2
Birofel'd Rus. Fed. 82 D2
Bir Ounâne well Mali 122 E5
Birpur India 97 E4
Bîr Qasîr el Sirr well Egypt 106 A5
Bîr Quleib well Egypt 121 G3
Birr Rep. of Ireland 47 E10
Birrie r. Australia 147 E2
Birrindudu Australia 148 A3
Birrîyet el Aṣeifar Egypt 108 B6
Bîr Rôd Sâlim well Egypt 108 E7
Bir Roumi well Alg. 123 G2
Bi'r Sābil Iraq 107 E4
Bîr Sahara well Egypt 121 F4
Bir Salala well Sudan 121 G4
Birsay U.K. 46 I4
Bîr Shalatein Egypt 121 G4
Bi'r Shamandūr well Syria 109 K1
Birshoghyr Kazakh. see Berchogur
Bi'r Simād waterhole Iraq 109 O3
Birsk Rus. Fed. 40 J5
Bir Sohanit well Sudan 104 A3
Birštonas Lith. 42 F7
Bîr Tâba Egypt 108 F8
Bir Ṭalḥah well Saudi Arabia 105 D3
Bir Tanguer well Alg. 123 H3
Bi'r Tānjidar well Libya 120 D2
Bîr Tarfâwi well Egypt 121 F4
Bi'r Ṭarūfāwī waterhole Iraq 109 O4
Bîr Thâl well Egypt 108 E8
Birthday Mountain hill Australia 149 D2
Birtle Canada 167 K5
Biru China 89 F6
also known as Biruxiong
Bîr Udeib well Egypt 108 D8
Biruintsa Moldova see Ştefan Vodă
Bi'r Umm el Gharānīq Libya 120 C2
Bîr Umm Fawâkhîr well Egypt 104 A2
Bi'r Umm Missā well Saudi Arabia 104 B2
Bîr Ungât well Egypt 121 G4
Biruni Uzbek. see Beruni
Birur India 94 B3
Bi'r Usaylīlah well Saudi Arabia 105 D3
Biruxiong China see Biru
Bir Wario well Sudan 121 G5
Bi'r Wedeb well Libya 120 B3
Bi'r Wurshah well Saudi Arabia 104 C3
Biryakovo Rus. Fed. 43 V2
Biržai Lith. 42 F5
Bir Zar well Tunisia 123 H3
Bisa i. Indon. 75 C3
Bisalpur India 96 C3
Bisau India 96 B3
Bisbee U.S.A. 181 E7
Biscarrosse France 50 E8
Biscarrosse et de Parentis, Étang de l. France 50 E8
Biscay, Bay of sea France/Spain 50 A7
Biscayne Bay U.S.A. 175 D7
Biscayne National Park U.S.A. 175 D7
Bischofshofen Austria 49 K8
Bischofswerda Germany 49 L4
Biscoe Islands Antarctica 222 T2
Biscotasing Canada 168 D4
Bisert' r. Rus. Fed. 40 K4
Bisertsi Bulg. 58 H5
Biševo i. Croatia 56 H6
Bisezhai China 86 B4
Bisha Eritrea 121 H6
Bīshah reg. Saudi Arabia 104 C4
Bīshah, Wādī watercourse Saudi Arabia 104 D3
Bishan China 86 C2
also known as Bicheng
Bishbek Kyrg. see Bishkek

▶Bishkek Kyrg. 103 H4
Capital of Kyrgyzstan. Also spelt Bishbek or Pishpek; formerly known as Frunze.

Bishnupur India 97 E5
Bisho S. Africa 133 L9
Bishop U.S.A. 182 F4
Bishop Auckland U.K. 47 K9
Bishop Lake Canada 167 G1
Bishop's Stortford U.K. 47 M12
Bishopville U.S.A. 175 D5
Bishrī, Jabal hills Syria 109 K2
Bishti i Pallës pt Albania 58 A7
Bishui China 82 A1
Bishui China see Biyang
Bisi S. Africa 133 N7
Bisinaca Col. 198 D3
Biskra Alg. 123 G2
also spelt Beskra
Biskupiec Poland 49 R2
Bislig Phil. 74 C4
Bislig Bay Phil. 74 C4

▶Bismarck U.S.A. 178 B2
State capital of North Dakota.

Bismarck Archipelago is P.N.G. 73 K7
Bismarck Sea P.N.G. 73 K7
Bismil Turkey 107 E3
Bismo Norway 45 J3
Bison U.S.A. 178 B2
Bīsotūn Iran 100 A3
Bispgården Sweden 44 L3
Bissa, Djebel mt. Alg. 55 M8
Bissamcuttak India 95 D2

▶Bissau Guinea-Bissau 124 B4
Capital of Guinea-Bissau.

Bissaula Nigeria 125 H5
Bissett Canada 167 M5
Bissikrima Guinea 124 C4
Bissorã Guinea-Bissau 124 B3
Bistcho Lake Canada 166 G3
Bistra mt. Macedonia 58 B7
Bistra r. Romania 58 D3
Bistra mt. Yugo. 58 B6
Bistreț Romania 58 E5
Bistreț, Lacul l. Romania 58 E5

index B

Bistrița Romania **58** F1
Bistrița *r.* Romania **58** F1
Bistrița *r.* Romania **58** H2
Bistrița Bârgăului Romania **58** F1
Bistrițel, Munții *mts* Romania **58** G1
Bistritsa *r.* Bulg. **58** E7
Biswan India **96** D4
Bisztynek Poland **49** R1
Bitam Gabon **126** A4
Bitata Eth. **128** C3
Bitburg Germany **48** D6
Bitche France **51** N3
Bitik Kazakh. **102** B2
Bitkine Chad **126** C2
Bitlis Turkey **107** E3
Bitola Macedonia **58** C7
formerly known as Manastir *or* Monastir; *formerly spelt* Bitolj
Bitolj Macedonia *see* **Bitola**
Bitonto Italy **56** I7
Bitrān, Jabal *hill* Saudi Arabia **105** D3
Bitra Par *reef* India **94** B4
Bitter Creek *r. UT* U.S.A. **183** O2
Bitter Creek *r. WY* U.S.A. **180** E4
Bitterfontein S. Africa **132** C8
Bitterroot *r.* U.S.A. **180** D3
Bitterroot Range *mts* U.S.A. **180** D3
Bitterwater U.S.A. **182** D5
Bittou Burkina **125** E4
Bituca Brazil **202** A4
Bitung Indon. **75** C2
Bityi S. Africa **133** M8
Bityug *r.* Rus. Fed. **41** F6
Biu Nigeria **125** I4
Biula Angola **127** D7
Bivane *r.* S. Africa **133** P4
Biwabik U.S.A. **172** A3
Biwa-ko *l.* Japan **91** D7
Bixad Romania **58** G2
Biyala Egypt **108** C6
Biyang China *see* **Yixian**
Biyang China **87** E1
also known as Bishui
Biye K'obē Eth. **128** D2
Biylikol', Ozero *l.* Kazakh. **103** G4
also known as Biliköl
Biyo Ado *well* Eth. **128** E3
Biysk Rus. Fed. **80** D2
Bizana S. Africa **133** N7
Bizen Japan **91** D7
Bizerta Tunisia *see* **Bizerte**
Bizerte Tunisia **123** H1
English form Bizerta; *also known as* Banzart; *historically known as* Hippo Zarytus
Bizhanābād Iran **100** D5

▶**Bjargtangar** *hd* Iceland **44** [inset] A2
Most westerly point of Europe.

Bjarkøy Norway **44** L1
Bjästa Sweden **44** L3
Bjelasica *mts* Yugo. **58** A6
Bjelašnica *mts* Bos.-Herz. **56** K5
Bjelovar Croatia **56** I3
Bjerkvik Norway **44** L1
Bjerringbro Denmark **45** J4
Bjøllånes Norway **44** K2
Bjoneroa Norway **45** J3
Björbo Sweden **45** K3
Bjørkelangen Norway **45** J4
Björkfjället *mts* Sweden **44** L2
Björklinden Sweden **44** L1
Björklinge Sweden **45** L3
Björksele Sweden **44** L2
Bjorli Norway **44** J3
Björna Sweden **44** L3
Bjørnafjorden *b.* Norway **45** I3
Björneborg Fin. *see* **Pori**
Bjørnevatn Norway **44** O1
Bjørnfjell Norway **44** L1

▶**Bjørnøya** *i.* Arctic Ocean **38** B2
Part of Norway. English form Bear Island.

Bjørnstad Norway **44** O1
Bjurholm Sweden **44** L3
Bjurõklubb *pt* Sweden **44** M2
Bjursås Sweden **45** K3
Bla Mali **124** D3
Blace *Kosovo, Srbija* Yugo. **58** B6
Blace *Srbija* Yugo. **58** C5
Blachownia Poland **49** P5
Black *r. Man.* Canada **167** L5
Black *r. Ont.* Canada **168** D3
Black *r. Ont.* Canada **172** G2
Black *r. AR* U.S.A. **174** B5
Black *r. AZ* U.S.A. **183** N8
Black *r. MI* U.S.A. **173** K8
Black *r. SC* U.S.A. **175** E5
Black *r. WI* U.S.A. **172** B6
Blackall Australia **149** E5
Black Bay *Ont.* Canada **168** B3
Black Bay *Sask.* Canada **167** I3
Blackbear *r.* Canada **168** B2
Blackbull Australia **149** D3
Blackburn U.K. **47** J10
Black Butte *mt.* U.S.A. **182** B2
Black Butte Lake U.S.A. **182** B2
Black Canyon *gorge* U.S.A. **183** J6
Black Canyon of the Gunnison National Park U.S.A. **181** F5
Black Coast Antarctica **222** T2
Black Creek U.S.A. **172** E6
Black Creek *watercourse* U.S.A. **183** O6
Black Dome *mt.* Canada **166** E4
Blackdown Tableland National Park Australia **149** F4
Blackfeet Indian Reservation *res.* U.S.A. **180** D2
Blackfoot U.S.A. **180** D4
Black Foot *r.* U.S.A. **180** D3
Blackfoot Reservoir U.S.A. **180** E4
Black Forest *mts* Germany **48** F8
also known as Schwarzwald
Black Hill Range *hills* Australia **148** B5
Black Hills *SD* U.S.A. **180** F3
Black Island Canada **167** L5
Black Lake Canada **167** J3
Black Lake *l.* Canada **167** J3
Black Lake *l.* U.S.A. **173** I5
Black Mesa *mt.* U.S.A. **183** O8
Black Mesa *ridge* U.S.A. **183** N5
Black Mountain *hill* U.K. **47** I12
Black Mountain *CA* U.S.A. **182** G6
Black Mountain *KY* U.S.A. **176** C9
Black Mountains *hills* U.K. **47** I12
Black Mountains U.S.A. **183** J6
Black Nossob *watercourse* Namibia **130** C4
also known as Swart Nossob
Black Pagoda India *see* **Konarka**
Black Point *Hong Kong* China **87** [inset]
also known as Lan Kok Tsui
Blackpool U.K. **47** I10
Black Range State Park *nature res.* Australia **147** D4
Black River Jamaica **186** D3
Black River U.S.A. **177** J1
Black River *r.* Vietnam **78** D3
also known as Đa, Sông
Black River Falls U.S.A. **172** C6
Black Rock *hill* Jordan *see* **'Unāb, Jabal al**
Black Rock Desert U.S.A. **182** E1
Blacksburg U.S.A. **176** E8
Black Sea Asia/Europe **41** F8
also known as Chernoye More *or* Kara Deniz
Blacks Fork *r.* U.S.A. **180** E4
Blackshear U.S.A. **175** D6
Blacksod Bay Rep. of Ireland **47** B9
Black Springs U.S.A. **182** E2
Blackstone *r. N.W.T.* Canada **166** F2
Blackstone *r. Y.T.* Canada **166** B1
Blackstone U.S.A. **176** G8
Black Sturgeon *r.* Canada **172** E2
Black Sugarloaf *mt.* Australia **147** F2
Black Tickle Canada **169** K2
Black Umfolozi *r.* S. Africa **133** P5
Black Volta *r.* Africa **124** E4
also known as Mouhoun; *also known as* Volta Noire
Blackwater Australia **149** F4
Blackwater *watercourse* Australia **149** E5
Blackwater *r.* Canada **166** E2
Blackwater *r.* Rep. of Ireland **47** E11
Blackwater *r.* U.S.A. **177** I9
Blackwater *watercourse* U.S.A. **179** B5
Blackwater Lake Canada **166** F2
Blackwood National Park Australia **149** E4
Bladensburg National Park Australia **149** D4
Blåfjellshatten *mt.* Norway **44** K2
Blagodarnyy Rus. Fed. **41** G7
Blagodatnoye Kazakh. **103** H2
Blagoevgrad Bulg. **58** E6
formerly known as Gorna Dzhumaya
Blagoveshchensk Rus. Fed. **103** I1
Blagoveshchensk Rus. Fed. **82** B2
Blagoveshchensk Rus. Fed. **40** K5
Blagoveshchenskoye Kazakh. **103** H4
Blaiklston, Mount Canada **167** H5
Blain France **50** E5
Blain U.S.A. **176** H5
Blaine U.S.A. **176** B9
Blaine Lake Canada **167** J4
Blair *NE* U.S.A. **178** C3
Blair *WI* U.S.A. **172** B6
Blair Athol Australia **149** E4
Blair Atholl U.K. **46** I7
Blairbeth S. Africa **133** K2
Blairgowrie U.K. **46** I7
Blairs U.S.A. **176** F9
Blairsden U.S.A. **182** D2
Blairsville U.S.A. **174** D5
Blaj Romania **58** E2
Blak Rus. Fed. **103** E2
Blakang Mati, Pulau *i.* Sing. *see* **Sentosa**
Blakely U.S.A. **175** C6
Blake Point U.S.A. **172** E2
Blakeslee U.S.A. **177** J4
Blama Sierra Leone **124** C5
Blambangan, Semenanjung *pen.* Indon. **77** F5
Blambangan Nature Reserve Indon. **77** F5

▶**Blanc, Mont** *mt.* France/Italy **51** M7
5th highest mountain in Europe. Also known as Bianco, Monte.
europe [landscapes] ➡ 30–31

Blanca, Bahía *b.* Arg. **204** E5
Blanca, Cordillera *mts* Peru **200** A2
Blanca, Sierra *mt.* U.S.A. **181** F6
Blanca Peak U.S.A. **181** F5
Blanche, Lake *salt flat S.A.* Australia **146** C2
Blanche, Lake *salt flat W.A.* Australia **150** C4
Blanchester U.S.A. **176** B6
Blanchetown Australia **146** C3
Blanco *r.* Arg. **204** C3
Blanco *r.* Bol. **201** E3
Blanco *r.* Peru **198** C6
Blanco S. Africa **132** G10
Blanco *r.* Spain **54** F7
Blanco, Cabo *c.* Costa Rica **186** B5
Blanco, Cape U.S.A. **180** A4
Blanc-Sablon Canada **169** J3
Bland *r.* Australia **147** E3
also known as Yeo Yeo
Bland U.S.A. **176** D8
Blanda *r.* Iceland **44** [inset] B2
Blandford Forum U.K. **47** J13
Blanding U.S.A. **183** O4
Blanes Spain **55** N3
Blaney Park U.S.A. **172** H4
Blangah, Telok *b.* Sing. **76** [inset]
Blangkejeren Indon. **76** B2
Blangpidie Indon. **76** B2
Blangy-sur-Bresle France **50** H3
Blanice *r.* Czech Rep. **49** L6
Blankenheim Germany **48** D5
Blanquefort France **50** F8
Blanquilla, Isla *i.* Venez. **199** E2
Blansko Czech Rep. **49** N6
Blantyre Malawi **129** B8
Blarney Rep. of Ireland **47** D12
Blåsjø *l.* Norway **45** I4
Blaskavlen *mt.* Norway **45** I3
Blåstöten *mt.* Sweden **44** K3
Błaszki Poland **49** P4
Blatná Czech Rep. **49** K6
Blattniksele Sweden **44** L2
Blau Indon. **75** B2
Blaubeuren Germany **48** G7
Blåvands Huk *pt* Denmark **45** J5
Blavet *r.* France **50** C5
Blåviksjön Sweden **40** A2
Blaydon U.K. **47** K9
Blaye France **50** F7
Blayeul Sommet *mt.* France **51** M8
Blayney Australia **147** F3
Blaze, Point Australia **148** A2
Błażowa Poland **49** T6
Blega Indon. **77** F4
Bleik Norway **44** K1
Bleilochtalsperre *resr* Germany **51** R2
Blekinge *county* Sweden **45** K4
Blenheim Canada **168** D5
Blenheim N.Z. **152** H9
Blenheim Palace *tourist site* U.K. **47** K12
Bléré France **50** G5
Blesmanspos S. Africa **132** I4
Bletoppen *mt.* Norway **45** J4
Bleu, Lac *l.* Canada **173** O4
Bleus, Monts *mts* Dem. Rep. Congo **126** F4
Blida Alg. **123** F1
also spelt El Boulaïda
Bligh Sound *inlet* N.Z. **153** B12
Bligh Water *b.* Fiji **145** G3
Blind River Canada **168** D4
Blinkwater S. Africa **133** K9
Blinman Australia **146** C2
Bliss U.S.A. **180** D4
Blissfield *MI* U.S.A. **173** J9
Blissfield *OH* U.S.A. **176** D5
Blitar Indon. **77** F5
Block Island U.S.A. **177** N4
Block Island *i.* U.S.A. **177** N4
Block Island Sound *sea chan.* U.S.A. **177** N4
Bloedrivier S. Africa **133** O4
Bloemfontein S. Africa **133** K6
Bloemhof S. Africa **133** J4
Bloemhof Dam S. Africa **133** J4
Bloemhof Dam Nature Reserve S. Africa **133** J4
Blois France **50** H5
Blomberg se Vloer *salt pan* S. Africa **132** E7
Blönduós *l.* Iceland **44** [inset] C2
Blönduós Iceland **44** [inset] B2
Blongas Indon. **77** G5
Błonie Poland **49** R3
Bloods Range *mts* Australia **148** A5
Bloodsworth Island U.S.A. **177** I7
Bloodvein *r.* Canada **167** L5
Bloody Foreland *pt* Rep. of Ireland **47** D8
Bloomer U.S.A. **172** B5
Bloomfield Canada **173** P7
Bloomfield *IA* U.S.A. **174** A3
Bloomfield *IN* U.S.A. **174** C4
Bloomfield *MO* U.S.A. **174** B4
Bloomfield *NM* U.S.A. **181** F5
Blooming Prairie U.S.A. **174** A3
Bloomington *IL* U.S.A. **174** B3
Bloomington *IN* U.S.A. **174** C4
Bloomington *MN* U.S.A. **174** A2
Bloomsburg U.S.A. **177** I4
Bloomsbury Australia **149** F4
Blora Indon. **77** E4
Blossburg U.S.A. **177** H4
Blosseville Kyst *coastal area* Greenland **165** Q3
Blossom, Mys *pt* Rus. Fed. **39** R2
Blouberg Nature Reserve S. Africa **131** F4
Blountstown U.S.A. **175** C6
Blowing Rock U.S.A. **176** D9
Bludenz Austria **48** G8
Blue *r.* Canada **166** D3
Blue *r.* U.S.A. **179** D5
Blue *watercourse* U.S.A. **183** O8
Blue Bell Knoll *mt.* U.S.A. **183** M3
Blueberry *r.* Canada **166** F3
Blue Cliff S. Africa **133** J10
Blue Creek *r.* Mex. *see* **Azul**
Blue Diamond U.S.A. **183** I5
Blue Earth U.S.A. **178** D3
Blue Earth *r.* U.S.A. **178** D2
Bluefield U.S.A. **176** D8
Bluefields Nicaragua **186** C4
Bluegums S. Africa **133** L7
Blue Hill U.S.A. **177** Q1
Blue Hills Turks and Caicos Is **187** E2
Blue Knob *hill* U.S.A. **176** G5
Blue Lagoon National Park Zambia **127** E8
Blue Mountain *hill* Canada **169** J3
Blue Mountain India **97** G5
Blue Mountain Pass Lesotho **133** L6
Blue Mountains Australia **147** F3
Blue Mountains N.Z. **153** D14
Blue Mountains U.S.A. **180** C3
Blue Mountains National Park Australia **147** F3
Blue Mud Bay Australia **148** C2
Blue Nile *r.* Eth./Sudan **104** A5
also known as Ābay Wenz (Ethiopia), Azraq, Bahr el (Sudan)
Blue Nile *state* Sudan **128** B2
Bluenose Lake Canada **164** H3
Blue Rapids U.S.A. **178** C4
Blue Ridge *GA* U.S.A. **174** C5
Blue Ridge *VA* U.S.A. **176** F8
Blue Ridge *mts* U.S.A. **176** E9
Blue River Canada **166** G4
Blue Stack Mountains *hills* Rep. of Ireland **47** D9
Bluestone Lake U.S.A. **176** E8
Bluff Australia **149** F4
Bluff N.Z. **153** C14
Bluff City U.S.A. **176** C9
Bluffdale U.S.A. **183** M1
Bluff Face Range *hills* Australia **150** D3
Bluff Harbour N.Z. **153** C14
Bluff Island *Hong Kong* China **87** [inset]
also known as Sha Tong Hau Shan
Bluff Knoll *mt.* Australia **151** B7
Bluffton *IN* U.S.A. **174** C3
Bluffton *OH* U.S.A. **176** B5
Blumberg Germany **48** F8
Blumenau Brazil **203** B8
Blustry Mountain Canada **166** F5
Blyde River Nature Reserve S. Africa **133** O1
Blyth *r.* Australia **148** B2
Blyth Canada **173** L7
Blythdale Beach S. Africa **133** P6
Blythe U.S.A. **183** J8
Blytheville U.S.A. **174** B5
Blyth Range *hills* Australia **151** E5
Bo Norway **45** J4
Bo Sierra Leone **124** C5
Boac Phil. **74** B3
Boaco Nicaragua **186** B4
Boa Esperança *Minas Gerais* Brazil **203** C7
Boa Esperança *Roraima* Brazil **199** F4
Boa Esperança, Açude *resr* Brazil **202** D3
Boa Esperança do Sul Brazil **206** E8
Boa Hora Brazil **200** D2
Bo'ai *Henan* China **85** G5
also known as Qinghua
Bo'ai *Yunnan* China **86** C4
Boal Spain **54** E1
Boali Cent. Afr. Rep. **126** C3
Boalsburg U.S.A. **176** H5
Boane Moz. **133** Q3
Boano *i.* Indon. **75** C3
Boano, Selat *sea chan.* Indon. **75** C3
Boa Nova Brazil **202** D5
Boardman U.S.A. **176** E4
Boatlaname Botswana **131** E4
Boatman Australia **147** E1
Boa Viagem Brazil **202** E3
Boa Vista *Amazonas* Brazil **198** C6
Boa Vista *Amazonas* Brazil **199** E5
Boa Vista *Pará* Brazil **199** H5
Boa Vista *Roraima* Brazil **199** F4
Boa Vista *i.* Cape Verde **124** [inset]
Bobadah Australia **147** E3
Bobai China **87** D4
Bobaomby, Tanjona *c.* Madag. **131** [inset] K1
formerly known as Ambre, Cap d'
Bobbili India **95** D2
Bobbio Italy **56** B4
Bobcaygeon Canada **173** O6
Bobia *mt.* Spain **54** E1
Bobigny France **51** I4
Bobkovo Rus. Fed. **43** U6
Bobo-Dioulasso Burkina **124** D4
Bobolice Poland **49** N2
Bobon Phil. **74** C3
Bobonong Botswana **131** F4
Boborás Spain **54** C2
Bobotov Kuk *mt.* Yugo. *see* **Durmitor**
Bobovdol Bulg. **58** E6
Boboyob, Gora *mt.* Uzbek. **103** G4
Bobr Belarus **43** K7
Bobr *r.* Belarus **43** J7
Bóbr *r.* Poland **49** M3
Bobriki Rus. Fed. *see* **Novomoskovsk**
Bobrinets Ukr. *see* **Bobrynets'**
Bobrov Rus. Fed. **41** G6
Bobrovitsa Ukr. *see* **Bobrovytsya**
Bobrovytsya Ukr. **41** D6
also spelt Bobrovitsa
Bobruysk Belarus *see* **Babruysk**
Bobryk *r.* Belarus **42** H9
Bobrynets' Ukr. **41** E6
also spelt Bobrinets
Bobs Lake Canada **173** Q6
Bobso China **86** B1
Bobuk Sudan **128** B2
Boburés Venez. **198** D2
Boby *mt.* Madag. **131** [inset] J4
Boca Chica Key *i.* U.S.A. **175** D7
Boca de la Travesía Arg. **204** D6
Boca del Pao Venez. **199** E2
Boca del Río Mex. **185** F5
Boca de Macareo Venez. **199** F2
Boca de Uracoa Venez. **199** F2
Boca do Acre Brazil **200** D2
Boca do Capanã Brazil **199** F6
Boca do Curuquetê Brazil **200** D2
Boca do Jari Brazil **199** I5
Boca do Moaco Brazil **200** C1
Boca Grande *r. mouth* Trin. and Tob./Venez. **187** H5
Bocaina de Minas Brazil **207** I9
Bocaiúva Brazil **203** D6
Bocaiúva do Sul Brazil **203** B8
Bocanó Venez. **199** E4
Bocanda Côte d'Ivoire **124** D5
Bocaranga Cent. Afr. Rep. **126** B3
Boca Raton U.S.A. **175** D7
Bocas del Toro Panama **186** C5
Bochinche Venez. **199** F3
Bochnia Poland **49** R6
Bocholt Germany **48** D4
Bochum Germany **48** E4
Bochum S. Africa **131** F4
Bockenem Germany **48** H3
Bocoio Angola **127** B8
formerly known as Sousa Lara
Bocșa Romania **58** C3
Boda Cent. Afr. Rep. **126** C3
Böda Sweden **45** L4
Bodalla Australia **147** F4
Bodallin Australia **151** B6
Bodaybo Rus. Fed. **39** L4
Bodden Town Cayman Is **186** C3
Bode *r.* Germany **48** I4
Bodega Head U.S.A. **182** A3
Bodélé *reg.* Chad **120** C6
Boden Sweden **44** M2
Bodensee *l.* Germany/Switz. *see* **Constance, Lake**
Bode-Sadu Nigeria **125** G4
Bodești Romania **58** H1
Bodfish U.S.A. **182** F6
Bodhan India **94** C2
Bodh Gaya India **97** E4
Bodie U.S.A. **182** E3
Bodinayakkanur India **94** C4
Bodión *r.* Spain **54** E6
Bodmin U.K. **47** H13
Bodø Norway **44** K2
Bodocó Brazil **202** E3
Bodonchiyn Gol *watercourse* Mongolia **84** B2
Bodoquena *Mato Grosso do Sul* Brazil **201** F4
Bodoquena *Mato Grosso do Sul* Brazil **201** F5
Bodoquena, Serra da *hills* Brazil **201** F5
Bodoukpa Cent. Afr. Rep. **126** C3
Bodrog *r.* Hungary **49** S7
Bodrum Turkey **106** A3
historically known as Halicarnassus
Bodsjö Sweden **44** K3
Bódva *r.* Hungary **49** R7
Bodva *r.* Slovakia **49** R7
Boechout Belgium **51** K1
Boedo *r.* Spain **54** G2
Boende Dem. Rep. Congo **126** D5
Bo Epinang Indon. **75** B4
Boerne U.S.A. **179** C6
Boesmans *r.* S. Africa **133** K10
Boesmans hoekpas *pass* S. Africa **133** K8
Boeuf *r.* U.S.A. **175** B6
Bofete Brazil **206** E10
Boffa Guinea **124** B4
Boftsa Norway **44** O1
Bogale Myanmar **78** A4
Bogale *r.* Myanmar **78** A5
Bogalusa U.S.A. **175** B6
Bogan *r.* Australia **147** E2
Bogandé Burkina **125** E3
Bogan Gate Australia **147** E3
Bogangolo Cent. Afr. Rep. **126** C3
Bogantungan Australia **149** E4
Bogatić *Srbija* Yugo. **58** A4
Boğazlıyan Turkey **106** C3
Bogbonga Dem. Rep. Congo **126** C4
Bogcang Zangbo *r.* China **89** D6
Bogda Feng *mt.* China **88** E3
Bogdan *mt.* Bulg. **58** F6
Bogdana Romania **58** G5
Bogdanci Macedonia **58** D7
Bogdanovka Rus. Fed. **102** C1
Bogda Shan *mts* China **88** E3
Bogembay Kazakh. **103** H1
Bogen Norway **44** L1
Boggeragh Mountains *hills* Rep. of Ireland **47** C11
Boggola *hill* Australia **150** B4
Boghar Alg. **55** N9
Boghari Alg. *see* **Ksar el Boukhari**
Bogia P.N.G. **73** J7
Bogie *r.* Australia **149** E4
Bogny-sur-Meuse France **51** K3
Bogo Phil. **74** C4
Bogodukhov Ukr. *see* **Bohodukhiv**
Bogodukhovka Kazakh. **103** G1
Bogol Manya Eth. **128** D3
Bogolyubovo *Smolenskaya Oblast'* Rus. Fed. **43** N6
Bogolyubovo *Vladimirskaya Oblast'* Rus. Fed. **43** V5
Bogong, Mount Australia **147** E4
Bogopol' Rus. Fed. **90** D2
Bogor Indon. **77** D4
Bogoroditsk Rus. Fed. **43** T8
Bogoroditskoye Rus. Fed. **43** Q8
Bogorodsk Rus. Fed. **82** F1
Bogorodskoye Rus. Fed. **40** I4
Bogoslof Island U.S.A. **164** C4

▶**Bogotá** Col. **198** C3
Capital of Colombia and 5th most populous city in South America. Long form Santa Fé de Bogotá.
world [cities] ➡ 24–25

Bogotol Rus. Fed. **80** D1
Bogovarovo Rus. Fed. **40** H4
Bogoyavlenskoye Rus. Fed. *see* **Pervomayskiy**
Bogra Bangl. **97** F4
Boguchany Rus. Fed. **39** J4
Boguchar Rus. Fed. **41** G6
Bogué Mauritania **124** B2
Boh *r.* Indon. **77** F2
Bo Hai *g.* China **85** H4
English form Chihli, Gulf of; *formerly spelt* Po Hai
Bohai Haixia *sea chan.* China **85** I4
formerly known as Laotieshan Shuidao
Bohain-en-Vermandois France **51** J3
Bohai Wan *b.* China **85** H4
Bohemia *reg.* Czech Rep. **49** L5
also known as Böhmen
Bohemia Downs Australia **150** D3
Bohemia Downs Aboriginal Reserve Australia **150** D3
Bohemian Forest *mts* Germany *see* **Böhmer Wald**
Bohicon Benin **125** F5
Bohinskaye, Vozyera *l.* Belarus **42** H6
Bohlokong S. Africa **133** M5
Böhmen *reg.* Czech Rep. *see* **Bohemia**
Böhmer Wald *mts* Germany **49** J6
English form Bohemian Forest
Bohodukhiv Ukr. **41** E6
also spelt Bogodukhov
Bohol *i.* Phil. **74** C4
Bohol Sea Phil. **74** C4
Bohol Strait Phil. **74** B4
Böhöt Mongolia **85** F2
Bohu China **88** D3
also known as Bagrax
Boi, Ponta do *pt* Brazil **207** H10
Boiaçu Brazil **199** F5
Boichoko S. Africa **132** H5
Boigu Island Australia **73** J8
Boikhutso S. Africa **133** K3
Boila Moz. **131** H3
Boileau, Cape Australia **150** C3
Boim Brazil **199** H5
Boin *r.* Myanmar **78** A3
Boipeba, Ilha *i.* Brazil **202** E5
Boiro Spain **54** C2
Bois *r.* Brazil **206** C5
Bois, Lac des *l.* Canada **166** E1
Bois Blanc Island U.S.A. **173** I5
Bois de Sioux *r.* U.S.A. **178** C2

▶**Boise** U.S.A. **180** C4
State capital of Idaho.

Boise *r.* U.S.A. **180** C4
Boise City U.S.A. **178** B4
Boissevain Canada **167** K5
Boite *r.* Italy **56** E2
Boitumelong S. Africa **133** J4
Boituva Brazil **206** F10
Boizenburg Germany **48** H2
Bojano Italy **56** G7
Bojeador, Cape Phil. **74** B2
Bojnik *Srbija* Yugo. **58** C5
Bojnūrd Iran **100** D2
Bojonegoro Indon. **77** E4
Bojuru Brazil **204** H3
Bokada Dem. Rep. Congo **126** C3
Bokadaban Feng *mt.* China **89** E4
Bokajan India **97** G4
Bokanda Congo **126** C5
Bokaro India **97** E5
Bokat Indon. **75** B2
Bokatola Dem. Rep. Congo **126** C5
Boké Guinea **124** B4
Bokfontein S. Africa **132** D9
Bokhara *r.* Australia **147** E2
Boknafjorden *sea chan.* Norway **45** I4
Boko Congo **126** B6
Boko Dem. Rep. Congo **127** C6
Bokoko Dem. Rep. Congo **126** E3
Bokolo Gabon **126** A5
Bokombayevskoye Kyrg. *see* **Bökönbaev**
Bökönbaev Kyrg. **103** I4
also known as Bokombayevskoye *or* Bokonbayevo
Bokonbayevo Kyrg. *see* **Bökönbaev**
Bokong Lesotho **133** M6
Bokoro Chad **120** C6
Bokoro Dem. Rep. Congo **126** C5
Bokote Dem. Rep. Congo **126** D5
Bokovskaya Rus. Fed. **41** G6
Bokpunt *pt* S. Africa **132** C10
Bokpyin Myanmar **79** B6
Boksburg S. Africa **133** M3
Boksitogorsk Rus. Fed. **43** O2
Bokspits S. Africa **132** E3
Boktor Rus. Fed. **82** E2
Bokungu Dem. Rep. Congo **126** D5
Bokurdak Turkm. *see* **Bakhardok**
Bokwankusu Dem. Rep. Congo **126** D5
Bol Chad **120** B6
Bola, Bahr *watercourse* Chad **126** C2
Bolaang Indon. **75** B3
Bolaiti Dem. Rep. Congo **126** E5
Bolama Guinea-Bissau **124** B4
Bolan *r.* Pak. **101** F4
Bolanda, Jebel *mt.* Sudan **126** E3
Bolaños de Calatrava Spain **54** H6
Bolan Pass Pak. **101** F4
Bolbec France **50** G3
Boldājī Iran **100** B4
Boldu Romania **58** I3
Boldumsaz Turkm. **102** D4
formerly known as Kalinin
Bole China **88** C2
also known as Bortala
Bole Ghana **124** E4
Boleko Dem. Rep. Congo **126** C5
Bolesławiec Poland **49** M4
Bolgar Rus. Fed. **40** I5
also known as Kuybyshev; *also spelt* Bulgar
Bolgatanga Ghana **125** E4
Bolgatovo Rus. Fed. **43** J5
Bolgrad Ukr. *see* **Bolhrad**
Bolhrad Ukr. **41** D7
also spelt Bolgrad
Boli China **82** C3
Boli Sudan **126** F3
Bolia Dem. Rep. Congo **126** C5
Boliden Sweden **44** M2
Bolinao Phil. **74** A2
Bolintin-Vale Romania **58** G4
Bolívar *Antioquia* Col. **198** B3
Bolívar *Cauca* Col. **198** B4
Bolívar *dept* Col. **198** C2
Bolívar Peru **200** A1
Bolivar *MO* U.S.A. **178** D4
Bolivar *NY* U.S.A. **176** G3
Bolivar *TN* U.S.A. **174** B5
Bolívar *state* Venez. **199** E3
Bolivia Cuba **175** E8

▶**Bolivia** *country* S. America **200** D4
5th largest country in South America.
world [land images] ➡ 12–13
southamerica [countries] ➡ 192–193
southamerica [impacts] ➡ 196–197

Boljevac *Srbija* Yugo. **58** C5
Bolkhov Rus. Fed. **43** R8
Bolkow Canada **173** J2
Bolków Poland **49** N5
Bollène France **51** K8
Bollnäs Sweden **45** L3
Bollon Australia **147** E2
Bollstabruk Sweden **44** L3
Bolmen *l.* Sweden **45** K4
Bolnisi Georgia **107** F2
Bolobo Dem. Rep. Congo **126** C5
Bolod Islands Phil. **74** B5
Bologna Italy **56** D4
historically known as Bononia *or* Felsina
Bolognesi *Loreto* Peru **198** C6
Bolognesi *Ucayali* Peru **200** B2
Bologovo Rus. Fed. **43** M5
Bologoye Rus. Fed. **43** P4
Bolokanang S. Africa **133** J6
Bolokhovo Rus. Fed. **43** S7
Bolomba Dem. Rep. Congo **126** C4
Bolombo *r.* Dem. Rep. Congo **126** D4
Bolon' Rus. Fed. *see* **Achan**
Bolonchén de Rejón Mex. **185** H4
Bolondo Dem. Rep. Congo **126** C5
Bolondo Equat. Guinea **125** H6
Bolong Phil. **74** B5
Bolongongo Angola **127** B7
Bolotana *Sardegna* Italy **57** A8
Bolotnoye Rus. Fed. **80** C1
Bolotovo Rus. Fed. **43** N2
Bolovens, Phouphieng *plat.* Laos **79** D5
Bolozo Congo **126** B4
Bolpur India **97** E5
Bolsa, Cerro *mt.* Arg. **204** C3
Bolsena, Lago di *l.* Italy **56** D6
Bol'shakovo Rus. Fed. **42** C7
Bol'shaya Rus. Fed. **43** U1
Bol'shaya Bereyka Rus. Fed. **43** T9
Bol'shaya Chernigovka Rus. Fed. **102** B1
Bol'shaya Churakovka Kazakh. **103** F1
Bol'shaya Glushitsa Rus. Fed. **102** B1
Bol'shaya Imandra, Ozero *l.* Rus. Fed. **40** E2
Bol'shaya Kokshaga *r.* Rus. Fed. **40** H4
Bol'shaya Kosha Rus. Fed. **43** O5
Bol'shaya Rogovaya *r.* Rus. Fed. **40** L2
Bol'shaya Synya *r.* Rus. Fed. **40** K2
Bol'shaya Tsarevshchina Rus. Fed. *see* **Volzhskiy**
Bol'shaya Usa Rus. Fed. **40** J4
Bol'shaya Vishera Rus. Fed. **43** N3
Bol'shaya Vladimirovka Kazakh. **103** I2
also known as Ülken Vladīmīrovka
Bol'shenarymskoye Kazakh. **88** D1
Bol'she-Ploskoye Rus. Fed. **43** Q4
Bol'sheretsk Rus. Fed. **39** P4
Bol'shevik, Ostrov *i.* Rus. Fed. **39** K2
Bol'shezemel'skaya Tundra *lowland* Rus. Fed. **40** J2
Bol'shiye Barsuki, Peski *des.* Kazakh. **102** D3
Bol'shiye Chirki Rus. Fed. **40** H3
Bol'shiye Kozly Rus. Fed. **40** F2
Bol'shiye Medvedki Rus. Fed. **43** S8
Bol'shiye Peshnyye, Ostrova *is* Kazakh. **102** B3
formerly known as Peshnyye, Ostrova
Bol'shoy Aksu Kazakh. **103** I4
Bol'shoy Aksuat, Ozero *salt l.* Kazakh. **103** F2
formerly known as Aksuat, Ozero
Bol'shoy Aluy *r.* Rus. Fed. **39** P3
Bol'shoy Anyuy *r.* Rus. Fed. **39** Q3
Bol'shoy Begichev, Ostrov *i.* Rus. Fed. **39** L2
also known as Begicheva, Ostrov
Bol'shoy Berezovyy, Ostrov *i.* Rus. Fed. **43** J1
Bol'shoy Bukon' Kazakh. **88** C1
Bol'shoye Alekseyevskoye Rus. Fed. **43** T6
Bol'shoye Beresnevo Rus. Fed. **43** N6
Bol'shoye Korovino Rus. Fed. **43** U7
Bol'shoye Mikhaylovskoye Rus. Fed. **43** T5
Bol'shoye Murashkino Rus. Fed. **40** H5
Bol'shoye Ozerko Rus. Fed. **44** P1
Bol'shoye Polpino Rus. Fed. **43** P8
Bol'shoye Popovo Rus. Fed. **43** U9
Bol'shoye Topol'noye, Ozero *salt l.* Rus. Fed. **103** I1
Bol'shoye Zaborov'ye Rus. Fed. **43** O3
Bol'shoye Zhokovo Rus. Fed. **43** T7
Bol'shoy Ik *r.* Rus. Fed. **102** C2
Bol'shoy Irgiz *r.* Rus. Fed. **102** A2
Bol'shoy Kamen' Rus. Fed. **82** D4
Bol'shoy Kavkaz *mts* Asia/Europe *see* **Caucasus**
Bol'shoy Kokovichi Rus. Fed. **43** O1
Bol'shoy Lug Rus. Fed. **84** E1
Bol'shoy Lyakhovskiy, Ostrov *i.* Rus. Fed. **39** O2
Bol'shoy Porog Rus. Fed. **39** J3
Bol'shoy Shantar, Ostrov *i.* Rus. Fed. **82** E1
Bol'shoy Tokmak Kyrg. *see* **Tokmak**
Bol'shoy Tokmak Ukr. *see* **Tokmak**
Bol'shoy Tuder *r.* Rus. Fed. **43** M4
Bol'shoy Uzen' *r.* Kazakh./Rus. Fed. **102** B2
also known as Ülkenözen
Bol'shoy Yug *r.* Rus. Fed. **43** T2
Bol'shoy Zelenchuk *r.* Rus. Fed. **107** E1
Bolsward Neth. **48** C2
Bolton Canada **173** N7
Bolton Phil. **74** C5
Bolton U.K. **47** J10
Boltutino Rus. Fed. **43** N7
Bolu Turkey **106** B2
Bolungarvík Iceland **44** [inset] B2
Boluntay China **84** B4
Boluo China **87** E4
also known as Luoyang
Bolus Head Rep. of Ireland **47** B12
Bolva *r.* Rus. Fed. **43** P8
Bolvadin Turkey **106** B3
Bolvanskiy Nos, Mys *c.* Rus. Fed. **40** K1
Bolyarovo Bulg. **58** H6
Bolzano Italy **56** D2
also known as Bozen
Boma Dem. Rep. Congo **127** B6
Bomaderry Australia **147** F3
Bomai China **86** A2
formerly known as Bowo
Bombala Australia **147** F4
Bombarral Port. **54** B5
Bombay India *see* **Mumbai**
Bombay N.Z. **152** I5
Bombay Beach U.S.A. **183** I8
Bomberai, Semenanjung *pen.* Indon. **73** H7
English form Bomberai Peninsula
Bomberai Peninsula Indon. *see* **Bomberai, Semenanjung**
Bombo *r.* Dem. Rep. Congo **126** B5
Bombo Uganda **128** B4
Bom Comércio Brazil **200** D2
Bom Despacho Brazil **207** H6
Bomdila India **97** G4
Bomi China **80** F7
also known as Bowo *or* Zhamo
Bomili Dem. Rep. Congo **126** E4
Bom Jardim Brazil **200** D2
Bom Jardim de Goiás Brazil **206** A3
Bom Jardim de Minas Brazil **207** I8
Bom Jesus *Piauí* Brazil **202** C4
Bom Jesus *Rio Grande do Sul* Brazil **203** B9
Bom Jesus da Gurgueia, Serra do *hills* Brazil **202** D4
Bom Jesus da Lapa Brazil **202** D5
Bom Jesus de Goiás Brazil **206** D5
Bom Jesus do Itabapoana Brazil **203** D7
Bømlo *i.* Norway **45** I4
Bomokandi *r.* Dem. Rep. Congo **126** E4
Bompas France **51** I10
Bom Retiro Brazil **203** B8
Bom Sucesso *Minas Gerais* Brazil **207** I8
Bom Sucesso *Paraná* Brazil **206** B10
Bon, Cap *c.* Tunisia **123** H1
Bona Alg. *see* **Annaba**
Bona, Mount U.S.A. **166** A2
Bonāb Iran **100** A2
Bona Bona Island P.N.G. **149** F1
Bon Air U.S.A. **176** H8
Bonaire *i.* Neth. Antilles **187** F4
Bonandolok Indon. **76** B2
Bonanza Nicaragua **186** B4
Bonaparte Archipelago *is* Australia **150** D2
Bonaparte Lake Canada **166** F5
Bonasse Trin. and Tob. **187** H5
Bonavista Canada **169** K3
Bonavista Bay Canada **169** K3
Bon Bon Australia **146** B2
Bondo *Équateur* Dem. Rep. Congo **126** D5
Bondo *Orientale* Dem. Rep. Congo **126** D4
Bondoc Peninsula Phil. **74** B3
Bondokodi Indon. **75** A5
Bondoukou Côte d'Ivoire **124** E4
Bondoukui Burkina **124** E4
Bondowoso Indon. **77** F4
Bonduel U.S.A. **172** E6
Bondyuzhskiy Rus. Fed. *see* **Mendeleyevsk**
Bône Alg. *see* **Annaba**
Bone Indon. **75** B4
Bone, Teluk *b.* Indon. **75** B4
Bonekraal S. Africa **132** E8
Bone Lake U.S.A. **172** A5
Bonelipu Indon. **75** B4
Bonerate Indon. **75** B4
Bonerate *i.* Indon. **75** B4
Bonerate, Kepulauan *is* Indon. **75** B4

▶Bonete, Cerro mt. Arg. 204 C2
3rd highest mountain in South America.

Bonfim Brazil 207 I7
Bonfim r. Brazil 206 A4
Bonfinópolis de Minas Brazil 202 C6
Bonga Eth. 128 C3
Bongabong Phil. 74 B3
Bongaigaon India 97 F4
Bongandanga Dem. Rep. Congo 126 D4
Bongani S. Africa 132 H6
Bongao Phil. 74 A5
Bongba China 89 C5
Bong Co l. China 89 E6
Bongka r. Indon. 75 B3
Bongo i. Phil. 74 C5
Bongo, Massif des mts Cent. Afr. Rep. 126 D2
Bongo, Serra do mts Angola 127 B7
Bongolava mts Madag. 131 [inset] J3
Bongor Chad 126 B2
Bongouanou Côte d'Ivoire 124 D5
Bông Son Vietnam 79 E5
Bonham U.S.A. 179 C5
Bönhamn Sweden 44 L3
Boni Mali 125 E3
Bonifacio Corse France 52 D3
Bonifacio, Bocche di strait France/Italy see Bonifacio, Strait of
Bonifacio, Bouches de strait France/Italy see Bonifacio, Strait of
Bonifacio, Strait of France/Italy 56 A7
also known as Bonifacio, Bocche di or Bonifacio, Bouches de
Boni National Reserve nature res. Kenya 128 D5

▶Bonin Islands N. Pacific Ocean 220 D4
Part of Japan. Also known as Ogasawara-shotō.

Bonita Springs U.S.A. 175 D7
Bonito Mato Grosso do Sul Brazil 201 F5
Bonito Minas Gerais Brazil 207 I2
Bonito r. Brazil 206 B3
Bonito r. Brazil 206 G2

▶Bonn Germany 48 E5
Former capital of Germany. Historically known as Bonna.

Bonna Germany see Bonn
Bonnat France 51 H6
Bonners Ferry U.S.A. 180 C2
Bonnet, Lac du resr Canada 167 M5
Bonnet Plume r. Canada 166 C1
Bonneval France 50 H4
Bonneville France 51 M6
Bonney, Lake Australia 146 D4
Bonnie Rock Australia 151 B6
Bonny Glen Aboriginal Holding res. Australia 149 E3
Bonny Ridge S. Africa 133 N7
Bonnyville Canada 167 I4
Bono Sardegna Italy 57 B8
Bōno-misaki pt Japan 91 B9
Bonom Mhai mt. Vietnam 79 D6
Bononia Italy see Bologna
Bonorva Sardegna Italy 57 A8
Bonoua Côte d'Ivoire 124 E5
Bonpland, Mount N.Z. 153 C12
Bonsall U.S.A. 183 G8
Bonshaw Australia 147 F2
Bontberg mts S. Africa 132 F9
Bonteberg mts S. Africa 132 D10
Bontebok National Park S. Africa 132 E11
Bonthe Sierra Leone 124 B5
Bontoc Phil. 74 B2
Bontomatane Indon. 75 B4
Bontosunggu Indon. 75 A4
Bontrand S. Africa 133 N7
Bontrug S. Africa 133 J10
Bonvouloir Islands P.N.G. 149 F1
Bonyhád Hungary 49 P9
Boo Sweden 45 L4
Boo, Kepulauan is Indon. 75 D3
Boodie Boodie Range hills Australia 151 C5
Bookabie Australia 146 B2
Book Cliffs ridge U.S.A. 183 O2
Booker U.S.A. 178 B4
Boola Guinea 124 C4
Booleroo Centre Australia 146 C3
Booligal Australia 147 E3
Boologooro Australia 151 A5
Boomi Australia 147 F2
Boon U.S.A. 172 H6
Boonah Australia 147 G1
Boone IA U.S.A. 174 A3
Boone NC U.S.A. 176 D9
Boone Lake U.S.A. 176 C9
Boones Mill U.S.A. 176 F8
Booneville AR U.S.A. 179 D5
Booneville KY U.S.A. 176 B8
Booneville MS U.S.A. 174 B5
Boons S. Africa 133 L2
Boonsboro U.S.A. 176 H6
Bööн Tsagaan Nuur salt l. Mongolia 84 C2
Boonville CA U.S.A. 182 A3
Boonville IN U.S.A. 174 C4
Boonville MO U.S.A. 178 D4
Boopi r. Bol. 200 D3
Boorabin National Park Australia 151 C6
Boorama Somalia 128 D2
Booroorban Australia 147 E3
Boorowa Australia 147 F3
Boosaaso Somalia 128 F2
Boothbay Harbor U.S.A. 177 P2
Boothby, Cape Antarctica 223 D2
Boothia, Gulf of Canada 165 K3
Boothia Peninsula Canada 165 J2
Booué Gabon 126 A5
Bopolu Liberia 124 C5
Boppard Germany 48 E5
Boqê China 89 E6
Boqueirão Brazil 204 G3
Boqueirão, Serra do hills Brazil 202 C5
Bor Rus. Fed. 40 H4
Bor Sudan 128 A3
Bor Turkey 106 C3
Bor Srbija Yugo. 58 D4
Boragi waterhole Kenya 128 C5
Borah Peak U.S.A. 180 D3
Borakalalo Nature Reserve S. Africa 133 L2
Boran Kazakh. see Buran
Boraraigh i. U.K. see Boreray
Borås Sweden 45 K4
Borasambar India 95 D1
Borāzjān Iran 100 B4
Borba Brazil 199 G6
Borba Port. 54 D6
Borbollón, Embalse del resr Spain 54 E4
Borbon Phil. 74 C4
Borborema Brazil 206 D8
Borborema, Planalto da plat. Brazil 202 E3
Borca Romania 58 G1
Borcea, Braţul watercourse Romania 58 I4
Borchalo Georgia see Marneuli
Borchgrevink Coast Antarctica 223 K2
Borçka Turkey 107 E2
also known as Yeniyol
Borda, Cape Australia 150 C3
Borda da Mata Brazil 207 G9
Bor Dağı mt. Turkey 59 K11
Bordeaux France 50 F8
historically known as Burdigala
Bordehi India 96 C5
Bordein Sudan 121 G6
Borden Canada 169 I4
Borden Island Canada 165 H2
Borden Peninsula Canada 165 K2
Bordentown U.S.A. 177 K5
Border Ranges National Park Australia 147 G2
Bordertown Australia 146 D4
Borðeyri Iceland 44 [inset] B2
Bordj Bou Arréridj Alg. 123 G1
Bordj Bounaama Alg. 55 M9
Bordj Flye Ste-Marie Alg. 123 E4
Bordj Messaouda Alg. 123 H3
Bordj Mokhtar Alg. 123 F5
Bordj Omar Driss Alg. see Bordj Omer Driss
Bordj Omer Driss Alg. 123 G3
formerly known as Fort Flatters or Zaouet el Kahla; formerly spelt Bordj Omar Driss
Bordj Zemoura Alg. 55 P8
Borðoy i. Faroe Is 46 F1
Bordu Kyrg. 103 H4
also known as Bordunskiy
Bordunskiy Kyrg. see Bordu
Borduşani Romania 58 I4
Boré Mali 124 E3
Boreas Nunatak Antarctica 223 X2
Borel r. Canada 169 G1
Borensberg Sweden 45 K4
Boreray i. U.K. 46 D6
also spelt Boraraigh
Borgå Fin. see Porvoo
Borgarfjäll Sweden 44 K2
Borgarfjörður Iceland 44 [inset] D2
Borgarnes Iceland 44 [inset] B2
Børgefjell Nasjonalpark nat. park Norway 44 K2
Borger U.S.A. 179 B5
Borgholm Sweden 45 L4
Borgo Corse France 51 P10
Borgo a Mozzano Italy 56 C5
Borgomanero Italy 56 A3
Borgo San Dalmazzo Italy 51 N8
Borgo San Lorenzo Italy 56 D5
Borgosesia Italy 56 A3
Borgo Val di Taro Italy 56 B4
Borgo Valsugana Italy 56 D2
Borgsjåbrotet mt. Norway 45 J3
Bori India 94 C1
Bori r. India 96 B5
Borili Kazakh. see Burli
Borilovo Rus. Fed. 43 Q8
Borino Bulg. 58 F7
Borinskoye Rus. Fed. 43 U9
Borisoglebsk Rus. Fed. 41 G6
Borisoglebskiy Rus. Fed. 43 U4
Borisov Belarus see Barysaw
Borisovka Rus. Fed. 41 F6
Borisovo-Sudskoye Rus. Fed. 43 R2
Borispol' Ukr. see Boryspil'
Bo River Post Sudan 126 E3
Boriziny Madag. 131 [inset] J2
Borja mts Bos.-Herz. 56 J4
Borja Peru 198 B6
Borjas Blancas Spain see Les Borges Blanques
Borj Bourguiba Tunisia 123 H2
Borjomis Nakrdzali nature res. Georgia 107 E2
Borkavichy Belarus 43 J6
Borken Germany 48 D4
Borkenes Norway 44 L1
Borki Rus. Fed. 43 T9
Borkou-Ennedi-Tibesti pref. Chad 120 C5
Borkovskaya Rus. Fed. 40 I2
Borkum Germany 48 D2
Borkum i. Germany 48 D2
Borlänge Sweden 45 K3
Borlaug Norway 45 I3
Borlu Turkey 106 B3
Borna Germany 49 J4
Born-Berge hill Germany 48 H4
Borne Alg. 123 G4

▶Borneo i. Asia 77 F2
Largest island in Asia and 3rd in the world.
asia [landscapes] ▶ 62–63

Bornes mts France 51 M7
Bornholm i. Denmark 45 K5
Bornholmsgattet strait Denmark/Sweden 45 K5
Borno state Nigeria 125 I4
Bornova Turkey 106 A3
Borobudur tourist site Indon. 77 E4
Borodino Krasnoyarskiy Kray Rus. Fed. 39 I3
Borodino Moskovskaya Oblast' Rus. Fed. 43 Q6
Borodino Ukr. 58 K2
Borodinskoye Rus. Fed. 43 K1
Borodyanka Ukr. 41 D6
Borogontsy Rus. Fed. 39 N3
Borohoro Shan mts China 88 C2
Borok Rus. Fed. 43 T3
Boroko Indon. 75 B2
Borok-Sulezhskiy Rus. Fed. 43 R4
Boromo Burkina 124 E4
Boron Mali 124 D3
Boron U.S.A. 182 G7
Borongan Phil. 74 C4
Boroon Australia 149 F5
Borovan Bulg. 58 E5
Borovenka Rus. Fed. 43 O3
Borovichi Rus. Fed. 43 O3
Borovo Selo Croatia 56 K3
Borovoy Kirovskaya Oblast' Rus. Fed. 40 I4
Borovoy Respublika Kareliya Rus. Fed. 40 E2
Borovoy Respublika Komi Rus. Fed. 40 J3
Borovoye Kazakh. 103 G1
Borovsk Rus. Fed. 43 R6
Borovskoy Kazakh. 103 F1
Borrachudo r. Brazil 207 H5
Borrazópolis Brazil 206 B10
Borrego Springs U.S.A. 183 H8
Borroloola Australia 148 C3
Børsa Norway 44 J3
Borşa Romania 58 E2
Borşa Romania 53 G2
Borsad India 96 B5
Borsec Romania 58 G2
Børselv Norway 44 N1
Borshchiv Ukr. 41 C6
Borshchovochnyy Khrebet mts Rus. Fed. 85 F1
Borsippa tourist site Iraq 107 F4
Borskoye Rus. Fed. 102 B1
Börßum Germany 48 H3
Bortala China see Bole
Bortala He r. China 88 C2
Bort-les-Orgues France 51 I7
Bor-Üdzüür Mongolia 84 B2
Borūjen Iran 100 B4
Borūjerd Iran 100 B3
Bor UI Shan mts China 84 C3
Borun Iran 100 D3
Borushtitsa Bulg. 58 G6
Boryspil' Ukr. 40 D6
also spelt Borispol'
Borzna Ukr. 41 E6
Börzsönyi park Hungary 49 P8
Borzya Rus. Fed. 85 H1
Borzya r. Rus. Fed. 85 G1
Bosa Sardegna Italy 57 A8
Bosaga Kazakh. 103 H3
also spelt Bosagha; formerly known as Bosaginskiy
Bosagha Kazakh. see Bosaga
Bosaginskiy Kazakh. see Bosaga
Bosanska Dubica Bos.-Herz. 56 I3
also known as Kozarska Dubica
Bosanska Gradiška Bos.-Herz. 56 J3
also known as Gradiška
Bosanska Kostajnica Bos.-Herz. 56 I3
also known as Srpska Kostajnica
Bosanska Krupa Bos.-Herz. 56 I4
also known as Krupa or Krupa na Uni
Bosanski Brod Bos.-Herz. 56 K3
also known as Srpski Brod
Bosanski Novi Bos.-Herz. 56 I3
also known as Novi Grad
Bosanski Petrovac Bos.-Herz. 56 I4
also known as Petrovac
Bosanski Šamac Bos.-Herz. 56 K3
also known as Šamac
Bosberg mt. S. Africa 133 K9
Bosbokrand S. Africa 133 P1
Boscawen U.S.A. 177 N2
Boscawen Island Tonga see Niuatoputopu
Bosch Arg. 204 F5
Boscobel U.S.A. 172 C7
Bosduiflaagte salt pan S. Africa 132 E6
Bose China 86 C4
Bosencheve, Parque Nacional nat. park Mex. 185 E5
Boshchakul' Kazakh. see Bozshakol'
Boshnyakovo Rus. Fed. 82 F2
Boshoek S. Africa 133 L2
Boshof S. Africa 133 J5
Boshrūyeh Iran 100 D3
Bosilegrad Srbija Yugo. 58 D6
formerly spelt Bosiljgrad
Bosiljgrad Srbija Yugo. see Bosilegrad
Boskol' Kazakh. 103 E1
also spelt Bozköl; formerly spelt Buskul'
Boskovice Czech Rep. 49 N6
Boslanti Suriname 199 H3
Bosna r. Bos.-Herz. 56 K3
Bosna hills Bulg. 58 I6
Bosna i Hercegovina country Europe see Bosnia-Herzegovina
Bosna Saray Bos.-Herz. see Sarajevo
▶Bosnia-Herzegovina country Europe 56 J4
known as Bosna i Hercegovina in Bosnian
europe [countries] ▶ 32–35
Boso Dem. Rep. Congo 126 D4
Bosobogolo Pan salt pan Botswana 132 G2
Bosobolo Dem. Rep. Congo 126 C3
Bōsō-hantō pen. Japan 91 G7
Bosomo Dem. Rep. Congo 126 D3
Bospoort S. Africa 133 K3
▶Bosporus strait Turkey 106 B2
also known as İstanbul Boğazı
europe [countries] ▶ 32–33
Bosque Spain 54 C1
Bossaga Turkm. see Basaga
Bossangoa Cent. Afr. Rep. 126 C3
Bossembélé Cent. Afr. Rep. 126 C3
Bossemptele Cent. Afr. Rep. see Bossentélé
Bossentélé Cent. Afr. Rep. 126 C3
formerly spelt Bossemptélé
Bossiekom S. Africa 132 E6
Bossier City U.S.A. 179 D5
Bossiesvlei Namibia 130 C5
Bosspruit S. Africa 133 L2
Bossut, Cape Australia 150 C3
Bostan China 89 D4
Bostān Iran 100 A4
Bosten Hu l. China 88 D3
also known as Bagrax Hu
Boston U.K. 47 L11

▶Boston U.S.A. 177 N3
State capital of Massachusetts.

Boston Creek Canada 173 N2
Boston Mountains U.S.A. 179 D5
Bosut r. Croatia 56 L3
Boswell IN U.S.A. 172 F10
Boswell PA U.S.A. 176 F5
Botad India 96 A5
Botany Bay Australia 147 F3
Botata Liberia 124 C5
Boteå Sweden 44 L3
Boteler Point S. Africa 133 Q3
Boteni Romania 58 G3
Boteti r. Botswana 131 E4
Botev mt. Bulg. 58 F6
Botevgrad Bulg. 58 E6
Bothaville S. Africa 133 K4
Bothell U.S.A. 180 B3
Bothnia, Gulf of Fin./Sweden 44 L3
Bothwell Australia 147 E5
Bothwell Canada 173 L8
Boticas Port. 54 D3
Botin mt. Bos.-Herz. 56 K5
Botkins U.S.A. 176 A5
Botlikh Rus. Fed. 102 A4
Botna r. Moldova 58 K2
Botoşani Romania 53 H2
Botou China 85 H4
Bô Trach Vietnam 78 D4
Botro Côte d'Ivoire 124 D5
Botshabelo S. Africa 133 K6
Botsmark Sweden 44 M2
▶Botswana country Africa 130 D4
formerly known as Bechuanaland
world [population] ▶ 22–23
africa [countries] ▶ 114–117
Bottenviken g. Fin./Sweden 44 M2
Bottineau U.S.A. 178 B1
Bottle Creek Turks and Caicos Is 187 E2
Bottom Neth. Antilles 187 H3
Bottrop Germany 48 D4
Botucatu Brazil 206 E9
Botumirim Brazil 207 J3
Bouaflé Côte d'Ivoire 124 D5
Bou Ahmed Morocco 54 G9
Bouaké Côte d'Ivoire 124 D5
Boualem Alg. 123 F2
Bouandougou Côte d'Ivoire 124 D4
formerly spelt Buandougou
Bouanga Congo 126 C5
Bouar Cent. Afr. Rep. 126 B3
Bou Arada Tunisia 57 B12
Bouârfa Morocco 123 E2
Bou Aroua Alg. 123 G2
Boubandjida, Parc National de nat. park Cameroon 125 I4
Boubin mt. Czech Rep. 49 K6
Boû Bleï'îne well Mauritania 124 C2
Boubout well Alg. 122 D4
Bouca Cent. Afr. Rep. 126 C3
Boucau France 50 E9
Boucaut Bay Australia 148 B2
Bouchette Canada 173 R4
Bouctouche Canada 169 H4
Boudinar Morocco 54 H9
Boû Djébéha well Mali 124 E2
Boudoua Cent. Afr. Rep. 126 C3
Boudry Switz. 51 M6
Bouenza admin. reg. Congo 126 B6
Bouenza r. Congo 126 B6
Boufore Cent. Afr. Rep. 126 C3
Bougainville, Cape Australia 150 D2
Bougainville Island P.N.G. 145 E2
Bougaroûn, Cap c. Alg. 123 G1
Boughessa Mali 125 F2
formerly spelt Bouressa
Bougie Alg. see Bejaïa
Bougoumen Chad 126 B2
Bougouni Mali 124 D4
Bougtob Alg. 123 F2
Boû Guendoûz well Mali 124 D2
Bouguirat Alg. 55 L9
Bougzoul Alg. 55 N9
Bouillon Belgium 51 L3
Bouira Alg. 123 F1
Bou Izakarn Morocco 122 C3
Boujdour W. Sahara 122 B4
Bou Kahil, Djebel mts Alg. 123 F2
Boukoumbé Benin 125 F4
Boukta Chad 126 C2
Boulder Australia 151 C6
Boulder CO U.S.A. 180 F4
Boulder MT U.S.A. 180 D3
Boulder UT U.S.A. 183 M4
Boulder Canyon gorge U.S.A. 183 J5
Boulder City U.S.A. 183 J6
Bou Legmaden, Oued watercourse Alg./Morocco 122 C3
Boulemane Morocco 122 D2
Boulemane Morocco 122 D2
Boulevard U.S.A. 183 H9
Boulhaut Morocco see Ben Slimane
Boulia Australia 148 C4
Boulogne France see Boulogne-sur-Mer
Boulogne r. France 50 E5
Boulogne-Billancourt France 51 I4
Boulogne-sur-Mer France 50 H2
historically known as Gesoriacum; short form Boulogne
Boulou r. Cent. Afr. Rep. 126 E3
Boulouba Cent. Afr. Rep. 126 D3
Boulouparì New Caledonia 145 F4
Boulsa Burkina 125 E3
Boultoum Niger 125 H3
Boumango Gabon 126 B5
Boumba r. Cameroon 125 I6
Boumbé I r. Cent. Afr. Rep. 126 B3
Boumerdes Alg. 123 F1
Bouna Côte d'Ivoire 124 E4
Bou Naceur, Jbel mt. Morocco 122 E2
Boû Nâga Mauritania 124 B2
Boundary U.S.A. 166 A1
Boundary Peak U.S.A. 182 F4
Boundiali Côte d'Ivoire 124 D4
Boung r. Vietnam 79 E4
Boungou r. Cent. Afr. Rep. 126 D3
Bountiful U.S.A. 183 M1
Bounty Islands N.Z. 145 G6
Bourail New Caledonia 145 F4
Bourbince r. France 51 K6
Bourbon terr. Indian Ocean see Réunion
Bourbon-Lancy France 51 J6
Bourbonne-les-Bains France 51 L5
Bourbriac France 50 C4
Bourem Mali 125 E2
Bouressa Mali see Boughessa
Bourg France 50 F7
Bourganeuf France 50 H7
Bourg-en-Bresse France 51 L6
Bourges France 51 I5
historically known as Avaricum
Bourgmont Canada 173 R2
Bourgneuf, Baie de b. France 50 D5
Bourgogne admin. reg. France 51 K5
Bourgoin-Jallieu France 51 L7
Bourg-St-Andéol France 51 K8
Bourg-St-Maurice France 51 M7
Bourke Australia 147 E2
Bourkes Canada 173 M2
Bournemouth U.K. 47 K13
Bouroum-Bouroum Burkina 124 E4
Bourtoutou Chad 126 D2
Bourzanga Burkina 125 E3
Bou Saâda Alg. 123 G2
Bou Salem Tunisia 57 A12
Bouse U.S.A. 183 J8
Bouse Wash watercourse U.S.A. 183 J7
Boussé Burkina 125 E3
Bousso Chad 126 C2
Boû Tezâya well Mauritania 124 C2
Boutilimit Mauritania 124 B2
Boutougou Fara Senegal 124 B3
Bouvet Island terr. S. Atlantic Ocean see Bouvetøya

▶Bouvetøya terr. S. Atlantic Ocean 217 O9
Dependency of Norway. English form Bouvet Island.

Boven Kapuas Mountains Indon./Malaysia see Kapuas Hulu, Pegunungan
Bow r. Australia 150 E3
Bow r. Alta Canada 167 I5
Bowa China see Muli
Bowbells U.S.A. 178 B1
Bowden U.S.A. 176 F7
Bowditch atoll Tokelau see Fakaofo
Bowen Arg. 204 D4
Bowen Australia 149 F4
Bowen r. Australia 149 E4
Bowen, Mount Australia 147 F4
Bowen Downs Australia 149 E4
Bowen Strait Australia 148 B1
Bowers Mountains Antarctica 223 K2
Bowie AZ U.S.A. 183 O9
Bowie TX U.S.A. 179 C5
Bow Island Canada 167 I5
Bowkan Iran 100 A2
Bowling Green KY U.S.A. 174 C4
Bowling Green MO U.S.A. 174 B4
Bowling Green OH U.S.A. 176 B4
Bowling Green VA U.S.A. 177 H7
Bowling Green Bay Australia 149 E3
Bowling Green Bay National Park Australia 149 E3
Bowman U.S.A. 178 B2
Bowman, Mount Canada 166 F5
Bowman Coast Antarctica 222 T2
Bowman Island Antarctica 223 G2
Bowman Peninsula Antarctica 222 T2
Bowmanville Canada 173 O7
Bown Somalia 128 D2
Bowo China see Bomai
Bowo China see Bomi
Bow River Aboriginal Reserve Australia 150 D3
Bowron r. Canada 166 F4
Bowron Lake Provincial Park Canada 166 F4
Bowser Lake Canada 166 D3
Boxberg Germany 48 G6
Box Elder U.S.A. 178 B2
Box Elder r. U.S.A. 178 B2
Boxholm Sweden 45 K4
Boxing China 85 H4
Boxtel Neth. 48 C4
Boyabat Turkey 106 C2
Boyacá dept Col. 198 C3
Boyadzhik Bulg. 58 H6
Boyalica Turkey 58 K8
Boyalık Turkey see Çiçekdağı
Boyana tourist site Bulg. 58 E6
Boyang China 87 F2
formerly known as Poyang
Boyanovichi Rus. Fed. 43 P8
Boyanovo Bulg. 58 H6
Boyd r. Australia 147 G2
Boyd Lagoon salt flat Australia 151 D5
Boyd Lake Canada 167 K2
Boydton U.S.A. 176 G9
Boyer r. U.S.A. 178 D3
Boyera Dem. Rep. Congo 126 C5
Boyertown U.S.A. 177 J5
Boykins U.S.A. 177 H9
Boyle Canada 167 H4
Boyle Rep. of Ireland 47 D10
Boyne r. Qld Australia 149 F4
Boyne r. Qld Australia 149 F5
Boyne r. Rep. of Ireland 47 F10
Boyne City U.S.A. 173 H5
Boyni Qara Afgh. 101 F2
Boyo Cent. Afr. Rep. 126 D3
Boyoma, Chutes waterfall Dem. Rep. Congo see Boyoma Falls
Boyoma Falls Dem. Rep. Congo 126 E4
also known as Boyoma, Chutes; formerly known as Stanley, Chutes
Boysun Uzbek. see Baysun
Boyuibe Bol. 201 E5
Böyük Hinaldağ mt. Azer. 100 A1
Boyup Brook Australia 151 B7
Bozashy Tübegi pen. Kazakh. see Buzachi, Poluostrov
Bozburun Turkey 106 B3

▶Bozcaada i. Turkey 106 A3
Most westerly point of Asia. Also known as Tenedos.

Bozdağ mt. Turkey 59 H10
Bozdağ mt. Turkey 109 H1
Boz Dağları mts Turkey 106 A3
Bozdoğan Turkey 106 B3
Bozeman U.S.A. 180 E3
Bozen Italy see Bolzano
Bozhou China 87 E1
Bozkir Turkey 106 C3
also known as Silistat
Bozköl Kazakh. see Boskol'
Bozkurt Turkey 59 K11
Bozouls France 51 I8
Bozoum Cent. Afr. Rep. 126 C3
Bozova Turkey 107 D3
also known as Hüvek
Bozovici Romania 58 D4
Bozqūsh, Kūh-e mts Iran 100 A2
Bozshakol' Kazakh. 103 H2
formerly spelt Boshchakul'
Boztumsyk Kazakh. 103 F2
Bozüyük Turkey 106 B3
Bozyazı Turkey 108 D1
Bra Italy 51 N8
Brabant Island Antarctica 222 T2
Brač i. Croatia 56 I5
Bracara Port. see Braga
Bracciano Italy 56 E6
Bracciano, Lago di l. Italy 56 E6
Bracebridge Canada 168 E4
Brachet, Lac au l. Canada 169 G3
Bräcke Sweden 44 K3
Brackettville U.S.A. 179 B6
Bracki Kanal sea chan. Croatia 56 I5
Bracknell U.K. 47 L12
Braço Norte r. Brazil 201 G2
Brad Romania 58 D2
Bradano r. Italy 57 I8
Bradenton U.S.A. 175 D7
Bradford Canada 173 N6
Bradford U.K. 47 K10
Bradford PA U.S.A. 176 G4
Bradford VT U.S.A. 177 M2
Bradley U.S.A. 172 F9
Bradner U.S.A. 176 B4
Bradshaw U.S.A. 176 D8
Brady U.S.A. 179 C6
Brady Creek r. U.S.A. 179 C6
Brady Glacier U.S.A. 166 B3
Braemar U.K. 46 I6
Braga Port. 54 C3
historically known as Bracara
Braga admin. dist. Port. 54 C3
Bragado Arg. 204 E4
Bragança Brazil 202 C2
Bragança Port. 54 E3
Bragança admin. dist. Port. 54 E3
Bragança Paulista Brazil 206 G9
Brahin Belarus 41 D6
Brahmakund India 97 H4
Brahmanbaria Bangl. 97 F5
Brahmani r. India 95 E1
Brahmapur India 95 E2
Brahmaputra r. China/India 89 D6
also known as Dihang (India) or Yarlung Zangbo (China)
Braidwood Australia 147 F3
Braidwood U.S.A. 172 E9
Brăila Romania 58 I3
Brăilei, Insula Mare a i. Romania 58 I4
Braine France 51 J3
Brainerd U.S.A. 178 D2
Braintree U.K. 47 M12
Braithwaite Point Australia 148 B1
Braives Belgium 51 L2
Brak r. S. Africa 132 E10
Brake watercourse S. Africa 132 C5
Brake (Unterweser) Germany 48 F2
Brâkna admin. reg. Mauritania 124 B2
Brakpoort S. Africa 132 H8
Brakspruit S. Africa 133 K3
Brakwater Namibia 130 C4
Bralorne Canada 166 F5
Bramhapuri India 94 C1
Bramming Denmark 45 J5
Brampton Canada 168 E5
Brampton U.K. 47 J9
Bramsche Germany 48 F3
Bramsöfjärden l. Sweden 45 L3
Brancaleone Italy 57 I11
Branch Canada 169 K4
Branco r. Mato Grosso Brazil 201 E2
Branco r. Roraima Brazil 199 F5
Branco i. Cape Verde 124 [inset]
Brandberg mt. Namibia 130 B4
Brändbo Sweden 45 L3
Brandbu Norway 45 J3
Brande Denmark 45 J5
Brandenburg Germany 49 J3
Brandenburg land Germany 49 K3
Brandenburg U.S.A. 174 C4
Brandenburger Wald- und Seengebiet park Germany 49 J3
Brandfort S. Africa 133 K5
Brandkop S. Africa 132 D8
Brändö Fin. 45 M3
Brandon Canada 167 L5
Brandon MS U.S.A. 175 B5
Brandon SD U.S.A. 178 C3
Brandon VT U.S.A. 177 L2
Brandon Head Rep. of Ireland 47 B11
Brandon Mountain hill Rep. of Ireland 47 B11
Brandonville U.S.A. 176 F6
Brandvlei S. Africa 132 E7
Brandvlei Dam resr S. Africa 132 D10
Brandvoll Norway 44 L1
Brani, Pulau i. Sing. 76 [inset]
Braniewo Poland 49 Q1
Brännberg Sweden 44 M2
Brannenburg Germany 48 J8
Bransfield Strait Antarctica 222 T2
Braniewo Poland 49 T3
Brantas r. Indon. 77 F4
Brantford Canada 168 D5
Brantôme France 50 G7
Brantwood U.S.A. 172 C5
Brás Brazil 199 G5
Brasaljce Kosovo, Srbija Yugo. 58 C6
Bras d'Or Lake Canada 169 I4
Brasil Brazil 198 D6
Brasil country S. America see Brazil
Brasil, Planalto do plat. Brazil 203 D6
Brasilândia Mato Grosso do Sul Brazil 206 A8
Brasilândia Minas Gerais Brazil 206 E2
Brasilândia Minas Gerais Brazil 207 G4
Brasileia Brazil 200 C2

▶Brasília Brazil 206 F2
Capital of Brazil.
southamerica [countries] ▶ 192–193

Brasília de Minas Brazil 202 C6
Brasília Legal Brazil 199 H5
Brasla r. Latvia 42 F4
Braslav Belarus see Braslaw
Braslaw Belarus 42 I6
also spelt Braslav
Braşov Romania 58 G3
formerly known as Oraşul Stalin; historically known as Kronstadt
Brasovo Rus. Fed. 43 P9
Brassey, Banjaran mts Sabah Malaysia 77 G1
Brassey, Mount Australia 148 B4
Brassey Range hills Australia 151 C5
Bratan mt. Bulg. 58 G6
Bratca Romania 58 D2

▶Bratislava Slovakia 49 O7
Capital of Slovakia. Also known as Pozsony; formerly known as Pressburg.

Bratsk Rus. Fed. 80 G1
Bratskoye Vodokhranilishche resr Rus. Fed. 80 G1
Brattleboro U.S.A. 177 M3
Brattmon Sweden 45 K3
Brattvåg Norway 44 I3
Bratunac Bos.-Herz. 56 L4
Braulio Carrillo, Parque Nacional nat. park Costa Rica 186 C5
Braúnas Brazil 207 K6
Braunau am Inn Austria 49 K7
Braunsbedra Germany 48 I4
Braunschweig Germany 48 H3
historically known as Brunswick
Brava i. Cape Verde 124 [inset]
Brave U.S.A. 176 E6
Bråviken inlet Sweden 45 L4
Bravo, Cerro mt. Bol. 201 D4
Bravo del Norte, Río r. Mex./U.S.A. 185 F3
also known as Rio Grande
Brawley U.S.A. 183 I9
Bray Rep. of Ireland 47 F10
also spelt Bré
Bray S. Africa 132 H2
Braye r. France 50 G5
Bray Island Canada 165 L3
Bray-sur-Seine France 51 J4
Brazeau r. Canada 167 H4
Brazeau, Mount Canada 167 G4

▶Brazil country S. America 202 B4
Largest country in South America and 5th in the world. Most populous country in South America and 5th in the world. Spelt Brasil in Portuguese.
world [countries] ▶ 10–11
world [population] ▶ 22–23
southamerica [countries] ▶ 192–193

Brazil U.S.A. 174 C4
Brazos r. U.S.A. 179 D6

▶Brazzaville Congo 126 B6
Capital of Congo.

Brčko Bos.-Herz. 56 K4
Brda r. Poland 49 P2
Brdy hills Czech Rep. 49 K6
Bré Rep. of Ireland see Bray
Breakfast Vlei S. Africa 133 K10
Breaksea Sound inlet N.Z. 153 A13
Breaksea Spit Australia 149 G5
Bream Bay N.Z. 152 I3
Bream Head N.Z. 152 I3
Bream Tail c. N.Z. 152 I4
Breas Chile 204 C2
Breaza Romania 58 G3
Brebes Indon. 77 E4
Brechin U.K. 46 J7
Brecht Belgium 51 K1
Breckenridge CO U.S.A. 180 F5
Breckenridge MN U.S.A. 178 C2
Breckenridge TX U.S.A. 179 C5
Brecknock, Peninsula pen. Chile 205 B9
Břeclav Czech Rep. 49 N7
Brecon U.K. 47 I12
also known as Aberhonddu
Brecon Beacons reg. U.K. 47 I12
Brecon Beacons National Park U.K. 47 I12
Breda Neth. 48 B4
Bredasdorp S. Africa 132 E11
Bredbo Australia 147 F3
Bredviken Sweden 44 K2
Bredy Rus. Fed. 103 E1
Breede r. S. Africa 132 E11
Bregalnica r. Macedonia 58 C7
Bregenz Austria 48 G8
Bregovo Bulg. 58 D4
Bréhal France 50 E4
Breiðafjörður b. Iceland 44 [inset] A2
Breiðdalsvík Iceland 44 [inset] D2
Breil-sur-Roya France 51 N9
Breipaal S. Africa 133 K7
Breisach am Rhein Germany 48 E7
Breivikbotn Norway 44 M1
Breivikeidet Norway 44 L1
Brejinho de Nazaré Brazil 202 B4
Brejo Brazil 202 D2
Brejo r. Brazil 202 D4
Brejo da Porta Brazil 202 C4
Brekstad Norway 44 J3
Bremen Germany 48 F2
Bremen GA U.S.A. 175 C5
Bremen OH U.S.A. 176 C6
Bremer Bay Australia 151 B7
Bremerhaven Germany 48 F2
Bremer Range hills Australia 151 C7
Bremersdorp Swaziland see Manzini
Bremerton U.S.A. 180 B3
Bremervörde Germany 48 G2
Breń r. Poland 49 S5
Brenham U.S.A. 179 C6
Brenna Norway 44 K2
Brennero Italy 56 D2
Brennero, Passo di pass Austria/Italy see Brenner Pass
Brennerpaß pass Austria/Italy see Brenner Pass
Brenner Pass pass Austria/Italy 48 I9
also known as Brennero, Passo di or Brennerpaß
Breno Italy 56 C3
Brenta r. Italy 56 E3
Brenta, Gruppo di mts Italy 56 C2
Brentwood U.K. 47 M12
Brenzone Italy 56 C3
Brescia Italy 56 C3
historically known as Brixia
Breslau Poland see Wrocław
Bresle r. France 50 H2
Bresolles, Lac l. Canada 169 G2
Bressanone Italy 56 D2
Bressay i. U.K. 46 K3
Bressuire France 50 F6
Brest Belarus 42 E9
formerly known as Brest-Litovsk or Brześć nad Bugiem
Brest France 50 B4
Brest-Litovsk Belarus see Brest
Brest Oblast admin. div. Belarus see Brestskaya Voblasts'
Brestovac Srbija Yugo. 58 C5
Brestskaya Oblast' admin. div. Belarus see Brestskaya Voblasts'
Brestskaya Voblasts' admin. div. Belarus 42 G9
English form Brest Oblast; also known as Brestskaya Oblast'
Bretagne admin. reg. France 50 D4
English form Brittany
Bretagne reg. France see Brittany
Bretana Peru 198 C6
Bretcu Romania 58 H2
Breteuil Haute-Normandie France 50 G4
Breteuil Picardie France 51 I3
Brétigny-sur-Orge France 51 I4
Breton Canada 167 H4
Breton Sound b. U.S.A. 175 B6
Bretten Germany 48 F6
Breu r. Brazil/Peru 200 B2
Breueh, Pulau i. Indon. 76 A1
Brevard U.S.A. 174 D5
Breves Brazil 202 B2
Brewarrina Australia 147 E2
Brewer U.S.A. 177 Q1
Brewerville Liberia 124 C5
Brewster NE U.S.A. 178 C3
Brewster OH U.S.A. 176 D5
Brewster WA U.S.A. 180 C2
Brewster, Kap c. Greenland see Kangikajik
Brewster, Lake imp. l. Australia 147 E3

index

B C

Brewton U.S.A. 175 C6
Breyten S. Africa 133 N3
Breytovo Rus. Fed. 43 S3
Brezhnev Rus. Fed. see Naberezhnyye Chelny
Brežice Slovenia 56 H3
Breznik Bulg. 58 D6
Breznita-Motru Romania 58 E4
Breznitsa Bulg. 58 E7
Brezno Slovakia 49 Q7
Brezovo Bulg. 58 G6
Brezovo Polje hill Croatia 56 J3
Bria Cent. Afr. Rep. 126 D3
Briakan Rus. Fed. 82 D1
Briançon France 51 M8
Brian Head mt. U.S.A. 183 L4
Briare France 51 I5
Bribie Island Australia 149 G5
Briceni Moldova 41 C6
formerly spelt Brichany
Brichany Moldova see Briceni
Bricquebec France 50 E3
Bridgehampton U.S.A. 177 M5
Bridgeman U.S.A. 172 G9
Bridgend U.K. 47 I12
also known as Pen-y-Bont ar Ogwr
Bridgeport AL U.S.A. 174 C5
Bridgeport CA U.S.A. 182 E3
Bridgeport CT U.S.A. 177 L4
Bridgeport MI U.S.A. 173 J7
Bridgeport NE U.S.A. 178 B3
Bridgeport TX U.S.A. 179 C5
Bridgeport Reservoir U.S.A. 182 E3
Bridger Peak U.S.A. 180 F4
Bridgeton U.S.A. 177 J6
Bridgetown Australia 151 B7

▶Bridgetown Barbados 187 I4
Capital of Barbados.

Bridgetown Canada 169 H4
Bridgeville U.S.A. 177 J7
Bridgewater Australia 147 E5
Bridgewater Canada 169 H4
Bridgewater MA U.S.A. 177 O4
Bridgewater NY U.S.A. 177 J3
Bridgewater VA U.S.A. 176 G7
Bridgton U.S.A. 177 O1
Bridgwater U.K. 47 I12
Bridgwater Bay U.K. 47 I12
Bridlington U.K. 47 L9
Bridport Australia 147 E5
Bridport U.K. 47 J13
Brie reg. France 51 I4
Briec France 50 C4
Brie-Comte-Robert France 51 I4
Brieg Poland see Brzeg
Brienne-le-Château France 51 K4
Brienzer See l. Switz. 51 N6
Briery Knob mt. U.S.A. 176 E7
Brig Switz. 51 N6
Briggsville U.S.A. 172 D7
Brigham City U.S.A. 180 D4
Brighton Canada 173 P6
Brighton N.Z. 153 E13
Brighton U.K. 47 L13
Brighton CO U.S.A. 180 F5
Brighton IA U.S.A. 172 B9
Brighton MI U.S.A. 173 J8
Brighton NY U.S.A. 176 H2
Brighton WV U.S.A. 176 C7
Brighton Downs Australia 149 D4
Brignoles France 51 M9
Brihuega Spain 55 I4
Brikama Gambia 124 A3
Brillion U.S.A. 172 E6
Brilon Germany 48 F4
Brimley U.S.A. 173 I4
Brimnes Iceland 44 [inset] D2
Brimson U.S.A. 172 B3
Brindisi Italy 57 J8
historically known as Brundisium
Brinje Croatia 56 H3
Brinkley U.S.A. 174 B5
Brinkworth Australia 146 C3
Brion, Île i. Canada 169 I4
Brionne France 50 G3
Brioude France 51 J7
Brisay Canada 169 G2

▶Brisbane Australia 147 G1
State capital of Queensland and 3rd most populous city in Oceania.
world [cities] ▬▶ 24–25

Brisighella Italy 56 D4
Bristol U.K. 47 J12
Bristol CT U.S.A. 177 M4
Bristol FL U.S.A. 175 C6
Bristol NH U.S.A. 177 N2
Bristol RI U.S.A. 177 N4
Bristol TN U.S.A. 176 C9
Bristol VT U.S.A. 177 L1
Bristol Bay U.S.A. 164 C4
Bristol Channel est. U.K. 47 H12
Bristol Lake U.S.A. 183 I7
Bristol Mountains U.S.A. 183 H7
Britânia Brazil 206 B2
Britannia Island New Caledonia see Maré
British Antarctic Territory Antarctica 222 S2
British Columbia prov. Canada 166 F5
British Empire Range mts Canada 165 K1

British Guiana country S. America see Guyana
British Honduras country Central America see Belize

▶British Indian Ocean Territory terr. Indian Ocean 218 L6
United Kingdom Overseas Territory.
asia [countries] ▬▶ 64–67

British Solomon Islands country S. Pacific Ocean see Solomon Islands
Brito Godins Angola see Kiwaba N'zogi
Brits S. Africa 133 L2
Britstown S. Africa 132 H7
Brittany admin. reg. France see Bretagne
Brittany reg. France 50 C4
also known as Bretagne
Britton U.S.A. 178 C2
Brive-la-Gaillarde France 50 H7
Briviesca Spain 55 H2
Brixham U.K. 47 I13
Brixia Italy see Brescia
Brlik Kazakh. see Birlik
Brlik Kazakh. 103 H4
also spelt Birlik
Brno Czech Rep. 49 N6
formerly spelt Brünn
Broach India see Bharuch
Broad r. U.S.A. 174 D5
Broadalbin U.S.A. 177 K2
Broad Arrow Australia 151 C6
Broadback r. Canada 168 E3
Broad Bay U.K. 46 F5
also known as Tuath, Loch a'
Broadford U.K. 46 G6
Broad Law hill U.K. 46 I8
Broadmere Australia 148 B3
Broad Sound sea chan. Australia 149 F4
Broad Sound Channel Australia 149 F4
Broadsound Range hills Australia 149 F4
Broadus U.S.A. 180 F3
Broadview Canada 167 K5
Broadwater U.S.A. 178 B3
Broadway U.S.A. 176 G7
Broadwood N.Z. 152 H3
Broby Sweden 45 K4
Broceni Latvia 42 D5
Brochet Canada 167 K3
Brocken mt. Germany 48 H4
Brockman, Mount Australia 150 B4
Brockport NY U.S.A. 176 H2
Brockport PA U.S.A. 176 G4
Brockton U.S.A. 177 N3
Brockville Canada 168 F4
Brockway U.S.A. 176 G4
Brod Macedonia 58 C7
Broderick Falls Kenya see Webuye
Brodeur Peninsula Canada 165 K2
Brodhead KY U.S.A. 176 A8
Brodhead WI U.S.A. 172 D8
Brodheadsville U.S.A. 177 J5
Brodick U.K. 46 G8
Brodnax U.S.A. 176 G9
Brodnica Poland 49 Q2
Brody Ukr. 41 C6
Broedersput S. Africa 133 J3
Brok r. Poland 49 S3
Broke Inlet Australia 151 B7
Broken Arrow U.S.A. 179 D4
Broken Bay Australia 147 F3
Broken Bow NE U.S.A. 178 C3
Broken Bow OK U.S.A. 179 D5
Broken Bow Reservoir U.S.A. 179 D5
Brokenburg U.S.A. 176 H7
Brokenhead r. Canada 167 L5
Broken Hill Australia 146 D2
Broken Hill Zambia see Kabwe
Brokopondo Suriname 199 H3
Brokopondo Stuwmeer resr Suriname see Professor van Blommestein Meer
Bromberg Poland see Bydgoszcz
Brømnes Norway 44 L1
Bromo Tengger Semeru National Park Indon. 77 F4
Bromsgrove U.K. 47 J11
Brønderslev Denmark 45 J4
Brong-Ahafo admin. reg. Ghana 125 E5
Bronkhorstspruit S. Africa 133 M2
Bronnitsy Rus. Fed. 43 T6
Brønnøysund Norway 44 K2
Bronson FL U.S.A. 175 D6
Bronson MI U.S.A. 173 H9
Bronte Sicilia Italy 57 G11
Brooke U.S.A. 176 H7
Brooke's Point Phil. 74 A4
Brookfield MO U.S.A. 178 D4
Brookfield WI U.S.A. 172 E7
Brookhaven U.S.A. 175 B6
Brookings OR U.S.A. 180 A4
Brookings SD U.S.A. 178 C2
Brookline U.S.A. 177 N3
Brooklyn U.S.A. 173 I8
Brooklyn Park U.S.A. 174 A2
Brookneal U.S.A. 176 G8
Brooks Canada 167 I5
Brooks ME U.S.A. 177 P1
Brooks WV U.S.A. 176 E8
Brooks, Cape Antarctica 222 T2
Brooks Brook Canada 166 C2
Brooks Range mts U.S.A. 164 E3
Brookston IN U.S.A. 172 G10
Brookston MN U.S.A. 172 A4
Brooksville FL U.S.A. 175 D6
Brooksville KY U.S.A. 176 A7
Brookton Australia 151 B7
Brookville U.S.A. 176 F4
Broom, Loch inlet U.K. 46 G6
Broome Australia 150 C3
Broomehill Australia 151 B7
Broons France 50 D4
Brora U.K. 46 I5
Brora r. U.K. 46 I5
Brøstadbotn Norway 44 L1
Broşteni Romania 58 G1
Brosville U.S.A. 176 F9
Brotas Brazil 206 F9
Brotas de Macaúbas Brazil 202 D5
Brothers U.S.A. 180 B4
Brou France 50 H4
Broughton Island Canada see Qikiqtarjuaq
Broulkou well Chad 120 C5
Brovary Ukr. 41 D6
Brown, Lake salt flat Australia 151 B6
Brown, Mount hill Australia 146 C3
Brown, Point Australia 146 B3
Brown City U.S.A. 173 K7
Brown Creek r. Australia 149 D3
Brown Deer U.S.A. 172 F7
Browne Range hills Australia 151 D5
Brownfield U.S.A. 179 B5
Brown Mountain U.S.A. 183 G6
Brown's Town Jamaica 186 D3
Brownstown U.S.A. 174 C4
Brownsville PA U.S.A. 176 F5
Brownsville TN U.S.A. 174 B5
Brownsville TX U.S.A. 179 C7
Brownsweg Suriname 199 H3
Brownwood U.S.A. 179 C6
Browse Island Australia 150 C2
Brozas Spain 54 E5
Brozha Belarus 43 K9
Bruay-la-Bussière France 51 I2
Bruce MS U.S.A. 174 B5
Bruce WI U.S.A. 172 B5
Bruce, Mount Australia 150 B4
Bruce Peninsula Canada 173 L6
Bruce Peninsula National Park Canada 173 L5
Bruce Rock Australia 151 B6
Bruchsal Germany 48 F6
Bruck an der Leitha Austria 49 N7

Bruck an der Mur Austria 49 M8
Bruges Belgium see Brugge
Brugge Belgium 51 J1
also spelt Bruges
Bruhagen Norway 44 I3
Bruin KY U.S.A. 176 B7
Bruin PA U.S.A. 176 F4
Bruin Point mt. U.S.A. 183 N2
Bruint India 97 H3
Brûk, Wâdi el watercourse Egypt 108 E7
Brukkaros Namibia 130 C5
Brukkaros, Mount Namibia 132 B2
Brûlé Canada 166 G4
Brule U.S.A. 172 B4
Brûlé, Lac l. Canada 169 I2
also known as Burnt Lake
Brumadinho Brazil 207 I7
Brumado Brazil 202 D5
Brumath France 51 N4
Brumer Islands P.N.G. 149 F1
Brumunddal Norway 45 J3
Brú Na Bóinne tourist site Rep. of Ireland 47 F10
Brundisium Italy see Brindisi
Bruneau r. U.S.A. 180 D4
Bruneau, West Fork r. U.S.A. 180 D4
▶Brunei country Asia 77 F1
asia [countries] ▬▶ 64–67
Brunei Brunei see Bandar Seri Begawan
Brunei Bay Malaysia 77 F1
Brunette Downs Australia 148 B3
Brunette Island Canada 169 K4
Brunflo Sweden 44 K3
Brunico Italy 56 D2
Brünn Czech Rep. see Brno
Brunna Sweden 45 L4
Brunner, Lake N.Z. 153 F10
Bruno Canada 167 J4
Bruno U.S.A. 172 A4
Brunsbüttel Germany 48 G2
Brunswick Germany see Braunschweig
Brunswick GA U.S.A. 175 D6
Brunswick MD U.S.A. 176 H6
Brunswick ME U.S.A. 177 P2
Brunswick MO U.S.A. 178 D4
Brunswick OH U.S.A. 176 D4
Brunswick, Peninsula de pen. Chile 205 C9
Brunswick Bay Australia 150 D2
Brunswick Head Australia 147 G2
Brunswick Junction Australia 151 A7
Brunswick Lake Canada 168 D3
Bruntál Czech Rep. 49 O6
Brunt Ice Shelf Antarctica 222 W2
Bruny Island Australia 147 E5
Brus Srbija Yugo. 58 C5
Brusa Turkey see Bursa
Brush U.S.A. 178 B3
Brushton U.S.A. 177 K1
Brusovo Rus. Fed. 43 Q4
Brusque Brazil 203 B8
Brussel Belgium see Brussels

▶Brussels Belgium 51 K2
Capital of Belgium. Also spelt Brussel or Bruxelles.
europe [issues] ▬▶ 34–35

Brusturi-Drăgăneşti Romania 58 H1
Brusy Poland 49 O2
Bruthen Australia 147 E4
Bruxelles Belgium see Brussels
Bruyères France 51 M4
Bruzual Venez. 198 D2
Bryan OH U.S.A. 176 A4
Bryan TX U.S.A. 179 C6
Bryan, Mount hill Australia 146 C3
Bryan Coast Antarctica 222 S2
Bryansk Rus. Fed. 43 P8
Bryanskaya Oblast' admin. div. Rus. Fed. 43 O8
English form Bryansk Oblast
Bryansk Oblast admin. div. Rus. Fed. see Bryanskaya Oblast'
Bryanskoye Rus. Fed. 102 A3
Bryant AR U.S.A. 179 D5
Bryant WI U.S.A. 172 D5
Bryant Creek r. U.S.A. 178 D4
Bryant Pond U.S.A. 177 O1
Bryce Canyon National Park U.S.A. 183 L4
Bryce Mountains U.S.A. 183 O8
Bryn' Rus. Fed. 43 Q8
Bryne Norway 45 I4
Bryson, Lac l. Canada 173 P4
Bryukhovetskaya Rus. Fed. 41 F7
Brzava r. Yugo. 58 B3
Brzeg Poland 49 O5
historically known as Brieg
Brzeg Dolny Poland 49 N4
Brześć nad Bugiem Belarus see Brest
Brzozów Poland 49 T6
Bû well Yemen 105 D4
Bua Angola 127 B6
Bua Sweden 45 K4
Bu'aale Somalia 128 D4
Buad i. Phil. 74 C4
Buala Solomon Is 145 E2
Buandougou Côte d'Ivoire see Bouandougou
Buang i. Indon. 75 C2
Buatan Indon. 76 C2
Bū Athlah well Libya 120 D2
Bu'ayj well Saudi Arabia 105 E2
Bu'ayrāt al Hasūn Libya 120 B2
Bubanza Burundi 126 F5
Bubi r. Zimbabwe 131 F4
Būbīyān Island Kuwait 107 G5
Bubuan i. Phil. 74 B5
Bubuan i. Phil. 74 B5
Buca Turkey 59 I10
Bucak Turkey 106 B3
Bucaramanga Col. 198 C3
Bucas Grande i. Phil. 74 C4
Buccaneer Archipelago is Australia 150 C3
Bucegi, Munţii mts Romania 58 G3
Buchan Australia 147 F4
Buchanan Liberia 124 C5
Buchanan MI U.S.A. 172 G9
Buchanan VA U.S.A. 176 F8
Buchanan, Lake salt flat Australia 149 E4
Buchanan, Lake U.S.A. 179 C6
Buchan Gulf Canada 165 L2
Buchans Canada 169 J3

▶Bucharest Romania 58 H4
Capital of Romania. Also spelt Bucureşti or Bükreş.

Buchen (Odenwald) Germany 48 G6
Bucholz in der Nordheide Germany 48 G2
Buchon, Point U.S.A. 182 D6
Buchy France 50 H3
Bucin, Pasul pass Romania 58 G2
Buckburn Draw watercourse U.S.A. 179 B6
Bückeburg Germany 48 G3
Buckeye U.S.A. 183 L8
Buckhannon U.S.A. 176 E7
Buckhannon r. U.S.A. 176 F6
Buckhaven U.K. 46 I7
Buckhorn Canada 173 O6
Buckhorn Lake Canada 173 O6
Buckie U.K. 46 J6
Buckingham Canada 173 R5
Buckingham U.K. 47 L11
Buckingham PA U.S.A. 177 J5
Buckingham VA U.S.A. 176 G8
Buckland U.S.A. 164 C3
Bucklands S. Africa 132 H6
Buckland Tableland reg. Australia 149 F5
Buckleboo Australia 146 C3
Buckle Island Antarctica 223 K2
Buckley watercourse Australia 148 C4

Buckley U.S.A. 172 E10
Buckley Bay Antarctica 223 J2
Buckskin Mountains U.S.A. 183 K7
Bucks Mountain U.S.A. 182 C2
Bucksport U.S.A. 177 Q1
Bučovice Czech Rep. 49 O6
Bucşani Romania 58 G4
Bucureşti Romania see Bucharest
Bucyrus U.S.A. 176 C5
Bud Norway 44 I3
Buda Rus. Fed. 43 P8
Buda, Illa de i. Spain 55 L4
Budai park Hungary 49 P8
Buda-Kashalyova Belarus 43 L9
Budalin Myanmar 78 A3

▶Budapest Hungary 49 Q8
Capital of Hungary. Historically known as Aquincum.

Budaun India 96 C3
Budayyi'ah well Saudi Arabia 104 C3
Bud Bud Somalia 128 E3
Budd Coast Antarctica 223 H2
Buddi Eth. 128 D3
Buddusò Sardegna Italy 57 B8
Bude U.K. 47 H13
Budennovsk Rus. Fed. 41 H7
Buderim Australia 149 G5
Budeşti Romania 58 H4
Budhiya, Gebel hills Egypt 108 E8
Budogoshch' Rus. Fed. 43 N2
Budongquan China 84 B5
Budoni Sardegna Italy 57 B8
Büdszentmihály Hungary see Tiszavasvári
Budū', Sabkhat al salt pan Saudi Arabia 105 E3
Budureasa Romania 58 D2
Budva Crna Gora Yugo. 56 K6
Budweis Czech Rep. see České Budějovice
Budzilava Belarus 43 K6
Buea Cameroon 125 H5
Buëch r. France 51 L8
Buellton U.S.A. 182 D7
Buena Esperanza Arg. 204 D4
Buenaventura Col. 198 B4
Buenaventura Mex. 184 D2
Buena Vista Bol. 201 E4
Buenavista Mex. 185 E5
Buena Vista i. N. Mariana Is see Tinian
Buenavista Phil. 74 B3
Buena Vista CO U.S.A. 180 F5
Buena Vista GA U.S.A. 175 C5
Buena Vista VA U.S.A. 176 F8
Buena Vista, Bahía de b. Cuba 186 D2
Buendia, Embalse de resr Spain 55 I4
Buenga r. Angola 127 B6
Buengas Angola 127 B6
formerly known as Nova Esperança
Buenolândia Brazil 206 C2
Buenópolis Brazil 203 C6

▶Buenos Aires Arg. 204 F4
Capital of Argentina. 2nd most populous city in South America and 10th in the world.
world [cities] ▬▶ 24–25

Buenos Aires prov. Arg. 204 E5
Buenos Aires Brazil 200 B2
Buenos Aires Amazonas Col. 198 D5
Buenos Aires Guaviare Col. 198 C4
Buenos Aires Costa Rica 186 C5
Buenos Aires, Lago l. Arg./Chile 205 B7
Buenos Aires National Wildlife Refuge nature res. U.S.A. 181 E7
Buen Pasto Arg. 205 C7
Buen Tiempo, Cabo c. Arg. 205 C8
Buerarema Brazil 202 E5
Buesaco Col. 198 B4
Bueu Spain 54 C2
Buey, Cabeza de mt. Spain 55 H6
Búfalo Mex. 184 D3
Buffalo r. Canada 167 H2
Buffalo MO U.S.A. 178 D4
Buffalo NY U.S.A. 176 G3
Buffalo OH U.S.A. 176 D6
Buffalo OK U.S.A. 178 C4
Buffalo SD U.S.A. 180 G3
Buffalo TX U.S.A. 179 C6
Buffalo WI U.S.A. 172 B6
Buffalo WY U.S.A. 180 F3
Buffalo r. AR U.S.A. 179 D4
Buffalo r. TN U.S.A. 174 C5
Buffalo r. WI U.S.A. 172 B6
Buffalo Head Hills Canada 167 G3
Buffalo Head Prairie Canada 167 G3
Buffalo Hump mt. U.S.A. 180 D3
Buffalo Lake Alta Canada 167 H4
Buffalo Lake N.W.T. Canada 167 H2
Buffalo Narrows Canada 167 I4
Buffalo Range Zimbabwe 131 F4
Buffalo Valley U.S.A. 183 G1
Buffels r. Kwazulu-Natal S. Africa 133 O5
Buffels r. W. Cape S. Africa 132 E10
Buffels watercourse S. Africa 132 B6
Buffels Drift S. Africa 131 E4
Buford U.S.A. 175 C5
Buftea Romania 58 G4
Bug r. Poland 49 U4
Buga Col. 198 B4
Buga Mongolia 84 B2
Buga Nigeria 125 G4
Bugala Island Uganda 128 B5
Bugana Nigeria 125 G5
Bugant Mongolia 85 E1
Bugarach, Pic de mt. France 51 I10
Bugaz Ukr. see Zatoka
Bugdayli Turkm. 102 C5
Bugeat France 51 H7
Bugel, Tanjung pt Indon. 77 E4
Bugojno Bos.-Herz. 56 J4
Bugøyfjord Norway 44 O1
Bugrino Rus. Fed. 40 I1
Bugsuk i. Phil. 74 A4
Bugt China 85 I1
Buguey Phil. 74 B2
Bugui Point Phil. 74 B3
Bugul'ma Rus. Fed. 40 J5
Bugun' Kazakh. 103 E3
Bügür China see Luntai
Buguruslan Rus. Fed. 41 J5
Būhābād Iran 100 C4
Buharkent Turkey 59 J11
Buhera Zimbabwe 131 F3
Buh He r. China 84 C4
Buhi Phil. 74 B3
Bühl Germany 48 F7
Buhl ID U.S.A. 180 D4
Buhl MN U.S.A. 172 A3
Buhoro Flats plain Tanz. 129 B7
Buhriz Iraq 109 P4
Buhu r. Tanz. 129 B6
Buhuşi Romania 58 H2
Buia Italy 56 F2
Buick Canada 166 F3
Builth Wells U.K. 47 I11
Buin P.N.G. 145 E2
Bui National Park Ghana 124 E4
Buinsk Rus. Fed. 40 I5
Bu'in Zahrā Iran 100 B3
Buir Nur l. Mongolia 85 H2
Buitepos Namibia 130 C4
Būivydžiai Lith. 42 G7
Bujalance Spain 54 G7
Bujanovac Srbija Yugo. 58 C6
Bujoru Romania 58 G5

▶Bujumbura Burundi 126 F5
Capital of Burundi. Formerly known as Usumbura.

Buk Poland 49 N3

Bukachacha Rus. Fed. 81 J2
Buka Island P.N.G. 145 E2
Bukama Dem. Rep. Congo 127 E7
Bukan' Rus. Fed. 43 P8
Būkand Iran 100 C4
Bukanskoye Rus. Fed. 103 J1
Bukantau, Gory hills Uzbek. 103 E4
Bukavu Dem. Rep. Congo 126 F5
formerly known as Costermansville
Bukedi Dem. Rep. Congo 127 C6
Bukene Tanz. 129 B6
Bukeya Dem. Rep. Congo 127 E7
Bukhara Uzbek. 103 F5
also spelt Bukhoro
Bukhara Oblast admin. div. Uzbek. see Bukharskaya Oblast'
Bukharskaya Oblast' admin. div. Uzbek. 103 E4
English form Bukhara Oblast; also known as Bukhoro Wiloyati
Bukhava Belarus 43 K6
Bukhoro Uzbek. see Bukhara
Bukhoro Wiloyati admin. div. Uzbek. see Bukharskaya Oblast'
Bukhtarminskoye Vodokhranilishche resr Kazakh. 88 D1
also known as Buqtyrma Bögeni
Bukide i. Indon. 75 C2
Bukima Tanz. 128 B5
Bukit Baka Bukit Raya National Park Indon. 77 F3
Bukit Timah Sing. 76 [inset]
Bukit Timah hill Sing. 76 [inset]
Bukittinggi Indon. 76 C3
also known as Fort de Kock
Bükk mts Hungary 49 R7
Bukkapatnam India 94 C3
Bükki nat. park Hungary 49 R7
Bükkzsérc Hungary 49 R8
Bukoba Tanz. 128 A5
Bukonys Lith. 42 F6
Bukowa r. Poland 49 T5
Bukowo, Jezioro lag. Poland 49 N1
Bükreş Romania see Bucharest
Buku, Tanjung pt Indon. 76 D3
Bukum, Pulau i. Sing. 76 [inset]
Būl, Kūh-e mt. Iran 100 C4
Bula Guinea-Bissau 124 B3
Bula Indon. 73 H7
Bülach Switz. 51 O5
Bulag Mongolia 85 F1
Bulagtay Mongolia 85 E1
Bulahdelal Australia 147 G3
Bulalacao i. Phil. 74 B4
Bulan Phil. 74 B3
Bulan i. Phil. 74 C5
Bulancak Turkey 107 D2
Bulandshahr India 96 C3
Bulanık Turkey 107 E3
Bulanovo Rus. Fed. 102 C1
Bulava Rus. Fed. 82 F2
Bulawa, Gunung mt. Indon. 75 B2
Bulawayo Zimbabwe 131 F4
Bulbula waterhole Kenya 128 C5
Buldan Turkey 106 B3
Buldana India 94 C1
Buldibuyo Peru 200 A2
Buleda reg. Pak. 101 E5
Bulei well Eth. 128 E3
Bulembu Swaziland 133 P2
formerly known as Havelock
Bulgan Bulgan Mongolia 84 D1
Bulgan Mongolia see Bürenhayrhan
Bulgan Hovd Mongolia 84 B2
formerly known as Darvi
Bulgan Hövsgöl Mongolia 84 D1
Bulgan Ömnögovĭ Mongolia 84 D2
Bulgan prov. Mongolia 84 D1
Bulgan Gol r. Mongolia 84 A2
Bulgar Rus. Fed. see Bolgar
Bŭlgarevo Bulg. 58 J5
▶Bulgaria country Europe 58 F6
spelt Bŭlgariya in Bulgarian
europe [countries] ▬▶ 32–35
Bŭlgariya country Europe see Bulgaria
Bulghah Saudi Arabia 104 C2
Buli Indon. 75 D2
Buli, Teluk b. Indon. 75 D2
Buliluyan, Cape Phil. 74 A4
Bulkley Ranges mts Canada 166 D4
Bullaque r. Spain 54 G6
Bullas Spain 55 J6
Bullaxaar Somalia 128 E2
Bulle Switz. 51 N6
Bullea, Lake salt flat Australia 146 D2
Bullen r. Canada 167 K1
Buller r. N.Z. 153 F9
Bulleringa National Park Australia 149 D3
Bullfinch Australia 151 B6
Bullhead City U.S.A. 183 J6
Bullion Mountains U.S.A. 183 H7
Bullmark Sweden 44 M2
Bullo r. Australia 148 A2
Bulloo watercourse Australia 147 D2
Bulloo Downs Australia 147 D2
Bulloo Lake salt flat Australia 147 D2
Bulls N.Z. 152 J8
Bull Shoals Lake U.S.A. 179 D4
Büllsport Namibia 130 C5
Bully Choop Mountain U.S.A. 182 B1
Bulman Australia 148 B2
Bulman Gorge Australia 148 B2
Bulmer Lake Canada 166 F2
Buloh, Pulau i. Sing. 76 [inset]
Buloke, Lake dry lake Australia 147 D4
Bulolo P.N.G. 73 K8
Bulqizë Albania 58 B7
Bultfontein S. Africa 133 K5
Bulu, Gunung mt. Indon. 77 G2
Buluan Phil. 74 C5
Buluan Indon. 75 B4
Buluk well Kenya 128 C3
Bulukumba Indon. 75 B4
Bulun Rus. Fed. 39 M2
Bulungu Bandundu Dem. Rep. Congo 126 C6
Bulungu Kasai Occidental Dem. Rep. Congo 127 D6
Bulungur Uzbek. 103 F5
formerly known as Krasnogvardeysk
Busan Phil. 74 C3
Bulwer S. Africa 133 N6
Bumba Bandundu Dem. Rep. Congo 127 C6
Bumba Equateur Dem. Rep. Congo 126 D4
Bumbah, Khalij b. Libya 120 D1
Bumbat Mongolia 84 E2
Bumbeşti-Jiu Romania 58 E3
Bumbuna Sierra Leone 124 C4
Bumhkang Myanmar 78 B2
Bumpha Bum mt. Myanmar 78 B2
Buna Dem. Rep. Congo 126 C5
Buna Kenya 128 C4
Bunayyān well Saudi Arabia 105 E3
Bunazi Tanz. 128 A5
Bunbury Australia 151 A7
Bunclody Rep. of Ireland 47 F11
formerly known as Newtownbarry
Buncrana Rep. of Ireland 47 E8
Bunda Tanz. 128 B5
Bundaberg Australia 149 G5
Bundaleer Australia 147 E2
Bundey watercourse Australia 148 B4
Bundi India 96 B4
Bundibugyo Uganda 128 A4
Bundjalung National Park Australia 147 G2
Bundoran Rep. of Ireland 47 D9
Bundu India 97 E5
Bunduqiya Sudan 128 A3
Bunë r. Albania/Yugo. 58 A7
Buner reg. Pak. 101 H3
Bunga r. Nigeria 125 H3
Bungalaut, Selat sea chan. Indon. 76 B3

Bung Boraphet l. Thai. 79 C5
Bungendore Australia 147 F3
Bunger Hills Antarctica 223 G2
Bungi Indon. 75 B4
Bungil Creek r. Australia 149 F5
Bungle Bungle National Park Australia see Purnululu National Park
Bungo Angola 127 B6
Bungoma Kenya 128 B4
Bungo-suidō sea chan. Japan 91 C8
Bungo-takada Japan 91 B8
Bunguran, Kepulauan is Indon. see Natuna, Kepulauan
Bunguran, Pulau i. Indon. see Natuna Besar
Bunia Dem. Rep. Congo 126 F4
Buningonia well Australia 151 C6
Bunji Jammu and Kashmir 96 B2
Bunker Group atolls Australia 149 G4
Bunkeya Dem. Rep. Congo 127 E7
Bunkie U.S.A. 179 D6
Bunkris Sweden 45 K3
Bunnell U.S.A. 175 D6
Bunnythorpe N.Z. 152 J8
Buñol Spain 55 K5
Bünsum China 89 C6
Bunsuru watercourse Nigeria 125 G3
Buntok Indon. 77 F3
Buntokecil Indon. 77 F3
Bununu Nigeria 125 H4
Bunya Mountains National Park Australia 149 F5
Bünyan Turkey 106 C3
Bunyu i. Indon. 77 G2
Bunza Nigeria 125 G3
Buoač Bos.-Herz. 56 J4
Buoddobohki Fin. see Patoniva
Buonconvento Italy 56 D5
Buôn Mê Thuôt Vietnam 79 E5
Buorkhaya, Guba b. Rus. Fed. 39 N2
Bup r. China 89 D6
Buqayq Saudi Arabia see Abqaiq
Buqbuq Egypt 121 E2
Buqtyrma Bögeni resr Kazakh. see Bukhtarminskoye Vodokhranilishche
Bura Kenya 128 C5
Buraan Somalia 128 F2
Burakin Australia 151 B6
Buram Sudan 126 E2
Buran Kazakh. 88 D1
also spelt Boran
Buran Darat reef Sing. 76 [inset]
Buranhaém r. Brazil 207 N3
Burannoye Rus. Fed. 102 C2
Burano r. Italy 56 E5
Burao Somalia 128 E2
Burauen Phil. 74 C4
Buraydah Saudi Arabia 104 C2
Burayevo Rus. Fed. 40 J5
Burbach Germany 48 F5
Burbank U.S.A. 182 F7
Burchell Lake Canada 172 C2
Burcher Australia 147 E3
Burdalyk Turkm. 103 F5
Burdekin r. Australia 149 E3
Burdekin Falls Australia 149 E4
Burdigala France see Bordeaux
Burdur Turkey 106 B3
Burdur Gölü l. Turkey 106 B3
Burdwan India see Barddhaman
Burē Eth. 128 C2
Bure r. U.K. 47 N11
Bureå Sweden 44 M2
Bureinskiy Khrebet mts Rus. Fed. 82 D2
English form Bureya Range
Bureiqa well Sudan 121 F5
Bürenhayrhan Mongolia 84 A2
formerly known as Bulgan
Bürentsogt Mongolia 85 F2
Bureya r. Rus. Fed. 82 C2
Bureya-Pristan' Rus. Fed. see Novobureyskiy
Bureya Range mts Rus. Fed. see Bureinskiy Khrebet
Bureyinskiy Zapovednik nature res. Rus. Fed. 82 D2
Burgaltay Mongolia 84 E1
Burgas Bulg. 58 I6
Burgaw U.S.A. 174 E5
Burg bei Magdeburg Germany 48 I3
Burgdorf Niedersachsen Germany 48 H3
Burgdorf Niedersachsen Germany 48 H3
Burgdorf Switz. 51 N5
Burg el 'Arab Egypt 108 A7
Burgeo Canada 169 J4
Burgersdorp S. Africa 133 K7
Burgersfort S. Africa 133 O1
Burgerville S. Africa 133 I7
Burges, Mount hill Australia 151 C6
Burgess U.S.A. 177 I8
Burget Tuyur waterhole Sudan 121 E4
Burghausen Germany 49 J7
Burghūth, Sabkhat al salt l. Syria 109 M3
Burgin U.S.A. 176 A8
Burglengenfeld Germany 48 J6
Burg Migheizil Egypt 108 B6
Burgos Mex. 185 F3
Burgos Spain 55 H2
Burgsvik Sweden 45 L4
Burhabalanga r. India 97 E5
Burhan Budai Shan mts China 84 B5
Burhaniye Turkey 106 A3
Burhanpur India 96 C5
Burhar-Dhanpuri India 97 D5
Burhave (Butjadingen) Germany 48 F2
Burhi Gandak r. India 97 E4
Buri Brazil 206 E10
Burias i. Phil. 74 B3
Buriat-Mongol Republic aut. rep. Rus. Fed. see Buryatiya, Respublika
Buribay Rus. Fed. 102 D2
Burica, Punta pt Costa Rica 186 C5
Burin Canada 169 K4
Burin Peninsula Canada 169 K4
Buriram Thai. 79 C5
Buritama Brazil 206 C8
Buriti Brazil 202 D2
Buriti r. Brazil 201 F3
Buriti Alegre Brazil 206 D5
Buriti Bravo Brazil 202 D3
Buritirama Brazil 202 D4
Buritis Brazil 206 G2
Buritizeiro Brazil 207 I4
Burjassot Spain 55 K5
Burkan-Suu r. Kyrg. 103 I4
also known as Buurakan
Burkburnett U.S.A. 179 C5
Burke watercourse Australia 149 C4
Burke U.S.A. 178 C3
Burke Channel Canada 166 E5
Burke Island Antarctica 222 Q2
Burke Pass N.Z. 153 E12
Burkesville U.S.A. 174 C4
Burketown Australia 148 C3
Burkeville U.S.A. 176 G8
Burkhala Rus. Fed. 39 O3
▶Burkina country Africa 125 E3
formerly known as Upper Volta or Haute-Volta; long form Burkina Faso
africa [countries] ▬▶ 114–117
Burkina Faso country Africa see Burkina
Burk's Falls Canada 168 E4
Burla Rus. Fed. 103 I1
Burley U.S.A. 180 D4
Burli Kazakh. 103 E1
also spelt Börili
Burlin Kazakh. 102 C2
Burlington Canada 168 E5
Burlington CO U.S.A. 178 B4
Burlington IA U.S.A. 174 B3
Burlington KS U.S.A. 178 D4
Burlington NC U.S.A. 176 F9
Burlington VT U.S.A. 177 L1

Burlington *WA* U.S.A. **180** B2
Burlington *WI* U.S.A. **172** E8
Burly Rus. Fed. **40** K5
Burma *country* Asia *see* **Myanmar**
Burmakino Rus. Fed. **43** V4
Burnaby Canada **166** F5
Burnet U.S.A. **179** C6
Burnett *r.* Australia **149** G5
Burney U.S.A. **182** C1
Burney, Monte *vol.* Chile **205** B9
Burnham U.S.A. **177** P1
Burnie Australia **147** E5
Burning Springs U.S.A. **176** B8
Burnley U.K. **47** J10
Burnoye Kazakh. *see* **Bauyrzhan Momysh-Uly**
Burns U.S.A. **180** C4
Burnside *r.* Canada **167** I1
Burnside U.S.A. **176** A9
Burnside, Lake *salt flat* Australia **151** C5
Burns Junction U.S.A. **180** C4
Burns Lake Canada **166** E4
Burnsville U.S.A. **176** E7
Burnt *r.* U.S.A. **180** C3
Burnt Lake Canada *see* **Brûlé, Lac**
Burntwood *r.* Canada **167** L4
Burntwood Lake Canada **167** K4
Burog Co *l.* China **89** D5
Buron *r.* Canada **169** G1
Burovoy Uzbek. **103** E4
Burqin China **88** D2
Burqin *r.* China **88** D2
Burqu' Jordan **109** J5
Burra Australia **146** C3
Burra *i.* U.K. **46** K3
Burrel Albania **58** B7
Burrel U.S.A. **182** E5
Burren *reg.* Rep. of Ireland **47** C10
Burrendong Reservoir Australia **147** F3
Burren Junction Australia **147** F2
Burriana Spain **55** K5
Burrinjuck Reservoir Australia **147** F3
Burro, Serranías del *mts* Mex. **185** E2
Burr Oak U.S.A. **172** B7
Burr Oak Reservoir U.S.A. **176** C6
Burro Creek *watercourse* U.S.A. **183** K7
Burrow Head U.K. **47** H9
Burruyacú Arg. **204** D2
Bursa Turkey **106** B2
historically known as Brusa *or* Prusa
Bursa *prov.* Turkey **59** J8
Būr Safāga Egypt **121** G3
Būr Sa'īd Egypt *see* **Port Said**
Būr Sa'īd *governorate* Egypt **108** D6
Bursinskoye Vodokhranilishche *resr* Rus. Fed. **82** C2
Būr Sudan Sudan *see* **Port Sudan**
Burt Lake U.S.A. **173** I5
Burtnieku ezers *l.* Latvia **42** G4
Burton U.S.A. **173** J8
Burton, Lac *l.* Canada **168** E2
Burton upon Trent U.K. **47** K11
Burträsk Sweden **44** M2
Burtundy Australia **147** D3
Burt Well Australia **148** B4
Buru *i.* Indon. **75** C3
Burubaytal Kazakh. **88** A2
also spelt Bürylbaytal
Burullus, Bahra el *lag.* Egypt *see* **Burullus, Lake**
Burullus, Lake *lag.* Egypt **108** B6
also known as Burullus, Bahra el
Burultokay China *see* **Fuhai**
Burûn, Râs *pt* Egypt **108** E6
▶ **Burundi** *country* Africa **126** F5
formerly known as Urundi
africa [countries] → 114–117
Burunniy Rus. Fed. *see* **Tsagan Aman**
Bururi Burundi **126** F5
Burwash Landing Canada **166** B2
Burwell U.S.A. **178** C3
Burwick U.K. **46** J5
Buryatia *aut. rep.* Rus. Fed. *see* **Buryatiya, Respublika**
Buryatiya, Respublika *aut. rep.* Rus. Fed. **84** D1
English form Buryatia; *formerly known as* Buriat-Mongol Republic *or* Buryatskaya Mongolskaya A.S.S.R.
Buryatskaya Mongolskaya A.S.S.R. *aut. rep.* Rus. Fed. *see* **Buryatiya, Respublika**
Bürylbaytal Kazakh. *see* **Burubaytal**
Buryn' Ukr. **41** E6
Burynshyk Kazakh. **102** B3
Bury St Edmunds U.K. **47** M11
Burzil Pass Jammu and Kashmir **96** B2
Busalla Italy **56** A4
Busan S. Korea *see* **Pusan**
Būs'ān Yemen **104** C5
Busan Bay Phil. **74** B5
Busanga Dem. Rep. Congo **126** D5
Busca Italy **51** N8
Buseire Syria *see* **Al Buşayrah**
Būshehr Iran **100** B4
formerly spelt Bushire
Būshehr *prov.* Iran **100** B4
Bushenyi Uganda **128** A5
Bushire Iran *see* **Būshehr**
Bushkill U.S.A. **177** J4
Bushnell *FL* U.S.A. **175** D6
Bushnell *IL* U.S.A. **172** C10
Bushuikha Rus. Fed. **43** V2
Busia Kenya **128** B4
Busing, Pulau *i.* Sing. **76** [inset]
Businga Dem. Rep. Congo **126** D4
Busira *r.* Dem. Rep. Congo **126** C5
Buskerud *county* Norway **45** J3
Busko-Zdrój Poland **49** R5
Buskul' Kazakh. *see* **Boskol'**
Busobuso Indon. **75** D2
Busselton Australia **151** A7
Bussol', Proliv *strait* Rus. Fed. **81** Q3
Bustamante Mex. **185** E3
Buşteni Romania **58** G3
Bustillos, Lago *l.* Mex. **184** D2
Busto Arsizio Italy **56** A3
Busuanga Phil. **74** A3
Busuanga *i.* Phil. **74** A3
Busu-Djanoa Dem. Rep. Congo **126** D4
Büsum Germany **48** F1
Busu Modanda Dem. Rep. Congo **126** C4
Buta Dem. Rep. Congo **126** E4
Butajira Eth. **128** C2
Butan Bulg. **58** E5
Butang Group *is* Thai. **79** B7
Buta Ranquil Arg. **204** C5
Butare Rwanda **126** F5
formerly known as Astrida
Butaritari *atoll* Kiribati **220** F6
also known as Makin
Butauanan *pt* Phil. **74** B3
Bute *i.* U.K. **46** G8
Butea Romania **58** H1
Butedale Canada **166** D4
Bute Inlet Canada **166** E5
Butembo Dem. Rep. Congo **126** F4
Butha Buthe Lesotho **133** M5
Butha Qi China *see* **Zalantun**
Buthidaung Myanmar **78** A3
Butiá Brazil **203** B9
Butiaba Uganda **128** A4
Butler *AL* U.S.A. **175** B5
Butler *GA* U.S.A. **175** C5
Butler *IN* U.S.A. **176** A4
Butler *KY* U.S.A. **176** A7
Butler *MO* U.S.A. **178** D4
Butler *PA* U.S.A. **176** F5
Buton *i.* Indon. **75** B4
Buton, Selat *sea chan.* Indon. **75** B4
Butrimonys Lith. **42** G7
Butrintit, Liqeni i *l.* Albania **59** B9
Buttahatchee *r.* U.S.A. **175** B5
Butte *MT* U.S.A. **180** D3
Butte *NE* U.S.A. **178** C3
Butternut U.S.A. **172** C4
Butterworth Malaysia **76** C1
Butterworth S. Africa **133** M9
Buttes, Sierra *mt.* U.S.A. **182** D2
Butt of Lewis *hd* U.K. **46** F5
also known as Robhanais, Rubha
Button Bay Canada **167** M3
Button Islands Canada **165** M3
Buttonwillow U.S.A. **182** E6
Butuan Phil. **74** C4
Butuan Bay Phil. **74** C4
Butuo China **86** B3
also known as Temuli
Buturlinovka Rus. Fed. **41** G6
Butwal Nepal **97** D4
Butzbach Germany **48** F5
Bützow Germany **48** I2
Buuhoodle Somalia **128** E2
Buulobarde Somalia **128** E4
Buurakan *r.* Kyrg. *see* **Burkan-Suu**
Buur Gaabo Somalia **128** D5
Buurhabaka Somalia **128** E4
Buvåg Norway **44** K1
Buvuma Island Uganda **128** B4
Buwārah, Jabal *mt.* Saudi Arabia **108** F9
Buwāṭah Saudi Arabia **104** B2
Buxar India **97** E4
Buxtehude Germany **48** G2
Buxton U.K. **47** K10
Buy Rus. Fed. **40** G4
Buy *r.* Rus. Fed. **40** J4
Buyant *Bayanhongor* Mongolia **84** C2
Buyant *Bayan-Ölgiy* Mongolia **84** A1
Buyant *Hentiy* Mongolia **85** F2
Buyant Gol *r.* Mongolia **84** A1
Buyant Gol *r.* Mongolia **84** C2
Buyant-Ovoo Mongolia **85** E2
Buyant-Uhaa Mongolia **85** F2
Buyck U.S.A. **172** A2
Buynaksk Rus. Fed. **102** A4
Buyo Côte d'Ivoire **124** D5
Buyo, Lac de *l.* Côte d'Ivoire **124** D5
Buyuan Jiang *r.* China **86** B4
Büyükada *i.* Turkey **58** K8
Büyük Egri Dağ *mt.* Turkey **108** E1
Büyükkarıştıran Turkey **58** I7
Büyükkonak Turkey **59** K11
Büyükmenderes *r.* Turkey **106** A3
Büyükorhan Turkey **59** J9
Büyükşahinbey Turkey **109** I1
Buyun Shan *mt.* China **85** I3
Buzachi, Poluostrov *pen.* Kazakh. **102** B3
also known as Bozashy Tübegi
Buzançais France **50** H6
Buzău Romania **58** H3
Buzău *r.* Romania **58** H3
Buzaymah *oasis* Libya **120** D3
Buzdyak Rus. Fed. **40** J5
Buzha *r.* Rus. Fed. **43** V6
Búzi Moz. **131** G3
Búzi *r.* Moz. **131** G3
Buziaş Romania **58** C3
Búzios, Cabo dos *c.* Brazil **207** L9
Búzios, Ilha dos *i.* Brazil **207** H10
Büzmeyin Turkm. *see* **Byuzmeyin**
Buzuluk Rus. Fed. **102** C1
Buzuluk *r.* Rus. Fed. **41** G6
Buzzards Bay U.S.A. **177** O4
Bwagaoia P.N.G. **149** G1
Byadgi India **94** B3
Byahoml' Belarus **42** J7
Byakar Bhutan *see* **Jakar**
Byala Bulg. **58** G5
Byala Bulg. **58** I6
Byala Slatina Bulg. **58** E5
Byalynichy Belarus **43** K8
Byalynkavichy Belarus **43** N8
Byam Martin Island Canada **165** I2
Byarezina *r.* Belarus **42** G8
Byarezina *r.* Belarus **43** L9
Byarezinski Biyasfyerny Zapavyednik *nature res.* Belarus **43** J7
Byaroza Belarus **42** F9
also spelt Bereza
Byarozawka Belarus **42** G8
also spelt Berëzovka
Byblos *tourist site* Lebanon **108** G3
Bychawa Poland **49** T4
Byczyna Poland **49** P4
Bydgoszcz Poland **49** P2
historically known as Bromberg
Byelaazyorsk Belarus **42** G9
also spelt Beloozersk
Byelavyezhskaya Pushcha *park* Belarus **42** E9
Byelitsk Belarus **43** L9
Byel'ki Belarus **42** I6
Byelorussia *country* Europe *see* **Belarus**
Byerastavitsa Belarus *see* **Pahranichny**
Byerazino Belarus **43** J8
also spelt Berezino
Byerazino Belarus **43** J7
also spelt Berezino
Byerazynyaki Belarus **42** I9
Byers U.S.A. **180** F5
Byershty Belarus **42** F8
Byeshankovichy Belarus **43** K6
Byesville U.S.A. **176** D6
Byesyedz' *r.* Belarus **43** M9
Byfield Australia **149** F4
Byfield National Park Australia **149** F4
Bygdeå Sweden **44** M2
Byglandsfjord Norway **45** I4
Bykhaw Belarus **43** L8
also spelt Bykhov
Bykhov Belarus *see* **Bykhaw**
Bykle Norway **45** I4
Bykovo Rus. Fed. **41** H6
Bykovskiy Rus. Fed. **39** M2
Bylas U.S.A. **183** N8
Bylot Island Canada **165** L2
Byng Inlet Canada **173** M5
Bynoe *r.* Australia **149** D3
Bynoe Harbour Australia **150** E2
Byramgore Reef India **94** A4
also known as Chereapani
Byrd Glacier Antarctica **223** K1
Byrka Rus. Fed. **85** H1
Byrkjelo Norway **45** I3
Byrock Australia **147** E2
Byron *IL* U.S.A. **172** D8
Byron *ME* U.S.A. **177** O1
Byron Bay Australia **147** G2
Byron Island Kiribati *see* **Nikunau**
Byrranga, Gory *mts* Rus. Fed. **39** J2
Byryne Ukr. **43** O9
Byske Sweden **44** M2
Byskeälven *r.* Sweden **44** M2
Byssa *r.* Rus. Fed. **82** C1
Bystrá *mt.* Slovakia **49** Q6
Bystretsovo Rus. Fed. **43** J4
Bystřice nad Pernštejnem Czech Rep. **49** N6
Bystrinskiy Golets, Gora *mt.* Rus. Fed. **85** F1
Bystrovka Kyrg. *see* **Kemin**
Bystryy Tanyp *r.* Rus. Fed. **40** J5
Bystrzyca *r.* Poland **49** N4
Bystrzyca *r.* Poland **49** T4
Bytantay *r.* Rus. Fed. **39** N3
Bytča Slovakia **49** P6
Bytom Poland **49** P5
historically known as Beuthen
Bytosh' Rus. Fed. **43** P8
Bytów Poland **49** O1
Byumba Rwanda **126** F5
Byurgyutli Turkm. **102** C5
Byuzmeyin Turkm. **102** D5
also spelt Büzmeyin; *formerly spelt* Bezmein
Byxelkrok Sweden **45** L4
Byzantium Turkey *see* **İstanbul**
Bzura *r.* Poland **49** R3

↓ C

Ca, Sông *r.* Vietnam **78** D4
Caacupé Para. **201** F6
Caaguazú Para. **201** F6
Caaguazú, Cordillera de *hills* Para. **201** G6
Caála Angola **127** B8
formerly known as Robert Williams
Caapiranga Brazil **199** F5
Caapucú Para. **201** F6
Caarapó Brazil **203** A7
Caatiba Brazil **207** M2
Caatinga Brazil **207** H4
Caazapá Para. **201** F6
Cabaçal *r.* Brazil **201** F3
Cabaiguán Cuba **186** D2
Caballas Peru **200** B3
Caballo *mt.* Spain **55** H7
Caballococha Peru **198** D5
Cabana *Ancash* Peru **200** A2
Cabana *Ayacucho* Peru **200** B3
Cabanaconde Peru **200** C3
Cabañaquinta Spain **54** F1
Cabanatuan Phil. **74** B3
Cabanères *hill* France **50** H9
Cabano Canada **169** G4
Čabar Croatia **56** G3
Cabdul Qaadir Somalia **128** D2
Cabeceiras Brazil **206** G2
Cabeço Rainha *mt.* Port. **54** D5
Cabedelo Brazil **202** F3
Cabeza del Buey Arg. **205** C6
Cabeza del Buey Spain **54** F6
Cabeza de Vaca, Punta *pt* Chile **204** C2
Cabeza Prieta National Wildlife Refuge *nature res.* U.S.A. **183** K9
Cabezas Bol. **201** E4
Cabezo Gordo *hill* Spain **54** D7
Cabimas Venez. **198** D2
Cabinda Angola **127** B6
Cabinda *prov.* Angola **127** B6
Cabinet Inlet Antarctica **222** T2
Cabinet Mountains U.S.A. **180** D2
Cabingan *i.* Phil. **74** B5
Cabistra Turkey *see* **Ereğli**
Cable U.S.A. **172** B4
Cabo Brazil **202** F4
Cabo Blanco Arg. **205** D7
Cabo Delgado *prov.* Moz. **131** H2
Cabo Frio Brazil **203** D7
Cabo Frio, Ilha do *i.* Brazil **207** L10
Cabonga, Réservoir Canada **168** E4
Cabool U.S.A. **178** D4
Caboolture Australia **147** G1
Cabo Orange, Parque Nacional de *nat. park* Brazil **199** I4
Cabo Pantoja Peru **198** C5
Cabora Bassa, Lake *resr* Moz. **131** F2
also known as Cahora Bassa, Lago de
Cabo Raso Arg. **205** D7
Caborca Mex. **184** B2
Cabot Head Canada **173** L5
Cabot Strait Canada **169** I4
Cabo Verde *country* N. Atlantic Ocean *see* **Cape Verde**
Cabo Verde, Ilhas do *is* N. Atlantic Ocean **124** [inset]
Cabo Yubi Morocco *see* **Tarfaya**
Cabra *i.* Phil. **74** B3
Cabra Spain **54** G7
Cabra *r.* Spain **54** H7
Cabral Dom. Rep. **187** F3
Cabral, Serra do *mts* Brazil **203** C6
Cabras *Sardegna* Italy **57** A9
Cäbrayıl Azer. **107** F3
Cabred Arg. **204** F3
Cabreira *mt.* Port. **54** C3
Cabrera Dom. Rep. **187** F3
Cabrera *i.* Spain **55** N5
Cabri Canada **167** I5
Cabriel *r.* Spain **55** J5
Cabrobó Brazil **202** E4
Cabruta Venez. **199** E3
Cabugao Phil. **74** B2
Čabulja *mt.* Bos.-Herz. **56** J5
Cabullona Mex. **184** C2
Caçador Brazil **203** B8
Cacagoin China *see* **Qagca**
Cacahuatepec Mex. **185** F5
Čačak *Srbija* Yugo. **58** B5
Cacao Fr. Guiana **199** H3
Caçapava Brazil **207** H10
Caçapava do Sul Brazil **203** A9
Cacapon *r.* U.S.A. **176** G6
Cáceres Col. **198** C3
Caccia, Capo *c. Sardegna* Italy **57** A8
Cacém Port. **54** B6
Cáceres Brazil **201** F4
Cáceres Spain **54** E5
Cachal Bol. **200** D3
Cache *r.* U.S.A. **174** B4
Cacheau *r.* Guinea-Bissau **124** A3
Cache Creek Canada **166** F5
Cache Creek *r.* U.S.A. **182** C3
Cache la Poudre *r.* U.S.A. **180** F4
Cacheu Guinea-Bissau **124** A3
Cachi Arg. **204** D2
Cachi, Nevados de *mts* Arg. **200** D6
Cachimbo Brazil **202** A4
Cachimbo, Serra do *hills* Brazil **202** A4
Cachimo Angola **127** D7
Cachina *r.* Chile **204** C2
Cachingues Angola **127** C8
Cáchira Col. **198** C3
Cachoeira *Bahia* Brazil **202** E5
Cachoeira *Mato Grosso do Sul* Brazil **206** B6
Cachoeira Alta Brazil **206** C5
Cachoeira de Goiás Brazil **206** C3
Cachoeira do Arari Brazil **202** B2
Cachoeira do Sul Brazil **203** A9
Cachoeiras de Macacu Brazil **207** K9
Cachoeiro de Itapemirim Brazil **203** D7
Cachos, Punta de *pt* Chile **204** C2
Cachuela Esperanza Bol. **200** D2
Cacine Guinea-Bissau **124** B4
Cacolo Angola **127** C7
Caconda Angola **127** B8
Cacongo Angola **127** B6
formerly known as Guilherme Capelo *or* Landana
Cactus U.S.A. **179** B4
Cactus Range *mts* U.S.A. **183** G4
Caçu Brazil **206** B5
Cacuaco Angola **127** B7
Cacula Angola **127** B8
Caculama Angola **127** C7
Caculé Brazil **202** D5
Cacumba, Ilha *i.* Brazil **207** N4
Cacuso Angola **127** B7
Cadale Somalia **128** E4
Čadca Slovakia **49** P6
Caddabassa *i.* Eth. **128** D2
Caddo Lake U.S.A. **179** D5
Cadell *r.* Australia **148** B2
Cadell Creek *watercourse* Australia **149** D4
Cadenberge Germany **48** G2
Cadereyta Mex. **185** E3
Cadí, Serra de *mts* Spain **55** M2
Cadibarrawirracanna, Lake *salt flat* Australia **146** B2
Cadig Mountains Phil. **74** B3
Cadillac *Que.* Canada **173** O2
Cadillac *Sask.* Canada **167** J5
Cadillac U.S.A. **172** H6
Cadillal, Embalse el *resr* Arg. **204** D2
Cadiz Phil. **74** B4
Cádiz Spain **54** E8
historically known as Gades
Cadiz *CA* U.S.A. **183** I7
Cadiz *KY* U.S.A. **174** C4
Cadiz *OH* U.S.A. **176** E5
Cádiz, Bahía de *b.* Spain **54** E8
Cádiz, Golfo de *g.* Spain **54** D8
Cadiz Lake U.S.A. **183** I7
Cadomin Canada **167** G4
Cadott U.S.A. **172** B6
Cadotte *r.* Canada **167** G3
Cadoux Australia **151** B6
Caen France **50** F3
Caerdydd U.K. *see* **Cardiff**
Caere Italy *see* **Cerveteri**
Caerfyrddin U.K. *see* **Carmarthen**
Caergybi U.K. *see* **Holyhead**
Caernarfon U.K. **47** H10
formerly spelt Caernarvon; *historically known as* Segontia *or* Segontium
Caernarfon Bay U.K. **47** H10
Caernarfon Castle *tourist site* U.K. **47** H10
Caernarvon U.K. *see* **Caernarfon**
Caesaraugusta Spain *see* **Zaragoza**
Caesarea Alg. *see* **Cherchell**
Caesarea *tourist site* Israel **108** F5
Caesarea Cappadociae Turkey *see* **Kayseri**
Caesarea Philippi Syria *see* **Bāniyās**
Caesarodunum France *see* **Tours**
Caesaromagus U.K. *see* **Chelmsford**
Caeté Brazil **207** J6
Caeté *r.* Brazil **200** C2
Caetité Brazil **202** D5
Cafayate Arg. **204** D2
Cafelândia Brazil **206** D8
Caffa Ukr. *see* **Feodosiya**
Cafuini *r.* Brazil **199** G4
Cagayan *i.* Phil. **74** B4
Cagayan *r.* Phil. **74** B2
Cagayan de Oro Phil. **74** C4
Cagayan Islands Phil. **74** B4
Cagli Italy **56** E5
Cagliari *Sardegna* Italy **57** B9
historically known as Carales *or* Caralis
Cagliari, Golfo di *b. Sardegna* Italy **57** B9
Cagnano Varano Italy **56** H7
Cagnes-sur-Mer France **51** N9
Caguán *r.* Col. **198** C5
Caguas Puerto Rico **187** G3
Cahaba *r.* U.S.A. **175** C5
Cahama Angola **127** B9
Caha Mountains *hills* Rep. of Ireland **47** C12
Cahersiveen Rep. of Ireland **47** B12
also spelt Cahirciveen
Cahir Rep. of Ireland **47** E11
Cahirciveen Rep. of Ireland *see* **Cahersiveen**
Cahora Bassa, Lago de *resr* Moz. *see* **Cabora Bassa, Lake**
Cahore Point Rep. of Ireland **47** F11
Cahors France **50** H8
Cahuapanas Peru **198** B6
Cahul Moldova **58** J3
formerly spelt Kagul *or* Kakhul
Caia Moz. **131** G3
formerly known as Vila Fontes
Caia *r.* Port. **54** D6
Caia, Barragem do *resr* Port. **54** D5
Caiabis, Serra dos *hills* Brazil **201** F3
Caianda Angola **127** D7
Caiapó *r.* Brazil **206** B2
Caiapó, Serra do *mts* Brazil **206** A4
Caiapônia Brazil **206** B3
Caiaza Angola **127** D7
Caibarién Cuba **186** D2
Cai Bâu, Đao *i.* Vietnam **78** D3
Cai Be Vietnam **79** D6
Caicara Venez. **199** E3
Caicó Brazil **202** E3
Caicos Islands Turks and Caicos Is **187** F2
Caicos Passage Bahamas/Turks and Caicos Is **187** E2
Caidian China **87** E2
formerly known as Hanyang
Caidu China *see* **Shangcai**
Caifuche Angola **127** D7
Caiguna Australia **151** D7
Caihua China **87** D2
Cailloma Peru **200** C3
Caimanero, Laguna del *lag.* Mex. **184** D4
Caiman Point Phil. **74** A3
Caimbambo Angola **127** B8
Caimodorro *mt.* Spain **55** J4
Cainde Angola **127** B8
Căineni Romania **58** F3
Caineville U.S.A. **183** M3
Cainnyigoin China **86** B1
Cains Store U.S.A. **176** A8
Caipe Arg. **200** C6
Caird Coast Antarctica **222** W1
Cairngorm Mountains U.K. **46** I6
Cairns Australia **149** E3
Cairnsmore of Carsphairn *hill* U.K. **47** H8

▶ **Cairo** Egypt **121** F2
Capital of Egypt and 2nd most populous city in Africa. Also known as El Qâhira or Al Qāhirah or Le Caire.
world [cities] → 24–25
africa [locations] → 118–119

Cairo *GA* U.S.A. **175** C6
Cairo *IL* U.S.A. **174** B4
Cairo, Monte *mt.* Italy **56** F7
Cairo Montenotte Italy **56** A4
Caisleán an Bharraigh Rep. of Ireland *see* **Castlebar**
Caistor U.K. **47** L10
Caitou Angola **127** B8
Caiundo Angola **127** C8
Caiwarro Australia **147** E2
Caixi China **87** F3
Caiyuanzhen China *see* **Shengsi**
Caiza Bol. **200** D5
Caizi Hu *l.* China **87** F2
Cajabamba Peru **200** A1
Cajamarca Peru **200** A1
Cajamarca *dept* Peru **198** B6
Cajapió Brazil **202** C2
Cajarc France **50** H8
Cajari Brazil **202** C2
Cajatambo Peru **200** A2
Cajàzeiras Brazil **202** E3
Ćajetina *Srbija* Yugo. **58** A5
Cajidiocan Phil. **74** B3
Čajniče Bos.-Herz. **56** L5
Cajones, Cayos *is* Hond. **186** C3
Cajuata Bol. **200** D4
Cajuru Brazil **206** F8
Caka China **84** C4
Caka'lho China *see* **Yanjing**
Caka Yanhu *l.* China **84** C4
Čakovec Croatia **56** I2
Çal Turkey **106** B3
Çal Turkey *see* **Çukurca**
Cala S. Africa **133** L8
Cala *r.* Spain **54** E7
Calabar Nigeria **125** H5
Calabogie Canada **173** Q5
Calabozo Venez. **199** E2
Calabria *admin. reg.* Italy **57** I10
Calabria, Parco Nazionale della *nat. park* Italy **57** I9
Calaburra, Punta de *pt* Spain **54** G8
Calacoto Bol. **200** C4
Calaf Spain **55** M3
Calafat Romania **58** D5
Calafate Arg. **205** B8
Cala Figuera, Cap de *c.* Spain **55** N5
Calagnaan *i.* Phil. **74** B4
Calagua Mex. **184** C3
Calagua Islands Phil. **74** B3
Calagurris Spain *see* **Calahorra**
Calahorra Spain **55** J2
historically known as Calagurris
Calai Angola **127** C9
Calais France **51** H2
Calais U.S.A. **174** H2
Calalasteo, Sierra de *mts* Arg. **204** D2
Calama Brazil **201** E2
Calama Chile **200** C5
Calamajué Mex. **181** D7
Calamar Col. **198** C4
Calamarca Bol. **200** C4
Calamian Group *is* Phil. **74** A4
Calamocha Spain **55** J4
Călan Romania **58** E3
Calanaque Brazil **199** E5
Calañas Spain **54** E7
Calanda Spain **55** K4
Calandagan *i.* Phil. **74** B4
Calandula Angola **127** C7
also spelt Kalandula; *formerly known as* Duque de Bragança
Calang Indon. **76** A1
Calanscio Sand Sea *des.* Libya **120** D2
Calapan Phil. **74** B3
Calapas *pass* S. Africa **133** L8
Calar Alta *mt.* Spain **55** I7
Călăraşi Moldova **58** J1
formerly spelt Kalarash
Călăraşi Romania **58** I4
Cala Santa Galdana Spain **55** O5
Calatafimi *Sicilia* Italy **57** E11
Calatayud Spain **55** J3
Calau Germany **49** K4
Calauag Phil. **74** B3
Calavà, Capo *c. Sicilia* Italy **57** G10
Calavite Passage Phil. **74** B3
Calawit *i.* Phil. **74** A3
Calayan *i.* Phil. **74** B2
Calbayog Phil. **74** C3
Calbiga Phil. **74** C4
Calca Peru **200** C3
Calcanhar, Ponta do *pt* Brazil **202** F3
Calcasieu *r.* U.S.A. **179** D6
Calcasieu Lake U.S.A. **179** D6
Calceta Ecuador **198** A5
Calchaquí Arg. **204** E3
Calcutta India *see* **Kolkata**
Căldăraru Romania **58** F4
Caldas *dept* Col. **198** C3
Caldas da Rainha Port. **54** B5
Caldas de Mombuy Spain *see* **Caldes de Montbui**
Caldas Novas Brazil **206** E4
Caldeirão Brazil **201** D2
Calder *r.* Canada **167** G1
Caldera Chile **204** C2
Calderitas Mex. **185** H5
Caldervale Australia **149** E5
Caldes de Montbui Spain **55** N3
also spelt Caldas de Mombuy
Çaldıran Turkey **107** E3
Caldwell *ID* U.S.A. **180** C4
Caldwell *KS* U.S.A. **178** C4
Caldwell *OH* U.S.A. **176** D6
Caldwell *TX* U.S.A. **179** C6
Caledon Canada **173** N7
Caledon *r.* Lesotho/S. Africa **133** K7
Caledon S. Africa **132** D11
Caledon Bay Australia **148** C2
Caledonia *N.S.* Canada **169** H4
Caledonia *Ont.* Canada **173** N7
Caledonia *admin. div.* U.K. *see* **Scotland**
Caledonia *MI* U.S.A. **172** H8
Caledonia *MN* U.S.A. **174** B3
Caledonia *NY* U.S.A. **176** H3
Caledon Nature Reserve S. Africa **133** K6
Calella Spain **55** N3
Calen Australia **149** F4
Calenzana *Corse* France **51** O10
Calera U.S.A. **175** C5
Caleta el Cobre Chile **200** C6
Caleta Josefina Chile **205** C9
Caleta Lobos Chile **200** C5
Caleta Pabellón de Pica Chile **200** C5
Caleufú Arg. **204** D4
Calexico U.S.A. **183** J9
Calf of Man *i.* Isle of Man **47** H9
Calgary Canada **167** H5
Calhoun U.S.A. **174** C5
Cali Col. **198** B4
Çalı Turkey **59** J8
Calicoan *i.* Phil. **74** C4
Calicut India **94** B4
also known as Kozhikode
Caliente U.S.A. **183** J4
California U.S.A. **178** D4
▶ **California** *state* U.S.A. **182** D4
world [earthquakes] → 14–15
northamerica [environments] → 162–163
California, Golfo de *g.* Mex. *see* **California, Gulf of**
California, Gulf of Mex. **184** B2
also known as California, Golfo de; *historically known as* Cortes, Sea of
California Aqueduct U.S.A. **182** D5
California Aqueduct *canal* U.S.A. **182** C4
Cälilabad Azer. **107** G3
also spelt Dzhalalabad; *formerly known as* Astrakhan' Bazar
Calilegua Arg. **201** D5
Călimăneşti Romania **58** F3
Călimani, Munţii *mts* Romania **58** F1
Calingasta Arg. **204** C3
Calistoga U.S.A. **182** B3
Calitri Italy **56** H8
Calitzdorp S. Africa **132** F10
Çalkaya Turkey **108** B1
Calkiní Mex. **185** H4
Callabonna, Lake *salt flat* Australia **146** D2
Callabonna Creek *watercourse* Australia **146** D2
Callac France **50** C4
Callaghan U.S.A. **176** E8
Callaghan, Mount U.S.A. **183** H2
Callan Rep. of Ireland **47** E11
Callander Canada **168** E4
Callander U.K. **46** H7
Callands U.S.A. **176** F9
Callang Phil. **74** B2
Callao Peru **200** A3
Callao U.S.A. **183** K2
Callawa Aboriginal Reserve Australia **150** C4
Calles Mex. **185** F4
Callicoon U.S.A. **177** J4
Callide Australia **149** F5
Calling Lake Canada **167** H4
Calling Lake *l.* Canada **167** H4
Calliope Australia **149** F5
Callipolis Turkey *see* **Gallipoli**
Callosa d'En Sarrià Spain **55** K6
Callosa de Segura Spain **55** K6
Callum Canada **173** M4
Callyharra Springs Australia **151** A5
Calmar Canada **167** H4
Calmar U.S.A. **174** B3
Călmăţui *r.* Romania **58** G5
Călniştea *r.* Romania **58** G4
Calolziocorte Italy **56** B3
Caloosahatchee *r.* U.S.A. **175** D7
Calore *r.* Italy **56** G7
Calotmul Mex. **185** H4
Caloundra Australia **149** G5
Calovo Slovakia *see* **Veľký Meder**
Calpe Spain **55** L6
Calpulálpan Mex. **185** F5
Calstock Canada **168** C3
Caltagirone *Sicilia* Italy **57** G11
Caltanissetta *Sicilia* Italy **57** G11
Çaltıbozkır Turkey **108** E1
Calucinga Angola **127** C7
Caluire-et-Cuire France **51** K7
Calulo Angola **127** B7
Calumet U.S.A. **172** E3
Calunda Angola **127** D8
Calunga Angola **127** C9
Caluquembe Angola **127** B8
Calusa *i.* Phil. **74** B4
Caluula Somalia **128** F2
Caluula, Raas *pt* Somalia **128** F2
Calvert *r.* Australia **148** C3
Calvert Hills Australia **148** C3
Calvert Island Canada **166** D5
Calvert Range *hills* Australia **150** C4
Calvi *Corse* France **51** O10
Calvià Spain **55** N5
Calvinia S. Africa **132** D8
Calvitero *mt.* Spain **54** F4
Calzada de Calatrava Spain **54** H6
Cam *r.* U.K. **47** M11
Camabatela Angola **127** B7
Camacã Brazil **207** N2
Camaçari Brazil **202** E5
Camache Reservoir U.S.A. **182** D3
Camachigama *r.* Canada **168** E4
Camachigama, Lac *l.* Canada **173** Q3
Camacho Mex. **185** E3
Camacuio Angola **127** B8
Camacupa Angola **127** C8
formerly known as General Machado
Camaguán Venez. **199** E2
Camagüey Cuba **186** D2
Camagüey, Archipiélago de *is* Cuba **186** D2
Camah, Gunung *mt.* Malaysia **76** C1
Camaiú *r.* Brazil **199** G6
Camajuaní Cuba **186** D2
Camalan Turkey *see* **Gülek**
Camamu Brazil **202** E5
Camana Peru **200** B4
Camaná *r.* Peru **200** B4
Camanongue Angola **127** D7
formerly known as Vila Bugaço; *formerly spelt* Kamenongue
Camapuã Brazil **203** A6
Camaquã Brazil **203** B9
Camaquã *r.* Brazil **204** H3
Camăr Romania **58** D1
Camará Brazil **199** F5
Camarão Brazil **198** D4
Camararé *r.* Brazil **201** F3
Camargo Bol. **200** D5
Camargo Mex. **185** F3
Camargo, Parque Natural *nature res.* Mex. **185** F3
Camargue, Parc Naturel Régional de *nature res.* France **51** K9
Camarillo U.S.A. **182** E7
Camariñas Spain **54** B1
Camarón, Cabo *c.* Hond. **186** B4
Camarones Arg. **205** D7
Camarones, Bahía *b.* Arg. **205** D7
Camas U.S.A. **180** B3
Camas *r.* U.S.A. **180** D4
Camas Creek *r.* U.S.A. **180** D4
Ca Mau Vietnam **79** D6
formerly known as Quan Long
Camaxilo Angola **127** C7
Cambara Brazil **201** F4
Cambará Brazil **206** C10
Cambay India *see* **Khambhat**
Cambay, Gulf of India *see* **Khambhat, Gulf of**
Cambé Brazil **206** B10
▶ **Cambodia** *country* Asia **79** C5
formerly known as Kampuchea *or* Khmer Republic
asia [countries] → 64–67
Camborne U.K. **47** G13
Cambrai Australia **146** C3
Cambrai France **51** J2
Cambre Spain **54** C1
Cambria S. Africa **133** I10
Cambria *admin. div.* U.K. *see* **Wales**
Cambria U.S.A. **182** C6
Cambrian Mountains *hills* U.K. **47** I11
Cambridge Canada **168** D5
Cambridge N.Z. **152** J5
Cambridge U.K. **47** M11
Cambridge *IL* U.S.A. **174** B3
Cambridge *MA* U.S.A. **177** N3
Cambridge *MD* U.S.A. **177** I7
Cambridge *MN* U.S.A. **174** A2
Cambridge *NY* U.S.A. **177** L2
Cambridge *OH* U.S.A. **176** D5
Cambridge *VT* U.S.A. **177** M1
Cambridge *WI* U.S.A. **172** D7
Cambridge Bay Canada **165** I3
Cambridge Gulf Australia **150** E2
Cambridge Springs U.S.A. **176** E4
Cambrien, Lac *l.* Canada **169** G1
Cambrils Spain **55** M3
Cambuí Brazil **207** G9
Cambulo Angola **127** D6
Cambundi-Catembo Angola **127** C7
formerly known as Nova Gaia
Cambuquira Brazil **207** H8
Cambutal, Cerro *mt.* Panama **186** C6
Cam Co *l.* China **89** C5
Camden Australia **147** F3
Camden *AL* U.S.A. **175** C5
Camden *AR* U.S.A. **179** D5
Camden *DE* U.S.A. **177** J6
Camden *ME* U.S.A. **177** P1
Camden *NC* U.S.A. **177** I9
Camden *NJ* U.S.A. **177** J6
Camden *NY* U.S.A. **177** J2
Camden *OH* U.S.A. **176** A6
Camden *SC* U.S.A. **175** D5
Camden *TN* U.S.A. **174** B4
Camden Bay U.S.A. **164** E2
Camden Sound *sea chan.* Australia **150** D2
Camdenton U.S.A. **178** D4
Cameia Angola **127** D7
Cameia, Parque Nacional da *nat. park* Angola **127** D7
also spelt Kameia, Parque Nacional de
Çameli Turkey **59** K11
Cameron *AZ* U.S.A. **183** M6
Cameron *LA* U.S.A. **179** D6
Cameron *MO* U.S.A. **178** D4
Cameron *TX* U.S.A. **179** C6
Cameron *WI* U.S.A. **172** B5
Cameron *WV* U.S.A. **176** E6
Cameron Highlands Malaysia **76** C1
Cameron Highlands *mts* Malaysia **76** C1
Cameron Hills Canada **167** G3
Cameron Island Canada **165** I2
Cameron Mountains N.Z. **153** A14
Cameron Park U.S.A. **182** D3
▶ **Cameroon** *country* Africa **125** H5
spelt Cameroun *in French*
africa [countries] → 114–117
Cameroun *country* Africa *see* **Cameroon**
Cameroun, Mont *vol.* Cameroon **125** H5
Cametá *Amazonas* Brazil **199** E6
Cametá *Pará* Brazil **202** B2
Camfield *r.* Australia **148** A3
Çamiçi Gölü *l.* Turkey **106** A3
Camiguin *i.* Phil. **74** B2
Camiguin *i.* Phil. **74** C4
Camiling Phil. **74** B3
Camilla U.S.A. **175** C6
Camiña Chile **200** C4
Camiranga Brazil **202** C2
Camiri Bol. **201** E5
Camisea Peru **200** B3
Camisea *r.* Peru **200** B2
Camissombo Angola **127** D7
formerly known as Veríssimo Sarmento

index

C

Cammarata, Monte *mt. Sicilia* Italy **57** F11
Cammin Poland *see* **Kamień Pomorski**
Camocim Brazil **202** D2
Camooweal Australia **148** C3
Camooweal Caves National Park Australia **148** C4
Camopi Brazil **199** H4
Camorta *i.* India **95** G4
Camotes Sea *g.* Phil. **74** C4
Campagna Italy **57** H8
Campamento Hond. **186** B4
Campana, Isla *i.* Chile **205** B8
Campanário *Mato Grosso do Sul* Brazil **201** G5
Campanário *Minas Gerais* Brazil **203** D6
Campanella, Punta *pt* Italy **57** G8
Campania *admin. reg.* Italy **56** G7
Campania Island Canada **166** D4
Campanquiz, Cerro *hills* Peru **198** B6
Campaspe *r.* Australia **149** E4
Campbell S. Africa **132** H5
Campbell U.S.A. **176** E4
Campbell, Cape N.Z. **153** I9
Campbellford Canada **168** E4
Campbell Hill *hill* U.S.A. **176** B5
Campbell Island Myanmar **79** B6
Campbell Island N.Z. **220** F9
also known as Motu Ihupuku
Campbell Lake Canada **167** J2
Campbell Range *hills* Australia **150** D2
Campbell River Canada **166** E5
Campbellsport U.S.A. **172** E7
Campbellstown U.S.A. **176** A6
Campbellsville U.S.A. **174** C4
Campbellton Canada **169** H4
Campbelltown Australia **147** F3
Campbell Town Australia **147** E5
Campbeltown U.K. **46** G8
Camp Creek U.S.A. **176** D8
Campeche Mex. **185** H5
Campeche *state* Mex. **185** H5
Campeche, Bahía de *g.* Mex. **185** G5
Campechuela Cuba **186** D2
Câmpeni Romania **58** E2
formerly spelt Cîmpeni
Camperdown Australia **147** D4
Camperdown S. Africa **133** O6
Campestre Brazil **207** G8
Campia U.S.A. **172** B5
Câmpia Turzii Romania **58** E2
formerly spelt Cîmpia Turzii
Campiglia Marittima Italy **56** C5
Campillos Spain **54** G7
Campina Brazil **201** H1
Câmpina Romania **58** G3
formerly spelt Cîmpina
Campinaçu Brazil **202** B5
Campina Grande Brazil **202** F3
Campinas Brazil **206** F9
Campina Verde Brazil **206** D6
Camplong Indon. **75** B5
Campo Cameroon **125** H6
Campo *r.* Cameroon *see* **Ntem**
Campo, Réserve de *nature res.* Cameroon **125** H6
Campoalegre Col. **198** C4
Campo Alegre de Lourdes Brazil **202** D4
Campobasso Italy **56** G7
Campobello di Licata *Sicilia* Italy **57** F11
Campobello di Mazara *Sicilia* Italy **57** E11
Campo Belo Brazil **203** C7
Campo de Criptana Spain **55** H5
Campo de Diauarum Brazil **202** A4
Campodolcino Italy **56** B2
Campo Erê Brazil **203** A8
Campo Esperanza Para. **201** F5
Campo Florido Brazil **206** E6
Campo Formoso Brazil **202** D4
Campo Gallo Arg. **204** E2
Campo Grande *Amazonas* Brazil **201** F2
Campo Grande *Mato Grosso do Sul* Brazil **203** A7
Campolândia Brazil **206** B3
Campo Largo Brazil **203** B8
Campo Maior Brazil **202** D3
Campo Maior Port. **54** D5
Campomarino Italy **56** H7
Campo Mourão Brazil **206** A11
Campo Novo Brazil **203** A8
Campos Brazil **203** D7
Campos Altos Brazil **203** C6
Campos Belos Brazil **202** C5
Campos del Puerto Spain **55** O5
Campos do Jordão Brazil **207** H9
Campo Serio Peru **198** C5
Campos Gerais Brazil **207** H8
Campos Novos Paulista Brazil **206** D9
Campos Sales Brazil **202** D3
Campo Tencia *mt.* Switz. **51** O6
Campo Troco Col. **199** D3
Camprodon Spain **55** N2
Campton U.S.A. **176** B8
Câmpulung Romania **58** G3
formerly spelt Cîmpulung
Câmpulung Moldovenesc Romania **41** C7
formerly spelt Cîmpulung Moldovenesc
Campuya Peru **198** C5
Campuya *r.* Peru **198** C5
Camp Verde U.S.A. **183** M7
Cam Ranh Vietnam **79** E6
Camrose Canada **167** H4
Camsell Lake Canada **167** I2
Camsell Range *mts* Canada **166** F2
Camulodunum U.K. *see* **Colchester**
Çamuzkışlası Turkey **109** H1
Çan Turkey **106** A2
Canaan *r.* Canada **169** H4
Canaan Trin. and Tob. **187** H5
Canaan U.S.A. **177** L3
Canaan Peak U.S.A. **183** M4
Canabrava Brazil **207** H4
Cana Brava *r.* Brazil **202** A3
Cana Brava, Serra da *hills* Brazil **207** N3
Canabungan *i.* Phil. **74** A4
Canacona India **94** B3

▶**Canada** *country* N. America **164** G3
Largest country in North America and 2nd in the world. 3rd most populous country in North America.
world [countries] ▶ 10–11
world [changes] ▶ 20–21
northamerica [countries] ▶ 158–159

Cañada Honda Arg. **204** C3
Canadian U.S.A. **179** B5
Canadian *r.* U.S.A. **179** D5
Cañadón de las Vacas Arg. **205** C8
Cañadon Grande, Sierra *mts* Arg. **205** C7
Canaima, Parque Nacional *nat. park* Venez. **199** F3
Canajoharie U.S.A. **177** K3
Çanakkale Turkey **106** A2
formerly known as Chanak
Çanakkale *prov.* Turkey **59** H8
Çanakkale Boğazı *strait* Turkey *see* **Dardanelles**
Canal Flats Canada **167** H5
Canals Spain **55** K6
Canal Winchester U.S.A. **176** C6
Canamari Brazil **200** C2
Canandaigua U.S.A. **177** H3
Canandaigua Lake U.S.A. **177** H3
Cananea Mex. **184** C2
Cananéia Brazil **203** C8
Canapiare, Cerro *hill* Col. **198** D4
Canápolis Brazil **206** D5
Cañar Ecuador **198** B5
Cañar *prov.* Ecuador **198** B5
Canarana Brazil **202** A5
Canarias, Islas *is* N. Atlantic Ocean **122** A3
also known as Canary Islands
Canarias, Islas *terr.* N. Atlantic Ocean *see* **Canary Islands**
Canary Islands *is* N. Atlantic Ocean *see* **Canarias, Islas**

▶**Canary Islands** *terr.* N. Atlantic Ocean **122** A3
Autonomous Community of Spain. Also known as Canarias, Islas.
africa [countries] ▶ 114–117

Canasayab Mex. **185** H5
Canaseraga U.S.A. **176** H3
Canastota U.S.A. **177** J2
Canastra, Serra da *mts* Brazil **206** G6
Canatlán Mex. **184** D3
Canaveral, Cape U.S.A. **175** D6
formerly known as Kennedy, Cape
Canaveral National Seashore *nature res.* U.S.A. **175** D6
Canavieiras Brazil **202** E5
Cañazas Panama **186** C5
Canbelego Australia **147** E2

▶**Canberra** Australia **147** F3
Capital of Australia.

Canby *CA* U.S.A. **180** B4
Canby *MN* U.S.A. **178** C2
Cancale France **50** E4
Canchas Chile **204** C2
Canchyuaya, Cerros de *hills* Peru **198** C6
Cancún Mex. **185** I4
Çandar Turkey *see* **Kastamonu**
Candarave Peru **200** C4
Çandarlı Turkey **106** A3
Candás Spain **54** F1
Candé France **50** E5
Candeias Brazil **203** C7
Candeias *r.* Brazil **201** E2
Candela *r.* Mex. **179** B7
Candelaria Arg. **204** D2
Candelaria Mex. **185** H5
Candelaria Venez. **199** E3
Candelaro *r.* Italy **56** H7
Candeleda Spain **54** F4
Candelo Australia **147** F4
Candia Greece *see* **Iraklion**
Cândido Mendes Brazil **202** C2
Cândido Sales Brazil **207** L2
Çandır Turkey **106** C2
Candle Lake Canada **167** J4
Candle Lake *l.* Canada **167** J4
Candlewood, Lake U.S.A. **177** L4
Cando U.S.A. **178** C1
Candon Phil. **74** B2
Candover S. Africa **133** P4
Cândrelu, Vârful *mt.* Romania **58** E3
Cane *r.* Australia **150** A4
Canea Greece *see* **Chania**
Canela Baja Chile **204** C3
Canelli Italy **56** A4
Canelones Uruguay **204** F4
Canelos Ecuador **198** B5
Cañete Chile **204** B5
Caney U.S.A. **178** D4
Caney *r.* U.S.A. **178** D4
Cangalha Brazil **206** G3
Cangallo Peru **200** B3
Cangamba Angola **127** C8
formerly known as Vila de Aljustrel
Cangandala Angola **127** C7
Cangandala, Parque Nacional de *nat. park* Angola **127** C7
also spelt Kangandala, Parque Nacional de
Çangarâfa Mauritania **124** B2
Cangas Spain **54** C2
Cangas del Narcea Spain **54** E1
Cango Caves S. Africa **132** G10
Cangola Angola **127** B7
Cangombe Angola **127** D8
Cangshan China **87** F1
also known as Bianzhuang
Canguaretama Brazil **202** F3
Canguçu Brazil **204** G3
Canguçu, Serra do *hills* Brazil **204** G3
Cangzhou China **85** H4
Caniapiscau Canada **169** G2
Caniapiscau *r.* Canada **169** G1
Caniapiscau, Lac *l.* Canada **169** G2
Caniçado Moz. *see* **Guija**
Canicatti *Sicilia* Italy **57** F11
Canicattini Bagni *Sicilia* Italy **57** H11
Canigao Channel Phil. **74** C4
Canigou, Pic du *mt.* France **51** I10
Caniles Spain **55** I7
Canim Lake Canada **166** F5
Canindé *Ceará* Brazil **202** E3
Canindé *Pará* Brazil **202** C2
Canindé *r.* Brazil **202** D3
Canino Italy **56** D6
Canisteo U.S.A. **176** H3
Canisteo *r.* U.S.A. **176** H3
Canisteo Peninsula Antarctica **222** R2
Canister Falls Guyana **199** G3
Cañitas de Felipe Pescador Mex. **185** E4
Çankırı Turkey **106** C2
historically known as Gangra
Cankuzo Burundi **126** F5
Canlaon Phil. **74** B4
Canna *i.* U.K. **46** F6
Cannanore India **94** B4
also known as Kannur
Cannanore Islands India **94** B4
Cannes France **51** N9
Cannich U.K. **46** H6
Canning Hill *hill* Australia **151** B6
Cannobio Italy **56** A2
Cannonball *r.* U.S.A. **178** B2
Cannon Beach U.S.A. **180** B3
Cannon Rocks S. Africa **133** K10
Cannonsburg U.S.A. **176** C7
Cann River Australia **147** F4
Canoa Ecuador **198** A5
Canoas Brazil **203** B9
Caño Colorado Col. **198** D4
Caño Colorado Venez. **187** H5
Canoeiros Brazil **203** C6
Canoe Lake Canada **167** I4
Canoe Lake *l.* Canada **167** I4
Canoinhas Brazil **203** B8
Canon City U.S.A. **181** F5
Cañón del Río Blanco, Parque Nacional *nat. park* Mex. **185** F5
Cañón del Sumidero, Parque Nacional *nat. park* Mex. **185** G5
Cañon Largo *watercourse* U.S.A. **181** F5
Canoochia *r.* U.S.A. **175** D6
Canoona Australia **149** F4
Canora Canada **167** K5
Caño Riecito Venez. **198** D3
Canosa di Puglia Italy **56** I7
historically known as Canusium
Canouan *i.* St Vincent **187** H4
Canowindra Australia **147** F3
Cansado W. Sahara **122** A5
Canso Canada **169** I4
Canso, Cape Canada **169** I4
Canso, Strait of Canada **169** I4
Canta Peru **200** A2
Cantabria *aut. comm.* Spain **54** G1
Cantabrian Mountains Spain *see* **Cantábrica, Cordillera**
Cantabrian Sea Spain *see* **Cantábrico, Mar**
Cantábrica, Cordillera *mts* Spain **54** G1
English form Cantabrian Mountains
Cantábrico, Mar *sea* Spain **54** E1
English form Cantabrian Sea
Cantagalo Brazil **199** G6
Cantalejo Spain **54** H3
Cantanhede Port. **54** C4
Canteras *hill* Spain **55** I5
Canterbury *admin. reg.* N.Z. **153** G11
Canterbury U.K. **47** N12
historically known as Cantuaria *or* Durovernum
Canterbury Bight *b.* N.Z. **153** F12
Canterbury Plains N.Z. **153** F11
Cân Thơ Vietnam **79** D6
Cantil U.S.A. **182** G6
Cantilan Phil. **74** C4
Cantillana Spain **54** F7
Canto do Buriti Brazil **202** D4
Canton China *see* **Guangzhou**
Canton *GA* U.S.A. **175** C5
Canton *IL* U.S.A. **174** B3
Canton *MO* U.S.A. **174** B3
Canton *MS* U.S.A. **175** B5
Canton *NY* U.S.A. **177** J1
Canton *OH* U.S.A. **176** D5
Canton *PA* U.S.A. **177** I4
Canton *SD* U.S.A. **178** C3
Canton *TX* U.S.A. **179** D5
Canton *WI* U.S.A. **172** B5
Canton Island Kiribati *see* **Kanton**
Cantu *r.* Brazil **201** G6
Cantù Italy **56** B3
Cantu, Serra do *hills* Brazil **203** B8
Cantuaria U.K. *see* **Canterbury**
Canudos Brazil **202** E4
Cañuelas Arg. **204** F4
Canumã *Amazonas* Brazil **199** F6
Canumã *Amazonas* Brazil **199** G6
Canunda National Park Australia **146** D4
Canusium Italy *see* **Canosa di Puglia**
Canutama Brazil **199** E6
Canvastown N.Z. **152** H9
Canwood Canada **167** J4
Cany-Barville France **50** G3
Cànyoles *r.* Spain **55** K5
Canyon Canada **166** B2
Canyon U.S.A. **179** B5
Canyon City U.S.A. **180** C3
Canyon Creek *r.* U.S.A. **182** C2
Canyondam U.S.A. **182** C1
Canyon de Chelly National Monument *nat. park* U.S.A. **183** O5
Canyon Ferry Lake U.S.A. **180** E3
Canyon Lake U.S.A. **183** M8
Canyonlands National Park U.S.A. **183** O3
Canyon Ranges *mts* Canada **166** E2
Canyonville U.S.A. **180** B4
Canzar Angola **127** D6
Cao *r.* China **83** B4
Cao Băng Vietnam **78** D3
Caocheng China *see* **Caoxian**
Caohe China *see* **Qichun**
Caohu China **88** D3
Caojiahe China *see* **Qichun**
Caojian China **86** A3
Caombo Angola **127** C7
Cao Nguyên Đăc Lăc *plat.* Vietnam **79** E5
Caorle Italy **56** E3
Caoxian China **87** E1
also known as Caocheng
Caozhou China *see* **Heze**
Cap *i.* Phil. **74** B5
Capac U.S.A. **173** K7
Capaccio Italy **57** H8
Capaci *Sicilia* Italy **57** F10
Cap-à-Foux *c.* Haiti **187** E3
Capaia Angola **127** D7
Çapakçur Turkey *see* **Bingöl**
Capalulu, Selat *sea chan.* Indon. **75** C3
Capana Brazil **198** D5
Capanaparo *r.* Venez. **199** E3
Capanema Brazil **202** C2
Capanne, Monte *mt.* Italy **56** C6
Capão Bonito Brazil **206** E11
Caparaó, Serra do *mts* Brazil **207** L7
Caparo *r.* Venez. **198** D3
Capas Phil. **74** B3
Căpăţânii, Munţii *mts* Romania **58** E3
Capatárida Venez. **198** D2
Cap-aux-Meules Canada **169** I4
Capbreton France **50** E9
Cap-Chat Canada **169** H3
Cap-de-la-Madeleine Canada **169** F4
Capdenac-Gare France **51** I8
Capdepera Spain **55** O5
Cape *r.* Australia **149** E4
Cape Arid National Park Australia **151** C7
Cape Bald Canada *see* **Cap-Pelé**
Cape Barren Island Australia **147** F5
Cape Borda Australia **146** C3
Cape Bougainville Aboriginal Reserve Australia **150** D2
Cape Breton Highlands National Park Canada **169** I4
Cape Breton Island Canada **169** I4
historically known as Royale, Île
Cape Charles Canada **169** K2
Cape Charles U.S.A. **177** I8
Cape Coast Ghana **125** E5
also known as Cape Coast Castle
Cape Coast Castle Ghana *see* **Cape Coast**
Cape Cod Bay U.S.A. **177** O4
Cape Cod National Seashore *nature res.* U.S.A. **174** G3
Cape Coral U.S.A. **175** D7
Cape Crawford Australia **148** B3
Cape Croker Canada **173** L6
Cape Dorset Canada **165** L3
Cape Elizabeth U.S.A. **177** O2
Cape Fear *r.* U.S.A. **174** E5
Cape Gantheaume Conservation Park *nature res.* Australia **146** C3
Cape George Canada **169** I4
Cape Girardeau U.S.A. **174** B4
Cape Juby Morocco *see* **Tarfaya**
Cape Krusenstern National Monument *nat. park* U.S.A. **164** C3
Capel Australia **151** A7
Cape Le Grand National Park Australia **151** C7
Capelinha Brazil **203** D6
Capella Australia **149** F4
Capelle aan de IJssel Neth. **48** B4
Capelongo Angola **127** B8
formerly known as Folgares
Capelongo Angola *see* **Kuvango**
Cape May U.S.A. **177** K7
Cape May Court House U.S.A. **177** K6
Cape May Point U.S.A. **177** K7
Cape Melville National Park Australia **149** E2
Capenda-Camulemba Angola **127** C7
Cape of Good Hope Nature Reserve S. Africa **132** C11
Cape Palmerston National Park Australia **149** F4
Cape Range *hills* Australia **150** A4
Cape Range National Park Australia **150** A4
Cape Romain National Wildlife Refuge *nature res.* U.S.A. **175** E5
Cape Sable Island Canada **169** H5
Cape St George Canada **169** J3
Capesterre Guadeloupe **187** H3

▶**Cape Town** S. Africa **132** C10
Legislative capital of South Africa. Also known as Kaapstad.
world [countries] ▶ 10–11
africa [locations] ▶ 118–119

Cape Tribulation National Park Australia **149** E2
Cape Upstart National Park Australia **149** E3
▶**Cape Verde** *country* N. Atlantic Ocean **124** [inset]
also known as Cabo Verde
africa [countries] ▶ 114–117
Cape Vincent U.S.A. **177** I1
Cape Wolfe Canada **169** H4
Cape York Peninsula Australia **149** D2
Cap-Haïtien Haiti **187** E3
Capibara Venez. **199** E4
Capim Brazil **202** C2
Capim *r.* Brazil **202** B2
Capinópolis Brazil **206** D5
Capinota Bol. **200** D4
Capitán Arturo Prat *research station* Antarctica **222** U2
Capitão Enéas Brazil **207** J3
Capitari Brazil **199** F6

▶**Capitol Hill** N. Mariana Is **73** K3
Capital of the Northern Mariana Islands, on Saipan.

Capitol Reef National Park U.S.A. **183** M3
Capivara, Represa *resr* Brazil **206** B9
Capivari *r. Bahia* Brazil **202** E5
Capivari *r. São Paulo* Brazil **206** F9
Capixaba Brazil **202** D4
Čapljina Bos.-Herz. **56** J5
Capnoyan *i.* Phil. **74** B4
Capoche *r.* Moz./Zambia **131** G2
Capo d'Orlando *Sicilia* Italy **57** G10
Capoeira Brazil **199** G6
Capoeiras, Cachoeira das *waterfall* Brazil **199** G6
Capoterra *Sardegna* Italy **57** A9
Cap-Pelé Canada **169** H4
formerly known as Cape Bald
Capraia, Isola di *i.* Italy **56** B5
Caprera, Isola *i. Sardegna* Italy **56** B7
Capri Italy **57** G8
Capri, Isola di *i.* Italy **57** G8
Capricorn, Cape Australia **149** F4
Capricorn Channel Australia **149** F4
Capricorn Group *atolls* Australia **149** G4
Caprivi *admin. reg.* Namibia **130** D3
Caprivi Game Park *nature res.* Namibia **130** D3
Caprivi Strip *reg.* Namibia **130** D2
Capsa Tunisia *see* **Gafsa**
Captain Cook U.S.A. **181** [inset] Z2
Captieux France **50** F8
Capuava Brazil **206** F11
Capuna Angola **127** C8
Capunda Cavilongo Angola **127** B8
formerly known as Olivença-a-Nova
Caqueta *dept* Col. **198** C4
Caquetá *r.* Col. **198** D5
Cáqueza Col. **198** C3
Carabao *i.* Phil. **74** B3
Carabaya, Cordillera de *mts* Peru **200** C3
Carabinani *r.* Brazil **199** F5
Carabobo *state* Venez. **199** E2
Caracal Romania **58** F4
Caracarai Brazil **199** F4

▶**Caracas** Venez. **199** E2
Capital of Venezuela.

Caracol *Mato Grosso do Sul* Brazil **201** F5
Caracol *Piauí* Brazil **202** D4
Caracol *Rondônia* Brazil **201** D2
Caracolí Col. **187** E5
Caracollo Bol. **200** D4
Caraga Phil. **74** C5
Caragabal Australia **147** E3
Caraguatatuba Brazil **207** H10
Carahue Chile **204** B5
Caraí Brazil **207** L4
Caraiva Brazil **207** N3
Carajari Brazil **199** H6
Carajás Brazil **202** B3
Carajás, Serra dos *hills* Brazil **199** I6
Carales *Sardegna* Italy *see* **Cagliari**
Caralis *Sardegna* Italy *see* **Cagliari**
Caramoan Peninsula Phil. **74** B3
Caramulo *mt.* Port. **54** C4
Caranavi Bol. **200** D3
Carandaí Brazil **203** D7
Carandaiti Bol. **201** E5
Carandazal Brazil **201** F4
Carangola Brazil **203** D7
Caransebeş Romania **58** D3
Carapajó Brazil **202** B2
Cara Paraná *r.* Col. **198** C5
Carapeguá Para. **201** F6
Carapelle *r.* Italy **56** H7
Carappee Hill *hill* Australia **146** C3
Caraquet Canada **169** H4
Caráquez Ecuador **198** A5
Carare *r.* Col. **198** C3
Caraşova Romania **58** C3
Carat, Tanjung *pt* Indon. **76** D3
Caratasca Hond. **186** C4
Caratasca, Laguna *lag.* Hond. **186** C4
Caratinga Brazil **203** D6
Caratué *r.* Col. **198** D5
Carauari Brazil **199** E6
Caraúbas Brazil **202** E3
Carauná *mt.* Brazil *see* **Grande, Serra**
Caravaca de la Cruz Spain **55** J6
Caravelas Brazil **203** E6
Caravelí Peru **200** B3
Carballiño Spain **54** C2
Carballo Spain **54** C1
Carberry Canada **167** L5
Carbó Mex. **184** C2
Carbon, Cap *c.* Alg. **55** K9
Carbonara, Capo *c. Sardegna* Italy **57** B9
Carbondale *CO* U.S.A. **180** F5
Carbondale *IL* U.S.A. **174** B4
Carbondale *PA* U.S.A. **177** J4
Carbonear Canada **169** K4
Carboneras Spain **55** J8
Carbonero El Mayor Spain **54** G3
Carbonia *Sardegna* Italy **57** A9
Carbonita Brazil **203** D6
Carbonne France **50** H9
Carcaixent Spain **55** K5
Carcajou Canada **167** G3
Carcajou *r.* Canada **166** D1
Carcaliu Romania **58** J3
Carcar Phil. **74** B4
Carcare Italy **56** A4
Carcassonne France **51** I9
Carcastillo Spain **55** J2
Carchi *prov.* Ecuador **198** B4
Carcross Canada **166** C2
Çardak Turkey **59** K11
Cardamomes, Chaîne des *mts* Cambodia *see* **Cardamom Range**
Cardamom Mountains Cambodia *see* **Cardamom Range**
Cardamom Range *mts* Cambodia **79** C5
also known as Cardamom Chain *or* Cardamomes, Chaîne des *or* Cardamom Mountains *or* Banthat *or* Krâvanh, Chuŏr Phnum
Cardamon Hills India **94** C4
Cardeña Spain **54** G6
Cárdenas Cuba **186** C2
Cárdenas *San Luis Potosí* Mex. **185** F4
Cárdenas *Tabasco* Mex. **185** G5
Cardenyabba *watercourse* Australia **147** D2
Çardi Turkey *see* **Harmancık**
Cardiel, Lago *l.* Arg. **205** C8

▶**Cardiff** U.K. **47** I12
Capital of Wales. Also spelt Caerdydd.

Cardiff U.S.A. **177** I6
Cardigan U.K. **47** H11
also known as Aberteifi
Cardigan Bay U.K. **47** H11
Cardinal Canada **177** J1
Cardinal Lake Canada **167** G3
Cardington U.S.A. **176** C5
Cardón, Cerro *hill* Mex. **184** B3
Cardona Spain **55** M3
Cardona Uruguay **204** F4
Cardoner *r.* Spain **55** M3
Cardoso Brazil **206** D7
Cardoso, Ilha do *i.* Brazil **203** C8
Cardrona N.Z. **153** D12
Cardston Canada **167** H5
Cardwell Australia **149** E3
Careaçu Brazil **207** H9
Careen Lake Canada **167** I3
Carega, Cima *mt.* Italy **56** D3
Carei Romania **49** T8
Careiro Brazil **199** G5
Careiro do Castanho Brazil **199** F5
Carén Chile **204** C3
Carentan France **50** E3
Carey U.S.A. **176** B5
Carey, Lake *salt flat* Australia **151** C6
Carey Downs Australia **151** A5
Carey Lake Canada **167** K2
Cargados Carajos Islands Mauritius **218** L7
Carhaix-Plouguer France **50** C4
Carhuamayo Peru **200** A2
Carhué Arg. **204** E5
Cariacica Brazil **203** D7
Cariaco Venez. **187** H5
Cariamanga Ecuador **198** B6
Cariango Angola **127** B7
Cariati Italy **57** I9
Caribbean Sea N. Atlantic Ocean **171** J8
Cariboo Mountains Canada **166** F4
Caribou *r. Man.* Canada **167** M3
Caribou *r. N.W.T.* Canada **166** E2
Caribou U.S.A. **174** G2
Caribou Island Canada **172** H3
Caribou Islands Canada **167** H2
Caribou Mountains Canada **167** H3
Carichic Mex. **184** D3
Carigara Phil. **74** C4
Carigara Bay Phil. **74** C4
Carignan France **51** L3
Carinda Australia **147** E2
Cariñena Spain **55** J3
Carinhanha Brazil **202** D5
Carinhanha *r.* Brazil **202** D5
Caripande Angola **127** D8
Cariparé Brazil **202** C4
Caripe Venez. **199** F2
Caripito Venez. **199** F2
Cariris Novos, Serra dos *hills* Brazil **202** D3
Caris *r.* Venez. **199** F2
Caritianas Brazil **201** E2
Carlabhagh U.K. *see* **Carloway**
Carleton U.S.A. **173** J8
Carleton, Mount *hill* Canada **169** H4
Carleton Place Canada **168** E4
Carletonville S. Africa **133** L3
Carlin U.S.A. **183** H1
Carlindie Aboriginal Reserve Australia **150** B4
Carlinville U.S.A. **174** B4
Carlisle U.K. **47** J9
Carlisle *KY* U.S.A. **176** A7
Carlisle *NY* U.S.A. **177** K3
Carlisle *PA* U.S.A. **177** H5
Carlisle Bridge S. Africa **133** K10
Carlisle Lakes *salt flat* Australia **151** D6
Carlit, Pic *mt.* France **50** H10
Carloforte *Sardegna* Italy **57** A9
Carlópolis Brazil **206** D10
Carlos Casares Arg. **204** E4
Carlos Chagas Brazil **203** D6
Carlos Tejedor Arg. **204** E4
Carlow Rep. of Ireland **47** F11
also spelt Ceatharlach
Carloway U.K. **46** F5
also spelt Carlabhagh
Carlsbad Czech Rep. *see* **Karlovy Vary**
Carlsbad *CA* U.S.A. **183** G8
Carlsbad *NM* U.S.A. **181** F6
Carlsbad *TX* U.S.A. **179** B6
Carlsbad Caverns National Park U.S.A. **181** F6
Carlson Inlet Antarctica **222** S1
Carlton U.S.A. **174** A2
Carlton Hills S. Africa **133** I8
Carlyle Canada **167** K5
Carlyle U.S.A. **174** B4
Carlyle Lake U.S.A. **174** B4
Carmacks Canada **166** B2
Carmagnola Italy **51** N8
Carman Canada **167** L5
Carmana Iran *see* **Kermān**
Carmarthen U.K. **47** H12
also known as Caerfyrddin
Carmarthen Bay U.K. **47** H12
Carmaux France **51** I8
Carmel *IN* U.S.A. **174** C4
Carmel *ME* U.S.A. **177** P1
Carmel, Mount *hill* Israel **108** G5
also known as Har Karmel
Carmel-by-the-Sea U.S.A. **182** C5
Carmel Head U.K. **47** H10
Carmelita Guat. **185** H5
Carmelo Uruguay **204** F4
Carmel Valley U.S.A. **182** C5
Carmen Col. **198** C2
Carmen *r.* Mex. **184** D2
Carmen Phil. **74** C4
Carmen Uruguay **204** F4
Carmen, Isla *i.* Mex. **184** C3
Carmen, Isla del *i.* Mex. **185** H5
Carmen Alto Chile **200** C5
Carmen de Areco Arg. **204** F4
Carmen del Paraná Para. **201** F6
Carmen de Patagones Arg. **204** E6
Carmi U.S.A. **174** B4
Carmichael U.S.A. **182** C3
Carmila Australia **149** F4
Carmo Brazil **207** K8
Carmo da Cachoeira Brazil **207** H8
Carmo de Minas Brazil **207** H9
Carmo do Paranaíba Brazil **207** G5
Carmody, Lake *salt flat* Australia **151** B7
Carmona Angola *see* **Uíge**
Carmona Costa Rica **186** B5
Carmona Spain **54** F7
Carmópolis do Minas Brazil **207** I7
Carnamah Australia **151** A6
Carnarvon Australia **151** A5
Carnarvon S. Africa **132** G7
Carnarvonleegte *salt pan* S. Africa **132** F7
Carnarvon National Park Australia **149** E5
Carnarvon Range *hills* Australia **151** C5
Carnarvon Range *mts* Australia **149** F5
Carnegie Australia **151** C5
Carnegie, Lake *salt flat* Australia **151** C5
Carn Eighe *mt.* U.K. **46** G6
Carnero, Bahía del *b.* Chile **204** B5
Carnes Australia **146** B2
Carnesville U.S.A. **174** D5
Carney U.S.A. **172** F5
Carney Island Antarctica **222** P2
Car Nicobar *i.* India **95** G4
Carnikava Latvia **42** F4
Carnot Cent. Afr. Rep. **126** B3
Carnot Bay Australia **150** C3
Carnoustie U.K. **46** J7
Carnsore Point Rep. of Ireland **47** F11
Caro U.S.A. **173** J7
Caroaebe *r.* Brazil **199** F4
Caroch *mt.* Spain *see* **El Caroche**
Carola Cay *reef* Australia **149** G3
Carol City U.S.A. **175** D7
Carolina Brazil **202** C3
Carolina S. Africa **133** O3
Carolina Beach U.S.A. **175** E5
Caroline Canada **167** H4
Caroline Island Kiribati **221** H6
also known as Millenium Island
Caroline Islands N. Pacific Ocean **73** J5
Caroline Peak N.Z. **153** B13
Carondelet Ecuador **198** B4
Caroní *r.* Venez. **199** F2
Carora Venez. **198** D2
C. A. Rosetti Romania **58** K3
Carpathian Mountains Europe **49** Q6
also known as Carpaţii *or* Karpaty
Carpaţii *mts* Europe *see* **Carpathian Mountains**
Carpaţii Meridionali *mts* Romania *see* **Transylvanian Alps**
Carpentaria, Gulf of Australia **148** C2
Carpentaria Downs Australia **149** E3
Carpentras France **51** L8
Carpi Italy **56** C4
Carpina Brazil **202** F3
Cărpiniş Romania **58** B3
Carpinteria U.S.A. **182** E7
Carp Lake Provincial Park Canada **166** F4
Carquefou France **50** E5
Carquesa *hill* Spain **54** E5
Carrabelle U.S.A. **175** C6
Carraig na Siuire Rep. of Ireland *see* **Carrick-on-Suir**
Carraipía Col. **198** C2
Carrantuohill *mt.* Rep. of Ireland **47** C12
Carrara Italy **56** C4
Carrasco, Parque Nacional *nat. park* Bol. **200** D4
Carrazeda de Ansiães Port. **54** D3
Carr Boyd Range *hills* Australia **150** E3
Carrbridge U.K. **46** I6
Carregal do Sal Port. **54** D4
Carrhae Turkey *see* **Harran**
Carriacou *i.* Grenada **187** H4
Carrickmacross Rep. of Ireland **47** F10
Carrick-on-Shannon Rep. of Ireland **47** D10
Carrick-on-Suir Rep. of Ireland **47** E11
also known as Carraig na Siuire
Carrieton Australia **146** C3
Carrillo Mex. **184** E3
Carrington U.S.A. **178** C2
Carrion *r.* Spain **54** G2
Carrión de los Condes Spain **54** G2
Carrizal Col. **198** C2
Carrizal Bajo Chile **204** C3
Carrizo U.S.A. **183** N7
Carrizo Creek *r.* U.S.A. **179** B4
Carrizo Creek *watercourse AZ* U.S.A. **183** N8
Carrizo Creek *watercourse CA* U.S.A. **183** I8
Carrizos Mex. **185** F3
Carrizo Springs U.S.A. **179** C6
Carrizo Wash *watercourse* U.S.A. **183** O7
Carrizozo U.S.A. **181** F6
Carroll U.S.A. **178** D3
Carrollton *AL* U.S.A. **175** B5
Carrollton *GA* U.S.A. **175** C5
Carrollton *IL* U.S.A. **174** B4
Carrollton *KY* U.S.A. **174** C4
Carrollton *MO* U.S.A. **178** D4
Carrollton *MS* U.S.A. **175** B5
Carrolltown U.S.A. **176** G5
Carron *r.* Australia **149** D3
Carron *r.* U.K. **46** H6
Carrot *r.* Canada **167** K4
Carrot River Canada **167** K4
Carrsville U.S.A. **177** I9
Carruthersville U.S.A. **174** B4
Carry Falls Reservoir U.S.A. **177** K1
Çarşamba Turkey **107** D2
Carson *r.* Australia **150** D2
Carson U.S.A. **178** B2
Carson *r.* U.S.A. **182** E2
Carson City *MI* U.S.A. **173** I7

▶**Carson City** *NV* U.S.A. **182** E2
State capital of Nevada.

Carson Escarpment Australia **150** D2
Carson Lake U.S.A. **182** F2
Carson River Aboriginal Reserve Australia **150** D2
Carson Sink *l.* U.S.A. **182** F2
Carsonville U.S.A. **173** K7
Carstensz-top *mt.* Indon. *see* **Jaya, Puncak**
Carswell Lake Canada **167** I3
Cartagena Chile **204** C4
Cartagena Col. **198** C2
Cartagena Spain **55** K7
historically known as Carthago Nova
Cartago Col. **198** C3
Cartago Costa Rica **186** C5
Cártama Spain **54** G8
Cartaxo Port. **54** C5
Cartaya, Cap *c.* France **51** M9
Carter, Mount *hill* Australia **149** D2
Carteret Group *is* P.N.G. *see* **Kilinailau Islands**
Carteret Island Solomon Is *see* **Malaita**
Carters Range *hills* Australia **149** D4
Cartersville U.S.A. **175** C5
Carterton N.Z. **152** J9
Carthage *tourist site* Tunisia **123** H1
historically known as Carthago
Carthage *IL* U.S.A. **174** B3
Carthage *MO* U.S.A. **178** D4
Carthage *NC* U.S.A. **174** E5
Carthage *NY* U.S.A. **177** J2
Carthage *TN* U.S.A. **174** C4
Carthage *TX* U.S.A. **179** D5
Carthago *tourist site* Tunisia *see* **Carthage**
Carthago Nova Spain *see* **Cartagena**
Cartier Canada **173** L4
Cartier Island Australia **150** C2
Cartwright *Man.* Canada **167** L5
Cartwright *Nfld.* Canada **169** J2
Caruachi Venez. **199** F2
Caruarú Brazil **202** F4
Caruçambaba Brazil **202** B2
Cărunta, Vârful *mt.* Romania **58** H2
Carúpano Venez. **199** F2
Carutapera Brazil **202** C2
Carvalho Brazil **199** I5
Carver U.S.A. **176** B8
Carvin France **51** I2
Carvoeiro Brazil **199** F5
Carvoeiro, Cabo *c.* Port. **54** B5

Carwell Australia **149** E5
Cary U.S.A. **174** E5
Caryapundy Swamp Australia **147** D2
Caryville TN U.S.A. **176** A9
Caryville WI U.S.A. **172** B6
Casabindo, Cerro de mt. Arg. **200** D5
Casablanca Chile **204** C4

▶**Casablanca** Morocco **122** D2
5th most populous city in Africa. Also known as Dar el Beida.
world [cities] ▶ 24–25

Casa Branca Brazil **206** F8
Casa de Janos Mex. **184** C2
Casa de Piedra, Embalse resr Arg. **204** D5
Casa Grande U.S.A. **183** M9
Casale Monferrato Italy **56** A3
Casalins Arg. **204** F5
Casalmaggiore Italy **56** C4
Casalpusterlengo Italy **56** B3
Casalvasco Brazil **201** E3
Casamance r. Senegal **124** A3
Casanare dept Col. **198** D3
Casanare r. Col. **198** D3
Casares Nicaragua **186** B5
Casas Grandes Mex. **184** D2
Casas Grandes r. Mex. **184** D2
Casas-Ibáñez Spain **55** J5
Casbas Arg. **204** E5
Casca Brazil **203** A9
Cascada de Bassaseachic, Parque Nacional nat. park Mex. **184** C2
Cascade Australia **151** C7
Cascade r. N.Z. **153** C12
Cascade IA U.S.A. **174** B3
Cascade ID U.S.A. **180** C3
Cascade Point N.Z. **153** C12
Cascade Range mts Canada/U.S.A. **164** G5
Cascade Reservoir U.S.A. **180** C3
Cascais Port. **54** B6
Cascal, Paso del pass Nicaragua **186** B5
Cascapédia r. Canada **169** H3
Cascavel Ceará Brazil **202** E3
Cascavel Paraná Brazil **203** A8
Căscioarele Romania **58** H4
Casco U.S.A. **172** F6
Casco Bay U.S.A. **177** P2
Caserta Italy **56** G7
Caseville U.S.A. **173** J7
Casey research station Antarctica **223** H2
Casey Bay Antarctica **223** D2
Caseyr, Raas c. Somalia **128** F2
English form Guardafui, Cape
Cashel Rep. of Ireland **47** E11
Cashmere Australia **147** F1
Cashton U.S.A. **172** C7
Casigua Falcón Venez. **198** D2
Casigua Zulia Venez. **198** C2
Casiguran Phil. **74** B2
Casiguran Sound sea chan. Phil. **74** B2
Casilda Arg. **204** E4
Casimcea Romania **58** J4
Casimcea r. Romania **58** J4
Casimiro de Abreu Brazil **207** K9
Casino Australia **147** G2
Casinos Spain **55** K5
Casita Mex. **181** E7
Čáslav Czech Rep. **49** M6
Casma Peru **200** A2
Casnewydd U.K. see **Newport**
Casnovia U.S.A. **172** H7
Casogoran Bay Phil. **74** C4
Casoli Italy **56** G6
Caspe Spain **55** K3
Casper U.S.A. **180** F4
Caspian U.S.A. **172** E4
Caspian Lowland Kazakh./Rus. Fed. **102** A3
also known as Kaspīy Mangy Oypaty or Prikaspiyskaya Nizmennost'

▶**Caspian Sea** Asia/Europe **102** B4
Largest lake in the world and in Asia/Europe. Lowest point in Europe. Also known as Kaspiyskoye More.
world [physical features] ▶ 8–9

Castelló d'Empúries Spain **55** O2
also spelt Castello de Ampurias
Castellón de la Plana Spain see **Castelló de la Plana**
Castelnaudary France **51** H9
Castelnau-de-Médoc France **50** F7
Castelnovo ne'Monti Italy **56** C4
Castelo Brazil **207** L7
Castelo Branco Port. **54** D5
Castelo Branco admin. dist. Port. **54** D4
Castelo de Vide Port. **54** D5
Castelo do Piauí Brazil **202** D3
Castèl San Pietro Terme Italy **56** D4
Castelsardo Sardegna Italy **56** A8
Castelsarrasin France **50** H8
Casteltermini Sicilia Italy **57** F11
Castelvetrano Sicilia Italy **57** E11
Castèl Volturno Italy **56** F7
Casterton Australia **146** D4
Castets France **50** E9
Castiglione dei Pepoli Italy **56** D4
Castiglione del Lago Italy **56** E5
Castiglione della Pescaia Italy **56** C6
Castiglione delle Stiviere Italy **56** C3
Castiglion Fiorentino Italy **56** D5
Castile U.S.A. **176** G3
Castilho Brazil **206** B7
Castilla Chile **204** C2
Castilla Peru **198** A6
Castilla - La Mancha aut. comm. Spain **55** H5
Castilla y León aut. comm. Spain **55** G3
Castillejo Venez. **199** F3
Castilletes Col. **198** D2
Castillo, Canal del sea chan. Chile **205** B8
Castillo, Pampa del hills Arg. **205** C7
Castillos Uruguay **204** G4
Castillos, Lago de l. Uruguay **204** G4
Castlebar Rep. of Ireland **47** C10
also known as Caisleán an Bharraigh
Castleblayney Rep. of Ireland **47** F9
Castle Dale U.S.A. **183** M2
Castle Danger U.S.A. **172** B3
Castle Dome Mountains U.S.A. **183** J8
Castle Douglas U.K. **47** I9
Castlegar Canada **166** G5
Castle Island Bahamas **187** E2
Castleisland Rep. of Ireland **47** C11
Castlemaine Australia **147** E4
Castle Mountain Canada **166** H5
formerly known as Eisenhower, Mount
Castle Mountain U.S.A. **182** D6
Castle Peak hill Hong Kong China **87** [inset]
also known as Tsing Shan
Castle Peak Bay Hong Kong China **87** [inset]
also known as Tsing Shan Wan
Castlepoint N.Z. **152** K8
Castlepollard Rep. of Ireland **47** E10
Castlerea Rep. of Ireland **47** D10
Castlereagh r. Australia **147** E2
Castle Rock CO U.S.A. **180** F5
Castle Rock WA U.S.A. **180** B3
Castle Rock Lake U.S.A. **172** C7
Castor Canada **167** I4
Castor, Rivière du r. Canada **168** E2
Castor Creek r. U.S.A. **179** D6
Castra Regina Germany see **Regensburg**
Castres France **51** I9
Castricum Neth. **48** B3

▶**Castries** St Lucia **187** H4
Capital of St Lucia.

Castro Brazil **203** B8
Castro Chile **205** B6
Castro Alves Brazil **202** E5
Castrocaro Terme Italy **56** D4
Castro del Río Spain **54** G7
Castro de Rei Spain **54** D1
Castro Marim Port. **54** D7
Castro-Urdiales Spain **55** H1
Castro Verde Port. **54** C7
Castrovillari Italy **57** I9
Castroville U.S.A. **182** C5
Castrovirreyna Peru **200** B3
Castuera Spain **54** F6

largest lakes

	lake	area sq km	area sq miles	location	page#
1 ▶	Caspian Sea	371 000	143 243	Asia/Europe	102 B4
2 ▶	Lake Superior	82 100	31 698	North America	172 F3
3 ▶	Lake Victoria	68 800	26 563	Africa	128 B5
4 ▶	Lake Huron	59 600	23 011	North America	173 J5
5 ▶	Lake Michigan	57 800	22 316	North America	172 F7
6 ▶	Aral Sea	33 640	12 988	Asia	102 D3
7 ▶	Lake Tanganyika	32 900	12 702	Africa	127 F6
8 ▶	Great Bear Lake	31 328	12 095	North America	166 F1
9 ▶	Lake Baikal	30 500	11 776	Asia	81 H2
10 ▶	Lake Nyasa	30 044	11 600	Africa	129 B7

Cass r. U.S.A. **173** J7
Cassacatiza Moz. **131** G2
Cassadaga U.S.A. **176** F3
Cassai Angola **127** D7
Cassamba Angola **127** D8
Cassano allo Ionio Italy **57** I9
Cassara Brazil **201** E3
Cass City U.S.A. **173** J7
Casselman Canada **168** F4
Casselton U.S.A. **178** C2
Cássia Brazil **206** G7
Cassiar Mountains Canada **166** D3
Cassilândia Brazil **206** B6
Cassilis Australia **147** F3
Cassinga Angola **127** C8
also spelt Kassinga
Cassino Brazil **204** G4
Cassino Italy **56** F7
Cassis France **51** L9
Cassley r. U.K. **46** H6
Cassongue Angola **127** B7
Cassopolis U.S.A. **172** G9
Cassville MO U.S.A. **178** D4
Cassville WI U.S.A. **172** C8
Castalla Spain **55** K6
Castanhal Amazonas Brazil **199** F6
Castanhal Pará Brazil **202** C2
Castanheira de Pêra Port. **54** C4
Castanheiro Brazil **199** E5
Castanho Brazil **201** E1
Castaño Nuevo Arg. **204** C3
Castaños Mex. **185** E3
Castejón, Montes de mts Spain **55** J3
Castèl di Sangro Italy **56** G7
Castelfiorentino Italy **56** C5
Castelfranco Emilia Italy **56** D4
Castelfranco Veneto Italy **56** D3
Casteljaloux France **50** G8
Castellammare, Golfo di b. Sicilia Italy **57** E10
Castellammare di Stabia Italy **57** G8
Castellane France **51** M9
Castellaneta Italy **57** I8
Castellanos mt. Spain **55** I6
Castellar de la Frontera Spain **54** F8
Castelldefels Spain **55** M3
Castell de Ferro Spain **55** H8
Castelli Buenos Aires Arg. **204** F5
Castelli Chaco Arg. **204** E2
Castell-nedd U.K. see **Neath**
Castell Newydd Emlyn U.K. see **Newcastle Emlyn**
Castello de Ampurias Spain see **Castelló d'Empúries**
Castelló de la Plana Spain **55** K5
also spelt Castellón de la Plana

Cast Uul mt. Mongolia **84** A1
Caswell Sound inlet N.Z. **153** B12
Çat Turkey **107** E3
Catabola Angola **127** C8
formerly known as Nova Sintra
Catacamas Hond. **186** B4
Catacaos Peru **198** A6
Catacocha Ecuador **198** B6
Cataguases Brazil **207** K8
Catahoula Lake U.S.A. **179** D6
Cataiñgan Phil. **74** B3
Çatak Turkey **107** E3
Catalão Brazil **206** F5
Çatalca Turkey **58** J7
Çatalca Yarımadası pen. Turkey **58** J7
Catalina U.S.A. **183** N9
Catalonia aut. comm. Spain see **Cataluña**
Cataluña aut. comm. Spain **55** M3
English form Catalonia; also spelt Catalunya
Catalunya aut. comm. Spain see **Cataluña**
Çatalzeytin Turkey **106** C2
Catamarca Arg. **204** D3
Catamarca prov. Arg. **204** D2
Catambia Moz. see **Catandica**
Catana Sicilia Italy see **Catania**
Catanauan Phil. **74** B3
Catandica Moz. **131** G3
formerly known as Catambia or Vila Gouveia
Catanduanes i. Phil. **74** C3
Catanduva Brazil **206** D8
Catanduvas Brazil **203** A8
Catania Sicilia Italy **57** H11
historically known as Catana
Catania, Golfo di g. Sicilia Italy **57** H11
Catán Lil Arg. **204** C5
Catanzaro Italy **57** I10
Cataqueamã Brazil **201** E2
Cataract U.S.A. **172** C6
Cataract Creek watercourse U.S.A. **183** L5
Catarina Brazil **202** E3
Catarina U.S.A. **179** C6
Catarino Rodriguez Mex. **185** E3
Catarman Phil. **74** C3
Catarroja Spain **55** K5
Catastrophe, Cape Australia **146** B3
Catata Nova Angola **127** B8
Catatumbo Bari nat. park Col. **198** C2
Catavi Bol. **200** D4
Catawba U.S.A. **172** C5
Catawba r. U.S.A. **174** D5
Catawissa U.S.A. **177** I5
Cat Ba, Đao i. Vietnam **78** D3
Catbalogan Phil. **74** C4
Cateel Phil. **74** C5
Cateel Bay Phil. **74** C5

Catemaco Mex. **185** G5
Catembe Moz. **133** Q3
Catengue Angola **127** B8
Catete Angola **127** B7
Catete r. Brazil **199** H6
Cathcart S. Africa **133** L9
Cathedral City U.S.A. **183** H8
Cathedral Peak Lesotho **133** N5
Cathedral Provincial Park Canada **166** F5
Catherine, Mount U.S.A. **183** L3
Catheys Valley U.S.A. **182** D4
Cathlamet U.S.A. **180** B3
Catió Guinea-Bissau **124** B4
Catisimiña Venez. **199** F3
Cat Island Bahamas **187** E1
Catlins Forest Park nature res. N.Z. **153** D14
Catoche, Cabo c. Mex. **185** I4
Catolé do Rocha Brazil **202** E3
Catolé Grande r. Brazil **207** M2
Catolo Angola **127** C7
Catorce Mex. **185** E4
Catota Angola **127** C8
Catoute mt. Spain **54** E2
Catria, Monte mt. Italy **56** E5
Catriló Arg. **204** E5
Catrimani Brazil **199** F4
Catrimani r. Brazil **199** F4
Catskill U.S.A. **177** L3
Catskill Mountains U.S.A. **177** K3
Cattenom France **51** M3
Cattle Creek N.Z. **153** E12
Cattolica Italy **56** E5
Catúa Arg. **200** D5
Catuane Moz. **131** G5
Catur Moz. **129** B8
Cauaxi r. Brazil **202** B2
Cauayan Phil. **74** B4
Caubvick, Mount Canada **169** I1
Cauca dept Col. **198** B4
Cauca r. Col. **198** C2
Caucaia Brazil **202** E2
Caucasia Col. **198** C3
▶**Caucasus** mts Asia/Europe **107** E2
also known as Bol'shoy Kavkaz
europe [countries] ▶ 32–33
Caucete Arg. **204** C3
Cauchari, Salar de salt flat Arg. **200** D5
Cauchon Lake Canada **167** L4
Caucomgomoc Lake U.S.A. **174** G2
Caudete Spain **55** K6
Caudry France **51** J2
Cauit Point Phil. **74** C4
Caulnes France **50** D4
Caulonia Italy **57** I10
Caunao r. Cuba **186** D2
Caungula Angola **127** C7
Cauno Angola **127** C9
Cauquenes Chile **204** B4
Caura r. Venez. **199** E3
Caurés r. Brazil **199** F5
Causapscal Canada **169** H3
Căuşeni Moldova **58** K2
formerly spelt Kaushany
Căuşeni prov. Moldova **53** H2
Caussade France **50** H8
Cautário r. Brazil **201** D3
Caution, Cape Canada **166** E5
Cauto r. Cuba **186** D2
Cava de'Tirreni Italy **57** G8
Cávado r. Port. **54** C3
Cavaglià Italy **56** A3
Cavaillon France **51** L9
Cavalcante Goiás Brazil **202** C5
Cavalcante Rondônia Brazil **201** E2
Cavalier U.S.A. **178** C1
Cavalleria, Cap de c. Spain **55** P4
Cavalli Islands N.Z. **152** H2
Cavally r. Côte d'Ivoire **124** D5
Cavan Rep. of Ireland **47** E10
Çavdarhisar Turkey **59** K9
Çavdır Turkey **106** B3
Cave N.Z. **153** E12
Cave City AR U.S.A. **174** B4
Cave City KY U.S.A. **174** C4
Cave Creek U.S.A. **183** M8
Caveira Brazil **207** J3
Cavenagh Range hills Australia **151** E5
Cavera, Serra do hills Brazil **203** A9
Cavernoso, Serra do mts Brazil **203** A8
Cave Run Lake U.S.A. **176** B7
Caviana, Ilha i. Brazil **202** B1
Cavili reef Phil. **74** B4
Cavite Phil. **74** B3
Cavo, Monte hill Italy **56** E7
Cavone r. Italy **57** I8
Cavongo Angola **127** C8
Çavuşçu Turkey **106** B3
Çavuşköy Turkey **108** B1
Cawndilla Lake imp. l. Australia **147** D3
Cawnpore India see **Kanpur**
Cawood U.S.A. **176** B9
Caxambu Brazil **207** I8
Caxias Amazonas Brazil **198** D6
Caxias Maranhão Brazil **202** D3
Caxias do Sul Brazil **203** B9
Caxito Angola **127** B7
Caxiuana, Baía de l. Brazil **199** I5
Çay Turkey **106** B3
Cayambe-Coca, Parque Nacional nat. park Ecuador **198** B5
Çaybaşı Turkey see **Çayeli**
Cayce U.S.A. **175** D5
Çaycuma Turkey **106** C2
Çayeli Turkey **107** E2
also known as Çaybaşı

▶**Cayenne** Fr. Guiana **199** H3
Capital of French Guiana.

Cayey Puerto Rico **187** G3
Çaygören Barajı resr Turkey **59** J9
Çayhan Turkey **106** C3
Çayhisar Turkey **59** J12
Çayırhan Turkey **106** B2
Caylus France **50** H8
Cayman Brac i. Cayman Is **186** D3

▶**Cayman Islands** terr. West Indies **186** C3
United Kingdom Overseas Territory.
oceania [countries] ▶ 138–139

Cay Sal i. Bahamas **186** C2
Cay Santa Domingo i. Bahamas **186** E2
Cayucos U.S.A. **182** D6
Cayuga Canada **173** N8
Cayuga Heights U.S.A. **177** I3
Cayuga Lake U.S.A. **177** I3
Cazage Angola **127** D7
also spelt Cazaje
Cazaje Angola see **Cazage**
Cazalla de la Sierra Spain **54** F7
Căzănești Romania **58** I4
Caza Pava Arg. **204** F3
Cazaux et de Sanguinet, Étang de l. France **50** E8
Cazê China **89** D6
Cazenovia U.S.A. **177** J3
Cazères France **50** H9
Cažma Croatia **56** I3
Cazombo Angola **127** D7
Cazorla Spain **55** I7
Cazula Moz. **131** G2
Cea r. Spain **54** F2
Ceadâr-Lunga Moldova see **Ciadîr-Lunga**
Ceanannus Mór Rep. of Ireland see **Kells**
Ceará Brazil see **Fortaleza**
Ceará state Brazil **202** E3
Ceatalchioi Romania **58** J3
Ceatharlach Rep. of Ireland see **Carlow**
Ceballos Mex. **184** D3
Cebireis Dağı mt. Turkey **108** D1
Cebollar Arg. **204** D3

Ceboruco, Volcán vol. Mex. **184** D4
Cebreros Spain **54** G4
Cebu Phil. **74** B4
Cebu i. Phil. **74** B4
Ceccano Italy **56** F7
Cecil U.S.A. **172** E6
Cecil Plains Australia **147** F1
Cecil Rhodes, Mount hill Australia **151** C5
Cecilton U.S.A. **177** J6
Cecina Italy **56** C5
Cecina r. Italy **56** C5
Ceclavín Spain **54** E5
Cedar r. MI U.S.A. **173** I7
Cedar r. ND U.S.A. **178** B2
Cedar r. NE U.S.A. **178** C3
Cedarberg mts S. Africa **132** C9
Cedar Bluff U.S.A. **176** D8
Cedar City U.S.A. **183** K4
Cedar Creek Reservoir U.S.A. **179** C5
Cedaredge U.S.A. **180** F5
Cedar Falls U.S.A. **174** A3
Cedar Grove CA U.S.A. **182** F5
Cedar Grove IN U.S.A. **176** A6
Cedar Grove WI U.S.A. **172** F7
Cedar Grove WV U.S.A. **176** D7
Cedar Island U.S.A. **177** J8
Cedar Lake Man. Canada **167** K4
Cedar Lake Ont. Canada **173** O4
Cedar Point U.S.A. **176** B4
Cedar Rapids U.S.A. **174** B3
Cedar Ridge U.S.A. **183** M5
Cedar River U.S.A. **172** F5
Cedar Run U.S.A. **177** K6
Cedar Springs Canada **173** K8
Cedar Springs U.S.A. **172** H7
Cedarville S. Africa **133** N7
Cedarville IL U.S.A. **172** D8
Cedarville MI U.S.A. **173** I5
Cedarville OH U.S.A. **176** B6
Cedegolo Italy **56** C2
Cedeira Spain **54** C1
Cedeño Hond. **186** B4
Cedral Quintana Roo Mex. **185** I4
Cedral San Luis Potosí Mex. **185** E4
Cedro Brazil **202** E3
Cedros Hond. **186** B4
Cedros Mex. **185** E3
Cedros, Cerro mt. Mex. **181** D7
Cedros, Isla i. Mex. **184** B2
Ceduna Australia **146** B3
Cée Spain **54** B2
Ceelayo Somalia **128** F2
Ceelbuur Somalia **128** E3
Ceel Dhaab Somalia **128** E2
Ceeldheere Somalia **128** E4
Ceel Gaal Bari Somalia **128** F2
Ceel Gaal Woqooyi Galbeed Somalia **128** D2
Ceel Huur Somalia **128** F3
Ceel Walaaq well Somalia **128** D4
Ceerigaabo Somalia **128** E2
Cefalù Sicilia Italy **57** G10
historically known as Cephaloedium
Cega r. Spain **54** G3
Cegléd Hungary **49** Q8
Čegrane Macedonia **58** B7
Ceheng China **86** C3
also known as Zhelou
Cehu Silvaniei Romania **58** E1
Ceira r. Port. **54** C4
Çekerek Turkey **106** C2
also known as Hacıköy
Celah, Gunung mt. Malaysia **76** C1
Celano Italy **56** F6
Celaque, Parque Nacional nat. park Hond. **186** A4
Celaya Mex. **185** E4
Celbridge Rep. of Ireland **47** F10
Célé r. France **50** H8

▶**Celebes** i. Indon. **75** B3
4th largest island in Asia. Also known as Sulawesi.
asia [landscapes] ▶ 62–63

Celebes Sea Indon./Phil. **75** B2
Celendín Peru **198** B6
Celina OH U.S.A. **176** A5
Celina TN U.S.A. **174** C4
Celje Slovenia **56** H2
Cella Spain **55** J4
Celldömölk Hungary **49** O8
Celle Germany **48** H3
Celles-sur-Belle France **50** F6
Cellina r. Italy **56** E2
Celone r. Italy **56** H7
Celovec Austria see **Klagenfurt**
Celtic Sea Rep. of Ireland/U.K. **47** F13
Cemaru, Gunung mt. Indon. **77** F2
Cemilbey Turkey **106** C2
Çemişgezek Turkey **107** D3
Čempi, Teluk b. Indon. **77** G5
Cenad Romania **58** B2
Cenajo, Embalse del resr Spain **55** J6
Cencenighe Agordino Italy **56** D2
Cenderawasih, Teluk b. Indon. **73** I7
also known as Irian, Teluk
Cenei Romania **58** B3
Cenis, Col du Mont pass France **51** M7
Ceno r. Italy **56** C4
Cenon France **50** F8
Čenta Vojvodina, Srbija Yugo. **58** B3
Centane S. Africa see **Kentani**
Centenário do Sul Brazil **206** B9
Centenary Zimbabwe **131** F3
Centennial Wash watercourse U.S.A. **183** L8
Center ND U.S.A. **178** B2
Center NE U.S.A. **178** C3
Center TX U.S.A. **179** D6
Centerburg U.S.A. **176** C5
Center City U.S.A. **178** D2
Centereach U.S.A. **177** L5
Center Hill Lake resr U.S.A. **174** C5
Center Point U.S.A. **175** C5
Centerville AL U.S.A. **175** C5
Centerville IA U.S.A. **174** A3
Centerville MO U.S.A. **174** B4
Centerville NC U.S.A. **176** G9
Centerville OH U.S.A. **176** C7
Centerville PA U.S.A. **176** F4
Centerville TN U.S.A. **174** C5
Centerville TX U.S.A. **179** D6
Centerville WV U.S.A. **176** E6
Cento Italy **56** D4
Centrafricaine, République country Africa see **Central African Republic**
Central admin. dist. Botswana **131** E4
Central Brazil **202** D4
Central Chile **200** C5
Central admin. reg. Ghana **125** E5
Central prov. Kenya **128** C5
Central admin. reg. Malawi **129** B8
Central U.S.A. **181** E6
Central prov. Zambia **127** F8
Central, Cordillera mts Bol. **200** D4
Central, Cordillera mts Col. **198** B4
Central, Cordillera mts Dom. Rep. **187** F3
Central, Cordillera mts Panama **186** C5
Central, Cordillera mts Peru **200** A2
Central, Cordillera mts Phil. **74** B2
Central African Empire country Africa see **Central African Republic**
▶**Central African Republic** country Africa **126** C3
known as Centrafricaine, République in French; formerly known as Central African Empire or Ubangi-Shari
africa [countries] ▶ 114–117
Central Australia Aboriginal Reserve Australia **150** E4
Central Brahui Range mts Pak. **101** F4
Central Butte Canada **167** J5
Central City IA U.S.A. **174** B3

Central City NE U.S.A. **178** C3
Central City PA U.S.A. **176** G5
Central de Minas Brazil **207** L5
Central Desert Aboriginal Land res. Australia **148** A4
Central Falls U.S.A. **177** N4
Centralia IL U.S.A. **174** B4
Centralia WA U.S.A. **180** B3
Central Islip U.S.A. **177** L5
Central Kalahari Game Reserve nature res. Botswana **131** D4
Central Makran Range mts Pak. **101** F5
Central Mount Wedge Australia **148** A4
Central'noolesnoy Zapovednik nature res. Rus. Fed. **43** N5
Central Plateau Conservation Area nature res. Australia **147** E5
Central Provinces state India see **Madhya Pradesh**
Central Range mts Lesotho **133** M6
Central Range mts P.N.G. **73** J7
Central Russian Upland hills Rus. Fed. **43** R7
also known as Sredne-Russkaya Vozvyshennost'
Central Siberian Plateau Rus. Fed. **39** L3
also known as Siberia or Sredne-Sibirskoye Ploskogor'ye
Central Square U.S.A. **177** I2
Central Valley U.S.A. **182** B1
Centre prov. Cameroon **125** H5
Centre admin. reg. France **50** H5
Centre U.S.A. **175** C5
Centreville MD U.S.A. **177** I6
Centreville VA U.S.A. **176** H7
Centurion S. Africa **133** M2
formerly known as Verwoerdburg
Cenxi China **87** D4
Ceos i. Greece see **Kea**
Céou r. France **50** H8
Cephaloedium Sicilia Italy see **Cefalù**
Cephalonia i. Greece **59** B10
also known as Kefallinía; also spelt Kefallonia
Čepin Croatia **56** K3
Čepkelių nature res. Lith. **42** F8
Ceprano Italy **56** F7
Cepu Indon. **77** E4
Cer hills Yugo. **58** A4
Ceram i. Indon. see **Seram**
Ceram Sea Indon. see **Seram Sea**
Cerbat Mountains U.S.A. **183** J6
Cerbol r. Spain see **Servol**
Cercal hill Port. **54** C7
Čerchov mt. Czech Rep. **49** J6
Cère r. France **51** H8
Cerea Italy **56** D3
Cereal Canada **167** I5
Cereales Arg. **204** E5
Ceres Arg. **204** E3
Ceres Brazil **206** D2
Ceres S. Africa **132** D10
Ceres U.S.A. **182** D4
Céret France **51** I10
Cereté Col. **198** C2
Cerf, Lac du l. Canada **173** R4
Cerignola Italy **56** H7
Cerigo i. Greece see **Kythira**
Çerikli Turkey **106** C3
Cêringgolêb China see **Dongco**
Çerkeş Turkey **106** C2
Çerkezköy Turkey **58** J7
Cerknica Slovenia **56** G3
Cermei Romania **58** C2
Çermik Turkey **107** D3
Cerna Romania **58** J3
Cerna r. Romania **58** D3
Cerna r. Romania **58** D4
Cerna r. Romania **58** F4
Cernat Romania **58** H3
Cernăuţi Ukr. see **Chernivtsi**
Cernavodă Romania **58** J4
Cernay France **51** N5
Cerqueira César Brazil **206** D10
Cerralvo Mex. **185** F3
Cerralvo, Isla i. Mex. **184** C3
Cërrik Albania **58** A7
Cerrillos Arg. **200** D6
Cerritos Mex. **185** E4
Cerro Azul Brazil **203** B8
Cerro Azul Mex. **185** F4
Cerro de Pasco Peru **200** A2
Cerro Hoya, Parque Nacional nat. park Panama **186** C6
Cerro Manantiales Chile **205** C9
Cerrón mt. Spain **55** H8
Cerrón, Cerro mt. Venez. **198** D2
Cerro Negro Chile **200** C5
Cerros Colorados, Embalse resr Arg. **204** C5
Cerros de Amotape, Parque Nacional nat. park Peru **198** A5
Certaldo Italy **56** D5
Certeju de Sus Romania **58** D3
Cervantes Australia **151** A6
Cervantes, Cerro mt. Arg. **205** B8
Cervaro r. Italy **56** H7
Cervati, Monte mt. Italy **57** H8
Cervenia Romania **58** G5
Cervera Spain **55** M3
Cervera de Pisuerga Spain **54** G2
Cerveteri Italy **56** E7
historically known as Caere
Cervia Italy **56** E4
Cervialto, Monte mt. Italy **57** H8
Cervignano del Friuli Italy **56** F3
Cervina, Punta mt. Italy **56** D2
Cervione Corse France **51** P10
Cervo Spain **54** D1
César dept Col. **198** C2
César r. Col. **198** C2
Cesarò Sicilia Italy **57** G11
Cesena Italy **56** E4
Cesenatico Italy **56** E4
Cēsis Latvia **42** G4
historically known as Wenden
Česká Lípa Czech Rep. **49** L5
Česká Republika country Europe see **Czech Republic**
České Budějovice Czech Rep. **49** L7
formerly known as Budweis
České Středohoří hills Czech Rep. **49** K5
Českomoravská Vysočina hills Czech Rep. **49** L6
Český Krumlov Czech Rep. **49** L7
Český Les mts Czech Rep./Germany **49** J6
Český Těšín Czech Rep. **49** P6
Česma r. Croatia **56** I3
Çeşme Turkey **106** A3
Cessnock Australia **147** F3
Cesson-Sévigné France **50** E4
Cestas France **50** F8
Cestos r. Liberia **124** C5
Cesuras Spain **54** C1
Cesvaine Latvia **42** H5
Cêtar China **84** D4
formerly known as Qaidar
Cetate Romania **58** E4
Cetatea Albă Ukr. see **Bilhorod-Dnistrovs'kyy**
Cetina r. Croatia **56** I5
Cetinje Crna Gora Yugo. **56** K6
Cetraro Italy **57** H9

▶**Ceuta** N. Africa **54** F9
Spanish Territory.
africa [countries] ▶ 114–117

Ceva-i-Ra reef Fiji **145** G4
also spelt Theva-i-Ra
Cévennes mts France **51** J9
Cévennes, Parc National des nat. park France **51** J8

Čevetjävri Fin. see **Sevettijärvi**
Cevizli Turkey **109** I1
Cevizlik Turkey see **Maçka**
Ceyhan Turkey **106** C3
Ceyhan r. Turkey **107** C3
Ceyhan Boğazı r. mouth Turkey **108** G1
Ceylanpınar Turkey **107** E3
also known as Resülayn
Ceylon country Asia see **Sri Lanka**
Cèze r. France **51** K8
Chaacha Turkm. **102** E5
also spelt Chäche
Chābahār Iran **101** E5
Chablais mts France **51** M6
Chablé Mex. **185** H5
Chablis France **51** J5
Chabre ridge France **51** L8
Chabrol i. New Caledonia see **Lifou**
Chabyêr Caka salt l. China **89** D6
Chaca Chile **200** C4
Chacabuco Arg. **204** E4
Chacarilla Bol. **200** C4
Chachahuén, Sierra mt. Arg. **204** C5
Chachapoyas Peru **198** B6
Chachaura-Binaganj India **96** C4
Chäche Turkm. see **Chaacha**
Chachersk Belarus **43** L9
Chachevichy Belarus **43** K8
Chachoengsao Thai. **79** C5
Chaco prov. Arg. **204** E2
formerly known as Presidente Juan Perón
Chaco Boreal reg. Para. **201** F5
Chaco Culture National Historical Park nat. park U.S.A. **181** F5
Chacon, Cape U.S.A. **166** C4
Chacorão, Cachoeira da waterfall Brazil **199** G6
Chacra de Piros Peru **200** B2

▶**Chad** country Africa **120** C6
5th largest country in Africa. Also spelt Tchad or Tshad.
africa [countries] ▶ 114–117

▶**Chad, Lake** Africa **120** B6
4th largest lake in Africa.
africa [landscapes] ▶ 112–113

Chadaasan Mongolia **84** D2
Chadan Rus. Fed. **84** A1
Chadileo r. Arg. **204** D5
Chadron U.S.A. **178** B3
Chadyr-Lunga Moldova see **Ciadîr-Lunga**
Chae Hom Thai. **78** B4
Chaek Kyrg. **103** H4
also spelt Chayek
Chaeryŏng N. Korea **83** B5
Chae Son National Park Thai. **78** B4
Chaffee U.S.A. **174** B4
Chaffers, Isla i. Chile **205** B7
Chaffey U.S.A. **172** A4
Chafurray Col. **198** C4
Chagai Pak. **101** F4
Chagai Hills Afgh./Pak. **101** E4
Chagalamarri India **94** C3
Chagan Kzyl-Ordinskaya Oblast' Kazakh. **103** F3
Chagan Vostochnyy Kazakhstan Kazakh. **103** I2
also spelt Shaghan
Chaganuzun Rus. Fed. **84** A1
Chagdo Kangri reg. China **89** D5
Chaghā Khūr mt. Iran **100** B4
Chaghcharān Afgh. **101** F3
Chaglinka r. Kazakh. **103** G1
Chagny France **51** K6
Chagoda Rus. Fed. **43** Q2
Chagoda r. Rus. Fed. **43** Q2
Chagodoshcha r. Rus. Fed. **43** R3
Chagos Archipelago is Indian Ocean **218** L6
Chagoyan Rus. Fed. **82** C1
Chagra r. Rus. Fed. **102** B1
Chagrayskoye Plato plat. Kazakh. see **Shagyray, Plato**
Chagres, Parque Nacional nat. park Panama **186** D5
Chaguanas Trin. and Tob. **187** H5
Chaguaramas Venez. **199** E2
Chagyl Turkm. **102** C4
Chagyllyshor, Vpadina depr. Turkm. **102** C4
Chaha r. Ukr. **58** K3
Chahah Burjal Afgh. **101** E4
Chāh Ākhvor Iran **101** D3
Chaharbagh Afgh. **101** G3
Chahār Maḩāll vā Bakhtīārī prov. Iran **100** B3
Chah Baba well Iran **100** C3
Chāh Bahār, Khalīj-e b. Iran **101** E5
Chahbounia Alg. **55** N9
Chāh-e'Asalū well Iran **100** C4
Chāh-e Bābā well Iran **100** D3
Chāh-e Gonbad well Iran **100** C3
Chāh-e Kavīr well Iran **100** D3
Chāh-e Khorāsān well Iran **100** C3
Chāh-e Malek well Iran **100** C3
Chāh-e Malek Mīrzā well Iran **100** C4
Chāh-e Mirzā well Iran **100** C3
Chāh-e Mūjān well Iran **100** C3
Chāh-e Nūklok Iran **100** C3
Chāh-e Nūklok well Iran **100** C3
Chāh-e Pansu well Iran **100** C3
Chāh-e Qeyşar well Iran **100** C4
Chāh-e Qobād well Iran **100** C3
Chāh-e Raḩmān well Iran **101** D4
Chāh-e Shūr well Iran **100** C3
Chāh-e Ţāqestān well Iran **100** C4
Chāh-e Tūnī well Iran **100** D3
Chāh Haji Abdulla well Iran **100** C3
Chāh Ḩaqq Iran **100** C4
Chah-i-Ab Afgh. **101** G2
Chāh Pās well Iran **100** C3
Chāh Ru'ī well Iran **101** D4
Chah Sandan Pak. **101** E4
Chahuites Mex. **185** G5
Chai r. China **82** A4
Chaibasa India **97** E5
Chaigneau, Lac l. Canada **169** H2
Chaigoubu China see **Huai'an**
Chaillu, Massif du mts Gabon **126** A5
Chainat Thai. **79** C5
Chainjoin Co l. China **89** D5
Chai Si r. Thai. **79** C5
Chaitén Chile **205** B6
Chai Wan Hong Kong China **87** [inset]
Chaiwopu China **88** D3
Chaiya Thai. **79** B6
Chaiyaphum Thai. **79** C5
Chajarí Arg. **204** F3
Chakai India **97** E4
Chakar r. Pak. **101** G4
Chakari Zimbabwe **131** F3
Chake Chake Tanz. **129** C6
Chakhānsūr Afgh. **101** E4
Chakia India **97** D4
Chak Jhumra Pak. **101** H4
Chakonipau, Lake Canada **169** G1
Chakradharpur India **97** E5
Chakulia India **97** E5
Chakwal Pak. **101** H3
Chala Peru **200** B3
Chala Tanz. **129** A6
Chalais France **50** G7
Chalap Dalan mts Afgh. **101** F3
Chalatenango El Salvador **185** H6
Chaláua Moz. **131** H3
Chalaxung China **86** A1
Chalbi Desert Kenya **128** C4
Chalcedon Turkey see **Kadıköy**
Chalengkou China **84** B4
Chaleur Bay inlet Canada **169** H3
also known as Chaleurs, Baie de

Chaleurs, Baie de *inlet* Canada *see* Chaleur Bay
Chalia *r.* Arg. 205 C8
Chalîb Abū Munṭar *watercourse* Iraq 109 L5
Chaling China 87 E3
Chalinze Tanz. 129 C6
Chalisgaon India 94 B1
Chalisseri India 94 C4
Chalkar, Ozero *salt l.* Kazakh. *see* Shalkar, Ozero
Chalki Greece 59 I12
Chalki *i.* Greece 59 J12
  also spelt Khálki
Chalkida Greece 59 E10
  also known as Khalkis
Chalkudysu Kazakh. 103 I4
Chalky Inlet N.Z. 153 A14
Challakere India 94 C3
Challans France 50 D3
Challapata Bol. 200 D4

▶ Challenger Deep *sea feature* N. Pacific Ocean 220 D5
  Deepest point in the world (Mariana Trench).
  oceans [features] ▶▶ 210–211

Challis U.S.A. 180 D3
Chalmette U.S.A. 175 B6
Chal'mny-Varre Rus. Fed. 40 F2
Chalones-sur-Loire France 50 F5
Châlons-en-Champagne France 51 K4
  formerly known as Châlons-sur-Marne
Châlons-sur-Marne France *see* Châlons-en-Champagne
Chalon-sur-Saône France 51 K6
Chalt Jammu and Kashmir 96 B1
Chalûs France 50 G7
Chālūs Iran 100 B2
Cham Germany 49 J6
Chama U.S.A. 181 F5
Chama *r.* U.S.A. 181 F5
Chamamba Tanz. 129 B6
Chaman Pak. 101 F4
Chaman Bid Iran 100 D2
Chamao, Khao *mt.* Thai. 79 C5
Chamba India 96 C2
Chamba Tanz. 129 C7
Chambal *r.* India 96 C4
Chambas Cuba 186 D2
Chambeaux, Lac *l.* Canada 169 G2
Chamberlain *r.* Australia 150 D3
Chamberlain Canada 167 J5
Chamberlain U.S.A. 178 C3
Chamberlain Lake U.S.A. 174 G2
Chambers U.S.A. 183 O6
Chambers Bay Australia 150 D3
Chambersburg U.S.A. 176 H6
Chambers Island U.S.A. 172 F5
Chambéry France 51 L7
Chambeshi Zambia 127 F8
Chambeshi *r.* Zambia 127 F8
Chambi, Jebel *mt.* Tunisia 123 H2
Chambira *r.* Peru 198 C6
Chambord Canada 169 F3
Chambri Lake P.N.G. 73 J7
Chamdo China *see* Qamdo
Chame Panama 186 D5
Chamela Mex. 184 D5
Chami *well* Mauritania 122 B5
Chamical Arg. 204 D3
Chamili *i.* Greece 59 H13
Ch'amo Hāyk' *l.* Eth. 128 C3
Chamoli India *see* Gopeshwar
Chamonix-Mont-Blanc France 51 M7
Chamouchouane *r.* Canada *see* Ashuapmushuan
Chamouse, Montagne de *mt.* France 51 L8
Champa India 97 E5
Champagne Castle *mt.* S. Africa 133 N6
Champagnole France 51 L6
Champagny Islands Australia 150 D3
Champaign U.S.A. 174 B3
Champaqui, Cerro *mt.* Arg. 204 D3
Champara *mt.* Peru 200 A2
Champasak Laos 79 D5
Champdoré, Lac *l.* Canada 169 H2
Champhai India 97 G5
Champion Canada 167 H5
Champlain NY U.S.A. 177 L1
Champlain VA U.S.A. 177 I7
Champlain, Lake Canada/U.S.A. 174 F2
Champlain U.S.A. 177 L2
Champlitte France 51 L5
Champneuf Canada 173 P2
Champotón Mex. 185 H5
Chamrajnagar India 94 C4
Cham Siyāh Iran 100 C4
Chamusca Port. 54 C5
Chamzinka Rus. Fed. 41 H5
Chan, Ko *i.* Thai. 79 B6
Chana Thai. 79 C7
Chanak Turkey *see* Çanakkale
Chanal Mex. 185 G5
Chañar Arg. 204 C4
Chañaral Chile 204 C2
Chañaral, Isla *i.* Chile 204 C3
Chañarén Iran 101 D2
Chañaro, Cerro *mt.* Venez. 199 F3
Chança *r.* Port./Spain *see* Chanza
Chancay Peru 200 A2
Chanco Chile 204 B4
Chancos Peru 200 A2
Chanda India *see* Chandrapur
Chandalar *r.* U.S.A. 164 E3
Chandama Tanz. 129 C6
Chandausi India 96 C3
Chandbali India 95 E1
Chandeless Islands U.S.A. 175 B6

Chanderi India 96 C4
Chandia India 96 D5
Chandigarh India 96 C3
Chandil India 97 E5
Chandler Canada 169 H3
Chandler AZ U.S.A. 183 M8
Chandler OK U.S.A. 179 C5
Chandless *r.* Brazil 200 C2
Chandmany Mongolia 84 C2
Chandos Lake Canada 173 P6
Chandpur Bangl. 97 F5
Chandpur India 96 C3
Chandragiri India 94 C3
Chandrapur India 94 C2
  formerly known as Chanda
Chandur India 94 C1
Chandvad India 94 B1
Chandyr *r.* Turkm. 102 C5
  also spelt Chendir
Chang, Ko *i.* Thai. 79 C5
Changalane Moz. 133 Q3
Chang'an China *see* Rong'an
Chang'an China 87 D1
  also known as Weiqu
Chang-an S. Korea 91 A7
Changane *r.* Moz. 131 G5
Changara Moz. 131 G3
Changbai China 82 C4
Changbai Shan *mts* China/N. Korea 82 B4
Chang Cheng *research station* Antarctica *see* Great Wall
Changchow China *see* Zhangzhou
Changchow China *see* Changzhou
Changchun China 82 B4
  historically known as Hsinking
Changdao China 85 I4
  also known as Nanchangshan; *formerly known as* Sihou
Changde China 87 D2
  formerly spelt Changteh
Changfeng China 87 F1
Changge China 87 F1
Changgi-ap *pt* S. Korea 83 C5
Changgo China 89 D6
Changhai China 85 I4
  also known as Sikuaishi
Chang Hu *l.* China 87 E2
Changhua Taiwan 87 G3
  also spelt Zhanghua
Changhua Jiang *r.* China 87 D5
Changhung S. Korea 83 B6
Changi Sing. 76 [inset]
Changji China 88 D3
Changjiang China 87 D5
  also known as Shiliu
Chang Jiang *r.* China *see* Yangtze
Changjiang Kou *r. mouth* China *see* Yangtze, Mouth of the
Changjin N. Korea 83 B4
Changjin-gang *r.* N. Korea 83 B4
Changkiang China *see* Zhanjiang
Changle China 87 F3
Changleng China *see* Xinjian
Changli China 85 H3
Changling China 85 I4
Changliushui China 85 E4
Changlun Jammu and Kashmir 96 C2
Changning Hunan China 87 E3
Changning China *see* Xunwu
Changning Sichuan China 86 C2
Changnyŏn N. Korea 83 B5
Ch'ang-pai Shan *mts* China/N. Korea *see* Changbai Shan
Changping China 85 H3
Changpu China *see* Suining
Changsan-got *pt* N. Korea 83 B5
Changsha China 87 E2
Changshan Qundao *is* China 85 I4
Changshi China 86 C3
Changshou China 86 C2
Changshoujie China 87 E2
Changshu China 87 G2
Changsŏng S. Korea 83 B6
Changtai China 87 F3
  also known as Wu'an
Changteh China *see* Changde
Changting Fujian China 87 F3
  also known as Tingzhou
Changting Heilong. China 82 C3
Changtu China 82 B4
Changuinola Panama 186 C5
Ch'angwŏn S. Korea 83 C6
Changwu China 85 E5
  also known as Zhaoren
Changxing China 87 F2
  also known as Zhicheng
Changxing Dao *i.* China 85 I4
Changyang China 87 D2
  also known as Longzhouping
Changyi China 85 H4
Changyuan China *see* Rongchang
Changyuan China 85 G5
Changzhi Shanxi China 85 G4
Changzhi Shanxi China 85 G5
  also known as Handian
Changzhou China 87 F2
  also known as Wujin; *formerly spelt* Changchow
Chani, Nevado de *mt.* Arg. 200 D6
Chania Greece 59 F13
  also spelt Khaniá; *historically known as* Canea *or* Cydonia
Chanion, Kolpos *b.* Greece 59 E13
Chankou China 84 E5
Channagiri India 94 C3
Channapatna India 94 C3
Channel Islands English Chan. 50 D3
  also known as Normandes, Îles
Channel Islands U.S.A. 182 E7
Channel Islands National Park U.S.A. 182 E7
Channel-Port-aux-Basques Canada 169 J4
Channel Rock *i.* Bahamas 186 D2
Channel Tunnel France/U.K. 50 H1
Channing U.S.A. 172 E4
Chantada Spain 54 D2
Chantal'skiy *mt.* Rus. Fed. 39 R3
Chanthaburi Thai. 79 C5
Chantonnay France 50 E3
Chantilly France 51 I3
Chanumla India 95 G4
Chanute U.S.A. 178 D4
Chany, Ozero *salt l.* Rus. Fed. 80 B2
Chanza *r.* Port./Spain 54 D7
  also spelt Chança
Chao Peru 200 A1
Chaobai Xinhe *r.* China 85 I4
Chaohu China 87 F2
Chao Hu *l.* China 87 F2
Chao Phraya *r.* Thai. 79 C5
Chaor China 85 I1
Chaor *r.* China 85 I2
Chaouèn Morocco 122 D2
Chaoyang Guangdong China 87 F4
Chaoyang China *see* Jiayin
Chaoyang China *see* Huinan
Chaoyang Liaoning China 85 I3
Chaozhong China 85 I1
Chaozhou China 87 F4
Chapada Diamantina, Parque Nacional *nat. park* Brazil 202 D5
Chapada dos Guimarães Brazil 201 F3
Chapada dos Veadeiros, Parque Nacional da *nat. park* Brazil 202 C5
Chapadão do Céu Brazil 206 A3
Chapadão do Sul Brazil 206 A5
Chapadinha Brazil 202 D2
Chapais Canada 169 F3
Chapak Guzar Afgh. 101 F2

Chapala Mex. 185 E4
Chapala, Laguna de *l.* Mex. 185 E4
Chapare *r.* Bol. 200 D3
Chaparral Col. 198 C3
Chapayev Kazakh. 102 B2
Chapayevsk Rus. Fed. 102 B1
Chapayevskoye Kazakh. 103 H1
Chapecó Brazil 203 A8
Chapecó *r.* Brazil 203 A8
Chapel Hill U.S.A. 174 E5
Chapicuy Uruguay 204 F3
Chapimarca Peru 200 B3
Chapleau Canada 168 D4
Chapleau Crown Game Reserve *nature res.* Canada 168 D4
Chaplin Canada 167 J5
Chaplin Lake *dry lake* Canada 167 J5
Chaplino Rus. Fed. 41 F6
Chaplygin Rus. Fed. 41 F5
Chapman, Mount Canada 166 G5
Chapman, *PA* U.S.A. 174 C5
Chapmanville WV U.S.A. 176 C8
Chappell U.S.A. 178 B3
Chappell Islands Australia 147 E5
Chapra India *see* Chhapra
Chapri Pass Afgh. 101 F3
Charadai Arg. 204 F2
Charagua Bol. 201 E4
Charana Bol. 200 C4
Charapita Col. 198 C5
Charata Arg. 204 E2
Charbonnel, Pointe de *mt.* France 51 N7
Charcas Mex. 185 E4
Charcot Island Antarctica 222 S2
Chard Canada 167 I4
Chard U.K. 47 J11
Chardara Kazakh. *see* Shardara
Chardarinskoye Vodokhranilishche *resr* Kazakh./Uzbek. 103 G4
  also known as Shardara Bögeni
Chardon U.S.A. 176 D4
Chardzhev Turkm. 103 E5
  also known as Turkmenabat; *also spelt* Chärjew; *formerly spelt* Chardzhou
Chardzhou Turkm. *see* Chardzhev
Chardzhouskaya Oblast' *admin. div.* Turkm. *see* Lebapskaya Oblast'
Char Chu *r.* Xizang China 89 F6
Charente *r.* France 50 F7
Charg Iran 100 C4
Chari *r.* Cameroon/Chad 125 I3
  also spelt Shari
Chari-Baguirmi *pref.* Chad 126 C2
Chārīkār Afgh. 101 G3
Charikot Nepal 97 E4
Chariton U.S.A. 174 A3
Chariton *r.* U.S.A. 174 A4
Chärjew Turkm. *see* Chardzhev
Charkayuvom Rus. Fed. 40 J2
Charkhari India 96 C4
Charkhi Dadri India 96 C3
Charkhlik China *see* Ruoqiang
Charleroi Belgium 51 K2
Charles, Cape U.S.A. 177 J8
Charlesbourg Canada 169 G4
Charles City IA U.S.A. 174 A3
Charles City VA U.S.A. 177 H8
Charles de Gaulle *airport* France 51 I3
Charles Lake Canada 167 I3
Charles M. Russell National Wildlife Refuge *nature res.* U.S.A. 180 F3
Charles Point Australia 148 A2
Charleston N.Z. 153 F9
Charleston IL U.S.A. 174 B4
Charleston MO U.S.A. 174 B4
Charleston MS U.S.A. 175 B5
Charleston SC U.S.A. 175 E5

▶ Charleston WV U.S.A. 176 D7
  State capital of West Virginia.

Charleston Peak U.S.A. 183 I5
Charleston St Kitts and Nevis 187 H3
Charlestown NH U.S.A. 177 M2
Charlestown RI U.S.A. 177 N4
Charles Town U.S.A. 176 H6
Charleville Australia 149 E5
Charleville Rep. of Ireland *see* Rathluirc
Charleville-Mézières France 51 K3
Charlevoix U.S.A. 172 H5
Charlie Lake Canada 166 F3
Charlotte MI U.S.A. 173 I8
Charlotte NC U.S.A. 174 D5

▶ Charlotte Amalie Virgin Is (U.S.A.) 187 G3
  Capital of the U.S. Virgin Islands.

Charlotte Bank *sea feature* S. China Sea 77 D1
Charlotte Court House U.S.A. 176 G8
Charlotte Harbor b. U.S.A. 175 D7
Charlotte Lake Canada 166 E4
Charlottenberg Sweden 45 K4
Charlottesville U.S.A. 176 G7

▶ Charlottetown Canada 169 I4
  Provincial capital of Prince Edward Island.

Charlton Australia 147 D4
Charlton Island Canada 168 E2
Charmes France 51 M4
Charnitsa *r.* Belarus 43 J7
Charny *r.* Australia 150 D3
Charolles France 51 K6
Charoum Kazakh. *see* Sharyn
Charomeskoye Rus. Fed. 43 T2
Charozero Rus. Fed. 43 T1
Charron Lake Canada 167 M4
Charsadda Pak. 101 G3
Charshanga Turkm. 103 F5
Charsk Kazakh. *see* Shar
Charters U.S.A. 176 B7
Charters Towers Australia 149 E4
Chartres France 50 H4
Charvakskoye Vodokhranilishche *resr* Kazakh./Uzbek. 103 G4
Charyn Kazakh. 103 I4
Charyn *r.* Kazakh. 103 I4
  also spelt Sharyn
Charysh *r.* Rus. Fed. 103 J1
Charyshskoye Rus. Fed. 88 E1
Chas India 97 E5
Châs *mt.* Port. 54 C3
Chascomús Arg. 204 F4
Chaschull Arg. 204 C2
Chase Canada 166 G5
Chase U.S.A. 172 H7
Chase City U.S.A. 176 G9
Chashkeh-ye Ab-e Garm *spring* Iran 100 D3
Chashmeh-ye Garm Ab *spring* Iran 100 D3
Chashmeh-ye Magu *well* Iran 100 D3
Chashmeh-ye Safid *spring* Iran 100 C3
Chashmeh-ye Shotoran *well* Iran 100 C3
Chashniki Belarus 43 K7
Chasia *reg.* Greece 59 C9
Chasico Arg. 205 D6
Chaska U.S.A. 178 D2
Chaslands Mistake *c.* N.Z. 153 D14
Chasovenskaya Rus. Fed. 43 O1
Chasôvoye Rus. Fed. 43 T2
Chassiron, Pointe de France 50 E6
Chastab, Küh-e *mts* Iran 100 C3
Chastyye Rus. Fed. 40 J4
Chasuta Peru 198 C5
Chāt Iran 100 C2
Chatang China *see* Zhanang
Château-Arnoux France 51 L8

Châteaubriant France 50 E5
Château-Chinon France 51 J5
Château-du-Loir France 50 G5
Chateaugay U.S.A. 177 K1
Châteaugiron France 50 E5
Château-Gontier France 50 F5
Châteaulin France 50 B4
Châteauneuf-en-Thymerais France 50 H4
Châteauneuf-sur-Loire France 51 I5
Chateau Pond *l.* Canada 169 J2
Châteauponsac France 50 H6
Château-Renault France 50 G5
Châteauroux France 50 H6
Château-Salins France 51 M4
Château-Thierry France 51 J3
Châtelaillon-Plage France 50 E6
Châtelet Belgium 51 K2
Châtellerault France 50 G6
Châtenois France 51 L4
Chatfield U.S.A. 178 D3
Chatham N.B. Canada 169 H4
Chatham Ont. Canada 168 D5
Chatham U.K. 47 M12
Chatham MA U.S.A. 177 P4
Chatham MI U.S.A. 172 G4
Chatham NY U.S.A. 177 L3
Chatham VA U.S.A. 176 F9
Chatham, Isla *i.* Chile 205 B8
Chatham Island Samoa *see* Savai'i
Chatham Island S. Pacific Ocean 145 H6
  also known as Rekohua
Chatham Islands S. Pacific Ocean 145 H6
Chatham Sound *sea chan.* Canada 166 D4
Chatham Strait U.S.A. 166 C3
Châtillon-sur-Indre France 50 H6
Châtillon-sur-Seine France 51 K5
Chatkal *mts* Kyrg. 103 G4
Chatkal *r.* Kyrg. 103 G4
Chatom U.S.A. 175 B6
Chatra India 97 E4
Chatra Nepal 97 E4
Chatsu India 96 B4
Chatsworth Australia 149 D4
Chatsworth Canada 173 M6
Chatsworth GA U.S.A. 174 C5
Chatsworth IL U.S.A. 172 E10
Chatsworth NJ U.S.A. 177 K6
Chatsworth Zimbabwe 131 F4
Chattagam Bangl. *see* Chittagong
Chattahoochee U.S.A. 175 C6
Chattahoochee *r.* U.S.A. 179 F6
Chattanooga U.S.A. 174 C5
Chatto Creek N.Z. 153 D13
Chatturat Thai. 79 C5
Chatyrkël', Ozero *l.* Kyrg. *see* Chatyr-Köl
Chatyr-Köl *l.* Kyrg. 103 H4
  also known as Chatyrkël', Ozero
Chatyr-Tash Kyrg. 103 I4
Châu Đôc Vietnam 79 D6
  formerly known as Chau Phu
Chauffailles France 51 K6
Chauhtan India 96 A4
Chauk Myanmar 78 A3
Chauka *r.* India 96 D4
Chaukhamba *mts* India *see* Badrinath Peaks
Chau Kung To *i.* Hong Kong China *see* Sunshine Island
Chaumont France 51 L4
Chauncey U.S.A. 176 C7
Chaungwabyin Myanmar 79 B5
Chaunskaya Guba *b.* Rus. Fed. 39 Q3
Chauny France 51 J3
Chau Phu Vietnam *see* Châu Đôc
Chaurai India 96 C5
Chausey, Îles *is* France 50 E4
Chausy Belarus *see* Chavusy
Chautauqua, Lake U.S.A. 176 F3
Chauvay Kyrg. 103 H4
Chauvigny France 50 G6
Chauvin Canada 167 I4
Chavakachcheri Sri Lanka 94 D4
Chaval Brazil 202 D2
Chavan'ga Rus. Fed. 40 F2
Chavar Iran 100 A3
Chaves Brazil 202 B2
Chaves Port. 54 D3
Chaves Valdivia Peru 198 B6
Chavigny, Lac *l.* Canada 169 F1
Chaviva Col. 198 D3
Chavusy Belarus 43 L8
  also known as Chausy
Chawal *r.* Pak. 101 F4
Chay *r.* Vietnam 78 D3
Chayan Kazakh. *see* Shayan
Chayanta *r.* Bol. 200 D4
Chayek Kyrg. *see* Chaek
Chayevo Rus. Fed. 43 S4
Chaykovskiy Rus. Fed. 40 J4
Chazhegovo Rus. Fed. 40 J3
Chazón Arg. 204 E4
Chazy U.S.A. 177 L1
Cheat *r.* U.S.A. 176 F6
Cheb Czech Rep. 49 J5
Chebanse U.S.A. 172 F9
Chebbi *salt l.* Alg. 123 H4
Cheboksary Rus. Fed. 40 H4
Cheboygan U.S.A. 173 I6
Chebsara Rus. Fed. 43 T3
Ch'ech'ŏng Taiwan 87 C4
Chechenia *aut. rep.* Rus. Fed. *see* Chechenskaya Respublika
Chechenskaya Respublika *aut. rep.* Rus. Fed. 41 H8
  short form Chechnya; *English form* Chechenia *or* Chechnia; *also known as* Ichkeria
Cheche Pass Lesotho 133 M6
Chechnya *aut. rep.* Rus. Fed. *see* Chechenskaya Respublika
Chech'ŏn S. Korea 83 C5
  also spelt Jecheon
Chęciny Poland 49 R5
Checotah U.S.A. 179 D5
Cheder Rus. Fed. 84 B1
Cheduba Island Myanmar 78 A4
Cheduba Strait Myanmar 78 A4
  also known as Man-aung Kyun
Chee *r.* France 51 K4
Cheektowaga U.S.A. 176 G3
Cheepie Australia 149 E5
Cheetham, Cape Antarctica 223 K2
Chef-Boutonne France 50 F6
Cheffadène *well* Niger 125 I2
Chegga Mauritania 122 D4
Chéggué *watercourse* Mauritania 124 C2
Chegguet Ti-n-Kerkâz *des.* Mauritania 124 D2
Chegutu Zimbabwe 131 F3
  formerly known as Hartley
Chehalis U.S.A. 180 B3
Chehalis *r.* U.S.A. 180 B3
Chehardeh Iran 100 D3
Chehariz *tourist site* Iraq 107 F4
Chehel Chashmeh, Kūh-e *hill* Iran 100 A3
Chehel Dokhtarān, Kūh-e *mt.* Iran 101 E3
Cheikria *well* Alg. 123 G2
Cheil Nerei-Beușnița *nat. park* Romania 58 C3

Cheiron, Cime du *mt.* France 51 M9
Cheju S. Korea 83 B6
Cheju-do *i.* S. Korea 83 B6
  English form Quelpart Island
Cheju-haehyŏp *sea chan.* S. Korea 83 B6
Chekalin Rus. Fed. 43 R7
Chek Chau *i.* Hong Kong China *see* Port Island
Chekhov Rus. Fed. 43 S6
Chekhov Rus. Fed. 82 F3
  formerly known as Lopasnya
Chekhov Rus. Fed. 82 F3
Chekiang *prov.* China *see* Zhejiang
Chek Jawa, Tanjong *pt* Sing. 76 [inset]
Chek Lap Kok *i.* Hong Kong China 87 [inset]
Chek Mun Hoi Hap *sea chan.* Hong Kong China *see* Tolo Channel
Chekshino Rus. Fed. 43 V2
Chela, Serra da *mts* Angola 127 B9
Chelan U.S.A. 180 B3
Chelan, Lake U.S.A. 180 B2
Cheleken Turkm. 102 C5
Chelford Arg. 204 D5
Chélif, Oued *r.* Alg. 55 L8
Chellal Alg. 55 P9
Chełm Poland 53 L1
  historically known as Kholm
Chelmer *r.* U.K. 47 M12
Chelmno Poland 49 P2
Chelmsford U.K. 47 M12
  historically known as Caesaromagus
Chelmsford U.S.A. 177 N3
Chelmsford Dam S. Africa 133 N4
Chelmsford Public Resort Nature Reserve S. Africa 133 N4
Chełmża Poland 49 P2
Chelsea U.S.A. 173 I8
Cheltenham U.K. 47 J12
Chelva Spain 55 K5
Chelyabinsk Rus. Fed. 38 G4
Chelyabinskaya Oblast' *admin. div.* Rus. Fed. 103 G1
  English form Chelyabinsk Oblast
Chelyabinsk Oblast *admin. div.* Rus. Fed. *see* Chelyabinskaya Oblast'
Chelyan U.S.A. 176 D7
Chelyuskin Rus. Fed. 39 K2
Chelyuskin, Mys *c.* Rus. Fed. 39 K2
Chemaïs Morocco 122 C2
Chemax Mex. 185 I4
Chembe Zambia 127 F7
Chemchām, Sebkhet *salt flat* Mauritania 122 B5
Chem Co *l.* China 89 B5
Chemenliti Turkm. 101 E3
Chemillé France 50 F5
Chemmis Egypt *see* Akhmim
Chemnitz Germany 49 J5
  formerly known as Karl-Marx-Stadt
Chemult S. Korea *see* Inch'ŏn
Chemult U.S.A. 180 B4
Chemung U.S.A. 177 I4
Chenab *r.* India/Pak. 96 A3
Chenachane Alg. 122 D4
Chenachane, Oued *watercourse* Alg. 122 E4
Chenango *r.* U.S.A. 177 J3
Chenango Bridge U.S.A. 177 J3
Ch'ench'a Eth. 128 C3
Chendir *r.* Turkm. *see* Chandyr
Cheney U.S.A. 180 C3
Cheney Reservoir U.S.A. 178 C4
Chengalpattu India 94 D3
  formerly known as Chingleput
Chengam India 94 C3
Cheng'an China 85 G4
Chengbihe Shuiku *resr* China 86 C3
Chengbu China 87 D3
  also known as Rulin
Chengcheng China 85 F4
Chengchow China *see* Zhengzhou
Chengde China 85 H3
Chengdu China 86 C2
  formerly spelt Chengtu
Chengel'dy Kazakh. *see* Shengel'dy
Chenggong China 86 B3
  also known as Longcheng
Chenghai China 87 F4
Cheng Hai *l.* China 86 B3
Chengjiang China 86 B3
  also known as Taihe
Chengkou China 87 D2
  also known as Gecheng
Chengqian China 85 H5
Chengshou China *see* Yingshan
Chengtu China *see* Chengdu
Chengwu China 87 E1
Chengxian China 86 C1
Chengxian China *see* Fuquan
Chengxiang China *see* Wuxi
Chengxiang China *see* Quannan
Chengxiang China *see* Tianquan
Chengxiang China *see* Mianning
Chengyang China *see* Juxian
Chengzhong China *see* Ningming
Cheniu Shan *i.* China 85 H5
Chennai India 94 D3
  formerly known as Madras
Chenoa U.S.A. 172 E10
Chenstokhov Poland *see* Częstochowa
Chentejn Nuruu *mts* Mongolia 85 E1
Chenting, Tanjong *pt* Sing. 76 [inset]
Chenxi China 87 D3
  also known as Chenyang
Chenyang China *see* Wannian
Chenying China *see* Wannian
Chenzhou China 87 E3
Cheom Ksan Cambodia *see* Chŏâm Khsant
Chepelare Bulg. 58 F7
Chepén Peru 200 A1
Chepo Panama 186 D5
Chepstow U.K. 47 J12
Cheptsa *r.* Rus. Fed. 40 I4
Chequamegon Bay U.S.A. 172 B4
Cher *r.* France 50 H5
Chera *state* India *see* Kerala
Cherán Mex. 185 E5
Cherangany Hills Kenya 128 B4
Cheraw U.S.A. 174 E5
Cherbaniani Reef India 94 A3
  also known as Beleapani
Cherbourg France 50 E3
  historically known as Caesaris
Cherchen China *see* Qiemo
Cherchen Rus. Fed. 40 K3
Chère *r.* France 50 E5
Chereapani *reef* India *see* Byramgore Reef
Cherekha *r.* Rus. Fed. 43 J4
Cheremisinovo Rus. Fed. 41 F6
Cheremkhovo Rus. Fed. 80 D2
  formerly known as Sinancha
Cheremukhinka Rus. Fed. 80 D2
Cherepanovo Rus. Fed. 80 C2
Cherepovets Rus. Fed. 43 S3
Cherevkovo Rus. Fed. 40 H3
Cherikov Belarus *see* Cherykaw
Chéria Alg. 123 G2
Cherlal India 94 C2
Cheriton U.S.A. 177 J8
Cheriyam *i.* India 94 B4
Chérkira Rus. Fed. 40 J4

Cherkasy Ukr. 41 E6
  also spelt Cherkassy
Cherkeskk Rus. Fed. 41 G7
Cherkutino Rus. Fed. 43 U5
Cherla India 94 D2
Chermenze Angola 127 C8
Chermoz Rus. Fed. 40 K4
Chern' Rus. Fed. 43 R8
Chernak Kazakh. 103 G4
  also spelt Shornaq
Chernaya Rus. Fed. 40 K1
Chernaya *r.* Rus. Fed. 40 K1
Chernaya *r.* Rus. Fed. 40 K1
Chernaya *r.* Rus. Fed. 40 I4
Chernaya Lipetskaya Oblast' Rus. Fed. 43 T9
Chernava Ryazanskaya Oblast' Rus. Fed. 43 U8
Chernaya Kholunitsa Rus. Fed. 40 I4
Chernevo Moskovskaya Oblast' Rus. Fed. 43 T7
Chernevo Pskovskaya Oblast' Rus. Fed. 43 J3
Chernigov Ukr. *see* Chernihiv
Chernigovka Rus. Fed. 82 D3
Chernihiv Ukr. 41 E6
  also spelt Chernigov
Cherni Lom *r.* Bulg. 58 G5
Cherni Vrŭkh *mt.* Bulg. 58 E6
Chernivtsi Ukr. 41 C6
  also known as Czernowitz; *also spelt* Chernovtsy; *historically known as* Cernăuţi
Chernobyl' Ukr. *see* Chornobyl'
Chernoostrovskoye Rus. Fed. 39 I3
Chernorechenskiy Rus. Fed. 40 I3
Chernoretskoye Kazakh. 103 I1
Chernushevo Rus. Fed. 43 N1
Chernovtsy Ukr. *see* Chernivtsi
Chernoye More *sea* Asia/Europe *see* Black Sea
Chernushka Rus. Fed. 40 K4
Chernyakhiv Ukr. 41 D6
Chernyakhovsk Rus. Fed. 42 C7
  historically known as Insterburg
Chernyanka Rus. Fed. 41 F6
Chernyayeve Rus. Fed. 82 B1
Chernysheva, Zaliv *b.* Kazakh. 102 D3
Chernyshevsk Rus. Fed. 81 J2
Chernyshevskiy Rus. Fed. 39 L3
Chernyshkovskiy Rus. Fed. 41 G6
Chernyy, Mys *c.* Rus. Fed. 40 J1
Chernyye Zemli *reg.* Rus. Fed. 41 H7
Chernyy Irtysh *r.* China/Kazakh. *see* Ertix He
Chernyy Otrog Rus. Fed. 102 C2
Chernyy Porog Rus. Fed. 40 E3
Chernyy Rynok Rus. Fed. *see* Kochubey
Chernyy Yar Rus. Fed. 102 A2
Cherokee IA U.S.A. 178 D3
Cherokee TX U.S.A. 178 C4
Cherokee Lake U.S.A. 178 B9
Cherokees, Lake o' the U.S.A. 178 D4
Cherokee Sound Bahamas 186 D1
Cherpessa Rus. Fed. 43 L5

▶ Cherrapunji India 97 F4
  Highest recorded annual rainfall in the world.
  world [climate and weather] ▶▶ 16–17

Cherry Creek *r.* U.S.A. 178 B2
Cherry Creek Mountains U.S.A. 183 J1
Cherryfield U.S.A. 177 R1
Cherry Hill U.S.A. 177 K6
Cherry Island Solomon Is 145 F3
Cherry Lake U.S.A. 182 E3
Cherry Valley Canada 173 P7
Cherskaya Rus. Fed. 43 J4
Cherskiy Rus. Fed. 39 Q3
Cherskiy Range *mts* Rus. Fed. *see* Cherskogo, Khrebet
Cherskogo, Khrebet *mts* Rus. Fed. 85 F1
  English form Cherskiy Range
Cherskogo, Khrebet *mts* Rus. Fed. 81 J2
Chersonisos Methano *pen.* Greece 59 E11
Cherthala India *see* Shertally
Chertkov Ukr. *see* Chortkiv
Chertkovo Rus. Fed. 41 G6
Chertolino Rus. Fed. 43 O5
Chertsey N.Z. 153 F11
Cherusti Rus. Fed. 43 V6
Chervonoarmeyskoye Ukr. *see* Vil'nyans'k
Chervonoarmiys'k Ukr. *see* Krasnoarmiys'k
Chervonograd Ukr. *see* Chervonohrad
Chervonohrad Ukr. 41 C6
  formerly known as Kristinopol' *or* Krystynopol
Chervonozavods'ke Ukr. 41 E6
Chervonoznam"yanka Ukr. 58 L1
Chervyen' Belarus 43 J8
Cherykaw Belarus 43 M8
Chesaning U.S.A. 173 I7
Chesapeake U.S.A. 177 I9
Chesapeake Bay U.S.A. 177 I7
Chesapeake Beach U.S.A. 177 I7
Cheshire U.S.A. 177 L3
Cheshme Vtoroy Turkm. 102 E5
Cheshskaya Guba *b.* Rus. Fed. 40 I2
Chesht-e Sharīf Afgh. 101 E3
Chesma Rus. Fed. 103 E1
Chesnokovka Rus. Fed. *see* Novoaltaysk
Chester Canada 182 C1
Chester CA U.S.A. 182 C1
Chester IL U.S.A. 174 B4
Chester MT U.S.A. 180 E2
Chester NJ U.S.A. 177 K5
Chester OH U.S.A. 176 D6
Chester PA U.S.A. 177 J6
Chester SC U.S.A. 174 D5
Chester VA U.S.A. 176 H8
Chester *r.* U.S.A. 177 K10
Chesterfield U.K. 47 K10
Chesterfield MO U.S.A. 174 B4
Chesterfield SC U.S.A. 174 D5
Chesterfield VA U.S.A. 176 H8
Chesterfield, Îles *is* New Caledonia 145 E3
Chesterfield Inlet Canada 167 N2
  also known as Igluligaarjuk
Chesterfield Inlet *inlet* Canada 167 M2
Chestertown U.S.A. 177 I6
Chestnut Ridge U.S.A. 176 F5
Chesuncook Lake U.S.A. 174 G2
Chetek U.S.A. 172 B5
Chéticamp Canada 169 I4
Chetlat *i.* India 94 B4
Chetopa U.S.A. 178 D4
Chetumal Mex. 185 H5
Chetwode Islands N.Z. 152 I8
Chetwynd Canada 166 F4
Chevelon Creek *r.* U.S.A. 183 N7
Cheviot N.Z. 153 H10
Cheviot U.S.A. 176 A6
Cheviot Hills U.K. 47 J8
Cheviot Range *hills* Australia 149 D5
Chevreulx *r.* Canada 169 F2
Che'w Bahir *salt l.* Eth. 128 C3
Che'w Bahir Wildlife Reserve *nature res.* Eth. 128 C3
Chewelah U.S.A. 180 C2
Cheyenne OK U.S.A. 179 C5

▶ Cheyenne WY U.S.A. 180 F4
  State capital of Wyoming.

Cheyenne *r.* U.S.A. 178 B2

Cheyenne River Indian Reservation *res.* U.S.A. **178** B2
Cheyenne Wells U.S.A. **178** B4
Cheyne Bay Australia **151** B7
Cheyur India **94** D3
Cheyyar *r.* India **94** C3
Chezacut Canada **166** E4
Chhabra India **96** C4
Chhapar India **96** B4
Chhapra India **97** E4
formerly spelt Chapra
Chhata India **96** C4
Chhatak Bangl. **97** F4
Chhatarpur *Jharkhand* India **97** E4
Chhatarpur *Madhya Pradesh* India **96** C4
Chhatrapur India **95** E2
Chhattisgarh *state* India **97** D5
Chhay Arêng, Stœng *r.* Cambodia **79** C6
Chhibramau India **96** C4
Chhindwara India **96** C5
Chhipa Barod India **96** C4
Chhlong, Prêk *r.* Cambodia **79** D5
Chhota Chhindwara India **96** C5
Chhota Udepur India **96** B5
Chhuikhadan India **96** D5
Chhuk Cambodia *see* **Phumĭ Chhuk**
Chhukha Bhutan **97** F4
Chiai Taiwan **87** G4
also spelt Jiayi
Ch'iak-san National Park S. Korea **83** C5
Chiang Dao Thai. **78** B4
Chiange Angola **127** B8
formerly known as Vila de Almoster
Chiang Kham Thai. **78** C4
Chiang Khan Thai. **78** C4
Chiang Mai Thai. **78** B4
also spelt Chiengmai
Chiang Rai Thai. **78** B4
Chiani *r.* Italy **56** E6
Chiapa Mex. **185** G5
Chiapas *state* Mex. **185** G5
Chiat'ura Georgia **107** E2
Chiautla Mex. **185** F5
Chiavari Italy **56** B4
Chiavenno Italy **56** B2
Chiba Japan **91** G7
Chiba *pref.* Japan **90** G7
Chibemba Angola **127** B8
Chibi China **87** E2
Chibia Angola **127** B8
formerly known as João de Almeida
Chibit Rus. Fed. **88** D1
Chibizovka Rus. Fed. *see* **Zherdevka**
Chiboma Moz. **131** G4
Chibougamau Canada **169** F3
Chibougamau, Lac *l.* Canada **169** F3
Chibu-Sangaku National Park Japan **91** E6
English form Japan Alps National Park
Chibuto Moz. **131** G5
Chibuzhang Hu *l.* China **89** E5
Chibwe Zambia **127** F8
Chicacole India *see* **Srikakulam**

▶**Chicago** U.S.A. **174** C3
4th most populous city in North America.
world [cities] ▶ 24–25

Chicago Heights U.S.A. **172** F9
Chicala Angola **127** C7
Chicamba Moz. **131** G3
Chicapa *r.* Angola **127** D6
Chic-Chocs, Monts *mts* Canada **169** H3
Chic-Chocs, Réserve Faunique des *nature res.* Canada **169** H3
Chicera Hamba *hill* Romania **58** F3
Chicha *well* Chad **120** C5
Chichagof Island U.S.A. **164** F4
Chichak *r.* Pak. **101** F5
Chichaoua Morocco **122** C3
Chichas, Cordillera de *mts* Bol. **200** D5
Chicheng China **85** G3
Chicheng China *see* **Pengxi**
Chichén Itzá *tourist site* Mex. **185** H4
Chichester U.K. **47** L13
Chichester Range *mts* Australia **150** B4
Chichgarh India **94** D1
Chichibu Japan **83** E6
Chichibu-Tama National Park Japan **91** F7
Chichijima-rettō *is* Japan **73** J1
Chichiriviche Venez. **199** D2
Chicholi India **96** C5
Chickahominy *r.* U.S.A. **177** I8
Chickasawhay *r.* U.S.A. **175** B6
Chickasha U.S.A. **179** C5
Chiclana de la Frontera Spain **54** E8
Chiclayo Peru **198** B6
Chico *r.* *Chubut* Arg. **205** C6
Chico *r.* *Chubut* Arg. **205** D7
Chico *r.* *Santa Cruz* Arg. **205** C8
Chico U.S.A. **182** C2
Chicoa Moz. **131** G2
Chicobea *i.* Fiji *see* **Cikobia**
Chicobi, Lac *l.* Canada **173** O2
Chicomba Angola **127** B8
Chicomo Moz. **131** G5
Chicomucelo Mex. **185** G6
Chiconono Moz. **129** B8
Chicopee U.S.A. **177** M3
Chico Sapocoy, Mount Phil. **74** B2
Chicoutimi Canada **169** G3
Chicoutimi *r.* Canada **169** G3
Chicualacuala Moz. **131** F4
formerly known as Malvérnia
Chicuma Angola **127** B8
Chidambaram India **94** C4
Chido S. Korea **83** B6
Chiede Angola **127** C9
Chiefland U.S.A. **175** D6
Chiemsee *l.* Germany **49** J8
Chiengi Zambia **127** F7
Chiengmai Thai. *see* **Chiang Mai**
Chienti *r.* Italy **56** F5
Chieo Lan Reservoir Thai. **79** B6
Chieri Italy **51** N7
Chiers *r.* France **51** L3
Chiese *r.* Italy **56** C3
Chieti Italy **56** G6
historically known as Teate
Chifeng China **85** H3
also known as Ulanhad
Chifre, Serra do *mts* Brazil **203** D6
Chifunde Moz. **131** G2
formerly known as Tembué
Chiganak Kazakh. **103** H3
also spelt Shyghanaq
Chiginagak, Mount *vol.* U.S.A. **164** D4
Chignecto Bay Canada **169** H4
Chignecto Game Sanctuary *nature res.* Canada **169** H4
Chignik U.S.A. **164** D4
Chigorodó Col. **198** B3
Chigu China **89** E6
Chiguana Bol. **200** D5
Chigubo Moz. **131** G4
Chigu Co *l.* China **89** E6
Chihli, Gulf of China *see* **Bo Hai**
Chihuahua Mex. **184** D2
Chihuahua *state* Mex. **184** D2
Chilli Kazakh. **103** F3
also spelt Shieli
Chijinpu China **84** C3
Chikalda India **96** C5
Chikan China **87** D4
Chikaskia *r.* U.S.A. **178** C4
Chik Ballapur India **94** C3
Chikhachevo Rus. Fed. **43** K4
Chikhali Kalan Parasia India **96** C5
Chikhli India **94** C1
Chikmagalur India **94** B3
Chikodi India **94** B2
Chikodi Road India **94** B2
Chikoy Rus. Fed. **85** E1
Chikoy *r.* Rus. Fed. **85** E1
Chikugo Japan **91** B8
Chikuma-gawa *r.* Japan **90** F6
Chikushino Japan **91** B8
Chikwa Zambia **129** B7
Chikwawa Malawi **129** B9
Chikyū-misaki *pt* Japan **90** G3
Chila Angola **127** B8
Chilanko *r.* Canada **166** F4
Chilanko Forks Canada **166** E4
Chilapa Mex. **185** F5
Chilas Jammu and Kashmir **96** B2
Chilaw Sri Lanka **94** C5
Chilca Peru **200** A3
Chilcaya Chile **200** C4
Chilcotin *r.* Canada **166** F5
Chilcott Island Australia **149** F3
Childers Australia **149** G5
Childress U.S.A. **179** B5
▶**Chile** *country* S. America **205** B7
southamerica [countries] ▶ 192–193
Chile Chico Chile **205** C7
Chilecito Arg. **204** D3
Chilengue, Serra do *mts* Angola **127** B8
Chilete Peru **200** A1
Chilhowie U.S.A. **176** D9
Chilia-Nouă Ukr. *see* **Kiliya**
Chilia Veche Romania **58** K3
Chilik Kazakh. **103** I4
also spelt Shelek
Chilik *r.* Kazakh. **103** I3
Chilika Lake India **95** E2
Chililabombwe Zambia **127** E8
formerly known as Bancroft
Chilimodi Greece **59** D11
also known as Khiliomódhion
Chilko *r.* Canada **166** F4
Chilko Lake Canada **166** E5
Chilkoot Trail National Historic Site *nat. park* U.S.A. **164** F4
Chillagoe Australia **149** E3
Chillán Chile **204** B5
Chillar Arg. **204** F5
Chillicothe *IL* U.S.A. **172** D10
Chillicothe *MO* U.S.A. **178** D4
Chillicothe *OH* U.S.A. **176** C6
Chillicolpo Peru **200** C4
Chillinji Jammu and Kashmir **96** B1
Chilliwack Canada **166** F5
Chil'mamedkum, Peski *des.* Turkm. **102** C4
Chilmari Bangl. **97** F4
Chiloé, Isla de *i.* Chile **205** B6
long form Chiloé, Isla Grande de
Chiloé, Isla Grande de *i.* Chile *see* **Chiloé, Isla de**
Chilombo Angola **127** D8
Chilonga Zambia **127** F8
Chiloquin U.S.A. **180** B4
Chilpancingo Mex. **185** F5
Chiltern Australia **147** E4
Chiltern Hills U.K. **47** L12
Chilton U.S.A. **172** E6
Chiluage Angola **127** D7
Chilubi Zambia **127** F7
Chilumba Malawi **129** B7
Chilung Taiwan **87** G3
English form Keelung; *also spelt* Jilong
Chilung Pass Jammu and Kashmir **96** C2
Chilwa, Lake Malawi **129** B8
Chimala Tanz. **129** B7
Chimaltenango Guat. **185** H6
Chimán Panama **186** D5
Chimanimani Zimbabwe **131** G3
formerly known as Mandidzuzure *or* Melsetter
Chi Ma Wan *Hong Kong* China **87** [inset]
Chimbe Zambia **127** F7
Chimbas Arg. **204** C3
Chimbay Uzbek. **102** D4
also spelt Chimboy
Chimborazo *mt.* Ecuador **198** B5
Chimborazo *prov.* Ecuador **198** B5
Chimbote Peru **200** A2
Chimboy Uzbek. *see* **Chimbay**
Chimian Pak. **101** H4
Chimichaguá Col. **187** E5
Chimion Uzbek. **103** G4
Chimishliya Moldova *see* **Cimişlia**
Chimkent Kazakh. *see* **Shymkent**
Chimkentskaya Oblast' *admin. div.* Kazakh. *see* **Yuzhnyy Kazakhstan**
Chimoio Moz. **131** G3
formerly known as Vila Pery
Chimorra *hill* Spain **54** G6
Chimpay Arg. **204** D5
Chimtargha, Qullai *mt.* Tajik. **101** G2
also known as Chimtorga, Gora
Chimtorga, Gora *mt.* Tajik. *see* **Chimtargha, Qullai**
Chin *state* Myanmar **78** A3

▶**China** *country* Asia **80** D5
Most populous country in the world and in Asia. 2nd largest country in Asia and 4th largest in the world. Known in Chinese as Zhongguo; long form Zhongguo Renmin Gongheguo or Chung-hua Jen-min Kung-ho-kuo.
world [countries] ▶ 10–11
world [population] ▶ 22–23
asia [countries] ▶ 64–67

Chinghwa N. Korea **83** B5
Chingirlau Kazakh. **102** C2
also spelt Shyngghyrlaū
Chingiz-Tau, Khrebet *mts* Kazakh. **103** I2
Chingleput India *see* **Chengalpattu**
Chingola Zambia **127** E8
Chinguar Angola **127** C8
Chinguetti Mauritania **122** B5
Chinguil Chad **126** C2
Chinhae S. Korea **83** C6
Chinhanda Moz. **131** G2
Chinhoyi Zimbabwe **131** F3
formerly spelt Sinoia
Chini India *see* **Kalpa**
Chiniljo Bol. **200** C3
Chining China *see* **Jining**
Chiniot Pak. **101** H4
Chinipas Mex. **184** C3
Chinit, Stœng *r.* Cambodia **79** D5
Chinju S. Korea **83** C6
Chinko *r.* Cent. Afr. Rep. **126** D3
Chinle U.S.A. **183** O5
Chinle Valley U.S.A. **183** O5
Chinle Wash *watercourse* U.S.A. **183** O5
Chinmen Taiwan **87** F3
also spelt Jinmen *or* Kinmen
Chinmen Tao *i.* Taiwan **87** F3
English form Quemoy
Chinna Ganjam India **94** D3
Chinnamanur India **94** C4
Chinnamp'o N. Korea *see* **Namp'o**
Chinna Salem India **94** C4
Chinnur India **94** C2
Chino Japan **91** F7
Chino U.S.A. **182** G7
Chino Creek *watercourse* U.S.A. **183** L7
Chinocup, Lake *salt flat* Australia **151** B7
Chinocup Nature Reserve Australia **151** B7
Chinon France **50** G5
Chinook U.S.A. **180** E2
Chino Valley U.S.A. **183** L7
Chinoz Uzbek. *see* **Chinaz**
Chinsali Zambia **129** B7
Chintalnar India **94** D2
Chintamani India **94** C3
Chinteni Romania **58** E2
Chinú Col. **198** C2
Chinyama Litapi Zambia **127** D8
Chin'yavoryk Rus. Fed. **40** J3
Chioco Moz. **131** G3
Chioggia Italy **56** E3
Chiona Tanz. **129** B6
Chios Greece **59** H10
Chios *i.* Greece **59** G10
also spelt Khíos
Chios Strait Greece **59** H10
English form Khios Strait
Chipanga Moz. **131** G3
Chipata Zambia **129** B8
formerly known as Fort Jameson
Chipchihua, Sierra de *mts* Arg. **205** C6
Chipili Zambia **127** F7
Chipindo Angola **127** B8
Chiping China **85** H4
Chipinga Zimbabwe *see* **Chipinge**
Chipinge Zimbabwe **131** G4
formerly spelt Chipinga
Chipiona Spain **54** E8
Chipley U.S.A. **175** C6
Chiplun India **94** B2
Chipman Canada **169** H4
Chipoia Angola **127** C8
Chippenham U.K. **47** J12
Chipperone, Monte *mt.* Moz. **131** G3
Chippewa *r. MN* U.S.A. **178** D2
Chippewa *r. WI* U.S.A. **172** A6
Chippewa, Lake U.S.A. **172** B5
Chippewa Falls U.S.A. **172** B6
Chipping Norton U.K. **47** K12
Chiprovtsi Bulg. **58** D5
Chipundu Zambia **127** F8
Chipuriro Zimbabwe *see* **Guruve**
Chipurupalle *Andhra Pradesh* India **95** D2
Chipurupalle *Andhra Pradesh* India **95** D2
Chiquian Peru **200** A2
Chiquibul, Parque Nacional *nat. park* Belize **185** H5
Chiquilá Mex. **185** I4
Chiquimula Guat. **185** H6
Chiquinquira Col. **198** C3
Chiquintirca Peru **200** B3
Chiquita, Mar *l.* Arg. **204** E4
Chiquitos, Llanos de *plain* Bol. **201** E4
Chiquitos Jesuit Missions *tourist site* Brazil **201** E4
Chir *r.* Rus. Fed. **41** G6
Chirada India **94** D3
Chiradzulu Malawi **129** B8
Chirala India **94** D3
Chiramba Moz. **131** G3
Chirambirá, Punta *pt* Col. **198** B3
Chiras Afgh. **101** F3
Chirawa India **89** A6
Chirchik Uzbek. **103** G4
Chirchik *r.* Uzbek. **103** G4
Chiredzi Zimbabwe **131** F4
Chire Wildlife Reserve *nature res.* Eth. **128** C1
Chirfa Niger **125** I1
Chirgua *r.* Venez. **199** E2

Chisholm *MN* U.S.A. **178** D2
Chishtian Mandi Pak. **101** H4
Chishui China **86** C2
Chishuihe China **86** C3
Chishui He *r.* China **86** C2
Chisimaio Somalia *see* **Kismaayo**

▶**Chişinău** Moldova **58** J1
Capital of Moldova. Formerly spelt Kishinev.

Chişineu-Criş Romania **58** C2
Chisone *r.* Italy **51** N8
Chistopol' Rus. Fed. **40** I5
Chistopol'ye Kazakh. **103** F1
Chistyakovskoye Kazakh. **103** G1
Chita Bol. **200** D5
Chita Col. **198** C3
Chita Rus. Fed. **85** G1
Chita Tanz. **129** B7
Chitado Angola **127** B9
Chitaldrug India *see* **Chitradurga**
Chitalwana India **96** A4
Chita Oblast *admin. div.* Rus. Fed. *see* **Chitinskaya Oblast'**
Chitato Angola **127** D6
formerly known as Portugália
Chitayevo Rus. Fed. **40** I3
Chitek Lake Canada **167** J4
Chitek Lake *l.* Canada **167** L4
Chitembo Angola **127** C8
Chitinskaya Oblast' *admin. div.* Rus. Fed. **85** H1
English form Chita Oblast
Chitipa Malawi **129** B7
Chitobe Moz. **131** G4
formerly known as Machaze
Chitokoloki Zambia **127** D8
Chitongo Zambia **127** E9
Chitor India *see* **Chittaurgarh**
Chitose Japan **90** G3
Chitradurga India **94** C3
formerly known as Chitaldrug
Chitrakut India **96** D4
Chitral Pak. **101** G3
Chitral *r.* Pak. **101** G3
Chitravati *r.* India **94** C3
Chitré Panama **186** C6
Chitrod India **96** A5
Chittagong Bangl. **97** F5
also spelt Chattagam
Chittagong *admin. div.* Bangl. **97** F5
Chittaranjan India **97** E5
formerly known as Mihidjan
Chittaurgarh India **96** B4
formerly known as Chitor; *formerly spelt* Chittorgarh
Chittoor India **94** C3
Chittorgarh India *see* **Chittaurgarh**
Chittur India **94** C4
Chitungulu Zambia **129** B8
Chitungwiza Zimbabwe **131** F3
Chiu Lung *Hong Kong* China *see* **Kowloon**
Chiume Angola **127** D8
Chiúre Novo Moz. **131** H2
Chiusa Sclafani *Sicilia* Italy **57** F11
Chiúta Moz. **131** G2
Chiva Spain **55** K5
Chivasso Italy **56** A3
Chivato, Punta *pt* Mex. **184** C3
Chivay Peru **200** C3
Chive Bol. **200** C3
Chivela Mex. **185** G5
Chivhu Zimbabwe **131** F3
formerly known as Enkeldoorn
Chivilcoy Arg. **204** E4
Chiyirchik, Pereval *pass* Kyrg. *see* **Ashusuu**
Chizarira Hills Zimbabwe **131** E3
Chizarira National Park Zimbabwe **131** E3
Chizha Vtoraya Kazakh. **102** B2
Chizu Japan **91** D7
Chkalov Rus. Fed. *see* **Orenburg**
Chkalovo Kazakh. **103** G1
Chkalovsk Rus. Fed. **40** G4
Chkalovskaya Oblast' *admin. div.* Rus. Fed. *see* **Orenburgskaya Oblast'**
Chkalovskiy Rus. Fed. **44** P2
Chkalovskoye Rus. Fed. **82** D3
Chlef Alg. *see* **Ech Chélif**
Chloride U.S.A. **183** J6
Chlumec nad Cidlinou Czech Rep. **49** M5
Chlya, Ozero *l.* Rus. Fed. **82** F1
Chmielnik Poland **49** R5
Choa Chu Kang Sing. **76** [inset]
Choa Chu Kang *hill* Sing. **76** [inset]
Chŏâm Khsant Cambodia **79** D5
also spelt Cheom Ksan
Choapa *r.* Chile **204** C3
Chobe *admin. dist.* Botswana **131** E3
Chobe National Park Botswana **131** E3
Choch'iwŏn S. Korea **83** B5
Chocianów Poland **49** M4
Chociwel Poland **49** M2
Chocó *dept* Col. **198** B3
Chocolate Mountains U.S.A. **183** I8
Choconta Col. **198** C3
Choctawhatchee *r.* U.S.A. **175** C6
Chodavaram India **94** D2
Chodecz Poland **49** Q3
Chodelka *r.* Poland **49** S4
Cho-do *i.* N. Korea **83** B5
Chodro Rus. Fed. **84** A1
Choduralyg Rus. Fed. **84** C1
Chodzież Poland **49** N3
Choele Choel Arg. **204** D5
Chofombo Moz. **131** F2
Choghādak Iran **100** B4
Chogo Lungma Glacier Jammu and Kashmir **96** B2
Chograyskoye Vodokhranilishche *resr* Rus. Fed. **41** H7
Choiceland Canada **167** J4
Choique Arg. **204** E5
Choiseul *i.* Solomon Is **145** E2
formerly known as Lauru
Choiseul Sound *sea chan.* Falkland Is **205** F8
Choix Mex. **184** C3
Chojna Poland **49** L3
Chojnice Poland **49** O2
Chojnów Poland **49** M4
Chōkai-san *vol.* Japan **90** G5
Ch'ok'ē Mountains Eth. **128** C2
Chokpar Kazakh. **103** H4
also spelt Shokpar *or* Shoqpar
Choksum China **89** D6
Chokue Moz. *see* **Chókwè**
Chokurdakh Rus. Fed. **39** O2
Chókwè Moz. **131** G5
formerly known as Vila de Trego Morais; *formerly spelt* Chokue
Cho La *pass* China **86** A2
Cholame U.S.A. **182** D6
Cholame Creek *r.* U.S.A. **182** D6
Chola Shan *mts* China **86** A1
Cholet France **50** F5
Choloma Hond. **186** B4
Cholpon-Ata Kyrg. **103** I4
Cholula Mex. **185** F5
Choluteca Hond. **186** B4
Choma Zambia **127** E9
Chŏmch'ŏn S. Korea **83** C5
Chomo China *see* **Yadong**
Chomo Ganggar *mt.* China **89** E6
Chomo Lhari *mt.* Bhutan **97** F4
Chomo Yummo *mt.* China/India **97** F3
Chomun India **96** B4
Chomutov Czech Rep. **49** K5
Chona *r.* Rus. Fed. **39** K3
Ch'ŏnan S. Korea **83** B5
Chon Buri Thai. **79** C5
also known as Ban Phla Soi
Chonchi Chile **205** B6

Chone Ecuador **198** A5
Chong'an China *see* **Wuyishan**
Ch'ŏngch'ŏn-gang *r.* N. Korea **83** B5
Ch'ongdo S. Korea **83** C6
Chonggye China *see* **Qonggyai**
Chŏngjin S. Korea **91** A7
Ch'ŏngjin N. Korea **82** C4
Chŏngju N. Korea **83** B5
Ch'ŏngju S. Korea **83** B5
Chongkü China **86** A2
Chongli China **85** G3
also known as Xiwanzi
Chonglong China *see* **Zizhong**
Chongming China **87** G2
also known as Chengqiao
Chongming Dao *i.* China **87** G2
Chongoroi Angola **127** B8
Chŏngp'yŏng N. Korea **83** B5
Chongqing China **86** C2
formerly spelt Chungking
Chongqing China *see* **Chongzhou**
Chongqing *municipality* China **87** C2
Chongren China **87** E3
also known as Bashan
Chŏngŭp S. Korea **83** B6
Chongwe Zambia **127** F8
Chongyang China **87** E2
also known as Tiancheng
Chongyang Xi *r.* China **87** F3
Chongyi China **87** E3
also known as Hengshui
Chongyz-Tayga, Gora *mt.* Rus. Fed. **84** B1
Chongzhou China **86** B2
formerly known as Chongqing
Chongzuo China **87** C4
also known as Taiping
Chŏnju S. Korea **83** B6
Chonogol Mongolia **85** G2
Chontalpa Mex. **185** G5
Chơn Thành Vietnam **79** D6

▶**Cho Oyu** *mt.* China/Nepal **97** E3
6th highest mountain in the world and in Asia.
world [physical features] ▶ 8–9

Chop Ukr. **49** T7
Chopan India **97** D4
Chopda India **96** B5
Chơ Phươc Hai Vietnam **79** D6
Chopimzinho Brazil **203** A8
Choptank *r.* U.S.A. **177** I7
Choquecamata Bol. **200** D4
Chor Pak. **101** G5
Chora Greece **59** C11
also spelt Khóra
Chorley U.K. **47** J10
Chornobyl' Ukr. **41** D6
also spelt Chernobyl'
Chornomors'ke Ukr. **41** E7
Chornomors'kyy Zapovidnyk *nature res.* Ukr. **41** D7
Choroszcz Poland **49** T2
Chorrochó Brazil **202** E4
Chortkiv Ukr. **41** C6
also spelt Chertkov
Chorwad India **94** A1
Ch'ŏrwŏn S. Korea **83** B5
Chorzele Poland **49** R2
Ch'osan N. Korea **83** B4
Chōsen-kaikyō *sea chan.* Japan/S. Korea *see* **Nishi-suidō**
Chōshi Japan **91** G7
Choshuenco, Volcán *vol.* Chile **204** B5
Chosica Peru **200** A2
Chos Malal Arg. **204** C5
Chosmes Arg. **204** D4
Choszczno Poland **49** M2
Chota Peru **198** B6
Chota Nagpur *reg.* India **97** D5
Choteau U.S.A. **180** D3
Chotila India **96** A5
Choûm Mauritania **122** B5
Chowan *r.* U.S.A. **177** I9
Chowchilla U.S.A. **182** D4
Chowghat India **94** B4
Chowilla Regional Reserve *nature res.* Australia **146** D3
Chown, Mount Canada **166** G4
Choya Arg. **204** D3
Choybalsan Mongolia **85** G2
Choyr Mongolia **85** F2
Chozi Zambia **129** B7
Chreirik *well* Mauritania **122** B5
Chřiby *hills* Czech Rep. **49** O6
Chrisman U.S.A. **174** C4
Chrissiesmeer S. Africa **133** O3
Christchurch N.Z. **153** G11
Christiana S. Africa **133** J4
Christiania Norway *see* **Oslo**
Christian Island Canada **173** M6
Christiansburg U.S.A. **176** E8
Christianshåb Greenland *see* **Qasigiannguit**
Christian Sound *sea chan.* U.S.A. **166** C4
Christiansted Virgin Is (U.S.A.) **187** G3
Christie U.S.A. **172** C6
Christie Bay Canada **167** I2
Christina *r.* Canada **167** I3
Christmas Creek Australia **150** D3
Christmas Creek *r.* Australia **150** D3

▶**Christmas Island** *terr.* Indian Ocean **218** O6
Australian External Territory.
asia [countries] ▶ 64–67

Christopher, Lake *salt flat* Australia **151** D5
Christos Greece **59** H11
also spelt Hristós
Chrudim Czech Rep. **49** M6
Chrysi *i.* Greece **59** G14
Chrysochou Bay Cyprus **108** D2
also known as Chrysochous, Kolpos; *also spelt* Khrysokhou Bay
Chrysochous, Kolpos *b.* Cyprus *see* **Chrysochou Bay**
Chrysoupoli Greece **58** F8
also known as Khrisoúpolis
Chu Kazakh. *see* **Shu**
Chu *r.* Kazakh. **103** F3
Chuadanga Bangl. **97** F5
Chuali, Lago *l.* Moz. **133** Q1
Chuansha China **87** G2
Chubalung China **86** A2
Chubarovka Ukr. *see* **Polohy**
Chubarovo Rus. Fed. **43** R6
Chubartau Kazakh. *see* **Barshatas**
Chubbuck U.S.A. **180** D4
Chubut *prov.* Arg. **205** C6
Chubut *r.* Arg. **205** D6
Chuchkovo Rus. Fed. **41** G5
Chuckwalla Mountains U.S.A. **183** I8
Chucul Arg. **204** D4
Chucunaque *r.* Panama **186** D5
Chudniv Ukr. **41** D6
Chudovo Rus. Fed. **43** M2
Chudskoye, Ozero *l.* Estonia/Rus. Fed. *see* **Peipus, Lake**
Chudzin Belarus **42** H9
Chudz"yavr, Ozero *l.* Rus. Fed. **44** P1
Chugach Mountains U.S.A. **164** E3
Chūgoku-sanchi *mts* Japan **91** C7
Chugqênsumdo China *see* **Jigzhi**
Chuguchak China *see* **Tacheng**
Chuguyev Ukr. *see* **Chuhuyiv**
Chuguyevka Rus. Fed. **82** D3
Chuhai China *see* **Zhuhai**
Chuhuyiv Ukr. **41** F6
also spelt Chuguyev
Chu-Iliyskiye Gory *mts* Kazakh. **103** H3
Chuka China **86** A2
Chukai Malaysia *see* **Cukai**
Chukchagirskoye, Ozero *l.* Rus. Fed. **82** E1

Chukchi Peninsula Rus. Fed. *see* **Chukotskiy Poluostrov**
Chukchi Sea Rus. Fed./U.S.A. **164** B3
Chukhloma Rus. Fed. **40** G4
Chukotskiy, Mys *c.* Rus. Fed. **39** S3
Chukotskiy Poluostrov *pen.* Rus. Fed. **39** S3
English form Chukchi Peninsula
Chulakkurgan Kazakh. *see* **Sholakkorgan**
Chulaktau Kazakh. *see* **Karatau**
Chulasa Rus. Fed. **40** H2
Chula Vista U.S.A. **183** G9
Chulkovo Rus. Fed. **43** R8
Chulucanas Peru **198** A6
Chulung Pass Pak. **96** C2
Chuluut Gol *r.* Mongolia **84** D1
Chulym Rus. Fed. **80** C1
Chulyshman *r.* Rus. Fed. **84** A1
Chulyshmanskoye Ploskogor'ye *plat.* Rus. Fed. **84** A1
Chum Rus. Fed. **40** L2
Chuma Bol. **200** C3
Chumba Eth. **128** C3
Chumbicha Arg. **204** D3
Chumda China **86** A1
Chumerna *mt.* Bulg. **58** G6
Chumikan Rus. Fed. **82** D1
Chum Phae Thai. **78** C4
Chumphon Thai. **79** B6
Chum Saeng Thai. **78** C5
Chuna *r.* Rus. Fed. **39** J4
Chuña Huasi Arg. **204** D3
Chun'an China **87** F2
also known as Pailing
Chuna-Tundra *plain* Rus. Fed. **44** P2
Ch'unch'ŏn S. Korea **83** B5
Chundzha Kazakh. **103** I4
also spelt Shonzha
Chunga Zambia **127** E8
Chung-hua Jen-min Kung-ho-kuo *country* Asia *see* **China**
Chung-hua Min-kuo *country* Asia *see* **Taiwan**
Ch'ungju S. Korea **83** B5
Chungking China *see* **Chongqing**
Ch'ungmu S. Korea *see* **T'ongyŏng**
Chŭngsan N. Korea **83** B5
Chungu Tanz. **129** C7
Chungyang Shanmo *mts* Taiwan **87** G4
also known as Taiwan Shan
Chunhua China **82** C4
Chunhuhux Mex. **185** H5
Chunxi China *see* **Gaochun**
Chunya *r.* Rus. Fed. **39** J3
Chunya Tanz. **129** B7
Chu Oblast *admin. div.* Kyrg. *see* **Chüy**
Chuŏr Phnum Dângrêk *mts* Cambodia/Thai. **79** D5
Chuosijia China *see* **Guanyinqiao**
Chupa Rus. Fed. **44** P2
Chūplū Iran **100** A2
Chuquicamata Chile **200** C5
Chuquisaca *dept* Bol. **201** D5
Chuquing China *see* **Chindu**
Chur Rus. Fed. **40** J4
Chur Switz. **51** P6
also spelt Coire; *historically known as* Curia
Churachandpur India **97** G4
Chūrān Iran **100** C4
Churapcha Rus. Fed. **39** N3
Churayevo Rus. Fed. **40** J5
Church Hill *MD* U.S.A. **177** J6
Church Hill *TN* U.S.A. **176** C9
Churchill Canada **167** M3
Churchill *r.* *Man.* Canada **167** M3
Churchill *r.* *Nfld.* Canada **169** I2
formerly known as Hamilton
Churchill, Cape Canada **167** M3
Churchill Falls Canada **169** I2
Churchill Lake Canada **167** I4
Churchill Mountains Antarctica **223** K1
Churchill Peak Canada **166** E3
Churchill Sound *sea chan.* Canada **168** E1
Churchville U.S.A. **176** F7
Chureg-Tag, Gora *mt.* Rus. Fed. **84** A1
Churia Ghati Hills Nepal **97** E4
Churilovo Rus. Fed. **43** L6
Churin Peru **200** A2
Churov Rus. Fed. **40** H4
Churovichi Rus. Fed. **43** N9
Churu India **96** B3
Churubay Nura Kazakh. *see* **Abay**
Churuguara Venez. **198** D2
Chūrui Japan **90** H3
Churumuco Mex. **185** E5
Chushul Jammu and Kashmir **96** C2
Chuska Mountains U.S.A. **183** O5
Chusovaya *r.* Rus. Fed. **40** K4
Chusovoy Rus. Fed. **40** K4
Chust Ukr. *see* **Khust**
Chust Uzbek. **103** G4
Chute-Rouge Canada **173** Q4
Chutung Taiwan **87** G3
also known as Zhudong
Chuuk *i.* Micronesia **220** E5
Chuvashia *aut. rep.* Rus. Fed. *see* **Chuvashskaya Respublika**
Chuvashskaya A.S.S.R. *aut. rep.* Rus. Fed. *see* **Chuvashskaya Respublika**
Chuvashskaya Respublika *aut. rep.* Rus. Fed. **40** H5
English form Chuvashia; *formerly known as* Chuvashskaya A.S.S.R.
Chuwang-san National Park S. Korea **83** C5
Chuxiong China **86** B3
Chüy *admin. div.* Kyrg. **103** H4
English form Chu Oblast; *also known as* Chuyskaya Oblast'
Chuy Uruguay **204** G4
Chư Yang Sin *mt.* Vietnam **79** E5
Chuyskaya Oblast' *admin. div.* Kyrg. *see* **Chüy**
Chuzhou China **87** F1
Chyganak Kazakh. **103** G3
Chyhirynskaye Vodaskhovishcha *resr* Belarus **43** K8
Chymyshliya Moldova *see* **Cimişlia**
Chyrvonaya Slabada Belarus **43** J9
Chyrvonaye, Vozyera *l.* Belarus **42** I9
Chyulu Range *mts* Kenya **128** C5
Ciacova Romania **58** C3
Ciadâr-Lunga Moldova *see* **Ciadîr-Lunga**
Ciadîr-Lunga Moldova **58** J2
formerly spelt Ceadâr-Lunga *or* Ciadâr-Lunga *or* Chadyr-Lunga
Ciamis Indon. **77** E4
Ciampino *airport* Italy **56** E7
Cianjur Indon. **77** D4
Cianorte Brazil **206** A10
Cibadak Indon. **77** D4
Cibatu Indon. **77** E4
Cibecue U.S.A. **183** N7
Cibinong Indon. **77** D4
Cibitoke Burundi **126** F5
Cibolo Creek *r.* U.S.A. **179** C6
Ci Buni *r.* Indon. **77** D4
Cibuta, Sierra *mt.* Mex. **184** C2
Čićarija *mts* Croatia **56** F3
Çiçekdağı Turkey **106** C3
also known as Boyalık
Çiçekli Turkey **108** G1
Çiçekli Turkey **59** J9
Cicero U.S.A. **172** F9
Cícero Dantas Brazil **202** E4
Ćićevac *Srbija* Yugo. **58** C5
Cidacos *r.* Spain **55** J2
Cide Turkey **106** C2
Cidlina *r.* Czech Rep. **49** M5
Ciechanów Poland **49** R3
Ciechanowiec Poland **49** T3
Ciechocinek Poland **49** P3
Ciego de Avila Cuba **186** D2
Ciénaga Col. **198** C2

China Mex. **185** F3
China, Republic of *country* Asia *see* **Taiwan**
China Bakir *r.* Myanmar *see* **To**
Chinacates Mex. **184** D3
China Lake U.S.A. **177** P1
Chinandega Nicaragua **186** B4
China Point U.S.A. **182** F9
Chinati Peak U.S.A. **181** F7
Chinaz Uzbek. **103** G4
also spelt Chinoz
Chincha Alta Peru **200** A3
Chinchaga *r.* Canada **166** G3
Chinchāl, Nahr *r.* Iraq **109** P3
Chinchilla Australia **149** F5
Chincholi India **94** C2
Chinchorro, Banco *sea feature* Mex. **185** I5
Chincolco Chile **204** C4
Chincoteague U.S.A. **177** J8
Chincoteague Bay U.S.A. **177** J8
Chinde Moz. **131** H3
Chin-do *i.* S. Korea **83** B6
Chindu China **86** A1
also known as Chuqung
Chindwin *r.* Myanmar **78** A3
Chineni Jammu and Kashmir **96** B2
Chinese Turkestan *aut. reg.* China *see* **Xinjiang Uygur Zizhiqu**
Chingaza, Parque Nacional *nat. park* Col. **198** C3
Chinghai *prov.* China *see* **Qinghai**

Chiricahua National Monument *nat. park* U.S.A. **183** O9
Chiricahua Peak U.S.A. **181** E7
Chiriguaná Col. **198** C2
Chirikof Island U.S.A. **164** D4
Chiriquí, Golfo de *b.* Panama **186** C5
Chiriquí, Laguna de *b.* Panama **186** C5
Chiriquí Grande Panama **186** C5
Chiri-san *mt.* S. Korea **83** B6
Chiri-san National Park S. Korea **83** B6
Chirka-Kem' *r.* Rus. Fed. **44** P2
Chirnside U.K. **46** J8
Chirpan Bulg. **58** G6
Chirripó, Parque Nacional *nat. park* Costa Rica **186** C5
Chirundu Zimbabwe **131** F3
Chirūyeh Iran **100** C5
Chisamba Zambia **127** F8
Chisana *r.* U.S.A. **166** A2
Chisasa Zambia **127** E8
Chisasibi Canada **168** E2
Chisec Guat. **185** H6
Chisekesi Zambia **127** E9
Chiselet Romania **58** H4
Chisenga Malawi **129** B7
Chishima-retto *is* Rus. Fed. *see* **Kuril Islands**
Chishmy Rus. Fed. **40** J5
Chisholm Canada **167** H4
Chisholm *ME* U.S.A. **177** O1

	country	population	location		page#
largest populations					
1	China	1 260 137 000	Asia	▶	80 D5
2	India	1 008 937 000	Asia	▶	93 E6
3	USA	283 230 000	North America	▶	170 E3
4	Indonesia	212 092 000	Asia	▶	72 D8
5	Brazil	170 406 000	South America	▶	202 B4
6	Russian Federation	145 491 000	Asia/Europe	▶	38 F3
7	Pakistan	141 256 000	Asia	▶	101 F4
8	Bangladesh	137 439 000	Asia	▶	97 F4
9	Japan	127 096 000	Asia	▶	90 E5
10	Nigeria	113 862 000	Africa	▶	125 G4

index C

Ciénagas del Catatumbo nat. park Venez. 198 D2
Cienfuegos Cuba 186 C2
Cíes, Illas is Spain 54 C2
Cieszanów Poland 49 U5
Cieszyn Poland 49 P6
Cieza Spain 55 J6
Çiftlikköy Turkey 109 I1
Çiftlik Turkey see Kelkit
Çiftlikköy Turkey 58 J7
Cifuentes Spain 55 I4
Cigeulis Indon. 77 D4
Cigüela r. Spain 55 H5
Cihanbeyli Turkey 106 C3
also known as İnevi
Cihangazi Turkey 59 K9
Cihuatlán Mex. 184 D5
Cijara, Embalse de resr Spain 54 G5
Cikai China see Gongshan
Çikes, Maja e mt. Albania 59 A8
Cikobia i. Fiji 145 H3
also spelt Thikombia; formerly spelt Chicobea or Ticumbia or Tikumbia
Čikola r. Croatia 56 I5
Cilacap Indon. 77 E4
Cilangkahan Indon. 77 D4
Çıldır Turkey 107 E2
also known as Zurzuna
Çıldır Gölü l. Turkey 107 E2
Çıldıroba Turkey 109 I1
Ciledug Indon. 77 E4
Cilento e del Vallo di Diano, Parco Nazionale del nat. park Italy 57 H8
Cili China 87 D2
Cilician Gates pass Turkey see Gülek Boğazı
Cilieni Romania 58 F5
Cill Airne Rep. of Ireland see Killarney
Cill Chainnigh Rep. of Ireland see Kilkenny
Cill Mhantáin Rep. of Ireland see Wicklow
Cilo Dağı mt. Turkey 107 F3
Çiloy Adası i. Azer. 107 G2
Cima U.S.A. 183 I6
Cimahi Indon. 77 D4
Cimarron KS U.S.A. 178 B4
Cimarron NM U.S.A. 181 F5
Cimarron r. U.S.A. 179 C4
Cimarron Creek r. U.S.A. 181 F5
Cimino, Monte mt. Italy 56 E6
Cimișlia Moldova 58 J2
formerly spelt Chimishliya or Chymyshliya
Cimone, Monte mt. Italy 56 C4
Cîmpeni Romania see Câmpeni
Cîmpia Turzii Romania see Câmpia Turzii
Cîmpina Romania see Câmpina
Cîmpulung Romania see Câmpulung
Cîmpulung Moldovenesc Romania see Câmpulung Moldovenesc
Cina, Tanjung c. Indon. 76 D4
Çınar Turkey 107 E3
also known as Hanakpınar
Çınarcık Turkey 58 K8
Cinaruco r. Venez. 198 E3
Cinaruco-Capanaparo, Parque Nacional nat. park Venez. 199 E3
Cinca r. Spain 55 L3
Cincar mt. Bos.-Herz. 56 J5
Cincinnati U.S.A. 176 A6
Cincinnatus U.S.A. 177 J3
Cinco-Balas, Cayos is Cuba 186 D2
Cinco de Outubro Angola see Xá-Muteba
Cincu Romania 58 F3
Çine Turkey 106 B3
Çine r. Turkey 59 I11
Ciney Belgium 51 L2
Cinfães Port. 54 C3
Cingoli Italy 56 F5
Cinque Island India 95 G4
Cintalapa Mex. 185 G5
Cinto, Monte mt. France 51 O10
Cintruénigo Spain 55 J2
Cinzas r. Brazil 206 C10
Ciolpani Romania 58 H4
Čiovo i. Croatia 56 I5
Cipatuja Indon. 77 E4
Ciping China see Jinggangshan
Cipó Brazil 202 E4
Cipó r. Brazil 207 I5
Cipolletti Arg. 204 D5
Cipotânea Brazil 207 J7
Circeo, Monte hill Italy 56 F7
Circeo, Parco Nazionale del nat. park Italy 56 E7
Circle AK U.S.A. 164 E3
Circle MT U.S.A. 180 F3
Circleville OH U.S.A. 176 C6
Circleville UT U.S.A. 183 L3
Cirebon Indon. 77 E4
formerly spelt Tjirebon
Cirencester U.K. 47 K12
historically known as Corinium
Cirene tourist site Libya see Cyrene
Ciriè Italy 51 N7
Cirišs l. Latvia 42 H5
Cirò Marina Italy 57 J9
Ciron r. France 50 F8
Cirque Mountain Canada 169 I1
Cirta Alg. see Constantine
Cisco U.S.A. 183 O3
Cisnădie Romania 58 F3
Cisterna di Latina Italy 56 E7
Cistierna Spain 54 F2
Citadelle Laferrière tourist site Haiti 187 E3
Citlaltépetl vol. Mex. see Orizaba, Pico de
Čitluk Bos.-Herz. 56 J5
Citronelle U.S.A. 175 B6
Citrusdal S. Africa 132 D9
Citrus Heights U.S.A. 182 C3
Cittadella Italy 56 D3
Città di Castello Italy 56 E5
Cittanova Italy 57 I10
City of Derry airport U.K. 47 E8
Ciucaș, Vârful mt. Romania 58 G3
Ciucea Romania 58 D2
Ciudad Acuña Mex. 185 E2
Ciudad Altamirano Mex. 185 E5
Ciudad Bolívar Venez. 199 F2
Ciudad Camargo Mex. 184 D3
Ciudad Constitución Mex. 184 C3
also known as Villa Constitución
Ciudad Cuauhtémoc Mex. 185 H6
Ciudad del Carmen Mex. 185 H5
Ciudad del Este Para. 201 G6
formerly known as Puerto Presidente Stroessner
Ciudad Delicias Mex. 184 D2
Ciudad del Maíz Mex. 185 F4
Ciudad de Valles Mex. 185 F4
Ciudad Guayana Venez. 199 F2
Ciudad Guzmán Mex. 184 E5
Ciudad Hidalgo Mex. 185 E5
Ciudad Ixtepec Mex. 185 G5
Ciudad Juárez Mex. 184 D2
Ciudad Lerdo Mex. 184 E3
Ciudad Madero Mex. 185 F4
Ciudad Mante Mex. 185 F4
Ciudad Mendoza Mex. 185 F5
Ciudad Mier Mex. 185 F3
Ciudad Obregón Mex. 184 C3
Ciudad Piar Venez. 199 F3
Ciudad Real Spain 54 H6
Ciudad Río Bravo Mex. 185 F3
Ciudad Rodrigo Spain 54 E4
Ciudad Trujillo Dom. Rep. see Santo Domingo
Ciudad Victoria Mex. 185 F4
Ciudanovița Romania 58 C3
Ciumani Romania 58 G2
Ciutadella de Menorca Spain 55 O4
Civa Burnu pt Turkey 107 D2
Civetta, Monte mt. Italy 56 E2
Cividale del Friuli Italy 56 F2
Civita Castellana Italy 56 E6
historically known as Falerii
Civitanova Marche Italy 56 F5
Civitavecchia Italy 56 D6
Civitella Roveto Italy 56 F7
Civray France 50 G6
Çivril Turkey 106 B3
Cixi China 87 G2
also known as Hushan
Cixian China 85 G4
also known as Cizhou
Ciyao China 85 H5
Cizhou China see Cixian
Cizre Turkey 107 E3
Clackamas r. U.S.A. 180 B3
Clacton-on-Sea U.K. 47 N12
Clain r. France 50 G6
Claire, Lake Canada 167 H3
Clair Engle Lake resr U.S.A. 180 B4
Clairfont Canada 166 G4
Claise r. France 50 G6
Clam Lake U.S.A. 172 C4
Clan Alpine Mountains U.S.A. 182 G2
Clanton U.S.A. 175 C5
Clanville S. Africa 133 L8
Clanwilliam S. Africa 132 C9
Clanwilliam Dam S. Africa 132 C9
Clara r. Australia 149 D3
Clara Rep. of Ireland 47 E10
Clara Island Myanmar 79 B6
Claraville Australia 149 D3
Clare N.S.W. Australia 147 D3
Clare S.A. Australia 146 C3
Clare r. Rep. of Ireland 47 C10
Clare U.S.A. 173 I7
Clare Island Rep. of Ireland 47 B10
Claremont U.S.A. 177 M2
Claremont Isles Australia 149 D2
Claremore U.S.A. 179 D4
Claremorris Rep. of Ireland 47 D10
Clarence r. Australia 147 G2
Clarence N.Z. 153 H10
Clarence r. N.Z. 153 H10
Clarence U.S.A. 172 B9
Clarence, Isla i. Chile 205 C9
Clarence Island Antarctica 222 U2
Clarence Strait Australia 148 A1
Clarence Strait U.S.A. 166 C3
Clarence Town Bahamas 187 E2
Clarendon N.Z. 153 E14
Clarendon AR U.S.A. 174 B5
Clarendon PA U.S.A. 176 F4
Clarendon TX U.S.A. 179 B5
Clarenville Canada 169 K3
Claresholm Canada 167 H5
Clarinda U.S.A. 178 D3
Clarington U.S.A. 176 E6
Clarion IA U.S.A. 174 A3
Clarion PA U.S.A. 176 F4
Clarion r. U.S.A. 176 F4
Clarión, Isla i. Mex. 184 B5
Claris N.Z. 152 J4
Clark U.S.A. 178 C2
Clark, Mount Canada 166 F1
Clarkdale U.S.A. 183 L7
Clarke r. Australia 149 E3
Clarkebury S. Africa 133 M8
Clarke Range mts Australia 149 E4
Clarke River Australia 149 E3
Clarkes Creek r. Australia 149 D3
Clarke's Head Canada 169 K3
Clark Fork r. ID U.S.A. 180 C2
Clark Fork r. MT U.S.A. 180 C2
Clark Hill Reservoir U.S.A. 175 D5
Clark Mountain U.S.A. 183 I6
Clark Mountains Antarctica 222 O1
Clark Point Canada 168 D4
Clarksburg U.S.A. 176 E6
Clarksdale U.S.A. 174 B5
Clark's Fork Yellowstone r. U.S.A. 180 E3
Clarks Junction N.Z. 153 E13
Clarkson S. Africa 133 I11
Clarkston U.S.A. 180 C3
Clarksville AR U.S.A. 179 D5
Clarksville TN U.S.A. 174 C4
Clarksville TX U.S.A. 179 D5
Claro r. Goiás Brazil 206 C6
Claro r. Mato Grosso Brazil 206 B2
Clatskanie U.S.A. 180 B3
Claude U.S.A. 179 B5
Cláudio Brazil 203 C7
Claveria Phil. 74 B2
Clavering Ø i. Greenland 165 Q2
Claxton U.S.A. 175 D5
Clay U.S.A. 176 D7
Clayburg U.S.A. 177 L1
Clay Center KS U.S.A. 178 C4
Clay Center NE U.S.A. 178 C3
Clay City U.S.A. 176 B8
Clayhole Wash watercourse U.S.A. 183 K4
Claymont U.S.A. 177 J6
Claypool U.S.A. 183 N8
Clay Springs U.S.A. 183 N7
Clayton DE U.S.A. 177 J6
Clayton GA U.S.A. 174 D5
Clayton NM U.S.A. 178 B4
Clayton NY U.S.A. 177 I1
Claytor Lake U.S.A. 176 E8
Clearco U.S.A. 176 E7
Clear Creek Canada 173 M8
Clear Creek U.S.A. 183 M2
Clear Creek r. AZ U.S.A. 183 N7
Clear Creek r. WY U.S.A. 180 F3
Clearfield PA U.S.A. 176 G4
Clearfield UT U.S.A. 180 D4
Clear Fork Brazos r. U.S.A. 179 C5
Clear Hills Canada 166 G3
Clear Island Rep. of Ireland 47 C12
Clear Lake IA U.S.A. 174 A3
Clear Lake SD U.S.A. 178 C2
Clear Lake WI U.S.A. 172 A5
Clear Lake l. CA U.S.A. 182 B2
Clear Lake l. UT U.S.A. 183 L2
Clearlake Oaks U.S.A. 182 B2
Clear Lake Reservoir U.S.A. 180 B4
Clearmont U.S.A. 180 F3
Clear Spring U.S.A. 176 H6
Clearwater Canada 166 G5
Clearwater r. Alta Canada 167 H4
Clearwater r. Alta/Sask. Canada 167 I3
Clearwater U.S.A. 175 D7
Clearwater r. ID U.S.A. 180 C3
Clearwater r. MN U.S.A. 178 C2
Clear Water Bay Hong Kong China 87 [inset]
also known as Tsing Shui Wan
Clearwater Lake l. Canada 167 K4
Clearwater Lake U.S.A. 172 D5
Clearwater Lake Provincial Park Canada 167 K4
Clearwater Mountains U.S.A. 180 D3
Clearwater River Provincial Park Canada 167 I3
Cleburne U.S.A. 179 C5
Cle Elum U.S.A. 180 B3
Cléguérec France 50 C4
Clejani Romania 58 G4
Clément Fr. Guiana 199 H4
Clementi Sing. 76 [inset]
Clementina Brazil 206 C8
Clemmons U.S.A. 176 E9
Clemson U.S.A. 174 D5
Clendenin U.S.A. 176 D7
Clendening Lake U.S.A. 176 D5
Cleopatra Needle mt. Phil. 74 A4
Clères France 50 H3
Clerf Lux. see Clervaux
Cléricy Canada 173 O2
Clerke Reef Australia 150 B3
Clermont Australia 149 E4
Clermont France 51 I3
Clermont U.S.A. 175 D6
Clermont-en-Argonne France 51 L3
Clermont-Ferrand France 51 J7
Clermont-l'Hérault France 51 J9
Clervaux Lux. 51 M2
also known as Clerf
Cles Italy 56 D2
Cleve Australia 146 C3
Cleveland r. Canada 167 O1
Cleveland GA U.S.A. 174 D5
Cleveland MS U.S.A. 175 B5
Cleveland OH U.S.A. 176 D4
Cleveland TN U.S.A. 174 C5
Cleveland TX U.S.A. 179 D6
Cleveland UT U.S.A. 183 N2
Cleveland VA U.S.A. 176 C9
Cleveland WI U.S.A. 172 F7
Cleveland, Cape Australia 149 E3
Cleveland, Mount U.S.A. 180 D2
Cleveland Bay Australia 149 E3
Cleveland Hills U.K. 47 K9
Clevelândia do Norte Brazil 199 I4
Cleveland Peninsula U.S.A. 166 C4
Cleves Germany see Kleve
Clew Bay Rep. of Ireland 47 C10
Clewiston U.S.A. 175 D7
Clifden Rep. of Ireland 47 B10
Cliffdale r. Australia 148 C3
Clifford S. Africa 133 L8
Clifftop U.S.A. 176 E7
Clifton Australia 147 F1
Clifton AZ U.S.A. 183 O8
Clifton IL U.S.A. 172 F10
Clifton Beach Australia 149 E3
Clifton Forge U.S.A. 176 F8
Clifton Hills Australia 146 C1
Clifton Park U.S.A. 177 L3
Climax Canada 167 I5
Climax U.S.A. 172 H8
Clinch r. U.S.A. 176 B9
Clinchco U.S.A. 176 C8
Clinch Mountain mts U.S.A. 176 C9
Clinchport U.S.A. 176 C9
Cline River Canada 167 G4
Clinton Canada 168 D5
Clinton N.Z. 153 D14
Clinton AR U.S.A. 179 D5
Clinton IA U.S.A. 174 B3
Clinton KY U.S.A. 174 B4
Clinton LA U.S.A. 175 B6
Clinton ME U.S.A. 177 P1
Clinton MI U.S.A. 173 J8
Clinton MO U.S.A. 178 D4
Clinton MS U.S.A. 175 B5
Clinton NC U.S.A. 174 E5
Clinton NY U.S.A. 177 J2
Clinton OK U.S.A. 179 C5
Clinton TN U.S.A. 176 A9
Clinton-Colden Lake Canada 167 J1
Clinton Creek Canada 166 A1
Clintonville WI U.S.A. 172 E6
Clintonville WV U.S.A. 176 E8
Clintwood U.S.A. 176 C8
Clio U.S.A. 173 J7

▶Clipperton, Île terr. N. Pacific Ocean 221 K5
French Overseas Territory. Most easterly point of Oceania. English form Clipperton Island.
oceania [countries] → 138–139

Clipperton Island terr. N. Pacific Ocean see Clipperton, Île
Clisham hill U.K. 46 F6
Clisson France 50 E5
Clitheroe U.K. 47 J10
Clive N.Z. 152 K7
Clive Lake Canada 167 G2
Cliza Bol. 200 D4
Cloates, Point Australia 150 A4
Clocolan S. Africa 133 L5
Clonagh Australia 149 D4
Clonakilty Rep. of Ireland 47 D12
Cloncurry Australia 149 D4
Cloncurry r. Australia 149 D3
Clones Rep. of Ireland 47 E9
Clonmel Rep. of Ireland 47 E11
also spelt Cluain Meala
Cloppenburg Germany 48 F3
Cloquet U.S.A. 174 A2
Cloquet r. U.S.A. 174 A2
Clorinda Arg. 204 F2
Cloud Bay Canada 172 D2
Cloud Peak WY U.S.A. 180 F3
Cloudy Bay N.Z. 152 I9
Clova Canada 168 F3
Clover U.S.A. 183 L1
Cloverdale U.S.A. 182 A3
Clovis CA U.S.A. 182 E5
Clovis NM U.S.A. 179 B5
Cloyes-sur-le-Loir France 50 H5
Cloyne Canada 173 P6
Cluain Meala Rep. of Ireland see Clonmel
Cluanie, Loch l. U.K. 46 G6
Cluff Lake Mine Canada 167 I3
Cluj-Napoca Romania 58 E2
also known as Kolozsvár
Cluny Australia 148 C5
Cluny France 51 K6
Cluses France 51 M6
Clustor Springs U.S.A. 176 G9
Clutha r. N.Z. 153 D14
Clut Lake Canada 167 G1
Clutterbuck Hills hill Australia 151 D5
Clwydian Range hills U.K. 47 I10
Clyde Canada 167 H4
Clyde r. U.K. 46 H8
Clyde NY U.S.A. 177 I2
Clyde OH U.S.A. 176 C4
Clyde, Firth of est. U.K. 46 H8
Clydebank U.K. 46 H8
Clyde River Canada 165 M2
Clydevale N.Z. 153 D14
Clyman U.S.A. 172 E7
Clymer U.S.A. 176 F5
Cnossus tourist site Greece see Knossos
Côa r. Port. 54 D3
Coachella Canal U.S.A. 183 I9
Coachella U.S.A. 183 H8
Coahuayutla de Guerrero Mex. 185 E5
Coahuila state Mex. 185 E3
Coal r. Canada 166 E3
Coal City U.S.A. 172 E9
Coaldale Canada 167 H5
Coalgate U.S.A. 179 C5
Coal Grove U.S.A. 176 C7
Coal Harbour Canada 166 E5
Coalinga U.S.A. 182 D5
Coalport U.S.A. 176 G5
Coal River Canada 166 E3
Coal Valley U.S.A. 183 I4
Coalville U.S.A. 183 M1
Coamo Puerto Rico 187 G3
Coaraci Brazil 207 N1
Coari Brazil 199 F6
Coari r. Brazil 199 F6
Coari, Lago l. Brazil 199 F6
Coarsegold U.S.A. 182 E4
Coast prov. Kenya 128 D5
Coast admin. reg. Tanz. see Pwani
Coastal Plain U.S.A. 175 A6
Coast Mountains Canada 166 E4
Coast Range hills Australia 149 F5
Coast Ranges mts U.S.A. 182 A1
Coatepec Mex. 185 F5
Coatepeque Guat. 185 H6
Coatesville U.S.A. 177 J6
Coaticook Canada 169 G4
Coats Island Canada 165 K3
Coats Land reg. Antarctica 222 V1
Coatzacoalcos Mex. 185 G5
formerly known as Puerto México
Coatzintla Mex. 185 F4
Cobadin Romania 58 J4
Cobalt Canada 173 N3
Cobán Guat. 185 H6
Cobar Australia 147 E2
Cobargo Australia 147 F4
Cobb, Lake salt flat Australia 150 D5
Cobden Canada 173 Q5
Cóbh Rep. of Ireland 47 D12
also spelt An Cóbh; formerly known as Queenstown
Cobham r. Canada 167 M4
Cobija Bol. 200 C2
Cobija Chile 200 C5
Coblenz Germany see Koblenz
Cobleskill U.S.A. 177 K3
Cobos Mex. 185 F4
Cobourg Canada 168 E5
Cobourg Peninsula Australia 148 B1
Cobquecura Chile 204 B5
Cobra Australia 150 B5
Cobram Australia 147 E3
Cobres Arg. 200 D5
Cóbuè Moz. 129 B8
Coburg Germany 48 H5
Coburg Island Canada 165 L2
Coca Spain 54 G3
Cocachacra Peru 200 C4
Cocal Brazil 202 D2
Cocalinho Brazil 202 B5
Cocanada India see Kakinada
Cocapata Bol. 200 D4
Cocentaina Spain 55 K6
Cochabamba Bol. 200 D4
Cochabamba dept Bol. 200 D4
Cochamó Chile 205 B6
Coche, Isla i. Venez. 199 F2
Cochem Germany 48 E5
Co Chiên, Sông r. mouth Vietnam 79 D6
Cochin India 94 C4
also known as Kochi
Cochin reg. Vietnam 79 D6
Cochinos, Bahía de b. Cuba see Pigs, Bay of
Cochise U.S.A. 183 O9
Cochise Head mt. U.S.A. 183 O9
Cochran U.S.A. 175 D5
Cochrane Alta Canada 167 H5
Cochrane Ont. Canada 168 D3
Cochrane r. Canada 167 K3
Cochrane Chile 205 B7
Cochrane, Lago l. Arg./Chile 205 B7
Cochranton U.S.A. 176 E4
Cochranville U.S.A. 177 J6
Cockaleechie Australia 146 B3
Cockburn Australia 146 D3
Cockburn Harbour Turks and Caicos Is 187 F2
Cockburn Island Canada 168 D4
Cockburn Town Bahamas 187 E1
Cockburn Town Turks and Caicos Is see Grand Turk
Cockermouth U.K. 47 I9
Cocklebiddy Australia 151 D7
Cockscomb mt. S. Africa 133 I10
Coclé del Norte Panama 186 C5
Coco r. Brazil 202 B4
Coco r. Hond./Nicaragua 186 C4
also known as Segovia
Coco, Cayo i. Cuba 186 D2
Coco, Isla de i. N. Pacific Ocean 221 M5
Cocobeach Gabon 126 A4
Coco Channel India 95 G3
Coconino Plateau U.S.A. 183 K6
Cocopara National Park Australia 147 E3
Cocorná Col. 198 C3
Cocos Brazil 202 C5

▶Cocos Islands terr. Indian Ocean 218 N6
Australian External Territory. Also known as Keeling Islands.
asia [countries] → 64–67

Cocula Mex. 184 E4
Cod, Cape U.S.A. 177 O4
Codăești Romania 58 I2
Codajás Brazil 199 F5
Codera, Cabo c. Venez. 199 E2
Coderre Canada 167 J5
Codigoro Italy 56 E4
Cod Island Canada 169 I1
Codlea Romania 58 G3
Codó Brazil 202 D3
Codogno Italy 56 B3
Codrington Antigua and Barbuda 187 H3
Codrington, Mount Antarctica 223 D2
Codroipo Italy 56 E3
Codru Moldova 58 J2
Cody U.S.A. 180 E3
Coeburn U.S.A. 176 C9
Coega S. Africa 133 J10
Coelho Neto Brazil 202 D3
Coen Australia 149 D2
Coen r. Australia 149 D2
Coerney S. Africa 133 J10
Coeroeni r. Suriname 199 G4
Coesfeld Germany 48 E4
Coetzeesberg mts S. Africa 133 I9
Coetzersdam S. Africa 133 I3
Coeur d'Alene U.S.A. 180 C3
Coeur d'Alene r. U.S.A. 180 C3
Coeur d'Alene Indian Reservation res. U.S.A. 180 C3
Coeur d'Alene Lake U.S.A. 180 C3
Coffee Bay S. Africa 133 N8
Coffee Creek Canada 166 B2
Coffeyville U.S.A. 178 D4
Coffin Bay Australia 146 B3
Coffin Bay b. Australia 146 B3
Coffin Bay National Park Australia 146 B3
Coffin Bay Peninsula Australia 146 B3
Coffs Harbour Australia 147 G2
Cofimvaba S. Africa 133 L9
formerly known as St Mark's
Cofre de Perote, Parque Nacional nat. park Mex. 185 F5
Cogălniceanu airport Romania see Kogălniceanu
Cogealac Romania 58 J4
Coggon U.S.A. 172 B8
Coghinas r. Sardegna Italy 57 A8
Coghlan S. Africa 133 M8
Coghlan, Mount hill Australia 150 D3
Cognac France 50 F7
Cogo Equat. Guinea 125 H6
Cogolin France 51 M9
Coguno Moz. 131 G5
Čohkkiras Sweden see Jukkasjärvi
Cohocton r. U.S.A. 177 H3
Cohoes U.S.A. 177 L3
Cohuna Australia 147 E3
Coiba, Isla i. Panama 186 C6
Coihaique Chile 205 B7
Coihaique Alto Chile 205 C7
Coimbatore India 94 C4
Coimbra Port. 54 C4
Coimbra admin. dist. Port. 54 C4
Coín Spain 54 G8
Coipasa, Salar de salt flat Bol. 200 C4
Coire Switz. see Chur
Cojasca Romania 58 G4
Cojata Peru 200 C3
Cojedes state Venez. 198 D2
Cojoro Venez. 187 F5
Cojudo Blanco, Cerro mt. Arg. 205 C7
Colac Australia 147 D4
Colac N.Z. 153 B14
Colair Lake India see Kolleru Lake
Çolaklı Turkey 108 C1
Colares Brazil 202 B2
Colatina Brazil 203 D6
Colborne Canada 173 P7
Colby KS U.S.A. 178 B4
Colby WI U.S.A. 172 C6
Colca r. Peru 200 B3
Colceag Romania 58 H4
Colchester S. Africa 133 J10
Colchester U.K. 47 M12
historically known as Camulodunum
Colchester U.S.A. 177 M4
Cold Bay U.S.A. 164 C4
also known as Fort Randall
Cold Lake Canada 167 I4
Cold Lake l. Canada 167 I4
Coldspring U.S.A. 179 D6
Cold Springs U.S.A. 182 G2
Coldstream Canada 166 G5
Coldstream N.Z. 153 F12
Coldstream U.K. 46 J8
Coldwater Canada 173 N6
Coldwater KS U.S.A. 178 C4
Coldwater MI U.S.A. 173 I9
Coldwater Creek r. U.S.A. 179 B4
Coldwell Canada 172 G2
Colebrook U.S.A. 177 N1
Coleford S. Africa 133 N6
Coleman r. Australia 149 D2
Coleman MI U.S.A. 173 I7
Coleman TX U.S.A. 179 C6
Coleman WI U.S.A. 172 E5
Çölemerik Turkey see Hakkâri
Colenso S. Africa 133 N5
Colentina r. Romania 58 G4
Cole Peninsula Antarctica 222 T2
Coleraine Australia 146 D4
Coleraine U.K. 47 F8
Coleroon r. India 94 C4
Coles, Punta de pt Peru 200 C4
Coles Bay Australia 147 F5
Colesberg S. Africa 133 J7
Colesburg U.S.A. 172 B8
Coleville U.S.A. 182 E3
Colfax CA U.S.A. 182 D2
Colfax LA U.S.A. 179 D6
Colfax WA U.S.A. 180 C3
Colfax WI U.S.A. 172 B6
Colhué Huapí, Lago l. Arg. 205 C7
Colibași Romania 58 F4
Colico Italy 56 B2
Coligny S. Africa 133 K3
Colima Mex. 184 E5
Colima state Mex. 184 E5
Colima, Nevado de vol. Mex. 184 E4
Colina Brazil 206 E7
Colinas Brazil 202 C3
Coliseu r. Brazil 202 A5
Coll i. U.K. 46 F7
Collado Bajo mt. Spain 55 J4
Collado Villalba Spain 54 H4
Collahuasi Chile 200 C5
Collalto mt. Austria/Italy 48 J9
also known as Hochgall
Collarenebri Australia 147 F2
Collecchio Italy 56 C4
Colle di Val d'Elsa Italy 56 D5
College Corner U.S.A. 176 A6
College Hill U.S.A. 176 A6
College Park U.S.A. 175 C5
College Station U.S.A. 179 C6
Collerina Australia 147 E2
Collesalvetti Italy 56 C5
Collie Australia 151 B7
Collier Bay Australia 150 D3
Collier Range hills Australia 151 B5
Collier Range National Park Australia 151 B5
Collierville U.S.A. 174 B5
Collingwood Canada 168 D4
Collingwood N.Z. 152 G8
Collins U.S.A. 175 B6
Collins Glacier Antarctica 223 E2
Collins Lake U.S.A. 182 C2
Collinson Peninsula Canada 165 I2
Collinsville Australia 149 E4
Collinsville OK U.S.A. 179 D4
Collinsville VA U.S.A. 176 F9
Collipulli Chile 204 B5
Collmberg hill Germany 49 K4
Collooney Rep. of Ireland 47 D9
Colmar France 51 N4
Colmena Arg. 204 E3
Colmenar de Oreja Spain 55 H4
Colmenar Viejo Spain 54 H4
Colne U.K. 47 J10
Colo r. Australia 147 F3
Cologne Germany 48 D5
also spelt Köln; historically known as Colonia Agrippina
Coloma MI U.S.A. 172 G8
Coloma WI U.S.A. 172 D6
Colomb-Béchar Alg. see Béchar
Colômbia Brazil 206 E7
Colombia Col. 198 C4
Colombia Mex. 185 F3

▶Colombia country S. America 198 C4
2nd most populous and 4th largest country in South America.
southamerica [countries] → 192–193

▶Colombo Sri Lanka 94 C5
Former capital of Sri Lanka.

Colombourg Canada 173 N2
Colomiers France 50 H9
Colón Buenos Aires Arg. 204 E4
Colón Entre Ríos Arg. 204 F4
Colón Cuba 186 C2
Colón Panama 186 D5
Colon U.S.A. 172 H9
Colón, Archipiélago de is Pacific Ocean see Galapagos Islands
Colón, Isla de i. Panama 186 C5
Colona Australia 146 B2
Colonelganj India 97 D4
Colonel Hill Bahamas 187 E2
Colonet, Cabo c. Mex. 184 A2
Colonia Arg. 204 E2
Colônia r. Brazil 207 N1
Colonia Micronesia 73 I5
Colonia Agrippina Germany see Cologne
Colonia del Sacramento Uruguay 204 F4
Colonia Dora Arg. 204 E3
Colonia Emilio Mitre Arg. 204 D5
Colonia Julia Fenestris Italy see Fano
Colonia Las Heras Arg. 205 C7
Colonial Heights U.S.A. 176 H8
Colonia Suiza Uruguay 204 F4
Colonna, Capo c. Italy 57 J9
Colonsay i. U.K. 46 F7
Colorado r. La Rioja Arg. 204 D3
Colorado r. San Juan Arg. 204 C3
Colorado r. Arg. 204 E5
Colorado Brazil 206 B9
Colorado r. Mex./U.S.A. 184 B2
Colorado r. U.S.A. 179 C6
Colorado state U.S.A. 183 P2
Colorado City AZ U.S.A. 183 K5
Colorado City TX U.S.A. 179 B5
Colorado Desert U.S.A. 183 H8
Colorado National Monument nat. park U.S.A. 183 P2
Colorado Plateau U.S.A. 183 O4
Colorado River Aqueduct canal U.S.A. 183 J7
Colorado River Indian Reservation res. U.S.A. 183 J8
Colorados, Cerro mt. Arg. 204 C2
Colorado Springs U.S.A. 180 F5
Colorno Italy 56 C4
Colossae Turkey see Honaz
Colotlán Mex. 185 E4
Colquechaca Bol. 200 D4
Colquiri Bol. 200 D4
Colquitt U.S.A. 175 C6
Colson U.S.A. 176 C8
Colstrip U.S.A. 180 F3
Colton CA U.S.A. 183 G7
Colton NY U.S.A. 177 K1
Colton UT U.S.A. 183 M2
Columbia KY U.S.A. 174 C4
Columbia LA U.S.A. 179 D5
Columbia MD U.S.A. 177 I6
Columbia MO U.S.A. 178 D4
Columbia MS U.S.A. 175 B6
Columbia NC U.S.A. 174 E5
Columbia NJ U.S.A. 177 J5
Columbia PA U.S.A. 177 I5

▶Columbia SC U.S.A. 175 D5
State capital of South Carolina.

Columbia TN U.S.A. 174 C5
Columbia r. U.S.A. 180 B3
Columbia, Cape Canada 165 L1
Columbia, Mount Canada 167 G4
Columbia, Sierra mts Mex. 184 B2
Columbia City U.S.A. 174 C3
Columbia Falls ME U.S.A. 177 R1
Columbia Falls MT U.S.A. 180 D2
Columbia Mountains Canada 166 F4
Columbia Plateau U.S.A. 180 C3
Columbine, Cape S. Africa 132 B9
Columbretes, Islas is Spain 55 L5
Columbus GA U.S.A. 175 C5
Columbus IN U.S.A. 174 C4
Columbus KS U.S.A. 178 D4
Columbus MS U.S.A. 175 B5
Columbus MT U.S.A. 180 E3
Columbus NC U.S.A. 174 D5
Columbus NE U.S.A. 178 C3

▶Columbus OH U.S.A. 176 B6
State capital of Ohio.

Columbus PA U.S.A. 176 F4
Columbus TX U.S.A. 179 C6
Columbus WI U.S.A. 172 D7
Columbus Grove U.S.A. 176 A5
Columbus Junction U.S.A. 172 B9
Columbus Salt Marsh U.S.A. 182 F3
Coluna Brazil 207 K5
Colunga Spain 54 F1
Colusa U.S.A. 182 B2
Colville N.Z. 152 J4
Colville U.S.A. 180 C2
Colville r. U.S.A. 164 D2
Colville, Cape N.Z. 152 J4
Colville Channel N.Z. 152 J4
Colville Indian Reservation res. U.S.A. 180 C2
Colville Lake Canada 166 E1
Colwyn Bay U.K. 47 I10
also known as Bae Colwyn
Comacchio Italy 56 E4
Comacchio, Valli di lag. Italy 56 E4
Comai China 89 E6
also known as Damxoi
Comalcalco Mex. 185 G5
Comallo Arg. 204 C6
Comana Romania 58 H4
Comanche U.S.A. 179 C6
Comandante Ferraz research station Antarctica 222 U2
Comandante Fontana Arg. 204 F2
Comandante Luis Piedra Buena Arg. 205 C8
Comandante Salas Arg. 204 C4
Comănești Romania 58 H2
Comarnic Romania 58 G3
Comayagua Hond. 186 B4
Combahee r. U.S.A. 175 D5
Combarbalá Chile 204 C3
Comber U.K. 47 G9
Combermere Canada 173 P5
Combermere Bay Myanmar 78 A4
Combol i. Indon. 76 C2
Combourg France 50 E4
Comendador Gomes Brazil 206 D6
Comercinho Brazil 207 L3
Comet Australia 149 F4
Comet r. Australia 149 F4
Comfort TX U.S.A. 179 C6
Comfort WV U.S.A. 176 D7
Comilla Bangl. 97 F5
Comino i. Malta see Kemmuna
Comino, Capo c. Sardegna Italy 57 B8
Comiso Sicilia Italy 57 G12
Comitán de Domínguez Mex. 185 G5
Commanda Canada 173 N5
Commentry France 51 I6
Commissioner's Salt Pan S. Africa 132 D7
Committee Bay Canada 165 K3
Commondale S. Africa 133 O4
Commonwealth Bay Antarctica 223 J2
Commonwealth Territory admin. div. Australia see Jervis Bay Territory
Como Italy 56 B3
Como, Lago di l. Italy see Como, Lake
Como, Lake Italy 56 B3
also known as Como, Lago di
Como Chamling l. China 89 E6
Comodoro Rivadavia Arg. 205 D7
Comoé r. Côte d'Ivoire see Komoé
Comonfort Mex. 185 E4
Comores country Africa see Comoros
Comorin, Cape India 94 C4
also known as Kanniya Kumari

▶Comoros country Africa 129 D7
known as Al Qumur in Arabic; also spelt Comores in French
africa [countries] → 114–117

Comox Canada 166 E5
Compiègne France 51 I3
Compostela Mex. 184 D4
Compostela Phil. 74 C5
Comprida, Ilha i. Brazil 203 C8
Compton CA U.S.A. 182 F8
Compton IL U.S.A. 172 D9

Comrat Moldova **58** J2
formerly spelt Komrat
Con, Sông *r.* Vietnam **78** D4
Cona China **89** E7
also spelt Tsona

Conakry Guinea **124** B4
Capital of Guinea.

Conambo Ecuador **198** B5
Conambo *r.* Ecuador **198** B5
Cona Niyeo Arg. **205** D6
Conay Chile **204** C3
Concarán Arg. **204** D4
Concarneau France **50** C5
Conceição *Amazonas* Brazil **199** F5
Conceição *Mato Grosso* Brazil **201** F1
Conceição *Paraíba* Brazil **202** E3
Conceição *Rondônia* Brazil **201** E2
Conceição *Roraima* Brazil **199** F4
Conceição *r.* Brazil **207** H3
Conceição da Barra Brazil **203** E6
Conceição das Alagoas Brazil **206** E6
Conceição de Macabu Brazil **207** L9
Conceição do Araguaia Brazil **202** B4
Conceição do Coité Brazil **202** E4
Conceição do Mato Dentro Brazil **203** D6
Conceição do Maú Brazil **199** G4
Concepción *Corrientes* Arg. **204** F3
Concepción *Tucumán* Arg. **204** D2
Concepción *Beni* Bol. **200** D2
Concepción *Santa Cruz* Bol. **201** E4
Concepción Chile **204** B5
Concepción Mex. **185** E3
Concepción *r.* Mex. **184** B2
Concepción Panama **186** C5
Concepción Para. **201** F5
Concepción, Canal *sea chan.* Chile **205** B8
Concepción, Punta *pt* Mex. **184** C3
Concepción del Uruguay Arg. **204** F4
Conception, Point U.S.A. **182** D7
Conception Bay Namibia **130** B4
Concesio Italy **56** C3
Concession Zimbabwe **131** F3
Concha Mex. **184** D4
Conchas Brazil **206** E9
Conchas Lake U.S.A. **181** F6
Conches-en-Ouche France **50** G4
Conchi Chile **200** C5
Concho Mex. **184** D3
Concho U.S.A. **183** O7
Concho *r.* U.S.A. **179** C6
Conchos *r. Chihuahua* Mex. **184** D2
Conchos *r. Nuevo León/Tamaulipas* Mex. **185** F3
Concord *CA* U.S.A. **182** B4
Concord *MI* U.S.A. **173** I8
Concord *NC* U.S.A. **174** D5

Concord *NH* U.S.A. **177** N2
State capital of New Hampshire.

Concord *PA* U.S.A. **176** H5
Concord *VA* U.S.A. **176** G8
Concord *VT* U.S.A. **177** N1
Concordia Arg. **204** F3
Concórdia *Amazonas* Brazil **199** E6
Concórdia *Santa Catarina* Brazil **203** A8
Concordia *Antioquia* Col. **198** C3
Concordia *Meta* Col. **198** C4
Concordiá Mex. **184** D4
Concordia Peru **198** C6
Concordia S. Africa **132** B6
Concordia U.S.A. **178** C4
Concord Peak Afgh. **101** H2
Con Cuông Vietnam **78** D4
Conda Angola **127** B7
Condamine Australia **149** F5
Condamine *r.* Australia **147** F1
Conde Brazil **202** E4
Condega Nicaragua **186** B4
Condeixa Brazil **202** B2
Condé-sur-Noireau France **50** F4
Condeúba Brazil **202** D5
Condobolin Australia **147** E3
Condoe Moz. **131** G3
Condom France **50** G9
Condon U.S.A. **180** B3
Condor, Cordillera del *mts* Ecuador/Peru **198** B6
Conecuh *r.* U.S.A. **175** C6
Conejos Mex. **184** E3
Conejos U.S.A. **181** F5
Conejos *r.* U.S.A. **181** F5
Conemaugh *r.* U.S.A. **176** F5
Conero, Monte *hill* Italy **56** F5
Conestogo Lake Canada **173** M7
Conesus Lake U.S.A. **176** H3
Conesville *IA* U.S.A. **172** B9
Conesville *OH* U.S.A. **176** D5
Coney Island Sing. *see* **Serangoon, Pulau**
Coney Island U.S.A. **177** L5
Conflict Group *is* P.N.G. **149** F1
Confluence U.S.A. **176** F6
Confoederatio Helvetica *country* Europe *see* **Switzerland**
Confolens France **50** G6
Confusion Range *mts* U.S.A. **183** K3
Confuso *r.* Para. **201** F6
Congdü China *see* **Nyalam**
Conghua China **87** E4
Congjiang China **87** D3
also known as Bingmei
Congleton U.K. **47** J10
Congo *country* Africa **126** B5
formerly known as Congo (Brazzaville) *or* French Congo *or* Middle Congo *or* Moyen Congo; *long form* Congo, Republic of
africa [countries] ➡ 114–117

Congo *r.* Congo/Dem. Rep. Congo **127** B6
2nd longest river in Africa and 8th in the world. Formerly known as Zaire.
africa [landscapes] ➡ 112–113

Congo (Brazzaville) *country* Africa *see* **Congo**
Congo (Kinshasa) *country* Africa *see* **Congo, Democratic Republic of**

Congo, Democratic Republic of *country* Africa **126** D5
3rd largest and 4th most populous country in Africa. Formerly known as Zaire or Belgian Congo or Congo (Kinshasa) or Congo Free State.
africa [countries] ➡ 114–117

Congo, Republic of *country* Africa *see* **Congo**
Congo Basin Dem. Rep. Congo **126** D5
Congo Free State *country* Africa *see* **Congo, Democratic Republic of**
Congonhas Brazil **207** J7
Congonhinhas Brazil **206** C10
Congress U.S.A. **183** L7
Conguillo, Parque Nacional *nat. park* Chile **204** C5
Conhuas Mex. **185** H5
Cónico, Cerro *mt.* Arg. **205** C6
Conil de la Frontera Spain **54** E8
Coniston Canada **173** M4
Coniston U.K. **47** I9
Conjuboy Australia **149** E3
Conkal Mex. **185** H4
Conklin Canada **167** I4
Conkouati, Réserve de Faune *nature res.* Congo **126** A5
Conlara *r.* Arg. **204** D4
Conn *r.* Canada **168** E2
Conn, Lough *l.* Rep. of Ireland **47** C9
Connacht *reg.* Rep. of Ireland *see* **Connaught**

Connaught Canada **173** M2
Connaught *reg.* Rep. of Ireland **47** C10
also spelt Connacht
Conneaut U.S.A. **176** E4
Conneaut Lake U.S.A. **176** E4
Conneautville U.S.A. **176** E4
Connecticut *r.* U.S.A. **177** M4
Connecticut *state* U.S.A. **177** M4
Connel U.K. **46** G7
Connells Lagoon Conservation Reserve *nature res.* Australia **148** C3
Connemara Australia **149** D5
Connemara *reg.* Rep. of Ireland **47** C10
Connemara National Park Rep. of Ireland **47** C10
Conner, Mount *hill* Australia **148** A5
Connersville U.S.A. **174** C4
Connolly, Mount Canada **166** C2
Connors Range *hills* Australia **149** F4
Cononaco Ecuador **198** C5
Cononaco *r.* Ecuador **198** C5
Conover U.S.A. **172** D4
Conquista Bol. **200** D2
Conquista Brazil **206** F6
Conrad U.S.A. **180** E2
Conroe U.S.A. **179** D6
Conroe, Lake U.S.A. **179** D6
Consecon Canada **173** P6
Consejo Belize **186** A3
Conselheiro Lafaiete Brazil **203** D7
Conselheiro Pena Brazil **203** D6
Conselice Italy **56** D4
Consett U.K. **47** K9
Consolación del Sur Cuba **186** C2
Côn Sơn *i.* Vietnam **79** D6
Consort Canada **167** I4
Constance Germany *see* **Konstanz**
Constance, Lake Germany/Switz. **51** P5
also known as Bodensee
Constância dos Baetas Brazil **199** F6
Constanța Romania **58** J4
also spelt Küstence; *historically known as* Tomi
Constanța *airport* Romania *see* **Kogălniceanu**
Constantia *tourist site* Cyprus *see* **Salamis**
Constantia Germany *see* **Konstanz**
Constantina Spain **54** F7
Constantine Alg. **123** G1
also known as Qacentina; *historically known as* Cirta
Constantine U.S.A. **172** H9
Constantine, Cape U.S.A. **164** D4
Constantinople Turkey *see* **İstanbul**
Constitución de 1857, Parque Nacional *nat. park* Mex. **184** B1
Consuelo Australia **149** F5
Consuelo Brazil **201** E3
Consul Canada **167** I5
Consul *r.* Canada **167** K1
Contagem Brazil **207** I6
Contamana Peru **200** B1
Contarina Italy **56** E3
Contas *r.* Brazil **202** E5
Conthey Switz. **51** N6
Contoocook *r.* U.S.A. **177** N2
Contoy, Isla *i.* Mex. **186** B2
Contratacion Col. **198** C3
Contreras, Embalse de *resr* Spain **55** J5
Contreras, Isla *i.* Chile **205** B8
Contres France **50** H5
Contria Brazil **207** I5
Contwoyto Lake Canada **167** I1
Convención Col. **198** C2
Convent U.S.A. **175** B6
Convoy U.S.A. **176** A5
Conway S. Africa **133** J8
Conway *AR* U.S.A. **179** D5
Conway *KY* U.S.A. **176** A8
Conway *NC* U.S.A. **177** H9
Conway *NH* U.S.A. **177** N2
Conway *SC* U.S.A. **175** E5
Conway, Cape Australia **149** F4
Conway, Lake *salt flat* Australia **146** B2
Conway National Park Australia **149** F4
Conway Springs U.S.A. **178** C4
Coober Pedy Australia **146** B2
Cooch Behar India *see* **Koch Bihar**
Coogoon *r.* Australia **147** F1
Cook Australia **146** A2
Cook U.S.A. **172** A3
Cook, Bahía de *b.* Chile **205** C9
Cook, Cape Canada **166** E5
Cook, Mount Canada/U.S.A. **166** B2
oceania [landscapes] ➡ 136–137

Cook, Mount N.Z. **153** E11
Highest mountain in New Zealand. Also known as Aoraki or Aorangi.

Cook Atoll Kiribati *see* **Tarawa**
Cookes Peak U.S.A. **181** F6
Cookeville U.S.A. **174** C4
Cookhouse S. Africa **133** J9
Cook Ice Shelf Antarctica **223** K2
Cook Inlet *sea chan.* U.S.A. **164** D3

Cook Islands S. Pacific Ocean **221** H7
Self-governing New Zealand Territory.
oceania [countries] ➡ 138–139

Cooksburg U.S.A. **177** K3
Cooks Passage Australia **149** E2
Cookstown U.K. **47** F9
Cook Strait N.Z. **152** I8
Cooktown Australia **149** E2
Coolabah Australia **147** E2
Cooladdi Australia **149** E5
Coolah Australia **147** F2
Coolamon Australia **147** E3
Coolgardie Australia **151** C6
Coolibah Australia **148** A2
Coolimba Australia **151** A6
Cooloola National Park Australia **149** G5
Coolum Beach Australia **149** G5
Cooma Australia **147** F4
Coombah Australia **146** D3
Coonabarabran Australia **147** F2
Coonalpyn Australia **146** C3
Coonamble Australia **147** F2
Coonana Aboriginal Reserve Australia **151** C6
Coondambo Australia **146** B2
Coondapoor India *see* **Kundapura**
Coongan *r.* Australia **150** B4
Coongan Aboriginal Reserve Australia **150** B4
Coongoola Australia **147** E1
Coon Rapids U.S.A. **174** A2
Cooper *r.* Australia **148** B2
Cooper U.S.A. **179** D5
Cooper Creek *watercourse* Australia **146** C2
also known as Barcoo Creek
Cooperdale U.S.A. **176** C5
Coopernook Australia **147** G2
Coopersburg U.S.A. **177** J5
Coopers Mills U.S.A. **177** P1
Cooper's Town Bahamas **186** D1
Cooperstown *ND* U.S.A. **178** C2
Cooperstown *NY* U.S.A. **177** K3
Coopracambra National Park Australia **147** F4
Coor-de-Wandy *hill* Australia **151** B5
Coorong National Park Australia **146** C4
Coorow Australia **151** B6
Cooroy Australia **149** G5
Coosa *r.* U.S.A. **175** C5
Coos Bay U.S.A. **180** A4
Coos Bay *b.* U.S.A. **180** A4
Cootamundra Australia **147** F3
Cooum *r.* India **94** D3
Copahue, Volcán *vol.* Chile **204** C5
Copainalá Mex. **185** G5

Copala Mex. **185** F5
Copal Urcu Peru **198** C5
Copán *tourist site* Hond. **186** A4
Cope, Cabo *c.* Spain **55** J7
Copemish U.S.A. **172** H6

Copenhagen Denmark **45** K5
Capital of Denmark. Also known as København.

Copere Bol. **201** E4
Copetonas Arg. **204** E5
Copeton Reservoir Australia **147** F2
Cô Pi, Phou *mt.* Laos/Vietnam **78** D4
Copiapó Chile **204** C2
Copiapo, Volcán *vol.* Chile **204** C2
Copley Australia **146** C2
Coporaque Peru **200** C3
Copparo Italy **56** D4
Coppename *r.* Suriname **199** G3
Copperbelt *prov.* Zambia **127** E8
formerly known as Western Province
Copperfield *r.* Australia **149** D3
Copper Harbor U.S.A. **172** F3
Coppermine Canada *see* **Kugluktuk**
Coppermine *r.* Canada **167** H1
Coppermine Point Canada **168** C4
Copperton S. Africa **132** G6
Copperton U.S.A. **183** L1
Copp Lake Canada **167** H2
Copșa Mică Romania **58** F2
Coqên China **89** D6
Coquilhatville Dem. Rep. Congo *see* **Mbandaka**
Coquille *i.* Micronesia *see* **Pikelot**
Coquille U.S.A. **180** A4
Coquimbo Chile **204** C3
Coquimbo *admin. reg.* Chile **204** C3
Coquitlam Canada **166** F5
Corabia Romania **58** F5
Coração de Jesus Brazil **202** C6
Coracesium Turkey *see* **Alanya**
Coracora Peru **200** B3
Coral Bay Australia **150** A4
Coral Harbour Canada **165** K3
Coral Sea S. Pacific Ocean **145** E3

Coral Sea Islands Territory *terr.* Australia **145** E3
Australian External Territory.
oceania [countries] ➡ 138–139

Coralville U.S.A. **172** B9
Corangamite, Lake Australia **147** D4
Corantijn *r.* Suriname *see* **Courantyne**
Coraopolis U.S.A. **176** E5
Corato Italy **56** I7
Corbett National Park India **96** C3
Corbie France **51** I3
Corbin U.S.A. **176** A9
Corbones *r.* Spain **54** F7
Corbu Romania **58** J4
Corby U.K. **47** L11
Corcaigh Rep. of Ireland *see* **Cork**
Córcoles *r.* Spain **55** H5
Corcoran U.S.A. **182** E5
Corcovado Arg. **205** C6
Corcovado, Golfo de *sea chan.* Chile **205** B6
Corcovado, Parque Nacional *nat. park* Costa Rica **186** C5
Corcyra *i.* Greece *see* **Corfu**
Cordeiro Brazil **207** K9
Cordele U.S.A. **175** D6
Cordelia U.S.A. **182** B3
Cordell U.S.A. **179** C5
Cordillera de los Picachos, Parque Nacional *nat. park* Col. **198** C4
Cordilleras Range *mts* Phil. **74** B4
Cordillo Downs Australia **149** D5
Cordisburgo Brazil **207** I6
Córdoba *Córdoba* Arg. **204** D3
Córdoba *Río Negro* Arg. **204** C6
Córdoba *prov.* Arg. **204** E4
Córdoba *dept* Col. **198** C2
Córdoba *Durango* Mex. **185** E3
Córdoba *Veracruz* Mex. **185** F5
Córdoba Spain **54** G7
historically known as Cordova *or* Corduba *or* Karmona
Córdoba, Sierras de *mts* Arg. **204** D4
Cordova Peru **200** B3
Cordova Spain *see* **Córdoba**
Cordova *AK* U.S.A. **164** E3
Cordova *IL* U.S.A. **172** C9
Cordova Bay U.S.A. **166** C4
Corduba Spain *see* **Córdoba**
Coreaú Brazil **202** D2
Corella *r.* Australia **149** D3
Corella Lake *salt flat* Australia **148** B3
Corfield Australia **149** D4
Corfu *i.* Greece **59** A9
also known as Kerkyra; *also spelt* Kérkira; *historically known as* Corcyra
Corguinho Brazil **203** A6
Coria Spain **54** E5
Coria del Río Spain **54** E7
Coribe Brazil **202** C5
Coricudgy *mt.* Australia **147** F3
Corigliano, Golfo di *b.* Italy **57** I9
Corigliano Calabro Italy **57** I9
Coringa Islands Australia **149** F3
Corinium U.K. *see* **Cirencester**
Corinne Canada **167** J5
Corinth Greece **59** D11
also spelt Korinthos; *historically known as* Corinthus
Corinth *MS* U.S.A. **174** B5
Corinth *NY* U.S.A. **177** L2
Corinth, Gulf of *sea chan.* Greece **59** D10
also known as Korinthiakos Kolpos
Corinthus Greece *see* **Corinth**
Corinto Brazil **203** C6
Corinto Nicaragua **186** B4
Corixa Grande *r.* Bol./Brazil **201** F4
Corixinha *r.* Brazil **201** F4
Cork Rep. of Ireland **47** D12
also spelt Corcaigh
Corlay France **50** C4
Corleone *Sicilia* Italy **57** F11
Çorlu Turkey **106** A2
Çorlu *r.* Turkey **58** I7
Cormeilles France **50** G3
Cormorant Canada **167** K4
Cormorant Lake Canada **167** K4
Cormorant Provincial Forest *nature res.* Canada **167** K4
Cornacchia, Monte *mt.* Italy **56** H7
Cornelia S. Africa **133** M4
Cornelia U.S.A. **179** G5
Cornélio Procópio Brazil **206** C10
Corneliskondre Suriname **199** G3
Cornell U.S.A. **172** B5
Cornellà de Llobregat Spain **55** N3
Corner Brook Canada **169** J3
Corneto Italy *see* **Tarquinia**
Cornetto *mt.* Italy **56** D3
Cornettsville U.S.A. **176** B8
Cornia *r.* Italy **56** C6
Corning *AR* U.S.A. **174** B4
Corning *CA* U.S.A. **182** B2
Corning *IA* U.S.A. **178** D3
Corning *NY* U.S.A. **177** H3
Corning *OH* U.S.A. **176** C6
Cornish *watercourse* Australia **149** E4
Cornish, Estrada *b.* Chile **205** B7
Corn Islands *is* Nicaragua *see* **Maíz, Islas del**
Corno, Monte *mt.* Italy **56** F6
Cornouaille *reg.* France **50** B4
Cornucopia U.S.A. **172** B4
Cornwall *Ont.* Canada **169** F4

Cornwall *P.E.I.* Canada **169** I4
Cornwall U.S.A. **177** I5
Cornwallis Island Canada **165** J2
Cornwall Island Canada **165** J2
Corny Point Australia **146** C3
Coro Venez. **198** D2
Coroaci Brazil **203** D6
Coroatá Brazil **202** C3
Corocoro Bol. **200** C4
Corocoro, Isla *i.* Venez. **199** F2
Coroglen N.Z. **152** J4
Coroico Bol. **200** D4
Corolla U.S.A. **177** J9
Coromandel Brazil **206** F5
Coromandel N.Z. **152** J4
Coromandel Coast India **94** D4
Coromandel Forest Park *nature res.* N.Z. **152** J5
Coromandel Peninsula N.Z. **152** J4
Coromandel Range *hills* N.Z. **152** J4
Coron Phil. **74** B3
Corona *CA* U.S.A. **182** G8
Corona *NM* U.S.A. **181** F6
Coronado U.S.A. **183** G9
Coronado, Bahía de *b.* Costa Rica **186** C5
Coronation Canada **167** I4
Coronation Gulf Canada **165** H3
Coronation Island S. Atlantic Ocean **222** U2
Coronation Islands Australia **150** D2
Coron Bay Phil. **74** B4
Coronda Arg. **204** E3
Coronel Brandsen Arg. **204** F4
Coronel Dorrego Arg. **204** E5
Coronel Fabriciano Brazil **203** D6
Coronel Francisco Sosa Arg. **204** D6
Coronel Moldes Arg. **204** D2
Coronel Murta Brazil **207** K3
Coronel Oviedo Para. **201** F6
Coronel Portillo Peru **198** B5
Coronel Pringles Arg. **204** E5
Coronel Sapucaia Brazil **201** G5
Coronel Suárez Arg. **204** E5
Coronel Vidal Arg. **204** F5
Çorovodë Albania **58** B8
Corowa Australia **147** E3
Corozal Belize **185** H5
Corozal Venez. **187** H5
Corozo Pando Venez. **199** E2
Corpen Aike Arg. **205** C8
Corpus Christi U.S.A. **179** C7
Corpus Christi, Lake U.S.A. **179** C6
Corque Bol. **200** D4
Corral Chile **204** B5
Corral de Almaguer Spain **55** H5
Corral de Cantos *mt.* Spain **54** G5
Corralilla Cuba **186** C2
Corralitos U.S.A. **182** C5
Corrandibby Range *hills* Australia **151** A5
Corrane Moz. **131** H2
Corrasi, Punta *mt. Sardegna* Italy **57** B8
Corraun Peninsula Rep. of Ireland **47** C10
Córrego do Ouro Brazil **206** C3
Córrego Novo Brazil **207** K6
Correntes Brazil **202** C4
Corrente *r. Bahia* Brazil **202** D5
Corrente *r. Minas Gerais* Brazil **206** C6
Corrente Grande *r.* Brazil **207** K6
Correntes Brazil **203** A6
Correntes *r.* Brazil **201** G4
Correnti, Isola delle *i. Sicilia* Italy **57** H12
Correntina Brazil **202** C5
Correntina *r.* Brazil *see* **Éguas**
Corrèze France **50** H7
Corrèze *r.* France **51** H7
Corrib, Lough *l.* Rep. of Ireland **47** C10
Corrientes Arg. **204** F2
Corrientes *prov.* Arg. **204** F3
Corrientes *r.* Arg. **204** F3
Corrientes *r.* Peru **198** C5
Corrientes, Cabo *c.* Arg. **204** F5
Corrientes, Cabo *c.* Col. **198** B3
Corrientes, Cabo *c.* Cuba **186** B2
Corrientes, Cabo *c.* Mex. **184** D4
Corrigan U.S.A. **179** D6
Corrigin Australia **151** B7
Corriverton Guyana **199** G3
Corrubedo, Cabo *c.* Spain **54** B2
Corry U.S.A. **176** F4
Corryong Australia **147** E4
Corsaglia *r.* Italy **51** N8
Corse *admin. reg.* France **56** B6
Corse *i.* France *see* **Corsica**
Corse, Cap *c. Corse* France **51** P9

Corsica *i.* France **51** O10
also known as Corse
europe [environments] ➡ 36–37

Corsicana U.S.A. **179** C5
Corsico, Baie de *b.* Gabon **126** A4
Cort Adelaer, Kap *c.* Greenland *see* **Kangeq**
Cortale Italy **57** I10
Corte *Corse* France **51** P10
Cortegana Spain **54** E7
Cortes Spain **55** J3
Cortes, Sea of *g.* Mex. *see* **California, Gulf of**
Cortes de la Frontera, Reserva Nacional de *nature res.* Spain **54** F8
Cortez U.S.A. **181** E5
Cortez Mountains U.S.A. **183** H1
Cortina d'Ampezzo Italy **56** E2
Cortland *NY* U.S.A. **177** I3
Cortland *OH* U.S.A. **176** E4
Cortona Italy **56** D5
Corubal *r.* Guinea-Bissau **124** B4
Coruche Port. **54** C6
Çoruh Turkey *see* **Artvin**
Çoruh *r.* Turkey **107** E2
Çorum Turkey **106** C2
Corumbá Brazil **201** F4
Corumbá *r.* Brazil **206** E5
Corumbá de Goiás Brazil **206** E2
Corumbaíba Brazil **206** E5
Corumbataí *r.* Brazil **206** B10
Corumbaú, Ponta *pt* Brazil **207** N3
Corund Romania **58** G2
Corunna Canada **173** K8
Corunna Spain *see* **A Coruña**
Corunna U.S.A. **173** I8
Coruripe Brazil **202** E4
Corvallis U.S.A. **180** B3
Corwen U.K. **47** I11
Corydon *IA* U.S.A. **174** A3
Corydon *IN* U.S.A. **174** C4
Coryville U.S.A. **176** G4
Cos *i.* Greece *see* **Kos**
Cosalá Mex. **184** D3
Cosamaloapan Mex. **185** G5
Coscaya Chile **200** C4
Cosentia Italy *see* **Cosenza**
Cosenza Italy **57** I9
historically known as Cosentia
Coșereni Romania **58** H4
Coshocton U.S.A. **176** D5
Cosmoledo Atoll Seychelles **129** E7
Cosmo Newbery Aboriginal Reserve Australia **151** C6
Cosmópolis Brazil **206** F9
Cosne-Cours-sur-Loire France **51** I5
Cosquín Arg. **204** D3
Cossato Italy **56** A3
Cossé-le-Vivien France **50** F5
Costa Brazil **202** D3
Costa Blanca *coastal area* Spain **55** K6
Costa Brava *coastal area* Spain **55** O3
Costache Negri Romania **58** I3
Costa de la Luz *coastal area* Spain **54** D7
Costa del Azahar *coastal area* Spain **55** K5
Costa del Sol *coastal area* Spain **54** F8
Costa Dorada *coastal area* Spain **55** N3
Costa Marques Brazil **201** D3
Costa Rica Brazil **203** A6

Costa Rica *country* Central America **186** B5
northamerica [countries] ➡ 158–159
Costa Rica Mex. **184** D3
Costa Verde *coastal area* Spain **54** E1
Costermansville Dem. Rep. Congo *see* **Bukavu**
Costești Romania **58** F4
Costești Romania **58** I2
Costigan Lake Canada **167** J3
Cosușțea *r.* Romania **58** E4
Cotabambas Peru **200** B3
Cotabato Phil. **74** C5
Cotacajes *r.* Bol. **200** D4
Cotagaita Bol. **200** D5
Cotahuasi Peru **200** B3
Cotaxé *r.* Brazil **203** D6
Cote, Mount U.S.A. **166** D3
Coteau des Prairies *slope* U.S.A. **178** C2
Coteau du Missouri *slope ND* U.S.A. **178** B1
Coteau du Missouri *slope SD* U.S.A. **178** B2
Coteaux Haiti **187** E3
Côte d'Azur *coastal area* France **51** N9
Côte d'Ivoire *country* Africa **124** D4
formerly known as Ivory Coast
africa [countries] ➡ 114–117
Côte Française de Somalis *country* Africa *see* **Djibouti**
Cotegipe Brazil **202** C4
Cotentin *pen.* France **50** E3
Côtes de Meuse *ridge* France **51** K3
Coti *r.* Brazil **200** D2
Cotiaeum Turkey *see* **Kütahya**
Cotiella *mt.* Spain **55** L2
Cotingo *r.* Brazil **199** F4
Cotmeana *r.* Romania **58** F4
Cotonou Benin **125** F5
Cotopaxi *prov.* Ecuador **198** B5
Cotopaxi, Volcán *vol.* Ecuador **198** B5
Cotovsc Moldova *see* **Hîncești**
Cotswold Hills U.K. **47** J12
Cottage Grove U.S.A. **180** B4
Cottbus Germany **49** L4
Cotteliar *r.* India **94** D3
Cottian Alps *mts* France/Italy **51** M8
also known as Cottiennes, Alpes *or* Cozie, Alpi
Cottica Suriname **199** H4
Cottiennes, Alpes *mts* France/Italy *see* **Cottian Alps**
Cotton U.S.A. **172** A3
Cottonbush Creek *watercourse* Australia **148** C4
Cottonwood *AZ* U.S.A. **183** L7
Cottonwood *CA* U.S.A. **182** B1
Cottonwood *r. KS* U.S.A. **178** C4
Cottonwood *r. MN* U.S.A. **178** D2
Cottonwood Creek *watercourse* U.S.A. **181** G7
Cottonwood Falls U.S.A. **178** C4
Cottonwood Wash *watercourse* U.S.A. **183** N7
Cotuí Dom. Rep. **187** F3
Cotulla U.S.A. **179** C6
Couchman Range *hills* Australia **150** D2
Coudersport U.S.A. **176** G4
Coudres, Île aux *i.* Canada **169** G4
Couëdic, Cape de Australia **146** C4
Couesnon *r.* France **50** E4
Couiza France **51** I10
Coulee Dam U.S.A. **180** C3
Coulman Island Antarctica **223** L2
Coulogne France **51** H2
Couloir 1 *well* Alg. **123** H4
Coulommiers France **51** J4
Coulonge *r.* Canada **168** E4
Coulterville U.S.A. **182** D4
Council U.S.A. **180** C3
Council Bluffs U.S.A. **178** D3
Council Grove U.S.A. **178** C4
Councillor Island Australia **147** E4
Coupeville U.S.A. **180** B2
Courageous Lake Canada **167** I1
Courantyne *r.* Guyana **199** G3
Courland Lagoon *b.* Lith./Rus. Fed. **42** C6
also known as Kurshskiy Zaliv *or* Kurskiy Zaliv *or* Kuršių marios
Cournon-d'Auvergne France **51** J7
Coursan France **51** J9
Courtenay Canada **166** E5
Courthézon France **51** K8
Courtland U.S.A. **177** H9
Courtrai Belgium *see* **Kortrijk**
Coushatta U.S.A. **179** D5
Coutances France **50** E3
Coutinho Moz. *see* **Ulongue**
Couto de Magalhães de Minas Brazil **207** J5
Coutras France **50** F7
Coutts Canada **167** I5
Couvin Belgium **51** K2
Couzeix France **50** H7
Covadea Spain **55** I3
Covasna Romania **58** H3
Cove Fort U.S.A. **183** L3
Cove Island Canada **173** L5
Covelo U.S.A. **182** A2
Cove Mountains *hills* U.S.A. **176** G6
Covendo Bol. **200** D3
Coventry U.K. **47** K11
Covesville U.S.A. **176** G8
Covilhã Port. **54** D4
Covington *GA* U.S.A. **175** D5
Covington *IN* U.S.A. **174** C3
Covington *KY* U.S.A. **176** A6
Covington *LA* U.S.A. **175** B6
Covington *OH* U.S.A. **176** A5
Covington *TN* U.S.A. **174** B5
Covington *VA* U.S.A. **176** E8
Cow *r.* Canada **173** J3
Cowal, Lake *dry lake* Australia **147** E3
Cowan U.S.A. **176** B7
Cowan, Lake *salt flat* Australia **151** C6
Cowcowing Lakes *salt flat* Australia **151** B6
Cowdenbeath U.K. **46** I7
Cowell Australia **146** C3
Cowen U.S.A. **176** E7
Cowes Australia **147** E4
Cowley Australia **149** E5
Cowlitz *r.* U.S.A. **180** B3
Cowpasture *r.* U.S.A. **176** F8
Cowra Australia **147** F3
Cox *r.* Australia **148** B2
Coxá *r.* Brazil **207** I1
Coxen Hole Hond. *see* **Roatán**
Coxilha de Santana *hills* Brazil/Uruguay **204** G3
Coxilha Grande *hills* Brazil **203** A9
Coxim Brazil **203** A6
Coxim *r.* Brazil **203** A6
Coxsackie U.S.A. **177** L3
Cox's Bazar Bangl. **97** F5
Coyah Guinea **124** B4
Coy Aike Arg. **205** C8
Coyame Mex. **181** F7
Coyanosa Creek *watercourse* U.S.A. **179** B6
Coyote *r.* Mex. **181** D7
Coyote, Punta *pt* Mex. **184** C3
Coyote Lake U.S.A. **183** H6
Coyote Peak *hill* U.S.A. **183** J9
Coyote Peak U.S.A. **182** F5
Coyotitán Mex. **184** D4
Coyuca de Benítez Mex. **185** E5
Coyuca de Catalán Mex. **185** E5
Cozad U.S.A. **178** C3
Cozia, Vârful *mt.* Romania **58** F3
Cozie, Alpi *mts* France/Italy *see* **Cottian Alps**
Cozumel Mex. **185** I4
Cozumel, Isla de *i.* Mex. **185** I4
Cozzo del Pellegrino *mt.* Italy **57** I9
Crab Island Australia **149** D1

Crab Orchard U.S.A. **176** A8
Cracovia Poland *see* **Kraków**
Cracow Australia **149** F5
Cracow Poland *see* **Kraków**
Cradle Mountain Lake St Clair National Park Australia **147** E5
Cradock Australia **146** C2
Cradock S. Africa **133** J9
Crafthole S. Africa **132** I3
Craig *AK* U.S.A. **166** C4
Craig *CO* U.S.A. **180** F4
Craigavon U.K. **47** F9
Craigieburn Australia **147** E4
Craigieburn N.Z. **153** F11
Craigieburn Forest Park *nature res.* N.Z. **153** F11
Craignure U.K. **46** G7
Craigsville *VA* U.S.A. **176** F7
Craigsville *WV* U.S.A. **176** E7
Crail U.K. **46** J7
Crailsheim Germany **48** H6
Craiova Romania **58** E4
Cramlington U.K. **47** K8
Cramond S. Africa **132** F4
Cranberry Junction Canada **166** D4
Cranberry Lake U.S.A. **177** K1
Cranberry Portage Canada **167** K4
Cranbourne Australia **147** E4
Cranbrook Canada **167** H5
Crandon U.S.A. **172** E5
Crane *OR* U.S.A. **180** C4
Crane *TX* U.S.A. **179** B6
Crane Lake *l.* Canada **167** I5
Crane Lake U.S.A. **172** A2
Cranston *KY* U.S.A. **176** B7
Cranston *RI* U.S.A. **177** N4
Cranz Rus. Fed. *see* **Zelenogradsk**
Craolândia Brazil **202** C3
Craon France **50** F5
Crary Ice Rise Antarctica **223** M1
Crary Mountains Antarctica **222** P1
Crasna Romania **58** D1
Crasna *r.* Romania **58** D1
Crater Lake National Park U.S.A. **180** B4
Crater Peak U.S.A. **182** C1
Craters of the Moon National Monument *nat. park* U.S.A. **180** D4
Crateús Brazil **202** D3
Crato Brazil **202** E3
Crato Port. **54** D5
Cravari *r.* Brazil **201** F3
Cravinhos Brazil **206** F8
Cravo Norte Col. **198** D3
Crawford U.S.A. **178** B3
Crawford Point Phil. **74** A4
Crawford Range *hills* Australia **148** B4
Crawfordsville U.S.A. **174** C3
Crawfordville U.S.A. **175** C6
Crawley U.K. **47** L12
Crazy Mountains U.S.A. **180** E3
Crean Lake Canada **167** J4
Crécy-en-Ponthieu France **51** H2
Crediton U.K. **47** I13
Cree *r.* Canada **167** J3
Creede U.S.A. **181** F5
Creedmoor U.S.A. **176** G9
Creel Mex. **184** D3
Cree Lake Canada **167** J3
Creighton Canada **167** K4
Creighton S. Africa **133** N7
Creil France **51** I3
Crema Italy **56** B3
Cremona Canada **167** H5
Cremona Italy **56** C3
Crepori *r.* Brazil **199** G6
Crépy-en-Valois France **51** I3
Cres Croatia **56** G4
Cres *i.* Croatia **56** G4
Crescent City U.S.A. **180** A4
Crescent Group *is* Paracel Is **72** D3
Crescent Head Australia **147** G2
Crescent Junction U.S.A. **183** O3
Crescent Lake National Wildlife Refuge *nature res.* U.S.A. **178** B3
Crescent Peak U.S.A. **183** I6
Crescent Valley U.S.A. **183** H1
Cresco U.S.A. **174** A3
Crespo Arg. **204** E4
Cresswell *watercourse* Australia **148** B3
Cresswell Downs Australia **148** B3
Crest France **51** L8
Crest Hill *hill Hong Kong* China **87** [inset]
also known as Tai Shek Mo
Crestline U.S.A. **176** C5
Creston Canada **167** G5
Creston *IA* U.S.A. **178** D3
Creston *WY* U.S.A. **180** F4
Crestview U.S.A. **175** C6
Creta *i.* Greece *see* **Crete**
Crêt de la Neige *mt.* France **51** L6
Crete *i.* Greece **59** F13
also spelt Kriti; *historically known as* Creta
Crete U.S.A. **178** C3
Crêt Monniot *mt.* France **51** M5
Creus, Cap de *c.* Spain **55** O2
Creuse *r.* France **51** G5
Crevalcore Italy **56** D4
Crevasse Valley Glacier Antarctica **222** O1
Crevillente Spain **55** K6
Crewe U.K. **47** J10
Crewe U.S.A. **176** G8
Crianlarich U.K. **46** H7
Criccieth U.K. **47** H11
Criciúma Brazil **203** B9
Cricova Moldova **58** J1
formerly spelt Krikovo
Cricovu Sărat *r.* Romania **58** H4
Cridersville U.S.A. **176** A5
Crieff U.K. **46** I7
Criffell *hill* U.K. **47** I9
Crikvenica Croatia **56** G3
Crillon, Mount U.S.A. **166** B3
Crimea *pen.* Ukr. **41** E7
also known as Kryms'kyy Pivostriv; *short form* Krym'
Crimmitschau Germany **49** J5
Cripple Creek U.S.A. **180** F5
Crișan Romania **58** K3
Crisfield U.S.A. **177** J8
Cristais, Serra dos *mts* Brazil **206** F4
Cristal, Monts de *mts* Equat. Guinea/Gabon **125** H6
Cristalândia Brazil **202** B4
Cristalina Brazil **206** F3
Cristalino *r.* Brazil **201** G2
Cristalino *r.* Brazil *see* **Mariembero**
Cristianópolis Brazil **206** E4
Cristina Brazil **207** H9
Cristino Castro Brazil **202** C4
Cristuru Secuiesc Romania **58** G2
Crișul Alb *r.* Romania **58** C2
Crișul Negru *r.* Romania **58** C2
Crișul Repede *r.* Romania **58** C1
Crișurilor, Câmpia *plain* Romania **58** C2
Criterion *mt.* Peru **200** B3
Criuleni Moldova **58** K1
formerly spelt Kriulyany
Crivitz Germany **48** I2
Crivitz U.S.A. **172** E5
Crixás Brazil **202** B5
Crixás Açu *r.* Brazil **202** B5
Crixás Mirim *r.* Brazil **202** B5
Crna *r.* Macedonia **58** C7
Crna Glava *mt.* Yugo. **58** A6
Crna Gora *mts* Macedonia/Yugo. **58** C6
Crna Gora *aut. rep.* Yugo. **58** A6
English form Montenegro
Crna Trava *Srbija* Yugo. **58** D6
Crni Drim *r.* Macedonia **58** B7
Crni Timok *r.* Yugo. **58** D5
Črni vrh *mt.* Slovenia **56** H2
Črnomelj Slovenia **56** H3

index
C D

Crnook mt. Yugo. 58 D6
Croajingolong National Park Australia 147 F4
Croatia country Europe 56 H3
known as Hrvatska in Croatian
europe [countries] 32–35
Crocco, Monte mt. Italy 57 I10
Crocker, Banjaran mts Malaysia 77 F1
Crocker Range National Park Sabah Malaysia 77 G1
Crockett U.S.A. 179 D6
Croghan U.S.A. 177 J2
Croisette, Cap c. France 51 L9
Croisic, Pointe de pt France 50 D5
Croisilles France 51 I2
Croker, Cape Australia 148 B1
Croker, Cape Canada 173 M6
Croker Island Australia 148 B1
Cromarty U.K. 46 H6
Cromer U.K. 47 N11
Cromwell N.Z. 153 D13
Cromwell U.S.A. 172 A4
Cronadun N.Z. 153 F10
Crooked r. U.S.A. 180 B3
Crooked Creek U.S.A. 166 A1
Crooked Harbour b. Hong Kong China 87 [inset]
also known as Kat O Hoi
Crooked Island Bahamas 187 E2
Crooked Island Hong Kong China 87 [inset]
also known as Kat O Chau
Crooked Island Passage Bahamas 187 E2
Crooked Lake Canada/U.S.A. 172 B2
Crooked River Canada 167 K4
Crookston U.S.A. 178 C2
Crooksville U.S.A. 176 C6
Crookwell Australia 147 F3
Crosbie r. Australia 149 D2
Crosby U.K. 47 I10
Crosby MN U.S.A. 174 A2
Crosby ND U.S.A. 178 B1
Crosbyton U.S.A. 179 B5
Cross r. Nigeria 125 H5
Cross Bay Canada 167 M2
Cross City U.S.A. 175 D6
Crosse, Île-à-la- Canada 167 J4
Crossett U.S.A. 175 A5
Cross Fell hill U.K. 47 J9
Crossfield Canada 167 H5
Cross Harbour b. Bahamas 186 D1
Cross Lake Canada 167 L4
Cross Lake l. Canada 167 L4
Cross Lake l. U.S.A. 173 Q7
Crossman Peak U.S.A. 183 J7
Cross River state Nigeria 125 H5
Cross Sound sea chan. U.S.A. 166 B3
Crosswell U.S.A. 173 K7
Crotch Lake Canada 173 Q6
Croton Italy see Crotone
Crotone Italy 57 J9
historically known as Croton
Crow r. Canada 166 E3
Crow Agency U.S.A. 180 F3
Crowal watercourse Australia 147 E2
Crow Creek r. U.S.A. 180 F4
Crow Creek Indian Reservation res. U.S.A. 178 C2
Crowdy Bay National Park Australia 147 G2
Crowell U.S.A. 179 C5
Crow Indian Reservation res. U.S.A. 180 F3
Crowl watercourse Australia 147 E3
Crowley U.S.A. 179 D6
Crowley, Lake U.S.A. 182 F4
Crown Point IN U.S.A. 174 C3
Crownpoint U.S.A. 181 E6
Crown Point NY U.S.A. 177 L2
Crown Prince Olav Coast Antarctica 223 C2
Crown Princess Martha Coast Antarctica 223 W1
Crows Nest Australia 147 G1
Crowsnest Pass Canada 167 H5
Crowsnest Pass pass Canada 167 H5
Crow Wing r. U.S.A. 178 D2
Croydon Australia 149 D3
Crozet U.S.A. 176 G7
Crozet, Îles is Indian Ocean 219 K9
English form Crozet Islands
Crozet Islands Indian Ocean see Crozet, Îles
Crozier Channel Canada 165 G2
Crozon France 50 B4
Crucea Romania 58 G1
Crucero Peru 200 C3
Cruces Cuba 186 C2
Cruces, Punta pt Col. 198 B3
Cruillas Mex. 185 F3
Crum U.S.A. 176 C8
Cruz mt. Spain 55 I5
Cruz Venez. 199 E2
Cruz, Cabo c. Cuba 186 D3
Cruz Alta Brazil 203 A9
Cruz del Eje Arg. 204 D3
Cruzeiro Brazil 203 C7
Cruzeiro do Sul Brazil 200 B1
Cruzen Island Antarctica 222 O2
Cruz Grande Mex. 185 F5
Crvenka Vojvodina, Srbija Yugo. 58 A3
Cry Lake Canada 166 D3
Crysdale, Mount Canada 166 F4
Crystal U.S.A. 183 P5
Crystal Brook Australia 146 C3
Crystal City Canada 167 L5
Crystal City MO U.S.A. 174 B4
Crystal City TX U.S.A. 179 C6
Crystal Falls U.S.A. 172 E4
Crystal Lake U.S.A. 172 E8
Crystal River U.S.A. 175 D6
Crystal Springs U.S.A. 175 B6
Csabrendek Hungary 49 O8
Csanádpalota Hungary 49 R9
Csépa Hungary 49 R9
Cserhát hills Hungary 49 Q8
Cserszegtomaj Hungary 49 O9
Csongrád Hungary 49 R9
Csorna Hungary 49 O8
Csorvás Hungary 49 R9
Csóványos hill Hungary 49 P8
Csurgó Hungary 49 O9
Ctesiphon tourist site Iraq 107 F4
also known as Tayspun
Cua r. Spain 54 E2
Cu'a Đinh An r. mouth Vietnam 79 D6
Cuadrada, Sierra hills Arg. 205 C7
Cuale Angola 127 C7
Cualedro Spain 54 D3
Cuamato Angola 127 B9
Cuamba Moz. 131 H2
formerly known as Nova Freixa
Cuando r. Angola/Zambia 127 D9
Cuando Cubango prov. Angola 127 C8
Cuangar Angola 127 C9
Cuango Cuando Cubango Angola 127 C8
Cuango Lunda Norte Angola 127 C7
Cuango Uíge Angola 127 C6
Cuango r. Angola 127 C6
also spelt Kwango
Cuanza r. Angola 127 B7
also spelt Kwanza
Cuanza Norte prov. Angola 127 B7
Cuanza Sul prov. Angola 127 B7
Cuareim r. Uruguay 204 F3
Cuaró Uruguay 204 F3
Cuarto r. Arg. 204 E4
Cuatir r. Angola 127 C9
Cuatro Ciénegas Mex. 185 E3
Cuatro Ojos Bol. 201 E4
Cuauhtémoc Mex. 184 D2
Cuautla Mex. 185 F5
Cuba Port. 54 D6
Cuba NY U.S.A. 176 G3
Cuba OH U.S.A. 176 B6
Cuba country West Indies 186 C2
5th largest island and 5th most populous country in North America.
northamerica [landscapes] 156–157
northamerica [countries] 158–159
Cubagua, Isla i. Venez. 199 E2
Cubal Angola 127 B8
Cubal r. Angola 127 B7
Cubango r. Angola/Namibia 127 D9
Cubara Col. 198 C3
Cubatão Brazil 206 G10
Cub Hills Canada 167 J4
Cubillas r. Spain 55 H7
Çubuk Turkey 106 C2
Cuchi Angola 127 C8
Cuchilla Grande hills Uruguay 204 G4
Cuchilla Grande Inferior hills Uruguay 204 F4
Cuchillo-Có Arg. 204 D5
Cucu, Vârful mt. Romania 58 G2
Cucuí Brazil 199 E4
Cucumbi Angola 127 C7
Cucurrupí Col. 198 B3
Cúcuta Col. 198 C3
Cucutas hill Spain 55 K3
Cudalbi Romania 58 I3
Cuddalore India 94 C4
Cuddapah India 94 C3
Cuddapan, Lake salt flat Australia 149 D5
Cuddeback Lake U.S.A. 182 G6
Cudi watercourse Turkey 109 K1
Cudi Dağı hill Turkey 109 J1
Cudillero Spain 54 E1
Cue Australia 151 B5
Cuebe r. Angola 127 C8
Cuelo r. Angola 127 D8
Cuéllar Spain 54 G3
Cuemba Angola 127 C8
Cuenca Ecuador 198 B5
Cuenca Phil. 74 B3
Cuenca Spain 55 I4
Cuenca, Serranía de mts Spain 55 I4
Cuencamé Mex. 184 E3
Cuernavaca Mex. 185 F5
Cuero U.S.A. 179 C6
Cuers France 51 M9
Cuervos Mex. 183 J9
Cueto Cuba 186 E2
Cuevo Bol. 201 E5
Cugir Romania 58 E3
Cugir r. Romania 58 E3
Cuglieri Sardegna Italy 57 A8
Cugnaux France 50 H9
Cugo r. Angola 127 C6
Cuiabá Brazil 201 F3
Cuiabá r. Brazil 201 F4
Cuicatlan Mex. 185 F5
Cuihua China see Daguan
Cuijiang China see Ninghua
Cuilapa Guat. 185 H6
Cuilcagh hill Rep. of Ireland/U.K. 47 E9
Cuillin Hills U.K. 46 F6
Cuillin Sound sea chan. U.K. 46 F6
Cuilo Angola 127 C7
Cuilo-Futa Angola 127 B6
Cuiluan China 82 C3
Cuimba Angola 127 B6
Cuité r. Brazil 207 L6
Cuitláhuac Mex. 185 F5
Cuito r. Angola 127 D9
Cuito Cuanavale Angola 127 C8
Cuitzeo, Laguna de l. Mex. 185 E5
Cuiuni r. Brazil 199 F5
Cuivre r. U.S.A. 174 B4
Cujangan i. Phil. 74 B5
Cujmir Romania 58 D4
Cukai Malaysia 76 C1
also spelt Chukai
Çukë Albania 59 B9
Çukurca Turkey 107 E3
also known as Çal
Çukurova plat. Turkey 108 G1
Čula r. Moldova 58 J1
formerly spelt Kula
Culai Shan mt. China 85 H4
Cu Lao Cham i. Vietnam 78 E5
Cu Lao Re i. Vietnam 79 E5
Cu Lao Thu i. Vietnam 79 E6
Culasi Phil. 74 B4
Culbertson U.S.A. 180 F2
Culcairn Australia 147 E3
Culebras Peru 200 A2
Culfa Azer. 107 F3
also spelt Dzhul'fa
Culiacán Mex. 184 D3
Culion Phil. 74 A4
Culion i. Phil. 74 A4
Cúllar-Baza Spain 55 I7
Cullen U.S.A. 179 D5
Cullen Point Australia 149 D1
Cullera Spain 55 K5
Cullinan S. Africa 133 M2
Cullman U.S.A. 174 C5
Cul Mor hill U.K. 46 G5
Culpeper U.S.A. 176 H7
Culuene r. Brazil 202 A4
Culver, Point Australia 151 D7
Culverden N.Z. 153 G10
Cumã, Baía do inlet Brazil 202 C2
Cumaná Venez. 199 E2
Cumbal, Nevado de vol. Col. 198 B4
Cumberland KY U.S.A. 176 C9
Cumberland MD U.S.A. 176 G6
Cumberland OH U.S.A. 176 D6
Cumberland VA U.S.A. 176 G8
Cumberland WI U.S.A. 172 A5
Cumberland r. U.S.A. 176 B9
Cumberland Bay S. Georgia 205 [inset]
Cumberland House Canada 167 K4
Cumberland Islands Australia 149 F4
Cumberland Mountain mts U.S.A. 176 B9
Cumberland Peninsula Canada 165 M3
Cumberland Plateau U.S.A. 174 C5
Cumberland Point U.S.A. 172 D3
Cumberland Sound sea chan. Canada 165 M3
Cumbernauld U.K. 46 I8
Cumbre Negro mt. Arg. 205 C7
Cumbres de Majalca, Parque Nacional nat. park Mex. 184 D2
Cumbum India 94 C3
Cuminá Brazil 199 G5
Cuminapanema r. Brazil 199 H5
Cummins Australia 146 B3
Cummins Range hills Australia 150 D3
Cumnock U.K. 46 H8
Cumpas Mex. 184 C2
Çumra Turkey 106 C3
Cumuruxatiba Brazil 207 N4
Cunani Brazil 199 I4
Cuñaré Col. 198 C4
Cundeelee Aboriginal Reserve Australia 151 C6
Cunderdin Australia 151 B6
Cundinamarca dept Col. 198 C3
Cunene prov. Angola 127 B9
Cunene r. Angola 127 A9
also spelt Kunene
Cuneo Italy 51 N8
Cung Son Vietnam 79 E5
Çüngüş Turkey 107 D3
Cunha Brazil 207 I10
Cunhinga Angola 127 C8
formerly known as Vouga
Cunnamulla Australia 147 E2
Cunshamayo Peru 200 B1
Cunuma r. Romania 58 C4
Čuokkarašša mt. Norway 44 N1
Cuorgnè Italy 51 N7
Cupar U.K. 46 I7
Cupari r. Brazil 199 H5
Cupica Col. 198 B3
Cupra Marittima Italy 56 F5
Ćuprija Srbija Yugo. 58 C5
Cupula, Pico mt. Mex. 184 C3
Curaça Brazil 202 E4
Curaçá r. Brazil 198 D6
Curaçao i. Neth. Antilles 187 F4
Curacautín Chile 204 C5
Curacó r. Arg. 204 D5
Curaculo Angola 127 B8
Curahuara de Carangas Bol. 200 C4
Curanilahue Chile 204 B5
Curanja r. Peru 200 C2
Curaray r. Ecuador 198 C5
Curatabaca Venez. 199 F3
Curaya r. Arg. 204 F3
Curdlawidny Lagoon salt flat Australia 146 C2
Curé r. Col. 198 D5
Cure r. France 51 J5
Curia Switz. see Chur
Curiapo Venez. 199 F2
Curicó Chile 204 C4
Curicuriari, Serra hill Brazil 199 E5
Curieuriari r. Brazil 199 E5
Curimata Brazil 202 C4
Curiplaya Col. 198 C4
Curitiba Brazil 203 B8
Curitibanos Brazil 203 B8
Curiúva Brazil 206 C11
Curnamona Australia 146 C2
Curoca r. Angola 127 A8
Curral de Dentro Brazil 207 L2
Curralinho Brazil 202 B2
Curralulla watercourse Australia 148 B5
Curral Velho Cape Verde 124 [inset]
Currawilla Australia 149 D5
Currawinya National Park Australia 147 E2
Current Bahamas 186 D1
Current r. U.S.A. 174 B4
Currie Australia 147 D4
Currie U.S.A. 183 J1
Currituck U.S.A. 177 I9
Currituck Sound inlet U.S.A. 177 J9
Curtea de Argeş Romania 58 F3
Curtici Romania 58 C2
Curtis Channel Australia 149 G5
Curtis Group is Australia 147 E4
Curtis Island Australia 149 F4
Curtis Island N.Z. 145 H5
Curuá Brazil 199 H5
Curuá r. Brazil 199 H6
Curuaés r. Brazil 202 A3
Curuai Brazil 199 H5
Curuapanema r. Brazil 199 H5
Curuá Una r. Brazil 199 H5
Curuçá Brazil 202 C2
Curumu Brazil 199 I5
Curup Indon. 76 C3
Curupira, Serra mts Brazil/Venez. 199 E4
Curuguaty? Curupira r. Brazil 199 F5
Cururú Bol. 201 E3
Cururu r. Brazil 201 F1
Cururupu Brazil 202 C2
Curutú, Cerro mt. Venez. 199 F3
Curuzú Cuatiá Arg. 204 F3
Curvelo Brazil 203 C6
Cushendun U.K. 47 F8
Cushing U.S.A. 179 C4
Cusset France 51 J6
Cusseta U.S.A. 175 C5
Custer MT U.S.A. 180 F3
Custer SD U.S.A. 178 B3
Cutato Angola 127 C8
Cut Bank U.S.A. 180 D2
Cut Bank Creek r. U.S.A. 180 D2
Cuthbert U.S.A. 175 C6
Cuthbertson Falls Australia 148 B2
Cutler U.S.A. 182 E5
Cutler Ridge U.S.A. 175 D7
Cut Off U.S.A. 175 B6
Cutral-Có Arg. 204 C5
Cutro Italy 57 I9
Cuttaburra Creek r. Australia 147 E2
Cuttack India 95 E1
Cuvelai Angola 127 B8
Cuvette admin. reg. Congo 126 B5
Cuvette Ouest admin. reg. Congo 126 B4
Cuvier, Cape Australia 151 A5
Cuvier Island N.Z. 152 J4
Cuvillier, Lac l. Canada 173 Q2
Cuxhaven Germany 48 F2
Cuya Chile 200 C4
Cuyahoga Valley National Recreation Area park U.S.A. 176 D4
Cuyama U.S.A. 182 E7
Cuyama r. U.S.A. 182 D7
Cuyapo Phil. 74 B3
Cuyo Phil. 74 B4
Cuyo i. Phil. 74 B4
Cuyo East Passage Phil. 74 B4
Cuyo Islands Phil. 74 B4
Cuyo West Passage Phil. 74 B4
Cuyuni r. Guyana 199 G3
Cuyutingni Nicaragua see Kuyu Tingni
Cuzco Peru see Cusco
Cuzco Peru 200 A1
Cuzna r. Spain 54 G6
Cwmbran U.K. 47 I12
Cyangugu Rwanda 126 F5
Cybinka Poland 49 L3
Cyclades is Greece 59 F11
also spelt Kikládhes or Kyklades
Cydonia Greece see Chania
Cygnet U.S.A. 176 B4
Cymru admin. div. U.K. see Wales
Cynthiana U.S.A. 176 A7
Cypress Hills Canada 167 I5
Cypress Hills Provincial Park Canada 167 I5
Cyprus country Asia 108 D3
spelt Kypros in Greek or Kibris in Turkish; historically known as Alashiya
asia [countries] 64–67
Cyrenaica reg. Libya 120 D3
Cyrene tourist site Libya 120 D1
also spelt Cirene
Cythera i. Greece see Kythira
Czaplinek Poland 49 N2
Czar Canada 167 I4
Czarna r. Poland 49 Q4
Czarna r. Poland 49 S5
Czarna Białostocka Poland 49 U2
Czarna Nida r. Poland 49 R5
Czarna Struga r. Poland 49 O3
Czarne Poland 49 N2
Czarnków Poland 49 N3
Czechoslovakia
Divided in 1993 into the Czech Republic and Slovakia.
Czechowice-Dziedzice Poland 49 Q6
Czech Republic country Europe 49 K6
also known as Česká Republika
europe [countries] 32–35
Czempiń Poland 49 N3
Czerniejewo Poland 49 O3
Czernowitz Ukr. see Chernivtsi
Czersk Poland 49 O2
Czerwieńsk Poland 49 M3
Częstochowa Poland 49 Q5
formerly known as Chenstokhov
Człopa Poland 49 N2
Człuchów Poland 49 O2

D

Đa, Sông r. Vietnam see Black River
Da'an China 85 J2
formerly known as Dalai
Daanbantayan Phil. 74 B4
Ḍabāb, Jabal aḍ mt. Jordan 108 G6
Dabaga Tanz. 129 B7
Dabajuro Venez. 198 D2
Dabakala Côte d'Ivoire 124 D4
Daban China 85 H3
also known as Bairin Youqi
Daban Shan mts China 84 D4
Dabao China 86 B2
Dabas Hungary 49 Q8
Daba Shan mts China 87 D1
Dabat Eth. 104 B5
Dabba China see Daocheng
Dabeiba Col. 198 B3
Dabein Myanmar 78 B4
Dabhoi India 96 B5
Dabhol India 94 B2
Dab'i, Wādī aḍ watercourse Jordan 109 H6
Dąbie, Jezioro l. Poland 49 L2
Dabie Shan mts China 87 E2
Dąbki Poland 49 N1
Dabl, Wādī watercourse Saudi Arabia 109 H8
Daboh India 96 C4
Dabola Guinea 124 C4
Dabou Côte d'Ivoire 124 D5
Daboya Ghana 125 E4
Dabqig China 85 F4
also known as Uxin Qi
Dabra India 96 C4
Dabraslawka Belarus 42 H9
Dąbrowa Białostocka Poland 49 U2
Dąbrowa Górnicza Poland 49 Q5
formerly known as Dombrowa; historically known as Dombrau
Dąbrowa Tarnowska Poland 49 R5
Dabsan Hu salt l. China 84 B4
Dabu China 87 F3
also known as Huliao
Dăbuleni Romania 58 F5
Dacca Bangl. see Dhaka
Dachau Germany 48 I7
Dachechang China 84 D4
Dachengzi China 85 H3
also known as Harqin Zuoqi Mongolzu Zizhixian
Dachepalle India 94 C2
Dacre Canada 173 Q5
Dadaj, Jezioro l. Poland 49 R2
Dadanawa Guyana 199 G4
Daday Turkey 106 C2
Daddato Djibouti 128 D1
Dade City U.S.A. 175 D6
Dadeville U.S.A. 175 C5
Dadhar Pak. 101 F4
Dadkan Iran 101 E5
Dadong China see Donggang
Dadou r. France 51 H9
Dadra India 94 B1
Dadra India see Achalpur
Dadra and Nagar Haveli union terr. India 94 B1
Dadu Pak. 101 F5
Dadu He r. China 86 B2
Đa Dung r. Vietnam 79 D6
Daedalus Reef Saudi Arabia 104 B2
Daet Phil. 74 B3
Dafang China 86 C3
Dafdaf, Jabal mt. Saudi Arabia 108 G9
Dafeng China 87 G1
formerly known as Dazhongji
Dafir U.A.E. 105 F3
Dafla Hills India 97 G4
Dafni Greece 59 F8
Dafnoudi, Akra pt Greece 59 B10
Dafoe r. Canada 167 M4
Dafra Chad 126 C2
Dafter U.S.A. 173 I4
Dag India 96 B5
Daga Medo Eth. 128 D3
Dagana Senegal 124 B2
Daga Post Sudan 128 B2
Dagash Sudan 121 G5
Dagcanglhamo China 86 B1
also known as Langmusi
Dagda Latvia 42 I5
Dage China see Fengning
Dagestan, Respublika aut. rep. Rus. Fed. 102 A4
also known as Daghestan; formerly known as Dagestanskaya A.S.S.R.
Dagestanskaya A.S.S.R. aut. rep. Rus. Fed. see Dagestan, Respublika
Dagezhen China see Fengning
Daggaboersnek S. Africa 133 J9
Dagg Sound inlet N.Z. 153 A13
Daghestan aut. rep. Rus. Fed. see Dagestan, Respublika
Daghmar Oman 105 G3
Dağlıq Qarabağ aut. reg. Azer. 107 F3
English form Nagorno-Karabakh; also known as Nagornyy Karabakh or Artsakh
Daglung China 89 E6
Dagmersellen Switz. 51 N5
Dagö i. Estonia see Hiiumaa
Dagon Myanmar see Rangoon
Dagon mt. N.Z. 153 C12
Dagrag Zangbo r. China 89 D6
Dagu China 85 H4
Dagu r. China 85 I4
Daguan China 86 B3
also known as Cuihua
Daguéla Chad 126 C2
Daguokui Shan hill China 82 C3
Dagupan Phil. 74 B2
Daguragu Aboriginal Land res. Australia 148 A3
Dagwin Myanmar 78 B4
Dagxoi China see Yidun
Dagxoi China see Sowa
Dagzê China 89 E6
also known as Dêqên
Dagzê Co salt l. China 89 D6
Dagzhuka China 89 E6
Dahab Egypt 121 G2
Dahab, Marsa b. Egypt 108 F9
Dahabān Saudi Arabia 104 B3
Dahadinni r. Canada 166 E2
Dahalach, Isole is Eritrea see Dahlak Archipelago
Dahana des. Saudi Arabia see Ad Dahnā'
Dahanu India 94 B2
Dahe China see Ziyuan
Dahei r. China 85 F3
Daheiding Shan mt. China 82 C3
Dahei Shan mt. China 84 B3
Dahei Shan mts China 82 B4
Daheng China 87 F3
Daheyan China see Turpan Zhan
Dahezhen China 82 D3
Dahin, Ḥarrāt ad lava field Saudi Arabia 104 C4
Da Hinggan Ling mts China 85 H3
English form Greater Khingan Mountains
Dahivadi India 94 B2
Dahlak Archipelago is Eritrea 121 I6
formerly known as Dahalach, Isole
Dahlak Marine National Park Eritrea 121 I5
Daḥl al Furayy well Saudi Arabia 105 D2
Dahlem Germany 48 D5
Dahlia Zimbabwe 131 E3
Daḥl Iftākh well Saudi Arabia 105 D2
Dahlonega U.S.A. 174 D5
Dahmani Tunisia 123 H2
Dahme Germany 49 K4
Dahod India 96 B5
also spelt Dohad
Dahomey country Africa see Benin
Dahongliutan Aksai Chin 89 B5
Dahra Senegal see Dara
Dahshūr Egypt 108 C8
Dahūk Iraq 107 E3
Dahūk governorate Iraq 107 E3
Daḥyah, Wādī r. Yemen 105 E4
Dai i. Indon. 75 D4
Daicheng China 85 H4
also known as Pingshu
Daido r. N. Korea see Taedong-gang
Dai Hai l. China 85 G3
Daik Indon. 76 D3
Daikanvik Sweden 44 L2
Daik-u Myanmar 78 B4
Dailekh Nepal 97 D3
Dailey U.S.A. 176 F7
Daim Iran 100 D3
Daimanji-san hill Japan 83 D5
Daimiel Spain 55 H5
Daingerfield U.S.A. 179 D5
Dainichiga-take vol. Japan 91 E6
Dainkog China 86 A1
Daintree Australia 149 E3
Daintree National Park Australia 149 E3
Daiō-zaki pt Japan 91 E7
Daiquiri Cuba 186 E3
Daireaux Arg. 204 E5
Dairen China see Dalian
Dairūt Egypt 121 F3
Dairyland U.S.A. 172 A4
Dai-sen vol. Japan 91 C7
Daisen-Oki National Park Japan 91 C7
Daisetsu-zan National Park Japan 90 H3
Daishan China 87 G2
also known as Gaotingzhen
Daiyue China see Shanyin
Daiyun Shan mts China 87 F3
Dajarra Australia 148 C4
Dajie China see Jiangchuan
Dajin Chuan r. China 86 B2
Dajing China 84 D4
Da Juh China 84 B4
Dakar Senegal 124 A3
Capital of Senegal.
Dakar el Arak well Sudan 121 F5
Dakhal, Wâdi el watercourse Egypt 108 D9
Dakhin Shahbazpur Island Bangl. 97 F5
Dakhla W. Sahara see Ad Dakhla
Dakhla Oasis Egypt 121 F3
Dakhlet Nouâdhibou admin. reg. Mauritania 122 A5
Dakingari Nigeria 125 G4
Dak Kon Vietnam 79 D5
Đak Nghe r. Vietnam 79 D5
Dakoank India 95 G5
Dakol'ka r. Belarus 43 J9
Dakor India 96 B5
Dakoro Niger 125 G3
Dakota City IA U.S.A. 178 D3
Dakota City NE U.S.A. 178 C3
Đakovica Kosovo, Srbija Yugo. 58 B6
also spelt Djakovica
Đakovo Croatia 56 K3
Dala Angola 127 D7
Dalaba Guinea 124 B4
Dalad Qi China see Shulinzhao
Dalai China see Da'an
Dalain Hob China 84 D3
also known as Ejin Qi
Dalai Nur l. China 85 H3
Dālā Khānī, Kūh-e mt. Iran 100 A3
Dālaki Iran 100 B4
Dālaki, Rūd-e r. Iran 100 B4
Dalälven r. Sweden 45 L3
Dalamamiao China 85 G3
Dalaman Turkey 106 B3
Dalaman r. Turkey 106 B3
Dalandzadgad Mongolia 84 E3
Dalanganem Islands Phil. 74 B4
Dalaoba China 88 C3
Dalap-Uliga-Darrit Marshall Is see Delap-Uliga-Djarrit
Dalarna county Sweden 45 K3
formerly known as Kopparberg
Dalarna reg. Sweden 45 K3
Dalat Sarawak Malaysia 77 E2
Đa Lat Vietnam 79 E6
Dalatando Angola see N'dalatando
Dalay Mongolia 84 D3
Dalbandin Pak. 101 F4
Dalbeg Australia 149 E4
Dalbosjön l. Sweden 45 K4
Dalby Australia 147 F1
Dalby Sweden 45 K5
Dalcahue Chile 205 B6
Dale Hordaland Norway 45 I3
Dale Sogn og Fjordane Norway 45 I3
Dale City U.S.A. 177 H7
Dale Hollow Lake U.S.A. 174 C4
Daletme Myanmar 78 A3
Dalfors Sweden 45 K3
Dalgaranger, Mount hill Australia 151 B5
Dalgety r. Australia 151 A5
Dalhart U.S.A. 179 B4
Dalhousie Canada 169 H3
Dalhousie, Cape Canada 164 G2
Dali Shaanxi China 87 D1
Dali Yunnan China 86 B3
also known as Xiaguan
Dali r. China 85 F4
Dalian China 85 I4
formerly known as Dairen or Dalny or Lüda
Daliang China see Shunde
Daliang China 84 D4
Daliang Shan mts China 86 B2
Dalian Wan b. China 85 I4
Dalin China 85 I3
Daling r. China 85 I3
Dalinghe China see Linhai
Dalizi China 82 B4
Dalj Croatia 56 K3
Dalkola India 97 E4
Dallas OR U.S.A. 180 B3
Dallas TX U.S.A. 179 C5
Dallas City U.S.A. 172 B10
Dalles City U.S.A. see The Dalles
Dall Island U.S.A. 164 F4
Dallol Bosso watercourse Mali/Niger 125 F3
Dalmā i. U.A.E. 105 F2
Dalmacija reg. Croatia see Dalmatia
Dalmally U.K. 46 H7
Dalman India 96 D4
Dalmas, Lac l. Canada 169 G2
Dalmatia reg. Croatia 56 H4
also spelt Dalmacija
europe [landscapes] 30–31
Dalmellington U.K. 46 H8
Dalmeny Canada 167 J4
Dal'negorsk Rus. Fed. 82 D3
formerly known as Tetyukhe
Dal'nerechensk Rus. Fed. 82 D3
formerly known as Iman
Dal'niye Zelentsy Rus. Fed. 40 F1
Dalny China see Dalian
Daloa Côte d'Ivoire 124 D5
Dalol Eth. 128 D1
Highest recorded annual mean temperature in the world.
world [climate and weather] 16–17
Dalou Shan mts China 86 C3
Dalqān well Saudi Arabia 105 D2
Dalrymple, Lake Australia 149 E4
Dalrymple, Mount Australia 149 F4
Dalsbruk Fin. 42 D1
Daltenganj India 97 E4
formerly spelt Daltonganj
Dalton Canada 168 C3
Dalton S. Africa 133 O6
Dalton GA U.S.A. 174 C5
Dalton MA U.S.A. 177 L3
Dalton OH U.S.A. 176 D5
Dalton PA U.S.A. 177 J4
Daltonganj India see Daltenganj
Dalton Iceberg Tongue Antarctica 223 I2
Dalton Mills Canada 173 I2
Daludalu Indon. 76 C2
Daluo Shan mt. China 87 E4
Dalupiri i. Phil. 74 B2
Dalvík Iceland 44 [inset] C2
Dalwallinu Australia 151 B6
Dalwhinnie U.K. 46 H7
Daly r. Australia 148 A2
Daly City U.S.A. 182 B4
Daly River Australia 148 A2
Daly River/Port Keats Aboriginal Land res. Australia 148 A2
Daly Waters Australia 148 B3
Damagaram Takaya Niger 125 H3
Damaliques de Leshwe nature res. Dem. Rep. Congo 127 F8
Daman India 94 B1
formerly spelt Damão
Daman and Diu union terr. India 94 A1
Damanava Belarus 42 G9
Damâne well Mauritania 124 B2
Dāmaneh Iran 100 B3
Damanhûr Egypt 121 F2
Damant Lake Canada 167 J2
Damão India see Daman
Damaq Iran 100 B3
Damaqun Shan mts China 85 G3
Damar Indon. 75 C2
Damar i. Moluccas Indon. 75 D3
Damar i. Moluccas Indon. 75 D4
Damara Cent. Afr. Rep. 126 C3
Damaraland reg. Namibia 130 C4
Damariscotta Lake U.S.A. 177 P1
Damar Laut, Pulau i. Sing. 76 [inset]
Damas Syria see Damascus
Damasak Nigeria 125 I3
Damascus Syria 109 H4
Capital of Syria. Also known as Ash Sham or Damas; also spelt Dimashq.
Damascus MD U.S.A. 177 H6
Damascus VA U.S.A. 176 D9
Damaturu Nigeria 125 H4
Damāvand Iran 100 C3
Damāvand, Qolleh-ye mt. Iran 100 C3
English form Demavend
Damba Angola 127 B6
Dambai Ghana 125 F4
Dambatta Nigeria 125 H3
Damboa Nigeria 125 I4
Dâmboviţa r. Romania 58 G4
Damdama India 97 G4
Damdy Kazakh. 103 F2
formerly known as Zhalanash
Dame Marie Haiti 187 E3
Damghan Iran 100 C2
Damietta Egypt see Dumyāṭ
Daming China 85 G4
Daming Shan mt. China 87 D4
Damjong China 97 G2
Damlasu Turkey 109 K1
Dammai i. Phil. 74 B5
Dammam Saudi Arabia 105 E2
also spelt Ad Dammām
Dammastock mt. Switz. 51 O6
Damme Germany 48 F3
Damoh India 96 C5
Damongo Ghana 125 E4
Damour Lebanon 108 G4
Dampelas, Tanjung pt Indon. 75 A2
Dampier Australia 150 B4
Dampier Archipelago is Australia 150 B4
Dampier Island P.N.G. see Karkar Island
Dampier Land reg. Australia 150 C3
Dampierre-sur-Salon France 51 L5
Dampier Strait P.N.G. 145 D2
Dampir, Selat sea chan. Indon. 73 H7
Dampit Indon. 77 F5
Damqoq Zangbo r. China see Maquan He
Dam Qu r. China 97 G2
Dâmrei, Chuŏr Phnum mts Cambodia 79 D6
Damroh India 97 G3
Damxoi China see Comai
Damxung China 89 E6
also known as Gongtang
Dan r. U.S.A. 176 G9
Dana i. Indon. 75 B5
Dana Nepal 97 D3
Dana, Mount U.S.A. 182 E4
Danakil reg. Eritrea/Eth. see Denakil
Danané Côte d'Ivoire 124 C5
Đa Năng Vietnam 78 E4
formerly known as Tourane
Đa Nang, Vinh b. Vietnam 78 E4
Danahu China 84 B3
Danao Phil. 74 C4
Danata Turkm. 102 C5
Danba China 86 B2
also known as Rongzhag or Zhanggu

Danbury CT U.S.A. 177 L4
Danbury NC U.S.A. 176 E9
Danbury NH U.S.A. 177 N2
Danbury WI U.S.A. 172 A4
Danby U.S.A. 177 M2
Danby Lake U.S.A. 183 I7
Dancheng China 87 E1
Dancheng China see Xiangshan
Dande r. Angola 127 B7
Dande Eth. 128 C3
Dandel'dhura Nepal 96 D3
Dandeli India 94 B3
Dando Angola 127 C7
Dandong China 83 B4
formerly known as Andong
Dandridge U.S.A. 174 D4
Danė r. Lith. 42 C6
Daneborg Greenland 165 Q2
Daneţi Romania 58 F5
Dänew Turkm. see Dyanev
Danfeng China 87 D1
also known as Longjuzhai
Danfeng China see Shizong
Dangan Liedao i. China 87 E4
Dangara Tajik. see Danghara
Dangbizhen Rus. Fed. 82 C3
Dangchang China 86 C1
Dangchengwan China see Subei
Dange Angola 127 B6
formerly known as Quitexe
Danger Islands atoll Cook Is see Pukapuka
Danger Point S. Africa 132 D11
Dangé-St-Romain France 50 G6
Danggali Conservation Park nature res. Australia 146 D3
Danghara Tajik. 101 G2
also spelt Dangara
Danghe Nanshan mts China 84 B4
Dangila Eth. 128 C2
Dangjin Shankou pass China 84 B4
Dangla Shan mts China see Tanggula Shan
Dan Gorayo Somalia 128 F2
Dangori India 97 G4
Dangqên China 89 E6
Dangriga Belize 185 H5
formerly known as Stann Creek
Dangshan China 87 F1
Dangtu China 87 F2
Dan-Gulbi Nigeria 125 G4
Dangur Eth. 128 B2
Dangur Mountains Eth. 128 B2
Dangyang China 87 D2
Daniel's Harbour Canada 169 J3
Daniëlskuil S. Africa 132 H5
Danielson U.S.A. 177 N4
Danielsrus S. Africa 133 M4
Danielsville U.S.A. 175 D5
Danilkovo Rus. Fed. 43 S2
Danilov Rus. Fed. 43 V3
Danilovgrad Crna Gora Yugo. 58 A6
Danilovka Kazakh. 103 G1
Danilovka Rus. Fed. 41 H6
Danilovskaya Vozvyshennost' hills Rus. Fed. 40 F4
Daning China 85 F4
Dänizkänarı Azer. 107 G2
Danjiang China see Leishan
Danjiangkou China 87 D1
formerly known as Junxian
Danjiangkou Shuiku resr China 87 D1
Danjo-guntō is Japan 91 A8
Dank Oman 105 G3
Dankalia prov. Eritrea 104 C5
Dankov Rus. Fed. 43 U8
Dankova, Pik mt. Kyrg. 103 I4
Danleng China 86 B2
Danlí Hond. 186 B4
Danmark Fjord inlet Greenland 165 Q1
English form Denmark Fjord
Dannebrog Ø i. Greenland see Qillak
Dannemora U.S.A. 177 L1
Dannenberg (Elbe) Germany 48 I2
Dannet well Niger 125 G2
Dannevirke N.Z. 152 K8
Dannhauser S. Africa 133 O5
Dan Sai Thai. 78 C4
Danshui Taiwan see Tanshui
Dansville U.S.A. 176 H3
Danta Gujarat India 96 B4
Danta Rajasthan India 89 A7
Dantewara India 94 D2
Dantu China 87 F1
also known as Zhenjiang

Danube r. Europe 58 J3
2nd longest river in Europe. Also spelt Donau (Austria/Germany) or Duna (Hungary) or Dunaj (Slovakia) or Dunărea (Romania) or Dunav (Bulgaria/Croatia/Yugoslavia) or Dunay (Ukraine).
europe [landscapes] 30–31

Danube Delta Romania 58 K3
also known as Dunării, Delta
Danubyu Myanmar 78 A4
Danumparai Indon. 77 F2
Danum Valley Conservation Area nature res. Sabah Malaysia 77 G1
Danville AR U.S.A. 179 D5
Danville IL U.S.A. 174 C3
Danville IN U.S.A. 174 C4
Danville KY U.S.A. 176 A8
Danville OH U.S.A. 176 C5
Danville VA U.S.A. 176 F9
Danville VT U.S.A. 177 M1
Danxian China see Danzhou
Danyang China 87 F2
Danzhai China 87 C3
also known as Longquan
Danzhou Guangxi China 87 D3
Danzhou Hainan China 87 D5
also known as Nada; formerly known as Danxian
Danzhou China see Yichuan
Danzig Poland see Gdańsk
Danzig, Gulf of Poland/Rus. Fed. see Gdańsk, Gulf of
Dao Phil. 74 B4
Dão r. Port. 54 C4
Daocheng China 86 B2
also known as Dabba or Jinzhu
Daojiang China see Daoxian
Daokou China see Huaxian
Daoshiping China 87 D2
Daotanghe China 84 D4
Dao Tay Sa is S. China Sea see Paracel Islands
Dao Timmi Niger 125 I1
Daoud Alg. see Aïn Beïda
Daoudi well Mauritania 124 D3
Daoukro Côte d'Ivoire 124 E5
Daoxian China 87 D3
also known as Daojiang
Daozhen China 87 C2
also known as Yuxi
Dapa Phil. 74 C4
Dapaong Togo 125 F4
Dapchi Nigeria 125 H3
Daphabum mt. India 97 H4
Daphnae tourist site Egypt 108 D7
also known as Kawm Dafanah
Daphne U.S.A. 175 C6
Dapiak, Mount Phil. 74 B4
Dapingdi China see Yanbian
Dapitan Phil. 74 B4
Daqahlīya governorate Egypt 108 C6
Da Qaidam Zhen China 84 B4
Daqiao China 86 B3
Daqing China 82 B3
also known as Anda; formerly known as Sartu
Daqing Shan mts China 85 F3
Daqin Tal China 85 I3
also known as Naiman Qi
Daqiu China 87 F3
Daqq-e Patargān salt flat Iran 101 E3
Daqq-e-Tundi, Dasht-e imp. l. Afgh. 101 E3
Daquan China 84 B3
Daquanwan China 84 B3
Dāqūq Iraq 107 F4
Daqu Shan i. China 87 G2
Dara Senegal 124 B3
formerly spelt Dahra
Dar'ā Syria 108 H5
Dar'ā governorate Syria 108 H5
Dāra, Gebel mt. Egypt 106 C6
Daraá r. Brazil 199 E5
Dārāb Iran 100 C4
Daraga Phil. 74 B3
Darahanava Belarus 43 J8
Daraim Afgh. 96 A1
Daraina Madag. 131 [inset] K2
Daraj Libya 120 A2
Daram i. Phil. 74 C4
Dārān Iran 100 B3
Đa Răng, Sông r. Vietnam 79 E5
Darasun Rus. Fed. 85 G1
Daraut-Kurgan Kyrg. see Daroot-Korgan
Daravica mt. Yugo. 58 B6
Darazo Nigeria 125 H4
Darb Saudi Arabia 104 C4
Darband Iran 100 D4
Darband Uzbek. see Derbent
Darband, Kūh-e mt. Iran 100 D4
Darb-e Behesht Iran 100 D4
Darbėnai Lith. 42 C5
Dar Ben Karricha el Behri Morocco 54 F9
Darbhanga India 97 E4
Darcang China 86 A1
Dar Chabanne Tunisia 57 C12
Dar Chaoui Morocco 54 F9
D'Arcy Canada 166 F5
Darda Croatia 56 K3
Dardanelle AR U.S.A. 179 D5
Dardanelle CA U.S.A. 182 E3
Dardanelle, Lake U.S.A. 179 D5
Dardanelles strait Turkey 106 A2
also known as Çanakkale Boğazi; historically known as Hellespont
Dardo China see Kangding
Dar el Beida Morocco see Casablanca
Darende Turkey 107 D3

Dar es Salaam Tanz. 129 C6
Former capital of Tanzania.

Dārestān Iran 100 C4
Darfield N.Z. 153 G11
Darfo Boario Terme Italy 56 C3
Dargai Pak. 101 G3
Darganata Turkm. 103 E4
Dargaville N.Z. 152 H3
Dargin, Jezioro l. Poland 49 S1
Dargo Australia 147 E4
Darhan Mongolia 85 E1
Darhan Muminggan Lianheqi China see Bailingmiao
Darıca Turkey 58 K8
Darıcı Turkey 59 J9
Darien CT U.S.A. 177 L4
Darien GA U.S.A. 175 D6
Darién, Golfo del g. Col. 198 B2
Darién, Parque Nacional de nat. park Panama 186 D6
Darién, Serranía del mts Panama 186 D5
Dar'inskiy Kazakh. 103 H2
also known as Darīya
Dar'inskoye Kazakh. 102 B2
Dario Nicaragua 186 B4
Darīya Kazakh. see Dar'inskiy
Dariz Oman 105 G3
Darjeeling India 97 F4
also spelt Darjiling
Darjiling India see Darjeeling
Dārkhovīn Iran 100 B4
Darlag China 86 A1
also known as Gyümai

Darling r. Australia 147 D3
2nd longest river in Oceania. Part of the longest (Murray-Darling).
oceania [landscapes] 136–137

Darling S. Africa 132 C10
Darling Downs hills Australia 147 F1
Darling Range hills Australia 151 A7
Darlington U.K. 47 K9
Darlington SC U.S.A. 175 E5
Darlington WI U.S.A. 172 C8
Darlington Dam resr S. Africa 133 J10
Darlington Point Australia 147 E3
Darlot, Lake salt flat Australia 151 C5
Darłowo Poland 49 N1
Dărmăneşti Romania 58 H2
Darma Pass China/India 89 C6
Darmaraopet India 94 C2
Darmstadt Germany 48 F6
Darna r. India 94 B1
Darnah Libya 120 D1
also spelt Derna
Darnall S. Africa 133 P6
Darnick Australia 147 D3
Darnley, Cape Antarctica 223 E2
Darnley Bay Canada 164 G3
Daroca Spain 55 J3
Daroot-Korgan Kyrg. 103 H5
also spelt Daraut-Kurgan
Darovskoy Rus. Fed. 40 H4
Dar Pahn Iran 100 D5
Darr watercourse Australia 149 D4
Darregueira Arg. 204 E5
Darreh Bīd Iran 100 D3
Darreh Gaz Iran 101 D2
also known as Moḩammadābād
Darreh Gozaru r. Iran see Gīzeh Rūd
Darreh-ye Bāhābād Iran 100 C4
Darreh-ye Shahr Iran 100 A3
Darreh-ye Shekārī r. Afgh. 101 G3
Darreh-ye Shekārī r. Afgh. 101 G3
Darro watercourse Eth. 128 D3
Darsa i. Yemen 105 F5
Darsi India 94 C3
Darß pen. Germany 49 J1
Darßer Ort c. Germany 49 J1
Darta Turkm. 102 C4
formerly known as Kianly; formerly spelt Tarta
Dār Ta'izzah Syria 109 H1
Dartang China see Baqên
Dartford U.K. 47 M12
Dartmoor Australia 146 D4
Dartmoor hills U.K. 47 H13
Dartmoor National Park U.K. 47 I13
Dartmouth Canada 169 I4
Dartmouth U.K. 47 I13
Dartmouth, Lake salt flat Australia 149 E5
Dartmouth Reservoir Australia 147 E4
Daru P.N.G. 73 J8
Daru waterhole Sudan 121 G5
Daruba Indon. 75 D2
Daruvar Croatia 56 J3
Darvaza Turkm. 102 D4
also spelt Derweze
Darvi Mongolia 84 B2
Darvi Mongolia see Bulgan
Darvinskiy Gosudarstvennyy Zapovednik nature res. Rus. Fed. 43 S3
Darvoz, Qatorkŭhi mts Tajik. 101 G2
Darwendale Zimbabwe 131 F3
Darwha India 94 C1

Darwin Australia 148 A2
Capital of Northern Territory. Historically known as Palmerston.

Darwin Falkland Is 205 F8
Darwin, Canal sea chan. Chile 205 B7
Darwin, Monte mt. Chile 205 C9
Darya Khan Pak. 101 G4
Dar'yalyktakyr, Ravnina plain Kazakh. 103 F3
Daryānah Libya 120 D1
Dar"yoi Amu r. Asia see Amudar'ya
Dar"yoi Sir r. Asia see Syrdar'ya
Dārzin Iran 100 D4
Dās i. U.A.E. 105 F2
Dasada India 96 A5
Dasha r. China 85 G4
Dashbalbar Mongolia 85 G1
Dashhowuz Turkm. see Dashkhovuz
Dashiqiao China 85 I3
formerly known as Yingkou
Dashitou China 88 E3
Dashizhai China 85 I2
Dashkawka Belarus 43 L8
Dashkesan Azer. see Daşkäsän
Dashkhovuz Turkm. 102 D4
also known as Dashoguz; also spelt Dashhowuz; formerly known as Tashauz
Dashkhovuz Oblast admin. div. Turkm. see Dashkhovuzskaya Oblast'
Dashkhovuzskaya Oblast' admin. div. Turkm. 102 D4
English form Dashkhovuz Oblast; formerly known as Tashauzskaya Oblast'
Dashköpri Turkm. see Tashkepri
Dashoguz Turkm. see Dashkhovuz
Dasht Iran 100 D2
Dasht r. Pak. 101 E5
Dashtak Qaléhsi Iran 100 D2
formerly spelt Dashtak Qal'ehsi
Dashtak Qal'ehsi Iran see Dashtak Qaléhsi
Dasht-e Bar Iran 100 D4
Dasht-e Palang r. Iran 100 C4
Dashtiari Iran 101 E5
Dashuikeng China 85 E4
Dashuiqiao China 84 C4
Dashuitou China 84 E4
Daska Pak. 101 H3
Daşkäsän Azer. 107 F2
also spelt Dashkesan
Daskop S. Africa 132 G10
Dasongshu China 86 C3
Daspar mt. Pak. 101 H2
Dassa Benin 125 F5
Dassalan i. Phil. 74 B5
Dassen Island S. Africa 132 C10
Dastakān, Ra's-e pt Iran 100 C5
Da Suifen He r. China 82 C4
Dasuya India 96 B3
Dasville S. Africa 133 M3
Datadian Indon. 77 F2
Datça Turkey 106 A3
Date Japan 90 G3
Date Creek watercourse U.S.A. 183 K7
Dateland U.S.A. 183 K9
Datha India 96 B5
Datia India 96 C4
Datian China 87 F3
also known as Junxi
Datian Ding mt. China 87 D4
Datong China see Tong'an
Datong Heilong. China 82 B3
Datong Qinghai China 84 D4
also known as Qiaotou
Datong Shanxi China 85 G3
Datong He r. China 84 D4
Datong Shan mts China 84 C4
Datta Rus. Fed. 82 F2
Datu i. Indon. 77 E2
Datu, Tanjung c. Indon./Malaysia 77 E2
Datuk, Tanjung pt Indon. 76 C3
Datu Piang Phil. 74 C5
also known as Dulawan
Daudkandi Bangl. 97 F5
Daud Khel Pak. 101 G3
Daudnagar India 97 E4
Daudzeva Latvia 42 G5
Daugai Lith. 42 F7
Daugailiai Lith. 42 G6
Daugava r. Latvia 42 F4
Daugavpils Latvia 42 H6
also known as Dvinsk; formerly known as Dünaburg
Daugyvenė r. Lith. 42 E5
Daulatabad Afgh. 101 F2
Daulatabad Iran see Malāyer
Daulatpur Bangl. 97 F5
Daule Ecuador 198 B5
Daun Germany 48 D5
Daund India 94 B2
Daung Kyun i. Myanmar 79 B5
also known as Ross Island
Daungyu r. Myanmar 78 A3
Dauphin Canada 167 K5
Dauphiné reg. France 51 L7
Dauphiné, Alpes du mts France 51 L8
Dauphin Island U.S.A. 175 B6
Dauphin Lake Canada 167 L5
Daura Nigeria 125 H3
Daurie Creek r. Australia 151 A5
Dauriya Rus. Fed. 85 H1
Daurskiy Khrebet mts Rus. Fed. 85 F1
Dausa India 96 C4
Dâu Tiêng, Hô resr Vietnam 79 D6
Däväçi Azer. 107 G2
also spelt Divichi
Davangere India 94 B3
Davao Phil. 74 C5
Davao Gulf Phil. 74 C5
Dāvarān Iran 100 D4
Dāvar Panāh Iran 101 E5
also known as Dizak
Davel S. Africa 133 N3
Davenport IA U.S.A. 174 B3
Davenport NY U.S.A. 177 K3
Davenport WA U.S.A. 180 C3
Davenport Downs Australia 149 D5
Davenport Range hills Australia 148 B4
Daveyton S. Africa 133 M3
David Panama 186 C5
David City U.S.A. 178 C3
Davidson Canada 167 J5
Davidson, Mount hill Australia 148 A4
Davidson Lake Canada 167 L4
Davies, Mount Australia 146 A1
Davinópolis Brazil 206 F5
Davis research station Antarctica 223 F2
Davis r. Australia 150 C4
Davis i. Myanmar see Than Kyun
Davis CA U.S.A. 182 C3
Davis WV U.S.A. 176 F6
Davis, Mount hill U.S.A. 176 F6
Davis Bay Antarctica 223 I2
Davis Dam U.S.A. 183 J6
Davis Dam dam U.S.A. 183 J6
Davis Inlet Canada 169 I2
Davison U.S.A. 173 J7
Davis Sea Antarctica 223 G2
Davis Strait Canada/Greenland 165 N3
Davlekanovo Rus. Fed. 40 J5
Davlia Greece 59 D10
also spelt Dhávlia
Davos Switz. 51 P6
Davutlar Turkey 59 I11
Davy U.S.A. 176 D8
Davyd-Haradok Belarus 42 I9
Davydkovo Rus. Fed. see Tolbukhino
Davydovo Rus. Fed. 43 T4
Davy Lake Canada 167 I3
Dawa China 85 I3
Dawa Co l. China 89 D6
Dawāsir reg. Saudi Arabia 104 D3
Dawāsir, Wādī ad watercourse Saudi Arabia 104 D3
Dawa Wenz r. Eth. 128 D3
Dawaxung China 89 D6
Dawê China 86 B2
Dawei Myanmar see Tavoy
Dawei r. Myanmar see Tavoy
Dawen r. China 85 H5
Dawera i. Indon. 75 D4
Dawhat Bilbul b. Saudi Arabia 105 E2
Dawhinava Belarus 42 I7
Dawna Range mts Myanmar/Thai. 78 B4
Dawqah Oman 105 F4
Dawqah Saudi Arabia 104 C4
Dawrān Yemen 104 D5
Dawson r. Australia 149 F4
Dawson Canada 166 B1
Dawson GA U.S.A. 175 C6
Dawson ND U.S.A. 180 H3
Dawson, Isla i. Chile 205 C9
Dawson, Mount Canada 167 G5
Dawson Bay Canada 167 K4
Dawson Creek Canada 166 F4
Dawson Inlet Canada 167 M2
Dawson Range mts Canada 166 A2
Dawsons Landing Canada 166 E5
Dawu Hubei China 87 E2
Dawu China see Maqên
Dawu Sichuan China 86 B2
also known as Xianshui
Dawu Taiwan see Tawu
Dawukou China see Shizuishan
Dawu Shan hill China 87 E2
Dawwah Oman 105 G3
Dax France 50 E9
Daxian China see Dazhou
Daxiang Ling mts China 86 B2
Daxihaizi Shuiku l. China 88 D3
Daxin China 87 C4
also known as Taocheng
Daxing China see Ninglang
Daxing China see Lüchun
Daxue China see Wencheng
Daxue Shan mts China 86 B2
Dayan China see Lijiang
Dayang r. China 85 I4
Dayangshu China 85 J1
Dayan Nuur l. Mongolia 84 A1
Dayao China 86 B3
also known as Jinbi
Dayao Shan mts China 87 D4
Dâyat en Nahârât well Mali 124 E2
Daye China 87 E2
Dayi China 86 B2
also known as Jinyuan
Daying Jiang r. China 86 A3
Dayishan China see Guanyun
Dayl Oman 105 G2
Daylesford Australia 147 E4
Dayong China 87 D2
formerly known as Zhangjiajie
Dayr Abū Sa'īd Jordan 108 G5
Dayr az Zawr Syria 109 L2
also spelt Deir-ez-Zor
Dayr az Zawr governorate Syria 109 L2
Dayr Ḥāfir Syria 109 I1
Daysland Canada 167 H4
Dayton OH U.S.A. 176 A6
Dayton TN U.S.A. 174 C5
Dayton TX U.S.A. 179 D6
Dayton VA U.S.A. 176 G7
Dayton WA U.S.A. 180 C3
Daytona Beach U.S.A. 175 D6
Dayu China 87 E3
also known as Nan'ao
Dayu Indon. 77 F3
Dayu Ling mts China 87 E3
Da Yunhe canal China 87 F1
English form Grand Canal
Dayyīna i. U.A.E. 105 F2
Dazaifu Japan 91 B8
Dazhe China see Pingyuan
Dazhongji China see Dafeng
Dazhou China 87 C2
formerly known as Daxian
Dazhou Dao i. China 87 D5
Dazhu China 87 C2
also known as Zhuyang
Dazu China 86 C2
also known as Longgang
De Aar S. Africa 132 I7
Dead r. U.S.A. 172 F4
Deadman's Cay Bahamas 187 E2
Dead Mountains U.S.A. 183 J7

Dead Sea salt l. Asia 98 B3
Lowest point in the world and in Asia. Also known as Bahrat Lut or HaMelah, Yam.

Deadwood U.S.A. 178 B2
Deakin Australia 151 E6
Deal U.K. 47 N12
Dealesville S. Africa 133 J5
Dean r. Canada 166 E4
De'an China 87 E2
also known as Puting
Dean Channel Canada 166 E4
Deán Funes Arg. 204 D3
Deanuvuotna inlet Norway see Tanafjorden
Dearborn U.S.A. 173 J8
Dease r. B.C. Canada 166 D3
Dease r. N.W.T. Canada 167 G1
Dease Arm b. Canada 166 F1
Dease Lake Canada 166 D3
Dease Lake l. Canada 166 D3
Dease Strait Canada 165 I3
Death Valley U.S.A. 183 H5

Death Valley depr. U.S.A. 183 G5
Lowest point in the Americas.
northamerica [landscapes] 156–157

Death Valley Junction U.S.A. 183 H5
Death Valley National Park U.S.A. 183 G5
Deauville France 50 G3
Deaver U.S.A. 180 E3
Debagram India 97 F5
Debak Sarawak Malaysia 77 E2
Debao China 86 C4
Debar Macedonia 58 B7
Debark Eth. 128 C1
Debay well Yemen 105 E4
Debden Canada 167 J4
De Beers Pass S. Africa 133 N5
Debert Canada 169 I4
Debesy Rus. Fed. 40 J4
Dębica Poland 49 S5
De Biesbosch, Nationaal Park nat. park Neth. 48 B4
Debila Alg. 123 G2
Debin Rus. Fed. 39 P3
Dęblin Poland 49 S4
Dębno Poland 49 L3
Débo, Lac l. Mali 124 D3
Deborah East, Lake salt flat Australia 151 B6
Deborah West, Lake salt flat Australia 151 B6
Deboyne Islands P.N.G. 149 G1
Debre Birhan Eth. 128 C2
Debrecen Hungary 49 S8
Debre Markos Eth. 128 C2
Debre Sina Eth. 128 C2
Debre Tabor Eth. 128 C2
Debre Werk' Eth. 128 C2
Debre Zeyit Eth. 128 C2
Debrzno Poland 49 O2
Deçan Kosovo, Srbija Yugo. see Dečani
Dečani Kosovo, Srbija Yugo. 58 B6
also spelt Deçan
Decatur AL U.S.A. 174 C5
Decatur GA U.S.A. 175 C5
Decatur IL U.S.A. 174 B4
Decatur IN U.S.A. 176 A5
Decatur MI U.S.A. 172 H8
Decatur MS U.S.A. 175 B5
Decatur TN U.S.A. 174 C5
Decatur TX U.S.A. 179 C5
Decazeville France 51 I8

Deccan plat. India 94 C2
Plateau making up most of southern and central India.

Deception watercourse Botswana 130 E4
Deception Bay Australia 147 G1
Dechang China 86 B3
also known as Dezhou
Decheng China see Deqing
Děčín Czech Rep. 49 L5
Decize France 51 J6
Decorah U.S.A. 174 B3
Dedap i. Indon. see Penasi, Pulau
Dedaye Myanmar 78 A4
Dedebağı Turkey 59 K11
Dedegöl Dağları mts Turkey 106 B3
Deder Eth. 128 D2
Dedinovo Rus. Fed. 43 U6
Dedo de Deus mt. Brazil 206 F11
Dedop'listsqaro Georgia 107 F2
formerly known as Tsiteli Tskaro
Dédougou Burkina 124 E3
Dedovichi Rus. Fed. 43 K4
Dedu China 82 B2
also known as Qingshan
Dedurovka Rus. Fed. 102 C2
Dedza Malawi 129 B8
Dedza Mountain Malawi 131 G2
Dee r. England/Wales U.K. 47 I10
Dee r. Scotland U.K. 46 J6
Deeg India 96 C4
Deelfontein S. Africa 132 H7
Deep Bay Hong Kong China 87 [inset]
also known as Shenzhen Wan
Deep Bight inlet Australia 150 D2
Deep Creek Lake U.S.A. 176 F6
Deep Creek Range mts U.S.A. 183 K2
Deep Gap U.S.A. 176 D9
Deep River Canada 168 E4
Deep River U.S.A. 177 M4
Deer Creek r. U.S.A. 182 B2
Deer Creek Reservoir U.S.A. 183 M1
Deeri Somalia 128 E3
Deering, Mount Australia 151 E5
Deer Island Canada 169 H4
Deer Island AK U.S.A. 164 C4
Deer Island ME U.S.A. 177 Q1
Deer Isle U.S.A. 177 Q1
Deer Lake Nfld. Canada 169 J3
Deer Lake Ont. Canada 167 M4
Deer Lake l. Canada 167 M4
Deer Lodge U.S.A. 180 D3
Deer Park U.S.A. 180 C3
Deerpass Bay Canada 166 F1
Deesa India see Disa
Defeng China see Liping
Defensores del Chaco, Parque Nacional nat. park Para. 201 E5
Defiance U.S.A. 176 A4
Defiance Plateau U.S.A. 183 O6
Défirou well Niger 125 H1
De Funiak Springs U.S.A. 175 C6
Degana India 96 B4
Degano r. Italy 56 E2
Dêgê China 86 A2
also known as Gengqing
Degebe r. Port. 54 D6
Degeberga Sweden 45 K5
Degeh Bur Eth. 128 D2
Dégelis Canada 169 G4
formerly known as Ste-Rose-du-Dégelé
Degema Nigeria 125 G5
Degerfors Sweden 45 K4
Deggendorf Germany 49 J7
Degh r. Pak. 101 H4
Değirmencik r. Turkey 59 J9
Değirmenlik Cyprus see Kythrea
Degodia reg. Eth. 128 D3
De Grey Australia 150 B4
De Grey r. Australia 150 B4
Degtevo Rus. Fed. 41 G6
Degtyarevka Rus. Fed. 43 N8
Dehaj Iran 100 C4
Dehak Iran 101 E5
Dehalak Deset i. Eritrea 121 I6
Deh Bakrī Iran 100 D4
Deh Barez Iran see Fāryāb
Deh Bīd Iran 100 C4
Deh-Dasht Iran 100 B4
Dehdez Iran 100 B4
Dehej India 96 B5
Deh-e Khalīfeh Iran 100 B4
Deh-e Kohneh Iran 100 B4
Dehel Island Eritrea 104 B5
Dehgāh Iran 100 B2
Deh Golān Iran 100 A3
Dehi Afgh. 101 F3
Deh Khvājeh Iran 100 C4
Dehkūyeh Iran 100 C5
Dehlorān Iran 100 A3
Deh Mollā Iran 100 B4
De Hoge Veluwe, Nationaal Park nat. park Neth. 48 C3
De Hoop Nature Reserve S. Africa 132 E11
De Hoop Vlei l. S. Africa 132 E11
Dehqonobod Uzbek. see Dekhkanabad
Dehra Dun India 96 C3
Dehri India 97 E4
Deh Shū Afgh. 101 E4
Dehua China 87 F3
also known as Longxun
Dehui China 82 B3
Deim Zubeir Sudan 126 E3
Deinze Belgium 51 J2
Deir el Qamar Lebanon 108 G4
Deir-ez-Zor Syria see Dayr az Zawr
Dej Romania 58 E1
Dejë, Mal mt. Albania 58 B7
Dejen Eth. 128 C2
Deji China see Rinbung
Dejiang China 87 D2
also known as Jiangsi
Deka Drum Zimbabwe 131 E3
De Kalb IL U.S.A. 174 B3
De Kalb MS U.S.A. 175 B5
De Kalb TX U.S.A. 179 D5
De Kalb Junction U.S.A. 177 J1
De-Kastri Rus. Fed. 82 F2
Dekemhare Eritrea 121 H6
Dekese Dem. Rep. Congo 126 D5
Dekhkanabad Uzbek. 103 F5
also spelt Dehqonobod
Dékoa Cent. Afr. Rep. 126 C3
Delaki Indon. 75 C5
Delamar Lake U.S.A. 183 J4
Delami Sudan 128 A2
De Land U.S.A. 175 D6
Delano U.S.A. 182 E6
Delano Peak U.S.A. 183 L3

Delap-Uliga-Djarrit Marshall Is 220 F5
Capital of the Marshall Islands, on Majuro atoll. Also spelt Dalap-Uliga-Darrit or Djarrit-Uliga-Dalap.

Delārām Afgh. 101 E3
Delareyville S. Africa 133 J3
Delaronde Lake Canada 167 J4
Delavan U.S.A. 172 E8
Delaware U.S.A. 176 B5
Delaware r. KS U.S.A. 178 D4
Delaware r. NJ/PA U.S.A. 177 J6
Delaware state U.S.A. 177 J7
Delaware, East Branch r. U.S.A. 177 J4
Delaware, West Branch r. U.S.A. 177 J4
Delaware Bay U.S.A. 177 J6
Delaware City U.S.A. 177 J6
Delaware Water Gap National Recreational Area park U.S.A. 177 K4
Delay r. Canada 169 G1
Delbarton U.S.A. 176 C8
Delbeng Sudan 126 F3
Del Bonita Canada 167 H5
Delburne Canada 167 H4
Delčevo Macedonia 58 D7
Delegate Australia 147 F4
Delémont Switz. 51 N5
Delevan CA U.S.A. 182 B2
Delevan NY U.S.A. 176 G3
Delfinópolis Brazil 206 G7
Delft Neth. 48 B3
Delft Island Sri Lanka 94 C4
Delfzijl Neth. 48 D2
Delgado, Cabo c. Moz. 129 D7
Delgermörön Mongolia 84 C2
Delger Mörön r. Mongolia 84 D1
Delgo Sudan 121 F4
Delhi Canada 173 M8
Delhi China 84 C4
formerly known as Delingha

Delhi India 96 C3
world [cities] 24–25

Delhi admin. div. India 89 B6
Delhi CA U.S.A. 182 D4
Delhi LA U.S.A. 175 B5
Delhi NY U.S.A. 177 K3
Deli i. Indon. 77 D4
Deli r. Turkey 107 E3
Delice Turkey 106 C3
Delice r. Turkey 106 C2
Délices Fr. Guiana 199 H3
Delījān Iran 100 B3
Deliktaş Turkey 59 H10
Déline Canada 166 F1
formerly known as Fort Franklin
Delingha China see Delhi
Delisle Canada 167 J5
Delitua Indon. 76 B2
Delitzsch Germany 49 J4
Dellys Alg. 123 F1
Del Mar U.S.A. 183 G9
Delmar DE U.S.A. 177 J7
Delmar IA U.S.A. 172 C8
Delmas S. Africa 133 M3
Delmenhorst Germany 48 F2
Delmont U.S.A. 176 F5
Delmore Downs Australia 148 B4
Delnice Croatia 56 G3
Del Norte U.S.A. 181 F5
Delong China 86 C4
De-Longa, Ostrova is Rus. Fed. 39 P2
English form De Long Islands
De Long Islands Rus. Fed. see De-Longa, Ostrova
De Long Mountains U.S.A. 164 C3
De Long Strait Rus. Fed. see Longa, Proliv
Deloraine Australia 147 E5
Deloraine Canada 167 K5
Delphi tourist site Greece 59 D10
Delphi U.S.A. 174 C3
Delphos U.S.A. 176 A5
Delportshoop S. Africa 133 I5
Delray Beach U.S.A. 175 D7
Del Río Mex. 184 C2
Del Rio U.S.A. 179 B6
Delsbo Sweden 45 L3
Delta state Nigeria 125 G5
Delta CO U.S.A. 181 E5
Delta OH U.S.A. 176 A4
Delta UT U.S.A. 183 L2
Delta Amacuro state Venez. 199 F2
Delta du Saloum, Parc National du nat. park Senegal 124 A3
Delta Junction U.S.A. 164 E3
Delta National Wildlife Refuge nature res. U.S.A. 175 B6
Delta Reservoir U.S.A. 177 J2
Deltona U.S.A. 175 D6
Delungra Australia 147 F2
Delvada India 94 A1
Delvinë Albania 59 B9
Dema r. Rus. Fed. 102 C1
Demak Indon. 77 E4
Demavend mt. Iran see Damāvand, Qolleh-ye
Demba Dem. Rep. Congo 127 D6
Dembava Lith. 42 F6
Dembia Cent. Afr. Rep. 126 E3
Dembī Dolo Eth. 128 B2
Demerara Guyana see Georgetown
Demidov Rus. Fed. 43 M6
Deming U.S.A. 181 F6
Demini r. Brazil 199 F5
Demini, Serras do mts Brazil 199 F4
Demirci Turkey 106 B3
Demir Hisar Macedonia 58 C7
Demirköprü Barajı resr Turkey 106 B3
Demirköy Turkey 58 I7
Demirler r. Turkey 59 K10
Demistkraal S. Africa 133 I10
Demmin Germany 49 K2
Democracia Brazil 199 F6
Demopolis U.S.A. 175 C5
Dempo, Gunung vol. Indon. 76 C4
Dempster Highway Canada 166 B1
Demqog Jammu and Kashmir 96 C2
Demyakhi Rus. Fed. 43 N6
Dem'yanovo Rus. Fed. 40 H3
Demyansk Rus. Fed. 43 N4
De Naawte S. Africa 132 F7
Denair U.S.A. 182 D4
Denakil reg. Eritrea/Eth. 121 I6
also spelt Danakil
Denali National Park and Preserve U.S.A. 164 D3
formerly known as Mount McKinley National Park
Denan Eth. 128 D3
Denare Beach Canada 167 K4
Denau Uzbek. 103 F5
also spelt Denow
Denbigh Canada 168 E4
Denbigh U.K. 47 I10
also spelt Dinbych
Den Bosch Neth. see 's-Hertogenbosch
Den Burg Neth. 48 B2
Den Chai Thai. 78 C4
Dendang Indon. 77 D3
Dendâra Mauritania 124 D2
Dendermonde Belgium 51 K1
Đeneral Janković Kosovo, Srbija Yugo. 58 C6
also spelt Djeneral Janković
Denezhkin Kamen', Gora mt. Rus. Fed. 40 K3
Dengas Niger 125 H3
Denge Nigeria 125 G3
Dengfeng China 87 E1
Dênggar China 89 D6
Dengjiabu China see Yujiang
Dêngka China see Têwo
Dêngkagoin China see Têwo
Dengkou China 85 E3
also known as Bayan Gol
Dêngqên China 97 G3
also known as Gyamotang
Dengta China 87 E4
Denguiro Cent. Afr. Rep. 126 D3
Dengxian China see Dengzhou
Dengzhou China 87 E1
formerly known as Dengxian
Dengzhou China see Penglai
Den Haag Neth. see The Hague
Denham Australia 151 A5
Denham r. Australia 150 E2
Denham Range mts Australia 149 F4
Denham Sound sea chan. Australia 151 A5
Den Helder Neth. 48 B3
Denholm Canada 167 I4
Denia Spain 55 L6

index D

Denial Bay Australia **146** B3
Deniliquin Australia **147** E3
Deniskovichi Rus. Fed. **43** M9
Denison *IA* U.S.A. **178** D3
Denison *TX* U.S.A. **179** C5
Denison, Cape Antarctica **223** J2
Denison Plains Australia **150** E3
Denisovka Kazakh. *see* **Ordzhonikidze**
Denizli Turkey **106** B3
historically known as Laodicea or Laodicea ad Lycum
Denizli *prov.* Turkey **59** K11
Denman Australia **147** F3
Denman Glacier Antarctica **223** G2
Denmark Australia **151** B7
▶**Denmark** *country* Europe **45** J5
europe [countries] ➡ 32–35
Denmark U.S.A. **172** F6
Denmark Fjord *inlet* Greenland *see* **Danmark Fjord**
Denmark Strait Greenland/Iceland **165** Q3
Dennilton S. Africa **133** N2
Dennis, Lake *salt flat* Australia **150** E4
Dennison U.S.A. **176** D5
Dennisville U.S.A. **177** K6
Denow Uzbek. *see* **Denau**
Denpasar Indon. **77** F5
Densongi Indon. **75** B3
Denton *MD* U.S.A. **177** J7
Denton *TX* U.S.A. **179** C5
D'Entrecasteaux, Point Australia **151** A7
D'Entrecasteaux, Récifs *reef* New Caledonia **145** F3
D'Entrecasteaux Islands P.N.G. **145** E2
D'Entrecasteaux National Park Australia **151** A7
Dents du Midi *mt.* Switz. **51** M6

▶**Denver** U.S.A. **180** F5
State capital of Colorado.

Denys *r.* Canada **168** E2
Deo India **97** E4
Deoband India **96** C3
Deobhog India **95** D2
Deogarh *Orissa* India **97** E5
Deogarh *Rajasthan* India **96** B4
Deogarh *mt.* India **97** D5
Deoghar India **97** E4
also spelt Devghar
Deoli India **94** C1
Déols France **50** H6
Deori India **96** C5
Deoria India **97** D4
Deosai, Plains of Jammu and Kashmir **96** B2
Dep *r.* Rus. Fed. **82** B1
Depalpur India **96** B5
De Pas, Rivière *r.* Canada **169** H2
De Pere U.S.A. **172** E6
Depew U.S.A. **176** G3
Deposit U.S.A. **177** J3
Depot-Forbes Canada **173** Q3
Depot-Rowanton Canada **173** P4
Depsang Point *hill* Aksai Chin **89** B5
Depue U.S.A. **172** D9
Deputatskiy Rus. Fed. **39** N3
Dêqên *Xizang* China **89** E6
Dêqên *Xizang* China **89** E6
Dêqên China *see* **Dagzê**
Dêqên *Yunnan* China **86** A2
also known as Kaiping
Deqing *Guangdong* China **87** D4
also known as Decheng
Deqing *Zhejiang* China **87** G2
De Queen U.S.A. **179** D5
De Quincy U.S.A. **179** D6
Der, Lac du *l.* France **51** K4
Dera Eth. **128** C2
Dera Bugti Pak. **101** G4
Dera Ghazi Khan Pak. **101** G4
Deraheib *reg.* Sudan **121** G4
Dera Ismail Khan Pak. **101** G3
Derajat *reg.* Pak. **101** G4
Deram, Mount Antarctica **223** G2
Derbent Rus. Fed. **102** B4
Derbent Turkey **59** J10
Derbent Uzbek. **103** F5
formerly spelt Darband
Derbesiye Turkey *see* **Şenyurt**
Derby Australia **150** C3
Derby S. Africa **133** L2
Derby U.K. **47** K11
Derby *CT* U.S.A. **177** L4
Derby *KS* U.S.A. **178** C4
formerly known as El Paso
Derby Line U.S.A. **177** M1
Derecske Hungary **49** S8
Dereköy Turkey **108** D1
Dereköy Turkey **59** K11
Dereva Rus. Fed. **43** N2
Derg, Lough *l.* Rep. of Ireland **47** D11
Dergachi Rus. Fed. **102** B2
Dergachi Ukr. *see* **Derhachi**
Dergholm State Park *nature res.* Australia **146** D4
Derhachi Ukr. **41** F6
also spelt Dergachi
De Ridder U.S.A. **179** D6
Derik Turkey **107** E3
Derinkuyu Turkey **106** C3
Derkali *well* Kenya **128** D4
Derna Libya *see* **Darnah**
Dêrong China **86** A2
also known as Songmai
Derow Iran **102** B5
Derre Moz. **131** H3
Derry U.K. *see* **Londonderry**
Derry U.S.A. **177** N3
Derryveagh Mountains *hills* Rep. of Ireland **47** D9
Derstei China **84** D3
Dêrub China *see* **Rutog**
Derudeb Sudan **121** H5
De Rust S. Africa **132** G10
Deruta Italy **56** E6
Derventa Bos.-Herz. **56** J4
Derwent *r.* Australia **147** E5
Derwent *r. Derbyshire, England* U.K. **47** K11
Derwent *r. England* U.K. **47** L10
Derweze Turkm. *see* **Darvaza**
Deryugino Rus. Fed. **43** Q9
Derza *r.* Rus. Fed. **43** P5
Derzhavino Rus. Fed. **102** C1
Derzhavinsk Kazakh. **103** F2
formerly known as Derzhavinskiy
Derzhavinskiy Kazakh. *see* **Derzhavinsk**
Desa Romania **58** E5
Desaguadero *r.* Arg. **204** D4
Desaguadero *r.* Bol. **200** C4
Désappointement, Îles du *is* Fr. Polynesia **221** I6
English form Disappointment Islands
Des Arc U.S.A. **174** B5
Desatoya Mountains U.S.A. **182** G2
Desbarats Canada **173** J4
Descalvado *Mato Grosso* Brazil **201** F4
Descalvado *São Paulo* Brazil **206** F8
Descartes France **50** G6
Deschambault Lake Canada **167** K4
Deschambault Lake *l.* Canada **167** K4
Deschutes *r.* U.S.A. **170** B2
Desē Eth. **128** C2
formerly spelt Dessye
Deseada Chile **200** C5
Deseado Arg. **205** D7
Deseado *r.* Arg. **205** D7
Desembarco Del Granma National Park *tourist site* Cuba **186** D3
Desemboque Mex. **184** B2
Desengaño, Punta *pt* Arg. **205** D8
Deseret U.S.A. **183** L2
Deseret Peak U.S.A. **183** L1
Deseronto Canada **173** P6
Désert, Lac *l.* Canada **173** Q4
Desertas, Ilhas *is* Madeira **122** A2
Desert Canal Pak. **101** G4
Desert Center U.S.A. **183** I8
Desert Hot Springs U.S.A. **183** H8
Desertines France **51** I6
Desert Lake U.S.A. **183** I5
Desert National Wildlife Refuge *nature res.* U.S.A. **183** I5
Desert View U.S.A. **183** M5
Deshler U.S.A. **176** B4
Deshnok India **96** B4
Desiderio Tello Arg. **204** D3
Desierto Central de Baja California, Parque Natural del *nature res.* Mex. **184** B2
Desierto de Sechura *des.* Peru **198** A6
Deskati Greece **59** C9
also spelt Dheskáti
De Smet U.S.A. **178** C2

▶**Des Moines** *IA* U.S.A. **174** A3
State capital of Iowa.

Des Moines *NM* U.S.A. **178** B4
Des Moines *r.* U.S.A. **178** D3
Desna *r.* Rus. Fed./Ukr. **41** D6
Desnățui *r.* Romania **58** E5
Desnogorsk Rus. Fed. **43** O7
Desnogorskoye Vodokhranilishche *resr* Rus. Fed. **43** O7
Desnudo, Cerro *mt.* Arg. **205** C7
Desolación, Isla *i.* Chile **205** B9
Desolation Point Phil. **74** C4
DeSoto U.S.A. **172** B7
Despatch S. Africa **133** J10
Despen Rus. Fed. **84** B1
Des Plaines U.S.A. **172** F8
Despotovac *Srbija* Yugo. **58** C4
Dessau Germany **49** J4
Dessye Eth. *see* **Desē**
Destor Canada **173** O2
D'Estrees Bay Australia **146** C3
Destruction Bay Canada **166** B2
Desvres France **51** H2
Deta Romania **58** C3
Detah Canada **167** H2
Detchino Rus. Fed. **43** R7
Dete Zimbabwe **131** E3
formerly spelt Dett
De Teut Natuurreservaat *nature res.* Belgium **51** L2
Deti Jon *b.* Albania/Greece **59** A8
Đetinja *r.* Yugo. **58** B5
Detmold Germany **48** F4
Detour, Point U.S.A. **172** G5
De Tour Village U.S.A. **173** J5
Detrital Wash *watercourse* U.S.A. **183** J5
Detroit U.S.A. **173** J8
Detroit Lakes U.S.A. **178** D2
Dett Zimbabwe *see* **Dete**
Det Udom Thai. **79** D5
Detva Slovakia **49** Q7
Deua National Park Australia **147** F3
Deurne Neth. **48** C4
Deutschland *country* Europe *see* **Germany**
Deutschlandsberg Austria **49** M9
Deutsch-Luxemburgischer Naturpark *nature res.* Germany **48** D6
Deux-Rivières Canada **173** O4
Deva Romania **58** D3
Deva U.K. *see* **Chester**
Devadurga India **94** C2
Devakottai India **94** C4
Devana U.K. *see* **Aberdeen**
Devanhalli India **94** C3
Devarkonda India **94** C2
Deve Bair *pass* Macedonia *see* **Velbŭzhdki Prokhod**
Devecser Hungary **49** O8
Develi Turkey **106** C3
also known as Everek
Deveron *r.* U.K. **46** J6
Devesel Romania **58** D4
Devét Skal *hill* Czech Rep. **49** N6
Devgadh Bariya India **96** B5
Devghar India *see* **Deoghar**
Devikot India **96** A4
Devil River Peak N.Z. **152** G8
Devils *r.* U.S.A. **179** B6
Devil's Bridge U.K. **47** I11
Devil's Gate *pass* U.S.A. **182** E3
Devil's Island U.S.A. **172** C3
Devils Lake U.S.A. **178** C1
Devil's Lake *l.* U.S.A. **179** B6
Devil's Paw *mt.* U.S.A. **164** F4
Devil's Peak U.S.A. **182** E4
Devil's Point Bahamas **187** E1
Devil's Thumb *mt.* Canada/U.S.A. **166** C3
Devin Bulg. **58** F7
Devine U.S.A. **179** C6
Devizes U.K. **47** K12
Devli India **96** B4
Devnya Bulg. **58** I5
Devoll *r.* Albania **58** A8
Dévoluy *mts* France **51** L8
Devon *Alta* Canada **180** D1
Devon *Ont.* Canada **173** J3
Devon S. Africa **133** M3
Devon Island Canada **165** J2
Devonport Australia **147** E5
Devore U.S.A. **182** G7
Devrek Turkey **106** B2
Devrez *r.* Turkey **106** C2
Devrukh India **94** B2
Dewa, Tanjung *pt* Indon. **76** A2
Dewakang Besar *i.* Indon. **77** G4
Dewanganj Bangl. **97** F4
Dewangiri Bhutan **97** F4
Dewas India **96** C5
De Weerribben, Nationaal Park *nat. park* Neth. **48** D3
Dewelē Eth. **128** D2
Dewetsdorp S. Africa **133** K6
De Witt *AR* U.S.A. **174** B5
De Witt *IA* U.S.A. **174** B3
Dexing China **87** F2
formerly known as Yincheng
Dexter *MI* U.S.A. **173** J8
Dexter *MO* U.S.A. **174** B4
Dexter *NM* U.S.A. **181** F6
Dexter *NY* U.S.A. **177** I1
Deyang China **86** C2
Dey-Dey Lake *salt flat* Australia **146** A2
Deyhuk Iran **100** D3
Deynau Turkm. *see* **Dyanev**
Deyong, Tanjung *pt* Indon. **73** I8
Dêyü Co *l.* China **89** D5
Deyyer Iran **100** B5
Dez *r.* Iran **100** B4
Dez, Sadd-e *resr* Iran **107** G4
formerly known as Mohammad Reza Shah Pahlavi Dam
Dezadeash Canada **166** B2
Dezadeash Lake Canada **166** B2
Dezfūl Iran **100** B3

▶**Dezhneva, Mys** *c.* Rus. Fed. **39** T3
Most easterly point of Asia. English form East Cape.

Dezhou China **85** H4
Dezhou China *see* **Dechang**
Dezh Shāhpūr Iran *see* **Marīvān**
Dhading Nepal **97** E4
Dhahab, Wādī adh *r.* Syria **108** G5
Dhāhiriya West Bank **108** F6
Dhahlān, Jabal *hill* Saudi Arabia **104** D2
Dhahran Saudi Arabia **105** E2
also spelt Aẓ Ẓahrān

▶**Dhaka** Bangl. **97** F5
Capital of Bangladesh and 5th most populous city in Asia. Formerly spelt Dacca.
world [cities] ➡ 24–25

Dhaka *admin. div.* Bangl. **97** F5
Dhalbhum *reg.* India **97** E5
Dhaleswari *r.* Bangl. **97** F5
Dhaleswari *r.* India **97** G4
Dhalgaon India **94** B2
Dhamār Yemen **104** D5
Dhamār *governorate* Yemen **104** D5
Dhamnod India **96** B5
Dhampur India **96** C3
Dhamtari India **94** D1
Dhanbad India **97** E5
Dhandhuka India **96** B5
Dhanera India **96** B4
Dhangarhi Nepal **96** D3
Dhang Range *mts* Nepal **97** D3
Dhankuta Nepal **97** E4
Dhar India **96** B5
Dhar Adrar *hills* Mauritania **124** B2
Dharampur India **94** B1
Dharan Bazar Nepal **97** E4
Dharapuram India **94** C4
Dhari India **96** A5
Dharmanagar India **97** G4
Dharmapuri India **94** C3
Dharmavaram India **94** C3
Dharmjaygarh India **97** D5
also known as Rabkob
Dharmkot India **96** B3
Dharoor *watercourse* Somalia **128** F2
Dhar Oualâta *hills* Mauritania **124** D2
Dhar Tichît *hills* Mauritania **124** C2
Dharug National Park Australia **147** F3
Dharur India **94** C2
Dharwad India **94** B3
formerly known as Dharwar
Dharwar India *see* **Dharwad**
Dhasa India **96** A5
Dhasan *r.* India **96** C4

▶**Dhaulagiri** *mt.* Nepal **97** D3
7th highest mountain in the world and in Asia. Also spelt Dhawlagiri.
world [physical features] ➡ 8–9

Dhaulpur India **96** C4
Dhaurahra India **96** D4
Dhávlia Greece *see* **Davlia**
Dhawlagiri *mt.* Nepal *see* **Dhaulagiri**
Dhebar Lake India **96** B4
Dhekelia Sovereign Base Area *military base* Cyprus **108** E2
Dhekiajuli India **97** G4
Dhenkanal India **95** E1
Dheskáti Greece *see* **Deskati**
Dhiafánion Greece *see* **Diafani**
Dhībān Jordan **108** G6
Dhidhimótikhon Greece *see* **Didymoteicho**
Dhing India **97** G4
Dhī Qār *governorate* Iraq **107** F5
Dhirwāh, Wādī adh *watercourse* Jordan **109** H6
Dhodhekánisos *is* Greece *see* **Dodecanese**
Dhofar *admin. reg.* Oman *see* **Ẓufār**
Dhokós *i.* Greece *see* **Dokos**
Dhola India **96** A5
Dholka India **96** B5
Dhomokós Greece *see* **Domokos**
Dhone India **94** C3
Dhoomadheere Somalia **128** D4
Dhoraji India **96** A5
Dhori India **96** A5
Dhragonádha *i.* Greece *see* **Dragonada**
Dhragónisos *i.* Greece *see* **Dragonisi**
Dhrangadhra India **96** A5
Dhrol India **96** A5
Dhrosiá Greece *see* **Drosia**
Dhubāb Yemen **104** C5
Dhubri India *see* **Dhuburi**
Dhuburi India **97** F4
also spelt Dhubri
Dhule India **94** B1
formerly known as Dhulia
Dhulia India *see* **Dhule**
Dhulian India **97** E4
Dhuma India **96** C5
Dhunche Nepal **97** E4
Dhuudo Somalia **128** F2
Dhuusa Marreeb Somalia **128** E3
Dhuwaybān *basin* Saudi Arabia **104** B2
Dhytikí Ellás *admin. reg.* Greece *see* **Dytiki Ellas**
Dhytikí Makedhonía *admin. reg.* Greece *see* **Dytiki Makedonia**
Dia *i.* Greece **59** G13
Diablo, Mount U.S.A. **182** C4
Diablo Range *mts* U.S.A. **182** C4
Diaca Moz. **129** C7
Diafani Greece **59** I13
also known as Dhiafánion
Diafarabé Mali **124** D3
Diaka *r.* Mali **124** D3
Dialakoto Senegal **124** B3
Diallassagou Mali **124** E3
Diamante Arg. **204** E4
Diamante *r.* Arg. **204** D4
Diamante Italy **57** H9
Diamantina *watercourse* Australia **149** C5
Diamantina *Amazonas* Brazil **199** F6
Diamantina *Minas Gerais* Brazil **203** D6
Diamantina, Chapada *plat.* Brazil **202** D5
Diamantina Gates National Park Australia **149** D4
Diamantina Lakes Australia **149** D4
Diamantino *Mato Grosso* Brazil **201** F3
Diamantino *Mato Grosso* Brazil **202** A6
Diamantino *r.* Brazil **206** A3
Diamond Harbour India **97** F5
Diamond Islets Australia **149** F3
Diamond Peak U.S.A. **183** I2
Diamond Springs U.S.A. **182** D3
Diamondville U.S.A. **180** E4
Diamou Mali **124** C3
Diamounguél Senegal **124** B3
Dianbai China **87** D4
also known as Shuidong
Dianbu China *see* **Feidong**
Diancang Shan *mt.* China **86** B3
Dian Chi *l.* China **86** B3
Diandioumé Mali **124** C3
Diane Bank *sea feature* Australia **149** F2
Diangounté Kamara Mali **124** C3
Diani *r.* Guinea **124** C5
Dianjiang China **87** C2
also known as Guixi
Diano Marina Italy **56** A5
Dianópolis Brazil **202** C4
Dianra Côte d'Ivoire **124** D4
Diaobingshan China *see* **Tiefa**
Diaokou China **85** H4
Diaoling China **82** C3
Diapaga Burkina **125** F3
Diaporioi *i.* Greece **59** E11
Diarizos *r.* Cyprus **108** D3
Diatifèrè Guinea **124** C4
Diavolo, Mount *hill* India **95** G3
Diaz Point Namibia **130** B5
Dib, Râs *pt* Egypt **108** E9
Dibā al Ḥiṣn U.A.E. **105** G2
Dibab Oman **105** G3
Dibang *r.* India *see* **Dingba Qu**
Dibaya Dem. Rep. Congo **127** D6
Dibbis Sudan **120** E6
Dibek Dağı *mt.* Turkey **59** J10
Dibella *well* Niger **125** I2
Dibeng S. Africa **132** G4
Dībīlē Eth. **128** D2
Dibis Iraq **109** P2
Dibiy, Jabal *hills* Saudi Arabia **104** C2
Dibrugarh India **97** G4
Dibulla Col. **198** C2
Dickens U.S.A. **179** B5
Dickeyville U.S.A. **172** C8
Dickinson U.S.A. **178** B2
Dickson U.S.A. **174** C4
Dicle *r.* Turkey **107** E3 *see* **Tigris**
Dida Galgalu *reg.* Kenya **128** C4
Didah *well* Saudi Arabia **104** D2
Dīdī, Jabal ad *hill* Syria **109** K2
Didicas *i.* Phil. **74** B2
Didiéni Mali **124** C3
Didinga Hills Sudan **128** B3
Dido *waterhole* Kenya **128** D5
Didsbury Canada **167** H5
Didwana India **96** B4
Didymoteicho Greece **58** H7
also known as Dhidhimótikhon
Didžiasalis Lith. **42** H6
Didžiulis *l.* Lith. **42** F7
Die France **51** L8
Die Berg *mt.* S. Africa **133** O2
Diébougou Burkina **124** E4
Dieburg Germany **48** F6
Diedenhofen France *see* **Thionville**
Diefenbaker, Lake Canada **167** I5
Diège *r.* France **51** I7
Diego de Almagro, Isla *i.* Chile **205** B8
Diego Garcia *i.* British Indian Ocean Terr. **218** L6
Diego Martin Trin. and Tob. **187** H5
Diégo Suarez Madag. *see* **Antsirañana**
Diégråga *well* Mauritania **124** C3
Diéké Guinea **124** C5
Diekirch Lux. **51** M3
Diéma Mali **124** C3
Diemelsee *park* Germany **48** F4
Điện Châu Vietnam **78** D4
Dienvidsusēja *r.* Latvia **42** F5
Diepholz Germany **48** F3
Dieppe France **50** H3
Dierks U.S.A. **179** D5
Di'er Nonchang Qu *r.* China **85** E4
Di'er Songhua Jiang *r.* China **82** B3
Diest Belgium **51** L2
Dietikon Switz. **51** O5
Dieveniškės Lith. **42** G7
Diffa Niger **125** I3
Diffa *dept* Niger **125** I2
Difnein Island Eritrea **104** B4
Dig *well* Eth. **128** E3
Diga Diga *well* Niger **125** F3
Digapahandi India **95** E2
Digba Dem. Rep. Congo **126** E3
Digboi India **97** G4
Digby Canada **169** H4
Digerbergen *hill* Sweden **45** K3
Digerberget *hill* Sweden **45** K3
Diggi India **96** B4
Dighton U.S.A. **178** B4
Diglur India **94** C2
Digne-les-Bains France **51** M8
Digoin France **51** J6
Digos Phil. **74** C5
Digras India **94** C1
Digri Pak. **101** G5
Digul *r.* Indon. **73** I8
Digya National Park Ghana **125** E5
Dihang *r.* India **97** G3 *see* **Brahmaputra**
Diib, Wadi *watercourse* Sudan **104** B3
Diinsoor Somalia **128** D4
Dijlah, Nahr *r.* Iraq/Syria **107** F4 *see* **Tigris**
Dijlah - Ath Tharthār, Qanāt *canal* Iraq **109** O4
English form Tharthār Canal
Dijon France **51** L5
Dik Chad **126** C2
Dikanäs Sweden **44** L2
Diken India **96** B4
Dikhil Djibouti **128** D2
Dikho *r.* India **97** G4
Dikili Turkey **106** A3
Diksal India **94** B2
Diksmuide Belgium **51** I1
Dikson Rus. Fed. **39** I2
Dikwa Nigeria **125** I3
Dila Eth. **128** C3
Dilaram Iran **100** D4
Dilek Yarımadası Milli Parkı *nat. park* Turkey **59** I11
Dili Dem. Rep. Congo **126** E4

▶**Dili** East Timor **75** C5
Capital of East Timor.

Dilia *watercourse* Niger **125** I3
Dilijan Armenia **107** F2
also spelt Dilizhan
Dilijan Argelanots' *nature res.* Armenia **107** F2
Di Linh Vietnam **79** E6
Dillon Cone *mt.* N.Z. **153** H10
Dilizhan Armenia *see* **Dilijan**
Dillenburg Germany **48** F5
Dilley U.S.A. **179** C6
Dilli Mali **124** D3
Dilling Sudan **121** F6
Dillingen an der Donau Germany **48** H7
Dillingham U.S.A. **164** D4
Dillinya Aboriginal Land *res.* Australia **148** B2
Dillon Canada **167** I4
Dillon *r.* Canada **167** I4
Dillon *MT* U.S.A. **180** D3
Dillon *SC* U.S.A. **174** E5
Dillsburg U.S.A. **177** H5
Dillwyn U.S.A. **176** G8
Dilolo Dem. Rep. Congo **127** D7
Dilos *i.* Greece **59** G11
Diltāwa Iraq **107** F4
Dimako Cameroon **125** I5
Dimapur India **97** G4
Dimas Mex. **184** D4
Dimashq Syria *see* **Damascus**
Dimashq *governorate* Syria **109** I4
Dimbelenge Dem. Rep. Congo **127** D6
Dimbokro Côte d'Ivoire **124** D5
Dimboola Australia **147** D4
Dimbulah Australia **149** E3
Dimitrovgrad Bulg. **58** G6
Dimitrovgrad Rus. Fed. **41** I5
formerly known as Melekess
Dimitrovgrad *Srbija* Yugo. **58** D5
formerly known as Tsaribrod
Dimitrovo Bulg. *see* **Pernik**
Dimmitt U.S.A. **179** B5
Dīmona Israel **108** G6
Dinagat *i.* Phil. **74** C4
Dinagat Sound *sea chan.* Phil. **74** C4
Dinajpur Bangl. **97** F4
Dinan France **50** D4
Dinanagar India **96** B2
Dinangourou Mali **125** E3
Dinant Belgium **51** K2
Dinapur India **97** E4
Dinar Turkey **106** B3
historically known as Apamea
Dīnār, Kūh-e *mt.* Iran **100** B4
Dinara *mt.* Bos.-Herz. **56** I4
Dinara Planina *mts* Bos.-Herz./Croatia *see* **Dinaric Alps**
Dinard France **50** D4
Dinaric Alps *mts* Bos.-Herz./Croatia **56** I4
also known as Dinara Planina
Dinas *well* Kenya **128** C4
Dinbych U.K. *see* **Denbigh**
Dinbych-y-Pysgod U.K. *see* **Tenby**
Dinder *r.* Sudan **121** G6
Dinder el Agaliyin *r.* Sudan **104** A5
Dinder National Park Sudan **121** G6
Dindi *r.* India **94** C2
Dindigul India **94** C4
Dindima Nigeria **125** H4
Dindiza Moz. **131** G4
Dindori *Madhya Pradesh* India **96** D5
Dindori *Maharashtra* India **94** B1
Dinek Turkey **106** C3
Dinga Dem. Rep. Congo **127** C6
Dinga Pak. **101** H3
Dingalan Bay Phil. **74** B3
Dingba Qu *r.* India **97** G4
also known as Dibang
Dingbian China **85** E4
Dingbujie China **87** E2
Dingelstädt Germany **48** H4
Dingin, Bukit *mt.* Indon. **76** C3
Dingla Nepal **97** E4
Dingle Rep. of Ireland **47** B11
Dingle Bay Rep. of Ireland **47** B11
Dingnan China **87** E3
also known as Lishi
Dingo Australia **149** F4
Dingolfing Germany **49** J7
Dingping China *see* **Linshui**
Dingras Phil. **74** B2
Dingtao China **85** G5
Dinguiraye Guinea **124** C4
Dingwall Canada **169** I4
Dingwall U.K. **46** H6
Dingxi China **84** E5
Dingxian China *see* **Dingzhou**
Dingxiang China **85** G4
Dingxin China **84** C3
Dingxing China **85** G4
Dingyuan China **87** F1
Dingzhou China **85** G4
formerly known as Dingxian
Dingzi Gang *b.* China **85** I4
Dingzikou China **84** B4
Dinhata India **97** F4
Dinh Lâp Vietnam **78** D3
Dinkel *r.* Neth. **48** D3
Dinkelsbühl Germany **48** H6
Dinnebito Wash *watercourse* U.S.A. **183** M6
Dinngyê China **89** D6
also known as Gyangkar
Dinokwe Botswana **131** E4
Dinosaur U.S.A. **183** O1
Dinosaur National Monument *nat. park* U.S.A. **183** O1
Dintiteladas Indon. **77** D4
Dinuba U.S.A. **182** E5
Dinwiddie U.S.A. **176** H8
Dioïla Mali **124** D3
Diois, Massif du *mts* France **51** L8
Dion *r.* Guinea **124** C4
Dionísio Brazil **207** K6
Dionísio Cerqueira Brazil **203** A8
Diorama Brazil **206** B3
Dioscurias Georgia *see* **Sokhumi**
Diosig Romania **58** D1
Diospolis Magna *tourist site* Egypt *see* **Thebes**
Dioulouou Senegal **124** A3
Dioumara Mali **124** C3
Dioundiou Niger **125** F3
Dioura Mali **124** D3
Diourbel Senegal **124** A3
Dipalpur Pak. **101** H4
Dipayal Nepal **96** D3
Diphu India **97** G4
Dipkarpaz Cyprus *see* **Rizokarpason**
Diplo Pak. **101** G5
Dipolog Phil. **74** B4
Dipperu National Park Australia **149** F4
Dipton N.Z. **153** C13
Dipu China *see* **Anji**
Dir Pak. **101** G3
Dir *reg.* Pak. **101** H3
Dīrah U.A.E. **105** F2
Dirang India **97** G4
Diré Mali **124** E3
Direction, Cape Australia **149** D2
Dirē Dawa Eth. **128** D2
Dirfys *mts* Greece **59** E10
Dirhami Estonia **42** E2
Diriamba Nicaragua **186** B5
Dirico Angola **127** D9
Dirillo *r. Sicilia* Italy **57** G11
Dirimil Geçidi *pass* Turkey **108** A1
Dirk Hartog Island Australia **151** A5
Dirkou Niger **125** I2
Dirranbandi Australia **147** F2
Dirs Saudi Arabia **104** C4
Dirschau Poland *see* **Tczew**
Dirty Devil *r.* U.S.A. **183** N4
Disa India **96** B4
formerly spelt Deesa
Disang *r.* India **97** G4
Disappointment, Cape Antarctica **222** T2
Disappointment, Cape S. Georgia **205** [inset]
Disappointment, Cape U.S.A. **180** A3
Disappointment, Lake *salt flat* Australia **150** C4
Disappointment Islands Fr. Polynesia *see* **Désappointement, Îles du**
Disappointment Lake Canada **169** I2
Discovery Bay Australia **146** D4
Discovery Bay *Hong Kong* China **87** [inset]
also known as Tai Pak Wan
Discovery Bay Coastal Park *nature res.* Australia **146** D4
Disentis Muster Switz. **51** O6
Disgrazia, Monte *mt.* Italy **56** B2
Dishna Egypt **121** G3
Disko *i.* Greenland *see* **Qeqertarsuaq**
Disko Bugt *b.* Greenland *see* **Qeqertarsuup Tunua**
Dismal Lakes Canada **167** G1
Dismal Mountains Antarctica **223** D2
Dismal Swamp U.S.A. **177** I9
Disneyland Paris *tourist site* France **51** I4
Dispur India **97** F4
Disputanta U.S.A. **177** H8
Disraëli Canada **169** G4
Diss U.K. **47** N11
Dissān Island Saudi Arabia **104** C4
Distrito Federal *admin. dist.* Brazil **206** F2
English form Federal District
Distrito Federal *admin. dist.* Mex. **185** F5
Distrito Federal *admin. dist.* Venez. **199** E2
English form Federal District
Disūq Egypt **108** B6
Ditloung S. Africa **132** G5
Dittaino *r. Sicilia* Italy **57** H11
Diu India **94** A1
Diuata Mountains Phil. **74** C4
Diuata Point Phil. **74** C4
Dīvān Darreh Iran **100** A3
Divehi *country* Indian Ocean *see* **Maldives**
Divénié Congo **126** B5
Dives *r.* France **50** F3
Divichi Azer. *see* **Dăvăçi**
Divide Mountain U.S.A. **166** A2
Divilacan Bay Phil. **74** B2
Divinésia Brazil **207** J7
Divinópolis Brazil **203** C7
Divisões, Serra das *mts* Brazil **206** B4
also known as Santa Marta, Serra de
Divisor, Sierra de *mts* Peru *see* **Ultraoriental, Cordillera**
Divjaka *nat. park* Albania **58** A8
Divnoye Rus. Fed. **41** G7
Divo Côte d'Ivoire **124** D5
Divo Rus. Fed. **43** M6
Divor *r.* Port. **54** C6
Divounia *i.* Greece **59** H13
Divriği Turkey **107** D3
Divuma Dem. Rep. Congo **127** D7
Div'ya Rus. Fed. **40** K4
Dīwaniyah Iraq *see* **Ad Dīwānīyah**
Dixcove Ghana **125** E5
Dixfield U.S.A. **177** O1
Dix Milles, Lac des *l.* Canada **173** S3
Dixmont U.S.A. **177** P1
Dixon *CA* U.S.A. **182** C3
Dixon *IL* U.S.A. **174** B3
Dixon Entrance *sea chan.* Canada/U.S.A. **164** F4
Dixon's Bahamas **175** F7
Dixonville Canada **167** G3
Diyadin Turkey **107** E3
Diyālā *governorate* Iraq **107** F4
Diyarbakır Turkey **107** E3
historically known as Amida
Diyodar India **96** A4
Diz Pak. **101** E5
Dizak Iran *see* **Dāvar Panāh**
Dizangué Cameroon **125** H6
Diz Chah Iran **100** C3
Dize Turkey *see* **Yüksekova**
Dizney U.S.A. **176** B9
Dja *r.* Cameroon **125** I6
Dja, Réserve du *nature res.* Cameroon **125** I6
Djado Niger **125** I1
Djado, Plateau du Niger **125** I1
Djakarta Indon. *see* **Jakarta**
Djakovica *Kosovo, Srbija* Yugo. *see* **Đakovica**
Djamâa Alg. **123** G2
Djamba Dem. Rep. Congo **127** D7
Djambala Congo **126** B5
Djampie Dem. Rep. Congo **126** C5
Djampiel Cameroon **125** I5
Djanet Alg. **123** H4
formerly known as Fort Charlet
Djarrit-Uliga-Dalap Marshall Is *see* **Delap-Uliga-Djarrit**
Djebr *mt.* Alg. **123** F4
Djébrène Chad **126** C2
Djédaa Chad **120** C6
Djedid *well* Alg. **123** E4
Djelfa Alg. **123** F2
Djéma Cent. Afr. Rep. **126** E3
Djèmber Chad **126** C2
Djeneral Janković *Kosovo, Srbija* Yugo. *see* **Đeneral Janković**
Djenné Mali **124** D3
also spelt Jenne
Djerdap *nat. park* Yugo. **58** D4
Djermaya Chad **120** B6
Djia Dem. Rep. Congo **126** D5
Djibo Burkina **125** E3
Djiborosso Côte d'Ivoire **124** D4

▶**Djibouti** *country* Africa **128** D3
spelt Jībūtī in Arabic; *formerly known as* Côte Française de Somalis in French or French Somaliland or French Territory of the Afars and Issas
africa [countries] ➡ 114–117

▶**Djibouti** Djibouti **128** D2
Capital of Djibouti. Also spelt Jibuti.

Djidjelli Alg. *see* **Jijel**
Djiguéni Mauritania **124** C3
Djinet, Cap *c.* Alg. **55** O8
Djoli-Kera, Forêt classée de *nature res.* Chad **126** C2
Djolu Dem. Rep. Congo **126** D4
Djombo Kibbit Chad **120** C6
Djoua *r.* Congo/Gabon **126** B4
Djoubissi Cent. Afr. Rep. **126** D3
Djougou Benin **125** F4
Djoum Cameroon **125** I6
Djugu Dem. Rep. Congo **126** F4
Djuma Dem. Rep. Congo **126** C6
Djúpivogur Iceland **44** [inset] D2
Djurås Sweden **45** K3
Djurdjura National Park Alg. **55** P8
Djurö nationalpark *nat. park* Sweden **45** K4
Dlairi India **96** B3
Dmitriya Lapteva, Proliv *sea chan.* Rus. Fed. **39** O2
Dmitriyevka *Primorskiy Kray* Rus. Fed. **90** C2
Dmitriyevka *Samarskaya Oblast'* Rus. Fed. **102** B1
Dmitriyev-L'govskiy Rus. Fed. **43** Q9
Dmitriyevsk Ukr. *see* **Makiyivka**
Dmitriyevskoye Rus. Fed. **43** S7
Dmitrov Rus. Fed. **43** S5
Dmitrovo Rus. Fed. **43** O8
Dmitrovskiy Pogost Rus. Fed. **43** U6
Dmitrovsk-Orlovskiy Rus. Fed. **43** Q9
Dmytriyevs'k Ukr. *see* **Makiyivka**
Dnepr *r.* Rus. Fed. *see* **Dnieper**
Dneprodzerzhinsk Ukr. *see* **Dniprodzerzhyns'k**
Dnepropetrovsk Ukr. *see* **Dnipropetrovs'k**
Dneprorudnoye Ukr. *see* **Dniprorudne**
Dneprovskoye Rus. Fed. **43** O6
formerly known as Andreyevskoye
Dnestrovsc Moldova **58** K2

▶**Dnieper** *r.* Europe **41** D6
3rd longest river in Europe. Also spelt Dnepr (Rus. Fed.) or Dnipro (Ukraine) or Dnyapro (Belarus).
europe [landscapes] ➡ 30–31

Dniester *r.* Moldova **58** L2
also spelt Nistru
Dniester *r.* Ukr. **41** D6
also spelt Dnister (Ukraine) or Nistru (Moldova)
Dnipro *r.* Ukr. **41** D6 *see* **Dnieper**
Dniprodzerzhyns'k Ukr. **41** E6
also spelt Dneprodzerzhinsk; *formerly known as* Kamenskoye
Dnipropetrovs'k Ukr. **41** E6
also spelt Dnepropetrovsk; *formerly known as* Yekaterinoslav
Dniprorudne Ukr. **41** E7
also spelt Dneprorudnoye
Dnister *r.* Ukr. **41** C6 *see* **Dniester**
Dnistrov'ky Lyman *l.* Ukr. **58** L2
Dno Rus. Fed. **43** K4

Dnyapro r. Belarus 41 D5 see Dnieper
Dnyaprowska-Buhski, Kanal canal Belarus 42 F9
Doa Moz. 131 G3
Doabi Mekh-i-Zarin Afgh. 101 F3
Doaktown Canada 169 H4
Doangdoangan Besar i. Indon. 77 G4
Doangdoangan Kecil i. Indon. 77 G4
Doany Madag. 131 [inset] K2
Doba Chad 126 C2
Doba China see Toiba
Dobasna r. Belarus 43 L9
Dobbertiner Seenlandschaft park Germany 49 J2
Dobbs, Cape Canada 167 O1
Dobczyce Poland 49 R6
Dobele Latvia 42 E5
Döbeln Germany 49 K4
Doberai, Jazirah pen. Indon. 73 H7
English form Doberai Peninsula; formerly known as Vogelkop Peninsula
Doberai Peninsula Indon. see Doberai, Jazirah
Döbern Germany 49 L4
Dobiegniew Poland 49 M3
Doblas Arg. 204 D5
Dobo Indon. 73 H8
Doboj Bos.-Herz. 56 K4
Do Borji Iran 100 C4
Dobra Poland 49 P4
Dobre Miasto Poland 49 R2
Dobrești Romania 58 D2
Dobrich Bulg. 58 I5
formerly known as Tolbukhin
Dobrinka Rus. Fed. 41 G5
Dobříš Czech Rep. 49 L6
Dobromyl' Ukr. 49 T6
Dobrotești Romania 58 F4
Dobrovăț Romania 58 I2
Dobrovol'sk Rus. Fed. 42 D7
Dobroye Rus. Fed. 43 U9
Dobruchi Rus. Fed. 42 I3
Dobrudzhansko Plato plat. Bulg. 58 I5
Dobrun Romania 58 F4
Dobrush Belarus 43 M9
Dobryanka Rus. Fed. 40 K4
Dobryanka Ukr. 43 M9
Dobrynikha Rus. Fed. 43 S6
Dobskie, Jezioro l. Poland 49 S1
Dobson N.Z. 153 F10
Dobson r. N.Z. 153 D12
Dobzha China 89 E6
Doc Can reef Phil. 74 A5
Doce r. Espírito Santo Brazil 203 E6
Doce r. Goiás Brazil 206 B5
Do China Qala Afgh. 101 G4
Doctor Arroyo Mex. 185 E4
Doctor Belisario Domínguez Mex. 184 D2
Doctor Hicks Range hills Australia 151 D6
Doctor Petru Groza Romania see Ștei
Doda Tanz. 129 C6
Dod Ballapur India 94 C3
Dodecanese is Greece 59 I13
also spelt Dodekanisos or Dhodhekánisos
Dodekanisos is Greece see Dodecanese
Dodge Center U.S.A. 174 A2
Dodge City U.S.A. 178 B4
Dodgeville U.S.A. 172 C8
Dodman Point U.K. 47 H13
Dodola Eth. 128 C3

▶Dodoma Tanz. 129 B6
Capital of Tanzania.

Dodoma admin. reg. Tanz. 129 B6
Dodori National Reserve nature res. Kenya 128 D5
Dodsonville U.S.A. 176 B6
Doetinchem Neth. 48 D4
Dofa Indon. 75 C3
Doftana r. Romania 58 G3
Dog r. Canada 168 B3
Dogai Coring salt l. China 89 E5
Dogaicoring Qangco salt l. China 89 E5
Doğanbey Aydın Turkey 59 I11
Doğanbey İzmir Turkey 59 H10
Doğanşehir Turkey 107 D3
Dog Creek Canada 166 F5
Doghārūn Iran 101 E3
Dog Island Canada 169 I1
Dog Lake Man. Canada 167 L5
Dog Lake Ont. Canada 168 B3
Dog Lake Ont. Canada 168 C3
Dognecea Romania 58 C3
Dōgo i. Japan 91 C6
Dogoble well Somalia 128 E2
Dogondoutchi Niger 125 G3
Dogoumbo Chad 126 C2
Dōgo-yama mt. Japan 91 C7
Dog Rocks is Bahamas 186 D1
Doğubeyazıt Turkey 107 F3
Doğu Menteşe Dağları mts Turkey 106 B3
Doguxung Zangbo r. China 89 D6
also known as Raka Zangbo

▶Doha Qatar 105 E2
Capital of Qatar. Also spelt Ad Dawḥah

Dohad India see Dahod
Dohazari Bangl. 78 A3
Dohrighat India 89 C7
Doi i. Fiji 145 H4
also spelt Ndoi
Doi Inthanon National Park Thai. 78 B4
Doi Luang National Park Thai. 78 B4
Doilungdêqên China 89 E6
also known as Namka
Doïranis, Limni l. Greece/Macedonia see Dojran, Lake
Doire U.K. see Londonderry
Doi Saket Thai. 78 B4
Doisanagar India 97 E5
Dois Córregos Brazil 206 E9
Dois Irmãos, Serra dos hills Brazil 202 D4
Dojran, Lake Greece/Macedonia 58 D7
also known as Doïranis, Limni or Dojransko, Ezero
Dojransko Ezero l. Greece/Macedonia see Dojran, Lake
Doka Sudan 121 G6
Dokali Iran 100 C3
Dokhara, Dunes de des. Alg. 123 G2
Dokkum Neth. 48 C2
Dokos i. Greece 59 E11
also spelt Dhokós
Dokri Pak. 101 G5
Dokshukino Rus. Fed. see Nartkala
Dokshytsy Belarus 42 I7
Doksy Czech Rep. 49 L5
Dokuchayeva, Mys c. Rus. Fed. 90 J2
Dokuchayevka Kazakh. 103 F2
Dokuchayevs'k Ukr. 41 F7
formerly known as Olenivs'ki Kar"yery or Yelenovskiye Kar'yery
Dolak, Pulau i. Indon. 73 I8
also known as Yos Sudarso
Dolan Springs U.S.A. 183 J6
Dolavón Arg. 205 D6
Dolbeau Canada 169 F3
Dol-de-Bretagne France 50 E4
Dole France 51 L5
Dolgellau U.K. 47 I11
Dolgeville U.S.A. 177 K2
Dolgiy, Ostrov i. Rus. Fed. 40 K1
Dolgorukovo Rus. Fed. 43 T9
Dolgoye Lipetskaya Oblast' Rus. Fed. 43 U8
Dolgoye Orlovskaya Oblast' Rus. Fed. 43 S9
Dolgusha Rus. Fed. 43 T9
Dolhasca Romania 58 H1
Dolianova Sardegna Italy 57 B9
Dolinsk Rus. Fed. 82 F3
Dolisie Congo see Loubomo

Dolit Indon. 75 C3
Doljevac Srbija Yugo. 58 C5
Dolleman Island Antarctica 222 T2
Dolna Lipnitska Bulg. 58 G5
Dolni Chiflik Bulg. 58 I6
formerly known as Georgi Traykov
Dolni Dŭbnik Bulg. 58 F5
Dolno Kamartsi Bulg. 58 E6
Dolno Levski Bulg. 58 F6
Dolný Kubín Slovakia 49 Q6
Dolo Indon. 75 A3
Dolomites mts Italy 56 D3
also known as Dolomiti or Dolomitiche, Alpi
Dolomiti mts Italy see Dolomites
Dolomiti Bellunesi, Parco Nazionale delle nat. park Italy 56 D2
Dolomitiche, Alpi mts Italy see Dolomites
Dolon, Pereval pass Kyrg. see Dolon Ashuusu
Dolon Ashuusu pass Kyrg. 103 H4
also known as Dolon, Pereval
Dolonnur China see Duolun
Dolo Odo Eth. 128 D3
Doloon Mongolia 85 E2
Dolores Arg. 204 F5
Dolores Guat. 185 H5
Dolores Mex. 184 C3
Dolores Uruguay 204 F4
Dolores r. U.S.A. 183 O3
Dolores Hidalgo Mex. 185 E4
Dolovo Vojvodina, Srbija Yugo. 58 B4
Dolphin, Cape Falkland Is 205 F8
Dolphin and Union Strait Canada 164 H3
Dolphin Head Namibia 130 B5
Dolphin Island Nature Reserve Australia 150 B4
Đô Lương Vietnam 78 D4
Dolzhitsy Rus. Fed. 43 K3
Dom, Gunung mt. Indon. 73 I7
Domaniç Turkey 106 B3
also known as Hisarköy
Domar Bangl. 97 F4
Domartang China see Banbar
Domažlice Czech Rep. 49 J6
Domba China 97 G2
Dombarovskiy Rus. Fed. 102 D2
Dombås Norway 45 J3
Dombe Moz. 131 G3
Dombe Grande Angola 127 B8
Dombegyház Hungary 49 S9
Dombóvár Hungary 49 P9
Dombra Angola 127 C8
Dombrau Poland see Dąbrowa Górnicza
Dombrovitsa Ukr. see Dubrovytsya
Dombrowa Poland see Dąbrowa Górnicza
Dom Cavati Brazil 207 K6
Domda China see Qingshuihe
Dome Argus ice feature Antarctica 223 F1
Dome Charlie ice feature Antarctica 223 H2
also known as Dome Circe
Dome Circe ice feature Antarctica see Dome Charlie
Dome Fuji research station Antarctica 223 C1
Domeikava Lith. 42 E7
Domel Island Myanmar see Letsok-aw Kyun
Dome Rock Mountains U.S.A. 183 J8
Domett, Cape Australia 150 E2
Domett, Mount N.Z. 152 G9
Domeyko Chile 204 C3
Dom Feliciano Brazil 203 A9
Domfront France 50 F4
Domingos Martins Brazil 207 M7
▶Dominica country West Indies 187 H4
northamerica [countries] 158–159
Dominical Costa Rica 186 C5
Dominicana, República country West Indies see Dominican Republic
▶Dominican Republic country West Indies 187 F3
also known as Dominicana, República; historically known as Santo Domingo
northamerica [countries] 158–159
Dominica Passage Dominica/Guadeloupe 187 H4
Dominion, Cape Canada 165 L3
Dominique i. Fr. Polynesia see Hiva Oa
Domiongo Dem. Rep. Congo 126 D6
Dom Joaquim Brazil 207 J5
Domka Bhutan 97 F4
Domnești Romania 58 F3
Domnești Romania 58 G4
Domo Eth. 128 E3
Domodedovo Rus. Fed. 43 S6
Domodossola Italy 56 A2
Domokos Greece 59 D9
also spelt Dhomokós
Domoni Comoros 129 E8
Domozhirovo Rus. Fed. 43 O1
Dom Pedrito Brazil 203 A9
Dom Pedro Brazil 202 C3
Dompu Indon. 77 G5
Domula China 89 C5
Domusnovas Sardegna Italy 57 A9
Domuyo, Volcán vol. Arg. 204 C5
Domville, Mount hill Australia 147 F2
Domžale Slovenia 56 G2
Don r. Australia 149 F3
Don r. India 94 C2
Don Mex. 184 C3

▶Don r. Rus. Fed. 43 U9
5th longest river in Europe.
europe [landscapes] 30–31

Don r. U.K. 46 J6
Don, Xé r. Laos 79 D5
Donadeu Arg. 204 E2
Donald Australia 147 D4
Donaldsonville U.S.A. 175 B6
Donalnes, Cerro mt. Chile 204 C2
Donalsonville U.S.A. 175 C6
Doñana, Parque Nacional de nat. park Spain 54 E8
Donau r. Austria/Germany 49 L7 see Danube
Donaueschingen Germany 48 F8
Donauwörth Germany 48 H7
Don Benito Spain 54 F6
Doncaster U.K. 47 K10
Dondo Angola 127 B7
Dondo Moz. 131 G3
Dondo, Tanjung pt Indon. 75 B2
Dondo, Teluk b. Indon. 75 B2
Dondonay i. Phil. 74 B4
Dondra Head Sri Lanka 94 D5
Donegal Rep. of Ireland 47 D9
Donegal Bay Rep. of Ireland 47 D9
Dönenbay Kazakh. see Dunenbay
Donets'k Ukr. 41 F7
formerly known as Stalino or Yuzovka
Donets'kyy Kryazh hills Rus. Fed./Ukr. 41 F6
Donfoss Norway 45 J3
Donga r. Cameroon/Nigeria 125 H4
Donga Nigeria 125 H5
Dong'an China 87 D3
also known as Baiyashi
Dongara Australia 151 A6
Dongargaon India 94 D1
Dongargarh India 96 D5
Dongbatu China 84 B3
Dongbo China see Mêdog
Dongchuan China 86 B3
formerly known as Xincun
Dongchuan China see Yao'an
Dongco China 89 D5
also known as Cêringgolêb
Dong Co l. China 89 D5
Dongcun China see Haiyang
Dongcun China see Lanxian

Dong'e China 85 H4
also known as Tongcheng
Dongfang China 87 D5
also known as Basuo
Dongfanghong China 82 D3
Dongfeng China 82 B4
Donggala Indon. 75 A3
Donggang China 83 B5
formerly known as Dadong or Donggou
Donggi Cona l. China 84 C5
Donggou China see Donggang
Donggu China 87 E3
Dongguan China 87 E4
Đông Hà Vietnam 78 D4
Donghai China 87 F1
also known as Niushan
Dong Hai sea N. Pacific Ocean see East China Sea
Donghai Dao i. China 87 D4
Dong He r. China 86 C2
Dong He watercourse China 84 D3
Đông Hồi Vietnam 78 D4
Dong Jiang r. China 87 E4
Dongjingcheng China 82 C3
Dongkait, Tanjung pt Indon. 75 A3
Dongkou China 87 D3
Donglan China 87 C3
Dongle China 84 D4
Dongliao r. China 85 I3
Donglük China 88 E4
Dongmen China see Luocheng
Dongming China 85 G5
Dongning China 82 C3
Dongo Angola 127 B8
Dongo Italy 56 B2
Dongobesh Tanz. 129 B6
Dongola Sudan 121 F5
Dongotona Mountains Sudan 128 B3
Dongou Congo 126 C4
Dong Phraya Fai mts Thai. 78 C4
Dong Phraya Yen esc. Thai. 79 C5
Dongping Guangdong China 87 E4
Dongping Shandong China 85 H5
Dongping Hu l. China 85 H4
Dongpo China see Meishan
Dongqiao China 89 E6
Dongshan Fujian China 87 F4
also known as Xibu
Dongshan China see Jiangning
Dongshan Jiangsu China 87 G2
Dongshan China see Shangyou
Dongshao China 87 E3
Dongsha Qundao is China 81 J8
English form Pratas Islands
Dongsheng China 85 F4
Dongshuan China see Tangdan
Dongtai China 87 G1
Dongtai r. China 87 G1
Dongting Hu l. China 84 B4
Dongting Hu l. China 87 E2
Dongtou China 87 G3
also known as Bei'ao
Donguena Angola 127 B9
Donguila Gabon 126 A4
Dong Ujimqin Qi China see Uliastai
Dongxiang China see Xuanhan
Dongxiangzu China see Xiaonan
Dongxing China 82 B3
Dongyang China 87 G2
Dongying China 85 H4
Dongzhen China 84 D4
Dongzhi China 87 F2
Doniphan U.S.A. 174 B4
Donja Dubnica Kosovo, Srbija Yugo. 58 C6
Donjek r. Canada 166 A2
Donji Miholjac Croatia 56 K3
Donji Milanovac Srbija Yugo. 58 D4
Donji Vakuf Bos.-Herz. 56 J4
also known as Srbobran
Donji Zemunik Croatia 56 H4
Donkerpoort S. Africa 133 J7
Donmanick Islands Bangl. 97 F5
Dønna i. Norway 44 K2
Donnacona Canada 169 G4
Donnelly Canada 167 G4
Donnellys Crossing N.Z. 152 H3
Donner Pass U.S.A. 182 D2
Donnersberg hill Germany 48 E6
Donnybrook Australia 151 A7
Donostia - San Sebastián Spain 55 J1
Donousa Greece 59 G11
Donousa i. Greece 59 G11
Donovan U.S.A. 172 F10
Donskoy Rus. Fed. 43 T8
Donskoye Lipetskaya Oblast' Rus. Fed. 43 T9
formerly known as Vodopyanovo
Donskoye Stavropol'skiy Kray Rus. Fed. 41 G7
Donsol Phil. 74 B3
Donthami r. Myanmar 78 B4
Donzenac France 50 H7
Doomadgee Australia 148 C3
Doomadgee Aboriginal Reserve Australia 148 C3
Doon Doon Aboriginal Reserve Australia 150 E3
Door Peninsula U.S.A. 172 F6
Dooxo Nugaaleed valley Somalia 128 F2
Do Qu r. China 86 B2
Dor watercourse Afgh. 101 E4
also known as Pudai
Dor Rus. Fed. 43 Q6
Dora, Lake salt flat Australia 150 C4
Dorado Mex. 184 D3
Do Rāhak Iran 100 B5
Dorah Pass Pak. 101 G2
Doramarkog China 86 A1
Doran Lake Canada 167 I2
Dora Riparia r. Italy 51 N7
D'Orbigny Bol. 201 E5
Dorbiljin China see Emin
Dorbod China see Taikang
Dorbod Qi China see Ulan Hua
Đorče Petrov Macedonia 58 C6
Dorchester U.K. 47 J13
Dordabis Namibia 130 C4
Dordogne r. France 51 F7
Dordrecht Neth. 48 B4
Dordrecht S. Africa 133 L8
Doré Lake Canada 167 J4
Doré Lake l. Canada 167 J4
Dores de Guanhães Brazil 207 K6
Dores do Indaiá Brazil 203 C6
Dorey Mali 125 E3
Dorfen Germany 48 J7
Dorfmark Germany 48 G3
Dorgali Sardegna Italy 57 B8
Dörgön Mongolia 84 B1
Dori r. Afgh. 101 F4
Dori Burkina 125 E3
Doring r. S. Africa 132 C8
Doring r. S. Africa 132 D9
Doringbaai S. Africa 132 C8
Doringbos S. Africa 132 D8
Dorisvale Australia 148 A2
Dormaa-Ahenkro Ghana 124 E5
Dormans France 51 J3
Dormidontovka Rus. Fed. 82 D3
Dornakal India 94 D2
Dornbirn Austria 48 G8
Dornoch U.K. 46 H6
Dornoch Firth est. U.K. 46 H6
Dornod prov. Mongolia 85 G1
Dornogovĭ prov. Mongolia 85 F2
Doro Mali 125 E2
Dorobanțu Romania 58 H4
Dorobino Rus. Fed. 43 S8
Dorog Hungary 49 P8
Dorogobuzh Rus. Fed. 43 O7
Dorohoi Romania 53 H2

Dorokhovo Rus. Fed. 43 R6
Dorokhsh Iran 101 D3
Döröö Nuur salt l. Mongolia 84 B2
Dorostol Bulg. see Silistra
Dorotea Sweden 44 L2
Dorowa Zimbabwe 131 F3
Dorpat Estonia see Tartu
Dorre Island Australia 151 A5
Dorrigo Australia 147 G2
Dorris U.S.A. 180 B4
Dorsale Camerounaise slope Cameroon/Nigeria 125 H5
Dorset Canada 173 O5
Dorsoidong Co l. China 89 E5
Dortmund Germany 48 E4
Dorton U.S.A. 176 C8
Dörtyol Turkey 106 D3
Doruma Dem. Rep. Congo 126 E3
Dorūneh Iran 100 D3
Dorylaeum Turkey see Eskişehir
Do Sārī Iran 100 D4
Dos Bahías, Cabo c. Arg. 205 D7
Dos Cabezas Mountains U.S.A. 183 O9
Dos de Mayo Peru 198 C6
Doshakh, Koh-i- mt. Afgh. 101 E3
Dos Hermanas Spain 54 F7
Dos Lagunos Guat. 185 H5
Đo Son Vietnam 78 D3
Dos Palos U.S.A. 182 D5
Dospat Bulg. 58 F7
Dospat r. Bulg. 58 F7
Dos Pozos Arg. 205 D6
Dosse r. Germany 49 J3
Dosso Niger 125 F3
Dosso dept Niger 125 F3
Dosso, Réserve Partielle de nature res. Niger 125 F3
Dossor Kazakh. 102 C3
Dostyk Kazakh. 88 C2
also spelt Dostyq; formerly known as Druzhba
Dostyq Kazakh. see Dostyk
Dothan U.S.A. 175 C6
Dötlingen Germany 48 F3
Douai France 51 J2
Douako Guinea 124 C4
Douala Cameroon 125 H5
Douala-Edéa, Réserve nature res. Cameroon 125 H6
Douarnenez France 50 B4
Douarnenez, Baie de b. France 50 B4
Double Headed Shot Cays is Bahamas 186 C2
Double Island Hong Kong China 87 [inset]
also known as Wong Wan Chau
Double Island Point Australia 149 G5
Double Mountain Fork r. U.S.A. 179 B5
Double Peak U.S.A. 182 F6
Double Point Australia 149 E3
Double Springs U.S.A. 174 C5
Doubs r. France/Switz. 51 L6
Doubtful Bay Australia 150 D2
Doubtful Island Bay Australia 151 B7
Doubtful Sound N.Z. 153 B13
Doué-la-Fontaine France 50 F5
Douentza Mali 124 E3
Dougga tourist site Tunisia 123 H1
Doughboy Bay N.Z. 153 B15

▶Douglas Isle of Man 47 H9
Capital of the Isle of Man.

Douglas N.Z. 152 I7
Douglas S. Africa 132 H6
Douglas AZ U.S.A. 181 E7
Douglas GA U.S.A. 175 D6
Douglas WY U.S.A. 180 F4
Douglas Apsley National Park Australia 147 F5
Douglas Channel Canada 166 D4
Douglas City U.S.A. 182 B1
Douglas Creek watercourse Australia 146 C2
Douglas Creek r. U.S.A. 183 P1
Douglas Range mts Antarctica 222 T2
Douglas Reef i. Japan see Okino-Tori-shima
Douglasville U.S.A. 175 C5
Dougoulé well Niger 125 H3
Douhi Chad 120 C5
Douhudi China see Gong'an
Doukato, Akra pt Greece 59 B10
Doulaincourt-Saucourt France 51 L4
Douliu Taiwan see Touliu
Doullens France 51 I2
Doumè Benin 125 F4
Doumé Cameroon 125 I5
Doumé r. Cameroon 125 I5
Doumen China 87 E4
also known as Jing'an
Douna Mali 125 E3
Dounkassa Benin 125 F4
Doupovské Hory mts Czech Rep. 49 K5
Dourada, Cachoeira waterfall Brazil 206 D5
Dourada, Serra hills Brazil 206 C3
Dourada, Serra mts Brazil 202 B5
Dourados Brazil 203 A7
Dourados r. Brazil 203 A7
Dourados, Serra dos hills Brazil 203 A7
Dourbali Chad 126 B2
Dourdou r. France 51 I8
Dourdoura Chad 126 D2
Douro r. Port. 54 C3
also spelt Duero (Spain)
Doushi China see Gong'an
Doushui Shuiku resr China 87 E3
Doutor Camargo Brazil 206 A10
Douve r. France 50 E3
Douz Tunisia 123 H2
Douze r. France 50 F9
Douziat Chad 120 C6
Dove r. U.K. 47 K11
Dove Brook Canada 169 J2
Dove Bugt b. Greenland 165 Q2
Dove Creek U.S.A. 183 P4
Dover U.K. 47 N12
historically known as Dubris

▶Dover DE U.S.A. 177 J6
State capital of Delaware.

Dover NH U.S.A. 177 O2
Dover NJ U.S.A. 177 K5
Dover OH U.S.A. 176 D5
Dover TN U.S.A. 174 C4
Dover, Point Australia 151 D7
Dover, Strait of France/U.K. 50 H2
also known as Pas de Calais
Dover-Foxcroft U.S.A. 174 G2
Dover Plains U.S.A. 177 L4
Dovey r. U.K. see Dyfi
Doveyrīch, Rūd-e r. Iran/Iraq 107 G5
Dovnsklint cliff Denmark 48 H1
Dovrefjell mts Norway 44 J3
Dovrefjell Nasjonalpark nat. park Norway 44 J3
Dow, Lake Botswana see Xau, Lake
Dowa Malawi 129 B8
Dowagiac U.S.A. 172 G9
Dowgha'i Iran 100 D2
Dowi, Tanjung pt Indon. 76 B2
Dowlatābād Afgh. 101 F2
Dowlatābād Fārs Iran 100 B4
Dowlatābād Fārs Iran 100 C4
Dowlatābād Khorāsan Iran 100 D2
Dowlatābād Khorāsan Iran 101 D3
Dowlatābād Khorāsan Iran 101 E2
Dowl at Yār Afgh. 101 F3
Downey CA U.S.A. 182 F8
Downey IA U.S.A. 172 B9
Downham Market U.K. 47 M11
Downieville U.S.A. 182 D2

Downpatrick U.K. 47 G9
Downs U.S.A. 178 C4
Downsville NY U.S.A. 177 K3
Downsville WI U.S.A. 172 B6
Downton, Mount Canada 166 E4
Dow Rūd Iran 100 B3
Dow Sar Iran 100 A3
Dowshī Afgh. 101 G3
Dowsk Belarus 43 L8
Dowzha Belarus 43 L6
Doyle U.S.A. 182 D1
Doyles Canada 169 J4
Doyrentsi Bulg. 58 F5
Dozdān r. Iran 100 D5
Dōzen is Japan 91 C6
Dozois, Réservoir Canada 168 E4
Dozulé France 50 F3
Drâa, Oued watercourse Morocco 122 C3
Dracena Brazil 206 B8
Drachkava Belarus 42 J8
Drachten Neth. 48 D2
Dragalina Romania 58 I4
Dragan l. Sweden 44 K2
Drăgănești-Olt Romania 58 F4
Drăgănești-Vlașca Romania 58 G4
Drăgășani Romania 58 F4
Dragboender S. Africa 132 G6
Dragoman Bulg. 58 D6
Dragonada i. Greece 59 H13
also spelt Dhragonádha
Dragonera, Isla i. Spain see Sa Dragonera
Dragones Arg. 201 E5
Dragonisi i. Greece 59 G11
also known as Dhragónisos
Dragon Rocks Nature Reserve Australia 151 B7
Dragon's Mouths strait Trin. and Tob./Venez. 187 H5
Dragoon U.S.A. 183 N9
Dragør Denmark 45 K5
Dragoș Vodă Romania 58 I4
Dragsfjärd Fin. 45 M3
Draguignan France 51 M9
Drăgușeni Romania 58 I3
Drahichyn Belarus 42 G9
also spelt Drogichin
Drakensberg mts Lesotho/S. Africa 133 M6
Drakensberg mts S. Africa 131 F5
Drakensberg Garden S. Africa 133 N6
Draken's Rock mt. S. Africa 133 M7
Drakes Bay U.S.A. 182 A4
Drakulya r. Ukr. 58 K3
Drama Greece 58 F7
Drammen Norway 45 J4
Drang, Prêk r. Cambodia 79 D5
Drangajökull ice cap Iceland 44 [inset] B2
Drangedal Norway 45 J4
Drangme Chhu r. Bhutan 97 F4
Dranov, Lacul l. Romania 58 K4
Dranske Germany 49 K1
Draper U.S.A. 183 M1
Draper, Mount U.S.A. 166 B3
Drapsaca Afgh. see Kondūz
Dras Jammu and Kashmir 96 B2
Drau r. Austria 49 L9
also spelt Drava or Dráva
Drava r. Croatia/Slovenia 49 N9
also spelt Drau or Dráva
Dráva r. Hungary 56 K3
also spelt Drau or Drava
Dravinja r. Slovenia 56 H2
Dravograd Slovenia 56 H2
Drawa r. Poland 49 M3
Drawieński Park Narodowy nat. park Poland 49 M2
Drawno Poland 49 M2
Drawsko, Jezioro l. Poland 49 N2
Drawsko Pomorskie Poland 49 M2
Drayton Valley Canada 167 H4
Drebber Germany 48 F3
Dreieich Germany 48 F5
Dreistelzberge hill Germany 48 G5
Drenovci Croatia 56 K4
Drenovets Bulg. 58 D5
Drepano, Akra pt Greece 59 E9
Dresden Canada 173 K8
Dresden Germany 49 K4
Dresden U.S.A. 174 B4
Dretun' Belarus 43 K6
Dreux France 50 H4
Drevsjø Norway 45 K3
Drewryville U.S.A. 177 H9
Drezdenko Poland 49 M3
Drīceni Latvia 42 I5
Driďža l. Latvia 42 I6
Driftwood U.S.A. 176 G4
Driggs U.S.A. 180 E4
Drillham Australia 149 F5
Drin r. Albania 58 A6
Drina r. Bos.-Herz./Yugo. 56 L4
Drincea r. Romania 58 D4
Drini i Zi r. Albania 58 B6
Drinit, Gjiri i b. Albania 58 A7
Drino r. Albania 59 B8
Driscoll Island Antarctica 222 O1
Drissa Belarus see Vyerkhnyadzvinsk
Drniš Croatia 56 I5
Drobeta - Turnu Severin Romania 58 D4
also known as Turnu Severin
Drochtersen Germany 48 G2
Drogheda Rep. of Ireland 47 F10
also known as Droichead Átha
Drogichin Belarus see Drahichyn
Drogobych Ukr. see Drohobych
Drohiczyn Poland 49 T3
Drohobych Ukr. 53 G2
also spelt Drogobych
Droichead Átha Rep. of Ireland see Drogheda
Droitwich U.K. 47 J11
Dronne r. France 50 F7
Dronning Ingrid Land reg. Greenland 165 O3
Dronning Louise Land reg. Greenland 165 Q2
Dronning Maud Land reg. Antarctica see Queen Maud Land
Droogmakerij de Beemster tourist site Neth. 48 B3
Dropt r. France 50 F8
Drosh Pak. 101 G3
Drosia Greece 59 E10
also spelt Dhrosiá
Droskovo Rus. Fed. 43 S9
Drovyanaya Rus. Fed. 85 G1
Drowning r. Canada 168 C3
Drūkšių ežeras l. Belarus/Lith. 42 H6
also known as Drysyvaty Vozyera
Druk-Yul country Asia see Bhutan
Drumheller Canada 167 H5
Drummond atoll Kiribati see Tabiteuea
Drummond, Lake U.S.A. 177 I9
Drummond Island Kiribati see McKean
Drummond Island U.S.A. 173 J5
Drummond Range hills Australia 149 E5
Drummondville Canada 169 F4
Drummore U.K. 47 H9
Drumnadrochit U.K. 46 H6
Drury Lake Canada 166 C2
Druskieniki Lith. see Druskininkai
Druskininkai Lith. 42 F8
formerly known as Druskieniki
Drusti Latvia 42 G4
Druts' r. Belarus 43 L8
Druya Belarus 42 I6
Druzhba Kazakh. see Dostyk
Druzhba Ukr. 43 O9
Druzhina Rus. Fed. 39 O3
Druzhnoye, Ozero l. Rus. Fed. 43 S1
Druzhnaya Gorka Rus. Fed. 43 L2
Druzhylavichy Belarus 42 G9
Drwęca r. Poland 49 P2

Dry r. Australia 148 B2
Dryanovo Bulg. 58 G6
Dryazhno Rus. Fed. 43 J3
Dry Bay U.S.A. 166 B3
Dryberry Lake Canada 168 A3
Drybin Belarus 43 M7
Dry Cimarron r. U.S.A. 178 B4
Dryden Canada 168 A3
Dryden NY U.S.A. 177 I3
Dryden VA U.S.A. 176 C9
Dry Fork r. U.S.A. 180 F4
Drygalski Fjord inlet S. Georgia 205 [inset]
Drygalski Ice Tongue Antarctica 223 L1
Drygalski Island Antarctica 223 G2
Drygarn Fawr hill U.K. 47 I11
Dry Harts r. S. Africa 133 I4
Dry Lake U.S.A. 183 J5
Dry Lake l. U.S.A. 182 G2
Dry Ridge U.S.A. 176 A7
Drysa r. Belarus 43 I6
Drysdale r. Australia 150 D2
Drysdale Island Australia 148 B1
Drysdale River National Park Australia 150 D2
Drysyvaty Vozyera l. Belarus/Lith. see Drūkšių ežeras
Dry Tortugas is U.S.A. 175 D7
Drzewica Poland 49 R4
Dschang Cameroon 125 H5
Dua r. Dem. Rep. Congo 126 D4
Dūāb r. Iran 100 B3
Du'an China 87 D4
also known as Anyang
Duancun China see Wuxiang
Duaringa Australia 149 F4
Duars reg. India 97 F4
Duarte, Pico mt. Dom. Rep. 187 F3
formerly known as Trujillo, Monte
Dubā Saudi Arabia 104 A2
Dubai U.A.E. 105 F2
also spelt Dubayy
Dubakella Mountain U.S.A. 182 A1
Dubăsari Moldova 58 K1
formerly spelt Dubesar' or Dubossary
Dubăsari prov. Moldova 53 H2
Dubawnt r. Canada 167 L2
Dubawnt Lake Canada 167 K2
Dubayy U.A.E. see Dubai
Dubbagh, Jabal ad mt. Saudi Arabia 104 A2
Dubbo Australia 147 F3
Dube r. Liberia 124 D5
Dübendorf Switz. 51 O5
Dübener Heide park Germany 49 J4
Dubesar' Moldova see Dubăsari
Dubets Rus. Fed. 43 T3
Dubičiai Lith. 42 F7
Dubinës, Maja e mt. Albania 58 A6
Dubingiai Lith. 42 G6
Dublán Mex. 184 D2
Dublin Canada 172 F2

▶Dublin Rep. of Ireland 47 F10
Capital of the Republic of Ireland. Also known as Baile Átha Cliath.

Dublin GA U.S.A. 175 D5
Dublin VA U.S.A. 176 E8
Dubna r. Latvia 42 H5
Dubna Moskovskaya Oblast' Rus. Fed. 43 S5
Dubna Tul'skaya Oblast' Rus. Fed. 43 R7
Dubnica nad Váhom Slovakia 49 P7
Dubno Ukr. 41 C6
Dubois U.S.A. 180 D3
Du Bois U.S.A. 176 G4
Dubossary Moldova see Dubăsari
Dubovaya Roshcha Rus. Fed. 43 R8
Dubovka Tul'skaya Oblast' Rus. Fed. 43 T8
Dubovka Volgogradskaya Oblast' Rus. Fed. 41 H6
Dubovoye, Ozero l. Rus. Fed. 43 V6
Dubovskoye Rus. Fed. 41 G7
Dūbrar Pass Azer. 107 G2
Dubréka Guinea 124 B4
Dubris U.K. see Dover
Dubrovichi Rus. Fed. 43 U7
Dubrovka Bryanskaya Oblast' Rus. Fed. 43 O8
Dubrovka Pskovskaya Oblast' Rus. Fed. 43 J5
Dubrovka Pskovskaya Oblast' Rus. Fed. 43 K4
Dubrovnik Croatia 56 K6
historically known as Ragusa
Dubrovytsya Ukr. 41 C6
formerly known as Dombrovitsa
Dubrowna Belarus 43 L7
Dubun Kazakh. 103 J4
Dubuque U.S.A. 174 B3
Dubysa r. Lith. 42 E6
Duc de Gloucester, Îles du is Fr. Polynesia 221 I7
English form Duke of Gloucester Islands
Ducey France 50 E4
Duchang China 87 F2
Duchateau Entrance sea chan. P.N.G. 149 G1
Ducherow Germany 49 K2
Duchesne U.S.A. 183 N1
Duchesne r. U.S.A. 183 O1
Duchess Australia 148 C4
Duchess Canada 167 I5
Ducie Island Pitcairn Is 221 J7
Duck r. U.S.A. 174 C4
Duck Bay Canada 167 K4
Duck Creek r. Australia 150 B4
Duck Lake Canada 167 J4
Duck Valley Indian Reservation res. U.S.A. 180 C4
Duckwater U.S.A. 183 I3
Duckwater Peak U.S.A. 183 I3
Đức Trọng Vietnam 79 E6
Duda r. Col. 198 C4
Duderstadt Germany 48 H4
Dudești Vechi Romania 58 B2
Dudhi India 97 D4
Dudinka Rus. Fed. 39 I3
Dudley U.K. 47 J11
Dudleyville U.S.A. 183 N9
Dudna r. India 94 C2
Dudorovskiy Rus. Fed. 43 Q8
Duduza S. Africa 133 M3
Duékoué Côte d'Ivoire 124 D5
Duen, Bukit vol. Indon. 76 C3
Dueré Brazil 202 B4
Duerna r. Spain 54 F2
Duero r. Spain 55 E3
also spelt Douro (Portugal)
Dufault, Lac l. Canada 173 O2
Dufferin, Cape Canada 168 E1
Duffer Peak U.S.A. 180 C4
Duffield U.S.A. 176 C9
Duff Islands Solomon Is 145 F2
Duffreboy, Lac l. Canada 169 G1
Dufftown U.K. 46 I6
Dufourspitze mt. Italy/Switz. 56 A3
Dufrost Canada 167 L5
Dugab Uzbek. 103 F5
also spelt Dughoba
Dugald r. Australia 149 D3
Duga Resa Croatia 56 H3
Duga-Zapadnaya, Mys c. Rus. Fed. 39 O4
Dugdash mts Saudi Arabia 109 H8
Dughoba Uzbek. see Dugab
Dugi Otok i. Croatia 56 H4
Dugi Rat Croatia 56 I5
Dugna Rus. Fed. 43 R7
Dugopolje Croatia 56 I5
Dugo Selo Croatia 56 I3
Dugui Qarag China 85 F4
Düğüncübaşı Turkey 58 I7
Dugway U.S.A. 183 L1
Du He r. China 87 D1

D E

Duhūn Tārsū mts Chad/Libya 120 C4
Duida-Marahuaca, Parque Nacional nat. park Venez. 199 E4
Duifken Point Australia 149 D2
Duisburg Germany 48 D4
Duitama Col. 198 C3
Dujiangyan China 86 B2
formerly known as Guanxian
Dukān Dam Iraq 107 F4
Dukat Rus. Fed. 39 P3
Dukat mt. Yugo. 58 D6
Dukathole S. Africa 133 K7
Dukat i Ri Albania 59 A8
Duke Island U.S.A. 166 D4
Duke of Clarence atoll Tokelau see Nukunonu
Duke of Gloucester Islands Fr. Polynesia see Duc de Gloucester, Îles du
Duke of York atoll Tokelau see Atafu
Duk Fadiat Sudan 128 A3
Duk Faiwil Sudan 128 A3
Dukhān Qatar 105 E2
Dukhnah Saudi Arabia 104 C2
Dukhovnitskoye Rus. Fed. 102 B1
Dukhovshchina Rus. Fed. 43 N6
Dukhovshehinskaya Vozvyshennost' hills Rus. Fed. 43 M6
Duki Rus. Fed. 82 D2
Duki r. Rus. Fed. 82 D2
Dukku Nigeria 125 H4
Dukla Poland 49 S6
Dukou China see Panzhihua
Dūkštas Lith. 42 H6
Dukwe Botswana 131 E4
Dulaanhaan Mongolia 85 E1
Dulac U.S.A. 175 B6
Dulan China 84 C4
also known as Qagan Us
Dulawan Phil. see Datu Piang
Dulce r. Arg. 204 E3
Dulce r. Spain 55 I4
Dulce U.S.A. 181 F5
Dulce, Golfo b. Costa Rica 186 C5
Dulce Nombre de Culmí Hond. 186 B4
Dulcinea Chile 204 C2
Dul'durga Rus. Fed. 85 G1
Dulgalakh r. Rus. Fed. 39 N3
Dŭlgopol Bulg. 58 I5
Dulhunty r. Australia 149 D1
Dulishi Hu salt l. China 89 C5
Dulit, Pegunungan mts Sarawak Malaysia 77 F2
Duliu Jiang r. China 87 D3
Duljugan Point Phil. 74 C4
Dullabchara India 97 G4
Dullstroom S. Africa 133 O2
Dülmen Germany 48 E4
Dulovka Rus. Fed. 43 J4
Dulovo Bulg. 58 I5
Duluth U.S.A. 174 A2
Dulyapino Rus. Fed. 43 V4
Dūmā Syria 109 H4
Dumago Bone National Park Indon. 75 B2
Dumaguete Phil. 74 B4
Dumai Indon. 76 C2
Dumanquilas Bay Phil. 74 B5
Dumaran i. Phil. 74 B4
Dumarchen i. Indon. 75 C1
Dumaresq r. Australia 147 F2
Dumas AR U.S.A. 174 B5
Dumas TX U.S.A. 179 B5
Ḑumayr Syria 107 D4
Ḑumayr, Jabal mts Syria 109 H4
Dumbarton U.K. 46 H8
Dumbe S. Africa 133 O4
Dumbéa New Caledonia 145 F4
Ďumbier mt. Slovakia 49 Q7
Dumbleyung Australia 151 B7
Dumbleyung, Lake salt flat Australia 151 B7
Dumbo Cameroon 125 H5
Dumbrăveni Romania 58 F2
Dumbrăveni Romania 58 I3
Dumbrăvița Romania 58 G3
Dumdum i. Indon. 77 D2
Dum Duma India 97 G4
Dumeşti Romania 58 I2
Dumfries U.K. 47 I8
Duminichi Kaluzhskaya Oblast' Rus. Fed. 43 Q8
Duminichi Kaluzhskaya Oblast' Rus. Fed. 43 Q8
Dumitra Romania 58 F1
Dumka India 97 E4
Dummagudem India 94 D2
Dümmer, Naturpark nature res. Germany 48 F3
Dummerstorf Germany 49 J2
Dumoga Indon. 75 C2
Dumoine r. Canada 168 E4
Dumoine, Lac l. Canada 173 P4
Dumont, Lac l. Canada 173 Q4
Dumont d'Urville research station Antarctica 223 J2
Dumont d'Urville Sea Antarctica 223 I2
Dumraon India 97 E4
Dumsuk i. Saudi Arabia 104 C4
Dumyât Egypt 121 F2
English form Damietta
Dumyât governorate Egypt 108 C6
Dumyât, Masabb est. Egypt 108 C6
Duna r. Hungary 49 P9 see Danube
Dünaburg Latvia see Daugavpils
Dunaföldvár Hungary 49 P9
Dunaj r. Slovakia 49 O8 see Danube
Dunajec r. Poland 49 R5
Dunajská Streda Slovakia 49 O8
Dunajs'ki Plavni nature res. Ukr. 58 K3
Dunakeszi Hungary 49 Q8
Dunanbay Kazakh. see Dunenbay
Dunany Point Rep. of Ireland 47 F10
Dunapataj Hungary 49 Q9
Dunărea r. Romania 58 J3 see Danube
Dunării, Delta Romania see Danube Delta
Dunaszekcső Hungary 49 P9
Dunaújváros Hungary 49 P9
formerly known as Sztálinváros
Dunav r. Bulg./Croatia/Yugo. 58 H5 see Danube
Dunavtsi Bulg. 58 D5
Dunay Rus. Fed. 90 C3
Dunay r. Ukr. 58 J3 see Danube
Dunay, Ostrova is Rus. Fed. 39 M2
Dunayivtsi Ukr. 41 C6
Dunback N.Z. 153 E13
Dunbar Australia 149 D3
Dunbar PA U.S.A. 176 F6
Dunbar WI U.S.A. 172 E5
Dunbar WV U.S.A. 176 D7
Dunbeath U.K. 46 I5
Duncan Canada 166 F5
Duncan AZ U.S.A. 181 E6
Duncan OK U.S.A. 179 C5
Duncan, Cape Canada 168 D2
Duncan Lake B.C. Canada 167 G5
Duncan Lake N.W.T. Canada 167 H2
Duncannon U.S.A. 177 H5
Duncan Passage India 95 G4
Duncansby Head U.K. 46 I5
Duncan Town Bahamas 186 E2
Dundaga Latvia 42 D4
Dundalk Rep. of Ireland 47 F9
also spelt Dún Dealgan
Dundalk U.S.A. 177 I6
Dundalk Bay Rep. of Ireland 47 F10
Dundas Canada 173 N7
Dundas Greenland 165 M2
also known as Uummannaq
Dundas, Lake salt flat Australia 151 C7
Dundas Island Canada 166 D4
Dundas Nature Reserve Australia 151 C7
Dundas Peninsula Canada 165 H2
Dundas Strait Australia 148 A1
Dundbürd Mongolia 85 F2
Dún Dealgan Rep. of Ireland see Dundalk
Dundee S. Africa 133 O5
Dundee U.K. 46 J7
Dundee U.S.A. 177 I3
Dundgovĭ prov. Mongolia 85 E2
Dund Hot China 85 H3
also known as Xulun Hoh Qi or Zhenglan Qi
Dundoo Australia 147 E1
Dundrum Bay U.K. 47 G9
Dundwa Range mts India/Nepal 97 D4
Dune, Lac l. Canada 169 F1
Dunedin N.Z. 153 E13
Dunedin U.S.A. 175 D6
Dunenbay Kazakh. 103 J2
also spelt Dönenbay; formerly spelt Dunanbay
Dunfermline U.K. 46 I7
Dungannon U.K. 47 F9
Dún Garbhán Rep. of Ireland see Dungarvan
Dungargarh India 96 B3
Dungarpur India 96 B5
Dungarvan Rep. of Ireland 47 E11
also spelt Dún Garbhán
Dung Co l. China 89 E6
Dungeness hd U.K. 47 M13
Dungeness, Punta pt Arg. 205 C9
Dungu Dem. Rep. Congo 126 F4
Dungun Malaysia 76 C1
formerly known as Kuala Dungun
Dungunab Sudan 104 B3
Dunhou China see Ji'an
Dunhua China 82 C4
Dunhuang China 84 B3
Dunkeld Australia 149 F5
Dunkeld U.K. 46 I7
Dunkerque France see Dunkirk
Dunkirk France 51 I1
also spelt Dunkerque
Dunkirk U.S.A. 176 F3
Dunkwa Ghana 125 E5
Dún Laoghaire Rep. of Ireland 47 F10
Dunlap IA U.S.A. 178 D3
Dunlap IN U.S.A. 172 H9
Dunlap TN U.S.A. 174 C5
Dunluce tourist site U.K. 47 F8
Dunmanway Rep. of Ireland 47 C12
Dunmarra Australia 148 B3
Dunmore PA U.S.A. 177 J4
Dunmore WV U.S.A. 176 F7
Dunmore Town Bahamas 186 D1
Dunn U.S.A. 174 E5
Dunnet Head U.K. 46 I5
Dunnigan U.S.A. 182 C3
Dunning U.S.A. 178 B3
Dunn Rock Nature Reserve Australia 151 B7
Dunnville Canada 173 N8
Dunolly Australia 147 D4
Dunphy U.S.A. 183 H1
Duns U.K. 46 J8
Dunsandel N.Z. 153 G11
Dunsborough Australia 151 A7
Dunsmuir U.S.A. 180 B4
Dunstan Mountains N.Z. 153 D13
Duntroon N.Z. 153 E12
Dunvegan U.K. 46 F6
Dunvegan Lake Canada 167 J2
Dunyapur Pak. 101 G4
Duobukur r. China 85 J1
Duolun China 85 H3
also known as Dolonnur
Dupadu India 94 C3
Dupang Ling mts China 87 D3
Duparquet Canada 173 N2
Duparquet, Lac l. Canada 173 N2
Duperré Alg. see Aïn Defla
Dupnitsa Bulg. 58 E6
formerly known as Stanke Dimitrov
Dupree U.S.A. 178 B2
Dupuy, Cape Australia 150 A4
Duqaylah i. Saudi Arabia 104 C4
Duque de Bragança Angola see Calandula
Duque de Caxias Brazil 207 J9
Duque de York, Isla i. Chile 205 B8
Duquette U.S.A. 172 A4
Dura r. Eth. 128 C2
Dūrā West Bank 108 G6
Durack r. Australia 150 D2
Durack Range hills Australia 150 D3
Dura Europos Syria see Aş Şālihīyah
Durağan Turkey 106 C2
Durance r. France 51 K9
Durand MI U.S.A. 173 J8
Durand WI U.S.A. 172 B6
Duranes hill Spain 54 G6
Durango Baja California Norte Mex. 183 I9
Durango Durango Mex. 184 D3
Durango state Mex. 184 D3
Durango Spain 55 I1
Durango U.S.A. 181 F5
Durani reg. Afgh. 101 F4
Durankulak Bulg. 58 J5
Duranno, Monte mt. Italy 56 E2
Durant IA U.S.A. 172 C9
Durant MS U.S.A. 175 B5
Durant OK U.S.A. 179 C5
Duratón r. Spain 54 G3
Durazno Arg. 204 C3
Durazno Uruguay 204 F4
Durazzo Albania see Durrës
Durban S. Africa 133 P6
Durban-Corbières France 51 I10
Durbanville S. Africa 132 C10
Durbin U.S.A. 176 F7
Durbuy Belgium 51 L2
Dúrcal Spain 55 H8
Đurđevac Croatia 56 J2
Durdura, Raas pt Somalia 128 F2
Düre China 84 A2
Düren Germany 48 D5
Dūren Iran 100 D3
Duren, Kūh-e mt. Iran 100 D3
Durg India 97 D5
Durgapur Bangl. 97 F4
Durgapur India 97 E5
Durham Canada 173 M6
Durham U.K. 47 K9
Durham CA U.S.A. 182 C2
Durham NC U.S.A. 174 E5
Durham NH U.S.A. 177 O2
Durham Downs Australia 146 D1
Durhi well Eth. 128 D3
Duri Indon. 76 C2
Durlas Rep. of Ireland see Thurles
Durleşti Moldova 58 J1
Durmitor mt. Yugo. 58 A5
also known as Bobotov Kuk
Durmitor nat. park Yugo. 58 A5
Durness U.K. 46 H5
Durocortorum France see Reims
Durostorum Bulg. see Silistra
Durovernum U.K. see Canterbury
Durrës Albania 58 A7
formerly spelt Durazzo; historically known as Dyrrhachium or Epidamnus
Dursey Island Rep. of Ireland 47 B12
Dursunbey Turkey 106 B3
Durtal France 50 F5
Duru China see Wuchuan
Duru r. Dem. Rep. Congo 126 F4
Duru reg. Oman 105 G3
Dūruḩ Iran 101 E3
Durukhsi Somalia 128 E2
Durusu Gölü l. Turkey 58 J7
Durūz, Jabal ad mt. Syria 109 H5
D'Urville, Tanjung pt Indon. 73 I7
D'Urville Island N.Z. 152 H8
Durzab Afgh. 101 F3
Dusetos Lith. 42 G6
Dushak Turkm. 102 D5
Dushan China 87 C3

▶Dushanbe Tajik. 101 G2
Capital of Tajikistan. Formerly known as Stalinabad.

Dushanzi China 88 D2
also known as Maytag
Dushore U.S.A. 177 I4
Dusia l. Lith. 42 E7
Dusky Sound inlet N.Z. 153 A13
Dussejour, Cape Australia 150 E2
Düsseldorf Germany 48 D4
Dusti Tajik. 101 G2
formerly known as Pyandzh
Dustlik Uzbek. 103 G4
Dusty U.S.A. 180 C3
Duszniki-Zdrój Poland 49 N5
Dutch East Indies country Asia see Indonesia
Dutch Guiana country S. America see Suriname
Dutch Mountain U.S.A. 183 K1
Dutch New Guinea prov. Indon. see Irian Jaya
Dutch West Indies terr. West Indies see Netherlands Antilles
Dutsan-Wai Nigeria 125 H4
Dutse Nigeria 125 H4
Dutsin-Ma Nigeria 125 G3
Dutton r. Australia 149 D4
Dutton Canada 173 L8
Dutton, Lake salt flat Australia 146 C2
Dutton, Mount U.S.A. 183 L3
Duval Canada 167 J5
Duved Sweden 44 K3
Duvergé Dom. Rep. 187 F3
Duvert, Lac l. Canada 169 G1
Duvno Bos.-Herz. see Tomislavgrad
Duweihin well Saudi Arabia 100 B5
Duweihin, Khor b. Saudi Arabia/U.A.E. 105 E2
Duwin Iraq 107 F3
Duyinzeik Myanmar 78 B4
Duyun China 87 C3
Duzab Pak. 101 E5
Düzce Turkey 106 B2
Duzdab Iran see Zāhedān
Dvarets Belarus 42 H9
Dve Mogili Bulg. 58 G5
Dviete Latvia 42 H5
Dvinitsa r. Rus. Fed. 43 V2
Dvinsk Latvia see Daugavpils
Dvinskaya Guba g. Rus. Fed. 40 F2
Dvin'ye, Ozero l. Rus. Fed. 43 M5
Dvor Croatia 56 I3
Dvoriki Rus. Fed. 43 T5
Dvoryanka Rus. Fed. 90 B2
Dvoyni Rus. Fed. 43 U6
Dwangwa Malawi 129 B8
Dwarka India 96 A5
Dwarsberg S. Africa 133 K1
Dwellingup Australia 151 B7
Dwesa Nature Reserve S. Africa 133 M9
Dweshula S. Africa 133 O7
Dwight U.S.A. 172 E9
Dwingelderveld, Nationaal Park nat. park Neth. 48 D3
Dwyka S. Africa 132 F10
Dwyka r. S. Africa 132 F10
D'yakonovo Rus. Fed. 43 V3
Dyanev Turkm. 103 E5
also spelt Dänew; formerly spelt Deynau
Dyankovo Bulg. 58 H5
Dyat'kovo Rus. Fed. 43 P8
Dyce U.K. 46 J6
Dyer, Cape Canada 165 M3
Dyer Bay Canada 173 L5
Dyer Plateau Antarctica 222 T2
Dyersburg U.S.A. 174 B4
Dyersville U.S.A. 172 B8
Dyfi r. U.K. 47 I11
also spelt Dovey
Dyje r. Austria/Czech Rep. 49 N7

▶Dykh-Tau, Gora mt. Rus. Fed. 41 G8
2nd highest mountain in Europe.
europe [landscapes] ➠ 30–31

Dylewska Góra hill Poland 49 Q2
Dymi Rus. Fed. 43 O2
Dynevor Downs Australia 147 E2
Dynów Poland 49 T6
Dyoki S. Africa 133 M8
Dyrrhachium Albania see Durrës
Dysart Australia 149 F4
Dysna r. Lith. 42 H6
Dysnų ežeras l. Lith. 42 H6
Dysselsdorp S. Africa 132 G10
Dytiki Ellas admin. reg. Greece 59 B10
also spelt Dhytikí Ellás
Dytiki Makedonia admin. reg. Greece 59 C8
also spelt Dhytikí Makedhonía
Dyuendyu Rus. Fed. 39 N3
Dyulino Bulg. 58 I6
Dyurtyuli Rus. Fed. 40 J5
Dyviziya Ukr. 58 K3
Dzaanhushuu Mongolia 84 D2
Dzadgay Mongolia 84 C2
Dzag Gol r. Mongolia 84 C2
Dzalaa Mongolia 84 C2
Dzamïn Üüd Mongolia 85 F3

▶Dzaoudzi Mayotte 129 E8
Capital of Mayotte.

Dzaudzhikau Rus. Fed. see Vladikavkaz
Dzavhan prov. Mongolia 84 B1
Dzavhan Gol r. Mongolia 84 B1
Džbán mts Czech Rep. 49 K5
Dzegstey Mongolia 84 D2
Dzelter Mongolia 85 E1
Dzeņi Latvia 42 H4
Dzerzhinsk Belarus see Dzyarzhynsk
Dzerzhinsk Rus. Fed. 40 G4
Dzerzhinskoye Kazakh. see Kabanbay
Dzhagdy, Khrebet mts Rus. Fed. 82 C1
Dzhaki-Unakhta Yakbyyana, Khrebet mts Rus. Fed. 82 D2
Dzhaksy Kazakh. see Zhaksy
Dzhakul', Gora mt. Rus. Fed. 84 B1
Dzhalagash Kazakh. 103 F3
also spelt Zhalaghash
Dzhalalabad Azer. see Cälilabad
Dzhalal-Abad Kyrg. see Jalal-Abad
Dzhalal-Abadskaya Oblast' admin. div. Kyrg. see Jalal-Abad
Dzhalil' Rus. Fed. 40 J5
Dzhalinda Rus. Fed. 82 A1
Dzhaltyr Kazakh. see Zhaltyr
Dzhambeyty Kazakh. see Zhympity
Dzhambul Kazakh. see Taraz
Dzhambulskaya Oblast' admin. div. Kazakh. see Zhambylskaya Oblast'
Dzhanga Turkm. 102 C4
also spelt Jangnga
Dzhangala Kazakh. 102 B2
formerly known as Kisykkamys
Dzhangel'dy Uzbek. 103 E4
also spelt Jangeldi; formerly spelt Dzhankel'dy or Dzhingil'dy
Dzhankel'dy Uzbek. see Dzhangel'dy
Dzhankoy Ukr. 41 E7
Dzhansugurov Kazakh. 103 I3
also spelt Zhansügirov
Dzhanybek Kazakh. 102 A2
also known as Zhänibek
Dzharkent Kazakh. see Zharkent
Dzharkurgan Uzbek. 103 F5
also spelt Jarqŭrghon
Dzhebariki-Khaya Rus. Fed. 39 N3
Dzhebel Bulg. 58 G7
Dzhebel Turkm. 102 C5
also spelt Jebel
Dzheksona, Ostrov i. Rus. Fed. 38 F1
English form Jackson Island
Dzhelondi Tajik. see Dzhilandy
Dzheltulak Rus. Fed. 82 B1
Dzhergalan Kyrg. see Jyrgalang
Dzhetygara Kazakh. see Zhitikara
Dzhetymtau, Gory hills Uzbek. 103 F4
Dzhetysay Kazakh. see Zhetysay
Dzheykhun Turkm. 103 E5
also spelt Jeyhun; formerly known as Farab-Pristan'
Dzhezdy Kazakh. see Zhezdy
Dzhezkazgan Kazakh. see Zhezkazgan
Dzhida Rus. Fed. 85 E1
Dzhida r. Rus. Fed. 84 E1
Dzhidinskiy, Khrebet mts Mongolia/Rus. Fed. 84 D1
Dzhigirbent Turkm. 103 E4
also spelt Jigerbent
Dzhilandy Tajik. 101 H2
also spelt Dzhelondi or Jelondí
Dzhingil'dy Uzbek. see Dzhangel'dy
Dzhirgatal' Tajik. see Jirgatol
Dzhizak Uzbek. 103 F4
also spelt Jizzakh
Dzhizak Oblast admin. div. Uzbek. see Dzhizakskaya Oblast'
Dzhizakskaya Oblast' admin. div. Uzbek. 103 F5
English form Dzhizak Oblast; also known as Jizzakh Wiloyati
Dzhokhar Ghala Rus. Fed. see Groznyy
Dzhubga Rus. Fed. 41 F7
Dzhu-Dzhu-Klu Turkm. 102 E5
Dzhugdzhur, Khrebet mts Rus. Fed. 39 N4
Dzhul'fa Azer. see Culfa
Dzhuma Uzbek. 103 F5
also spelt Juma
Dzhungarskiy Alatau, Khrebet mts China/Kazakh. 88 B2
Dzhurun Kazakh. see Zhuryn
Dzhusaly Kazakh. 103 F3
also spelt Zhosaly
Działdowo Poland 49 R2
Dzibalchén Mex. 185 H5
Dzierzgoń Poland 49 Q2
Dzierżoniów Poland 49 N5
Dzilam de Bravo Mex. 185 H4
Dzioua Alg. 123 G2
Dzisna Belarus 43 J6
Dzitás Mex. 185 H4
Dzitva r. Belarus 42 G8
Dzodze Ghana 125 F5
Dzogsool Mongolia 85 E2
Dzöölön Mongolia 84 C1
Dzūkija nat. park Lith. 42 F7
Dzungarian Basin China see Junggar Pendi
Dzungarian Gate pass China/Kazakh. 88 C2
also known as Alataw Shankou
Dzur Mongolia 84 B1
Dzüünbayan Mongolia 85 F2
Dzüünharaa Mongolia 85 E1
Dzuunmod Mongolia 85 E2
Dzüyl Mongolia 84 B2
formerly known as Tonhil
Dzyaniskavichy Belarus 42 H9
Dzyarazhnya Belarus 43 M8
Dzyarazhnya r. Belarus 43 N8
Dzyarechyn Belarus 42 F8
Dzyarzhynsk Belarus 42 I8
also spelt Dzerzhinsk; formerly known as Kaydanovo
Dzyatlava Belarus 42 G8
Dzyatlavichy Belarus 42 H9
Dzyerkawshchyna Belarus 42 I6

↓ E

Eabamet Lake Canada 168 C3
Eads U.S.A. 178 B4
Eagar U.S.A. 183 O7
Eagle r. Canada 169 J2
Eagle AK U.S.A. 166 A1
Eagle CO U.S.A. 180 F5
Eagle Cap mt. U.S.A. 180 C3
Eagle Crags mt. U.S.A. 183 G6
Eagle Creek r. Canada 167 J4
Eagle Lake CA U.S.A. 182 D1
Eagle Lake ME U.S.A. 174 G2
Eagle Mountain U.S.A. 183 I8
Eagle Mountain hill U.S.A. 174 B2
Eagle Pass U.S.A. 179 B6
Eagle Passage Falkland Is 205 F9
Eagle Peak U.S.A. 181 F7
Eagle Plain Canada 164 F3
Eagle Rock U.S.A. 176 F8
Eaglesham Canada 167 G4
Eagle Tail Mountains U.S.A. 183 K8
Eagle Village U.S.A. 166 A1
Eap i. Micronesia see Yap
Earaheedy Australia 151 C5
Ear Falls Canada 168 A3
Earlimart U.S.A. 182 E6
Earl Mountains N.Z. 153 B13
Earlton Canada 173 N3
Earn r. U.K. 46 I7
Earnscleugh N.Z. 153 D13
Earnslaw, Mount N.Z. 153 C12
also known as Pikirakatahi
Earp U.S.A. 183 J7
Earth U.S.A. 179 B5
Easley U.S.A. 174 D5
East, Mount hill Australia 151 C6
East Alligator r. Australia 148 B2
East Antarctica reg. Antarctica 223 H1
East Ararat U.S.A. 177 J4
East Aurora U.S.A. 176 G3
East Baines r. Australia 148 A2
East Bay U.S.A. 175 B6
East Bay inlet U.S.A. 175 C6
East Bengal country Asia see Bangladesh
East Berlin U.S.A. 177 I6
Eastbourne N.Z. 152 I9
Eastbourne U.K. 47 M13
East Brady U.S.A. 176 F5
East Branch U.S.A. 177 J4
East Branch Clarion River Reservoir U.S.A. 176 G4
East Caicos i. Turks and Caicos Is 187 F2
East Cape N.Z. 152 M5
East Cape Rus. Fed. see Dezhneva, Mys
East Carbon City U.S.A. 183 N2
East Chicago U.S.A. 172 F9
East China Sea N. Pacific Ocean 81 L6
also known as Dong Hai
East Coast Bays N.Z. 152 I4
East Dereham U.K. 47 M11
East Dubuque U.S.A. 172 C8
Eastend Canada 167 I5
Easter Group is Australia 151 A6

▶Easter Island S. Pacific Ocean 221 K7
Part of Chile. Also known as Pascua, Isla de.

Eastern admin. reg. Ghana 125 E5
Eastern prov. Kenya 128 C5
Eastern prov. Sierra Leone 124 C4
Eastern prov. Zambia 127 F8
Eastern Cape prov. S. Africa 133 K8
Eastern Creek r. Australia 149 D4
Eastern Desert Egypt 121 G3
also known as Şaḩara el Sharqîya
Eastern Equatoria state Sudan 128 B3
Eastern Ghats mts India 94 C4

▶Eastern Island HI U.S.A. 220 G4
Most northerly point of Oceania.

Eastern Lesser Sunda Islands prov. Indon. see Nusa Tenggara Timur
Eastern Nara canal Pak. 101 G5
Eastern Samoa terr. S. Pacific Ocean see American Samoa
Eastern Sayan Mountains Rus. Fed. see Vostochnyy Sayan
Eastern Taurus plat. Turkey see Güneydoğu Toroslar
Eastern Transvaal prov. S. Africa see Mpumalanga
Easterville Canada 167 L4
East Falkland i. Falkland Is 205 F9
East Frisian Islands Germany 48 E2
also known as Ostfriesische Inseln
East Grand Forks U.S.A. 178 C2
East Grand Rapids U.S.A. 172 H8
Easthampton U.S.A. 177 M3
East Hampton U.S.A. 177 M5
East Hartford U.S.A. 177 M4
East Haydon Australia 149 D3
East Holden U.S.A. 177 Q1
East Island P.N.G. 149 G1
East Jamaica U.S.A. 177 M2
East Jordan U.S.A. 173 H5
East Kazakhstan Oblast admin. div. Kazakh. see Vostochnyy Kazakhstan
East Kilbride U.K. 46 H8
East Lamma Channel Hong Kong China 87 [inset]
also known as Tung Pok Liu Hoi Hap
Eastland U.S.A. 179 C5
East Lansing U.S.A. 173 I8
Eastleigh U.K. 47 K13
East Linton U.K. 46 J8
East Liverpool U.S.A. 176 E5
East London S. Africa 133 L10
also known as Oos-Londen
East Longmeadow U.S.A. 177 M3
Eastmain Canada 168 E2
Eastmain r. Canada 168 E2
Eastman U.S.A. 175 D5
East Middlebury U.S.A. 177 L2
East Millinocket U.S.A. 174 G2
East Naples U.S.A. 175 D7
Easton CA U.S.A. 182 E5
Easton MD U.S.A. 177 I7
Easton PA U.S.A. 177 J5
East Pakistan country Asia see Bangladesh
East Park Reservoir U.S.A. 182 B2
East Peoria U.S.A. 172 D10
East Point Canada 169 I4
Eastport ME U.S.A. 174 H2
Eastport MI U.S.A. 172 H5
East Range mts U.S.A. 182 G1
East Retford U.K. see Retford
East Ridge U.S.A. 174 C5
East St Louis U.S.A. 174 B4
East Sea N. Pacific Ocean see Japan, Sea of
East Shoal Lake Canada 167 L5
East Siberian Sea Rus. Fed. 39 O2
also known as Vostochno-Sibirskoye More
East Side Canal r. U.S.A. 182 E6
East Tavaputs Plateau U.S.A. 183 O2
East Tawas U.S.A. 173 J6

▶East Timor terr. Asia 75 C5
Former Portuguese territory. Part of Indonesia 1976-1999, awaiting independence. Formerly known as Portuguese Timor or Timor Timur.
asia [countries] ➠ 64–67

East Tons r. India 97 E4
East Troy U.S.A. 172 E8
East Verde r. U.S.A. 183 M7
Eastview Canada see Vanier
East Walker r. U.S.A. 182 E3
East York Canada 173 N7
Eateringinna Creek watercourse Australia 148 B5
Eaton CO U.S.A. 180 F4
Eaton OH U.S.A. 176 A6
Eatonia Canada 167 I5
Eaton Rapids U.S.A. 173 I8
Eatonton U.S.A. 175 D5
Eatonville U.S.A. 180 B3
Eau Claire U.S.A. 172 B6
Eau Claire r. U.S.A. 172 B6
Eauripik atoll Micronesia 73 J5
also spelt Eaurypyg
Eaurypyg atoll Micronesia see Eauripik
Eauze France 50 G9
Ebagoola Australia 149 D2
Eban Nigeria 125 G4
Ebano Mex. 185 F4
Ebbw Vale U.K. 47 I12
Ebebiyin Equat. Guinea 125 H6
Ebeltoft Denmark 45 J4
Ebenerde Namibia 130 C5
Ebensburg U.S.A. 176 G5
Ebensee Austria 49 K8
Eberndorf Austria 49 L9
Eberswalde-Finow Germany 49 K3
Ebetsu Japan 90 G3
Ebian China 86 B2
also known as Shaping
Ebino Japan 91 B8
Ebi Nor salt l. China see Ebinur Hu
Ebinur Hu salt l. China 88 C2
also known as Ebi Nor
Ebla tourist site Syria 109 H2
Ebnat-Kappel Switz. 51 P5
Ebo Angola 127 B7
Ebola r. Dem. Rep. Congo 126 D4
Ebolowa Cameroon 125 H6
Ebony Namibia 130 B4
Ebonyi state Nigeria 125 H5
Ebre r. Spain see Ebro
Ebro r. Spain 55 L4
also spelt Ebre
Ebro, Embalse del resr Spain 54 H1
Eburacum U.K. see York
Ebusus i. Spain see Ibiza
Ecbatana Iran see Hamadān
Eccles U.S.A. 176 D8
Eceabat Turkey 59 H8
also known as Maydos
Echague Phil. 74 B2
Echarri-Aranaz Spain 55 I2
also spelt Etxarri-Aranatz
Ech Chélif Alg. 123 F1
also spelt Chlef; formerly known as El Asnam or Orléansville
Ech Cherita, Sebkhet salt pan Tunisia 57 C13
Echeng China see Ezhou
Echinades i. Greece 59 B10
Echinos Greece 58 F7
also spelt Ekhínos
Echizen-misaki pt Japan 91 D7
Echmiadzin Armenia see Ejmiatsin
Echo Bay N.W.T. Canada 167 G1
formerly known as Port Radium
Echo Bay Ont. Canada 168 C4
Echo Cliffs esc. U.S.A. 183 M5
Echoing r. Canada 167 M4
Échouani, Lac l. Canada 173 R3
Echternach Lux. 51 M3
Echuca Australia 147 E4
Écija Spain 54 F7
Ečka Vojvodina, Srbija Yugo. 58 B3
Eckerman U.S.A. 173 H4
Eckernförde Germany 48 G1
Eckerö Fin. 45 L3
Eckerö i. Fin. 42 A1
Eckman U.S.A. 176 D8
Eclipse Sound sea chan. Canada 165 K2
Ecoporanga Brazil 207 M5
Écrins, Parc National des nat. park France 51 M8

▶Ecuador country S. America 198 B5
southamerica [countries] ➠ 192–193
southamerica [contrasts] ➠ 194–195

Écueillé France 50 H5
Ed Eritrea 121 I6
Ed Sweden 45 J4
Eday i. U.K. 46 J4
Ed Da'ein Sudan 126 E2
Ed Dair, Jebel mt. Sudan 121 F6
Ed Damazin Sudan 128 B2
Ed Damer Sudan 121 G5
also spelt Ad Damir
Ed Debba Sudan 121 F5
also spelt Ad Dabbah
Eddeki well Chad 120 C5
Eddies Cove Canada 169 J3
Ed Dueim Sudan 121 G6
also spelt Ad Duwaym
Eddystone Point Australia 147 F5
Eddyville U.S.A. 174 B4
Ede Neth. 48 C3
Edéa Cameroon 125 H6
Edehon Lake Canada 167 L2
Edéia Brazil 206 D4
Eden Australia 147 F4
Eden r. U.K. 47 I9
Eden NC U.S.A. 176 F9
formerly known as Leaksville
Eden TX U.S.A. 179 C6
Edenburg S. Africa 133 J6
Edendale N.Z. 153 C14
Edendale S. Africa 133 O6
Edenderry Rep. of Ireland 47 E10
Edenhope Australia 146 D4
Edenton U.S.A. 177 I9
Edenvale S. Africa 133 M3
Edenville S. Africa 133 L4
Eder r. Germany 48 G4
Eder-Stausee resr Germany 51 O1
Edessa Greece 58 D8
also spelt Édhessa
Edessa Turkey see Şanlıurfa
Edevik Sweden 44 K3
Edfu Egypt see Idfu
Edgar Ranges hills Australia 150 C3
Edgartown U.S.A. 177 O4
Edgecumbe N.Z. 152 K5
Edgecumbe Island Solomon Is see Utupua
Edgefield U.S.A. 175 D5
Edge Island Svalbard see Edgeøya
Edgeøya i. Svalbard 38 C2
English form Edge Island
Edgerton Canada 167 I4
Edgerton OH U.S.A. 176 A4
Edgerton VA U.S.A. 176 H9
Edgerton WI U.S.A. 172 D8
Edgewood U.S.A. 177 I6
Édhessa Greece see Edessa
Edievale N.Z. 153 D13
Edigan Rus. Fed. 88 D1
Édîkel well Niger 125 G2
Edina U.S.A. 174 A3
Edinboro U.S.A. 176 E4
Edinburg TX U.S.A. 179 C7
Edinburg VA U.S.A. 176 G7

▶Edinburgh U.K. 46 I8
Capital of Scotland.

Edincik Turkey 59 I8
Edineț Edineț Moldova 41 D7
Edineț prov. Moldova 53 H2
Edingeni Malawi 129 B8
Edirne Turkey 106 A2
historically known as Adrianople or Adrianopolis
Edirne prov. Turkey 58 H8
Edisto r. U.S.A. 175 D5
Edith, Mount U.S.A. 180 E3
Edithburgh Australia 146 C3
Edith Cavell, Mount Canada 166 G4
Edith Ronne Land ice feature Antarctica see Ronne Ice Shelf
Edith Withnell, Lake salt flat Australia 151 C5
Edjeleh Libya 120 A3
Édjérir watercourse Mali 125 F2
Edjudina Australia 151 C6
Edmond U.S.A. 179 C5
Edmonds U.S.A. 180 B3
Edmonton Australia 149 E3

▶Edmonton Canada 167 H4
Provincial capital of Alberta.

Edmonton U.S.A. 174 C4
Edmore U.S.A. 173 H7
Edmund Lake Canada 167 M4
Edmundston Canada 169 G4
Edna U.S.A. 179 C6
Edo Japan see Tōkyō
Edo state Nigeria 125 G5
Edolo Italy 56 C2
Edom reg. Israel/Jordan 108 G7
Edremit Turkey 106 A3
historically known as Adramyttium
Edremit Körfezi b. Turkey 106 A3
historically known as Adramyttium, Gulf of
Edrengiyn Nuruu mts Mongolia 84 C2
Edsbro Sweden 45 L4

Edsbyn Sweden 45 K3
Edsele Sweden 44 L3
Edson Canada 167 G4
Eduardo Castex Arg. 204 D4
Eduni, Mount Canada 166 D1
Edward r. N.S.W. Australia 147 E3
Edward r. Qld Australia 149 D2
Edward, Lake Dem. Rep. Congo/Uganda 126 F5
also known as Rutanzige, Lake; formerly known as Idi Amin Dada, Lake
Edward, Mount Antarctica 222 T1
Edwardesabad Pak. see Bannu
Edward Island Australia 148 B2
Edward Island Canada 172 E2
Edward River Aboriginal Reserve Australia 149 D2
Edwards U.S.A. 177 J1
Edwards Plateau U.S.A. 179 B6
Edwardsville U.S.A. 174 B4
Edward VIII Bay Antarctica 223 D2
Edward VII Peninsula Antarctica 223 N1
Edwin B. Forsythe National Wildlife Refuge nature res. U.S.A. 177 K6
Edziza, Mount Canada 166 D3
Edzo Canada see Rae-Edzo
Eel r. U.S.A. 182 A1
Eel, South Fork r. U.S.A. 182 A1
Eendekuil S. Africa 132 C9
Eenzamheid Pan salt pan S. Africa 132 E4
Eesti country Europe see Estonia
Éfaté i. Vanuatu 145 F3
also spelt Vaté; formerly known as Sandwich Island
Efes tourist site Turkey see Ephesus
Effingham U.S.A. 174 B4
Eflâni Turkey 106 C2
Efsus Turkey see Afşin
Eftimie Murgu Romania 58 D4
Eg Mongolia 85 F1
Ega r. Spain 55 J2
Egadi, Isole is Sicilia Italy 57 D10
English form Egadi Islands
Egadi Islands is Sicilia Italy see Egadi, Isole
Egan Range mts U.S.A. 183 J3
Eganville Canada 173 P5
Egbe Nigeria 125 G4
Egedesminde Greenland see Aasiaat
Egentliga Finland reg. Fin. see Varsinais-Suomi
Eger r. Germany 49 J5
Eger Hungary 49 R8
Egersund Norway 45 I4
Egerton, Mount hill Australia 151 B5
Eggenfelden Germany 49 J7
Egg Harbor U.S.A. 172 F5
Egg Harbor City U.S.A. 177 K6
Egg Lake Canada 167 J4
Eggum Norway 44 K1
Egilsstaðir Iceland 44 [inset] D2
Eğin Turkey see Kemaliye
Eginbah Australia 150 B4
Egindibulaq Kazakh. see Yegindybulak
Egindy Kazakh. 103 H2
Eğirdir Turkey 106 B3
Eğirdir Gölü l. Turkey 106 B3
Egiyn Gol r. Mongolia 84 D1
Égletons France 51 I7
Eglinton Island Canada 165 H2
Eglisau Switz. 51 O5
Egmont, Cape N.Z. 152 H7
Egmont, Mount vol. N.Z. see Taranaki, Mount
Egmont National Park N.Z. 152 I7
Egmont Village N.Z. 152 I7
Egua Col. 199 E3
Éguas r. Brazil 202 C5
also known as Correntina
Egvekinot Rus. Fed. 39 S3

▶Egypt country Africa 121 F3
2nd most populous country in Africa. Known as Misr or Mudraya in Arabic; formerly known as United Arab Republic; historically known as Aegyptus.
africa [countries] ▶ 114–117

Ehcel well Mali see Agous-n-Ehsel
Ehen Hudag China 84 D4
also known as Alxa Youqi
Ehime pref. Japan 91 C8
Ehingen (Donau) Germany 48 G7
Ehrenberg U.S.A. 183 J8
Ehrenberg Range hills Australia 148 A4
Eibar Spain 55 I1
Eibergen Neth. 48 D3
Eichstätt Germany 48 I7
Eide Norway 44 I3
Eider r. Germany 48 F1
Eidfjord Norway 45 I3
Eiði Faroe Is 46 E1
Eidsvåg Norway 44 J3
Eidsvold Australia 149 F5
Eidsvoll Norway 45 J3
Eifel hills Germany 48 D5
Eigg i. U.K. 46 F7
Eight Degree Channel India/Maldives 94 B5
Eights Coast Antarctica 222 R2
Eighty Mile Beach Australia 150 C3
Eilat Israel 108 F8
also spelt Elat
Eildon, Lake Australia 147 E4
Eildon State Park nature res. Australia 147 E4
Eileen Lake Canada 167 J2
Eilenburg Germany 49 J4
Eilerts de Haan, Natuurreservaat nature res. Suriname 199 G4
Eilerts de Haan Gebergte mts Suriname 199 G4
Eil Malk i. Palau 73 H5
also known as Mecherchar
Einasleigh Australia 149 E3
Einasleigh r. Australia 149 D3
Einbeck Germany 48 G4
Eindhoven Neth. 48 C4
Eindpaal Namibia 132 D2
Einme Myanmar 78 A4
Einsiedeln Switz. 51 O5
Éire country Europe see Ireland, Republic of
Eiriosgaigh i. U.K. see Eriskay
Eiru r. Brazil 198 D6
Eirunepé Brazil 198 D6
Eisberg hill Germany 48 G4
Eiseb watercourse Namibia 130 D3
Eisenach Germany 48 H5
Eisenerz Austria 49 L8
Eisenerzer Alpen mts Austria 49 L8
Eisenhower, Mount Canada see Castle Mountain
Eisenhüttenstadt Germany 49 L3
Eisenstadt Austria 49 N8
Eišiškės Lith. 42 F7
Eisleben Lutherstadt Germany 48 I4
Eistow N.Z. 152 J5
Eitape P.N.G. see Aitape
Eivinvik Norway 45 I3
Eivissa Spain see Ibiza
Eivissa i. Spain see Ibiza
Ejea de los Caballeros Spain 55 J2
Ejeda Madag. 131 [inset] J5
Ejin Horo Qi China see Altan Shiret
Ejin Qi China see Dalain Hob
Ej Jill, Sebkhet salt flat Mauritania 122 B5
Ejmiadzin Armenia see Ejmiatsin
Ejmiatsin Armenia 107 F2
formerly spelt Echmiadzin or Ejmiadzin
Ejura Ghana 125 E5
Ekalaka U.S.A. 180 F3
Ekang Nigeria 125 H5
Ekangala S. Africa 133 M2
Ékata Gabon 126 B4
Ekawasaki Japan 91 C8
Ekenäs Fin. 45 M4
also known as Tammisaari
Ekenäs Sweden 45 K4
Ekenäs skärgårds Nationalpark nat. park Fin. 45 M4
also known as Tammisaaren Saariston Kansallispuisto
Ekerem Turkm. see Okarem
Eket Nigeria 125 G5
Eketahuna N.Z. 152 J8
Ekhinos Greece see Echinos
Ekhmîm Egypt see Akhmîm
Ekibastuz Kazakh. 103 H2
Ekimchan Rus. Fed. 82 D1
Ekinyazı Turkey 109 K1
Ekiti state Nigeria 125 G5
Ekka Island Canada 166 F1
Ekoli Dem. Rep. Congo 126 E5
Ekonda Rus. Fed. 39 K3
Ekondo Titi Cameroon 125 H5
Ekostrovskaya Imandra, Ozero l. Rus. Fed. 44 P2
Ekouamou Congo 126 C4
Ekpoma Nigeria 125 G5
Eksere Turkey see Gündoğmuş
Ekshärad Sweden 45 K3
Eksjö Sweden 45 K4
Ekskavatornyy Rus. Fed. 82 A1
Ekstenfontein S. Africa 132 B5
Ekström Ice Shelf Antarctica 223 X2
Ekträsk Sweden 44 L2
Ekwan r. Canada 168 D2
Ekwan Point Canada 168 D2
Ela Myanmar 78 B4
El Aaiún W. Sahara see Laâyoune
El Abbasiya Sudan 121 F6
Elafonisos i. Greece 59 D12
Elafonisou, Steno sea chan. Greece 59 D12
El 'Agrûd well Egypt 108 F7
Elaia, Cape Cyprus 108 F2
also known as Zeytin Burnu; also spelt Elea, Cape
El Aiadia well Sudan 121 G5
El 'Aiyat Egypt 108 C8
El 'Alamein Egypt 121 F2
also spelt Al 'Alamayn
El Alamo Mex. 184 A2
El Alia Alg. 123 G2
El Alia Tunisia 57 B11
El Alto Peru 198 A6
El 'Âmiriya Egypt 108 A6
El Amria Alg. 55 J9
Elands r. S. Africa 133 N1
Elands r. S. Africa 133 O2
Elandsberg mt. S. Africa 133 K9
Elandsdoorn S. Africa 133 N2
Elandsdrif S. Africa 133 J9
Elandskraal S. Africa 133 O5
Elandslaagte S. Africa 133 N5
Elandsputte S. Africa 133 K2
El Aouinet Alg. 57 A13
El Arahal Spain 54 F7
El Araïche Morocco see Larache
El Arco Mex. 184 B2
El Aricha Alg. 123 E2
El 'Arîsh Egypt 121 G2
Elasa i. Greece 59 H13
El Ashmûnein Egypt 121 F3
historically known as Hermopolis Magna
El Asnam Alg. see Ech Chélif
Elassona Greece 59 D9
El Astillero Spain 54 H1
Elat Israel see Eilat
El 'Aţf reg. W. Sahara 122 B5
Elati mt. Greece 59 B10
Elato atoll Micronesia 73 K5
Elazığ Turkey 107 D3
Elba U.S.A. 175 C6
Elba, Isola d' i. Italy 56 C6
historically known as Ilva
El Bahr El Ahmar governorate Egypt 108 C9
El'ban Rus. Fed. 82 E2
El Banco Col. 198 C2
El Bânoûn well Mauritania 124 D2
El Barco de Ávila Spain 54 F4
El Barco de Valdeorras Spain see O Barco
El Barreal salt l. Mex. 184 D2
El Barun Sudan 128 B2
Elbasan Albania 58 B7
Elbaşı Turkey 106 C3
El Bauga Sudan 121 G5
El Baúl Venez. 199 D2
El Bayadh Alg. 123 F2
formerly known as Géryville
Elbe r. Germany 48 G2
also known as Labe (Czech Republic)
'Elb el Fçâl des. Mauritania 124 C2
El Beqa'a valley Lebanon 109 H3
El Berié well Mauritania 124 C2
Elberta U.S.A. 183 M2
Elberton U.S.A. 175 D5
El Beru Hagia Somalia 128 D4
Elbeuf France 50 H3
Elbeyli Turkey 109 I1
El Beyyed well Mauritania 122 C5
El Beyyed well Mauritania 124 C2
El Billete, Cerro mt. Mex. 185 E5
Elbing Poland see Elbląg
Elbistan Turkey 107 D3
Elbląg Poland 49 Q1
historically known as Elbing
Elbląski, Kanał canal Poland 49 Q1
El Bluff Nicaragua 186 C4
El Bolsón Arg. 205 C6
El Bordj Alg. 55 L9
El Borma Tunisia 123 H3
El Bouláida Alg. see Blida
Elbow Canada 167 J5
Elbow Lake U.S.A. 178 C2
El Bozal Mex. 185 E4

▶Elbrus mt. Rus. Fed. 41 G8
Highest mountain in Europe.
europe [landscapes] ▶ 30–31

El Buheyrat state Sudan 126 F3
El Buitre mt. Spain 55 J6
El Burg Egypt 108 C6
El Burgo de Osma Spain 55 H3
El Burumbul Egypt 108 C8
Elburz Mountains Iran 100 B2
also known as Alborz, Reshteh-ye
El Cain Arg. 205 C6
El Cajon U.S.A. 183 H9
El Callao Venez. 199 F3
El Campo U.S.A. 179 C6
El Canton Venez. 198 D2
El Capulin r. Mex. 179 B7
El Carmelo Venez. 198 D2
El Carmen Arg. 200 D6
El Carmen Beni Bol. 201 E3
El Carmen Santa Cruz Bol. 201 F4
El Carmen Ecuador 198 B5
El Carmen Venez. 199 E4
El Caroche mt. Spain 55 K5
also spelt Caroch
El Casco Mex. 184 D3
El Cebú, Cerro mt. Mex. 185 G6
El Centro U.S.A. 183 I9
El Cerro Bol. 201 E4
El Chaparro Venez. 199 E2
Elche Spain 55 K6
historically known as Ilici
El Chichónal vol. Mex. 185 G5
El Chilicote Mex. 184 D2
Elcho U.S.A. 172 D5
Elcho Island Australia 148 B1
El Coca Ecuador see Puerto Francisco de Orellana
El Cocuy, Parque Nacional nat. park Col. 198 C3
El Collado hill Spain 54 G6
El Contador, Puerto de pass Spain 55 I7
El Cotorro Cuba 186 C2
El Cuy Arg. 204 C5
El Cuyo Mex. 185 I4
Elda Spain 55 K6
El Dab'a Egypt 53 H5
El Dalgamûn Egypt 108 B7
Eldama Ravine Kenya 128 B4
Elde r. Germany 48 I2
El Debb well Eth. 128 D3
Eldee Canada 173 N4
El Deir Egypt 108 C7
Eldena U.S.A. 172 D9
Elderon U.S.A. 172 D6
El Desemboque Mex. 181 D7
Eldhraun lava field Iceland 44 [inset] C3
El Diamante Mex. 184 E2
El Difícil Col. 198 C2
El'dikan Rus. Fed. 39 N3
El Diviso Col. 198 B4
El Djezair Alg. see Algiers
El Doctor Mex. 184 B2
Eldon U.S.A. 178 D4
Eldorado Arg. 204 G2
Eldorado Brazil 203 B8
El Dorado Col. 198 D4
El Dorado Mex. 184 D3
El Dorado AR U.S.A. 179 D5
El Dorado KS U.S.A. 178 C4
Eldorado U.S.A. 179 B6
El Dorado Venez. 199 F3
Eldorado Mountains U.S.A. 183 J6
Eldoret Kenya 128 B4
Eldridge U.S.A. 172 C9
Eldridge, Mount U.S.A. 166 A1
Elea, Cape Cyprus see Elaia, Cape
Eleanor U.S.A. 176 D7
Electric Peak U.S.A. 180 E3
El Eglab plat. Alg. 122 D4
El 'Ein well Sudan 121 F5
Eleja Latvia 42 E5
El Ejido Spain 55 I8
Elek Hungary 49 S9
Elek r. Rus. Fed. see Ilek
Elekmonar Rus. Fed. 88 D1
Elektrėnai Lith. 42 F7
Elektrogorsk Rus. Fed. 43 T6
Elektrostal' Rus. Fed. 43 T6
Elektrougli Rus. Fed. 43 T6
Elele Nigeria 125 G5

▶Elemi Triangle terr. Africa 128 B3
Disputed territory (Ethiopia/Kenya/Sudan) administered by Kenya.

Elena Bulg. 58 G6
El Encanto Col. 198 C5
El Encinal Mex. 183 H9
Elephanta Caves tourist site India 94 B2
Elephant Butte Reservoir U.S.A. 181 F6
Elephant Island Antarctica 222 U2
Éléphants de Kaniama, Réserve des nature res. Dem. Rep. Congo 127 E6
Éléphants de Sakania, Réserve Partielle aux nature res. Dem. Rep. Congo 127 F7
Eleshnitsa Bulg. 58 E7
Eleşkirt Turkey 107 E3
also known as Aleşkirt
El Espinar Spain 54 G4
El Estor Guat. 185 H6
Eleuthera i. Bahamas 186 D1
Eleva U.S.A. 172 B6
Eleven Point r. U.S.A. 178 E4
El Fahs Tunisia 57 B12
El Faiyûm Egypt 121 F2
also spelt Al Fayyūm
El Faiyûm governorate Egypt 108 B8
El Faouar Tunisia 123 H2
El Fasher Sudan 120 E6
El Fashn Egypt 106 B5
El Fendek Morocco 54 F9
El Ferrol Spain see Ferrol
El Ferrol del Caudillo Spain see Ferrol
El Fud Eth. 128 D3
El Fuerte Mex. 184 C3
El Fula Sudan 126 F2
Elgå Norway 45 J3
Elgal waterhole Kenya 128 C4
El Gamâliya Egypt 108 C6
El Gçaib well Mali 122 D5
formerly known as El Ksaib Ounane
El Geili Sudan 121 G6
El Geneina Sudan 120 D6
El Geteina Sudan 121 G6
El Gezira state Sudan 121 G6
El Ghaba Sudan 121 F5
El Ghalla, Wadi watercourse Sudan 126 E2
El Ghallâouîya well Mauritania 122 C5
El Gheddiya Mauritania 124 C2
El Ghor plain Jordan/West Bank see Al Ghawr
Elgin U.K. 46 I6
Elgin IL U.S.A. 178 E3
Elgin NV U.S.A. 183 J4
Elgin OR U.S.A. 180 C3
Elgin TX U.S.A. 179 C6
Elgin Down Australia 149 E4
El'ginskiy Rus. Fed. 39 O3
El Gir well Sudan 121 F5
El Gîza Egypt see Giza
El Gîza governorate Egypt 108 A9
El Gogorrón, Parque Nacional nat. park Mex. 185 E4
El Goléa Alg. 123 F3
El Golfo de Santa Clara Mex. 184 B2
Elgon, Mount Uganda 128 B4
Elgoras, Gora hill Rus. Fed. 44 O1
El Guante Mex. 184 D2
El Guetar Tunisia 123 H2
El Guettâra well Mali 123 E5
El'gyay Rus. Fed. 39 L3
El Haddâd Egypt 108 B6
El Hamma Tunisia 123 H2
El Hammâm Egypt 121 F2
El Hammâmi reg. Mauritania 122 C5
El Hâmûl Egypt 108 C6
El Hank reg. Alg. 122 D4
El Ḫank esc. Mali/Mauritania 122 C5
El Haouaria Tunisia 57 D11
El Harra Egypt 121 F2
El Hasira Sudan 104 A5
El Hato del Volcán Panama 186 C5
El Hawata Sudan 121 G6
El Heiz Egypt 106 B5
El Hierro i. Canary Is 122 A4
El Higo Mex. 185 F4
El Hilla Sudan 121 E6
El Homr Alg. 123 F3
El Homra Sudan 121 F6
El Houeïtat well Mauritania 124 C2
El Huecu Arg. 204 C5
El Huseiniya Egypt 108 C7
Elias Garcia Angola 127 D7
Elías Piña Dom. Rep. 187 F3
Elichpur India see Achalpur
Elihu U.S.A. 176 A8
Elila Dem. Rep. Congo 126 E5
Elila r. Dem. Rep. Congo 126 E5
El 'Ilw el Ahmar el Qibli hill Egypt 108 B9
Elim S. Africa 132 D11
Elim U.S.A. 164 C3
Elimäki Fin. 42 H1
Elimberrum France see Auch
Elin Pelin Bulg. 58 E6
Eliot, Mount Canada 169 I1
Eliozondo Spain 55 J1
Elipa Dem. Rep. Congo 126 E5
Elisabetha Dem. Rep. Congo 126 D4
also known as Lokutu
Élisabethville Dem. Rep. Congo see Lubumbashi
Eliseu Martins Brazil 202 D4
El Iskandarîya Egypt see Alexandria
El Iskandarîya governorate Egypt 108 A6
Elista Rus. Fed. 41 H7
formerly known as Stepnoy
Elizabeth U.S.A. 177 K5
Elizabeth, Mount hill Australia 150 D3
Elizabeth City U.S.A. 177 I9
Elizabeth Creek r. Australia 148 C3
Elizabeth Island Pitcairn Is see Henderson Island
Elizabeth Islands U.S.A. 177 O4
Elizabeth Point Namibia 130 B5
Elizabeth Reef Australia 145 E4
Elizabethton U.S.A. 176 C9
Elizabethtown KY U.S.A. 174 C4
Elizabethtown NC U.S.A. 174 E5
Elizabethtown NY U.S.A. 177 L1
Elizabethville U.S.A. 177 I5
Elizavety, Mys c. Rus. Fed. 39 O4
El Jadida Morocco 122 C2
formerly known as Mazagan
El Jaralito Mex. 184 D3
El Jebelein Sudan 121 G6
El Jem Tunisia 123 H2
El Jicaro Nicaragua 186 B4
El Julie Mex. 185 G5
Elk r. Canada 167 H5
Ełk Poland 49 T2
historically known as Lyck
Ełk r. Poland 49 T2
Elk r. MD U.S.A. 177 J6
Elk r. TN U.S.A. 174 C5
El Kaa Lebanon see Qaa
El Kab Sudan 121 G5
Elkader U.S.A. 174 B3
El Kala Alg. 123 H1
formerly spelt La Calle
El Kamlin Sudan 121 G6
El Karabi Sudan 121 G5
Elkas kalns hill Latvia 42 G4
Elk City U.S.A. 179 C5
Elk Creek U.S.A. 182 B2
Elkedra Australia 148 B4
Elkedra watercourse Australia 148 C4
El Kelaâ des Srarhna Morocco 122 D2
El Kere Eth. 128 D3
Elkford Canada 167 H5
Elk Grove U.S.A. 182 C3
El Khalil West Bank see Hebron
El Khandaq Sudan 121 F5
El Khârga Egypt 121 F3
also spelt Al Khārijah
Elkhart IN U.S.A. 174 C3
Elkhart KS U.S.A. 178 B4
El Khartûm Sudan see Khartoum
El Khatatba Egypt 108 B7
El Khenachich esc. Mali see El Khnâchîch
El Khnâchîch esc. Mali 122 D5
also spelt El Khenachich
Elkhorn U.S.A. 172 E8
Elkhorn r. U.S.A. 178 C3
Elkhorn City U.S.A. 176 C8
Elkhovo Bulg. 58 H6
Elki Turkey see Beytüşşebap
Elkin U.S.A. 176 E9
Elkins U.S.A. 176 F7
Elk Island National Park Canada 167 H4
Elk Lake Canada 168 D4
Elk Lake l. U.S.A. 172 H6
Elkland U.S.A. 177 H4
Elk Mountain U.S.A. 180 F4
Elko Canada 167 H5
Elko U.S.A. 183 I1
El K'oran Eth. 128 E3
Elk Park U.S.A. 176 D9
Elk Point Canada 167 I4
Elk Point U.S.A. 178 C3
Elk River U.S.A. 174 A2
El Ksaib Ounane well Mali see El Gçaib
El Ksour Tunisia 57 A13
Elk Springs U.S.A. 183 P1
Elkton KY U.S.A. 174 C4
Elkton MD U.S.A. 177 J6
Elkton VA U.S.A. 176 G7
Elkview U.S.A. 176 D7
El Lagowa Sudan 126 F2
Ellas country Europe see Greece
Ellavalla Australia 151 A5
Ellaville U.S.A. 175 C5
Ell Bay Canada 167 O1
Ellef Ringnes Island Canada 165 I2
El Lēh Eth. 128 C4
El Lein well Kenya 128 D5
Elleker Australia 151 B7
Elléloyé well Chad 120 C5
Ellen, Mount U.S.A. 183 N3
Ellenabad India 96 B3
Ellenboro U.S.A. 176 D6
Ellenburg Depot U.S.A. 177 L1
Ellendale DE U.S.A. 177 J7
Ellendale ND U.S.A. 178 C2
Ellensburg U.S.A. 180 B3
Ellenville U.S.A. 177 K4
El León, Cerro mt. Mex. 184 D3
Ellesmere N.Z. 153 G11
Ellesmere, Lake N.Z. 153 G11

▶Ellesmere Island Canada 165 K2
4th largest island in North America and 10th in the world.
northamerica [landscapes] ▶ 156–157

Ellesmere Island National Park Reserve Canada 165 L1
Ellesmere Port U.K. 47 J10
Ellice r. Canada 167 K1
Ellice Island atoll Tuvalu see Funafuti
Ellice Islands country S. Pacific Ocean see Tuvalu
Ellicott City U.S.A. 177 I6
Ellicottville U.S.A. 176 G3
Ellijay U.S.A. 174 C5
El Limón Mex. 185 F4
Elliot Australia 148 B3
Elliot S. Africa 133 L8
Elliot, Mount Australia 149 E3
Elliotdale S. Africa 133 M8
also known as Xhora
Elliot Knob mt. U.S.A. 176 F7
Elliot Lake Canada 168 D4
Elliot Price Conservation Park nature res. Australia 146 C2
Ellis U.S.A. 178 C4
Ellisras S. Africa 131 E4
Elliston Australia 146 B3
Elliston U.S.A. 176 E8
Ellisville U.S.A. 175 B6
Ellon U.K. 46 J6
Ellora Caves tourist site India 94 B1
Ellsworth KS U.S.A. 178 C4
Ellsworth ME U.S.A. 177 Q1
Ellsworth WI U.S.A. 174 A2
Ellsworth Land reg. Antarctica 222 R1
Ellsworth Mountains Antarctica 222 S1
Ellwangen (Jagst) Germany 48 H7
El Macao Dom. Rep. 187 F3
El Mahalla el Kubra Egypt 108 C7
El Mahâriq Egypt 121 F3
El Maharraqa Egypt 108 C8
El Mahia reg. Mali 123 E5
El Maitén Arg. 205 C6
El Maks el Bahari Egypt 121 F3
Elmakuz Dağı mt. Turkey 108 E1
Elmalı Turkey 106 B3
El Mallâha marsh Egypt 108 E9
El Malpais National Monument nat. park U.S.A. 181 F6
El Ma'mûra Egypt 108 B6
El Manaqil Sudan 121 G6
El Mango Venez. 199 E4
El Mansûra Egypt 121 F2
also spelt Al Manşūrah
El Mansûriya Egypt 108 C7
El Manteco Venez. 199 F3
El Manzla Morocco 54 F9
El Marsa Tunisia 57 C12
El Matarîya Egypt 108 D6
El Medo Eth. 128 D3
El Meghaïer Alg. 123 G2
El Melemm Sudan 126 F2
El Melhes well Mauritania 124 B2
El Mesellemiya Sudan 121 G6
El Messir well Chad 120 C6
El Mex Egypt 108 A6
El Miamo Venez. 199 F3
Elmina Ghana 125 E5
also known as São Jorge da Mina
El Mîna Lebanon 108 G3
El Minya Egypt 108 C8
El Minya Egypt 121 F2
El Minya governorate Egypt 108 B9
Elmira Ont. Canada 173 M7
Elmira P.E.I. Canada 169 I4
Elmira MI U.S.A. 173 I5
Elmira NY U.S.A. 177 I3
El Mirage U.S.A. 183 L8
El Moïnane well Mauritania 124 C2
Elmore Australia 147 E4
El Morro mt. Arg. 204 D4
El Mraïfig well Mauritania 124 C3
El Mraïti well Mali 125 E2
El Mreyyé reg. Mauritania 124 D2
Elmshorn Germany 48 G2
El Muglad Sudan 126 E2
El Mugrón mt. Spain 55 J6
Elmwood U.S.A. 172 C10
El Mzereb well Mali 122 D4
Elne France 51 I10
Elnesvågen Norway 44 I3
El Nido Phil. 74 A4
El Oasis Mex. 183 I9
El Obeid Sudan 121 F6
El Ocote, Parque Natural nature res. Mex. 185 G5
El Odaiya Sudan 121 F6
El Oro prov. Ecuador 198 B5
El Oro Mex. 184 E3
Elos Greece 59 E13
El Oued Alg. 123 G2
Eloy U.S.A. 183 M9
El Palmar Venez. 199 F3
El Palmito Mex. 184 D3
El Pao Bolívar Venez. 199 F2
El Pao Cojedes Venez. 198 D2
Elpaputih, Teluk b. Indon. 75 D3
El Paraíso Hond. 186 B4
El Paso IL U.S.A. 174 B3
El Paso KS U.S.A. see Derby
El Paso TX U.S.A. 181 F7
El Peñón Arg. 204 D2
El Perelló Spain 55 L4
Elphinstone i. Myanmar see Thayawthadangyi Kyun
El Pilar Venez. 199 F2
El Pino, Sierra mts Mex. 185 E2
El Pintado Arg. 201 E6
El Pluma Arg. 205 C7
El Pocito Bol. 201 E3
El Portele b. Col. 198 C1
El Porvenir Col. 198 D3
El Porvenir Mex. 183 I9
El Porvenir Mex. 184 D2
El Porvenir Panama 186 D5
El Prat de Llobregat Spain 55 N3
also known as Prat de Llobregat
El Progreso Guat. 185 H6
also known as Guastatoya
El Puente Bol. 200 D5
El Puente Nicaragua 186 B4
El Puerto de Santa María Spain 54 E8
El Qâ' valley Egypt 108 E9
El Qâhira Egypt see Cairo
El Qâhira governorate Egypt 108 C8
El Qanâtir el Qahiriya Egypt 108 C7
El Qantara Egypt 106 C5
El Qantara el Sharqîya Egypt 108 D7
El Qasimiye r. Lebanon 108 G4
El Qasr Egypt 121 F3
El Quds Israel/West Bank see Jerusalem
El Quebrachal Arg. 204 D2
El Quss Abû Sa'îd plat. Egypt 121 E3
El Real Panama 186 D5
El Regocijo Mex. 184 D4
El Reno U.S.A. 179 C5
El Retorno Mex. 185 E4
El Rey, Parque Nacional nat. park Arg. 201 D6
El Ridisîya Bahari Egypt 121 G3
El Rio U.S.A. 182 E7
El Rôda Egypt 108 B8
El Rosario watercourse Mex. 181 D7
Elrose Canada 167 I5
Elroy U.S.A. 172 C7
El Rucio Mex. 185 E4
Elsa Canada 166 C2
Elsa r. Italy 56 C5
El Saff Egypt 121 F2
El Sahuaro Mex. 184 B2
El Salado Arg. 205 D8
El Salado Mex. 185 E3
El Sâlhîya Egypt 108 D7
El Salto Mex. 184 D4

▶El Salvador country Central America 185 H6
also known as Salvador
northamerica [countries] ▶ 158–159

El Salvador Chile 204 C2
El Salvador Mex. 185 E3
El Salvador Phil. 74 C4
El Samán de Apure Venez. 198 D3
Elsas Canada 173 K2
El Sauz Mex. 184 D2
El Seibo Dom. Rep. 187 F3
Elsen Nur l. China 84 B5
El Serrat Andorra 55 M2
El Shab well Egypt 121 F4
El Shâyib hill Egypt 108 B8
El Shuhada Egypt 108 B7
Elsie U.S.A. 173 I7
Elsinore Denmark see Helsingør
Elsinore CA U.S.A. 183 G8
Elsinore UT U.S.A. 183 L3
Elsinore Lake U.S.A. 183 G8
Elsnes Norway 44 M1
El Sosneado Arg. 204 C4
Elsterniederung und Westliche Oberlausitzer Heide park Germany 49 K4
Elsterwerda Germany 49 K4
El Sueco Mex. 184 D2
El Suweis Egypt see Suez
El Suweis governorate Egypt 108 C8
El Tajín tourist site Mex. 185 F4
El Tama, Parque Nacional nat. park Venez. 198 C3
El Tarabil hill Egypt 108 D8
El Tarf Alg. 123 H1
El Teleno mt. Spain 54 E2
El Temascal Mex. 185 F3
Eltham N.Z. 152 I7
El Thamad Egypt 121 G2
El Tigre Venez. 199 E2
El Tigre, Parque Nacional nat. park Guat. 185 H5
El Tocuyo Venez. 198 D2
El'ton Rus. Fed. 102 A2
El'ton, Ozero l. Rus. Fed. 102 A2
El Toro Chile 204 C3
El Totumo Venez. 198 C2
El Trébol Arg. 204 E4
El Tren Mex. 184 B2
El Triunfo Mex. 184 C4
El Tunal Arg. 204 D2
El Tuparro, Parque Nacional nat. park Col. 198 D3
El Tûr Egypt 121 G2
El Turbio Chile 205 B8
El Turbón mt. Spain 55 L2
El Uqşur Egypt see Luxor
Eluru India 94 D2
El 'Uteishan well Sudan 121 G5
Elva Estonia 42 H3
El Vallecillo Mex. 184 C2
Elvanlı Turkey see Tömük
Elvas Port. 54 D6
Elvebakken Norway 44 M1
Elven France 50 D5
El Vendrell Spain 55 M3
also spelt Vendrell
Elvenes Norway 44 O1
Elverum Norway 45 J3
El Viejo mt. Col. 198 C3
El Viejo Nicaragua 186 B4
El Vigía, Cerro mt. Mex. 184 D4
Elvira Brazil 198 C6
Elvire r. Australia 150 E3
Elvire Aboriginal Reserve Australia 150 D3
Elvo r. Italy 56 A3
El Wâdi El Jadîd governorate Egypt 106 A6
El Wak Kenya 128 D4
El Wasta Egypt 108 C8
El Watya well Egypt 121 E2
Elwood IN U.S.A. 174 C3
Elwood NE U.S.A. 178 C3
Elwood NJ U.S.A. 177 K6
El Wuz Sudan 121 F6
Ely U.K. 47 M11
Ely MN U.S.A. 174 B2
Ely NV U.S.A. 183 J2
El Yagual Venez. 198 D3
El Yibo well Kenya 128 C3
Elyria U.S.A. 176 C4
Elysburg U.S.A. 177 I5
El Zacatón, Cerro mt. Mex. 185 F5
El Zape Mex. 184 D3
El Zawâmil Egypt 108 C7
Emajõgi r. Estonia 42 I3
Emām Qolī Iran 100 D2
Emāmrūd Iran 100 C2
formerly known as Shāhrūd
Emām Şaḩēb Afgh. 101 G2
Emām Taqī Iran 101 D2
formerly known as Shāh Taqī
Emangusi S. Africa 133 Q3
E. Martínez Mex. see Emiliano Martínez
Emas, Parque Nacional das nat. park Brazil 206 A5
Emazar Kazakh. 88 C2
Emba Kazakh. 102 D2
also known as Embi or Zhem
Emba r. Kazakh. 102 C3
Embalenhle S. Africa 133 N3
Embarcación Arg. 201 D5
Embarras Portage Canada 167 I3
Embarrass U.S.A. 172 A3
Embetsu Japan see Enbetsu
Embi Kazakh. see Emba
Embiah, Mount hill Sing. 76 [inset]
Embira r. Brazil see Envira
Émbonas Greece see Emponas
Emborcação, Represa de resr Brazil 206 F5
Emborion Greece see Emporeio
Embu Brazil 206 G10
Embu Kenya 128 C5
Embundo Angola 127 C9
Emden Germany 48 E2
Emecik Turkey 59 I12
Emei China see Emeishan
Emeishan China 86 B2
formerly known as Emei
Emei Shan mt. China 86 B2
Emel' r. Kazakh. 88 C2
Emerald Australia 149 F4
Emeril Canada 169 H2
Emerita Augusta Spain see Mérida
Emerson Canada 167 L5
Emerson U.S.A. 176 B7
Emery U.S.A. 183 M3
Emesa Syria see Homs
Emet Turkey 106 B3
Emigrant Gap U.S.A. 182 D2
Emigrant Pass U.S.A. 183 H1
Emigrant Valley U.S.A. 183 I4
eMijindini S. Africa 133 P2
Emi Koussi mt. Chad 120 C5
Emile r. Canada 167 G2
Emiliano Martínez Mex. 184 D3
short form E. Martínez
Emiliano Zapata Mex. 185 H5
Emilia-Romagna admin. reg. Italy 56 D4
Emin China 88 C2
also known as Dorbiljin
Emine, Nos pt Bulg. 58 I6
Eminence U.S.A. 174 B4
Emin He r. China 88 C2
Eminska Planina hills Bulg. 58 I6
Emirdağ Turkey 106 B3
Emir Dağı mt. Turkey 106 B3
Emlenton U.S.A. 176 F4
Emmaboda Sweden 45 K4
Emmahaven Indon. see Telukbayur
Emmaste Estonia 42 D3
Emmaus Rus. Fed. 43 R5
Emmaus U.S.A. 177 J5
Emmeloord Neth. 48 C3
Emmelshausen Germany 48 E5
Emmen Neth. 48 D3
Emmen Switz. 51 O5
Emmendingen Germany 48 E7
Emmerich Germany 48 D4
Emmet Australia 149 E5
Emmetsburg U.S.A. 178 D3
Emmett U.S.A. 180 C4
Emmiganuru India 94 C3
formerly spelt Yemmiganur
Emmitsburg U.S.A. 177 H6
Emo Canada 168 A3
Emőd Hungary 49 R8
Emona Slovenia see Ljubljana
Emory U.S.A. 179 D5
Emory Peak U.S.A. 179 B6
Empada Guinea-Bissau 124 B4
Empalme Mex. 184 C3
Empanadas mt. Spain 55 I7
Empangeni S. Africa 133 P5
Empedrado Arg. 204 F2
Empexa, Salar de salt flat Bol. 200 C5
Empire U.S.A. 172 G6
Empoli Italy 56 C5
Emponas Greece 59 I12
also spelt Émbonas
Emporeio Greece 59 G12
also known as Emborion
Emporia KS U.S.A. 178 C4
Emporia VA U.S.A. 176 H9
Emporium U.S.A. 176 G4
Empress Canada 167 I5
Empress Mine Zimbabwe 131 F3
Empty Quarter des. Saudi Arabia see Rub' al Khālī
'Emrānī Iran 100 D3
Ems r. Germany 48 E2
Emsdale Canada 173 N5
Emsdetten Germany 48 E3
Ems-Jade-Kanal canal Germany 48 E2
Emthonjeni S. Africa 133 O2
Emu Creek r. Australia 149 D3
Emumägi hill Estonia 42 I3
Emu Park Australia 149 F4
Emur r. China 82 B1
Emur Shan mts China 82 A1
Emzinoni S. Africa 133 N3
Ena Japan 91 E7
Enafors Sweden 44 K3
Enambú Col. 198 D4

index

E

Enamuna Brazil 199 F3
Enarotali Indon. 73 I7
Ena-san mt. Japan 91 E7
Enbetsu Japan 90 G2
also spelt Embetsu
Encanadé mt. Spain 55 L4
Encantadas, Serra das hills Brazil 203 A9
Encanto, Cape Phil. 74 B3
Encarnación Mex. 185 E4
Encarnación Para. 201 G6
Enchi Ghana 124 E5
Encinas mt. Spain 54 H6
Encinitas U.S.A. 183 G8
Encino U.S.A. 181 F6
Encón Arg. 204 D4
Encontrados Venez. 198 C2
Encounter Bay Australia 146 C3
Encruzilhada Brazil 202 D5
Encruzilhada do Sul Brazil 203 A9
Encs Hungary 49 S7
Endako Canada 166 E4
Endau Malaysia 76 C2
Endau r. Malaysia 76 C2
Endeavour Strait Australia 149 D1
Endeh Indon. 75 B5
Enderbury i. Kiribati 145 H2
Enderby Canada 166 G5
Enderby Land reg. Antarctica 223 D2
Endicott Mountains U.S.A. 164 D3
Endimari r. Brazil 200 D2
Endla riiklik looduskaitseala nature res. Estonia 42 H3
Endom Cameroon 125 I6
Endwell U.S.A. 177 I3
Endzele Latvia 42 G4
Ene r. Peru 200 B2
Eneabba Australia 151 A6
Enebakk Norway 45 J4
Enemutu Brazil 199 G3
EnenKio terr. N. Pacific Ocean see Wake Atoll
Energeticheskiy Kazakh. 103 I4
Energetik Rus. Fed. 102 D2
Energía Arg. 204 F5
Enewetak atoll Marshall Is 220 E5
Enez Turkey 106 A2
historically known as Aenus
Enfião, Ponta do pt Angola 127 A8
Enfidaville Tunisia 57 C12
Enfield Canada 169 I4
Enfield U.S.A. 174 E4
Engan Norway 44 J3
Engaño, Cabo c. Dom. Rep. 187 F3
Engaños, Río de los r. Col. see Yari
Engaru Japan 90 H2
Engcobo S. Africa 133 L8
Engelhard U.S.A. 174 F5
Engel's Rus. Fed. 102 A2
also known as Pokrovsk
Engelschmangat sea chan. Neth. 48 B2
Engenheiro Beltrão Brazil 206 A10
Engenheiro Navarro Brazil 207 J4
Engenina watercourse Australia 146 B2
Engerdal Norway 45 J3
Enggano i. Indon. 76 C4
Enghershatu mt. Eritrea 121 H5
Engineer Canada 166 C3
Engkilili Sarawak Malaysia 77 E2
England admin. div. U.K. 47 K11
Englee Canada 169 K3
Englehart Canada 168 E4
Englewood FL U.S.A. 175 D7
Englewood OH U.S.A. 176 A6
English r. Canada 167 M5
English U.S.A. 174 C4
English Bazar India see Ingraj Bazar
English Channel France/U.K. 47 K14
also known as La Manche
English Coast Antarctica 222 S2
Engozero Rus. Fed. 40 E2
Engstingen Germany 48 G7
Engure Latvia 42 E4
Engures ezers l. Latvia 42 E4
Enguri r. Georgia 107 E2
Enhlalakahle S. Africa 133 O6
Enid U.S.A. 179 C4
Enipefs r. Greece 59 D9
Eniwa Japan 90 G3
eNjesuthi mt. S. Africa 133 N6
Enkan, Mys pt Rus. Fed. 39 O4
Enkeldoorn Zimbabwe see Chivhu
Enkhuizen Neth. 48 C3
Enköping Sweden 45 L4
Enle China see Zhenyuan
Enna Sicilia Italy 57 G11
Ennadai Lake Canada 167 K2
En Nahud Sudan 121 F6
En Namous, Oued watercourse Alg. 123 E3
E-n-Nassamé well Niger 125 H3
Enné, Ouadi watercourse Chad 120 C6
Ennedi, Massif mts Chad 120 D5
Enneri Achelouma watercourse Niger 123 I5
Enneri Maro watercourse Chad 120 C5
Enneri Yebigué watercourse Chad 120 C4
Ennery Haiti 187 E3
Enngonia Australia 147 E2
Ennis Rep. of Ireland 47 D11
also spelt Inis
Ennis MT U.S.A. 180 E3
Ennis TX U.S.A. 179 C5
Enniscorthy Rep. of Ireland 47 F11
also spelt Inis Córthaidh
Enniskerry Rep. of Ireland 47 F10
Enniskillen U.K. 47 E9
Ennistymon Rep. of Ireland 47 C11
Enn Nâqoûra Lebanon 108 G4
Enns Austria 49 L7
Enns r. Austria 49 L7
Eno Fin. 44 O3
Enoch U.S.A. 183 K4
Enonkoski Fin. 44 O3
Enontekiö Fin. 44 M1
Enoree r. U.S.A. 174 D5
Enosburg Falls U.S.A. 177 M1
Enping China 87 E4
Enrekang Indon. 75 A3
Enrile Phil. 74 B2
Enriquillo Dom. Rep. 187 F3
Enriquillo, Lago de l. Dom. Rep. 187 F3
Enschede Neth. 48 D3
Ensenada Baja California Norte Mex. 184 A2
Ensenada Baja California Sur Mex. 184 C4
Ensenada de Utria nat. park Col. 198 B3
Enshi China 87 D2
Ensley U.S.A. 175 C6
Entebbe Uganda 128 B4
Enterprise Canada 167 G2
Enterprise AL U.S.A. 175 C6
Enterprise OR U.S.A. 180 C3
Enterprise UT U.S.A. 183 K4
Enterprise Point Phil. 74 A4
Entrance Canada 167 G4
Entrepeñas, Embalse de resr Spain 55 I4
Entre Ríos prov. Arg. 204 F4
Entre Ríos Bol. 201 D5
Entre Rios Bahia Brazil 202 E4
Entre Rios Pará Brazil 199 H6
Entre Rios Moz. see Malema
Entre Rios de Minas Brazil 203 C7
Entroncamento Port. 54 C5
Entuba Zimbabwe 131 E3
Entumeni S. Africa 133 P5
Enugu Nigeria 125 G5
Enugu state Nigeria 125 G5
Enurmino Rus. Fed. 39 S3
Envigado Col. 198 C3
Envira Brazil 200 C1
Envira r. Brazil 200 C1
also known as Embira
Enying Hungary 49 P9
Enys, Mount N.Z. 153 F11
Enzan Japan 91 F7
Eo r. Spain 54 D1
Eochaill Rep. of Ireland see Youghal
Eokuk Lake Canada 167 H1
Eooa i. Tonga see Eua
Epe Nigeria 125 F5
Epéna Congo 126 C4
Épernay France 51 J3
Ephesus tourist site Turkey 59 I11
also known as Efes
Ephraim U.S.A. 183 M2
Ephrata PA U.S.A. 177 I5
Ephrata WA U.S.A. 180 C3
Epidamnus Albania see Durrës
Epidavros tourist site Greece 59 E11
Epidavrou Limiras, Kolpos b. Greece 59 E12
Épila Spain 55 J3
Épinac France 51 K6
Épinal France 51 M4
Epirus admin. reg. Greece see Ipeiros
Episkopi Cyprus 108 D3
Episkopi Bay Cyprus 108 D3
also known as Episkopis, Kolpos
Episkopis, Kolpos b. Cyprus see Episkopi Bay
Epping U.K. 47 M12
Epping U.S.A. 177 N2
Epping Forest National Park Australia 149 E4
Eppynt, Mynydd hills U.K. 47 I11
Epsom U.K. 47 L12
Epte r. France 50 H3
Epu-pel Arg. 204 D5
Epuyén Arg. 205 C6
Eqlīd Iran 100 C4
Équateur prov. Dem. Rep. Congo 126 D4
▶Equatorial Guinea country Africa 125 H6
known as Guinea Ecuatorial in Spanish; formerly known as Spanish Guinea
africa [countries] ▶ 114–117
Equeipa Venez. 199 F3
Équerdreville-Hainneville France 50 E3
Era r. Italy 56 C5
Erac Creek watercourse Australia 149 E5
Eraclea Italy 56 E3
Erakurri mt. Spain 55 J1
Eran Bay Phil. 74 A4
Erandol India 94 B1
Erawadi r. Myanmar see Irrawaddy
Erawan National Park Thai. 79 B5
Erba, Jebel mt. Sudan 121 H4
Erbaa Turkey 107 D2
Erbendorf Germany 48 J6
Erbeskopf hill Germany 48 E6
Ercan airport Cyprus 108 E2
Erçek Turkey 107 E3
Erciş Turkey 107 E3
Erciyes Dağı mt. Turkey 106 C3
Ercsi Hungary 49 P8
Érd Hungary 49 P8
Erdalsfjellet hill Norway 44 N1
Erdaobaihe China see Baihe
Erdaogou China 84 B5
Erdao Jiang r. China 82 B4
Erdek Turkey 106 A2
Erdemli Turkey 106 C3
also known as Yağda
Erdenet Hövsgöl Mongolia 84 C1
Erdenet Orhon Mongolia 84 E1
Erdenetsogt Bayanhongor Mongolia 84 D2
Erdenetsogt Ömnögovĭ Mongolia 85 E3
Erding Germany 48 I7
Erdniyevskiy Rus. Fed. 102 A3
Erdre r. France 50 E5
Eré Peru 198 C5
Eré, Campos hills Brazil 206 A11
Erebato r. Venez. 199 E3
Erebus, Mount vol. Antarctica 223 L1
Erech tourist site Iraq 107 F5
also spelt Uruk
Erechim Brazil 203 A8
Ereentsav Mongolia 85 G1
Ereğli Konya Turkey 106 C3
historically known as Cabistra or Heraclea
Ereğli Zonguldak Turkey 106 B2
historically known as Heraclea Pontica
Erego Moz. see Errego
Erei, Monti mts Sicilia Italy 57 G11
Ereikoussa i. Greece 59 A9
also spelt Erikoússa
Erementaū Kazakh. see Yereymentau
Eréndira Mex. 185 E5
Erenhaberga Shan mts China 88 D3
Erenhot China 85 G3
Erenik r. Yugo. 58 B6
Erenköy Cyprus see Kokkina
Eresk Iran 100 D3
Eresma r. Spain 54 G3
Eresos Greece 59 G9
Eretria Greece 59 E10
Erevan Armenia see Yerevan
Erfenis Dam resr S. Africa 133 K5
Erfenis Dam Nature Reserve S. Africa 133 K5
Erfoud Morocco 122 D3
Erfurt Germany 48 I5
Ergani Turkey 107 D3
Erg Atouila des. Mali 122 D5
Erg Azennezal des. Alg. 123 E5
Erg Bourarhet des. Alg. 123 H4
'Erg Chech des. Alg./Mali 123 D5
Erg d' Amer des. Alg. 123 H4
Erg du Djourab des. Chad 120 C6
Erg du Ténéré des. Niger 125 H2
Ergel Mongolia 85 F3
Ērģeme Latvia 42 G4
Ergene r. Turkey 106 A2
Erg Iabès des. Alg. 123 E4
Erg Iguidi des. Alg./Mauritania 122 D4
'Erg I-n-Sâkâne des. Mali 123 E5
Erg Issaouane des. Alg. 123 G4
Erg Kilian des. Alg. 123 H5
Ērgļi Latvia 42 G5
Erg Mehedjibat des. Alg. 123 F4
Erg Tassedjefit des. Alg. 123 F4
Erguig r. Chad 126 B2
Ergun China 85 I1
formerly known as Ergun Youqi or Labudalin
Ergun He r. China/Rus. Fed. see Argun'
Ergun Youqi China see Ergun
Er Hai l. China 86 B3
Erheib Sudan 104 B4
Eria r. Spain 54 F2
Erice Sicilia Italy 57 E10
Ericht, Loch l. U.K. 46 H7
Erickson Man. Canada 167 L5
Erie KS U.S.A. 178 D4
Erie PA U.S.A. 176 E3
Erie, Lake Canada/U.S.A. 173 M8
'Erîgât des. Mali 124 D2
Erik Eriksenstretet sea chan. Svalbard 38 C2
Erikoússa i. Greece see Ereikoussa
Eriksdale Canada 167 L5
Erillas hill Spain 54 F6
Erimo Japan 90 H3
Erimo-misaki c. Japan 90 H4
Erin Canada 173 M7
Erin U.S.A. 174 C4
Eriskay i. U.K. 46 E6
also spelt Eiriosgaigh
Erithraí Greece see Erythres
Erithropótamos r. Greece see Erydropotamos
▶Eritrea country Africa 121 H6
africa [countries] ▶ 114–117
Erkech-Tam Kyrg. 103 H5
formerly spelt Irkeshtam
Erkner Germany 49 K3
Erkowit Sudan 104 B4
Erlangen Germany 48 I6
Erlangping China 87 D1
Erldunda Australia 148 B5
Erlong Shan mt. China 82 C4
Ermak Kazakh. see Aksu
Ermana, Khrebet mts Rus. Fed. 85 G1
Ermelo S. Africa 133 N3
Ermenek Turkey 106 C3
Ermenek r. Turkey 108 E1
Ermil Sudan 121 E6
Ermioni Greece 59 E11
Ermoupoli Greece 59 F11
Ernakulam India 94 C4
Erne r. Rep. of Ireland/U.K. 47 D9
Ernée France 50 F4
Ernest Giles Range hills Australia 151 C5
Ernest Sound sea chan. U.S.A. 166 C4
Erode India 94 C4
Eromanga Australia 149 D5
Erongo admin. reg. Namibia 130 B4
Erpu China 84 B3
Erqu China see Zhouzhi
Errabiddy Hills Australia 151 A5
Er Rachidia Morocco 122 D3
formerly known as Ksar-es-Souk
Er Rahad Sudan 121 F6
Erramala Hills India 94 C3
Er Raoui des. Alg. 123 E3
Errego Moz. 131 H3
formerly spelt Erego
Er Renk Sudan 128 B2
Errigal hill Rep. of Ireland 47 D8
Errinundra National Park Australia 147 F4
Erris Head Rep. of Ireland 47 B9
Erro r. Spain 55 J2
Er Rogel Sudan 121 G5
Erromango i. Vanuatu 145 F3
Erronan i. Vanuatu see Futuna
Er Roseires Sudan 128 B2
Er Rua'at Sudan 121 G6
Ersekë Albania 59 B8
Erta Ale vol. Eth. 128 D1
Ertai China 84 A2
Ertil' Rus. Fed. 41 G6
Ertis Kazakh. see Irtyshsk
Ertis r. Kazakh./Rus. Fed. see Irtysh
Ertix He r. China/Kazakh. 88 D1
also known as Chernyy Irtysh or Qara Ertis
Erufu Nigeria 125 G4
Eruh Turkey 107 E3
Eru laht b. Estonia 42 G2
Eruwa Nigeria 125 F5
Erval Brazil 204 G4
Ervália Brazil 207 K7
Erve r. France 50 F5
Erwin U.S.A. 178 G4
Erwitte Germany 48 F4
Erydropotamos r. Greece 58 H7
also spelt Erithropótamos
Erythres Greece 59 E10
also known as Erithraí
Eryuan China 86 A3
also known as Yuhu
Erzen r. Albania 58 A7
Erzerum Turkey see Erzurum
Erzgebirge mts Czech Rep./Germany 49 K5
historically known as Ore Mountains
Erzhan China 82 B2
Erzin Rus. Fed. 84 B1
Erzin Turkey 106 D3
Erzincan Turkey 107 D3
Erzurum Turkey 107 E3
also spelt Erzerum
Eržvilkas Lith. 42 D6
Esa-ala P.N.G. 145 E2
Esan-misaki pt Japan 90 G4
Esashi Hokkaidō Japan 90 H2
Esashi Iwate Japan 90 G5
Esbjerg Denmark 45 J5
Esbo Fin. see Espoo
Escada Brazil 202 F4
Escalante Phil. 74 B4
Escalante r. U.S.A. 183 N4
Escalante Desert U.S.A. 183 K4
Escalón Mex. 184 D3
Escalon U.S.A. 182 D4
Escambia r. U.S.A. 175 C6
Escanaba U.S.A. 172 F5
Escandón, Puerto de pass Spain 55 K4
Escárcega Mex. 185 H5
Escarpada Point Phil. 74 B2
Escaut r. Belgium 51 J2
Eschede Germany 48 H3
Esch-sur-Alzette Lux. 51 L3
Eschwege Germany 48 H4
Eschweiler Germany 48 D5
Escocesa, Bahía b. Dom. Rep. 187 F3
Escoma Bol. 200 C3
Escondido r. Mex. 179 B6
Escondido r. Nicaragua 186 C4
Escondido U.S.A. 183 G8
Escudilla mt. U.S.A. 183 O8
Escuinapa Mex. 184 D4
Escuintla Guat. 185 H6
Escuintla Mex. 185 G6
Escuque Venez. 198 D2
Escurso r. Brazil 206 G4
Escusa mt. Spain 54 G4
Eséka Cameroon 125 H6
Ese-Khayya Rus. Fed. 39 N3
Eşen Turkey 106 B3
Eşen r. Turkey 59 K12
Esence Turkey 59 J8
Esenguly Turkm. 102 C5
formerly spelt Gasan-Kuli or Hasan Guli
Esenköy Turkey 58 J8
Esenyurt Turkey 58 J7
Ésera r. Spain 55 L2
Eşfahān Iran 100 B3
English form Isfahan; formerly spelt Ispahan
Eşfahān prov. Iran 100 C3
Esfandak Iran 101 E5
Esfarayen, Reshteh-ye mts Iran 100 D2
Esfīdeh Iran 101 D3
Esgueva r. Spain 54 G3
Eshan China 86 B3
also known as Shuangjiang
Eshanguzar Kyrg. 103 I4
formerly known as imeni Voroshilova or Kalinin
Eshimba Dem. Rep. Congo 127 E6
Eshkamesh Afgh. 101 G2
Eshowe S. Africa 133 P5
Esigodini Zimbabwe 131 F4
formerly known as Essexvale
Esikhawini S. Africa 133 Q5
Esil Kazakh. see Yesil'
Esil r. Kazakh./Rus. Fed. see Ishim
Esino r. Italy 56 F5
eSizameleni S. Africa 133 O4
Esk Australia 147 G1
Esk r. Australia 147 E5
Esk r. U.K. 47 I9
Eskdale N.Z. 152 K7
Esker Canada 169 H2
Eskifjörður Iceland 44 [inset] D2
Eski Gediz Turkey 106 B3
Eskilstuna Sweden 45 L4
Eskimo Lakes Canada 164 F3
Eskimo Point Canada see Arviat
Eski Mosul Iraq 107 E3
Eski-Nookat Kyrg. 103 H4
formerly spelt Iski-Naukat
Eskipazar Turkey 106 C2
Eskişehir Turkey 106 B3
historically known as Dorylaeum
Esla r. Spain 54 E3
Esla, Embalse de resr Spain see Ricobayo, Embalse de
Eslāmābād-e Gharb Iran 100 A3
formerly known as Shāhābād
Esler Dağı mt. Turkey 59 K11
Eslöv Sweden 45 K5
Esmā'īlī-ye Soflá Iran 100 D4
Eşme Turkey 106 B3
Esmeralda Cuba 186 D2
Esmeralda, Isla i. Chile 205 B8
Esmeraldas Brazil 207 I6
Esmeraldas Ecuador 198 B4
Esmeraldas prov. Ecuador 198 B4
Esmeraldo r. Bol. 200 D3
Esmont U.S.A. 176 G8
Esnagi Lake Canada 173 I2
Espakeh Iran 101 E5
Espalha r. Brazil see São Francisco
Espalion France 51 I8
Espalmador, Isla i. Spain see S'Espalmador
España country Europe see Spain
Espanola Canada 168 D4
Espanola U.S.A. 181 F5
Esparreguera Spain 55 M3
Esparta Hond. 186 B4
Esparto U.S.A. 182 B3
Espe Kazakh. 103 H4
Espelette France 50 E9
Esperance Australia 151 C7
Esperance Bay Australia 151 C7
Esperantinópolis Brazil 202 C3
Esperanza research station Antarctica 222 U2
Esperanza Santa Cruz Arg. 205 C8
Esperanza Santa Fé Arg. 204 E3
Esperanza Mex. 184 C3
Esperanza Peru 200 C2
Esperanza Phil. 74 C4
Espichel, Cabo c. Port. 54 B6
Espiel Spain 54 G6
Espigão, Serra do mts Brazil 203 B8
Espinazo Mex. 185 E3
Espinhaço, Serra do mts Brazil 203 D6
Espinheira Angola 127 B9
Espinheira hill Port. 54 D6
Espinho Port. 54 C3
Espinilho, Serra do hills Brazil 203 A9
Espino Venez. 199 E2
Espinosa Brazil 202 D5
Espinosa de los Monteros Spain 55 H1
Espirito Santo Brazil see Vila Velha
Espírito Santo state Brazil 203 D6
Espiritu Phil. 74 B2
Espiritu Santo Bol. 200 D4
Espíritu Santo i. Vanuatu 145 F3
Espíritu Santo, Bahía del b. Mex. 185 I5
Espíritu Santo, Isla i. Mex. 184 C3
Espita Mex. 185 H4
Esplanada Brazil 202 E4
Espoo Fin. 45 N3
also spelt Esbo
Espuña mt. Spain 55 J7
Espungabera Moz. 131 G4
Esqueda Mex. 184 C2
Esquel Arg. 205 C6
Esquimalt Canada 166 F5
Esquina Arg. 204 F3
Esquipulas Guat. 185 H6
Esrange Sweden 44 M2
Essaouira Morocco 122 C3
formerly known as Mogador
Essé Cameroon 125 H5
Es Semara W. Sahara 122 C4
▶Essen Germany 48 E4
4th most populous city in Europe.
world [cities] ▶ 24–25
Essendon, Mount hill Australia 151 C5
Essex Canada 173 K8
Essex CA U.S.A. 183 I7
Essex MA U.S.A. 177 O3
Essex MD U.S.A. 177 I6
Essex NY U.S.A. 177 L1
Essex Junction U.S.A. 177 L1
Essexvale Zimbabwe see Esigodini
Essexville U.S.A. 173 J7
Esslingen am Neckar Germany 48 G7
Esso Rus. Fed. 39 P4
Essonne r. France 51 I4
Essu Estonia 42 H2
Es Suaifi well Sudan 121 F5
Es Suki Sudan 121 G6
Est prov. Cameroon 125 I5
Estaca de Bares, Punta da pt Spain 54 D1
Estación Coahuila Mex. 183 J9
Estagno Point Phil. 74 B2
Eşţahbān Iran 100 C4
also known as Savanat
Estaire Canada 173 M4
Estância Goiás Brazil 206 B4
Estância Sergipe Brazil 202 E4
Estancia U.S.A. 181 F6
Estancia Camerón Chile 205 C9
Estancia Carmen Arg. 205 C9
Estand, Kūh-e mt. Iran 101 E4
Estarreja Port. 54 C4
Estats, Pic d' mt. France/Spain 55 M2
Estcourt S. Africa 133 N6
Este Italy 56 D3
Este, Parque Nacional del nat. park Dom. Rep. 187 F3
Esteban hill Spain 55 K3
Esteban de Urizar Arg. 201 D5
Estelí Nicaragua 186 B4
Estella Spain 55 I2
also known as Lizarra
Estena r. Spain 54 G5
Estepa Spain 54 G7
Estepona Spain 54 F8
Esteras r. Spain 54 G6
Esterel reg. France 51 M9
Esterhazy Canada 167 K5
Estero Bay U.S.A. 182 C6
Esteros Para. 201 E5
Estes Park U.S.A. 180 F4
Este Sudeste, Cayos del is Col. 198 A1
Estevan Canada 167 K5
Estevan Group is Canada 166 D4
Estherville U.S.A. 178 D3
Estill U.S.A. 175 D5
Estiva Brazil 207 G9
Estiva r. Brazil 202 C3
Eston Canada 167 I5
▶Estonia country Europe 42 F3
known as Eesti in Estonian; formerly known as Estonskaya S.S.R.
europe [countries] ▶ 32–35
Estonskaya S.S.R. country Europe see Estonia
Estreito Brazil 204 H3
Estrela, Serra da mts Port. 54 D4
Estrela do Indaiá Brazil 207 H6
Estrela do Sul Brazil 206 F5
Estrella mt. Spain 55 H6
Estrella, Punta pt Mex. 184 B2
Estrella, Sierra mts U.S.A. 183 L8
Estrema Brazil 200 D2
Estremadura reg. Port. 54 B5
Estremoz Port. 54 D6
Estrondo, Serra hills Brazil 202 B4
Estuaire prov. Gabon 126 A4
Estuario do Sado, Reserva Natural do nature res. Port. 54 C6
Estuario do Tejo, Reserva Natural nature res. Port. 54 C6
Estūh Iran 100 B3
Esztergom Hungary 49 P8
also known as Gran
Étables-sur-Mer France 50 D4
Etadunna Australia 146 C2
Etah India 96 C4
Étain France 51 L3
Etamamiou Canada 169 J3
Étampes France 51 I4
Etamunbanie, Lake salt flat Australia 148 C5
Étaples France 50 H2

highest mountains

	mountain	height	location		page#
1 ▶	Mount Everest	8 848m / 29 028ft	China/Nepal Asia	▶	97 E4
2 ▶	K2	8 611m / 28 251ft	China/Jammu and Kashmir Asia	▶	96 C2
3 ▶	Kangchenjunga	8 586m / 28 169ft	India/Nepal Asia	▶	97 F4
4 ▶	Lhotse	8 516m / 27 939ft	China/Nepal Asia	▶	97 E3
5 ▶	Makalu	8 463m / 27 765ft	China/Nepal Asia	▶	97 E4
6 ▶	Cho Oyu	8 201m / 26 906ft	China/Nepal Asia	▶	97 E3
7 ▶	Dhaulagiri	8 167m / 26 794ft	Nepal Asia	▶	97 D3
8 ▶	Manaslu	8 163m / 26 781ft	Nepal Asia	▶	97 E3
9 ▶	Nanga Parbat	8 126m / 26 660ft	Jammu and Kashmir Asia	▶	96 B2
10 ▶	Annapurna I	8 091m / 25 545ft	Nepal Asia	▶	97 D3

Etawah Rajasthan India 96 C4
Etawah Uttar Pradesh India 96 C4
Etchojoa Mex. 184 C3
Etelä-Suomi prov. Fin. 45 N3
eThandakukhanya S. Africa 133 O3
Ethel watercourse Australia 151 B5
Ethelbert Canada 167 K5
Ethel Creek Australia 150 C4
E'Thembini S. Africa 132 G6
Etheridge r. Australia 149 D3
▶Ethiopia country Africa 128 C2
3rd most populous country in Africa. Spelt Ityopia in Amharic; historically known as Abyssinia.
africa [countries] ▶ 114–117
Ethiopian Highlands mts Eth. 128 C2
Etili Turkey 59 H9
also known as Gölçük
Etimesğut Turkey 106 C3
Etna r. Norway 45 J3
Etna, Monte vol. Sicilia Italy see Etna, Mount
Etna, Mount vol. Sicilia Italy 57 H11
also known as Etna, Monte
Etna, Parco dell' park Sicilia Italy 57 G11
Etne Norway 45 I4
Etobicoke Canada 173 N7
Etolin Island U.S.A. 164 F4
Eton Australia 149 F4
Etorofu-tō i. Rus. Fed. see Iturup, Ostrov
Etosha National Park Namibia 130 B3
Etosha Pan salt pan Namibia 130 C3
Etoumbi Congo 126 B4
Etowah r. U.S.A. 179 F5
Etrek r. Iran/Turkm. see Atrek
Étrépagny France 50 H3
Etropole Bulg. 58 F6
Etsha Botswana 130 D3
Ettelbruck Lux. 51 M3
Etten-Leur Neth. 48 B4
Ettlingen Germany 48 F7
Ettumanur India 94 C4
Etxarri-Aranatz Spain see Echarri-Aranaz
Etzatlán Mex. 184 D4
Etzicom Coulee r. Canada 167 I5
Eua i. Tonga 145 H4
formerly spelt Eooa
Euabalong Australia 147 E3
Eubank U.S.A. 176 A8
Euboea i. Greece see Evvoia
Eucla Australia 151 E6
Euclid U.S.A. 176 D4
Euclides da Cunha Brazil 202 E4
Eucumbene, Lake Australia 147 F4
Eudora U.S.A. 175 B5
Eudunda Australia 146 C3
Eufaula AL U.S.A. 175 C6
Eufaula OK U.S.A. 179 D5
Eufaula Lake resr U.S.A. 179 D5
Eugene U.S.A. 180 B3
Eugênia r. Brazil 201 F2
Eugenia, Punta pt Mex. 184 B3
Eulo Australia 147 E2
Eungella Australia 149 F4
Eungella National Park Australia 149 F4
Eunice LA U.S.A. 179 D6
Eunice NM U.S.A. 179 B5
▶Euphrates r. Asia 107 F5
Longest river in western Asia. Also known as Al Furāt (Iraq/Syria) or Fırat (Turkey).
Eupora U.S.A. 175 B5
Eura Fin. 45 M3
Eure r. France 50 H3
Eureka N.W.T. Canada 172 D10
Eureka CA U.S.A. 180 A4
Eureka IL U.S.A. 168 B5
Eureka KS U.S.A. 178 C4
Eureka MT U.S.A. 180 D2
Eureka NV U.S.A. 183 I2
Eureka OH U.S.A. 176 C7
Eureka SD U.S.A. 178 C2
Eureka UT U.S.A. 183 L2
Eureka Sound sea chan. Canada 165 K2
Eureka Springs U.S.A. 179 D4
Eureka Valley U.S.A. 182 G4
Euriápolis Brazil 207 N3
Eurinilla watercourse Australia 146 D2
Euriowie Australia 146 D2
Euroa Australia 147 E4
Eurombah Australia 149 F5
Eurombah Creek r. Australia 149 F5
Europa, Île i. Indian Ocean 218 J7
English form Europa Island
Europa, Picos de mts Spain 54 F1
Europa, Punta de pt Gibraltar see Europa Point
Europa Island Indian Ocean see Europa, Île
Europa Point Gibraltar 54 F8
also known as Europa, Punta de
Eustis U.S.A. 175 D6
Euston Australia 147 D3
Eutaw U.S.A. 175 C5
Eutin Germany 48 H1
Eutsuk Lake Canada 166 E4
Evale Angola 127 B9
Evans, Lac l. Canada 168 E3
Evansburg Canada 167 H4
Evans City U.S.A. 176 E5
Evans Ice Stream Antarctica 222 S1
Evans Strait Canada 165 K3
Evanston IL U.S.A. 174 C3
Evanston WY U.S.A. 180 E4
Evansville Canada 168 D4
Evansville IN U.S.A. 174 C4
Evansville WI U.S.A. 172 D8
Evansville WY U.S.A. 180 F4
Eva Perón Arg. see La Plata
Eva Perón prov. Arg. see La Pampa
Evart U.S.A. 172 H7
Evaton S. Africa 133 L3
Evaz Iran 100 C5
Evcili Turkey 108 F1
Eveleth U.S.A. 172 A3
Evening Shade U.S.A. 174 B4
Evensk Rus. Fed. 39 P3
Evenskjær Norway 44 L1
Everard, Cape Australia 147 F4
Everard, Lake salt flat Australia 146 B2
Everard, Mount N.T. Australia 148 B4
Everard, Mount S.A. Australia 148 B5
Everard Range hills Australia 146 B1
Everek Turkey see Develi
▶Everest, Mount China/Nepal 97 E4
Highest mountain in the world and in Asia. Also known as Qomolangma Feng or Sagarmatha.
world [physical features] ▶ 8–9
Everett PA U.S.A. 176 G5
Everett WA U.S.A. 180 B3
Evergem Belgium 51 J1
▶Everglades swamp U.S.A. 175 D7
world [land cover] ▶ 18–19
Everglades National Park U.S.A. 175 D7
Evergreen U.S.A. 175 C6
Everman, Volcán vol. Mex. 184 C5
Everson U.S.A. 180 B2
Evertsberg Sweden 45 K3
Evesham Australia 149 D4
Evesham U.K. 47 K11
Évian-les-Bains France 51 M6
Evijärvi Fin. 44 M3
Evinayong Equat. Guinea 125 H6
Evington U.S.A. 176 F8
Evinos r. Greece 59 C10
Evje Norway 45 I4
Evolène Switz. 51 N6
Évora Port. 54 D6
Évora admin. dist. Port. 54 D6
Evoron, Ozero l. Rus. Fed. 82 E2
Evosmo Greece 58 D8
Evowghlī Iran 100 A2
Évreux France 50 H3
Évron France 50 F4
Evros r. Greece/Turkey 58 H8
also known as Meriç; also spelt Hebros
Evrotas r. Greece 59 D12
Évry France 51 I4
Evrychou Cyprus 108 D2
also spelt Evrykhou
Evrykhou Cyprus see Evrychou
Evvoia i. Greece 59 F10
English form Euboea; also known as Negroponte
Ewa Beach U.S.A. 181 [inset] Z1
Ewan Australia 149 E3
Ewaso Ngiro r. Kenya 128 D4
Ewbank S. Africa 132 H3
Ewe, Loch b. U.K. 46 G6
Ewen U.S.A. 172 D4
Ewenkizu Zizhiqi China see Bayan Tohoi
Ewing Island Antarctica 222 T2
Ewirgol China 88 D3
Ewo Congo 126 B5
Exaltación Bol. 200 D3
Excelsior S. Africa 133 L5
Excelsior Mountain U.S.A. 182 E3
Excelsior Mountains U.S.A. 182 F3
Excelsior Springs U.S.A. 178 D4
Exe r. U.K. 47 I13
Executive Committee Range mts Antarctica 222 P1
Exeland U.S.A. 172 B5
Exeter Canada 173 L7
Exeter U.K. 47 I13
Exeter CA U.S.A. 182 E5
Exeter NH U.S.A. 177 O3
Exeter Lake Canada 167 I1
Exmoor hills U.K. 47 I12
Exmoor National Park U.K. 47 I12
Exmore U.S.A. 177 J8
Exmouth Australia 150 A4
Exmouth U.K. 47 I13
Exmouth, Mount Australia 147 F2
Exmouth Gulf Australia 150 A4
Exmouth Lake Canada 167 H1
Expedition National Park Australia 149 F5
Expedition Range mts Australia 149 F5
Exploits r. Canada 169 K3
Exton U.S.A. 177 J5
Extremadura aut. comm. Spain 54 H5
Extrême-Nord prov. Cameroon 125 I4
Exuma Cays is Bahamas 186 D1
Exuma Sound sea chan. Bahamas 186 E1
Eya r. Rus. Fed. 41 F7
Eyangu Dem. Rep. Congo 126 D5
Eyasi, Lake salt l. Tanz. 129 B5
Eyawadi r. Myanmar see Irrawaddy
Eydehavn Norway 45 J4
Eyeberry Lake Canada 167 J2
Eyelenoborsk Rus. Fed. 40 L2
Eyemouth U.K. 46 J8
Eyjafjallajökull ice cap Iceland 44 [inset] C3
Eyjafjörður inlet Iceland 44 [inset] C2
Eyl Somalia 128 F3
Eylau Rus. Fed. see Bagrationovsk
Eymet France 50 G8
Eymir Turkey 59 J11
Eymoutiers France 50 H7
Eyre r. France 50 E8
Eyre (South), Lake salt flat Australia 146 C2
▶Eyre, Lake salt flat Australia 146 C2
Largest lake in Oceania and lowest point.
oceania [landscapes] ▶ 136–137
oceania [features] ▶ 142–143
Eyre Creek watercourse Australia 148 C5

Eyre Mountains N.Z. 153 C13
Eyre Peak N.Z. 153 C13
Eyre Peninsula Australia 146 B3
Eyrieux r. France 51 K8
Eysturoy i. Faroe Is 46 F1
Eyuku waterhole Kenya 128 C5
Eyumojok Cameroon 125 H5
Eyvānekī Iran 100 C3
Ezakheni S. Africa 133 O5
eZamokuhle S. Africa 133 N3
'Ezbet el Burg Egypt 108 C6
Ezbet el Gezîra Egypt 108 C6
Ezbet Gamasa el Gharbîya Egypt 108 C6
Ezel U.S.A. 176 B8
Ezenzeleni S. Africa 133 M4
Ezequiel Ramos Mexía, Embalse resr Arg. 204 C5
Ezernieki Latvia 42 I5
Ezhou China 87 E2
formerly known as Echeng
Ezhva Rus. Fed. 40 I3
formerly known as Sloboda
Ezine Turkey 106 A3
Ezinepazar Turkey 106 D2
Ezo i. Japan see Hokkaidō
Ezousa r. Cyprus 108 D3
Ezra's Tomb tourist site Iraq 107 F5

F

Faadhippolhu Atoll Maldives 94 B5
Fabens U.S.A. 181 F7
Faber, Mount hill Sing. 76 [inset]
Faber Lake Canada 167 G2
Fabero Spain 54 E2
Fåborg Denmark 45 J5
Fabriano Italy 56 E5
Facatativá Col. 198 C3
Fachi Niger 125 H2
Factoryville U.S.A. 177 J4
Facundo Arg. 205 C7
Fada Chad 120 D5
Fada-Ngourma Burkina 125 F3
Faḍilah well Saudi Arabia 105 E3
Faḍli reg. Yemen 105 D5
Fadnoun, Plateau du Alg. 123 H4
Faenza Italy 56 D4
Færingehavn Greenland see Kangerluarsoruseq
Færoerne terr. N. Atlantic Ocean see Faroe Islands
Faeroes terr. N. Atlantic Ocean see Faroe Islands
Fafa r. Cent. Afr. Rep. 126 C3
Fafanlap Indon. 73 H7
Fafe Port. 54 C3
Fafen Shet' watercourse Eth. 128 E3
Fafi waterhole Kenya 128 D5
Faga watercourse Burkina 125 F3
Făgăraş Romania 58 F3

▶Fagatogo American Samoa 145 H3
Capital of American Samoa.

Fagersta Sweden 45 K4
Făget Romania 58 D3
Fagnano, Lago l. Arg./Chile 205 C9
Fagne reg. Belgium 51 K2
Fagochia well Niger 125 G2
Faguibine, Lac l. Mali 124 D2
Fagurhólsmýri Iceland 44 [inset] C3
Fagwir Sudan 128 A2
Fahliān, Rūdkhāneh-ye watercourse Iran 100 B4
Fahraj Iran 100 C4
Fahūd, Jabal hill Oman 105 G3
Faillon, Lac l. Canada 173 Q2
Fairbanks U.S.A. 164 E3
Fairborn U.S.A. 176 A6
Fairbury U.S.A. 178 C3
Fairchild U.S.A. 172 C6
Fairfax N.Z. 153 C14
Fairfax IA U.S.A. 172 B9
Fairfax VA U.S.A. 177 H7
Fairfax VT U.S.A. 177 L1
Fairfield CA U.S.A. 182 B3
Fairfield IA U.S.A. 174 B3
Fairfield ID U.S.A. 180 D4
Fairfield IL U.S.A. 174 B4
Fairfield OH U.S.A. 176 A6
Fairfield TX U.S.A. 179 C6
Fairfield UT U.S.A. 183 L1
Fairfield VA U.S.A. 176 F8
Fairgrove U.S.A. 173 J7
Fairhaven U.S.A. 177 O4
Fair Haven U.S.A. 177 L2
Fair Head U.K. 47 F8
Fair Hill U.S.A. 177 J6
Fair Isle i. U.K. 46 K4
Fairlee U.S.A. 177 M2
Fairlie N.Z. 153 E12
Fairmont MN U.S.A. 178 D3
Fairmont WV U.S.A. 176 E6
Fairmont Hot Springs Canada 167 H5
Fairplay U.S.A. 180 F5
Fairview Australia 149 E2
Fairview Canada 166 G3
Fairview IL U.S.A. 172 C10
Fairview KY U.S.A. 176 B7
Fairview MI U.S.A. 173 I6
Fairview OK U.S.A. 179 C4
Fairview PA U.S.A. 176 E3
Fairview UT U.S.A. 183 M2
Fairview WI U.S.A. 172 C7
Fairview Park Hong Kong China 87 [inset]
Fairweather, Cape U.S.A. 166 B3
Fairweather, Mount Canada/U.S.A. 164 F4
Fais i. Micronesia 73 J5
formerly known as Tromelin Island
Faisalabad Pak. 101 H4
formerly known as Lyallpur
Faizabad Afgh. see Feyzābād
Faizabad Afgh. 101 F2
Faizabad India 97 D4
Fāj aş Şulubī watercourse Saudi Arabia 109 M7
Fajj, Wādī al watercourse Iraq 109 O5
Fajr, Wādī watercourse Saudi Arabia 107 D5
Fakaofo atoll Tokelau 145 H2
also spelt Fakaofu; formerly known as Bowditch
Fakaofu atoll Tokelau see Fakaofo
Fakel Rus. Fed. 40 J4
formerly known as Sergiyevskiy
Fakenham U.K. 47 M11
Fåker Sweden 44 K3
Fakfak Indon. 73 H7
Fakhrabad Iran 100 C4
Fakiragram India 97 F4
Fakiyska Reka r. Bulg. 58 I6
Fakse Denmark 45 K5
Fakse Bugt b. Denmark 45 K5
Faku China 85 I3
Falaba Sierra Leone 124 C4
Falagountou Burkina 125 F3
Falaise France 50 F4
Falaise Lake Canada 167 G2
Falakata India 97 F4
Falam Myanmar 78 A3
Falavarjan Iran 100 B3
Falcarragh Rep. of Ireland 47 D8
Falces Spain 55 J2
Fălciu Romania 58 J2
Falcón state Venez. 198 D2
Falcon, Cap c. Alg. 55 K9
Falconara Marittima Italy 56 F5
Falcone, Capo del c. Sardegna Italy 56 A8
Falcon Island Tonga see Fonuafo'ou
Falcon Lake Canada 167 M5
Falcon Lake l. Mex./U.S.A. 185 F3
Falelima Samoa 145 H3
Falémé r. Mali/Senegal 124 B3
Falerii Italy see Civita Castellana
Falfurrias U.S.A. 179 C7
Falher Canada 167 G4
Falkat watercourse Eritrea 104 B4
Falkenberg Germany 49 K4
Falkenberg Sweden 45 K4
Falkensee Germany 49 K3
Falkirk U.K. 46 I8

▶Falkland Islands terr. S. Atlantic Ocean 205 F8
United Kingdom Overseas Territory. Also known as Malvinas, Islas.
southamerica [countries] ▶▶ 192–193

Falkland Sound sea chan. Falkland Is 205 E9
Falkner Arg. 204 D6
Falkonera i. Greece 59 E12
Falköping Sweden 45 K4
Fall r. U.S.A. 178 D4
Fall Branch U.S.A. 176 C9
Fallbrook U.S.A. 183 G8
Fall Creek U.S.A. 172 B6
Fallieres Coast Antarctica 222 T2
Fallon U.S.A. 182 F2
Fall River U.S.A. 177 N4
Fall River Pass U.S.A. 180 F4
Falls City U.S.A. 178 D3
Falls Creek U.S.A. 176 G4
Falmouth Antigua and Barbuda 187 H3
Falmouth Jamaica 186 D3
Falmouth U.K. 47 G13
Falmouth KY U.S.A. 176 A7
Falmouth MA U.S.A. 177 O4
Falmouth ME U.S.A. 177 O2
Falmouth VA U.S.A. 176 H7
Falou Mali 124 D3
False r. Canada 169 G1
False Bay S. Africa 132 C11
False Bay Park S. Africa 133 Q4
False Point India 95 E1
Falso, Cabo c. Dom. Rep. 187 F3
Falso, Cabo c. Hond. 186 C4
Falso Cabo de Hornos c. Chile 205 C9
Falster i. Denmark 45 J5
Fălticeni Romania 58 H1
Falun Sweden 45 K3
Falzarego, Passo di pass Italy 56 E2
Famagusta Cyprus 108 E2
also known as Ammochostos or Gazimağusa or Magosa
Famagusta Bay Cyprus see Ammochostos Bay
Famatina Arg. 204 D3
Famatina, Sierra de mts Arg. 204 C3
Famenin Iran 100 B3
Fame Range hills Australia 151 C5
Family Lake Canada 167 M5
Family Well Australia 150 D4
Fana Mali 124 D3
Fanad Head Rep. of Ireland 47 E8
Fanambana Madag. 131 [inset] K2
Fanandrana Madag. 131 [inset] K3
Fanari, Akra pt Greece 59 H11
Fanchang China 87 F2
Fandriana Madag. 131 [inset] J4
Fang Thai. 78 B4
Fangak Sudan 128 A2
Fangcheng China see Fangchenggang
Fangcheng China 87 E1
Fangchenggang China 87 D4
formerly known as Fangcheng
Fangdou Shan mts China 87 D2
Fangliao Taiwan 87 G4
Fangshan Taiwan 87 G4
Fangxian China 87 D1
Fangzheng China 82 C3
Fani i Vogël r. Albania 58 A7
Fanipal' Belarus 42 I8
Fankuai China 87 D2
formerly known as Fankuaidian
Fankuaidian China see Fankuai
Fanling Hong Kong China 87 [inset]
Fannrem Norway 44 J3
Fannūj Iran 101 D5
Fanø i. Denmark 45 J5
Fano Italy 56 F5
historically known as Colonia Julia Fenestris or Fanum Fortunae
Fanoualie i. Tonga see Fonualei
Fanshan Anhui China 87 F2
Fanshan Zhejiang China 87 G3
Fanshi China 85 G4
Fan Si Pan mt. Vietnam 78 C3
Fanum Fortunae Italy see Fano
Fanxian China 85 G5
also known as Yingtaoyuan
Farab Turkm. see Farap
Faraba Mali 124 C3
Farab-Pristan' Turkm. see Dzheykhun
Faradje Dem. Rep. Congo 126 F4
Faradofay Madag. see Tôlañaro
Farafangana Madag. 131 [inset] J4
Farafenni Gambia 124 B3
Farafra Oasis Egypt 121 F3
Farāgheh Iran 100 C4
Farāh Afgh. 101 E3
historically known as Alexandria Prophthasia
Farāh prov. Afgh. 101 E3
Farahābād Iran see Khezerābād
Farah Rūd watercourse Afgh. 101 E4
Farakhulm Afgh. 101 G3
Farallon de Medinilla i. N. Mariana Is 73 K3
also known as Bird Island
Farallon de Pajaros vol. N. Mariana Is 73 J2
Farallones de Cali, Parque Nacional nat. park Col. 198 B4
Farallon National Wildlife Refuge nature res. U.S.A. 182 A4
Faramuti i. Sudan 126 E2
Faranah Guinea 124 C4
Faraoani Romania 58 H2
Far'aoun well Mauritania 124 B2
Farap Turkm. 103 E5
formerly spelt Farab
Fararah Oman 105 F4
Farasān Saudi Arabia 104 C4
Farasān, Jazā'ir is Saudi Arabia 104 C4
Faratsiho Madag. 131 [inset] J3
Faraulep atoll Micronesia 73 J5
also known as Fattoilep; also spelt Foraulep; formerly known as Gardner
Fardes r. Spain 55 I7
Farewell, Cape Greenland 165 O3
also known as Farvel, Kap or Nunap Isua or Uummannarsuaq
Farewell, Cape N.Z. 152 G8
Farewell Spit N.Z. 152 G8
Färgelanda Sweden 45 K4
Farghona Uzbek. see Fergana
Farghona Wiloyati admin. div. Uzbek. see Ferganskaya Oblast'
Fargo U.S.A. 178 C2
Faribault U.S.A. 174 A2
Faribault, Lac l. Canada 169 G1
Faridabad India 96 C3
Faridkot India 96 B3
Faridpur Bangl. 97 F5
Faridpur India 96 C3
Fārīğ Iran 100 D2
Fārigh, Wādī al watercourse Libya 120 C2
Färila Sweden 45 K3
Farim Guinea-Bissau 124 B3
Farīmān Iran 101 D3
Farinha r. Brazil 202 C3
Farish Uzbek. 103 F4
also spelt Forish
Fâriskûr Egypt 108 C6
Färjestaden Sweden 45 L4
Farkadhon Greece 59 D9
Farkhar Afgh. see Farkhato
Farkhato Afgh. 101 G2
also known as Farkhar
Farkhor Tajik. 101 G2
also spelt Parkhar
Farley U.S.A. 172 B8
Farmahin Iran 100 B3
Farmakonisi i. Greece 59 I11
Farmer City U.S.A. 174 B3
Farmer Island Canada 168 D1
Farmerville U.S.A. 179 D5
Farmington Canada 166 F4
Farmington IA U.S.A. 172 B10
Farmington IL U.S.A. 172 C10
Farmington ME U.S.A. 177 O1
Farmington MO U.S.A. 174 B4
Farmington NH U.S.A. 177 N2
Farmington NM U.S.A. 181 E5
Farmington UT U.S.A. 180 E4
Farmington Hills U.S.A. 173 J8
Far Mountain Canada 166 E4
Farmville U.S.A. 176 G8
Farne Islands U.K. 46 K8
Farnham U.S.A. 177 I8
Farnham, Lake salt flat Australia 151 D5
Farnham, Mount Canada 167 G5
Faro Brazil 199 G5
Faro r. Cameroon 125 I4
Faro Canada 166 C2
Faro Port. 54 D7
Faro admin. dist. Port. 54 C7
Fårö i. Sweden 45 L4
Faro, Réserve du nature res. Cameroon 125 I4
Faro, Serra do mts Spain 54 D2

▶Faroe Islands terr. N. Atlantic Ocean 46 E2
Self-governing Danish Territory. Also spelt Faeroes; also known as Færoerne or Føroyar.
europe [countries] ▶▶ 32–35

Fårösund Sweden 45 L4
Farquhar Atoll Seychelles 129 F7
Farquhar Islands Seychelles 129 F7
Farquharson Tableland hills Australia 151 C5
Farrandsville U.S.A. 176 H4
Farrars Creek watercourse Australia 149 D5
Farrāsh, Jabal al hill Saudi Arabia 104 C4
Farrashband Iran 100 C4
Farr Bay Antarctica 223 G2
Farrellton Canada 173 R5
Farrokhī Iran 101 D3
Farrukhabad India see Fatehgarh
Fārs prov. Iran 100 C4
historically known as Pars or Parsa or Persis
Farsakh Iran 100 C3
Farsala Greece 59 D9
Farsaliotis r. Greece 59 D9
Fārsī, Jazīreh-ye i. Iran 107 G6
Farsi Afgh. 101 E3
Farsund Norway 45 I4
Fartak, Jabal mts Yemen 105 E5
Fartak, Ra's c. Yemen 105 F5
Fărtăneşti Romania 58 I3
Fartura r. Brazil 206 C3
Fartura, Serra da mts Brazil 203 A8
Farvel, Kap c. Greenland see Farewell, Cape
Farwell MI U.S.A. 173 I7
Farwell TX U.S.A. 179 B5
Fāryāb prov. Afgh. 101 F2
Fāryāb Hormozgan Iran 100 D5
also known as Deh Barez
Fāryāb Kermān Iran 100 D4
Farynava Belarus 43 J6
Fasā Iran 100 C4
Fasano Italy 56 J8
Fåset Norway 45 J3
Faşikan Geçidi pass Turkey 108 D1
Fasil Ghebbi and Gonder Monuments tourist site Eth. 128 C1
Fāsteh, Ra's-e pt Iran 101 E5
Fastiv Ukr. 41 D6
also spelt Fastov
Fastov Ukr. see Fastiv
Fatehabad India 96 B3
Fatehgarh Madhya Pradesh India 96 C4
Fatehgarh Uttar Pradesh India 96 C4
formerly known as Farrukhabad
Fatehnagar India 96 B4
Fatehpur Rajasthan India 96 B4
Fatehpur Uttar Pradesh India 96 D4
Fatehpur Sikri India 96 C4
Fateyevka Rus. Fed. 43 P9
Fatezh Rus. Fed. 43 Q9
Fatḥābād Iran 100 C4
Fathai Sudan 128 A2
Fati, Lac l. Mali 124 E2
Fatick Senegal 124 A3
Fattoilep atoll Micronesia see Faraulep
Fatuma Dem. Rep. Congo 127 F6
Faulkton U.S.A. 178 C2
Faulquemont France 51 M3
Fauquier Canada 166 G5
Fauresmith S. Africa 133 J6
Fauske Norway 44 K2
Faust Canada 167 H4
Favalto, Monte mt. Italy 56 E5
Favignana Sicilia Italy 57 E11
Favignana, Isola i. Sicilia Italy 57 E11
Fawcett Canada 167 H4
Fawn r. Canada 168 B2
Fawnleas S. Africa 133 O6
Fawwārah Saudi Arabia 104 C2
Faxaflói b. Iceland 44 [inset] B2
Faxälven r. Sweden 44 L3
Faxian Hu l. China 86 B3
Faya Chad 120 C5
also known as Largeau
Fayaoué New Caledonia 145 F4
Faydat al Adyān waterhole Iraq 109 M6
Faydat al Habbārīyah waterhole Iraq 109 N5
Fayette AL U.S.A. 175 C5
Fayette IA U.S.A. 172 B8
Fayette MI U.S.A. 172 G5
Fayette MO U.S.A. 178 D4
Fayette MS U.S.A. 175 B6
Fayette OH U.S.A. 176 A4
Fayetteville AR U.S.A. 179 D4
Fayetteville GA U.S.A. 175 C5
Fayetteville NC U.S.A. 174 E5
Fayetteville NY U.S.A. 177 I2
Fayetteville PA U.S.A. 176 H6
Fayetteville TN U.S.A. 174 C5
Fayetteville WV U.S.A. 176 D7
Fayfā Saudi Arabia 104 C4
Fayḥālah, Wādī watercourse Saudi Arabia 109 O8
Fâyid Egypt 108 D7
Faylakah i. Kuwait 107 G5
Fayl-la-Forêt France 51 L5
Fazair al Ghrazi watercourse Saudi Arabia 109 H8
Fazao Malfakassa, Parc National de nat. park Togo 125 F4
Fazel well Niger 125 H2
Fazilka India 96 B3
Fazrān, Jabal hill Saudi Arabia 105 E2
Fdérik Mauritania 122 B5
formerly known as Fort Gouraud
Fead Group is P.N.G. see Nuguria Islands
Feale r. Rep. of Ireland 47 C11
Fear, Cape U.S.A. 175 E5
Feather r. U.S.A. 182 C3
Feather, North Fork r. U.S.A. 182 C2
Featherston N.Z. 152 J9
Fécamp France 50 G3
Federacija Bosna i Hercegovina aut. div. Bos.-Herz. 56 K4
English form Federation of Bosnia and Herzegovina; also known as Muslim-Croat Federation
Federal Arg. 204 F3
Federal Capital Territory admin. div. Nigeria 125 G4
Federal District admin. dist. Brazil see Distrito Federal
Federal District admin. dist. Venez. see Distrito Federal
Federalsburg U.S.A. 177 J7
Federated Malay States country Asia see Malaysia
Federation of Bosnia and Herzegovina aut. div. Bos.-Herz. see Federacija Bosna i Hercegovina
Fedorov Kazakh. see Fedorovka
Fedorovka Kustanayskaya Oblast' Kazakh. 103 E1
Fedorovka Pavlodarskaya Oblast' Kazakh. 103 I1
Fedorovka Zapadnyy Kazakhstan Kazakh. 102 B2
also known as Fedorov
Fedorovka Rus. Fed. 102 C1
Fedorovskoye Rus. Fed. 43 U5
Fehérgyarmat Hungary 49 T8
Fehet Lake Canada 167 M1
Fehmarn i. Germany 48 I1
Fehmarn Belt strait Denmark/Germany 45 J5
also known as Femer Bælt
Fehrbellin Germany 49 J3
Feia, Lagoa lag. Brazil 203 D7
Feicheng China see Feixian
Feidong China 87 F2
also known as Dianbu
Feijó Brazil 200 C2
Feilding N.Z. 152 J8
Fei Ngo Shan hill Hong Kong China see Kowloon Peak
Feio r. Brazil see Aguapeí
Feira Zambia see Luangwa
Feira de Santana Brazil 202 E5
Feira do Monte Spain 54 D1
Feirān well Egypt 108 E9
Feirān, Wâdi watercourse Egypt 108 E9
Feirâni, Gebel mt. Egypt 108 F9
Feixi China 87 F2
also known as Shangpai; formerly known as Shangpaihe
Feixian China 85 H5
also known as Feicheng
Feixiang China 85 G4
Fejaj, Chott el salt l. Tunisia 123 H2
Fejø i. Denmark 48 I1
Feke Turkey 106 C3
Felanitx Spain 55 O5
Felaou well Alg. 125 G2
Feldberg mt. Ger. 51 N5
Feldkirch Austria 48 G8
Feldkirchen in Kärnten Austria 49 L9
Feldru Romania 58 F1
Feliciano r. Arg. 204 F3
Felicity U.S.A. 176 A7
Felidhu Atoll Maldives 93 D10
Felipe C. Puerto Mex. 185 H5
Felixlândia Brazil 203 C6
Felixstowe U.K. 47 N12
Felletin France 51 I7
Fellowsville U.S.A. 176 F6
Felsberg Germany 48 G4
Felsina Italy see Bologna
Feltre Italy 56 D2
Femeas r. Brazil 202 C5
Femer Bælt strait Denmark/Germany see Fehmarn Belt
Femminamorta, Monte mt. Italy 57 I9
Femø i. Denmark 48 I1
Femundsmarka Nasjonalpark nat. park Norway 44 K3
Fen r. China 85 F5
Fenambosy, Lohatanjona pt Madag. 131 [inset] J5
Fenelon Falls Canada 173 O6
Fener Burnu hd Turkey 108 G1
also known as Karataş Burnu
Fénérive Madag. see Fenoarivo Atsinanana
Fengari mt. Greece 59 G8
Fengcheng China see Lianjiang
Fengcheng China see Yongding
Fengcheng China see Anxi
Fengcheng China see Xinfeng
Fengcheng China see Fengshan
Fengcheng Jiangxi China 87 E2
Fengcheng Liaoning China 83 B4
Fengchuan China see Fengxin
Fengdu China 87 C2
also known as Xiucaiwan; formerly known as Mingshan
Fenggang China see Shaxian
Fenggang China 87 C3
also known as Longquan
Fenggeling China 86 C1
Fenghua China 87 G2
Fenghuang China 87 D3
also known as Tuojiang
Fengjiaba China see Wangcang
Fengjie China 87 D2
also known as Yong'an
Fengkai China 87 D4
also known as Jiangkou
Fenglin Taiwan 87 G4
Fengming China see Qishan
Fengnan China 85 H4
Fengning China 85 H3
also known as Dage or Dagezhen
Fengqi China see Luochuan
Fengqing China 86 A3
also known as Fengshan
Fengqiu China 87 E1
Fengrun China 85 H4
Fengshan China see Luoyuan
Fengshan China 86 C3
also known as Fengcheng
Fengshan China see Luotian
Fengshan China see Fengqing
Fengshuba Shuiku resr China 87 E3
Fengshui Shan mt. China 82 A1
Fengtai China 87 F1
Fengtongzai Giant Panda Reserve nature res. China 86 B2
Fengxian Jiangsu China 87 F1
Fengxian Shaanxi China 86 C1
also known as Shuangshipu
Fengxian Shanghai China 87 G2
also known as Nanqiao
Fengxiang China see Luobei
Fengxiang China see Lincang
Fengxin China 87 E2
also known as Fengchuan
Fengyang China 87 F1
also known as Fucheng
Fengyi China see Zheng'an
Fengyi China see Maoxian
Fengyüan Taiwan 87 G3
Fengzhen China 85 G3
Fenhe Shuiku resr China 85 F4
Feni Bangl. 97 F5
Feni Islands P.N.G. 145 E2
Fenny r. Bangl./India 97 F5
Feno, Capo di c. Corse France 56 A7
Fenoarivo Atsinanana Madag. 131 [inset] K3
formerly known as Fénérive
Fenoarivo Be Madag. 131 [inset] J3
Fenton U.S.A. 173 J8
Fenua Ura atoll Fr. Polynesia see Manuae
Fenwick U.S.A. 176 E7
Fenyang China 85 F4
Fenyi China 87 E3
Feodosiya Ukr. 41 E7
also known as Caffa or Kafa or Kefe; historically known as Theodosia
Fer, Cap de c. Alg. 123 G1
Férai Greece see Feres
Ferapontovo Rus. Fed. 43 T2
Ferdinandshof Germany 49 K2
Ferdows Iran 100 D3
Fère-Champenoise France 51 J4
Feres Greece 58 H8
also known as Férai
Fērfēr Somalia 128 E3
Fergana Uzbek. 103 G4
also spelt Farghona; formerly known as Novyy Margelan or Skobelev
Fergana Oblast admin. div. Uzbek. see Ferganskaya Oblast'
Fergana Range mts Kyrg. see Fergana Too Tizmegi
Fergana Too Tizmegi mts Kyrg. 103 H4
English form Fergana Range; also known as Ferganskiy Khrebet
Ferganskaya Oblast' admin. div. Uzbek. 103 G4
English form Fergana Oblast; also known as Farghona Wiloyati
Ferganskiy Khrebet mts Kyrg. see Fergana Too Tizmegi
Fergus Canada 173 M7
Fergus Falls U.S.A. 178 C2
Ferguson Lake Canada 167 L2
Fergusson r. Australia 148 A2
Fergusson Island P.N.G. 145 E2
Fériana Tunisia 123 H2
Ferjukot Iceland 44 [inset] B2
Ferkessédougou Côte d'Ivoire 124 D4
Ferlach Austria 49 L9
Ferlo, Vallée du watercourse Senegal 124 B3
Ferlo-Nord, Réserve de Faune du nature res. Senegal 124 B3
Ferlo-Sud, Réserve de Faune du nature res. Senegal 124 B3
Fermo Italy 56 F5
historically known as Firmum or Firmum Picenum
Fermont Canada 169 H2
Fermoselle Spain 54 E3
Fermoy Rep. of Ireland 47 D11
Fernandina Beach U.S.A. 175 D6
Fernando de Magallanes, Parque Nacional nat. park Chile 205 B9
Fernando de Noronha i. Brazil 216 L6
Fernandópolis Brazil 206 C7
Fernando Poó i. Equat. Guinea see Bioco
Fernão Dias Brazil 207 I3
Fernão Veloso Moz. 131 I2
Ferndale U.S.A. 180 B2
Ferndown U.K. 47 K13
Fernhill N.Z. 152 K7
Fernie Canada 167 H5
Fernley U.S.A. 182 E2
Ferns Rep. of Ireland 47 F11
Ferozepore India see Firozpur
Ferrara Italy 56 D4
Ferrato, Capo c. Sardegna Italy 57 B9
Ferreira Spain 54 D1
Ferreira do Alentejo Port. 54 C6
Ferrelsburg U.S.A. 176 C7
Ferreñafe Peru 198 B6
Ferriday U.S.A. 175 B6
Ferro, Capo c. Sardegna Italy 56 B7
Ferrol Spain 54 C1
also known as El Ferrol; long form El Ferrol del Caudillo
Ferron U.S.A. 183 M2
Ferros Brazil 203 D6
Ferrum U.S.A. 176 E9
Ferryland Canada 169 K4
Ferryville Tunisia see Menzel Bourguiba
Fertő-tavi nat. park Hungary 49 N8
Ferzikovo Rus. Fed. 43 R7
Fès Morocco 122 D2
also spelt Al Fas or Fez
Feshi Dem. Rep. Congo 127 C6
Fessenden U.S.A. 178 C2
Fet Dom, Tanjung pt Indon. 75 D3
Fété Bowé Senegal 124 B3
Feteşti Romania 58 I4
Feteşti-Gară Romania 58 I4
Fethard Rep. of Ireland 47 E11
Fethiye Turkey see Yazıhan
Fethiye Turkey 106 B3
Fetisovo Kazakh. 102 C4
Fetlar i. U.K. 46 L3
Feuilles, Rivière aux r. Canada 169 G1
Feurs France 51 K7
Fevral'sk Rus. Fed. 82 C1
Fevzipaşa Turkey 107 D3
Feyzābād Afgh. 101 G2
also spelt Faizabad
Feyzābād Iran 100 C4
Fez Morocco see Fès
Fiambalá Arg. 204 D2
Fiambala r. Arg. 204 D2
Fian Ghana 124 E4
Fianarantsoa Madag. 131 [inset] J4
Fianarantsoa prov. Madag. 131 [inset] J4
Fianga Chad 126 B2
Fiano Romano Italy 56 E6
Ficalho hill Port. 54 D7
Fichē Eth. 128 C2
Fichtelgebirge hills Germany 51 S2
Fichtelgebirge park Germany 48 J5
Ficksburg S. Africa 133 L5
Fidā oasis Saudi Arabia 105 F4
Fidenza Italy 56 C4
Fidīmīn Egypt 108 B8
Fidjeland Norway 45 I4
Fidlův Kopec hill Czech Rep. 49 O6
Field B.C. Canada 167 G5
Field Ont. Canada 173 M4
Field U.S.A. 176 B9
Field Island Australia 148 B2
Fiemanka r. Latvia 42 H5
Fieni Romania 58 G3
Fier Albania 58 A8
Fiery Creek r. Australia 148 C3
Fierzes, Liqeni i resr Albania 58 B6
Fife Lake U.S.A. 172 H6
Fife Ness pt U.K. 46 J7
Fifield U.S.A. 172 C5
Fifteenth of May City Egypt see Medinet 15 Mayo
Fifth Cataract rapids Sudan see 5th Cataract
Fifth Meridian Canada 167 H3
Figalo, Cap c. Alg. 55 J9
Figari, Capo c. Sardegna Italy 56 B8
Figeac France 51 I8
Figueira r. Port. 54 C6
Figueira da Foz Port. 54 C4
Figueiró dos Vinhos Port. 54 C5
Figueras Spain see Figueres
Figueres Spain 55 N2
also spelt Figueras
Figuig Morocco 123 E2
Figuil Cameroon 125 I4

▶Fiji country S. Pacific Ocean 145 G3
4th most populous and 5th largest country in Oceania.
oceania [countries] ▶▶ 138–139

Fīk' Eth. 128 D2
Filabusi Zimbabwe 131 F4
Filadelfia Costa Rica 186 B5
Filadelfia Italy 57 I10
Filadelfia Para. 201 E5
Fiľakovo Slovakia 49 Q7
Filamana Mali 124 D4
Filchner Ice Shelf Antarctica 222 V1
Filey U.K. 47 L9
Filiaşi Romania 58 E4
Filiates Greece 59 B9
Filiatra Greece 59 C11
Filibe Bulg. see Plovdiv
Filicudi, Isola i. Isole Lipari Italy 57 G10
Filingué Niger 125 F3
Filiouri r. Greece 58 G8
Filipinas country Asia see Philippines
Filippa, Mys hd Rus. Fed. 82 E1
Filippiada Greece 59 B9
Filippoi tourist site Greece 58 F7
Filipstad Sweden 45 K4
Fillan Norway 44 J3
Fillira Greece see Fillyra
Fillmore CA U.S.A. 182 F7
Fillmore UT U.S.A. 183 L3
Fillyra Greece 58 G7
also spelt Fillira
Filtu Eth. 128 D3
Fimbull Ice Shelf Antarctica 223 A2
Fina, Réserve de nature res. Mali 124 C3
Finale Ligure Italy 56 A4
Fincastle U.S.A. 176 F8
Finch'a'ā Hāyk' l. Eth. 128 C2
Findhorn r. U.K. 46 I6
Fındık Turkey 107 E3
also known as Parona
Findlay U.S.A. 176 B4
Fine U.S.A. 177 J1
Finger Lake Canada 167 M4
Finger Lakes U.S.A. 177 I3
Fingeshwar India 94 D1
Fingoè Moz. 131 F2
Finiels, Sommet de mt. France 51 J8
Finike Turkey 106 B3
Finike Körfezi b. Turkey 106 B3
Finisterre Spain see Fisterra
Finisterre, Cabo c. Spain see Finisterre, Cape
Finisterre, Cape Spain 54 B2
also known as Finisterre, Cabo or Fisterra, Cabo
Finke Australia 148 B5
Finke watercourse Australia 148 B5
Finke, Mount hill Australia 146 B2
Finke Aboriginal Land res. Australia 148 C5
Finke Bay Australia 148 A2
Finke Flood Flats lowland Australia 148 B5
Finke Gorge National Park Australia 148 B5

▶Finland country Europe 44 M3
known as Suomi in Finnish
europe [countries] ▶▶ 32–35
europe [environments] ▶▶ 36–37

Finland U.S.A. 172 B3
Finland, Gulf of Europe 42 D2
Finlay r. Canada 166 E3
Finlay, Mount Canada 166 E3
Finlay Forks Canada 166 F4
Finlayson U.S.A. 172 A4
Finley Australia 147 E3
Finley U.S.A. 178 C2
Finmark Canada 172 D2
Finn r. Rep. of Ireland 47 E9
Finne ridge Germany 48 I4
Finnigan, Mount Australia 149 E2
Finniss r. Australia 148 A2
Finniss, Cape Australia 146 B3
Finniss Springs Aboriginal Land res. Australia 146 C2
Finnmark county Norway 44 N1
Finnmarksvidda reg. Norway 44 M1
Finnskog Norway 45 K3
Finnsnes Norway 44 L1
Finschhafen P.N.G. 73 K8
Finspång Sweden 45 K4
Finsteraarhorn mt. Switz. 51 O6
Finsterwalde Germany 49 K4
Finström Fin. 42 A1
Fintona U.K. 47 E9
Finucane Range hills Australia 149 D4
Fiora r. Italy 56 D6
Fiordland National Park N.Z. 153 B13
Fiorenzuola d'Arda Italy 56 B4
Fīr reg. Saudi Arabia 105 D1
Frat r. Turkey 107 D3 see Euphrates
Firavahana Madag. 131 [inset] J3
Firebaugh U.S.A. 182 D5
Firedrake Lake Canada 167 J2
Firenze Italy see Florence
Fire River Canada 173 J2
Fireside Canada 166 E3
Firesteel Creek r. U.S.A. 178 C3
Firiña Venez. 199 E3
Firk, Sha'ib watercourse Iraq 107 F5
Firkachi well Niger 125 I3
Firmat Arg. 204 E4
Firmino Alves Brazil 207 N1
Firminópolis Brazil 206 C3
Firminy France 51 K7
Firmum Italy see Fermo
Firmum Picenum Italy see Fermo
Firovo Rus. Fed. 43 O4
Firozabad India 96 C4
Firozkoh reg. Afgh. 101 F3
Firozpur Haryana India 96 C4
Firozpur Punjab India 96 B3
formerly spelt Ferozepore
First Cataract rapids Egypt see 1st Cataract
First Three Mile Opening sea chan. Australia 149 E2
Firuzabad Iran see Rāsk
Fīrūzābād Iran 100 C4
Fīrūzeh Iran 100 D2
Firūzkūh Iran 100 C3
Fischersbrunn Namibia 130 B5
Fish watercourse Namibia 130 C6
Fish r. S. Africa 132 E7
Fisher Australia 146 A2
Fisher Bay Antarctica 223 J2
Fisher Glacier Antarctica 223 E2
Fisher River Canada 167 L5
Fisher Strait Canada 165 K3
Fishersville U.S.A. 176 G7
Fishguard U.K. 47 H12
also known as Abergwaun
Fishing Creek U.S.A. 177 I7
Fishing Lake Canada 167 M4
Fish Lake Canada 166 F2
Fish Lake MN U.S.A. 172 A4
Fish Lake UT U.S.A. 183 M3
Fish Point U.S.A. 173 J7
Fiska Norway 44 I3
Fiske, Cape Antarctica 222 T2
Fiskebøl Norway 44 K1
Fiskenæsset Greenland see Qeqertarsuatsiaat
Fismes France 51 J3
Fisterra Spain 54 B2
also spelt Finisterre
Fisterra, Cabo c. Spain see Finisterre, Cape
Fitampito Madag. 131 [inset] J4
Fitchburg MA U.S.A. 177 N3
Fitchburg WI U.S.A. 172 D8
Fitchville U.S.A. 176 C4
Fitiai Greece see Fyteies
Fitjar Norway 45 I4
Fitri, Lac l. Chad 120 C6
Fitzcarrald Peru 200 B2
Fitzgerald U.S.A. 175 D6
Fitzgerald River National Park Australia 151 B7
Fitz Hugh Sound sea chan. Canada 166 D5
Fitzmaurice r. Australia 148 A2
Fitz Roy Arg. 205 D7
Fitzroy r. Qld Australia 149 F4
Fitzroy r. W.A. Australia 150 C3
Fitz Roy, Cerro mt. Arg. 205 B8
Fitzroy Aboriginal Land res. Australia 148 A2
Fitzroy Crossing Australia 150 D3
Fitzwilliam Island Canada 168 D4
Fiume Croatia see Rijeka
Fiumefreddo di Sicilia Sicilia Italy 57 H11
Five Fingers Peninsula N.Z. 153 A13
Five Forks N.Z. 153 E13
Five Points U.S.A. 182 D5
Fivizzano Italy 56 C4
Fizi Dem. Rep. Congo 126 F6
Fizuli Azer. see Füzuli
Fjällsjönäs Sweden 44 L2
Fjellbu Norway 44 L1
Fjerritslev Denmark 45 J4
Fkih Ben Salah Morocco 122 D2
Flå Norway 45 J3
Flaga Iceland 44 [inset] C3

index F G

Flagstaff S. Africa 133 N8
also known as Siphaqeni
Flagstaff U.S.A. 183 M6
Flagstaff Lake U.S.A. 174 G2
Flaherty Island Canada 168 E1
Flakaberg Sweden 44 M2
Flåm Norway 45 I3
Flambeau r. U.S.A. 172 B5
Flamborough Head U.K. 47 L9
Flamenco, Isla i. Arg. 204 E6
Fläming hills Germany 49 J3
Flaming Gorge Reservoir U.S.A. 180 E4
Flaminksvlei salt pan S. Africa 132 F7
Flanagan r. Canada 167 M4
Flandreau U.S.A. 178 C2
Flannagan Lake U.S.A. 176 C8
Flannan Isles U.K. 46 E5
Fläsjön l. Sweden 44 K2
Flat r. Canada 166 E2
Flat r. U.S.A. 172 H8
Flateyjardalsheiði reg. Iceland 44 [inset] C2
Flathead r. U.S.A. 180 D2
Flathead, Middle Fork r. U.S.A. 167 H5
Flathead Indian Reservation res. U.S.A. 180 D3
Flathead Lake U.S.A. 180 D3
Flatiron mt. U.S.A. 180 D3
Flat Island Mauritius 72 E4
Flat Lick U.S.A. 176 B9
Flat Point N.Z. 152 J9
Flattery, Cape Australia 149 E2
Flattery, Cape U.S.A. 180 A2
Flat Top mt. Canada 166 B2
Flatwillow Creek r. U.S.A. 180 F3
Flatwoods KY U.S.A. 176 C7
Flatwoods WV U.S.A. 176 E7
Flechtinger Höhenzug park Germany 48 I3
Fleetwood U.K. 47 I10
Fleetwood U.S.A. 177 J5
Flekkefjord Norway 45 I4
Flemingsburg U.S.A. 176 B7
Flemington U.S.A. 177 K5
Flen Sweden 45 L4
Flensborg Fjord inlet Denmark/Germany 45 J5
also known as Flensburger Förde
Flensburg Germany 48 G1
Flensburger Förde inlet Denmark/Germany see Flensborg Fjord
Flers France 50 F4
Flesherton Canada 173 M6
Flesko, Tanjung pt Indon. 75 C2
Fletcher Lake Canada 167 I2
Fletcher Peninsula Antarctica 222 S2
Fletcher Pond l. U.S.A. 173 J6
Fleurance France 50 G9
Fleur de Lys Canada 169 J3
Fleur-de-May, Lac l. Canada 169 H3
Fleury-les-Aubrais France 51 H5
Flinders r. Australia 149 D3
Flinders Bay Australia 151 A7
Flinders Chase National Park Australia 146 C3
Flinders Group is Australia 149 E2
Flinders Group National Park Australia 149 E2
Flinders Island S.A. Australia 146 B3
Flinders Island Tas. Australia 147 F4
Flinders Passage Australia 149 F3
Flinders Ranges mts Australia 146 C3
Flinders Ranges National Park Australia 146 C2
Flinders Reefs Australia 149 F3
Flin Flon Canada 167 K4
Flint U.K. 47 I10
also known as Y Fflint
Flint U.S.A. 173 J7
Flint r. GA U.S.A. 175 C6
Flint r. MI U.S.A. 173 J7
Flint Island Kiribati 221 H6
Flintstone U.S.A. 176 G6
Flisa Norway 45 K3
Flisa r. Norway 45 K3
▶ Flissingskiy, Mys c. Rus. Fed. 38 G2
Most easterly point of Europe.
Flix Spain 55 L3
Flöha Germany 49 K5
Flood Range mts Antarctica 222 P1
Flora r. Australia 148 A2
Flora U.S.A. 172 G10
Florac France 51 J8
Florala U.S.A. 175 C6
Flora Reef Australia 149 E3
Floraville Australia 148 C3
Flor de Punga Peru 198 C6
Florence Italy 56 D5
also known as Firenze; historically known as Florentia
Florence AL U.S.A. 174 C5
Florence AZ U.S.A. 183 M8
Florence CO U.S.A. 181 F5
Florence KY U.S.A. 176 A7
Florence OR U.S.A. 180 A4
Florence SC U.S.A. 175 E5
Florence Junction U.S.A. 183 M8
Florencia Arg. 204 F3
Florencia Col. 198 C4
Florentia Italy see Florence
Florentino Ameghino Arg. 205 D6
Florentino Ameghino, Embalse resr Arg. 205 D6
Flores Brazil 202 D3
Flores Guat. 185 H5
Flores i. Indon. 75 B5
Florescência Brazil 200 C2
Flores de Goiás Brazil 202 C5
Flores Island Canada 166 E5
Flores Sea Indon. 75 A4
Floresta Brazil 202 E4
Floresville U.S.A. 179 C6
Floriano Brazil 202 D3
Floriano Peixoto Brazil 200 D2
Florianópolis Brazil 203 B8
Florida Bol. 201 E4
Florida Chile 204 B5
Florida Cuba 186 D2
Florida Uruguay 204 F4
Florida state U.S.A. 175 D6
Florida, Straits of Bahamas/U.S.A. 186 C2
Florida Bay U.S.A. 175 D7
Florida Keys is U.S.A. 175 D7
Florida Negra Arg. 205 D8
Flórida Paulista Brazil 206 B8
Floridia Sicilia Italy 57 H11
Florii, Vârful hill Romania 58 E1
Florin U.S.A. 182 C3
Florina Greece 58 C8
Florínia Brazil 206 C9
Floriskraaldam l. S. Africa 132 F10
Florissant U.S.A. 174 B4
Florø Norway 45 I3
Flour Lake Canada 169 H2
Floyd U.S.A. 176 E9
Floyd, Mount U.S.A. 183 L6
Floydada U.S.A. 179 B5
Fluchthorn mt. Austria/Switz. 51 Q6
Fluk Indon. 75 C3
Flums Switz. 51 P5
Flushing Neth. see Vlissingen
Flushing OH U.S.A. 176 D5
Fluvià r. Spain 55 O2
Fly r. P.N.G. 73 J8
Flying Fish, Cape Antarctica 222 R2
Flying Fox Creek r. Australia 148 B2
Foam Lake Canada 167 K5
Foča Bos.-Herz. 56 K5
also known as Srbinje
Foça Turkey 106 A3
Focșani Romania 58 I3
Focuri Romania 58 I1
Fodé Cent. Afr. Rep. 126 D3
Foelsche r. Australia 148 C2
Fogang China 87 E4
also known as Shijiao
Fog Bay Australia 148 A2
Fogelsville U.S.A. 177 J5
Foggâret el Arab Alg. 123 F4
Foggia Italy 56 H7
Fogi Indon. 75 C3
Foglia r. Italy 56 E5
Föglö Fin. 45 M3
Fogo i. Cape Verde 124 [inset]
Fogo Island Canada 169 K3
Fogoleva Kazakh. 103 G4
Föhr i. Germany 48 F1
Foinaven hill U.K. 46 H5
Foix France 50 H10
Fokino Rus. Fed. 43 P8
formerly known as Tsementnyy
Fokku Nigeria 125 G4
Folarskarnuten mt. Norway 45 I3
Folda sea chan. Norway 44 K2
Foldereid Norway 44 K2
Foldfjorden sea chan. Norway 44 J2
Folegandros Greece 59 F12
Folegandros i. Greece 59 F12
Foley Botswana 131 E4
Foley AL U.S.A. 175 C6
Foley MN U.S.A. 174 A2
Foleyet Canada 168 D3
Foley Island Canada 165 L3
Folgares Angola see Capelongo
Folger, Cape Antarctica 223 H2
Foligno Italy 56 E6
Folkestone U.K. 47 N12
Folkston U.S.A. 175 D6
Folldal Norway 45 J3
Folletts U.S.A. 172 C9
Föllinge Sweden 44 K3
Follonica Italy 56 C6
Folsom U.S.A. 176 E6
Folsom Lake U.S.A. 182 C3
Fomboni Comoros 129 D8
Fómento Cuba 186 D2
Fomin Rus. Fed. 41 G7
Fominskoye Rus. Fed. 40 G4
Fonda U.S.A. 177 K3
Fond-du-Lac Canada 167 J3
Fond du Lac r. Canada 167 J3
Fond du Lac U.S.A. 172 E7
Fond du Lac Indian Reservation res. U.S.A. 174 A2
Fonde U.S.A. 176 B9
Fondevila Spain 54 C3
Fondi Italy 56 F7
historically known as Fundi
Fon Going ridge Guinea 124 C4
Fonni Sardegna Italy 57 B8
Fonsagrada Spain see A Fonsagrada
Fonseca Col. 198 C2
Fontainebleau France 51 I4
Fontanges Canada 169 G2
Fontas Canada 166 F3
Fontas r. Canada 166 F3
Fonte Boa Brazil 199 E5
Fonte do Pau-d'Agua Brazil 201 F3
Fontenay-le-Comte France 50 F6
Fonteneau, Lac l. Canada 169 I3
Fontur pt Iceland 44 [inset] D2
Fonuafo'ou i. Tonga 145 H4
also known as Falcon Island; also spelt Fonuafu'u
Fonuafu'u i. Tonga see Fonuafo'ou
Fonualei i. Tonga 145 H3
also spelt Fanoualie; formerly known as Amargura Island
Fonyód Hungary 49 O9
Foochow China see Fuzhou
Fool Creek Reservoir U.S.A. 183 L2
Foot's Bay Canada 173 N5
Foping China 87 D1
also known as Yuanjiazhuang
Foraker, Mount U.S.A. 164 D3
Forat Iran 100 C3
Foraulep atoll Micronesia see Faraulep
Forbes Australia 147 F3
Forbesganj India 97 E4
Forbes Reef Swaziland 133 P3
Forchheim Germany 48 I6
Ford r. Canada 169 H1
Ford r. U.S.A. 172 F5
Ford City CA U.S.A. 182 E6
Ford City PA U.S.A. 176 F5
Førde Hordaland Norway 45 I4
Førde Sogn og Fjordane Norway 45 I3
Forde Lake Canada 167 L2
Fordell N.Z. 152 J7
Fordingbridge U.K. 50 E2
Ford Range mts Antarctica 222 O1
Fords Bridge Australia 147 E2
Fordyce U.S.A. 179 D5
Forécariah Guinea 124 B4
Forel, Mont mt. Greenland 165 P3
Foreman U.S.A. 179 D5
Foremost Canada 167 I5
Foresight Mountain Canada 166 E4
Forest Canada 166 D5
Forest MS U.S.A. 175 B5
Forest OH U.S.A. 176 B5
Forest VA U.S.A. 176 F8
Forestburg Canada 167 H4
Forest City U.S.A. 177 J4
Forest Creek r. Australia 149 D3
Foresthill U.S.A. 182 D2
Forest Junction U.S.A. 172 E6
Forest Lake U.S.A. 172 A5
Forest Lakes U.S.A. 183 N7
Forest Park U.S.A. 175 C5
Forest Ranch U.S.A. 182 C2
Forestville Canada 169 G3
Forestville CA U.S.A. 182 B3
Forestville MI U.S.A. 173 K7
Forestville NY U.S.A. 176 F3
Forêt des Deux Balé nat. park Burkina 124 E4
Forêt de Togodo nature res. Togo 125 F5
Forfar U.K. 46 J7
Forges-les-Eaux France 50 H3
Forillon, Parc National de nat. park Canada 169 H3
Forish Uzbek. see Farish
Forked River U.S.A. 177 K6
Forks U.S.A. 180 A3
Forksville U.S.A. 177 I4
Fork Union U.S.A. 176 G8
Forlì Italy 56 E4
Forman U.S.A. 178 C2
Formby U.K. 47 I10
Formentera i. Spain 55 M6
Formentor, Cap de c. Spain 55 O5
Formerie France 50 H3
Former Yugoslav Republic of Macedonia country Europe see Macedonia
Formia Italy 56 F7
Formiga Brazil 203 C7
Formigine Italy 56 C4
Formosa Arg. 204 F2
Formosa prov. Arg. 204 F2
Formosa country Asia see Taiwan
Formosa Brazil 206 F2
Formosa, Serra hills Brazil 201 G3
Formosa do Rio Preto Brazil 202 C4
Formosa Strait China/Taiwan see Taiwan Strait
Formoso Brazil 202 B4
Formoso r. Bahia Brazil 202 C5
Formoso r. Goiás Brazil 206 A5
Formoso r. Tocantins Brazil 202 B4
also known as Javaés
Fornos Moz. 131 G4
Forolshogna mt. Norway 44 J3
Foroyar terr. N. Atlantic Ocean see Faroe Islands
Forres U.K. 46 I6
Forrest Australia 151 E6
Forrest r. Australia 150 E2
Forrest U.S.A. 174 B3
Forrestal Range mts Antarctica 222 U1
Forrest City U.S.A. 174 B5
Forrest Lakes salt flat Australia 151 E6
Forreston U.S.A. 172 D8
Forsand Norway 45 I4
Forsayth Australia 149 D3
Forsbakken Norway 44 L1
Forshaga Sweden 45 K4
Forssa Fin. 45 M3
Forst Germany 49 L4
Forster Australia 147 G3
Forsyth GA U.S.A. 175 D5
Forsyth MO U.S.A. 178 D4
Forsyth MT U.S.A. 180 F3
Forsythe Canada 173 Q2
Forsyth Islands Australia 148 C3
Forsyth Range hills Australia 149 D4
Fort Abbas Pak. 101 H4
Fort Albany Canada 168 D2
Fortaleza Pando Bol. 200 D2
Fortaleza Pando Bol. 200 D3
Fortaleza Brazil 202 E2
formerly known as Ceará
Fortaleza de Santa Teresa Uruguay 204 G4
Fort Apache Indian Reservation res. U.S.A. 183 N8
Fort Archambault Chad see Sarh
Fort Ashby U.S.A. 176 G6
Fort Assiniboine Canada 167 H4
Fort Atkinson U.S.A. 172 E8
Fort Augustus U.K. 46 H6
Fort Babine Canada 166 E4
Fort Beaufort S. Africa 133 K9
Fort Belknap Indian Reservation res. U.S.A. 180 E2
Fort Benton U.S.A. 180 E3
Fort Berthold Indian Reservation res. U.S.A. 178 B2
Fort Black Canada 167 J4
Fort Brabant Canada see Tuktoyaktuk
Fort Bragg U.S.A. 182 A2
Fort Carillon U.S.A. see Ticonderoga
Fort Carnot Madag. see Ikongo
Fort Charlet Alg. see Djanet
Fort Chimo Canada see Kuujjuaq
Fort Chipewyan Canada 167 I3
Fort Collins U.S.A. 180 F4
Fort Constantine Australia 149 D4
Fort-Coulonge Canada 168 E4
Fort Covington U.S.A. 177 K1
Fort Crampel Cent. Afr. Rep. see Kaga Bandoro
Fort-Dauphin Madag. see Tôlañaro
Fort Davis U.S.A. 179 B6
▶ Fort-de-France Martinique 187 H4
Capital of Martinique.
Fort de Kock Indon. see Bukittinggi
Fort de Polignac Alg. see Illizi
Fort Deposit U.S.A. 175 C5
Fort Dodge U.S.A. 178 D3
Fort Donald S. Africa 133 N7
Fort Duchesne U.S.A. 183 O1
Forte, Monte hill Sardegna Italy 57 A8
Fort Edward U.S.A. 177 L2
Forte Nordeste Angola 127 D6
Fort Erie Canada 173 O8
Fortescue r. Australia 150 B4
Forte Veneza Brazil 199 H6
Fortezza, Monte della hill Italy 56 C6
Fort Flatters Alg. see Bordj Omer Driss
Fort Foureau Cameroon see Kousséri
Fort Franklin Canada see Déline
Fort Gaines U.S.A. 175 C6
Fort Gardel Alg. see Zaouatallaz
Fort Garland U.S.A. 181 F5
Fort Gay U.S.A. 176 C7
Fort Gibson Lake U.S.A. 179 D5
Fort Good Hope Canada 166 D1
Fort Gouraud Mauritania see Fdérik
Forth r. U.K. 46 I7
Forth, Firth of est. U.K. 46 I7
Fort Hall Kenya see Muranga
Fort Hall Indian Reservation res. U.S.A. 180 D4
Fort Hertz Myanmar see Putao
Fortification Range mts U.S.A. 183 J3
Fortín Aroma Para. 201 E5
Fortín Avalos Sánchez Para. 201 E5
Fortín Boquerón Para. 201 F5
Fortín Capitán Demattei Para. 201 E5
Fortín Carlos Antonio López Para. 201 F5
Fortín Coronel Bogado Para. 201 F5
Fortín Coronel Eugenio Garay Para. 201 E5
Fortín Galpón Para. 201 F4
Fortín General Caballero Para. 201 F6
Fortín General Díaz Para. 201 E5
Fortín General Mendoza Para. 201 E5
Fortín Hernandarias Para. 201 E5
Fortín Infante Rivarola Para. 201 E5
Fortín Juan de Zalazar Para. 201 F5
Fortín Lagerenza Para. 201 E5
Fortín Lavalle Arg. 204 E2
Fortín Leonardo Britos Para. 201 E5
Fortín Leonida Escobar Para. 201 E5
Fortín Linares Para. 201 E5
Fortín Madrejón Para. 201 F5
Fortín May Alberto Gardel Para. 201 E5
Fortín Nueva Asunción Para. 201 E5
Fortín Pilcomayo Arg. 201 E5
Fortín Presidente Ayala Para. 201 F5
Fortín Ravelo Bol. 201 E4
Fortín Suárez Arana Bol. 201 E4
Fortín Teniente Juan Echauri López Para. 201 E5
Fortín Teniente Mountania Para. 201 F5
Fortín Teniente Primero hill Mendoza Para. 201 F4
Fortín Teniente Rojas Silva Para. 201 E6
Fort Jameson Zambia see Chipata
Fort Johnston Malawi see Mangochi
Fort Kent U.S.A. 174 G2
Fort Laperrine Alg. see Tamanrasset
Fort Lauderdale U.S.A. 175 D7
also known as Port Everglades
Fort Liard Canada 166 F2
Fort Liberté Haiti 187 F3
Fort Loudon U.S.A. 176 H6
Fort Mackay Canada 167 I3
Fort Macleod Canada 167 H5
formerly known as MacLeod
Fort Madison U.S.A. 174 B3
Fort Manning Malawi see Mchinji
Fort McCoy U.S.A. 172 C6
Fort McMurray Canada 167 I3
Fort McPherson Canada 164 F3
Fort Morgan U.S.A. 178 B3
Fort Mtombeni S. Africa 133 O6
Fort Myers U.S.A. 175 D7
Fort Nelson Canada 166 F3
Fort Nelson r. Canada 166 F3
Fort Norman Canada see Tulít'a
Fort Orange U.S.A. see Albany
Fortore r. Italy 56 H7
Fort Payne U.S.A. 174 C5
Fort Peck Indian Reservation res. U.S.A. 180 F2
Fort Peck Reservoir U.S.A. 180 F3
Fort Pierce U.S.A. 175 D7
Fort Pierre U.S.A. 178 B2
Fort Portal Uganda 128 A4
Fort Providence Canada 167 G2
Fort Qu'Appelle Canada 167 K5
Fort Randall U.S.A. see Cold Bay
Fort Recovery U.S.A. 176 A5
Fort Resolution Canada 167 H2
Fortrose N.Z. 153 C14
Fortrose U.K. 46 H6
Fort Rosebery Zambia see Mansa
Fort Rousset Congo see Owando
Fort Rupert Canada see Waskaganish
Fort St James Canada 166 E4
Fort St John Canada 166 F3
Fort Sandeman Pak. see Zhob
Fort Saskatchewan Canada 167 H4
Fort Scott U.S.A. 178 D4
Fort Severn Canada 168 C1
Fort-Shevchenko Kazakh. 102 B3
Fort Simpson Canada 166 F2
Fort Smith Canada 167 H2
Fort Smith U.S.A. 179 D5
Fort Stockton U.S.A. 179 B6
Fort Sumner U.S.A. 181 F6
Fort Totten (Devils Lake Sioux) Indian Reservation res. U.S.A. 178 C2
Fort Trinquet Mauritania see Bîr Mogreïn
Fortuna U.S.A. 180 A4
Fortune Bay Canada 169 K4
Fort Valley U.S.A. 175 D5
Fort Vermilion Canada 167 G3
Fort Victoria Zimbabwe see Masvingo
Fort Walton U.S.A. see Fort Walton Beach
Fort Walton Beach U.S.A. 175 C6
formerly known as Fort Walton
Fort Ware Canada see Ware
Fort Wayne U.S.A. 174 C3
Fort Wellington Guyana 199 G3
Fort White Myanmar 78 A3
Fort William U.K. 46 G7
Fort Worth U.S.A. 179 C5
Fort Yates U.S.A. 178 B2
Fortymile r. Canada/U.S.A. 166 A1
Forty Mile Scrub National Park Australia 149 E3
Forty-Second Hill S. Africa see 42nd Hill
Fort Yukon U.S.A. 164 E3
Forum Iulii France see Fréjus
Forūr, Jazīreh-ye i. Iran 100 C5
Forvik Norway 44 K2
Fos, Golfe de b. France 51 K9
Foshan China 87 E4
Fo Shek Chau i. Hong Kong China see Basalt Island
Foskvallen Sweden 45 K3
Fosna pen. Norway 44 J3
Foso Ghana 125 E5
Foss Iceland 44 [inset] C3
Fossano Italy 51 N8
Fosshóll Iceland 44 [inset] C2
Fossil U.S.A. 180 B3
Fossil Downs Australia 150 D3
Fossombrone Italy 56 E5
Fos-sur-Mer France 51 K9
Foster Australia 147 E4
Foster U.S.A. 176 A7
Foster, Mount Canada/U.S.A. 166 C3
Foster Bugt b. Greenland 165 Q2
Foster Lakes Canada 167 J3
Fostoria U.S.A. 176 B4
Fotadrevo Madag. 131 [inset] J5
Fotuna i. Vanuatu see Futuna
Fouesnant France 50 B5
Fougamou Gabon 126 A5
Fougères France 50 E4
Foula i. U.K. 46 J3
Foulamôri Guinea 124 B3
Foul Bay Egypt 121 G4
Foulenzem Gabon 126 A5
Foulness Point U.K. 47 M12
Foul Point Sri Lanka 94 D4
Foulpointe Madag. see Mahavelona
Foulwind, Cape N.Z. 153 F9
Foumban Cameroon 125 H5
Foumbot Cameroon 125 H5
Foum Zguid Morocco 122 D3
Foundation Ice Stream glacier Antarctica 222 T1
Founougo Benin 125 F4
Fount U.S.A. 176 B9
Fountain Green U.S.A. 183 M2
Fountains Abbey tourist site U.K. 47 K9
Four, Pointe de pt Alg. 55 N8
Fourchambault France 51 J5
Fourches, Mont des hill France 51 L4
Four Corners U.S.A. 182 G7
Fouriesburg S. Africa 133 M5
Fournier, Lac l. Canada 169 H3
Fournoi Greece 59 H11
Fournoi i. Greece 59 H11
Fourteen Mile Point U.S.A. 172 D4
Fourth Cataract rapids Sudan see 4th Cataract
Fouta Djallon reg. Guinea 124 B4
Foveaux Strait N.Z. 153 B14
Fowl Cay i. Bahamas 175 E7
Fowler CA U.S.A. 182 E5
Fowler CO U.S.A. 181 F5
Fowler IN U.S.A. 174 C3
Fowler MI U.S.A. 173 I7
Fowler Ice Rise Antarctica 222 S1
Fowlers Bay Australia 146 B2
Fowlers Bay b. Australia 146 B3
Fowlerville U.S.A. 173 I8
Fox r. B.C. Canada 166 E3
Fox r. Man. Canada 167 M3
Fox r. IL U.S.A. 174 B3
Fox r. WI U.S.A. 172 D7
Foxas Spain 54 C1
Fox Creek Canada 167 G4
Foxe Basin g. Canada 165 L3
Foxe Channel Canada 165 K3
Foxen l. Sweden 45 J4
Foxe Peninsula Canada 165 L3
Fox Glacier N.Z. 153 E11
Fox Islands U.S.A. 164 C4
Fox Lake Canada 167 H3
Fox Mountain Canada 166 C2
Foxton N.Z. 152 J8
Foxton Beach N.Z. 152 J8
Fox Valley Canada 167 I5
Foyle r. Rep. of Ireland/U.K. 47 E9
Foyle, Lough b. Rep. of Ireland/U.K. 47 E8
Foz Spain 54 D1
Foz de Areia, Represa de resr Brazil 203 B8
Foz de Gregório Brazil 198 D6
Foz do Copeá Brazil 199 F5
Foz do Cunene Angola 127 A9
Foz do Iguaçu Brazil 203 A8
Foz do Jamari Brazil 201 E2
Foz do Jutaí Brazil 199 E5
Foz do Mamoriá Brazil 199 E5
Foz do Riosinho Brazil 200 C1
Frackville U.S.A. 177 I5
Fraga Arg. 204 D4
Fraga Spain 55 L3
Fraile Muerto Uruguay 204 G4
Frakes, Mount Antarctica 222 Q1
Framingham U.S.A. 177 N3
Framnes Mountains Antarctica 223 E2
Fram Peak Antarctica 223 D2
Franca Brazil 206 F7
Français, Récif des reef New Caledonia 145 F3
Francavilla al Mare Italy 56 G6
Francavilla Fontana Italy 57 J8
▶ France country Europe 50 F5
3rd largest and 4th most populous country in Europe. Historically known as Gallia or Gaul.
europe [countries] 32–35
France, Île de i. Greenland 165 R2
Frances Australia 146 D4
Frances r. Canada 166 D2
Francés, Punta pt Cuba 186 C2
Frances Lake Canada 166 D2
Frances Lake l. Canada 166 D2
Francesville U.S.A. 172 G10
Franceville Gabon 126 B5
also known as Masuku
Franche-Comté admin. reg. France 51 M5
Francis Canada 167 K5
Francis atoll Kiribati see Beru
Francisco de Orellana Ecuador see Puerto Francisco de Orellana
Francisco de Orellana Peru 198 C5
Francisco I. Madero Coahuila Mex. 185 E3
Francisco I. Madero Durango Mex. 184 D3
Francisco Meeks Arg. 204 F5
Francisco Sá Brazil 202 D6
Francisco Zarco Mex. 184 A1
Francistown Botswana 131 E4
Franco da Rocha Brazil 206 G10
Francofonte Sicilia Italy 57 G11
François Lake Canada 166 E4
Francois Peron National Park Australia 151 A5
Francs Peak U.S.A. 180 E4
Frankenberg (Eder) Germany 48 F4
Frankenhöhe park Germany 48 H6
Frankenmuth U.S.A. 173 J7
Frankenthal (Pfalz) Germany 48 F6
Frankenwald mts Germany 48 I5
Frankenwald park Germany 48 I5
Frankford Canada 173 P6
Frankfort S. Africa 133 M4
Frankfort IN U.S.A. 174 C3
▶ Frankfort KY U.S.A. 176 A7
State capital of Kentucky.
Frankfort MI U.S.A. 172 G6
Frankfort OH U.S.A. 176 B6
Frankfurt am Main Germany 48 F5
Frankfurt an der Oder Germany 49 L3
Frank Hann National Park Australia 151 C7
Franklin Lake U.S.A. 183 I1
Fränkische Alb hills Germany 48 H7
Fränkische Schweiz reg. Germany 48 I6
Fränkische Schweiz Veldensteiner Forst park Germany 48 I5
Frankland r. Australia 151 B7
Frankland, Cape Australia 147 E4
Franklin S. Africa 133 N7
Franklin AZ U.S.A. 183 O9
Franklin IN U.S.A. 174 C4
Franklin KY U.S.A. 174 C4
Franklin LA U.S.A. 175 B6
Franklin MA U.S.A. 177 N3
Franklin ME U.S.A. 177 Q1
Franklin NC U.S.A. 174 D5
Franklin NE U.S.A. 178 C3
Franklin NH U.S.A. 177 N2
Franklin NJ U.S.A. 177 K4
Franklin OH U.S.A. 176 A6
Franklin PA U.S.A. 176 F4
Franklin TN U.S.A. 174 C5
Franklin TX U.S.A. 179 C6
Franklin VA U.S.A. 177 I9
Franklin WI U.S.A. 172 E8
Franklin WV U.S.A. 176 F7
Franklin Bay Canada 164 G3
Franklin D. Roosevelt Lake U.S.A. 180 C2
Franklin Furnace U.S.A. 176 C7
Franklin-Gordon National Park Australia 147 E5
Franklin Grove U.S.A. 172 D9
Franklin Island Antarctica 223 L1
Franklin Lake Canada 167 M1
Franklin Mountains Canada 166 F2
Franklin Mountains N.Z. 153 B12
Franklin Sound sea chan. Australia 147 E5
Franklin Strait Canada 165 J2
Franklinton LA U.S.A. 175 B6
Franklinton NC U.S.A. 176 G9
Franklinville U.S.A. 176 G3
Frankrike Sweden 44 K3
Frankston Australia 147 E4
Fransenhof S. Africa 132 G6
Fransfontein Namibia 130 B4
Franske Øer is Greenland 165 R2
Fränsta Sweden 44 L3
Frantsa-Iosifa, Zemlya is Rus. Fed. 38 F2
English form Franz Josef Land
Franz Canada 168 C3
Franz Josef Glacier N.Z. 153 E11
Franz Josef Land is Rus. Fed. see Frantsa-Iosifa, Zemlya
Frasca, Capo della c. Sardegna Italy 57 A9
Frascati Italy 56 E7
Fraser r. Australia 150 C3
Fraser r. B.C. Canada 166 F5
Fraser r. Nfld. Canada 169 I1
Fraser, Mount hill Australia 151 B5
Fraserburg S. Africa 132 F8
Fraserburgh U.K. 46 J6
Fraserdale Canada 168 D3
Fraser Island Australia 149 G5
also known as Great Sandy Island
Fraser Island National Park Australia 149 G5
Fraser Lake Canada 166 E4
Fraser National Park Australia 147 E4
Fraser Plateau Canada 166 E4
Fraser Range Australia 151 C7
Fraser Range hills Australia 151 C7
Frasertown N.Z. 152 L6
Frater Canada 173 I3
Frătești Romania 58 G5
Frauenfeld Switz. 51 O5
Fray Bentos Uruguay 204 F4
Fray Marcos Uruguay 204 G4
Frazeysburg U.S.A. 176 C5
Frazier Downs Aboriginal Reserve Australia 150 C3
Frazier Park U.S.A. 182 F7
Frecăţei Romania 58 J4
Frederic MI U.S.A. 173 I6
Frederic WI U.S.A. 172 A5
Frederica U.S.A. 177 J6
Fredericia Denmark 45 J5
Frederick r. Australia 150 B5
Frederick MD U.S.A. 176 H6
Frederick OK U.S.A. 179 C5
Frederick E. Hyde Fjord inlet Greenland 165 P1
Frederick Hills Australia 148 B2
Frederick Reef Australia 149 G4
Fredericksburg TX U.S.A. 179 C6
Fredericksburg VA U.S.A. 176 H7
Frederick Sound sea chan. U.S.A. 166 C3
Fredericktown MO U.S.A. 174 B4
Fredericktown OH U.S.A. 176 C5
▶ Fredericton Canada 169 H4
Provincial capital of New Brunswick.
Fredericton airport Canada 174 H2
Frederikshåb Greenland see Paamiut
Frederikshavn Denmark 45 J4
Frederikssund Denmark 45 K5
Frederiksted Virgin Is (U.S.A.) 187 G3
Frederiksværk Denmark 45 K5
Fredonia AZ U.S.A. 183 L5
Fredonia KS U.S.A. 178 D4
Fredonia NY U.S.A. 176 F3
Fredonia PA U.S.A. 176 E4
Fredonia WI U.S.A. 172 F7
Fredrika Sweden 44 L2
Fredriksberg Sweden 45 K3
Fredrikshamn Fin. see Hamina
Fredrikstad Norway 45 J4
Freedonyer Peak U.S.A. 182 D1
Freehold U.S.A. 177 K5
Freeland U.S.A. 177 J4
Freeling Heights hill Australia 146 C2
Freel Peak U.S.A. 182 E3
Freels, Cape Canada 169 K3
Freeman U.S.A. 178 C3
Freeman, Lake U.S.A. 172 G10
Freeport IL U.S.A. 174 B3
Freeport ME U.S.A. 177 O2
Freeport PA U.S.A. 176 F5
Freeport TX U.S.A. 179 D6
Freeport City Bahamas 186 D1
Freer U.S.A. 179 C7
Freesoil U.S.A. 172 G6
Free State prov. S. Africa 133 K5
formerly known as Orange Free State
▶ Freetown Sierra Leone 124 B4
Capital of Sierra Leone.
Freewood Acres U.S.A. 177 K5
Fregenal de la Sierra Spain 54 E6
Fregon Australia 146 B1
Fréhel, Cap c. France 50 D4
Freiberg Germany 49 K5
Freiburg Switz. see Fribourg
Freiburg im Breisgau Germany 48 E7
Frei Gonzaga Brazil 207 L4
Frei Inocêncio Brazil 207 L5
Freising Germany 48 I7
Freistadt Austria 49 L7
Freital Germany 49 K5
Freixo de Espada à Cinta Port. 54 E3
Fréjus France 51 M9
historically known as Forum Iulii
Frekhaug Norway 45 I3
Fremantle Australia 151 A7
Fremont CA U.S.A. 182 C4
Fremont IN U.S.A. 176 A4
Fremont MI U.S.A. 172 H7
Fremont NE U.S.A. 178 C3
Fremont OH U.S.A. 176 B4
Fremont WI U.S.A. 172 E6
Fremont r. U.S.A. 183 N3
Fremont Junction U.S.A. 183 M3
Frenchburg U.S.A. 176 B8
French Congo country Africa see Congo
French Creek r. U.S.A. 176 F4
▶ French Guiana terr. S. America 199 H4
French Overseas Department. Known as Guyane Française in French.
southamerica [countries] 192–193
French Guinea country Africa see Guinea
French Island Australia 147 E4
Frenchman r. U.S.A. 180 F2
Frenchman Bay U.S.A. 177 Q1
Frenchman Creek r. U.S.A. 178 B3
Frenchman Lake CA U.S.A. 182 D2
Frenchman Lake NV U.S.A. 183 I5
French Pass N.Z. 152 H8
▶ French Polynesia terr. S. Pacific Ocean 221 I7
French Overseas Territory. Known as Polynésie Française in French.
world [land images] 12–13
oceania [countries] 138–139
oceania [issues] 140–141
French Somaliland country Africa see Djibouti
▶ French Southern and Antarctic Lands terr. Indian Ocean 218 L8
French Overseas Territory. Known as Terres Australes et Antarctiques Françaises in French.
asia [countries] 64–67
French Sudan country Africa see Mali
French Territory of the Afars and Issas country Africa see Djibouti
Frenchtown U.S.A. 177 J5
Frenda Alg. 123 F2
Frenštát pod Radhoštěm Czech Rep. 49 P6
Frere S. Africa 133 N5
Fresco r. Brazil 199 I6
Fresco Côte d'Ivoire 124 D5
Freshfield, Cape Antarctica 223 K2
Fresnillo Mex. 185 E4
Fresno U.S.A. 182 E5
Fresno r. U.S.A. 182 D5
Fressel, Lac l. Canada 169 F2
Fresvikbreen glacier Norway 45 I3
Freu, Cap des c. Spain 55 O5
Freudenstadt Germany 48 F7
Frew watercourse Australia 148 B4
Frewsburg U.S.A. 176 F3
Freycinet Estuary inlet Australia 151 A5
Freycinet Peninsula Australia 147 F5
Freyming-Merlebach France 51 M3
Freyre Arg. 204 E3
Freyung Germany 49 K7
Fria Guinea 124 B4
Fria, Cape Namibia 130 B3
Friant U.S.A. 182 E5
Friant-Kern Canal U.S.A. 182 E6
Frias Arg. 204 D3
Fribourg Switz. 51 N6
also known as Freiburg
Frick Switz. 51 O5
Friday Harbor U.S.A. 180 B2
Fridtjof Nansen, Mount Antarctica 223 M1
Friedberg Germany 48 H7
Friedens U.S.A. 176 G5
Friedland Germany 49 K2
Friedland Rus. Fed. see Pravdinsk
Friedrichshafen Germany 48 G8
Friend U.S.A. 178 C3
Friendly Islands country S. Pacific Ocean see Tonga
Friendship U.S.A. 176 G3
Friesach Austria 49 L9

Friesack Germany 49 J3
Friesoythe Germany 48 E2
Friggesund Sweden 45 L3
Frio r. TX U.S.A. 179 C6
Frio watercourse U.S.A. 179 B5
Friol Spain 54 D1
Frisco U.S.A. 180 F5
Frisco Mountain U.S.A. 183 K3
Frissell, Mount hill U.S.A. 177 L3
Friuli - Venezia Giulia admin. reg. Italy 56 F2
Friza, Proliv strait Rus. Fed. 81 P3
Froan nature res. Norway 44 J2
Frobisher Bay Canada see Iqaluit
Frobisher Bay b. Canada 165 M3
Frobisher Lake Canada 167 I3
Frohavet b. Norway 44 J3
Frohburg Germany 49 J4
Frohnleiten Austria 49 M8
Frolovo Rus. Fed. 41 G6
Frombork Poland 49 Q1
Frome watercourse Australia 146 C2
Frome U.K. 47 J12
Frome, Lake salt flat Australia 146 C2
Fromveur, Passage du strait France 50 A4
Fronteira Port. 54 D5
Fronteiras Brazil 202 D3
Frontera Coahuila Mex. 185 E3
Frontera Tabasco Mex. 185 G5
Frontera, Punta pt Mex. 185 G5
Fronteras Mex. 184 C2
Frontignan France 51 J9
Front Royal U.S.A. 176 G7
Frosinone Italy 56 F7
historically known as Frusino
Frosta Norway 44 J3
Frostburg U.S.A. 176 G6
Frost Glacier Antarctica 223 I2
Frøya i. Norway 44 J3
Fruges France 51 I2
Fruita U.S.A. 183 P2
Fruitland IA U.S.A. 172 B9
Fruitland MD U.S.A. 177 J7
Fruitland UT U.S.A. 183 N1
Fruitport U.S.A. 172 G7
Fruitvale U.S.A. 183 P2
Fruktovaya Rus. Fed. 43 U7
Frunze Kyrg. 103 G4
also known as Frunzenskoye
Frunze Kyrg. see Bishkek
Frunzenskoye Kyrg. see Frunze
Frunzivka Ukr. 58 K1
Frusino Italy see Frosinone
Fruska Gora nat. park Yugo. 58 A3
Frutigen Switz. 51 N6
Frutillar Chile 205 B6
Frutuoso Brazil 201 E3
Fryanovo Rus. Fed. 43 T5
Fryazino Rus. Fed. 43 T6
Frýdek-Místek Czech Rep. 49 P6
Fryeburg U.S.A. 177 O1
Fu'an China 87 F3
Fucheng China see Fengyang
Fucheng China see Fuxian
Fuchū Japan 91 C7
Fuchuan China 87 D3
also known as Fuyang
Fuchun Jiang r. China 87 G2
Fudai Japan 90 G4
Fude China 87 F3
Fuding China 87 G3
Fudua waterhole Kenya 128 C5
Fudul reg. Saudi Arabia 105 D3
Fuengirola Spain 54 G8
Fuenlabrada Spain 54 H4
Fuente-Álamo Spain 55 J6
Fuente Álamo Spain 55 J7
Fuente Albilla, Cerro de mt. Spain 55 J6
Fuente de Cantos Spain 54 E6
Fuente Obejuna Spain 54 F6
Fuentesaúco Spain 54 F3
Fuentes de Ebro Spain 55 K3
Fuerte Olimpo Para. 201 F5
Fuerteventura i. Canary Is 122 B3
Fuga i. Phil. 74 B2
Fugloy i. Faroe Is 46 F1
Fuglstad Norway 44 K2
Fugou China 87 E1
Fugu China 85 F4
Fuguo China see Zhanhua
Fuhai China 88 D2
also known as Burultokay
Fuhaymī Iraq 109 N3
Fujairah U.A.E. 105 G2
also spelt Al Fujayrah or Fujeira
Fujeira U.A.E. see Fujairah
Fuji China see Luxian
Fuji Japan 91 F7
Fujian prov. China 87 F3
English form Fukien
Fu Jiang r. China 86 C2
Fujieda Japan 91 F7
Fuji-Hakone-Izu National Park Japan 91 F7
Fujiidera Japan 91 D7
Fujin China 82 C3
Fujinomiya Japan 91 F7
Fujioka Japan 91 F6
Fuji-san vol. Japan 91 F7
Fujiyoshida Japan 91 F7
Fūka Egypt 106 A5
Fukagawa Japan 90 H3
Fukang China 88 D2
Fukaura Japan 90 F4
Fukaya Japan 91 F6
Fukien prov. China see Fujian
Fukuchiyama Japan 91 D7
Fukue Japan 91 A8
Fukue-jima i. Japan 91 A8
Fukui Japan 91 E6
Fukui pref. Japan 91 E7
Fukuno Japan 91 E6
Fukuoka Japan 91 B8
Fukuoka pref. Japan 91 B8
Fukushima Fukushima Japan 90 G6
Fukushima Hokkaidō Japan 90 G4
Fukushima pref. Japan 90 G6
Fukuyama Japan 91 B9
Fūl, Gebel hill Egypt 108 D8
Fulacunda Guinea-Bissau 124 B4
Fūlād Maialleh Iran 100 C2
also known as Amirabad
Fulayj Oman 105 G3
Fulchhari Bangl. 97 F4
Fulda Germany 48 G5
Fulda r. Germany 48 G4
Fule China 86 C3
Fuli China see Jixian
Fuliji China 87 F1
Fulin China see Hanyuan
Fuling China 87 C2
Fulitun China see Jixian
Fullerton CA U.S.A. 182 G8
Fullerton NE U.S.A. 178 C3
Fullerton, Cape Canada 167 N2
Fulnek Czech Rep. 49 O6
Fulton KY U.S.A. 174 B4
Fulton MO U.S.A. 174 B4
Fulton MS U.S.A. 174 B5
Fulton NY U.S.A. 177 I2
Fulufjället naturreservat nature res. Sweden 45 K3
Fulunäs Sweden 45 K3
Fumay France 51 K3
Fumel France 50 G8
Fumin China 86 B3
also known as Yongding
Funabashi Japan 91 F7
Funafuti atoll Tuvalu 145 G2
formerly known as Ellice Island
Funan China 87 E1
Funan China see Fusui
Funäsdalen Sweden 44 K3

Funchal Madeira 122 A2
Capital of Madeira.

Fundación Col. 198 C2
Fundão Brazil 203 D6
Fundão Port. 54 D4
Fundi Italy see Fondi
Fundición Mex. 184 C3
Fundo das Figuerias Cape Verde 124 [inset]
Fundulea Romania 58 H4
Fundy, Bay of g. Canada 169 H4
Fünen i. Denmark see Fyn
Funeral Peak U.S.A. 183 H5
Fünfkirchen Hungary see Pécs
Fung Wong Shan hill Hong Kong China see Lantau Peak
Funhalouro Moz. 131 G4
Funing Jiangsu China 87 F1
Funing Yunnan China 86 C4
also known as Xinhua
Funiu Shan mts China 87 D1
Funnel Creek r. Australia 149 F4
Funsi Ghana 125 E4
Funtua Nigeria 125 G4
Funzie U.K. 46 L3
Fuping China 85 G4
Fuqing China 87 F3
Fuquan China 87 C3
also known as Chengxian
Furancungo Moz. 131 G2
Furano Japan 90 H3
Fürgun, Küh-e mt. Iran 100 D5
Furmanov Rus. Fed. 40 G4
Furmanovka Kazakh. see Moyynkum
Furmanovo Kazakh. see Zhalpaktal
Furmanovo Rus. Fed. 90 D3
Furnas, Represa resr Brazil 207 G8
Furneaux Group is Australia 147 F5
Furnes Belgium see Veurne
Furong China see Wan'an
Fürstenau Germany 48 E3
Fürstenberg Germany 49 K2
Fürstenfeld Austria 49 N8
Fürstenfeldbruck Germany 48 I7
Fürstenwalde Germany 49 L3
Fürth Germany 48 H6
Furth im Wald Germany 49 J6
Furubira Japan 90 G3
Furudal Sweden 45 K3
Furukawa Japan 90 G5
Fury and Hecla Strait Canada 165 K3
Fusagasugá Col. 198 C3
Fusan S. Korea see Pusan
Fushan Shandong China 85 I4
Fushan Shanxi China 85 F5
Fushë-Krujë Albania 58 A7
Fushun Liaoning China 82 A4
Fushun Sichuan China 86 C2
Fusong China 82 B4
Fusui China 87 C4
also known as Xinning; formerly known as Funan
Futago-san vol. Japan 91 B8
Futaleufú Chile 205 C6
Fu Tau Pun Chau i. Hong Kong China 87 [inset]
Futog Vojvodina, Srbija Yugo. 58 A3
Futtsu Japan 91 F7
Futuna i. Vanuatu 145 G3
formerly spelt Fotuna; formerly known as Erronan
Futuna, Île i. Wallis and Futuna Is 145 H3
Futuna Islands Wallis and Futuna Is 145 H3
English form Hoorn Islands; also known as Hoorn, Îles de or Horne, Îles de.
Futun Xi r. China 87 F3
Fuwa Egypt 108 B6
Fuwayriț Qatar 105 E2
Fuxian China see Wafangdian
Fuxian China 85 F5
also known as Fucheng
Fuxin Liaoning China 85 I3
also known as Fuxinzhen
Fuxin Liaoning China 85 I3
Fuxing China see Wangmo
Fuxinzhen China see Fuxin
Fuya Japan 90 F5
Fuyang Anhui China 87 E1
Fuyang China see Fuchuan
Fuyang Zhejiang China 87 F2
Fuyang r. China 85 H4
Fuying Dao i. China 87 G3
Fuyu Heilong. China 85 J2
Fuyu China see Songyuan
Fuyu Jilin China 82 B3
formerly known as Sanchahe
Fuyuan Heilong. China 82 D2
Fuyuan Yunnan China 86 C3
also known as Zhong'an
Fuyun China 84 A2
also known as Koktokay
Füzesabony Hungary 49 R8
Füzesgyarmat Hungary 49 S8
Fuzhou China 87 F3
formerly spelt Foochow
Fuzhou China see Linchuan
Füzuli Azer. 107 F3
also spelt Fizuli; formerly known as Karyagino
Fwamba Dem. Rep. Congo 127 D6
Fyn county Denmark 45 J5
Fyn i. Denmark 38 B4
also known as Fünen
Fyne, Loch inlet U.K. 46 G8
Fyresvatn l. Norway 45 J4
F.Y.R.O.M. country Europe see Macedonia
Fyteies Greece 59 C10
also known as Fitíai

↓ G

Gaâfour Tunisia 57 B12
Gaalkacyo Somalia 128 E3
Ga'âr, Birket el salt l. Egypt 108 B7
Gaat r. Sarawak Malaysia 77 F2
Gab watercourse Namibia 132 B4
Gabakly Turkm. see Kabakly
Gabangab well Eth. 128 E3
Gabas r. France 50 F9
Gabasumdo China see Tongde
Gabbac, Raas pt Somalia 128 F2
Gabbs Valley Range mts U.S.A. 182 F3
Gabd Pak. 101 E5
Gabela Angola 127 B7
Gaberones Botswana see Gaborone
Gabès Tunisia 123 H2
Gabès, Golfe de g. Tunisia 123 H2
English form Gabès, Gulf of
Gabès, Gulf of Tunisia see Gabès, Golfe de
Gabgaba, Wadi watercourse Sudan 121 G4
Gable End Foreland hd N.Z. 152 M6
Gabon country Africa 126 A5
africa [countries] 114–117
Gabon, Estuaire du est. Gabon 126 A4

Gaborone Botswana 131 E5
Capital of Botswana. Formerly spelt Gaberones.

Gabou Senegal 124 B3
Gabriel Vera Bol. 200 D4
Gabriel y Galán, Embalse de resr Spain 54 E4
Gābrik Iran 100 D5
Gābrik watercourse Iran 100 D5
Gabrovnitsa Bulg. 58 E5
Gabrovo Bulg. 58 G6
Gabú Guinea-Bissau 124 B3
Gabuli vol. Eth. 128 D1
Gacé France 50 G4
Gacko Bos.-Herz. 56 K5
Gādābāy Azer. 107 F2
Gadabedji, Réserve Totale de Faune de nature res. Niger 125 G3

Gadag India 94 B3
Gadaisu P.N.G. 149 F1
Gäddede Sweden 44 K2
Gadê China 86 A1
also known as Pagqên
Gadebusch Germany 48 I2
Gades Spain see Cádiz
Gadhada India 96 A5
Gadhra India 94 A1
Gadsden U.S.A. 175 C5
Gadwal India 94 C2
Gadyach Ukr. see Hadyach
Gadyn Turkm. 103 E5
Gadzi Cent. Afr. Rep. 126 C3
Gadžin Han Srbija Yugo. 58 D5
Gæi'dnuvuop'pi Norway 44 M1
Gael Hamke Bugt b. Greenland 165 Q2
Găeşti Romania 58 G4
Gaeta Italy 56 F7
Gaeta, Golfo di g. Italy 56 F7
Gafanha da Nazaré Port. 54 C4
Gaferut i. Micronesia 73 K5
Gaffney U.S.A. 174 D5
Gafra, Wādī el watercourse Egypt 108 C7
Gafsa Tunisia 123 H2
historically known as Capsa
Gag i. Indon. 75 D3
Gagal Chad 126 B2
Gagaon India 96 B5
Gagarin Rus. Fed. 43 Q6
formerly known as Gzhatsk
Gagarin Uzbek. 103 G4
formerly known as Yerzhar
Gagere watercourse Nigeria 125 G3
Gagliano del Capo Italy 57 K9
Gagnoa Côte d'Ivoire 124 D5
Gagnon Canada 169 G3
Gago Coutinho Angola see Lumbala N'guimbo
Gagra Georgia 107 E2
Gaià r. Spain 55 M3
also spelt Gayá
Gaiab watercourse Namibia 130 C6
Gaibandha Bangl. 97 F4
Găiceana Romania 58 I2
Gaifi, Wâdi el watercourse Egypt 108 F7
Gail r. Austria 49 K9
Gail U.S.A. 179 B5
Gaillac France 50 H9
Gaillimh Rep. of Ireland see Galway
Gaillon France 50 H3
Gaindaingoinkor China see Lhünzhub
Gainesboro U.S.A. 178 F4
Gainesville FL U.S.A. 175 D6
Gainesville GA U.S.A. 174 D5
Gainesville MO U.S.A. 178 D4
Gainesville TX U.S.A. 179 C5
Gainsborough U.K. 47 L10
Gairdner r. Australia 151 B7
Gairdner, Lake salt flat Australia 146 B2
Gairloch U.K. 46 G6
Gairo Tanz. 129 C6
Gaixian China see Gaizhou
Gaizhou China 85 I3
formerly known as Gaixian
Gaizinkalns hill Latvia 42 G5
Gaja r. Hungary 49 P8
Gajah Hutan, Bukit hill Malaysia 76 C1
Gajapatinagaram India 95 D2
Gaji r. Nigeria 125 H4
Gajiram Nigeria 125 I3
Gajol India 97 F4
Gajos well Kenya 128 C4
Gakarosa mt. S. Africa 132 H4
Gakem Nigeria 125 H5
Gakuch Jammu and Kashmir 96 B1
Gala China 89 E6
Galaasiya Uzbek. 103 F5
also spelt Galaosiyo
Galâla el Baharîya, Gebel el plat. Egypt 108 C8
Galán, Cerro mt. Arg. 204 D2
Galana r. Kenya 128 D5
Galand Iran 100 C2
Galang Besar i. Indon. 76 D2
Galangue Angola 127 C8
Galanta Slovakia 49 O7
Galaosiyo Uzbek. see Galaasiya
Galápagos, Islas is Pacific Ocean see Galapagos Islands

Galapagos Islands is Pacific Ocean 221 M6
Part of Ecuador. Most westerly point of South America. Also known as Galápagos, Islas or Colón, Archipiélago de.
southamerica [contrasts] 194–195

Galashiels U.K. 46 J8
Galata Bulg. 58 I5
Galatea N.Z. 152 K6
Galați Romania 58 J3
Galatina Italy 57 K8
Galatini Greece 59 C8
Galatista Greece 59 E8
Galatone Italy 57 K8
Galax U.S.A. 176 E9
Galaymor Turkm. see Kala-I-Mor
Galdhøpiggen mt. Norway 45 J3
Galeana Chihuahua Mex. 184 D2
Galeana Nuevo León Mex. 185 E3
Galegu Sudan 121 G6
Galela Indon. 75 C2
Galena AK U.S.A. 164 D3
Galena IL U.S.A. 174 B3
Galena KS U.S.A. 178 D4
Galena MD U.S.A. 177 J6
Galena MO U.S.A. 178 D4
Galena Bay Canada 166 G5
Galera, Punta pt Chile 204 B6
Galera, Punta pt Ecuador 198 A4
Galera, Punta pt Mex. 185 F6
Galera Point Trin. and Tob. 187 H5
Galeras vol. Col. 198 B4
Galesburg IL U.S.A. 174 B3
Galesburg MI U.S.A. 172 H8
Galeshewe S. Africa 133 I5
Galesville U.S.A. 172 B6
Galeton U.S.A. 176 H4
Galga r. Hungary 49 Q8
Galguduud admin. reg. Somalia 128 E3
Gal Hareeri Somalia 128 E3
Gália Brazil 206 D9
Galicea Mare Romania 58 E4
Galich Rus. Fed. 40 G4
Galichskaya Vozvyshennost' hills Rus. Fed. 40 G4
Galicia aut. comm. Spain 54 D2
Galičica nat. park Macedonia 58 B7
Galilee, Sea of l. Israel 108 G5
also known as Tiberias, Lake or Kinneret, Yam
Galiléia Brazil 207 L6
Galissas Greece 59 F11
Galitsa Rus. Fed. 43 S8
Galiuro Mountains U.S.A. 183 N9
Galiwinku Australia 148 B2
Gallabat Sudan 121 H6
Gallarate Italy 56 A3
Gallatin MO U.S.A. 178 D4
Gallatin TN U.S.A. 174 C4
Gallatin r. U.S.A. 180 E3
Galle Sri Lanka 94 D5
Gállego r. Spain 55 K3
Gallegos r. Arg. 205 C8
Gallegos, Cabo c. Chile 205 B7
Gallia country Europe see France

Gallinas, Punta pt Col. 198 D1
Most northerly point of South America.

Gallipoli Italy 57 K8
Gallipoli Turkey 106 A2
also spelt Gelibolu; historically known as Callipolis

Gallipolis U.S.A. 176 C7
Gällivare Sweden 44 M2
Gallneukirchen Austria 49 L7
Gallo r. Spain 55 I4
Gällö Sweden 44 K3
Gallo, Capo c. Sicilia Italy 57 F10
Gallup KY U.S.A. 176 C7
Gallup NM U.S.A. 181 E6
Gallur Spain 55 J3
Gallura reg. Sardegna Italy 56 A8
Gallyaaral Uzbek. 103 F4
also spelt Ghallaorol
Galma watercourse Nigeria 125 G4
Galoya Sri Lanka 94 D4
Gal Oya National Park Sri Lanka 94 D5
Gal Shiikh Somalia 128 E2
Galt U.S.A. 182 C3
Gal Tardo Somalia 128 E4
Galtat Zemmour W. Sahara 122 B4
Galtee Mountains hills Rep. of Ireland 47 D11
Galtymore hill Rep. of Ireland 47 D11
Galūgāh, Kūh-e mts Iran 100 C4
Galūgāh-e Āsīyeh Iran 101 D3
Galunggung, Gunung vol. Indon. 77 E4
Galva U.S.A. 172 C9
Galveias Port. 54 D5
Galveston IN U.S.A. 172 G10
Galveston TX U.S.A. 179 D6
Galveston Bay U.S.A. 179 D6
Gálvez Arg. 204 E4
Galwa Nepal 97 D3
Galway Rep. of Ireland 47 C10
also spelt Gaillimh
Galway Bay Rep. of Ireland 47 C10
Gâm r. Vietnam 78 D3
Gamá Brazil 206 E3
Gama, Isla i. Arg. 204 E6
Gamaches France 50 H3
Gamagōri Japan 91 E7
Gamalakhe S. Africa 133 O7
Gamalama vol. Indon. 75 C2
Gamarra Col. 198 C2
Gåmas Fin. see Kaamanen
Gamawa Nigeria 125 H3
Gamay Bay Phil. 74 C3
Gamba China 89 E6
also known as Gongbalou
Gamba Gabon 126 A5
Gambēla Eth. 128 B2
Gambēla admin. reg. Eth. 128 B3
Gambēla National Park Eth. 128 B3
Gambell U.S.A. 164 B3
Gambia country Africa 124 A3
africa [countries] 114–117
Gambia r. Gambia 124 B3
Gambie r. Senegal 124 B3
Gambier, Îles is Fr. Polynesia 221 J7
English form Gambier Islands; also known as Mangareva Islands
Gambier Islands Australia 146 C3
Gambier Islands Fr. Polynesia see Gambier, Îles
Gambo Canada 169 K3
Gamboma Congo 126 B5
Gamboola Australia 149 D3
Gamboula Cent. Afr. Rep. 126 B3
Gamda China see Zamtang
Gamka r. S. Africa 132 F10
Gamkunoro, Gunung vol. Indon. 75 C2
Gamlakarleby Fin. see Kokkola
Gamleby Sweden 45 L4
Gammams well Sudan 121 G5
Gammelstaden Sweden 44 M2
Gammon Ranges National Park Australia 146 C2
Gamoep S. Africa 132 C6
Gamova, Mys pt Rus. Fed. 82 C4
Gampaha Sri Lanka 94 D5
Gampola Sri Lanka 94 D5
Gams Switz. 51 P5
Gamshadzai Kūh mts Iran 101 E4
Gamtog China 86 A2
Gamtoos r. S. Africa 133 J10
Gamud mt. Eth. 128 C3
Gamvik Norway 44 O1
Gan r. China 85 J1
Gana China see Gengda
Ganado U.S.A. 183 O6
Ganāg Egypt 108 B7
Gananoque Canada 168 E4
Ganāveh Iran 100 B4
Gäncä Azer. 107 F2
also spelt Gandzha; formerly known as Kirovabad; formerly spelt Gyandzha
Gand Belgium see Ghent
Ganda Angola 127 B8
formerly known as Mariano Machado
Gandadiwata, Bukit mt. Indon. 75 A3
Gandai India 96 D5
Gandajika Dem. Rep. Congo 127 D6
Gandara Spain 54 C1
Gandarbal Jammu and Kashmir 96 B2
Gandari Mountain Pak. 101 G4
Gandava Pak. 101 F4
Gander Canada 169 K3
Gander r. Nfld. Canada 159 K3
Ganderkesee Germany 48 F2
Gander Lake Canada 169 K3
Gandesa Spain 55 L3
Gandevi India 94 B1
Gandhidham India 96 A5
Gandhinagar India 96 B5
Gandhi Sagar resr India 96 B4
Gandi, Wadi watercourse Sudan 126 E2
Gandía Spain 55 K6
Gand-i-Zureh plain Afgh. 101 E4
Gandomān Iran 100 B4
Gandu Brazil 202 E5
Gandvik Norway 44 O1
Gandzha Azer. see Gäncä
Ganeb well Mauritania 124 C2
Ganga r. Bangl./India see Ganges
Ganga Nigeria 125 G4
Ganga r. Sri Lanka 94 D5
Gangakher India 94 C2
Gangán Arg. 205 C6
Gangán, Pampa de plain Arg. 205 C6
Ganganagar India 96 B3
Gangapur Maharashtra India 94 B2
Gangapur Rajasthan India 96 B4
Gangapur Rajasthan India 96 C4
Gangara Niger 125 H3
Gangavali r. India 94 B3
Gangaw Myanmar 78 A3
Gangawati India 94 C3
Gangaw Range mts Myanmar 78 B3
Gangca China 84 D4
also known as Shaliuhe
Gangdhar India 96 B5
Gangdisê Shan mts China 89 C6
English form Kailas Range
Ganges r. Bangl./India 96 F5
also known as Ganga or Padma (Bangl.)
Ganges France 51 J9
Ganges, Mouths of the Bangl./India 97 F5
asia [landscapes] 62–63
Gangi Sicilia Italy 57 G11
Ganglota Liberia 124 C5
Gangouyi China 85 E5
Gangra Turkey see Çankırı
Gangtok India 97 F4
Gangu China 86 C1
Gangziyao China 85 G4
Ganhezi China 88 E2
Gani Indon. 75 D3
Ganiakali Guinea 124 C4
Ganjam India 95 E2
Gan Jiang r. China 87 F2
Ganjig China 85 I3
also known as Horqin Zuoyi Houqi
Gankovo Rus. Fed. 43 O2

Ganluo China 86 B2
also known as Xinshiba
Gannan China 85 I2
Gannat France 51 J6
Gannett Peak U.S.A. 180 E4
Ganq China 84 B4
Ganquan China 85 F4
Gansbaai S. Africa 132 D11
Gänserndorf Austria 49 N7
Ganshui China 86 C2
Ganskuil S. Africa 133 K1
Gansu prov. China 84 C3
English form Kansu
Gantamaa Somalia 128 D4
Gantapara India 95 D1
Gantheaume Point Australia 150 C3
Gant'iadi Georgia 107 E2
formerly known as Pilenkovo
Ganting China see Huxian
Gantsevichi Belarus see Hantsavichy
Ganxian China 87 E3
also known as Meilin
Ganyal r. India 94 C1
Ganye Nigeria 125 I4
Ganyesa S. Africa 132 I3
Ganyu China 87 F1
also known as Qingkou
Ganyushkino Kazakh. 102 B3
Ganzhe China see Minhou
Ganzhou China 87 E3
Ganzi Sudan 128 A3
Ganzurino Rus. Fed. 85 E1
Gao Mali 125 E2
Gao admin. reg. Mali 125 F2
Gao'an China 87 E2
Gaocheng China 85 G4
Gaocheng China see Litang
Gaochun China 87 F2
also known as Chunxi
Gaocun China see Mayang
Gaohebu China 87 F2
Gaojian China 87 G2
Gaolan China 84 D4
formerly known as Shidongsi
Gaoleshan China see Xianfeng
Gaoliangjian China see Hongze
Gaoligong Shan mts China 86 A3
Gaoling China 87 D1
also known as Luyuan
Gaomi China 85 H4
Gaomutang China 87 D3
Gaoping China 85 G5
Gaoqing China 85 H4
also known as Tianzhen
Gaotai China 84 C4
Gaotang China 85 H4
Gaotangling China see Wangcheng
Gaotingzhen China see Daishan
Gaotouyao China 85 F4
Gaoua Burkina 124 E4
Gaoual Guinea 124 B4
Gaoxian China 86 C2
also known as Wenjiang
Gaoxiong Taiwan see Kaohsiung
Gaoyang China 85 G4
Gaoyi China 85 G4
Gaoyou China 87 F1
Gaoyou Hu l. China 87 F1
Gaozhou China 87 D4
Gap France 51 M8
Gapan Phil. 74 B3
Gapuwiyak Australia 148 B2
Gaqoi China 89 C6
Gar China 99 K3
also known as Gargunsa or Shiquanhe
Gar Pak. 101 E5
Gar' r. Rus. Fed. 82 C1
Gara Tebourt well Tunisia 123 H3
Garabekevyul Turkm. 103 F5
formerly spelt Karabekaul
Garabil Belentligi hills Turkm. see Karabil', Vozvyshennost'
Garabinzam Congo 126 B4
Garabogazköl Aylagy b. Turkm. see Kara-Bogaz-Gol, Zaliv
Garabogazköl Bogazy sea chan. Turkm. see Kara-Bogaz-Gol, Proliv
Garacad Somalia 128 F3
Garachiné Panama 186 D5
Garachiné, Punta pt Panama 186 D5
Garadag Somalia 128 E2
Gara Ekar hill Alg. 123 G6
Garagoa Col. 198 C3
Garagum des. Kazakh. see Karakum Desert
Garagum des. Turkm. see Karakum Desert
Garah Australia 147 F2
Garah Mali 124 D4
Garamätnyyaz Turkm. see Karamet-Niyaz
Garamba r. Dem. Rep. Congo 126 F4
Garanhuns Brazil 202 E4
Ga-Rankuwa S. Africa 133 L2
Garapu Brazil 202 A5
Garapuava Brazil 206 G3
Garar, Plaine de plain Chad 126 D2
Garawa Aboriginal Land res. Australia 148 C3
Garba Cent. Afr. Rep. 126 D2
Garbahaarey Somalia 128 D4
Garba Tula Kenya 128 C4
Garberville U.S.A. 182 A1
Garbo China see Lhozhag
Garbosh, Kūh-e mt. Iran 100 B3
Gârbova, Vârful hill Romania 58 H3
Garbsen Germany 48 G3
Garça Brazil 206 D9
Garças, Rio das r. Brazil 206 A2
Gârceni Romania 58 I2
Garcias Brazil 206 A7
Garcia Sola, Embalse de resr Spain 54 F5
Gârcina Romania 58 H2
Gard r. France 51 K9
Garda Italy 56 C3
Garda, Lago di l. Italy see Garda, Lake
Garda, Lake Italy 56 C3
also known as Garda, Lago di
Gardabani Georgia 107 F2
Gârda de Sus Romania 58 D2
Garde Lake Canada 167 J2
Gardelegen Germany 48 I3
Garden City U.S.A. 178 B4
Garden Corners U.S.A. 172 G5
Garden Grove U.S.A. 182 G8
Garden Hill Canada 167 M4
Garden Island U.S.A. 172 H5
Garden Mountain U.S.A. 176 D8
Gardermoen airport Norway 45 J3
also known as Oslo
Gardez Afgh. 101 G3
Gardinas Belarus see Hrodna
Gardiner U.S.A. 177 P1
Gardiner, Mount Australia 148 B4
Gardiner Range hills Australia 148 A3
Gardiners Island U.S.A. 177 M4
Gardiner's Range mts Australia 148 B4
Gardner atoll Micronesia see Faraulep
Gardner IL U.S.A. 172 E9
Gardner MA U.S.A. 177 N3
Gardner Inlet Antarctica 222 T1
Gardner Island Kiribati see Nikumaroro
Gardner Pinnacles is U.S.A. 221 G4
formerly known as Man-of-War Rocks or Pollard Islands
Gardnerville U.S.A. 182 E3
Gardno, Jezioro lag. Poland 49 O1
Gárdony Hungary 49 P8
Gardsjönås Sweden 44 L2
Gärdslösa Sweden 45 L4
Gáregasnjárga Fin. see Karigasniemi
Gares Spain see Puente la Reina
Garešnica Croatia 56 I3
Garet El Djenoun mt. Alg. 123 G4
Gare Tigre Fr. Guiana 199 H3
Garfield U.S.A. 181 F5

Garforth U.K. 47 K10
Gargalianoi Greece 59 C11
Gargáligas r. Spain 54 F5
Gargano, Parco Nazionale del nat. park Italy 56 H7
Gargantua, Cape Canada 168 C4
Gargunsa China see Gar
Gargždai Lith. 42 C6
Garhakota India 96 C5
Garhbeta India 97 E5
Garhchiroli India 94 D1
Garhi India 96 B5
Garhi Khairo Pak. 101 F4
Garhi Malehra India 96 C4
Garhmuktesar India 96 C3
Garhshankar India 96 C3
Garibaldi Brazil 203 B9
Garibaldi Canada 166 F5
Garibaldi, Mount Canada 166 F5
Garibaldi Provincial Park Canada 166 F5
Gariep Dam resr S. Africa 133 J7
Gariep Dam Nature Reserve S. Africa 133 J7
Garies S. Africa 132 B7
Garissa Kenya 128 C5
Garkalne Latvia 42 F4
Garkung Caka l. China 89 D5
Garland U.S.A. 179 C5
Garliava Lith. 42 E7
Gârliciu Romania 58 J4
Garlin France 50 F9
Garm Tajik. see Gharm
Garmab Afgh. 101 F3
Garmdasht Iran 100 B4
Garmeh Iran 100 D2
Garmī Iran 100 B2
Garmisch-Partenkirchen Germany 48 I8
Garmo, Qullai mt. Tajik. 101 G2
also known as Kommunizma, Pik or Kommunizm, Qullai
Garmsar Iran 100 C3
Garmsel reg. Afgh. 101 E4
Garner IA U.S.A. 174 A3
Garner KY U.S.A. 176 C8
Garnett U.S.A. 178 D4
Garnpung Lake imp. l. Australia 147 D3
Garo Hills India 97 F4
Garonne r. France 50 F8
Garoowe Somalia 128 F2
Garoth India 96 B4
Garou, Lac l. Mali 124 E2
Garoua Cameroon 125 I4
Garoua Boulai Cameroon 125 I5
Garqêntang China see Sog
Garrett U.S.A. 173 H9
Garrison KY U.S.A. 176 B7
Garrison ND U.S.A. 178 B2
Garrucha Spain 55 J7
Garrygala Turkm. 102 D5
formerly spelt Kara-Kala
Garry Lake Canada 167 K1
Garryowen S. Africa 133 L8
Garsen Kenya 128 D5
Garshy Turkm. see Karshi
Garsila Sudan 120 D6
Gartar China see Qianning
Gartempe r. France 50 G6
Gartog China see Markam
Gartok China see Garyarsa
Garut Indon. 77 D4
Garvie Mountains N.Z. 153 C13
Garwa India 97 D4
Garwolin Poland 49 S4
Gar Xincun China 89 C5
Gary IN U.S.A. 174 C3
Gary WV U.S.A. 176 D8
Garyarsa China 89 C6
also known as Gartok
Garyi China 86 A2
Garyū-zan mt. Japan 91 C7
Garza Arg. 204 E3
Gar Zangbo r. China 89 B5
Garzê China 86 A2
Garzón Col. 198 C4
Gasan-Kuli Turkm. see Esenguly
Gasan-Kuliyskiy Zapovednik nature res. Turkm. 102 C5
Gascogne reg. France see Gascony
Gascogne, Golfe de g. France/Spain see Gascony, Gulf of
Gasconade r. U.S.A. 174 B4
Gascony reg. France 50 F9
also spelt Gascogne
Gascony, Gulf of France/Spain 50 D9
also known as Gascogne, Golfe de or Gascuña, Golfo de
Gascoyne r. Australia 151 A5
Gascoyne, Mount hill Australia 151 B5
Gascoyne Junction Australia 151 A5
Gascuña, Golfo de g. France/Spain see Gascony, Gulf of
Gash and Setit prov. Eritrea 104 B5
Gasherbrum mt. Jammu and Kashmir 96 C2
Gash Setit Wildlife Reserve nature res. Eritrea 121 H6
Gasht Iran 101 E5
Gas Hu salt l. China 88 E4
Gashua Nigeria 125 H3
Gaspar Cuba 186 D2
Gaspar, Selat sea chan. Indon. 77 D3
Gaspé Canada 169 H3
Gaspé, Baie de b. Canada 169 H3
Gaspé, Cap c. Canada 169 H3
Gaspé, Péninsule de pen. Canada 169 H3
Gassan Burkina 124 E3
Gassan vol. Japan 90 G5
Gassane Senegal 124 B3
Gassaway U.S.A. 176 E7
Gassol Nigeria 125 H4
Gass Peak U.S.A. 183 I5
Gasteiz Spain see Vitoria-Gasteiz
Gastello Rus. Fed. 82 F2
Gaston U.S.A. 176 H9
Gaston, Lake U.S.A. 176 H9
Gastonia U.S.A. 174 D5
Gastouni Greece 59 C11
Gastre Arg. 205 C6
Gata, Cabo de c. Spain 55 I8
Gata, Cape Cyprus 108 E3
also known as Gatas, Akra
Gata, Sierra de mts Spain 54 E4
Gataga r. Canada 166 E3
Gătaia Romania 58 C3
Gatas, Akra c. Cyprus see Gata, Cape
Gatchina Rus. Fed. 43 L2
Gateshead U.K. 47 K9
Gates of the Arctic National Park and Preserve U.S.A. 164 D3
Gatesville U.S.A. 179 C6
Gateway U.S.A. 183 P3
Gatico Chile 200 C5
Gatineau Canada 168 F4
Gatineau r. Canada 168 F4
Gatlinburg U.S.A. 179 G5
Gatong China see Jomda
Gatooma Zimbabwe see Kadoma
Gatton Australia 147 G1
Gatún Panama 186 D5
Gatún, Lago l. Panama 186 C5
Gatvand Iran 100 B3
Gatwick airport U.K. 47 L12
Gaúcha do Norte Brazil 202 A5
Gaud-i-Zirreh depr. Afgh. 101 E4
Gauer Lake Canada 167 L3
Gauhati India see Guwahati
Gauja r. Latvia 42 F4
Gaujas nacionālais parks nat. park Latvia 42 G4
Gaul country Europe see France
Gaula r. Norway 44 J3
Gauley Bridge U.S.A. 176 D7
Gaupne Norway 45 I3
Gaurdak Turkm. see Govurdak

G index

Gaurella India 97 D5
Gauribidanur India 94 C3
Gaurnadi Bangl. 97 F5
Gauteng prov. S. Africa 133 M3 formerly known as Pretoria-Witwatersrand-Vereeniging
Gavà Spain 55 N3
Gavarr Armenia see Kamo
Gavāter Iran 101 E5
Gāvbandī Iran 100 C5
Gāvbūs, Kūh-e mts Iran 100 C5
Gavdopoula i. Greece 59 F14

▶Gavdos i. Greece 59 F14
Most southerly point of Europe.

Gave r. France 50 E9
Gāveh Rūd r. Iran 100 A3
Gavião r. Brazil 202 D5
Gavião Port. 54 D5
Gävle Sweden 45 L3
Gävleborg county Sweden 45 K3
Gävlebukten b. Sweden 45 L3
Gavrilovka Vtoraya Rus. Fed. 41 G5
Gavrilov Posad Rus. Fed. 43 V5
Gavrilov-Yam Rus. Fed. 43 U4
Gavrio Greece 59 F11
Gawachab Namibia 130 C5
Gawai Myanmar 78 B2
Gawan India 97 E4
Gawat well Libya 120 B3
Gawilgarh Hills India 96 C5
Gawler Australia 146 C3
Gawler Ranges hills Australia 146 B3
Gäwür watercourse Turkm. see Gyaur
Gaxun Nur salt l. China 84 D3
Gay Rus. Fed. 102 D2
Gay U.S.A. 172 E3
Gaya r. China 82 C4
Gaya India 97 E4
Gaya i. Sabah Malaysia 77 G1
Gaya Niger 125 F4
Gayá r. Spain see Gaià
Gaya, Pulau i. Sabah Malaysia 77 G1
Gayam Indon. 77 F4
G'Aydat al Jhoucha ridge W. Sahara 122 C4
Gayéri Burkina 125 F3
Gaylord MI U.S.A. 173 I5
Gaylord MN U.S.A. 178 D2
Gayndah Australia 149 F5
Gaynovo Rus. Fed. 43 R4
Gayny Rus. Fed. 40 J3
Gaysin Ukr. see Haysyn
Gayutino Rus. Fed. 43 T3
Gaz Iran 100 D5

▶Gaza terr. Asia 108 F6
Semi-autonomous region.
asia [countries] ▶▶ 64–67

▶Gaza Gaza 108 F6
Capital of Gaza. Also spelt 'Azza.

Gaza prov. Moz. 131 G4
Gaz-Achak Turkm. 103 E4 also spelt Gazojak
Gazalkent Uzbek. 103 G4 also spelt Ghazalkent
Gazandzhyk Turkm. 102 C5 formerly spelt Kazandzhik
Gazawa Cameroon 125 I4
Gaziantep Turkey 107 D3 also known as Aintab
Gazibenli Turkey see Yahyalı
Gazik Iran 101 E3
Gazimağusa Cyprus see Famagusta
Gazimuro-Ononskiy Khrebet mts Rus. Fed. 85 F1
Gazimurskiy Zavod Rus. Fed. 85 H1
Gazipaşa Turkey 106 C3
Gazivode Jezero l. Yugo. 58 B6
Gazli Uzbek. 103 E4
Gazojak Turkm. see Gaz-Achak
Gbaaka Liberia 124 D5
Gbangbatok Sierra Leone 124 B5
Gbarnga Liberia 124 C5
Gbatala Liberia 124 C5
Gbéroubouè Benin 125 F4
Gboko Nigeria 125 H5
Gbwado Dem. Rep. Congo 126 D4
Gdańsk Poland 49 P1 historically known as Danzig
Gdańsk, Gulf of Poland/Rus. Fed. 49 Q1 also known as Gdańska, Zatoka; formerly known as Danzig, Gulf of
Gdańska, Zatoka g. Poland/Rus. Fed. see Gdańsk, Gulf of
Gdingen Poland see Gdynia
Gdov Rus. Fed. 42 I3
Gdyel Alg. 55 K9
Gdynia Poland 49 P1 historically known as Gdingen or Gotenhafen
Gearhart Mountain U.S.A. 180 B4
Gebe i. Indon. 75 D2
Gebeit Sudan 121 H5
Gebeit Mine Sudan 121 H4
Gebel Iweibid Egypt 108 D7
Gebre Guracha Eth. 128 C2
Gebze Turkey 58 K8
Gech'a Eth. 128 B3
Gecheng China see Chengkou
Gedang, Gunung mt. Indon. 76 C3
Gedanonių kalnas hill Lith. 42 F7
Gedaref Sudan 121 G6
Gedaref state Sudan 121 G6
Gedern Germany 48 G5
Gediz Turkey 59 K10
Gediz r. Turkey 106 A3
Gedlegubē Eth. 128 E3
Gēdo Eth. 128 C2
Gedo admin. reg. Somalia 128 D4
Gedong, Tanjong pt Sing. 76 [inset]
Gedser Denmark 45 J5

Gedungpakuan Indon. 76 D4
Geel Belgium 51 L1
Geelong Australia 147 E4
Geelvink Channel Australia 151 A6
Geel Vloer salt pan S. Africa 132 E6
Geesthacht Germany 48 H2
Gefersa Eth. 128 C2
Gėgė r. Lith. 42 C6
Gegužinė Lith. 42 F7
Gê'gyai China 89 C5
Ge Hu l. China 87 F2
Geidam Nigeria 125 H3
Geiersberg hill Germany 48 G6
Geikie r. Canada 167 K3
Geikie Island Canada 168 B3
Geikie Range hills Australia 149 D2
Geilo Norway 45 J3
Geiselhöring Germany 49 J7
Geislingen an der Steige Germany 48 G7
Geisūm, Gezā'ir is Egypt see Qeisūm, Gezâ'ir
Geita Tanz. 128 B5
Gejiu China 86 B4
Gekdepe Turkm. 102 D5 also spelt Gökdepe; formerly spelt Geok-Tepe
Gel r. Sudan 128 A3
Gel watercourse Sudan 126 F2
Gela Sicilia Italy 57 G11
Gela r. Sicilia Italy 57 G11
Gela, Golfo di g. Sicilia Italy 57 G11
Geladaindong mt. China 89 E5
Geladī Eth. 128 E3
Gelai vol. Tanz. 128 C5
Gelam i. Indon. 77 E3
Geldern Germany 48 D4
Gelembe Turkey 59 I9
Gelemso Eth. 128 D2
Gelendzhik Rus. Fed. 41 F7
Gelephu Bhutan 97 F4 also known as Hatisar
Gelibolu Turkey see Gallipoli
Gelibolu Yarımadası pen. Turkey 59 H8
Gelibolu Yarımadası Tarihi Milli Parkı nat. park Turkey 59 H8
Gelidonya Burnu pt Turkey see Yardımcı Burnu
Gelincik Dağı mt. Turkey 106 B3
Gelinsoor Somalia 128 E3
Gelmord Iran 100 D3
Gelnica Slovakia 49 R7
Gelsenkirchen Germany 48 E4
Gemas Malaysia 76 C2
Gembu Nigeria 125 H5
Gemena Dem. Rep. Congo 126 C4
Gemenci park Hungary 49 P9
Gemerek Turkey 106 D3
Gemlik Turkey 106 B2
Gemlik Körfezi b. Turkey 58 J8
Gemlufall Iceland 44 [inset] B2
Gemona del Friuli Italy 56 F2
Gémozac France 50 F7
Gemsa Egypt 121 G3
Gemsbok National Park Botswana 130 D5
Gemsbokplein well S. Africa 132 E3
Gemsbokvlakte S. Africa 133 I2
Gen r. China 85 H1
Genale Wenz r. Eth. 128 D3
Genalē Wenz r. Eth. 128 D3
Gençay France 50 G6
Gendoe r. Eth. 104 B5
General Acha Arg. 204 D5
General Alvear Buenos Aires Arg. 204 E5
General Alvear Mendoza Arg. 204 D4
General Artigas Para. 201 F6
General Belgrano Arg. 204 F4
General Belgrano II research station Antarctica see Belgrano II
General Bernardo O'Higgins research station Antarctica 222 U2
General Cabrera Arg. 204 E4
General Carneiro Brazil 206 A2

▶General Carrera, Lago l. Arg./Chile 205 B7
Deepest lake in South America.

General Conesa Arg. 204 D6
General Escobeda Mex. 185 E3
General Freire Angola see Muxaluando
Generalísimo, Embalse del resr Spain 55 J5
General José de San Martín Arg. 204 F2
General Juan Madariaga Arg. 204 F5
General Lagos Chile 200 C4
General La Madrid Arg. 204 E5
General Luna Phil. 74 C4
General MacArthur Phil. 74 C4
General Machado Angola see Camacupa
General Martín Miguel de Güemes Arg. 200 D6
General Paz Arg. 204 F2
General Pico Arg. 204 E4
General Pinto Arg. 204 E4
General Roca Arg. 204 D5
General Saavedra Bol. 201 E4
General Salgado Brazil 206 C7
General San Martín research station Antarctica see San Martín
General Santos Phil. 74 C5
General Simón Bolívar Mex. 185 E3
General Terán Mex. 185 F3
General Toshevo Bulg. 58 J5
General Trías Mex. 184 D2
General Villegas Arg. 204 E4
Genesee U.S.A. 176 H4
Genesee r. U.S.A. 176 H2
Geneseo IL U.S.A. 172 C9
Geneseo NY U.S.A. 176 H3
Genet Eth. 128 C2
Geneva Switz. 51 M6 also spelt Genève or Genf
Geneva AL U.S.A. 175 C6
Geneva IL U.S.A. 172 E9
Geneva NE U.S.A. 178 C3
Geneva NY U.S.A. 177 H3
Geneva OH U.S.A. 176 E4
Geneva, Lake France/Switz. 51 M6 also known as Léman, Lac
Genève Switz. see Geneva
Genf Switz. see Geneva
Gengda China 86 B1 formerly known as Gana
Gengenbach Germany 48 F7
Genglou China 87 E4
Gengqing China see Dêgê
Geni r. Sudan 128 B3
Genil r. Spain 54 F7
Genisea Greece 58 F7 also spelt Yeniséa
Genk Belgium 51 L2
Genkai-nada b. Japan 91 B8
Gennargentu, Monti del mts Sardegna Italy 57 B9
Gennes France 50 F5
Genoa Australia 147 F4
Genoa Italy 56 A4 also spelt Genova; historically known as Genua
Genoa U.S.A. 172 E8
Genoa, Gulf of Italy 56 A4 also known as Genova, Gulf of
Genova Italy see Genoa
Genova, Gulf of Italy see Genoa, Gulf of
Gent Belgium see Ghent
Genteng Indon. 77 D4
Genteng i. Indon. 77 F4
Genthin Germany 49 J3
Gentio do Ouro Brazil 202 D4
Genua Italy see Genoa
Genzano di Roma Italy 56 E7
Geoagiu r. Romania 58 E2
Geographe Bay Australia 151 A7
Geographe Channel Australia 151 A5

Geographical Society Ø i. Greenland 165 Q2
Geok-Tepe Turkm. see Gekdepe
Georga, Zemlya i. Rus. Fed. 38 E1 English form George Land
George r. Canada 169 H1
George S. Africa 132 G10
George, Lake N.S.W. Australia 147 F3
George, Lake S.A. Australia 146 C4
George, Lake salt flat Australia 150 C4
George, Lake Uganda 128 A4
George, Lake FL U.S.A. 175 D6
George, Lake NY U.S.A. 177 L2
George Gills Range mts Australia 148 A4
George Land i. Rus. Fed. see Georga, Zemlya
Georges Mills U.S.A. 177 M2
George Sound inlet N.Z. 153 B12
Georgetown Australia 149 D3
George Town Australia 147 E5
George Town Bahamas 186 E2
Georgetown Canada 173 N7

▶George Town Cayman Is 186 C3
Capital of the Cayman Islands.

Georgetown Gambia 124 B3

▶Georgetown Guyana 199 G3
Capital of Guyana. Formerly known as Demerara; historically known as Stabroek.

George Town Malaysia 76 C1 also known as Pinang
Georgetown DE U.S.A. 177 J7
Georgetown GA U.S.A. 175 C6
Georgetown KY U.S.A. 176 A7
Georgetown OH U.S.A. 176 B7
Georgetown SC U.S.A. 175 E5
Georgetown TX U.S.A. 179 C6
George VI Sound sea chan. Antarctica 222 T2
George V Land reg. Antarctica 223 K2
George West U.S.A. 179 C6
▶Georgia country Asia 107 E2 known as Sakartvelo in Georgian; formerly known as Gruzinskaya S.S.R.
asia [countries] ▶▶ 64–67
Georgia state U.S.A. 175 D5
Georgia, Strait of Canada 166 E5
Georgian Bay Canada 168 D4
Georgian Bay Islands National Park Canada 173 N6
Georgi Dimitrov, Yazovir resr Bulg. see Koprinka, Yazovir
Georgina watercourse Australia 148 C5
Georgi Traykov Bulg. see Dolni Chiflik
Georgiu-Dezh Rus. Fed. see Liski
Georgiyevka Aktyubinskaya Oblast' Kazakh. 102 D2
Georgiyevka Vostochnyy Kazakhstan Kazakh. 103 J2
Georgiyevka Kazakh. see Korday
Georgiyevsk Rus. Fed. 41 G7
Georgiyevskoye Kostromskaya Oblast' Rus. Fed. 40 H4
Georgiyevskoye Vologod. Obl. Rus. Fed. 43 R2
Georg von Neumayer research station Antarctica see Neumayer
Gera Germany 48 J5
Gerakarou Greece 58 E8 also spelt Yerakaroú
Geraki Greece 59 D12 also known as Yerákion
Geraki, Akra pt Greece 59 B11 also spelt Yeráki, Ákra
Geral de Goiás, Serra hills Brazil 202 C4
Geraldine N.Z. 153 F12
Geral do Paraná, Serra hills Brazil 206 F2
Geraldton Australia 151 A6
Gerama i. Indon. 75 C1
Geraneia mts Greece 59 E11
Gerar watercourse Israel 108 F6
Gérardmer France 51 M4
Gerāsh Iran 100 C5
Gerber U.S.A. 182 B1
Gercüş Turkey 107 E3
Gerdau S. Africa 133 K3
Gerdauen Rus. Fed. see Zheleznodorozhnyy
Gerecsei park Hungary 49 P8
Gerede Turkey 106 C2
Gerede r. Turkey 106 C2
Gereshk Afgh. 101 F4
Geretsried Germany 48 I8
Gergovie tourist site France 51 J7
Gerik Malaysia 76 C1 formerly spelt Grik
Gerimenj Iran 100 D3
Gering U.S.A. 178 B3
Gerlach U.S.A. 182 E1
Gerlachovský štít mt. Slovakia 49 R6
Gerlospaß pass Austria 48 J8
Germaine, Lac l. Canada 169 H2
Germania country Europe see Germany
Germania Land reg. Greenland 165 R2
Germanicea Turkey see Kahramanmaraş
Germansen Landing Canada 166 E4
German South-West Africa country Africa see Namibia
Germantown MD U.S.A. 177 H6
Germantown TN U.S.A. 174 B5
Germantown WI U.S.A. 172 E7

▶Germany country Europe 48 F5
2nd most populous country in Europe. Known as Deutschland in German; historically known as Germania.
europe [countries] ▶▶ 32–35

Germencik Turkey 59 I11
Germersheim Germany 48 F6
Germiston S. Africa 133 M3
Gernika-Lumo Spain 55 I1 also known as Guernica
Gerolstein Germany 48 D5
Gerolzhofen Germany 48 H6
Gerona Spain see Girona
Gerrit Denys is P.N.G. see Lihir Group
Gers r. France 50 G8
Gersfeld (Rhön) Germany 48 G5
Gersoppa India 94 B3
Géryville Alg. see El Bayadh
Gêrzê China 89 D5 also known as Luring
Gerze Turkey 106 C2
Geschriebenstein hill Austria 49 N8
Gesoriacum France see Boulogne-sur-Mer
Gessler Arg. 204 E3
Geta Fin. 45 L3
Getafe Spain 55 H4
Getcheh, Kūh-e hills Iran 100 C3
Gete r. Belgium 51 L2
Getic, Podișul plat. Romania 58 E4
Gettysburg PA U.S.A. 177 H6
Gettysburg SD U.S.A. 178 C2
Gettysburg National Military Park nat. park U.S.A. 177 H6
Getu He r. China 86 C3
Getulina Brazil 206 D8
Getúlio Vargas Brazil 203 A8
Getz Ice Shelf Antarctica 222 P2
Geumapang r. Indon. 76 B2
Geureudong, Gunung vol. Indon. 76 B1
Gevān-e Tāleb Khānī Iran 101 D5
Gevaş Turkey 107 E3 also known as Vastan
Gevgelija Macedonia 58 D7
Gevrai India 94 B2
Gevrey-Chambertin France 51 K5
Gewanē Wildlife Reserve nature res. Eth. 128 D2

Gex France 51 M6
Gexianzhuang China see Qinghe
Gey Iran see Nīkshahr
Geydik Dağları mts Turkey 108 D1
Geyikli Turkey 59 H9
Geylang Sing. 76 [inset]
Geylang r. Sing. 76 [inset]
Geyserville U.S.A. 182 B3
Gezarina Brazil 206 D3
Ghaap Plateau S. Africa 132 H4
Ghabeish Sudan 121 E6
Ghadaf, Wādī al watercourse Iraq 107 E4
Ghadaf, Wādī al watercourse Jordan 109 H6
Ghadamès Libya see Ghadāmis
Ghadāmis Libya 120 A2 also spelt Ghudamis; formerly spelt Ghadamès
Ghaddūwah Libya 120 B3
Ghadīr al Khayl waterhole Iraq 109 N6
Ghadīr al Mulūsī well Iraq 109 K4
Ghaem Shahr Iran 100 C2
Ghaggar, Dry Bed of watercourse Pak. 101 H4
Ghaghara r. India 97 E4
Ghaghra India 97 E5 formerly spelt Gogra
Ghaghra India 97 E5 formerly spelt Gogra
Ghāidah watercourse Iraq 109 M5
Ghalkarteniz, Solonchak salt marsh Kazakh. 103 E2
Ghallaorol Uzbek. see Gallyaaral
▶Ghana country Africa 125 E4 formerly known as Gold Coast
africa [countries] ▶▶ 114–117
Ghanādah, Rās pt U.A.E. 105 F2
Ghānah well Oman 105 G4
Ghanīm well Saudi Arabia 105 F4
Ghanliala India 96 B4
Ghantwar India 94 A1
Ghanwā Saudi Arabia 105 E2
Ghanzi Botswana 130 D4
Ghanzi admin. dist. Botswana 130 D4
Ghap'an Armenia see Kapan
Gharāmil, Jabal al hill Saudi Arabia 104 C3
Gharandal Jordan 108 G7
Gharandal, Wādī watercourse Egypt 108 D8
Gharāt Tāris hill Syria 109 M2
Gharbīya governorate Egypt 108 C7
Ghardaïa Alg. 123 F2
Ghardimaou Tunisia 57 A12
Ghar el Melh Tunisia 57 C11
Gharghoda India 97 D5
Ghārib, Gebel mt. Egypt 121 G2
Ghārib, Rās pt Egypt 108 E9
Gharm Tajik. 101 G2 also spelt Garm
Gharo Pak. 101 F5
Gharyān Libya 120 B1
Gharz, Wādī al watercourse Syria 109 I5
Ghāt Libya 120 A3
Ghatampur India 96 D4
Ghatgan India 97 E5
Ghatol India 96 B5
Ghatsila India 97 E5
Ghauspur Pak. 101 G4
Ghawdex i. Malta see Gozo
Ghawr, Wādī al watercourse Syria 109 L3
Ghaymān Yemen 104 D5
Ghazal, Bahr el watercourse Chad 120 C6
Ghazal, Bahr el r. Sudan 128 A2
Ghazalkent Uzbek. see Gazalkent
Ghazaouet Alg. 123 E2 formerly known as Nemours
Ghaziabad India 96 C3
Ghazīlah, Wādī watercourse Iraq 109 O3
Ghazipur India 97 D4
Ghazira, Ghubbat al inlet Oman 105 G2 English form Malcolm Inlet
Ghazna Afgh. see Ghaznī
Ghaznī Afgh. 101 G3 also spelt Ghazna; historically known as Alexandria
Ghaznī prov. Afgh. 101 F3
Ghazni r. Afgh. 101 F3
Ghazzālah Saudi Arabia 104 C2
Ghelari Romania 58 D3
Ghelința Romania 58 H3
Ghemeis, Ras pt U.A.E. 105 E2
Ghent Belgium 51 J1 also spelt Gent or Gand
Ghent U.S.A. 176 D8
Gheorghe Gheorghiu-Dej Romania see Onești
Gheorghe Lazăr Romania 58 I4
Gheorgheni Romania 58 G2
Gherdi India 94 B2
Gherla Romania 58 E1 formerly known as Armenopolis
Ghijduwon Uzbek. see Gizhduvan
Ghilzai reg. Afgh. 101 F4
Ghīnah, Wādī al watercourse Saudi Arabia 107 D5
Ghioroiu Romania 58 E4
Ghisonaccia Corse France 52 D3
Ghizao Afgh. 101 F3
Ghizar Jammu and Kashmir 96 B1
Ghizri Creek inlet Pak. 101 F5
Ghod India 94 B2
Ghod r. India 94 B2
Gholvad India 94 B1
Ghoraghat Bangl. 97 F4
Ghorak Afgh. 101 F3
Ghorband r. Afgh. 101 G3
Ghost Lake Canada 167 H2
Ghotaru India 96 A4
Ghotki Pak. 101 G5
Ghowr prov. Afgh. 101 F3
Ghuari r. India 97 E4
Ghubbah Yemen 105 F5
Ghudamis Libya see Ghadāmis
Ghugus India 94 C2
Ghulam Mohammed Barrage Pak. 101 G5
Ghurayfah hill Saudi Arabia 109 I6
Ghūrī Iran 100 C4
Ghurian Afgh. 101 E3
Ghurrab, Jabal hill Saudi Arabia 104 D2
Ghurūb, Jabal hill Saudi Arabia 104 C3
Ghuzayn Oman 105 G3
Ghuzayyil, Sabkhat salt marsh Libya 120 C2
Ghuzor Uzbek. see Guzar
Gia Đinh Vietnam 79 D6
Giaginskaya Rus. Fed. 41 G7
Gialias r. Cyprus 108 E2
Giang r. Vietnam 78 D4
Gia Nghia Vietnam 79 D5
Giannitsa Greece 58 D8 also known as Yenije-i-Vardar; also spelt Yiannitsá
Giannutri, Isola di i. Italy 56 D6
Giant's Causeway lava field U.K. 47 F8
Gianyar Indon. 77 F5
Gianysada i. Greece 59 H13 also spelt Yianisádha
Giarmata Romania 58 C3
Giarre Sicilia Italy 57 H11
Giaveno Italy 51 N7
Gibara Cuba 186 D2
Gibarrayo hill Spain 54 F7
Gibb r. Australia 150 D2
Gibbon U.S.A. 178 C3
Gibb River Australia 150 D3
Gibb River Aboriginal Reserve Australia 150 D3
Gibeon Namibia 130 C5
Gibraleón Spain 54 E7

▶Gibraltar Europe 54 F8
United Kingdom Overseas Territory.
europe [countries] ▶▶ 32–35

▶Gibraltar, Strait of Morocco/Spain 54 E9
europe [countries] ▶▶ 32–33

Gibraltar Range National Park Australia 147 G2
Gibson Australia 151 C7
Gibson City U.S.A. 174 B3
▶Gibson Desert Australia 150 C5
oceania [landscapes] ▶▶ 136–137
Gibson Desert Nature Reserve Australia 151 D5
Gibsons Canada 166 F5
Gichgeniyn Nuruu mts Mongolia 84 B2
Gīdamī Eth. 128 B2
Gidda Eth. 128 B2
Giddalur India 94 C3
Giddi, Gebel el hill Egypt 121 G2 English form Giddi Pass
Giddings U.S.A. 179 C6
Giddi Pass hill Egypt see Giddi, Gebel el
Gideälven r. Sweden 44 L3
Gīdolē Eth. 128 C3
Gien France 51 I5
Giesecke Isfjord inlet Greenland see Kangerlussuaq
Gießen Germany 48 F5
Gīfan Iran 100 D2
Gifatīn, Gezîret i. Egypt 104 A2 English form Gifatin Island
Gifatin Island Egypt see Gifatīn, Gezîret
Giffou r. France 51 I8
Gifhorn Germany 48 H3
Gift Lake Canada 167 H4
Gifu Japan 91 E7
Gifu pref. Japan 91 E7
Gigant Rus. Fed. 41 G7
Giganta, Cerro mt. Mex. 184 C3
Gigante Col. 198 C4
Gigha i. U.K. 46 G8
Ghighera Romania 58 E5
Giglio, Isola del i. Italy 56 C6
Gijón Spain 54 F1 also spelt Xixón
Gikongoro Rwanda 126 F5
Gila r. U.S.A. 183 J9
Gila, Tanjung pt Indon. 75 D2
Gila Bend U.S.A. 183 L9
Gila Bend Mountains U.S.A. 183 K8
Gila Mountains U.S.A. 183 J9
Gīlān prov. Iran 100 B2
Gīlān-e Gharb Iran 100 A3
Gila River Indian Reservation res. U.S.A. 183 M8
Gilău Romania 58 E2
Giläzi Azer. 107 G2 also spelt Kilyazi
Gilbert r. Australia 149 D3
Gilbert AZ U.S.A. 183 M8
Gilbert MN U.S.A. 172 A3
Gilbert WV U.S.A. 176 D8
Gilbert Islands country Pacific Ocean see Kiribati
Gilbert Range mts Australia 149 D3
Gilbert River Australia 149 D3
Gilbués Brazil 202 C4
Gilé Moz. 131 H3
Gilead reg. Jordan see Jil'ād
Giles Creek r. Australia 148 A3
Giles Meteorological Station Australia 151 E5
Gilf Kebir Plateau Egypt 121 E4 also known as Jilf al Kabīr, Haḍabat al
Gilgandra Australia 147 F2
Gil Gil Creek r. Australia 147 F2
Gilgit Jammu and Kashmir 96 B2
Gilgit r. Jammu and Kashmir 96 B2
Gilgunnia Australia 147 E3
Gili Iyang i. Indon. 77 F4
Gilimanuk Indon. 77 F5
Gilindire Turkey see Aydıncık
Gillam Canada 167 M3
Gillen watercourse Australia 148 B4
Gillen, Lake salt flat Australia 151 D5
Gilles, Lake salt flat Australia 146 C3
Gillespies Point N.Z. 153 D11
Gillett PA U.S.A. 177 I4
Gillett WI U.S.A. 172 E6
Gillette U.S.A. 180 F3
Gillhov Sweden 44 K3
Gilliat Australia 149 D4
Gilliat r. Australia 149 D4
Gillingham U.K. 47 M12
Gilman IL U.S.A. 174 C3
Gilman WI U.S.A. 172 C5
Gilmer U.S.A. 179 D5
Gilort r. Romania 58 E4
Gilroy U.S.A. 182 C4
Giluwe, Mount P.N.G. 73 J8
Gīmbī Eth. 128 B2
Gimli Canada 167 L5
Gimo Sweden 45 L3
Gimont France 50 G9
Ginda Eritrea 121 H6
Gindie Australia 149 F4
Ginebra, Laguna l. Bol. 200 D3
Gineina, Râs el mt. Egypt 108 E8
Gingee India 94 C3
Gin Gin Australia 149 F5
Gingin Australia 151 A6
Gingindlovu S. Africa 133 P6
Gingoog Phil. 74 C4
Gīnīr Eth. 128 D3
Ginkūnai Lith. 42 E6
Ginzo de Limia Spain see Xinzo de Limia
Gioia, Golfo di b. Italy 57 H10
Gioia del Colle Italy 57 I8
Gioia Tauro Italy 57 H10
Gioura i. Greece 59 F9 also spelt Yioúra
Gipouloux r. Canada 169 F2
Gippsland reg. Australia 147 E4
Girā, Wādī watercourse Egypt 108 E8
Girab India 96 A4
Girān Rig mt. Iran 101 D4
Girar India 94 C1
Girard KS U.S.A. 178 D4
Girard OH U.S.A. 176 E4
Girard PA U.S.A. 176 E3
Girardin, Lac l. Canada 169 H1
Girdar Dhor r. Pak. 101 F5 also known as Hingol
Girdi Iran 101 E4
Giresun Turkey 107 D2
Girga Egypt 121 F3
Girgenti Sicilia Italy see Agrigento
Giri r. Dem. Rep. Congo 126 C4
Giridih India 97 E4
Girilambone Australia 147 E2
Girna r. India 96 B5
Gir National Park India 96 A5
Girne Cyprus see Kyrenia
Giromagny France 51 M5
Girón Ecuador 198 B5
Girón Sweden see Kiruna
Girona Spain 55 N3 also spelt Gerona
Gironde est. France 50 F7
Girou r. France 50 H9
Giruá Brazil 203 A9
Girvan U.K. 47 H8
Girvas Rus. Fed. 40 E3
Gisborne N.Z. 152 M6
Gisborne admin. reg. N.Z. 152 M6
Giscome Canada 166 F4
Gisenyi Rwanda 126 F5
Gislaved Sweden 45 K4
Gisors France 50 H3
Gissar Tajik. see Hisor
Gissar Range mts Tajik./Uzbek. 101 F2 also known as Gissarskiy Khrebet or Hisor Tizmasi
Gissarskiy Khrebet mts Tajik./Uzbek. see Gissar Range

Gissarskiy Zapovednik nature res. Uzbek. 103 F5
Gitarama Rwanda 126 F5
Gitega Burundi 126 F5
Giuba r. Somalia see Jubba
Giubega Romania 58 E4
Giubiasco Switz. 51 P6
Giugliano in Campania Italy 56 G8
Giulianova Italy 56 F6
Giurgeului, Munții mts Romania 58 G2
Giurgiu Romania 58 G5 also spelt Yergoğu
Givar Iran 100 D2
Give Denmark 45 J5
Givors France 51 K7
Giyani S. Africa 131 F4
Giyon Eth. 128 C2
Giza Egypt 121 F2 also spelt El Gîza or Al Jīzah
▶Giza Pyramids tourist site Egypt 121 F2 also known as Ahrāmāt el Jīzah
africa [locations] ▶▶ 118–119
Gīzeh Rūd r. Iran 100 A3 also known as Darreh Gozaru
Gizhduvan Uzbek. 103 F4 also spelt Ghijduwon
Gizhiga Rus. Fed. 39 Q3
Gizo Solomon Is 145 E2
Giżycko Poland 49 S1
Gjalicë e Lumës, Mal mt. Albania 58 B6
Gjerde Norway 45 I3
Gjerstad Norway 45 J4
Gjirokastër Albania 59 B8 formerly known as Argyrokastron
Gjoa Haven Canada 165 J3
Gjögur Iceland 44 [inset] B2
Gjøra Norway 44 J3
Gjøvik Norway 45 J3
Gjuhëzës, Kepi i pt Albania 58 A8
Glace Bay Canada 169 J4
Glacier Bay U.S.A. 166 C3
Glacier Bay National Park and Preserve U.S.A. 164 F4
Glacier National Park Canada 167 G5
Glacier National Park U.S.A. 180 D2
Glacier Peak vol. U.S.A. 180 B2
Glade Spring U.S.A. 176 D9
Gladstone Qld Australia 149 F4
Gladstone S.A. Australia 146 C3
Gladstone Canada 167 L5
Gladstone N.Z. 152 J9
Gladstone MI U.S.A. 172 F5
Gladstone VA U.S.A. 176 G8
Gladwin U.S.A. 173 I7
Gladys U.S.A. 176 F8
Gladys Lake Canada 166 C3
Glamis U.K. 46 I7
Glamis U.S.A. 183 I9
Glamoč Bos.-Herz. 56 I4
Glan r. Austria 49 L9
Glan r. Germany 48 E6
Glan Phil. 74 C5
Glan l. Sweden 45 K4
Glarner Alpen mts Switz. 51 O6
Glarus Switz. 51 P5
Glasfjorden l. Sweden 45 K4
Glasford U.S.A. 172 D10
Glasgow U.K. 46 H8
Glasgow KY U.S.A. 174 C4
Glasgow MT U.S.A. 180 F2
Glasgow VA U.S.A. 176 F8
Glaskogens naturreservat nature res. Norway 45 K4
Glaslyn Canada 167 I4
Glassboro U.S.A. 177 J6
Glass Mountain U.S.A. 182 F4
Glass Peninsula U.S.A. 166 C3
Glauchau Germany 49 J5
Glavacioc r. Romania 58 G4
Glavan Bulg. 58 H6
Glăvănești Romania 58 I2
Glavinitsa Bulg. 58 H5
Glavnik Kosovo, Srbija Yugo. 58 C6
Glazoué Benin 125 F5
Glazov Rus. Fed. 40 J4
Glazunovka Rus. Fed. 43 R9
Glazunovo Rus. Fed. 43 L6
Gleason U.S.A. 172 D5
Gleichen Canada 167 H5
Gleisdorf Austria 49 M8
Gleiwitz Poland see Gliwice
Glen Sweden 44 K3
Glen U.S.A. 177 N1
Glen Afton Canada 173 M4
Glen Afton N.Z. 152 J5
Glen Allen U.S.A. 176 H8
Glénan, Îles de is France 50 C5
Glen Arbor U.S.A. 172 G6
Glenavy N.Z. 153 F12
Glenboro Canada 167 L5
Glen Burnie U.S.A. 177 I6
Glen Canyon gorge U.S.A. 183 M4
Glen Canyon Dam U.S.A. 183 M5
Glencoe S. Africa 133 O5
Glencoe KY U.S.A. 176 A7
Glencoe MN U.S.A. 178 D2
Glenconnor S. Africa 133 J10
Glen Cove U.S.A. 177 L5
Glendale Canada 173 I4
Glendale AZ U.S.A. 183 L8
Glendale CA U.S.A. 182 F7
Glendale UT U.S.A. 183 L4
Glendale Lake U.S.A. 176 G5
Glendale Springs U.S.A. 176 D9
Glendambo Australia 146 B2
Glendive U.S.A. 180 F3
Glendon Canada 167 I4
Glendo Reservoir U.S.A. 180 F4
Glenelg r. Australia 146 D4
Glenfield U.S.A. 177 J2
Glenfinnan U.K. 46 G7
Glengarry Range hills Australia 151 B5
Glengyle Australia 148 C5
Glen Hill Aboriginal Reserve Australia 150 E3
Glen Innes Australia 147 F2
Glenlyon Peak Canada 166 C2
Glen Massey N.Z. 152 I5
Glen More valley U.K. 46 H6
Glenmorgan Australia 147 F1
Glen Murray N.Z. 152 I5
Glenn U.S.A. 182 B2
Glennallen U.S.A. 164 E3
Glennie U.S.A. 173 J6
Glenns U.S.A. 177 I8
Glenns Ferry U.S.A. 180 D4
Glenora Canada 166 D3
Glenore Australia 149 D3
Glenormiston Australia 148 C4
Glenorn Aboriginal Reserve Australia 151 C6
Glen Rock U.S.A. 177 I6
Glen Rogers U.S.A. 176 D8
Glen Rose U.S.A. 179 C5
Glenrothes U.K. 46 I7
Glenroy Australia 150 D3
Glens Falls U.S.A. 177 L2
Glen Shee valley U.K. 46 I7
Glenties Rep. of Ireland 47 D9
Glentunnel N.Z. 153 F11
Glenveagh National Park Rep. of Ireland 47 E8
Glenville U.S.A. 176 E7
Glenwater Canada 172 D2
Glen Wilton U.S.A. 176 F8
Glenwood AR U.S.A. 179 D5
Glenwood IA U.S.A. 178 D3
Glenwood MN U.S.A. 178 D2
Glenwood UT U.S.A. 183 M3
Glenwood WV U.S.A. 176 C7
Glenwood City U.S.A. 172 A5
Glenwood Springs U.S.A. 180 F5

Glevum U.K. see Gloucester
Glina r. Bos.-Herz./Croatia 56 I3
Glina Croatia 56 I3
Glinka Rus. Fed. 43 N7
Glittertinden mt. Norway 45 J3
Gliwice Poland 49 P5
historically known as Gleiwitz
Globe U.S.A. 183 N9
Glodeanu-Sărat Romania 58 H4
Glodeni Romania 58 H4
Glogau Poland see Głogów
Gloggnitz Austria 49 M8
Glogovac Kosovo, Srbija Yugo. 58 B6
Głogów Poland 49 N4
historically known as Glogau
Głogówek Poland 49 O5
Głogów Małopolski Poland 49 S5
Glomfjord Norway 44 K2
Glomma r. Norway 45 J4
Glommersträsk Sweden 44 L2
Glória Brazil 202 E4
Glorieuses, Îles is Indian Ocean 129 E7
English form Glorioso Islands
Glorioso Islands Indian Ocean see
Glorieuses, Îles
Gloucester Australia 147 F2
Gloucester P.N.G. 145 D2
Gloucester U.K. 47 J12
historically known as Glevum
Gloucester MA U.S.A. 177 O3
Gloucester VA U.S.A. 177 I8
Gloucester Island Australia 149 F4
Gloucester Point U.S.A. 177 I8
Glover Reef Belize 185 I5
Gloversville U.S.A. 177 K3
Glovertown Canada 169 K3
Glöwen Germany 48 J3
Głowno Poland 49 R3
Głubczyce Poland 49 O5
Glubinnoye Rus. Fed. 82 D3
Glubokiy Rus. Fed. 41 G6
Glubokoye Belarus see Hlybokaye
Glubokoye Kazakh. 88 C1
Glubokoye, Ozero l. Rus. Fed. 43 K1
Glücksburg (Ostsee) Germany 48 G1
Glückstadt Germany 48 G2
Gluggarnir Hill Faroe Is 46 F2
Glukhov Ukr. see Hlukhiv
Gmelinka Rus. Fed. 102 J4
Gmünd Austria 49 L7
Gmunden Austria 49 L8
Gnarp Sweden 45 L3
Gnarrenburg Germany 48 G2
Gnesen Poland see Gniezno
Gniew Poland 49 P2
Gniewkowo Poland 49 P3
Gniezno Poland 49 O3
historically known as Gnesen
Gnisvärd Sweden 45 L4
Gnjilane Kosovo, Srbija Yugo. 58 C6
Gnoien Germany 49 J2
Gnowangerup Australia 151 B7
Gnows Nest Range hills Australia 151 B6
Goa state India 94 B3
Goageb Namibia 130 C5
Goalpara India 97 F4
Goang Indon. 75 A5
Goaso Ghana 124 E5
Goat Fell hill U.K. 46 G8
Goba Eth. 128 D3
Gobabis Namibia 130 C4
Gobannium U.K. see Abergavenny
Gobas Namibia 130 C5
Gobernador Crespo Arg. 204 E3
Gobernador Duval Arg. 204 D5
Gobernador Gregores Arg. 205 C8
Gobernador Mayer Arg. 205 D8
Gobernador Virasoro Arg. 204 F3
Gobi des. China/Mongolia 85 G2
English form Gobi Desert
Gobi Desert China/Mongolia see Gobi
Gobiki Rus. Fed. 43 O8
Gölberg hill Germany 43 K7
Gobō Japan 91 D8
Goch Germany 48 D4
Gochas Namibia 130 C4
Go Công Vietnam 79 D6
Godagari Bangl. 97 F4
Godavari r. India 94 C2
Godbout Canada 169 H3
Godbout r. Canada 169 H3
Godda India 97 E4
Goddard, Mount U.S.A. 182 F4
Godē Eth. 128 D3
Godeal Hill Port. 54 C6
Godech Bulg. 58 E5
Goderich Canada 168 D5
Goderville France 50 H3
Godhavn Greenland see Qeqertarsuaq
Godhra India 96 B5
Godinlabe Somalia 128 E3
Godo, Gunung mt. Indon. 75 C3
Gödöllő Hungary 49 Q8
Gods r. Canada 167 M3
God's Mercy, Bay of Canada 167 O2
Godthåb Greenland see Nuuk
Godučohkka mt. Sweden 44 L1
also spelt Kátottjåkka
Godwin-Austen, Mount
China/Jammu and Kashmir see K2
Goedemoed S. Africa 133 K7
Goedgegun Swaziland see Nhlangano
Goéland, Lac au l. Canada 168 F3
Goélands, Lac aux l. Canada 169 I2
Goes Neth. 48 A4
Goetzville U.S.A. 173 I4
Goffstown U.S.A. 177 N2
Gogama Canada 168 D4
Gogebic, Lake U.S.A. 172 D4
Gogebic Range hills U.S.A. 172 D4
Göğeç Turkey 109 K1
Gogland, Ostrov i. Rus. Fed. 42 H1
Gogoi Moz. 131 G2
Gogolevka Rus. Fed. 43 M7
Gogosu Romania 58 D4
Gogounou Benin 125 F4
Gogra r. India see Ghaghara
Gogra r. India see Ghaghara
Gogrial Sudan 126 F2
Gogunda India 96 B4
Gohad India 96 C4
Gohana India 96 C3
Goharganj India 96 C5
Goiana Brazil 202 F3
Goianésia Brazil 206 C2
Goiânia Brazil 206 C2
Goianinha Brazil 202 F3
Goiatira Brazil 206 B3
Goiás Brazil 206 C2
Goiás state Brazil 206 C3
Goiatuba Brazil 206 D5
Goincang China 86 B1
Goio-Erê Brazil 203 A8
Goito Italy 56 C3
Gojeb Wenz r. Eth. 128 C3
Gojra India 94 B2
Gokak India 94 B3
Gökçay r. Turkey 108 D1
Gökçeada i. Turkey 106 A2
also known as İmroz
Gökçedağ Turkey 106 C3
Gökçeören Turkey 59 J10
Gökçedepe Turkm. see Gekdepe
Gökdere r. Turkey 108 D1
Goklenkuyu, Solonchak salt l. Turkm. 102 D4
Gökova Turkey see Ula

Granvin Norway 45 I3
Grão Mogol Brazil 202 D6
Grapevine Mountains U.S.A. 183 G5
Gras, Lac de l. Canada 167 I1
Graskop S. Africa 133 O1
Gräsö i. Sweden 45 L3
Grasplatz Namibia 130 B5
Grass r. Canada 167 L3
Grass r. U.S.A. 177 K1
Grasse France 51 M9
Grassflat U.S.A. 176 G4
Grass Lake U.S.A. 173 I8
Grasslands National Park Canada 167 J5
Grass Patch Australia 151 C7
Grassrange U.S.A. 180 E3
Grassridgedam l. S. Africa 133 J8
Grass River Provincial Park Canada 167 K4
Grass Valley U.S.A. 182 C2
Grassy Australia 147 E5
Grassy Creek r. Bahamas 186 D2
Grästorp Sweden 45 K4
Gratiot U.S.A. 172 C8
Gratkorn Austria 49 M8
Graudenz Poland see Grudziądz
Graulhet France 51 H9
Graus Spain 55 L2
Gravatá Brazil 202 F4
Gravataí Brazil 203 B9
Gravdal Norway 44 K1
Grave, Pointe de pt France 50 E7
Gravelbourg Canada 167 J5
Gravenhurst Canada 168 E4
Grave Peak U.S.A. 180 D3
Grāveri Latvia 42 I5
Gravesend Australia 147 F2
Gravette U.S.A. 179 D4
Gravina in Puglia Italy 57 I8
Gravina Island U.S.A. 166 D4
Gravois, Pointe-à- pt Haiti 187 E3
Grawn U.S.A. 172 H6
Gray France 51 L5
Gray GA U.S.A. 175 D5
Gray KY U.S.A. 176 A9
Gray ME U.S.A. 177 O2
Gray TN U.S.A. 176 C9
Grayback Mountain U.S.A. 180 B4
Gray Lake Canada 167 I2
Grayling r. Canada 166 E3
Grayling U.S.A. 173 I6
Grays Harbor inlet U.S.A. 180 A3
Grays Lake U.S.A. 180 E4
Grayville U.S.A. 174 C4
Graz Austria 49 M8
Grdelica Srbija Yugo. 58 D6
Greasy Lake Canada 166 F2
Great Abaco i. Bahamas 186 D1
Great Australian Bight g. Australia 146 A3
Great Bahama Bank sea feature Bahamas 186 D1
Great Barrier Island N.Z. 152 J4
▶Great Barrier Reef Australia 149 E1
oceania [landscapes] ▶ 136–137
oceania [features] ▶ 142–143
Great Barrier Reef Marine Park (Cairns Section) Australia 149 E3
Great Barrier Reef Marine Park (Capricorn Section) Australia 149 F4
Great Barrier Reef Marine Park (Central Section) Australia 149 F3
Great Barrier Reef Marine Park (Far North Section) Australia 149 E2
Great Barrington U.S.A. 177 L3
Great Basalt Wall National Park Australia 149 E3
Great Basin U.S.A. 183 H2
Great Basin National Park U.S.A. 183 J3
Great Bear r. Canada 166 E1

▶Great Bear Lake Canada 166 F1
4th largest lake in North America and 8th in the world.
northamerica [landscapes] ▶ 156–157

Great Belt sea chan. Denmark 45 J5
also known as Store Bælt
Great Bend KS U.S.A. 178 C4
Great Bend PA U.S.A. 177 J4
Great Bitter Lake Egypt 121 G2
also known as Murrat el Kubra, Buheirat
Great Blasket Island Rep. of Ireland 47 B11

▶Great Britain i. U.K. 47 J9
Largest island in Europe and 8th in the world.
europe [landscapes] ▶ 30–31

Great Coco Island Cocos Is 79 A5
Great Dismal Swamp National Wildlife Refuge nature res. U.S.A. 177 I9
Great Dividing Range mts Australia 145 D5
Great Driffield U.K. 47 L9
Great Duck Island Canada 173 K5
Great Eastern Erg des. Alg. see Grand Erg Oriental
Great Egg Harbor Inlet U.S.A. 177 K6
Greater Accra admin. reg. Ghana 125 F5
Greater Antilles is Caribbean Sea 171 J7
Greater Khingan Mountains China see Da Hinggan Ling
Greater Tunb i. The Gulf 105 F2
also known as Tonb-e Bozorg, Jazīreh-ye or Ṭunb al Kubrá
Great Exhibition Bay N.Z. 152 H2
Great Exuma i. Bahamas 186 E2

Great Falls U.S.A. 180 E3
Great Fish r. S. Africa 133 L10
Greatford N.Z. 152 J8
Great Gandak r. India 97 E4
Great Ganges atoll Cook Is see Manihiki
Great Guana Cay i. Bahamas 186 D1
Great Harbour Cay i. Bahamas 186 D1
Great Inagua i. Bahamas 187 E2
Great Karoo plat. S. Africa 132 H9
also known as Karroo
Great Kei r. S. Africa 133 M9
Great Lake Australia 147 E5

▶Great Lakes Canada/U.S.A. 172
Consist of Lakes Erie, Huron, Michigan, Ontario and Superior.

Great Mercury Island N.Z. 152 J4
Great Miami r. U.S.A. 176 A6
Great Namaqualand reg. Namibia 130 C5
Great Nicobar i. India 95 G5
Great North East Channel Australia/P.N.G. 144 D2
Great Ouse r. U.K. 47 M11
Great Oyster Bay Australia 147 F5
Great Palm Island Australia 149 E3
Great Peconic Bay U.S.A. 177 M5
Great Plain of the Koukdjuak Canada 165 L3
Great Plains U.S.A. 178 B3
Great Point U.S.A. 177 O4
Great Rift Valley Africa 128 C5
Great Ruaha r. Tanz. 129 C6
Great Sacandaga Lake U.S.A. 177 K2
Great St Bernard Pass Italy/Switz. 51 N7
also known as Grand St Bernard, Col du or Gran San Bernardo, Colle del
Great Salt Lake U.S.A. 183 L1
Great Salt Lake Desert U.S.A. 183 K1
Great Sand Hills Canada 167 I5
Great Sand Sea des. Egypt/Libya 120 E2
Great Sandy Desert Australia 150 C4
Great Sandy Island Australia see Fraser Island
Great Sandy Island Nature Reserve Australia 150 A4
Great Sea Reef Fiji 145 G3

▶Great Slave Lake Canada 167 H2
Deepest and 5th largest lake in North America.
northamerica [landscapes] ▶ 156–157

Great Smoky Mountains U.S.A. 174 C5
Great Smoky Mountains National Park U.S.A. 174 D5
Great Snow Mountain Canada 166 E3
Great South Bay U.S.A. 177 L5
Great Usutu r. Africa see Usutu
Great Victoria Desert Australia 151 E6
Great Victoria Desert Conservation Park nature res. Australia 146 A2
Great Victoria Desert Nature Reserve Australia 151 E6
Great Wall research station Antarctica 222 U2
also known as Chang Cheng
▶Great Wall tourist site China 85 H3
asia [countries] ▶ 64–65
Great Western Erg des. Alg. see Grand Erg Occidental
Great West Torres Islands Myanmar 79 B6
Great Winterhoek mt. S. Africa 132 D10
Great Yarmouth U.K. 47 N11
short form Yarmouth
Great Zab r. Iraq see Zāb al Kabīr, Nahr az
Great Zimbabwe National Monument tourist site Zimbabwe 131 F4
short form Zimbabwe
Grebbestad Sweden 45 J4
Grebenkovskiy Ukr. see Hrebinka
Grebnevo Rus. Fed. 43 U7
Grebyonka Ukr. see Hrebinka
Greci, Vârful hill Romania 58 J3
Greco, Cape Cyprus see Greko, Cape
Greco, Monte mt. Italy 56 F7
Gredos, Sierra de mts Spain 54 F4
Greec Chile 205 C9
▶Greece country Europe 59 C10
known as Ellas in Greek; historically known as Hellas
europe [countries] ▶ 32–35
Greece U.S.A. 176 H2
Greeley U.S.A. 180 F4
Greely Center U.S.A. 178 C3
Greely Fiord inlet Canada 165 K1
Greem-Bell, Ostrov i. Rus. Fed. 39 G1
English form Graham Bell Island
Green r. Canada 171 M2
Green r. KY U.S.A. 174 C4
Green r. ND U.S.A. 178 B2
Green r. WY U.S.A. 183 O3
Green Bay U.S.A. 172 E6
Green Bay b. U.S.A. 172 F5
Greenbrier r. U.S.A. 176 E8
Greenbushes Australia 151 B7
Greencastle Bahamas 175 E7
Greencastle IN U.S.A. 174 C4
Greencastle PA U.S.A. 176 H6
Green Cove Springs U.S.A. 175 D6
Greendale IN U.S.A. 176 A6
Greendale KY U.S.A. 176 A7
Greene ME U.S.A. 177 O1
Greene NY U.S.A. 177 J3
Greeneville U.S.A. 176 C9
Greenfield CA U.S.A. 182 C5
Greenfield IA U.S.A. 178 D3
Greenfield IN U.S.A. 174 C4
Greenfield MA U.S.A. 177 M3
Greenfield MO U.S.A. 178 D4
Greenfield OH U.S.A. 176 B6
Greenfield WI U.S.A. 172 E8
Green Head Australia 151 A6
Greenhill Island Australia 148 B1
Greenhills N.Z. 153 C14
Greening Canada 173 S2
Green Island i. Taiwan see Lü Tao
Green Island U.S.A. 172 C8
Green Island Bay Phil. 74 A4
Green Islands P.N.G. 145 E2
Green Lake Canada 167 J4
Green Lake l. Canada 166 F5
Green Lake U.S.A. 172 E7

▶Greenland terr. N. America 165 O2
Self-governing Danish Territory. Largest island in the world and in North America. 3rd largest political entity in North America. Known as Grønland in Danish or Kalaallit Nunaat in Greenlandic.
world [physical features] ▶ 8–9
world [land images] ▶ 12–13
oceania [countries] ▶ 138–139
northamerica [environments] ▶ 162–163

Greenland U.S.A. 172 D4
Greenly Island Australia 146 B3
Green Mountains U.S.A. 177 M1
Greenock U.K. 46 H8
Greenough Australia 151 A6
Greenough r. Australia 151 A6
Greenport U.S.A. 177 M4
Green River WY U.S.A. 180 E4
Greensboro AL U.S.A. 175 C5
Greensboro GA U.S.A. 175 D5
Greensboro MD U.S.A. 177 J7
Greensboro NC U.S.A. 176 F9
Greensburg IN U.S.A. 174 C4
Greensburg KS U.S.A. 178 C4
Greensburg KY U.S.A. 174 C4
Greensburg LA U.S.A. 175 B6
Greensburg PA U.S.A. 176 F5
Greens Peak U.S.A. 183 O7
Green Swamp U.S.A. 175 E5
Greenup IL U.S.A. 174 B4
Greenup KY U.S.A. 176 C7
Greenvale Australia 149 E3
Green Valley U.S.A. 181 E7
Greenville Canada 166 D4
Greenville Liberia 124 C5
Greenville AL U.S.A. 175 C6
Greenville CA U.S.A. 182 D1
Greenville IL U.S.A. 174 B4
Greenville KY U.S.A. 174 C4
Greenville ME U.S.A. 174 G2
Greenville MI U.S.A. 172 H7
Greenville MO U.S.A. 174 B4
Greenville MS U.S.A. 175 B5
Greenville NC U.S.A. 174 E5
Greenville NH U.S.A. 177 N3
Greenville OH U.S.A. 176 A5
Greenville PA U.S.A. 176 E4
Greenville SC U.S.A. 174 D5
Greenville TX U.S.A. 179 C5
Greenwater Lake Canada 172 C2
Greenwater Provincial Park Canada 167 K4
Greenwich atoll Micronesia see Kapingamarangi
Greenwich CT U.S.A. 177 L4
Greenwich NY U.S.A. 177 L2
Greenwich OH U.S.A. 176 C4
Greenwood AR U.S.A. 179 D5
Greenwood IN U.S.A. 174 C4
Greenwood MS U.S.A. 175 B5
Greenwood SC U.S.A. 175 D5
Greenwood WI U.S.A. 172 C6
Greer U.S.A. 174 D5
Greers Ferry Lake U.S.A. 179 D5
Gregório r. Brazil 198 D6
Gregory r. Australia 148 C3
Gregory MI U.S.A. 173 I8
Gregory SD U.S.A. 178 C3
Gregory, Lake salt flat S.A. Australia 146 C2
Gregory, Lake salt flat W.A. Australia 150 D4
Gregory, Lake salt flat W.A. Australia 151 B5
Gregory Downs Australia 148 C3
Gregory National Park Australia 148 A3
Gregory Range hills Qld Australia 149 D3
Gregory Range hills W.A. Australia 150 C4
Greifswald Germany 49 K1
Greifswalder Bodden b. Germany 49 K1
Greifswalder Oie i. Germany 49 K1
Greiz Germany 49 J5
Greko, Cape Cyprus 108 F3
also spelt Greco, Cape
Gremikha Rus. Fed. 40 F1
Gremyachev Rus. Fed. 43 T7
Gremyachinsk Rus. Fed. 40 K4
Gremyachinsk Rus. Fed. 81 H2
Grenå Denmark 45 J4
Grenada U.S.A. 175 B5
▶Grenada country West Indies 187 H4
northamerica [countries] ▶ 158–159
Grenade France 50 H9
Grenade-sur-l'Adour France 50 F9
Grenchen Switz. 51 N5
Grenen spit Denmark 45 J4
English form The Skaw
Grenfell Australia 147 F3
Grenfell Canada 167 K5
Grenoble France 51 L7
Grense-Jakobselv Norway 44 O1
Grenville Grenada 187 H4
Grenville, Cape Australia 149 D1
Grenville Island Fiji see Rotuma
Greshak Pak. 101 F5
Gresham U.S.A. 180 B3
Gresik Indon. 77 F4
Gressåmoen Nasjonalpark nat. park Norway 44 K2
Gretna LA U.S.A. 175 B6
Gretna VA U.S.A. 176 F9
Grevelingen sea chan. Neth. 48 A4
Greven Germany 48 E3
Grevena Greece 59 C8
Grevenbroich Germany 48 D4
Grevenmacher Lux. 51 M3
Grevesmühlen Germany 48 I2
Grey r. N.Z. 153 F10
also known as Māwheranui
Grey, Cape Australia 148 C2
Greybull U.S.A. 180 E3
Greybull r. U.S.A. 180 E3
Grey Hunter Peak Canada 166 C2
Grey Islands Canada 169 K3
Greylock, Mount U.S.A. 177 L3
Greymouth N.Z. 153 F10
Grey Range hills Australia 147 D2
Grey's Plains Australia 151 A5
Greystone Zimbabwe 131 F4
Greytown S. Africa 133 O6
Grez-Doiceau Belgium 51 K2
Gria, Akra pt Greece 59 F11
Gribanovskiy Rus. Fed. 41 G6
Gribingui r. Cent. Afr. Rep. 126 C2
Gribingui-Bamingui, Réserve de Faune du nature res. Cent. Afr. Rep. 126 C3
Gridley CA U.S.A. 182 C2
Gridley IL U.S.A. 172 E10
Grieskirchen Austria 49 K7
Griffin U.S.A. 175 C5
Griffith Australia 147 E3
Griffith Canada 173 P5
Griffiths Point Canada 165 G2
Griffithsville U.S.A. 176 D7
Grigan i. N. Mariana Is see Agrihan
Grigiškės Lith. 42 G7
Grignols France 50 F8
Grigoriopol Moldova 58 K1
Grik Malaysia see Gerik
Grim, Cape Australia 147 E5
Grimari Cent. Afr. Rep. 126 D3
Grimma Germany 49 J4

Grimmen Germany 49 K1
Grimsby Canada 173 N7
Grimsby U.K. 47 L10
Grímsey i. Iceland 44 [inset] C2
Grimshaw Canada 167 G3
Grímsstaðir Iceland 44 [inset] C2
Grimstad Norway 45 J4
Grindaheim Norway 45 J3
Grindavík Iceland 44 [inset] B3
Grindsted Denmark 45 J5
Grindu Romania 58 H4
Grindu Romania 58 J3
Grindul Chituc spit Romania 58 J4
Grindușu, Vârful mt. Romania 58 H2
Grinevo Rus. Fed. 43 O9
Grinnell U.S.A. 174 A3
Grinnell Peninsula Canada 165 J2
Grinties Romania 58 G1
Grintovec mt. Slovenia 56 G2
Griqualand East reg. S. Africa 133 N7
Griqualand West reg. S. Africa 132 H5
Griquatown S. Africa 132 H5
Grise Fiord Canada 165 K2
Grishino Ukr. see Krasnoarmiys'k
Grisik Indon. 76 C3
Gris Nez, Cap c. France 50 H2
Grisolles France 50 H9
Grisslehamn Sweden 45 L3
Gritley U.K. 46 J5
Grizim well Alg. 123 E4
Grizzly Bear Mountain hill Canada 166 F1
Grmeč mts Bos.-Herz. 56 I4
Groais Island Canada 169 K3
Grobbendonk Belgium 51 K1
Grobiņa Latvia 42 C5
Groblersdal S. Africa 133 N2
Groblershoop S. Africa 132 G5
Gröbming Austria 49 K8
Grocka Srbija Yugo. 58 B4
Grodekovo Rus. Fed. 82 C3
Grodków Poland 49 O5
Grodnenskaya Oblast' admin. div. Belarus see Hrodzyenskaya Voblasts'
Grodno Belarus see Hrodna
Grodno Oblast admin. div. Belarus see Hrodzyenskaya Voblasts'
Grodzisk Mazowiecki Poland 49 R3
Grodzisk Wielkopolski Poland 49 N3
Groen watercourse N. Cape S. Africa 132 H7
Groen watercourse N. Cape/W. Cape S. Africa 132 B7
Groesbeck U.S.A. 179 C6
Gröf Iceland 44 [inset] B2
Groganville Australia 149 E3
Groix, Île de i. France 50 C5
Grójec Poland 49 R4
Grombalia Tunisia 57 C12
Grömitz Germany 48 H1
Gronau (Westfalen) Germany 48 E3
Grong Norway 44 K2
Groningen Neth. 48 D2
Groningen Suriname 199 H3
Grønland terr. N. America see Greenland
Grønnedal Greenland see Kangilinnguit
Groom Lake U.S.A. 183 I4
Groot r. E. Cape S. Africa 132 I10
Groot r. W. Cape S. Africa 132 D9
Groot r. W. Cape S. Africa 132 F10
Groot-Aar Pan salt pan S. Africa 132 E4
Groot Berg r. S. Africa 132 C9
Groot Brak r. S. Africa 133 J8
Groot Brakrivier S. Africa 132 G11
Grootdraaidam dam S. Africa 133 N3
Grootdrink S. Africa 132 F5
Groote Eylandt i. Australia 148 C2
Groote Eylandt Aboriginal Land res. Australia 148 C2
Grootfontein Namibia 130 C3
Groot-Grannapan salt pan S. Africa 133 J5
Groot Karas Berg plat. Namibia 130 C5
Groot Letaba r. S. Africa 131 F4
Grootmis S. Africa 132 B6
Grootpan S. Africa 133 K2
Grootrivierhoogte mts S. Africa 132 H10
Groot Swartberge mts S. Africa 132 F10
Grootvaalgraspan salt pan Namibia 132 C3
Grootvloer salt pan S. Africa 132 E6
Groot Winterberg mt. S. Africa 133 K9
Groot-Winterhoekberge mts S. Africa 133 I10
Gropeni Romania 58 I3
Grosa, Isla i. Spain 55 K7
Gros Islet St Lucia 187 H4
Gros Morne National Park Canada 169 J3
Grosne r. France 51 K6
Gross Barmen Namibia 130 C4
Großenhain Germany 49 K4
Großenkneten Germany 48 F3
Großenlüder Germany 48 G5
Großer Arber mt. Germany 49 K6
Großer Beerberg hill Germany 48 H5
Grösser Bösenstein mt. Austria 49 L8
Grosser Priel mt. Austria 49 L8
Großer Rachel mt. Germany 49 K7
Grosser Speikkofel mt. Austria 49 K9
Grosser Speikkogel mt. Austria 49 L9
Grosseto Italy 56 D6
Groß-Gerau Germany 48 F6
Großglockner mt. Austria 49 J8
Groß-Hesepe Germany 48 E3
Großräschen Germany 49 L4
Groß Schönebeck Germany 49 K3
Gross Umis Namibia 130 C4
Großvenediger mt. Austria 49 J8
Grosuplje Slovenia 56 G3
Grosvenor Mountains Antarctica 223 L1
Gros Ventre Range mts U.S.A. 180 E4
Groswater Bay Canada 169 J2
Groton CT U.S.A. 177 M4
Groton NY U.S.A. 177 I3
Groton SD U.S.A. 178 C2
Grottoes U.S.A. 176 G7
Grouard Lake Canada 167 G1
Grouard Mission Canada 167 G4
Grouin, Pointe du pt France 50 E4
Groumania Côte d'Ivoire 124 E5
Groundhog r. Canada 168 D3
Grove U.S.A. 178 D4
Grove City OH U.S.A. 176 B6
Grove City PA U.S.A. 176 E4
Grove Hill U.S.A. 175 C6
Grövelsjön Sweden 45 K3
Grove Mountains Antarctica 223 F2
Grover Beach U.S.A. 182 D6
Groveton NH U.S.A. 177 N1
Groveton TX U.S.A. 179 D6
Grovfjord Norway 44 L1
Growler Mountains U.S.A. 183 K9
Groz'dovo Bulg. 58 I5
Groznyy Rus. Fed. 41 H8
also known as Dzhokhar Ghala
Grubišno Polje Croatia 56 J3
Grudovo Bulg. see Sredets
Grudziądz Poland 49 P2
historically known as Graudenz
Grumăzești Romania 58 H1
Grums Sweden 45 K4
Grünau Namibia 130 C5
Grünau-Grünheider Wald und Seengebiet park Germany 49 K3
Grünberg Poland see Zielona Góra
Grundagssätern Sweden 45 K3
Grundarfjörður Iceland 44 [inset] B2
Grundforsen Sweden 45 K3
Grundlsee nature res. Austria 49 K8
Grundorner Namibia 132 B2
Grundsuna Sweden 44 L3
Grundy U.S.A. 176 C8
Gruñidora Mex. 185 E3
Gruver U.S.A. 179 B4
Gruzdžiai Lith. 42 E5

Gruzinskaya S.S.R. country Asia see Georgia
Gryazi Rus. Fed. 41 F5
Gryaznoye Rus. Fed. 43 U7
Gryazovets Rus. Fed. 43 V3
Grybów Poland 49 R6
Gryfice Poland 49 M2
Gryfino Poland 49 L2
Gryfów Śląski Poland 49 M4
Gryllefjord Norway 44 L1
Grytviken S. Georgia 205 [inset]
Guà r. Italy 56 D3
Guabito Panama 186 C5
Guacanayabo, Golfo de b. Cuba 186 D2
Guacara Venez. 187 G5
Guacharía r. Col. 198 D3
Guaçu Brazil 203 A7
Guaçuí Brazil 207 L7
Guadaira r. Spain 54 E7
Guadajira r. Spain 54 E6
Guadajoz r. Spain 54 G7
Guadalajara Mex. 185 E4
Guadalajara Spain 55 H4
Guadalaviar r. Spain 55 J4
Guadalcacín, Embalse de resr Spain 54 F8
Guadalcanal i. Solomon Is 145 F2
Guadalcanal Spain 54 F6
Guadalén r. Spain 55 H6
Guadales Arg. 204 D4
Guadalhorce r. Spain 54 G8
Guadalhorce, Embalse de resr Spain 54 G8
Guadalimar r. Spain 55 H7
Guadalmez r. Spain 54 G6
Guadalope r. Spain 55 K3
Guadalquivir r. Spain 55 E8
Guadalupe Brazil 202 D3
Guadalupe Nuevo León Mex. 185 E3
Guadalupe Zacatecas Mex. 185 E4
Guadalupe i. Mex. 170 C6
Guadalupe watercourse Mex. 183 H9
Guadalupe Peru 200 A1
Guadalupe Spain 54 F5
Guadalupe AZ U.S.A. 183 M8
Guadalupe CA U.S.A. 182 D7
Guadalupe r. TX U.S.A. 179 C6
Guadalupe, Sierra de mts Spain 54 F5
Guadalupe Aguilera Mex. 184 D3
Guadalupe Mountains National Park U.S.A. 181 F7
Guadalupe Victoria Baja California Norte Mex. 183 I9
Guadalupe Victoria Durango Mex. 184 D3
Guadamez r. Spain 54 F6
Guadarrama r. Spain 54 G5
Guadarrama Venez. 199 D2
Guadarrama, Puerto de pass Spain 54 G4
Guadarrama, Sierra de mts Spain 54 G4
Guadazaón r. Spain 55 J5

▶Guadeloupe terr. West Indies 187 H3
French Overseas Department.
oceania [countries] ▶ 138–139

Guadeloupe Passage Caribbean Sea 187 H3
Guadiamar r. Spain 54 E8
Guadiana r. Port./Spain 54 D7
Guadiana, Bahía de b. Cuba 186 B2
Guadiana Menor r. Spain 55 H7
Guadiaro r. Spain 54 F8
Guadiato r. Spain 54 F7
Guadiela r. Spain 55 I4
Guadiervas r. Spain 54 F4
Guadix Spain 55 H7
Guafo, Isla i. Chile 205 B6
Guagua Phil. 74 B3
Guaíba Brazil 203 B9
Guaiçuí Brazil 203 C6
Guaicuras Brazil 201 F5
Guaillabamba r. Ecuador 198 B4
Guáimaro Cuba 186 D2
Guaina Venez. 199 F3
Guainía dept Col. 198 D4
Guainía r. Col./Venez. 198 E4
Guaiquinima, Cerro mt. Venez. 199 F3
Guaira Brazil 203 A8
Guaíra Brazil 206 E7
Guairaçá Brazil 206 A9
Guaitecas, Islas is Chile 205 B6
Guajará Açu Brazil 202 B2
Guajará Mirim Brazil 200 D2
Guajaratuba Brazil 199 F6
Guajarraã Brazil 200 D1
Guaje, Laguna de l. Mex. 185 E2
Guaje, Llano de plain Mex. 185 E3
Guajira dept Col. 198 C2
Gualaceo Ecuador 198 B5
Gualala U.S.A. 182 A3
Gualán Guat. 185 H6
Gualaquiza Ecuador 198 B5
Gualdo Tadino Italy 56 E5
Gualeguay Arg. 204 F4
Gualeguay r. Arg. 204 F4
Gualeguaychu Arg. 204 F4
Gualicho, Salina salt flat Arg. 204 D6
Gualjaina Arg. 205 C6
Guallatiri vol. Chile 200 C4

▶Guam terr. N. Pacific Ocean 73 J4
United States Unincorporated Territory.
oceania [countries] ▶ 138–139

Guamblin, Isla i. Chile 205 B7
Guamini Arg. 204 E5
Guamo Cuba 186 D2
Guampí, Sierra de mts Venez. 199 E3
Guamúchil Mex. 184 C3
Gu'an China 85 H4
Guan r. China 87 F1
Guanabacoa Cuba 186 C2
Guanabara Brazil 200 C2
Guanabara, Baía de b. Brazil 207 J9
Guanacaste, Parque Nacional nat. park Costa Rica 186 B5
Guanacevi Mex. 184 D3
Guanahacabibes, Península de pen. Cuba 186 B2
Guanaja Hond. 186 B3
Guanajay Cuba 186 C2
Guanajuato Mex. 185 E4
Guanajuato state Mex. 185 E4
Guanambi Brazil 202 D5
Guanare Venez. 198 D2
Guanare Viejo r. Venez. 198 E2
Guanarito Venez. 198 D2
Guanarito r. Venez. 198 D2
Guanay Bol. 200 D3
Guandacol Arg. 204 C3
Guandaokou China 87 D1
Guandi Shan mt. China 85 F4
Guandu r. Brazil 207 L6
Guandu China 87 E3
Guane Cuba 186 B2
Guang'an China 86 C2
Guangchang China 87 F3
also known as Xujiang
Guangde China 87 F2
also known as Taozhou
Guangdong prov. China 87 E4
English form Kwangtung
Guangfeng China 87 F2
also known as Yongfeng
Guanghai China 87 E4
Guanghan China 86 C2
Guanghua China see Laohekou
Guangling China 85 G4
Guangmao Shan mt. China 86 B3
Guangming China see Xide
Guangming Ding mt. China 87 F2

Guangnan China 86 C3
also known as Liancheng
Guangning China 87 E4
also known as Nanjie
Guangning China see Beining
Guangrao China 85 H4
Guangshan China 87 E2
Guangshui China 87 E2
Guangxi aut. reg. China see Guangxi Zhuangzu Zizhiqu
Guangxi Zhuangzu Zizhiqu aut. reg. China 87 D4
short form Guangxi; English form Kwangsi or Kwangsi Chuang Autonomous Region
Guangyuan China 86 C1
Guangze China 87 F3
also known as Hangchuan
Guangzhou China 87 E4
English form Canton; formerly spelt Kwangchow
Guanhães Brazil 203 D6
Guanhães r. Brazil 207 K6
Guanhe Kou r. mouth China 87 F1
Guánica Puerto Rico 187 G3
Guanipa r. Venez. 199 F2
Guanling China 86 C3
also known as Guansuo
Guanmian Shan mts China 87 D2
Guanpo China 87 D1
Guansuo China see Guanling
Guanta Venez. 199 E2
Guantánamo Cuba 187 E2
Guantao China 85 G4
Guanxian China see Dujiangyan
Guanyang China 87 D3
Guanyinqiao China 86 B2
formerly known as Chuosijia
Guanyun China 87 F1
also known as Yishan; formerly known as Dayishan
Guapay r. Bol. see Grande
Guapé Brazil 203 C7
Guapí Col. 198 B4
Guapiara Brazil 206 E11
Guápiles Costa Rica 186 C5
Guaporé r. Bol./Brazil 200 D2
Guaporé Brazil 203 B9
Guaporé state Brazil see Rondônia
Guaqui Bol. 200 C4
Guará Brazil 206 F7
Guará r. Brazil 202 C5
Guara, Sierra de mts Spain 55 K2
Guarabira Brazil 202 F3
Guaranda Ecuador 198 B5
Guarani Brazil 207 J8
Guarantã Brazil 206 D8
Guarapari Brazil 203 D7
Guarapuava Brazil 203 B8
Guararapes Brazil 206 C8
Guaratinga Brazil 202 E6
Guaratinguetá Brazil 207 H9
Guaratuba Brazil 203 B8
Guarayos Bol. 200 C3
Guarda Port. 54 D4
Guarda admin. dist. Port. 54 D4
Guardafui, Cape Somalia see Caseyr, Raas
Guardal r. Spain 55 I7
Guardamar del Segura Spain 55 K6
Guardatinajas Venez. 199 E2
Guardia Escolta Arg. 204 E3
Guardiagrele Italy 56 G6
Guardianes de la Patria Mex. 183 I9
Guardo Spain 54 G2
Guardunha, Serra de mts Port. 54 D5
Guareña Spain 54 E6
Guariba r. Brazil 201 E1
Guárico state Venez. 199 E2
Guarico, Punta pt Cuba 187 E2
Guarrojo r. Col. 198 D3
Guarujá Brazil 207 G10
Guarulhos Brazil 206 G10
Guasare r. Venez. 187 F5
Guasave Mex. 184 C3
Guasdualito Venez. 198 D3
Guasipati Venez. 199 F3
Guastatoya Guat. see El Progreso
Guasuba r. India 97 F5

▶Guatemala country Central America 185 H6
4th most populous country in North America.

Guatemala Guat. see Guatemala City

▶Guatemala City Guat. 185 H6
Capital of Guatemala. Also known as Guatemala.
northamerica [countries] ▶ 158–159

Guatimozin Arg. 204 E4
Guatrache Arg. 204 E5
Guatrochi Arg. 205 D6
Guaviare dept Col. 198 D4
Guaviare r. Col. 198 E3
Guaxupé Brazil 206 G8
Guayabal Col. 198 D3
Guayabal Cuba 186 D2
Guayaguas, Sierra da mts Arg. 204 D3
Guayama Puerto Rico 187 G3
Guayapo, Serranía mts Venez. 199 E3
Guayaquil Ecuador 198 B5
Guayaquil, Golfo de g. Ecuador 198 A5
Guayaramerín Bol. 200 D2
Guayas prov. Ecuador 198 A5
Guayatayoc, Lago de imp. l. Arg. 200 D5
Guaymas Mex. 184 C3
Guayquiraró r. Arg. 204 F3
Guazacapán Guat. 185 H6
Guba Eth. 128 B2
Gubadag Turkm. 102 D4
formerly known as Tel'mansk
Guba Dolgaya Rus. Fed. 40 K1
Gubakha Rus. Fed. 40 K4
Gûbâl, Gezîret i. Egypt 104 A2
English form Gûbâl Island
Gûbâl Island Egypt see Gûbâl, Gezîret
Guban plain Somalia 128 E2
Gubat Phil. 74 C3
Gubbi India 94 C3
Gubbio Italy 56 E5
historically known as Iguvium
Gubdor Rus. Fed. 40 K3
Gubed Binna b. Somalia 128 F2
Guben Germany 49 L4
formerly known as Wilhelm-Pieck-Stadt
Gübene Bulg. 58 G6
Gubin Poland 49 L4
Gubino Rus. Fed. 43 Q6
Gubio Nigeria 125 I3
Gubkin Rus. Fed. 41 F6
Gucheng Hebei China 85 G4
also known as Zhengkou; formerly known as Zhengjiakou
Gucheng Hubei China 87 D1
Gudalur India 94 C4
Gudar, Sierra de mts Spain 55 K4
Gudari India 95 D2
Gudaut'a Georgia 107 E2
Gudbrandsdalen valley Norway 45 J3
Guddu Barrage Pak. 101 G4
Gudermes Rus. Fed. 102 A4
Gudi Nigeria 125 H4
Gudivada India 94 D2
Gudiyattam India 94 C3
Gudong r. China 82 C4
Gudri r. Pak. 101 E5
Güdül Turkey 106 C2
Gudur Andhra Pradesh India 94 C3
Gudur Andhra Pradesh India 94 C3
Gudvangen Norway 45 I3
Gudzhal r. Rus. Fed. 82 D2

largest islands

	island	area sq km	area sq miles	location		page#
1 ▶	Greenland	2 175 600	840 004	North America	▶	165 O2
2 ▶	New Guinea	808 510	312 167	Oceania	▶	73 J8
3 ▶	Borneo	745 561	287 863	Asia	▶	77 F2
4 ▶	Madagascar	587 040	266 657	Africa	▶	131 J4
5 ▶	Baffin Island	507 451	195 927	North America	▶	165 L2
6 ▶	Sumatra	473 606	182 860	Asia	▶	76 B2
7 ▶	Honshū	227 414	87 805	Asia	▶	91 F6
8 ▶	Great Britain	218 476	84 354	Europe	▶	47 J9
9 ▶	Victoria Island	217 291	83 897	North America	▶	165 H2
10 ▶	Ellesmere Island	196 236	75 767	North America	▶	165 K2

Gudžiūnai Lith. **42** E6
Guè, Rivière du *r.* Canada **169** G1
Guebwiller France **51** N5
Guéckédou Guinea **124** C4
Guéguen, Lac *l.* Canada **173** P2
Guelb er Richât *hill* Mauritania **122** C5
Guélengdeng Chad **126** B2
Guelma Alg. **123** G1
Guelmine Morocco **122** C3
Guelph Canada **168** D5
Guémez Mex. **185** F4
Guendour *well* Mauritania **122** C6
Guéné Benin **125** F4
Guènt Paté Senegal **124** B3
Guer France **50** D5
Guéra *pref.* Chad **126** C2
Guéra, Massif du *mts* Chad **126** C2
Guérande France **50** D5
Guerara Alg. **123** G2
Guérard, Lac *l.* Canada **169** H1
Guercif Morocco **123** E2
Guéré *watercourse* Chad **120** C5
Guéréda Chad **120** D6
Guerende Libya **120** D4
Guéret France **50** H6
Guerneville U.S.A. **182** B3
Guernica Spain *see* **Gernika-Lumo**

▶**Guernsey** *terr.* Channel Is **50** D3
United Kingdom Crown Dependency.
europe [countries] ▶ 32–35

Guernsey U.S.A. **180** F4
Guérou Mauritania **124** C2
Guerrero *Coahuila* Mex. **179** B6
Guerrero *Tamaulipas* Mex. **185** F3
Guerrero *state* Mex. **185** E5
Guerrero Negro Mex. **184** B3
Guers, Lac *l.* Canada **169** H1
Guerzim Alg. **123** E3
Guețâțira *well* Mali **122** D4
Gueugnon France **51** K6
Guéyo Côte d'Ivoire **124** D5
Gufeng China *see* **Pingnan**
Gufu China *see* **Xingshan**
Gugē *mt.* Eth. **128** C3
Gügerd, Kūh-e *mts* Iran **100** C3
Guglieri Arg. **204** E3
Guguan *i.* N. Mariana Is **73** K3
Gugu Mountains Eth. **128** C2
Guhakolak, Tanjung *pt* Indon. **76** D4
Guhe China **87** F2
Gūh Kūh *mt.* Iran **100** D5
Guhuai China *see* **Pingyu**
Guia Brazil **201** F3
Guiana Highlands *mts* S. America **199** E3
Guichen France **50** E5
Guichi China **87** F2
Guichicovi Mex. **185** G5
Guichón Uruguay **204** F4
Guidan-Roumji Niger **125** G3
Guidari Chad **126** C2
Guide China **84** D5
also known as Heyin
Guidel France **50** C5
Guider Cameroon **125** I4
Guidiguir Niger **125** H3
Guidimaka *admin. reg.* Mauritania **124** B3
Guiding China **87** C3
Guidong China **87** E3
Guidonia-Montecelio Italy **56** E7
Guier, Lac de *l.* Senegal **124** B2
Guietsou Gabon **126** A5
Guigang China **87** D4
Guiglo Côte d'Ivoire **124** D5
Güigüe Venez. **187** G5
Guija Moz. **131** G5
formerly known as Caniçado *or* Vila Alferes Chamusca
Gui Jiang *r.* China **87** D4
Guiji Shan *mts* China **87** G2
Guijuelo Spain **54** F4
Guildford U.K. **47** L12
Guilford U.S.A. **174** G2
Guilherand France **51** K8
Guilherme Capelo Angola *see* **Cacongo**
Guilin China **87** D3
Guillaume-Delisle, Lac *l.* Canada **168** E1
Guillaumes France **51** M8
Guillestre France **51** M8
Guimarães Brazil **202** C2
Guimarães Port. **54** C3
Guimaras *i.* Phil. **74** B4
Guimaras Strait Phil. **74** B4
Guimeng Ding *mt.* China **85** H5
Guinagourou Benin **125** F4
Guinan China **84** D5
also known as Mangra
Guindulman Phil. **74** C4
▶**Guinea** *country* Africa **124** B4
also known as Guinea-Conakry; *spelt* Guinée *in French; formerly known as* French Guinea
africa [countries] ▶ 114–117
Guinea, Gulf of Africa **125** G6
▶**Guinea-Bissau** *country* Africa **124** B3
also spelt Guiné-Bissau; *formerly known as* Portuguese Guinea
africa [countries] ▶ 114–117
Guinea-Conakry *country* Africa *see* **Guinea**
Guinea Ecuatorial *country* Africa *see* **Equatorial Guinea**
Guiné-Bissau *country* Africa *see* **Guinea-Bissau**
Guinée *country* Africa *see* **Guinea**
Guinée-Forestière *admin. reg.* Guinea **124** C4
Guinée-Maritime *admin. reg.* Guinea **124** B4
Güines Cuba **186** C2
Guines France **51** H2
Guingamp France **50** C4
Guinguinéo Senegal **124** B3
Guiones, Punta *pt* Costa Rica **186** B5
Guipavas France **50** B4
Guiping China **87** D4
Güira de Melena Cuba **186** C2
Guiratinga Brazil **202** A6
Güiria Venez. **199** F2
Guisanbourg Fr. Guiana **199** I3
Guisborough U.K. **47** K9
Guise France **51** J3
Guishan China *see* **Xinping**
Guissefa *well* Mali **125** F2
Guitiriz Spain **54** D1
Guitri Côte d'Ivoire **124** D5
Guiuan Phil. **74** C4
Guivi *hill* Fin. **44** N1
Guixi China *see* **Dianjiang**
Guiyang *Guizhou* China **86** C3
formerly spelt Kweiyang
Guiyang *Hunan* China **87** E3
Guiyang *Hunan* China **87** E3
Guizhou *prov.* China **86** C3
English form Kweichow
Guizi China **87** D4
Gujan-Mestras France **50** E8
Gujarat *state* India **96** B5
formerly spelt Gujerat
Gujar Khan Pak. **101** H3
Gujba Nigeria **125** H4
Gujerat *state* India *see* **Gujarat**
Gujranwala Pak. **101** H3
Gujrat Pak. **101** H3
Gukou China **87** F3
Gukovo Rus. Fed. **41** F6
Gulabgarh Jammu and Kashmir **96** C2
Gulabie Uzbek. **102** D4
formerly known as Takhiatash
Gulang China **84** D4
Gulān Islands Egypt *see* **Qul'ān, Gezā'ir**
Gülbahçe Turkey **59** H10
Gul'bakhor Uzbek. **103** G4
Gulbarga India **94** C2
Gul Basin *dock* Sing. **76** [inset]
Gulbene Latvia **42** H4
Gul'cha Kyrg. *see* **Gülchö**
Gülchö Kyrg. **103** H4
also spelt Gul'cha
Gülek Turkey **106** C3
also known as Çamalan
Gülek Boğazı *pass* Turkey **106** C3
English form Cilician Gates
Gulf, The Asia **105** E1
also known as Persian Gulf *or* Arabian Gulf
Gulfport U.S.A. **175** B6
Gulf Shores U.S.A. **175** C6
Gulgong Australia **147** F3
Gulian China **82** A1
Gulin China **86** C3
Gulistan Pak. **101** F4
Gulistan Uzbek. **103** G4
also spelt Guliston; *formerly known as* Mirzachul
Guliston Uzbek. *see* **Gulistan**
Guliya Shan *mt.* China **85** I1
Gulja China *see* **Yining**
Gul Kach Pak. **101** G4
Gul'kevichi Rus. Fed. **41** G7
Gull *r.* Canada **168** B3
Gullbrå Norway **45** I3
Gullkrona fjärd *b.* Fin. **45** M4
Gull Lake Canada **167** I5
Gullrock Lake Canada **167** M5
Gullspång Sweden **45** K4
Gullträsk Sweden **44** M2
Güllübahçe Turkey **59** I11
Güllük Turkey **59** I11
Güllük Körfezi *b.* Turkey **106** A3
Gulmarg Jammu and Kashmir **96** B2
Gülnar Turkey **106** C3
also known as Anaypazari
Gülpınar Turkey **59** H9
Gulrip'shi Georgia **107** E2
Gülşehir Turkey **106** C3
also known as Arapsun
Gul'shad Kazakh. **103** H3
Gulü China *see* **Xincai**
Gulu Uganda **128** B4
Gülübovo Bulg. **58** G6
Gulumba Gana Nigeria **125** I4
Gulwe Tanz. **129** C6
Gulyantsi Bulg. **58** F5
Gulyayevskiye Koshki, Ostrova *is* Rus. Fed. **40** J1
Guma China *see* **Pishan**
Gumal *r.* Pak. **101** G4
Gumare Botswana **130** D3
Gumbinnen Rus. Fed. *see* **Gusev**
Gumbiri *mt.* Sudan **128** A3
Gumdag Turkm. **102** C5
formerly spelt Kum-Dag
Gumel Nigeria **125** H3
Gümgüm Turkey *see* **Varto**
Gumla India **97** E5
Gumma *pref.* Japan *see* **Gunma**
Gummersbach Germany **48** E4
Gumpang *r.* Indon. **76** B1
Gumsi Nigeria **125** H3
Gümüşhane Turkey **107** D2
Gümüşsuyu Turkey **59** I10
Gümüşyaka Turkey **58** J7
Guna India **96** C4
Gunan China *see* **Qijiang**
Guna Terara *mt.* Eth. **128** C2
Gund *r.* Tajik. **101** G2
also spelt Gunt
Gundagai Australia **147** F3
Gunderi India **94** C3
Gundji Dem. Rep. Congo **126** D4
Gundlakamma *r.* India **94** D3
Gundlupet India **94** C4
Gündoğmuş Turkey **106** C3
also known as Eksere
Güneşli Turkey **59** J9
Güney *Denizli* Turkey **59** K10
Güney *Kütahya* Turkey **59** J9
Güneydoğu Toroslar *plat.* Turkey **107** E3
English form Eastern Taurus
Güneyyurt Turkey **108** D1
Gungilap Myanmar **78** B2
Gungu Dem. Rep. Congo **127** C6
Gungue Angola **127** B8
Gunib Rus. Fed. **102** A4
Gunisao *r.* Canada **167** L4
Gunja Croatia **56** K4
Günlüce Turkey **59** K9
Gunma *pref.* Japan **91** F6
also spelt Gumma
Gunna, Gebel *mts* Egypt **108** F9
Gunnarn Sweden **44** L2
Gunnbjørn Fjeld *nunatak* Greenland **165** Q3
Gunnedah Australia **147** F2
Gunnison *CO* U.S.A. **181** F5
Gunnison *UT* U.S.A. **183** M2
Gunnison *r.* U.S.A. **183** P2
Gunn Point Australia **148** A2
Gunong Ayer *Sarawak* Malaysia *see* **Gunung Ayer**
Gunpowder Creek *r.* Australia **148** C3
Güns Hungary *see* **Kőszeg**
Gun Sangari India **94** C2
Gunt *r.* Tajik. *see* **Gund**
Guntakal India **94** C3
Guntersville U.S.A. **174** C5
Guntur India **94** D2
Gununa Australia **148** C3
Gunungapi *i.* Indon. **75** C4
Gunung Ayer *Sarawak* Malaysia **77** E2
formerly spelt Gunong Ayer
Gunung Gading National Park *Sarawak* Malaysia **77** E2
Gunung Leuser National Park Indon. **76** B2
Gunung Mulu National Park *Sarawak* Malaysia **77** F1
Gunung Niyut Reserve *nature res.* Indon. **77** E2
Gunung Palung National Park Indon. **77** E3
Gunung Rinjani National Park Indon. **77** G5
Gunungsitoli Indon. **76** B2
Gunungsugih Indon. **76** D4
Gunungtua Indon. **76** B2
Gunupur India **95** D2
Günyüzü Turkey **106** B3
also known as Kozağacı
Gunza Angola *see* **Porto Amboim**
Günzburg Germany **48** H7
Gunzenhausen Germany **48** H6
Guochengyi China **84** E4
Guo He *r.* China **87** E1
Guo He *r.* China **87** F1
Guoluezhen China *see* **Lingbao**
Guoyang China **87** F1
Guozhen China *see* **Baoji**
Gupis Jammu and Kashmir **96** B1
Gura Caliței Romania **58** H3
Gurais Jammu and Kashmir **96** B2
Gura Portiței *sea chan.* Romania **58** J4
Gurara *r.* Nigeria **125** G4
Gura Șuții Romania **58** G4
Gura Teghii Romania **58** H3
Gurba *r.* Dem. Rep. Congo **126** E4
Gurban Obo China **85** G3
Gurbantünggüt Shamo *des.* China **88** D2
Gurdaspur India **96** B2
Gurdim Iran **101** E5
Gurdon U.S.A. **179** D5
Güre Turkey **59** H9
Güre Turkey **106** B3
Gürgān Azer. **100** B1
Gurgan Iran *see* **Gorgān**
Gurgaon India **96** C3
Gurgei, Jebel *mt.* Sudan **120** E6
Gurghiu *r.* Romania **58** F2
Gurghiului, Munții *mts* Romania **58** F2
Gurgueia *r.* Brazil **202** D3
Gurha India **96** A4
Guri, Embalse de *resr* Venez. **199** F3
Gurig National Park Australia **148** B1
Gurinhatã Brazil **206** D6
Gurktaler Alpen *mts* Austria **49** K9
Gurlan Uzbek. *see* **Gurlen**
Gurlen Uzbek. **102** E4
also spelt Gurlan
Gurmatkal India **94** C2
Gurnee U.S.A. **172** F8
Guro Moz. **131** G3
Gürpınar Turkey **107** E3
also known as Kasrik
Gurramkonda India **94** C3
Gürsu Turkey **59** K8
also known as Kestel
Gurué Moz. **131** H2
formerly known as Vila de Junqueiro
Gürün Turkey **107** D3
Gurupá Brazil **199** I5
Gurupa, Ilha Grande de *i.* Brazil **199** I5
Gurupi Brazil **202** B4
Gurupi *r.* Brazil **202** C2
Gurupi, Cabo *c.* Brazil **202** C2
Gurupi, Serra do *hills* Brazil **202** B3
Guru Sikhar *mt.* India **96** B4
Guruve Zimbabwe **131** F3
also spelt Guruwe; *formerly known as* Chipuriro *or* Sipolilo
Guruwe Zimbabwe *see* **Guruve**
Guruzala India **94** C2
Gurvan Sayan Uul *mts* Mongolia **84** D3
Gur'yev Kazakh. *see* **Atyrau**
Gur'yevsk Rus. Fed. **42** B7
historically known as Neuhausen
Gur'yevskaya Oblast' *admin. div.* Kazakh. *see* **Atyrauskaya Oblast'**
Gusau Nigeria **125** G3
Gusev Rus. Fed. **42** D7
historically known as Gumbinnen
Gushgy Turkm. **101** E3
formerly spelt Kushka
Gushgy *r.* Turkm. **101** E2
Gushi China **87** E1
Gushiegu Ghana **125** E4
Gusinje *Crna Gora* Yugo. **58** A6
Gusino Rus. Fed. **43** M7
Gusinoozersk Rus. Fed. **85** E1
formerly known as Shakhty
Gusinoye, Ozero *l.* Rus. Fed. **85** E1
Guskara India **97** E5
Gus'-Khrustal'nyy Rus. Fed. **40** G5
Guspini *Sardegna* Italy **57** A9
Güssing Austria **49** N9
Gustav Holm, Kap *c.* Greenland *see* **Tasiilap Karra**
Gustavia West Indies **187** H3
Gustavo Sotelo Mex. **184** B2
Gustavus U.S.A. **166** C3
Gustine U.S.A. **182** D4
Güstrow Germany **49** J2
Gütersloh Germany **48** F4
Guthrie *AZ* U.S.A. **183** O9
Guthrie *KY* U.S.A. **174** C4
Guthrie *OK* U.S.A. **179** C5
Guthrie *TX* U.S.A. **179** B5
Guthrie Center U.S.A. **178** D3
Gutian *Fujian* China **87** F3
Gutian *Fujian* China **87** F3
also known as Xincheng
Gutian Shuiku *resr* China **87** F3
Gutiérrez Bol. **201** E4
Guting China *see* **Yutai**
Guttenberg U.S.A. **174** B3
Gutu Zimbabwe **131** F3
Guvertfjället *mts* Sweden **44** L2
Guwahati India **97** F4
also spelt Gauhati
Guwēr Iraq **107** E3
Guwlumayak Turkm. *see* **Kuuli-Mayak**
Guxian China **87** E3
▶**Guyana** *country* S. America **199** G3
formerly known as British Guiana
southamerica [countries] ▶ 192–193
Guyane Française *terr.* S. America *see* **French Guiana**
Guyang China *see* **Guzhang**
Guyang China **85** F3
Guyenne *reg.* France **50** F8
Guy Fawkes River National Park Australia **147** G2
Guyi China *see* **Sanjiang**
Guymon U.S.A. **178** B4
Güyom Iran **100** C4
Guyong China *see* **Jiangle**
Guyot Glacier Canada/U.S.A. **166** A2
Guyra Australia **147** F2
Guysborough Canada **169** I4
Guyu Zimbabwe **131** F4
Guyuan *Hebei* China **85** G3
also known as Pingdingbu
Guyuan *Ningxia* China **85** E5
Guzar Uzbek. **103** F5
also spelt Ghuzor
Güzelbağ Turkey **108** C1
Güzelhisar Barajı *resr* Turkey **59** I10
Güzeloluk Turkey **108** F1
Güzelyurt Cyprus *see* **Morfou**
Guzhang China **87** D2
also known as Guyang
Guzhen China **87** F1
Guzhou China *see* **Rongjiang**
Guzmán Mex. **184** D2
Guzmán, Lago de *l.* Mex. **184** D2
Gvardeysk Rus. Fed. **42** C7
historically known as Tapiau
Gvasyugi Rus. Fed. **82** E3
Gwa Myanmar **78** A4
Gwada Nigeria **125** G4
Gwadabawa Nigeria **125** G3
Gwadar Pak. **101** E5
formerly spelt Gwador
Gwadar West Bay Pak. **101** E5
Gwador Pak. *see* **Gwadar**
Gwaii Haanas National Park Reserve Canada **166** D4
Gwalior India **96** C4
Gwanda Zimbabwe **131** F4
Gwarzo Nigeria **125** G4
Gwatar Bay Pak. **101** E5
Gwayi Zimbabwe **131** E3
Gwayi *r.* Zimbabwe **131** E3
Gwda *r.* Poland **49** N2
Gweebarra Bay Rep. of Ireland **47** D9
Gweedore Rep. of Ireland **47** D8
Gwelo Zimbabwe *see* **Gweru**
Gweru Zimbabwe **131** F3
formerly spelt Gwelo
Gweta Botswana **131** E4
Gwinn U.S.A. **172** F4
Gwoza Nigeria **125** I4
Gwydir *r.* Australia **147** F2
Gyablung China **89** F6
Gyaca China **89** F6
also known as Ngarrab
Gyagartang China **86** B1
Gya'gya China *see* **Saga**
Gyaijêpozhanggê China *see* **Zhidoi**
Gyai Qu *r.* China **89** F6
Gyairong China **86** A1
Gyaisi China *see* **Jiulong**
Gyali *i.* Greece **59** I12
also spelt Yiali
Gyamotang China *see* **Dêngqên**
Gyamug China **89** C5
Gyandzha Azer. *see* **Gäncä**
Gyangkar China *see* **Dinngyê**
Gyangnyi Caka *salt l.* China **89** D5
Gyangrang China **89** D6
Gyangtse China *see* **Gyangzê**
Gyangzê China **89** E6
also spelt Gyangtse
Gyaring China **84** C5
Gyaring Co *l.* China **89** E6
Gyaring Hu *l.* China **86** A1
Gyaros Greece **59** F11
Gyaros *i.* Greece **59** F11
Gyaur *watercourse* Turkm. **102** C5
also spelt Gäwür
Gyaurs Turkm. *see* **Sakhra**
Gydan, Khrebet *mts* Rus. Fed. *see* **Kolymskiy, Khrebet**
Gydan Peninsula Rus. Fed. **39** H2
Gydopas *pass* S. Africa **132** D10
Gyêgu China *see* **Yushu**
Gyêmdong China **89** F6
Gyêsar Co *l.* China **89** D6
Gyêwa China **89** D6
also known as Zabqung
Gyigang China *see* **Zayü**
Gyimda China **89** F6
Gyirong *Xizang* China **89** D6
Gyirong *Xizang* China **89** D6
also known as Zongga
Gyitang China **86** A2
Gyixong China *see* **Gonggar**
Gyiza China **97** G2
Gyldenløve Fjord *inlet* Greenland *see* **Umiiviip Kangertiva**
Gyljen Sweden **44** M2
Gympie Australia **149** G5
Gyobingauk Myanmar **78** A4
Gyomaendrőd Hungary **49** R9
Gyöngyös Hungary **49** Q8
Győr Hungary **49** O8
historically known as Raab
Győrszentmárton Hungary *see* **Pannonhalma**
Gypsum Point Canada **167** H2
Gypsumville Canada **167** L5
Gytheio Greece **59** D12
also known as Yithion
Gyula Hungary **49** S9
Gyulafehérvár Romania *see* **Alba Iulia**
Gyümai China *see* **Darlag**
Gyumri Armenia **107** E2
also known as Kumayri; *formerly known as* Aleksandropol *or* Leninakan
Gyurgen Bair *hill* Turkey **58** H7
Gyzylarbat Turkm. **102** D5
formerly spelt Kizyl-Arbat
Gyzyletrek Turkm. **102** C5
formerly spelt Kizyl-Atrek
Gyzylsuw Turkm. *see* **Kizyl-Su**
Gzhat' *r.* Rus. Fed. **43** P6
Gzhatsk Rus. Fed. *see* **Gagarin**

↓ H

Ha Bhutan **97** F4
Haabneeme Estonia **42** F2
Häädemeeste Estonia **42** F3
Haag Austria **49** L7
Haanhöhiy Uul *mts* Mongolia **84** B1
Haanja Estonia **42** I4
Ha'ano *i.* Tonga **145** H3
Ha'apai Group *is* Tonga **145** H3
also spelt Habai Group
Haapajärvi Fin. **40** C3
Haapavesi Fin. **44** N2
Haapsalu Estonia **42** E3
Ha 'Arava *watercourse* Israel/Jordan *see* **'Arabah, Wādī al**
Haarlem Neth. **48** B3
Haarlem S. Africa **132** H10
Haarstrang *ridge* Germany **48** E4
Haast N.Z. **153** D11
Haast *r.* N.Z. **153** D11
Haasts Bluff Aboriginal Land *res.* Australia **148** A4
Haaway Somalia **128** D4
Hab *r.* Pak. **101** F5
Habahe China **88** D1
also known as Kaba
Habai Group *is* Tonga *see* **Ha'apai Group**
Habana Cuba *see* **Havana**
Habarōn *well* Saudi Arabia **105** E3
Habarūt Oman **105** F4
Habaswein Kenya **128** C4
Ḥabawnāh, Wādī *watercourse* Saudi Arabia **104** D4
Habay Canada **166** G3
Ḥabbān Yemen **105** D5
Ḥabbānīyah, Hawr al *l.* Iraq **107** E4
Habbah ash Shaykh, Ḥarrāt *lava field* Saudi Arabia **104** C4
Habicht *mt.* Austria **48** I8
Habichtswald *park* Germany **48** G4
Habiganj Bangl. **97** F4
Habirag China **85** G3
Ḥabīs, Wādī al *r.* Jordan **108** G6
Habo Sweden **45** K4
Habra India **97** F5
Ḥabshīyah, Jabal *mts* Yemen **105** E4
Hacha Col. **198** C5
Hachijō-jima *i.* Japan **91** F8
Hachiman Japan **91** E7
Hachimori Japan **90** F4
Hachinohe Japan **90** G4
Hachiōji Japan **91** F7
Hachiryū Japan **90** F4
Hacıbekir Turkey **59** K9
Hacıbektaş Turkey **106** C3
Hacıköy Turkey *see* **Çekerek**
Hacıpaşa Turkey **109** H1
Hacı Zeynalabdin Azer. **107** G2
formerly known as Nasosnyy
Hack, Mount Australia **146** C2
Hackberry U.S.A. **183** K6
Hacker Valley U.S.A. **176** E7
Hackettstown U.S.A. **177** K5
Ha Côi Vietnam **78** D3
Hacufera Moz. **131** G4
formerly known as Algueirao
Hadabat al Budū *plain* Saudi Arabia **105** E3
Hadagalli India **94** B3
Hada Mountains Afgh. **101** F4
Ḥadan, Ḥarrat *lava field* Saudi Arabia **104** C3
Hadano Japan **91** F7
Ḥadārah *i.* Saudi Arabia **104** C4
Hadārba, Rās *pt* Sudan **121** H4
Ḥadd, Ra's al *pt* Oman **105** G3
Haddad, Ouadi *watercourse* Chad **120** C6
Haddington U.K. **46** J8
Hadejia Nigeria **125** H3
Hadejia *watercourse* Nigeria **125** I3
Ḥadera Israel **108** F5
Ḥadera *r.* Israel **108** F5
Haderslev Denmark **45** J5
Hadgaon India **94** C2
Ḥādhah Saudi Arabia **104** C3
Ḥādh Banī Zaynān *des.* Saudi Arabia **105** E3
Hadhdhunmathi Atoll Maldives **93** D10
Hadhramaut *reg.* Yemen *see* **Ḥaḍramawt**
Ḥādī, Jabal al *mts* Jordan **109** H7
Hadībōh Yemen **105** F5
Hadilik China **88** D4
Hadım Turkey **106** C3
Hadjer Momou *mt.* Chad **120** D5
Hadley Bay Canada **165** I2
Ha Đông Vietnam **86** C4
Ḥadraj, Wādī *watercourse* Saudi Arabia **107** D5
Ḥaḍramawt *governorate* Yemen **105** E4
Ḥaḍramawt *reg.* Yemen **105** D5
also spelt Hadhramaut
Ḥaḍramawt, Wādī *watercourse* Yemen **105** E4
Hadranum *Sicilia* Italy *see* **Adrano**
Hadrian's Wall *tourist site* U.K. **47** J8
Hadrumetum Tunisia *see* **Sousse**
Hadseløy *i.* Norway **44** K1
Hadsten Denmark **45** J4
Hadsund Denmark **45** J4
Hadūs, Baḥr *canal* Egypt **108** D6
Hadyach Ukr. **41** E6
also spelt Gadyach
Hadzilavichy Belarus **43** L8
Haedo, Cuchilla de *hills* Uruguay **204** F4
Haeju N. Korea **83** B5
Haeju-man *b.* N. Korea **83** B5
Haena U.S.A. **181** [inset] Y1
Haenam S. Korea **83** B6
Ḥafar al 'Atk *well* Saudi Arabia **105** D2
Ḥafar al Bāṭin Saudi Arabia **105** D1
Haffküste *park* Germany **49** L2
Hafford Canada **167** J4
Hafik Turkey **107** D3
Ḥafīrah, Qā' al *depr.* Jordan **108** H6
Ḥafīrah, Wādī al *watercourse* Jordan **108** G6
Ḥafirat al'Aydā Saudi Arabia **104** B2
Hafirat Nasah Saudi Arabia **105** D2
Ḥafīt Oman **105** F3
Ḥafīt, Jabal *mt.* U.A.E. **105** F2
Hafizabad Pak. **101** H3
Haflong India **97** G4
Hafnarfjörður Iceland **44** [inset] B2
Haft Gel Iran **100** B4
Haftvān Iran **100** C5
Hafursfjörður *b.* Iceland **44** [inset] B2
Haga Myanmar *see* **Haka**
Hag Abdullah Sudan **121** G6
Haga-Haga S. Africa **133** M9
Hagar Canada **173** M4
Hagari *r.* India **94** C3
Hagar Nish Plateau Eritrea **121** H5

▶**Hagåtña** Guam **73** J4
Capital of Guam. Also known as Agana.

Hagen Germany **48** E4
Hagen, Mount P.N.G. **73** J8
Hagenow Germany **48** I2
Hagensborg Canada **166** E4
Hägere Hiywet Eth. **128** C2
Hagerhill U.S.A. **176** C8
Hagerstown U.S.A. **176** H6
Hagetmau France **50** F9
Häggenås Sweden **44** K3
Haggin, Mount U.S.A. **180** D3
Hagi Japan **91** B7
Ha Giang Vietnam **78** D3
Ha Giao, Sông *r.* Vietnam **79** E5
Hagiwara Japan **91** E7
HaGolan *hills* Syria *see* **Golan**
Hag's Head Rep. of Ireland **47** C11
Hague U.S.A. **177** L2
Haguenau France **51** N4
Hahajima-rettō *is* Japan **73** J1
Hai *r.* China **85** H4
Hai Tanz. **128** C5
Hai, Gebel el *hill* Egypt **108** C8
Hai'an China **87** G1
Haian Shanmo *mts* Taiwan *see* **T'aitung Shan**
Haib *watercourse* Namibia **130** C6
Haicheng China *see* **Haifeng**
Haicheng China **85** I3
Haicheng China *see* **Haiyuan**
Haidargarh India **97** D4
Hai Dương Vietnam **78** D3
Haifa Israel **108** F5
also spelt Hefa *or* Khefa
Haifa, Bay of Israel **108** G5
also known as Hefa, Mifraz
Haifeng China **87** E4
also known as Haicheng
Haikakan *country* Asia *see* **Armenia**
Haikang China *see* **Leizhou**
Haiki Japan **91** A8
Haikou China **87** D4
Hā'il Saudi Arabia **104** C2
Hā'il *prov.* Saudi Arabia **104** C2
Hailakandi India **97** G4
Hailar China **85** H1
also known as Hulun
Hailar *r.* China **85** H1
Hailey U.S.A. **180** D4
Haileybury Canada **168** E4
Hailin China **82** C3
Hailong China *see* **Meihekou**
Hails China **85** H3
Hailun China **82** B3
Hailuoto Fin. **44** N2
Hailuoto *i.* Fin. **44** N2
Haimen China **87** G2
Hainan *i.* China **87** D5
Hainan *prov.* China **81** H9
Hai-nang Myanmar **78** B3
Hainan Strait China **87** D5
also known as Qiongzhou Haixia
Hainaut *reg.* France **51** J2
Hainburg an der Donau Austria **49** N7
Haindi Liberia **124** C5
Haines U.S.A. **164** F4
Haines City U.S.A. **175** D6
Haines Junction Canada **166** B2
Haines Road Canada/U.S.A. **166** B2
Hainich *ridge* Germany **48** H4
Hainleite *ridge* Germany **48** H4
Haiphong Vietnam *see* **Hai Phong**
Hai Phong Vietnam **78** D3
English form Haiphong
Haiqing China **82** D3
Hairhan Namag China **84** D3
Haitan Dao *i.* China **87** F3
formerly known as Pingtan Dao
▶**Haiti** *country* West Indies **187** E3
historically known as St-Domingue
northamerica [countries] ▶ 158–159
Haiwee Reservoir U.S.A. **182** G5
Haiya Sudan **121** H5
Haiyaf *i.* Sudan **126** E2
Haiyan *Qinghai* China **84** D4
also known as Sanjiaocheng
Haiyan *Zhejiang* China **87** G2
also known as Wuyuan
Haiyang China *see* **Xiuning**
Haiyang China **85** I4
also known as Dongcun
Haiyou China *see* **Sanmen**
Haiyuan China **85** E4
also known as Haicheng
Haizhou Wan *b.* China **87** F1
Ḥaj Ali Qoli, Kavīr-e *salt l.* Iran **100** C3
Hajar, Jibāl *mts* Saudi Arabia **104** B2
Ḥajār, Oued el *well* Mali **124** E2
Hajdúböszörmény Hungary **49** S8
Hajdúnánás Hungary **49** S8
Hajdúszoboszló Hungary **49** S8
Hajeb El Ayoun Tunisia **57** B13
Ḥajhir *mt.* Yemen **105** F5
Hajiki-zaki *pt* Japan **90** F5
Hajipur India **97** E4
Hajir *reg.* Saudi Arabia **105** E2
Ḥājir Yemen **104** C5
Ḥajiyah, Wādī *watercourse* Iraq **109** N4
Ḥajjah Yemen **104** C5
Ḥajjah *governorate* Yemen **104** C4
Ḥājjīābād *Fārs* Iran **100** C4
Ḥājjīābād Iran **100** C2
Ḥājjīābād *Hormozgan* Iran **100** C4
Hajnówka Poland **49** U3
Hajo India **97** F4
Ḥājr, Wādī *watercourse* Yemen **105** E5
Ḥajrah Saudi Arabia **104** C3
Hajuu-Us Mongolia **85** E2
Haka Myanmar **78** A3
also spelt Haga *or* Hakha
Hakase-yama *mt.* Japan **90** F6
Hakataramea N.Z. **153** E12
Hakatere N.Z. **153** F11
Hakatere *r.* N.Z. *see* **Ashburton**
Hakelhuincul, Altiplanicie de *plat.* Arg. **204** C6
Hakha Myanmar *see* **Haka**
Hakippa, Har *hill* Israel **108** G7
Hakkâri Turkey **107** E3
also known as Çölemerik
Hakkas Sweden **44** M2
Hakken-zan *mt.* Japan **91** D7
Hakkōda-san *mt.* Japan **90** G4
Hako-dake *mt.* Japan **90** H2
Hakodate Japan **90** G4
Hakodate-wan *b.* Japan **90** G4
Hakos Mountains Namibia **130** C4
Hakseen Pan *salt pan* S. Africa **132** E3
Hakui Japan **91** E6
Haku-san *vol.* Japan **91** E6
Haku-san National Park Japan **91** E6
Hal Belgium *see* **Halle**
Hala Pak. **101** G5
Ḥalā', Jabal al *mt.* Jordan **108** G7
Ḥalab Syria *see* **Aleppo**
Ḥalab *governorate* Syria **109** I1
Halabān Saudi Arabia **104** D3
Halabja Iraq **107** F4
Halach Turkm. *see* **Khalach**
Halachó Mex. **185** H4
Halahai China **82** B3
Halaib Sudan **121** H4

▶**Halaib Triangle** *terr.* Egypt/Sudan **121** G4
Disputed territory (Egypt/Sudan) administered by Sudan.

Ḥalāl, Gebel *hill* Egypt **108** E7
Ḥalāniyāt, Juzur al *is* Oman **105** G4
English form Kuria Muria Islands
Ḥalāniyāt, Khalīj al *b.* Oman **105** F4
English form Kuria Muria Bay
Ḥālat 'Ammār Saudi Arabia **106** D5
Hălăucești Romania **58** H1
Halawa U.S.A. **181** [inset] Z1
Ḥalbā', Wādī al *watercourse* Saudi Arabia **109** M8
Halban Mongolia **84** C1
formerly known as Tsetserleg
Halberstadt Germany **48** I4
Halcon, Mount Phil. **74** B3
Halcyon Drift S. Africa **133** M7
Haldane *r.* Canada **166** F1
Halden Norway **45** J4
Haldensleben Germany **48** I3
Haldi *r.* India **97** F5
Haldia India **97** F5
Haldibari India **97** F4
Haldwani India **96** C3
Hale *watercourse* Australia **148** B5
Hale China **85** F3
Hale U.S.A. **173** J6
Hale, Mount *hill* Australia **151** B5
Haleakala National Park U.S.A. **181** [inset] Z1
Hāleh Iran **100** C5
Haleiwa U.S.A. **181** [inset] Y1
Halénia *well* Chad **120** D5
Halepanki Deresi *r.* Syria/Turkey *see* **Quwayq, Nahr**
Half Assini Ghana **124** E5
Halfeti Turkey **107** D3
Halfmoon Bay N.Z. **153** C14
Half Moon Bay U.S.A. **182** B4
Half Moon Lake *salt flat* Australia **146** B2
Halfway *r.* Canada **166** F3
Halfway U.S.A. **176** H6
Halfweg S. Africa **132** E7
Halhgol Mongolia **85** H2
Ḥalī, Wādī *watercourse* Saudi Arabia **104** C4
Ḥalib, Quwayrat al *hill* Iraq **109** N6
Haliburton Canada **173** O5
Haliburton Highlands *hills* Canada **168** E4
Halicarnassus Turkey *see* **Bodrum**
Halichy Rus. Fed. **43** N8

▶**Halifax** Canada **169** I4
Provincial capital of Nova Scotia.

Halifax U.K. **47** K10
Halifax *NC* U.S.A. **176** H9
Halifax *VA* U.S.A. **176** G9
Halifax, Mount Australia **149** E3
Halifax Bay Australia **149** E3
Halikko Fin. **42** E1
Halileh, Ra's-e *pt* Iran **100** B4
Halilulik Indon. **75** C5
Ḥalīmah *mt.* Lebanon/Syria **109** H3
Halimun National Park Indon. **77** D4
Halinor Lake *salt flat* Australia **146** A2
Haliut China *see* **Urad Zhongqi**
Ḥalīyā *well* Yemen **105** E4
Haliyal India **94** B3
Hall *atoll* Kiribati *see* **Maiana**
Hall U.S.A. **176** A8
Hälla Sweden **44** L3
Halland *county* Sweden **45** K4
Halla-san *mt.* S. Korea **83** B6
Halla-san National Park S. Korea **83** B6
Hall Beach Canada **165** K3
Halle Belgium **51** K2
also spelt Hal
Halle (Saale) Germany **48** I4
Halleck U.S.A. **183** I1
Hällefors Sweden **45** K4
Hälleforsnäs Sweden **45** L4
Hallein Austria **49** K8
Hallen Sweden **44** K3
Hallett, Cape Antarctica **223** L2
Hallettsville U.S.A. **179** C6
Hällevikstrand Sweden **45** J4
Halley *research station* Antarctica **222** W1
Hallgreen, Mount Antarctica **223** X2
Halliday Lake Canada **167** I2
Halligen *is* Germany **48** F1
Hallingdal *valley* Norway **45** J3
Hallingdalselva *r.* Norway **45** J4
Hall in Tirol Austria **48** I8
Hall Islands Micronesia **220** E5
Halliste *r.* Estonia **42** G3
Hällnäs Sweden **44** L2
Hallock U.S.A. **178** C1
Hall Peninsula Canada **165** M3
Hallsberg Sweden **45** K4
Halls Creek Australia **150** D3
Halls Lake Canada **173** O5
Hallstavik Sweden **45** L3
Hällvik Sweden **44** L2
Hällviken Sweden **44** K3
Hallyŏ Haesang National Park S. Korea **83** C6
Halmahera *i.* Indon. **75** D2
also known as Jailolo Gilolo
Halmahera Sea Indon. **75** D3
Halmstad Sweden **45** K4
Halol India **96** B5
Haloze *reg.* Slovenia **56** H2
Hals Denmark **45** J4
Hal Saflieni Hypogeum *tourist site* Malta **57** G13
Hälsingborg Sweden *see* **Helsingborg**
Halsua Fin. **44** N3
Haltang *r.* China **84** B4
Haltwhistle U.K. **47** J9
Ḥālūl *i.* Qatar **105** F2
Halvad India **96** A5
Halvmåneøya *i.* Svalbard **38** C2
Ḥalwān *hill* Saudi Arabia **109** K9
Ham France **51** J3
Ham *watercourse* Namibia **132** D5

H index

Ham, Oued el r. Alg. 55 O9
Hamab Namibia 132 D5
Hamada Japan 91 C7
Ḥamâda Çafia des. Mali 122 D5
Hamada ed Douakel plat. Alg. 122 D4
Ḥamâda El Ḥaricha des. Mali 122 D5
Hamadān Iran 100 B3
also known as Itagmatana; historically known as Ecbatana
Hamadān prov. Iran 100 B3
Ḥamâdat Murzuq plat. Libya 120 B3
Hamada Tounassine des. Alg. 122 D3
Hamaguir Alg. 123 E3
Ḥamāh Syria 109 H2
Ḥamāh governorate Syria 109 I2
Hamakita Japan 91 E7
Hamamasu Japan 90 G3
Hamamatsu Japan 91 E7
Hamapega hill Spain 54 F6
Hamar Iceland 44 [inset] B2
Hamar Norway 45 J3
Ḥamar Nafūr i. Oman 105 G4
Hamarøy Norway 44 K1
Hamarøy i. Norway 44 K1
Hamasaka Japan 91 D7
Hamasien prov. Eritrea 104 B5
Hamâta, Gebel mt. Egypt 121 G3
Hamatonbetsu Japan 90 H2
Hambantota Sri Lanka 94 D5
Hambidge Conservation Park nature res. Australia 146 B3
Hambleton U.S.A. 176 F6
Hamburg Germany 48 G2
Hamburg S. Africa 133 L10
Hamburg AR U.S.A. 175 B5
Hamburg IA U.S.A. 178 D3
Hamburg NJ U.S.A. 177 K4
Hamburg NY U.S.A. 176 G3
Hamburg PA U.S.A. 177 J5
Hamburgisches Wattenmeer, Nationalpark nat. park Germany 48 F2
Ḥamḍ, Wādī al watercourse Saudi Arabia 104 B2
Ḥamdah Saudi Arabia 104 C4
Hamdallay Niger 125 F3
Ḥamdānah Saudi Arabia 104 C4
Hamden U.S.A. 177 M4
Hamdibey Turkey 59 I9
Hamdili Turkey 108 G1
Hämeenkangas moorland Fin. 45 M3
Hämeenkoski Fin. 42 E1
formerly known as Koski
Hämeenkyrö Fin. 45 M3
Hämeenlinna Fin. 45 N3
also known as Tavastehus
HaMelaḥ, Yam salt l. Asia see Dead Sea
Hamelin Australia 151 A5
Hamelin Pool b. Australia 151 A5
Hameln Germany 48 G3
Hamero Hadad Eth. 128 D3
Hamersley Australia 150 B4
Hamersley Lakes salt flat Australia 151 B6
Hamersley Range mts Australia 150 B4
Hamgyŏng-sanmaek mts N. Korea 82 C4
Hamhŭng N. Korea 83 B5
Hami China 84 B3
also known as Kumul
Ḥamīd Iran 100 B4
Hamid Sudan 121 F4
Hamidiye Turkey 58 H7
Hamilton Qld Australia 149 D4
Hamilton S.A. Australia 148 B5
Hamilton Vic. Australia 147 D4
Hamilton watercourse Qld Australia 149 C4
Hamilton watercourse S.A. Australia 146 B1
▶Hamilton Bermuda 171 N5
Capital of Bermuda.
Hamilton Canada 168 E5
Hamilton r. Canada see Churchill
Hamilton N.Z. 152 J5
Hamilton U.K. 46 H8
Hamilton AL U.S.A. 174 C5
Hamilton MT U.S.A. 180 D3
Hamilton NY U.S.A. 177 J3
Hamilton OH U.S.A. 176 A6
Hamilton TX U.S.A. 179 C6
Hamilton, Mount CA U.S.A. 182 C4
Hamilton, Mount NV U.S.A. 183 I2
Hamilton Burn N.Z. 153 C13
Hamilton City U.S.A. 182 B2
Hamilton Downs Australia 148 B4
Hamilton Mountain hill U.S.A. 177 K2
Hamilton Sound sea chan. Canada 169 K3
Ḥamīm, Wādī al watercourse Libya 120 D2
Hamina Fin. 45 N3
also known as Fredrikshamn
Ḥāmir, Wādī al watercourse Saudi Arabia 107 E5
Hamirpur Himachal Pradesh India 96 C3
Hamirpur Uttar Pradesh India 96 D4
Hamitabat Turkey see Isparta
Hamlet U.S.A. 174 E5
Hamley Bridge Australia 146 C3
Hamlin PA U.S.A. 177 J4
Hamlin TX U.S.A. 179 B5
Hamlin Lake U.S.A. 172 G6
Ham Luông, Sông r. mouth Vietnam 79 D6
Hamm Germany 48 E4
Hammada du Drâa plat. Alg. 122 C3
Hammâdat Tingharat des. Libya 120 A2
Ḥammām al 'Alīl Iraq 107 E3
Hammam Boughrara Alg. 55 J9
Hammamet Tunisia 57 C12
Hammamet, Golfe de g. Tunisia 123 H1
Hammam-Lif Tunisia 57 C12
Ḥammār, Hawr al imp. l. Iraq 107 F5
Hammarland Fin. 42 A1
Hammarsdale S. Africa 133 O6
Hammarstrand Sweden 44 L3
Hammelburg Germany 48 G5
Hammerdal Sweden 44 K3
Hammerfest Norway 44 M1
Hammond IN U.S.A. 174 C3
Hammond LA U.S.A. 175 B6
Hammond Bay U.S.A. 173 I5
Hammondsport U.S.A. 177 H3
Hammonton U.S.A. 177 K6
Hamnbukt Norway 44 N1
Ham Ninh Vietnam 79 D6
Hamorton U.S.A. 177 J6
Hampden N.Z. 153 E13
Hampden Highlands U.S.A. 177 Q1
Hampden Sydney U.S.A. 176 G8
Hampi India 94 C3
also known as Vijayanagar
Hämpjäkk Sweden 44 M2
Hampstead U.S.A. 177 I6
Hampton Canada 169 H4
Hampton AR U.S.A. 179 D5
Hampton IA U.S.A. 174 A3
Hampton NH U.S.A. 177 O3
Hampton SC U.S.A. 175 D5
Hampton TN U.S.A. 176 C9
Hampton VA U.S.A. 177 I8
Hampton Bays U.S.A. 177 M5
Hampton Tableland reg. Australia 151 D7
Hamra, Vâdii watercourse Syria/Turkey see Ḥimār, Wādī al
Hamrat esh Sheikh Sudan 121 E6
Ḥamrīn, Jabal hills Iraq 107 F4
Hams Fork r. U.S.A. 180 E4
Ham Tân Vietnam 79 D6
Hamta Pass India 96 C2
Hāmūn-e-Chah Gheybī salt pan Iran 101 E4
Hāmūn-e Jaz Mūrīān salt marsh Iran 100 D5
Hāmūn Helmand salt flat Afgh./Iran 101 E4
Hamun-i-Lora dry lake Pak. 101 F4
Hamun-i-Mashkel salt flat Pak. 101 E4
Hāmūn Pu marsh Afgh. 101 E4
Hamur Turkey 107 E3
Hamwic U.K. see Southampton
Hamza Uzbek. see Khamza
Haná r. Czech Rep. 49 O6
Hana U.S.A. 181 [inset] Z1
Hanábana r. Cuba 175 D8
Hanahai watercourse Botswana/Namibia 130 D4
Hanakpınar Turkey see Çınar
Ḥanalc Saudi Arabia 104 B2
Hanamaki Japan 90 G5
Hanamanioa, Cape U.S.A. 181 [inset] Z1
Hanam Plateau Namibia 132 B2
Hanang mt. Tanz. 129 B6
Hananui hill N.Z. see Anglem, Mount
Hanapepe U.S.A. 181 [inset] Y1
Hanau Germany 48 F5
Hânceşti Moldova see Hînceşti
Hanchary Belarus 42 G8
Hancheng China 85 F5
Hanchuan China 87 E2
Hancock MD U.S.A. 176 G6
Hancock MI U.S.A. 172 E3
Hancock NY U.S.A. 177 J4
Handa Japan 91 E7
Handan China 85 G4
Handeni Tanz. 129 C6
Handian China see Changzhi
Handlová Slovakia 49 P7
HaNegev des. Israel see Negev
Haneqarot watercourse Israel 108 G7
Hanerau-Hademarschen Germany 48 G1
Hanfeng China see Kaixian
Hanford U.S.A. 182 E5
Hangal India 94 B3
Hangan Myanmar 79 B5
Han-gang r. S. Korea 83 B5
Hangayn Nuruu mts Mongolia 84 C1
Hangchow China see Hangzhou
Hangchuan China see Guangze
Hanggin Houqi China see Xamba
Hanggin Qi China see Xin
Hangö Fin. see Hanko
Hangö östra fjärd b. Fin. 42 E2
Hangö västra fjärd b. Fin. 42 D2
Hangu China 85 H4
Hangu Pak. 101 G3
Hangya China 84 C4
Hangzhou China 87 G2
formerly spelt Hangchow
Hangzhou Wan b. China 87 G2
Hani Turkey 107 E3
Ḥanīdh Saudi Arabia 105 E2
Hanife r. Turkey 59 J8
Hanish Kabir i. Yemen 104 C5
Hanjia China see Pengshui
Hanjiang China 87 F1
also known as Yangzhou
Han Jiang r. China 87 F4
Hanjiaoshui China 85 E4
Hankasalmi Fin. 44 N3
Hankey S. Africa 133 I10
Hanko Fin. 45 M4
also spelt Hangö
Hanksville U.S.A. 183 N3
Hanle Jammu and Kashmir 96 C2
Hanley Canada 167 J5
Hanmer Forest Park nature res. N.Z. 153 G10
Hanmer Springs N.Z. 153 G10
Hann r. Qld Australia 149 E2
Hann r. W.A. Australia 150 D3
Hann, Mount hill Australia 150 D2
Hanna Canada 167 I5
Hannagan Meadow U.S.A. 183 O8
Hannah Bay Canada 168 D3
Hannibal MO U.S.A. 174 B4
Hannibal NY U.S.A. 177 I2
Hannibal OH U.S.A. 176 E6
Hannik well Sudan 121 G5
Hannover Germany 48 G3
English form Hanover
Hannoversch Münden Germany 48 G4
Hann Range mts Australia 148 B4
Hanöbukten b. Sweden 45 K5
▶Ha Nôi Vietnam 78 D3
Capital of Vietnam. English form Hanoi.
Hanoi Vietnam see Ha Nôi
Hanover Canada 168 D4
Hanover Germany see Hannover
Hanover S. Africa 133 I8
Hanover NH U.S.A. 177 M2
Hanover OH U.S.A. 176 C5
Hanover PA U.S.A. 177 I6
Hanover VA U.S.A. 176 H8
Hanover, Isla i. Chile 205 B8
Hanover Road S. Africa 133 I7
Hansen Mountains Antarctica 223 D2
Hanshou China 87 D2
Han Shui r. China 87 E2
Hansi India 96 C3
Hansnes Norway 44 L1
Hanson watercourse Australia 148 B4
Hanson, Lake salt flat Australia 146 C2
Hansonville U.S.A. 176 C9
Hanstholm Denmark 45 J4
Han Sum China 85 H2
Hantengri Feng mt. Kazakh./Kyrg. see Khan-Tengri, Pik
Hantsavichy Belarus 42 H9
also spelt Gantsevichi
Hanumana India 97 D4
Hanumangarh India 96 B3
also known as Bhatnair
Hanun well Oman 105 F4
Hanuy Gol r. Mongolia 84 D1
Hanyang China see Caidian
Hanyin China 87 D1
Hanyuan China see Xihe
Hanyuan China 86 B2
also known as Fulin
Hanzhong China 86 C1
Hao atoll Fr. Polynesia 221 I7
Haomen China see Menyuan
Haora India 97 F5
formerly spelt Howrah
Haoud el Hamra Alg. 123 G2
Haouza W. Sahara 122 C4
Haparanda Sweden 44 N2
Haparanda skärgård nationalpark nat. park Sweden 44 M2
Hapch'ŏn S. Korea 91 A7
Hapoli India 97 G4
Happy Jack U.S.A. 183 M7
Happy Valley - Goose Bay Canada 169 I2
also known as Goose Bay
Hapsu N. Korea 83 C4
Hapur India 96 C3
Ḥaql Saudi Arabia 106 C5
Ḥaqshah well Saudi Arabia 105 E3
Hara Alol mt. Djibouti 128 D2
Ḥaraḍ well Saudi Arabia 105 E2
Ḥaraḍ Yemen 104 C4
Ḥarad, Jabal al mt. Jordan 108 G8
Haradah Saudi Arabia 105 D3
Ḥaraḍh Saudi Arabia 105 E2
Haradok Belarus 42 H7
also spelt Gorodok
Haradok Belarus 43 K6
also spelt Gorodok
Haradotskaye Wzvyshsha hills Belarus 43 K6
Harads Sweden 44 M2
Haradzishcha Belarus 42 H8
Haradzishcha Belarus 43 K8
Haradzyeya Belarus 42 H8
Haraiya India 97 D4
Ḥarajā Saudi Arabia 104 C4
Haramachi Japan 90 G6
Haramukh mt. Jammu and Kashmir 96 B2
Haran Turkey see Harran
Harany Belarus 43 K6
Harappa Road Pak. 101 H4
▶Harare Zimbabwe 131 F3
Capital of Zimbabwe. Formerly known as Salisbury.
Ha Rasebi S. Africa 133 J6
Ḥarāsīs, Jiddat al des. Oman 105 F4
also known as a-Jiddét
Harāt Iran 100 C4
Harat Island Eritrea 121 H5
Haraym well Saudi Arabia 105 F4
Har-Ayrag Mongolia 85 F2
Haraz-Djombo Chad 120 C6
Haraze-Mangueigne Chad 126 D2
Harbacheva Belarus 43 K6
Harbel Liberia 124 C5
Harbin China 82 B3
Harbke-Allertal park Germany 48 I3
Harboi Hills Pak. 101 F4
Harbor Beach U.S.A. 173 K7
Harbor Springs U.S.A. 173 I5
Harbour Breton Canada 169 K4
Harbutt Range hills Australia 150 C4
Harcuvar Mountains U.S.A. 183 K8
Harda Khas India 96 C5
Hardangerfjorden sea chan. Norway 45 I4
Hardangervidda Nasjonalpark nat. park Norway 45 I3
Hardap admin. reg. Namibia 130 C5
Hardap Dam Namibia 130 C5
Hardbakke Norway 45 I3
Harden, Bukit mt. Indon. 77 F1
Hardenberg Neth. 48 D3
Harderwijk Neth. 48 C3
Hardeveld mts S. Africa 132 C8
Hardey r. Australia 150 B4
Hardin IL U.S.A. 174 B4
Hardin MT U.S.A. 180 F3
Harding r. Australia 150 B4
Harding S. Africa 133 N7
Harding Range hills W.A. Australia 150 D3
Harding Range hills W.A. Australia 151 B5
Hardoi India 96 D4
Hardwar India see Haridwar
Hardwick GA U.S.A. 175 D5
Hardwick VT U.S.A. 177 M1
Hardwicke Bay Australia 146 C3
Hardy U.S.A. 174 B4
Hardy, Mount N.Z. see Rangipoua
Hardy, Peninsula pen. Chile 205 C9
Hare Bay Canada 169 K3
Hareid Norway 44 I3
Hareidin, Wâdi watercourse Egypt 108 E7
Hare Indian r. Canada 166 D1
Haren (Ems) Germany 48 E3
Hareøen i. Greenland see Qeqertarsuatsiaq
Hārer Eth. 128 D2
Hārer Wildlife Sanctuary nature res. Eth. 128 D2
Haret el Mreffi mt. Lebanon 108 G4
Hargant China 85 H1
Hargeisa Somalia see Hargeysa
Hargele Eth. 128 D3
Hargeysa Somalia 128 E2
also spelt Hargeisa
Harghita, Munții mts Romania 58 G2
Harghita-Mădăraş, Vârful mt. Romania 58 G2
Hargigo Eritrea 104 B5
Harhal Dağları mts Turkey 107 E3
Harhatan China 85 E4
Harhorin Mongolia 84 D2
Har Hu l. China 84 C4
Harib Yemen 105 D5
Haribomo, Lac l. Mali 124 E2
Haridwar India 96 C3
formerly spelt Hardwar
Harif, Har mt. Israel 108 F7
also known as Kharuf, Ra's
Harihar India 94 B3
Harihari N.Z. 153 E11
Hariharpur India 94 B3
Harij India 96 A5
Hari kurk sea chan. Estonia 42 D2
Ḥārim Syria 109 H1
Harima-nada b. Japan 91 D7
Haringhat r. Bangl. 97 F5
Haringvliet est. Neth. 48 B4
Haripad India 94 C4
Haripur Pak. 101 H3
Ḥārim, Wādī adh r. Syria 108 H5
Hari Rūd r. Afgh./Iran 101 E2
Ḥarjab, Wādī watercourse Saudi Arabia 104 C4
Härjåsjön Sweden 45 K3
Harjavalta Fin. 45 M3
Härjedalen reg. Sweden 45 K3
Harjufjärden b. Sweden 44 M2
Hårkan r. Sweden 44 K3
Har Karmel hill Israel see Carmel, Mount
Harlan U.S.A. 176 B9
Harlan County Lake U.S.A. 178 C3
Hârlău Romania 58 H1
formerly spelt Hîrlău
Harlem U.S.A. 180 E2
Harlingen Neth. 48 C2
Harlingen U.S.A. 179 C7
Harlow U.K. 47 M12
Harlowton U.S.A. 180 E3
Harman U.S.A. 176 F7
Harmancık Turkey 106 B3
also known as Çardi
Harmil i. Eritrea 121 I5
Harnahalli India 94 C3
Harnai India 94 B2
Harnai Pak. 101 F4
Harney Basin U.S.A. 180 C4
Harney Lake U.S.A. 180 C4
Härnösand Sweden 44 L3
Har Nur China 85 I2
Har Nuur l. Mongolia 84 B1
Har Nuur l. Mongolia 84 C1
Haro Spain 55 I2
Harochychy Belarus 43 K9
Harold U.S.A. 176 C8
Haroldswick U.K. 46 L3
Harpanahalli India 94 B3
Harper Liberia 124 D5
Harper U.S.A. 178 C4
Harper, Mount Canada 166 B1
Harper Creek r. Canada 167 H3
Harper Lake U.S.A. 183 G6
Harpers Ferry U.S.A. 176 H6
Harp Lake Canada 169 I2
Harpstedt Germany 48 F3
Harqin Qi China see Jinshan
Harqin Zuoqi Mongolzu Zizhixian China see Dachengzi
Harquahala Mountains U.S.A. 183 K8
Harrai India 96 C5
Harran Turkey 109 K1
also spelt Haran; historically known as Carrhae
Harras of Dhamar vol. Yemen 104 D5
Ḥarrāt Kishb lava field Saudi Arabia 104 C3
Harricanaw r. Canada 168 E3
Harriman U.S.A. 177 K4
Harriman Reservoir U.S.A. 177 M3
Harrington Australia 147 G2
Harrington DE U.S.A. 177 J7
Harrington ME U.S.A. 177 R1
Harris reg. U.K. 46 F6
Harris, Lake salt flat Australia 146 B2
Harris, Mount Australia 148 A5
Harris, Sound of sea chan. U.K. 46 E6
Harrisburg AR U.S.A. 174 B5
Harrisburg IL U.S.A. 174 B4
Harrisburg NE U.S.A. 178 B3
Harrisburg OH U.S.A. 176 B6
▶Harrisburg PA U.S.A. 177 I5
State capital of Pennsylvania.
Harrismith S. Africa 133 N5
Harris Mountains N.Z. 153 C12
Harrison AR U.S.A. 179 D4
Harrison MI U.S.A. 173 I6
Harrison NE U.S.A. 178 B3
Harrison OH U.S.A. 176 A6
Harrison, Cape Canada 169 J2
Harrison Bay U.S.A. 164 D2
Harrisonburg LA U.S.A. 175 B6
Harrisonburg VA U.S.A. 176 G7
Harrison Lake Canada 166 F5
Harrisonville U.S.A. 178 D4
Harriston Canada 173 M7
Harrisville NY U.S.A. 177 J1
Harrodsburg U.S.A. 176 A8
Harrodsville N.Z. see Otorohanga
Harrogate U.K. 47 K10
Harrowsmith Canada 173 Q6
Harry S. Truman Reservoir U.S.A. 178 D4
Harsa Sweden 45 K3
Har Sai Shan mt. China 84 C5
Hârşeşti Romania 58 F4
Harsin Iran 100 A3
Harşit r. Turkey 107 D2
Hârşova Romania 58 I4
formerly spelt Hîrşova
Harstad Norway 44 L1
Harsud India 96 C5
Harsvik Norway 44 J2
Hart r. Canada 166 B1
Hart U.S.A. 172 G7
Hart, Lake salt flat Australia 146 C2
Hart, Mount hill Australia 150 D3
Hartao China 85 I3
Hartbees watercourse S. Africa 132 E5
Hartbeesfontein S. Africa 133 K3
Hartbeespoort S. Africa 133 L2
Hartberg Austria 49 M8
Harteigan mt. Norway 45 I3
Hartford Liberia 124 C5
▶Hartford CT U.S.A. 177 M4
State capital of Connecticut.
Hartford KY U.S.A. 174 C4
Hartford MI U.S.A. 172 G8
Hartford SD U.S.A. 178 C3
Hartford WI U.S.A. 172 E7
Hartford City U.S.A. 174 C3
Hartibaciu r. Romania 58 F3
Hartington U.S.A. 178 C3
Hartland Canada 169 H4
Hartland U.S.A. 177 P1
Hartland Point U.K. 47 H12
Hartlepool U.K. 47 K9
Hartley U.S.A. 181 G6
Hartley Zimbabwe see Chegutu
Hartley Bay Canada 166 D4
Hart Mountain National Wildlife Refuge nature res. U.S.A. 180 C4
Hartola Fin. 45 N3
Harts r. S. Africa 133 I5
Hartseer Namibia 130 C4
Hartselle U.S.A. 174 C5
Härtsfeld hills Germany 48 H7
Hartshorne U.S.A. 179 D5
Harts Range Australia 148 B4
Harts Range mts Australia 148 B4
Hartsville SC U.S.A. 174 D5
Hartsville TN U.S.A. 174 C4
Hartswater S. Africa 133 I4
Hartville MO U.S.A. 178 D4
Hartville OH U.S.A. 176 D5
Hartwell U.S.A. 174 D5
Hartwell Reservoir U.S.A. 174 D5
Hartz Mountains National Park Australia 147 E5
Haruku i. Indon. 75 D3
Harur India 94 C3
Har Us Nuur l. Mongolia 84 B2
Har Us Nuur salt l. Mongolia 84 B1
Harut watercourse Afgh. 101 E4
Harūt Yemen 105 F4
Haruuhin Gol r. Mongolia 84 E1
Harūz-e Bālā Iran 100 D4
Harvard U.S.A. 172 E8
Harvard, Mount U.S.A. 180 F5
Harvey Canada 169 H4
Harvey MI U.S.A. 172 F4
Harvey ND U.S.A. 178 B2
Harvey Mountain U.S.A. 182 C1
Harwich U.K. 47 N12
Harwich Port U.S.A. 177 O4
Haryana state India 96 C3
Harz hills Germany 48 H4
Harz nat. park Germany 48 H4
Har Zin Israel 108 G7
Ḥaşāh, Wādī al watercourse Jordan 108 G7
Ḥaşāh, Wādī al watercourse Jordan/Saudi Arabia 109 I7
Hasalbag China 88 B4
Hasana, Wādī watercourse Egypt 108 E7
Hasan Dağı mts Turkey 106 C3
Hasan Guli Turkm. see Esenguly
Hasankeyf Turkey 107 E3
Ḥasan Langī Iran 100 D5
Hasanparti India 94 C2
Hasan Sālārān Iran 100 A2
Hasanur India 94 C4
Hasbaïya Lebanon 108 G4
Hasbani r. Lebanon 106 C4
Hasbek Turkey 106 C3
Hasdo r. India 97 D5
Hase r. Germany 48 E3
Hashaat Mongolia 84 E2
HaSharon plain Israel see Sharon, Plain of
Hashimoto Japan 91 D7
Ḥāshiṣh, Ghubbat b. Oman 105 G3
Hashtgerd Iran 100 B3
Hashtpar Iran 100 B2
formerly known as Tālesh
Hashtrud Iran 100 A2
formerly known as Azaran or Sar Eskandar
Hasić Bos.-Herz. see Srnice
Ḥāsik Oman 105 F4
Hasilpur Pak. 101 H4
Haskell U.S.A. 179 C5
Hasle Denmark 45 K5
Haslemere U.K. 47 L12
Haslev Denmark 45 J5
Hăşmaşul Mare mt. Romania 58 G2
Hasparren France 50 E9
Ḥaşş, Jabal al hills Syria 109 I1
Hassa Turkey 109 H1
Hassan India 94 C3
Hassayampa watercourse U.S.A. 183 L8
Haßberge park Germany 48 H5
Hasselt Belgium 51 L2
Hassi Aridal well W. Sahara 122 B4
Hassi Bahbah Alg. 55 O9
Hassi Bedjedjene well Alg. 123 H4
Hassi Bel Guebbour Alg. 123 G3
Hassi Bou Bernous well Alg. 123 E4
Hassi Bourahla well Alg. 123 H4
Hassi Chebbaba well Alg. 123 F3
Hassi Dalaa Alg. 123 F2
Hassi Doumas well W. Sahara 122 B5
Hassi el Ahmar well Alg. 123 F3
Hassi el Krenig well Alg. 123 F4
Hassi Fahl well Alg. 123 F3
Hassi Habadra well Alg. 123 G4
Hassi Ifertas well Libya 120 A2
Hassi I-n-Akeouet well Alg. 123 H4
Hassi I-n-Belrem well Alg. 123 F4
Hassi Inifel Alg. 123 F3
Hassi Khanem well Alg. 123 F3
Hassi Mdakene well Alg. 123 E3
Hassi Messaoud Alg. 123 G3
Hassi Msegguem well Alg. 123 G3
Hassi Nebka well Alg. 123 F3
Hassi Ntsel well Alg. 123 G4
Hassi Sebbakh well Alg. 123 G3
Hassi Tabelbalet well Alg. 123 G4
Hassi Tiguentourine well Alg. 123 F4
Hassi Ti-n Fouchaye well Alg. 123 H3
Hässleholm Sweden 45 K4
Hastière-Lavaux Belgium 51 K2
Hastings Australia 147 E4
Hastings Canada 173 P6
Hastings N.Z. 152 K7
Hastings U.K. 47 M13
Hastings MI U.S.A. 172 H8
Hastings MN U.S.A. 174 A2
Hastings NE U.S.A. 178 C3
Hastings Island P.N.G. 149 F1
Hasvik Norway 44 M1
Ḥaşwayl Yemen 105 F5
Ḥasy Haghe well Libya 120 A3
Hata India 97 D4
Hatansuudal Mongolia 84 D2
Hatay Turkey see Antakya
Hatay prov. Turkey 108 H1
Hatch U.S.A. 183 L4
Hatches Creek Australia 148 B4
Hatchie r. U.S.A. 174 B5
Hat Creek U.S.A. 182 C1
Hațeg Romania 58 D3
Hatepe N.Z. 152 K6
Hatfield Australia 147 D3
Hatgal Mongolia 84 D1
Hat Head National Park Australia 147 G2
Hathras India 96 C4
Hatia Bangl. 97 F5
Hatia Nepal 97 E4
Ḥāṭibah, Ra's pt Saudi Arabia 104 B3
Ha Tiên Vietnam 79 D6
Ha Tinh Vietnam 78 D4
Hatisar Bhutan see Gelephu
Hato Corozal Col. 198 D3
Hatohud East Timor 75 C5
formerly known as Hotahudo; formerly spelt Hato Hud
Hato Hud East Timor see Hatohud
Hato la Vergareña Venez. 199 F3
Hato Mayor Dom. Rep. 187 F3
Hat Piplia India 96 C5
Hatra Iraq 107 E4
also known as Al Ḥaḍr
Hatsukaichi Japan 91 C7
Hatta Madhya Pradesh India 96 C4
Hatta Madhya Pradesh India 96 D5
Hattah Australia 147 D3
Hatteras, Cape U.S.A. 174 F5
Hattfjelldal Norway 44 K2
Hatti r. India 95 D2
Hattiesburg U.S.A. 175 B6
Hattingen Germany 48 E4
Hatton, Gunung hill Sabah Malaysia 77 G1
Hattras Passage Myanmar 79 B5
Hattula Fin. 45 N3
Hatvan Hungary 49 Q8
Hat Yai Thai. 79 C7
Haud reg. Eth. 128 E2
Hauge Norway 45 I4
Haugesund Norway 45 I4
Hâu Giang, Sông r. Vietnam 79 D6
Hauho Fin. 45 N3
Hauhungaroa Range mts N.Z. 152 J6
Haukeligrend Norway 45 I4
Haukipudas Fin. 44 N2
Haukivesi l. Fin. 44 O3
Haukivuori Fin. 45 N3
Haultain r. Canada 167 J4
Haungpa Myanmar 78 B2
Haupt̄rus S. Africa 133 K3
Hauraki Gulf N.Z. 152 J4
Hauraki Gulf Maritime Park nature res. N.Z. 152 I4
Haurangi Forest Park nature res. N.Z. 152 J9
Hauroko, Lake N.Z. 153 B14
Hausach Germany 48 F7
Hausjärvi Fin. 42 F1
Haut, Isle au i. U.S.A. 177 Q1
Hautajärvi Fin. 44 O2
Haut Atlas mts Morocco 122 C3
English form High Atlas; also known as Grand Atlas
Haut-Congo prov. Dem. Rep. Congo see Orientale
Hautefort France 50 H7
Haute-Guinée admin. reg. Guinea 124 C4
Haute-Kotto pref. Cent. Afr. Rep. 126 D3
Haute-Normandie admin. reg. France 50 H3
Hauterive Canada 169 G3
Hauteurs de la Gâtine reg. France 50 F6
Haute-Volta country Africa see Burkina
Haut-Folin hill France 51 K6
Haut Jura, Parc Naturel Régional du nature res. France 51 L6
Haut-Languedoc, Parc Naturel Régional du nature res. France 51 I9
Haut-Mbomou pref. Cent. Afr. Rep. 126 E3
Haut-Ogooué prov. Gabon 126 B5
Hauts Plateaux Alg. 123 E2
Haut-Zaïre prov. Dem. Rep. Congo see Orientale
Hauvo Fin. see Nagu
Hauwai N.Z. 153 I9
Hauzenberg Germany 49 K7
▶Havana Cuba 186 C2
Capital of Cuba. Also spelt Habana or La Habana.
Havana U.S.A. 174 B3
Havant U.K. 47 L13
Havasu, Lake U.S.A. 183 J7
Havel r. Germany 49 I3
Havelberg Germany 49 J3
Haveli Pak. 101 H4
Havelian Pak. 101 H3
Havelock Canada 173 P6
Havelock N.Z. 152 H9
Havelock Swaziland see Bulembu
Havelock U.S.A. 174 E5
Havelock Falls Australia 148 B2
Havelock Island India 95 G4
Havelock North N.Z. 152 K7
Haven U.S.A. 178 C4
Haverdal Sweden 45 K4
Haverfordwest U.K. 47 H12
also known as Hwlffordd
Haverhill U.K. 47 M11
Haverhill U.S.A. 177 N3
Haveri India 94 B3
Haverö Sweden 44 K3
Haverstraw U.S.A. 177 L4
Havlíčkův Brod Czech Rep. 49 M6
Havøysund Norway 44 N1
Havran Turkey 59 I9
Havran r. Turkey 59 H9
Havre U.S.A. 180 E2
Havre Aubert Canada 169 I4
Havre Aubert, Île du i. Canada 169 I4
Havre de Grace U.S.A. 177 I6
Havre Rock i. N.Z. 145 H5
Havre-St-Pierre Canada 169 I3
Havsa Turkey 58 H7
Havutlu Turkey 108 G1
Havza Turkey 106 C2
Hawaii i. U.S.A. 181 [inset] Z1
▶Hawaii state U.S.A. 181 [inset] Z1
northamerica [environments] ▶ 162–163
Hawaii Volcanoes National Park U.S.A. 181 [inset] Z2
Ḥawallī Kuwait 107 G5
Hawar i. The Gulf see Ḥuwār
Hawashīya, Wâdi watercourse Egypt 108 D9
Hawea, Lake N.Z. 153 D12
Hawea Flat N.Z. 153 D12
Hawera N.Z. 152 I7
Hawes U.K. 47 J9
Hawesville U.S.A. 174 C4
Hawick U.K. 46 J8
Ḥawīzah, Hawr al imp. l. Iraq 107 F5
Hawkdun Range mts N.Z. 153 D12
Hawke Bay N.Z. 152 L7
Hawke Island Canada 169 K2
Hawker Australia 146 C2
Hawkers Gate Australia 146 D2
Hawkes Bay Canada 169 J3
Hawke's Bay admin. reg. N.Z. 152 K7
Hawkins Peak U.S.A. 183 K4
Hawk Junction Canada 173 I2
Haw Knob mt. U.S.A. 174 C5
Hawksbill Cay i. Bahamas 175 E7
Hawksnest Point Bahamas 186 E1
Hawkswood N.Z. 153 H10
Hawlêr Iraq see Arbīl
Hawley U.S.A. 177 J4
Hawng Luk Myanmar 78 B3
Ḥawrā' Yemen 105 E5
Ḥawrān, Wādī watercourse Iraq 107 E4
Haw River U.S.A. 176 F9
Ḥawşal hills Saudi Arabia 108 G9
Ḥawshah, Jibāl al mts Saudi Arabia 104 D3
Hawthorne U.S.A. 182 F3
Hawya r. Belarus 42 G8
Hawzēn Eth. 104 B5
Hay Australia 147 E3
Hay watercourse Australia 148 C5
Hay r. Canada 167 H2
Hay r. U.S.A. 172 B6
Haya China 84 D3
Haya Indon. 75 D3
Hayachine-san mt. Japan 90 G5
Hayakita Japan 90 G3
Hayang S. Korea 91 A7
Haydān, Wādī al r. Jordan 108 G6
also known as Heidan
Haydarābad Iran 100 A2
Haydarobа Turkey 59 I9
Hayden CO U.S.A. 180 F4
Hayden ID U.S.A. 180 C3
Hayes r. Man. Canada 167 M3
Hayes r. Nunavut Canada 165 J3
Hayes Center U.S.A. 178 B3
Hayes Creek Australia 148 A2
Hayes Halvø pen. Greenland 165 M2
Hayesville U.S.A. 174 D5
Ḥayf Yemen 105 F5
Hayfield Reservoir U.S.A. 183 I8
Hayfork U.S.A. 182 A1
Ḥayl Oman 105 G2
Ḥayl, Wādī watercourse Syria 109 I4
Ḥayl, Wādī al watercourse Syria 109 K3
Haylaastay Mongolia 85 G2
Haymā' Oman 105 G4
Haymana Turkey 106 C3
Haymarket U.S.A. 176 H7
Hayna r. Belarus 42 J7
Haynesville U.S.A. 179 D5
Hayneville U.S.A. 175 C5
Hayotboshi Toghi mt. Uzbek. see Khayatbashi, Gora
Hayrabolu Turkey 106 A2
Hay River Canada 167 H2
Hay River Reserve Canada 167 H2
Hays U.S.A. 178 C4
Ḥays Yemen 104 C5
Hayshah, Sabkhat al salt pan Libya 120 B2
Haysi U.S.A. 176 C8
Hays Mountains Antarctica 223 N1
Haysville U.S.A. 178 C4
Haysyn Ukr. 41 D6
also spelt Gaysin
Hayti U.S.A. 178 C2
Hayward CA U.S.A. 182 B4
Hayward WI U.S.A. 172 B4
Haywards Heath U.K. 47 L13
Ḥayy well Oman 105 G3
Hazarajat reg. Afgh. 101 F3
Hazard U.S.A. 176 B8
Hazaribag India 97 E5
Hazaribagh Range mts India 97 D5
Hazār Masjed, Kūh-e mts Iran 101 D2
Hazebrouck France 51 I2
Hazel Green U.S.A. 172 C8
Hazelhurst U.S.A. 172 D5
Hazelton Canada 166 E4
Hazen U.S.A. 178 B2
Hazen, Lake Canada 165 L1
Hazen Strait Canada 165 H2
Hazhdanahr reg. Afgh. 101 F2
Ḥazīmī, Wādī al watercourse Iraq 109 L5
Hazlehurst GA U.S.A. 175 D6
Hazlehurst MS U.S.A. 175 B6
Hazleton U.S.A. 177 J5
Hazlett, Lake salt flat Australia 150 E4
Hazorasp Uzbek. see Khazarasp
Hazrat Sultan Afgh. 101 F2
Hazro Pak. 101 H3
Hazro Turkey 107 E3
H. Bouchard Arg. 204 E4
Headingly Australia 148 C4
Head of Bight b. Australia 146 A2
Heafford Junction U.S.A. 172 D5
Healdsburg U.S.A. 182 B3
Healdton U.S.A. 179 C5
Healesville Australia 147 E4
Healing Springs U.S.A. 176 F8
▶Heard and McDonald Islands terr. Indian Ocean 219 L9
Australian External Territory.
asia [countries] ▶ 64–67
Heard Island Indian Ocean 219 L9
Hearne U.S.A. 179 C6
Hearne Lake Canada 167 H2
Hearst Canada 168 D3

Hearst Island Antarctica 222 T2
Heart r. U.S.A. 178 B2
Heath r. Bol./Peru 200 C3
Heathcote Australia 147 E4
Heathfield U.K. 47 M13
Heathrow airport U.K. 47 L12
Heathsville U.S.A. 177 I8
Heavener U.S.A. 179 D5
Hebbronville U.S.A. 179 C7
Hebei prov. China 85 G4
English form Hopei
Hebel Australia 147 E2
Heber AZ U.S.A. 183 N7
Heber CA U.S.A. 183 I9
Heber City U.S.A. 183 M1
Heber Springs U.S.A. 179 D5
Hebgen Lake U.S.A. 180 E3
Hebi China 85 G5
Hebian China 85 G4
Hebron Canada 169 I1
Hebron IN U.S.A. 172 F9
Hebron MD U.S.A. 177 J7
Hebron NE U.S.A. 178 C3
Hebron West Bank 108 G6
also known as Al Khalil or El Khalil; also spelt Hevron
Hebron Fiord inlet Canada 169 I1
Hebros r. Greece/Turkey see Evros
Heby Sweden 45 L4
Hecate Strait Canada 166 D4
Hecelchakán Mex. 185 H4
Hecheng China see Zixi
Hecheng China see Qingtian
Hechi China 87 D3
also known as Jinchengjiang
Hechingen Germany 48 F7
Hechuan China 86 C2
Hechuan China see Yongxing
Hecla Island Canada 167 L5
Hector U.S.A. 178 D2
Hector Mountain mts N.Z. 153 C13
Hedberg Sweden 44 L2
Hede China see Sheyang
Hédé France 50 E4
Hede Sweden 44 K3
Hedemora Sweden 45 K3
Hedenäset Sweden 44 M2
Hede Shuiku resr China 87 D4
Hedesunda Sweden 45 L3
He Devil Mountain U.S.A. 180 C3
Hedgehope N.Z. 153 C14
Hedmark county Norway 45 J3
Heerenveen Neth. 48 C3
Heerhugowaard Neth. 48 B3
Heerlen Neth. 48 C5
Ḥefa Israel see Haifa
Ḥefa, Mifraz b. Israel see Haifa, Bay of
Hefei China 87 F2
Hefeng China 87 D2
also known as Rongmei
Heflin U.S.A. 175 C5
Hegang China 82 C3
Heggadadevankote India 94 C3
Heggenes Norway 45 J3
Hegura-jima i. Japan 90 E6
Heguri-jima i. Japan 91 C8
Heho Myanmar 78 B3
Heiban Sudan 128 A2
Heidan r. Jordan see Haydān, Wādī al
Heide Germany 48 G1
Heidelberg Germany 48 F6
Heidelberg Gauteng S. Africa 133 M3
Heidelberg W. Cape S. Africa 132 E11
Heidenheim an der Brenz Germany 48 H7
Heihe China 82 B2
formerly known as Aihui
Heilbron S. Africa 133 L4
Heilbronn Germany 48 G6
Heiligenbeil Rus. Fed. see Mamonovo
Heiligenhafen Germany 48 H1
Hei Ling Chau i. Hong Kong China 87 [inset]
Heilongjiang prov. China 85 I2
English form Heilungkiang
Heilong Jiang r. China 82 D2
also known as Amur
Heilungkiang prov. China see Heilongjiang
Heimaey i. Iceland 44 [inset] B3
Heinävesi Fin. 44 O3
Heinola Fin. 45 N3
Heinrichswalde Rus. Fed. see Slavsk
Heinze Bay Myanmar 79 B5
Heinze Islands Myanmar 79 B5
Heishan China 85 I3
Heishantou China 85 H1
Heishi Beihu l. China 89 C5
Heishui China 86 B1
also known as Luhua
Heisker Islands U.K. see Monach Islands
Heitân, Gebel hill Egypt 108 E7
Heituo Shan mt. China 85 G4
Hejaz reg. Saudi Arabia see Hijaz
Hejian China 85 H4
Hejiang China 86 C2
He Jiang r. China 87 D4
Hejin China 85 F5
Hejing China 88 D3
Heka China 84 C5
Hekimhan Turkey 107 D3
Hekla vol. Iceland 44 [inset] C3
Hekou Gansu China 84 D4
Hekou Hubei China 87 E2
Hekou China see Yanshan
Hekou China see Yajiang
Hekou Yunnan China 86 B4
Hekpoort S. Africa 133 L2
Hel Poland 49 P1
Helagsfjället mt. Sweden 44 K3
Helan Shan mts China 85 E4
Helegiu Romania 58 H2
Helem India 97 G4
Helen i. Palau 73 H6
Helen, Mount U.S.A. 183 H4
Helena AR U.S.A. 174 B5

▶Helena MT U.S.A. 180 D3
State capital of Montana.

Helena OH U.S.A. 176 B4
Helen Reef Palau 73 H6
Helensburgh U.K. 46 H7
Helensville N.Z. 152 I4
Helenwood U.S.A. 176 A9
Helgoland i. Germany 48 E1
English form Heligoland
Helgoländer Bucht b. Germany 48 F1
English form Heligoland Bight
Helgum Sweden 44 L3
Heligoland i. Germany see Helgoland
Heligoland Bight b. Germany see Helgoländer Bucht
Helixi China see Ningguo
Hella Iceland 44 [inset] B3
Hellas country Europe see Greece
Helleh r. Iran 100 B4
Hellertown U.S.A. 177 J5
Hellespont strait Turkey see Dardanelles
Hellevoetsluis Neth. 48 B4
Hellhole Gorge National Park Australia 149 E5
Helligskogen Norway 44 M1
Hellín Spain 55 J6
Hells Canyon gorge U.S.A. 180 C3
Hell-Ville Madag. see Andoany
Helm U.S.A. 182 D5
Helmand prov. Afgh. 101 E4
Helmand r. Afgh. 101 E4
Helmantica Spain see Salamanca
Helmbrechts Germany 48 I5
Helme r. Germany 48 I4
Helmeringhausen Namibia 130 C5
Helmond Neth. 48 C4
Helmsdale U.K. 46 I5
Helmsdale r. U.K. 46 I5
Helmsley U.K. 47 K9
Helmsley Aboriginal Holding res. Australia 149 D2
Helmstedt Germany 48 I3
Helodrano Antongila b. Madag. 131 [inset] K2
Helong China 82 C4
Helper U.S.A. 183 N2
Helpmekaar S. Africa 133 O5
Helsingborg Sweden 45 K4
formerly spelt Hälsingborg
Helsingfors Fin. see Helsinki
Helsingør Denmark 45 K4
historically known as Elsinore

▶Helsinki Fin. 45 N3
Capital of Finland. Also known as Helsingfors.

Helston U.K. 47 G13
Heltermaa Estonia 42 E3
Helvacı Turkey 59 I10
Helvécia Brazil 203 E6
Helvetic Republic country Europe see Switzerland
Helvetinjärven kansallispuisto nat. park Fin. 45 M3
Helwân Egypt 121 F2
also spelt Ḥulwān
Hemel Hempstead U.K. 47 L12
Hemet U.S.A. 183 H8
Hemlo Canada 172 H2
Hemlock Lake U.S.A. 176 H3
Hemmoor Germany 48 G2
Hemnesberget Norway 44 K2
Hemphill U.S.A. 179 D6
Hempstead U.S.A. 179 C6
Hemse Sweden 45 L4
Hemsedal Norway 45 J3
Hemsedal valley Norway 45 J3
Henan China 86 B1
also known as Yêgainnyin
Henan prov. China 87 E1
English form Honan
Hen and Chickens Islands N.Z. 152 I3
Henares r. Spain 55 H4
Henashi-zaki pt Japan 90 F4
Henbury Australia 148 B5
Hendawashi Tanz. 129 B5
Henderson KY U.S.A. 174 C4
Henderson LA U.S.A. 179 E6
Henderson NC U.S.A. 176 G9
Henderson NV U.S.A. 183 J5
Henderson NY U.S.A. 177 I2
Henderson TN U.S.A. 174 B5
Henderson TX U.S.A. 179 D5
Henderson Island Antarctica 223 G2
Henderson Island Pitcairn Is 221 J7
historically known as Elizabeth Island
Hendersonville NC U.S.A. 174 D5
Hendersonville TN U.S.A. 174 C4
Henderville atoll Kiribati see Aranuka
Hendījān Iran 100 B4
Hendorābī i. Iran 100 C5
Hendriksdal S. Africa 133 O2
Hendrina S. Africa 133 N3
Hengām, Jazīreh-ye i. Iran 100 C5
Hengch'un Taiwan 87 G4
Hengdong China 87 E3
Hengduan Shan mts China 86 A2
Hengelo Neth. 48 D3
Hengnan China see Hengyang
Hengshan Heilong. China 82 C3
Hengshan Hunan China 87 E3
Hengshan Shaanxi China 85 F4
Heng Shan mt. China 87 E3
Heng Shan mts China 85 G4
Hengshui China 85 G4
Hengshui China see Chongyi
Hengxian China 87 D4
also known as Hengzhou
Hengyang Hunan China 87 E3
also known as Hengnan
Hengyang Hunan China 87 E3
also known as Xidu
Hengzhou China see Hengxian
Henlopen, Cape U.S.A. 177 J7
Hennebont France 50 C5
Hennef (Sieg) Germany 48 E5
Hennenman S. Africa 133 L4
Hennessey U.S.A. 179 C4
Hennigsdorf Berlin Germany 49 K3
Henniker U.S.A. 177 N2
Henrichemont France 51 I5
Henrietta U.S.A. 179 C5
Henrietta Maria, Cape Canada 168 D2
Henrique de Carvalho Angola see Saurimo
Henry r. Australia 150 A4
Henry U.S.A. 172 D9
Henry, Cape U.S.A. 177 I9
Henryetta U.S.A. 179 D5
Henry Ice Rise Antarctica 222 T1
Henryk Arctowski research station Antarctica see Arctowski
Henry Kater, Cape Canada 165 M3
Henry Mountains U.S.A. 183 N3
Henrys Fork r. U.S.A. 180 E4
Hensall Canada 173 L7
Henshaw, Lake U.S.A. 183 H8
Henstedt-Ulzburg Germany 48 G2
Hentiesbaai Namibia 130 B4
Hentiy prov. Mongolia 85 F2
Henzada Myanmar 78 A4
also spelt Hinthada
Heping China see Huishui
Heping China see Yanhe
Hepo China see Jiexi
Heppner U.S.A. 180 C3
Hepu China 87 D4
also known as Lianzhou
Heqiaoyi China 84 D4
Heqing Guangdong China 87 E4
Heqing Yunnan China 86 B3
also known as Yunhe
Hequ China 85 F4
Heraclea Turkey see Ereğli
Heraclea Pontica Turkey see Ereğli
Heraklion Greece see Iraklion
Herald Cays atolls Australia 149 F3
Herāt Afgh. 101 E3
historically known as Alexandria Areion
Herāt prov. Afgh. 101 E3
Hérault r. France 51 J9
Herbagat Sudan 104 B4
Herbert r. Australia 149 E3
Herbert watercourse Australia 148 C3
Herbert Canada 167 J5
Herbert N.Z. 153 E13
Herbert Downs Australia 148 C4
Herberton Australia 149 E3
Herbert River Falls National Park Australia 149 E3
Herbertsdale S. Africa 132 F11
Herbertville N.Z. 152 K8
Herbert Wash salt flat Australia 151 D5
Herbignac France 50 D5
Herbstein Germany 48 G5
Herceg-Novi Crna Gora Yugo. 56 K6
Herculândia Brazil 206 C8
Hercules Dome ice feature Antarctica 223 Q1
Heredia Costa Rica 186 B5
Hereford U.K. 47 J11
Hereford U.S.A. 179 B5
Herekino N.Z. 152 H3
Heretaniwha Point N.Z. 153 D11
Herford Germany 48 F3
Héricourt France 51 M5
Herington U.S.A. 178 C4
Heriot N.Z. 153 D13
Herisau Switz. 51 P5
Heritage Range mts Antarctica 222 S1
Herkimer U.S.A. 177 K2
Herlen Mongolia 85 F2
Herlen Gol r. China/Mongolia see Kerulen
Herlen He r. China/Mongolia see Kerulen
Herlong U.S.A. 182 D1
Hermagor Austria 49 K9
Herma Ness hd U.K. 46 L3
Hermann U.S.A. 174 B4
Hermannsburg Australia 148 B4
Hermanus S. Africa 132 D11
Hermel Lebanon 109 H3
Hermes, Cape S. Africa 133 N8
Hermidale Australia 147 E2
Hermitage MO U.S.A. 178 D4
Hermitage PA U.S.A. 176 E4
Hermitage Bay Canada 169 J4
Hermite, Islas is Chile 205 D9
Hermit Islands P.N.G. 73 K7
Hermon, Mount Lebanon/Syria 108 G4
also known as Sheikh, Jebel esh
Hermonthis Egypt see Armant
Hermopolis Magna Egypt see El Ashmûnein
Hermosa, Valle valley Arg. 205 C7
Hermosillo Mex. 184 C2
Hernád r. Hungary 49 R8
also spelt Hornád (Slovakia)
Hernandarias Para. 201 G6
Hernando U.S.A. 174 B5
Hernani Spain 55 J1
Herndon CA U.S.A. 182 E5
Herndon WV U.S.A. 176 D8
Herne Germany 48 E4
Herning Denmark 45 J4
Heroica Nogales Mex. see Nogales
Heron Bay Canada 172 G2
Herong China 87 E2
Hérouville-St-Clair France 50 F3
Herowābād Iran see Khalkhāl
Herradura Mex. 185 E4
Herrenberg Germany 48 F7
Herrera Arg. 204 E3
Herrera del Duque Spain 54 F5
Herrero, Punta pt Mex. 185 I5
Herrieden Germany 48 H6
Herrin U.S.A. 174 B4
Herrljunga Sweden 45 K4
Herrvik Sweden 45 L4
Hers r. France 50 H9
Herschel S. Africa 133 L7
Herschel Island Canada 164 F3
Hershey U.S.A. 177 I5
Hertel U.S.A. 172 A5
Hertford U.K. 47 L12
Hertford U.S.A. 177 I9
Hertzogville S. Africa 133 J5
Hervey Bay Australia 149 G5
Hervey Islands Cook Is 221 H7
Herzberg Germany 49 K4
Herzliyya Israel 108 F5
Herzogenaurach Germany 48 H6
Herzogenburg Austria 49 M7
Ḥesār Iran 100 B4
Ḥeṣār Iran 100 B3
Hesdin France 51 I2
Heshan China 87 D4
Heshengqiao China 87 E2
Heshui China 85 F5
also known as Xihuachi
Heshun China 85 G4
Hesperia CA U.S.A. 183 G7
Hesperia MI U.S.A. 172 G7
Hesquiat Canada 166 E5
Hess r. Canada 166 C2
Hesse land Germany see Hessen
Hessel U.S.A. 173 I4
Hesselberg hill Germany 48 H6
Hessen land Germany 48 G5
English form Hesse
Hessischer Spessart, Naturpark nature res. Germany 48 G5
Hessisch Lichtenau Germany 48 G4
Hess Mountains Canada 166 C2
Hester Malan Nature Reserve S. Africa 132 C6
Hestvika Norway 44 J3
Het r. Laos 78 D3
Hetch Hetchy Aqueduct canal U.S.A. 182 B4
Hettinger U.S.A. 178 B2
Hettstedt Germany 48 I4
Heung Kong Tsai Hong Kong China see Aberdeen
Heuningneskloof S. Africa 133 I6
Heuningspruit S. Africa 133 L4
Heuningvlei salt pan S. Africa 132 H3
Heuvelton U.S.A. 177 J1
Heves Hungary 49 R8
Ḥevron West Bank see Hebron
Hewlett U.S.A. 176 H8
Hexenkopf mt. Austria 48 H8
Hexham U.K. 47 J9
Hexian China 87 F2
Hexigten Qi China see Jingpeng
Hexipu China 84 D4
Hexrivierberg mts S. Africa 132 D10
Heyang China see Nanhe
Heyang China 85 F5
Heydebreck Poland see Kędzierzyn-Koźle
Heydon S. Africa 133 I8
Heygali well Eth. 128 E3
Heyin China see Guide
Heyshope Dam S. Africa 133 O3
Heyuan China 87 E4
Heywood Australia 146 D4
Heze China 85 G5
also known as Caozhou
Hezhang China 86 C3
Hezheng China 84 D5
Hezhou China 87 D3
also known as Babu
Hezuozhen China 84 D5
Hhohho reg. Swaziland 133 P3
Hialeah U.S.A. 175 D7
Hiawassee U.S.A. 174 D5
Hiawatha U.S.A. 178 D4
Hibata reg. Saudi Arabia 104 C4
Hibberdene S. Africa 133 O7
Hibbing U.S.A. 174 A2
Hibbs, Point Australia 147 E5
Hibernia Reef Australia 150 C2
Hibiki-nada b. Japan 91 B7
Hichān Iran 101 E5
Hickman U.S.A. 174 B4
Hickory U.S.A. 174 D5
Hicks Bay N.Z. 152 M5
Hicks Cays is Belize 185 H5
Hicksville NY U.S.A. 177 L5
Hicksville OH U.S.A. 176 A4
Hico U.S.A. 179 C5
Hidaka Japan 90 H3
Hidaka-sanmyaku mts Japan 90 H3
Hidalgo Coahuila Mex. 185 F3
Hidalgo Tamaulipas Mex. 185 F3
Hidalgo state Mex. 185 F4
Hidalgo del Parral Mex. 184 D3
Hidalgo Yalalag Mex. 185 F5
Hidasnémeti Hungary 49 S7
Hiddensee i. Germany 49 K1
Hidişelu de Sus Romania 58 D2
Hidrolândia Brazil 206 D3
Hierosolyma Israel/West Bank see Jerusalem
Hietaniemi Fin. 44 O2
Higashi-Hiroshima Japan 91 C7
Higashi-matsuyama Japan 91 F6
Higashine Japan 90 G5
Higashi-ōsaka Japan 91 D7
Higashi-suidō sea chan. Japan 91 A8
Higgins Bay U.S.A. 177 K2
Higgins Lake U.S.A. 173 I6
Higg's Hope S. Africa 132 H6
High Atlas mts Morocco see Haut Atlas
High Desert U.S.A. 180 B4
High Falls Reservoir U.S.A. 172 E5
Highflats S. Africa 133 O7
High Island i. Hong Kong China 87 [inset]
also known as Leung Shuen Wan Chau
High Island U.S.A. 179 D6
High Island i. U.S.A. 172 H5
High Island Reservoir Hong Kong China 87 [inset]
Highland CA U.S.A. 183 G7
Highland MN U.S.A. 172 B3
Highland NY U.S.A. 177 L4
Highland WI U.S.A. 172 C7
Highland Beach U.S.A. 177 I7
Highland Peak CA U.S.A. 182 E3
Highland Peak NV U.S.A. 183 J4
Highlands U.S.A. 177 L5
Highland Springs U.S.A. 177 H8
High Level Canada 167 G3
High Level Canal India 95 E1
Highline Canal U.S.A. 183 I9
Highmore U.S.A. 178 C2
High Point U.S.A. 174 E5
High Point hill U.S.A. 177 K4
High Prairie Canada 167 G4
High River Canada 167 H5
High Rock Bahamas 186 D1
Highrock Lake Canada 167 K4
High Rocky Point Australia 147 E5
High Springs U.S.A. 175 D6
High Tatras mts Poland/Slovakia see Tatra Mountains
Hightstown U.S.A. 177 K5
High Wycombe U.K. 47 L12
Higlale well Eth. 128 E3
Higuera de Abuya Mex. 184 D3
Higuera de Zaragoza Mex. 184 C3
Higüey Dom. Rep. 187 F3
Hihifo Tonga 145 H3
Hihnavaara Fin. 44 O2
Hiidenportin kansallispuisto nat. park Fin. 44 O3
Hiidenvesi l. Fin. 42 F1
Hiiraan Somalia 128 E3
Hiiraan admin. reg. Somalia 128 E3
Hiiumaa i. Estonia 42 D3
also known as Dagö; historically known as Oesel or Ösel
Hijānah, Buḥayrat al imp. l. Syria 109 H4
Hijānah, Wādī watercourse Syria 109 K3
Hijau, Gunung mt. Indon. 76 C3
Hijaz reg. Saudi Arabia 104 B2
English form Hejaz
Hiji Japan 91 B8
Hijo Phil. 74 C5
Hikari Japan 91 B8
Hiketa Japan 91 D7
Hikone Japan 91 E7
Hikurangi mt. N.Z. 152 M5
Hila Indon. 75 C4
Hilahila Indon. 75 B4
Hilaricos Chile 200 C5
Hilary Coast Antarctica 223 K1
Hildale U.S.A. 183 K4
Hildburghausen Germany 48 H5
Hilders Germany 48 H5
Hildesheim Germany 48 G3
Ḥilf, Ra's c. Oman 105 G3
Hili Bangl. 97 F4
Ḥillah Iraq 107 F4
also spelt Al Ḥillah
Hillandale S. Africa 132 E10
Hillard U.S.A. 176 B5
Hill City U.S.A. 178 C4
Hill Creek r. U.S.A. 183 O2
Hillerød Denmark 45 K5
Hillersden N.Z. 153 H9
Hillerse Germany 48 H3
Hillerstorp Sweden 45 K4
Hillesheim Germany 48 D5
Hillgrove Australia 149 E3
Hill Island Lake Canada 167 I2
Hillman U.S.A. 173 J5
Hillman, Lake salt flat Australia 151 B6
Hillsboro IL U.S.A. 174 B4
Hillsboro MO U.S.A. 174 B4
Hillsboro ND U.S.A. 178 C2
Hillsboro NH U.S.A. 177 N2
Hillsboro OH U.S.A. 176 B6
Hillsboro OR U.S.A. 180 B3
Hillsboro TX U.S.A. 179 C5
Hillsboro WI U.S.A. 172 C7
Hillsboro Canal U.S.A. 175 D7
Hillsborough Grenada 187 H4
Hillsborough U.S.A. 176 F9
Hillsborough, Cape Australia 149 F4
Hillsdale MI U.S.A. 173 I9
Hillsdale NY U.S.A. 177 L3
Hillsgrove U.S.A. 177 I4
Hillside Australia 150 B4
Hillsport Canada 168 C3
Hillston Australia 147 E3
Hillsville U.S.A. 176 E9
Hillswick U.K. 46 K3
Hilo U.S.A. 181 [inset] Z2
Hilton Australia 148 C4
Hilton U.S.A. 176 H2
Hilton Beach Canada 173 J4
Hilton Head Island U.S.A. 175 D5
Hilvan Turkey 107 D3
also known as Karacurun
Hilversum Neth. 48 C3
Ḥimá well Saudi Arabia 104 D4
Himachal Pradesh state India 96 C3
Ḥimā Ḍarīyah, Jabal mt. Saudi Arabia 104 C2
▶Himalaya mts Asia 97 C2
world (physical features) ⟶ 8–9
asia (landscapes) ⟶ 62–63
Himalchuli mt. Nepal 97 E3
Himanka Fin. 44 M2
Ḥimār, Wādī al watercourse Syria/Turkey 109 K1
also known as Hamra, Vâdii
Himarë Albania 59 A8
Ḥimār Umm Khunṣur hill Saudi Arabia 109 M7
Himatangi Beach N.Z. 152 J8
Himatnagar India 96 B5
Himbirti Eritrea 104 B5
Himeji Japan 91 D7
Himekami-dake mt. Japan 90 G5
Himeville S. Africa 133 N6
Hime-zaki pt Japan 90 F5
Himi Japan 91 E6
Himora Eth. 128 C1
Ḥimṣ Syria see Homs
Ḥimṣ governorate Syria 109 J2
Ḥimṣ, Baḥrat resr Syria see Qaṭṭīnah, Buḥayrat
Hinako i. Indon. 76 B2
Hinakura N.Z. 152 J9
Hinatuan Phil. 74 C4
Hinatuan Passage Phil. 74 C4
Hînceşti Moldova 58 J2
formerly known as Cotovsc or Kotovsk; formerly spelt Hănceşti or Khynchest' or Khynchesty
Hinche Haiti 187 E3
Hinchinbrook Island Australia 149 E3
Hinckley U.K. 47 K11
Hinckley IL U.S.A. 172 E9
Hinckley ME U.S.A. 177 P1
Hinckley MN U.S.A. 174 A2
Hinckley UT U.S.A. 183 L2
Hinckley Reservoir U.S.A. 177 J2
Hind, Wādī al watercourse Saudi Arabia 108 G8
Hinda Congo 126 B6
Hindan r. India 89 B6
Hindaun India 96 C4
Hindelang Germany 48 H8
Hindenburg Poland see Zabrze
Hindman U.S.A. 176 C8
Hindmarsh, Lake dry lake Australia 146 D4
Hindola India 95 E1
Hindoli India 96 B4
Hindoria India 96 C5
Hindri r. India 94 C3
Hinds N.Z. 153 F12
Hindu Kush mts Afgh./Pak. 101 F3
Hindupur India 94 C3
Hines Creek Canada 166 G3
Hinesville U.S.A. 175 D6
Hinganghat India 94 C1
Hingol r. Pak. 101 F5
Hingol r. Pak. see Girdar Dhor
Hınıs Turkey 107 E3
Hinks Conservation Park nature res. Australia 146 C3
Hinnøya i. Norway 44 K1
Hino Japan 91 C7
Hinobaan Phil. 74 B4
Hinojedo mt. Spain 55 I3
Hinojosa del Duque Spain 54 F6
Hino-misaki pt Japan 91 C7
Hinsdale U.S.A. 177 M3
Hinterzarten Germany 48 F8
Hinthada Myanmar see Henzada
Hinton KY U.S.A. 176 A7
Hinton OK U.S.A. 179 C5
Hinton WV U.S.A. 176 E8
Hinuera N.Z. 152 J5
Hiort i. U.K. see Hirta
Hipólito Mex. 185 E3
Hipponium Italy see Vibo Valentia
Hippopotames, Réserve de nature res. Dem. Rep. Congo 126 F6
Hippopotames, Réserve de Faune des nature res. Dem. Rep. Congo 126 E5
Hippopotames de Sakania, Réserve de nature res. Dem. Rep. Congo 127 F8
Hippo Regius Alg. see Annaba
Hippo Zarytus Tunisia see Bizerte
Hirabit Dağ mt. Turkey 107 F3
Hirado Japan 91 A8
Hirado-shima i. Japan 91 A8
Hirafok Alg. 123 G5
Hirakud Reservoir India 97 D5
Hiraman watercourse Kenya 128 C5
Hirata Japan 91 C7
Hiré-Watta Côte d'Ivoire 124 D5
Hiriyur India 94 C3
Hîrlău Romania see Hârlău
Hiroo Japan 90 H3
Hirosaki Japan 90 G4
Hirose Japan 91 C7
Hiroshima Japan 91 C7
Hiroshima airport Japan 91 C7
Hiroshima pref. Japan 91 C7
Hirota-wan b. Japan 90 G5
Hirschaid Germany 48 I6
Hirschberg Germany 48 I5
Hirschberg Poland see Jelenia Góra
Hirsingue France 51 N5
Hirson France 51 K3
Hîrşova Romania see Hârşova
Hirta i. U.K. 46 D6
also known as Hiort
Hirtshals Denmark 45 J4
Hisai Japan 91 E7
Hisaka-jima i. Japan 91 A8
Hisar India 96 B3
also spelt Hissar
Hisar, Koh-i- mts Afgh. 101 F3
Hisarcık Turkey 59 K9
Hisarköy Turkey see Domaniç
Hisarönü Turkey 106 C2
Hisarönü Körfezi b. Turkey 59 I12
Ḥisb, Sha'īb watercourse Iraq 107 F5
Ḥiṣn al Fuḍūl Yemen 105 E4
Hisor Tajik. 101 G2
also known as Gissar
Hisor Tizmasi mts Tajik./Uzbek. see Gissar Range
Hispalis Spain see Seville
Hispania country Europe see Spain

▶Hispaniola i. Caribbean Sea 171 L7
Consists of the Dominican Republic and Haiti.

Hispur Glacier Jammu and Kashmir 96 B1
Hissar India see Hisar
Hisua India 97 E4
Hīt Iraq 107 E4
Hita Japan 91 B8
Hitachi Japan 91 G6
Hitachinaka Japan 91 G6
Hitachi-ōta Japan 91 G6
Hitoyoshi Japan 91 B8
Hitra i. Norway 44 J3
Hiuchi-nada b. Japan 91 C7
Hiva Oa i. Fr. Polynesia 221 I6
formerly known as Dominique
Hiwasa Japan 91 D8
Hixon Canada 166 F4
Hixson Cay reef Australia 149 G4
Hixton U.S.A. 172 B6
Hiyon watercourse Israel 108 G7
Hizan Turkey 107 E3
also known as Karasu
Hjallerup Denmark 45 J4
Hjälmaren l. Sweden 45 K4
Hjelle Norway 45 I3
Hjellestad Norway 46 R3
Hjelmeland Norway 45 I4
Hjerkinn Norway 44 J3
Hjo Sweden 45 K4
Hjørring Denmark 45 J4
Hjuvik Sweden 45 J4
Hka, Nam r. Myanmar 78 B3
Hkakabo Razi mt. Myanmar 78 B1
Hkok r. Myanmar 78 B3
Hkring Bum mt. Myanmar 78 B2
Hlabisa S. Africa 133 P5
Hlaing r. Myanmar 78 B4
Hlako Kangri mt. China see Lhagoi Kangri
Hlane Game Sanctuary nature res. Swaziland 133 P3
Hlatikulu Swaziland 133 P3
Hlazove Ukr. 43 O9
Hlegu Myanmar 78 B4
Hlinsko Czech Rep. 49 M6
Hlohlowane S. Africa 133 L5
Hlohovec Slovakia 49 O7
Hlotse Lesotho 133 M5
Hlučín Czech Rep. 49 P6
Hluhluwe S. Africa 133 Q5
Hluhluwe Game Reserve nature res. S. Africa 133 Q5
Hlukhiv Ukr. 41 E6
also spelt Glukhov
Hlung-Tan Myanmar 78 B3
Hlusha Belarus 43 J8
Hlusk Belarus 43 J9
Hlybokaye Belarus 42 I6
also spelt Glubokoye
Hnilec r. Slovakia 49 R7
Hnúšťa Slovakia 49 Q7
Ho Ghana 125 F5
Hoa Binh Vietnam 78 D3
Hoachanas Namibia 130 C4
Hoang Liên Sơn mts Vietnam 78 C3
Hoang Sa is S. China Sea see Paracel Islands
Hoanib watercourse Namibia 130 B3
Hoarusib watercourse Namibia 130 B3

▶Hobart Australia 147 E5
State capital of Tasmania.

Hobart U.S.A. 179 C5
Hobbs U.S.A. 179 B5
Hobbs Coast Antarctica 222 P1
Hobe Sound U.S.A. 175 D7
Hobhouse S. Africa 133 L6
Hobo Col. 198 C4
Hoboksar China 88 D2
Hobor China 85 G3
also known as Qahar Youyi Zhongqi
Hobot Xar Qi China see Xin Bulag
Hobro Denmark 45 J4
Hoburg Sweden 45 L4
Hoburgen pt Sweden 45 L4
Hobyo Somalia 128 F3
formerly spelt Obbia
Hochfeiler mt. Austria/Italy see Gran Pilastro
Hochfeld Namibia 130 C4
Hochgall mt. Austria/Italy see Collalto
Hochgolling mt. Austria 49 K8
Hochharz nat. park Germany 48 H4
Hô Chi Minh Vietnam see Ho Chi Minh City
Ho Chi Minh City Vietnam 79 D6
also known as Hô Chi Minh; formerly known as Saigon
Hochobir mt. Austria 49 L9
Hochschwab mt. Austria 49 M8
Hochtaunus nature res. Germany 48 F5
Hochtor mt. Austria 49 L8
Hocking r. U.S.A. 176 D6
Hôd reg. Mauritania 124 C2
Hodal India 96 C4
Hodda mt. Somalia 128 F2
Hodeidah Yemen 104 C5
also spelt Al Ḥudaydah
Hodein, Wâdi watercourse Egypt 121 G4
Hodgesville U.S.A. 176 E6
Hodgson Downs Australia 148 B2
Hodgson Downs Aboriginal Land res. Australia 148 B2
Hodh Ech Chargui admin. reg. Mauritania 124 D2
Hodh El Gharbi admin. reg. Mauritania 124 C2
Hódmezővásárhely Hungary 49 R9
Hodmo watercourse Somalia 128 E2
Hodna, Chott el salt l. Alg. 123 G2
Hodonín Czech Rep. 49 O7
Hodoşa Romania 58 F2
Hödrögö Mongolia 84 C1
Hodsons Peak Lesotho 133 N6
Hoek van Holland Neth. see Hook of Holland
Hoeryŏng N. Korea 82 C4
Hoeyang N. Korea 83 B5
Hof Germany 48 I5
Hoffman Mountain U.S.A. 177 L2
Hoffman's Cay i. Bahamas 186 D1
Hofmeyr S. Africa 133 J8
Höfn Iceland 44 [inset] D2
Hofors Sweden 45 L3
Hofsjökull ice cap Iceland 44 [inset] C2
Hofsós Iceland 44 [inset] C2
Hōfu Japan 91 B7
Hofuf Saudi Arabia see Al Hufūf
Höganäs Sweden 45 K4
Hogan Group is Australia 147 E4
Hogansburg U.S.A. 177 K1
Hoganthulla Creek r. Australia 149 E5
Hogg, Mount Canada 166 C2
▶Hoggar plat. Alg. 123 G5
also spelt Ahaggar
world (land cover) ⟶ 18–19
Hog Island U.S.A. 177 J8
Högsby Sweden 45 L4
Høgste Breakulen mt. Norway 45 I3
Hogsty Reef Bahamas 187 E2
Högyész Hungary 49 P9
Hoh r. U.S.A. 180 A3
Hohenems Austria 48 G8
Hohenloher Ebene plain Germany 48 G6
Hohe Nock mt. Austria 49 L8
Hohensalza Poland see Inowrocław
Hohenwald U.S.A. 174 C5
Hohenwartetalsperre resr Germany 51 R2
Hoher Dachstein mt. Austria 49 K8
Hoh Ereg China see Wuchuan
Hoher Göll mt. Austria/Germany 49 K8
Hohe Rhön mts Germany 48 G5
Hohe Tauern mts Austria 49 J8
Hohe Tauern, Nationalpark nat. park Austria 49 J8
Hohe Venn moorland Belgium 51 M2
Hohhot China 85 F3
also spelt Huhhot; formerly spelt Huhehot
Hohoe Ghana 125 F5
Ho Ho Shak Hong Kong China 87 [inset]
Hōhoku Japan 91 B7
Hoh Xil Hu salt l. China 89 E5
Hoh Xil Shan mts China 80 D5
Hôi An Vietnam 78 E5
Hoima Uganda 128 A4
Hoisdorf Germany 48 H2
Hoisington U.S.A. 178 C4
Hoit Taria China 84 C4
Hôi Xuân Vietnam 78 D3
Hojai India 97 G4
Hojambaz Turkm. see Khodzhambaz
Hōjo Japan 91 C8
Hökensås hills Sweden 45 K4
Hokio Beach N.Z. 152 J8
Hokitika N.Z. 153 E10
Hokkaidō i. Japan 81 O4
historically known as Ezo or Yezo
Hokkaidō pref. Japan 90 H3
Hokksund Norway 45 J4
Hokmābād Iran 100 D2
Hokonui N.Z. 153 C14
Hokonui Hills N.Z. 153 C13
Hokota Japan 91 G6
Hoktemberyan Armenia 107 F2
formerly spelt Oktemberyan
Hol Buskerud Norway 45 J3
Hol Nordland Norway 44 L1
Hola Kenya 128 C5
Holalkere India 94 C3
Holanda Bol. 200 D3
Holbæk Denmark 45 J5
Holberg Canada 166 D5
Holbrook Australia 147 E3
Holbrook U.S.A. 183 N7
Holcombe U.S.A. 172 B5
Holcombe Flowage resr U.S.A. 172 B5
Holden Canada 167 H4
Holden U.S.A. 183 L2
Holdenville U.S.A. 179 C5
Holdich Arg. 205 C7
Holdrege U.S.A. 178 C3
Hole Narsipur India 94 C3
Holgat watercourse S. Africa 132 A5
Holgate U.S.A. 176 A4
Holguín Cuba 186 D2
Holič Slovakia 49 O7
Höljes Sweden 45 K3
Hollabrunn Austria 49 N7
Holland country Europe see Netherlands
Holland MI U.S.A. 172 G8
Holland NY U.S.A. 176 G3
Hollandale U.S.A. 175 B5
Hollandia Indon. see Jayapura
Hollands Diep est. Neth. 48 B4
Hollick-Kenyon Peninsula Antarctica 222 T2
Hollick-Kenyon Plateau Antarctica 222 Q1
Hollis U.S.A. 179 C5
Hollister U.S.A. 182 C5
Hollóháza Hungary 49 S7
Hollola Fin. 45 N3
Hollum Neth. 48 C2
Holly U.S.A. 173 J8
Holly Springs U.S.A. 174 B5

H index

Hollywood U.S.A. **175** D7
Holm Norway **44** K2
Holman Canada **165** H2
also known as Uluqsaqtuuq
Holmdene S. Africa **133** N3
Holmes Reef Australia **149** E3
Holmestrand Norway **45** J4
Holmgard Rus. Fed. see **Velikiy Novgorod**
Holm Ø i. Greenland see **Kiatassuaq**
Holmöarna naturreservat nature res. Sweden **44** M3
Holmön i. Sweden **44** M3
Holmsund Sweden **44** M3
Holmudden pt Sweden **45** L4
Holod r. Romania **58** D2
Ḥolon Israel **108** F5
also spelt Kholon
Holoog Namibia **130** C5
Holothuria Banks reef Australia **150** D2
Holovets'ko Ukr. **49** T6
Holroyd r. Australia **149** D2
Holroyd Bluff hills Australia **151** C5
Holspruit r. S. Africa **133** M4
Holstebro Denmark **45** J4
Holsted Denmark **45** J5
Holstein U.S.A. **178** D3
Holsteinsborg Greenland see **Sisimiut**
Holston r. U.S.A. **176** B9
Holston Lake U.S.A. **176** D9
Holt U.S.A. **173** I8
Holton KS U.S.A. **178** D4
Holton MI U.S.A. **172** G7
Holtville U.S.A. **183** I9
Holtwood U.S.A. **177** I6
Holy Cross, Mount of the U.S.A. **180** F5
Holyhead U.K. **47** H10
also known as Caergybi
Holy Island England U.K. **46** K8
also known as Lindisfarne
Holy Island Wales U.K. **47** H10
Holyoke CO U.S.A. **178** B3
Holyoke MA U.S.A. **177** M3
Holy See Europe see **Vatican City**
Holzkirchen Germany **48** I8
Holzminden Germany **48** G4
Hom watercourse Namibia **132** C5
Homa Bay Kenya **128** B5
Homalin Myanmar **78** A2
Homathko r. Canada **166** E5
Homāyūnshahr Iran see **Khomeynīshahr**
Homberg (Efze) Germany **48** G4
Hombetsu Japan see **Honbetsu**
Hombori Mali **125** E3
Hombre Muerto, Salar del salt flat Arg. **204** D2
Homburg Germany **48** E6
Home Bay Canada **165** M3
Home Hill Australia **149** E3
Home Point N.Z. **152** I3
Homer AK U.S.A. **164** D4
Homer GA U.S.A. **174** D5
Homer LA U.S.A. **179** D5
Homer MI U.S.A. **173** I8
Homer City U.S.A. **176** F5
Homerville U.S.A. **175** D6
Homestead Australia **149** E4
Homestead U.S.A. **175** D7
Homewood N.Z. **152** J9
Homewood U.S.A. **175** C5
Hommelvik Norway **44** J3
Homnabad India **94** C2
Homocea Romania **58** I2
Homodji well Niger **125** I2
Homoine Moz. **131** G4
Homs Libya see **Al Khums**
Homs Syria **109** H3
also spelt Ḥimş; historically known as Emesa
Homyel' Belarus **43** M9
also spelt Gomel'
Homyel Oblast admin. div. Belarus see **Homyel'skaya Voblasts'**
Homyel'skaya Voblasts' admin. div. Belarus **43** K9
English form Homyel Oblast or Gomel Oblast; also known as Gomel'skaya Oblast'
Honaker U.S.A. **176** D8
Honan prov. China see **Henan**
Honavar India **94** B3
Honaz Turkey **59** K11
historically known as Colossae
Hon Bai Canh i. Vietnam **79** D6
Honbetsu Japan **90** H3
also spelt Hombetsu
Hon Chông Vietnam **79** D6
Hon Chuôi i. Vietnam **79** D6
Honda Col. **198** C3
Honda India **97** E5
Honda, Bahía b. Col. **198** C1
Honda Bay Phil. **74** A4
Hondapa India **95** E1
Hondeblaf r. S. Africa **133** I7
Hondeklipbaai S. Africa **132** B7
Hondo r. Belize/Mex. **185** H5
Hondo Japan **91** B8
Hondo NM U.S.A. **181** F6
Hondo TX U.S.A. **179** C6
Hondo r. U.S.A. **181** F6
▶**Honduras** country Central America **186** B4
northamerica [countries] ▶ 158–159
Honduras, Gulf of Belize/Hond. **186** B3
Hønefoss Norway **45** J3
Honesdale U.S.A. **177** J4
Honey Brook U.S.A. **177** J5
Honey Lake U.S.A. **182** D1
Honfleur France **50** G3
Hông, Sông r. Vietnam see **Red River**
Hong'an China **87** E2
Hongch'ŏn S. Korea **83** B5
Hongde China **85** E4
Hông Gai Vietnam **78** D3
Honggouzi China **88** E4
Honggu China **84** D4
formerly known as Yaojie
Honghai Wan b. China **87** E4
Honghe China **86** B4
also known as Yisa
Hong He r. China **87** E1
Honghu China **87** E2
formerly known as Xindi
Hong Hu l. China **87** E2
Hongjialou China see **Licheng**
Hongjiang China **87** D3
Hongjiang China see **Wangcang**
▶**Hong Kong** Hong Kong China **87** [inset]
also known as Hsiang Kang or Xianggang
world [cities] ▶ 24–25
Hong Kong special admin. reg. China **87** [inset]
long form Xianggang Tebie Xingzhengqu
Hong Kong Harbour sea chan. Hong Kong China **87** [inset]
also known as Victoria Harbour
Hong Kong Island Hong Kong China **87** [inset]
also known as Hsiang Chang
Hongliu r. China **85** F4
Hongliu Daquan well China **84** C3
Hongliuwan China see **Aksay**
Hongliuyuan Gansu China **84** B3
Hongliuyuan Gansu China **84** D4
Hông Ngư Vietnam **79** D6
Hongor Mongolia **85** G2
Hongqiao China see **Qidong**
Hongqizhen China see **Tongshi**
Hongshan China **86** A2
formerly known as Mabating
Hongshui He r. China **87** D4
Hongtong China **85** F4
Hongū Japan **91** D8
Honguedo, Détroit d' sea chan. Canada **169** H3
Hongwansi China see **Sunan**
Hongwŏn N. Korea **83** B4
Hongyuan China **86** B1
also known as Qiongxi
Hongze China **87** F1
also known as Gaoliangjian
Hongze Hu l. China **87** F1
▶**Honiara** Solomon Is **145** E2
Capital of the Solomon Islands.
Honiton U.K. **47** I13
Honjō Japan **90** G5
Honkajoki Fin. **45** M3
Hon Khoai i. Vietnam **79** D6
Hon Mê i. Vietnam **78** D4
Hon Minh Hoa i. Vietnam **79** D6
Honnali India **94** B3
Honningsvåg Norway **44** N1
Honokaa U.S.A. **181** [inset] Z1
▶**Honolulu** U.S.A. **181** [inset] Z1
State capital of Hawaii.
Honor U.S.A. **172** G6
Hon Rai i. Vietnam **79** D6
▶**Honshū** i. Japan **91** F6
3rd largest island in Asia and 7th in the world.
asia [landscapes] ▶ 62–63
Honwad India **94** B2
Hood r. Canada **167** I1
Hood, Mount vol. U.S.A. **180** B3
Hood Point Australia **151** B7
Hood River U.S.A. **180** B3
Hoogeveen Neth. **48** D3
Hoogezand-Sappemeer Neth. **48** D2
Hooghly r. mouth India see **Hugli**
Hooker U.S.A. **178** B4
Hooker Creek Aboriginal Land res. Australia **148** A3
Hook Head Rep. of Ireland **47** F11
Hook of Holland Neth. **48** B4
also known as Hoek van Holland
Hook Reef Australia **149** F3
Hoolt Mongolia **84** D2
Hoonah U.S.A. **164** F4
Hoopa Valley Indian Reservation res. U.S.A. **180** B4
Hooper Bay U.S.A. **164** C3
Hooper Island U.S.A. **177** I7
Hoopstad S. Africa **133** J4
Hoorn Neth. **48** C3
Hoorn, Îles de is Wallis and Futuna Is see **Futuna Islands**
Hoorn Islands Wallis and Futuna Is see **Futuna Islands**
Hoosick U.S.A. **177** L3
Hoover Dam U.S.A. **183** J5
Hoover Memorial Reservoir U.S.A. **176** C5
Höövör Mongolia **84** D2
Hóp lag. Iceland **44** [inset] B2
Hopa Turkey **107** E2
Hope Canada **166** F5
Hope N.Z. **152** H9
Hope r. N.Z. **153** G10
Hope U.S.A. **179** D5
Hope, Lake salt flat S.A. Australia **146** C2
Hope, Lake salt flat W.A. Australia **151** C7
Hope, Point U.S.A. **164** C3
Hopedale Canada **169** I2
Hopefield S. Africa **132** C10
Hopei prov. China see **Hebei**
Hopelchén Mex. **185** H5
Hope Mountains Canada **169** I2
Hopen i. Svalbard **38** C2
Hopes Advance, Baie b. Canada **169** G1
Hopes Advance, Cap c. Canada **165** M3
Hopes Advance Bay Canada see **Aupaluk**
Hopetoun Vic. Australia **147** D3
Hopetoun W.A. Australia **151** C7
Hopetown S. Africa **132** I6
Hope Vale Aboriginal Reserve Australia **149** E2
Hope Valley U.S.A. **177** N4
Hopewell U.S.A. **177** H8
Hopewell Islands Canada **168** E1
Hopi Indian Reservation res. U.S.A. **183** N6
Hopin Myanmar **78** B2
Hopkins r. Australia **147** D4
Hopkins, Lake salt flat Australia **150** E5
Hopkinsville U.S.A. **174** C4
Hopland U.S.A. **182** A3
Hopong Myanmar **78** B3
Hopseidet Norway **44** N1
Hoquiam U.S.A. **180** B3
Hor Qinghai China **84** D5
Hor Xizang China **89** C6
also spelt Huoer
Horadiz Azer. **107** F3
also spelt Goradiz
Horasan Turkey **107** E2
Horažďovice Czech Rep. **49** K6
Horb am Neckar Germany **48** F7
Hörby Sweden **45** K5
Horcajo de Santiago Spain **55** I5
Horcasitas Mex. **184** D2
Horcón hill Spain **54** G6
Horcones r. Arg. **204** D2
Horda Norway **45** I4
Hordaland county Norway **45** I3
Horezu Romania **58** E3
Horgo Mongolia **84** C1
Horgoš Vojvodina, Srbija Yugo. **58** A2
Hörh Uul mts Mongolia **85** E3
Horia Romania **58** J3
Horicon U.S.A. **172** E7
Horinger China **85** F3
Horiult Mongolia **84** D2
▶**Horizon Deep** sea feature S. Pacific Ocean **220** G7
2nd deepest point in the world (Tonga Trench).
Horki Belarus **43** L7
also spelt Gorki
Horlick Mountains Antarctica **223** Q1
Horlivka Ukr. **41** F6
also spelt Gorlovka
Hormak Iran **101** E4
Hormoz i. Iran **100** D5
Hormoz, Kūh-e mt. Iran **100** C5
Hormozgan prov. Iran **100** D5
Hormūd-e Bāgh Iran **100** C5
Hormūd-e Mīr Khūnd Iran **100** C5
Hormuz, Strait of Iran/Oman **105** G2
Horn Austria **49** M7
Horn r. Canada **167** G2
Horn c. Iceland **44** [inset] B2
also known as Nord Kap
▶**Horn, Cape** Chile **205** D9
Most southerly point of South America. Also known as Hornos, Cabo de.
Hornád r. Slovakia **49** R7
also spelt Hernád (Hungary)
Hornavan l. Sweden **44** L2
Hornbrook U.S.A. **180** B4
Horndal Sweden **45** L3
Horne, Îles de is Wallis and Futuna Is see **Futuna Islands**
Hörnefors Sweden **44** L3
Hornell U.S.A. **176** H3
Hornepayne Canada **168** C3
Hornillos Mex. **184** C3
Hornindal Norway **45** I3
Horn Island U.S.A. **175** B6
Hornkranz Namibia **130** C4
Horn Mountains Canada **166** F2
Hornos, Cabo de c. Chile see **Horn, Cape**
Hornos, Parque Nacional de nat. park Chile **205** D9
Hornoy-le-Bourg France **51** H3
Horn Peak Canada **166** D2
Hornsby Australia **147** F3
Hornsea U.K. **47** L10
Hornslandet pen. Sweden **45** L3
Hornslet Denmark **45** J4
Hornstrandir reg. Iceland **44** [inset] B2
Horodenka Ukr. **41** C6
also spelt Gorodenka
Horodnya Ukr. **41** D6
Horodok Ukr. **41** C6
also spelt Gorodok
Horokanai Japan **90** H2
Horo Shan mts China **88** C3
Horoshiri-dake mt. Japan **90** H3
Horqin Shadi reg. China **85** I3
Horqin Youyi Qianqi China see **Ulanhot**
Horqin Zuoyi Houqi China see **Ganjig**
Horqin Zuoyi Zhongqi China see **Baokang**
Horqueta Para. **201** F5
Horru China **89** E6
Horse Creek r. U.S.A. **180** F4
Horsefly Canada **166** F4
Horseheads U.S.A. **177** I3
Horse Lake U.S.A. **182** D1
Horsens Denmark **45** J5
Horseshoe Bend Australia **148** B5
Horseshoe Reservoir U.S.A. **183** M7
Horsham Australia **147** D4
Horsham U.K. **47** L12
Horten Norway **45** J4
Hortobágyi nat. park Hungary **49** S8
Horton r. Canada **164** G3
Horwood Lake Canada **168** D3
Ho Sai Hu l. China **84** B5
Hosa'ina Eth. **128** C3
Hosdurga India **94** C3
Hose, Pegunungan mts Sarawak Malaysia **77** F2
Hosenofu well Libya **120** D4
Ḥoseynābād Iran **100** A3
Ḥoseynīyeh Iran **100** B4
Hoshab Pak. **101** E5
Hoshangabad India **96** C5
Hoshiarpur India **96** B3
Hôsh'îsa Egypt **108** B7
Höshööt Arhangay Mongolia **84** D1
Höshööt Bayan-Ölgiy Mongolia **84** A1
Hoskins P.N.G. **145** E2
Hoşköy Turkey **58** I8
Hospet India **94** C3
Hosséré Vokre mt. Cameroon **125** I4
Hosszúpályi Hungary **49** S8
Hoste, Isla i. Chile **205** C9
Hosur India **94** C3
Hotahudo East Timor see **Hatohud**
Hotan China **89** C4
formerly spelt Khotan
Hotan He watercourse China **88** C3
Hotazel S. Africa **132** G4
Hot Creek r. U.S.A. **183** H3
Hot Creek Range mts U.S.A. **183** H3
Hotham r. Australia **151** B7
Hotham, Cape Australia **148** A2
Hoting Sweden **44** L2
Hot Springs AR U.S.A. **179** D5
Hot Springs U.S.A. see **Truth or Consequences**
Hot Springs SD U.S.A. **178** B3
Hot Sulphur Springs U.S.A. **180** F4
Hottah Lake Canada **167** G1
Hottentots-Holland Nature Reserve S. Africa **132** C10
Hottentots Point Namibia **130** B5
Houaïlu New Caledonia **145** F4
Houdan France **50** H4
Houffalize Belgium **51** L2
Hougang Sing. **76** [inset]
Houghton MI U.S.A. **172** E3
Houghton NY U.S.A. **176** G3
Houghton Lake U.S.A. **173** I6
Houghton Lake l. U.S.A. **173** I6
Houghton le Spring U.K. **47** K9
Houie Moc, Phou mt. Laos **78** C3
Houlton U.S.A. **174** H2
Houma China **85** F5
Houma U.S.A. **175** B6
Houmen China **87** E4
Houmt Souk Tunisia **123** H2
Houndé Burkina **124** E4
Hourtin et de Carcans, Étang d' l. France **50** E7
Housatonic U.S.A. **177** L3
Housatonic r. U.S.A. **177** L4
House Range mts U.S.A. **183** K2
Housesteads tourist site U.K. **47** J8
historically known as Vercovicium
Houston Canada **166** E4
Houston MN U.S.A. **172** B7
Houston MO U.S.A. **174** B4
Houston MS U.S.A. **175** B5
Houston TX U.S.A. **179** D6
Hout Bay S. Africa **132** C11
Houtkraal S. Africa **132** I7
Houtman Abrolhos is Australia **151** A6
Houtskär Fin. **42** C1
Houwater S. Africa **132** H7
Houxia China **88** D3
Houzhai China see **Nan'ao**
Hov Denmark **45** J5
Hov Norway **45** J3
Hova Sweden **45** K4
Hovd Hovd Mongolia **84** A2
also known as Jargalant
Hovd Övörhangay Mongolia **84** D2
Hovd prov. Mongolia **84** B2
Hovden park Norway **45** I4
Hovd Gol r. Mongolia **84** B1
Hoveyzeh Iran **107** G5
Hovland U.S.A. **172** D3
Hovmantorp Sweden **45** K4
Hövsgöl Mongolia **85** F3
Hövsgöl prov. Mongolia **84** D1
Hövsgöl Nuur l. Mongolia **84** D1
Hövüün Mongolia **84** D3
Howa, Ouadi watercourse Chad/Sudan **120** D6
Howakil Bay Eritrea **104** C5
Howakil Island Eritrea **104** C5
Howar, Wadi watercourse Sudan **120** E5
Howard Australia **149** G5
Howard KS U.S.A. **178** C4
Howard SD U.S.A. **178** C2
Howard WI U.S.A. **172** E6
Howard City U.S.A. **172** H7
Howard Island Australia **148** B2
Howard Springs Australia **148** A2
Howden U.K. **47** L10
Howe, Cape Australia **147** F4
Howe, Mount Antarctica **223** O1
Howell U.S.A. **173** J8
Howes U.S.A. **180** G3
Howick S. Africa **133** O6
Howitt, Lake salt flat Australia **146** C1
Howland U.S.A. **174** G2
▶**Howland Island** N. Pacific Ocean **145** H1
United States Unincorporated Territory.
oceania [countries] ▶ 138–139
Howlong Australia **147** E3
Howrah India see **Haora**
Ḥowz well Iran **100** D3
Ḥowz-e Panj Iran **100** D4
Ḥowz-e Panj waterhole Iran **100** C3
Ḥowz-i-Khan well Iran **100** D3
Howz i-Mian i-Tak Iran **100** C3
Hoxie U.S.A. **178** B4
Höxter Germany **48** G4
Hoxtolgay China **88** D2
Hoxud China **88** D3
Hoy i. U.K. **46** I5
Høyanger Norway **45** I3
Hoyerswerda Germany **49** L4
Høylandet Norway **44** K2
Hoyle Canada **173** L2
Höytiäinen l. Fin. **44** O3
Hoyt Peak U.S.A. **183** M1
Hozat Turkey **107** D3
Hozha Belarus **42** E8
Hpa-an Myanmar see **Pa-an**
Hradec Králové Czech Rep. **49** M5
Hradiště hill Czech Rep. **49** K5
Hradzyanka Belarus **43** J8
Hrasnica Bos.-Herz. **56** K5
Hraun Iceland **44** [inset] B2
Hraun slope Iceland **44** [inset] D2
Hrawzhyshki Belarus **42** G7
Hrazdan Armenia **107** F2
also spelt Razdan; formerly known as Akhta
Hrazený hill Czech Rep. **49** L5
Hrebinka Ukr. **41** E6
also spelt Grebyonka; formerly known as Grebenkovskiy
Hrem"yach Ukr. **43** O9
Hristós Greece see **Christos**
Hrodna Belarus **42** E8
also known as Gardinas; also spelt Grodno
Hrodna Oblast admin. div. Belarus see **Hrodzyenskaya Voblasts'**
Hrodzyenskaya Voblasts' admin. div. Belarus **42** G8
English form Hrodna Oblast or Grodno Oblast; also known as Grodnenskaya Oblast'
Hron r. Slovakia **49** P8
Hrvatska country Europe see **Croatia**
Hrvatska Kostajnica Croatia **56** I3
Hsenwi Myanmar **78** B3
Hsiang Chang i. Hong Kong China see **Hong Kong Island**
Hsiang Kang Hong Kong China see **Hong Kong**
Hsi-hseng Myanmar **78** B3
Hsin, Nam r. Myanmar **78** B3
Hsin-chia-p'o country Asia see **Singapore**
Hsin-chia-p'o Sing. see **Singapore**
Hsinchu Taiwan **87** G3
also spelt Xinzhu
Hsinking China see **Changchun**
Hsinying Taiwan **87** G4
also spelt Xinying
Hsipaw Myanmar **78** B3
Hsi-sha Ch'un-tao is S. China Sea see **Paracel Islands**
Hsiyüp'ing Yü i. Taiwan **87** F4
Hsüeh Shan mt. Taiwan **87** G3
Hua'an China **87** F3
also known as Huafeng
Huab watercourse Namibia **130** B4
Huacaibamba Peru **200** A2
Huacaraje Bol. **201** E3
Huacaya Bol. **201** E5
Huacheng China **87** E3
Huachi Bol. **201** E3
Huachi China **85** F4
also known as Rouyuan; formerly known as Rouyuanchengzi
Huachinera Mex. **184** C2
Huacho Peru **200** A2
Huachón Peru **200** B2
Huachuan China **82** C3
also known as Yuelai
Huacrachuco Peru **200** A2
Huacullani Peru **200** C4
Huade China **85** G3
Huadian China **82** B4
Huadu China **87** E4
formerly known as Huaxian or Xinhua
Huafeng China see **Hua'an**
Huahaizi China **84** B4
Hua Hin Thai. **79** B5
Huai'an Hebei China **85** G3
also known as Chaigoubu
Huai'an Jiangsu China **87** F1
Huaibei China **87** F1
Huaibin China **87** E1
formerly known as Wulongji
Huaicheng China see **Huaiji**
Huaide China see **Gongzhuling**
Huaidian China see **Shenqiu**
Huai Had National Park Thai. **78** D4
Huai He r. China **87** F1
Huaihua China **87** D3
also known as Yushuwan
Huaiji China **87** E4
also known as Huaicheng
Huai-kha-khaeng Wildlife Reserve nature res. Thai. **79** B5
Huailai China **85** G3
also known as Shacheng
Huai Luang r. Thai. **78** C4
Huainan China **87** F1
Huaining China **87** F2
also known as Shipai
Huairen China **85** G4
Huairou China **85** H3
Huai Samran r. Thai. **79** D5
Huaiyang China **87** E1
Huaiyin Jiangsu China **87** F1
also known as Wangying
Huaiyin Jiangsu China **87** F1
formerly known as Qingjiang
Huaiyuan Anhui China **87** F1
Huaiyuan Guangxi China **87** D3
Huajialing China **84** E5
Huajuápan de León Mex. **185** F5
Huaki Indon. **75** C4
Hualahuises Mex. **185** F3
Hualapai Indian Reservation res. U.S.A. **183** K6
Hualapai Peak U.S.A. **183** K6
Hualfín Arg. **204** D2
Hualien Taiwan **87** G3
Hualla Peru **200** B3
Huallaga r. Peru **198** C6
Hualong China **84** D4
also known as Bayan
Huamachuco Peru **200** A1
Huamani Peru **200** B3
Huambo Angola **127** B8
formerly known as Nova Lisboa
Huambo prov. Angola **127** B8
Huams watercourse Namibia **132** B2
Huanan China **82** C3
Huancabamba r. Peru **198** B6
Huancache, Sierra mts Arg. **205** C6
Huancapi Peru **200** B3
Huancavelica Peru **200** B3
Huancavelica dept Peru **200** B3
Huancayo Peru **200** B3
Huancheng China see **Huanxian**
Huangbei China **87** E3
Huangcaoba China see **Xingyi**
Huangchuan China **87** E1
Huanggang China **87** E2
also known as Huangzhou
Huang He r. China see **Yellow River**
Huanghe Kou r. mouth China **85** H4
Huanghua China **85** H4
Huangjiajian China **87** G1
Huangling China **85** F5
also known as Qiaoshan
Huangliu China **87** D5
Huanglong China **85** F5
also known as Shipu
Huanglongsi China see **Kaifeng**
Huangmao Jian mt. China **87** F3
Huangmei China **87** E2
Huangnihe China **82** B4
Huangpi China **87** E2
Huangping China **87** C3
also known as Xinzhou
Huangqi China **87** F3
Huangshan China **87** F2
also known as Tunxi
Huang Shan mts China **87** F2
Huangshengguan China **86** B1
Huangshi China **87** E2
Huang Shui r. China **84** D4
Huangtu Gaoyuan plat. China **85** E4
Huangxian China **85** I4
Huangyan China **87** G2
Huangyangzhen China **84** D4
Huangyuan China **84** D4
Huangzhong China **84** D4
also known as Lushar
Huangzhou China see **Huanggang**
Huaning China **86** B3
also known as Ningzhou
Huanjiang China **87** D3
also known as Si'en
Huan Jiang r. China **85** E4
Huanren China **82** B4
Huanshan China see **Yuhuan**
Huanta Peru **200** B3
Huantai China **85** H4
also known as Suozhen
Huánuco Peru **200** A2
Huánuco dept Peru **200** A2
Huanuhuanu Peru **200** B3
Huanuni Bol. **200** D4
Huanxian China **85** E4
also known as Huancheng
Huaping China **86** B3
also known as Zhongxin
Huap'ing Yü i. Taiwan **87** G3
Huar Bol. **200** D4
Huaral Peru **200** A2
Huaráz Peru **200** A2
Huari Peru **200** A2
Huariaca Peru **200** A2
Huarmey Peru **200** A2
Huarochiri Peru **200** A3
Huaron Peru **200** A2
Huarong China **87** E2
Huasaga r. Peru **198** B5
Huascarán, Parque Nacional nat. park Peru **200** A2
Huasco Chile **204** C3
Hua Shan mt. China **87** D1
Huashaoying China **85** G3
Huashixia China **84** C5
also known as Zogainrawar
Huashugou China see **Jingtieshan**
Huatabampo Mex. **184** C3
Huatusco Mex. **185** F5
Huauchinango Mex. **185** F4
Huauru, Islas de is Peru **200** A2
Huautla Mex. **185** F5
Huaxian China see **Huadu**
Huaxian Henan China **85** G5
also known as Daokou
Huaxian Shaanxi China **87** D1
Huayacocotla Mex. **185** F4
Huayang China see **Jixi**
Huaylas Peru **200** A2
Huayuan China see **Xiaochang**
Huayuan China **87** D2
Huazangsi China see **Tianzhu**
Huazhaizi China **84** D4
Huazhou China **87** D4
Hubbard, Mount Canada/U.S.A. **166** B2
Hubbard, Pointe pt Canada **169** H1
Hubbard Lake U.S.A. **173** J6
Hubbart Point Canada **167** M3
Hubei prov. China **87** E2
English form Hupeh
Hubli India **94** B3
Hucal Arg. **204** D5
Huch'ang N. Korea **82** B4
Hückelhoven Germany **48** D4
Huḍb Ḥumar mts Saudi Arabia **104** B2
Huddersfield U.K. **47** K10
Huder China **85** I1
Hudiksvall Sweden **45** L3
Hudson MA U.S.A. **177** N3
Hudson MD U.S.A. **177** I7
Hudson MI U.S.A. **173** I9
Hudson NH U.S.A. **177** N3
Hudson NY U.S.A. **177** L3
Hudson r. U.S.A. **177** L5
Hudson, Baie d' sea Canada see **Hudson Bay**
Hudson, Cerro mt. Chile **205** B7
Hudson, Détroit d' strait Canada see **Hudson Strait**
Hudson Bay Canada **167** K4
Hudson Bay sea Canada **165** K4
also known as Hudson, Baie d'
Hudson Falls U.S.A. **177** L2
Hudson Island Tuvalu see **Nanumanga**
Hudson Land reg. Greenland **165** Q2
Hudson's Hope Canada **166** F3
Hudson Strait Canada **165** L3
also known as Hudson, Détroit d'
Huê Vietnam **78** D4
Huebra r. Spain **54** E4
Huechucuicui, Punta pt Chile **205** B6
Huedin Romania **58** E2
Huehuetán Mex. **185** G6
Huehuetenango Guat. **185** H6
Huehueto, Cerro mt. Mex. **184** D3
Huejuqilla Mex. **184** E4
Huejutla Mex. **185** F4
Huelgoat France **50** C4
Huelma Spain **55** H7
Huelva Spain **54** E7
Huelva r. Spain **54** E7
Huentelauquén Chile **204** C3
Huépac Mex. **184** C2
Huércal-Overa Spain **55** J7
Huerfano r. U.S.A. **181** F5
Huertecillas Mex. **185** E3
Huerva r. Spain **55** K3
Huesca Spain **55** K2
Huéscar Spain **55** I7
Huétamo Mex. **185** E5
Huete Spain **55** I4
Hueytown U.S.A. **175** C5
Huftarøy i. Norway **46** R3
Hugeilig l. Sudan **126** E2
Hugh watercourse Australia **148** B5
Hughenden Australia **149** E4
Hughes Australia **146** A2
Hughes r. Canada **167** K3
Hughes Bay Antarctica **222** T2
Hughesville MD U.S.A. **177** I7
Hughesville PA U.S.A. **177** I4
Hughson U.S.A. **182** D4
Hugli r. mouth India **97** E5
also spelt Hooghly
Hugli-Chunchura India **97** F5
Hugo CO U.S.A. **178** B4
Hugo OK U.S.A. **179** D5
Hugoton U.S.A. **178** B4
Huhehot China see **Hohhot**
Huhhot China see **Hohhot**
Huhucunya Venez. **199** E3
Huhudi S. Africa **133** I3
Huhus Fin. **44** O3
Hui'an China **87** F3
also known as Luocheng
Hui'anpu China **85** E4
Huiarau Range mts N.Z. **152** K6
Huib-Hoch Plateau Namibia **130** C5
Huichang China **87** E3
also known as Xiangjiang
Huichapán Mex. **185** F4
Huicheng China see **Shexian**
Huicheng China see **Huilai**
Huich'ŏn N. Korea **83** B4
Huidong Guangdong China **87** E4
also known as Pingshan
Huidong Sichuan China **86** B3
Huifa r. China **82** B4
Huihe China **85** H1
Huiji r. China **87** E1
Huíla prov. Angola **127** B8
Huila dept Col. **198** C4
Huila, Nevado de vol. Col. **198** C4
Huilai China **87** F4
also known as Huicheng
Huíla Plateau Angola **127** B8
Huili China **86** B3
Huilongzhen China see **Qidong**
Huimanguillo Mex. **185** G5
Huimin China **85** H4
Huinahuaca Arg. **200** D5
Huiñaimarca, Lago de l. Bol./Peru **200** C4
Huinan China **82** B4
also known as Chaoyang
Huinan China see **Nanhui**
Huinca Renancó Arg. **204** D4
Huining China **84** E5
also known as Huishi
Huishi China see **Huining**
Huishui China **86** C3
also known as Heping
Huisne r. France **50** G4
Huiten Nur l. China **89** E5
Huitong China **87** D3
also known as Lincheng
Huittinen Fin. **45** M3
Huixian Gansu China **86** C1
Huixian Henan China **85** G5
Huixtla Mex. **185** G6
Huiyang China see **Huizhou**
Huize China **86** B3
also known as Zhongping
Huizhou China **87** E4
also known as Huiyang
Hujirt Arhangay Mongolia **84** D1
Hujirt Övörhangay Mongolia **84** D2
Hujirt Töv Mongolia **84** E2
Hukanui N.Z. **152** J8
Hukawng Valley Myanmar **78** B2
Hukou China **87** F2
also known as Shuangzhong
Hukuntsi Botswana **130** D4
Hulan China **82** B3
Hulan r. China **82** B3
Hulan Ergi China **85** I2
Ḥulayfah Saudi Arabia **104** C2
Ḥulayḥilah well Syria **109** J3
Hulbert U.S.A. **173** H4
Hulbert Lake U.S.A. **173** H4
Hulen U.S.A. **176** B9
Huliao China see **Dabu**
Hulin China **82** D3
Hull Canada **168** F4
Hull U.K. see **Kingston upon Hull**
Hull U.S.A. **177** O3
Hull Island Kiribati see **Orona**
Hullo Estonia **42** E3
Hultsfred Sweden **45** K4
Hulu r. China **85** F5
Huludao China **85** I3
Hulun China see **Hailar**
Hulun Nur l. China **85** H1
Ḥulwān Egypt see **Helwân**
Hulyaypole Ukr. **41** F7
Huma China **82** B2
Huma r. China **82** B2
Humacao Puerto Rico **187** G3
Humaita Bol. **200** D2
Humaitá Brazil **201** E1
Humaitá Para. **201** F6
Humansdorp S. Africa **133** I11
Humay Peru **200** B3
Humaym well U.A.E. **105** F3
Humayyān, Jabal hill Saudi Arabia **104** D2
Humbe Angola **127** B9
Humbe, Serra do mts Angola **127** B8
Humber, Mouth of the U.K. **47** M10
Humberside airport U.K. **47** L10
Humberstone Chile **200** C5
Humberto de Campos Brazil **202** D2
Humboldt Canada **167** J4
Humboldt AZ U.S.A. **183** L7
Humboldt NE U.S.A. **178** D3
Humboldt NV U.S.A. **182** F1
Humboldt TN U.S.A. **174** B5
Humboldt r. U.S.A. **182** F1
Humboldt, Mont mt. New Caledonia **145** F4
Humboldt Bay U.S.A. **180** A4
Humboldt Gletscher glacier Greenland see **Sermersuaq**
Humboldt Lake U.S.A. **182** F1
Humboldt Mountain mts N.Z. **153** C12
Humboldt Range mts U.S.A. **182** F1
Humbolt Salt Marsh U.S.A. **182** G2
Hume r. Canada **166** D1
Humeburn Australia **147** E1
Humeda plain Arg. **204** E5
Hu Men sea chan. China **87** E4
Humenné Slovakia **49** S7
Hume Reservoir Australia **147** E3
Humina reg. Bos.-Herz. **56** J5
Humka, Gora hill Croatia **56** I3
Humos, Cabo c. Chile **204** B4
Humpata Angola **127** B8
Humphrey Island atoll Cook Is see **Manihiki**
Humphreys, Mount U.S.A. **182** F4
Humphreys Peak U.S.A. **183** M6
Humpolec Czech Rep. **49** M6
Humppila Fin. **45** M3
Humpty Doo Australia **148** A2

Hun r. China 85 I3
Hūn Libya 120 B2
Húnaflói b. Iceland 44 [inset] B2
Hunan prov. China 87 D3
Hunchun China 82 C4
Hunchun r. China 82 C4
Hundorp Norway 45 J3
Hundred U.S.A. 176 E6
Hunedoara Romania 58 D3
Hünfeld Germany 48 G5
Hungary country Europe 49 P8
known as Magyar Köztársaság in Hungarian
europe [countries] 32–35
Hungerford Australia 147 E2
Hungerford U.K. 47 K12
Hung Fa Leng hill Hong Kong China see Robin's Nest
Hüngiy Gol r. Mongolia 84 B1
Hüngnam N. Korea 83 B5
Hungry Horse Reservoir U.S.A. 180 D2
Hung Shui Kiu Hong Kong China 87 [inset]
Hungund India 94 C2
Hunissout Pan salt pan S. Africa 132 D7
Hunjiang China see Baishan
Hun Jiang r. China 82 B4
Hunnebostrand Sweden 45 J4
Huns Mountains Namibia 132 B4
Hunstanton U.K. 47 M11
Hunsur India 94 C3
Hunta Canada 173 L1
Hunte r. Germany 48 F2
Hunter r. Australia 147 F3
Hunter N.Z. 153 F12
Hunter r. N.Z. 153 D12
Hunterganj India 97 E4
Hunter Island Australia 147 E5
Hunter Island Canada 166 D5
Hunter Island S. Pacific Ocean 145 G4
Hunter Islands Australia 147 E5
Hunter Mountains N.Z. 153 B13
Hunter's Bay Myanmar 78 A4
Huntingdon U.K. 47 L11
Huntingdon PA U.S.A. 176 H5
Huntingdon TN U.S.A. 174 B4
Huntington IN U.S.A. 174 C3
Huntington UT U.S.A. 183 N2
Huntington WV U.S.A. 176 C7
Huntington Beach U.S.A. 182 F8
Huntington Creek r. U.S.A. 183 I1
Huntly N.Z. 152 J5
Huntly U.K. 46 J6
Hunt Mountain U.S.A. 180 F3
Hunt Peninsula Australia 146 C2
Huntsville Canada 168 E4
Huntsville AL U.S.A. 174 C5
Huntsville AR U.S.A. 179 D4
Huntsville MO U.S.A. 178 D4
Huntsville TX U.S.A. 179 D6
Hunucmá Mex. 185 H4
Hunyani r. Moz./Zimbabwe see Manyame
Hunyuan China 85 G4
Hunza Jammu and Kashmir 96 B1
Hunza reg. Jammu and Kashmir 96 B1
Hunza r. Pak. 101 H3
Hunze r. Neth. 48 D2
Huocheng China 88 C2
also known as Shuiding
Huoer China see Hor
Huojia China 85 G5
Huolin r. China 85 J2
Huolongmen China 82 B2
Huolu China see Luquan
Huong Thuy Vietnam 78 D4
Huon Peninsula P.N.G. 73 K8
Huonville Australia 147 E5
Huoqiu China 87 F1
Huoshan China 87 F2
Huo Shan mt. China 87 F2
Huoshao Tao i. Taiwan see Lü Tao
Huotsaus waterhole Namibia 130 B4
Huoxian China see Huozhou
Huozhou China 85 F4
formerly known as Huoxian
Hupeh prov. China see Hubei
Hupnik r. Turkey 109 H1
Ḥūr Iran 100 D4
Hurault, Lac l. Canada 169 G2
Ḥuraymilā Saudi Arabia 105 D2
Huraysān reg. Saudi Arabia 105 D3
Hurbanovo Slovakia 49 P8
Hurd, Cape Canada 168 D4
Hurd Island Kiribati see Arorae
Hurdiyo Somalia 128 F2
Hure China 85 I3
also known as Hure Qi
Hüremt Mongolia 84 D1
Hürent Mongolia 84 D2
Hure Qi China see Hure
Hurghada Egypt 121 G3
also known as Al Ghardaqah
Huri mt. Kenya 128 C4
Huriel France 51 I6
Hurkett Canada 172 E2
Hurley U.S.A. 177 K4
Hurlock U.S.A. 177 J7
Huron CA U.S.A. 182 D5
Huron SD U.S.A. 178 C2
Huron, Lake Canada/U.S.A. 173 J5
2nd largest lake in North America and 4th in the world.
northamerica [landscapes] 156–157
Huron Bay U.S.A. 172 E4
Huron Beach U.S.A. 173 I5
Huronian Canada 172 C2
Huron Mountains hills U.S.A. 172 F4
Hurricane U.S.A. 183 K4
Hurricane Flats sea feature Bahamas 175 E8
Hurtado Chile 204 C3
Hurung, Gunung mt. Indon. 77 F2
Hurunui r. N.Z. 153 H10
Hurup Denmark 45 J4
Husain Nika Pak. 101 G4
Húsavík Norðurland eystra Iceland 44 [inset] C2
Húsavík Vestfirðir Iceland 44 [inset] B2
Husayn reg. Yemen 105 D4
Huseyinabat Turkey see Alaca
Huseyinli Turkey see Kızılırmak
Hushan China see Wuyi
Hushan China see Cixi
Husheib Sudan 121 G6
Huşi Romania 58 J2
Huskvarna Sweden 45 K4
Husn Jordan see Al Ḥiṣn
Ḥusn Āl 'Abr Yemen 105 D4
Husnes Norway 45 I4
Husøy i. Norway 46 Q2
Hussainabad India 97 E4
Hustopeče Czech Rep. 49 N7
Husum Germany 48 G1
Husum Sweden 44 L3
Husvik S. Georgia 205 [inset]
Hutag Mongolia 84 D1
Hūtak Iran 100 D4
Hutanopan Indon. 76 B2
Hutaym, Ḥarrat lava field Saudi Arabia 104 C2
Hutchinson S. Africa 132 H8
Hutchinson KS U.S.A. 178 C4
Hutchinson MN U.S.A. 178 D2
Hutch Mountain U.S.A. 183 M7
Ḥūth Yemen 104 C4
Hutou China 82 D3
Huttah Kulkyne National Park Australia 147 D3
Hutton, Mount hill Australia 149 F5
Hutton Range hills Australia 151 C5
Hutubi China 88 D2
Hutubi He r. China 88 D2
Hutuo r. China 85 H4
Hutup watercourse Namibia 132 B2
Huu Đô Vietnam 78 D3
Huvadhu Atoll Maldives 93 D10
Hūvār Iran 101 E5
Hüvek Turkey see Bozova
Hüvīān, Kūh-e mts Iran 101 D5
Huwār i. The Gulf 105 E2
also spelt Hawar
Ḥuwaymī, Sha'īb al watercourse Iraq 109 P7
Huwaytat reg. Saudi Arabia 107 D5
Huxi China 87 E3
Huxian China 87 D1
also known as Ganting
Huxley, Mount hill Australia 150 D3
Huxley, Mount N.Z. 153 D12
Huy Belgium 51 L2
Hüzgān Iran 100 B4
Huzhen China 87 G2
Huzhou China 87 G2
formerly known as Wuxing
Huzhu China 84 D4
also known as Weiyuan
Huzurnagar India 94 C2
Hvalnes Iceland 44 [inset] D2
Hvammsfjörður inlet Iceland 44 [inset] B2
Hvannadalshnúkur vol. Iceland 44 [inset] C2
Hvar Croatia 56 I5
Hvar i. Croatia 56 I5
Hvardiys'ke Ukr. 41 E7
Hvarski Kanal sea chan. Croatia 56 I5
Hveragerði Iceland 44 [inset] B2
Hvide Sande Denmark 45 J4
Hvíta r. Iceland 44 [inset] B3
Hvítárvatn l. Iceland 44 [inset] C2
Hwadae N. Korea 83 C4
Hwange Zimbabwe 131 E3
formerly spelt Wankie
Hwange National Park Zimbabwe 131 E3
Hwang Ho r. China see Yellow River
Hwangju N. Korea 83 B5
Hwayang S. Korea 91 A7
Hwedza Zimbabwe 131 F3
Hwlffordd U.K. see Haverfordwest
Hyannis MA U.S.A. 177 O4
Hyannis NE U.S.A. 178 B3
Hyargas Nuur salt l. Mongolia 84 B1
Hyco Lake U.S.A. 176 F9
Hyde N.Z. 153 E13
Hyden Australia 151 B7
Hyden U.S.A. 176 B8
Hyderabad India 94 C2
Hyderabad Pak. 101 G5
Hydra i. Greece see Ydra
Hyères France 51 M9
Hyères, Îles d' is France 51 M10
Hyermanavichy Belarus 42 I6
Hyesan N. Korea 82 C4
Hyland r. Canada 166 D3
Hyland, Mount Australia 147 G2
Hyland Bay Australia 148 A2
Hyland Post Canada 166 D3
Hyllekrog i. Denmark 48 I1
Hyllestad Norway 45 I3
Hyltebruk Sweden 45 K4
Hyndman U.S.A. 176 G6
Hyndman Peak U.S.A. 180 D4
Hyōgo pref. Japan 91 D7
Hyōno-sen mt. Japan 91 D7
Hyrcania Iran see Gorgān
Hyrra Banda Cent. Afr. Rep. see Ira Banda
Hyrynsalmi Fin. 44 O2
Hysham U.S.A. 180 F3
Hythe Canada 166 G4
Hyūga Japan 91 B8
Hyvinkää Fin. 45 N3

↓ I

Ia A Dun r. Vietnam 79 E5
Iacanga Brazil 206 D8
Iaciara Brazil 202 C5
Iaco r. Brazil 200 C2
Iacobeni Romania 58 F2
Iacobeni Romania 58 G1
Iacri Brazil 206 C8
Iaçu Brazil 202 D5
Iadera Croatia see Zadar
Iaeger U.S.A. 176 D8
Iakora Madag. 131 [inset] J4
Ialomiţa r. Romania 58 I4
Ialomiţei, Balta marsh Romania 58 I4
Ialoveni Moldova 58 J2
formerly known as Kutuzov; formerly spelt Yaloven'
Ialpug r. Moldova 58 J3
formerly spelt Yalpukh
Ianca Romania 58 I3
Ian Calder Lake Canada 167 L1
Iancu Jianu Romania 58 F4
Iapu Brazil 207 K6
Iara r. Romania 58 E2
Iarauarune, Serra mts Brazil 199 F4
Iargara Moldova 58 J2
formerly spelt Yargara
Iaşi Romania 58 I1
also known as Jassy; also spelt Yaş
Iasmos Greece 58 G7
Iba Phil. 74 A3
Ibadan Nigeria 125 F5
Ibagué Col. 198 C3
Ibaiti Brazil 206 C10
Ibanda Uganda 128 A5
Ibăneşti Romania 58 F2
Ibañeta, Puerto de pass Spain 55 J1
Ibanga Kasai Occidental Dem. Rep. Congo 127 D6
Ibanga Sud-Kivu Dem. Rep. Congo 126 E5
Ibapah U.S.A. 183 K1
Ibar r. Yugo. 58 B5
Ibara Japan 91 C7
Ibaraki pref. Japan 91 G6
Ibarra Ecuador 198 B4
Ibarreta Arg. 204 F2
Ibaté Brazil 206 F8
Ibb Yemen 104 D5
Ibb governorate Yemen 104 D5
Ibba watercourse Sudan 126 F3
Ibbenbüren Germany 48 E3
Ibdeqqene watercourse Mali 125 F2
Iberá, Esteros del marsh Arg. 204 F3
Iberá, Lago l. Arg. 204 F3
Iberia Loreto Peru 198 C6
Iberia Madre de Dios Peru 200 C2
Iberian Peninsula Europe 54
Consists of Portugal, Spain and Gibraltar.
Ibertioga Brazil 207 J8
Iberville, Lac d' l. Canada 169 F2
also known as Upper Seal Lake
Ibestad Norway 44 L1
Ibeto Nigeria 125 G4
Ibi Indon. 76 B1
Ibi Nigeria 125 H4
Ibi Spain 55 K6
Ibiá Brazil 206 G6
Ibiapaba, Serra da hills Brazil 202 D2
Ibias r. Spain 54 E1
Ibicaraí Brazil 202 E5
Ibicuí Bahia Brazil 207 N1
Ibicuí Rio Grande do Sul Brazil 204 F3
Ibicuí r. Brazil 203 A9
Ibigawa Japan 91 E7
Ibimirim Brazil 202 E4
Ibina r. Dem. Rep. Congo 126 F4
Ibiporã Brazil 206 B10
Ibirá Brazil 206 D8
Ibiraçu Brazil 207 M6
Ibiranhém Brazil 207 M4
Ibitiara Brazil 202 D5
Ibitinga Brazil 206 E8
Ibiúna Brazil 206 F10
Ibiza Spain 55 M6
also spelt Eivissa
Ibiza i. Spain 55 M5
also spelt Eivissa; formerly spelt Iviza; historically known as Ebusus
Iblei, Monti mts Sicilia Italy 57 G11
İblis Burnu pt Turkey 59 J12
Ibn Buşayyiş well Saudi Arabia 105 D2
Ibn Hādī Saudi Arabia 104 C4
Ibotirama Brazil 202 D5
Iboundji, Mont hill Gabon 126 A5
Ibra, Wadi watercourse Sudan 126 E2
Ibrāt, Wādī watercourse Iraq 109 N2
Ibresi Rus. Fed. 40 H5
'Ibrī Oman 105 G3
Ibu Indon. 75 C2
Ibuhos i. Phil. 74 B1
Ibusuki Japan 91 B9
Içá r. Brazil 198 E5
Ica Peru 200 B3
Ica dept Peru 200 B3
Icabarú Venez. 199 F3
Icaiché Mex. 185 H5
Içana Brazil 199 E4
Içana r. Brazil 198 E4
Icaraí Brazil 202 E2
Icaria i. Greece see Ikaria
Icatu Brazil 202 C2
Iceberg Canyon gorge U.S.A. 183 J5
İçel Turkey 106 C3
also known as Mersin
İçel prov. Turkey 108 E1
Iceland country Europe 44 [inset] B2
2nd largest island in Europe. Known as Ísland in Icelandic.
europe [landscapes] 30–31
europe [countries] 32–35
europe [environments] 36–37
Icem Brazil 206 D7
Ichak India 97 E4
Ichalkaranji India 94 B2
Ichchapuram India 95 E2
Ichihara Japan 91 G7
Ichilo r. Bol. 201 D4
Ichinoseki Japan 90 G5
Ichinskiy, Vulkan vol. Rus. Fed. 39 P4
Ichkeria aut. rep. Rus. Fed. see Chechenskaya Respublika
Ichkeul National Park Tunisia 57 B11
Ichnya Ukr. 41 E6
Ich'ŏn N. Korea 83 B5
Ich'ŏn S. Korea 83 B5
Ichuña Peru 200 C4
İçikler Turkey 59 J10
İçmeler Turkey 59 J12
Icó Brazil 202 E3
Iconha Brazil 207 M7
Iconium Turkey see Konya
Icosium Alg. see Algiers
Iculisma France see Angoulême
Icy Bay U.S.A. 166 A3
Icy Strait U.S.A. 166 C3
Ida, Mount N.Z. 153 E12
Idabdaba well Niger 125 H2
Idabel U.S.A. 179 D5
Idaga Hamus Eth. 104 B5
Ida Grove U.S.A. 178 D3
Idah Nigeria 125 G5
Idaho state U.S.A. 180 D3
Idaho City U.S.A. 180 D4
Idaho Falls U.S.A. 180 D4
Idalia National Park Australia 149 E5
Idanha-a-Nova Port. 54 D5
Idar India 96 B5
Idar-Oberstein Germany 48 E6
Ida Valley N.Z. 153 D13
Idday well Niger 125 H3
Iddan Somalia 128 F3
Idd el Asoda well Sudan 121 F6
Idd el Chanam Sudan 126 E2
Idd esh Shurak well Sudan 121 F5
Idefjorden inlet Norway/Sweden 45 J4
Ider Mongolia 84 C1
Ideriyn Gol r. Mongolia 84 D1
Idfina Egypt 108 B6
Idfu Egypt 121 G3
also spelt Edfu; historically known as Apollinopolis Magna
Idhān Awbārī des. Libya 120 A3
Idhān Murzūq des. Libya 120 B3
Idhra i. Greece see Ydra
Ídhras, Kólpos sea chan. Greece see Ydras, Kolpos
Idi Amin Dada, Lake Dem. Rep. Congo/Uganda see Edward, Lake
Idice r. Italy 56 D4
Idiofa Dem. Rep. Congo 126 C6
Idku Egypt 121 F2
Idlib Syria 109 H2
Idlib governorate Syria 109 H2
Idra i. Greece see Ydra
Idracowra Australia 148 B5
Idre Sweden 45 K3
Idrija Slovenia 56 G2
Idrijca r. Slovenia 56 F2
Idritsa Rus. Fed. 43 J5
Idstein Germany 48 F5
Idugala Tanz. 129 B6
Idukki India 94 C4
Idutywa S. Africa 133 M9
Idyllwild U.S.A. 183 H8
Idzhevan Armenia see Ijevan
Iecava Latvia 42 F5
Iecava r. Latvia 42 E5
Iepê Brazil 206 B9
Ieper Belgium 51 I2
also spelt Ypres
Ier r. Romania 49 T8
Ierapetra Greece 59 G13
Ierissou, Kolpos b. Greece 59 E8
Ifakara Tanz. 129 C7
'Ifāl, Wādī watercourse Saudi Arabia 104 A1
also known as Afal
Ifalik atoll Micronesia 73 J5
also spelt Ifaluk; formerly known as Wilson
Ifaluk atoll Micronesia see Ifalik
Ifanadiana Madag. 131 [inset] J4
Ifanirea Madag. 131 [inset] J4
Ife Nigeria 125 G5
Ifenat Chad 120 C6
Iferouâne Niger 125 H2
Ifetesene mt. Alg. 123 G4
Iffley Australia 149 D3
Ifjord Norway 44 N1
Ifôghas, Adrar des hills Mali 125 F2
also known as Iforas, Adrar des; short form Adrar
Ifon Nigeria 125 G5
Iforas, Adrar des hills Mali see Ifôghas, Adrar des
Ifould Lake salt flat Australia 146 B2
Ifrane Morocco 122 D2
Ifumo Dem. Rep. Congo 126 D5
Ifunda Tanz. 129 B7
Igan Sarawak Malaysia 72 D6
Igan r. Sarawak Malaysia 77 E2
Iganga Uganda 128 B4
Igarapava Brazil 206 F7
Igarapé Açú Brazil 202 C2
Igarapé Grande Brazil 202 C3
Igarapé Miri Brazil 202 B2
Igaratá Brazil 207 G10
Igarité Brazil 202 D4
Igarka Rus. Fed. 39 I3
Igatpuri India 94 B2
Igbeti Nigeria 125 G4
Igboho Nigeria 125 F4
Iğdır Turkey 107 F3
Iggesund Sweden 45 L3
Ighiu Romania 58 E2
Iglesia Arg. 204 C3
Iglesias Sardegna Italy 57 A9
Igli Alg. 123 E3
Iglino Rus. Fed. 40 K5
Igloolik Canada 165 K3
Igluligaarjuk Canada see Chesterfield Inlet
'Igma, Gebel el plat. Egypt 108 E8
Ignace Canada 168 B3
Ignacio Zaragosa Mex. 184 D2
Ignacio Zaragoza Mex. 185 F4
Ignalina Lith. 42 H6
İğneada Turkey 106 A2
İğneada Burnu pt Turkey 106 B2
Igoma Tanz. 129 B6
Igombe r. Tanz. 129 A6
Igorevskaya Rus. Fed. 43 O6
Igoumenitsa Greece 59 B9
Igra Rus. Fed. 40 J4
Igrim Rus. Fed. 38 G3
Iguaçu r. Brazil 203 A8
Iguaçu, Parque Nacional do nat. park Brazil 203 A8
Iguaçu, Saltos do waterfall Arg./Brazil see Iguaçu Falls
Iguaçu Falls Arg./Brazil 204 G2
also known as Iguazú, Cataratas do or Iguaçu, Saltos do
Iguaí Brazil 202 D5
Iguala Mex. 185 F5
Igualada Spain 55 M3
Iguape Brazil 203 C8
Iguaraçu Brazil 206 B10
Iguarapé Brazil 207 I7
Iguatemi Brazil 203 A7
Iguatemi r. Brazil 203 A7
Iguatu Brazil 202 E3
Iguazú, Cataratas do waterfall Arg./Brazil see Iguaçu Falls
Iguazú, Parque Nacional del nat. park Arg. 204 G2
Iguéla Gabon 126 A5
Igueña Spain 54 E2
Iguetti, Sebkhet salt flat Mauritania 122 C4
Igunga Tanz. 129 B6
Iguobazuwa Nigeria 125 G5
Igusule Tanz. 129 B5
Iguvium Italy see Gubbio
Iharaña Madag. 131 [inset] K2
formerly known as Vohémar or Vohimarina
Ihavandhippolhu Atoll Maldives 94 B5
Ihbulag Mongolia 85 E3
Ihhayrhan Mongolia 85 E2
Ihiala Nigeria 125 G5
Ihirène, Oued watercourse Alg. 123 G5
Ihosy Madag. 131 [inset] J4
Ihsuuj Mongolia 85 E1
Ih Tal China 85 I3
Iida Japan 91 E7
Iide-san mt. Japan 90 F6
Iijoki r. Fin. 44 N2
Iisalmi Fin. 44 N3
Iitti Fin. 42 H1
Iiyama Japan 91 F6
Iizuka Japan 91 B8
Ijâfene des. Mauritania 122 C5
Ijara Kenya 128 D5
Ijebu-Ode Nigeria 125 F5
Ijevan Armenia 107 F2
also spelt Idzhevan
IJmuiden Neth. 48 B3
Ijnâouene well Mauritania 124 B2
Ijoubbâne des. Mali 122 D5
IJssel r. Neth. 48 C3
IJsselmeer l. Neth. 48 C3
formerly known as Zuider Zee
Ijuí Brazil 203 A9
Ijuí r. Brazil 203 A8
IJzer r. Belgium 51 I2
also known as Yser (France)
Ikaahuk Canada see Sachs Harbour
Ikaalinen Fin. 45 M3
Ikageleng S. Africa 133 K2
Ikageng S. Africa 133 L3
Ikahavo hill Madag. 131 [inset] J3
Ikalamavony Madag. 131 [inset] J4
Ikamatua N.Z. 153 F10
Ikang Nigeria 125 H5
Ikare Nigeria 125 G5
Ikaria i. Greece 59 H11
English form Icaria
Ikast Denmark 45 J4
Ikawai N.Z. 153 E12
Ikawhenua Range mts N.Z. 152 K6
Ikeda Hokkaidō Japan 90 H3
Ikeda Tokushima Japan 91 C7
Ikeja Nigeria 125 F5
Ikela Dem. Rep. Congo 126 D5
Ikelemba r. Dem. Rep. Congo 126 C4
Ikelenge Zambia 127 E7
Ikengo Dem. Rep. Congo 126 C5
Ikénguе Gabon 126 A5
Ikere Nigeria 125 G5
also spelt Ikerre
Ikerre Nigeria see Ikere
Ikhtiman Bulg. 58 E6
Ikhutseng S. Africa 133 I5
Iki i. Japan 91 A8
Iki-Burul Rus. Fed. 41 H7
Ikimba, Lake Tanz. 128 A5
Ikire Nigeria 125 G5
Iki-suidō sea chan. Japan 91 A8
Ikla Estonia 42 F4
Ikom Nigeria 125 H5
Ikoma Tanz. 128 B5
Ikongo Madag. 131 [inset] J4
formerly known as Fort Carnot
Ikopa r. Madag. 131 [inset] J3
Ikorodu Nigeria 125 F5
Ikosi Dem. Rep. Congo 126 E5
Ikot Ekpene Nigeria 125 G5
Ikouhaouene, Adrar mt. Alg. 123 H4
Iksan S. Korea 83 B6
formerly known as Iri
Ikungu Tanz. 129 B6
Ila Nigeria 125 G4
Ilaferh, Oued watercourse Alg. 123 F5
Ilagala Tanz. 129 A6
Ilagan Phil. 74 B2
Ilaisamis Kenya 128 C4
Ilaiyankudi India 94 C4
Ilaka Atsinanana Madag. 131 [inset] K3
Īlām Iran 100 A3
Īlām prov. Iran 100 A3
Ilam Nepal 97 E4
Ilan Taiwan 87 G3
also spelt Yilan
Ilanz Switz. 51 P6
Ilaro Nigeria 125 F5
Ilave Peru 200 C4
Iława Poland 49 Q2
Ilazārān, Kūh-e mt. Iran 100 D4
Il Bogd Uul mts Mongolia 84 C2
Ile r. China/Kazakh. 88 B3
Île-à-la-Crosse, Lac l. Canada 167 J4
Ilebo Dem. Rep. Congo 126 D6
formerly known as Port Francqui
Île-de-France admin. reg. France 51 I4
Ileje Tanz. 129 B7
Ilek Kazakh. 102 C2
Ilek r. Rus. Fed. 102 C2
also spelt Elek
Ilen r. Rep. of Ireland 47 C12
Ileret Kenya 128 C3
Ilesa Nigeria 125 G5
also spelt Ilesha
Ilesha Nigeria see Ilesa
Ilet' r. Rus. Fed. 40 I5
Ileza Rus. Fed. 40 G3
Ilford Canada 167 M3
Ilfracombe Australia 149 E4
Ilfracombe U.K. 47 H12
Ilgaz Turkey 106 C2
Ilgaz Dağları mts Turkey 106 C2
Ilgın Turkey 106 B3
Ilhabela Brazil 203 C7
Ilha Grande Brazil 199 E5
Ilha Grande, Baía da b. Brazil 207 I10
Ilha Grande, Represa resr Brazil 203 A7
Ilha Solteira, Represa resr Brazil 206 B7
Ílhavo Port. 54 C4
Ilhéus Brazil 202 E5
Ili Kazakh. see Kapchagay
Ilia Romania 58 D3
Iliamna Lake U.S.A. 164 D4
İliç Turkey 107 D3
Il'ich Kazakh. 103 G4
Il'ichevsk Azer. see Şärur
Ilici Spain see Elche
Iligan Phil. 74 C4
Iligan Bay Phil. 74 C4
Iligan Point Phil. 74 B2
Ilijaš Bos.-Herz. 56 K5
Ilimananngip Nunaa i. Greenland 165 Q2
also known as Milne Land
Ilimpeya r. Rus. Fed. 39 K3
Il'inka Kazakh. 102 D2
Il'inka Kaluzhskaya Oblast' Rus. Fed. 43 R7
Il'inka Respublika Altay Rus. Fed. 88 D1
Il'inka Respublika Buryatiya Rus. Fed. 85 E1
Il'inka Respublika Tyva Rus. Fed. 84 B1
Il'ino Rus. Fed. 43 M6
Il'inskiy Permskaya Oblast' Rus. Fed. 40 J4
Il'inskiy Respublika Kareliya Rus. Fed. 43 N1
Il'inskiy Sakhalin Rus. Fed. 82 F3
Il'insko-Podomskoye Rus. Fed. 40 H3
Il'inskoye Orlovskaya Oblast' Rus. Fed. 43 Q8
Il'inskoye Tverskaya Oblast' Rus. Fed. 43 S5
Il'inskoye Yaroslavskaya Oblast' Rus. Fed. 43 T4
Il'inskoye-Khovanskoye Rus. Fed. 43 U5
Ilin Strait Phil. 74 B3
Iliomar East Timor 75 C5
Ilion U.S.A. 177 J2
Ilirska Bistrica Slovenia 56 G3
Ilium tourist site Turkey see Troy
Iliya r. Belarus 42 I7
Iliysk Kazakh. see Kapchagay
Ilk Hungary 49 T7
Il'ka Rus. Fed. 85 F1
Ilkal India 94 C3
Ill r. France 51 N4
Illana Bay Phil. 74 B5
Illapel Chile 204 C3
Illapel r. Chile 204 C3
Illbillee, Mount hill Australia 146 B1
Ille r. France 50 E4
Illela Nigeria 125 G3
Iller r. Germany 48 G7
Illertissen Germany 48 H7
Illescas Spain 54 H4
Illescas Uruguay 204 G4
Illimani, Nevado de mt. Bol. 200 D4
Illinois r. U.S.A. 174 B4
Illinois state U.S.A. 174 B4
Illinois and Mississippi Canal U.S.A. 172 D9
Illizi Alg. 123 H4
formerly known as Fort de Polignac
Illogwa watercourse Australia 148 B5
Illueca Spain 55 J3
Ilm r. Germany 48 I4
Ilma, Lake salt flat Australia 151 D6
'Ilmān, Jabal al hill Saudi Arabia 104 D4
Il'men', Ozero l. Rus. Fed. 43 M3
Ilmenau Germany 48 H5
Ilmtal park Germany 48 I5
Ilo Peru 200 C4
Ilobu Nigeria 125 G5
Iloc i. Phil. 74 A4
Iloilo Phil. 74 B4
Iloilo Strait Phil. 74 B4
Ilomantsi Fin. 44 O3
Ilongero Tanz. 129 B6
Ilorin Nigeria 125 G4
Ilova r. Croatia 56 I3
Ilovatka Rus. Fed. 41 H6
Ilovik i. Croatia 56 G4
Ilovlya Rus. Fed. 41 G6
Ilovlya r. Rus. Fed. 41 G6
Iłowa Poland 49 M4
Il-Ponta ta' Benghajsa pt Malta see Benghisa Point
Il'pyrskiy Rus. Fed. 39 Q3
formerly known as Il'pyrskoye
Il'pyrskoye Rus. Fed. see Il'pyrskiy
Ilūkste Latvia 42 H6
Ilulissat Greenland 165 N3
also known as Jakobshavn
Ilunde Tanz. 129 B6
Ilungu Tanz. 129 B6
Ilva i. Italy see Elba, Isola d'
Il'ya Belarus 42 I7
Il'yaly Turkm. see Yylanly
Ilych r. Rus. Fed. 40 K3
Iłżanka r. Poland 49 S4
Imabari Japan 91 C7
Imabetsu Japan 90 G4
Imabū r. Brazil 199 G5
Imagane Japan 90 G3
Imaichi Japan 91 F6
Imala Moz. 131 H2
Imām al Ḥamzah Iraq 107 F5
Imam-baba Turkm. 103 E5
İmamoğlu Turkey 106 C3
Iman Rus. Fed. see Dal'nerechensk
Iman r. Rus. Fed. 82 D3
Imantau, Ozero l. Kazakh. 103 G1
Imari Japan 91 A8
Imasgo Burkina 125 E3
also spelt Imassogo
Imassogo Burkina see Imasgo
Imata Peru 200 C3
Imataca, Serranía de mts Venez. 199 F3
Imatra Fin. 45 O3
Imavere Estonia 42 G3
Imazu Japan 91 E7
Imbabura prov. Ecuador 198 B4
Imbaimadai Guyana 199 F3
Imbituba Brazil 203 B9
imeni 26 Bakinskikh Komissarov Azer. see 26 Bakı Komissarı
imeni 26 Bakinskikh Komissarov Turkm. 102 C5
imeni Babushkina Rus. Fed. 40 G4
imeni C. A. Niyazova Turkm. 103 E5
formerly known as imeni Chapayevka
imeni Chapayevka Turkm. see imeni C. A. Niyazova
imeni Gastello Rus. Fed. 39 O3
imeni Kalinina Tajik. 101 H2
imeni Kerbabayeva Turkm. 102 E5
formerly known as Karrychirla
imeni Khamzy Khakikmzade Uzbek. see Khamza
imeni Kirova Kazakh. see Kopbirlik
imeni Kuybysheva Turkm. 103 E5
also known as Kuybyshew Adyndaky
imeni Petra Stuchki Latvia see Aizkraukle
imeni Poliny Osipenko Rus. Fed. 82 E1
imeni Voroshilova Kyrg. see Eshanguzar
imeni Zhelyabova Rus. Fed. 43 R3
Imeri, Serra mts Brazil 199 E4
Imese Dem. Rep. Congo 126 C4
Īmī Eth. 128 D3
Imishli Azer. see İmişli
İmişli Azer. 107 G3
also spelt Imishli
Imit Jammu and Kashmir 96 B1
Imja-do i. S. Korea 83 B6
Imjin-gang r. N. Korea/S. Korea 83 B5
Imlay U.S.A. 182 F1
Imlay City U.S.A. 173 J7
Imlili W. Sahara 122 B5
Immokalee U.S.A. 175 D7
Imo state Nigeria 125 G5
Imola Italy 56 D4
Imotski Croatia 56 J5
Imperatriz Brazil 202 C3
Imperia Italy 56 A5
Imperial Peru 200 A3
Imperial CA U.S.A. 183 I9
Imperial NE U.S.A. 178 B3
Imperial Beach U.S.A. 183 G9
Imperial Dam U.S.A. 183 J9
Imperial Valley plain U.S.A. 183 I9
Imperieuse Reef Australia 150 B3
Impfondo Congo 126 C4
Imphal India 97 G4
formerly known as Manipur
İmralı Adası i. Turkey 58 J8
Imrān Yemen 104 D5
İmroz Turkey 106 A2
İmroz i. Turkey see Gökçeada
Imrun Turkey see Pütürge
Imsil S. Korea 83 B6
Imst Austria 48 H8
Imtān Syria 109 H5
Imuris Mex. 184 C2
Imuruan Bay Phil. 74 A4
Imzouren Morocco 54 H9
In r. Rus. Fed. 82 D2
Ina Japan 91 E7
Ina r. Poland 49 L2
I-n-Abanghanit well Niger 125 G2
Inabu Japan 91 E7
In Afaleleh well Alg. 123 H5
Inagauan Phil. 74 A4
Inago Moz. 131 H2
Inahuaya Peru 200 B1
Inajá Brazil 202 E4
Inaja, Serra do hills Brazil 201 H2
I-n-Akhmed well Mali 125 E2
I-n-Alchi well Mali 125 E2
I-n-Aleï well Mali 124 E2
Inamba-jima i. Japan see Inanba-jima
Inambari Peru 200 C3
Inambari r. Peru 200 C3
I-n-Amedé well Mali 124 D2
In Aménas Alg. 123 H3
In Amguel Alg. 123 G5
Inanba-jima i. Japan 91 F8
also spelt Inamba-jima
Inanda S. Africa 133 O6
Inangahua Junction N.Z. 153 F9
Inanwatan Indon. 73 H7
Iñapari Peru 200 C2
Inari Fin. 44 N1
also known as Aanaar or Anár
Inarigda Rus. Fed. 39 K3
Inarijärvi l. Fin. 44 N1
Inarijoki r. Fin./Norway 44 N1
I-n-Arouinat well Niger 125 G2
I-n-Atankarer well Mali 125 F2
Inauini r. Brazil 200 D2
Inawashiro-ko l. Japan 90 G6
I-n-Azaoua well Alg. 123 G4
In-Azaoua well Alg. 123 G5
I-n-Azaoua watercourse Niger 125 G1
In Azar well Libya 120 A2
In Azāwah well Libya 120 A3
I-n-Azerraf well Mali 125 F2
In Belbel Alg. 123 F4
Inca Spain 55 N5
Inca de Oro Chile 204 C2
İnce Burnu pt Turkey 58 I8
İnce Burun pt Turkey 106 C2
İnceler Turkey 59 K11
Inchbonnie N.Z. 153 F10
Incheh Iran 100 D2
Inch'īnī Terara mt. Eth. 128 C3
Inchiri admin. reg. Mauritania 122 B5
Inch'ŏn S. Korea 83 B5
also known as Jinsen; formerly known as Chemulpo
Inchope Moz. 131 G3
I-n-Chaouâguene well Mali 125 F2
Incirli Turkey see Karasu
İncirlik Turkey 108 G1
Incomati r. Moz. 131 G5
Incudine, Monte mt. France 56 B7
Inčukalns Latvia 42 F4
Indaiá r. Brazil 207 H5
Indaiá Grande r. Brazil 206 A6
Indaiatuba Brazil 206 F10
Indalsälven r. Sweden 44 L3
Indalstø Norway 45 I3
Indargarh Madhya Pradesh India 96 C4
Indargarh Rajasthan India 96 C4
Inda Silasē Eth. 128 C1
Indawgyi, Lake Myanmar 78 B2
Indé Mex. 184 D3
I-n-Délimane well Mali 125 F3
Independence CA U.S.A. 182 F5
Independence IA U.S.A. 174 B3
Independence KS U.S.A. 178 D4
Independence KY U.S.A. 176 A7
Independence MO U.S.A. 178 D4
Independence VA U.S.A. 176 D9
Independence WI U.S.A. 172 B6
Independence Fjord inlet Greenland 165 Q1
Independence Mountains U.S.A. 180 C4
Independencia Bol. 200 D4
Independenţa Romania 58 I4
Independenţa Romania 58 J5
Independenţa Romania 58 I3
Inder China 85 I2
also known as Jalaid
Inder, Ozero salt l. Kazakh. 102 B2
Inderborskiy Kazakh. 102 B2
Indi India 94 C2
India country Asia 93 E6
2nd most populous country in the world and in Asia. 3rd largest country in Asia and 7th in the world. Known as Bharat in Hindi.
world [countries] 10–11
world [population] 22–23
asia [landscapes] 62–63
asia [countries] 64–67
Indian r. U.S.A. 172 G4
Indiana U.S.A. 176 F5
Indiana state U.S.A. 174 C3
Indianapolis U.S.A. 174 C4
State capital of Indiana.
Indian Cabins Canada 167 G3
Indian Desert India/Pak. see Thar Desert
Indian Fields U.S.A. 176 B8
Indian Harbour Canada 169 J2
Indian Head Canada 167 K5
Indian Lake U.S.A. 177 K2
Indian Lake l. MI U.S.A. 172 G5
Indian Lake l. NY U.S.A. 177 K2
Indian Lake l. OH U.S.A. 176 B5
Indian Lake l. PA U.S.A. 176 G5
Indian Ocean 218 M7
3rd largest ocean in the world.
oceans [features] 210–211
Indianola IA U.S.A. 174 A3
Indianola MS U.S.A. 175 B5
Indian Peak U.S.A. 183 I3
Indian Springs U.S.A. 183 I5

Indian Wells U.S.A. 183 N6
Indiara Brazil 206 C4
Indiaroba Brazil 202 E4
Indibir Eth. 128 C2
Indiga Rus. Fed. 40 I2
Indigirka r. Rus. Fed. 39 O2
Indigskaya Guba b. Rus. Fed. 40 I2
Inđija Vojvodina, Srbija Yugo. 58 B3
Indin Myanmar 78 A3
Indin Lake Canada 167 H1
Indio r. Nicaragua 186 C5
Indio U.S.A. 183 H8
Indispensable Reefs Solomon Is 145 F3
Indo-China reg. Asia 72 C3
Indomanka r. Rus. Fed. 43 S1

Indonesia country Asia 72 D8
4th most populous country in the world and Asia. 5th largest country in Asia. Formerly known as Dutch East Indies.
world [population] 22–23
asia [countries] 64–67

Indore India 96 B5
Indragiri r. Indon. 76 C3
Indramayu Indon. 77 E4
Indramayu, Tanjung pt Indon. 77 E4
Indrapura, Gunung vol. Indon. see Kerinci, Gunung
Indrapura, Tanjung pt Indon. 76 C3
Indravati r. India 95 D2
Indre r. France 51 G5
Indulkana Australia 146 B1
Indur India see Nizamabad
Indura Belarus 42 E8
Indurti India 94 C2
Indus r. China/Pakistan 89 C5
also known as Shiquan He
Indus, Mouths of the Pak. 101 F5
Indwe S. Africa 133 L8
Indwe r. S. Africa 133 L9
Indzhe Voyvoda Bulg. 58 I6
In Ebeggi well Alg. 123 G5
İnebolu Turkey 106 C2
I-n-Échaï well Mali 123 E5
İnegöl Turkey 106 B2
In Ekker Alg. 123 G4
Inerie vol. Indon. 75 B5
Ineu Romania 58 C2
Inevi Turkey see Cihanbeyli
Inez U.S.A. 176 C8
In Ezzane well Alg. 123 H5
Infanta, Cape S. Africa 132 E11
Infantas Col. 187 E6
Infantes Spain see Villanueva de los Infantes
Infernao, Cachoeira waterfall Brazil 201 E2
Infieles, Punta pt Chile 204 C2
Infiernillo, Presa resr Mex. 185 E5
Infiesto Spain 54 F1
Ing, Mae Nam r. Thai. 78 C3
Inga Dem. Rep. Congo 127 B6
Ingå Fin. 45 N3
Ingabu Myanmar 78 A4
Ingal Niger 125 G2
Ingallanna watercourse Australia 148 B4
Ingalls, Mount U.S.A. 182 D2
Inganda Dem. Rep. Congo 126 D5
Ingelstad Sweden 45 K4
Ingende Dem. Rep. Congo 126 C5
Ingeniero Guillermo Nueva Juárez Arg. 201 E5
Ingeniero Jacobacci Arg. 204 C6
Ingenika r. Canada 166 E3
Ingenio r. Peru 200 B3
Ingersoll Canada 173 M7
Ingessana Hills Sudan 128 B2
Ingettolgoy Mongolia 84 D1
Ingezi Zimbabwe see Ngezi
Ingham Australia 149 E3
Ingichka Uzbek. 103 F5
formerly known as Rudnik Ingichka
Inglefield Land reg. Greenland 165 L2
Inglewood Qld Australia 147 F2
Inglewood Vic. Australia 147 D4
Inglewood N.Z. 152 I7
Inglewood U.S.A. 182 F8
Ingoda r. Rus. Fed. 85 G1
Ingoka Pum mt. Myanmar 78 B2
Ingolf Fjord inlet Greenland 165 R1
Ingolstadt Germany 48 I7
Ingomar Australia 146 B2
Ingonish Canada 169 I4
Ingraj Bazar India 97 F4
formerly known as English Bazar
Ingram VA U.S.A. 176 F9
Ingram WI U.S.A. 172 C5
Ingray Lake Canada 167 G1
Ingrid Christensen Coast Antarctica 223 F2
I-n-Guezzam Alg. 123 G6
I-n-Guita well Mali 125 F3
Ingulets Ukr. see Inhulets'
Ingulsvatn Norway 44 K2
Ingushetia aut. rep. Rus. Fed. see Ingushetiya, Respublika
Ingushetiya, Respublika aut. rep. Rus. Fed. 41 H8
English form Ingushetia or Ingush Republic
Ingush Republic aut. rep. Rus. Fed. see Ingushetiya, Respublika
Ingwavuma S. Africa 133 Q4
Ingwavuma r. Swaziland see Ngwavuma

Ingwe Zambia 127 E8
Inhaca Moz. 133 Q2
Inhaca, Peninsula pen. Moz. 131 G5
Inhafenga Moz. 131 G4
Inhambane Moz. 131 G4
Inhambane prov. Moz. 131 G4
Inhambupe Brazil 202 E4
Inhamitanga Moz. 131 G3
Inhapim Brazil 203 D6
Inharrime Moz. 131 G5
Inhassoro Moz. 131 G4
Inhaúmas Brazil 202 C5
I-n-Hihaou, Adrar hills Alg. 123 F5
Inhobim Brazil 207 M2
Inhulets' Ukr. 41 E7
also spelt Ingulets
Inhumas Brazil 206 D3
Inielika vol. Indon. 75 B5
Iniesta Spain 55 J5
Inimutaba Brazil 207 I5
Iniö Fin. 42 C1
Inírida r. Col. 198 E4
Inis Rep. of Ireland see Ennis
Inis Córthaidh Rep. of Ireland see Enniscorthy
Inishark i. Rep. of Ireland 47 B10
Inishbofin i. Rep. of Ireland 47 B10
Inishmore i. Rep. of Ireland 47 C10
Inishmurray i. Rep. of Ireland 47 D9
Inishowen pen. Rep. of Ireland 47 E8
Inishowen Head Rep. of Ireland 47 F8
Inishtrahull i. Rep. of Ireland 46 E8
Inishturk i. Rep. of Ireland 47 B10
Injgan Sum China 85 H2
Injibara Eth. 128 C2
Injune Australia 149 F5
Inkardar'ya Kazakh. 103 F3
I-n-Kerchef well Mali 124 D2
Inkerman Australia 149 D3
Inklin Canada 166 C3
Inklin r. Canada 166 C3
Inkylap Turkm. 103 E5
Inland Kaikoura Range mts N.Z. 153 H10
Inland Sea Japan see Seto-naikai
Inlet U.S.A. 177 K2
I-n-Milach well Mali 125 E2
Inn r. Europe 48 H9
Innaanganeq c. Greenland 165 M2
also known as York, Kap
Innai Japan 91 B8
Innamincka Australia 146 D1
Innamincka Regional Reserve nature res. Australia 146 D1
Inndyr Norway 44 K2
Inner Mongolia aut. reg. China see Nei Mongol Zizhiqu
Inner Sound sea chan. U.K. 46 G6
Innes National Park Australia 146 C3
Innisfail Australia 149 E3
Innisfail Canada 167 H4
Innokent'yevka Rus. Fed. 82 C2
Innoshima Japan 91 C7
Innsbruck Austria 48 I8
Innuksuak r. Canada 168 E1
Inny r. Rep. of Ireland 47 E10
Ino Japan 91 C8
Inobonto Indon. 75 C2
Inocência Brazil 206 B6
Inongo Dem. Rep. Congo 126 C5
Inoni Congo 126 B5
Inonias Peru 198 C5
İnönü Turkey 106 B3
Inosu Col. 198 D1
Inoucdjouac Canada see Inukjuak
Inovec mt. Slovakia 49 P7
Inowrocław Poland 49 P3
historically known as Hohensalza
Inquisivi Bol. 200 D4
In Salah Alg. 123 F4
also spelt Aïn Salah

Inscription, Cape Australia 151 A5
Most westerly point of Oceania.

Insein Myanmar 78 B4
Insel Usedom park Germany 49 L2
Ińsko Poland 49 M2
In Sokki, Oued watercourse Alg. 123 F3
Insterburg Rus. Fed. see Chernyakhovsk
Instruch r. Rus. Fed. 42 C7
Însurăţei Romania 58 I4
Insuza r. Zimbabwe 131 E3
Inta Rus. Fed. 40 L2
I-n-Tadéra well Niger 125 H1
I-n-Tadrof well Niger 125 H2
In Takoufi, Oued watercourse Alg. 123 G4
I-n-Tassit well Mali 125 F2
I-n-Tebezas Mali 125 F2
I-n-Téguift well Mali 125 F2
I-n-Telli well Mali 125 F2
I-n-Témeguí well Mali 125 F2
İntepe Turkey 59 H8
Interamna Italy see Teramo
Interlaken Switz. 51 N6
International Falls U.S.A. 174 A1
Interview Island India 95 G3
Intich'o Eth. 104 B5
Întorsura Buzăului Romania 58 H3
I-n-Touft well Mali 125 F2
Intracoastal Waterway canal U.S.A. 179 D6
Intutu Peru 198 C5
Inubō-zaki pt Japan 91 G7
Inukai Japan 91 B8
Inukjuak Canada 168 E1
formerly known as Port Harrison; formerly spelt Inoucdjouac
Inútil, Bahía b. Chile 205 C9
Inuvik Canada 164 F3
Inuya r. Peru 200 B2
In'va r. Rus. Fed. 40 K4
Inveraray U.K. 46 G7
Inverbervie U.K. 46 J7
Invercargill N.Z. 153 C14
Inverell Australia 147 F2
Inverleigh Australia 149 D3
Inverness Canada 169 I4
Inverness U.K. 46 H6
Inverness CA U.S.A. 182 B3
Inverness FL U.S.A. 175 D6
Inverurie U.K. 46 J6
Inverway Australia 148 A3
Investigator Channel Myanmar 79 B5
Investigator Group is Australia 146 B3
Investigator Strait Australia 146 C3
Inwood U.S.A. 176 G6
Inxu r. S. Africa 133 M8
Inya Rus. Fed. 88 D1
Inyanga Zimbabwe see Nyanga
Inyanga Mountains Zimbabwe 131 G3
Inyanga National Park Zimbabwe see Nyanga National Park
Inyangani mt. Zimbabwe 131 G3
Inyati Zimbabwe see Nyathi
Inyazura Zimbabwe see Nyazura
Inyokern U.S.A. 182 G6
Inyo Mountains U.S.A. 182 F4
Inyonga Tanz. 129 B6
Inza Rus. Fed. 41 H5
Inzer r. Rus. Fed. 40 K5
Inzhavino Rus. Fed. 41 G5
Ioannina Greece 59 B9
also spelt Yannina
Ioanninon, Limni l. Greece 59 B9
Iōf di Montasio mt. Italy 56 F2
Iō-jima i. Kazan-rettō Japan 73 J2
also known as Iō-tō; also spelt Iwo Jima
Iō-jima i. Japan 91 B9
also spelt Iō-shima
Iokanga r. Rus. Fed. 40 F2
Iola KS U.S.A. 178 D4
Iola WI U.S.A. 172 D6
Iolgo, Khrebet mts Rus. Fed. 88 D1

Iolotan' Turkm. see Yeloten
Iona Angola 127 B9
Iona Canada 169 I4
Iona i. U.K. 46 F7
Iona, Parque Nacional do nat. park Angola 127 B9
Iona Abbey tourist site U.K. 46 F7
Ione U.S.A. 182 G3
Ioneşti Romania 58 F4
Ionia U.S.A. 173 H8
Ionian Islands admin. reg. Greece see Ionioi Nisoi
Ionian Islands reg. Greece 59 A9
also known as Ionioi Nisoi
Ionian Sea Greece/Italy 59 A11
Ionioi Nisoi admin. reg. Greece 59 A10
English form Ionian Islands
Ionioi Nisoi reg. Greece see Ionian Islands
Iony, Ostrov i. Rus. Fed. 39 O4
Iordan Uzbek. 101 G1
also spelt Yordon; formerly spelt Yardan
Iori r. Georgia 107 F2
Ios Greece 59 G12
Ios i. Greece 59 G12
Iō-shima i. Japan see Iō-jima
Iō-tō i. Japan see Iō-jima
Iouîk Mauritania 124 A2
Iowa r. U.S.A. 174 B3
Iowa state U.S.A. 174 A3
Iowa City U.S.A. 174 B3
Iowa Falls U.S.A. 174 A3
Ipameri Brazil 206 E4
Ipanema Brazil 203 D6
Ipanema r. Brazil 202 E4
Iparía Peru 200 B2
Ipatinga Brazil 203 D6
Ipatovo Rus. Fed. 41 G7
Ipauçu Brazil 206 D10
Ipeiros admin. reg. Greece 59 B9
English form Epirus; also spelt Ípiros
Ipeľ r. Slovakia 49 P8
Ipelegeng S. Africa 133 J4
Ipiaçu Brazil 206 D5
Ipiales Col. 198 B4
Ipiaú Brazil 202 E5
Ipirá Brazil 202 E5
Ipiranga Amazonas Brazil 198 D5
Ipiranga Amazonas Brazil 199 F6
Ípiros admin. reg. Greece see Ipeiros
Ipixuna Brazil 200 B1
Ipixuna r. Amazonas Brazil 199 F6
Ipixuna r. Amazonas Brazil 200 B1
Ipoh Malaysia 76 C1
Ipoly r. Hungary/Slovakia 49 P8
Ipopeng S. Africa 133 J6
Iporá Brazil 206 B3
Ippy Cent. Afr. Rep. 126 D3
İpsala Turkey 58 H8
Ipswich Australia 147 G1
Ipswich U.K. 47 N11
Ipswich U.S.A. 178 C2
Ipu Brazil 202 D3
Ipuã Brazil 206 F7
Ipueiras Brazil 202 D3
Ipuh Indon. 76 C3
Ipupiara Brazil 202 D4
Iput' r. Rus. Fed. 43 M9

Iqaluit Canada 165 M3
Territorial capital of Nunavut. Formerly known as Frobisher Bay.

Iqe He r. China 84 B4
Iquê r. Brazil 201 F3
also known as Languiaru
Iquique Chile 200 C5
Iquiri r. Brazil see Ituxi
Iquitos Peru 198 C5
Ira Banda Cent. Afr. Rep. 126 D3
formerly spelt Hyrra Banda
Iracoubo Fr. Guiana 199 H3
Īrafshān reg. Iran 101 E5
Iraí Brazil 203 A8
Irai Island P.N.G. 149 F1
Irakleia Greece 58 F7
Irakleia i. Greece 59 G12
also spelt Iráklia
Irakleio Greece see Iraklion
Irakleiou, Kolpos b. Greece 59 G13
Iráklia i. Greece see Irakleia
Iraklion Greece 59 G13
also spelt Herakleion or Irakleio; historically known as Candia
Irala Para. 201 G6
Iramaia Brazil 202 D5
Iran country Asia 100 C4
formerly known as Persia
asia [countries] 64–67
Iran, Pegunungan mts Indon. 77 F2
Īrānshāh Iran 100 A2
Īrānshahr Iran 101 E5
Irapuato Mex. 185 E4
Iraq country Asia 107 E4
asia [countries] 64–67
Irarrarene reg. Alg. 123 G4
Irasville U.S.A. 177 M1
Iratapuru r. Brazil 199 H5
Irati Brazil 203 B8
Irati r. Spain 55 J2
Irayel' Rus. Fed. 40 J2
Irazú, Volcán vol. Costa Rica 186 C5
Irbe r. Latvia 42 D4
Irbes šaurums sea chan. Estonia/Latvia see Irbe Strait
Irbe Strait Estonia/Latvia 42 D4
also known as Irbe väin or Irbes šaurums or Kura kurk or Sõrve väin
Irbe väin sea chan. Estonia/Latvia see Irbe Strait
Irbid Jordan 108 G5
Irbil Iraq see Arbīl
Irbit Rus. Fed. 38 G4
Irebu Dem. Rep. Congo 126 C5
Irecê Brazil 202 D4
Iregua r. Spain 55 I2

Ireland i. International Feature 47 C11
4th largest island in Europe.
europe [landscapes] 30–31

Ireland, Republic of country Europe 47 D10
known as Éire in Irish; formerly known as Irish Free State
europe [countries] 32–35

Iren' r. Rus. Fed. 40 K4
Irene Arg. 204 E5
Irene, Mount N.Z. 153 B13
Ireng r. Guyana/Venez. 199 G4
Iretama Brazil 206 A11
Irgiz Kazakh. 103 E2
also spelt Yrghyz
Irgiz r. Kazakh. 102 E2
Irharrhar, Oued watercourse Alg. 123 G3
Irharrhar, Oued watercourse Alg. 123 G5
Irherm Morocco 122 C3
Irhil M'Goun mt. Morocco 122 D3
Irhzer Ediessane watercourse Alg. 120 A3
Iri S. Korea see Iksan
Irian, Teluk b. Indon. see Cenderawasih, Teluk
Irian Barat prov. Indon. see Irian Jaya
Irian Jaya prov. Indon. 75 D3
also known as West Papua; formerly known as Dutch New Guinea or Irian Barat or West Irian
Irian Jaya reg. Indon. 73 I7
Iriba Chad 120 D6
Iricoumé, Serra hills Brazil 199 G4
Īrī Dāgh mt. Iran 100 A2
Iriga Phil. 74 B3
Iriklinskiy Rus. Fed. 102 D2

Iriklinskoye Vodokhranilische resr Rus. Fed. 102 D2
Iringa Tanz. 129 B6
Iringa admin. reg. Tanz. 129 B7
Iriri r. Brazil 199 H5
Iriri Novo r. Brazil 202 A4
Irish Free State country Europe see Ireland, Republic of
Irish Sea Rep. of Ireland/U.K. 47 G10
Irituia Brazil 202 C2
'Irj well Saudi Arabia 105 E2
Irkeshtam Kyrg. see Erkech-Tam
Irkut r. Rus. Fed. 84 D1
Irkutsk Rus. Fed. 80 G2
Irkutskaya Oblast' admin. div. Rus. Fed. 84 D1
English form Irkutsk Oblast
Irkutsk Oblast admin. div. Rus. Fed. see Irkutskaya Oblast'
Irma U.S.A. 172 D5
Irmak Turkey 106 C3
Irminio r. Sicilia Italy 57 G12
Irmo U.S.A. 175 D5
Irnijärvi l. Fin. 44 O2
Iro, Lac l. Chad 126 C2
Iroise, Mer d' g. France 50 B4
Iron Baron Australia 146 C3
Iron Bridge Canada 173 J4
Irondequoit U.S.A. 176 H2
Iron Junction U.S.A. 172 A3
Iron Knob Australia 146 C3
Iron Mountain U.S.A. 172 E5
Iron Mountain mt. U.S.A. 183 K4
Iron Range National Park Australia 149 D2
Iron River MI U.S.A. 172 E4
Iron River WI U.S.A. 172 B4
Ironton MO U.S.A. 174 B4
Ironton OH U.S.A. 176 C7
Ironwood U.S.A. 172 C4
Iroquois Canada 177 J1
Iroquois r. U.S.A. 172 F9
Iroquois Falls Canada 168 D3
Irosin Phil. 74 C3
Irō-zaki pt Japan 91 F7
Irpen' Ukr. see Irpin'
Irpin' Ukr. 41 D6
also spelt Irpen'
Irqah Yemen 105 D5
'Irq al Ḩarūrī des. Saudi Arabia 105 D2
Irq al Mazhūr des. Saudi Arabia 104 C2
'Irq Banbān des. Saudi Arabia 105 D2
'Irq Jahām des. Saudi Arabia 105 D2
'Irq Subay des. Saudi Arabia 104 C3
Irramarne Aboriginal Land res. Australia 148 C4
Irrawaddy admin. div. Myanmar 78 A4
Irrawaddy r. Myanmar 78 A5
also spelt Ayeyarwady or Erawadi or Eyawadi
Irrawaddy, Mouths of the Myanmar 79 A5
Irsarybaba, Gory hills Turkm. 102 C4
also known as Ärsarybaba Erezi
Irshad Pass Afgh./Pak. 101 H2

Irtysh r. Kazakh./Rus. Fed. 38 G3
5th longest river in Asia and 10th in the world. Part of the 2nd longest river in Asia (Ob'-Irtysh). Also spelt Ertis.
asia [landscapes] 62–63

Irtyshsk Kazakh. 103 H1
also known as Ertis; formerly known as Irtyshskoye
Irtyshskoye Kazakh. see Irtyshsk
Iruma Japan 91 F7
Irumu Dem. Rep. Congo 126 F4
Irún Spain 55 J1
Iruña Spain see Pamplona
Irupana Bol. 200 D4
Irvine U.K. 46 H8
Irvine CA U.S.A. 182 G8
Irvine KY U.S.A. 176 B8
Irvine Glacier Antarctica 222 T2
Irving U.S.A. 179 C5
Irwin r. Australia 151 A6
Irwinton U.S.A. 175 D5
Isa Nigeria 125 G3
'Īsá, Ra's pt Yemen 104 C5
Isaac r. Australia 149 F4
Isaac Lake Canada 166 F4
Isabela Negros Phil. 74 B4
Isabela Phil. 74 B5
Isabela, Cabo c. Dom. Rep. 187 F3
Isabelia, Cordillera mts Nicaragua 186 B4
Isabella U.S.A. 172 B3
Isabella Indian Reservation res. U.S.A. 173 I7
Isabella Lake U.S.A. 182 F6
Isabelle, Point U.S.A. 172 F3
Isabey Turkey 59 K11
Isaccea Romania 58 J3
Isachenko, Ostrov i. Rus. Fed. 39 I2
Isachsen, Cape Canada 165 I2
Ísafjarðardjúp est. Iceland 44 [inset] B2
Ísafjörður Iceland 44 [inset] B2
Isagarh India 96 C4
Isahaya Japan 91 B8
Isai Kalat Pak. 101 F5
Isà Khel Pak. 101 G3
Isakogorka Rus. Fed. 40 G2
Isakovo Rus. Fed. 43 P6
Isalniţa Romania 58 E4
Isana r. Col. 198 D4
Isanga Dem. Rep. Congo 126 D5
Isangano National Park Zambia 127 F7
Isaouane-n-Tifernine des. Alg. 123 G4
Isar r. Germany 48 J7
Isbister U.K. 46 K3
Iscar Spain 54 G3
Iscayachi Bol. 200 D5
Ischia Italy 57 F8
Ischia, Isola d' i. Italy 57 F8
Isdell r. Australia 150 D3
Ise Japan 91 E7
formerly known as Ujiyamada
Isefjord b. Denmark 45 J5
Iseke Tanz. 129 B6
Isel r. Austria 49 J9
Isengi Dem. Rep. Congo 126 E4
Iseo, Lago d' l. Italy 56 C3
Isère r. France 51 K8
Isère, Pointe pt Fr. Guiana 199 H3
Iserlohn Germany 48 E4
Isernhagen Germany 48 G3
Isernia Italy 56 G7
historically known as Aesernia
Ise-shima National Park Japan 91 E7
Ise-wan b. Japan 91 E7
Iseyin Nigeria 125 F5
Isfahan Iran see Eşfahān
Isfana Kyrg. 103 G5
Isfandaqeh Iran see Sangū'īyeh
Isfara Tajik. 101 G1
Isherim, Gora mt. Rus. Fed. 40 K3
Isherton Guyana 199 G4
Isheyevka Rus. Fed. 41 I5
Ishikari Japan 90 G3
Ishikari-gawa r. Japan 90 G3
Ishikari-wan b. Japan 90 G3
Ishikawa pref. Japan 91 E6
Ishim r. Kazakh./Rus. Fed. 103 F1
also known as Esil
Ishim Rus. Fed. 38 G4
Ishimbay Rus. Fed. 102 D1
Ishinomaki Japan 90 G5
Ishioka Japan 91 G6
Ishizuchi-san mt. Japan 91 C8
Ishkaft, Jabal hill Iraq 109 N1
Ishkoshim Tajik. 101 G2
Ishkuman Jammu and Kashmir 96 B1
Ishnya Rus. Fed. 43 U4
Ishpeming U.S.A. 172 F4

Ishtikhon Uzbek. see Ishtykhan
Ishtragh Afgh. 101 G2
Ishtykhan Uzbek. 103 F5
also spelt Ishtikhon
Ishurdi Bangl. 97 F4
Isiboro r. Bol. 200 D3
Isiboro Sécure, Parque Nacional nat. park Bol. 200 D4
Isigny-sur-Mer France 50 E3
Işıklı Turkey 106 B3
Isil'kul' Rus. Fed. 38 H4
Isimbira Tanz. 129 B6
Isinliví Ecuador 198 B5
Isiolo Kenya 128 C4
Isipingo S. Africa 133 O6
Isiro Dem. Rep. Congo 126 E4
formerly known as Paulis
Isisford Australia 149 E5
Iskabad Canal Afgh. 101 F2
Iskateley Rus. Fed. 40 J2
İskele Cyprus see Trikomon
İskenderun Turkey 106 D3
historically known as Alexandretta
İskenderun Körfezi b. Turkey 106 C3
İskilip Turkey 106 C2
Iski-Naukat Kyrg. see Eski-Nookat
Iskine Kazakh. 102 C3
Iskitim Rus. Fed. 80 C2
Iskra Rus. Fed. 43 U7
Iskŭr r. Bulg. 58 F5
Iskŭr, Yazovir resr Bulg. 58 E6
Iskushuban Somalia 128 F2
Iskut r. Canada 166 D3
Isla r. U.K. 46 I7
Isla, Wâdi el watercourse Egypt 108 E9
Isla Cristina Spain 54 D7
Isla de Salamanca, Parque Nacional nat. park Col. 198 C2
Isla Gorge National Park Australia 149 F5
İslahiye Turkey 107 D3
Islamabad Jammu and Kashmir see Anantnag

Islamabad Pak. 101 H3
Capital of Pakistan.

Isla Magdalena, Parque Nacional nat. park Chile 205 B7
Islamkot Pak. 101 G5
Islamorada U.S.A. 175 D7
Islampur India 97 E4
Island r. Canada 166 F2
Ísland country Europe see Iceland
Island Bay Phil. 74 A4
Island Lagoon salt flat Australia 146 C2
Island Lake Canada 167 M4
Island Lake l. Canada 167 M4
Island Lake l. U.S.A. 172 A3
Island Magee pen. U.K. 47 G9
Island Pond U.S.A. 177 N1
Islands, Bay of N.Z. 152 I3
Islas Baleares aut. comm. Spain 55 N5
Islas de Bahá, Parque Nacional nat. park Hond. 186 B3
Islay i. U.K. 46 F8
Islaz Romania 58 F5
Isle r. France 50 F8

Isle of Man i. Irish Sea 47 H9
United Kingdom Crown Dependency.
europe [countries] 32–35

Isle of Wight U.S.A. 177 I9
Isle Royale National Park U.S.A. 172 E3
Isluga, Parque Nacional nat. park Chile 200 C4
Ismail Ukr. see Izmayil
Ismâ'ilîya Egypt 121 G2
also spelt Al Ismā'īlīyah
Ismâ'ilîya governorate Egypt 108 D7
Ismâ'ilîya, Tir'at el canal Egypt 108 D7
Ismailly Azer. see İsmayıllı
İsmayıllı Azer. 107 G2
also spelt Ismailly
Isna Egypt 121 G3
Isoanala Madag. 131 [inset] J4
Isojoki Fin. 45 M3
Isoka Zambia 129 B7
Isokylä Fin. 44 N2
Isokyrö Fin. 44 M3
Isola del Liri Italy 56 F7
Isola di Capo Rizzuto Italy 57 J10
Isonzo r. Italy 56 F3
also known as Soča
Isopa Tanz. 129 A7
Isorana Madag. 131 [inset] J4
Iso-Syöte hill Fin. 44 N2
Ispahan Iran see Eşfahān
Isparta Turkey 106 B3
also known as Hamitabat
Isperikh Bulg. 58 H5
Ispica Sicilia Italy 57 G12
Ispir Turkey 107 E2
Ispisar Tajik. see Khŭjand

Israel country Asia 108 F5
spelt Yizra'el in Hebrew or Isrā'īl in Arabic
asia [countries] 64–67

Israelândia Brazil 206 C3
Israelite Bay Australia 151 C7
Isrā'īl country Asia see Israel
Issa Croatia see Vis
Issa r. Rus. Fed. 43 J5
Issano Guyana 199 G3
Issia Côte d'Ivoire 124 D5
Issimu Indon. 75 B2
Issin tourist site Iraq 107 F5
Issoire France 51 J7
Issoudun France 51 H6
Issuna Tanz. 129 B6
Is-sur-Tille France 51 L5
Issyk-Kul' Kyrg. see Balykchy
Issyk-Kul', Ozero salt l. Kyrg. see Ysyk-Köl
Issyk-Kul Oblast admin. div. Kyrg. see Ysyk-Köl
Issyk-Kul'skaya Oblast' admin. div. Kyrg. see Ysyk-Köl
Ista r. Rus. Fed. 43 R8
Iştabl 'Antar Saudi Arabia 104 B2
Iştablāt tourist site Iraq 107 E4
İstanbul Turkey 106 B2
historically known as Byzantium or Constantinople
İstanbul prov. Turkey 58 J7
İstanbul Boğazı sea chan. Turkey see Bosporus
İstanbul Boğazı strait Turkey see Bosporus
Isten dombja hill Hungary 49 N9
Īstgāh-e Eznā Iran 100 B3
Isthilart Arg. 204 F3
Istiaia Greece 59 E10
Istik r. Tajik. 101 H2
Istmina Col. 198 B3
Istok Kosovo, Srbija Yugo. 58 B6
Istokpoga, Lake U.S.A. 175 D7
Istra pen. Croatia see Istria
Istra Rus. Fed. 43 R6
Istres France 51 K9
Istria pen. Croatia 56 F3
also spelt Istra
Istria Romania 58 J4
Istriţa, Dealul hill Romania 58 H3
Ist'ya r. Rus. Fed. 43 V7
Isuela r. Spain 55 J3
Iswaripur Bangl. 97 F5
Iswepe S. Africa 133 O3
Isyangulovo Rus. Fed. 102 D1
Isyk Kazakh. 103 I4
Itabaianinha Brazil 202 E4
Itabapoana Brazil 207 M8
Itabapoana r. Brazil 207 M8
Itaberá Brazil 206 D10

Itaberaba Brazil 202 D5
Itaberaí Brazil 206 D3
Itabira Brazil 203 D6
Itabirito Brazil 203 D7
Itaboca Brazil 199 F6
Itaboraí Brazil 207 K9
Itabuna Brazil 202 E5
Itacaiuna r. Brazil 202 B3
Itacajá Brazil 202 C4
Itacambira Brazil 207 J4
Itacarambi Brazil 202 C5
Itacaré Brazil 202 E5
Itacayunas, Serra hills Brazil 201 H1
Itacoatiara Brazil 199 G5
Itacuaí r. Brazil 198 D6
Itaetê Brazil 202 D5
Itagmatana Iran see Hamadān
Itagmirim Brazil 207 N3
Itaguaçu Brazil 203 D6
Itaguaí Brazil 207 J9
Itaguajé Brazil 206 B9
Itaguara Brazil 207 I7
Itahuania Peru 200 C3
Itaí Brazil 206 D10
Itaim r. Brazil 202 D3
Itaiópolis Brazil 203 B8
Itaipu, Represa de resr Brazil 203 A8
Itäisen Suomenlahden kansallispuisto nat. park Fin. 45 N3
Itaituba Brazil 199 G6
Itajá Brazil 206 B6
Itajaí Brazil 203 B8
Itajobi Brazil 206 D8
Itajubá Brazil 203 C7
Itaju de Colônia Brazil 207 N2
Itajuípe Brazil 202 E5
Itaki India 97 E5
Itala Nature Reserve S. Africa 133 P4
Italia country Europe see Italy

Italy country Europe 56 C4
5th most populous country in Europe. Known as Italia in Italian.
europe [countries] 32–35

Itamaracá, Ilha de i. Brazil 202 F3
Itamaraju Brazil 203 E6
Itamarandiba Brazil 203 D6
Itamataré Brazil 202 C2
Itambacuri Brazil 207 L5
Itambacuri r. Brazil 207 L5
Itambé Brazil 202 D5
Itambé, Pico de mt. Brazil 203 D6
Itami airport Japan 91 D7
Itamirim Brazil 207 K1
Itampolo Madag. 131 [inset] I5
Itanagar India 97 G4
Itanguari r. Brazil 207 H1
Itanhaém Brazil 206 G11
Itanhauã r. Brazil 199 F6
Itanhém Brazil 203 D6
Itanhém r. Brazil 203 E6
Itanhomi Brazil 207 L6
Itany r. Fr. Guiana/Suriname 199 H4
Itaobim Brazil 202 D6
Itaocara Brazil 207 K8
Itapaci Brazil 206 D1
Itapajipe Brazil 206 D6
Itaparaná r. Brazil 199 F6
Itaparica, Represa de resr Brazil 202 E4
Itapé Brazil 207 N1
Itapebi Brazil 202 E5
Itapebí Uruguay 204 F3
Itapecerica Brazil 207 H7
Itapemirim Brazil 203 D7
Itaperuna Brazil 203 D7
Itapetinga Brazil 202 D5
Itapetininga Brazil 206 E10
Itapeva Brazil 206 E10
Itapeva, Lago l. Brazil 203 B9
Itapi r. Brazil 199 G5
Itapicuru Brazil 202 D4
Itapicuru r. Brazil 202 C2
Itapicuru r. Brazil 202 E4
Itapicuru, Serra de hills Brazil 202 C3
Itapicuru Mirim Brazil 202 C2
Itapicuru Mirim r. Brazil 202 E4
Itapinima Brazil 199 F6
Itapipoca Brazil 202 E2
Itapira Brazil 206 G9
Itapiranga Brazil 199 G5
Itapirapuã Brazil 206 C2
Itapiúna Brazil 202 E3
Itápolis Brazil 206 E8
Itaporanga Paraíba Brazil 202 E3
Itaporanga São Paulo Brazil 206 D10
Itapuã Brazil 203 B9
Itapuranga Brazil 206 D2
Itaquaquecetuba Brazil 207 G10
Itaqui Brazil 204 F3
Itarana Brazil 207 M6
Itarantim Brazil 207 M2
Itararé Brazil 206 D11
Itararé r. Brazil 206 D10
Itarsi India 96 C5
Itarumã Brazil 206 B5
Itā-Suomi prov. Fin. 44 O3
Itatiba Brazil 206 G10
Itatinga Brazil 206 E10
Itatuba Brazil 199 F6
Itatupã Brazil 199 I5
Itaúçu Brazil 206 D3
Itaueira r. Brazil 202 D3
Itaúna Amazonas Brazil 199 E5
Itaúna Minas Gerais Brazil 203 C7
Itaúnas Brazil 207 N5
Itbayat i. Phil. 74 B1
Itchen Lake Canada 167 H1
Ite Peru 200 C4
Itea Greece 59 D10
Itebero Dem. Rep. Congo 126 F5
Itemgen, Ozero l. Kazakh. 103 G1
Itende Tanz. 129 B6
Itezhi-Tezhi Dam Zambia 127 E8
Ithaca Greece see Ithaki
Ithaca i. Greece see Ithaki
Ithaca MI U.S.A. 173 I7
Ithaca NY U.S.A. 177 I3
Ithaki Greece 59 B10
English form Ithaca; also known as Vathí
Ithaki i. Greece 59 B10
English form Ithaca
Ithakis, Steno sea chan. Greece 59 B10
Ith Hils ridge Germany 48 G3
Ithil, Wādī al watercourse Saudi Arabia 109 H9
Itigi Tanz. 129 B6
Itihusa-yama mt. Japan 91 B8
Itilleq Greenland 165 N3
Itimbiri r. Dem. Rep. Congo 126 D4
Itinga Brazil 202 D6
Itiquira Brazil 203 A6
Itiquira r. Brazil 201 F4
Itirapina Brazil 206 F9
Itirapuã Brazil 206 F7
Itiúba Brazil 202 E4
Itiúba, Serra de hills Brazil 202 E4
Itiyura r. Arg. 201 E5
Itkhari India 97 E4
Itmurinkol', Ozero l. Kazakh. 102 C2
Itō Japan 91 F7
Itoculo Moz. 131 I2
Itoigawa Japan 90 E6
Itoko Dem. Rep. Congo 126 D5
Iton r. France 50 H3
Itongafeno mt. Madag. 131 [inset] J4
Itororó Brazil 207 M2
Itsuki Japan 91 B8
Itsukushima Shrine tourist site Japan 91 C7
Ittiri Sardegna Italy 57 A8
Ittoqqortoormiit Greenland 165 Q2
also known as Scoresbysund

Itu Brazil 206 F10
Itu Nigeria 125 G5
Itu Abu Island S. China Sea 72 D4
Ituaçu Brazil 202 D5
Ituberá Brazil 202 E5
Ituí r. Brazil 198 D6
Ituiutaba Brazil 206 D5
Itula Dem. Rep. Congo 126 E5
Itumba Tanz. 129 B6
Itumbiara Brazil 206 D5
Itumbiara, Barragem resr Brazil 206 D5
Itungi Port Malawi 129 B7
Ituni Guyana 199 G3
Itupiranga Brazil 202 B3
Iturama Brazil 206 C6
Iturbe Para. 201 F6
Iturbide Campeche Mex. 185 H5
Iturbide Nuevo León Mex. 185 F3
Ituri r. Dem. Rep. Congo 126 E4
Iturup, Ostrov i. Rus. Fed. 82 G3
also known as Etorofu-tō
Itutinga Brazil 207 I8
Ituverava Brazil 206 F7
Ituxi r. Brazil 200 D1
also known as Iquiri
Ituzaingo Arg. 204 F2
Ityopia country Africa see Ethiopia
Itzehoe Germany 48 G2
Iuaretê Brazil 198 D4
Iuka U.S.A. 174 B5
Iul'tin Rus. Fed. 39 S3
Iuluti Moz. 131 H2
Iúna Brazil 207 L7
Iutica Brazil 198 D4
Ivaí r. Brazil 206 A10
Ivaiporã Brazil 206 B11
Ivakoany mt. Madag. 131 [inset] J4
Ivalo Fin. 44 N1
also known as Avveel or Avvil
Ivalojoki r. Fin. 44 N1
Ivanava Belarus 42 G9
also spelt Ivanovo
Ivanec Croatia 56 I2
Ivangorod Rus. Fed. 43 J2
Ivangrad Crna Gora Yugo. see Berane
Ivanhoe N.S.W. Australia 147 E3
Ivanhoe W.A. Australia 150 E2
Ivanhoe r. Canada 168 D3
Ivanhoe CA U.S.A. 182 E5
Ivanhoe MN U.S.A. 178 C2
Ivanhoe VA U.S.A. 176 E9
Ivanhoe Lake N.W.T. Canada 167 J2
Ivanhoe Lake Ont. Canada 173 K2
Ivanić-Grad Croatia 56 I3
Ivanishchi Rus. Fed. 43 V6
Ivanivka Ukr. 58 L2
Ivanjica Srbija Yugo. 58 B5
Ivankiv Ukr. 41 D6
Ivankovo Croatia 56 K3
Ivan'kovo Rus. Fed. 43 S7
Ivan'kovskiy Rus. Fed. 43 V5
Ivan'kovskoye Vodokhranilishche resr Rus. Fed. 43 R5
Ivankovtsy Rus. Fed. 82 D2
Ivano-Frankivs'k Ukr. 41 C6
also spelt Ivano-Frankovsk; formerly known as Stanislav
Ivano-Frankovsk Ukr. see Ivano-Frankivs'k
Ivanovka Kazakh. see Kokzhayyk
Ivanovka Amurskaya Oblast' Rus. Fed. 82 B2
Ivanovka Orenburgskaya Oblast' Rus. Fed. 102 C1
Ivanovo Belarus see Ivanava
Ivanovo tourist site Bulg. 58 G5
Ivanovo Ivanovskaya Oblast' Rus. Fed. 40 G4
Ivanovo Pskovskaya Oblast' Rus. Fed. 43 L5
Ivanovo Tverskaya Oblast' Rus. Fed. 43 S3
Ivanovo Oblast admin. div. Rus. Fed. see Ivanovskaya Oblast'
Ivanovskaya Oblast' admin. div. Rus. Fed. 43 U4
English form Ivanovo Oblast
Ivanovskiy Khrebet mts Kazakh. 88 C1
Ivanovskoye Orlovskaya Oblast' Rus. Fed. 43 R8
Ivanovskoye Yaroslavskaya Oblast' Rus. Fed. 43 U5
Ivanpah Lake U.S.A. 183 I6
Ivanšćica mts Croatia 56 H2
Ivanski Bulg. 58 I5
Ivanteyevka Rus. Fed. 102 B1
Ivantsevichi Belarus see Ivatsevichy
Ivato Madag. 131 [inset] J4
Ivatsevichy Belarus 42 G9
also spelt Ivantsevichi
Ivaylovgrad Bulg. 58 H7
Ivaylovgrad, Yazovir resr Bulg. 58 G7
Ivdel' Rus. Fed. 38 G3
Iveşti Romania 58 I3
Iveşti Romania 58 I2
Ivi, Cap c. Alg. 55 L8
Ivindo r. Gabon 126 B5
Ivinheima Brazil 203 A7
Ivittuut Greenland 165 O3
Iviza i. Spain see Ibiza
Ivohibe Madag. 131 [inset] J4
Ivolândia Brazil 206 C3
Ivolginsk Rus. Fed. 85 E1
Ivón Bol. 200 D2
Ivor U.S.A. 177 I9
Ivory Coast country Africa see Côte d'Ivoire
Ivösjön l. Sweden 45 K4
Ivot Rus. Fed. 43 P8
Ivrea Italy 51 N7
İvrindi Turkey 59 I9
Ivris Ugheltekhili pass Georgia 107 F2
Ivugivik Canada see Ivujivik
Ivujivik Canada 165 L3
formerly spelt Ivugivik
Ivuna Tanz. 129 B7
Ivvavik National Park Canada 164 F3
Ivyanyets Belarus 42 H8
Ivydale U.S.A. 176 D7
Iwaizumi Japan 90 G5
Iwaki Japan 90 G6
Iwaki-san vol. Japan 90 G4
Iwakuni Japan 91 C7
Iwamatsu Japan 91 C8
Iwamizawa Japan 90 G3
Iwan r. Indon. 77 F2
Iwanai Japan 90 G3
Iwanda Tanz. 129 B7
Iwanuma Japan 90 G5
Iwata Japan 91 E7
Iwate Japan 90 G5
Iwate pref. Japan 90 G5
Iwate-san vol. Japan 90 G5
Iwo Nigeria 125 G5
Iwo Jima i. Japan see Iō-jima
Iwupataka Aboriginal Land res. Australia 148 B4
Iwye Belarus 42 G8
Ixcamilpa Mex. 185 F5
Ixiamas Bol. 200 C3
Ixmiquilpán Mex. 185 F4
Ixopo S. Africa 133 O7
Ixtacomitán Mex. 185 G5
Ixtlán Nayarit Mex. 184 D4
Ixtlán Oaxaca Mex. 185 F5
Iya i. Indon. 75 B5
Iya r. Rus. Fed. 80 G1
Iyayi Tanz. 129 B7
İyirmi Altı Bakı Komissarı Azer. see 26 Bakı Komissarı
Iyo Japan 91 C8
Iyomishima Japan 91 C8
Iyo-nada b. Japan 91 C8
Izabal, Lago de l. Guat. 185 H6
Izamal Mex. 185 H4
Izapa tourist site Mex. 185 G6
Izari-dake mt. Japan 90 G3
Izazi Tanz. 129 B6
Izbăşeşti hill Romania 58 F3
Izberbash Rus. Fed. 102 A4
Izdeshkovo Rus. Fed. 43 O6
Izeh Iran 100 B4
Izgagane well Niger 125 H2
Izhevsk Rus. Fed. 40 J4
formerly known as Ustinov
Izhma Rus. Fed. 40 J2
Izhma Rus. Fed. see Sosnogorsk
Izhma r. Rus. Fed. 40 J2
Izkī Oman 105 G3
Izmail Ukr. see Izmayil
Izmalkovo Rus. Fed. 43 S9
Izmayil Ukr. 41 D7
also spelt Izmail; formerly spelt Ismail
Izmeny, Proliv sea chan. Japan/Rus. Fed. see Notsuke-suidō
İzmir Turkey 106 A3
historically known as Smyrna
İzmir prov. Turkey 59 I10
İzmir Körfezi g. Turkey 106 A3
İzmit Turkey see Kocaeli
İzmit Körfezi b. Turkey 106 B2
Izmorene Morocco 54 H9
Iznajar, Embalse de resr Spain 54 G7
Iznalloz Spain 55 H7
İznik Turkey 58 K8
historically known as Nicaea
İznik Gölü l. Turkey 106 B2
Iznoski Rus. Fed. 43 Q7
Izoard, Col d' pass France 51 M8
Izobil'noye Rus. Fed. see Izobil'nyy
Izobil'nyy Rus. Fed. 41 G7
formerly known as Izobil'noye
Izola Slovenia 56 F3
Izoplit Rus. Fed. 43 R5
Izozog Bajo Bol. 201 E4
Izra' Syria 108 H5
Iztochni Rodopi mts Bulg. 58 G7
Izúcar de Matamoros Mex. 185 F5
Izu-hantō pen. Japan 91 F7
Izuhara Japan 91 A7
Izumi Japan 91 B8
Izumisano Japan 91 D7
Izumo Japan 91 C7

Izu-Ogasawara Trench sea feature N. Pacific Ocean 220 D3
5th deepest trench in the world.

Izu-shotō is Japan 91 F7
Izu-tobu vol. Japan 91 F7
Izvestiy Tsentral'nogo Ispolnitel'nogo Komiteta, Ostrova is Rus. Fed. 39 I2
Izvestkovyy Rus. Fed. 82 C2
Izvoarele Romania 58 G4
Izvoarele Romania 58 F4
Izvoarele Romania 58 H3
Izvoru Romania 58 G4
Izyaslav Ukr. 41 C6
Iz"yayu Rus. Fed. 40 K2
Izyndy Kazakh. 102 D3
Izyum Ukr. 41 F6

↓ J

Jaama Estonia 42 I2
Ja'ar Yemen 105 D5
Jaba watercourse Iran 100 D3
Jabal as Sirāj Afgh. 101 G3
Jabal Dab Saudi Arabia 105 E3
Jabalón r. Spain 54 G6
Jabalpur India 96 C5
formerly spelt Jubbulpore
Jabbārah Fara Islands Saudi Arabia 104 C4
Jabbūl, Sabkhat al salt flat Syria 109 I2
Jabiluka Aboriginal Land res. Australia 148 B2
Jabir reg. Oman 105 G3
Jabiru Australia 148 B2
Jablah Syria 108 G2
Jablanica Bos.-Herz. 56 J5
Jablanica r. Yugo. 58 C5
Jablonec nad Nisou Czech Rep. 49 M5
Jabłonowo Pomorskie Poland 49 Q2
Jablunkov Czech Rep. 49 P6
Jaboticabal Brazil 206 E8
Jaboticatubas Brazil 207 J6
Jabuka i. Croatia 56 H5
Jabuka Vojvodina, Srbija Yugo. 58 B4
Jabung, Tanjung pt Indon. 76 D3
Jaburu Brazil 199 E6
Jabuti Brazil 199 G6
Jaca Spain 55 K2
Jacala Mex. 185 F4
Jacaraci Brazil 207 K1
Jacaré Mato Grosso Brazil 202 A5
Jacaré Rondônia Brazil 201 D2
Jacaré r. Brazil 199 F6
Jacaré r. Brazil 202 D4
Jacareacanga Brazil 199 G6
Jacareí Brazil 207 G10
Jacaretinga Brazil 201 F2
Jacarézinho Brazil 206 D10
Jáchal r. Arg. 204 D3
Jaciara Brazil 202 A5
Jacinto Brazil 202 D6
Jaciparaná Brazil 201 D2
Jaciparaná r. Brazil 201 D2
Jack r. Australia 149 E2
Jackfish Canada 172 G2
Jackfish Lake Canada 167 I4
Jack Lee, Lake resr U.S.A. 179 D5
Jacksboro TN U.S.A. 176 A9
Jacksboro TX U.S.A. 179 C5
Jackson Australia 149 F5
Jackson AL U.S.A. 175 C6
Jackson CA U.S.A. 182 D3
Jackson GA U.S.A. 175 D5
Jackson KY U.S.A. 176 B8
Jackson MI U.S.A. 173 I8
Jackson MN U.S.A. 178 D3
Jackson MO U.S.A. 174 B4

Jackson MS U.S.A. 175 B5
State capital of Mississippi.

Jackson NC U.S.A. 176 H9
Jackson OH U.S.A. 176 C6
Jackson TN U.S.A. 174 B5
Jackson WI U.S.A. 172 E7
Jackson WY U.S.A. 180 E4
Jackson, Cape N.Z. 152 I8
Jackson, Mount Antarctica 222 T2
Jackson Bay N.Z. 153 C11
Jackson Bay b. N.Z. 153 C11
also known as Okahu
Jackson Head N.Z. 153 C11
Jackson Island Rus. Fed. see Dzheksona, Ostrov
Jackson Lake U.S.A. 180 E4
Jacksonport U.S.A. 172 E6
Jacksons N.Z. 153 F10
Jackson's Arm Canada 169 J3
Jacksonville AL U.S.A. 175 C5
Jacksonville AR U.S.A. 179 D5
Jacksonville FL U.S.A. 175 D6
Jacksonville IL U.S.A. 174 B4
Jacksonville NC U.S.A. 174 E5
Jacksonville OH U.S.A. 176 C6
Jacksonville TX U.S.A. 179 D6
Jacksonville Beach U.S.A. 175 D6
Jack Wade U.S.A. 166 A1
Jacmel Haiti 187 E3
Jaco i. East Timor see Jako
Jacobabad Pak. 101 G4
Jacobina Brazil 202 D4
Jacob Lake U.S.A. 183 L5
Jacobsdal S. Africa 133 I6
Jacques-Cartier, Détroit de sea chan. Canada 169 H3
also known as Jacques Cartier Passage
Jacques Cartier, Mont mt. Canada 169 H3
Jacques Cartier Passage Canada see Jacques-Cartier, Détroit de
Jacquet River Canada 169 H4
Jacuba r. Brazil 206 A5
Jacuí Brazil 206 G8
Jacuí r. Brazil 203 B9
Jacuípe r. Brazil 202 E5
Jacunda Brazil 202 B3
Jacundá r. Brazil 202 B2
Jacupemba Brazil 207 M6
Jacupiranga Brazil 203 C8
Jacura Venez. 198 D2
Jadar r. Bos.-Herz. 56 L4
Jadar r. Yugo. 58 A4
Jadcherla India 94 C2
Jaddangi India 95 D2
Jaddi, Ras pt Pak. 101 E5
Jadebusen b. Germany 48 F2
Jadhdhānah Saudi Arabia 104 C4
Jādib Yemen 105 F4
J. A. D. Jensen Nunatakker nunataks Greenland 165 O3
Jadotville Dem. Rep. Congo see Likasi
Jadova r. Croatia 56 H4
Jadovnik mt. Bos.-Herz. 56 I4
Jaén Peru 198 B6
Jaen Phil. 74 B3
Jaén Spain 54 H7
Jæren reg. Norway 45 I4
Ja'farābād Ardabīl Iran 100 B2
Ja'farābād Khorāsan Iran 100 D2
Jaffa Israel see Tel Aviv-Yafo
Jaffa, Cape Australia 146 C4
Jaffna Sri Lanka 94 C4
Jaffrey U.S.A. 177 M3
Jafr, Qa' al imp. l. Jordan 109 H7
Jagadhri India 96 C3
Jägala r. Estonia 42 G2
Jagalur India 94 C3
Jagdalak Afgh. 101 G3
Jagdalpur India 94 D2
Jagdaqi China 85 J1
Jagdishpur India 89 C7
Jagdispur India 97 E4
Jagersfontein S. Africa 133 J6
Jaggang China 89 B5
Jaggayyapeta India 94 D2
Jaghin Iran 100 D5
Jaghjaghah, Nahr r. Syria/Turkey 109 M1
Jagin watercourse Iran 100 D5
Jagkolk Vloer salt pan S. Africa 132 E6
Jagodina Srbija Yugo. 58 C5
formerly known as Svetozarevo
Jagok Tso salt l. China see Urru Co
Jagsamka China see Luding
Jagst r. Germany 48 G6
Jagtial India 94 C2
Jaguapitã Brazil 206 B10
Jaguarão r. Brazil/Uruguay 204 G4
also known as Yaguarón
Jaguarão Uruguay 204 G4
Jaguarari Brazil 202 D4
Jaguaretama Brazil 202 E3
Jaguari Brazil 203 A9
Jaguariaíva Brazil 206 D11
Jaguaribe Brazil 202 E3
Jaguaribe r. Brazil 202 E3
Jaguaruana Brazil 202 E3
Jagüe Arg. 204 C3
Jagüey Grande Cuba 186 C2
Jahanabad India 97 E4
formerly spelt Jehanabad
Jahān Dāgh mt. Iran 100 B2
Jahleel, Point Australia 148 A1
Jahmah well Iraq 107 F5
Jahrom Iran 100 C4
Jāhyad Iran 100 D5
Jaicós Brazil 202 D3
Jaigarh India 94 B2
Jailolo Indon. 75 C2
Jailolo, Selat sea chan. Indon. 75 D3
Jailolo Gilolo i. Indon. see Halmahera
Jaiña Chile 200 C4
Jainca China 84 D5
also known as Magitang
Jaintiapur Bangl. 97 G4
Jaipur India 96 B4
Jaipurhat Bangl. 97 F4
Jais India 97 D4
Jaisalmer India 96 A4
Jaisinghnagar India 97 D5
Jaitaran India 96 B4
Jaitgarh hill India 94 C1
Jaitpur India 96 C4
Jajarkot Nepal 97 D3
Jajce Bos.-Herz. 56 J4
Jajnagar state India see Orissa
Jakar Bhutan 97 F4
also known as Byakar

Jakarta Indon. 77 D4
Capital of Indonesia. Formerly spelt Djakarta; historically known as Batavia or Sunda Kalapa.
world [cities] 24–25

Jakhan India 101 G6
Jakharrah Libya 120 D2
Jakin mt. Afgh. 101 F4
Jakkalsberg Namibia 130 C3
Jakkalsberg hills Namibia 132 A5
Jakki Kowr Iran 101 E5
Jäkkvik Sweden 44 L2
Jaklat India 96 B3
Jako i. East Timor 75 C5
also known as Jaco
Jakobshavn Greenland see Ilulissat
Jakobstad Fin. 44 M3
also known as Pietersaari
Jakupica mts Macedonia 58 C7
Jal U.S.A. 179 B5
Jalaid China see Inder
Jalājil Saudi Arabia 105 D2
Jalālābād Afgh. 101 G3
Jalalabad Punjab India 96 B3
Jalalabad Uttar Pradesh India 96 C3
Jalalabad Uttar Pradesh India 96 C4
Jalal-Abad Kyrg. 103 H4
also spelt Dzhalal-Abad
Jalal-Abad admin. div. Kyrg. 103 H4
English form Jalal-Abad Oblast; also known as Dzhalal-Abadskaya Oblast'
Jalal-Abad Oblast admin. div. Kyrg. see Jalal-Abad
Jalalpur Gujarat India 94 B1
Jalalpur Uttar Pradesh India 97 D4
Jalāmīd, Ḩazm al ridge Saudi Arabia 107 D5
Ja'lān, Jabal mts Oman 105 G3
Jalandhar India 96 B3
formerly spelt Jullundur
Jalan Kayu Sing. 76 [inset]
Jalapa Mex. 185 G5
Jalapa Nicaragua 186 B4
Jalapa Enríquez Mex. 185 F5
also known as Xalapa
Jalapur Pak. 101 H3
Jalapur Pirwala Pak. 101 G4
Jalasjärvi Fin. 44 M3
Jalaun India 96 C4
Jalawlā' Iraq 107 F4
also spelt Jalūlā
Jalbol r. Australia 148 B2
Jaldak Afgh. 101 F4
Jaldhaka r. Bangl. 97 F4
Jaldrug India 94 C2
Jales Brazil 206 C7
Jalesar India 96 C4
Jaleshwar India 97 E5
Jaleshwar Nepal see Jaleswar
Jaleswar Nepal 97 E4
also spelt Jaleshwar
Jalgaon India 96 B5
Jalībah Iraq 107 F5
Jalingo Nigeria 125 H4
Jalisco state Mex. 184 D5
Jallābī Iran 100 D5
Jalna India 94 B2
Jālo Iran 101 E5
Jalón r. Spain 55 J3
Jalor India 96 B4
Jalostotitlán Mex. 185 E4
Jalovik Srbija Yugo. 58 A4
Jalpa Mex. 185 E4
Jalpaiguri India 97 F4
Jalpan Mex. 185 F4
Jalrez Afgh. 101 G3
Jālū Libya 120 D2
Jalūlā Iraq see Jalawlā'
Jālū Oasis Libya 120 D2
Jām r. Iran 101 E3
Jām reg. Iran 101 E3
Jamaica Cuba 187 E2

Jamaica country West Indies 186 D3
northamerica [countries] 158–159

Jamaica Channel Haiti/Jamaica 187 E3
Jämaja Estonia 42 D3
Jamalpur Bangl. 97 F4
Jamalpur India 97 E4
Jamanxim r. Brazil 199 G6
Jamari Brazil 201 E2
Jamba Angola 127 C8
Jambi Indon. 76 C3
also known as Telanaipura
Jambi prov. Indon. 76 C3
Jambin Australia 149 F5
Jambo India 96 B4
Jamboaye r. Indon. 76 B1
Jambongan i. Sabah Malaysia 77 G1
Jambuair, Tanjung pt Indon. 76 B1
Jambūr Iraq 109 P2
Jambusar India 96 B5
Jamekunte India 94 C2
James watercourse Australia 148 C4
James r. Canada 167 I1
James r. MO U.S.A. 178 D4
James r. ND/SD U.S.A. 178 C3
James r. VA U.S.A. 177 I8
James, Isla i. Chile 205 B7
Jamesabad Pak. 101 G5
James Bay Canada 168 D2
Jamesburg U.S.A. 177 K5
James Cistern Bahamas 186 D1
Jameson Land reg. Greenland 165 Q2
Jameson Range hills Australia 151 D5
James Peak N.Z. 153 C13
James Ranges mts Australia 148 B5
James Ross Island Antarctica 222 U2
James Ross Strait Canada 165 J3
Jamestown Australia 146 C3
Jamestown Canada see Wawa
Jamestown S. Africa 133 K8

Jamestown St Helena 216 N7
Capital of St Helena and Dependencies.

Jamestown CA U.S.A. 182 D4
Jamestown KY U.S.A. 174 C4
Jamestown ND U.S.A. 178 C2
Jamestown NY U.S.A. 176 F3
Jamestown PA U.S.A. 176 E4
Jamestown TN U.S.A. 176 A9
Jämijärvi Fin. 45 M3
Jamiltepec Mex. 185 F5
Jamkhandi India 94 B2
Jamkhed India 94 B2
Jammalamadugu India 94 C3
Jammerbugten b. Denmark 45 J4
Jammu Jammu and Kashmir 96 B2

Jammu and Kashmir terr. Asia 96 C2
Disputed territory (India/Pakistan). Short form Kashmir.
asia [countries] 64–67

Jamnagar India 96 A5
formerly known as Navangar
Jamner India 94 B1
Jamni r. India 96 C4
Jamno, Jezioro lag. Poland 49 N1
Jampang Kulon Indon. 77 D4
Jampur Pak. 101 G4
Jämsä Fin. 45 N3
Jämsänkoski Fin. 45 N3
Jamshedpur India 97 E5
Jamtara India 97 E5
Jamtari Nigeria 125 H5
Jämtland county Sweden 44 K3
Jamui India 97 E4
Jamuk, Gunung mt. Indon. 77 G2
Jamu Mare Romania 58 C3
Jamuna r. Bangl. 97 F5
Jamuna r. India 97 G4
Janā i. Saudi Arabia 105 E2
Janāb, Wādī al watercourse Jordan 109 H6
Janakpur India 97 D5
Janakpur Nepal 97 E4
Janaúba Brazil 202 D5
Jandaia Brazil 206 C4
Jandaia do Sul Brazil 206 B10
Jandaq Iran 100 C3
Jandiala India 96 B3
Jandiatuba r. Brazil 198 D5
Jandongi Dem. Rep. Congo 126 D4
Jandowae Australia 149 F5
Jándula r. Spain 54 G6
Jandulilla r. Spain 55 H7
Janeiro r. Brazil 202 C5
Janesville CA U.S.A. 182 D1
Janesville WI U.S.A. 172 D8
Jang, Tanjung pt Indon. 76 D3
Jangal Iran 101 D3
Jangamo Moz. 131 G5
Jangaon India 94 C2
Jangeldi Uzbek. see Dzhangel'dy
Jangipur India 97 F4
Jangnga Turkm. see Dzhanga
Jangngai Ri mts China 89 D5
Jangngai Zangbo r. China 89 D5
Jānī Beyglū Iran 100 A2
Janikowo Poland 49 P3
Janiópolis Brazil 206 A11
Janja Bos.-Herz. 56 L4
Janja r. Bos.-Herz. 56 L4
Janjevo Kosovo, Srbija Yugo. 58 C6
Jan Kempdorp S. Africa 133 I4
formerly known as Andalusia
Jankov Kamen mt. Yugo. 58 B5

Jan Mayen i. Arctic Ocean 224 X2
Part of Norway.

Jänmuiža Latvia 42 G4
Jannatābād Iran 100 B3
Jañona mt. Spain 54 E4
Janos Mex. 184 C2
Jánoshalma Hungary 49 Q9
Jánossomorja Hungary 49 O8
Janów Lubelski Poland 49 T5
Jans Bay Canada 167 I4
Jansenville S. Africa 133 I9
Jânua Coeli Brazil 202 B2
Januária Brazil 202 C5
Janūbī, Al Fulayj al watercourse Saudi Arabia 105 D1
Janūb Sīnā' governorate Egypt 108 E8
English form South Sinai; also known as Sinai al Janûbîya
Janwada India 94 C2
Janzar mt. Pak. 101 E5
Janzé France 50 E5
Jaora India 96 B5

Japan country Asia 90 E5
9th most populous country in the world. Known as Nihon or Nippon in Japanese.
world [population] 22–23
asia [countries] 64–67

Japan, Sea of N. Pacific Ocean 83 D5
also known as East Sea or Nippon Hai
Japan Alps National Park Japan see Chibu-Sangaku National Park
Japón Hond. 186 B4
Japurá r. Brazil 198 E5
Japvo Mount India 97 G4
Jaqué Panama 186 D6
Jarabacoa Dom. Rep. 187 F3
Jarābulus Syria 109 J1
Jarad Saudi Arabia 104 C4
Jaraguá Brazil 206 D2
Jaraguá do Sul Brazil 203 B8
Jaraguari Brazil 203 A7
Jaraiz de la Vera Spain 54 F4
Jarama r. Spain 55 H4
Jarash Jordan 108 G5
Jarauçu r. Brazil 199 H5
Järbo Sweden 45 L3
Jarboesville U.S.A. see Lexington Park
Jar-bulak Kazakh. see Kabanbay
Jardim Ceará Brazil 202 E3
Jardim Mato Grosso do Sul Brazil 201 F5
Jardín r. Spain 55 I6
Jardine River National Park Australia 149 D1
Jardinópolis Brazil 206 F8
Jargalant Arhangay Mongolia 84 D2
Jargalant Bayanhongor Mongolia 84 C2
Jargalant Bayan-Ölgiy Mongolia 84 A2
Jargalant Dornod Mongolia 85 G2
Jargalant Govĭ-Altay Mongolia 84 C2
Jargalant Mongolia see Hovd
Jargalant Töv Mongolia 85 E1
Jargalant Hayrhan mt. Mongolia 84 B2
Jargalthaan Mongolia 85 F2
Jari r. Brazil 199 I5
Jaria Jhanjail Bangl. 97 F4
Jarmen Germany 49 K2
Järna Dalarna Sweden 45 K3
Järna Stockholm Sweden 45 L4
Jarnac France 50 F7
Jarocin Poland 49 O4
Jaroměř Czech Rep. 49 M5
Jarosław Poland 49 T5
Järpen Sweden 44 K3
Jarqürghon Uzbek. see Dzharkurgan
Jarrāh, Wādī watercourse Syria 109 M1
Jarrāhi watercourse Iran 100 B4
Jarratt U.S.A. 176 H9
Jarrettsville U.S.A. 177 I6
Jartai China 85 E4
Jartai Yanchi salt l. China 84 E4
Jarú Brazil 201 E2
Jarūb Yemen 105 F4
Jarud China see Lubei
Jarut mt. Yugo. 58 B5
Järvakandi Estonia 42 F3
Järvenpää Fin. 45 N3

Jarvis Island terr. N. Pacific Ocean 221 H6
United States Unincorporated Territory.
oceania [countries] 138–139

Järvsand Sweden 44 K2
Järvsö Sweden 45 L3
Jarwa India 97 D4
Jasdan India 96 A5
Jashpurnagar India 97 E5
Jasień Poland 49 M4
Jasiołka r. Poland 49 S6
Jāsk Iran 100 D5
Jāsk-e Kohneh Iran 100 D5
Jasliq Uzbek. see Zhaslyk
Jasło Poland 49 S6
Jašlūnai Lith. 42 G7
Jasmund pen. Germany 49 K1
Jasmund, Nationalpark nature res. Germany 49 K1
Jason Peninsula Antarctica 222 T2
Jasper Canada 166 G4
Jasper AL U.S.A. 175 C5
Jasper AR U.S.A. 179 D4
Jasper FL U.S.A. 175 D6
Jasper GA U.S.A. 174 C5
Jasper IN U.S.A. 174 C4
Jasper NY U.S.A. 176 H3
Jasper OH U.S.A. 176 B6
Jasper TN U.S.A. 174 C5
Jasper TX U.S.A. 179 D6
Jasper National Park Canada 167 G4
Jaşşān Iraq 107 F4
Jassy Romania see Iaşi
Jastarnia Poland 49 P1
Jastrebarsko Croatia 56 H3
Jastrowie Poland 49 N2
Jastrzębie-Zdrój Poland 49 P6
historically known as Bad Königsdorff
Jászárokszállás Hungary 49 Q8
Jászberény Hungary 49 Q8
Jataí Brazil 206 B4
Jatapu r. Brazil 199 G5
Jatara India 96 C4
Jati Pak. 101 G5
also known as Mughalbhin
Jatibarang Indon. 77 E4
Jatibonico Cuba 186 D2
Játiva Spain see Xátiva
Jatiwangi Indon. 77 E4
Jatobá Brazil 202 A5
Jatoi Pak. 101 G4
Jättendal Sweden 45 L3
Jatuarana Brazil 201 E1
Jaú Brazil 206 E9
Jaú r. Brazil 199 F5
Jaú, Parque Nacional do nat. park Brazil 199 F5
Jauaperi r. Brazil 199 F5
Jaua Sarisariñama, Parque Nacional nat. park Venez. 199 E3
Jauco Cuba 187 E2
Jauja Peru 200 B2
Jaumave Mex. 185 F4
Jauna r. Brazil 199 F6
Jaunanna Latvia 42 I4
Jaunay-Clan France 50 G6
Jaunjelgava Latvia 42 G5
Jaunkalsnava Latvia 42 G5
Jaunlutriņi Latvia 42 D5
Jaunmārupe Latvia 42 E5
Jaunpiebalga Latvia 42 H4
Jaunpils Latvia 42 E5
Jaunpur India 97 D4
Jaupaci Brazil 206 C3
Jauru Brazil 203 A6
Jauru r. Brazil 201 F4

Java i. Indon. 77 D5
5th largest island in Asia. Also spelt Jawa.
asia [landscapes] 62–63

Javadi Hills India 94 C3
Javaés r. Brazil see Formoso
Javaés, Serra dos hills Brazil 202 B4
Javalambre mt. Spain 55 K4
Javalambre, Sierra de mts Spain 55 J4
Javand Afgh. 101 F3
Javari r. Brazil 198 D6
also spelt Yavari
Javarthushuu Mongolia 85 G1
Java Sea Indon. 77 E4

Java Trench sea feature Indian Ocean 218 N6
Deepest point in the Indian Ocean.
oceans [features] 210–211

Jávea Spain 55 L6
Javier, Isla i. Chile 205 B7
Javor mts Yugo. 58 B5
Javořice hill Czech Rep. 49 M6
Javorie mt. Slovakia 49 Q7
Javorník mt. Slovenia 56 H2
Javorníky mts Slovakia 49 P6
Jävre Sweden 44 M2
Jawa i. Indon. see Java
Jawa Barat prov. Indon. 77 D4
Jawad India 96 B4
Jawai r. India 96 A4
Jawala Mukhi India 96 C3
Jawar India 96 C5
Jawa Tengah prov. Indon. 77 E4
Jawa Timur prov. Indon. 77 F4
Jawbān Bayk Syria 109 I1
Jawf, Wādī al watercourse Yemen 104 D5
Jawhar India 94 B2
Jawhar Somalia 128 E4
Jawor Poland 49 N4
Jaworzno Poland 49 Q5
Jawoyn Aboriginal Land res. Australia 148 B2
Jay U.S.A. 179 D4

Jaya, Puncak mt. Indon. 73 I7
Highest mountain in Oceania. Formerly known as Carstensz-top or Puntjak Sukarno.
oceania [landscapes] 136–137

Jayanca Peru 198 B6
Jayanti India 97 F4
Jayapura Indon. 73 J7
formerly known as Hollandia or Sukarnapura
Jayb, Wādī al watercourse Israel/Jordan 108 G6
Jaynagar Bihar India 97 E4
Jaynagar W. Bengal India 97 F5
Jaypur India 95 D2
Jayrūd Syria 109 H4
Jayton U.S.A. 179 B5
Jazīrat al Ḩamrā U.A.E. 105 F2
Jazminal Mex. 185 E3
Jbail Lebanon 108 G3
historically known as Biblos
J. C. Murphey Lake U.S.A. 172 F9
Jean U.S.A. 183 I6
Jeanerette U.S.A. 175 B6
Jean Marie River Canada 166 F2
Jebāl Bārez, Kūh-e mts Iran 100 D4
Jebel Libya 120 C2
Jebel Romania 58 C3
Jebel Turkm. see Dzhebel
Jebel Abyad Plateau Sudan 121 F5
Jebel Ali U.A.E. see Mina Jebel Ali
Jebel, Bahr el r. Sudan/Uganda see White Nile
Jeberos Peru 198 B6
Jebha Morocco 54 G9
Jebus Indon. 77 D3
Jedburgh U.K. 46 J8
Jeddah Saudi Arabia 104 B3
also spelt Jiddah
Jeddore Lake Canada 169 K3
Jedeida Tunisia 57 B12
Jędrzejów Poland 49 R5
Jedwabne Poland 49 T2
Jeetze r. Germany 48 I2
Jefferson IA U.S.A. 178 D3
Jefferson NC U.S.A. 176 D9
Jefferson OH U.S.A. 176 E4
Jefferson TX U.S.A. 179 D5
Jefferson WI U.S.A. 172 E8
Jefferson r. U.S.A. 180 E3
Jefferson, Mount U.S.A. 183 H3
Jefferson, Mount vol. U.S.A. 180 B3

Jefferson City MO U.S.A. 178 D4
State capital of Missouri.

Jefferson City TN U.S.A. 176 B9
Jeffersonton U.S.A. 176 H7
Jeffersonville IN U.S.A. 174 C4
Jeffersonville KY U.S.A. 176 B8
Jeffersonville OH U.S.A. 176 B6
Jeffrey U.S.A. 176 D8
Jeffrey's Bay S. Africa 133 I11
Jega Nigeria 125 G3
Jehanabad India see Jahanabad
Jēkabpils Latvia 42 G5
Jelbart Ice Shelf Antarctica 223 X2
Jelcz-Laskowice Poland 49 O4
Jeldēsa Eth. 128 D2
Jelenia Góra Poland 49 M5
historically known as Hirschberg
Jelep La pass China/India 89 E7
Jelgava Latvia 42 E5
Jellico U.S.A. 176 A9
Jellicoe Canada 168 C3
Jelloway U.S.A. 176 C5
Jelondī Tajik. see Dzhilandy
Jelow Gīr Iran 100 A3
Jemaja i. Indon. 77 D2
Jember Indon. 77 F5
Jemez Pueblo U.S.A. 181 F6
Jeminay China 88 D2
also known as Topterek
Jeminay Kazakh. 88 D2
Jemma Bauchi Nigeria 125 H4
Jemma Kaduna Nigeria 125 H4
Jemmel Tunisia 57 C13
Jemnice Czech Rep. 49 M6
Jempang, Danau l. Indon. 77 G3
Jena Germany 48 I5
Jena U.S.A. 179 D6
Jenda Malawi 129 B8
Jendouba Tunisia 123 H1
Jengish Chokusu mt. China/Kyrg. see Pobeda Peak
Jenīn West Bank 108 G5
Jenipapo Brazil 199 F6
Jenkinjones U.S.A. 176 D8
Jenkins U.S.A. 176 C8
Jenkintown U.S.A. 177 J5
Jenne Mali see Djenné
Jenner Canada 167 I5
Jennersdorf Austria 49 N9
Jennings r. Canada 166 C3
Jennings U.S.A. 179 D6
Jenpeg Canada 167 L4
Jepara Indon. 77 E4
Jeparit Australia 147 D4
Jeppo Fin. 44 M3
Jequié Brazil 202 D5
Jequitaí Brazil 203 C6
Jequitaí r. Brazil 207 I4
Jequitinhonha Brazil 202 D6
Jequitinhonha r. Brazil 207 O2
Jerba, Île de i. Tunisia 123 H2
Jerbar Sudan 128 A3
Jereh Iran 107 G5
Jérémie Haiti 187 E3
Jeremoabo Brazil 202 E4
Jerer Shet' watercourse Eth. 128 D3
Jereweh Indon. 77 G5
Jerez Mex. 185 E4
Jerez de la Frontera Spain 54 E8
Jerez de los Caballeros Spain 54 E6
Jerfojaur Sweden 44 L2
Jergucat Albania 59 B9
Jericho Australia 149 E4
Jericho West Bank 108 G6
also known as Arīḩā; also spelt Yeriḩo; historically known as Tell es-Sultan

index J K

Jerid, Chott el salt l. Tunisia 123 H2
Jerijih, Tanjong pt Sarawak Malaysia 77 E2
Jerilderie Australia 147 E3
Jermyn U.S.A. 177 J4
Jerome AZ U.S.A. 183 L7
Jerome ID U.S.A. 180 D4
Jerramungup Australia 151 B7

▶**Jersey** terr. Channel Is 50 D3
United Kingdom Crown Dependency.
europe [countries] ➡ 32–35

Jersey City U.S.A. 177 K5
Jerseyville U.S.A. 174 B4
Jerte r. Spain 54 E5
Jerumenha Brazil 202 D3

▶**Jerusalem** Israel/West Bank 108 G6
Capital of Israel. Also known as El Quds; also spelt Yerushalayim; historically known as Aelia Capitolina or Hierosolyma.
asia [issues] ➡ 66–67

Jerusalem N.Z. 152 J7
Jervis Bay Australia 147 F3
Jervis Bay Territory admin. div. Australia 147 F3
also known as Commonwealth Territory
Jervois Range hills Australia 148 B4
Jesenice Slovenia 56 G2
Jeseník Czech Rep. 49 O5
Jesi Italy 56 F5
Jesmond Canada 166 F5
Jesolo Italy 56 E3
Jesselton Sabah Malaysia see **Kota Kinabalu**
Jessen Germany 49 J4
Jessheim Norway 45 J3
Jessore Bangl. 97 F5
Jesu Maria Island P.N.G. see **Rambutyo Island**
Jesup U.S.A. 175 D6
Jesús Carranza Mex. 185 G5
Jesús María Arg. 204 D3
Jesús María, Barra spit Mex. 185 F3
Jetalsar India 96 A5
Jethro tourist site Saudi Arabia 104 A1
also known as Maghā'ir Shu'ayb
Jetmore U.S.A. 178 C4
Jevnaker Norway 45 J3
Jewett City U.S.A. 177 N4
Jewish Autonomous Oblast admin. div. Rus. Fed. see **Yevreyskaya Avtonomnaya Oblast'**
Jeyhun Turkm. see **Dzheykhun**
Jeziorak, Jezioro l. Poland 49 Q2
Jeziorany Poland 49 R2
Jeziorka r. Poland 49 S3
Jeziorsko, Jezioro l. Poland 49 P4
Jezzine Lebanon 108 G4
Jhabua India 96 B5
Jha Jha India 97 E4
Jhajjar India 96 C3
Jhajju India 96 B4
Jhal Pak. 101 F4
Jhalakati Bangl. 97 F5
Jhalawar India 96 C4
Jhalida India 97 E5
Jhalrapatan India 96 C4
Jhang Pak. 101 H4
Jhanjharpur India 97 E4
Jhansi India 96 C4
Jhanzi r. India 97 G4
Jhapa Nepal 97 E4
Jhargram India 97 E5
Jharia India 97 E5
Jharkhand state India 97 E5
Jharsuguda India 97 E5
Jhatpat Pak. 101 G4
Jhawani Nepal 97 E4
Jhelum r. India/Pak. 96 B3
Jhelum Pak. 101 H3
Jhenaidaha Bangl. see **Jhenida**
Jhenida Bangl. 97 F5
also known as Jhenaidaha
Jhinjhuvada India 96 A5
Jhinkpani India 97 E5
Jhudo Pak. 101 G5
Jhumritilaiya India 97 E4
Jhunjhunun India 96 B3
Jhusi India 97 D4
Jiachuan China 86 C1
formerly known as Jiachuanzhen
Jiachuanzhen China see **Jiachuan**
Jiading China see **Xinfeng**
Jiading China 87 G2
Jiahe China 87 E3
Jiajiang China 86 B2
Jialing Jiang r. China 86 C2
Jialu China see **Jiaxian**
Jialu r. China 87 E1
Jiamusi China 82 C3
Ji'an Jiangxi China 87 E3
also known as Dunhou
Ji'an Jiangxi China 87 E3
Ji'an Jilin China 83 B4
Jianchang China see **Nancheng**
Jianchang China 85 H3
Jianchuan China 86 A3
also known as Jinhua
Jiandaoyu China see **Zigui**
Jiande China 87 F2
Jiang'an China 86 C2
Jiangbei China see **Yubei**
Jiangcheng China 86 B4
also known as Menglie
Jiangchuan China 86 B3
also known as Dajie
Jiangcun China 87 D3
Jiangdu China 87 F1
formerly known as Xiannümiao
Jiange China 86 C2
also known as Pu'an
Jiangjiehe China 87 C3
Jiangjin China 86 C2
Jiangjunmiao China 88 E2
Jiangjunmu China 85 G4
Jiangjuntai China 84 C3
Jiangkou China see **Fengkai**
Jiangkou Guizhou China 87 D3
also known as Shuangjiang
Jiangkou Shaanxi China 86 C1
Jiangkou China see **Pingchang**
Jiangle China 87 F3
also known as Guyong
Jiangling China see **Jingzhou**
Jiangluozhen China 86 C1
Jiangmen China 87 E4
Jiangna China see **Yanshan**
Jiangning China 87 F2
also known as Dongshan
Jiangshan China 87 F2
Jiangsi China see **Dejiang**
Jiangsu prov. China 87 F1
English form Kiangsu
Jiangtaibu China 85 E5
Jiangxi prov. China 87 E3
English form Kiangsi
Jiangxia China see **Wuchang**
Jiangxian China 85 F5
Jiangxigou China 84 D4
Jiangyan China 87 G1
formerly known as Taixian
Jiangyin China 87 G2
Jiangyong China 87 D3
Jiangyou China 86 C2
formerly known as Zhongba
Jiangyu China 85 H4
Jiangzhesongrong China 89 D6
Jianhu China 87 F1
Jian Jiang r. China 87 D4
Jianjun China see **Yongshou**
Jianli China 87 E2
also known as Rongcheng
Jianning China 87 F3
also known as Suicheng
Jian'ou China 87 F3
Jianping Liaoning China 85 H3
also known as Yebaishou
Jianping Liaoning China 85 H3
Jianshe China 86 A1
Jianshe China see **Baiyü**
Jianshi China 87 D2
also known as Yezhou
Jianshui China 86 B4
also known as Lin'an
Jianxing China 86 C2
Jianyang Fujian China 87 F3
Jianyang Sichuan China 86 C2
Jiaochang China 86 B1
formerly known as Jiaochangba
Jiaochangba China see **Jiaochang**
Jiaocheng China see **Jiaoling**
Jiaocheng China 85 G4
Jiaohe Hebei China 85 H4
Jiaohe Jilin China 82 B4
Jiaojiang China see **Taizhou**
Jiaokou China 85 F4
Jiaokui China see **Yiliang**
Jiaolai r. China 85 H4
Jiaolai r. China 85 I3
Jiaoling China 87 F3
also known as Jiaocheng
Jiaonan China 85 H5
formerly known as Wanggezhuang
Jiaowei China 87 F3
Jiaozhou China 85 I4
Jiaozhou Wan b. China 85 I4
Jiaozuo China 85 G5
Jiapigou China 82 B4
Jiasa China 86 B3
Jiashan China see **Mingguang**
Jiashi China 88 B4
also known as Payzawat
Jia Tsuo La pass China 89 D6
Jiaxian Henan China 87 E1
Jiaxian Shaanxi China 85 F4
also known as Jialu
Jiaxiang China 85 H5
Jiaxing China 87 G2
Jiayi Taiwan see **Chiai**
Jiayin China 82 C2
also known as Chaoyang
Jiayu China 87 E2
also known as Yuyue
Jiayuguan China 84 C4
Jiazi China 87 F4
Jibou Romania 58 E1
Jibsh, Ra's c. Oman 105 G3
Jībūtī country Africa see **Djibouti**
Jibuti Djibouti see **Djibouti**
Jicarilla Apache Indian Reservation res. U.S.A. 181 F5
Jičín Czech Rep. 49 M5
Jiddah Saudi Arabia see **Jeddah**
Jidong China 82 C3
Jiehkkevarri mt. Norway 44 L1
Jiehu China see **Yinan**
Jieshi China 87 E4
Jieshi Wan b. China 87 E4
Jieshou China 87 E1
Jiesia r. Lith. 42 E7
Ješjávri l. Norway 44 N1
Jiexi China 87 E4
also known as Hepo
Jiexiu China 85 F4
Jieyang China 87 F4
Jieznas Lith. 42 F7
Jigalong Aboriginal Reserve Australia 150 C4
Jigawa state Nigeria 125 H3
Jigerbent Turkm. see **Dzhigirbent**
Jiggalong Australia 150 C4
Jiggs U.S.A. 183 I1
Jiguaní Cuba 186 D2
Jigzhi China 86 B1
also known as Chugqênsumdo
Jiḥār, Wādī al watercourse Syria 109 I3
Jihlava Czech Rep. 49 M6
Jihlava r. Czech Rep. 49 N7
Jijel Alg. 123 G1
formerly spelt Djidjelli
Jijia r. Romania 58 J2
Jijiga Eth. 128 D2
Jijona Spain 55 K6
Jiju China 86 B2
Jil'ād reg. Jordan 108 G5
English form Gilead
Jīlān ash Shuwayḥīṭīyah esc. Saudi Arabia 109 K7
Jilava Romania 58 H4
Jilbadji Nature Reserve Australia 151 B6
Jilf al Kabīr, Haḍabat al plat. Egypt see **Gilf Kebir Plateau**
Jilga r. Afgh. 101 G3
Jilh al 'Ishār plain Saudi Arabia 105 D2
Jilib Somalia 128 D4
Jili Hu l. China 88 D2
Jilin China 82 B4
also known as Kirin
Jilin prov. China 85 J3
English form Kirin
Jiling China 84 D4
Jilin Handa Ling mts China 82 B4
Jiloca r. Spain 55 J3
Jilong Taiwan see **Chilung**
Jīma Eth. 128 C3
Jima Ali well Eth. 128 E3
Jimani Haiti 187 F3
Jimbo Tanz. 129 C6
Jimbolia Romania 58 B3
Jimda China see **Zindo**
Jimena de la Frontera Spain 54 F8
Jiménez Chihuahua Mex. 184 D3
Jiménez Coahuila Mex. 185 E2
Jiménez Tamaulipas Mex. 185 F3
Jimeta Nigeria 125 I4
Jimi r. P.N.G. 73 J7
Jim Jim Creek r. Australia 148 B2
Jimo China 85 I4
Jimsar China 88 E3
Jina Romania 58 E3
Jinan China 85 H4
formerly spelt Tsinan
Jin'an China see **Songpan**
Jinbi China see **Dayao**
Jinchang China 84 D4
formerly known as Jinchuan
Jincheng China 85 G5
Jincheng China see **Leibo**
Jincheng China see **Yilong**
Jincheng China see **Wuding**
Jinchengjiang China see **Hechi**
Jinchuan China see **Jinchang**
Jinchuan China see **Xingan**
Jinchuan China 86 B2
also known as Quqên
Jind India 96 C3
Jindřichův Hradec Czech Rep. 49 M6
Jin'e China see **Longchang**
Jinfosi China 84 C4
Jing China see **Jinghe**
Jing r. China 87 D1
Jing'an China see **Doumen**
Jingbian China 85 F4
also known as Zhangjiapan
Jingchuan China 85 E5
Jingde China 87 F2
also known as Jingyang
Jingdezhen China 87 F2
Jingdong China 86 B3
also known as Jinping
Jinggangshan China 87 E3
formerly known as Ciping
Jinggang Shan hill China 87 E3
Jinggongqiao China 87 F2
Jinggu China 86 B4
also known as Weiyuan
Jinghai China 85 H4
Jinghe China 88 C2
also known as Jing
Jinghong China 86 B4
formerly known as Yunjinghong
Jingjiang China 87 G1
Jingle China 85 G4
Jingmen China 87 E2
Jingning China 85 E5
Jingpeng China 85 H3
also known as Hexigten Qi
Jingpo Hu resr China 82 C4
Jingshan China 87 E2
also known as Xinshi
Jingtai China 84 D4
also known as Yitiaoshan
Jingtieshan China 84 C4
formerly known as Huashugou
Jingxi China 86 C4
also known as Xinjing
Jingxian China 87 F2
Jingxian China see **Jingzhou**
Jingxin China see **Yongshan**
Jingyan China 86 C2
also known as Yancheng
Jingyang China see **Jingde**
Jingyu China 82 B4
Jingyuan China 84 E4
Jingzhou Hubei China 87 E2
formerly known as Jiangling
Jingzhou Hubei China 87 E2
formerly known as Shashi
Jingzhou Hunan China 87 D3
also known as Quyang; formerly known as Jingxian
Jinhe China see **Jinping**
Jinhua China see **Jianchuan**
Jinhua China 87 F2
Jining Nei Mongol China 85 G3
also spelt Tsining
Jining Shandong China 85 H5
formerly known as Chining
Jinja Uganda 128 B4
Jinjiang Fujian China 87 F3
Jinjiang China see **Chengmai**
Jinjiang Yunnan China 86 B3
Jin Jiang r. China 87 D3
Jin Jiang r. China 87 E2
Jinka Eth. 128 C3
Jinkouhe China 86 B2
Jinmen Taiwan see **Chinmen**
Jinmu Jiao pt China 87 D5
Jinning China 86 B3
also known as Kunyang
Jinotega Nicaragua 186 B4
Jinotepe Nicaragua 186 B5
Jinping Guizhou China 87 D3
also known as Sanjiang
Jinping China see **Jingdong**
Jinping Yunnan China 86 B4
also known as Jinhe
Jinping China see **Qiubei**
Jinping Shan mts China 86 B3
Jinsen S. Korea see **Inch'ŏn**
Jinsha China 86 C3
Jinsha Jiang r. China 78 B1
Jinsha Jiang r. China see **Yangtze**
Jinshan Nei Mongol China 85 H3
also known as Harqin Qi
Jinshan Shanghai China 87 G2
also known as Zhujing
Jinshan China see **Lufeng**
Jinshi China 87 D2
Jinshi China see **Xinning**
Jinta China 84 C4
Jintan China 87 F2
Jintang China 86 C2
also known as Zhaozhen
Jintotolo Channel Phil. 74 B4
Jintur India 94 C2
Jinxi China 87 F3
also known as Xiugu
Jinxi China see **Lianshan**
Jin Xi r. China 87 F3
Jinxian China 87 F2
also known as Minhe
Jinxian China see **Linhai**
Jinxiang Shandong China 85 H5
Jinxiang Zhejiang China 87 G3
Jinxiu China 87 D3
Jinyang China 86 B3
also known as Tiandiba
Jinyuan China see **Dayi**
Jinyun China 87 G2
also known as Wuyun
Jinz, Qa' al salt flat Jordan 108 H7
Jinzhai China 87 E2
also known as Meishan
Jinzhong China 85 G4
Jinzhou Liaoning China 85 I3
Jinzhou Liaoning China 85 I4
Jinzhou Wan b. China 85 I4
Jinzhu China see **Daocheng**
Ji-Paraná Brazil 201 E2
Jiparaná r. Brazil 201 E2
Jipijapa Ecuador 198 A5
Jiquilisco El Salvador 185 H6
Jiquilpan de Juárez Mex. 185 E5
Jiquitaia Brazil 207 N4
Jírau Brazil 200 D2
Jirgatol Tajik. 101 G2
also spelt Dzhirgatal'
Jiri r. India 97 G4
Jirin Gol China 85 H2
Jirkov Czech Rep. 49 K5
Jīroft Iran 100 D4
also known as Sabzvārān
Jirriiban Somalia 128 F3
Jirwān Saudi Arabia 105 E3
Jirzah Egypt 108 C8
Jishan China 85 F5
Jishi China see **Xunhua**
Jishou China 87 D2
Jishui China see **Yongfeng**
Jisr ash Shughūr Syria 108 H2
Jitian China see **Lianshan**
Jitra Malaysia 76 C1
Jiu r. Romania 58 E5
Jiudengkou China 85 E4
Jiuding Shan mt. China 86 B2
Jiugong Shan mt. China 87 E2
Jiujiang Jiangxi China 87 E2
also known as Shahejie; formerly known as Shahezhen
Jiujiang Jiangxi China 87 F2
Jiulian China see **Mojiang**
Jiuling Shan mts China 87 E2
Jiulong Hong Kong China see **Kowloon**
Jiulong China 86 B2
also known as Gyaisi
Jiulong China see **Yuechi**
Jiuquan China 84 C4
formerly known as Suzhou
Jiutai China 82 B3
Jiuxian China 85 F4
Jiuxu China 87 C3
Jiuzhen China 87 F3
Jiwani Pak. 101 E5
Jiwen China 85 I1
Jixi Anhui China 87 F2
also known as Huayang
Jixi Heilong. China 82 C3
Jixian China see **Jizhou**
Jixian Heilong. China 82 C3
also known as Fuli; formerly known as Fulitun
Jixian China see **Weihui**
Jixian Shanxi China 85 F4
Jiyuan China 85 G5
Jiz, Wādī al r. Yemen 105 F4
Jīzān Saudi Arabia 104 C4
Jīzān prov. Saudi Arabia 104 C4
Jizera r. Czech Rep. 49 L5
Jizerské Hory mts Czech Rep. 49 M5
Jizhou China 85 G4
formerly known as Jixian
Jizl watercourse Saudi Arabia 104 B2
Jizō-zaki pt Japan 91 C7
Jizzakh Uzbek. see **Dzhizak**
Jizzakh Wiloyati admin. div. Uzbek. see **Dzhizakskaya Oblast'**
Joaçaba Brazil 203 B8
Joachimsthal Germany 49 K3
Joaíma Brazil 202 D6
Joal-Fadiout Senegal 124 A3
Joana Peres Brazil 202 B2
João Belo Moz. see **Xai-Xai**
João de Almeida Angola see **Chibia**
João Monlevade Brazil 207 J6
João Pessoa Brazil 202 F3
João Pinheiro Brazil 203 C6
Joaquim Felício Brazil 207 I4
Joaquin V. González Arg. 204 D2
Jobabo Cuba 186 D2
Jobat India 96 B5
Job Peak U.S.A. 182 F2
Jockfall Sweden 44 M2
Jocoli Arg. 204 C4
Joda India 97 E5
Jódar Spain 55 H7
Jodhpur India 96 B4
Jodiya India 96 A5
Joe Batt's Arm Canada 169 K3
Joensuu Fin. 44 O3
Joesjö Sweden 44 K2
Jōetsu Japan 90 F6
Jofane Moz. 131 G4
Joffre, Mount Canada 167 H5
Jogbani India 97 E4
Jogbura Nepal 96 D3
Jõgeva Estonia 42 H3
Jogighopa India 97 F4
Jogindarnagar India 96 C3
Jogjakarta Indon. see **Yogyakarta**
Jõgua Estonia 42 I2
Johannesburg S. Africa 133 L3
Johan Peninsula Canada 165 L2
Jōhen Japan 91 C8
Johilla r. India 96 D5
John Day U.S.A. 180 C3
John Day r. U.S.A. 180 B3
John Day, Middle Fork r. U.S.A. 180 C3
John Day, North Fork r. U.S.A. 180 C3
John d'Or Prairie Canada 167 H3
John F. Kennedy airport U.S.A. 177 L5
John hill Kerr Reservoir U.S.A. 176 G9
John Jay, Mount Canada/U.S.A. 166 D3
Johnny Hoe r. Canada 166 F1
John o'Groats U.K. 46 I5
Johnson U.S.A. 177 M1
Johnsonburg U.S.A. 176 G4
Johnson City NY U.S.A. 177 J3
Johnson City TN U.S.A. 176 C9
Johnson City TX U.S.A. 179 C6
Johnsondale U.S.A. 182 F6
Johnston U.S.A. 175 D5
Johnston, Lake salt flat Australia 151 C7
Johnston and Sand Islands atoll N. Pacific Ocean see **Johnston Atoll**

▶**Johnston Atoll** N. Pacific Ocean 220 G4
United States Unincorporated Territory. Also known as Johnston and Sand Islands.
oceania [countries] ➡ 138–139

Johnstone Lake Canada see **Old Wives Lake**
Johnstone Strait Canada 166 E5
Johnston Range hills Australia 151 B6
Johnstown NY U.S.A. 177 K2
Johnstown OH U.S.A. 176 C5
Johnstown PA U.S.A. 176 G5
Johor state Malaysia 76 C2
Johor, Selat strait Malaysia/Sing. 76 [inset]
Johor, Sungai Malaysia 76 [inset]
Johor Bahru Malaysia 76 C2
Jõhvi Estonia 42 I2
Joigny France 51 J5
Joinville Brazil 203 B8
Joinville France 51 L4
Joinville Island Antarctica 222 U2
Jojutla Mex. 185 F5
Jokela Fin. 42 F1
Jøkelbugten b. Greenland 165 Q2
Jokioinen Fin. 45 M3
Jokiperä Fin. 44 M3
Jokkmokk Sweden 44 L2
Jökulbunga hill Iceland 44 [inset] B2
Jökulfirðir inlet Iceland 44 [inset] B2
Jökulsá á Dál r. Iceland 44 [inset] D2
Jökulsá á Fjöllum r. Iceland 44 [inset] C2
Jolarpettai India 94 C3
Jolfā Iran 107 G4
Joliet U.S.A. 174 B3
Joliet, Lac l. Canada 168 E3
Joliette Canada 169 F4
Jolly Lake Canada 167 H1
Jolo Phil. 74 B5
Jolo i. Phil. 74 B5
Jomala Fin. 42 A1
Jomalig i. Phil. 74 B3
Jomard Entrance sea chan. P.N.G. 149 F1
Jombang Indon. 77 F4
Jomda China 86 A2
also known as Gatong
Jømna Norway 45 J3
Jomsom Nepal 97 D3
Jonāḩ Iran 100 C5
Jonancy U.S.A. 176 C8
Jonathán Point Belize 185 H5
Jonava Lith. 42 F6
Jondal Norway 45 I3
Jonê China 86 B1
also known as Liulin
Jonesboro AR U.S.A. 174 B5
Jonesboro IL U.S.A. 174 B4
Jonesboro LA U.S.A. 179 D5
Jonesboro TN U.S.A. 176 C9
Jones Mills U.S.A. 176 F5
Jones Mountains Antarctica 222 R2
Jonesport U.S.A. 174 H2
Jones Sound sea chan. Canada 165 K2
Jonestown KY U.S.A. 176 A8
Jonestown PA U.S.A. 177 I5
Jonesville LA U.S.A. 175 B6
Jonesville NC U.S.A. 176 E9
Jonesville VA U.S.A. 176 B9
Jonglei Sudan 128 A3
Jonglei state Sudan 128 B3
Jonglei Canal Sudan 128 A3
Joniškėlis Lith. 42 F5
Joniškis Lith. 42 E5
Jonk r. India 97 D5
Jönköping Sweden 45 K4
Jönköping county Sweden 45 K4
Jonquière Canada 169 G3
Jonuta Mex. 185 G5
Jonzac France 50 F7
Joplin U.S.A. 178 D4
Joppa Israel see **Tel Aviv-Yafo**
Jora India 96 C4
▶**Jordan** country Asia 108 G7
known as Al 'Urdun in Arabic
asia [countries] ➡ 64–67
Jordan r. Asia 108 G6
Jordan MT U.S.A. 180 F3
Jordan NY U.S.A. 177 I2
Jordan r. OR U.S.A. 180 C4
Jordan r. UT U.S.A. 183 L1
Jordânia Brazil 207 M2
Jordet Norway 45 K3
Jorge Montt, Isla i. Chile 205 B8
Jorhat India 97 G4
Jorm Afgh. 101 G2
Jormvattnet Sweden 44 K2
Jörn Sweden 44 M2
Joroinen Fin. 44 N3
Jørpeland Norway 45 I4
Jos Nigeria 125 H4
Jose Abad Santos Phil. 74 C5
José Bonifácio Rondônia Brazil 201 E3
José Bonifácio São Paulo Brazil 206 D8
José Cardel Mex. 185 F5
José de Freitas Brazil 202 D3
José de San Martin Arg. 205 C7
José Enrique Rodó Uruguay 204 F4
Joselândia Brazil 201 F4
Jose Pañganiban Phil. 74 B3
José Pedro Varela Uruguay 204 G4
Joseph, Lac l. Canada 169 H2
Joseph Bonaparte Gulf Australia 150 E2
Joseph City U.S.A. 183 N7
Joshimath India 96 C3
Jōshinetsu-kōgen National Park Japan 91 F6
Joshipur India 97 E5
Joshua Tree U.S.A. 183 H7
Joshua Tree National Park U.S.A. 183 I8
Jos Plateau Nigeria 125 H4
Josselin France 50 D5
Jossund Norway 44 J2
Jostedalsbreen glacier Norway 45 I3
Jostedalsbreen Nasjonalpark nat. park Norway 45 I3
Josvainiai Lith. 42 E6
Jotunheimen mts Norway 45 J3
Jotunheimen Nasjonalpark nat. park Norway 45 J3
Joubertina S. Africa 132 H10
Jouberton S. Africa 133 K3
Joué-lès-Tours France 50 G5
Joukokylä Fin. 44 N2
Joûnié Lebanon 108 G4
Jourdanton U.S.A. 179 C6
Joussard Canada 167 H4
Joutsa Fin. 45 N3
Joutseno Fin. 45 O3
Joutsijärvi Fin. 44 N2
Jovellanos Cuba 186 C2
Jowai India 97 G4
Jowzjān prov. Afgh. 101 F2
Joy, Mount Canada 166 C2
Joya de Cerén tourist site El Salvador 185 H6
Jozini S. Africa 133 Q4
Jrayfiya well W. Sahara 122 B4
Jreïda Mauritania 124 A2
Juan Aldama Mex. 185 E3
Juancheng China 85 G5
Juan de Fuca Strait Canada/U.S.A. 164 G5
Juan de Garay Arg. 204 D5
Juan de Nova i. Indian Ocean 129 D9
Juan E. Barra Arg. 204 E5
Juan Escutia Mex. 184 D4
Juan Fernández, Archipiélago is S. Pacific Ocean see **Juan Fernández Islands**
Juan Fernández Islands S. Pacific Ocean 221 M8
also known as Juan Fernández, Archipiélago
Juangriego Venez. 199 F2
Juan Jorge Arg. 204 F3
Juanjuí Peru 200 A1
Juankoski Fin. 44 O3
Juan Mata Ortíz Mex. 184 C2
Juanshui China see **Tongcheng**
Juan Stuven, Isla i. Chile 205 B7
Juara Brazil 201 F2
Juaréz Mex. 185 E3
Juárez, Sierra de mts Mex. 184 A1
Juatinga, Ponta da pt Brazil 207 I10
Juàzeiro Brazil 202 D4
Juàzeiro do Norte Brazil 202 E3
Juazohn Liberia 124 C5
Juba r. Somalia see **Jubba**
Juba Sudan 128 A3
Juban Yemen 104 D5
Jubany research station Antarctica 222 U2
long form Teniente Jubany
Jubba r. Somalia 128 D5
also spelt Juba; formerly spelt Giuba
Jubbada Dhexe admin. reg. Somalia 128 D4
Jubbada Hoose admin. reg. Somalia 128 D4
Jubbah Saudi Arabia 104 C1
Jubbulpore India see **Jabalpur**
Jubilee Lake salt flat Australia 151 D6
Jubing Nepal 97 E4
Juby, Cap c. Morocco 122 B4
Júcar r. Spain 55 K5
Juçara Brazil 206 C2
Jucas Brazil 202 E3
Juchatengo Mex. 185 F5
Juchitán Mex. 185 G5
Juchitlán Mex. 184 D4
Jucuruçu Brazil 203 E6
Jucuruçu r. Brazil 207 N4
Judaberg Norway 45 I4
Judaidat al Hamir Iraq 107 E5
Judaydah waterhole Iraq 109 M5
Judaydah Syria 109 K2
Judayyidat 'Ar'ar well Iraq 107 E5
Judenburg Austria 49 L8
Judian China 86 A3
Judith r. U.S.A. 180 E3
Judith Gap U.S.A. 180 E3
Juegang China see **Rudong**
Juego de Bolos mt. Spain 55 H6
Juelsminde Denmark 45 J5
Juerana Brazil 207 N4
Jufari r. Brazil 199 F5
Jugon-les-Lacs France 50 D4
Jugoslavija country Europe see **Yugoslavia**
Juh China 85 F4
Juhaynah reg. Saudi Arabia 104 B2
Juigalpa Nicaragua 186 B4
Juillac France 50 H7
Juillet, Lac l. Canada 169 I2
Juína Brazil 201 F2
Juina r. Brazil 201 F3
Juist i. Germany 48 E2
Juiz de Fora Brazil 203 D7
Jujuhan r. Indon. 76 C3
Jujuy prov. Arg. 200 D5
Jukkasjärvi Sweden 44 M2
also known as Čohkkiras
Julaca Bol. 200 D5
Julesburg U.S.A. 178 B3
Juli Peru 200 C4
Julia Brazil 199 E5
Juliaca Peru 200 C3
Julia Creek Australia 149 D4
Julian U.S.A. 183 H8
Julian, Lac l. Canada 168 E2
Julian Alps mts Slovenia see **Julijske Alpe**
Julianatop mt. Indon. see **Mandala, Puncak**
Juliana Top mt. Suriname 199 G4
Julianehåb Greenland see **Qaqortoq**
Julijske Alpe mts Slovenia 56 F2
English form Julian Alps
Julimes Mex. 184 D2
Júlio de Castilhos Brazil 203 A9
Juliomagus France see **Angers**
Júlio Mesquita Brazil 206 D9
Julius, Lake Australia 148 C4
Jullundur India see **Jalandhar**
Juma r. Brazil 199 E6
Juma r. China 85 G4
Juma Uzbek. see **Dzhuma**
Jumanggoin China 86 A1
Jumba Somalia 128 D5
Jumilla Spain 55 J6
Jumla Nepal 97 D3
Jumna r. India see **Yamuna**
Jump r. U.S.A. 172 B5
Jumprava Latvia 42 F5
Junagadh India 96 A5
Junagarh India 95 D2
Junan China 85 H5
also known as Shizilu
Jun Bulen China 85 H2
Junction TX U.S.A. 179 C6
Junction UT U.S.A. 183 L3
Junction Bay Australia 148 B1
Junction City KS U.S.A. 178 C4
Junction City KY U.S.A. 176 A8
Junction City OR U.S.A. 180 B3
Jundah Australia 149 D5
Jundiaí Brazil 206 G10

▶**Juneau** U.S.A. 164 F4
State capital of Alaska.

Juneau Icefield Canada 166 C3
Junee Australia 147 E3
Jūn el Khudr b. Lebanon 108 G4
Jungar Qi China see **Shagedu**
Jungfrau mt. Switz. 51 O6
Junggar Pendi basin China 88 D2
English form Dzungarian Basin
Jungshahi Pak. 101 F5
Junguls Sudan 128 B2
Juniata r. U.S.A. 177 H5
Junik Kosovo, Srbija Yugo. 58 B6
Junín Arg. 204 E4
Junín Peru 200 A2
Junín dept Peru 200 B2
Junior U.S.A. 176 F7
Juniper Mountains U.S.A. 183 K6
Junipero Serro Peak U.S.A. 182 C5
Junkerdalen Balvatnet nature res. Norway 44 K2
Junlian China 86 C2
Junnar India 94 B2
Junosuando Sweden 44 M2
Junqueirópolis Brazil 206 B8
Junsele Sweden 44 L3
Junshan Hu l. China 87 F2
Juntura U.S.A. 180 C4
Juntusranta Fin. 44 O2
Junxi China see **Datian**
Junxian China see **Danjiangkou**
Ju'nyung China 86 A1
formerly known as Ju'nyunggoin
Ju'nyunggoin China see **Ju'nyung**
Juodkrantė Lith. 42 C6
Juodšiliai Lith. 42 G7
Juodupė Lith. 42 G5
Juoksengi Sweden 44 M2
Juosta r. Lith. 42 F6
Juostinikai Lith. 42 F6
Juozapinės kalnas hill Lith. 42 G7
Jūpār Iran 100 D4
Juparanã, Lagoa l. Brazil 207 M6
Jupiá Brazil 206 B7
Jupía, Represa resr Brazil 206 B8
Jupiter U.S.A. 175 D7
Juquiá Brazil 206 F11
Juquiá r. Brazil 206 F11
Juquitiba Brazil 206 F10
Jur r. Sudan 126 F2
Jura mts France/Switz. 51 L7
Jūra r. Lith. 42 D6
Jura i. U.K. 46 G7
Jura, Sound of sea chan. U.K. 46 G8
Juradó Col. 198 B3
Juramento Brazil 207 J3
Juranda Brazil 206 A11
Jurbarkas Lith. 42 D6
Juremal Brazil 202 D4
Jurf ad Darāwīsh Jordan 108 G7
Jurgurra r. Australia 150 C3
Jurh China 85 I2
Jurhen Ul Shan mts China 97 F2
Jüri Estonia 42 F2
Jurien Australia 151 A6
Jurien Bay Australia 151 A6
Jurilovca Romania 58 J4
Juriti Velho Brazil 199 G5
Jūrmala Latvia 42 E5
Jurmu Fin. 44 N2
Jurong China 87 F2
Jurong Sing. 76 [inset]
Jurong, Selat strait Sing. 76 [inset]
Jurong, Sungai r. Sing. 76 [inset]
Jurong Island reg. Sing. 76 [inset]
Juruá Brazil 199 E5
Juruá r. Brazil 198 E5
Juruena Brazil 201 F3
Juruena r. Brazil 201 F1
Jurumirim, Represa de resr Brazil 206 E10
Jurupari r. Brazil 200 C1
Juruti Brazil 199 G5
Jurva Fin. 44 M3
Jūsan-ko l. Japan 90 G4
Jusepín Venez. 199 F2
Jūshqān Iran 100 D2
Jussarö i. Fin. 42 E2
Jussey France 51 L5
Justice U.S.A. 176 D8
Justo Daract Arg. 204 D4
Jutaí Brazil 198 D6
Jutaí r. Brazil 198 E5
Jüterbog Germany 49 K4
Juti Brazil 203 A7
Jutiapa Guat. 185 H6
Jutiapa Hond. 186 B4

Juticalpa Hond. 186 B4
Jutis Sweden 44 L2
Jutland pen. Denmark 45 J4
also spelt Jylland
Juuka Fin. 44 O3
Juupajoki Fin. 45 N3
Juurikorpi Fin. 42 H1
Juva Fin. 45 N3
Juwain Afgh. 101 E4
Juwana Indon. 77 E4
Juxian China 85 H5
also known as Chengyang
Juye China 85 H5
Jūymand Iran 100 D3
also known as Gonabad
Jūyom Iran 100 C4
Južnoukrajinsk Ukr. see Yuzhnoukrayinsk
Jwaneng Botswana 131 E5
Jylland pen. Denmark see Jutland
Jyrgalang Kyrg. 103 I4
also spelt Dzhergalan
Jyväskylä Fin. 44 N3

↓ K

▶K2 mt. China/Jammu and Kashmir 96 C2
2nd highest mountain in the world and in Asia. English form Godwin-Austen, Mount; also known as Qogir Feng.
world [physical features] ▶▶ 8–9

Ka r. Nigeria 125 G4
Kaabong Uganda 128 B4
Kaa-Iya, Parque Nacional nat. park Bol. 201 E4
Kaakhka Turkm. see Kaka
Kaalpan salt pan S. Africa 132 I6
Kaalrug S. Africa 133 P2
Kaamanen Fin. 44 N1
also known as Gámas
Kaambooni Kenya 128 D5
Kääpa Estonia 42 I4
Kaapamuiden S. Africa 133 P2
Kaapstad S. Africa see Cape Town
Kaarina Fin. 45 M3
Kaarta reg. Mali 124 C3
Kaavi Fin. 44 O3
Kaba China see Habahe
Kaba r. China/Kazakh. 88 D2
Kabaena i. Indon. 75 B4
Kabakly Turkm. 103 E5
also spelt Gabakly
Kabala Sierra Leone 124 C4
Kabale Uganda 128 A5
Kabalega Falls National Park Uganda see Murchison Falls National Park
Kabalo Dem. Rep. Congo 127 E6
Kabambare Dem. Rep. Congo 126 E6
Kabanbay Kazakh. 88 C2
also spelt Qabanbay; formerly known as Dzerzhinskoye or Jar-bulak or Zharbulak
Kabanga Dem. Rep. Congo 127 C6
Kabangu Dem. Rep. Congo 127 D7
Kabanjahe Indon. 76 B2
Kabansk Rus. Fed. 85 E1
Kabara i. Fiji 145 H3
also spelt Kambara; formerly known as Appalla
Kabardino-Balkarskaya A.S.S.R. aut. rep. Rus. Fed. see Kabardino-Balkarskaya Respublika
Kabardino-Balkarskaya Respublika aut. rep. Rus. Fed. 41 G8
formerly known as Kabardino-Balkarskaya A.S.S.R.
Kabardino-Balkarskiy Zapovednik nature res. Rus. Fed. 107 E2
Kabare Dem. Rep. Congo 126 F5
Kabarega National Park Uganda see Murchison Falls National Park
Kabasalan Phil. 74 B5
Kabaung r. Myanmar 78 B4
Kabaw Valley Myanmar 78 A3
Kabba Nigeria 125 G5
Kåbbani r. India 94 C3
Kåbdalis Sweden 44 M2
Kabd aş Şārim reg. Syria 109 K3
Kabd Warqah reg. Syria 109 K3
Kabélawa Niger 125 I3
Kabenung Lake Canada 173 I2
Kaberneeme Estonia 42 G2
Kabertene Alg. 123 F3
Kab-hegy hill Hungary 49 O8
Kabinakagami r. Canada 168 C3
Kabinakagami Lake Canada 168 C3
Kabinda Dem. Rep. Congo 127 E6
Kabīr r. Syria 108 G2
Kabīrkūh mts Iran 100 A3
Kabirwala Pak. 101 G4
Kabli Estonia 42 F3
Kabneshwar India 96 C5
Kabo Cent. Afr. Rep. 126 C3
Kabompo Zambia 127 E8
Kabompo r. Zambia 127 D8
Kabondo-Dianda Dem. Rep. Congo 127 E7
Kabongo Dem. Rep. Congo 127 E6
Kabosa Island Myanmar 79 B5
Kabou Cent. Afr. Rep. 126 D3
Kabou Togo 125 F4
Kabozha Rus. Fed. 43 Q3
Kabrousse Senegal 124 A3
Kabshah, Jabal hills Saudi Arabia 104 C2
Kabūdeh Iran 101 E3
Kabūd Gonbad Iran 101 D2
also known as Kalāt
Kabūd Rāhang Iran 100 B3
Kabugao Phil. 74 B2

▶Kābul Afgh. 101 G3
Capital of Afghanistan. Historically known as Ortospana.

Kābul prov. Afgh. 101 G3
Kābul r. Afgh. 101 H3
Kabunda Dem. Rep. Congo 127 F8
Kabunduk Indon. 75 A5
Kaburuang i. Indon. 75 C2
Kabushiya Sudan 121 G5
Kabūtar Khān Iran 100 D4
Kabwe Zambia 127 F8
formerly known as Broken Hill
Kabyrga r. Kazakh. 103 E2
also spelt Qabyrgha
Kačanik Kosovo, Srbija Yugo. 58 C6
Kacepi Indon. 75 D3
Kacha Kuh mts Iran/Pak. 101 E4
Kachalinskaya Rus. Fed. 41 H6
Kachchh, Great Rann of marsh India see Kachchh, Rann of
Kachchh, Gulf of India 96 A5
formerly known as Kutch, Gulf of
Kachchh, Rann of marsh India 96 A4
also known as Kachchh, Great Rann of; also spelt Kutch, Rann of
Kachh Pak. 101 F4
Kachhola India 96 B4
Kachhwa India 97 D4
Kachia Nigeria 125 G4
Kachin state Myanmar 78 B2
Kachiry Kazakh. 103 I1
Kachīsī Eth. 128 C2
Kacholola Zambia 127 F8
Kachug Rus. Fed. 80 H2
Kachung Uganda 128 B4
Kaçkar Dağı mt. Turkey 107 E2
Kaczawa r. Poland 49 N4
Kada Japan 91 D7
Kadaingti Myanmar 78 B4
Kadaiyanallur India 94 C4
Kadam mt. Uganda 128 B4
Kadana Chad 120 D6
Kadanai r. Afgh./Pak. 101 F4
Kadan Kyun i. Myanmar 79 B5
also known as King Island
Kadapongan i. Indon. 77 F4
Kadarkút Hungary 49 O9
Kadaura India 96 C4
Kadavu i. Fiji 145 G3
also spelt Kantavu
Kadavu Passage Fiji 145 G3
also known as Kedairu Passage; also spelt Kandavu Passage
Kadaya Rus. Fed. 85 H1
Kaddam l. India 94 C2
Kade Ghana 125 E5
Kadéï r. Cent. Afr. Rep. 125 J6
Kadgo, Lake salt flat Australia 151 D5
Kādhimain Iraq see Al Kāẓimīyah
Kadi India 96 B5
Kadiana Mali 124 D4
Kadiapattanam India 94 C4
Kadijica mt. Bulg. see Kadiytsa
Kadıköy Turkey 58 H8
Kadıköy Turkey 106 B2
historically known as Chalcedon
Kadina Australia 146 C3
Kading r. Laos 78 C4
Kadınhanı Turkey 106 C3
also known as Saiteli
Kadiolo Mali 124 D4
Kadiri India 94 C3
Kadirli Turkey 106 D3
Kadiyevka Ukr. see Stakhanov
Kadiytsa mt. Bulg. 58 D7
also spelt Kadijica
Kadmat i. India 94 B4
Kadnikov Rus. Fed. 43 V2
Kado Nigeria 125 H5
Ka-do i. N. Korea 83 B5
Kadok Malaysia 76 C1
Kadoka U.S.A. 178 B3
Kadoma Zimbabwe 131 F3
formerly spelt Gatooma
Kadonkani Myanmar 78 A5
Kadrina Estonia 42 H2
Kadugli Sudan 126 F2
Kaduna Nigeria 125 G4
Kaduna r. Nigeria 125 G4
Kaduna state Nigeria 125 G4
Kadur India 94 C3
Kadusam mt. China/India 86 A2
Kaduy Rus. Fed. 43 S2
Kadyy Rus. Fed. 40 G4
Kadzherom Rus. Fed. 40 J2
Kadzhi-Say Kyrg. see Kajy-Say
Kaechon N. Korea 83 B5
Kaédi Mauritania 124 B2
Kaegudeck Lake Canada 169 K3
Kaélé Cameroon 125 I4
Kaena Point U.S.A. 181 [inset] Y1
Kaeng Krachan National Park Thai. 79 B5
Kaeo N.Z. 152 H3
Kaesŏng N. Korea 83 B5
Kafa Ukr. see Feodosiya
Kafakumba Dem. Rep. Congo 127 D7
Kafan Armenia see Kapan
Kafanchan Nigeria 125 H4
Kafferrivier S. Africa 133 K6
Kaffin-Hausa Nigeria 125 H3
Kaffir r. S. Africa 133 J6
Kaffrine Senegal 124 B3
Kafia Kingi Sudan 126 E2
Kafiau i. Indon. 75 D3
Kafireas, Akra pt Greece 59 F10
Kafireos, Steno sea chan. Greece 59 F11
Kafiristan reg. Pak. 101 G3
Kafirnigan Tajik. see Kofarnihon
Kåfjordbotn Norway 44 M1
Kafolo Côte d'Ivoire 124 D4
Kafr el Battikh Egypt 108 C6
Kafr el Dauwâr Egypt 108 B6
Kafr el Garâyda Egypt 108 C8
Kafr el Sheikh Egypt 121 F2
Kafr el Sheikh governorate Egypt 108 B6
Kafr el Zaiyât Egypt 108 B7
Kafr Rihama Egypt 121 E2
Kafr Silîm Egypt 108 B6
Kafu r. Uganda 128 B4
Kafue Zambia 127 F8
Kafue r. Zambia 127 F8
Kafue Flats marsh Zambia 127 E8
Kafue National Park Zambia 127 E8
Kaga Japan 91 E6
Kaga Bandoro Cent. Afr. Rep. 126 C3
formerly known as Fort Crampel
Kagan Uzbek. 103 F5
also spelt Kogon
Kagang China 84 C5
Kaganovich Rus. Fed. see Tovarkovskiy
Kaganovichabad Tajik. see Kolkhozobod
Kaganovichi Pervyye Ukr. see Polis'ke
Kagarlyk Ukr. see Kaharlyk
Kagawa pref. Japan 91 D7
Kagawong Canada 173 K5
Kåge Sweden 44 M2
Kagera admin. reg. Tanz. 128 A5
Kagera, Parc National de la nat. park Rwanda see Akagera National Park
Kagiso S. Africa 133 L3
Kağızman Turkey 107 E2
Kagmar Sudan 121 F6
Kagologolo Indon. 76 B3
Kagoshima Japan 91 B9
Kagoshima airport Japan 91 B9
Kagoshima pref. Japan 91 B9
Kagoshima-wan b. Japan 91 B9
Kagul Moldova see Cahul
Kāhak Iran 100 D2
Kahalīya, Gebel hill Egypt 108 D8
Kahama Tanz. 129 B5
Kaharlyk Ukr. 41 D6
also spelt Kagarlyk
Kahatola i. Indon. 75 C2
Kahawero waterhole Namibia 130 B4
Kahayan r. Indon. 77 F3
Kahemba Dem. Rep. Congo 127 C6
Kaherekoau Mountains N.Z. 153 B13
Kahla Germany 48 I5
Kahntah Canada 166 F3
Kahnu Iran see Kahnūj
Kahnūj Iran 100 D5
also known as Kahnu
Kahnwia Liberia 124 C5
Kahoe N.Z. 152 H3
Kahoka U.S.A. 174 B3
Kahoolawe i. U.S.A. 181 [inset] Z1
also spelt Kahulaui; formerly known as Tahaurawe
Kahperusvaarat mts Fin. 38 C3
Kahramanmaraş Turkey 107 D3
formerly known as Maraş; historically known as Germanicea
Kahror Pak. 101 G4
Kahta Turkey 107 D3
also known as Kölük
Kahugish well Iran 100 D3
Kahuku Point U.S.A. 181 [inset] Y1
Kahul, Ozero l. Ukr. 58 J3
Kahulaui i. U.S.A. see Kahoolawe
Kahului U.S.A. 181 [inset] Z1
Kahūrak Iran 101 D4
Kahurangi National Park N.Z. 152 G9
formerly known as North West Nelson Forest Park
Kahuta Pak. 101 H3
Kahuzi-Biega, Parc National du nat. park Dem. Rep. Congo 126 E5
Kai, Kepulauan is Indon. 73 H8
Kaia r. Sudan 128 A3
Kaiama Nigeria 125 F4
Kaiapit P.N.G. 73 K8
Kaiapoi N.Z. 153 G11
Kaibab U.S.A. 183 L5
Kaibamardang China 84 C4
Kaibara Japan 91 D7
Kai Besar i. Indon. 73 H8
Kaibito Plateau U.S.A. 183 M5
Kaidu He r. China 88 D3
also known as Karaxahar
Kaieteur Falls Guyana 199 G3
Kaifeng Henan China 87 E1
also known as Huanglongsi
Kaifeng Henan China 87 E1
Kaihu N.Z. 152 H3
Kaihua China see Wenshan
Kaihua China 87 F2
Kaiingveld reg. S. Africa 132 F6
Kaijiang China 87 C2
also known as Xinning
Kai Kecil i. Indon. 73 H8
Kai Keung Leng Hong Kong China 87 [inset]
Kaikohe N.Z. 152 H3
Kaikoura N.Z. 153 H10
Kaikoura Peninsula N.Z. 153 H10
Kailahun Sierra Leone 124 C4
Kailas mt. China see Kangrinboqê Feng
Kailas Range mts China see Gangdisê Shan
Kaili China 87 C3
Kailongong waterhole Kenya 128 B3
Kailu China 85 I3
Kailua U.S.A. 181 [inset] Z1
Kailua Kona U.S.A. 181 [inset] Z2
Kaimai-Mamaku Forest Park nature res. N.Z. 152 J5
Kaimai Range hills N.Z. 152 J5
Kaimana Indon. 73 H7
Kaimanawa Forest Park nature res. N.Z. 152 K6
Kaimanawa Mountains N.Z. 152 J7
Kaimar China 97 G2
Kaimganj India 96 C4
Kaimon-dake hill Japan 91 B9
Kaimur Range hills India 97 D4
Käina Estonia 42 D3
Kainan Tokushima Japan 91 D8
Kainan Wakayama Japan 91 D7
Kainda Kyrg. see Kayyngdy
Kaindy Kyrg. see Kayyngdy
Kaingaroa Forest N.Z. 152 K6
Kaingiwa Nigeria 125 F3
Kainji Lake National Park Nigeria 125 G4
Kainji Reservoir Nigeria 125 G4
Kaintaragarh India 95 E1
Kaipara Harbour N.Z. 152 I4
Kaiparowits Plateau U.S.A. 183 M4
Kaiping China 87 E4
Kaiping China see Dêqên
Kaipokok Bay Canada 169 J2
Kaira India see Kheda
Kairakau Beach N.Z. 152 K7
Kairala Fin. 44 N2
Kairana India 96 C3
Kairatu Indon. 75 D3
Kairouan Tunisia 123 H2
Kaisepakte Sweden 44 L1
Kaiserslautern Germany 48 E6
Kaiser Wilhelm II Land reg. Antarctica 223 F2
Kaishantun China 82 C4
Kaišiadorys Lith. 42 F7
Kait, Tanjung pt Indon. 77 D3
Kaitaia N.Z. 152 H3
Kaitangata N.Z. 153 D14
Kaitawa N.Z. 152 L6
Kaitha India 96 C5
Kaithal India 96 C3
Kaitong China see Tongyu
Kaitum Sweden 44 M2
Kaitumälven r. Sweden 44 M2
Kaiwatu Indon. 75 C5
Kaiwi Channel U.S.A. 181 [inset] Z1
Kaixian China 87 D2
also known as Hanfeng
Kaiyang China 86 C3
Kaiyuan Liaoning China 85 J3
Kaiyuan Yunnan China 86 B4
Kajaani Fin. 44 N2
Kajabbi Australia 149 D4
Kajaki Afgh. 101 F3
Kajang Malaysia 76 C2
Kajdar Iran 101 E5
Kajiado Kenya 128 C5
Kajo Kaji Sudan 128 A4
Kaju Iran 100 A2
Kajuligah Nature Reserve Australia 147 E3
Kajy-Say Kyrg. 103 I4
also spelt Kadzhi-Say
Kak, Ozero salt l. Kazakh. 103 F1
also known as Qaq Köli
Kaka Sudan 128 B2
Kaka Turkm. 102 D5
formerly spelt Kaakhka
Kakaban i. Indon. 77 G2
Kakabeka Falls Canada 168 B3
Kakabia i. Indon. 75 B4
Kakadu Aboriginal Land res. Australia 148 B2
Kakadu National Park Australia 148 B2
Kakagi Lake Canada 168 A3
Kakal r. Phil. 74 C5
Kakamas S. Africa 132 E5
Kakamega Kenya 128 B4
Kakamigahara Japan 91 E7
Kakamoéka Congo 126 A6
Kakana India 95 G4
Kakanj Bos.-Herz. 56 K4
Kakanui Mountains N.Z. 153 E13
Kakarahil well Niger 125 H3
Kakaramea N.Z. 152 I7
Kakaramea vol. N.Z. 152 J6
Kakata Liberia 124 C5
Kakatahi N.Z. 152 J7
Kakching India 97 G4
Kake Japan 91 C7
Kakenge Dem. Rep. Congo 126 D6
Kakesio Tanz. 128 B5
Kakhi Azer. see Qax
Kakhovs'ke Vodoskhovyshche resr Ukr. 41 E7
Kakhul Moldova see Cahul
Kākī Iran 100 B4
Kakinada India 95 D2
also spelt Cocanada
Kakinjës, Maja e mt. Albania 58 A6
Kakisa Canada 167 G2
Kakisa r. Canada 167 G2
Kakisa Lake Canada 167 G2
Kākiške Latvia 42 C5
Kakogawa Japan 91 D7
Kakonko Tanz. 128 A5
Kakpin Côte d'Ivoire 124 E4
Kakrala India 96 C4
Kakrima r. Guinea 124 B4
Kakshaal-Too mts China/Kyrg. see Kokshaal-Tau
Kakuda Japan 90 G6
Kakuma Kenya 128 B4
Kakus r. Sarawak Malaysia 77 F2
Kakwa r. Canada 166 G4
Kal hill Croatia 56 G3
Kala Nigeria 125 I3
Kala Tanz. 129 A7
Kalaå Kebira Tunisia 123 H2
Kalaallit Nunaat terr. N. America see Greenland
Kalabagh Pak. 101 G3
Kalabahi Indon. 75 C5
Kalabak mt. Bulg./Greece see Radomir
Kalabáka Greece see Kalampaka
Kalabakan Sabah Malaysia 77 G1
Kalabaydh Togdheer Somalia 128 E2
Kalabaydh Woqooyi Galbeed Somalia 128 D2
Kalabo Zambia 127 D8
Kalach Rus. Fed. 41 G6
Kalacha Dida Kenya 128 C4
Kalach-na-Donu Rus. Fed. 41 G6
Kaladan r. India/Myanmar 95 G1
Kaladar Canada 168 E4
Kaladgi India 94 B2
Kalaena r. Indon. 75 B3
Kalagwe Myanmar 78 B3
▶Kalahari Desert Africa 130 D4
world [population] ▶▶ 22–23
Kalahari Gemsbok National Park S. Africa 132 E2
Kalaikhum Tajik. see Qal'aikhum
Kalai-Khumb Tajik. see Qal'aikhum
Kala-I-Mor Turkm. 101 E3
also spelt Galaymor
Kalaiya Nepal 97 E4
Kalajoki Fin. 44 M2
Kalajoki r. Fin. 44 M2
Kalak Norway 44 N1
Kalakoch hill Bulg. 58 H5
Kalalé Benin 125 F4
Kalaliok Indon. 75 B3
Kalalusu i. Indon. 75 C1
Kalam India 94 C1
Kalam Pak. 101 H3
Kalámai Greece see Kalamata
Kalamaria Greece 58 D8
Kalamata Greece 59 D11
also known as Kalámai
Kalamazoo U.S.A. 172 H8
Kalamazoo r. U.S.A. 172 G8
Kalambau i. Indon. 77 F4
Kalamnuri India 94 C2
Kalamos i. Greece 59 B10
Kalamos, Akra pt Greece 59 G12
Kalampaka Greece 59 C9
also spelt Kalabáka
Kalana Estonia 42 D3
Kalana Mali 124 C4
Kalanaur Haryana India 89 B6
Kalanaur Punjab India 96 B3
Kalanchak Ukr. 41 E7
Kalandula Angola see Calandula
Kalangala Uganda 128 B5
Kalangali Tanz. 129 B6
Kalanguy Rus. Fed. 85 H1
Kalannie Australia 151 B6
Kalanwali India 96 B3
Kalao i. Indon. 75 B4
Kalaoa U.S.A. 181 [inset] Z2
Kalaong Phil. 74 C5
Kalaotoa i. Indon. 75 B4
Kala Oya r. Sri Lanka 94 C4
Kalapana U.S.A. 181 [inset] Z2
Kalar watercourse Iran 101 E5
Kalār Iraq 107 F4
Kalarash Moldova see Călărași
Kalashnikovo Rus. Fed. 43 Q4
Kalasin Thai. 78 C4
Kalāt Iran 101 D5
Kalāt Iran see Kabūd Gonbad
Kalat Balochistān Pak. 101 F4
Kalat Balochistān Pak. 101 F5
Kalat, Kūh-e mt. Iran 100 D3
Kalaus r. Rus. Fed. 41 H7
Kalavad India 96 A5
Kalavryta Greece 59 D10
Kalb, Ra's al c. Yemen 105 E5
Kalbā U.A.E. 105 G2
Kalbăcăr Azer. 107 F2
Kalbarri Australia 151 A5
Kalbarri National Park Australia 151 A5
Kalbaskraal S. Africa 132 C10
Kalbinskiy Khrebet mts Kazakh. 88 C1
also known as Qalbi Zhotasy
Kalbū Iran 100 D3
Kaldırım Turkey 108 G1
Kaldygayty r. Kazakh. 102 C2
Kale Turkey 106 B3
Kalecik Turkey 106 C2
Kaledupa i. Indon. 75 B4
Kalegauk Island Myanmar 79 B5
Kaleindaung inlet Myanmar 78 A4
Kalema Dem. Rep. Congo 126 E6
Kalémié Dem. Rep. Congo 127 F6
formerly known as Albertville
Kalemyo Myanmar 78 A3
Kalenoye Kazakh. 102 B2
Kalesija Bos.-Herz. 56 K4
Kalevala Rus. Fed. 44 O2
formerly known as Ukhta
Kalewa Myanmar 78 A3
Kaleybar Iran 100 A2
Kalga Rus. Fed. 85 H1
Kalgan r. Australia 151 B7
Kalgan China see Zhangjiakou
Kalghatgi India 94 B3
Kalgoorlie Australia 151 C6
Kalguéri Niger 125 H3
Kali Croatia 56 H4
Kali r. India/Nepal 96 D3
Kaliakra, Nos pt Bulg. 58 J5
Kalianda Indon. 77 D4
Kalibo Phil. 74 B4
Kaliet Indon. 76 B3
Kali Gandaki r. Nepal 97 E4
Kaligiri India 94 C3
Kalikino Rus. Fed. 43 U9
Kalima Dem. Rep. Congo 126 E5
Kalimantan reg. Indon. 77 E3
Kalimantan Barat prov. Indon. 77 E2
Kalimantan Selatan prov. Indon. 77 F3
Kalimantan Tengah prov. Indon. 77 F3
Kalimantan Timur prov. Indon. 77 G2
Kalimedence park Hungary 49 O9
Kálimnos i. Greece see Kalymnos
Kalimpang India 97 F4
Kalinadi r. India 94 B3
Kali Nadi r. India 96 D4
Kalingapatnam India 95 E2
Kalinin Kyrg. see Eshanguzar
Kalinin Rus. Fed. see Tver'
Kalinin Turkm. see Boldumsaz
Kalininabad Tajik. see Kalininobod
Kaliningrad Rus. Fed. 42 B7
historically known as Königsberg
Kaliningrad Oblast admin. div. Rus. Fed. see Kaliningradskaya Oblast'
Kaliningradskaya Oblast' admin. div. Rus. Fed. 42 C7
English form Kaliningrad Oblast
Kaliningradskiy Zaliv b. Rus. Fed. 42 A7
Kalinino Armenia see Tashir
Kalinino Kostromskaya Oblast' Rus. Fed. 40 G4
Kalinino Omskaya Oblast' Rus. Fed. 103 H1
Kalinino Permskaya Oblast' Rus. Fed. 40 K4
Kalininobod Tajik. 101 G2
also spelt Kalininabad
Kalininsk Rus. Fed. 41 H6
formerly known as Balanda
Kalininskaya Rus. Fed. 41 F7
formerly known as Popovichskaya
Kalininskaya Oblast' admin. div. Rus. Fed. see Tverskaya Oblast'
Kalinjara India 96 B5
Kalinkavichy Belarus 43 K9
also spelt Kalinkovichi
Kalinkovichi Belarus see Kalinkavichy
Kalinovka Kazakh. 102 C2
Kalinovik Bos.-Herz. 56 K5
Kaliro Uganda 128 B4
Kalis Somalia 128 F2
Kalisat Indon. 77 F5
Kalisch Poland see Kalisz
Kali Sindh r. India 99 J4
Kalispell U.S.A. 180 D2
Kalisz Poland 49 P4
historically known as Kalisch
Kalisz Pomorski Poland 49 M2
Kalitva r. Rus. Fed. 41 G6
Kaliua Tanz. 129 A6
Kalix Sweden 44 M2
Kalixälven r. Sweden 44 M2
Kalka India 96 C3
Kalkan Turkey 106 B3
Kalkaringi Australia 148 A3
Kalkaska U.S.A. 173 H6
Kalkfeld Namibia 130 C4
Kalkfonteindam dam S. Africa 133 J6
Kalkfontein Dam Nature Reserve S. Africa 133 J6
Kalkwerf S. Africa 132 F5
Kallakkurichchi India 94 C4
Kallakoopah Creek watercourse Australia 146 C1
Kallaktjåkkå mt. Sweden 44 L2
Kallam India 94 C2
Kallang Sing. 76 [inset]
Kallang r. Sing. 76 [inset]
Kallaste Estonia 42 I3
Kallavesi l. Fin. 44 N3
Kållberget Sweden 44 K3
Kallfjärden b. Sweden 44 M2
Kallifoni Greece 59 C9
Kallmet i Madh Albania 58 A7
Kalloni Greece 59 G11
Kallonis, Kolpos b. Greece 59 H9
Kallsjön l. Sweden 44 K3
Kallur India 94 C2
Kalmakkyrgan watercourse Kazakh. 103 F3
Kalmar Sweden 45 L4
Kalmar county Sweden 45 L4
Kalmarsund sea chan. Sweden 45 L4
Kalmthoutse Heide Natuurreservaat nature res. Belgium 51 K1
Kalmūkh Qal'eh Iran 100 D2
Kalmunai Sri Lanka 94 D5
Kalmykia aut. rep. Rus. Fed. see Kalmykiya - Khalm'g-Tangch, Respublika
Kalmykiya - Khalm'g-Tangch, Respublika aut. rep. Rus. Fed. 41 H7
English form Kalmykia; formerly known as Kalmytskaya Avtonomnaya Oblast'
Kalmykovo Kazakh. see Taypak
Kalmytskaya Avtonomnaya Oblast' aut. rep. Rus. Fed. see Kalmykiya - Khalm'g-Tangch, Respublika
Kalnai India 97 D5
Kalnciems Latvia 42 E5
Kalni r. Bangl. 97 F4
Kalnik mts Croatia 56 I2
Kalo Chorio Greece 59 G13
Kalocsa Hungary 49 P9
Kalodnaye Belarus 41 C6
Kaloko Dem. Rep. Congo 127 E6
Kalol Gujarat India 96 B5
Kalol Gujarat India 96 B5
Kaloma i. Indon. 75 C2
Kaloma Tanz. 129 A6
Kalomo Zambia 127 E9
Kalona U.S.A. 172 B9
Kalone Peak Canada 166 E4
Kalopanagiotis Cyprus 108 D3
Kalozhnoye, Ozero l. Rus. Fed. 44 O2
Kalpa India 96 C3
formerly known as Chini
Kalpeni i. India 94 B4
Kalpetta India 94 C4
Kalpi India 96 C4
Kalpin China 88 B3
Kalquduq Uzbek. see Kulkuduk
Kāl-Shūr, Rūd-e r. Iran 100 D2
Kaltanėnai Lith. 42 G6
Kaltenkirchen Germany 48 G2
Kaltinėnai Lith. 42 D6
Kaltukatjara Australia 148 A5
Kaltungo Nigeria 125 H4
Kalu India 96 B3
Kalu r. India 94 B2
Kaluderica Srbija Yugo. 58 B4
Kaluga Rus. Fed. 43 R7
Kaluga Oblast admin. div. Rus. Fed. see Kaluzhskaya Oblast'
Kalukalukuang i. Indon. 77 G4
Kaluku Indon. 75 A3
Kalulong, Bukit mt. Sarawak Malaysia 77 F2
Kalulushi Zambia 127 F8
Kalumburu Australia 150 D2
Kalumburu Aboriginal Reserve Australia 150 D2
Kalundborg Denmark 45 J5
Kalupis Falls Sabah Malaysia 77 G1
Kalur Kot Pak. 101 G3
Kalush Ukr. 41 C6
Kałuszyn Poland 49 S3
Kalutara Sri Lanka 94 C5
Kaluzhskaya Oblast' admin. div. Rus. Fed. 43 Q7
English form Kaluga Oblast
Kalvåg Norway 45 I3
Kalvan India 94 B1
Kalvarija Lith. 42 E7
Kalveliai Lith. 42 G7
Kälviä Fin. 44 M3
Kalvitsa Fin. 45 N3
Kalvola Fin. 45 N3
Kalwakurti India 94 C2
Kalyan India 94 B2
Kalyandurg India 94 C3
Kalyani India 94 C2
Kalyansingapuram India 95 D2
Kalyazin Rus. Fed. 43 S4
Kalymnos Greece 59 H12
Kalymnos i. Greece 59 H11
also spelt Kálimnos
Kalyshki Belarus 43 L6
Kama Dem. Rep. Congo 126 E5
Kama Myanmar 78 A4

▶Kama r. Rus. Fed. 40 J4
4th longest river in Europe.
europe [landscapes] ▶▶ 30–31

Kamaishi Japan 90 G5
Kamakura Japan 91 F7
Kamakusa Guyana 199 G3
Kamakwie Sierra Leone 124 B4
Kamal Chad 120 C4
Kamalapuram India 94 C3
Kamalia Pak. 101 H4
Kamamaung Myanmar 78 B4
Kaman India 96 C4
Kaman Turkey 106 C3
Kamanassie r. S. Africa 132 G10
Kamanassieberg mts S. Africa 132 G10
Kamaniskeg Lake Canada 173 P5
Kamanjab Namibia 130 B3
Kamaran Yemen 104 C5
Kamarān i. Yemen 104 C5
English form Kamaran Island
Kamarang Guyana 199 F3
Kamaran Island Yemen see Kamarān
Kamard reg. Afgh. 101 F3
Kamarde Latvia 42 F5
Kamareddi India 94 C2
Kamares Dytiki Ellas Greece 59 C10
Kamares Sifnos Greece 59 F12
Kamaria Falls Guyana 199 G3
Kamarlu Armenia see Artashat
Kamas U.S.A. 183 M1
Kamashi Uzbek. 103 F5
also spelt Qamashi
Kamativi Zimbabwe 131 E3
Kamba Nigeria 125 F4
Kamba Kota Cent. Afr. Rep. 126 C3
Kambalda Australia 151 C6
Kambam India 94 C4
Kambang Indon. 76 C3
Kambangan i. Indon. 77 E5
Kambara i. Fiji see Kabara
Kambarka Rus. Fed. 40 J4
Kambia Sierra Leone 124 B4
Kambing, Pulau i. East Timor see Atauro
Kambo-san mt. N. Korea see Kwanmo-bong
Kambove Dem. Rep. Congo 127 E7
Kamburovo Bulg. 58 H5
Kambūt Libya 120 E2
Kamchatka r. Rus. Fed. 39 Q4
Kamchatka, Poluostrov pen. Rus. Fed. see Kamchatka Peninsula
▶Kamchatka Peninsula Rus. Fed. 39 P4
also known as Kamchatka, Poluostrov
asia [threats] ▶▶ 70–71
Kamchatskiy Proliv strait Rus. Fed. 39 Q4
Kamchatskiy Zaliv b. Rus. Fed. 39 Q4
Kamchiya r. Bulg. 58 I5
Kamchiyska Planina hills Bulg. 58 I6
Kamdesh Afgh. 101 G3
Kameia, Parque Nacional de nat. park Angola see Cameia, Parque Nacional da
Kamelik r. Rus. Fed. 102 B1
Kamen Bulg. 58 G5
Kamen', Gory mts Rus. Fed. 39 J3
Kamende Dem. Rep. Congo 127 E6
Kamenets-Podol'skiy Ukr. see Kam"yanets'-Podil's'kyy
Kamenitsa r. Bulg. 58 F5
Kamenjak, Rt pt Croatia 56 F4
Kamenka Kazakh. 102 B2
Kamenka Arkhangel'skaya Oblast' Rus. Fed. 40 H2
Kamenka Kaluzhskaya Oblast' Rus. Fed. 43 Q7
Kamenka Leningradskaya Oblast' Rus. Fed. 43 K1
Kamenka Lipetskaya Oblast' Rus. Fed. 43 T9
Kamenka Penzenskaya Oblast' Rus. Fed. 41 H5
Kamenka Primorskiy Kray Rus. Fed. 82 E3
Kamenka Smolenskaya Oblast' Rus. Fed. 43 N6
Kamenka-Bugskaya Ukr. see Kam"yanka-Buz'ka
Kamenka-Strumilovskaya Ukr. see Kam"yanka-Buz'ka
Kamenki Rus. Fed. 43 S5
Kamen'-na-Obi Rus. Fed. 80 C2
Kamenniki Rus. Fed. 43 T3
Kamennogorsk Rus. Fed. 43 K1
Kamennomostskiy Rus. Fed. 41 G7
Kamennoye, Ozero l. Rus. Fed. 44 O2
Kameno Bulg. 58 I6
Kamenongue Angola see Camanongue
Kamen'-Rybolov Rus. Fed. 82 D3
Kamenskiy Rus. Fed. 41 H6
Kamenskoye Koryakskiy Avtonomnyy Okrug Rus. Fed. 39 Q3
Kamenskoye Lipetskaya Oblast' Rus. Fed. 43 T9
Kamenskoye Ukr. see Dniprodzerzhyns'k
Kamensk-Shakhtinskiy Rus. Fed. 41 G6
Kamensk-Ural'skiy Rus. Fed. 38 G4
Kamenz Germany 49 L4
Kameoka Japan 91 D7
Kamet mt. China 89 B6
Kameyama Japan 91 E7
Kamëz Albania 58 A7
Kamiah U.S.A. 180 C3
Kamienna r. Poland 49 S4
Kamienna Gora Poland 49 N5
Kamień Pomorski Poland 49 L2
historically known as Cammin
Kamiesberg S. Africa 132 C7
Kamiesberge mts S. Africa 132 C7
Kamieskroon S. Africa 132 B7
Kamifurano Japan 90 H3
Kamikawa Japan 90 H3
Kamileroi Australia 149 D3
Kamina Dem. Rep. Congo 127 E7
Kamina Base Dem. Rep. Congo 127 E7
Kaminak Lake Canada 167 M2
Kaminokuni Japan 90 G4
Kaminoyama Japan 90 G5
Kaminške in Savinjske Alpe mts Slovenia 56 G2
Kaminuriak Lake Canada see Qamanirjuaq Lake
Kamioka Japan 91 E6
Kamiros Greece 59 I12
Kamishihoro Japan 90 H3
Kamitsushima Japan 91 A7
Kamituga Dem. Rep. Congo 126 F5
Kamkaly Kazakh. 103 G3
Kamla r. India 97 E4
Kamla r. India 97 F4
Kamloops Canada 166 F5
Kamloops Lake Canada 166 F5
Kammuri-yama mt. Japan see Kanmuri-yama
Kamnik Slovenia 56 G2
Kamo Armenia 107 F2
formerly known as Gavarr or Nor-Bayazet
Kamo N.Z. 152 I3
Kamob Sanha Sudan 121 H5
Kamoenai Japan 90 G3
Kamogawa Japan 91 G7
Kamoke Pak. 101 H4
Kamola Dem. Rep. Congo 127 E6
Kamonanira Tanz. 129 A6
Kamp r. Austria 49 M7

▶Kampala Uganda 128 B4
Capital of Uganda.

Kampanos, Akra pt Greece 59 F10
Kampar r. Indon. 76 C2
Kampar Malaysia 76 C1
Kamparkalns hill Latvia 42 D4
Kamparkiri r. Indon. 76 C2
Kampen Neth. 48 C3
Kampene Dem. Rep. Congo 126 E5
Kamphaeng Phet Thai. 78 B4
Kampi Katoto Tanz. 129 B6
Kampinoski Park Narodowy nat. park Poland 49 R3
Kampli India 94 C3
Kamp'o S. Korea 91 A7
Kampolombo, Lake Zambia 127 F7
Kâmpóng Cham Cambodia 79 D6
also spelt Kompong Cham
Kâmpóng Chhnăng Cambodia 79 D5
also spelt Kompong Chhnang
Kâmpóng Khleăng Cambodia 79 D5
also spelt Kompong Kleang
Kâmpóng Saôm Cambodia see Sihanoukville
Kâmpóng Spœ Cambodia 79 D6
also spelt Kompong Speu
Kâmpóng Thum Cambodia 79 D5
also spelt Kompong Thom
Kâmpôt Cambodia 79 D6
Kampuchea country Asia see Cambodia
Kamrau, Teluk b. Indon. 73 H7
Kamroneskoye, Ozero l. Rus. Fed. 43 V1
Kamsack Canada 167 K5
Kamsar Guinea 124 B4
Kamskoye Vodokhranilishche resr Rus. Fed. 40 K4
Kamsuuma Somalia 128 D4
Kamtha India 96 D5
Kamui-dake mt. Japan 90 H3
Kamuli Uganda 128 B4
Kamungu Dem. Rep. Congo 127 E6
Kam"yanets'-Podil's'kyy Ukr. 41 C6
also spelt Kamenets-Podol'skiy
Kam"yanka-Buz'ka Ukr. 41 C6
also known as Kamenka-Bugskaya; formerly known as Kamenka-Strumilovskaya
Kam"yans'ke Ukr. 58 K3
Kamyanets Belarus 42 E9
Kamyanyuki Belarus 42 E9
Kāmyārān Iran 100 A3
Kamyen' Belarus 43 J6
Kamyshin Rus. Fed. 41 H6

index K

Kamyshla Rus. Fed. 41 J5
Kamyshlybash Kazakh. 103 E3 also spelt Qamystybas; formerly spelt Kamyslybas
Kamysh-Samarskiye Ozera l. Kazakh. 102 B2
Kamysknoye Kazakh. 103 E2
Kamyslybas Kazakh. see Kamyshlybash
Kamyslybas, Ozero l. Kazakh. 103 E3
Kamyzyak Rus. Fed. 102 B3
Kamzar Oman 105 G2
Kan r. Rus. Fed. 80 F2
Kan Sudan 128 A2
Kana r. Zimbabwe 131 E3
Kana, Bukit mt. Sarawak Malaysia 77 F2
Kanaaupscow r. Canada 169 E2
Kanab U.S.A. 183 L4
Kanab Creek r. U.S.A. 183 L5
Kanagawa pref. Japan 90 F7
Kanagi Japan 90 G4
Kanaima Falls Guyana 199 F3
Kanairiktok r. Canada 169 J2
Kanakapura India 94 C3
Kanala Greece 59 F11
Kanallaki Greece 59 B9
Kanan Sweden 44 K2
Kanana S. Africa 133 K3
Kananga Dem. Rep. Congo 127 D6 formerly known as Luluabourg
Kanangra-Boyd National Park Australia 147 F3
Kanarak India see Konarka
Kanarraville U.S.A. 183 K4
Kanas watercourse Namibia 132 B4
Kanash Rus. Fed. 40 H5
Kanas Köl l. China 88 D1
Kanawha r. U.S.A. 176 C7
Kanazawa Japan 91 E6
Kanbalu Myanmar 78 A3
Kanchanaburi Thai. 79 B5
Kanchanjanga mt. India/Nepal see Kangchenjunga
Kanchipuram India 94 C3
Kańczuga Poland 49 T6
Kand mt. Pak. 101 F4
Kandahār Afgh. 101 F4 also spelt Qandahar; historically known as Alexandria Arachoton
Kandahār prov. Afgh. 101 F4
Kandahar India 94 C2
Kandalaksha Rus. Fed. 44 P2
Kandalakshskiy Zaliv g. Rus. Fed. 40 E2
Kandalakshskiy Zapovednik nature res. Rus. Fed. 44 P2
Kandang Indon. 76 B2
Kandangan Indon. 77 F3
Kandava Latvia 42 D4
Kandavu Passage Fiji see Kadavu Passage
Kandé Togo 125 F4
Kandhkot Pak. 101 G4
Kandi Benin 125 F4
Kandi, Tanjung pt Indon. 75 B2
Kandiaro Pak. 101 G5
Kandila Dytiki Ellas Greece 59 B10
Kandila Peloponnisos Greece 59 D11
Kandil Bouzou well Niger 125 H3
Kandıra Turkey 106 B2
Kandja Cent. Afr. Rep. 126 D3
Kandla India 96 A5
Kandos Australia 147 F3
Kandra India 95 E1
Kandreho Madag. 131 [inset] J3
Kandri India 97 D5
Kandrian P.N.G. 145 D2
Kandukur India 94 C3
Kandy Sri Lanka 94 D5
Kandyagash Kazakh. 102 D2 also spelt Qandyaghash; formerly known as Oktyabr' or Oktyabr'sk
Kane U.S.A. 176 G4
Kane Basin b. Greenland see Kane Bassin
Kane Bassin b. Greenland 165 M2 English form Kane Basin
Kaneh watercourse Iran 100 C5
Kanem pref. Chad 120 B6
Kaneohe U.S.A. 181 [inset] Z1
Kanevskaya Rus. Fed. 41 F7
Kaneyama Japan 90 G5
Kang Botswana 130 D4
Kanga r. Bangl. 97 F5
Kangaamiut Greenland 165 N3
Kangaarsussuaq c. Greenland 165 L2 also known as Parry, Kap
Kangaatsiaq Greenland 165 N3
Kangaba Mali 124 C4
Kangal Turkey 107 D3
Kangalassy Rus. Fed. 39 M3
Kangān Būshehr Iran 100 C5
Kangān Hormozgan Iran 100 D5
Kangan Aboriginal Reserve Australia 150 B4
Kangandala, Parque Nacional de nat. park Angola see Cangandala, Parque Nacional de
Kangar Malaysia 76 C1
Kangaré Mali 124 C4
Kangaroo Island Australia 146 C3
Kangaroo Point Australia 148 C3
Kangaruma Guyana 199 G3
Kangasala Fin. 45 N3
Kangaslampi Fin. 44 O3
Kangasniemi Fin. 45 N3
Kangāvar Iran 100 A3
Kangayam India 94 C4
Kangbao China 85 G3

▶ Kangchenjunga mt. India/Nepal 97 F4
3rd highest mountain in the world and in Asia. Also spelt Kanchanjanga.
world [physical features] ➡ 8–9

Kangding China 86 B2 also known as Dardo or Lucheng
Kangean, Kepulauan is Indon. 77 F4
Kangen r. Sudan 128 B3
Kangeq c. Greenland 165 O3 also known as Cort Adelaer, Kap
Kangerluarsoruseq Greenland 165 N3 also known as Færingehavn
Kangerlussuaq Greenland 165 N3 also known as Søndre Strømfjord
Kangerlussuaq inlet Greenland 165 N2 also known as Giesecke Isfjord
Kangerlussuaq inlet Greenland 165 N3 also known as Søndre Strømfjord
Kangerlussuaq inlet Greenland 165 P3
Kangerlussuatsiaq inlet Greenland 165 O3 also known as Lindenow Fjord
Kangersuatsiaq Greenland 165 N2 also known as Prøven
Kangertittivaq sea chan. Greenland 165 Q2 also known as Scoresby Sund
Kangertittivatsiaq inlet Greenland 165 P3
Kangetet Kenya 128 C4
Kanggye N. Korea 83 B4
Kangikajik c. Greenland 165 Q2 also known as Brewster, Kap
Kangilinnguit Greenland 165 O3 also known as Grønnedal
Kangiqsualujjuaq Canada 169 H1 formerly known as Port-Nouveau-Québec
Kangiqsujuaq Canada 165 L3 formerly known as Maricourt or Wakeham
Kangirsuk Canada 165 L3 formerly known as Bellin or Payne
Kang Krung National Park Thai. 79 B6
Kangle China 84 D5
Kangle China see Wanzai
Kanglong China 86 A1
Kangmar China 89 E6
Kangnŭng S. Korea 83 C5
Kango Gabon 126 A4
Kangping China 85 I3
Kangra India 96 C2
Kangri Karpo Pass China/India 86 A2
Kangrinboqê Feng mt. China 89 C6 also known as Kailas
Kangsangdobdê China see Xainza
Kang Tipayan Dakula i. Phil. 74 B5
Kangto mt. China/India 89 F7
Kangtog China 89 D5
Kangxian China 86 C1 also known as Zuitai; formerly known as Zuitaizi
Kangxiwar China 89 B4
Kangyidaung Myanmar 78 A4
Kanhan r. India 96 C5
Kanhar r. India 97 D4
Kanhargaon India 94 C2
Kani Côte d'Ivoire 124 D4
Kani Myanmar 78 A3
Kaniama Dem. Rep. Congo 127 E6
Kanibadam Tajik. 101 G1 also spelt Konibodom
Kanibongan Sabah Malaysia 77 G1
Kaniere N.Z. 153 F10
Kanifing Gambia 124 A3
Kanigiri India 94 C3
Kanimekh Uzbek. 103 F4 also spelt Konimekh
Kanin, Poluostrov pen. Rus. Fed. 40 H2
Kanin Nos Rus. Fed. 40 G1
Kanin Nos, Mys c. Rus. Fed. 40 G1
Kaninskiy Bereg coastal area Rus. Fed. 40 G2
Kanita Japan 90 G4
Kaniva Australia 146 D4
Kanjiroba mt. Nepal 97 D3
Kanjiža Vojvodina, Srbija Yugo. 58 B2 also known as Magyarkanizsa
Kankaanpää Fin. 45 M3
Kankakee U.S.A. 174 C3
Kankakee r. U.S.A. 174 B3
Kankan Guinea 124 C4
Kankan, Réserve Naturelle de nature res. Guinea 124 C4
Kanker India 94 D1
Kankesanturai Sri Lanka 94 D4
Kankiya Nigeria 125 G3
Kankossa Mauritania 124 C3
Kanmaw Kyun i. Myanmar 79 B6 also known as Kisseraing Island
Kanmuri-yama mt. Japan 91 C7 also spelt Kammuri-yama
Kannad India 94 B1
Kannapolis U.S.A. 174 D5
Kannauj India 96 C4 also known as Kanyakubja
Kanniyakumari India 94 C4
Kanniya Kumari c. India see Comorin, Cape
Kannod India 96 C5
Kannonkoski Fin. 44 N3
Kannur India see Cannanore
Kannus Fin. 44 M3
Kannuskoski Fin. 42 I1
Kano Nigeria 125 H3
Kano r. Nigeria 125 H4
Kano state Nigeria 125 H4
Kanona Zambia 127 F8
Kanonerka Kazakh. 103 I2
Kan-onji Japan 91 C7
Kanonpunt pt S. Africa 132 F11
Kanor India 96 B4
Kanosh U.S.A. 183 L3
Kanovlei Namibia 130 C3
Kanowit Sarawak Malaysia 77 F2
Kanoya Japan 91 B9
Kanpur India 96 D4 formerly spelt Cawnpore
Kanpur Pak. 101 G4
Kanrach reg. Pak. 101 F5
Kansai airport Japan 91 D7
Kansanshi Zambia 127 E8
Kansas r. U.S.A. 178 D4
Kansas state U.S.A. 178 C4
Kansas City KS U.S.A. 178 D4
Kansas City MO U.S.A. 178 D4
Kansenia Dem. Rep. Congo 127 E7
Kansk Rus. Fed. 80 F1
Kansu China 88 A4
Kansu prov. China see Gansu
Kanta mt. Eth. 128 B3
Kantala Fin. 44 N3
Kantang Thai. 79 B7
Kantara hill Cyprus 108 E2
Kantaralak Thai. 79 D5
Kantavu i. Fiji see Kadavu
Kantchari Burkina 125 F3
Kantemirovka Rus. Fed. 41 F6
Kanth India 96 C3
Kanti India 97 E4
Kantilo India 95 E1
Kantishna r. U.S.A. 164 D3
Kanton i. Kiribati 145 H2 also known as Abariringa; formerly spelt Canton Island
Kan-Too, Pik mt. Kazakh./Kyrg. see Khan-Tengri, Pik
Kanto-sanchi mts Japan 91 F7
Kantserava Belarus 45 O5
Kanttaji Aboriginal Land res. Australia 148 B3
Kanturk Rep. of Ireland 47 D11
Kanturrpa Aboriginal Land res. Australia 148 B3
Kanuku Mountains Guyana 199 G4
Kanuma Japan 91 F6
Kanur India 94 C3 also known as Vajrakarur
Kanus Namibia 132 C4
Kanuwe r. P.N.G. 73 J8
Kanyakubja India see Kannauj
KaNyamazane S. Africa 133 P2
Kanye Botswana 131 E5
Kanyemba Zimbabwe 131 F2
Kanyutino Rus. Fed. 43 O6
Kao Indon. 75 C2
Kao Niger 125 G3
Kao i. Tonga 145 H3
Kao, Teluk b. Indon. 75 C2
Kaohsiung Taiwan 87 G4 also spelt Gaoxiong
Kaôh Tang i. Cambodia 79 C6
Kaokoveld plat. Namibia 130 B3
Kaolack Senegal 124 A3
Kaoma Zambia 127 E8
Kaouadja Cent. Afr. Rep. 126 D3
Kapaa U.S.A. 181 [inset] Y1
Kapaau U.S.A. 181 [inset] Z1
Kapal Kazakh. 103 I3 also spelt Qapal
Kapalabuaya Indon. 75 C3
Kapa Moračka mt. Yugo. 58 A6
Kapan Armenia 107 F3 formerly spelt Ghap'an or Kafan
Kapanga Dem. Rep. Congo 127 D7
Kapareli Greece 59 E10
Kapatkyevichy Belarus 43 J9
Kapatu Zambia 127 F7
Kapchagay Kazakh. 103 I4 also spelt Qapshagay; formerly known as Ili or Iliysk
Kapchagayskoye Vodokhranilishche resr Kazakh. 103 I4 also known as Qapshagay Bögeni
Kapchorwa Uganda 128 B4
Kapčiamiestis Lith. 42 E8
Kap Dan Greenland see Kulusuk
Kapellen Belgium 51 K1
Kapello, Akra pt Greece 59 E12
Kapellskär Sweden 45 L4 also spelt Kapelskär
Kapelskär Sweden see Kapellskär
Kapfenberg Austria 49 M8
Kapıdağı Yarımadası pen. Turkey 58 I8
Kapili r. India 97 F4
Kapingamarangi atoll Micronesia 145 E1 formerly known as Greenwich
Kapıorman Dağları mts Turkey 106 B2
Kapiri Mposhi Zambia 127 F8
Kāpīsā prov. Afgh. 101 G3
Kapisillit Greenland 165 N3
Kapiskau r. Canada 168 D2
Kapiskong Lake Canada 173 L3
Kapit Sarawak Malaysia 77 F2
Kapiti Island N.Z. 152 I8
Kapiting Brazil 199 H4
Kapka well Chad 120 D5
Kapka, Massif du mts Chad 120 D6
Kaplamada, Gunung mt. Indon. 75 C3
Kaplankyr, Chink hills Turkm./Uzbek. 102 C4
Kaplankyrskiy Gosudarstvennyy Zapovednik nature res. Turkm. 102 D4
Kaplice Czech Rep. 49 L7
Kapoe Thai. 79 B6
Kapoeta Sudan 128 B3
Kapondai, Tanjung pt Indon. 75 B5
Kaponga N.Z. 152 I7
Kapos r. Romania 49 P9
Kaposvár Hungary 49 O9
Kappar Pak. 101 E5
Kappeln Germany 48 G1
Kapran India 96 C4
Kapsabet Kenya 128 B4
Kap Salt Swamp Pak. 101 E5
Kapsan N. Korea 83 C4
Kapsha r. Rus. Fed. 43 O2
Kapsukas Lith. see Marijampolė
Kaptai Bangl. 97 G5
Kaptsegaytuy Rus. Fed. 85 H1
Kaptsevichy Belarus 43 J9
Kapuas r. Indon. 77 E3
Kapuas r. Indon. 77 F3
Kapuas Hulu, Pegunungan mts Indon./Malaysia 77 F2 also known as Boven Kapuas Mountains
Kapunda Australia 146 C3
Kapuriya India 96 B4
Kapurthala India 96 B3
Kapuskasing Canada 168 D3
Kapuskasing r. Canada 168 D3
Kapustin Yar Rus. Fed. 41 H6
Kaputa Zambia 127 F7
Kaputar mt. Australia 147 F2
Kaputir Kenya 128 B4
Kapuvár Hungary 49 O8
Kapydzhik, Gora mt. Armenia/Azer. see Qazangödağ
Kapyl' Belarus 42 I8 also spelt Kopyl'
Kap'yŏng S. Korea 83 B5
Kapyrevshchina Rus. Fed. 43 N6
Ka Qu r. China 89 F6
Kaqung China 88 B4
Kara India 97 D4
Kara r. Rus. Fed. 40 M1
Kara Togo 125 F4
Kara r. Turkey 107 E3
Kara Ada i. Turkey 59 H10
Karaali Turkey 106 C3
Kara Art Pass China 88 A4
Karaaul Kazakh. see Karaul
Kara-Balta Kyrg. 103 H4
Karabanovo Rus. Fed. 43 T5
Karabas Kazakh. 103 H2 also spelt Qarabas
Karabekaul Turkm. see Garabekevyul
Karabiga Turkey 106 A2
Karabil', Vozvyshennost' hills Turkm. 103 E5 also known as Garabil Belentligi
Kara-Bogaz-Gol Turkm. see Karabogazkel'
Kara-Bogaz-Gol, Proliv sea chan. Turkm. 102 C4 also known as Garabogazköl Bogazy

▶ Kara-Bogaz-Gol, Zaliv b. Turkm. 102 C4
also known as Garabogazköl Aylagy
asia [changes] ➡ 68–69

Karabogazkel' Turkm. 102 C4 formerly spelt Kara-Bogaz-Gol
Karabük Turkey 106 C2
Karabulak Almatinskaya Oblast' Kazakh. 103 I3 also spelt Qarabulaq
Karabulak Vostochnyy Kazakhstan Kazakh. 88 D2
Karabulakskaya Kazakh. 103 H2
Karabura China see Yumin
Karaburun Turkey 106 A3
Karabutak Kazakh. 102 E2 also spelt Qarabutaq
Karacabey Turkey 106 B2
Karacadağ mts Turkey 106 C3
Karacakılavuz Turkey 58 I7
Karacaköy Turkey 106 B2
Karacalı Dağ mt. Turkey 107 D3
Karaçal Tepe mt. Turkey 108 D1
Karacasu Turkey 59 J11
Karaca Yarımadası pen. Turkey 108 B1
Karachay-Cherkess Republic aut. rep. Rus. Fed. see Karachayevo-Cherkesskaya Respublika
Karachayevo-Cherkesskaya A.S.S.R. aut. rep. Rus. Fed. see Karachayevo-Cherkesskaya Respublika
Karachayevo-Cherkesskaya Respublika aut. rep. Rus. Fed. 41 G8 English form Karachay-Cherkess Republic; formerly known as Karachayevo-Cherkesskaya A.S.S.R.
Karachayevsk Rus. Fed. 41 G8 formerly known as Klukhori
Karachev Rus. Fed. 43 P8

▶ Karachi Pak. 101 F5
world [cities] ➡ 24–25

Karaçoban Turkey 107 E3 also known as Karaköprü
Karaçulha Turkey 59 K12
Karacurun Turkey see Hilvan
Karad India 94 B2
Kara Dağ hill Turkey 59 H8
Kara Dağ hill Turkey 109 J1
Kara Dağ mt. Turkey 106 C3
Kara-Darya r. Kyrg. 103 H4 also spelt Qoradaryo
Kara-Dar'ya Uzbek. see Payshanba
Kara Deniz sea Asia/Europe see Black Sea
Karaga Ghana 125 E4
Karaganda Kazakh. 103 H2 also spelt Qaraghandy
Karaganda Oblast admin. div. Kazakh. see Karagandinskaya Oblast'
Karagandinskaya Oblast' admin. div. Kazakh. 103 H2 English form Karaganda Oblast; also known as Qaraghandy Oblysy
Karagash Kazakh. 103 I3
Karagay Rus. Fed. 40 J4
Karagayly Kazakh. 103 H2 also spelt Qaraghayly
Karagez Turkm. 102 C5
Karaginskiy, Ostrov i. Rus. Fed. 39 Q4
Karagiye, Vpadina depr. Kazakh. 102 B4
Karaguzhikha Kazakh. 88 C1 also known as Qaraqozha
Karagwe Tanz. 128 A5
Karahalil Turkey 58 I7
Karahallı Turkey 59 K10
Karahasanlı Turkey 106 C3
Karahisar Turkey 59 J11
Karaidel' Rus. Fed. 40 K5
Karaikal India 94 C4
Karaikkudi India 94 C4
Kara Irtysh r. Kazakh. 88 D2
Karaisalı Turkey 106 C3
Karaj Iran 100 B3
Karak Jordan see Al Karak
Kara-Kala Turkm. see Garrygala
Karakalli Turkey see Özalp
Karakalpakistan, Respublika aut. rep. Uzbek. 102 D4 also known as Karakalpakskaya Respublika or Karakalpakstan or Qaraqalpaqstan Respublikasy or Qoraqalpoghiston Respublikasi
Karakalpakiya Uzbek. 102 D3 also known as Qoraqalpoghiston
Karakalpakskaya Respublika aut. rep. Uzbek. see Karakalpakistan, Respublika
Karakalpakstan aut. rep. Uzbek. see Karakalpakistan, Respublika
Kara Kara State Park nature res. Australia 147 D4
Karakatinskaya, Vpadina depr. Uzbek. 103 F4
Karakax China see Moyu
Karakax He r. China 89 C4
Karakax Shan mts China 89 C5
Karakeçi Turkey 107 D3 also known as Mizar
Karakeçili Turkey 106 C3
Karakelong i. Indon. 75 C1
Kara-Khol' Rus. Fed. 88 E1
Karaki China 89 C4
Karakitang i. Indon. 75 C2
Karaklis Armenia see Vanadzor
Karakoçan Turkey 107 E3 also known as Tepeköy
Karakoin salt l. Kazakh. see Karakoyyn, Ozero
Karakol' Kazakh. 102 C2 also spelt Qaraköl
Kara-Köl Kyrg. 103 H4 also spelt Kara Kul'
Karakol Ysyk-Köl Kyrg. 103 I4 also known as Karakolka
Karakol Ysyk-Köl Kyrg. 103 I4 formerly known as Przheval'sk
Karakolka Kyrg. see Karakol
Karaköprü Turkey see Karaçoban
Karakoram mts Asia 99 J2
Karakoram Pass China/Jammu and Kashmir 89 B5
Kara K'orē Eth. 128 C2
Karakoro r. Mali/Mauritania 124 B3
Karaköse Turkey see Ağrı
Karakoyyn, Ozero salt l. Kazakh. 103 G3 also known as Karakoin or Qaraqoyyn Köli
Karaksar Rus. Fed. 85 G1
Karakubbud Ukr. see Komsomol's'ke
Kara Kul' Kyrg. see Kara-Köl
Karakul' Bukharskaya Oblast' Uzbek. 103 E5
Karakul' Bukharskaya Oblast' Uzbek. 103 E5
Karakul', Ozero l. Tajik. see Qarokŭl
Kara-Kul'dzha Kyrg. see Kara-Kulja
Karakulino Rus. Fed. 40 J4
Kara-Kulja Kyrg. 103 H4 also spelt Kara-Kul'dzha
Karakum Kazakh. 103 I3
Karakum Desert Kazakh. 102 C3 also known as Garagum or Peski Karakum or Qaraqum
Karakum Desert Turkm. 102 E5 also known as Garagum or Peski Karakumy or Qaraqum
Karakumskiy Kanal canal Turkm. 103 E5
Karakurt Turkey 107 E2
Karakurt Turkey 59 I9
Karala Estonia 42 C3
Karalı Turkey 108 H1
Karalundi Australia 151 B5
Karama r. Indon. 75 A3
Karaman Turkey 106 C3 historically known as Laranda
Karaman prov. Turkey 108 D1
Karamanbeyli Geçidi pass Turkey 108 B1
Karamanlı Turkey 106 B3
Karamay China 88 D2
Karambar Pass Afgh./Pak. 101 H2
Karamea N.Z. 152 G9
Karamea r. N.Z. 152 G9
Karamea Bight b. N.Z. 152 F9
Karamet-Niyaz Turkm. 103 F5 also spelt Garamätnyyaz
Karamian i. Indon. 77 F4
Karamiran China 89 D4
Karamiran He r. China 89 D4
Karamiran Shankou pass China 89 D4
Karamken Rus. Fed. 39 P3
Karamürsel Turkey 58 K8
Karamyshevo Rus. Fed. 43 J4
Karan r. Afgh. 101 G2
Karan state Myanmar see Kayin
Karān i. Saudi Arabia 105 E2
Karang Senegal 124 A3
Karang, Tanjung pt Indon. 75 A3
Karangagung Indon. 76 D3
Karangan Indon. 76 D4
Karangarua N.Z. 153 D11
Karangasem Indon. 77 F5
Karangetang vol. Indon. 75 C2
Karangoua r. Congo 126 B4
Karanja India 94 C1
Karanja r. India 94 C2
Karanjia India 97 E5
Karanpura India 96 B3
Karaoba Kazakh. 103 I1
Karaova Turkey 59 I11
Karaoy Almatinskaya Oblast' Kazakh. 103 H3
Karaoy Almatinskaya Oblast' Kazakh. 103 H3 also spelt Qaraoy
Karapelit Bulg. 58 I5
Karapınar Turkey 106 C3 also known as Sultanıye
Karapürçek Turkey 59 J9
Karaqi China 88 B3
Karas admin. reg. Namibia 130 C5
Karas mts Namibia 132 B4
Karaşar Turkey 106 B2
Karasay China 89 C4
Kara-Say Kyrg. 103 I4
Karasburg Namibia 130 C6
Kara Sea Rus. Fed. 39 H2 also known as Karskoye More
Karash Rus. Fed. 43 U5
Karashoky Kazakh. 103 H2
Karašica r. Croatia 56 K3
Karasica r. Hungary/Romania 56 K3
Kárášjohka Norway 44 N1 also spelt Karasjok
Kárášjohka r. Norway 44 N1 also spelt Karasjokka
Karasjok Norway see Kárášjohka
Karasjokka r. Norway see Kárášjohka
Karasor, Ozero salt l. Karagandinskaya Oblast' Kazakh. 103 H2
Karasor, Ozero salt l. Pavlodarskaya Oblast' Kazakh. 103 H2
Kara Strait Rus. Fed. see Karskiye Vorota, Proliv
Karasu Karagandinskaya Oblast' Kazakh. 103 H3
Karasu Kustanayskaya Oblast' Kazakh. 103 E2
Karasu Kustanayskaya Oblast' Kazakh. 103 F1 also spelt Qarasū
Karasu r. Kazakh. 103 H1
Karasu r. Syria/Turkey 109 H1 also known as Qara Şū Chāy
Karasu Turkey see Hizan
Karasu Turkey 106 B2 also known as Incirli
Karasu r. Turkey 107 E3
Karasubazar Ukr. see Bilohirs'k
Kara-Sug Rus. Fed. 84 B1
Karasuk Rus. Fed. 80 B2
Karasulak r. Ukr. 58 J3
Kara-Suu Kyrg. 103 H4
Karāt Iran 101 E3
Karatan Kazakh. 88 D2
Karataş Turkey 106 C3
Karataş Burnu hd Turkey see Fener Burnu
Karatau Kazakh. 103 G4 also spelt Qaratau; formerly known as Chulaktau
Karatau, Khrebet mts Kazakh. 103 F3 also known as Qaratau Zhotasy
Karatayka Rus. Fed. 40 L1
Karathuri Myanmar 79 B6
Karativu i. Sri Lanka 94 C4
Karatj l. Sweden 44 L2
Karatobe Kazakh. 102 C2 also spelt Qaratöbe
Karatobe, Mys pt Kazakh. 102 D3
Karatogay Kazakh. 102 D2 also spelt Qaratoghay
Karatol r. Kazakh. 103 I3
Karatomarskoye Vodokhranilishche resr Kazakh. 103 E1 also known as Qaratomar Bögeni
Karaton Kazakh. 102 C3 also spelt Qaraton
Karatsu Japan 91 A8
Karatünggü China 84 A2
Karatup, Poluostrov pen. Kazakh. 102 D3
Kara-Turgey r. Kazakh. 103 F2
Karaul Kazakh. 103 I2 also spelt Qaraüyl; formerly known as Abay; formerly spelt Karaaul
Karaulbazar Uzbek. 103 F5 also spelt Qorowulbozor
Karauli India 96 C4
Karaulkel'dy Kazakh. see Bayganin
Karaurgan Turkey 107 E2
Karauzyak Uzbek. 102 D4 also spelt Qara Özek or Qoraŭzak
Karavan Kyrg. see Kerben
Karavas Greece 59 D12
Karavastasë, Gjiri i b. Albania 58 A8
Karavastasë, Laguna e lag. Albania 58 A8
Karavatsichy Belarus 43 L9
Karavayevo Rus. Fed. 43 V4
Karavi i. Greece 59 E12
Karavonisia i. Greece 59 H13
Karawa Dem. Rep. Congo 126 D4
Karawang Indon. 77 D4
Karaxahar r. China see Kaidu He
Karayılan Turkey 108 H1
Karayulgan China 88 C3
Karazhal Kazakh. 103 G2 also spelt Qarazhal
Karazhar Uzbek. 102 D4
Karazhingil Kazakh. 103 H3
Karbalā' Iraq 107 F4 also spelt Kerbela
Karbalā' governorate Iraq 107 E4
Karbushevka Kazakh. 103 H2
Karcag Hungary 49 R8
Kardam Bulg. 58 J5
Kardamaina Greece 59 I12 also spelt Kardhaámaina
Kardeljevo Croatia see Ploče
Kardhaámaina Greece see Kardamaina
Kardhítsa Greece see Karditsa
Kardis Sweden 44 M2
Karditsa Greece 59 C9 also spelt Kardhítsa
Kärdla Estonia 42 D3
Kardymovo Rus. Fed. 43 N7
Karee S. Africa 133 K5
Kareeberge mts S. Africa 132 F7
Kareebospoort pass S. Africa 132 G7
Kareedouw S. Africa 133 I10
Kareha, Jebel mt. Morocco 54 F9
Kareima Sudan 121 F5
Karelaksha Rus. Fed. 44 P2
Kareli India 96 C5
Karelia aut. rep. Rus. Fed. see Kareliya, Respublika
Karelichy Belarus 42 H8
Kareliya, Respublika aut. rep. Rus. Fed. 44 P3 English form Karelia; formerly known as Karel'skaya A.S.S.R.
Karel'skaya A.S.S.R. aut. rep. Rus. Fed. see Kareliya, Respublika
Karel'skiy Bereg coastal area Rus. Fed. 40 E2
Karema Dodoma Tanz. 129 B6
Karema Rukwa Tanz. 129 A6
Karen state Myanmar see Kayin
Karenga r. Rus. Fed. 81 J2
Karera India 96 C4
Karesuando Sweden 44 M1
Kārevāndar Iran 101 E5
Kargala Rus. Fed. 102 C2
Kargalinskaya Rus. Fed. 102 A4 also known as Kargalinski
Kargalinski Rus. Fed. see Kargalinskaya
Kargalinskoye Kazakh. 102 D2 formerly known as Zhilyanka
Kargapazarı Dağları mts Turkey 107 E3
Karghalik China see Yecheng
Kargı Turkey 106 C2
Kargil Jammu and Kashmir 96 C2
Kargilik China see Yecheng
Kargıpınarı Turkey 108 F1
Kargopol' Rus. Fed. 40 F3
Kargowa Poland 49 M3
Kargūshkī Iran 100 D5
Karhal India 96 C4
Kari Nigeria 125 H4
Karīān Iran 100 D5
Kariba Zimbabwe 131 F3
Kariba, Lake resr Zambia/Zimbabwe 127 E9
Kariba Dam Zambia/Zimbabwe 127 F9
Kariba-yama vol. Japan 90 F3
Karibib Namibia 130 B4
Kariega r. S. Africa 132 H10
Karīf Salāsil well Yemen 105 E4
Karigasniemi Fin. 44 N1 also known as Gáregasnjárga
Karijini National Park Australia 150 B4
Karikari, Cape N.Z. 152 H2
Karīmābād Iran 100 C3
Karimata i. Indon. 77 E3
Karimata, Pulau-pulau is Indon. 77 E3
Karimata, Selat strait Indon. 77 E3
Karimganj India 97 G4
Karim Khanch Iran 100 B3
Karimnagar India 94 C2
Karimun Besar i. Indon. 76 C2
Karimunjawa i. Indon. 77 E4
Karimunjawa, Pulau-pulau is Indon. 77 E4
Karin Somalia 128 E2
Karinainen Fin. 45 M3
Käringsjön Sweden 44 K3
Karino S. Africa 133 P2
Karioi hill N.Z. 152 I5
Karis Fin. 45 M3 also known as Karjaa
Karisimbi, Mont vol. Rwanda 126 F5
Káristos Greece see Karystos
Karit Iran 100 D3
Karitsa Greece 59 D8
Kariya Japan 91 E7
Kariyangwe Zimbabwe 131 E3
Karjaa Fin. see Karis
Karjalohja Fin. 42 E1
Karjan India 96 B5
Karjat India 94 B2
Karkai r. India 97 E5
Karkal India 94 B3
Karkamb India 94 B2
Karkams S. Africa 132 B7
Karkaralinsk Kazakh. 103 H2 also known as Qarqaraly
Karkaralong, Kepulauan is Indon. 75 C1
Karkar Island P.N.G. 73 K7 also known as Dampier Island
Karkas, Kūh-e mts Iran 100 B3
Karkh Pak. 101 F5
Karkheh, Rūdkhāneh-ye r. Iran 100 A4
Karkinits'ka Zatoka g. Ukr. 41 E7
Karkkila Fin. 45 N3
Kärkölä Fin. 45 N3
Karkonoski Park Narodowy nat. park Czech Rep./Poland see Krkonošský narodní park
Karksi-Nuia Estonia 42 G3
Karkūmā, Ra's hd Saudi Arabia 104 B2
Karlantijpa North Aboriginal Land res. Australia 148 B3
Karlantijpa South Aboriginal Land res. Australia 148 B4
Karlik Shan mt. China 84 B3
Karlino Poland 49 M1
Karlıova Turkey 107 E3
Karlivka Ukr. 41 E6 also spelt Karlovka
Karl Marks, Qullai mt. Tajik. 101 H2
Karl-Marx-Stadt Germany see Chemnitz
Karlovac Croatia 56 H3
Karlovka Ukr. see Karlivka
Karlovo Bulg. 58 F6 formerly known as Levskigrad
Karlovy Vary Czech Rep. 49 J5 historically known as Carlsbad
Karlsberg Sweden 45 K3
Karlsborg Sweden 45 K4
Karlsburg Romania see Alba Iulia
Karlshamn Sweden 45 K4
Karlskoga Sweden 45 K4
Karlskrona Sweden 45 K4
Karlsruhe Germany 48 F6
Karlstad Sweden 45 K4
Karlstadt Germany 48 G6
Karlyuk Turkm. 103 F5
Karma Belarus 43 L8
Karma Niger 125 F3
Karma, Ouadi watercourse Chad 120 C6
Karmala India 94 B2
Karmanovka Kazakh. 102 B2
Karmanovo Rus. Fed. 43 P6
Karmas Sweden 44 L2
Karmona Spain see Córdoba
Karnabchul', Step' plain Uzbek. 103 F5
Karnafuli Reservoir Bangl. 97 G5
Karnal India 96 C3
Karnali r. Nepal 97 D3
Karnaprayag India 96 C3
Karnataka state India 94 B3 formerly known as Mysore
Karnes City U.S.A. 179 C6
Karnobat Bulg. 58 H6 formerly known as Polyanovgrad
Karodi Pak. 101 F5
Karoi Zimbabwe 131 F3
Karokpi Myanmar 78 B5
Karo La pass China 89 E6
Karong India 97 G4
Karonga Malawi 129 B7
Karonie Australia 151 C6
Karoo National Park S. Africa 132 G9
Karoonda Australia 146 C3
Karor Pak. 101 G4
Karora Eritrea 121 H5
Káros i. Greece see Keros
Karossa Indon. 75 A3
Karossa, Tanjung pt Indon. 77 G5
Karotis Greece 58 H7
Karouassa well Mali 125 E2
Karpasia pen. Cyprus 108 F2 also known as Karpas Peninsula; also spelt Kırpaşa
Karpas Peninsula Cyprus see Karpasia
Karpathos Greece 59 I13
Karpathos i. Greece 59 I13 formerly known as Scarpanto
Karpathou, Steno sea chan. Greece 59 I12
Karpaty mts Europe see Carpathian Mountains
Karpenisi Greece 59 C10
Karpilovka Belarus see Aktsyabrski
Karpinsk Rus. Fed. 38 G4
Karpogory Rus. Fed. 40 H2
Karpovychi Ukr. 43 N9
Karpuz r. Turkey 108 C1
Karpuzlu Aydın Turkey 59 I11
Karpuzlu Edirne Turkey 58 H8
Karratha Australia 150 B4
Karrats Fjord inlet Greenland see Nuugaatsiaap Imaa
Karrī Iran 100 B4
Karringmelkspruit S. Africa 133 L7
Karroo plat. S. Africa see Great Karoo
Karroun Hill Nature Reserve Australia 151 B6
Karrukh Afgh. 101 E3
Karrychirla Turkm. see imeni Kerbabayeva
Kars Turkey 107 E2
Karsakpay Kazakh. 103 F3 also spelt Qarsaqbay
Kärsämäki Fin. 44 N3
Kārsava Latvia 42 I5
Karshi Turkm. 102 C4 also spelt Garshy
Karshi Uzbek. 103 F5 also spelt Qarshi; historically known as Nautaca
Karshinskaya Step' plain Uzbek. 103 F5 also known as Qarshi Chŭli
Karşıyaka Balıkesir Turkey 58 J8
Karşıyaka İzmir Turkey 59 I10
Karsiyang India 97 F4
Karskiye Vorota, Proliv strait Rus. Fed. 40 K1 English form Kara Strait
Karskoye More sea Rus. Fed. see Kara Sea
Karstädt Germany 48 I2
Karsu Turkey 109 H1
Karsun Rus. Fed. 41 H5
Kartal Turkey 106 B2
Kartala vol. Comoros 129 D7
Kartaly Rus. Fed. 103 E1

Kartarpur India 96 B3
Kartena Lith. 42 C6
Karthaus U.S.A. 176 G4
Kartsevo Rus. Fed. 43 L5
Kartsino, Akra pt Greece 59 F10
Karttula Fin. 44 N3
Kartuni Guyana 199 G3
Kartuzy Poland 49 P1
Karubwe Zambia 127 F8
Kārūkh, Jabal mt. Iraq 109 P1
Karumai Japan 90 G4
Karumba Australia 149 D3
Karun, Kūh-e hill Iran 100 B4
Kārūn, Rūd-e r. Iran 100 B4
Karunagapalli India 94 C4
Karungi Sweden 44 M2
Karungu Kenya 128 B5
Karuni Indon. 75 A5
Karunjie Australia 150 D3
Karup Denmark 45 J4
Karur India 94 C4
Karuzi Burundi 126 F5
Karvetnagar India 94 C3
Karvia Fin. 45 M3
Karviná Czech Rep. 49 P6
Karwar India 94 B3
Karwendelgebirge nature res. Austria 48 I8
Karwi India 96 D4
Karya Greece 59 B10
Karyagino Azer. see Füzuli
Karyes Greece 59 F8
Karymskoye Rus. Fed. 85 G1
Karynzharyk, Peski des. Kazakh. 102 C4
Karystos Greece 59 F10
also spelt Káristos
Kaş Turkey 106 B3
Kasa India 94 B2
Kasaba Turkey see Turgutlu
Kasaba Lodge Zambia 127 F7
Kasabonika Canada 168 B2
Kasai r. Dem. Rep. Congo 127 C5
Kasai Japan 91 D7
Kasai, Plateau du Dem. Rep. Congo 127 D6
Kasai Occidental prov. Dem. Rep. Congo 127 D6
Kasai Oriental prov. Dem. Rep. Congo 126 E6
Kasaji Dem. Rep. Congo 127 D7
Kasama Japan 91 G6
Kasama Zambia 127 F7
Kasan Uzbek. 103 F5
also spelt Koson
Kasane Botswana 131 E3
Kasanga Tanz. 129 A7
Kasangulu Dem. Rep. Congo 126 B6
Kasanka National Park Zambia 127 F8
Kasansay Uzbek. 103 G4
also spelt Kosonsoy
Kasanza Dem. Rep. Congo 127 C6
Kasar, Ras pt Sudan 121 H5
Kasaragod India 94 B3
Kasari r. Estonia 42 E3
Kasatkino Rus. Fed. 82 C2
Kasba Lake Canada 167 K2
Kasba Tadla Morocco 122 D2
Kasbi Uzbek. 103 F5
Kaseda Japan 91 B9
Kasempa Zambia 127 E8
Kasenga Katanga Dem. Rep. Congo 127 D7
Kasenga Katanga Dem. Rep. Congo 127 F7
Kasenye Dem. Rep. Congo 126 F4
Kasese Dem. Rep. Congo 126 E5
Kasese Uganda 128 A4
Kasevo Rus. Fed. see Neftekamsk
Kasganj India 96 C4
Kasha China see Gonjo
Kasha waterhole Kenya 128 D5
Kashabowie Canada 168 B3
Kāshān Iran 100 B3
Kashary Rus. Fed. 41 G6
Kashechewan Canada 168 D2
Kashgar China see Kashi
Kashi China 88 B4
formerly known as Kashgar or Kaxgar
Kashihara Japan 91 D7
Kashima Japan 91 B8
Kashima-nada b. Japan 91 G6
Kashin Rus. Fed. 43 S4
Kashinka r. Rus. Fed. 43 S4
Kashiobwe Dem. Rep. Congo 127 F7
Kashipur India 96 C3
Kashira Rus. Fed. 43 T7
Kashirka r. Rus. Fed. 43 T7
Kashiwazaki Japan 90 F6
Kashkadar'inskaya Oblast' admin. div. Uzbek. 103 F5
English form Kashkadarya Oblast; also known as Qashqadaryo Wiloyati
Kashkadar'ya r. Uzbek. 101 F2
also known as Qashqadaryo
Kashkadarya Oblast admin. div. Uzbek. see Kashkadar'inskaya Oblast'
Kashkanteniz Kazakh. 103 H3
also spelt Kashken-Teniz or Qashqantengiz
Kashken-Teniz Kazakh. see Kashkanteniz
Kashkurino Rus. Fed. 43 M6
Kāshmar Iran 100 D3
Kashmir terr. Asia see Jammu and Kashmir
Kashmir, Vale of valley India 96 B2
Kashmor Pak. 101 G4
Kashmund reg. Afgh. 101 G3
Kashyukulu Dem. Rep. Congo 127 E6
Kasi India see Varanasi
Kasia India 97 D4
Kasilovo Rus. Fed. 43 O8
Kasimbar Indon. 75 A3
Kasimov Rus. Fed. 40 G5
Kasingi Dem. Rep. Congo 126 F4
Kasiruta i. Indon. 75 C3
Kaskaskia r. U.S.A. 174 B4
Kaskattama r. Canada 167 N3
Kaskelen Kazakh. 103 I4
also spelt Qaskelen
Kaskinen Fin. 44 M3
also known as Kaskö
Kas Klong i. Cambodia see Kŏng, Kaôh
Kaskö Fin. see Kaskinen
Kaslo Canada 167 G5
Kasmere Lake Canada 167 K3
Kasnya r. Rus. Fed. 43 P6
Kasomeno Dem. Rep. Congo 127 F7
Kasongan Indon. 77 F3
Kasongo Dem. Rep. Congo 126 E6
Kasongo-Lunda Dem. Rep. Congo 127 C6
Kasonguele Dem. Rep. Congo 127 E6
Kasos i. Greece 59 H13
Kasou, Steno sea chan. Greece 59 I13
Kaspi Georgia 107 F2
Kaspiy Mangy Oypaty lowland Kazakh./Rus. Fed. see Caspian Lowland
Kaspiysk Rus. Fed. 102 A4
Kaspiyskiy Rus. Fed. see Lagan'
Kaspiyskoye More sea Asia/Europe see Caspian Sea
Kasplya Rus. Fed. 43 M7
Kasplya r. Rus. Fed. 43 L6
Kasrawad India 96 B5
Kasrik Turkey see Gürpınar
Kassa Slovakia see Košice
Kassaare laht b. Estonia 42 D3
Kassala Sudan 121 H6
Kassala state Sudan 121 G6
Kassandra pen. Greece 59 E9
Kassandras, Akra pt Greece 59 E9
Kassandras, Kolpos b. Greece 59 E8
Kassandreia Greece 59 E8
Kassel Germany 48 G4
Kasserine Tunisia 123 H2
Kassinga Angola see Cassinga
Kassouloua well Niger 125 H3
Kastamonu Turkey 106 C2
also known as Çandar
Kastelli Kriti Greece 59 E13
also known as Kastéllion
Kastelli Kriti Greece 59 G13
Kastéllion Greece see Kastelli
Kastellorizon i. Greece see Megisti
Kastellou, Akra pt Greece 59 I13
Kastoria Greece 58 C8
Kastorias, Limni l. Greece 58 C8
Kastornoye Rus. Fed. 41 F6
Kastos i. Greece 59 B10
Kastrakiou, Techniti Limni resr Greece 59 C10
Kastre Estonia 42 I3
Kastrova Belarus 43 J5
Kastsyukovichy Belarus 43 N8
also spelt Kostyukovichi
Kastsyukowka Belarus 43 L9
Kasugai Japan 91 E7
Kasuku Dem. Rep. Congo 126 E5
Kasulu Tanz. 129 A6
Kasumiga-ura l. Japan 91 G6
Kasumkent Rus. Fed. 102 B4
Kasungu Malawi 129 B8
Kasungu National Park Malawi 129 B8
Kasur Pak. 101 H4
Kataba Zambia 127 E9
Katagum Nigeria 125 H3
Katahdin, Mount U.S.A. 174 G2
Kataklik Jammu and Kashmir 96 C2
Katako-Kombe Dem. Rep. Congo 126 E5
Katakolo, Akra pt Greece 59 C11
Katakwi Uganda 128 B4
Katanda Dem. Rep. Congo 127 D6
Katanga prov. Dem. Rep. Congo 127 E7
formerly known as Shaba
Katangi Madhya Pradesh India 96 C5
Katangi Madhya Pradesh India 96 C5
Katangli Rus. Fed. 82 F2
Katanning Australia 151 B7
Kata Pusht Iran 100 B2
Katashin Rus. Fed. 43 N9
Katastari Greece 59 B11
Katavi National Park Tanz. 129 A6
Katawaz Afgh. 101 G3
Katawaz reg. Afgh. 101 F3
Katchall i. India 95 G5
Katchamba Togo 125 F4
Katea Dem. Rep. Congo 127 E6
Katerini Greece 59 D8
Katesh Tanz. 129 B6
Kate's Needle mt. Canada/U.S.A. 164 F4
Katete Zambia 129 B8
Katghora India 97 D5
Katha Myanmar 78 B2
Katherina, Gebel mt. Egypt 121 G2
Katherine Australia 148 B2
Katherine r. Australia 148 A2
Katherine Gorge National Park Australia see Nitmiluk National Park
Kathi India 96 B5
Kathiawar pen. India 96 A5
Kathīb, Ra's al pt Yemen 104 C5
Kathīb el Henu des. Egypt 121 G2
Kathīb el Henu hill Egypt 108 D7
Kathīb el Makhāzin des. Egypt 108 D7
Kathleen Falls Australia 148 A2
Kathlehong S. Africa 133 M3

▶ Kathmandu Nepal 97 E4
Capital of Nepal. English form Katmandu.

Kathu S. Africa 132 H4
Kathua Jammu and Kashmir 96 B2
Kathua watercourse Kenya 128 C5
Kati Mali 124 C3
Katibas r. Sarawak Malaysia 77 F2
Kati-ér r. Hungary 49 S8
Katihar India 97 E4
Katikati N.Z. 152 J5
Kati-Kati S. Africa 133 L9
Katima Mulilo Namibia 131 E3
Katimik Lake Canada 167 L4
Katino Rus. Fed. 43 U8
Katiola Côte d'Ivoire 124 D4
Kā Tiritiri o te Moana mts N.Z. see Southern Alps
Katiti Aboriginal Land res. Australia 148 A5
Katkop Hills S. Africa 132 E7
Katlabukh, Ozero l. Ukr. 58 J3
Katma China 88 D4
Katmai National Park and Preserve U.S.A. 164 D4
Katmandu Nepal see Kathmandu
Kato Achaia Greece 59 C10
Kat O Chau i. Hong Kong China see Crooked Island
Katochi Greece 59 C10
Kato Figaleia Greece 59 C11
Kat O Hoi b. Hong Kong China see Crooked Harbour
Katol India 96 C5
Kåtölandet i. Fin. 44 M3
Katombe Dem. Rep. Congo 127 D6
Katompi Dem. Rep. Congo 127 E6
Katondwe Zambia 127 F8
Kato Nevrokopi Greece 58 E7
Katong Sing. 76 [inset]
Katonga r. Uganda 128 A4
Katon-Karagay Kazakh. 88 D1
also spelt Katonqaraghay
Katonqaraghay Kazakh. see Katon-Karagay
Katoomba Australia 147 F3
Katoposa, Gunung mt. Indon. 75 B3
Katosan India 96 B5
Kato Tithorea Greece 59 D10
Kåtotjåkka mt. Sweden see Goduĉohkka
Katowice Poland 49 Q5
formerly known as Stalinogród; historically known as Kattowitz
Katoya India 97 F5
formerly spelt Katwa
Katpur India 96 B5
Katrineholm Sweden 45 L4
Katse Dam Lesotho 133 M6
Katsepy Madag. 131 [inset] J2
Katsikas Greece 59 B9
Katsina Nigeria 125 G3
Katsina state Nigeria 125 G4
Katsina-Ala Nigeria 125 H5
Katsumoto Japan 91 A8
Katsuura Japan 91 G7
Katsuyama Japan 91 E6
Kattakurgan Uzbek. 103 F5
also spelt Kattaqŭrghon
Kattamudda Well Australia 150 D4
Kattaqŭrghon Uzbek. see Kattakurgan
Kattasang Hills Afgh. 101 F3
Kattavia Greece 59 I13
Kattegat strait Denmark/Sweden 45 J4
Kattisavan Sweden 44 L2
Kattowitz Poland see Katowice
Kattuputtur India 94 C4
Katumba Dem. Rep. Congo 127 E6
Katumbi Malawi 129 B7
Katun' r. Rus. Fed. 88 D1
Katunino Rus. Fed. 40 H4
Katunskiy Khrebet mts Rus. Fed. 88 D1
Katwa India see Katoya
Katwijk aan Zee Neth. 48 B3
Katyk Ukr. see Shakhtars'k
Katyn' Rus. Fed. 43 M7
Kąty Wrocławskie Poland 49 N4
Kauai i. U.S.A. 181 [inset] Y1
Kauai Channel U.S.A. 181 [inset] Y1
Kaudom Game Park nature res. Namibia 130 D3
Kaufbeuren Germany 48 H8
Kaufman U.S.A. 179 C5
Kauhajoki Fin. 44 M3
Kauhanevan-Pohjankankaan kansallispuisto nat. park Fin. 45 M3
Kauhava Fin. 44 M3
Kaukauna U.S.A. 172 E6
Kaukkwè Hills Myanmar 78 B2
Kaukonen Fin. 44 N2
Kauksi Estonia 42 I2
Kaulinranta Fin. 44 M2
Kaumajet Mountains Canada 169 I1
Kaunakakai U.S.A. 181 [inset] Z1
Kaunas Lith. 42 E7
formerly known as Kovno
Kaunata Latvia 42 I5
Kaundy, Vpadina depr. Kazakh. 102 C4
Kaunia Bangl. 97 F4
Kauno marios l. Lith. 42 F7
Kaupiri N.Z. 153 F10
Kaura-Namoda Nigeria 125 G3
Kau Sai Chau i. Hong Kong China 87 [inset]
Kaushany Moldova see Căuşeni
Kaustinen Fin. 44 M3
Kautokeino Norway 44 M1
Kau-ye Kyun i. Myanmar 79 B6
Kavacha Rus. Fed. 39 Q3
Kavadarci Macedonia 58 D7
Kavajë Albania 58 A7
Kavak Turkey 58 H8
Kavak Turkey 106 D2
Kavaklı Dağı hill Turkey 59 H9
Kavaklıdere Manisa Turkey 59 J10
Kavaklıdere Muğla Turkey 59 J11
Kavala Greece 58 F8
Kavalas, Kolpos b. Greece 58 F8
Kavalerovo Rus. Fed. 82 D3
Kavali India 94 D3
Kavalpatnam India 94 C4
Kavalyova Belarus 43 L6
Kavanayen Venez. 199 F3
Kavār Iran 100 C4
Kavaratti India 94 B4
Kavaratti i. India 94 B4
Kavarna Bulg. 58 J5
Kavarskas Lith. 42 F6
Kavendou, Mont mt. Guinea 124 B4
Kaveri r. India 94 C4
Kaveripatnam India 94 C3
Kavi India 96 B5
Kavieng P.N.G. 145 E2
Kavīr Iran 100 B3
Kavīr, Dasht-e des. Iran 100 C3
Kavīr-e Abarkūh des. Iran 100 C4
Kavīr-i-Namak salt flat Iran 100 D3
Kavīr Kūshk well Iran 100 D3
Kavirondo Gulf Kenya see Winam Gulf
Kavkazskiy Zapovednik nature res. Rus. Fed. 41 G8
Kaw Fr. Guiana 199 H3
Kawabe Japan 90 G5
Kawachi-nagano Japan 91 D7
Kawagama Lake Canada 168 E4
Kawagoe Japan 91 F7
Kawaguchi Japan 91 F7
Kawahara Japan 91 D7
Kawai Japan 90 G5
Kawaihae U.S.A. 181 [inset] Z1
Kawaihoa Point U.S.A. 181 [inset] Y1
Kawakawa N.Z. 152 I3
Kawamata Japan 90 G6
Kawambwa Zambia 127 F7
Kawaminami Japan 91 B8
Kawana Zambia 127 E8
Kawangkoan Indon. 75 C2
Kawanishi Japan 91 D7
Kawardha India 96 D5
Kawartha Lakes Canada 168 E4
Kawasa Dem. Rep. Congo 127 F7
Kawasaki Japan 91 F7
Kawashiri-misaki pt Japan 91 B7
Kawato Indon. 75 B3
Kawaura Japan 91 B8
Kawawachikamach Canada 169 H2
Kawe i. Indon. 75 D2
Kaweah, Lake U.S.A. 182 F5
Kaweka Forest Park nature res. N.Z. 152 K7
Kaweka Range mts N.Z. 152 K7
Kawene Canada 172 B2
Kawerau N.Z. 152 K6
Kawhia N.Z. 152 I6
Kawich Peak U.S.A. 183 H4
Kawich Range mts U.S.A. 183 H4
Kawinaw Lake Canada 167 L4
Kawio i. Indon. 75 C1
Kawkabān Yemen 104 C5
Kawkareik Myanmar 78 B4
Kaw Lake U.S.A. 178 C4
Kawlin Myanmar 78 A3
Kawludo Myanmar 78 B4
Kawmapyin Myanmar 79 B5
Kawm Dafanah tourist site Egypt see Daphnae
Kawngmeum Myanmar 78 B3
Kawthaung Myanmar 79 B6
Kawthoolei state Myanmar see Kayin
Kawthule state Myanmar see Kayin
Kaxgar China see Kashi
Kaxgar He r. China 88 B4
Kax He r. China 88 C3
Kaxtax Shan mts China 89 C4
Kaya Burkina 125 E3
Kaya S. Korea 91 A7
Kayacı Dağı hill Turkey 59 H9
Kayadibi Turkey 107 D3
Kayah state Myanmar 78 B4
Kayambi Zambia 129 A7
Kayan r. Indon. 77 E3
Kayan r. Indon. 77 G2
Kayan Myanmar 78 B4
Kayanaza Burundi 126 F5
Kayangel atoll Palau 73 H5
also known as Ngcheangel
Kayankulam India 94 C4
Kayar India 94 C2
Kayasa Indon. 75 C2
Kaya-san National Park S. Korea 91 A7
Kaybagar, Ozero l. Kazakh. see Koybagar, Ozero
Kaydanovo Belarus see Dzyarzhynsk
Kayenta U.S.A. 183 N5
Kayes Mali 124 C3
Kayes admin. reg. Mali 124 C3
Kayga Kazakh. 103 F2
also known as Qayghy; formerly known as Kaygy
Kaygy Kazakh. see Kayga
Kayin state Myanmar 78 B4
also known as Karan; formerly known as Karen or Kawthoolei or Kawthule
Kaymanachikha Kazakh. 103 H1
Kaymaz Turkey 106 B3
Kaynar Kazakh. 103 I2
also spelt Qaynar
Kaynar Turkey 107 D3
Kaynarlı r. Turkey 58 I7
Kayoa i. Indon. 75 C2
Kayrakkum Tajik. see Qayroqqum
Kayrakkumskoye Vodokhranilishche resr Tajik. see Obanbori Qayroqqum
Kayrakty Kazakh. 103 H2
also spelt Qayraqty
Kayseri Turkey 106 C3
historically known as Caesarea Cappadociae or Mazaca
Kaysersberg France 51 N4
Kayuadi i. Indon. 75 B4
Kayuagung Indon. 76 D3
Kayuyu Dem. Rep. Congo 126 E5
Kayyerkan Rus. Fed. 39 I3
Kayyngdy Kyrg. 103 H4
formerly spelt Kainda or Kaindy; formerly known as Molotovsk
Kazachka Rus. Fed. 43 T8
Kazach'ye Rus. Fed. 39 N2
Kazakh Azer. see Qazax
Kazakhdar'ya Uzbek. 102 D4
also spelt Qozoqdaryo
Kazakhskaya S.S.R. country Asia see Kazakhstan
Kazakhskiy Melkosopochnik plain Kazakh. 103 G2
Kazakhskiy Zaliv b. Kazakh. 102 C4
also known as Qazaq Shyghanaghy

▶ Kazakhstan country Asia 102 C2
4th largest country in Asia and 9th in the world. Also spelt Kazakstan or Qazaqstan in Kazakh; formerly known as Kazakhskaya S.S.R.
world [countries] ▶ 10–11
asia [countries] ▶ 64–67

Kazakhstan Kazakh. see Aksay
Kazaki Rus. Fed. 43 T9
Kazakstan country Asia see Kazakhstan
Kazalinsk Kazakh. 103 E3
also known as Qazaly
Kazan r. Canada 167 M2
Kazan' Rus. Fed. 40 I5
Kazanchunkur Kazakh. 103 J2
Kazancı Turkey 106 C3
Kazandzhik Turkm. see Gazandzhyk
Kazanje, Mal mt. Albania 58 B9
Kazanka r. Rus. Fed. 40 I5
Kazanketken Uzbek. 102 D4
also spelt Qozonketkan
Kazanlı Turkey 108 F1
Kazanlŭk Bulg. 58 G6
Kazanovka Rus. Fed. 43 T8
Kazanovo Rus. Fed. 85 G1
Kazan-rettō is N. Pacific Ocean see Volcano Islands
Kazatin Ukr. see Kozyatyn
Kazatskiy Kazakh. 102 D2
Kaza Wenz r. Eth. 128 C1

▶ Kazbek mt. Georgia/Rus. Fed. 107 F2
4th highest mountain in Europe. Also known as Mqinvartsveri.
europe [landscapes] ▶ 30–31

Kaz Dağı mts Turkey 106 A3
Kāzerūn Iran 100 B4
Kazgorodok Kazakh. 103 G1
Kazhim Rus. Fed. 40 I3
Kazhmak r. Pak. 101 E5
Kazıkbeli Geçidi pass Turkey 59 K11
Kazi Magomed Azer. see Qazımämmäd
Kazimierza Wielka Poland 49 R5
Kazimierz Dolne Poland 49 S4
Kazincbarcika Hungary 49 R7
Kazinka Lipetskaya Oblast' Rus. Fed. 43 U9
formerly known as Novaya Zhizn
Kazinka Ryazanskaya Oblast' Rus. Fed. 43 U8
Kaziranga National Park India 97 G4
Kazlowshchyna Belarus 42 G8
Kazlowshchyna Belarus 42 J6
Kazlų Rūda Lith. 42 E7
Kazo Japan 91 F6
Kaztalovka Kazakh. 102 B2
Kazuma Pan National Park Zimbabwe 131 E3
Kazumba Dem. Rep. Congo 127 D6
Kazungula Zambia 127 E9
Kazuno Japan 90 G4
Kazy Turkm. 102 D5
Kazyany Belarus 43 K6
Kazygurt Kazakh. 103 G4
also spelt Qazyqurt; formerly known as Lenin or Leninskoye
Kazym r. Rus. Fed. 38 G3
Kazymskiy Mys Rus. Fed. 38 G3
Kçirë Albania 58 A6
Kea Greece 59 F11
Kea i. Greece 59 F11
English form Ceos
Keaau U.S.A. 181 [inset] Z2
Keahole Point U.S.A. 181 [inset] Z2
Kealakekua Bay U.S.A. 181 [inset] Z2
Kealia U.S.A. 181 [inset] Z2
Keams Canyon U.S.A. 183 N6
Keamu i. Vanuatu see Anatom
Kearney U.S.A. 178 C3
Kearneysville U.S.A. 176 H6
Kearny U.S.A. 183 N8
Keas, Steno sea chan. Greece 59 F11
Keate's Drift S. Africa 133 O5
Keban Turkey 107 D3
Keban Barajı resr Turkey 107 D3
Kebatu i. Indon. 77 E3
Kebbi state Nigeria 125 F3
Kébémèr Senegal 124 A3
Kébi r. Cameroon 125 I4
Kébi Côte d'Ivoire 124 D4
Kebili Tunisia 123 H2
Kebīr, Nahr al r. Lebanon/Syria 108 G3
Kebkabiya Sudan 120 E6
Kebnekaise mt. Sweden 44 L2
K'ebrī Dehar Eth. 128 E3
Kebumen Indon. 77 E4
Kecel Hungary 49 Q9
Kech reg. Pak. 101 E5
K'ech'a Terara mt. Eth. 128 C3
Kéché Cent. Afr. Rep. 126 D2
Kechika r. Canada 166 E3
Keçiborlu Turkey 106 B3
Kecskemét Hungary 49 Q9
Kedah state Malaysia 76 C1
Kėdainiai Lith. 42 E6
Kedairu Passage Fiji see Kadavu Passage
Kédédéssé Chad 126 C2
Kedgwick Canada 169 H4
Kedian China 87 E2
Kediri Indon. 77 F4
Kedong China 82 B3
Kédougou Senegal 124 B3
Kedva r. Rus. Fed. 40 J2
Kędzierzyn-Koźle Poland 49 P5
historically known as Heydebreck
Keele r. Canada 166 E1
Keele Peak Canada 166 D2
Keeley Lake Canada 167 I4
Keeling Islands terr. Indian Ocean see Cocos Islands
Keelung Taiwan see Chilung
Keenapusan i. Phil. 74 A5
Keene CA U.S.A. 182 F6
Keene NH U.S.A. 177 M3
Keene OH U.S.A. 176 D5
Keep r. Australia 148 A2
Keepit, Lake resr Australia 147 F2
Keep River National Park Australia 148 A2
Keeromsberg mt. Free State S. Africa 133 K5
Keeromsberg mt. W. Cape S. Africa 132 D10
Keer-weer, Cape Australia 149 D2
Keetmanshoop Namibia 130 C5
Keewatin Canada 167 M5
Keewatin U.S.A. 174 A2
Kefallinia i. Greece see Cephalonia
Kefallonia i. Greece see Cephalonia
Kefalos Greece 59 H12
Kefalos, Akra pt Greece 59 F11
Kefamenanu Indon. 75 C5
Kefe Ukr. see Feodosiya
Keffi Nigeria 125 G4
Keflavík Iceland 44 [inset] B2
Kegalla Sri Lanka 94 D5
Kegayli Uzbek. see Kegeyli
Kegen Kazakh. 103 I4
Kegeyli Uzbek. 102 D4
also spelt Kegayli
Keglo, Baie de b. Canada 169 H1
Keg River Canada 167 G3
Kegul'ta Rus. Fed. 41 H7
Ķegums Latvia 42 F5
Keheili Sudan 121 G5
Kehl Germany 48 E7
Kehoula well Mauritania 124 C2
Kehra Estonia 42 G2
Kehsi Mansam Myanmar 78 B3
Kehtna Estonia 42 F3
Keibab Plateau U.S.A. 183 L5
Keighley U.K. 47 K10
Keihoku Japan 91 D7
Keila Estonia 42 F2
Keila r. Estonia 42 F2
Keilak Sudan 126 F2
Keili Sudan 128 B2
Kei Ling Ha Hoi b. Hong Kong China see Three Fathoms Cove
Keimoes S. Africa 132 E5
Kei Mouth S. Africa 133 M9
Kei Road S. Africa 133 L9
Keiskama r. S. Africa 133 L10
Keiskammahoek S. Africa 133 L9
Keïta Niger 125 G3
Kéïta, Bahr r. Chad 126 C2
Keitele Fin. 44 N3
Keitele l. Fin. 44 N3
Keith Australia 146 D4
Keith U.K. 46 J6
Keith, Cape Australia 148 A1
Keith Arm b. Canada 166 F1
Keithley Creek Canada 166 F4
Keithsburg U.S.A. 172 C9
Kejimkujik National Park Canada 169 H4
Kekaha U.S.A. 181 [inset] Y1
Kek-Art Kyrg. see Alaykuu
Kekava Latvia 42 F5
Kekaygyr Kyrg. see Kök-Aygyr
Kekerengu N.Z. 153 H10
Kékes mt. Hungary 49 R8
Kekova Adası i. Turkey 108 A1
Kekra Rus. Fed. 39 O4
Kekri India 96 B4
Kek-Tash Kyrg. see Kök-Tash
K'elafo Eth. 128 E3
Kelai atoll Maldives 94 B5
Kelan China 85 F4
Kelang i. Indon. 75 C3
Kelang Malaysia 76 C2
formerly spelt Klang
Kelantan r. Malaysia 76 C1
Kelantan state Malaysia 76 C1
Kelārdasht Iran 100 B2
Kelawar i. Indon. 77 E3
Kelbia, Sebkhet salt pan Tunisia 57 C13
Kele Uganda 128 B4
Kelekçi Turkey 59 K11
Keles Turkey 59 K9
Keles Uzbek. 103 G4
Kelheim Germany 48 I7
Kelibia Tunisia 123 H1
Kelif Turkm. 103 F5
Kelifskiy Uzboy marsh Turkm. 103 E5
Kelkit Turkey 107 D2
also known as Çiftlik
Kelkit r. Turkey 107 D2
Kellavere hill Estonia 42 H2
Kellé Congo 126 B5
Kellerberrin Australia 151 B6
Keller Lake Canada 166 F2
Kellerovka Kazakh. 103 G1
Kellett, Cape Canada 164 G2
Kelliher Canada 167 K5
Kellogg U.S.A. 180 C3
Kelloselkä Fin. 44 O2
Kells Rep. of Ireland 47 F10
also known as Ceanannus Mór
Kelly Lake Canada 166 E1
Kelly Range hills Australia 151 C5
Kelmė Lith. 42 D6
Kelo Chad 126 B2
Kelowna Canada 166 G5
Kelp Head Canada 166 E5
Kelsey U.S.A. 172 A3
Kelseyville U.S.A. 182 B3
Kelso N.Z. 153 C13
Kelso U.K. 46 J8
Kelso CA U.S.A. 183 I6
Kelso WA U.S.A. 180 B3
Kelti, Jebel mt. Morocco 54 F9
Keluang Malaysia 76 C2
formerly spelt Kluang
Kelujärvi Fin. 44 N2
Kelvington Canada 167 K4
Kelvin Island Canada 168 B3
Kelwara India 101 H5
Kem' Rus. Fed. 40 E2
Kem' r. Rus. Fed. 40 E2
Kema r. Rus. Fed. 43 S1
Ke Macina Mali see Massina
Kemah Turkey 107 D3
Kemaliye Turkey 58 H7
Kemaliye Turkey 107 D3
also known as Eğin
Kemalpaşa Turkey 59 I10
Kemano Canada 166 E4
Kembé Cent. Afr. Rep. 126 D3
Kembolcha Eth. 128 C2
Kemeneshát hills Hungary 49 O8
Kemer Antalya Turkey 106 B3
Kemer Antalya Turkey 108 A1
Kemer Muğla Turkey 106 B3
Kemer Barajı resr Turkey 106 B3
Kemerovo Rus. Fed. 80 D1
Kemerovo Oblast admin. div. Rus. Fed. see Kemerovskaya Oblast'
Kemerovskaya Oblast' admin. div. Rus. Fed. 80 D2
English form Kemerovo Oblast
Kemi Fin. 44 N2
Kemihaara Fin. 44 O2
Kemijärvi Fin. 44 N2
Kemijärvi l. Fin. 44 N2
Kemijoki r. Fin. 44 N2
Kemin Kyrg. 103 H4
formerly known as Bystrovka
Keminmaa Fin. 44 N2
Kemiö Fin. see Kimito
Kemir Turkm. 102 C5
formerly spelt Keymir
Kemlya Rus. Fed. 40 H5
Kemmerer U.S.A. 180 E4
Kemmuna i. Malta 57 G12
also known as Comino
Kémo pref. Cent. Afr. Rep. 126 C3
Kemp, Lake U.S.A. 179 C5
Kempazh r. Rus. Fed. 40 L2
Kempele Fin. 44 N2
Kempen reg. Belgium 51 K1
Kempendyay Rus. Fed. 39 L3
Kempisch Kanaal canal Belgium 51 L1
Kemp Land reg. Antarctica 223 D2
Kemp Peninsula Antarctica 222 U2
Kemp's Bay Bahamas 186 D1
Kempsey Australia 147 G2
Kempt, Lac l. Canada 169 F4
Kempten (Allgäu) Germany 48 H8
Kempton Australia 147 E5
Kempton Park S. Africa 133 M3
Kemptville Canada 173 R5
Kemujan i. Indon. 77 E4
Ken r. India 96 D4
Kenabeek Canada 173 N3
Kenai U.S.A. 164 D3
Kenai Fiords National Park U.S.A. 164 D4
Kenai Mountains U.S.A. 164 D4
Kenamu r. Canada 169 J2
Kenamuke Swamp Sudan 128 B3
Kenansville U.S.A. 174 E5
Kenawang, Bukit mt. Sarawak Malaysia 77 F2
Kenāyis, Râs el pt Egypt 121 E2
Kenbridge U.S.A. 176 G9
Kendal Indon. 77 E4
Kendal U.K. 47 J9
Kendall r. Australia 149 D2
Kendall U.S.A. 175 D7
Kendall, Cape Canada 167 O2
Kendall, Mount N.Z. 152 G9
Kendallville U.S.A. 172 H9
Kendari Indon. 75 B3
Kendawangan Indon. 77 E3
Kendawangan r. Indon. 77 E3
Kendégué Chad 126 C2
Kendrikí Makedhonía admin. reg. Greece see Kentriki Makedonia
Kendraparha India 95 E1
Kendrew S. Africa 133 I9
Kendrick Peak U.S.A. 183 M6
Kendua Bangl. 97 F4
Kendujhargarh India 97 E5
Kendyktas mts Kazakh. 103 H4
Kendyrli-Kayasanskoye, Plato plat. Kazakh. 102 C4
Kendyrlisor, Solonchak salt l. Kazakh. 102 C4
Kenedy U.S.A. 179 C6
Keneka r. S. Africa 133 N7
Kenema Sierra Leone 124 C5
Kenepai, Gunung mt. Indon. 77 E2
Keneurgench Turkm. 102 D4
also spelt Köneürgench; formerly spelt Kunya-Urgench
Kenga Bhutan 97 F4
Kenge Dem. Rep. Congo 126 C6
Kengere Dem. Rep. Congo 127 E7
Keng Hkam Myanmar 78 B3
Kengis Sweden 44 M2
Keng Lap Myanmar 78 C3
Keng Lon Myanmar 78 B3
Keng-Peli Uzbek. 102 D4
Keng Tawng Myanmar 78 B3
Kengtung Myanmar 78 B3
Kenhardt S. Africa 132 F6
Kéniéba Mali 124 C3
Kéniébaoulé, Réserve de nature res. Mali 124 C3
Kénitra Morocco 122 D2
formerly known as Port-Lyautrey
Kenli China 85 H4
Kenmare Rep. of Ireland 47 C12
Kenmare U.S.A. 178 B1
Kenmare River inlet Rep. of Ireland 47 B12
Kenmaur Zimbabwe 131 F3
Kenmore U.S.A. 176 G3
Kenn Germany 48 D6
Kennebec U.S.A. 178 C3
Kennebec r. U.S.A. 174 G2
Kennebunk U.S.A. 177 O2
Kennebunkport U.S.A. 177 O2
Kennedy Australia 149 E3
Kennedy r. Australia 149 E2
Kennedy, Cape U.S.A. see Canaveral, Cape
Kennedy Range hills Australia 151 A5
Kennedy Range National Park Australia 151 A5
Kennedy's Vale S. Africa 133 O1
Kennedy Town Hong Kong China 87 [inset]
Kennedyville U.S.A. 177 J6
Kenner U.S.A. 175 B6
Kennet r. U.K. 47 L12
Kenneth Range hills Australia 150 B4
Kennett U.S.A. 174 B4
Kennewick U.S.A. 180 C3
Kenogami r. Canada 168 C3
Kenogami Lake Canada 173 M2
Kenogamissi Lake Canada 173 L2
Keno Hill Canada 166 C2
Kenora Canada 167 M5
Kenosha U.S.A. 172 F8
Kenova U.S.A. 176 C7
Kenozero, Ozero l. Rus. Fed. 40 F3
Kensington Canada 169 I4
Kent OH U.S.A. 176 D4
Kent TX U.S.A. 181 F7
Kent VA U.S.A. 176 D9
Kent WA U.S.A. 180 B3
Kentani S. Africa 133 M9
also spelt Centane
Kentau Kazakh. 103 G4
Kent Group is Australia 147 E4
Kentland U.S.A. 174 C3
Kenton MI U.S.A. 172 E4
Kenton OH U.S.A. 176 B5
Kenton-on-Sea S. Africa 133 K10
Kent Peninsula Canada 165 I3
Kentriki Makedonia admin. reg. Greece 58 E8
also spelt Kendrikí Makedhonía
Kentucky r. U.S.A. 176 B8
Kentucky state U.S.A. 176 A8
Kentucky Lake U.S.A. 174 B4
Kentwood LA U.S.A. 175 B6
Kentwood MI U.S.A. 172 H8

▶ Kenya country Africa 128 C4
africa [countries] ▶ 114–117

▶ Kenya, Mount Kenya 128 C5
2nd highest mountain in Africa. Also known as Kirinyaga.
africa [landscapes] ▶ 112–113

Kenyir, Tasik resr Malaysia 76 C1
Kenzingen Germany 48 E7
Keokuk U.S.A. 174 B3
Keoladeo National Park India 96 C4
Keosauqua U.S.A. 174 B3
Keowee, Lake resr U.S.A. 174 D5
Kepa Rus. Fed. 44 P2
Kepa r. Rus. Fed. 44 P2
Kepahiang Indon. 76 C3
Kępice Poland 49 N1
Kepina r. Rus. Fed. 40 G2
Kepler Mountains N.Z. 153 B13
Kępno Poland 49 O4
Keppel Bay Australia 149 F4
Keppel Harbour sea chan. Sing. 76 [inset]
Keppel Island Tonga see Tafahi
Kepsut Turkey 106 B3
Kerala state India 94 B4
historically known as Chera
Kerang Australia 147 D3
Kerava Fin. 45 N3
Kerba Alg. 55 M8
Kerbau, Tanjung pt Indon. 76 C3
Kerbela Iraq see Karbalā'
Kerben Kyrg. 103 G4
also spelt Karavan
Kerbi r. Rus. Fed. 82 E1
Kerch Ukr. 41 F7
historically known as Panticapaeum
Kerchem'ya Rus. Fed. 40 J3
Kerchevskiy Rus. Fed. 40 K4
Kere Eth. 128 C3
Kerema P.N.G. 73 K8
Keremeos Canada 166 G5
Kerempe Burun pt Turkey 106 C2
Keren Eritrea 121 H6
Kerend Iran 100 A3
Kerepehi N.Z. 152 J5
Kerest' r. Rus. Fed. 43 M2
Keret' Rus. Fed. 44 P2
Keret' r. Rus. Fed. 44 P2
Keret', Ozero l. Rus. Fed. 44 P2
Kerewan Gambia 124 A3
Kerey watercourse Kazakh. 103 G2
formerly spelt Kirey
Kerey, Ozero salt l. Kazakh. 103 G2
formerly spelt Kirey, Ozero
Kergeli Turkm. 102 D5
Kerguélen, Îles is Indian Ocean 219 L9
English form Kerguelen Islands
Kerguelen Islands Indian Ocean see Kerguélen, Îles
Kericho Kenya 128 B5
Kerihun mt. Indon. 77 F2
Kerikeri N.Z. 152 H3
Kerimäki Fin. 45 O3
Kerinci, Danau l. Indon. 76 C3

index K

Kerinci, Gunung vol. Indon. 76 C3
formerly known as Gunung Indrapura or Kerintji
Kerinci Seblat National Park Indon. 76 C3
Kerintji vol. Indon. see Kerinci, Gunung
Kerio watercourse Kenya 128 C4
Keriya China see Yutian
Keriya He watercourse China 88 C4
Keriya Shankou pass China 89 C5
Kerka r. Romania 49 N9
Kerkebet Eritrea 104 B4
Kerkenah, Îles is Tunisia 123 H2
Kerki Turkm. 103 F5
Kerkichi Turkm. 103 F5
Kerkini Oros mts Bulg./Macedonia see Belasica
Kerkinitis, Limni l. Greece 58 E7
Kérkira i. Greece see Corfu
Kerkouane tourist site Tunisia 123 H1
Kerkyra Greece 59 A9
Kerkyra i. Greece see Corfu
Kerma Sudan 121 F5
Kermadec Islands S. Pacific Ocean 145 H5
▶Kermadec Trench sea feature S. Pacific Ocean 220 G8
4th deepest trench in the world.
Kermān Iran 100 D4
also spelt Kirman; historically known as Carmana
Kermān prov. Iran 100 D4
Kerman U.S.A. 182 D5
Kermān Desert Iran 101 D4
Kermānshāh Iran 100 A3
formerly known as Bākhtarān or Qahremānshahr
Kermānshāh prov. Iran 100 A3
formerly known as Bākhtarān or Kermānshāhān
Kermānshāhān prov. Iran see Kermānshāh
Kermine Uzbek. see Navoi
Kermit U.S.A. 179 B6
Kern r. U.S.A. 182 E6
Kern, South Fork r. U.S.A. 182 F6
Kernersville U.S.A. 176 E9
Kernertut, Cap c. Canada 169 H1
Kernot Range hills Australia 148 B5
Kernville U.S.A. 182 F6
Keros i. Greece 59 G12
also spelt Káros
Kérouané Guinea 124 C4
Kerpen Germany 48 D5
Kerr, Cape Antarctica 223 K1
Kerrobert Canada 167 I5
Kerrville U.S.A. 179 C6
Kerry Head Rep. of Ireland 47 C11
Kersa Dek Eth. 128 C3
Kershaw U.S.A. 174 D5
Kert, Oued r. Morocco 55 H9
Kerteminde Denmark 45 J5
Kertosono Indon. 77 F4
Kerulen r. China/Mongolia 85 H1
also known as Herlen Gol or Herlen He
Kerumutan Reserve nature res. Indon. 76 C3
Kerur India 94 B2
Kerva Rus. Fed. 43 U6
Keryneia Cyprus see Kyrenia
Kerzaz Alg. 123 E3
Kerzhenets r. Rus. Fed. 40 H4
Kesagami r. Canada 168 E3
Kesagami Lake Canada 168 D3
Kesälahti Fin. 44 O3
Keşan Turkey 106 A2
Keşap Turkey 107 D2
Kesarevo Bulg. 58 G5
Kesariya India 97 E4
Kesennuma Japan 90 G5
Keshan China 82 B2
Keshem Afgh. 101 G2
Keshendeh-ye Bala Afgh. 101 F2
Keshod India 96 A5
Keshorai Patan India 96 C4
Keskin Turkey 106 C3
Keskozero Rus. Fed. 40 E3
Kes'ma Rus. Fed. 43 S3
Kesova Gora Rus. Fed. 43 S4
Kesra Tunisia 57 B13
Kestel Turkey see Gürsu
Kestel Turkey 59 K8
Kestell S. Africa 133 M5
Kesten'ga Rus. Fed. 44 O2
Kestilä Fin. 44 N2
Keswick U.K. 47 I9
Keswick Dam U.S.A. 182 B1
Keszthely Hungary 49 O9
Ket' r. Rus. Fed. 39 I4
Keta Ghana 125 F5
Ketahun Indon. 76 C3
Ketam, Pulau i. Sing. 76 [inset]
Ketapang Jawa Timur Indon. 77 F4
Ketapang Kalimantan Barat Indon. 77 E3
Ketchikan U.S.A. 166 D4
Ketchum U.S.A. 180 D4
Kete Krachi Ghana 125 E5
Ketmen', Khrebet mts China/Kazakh. 88 C3
Kétou Benin 125 F5
Ketoy, Ostrov i. Rus. Fed. 81 Q3
Kętrzyn Poland 49 S1
Kette Cameroon 125 I5
Kettering U.K. 47 L11
Kettering U.S.A. 176 A6
formerly known as Van Buren
Kettle r. Canada 166 G5
Kettle r. U.S.A. 174 A2
Kettle Creek r. U.S.A. 176 H4
Kettle Falls U.S.A. 180 C2
Kettleman City U.S.A. 182 E5
Kettle River U.S.A. 172 A4
Kettle River Range mts U.S.A. 180 C2
Ketungau r. Indon. 77 E2
Keuka U.S.A. 177 H3
Keuka Lake U.S.A. 177 H3
Keumgang, Mount N. Korea see Kumgang-san
Keumsang, Mount N. Korea see Kumgang-san
Keur Massène Mauritania 124 A2
Keurusselkä l. Fin. 45 N3
Keuruu Fin. 44 N3
Kevelaer Germany 48 D4
Kevon luonnonpuisto nature res. Fin. 44 N1
Kew Turks and Caicos Is 187 E2
Kewanee U.S.A. 174 B3
Kewaskum U.S.A. 172 E7
Kewaunee U.S.A. 172 F6
Keweenaw Bay U.S.A. 172 E4
Keweenaw Bay b. U.S.A. 172 E4
Keweenaw Peninsula U.S.A. 172 E3
Keweenaw Point U.S.A. 172 F3
Keyala Sudan 128 B3
Keya Paha r. U.S.A. 178 C3
Key Harbour Canada 168 D4
Keyi China 88 C3
Keyihe China 85 I1
Key Largo U.S.A. 175 D7
Key Largo National Marine Sanctuary nature res. U.S.A. 175 D7
Keyling Inlet Australia 148 A2
Keymir Turkm. see Kemir
Keyser U.S.A. 176 G6
Keysers Ridge U.S.A. 176 F6
Keystone Lake OK U.S.A. 179 C4
Keystone Lake PA U.S.A. 176 F5
Keysville U.S.A. 176 G8
Keytesville U.S.A. 178 D4
Keytū Iran 100 B3
Keyvy, Vozvyshennost' hills Rus. Fed. 40 F2
Key West FL U.S.A. 175 D7
Key West IA U.S.A. 172 C8
Kez Rus. Fed. 40 J4
Kezar Falls U.S.A. 177 O2
Kezi Zimbabwe 131 F4
Kežmarok Slovakia 49 R6
Kgakala S. Africa 133 K4
Kgalagadi admin. dist. Botswana 130 D5
Kgatleng admin. dist. Botswana 131 E5
Kgotsong S. Africa 133 K4
Khabarī al Hajm salt pan Saudi Arabia 109 K6
Khabari al Khubub salt pan Iraq 109 K4
Khabarikha Rus. Fed. 40 J2
Khabarovo Rus. Fed. 40 L1
Khabarovsk Rus. Fed. 82 D2
Khabarovskiy Kray admin. div. Rus. Fed. 82 D2
English form Khabarovsk Kray
Khabarovsk Kray admin. div. Rus. Fed. see Khabarovskiy Kray
Khabb, Wādī watercourse Yemen 104 D4
Khabis Iran see Shahdād
Khabody Pass Afgh. 101 E3
Khabrā al 'Arn salt pan Saudi Arabia 104 C3
Khabrah Sāfiyah hill Saudi Arabia 109 K6
Khābūr, Nahr al r. Syria 109 L1
Khachmas Azer. see Xaçmaz
Khachrod India 96 B5
Khadar, Jabal mt. Oman 105 G3
Khadārah Saudi Arabia 104 C4
Khadari watercourse Sudan 126 E2
Khadun' Belarus 43 M8
Khadyzhensk Rus. Fed. 41 F7
Khadzhidimovo Bulg. 58 E7
Khadzhybeys'kyy Lyman l. Ukr. 58 L2
Khafī, Sha'īb al watercourse Iraq 109 N6
Khafs Banbān well Saudi Arabia 105 D2
Khaga India 96 D4
Khagaria India 97 E4
Khagaul India 97 E4
Khagrachari Bangl. 97 F5
also spelt Khagrachhari
Khagrachhari Bangl. see Khagrachari
Khairagarh Chhattisgarh India 96 D5
Khairagarh Uttar Pradesh India 89 B7
Khairpur Pak. 101 H4
Khairpur Pak. 101 G5
Khairwara India 96 B5
Khāīz, Kūh-e mt. Iran 100 B4
Khaja du Koh hill Afgh. 103 F5
Khakasiya, Respublika aut. rep. Rus. Fed. 80 E2
English form Khakassia; formerly known as Khakasskaya A.S.S.R.
Khakassia aut. rep. Rus. Fed. see Khakasiya, Respublika
Khakasskaya A.S.S.R. aut. rep. Rus. Fed. see Khakasiya, Respublika
Khāk-e Jabbar Afgh. 101 G3
Khakhea Botswana 130 D5
Khakīr Afgh. 101 F3
Khakriz reg. Afgh. 101 F4
Khalach Turkm. 103 F5
also spelt Halach
Khalajestan reg. Iran 100 B3
Khalamyer"ye Belarus 43 K6
Khalatse Jammu and Kashmir 96 C2
Khalidabad Iran 100 C3
Khalifat mt. Pak. 101 F4
Khalilabad India 97 D4
Khalilabad Iran 100 D3
Khallovo Rus. Fed. 102 D2
Khalkabad Turkm. 103 E4
Khalkabad Uzbek. 102 D4
Khalkhāl Iran 100 B2
formerly known as Herowābād
Khalki i. Greece see Chalki
Khalkis Greece see Chalkida
Khallikot India 95 E2
Khal'mer-Yu Rus. Fed. 40 M2
Khalopyenichy Belarus 43 J7
Khalqobod Uzbek. see Khalkabad
Khalte Nepal 97 E4
Khalturin Rus. Fed. see Orlov
Khamar-Daban, Khrebet mts Rus. Fed. 84 D1
Khamaria India 96 D5
Khambhaliya India 96 A5
Khambhat India 96 B5
formerly known as Cambay
Khambhat, Gulf of India 94 A2
also known as Cambay, Gulf of
Khamgaon India 94 C1
Khamir Iran 100 C5
Khamir Yemen 104 C4
Khami Ruins National Monument tourist site Zimbabwe 131 F4
Khamis Mushayţ Saudi Arabia 104 C4
Khamma well Saudi Arabia 105 D2
Khammam India 94 D2
Khampa Rus. Fed. 39 M3
Khampat Myanmar 78 A3
Khamra Rus. Fed. 39 L3
Khamseh reg. Iran 100 B3
Khamza Uzbek. 103 G4
also spelt Hamza; formerly known as imeni Khamzy Khakikmzade
Khan Afgh. 101 G3
Khan, Nam r. Laos 78 C4
Khānābād Afgh. 101 G2
Khanabad Uzbek. 103 H4
also spelt Khonobod; formerly known as Sovetabad
Khān al Baghdādī Iraq 107 E4
Khān al Ḩammād Iraq 109 P5
Khān al Maḩāwīl Iraq 107 F4
Khanapur Karnataka India 94 B3
Khanapur Maharashtra India 94 B2
Khānaqāh Iran 100 A2
Khān ar Raḩbah Iraq 107 F5
also spelt Khān Ruḩābah
Khanasur Pass Iran/Turkey 107 F3
Khanbalik China see Beijing
Khānch Iran 100 A2
Khandagayty Rus. Fed. 84 B1
Khandala India 94 B2
Khandud Afgh. 101 H2
Khandwa India 96 C5
Khandyga Rus. Fed. 39 N3
Khāneh Khowreh Iran 100 C4
Khanewal Pak. 101 G4
Khangarh Pak. 101 G4
Khanh Dương Vietnam 79 E5
Khan Hung Vietnam see Soc Trăng
Khani Rus. Fed. 39 M4
Khaniá Greece see Chania
Khaniadhana India 96 C4
Khanino Rus. Fed. 43 R7
Khānī Yek Iran 100 C4
Khanka Uzbek. 102 E4
also spelt Khonqa; formerly spelt Khanki
Khanka, Lake China/Rus. Fed. 82 D3
also known as Ozero Khanka or Xingkai Hu
Khanka, Ozero l. China/Rus. Fed. see Khanka, Lake
Khankendi Azer. see Xankändi
Khanki Uzbek. see Khanka
Khanna India 96 C3
Khannā, Qā' salt pan Jordan 109 H5
Khannfoussa hill Alg. 123 G4
Khanovey Rus. Fed. 40 L2
Khanpur Pak. 101 G4
Khān Ruḩābah Iraq see Khān ar Raḩbah
Khān Shaykhūn Syria 109 H2
Khansiir, Raas pt Somalia 128 E2
Khantau Kazakh. 103 H3
Khantayskoye, Ozero l. Rus. Fed. 39 J3
Khantayskoye Vodokhranilishche resr Rus. Fed. 39 I3
Khan-Tengri, Pik mt. Kazakh./Kyrg. 88 C3
also known as Hantengri Feng or Kan-Too,Pik
Khanty-Mansiysk Rus. Fed. 38 G3
Khanty-Mansiyskiy Avtonomnyy Okrug admin. div. Rus. Fed. 40 L3
English form Khanty-Mansy Autonomous Okrug
Khanty-Mansy Autonomous Okrug admin. div. Rus. Fed. see Khanty-Mansiyskiy Avtonomnyy Okrug
Khān Yūnis Gaza 108 F6
Khao-ang-runai Wildlife Reserve nature res. Thai. 79 C5
Khao Banthat Wildlife Reserve nature res. Thai. 79 B7
Khao Chum Thong Thai. 79 B6
Khaoen Si Nakarin National Park Thai. 79 B5
Khao Laem National Park Thai. 79 B5
Khao Laem Reservoir Thai. 79 B5
Khao Luang National Park Thai. 79 B6
Khao Pu-Khao Ya National Park Thai. 79 B7
Khao-soi-dao Wildlife Reserve nature res. Thai. 79 C5
Khao Sok National Park Thai. 79 B6
Khao Yai National Park Thai. 79 C5
Khapa India 96 C5
Khapcheranga Rus. Fed. 85 G1
Khaptad National Park Nepal 96 D3
Kharabali Rus. Fed. 102 A3
Kharaghoda India 96 A5
Kharagpur Bihar India 97 E4
Kharagpur W. Bengal India 97 E5
Kharakī Iran 100 D2
Khārān r. Iran 100 D5
Kharan Pak. 101 F4
Kharari India see Abu Road
Khardi India 94 B2
Khardung La pass Jammu and Kashmir 96 C2
also known as Laowohi
Kharfiyah Iraq 107 F5
Kharga r. Rus. Fed. 82 D1
Kharga Oasis Egypt 121 F3
also known as The Great Oasis
Khargapur India 96 C4
Khārg Islands Iran 100 B4
Khargon India 96 B5
Khari r. India 96 B4
Kharian Pak. 101 H3
Khariar India 95 D1
Kharīm, Gebel hill Egypt 108 E7
Kharkhara r. India 96 D5
Kharkhauda India 96 C3
Kharkiv Ukr. 41 F6
also spelt Khar'kov
Khar'kov Ukr. see Kharkiv
Khār Kūh mt. Iran 100 C4
Kharlu Rus. Fed. 40 D3
Kharmah, Ghubbat b. Yemen 105 F5
Kharmanli Bulg. 58 G7
Kharora India 97 D5
Kharoti reg. Afgh. 101 G3
Kharovsk Rus. Fed. 43 V2
Kharovskaya Gryada hills Rus. Fed. 43 V2
Kharsawan India 97 E5
Kharsia India 97 D5
▶Khartoum Sudan 121 G6
Capital of Sudan. Also spelt El Khartûm.
Khartoum state Sudan 121 G6
Khartoum North Sudan 121 G6
Kharuf, Ra's mt. Israel see Harif, Har
Kharwar reg. Afgh. 101 G3
Khasab, Khor b. Oman 105 F2
Khasardag, Gora mt. Turkm. 102 D5
Khasav'yurt Rus. Fed. 102 A4
Khash Afgh. 101 E4
Khāsh Iran 101 E4
also known as Vasht
Khash Desert Afgh. 101 E4
Khashgort Rus. Fed. 38 G3
Khashm el Girba Sudan 121 G6
Khashm el Girba Dam Sudan 121 G6
Khash Rūd r. Afgh. 101 E4
Khashuri Georgia 107 E2
Khasi Hills India 97 F4
Khaskovo Bulg. 58 G7
Khasm al Mu'aydi hill Saudi Arabia 105 E2
Khatam, Jabal al hill Saudi Arabia 104 B2
Khatanga Rus. Fed. 39 K2
Khatanga r. Rus. Fed. 39 K2
Khatanga, Gulf of Rus. Fed. see Khatangskiy Zaliv
Khatangskiy Zaliv b. Rus. Fed. 39 K2
English form Khatanga, Gulf of
Khategaon India 96 C5
Khatinza Pass Pak. 101 G2
Khatlon admin. div. Tajik. 101 G2
English form Khatlon Oblast
Khatlon Oblast admin. div. Tajik. see Khatlon
Khatmat al Malāha Oman 105 G2
Khatmia Pass Egypt 108 D7
Khātūnābād Iran 100 C4
Khatyrka Rus. Fed. 39 R3
Khavast Uzbek. 103 G4
also spelt Khowos; formerly known as Ursat'yevskaya
Khavda India 96 A5
Khawak Pass Afgh. 101 G3
Khawlaf, Ra's pt Yemen 105 F5
Khawr Shiban well Saudi Arabia 105 F4
Khawsh Saudi Arabia 104 C4
Khayamnandi S. Africa 133 J8
Khayatbashi, Gora mt. Uzbek. 103 F4
also known as Hayotboshi Toghi
Khaybar Saudi Arabia 104 B2
also known as Ash Shurayf
Khaydarken Kyrg. 103 G5
Khayelitsha S. Africa 132 D11
Khaypudyrskaya Guba b. Rus. Fed. 40 K1
Khayrān, Ra's al pt Oman 105 G3
Khazarasp Uzbek. 103 E4
also spelt Hazorasp
Khê Bo Vietnam 78 D4
Khed Maharashtra India 94 B2
Khed Maharashtra India 94 B2
Kheda India 96 B5
formerly known as Kaira
Khedbrahma India 96 B4
Khedrī Iran 100 D3
Khefa Israel see Haifa
Khehuene, Ponta pt Moz. 131 G4
Khelari India 97 E5
Khelyulya Rus. Fed. 44 O3
Khemchik r. Rus. Fed. 88 F1
Khemis Anjra Morocco 54 F9
Khemis Beni Arous Morocco 54 F9
Khemis Miliana Alg. 123 F1
formerly known as Affreville
Khemisset Morocco 122 D2
Khemmarat Thai. 78 D4
Khenchela Alg. 123 G2
Khenifra Morocco 122 D2
Khenjan Afgh. 101 G3
Kheralu India 96 B5
Kherāmeh Iran 100 C4
Kherli India 96 C4
Kherreh Iran 100 C5
Khersan r. Iran 100 B4
Kherson Ukr. 41 E7
Khe Sanh Vietnam 78 D4
Khesht Iran 100 B4
Kheta r. Rus. Fed. 39 K2
Khetolambina Rus. Fed. 44 P2
Kheyrābād Iran 100 C4
Khezerābād Iran 100 C2
formerly known as Farahābād
Khiaw, Khao mt. Thai. 79 C5
Khibiny mts Rus. Fed. 44 P2
Khidā, Jabal hill Saudi Arabia 104 D3
Khilchipur India 96 C4
Khiliomódhion Greece see Chiliomodi
Khilok Rus. Fed. 85 F1
Khilok r. Rus. Fed. 85 E1
Khimki Rus. Fed. 43 S6
Khingansk Rus. Fed. 82 C2
Khinganskiy Zapovednik nature res. Rus. Fed. 82 C2
Khíos i. Greece see Chios
Khios Strait Greece see Chios Strait
Khirbat Isrīyah Syria 109 I2
Khirkiya India 96 C5
Khirr, Wādī al watercourse Iraq 109 O6
Khisarya Bulg. 58 F6
Khislavichi Rus. Fed. 43 N7
Khitai Pass Aksai Chin 89 B5
Khiva Uzbek. 102 E4
also spelt Khiwa
Khiwa Uzbek. see Khiva
Khiyāv Iran 100 A2
Khlytola Rus. Fed. 45 O3
Khlepen' Rus. Fed. 43 P6
Khlevnoye Rus. Fed. 43 U9
Khlong, Mae r. Thai. 79 C5
Khlong-saeng Wildlife Reserve nature res. Thai. 79 B6
Khlong Wang Chao National Park Thai. 78 B4
Khlung Thai. 79 C5
Khmelezero Rus. Fed. 43 P1
Khmelinets Rus. Fed. 43 T9
Khmelita Rus. Fed. 43 O6
Khmel'nik Ukr. see Khmil'nyk
Khmel'nitskiy Ukr. see Khmel'nyts'kyy
Khmel'nyts'kyy Ukr. 41 C6
also spelt Khmel'nitskiy; formerly known as Proskurov
Khmer Republic country Asia see Cambodia
Khmes, Jebel mt. Morocco 54 F9
Khmil'nyk Ukr. 41 C6
also spelt Khmel'nik
Khobda Kazakh. 102 C2
formerly known as Novoalekseyevka
Khodā Āfarīd spring Iran 100 D3
Khodasy Belarus 43 M8
Khodzha Davlet Uzbek. 103 E5
Khodzha-Kala Turkm. 102 D5
also spelt Hojagala
Khodzhambaz Turkm. 103 F5
also spelt Hojambaz
Khodzhaolen Turkm. 102 D5
Khodzhapir'yakh, Gora mt. Uzbek. 92 C3
Khodzhavend Azer. see Xocavänd
Khodzhent Tajik. see Khŭjand
Khodzheyli Uzbek. 102 D4
also spelt Khŭjayli
Khodzhyder r. Ukr. 58 K3
Khogali Sudan 126 E3
Khojand Tajik. see Khŭjand
Khokhlovo Rus. Fed. 43 S2
Khokhol'skiy Rus. Fed. 41 F6
Kholapur India 94 C1
Kholbon Rus. Fed. 85 H1
Kholm Afgh. 101 F2
also known as Tāshqurghān
Kholm Poland see Chełm
Kholm Novgorodskaya Oblast' Rus. Fed. 43 M4
Kholm Smolenskaya Oblast' Rus. Fed. 43 M6
Kholmech Rus. Fed. 43 P9
Kholmogory Rus. Fed. 40 G2
Kholmsk Rus. Fed. 82 F3
Kholm-Zhirkovskiy Rus. Fed. 43 O6
Kholon Israel see Holon
Kholova r. Rus. Fed. 43 N3
Kholtoson Rus. Fed. 84 D1
Kholzun, Khrebet mts Kazakh./Rus. Fed. 88 D1
Khoman Iran 100 B2
Khomas admin. reg. Namibia 130 C4
Khomas Highland hills Namibia 130 B4
Khomeyn Iran 100 B3
Khomeynīshahr Iran 100 B3
formerly known as Homāyūnshahr
Khomutovo Rus. Fed. 43 S9
Khong, Mae Nam r. Myanmar see Salween
Khonj Iran 100 C5
Khonj, Kūh-e mts Iran 100 C5
Khon Kaen Thai. 78 C4
Khonobod Uzbek. see Khanabad
Khonqa Uzbek. see Khanka
Khonsa India 97 G4
Khonuu Rus. Fed. 39 O3
Khoper r. Rus. Fed. 41 G6
Khor Rus. Fed. 82 D3
Khor r. Rus. Fed. 82 D3
Khóra Greece see Chora
Khorāsan prov. Iran 100 D3
Khorat Plateau Thai. 78 C4
Khorazm Wiloyati admin. div. Uzbek. see Khorezmskaya Oblast'
Khordha India 95 E1
Khoreyver Rus. Fed. 40 K2
Khorezm Oblast admin. div. Uzbek. see Khorezmskaya Oblast'
Khorezmskaya Oblast' admin. div. Uzbek. 102 E4
English form Khorezm Oblast; also known as Khorazm Wiloyati
Khorinsk Rus. Fed. 81 H2
Khorixas Namibia 130 B4
formerly known as Welwitschia
Khor-Khut Kazakh. 103 E3
Khormūj, Kūh-e mt. Iran 100 B4
Khorog Tajik. see Khorugh
Khorol Rus. Fed. 82 D3
Khorol Ukr. 41 E6
Khorramābād Iran 100 B3
Khorram Darreh Iran 100 B2
Khorramshahr Iran 100 B4
formerly known as Khūninshahr or Muhammarah
Khorugh Tajik. 101 G2
also spelt Khorog
Khosedayu r. Rus. Fed. 40 K2
Khosf Iran 100 D3
Khosheutovo Rus. Fed. 102 A3
Khosravī Iran 100 B4
Khosrovi Argelanots' nature res. Armenia 107 F2
Khosta Rus. Fed. 41 F8
Khosūyeh Iran 100 C4
Khotan China see Hotan
Khotang Nepal 97 E4
Khotetovo Rus. Fed. 43 R9
Khot'kovo Rus. Fed. 43 S5
Khotsimsk Belarus 43 O8
Khotynets Rus. Fed. 43 Q8
Khouribga Morocco 122 D2
Khovaling Tajik. 101 G2
Khovu-Aksy Rus. Fed. 84 B1
Khowai India 97 F4
Khowos Uzbek. see Khavast
Khowrjān Iran 100 C4
Khowrnag, Kūh-e mt. Iran 100 C3
Khowst Afgh. 101 G3
also known as Matun
Khowst reg. Afgh./Pak. 101 G3
Khozap'ini, Tba l. Georgia 107 E2
Khozor Anghar Djibouti 104 C5
Khram, Ko i. Thai. 79 C5
Khri r. India 97 F4
Khrisoúpolis Greece see Chrysoupoli
Khristoforovo Rus. Fed. 40 H3
Khroma r. Rus. Fed. 39 O2
Khromtau Kazakh. 102 D2
Khru r. India 97 G4
Khrushchev Ukr. see Svitlovods'k
Khrushchevo Rus. Fed. 43 V7
Khrustalnyy Rus. Fed. 82 D3
Khrysokhou Bay Cyprus see Chrysochou Bay
Khubbāz, Wādī watercourse Iraq 109 N4
Khubelu r. Lesotho 133 M6
Khudan r. Rus. Fed. 85 F1
Khudat Azer. see Xudat
Khude Hills Pak. 101 F5
Khudian Pak. 101 H4
Khudrah, Wādī r. Yemen 105 E4
Khudzhand Tajik. see Khŭjand
Khufaysah, Khashm al hill Saudi Arabia 105 D3
Khuff Saudi Arabia 104 D2
Khugiana Afgh. see Pirzada
Khūh Lab, Ra's pt Iran 101 E5
Khuis Botswana 132 F3
Khŭjand Tajik. 101 G1
also spelt Khodzhent or Khojand or Khudzhand; formerly known as Ispisar or Leninabad or Leninobod
Khŭjand admin. div. Tajik. see Leninobod
Khŭjayli Uzbek. see Khodzheyli
Khu Khan Thai. 79 D5
Khulays Saudi Arabia 104 B3
Khuldabad India 94 B1
also known as Rauza
Khulga r. Rus. Fed. 40 L2
Khulkhuta Rus. Fed. 102 A3
Khulm r. Afgh. 101 G2
Khulna Bangl. 97 F5
Khulna admin. div. Bangl. 97 F5
Khuma S. Africa 133 K3
Khunayzīr, Jabal al mts Syria 109 I3
Khunayzīr, Wādī watercourse Iraq 109 M1
Khuneiqa watercourse Sudan 121 F6
Khūnīk Bālā Iran 101 D3
Khūnīnshahr Iran see Khorramshahr
Khunjerab Pass China/Jammu and Kashmir 89 A4
Khunsar Iran 100 B3
Khunti India 97 E5
Khūr Iran 100 D3
Khūr Iran 100 D3
Khurai India 96 C4
Khūran sea chan. Iran 100 C5
Khurays Saudi Arabia 105 E2
Khurd, Koh-i- mt. Afgh. 101 F3
Khureit Sudan 121 E6
Khuria Tank resr India see Maniari Tank
Khurja India 96 C3
Khurmalik Afgh. 101 E3
Khurmuli Rus. Fed. 82 E2
Khurr, Wādī al watercourse Saudi Arabia 107 E5
Khurvatan Uzbek. 103 F5
Khushab Pak. 101 H3
Khushshah, Wādī al watercourse Jordan/Saudi Arabia 109 H8
Khust Ukr. 53 G2
also spelt Chust
Khutar Belarus 43 J8
Khutgaon India 94 D1
Khutse Game Reserve nature res. Botswana 131 E4
Khutsong S. Africa 133 L3
Khutu r. Rus. Fed. 82 E2
Khuwei Sudan 121 F6
Khuzdar Pak. 101 F5
Khūzestān prov. Iran 100 B4
Khvāf reg. Iran 101 E3
Khvājeh Iran 100 A2
Khvalynsk Rus. Fed. 102 B1
Khvashchevka Rus. Fed. 43 Q6
Khvastovichi Rus. Fed. 43 Q8
Khvor Iran 100 C3
Khvord Nārvan Iran 100 D3
Khvormūj Iran 100 B4
Khvorostyanka Rus. Fed. 102 B1
Khvosh Maqām Iran 100 A2
Khvoshna Belarus 43 L6
Khvoy Iran 100 A2
Khvoynaya Rus. Fed. 43 P3
Khvoynyy Rus. Fed. 82 B1
Khwae Noi r. Thai. 79 B5
Khwahan Afgh. 101 G2
Khwaja Amran mt. Pak. 101 F4
Khwaja-i-Ghar Afgh. 101 G2
Khwaja Muhammad Range mts Afgh. 101 G2
Khyber Pass Afgh./Pak. 101 G3
Khynchest' Moldova see Hînceşti
Khynchesty Moldova see Hînceşti
Kia'i Iran 100 D5
Kiama Australia 147 F3
Kiamba Phil. 74 C5
Kiambi Dem. Rep. Congo 127 F6
Kiamichi r. U.S.A. 179 D5
Kiamika, Lac l. Canada 173 R4
Kiangsi prov. China see Jiangxi
Kiangsu prov. China see Jiangsu
Kiang West National Park Gambia 124 B3
Kianly Turkm. see Darta
Kiantajärvi l. Fin. 44 O2
Kiāseh Iran 100 C2
Kiatassuaq i. Greenland 165 N2
also known as Holm Ø
Kiato Greece 59 D10
Kibaha Tanz. 129 C6
Kibala Angola 127 B6
Kibale Uganda 128 A4
Kibali r. Dem. Rep. Congo 126 F4
Kibambi Dem. Rep. Congo 127 B6
Kibangou Congo 126 B5
Kibara Tanz. 128 B5
Kibara, Monts mts Dem. Rep. Congo 127 E7
Kibawe Phil. 74 C5
Kibaya Tanz. 129 C6
Kiberashi Tanz. 129 C6
Kiberege Tanz. 129 C6
Kiboga Uganda 128 A4
Kibombo Dem. Rep. Congo 126 E5
Kibondo Tanz. 128 A5
Kibray Uzbek. 103 G4
also spelt Qibray
Kibre Mengist Eth. 128 C3
Kibris country Asia see Cyprus
Kibrīt, Jabal al hill Saudi Arabia 108 F9
Kibungo Rwanda 126 F5
Kibuye Rwanda 126 F5
Kibwesa Tanz. 129 A6
Kičevo Macedonia 58 B7
Kichi-Kichi well Chad 120 C5
Kichmengskiy Gorodok Rus. Fed. 40 H4
Kichwamba Uganda 128 A5
Kicking Horse Pass Canada 167 G5
Kid, Wādī watercourse Egypt 108 F9
Kidal Mali 125 F2
Kidal admin. reg. Mali 125 F2
Kidatu Tanz. 129 C6
Kidderminster U.K. 47 J11
Kidd's Beach S. Africa 133 L10
Kidepo Valley National Park Uganda 128 B4
Kidete Tanz. 129 C6
Kidira Senegal 124 B3
Kidmang Jammu and Kashmir 96 C2
Kidnappers, Cape N.Z. 152 L7
Kiel Germany 48 H1
Kiel U.S.A. 172 E7
Kiel Canal Germany 48 G1
also known as Nord-Ostsee-Kanal
Kielce Poland 49 R5
Kielder Water resr U.K. 47 J8
Kieler Bucht b. Germany 48 H1
Kieler Förde g. Germany 48 H1
Kiembara Burkina 124 E3
Kienge Dem. Rep. Congo 127 E7
Kietrz Poland 49 P5
Kiev Kazakh. see Kiyevka
▶Kiev Ukr. 41 D6
Capital of Ukraine. Also spelt Kiyev or Kyiv or Kyyev or Kyyiv; historically known as Kǿnugard or Sambat.
Kiffa Mauritania 124 C2
Kifisia Greece 59 E10
Kifisos r. Greece 59 E10
Kifri Iraq 107 F4
Kifwanzondo Dem. Rep. Congo 126 C6
▶Kigali Rwanda 126 F5
Capital of Rwanda.
Kiği Turkey 107 E3
Kiglapait Mountains Canada 169 I1
Kiglikavik Lake Canada 167 H1
Kignan Mali 124 D4
Kigoma Tanz. 129 A6
Kigoma admin. reg. Tanz. 129 A6
Kigwe Tanz. 129 B6
Kihambatang Indon. 77 F3
Kihei U.S.A. 181 [inset] Z1
Kihikihi N.Z. 152 J6
Kihlanki Fin. 44 M2
Kihniö Fin. 45 M3
Kihnu i. Estonia 42 E3
Kiik Kazakh. 103 H3
Kiikala Fin. 42 E1
Kiiminki Fin. 44 N2
Kii-nagashima Japan 91 E7
Kii-sanchi mts Japan 91 D8
Kii-suidō sea chan. Japan 91 D8
Kijungu Well Tanz. 129 C6
Kikerino Rus. Fed. 43 K2
Kikerk Lake Canada 167 H1
Kikinda Vojvodina, Srbija Yugo. 58 B3
Kikki Pak. 101 E5
Kikládhes is Greece see Cyclades
Kiknur Rus. Fed. 40 H4
Kikonai Japan 90 G4
Kikondja Dem. Rep. Congo 127 E7
Kikongo Dem. Rep. Congo 126 C6
Kikori P.N.G. 73 J8
Kikori r. P.N.G. 73 J8
Kikuchi Japan 91 B8
Kikwit Dem. Rep. Congo 126 C6
Kil Sweden 45 K4
Kilafors Sweden 45 L3
Kilakkarai India 94 C4
Kīlan Iran 100 C3
Kilauea U.S.A. 181 [inset] Y1
▶Kilauea Crater U.S.A. 181 [inset] Z2
world [volcanoes] ▶ 14–15
Kilboghamn Norway 44 K2
Kilbotn Norway 44 L1
Kilchu N. Korea 83 C4
Kilcock Rep. of Ireland 47 F10
Kilcoy Australia 149 G5
Kildare Rep. of Ireland 47 F10
Kil'dinstroy Rus. Fed. 44 P1
Kildonan Zimbabwe 131 F3
Kilekale Lake Canada 166 F1
Kilemary Rus. Fed. 40 H4
Kilembe Dem. Rep. Congo 127 C6
Kilgore U.S.A. 179 D5
Kilgour r. Australia 148 B3
Kilia Ukr. see Kiliya
Kiliba Dem. Rep. Congo 126 F5
Kilibo Benin 125 F4
Kilifi Kenya 128 C5
Kilik Pass China 89 A4
Kilimanjaro admin. reg. Tanz. 129 C5
▶Kilimanjaro vol. Tanz. 128 C5
Highest mountain in Africa.
africa [landscapes] ▶ 112–113
Kilimanjaro National Park Tanz. 128 C5
Kilimatinde Tanz. 129 B6
Kilinailau Islands P.N.G. 145 E2
formerly known as Carteret Group or Nine Islands
Kilindoni Tanz. 129 C6
Kilingi-Nõmme Estonia 42 F3
Kılıs Turkey 107 D3
Kılıs prov. Turkey 109 I1
Kiliya Ukr. 58 K3
also known as Chilia-Nouă; also spelt Kilia
Kilkee Rep. of Ireland 47 C11
Kilkenny Rep. of Ireland 47 E11
also spelt Cill Chainnigh
Kilkis Greece 58 D8
Killala Rep. of Ireland 47 C9
Killala Bay Rep. of Ireland 47 C9
Killala Lake Canada 172 G1
Killaloe Rep. of Ireland 47 D11
Killaloe Station Canada 173 P5
Killam Canada 167 I4
Killarney Australia 147 G2
Killarney Canada 168 D4
Killarney Rep. of Ireland 47 C11
also spelt Cill Airne
Killarney National Park Rep. of Ireland 47 C12
Killarney Provincial Park Canada 173 L4
Killary Harbour b. Rep. of Ireland 47 C10
Killeen U.S.A. 179 C6
Killin U.K. 46 H7
Killinek Island Canada see Killiniq Island
Killíni mt. Greece see Kyllini
Killiniq Canada 165 M3
Killiniq Island Canada 165 M3
also spelt Killinek Island
Killorglin Rep. of Ireland 47 C11
Killybegs Rep. of Ireland 47 D9
Kilmarnock U.K. 46 H8
Kilmarnock U.S.A. 177 I8
Kil'mez' Rus. Fed. 40 I4
Kil'mez' r. Rus. Fed. 40 I4
Kilmore Australia 147 E4
Kilosa Tanz. 129 C6
Kilpisjärvi Fin. 44 M1
Kilpua Fin. 44 N2

Kilrush Rep. of Ireland 47 C11
Kilttan i. India 94 B4
Kilwa Dem. Rep. Congo 127 F7
Kilwa Masoko Tanz. 129 C7
Kilyazi Azer. see Giläzi
Kim Chad 126 B2
Kimambi Tanz. 129 C7
Kimanis, Teluk b. Sabah Malaysia 77 F1
Kimasozero Rus. Fed. 44 O2
Kimasozero, Ozero l. Rus. Fed. 44 O2
Kimba Australia 146 C3
Kimba Congo 126 B5
Kimball NE U.S.A. 178 B3
Kimbe P.N.G. 145 E2
Kimberley Canada 167 H5
Kimberley S. Africa 133 I5
Kimberley Downs Australia 150 D3
Kimberley Plateau Australia 150 D3
Kimberley Range hills Australia 151 B5
Kimbirila-Sud Côte d'Ivoire 124 D4
formerly known as Kinbirila
Kimch'aek N. Korea 83 C4
also known as Sŏngjin
Kimch'ŏn S. Korea 83 C5
Kimhae S. Korea 83 C6
Kími Greece see Kymi
Kimito Fin. 45 M3
also known as Kemiö
Kimje S. Korea 83 B6
Kimmirut Canada 165 M3
formerly known as Lake Harbour
Kimobetsu Japan 90 G3
Kimolos i. Greece 59 F12
Kimolou-Sifnou, Steno sea chan. Greece 59 F12
Kimongo Congo 126 B6
Kimovaara Rus. Fed. 44 O3
Kimovsk Rus. Fed. 43 T8
formerly known as Mikhaylovka
Kimpanga Dem. Rep. Congo 127 E6
Kimpangu Dem. Rep. Congo 127 B6
Kimparana Mali 124 D3
Kimper U.S.A. 176 C8
Kimpese Dem. Rep. Congo 127 B6
Kimpoko Dem. Rep. Congo 126 B6
Kimpoku-san mt. Japan see Kinpoku-san
Kimry Rus. Fed. 43 S5
Kimsquit Canada 166 E4
Kimvula Dem. Rep. Congo 127 B6
Kinabalu, Gunung mt. Sabah Malaysia 77 G1
Kinabalu National Park Sabah Malaysia 77 G1
Kinabatangan r. Sabah Malaysia 77 G1
Kınalıada i. Turkey 58 K8
Kinango Kenya 129 C6
Kinaros i. Greece 59 H12
Kinaskan Lake Canada 166 D3
Kinbasket Lake Canada 166 G4
also known as McNaughton Lake
Kinbirila Côte d'Ivoire see Kimbirila-Sud
Kinbrace U.K. 46 I5
Kincaid Canada 167 J5
Kincardine Canada 168 D4
Kinchang Myanmar 78 B2
Kinchega National Park Australia 147 D3
Kincolith Canada 166 D4
Kinda Dem. Rep. Congo 127 E7
Kindamba Congo 126 B5
Kindat Myanmar 78 A3
Kinde U.S.A. 173 K7
Kindembe Dem. Rep. Congo 127 C6
Kinder U.S.A. 179 D6
Kindersley Canada 167 I5
Kindia Guinea 124 B4
Kindongo-Mbe Dem. Rep. Congo 126 C5
Kindu Dem. Rep. Congo 126 E5
Kinel' Rus. Fed. 41 I5
Kinel'-Cherkasy Rus. Fed. 41 I5
Kineshma Rus. Fed. 40 G4
King r. N.T. Australia 148 B2
King r. W.A. Australia 150 E2
King U.S.A. 176 E9
King, Canal sea chan. Chile 205 B7
King, Lake salt flat Australia 151 C5
King and QueenCourthouse U.S.A. 177 I8
Kingaroy Australia 149 F5
King City U.S.A. 182 C5
Kingcome r. Canada 166 E5
King Creek watercourse Australia 148 C5
King Edward r. Australia 150 D2
Kingfisher U.S.A. 179 C5
King George Bay Falkland Is 205 E8
King George Island Antarctica 222 U2
King George Islands Canada 168 E1
King George Islands Fr. Polynesia see Roi Georges, Îles du
King George Sound b. Australia 151 B7
King George VI Falls Guyana 199 F3
Kingimbi Dem. Rep. Congo 126 B6
Kingisepp Rus. Fed. 43 J2
King Island Australia 147 D4
King Island Canada 166 E4
King Island Myanmar see Kadan Kyun
Kingisseppa Estonia see Kuressaare
King Kirkland Canada 173 N2
Kinglake National Park Australia 147 E4
King Leopold and Queen Astrid Coast Antarctica 223 F2
King Leopold Range National Park Australia 150 D3
King Leopold Ranges hills Australia 150 D3
Kingman AZ U.S.A. 183 J6
Kingman KS U.S.A. 178 C4
Kingman Reef N. Pacific Ocean 221 H5
United States Unincorporated Territory.
oceania [countries] 138–139
King Mountain Canada 166 D3
King Mountain hill U.S.A. 179 B6
Kingombe Mbali Dem. Rep. Congo 126 E5
Kingondji Dem. Rep. Congo 127 C6
Kingoonya Australia 146 B2
King Peak Antarctica 223 S1
King Peninsula Antarctica 222 R2
Kingri Pak. 101 G4
Kings r. CA U.S.A. 182 D5
Kings r. NV U.S.A. 180 C4
Kingsburg U.S.A. 182 E5
Kings Canyon Australia 148 A5
Kings Canyon National Park U.S.A. 182 F5
Kingscote Australia 146 C3
Kingscourt Rep. of Ireland 47 F10
Kingseat N.Z. 152 I5
King Sejong research station Antarctica 222 U2
Kingsford U.S.A. 172 E5
Kingsland GA U.S.A. 175 D6
Kingsland IN U.S.A. 173 H10
Kingsley S. Africa 133 O4
Kingsley U.S.A. 172 H6
King's Lynn U.K. 47 M11
short form Lynn
Kingsmill Group is Kiribati 145 G2
King Sound b. Australia 150 C3
Kings Peak U.S.A. 183 N1
Kingsport U.S.A. 176 C9
Kingston Australia 147 E5
Kingston Canada 168 E4
Kingston Jamaica 186 D3
Capital of Jamaica.
Kingston Norfolk I. 220 F7
Capital of Norfolk Island.
Kingston N.Z. 153 C13
Kingston MA U.S.A. 177 O4
Kingston MO U.S.A. 178 D4
Kingston NY U.S.A. 177 K4
Kingston OH U.S.A. 176 C6
Kingston PA U.S.A. 177 J4
Kingston TN U.S.A. 174 C5
Kingston Peak U.S.A. 183 I6
Kingston South East Australia 146 C4
Kingston upon Hull U.K. 47 L10
short form Hull
Kingstown St Vincent 187 H4
Capital of St Vincent.
Kingstree U.S.A. 175 E5
Kingsville U.S.A. 179 C7
Kingswood U.K. 47 J12
Kington U.K. 47 I11
Kingungi Dem. Rep. Congo 127 C6
Kingurutik r. Canada 169 I1
Kingussie U.K. 46 H6
King William Island Canada 165 J3
King William's Town S. Africa 133 L9
Kingwood TX U.S.A. 179 D6
Kingwood WV U.S.A. 176 F6
Kiniama Dem. Rep. Congo 127 F7
Kınık Antalya Turkey 59 K12
Kınık İzmir Turkey 59 I9
Kinkala Congo 126 B6
Kinka-san i. Japan 90 G5
Kinleith N.Z. 152 J6
Kinloch N.Z. 153 C12
Kinlochleven U.K. 46 H7
Kinmen Taiwan see Chinmen
Kinmount Canada 173 O6
Kinna Sweden 45 K4
Kinnarasani r. India 94 D2
Kinnarodden pt Norway 44 N1
Kinnegad Rep. of Ireland 47 E10
Kinneret, Yam l. Israel see Galilee, Sea of
Kinniyai Sri Lanka 94 D4
Kinnula Fin. 44 N3
Kinoje r. Canada 168 D2
Kino-kawa r. Japan 91 D7
Kinomoto Japan 91 E7
Kinoosao Canada 167 K3
Kinpoku-san mt. Japan 90 F5
also spelt Kimpoku-san
Kinross S. Africa 133 N3
Kinsale Rep. of Ireland 47 D12
Kinsale U.S.A. 177 I7
Kinsarvik Norway 45 I3
Kinsele Dem. Rep. Congo 126 C6
Kinshasa Dem. Rep. Congo 126 B6
Capital of the Democratic Republic of Congo and 3rd most populous city in Africa. Formerly known as Léopoldville.
world [cities] 24–25
Kinshasa municipality Dem. Rep. Congo 126 C6
Kinsley U.S.A. 178 C4
Kinston U.S.A. 174 E5
Kintai Lith. 42 C6
Kintampo Ghana 125 E4
Kintata Dem. Rep. Congo 127 B6
Kintinian Guinea 124 C4
Kintom Indon. 75 B3
Kintop Indon. 77 F3
Kintore Australia 148 A4
Kintore, Mount Australia 146 A1
Kintyre pen. U.K. 46 G8
Kinu Myanmar 78 A3
Kinushseo r. Canada 168 D2
Kinuso Canada 167 H4
Kinwat India 94 C2
Kinyangiri Tanz. 129 B6
Kinyeti mt. Sudan 128 B4
Kinzhaly Kazakh. 102 D2
Kiomboi Tanz. 129 B6
Kiosk Canada 173 O4
Kiowa CO U.S.A. 180 F5
Kiowa KS U.S.A. 178 C4
Kipahigan Lake Canada 167 K4
Kipahulu U.S.A. 181 [inset] Z1
Kiparissía Greece see Kyparissia
Kipawa, Lac l. Canada 168 E4
Kipchak Pass China 88 B3
Kipelovo Rus. Fed. 43 U2
Kipen' Rus. Fed. 43 K2
Kipengere Range mts Tanz. 129 B7
Kipili Tanz. 129 A6
Kipini Kenya 128 D5
Kipling Canada 167 K5
formerly known as Kipling Station
Kipling Station Canada see Kipling
Kiptopeke U.S.A. 177 J8
Kipungo Angola see Quipungo
Kipushi Dem. Rep. Congo 127 E7
Kipushia Dem. Rep. Congo 127 F8
Kirakat India 97 D4
Kirakira Solomon Is 145 F3
Kiran Dağları hills Turkey 59 H10
Kirandul India 94 D2
Kirané Mali 124 C3
Kirawsk Belarus 43 K8
Kiraz Turkey 59 J10
Kirbla Estonia 42 E3
Kirbyville U.S.A. 179 D6
Kirchdorf an der Krems Austria 49 L8
Kirdimi Chad 120 C5
Kirenga r. Rus. Fed. 81 H1
Kirensk Rus. Fed. 81 H1
Kirey watercourse Kazakh. see Kerey
Kirey, Ozero salt l. Kazakh. see Kerey, Ozero
Kireyevsk Rus. Fed. 43 S8
Kirghizia country Asia see Kyrgyzstan
Kirghiz Range mts Asia 88 A3
also known as Kirgizskiy Khrebet
Kirgiziya Kazakh. 103 I2
Kirgiz-Miyaki Rus. Fed. 102 C1
Kirgizskaya S.S.R. country Asia see Kyrgyzstan
Kirgizskiy Khrebet mts Asia see Kirghiz Range
Kirgizstan country Asia see Kyrgyzstan
Kiri Dem. Rep. Congo 126 C5
Kíria Greece see Kyria
Kiriákion Greece see Kyriaki
Kiribati country Pacific Ocean 145 G2
formerly known as Gilbert Islands
oceania [countries] 138–139
Kiridh Somalia 128 E2
Kırıkhan Turkey 106 D3
Kırıkkale Turkey 106 C3
Kirikkuduk China 84 A2
Kirikopuni N.Z. 152 I3
Kirillov Rus. Fed. 43 T2
Kirillovo Rus. Fed. 82 F3
Kirillovskoye Rus. Fed. 43 K1
Kirin China see Jilin
Kirin prov. China see Jilin
Kirinyaga mt. Kenya see Kenya, Mount
Kirishi Rus. Fed. 43 N2
Kirishima-Yaku National Park Japan 91 B9
Kirishima-yama vol. Japan 91 B9
Kiritimati i. Kiribati 221 H5
Kiriwina Islands P.N.G. see Trobriand Islands
Kırkağaç Turkey 59 I9
Kirk Bulāg Dāgh mt. Iran 100 A2
Kirkby U.K. 47 J10
Kirkby Stephen U.K. 47 J9
Kirkcaldy U.K. 46 I7
Kirkcudbright U.K. 47 H9
Kirkenær Norway 45 K3
Kirkenes Norway 44 O1
Kirkfield Canada 173 O6
Kirkkonummi Fin. 45 N3
Kirkland AZ U.S.A. 183 L7
Kirkland IL U.S.A. 172 E8
Kirkland Lake Canada 168 D3
Kırklareli Turkey 106 A2
Kırklareli prov. Turkey 59 I7
Kırklareli Barajı resr Turkey 58 I7
Kirkliston Range mts N.Z. 153 E12
Kirkonmaanselkä b. Fin. 42 I1
Kirkovo Bulg. 58 G7
Kirkpatrick, Mount Antarctica 223 L1
Kirksville U.S.A. 174 A3
Kirkuk Iraq see Kirkūk
Kirkūk Iraq 107 F4
English form Kirkuk
Kirkwall U.K. 46 J5
Kirkwood S. Africa 133 J10
Kirkwood U.S.A. 172 C10
Kirman Iran see Kermān
Kırmır r. Turkey 106 B2
Kırobası Turkey see Mağara
Kīrov Kazakh. see Balpyk Bi
Kirov Kyrg. see Kyzyl-Adyr
Kirov Kaluzhskaya Oblast' Rus. Fed. 43 P7
Kirov Kirovskaya Oblast' Rus. Fed. 40 I4
also known as Vyatka
Kirova, Zaliv b. Azer. see Qızılağac Körfäzi
Kirovabad Azer. see Gäncä
Kirovabad Tajik. see Panj
Kirovakan Armenia see Vanadzor
Kirovo Kazakh. 102 C2
Kirovo Ukr. see Kirovohrad
Kirovo Uzbek. see Besharyk
Kirov Oblast admin. div. Rus. Fed. see Kirovskaya Oblast'
Kirovo-Chepetsk Rus. Fed. 40 I4
formerly spelt Kirovo-Chepetskiy
Kirovo-Chepetskiy Rus. Fed. see Kirovo-Chepetsk
Kirovograd Ukr. see Kirovohrad
Kirovohrad Ukr. 41 E6
also spelt Kirovograd; formerly known as Kirovo or Yelizavetgrad or Zinoyevsk
Kirovsk Leningradskaya Oblast' Rus. Fed. 43 L2
formerly known as Nevdubstroy
Kirovsk Murmanskaya Oblast' Rus. Fed. 44 P2
Kirovsk Turkm. see Babadaykhan
Kirovskaya Oblast' admin. div. Rus. Fed. 40 I4
English form Kirov Oblast
Kirovskiy Kazakh. see Balpyk Bi
Kirovskiy Rus. Fed. 82 D3
Kirovskoye Kyrg. see Kyzyl-Adyr
Kırpaşa pen. Cyprus see Karpasia
Kirpili Turkm. 102 D5
Kirriemuir U.K. 46 I7
Kirs Rus. Fed. 40 J4
Kirsanov Rus. Fed. 41 G5
Kirsanovo Kazakh. 102 C2
Kırşehir Turkey 106 C3
Kirtachi Niger 125 F3
Kirthar National Park Pak. 101 F5
Kirthar Range mts Pak. 101 F5
Kiruna Sweden 44 M2
also spelt Giron
Kirundo Burundi 126 F5
Kirundu Dem. Rep. Congo 126 E5
Kirwan Escarpment Antarctica 223 X2
Kirya Rus. Fed. 40 H5
Kiryū Japan 91 F6
Kirzhach Rus. Fed. 43 T5
Kisa Sweden 45 K4
Kisakata Japan 90 F5
Kisaki Tanz. 129 C6
Kisama, Parque Nacional de nat. park Angola see Quicama, Parque Nacional do
Kisangani Dem. Rep. Congo 126 E4
formerly known as Stanleyville
Kisar i. Indon. 75 C5
Kisaran Indon. 76 B2
Kisarawe Tanz. 129 C6
Kisarazu Japan 91 F7
Kis-Balaton park Hungary 49 O9
Kisbér Hungary 49 P8
Kiselevsk Rus. Fed. 80 D2
Kiseljak Bos.-Herz. 56 K5
Kisel'nya Rus. Fed. 43 N1
Kisel'ovka Rus. Fed. 82 E2
Kishanganj India 97 E4
Kishangarh Rajasthan India 96 A4
Kishangarh Rajasthan India 96 B4
Kishen Ganga r. India/Pak. 96 B2
Kishi-Karoy, Ozero salt l. Kazakh. 103 G1
Kishika-zaki pt Japan 91 B9
Kishinev Moldova see Chişinău
Kishiözen r. Kazakh./Rus. Fed. see Malyy Uzen'
Kishiwada Japan 91 D7
Kishkenekol' Kazakh. 103 H1
formerly known as Kzyltu or Qyzyltū
Kishorganj Bangl. 97 F4
Kishtwar Jammu and Kashmir 96 B2
Kisi Nigeria 125 F4
Kisi Tanz. 129 A6
Kisigo r. Tanz. 129 B6
Kisii Kenya 128 B5
Kisiju Tanz. 129 C6
Kiskittogisu Lake Canada 167 L4
Kiskitto Lake Canada 167 L4
Kisko Fin. 45 M3
Kiskőrös Hungary 49 Q9
Kiskunfélegyháza Hungary 49 Q9
Kiskunhalas Hungary 49 Q9
Kiskunlacháza Hungary 49 Q8
Kiskunmajsa Hungary 49 Q9
Kiskunsági nat. park Hungary 49 Q8
Kislovodsk Rus. Fed. 41 G8
Kismaayo Somalia 128 D5
formerly spelt Chisimaio or Kismayu
Kismayu Somalia see Kismaayo
Kisofukushima Japan 91 E7
Kisoro Uganda 128 A5
Kiso-sanmyaku mts Japan 91 E7
Kispiox Canada 166 E4
Kispiox r. Canada 166 E4
Kissamou, Kolpos b. Greece 59 E13
Kisseraing Island Myanmar see Kanmaw Kyun
Kissidougou Guinea 124 C4
Kissimmee U.S.A. 175 D6
Kissimmee r. U.S.A. 175 D7
Kissimmee, Lake U.S.A. 175 D7
Kississing Lake Canada 167 K4
Kissu, Jebel mt. Sudan 120 E4
Kistanje Croatia 56 H5
Kistelek Hungary 49 Q9
Kistna r. India see Krishna
Kistrand Norway 44 N1
Kisújszállás Hungary 49 R8
Kisuki Japan 91 C7
Kisumu Kenya 128 B5
Kisvárda Hungary 49 T7
Kisykkamys Kazakh. see Dzhangala
Kit r. Sudan 128 A3
Kita Mali 124 C3
Kitab Uzbek. 103 F5
also spelt Kitob
Kita-Daitō-jima i. Japan 81 M7
Kitagawa Japan 91 B8
Kitahiyama Japan 90 F3
Kitaibaraki Japan 90 G6
Kita-Iō-jima vol. Japan 73 J1
Kitakami Japan 90 G5
Kitakami-gawa r. Japan 90 G5
Kitakata Japan 90 F6
Kita-Kyūshū Japan 91 B8
Kitale Kenya 128 B4
Kitami Japan 90 H3
Kitami-sanchi mts Japan 90 H2
Kitanda Dem. Rep. Congo 127 E6
Kitaura Japan 91 B8
Kitchener Canada 168 D5
Kitchigama r. Canada 168 E3
Kiteba Dem. Rep. Congo 127 E6
Kitee Fin. 44 O3
Kitendwe Dem. Rep. Congo 127 F6
Kitgum Uganda 128 B4
Kíthira i. Greece see Kythira
Kíthnos i. Greece see Kythnos
Kíthnou, Stenón sea chan. Greece see Kythnou, Steno
Kiti, Cape Cyprus see Kition, Cape
Kitimat Canada 166 D4
Kitinen r. Fin. 44 N2
Kition, Cape Cyprus 108 E3
also known as Kiti, Cape or Kitiou, Akra
Kitiou, Akra c. Cyprus see Kition, Cape
Kitkatla Canada 166 D4
Kitob Uzbek. see Kitab
Kitriani i. Greece 59 F12
Kitsa Rus. Fed. 44 P1
Kitsault Canada 166 D4
Kitscoty Canada 167 I4
Kitsuki Japan 91 B8
Kittanning U.S.A. 176 F5
Kittatinny Mountains hills U.S.A. 177 K5
Kittilä Fin. 44 N2
Kittur India 94 B3
Kitty Hawk U.S.A. 177 J9
Kitui Kenya 128 C5
Kitumbeine vol. Tanz. 128 C5
Kitumbini Tanz. 129 C7
Kitunda Tanz. 129 B6
Kitwanga Canada 166 D4
Kitwe Zambia 127 F8
Kitzbühel Austria 49 J8
Kitzbüheler Alpen mts Austria 49 J8
Kitzingen Germany 48 H6
Kiu Kenya 128 C5
Kiu Lom Dam Thai. 78 B4
Kiunga P.N.G. 73 J8
Kiunga Marine National Reserve nature res. Kenya 128 D5
Kiuruvesi Fin. 44 N3
Kivalo ridge Fin. 44 N2
Kiverichi Rus. Fed. 43 R4
Kivijärvi Fin. 44 N3
Kivijärvi l. Fin. 42 I1
Kivijärvi l. Fin. 44 N3
Kivilompolo Norway 44 M1
Kiviõli Estonia 42 H2
Kivivaara Fin. 44 O3
Kivi-Vigala Estonia 42 F3
Kivu, Lake Dem. Rep. Congo/Rwanda 126 F5
Kiwaba N'zogi Angola 127 C7
formerly known as Brito Godins
Kiwai Island P.N.G. 73 J8
Kiwawa Tanz. 129 C7
Kiwirrkurra Aboriginal Reserve Australia 150 D4
Kiyakty, Ozero salt l. Kazakh. 103 G2
Kiyāt Saudi Arabia 104 C4
Kiyev Ukr. see Kiev
Kiyevka Kazakh. 103 G2
also known as Kīev
Kiyevka Rus. Fed. 90 C3
Kiyevskiy Rus. Fed. 43 R6
Kiyevskoye Vodokhranilishche resr Ukr. see Kyyivs'ke Vodoskhovyshche
Kıyıköy Turkey 58 J7
also known as Midye
Kiyma Kazakh. 103 F2
also spelt Qīma
Kizel Rus. Fed. 40 K4
Kizema Rus. Fed. 40 H3
Kizhi, Ostrov i. Rus. Fed. 40 E3
Kizhinga Rus. Fed. 85 F1
Kiziba-Baluba, Réserve de nature res. Dem. Rep. Congo 127 E7
Kizigo Game Reserve nature res. Tanz. 129 B6
Kizil China 88 C3
Kızılcadağ Turkey 106 B3
Kızılca Dağ mt. Turkey 106 B3
Kızılcahamam Turkey 106 C2
also known as Yabanabat
Kızıldağ mt. Turkey 108 E1
Kızıldağ mt. Turkey 108 G1
Kızıl Dağı mt. Turkey 107 D3
Kızılırmak Turkey 106 C2
also known as Huseyınli
Kızılırmak r. Turkey 107 C2
Kızılören Turkey 106 C3
Kizil'skoye Rus. Fed. 102 D1
Kızıltepe Turkey 107 E3
also known as Koçhisar
Kizil"yurt Rus. Fed. 102 A4
Kızkalesi Turkey 108 F1
Kizlyar Rus. Fed. 102 A4
Kizlyarskiy Zaliv b. Rus. Fed. 102 A3
Kizner Rus. Fed. 40 I4
Kizreka Rus. Fed. 44 O2
Kizyl-Arbat Turkm. see Gyzylarbat
Kizyl-Atrek Turkm. see Gyzyletrek
Kizylayak Turkm. 103 F5
Kizyl Jilga Aksai Chin 89 B5
Kizyl-Su Turkm. 102 C5
also known as Gyzylsuw
Kjøllefjord Norway 44 N1
Kjøpsvik Norway 44 L1
Klaarstroom S. Africa 132 G10
Kladanj Bos.-Herz. 56 K4
Kladno Czech Rep. 49 L5
Kladovo Srbija Yugo. 58 D4
Klagan Sabah Malaysia 77 G1
Klagenfurt Austria 49 L9
also known as Celovec
Klagetoh U.S.A. 183 O6
Klaipėda Lith. 42 C6
historically known as Memel
Klaksvig Faroe Is see Klaksvík
Klaksvík Faroe Is 46 F1
also spelt Klaksvig
Klamath r. U.S.A. 180 A4
Klamath Falls U.S.A. 180 B4
Klamath Mountains U.S.A. 180 B4
Klampo Indon. 77 G2
Klang Malaysia see Kelang
Klappan r. Canada 166 D3
Klášterec nad Ohří Czech Rep. 49 K5
Klaten Indon. 77 E4
Klatovy Czech Rep. 49 K6
Klawer S. Africa 132 C8
Klawock U.S.A. 164 F4
Klazienaveen Neth. 48 D3
Kłecko Poland 49 O3
Kleczew Poland 49 P3
Kleides Islands Cyprus 108 F2
also known as Zafer Adaları; also spelt Klidhes Islands
Kleinbegin S. Africa 132 F5
Klein Doring r. S. Africa 132 D8
Kleinegga mt. Norway 44 J3
Klein Karas Namibia 132 C4
Kleinmachnow Germany 49 K3
Kleinmond S. Africa 132 D11
Klein Roggeveldberge mts S. Africa 132 E10
Kleinsee S. Africa 132 B6
Kleinseenplatte Neustrelitz park Germany 49 J2
Klein Swartberg mt. S. Africa 132 F10
Klein-Vet r. S. Africa 133 K5
Kleitoria Greece 59 D11
also spelt Klitória
Klekovača mt. Bos.-Herz. 56 I4
Klemtu Canada 166 D4
Kleppestø Norway 45 I3
Klerksdorp S. Africa 133 K3
Klerkskraal S. Africa 133 L3
Kleszczele Poland 49 U3
Kletnya Rus. Fed. 43 O8
Kletsk Belarus see Klyetsk
Kletskaya Rus. Fed. 41 G6
formerly known as Kletskiy
Kletskiy Rus. Fed. see Kletskaya
Kleve Germany 48 D4
historically known as Cleves
Klichaw Belarus 43 K8
Klichka Rus. Fed. 85 H1
Klidhes Islands Cyprus see Kleides Islands
Klienpoort S. Africa 133 I10
Klimatino Rus. Fed. 43 S4
Klimavichy Belarus 43 M8
also spelt Klimovichi
Klimawka Belarus 43 M9
Kliment Bulg. 58 I5
Klimovichi Belarus see Klimavichy
Klimovo Rus. Fed. 43 N9
Klimovsk Rus. Fed. 43 S6
Klimov Zavod Rus. Fed. 43 P7
Klimpfjäll Sweden 44 K2
Klin Rus. Fed. 43 R5
Klina Kosovo, Srbija Yugo. 58 B6
Klinaklini r. Canada 166 E5
Kling Phil. 74 C5
Klingkang, Banjaran mts Indon./Malaysia 77 E2
Klinsko-Dmitrovskaya Gryada ridge Rus. Fed. 43 R5
Klintehamn Sweden 45 L4
Klintsovka Rus. Fed. 102 B2
Klintsy Rus. Fed. 43 N9
Klip r. S. Africa 133 N4
Klipdale S. Africa 132 D11
Klipfontein S. Africa 133 J10
Klippan Sweden 45 K4
Klipplaat S. Africa 133 I10
Kliprand S. Africa 132 C7
Klipskool S. Africa 133 O2
Klipvoor Dam S. Africa 133 L2
Klis Croatia 56 I5
Klishino Moskovskaya Oblast' Rus. Fed. 43 T7
Klishino Novgorodskaya Oblast' Rus. Fed. 43 O2
Klitmøller Denmark 45 J4
Klitória Greece see Kleitoria
Ključ Bos.-Herz. 56 I4
Kłobuck Poland 49 P5
Kłodawa Poland 49 P3
Kłodzko Poland 49 N5
Klondike r. Canada 166 B1
Klondike Goldrush National Historical Park nat. park U.S.A. 166 C3
Klooga Estonia 42 F2
Klosterneuburg Austria 49 N7
Klosters Switz. 51 P6
Klötze (Altmark) Germany 48 I3
Kluane r. Canada 166 B2
Kluane Game Sanctuary nature res. Canada 166 A2
Kluane Lake Canada 166 B2
Kluane National Park Canada 166 B2
Kluang Malaysia see Keluang
Kluang, Tanjung pt Indon. 77 E3
Kluczbork Poland 49 P5
Klukhori Rus. Fed. see Karachayevsk
Klumpang, Teluk b. Indon. 77 G3
Klungkung Indon. 77 F5
Klupro Pak. 101 G5
Klyastsitsy Belarus 43 J6
Klyava r. Belarus 43 J8
Klyavlino Rus. Fed. 40 J5
Klyaz'ma r. Rus. Fed. 43 U5
Klyetsk Belarus 42 H8
also spelt Kletsk
Klyuchevskaya, Sopka vol. Rus. Fed. 39 Q4
asia [threats] 70–71
Klyuchi Rus. Fed. 103 I1
Klyuchi Rus. Fed. 39 Q4
Knapdaar S. Africa 133 K7
Knapp Mound hill U.S.A. 172 C6
Knaresborough U.K. 47 K9
Knee Lake Man. Canada 167 M4
Knee Lake Sask. Canada 167 J4
Knesebeck Germany 48 H3
Knetzgau Germany 48 H6
Kneževi Vinogradi Croatia 56 K3
Knezha Bulg. 58 F5
Knić Srbija Yugo. 58 B5
Knife r. U.S.A. 178 B2
Knife River U.S.A. 172 B4
Knight Inlet Canada 166 E5
Knighton U.K. 47 I11
Knights Landing U.S.A. 182 C3
Knin Croatia 56 I4
Knittelfeld Austria 49 L8
Knivsta Sweden 45 L4
Knizhovnik Bulg. 58 G7
Knjaževac Srbija Yugo. 58 D5
Knob Lake Canada see Schefferville
Knob Peak hill Australia 150 E2
Knockaboy hill Rep. of Ireland 47 C12
Knock Hill hill U.K. 46 J6
Knockmealdown Mountains hills Rep. of Ireland 47 D11
Knokke-Heist Belgium 51 J1
Knosos tourist site Greece see Knossos
Knossos tourist site Greece 59 G13
also spelt Knosos or Knossós; historically known as Cnossus
Knossós tourist site Greece see Knossos
Knowles, Cape Antarctica 222 T2
Knox IN U.S.A. 172 G9
Knox PA U.S.A. 176 F4
Knox, Cape Canada 166 C4
Knox Atoll Kiribati see Tarawa
Knox Coast Antarctica 223 G2
Knoxville GA U.S.A. 175 D5
Knoxville IA U.S.A. 174 A3
Knoxville IL U.S.A. 172 C10
Knoxville TN U.S.A. 174 D5
Knud Rasmussen Land reg. Greenland 165 M2
Knyahinin Belarus 42 I7
Knyazevo Rus. Fed. 43 J5
Knyazhikha Rus. Fed. 43 R4
Knyazhitsy Rus. Fed. 43 J3
Knyazhytsy Belarus 43 L7
Knysna S. Africa 132 H11
Knyszyn Poland 49 T2
Ko, Gora mt. Rus. Fed. 82 E3
Koani Tanz. 129 C6
Koartac Canada see Quaqtaq
Koa Valley watercourse S. Africa 132 D6
Koba Indon. 77 D3
Kobayashi Japan 91 B9
Kobbfoss Norway 44 O1
Kobe Indon. 75 C2
Kōbe Japan 91 D7
world [earthquakes] 14–15
København Denmark see Copenhagen
Kobenni Mauritania 124 C3
Kobi Indon. 75 D3
Koblenz Germany 48 E5
formerly spelt Coblenz
K'obo Eth. 128 C1
Koboldo Rus. Fed. 82 D1
Kobozha r. Rus. Fed. 43 R3
Kobrin Belarus see Kobryn
Kobroör i. Indon. 73 H8
Kobryn Belarus 42 F9
also spelt Kobrin
Kobuk Valley National Park U.S.A. 164 D3
K'obulet'i Georgia 107 E2
Kobyay Rus. Fed. 39 M3
Kocaafşar r. Turkey 59 J8
Koca Dağ mt. Turkey 59 K10
Kocaeli Turkey 106 B2
also known as İzmit; historically known as Astacus or Nicomedia
Kocaeli prov. Turkey 58 K8
Kocaeli Yarımadası pen. Turkey 58 K7
Kočani Macedonia 58 D7
Koçarlı Turkey 59 I11
Kocasu r. Turkey 106 B2
Kocatepe Turkey 109 I1
Koceljevo Srbija Yugo. 58 A4
Kočevje Slovenia 56 G3
Koch'ang S. Korea 83 B6
Koch Bihar India 97 F4
formerly spelt Cooch Behar
Kocher r. Germany 48 G6
Kocherinovo Bulg. 58 E6
Kochevo Rus. Fed. 40 J4
Kochi India see Cochin
Kōchi Japan 91 C8
Kōchi pref. Japan 91 C8
Koçhisar Turkey see Kızıltepe
Kochkor Kyrg. 103 H4
also known as Kochkorka
Kochkorka Kyrg. see Kochkor
Kochkurovo Rus. Fed. 41 H5
Kochubey Rus. Fed. 102 A3
formerly known as Chernyy Rynok
Kochylas hill Greece 59 F10
Kock Poland 49 T4
Kocs Hungary 49 P8
Kod India 94 B3
Kodaikanal India 94 C4
Kodala India 95 E2
Kodari Nepal 97 E4
Kodarma India 97 E4
Kodavere Estonia 42 I3
Kodiak U.S.A. 164 D4
Kodiak Island U.S.A. 164 D4
Kodinar India 94 A1
Kodino Rus. Fed. 40 F3
Kodiyakkarai India 94 C4
Kodok Sudan 128 B2
Kodomari Japan 90 G4
Kodori r. Georgia 107 E2
Kodumuru India 94 C3
Kodyma Ukr. 41 D6
Kodzhaele mt. Bulg./Greece 58 G7
Koedoesberg mts S. Africa 132 E9
Koedoeskop S. Africa 133 L1
Koegrabie S. Africa 132 F6
Koekenaap S. Africa 132 C8
Koës Namibia 130 C5
Kofa Mountains U.S.A. 183 K8
Kofa National Wildlife Refuge nature res. U.S.A. 183 J8
Kofarnihon Tajik. 101 G2
also spelt Kafirnigan; formerly known as Ordzhonikidzeabad or Orjonikidzeobod
Kofarnihon r. Tajik. 101 G2
Kofçaz Turkey 58 I7
Koffiefontein S. Africa 133 J6
Kofinas, Oros mt. Greece 59 G14
Köflach Austria 49 M8
Koforidua Ghana 125 E5
Kōfu Tottori Japan 91 C7
Kōfu Yamanashi Japan 91 F7
Kogălniceanu airport Romania 58 J4
also known as Cogălniceanu or Constanţa
Kogaluc r. Canada 168 E1
Kogaluc, Baie de b. Canada 168 E1
Kogaluk r. Canada 169 I1
Kögart Kyrg. see Alaykuu
Køge Denmark 45 K5
Kogel' r. Rus. Fed. 40 K3
Kogi state Nigeria 125 G4
Kogon Uzbek. see Kagan
Kogoni Mali 124 D3
Kōhaihai pt N.Z. see Gillespies Point
Kohat Pak. 101 G3
Kohila Estonia 42 F2
Kohima India 97 G4
Kohistan reg. Pak. 101 H3
Kohkīlūyeh va Būyer Ahmadī prov. Iran 100 B4
Kohler Range mts Antarctica 222 Q2
Kohls Ranch U.S.A. 183 M7
Kohlu Pak. 101 G4
Kohouro well Chad 120 D5
Kohrener Land park Germany 49 J4
Kohsan Afgh. 101 E3
Kohtla-Järve Estonia 42 I2
Kohyl'nyk r. Ukr. 58 K3
Koide Japan 90 F6
Koidern Canada 166 A2
Koidern Mountain Canada 166 A2
Koidu Sierra Leone see Sefadu
Koigi Estonia 42 G3
Koihoa India 95 G4
Koiingnaas S. Africa 132 B7
Koilkonda India 94 C2
Koilkuntla India 94 C3
Koin r. Rus. Fed. 40 I3
Koi Sanjaq Iraq 107 F3
Koitere l. Fin. 44 O3
Koivu Fin. 44 N2
Kŏje-do i. S. Korea 83 C6
Ko-jima i. Japan 90 F4
Ko-jima i. Japan 91 F8
Kojonup Australia 151 B7
Kok r. Thai. 78 C3
Kokalaat Kazakh. 103 F2
Kokand Uzbek. 103 G4
also spelt Qŭqon
Kokankishlak Uzbek. see Pakhtaabad
Kökar Fin. 45 M4
Kökar i. Fin. 42 B2
Kök-Art Kyrg. see Alaykuu
Kokatahi N.Z. 153 F10
Kök-Aygyr Kyrg. 103 H4
also spelt Këkaygyr
Kokcha r. Afgh. 101 G2
Kokchetav Kazakh. see Kokshetau
Kokemäki Fin. 45 M3
Kokerboom Namibia 130 C6
Kokhanava Belarus 43 K7
Koki Senegal 124 B3
Kök-Janggak Kyrg. 103 H4
also spelt Kok-Yangak
Kokkina Cyprus 108 D2
also known as Erenköy
Kokkola Fin. 44 M3
also known as Gamlakarleby
Kok Kuduk well China 88 D2
Koknese Latvia 42 G5
Koko Nigeria 125 G4
Kokofata Mali 124 C3
Kokolo-Pozo Côte d'Ivoire 124 D5
Kokomo U.S.A. 174 C3
Kokong Botswana 130 D5
Kokonoe Japan 91 B8
Kokora Estonia 42 I3
Kokorevka Rus. Fed. 43 P9
Kokorevo Rus. Fed. 43 K4
Kokoro Benin 125 F4
Kokoshkino Rus. Fed. 43 S6
Kokosi S. Africa 133 L3
Kokou mt. Guinea 124 B4
Kokpekti Kazakh. 88 C1
Koksan N. Korea 83 B5
Koksaray Kazakh. 103 G4
Kokshaal-Tau mts China/Kyrg. 88 B3
also known as Kakshaal-Too
Kokshetau Kazakh. 103 G1
formerly spelt Kokchetav
Koksoak r. Canada 169 G1
Kokstad S. Africa 133 N7
Koksu Almatinskaya Oblast' Kazakh. 103 I3
Koksu Yuzhnyy Kazakhstan Kazakh. 103 G4
Koktal Kazakh. 103 I3
Kök-Tash Kyrg. 103 H4
also spelt Këk-Tash
Kokterek Kazakh. 103 I3
Koktokay China 84 A2
Koktokay China see Fuyun
Koktuma Kazakh. 88 C2
Koku, Tanjung pt Indon. 75 B4
Kokubu Japan 91 B9
Kok-Yangak Kyrg. see Kök-Janggak
Kokyar China 88 B4

index

K

Kokzhayyk Kazakh. **88** C1
formerly known as Ivanovka
Kola Rus. Fed. **44** P1
Kola *r.* Rus. Fed. **44** P1
Kolab *r.* India *see* **Sabari**
Kolabira India **97** E5
Kolachi *r.* Pak. **101** F5
Kola Diba Eth. **104** B5
Kolaghat India **97** E5
Kolahoi *mt.* Jammu and Kashmir **96** B2
Kolaka Indon. **75** B4
Kolambugan Phil. **74** B4
Kolana Indon. **75** C5
Ko Lanta Thai. **79** B7
Kola Peninsula Rus. Fed. **40** E2
also known as Kol'skiy Poluostrov
Kolar *Chhattisgarh* India **94** D2
Kolar *Karnataka* India **94** C3
Kolaras India **96** C4
Kolar Gold Fields India **94** C3
Kolari Fin. **44** M2
Kolarovgrad Bulg. *see* **Shumen**
Kolašin *Crna Gora* Yugo. **58** A6
Kolayat India **96** B4
Kolbano Indon. **75** C5
Kolberg Poland *see* **Kołobrzeg**
Kolbio Kenya **128** D5
Kolchanovo Rus. Fed. **43** N1
Kol'chugino Rus. Fed. **43** U5
Kolda Senegal **124** B3
Koldere Turkey **59** I10
Kolding Denmark **45** J5
Kole *Kasai Oriental* Dem. Rep. Congo **126** D5
Kole *Orientale* Dem. Rep. Congo **126** E4
Koléa Alg. **55** N8
Kolendo Rus. Fed. **82** F1
Koler Sweden **44** M2
Kolga-Jaani Estonia **42** G3
Kolguyev, Ostrov *i.* Rus. Fed. **40** I1
Kolhan *reg.* India **97** E5
Kolhapur India **94** B2
Kolho Fin. **45** N3
Kolhumadulu Atoll Maldives **93** D10
Koliba *r.* Guinea/Guinea-Bissau **124** B3
Kolikata India *see* **Kolkata**
Kolima *l.* Fin. **44** N3
Kolín Czech Rep. **49** M5
Kolin kansallispuisto *nat. park* Fin. **44** O3
K'olīto Eth. **128** C3
Kõljala Estonia **42** D3
Kolkasrags *pt* Latvia **42** D4

▶**Kolkata** India **97** F5
3rd most populous city in Asia and 8th in the world. Also spelt Calcutta or Kolikata.
world [cities] ▶ 24–25

Kolkhozabad Tajik. *see* **Kolkhozobod**
Kolkhozobod Tajik. **101** G2
also spelt Kolkhozabad; *formerly known as* Kaganovichabad
Kollam India *see* **Quilon**
Kollegal India **94** C3
Kolleru Lake India **94** D2
also known as Colair Lake
Kollo Niger **125** F3
Köln Germany *see* **Cologne**
Kolno Poland **49** S2
Kolo Poland **49** P3
Kolo Tanz. **129** B6
Kołobrzeg Poland **49** M1
historically known as Kolberg
Kolodenskoye, Ozero *l.* Rus. Fed. **43** S2
Kologriv Rus. Fed. **40** H4
Kolokani Mali **124** C3
Kolokolkova, Guba *b.* Rus. Fed. **40** J1
Koloksha *r.* Rus. Fed. **43** V5
Kolombangara *i.* Solomon Is **145** E2
also known as Nduke
Kolomea Ukr. *see* **Kolomyya**
Kolomna Rus. Fed. **43** T6
Kolomonyi Dem. Rep. Congo **126** D6
Kolomyja Ukr. *see* **Kolomyya**
Kolomyya Ukr. **41** C6
also spelt Kolomea *or* Kołomyja
Kolondiéba Mali **124** D4
Kolonedale Indon. **75** B3
Kolonjë Albania **58** A8
Kolonkwane Botswana **130** D5
Kolono Indon. **75** B4
Koloshma *r.* Rus. Fed. **43** Q1
Kolowana Watobo, Teluk *b.* Indon. **75** B4
Kolozero, Ozero *l.* Rus. Fed. **44** P1
Kolozsvár Romania *see* **Cluj-Napoca**
Kolp' *r.* Rus. Fed. **43** R2
Kolpashevo Rus. Fed. **39** I4
Kolpino Rus. Fed. **43** L2
Kolpny Rus. Fed. **43** R9
Kol'shat Kazakh. **88** C3
Kol'skiy Poluostrov *pen.* Rus. Fed. *see* **Kola Peninsula**
Kölsvallen Sweden **45** K3
Koltubanovskiy Rus. Fed. **102** B1
Kolubara *r.* Yugo. **58** B4
Kölük Turkey *see* **Kahta**
Koluli Eritrea **121** I6
Koluton Kazakh. **103** G2
also known as Qalqutan
Kolva *r.* Rus. Fed. **40** K2
Kolva *r.* Rus. Fed. **40** K3
Kolvereid Norway **44** J2
Kolvik Norway **44** N1
Kolvitsa Rus. Fed. **44** P2
Kolvitskoye, Ozero *l.* Rus. Fed. **44** P2
Kolwa *reg.* Pak. **101** F5
Kolwezi Dem. Rep. Congo **127** E7
Kolya *r.* India **94** B2
Kolyma *r.* Rus. Fed. **39** Q3
Kolyma Lowland Rus. Fed. *see* **Kolymskaya Nizmennost'**
Kolyma Range *mts* Rus. Fed. *see* **Kolymskiy, Khrebet**
Kolymskaya Nizmennost' *lowland* Rus. Fed. **39** P3
English form Kolyma Lowland
Kolymskiy, Khrebet *mts* Rus. Fed. **39** Q3
English form Kolyma Range; *also known as* Gydan, Khrebet
Kolymskoye Vodokhranilische *resr* Rus. Fed. **39** O3
Kolyshley Rus. Fed. **41** H5
Kolyuchinskaya Guba *b.* Rus. Fed. **39** S3
Kolyvan' Rus. Fed. **88** C1
Kom *mt.* Bulg. **58** E5
Kom China **88** D1
Komadugu-gana *watercourse* Nigeria **125** I3
Komaga-take *mt.* Japan **90** F6
Komaga-take *vol.* Japan **90** G3
Komaggas S. Africa **132** B6
Komaggas Mountains S. Africa **132** B6
Komagvær Norway **44** O1
Komaki Japan **91** E7
Komandnaya, Gora *mt.* Rus. Fed. **82** E2
Komandorskiye Ostrova *is* Rus. Fed. **39** Q4
Komarichi Rus. Fed. **43** P9
Komárno Slovakia **49** P8
Komarovo *Leningradskaya Oblast'* Rus. Fed. **43** K1
Komarovo *Novgorodskaya Oblast'* Rus. Fed. **43** O3
Komary Rus. Fed. **43** O6
Komati *r.* Swaziland **133** P2
Komatipoort S. Africa **133** P2
Komatsu Japan **91** E6
Komatsushima Japan **91** D7
Komba Dem. Rep. Congo **126** E4
Komba *i.* Indon. **75** B4
Kombakomba Indon. **75** B3
Kombat Namibia **130** C3
Kombe Dem. Rep. Congo **126** E6
Kombe Tanz. **129** A6
Kombissiri Burkina **125** E3
Komering *r.* Indon. **76** D3
Komga S. Africa **133** L9
Kôm Hamâda Egypt **108** B7
Komi, Respublika *aut. rep.* Rus. Fed. **40** I3
English form Komi Republic; *formerly known as* Komi A.S.S.R.
Komi A.S.S.R. *aut. rep.* Rus. Fed. *see* **Komi, Respublika**
Kominato Japan **90** G4
Komintern Ukr. *see* **Marhanets'**
Kominternivs'ke Ukr. **41** D7
Komi-Permyak Autonomous Okrug *admin. div.* Rus. Fed. *see* **Komi-Permyatskiy Avtonomnyy Okrug**
Komi-Permyatskiy Avtonomnyy Okrug *admin. div.* Rus. Fed. **40** J3
English form Komi-Permyak Autonomous Okrug
Komi Republic *aut. rep.* Rus. Fed. *see* **Komi, Respublika**
Komiža Croatia **56** I5
Komkans S. Africa **132** C8
Komló Hungary **49** P9
Kommandokraal S. Africa **132** G10
Kommetjie S. Africa **132** C11
Kommissiepoort S. Africa **133** L6
Kommuna Turkm. *see* **Babadaykhan**
Kommunar *Kostromskaya Oblast'* Rus. Fed. **40** G4
Kommunar *Leningradskaya Oblast'* Rus. Fed. **43** L2
Kommunarsk Ukr. *see* **Alchevs'k**
Kommunizm, Qullai *mt.* Tajik. *see* **Garmo, Qullai**
Kommunizma, Pik *mt.* Tajik. *see* **Garmo, Qullai**
Komodo *i.* Indon. **75** A5
Komodo National Park Indon. **75** A5
Komodou Guinea **124** C4
Komoé *r.* Côte d'Ivoire **124** E5
also spelt Comoé
Kôm Ombo Egypt **121** G3
Komono Congo **126** B5
Komoran *i.* Indon. **73** I8
Komoro Japan **91** F6
Komotini Greece **58** G7
Kompong Cham Cambodia *see* **Kâmpóng Cham**
Kompong Chhnang Cambodia *see* **Kâmpóng Chhnăng**
Kompong Kleang Cambodia *see* **Kâmpóng Khleăng**
Kompong Som Cambodia *see* **Sihanoukville**
Kompong Som Bay Cambodia *see* **Sihanoukville, Chhâk**
Kompong Speu Cambodia *see* **Kâmpóng Spoe**
Kompong Thom Cambodia *see* **Kâmpóng Thum**
Komrat Moldova *see* **Comrat**
Komsberg *mt.* S. Africa **132** F9
Komsberg *mts* S. Africa **132** E9
Komsomol Kazakh. *see* **Komsomol'skiy**
Komsomol Kazakh. *see* **Komsomolets**
Komsomol Turkm. *see* **Komsomol'sk**
Komsomolets Kazakh. **103** E1
also known as Komsomol
Komsomolets, Ostrov *i.* Rus. Fed. **39** J1
Komsomolets, Zaliv *b.* Kazakh. **102** C3
Komsomol'sk *Ivanovskaya Oblast'* Rus. Fed. **43** V4
Komsomol'sk *Kaliningradskaya Oblast'* Rus. Fed. **42** B7
Komsomol'sk Turkm. **103** E5
also known as Komsomol
Komsomol's'k Ukr. **41** E6
Komsomol's'ke Ukr. **41** F7
formerly known as Karakubbud
Komsomol'skiy Kazakh. **102** C3
also known as Komsomol
Komsomol'skiy *Chukotskiy Avtonomnyy Okrug* Rus. Fed. **39** R3
Komsomol'skiy Rus. Fed. *see* **Yugorsk**
Komsomol'skiy *Respublika Kalmykiya - Khalm'g-Tangch* Rus. Fed. **41** H7
formerly known as Krasnyy Kamyshanik
Komsomol'skiy *Respublika Mordoviya* Rus. Fed. **41** H5
formerly known as Zavodskoy
Komsomol'sk-na-Amure Rus. Fed. **82** E2
Komsomol'skoye Kazakh. **103** E2
Komuniga Bulg. **58** G7
Kömürlü Turkey **107** E2
Kon India **97** D4
Konacık Turkey **108** G1
Konada India **95** D2
Konaklı Turkey **108** C1
Konakovo Rus. Fed. **43** R5
Konar *prov.* Afgh. **101** G3
Konarak India *see* **Konarka**
Konarka India **95** E2
also known as Black Pagoda; *formerly known as* Kanarak *or* Konarak
Konch India **96** C4
Konchanskoye-Suvorovskoye Rus. Fed. **43** P3
Konchezero Rus. Fed. **40** E3
Konchytsy Belarus **42** G9
Konda Rus. Fed. **44** P2
Kondagaon India **94** D2
Kondapalle India **94** D2
Kondaparinga Aboriginal Holding *res.* Australia **149** E3
Kondavid India **94** D2
Kondiaronk, Lac *l.* Canada **173** Q4
Kondinin Australia **151** B7
Kondinskoye Rus. Fed. *see* **Oktyabr'skoye**
Kondinskoye Rus. Fed. **38** G3
formerly known as Nakhrachi
Kondoa Tanz. **129** B6
Kondol' Rus. Fed. **41** H5
Kondopoga Rus. Fed. **40** E3
Kondoros Hungary **49** R9
Kondrat'yevo Rus. Fed. **43** J1
Kondrovo Rus. Fed. **43** Q7
Kondūz Afgh. **101** G2
also spelt Kunduz; *historically known as* Drapsaca
Kondūz *prov.* Afgh. **101** G2
Konečka Planina *mts* Macedonia **58** D7
Konetsbor Rus. Fed. **40** K2
Köneürgench Turkm. *see* **Keneurgench**
Konevits, Ostrov *i.* Rus. Fed. **43** L1
Kong Cameroon **125** I5
Kong Côte d'Ivoire **124** D4
Kŏng, Kaôh *i.* Cambodia **79** C6
formerly known as Kas Klong
Kŏng, Tônlé *r.* Cambodia **79** D5
Kong, Xé *r.* Laos **79** D5
Kongassambougou, Réserve de *nature res.* Mali **124** C3
Kongbo Cent. Afr. Rep. **126** D3
Kong Christian IX Land *reg.* Greenland **165** P3
Kong Christian X Land *reg.* Greenland **165** Q2
Kongelab *atoll* Marshall Is *see* **Rongelap**
Kong Frederik IX Land *reg.* Greenland **165** N3
Kong Frederik VIII Land *reg.* Greenland **165** Q2
Kong Frederik VI Kyst *coastal area* Greenland **165** O3
Kong Karls Land *is* Svalbard **38** C2
Kong Kat *hill* Indon. **77** G2
Kongkemul *mt.* Indon. **77** G2
Kongola Namibia **130** D3
Kongolo Dem. Rep. Congo **127** E6
Kong Oscars Fjord *inlet* Greenland **165** Q2
Kongoussi Burkina **125** E3
Kongsberg Norway **45** J4
Kongsfjord Norway **44** O1
Kongsøya *i.* Svalbard **38** C2
Kongsvinger Norway **45** K3
Kongur Shan *mt.* China **88** A4
also known as Kungur
Kongwa Tanz. **129** C6
Kong Wilhelm Land *reg.* Greenland **165** Q2
Konibodom Tajik. *see* **Kanibadam**
Koniecpol Poland **49** Q5
Königsberg Rus. Fed. *see* **Kaliningrad**
Königsbrunn Germany **48** H7
Königswartha Germany **49** L4
Königswinter Germany **48** E5
Königs Wusterhausen Germany **49** K3
Konimekh Uzbek. *see* **Kanimekh**
Konin Poland **49** P3
Konin *r.* Rus. Fed. **82** E1
Konitsa Greece **59** B8
Köniz Switz. **51** N6
Konj *mt.* Bos.-Herz. **56** I5
Konjic Bos.-Herz. **56** J5
Konjuh *mts* Bos.-Herz. **56** K4
Könkämäeno *r.* Fin./Sweden **44** M1
Konkiep *watercourse* Namibia **130** C6
Kon'-Kolodez' Rus. Fed. **43** U9
Konkwesso Nigeria **125** G4
Konna Mali **124** E3
Konnarock U.S.A. **176** D9
Konnevesi Fin. **44** N3
Konongo Ghana **125** E5
Konoplyane Ukr. **58** L1
Konosha Rus. Fed. **40** G3
Kōnosu Japan **91** F6
Konotop Ukr. **41** E6
Kon Plong Vietnam **79** E5
Konqi He *r.* China **88** E3
Końskie Poland **49** R4
Konso Eth. **128** C3
Konstantinograd Ukr. *see* **Krasnohrad**
Konstantinovka Rus. Fed. **82** B2
Konstantinovka Ukr. *see* **Kostyantynivka**
Konstantinovo Rus. Fed. **43** T5
Konstantinovskiy Rus. Fed. **43** U4
Konstanz Germany **48** G8
English form Constance; *historically known as* Constantia
Kontagora Nigeria **125** G4
Kontcha Cameroon **125** I5
Kontiolahti Fin. **44** O3
Kontiomäki Fin. **44** O2
Kontos, Akra *pt* Greece **59** F12
Konttila Fin. **44** N2
Kon Tum Vietnam **79** D5
Kontum, Plateau du Vietnam **79** E5
Konugard Ukr. *see* **Kiev**
Konushin, Mys *pt* Rus. Fed. **40** G2
Konya Turkey **106** C3
historically known as Iconium
Konyrat Kazakh. **103** H3
also spelt Qongyrat; *formerly known as* Kounradskiy
Konyrolen Kazakh. **103** I3
also spelt Qongyröleng
Konystanu Kazakh. **102** C2
also spelt Qonystanū
Konz Germany **48** D6
Konzhakovskiy Kamen', Gora *mt.* Rus. Fed. **40** K4
Koocanusa, Lake *resr* Canada/U.S.A. **167** H5
Kookynie Australia **151** C6
Kooline Australia **150** B4
Koolivoo, Lake *salt flat* Australia **148** C5
Koolkootinnie, Lake *salt flat* Australia **146** C2
Koolyanobbing Australia **151** B6
Koonga Estonia **42** F3
Koongie Park Aboriginal Reserve Australia **150** D3
Koonibba Australia **146** B2
Koopan-Suid S. Africa **132** E4
Koorawatha Australia **147** F3
Koorda Australia **151** B6
Koordarrie Australia **150** A4
Koorküla Estonia **42** G4
Koosa Estonia **42** I3
Kooskia U.S.A. **180** C3
Koosharem U.S.A. **183** M3
Kootenay *r.* Canada **167** G5
Kootenay Bay Canada **167** G5
Kootenay Lake Canada **167** G5
Kootenay National Park Canada **167** G5
Kootingal Australia **147** F2
Kootjieskolk S. Africa **132** E8
Kopa Kazakh. **103** H4
Kopa Zambia **127** F7
Kopanovka Rus. Fed. **102** A3
Kopaonik *mts* Yugo. **58** B5
Kopaonik *nat. park* Yugo. **58** B5
Kopargaon India **94** B2
Kópasker Iceland **44** [inset] C2
Kopbirlik Kazakh. **103** I3
formerly known as imeni Kirova
Koper Slovenia **56** F3
Kopet Dag *mts* Iran/Turkm. **100** D2
also known as Kopet-Dag, Khrebet; *also spelt* Koppeh Dāgh
Kopet-Dag, Khrebet *mts* Iran/Turkm. *see* **Kopet Dag**
Köping Sweden **45** L4
Koplik Albania **58** A6
Köpmanholmen Sweden **44** L3
Koporikha Rus. Fed. **43** P6
Koppa India **94** B3
Koppal India **94** C3
Koppang Norway **45** J3
Koppány *r.* Hungary **49** P9
Kopparberg Sweden **45** K4
Kopparberg *county* Sweden *see* **Dalarna**
Koppeh Dāgh *mts* Iran/Turkm. *see* **Kopet Dag**
Koppi *r.* Rus. Fed. **82** F2
Koppies S. Africa **133** L4
Koppies Dam Nature Reserve S. Africa **133** L4
Koppieskraal Pan *salt pan* S. Africa **132** E3
Koprinka, Yazovir *resr* Bulg. **58** G6
formerly known as Georgi Dimitrov, Yazovir
Koprivnica Croatia **56** I2
Köprü *r.* Turkey **106** B3
Köprübaşı Turkey **59** J10
Köprülü Turkey **106** C3
Köprülü Kanyon Milli Parkı *nat. park* Turkey **106** B3
Kopshorn *mt.* S. Africa **133** L8
Koptsi Belarus **43** L6
Kõpu Estonia **42** G3
Kõpu *r.* Estonia **42** G3
Kopyl' Belarus *see* **Kapyl'**
Kora India **96** D4
Korab *mts* Albania/Macedonia **58** B7
Korablino Rus. Fed. **43** V8
Koraf *well* Eth. **128** E3
K'orahē Eth. **128** E3
Koramlik China **89** D4
Korana *r.* Bos.-Herz./Croatia **56** H3
Korangal India **94** C2
Koraput India **95** D2
Korat Thai. *see* **Nakhon Ratchasima**
Koratla India **94** C2
Korba India **97** D5
Korba Tunisia **57** C12
Korbach Germany **48** F4
Korbenichi Rus. Fed. **43** P1
Korbous Tunisia **57** C12
Korbu, Gunung *mt.* Malaysia **76** C1
Korçë Albania **58** B8
formerly known as Koritsa
Korchino Rus. Fed. **103** J1
Korčula Croatia **56** J6
Korčula *i.* Croatia **56** I6
Korčulanski Kanal *sea chan.* Croatia **56** I5
Korday Kazakh. **103** H4
formerly known as Georgiyevka
Kordestān *prov.* Iran **100** A3
Kord Kūy Iran **100** C2
Kordon Rus. Fed. **40** K4
Kords *reg.* Iran **101** E5
▶**Korea, North** *country* Asia **83** B4
asia [countries] ▶ 64–67
▶**Korea, South** *country* Asia **83** B5
asia [countries] ▶ 64–67
Korea Bay *g.* China/N. Korea **83** B5
Korea Strait Japan/S. Korea **83** C6
also known as Tsushima-kaikyō
Koregaon India **94** B2
Korem Eth. **128** C1
Korenovsk Rus. Fed. **41** F7
formerly known as Korenovskaya
Korenovskaya Rus. Fed. *see* **Korenovsk**
Korets' Ukr. **41** C6
Korf Rus. Fed. **39** Q3
Körfez Turkey **106** B2
also known as Yarımca
Korff Ice Rise Antarctica **222** T1
Korfovskiy Rus. Fed. **82** D2
Korgas China **88** C2
Korgen Norway **44** K2
Korhogo Côte d'Ivoire **124** D4
Koriabo Guyana **199** G3
Koribundu Sierra Leone **124** C5
Kori Creek *inlet* India **96** A5
Koringberg S. Africa **132** C10
Koringplaas S. Africa **132** E9
Korinniti N.Z. **152** J7
Korinos Greece **59** D8
Korinthiakos Kolpos *sea chan.* Greece *see* **Corinth, Gulf of**
Korinthos Greece *see* **Corinth**
Kōris-hegy *hill* Hungary **49** O8
Korissia Greece **59** F11
Koritsa Albania *see* **Korçë**
Kōriyama Japan **90** G6
Korkana Fin. **44** O2
Korki Iran **100** D2
Korkino Rus. Fed. **38** G4
Korkodon *r.* Rus. Fed. **39** P3
Korkuteli Turkey **106** B3
Körkvere Estonia **42** E3
Korla China **88** D3
Kormakitis, Cape Cyprus **108** D2
Korman *mt.* Yugo. **58** A5
Körmend Hungary **49** N8
Kōrmōr Iraq **109** P2
Kornat *i.* Croatia **56** H5
Kornat *nat. park* Croatia **56** H5
Korneyevka *Karagandinskaya Oblast'* Kazakh. **103** H2
Korneyevka *Severnyy Kazakhstan* Kazakh. **103** G1
Korneyevka Rus. Fed. **102** B2
Kornsjø Norway **45** J4
Koro Côte d'Ivoire **124** D4
Koro *i.* Fiji **145** G3
also spelt Goro
Koro *r.* Indon. **75** B3
Koro Mali **124** E3
Korobets Rus. Fed. **43** O7
Koroc *r.* Canada **169** H1
Köroğlu Dağları *mts* Turkey **106** C2
Köroğlu Tepesi *mt.* Turkey **106** C2
Korogo *well* Eth. **128** D3
Korogwe Tanz. **129** C6
Korom, Bahr *watercourse* Chad **126** C2
Koroni Greece **59** C12
Koronowo Poland **49** O2
Koropi Greece **59** E11

▶**Koror** Palau **73** H5
Capital of Palau. Also known as Oreor.

Körös *r.* Romania **58** B2
Koro Sea *b.* Fiji **145** G3
Körösladány Hungary **49** S9
Korostelevo Rus. Fed. **43** R6
Korosten' Ukr. **41** D6
Korostyshiv Ukr. **41** D6
Korotaikha *r.* Rus. Fed. **40** L1
Korotnik *mt.* Albania **58** B6
Koro Toro Chad **120** C5
Korovou Solomon Is **145** E2
Korozhechna *r.* Rus. Fed. **43** T4
Korpilahti Fin. **45** N3
Korpilombolo Sweden **44** M2
Korpisel'kya Rus. Fed. **44** O3
Korpivaara Fin. **44** O3
Korpo Fin. **45** M3
also spelt Korppoo
Korppoo Fin. *see* **Korpo**
Korsakov Rus. Fed. **82** F3
Korsakovo Rus. Fed. **43** S8
Korsiki Rus. Fed. **43** N8
Korskrogen Sweden **45** K3
Korsnäs Fin. **44** M3
Korso Fin. **42** G1
Korsør Denmark **45** J5
Korsze Poland **49** S1
Kortala Sudan **121** F6
Kortesjärvi Fin. **44** M3
Korti Sudan **121** F5
Kortkeros Rus. Fed. **40** I3
Kortrijk Belgium **51** J2
also spelt Courtrai
Korucu Turkey **59** I9
Korumburra Australia **147** E4
Korup, Parc National de *nat. park* Cameroon **125** H5
Korvala Fin. **44** N2
Korwai India **96** C4
Koryakskaya, Sopka *vol.* Rus. Fed. **39** P4
Koryakskiy Khrebet *mts* Rus. Fed. **39** R3
Koryazhma Rus. Fed. **40** H3
Koryŏng S. Korea **83** C6
Korzhovka Golubovka Rus. Fed. **43** N9
Korzhun Kazakh. **102** C2
Kos Greece **59** I12
Kos *i.* Greece **59** I12
English form Cos
Kosa Rus. Fed. **40** J4
Kosa *r.* Rus. Fed. **40** J3
Kosagal Kazakh. **103** E2
Kosaka Japan **90** G4
Kosan N. Korea **83** B5
formerly known as Sin'gosan
Kosava Belarus **42** G9
Kosaya Gora Rus. Fed. **43** S7
Koschagyl Kazakh. **102** C3
also spelt Qosshaghyl
Kościan Poland **49** N3
Kościerzyna Poland **49** O1
Kosciusko U.S.A. **175** B5
Kosciusko, Mount Australia *see* **Kosciuszko, Mount**
Kosciusko Island U.S.A. **166** C3
Kosciuszko, Mount Australia **147** F4
formerly spelt Kosciusko, Mount
Kosciuszko National Park Australia **147** F4
Kose Estonia **42** G2
Köseçobanlı Turkey **108** E1
Köse Dağı *mt.* Turkey **107** D2
Kösedere Turkey **59** H9
Kosgi India **94** C2
Kosha Sudan **121** F4
Kosh-Agach Rus. Fed. **84** A1
Koshankol' Kazakh. **102** B2
Koshbulakskoye Vodokhranilische *resr* Turkm. **103** E4
Kosh-Döbö Kyrg. **103** H4
also spelt Koshtëbë
Koshikijima-rettō *is* Japan **91** A9
Koshiki-kaikyō *sea chan.* Japan **91** A9
Koshimizu Japan **90** I3
Koshk Afgh. **101** E3
Koshkak Iran **101** E3
Koshkarkol', Ozero *l.* Kazakh. **88** C2
formerly known as Uyaly, Ozero
Koshk-e Kohneh Afgh. **101** E3
Koshki Rus. Fed. **41** I5
Koshkonong, Lake U.S.A. **172** E8
Koshkupyr Uzbek. **102** E4
also spelt Qūshkūpir
Koshoba Turkm. **102** C4
also spelt Goshoba
Kōshoku Japan **91** F6
Koshrabad Uzbek. **103** F4
also spelt Qūshrabot
Koshtëbë Kyrg. *see* **Kosh-Döbö**
Kosi *r.* India **96** C3
Kosi Bay S. Africa **133** Q3
Kosi Bay Nature Reserve S. Africa **133** Q4
Košice Slovakia **49** S7
also known as Kassa
Kosigi India **94** C3
Kosi Reservoir Nepal **97** E4
Kos-Istek Kazakh. **102** D2
Kosjerić *Srbija* Yugo. **58** A5
Köşk Turkey **59** J11
Koski Fin. *see* **Hämeenkoski**
Koski Rus. Fed. **43** O7
Koskol' Kazakh. **103** F2
Kos'kovo Rus. Fed. **43** O1
Koskuduk Kazakh. **103** I3
Koskullskulle Sweden **44** M2
Koslan Rus. Fed. **40** I3
Köslin Poland *see* **Koszalin**
Kosma *r.* Rus. Fed. **40** I2
Kosmynino Rus. Fed. **43** V4
Košnica *r.* Croatia **56** K3
Koson Uzbek. *see* **Kasan**
Kosŏng N. Korea **82** C4
Kosŏng N. Korea **83** C5
Kosŏng S. Korea **91** A7
Kosonsoy Uzbek. *see* **Kasansay**
Kosorzha Rus. Fed. **43** R9
Kosova *prov.* Yugo. *see* **Kosovo**
▶**Kosovo** *prov.* Yugo. **58** B6
also known as Amselfeld; *also spelt* Kosova; *long form* Kosovo-Metohija
europe [issues] ▶ 34–35
Kosovo-Metohija *prov.* Yugo. *see* **Kosovo**
Kosovo Polje *Kosovo, Srbija* Yugo. **58** C6
Kosovo Polje *plain* Yugo. **58** B6
Kosovska Kamenica *Kosovo, Srbija* Yugo. **58** C6
Kosovska Mitrovica *Kosovo, Srbija* Yugo. **58** B6
formerly known as Titova Mitrovica; *short form* Mitrovica
Kosrae *atoll* Micronesia **220** E5
also known as Ualan; *formerly spelt* Kusaie
Kossa *well* Mauritania **124** D3
Kossatori *well* Niger **125** I3
Kösseine *hill* Germany **48** I6
Kossol Reef Palau **73** H5
Kossou, Lac de *l.* Côte d'Ivoire **124** D5
Kosta-Khetagurovo Rus. Fed. *see* **Nazran'**
Kostanay Kazakh. **103** E1
also spelt Qostanay; *formerly spelt* Kustanay
Kostenets Bulg. **58** E6
Koster S. Africa **133** K2
Kosterevo Rus. Fed. **43** U6
Kosti Sudan **121** G6
Kostinbrod Bulg. **58** E6
Kostino Rus. Fed. **39** I3
Kostobobriv Ukr. **43** N9
Kostolac *Srbija* Yugo. **58** C4
Kostomuksha Rus. Fed. **44** O2
Kostomukshskiy Zapovednik *nature res.* Rus. Fed. **44** O2
Kostopil' Ukr. **41** C6
also spelt Kostopol'
Kostopol' Ukr. *see* **Kostopil'**
Kostroma Rus. Fed. **43** V4
Kostroma *r.* Rus. Fed. **43** V4
Kostroma Oblast *admin. div.* Rus. Fed. *see* **Kostromskaya Oblast'**
Kostromskaya Oblast' *admin. div.* Rus. Fed. **40** G4
English form Kostroma Oblast
Kostrzyn Poland **49** L3
Kostrzyn *r.* Poland **49** T3
Kostyantynivka Ukr. **41** F6
also spelt Konstantinovka
Kostyri Rus. Fed. **43** O7
Kostyukovichi Belarus *see* **Kastsyukovichy**
Kostyzhitsy Rus. Fed. **43** K4
Kosubosu Nigeria **125** F4
Kos'yu Rus. Fed. **40** K2
Kos'yu *r.* Rus. Fed. **40** K2
Koszalin Poland **49** N1
historically known as Köslin
Kőszeg Hungary **49** N8
also known as Güns
Kota *Andhra Pradesh* India **94** D3
Kota *Chhattisgarh* India **97** D5
Kota *Rajasthan* India **96** B4
Kotaagung Indon. **76** D4
Kota Baharu Malaysia *see* **Kota Bharu**
Kotabaru *Kalimantan Barat* Indon. **77** E3
Kotabaru *Kalimantan Selatan* Indon. **77** G3
Kotabaru *Sumatra* Indon. **76** B2
Kota Belud *Sabah* Malaysia **77** G1
Kota Bharu Malaysia **76** C1
also spelt Kota Baharu
Kotabumi Indon. **76** D4
Kot Addu Pak. **101** G4
Kota Kinabalu *Sabah* Malaysia **77** G1
formerly known as Jesselton
Kotala Fin. **44** O2
Kotamobagu Indon. **75** C2
Kotaneelee Range *mts* Canada **166** E2
Kotanemel', Gora *mt.* Kazakh. **103** I3
Kotapinang Indon. **76** C2
Kotar India **96** D4
Kotari *r.* India **96** B4
Kota Samarahan *Sarawak* Malaysia **77** E2
formerly known as Muara Tuang
Kota Tinggi Malaysia **76** C2
Kotawaringin Indon. **77** E3
Kotchandpur Bangl. **97** F5
Kotcho *r.* Canada **166** F3
Kotcho Lake Canada **166** F3
Kot Diji Pak. **101** G5
Kotdwara India **96** C3
Koteasro Afgh. **96** A2
Kotel Bulg. **58** H6
Kotel'nich Rus. Fed. **40** I4
Kotel'nikovo Rus. Fed. **41** G7
Kotel'nyy, Ostrov *i.* Rus. Fed. **39** N2
Kotemaori N.Z. **152** L7
Kotgar India **95** D2
Kotgarh India **96** C3
Kothagudem India *see* **Kottagudem**
Köthen (Anhalt) Germany **48** I4
Kothi India **96** D4
Kotiari Naoude Senegal **124** B3
Kotido Uganda **128** B4
Kotka Fin. **45** N3
Kot Kapura India **96** B3
Kotkino Rus. Fed. **40** I2
Kotlas Rus. Fed. **40** H3
Kotli Pak. **101** H3
Kotlik U.S.A. **164** C3
Kotlina Sandomierska *basin* Poland **49** S5
Kotlovan Rus. Fed. **43** P3
Kötlutangi *pt* Iceland **44** [inset] C3
Kotly Rus. Fed. **43** J2
Koton-Karifi Nigeria **125** G4
Kotooka Japan **90** G4
Kotor *Crna Gora* Yugo. **56** K6
Kotorkoshi Nigeria **125** G3
Kotorosl' *r.* Rus. Fed. **43** U4
Kotorsko Bos.-Herz. **56** K4
Kotor Varoš Bos.-Herz. **56** J4
Kotouba Côte d'Ivoire **124** E4
Kotovo Rus. Fed. **41** H6
Kotovsk Moldova *see* **Hîncești**
Kotovsk Rus. Fed. **41** G5
Kotovs'k Ukr. **41** D7
Kot Putli India **96** C4
Kotra *r.* Belarus **42** F8
Kotri *r.* India **94** D2
Kotri Pak. **101** G5
Kotronas Greece **59** D12
Kotrtas Kazakh. **102** D2
Kot Sarae Pak. **101** F6
Kottagudem India **94** D2
also known as Bhadrachalam Road Station; *also spelt* Kothagudem
Kottayam *Kerala* India **94** C4
Kottayam *Pondicherry* India **94** B4
Kotte Sri Lanka *see* **Sri Jayewardenepura Kotte**
Kotto *r.* Cent. Afr. Rep. **126** D3
Kotturu India **94** C3
Kotuy *r.* Rus. Fed. **39** K2
Kotwar Peak India **97** D5
Kotzebue U.S.A. **164** C3
Kotzebue Sound *sea chan.* U.S.A. **164** C3
Kotzehoop S. Africa **132** B5
Kotzesrus S. Africa **132** B7
Kouango Cent. Afr. Rep. **126** D3
Kouba Olanga Chad **120** C6
Koubia Guinea **124** C4
Kouchibouguac National Park Canada **169** H4
Koudougou Burkina **124** E3
Kouebokkeveld *mts* S. Africa **132** D9
Kouéré Burkina **124** E4
Koueveldberge *mts* S. Africa **132** H9
Koufalia Greece **58** D8
Koufonisi *i. Kriti* Greece **59** H14
Koufonisi *i.* Greece **59** G12
Koufos Greece **59** E9
Kouga *r.* S. Africa **133** I10
Kougaberge *mts* S. Africa **132** H10
Koui Cent. Afr. Rep. **126** B3
Kouilou *admin. reg.* Congo **126** A6
Kouki Cent. Afr. Rep. **126** C3
Koukourou *r.* Cent. Afr. Rep. **126** C3
Koukourou-Bamingui, Réserve de Faune du *nature res.* Cent. Afr. Rep. **126** C3
Koulamoutou Gabon **126** B5
Koulbo Chad **120** D6
Koulikoro Mali **124** D3
Koulikoro *admin. reg.* Mali **124** D3
Kouloudia Chad **120** B6
Koum Cameroon **125** I4
Kouma *r.* Cent. Afr. Rep. **126** C3
Koumac New Caledonia **145** F4
Koumala Australia **149** F4
Koumameyong Gabon **126** A4
Koumbala Cent. Afr. Rep. **126** D2
Koumbia Burkina **124** E4
Koumbia Guinea **124** B4
Koumenzi China **84** B3
Koumogo Chad **126** C2
Koumra Chad **126** C2
Koundâra Guinea **124** B3
Koundian Mali **124** C3
Koundougou Burkina **124** D4
Koungheul Senegal **124** B3
Kounoupoi *i.* Greece **59** H12
Kounradskiy Kazakh. *see* **Konyrat**
Kounradskiy Kazakh. **103** H3
also known as Qongyrat
Kounsitél Guinea **124** B4
Kountchi *well* Niger **125** H3
Kountze U.S.A. **179** D6
Koup S. Africa **132** F10
Koupéla Burkina **125** E3
Kouqian China *see* **Yongji**
Kouridinga *well* Niger **125** I3
Kournas Greece **59** F13
Kourou Fr. Guiana **199** H3
Kourou *r.* Greece **58** G7
also spelt Kurú
Koûroudjél Mauritania **124** C2
Kouroussa Guinea **124** C4
Koussanar Senegal **124** B3
Koussané Mali **124** C3
Kousséri Cameroon **125** I3
formerly known as Fort Foureau
Koussountou Togo **125** F4
Koutiala Mali **124** D3
Kouto Côte d'Ivoire **124** D4
Kouvola Fin. **45** N3
Kouyou *r.* Congo **126** C5
Kovačica *Vojvodina, Srbija* Yugo. **58** B3
Kovarzino Rus. Fed. **43** T1
Kovda Rus. Fed. **44** P2
Kovdor Rus. Fed. **44** O2
Kovdozero Rus. Fed. **44** O2
Kovdozero, Ozero *l.* Rus. Fed. **44** P2
Kovel' Ukr. **41** C6
Kovernino Rus. Fed. **40** G4
Kovilj *Vojvodina, Srbija* Yugo. **58** B3
Kovilpatti India **94** C4
Kovin *Vojvodina, Srbija* Yugo. **58** B4
Kovno Lith. *see* **Kaunas**
Kovriga, Gora *hill* Rus. Fed. **40** I2
Kovrov Rus. Fed. **40** G4
Kovylkino Rus. Fed. **41** G5
Kovzha *canal* Rus. Fed. **43** S1
Kovzhskoye, Ozero *l.* Rus. Fed. **43** S1
Kowanyama Australia **149** D2
Kowanyama Aboriginal Reserve Australia **149** D2
Kowares *waterhole* Namibia **130** B3
Kowary Poland **49** M5
Kowbcha Belarus **43** K8
Kowhitirangi N.Z. **153** F10
Kowlī Kosh, Gardaneh-ye *pass* Iran **100** C4
Kowloon *Hong Kong* China **87** [inset]
also known as Chiu Lung *or* Jiulong
Kowloon Peak *hill Hong Kong* China **87** [inset]
also known as Fei Ngo Shan
Kowloon Peninsula *Hong Kong* China **87** [inset]

Kowr-e-Koja watercourse Iran 101 E5
Kox Kuduk well China 84 B3
Kōya Japan 91 D7
Kōyama-misaki pt Japan 91 B7
Koybagar, Ozero l. Kazakh. 103 F1
formerly known as Kaybagar, Ozero
Köyceğiz Turkey 106 B3
Köyceğiz Gölü l. Turkey 59 J12
Koygorodok Rus. Fed. 40 I3
Koymatdag, Gory hills Turkm. 102 C4
also known as Goymatdag
Koynare Bulg. 58 F5
Koyna Reservoir India 94 B2
Koyp, Gora mt. Rus. Fed. 40 K3
Koyukuk r. U.S.A. 164 D3
Koyulhisar Turkey 107 D2
Koza Rus. Fed. 43 U3
Kozağacı Turkey see Günyüzü
Kō-zaki pt Japan 91 A7
Kozan Turkey 106 C3
also known as Sis
Kozani Greece 59 C8
Kozar, Ras pt Eritrea 104 C5
Kozara mts Bos.-Herz. 56 I3
Kozara nat. park Bos.-Herz. 56 J3
Kozarska Dubica Bos.-Herz. see Bosanska Dubica
Kozel'sk Rus. Fed. 43 Q7
Kozen well Chad 120 C4
Kozhabakhy Kazakh. 103 E3
Kozhakol', Ozero l. Kazakh. 103 G2
also known as Qozhaköl
Kozhevnikovo Rus. Fed. 39 L2
Kozhikode India see Calicut
Kozhim-Iz, Gora mt. Rus. Fed. 40 K3
Kozhva Rus. Fed. 40 K2
Kozhva r. Rus. Fed. 40 K2
Kozhym r. Rus. Fed. 40 K2
Kozienice Poland 49 S4
Kozlikha Rus. Fed. 43 V1
Kozloduy Bulg. 58 E5
Kozlovka Chuvashskaya Respublika Rus. Fed. 40 I5
Kozlovka Voronezhskaya Oblast' Rus. Fed. 41 G6
Kozlovo Rus. Fed. 43 R5
Kozlu Turkey 106 B2
Kozluk Bos.-Herz. 56 L4
Koźmin Poland 49 O4
Koz'modem'yansk Rus. Fed. 40 H4
Kozmoldak Kazakh. 103 G4
Koznitsa mt. Bulg. 58 E6
Kożuchów Poland 49 M4
Kožuf mts Greece/Macedonia 58 D7
Kōzu-shima i. Japan 91 F7
Kozyatyn Ukr. 41 D6
also spelt Kazatin
Kozyörük Turkey 58 H7
Kpalimé Togo 125 F5
Kpandae Ghana 125 E4
Kpandu Ghana 125 F5
Kpungan Pass India/Myanmar 97 H4
Kra, Isthmus of Thai. 79 B6
Kraai r. S. Africa 133 K7
Kraankuil S. Africa 132 I6
Krabi Estonia 42 H4
Krabi Thai. 79 B6
Kra Buri Thai. 79 B6
Krâchéh Cambodia 79 D5
also spelt Kratie
Kräckelbäcken Sweden 45 K3
Kraftino, Ozero l. Rus. Fed. 43 P4
Kragan Indon. 77 E4
Kragerø Norway 45 J4
Kragujevac Srbija Yugo. 58 B4
Krajenka Poland 49 O2
Krakatau i. Indon. 77 D4
Krakatau Volcano National Park Indon. 76 D4
Krakau Poland see Kraków
Kråklivollen Norway 44 J3
Kraków Poland 49 Q5
historically known as Cracovia or Cracow or Krakau
Krakow U.S.A. 172 E6
Kralendijk Neth. Antilles 187 F4
Kraljeviča Croatia 56 G3
Kraljevo Srbija Yugo. 58 B5
formerly known as Rankovićevo
Kráľova hoľa mt. Slovakia 49 R7
Kráľovský Chlmec Slovakia 49 S7
Kralupy nad Vltavou Czech Rep. 49 L5
Kramators'k Ukr. 41 F6
Kramfors Sweden 44 L3
Krammer est. Neth. 48 B4
Kranidi Greece 59 E11
Kranj Slovenia 56 G2
Kranji Reservoir Sing. 76 [inset]
Kransfontein S. Africa 133 M5
Kranskop S. Africa 133 O5
Kranskop mt. S. Africa 133 N4
Krapanj Croatia 56 H5
Krapina Croatia 56 H2
Krapinske Toplice Croatia 56 H2
Krapivna Kaluzhskaya Oblast' Rus. Fed. 43 Q8
Krapivna Smolenskaya Oblast' Rus. Fed. 43 O7
Krapkowice Poland 49 O5
Krasavino Rus. Fed. 40 H3
Krasilov Ukr. see Krasyliv
Krasino Rus. Fed. 40 J1
Kraskino Rus. Fed. 82 C4
Krāslava Latvia 42 I6
Kraslice Czech Rep. 49 J5
Krasnapollye Belarus 43 M8
Krasnasyel'ski Belarus 42 F8
Krasnaya Gora Rus. Fed. 43 M8
Krasnaya Gorbatka Rus. Fed. 40 G5
Krasnaya Polyana Kazakh. 103 H2
Krasnaya Polyana Rus. Fed. 41 G8
Krasnaya Slabada Belarus 42 I9
Krasnaya Zarya Rus. Fed. 43 S9
Kraśnik Poland 49 T5
Krasnoarmeysk Kazakh. see Tayynsha
Krasnoarmeysk Moskovskaya Oblast' Rus. Fed. 43 T5
Krasnoarmeysk Saratovskaya Oblast' Rus. Fed. 41 H6
Krasnoarmeysk Ukr. see Krasnoarmiys'k
Krasnoarmeyskaya Rus. Fed. see Poltavskaya
Krasnoarmeyskiy Chukotskiy Avtonomnyy Okrug Rus. Fed. 39 R3
Krasnoarmeyskiy Rostovskaya Oblast' Rus. Fed. 41 G7
formerly known as Kuberle
Krasnoarmiys'k Ukr. 41 F6
also spelt Krasnoarmeysk; formerly known as Chervonoarmiys'k or Grishino or Postysheve
Krasnobarskiy Rus. Fed. 43 Q2
Krasnoborsk Rus. Fed. 40 H3
Krasnodar Rus. Fed. 41 F7
formerly known as Yekaterinodar
Krasnodar Kray admin. div. Rus. Fed. see Krasnodarskiy Kray
Krasnodarskiy Kray admin. div. Rus. Fed. 41 F7
English form Krasnodar Kray
Krasnodon Ukr. 41 F6
Krasnofarfornyy Rus. Fed. 43 M2
Krasnogorka Kazakh. see Ul'ken Sulutar
Krasnogorodskoye Rus. Fed. 43 J5
Krasnogorsk Rus. Fed. 43 S6
Krasnogorsk Rus. Fed. 82 F2
Krasnogorskoye Rus. Fed. 40 J4
Krasnograd Ukr. see Krasnohrad
Krasnogvardeysk Uzbek. see Bulungur
Krasnogvardeyskiy Rus. Fed. 43 V5
Krasnogvardeyskoye Rus. Fed. 41 G7
formerly known as Yevdokimovskoye
Krasnohrad Ukr. 41 E6
also spelt Krasnograd; formerly known as Konstantinograd
Krasnohvardiys'ke Ukr. 41 E7
Krasnokamensk Rus. Fed. 85 H1
Krasnokamsk Rus. Fed. 40 J4
Krasnokholm Rus. Fed. 102 C2
Krasnokutsk Kazakh. see Aktogay
Krasnokutskoye Kazakh. see Aktogay
Krasnolesnyy Rus. Fed. 41 F6
Krasnoles'ye Rus. Fed. 42 D7
Krasnomayskiy Rus. Fed. 43 P4
Krasnoostrovskiy Rus. Fed. 43 J1
Krasnoperekops'k Ukr. 41 E7
Krasnopol'ye Rus. Fed. 82 F2
Krasnorechenskiy Rus. Fed. 82 D3
Krasnosel'kup Rus. Fed. 39 I3
Krasnosel'skoye Rus. Fed. 43 K1
Krasnoslobodsk Rus. Fed. 41 G5
Krasnotur'insk Rus. Fed. 38 G4
Krasnoufimsk Rus. Fed. 40 K4
Krasnousol'skiy Rus. Fed. 40 K5
Krasnovishersk Rus. Fed. 40 K3
Krasnovodsk Turkm. see Turkmenbashi
Krasnovodskaya Oblast' admin. div. Turkm. see Balkanskaya Oblast'
Krasnovodskiy Gosudarstvenny Zapovednik nature res. Turkm. 102 C5
Krasnovodskiy Zaliv b. Turkm. 102 C5
Krasnovodskoye Plato plat. Turkm. 102 C4
Krasnoyar Kazakh. 102 C2
Krasnoyarovo Rus. Fed. 82 C2
Krasnoyarsk Rus. Fed. 80 E1
Krasnoyarskiy Rus. Fed. 102 D2
Krasnoyarskiy Kray admin. div. Rus. Fed. 80 E1
English form Krasnoyarsk Kray
Krasnoyarsk Kray admin. div. Rus. Fed. see Krasnoyarskiy Kray
Krasnoye Belgorodskaya Oblast' Rus. Fed. 41 F6
Krasnoye Bryanskaya Oblast' Rus. Fed. 43 O8
Krasnoye Lipetskaya Oblast' Rus. Fed. 43 T9
Krasnoye Pskovskaya Oblast' Rus. Fed. 43 K5
Krasnoye Rus. Fed. see Ulan Erge
Krasnoye Smolenskaya Oblast' Rus. Fed. 43 M7
Krasnoye, Ozero l. Rus. Fed. 39 R3
Krasnoye Plamya Rus. Fed. 43 T5
Krasnoye Znamya Rus. Fed. 43 Q4
Krasnozatonskiy Rus. Fed. 40 I3
Krasnozavodsk Rus. Fed. 43 T5
Krasnoznamensk Rus. Fed. 42 D7
Krasnoznamenskiy Kazakh. see Krasnoznamenskoye
Krasnoznamenskoye Kazakh. 103 G2
formerly known as Krasnoznamenskiy
Krasnystaw Poland 49 U5
Krasnyy Rus. Fed. 43 M7
Krasnyy Chikoy Rus. Fed. 85 F1
Krasnyye Baki Rus. Fed. 40 H4
Krasnyye Barrikady Rus. Fed. 102 A3
Krasnyye Tkachi Rus. Fed. 43 U4
Krasnyy Kamyshanik Rus. Fed. see Komsomol'skiy
Krasnyy Kholm Rus. Fed. 43 S3
Krasnyy Kut Rus. Fed. 102 A2
Krasnyy Luch Rus. Fed. 43 L4
Krasnyy Luch Ukr. 41 F6
Krasnyy Lyman Ukr. 41 F6
Krasnyy Oktyabr' Rus. Fed. 43 T5
Krasnyy Profintern Rus. Fed. 43 V4
Krasnyy Rog Bryanskaya Oblast' Rus. Fed. 43 O8
Krasnyy Rog Bryanskaya Oblast' Rus. Fed. 43 O9
Krasnyy Tekstil'shchik Rus. Fed. 41 H6
Krasnyy Yar Kazakh. 103 G1
Krasnyy Yar Rus. Fed. 102 B3
Krasyliv Ukr. 41 C6
also spelt Krasilov
Kratie Cambodia see Krâchéh
Kratovo Macedonia 58 D6
Krauja Latvia 42 H6
Kraul Mountains Antarctica 223 X2
Kraulshavn Greenland see Nuussuaq
Krâvanh, Chuŏr Phnum mts Cambodia see Cardamom Range
Kraynovka Rus. Fed. 102 A4
Krechevitsy Rus. Fed. 43 M3
Krefeld Germany 48 D4
Krekenava Lith. 42 F6
Kremaston, Techniti Limni resr Greece 59 C10
Kremen mt. Croatia 56 H4
Kremenchug Ukr. see Kremenchuk
Kremenchuk Ukr. 41 E6
also spelt Kremenchug
Kremenchuts'ka Vodoskhovyshche resr Ukr. 41 E6
Kremenki Rus. Fed. 43 S7
Kremenskoye Rus. Fed. 43 Q6
Kremges Ukr. see Svitlovods'k
Kreml' Rus. Fed. see Solovetskiy
Kremmidi, Akra pt Greece 59 E12
Kremmling U.S.A. 180 F4
Krems an der Donau Austria 49 M7
Kremsmünster Austria 49 L7
Krenitzin Islands U.S.A. 164 C4
Krepoljin Srbija Yugo. 58 C4
Kresna Bulg. 58 E7
Kresta, Zaliv g. Rus. Fed. 39 S3
Krestena Greece 59 C11
Krest-Khal'dzhayy Rus. Fed. 39 N3
Krestovka Rus. Fed. 40 J2
Kresttsy Rus. Fed. 43 N3
Kresty Moskovskaya Oblast' Rus. Fed. 43 S6
Kresty Pskovskaya Oblast' Rus. Fed. 43 M6
Kresty Tul'skaya Oblast' Rus. Fed. 43 T8
Krestyakh Rus. Fed. 39 L3
Kretinga Lith. 42 C6
Kreuth Germany 48 I8
Kreuzau Germany 48 D5
Kreuzeck Gruppe mts Austria 49 K9
Kreuzlingen Switz. 51 P5
Kreuztal Germany 48 E5
Kreva Belarus 42 H7
Kribi Cameroon 125 H6
Krichev Belarus see Krychaw
Krichim Bulg. 58 F6
Krieglach Austria 49 M8
Kriel S. Africa 133 N3
Krievukalns hill Latvia 42 C5
Krieza Greece 59 F10
Krikellos Greece 59 C10
Krikelos, Akra pt Greece 59 H12
Krikovo Moldova see Cricova
Kril'on, Mys c. Rus. Fed. 82 F3
Krios, Akra pt Greece 59 E13
Krishna r. India 94 D2
formerly known as Kistna
Krishnagiri India 94 C3
Krishnai r. India 97 F4
Krishnanagar India 97 F5
Krishnaraja Sagara l. India 94 C3
Krishnarajpet India 94 C3
Kristdala Sweden 45 L4
Kristiania Norway see Oslo
Kristiansand Norway 45 I4
Kristianstad Sweden 45 K4
Kristiansund Norway 44 I3
Kristiinankaupunki Fin. see Kristinestad
Kristinehamn Sweden 45 K4
Kristinestad Fin. 45 M3
also known as Kristiinankaupunki
Kristinopol' Ukr. see Chervonohrad
Kriti admin. reg. Greece 59 F14
Kriti i. Greece see Crete
Kriūkai Lith. 42 E6
Kriulyany Moldova see Criuleni
Kriusha Rus. Fed. 43 U7
Krivača mt. Yugo. 58 B5
Krivaja r. Bos.-Herz. 56 K4
Krivandino Rus. Fed. 43 U6
Kriva Palanka Macedonia 58 D6
Kriva Reka r. Macedonia 58 C6
Křivoklátská Vrchovina hills Czech Rep. 49 K6
Krivoles Rus. Fed. 43 N8
Krivoy Porog Rus. Fed. 40 E2
Krivoy Rog Ukr. see Kryvyy Rih
Križevci Croatia 56 I2
Krk mt. Bos.-Herz. 56 L4
Krk Croatia 56 G3
Krk i. Croatia 56 G3
Krka r. Croatia 56 H5
Krka r. Slovenia 56 H3
Krkonošský narodní park nat. park Czech Rep./Poland 49 M5
also known as Karkonoski Park Narodowy
Krnjača Srbija Yugo. 58 B4
Krnov Czech Rep. 49 O5
Krobia Poland 49 N4
Krohnwodoke Liberia 124 D5
Kroknes Norway 44 O1
Krokom Sweden 44 K3
Króksfjarðarnes Iceland 44 [inset] B2
Krokstadøra Norway 44 J3
Krolevets' Ukr. 41 E6
Kroma r. Rus. Fed. 43 Q9
Kromdraai S. Africa 133 N2
Kromy Rus. Fed. 43 Q9
Kronach Germany 48 I5
Kronfjell hill Norway 45 J4
Krŏng Kaôh Kŏng Cambodia 79 C6
Kronli India 97 G3
Kronoberg county Sweden 45 K4
Kronoby Fin. 44 M3
Kronotskiy Poluostrov pen. Rus. Fed. 39 Q4
Kronotskiy Zaliv b. Rus. Fed. 39 Q4
Kronotskoye Ozero l. Rus. Fed. 39 Q4
Kronprins Christian Land reg. Greenland 165 Q1
Kronprins Frederik Bjerge nunataks Greenland 165 P3
Kronshagen Germany 48 H1
Kronshtadt Rus. Fed. 43 K2
English form Kronstadt
Kronstadt Romania see Braşov
Kronstadt Rus. Fed. see Kronshtadt
Kroonstad S. Africa 133 L4
Kropotkin Rus. Fed. 41 G7
Kropp Germany 48 G1
Krosno Poland 49 S6
Krosno Odrzańskie Poland 49 M3
Krossen Norway 45 J4
Krotoszyn Poland 49 O4
Krotz Springs U.S.A. 175 B6
Krousonas Greece 59 F13
Kroya Indon. 77 E4
Krško Slovenia 56 H3
Krstača mt. Yugo. 58 B6
Krugerdrifdam resr S. Africa 133 K5
Kruger National Park S. Africa 133 P2
Krugersdorp S. Africa 133 L3
Krugerspos S. Africa 133 O1
Kruglyakov Rus. Fed. see Oktyabr'skiy
Kruhlaye Belarus 43 K7
Krui Indon. 76 C4
Kruidfontein S. Africa 132 F9
Kruisfontein S. Africa 133 I11
Krujë Albania 58 A7
Krumë Albania 58 B6
Krumovgrad Bulg. 58 G7
Krungkao Thai. see Ayutthaya
Krung Thep Thai. see Bangkok
Kruoja r. Lith. 42 E5
Krupa Bos.-Herz. see Bosanska Krupa
Krupa na Uni Bos.-Herz. see Bosanska Krupa
Krupanj Srbija Yugo. 58 A4
Krupina Slovakia 49 Q7
Krupki Belarus 43 K7
Kruševac Srbija Yugo. 58 C5
Kruševo Macedonia 58 C7
Krušné Hory mts Czech Rep. 49 J5
Krustkalnu rezervāts nature res. Latvia 42 H5
Kruszwica Poland 49 P3
Krutoye Orlovskaya Oblast' Rus. Fed. 43 S9
Krutoye Smolenskaya Oblast' Rus. Fed. 43 M6
Kruzof Island U.S.A. 166 C3
Krybinka r. Belarus 43 K6
Krychaw Belarus 43 M8
also spelt Krichev
Kryezi Albania 58 B6
Krym' pen. Ukr. see Crimea
Krymsk Rus. Fed. 41 F7
formerly known as Krymskaya
Krymskaya Rus. Fed. see Krymsk
Kryms'kyy Pivostriv pen. Ukr. see Crimea
Kryms'kyy Zapovidnyk nature res. Ukr. 106 C1
Krynica Poland 49 R6
Krynica Morska Poland 49 Q1
Krynki Belarus 43 L6
Krystynopol Ukr. see Chervonohrad
Krytiko Pelagos sea Greece 59 G12
Kryvichy Belarus 42 I7
Kryvyy Rih Ukr. 41 E7
also spelt Krivoy Rog
Krzepice Poland 49 P5
Krzna r. Poland 49 U3
Krzna Południowa r. Poland 49 T4
Krzyż Wielkopolski Poland 49 N3
Ksabi Alg. 123 E3
Ksar Chellala Alg. 55 N9
formerly known as Reïbell
Ksar el Boukhari Alg. 123 F2
formerly known as Boghari
Ksar el Hirane Alg. 123 F2
Ksar el Kebir Morocco 122 D2
formerly spelt Alcazarquivir
Ksar-es-Souk Morocco see Er Rachidia
Ksenofontova Rus. Fed. 40 J3
Kshen' r. Rus. Fed. 43 S9
Kskyrbulak Yuzhnyy, Gora hill Turkm. 102 C4
Ksour, Monts des mts Alg. 120 A1
Ksour, Monts des mts Tunisia 123 H2
Ksour Essaf Tunisia 123 H2
Kstovo Rus. Fed. 40 H4
Ktsyn' Rus. Fed. 43 Q8
Kū', Jabal al hill Saudi Arabia 105 D2
Ku, Wadi el watercourse Sudan 121 E6
Kuaidamao China see Tonghua
Kuala Belait Brunei 77 F1
Kuala Dungun Malaysia see Dungun
Kualajelai Indon. 77 E3
Kuala Kangsar Malaysia 76 C1
Kualakapuas Indon. 77 F3
Kuala Kerai Malaysia 76 C1
Kuala Kinabatangan r. mouth Sabah Malaysia 77 G1
Kualakuayan Indon. 77 F3
Kuala Kubu Baharu Malaysia 76 C2
Kualakurun Indon. 77 F3
Kuala Lipis Malaysia 76 C1

▶Kuala Lumpur Malaysia 76 C2
Capital of Malaysia.

Kualapembuang Indon. 77 F3
Kuala Penyu Sabah Malaysia 77 F1
Kuala Pilah Malaysia 76 C2
Kualapuu U.S.A. 181 [inset] Z1
Kualasampit Indon. 77 F3
Kualasimpang Indon. 76 B1
Kuala Terengganu Malaysia 76 C1
Kualatungal Indon. 76 C3
Kuamut Sabah Malaysia 77 G1
Kuamut r. Sabah Malaysia 77 G1
Kuancheng China 85 H3
Kuandian China 83 B4
Kuangyuan China see Yiliang
Kuanshan Taiwan 87 G4
Kuantan Malaysia 76 C2
Kuaotuou N.Z. 152 J4
Kuba Azer. see Quba
Kuban' r. Rus. Fed. 41 F7
Kubār Dayr az Zawr Syria 109 K2
Kubārah Oman 105 G3
Kübassaare poolsaar pen. Estonia 42 E3
Kubaysah Iraq 107 E4
Kubbum Sudan 126 D2
Kubena r. Rus. Fed. 43 U2
Kubenskoye Rus. Fed. 43 U2
Kubenskoye, Ozero l. Rus. Fed. 43 U2
Kuberle Rus. Fed. see Krasnoarmeyskiy
Kubinka Rus. Fed. 43 R6
Kubitzer Bodden b. Germany 49 K1
Kubnya r. Rus. Fed. 40 I5
Kubokawa Japan 91 C8
Kubor, Mount P.N.G. 73 J8
Kubrat Bulg. 58 H5
Kubrinsk Rus. Fed. 43 T5
Kubumesaäi Indon. 77 F2
Kučevo Srbija Yugo. 58 C4
Kuchaman India 96 B4
Kuchema Rus. Fed. 40 G2
Kuchera India 96 B4
Kuching Sarawak Malaysia 77 E2
also spelt Kucing
Kuchinotsu Japan 91 B8
Kuchukskoye, Ozero salt l. Rus. Fed. 103 I1
Kuchurhan r. Ukr. 58 K2
Kucing Sarawak Malaysia see Kuching
Kuçovë Albania 58 A8
formerly known as Qyteti Stalin
Küçükköy Turkey 59 H9
Küçükmenderes r. Turkey 59 H8
Küçükmenderes r. Turkey 59 I11
Kuda India 96 A5
Kudachi India 94 B2
Kudal India 94 B3
Kudamatsu Japan 91 B8
Kudap Indon. 76 C2
Kudara-Somon Rus. Fed. 85 E1
Kudev r. Rus. Fed. 42 J4
Kudever' Rus. Fed. 43 K5
Kudirkos Naumiestis Lith. 42 D7
Kudligi India 94 C3
Kudremukh mt. India 94 B3
Kudrinskaya Rus. Fed. 43 Q7
Kudu Nigeria 125 G4
Kudus Indon. 77 E4
Kudymkar Rus. Fed. 40 J4
Kueishan Tao i. Taiwan 87 G3
Kufstein Austria 48 J8
Kugaly Kazakh. 103 I3
also spelt Qoghaly
Kugesi Rus. Fed. 40 H4
Kugka Lhai China 89 E6
Kugluktuk Canada 165 H3
formerly known as Coppermine
Kugmallit Bay Canada 164 F3
Kūh, Ra's-al- pt Iran 100 D5
Kūhak Iran 101 E5
Kūhbonān Iran 100 D4
Kūhdasht Iran 100 A3
Kūhestak Iran 100 D5
Kūhīn Iran 100 B2
Kūhīrī Iran 101 E5
Kŭhistoni Badakhshon aut. rep. Tajik. 101 H2
also known as Gorno-Badakhshan or Gornyy Badakhshan; formerly known as Badakhshoni Kŭhí; short form Badakhshan
Kühlung park Germany 48 I1
Kuhmo Fin. 44 O2
Kuhmoinen Fin. 45 N3
Kūhpāyeh Iran 100 C3
Kūhpāyeh mt. Iran 100 D4
Kūhrān, Kūh-e mt. Iran 100 D5
Kūhrang r. Iran 100 B4
Kui Buri Thai. 79 B5
Kuimetsa Estonia 42 G2
Kuis Namibia 130 C5
Kuiseb watercourse Namibia 130 B4
Kuitan China 87 E4
Kuitin China see Kuytun
Kuito Angola 127 C8
formerly known as Bié
Kuiu Island U.S.A. 166 C3
Kuivaniemi Fin. 44 N2
Kuivastu Estonia 42 E3
Kuja r. Latvia 42 H5
Kujang India 95 E1
Kujang N. Korea 83 B5
Kuji Japan 90 G4
Kuji-wan b. Japan 90 G4
Kujū-san vol. Japan 91 B8
Kukālār, Kūh-e hill Iran 100 B4
Kukan Rus. Fed. 82 D2
Kukatush Canada 173 K2
Kukawa Nigeria 125 I3
Kukerin Australia 151 B7
Kukës Albania 58 B6
Kuki Japan 91 F6
Kukkola Fin. 44 N2
Kukmor Rus. Fed. 40 I4
Kukoboy Rus. Fed. 43 U3
Kukruse Estonia 42 I2
Kukshi India 96 B5
Kukunuru India 94 D2
Kukup Malaysia 76 C2
Kukurtli Turkm. 102 D5
formerly known as Sernyy Zavod
Kukusan, Gunung hill Indon. 77 F3
Kukushtan Rus. Fed. 40 K4
Kūl r. Iran 100 C5
Kula Bulg. 58 D5
Kula r. Moldova see Cula
Kula Nigeria 125 G5
Kula Turkey 106 B3
Kula Vojvodina, Srbija Yugo. 58 A3
Kula mt. Yugo. 58 A6
Kulabu, Gunung mt. Indon. 76 B2
Kulachi Pak. 101 G4
Kulagi Rus. Fed. 43 N9
Kulagino Kazakh. 102 B2
Kula Kangri mt. Bhutan 97 F3
Kulal, Mount Kenya 128 C4
Kulaly, Ostrov i. Kazakh. 102 B3
also known as Qulaly Araly
Kulandy Kazakh. 102 D3
also spelt Qulandy
Kulaneh reg. Pak. 101 E5
Kulanotpes watercourse Kazakh. 103 G2
also spelt Qulanötpes
Kulao r. Pak. 101 F4
Kular Rus. Fed. 39 N2
Kulassein i. Phil. 74 B5
Kulat, Gunung mt. Indon. 77 G2
Kulautuva Lith. 42 E7
Kulawi Indon. 75 A3
Kulb Sudan 121 F4
Kuldīga Latvia 42 C5
Kuldja China see Yining
Kul'dur Rus. Fed. 82 C2
Kul'dzhuktau, Gory hills Uzbek. 103 E4
also known as Quljuqtow Toghi
Kule Botswana 130 D4
Kulebaki Rus. Fed. 40 G5
Kuleshi Rus. Fed. 43 S9
Kûlet el Qrein hill Egypt 108 C8
Kulgera Australia 148 B5
Kulgunino Rus. Fed. 102 D1
Kuliai Lith. 42 C6
Kuligi Rus. Fed. 40 J4
Kulikovo Arkhangel'skaya Oblast' Rus. Fed. 40 H3
Kulikovo Lipetskaya Oblast' Rus. Fed. 43 U9
Kulim Malaysia 76 C1
Kulittalai India 94 C4
Kulkuduk Uzbek. 103 E4
also spelt Kalquduq
Kulkyne watercourse Australia 147 E2
Kullamaa Estonia 42 F3
Kullu India 96 C3
Kulmbach Germany 48 I5
Kŭlob Tajik. 101 G2
also spelt Kulyab
Kulotino Rus. Fed. 43 O3
Kuloy Rus. Fed. 40 G3
Kuloy r. Rus. Fed. 40 G2
Kulp Turkey 107 E3
also known as Pasur
Kul'sary Kazakh. 102 C3
also spelt Qulsary
Kulshabi Sudan 126 F2
Kultuk Rus. Fed. 84 D1
Kulu Turkey 106 C3
Kulübe Tepe mt. Turkey 106 B3
Kulunda Rus. Fed. 103 I1
Kulunda r. Rus. Fed. 103 I1
Kulundinskaya Step' plain Kazakh./Rus. Fed. 103 H1
Kulundinskoye, Ozero salt l. Rus. Fed. 103 I1
Kulusuk Greenland 165 P3
also known as Kap Dan
Külvand Iran 100 C4
Kulwin Australia 147 D3
Kulyab Tajik. see Kŭlob
Kuma r. Rus. Fed. 44 O2
Kuma r. Rus. Fed. 102 A3
Kumagaya Japan 91 F6
Kumai, Teluk b. Indon. 77 E3
Kumaishi Japan 90 F3
Kumak r. Rus. Fed. 102 D2
Kumaka Guyana 199 G4
Kumalar Dağı mts Turkey 106 B3
Kumamoto Japan 91 B8
Kumamoto pref. Japan 91 B8
Kumano Japan 91 E8
Kumanovo Macedonia 58 C6
Kumara N.Z. 153 F10
Kumara Junction N.Z. 153 F10
Kumarkhali Bangl. 97 F5
Kumasi Ghana 125 E5
Ku-Mayima S. Africa 133 M8
Kumayri Armenia see Gyumri
Kumba Cameroon 125 H5
Kumbağ Turkey 58 I8
Kumbakonam India 94 C4
Kümbet Turkey 106 B3
Kumbharli Ghat mt. India 94 B2
Kumbher Nepal 97 D3
Kumbla India 94 B3
Kumbo Cameroon 125 H5
Kumbri Latvia 42 D5
Kumchuru Botswana 130 D4
Kum-Dag Turkm. see Gumdag
Kumdah Saudi Arabia 105 D3
Kumel well Iran 100 C3
Kumertau Rus. Fed. 102 C1
Kŭm-gang r. S. Korea 83 B6
Kumgang-san mt. N. Korea 83 C5
English form Keumgang, Mount; formerly known as Keumsang, Mount
Kumguri India 97 F4
Kumharsain India 89 B6
Kumher India 96 C4
Kŭmho-gang r. S. Korea 83 C6
Kumi S. Korea 83 C5
Kumi Uganda 128 B4
Kumkale Turkey 59 H9
Kum Kuduk well China 88 E3
Kumla Sweden 45 K4
Kumlinge Fin. 45 M3
Kumlu Turkey 109 H1
Kumluca Turkey 108 B1
Kummerower See l. Germany 49 J2
Kumo Nigeria 125 H4
Kŭmŏ-do i. S. Korea 83 B6
Kumola watercourse Kazakh. 103 F3
also spelt Qumola
Kumon Range mts Myanmar 78 B2
Kumphawapi Thai. 78 C4
Kumputunturi hill Fin. 44 N2
Kumta India 94 B3
Kumu Dem. Rep. Congo 126 E4
Kumukahi, Cape U.S.A. 181 [inset] Z2
Kumul China see Hami
Kumund India 95 D1
Kümüx China 88 E3
Kumylzhenskaya Rus. Fed. see Kumylzhenskiy
Kumylzhenskiy Rus. Fed. 41 G6
formerly known as Kumylzhenskaya
Kumyshtag, Pik mt. Kyrg. see Kyumyush-Tak, Pik
Kun r. Myanmar 78 B4
Kunar r. Afgh. 101 G3
Kunashir, Ostrov i. Rus. Fed. 82 G3
Kunashirskiy Proliv sea chan. Japan/Rus. Fed. see Nemuro-kaikyō
Kunchaung Myanmar 78 B3
Kunda Dem. Rep. Congo 126 E5
Kunda Estonia 42 H2
Kunda r. Estonia 42 H2
Kunda India 97 D4
Kunda-dia-Baze Angola 127 C7
Kunda laht b. Estonia 42 H2
Kundapura India 94 B3
formerly spelt Coondapoor
Kundar r. Afgh./Pak. 101 G3
Kundat Sabah Malaysia 77 G1
Kundelungu, Parc National de nat. park Dem. Rep. Congo 127 E7
Kundelungu Ouest, Parc National de nat. park Dem. Rep. Congo 127 E7
Kundgol India 94 B3
Kundian Pak. 101 G3
Kundur i. Indon. 76 C2
Kunduz Afgh. see Kondūz
Kunene admin. reg. Namibia 130 B3
Kunene r. Namibia 127 A9
also spelt Cunene
Künes China see Xinyuan
Künes Chang China 88 C3
Künes He r. China 88 C3
Künes Linchang China 88 D3
Kungälv Sweden 45 J4
Kungei Alatau mts Kazakh./Kyrg. 103 I4
also spelt Küngöy Ala-Too
Kunggar China see Maizhokunggar
Kunghit Island Canada 166 D4
Küngöy Ala-Too mts Kazakh./Kyrg. see Kungei Alatau
Kungrad Uzbek. 102 D4
also spelt Qongrat or Qŭnghirot; formerly known as Zheleznodorozhnyy
Kungradkol' Uzbek. 102 E4
Kungsbacka Sweden 45 K4
Kungshamn Sweden 45 J4
Kungsör Sweden 45 L4
Kungu Dem. Rep. Congo 126 C4
Kungur mt. China see Kongur Shan
Kungur Rus. Fed. 40 K4
Kungyangon Myanmar 78 A4
Kunhegyes Hungary 49 R8
Kuni r. India 94 C2
Kunié i. New Caledonia see Pins, Île des
Kunigai India 94 C3
Kunimi-dake mt. Japan 91 B8
Kuningaküla Estonia 42 I2
Kuningan Indon. 77 E4
Kunisaki Japan 91 B8
Kunjabar India 95 E1
Kunlavav India 96 A5
Kunlong Myanmar 78 B3
Kunlui r. India/Nepal 97 F4
Kunlun Shan mts China 84 B5
Kunlun Shankou pass China 84 B5
Kunmadaras Hungary 49 R8
Kunming China 86 B3
Kunmunya Aboriginal Reserve Australia 150 D2
Kuno r. India 96 C4
Kunoy i. Faroe Is 46 F1
Kunsan S. Korea 83 B6
Kunshan China 87 G2
Kunszentmárton Hungary 49 R9
Kunszentmiklós Hungary 49 Q8
Kuntshankoie Dem. Rep. Congo 126 D5
Kununurra Australia 150 E2
Kunwak r. Canada 167 L2
Kunwari r. India 96 C4
Kun'ya Rus. Fed. 43 L5
Kun'ya r. Rus. Fed. 43 M4
Kunyang China see Yexian
Kunyang China see Jinning
Kunyang China see Pingyang
Kunya-Urgench Turkm. see Keneurgench
Kunyu Shan mts China 85 I4
Künzelsau Germany 48 G6
Kuocang Shan mts China 87 G2
Kuolayarvi Rus. Fed. 44 O2
Kuopio Fin. 44 N3
Kuosku Fin. 44 O2
Kupa r. Croatia/Slovenia 56 I3
Kupang Indon. 75 B5
Kupang, Teluk b. Indon. 75 B5
Kupanskoye Rus. Fed. 43 T5
Kupari India 97 E5
Kupiškis Lith. 42 F6
Kuprava Latvia 42 I4
Kupreanof Island U.S.A. 164 F4
Kupreanof Point U.S.A. 164 D4
Kupuy Rus. Fed. 43 L5
Kupwara Jammu and Kashmir 96 B2
Kup"yans'k Ukr. 41 F6
Kuqa China 88 C3
Kür r. Azer. 107 G3
Kür r. Georgia 107 F2
Kur r. Rus. Fed. 82 D2
Kura r. Azer./Georgia 107 F2
Kura r. Rus. Fed. 41 G8
Kurabuka r. Australia 150 B5
Kuragaty Kazakh. 103 H4
also spelt Qoraghaty
Kuragwi Nigeria 125 H4
Kurakh Rus. Fed. 102 A4
Kura kurk sea chan. Estonia/Latvia see Irbe Strait
Kuramā, Ḩarrat lava field Saudi Arabia 104 C2
Kurashasayskiy Kazakh. 102 D2
Kurashiki Japan 91 C7
Kurasia India 97 D5
Kura Soak well Australia 150 D3
Kurayn i. Saudi Arabia 105 E2
Kurayoshi Japan 91 C7
Kurayskiy Khrebet mts Rus. Fed. 84 A1
Kurba Rus. Fed. 43 U4
Kurban Dağı mt. Turkey 58 K8
Kurbin r. China 82 C2
Kurca r. Romania 58 B2
Kurchatov Rus. Fed. 41 E6
Kurchum Kazakh. 88 C1
also spelt Kürshim; formerly known as Kurmashkino
Kurchum r. Kazakh. 88 C1
Kürdämir Azer. 107 G2
also spelt Kyurdamir
Kurday Kazakh. 103 H4
also spelt Qorday
Kür Dili pt Azer. 107 G3
Kurduvadi India 94 B2
Kŭrdzhali Bulg. 58 G7
Kure Japan 91 C7
Küre Turkey 106 C2
Kure Atoll U.S.A. 220 G4
also known as Ocean Island
Kuressaare Estonia 42 D3
formerly known as Kingisseppa
Kureya r. Rus. Fed. 43 K3
Kureyskoye Vodokhranilische resr Rus. Fed. 39 I3
Kurgal'dzhino Kazakh. see Kurgal'dzhinskiy
Kurgal'dzhinskiy Kazakh. 103 G2
also known as Qorghalzhyn; formerly known as Kurgal'dzhino
Kurgan Rus. Fed. 38 G4
Kurganinsk Rus. Fed. 41 G7
formerly known as Kurgannaya
Kurgannaya Rus. Fed. see Kurganinsk
Kurgantyube Tajik. see Qŭrghonteppa
Kuri India 96 A4
Kuria is Kiribati 145 G1
Kuria Muria Bay Oman see Ḩalāniyāt, Khalīj al
Kuria Muria Islands Oman see Ḩalāniyāt, Juzur al
Kuridala Australia 149 D4
Kurigram Bangl. 97 F4
Kurikka Fin. 44 M3
Kurikoma-yama vol. Japan 90 G5
Kurile, Mal mt. Albania 58 A6
Kuril Islands Rus. Fed. 82 G3
also known as Kuril'skiye Ostrova or Chishima-retto
Kurilovka Rus. Fed. 102 B2
Kuril'sk Rus. Fed. 81 P3
Kuril'skiye Ostrova is Rus. Fed. see Kuril Islands
Kuriyama Japan 90 G3
Kurkino Rus. Fed. 43 T8
Kurkurabazhi, Gora mt. Rus. Fed. 84 A1
Kurlkuta Aboriginal Reserve Australia 150 D4
Kurlovskiy Rus. Fed. 40 G5
Kurmanayevka Rus. Fed. 102 B1
Kurmashkino Kazakh. see Kurchum
Kurmene Latvia 42 F5
Kurmuk Sudan 128 B2
Kurnool India 94 C3
Kurobe Japan 91 E6
Kuroishi Japan 90 G4
Kuroiso Japan 90 G6
Kuromatsunai Japan 90 G3
Kuror, Jebel mt. Sudan 121 F4
Kuro-shima i. Japan 91 A9
Kurovskiy Rus. Fed. 82 B1
Kurovskoy Rus. Fed. 43 R7
Kurovskoye Rus. Fed. 43 T6
Kurow N.Z. 153 E12
Kurram r. Afgh./Pak. 101 G3
Kurri Kurri Australia 147 F3
Kuršėnai Lith. 42 D5
Kursh, Jabal hill Saudi Arabia 104 C3
Kürshim Kazakh. see Kurchum
Kurshskiy Zaliv b. Lith./Rus. Fed. see Courland Lagoon
Kurshynavichy Belarus 42 H9
Kursīši Latvia 42 D5
Kuršių marios b. Lith./Rus. Fed. see Courland Lagoon
Kuršių neringos nacionalinis parkas nat. park Lith. 42 B6
Kursk Rus. Fed. 41 F6
Kurskaya Rus. Fed. 41 H7
Kurskaya Oblast' admin. div. Rus. Fed. 41 F6
English form Kursk Oblast
Kurskiy Zaliv b. Lith./Rus. Fed. see Courland Lagoon
Kursk Oblast admin. div. Rus. Fed. see Kurskaya Oblast'
Kuršumlija Srbija Yugo. 58 C5
Kurşunlu Turkey 106 C2
Kurtalan Turkey 107 E3
also known as Misraç
Kürti r. Kazakh. see Kurtty
Kurtoğlu Burnu pt Turkey 106 B3

Kurtpınar Turkey **108** G1
Kurttepe Turkey **108** G1
Kurtty *r.* Kazakh. **103** I3
also spelt Kürti *or* Kurty
Kurty *r.* Kazakh. *see* **Kurtty**
Kuru Fin. **45** M3
Kurú *r.* Greece *see* **Kourou**
Kuru India **97** E5
Kuru *watercourse* Sudan **126** E2
Kurucaşile Turkey **106** C2
Kurud India **94** D1
Kurukshetra India **96** C3
Kuruktag *mts* China **88** D3
Kuruman S. Africa **132** H4
Kuruman *watercourse* S. Africa **132** E3
Kuruman Hills S. Africa **132** H4
Kurume Japan **91** B8
Kurumkan Rus. Fed. **81** I2
Kurun *r.* Sudan **128** B3
Kurundi *watercourse* Australia **148** B4
Kurundvad India **94** B2
Kurunegala Sri Lanka **94** D5
Kurunzulay Rus. Fed. **85** H1
Kurupam India **95** D2
Kurupukari Guyana **199** G3
Kurush, Jebel *hills* Sudan **121** F4
Kur'ya Rus. Fed. **103** J2
Kur'ya Rus. Fed. **40** K3
Kuryk Kazakh. **102** B4
formerly known as Yeraliyev
Kuryongp'o S. Korea **91** A7
Kuşadası Turkey **106** A3
Kuşadası Körfezi *b.* Turkey **106** A3
Kusaie *atoll* Micronesia *see* **Kosrae**
Kusary Azer. *see* **Qusar**
Kusawa Lake Canada **166** B2
Kuşcenneti Milli Parkı *nat. park* Turkey **59** I8
Kuse Japan **91** C7
Kuş Gölü *l.* Turkey **106** A2
formerly known as Manyas Gölü
Kushalgarh India **96** B5
Kushalino Rus. Fed. **43** R4
Kūshank Iran **100** D3
Kusheriki Nigeria **125** G4
Kushida-gawa *r.* Japan **91** E7
Kushikino Japan **91** B9
Kushima Japan **91** B9
Kushimoto Japan **91** D8
Kushiro Japan **90** I3
Kushiro-Shitsugen National Park Japan **90** I3
Kushka Turkm. *see* **Gushgy**
Kushmurun Kazakh. **103** F1
also spelt Qusmuryn
Kushmurun, Ozero *salt l.* Kazakh. **103** F1
also known as Qusmuryn Köli
Kushnarenkovo Rus. Fed. **40** J5
Kushtagi India **94** C3
Kushtia Bangl. **97** F5
also spelt Kustia
Kushtih Iran **101** D4
Kushtozero, Ozero *l.* Rus. Fed. **43** R1
Kushui *r.* China **85** E4
Kushum Kazakh. **102** B2
Kushum *r.* Kazakh. **102** B2
Kuskan Turkey **108** E1
Kuskokwim *r.* U.S.A. **164** C3
Kuskokwim Bay U.S.A. **164** C4
Kuskokwim Mountains U.S.A. **164** D3
Kuskovo Rus. Fed. **43** Q6
Kuşluyan Turkey *see* **Gölköy**
Kusŏng N. Korea **83** B5
Kussharo-ko *l.* Japan **90** I3
Kustanay Kazakh. *see* **Kostanay**
Kustanay Oblast *admin. div.* Kazakh. *see* **Kustanayskaya Oblast'**
Kustanayskaya Oblast' *admin. div.* Kazakh. **103** E1
English form Kustanay Oblast; *also known as* Qostanay Oblysy
Kustavi Fin. **45** M3
Küstence Romania *see* **Constanţa**
Kustia Bangl. *see* **Kushtia**
Kusu Indon. **75** C2
Kut, Ko *i.* Thai. **79** C6
Kūt 'Abdollāh Iran **100** B4
Kutacane Indon. **76** B2
Kütahya Turkey **106** B3
historically known as Cotiaeum
Kütahya *prov.* Turkey **59** K9
Kutai National Park Indon. **77** G2
K'ut'aisi Georgia **107** E2
Kut-al-Imara Iraq *see* **Al Kūt**
Kutan Rus. Fed. **102** A3
Kutaraja Indon. *see* **Banda Aceh**
Kutarere N.Z. **152** L6
Kutayfat Ţurayf *vol.* Saudi Arabia **109** J6
Kutch, Gulf of India *see* **Kachchh, Gulf of**
Kutch, Rann of *marsh* India *see* **Kachchh, Rann of**
Kutchan Japan **90** G3
Kūt-e Gapu *tourist site* Iran **100** B3
Kutina Croatia **56** I3
Kutjevo Croatia **56** J3
Kutkai Myanmar **78** B3
Kutloanong S. Africa **133** K4
Kutná Hora Czech Rep. **49** M6
Kutno Poland **49** Q3
Kuttainen Sweden **44** M1
Kutu Dem. Rep. Congo **126** C5
Kutubdia Island Bangl. **97** F5

Kutum Sudan **120** E6
Kutuzov Moldova *see* **Ialoveni**
Kutztown U.S.A. **177** J5
Kuujjua *r.* Canada **165** H2
Kuujjuaq Canada **169** G1
formerly known as Fort Chimo
Kuujjuarapik Canada **168** E2
also known as Poste-de-la-Baleine
Kuuli-Mayak Turkm. **102** C4
also spelt Guwlumayak
Kuusajoki Fin. **44** N2
Kuusalu Estonia **42** G2
Kuusamo Fin. **44** O2
Kuusankoski Fin. **45** N3
Kuusjoki Fin. **42** E1
Kuutse mägi *hill* Estonia **42** H3
Kuvandyk Rus. Fed. **102** D2
Kuvango Angola **127** C8
formerly known as Artur de Paiva *or* Capelongo *or* Vila da Ponte
Kuvshinovo Rus. Fed. **43** P4
▶**Kuwait** *country* Asia **107** F5
spelt Al Kuwayt in Arabic
world [changes] ➔ 20–21
asia [countries] ➔ 64–67

▶**Kuwait** Kuwait **107** F5
Capital of Kuwait. Also spelt Al Kuwayt.

Kuwait Jun *b.* Kuwait **107** F5
Kuwajleen *atoll* Marshall Is *see* **Kwajalein**
Kuwana Japan **91** E7
Kūybyshev Kazakh. *see* **Kuybyshevskiy**
Kuybyshev Rus. Fed. **80** B1
Kuybyshev Rus. Fed. *see* **Bolgar**
Kuybyshev Rus. Fed. *see* **Samara**
Kuybysheve Ukr. **41** F7
Kuybyshevka-Vostochnaya Rus. Fed. *see* **Belogorsk**
Kuybyshevo Kazakh. *see* **Zhyngyldy**
Kuybyshevskaya Oblast' *admin. div.* Rus. Fed. *see* **Samarskaya Oblast'**
Kuybyshevskiy Kazakh. **103** F1
also known as Kūybyshev; *formerly known as* Trudovoy
Kuybyshevskoye Vodokhranilishche *resr* Rus. Fed. **40** I5
Kuybyshew Adyndaky Turkm. *see* **imeni Kuybysheva**
Kuye *r.* China **85** F4
Kuyeda Rus. Fed. **40** J4
Kuygan Kazakh. **103** H3
also spelt Quyghan
Küysu China **84** B3
Kuytun China **88** D2
also spelt Kuitin
Kuytun He *r.* China **88** C2
Kuyucak Turkey **59** J11
Kuyukkol', Ozero *salt l.* Kazakh. **103** F2
Kuyuluk Turkey **108** F1
Kuyus Rus. Fed. **88** D1
Kuyu Tingni Nicaragua **186** C4
also known as Cuyutingni
Kuyuwini *r.* Guyana **199** G4
Kuyvozi Rus. Fed. **43** L1
Kuzhenkino Rus. Fed. **43** O4
Kužiai Lith. **42** E6
Kuzino Rus. Fed. **43** T2
Kuz'minichi Rus. Fed. **43** O7
Kuz'minskoye Rus. Fed. **43** U7
Kuz'molovskiy Rus. Fed. **43** L1
Kuznechnoye Rus. Fed. **45** O3
Kuznetsk Rus. Fed. **41** H5
Kuznetsovo Rus. Fed. **90** F1
Kuznetsovs'k Ukr. **41** C6
Kuzomen' Rus. Fed. **40** F2
Kuzovatovo Rus. Fed. **41** H5
Kuzovka Rus. Fed. **43** T8
Kuzumaki Japan **90** G4
Kvænangen *sea chan.* Norway **44** M1
Kvaløya *i.* Norway **44** L1
Kvaløya *i.* Norway **44** M1
Kvalsund Norway **44** M1
Kvareli Georgia *see* **Qvareli**
Kvarkeno Rus. Fed. **102** D1
Kvarnberg Sweden **45** K3
Kvarner *g.* Croatia **56** G4
Kvarnerić *sea chan.* Croatia **56** G4
Kvėdarna Lith. **42** C6
Kvenvær Norway **44** J3
Kvichak Bay U.S.A. **164** D4
Kvikkjokk Sweden **44** L2
Kvinesdal Norway **45** I4
Kvissleby Sweden **45** L3
Kvitanosi *mt.* Norway **45** I3
Kvitegga *mt.* Norway **44** I3
Kvitøya *ice feature* Svalbard **38** D2
Kvitsøy Norway **45** I4
Kwa *r.* Dem. Rep. Congo **126** C5
Kwabhaca S. Africa *see* **Mount Frere**
KwaChibukhulu S. Africa **133** O3
Kwadacha Wilderness Provincial Park Canada **166** E3
KwaDela S. Africa **133** N3
Kwadelen *atoll* Marshall Is *see* **Kwajalein**
Kwaga Tanz. **129** A6
KwaGuga S. Africa **133** N2
Kwajalein *atoll* Marshall Is **220** F5
also spelt Kuwajleen *or* Kwadelen
Kwakoegron Suriname **199** H3
Kwakwani Guyana **199** G3
Kwakwatse S. Africa **133** L4
Kwale Kenya **129** C6
Kwale Nigeria **125** G5
KwaMashu S. Africa **133** O6
Kwa-Mbonambi S. Africa **133** Q5
Kwame Danso Ghana **125** E5
KwaMhlanga S. Africa **133** M2
Kwamouth Dem. Rep. Congo **126** C5
Kwa Mtoro Tanz. **129** B6
Kwandang Indon. **75** B2
Kwangchow China *see* **Guangzhou**
Kwangju S. Korea **83** B6
Kwango *r.* Dem. Rep. Congo **126** C5
also spelt Cuango
Kwangsi *aut. reg.* China *see* **Guangxi Zhuangzu Zizhiqu**
Kwangsi Chuang Autonomous Region *aut. reg.* China *see* **Guangxi Zhuangzu Zizhiqu**
Kwangtung *prov.* China *see* **Guangdong**
Kwangwazi Tanz. **129** C6
Kwania, Lake Uganda **128** B4
Kwanmo-bong *mt.* N. Korea **82** C4
also known as Kambo-san
Kwanobuhle S. Africa **133** J10
KwaNojoli S. Africa **133** J9
Kwanonqubela S. Africa **133** K10
Kwanonzame S. Africa **133** I8
Kwanza *r.* Angola *see* **Cuanza**
Kwa-Pita S. Africa **133** L9
Kwara *state* Nigeria **125** F4
KwaThandeka S. Africa **133** O3
Kwatinidubu S. Africa **133** K9
Kwawr Umm Wu'al *depr.* Saudi Arabia **109** K6
KwaZamokhule S. Africa **133** N3
Kwazamukucinga S. Africa **133** I9
Kwazamuxolo S. Africa **133** I8
KwaZanele S. Africa **133** N3
Kwazulu-Natal *prov.* S. Africa **133** O5
formerly known as Natal
Kweichow *prov.* China *see* **Guizhou**
Kweiyang China *see* **Guiyang**
Kwekwe Zimbabwe **131** F3
formerly spelt Que Que
Kwena Dam S. Africa **133** O2
Kweneng *admin. dist.* Botswana **131** E4
Kwenge *r.* Dem. Rep. Congo **127** C6
Kwetabohigan *r.* Canada **168** D3
Kwezi-Naledi S. Africa **133** L7
Kwiambana Nigeria **125** G4

Kwidzyn Poland **49** P2
historically known as Marienwerder
Kwīhā Eth. **104** B5
Kwikila P.N.G. **73** K8
Kwilu *r.* Angola/Dem. Rep. Congo **127** C5
Kwisa *r.* Poland **49** M4
Kwitaro *r.* Guyana **199** G4
Kwo Chau Kwan To *is* *Hong Kong* China *see* **Ninepin Group**
Kwoka *mt.* Indon. **73** H7
Kwoungo, Mont *mt.* Cent. Afr. Rep. **126** E3
Kwun Tong *Hong Kong* China **87** [inset]
Kyabé Chad **126** C2
Kyabra Australia **149** D5
Kyabra *watercourse* Australia **149** D5
Kyabram Australia **147** E4
Kyadet Myanmar **78** A3
Kyaiklat Myanmar **78** A4
Kyaikto Myanmar **78** B4
Kya-in Seikkyi Myanmar **78** B4
Kyakhta Rus. Fed. **85** E1
Kyalite Australia **147** D3
Kyancutta Australia **146** B3
Kyangin *Irrawaddy* Myanmar **78** A4
Kyangin *Mandalay* Myanmar **78** B4
Kyaukhnyat Myanmar **78** B4
Kyaukkyi Myanmar **78** B4
Kyaukme Myanmar **78** B3
Kyaukmyaung Myanmar **78** A3
Kyaukpadaung Myanmar **78** A3
Kyaukpyu Myanmar **78** A4
Kyaukse Myanmar **78** B3
Kyauktan Myanmar **78** B4
Kyauktaw Myanmar **78** A3
Kyaunggon Myanmar **78** A4
Kybartai Lith. **42** D7
Kybeyan Range *mts* Australia **147** F4
Ky Cung, Sông *r.* Vietnam **78** D3
Kyeburn N.Z. **153** E13
Kyeintali Myanmar **78** A4
Kyela Tanz. **129** B7
Kyelang India **96** C2
Kyenjojo Uganda **128** A4
Kyeraa Ghana **125** E5
Kyeylbelen, Gora *hill* Kazakh. **103** H3
Kyidaunggan Myanmar **78** B4
Kyikug China **84** D4
Kyinderi Ghana **125** E4
Kyiv Ukr. *see* **Kiev**
Kyjov Czech Rep. **49** O6
Kyklades *is* Greece *see* **Cyclades**
Kyle Canada **167** I5
Kyle of Lochalsh U.K. **46** G6
Kyll *r.* Germany **48** D6
Kyllini *mt.* Greece **59** D11
also spelt Killíni
Kyllinis, Akra *pt* Greece **59** C11
Kymi Greece **59** F10
also spelt Kími
Kymijoki *r.* Fin. **42** H1
Kymis, Akra *pt* Greece **59** F10
Kynna *r.* Norway **45** K3
Kynuna Australia **149** D4
Kyoga, Lake Uganda **128** B4
Kyōga-misaki *pt* Japan **91** D7
Kyogle Australia **147** G2
Kyom *watercourse* Sudan **126** F2
Kyondo Myanmar **78** B4
Kyŏnggi-man *b.* S. Korea **83** B5
Kyŏngju S. Korea **83** C6
Kyongju National Park S. Korea **83** C6
Kyonpyaw Myanmar **78** A4
Kyōto Japan **91** D7
Kyōto *pref.* Japan **91** D7
Kyōwa Japan **90** G5
Kyparissia Greece **59** C11
also spelt Kiparissía
Kyparissiakos Kolpos *b.* Greece **59** C11
Kypros *country* Asia *see* **Cyprus**
Kypshak, Ozero *salt l.* Kazakh. **103** G2
also known as Qypshaq Köli
Kyra Rus. Fed. **85** G1
Kyra Panagia *i.* Greece **59** F9
Kyren Rus. Fed. **84** D1
Kyrenia Cyprus **108** E2
also known as Girne; *also spelt* Keryneia
Kyrenia Mountains Cyprus *see* **Pentadaktylos Range**
▶**Kyrgyzstan** *country* Asia **103** H4
also spelt Kirgizstan; *formerly known as* Kirghizia *or* Kirgizskaya S.S.R.
asia [countries] ➔ 64–67
Kyrhyzh-Kytay *r.* Ukr. **58** K3
Kyria Greece **58** F7
also spelt Kíria
Kyriaki Greece **59** D10
also known as Kiriákion
Kyritz Germany **49** J3
Kyritz-Ruppiner Heide *park* Germany **49** J2
Kyrnychky Ukr. **58** K3
Kyrta Rus. Fed. **40** K3
Kysucké Nové Mesto Slovakia **49** P6
Kytalyktakh Rus. Fed. **39** N3
Kytay, Ozero *l.* Ukr. **58** K3
Kythira Greece **59** D12
Kythira *i.* Greece **59** D12
English form Cerigo; *also spelt* Kíthira; *historically known as* Cythera
Kythnos *i.* Greece **59** F11
also spelt Kíthnos
Kythnou, Steno *sea chan.* Greece **59** F11
also spelt Kíthnou, Stenón
Kythrea Cyprus **108** E2
also known as Değirmenlik
Kyumyush-Tak, Pik *mt.* Kyrg. **103** G4
also spelt Kumyshtag, Pik
Kyunglung China **89** C6
Kyungyaung Myanmar **79** B5
Kyunhla Myanmar **78** A3
Kyuquot Canada **166** E5
Kyurdamir Azer. *see* **Kürdämir**
Kyushe Kazakh. **102** D3
Kyūshū *i.* Japan **91** B9
Kyūshū-sanchi *mts* Japan **91** B8
Kyustendil Bulg. **58** D6
Kywebwe Myanmar **78** B4
Kywong Australia **147** E3
Kyyev Ukr. *see* **Kiev**
Kyyiv Ukr. *see* **Kiev**
Kyyivs'ke Vodoskhovyshche *resr* Ukr. **41** D6
also known as Kiyevskoye Vodokhranilishche
Kyyjärvi Fin. **44** N3
Kyyvesi *l.* Fin. **45** N3
Kyzan Kazakh. **102** C3
also spelt Qyzan
Kyzketken Uzbek. **102** D4
also spelt Qizqetkan
Kyzyl Moldova *see* **Ştefan Vodă**
Kyzyl Rus. Fed. **80** E2
Kyzyl-Adyr Kyrg. **103** G4
formerly known as Kirov *or* Kirovskoye
Kyzylagash Kazakh. **103** I3
also spelt Qyzylaghash
Kyzyl-Art, Pereval *pass* Kyrg./Tajik. *see* **Kyzylart Pass**
Kyzylart Pass Kyrg./Tajik. **101** H2
also known as Kyzyl-Art,Pereval *or* Qizil-Art, Aghbai
Kyzyl-Burun Azer. *see* **Siyäzän**
Kyzylkesek Kazakh. **88** C2
also spelt Qyzylkesek; *formerly known as* Kyzylkesken
Kyzylkesken Kazakh. *see* **Kyzylkesek**
Kyzyl-Khaya Rus. Fed. **88** E1
Kyzyl-Khem *r.* Rus. Fed. **84** C1
Kyzyl-Kiya Kyrg. *see* **Kyzyl-Kyya**
Kyzylkoga Kazakh. **102** C2
Kyzylkol', Ozero *l.* Kazakh. **103** E2
also known as Qyzylköl
Kyzylkum, Peski *des.* Kazakh./Uzbek. *see* **Kyzylkum Desert**

Kyzylkum Desert Kazakh./Uzbek. **103** F4
also known as Kyzylkum, Peski
Kyzyl-Kyya Kyrg. **103** H4
also spelt Kyzyl-Kiya
Kyzyl-Mazhalyk Rus. Fed. **84** A1
Kyzylorda Kazakh. **103** F3
also spelt Kzyl-Orda *or* Qyzylorda; *formerly known as* Ak-Mechet
Kyzyl-Orda Oblast *admin. div.* Kazakh. *see* **Kzyl-Ordinskaya Oblast'**
Kyzylrabot Tajik. *see* **Qizilrabot**
Kyzylsay Kazakh. **102** C4
formerly known as Özen *or* Uzen'
Kyzyl-Suu Kyrg. **103** I4
formerly known as Pokrovka
Kyzyl-Suu *r.* Kyrg. **103** G5
Kyzyltau Kazakh. **103** H3
also spelt Qyzyltaū
Kyzylzhar Kazakh. **103** G2
also spelt Qyzylzhar; *formerly spelt* Kzyl-Dzhar
Kzyl-Dzhar Kazakh. *see* **Kyzylzhar**
Kzyl-Orda Kazakh. *see* **Kyzylorda**
Kzyl-Ordinskaya Oblast' *admin. div.* Kazakh. **103** E3
English form Kzyl-Orda Oblast; *also known as* Qyzylorda Oblysy
Kzyl-Ordinskoye Vodokhranilishche *resr* Kazakh. **103** F3
Kzyltu Kazakh. *see* **Kishkenekol'**

↓ L

Laage Germany **49** J2
Laagri Estonia **42** F2
La Almunia de Doña Godina Spain **55** J3
La Amistad, Parque Internacional *nat. park* Costa Rica/Panama **186** C5
La Angostura, Presa de *resr* Mex. **185** G6
Lääniste Estonia **42** I3
Laanle *well* Somalia **128** F2
La Antigua, Salina *salt pan* Arg. **204** D3
La Araucania *admin. reg.* Chile **204** B5
La Ardilla, Cerro *mt.* Mex. **185** E4
Laas Aano Somalia **128** F3
Laascaanood Somalia **128** E2
formerly known as Las Anod
La Ascensión, Bahía de *b.* Mex. **185** I5
Laas Dawaco Somalia **128** F2
Laasgoray Somalia **128** F2
La Asunción Venez. **199** F2
Laau Point U.S.A. **181** [inset] Z1

▶**Laâyoune** W. Sahara **122** B4
Capital of Western Sahara. Formerly spelt El Aaiún.

Lab *r.* Yugo. **58** C6
Laba *r.* Rus. Fed. **41** G7
La Babia Mex. **185** E2
La Bahía, Islas de *is* Hond. **186** B3
English form Bay Islands
La Baie Canada **169** G3
formerly known as Port-Alfred
Labala Indon. **75** B5
La Baleine, Grande Rivière de *r.* Canada **168** E2
La Baleine, Petite Rivière de *r.* Canada **168** E2
La Baleine, Rivière à *r.* Canada **169** H1
also known as Whale
La Banda Arg. **204** D2
La Bañeza Spain **54** F2
Labang *Sarawak* Malaysia **77** F2
Labanoras Lith. **42** G6
Labao China *see* **Liujiang**
La Barthe-de-Neste France **50** G9
Labasa Fiji **145** G3
La Baule-Escoublac France **50** D5
Labaz, Ozero *l.* Rus. Fed. **39** J2
Labazhskoye Rus. Fed. **40** J2
Labe *r.* Czech Rep. **49** L5
also known as Elbe (Germany)
Labé Guinea **124** B4
Labelle Canada **169** F4
La Belle U.S.A. **175** D7
Labengke *i.* Indon. **75** B3
La Bénoué, Parc National de *nat. park* Cameroon **125** I4
Laberge, Lake Canada **166** C2
La Bernarde, Sommet de *mt.* France **51** M9
Labi Brunei **77** F1
Labian, Tanjong *pt* *Sabah* Malaysia **77** G1
La Biche *r.* Canada **166** F3
La Biche, Lac *l.* Canada **167** H4
Labin Croatia **56** G3
Labinsk Rus. Fed. **41** G7
Labis Malaysia **76** C2
La Bisbal d'Empordà Spain **55** O3
La Biznaga Mex. **184** C2
Labo Phil. **74** B3
La Bobia, Sierra de *mts* Spain **54** E1
Labobo *i.* Indon. **75** B3
La Bodera *mt.* Spain **55** I3
La Bomu, Réserve de Faune de *nature res.* Dem. Rep. Congo **126** D3
La Boquilla Mex. **184** D3
Labora Namibia **130** C4
Labouchere, Mount *hill* Australia **151** B5
La Boucle du Baoulé, Parc National de *nat. park* Mali **124** C3
Laboué Lebanon **109** H3
Labouheyre France **50** F8
Laboulaye Arg. **204** E4
Labrador *reg.* Canada **169** I2
Labrador City Canada **169** H2
Labrador Sea Canada/Greenland **165** N3
Labrang China *see* **Xiahe**
Lábrea Brazil **200** D1
La Brea Peru **198** A6
La Brède France **50** F8
La Brenne, Parc Naturel Régional de *nature res.* France **50** H6
Labruguière France **51** I9
Labuan Malaysia **77** F1
formerly known as Victoria
Labuan *i.* Malaysia **77** F1
Labuanbajo Indon. **75** B3
Labudalin China *see* **Ergun**
La Bufa, Cerro *mt.* Mex. **185** E5
Labuhan Indon. **77** D4
Labuhanbajo Indon. **75** A5
Labuhanbilik Indon. **76** C2
Labuhanmeringgai Indon. **77** D4
Labuhanruku Indon. **76** B2
Labuk *r.* *Sabah* Malaysia **77** G1
Labuk, Telukan *b.* *Sabah* Malaysia **77** G1
Labuna Indon. **75** C3
Labutta Myanmar **78** A4
Labyrinth, Lake *salt flat* Australia **146** B2
Labytnangi Rus. Fed. **38** G3
Laç Albania **58** A7
Lac *pref.* Chad **120** B6
La Cabrera, Sierra de *mts* Spain **54** E2
La Cadena Mex. **184** D3
La Calderina *mt.* Spain **54** H5
La Calera Chile **204** C4
Lac Allard Canada **169** I3
La Calle Alg. *see* **El Kala**
La Campana Spain **54** F7
Lacanau, Étang de *l.* France **50** E8
Lacandón, Parque Nacional *nat. park* Guat. **185** H5
Lacantún *r.* Mex. **185** H5
La Capelle France **51** J3
Lacapelle-Marival France **50** H8
Laćarak *Vojvodina, Srbija* Yugo. **58** A3
La Carlota Arg. **204** E4
La Carlota Phil. **74** B4
La Carlota Spain **54** G7

La Carolina Spain **55** H6
Laccadive, Minicoy and Amindivi Islands *union terr.* India *see* **Lakshadweep**
Laccadive Islands India **94** B4
also known as Lakshadweep
Lac du Bonnet Canada **167** L5
Lac du Flambeau U.S.A. **172** D5
Lacedaemon Greece *see* **Sparti**
La Ceiba Hond. **186** B4
Lacepede Bay Australia **146** C4
Lacepede Islands Australia **150** C3
Lacha, Ozero *l.* Rus. Fed. **40** F3
La Charité-sur-Loire France **51** J5
La Chartre-sur-le-Loir France **50** G5
La Chartreuse, Massif de *mts* France **51** L7
La Châtaigneraie France **50** F6
La Châtre France **51** H6
La Chaux-de-Fonds Switz. **51** M5
Lachine U.S.A. **173** J5

▶**Lachlan** *r.* Australia **147** D3
5th longest river in Oceania.
oceania [landscapes] ➔ 136–137

La Chorrera Col. **198** C5
La Chorrera Panama **186** D5
Lachung India **97** F4
Lachute Canada **169** F4
Lāči Latvia **42** H6
Laçın Azer. **107** F3
La Ciotat France **51** L9
La Ciudad Mex. **184** D4
Lackawanna U.S.A. **176** G3
Lac La Biche Canada **167** I4
Lac la Martre Canada *see* **Wha Ti**
Lac La Ronge Provincial Park Canada **167** J4
Lac-Mégantic Canada **169** G4
La Cocha Arg. **204** D2
La Cogulla *mt.* Spain **55** L3
La Colorada *Sonora* Mex. **184** C2
La Colorada *Zacatecas* Mex. **185** E4
Lacombe Canada **167** H4
La Comoé, Parc National de *nat. park* Côte d'Ivoire **124** E4
Lacon U.S.A. **174** B3
La Concordia Mex. **185** G5
Laconi *Sardegna* Italy **57** B9
Laconia U.S.A. **177** N2
La Corey Canada **167** I4
La Corne Canada **173** P2
La Corse, Parc Naturel Régional de *nature res.* *Corse* France **56** A6
La Coruña Spain *see* **A Coruña**
La Coubre, Pointe de *pt* France **50** E7
La Crescent U.S.A. **172** B7
La Crete Canada **167** G3
La Croix, Lac *l.* Canada/U.S.A. **172** B2
La Crosse *KS* U.S.A. **178** C4
La Crosse *VA* U.S.A. **176** G9
La Crosse *WI* U.S.A. **172** B7
La Cruz Arg. **204** F3
La Cruz Col. **198** B4
La Cruz Costa Rica **186** B5
La Cruz *Chihuahua* Mex. **184** D3
La Cruz *Sinaloa* Mex. **184** D4
La Cruz *Tamaulipas* Mex. **185** F3
La Cruz Nicaragua **186** B4
La Cruz Uruguay **204** F4
La Cruz, Cerro *mt.* Mex. **185** E5
Lac Thiên Vietnam **79** E5
La Cuenca Alta del Manzanares, Parque Regional de *park* Spain **54** H4
La Cuesta Mex. **185** E2
La Culebra, Sierra de *mts* Spain **54** E3
La Curva Mex. **181** F7
La Cygne U.S.A. **178** D4
Ladainha Brazil **207** L4
Ladakh *reg.* Jammu and Kashmir **96** C2
English form Little Tibet
Ladakh Range *mts* India **96** C2
L'Adamaoua, Massif de *mts* Cameroon **125** I5
Ladang *i.* Thai. **79** B7
Ladd U.S.A. **172** D9
Lądek-Zdrój Poland **49** N5
La Demajagua Cuba **186** C2
also known as Santa Bárbara
La Demanda, Sierra de *mts* Spain **55** H2
La Déroute, Passage de *strait* Channel Is/France **50** D3
La Désirade *i.* Guadeloupe **187** H3
Ladik Turkey **106** C2
Ladismith S. Africa **132** F10
Ladispoli Italy **56** E7
Lādīz Iran **101** E4
Ladnun India **96** B4

▶**Ladoga, Lake** Rus. Fed. **43** M1
2nd largest lake in Europe. Also known as Ladozhskoye Ozero.
europe [landscapes] ➔ 30–31

La Dôle *mt.* Switz. **51** M6
Ladon *r.* Greece **59** C11
Ladong China **87** D3
Ladozhskoye Ozero *l.* Rus. Fed. *see* **Ladoga, Lake**
Ladra *r.* Spain **54** D1
Ladrillero, Canal *sea chan.* Chile **205** A8
Ladrones *terr.* N. Pacific Ocean *see* **Northern Mariana Islands**
Ladrones, Islas *is* Panama **186** C6
Ladu *mt.* India **97** G4
Ladue *r.* Canada/U.S.A. **166** A2
Ladushkin Rus. Fed. **42** B7
historically known as Ludwigsort
Ladva Rus. Fed. **40** E3
Ladva-Vetka Rus. Fed. **40** E3
Ladwa India **96** C3
Lady Ann Strait Canada **165** K2
Lady Barron Australia **147** F5
Ladybrand S. Africa **133** L6
Lady Evelyn Lake Canada **173** M3
Lady Frere S. Africa **133** L8
Lady Grey S. Africa **133** L7
Lady Newnes Bay Antarctica **223** L2
Ladysmith Canada **166** F5
Ladysmith S. Africa **133** N5
Ladysmith U.S.A. **172** B5
Ladyzhenka Kazakh. **103** G2
Ladzhanurges Georgia *see* **Lajanurpekhi**
Lae P.N.G. **73** K8
Lae Thai. **78** C4
Laem Ngop Thai. **79** C5
La Encrucijada Venez. **187** G5
Lærdalsøyri Norway **45** I3
La Escala Spain *see* **L'Escala**
La Esmeralda Arg. **204** D3
La Esmeralda Bol. **201** E5
La Esmeralda Venez. **199** E4
Læsø *i.* Denmark **45** J4
La Esperanza Arg. **204** D5
La Esperanza *Beni* Bol. **200** D3
La Esperanza *Santa Cruz* Bol. **201** E3
La Esperanza Hond. **186** A4
La Estrella Bol. **201** E4
Laeva Estonia **42** H3
Lævvajåk Norway **44** N1
La Falda Arg. **204** D3
La Farge U.S.A. **172** C7
La Fargeville U.S.A. **177** J1
Lafayette *CA* U.S.A. **182** B4
Lafayette *CO* U.S.A. **180** F5
La Fayette U.S.A. **174** C5
Lafayette *IN* U.S.A. **174** C3
Lafayette *LA* U.S.A. **179** D6
Lafayette *NJ* U.S.A. **177** K4
Lafayette *OH* U.S.A. **176** B6
Lafayette *TN* U.S.A. **174** C4
Lafé Cuba **186** B2
Laferté Canada **173** O2

Laferte *r.* Canada **167** G2
La Ferté-Bernard France **50** G4
La Ferté-Gaucher France **51** J4
La Ferté-Macé France **50** F4
La Ferté-St-Aubin France **51** H5
La Ferté-sous-Jouarre France **51** J4
Lafia Nigeria **125** H4
Lafiagi Nigeria **125** G4
Laflamme *r.* Canada **173** P1
Lafleche Canada **167** J5
La Flèche France **50** F5
Lafnitz *r.* Austria **49** N9
La Follette U.S.A. **176** A9
La Fontaine U.S.A. **172** H10
Laforce Canada **173** O3
Laforest Canada **173** L3
La Forest, Lac *l.* Canada **169** G2
La Forêt d'Orient, Parc Naturel Régional de *nature res.* France **51** K4
Laforge Canada **169** F2
Laforge *r.* Canada **169** F2
Lafourche, Bayou *r.* U.S.A. **175** B6
Lafrançaise France **50** H8
La Frégate, Lac de *l.* Canada **169** F2
Lāft Iran **100** C5

▶**La Galite** *i.* Tunisia **123** H1
Most northerly point of Africa.

La Galite, Canal de *sea chan.* Tunisia **123** H1
La Gallareta Arg. **204** E3
Lagamar Brazil **206** G5
Lagan' Rus. Fed. **102** A3
formerly known as Kaspiyskiy
Lagan *r.* Sweden **45** K4
Lagana, Kolpos *b.* Greece **59** B11
Lagané *well* Niger **125** I3
La Garamba, Parc National de *nat. park* Dem. Rep. Congo **126** F3
Lagarto Brazil **202** E4
Lagarto, Serra do *hills* Brazil **206** A10
Lagbar Senegal **124** B3
Lagdo, Lac de *l.* Cameroon **125** I4
Lågen *r.* Norway **45** J3
Lågen *r.* Norway **45** J4
Lagh Bogal *watercourse* Kenya/Somalia **128** D4
Lagh Bor *watercourse* Kenya/Somalia **128** D4
Lagh Kutulo *watercourse* Kenya/Somalia **128** D4
Laghmān *prov.* Afgh. **101** G3
Laghouat Alg. **123** F2
La Gineta Spain **55** J5
Lagkadas Greece **58** E8
also spelt Langadhás
Lagkor Co *salt l.* China **89** D5
La Gloria Col. **198** C2
La Gloria Mex. **185** F3
Lago *prov.* Moz. *see* **Niassa**
Lagoa da Prata Brazil **207** H7
Lagoa Dourada Brazil **207** I7
Lagoa Formosa Brazil **206** G5
Lagoa Santa Brazil **207** J6
Lagoa Vermelha Brazil **203** B9
Lago Belgrano Arg. **205** B7
Lago Cardiel Arg. **205** C8
Lago da Pedra Brazil **202** C3
Lagodekhi Georgia **107** F2
Lagolândia Brazil **206** D2
La Gomera *i.* Canary Is **122** A3
La Gomera Guat. **185** H6
La Gonâve, Île de *i.* Haiti **187** E3
Lagong *i.* Indon. **77** E2
Lagonoy Gulf Phil. **74** B3
Lagoon Creek *r.* Australia **148** C3
Lago Posadas Arg. **205** C7
La Gorce Mountains Antarctica **223** O1

▶**Lagos** Nigeria **125** F5
Former capital of Nigeria. Most populous city in Africa and 6th in the world.
world [cities] ➔ 24–25

Lagos *state* Nigeria **125** F5
Lagos Port. **54** C7
Lagosa Tanz. **129** A6
Lagos de Moreno Mex. **185** E4
Lago Verde Brazil **201** E2
Lago Viedma Arg. **205** B8
Lagran Spain **55** I2
La Grande *r.* Canada **168** E2
La Grande U.S.A. **180** C3
La Grande 2, Réservoir Canada **168** E2
La Grande 3, Réservoir Canada **169** F2
La Grande 4, Réservoir *Que.* Canada **169** F2
La Grande Casse, Pointe de *mt.* France **51** M7
La Grande-Combe France **51** K8
Lagrange Australia **150** C3
La Grange *CA* U.S.A. **182** D4
La Grange *GA* U.S.A. **175** C5
Lagrange U.S.A. **172** H9
La Grange *TX* U.S.A. **179** C6
Lagrange Bay Australia **150** C3
La Gran Sabana *plat.* Venez. **199** F3
La Grita Venez. **198** D2
La Guajira, Península de *pen.* Col. **198** D2
La Guardia Arg. **204** D3
La Guardia Chile **204** C2
La Guardia Spain *see* **A Guardia**
Laguna Brazil **203** B9
Laguna U.S.A. **181** F6
Laguna, Ilha da *i.* Brazil **202** B2
Laguna Beach U.S.A. **182** G8
Laguna Dam U.S.A. **183** J9
Laguna de Laja, Parque Nacional *nat. park* Chile **204** C5
Laguna de Perlas Nicaragua **186** C4
Laguna de Temascal, Parque Natural *nature res.* Mex. **185** F5
Laguna Grande Arg. **205** C8
Laguna Lachua, Parque Nacional *nat. park* Guat. **185** H6
Laguna Mountains U.S.A. **183** H9
Lagunas Chile **200** C5
Lagunas Peru **198** C6
Laguna San Rafael, Parque Nacional *nat. park* Chile **205** B7
Lagunas de Catemaco, Parque Natural *nature res.* Mex. **185** G5
Lagunas de Chacahua, Parque Nacional *nat. park* Mex. **185** F6
Lagunas de Montebello, Parque Nacional *nat. park* Mex. **185** H5
Laguna Yema Arg. **201** E6
Lagunillas Bol. **201** E4
Lagunillas Venez. **198** D2
Laha China **85** J1
La Habana Cuba *see* **Havana**
La Habra U.S.A. **182** G8
Lahad Datu *Sabah* Malaysia **77** G1
Lahad Datu, Telukan *b.* *Sabah* Malaysia **77** G1
La Hague, Cap de *c.* France **50** E3
Lahar India **96** C4
La Harpe U.S.A. **172** C10
Laharpur India **96** D4
Lahat Indon. **76** C3
Lahemaa rahvuspark *nat. park* Estonia **42** G2
Lahepera laht *b.* Estonia **42** F2
La Hève, Cap de *c.* France **50** G3
Lahewa Indon. **76** B2
Laḩij Yemen **104** D5
Laḩij *governorate* Yemen **104** D5
Lahishyn Belarus **42** G9
Lahn *r.* Germany **48** E5
Lahnstein Germany **48** E5
Laholm Sweden **45** K4

Laholmsbukten b. Sweden 45 K4
Lahontan Reservoir U.S.A. 182 E2
Lahore Pak. 101 H4
La Horqueta Venez. 199 F3
La Hotte, Massif de mts Haiti 187 E3
Lahoysk Belarus 42 I7
Lahr (Schwarzwald) Germany 48 E7
Lahri Pak. 101 G4
Lahti Fin. 45 N3
La Huerta Mex. 184 D5
L'Ahzar, Vallée de watercourse Niger 125 F3
Laï Chad 126 C2
Lai'an China 87 F1
also known as Xin'an
Laibach Slovenia see Ljubljana
Laibin China 87 D4
Laie U.S.A. 181 [inset] Z1
Laifeng China 87 D2
also known as Xiangfeng
L'Aigle France 50 G4
Laihia Fin. 44 M3
Lai-hka Myanmar 78 B3
Lai-Hsak Myanmar 78 B3
Laingsburg S. Africa 132 E10
Laingsburg U.S.A. 173 I8
Lainioälven r. Sweden 44 M2
Lainsitz r. Austria 49 M7
Lair U.S.A. 176 A7
L'Aïr, Massif de mts Niger 125 H2
also known as Azbine
L'Aïr et du Ténéré, Réserve Naturelle Nationale de nature res. Niger 125 H2
Lairg U.K. 46 H5
Lais Indon. 76 C3
Lais Phil. 74 C5
La Isabela Cuba 186 C2
Laisälven r. Sweden 44 L2
Laishevo Rus. Fed. 40 I5
La Isla Col. 198 B3
La Isla, Salar de salt flat Chile 204 C2
Laitila Fin. 45 M3
Laivera well Tanz. 129 C6
Laives Italy 56 D2
Laiwu China 85 H4
Laiwui Indon. 75 C3
Laixi China 85 I4
formerly known as Shuiji
Laiyang China 85 I4
Laiyuan China 85 G4
Laizhou China 85 H4
formerly known as Yexian
Laizhou Wan b. China 85 H4
La Jagua Col. 198 C2
Lajamanu Australia 148 A3
Lajanurpekhi Georgia 107 E2
also known as Ladzhanurges
Lajeado Brazil 203 A9
Lajedo Brazil 202 E4
Laje dos Santos i. Brazil 207 G11
Lajes Brazil 203 B8
Lajinha Brazil 207 L7
Lajkovac Srbija Yugo. 58 B4
La Jolla Peak hill U.S.A. 182 F7
Lajosmizse Hungary 49 Q8
La Joya Mex. 184 D3
La Joya Peru 200 C4
La Joya de los Sachas Ecuador 198 B5
Lajta r. Austria/Hungary 49 O8
La Junta Bol. 201 E3
La Junta Mex. 184 D2
La Junta U.S.A. 178 B4
La Juventud, Isla de i. Cuba 186 C2
formerly known as Pines, Isle of or Pinos, Isla de
Lakadiya India 96 A5
L'Akagera, Parc National de nat. park Rwanda see Akagera National Park
Lakathah Saudi Arabia 104 C4
Lakatrask Sweden 44 M2
Lake KY U.S.A. 176 B8
Lake WY U.S.A. 180 E3
Lake Alice N.Z. 152 J8
Lake Andes U.S.A. 178 C3
Lake Arthur U.S.A. 179 D6
Lake Butler U.S.A. 175 D6
Lake Cargelligo Australia 147 E3
Lake Charles U.S.A. 179 D6
Lake City AR U.S.A. 174 B5
Lake City CO U.S.A. 181 F5
Lake City FL U.S.A. 175 D6
Lake City IA U.S.A. 178 D3
Lake City MN U.S.A. 168 A4
Lake City SC U.S.A. 175 E5
Lake City TN U.S.A. 176 A9
Lake Clark National Park and Preserve U.S.A. 164 D3
Lake Clear U.S.A. 177 K1
Lake Coleridge N.Z. 153 F11
Lake Cowichan Canada 166 E5
Lake District National Park U.K. 47 I9
Lake Eyre National Park Australia 146 C2
Lakefield Australia 149 E2
Lakefield Canada 168 E4
Lakefield National Park Australia 149 E2
Lake Fork r. U.S.A. 183 O1
Lake Frome Regional Reserve nature res. Australia 146 C2
Lake Gairdner National Park Australia 146 B2
Lake Geneva U.S.A. 172 E8
Lake Gilles Conservation Park nature res. Australia 146 C3
Lake Grace Australia 151 B7
Lake Gregory Aboriginal Reserve Australia 150 D4
Lake Harbour Canada see Kimmirut
Lake Havasu City U.S.A. 183 J7
Lakehurst U.S.A. 177 K5
Lake Isabella U.S.A. 182 F6
Lake Jackson U.S.A. 179 D6
Lake King Australia 151 B7
Lake King Nature Reserve Australia 151 B7
Lakeland Australia 149 E2
Lakeland FL U.S.A. 175 D7
Lakeland GA U.S.A. 175 D6
Lake Linden U.S.A. 172 E3
Lake Louise Canada 167 G5
Lake Mackay Aboriginal Land res. Australia 148 A4
Lake Magenta Nature Reserve Australia 151 B7
Lake Manyara National Park Tanz. 128 B5
Lake Mburo National Park Uganda 128 A5
Lake Mills U.S.A. 174 A3
Lake Nash Australia 148 C4
Lake Paringa N.Z. 153 D11
Lake Placid U.S.A. 177 L1
Lakeport CA U.S.A. 182 B2
Lakeport MI U.S.A. 173 K7
Lake Providence U.S.A. 175 B5
Lake Pukaki N.Z. 153 E12
La Kéran, Parc National de nat. park Togo 125 F4
Lake Range mts U.S.A. 182 E1
Lake River Canada 168 D2
Lake St Peter Canada 173 O5
Lakes Entrance Australia 147 F4
Lakeshore U.S.A. 182 E4
Lakeside AZ U.S.A. 183 O7
Lakeside CA U.S.A. 183 H9
Lakeside NJ U.S.A. 177 K4
Lake Sumner Forest Park nature res. N.Z. 153 G10
Lake Superior Provincial Park Canada 173 I3
Lake Tekapo N.Z. 153 E12
Lake Torrens National Park Australia 146 C2
Lake Traverse (Sisseton) Indian Reservation res. U.S.A. 178 C2
Lakeview OH U.S.A. 176 B5
Lakeview OR U.S.A. 180 B4
Lake Village U.S.A. 175 B5
Lakeville U.S.A. 174 A2
Lake Wales U.S.A. 175 D7
Lakewood CO U.S.A. 180 F5
Lakewood OH U.S.A. 176 D4
Lakewood WI U.S.A. 172 E5
Lakhdaria Alg. 55 O8
Lakhdenpokh'ya Rus. Fed. 45 O3
Lakheri India 96 C4
Lakhimpur India 96 D4
Lakhipur India 97 G4
Lakhisarai India see Luckeesarai
Lakhish r. Israel 108 F6
Lakhnadon India 96 C5
Lakhpat India 96 A5
Lakhtar India 96 A5
Lakhva r. Belarus 43 L8
Lakin U.S.A. 178 B4
Lakinsk Rus. Fed. 43 U5
formerly known as Lakinskiy
Lakinskiy Rus. Fed. see Lakinsk
Lakitusaki r. Canada 168 D2
Lakki Pak. 101 G3
Lakkoma Greece 59 G8
Lakonikos Kolpos b. Greece 59 D12
Lakor i. Indon. 75 D5
Lakota Côte d'Ivoire 124 D5
Lakota U.S.A. 178 C1
Laksefjorden sea chan. Norway 44 N1
Lakselv Norway 44 N1
Laksfors Norway 44 K2
Lakshadweep is India see Laccadive Islands
Lakshadweep union terr. India 94 B4
formerly known as Laccadive, Minicoy and Amindivi Islands
Laksham Bangl. 97 F5
Lakshettipet India 94 C2
Lakshmeshwar India 94 B3
Lakshmikantapur India 97 F5
Laktyshy Vodaskhovishcha resr Belarus 42 H9
Lala Phil. 74 B5
Lalago Tanz. 128 B5
La Laguna Arg. 204 E4
La Laguna, Picacho de mt. Mex. 184 C4
La Laguna Ojo de Liebre, Parque Natural de nature res. Mex. 184 B3
Lala Musa Pak. 101 H3
Lalapanzi Zimbabwe 131 F3
Lalapaşa Turkey 58 H7
Lalara Gabon 126 A4
Lalaua Moz. 131 H2
L'Albufera l. Spain 55 K5
La Léfini, Réserve de Chasse de nature res. Congo 126 B5
Laleham Australia 149 F4
Lāleh Zār, Kūh-e mt. Iran 100 D4
La Lékoli-Pandaka, Réserve de Faune de nature res. Congo 126 B4
Lalganj India 97 E4
Lalgudi India 94 C4
Lālī Iran 100 B3
Lalibela Eth. 128 C1
La Libertad Ecuador 198 A5
La Libertad El Salvador 185 H6
La Libertad Guat. 185 H5
La Libertad Nicaragua 186 B4
La Libertad dept Peru 200 A2
La Ligua Chile 204 C4
Laliki Indon. 75 C4
Lalimboee Indon. 75 B3
Lalin China 82 B3
Lalin r. China 82 B3
Lalín Spain 54 C2
Lalinde France 50 G8
La Línea de la Concepción Spain 54 F8
Lalitpur India 96 C4
Lalitpur Nepal see Patan
Lal-Lo Phil. 74 B2
Lalmanirhat Bangl. 97 F4
Lalmikor Uzbek. see Lyal'mikar
La Loche Canada 167 I3
La Loche, Lac l. Canada 167 I3
La Loire et de l'Allier, Plaines de plain France 51 J6
La Loma Bol. 201 D5
La Loma Negra, Planicie de plain Arg. 204 D5
La Loupe France 50 H4
La Louvière Belgium 51 K2
Lalpur India 96 A5
Lal'sk Rus. Fed. 40 H3
Lalsot India 96 C4
La Lufira, Lac de retenue de resr Dem. Rep. Congo 127 E7
Laluin i. Indon. 75 C3
Lalung La pass China 89 D6
Lama Bangl. 97 G5
La Macarena, Parque Nacional nat. park Col. 198 C4
La Maddalena Sardegna Italy 56 B7
La Madeleine, Îles de is Canada 169 I4
Lamag Sabah Malaysia 77 G1
La Maiko, Parc National de nat. park Dem. Rep. Congo 126 E5
Lamaing Myanmar 79 B5
La Malbaie Canada 169 G4
La Malinche, Parque Nacional nat. park Mex. 185 F5
La Mancha Mex. 185 E3
La Manche strait France/U.K. see English Channel
La Manga del Mar Menor Spain 55 K7
La Manika, Plateau de Dem. Rep. Congo 127 E7
La Máquina Mex. 184 D2
Lamar CO U.S.A. 178 B4
Lamar MO U.S.A. 178 D4
La Maraoué, Parc National de nat. park Côte d'Ivoire 124 D5
La Marche, Plateaux de France 50 H6
Lamard Iran 100 C5
La Margeride, Monts de mts France 51 J7
Lamarque Arg. 204 D5
La Marque U.S.A. 179 D6
La Martre, Lac l. Canada 167 G2
Lamas r. Turkey 108 F1
La Matanzilla, Pampa de plain Arg. 204 C5
La Mauricie, Parc National de nat. park Canada 169 F4
La Maya Cuba 186 E2
Lamballe France 50 D4
Lambaréné Gabon 126 A5
Lambayeque Peru 198 B6
Lambayeque dept Peru 198 B6
Lambay Island Rep. of Ireland 47 G10
Lambeng Indon. 77 F3
Lambert atoll Marshall Is see Ailinglapalap
Lambert, Cape Australia 150 B4

▶Lambert Glacier Antarctica 223 E2
Largest series of glaciers in the world.

Lambert's Bay S. Africa 132 C9
Lambertville U.S.A. 177 K5
Lambeth Canada 173 L8
Lambi India 96 B3
Lambina Australia 146 B1
Lambro r. Italy 56 B3
Lam Chi r. Thai. 78 D5
Lam Chi r. Thai. 79 C5
La Media Luna, Arrecife de reef Hond. 186 C4
La Medjerda, Monts de mts Alg. 57 A12
Lamego Port. 54 D3
La Mejorada Peru 200 B3
Lamen Vanuatu 145 F3
Lamèque, Île i. Canada 169 H4
La Merced Arg. 204 D3
La Merced Peru 200 B2
Lameroo Australia 146 D3
La Mesa U.S.A. 183 G9
Lamesa U.S.A. 179 B5
L'Ametlla de Mar Spain 55 L4
Lamezia Italy 57 I10
Lamhar Touil, Sabkhet imp. l. W. Sahara 122 A5
Lamia Greece 59 D10
Lamigan Point Phil. 74 C5
Lamington National Park Australia 147 G2
Lamir Iran 100 B2
La Mirada U.S.A. 182 F8
formerly known as Mirada Hills
La Misa Mex. 184 C2
La Misión Mex. 183 H9
Lamitan Phil. 74 B5
Lamma Island Hong Kong China 87 [inset]
also known as Pok Liu Chau
Lammerkop S. Africa 133 N2
Lammerlaw Range mts N.Z. 153 D13
Lammermuir Hills U.K. 46 J8
Lammhult Sweden 45 K4
Lammi Fin. 45 N3
Lammijärv lake channel Estonia/Rus. Fed. 42 I3
La Moille U.S.A. 172 D9
Lamoille r. U.S.A. 177 L1
La Moine r. U.S.A. 174 B4
La Mojonera Spain 55 I8
Lamon Bay Phil. 74 B3
Lamone r. Italy 56 E4
Lamongan Indon. 77 F4
Lamoni U.S.A. 174 A3
Lamont U.S.A. 182 F6
La Montagne d'Ambre, Parc National de nat. park Madag. 131 [inset] K2
La Montagne de Reims, Parc Naturel Régional de nature res. France 51 J3
La Morita Chihuahua Mex. 184 D2
La Morita Coahuila Mex. 185 E2
Lamotrek atoll Micronesia 73 K5
La Motte Canada 173 O2
Lamotte-Beuvron France 51 I5
La Motte-Servolex France 51 L7
La Mougalaba, Réserve de nature res. Gabon 126 A5
La Moure U.S.A. 178 C2
Lampa Peru 200 C3
Lampang Thai. 78 B4
Lam Pao Reservoir Thai. 78 C4
Lampasas U.S.A. 179 C6
Lampasas r. U.S.A. 179 C6
Lampazos Mex. 185 E3
Lampedusa, Isola di i. Sicilia Italy 57 E13
Lampeland Norway 45 J4
Lampeter U.K. 47 H11
also known as Llanbedr
Lamphun Thai. 78 B4
Lam Plai Mat r. Thai. 79 C5
Lampozhnya Rus. Fed. 40 H2
Lampsacus Turkey see Lâpseki
Lampung prov. Indon. 76 D4
Lampung, Teluk b. Indon. 76 D4
Lam Si Bai r. Thai. 79 D5
Lamta India 96 D5
Lam Tin Hong Kong China 87 [inset]
Lamu Kenya 128 D5
Lamu Myanmar 78 A4
La Muela mt. Spain 55 J5
La Mure France 51 L8
Lana Australia 149 D4
Lana Italy 56 D2
Lanai i. U.S.A. 181 [inset] Z1
also known as Ranai
Lanai City U.S.A. 181 [inset] Z1
La Nao, Cabo de c. Spain 55 L6
Lanao, Lake Phil. 74 C5
Lanark Canada 173 Q5
Lanark U.K. 46 I8
Lanark U.S.A. 172 D8
Lanas Sabah Malaysia 77 G1
Lanbi Kyun i. Myanmar 79 B6
also known as Sullivan Island
Lanboyan Point Phil. 74 B4
Lancang China 86 A4
also known as Menglang
Lancang Jiang r. China see Mekong
Lancaster Canada 177 J1
Lancaster U.K. 47 J9
Lancaster CA U.S.A. 182 F7
Lancaster KY U.S.A. 176 A8
Lancaster MO U.S.A. 174 A3
Lancaster NH U.S.A. 177 N1
Lancaster OH U.S.A. 176 C6
Lancaster PA U.S.A. 177 I5
Lancaster SC U.S.A. 174 D5
Lancaster VA U.S.A. 177 I8
Lancaster WI U.S.A. 172 C8
Lancaster Sound strait Canada 165 K2
Lancelin Australia 151 A6
Lanch'khut'i Georgia 107 E2
Lanchow China see Lanzhou
Lanciano Italy 56 G6
Lancing U.S.A. 176 A9
Lanco Chile 204 B5
Lancun China 85 I4
Łańcut Poland 49 T5
Lancy Switz. 51 M6
Landak r. Indon. 77 E3
Landana Angola see Cacongo
Landau an der Isar Germany 49 J7
Landau in der Pfalz Germany 48 F6
Landeck Austria 48 H8
Lander watercourse Australia 148 A4
Lander U.S.A. 180 E4
Landerneau France 50 B4
Landes reg. France 50 E8
Landes de Gascogne, Parc Naturel Régional des nature res. France 50 F8
Landes de Lanvaux reg. France 50 D5
Landes du Mené reg. France 50 D4
Landfall Island India 95 G3
Landik, Gunung mt. Indon. 76 C3
Landis Canada 167 I4
Landivisiau France 50 B4
Landless Corner Zambia 127 F8
Land O' Lakes U.S.A. 172 D4
Landön Sweden 44 K3
Landor Australia 151 B5
Landquart Switz. 51 P5
Landrienne Canada 173 P2
Landrum U.S.A. 174 D5
Landsberg Poland see Gorzów Wielkopolski
Landsberg am Lech Germany 48 H7
Landsborough r. N.Z. 153 D11
Land's End pt U.K. 47 G13
Landshut Germany 48 J7
Landskrona Sweden 45 K5
La Nedei mt. Romania 58 E3
La Negra Chile 200 C5
Lane Pool Reserve nature res. Australia 151 B7
La Neuveville Switz. 51 N5
Lanfeng China see Lankao
Lang, Nam r. Myanmar 78 B2
La Nga r. Vietnam 79 D6
Lan'ga Co l. China 89 C6
Langadhás Greece see Lagkadas
Langai r. India 97 G4
Långan r. Sweden 44 K3
Langao China 87 D1
Langar Badakhshān Afgh. 101 H2
Langar Parvān Afgh. 101 G3
Langar Iran 101 E3
Langar Uzbek. 103 F5
formerly spelt Lyangar
Langar Uzbek. see Lyangar
Langara Indon. 75 B4
Langberg mts S. Africa 132 G5
Langdon U.S.A. 178 C1
Langeac France 51 J7
Langeais France 50 G5
Langebaan S. Africa 132 C10
Langeberg mts S. Africa 132 D10
Langehorn S. Africa 133 I3
Langeland i. Denmark 45 J5
Langelands Bælt strait Denmark 45 J5
Längelmäki Fin. 45 N3
Längelmävesi l. Fin. 40 C3
Langen Germany 48 F2
Langenburg Canada 167 K5
Langenlois Austria 49 M7
Langenthal Switz. 51 N5
Langeoog Germany 48 E2
Langeoog i. Germany 48 E2
Langepas Rus. Fed. 38 H3
Langesund Norway 45 J4
Langfang China 85 H4
also known as Anci
Långfjallets naturreservat nature res. Sweden 45 K3
Langgapayung Indon. 76 C2
Langgar China 89 F6
Langgöns Germany 48 F5
Langham Canada 167 J4
Langhko Myanmar 78 B3
Langholm S. Africa 133 K10
Langholm U.K. 47 J8
Langjökull ice cap Iceland 44 [inset] B2
Langka Indon. 76 B1
Langkawi i. Malaysia 76 B1
Langkesi, Kepulauan is Indon. 75 C4
Lang Kha Toek, Khao mt. Thai. 79 B6
Langkip S. Africa 132 E5
Langkon Sabah Malaysia 77 G1
Langlade Canada 173 R2
Langley Canada 166 F5
Langley U.S.A. 176 C8
Langlo watercourse Australia 149 E5
Langmusi China see Dagcanglhamo
Langogne France 51 J8
Langon France 50 F8
Langong, Xé r. Laos 78 D4
Langøya i. Norway 44 K1
Langqi China 87 F3
Langreo Spain 54 F1
Langres France 51 L5
Langres, Plateau de France 51 K5
Langsa Indon. 76 B1
Langsa, Teluk b. Indon. 76 B1
Långsele Sweden 44 L3
Langshan China 85 E3
Lang Shan mts China 85 E3
Langslett Norway 44 M1
Lang Son Vietnam 78 D3
Langtang National Park Nepal 97 E3
Langtao Myanmar 78 B2
Långträsk Sweden 44 M2
Langtry TX U.S.A. 179 B6
Languan China see Lantian
Languedoc-Roussillon admin. reg. France 51 I10
Languiaru r. Brazil see Iquê
Languiñeo Arg. 205 C6
Langundu, Tanjung pt Indon. 77 G5
Långvinds bruk Sweden 45 L3
Langwedel Germany 48 G3
Langya Shan mt. China 85 G4
Langzhong China 86 C2
Laniel Canada 173 N3
Lanigan Canada 167 J5
Lanín, Parque Nacional nat. park Arg. 204 C5
Lanín, Volcán vol. Arg./Chile 204 C5
Lanjak, Bukit mt. Sarawak Malaysia 77 E2
Lanji India 96 D5
Lanka country Asia see Sri Lanka
Lankao China 87 E1
formerly known as Lanfeng
Länkäran Azer. 107 G3
also spelt Lenkoran'
Lan Kok Tsui pt Hong Kong China see Black Point
Lanlacuni Bajo Peru 200 C3
Lannemezan France 50 G9
Lannion France 50 C4
L'Annonciation Canada 169 F4
La Noria Bol. 201 E3
La Noria Mex. 184 D4
Lansdale U.S.A. 177 J5
L'Anse U.S.A. 172 E4
L'Anse-St-Jean Canada 169 G3
Lansford U.S.A. 177 J5
Lansing r. Canada 166 C2
Lansing IA U.S.A. 172 B7

▶Lansing MI U.S.A. 173 I8
State capital of Michigan.

Länsi-Suomi prov. Fin. 44 M3
Lansjärv Sweden 44 M2
Lanta, Ko i. Thai. 79 B7
Lantau Island Hong Kong China 87 [inset]
also known as Tai Yue Shan
Lantau Peak hill Hong Kong China 87 [inset]
also known as Fung Wong Shan
Lanterne r. France 51 M5
Lantian China see Lianyuan
Lantian China 87 D1
also known as Languan
Lanusei Sardegna Italy 57 B9
Lanuza Phil. 74 C4
Lanuza Bay Phil. 74 C4
Lanxi Heilong. China 82 B3
Lanxi Zhejiang China 87 F2
Lanxian China 85 F4
also known as Dongcun
Lanya Sudan 128 A3
Lanyi r. China 85 F4
Lan Yü i. Taiwan 87 G4
Lanzarote i. Canary Is 122 B3
Lanzhou China 84 D4
also spelt Lanchow
Lanzijing China 85 I2
Lanzo Torinese Italy 51 N7
Lao r. Italy 57 H9
Lao, Mae r. Thai. 78 B4
Laoag Phil. 74 B2
Laoang Phil. 74 C3
Laobie Shan mts China 86 A4
Laobukou China 87 D3
Lao Cai Vietnam 78 C3
Laodicea Syria see Latakia
Laodicea Turkey see Denizli
Laodicea ad Lycum Turkey see Denizli
Laodicea ad Mare Syria see Latakia
Laofengkou China 88 C2
Laoha r. China 85 I3
Laoheishan China 82 C4
Laohekou China 87 D1
formerly known as Guanghua
Laohutun China 85 I4
Laojunmiao China see Yumen
La Okapi, Parc National de nat. park Dem. Rep. Congo 126 E4
Lao Ling mts China 82 B4
Laolong China see Longchuan
Laon France 51 J3
Laona U.S.A. 172 E5
La Oroya Peru 200 B2

▶Laos country Asia 78 C4
asia [countries] ▶▶▶ 64–67

Laoshan China 85 I4
also known as Licun
Laoshan Shuidao sea chan. China see Bohai Haixia
Laotougou China 82 C4
Laotuding Shan hill China 82 B4
Laou, Oued r. Morocco 54 F9
La Ouandja-Vakaga, Réserve de Faune de nature res. Cent. Afr. Rep. 126 D2
Laoudi-Ba Côte d'Ivoire 124 E4
L'Aouk-Aoakole, Réserve de Faune de nature res. Cent. Afr. Rep. 126 D2
Laowohi pass Jammu and Kashmir see Khardung La
Laoximiao China 84 D3
Laoye Ling mts China 82 C4
Lapa Brazil 203 B8
Lapac i. Phil. 74 B5
Lapachito Arg. 204 F2
Lapai Nigeria 125 G4
Lapalisse France 51 J6
La Palma i. Canary Is 122 A3
La Palma Panama 186 D5
La Palma U.S.A. 183 M9
La Palma del Condado Spain 54 E7
La Paloma Uruguay 204 G4
La Pampa prov. Arg. 204 D5
formerly known as Eva Perón
La Panza Range mts U.S.A. 182 D6
La Paragua Venez. 199 F3
La Paramera, Puerto de pass Spain 54 G4
La Paramera, Sierra de mts Spain 54 F4
Laparan i. Phil. 74 A5
La Parata, Pointe de pt Corse France 56 A7
La Paya, Parque Nacional nat. park Col. 198 C4
La Paz Entre Ríos Arg. 204 F3
La Paz Mendoza Arg. 204 D4

▶La Paz Bol. 200 C4
Official capital of Bolivia.
world [countries] ▶▶▶ 10–11
southamerica [contrasts] ▶▶▶ 194–195

La Paz dept Bol. 200 C3
La Paz Hond. 186 B4
La Paz Mex. 184 C3
La Paz Nicaragua 186 B4
Lapaz U.S.A. 172 G9
La Paz Venez. 198 C2
La Paz, Bahía b. Mex. 184 C3
La Pedrera Col. 198 D5
Lapeer U.S.A. 173 J7
La Pelada Arg. 204 E3
La Peña Panama 186 C5
La Pendjari, Parc National de nat. park Benin 125 F4
La Perla Mex. 184 D2
La Pérouse Strait Japan/Rus. Fed. 90 G2
also known as Sōya-kaikyō
La Pesca Mex. 185 F4
La Piedad Mex. 185 E4
La Pila, Sierra de mts Spain 55 J6
La Pine U.S.A. 180 B4
Lapinig Phil. 74 C3
Lapinlahti Fin. 44 N3
La Pintada Panama 186 C5
Laplace U.S.A. 175 B6
Lap Lae Thai. 78 C4
La Plaine Ouanga, Réserve de nature res. Gabon 126 A5
Laplandskiy Zapovednik nature res. Rus. Fed. 44 P2
La Plata Arg. 204 F4
formerly known as Eva Perón
La Plata MD U.S.A. 177 I7
La Plata MO U.S.A. 178 D3
La Plata, Río de sea chan. Arg./Uruguay 204 F4
La Plaza Spain 54 E1
La Plonge, Lac l. Canada 167 J4
Lapmežciems Latvia 42 E4
La Pobla de Segur Spain 55 L2
La Pola de Gordón Spain 54 F2
La Poma Arg. 200 D6
Lapominka Rus. Fed. 40 G2
La Porte U.S.A. 174 C3
Laporte U.S.A. 177 I4
Laporte, Mount Canada 166 E2
Laposo, Bukit mt. Indon. 75 A4
La Potherie, Lac l. Canada 169 F1
Lapovo Srbija Yugo. 58 C4
La Poyata Col. 198 C3
Lappajärvi l. Fin. 44 M3
Lappeenranta Fin. 45 O3
Lappi Fin. 45 M3
Lappi prov. Fin. 44 N2
Lappland reg. Europe 44 L2
Lappohja Fin. 42 E2
Lappträsk Sweden 44 M2
La Prida Arg. 204 E5
La Pryor U.S.A. 179 C6
Lâpseki Turkey 106 A2
historically known as Lampsacus
Laptevo Rus. Fed. see Yasnogorsk
Laptev Sea Rus. Fed. 39 M2
also known as Laptevykh, More
Laptevykh, More sea Rus. Fed. see Laptev Sea
Lapua Fin. 44 M3
Lapuanjoki r. Fin. 44 M3
La Puebla Spain see Sa Pobla
La Puebla del Río Spain 54 E7
La Puebla de Montalbán Spain 54 G5
La Puerta Catamarca Arg. 204 D3
La Puerta Córdoba Arg. 204 E3
La Puerta Venez. 198 D2
Lapu-Lapu Phil. 74 B4
La Punilla, Cordillera de mts Chile 204 C3
Lapurdum France see Bayonne
Lăpuşnicu Mare Romania 58 C4
Lapušnik Kosovo, Srbija Yugo. 58 B6
Łapy Poland 49 T3
Laqiya Arbain well Sudan 121 F4
La Quiaca Arg. 200 D5
L'Aquila Italy 56 F6
La Quinta U.S.A. 183 H8
Lār Iran 100 C5
Lara Australia 147 E4
Lara state Venez. 198 D2
Laracha Spain 54 C1
Larache Morocco 122 D2
formerly spelt El Araïche; historically known as Lixus
Laragne-Montéglin France 51 L8
Lārak i. Iran 100 D5
Laramie U.S.A. 180 F4
Laramie r. U.S.A. 180 F4
Laramie Mountains U.S.A. 180 F4
Laranda Turkey see Karaman
Laranjal Brazil 199 G6
Laranjal Paulista Brazil 206 F10
Laranjeiras Brazil 202 E4
Laranjeiras do Sul Brazil 203 A8
Laranjinha r. Brazil 206 C9
Larantuka Indon. 75 B5
Larat i. Indon. 73 H8
La Raygat reg. W. Sahara 122 B5
Larba Alg. 55 O8
L'Arbresle France 51 K7
Lärbro Sweden 45 L4
L'Archipélago de Mingan, Réserve du Parc National de nat. park Canada 169 I3
Larchwood Canada 173 L4
L'Ardenne, Plateau de Belgium see Ardennes
Larder Lake Canada 173 N2
Larder Lake l. Canada 173 N2
Laredo Spain 55 H1
Laredo U.S.A. 179 C7
La Reforma Sonora Mex. 181 E7
La Reforma Veracruz Mex. 185 F4
La Reina Adelaida, Archipiélago de is Chile 205 B9
English form Queen Adelaide Islands
La Reine Canada 173 N2
La Réole France 50 F8
Largeau Chad see Faya
L'Argentière-la-Bessée France 51 M8
Largo U.S.A. 175 D7
Largo, Cayo i. Cuba 186 C2
Largs U.K. 46 H8
Lāri Iran 100 A2
L'Ariana Tunisia 123 H1
also spelt Aryanah
Lariang Indon. 75 A3
Lariang r. Indon. 75 A3
Larimore U.S.A. 178 C1
La Rinconada Spain 54 F7
Larino Italy 56 G7
La Rioja Arg. 204 D3
La Rioja prov. Arg. 204 D3
La Rioja aut. comm. Spain 55 I2
Larionovo Rus. Fed. 43 L1
Larisa Greece 59 D9
also known as Yenisehir; also spelt Larissa
Larissa Greece see Larisa
Laristan reg. Iran 100 D5
Larkana Pak. 101 G5
Lark Harbour Canada 169 J3
Lar Koh mt. Afgh. 101 E3
Lark Passage Australia 149 E2
L'Arli, Parc National de nat. park Burkina 125 F4
L'Arli, Réserve Partielle de nature res. Burkina 125 F4
Larnaca Cyprus 108 E3
also spelt Larnaka
Larnaka Cyprus see Larnaca
Larne U.K. 47 G9
Larned U.S.A. 178 C4
Laro Cameroon 125 I4
La Robe Noire, Lac de l. Canada 169 I3
La Robla Spain 54 F2
La Roche-en-Ardenne Belgium 51 L2
La Rochefoucauld France 50 G7
La Rochelle France 50 E6
La Roche-sur-Yon France 50 E6
La Roda Spain 55 I5
La Romana Dom. Rep. 187 F3
La Ronge Canada 167 J4
La Ronge, Lac l. Canada 167 J4
La Rosa Mex. 185 E3
La Rosa de Castilla Mex. 183 H9
La Rosita Mex. 185 E2
Larouco, Serra do mts Spain 54 D3
Larrey Point Australia 150 B3
Larrimah Australia 148 B2
Larrimah Aboriginal Land res. Australia 148 B2
also known as Wubalawun
Lars Christensen Coast Antarctica 223 E2

▶Larsen Ice Shelf Antarctica 222 T2
antarctica [features] ▶▶▶ 212–213

Larsnes Norway 44 I3
La Rubia Arg. 204 E3
Larvik Norway 45 J4
Lar'yak Rus. Fed. 39 I3
Larzac, Causse du plat. France 51 J8
La Sabana Arg. 204 F2
La Sabana Col. 198 D4
Las Adjuntas, Presa de resr Mex. 185 F4
La Sal U.S.A. 183 O3
La Sal, Cerros de mts Peru 200 B2
La Sal Junction U.S.A. 183 O3
La Salle Canada 169 F4
La Salle U.S.A. 174 B3
La Salonga Nord, Parc National de nat. park Dem. Rep. Congo 126 D5
La Salonga Sud, Parc National de nat. park Dem. Rep. Congo 126 D5
Las Animas U.S.A. 178 B4
Las Ánimas, Punta pt Mex. 184 B2
Las Anod Somalia see Laascaanood
La Sarre Canada 168 E3
La Sauvette hill France 51 M9
Las Aves, Islas is West Indies 187 G5
short form Aves
Las Avispas Arg. 204 E3
Las Avispas Mex. 184 C2
La Savonnière, Lac l. Canada 169 F2
Las Bonitas Venez. 199 E3
Las Breñas Arg. 204 E2
Las Chapas Arg. 205 D6
La Scie Canada 169 K3
Las Conchas Bol. 201 F4
Las Cruces Mex. 184 D2
Las Cruces CA U.S.A. 182 D7
Las Cruces NM U.S.A. 181 F6
La Selle mt. Haiti 187 F3
La Serena Chile 204 C3
La Serena, Embalse de resr Spain 54 F6
Las Esperanças Mex. 185 E3
Las Estancias, Sierra de mts Spain 55 I7
Las Flores Buenos Aires Arg. 204 F5
Las Flores Salta Arg. 201 E6
Lashburn Canada 167 I4
Las Heras Arg. 204 C4
Las Hermosas, Parque Nacional nat. park Col. 198 C4
Las Herreras Mex. 184 D3
Lashio Myanmar 78 B3
Lashkar Gāh Afgh. 101 F4
Las Horquetas Arg. 205 C8
La Sila reg. Italy 57 I9
Łasin Poland 49 Q2
Las Juntas Chile 204 C3
Las Lajas Arg. 204 C5
Las Lajitas Venez. 199 E3
Las Lavaderos Mex. 185 F4
Las Lomas Peru 198 A6
Las Lomitas Arg. 201 E6
Las Marismas marsh Spain 54 E7
Las Martinetas Arg. 205 D7
Las Médulas tourist site Spain 54 E2
Las Mercedes Venez. 199 E2
Las Mesteñas Mex. 184 D2
Las Minas Venez. 199 E2
Las Minas, Sierra de mts Guat. 185 H6
Las Mulatas is Panama see San Blas, Archipiélago de
Las Nieves Mex. 184 D3
Las Nopaleras, Cerro mt. Mex. 185 E3
La Solana Spain 55 H6
Lasolo, Teluk b. Indon. 75 B3
Las Orquídeas, Parque Nacional nat. park Col. 198 B3
La Souterraine France 50 H6
Las Ovejas Arg. 204 C5
Las Palmas watercourse Mex. 183 G9
Las Palmas Panama 186 C5

▶Las Palmas de Gran Canaria Canary Is 122 B3
Joint capital of the Canary Islands.

Las Perlas, Archipiélago de is Panama 186 D5
Las Petas Bol. 201 F4
La Spezia Italy 56 B4
Las Piedras Uruguay 204 F4
Las Piedras, Río de r. Peru 200 C3
Las Pipinas Arg. 204 F4
Las Planchas Hond. 186 B4
Las Plumas Arg. 205 D6
Laspur Pak. 101 H2
Las Rosas Arg. 204 E4
Las Rozas de Madrid Spain 54 H4
Las Salinas, Pampa de salt pan Arg. 204 D3
Lassance Brazil 207 I4
Lassay-les-Châteaux France 50 F4
Lassen Peak vol. U.S.A. 182 C1
Lassen Volcanic National Park U.S.A. 182 C1
Las Tablas Panama 186 C6
Las Tablas de Daimiel, Parque Nacional de nat. park Spain 55 H5
Lastarria, Parque Nacional de nat. park Chile 205 B7
Last Chance U.S.A. 178 B4
Las Termas Arg. 204 D2
Last Mountain Lake Canada 167 J5
Las Torres de Cotillas Spain 55 J6
Las Tórtolas, Cerro mt. Chile 204 C3

index

L

Lastoursville Gabon 126 B5
Lastovo i. Croatia 56 I6
Lastovski Kanal sea chan. Croatia 56 I6
Las Tres Vírgenes, Volcán vol. Mex. 184 B3
Las Trincheras Venez. 199 E3
Las Tunas Cuba 186 D2
Lasva Estonia 42 I4
Las Varas Col. 199 D3
Las Varas Chihuahua Mex. 184 D2
Las Varas Nayarit Mex. 184 D4
Las Varas Venez. 198 D3
Las Varillas Arg. 204 E3
Las Vegas NM U.S.A. 181 F6
Las Vegas NV U.S.A. 183 I5
Las Villuercas mt. Spain 54 F5
Las Yaras Peru 200 C4
Lata Solomon Is 145 F3
La Tabatière Canada 169 J3
Latacunga Ecuador 198 B5
Latady Island Antarctica 222 S2
La Tagua Col. 198 C5
Latakia Syria 108 G2
also known as Lattaquié; also spelt Al Lādhiqīyah; historically known as Laodicea or Laodicea ad Mare
Latalata i. Indon. 75 C3
Latchford Canada 173 N3
Latehar India 97 E5
La Teignouse, Passage de strait France 50 C5
Late Island Tonga 145 H3
also known as Late Island or Lette Island
Latemar mt. Italy 56 D2
La Teste France 50 E8
La Tetilla, Cerro mt. Mex. 184 D4
Latgales Augstiene reg. Latvia 42 I5
Latham Australia 151 B6
Lathi India 96 A5
Lathrop U.S.A. 182 C4
Lātīdān Iran 100 C5
Latimojong Mountains Reserve nature res. Indon. 75 B3
Latina Italy 56 E7
Latisana Italy 56 F3
La Toma Arg. 204 D4
La Tortue, Île de i. Haiti 187 E2
La Tortuga, Isla i. Venez. 199 E2
Latorytsya r. Ukr. 49 T7
Latouche Treville, Cape Australia 150 C3
Latouma well Niger 123 I5
La Tour-du-Pin France 51 L7
La Tranquera, Embalse de resr Spain 55 J3
La Tremblade France 50 E7
La Trinidad Nicaragua 186 B4
La Trinidad Phil. 74 B2
La Trinitaria Mex. 185 G5
La Trinité France 51 N9
Latrobe Australia 147 E5
Latrobe U.S.A. 176 F5
Latronico Italy 57 I8
La Troya r. Arg. 204 C3
La Truite, Lac à l. Canada 173 O3
Latskoye Rus. Fed. 43 T3
Lattaquié Syria see Latakia
Latte Island Tonga see Late Island
Lattes France 51 J9
Latulipe Canada 173 N3
La Tuque Canada 169 F4
Latur India 94 C2
Latvia country Europe 42 E5
spelt Latvija in Latvian; formerly known as Latviyskaya S.S.R.
europe [countries] 32–35
Latvija country Europe see Latvia
Latviyskaya S.S.R. country Europe see Latvia
Lau Nigeria 125 H4
Lau r. Sudan 128 A3
Laua r. India 97 E5
Lauban waterhole Namibia 130 D3
Lauca, Parque Nacional nat. park Chile 200 C4
Lauenburg (Elbe) Germany 48 H2
Lauf an der Pegnitz Germany 48 I6
Laufen Germany 49 J8
Laufen Switz. 51 N5
Laugarbakki Iceland 44 [inset] B2
Lauge Koch Kyst reg. Greenland 165 M2
Laughland Lake Canada 167 M1
Laughlen, Mount Australia 148 B4
Laughlin Peak U.S.A. 181 F5
Lauhanvuoren kansallispuisto nat. park Fin. 45 M3
Lauka Estonia 42 D3
Laukaa Fin. 44 N3
Laukuva Lith. 42 D6
Laun Thai. 79 B6
Launay Canada 173 O2
Launceston Australia 147 E5
Launceston U.K. 47 H13
Launglon Myanmar 79 B5
Launglon Bok Islands Myanmar 79 B5
La Unidad Mex. 185 G6
La Unión Bol. 201 E3
La Unión Chile 204 B6
La Unión Col. 198 B4
La Unión El Salvador 185 I6
La Unión Hond. 186 B4
La Unión Mex. 185 E5
La Unión Huánuco Peru 200 A2
La Unión Piura Peru 198 A6
La Unión Spain 55 K7
Laur Phil. 74 B3
Laura Australia 149 E2
La Urbana Venez. 199 E3
Laurel DE U.S.A. 177 J7
Laurel MS U.S.A. 175 B6
Laurel MT U.S.A. 180 E3
Laureldale U.S.A. 177 J5
Laureles Para. 201 F6
Laurel Hill hills U.S.A. 176 F6
Laurencekirk U.K. 46 J7
Laurens IA U.S.A. 178 D3
Laurens SC U.S.A. 174 D5
Laurentides, Réserve Faunique des nature res. Canada 169 G4
Lauri India 96 D4
Lauria Italy 57 H8
Laurie Island S. Atlantic Ocean 222 V2
Laurinburg U.S.A. 174 E5
Lauriston N.Z. 153 F11
Laurium U.S.A. 172 E3
Lauru i. Solomon Is see Choiseul
Lausanne Switz. 51 M6
Lausitzer Grenzwall park Germany 49 K4
Laut i. Indon. 77 E1
Laut i. Indon. 77 E3
Laut i. Indon. 77 G3
Laut, Selat sea chan. Indon. 77 F3
Lauta Germany 49 L4
Lautaro Chile 204 B5
Lautaro, Cerro vol. Chile 205 B8
Lautem East Timor 75 C5
Lauterbrunnen Switz. 51 N6
Lautersbach (Hessen) Germany 48 G5
Laut Kecil, Kepulauan is Indon. 77 F4
Lautoka Fiji 145 G3
Laut Taka Bonerate National Park Indon. 75 B4
Lauttawar, Danau l. Indon. 76 B1
Lauvsnes Norway 44 J2
Lauvuskylä Fin. 44 O3
Lauwersmeer l. Neth. 48 D2
Lava r. Rus. Fed. 49 S1
Lava Beds National Monument nat. park U.S.A. 180 B4
Lavaca r. U.S.A. 179 C6
Laval Canada 169 F4
Laval France 50 F4
Lavalette U.S.A. 176 C7
Lāvān Iran 100 C5
La Vanoise, Massif de mts France 51 M7
La Vanoise, Parc National de nat. park France 51 M7
Lavant r. Austria/Slovenia 49 L9
Lavapié, Punta pt Chile 204 B5
Lāvar Iran 100 B4
Lavara Greece 58 H7
Lavaraty Madag. 131 [inset] J4
Lavardac France 50 G8
Lāvar Meydān salt marsh Iran 100 C4
La Vassako-Bolo, Réserve National Intégral de nature res. Cent. Afr. Rep. 126 C2
Lavaur France 50 H9
Laveaga Peak U.S.A. 182 C5
La Vega Dom. Rep. 187 F3
La Vela Venez. 187 F5
La Vela, Cabo de c. Col. 198 C1
Lavello Italy 56 H7
La Venada r. Mex. 179 B6
Laveno Italy 56 A3
La Venta Hond. 186 B4
La Ventana, Sierra de mts Arg. 204 E5
Laventie France 51 I2
La Venturosa Col. 198 D3
La Vérendrye, Réserve Faunique de nature res. Canada 168 E4
Laverne U.S.A. 178 C4
Laverton Australia 151 C6
Lavia Fin. 45 M3
La Víbora Mex. 185 E3
La Victoria Venez. 187 G5
Lavieille, Lake Canada 173 O5
Lavigne Canada 173 M4
La Viña Arg. 204 D2
La Viña Peru 198 B6
Lavina U.S.A. 180 E3
La Virgen, Sierra de mts Spain 55 J3
Lavit France 50 G9
La Vôge reg. France 51 M4
Lavongai i. P.N.G. see New Hanover
Lavoriškės Lith. 42 G7
La Voulte-sur-Rhône France 51 K8
Lavras Brazil 203 C7
Lavrio Greece 59 F11
Lavrovo Orlovskaya Oblast' Rus. Fed. 43 R9
Lavrovo Vologod. Obl. Rus. Fed. 43 S2
Lavumisa Swaziland 133 P4
formerly known as Gollel
Lavushi-Manda National Park Zambia 127 F8
Lawa r. Liberia 124 C5
Lawa Myanmar 78 B2
Lawagamau r. Canada 168 E3
Lawan India 97 D5
Lawang i. Indon. 77 G5
Lawashi r. Canada 168 D2
Lawdar Yemen 105 D5
Law Dome ice feature Antarctica 223 H2
Lawele Indon. 75 B4
Lawik Reef P.N.G. 149 G1
Lawit, Gunung mt. Indon./Malaysia 77 F2
Lawit, Gunung mt. Malaysia 76 C1
Lawksawk Myanmar 78 B3
Lawn Hill Australia 148 C3
Lawn Hill Creek r. Australia 148 C3
Lawn Hill National Park Australia 148 C3
Lawqah Saudi Arabia 109 N8
Lawqah waterhole Saudi Arabia 121 I2
Lawra Ghana 124 E4
Lawrence N.Z. 153 D13
Lawrence r. N.Z. 153 E11
Lawrence KS U.S.A. 178 D4
Lawrence MA U.S.A. 177 N3
Lawrenceburg KY U.S.A. 176 A7
Lawrenceburg TN U.S.A. 174 C5
Lawrenceville IL U.S.A. 174 C4
Lawrenceville NJ U.S.A. 177 K5
Lawrenceville PA U.S.A. 177 H4
Lawrenceville VA U.S.A. 176 H9
Lawrence Wells, Mount hill Australia 151 C5
Lawton U.S.A. 179 C5
Lawu, Gunung vol. Indon. 77 E4
Lawz, Jabal al mt. Saudi Arabia 104 A1
Laxå Sweden 45 K4
Laxey S. Africa 132 H3
Lax Kw'alaams Canada 166 D4
formerly known as Port Simpson
Lay r. France 50 E6
Laya r. Rus. Fed. 40 K2
Layar, Tanjung pt Indon. 77 G4
La Yarada Peru 200 C4
La Yata-Ngaya, Réserve de Faune de nature res. Cent. Afr. Rep. 126 D2
Laydennyy, Mys c. Rus. Fed. 40 H1
Layeni Indon. 75 D4
Laylá Saudi Arabia 105 D3
Laylá salt pan Saudi Arabia 109 J6
Laylān Iraq 109 P2
Layon r. France 50 F5
L'Ayrolle, Étang de lag. France 51 J9
Laysan Island U.S.A. 221 G4
Laytonville U.S.A. 182 A2
La Zacatosa, Picacho mt. Mex. 184 C4
Lazarev Rus. Fed. 82 F1
formerly known as Mys Lazareva
Lazarevac Srbija Yugo. 58 B4
Lazarevo Rus. Fed. 43 S8
Lazarevskoye Rus. Fed. 107 D2
Lázaro, Sierra de San mts Mex. 184 C4
Lázaro Cárdenas Baja California Norte Mex. 184 B2
Lázaro Cárdenas Baja California Norte Mex. 184 B2
Lázaro Cárdenas Michoacán Mex. 185 E5
Lazcano Uruguay 204 G4
Lazdijai Lith. 42 E7
Lazinki Rus. Fed. 43 P7
Lazio admin. reg. Italy 56 E6
Lazise Italy 56 C3
Lazo Arg. 204 F4
Lazo Rus. Fed. 82 D4
Lazo Rus. Fed. 39 N3
La Zorra watercourse Mex. 179 B6
Leach Island Canada 173 I3
Leader Canada 167 I5
Leadville U.S.A. 180 F5
Leaf r. U.S.A. 175 B6
Leaf Bay Canada see Tasiujaq
Leaf Rapids Canada 167 K3
Leahy, Cape Antarctica 222 Q2
Leake, Mount hill Australia 150 D3
Leakesville U.S.A. 175 B6
Leakey U.S.A. 179 C6
Leaksville U.S.A. see Eden
Leal, Mount hill Australia 150 B4
Leales Arg. 204 D2
Leamington Canada 168 D5
Leamington Spa, Royal U.K. 47 K11
Le'an China 87 E3
also known as Aoxi
Leandra S. Africa 133 M3
Leandro N. Alem Arg. 204 G2
Leanja Madag. 131 [inset] J2
Leasburg U.S.A. 176 F9
L'Eau Claire, Lac à l. Canada 169 F1
Leava Wallis and Futuna Is see Sigave
Leavenworth KS U.S.A. 178 D4
Leavenworth WA U.S.A. 180 B3
Leavitt Peak U.S.A. 182 E3
Łeba Poland 49 O1
Lebach Germany 48 D6
Lebak Phil. 74 C5
Lebaleng S. Africa 133 J4
Lébamba Gabon 126 A5
Lebane Srbija Yugo. 58 C6
Lebanon country Asia 108 G3
spelt Lubnān in Arabic or Liban in French
asia [countries] 64–67
Lebanon IN U.S.A. 174 C3
Lebanon MO U.S.A. 178 D4
Lebanon NH U.S.A. 177 M2
Lebanon NJ U.S.A. 177 K5
Lebanon OH U.S.A. 176 A6
Lebanon OR U.S.A. 180 B3
Lebanon PA U.S.A. 177 I5
Lebanon TN U.S.A. 174 C4
Lebanon VA U.S.A. 176 C9
Lebap Turkm. 103 E4
Lebap Oblast admin. div. Turkm. see Lebapskaya Oblast'
Lebapskaya Oblast' admin. div. Turkm. 103 E5
English form Lebap Oblast; formerly known as Chardzhouskaya Oblast'
Lebda tourist site Libya see Leptis Magna
Lebec U.S.A. 182 F7
Lebedin Ukr. see Lebedyn
Lebedyan' Rus. Fed. 43 U8
Lebedyn Ukr. 41 E6
also spelt Lebedin
Lebel-sur-Quévillon Canada 168 E3
Lebiolali well Eth. 128 E3
Le Blanc France 50 H6
Lebo Dem. Rep. Congo 126 D3
Lebomboberge hills Moz. see Lebombomberg
Lebombomberg hills Moz. 133 Q3
also known as Lebomboberge
Lebonang S. Africa 133 M3
Łebork Poland 49 O1
Le Bourg-d'Oisans France 51 M7
Lebowakgomo S. Africa 131 F5
Lebrija Spain 54 E8
Łebsko, Jezioro lag. Poland 49 O1
Lebu Chile 204 B5
Le Bugue France 50 G8
Lebyazh'ye Kazakh. see Akku
Lebyazh'ye Kirovskaya Oblast' Rus. Fed. 40 I4
Lebyazh'ye Leningradskaya Oblast' Rus. Fed. 43 K2
Le Caire Egypt see Cairo
Lecce Italy 57 K8
Lecco Italy 56 B3
Lech r. Austria/Germany 48 H8
Lechaina Greece 59 C11
also spelt Lekhainá
Lechang China 87 E3
Le Chasseron mt. Switz. 51 M6
Le Château-d'Oléron France 50 E7
Lechinta Romania 58 F1
Lechința r. Romania 58 F2
Lechtaler Alpen mts Austria 48 H8
Leck Germany 48 F1
Lecompte U.S.A. 179 D6
L'Écorce, Lac de l. Canada 173 Q3
Le Coteau France 51 K6
Le Creusot France 51 K6
Lectoure France 50 G9
Lecumberri Spain 55 J1
Łęczna Poland 49 T4
Łęczyca Poland 49 Q3
Ledang, Gunung mt. Malaysia 76 C2
Ledava r. Slovenia 56 I2
Ledbury U.K. 47 J11
Ledeč nad Sázavou Czech Rep. 49 M6
Ledengskoye Rus. Fed. 40 H4
Ledesma Spain 54 F3
Lediba Dem. Rep. Congo 126 C5
Ledmozero Rus. Fed. 44 P2
Ledong Hainan China 87 D5
also known as Baoyou
Le Dorat France 50 H6
Ledu China 84 D4
also known as Nianbai
Leduc Canada 167 H4
Le Duffre mt. France 51 L8
Ledyanaya, Gora mt. Rus. Fed. 39 R3
Lee r. Rep. of Ireland 47 D12
Leechburg U.S.A. 176 F5
Leech Lake U.S.A. 178 D2
Leech Lake Indian Reservation res. U.S.A. 174 A2
Leeds U.K. 47 K10
Leek U.K. 47 J10
Leenane Rep. of Ireland 47 C10
Leeper U.S.A. 176 F4
Leer (Ostfriesland) Germany 48 E2
Leesburg FL U.S.A. 175 D6
Leesburg GA U.S.A. 175 C6
Leesburg KY U.S.A. 176 A7
Leesburg OH U.S.A. 176 B6
Leesburg VA U.S.A. 176 H6
Lees Summit U.S.A. 178 D4
Lee Steere Range hills Australia 151 C5
Leeston N.Z. 153 G11
Leesville U.S.A. 179 D6
Leesville Lake U.S.A. 176 F8
Leeton Australia 147 E3
Leeudoringstad S. Africa 133 K4
Leeu-Gamka S. Africa 132 F9
Leeukop mt. S. Africa 133 J5
Leeupoort S. Africa 133 L1
Leeuw r. S. Africa 132 F9
Leeuwarden Neth. 48 C2
Leeuwin, Cape Australia 151 A7
Lee Vining U.S.A. 182 E4
Leeward Islands Caribbean Sea 187 G3
Leewin-Naturaliste National Park Australia 151 A7
Le Faouët France 50 C4
Lefedzha r. Bulg. 58 G5
Lefka Cyprus 108 D2
also spelt Lefke
Lefkada Greece 59 B10
also known as Lefkás; formerly known as Leukas; historically known as Leucas
Lefkada i. Greece 59 B10
also known as Levkás or Santa Maura
Lefkás Greece see Lefkada
Lefke Cyprus see Lefka
Lefkimmi Greece 59 B9
also spelt Levkímmi
Lefkosia Cyprus see Nicosia
Lefkosia Cyprus see Nicosia
Lefroy, Lake salt flat Australia 151 C6
Łęg r. Poland 49 S5
Legarde r. Canada 168 C3
Legaspi Phil. 74 B3
Legé France 50 E6
Legges Tor mt. Australia 147 E5
Leggett U.S.A. 182 A2
Leghorn Italy see Livorno
Legionowo Poland 49 R3
Legnago Italy 56 D3
Legnica Poland 49 N4
historically known as Liegnitz
Legnone, Monte mt. Italy 56 B2
Le Grand U.S.A. 182 D4
Le Grand, Cape Australia 151 C7
Le Grand Coyer mt. France 51 M8
Le Grau-du-Roi France 51 K9
Leguena Chile 200 C5
Legune Australia 148 A2
Legwe r. Dem. Rep. Congo 126 E4
Leh Jammu and Kashmir 96 C2
Le Havre France 50 G3
Lehi U.S.A. 183 M1
Lehighton U.S.A. 177 J5
Lehliu-Gară Romania 58 H4
Lehlohonolo S. Africa 133 M7
Lehrte Germany 48 G3
Lehtimäki Fin. 44 M3
Lehututu Botswana 130 D4
Leiah Pak. 101 G4
Leibnitz Austria 49 M9
Leibo China 86 B2
also known as Jincheng
Leicester U.K. 47 K11
historically known as Ratae
Leichhardt r. Australia 148 C3
Leichhardt Falls Australia 148 C3
Leichhardt Range mts Australia 149 E4
Leiden Neth. 48 B3
historically known as Leyden
Leie r. Belgium 51 J1
Leie Estonia 42 H3
Leigh watercourse Australia 146 C2
Leigh N.Z. 152 I4
Leigh Creek Australia 146 C2
Leighlinbridge Rep. of Ireland 47 F11
Leikanger Norway 45 I3
Leiktho Myanmar 78 B4
Leine r. Germany 48 G3
Leinefelde Germany 48 H4
Leinster Australia 151 C6
Leinster reg. Rep. of Ireland 47 F10
Leinster, Mount hill Rep. of Ireland 47 F11
Leipalingis Lith. 42 E7
Leipojärvi Sweden 44 M2
Leipsic U.S.A. 176 B4
Leipsoi i. Greece 59 H11
also spelt Lipsoí
Leipzig Germany 49 J4
Leipzig-Halle airport Germany 49 J4
Leira Møre og Romsdal Norway 44 J3
Leira Oppland Norway 45 J3
Leirbotn Norway 44 M1
Leiria Port. 54 C5
Leiria admin. dist. Port. 54 C5
Leirvik Norway 45 I4
Leirvik Sogn og Fjordane Norway 45 I3
Leishan China 87 D3
also known as Danjiang
Lei Shui r. China 87 E3
Leisi Estonia 42 D3
Leisler, Mount hill Australia 148 A4
Leisler Hills Australia 146 A2
Leitchfield U.S.A. 174 C4
Leithfield N.Z. 153 G11
Leivonmäki Fin. 45 N3
Leiyang China 87 E3
Leizhou China 87 D4
formerly known as Haikang
Leizhou Bandao pen. China 87 D4
English form Luichow Peninsula
Leizhou Wan b. China 87 D4
Lek r. Neth. 48 B4
Leka i. Norway 44 J2
Lékana Congo 126 B5
Le Kef Tunisia 123 H1
historically known as Sicca Veneria
Lékéti r. Congo 126 B5
Lekhainá Greece see Lechaina
Lekhcheb Mauritania 124 C2
Lekkersing S. Africa 132 B6
Lekoes Norway 44 K1
Lékoni Gabon 126 B5
Lékoumou admin. reg. Congo 126 B5
Leksand Sweden 45 K3
Leksozero, Ozero l. Rus. Fed. 44 O3
Lek'suiri Georgia see Lentekhi
Leksura Georgia see Lentekhi
Leksvik Norway 44 J3
Lelai, Tanjung pt Indon. 75 D2
Le Lamentin Martinique 187 H4
Leland Norway 44 K2
Leland IL U.S.A. 172 E9
Leland MS U.S.A. 175 B5
Leläng l. Sweden 45 K4
Le Lavandou France 51 M9
Leleque Arg. 205 C6
Leli China see Tianlin
Lelija mt. Bos.-Herz. 56 K5
Leling China 85 H4
Le Locle Switz. 51 M5
Lelogama Indon. 75 B5
Léloúma Guinea 124 B4
Le Lude France 50 G5
Lelydorp Suriname 199 H3
Lelystad Neth. 48 C3
Le Maire, Estrecho de sea chan. Arg. 205 D9
Léman, Lac l. France/Switz. see Geneva, Lake
Le Mans France 50 G4
Le Mars U.S.A. 178 C3
LeMay Range mts Antarctica 222 T2
Lembeh i. Indon. 75 C2
Lemberg mt. Germany 48 F7
Lemberg Ukr. see L'viv
Lembu Indon. 77 G2
Lembu, Gunung mt. Indon. 76 B1
Lembubut Indon. 77 G1
Lemdiyya Alg. see Médéa
Leme Brazil 206 F9
Le Merlu Rocher mt. France 51 L8
Lemeshivka Ukr. 43 M9
Lemesos Cyprus see Limassol
Lemförde Germany 48 F3
Lemgo Germany 48 F3
Lemhi r. U.S.A. 180 D3
Lemhi Range mts U.S.A. 180 D3
Lemi Fin. 45 N3
Lemieux Islands Canada 165 M3
Lemland Fin. 45 L3
Lemmenjoen kansallispuisto nat. park Fin. 44 N1
Lemmon U.S.A. 178 B2
Lemmon, Mount U.S.A. 183 N9
Lemnos i. Greece see Limnos
Le Môle St Nicolas Haiti 187 E3
Lemoncove U.S.A. 182 E5
Le Mont-Dore New Caledonia 145 F4
Le Mont-St-Michel tourist site France 50 E4
also known as Mont St Michel
Lemoore U.S.A. 182 E5
Lempäälä Fin. 45 M3
Lemro r. Myanmar 78 A3
Lemtybozh Rus. Fed. 40 K3
Lemukutan i. Indon. 77 E2
Le Murge hills Italy 56 I7
Le Muy France 51 M9
Lemva r. Rus. Fed. 40 L2
Lemvig Denmark 45 J4
Lemyethna Myanmar 78 A4
Lem'yu r. Rus. Fed. 40 K3
Lena Norway 45 J3
Lena r. Rus. Fed. 80 H1
Lena IL U.S.A. 172 D8
Lena WI U.S.A. 172 E6
Lena, Mount U.S.A. 183 O1
Lénakel Vanuatu 145 F3
Lēnas Latvia 42 C5
Lencloître France 50 G6
Lençóis Maranhenses, Parque Nacional dos nat. park Brazil 202 D2
Lençóis Paulista Brazil 206 E9
Lenda r. Dem. Rep. Congo 126 F4
Lendava Slovenia 56 I2
Lendeh Iran 100 B4
Lendery Rus. Fed. 44 O3
Lendinara Italy 56 D3
Le Neubourg France 50 G3
Lengbarūt Iran 101 D4
Lenger Kazakh. 103 G4
Lengerich Germany 48 E3
Lenggries Germany 48 I8
Lenghuzhen China 84 B4
Lenglong Ling mts China 84 D4
Lengoué r. Congo 126 C5
Lengshuijiang China 87 D3
Lengshuitan China 87 D3
Lengua de Vaca, Punta pt Chile 204 C3
Lengwe National Park Malawi 129 B9
Lenhovda Sweden 45 K4
Lenin Kazakh. see Kazygurt
Lenin Tajik. 101 G2
Lenin, Qullai mt. Kyrg./Tajik. see Lenin Peak
Lenina, Kanal canal Rus. Fed. 41 H8
Lenina, Pik mt. Kyrg./Tajik. see Lenin Peak
Leninabad Tajik. see Khŭjand
Leninabad Uzbek. 102 D4
also spelt Leninobod
Leninabad Oblast admin. div. Tajik. see Leninobod
Leninakan Armenia see Gyumri
Lenin Atyndagy Choku mt. Kyrg./Tajik. see Lenin Peak
Lenine Ukr. 41 E7
also spelt Lenino; formerly known as Sem Kolodezey
Leningori Georgia see Akhalgori
Leningrad Rus. Fed. see St Petersburg
Leningrad Tajik. 101 G2
also known as Leningradskiy or Mū'minobod; formerly known as Muminabad
Leningrad Oblast admin. div. Rus. Fed. see Leningradskaya Oblast'
Leningradskaya Rus. Fed. 41 F7
Leningradskaya Oblast' admin. div. Rus. Fed. 43 N2
English form Leningrad Oblast
Leningradskiy Tajik. see Leningrad
Lenino Rus. Fed. 90 D2
Lenino Ukr. see Lenine
Leninobod Tajik. see Khŭjand
Leninobod admin. div. Tajik. 101 G2
English form Leninabad Oblast; also known as Khŭjand
Leninobod Uzbek. see Leninabad
Leninogor Kazakh. see Leninogorsk
Leninogorsk Kazakh. 88 C1
also known as Leninogor or Ridder
Leninogorsk Rus. Fed. 40 J5
formerly known as Novaya Pismyanka
Lenin Peak Kyrg./Tajik. 103 H5
also known as Lenina, Pik or Lenin, Qullai or Lenin Atyndagy Choku
Leninpol' Kyrg. 103 G4
Leninsk Kazakh. see Baykonur
Leninsk Rus. Fed. 41 H6
Leninsk Turkm. see Akdepe
Leninsk Uzbek. see Asaka
Leninskiy Kazakh. 102 D2
Leninskiy Rus. Fed. 43 S7
Leninsk-Kuznetskiy Rus. Fed. 80 D2
Leninskoye Kazakh. see Kazygurt
Leninskoye Kazakh. 103 E3
Leninskoye Rus. Fed. 40 H4
Leninskoye Rus. Fed. 82 D3
Lenkoran' Azer. see Länkäran
Lennard r. Australia 150 D3
Lenne r. Germany 51 N1
Lennox, Isla i. Chile 205 D9
Lennox-King Glacier Antarctica 223 L1
Lenoir U.S.A. 174 D5
Lenoir City U.S.A. 174 C5
Lenore U.S.A. 176 C8
Lenore Lake Canada 167 J4
Lenox U.S.A. 177 L3
Lens France 52 C1
Lensk Rus. Fed. 39 L3
formerly known as Mukhtuya
Lentekhi Georgia 107 E2
formerly known as Lek'suiri or Leksura
Lenti Hungary 49 N9
Lentini Sicilia Italy 57 H11
Lentua l. Fin. 44 O2
Lentvaravas Lith. see Lentvaris
Lentvaris Lith. 42 G7
also known as Lentvaravas
Lent'yevo Rus. Fed. 43 R3
Lenwood U.S.A. 183 G7
Lenya Myanmar 79 B6
Léo Burkina 125 E4
Leoben Austria 49 M8
Leodhais, Eilean i. U.K. see Lewis, Isle of
Léogane Haiti 187 E3
Leok Indon. 75 B2
Leola U.S.A. 178 C2
Leominster U.K. 47 J11
Leominster U.S.A. 177 N3
León Mex. 185 E4
León Nicaragua 186 B4
León Spain 54 F2
Leon U.S.A. 174 A3
Leon r. U.S.A. 179 C6
León, Montes de mts Spain 54 E2
Leonard U.S.A. 179 C5
Leonardo da Vinci airport Italy 56 E7
Leonardtown U.S.A. 177 I7
Leonardville Namibia 130 C4
Leona Vicario Mex. 185 I4
Leonforte Sicilia Italy 57 G11
Leongatha Australia 147 E4
Leonidi Greece 59 D11
Leonidovo Rus. Fed. 82 F2
Leonora Australia 151 C6
Leopold r. Australia 150 D3
Leopold U.S.A. 176 E6
Leopold Downs Australia 150 D3
Leopold Downs Aboriginal Reserve Australia 150 D3
Léopold II, Lac l. Dem. Rep. Congo see Mai-Ndombe, Lac
Leopoldina Brazil 203 D7
Leopoldo de Bulhões Brazil 206 E3
Léopoldville Dem. Rep. Congo see Kinshasa
Leoti U.S.A. 178 B4
Leova Moldova 58 J2
formerly spelt Leovo
Leoville Canada 167 J4
Leovo Moldova see Leova
Le Palais France 50 C5
Lepar i. Indon. 77 D3
Le Péage-de-Roussillon France 51 K7
Lepel' Belarus see Lyepyel'
Lepenoú Greece 59 C10
Lephepe Botswana 131 E4
Lephoi S. Africa 133 J7
Leping China 87 F2
Lep'lya r. Rus. Fed. 40 L3
Lepoglava Croatia 56 I2
Le Poiré-sur-Vie France 50 E6
Le Pontet France 51 K9
Lepontine, Alpi mts Italy/Switz. 56 A2
Leposavić Kosovo, Srbija Yugo. 58 B5
Leppävirta Fin. 44 N3
Lepreau, Point Canada 169 H4
Lepsa Kazakh. see Lepsy
Lepsa r. Kazakh. see Lepsy
Lepsi Kazakh. see Lepsinsk
Lepsinsk Kazakh. 103 J3
also known as Lepsi
Lepsy Kazakh. 103 I3
also known as Lepsa
Lepsy r. Kazakh. 103 I3
formerly known as Lepsa
Leptis Magna tourist site Libya 120 B1
also known as Lebda
Leptokarya Greece 59 D8
Le-Puy-en-Velay France 51 J7
Leqçeïba Mauritania 124 B2
Léraba r. Burkina/Côte d'Ivoire 124 D4
Lerala Botswana 131 E4
Leratswana S. Africa 133 L5
Lercara Friddi Sicilia Italy 57 F11
Lerderderg State Park nature res. Australia 147 E4
Léré Chad 126 B2
Léré Mali 124 D3
Lere Nigeria 125 H4
Lereh, Tanjung pt Indon. 77 G3
Le Relecq-Kerhuon France 50 B4
Lérida Col. 198 D5
Lérida Spain see Lleida
Lerik Azer. 107 G3
Lerma Mex. 185 H5
Lerma Spain 54 H2
Lermontov Rus. Fed. 107 E1
formerly known as Lermontovskiy
Lermontovka Rus. Fed. 82 D3
Lermontovskiy Rus. Fed. see Lermontov
Lerno, Monte mt. Sardegna Italy 57 B8
Le Robert Martinique 187 H4
Leros i. Greece 59 H11
Le Roy U.S.A. 176 H3
Lerum Sweden 45 K4
Lerwick U.K. 46 K3
Ler Zerai well Sudan 126 E2
Les Agudes mt. Spain 55 N3
Les Borges Blanques Spain 55 L3
also spelt Borjas Blancas
Lesbos i. Greece 59 G9
also known as Mytilene; also spelt Lesvos
L'Escala Spain 55 O2
also spelt La Escala
Les Cayes Haiti 187 E3
Le Sentier Switz. 51 M6
Les Escaldes Andorra 55 M2
Les Escoumins Canada 169 G3
Le Seu d'Urgell Spain 55 M2
also spelt Seo de Urgell
Leshan China 86 B2
Les Herbiers France 50 E6
Leshou China see Xianxian
Leshukonskoye Rus. Fed. 40 H2
Lesina, Lago di lag. Italy 56 H7
Lesja Norway 45 J3
Lesjöfors Sweden 45 K4
Leskhimstroy Ukr. see Syeverodonets'k
Lesko Poland 49 T6
Leskovac Srbija Yugo. 58 C6
Leskovik Albania 59 B8
Leskov Island Antarctica 223 F2
Leslie U.S.A. 173 I8
Les Méchins Canada 169 H3
Les Mées France 51 L8
Les Minquiers is Channel Is 50 D4
Leśna r. Poland 42 E9
Lesneven France 50 B4
Lesnoy Kirovskaya Oblast' Rus. Fed. 40 J4
Lesnoy Rus. Fed. see Umba
Lesnoy Smolenskaya Oblast' Rus. Fed. 43 M6
Lesnoy, Ostrov i. Rus. Fed. 43 J1
Lesnoye Rus. Fed. 43 Q3
Lesnyye Polyany Rus. Fed. 40 J4
Lesogorsk Rus. Fed. 82 F2
Lesogorskiy Rus. Fed. 43 J1
Lesopil'noye Rus. Fed. 82 D3
Lesosibirsk Rus. Fed. 39 J4
Lesotho country Africa 133 L6
formerly known as Basutoland
africa [countries] 114–117
Lesotho Highlands Water Scheme Lesotho 133 M6
Lesozavodsk Rus. Fed. 82 D3
Lesozavodskiy Rus. Fed. 44 P2
Lesparre-Médoc France 50 F7
L'Espérance Rock i. N.Z. 145 H5
Les Pieux France 50 E3
L'Espina mt. Spain 55 L4
Les Ponts-de-Cé France 50 F5
Les Sables-d'Olonne France 50 E6
Lesse r. Belgium 51 K2
Les Sept-Îles is France 50 C4
Lesser Antilles is Caribbean Sea 187 G4
Lesser Caucasus mts Asia 41 G8
also known as Malyy Kavkaz
Lesser Himalaya mts India/Nepal 96 C3
Lesser Khingan Mountains China see Xiao Hinggan Ling
Lesser Slave Lake Canada 167 H4
Lesser Slave Lake Provincial Park Canada 167 H4
Lesser Tunb i. The Gulf 105 F2
also known as Tonb-e Kūchek, Jazīreh-ye or Ţunb aş Şughrá
Lessingskop mt. S. Africa 133 K6
L'Est, Île de i. Canada 169 I4
L'Est, Pointe de pt Canada 169 I3
Lester U.S.A. 176 D8
Lestijärvi Fin. 44 N3
Lestijoki r. Fin. 44 M2
Les Triagoz is France 50 C4
Les Trois Rivieres Cent. Afr. Rep. 126 E3
Lesung, Bukit mt. Indon. 77 F2
Les Vans France 51 K8
Lesvos i. Greece see Lesbos
Leszno Poland 49 N4
historically known as Lissa
Le Teil France 51 K8
Le Télégraphe hill France 51 K5
Letenye Hungary 49 N9
Leteri India 96 C4
Lethabile S. Africa 133 L2
Letha Range mts Myanmar 78 A3
Lethbridge Alta Canada 167 H5
Lethbridge Nfld. Canada 169 K3
Lethem Guyana 199 G4
Le Thillot France 51 M5
Leti i. Indon. 75 C5
Leti, Kepulauan is Indon. 75 C5
Leticia Col. 198 D6
Leting China 85 H4
Letjiesbos S. Africa 132 G9
Letlhakane Botswana 131 E4
Letlhakeng Botswana 131 E5
Letnerechenskiy Rus. Fed. 40 E2
Letniy Navolok Rus. Fed. 40 F2
Le Touquet-Paris-Plage France 50 H2
Letpadan Myanmar 78 A4
Le Tréport France 50 H2
Letsbo Sweden 45 K3
Letsok-aw Kyun i. Myanmar 79 B6
also known as Domel Island
Letsopa S. Africa 133 J3
Lette Island Tonga see Late Island
Letterkenny Rep. of Ireland 47 E9
Letung Indon. 77 D2
Letwurung Indon. 75 D4
Lëtzebuerg country Europe see Luxembourg
Leu Romania 58 F4
Léua Angola 127 D7
Leucas Greece see Lefkada
Leucate, Étang de l. France 51 J10
also known as Salses, Étang de

Leukas Greece see Lefkada
Leung Shuen Wan Chau i. Hong Kong China see High Island
Leunovo Rus. Fed. 40 G2
Leupp U.S.A. 183 N6
Leura Australia 149 F4
Leuser, Gunung mt. Indon. 76 B2
Leutkirch im Allgäu Germany 48 H8
Leuven Belgium 51 K2
also spelt Louvain
Levadeia Greece 59 D10
Levan Albania 58 A8
Levanger Norway 44 J3
Levante, Riviera di coastal area Italy 56 A4
Levanto Italy 56 B4
Levanzo, Isola di i. Sicilia Italy 57 E10
Levashi Rus. Fed. 102 A4
Levelland U.S.A. 179 B5
Levels N.Z. 153 F12
Leven U.K. 46 J7
Levens France 51 N9
Lévêque, Cape Australia 150 C3
Leverburgh U.K. 46 E6
also known as An t-Ob
Levering U.S.A. 173 I5
Leverkusen Germany 48 D4
Leverville Dem. Rep. Congo see Lusanga
Lévézou mts France 51 I8
Levice Slovakia 49 P7
Levidi Greece 59 D11
Levin N.Z. 152 J8
Lévis Canada 169 G4
Levitha i. Greece 59 H12
Levittown U.S.A. 177 K5
Levka Bulg. 58 H7
Levkás i. Greece see Lefkada
Levkimmi Greece see Lefkimmi
Levoča Slovakia 49 R6
Levočské vrchy mts Slovakia 49 R6
Levroux France 50 H6
Levski Bulg. 58 G5
Levskigrad Bulg. see Karlovo
Lev Tolstoy Rus. Fed. 43 U8
Levuka Fiji 145 G3
Lévuo r. Lith. 42 F5
Lewa Indon. 75 A5
Lewe Myanmar 78 B4
Lewer watercourse Namibia 132 B2
Lewerberg mt. S. Africa 132 B6
Lewes U.K. 47 M13
Lewes U.S.A. 177 J7
Lewin Brzeski Poland 49 O5
Lewis U.S.A. 183 P4
Lewis r. U.S.A. 180 B3
Lewis, Isle of i. U.K. 46 F5
also known as Leodhais, Eilean
Lewis, Lake salt flat Australia 148 B4
Lewisburg OH U.S.A. 176 A6
Lewisburg PA U.S.A. 177 I5
Lewisburg TN U.S.A. 174 C5
Lewisburg WV U.S.A. 176 E8
Lewis Cass, Mount Canada/U.S.A. 166 D3
Lewis Hills hill Canada 169 J3
Lewis Inlet India 95 G3
Lewis Pass N.Z. 153 G10
Lewis Pass National Reserve nature res. N.Z. 153 G10
Lewisporte Canada 169 K3
Lewis Range hills Australia 150 E4
Lewis Range mts U.S.A. 180 D2
Lewis Smith, Lake U.S.A. 175 C5
Lewiston CA U.S.A. 182 B1
Lewiston ID U.S.A. 180 C3
Lewiston ME U.S.A. 177 O1
Lewiston MN U.S.A. 172 B7
Lewistown IL U.S.A. 174 B3
Lewistown MT U.S.A. 180 E3
Lewistown PA U.S.A. 176 H5
Lewisville U.S.A. 179 D5
Lewisville, Lake U.S.A. 179 C5
Lewitz park Germany 48 I2
Lewotobi, Gunung vol. Indon. 75 B5
Lexington GA U.S.A. 175 D5
Lexington IL U.S.A. 172 E10
Lexington KY U.S.A. 176 A7
Lexington MI U.S.A. 173 K7
Lexington MO U.S.A. 178 D4
Lexington MS U.S.A. 175 B5
Lexington NC U.S.A. 174 D5
Lexington NE U.S.A. 178 C3
Lexington OH U.S.A. 176 C5
Lexington SC U.S.A. 175 D5
Lexington TN U.S.A. 174 B5
Lexington VA U.S.A. 176 F8
Lexington Park U.S.A. 177 I7
formerly known as Jarboesville
Leyden Neth. see Leiden
Leye China 86 C3
also known as Tongle
Leyla Dāgh mt. Iran 100 A2
Leyte i. Phil. 74 C4
Leyte Gulf Phil. 74 C4
Leżajsk Poland 49 T5
Lèze r. France 50 H9
Lezha Rus. Fed. 43 V3
Lezha r. Rus. Fed. 43 V2
Lezhë Albania 58 A7
formerly known as Alessio
Lezhi China 86 C2
also known as Tianchi
Lézignan-Corbières France 51 I9
Lezuza Spain 55 I6
L'gov Rus. Fed. 41 E6
Lhagoi Kangri mt. China 89 D6
also known as Hlako Kangri
Lhari China 89 F6
also known as Sirdingka
Lharidon Bight b. Australia 151 A5
Lharigarbo China see Amdo
Lhasa China 89 E6
Lhasa He r. China 89 E6
Lhasoi China 89 F6
Lhatog China 86 A2
Lhazê Xizang China 89 D6
also known as Quxar
Lhazê Xizang China 97 G3
L'Herbaudière, Pointe de pt France 50 D5
Lhokseumawe Indon. 76 B1
Lhoksukon Indon. 76 B1
Lhorong China 97 G3
also known as Zito

▶Lhotse mt. China/Nepal 97 E3
4th highest mountain in the world and in Asia.
world [physical features] 8–9

Lhozhag China 89 E6
also known as Garbo
Lhuentse Bhutan 97 F4
Lhünzê China 89 F6
also known as Xingba
Lhünzhub China 89 E6
also known as Gaindaingoinkor
Liancheng China 87 F3
also known as Lianfeng
Liancheng China see Qinglong
Liancheng China see Guangnan
Liancourt Rocks i. N. Pacific Ocean 91 B6
also known as Take-shima or Tokdo or Tok-tō or Tokto-ri
Lianfeng China see Liancheng
Liang Indon. 75 B3
Lianga Phil. 74 C4
Lianga Bay Phil. 74 C4
Liangaz Hu l. China 87 E2
Liangcheng China 85 G3
Liangdang China 86 C1
Liangfeng China 87 D3
Lianghe China 86 A3
also known as Zhedao
Lianghekou Gansu China 86 C1
Lianghekou Sichuan China 86 B2

Liangjiayoufang China see Youyu
Liangping China 87 C2
also known as Liangshan
Liangpran, Bukit mt. Indon. 77 F2
Liangshan China see Liangping
Liang Shan mt. Myanmar 78 B2
Liangshi China see Shaodong
Liang Timur, Gunung mt. Malaysia 76 C2
Liangwang Shan mts China 86 B3
Liangzhen China 85 F4
Liangzhou China see Wuwei
Lianhe China see Qianjiang
Lianhua China 87 E3
also known as Qinting
Lianhua Shan mts China 87 E4
Lianjiang Fujian China 87 F3
also known as Fengcheng
Lianjiang Guangdong China 87 D4
Lianjiang China see Xingguo
Lianjiangkou China 87 E3
Lian Jiang r. China 78 D2
Liannan China 87 E3
also known as Sanjiang
Lianping China 87 E3
also known as Yuanshan
Lianran China see Anning
Lianshan Guangdong China 87 E3
Lianshan Liaoning China 85 I3
formerly known as Jinxi
Liant, Cape pt Thai. see Samae San, Laem
Liantang China see Nanchang
Liantuo China 87 D2
Lianxian China see Lianzhou
Lianyin China 82 A1
Lianyuan China 87 D3
formerly known as Lantian
Lianyungang China 87 F1
Lianzhou China 87 E3
formerly known as Lianxian
Lianzhou China see Hepu
Lianzhushan China 82 C3
Liao r. China 85 I3
Liaocheng China 85 G4
Liaodong Bandao pen. China 85 I3
Liaodong Wan b. China 85 I3
Liaodun China 84 B3
Liaodunzhan China 84 B3
Liaoning prov. China 85 I3
Liaoyang China 85 I3
Liaoyuan China 82 B4
Liaozhong China 85 I3
Liapades Greece 59 A9
Liaqatabad Pak. 101 G3
Liard r. Canada 166 F2
Liard Highway Canada 166 F2
Liard Plateau Canada 166 E3
Liard River Canada 166 E3
Liari Pak. 101 F5
Liat i. Indon. 77 D3
Liathach mt. U.K. 46 G6
Liban country Asia see Lebanon
Liban, Jebel mts Lebanon 108 H3
Libano Col. 198 C3
Libau Latvia see Liepāja
Libby U.S.A. 180 D2
Libenge Dem. Rep. Congo 126 C4
Liberal U.S.A. 178 B4
Liberdade Brazil 207 I9
Liberdade r. Amazonas Brazil 200 C1
Liberdade r. Mato Grosso Brazil 202 A4
Liberec Czech Rep. 49 M5
▶Liberia country Africa 124 C5
africa [countries] 114–117
Liberia Costa Rica 186 B5
Libertad Venez. 198 D2
Libertador General San Martín Arg. 201 D5
Liberty AK U.S.A. 166 A1
Liberty IN U.S.A. 176 A6
Liberty KY U.S.A. 176 A8
Liberty ME U.S.A. 177 P1
Liberty MO U.S.A. 178 D4
Liberty NY U.S.A. 177 K4
Liberty TX U.S.A. 179 D6
Libertyville U.S.A. 172 F8
Libmanan Phil. 74 B3
Libni, Gebel hill Egypt 108 E7
Libo China 87 C3
also known as Yuping
Libobo, Tanjung pt Indon. 75 D3
Libode S. Africa 133 N8
Libohovë Albania 59 B8
Liboi Kenya 128 D4
Libong, Ko i. Thai. 79 B7
Libourne France 50 F8
Libral Well Australia 150 D4
Librazhd Albania 58 B7
Libre, Sierra mts Mex. 184 C2

▶Libreville Gabon 126 A4
Capital of Gabon.

Libuganon r. Phil. 74 C5

▶Libya country Africa 120 B3
4th largest country in Africa. Spelt Al Lībīyah in Arabic.
africa [countries] 114–117

Libyan Desert Egypt/Libya 120 E3
Libyan Plateau Egypt 121 E2
Licantén Chile 204 B4
Licata Sicilia Italy 57 F11
Lice Turkey 107 E3
Lichas pen. Greece 59 D10
also known as Likhás
Licheng China see Xianyou
Licheng China see Lipu
Licheng Shandong China 85 H4
also known as Hongjialou
Licheng Shanxi China 85 G4
Lichfield N.Z. 152 J6
Lichfield U.K. 47 K11
Lichinga Moz. 129 B8
formerly known as Vila Cabral
Lichte Germany 48 I5
Lichtenburg S. Africa 133 K3
Lichtenfels Germany 48 I5
Lichuan Hubei China 87 D2
Lichuan Jiangxi China 87 F3
also known as Rifeng
Licínio de Almeida Brazil 207 K1
Licito Moz. 131 H3
Licking r. U.S.A. 176 A6
Lički Osik Croatia 56 H4
Licun China see Laoshan
Lid' r. Rus. Fed. 43 Q2
Lida Belarus 42 G8
Lidjombo Cent. Afr. Rep. 126 C4
Lidköping Sweden 45 K4
Lidsjöberg Sweden 44 K2
Lidumnieki Latvia 42 I5
Lidzbark Poland 49 Q2
Lidzbark Warmiński Poland 49 R1
Liebenbergs Vlei r. S. Africa 133 M4
Liebenwalde Germany 49 K3
Liebig, Mount Australia 148 A4
Liebling Romania 58 C3
▶Liechtenstein country Europe 51 P5
europe [countries] 32–35
Liège Belgium 51 L2
also known as Luik
Liegnitz Poland see Legnica
Lieksa Fin. 44 O3
Lielais Ludzas l. Latvia 42 I5
Lielupe r. Latvia 42 F4
Lielvārde Latvia 42 F5
Lien Sweden 44 L3
Lienz Austria 49 J9
Liepāja Latvia 42 C5
also spelt Liepaya; formerly spelt Libau

Liepaya Latvia see Liepāja
Liepna Latvia 42 I4
Liesjärven kansallispuisto nat. park Fin. 42 E1
Liestal Switz. 51 N5
Lieto Fin. 42 D1
Liétor Spain 55 J6
Lietuva country Europe see Lithuania
Liévin France 51 I2
Lièvre r. Canada 168 F4
Liezen Austria 49 L8
Lifamatola i. Indon. 75 C3
Lifanga Dem. Rep. Congo 126 D4
Liffey r. Rep. of Ireland 47 F10
Lifford Rep. of Ireland 47 E9
Liffré France 50 E4
Lifi Mahuida mt. Arg. 205 C6
Lifou i. New Caledonia 145 F4
also spelt Lifu; formerly known as Chabrol
Lifu i. New Caledonia see Lifou
Lifudzin Rus. Fed. see Rudnyy
Ligao Phil. 74 B3
Ligatne Latvia 42 G4
Lighthouse Reef Belize 185 I5
Lightning Ridge Australia 147 E2
Ligny-en-Barrois France 51 L4
Ligonha r. Moz. 131 H3
Ligonier IN U.S.A. 172 H9
Ligonier PA U.S.A. 176 F5
Ligoúrion Greece see Lygourio
Ligui Mex. 184 C3
Ligure, Mar sea France/Italy see Ligurian Sea
Liguria admin. reg. Italy 56 A4
Ligurian Sea France/Italy 51 O9
also known as Ligure, Mar or Ligurienne, Mer
Ligurienne, Mer sea France/Italy see Ligurian Sea
Ligurta U.S.A. 183 J9
Lihir Group is P.N.G. 145 E2
formerly known as Gerrit Denys
Lihou Reef and Cays Australia 149 F3
Lihue U.S.A. 181 [inset] Y1
Lihula Estonia 42 E3
Liivi laht b. Estonia/Latvia see Riga, Gulf of
Lijiang China 86 B3
also known as Dayan
Lijiang China see Yuanjiang
Lijiazhai China 87 E2
Lik, Nam r. Laos 78 C4
Lika reg. Croatia 56 H4
Likak Iran 100 B4
Likala Dem. Rep. Congo 126 C4
Likasi Dem. Rep. Congo 127 E7
formerly known as Jadotville
Likati Dem. Rep. Congo 126 D4
Likati r. Dem. Rep. Congo 126 E4
Likely Canada 166 F4
Likhachevo Ukr. see Pervomays'kyy
Likhachyovo Ukr. see Pervomays'kyy
Likhás pen. Greece see Lichas
Likhoslavl' Rus. Fed. 43 Q4
Likimi Dem. Rep. Congo 126 D4
Likino-Dulevo Rus. Fed. 43 T6
Likisia East Timor 75 C5
also spelt Liquiçá or Liquissa
Likma India 94 D1
Likolia Dem. Rep. Congo 126 D5
Likouala admin. reg. Congo 126 C4
Likouala r. Congo 126 C5
Likouala aux Herbes r. Congo 126 C5
Liku Indon. 77 E2
Liku Sarawak Malaysia 77 F1
Likupang Indon. 75 C2
L'Île d'Anticosti, Réserve Faunique de nature res. Canada 169 I3
L'Île-Rousse Corse France 51 O10
Lilienfeld Austria 49 M7
Lilienthal Germany 48 F2
Liling China 87 E3
Liljendal Fin. 42 H1
Lilla Pak. 101 H3
Lilla Edet Sweden 45 K4
Lilla Luleälven r. Sweden 44 M2
Lillblaiken hill Sweden 44 L2
Lille Belgium 51 K1
Lille France 51 J2
Lille Bælt sea chan. Denmark see Little Belt
Lillebonne France 50 G3
Lillehammer Norway 45 J3
Lillesand Norway 45 J4
Lillestrøm Norway 45 J4
Lilley U.S.A. 172 H7
Lillian, Point hill Australia 151 D5
Lillie Glacier Antarctica 223 L2
Lillington U.S.A. 174 E5
Lillooet Canada 166 F5
Lillooet r. Canada 166 F5
Lillooet Range mts Canada 166 F5
Lilo r. Dem. Rep. Congo 126 E5
Liloing India 97 G4

▶Lilongwe Malawi 129 B8
Capital of Malawi.

Lilo Viejo Arg. 204 E2
Liloy Phil. 74 B4
Lily U.S.A. 172 E5
Lim r. Yugo. 58 A5

▶Lima Peru 200 A3
Capital of Peru and 4th most populous city in South America.
world [cities] 24–25

Lima dept Peru 200 A2
Lima MT U.S.A. 180 D3
Lima NY U.S.A. 176 H3
Lima OH U.S.A. 176 A5
Limaão Brazil 199 F4
Lima Duarte Brazil 207 J8
Līmah Oman 105 G2
Lima Islands China see Wanshan Qundao
Liman Rus. Fed. 102 A3
Limanowa Poland 49 R6
Limar Indon. 75 C4
Limarí r. Chile 204 C3
Limas Indon. 76 D2
Limassol Cyprus 108 E3
also known as Lemesos
Limavady U.K. 47 F8
Limay r. Arg. 204 D5
Limay Mahuida Arg. 204 D5
Limbach-Oberfrohna Germany 49 J5
Limbang r. Sarawak Malaysia 77 F1
Limbani Peru 200 C3
Limbaži Latvia 42 F4
Limbdi India 96 A5
Limbe Cameroon 125 H5
formerly known as Victoria
Limboto Indon. 75 B2
Limboto, Danau l. Indon. 75 B2
Limbuè Moz. 131 H3
Limbungan Indon. 77 F3
Limbunya Australia 148 A3
Limburg an der Lahn Germany 48 F5
Lim Chu Kang Sing. 76 [inset]
Lim Chu Kang hill Sing. 76 [inset]
Lime Acres S. Africa 132 H5
Limehills N.Z. 153 C14
Limeira Brazil 206 F9
Limenaria Greece 58 F8
Limerick Rep. of Ireland 47 D11
also spelt Luimneach
Limestone U.S.A. 176 C9
Limestone Point Canada 167 L4
Limfjorden sea chan. Denmark 45 J4
Limia r. Spain 54 C3
Limin Chersonisou Greece 59 G13
Limingen Norway 44 K2
Limingen l. Norway 44 K2
Liminka Fin. 44 N2

Limmen Bight b. Australia 148 C2
Limmen Bight River r. Australia 148 B2
Limni Greece 59 E10
Limnos i. Greece 59 G9
also spelt Lemnos
Limoeiro Brazil 202 F3
Limoges France 50 H7
Limón Costa Rica 186 C5
Limón Hond. 186 B4
Limon U.S.A. 178 B4
Limonum France see Poitiers
Limoquije Bol. 200 D3
Limousin admin. reg. France 50 H7
Limousin, Plateaux du France 50 H7
Limoux France 51 I9
Limpopo r. S. Africa/Zimbabwe 131 G5
Limu China 87 D3
Limulunga Zambia 127 D8
Linaälven r. Sweden 44 M2
Linah Saudi Arabia 104 C1
Linakeng Lesotho 133 M6
Linakhamari Rus. Fed. 44 O1
Lin'an China see Jianshui
Lin'an China 87 F2
Linao Bay Phil. 74 C5
Linapacan i. Phil. 74 A4
Linapacan Strait Phil. 74 A4
Linares Chile 204 C4
Linares Mex. 185 F3
Linares Spain 55 H6
Linas, Monte mt. Sardegna Italy 57 A9
Linau Balui plat. Sarawak Malaysia 77 F2
Lincang China 86 B4
also known as Fengxiang
Lincheng China see Lingao
Lincheng China see Huitong
Linchuan China 87 F3
formerly known as Fuzhou
Linck Nunataks Antarctica 222 R1
Lincoln Arg. 204 E4
Lincoln U.K. 47 L10
historically known as Lindum
Lincoln CA U.S.A. 182 C3
Lincoln IL U.S.A. 174 B3
Lincoln KS U.S.A. 178 C4
Lincoln ME U.S.A. 174 G2
Lincoln MI U.S.A. 173 J6

▶Lincoln NE U.S.A. 178 C3
State capital of Nebraska.

Lincoln City U.S.A. 180 A3
Lincoln Island Paracel Is 72 D3
Lincoln National Park Australia 146 B3
Lincoln Sea Canada/Greenland 165 O1
Lincolnshire Wolds hills U.K. 47 L10
Linda, Serra hills Brazil 202 D5
Lindas Norway 46 R3
Lindau (Bodensee) Germany 48 G8
Lindeman Group is Australia 149 F4
Linden Canada 167 H5
Linden Guyana 199 G3
formerly known as Mackenzie
Linden AL U.S.A. 175 C5
Linden CA U.S.A. 182 C3
Linden NJ U.S.A. 177 K5
Linden TN U.S.A. 174 C5
Linden TX U.S.A. 179 D5
Lindenow Fjord inlet Greenland see Kangerlussuatsiaq
Lindesberg Sweden 45 K4
Lindhos Greece see Lindos
Lindi r. Dem. Rep. Congo 126 E4
Lindi Tanz. 129 C7
Lindi admin. reg. Tanz. 129 C7
Lindian China 85 J2
Lindisfarne i. U.K. see Holy Island
Lindley S. Africa 133 L4
Lindóia Brazil 206 G9
Lindome Sweden 45 K4
Lindong China 85 H3
also known as Bairin Zuoqi
Lindos Greece 59 J12
also spelt Lindhos
Lindos, Akra pt Greece 59 J12
Lindsay Canada 168 E4
Lindsay CA U.S.A. 182 E5
Lindsborg U.S.A. 178 C4
Lindsdal Sweden 45 L4
Lindside U.S.A. 176 E8
Lindum U.K. see Lincoln
Line Islands S. Pacific Ocean 221 H5
Linets Rus. Fed. 43 Q9
Linfen China 85 F4
Lingampalli India 94 D2
Linganamakki Reservoir India 94 B3
Lingao China 87 D5
also known as Lincheng
Lingayen Phil. 74 B2
Lingayen Gulf Phil. 74 B2
Lingbao China 87 D1
formerly known as Guoluezhen
Lingbi China 87 F1
Lingcheng China see Lingshan
Lingcheng China see Lingshui
Lingcheng China see Lingxian
Lingchuan Guangxi China 87 D3
Lingchuan Shanxi China 85 G5
Lingelethu S. Africa 133 L9
Lingelihle S. Africa 133 J9
Lingen (Ems) Germany 48 E3
Lingga i. Indon. 76 D3
Lingga, Kepulauan is Indon. 76 D3
Linggo Co l. China 89 E5
Lingig Phil. 74 C5
Lingle U.S.A. 180 F4
Lingomo Dem. Rep. Congo 126 D4
Lingqiu China 85 G4
Lingshan China 87 D4
also known as Lingcheng
Lingshan Wan b. China 85 I5
Lingshi Bhutan see Lingzhi
Lingshi China 85 F4
Lingshui China 87 D5
also known as Lingcheng
Lingsugur India 94 C2
Lingtai China 85 E5
also known as Zhongtai
Linguère Senegal 124 B3
Lingui China 87 D3
Lingxi China see Yongshun
Lingxian China see Yanling
Lingxian China 85 H4
also known as Lingcheng
Lingxiang China 87 E2
Lingyuan China 85 H3
Lingyun China 86 C3
also known as Sicheng
Lingzhi Bhutan 97 F4
also spelt Lingshi
Lingzi Thang Plains l. Aksai Chin 89 B5
Linhai Liaoning China 85 I3
also known as Dalinghe; formerly known as Jinxian
Linhai Zhejiang China 87 G2
Linhares Brazil 203 D6
Linh Cam Vietnam 78 D4
Linhe China 85 E3
Linhpa Myanmar 78 A2
Linidis Valley N.Z. 153 D12
Linjiang China see Shanghang
Linjiang China 82 B4
Linköping Sweden 45 K4
Linkou China 82 C3
Linksness U.K. 46 I5
Linkuva Lith. 42 E5
Linli China 87 D2
Linlü Shan mt. China 85 G4
Linmingguan China see Yongnian
Linn U.S.A. 174 B4

Linn, Mount U.S.A. 182 B1
Linnansaaren kansallispuisto nat. park Fin. 44 O3
Linnhe, Loch inlet U.K. 46 G7
Linosa, Isola di i. Sicilia Italy 57 E13
Linova Belarus 42 F9
Linqing China 85 G4
Linru China see Ruzhou
Lins Brazil 206 D8
Linsan Guinea 124 B4
Linshui China 86 C2
also known as Dingping
Linta r. Madag. 131 [inset] J5
Lintah, Selat sea chan. Indon. 75 A5
Lintan China 86 B1
Lintao China 84 D5
Linth r. Switz. 51 P5
Linthal Switz. 51 P6
Linton U.S.A. 178 B2
Lintong China 87 D1
also known as Lishan
Linville U.S.A. 176 D9
Linxi China 85 H3
Linxia China 84 D5
Linxian China see Linzhou
Linxian China 85 F4
Linxiang China 87 E2
Linyanti r. Botswana/Namibia 131 E3
Linyanti Swamp Namibia 130 D3
Linyi Shandong China 85 H4
Linyi Shandong China 85 H5
Linyi Shanxi China 85 F5
Linying China 87 E1
Linz Austria 49 L7
Linze China 84 D4
formerly known as Shahepu or Shahezhen
Linzhou China 85 G4
formerly known as Linxian
Lioma Moz. 131 H2
Lion, Golfe du g. France 51 J10
English form Lions, Gulf of
Lions, Gulf of France see Lion, Golfe du
Lions Den Zimbabwe 131 F3
Lion's Head Canada 173 L6
Lioua Chad 120 B6
Liouesso Congo 126 B4
Lipa Phil. 74 B3
Lipari Isole Lipari Italy 57 G10
Lipari, Isola i. Isole Lipari Italy 57 G10
Lipari, Isole is Italy 57 G10
Lipatkain Indon. 76 C2
Lipawki Belarus 42 I6
Liperi Fin. 44 O3
Lipetsk Rus. Fed. 43 U9
Lipetskaya Oblast' admin. div. Rus. Fed. 43 T9
English form Lipetsk Oblast
Lipetsk Oblast admin. div. Rus. Fed. see Lipetskaya Oblast'
Lipez, Cordillera de mts Bol. 200 D5
Lipiany Poland 49 L2
Lipin Bor Rus. Fed. 43 S1
Liping China 87 D3
also known as Defeng
Lipitsy Rus. Fed. 43 S8
Lipki Rus. Fed. 43 S8
Lipljan Kosovo, Srbija Yugo. 58 C6
Lipnaya Gorka Rus. Fed. 43 O2
Lipník nad Bečvou Czech Rep. 49 O6
Lipno Poland 49 Q3
Lipno, Vodní nádrž resr Czech Rep. 49 L7
Lipova Romania 58 C2
Lipovtsy Rus. Fed. 90 B2
Lipovu Romania 58 E4
Lippe r. Germany 48 D4
Lippstadt Germany 48 F4
Lipscomb U.S.A. 179 B4
Lipsk Poland 49 U2
Lipsko Poland 49 S4
Lipsoi i. Greece see Leipsoi
Lipti Lekh pass Nepal 96 D3
Liptovská Mara, Vodná nádrž resr Slovakia 49 Q6
Liptovský Hrádok Slovakia 49 Q6
Liptovský Mikuláš Slovakia 49 Q6
Liptrap, Cape Australia 147 E4
Liptsy Rus. Fed. 43 P6
Lipu China 87 D3
also known as Licheng
Lipusz Poland 49 O1
Liquiçá East Timor see Likisia
Liquissa East Timor see Likisia
Lira Uganda 128 B4
Liran i. Indon. 75 C4
Liranga Congo 126 C5
Liri r. Italy 56 F7
Liri, Jebel el mt. Sudan 128 A2
Lirung Indon. 75 C2
Lis Albania 58 B7
Lisa Romania 58 F3
Lisakovsk Kazakh. 103 E1
Lisala Dem. Rep. Congo 126 D4
L'Isalo, Massif de mts Madag. 131 [inset] J4
L'Isalo, Parc National de nat. park Madag. 131 [inset] J4
Lisboa Port. see Lisbon
Lisboa admin. dist. Port. 54 B5

▶Lisbon Port. 54 B6
Capital of Portugal. Also spelt Lisboa; historically known as Olisipo.

Lisbon IL U.S.A. 172 E9
Lisbon ME U.S.A. 177 O1
Lisbon ND U.S.A. 178 C2
Lisbon NH U.S.A. 177 N1
Lisbon OH U.S.A. 176 E5
Lisbon Falls U.S.A. 177 O2
Lisburn U.K. 47 F9
Liscannor Bay Rep. of Ireland 47 C11
Liscomb Game Sanctuary nature res. Canada 169 I4
Lisdoonvarna Rep. of Ireland 47 C10
Lisec mt. Macedonia 58 D7
L'Iseran, Col de pass France 51 N7
Lishan China see Lintong
Lishan Taiwan 87 G3
Lishe Jiang r. China 86 B3
Lishi China see Dingnan
Lishi China 85 F4
Lishtar-e Bālā Iran 100 B4
Lishu China 82 B4
Lishui Jiangsu China 87 F2
Lishui Zhejiang China 87 F2
Li Shui r. China 87 D2
Lisichansk Ukr. see Lysychans'k
Lisieux France 50 G3
Lisiy Nos Rus. Fed. 43 L1
Liskeard U.K. 47 H13
Liski Rus. Fed. 41 F6
formerly known as Georgiu-Dezh
L'Isle-en-Dodon France 50 G9
L'Isle-Jourdain France 50 H9
L'Isle-sur-la-Sorgue France 51 L9
L'Isle-sur-le-Doubs France 51 M5
Lismore Australia 147 G2
Lismore N.Z. 153 F11
Lismore Rep. of Ireland 47 E11
Lisne Ukr. 58 K2
Liss mt. Saudi Arabia 109 J6
Lissa Croatia see Vis
Lissa Poland see Leszno
Lisseri, Oued watercourse Tunisia 123 H2
Listafjorden b. Norway 45 I4
Lister, Mount Antarctica 223 K1
Listore watercourse Australia 148 C5
Listowel Canada 168 D5
Listowel Rep. of Ireland 47 C11
Listowel Downs Australia 149 E5
Listvyaga, Khrebet mts Kazakh./Rus. Fed. 88 D1

Listvyanka Rus. Fed. 84 E1
Liswarta r. Poland 49 P4
Lit Sweden 44 K3
Litang Guangxi China 87 D4
Litang Sichuan China 86 B2
also known as Gaocheng
Litang Qu r. China 86 B2
Litani r. Fr. Guiana/Suriname 199 H4
Lītāni r. Lebanon 108 G4
Litchfield CA U.S.A. 182 D1
Litchfield IL U.S.A. 174 B4
Litchfield MI U.S.A. 173 I8
Litchfield MN U.S.A. 178 D2
Litembe Tanz. 129 D7
Litene Latvia 42 I4
Līth, Wādī al watercourse Saudi Arabia 104 C3
Lithgow Australia 147 F3
Lithino, Akra pt Greece 59 F14
▶Lithuania country Europe 42 E6
known as Lietuva in Lithuanian; formerly known as Litovskaya S.S.R.
europe [countries] 32–35
Litija Slovenia 56 G2
Lititz U.S.A. 177 I5
Litochoro Greece 59 D8
Litoměřice Czech Rep. 49 L5
Litomyšl Czech Rep. 49 N6
Litovel Czech Rep. 49 O6
Litovko Rus. Fed. 82 D2
Litovskaya S.S.R. country Europe see Lithuania
Little r. LA U.S.A. 179 D6
Little r. OK U.S.A. 179 D5
Little r. TX U.S.A. 179 C6
Little Abaco i. Bahamas 186 D1
Little Abitibi r. Canada 168 D3
Little Abitibi Lake Canada 168 D3
Little Aden Yemen see 'Adan as Sughra
Little Andaman i. India 95 G4
Little Bahama Bank sea feature Bahamas 186 D1
Little Barrier i. N.Z. 152 J4
Little Bay de Noc U.S.A. 172 F5
Little Belt sea chan. Denmark 45 J5
also known as Lille Bælt
Little Belt Mountains U.S.A. 180 E3
Little Bighorn r. U.S.A. 180 F3
Little Bitter Lake Egypt 108 D7
also known as Murrat el Sughra, Buheirat
Little Blue r. U.S.A. 178 C4
Little Bow r. Canada 167 H5
Little Buffalo r. Canada 167 H2
Little Cayman i. Cayman Is 186 C3
Little Churchill r. Canada 167 M3
Little Coco Island Cocos Is 79 A5
Little Colorado r. U.S.A. 183 M5
Little Creek Peak U.S.A. 183 L4
Little Current Canada 168 D4
Little Current r. Canada 168 C3
Little Desert National Park Australia 146 D4
Little Egg Harbor inlet U.S.A. 177 K6
Little Exuma i. Bahamas 186 E2
Little Falls MN U.S.A. 178 D2
Little Falls NY U.S.A. 177 K2
Littlefield AZ U.S.A. 183 K5
Littlefield TX U.S.A. 179 B5
Little Fish r. S. Africa 133 K10
Little Fork r. U.S.A. 174 A1
Little Fort Canada 166 F5
Little Grand Rapids Canada 167 M4
Little Grass Valley Reservoir U.S.A. 182 C2
Little Inagua Island Bahamas 187 E2
Little Kanawha r. U.S.A. 176 D6
Little Karas Berg plat. Namibia 132 C4
Little Karoo plat. S. Africa 132 E10
Little Lake U.S.A. 182 G6
Little Mecatina r. Canada 169 I3
also known as Petit Mécatina
Little Mecatina Island Canada see Petit Mécatina, Île du
Little Miami r. U.S.A. 176 A6
Little Minch sea chan. U.K. 46 E6
Little Missouri r. U.S.A. 178 B2
Little Muskingum r. U.S.A. 176 D6
Little Nicobar i. India 95 G5
Little Olifants r. S. Africa 133 N2
Little Pamir mts Afgh. 101 H2
Little Pic r. Canada 172 G2
Little Powder r. U.S.A. 180 F3
Little Rann marsh India 96 A5
Little Red r. U.S.A. 179 E5
Little Red River Canada 167 H3
Little River N.Z. 153 G11
Little River U.S.A. 175 E5

▶Little Rock U.S.A. 179 D5
State capital of Arkansas.

Littlerock U.S.A. 182 G7
Little Sable Point U.S.A. 172 G7
Little Sachigo Lake Canada 168 A2
Little Salmon Lake Canada 166 C2
Little Salt Lake U.S.A. 183 L4
Little Sandy Desert Australia 150 B4
Little San Salvador i. Bahamas 186 E1
Little Sioux r. U.S.A. 178 C3
Little Smoky Canada 167 G4
Little Smoky r. Canada 167 G4
Little Snake r. U.S.A. 180 E4
Littlestown U.S.A. 177 I6
Little Tibet reg. Jammu and Kashmir see Ladakh
Littleton NC U.S.A. 176 H9
Littleton NH U.S.A. 177 N1
Littleton WV U.S.A. 176 E6
Little Traverse Bay U.S.A. 173 H5
Little Tupper Lake U.S.A. 177 K1
Little Turtle Lake Canada 172 A2
Little Valley U.S.A. 176 G3
Little Wabash r. U.S.A. 174 B4
Little Wanganui N.Z. 152 G9
Little White r. U.S.A. 178 B3
Little Wichita r. U.S.A. 179 C5
Little Wind r. U.S.A. 180 E4
Little Wood r. U.S.A. 180 D4
Little Zab r. Iraq see Zāb aş Şaghīr, Nahr az
Littoral prov. Cameroon 125 H5
Litunde Moz. 129 B8
Lituya Bay U.S.A. 166 B3
Litvínov Czech Rep. 49 K5
Liu r. China 85 H3
Liu r. China 85 I3
Liu Estonia 42 F3
Liuba China 86 C1
Liuchiu Yü i. Taiwan 87 G4
Liuchong He r. China 86 C3
Liuchow China see Liuzhou
Liugong Dao i. China 85 I4
Liugu r. China 85 I3
Liuhe China 82 B4
Liuheng Dao i. China 87 G2
Liujiachang China 87 D2
Liujiang China 87 D3
also known as Labao
Liujiaxia China see Yongjing
Liujiaxia Shuiku resr China 84 D5
Liulin China see Jonê
Liulin China 85 F4
Liupai China see Tian'e
Liupan Shan mts China 85 E5
Liupanshui China see Lupanshui
Liupo Moz. 131 H2
Liure Hond. 186 B4
Liushuquan China 84 B3
Liuwa Plain Zambia 127 D8
Liuwa Plain National Park Zambia 127 D8
Liuyang China 87 E2
Liuyang He r. China 87 E2
Liuzhangzhen China see Yuanqu

index L M

Liuzhou China 87 D3
formerly known as Liuchow
Livada, Akra *pt* Greece 59 G11
Livadi *i.* Greece 59 H12
Livadiya Rus. Fed. 82 D4
Līvāni Latvia 42 H5
Livanjsko Polje *plain* Bos.-Herz. 56 I4
Livarot France 50 G3
Livbērze Latvia 42 E5
Live Oak *CA* U.S.A. 182 C2
Live Oak *FL* U.S.A. 175 D6
Liveringa Australia 150 D3
Livermore U.S.A. 182 C4
Livermore, Mount U.S.A. 181 F7
Liverpool Australia 147 F3
Liverpool Canada 169 H4
Liverpool U.K. 47 J10
Liverpool U.S.A. 177 I2
Liverpool Bay Canada 164 F3
Liverpool Plains Australia 147 F2
Liverpool Range *mts* Australia 147 F2
Livingston U.K. 46 I8
Livingston *AL* U.S.A. 175 B5
Livingston *CA* U.S.A. 182 D4
Livingston *KY* U.S.A. 176 A8
Livingston *LA* U.S.A. 175 B6
Livingston *MT* U.S.A. 180 E3
Livingston *NJ* U.S.A. 177 K5
Livingston *TX* U.S.A. 179 D6
Livingston *WI* U.S.A. 172 C8
Livingston, Lake U.S.A. 179 D6
Livingstone Zambia 127 E9
also known as Maramba
Livingstonia Malawi 129 B7
Livingston Island Antarctica 222 T2
Livingston Manor U.S.A. 177 K4
Livingston Mountains N.Z. 153 C12
Livno Bos.-Herz. 56 J5
Livny Rus. Fed. 43 S9
Livo *r.* Rus. Fed. 44 O2
Livonia *MI* U.S.A. 173 J8
Livonia *NY* U.S.A. 176 H3
Livorno Italy 56 C5
historically known as Leghorn
Livradois, Monts du *mts* France 51 J7
Livradois Forez, Parc Naturel Régional du *nature res.* France 51 J7
Livramento do Brumado Brazil 202 D5
Livron-sur-Drôme France 51 K8
Liwā Oman 105 G2
Liwā', Wādī al *watercourse* Syria 109 H5
Liwale Tanz. 129 C7
Liwiec *r.* Poland 49 S3
Liwonde Malawi 129 B8
Liwonde National Park Malawi 129 B8
Liwu China *see* Lixian
Lixian *Gansu* China 86 C1
Lixian *Hebei* China 85 G4
also known as Liwu
Lixian *Hunan* China 87 D2
Lixian *Sichuan* China 86 B2
also known as Zagunao
Lixin China 87 F1
Lixouri Greece 59 B10
Lixus Morocco *see* Larache
Liyang China 87 F2
Liyuan China *see* Sangzhi
Liz *r.* Port. 54 C5
Lizarda Brazil 202 C4
Lizard Island Australia 149 E2
Lizard Point U.K. 47 G14
Lizarra Spain *see* Estella
Lizemores U.S.A. 176 D7
Liziping China 86 B2
Lizonne *r.* France 50 G7
Ljig *Srbija* Yugo. 58 B4
Ljubija Bos.-Herz. 56 I4

▶**Ljubljana** Slovenia **56** G2
Capital of Slovenia. Historically known as Emona or Laibach.

Ljubuški Bos.-Herz. 56 J5
Ljugarn Sweden 45 L4
Ljungå Sweden 44 L3
Ljungan *r.* Sweden 45 L3
Ljungaverk Sweden 44 L3
Ljungby Sweden 45 K4
Ljungskile Sweden 45 J4
Ljusdal Sweden 45 L3
Ljusnan *r.* Sweden 45 L3
Ljusne Sweden 45 L3
Ljutomer Slovenia 56 I2
Llagostera Spain 55 N3
Llaima, Volcán *vol.* Chile 204 C5
Llanbedr U.K. *see* Lampeter
Llançà Spain 55 O2
also spelt Llansá
Llancanelo, Salina *salt flat* Arg. 204 C4
Llandeilo U.K. 47 I12
Llandovery U.K. 47 I12
also known as Llanymddyfri
Llandrindod Wells U.K. 47 I11
Llandudno U.K. 47 I10
Llanelli U.K. 47 H12
Llanes Spain 54 G1
Llangollen U.K. 47 I11
Llangurig U.K. 47 I11
Llano Mex. 184 C2
Llano U.S.A. 179 C6
Llano *r.* U.S.A. 179 C6
Llano Estacado *plain* U.S.A. 179 B5
Llanos *plain* Col./Venez. 198 D3
Llanquihue, Lago *l.* Chile 205 B6
Llansá Spain *see* Llançà
Llanymddyfri U.K. *see* Llandovery
Llata Peru 200 A2
Lleida Spain 55 L3
also spelt Lérida
Llentrisca, Cap *c.* Spain 55 M6
Llerena Spain 54 E6
Llica Bol. 200 C4
Lliria Spain 55 K5
Llobregat *r.* Spain 55 M3
Llodio Spain 55 I1
Lloret de Mar Spain 55 N3
Llorgara *nat. park* Albania 59 A8
Lloyd Bay Australia 149 D2
Lloyd George, Mount Canada 166 E3
Lloyd Lake Canada 167 I3
Lloydminster Canada 167 I4
Lluchmayor Spain *see* Llucmajor
Llucmajor Spain 55 N5
also spelt Lluchmayor
Llullaillaco, Volcán *vol.* Chile 200 C6
Lô *r.* China/Vietnam 86 C4
Loa *r.* Chile 200 C5
Loa U.S.A. 183 M3
Loagan Bunut National Park *Sarawak* Malaysia 77 F2
Loakulu Indon. 77 G3
Loanda Brazil 203 A7
Loano Italy 56 A4
Loay Phil. 74 C4
Lob' *r.* Rus. Fed. 43 Q5
Loban' *r.* Rus. Fed. 40 I4
Lobanovo Rus. Fed. 43 T8
Lobata Indon. 75 B3
Lobatse Botswana 131 E5
Löbau Germany 49 L4
Lobaye *pref.* Cent. Afr. Rep. 126 C3
Lobaye *r.* Cent. Afr. Rep. 126 C4
Löbenberg *hill* Germany 49 J4
Loberia Arg. 204 F5
Łobez Poland 49 M2
Lobito Angola 127 B8
Lobitos Peru 198 A6
Lobnya Rus. Fed. 43 S5
Loboko Congo 126 C5
Lobón Spain 54 E6
Lobos Arg. 204 F4
Lobos, Cabo *c.* Mex. 184 B2
Lobos, Isla de *i.* Mex. 185 F4
Lobos de Afuera, Islas *is* Peru 198 A6
Lobos de Tierra, Isla *i.* Peru 198 A6
Loburg Germany 48 J3
Loburn N.Z. 153 G11
Łobżenica Poland 49 O2
Locarno Switz. 51 O6
Lochaline U.K. 46 G7
Lochaish Canada 173 I2
Lo Chau *i.* *Hong Kong* China *see* Beaufort Island
Loch Baghasdail U.K. *see* Lochboisdale
Lochboisdale U.K. 46 E6
also spelt Loch Baghasdail
Lochern National Park Australia 149 D5
Loches France 50 G5
Loch Garman Rep. of Ireland *see* Wexford
Lochgilphead U.K. 46 G7
Lochiel S. Africa 133 O3
Lochinvar National Park Zambia 127 E8
Lochinver U.K. 46 G5
Lochmaddy U.K. 46 E6
also known as Loch nam Madadh
Lochnagar *mt.* U.K. 46 I7
Loch nam Madadh U.K. *see* Lochmaddy
Łochów Poland 49 S3
Lochranza U.K. 46 G8
Lochsa *r.* U.S.A. 180 D3
Lochy, Loch *l.* U.K. 46 H7
Lock Australia 146 B3
Lockbourne U.S.A. 176 C6
Lockeford U.S.A. 182 C3
Lockerbie U.K. 47 I8
Lockhart Australia 147 E3
Lockhart U.S.A. 179 C6
Lockhart River Australia 149 D2
Lockhart River Aboriginal Reserve Australia 149 D2
Lock Haven U.S.A. 176 H4
Löcknitz *r.* Germany 48 I2
Lockport U.S.A. 176 G2
Lockminé France 50 D5
Lôc Ninh Vietnam 79 D6
Locorotondo Italy 57 J8
Locri Italy 57 I10
Locumba *r.* Peru 200 C4
Lod Israel 108 F6
also known as Lydda
Loddon *r.* Australia 147 D3
Lode Latvia 42 G4
Lodève France 51 J9
Lodeynoye Pole Rus. Fed. 43 O1
Lodge, Mount Canada/U.S.A. 166 B3
Lodge Creek *r.* Canada/U.S.A. 167 I5
Lodhikheda India 96 C5
Lodhran Pak. 101 G4
Lodi Italy 56 B3
Lodi *CA* U.S.A. 182 C3
Lodi *OH* U.S.A. 176 C4
Lodi *WI* U.S.A. 172 D7
Løding Norway 44 K2
Lødingen Norway 44 K1
Lodja Dem. Rep. Congo 126 D5
Lodomeria Rus. Fed. *see* Vladimir
Lodosa Spain 55 I2
Lodrani India 96 A5
Lodwar Kenya 128 B4
Lodz Poland *see* Łódź
Łódź Poland 49 Q4
English form Lodz
Loei Thai. 78 C4
Loerie S. Africa 133 J10
Loeriesfontein S. Africa 132 D7
Lofoten *is* Norway 44 K1
Lofsdalen Sweden 45 K3
Loftee S. Africa 133 J7
Lofty Range *hills* Australia 150 B5
Log Rus. Fed. 41 G6
Loga Niger 125 F3
Logageng S. Africa 133 I2
Logan *IA* U.S.A. 178 D3
Logan *NM* U.S.A. 181 G6
Logan *OH* U.S.A. 176 C6
Logan *UT* U.S.A. 180 E4
Logan *WV* U.S.A. 176 D8

▶**Logan, Mount** Canada **166** A2
2nd highest mountain in North America.
northamerica [landscapes] ▶ 156–157

Logan, Mount U.S.A. 180 B2
Logan Creek *r.* Australia 149 E4
Logan Creek *r.* U.S.A. 178 C3
Logandale U.S.A. 183 J5
Logan Lake Canada 166 F5
Logan Mountains Canada 166 D2
Logansport *IN* U.S.A. 174 C3
Logansport *LA* U.S.A. 179 D6
Logatec Slovenia 56 G3
Lögdeälven *r.* Sweden 44 L3
Loge *r.* Angola 127 B6
Logone *r.* Africa 126 B1
Logone Birni Cameroon 125 I4
Logone Occidental *pref.* Chad 126 B2
Logone Oriental *pref.* Chad 126 C2
Logreşti Romania 58 E4
Logroño Spain 55 I2
Løgstør Denmark 45 J4
Logtak Lake India 97 G4
Logudoro *reg. Sardegna* Italy 57 A8
Lohardaga India 97 E5
Loharu India 96 B3
Lohatlha S. Africa 132 H5
Lohawat India 96 B4
Lohil *r.* China/India *see* Zayü Qu
Lohilahti Fin. 45 O3
Lohiniva Fin. 44 N2
Lohja Fin. 45 N3
Lohjanjärvi *l.* Fin. 42 E1
Löhne Germany 48 F3
Lohne (Oldenburg) Germany 48 F3
Lohtaja Fin. 44 M2
Lohusuu Estonia 42 I3
Loi, Nam *r.* Myanmar 78 C3
Loikaw Myanmar 78 B4
Loi Lan *mt.* Myanmar/Thai. 78 B4
Loi-lem Myanmar 78 B3
Loimaa Fin. 45 M3
Loimaan kunta Fin. 42 D1
Loipyet Hills Myanmar 78 B2
Loir *r.* France 50 F5
Loir, Les Vaux du *valley* France 50 G5
Loire *r.* France 51 D5
Loisach *r.* Germany 48 I8
Loi Sang *mt.* Myanmar 78 B3
Loi Song *mt.* Myanmar 78 B3
Loita Plains Kenya 128 B5
Loja Ecuador 198 B6
Loja *prov.* Ecuador 198 B6
Loja Spain 54 G7
Lokan *r. Sabah* Malaysia 77 G1
Lokandu Dem. Rep. Congo 126 E5
Lokan tekojärvi *l.* Fin. 44 N2
Lokchim *r.* Rus. Fed. 40 I3
Lokeren Belgium 51 K1
Loki *vol.* Iceland 44 [inset] C2
Lokichar Kenya 128 B4
Lokichokio Kenya 128 B3
Lokilalaki, Gunung *mt.* Indon. 75 B3
Lokka Fin. 44 N2
Løkken Denmark 45 J4
Løkken Norway 44 J3
Loknya Rus. Fed. 43 L5
Lokofe Dem. Rep. Congo 126 D5
Lokoja Nigeria 125 G5
Lokolama Dem. Rep. Congo 126 C5
Lokolo *r.* Dem. Rep. Congo 126 C5
Lokomo Cameroon 125 I6
Lokoro *r.* Dem. Rep. Congo 126 C5
Lokosafa Cent. Afr. Rep. 126 C4
Lokossa Benin 125 F5
Lokot' Rus. Fed. 43 P9
Loksa Estonia 42 G2
Loksebotn Norway 44 L1
Loks Land *i.* Canada 165 M3
Lokutu Dem. Rep. Congo *see* Elisabetha
Lol Sudan 126 F3
Lol *watercourse* Sudan 126 F2
Lola Angola 127 B8
Lola Guinea 124 C5
Lola, Mount U.S.A. 182 D2
Lolland *i.* Denmark 45 J5
Lolle *watercourse* Sudan 128 A2
Lollondo Tanz. 128 B5
Lolo Dem. Rep. Congo 126 D4
Lolo U.S.A. 180 D3
Loloda Indon. 75 C2
Loloda Utara, Kepulauan *is* Indon. 75 C2
Lolodorf Cameroon 125 H6
Lolo Pass U.S.A. 180 D3
Lolowau Indon. 76 B2
Lolwane S. Africa 132 H3
Lom Bulg. 58 E5
Lom *r.* Bulg. 58 E5
Lom Norway 45 J3
Lom Rus. Fed. 43 U4
Loma U.S.A. 183 P2
Loma Alta Bol. 200 D2
Lomako *r.* Dem. Rep. Congo 126 D4
Lomaloma Fiji 145 H3
Lomami *r.* Dem. Rep. Congo 126 E4
Loma Mountains Sierra Leone 124 C4
Lomar Pass Afgh. 101 F3
Lomas Peru 200 B3
Lomas Coloradas *hills* Arg. 205 D6
Lomas de Zamora Arg. 204 F4
Lomati *r.* S. Africa *see* Mlumati
Lombarda, Serra *hills* Brazil 199 H4
Lombardia *admin. reg.* Italy 56 B3
Lombardina Australia 150 C3
Lomblen *i.* Indon. 75 B5
Lombok Indon. 77 G5
Lombok *i.* Indon. 77 G5
Lombok, Selat *sea chan.* Indon. 77 F5

▶**Lomé** Togo **125** F5
Capital of Togo.

Lomela *r.* Dem. Rep. Congo 126 D5
Lomié Cameroon 125 I6
Lomira U.S.A. 172 E7
Lommel Belgium 51 L1
Lomond Canada 169 J3
Lomond, Loch *l.* U.K. 46 H7
Lomonosov Rus. Fed. 43 K2
Lomont *hills* France 51 M5
Lomovoye Rus. Fed. 40 G2
Lomphat Cambodia *see* Lumphăt
Lompobattang, Gunung *mt.* Indon. 75 A4
Lompoc U.S.A. 182 D7
Lom Sak Thai. 78 C4
Lomsjö Sweden 44 L2
Łomża Poland 49 T2
Lonar India 94 C2
Lonato Italy 56 C3
Lonavale India 94 B2
Loncopue Arg. 204 C5
Londa Bangl. 97 F5
Londa India 94 B3
Londinium U.K. *see* London
Londoko Rus. Fed. 82 D2
London Canada 168 D5

▶**London** U.K. **47** L12
Capital of the United Kingdom and of England. 3rd most populous city in Europe. Historically known as Londinium.
world [cities] ▶ 24–25
europe [environments] ▶ 36–37

London *KY* U.S.A. 176 A8
London *OH* U.S.A. 176 B6
London City *airport* U.K. 47 M12
Londonderry U.K. 47 E9
also known as Derry *or* Doire
Londonderry U.S.A. 177 M2
Londonderry, Cape Australia 150 D2
Londonderry, Isla *i.* Chile 205 C9
Londres Arg. 204 D2
Londrina Brazil 206 B10
Lone Mountain U.S.A. 176 A9
Lone Pine U.S.A. 182 F5
Long Thai. 78 B4
Longa Angola 127 C8
Longa *r. Bengo/Cuanza Sul* Angola 127 B7
Longa *r. Cuando Cubango* Angola 127 C9
Longa Greece 59 C12
Longa, Proliv *sea chan.* Rus. Fed. 39 R2
English form De Long Strait
Longagung Indon. 77 F2
Long Akah *Sarawak* Malaysia 77 F2
Longa-Mavinga, Coutada Pública do *nature res.* Angola 127 D9
Long'an China 87 C4
Long'an China *see* Pingwu
Longarone Italy 56 E2
Longaví, Nevado de *mt.* Chile 204 C5
Long Bay U.S.A. 175 E5
Longbeach N.Z. 153 F12
Long Beach *CA* U.S.A. 182 F8
Long Beach *WA* U.S.A. 180 A3
Longbia Indon. 77 G2
Longboh Indon. 77 F2
Long Branch U.S.A. 177 L5
Longburn N.Z. 152 J8
Long Cay *i.* Bahamas 187 E2
Longchang China 86 C2
also known as Jin'e
Longcheng China *see* Xiaoxian
Longcheng China *see* Longmen
Longcheng China *see* Pengze
Longchuan China *see* Chenggong
Longchuan China 87 E3
also known as Laolong
Longchuan China *see* Nanhua
Longchuan Jiang *r.* China 86 A4
Long Creek *r.* Canada 167 K5
Long Eaton U.K. 47 K11
Longfellow, Mount N.Z. 153 G10
Longford Rep. of Ireland 47 E10
Longgang China *see* Dazu
Longgang China 87 E4
Longgi *r.* Indon. 77 G2
Long Harbour *Hong Kong* China 87 [inset]
also known as Tai Tan Hoi Hap
Longhope U.K. 46 I5
Longhua China 85 H3
Longhui China 87 D3
also known as Taohong; *formerly known as* Taohuaping
Longhurst, Mount Antarctica 223 K1
Longibau Indon. 77 G2
Longido Tanz. 128 C5
Longikis Indon. 77 G3
Longing, Cape Antarctica 222 U2
Longiram Indon. 77 F3
Long Island Bahamas 187 E2
Long Island *N.S.* Canada 169 H4
Long Island *Nunavut* Canada 168 E2
Long Island India 95 G3
Long Island P.N.G. 73 K8
Long Island U.S.A. 177 M5
Long Island Sound *sea chan.* U.S.A. 177 L4
Longjiang China 85 I2
Long Jiang *r.* China 87 D3
Longjin China *see* Qingliu
Longjin China *see* Anyi
Longjuzhai China *see* Danfeng
Longkou China 85 I4
Longkou Wan *b.* China 85 I4
Longlac Canada 168 C3
Long Lake *l.* Canada 168 C3
Long Lake U.S.A. 177 K2
Long Lake *l. MI* U.S.A. 172 H6
Long Lake *l. MI* U.S.A. 173 J5
Long Lake *l. NY* U.S.A. 177 K1
Longli China 86 C3
also known as Longshan
Longlin China 86 C3
also known as Xinzhou
Longmeadow U.S.A. 177 M3
Longmen China 87 E4
also known as Longcheng
Longmen Shan *mts* China 86 C1
Longming China 86 C4
Longmont U.S.A. 180 F4
Longnan China 87 E3
Longnawan Indon. 77 F2
Longobucco Italy 57 I9
Longonjo Angola 127 B8
Longotoma Chile 204 C4
Longpahangai Indon. 77 F2
Long Phu Vietnam 79 D6
Longping China *see* Luodian
Long Point Canada 168 D5
Long Point *pt Man.* Canada 167 L4
Long Point *pt Ont.* Canada 168 D5
Long Point Bay Canada 173 M8
Long Prairie U.S.A. 178 D2
Longpujungan Indon. 77 F2
Longquan China *see* Danzhai
Longquan China *see* Fenggang
Longquan China 87 F2
Longquan Xi *r.* China 87 G2
Long Range Mountains *Nfld.* Canada 169 J3
Longreach Australia 149 E4
Long Reef Australia 150 D2
Long Reef P.N.G. 149 F1
Longriba China 86 B1
Long Ridge U.S.A. 176 A7
Longshan China *see* Longli
Longshan China 87 D2
also known as Min'an
Longsheng China 87 D3
Longshou Shan *mts* China 84 D4
Longs Peak U.S.A. 180 F4
Long Teru *Sarawak* Malaysia 77 F2
Longtian China 87 D2
Longtom Lake Canada 167 G1
Long Tompas *pass* S. Africa 133 O2
Longtown U.K. 47 J8
Longué-Jumelles France 50 F5
Longue-Pointe Canada 169 H3
Longueuil Canada 169 F4
Longuyon France 51 L3
Longvale U.S.A. 182 A2
Long Valley U.S.A. 183 M7
Longview *TX* U.S.A. 179 D5
Longview *WA* U.S.A. 180 B3
Longwangmiao China 90 C2
Longwei Co *l.* China 89 E5
Longxi China 86 C1
Longxian China *see* Wengyuan
Longxian China 86 C1
Longxi Shan *mt.* China 87 F3
Longxun China *see* Dehua
Long Xuyên Vietnam 79 D6
Longyan China 87 F3
Longyao China 85 G4

▶**Longyearbyen** Svalbard **38** B2
Capital of Svalbard.

Longzhen China 82 B2
Longzhou China 86 C4
Longzhouping China *see* Changyang
Lonigo Italy 56 D3
Lonja *r.* Croatia 56 I3
Lonjsko Polje *plain* Croatia 56 I3
Lonkintsy Madag. 131 [inset] K3
Lonoke U.S.A. 174 B5
Lönsboda Sweden 45 K4
Lønsdalen *valley* Norway 44 K2
Lons-le-Saunier France 51 L6
Lontar *i.* Indon. 75 D4
Lonton Myanmar 78 B2
Lontra Brazil 199 I6
Lontra *r. Mato Grosso do Sul* Brazil 203 A7
Lontra *r. Tocantins* Brazil 202 B3
Loo Estonia 42 F2
Looc Phil. 74 B3
Loochoo Islands Japan *see* Ryukyu Islands
Looking Glass *r.* U.S.A. 173 I8
Lookout, Cape Canada 168 D2
Lookout, Cape U.S.A. 174 E5
Lookout, Point U.S.A. 173 J6
Lookout Mountain U.S.A. 182 F5
Lookout Point *Qld* Australia 149 E2
Lookout Point *W.A.* Australia 151 B7
Loolmalasin *vol. crater* Tanz. 128 B5
Looma Australia 150 D3
Loon Canada 168 B3
Loon *r.* Canada 167 H3
Loongana Australia 151 D6
Loon Lake Canada 167 I4
Loop Head Rep. of Ireland 47 C11
Lootsberg Pass S. Africa 133 I8
Lop China 89 C4
Lopandino Rus. Fed. 43 P9
Lopary Madag. 131 [inset] J4
Lopasnya Rus. Fed. *see* Chekhov
Lopasnya *r.* Rus. Fed. 43 S7
Lopatina, Gora *mt.* Rus. Fed. 82 F2
Lopatino Rus. Fed. 41 H5
Lopatinskiy Rus. Fed. 43 T6
Lopatka, Cape Rus. Fed. *see* Lopatka, Mys
Lopatka, Mys *c. Kamchatskaya Oblast'* Rus. Fed. 39 P4
Lopatka, Mys *c. Respublika Sakha (Yakutiya)* Rus. Fed. 39 P2
English form Lopatka, Cape
Lopatovo Rus. Fed. 43 J4
Lopazna Rus. Fed. 43 N8
Lop Buri Thai. 79 C5
also known as Tha Hin
Lopé-Okanda, Réserve de *nature res.* Gabon 126 A5
Lopez Phil. 74 B3
Lopez, Cap *c.* Gabon 126 A5
Lopnur China *see* Yuli
Lop Nur *salt l.* China 88 E3
Lopori *r.* Dem. Rep. Congo 126 C4
Lopphavet *b.* Norway 44 M1
Loppi Fin. 45 N3
Lora *r.* Afgh. 101 F4
Lora *watercourse* Australia 146 B2
Lora Norway 45 J3
Lora del Río Spain 54 F7
Lorain U.S.A. 176 C4
Loralai Pak. 101 G4
Loralai *r.* Pak. 101 G4
Lorca Spain 55 J7
Lord Howe Atoll Solomon Is *see* Ontong Java Atoll
Lord Howe Island Australia 145 E5
Lord Loughborough Island Myanmar 79 B6
Lordsburg U.S.A. 181 E6
Lore Lindu National Park Indon. 75 B3
Lorena Brazil 203 C7
Lorengau P.N.G. 73 K7
Lorentz *r.* Indon. 73 I8
Lorentz National Park Indon. 73 I7
Lorenzo del Real Mex. 185 F4
Lorenzo Geyres Uruguay 204 F4
Lorestān *prov.* Iran 100 B3
Loreto Brazil 202 C3
Loreto Italy 56 F5
Loreto Mex. 184 C3
Loreto Para. 201 F5
Loreto *dept* Peru 198 C5
Loreto Phil. 74 C4
Loretta U.S.A. 172 C5
Lorian Swamp Kenya 128 C4
Lorica Col. 198 C2
Lorient France 50 C5
Lorillard *r.* Canada 167 N1
Lormi India 97 D5
Lorn, Firth of *est.* U.K. 46 G7
Lorne *Qld* Australia 149 E5
Lorne *Vic.* Australia 147 D4
Loro *r.* China 89 F6
Loropéni Burkina 124 E4
Lörrach Germany 48 E8
Lorrain, Plateau France 51 M4
Lorraine Australia 148 C3
Lorraine *admin. reg.* France 51 M4
Lorraine, Parc Naturel Régional de *park* France 51 L4
Lort *r.* Australia 151 C7
Lörudden Sweden 45 L3
Los, Îles de *is* Guinea 124 B4
Losai National Reserve *nature res.* Kenya 128 C4
Losal India 96 B4
Los Alamitos, Sierra de *mt.* Mex. 185 E3
Los Alamos *CA* U.S.A. 182 D7
Los Alamos *NM* U.S.A. 181 F6
Los Alerces, Parque Nacional *nat. park* Arg. 205 C6
Los Amores Arg. 204 F3
Los Andes Chile 204 C4
Los Angeles Chile 204 B5

▶**Los Angeles** U.S.A. **182** F7
3rd most populous city in North America and 7th in the world.
world [cities] ▶ 24–25
northamerica [threats] ▶ 160–161

Los Angeles Aqueduct *canal* U.S.A. 182 F6
Los Antiguos Arg. 205 C7
Los Arabos Cuba 186 C2
Los Argallanes, Sierra de *hills* Spain 54 F6
Los Banos U.S.A. 182 D4
Los Barreros *mt.* Spain 55 I6
Los Barrios Spain 54 F8
Los Blancos Arg. 201 E5
Los Caballos Mesteños, Llano de *plain* Mex. 184 D2
Los Canarreos, Archipiélago de *is* Cuba 186 C2
Los Chiles Costa Rica 186 B5
Los Chonos, Archipiélago de *is* Chile 205 B7
Los Choros, Islas de *is* Chile 204 C3
Los Cisnes, Lagunas de *lakes* Arg. 204 E3
Los Corales del Rosario, Parque Nacional *nat. park* Col. 198 C2
Los Coronados, Golfo de *b.* Chile 205 B6
Los Coronados, Islas *is* Mex. 183 G9
Los Corrales de Buelna Spain 54 G1
Los Cusis *Beni* Bol. 200 D3
Los Cusis *Beni* Bol. 201 D3
Los Difuntos, Lago de *l.* Uruguay *see* Negra, Lago
Los Desventurados, Islas de *is* S. Pacific Ocean 221 M7
Los Estados, Isla de *i.* Arg. 205 D9
historically known as Staten Island
Losevo Rus. Fed. 41 G6
Loseya *well* Tanz. 129 C6
Los Gatos U.S.A. 182 C4
Los Glaciares, Parque Nacional *nat. park* Arg. 205 B8
Los Haitises *nat. park* Dom. Rep. 187 F3
Los Hoyos Mex. 184 C2
Los Huemules, Parque Nacional *nat. park* Chile 205 B7
Los Huicholes, Sierra de *mts* Mex. 184 D4
Łosice Poland 49 T3
Los Idolos Mex. 185 G5
Lošinj *i.* Croatia 56 G4
Los Jardines de la Reina, Archipiélago de *is* Cuba 186 D2
Los Juríes Arg. 204 E3
Loskop S. Africa 133 N5
Loskop Dam Nature Reserve S. Africa 133 N2
Los Lagos Chile 204 B5
Los Lagos *admin. reg.* Chile 204 B6
Loslau Poland *see* Wodzisław Śląski
Los Leones Mex. 184 D2
Los Lunas U.S.A. 181 F6
Los Mármoles, Parque Nacional *nat. park* Mex. 185 F4
Los Menucos Arg. 204 C6
Los Mexicanos, Lago de *l.* Mex. 184 D2
Los'mino Rus. Fed. 43 P6
Los Mochis Mex. 184 C3
Los Molinos U.S.A. 182 B1
Los Mosquitos, Golfo de *b.* Panama 186 C5
Los Navalmorales Spain 54 G5
Los Nevados, Parque Nacional *nat. park* Col. 198 C3
Los Nodales, Bahía de *b.* Arg. 205 D8
Los Organos, Sierra de *hills* Cuba 175 C8
Los Palacios Cuba 186 C2
Los Palacios y Villafranca Spain 54 F7
Lospatos East Timor 75 C5
Los Pedroches *plat.* Spain 54 F6
Los Picos de Europa, Parque Nacional de *nat. park* Spain 54 G1
Los Reyes Mex. 185 E5
Los Riachos, Islas de *is* Arg. 204 E6
Los Ríos *prov.* Ecuador 198 B5
Los Roques, Islas *is* Venez. 199 E2
Los Sauces Chile 204 B5
Lossiemouth U.K. 46 I6
Los Taques Venez. 198 D2
Lost Creek U.S.A. 176 B8
Los Telares Arg. 204 E3
Los Teques Venez. 199 E2
Los Testigos *is* Venez. 199 F2
Lost Hills U.S.A. 182 E6
Los Tigres Arg. 204 E2
Lost Trail Pass U.S.A. 180 D3
Losvida, Vozyera *l.* Belarus 43 L6
Los Vientos Chile 200 C6
Los Vilos Chile 204 C3
Los Yébenes Spain 54 H5
Lot *r.* France 51 G8
Lota Chile 204 B5
Lotagipi Swamp Kenya 128 B3
Lote Norway 45 I3
Løten Norway 45 J3
Lotfābād Turkm. 102 D5
Loth U.K. 46 J4
Lothagum Hills Sudan 128 B3
Lothair S. Africa 133 O3
L'Oti, Réserve de Faune de *nature res.* Togo 125 F4
Lotikipi Plain Kenya 128 B3
Loto Dem. Rep. Congo 126 D5
Lotoi *r.* Dem. Rep. Congo 126 C5
Lotoshino Rus. Fed. 43 Q5
Lot's Wife *i.* Japan *see* Sōfu-gan
Lotta *r.* Fin./Rus. Fed. 44 O1
also spelt Lutto
Louang Namtha Laos 78 C3
also spelt Luang Nam Tha
Louangphrabang Laos 78 C4
also spelt Luang Prabang
Louang Phrabang Range *mts* Laos/Thai. 78 C4
Loubomo Congo 126 B6
also known as Dolisie
Loučná *hill* Czech Rep. 49 K5
Loudéac France 50 D4
Loudi China 87 D3
Loudima Congo 126 B6
Loudon U.S.A. 174 C5
Loudonville U.S.A. 176 C5
Loudun France 50 G5
Louéssé *r.* Congo 126 B5
L'Ouest, Pointe de *pt* Canada 169 H3
Louga Senegal 124 A3
Loughborough U.K. 47 K11
Lougheed Island Canada 165 I2
Loughrea Rep. of Ireland 47 D10
Louhans France 51 L6
Louisa *KY* U.S.A. 176 C7
Louisa *VA* U.S.A. 176 H7
Louisa Downs Aboriginal Reserve Australia 150 D3
Louisbourg Canada 169 J4
formerly spelt Louisburg
Louisburg Canada *see* Louisbourg
Louisburg U.S.A. 176 G9
Louise Falls Canada 167 G2
Louis Gentil Morocco *see* Youssoufia
Louisiade Archipelago *is* P.N.G. 149 G1
Louisiana U.S.A. 174 B4
Louisiana *state* U.S.A. 175 B6
Louis Trichardt S. Africa 131 F4
Louisvale S. Africa 132 F5
Louisville *GA* U.S.A. 175 D5
Louisville *IL* U.S.A. 174 B4
Louisville *KY* U.S.A. 174 C4
Louisville *MS* U.S.A. 175 B5
Louisville *OH* U.S.A. 176 D5
Louis-XIV, Pointe *pt* Canada 168 E2
Loukhi Rus. Fed. 44 P2
Loukoléla Congo 126 C5
Loukouo Congo 126 B5
Loulé Port. 54 C7
Louloni Mali 124 D4
Loum Cameroon 125 H5
Louny Czech Rep. 49 K5
Loup *r.* U.S.A. 178 C3
Loup City U.S.A. 178 C3
Loups-Marins, Lacs des *lakes* Canada 169 F1
Lourdes Canada 169 J3
Lourdes France 50 F9
Lourenço Brazil 199 I4
Lourenço Marques Moz. *see* Maputo
Lourinhã Port. 54 B5
Lousã Port. 54 C4
Louterwater S. Africa 132 H10
Louth Australia 147 E2
Louth U.K. 47 L10
Loutra Greece 59 F11
Loutra Aidipsou Greece 59 E10
Loutraki Greece 59 D11
Louvain Belgium *see* Leuven
Louviers France 50 H3
Louwsburg S. Africa 133 P4
Lövånger Sweden 44 M2
Lovasberény Hungary 49 P8
Lovat' *r.* Rus. Fed. 43 M3
Lövberga Sweden 44 K3
Lovćen *mts* Yugo. 56 K6
Lovech Bulg. 58 F5
Loveland U.S.A. 180 F4
Lovell *ME* U.S.A. 177 O1
Lovell *WY* U.S.A. 180 E3
Lovelock U.S.A. 182 F1
Lovenia, Mount U.S.A. 183 N1
Lovere Italy 56 C3
Lovers' Leap *mt.* U.S.A. 176 E9
Loves Park U.S.A. 172 D8
Loviisa Fin. 45 N3
Lovington U.S.A. 179 B5
Lovozero Rus. Fed. 40 E1
Lovran Croatia 56 G3
Lovrin Romania 58 B3
Lövstabukten *b.* Sweden 45 L3
Lovtsy Rus. Fed. 43 U6
Lóvua Angola 127 D6
Lóvua Angola 127 D7
Low Canada 173 R5
Lowa Dem. Rep. Congo 126 E5
Lowa *r.* Dem. Rep. Congo 126 E5
Lowarai Pass Pak. 101 G3
Lowell *IN* U.S.A. 172 F9
Lowell *MA* U.S.A. 177 N3
Lowell *MI* U.S.A. 172 H8
Lowell *OR* U.S.A. 180 B4
Lowell *VT* U.S.A. 177 M1
Lowelli Sudan 128 B3
Löwen *watercourse* Namibia 132 B4
Lower Arrow Lake Canada 166 G5
Lower Brule Indian Reservation *res.* U.S.A. 178 C2
Lower California *pen.* Mex. *see* Baja California
Lower Garry Lake Canada 167 L1
Lower Glenelg National Park Australia 146 D4
Lower Granite Gorge U.S.A. 183 K6
Lower Hutt N.Z. 152 I9
Lower Klamath National Wildlife Refuge *nature res.* U.S.A. 180 B4
Lower Laberge Canada 166 C2
Lower Lake U.S.A. 182 B3
Lower Loteni S. Africa 133 N6
Lower Lough Erne *l.* U.K. 47 E9
Lower Peirce Reservoir Sing. 76 [inset]
Lower Pitseng S. Africa 133 M7
Lower Red Lake U.S.A. 178 D2
Lower Sabie S. Africa 133 P2
Lower Saxony *land* Germany *see* Niedersachsen
Lower Tunguska *r.* Rus. Fed. *see* Nizhnyaya Tunguska
Lower Zambezi National Park Zambia 127 F8

Lowestoft U.K. 47 N11
Lowgar prov. Afgh. 101 G3
Łowicz Poland 49 Q3
Low Island Kiribati see Starbuck Island
Lowmoor U.S.A. 176 F8
Lowsville U.S.A. 176 E6
Lowville U.S.A. 177 J2
Loxton Australia 146 D3
Loxton S. Africa 132 G8
Loyalsock Creek r. U.S.A. 177 I4
Loyalton U.S.A. 182 D2
Loyalty Islands New Caledonia see Loyauté, Îles
Loyang China see Luoyang
Loyauté, Îles is New Caledonia 145 F4
English form Loyalty Islands
Loyd U.S.A. 172 C7
Loyengo Swaziland 133 P3
Loyev Belarus see Loyew
Loyew Belarus 41 D6
also spelt Loyev
Loyno Rus. Fed. 40 J4
Loyola, Punta pt Arg. 205 C8
Løypskardtinden mt. Norway 44 K2
Lozère, Mont mt. France 51 J8
Loznica Srbija Yugo. 58 A4
Loznitsa Bulg. 58 H5
Lozova Ukr. 41 F6
also spelt Lozovaya
Lozovaya Kazakh. see Lozovoye
Lozovaya Ukr. see Lozova
Lozovik Srbija Yugo. 58 C4
Lozovoye Kazakh. 103 I1
formerly known as Lozovaya
Loz'va r. Rus. Fed. 40 L3
Ltyentye Apurte Aboriginal Land res. Australia 148 B5
also known as Santa Teresa Aboriginal Land
Lu r. China 85 F4
Luabo Moz. 131 H3
Luacano Angola 127 D7
Luachimo r. Angola/Dem. Rep. Congo 127 D6
Lua Dekere r. Dem. Rep. Congo 126 C4
Luakila Dem. Rep. Congo 126 E6
Luala r. Moz. 131 H3
Luambe National Park Zambia 129 B8
Luamssa r. Zambia 127 E8
Lu'an China 87 F2
Luanchuan China 87 D1
Luanco Spain 54 F1

▶Luanda Angola 127 B7
Capital of Angola.

Luanda prov. Angola 127 B7
Luando Angola 127 C7
Luando r. Angola 127 C7
Luando, Reserva Natural Integral do nature res. Angola 127 C7
Luang, Khao mt. Thai. 79 B6
Luanginga r. Zambia 127 D8
Luang Nam Tha Laos see Louang Namtha
Luang Prabang Laos see Louangphrabang
Luanguinga r. Angola 127 D8
Luangwa Zambia 127 F8
formerly known as Feira
Luangwa r. Zambia 127 F8
Luanhaizi China 84 B5
Luan He r. China 85 H4
Luannan China 85 H4
also known as Bencheng
Lua Nova Brazil 199 G6
Luanping China 85 H3
Luanshya Zambia 127 F8
Luanxian China 85 H4
also known as Luanzhou
Luanza Dem. Rep. Congo 127 F7
Luanzhou China see Luanxian
Luao Angola see Luau
Luapula prov. Zambia 127 F7
Luar, Danau l. Indon. 77 F2
Luarca Spain 54 E1
Luashi Dem. Rep. Congo 127 D7
Luatamba Angola 127 D8
Luau Angola 127 D7
formerly known as Teixeira de Sousa or Vila Teixeira de Sousa; formerly spelt Luao
Luba Equat. Guinea 125 H6
formerly known as San Carlos
Lubaczów Poland 49 U5
Lubalo Angola 127 C7
Lubań Poland 49 M4
Lubāna Latvia 42 H5
Lubānas ezers l. Latvia 42 H5
Lubang Phil. 74 B3
Lubang i. Phil. 74 B3
Lubang Islands Phil. 74 A3
Lubango Angola 127 B8
formerly known as Sá da Bandeira
Lubao Dem. Rep. Congo 127 E6
Lubartów Poland 49 T4
Lubawa Poland 49 Q2
Lübbecke Germany 48 F3
Lübben Germany 49 K4
Lübbenau Germany 49 K4
Lubbeskolk salt pan S. Africa 132 D6
Lubbock U.S.A. 179 B5
Lübeck Germany 48 H2
Lubeck U.S.A. 176 D6
Lübecker Bucht b. Germany 48 H1
Lubefu Dem. Rep. Congo 126 E6
Lubei China 85 I2
also known as Jarud
Lubelska, Wyżyna hills Poland 49 T4
Lüben Poland see Lubin
Lubenka Kazakh. 102 C2
Lubero Dem. Rep. Congo 126 F5
Lubéron, Montagne du ridge France 51 L9
Lubéron, Parc Naturel Régional du nature res. France 51 L9
Lubersac France 50 H7
Lubie, Jezioro l. Poland 49 M2
Lubienka r. Poland 49 P3
Lubień Kujawski Poland 49 Q3
Lubin Poland 49 N4
historically known as Lüben
Lubisi Dam resr S. Africa 133 L8
Lublin Poland 49 T4
Lubliniec Poland 49 P5
Lubnān country Asia see Lebanon
Lubny Ukr. 41 E6
Lubok Antu Sarawak Malaysia 77 E2
Luboń Poland 49 N3
Lubosalma Rus. Fed. 44 O3
Lubraniec Poland 49 P3
Lubrín Spain 55 I7
Lübtheen Germany 48 I2
Lubuagan Phil. 74 B2
Lubudi Dem. Rep. Congo 127 E7
Lubudi r. Dem. Rep. Congo 127 E7
Lubuklinggau Indon. 76 C3
Lubukpakam Indon. 76 B2
Lubuksikaping Indon. 76 C2
Lubumbashi Dem. Rep. Congo 127 E7
formerly known as Élisabethville
Lubunda Dem. Rep. Congo 127 E6
Lubungu Zambia 127 E8
Lubuta Zambia 127 D9
Lubutu Dem. Rep. Congo 126 E5
Lubutu r. Dem. Rep. Congo 126 E5
Lubwe Zambia 127 F7
Lubyanki Rus. Fed. 43 Q9
Lucala Angola 127 B7
Lucan Canada 173 L7
Lucanas Peru 200 B3
Lučani Srbija Yugo. 58 B5
Lucania, Mount Canada 166 A2
Lücaoshan China 84 B4
Lucapa Angola 127 D7
formerly known as Lukapa
Lucas Brazil 201 G3
Lucasville U.S.A. 176 C7
Lucca Italy 56 C5
Lucé France 50 H4
Lucea Jamaica 186 D3
Luce Bay U.K. 47 H9
Lucedale U.S.A. 175 B6
Lucélia Brazil 206 B8
Lucena Phil. 74 B3
Lucena Spain 54 G7
Lučenec Slovakia 49 Q7
Lucera Italy 56 H7
Lucerna Peru 200 C3
Lucerne Switz. 51 O5
also spelt Luzern
Lucerne U.S.A. 182 B2
Lucerne Valley U.S.A. 183 H7
Lucero Mex. 184 D2
Lucha r. Rus. Fed. 82 C1
Luchay Belarus 42 I6
Luchegorsk Rus. Fed. 82 D3
Lucheng China see Luchuan
Lucheng China 85 G4
Lucheng China see Kangding
Lucheringo r. Moz. 129 C7
Luchki Rus. Fed. 43 U5
Luchosa r. Belarus 43 L7
Lüchow Germany 48 I3
Luchuan China 87 D4
also known as Lucheng
Lüchun China 86 B4
also known as Daxing
Lucinda Australia 149 E3
Lucipara, Kepulauan is Indon. 75 C4
Lucira Angola 127 B8
Luciu Romania 58 I4
Łuck Ukr. see Luts'k
Luck U.S.A. 172 A5
Luckau Germany 49 K4
Luckeesarai India 97 E4
also spelt Lakhisarai
Luckenwalde Germany 49 K3
Luckhoff S. Africa 133 I6
Lucknow Canada 173 L7
Lucknow India 96 D4
Luçon France 50 E6
Lücongpo China 87 D2
Lucunga Angola 127 B6
Lucusse Angola 127 D8
Lucy Creek Australia 148 C4
Lüda China see Dalian
Luda Kamchiya r. Bulg. 58 I5
Ludbreg Croatia 56 I2
Lüdenscheid Germany 48 E4
Lüderitz Namibia 130 B5
Ludewa Tanz. 129 B7
Ludhiana India 96 B3
Ludian China 86 B3
also known as Wenping
Luding China 86 B2
also known as Jagsamka or Luqiao
Ludington U.S.A. 172 G7
Ludlow U.K. 47 J11
Ludlow CA U.S.A. 183 H7
Ludlow VT U.S.A. 177 M2
Ludogorie reg. Bulg. 58 H5
Ludogorsko Plato plat. Bulg. 58 H5
Ludoni Rus. Fed. 43 K3
Ludowici U.S.A. 175 D6
Luduș Romania 58 F2
Ludvika Sweden 45 K3
Ludwigsburg Germany 48 G7
Ludwigsfelde Germany 49 K3
Ludwigshafen am Rhein Germany 48 F6
Ludwigslust Germany 48 I2
Ludwigsort Rus. Fed. see Ladushkin
Ludza Latvia 42 I5
Luebo Dem. Rep. Congo 127 D6
Lueki Dem. Rep. Congo 126 E5
Lueki r. Dem. Rep. Congo 126 E5
Luembe Zambia 127 F8
Luena Angola 127 C7
formerly known as Luso
Luena Dem. Rep. Congo 127 E7
Luena Zambia 127 F7
Luena r. Zambia 127 D8
Luena Flats plain Zambia 127 D8
Luengé, Coutada Pública do nature res. Angola 127 D9
Luengue r. Angola 127 D9
Luenha r. Moz./Zimbabwe 131 G3
Luepa Venez. 199 F3
Lüeyang China 86 C1
Lufeng Guangdong China 87 E4
Lufeng China see Xupu
Lufeng Yunnan China 86 B3
also known as Jinshan
Lufira r. Dem. Rep. Congo 127 E7
Lufkin U.S.A. 179 D6
Lufu China see Lunan
Lug r. Yugo. 58 C4
Luga Rus. Fed. 43 K3
Luga r. Rus. Fed. 43 J2
Lugano Switz. 51 O6
Lugansk Ukr. see Luhans'k
Luganville Vanuatu 145 F3
Lugdunum France see Lyon
Lugela Moz. 131 H3
Lugela r. Moz. 131 H3
Lugenda r. Moz. 131 H1
Lugg r. U.K. 47 J11
Luggate N.Z. 153 D12
Luggudontsen mt. China 89 E6
Lughaye Somalia 128 D2
Lugo Italy 56 D4
Lugo Spain 54 D1
Lugoj Romania 58 C3
Lugovaya Rus. Fed. 43 S5
Lugovaya Proleyka Rus. Fed. see Primorsk
Lugovoy Kazakh. 103 H4
Lugovoye Kazakh. 103 H4
Lugus i. Phil. 74 B5
Luhanka Fin. 45 N3
Luhans'k Ukr. 41 F6
also spelt Lugansk; formerly known as Voroshilovgrad
Luhawskiya Belarus 43 L6
Luhe China 87 F1
Luḩfī, Wādī watercourse Jordan 109 H5
Luhin Sum China 85 H2
Luhit r. China/India see Zayü Qu
Luhit r. India 97 G3
Luhombero Tanz. 129 C7
Luhua China see Heishui
Luhuo China 86 B2
also known as Xindu or Zhaggo
Luhyny Ukr. 41 D6
Luia Angola 127 D7
Luia r. Angola 127 D6
Luia r. Moz. 131 G3
Luiana Angola 127 D9
Luiana r. Angola 127 D9
Luiana, Coutada Pública do nature res. Angola 127 D9
Luica Romania 58 H4
Luichow Peninsula China see Leizhou Bandao
Luik Belgium see Liège
Luilaka r. Dem. Rep. Congo 126 D5
Luimneach Rep. of Ireland see Limerick
Luing i. U.K. 46 G7
Luino Italy 56 A3
Luio r. Angola 127 D8
Luiro r. Fin. 44 N2
Luís Correia Brazil 202 D2
Luís Echeverría Álvarez Mex. 183 H9
Luís Gomes Brazil 202 E3
Luishia Dem. Rep. Congo 127 E7
Luis L. León, Presa resr Mex. 184 D2
Luis Moya Durango Mex. 184 E3
Luis Moya Zacatecas Mex. 185 E4
Luitpold Coast Antarctica 222 V1
Luiza Dem. Rep. Congo 127 D6
Luizi Dem. Rep. Congo 127 E6
Luján Arg. 204 F4
Luján de Cuyo Arg. 204 C4
Lujiang China 87 F2
Lukackek Rus. Fed. 82 D1
Lukala Dem. Rep. Congo 127 B6
Lukanga Dem. Rep. Congo 126 C6
Lukanga Swamps Zambia 127 E8
Lukapa Angola see Lucapa
Lukavac Bos.-Herz. 56 K4
Luke, Mount hill Australia 151 B5
Lukenga, Lac l. Dem. Rep. Congo 127 E7
Lukenie r. Dem. Rep. Congo 126 C5
Lukh r. Rus. Fed. 40 G4
Lukhovitsy Rus. Fed. 43 U7
Lŭki Bulg. 58 F7
Lukinskaya Rus. Fed. 43 P1
Luk Keng Hong Kong China 87 [inset]
Lukolela Équateur Dem. Rep. Congo 126 C5
Lukolela Kasai Oriental Dem. Rep. Congo 127 E6
Lukomskaye, Vozyera l. Belarus 43 K7
Lukou China see Zhuzhou
Lukovac r. Bos.-Herz. 56 L4
Lukovë Albania 59 A9
Lukovit Bulg. 58 F5
Lukovnikovo Rus. Fed. 43 P5
Łuków Poland 49 T4
Lukoyanov Rus. Fed. 40 H5
Luksagu Indon. 75 B3
Lukšiai Lith. 42 E7
Lukuga r. Dem. Rep. Congo 127 E6
Lukula Dem. Rep. Congo 127 B6
Lukuledi Tanz. 129 C7
Lukulu Zambia 127 D8
Lukumburu Tanz. 129 B7
Lukuni Dem. Rep. Congo 127 C6
Lukusashi r. Zambia 127 F8
Lukusuzi National Park Zambia 129 B8
Lula r. Dem. Rep. Congo 126 D5
Luleå Sweden 44 M2
Luleälven r. Sweden 44 M2
Lüleburgaz Turkey 106 A2
Lules Arg. 204 D2
Luliang China 86 B3
also known as Zhongshu
Lüliang Shan mts China 85 F4
Lulimba Dem. Rep. Congo 126 F6
Luling U.S.A. 179 C6
Lulong China 85 H4
Lulonga Dem. Rep. Congo 126 C4
Lulonga r. Dem. Rep. Congo 126 C4
Lulu r. Dem. Rep. Congo 126 D4
Luluabourg Dem. Rep. Congo see Kananga
Lülung China 89 D6
Lulworth, Mount hill Australia 151 B5
Lumachomo China 89 D6
Lumai Angola 127 D8
Lumajang Indon. 77 F5
Lumajangdong Co salt l. China 89 C5
Lumanda Estonia 42 D3
Lūmār Iran 107 F4
Lumbala Angola see Lumbala N'guimbo
Lumbala Angola see Lumbala Kaquengue
Lumbala Kaquengue Angola 127 D8
formerly known as Lumbala
Lumbala N'guimbo Angola 127 D8
formerly known as Gago Coutinho or Lumbala
Lumber r. U.S.A. 174 E5
Lumberton U.S.A. 174 E5
Lumbis Indon. 77 G1
Lumbrales Spain 54 E4
Lumding India 97 G4
Lumecha Tanz. 129 B7
Lumezzane Italy 56 C3
Lumi P.N.G. 73 J7
Lumijoki Fin. 44 N2
Lumina Romania 58 J4
Luminárias Brazil 207 I8
Lum-nan-pai Wildlife Reserve nature res. Thai. 78 B4
Lumparland Fin. 45 M3
Lumphăt Cambodia 79 D5
also spelt Lomphat
Lumpkin U.S.A. 175 C5
Lumsden Canada 167 J5
Lumsden N.Z. 153 C13
Lumut, Gunung mt. Indon. 77 F3
Lumut, Tanjung pt Indon. 77 D3
Lumwana Zambia 127 E7
Lün Mongolia 85 E2
Luna Phil. 74 B2
Luna hill Spain 54 F8
Luna r. Spain 54 F2
Lunan China 86 B3
also known as Lufu
Lunan Lake Canada 167 M1
Lunan Shan mts China 86 B3
Luna Pier U.S.A. 173 J9
Lunavada India 96 B5
Lunayyir, Ḩarrāt lava field Saudi Arabia 104 B2
Lunca Romania 58 F5
Lunca Bradului Romania 58 G2
Lunca Ilvei Romania 58 F1
Luncavăț r. Romania 58 F4
Lund Sweden 45 K5
Lund NV U.S.A. 183 I3
Lund UT U.S.A. 183 K3
Lunda Norte prov. Angola 127 C7
Lundar Canada 167 L5
Lunda Sul prov. Angola 127 D7
Lundazi Zambia 129 B8
Lundbreck Canada 167 H5
Lundi r. Zimbabwe see Runde
Lunds U.S.A. 172 E6
Lundu Tanz. 129 B7
Lundy Island U.K. 47 H12
Lune r. U.K. 47 J9
Lüneburg Germany 48 H2
Lüneburger Heide reg. Germany 48 H2
Lüneburger Heide, Naturpark nature res. Germany 48 H2
Lunel France 51 K9
Lünen Germany 48 E4
Lunenburg U.S.A. 176 G9
Lunestedt Germany 48 F2
Lunéville France 51 M4
Lunga Moz. 131 I2
Lunga r. Zambia 127 E8
Lunggar China 89 C6
Lunggar Shan mts China 89 C6
Lung Kwu Chau i. Hong Kong China 87 [inset]
Lungleh India see Lunglei
Lunglei India 97 G5
formerly spelt Lungleh
Lungmari mt. China 89 D6
Lungmu Co salt l. China 89 C5
Lungnaquilla Mountain hill Rep. of Ireland 47 F11
Lungro Italy 57 I9
Lungué-Bungo r. Angola 127 D8
Lungwebungu r. Zambia 127 D8
Lunh Nepal 97 D3
Luni India 96 A4
Luni r. India 96 B4
Luni r. Pak. 101 G4
Luninets Belarus see Luninyets
Lunino Rus. Fed. 41 H5
Luninyets Belarus 42 H9
also spelt Luninets
L'Union France 50 H9
Lunkaransar India 96 B3
Lunkha India 96 B3
Lunkho mt. Afgh./Pak. 101 H2
Lunkkaus Fin. 44 N2
Lunna Belarus 42 F8
Lunn Island P.N.G. 149 F1
Lunsar Sierra Leone 124 B4
Lunsemfwa r. Zambia 127 F8
Lunsklip S. Africa 131 F5
Luntai China 88 D3
also known as Bügür
Lunxhërisë, Mali i ridge Albania 59 B8
Lunyuk Indon. 77 G5
Lunzua Zambia 127 F7
Luo r. Henan China 87 E1
Luo r. Shaanxi China 87 D1
Luobei China 82 C3
also known as Fengxiang
Luobuzhuang China 88 E4
Luocheng China see Hui'an
Luocheng Gansu China 84 C4
Luocheng Guangxi China 87 D3
also known as Dongmen
Luochuan China 85 F5
also known as Fengqi
Luodian China 86 C3
also known as Longping
Luoding China 87 D4
Luodonselkä sea chan. Fin. 44 N2
Luodou Sha i. China 87 D4
Luohe China 87 E1
Luoma Hu l. China 87 F1
Luonan China 87 D1
Luoning China 87 D1
Luonnonsuojelualue nature res. Fin. 44 M3
Luonteri l. Fin. 45 N3
Luoping China 86 C3
also known as Luoxiong
Luopioinen Fin. 45 N3
Luoshan China 87 E1
Luotian China 87 E2
also known as Fengshan
Luovtejok Norway 44 O1
Luoxiao Shan mts China 87 E3
Luoxiong China see Luoping
Luoyang China see Boluo
Luoyang China 87 E1
formerly known as Loyang
Luoyang China see Taishun
Luoyuan China 87 F3
also known as Fengshan
Luozi Dem. Rep. Congo 126 B6
Luozigou China 82 C4
Lupa Market Tanz. 129 B7
Lupane Zimbabwe 131 E3
Lupanshui China 86 C3
also known as Shuicheng or Xiayingpan or Zhongshan; formerly spelt Liupanshui
Lupar r. Sarawak Malaysia 77 E2
Łupawa r. Poland 49 O1
L'Upemba, Parc National de nat. park Dem. Rep. Congo 127 E7
Lupeni Romania 58 G2
Lupeni Romania 58 E3
Luperón Dom. Rep. 187 F3
Lupilichi Moz. 129 B7
formerly known as Olivença
Lupire Angola 127 C8
Lupiro Tanz. 129 C7
Lupon Phil. 74 C5
Luppa Germany 49 J4
Lupton U.S.A. 183 O6
Lup'ya r. Rus. Fed. 40 J3
Luqiao China see Luding
Luqu China 86 B1
also known as Ma'ngê
Lu Qu r. China see Tao He
Luquan Hebei China 85 G4
also known as Huolu
Luquan Yunnan China 86 B3
also known as Pingshan
Luquembo Angola 127 C7
Lūrā Shīrīn Iran 107 F3
Luray U.S.A. 176 G7
Lure France 51 M5
Lure, Montagne de mt. France 51 L8
Lureco r. Moz. 129 C8
Luremo Angola 127 C7
Lurgan U.K. 47 F9
Lūrg-e Shotorān salt pan Iran 101 D3
Luribay Bol. 200 D4
Lurín Peru 200 A3
Luring China see Gêrzê
Lúrio Moz. 131 I2
Lurio r. Moz. 131 I2
Lursaskela park Norway 45 I4
Lusahunga Tanz. 128 A5
Lusaka Dem. Rep. Congo 127 F6

▶Lusaka Zambia 127 F8
Capital of Zambia.

Lusaka prov. Zambia 127 F8
Lusambo Dem. Rep. Congo 126 D6
Lusancay Islands and Reefs P.N.G. 145 E2
Lusanga Dem. Rep. Congo 126 C6
formerly known as Leverville
Lusangi Dem. Rep. Congo 126 E6
Luseland Canada 167 I4
Lusenga Plain National Park Zambia 127 F7
Lusewa Tanz. 129 C7
Lush, Mount hill Australia 150 D3
Lushan China 86 B2
also known as Luyang
Lushar China see Huangzhong
Lushi China 87 D1
Lushnjë Albania 58 A8
Lushoto Tanz. 129 C6
Lüshun China 85 I4
formerly known as Port Arthur or Ryojun
Lüsi China 87 G1
Lusi r. Indon. 77 E4
Lusignan France 50 G6
Lusikisiki S. Africa 133 N8
Lusiwasi Zambia 127 F8
Lusk U.S.A. 180 F4
Luso Angola see Luena
Lussac-les-Châteaux France 50 G6
Lussusso Angola 127 B7
Lusushwana r. Swaziland 133 P3
Lusutufu r. Africa see Usutu
Lut, Bahrat salt l. Asia see Dead Sea
Lut, Dasht-e des. Iran 100 D4
Lutai China see Ninghe
Lü Tao i. Taiwan 87 G4
English form Green Island; also known as Huoshao Tao
Lutécia Brazil 206 C9
Luterskie, Jezioro l. Poland 49 R2
Lutetia France see Paris
Lut-e Zangī Aḩmad des. Iran 100 D4
Luther Lake Canada 173 M7
Luthersburg U.S.A. 176 G4
Lutherstadt Wittenberg Germany 49 J4
also known as Wittenberg
Lutiba Dem. Rep. Congo 126 F5
Lütjenburg Germany 48 H1
Luton U.K. 47 L12
Lutong Sarawak Malaysia 77 F1
Lutope r. Zimbabwe 131 F3
Łutselk'e Canada 167 I2
formerly known as Snowdrift
Lutshi Dem. Rep. Congo 126 E6
Luts'k Ukr. 41 C6
formerly spelt Łuck
Luttig S. Africa 132 G9
Lutto r. Fin./Rus. Fed. see Lotta
Lutuai Angola 127 D8
Lutynia r. Poland 49 O3
Lutz U.S.A. 175 D6
Lützow-Holm Bay Antarctica 223 C2
Lutzputs S. Africa 132 E5
Lutzville S. Africa 132 C8
Luumäki Fin. 45 N3
Luuq Somalia 128 D4
Luve Swaziland 133 P3
Luverne AL U.S.A. 175 C6
Luverne MN U.S.A. 178 C3
Luvia Fin. 45 M3
Luvo Angola 127 B6
Luvozero Rus. Fed. 44 O2
Luvua r. Dem. Rep. Congo 127 E6
Luvuei Angola 127 D8
Luvuvhu r. S. Africa 131 F4
Luwegu r. Tanz. 129 C7
Luwero Uganda 128 B4
Luwingu Zambia 127 F7
Luwo i. Indon. 75 D2
Luwuk Indon. 75 B3
▶Luxembourg country Europe 51 L3
Letzeburgish form Lëtzebuerg; also spelt Luxemburg
europe [countries] ▶▶ 32–35

▶Luxembourg Lux. 51 M3
Capital of Luxembourg.

Luxemburg country Europe see Luxembourg
Luxemburg IA U.S.A. 172 B8
Luxemburg WI U.S.A. 172 F6
Luxeuil-les-Bains France 51 M5
Luxi Hunan China 87 D2
also known as Wuxi
Luxi Yunnan China 86 A3
also known as Mangshi
Luxi Yunnan China 86 B3
also known as Zhongshu
Luxian China 86 C2
also known as Fuji
Luxolweni S. Africa 133 J8
Luxor Egypt 121 G3
also spelt El Uqṣur or Al Uqṣur
Luyang China see Lushan
Luya Shan mts China 85 F4
Luy de France r. France 50 F9
Luyi China 87 E1
Luyuan China see Gaoling
Luz Brazil 207 H6
Luza Rus. Fed. 40 H3
Luza r. Rus. Fed. 40 H3
Luza r. Rus. Fed. 40 K2
Luzech France 50 H8
Luzern Switz. see Lucerne
Luzha r. Rus. Fed. 43 R7
Luzhai China 87 D3
Luzhi China 86 C3
also known as Xiayingpan
Luzhou China 86 C2
Luziânia Brazil 206 F3
Lužické Hory mts Czech Rep. 49 L5
Luzilândia Brazil 202 D2
Lūžņas Latvia 42 C4
Lužnice r. Czech Rep. 49 L6
Luzon i. Phil. 74 B3
Luzon Strait Phil. 74 B1
Luzy France 51 J6
Luzzi Italy 57 I9
L'viv Ukr. 41 C6
English form Lvov; also spelt L'vov; formerly spelt Lwów; historically known as Lemberg
L'vov Ukr. see L'viv
Lvov Ukr. see L'viv
L'vovskiy Rus. Fed. 43 S6
Lwów Ukr. see L'viv
Lwówek Poland 49 N3
Lyady Belarus 43 M7
Lyady Rus. Fed. 43 J3
Lyakhavichy Belarus 42 H8
also spelt Lyakhovichi
Lyakhovichi Belarus see Lyakhavichy
Lyakhovskiye Ostrova is Rus. Fed. 39 O2
Lyallpur Pak. see Faisalabad
Lyal'mikar Uzbek. 103 F5
also spelt Lalmikor
Lyamtsa Rus. Fed. 40 F2
Lyangar Uzbek. see Langar
Lyangar Uzbek. 103 F4
also spelt Langar
Lyapin r. Rus. Fed. 40 L3
Lyaskelya Rus. Fed. 44 O3
Lyaskovets Bulg. 58 G5
Lyasnaya Belarus 42 G9
Lyasnaya r. Belarus 42 E9
Lybster U.K. 46 I5
Lychkovo Rus. Fed. 43 N4
Lyck Poland see Ełk
Lycksele Sweden 44 L2
Lycopolis Egypt see Asyūt
Lydda Israel see Lod
Lyddan Island Antarctica 222 W2
Lydenburg S. Africa 133 O2
Lydia reg. Turkey 59 I10
Łydynia r. Poland 49 R3
Lyebyada r. Belarus 42 G8
Lyel'chytsy Belarus 41 D6
Lyell, Mount U.S.A. 182 E4
Lyell Island Canada 166 D4
Lyell Range mts N.Z. 153 G9
Lyenina Belarus 43 M9
Lyepyel' Belarus 43 J7
also spelt Lepel'
Lygourio Greece 59 E11
also known as Ligoúrion
Lygumai Lith. 42 E5
Lykens U.S.A. 177 I5
Lykoshino Rus. Fed. 43 O3
Lykso S. Africa 132 I4
Lyman Ukr. 58 K3
Lyman U.S.A. 180 E4
Lyman'ske Ukr. 58 K2
Lyme Bay U.K. 47 J13
Lymington U.K. 47 K13
Łyna r. Poland 49 S1
Lynch U.S.A. 176 C9
Lynchburg TN U.S.A. 174 C5
Lynchburg VA U.S.A. 176 F8
Lynches r. U.S.A. 175 E5
Lynch Station U.S.A. 176 F8
Lynchville U.S.A. 177 O1
Lynd r. Australia 149 D3
Lyndhurst Qld Australia 149 E3
Lyndhurst S.A. Australia 146 C2
Lyndon Australia 150 A4
Lyndon r. Australia 150 A4
Lyndon U.S.A. 178 D4
Lyndonville NY U.S.A. 176 G2
Lyndonville VT U.S.A. 177 M1
Lyngdal Norway 45 I4
Lyngen sea chan. Norway 44 M1
Lyngseidet Norway 44 M1
Lynher Reef Australia 150 C2
Lynn U.K. see King's Lynn
Lynn IN U.S.A. 176 A5
Lynn MA U.S.A. 177 O3
Lynn Canal sea chan. U.S.A. 166 C3
Lynndyl U.S.A. 183 L2
Lynn Haven U.S.A. 175 C6
Lynn Lake Canada 167 K3
Lynton U.K. 47 I12
Lyntupy Belarus 42 H6
Lynx Lake Canada 167 J2
Lynxville U.S.A. 172 B7
Lyon France 51 K7
English form Lyons; historically known as Lugdunum
Lyon Mountain U.S.A. 177 L1
Lyonnais, Monts du hills France 51 K7
Lyons Australia 146 B2
Lyons r. Australia 151 A5
Lyons France see Lyon
Lyons GA U.S.A. 175 D5
Lyons KS U.S.A. 178 C4
Lyons NY U.S.A. 177 I2
Lyons Falls U.S.A. 177 J2
Lyozna Belarus 43 L6
Lyra Reef P.N.G. 145 E2
Lysá Hora mt. Czech Rep. 49 P6
Lysekil Sweden 45 J4
Lyshchichi Rus. Fed. 43 N9
Łysica hill Poland 49 R5
Lyskovo Rus. Fed. 40 H4
Lys'va Rus. Fed. 40 K4
Lysychans'k Ukr. 41 F6
also spelt Lisichansk
Lysyye Gory Rus. Fed. 41 H6
Lytham St Anne's U.K. 47 I10
Lytkarino Rus. Fed. 43 S6
Lyttelton N.Z. 153 G11
Lytton Canada 166 F5
Lyuban' Belarus 42 J9
Lyuban' Rus. Fed. 43 M2
Lyubanskaye Vodaskhovishcha resr Belarus 42 J9
Lyubavichi Rus. Fed. 43 L7
Lyubazh Rus. Fed. 43 Q9
Lyubcha Belarus 42 H8
Lyubertsy Rus. Fed. 43 S6
Lyubeshiv Ukr. 41 C6
Lyubim Rus. Fed. 43 V3
Lyubimets Bulg. 58 H7
Lyubimovka Rus. Fed. 43 T8
Lyubishchytsy Belarus 42 G9
Lyubitovo Rus. Fed. 43 P3
Lyubokhna Rus. Fed. 43 P8
Lyubomirovo Rus. Fed. 43 T2
Lyubotin Ukr. see Lyubotyn
Lyubotyn Ukr. 53 J2
also spelt Lyubotin
Lyubyacha Belarus 42 I8
Lyubytino Rus. Fed. 43 O3
Lyudinovo Rus. Fed. 43 P8
Lyugovichi Rus. Fed. 43 O1
Lyulyakovo Bulg. 58 I6
Lyunda r. Rus. Fed. 40 H4
Lyusina Belarus 42 H9
Lyzha r. Rus. Fed. 40 K2
Lža r. Latvia 42 J4
Lzha r. Rus. Fed. 43 J4

↓ M

Ma r. Myanmar 78 B3
Ma, Nam r. Laos 78 C3
Ma, Sông r. Vietnam 78 D4
Maalhosmadulu Atoll Maldives 94 B5
Maamakundhoo i. Maldives see Makunudhoo
Maamba Zambia 127 E9
Ma'an Cameroon 125 H6
Ma'an Jordan 108 G7
Maaninka Fin. 44 N3
Maaninkavaara Fin. 44 O2
Maanselkä Fin. 44 O3
Ma'anshan China 87 F2
Maanyt Bulgan Mongolia 84 D1
Maanyt Töv Mongolia 85 E2
Maardu Estonia 42 G2
Maarianhamina Fin. see Mariehamn
Ma'arrat an Nu'mān Syria 109 H2
Maartenshoop S. Africa 133 O1
Maas r. Neth. 48 B4
also spelt Meuse (Belgium/France)
Maaseik Belgium 51 L1
Maasin Phil. 74 C4
Maas-Schwalm-Nette nat. park Germany/Neth. 48 C4
Maastricht Neth. 48 C5
Maatsuyker Group is Australia 147 E5
Maba China 87 F1
Maba Indon. 75 D2
Maba, Ouadi watercourse Chad 120 D6
Mabalacat Phil. 74 B3
Mabalane Moz. 131 G4
Mabana Dem. Rep. Congo 126 F4
Mabanda Gabon 126 A5
Ma'bar Yemen 104 D5
Mabaruma Guyana 199 G2
Mabating China see Hongshan
Mabein Myanmar 78 B3
Mabel Creek Australia 146 B2
Mabel Downs Australia 150 D3
Mabella Canada 168 B3
Maberly Canada 173 Q6
Mabian China 86 B2
also known as Minjian
Mablethorpe U.K. 47 M10
Mably France 51 K6
Mabopane S. Africa 133 M2
Mabote Moz. 131 G4
Mabou Canada 169 I4
Mabrak, Jabal mt. Jordan 108 G7
Mabrouk well Mali 125 E2
Mabrous well Niger 125 I1
Mabuasehube Game Reserve nature res. Botswana 130 D5
Mabudis i. Phil. 74 B1
Mabula S. Africa 133 L1
Ma'būs Yūsuf oasis Libya 120 D3
Mabutsane Botswana 130 D5
Macá, Monte mt. Chile 205 B7
Macachín Arg. 204 E5
Macadam Plains Australia 151 B5
Macadam Range hills Australia 148 A2
Macaé Brazil 203 D7
Macael Spain 55 I7
Macaíba Brazil 202 F3
Macajalar Bay Phil. 74 C4
Macajuba Brazil 202 D5
Macaloge Moz. 129 B8
formerly known as Miranda or Vila Miranda
MacAlpine Lake Canada 167 K1
Macamic Canada 168 E3
Macan, Kepulauan atolls Indon. see Taka'Bonerate, Kepulauan
Macandze Moz. 131 G4
Macaneta, Ponta de pt Moz. 133 Q2
Macao China see Macau
Macapá Amapá Brazil 199 I4
Macapá Amazonas Brazil 200 D2
Macará Ecuador 198 B6
Macaracas Panama 186 C6
Macarani Brazil 202 D5
Macarena, Cordillera mts Col. 198 C4
Macareo, Caño r. Venez. 199 F2
Macas Ecuador 198 B5
Maçãs r. Port./Spain 54 E3
Macassar Indon. see Ujung Pandang
Macassar Strait Indon. see Makassar Strait
Macau Brazil 202 E3
Macau China 87 E4
also known as Aomen; also spelt Macao
Macaúba Brazil 202 B4
Macaúbas Brazil 202 D5
Macauley Island N.Z. 145 H5
Macayari Col. 198 C4
Macbride Head Falkland Is 205 F8
Maccaretane Moz. 131 G5
Macclenny U.S.A. 175 D6
Macclesfield U.K. 47 J10
Macclesfield Bank sea feature S. China Sea 72 D3
also known as Zhongsha Qundao
Macdiarmid Canada 168 B3
Macdonald, Lake salt flat Australia 150 E4
MacDonnell Creek watercourse Australia 146 C2
Macdonnell Ranges mts Australia 148 A4
MacDowell Lake Canada 167 M4
Macedo de Cavaleiros Port. 54 E3
Macedon country Europe see Macedonia
▶Macedonia country Europe 58 C7
also spelt Makedonija in Macedonian; historically known as Macedon; long form Former Yugoslav Republic of Macedonia; short form F.Y.R.O.M.
europe [countries] ▶▶ 32–35
Maceió Brazil 202 F4
Maceio, Ponta da pt Brazil 202 E3
Macenta Guinea 124 C4
Macerata Italy 56 F5
Macfarlane, Lake salt flat Australia 146 C3

index M

Macgillycuddy's Reeks mts Rep. of Ireland 47 C12
Mach Pak. 101 F4
Macha Rus. Fed. 39 L3
Machacalis Brazil 207 M4
Machacamarca Bol. 200 D4
Machachi Ecuador 198 B5
Machadinho r. Brazil 201 E2
Machado Brazil 207 H8
Machadodorp S. Africa 133 O2
Machai Zambia 127 E8
Machaila Moz. 131 G4
Machakos Kenya 128 C5
Machala Ecuador 198 B5
Machali China see Madoi
Machanga Moz. 131 G4
Machareti Bol. 201 E5
Machar Marshes Sudan 128 B2
Machattie, Lake salt flat Australia 148 C5
Machatuine Moz. 133 Q2
Machaze Moz. see Chitobe
Machecoul France 50 E6
Macheng China 87 E2
Macherla India 94 C2
Machesney Park U.S.A. 172 D8
Machhiwara India 96 C3
formerly spelt Machiwara
Machhlishahr India 97 D4
Machias ME U.S.A. 174 H2
Machias NY U.S.A. 176 G3
Machico Madeira 122 A2
Machilipatnam India 94 D2
also known as Masulipatam; formerly known as Bandar
Machinga Malawi 129 B8
Machiques Venez. 198 C2
Machiwara India see Machhiwara
Māch Kowr Iran 101 E5
Macho, Arroyo del watercourse U.S.A. 181 F6
Machupicchu tourist site Peru 200 B3
Machupo r. Bol. 201 D3
Machynlleth U.K. 47 I11
Macia Moz. 131 G5
Macias Nguema i. Equat. Guinea see Bioco
Măcin Romania 58 J3
Macintyre r. Australia 147 F2
Macintyre Brook r. Australia 147 F2
Macizo de Tocate mts Peru 200 B3
Maçka Turkey 107 D2
also known as Cevizlik
Mackay Australia 149 F4
MacKay r. Canada 167 I3
Mackay, Lake salt flat Australia 150 E4
MacKay Lake Canada 167 I2
Mackay Mountains Antarctica 222 O1
Mackenzie r. Australia 149 F4
Mackenzie B.C. Canada 166 F4
Mackenzie Ont. Canada 172 E2
▶Mackenzie r. Canada 166 E2
northamerica [landscapes] ▶ 156–157
Mackenzie Guyana see Linden
Mackenzie atoll Micronesia see Ulithi
Mackenzie Bay Antarctica 223 E2
Mackenzie Bay Canada 164 F3
Mackenzie Bison Sanctuary nature res. Canada 167 G2
Mackenzie Highway Canada 167 G2
Mackenzie King Island Canada 165 H2
Mackenzie Mountains Canada 166 C1

▶Mackenzie-Peace-Finlay r. Canada 166
2nd longest river in North America.
northamerica [landscapes] ▶ 156–157

Mackillop, Lake salt flat Australia see Yamma Yamma, Lake
Mackinac, Straits of lake channel U.S.A. 173 H5
Mackinac Island U.S.A. 173 I5
Mackinaw r. U.S.A. 174 B3
Macklin Canada 167 I4
Macksville Australia 147 G2
Mackunda Creek watercourse Australia 149 D4
Maclean Australia 147 G2
Macleantown S. Africa 133 L9
Maclear S. Africa 133 M8
Macleay r. Australia 147 G2
MacLeod Canada see Fort Macleod
MacLeod, Lake imp. l. Australia 150 A5
Macmillan r. Canada 166 C2
Macmillan Pass Canada 166 D2
Maçobere Moz. 131 G4
Macocola Angola 127 C6
Macomb U.S.A. 174 B3
Macomer Sardegna Italy 57 A8
Mâcon France 51 K6
Macon GA U.S.A. 175 D5
Macon MO U.S.A. 178 D4
Macon MS U.S.A. 175 B5
Macon OH U.S.A. 176 B7
Macon, Bayou r. U.S.A. 175 B6
Macondo Angola 127 D8
Macossa Moz. 131 G3
Macotera Spain 54 F4
Macoun Lake Canada 167 K3
Macovane Moz. 131 G4
Macpherson Robertson Land reg. Antarctica see Mac. Robertson Land
Macquarie r. N.S.W. Australia 147 E2
Macquarie r. Tas. Australia 147 E5
Macquarie Harbour Australia 147 E5

▶Macquarie Island S. Pacific Ocean 220 E9
Part of Australia. Most southerly point of Oceania.

Macquarie Marshes Australia 147 E2
Macquarie Marshes Nature Reserve Australia 147 E2
Macquarie Mountain Australia 147 F3
Macraes Flat N.Z. 153 E13
MacRitchie Reservoir Sing. 76 [inset]
Mac. Robertson Land reg. Antarctica 223 E2
long form Macpherson Robertson Land
Macroom Rep. of Ireland 47 D12
Mactún Mex. 185 H5
Macú Brazil 198 D4
Macuira, Parque Nacional nat. park Col. 198 D1
Macuje Col. 198 C4
Macukull Albania 58 B7
Macumba Australia 146 B1
Macumba watercourse Australia 146 C1
Macururé Brazil 202 E4
Macusani Peru 200 C3
Macuspana Mex. 185 G5
Macuzari, Presa resr Mex. 184 C3
Macuze Moz. 131 H3
Mādabā Jordan 108 G6
Madadeni S. Africa 133 O4

▶Madagascar country Africa 131 [inset] J4
Largest island in Africa and 4th in the world.
africa [landscapes] ▶ 112–113
africa [countries] ▶ 114–117

Madagli Nigeria 125 I4
Madā'in Şāliḩ Saudi Arabia 104 B2
Madalena Brazil 202 E3
Madama Niger 123 I5
Madan Bulg. 58 F7
Madana Chad 126 C2
Madana well Chad 120 C5
Madanapalle India 94 C3
Madang P.N.G. 73 K8
Madaora India 96 C4
Madaoua Niger 125 G3
Mădăraş Romania 58 C2
Madaripur Bangl. 97 F5
Madarounfa Niger 125 G3
Madau Turkm. 102 C5
also spelt Madaw; formerly known as Suidzhikurmsy
Madaw Turkm. see Madau
Madawaska Canada 173 P5
Madawaska r. Canada 168 E4
Madaya Myanmar 78 B3
Maddalena, Isola i. Sardegna Italy 56 B7
Maddaloni Italy 56 G7
Madded India 94 D2
Maddur India 94 C3
Madeir Sudan 126 F3

▶Madeira r. Brazil 199 G5
4th longest river in South America.
southamerica [landscapes] ▶ 190–191

▶Madeira terr. N. Atlantic Ocean 122 A2
Autonomous Region of Portugal. Long form Madeira, Arquipélago da.
africa [countries] ▶ 114–117

Madeira, Arquipélago da terr. N. Atlantic Ocean see Madeira
Madeirinha r. Brazil 201 E2
Madeley U.K. 47 J11
Madeline Island U.S.A. 172 C4
Madel Ouèï Chad 126 C2
Maden Turkey 107 D3
Madeniyet Kazakh. 103 I3
Madera Mex. 184 C2
Madera U.S.A. 182 D5
Madgaon India 94 B3
formerly known as Margao
Madgoul Djibouti 128 D1
Madhavpur India 96 A5
Madhepura India 97 E4
Madhoganj India 89 C7
Madhubani India 97 E4
Madhugiri India 94 C3
Madhya Pradesh state India 96 C5
formerly known as Central Provinces
Madi, Dataran Tinggi plat. Indon. 77 F2
Madibogo S. Africa 133 J3
Madikeri India 94 B3
Madill U.S.A. 179 C5
Madimba Angola 127 B6
Madimba Dem. Rep. Congo 126 B6
Madinani Côte d'Ivoire 124 D4
Madīnat al 'Abīd Yemen 104 C5
Madīnat ash Sha'b Yemen 104 D5
formerly known as Al Ittihab
Madīnat ath Thawrah Syria 109 J2
also known as Ţabaqah
Madingo-Kayes Congo 126 A6
Madingou Congo 126 B6
Madingrin Cameroon 125 I4
Madini r. Bol. 200 D3
Madirovalo Madag. 131 [inset] J3
Madison AL U.S.A. 174 C5
Madison FL U.S.A. 175 D6
Madison GA U.S.A. 175 D5
Madison IN U.S.A. 174 C4
Madison ME U.S.A. 177 P1
Madison MN U.S.A. 178 C2
Madison NC U.S.A. 176 F9
Madison NE U.S.A. 178 C3
Madison OH U.S.A. 176 D4
Madison SD U.S.A. 178 C2
Madison VA U.S.A. 176 G7

▶Madison WI U.S.A. 172 D7
State capital of Wisconsin.

Madison WV U.S.A. 176 D7
Madison r. U.S.A. 180 E3
Madison Heights U.S.A. 176 F8
Madisonville KY U.S.A. 174 C4
Madisonville TN U.S.A. 174 C5
Madisonville TX U.S.A. 179 D6
Madita Indon. 75 B5
Madiun Indon. 77 E4
Madjingo Gabon 126 B4
Madley, Mount hill Australia 150 C5
Madliena Latvia 42 G5
Mado Dem. Rep. Congo 126 F4
Madoc Canada 168 E4
Mado Gashi Kenya 128 C4
Madoi China 86 A1
also known as Machali
Madona Latvia 42 H5
Madongo Pan salt pan Botswana 130 D4
Madonie mts Sicilia Italy 57 F11
Madra Dağı mts Turkey 106 A3
Madrakah Saudi Arabia 104 B3
Madrakah, Ra's c. Oman 105 G4
Madras India see Chennai
Madras state India see Tamil Nadu
Madras U.S.A. 180 B3
Madre, Laguna lag. Mex. 185 F3
Madre, Laguna lag. U.S.A. 179 C7
Madre, Sierra mts Mex. 185 G5
also known as Madre de Chiapas, Sierra or Soconusco, Sierra de
Madre, Sierra mt. Phil. 74 B2
Madre de Chiapas, Sierra mts Mex. see Madre, Sierra
Madre de Deus de Minas Brazil 207 I8
Madre de Dios dept Peru 200 C2
Madre de Dios, Isla i. Chile 205 B8
Madre del Sur, Sierra mts Mex. 185 E5
Madre Occidental, Sierra mts Mex. 184 C2
Madre Oriental, Sierra mts Mex. 185 E3
Madrès, Pic de mt. France 51 I10
Madrid Phil. 74 C4

▶Madrid Spain 54 H4
Capital of Spain.

Madrid aut. comm. Spain 54 H4
Madridejos Phil. 74 B4
Madridejos Spain 55 H5
Madrona, Sierra mts Spain 54 G6
Madruga Cuba 186 C2
Madrūsah Libya 120 B3
Maduda Dem. Rep. Congo 126 B6
Madugula India 95 D2
Madura Australia 151 D6
Madura i. Indon. 77 F4
Madura, Selat sea chan. Indon. 77 F4
Madurai India 94 C4
Madurantakam India 94 C3
Madvār, Kūh-e mt. Iran 100 C4
Madwas India 97 D4
Madzhalis Rus. Fed. 102 A4
Madzharovo Bulg. 58 G7
Madziwadzido Zimbabwe 131 F3
Madziwa Mine Zimbabwe 131 F3
Maebashi Japan 91 F6
Mae Hong Son Thai. 78 B4
Maelang Indon. 75 B2
Maella Spain 55 L3
Mae Ping National Park Thai. 78 B4
Mae Ramat Thai. 78 B4
Mae Rim Thai. 78 B4
Măeriște Romania 58 D1
Mae Sariang Thai. 78 B4
Maeser U.S.A. 183 O1
Maes Howe tourist site U.K. 46 I4
Mae Sot Thai. 78 B4
Maestra, Sierra mts Cuba 186 D3
Mae Suai Thai. 78 B4
Mae Tuen Wildlife Reserve nature res. Thai. 78 B4
Maevatanana Madag. 131 [inset] J3
Maéwo i. Vanuatu 145 F3
also spelt Maiwo; formerly known as Aurora Island
Mae Wong National Park Thai. 78 B5
Mae Yom National Park Thai. 78 C4
Mafa Indon. 75 C2
Mafeking Canada 167 K4
Mafeking S. Africa see Mafikeng
Mafeteng Lesotho 133 L6
Mafia Channel Tanz. 129 C7
Mafia Island Tanz. 129 C6
Mafikeng S. Africa 133 J2
formerly spelt Mafeking
Mafinga Tanz. 129 B7
Mafra Brazil 201 H6
Mafraq Jordan see Al Mafraq
Mafungabusi Plateau Zimbabwe 131 F3
Magabeni S. Africa 133 O7
Magacela hill Spain 54 F6
Magadan Rus. Fed. 39 P4
Magadi Kenya 128 C5
Magaliesburg S. Africa 133 L2
Magallanes Chile see Punta Arenas
Magallanes Phil. 74 B3
Magallanes, Estrecho de sea chan. Chile see Magellan, Strait of
Magallanes y Antártica Chilena admin. reg. Chile 205 B9
Magangue Col. 198 C2
Maganik mt. Yugo. 56 L6
Mağara Turkey 106 C3
also known as Kırobası
Mağarali Turkey 109 J1
Magaramkent Rus. Fed. 102 B4
Magaria Niger 125 H3
Magas Iran see Zābolī
Magas Rus. Fed. 107 F2
Magat r. Phil. 74 B2
Magazine Mountain hill U.S.A. 179 D5
Magbakele Dem. Rep. Congo 126 D4
Magburaka Sierra Leone 124 C4
Magdagachi Rus. Fed. 82 B1
Magdalena Bol. 201 D3
Magdalena dept Col. 198 C2
Magdalena r. Col. 198 C2
Magdalena Mex. 184 C2
Magdalena r. Mex. 184 C2
Magdalena, Bahía b. Col. 198 B3
Magdalena, Bahía b. Mex. 184 C3
Magdalena, Isla i. Chile 205 B7
Magdalena, Isla i. Mex. 184 B3
Magdalene, Gunung mt. Sabah Malaysia 77 G1
Magdeburg Germany 48 I3
Magdelaine Cays atoll Australia 149 F3
Magee U.S.A. 175 B6
Magelang Indon. 77 E4
Magellan, Strait of Chile 205 C9
also known as Magallanes, Estrecho de
Magenta Italy 56 A3
Magenta, Lake salt flat Australia 151 B7
Magerøya i. Norway 44 N1
Mage-shima i. Japan 91 B9
Maggia r. Switz. 51 O6
Maggiorasca, Monte mt. Italy 56 B4
Maggiore, Lago l. Italy see Maggiore, Lake
Maggiore, Lake Italy 56 A3
also known as Maggiore, Lago
Maggiore, Monte hill Sardegna Italy 57 B8
Maghâgha Egypt 121 F2
Maghā'ir Shu'ayb tourist site Saudi Arabia see Jethro
Maghama Mauritania 124 B3
Maghâra, Gebel hill Egypt 108 E7
Maghera U.K. 47 F9
Maghnia Alg. 123 E2
Maghor Afgh. 101 E3
Mágina, Sierra mts Spain 55 H7
Magingo Tanz. 129 B7
Magione Italy 56 E5
Magitang China see Jainca
Maglaj Bos.-Herz. 56 K4
Maglavit Romania 58 E4
Maglie Italy 57 K8
Magma U.S.A. 183 M8
Magna U.S.A. 183 L1
Magna Grande hill Italy 57 E12
Magnet Bay Antarctica 223 D2
Magnetic Island Australia 149 E3
Magnetic Passage Australia 149 E3
Magnitnyy Rus. Fed. 43 Q9
Magnitogorsk Rus. Fed. 102 D1
Magnolia AR U.S.A. 179 D5
Magnolia MS U.S.A. 175 B6
Magnor Norway 45 K4
Magny-en-Vexin France 50 H3
Mago Rus. Fed. 82 F1
Mágocs-ér r. Hungary 49 R9
Màgoé Moz. 131 F2
Magog Canada 169 F4
Magole Tanz. 129 C6
Mago National Park Eth. 128 C3
Magosa Cyprus see Famagusta
Magoye Zambia 127 E8
Magozal Mex. 185 F4
Magpie Canada 169 H3
Magpie r. Ont. Canada 168 C4
Magpie r. Que. Canada 169 H3
Magpie, Lac l. Canada 169 H3
Magpie-Ouest r. Canada 169 H3
Magrath Canada 167 H5
Magre r. Spain 55 K5
Magruder Mountain U.S.A. 182 G4
Magrur, Wadi watercourse Sudan 121 E5
Magţa' Laḩjar Mauritania 124 B2
Magu Tanz. 128 B5
Magu, Khrebet mts Rus. Fed. 82 E1
Maguan China 86 C4
Maguarinho, Cabo c. Brazil 202 B2
Magude Moz. 131 G5
Magudu S. Africa 133 P4
Magura Bangl. 97 F5
Magura mt. Slovakia 49 P7
Măgura Mare, Vârful hill Romania 58 D1
Măgurii, Vârful mt. Romania 58 D3
Maguse Lake Canada 167 M2
Magwali S. Africa 133 L9
Magway Myanmar see Magwe
Magway admin. div. Myanmar see Magwe
Magwe Myanmar 78 A3
also spelt Magway
Magwe admin. div. Myanmar 78 A3
also spelt Magway
Magwegqana watercourse Botswana 130 D3
Magyarkanizsa Vojvodina, Srbija Yugo. see Kanjiža
Magyar Köztársaság country Europe see Hungary
Magyichaung Myanmar 78 A3
Mahābād Iran 100 A2
also known as Sāūjbolāgh
Mahabaleshwar India 94 B2
Mahabe Madag. 131 [inset] J3
Mahabharat Range mts Nepal 97 E4
Mahabo Toliara Madag. 131 [inset] J4
Mahabo Toliara Madag. 131 [inset] J4
Mahaboboka Madag. 131 [inset] J4
formerly known as Maneva
Mahad India 94 B2
Mahaddayweyne Somalia 128 E4
Mahadeo Hills India 96 C5
Mahadeopur India 94 D2
Mahaffey U.S.A. 176 G5
Mahagi Dem. Rep. Congo 126 F4
Mahagi Port Dem. Rep. Congo 126 F4
Mahaicony Guyana 199 G3
Mahajan India 96 B3
Mahajanga Madag. 131 [inset] J2
formerly spelt Majunga
Mahajanga prov. Madag. 131 [inset] J3
Mahakam r. Indon. 77 G3
Mahalapye Botswana 131 E4
Mahale Mountain National Park Tanz. 129 A6
also known as Makari Mountain National Park
Mahalevona Madag. 131 [inset] K2
Mahallāt Iran 100 B3
Maham India 96 C3
Māhān Iran 100 D4
Mahanadi r. India 95 E1
Mahanoro Madag. 131 [inset] K3
Maharajganj Bihar India 97 E4
Maharajganj Uttar Pradesh India 97 D4
Maharajpur India 96 C4
Maharashtra state India 94 B2
Mahārlū, Daryācheh-ye salt l. Iran 100 C4
Maha Sarakham Thai. 78 C4
Mahash, Wādī al watercourse Egypt 108 E9
Mahasham, Wâdi el watercourse Egypt 108 F7
Mahatalaky Madag. 131 [inset] J5
Maḩaţţat Dab'ah Jordan 108 H6
Mahavavy r. Madag. 131 [inset] J2
Mahavelona Madag. 131 [inset] K3
formerly known as Foulpointe
Mahaweli Ganga r. Sri Lanka 94 D4
Mahazoma Madag. 131 [inset] J3
Mahbub Sudan 121 F6
Mahbubabad India 94 D2
Mahbubnagar India 94 C2
Mahd adh Dhahab Saudi Arabia 104 C3
Mahdah Oman 105 F2
Mahdia Alg. 123 F2
Mahdia Guyana 199 G3
Mahdia Tunisia 123 H2
also spelt Mehdia
Mahe China 84 E5
Mahe India 94 B4
Mahé Seychelles 218 K6
Mahendragarh India 96 C3
Mahendragiri mt. India 95 E2
Mahenge Tanz. 129 C7
Maheno N.Z. 153 E13
Mahesana India 96 B5
formerly spelt Mahsana
Maheshwar India 96 B5
Maḩfirhin Yemen 105 E5
Māhfūr well Saudi Arabia 109 K7
Mahgawan India 96 C4
Mahi r. India 96 B5
Māhī watercourse Iran 101 D4
Mahia N.Z. 152 L7
Mahia Peninsula N.Z. 152 L7
Mahilyow Belarus 43 L8
also spelt Mogilev
Mahilyow Oblast admin. div. Belarus see Mahilyowskaya Voblasts'
Mahilyowskaya Voblasts' admin. div. Belarus 43 L8
English form Mahilyow Oblast or Mogilev Oblast; also known as Mogilevskaya Oblast'
Mahim India 94 B2
Mahina Mali 124 C3
Mahkene mt. Sweden 44 K2
Mahlabatini S. Africa 133 P5
Mahlaing Myanmar 78 A3
Mahlangasi S. Africa 133 P4
Mahlatswetsa S. Africa 133 L5
Mahmudabad India 96 D4
Mahmudabad Iran 100 C2
Maḩmūd-e 'Erāqī Afgh. 101 G3
Mahmudia Romania 58 K3
Mahmudiye Turkey 59 H9
Mahmutlar Turkey 108 D1
Mahmutşevketpaşa Turkey 58 K7
Mahnomen U.S.A. 178 C2
Mahoba India 96 C4
Mahoenui N.Z. 152 I6
Maholi India 96 D4
Mahón Spain 55 P5
also spelt Maó
Mahone Bay Canada 169 H4
Mahongo Game Park nature res. Namibia 130 D3
Mahony Lake Canada 166 E1
Mahou Mali 124 D3
Mahrāt, Jabal mt. Yemen 105 E4
Mahrāt, Wādī r. Yemen 105 E4
Mahrauni India 96 C4
Mähren reg. Czech Rep. see Moravia
Mahrès Tunisia 123 H2
Māhrūd Iran 101 E3
Mahsana India see Mahesana
Mahuanggou China 84 B4
Mahur Assam India 97 G4
Mahur Maharashtra India 94 C2
Mahuta Tanz. 129 C7
Mahuva India 96 A5
Mahwa India 96 C4
Mahya Dağı mt. Turkey 58 I7
Mahyār Iran 100 B3
Mai i. Indon. 75 C4
Maia American Samoa 145 I3
Maia Port. 54 C3
Maiaia Moz. see Nacala
Maiana atoll Kiribati 145 G1
formerly known as Hall
Maibang India 97 G4
Maicao Col. 198 C2
Maicasagi r. Canada 168 E3
Maicasagi, Lac l. Canada 168 E3
Maîche France 51 M5
Maici r. Brazil 199 F6
Maicuru r. Brazil 199 H5
Maidens U.K. 46 H8
Maidi Indon. 75 C2
Maidstone Canada 167 I4
Maidstone U.K. 47 M12
Maiduguri Nigeria 125 I4
Maiella, Parco Nazionale della nat. park Italy 56 G6
Maieru Romania 58 F1
Maigmó mt. Spain 55 K6
Mai Gudo mt. Eth. 128 C3
Maihar India 96 D4
Maihiihi N.Z. 152 J6
Maijdi Bangl. 97 F5
Maiji Shan mt. China 86 C1
Maikala Range hills India 96 D5
Maiko r. Dem. Rep. Congo 126 E4
Mailan Hill mt. India 97 D5
Mailani India 96 D3
Maïlao Chad 126 B2
Mailsi Pak. 101 H4
Ma'īn tourist site Yemen 104 D4
Mainaguri India 97 F4
Main Brook Canada 169 K3
Mainburg Germany 48 I7
Main Channel lake channel Canada 173 L5
Maindargi India 94 C2
Mai-Ndombe, Lac l. Dem. Rep. Congo 126 C5
formerly known as Léopold II, Lac
Maine state U.S.A. 177 O1
Maine, Gulf of U.S.A. 177 P2
Mainé Hanari, Cerro hill Col. 198 C5
Maïné-Soroa Niger 125 I3
Maingkwan Myanmar 78 B2
Maingy Island Myanmar 79 B5
Mainit Phil. 74 C4
Mainit, Lake Phil. 74 C4
Mainkung China 86 A2
Mainland i. Orkney, Scotland U.K. 46 I4
Mainland i. Shetland, Scotland U.K. 46 K3
Mainling China 89 F6
also known as Tungdor
Mainoru Australia 148 B2
Mainoru r. Australia 148 B2
Mainpat reg. India 97 D5
Mainpuri India 96 C4
Main Range National Park Australia 147 G2
Maintenon France 50 H4
Maintirano Madag. 131 [inset] J3
Mainua Fin. 44 N2
Mainz Germany 48 F5
historically known as Mogontiacum
Maio i. Cape Verde 124 [inset]
Maipó, Volcán vol. Chile 204 C4
Maipú Buenos Aires Arg. 204 F5
Maipú Mendoza Arg. 204 C4
Maipures Col. 199 E3
Maipuri Landing Guyana 199 G3
Maiquetía Venez. 199 E2
Maiquinique Brazil 207 M2
Maiqu Zangbo r. China 89 D6
Mairi Brazil 202 D4
Mairiporã Brazil 206 G10
Mairipotaba Brazil 206 D4
Maisí Cuba 187 E2
Maišiagala Lith. 42 G7
Maiskhal Island Bangl. 97 F5
Maisons-Laffitte France 51 I4
Maitencillo Chile 204 C3
Maitengwe Botswana 131 E4
Maithon India 97 E5
Maitland N.S.W. Australia 147 F3
Maitland S.A. Australia 146 C3
Maitland r. Australia 150 B4
Maitland, Banjaran mts Sabah Malaysia 77 G1
Maitland, Lake salt flat Australia 151 C5
Maitri research station Antarctica 223 A2
Maiwo i. Vanuatu see Maéwo
Maiwok r. Australia 148 B2
Maíz, Islas del is Nicaragua 186 C4
also known as Corn Islands
Maizhokunggar China 89 E6
also known as Kunggar or Medu Kongkar
Maizuru Japan 91 D7
Maja Jezercë mt. Albania 58 A6
Majalgaon India 94 C2
Majari r. Brazil 199 F4
Majdaḩah Yemen 105 E5
Majdanpek Srbija Yugo. 58 C4
Majé Brazil 207 J9
Majene Indon. 75 A3
Majevica mts Bos.-Herz. 56 K4
Majhgawan India 96 D4
Majholi India 96 C5
Majḩūd well Saudi Arabia 105 E3
Majia r. China 85 H4
Majiang Guangxi China 87 D4
Majiang Guizhou China 87 C3
also known as Xingshan
Majōl country N. Pacific Ocean see Marshall Islands
Major, Puig mt. Spain 55 N5
also spelt Mayor, Puig
Majorca i. Spain 55 N5
also spelt Mallorca
Mājro atoll Marshall Is see Majuro
Majuli Island India 97 G4
Majunga Madag. see Mahajanga
Majuriã Brazil 200 D1
Majuro atoll Marshall Is 220 F5
also spelt Mājro; formerly spelt Meduro
Majwemasweu S. Africa 133 K5
Maka Senegal 124 B3
Makabana Congo 126 B5
Makahuena Point U.S.A. 181 [inset] Y1
Makak Cameroon 125 H6
Makale Indon. 75 A3
Makalehi i. Indon. 75 C2

▶Makalu mt. China/Nepal 89 D7
5th highest mountain in the world and in Asia.
world [physical features] ▶ 8–9

Makalu Barun National Park Nepal 97 E4
Makamba Burundi 126 F6
Makanchi Kazakh. 88 C2
also spelt Maqanshy
Makanjila Malawi 129 B8
Makanya Tanz. 129 C6
Makanza Dem. Rep. Congo 126 C4
also spelt Mankanza; formerly known as Nouvelle Anvers
Makaraingo Madag. 131 [inset] J3
Makarewa N.Z. 153 C14
Makari Cameroon 125 I3
Makari Mountain National Park Tanz. see Mahale Mountain National Park
Makarov Rus. Fed. 82 F2
Makarska Croatia 56 J5
Makar'ye Rus. Fed. 40 I4
Makassar Indon. see Ujung Pandang
Makassar Strait Indon. 75 A3
also spelt Macassar Strait
Makat Kazakh. 102 C3
also spelt Maqat
Makatini Flats lowland S. Africa 133 Q4
Makaw Myanmar 78 B2
Makay, Massif du mts Madag. 131 [inset] J4
Makedonija country Europe see Macedonia
Makeleketla S. Africa 133 K5
Makeni Sierra Leone 124 B4
Makete Tanz. 129 B7
Makeyevka Ukr. see Makiyivka
Makgadikgadi salt pan Botswana 131 E4
Makgadikgadi Pans National Park Botswana 131 E4
Makhachkala Rus. Fed. 102 A4
Makhaleng r. Lesotho 133 L7
Makhambet Kazakh. 102 B3
formerly known as Yamankhalinka
Makhāmir, Jabal al hill Saudi Arabia 104 C2
Makharadze Georgia see Ozurget'i
Makheka mt. Lesotho 133 N6
Makhfar al Ḩammām Syria 109 J2
Makhmal Turkm. 102 E5
Makhmūr Iraq 107 E4
Makhrūq, Khashm al hill Saudi Arabia 109 L7
Makhtal India 94 C2
Makhyah, Wādī r. Yemen 105 E4
Makian vol. Indon. 75 C2
Makikihi N.Z. 153 F12
Makin atoll Kiribati see Butaritari
Makindu Kenya 128 C5
Makinsk Kazakh. 103 G1
Makira i. Solomon Is see San Cristobal
Makiyivka Ukr. 41 F6
also spelt Makeyevka; formerly known as Dmitriyevsk or Dmytriyevs'k
Makkah Saudi Arabia see Mecca
Makkah prov. Saudi Arabia 104 C3
Makkaurhalvøya Naturreservat nature res. Norway 44 O1
Makkovik Canada 169 J2
Makkovik, Cape Canada 169 J2
Maklaki Rus. Fed. 43 P7
Makljen pass Bos.-Herz. 56 J5
Makó Hungary 53 G2
Makoa, Serra hills Brazil 199 G4
Makokou Gabon 126 B4
Makokskraal S. Africa 133 K3
Makonde Plateau Tanz. 129 C7
Makongolosi Tanz. 129 B7
Makopong Botswana 130 D5
Makoro Dem. Rep. Congo 126 F4
Makotipoko Congo 126 C5
Makoua Congo 126 B5
Makovnik mt. Croatia 56 H3
Maków Mazowiecki Poland 49 S3
Makra i. Greece 59 G12
Makrakomi Greece 59 D10
Makran reg. Iran/Pak. 101 E5
Makrana India 96 B4
Makran Coast Range mts Pak. see Talar-i-Band
Makronisi i. Greece 59 F11
Makronisi i. Greece 59 H11
Maksatikha Rus. Fed. 43 Q4
Maksi India 96 C5
Maksimovka Rus. Fed. 82 E3
Maksotag Iran 101 E4
Maksudangarh India 96 C5
Makthar Tunisia 57 B13
Mākū Iran 100 A2
Makum India 97 G4
Makumbako Tanz. 129 B7
Makumbi Dem. Rep. Congo 127 D6
Makundu i. Maldives see Makunudhoo
Makunduchi Tanz. 129 C6
Makung Taiwan 87 F4
Makunguwiro Tanz. 129 C7
Makunudhoo i. Maldives 94 B5
also known as Maamakundhoo; also spelt Makundu
Makurazaki Japan 91 B9
Makurdi Nigeria 125 H5
Makuri N.Z. 152 J8
Makuungo Somalia 128 D4
Makuyuni Tanz. 128 C5
Makwassie S. Africa 133 J4
Mal India 97 F4
Mala Peru 200 A3
Mala Rep. of Ireland see Mallow
Mala i. Solomon Is see Malaita
Malå Sweden 44 L2
Mala, Punta pt Panama 186 C6
Mala Aboriginal Land res. Australia 148 A4
Mal'ab, Râs pt Egypt 108 D8
Malabang Phil. 74 C5
Malabar Coast India 94 B3

▶Malabo Equat. Guinea 125 H6
Capital of Equatorial Guinea. Formerly known as Santa Isabel.

Malabuñgan Phil. 74 A4
Malaca Spain see Málaga
Malacacheta Brazil 207 K4
Malacca Malaysia see Melaka
Malacca state Malaysia see Melaka
Malacca, Strait of Indon./Malaysia 76 B1
Malacky Slovakia 49 O7
Malad r. U.S.A. 180 D4
Malad City U.S.A. 180 D4
Maladzyechna Belarus 42 H7
also spelt Molodechno
Malá Fatra nat. park Slovakia 49 Q6
Málaga Spain 54 G8
also spelt Malaca
Malaga NJ U.S.A. 177 J6
Malaga NM U.S.A. 181 F6
Malaga OH U.S.A. 176 D6
Malagarasi r. Burundi/Tanz. 129 A6
Malagarasi Tanz. 129 A6
Malagón Spain 54 H5
Malagon r. Spain 54 D7
Malahar Indon. 75 B5
Malaimbandy Madag. 131 [inset] J4
Mała Ina r. Poland 49 M2
Malaita i. Solomon Is 145 F2
also known as Mala; historically known as Carteret Island
Malaka mt. Indon. 77 G5
Malakal Sudan 128 A2
Malakanagiri India 94 D2
Mala Kapela mts Croatia 56 H3
Malakheti Nepal 96 D3
Malak Malak Aboriginal Land res. Australia 148 A2
Malakula i. Vanuatu 145 F3
Malakwal Pak. 101 H3
Malali Guyana 199 G3
Malamala Indon. 75 B3
Malamaui i. Phil. 74 B5
Malampaya Sound sea chan. Phil. 74 A4
Malan, Ras pt Pak. 101 F5
Malang Indon. 77 F4
Malanga Moz. 129 C8
Malangali Tanz. 129 B7
Malangana Nepal see Malangwa
Malange Angola see Malanje
Malangseidet Norway 44 L1
Malangwa Nepal 97 E4
also known as Malangana
Malanipa i. Phil. 74 B5
Malanje Angola 127 C7
formerly spelt Malange
Malanje prov. Angola 127 C7
Malanut Bay Phil. 74 A4
Malanville Benin 125 F4
Malanzán Arg. 204 D3
Malanzán, Sierra de mts Arg. 204 D3
Malappuram India 94 C4
Mälaren l. Sweden 45 L4
Malargüe Arg. 204 C4
Malaripo Brazil 199 H4
Malartic Canada 168 E3
Malartic, Lac l. Canada 173 O2
Malasoro, Teluk b. Indon. 75 A4
Malaspina Arg. 205 D7
Malaspina Glacier U.S.A. 166 A3
Malaspina Strait Canada 166 E5
Malatayur, Tanjung pt Indon. 77 F3
Malatya Turkey 107 D3
historically known as Melitene or Milid
Malaut India 96 B3
Malavalli India 94 C3
Malavate Fr. Guiana 199 H4
Malāvī Iran 100 A3
Malawali i. Sabah Malaysia 77 G1
▶Malawi country Africa 129 B7
formerly known as Nyasaland
africa [countries] ▶ 114–117
Malawi, Lake Africa see Nyasa, Lake
Malawi National Park Zambia see Nyika National Park
Malawiya Sudan 121 H6
Malax Fin. 44 M3
Malaya pen. Malaysia see Peninsular Malaysia
Malaya Byerastavitsa Belarus 42 E8
Malaya Pera Rus. Fed. 40 J2
Malaya Vishera Rus. Fed. 43 N3
Malaybalay Phil. 74 C4
Malāyer Iran 100 B3
also known as Daulatabad
Malay Reef Australia 149 F3

Malay Sary Kazakh. 103 I3
▶Malaysia country Asia 76 C1
formerly known as Federated Malay States
asia [countries] ▶ 64–67
Malaysia, Semenanjung pen. Malaysia see Peninsular Malaysia
Malazgirt Turkey 107 E3
Malbaie r. Canada 169 G4
Malbaza Niger 125 G3
Malbon Australia 149 D4
Malbork Poland 49 Q1
historically known as Marienburg
Malbrán Arg. 204 E3
Malchin Germany 49 J2
Malcolm Australia 151 C6
Malcolm, Point Australia 151 C7
Malcolm Inlet Oman see Ghazira, Ghubbat al
Maldegem Belgium 51 J1
Malden U.S.A. 174 B4
Malden Island Kiribati 221 H6
▶Maldives country Indian Ocean 93 D10
also known as Divehi
asia [countries] ▶ 64–67
Maldon U.K. 47 M12
Maldonado Uruguay 204 G4
Maldonado, Punta pt Mex. 185 F5

▶Male Maldives 93 D10
Capital of the Maldives.
world [countries] ▶ 10–11

Male Myanmar 78 B3
Maléa Guinea 124 C4
Maleas, Akra pt Lesbos Greece 59 H9
Maleas, Akra pt Greece 59 E12
Male Atoll Maldives 93 D10
Malebogo S. Africa 133 J5
Malegaon Maharashtra India 94 B1
Malegaon Maharashtra India 94 C2
Malei Moz. 131 H3
Malé Karpaty hills Slovakia 49 O7
Malek Sīāh, Kūh-e mt. Afgh. 101 E4
Malela Maniema Dem. Rep. Congo 126 E5
Malela Maniema Dem. Rep. Congo 126 E6
Malele Congo 126 B6
Malele Dem. Rep. Congo 127 B6
Malema Moz. 131 H2
formerly known as Entre Rios
Malendo watercourse Nigeria 125 G4
Malente Germany 48 H1
Maleoskop S. Africa 133 N2
Målerås Sweden 45 K4
Maler Kotla India 96 B3
Maleševske Planine mts Bulg./Macedonia 58 D7
Malesherbes France 51 I4
Malesina Greece 59 E10
Mālestān Afgh. 101 F3
Malestroit France 50 D5
Maleta Rus. Fed. 85 F1
Malevka Rus. Fed. 43 T8
Malgas S. Africa 132 E11
Malgobek Rus. Fed. 41 H8
Malgomaj l. Sweden 44 L2
Malha Sudan 121 E6
Malhada Brazil 202 D5
Malham Saudi Arabia 105 D2
Malhargarh India 96 B4
Malheur r. U.S.A. 180 C3
Malheur Lake U.S.A. 180 C4
Malheur National Wildlife Refuge nature res. U.S.A. 180 C4
▶Mali country Africa 124 E2
formerly known as French Sudan
africa [countries] ▶ 114–117
Mali Dem. Rep. Congo 126 E5
Mali Guinea 124 B3
Malia Greece 59 G13
also spelt Mallia
Malian r. China 85 E5
Maliana East Timor 75 C5
Malianjing Gansu China 84 B3
Malianjing Gansu China 84 D4
Malibamatso r. Lesotho 133 M6
Malibu U.S.A. 182 F7
Maligay Bay Phil. 74 B5
Malihabad India 89 C7
Mali Hka r. Myanmar 78 B2
Malikdin Afgh. 101 G3
Malik Naro mt. Pak. 101 E4
Maliku Indon. 75 B3
Mali Kyun i. Myanmar 79 B5
also known as Tavoy Island
Malili Indon. 75 B3
Mali Lošinj Croatia 56 G4
Malimba, Monts mts Dem. Rep. Congo 127 F6
Malin Rep. of Ireland 47 E8
Malin Ukr. see Malyn
Malindi Kenya 128 D5
Malines Belgium see Mechelen
Malinga Gabon 126 B5
Malin Head Rep. of Ireland 46 E8
Mălini Romania 58 H1
Malino Indon. 75 A4
Malino Rus. Fed. 43 T6
Malino, Gunung mt. Indon. 75 B2
Malinovka r. Rus. Fed. 82 D3
Malinovoye Ozero Rus. Fed. 103 I2
formerly known as Mikhaylovskiy
Malinyi Tanz. 129 C7
Malipo China 86 C4
Maliq Albania 58 B8
Mali Raginac mt. Croatia 56 H4
Malit, Qafa e pass Albania 58 B6
Malita Phil. 74 C5
Malitbog Phil. 74 C4
Maliwun Myanmar 79 B6
Maliya India 96 A5
Malka r. Rus. Fed. 41 H8
Malka Mary Kenya 128 D3
Malkapur Maharashtra India 94 B2
Malkapur Maharashtra India 94 C1
Malkara Turkey 106 A2
Mal'kavichy Belarus 42 H9
Malkhanskiy Khrebet mts Rus. Fed. 85 F1
Malko Tŭrnovo Bulg. 58 I7
Mallacoota Australia 147 F4
Mallacoota Inlet b. Australia 147 F4
Mallaig U.K. 46 G7
Mallanga well Chad 120 D5
Mallani reg. India 96 A4
Mallawi Egypt 121 F3
Mallee Cliffs National Park Australia 147 D3
Mållejus hill Norway 44 M1
Mallery Lake Canada 167 L1
Mallét Brazil 203 B8
Mallia Greece see Malia
Mallorca i. Spain see Majorca
Mallow Rep. of Ireland 47 D11
also spelt Mala
Mallowa Well Australia 150 D4
Malm Norway 44 J2
Malmberget Sweden 44 M2
Malmédy Belgium 51 M2
Malmesbury S. Africa 132 C10
Malmesbury U.K. 47 J12
Malmköping Sweden 45 L4
Malmö Sweden 45 K5
Malmö-Sturup airport Sweden 45 K5
Malmslätt Sweden 45 K4
Malmyzh Rus. Fed. 40 I4
Malo i. Indon. 75 C1
Maloarkhangel'sk Rus. Fed. 43 R9
Maloca Amazonas Brazil 199 F5
Maloca Pará Brazil 199 H4
Maloca Salamaim Brazil 201 E2
Malo Crniće Srbija Yugo. 58 C4
Malolos Phil. 74 B3
Malolotja Nature Reserve Swaziland 133 P3
Maloma Swaziland 133 P4
Malombe, Lake Malawi 129 B8
Malone U.S.A. 177 K1
Malong China 86 B3
also known as Tongquan
Malonga Dem. Rep. Congo 127 D7
Małopolska, Wyżyna hills Poland 49 R5
Maloshuyka Rus. Fed. 40 F3
Malovan pass Bos.-Herz. 56 J5
Malovăţ Romania 58 D4
Malowera Moz. 131 F2
formerly spelt Maluera
Måløy Norway 44 I3
Maloyaroslavets Rus. Fed. 43 R6
Maloye Borisovo Rus. Fed. 43 R2
Malozemel'skaya Tundra lowland Rus. Fed. 40 I2
Malpelo, Isla de i. N. Pacific Ocean 198 A4
Malpica Spain 54 C1
Mālpils Latvia 42 F4
Malprabha r. India 94 C2
Malpura India 96 B4
Malše r. Czech Rep. 49 L7
Malsiras India 94 B2
▶Malta country Europe 57 G13
europe [countries] ▶ 32–35
Malta Latvia 42 I5
Malta r. Latvia 42 I5
Malta i. Malta 57 G13
Malta U.S.A. 180 F2
Maltahöhe Namibia 130 C5
Maltam Cameroon 125 I3
Maltion luonnonpuisto nature res. Fin. 44 O2
Malton U.K. 47 L9
Maluera Moz. see Malowera
Malukken is Indon. see Moluccas
Maluku is Indon. see Moluccas
Maluku prov. Indon. 75 D3
Ma'lūlā, Jabal mts Syria 109 H4
Malului, Vârful hill Romania 58 D2
Malumfashi Nigeria 125 G4
Malundano Zambia 127 E9
Malung Sweden 45 K3
Maluti Mountains Lesotho 133 M6
Malu'u Solomon Is 145 F2
Malvan India 94 B2
Malvasia Greece see Monemvasia
Malvern AR U.S.A. 179 D5
Malvern OH U.S.A. 176 D5
Malvérnia Moz. see Chicualacuala
Malvinas, Islas terr. S. Atlantic Ocean see Falkland Islands
Malwa reg. India 96 C5
Malwal Sudan 128 A2
Malxe r. Germany 49 L4
Malý Dunaj r. Slovakia 49 P8
Malykay Rus. Fed. 39 L3
Malyn Ukr. 41 D6
also spelt Malin
Malyy, Ostrov i. Rus. Fed. 43 J1
Malyy Anyuy r. Rus. Fed. 39 Q3
Malyye Soli Rus. Fed. 43 V4
Malyy Irgiz r. Rus. Fed. 41 I5
Malyy Kavkaz mts Asia see Lesser Caucasus
Malyy Kunaley Rus. Fed. 85 E1
Malyy Lyakhovskiy, Ostrov i. Rus. Fed. 39 O2
Malyy Taymyr, Ostrov i. Rus. Fed. 39 K2
Malyy Uzen' r. Kazakh./Rus. Fed. 102 B2
also known as Kishiözen
Malyy Yenisey r. Rus. Fed. 84 B1
Malyy Zelenchuk r. Rus. Fed. 107 E1
Mama r. Rus. Fed. 39 O3
Mamadysh Rus. Fed. 40 I5
Mamafubedu S. Africa 133 M4
Mamahabane S. Africa 133 L5
Mamaranui N.Z. 152 H3
Mamasa Indon. 75 A3
Mambahenauhan i. Phil. 74 A5
Mambai Brazil 202 C5
Mambajao Phil. 74 C4
Mambal Cameroon 125 I5
Mambali Tanz. 129 B6
Mambasa Dem. Rep. Congo 126 F4
Mambéré r. Cent. Afr. Rep. 126 C4
Mambéré-Kadéï pref. Cent. Afr. Rep. 126 B3
Mambi Indon. 75 A3
Mambili r. Congo 126 C4
Mambolo Sierra Leone 124 B4
Mamboré Brazil 206 A11
Mambrui Kenya 128 D5
Mamburao Phil. 74 B3
Mamelodi S. Africa 133 M2
Mamers France 50 G4
Mamfé Cameroon 125 H5
Mamiá Brazil 199 F6
Mamili National Park Namibia 130 D3
Mamiña Chile 200 C5
Mamison Pass Georgia/Rus. Fed. 107 E2
Mammoth U.S.A. 183 N9
Mammoth Cave National Park U.S.A. 174 C4
Mammoth Lakes U.S.A. 182 F4
Mammoth Reservoir U.S.A. 182 E4
Mamonas Brazil 207 K2
Mamonovo Kaliningradskaya Oblast' Rus. Fed. 42 A7
historically known as Heiligenbeil
Mamonovo Ryazanskaya Oblast' Rus. Fed. 43 U8
Mamontovo Rus. Fed. 103 J1
Mamoré r. Bol./Brazil 200 D2
Mamori Brazil 199 E5
Mamori, Lago l. Brazil 199 F5
Mamoriá Brazil 200 D1
Mamou Guinea 124 B4
Mamoudzou Mayotte 129 E8
also spelt Mamoutsou or Mamutzu
Mamoutsou Mayotte see Mamoudzou
Mampikony Madag. 131 [inset] J3
Mampong Ghana 125 E5
Mamre S. Africa 132 C10
Mamry, Jezioro l. Poland 49 S1
Mamuju Indon. 75 A3
Ma'mūl Oman 105 F4
Mamuno Botswana 130 D4
Mamuras Albania 58 A7
Mamurogawa Japan 90 G5
Mamutzu Mayotte see Mamoudzou
Man Côte d'Ivoire 124 D5
Man r. India 94 B2
Man U.S.A. 176 D8

▶Man, Isle of i. Irish Sea 47 H9
United Kingdom Crown Dependency.
europe [countries] ▶ 32–35

Mana Fr. Guiana 199 H3
Mana U.S.A. 181 [inset] Y1
Mana Bárbara Venez. 198 C2
Manabí prov. Ecuador 198 B5
Manacacias r. Col. 198 C3
Manacapuru Brazil 199 F5
Manacor Spain 55 O5
Manado Indon. 75 C2

▶Managua Nicaragua 186 B4
Capital of Nicaragua.

Managua, Lago de l. Nicaragua 186 B4
Manah Oman 105 G3
Manaia N.Z. 152 I7
Manakara Madag. 131 [inset] J4
Manakau mt. N.Z. 153 H10
Manākhah Yemen 104 C5
Manali India 96 C2

▶Manama Bahrain 105 E2
Capital of Bahrain. Also spelt Al Manāmah.
world [countries] ▶ 10–11

Manamadurai India 94 C4
Manambaho r. Madag. 131 [inset] J3
Manambondro Madag. 131 [inset] J4
Manamelkudi India 94 C4
Manam Island P.N.G. 73 K7
also known as Vulcan Island
Manamo, Caño r. Venez. 199 F2
Manamoc i. Phil. 74 B4
Mananantañana r. Madag. 131 [inset] J4
Mananara r. Madag. 131 [inset] J4
Mananara, Parc National de nat. park Madag. 131 [inset] K3
Mananara Avaratra Madag. 131 [inset] K3
Manangoora Australia 148 C3
Mananjary Madag. 131 [inset] K4
Manankoliva Madag. 131 [inset] J5
Manankoro Mali 124 D4
Manantali, Lac de l. Mali 124 C3
Manantavadi India 94 C4
Manantenina Madag. 131 [inset] J5
Mana Pass China/India 89 B6
Mana Pools National Park Zimbabwe 131 F3
Manapouri N.Z. 153 B13

▶Manapouri, Lake N.Z. 153 B13
Deepest lake in Oceania.

Manapparai India 94 C4
Manarantsandry Madag. 131 [inset] J3
Manas China 88 D2
Manas r. India 97 F4
Manas, Gora mt. Uzbek. 103 G4
Manasa India 96 B4
Manas He r. China 88 D2
Manas Hu l. China 88 D2
Manāşir reg. U.A.E. 105 F3

▶Manaslu mt. Nepal 97 E3
8th highest mountain in the world and in Asia.
world [physical features] ▶ 8–9

Manasquan U.S.A. 177 K5
Manassas U.S.A. 176 H7
Manastir Macedonia see Bitola
Manas Wildlife Sanctuary nature res. Bhutan 97 F4
Manatang Indon. 75 C5
Manatuto East Timor 75 C5
Man-aung Kyun i. Myanmar see Cheduba Island
Manaus Brazil 199 F5
Manavgat Turkey 106 B3
Manavgat r. Turkey 108 C1
Manawa U.S.A. 172 E6
Manawar India 96 B5
Manawaru N.Z. 152 J5
Manawashei Sudan 120 E6
Manawatu r. N.Z. 152 J8
Manawatu-Wanganui admin. reg. N.Z. 152 J7
Manay Phil. 74 C5
Manayenki Rus. Fed. 43 R8
Manbazar India 97 E5
Manbij Syria 109 I1
Mancelona U.S.A. 173 H6
Manchar India 94 B2
Manchester U.K. 47 J10
Manchester CT U.S.A. 177 M4
Manchester IA U.S.A. 174 B3
Manchester KY U.S.A. 176 B8
Manchester MD U.S.A. 177 I6
Manchester MI U.S.A. 173 I8
Manchester NH U.S.A. 177 N3
Manchester OH U.S.A. 176 B7
Manchester TN U.S.A. 174 C5
Manchhar Lake Pak. 101 F5
Manciano Italy 56 D6
Mancılık Turkey 107 D3
Mancınık Dağı mts Turkey 59 I9
Mancos r. U.S.A. 183 P5
Mand Pak. 101 E5
Mand, Rūd-e r. Iran 100 B4
also known as Qara Āghach
Manda Bangl. 97 F4
Manda Malawi 129 B7
Manda Tanz. 129 B6
Manda, Jebel mt. Sudan 126 E2
Manda, Parc National de nat. park Chad 126 C2
Mandabe Madag. 131 [inset] J4
Mandaguaçu Brazil 206 A10
Mandaguari Brazil 206 B10
Mandai Sing. 76 [inset]
Mandal Afgh. 101 E3
Mandal Gujarat India 96 A5
Mandal Rajasthan India 96 B4
Mandal Bulgan Mongolia 84 D1
Mandal Töv Mongolia 85 E1
Mandal Norway 45 I4

▶Mandala, Puncak mt. Indon. 73 J7
3rd highest mountain in Oceania. Formerly known as Julianatop.
oceania [landscapes] ▶ 136–137

Mandalay Myanmar 78 B3
also spelt Mandale
Mandalay admin. div. Myanmar 78 A3
also spelt Mandale
Mandale Myanmar see Mandalay
Mandale admin. div. Myanmar see Mandalay
Mandalgarh India 96 B4
Mandalgovi Mongolia 85 E2
Mandalī Iraq 107 F4
Mandalt China 85 G3
also known as Sonid Zuoqi
Mandan U.S.A. 178 B2
Mandaon Phil. 74 B3
Mandapam India 94 C4
Mandar, Teluk b. Indon. 75 A3
Mandas Sardegna Italy 57 B9
Mandav Hills India 96 A5
Mandé, Mont de hill France 51 K6
Mandelieu-la-Napoule France 51 M9
Mandello del Lario Italy 56 B3
Mandera Kenya 128 D4
Manderfield U.S.A. 183 L3
Mandeville Jamaica 186 D3
Mandeville N.Z. 153 C13
Mandha India 96 A4
Mandheera Somalia 128 E2
Mandhoúdhion Greece see Mantoudi
Mandi India 96 C3
Mandiakui Mali 124 D3
Mandiana Guinea 124 C4
Mandi Burewala Pak. 101 H4
Mandidzuzure Zimbabwe see Chimanimani
Mandié Moz. 131 G3
Mandimba Moz. 131 G2
Manding, Monts mts Mali 124 C3
Mandioli i. Indon. 75 C3
Mandji Gabon 126 A5
Mandla India 96 D5
Mandor India 96 B4
Mandorah Australia 148 A2
Mandoro Dem. Rep. Congo 126 F3
Mandoro Madag. 131 [inset] J3
Mandor Reserve nature res. Indon. 77 E2
Mandouri Togo 125 F4
Mandra Greece 59 E10
Mandraki Greece 59 I12
Mandrare r. Madag. 131 [inset] J5
Mandrenska r. Bulg. see Sredetska Reka
Mandritsara Madag. 131 [inset] K2
Mandsaur India 96 B4
Mandul i. Indon. 77 G2
Mandurah Australia 151 A7
Manduria Italy 57 J8
Mandvi Gujarat India 96 A5
Mandvi Gujarat India 96 B5
Mandya India 94 C3
Manekwara India 96 A5
Manendragarh India 97 D5
Maner India 97 E4
Maner r. India 94 C2
Manerbio Italy 56 C3
Maneromango Tanz. 129 C6
Manesht Kūh mt. Iran 100 A3
Mănești Romania 58 G4
Maneva Madag. see Mahaboboka
Manevychi Ukr. 41 C6
Manfalūt Egypt 121 F3
Manfredonia Italy 56 H7
Manfredonia, Golfo di g. Italy 56 I7
Manga Brazil 202 D5
Manga Burkina 125 E4
Mangabeiras, Serra das hills Brazil 202 C4
Manga Grande Angola 127 B6
Mangai Dem. Rep. Congo 126 C6
Mangai, Réserve de Faune des Hippopotames de nature res. Dem. Rep. Congo 126 C5
Mangaia i. Cook Is 221 H7
also spelt Mangea
Mangakino N.Z. 152 J6
Mangalagiri India 94 D2
Mangaldai India 97 G4
Mangalia Romania 58 J5
Mangalmé Chad 120 C6
Mangalore India 94 B3
Mangalvedha India 94 B2
Mangamaunu N.Z. 153 H10
Mangamuka N.Z. 152 H3
Mangania Dem. Rep. Congo 126 D4
Manganui r. N.Z. 152 H3
Mangaon India 94 B2
Mangapet India 94 D2
Mangarakau N.Z. 152 G8
Mangaratiba Brazil 207 I9
Mangareva Islands Fr. Polynesia see Gambier, Îles
Mangatainoka N.Z. 152 J8
Mangatawhiri N.Z. 152 J5
Mangaung S. Africa 133 K6
Mangawan India 97 D4
Mangaweka N.Z. 152 J7
Mangawhai N.Z. 152 I4
Mangde Chhu r. Bhutan see Trongsa Chhu
Ma'ngê China see Luqu
Mangea i. Cook Is see Mangaia
Mangembe Dem. Rep. Congo 126 E6
Manger Norway 45 I3
Manggar Indon. 77 E3
Mangghyshlaq Kazakh. see Mangistau
Mangghystaū Kazakh. see Mangistau
Mangghystaū Oblysy admin. div. Kazakh. see Mangistauskaya Oblast'
Mangghyt Uzbek. see Mangit
Manghit Uzbek. see Mangit
Mangistau Kazakh. 102 B4
also spelt Mangghystaū; formerly known as Mangghyshlaq or Mangyshlak
Mangistau, Gory hills Kazakh. 102 B3
Mangistauskaya Oblast' admin. div. Kazakh. 102 C4
also known as Mangghystaū Oblysy; formerly known as Mangyshlak Oblast or Mangyshlakskaya Oblast'
Mangit Uzbek. 102 E4
also spelt Mangghyt or Manghit
Mangkalihat, Tanjung pt Indon. 77 G2
Mangkutup r. Indon. 77 F3
Manglares, Punta pt Col. 198 B4
Mangnai China 88 E4
Mangnai Zhen China 88 E4
Mangoaka Madag. 131 [inset] K2
Mangochi Malawi 129 B8
formerly known as Fort Johnston
Mangodara Burkina 124 D4
Mangoky r. Toliara Madag. 131 [inset] I4
Mangoky r. Toliara Madag. 131 [inset] J4
Mangole i. Indon. 75 C3
Mangole, Selat sea chan. Indon. 75 C3
Mangoli India 94 B2
Mangombe Dem. Rep. Congo 126 E5
Mangonui N.Z. 152 H3
Mangoro r. Madag. 131 [inset] K3
Mangqystaū Shyghanaghy b. Kazakh. see Mangyshlakskiy Zaliv
Mangra China see Guinan
Mangral India 96 A5
Mangrol India 96 C4
Mangrul India 94 C1
Mangshi China see Luxi
Mangualde Port. 54 D4
Manguari Brazil 198 D5
Manguchar Pak. 101 F4
Mangueira, Lago l. Brazil 204 G4
Mangueirinha Brazil 203 A8
Manguéni, Plateau du Niger 123 H5
Mangui China 82 A2
Manguinha, Pontal do pt Brazil 202 E4
Mangula Zimbabwe see Mhangura
Mangum U.S.A. 179 C5
Mangunça, Ilha i. Brazil 202 C2
Mangut Rus. Fed. 85 G1
Mangyshlak Kazakh. see Mangistau
Mangyshlak, Poluostrov pen. Kazakh. 102 B3
also known as Tüpqaraghan Tübegi
Mangyshlak Oblast admin. div. Kazakh. see Mangistauskaya Oblast'
Mangyshlakskaya Oblast' admin. div. Kazakh. see Mangistauskaya Oblast'
Mangyshlakskiy Zaliv b. Kazakh. 102 B3
also known as Mangqystaū Shyghanaghy
Manhan Mongolia see Tögrög
Manhan Mongolia 84 B1
Manhattan U.S.A. 178 C4
Manhattan Beach U.S.A. 182 F8
Manhica Moz. 133 Q2
Manhoca Moz. 133 Q3
Manhuaçu Brazil 203 D7
Manhuaçu r. Brazil 207 L6
Manhumirim Brazil 207 L7
Mani Chad 120 B6
Mani well Chad 120 C5
Mani China 89 D5
Mani Col. 198 C3
Mani Nigeria 125 G3
Mānī', Wādī al watercourse Iraq 109 M3
Mania r. Madag. 131 [inset] J3
Maniago Italy 56 E2
Maniakoi Greece 58 C8
Maniari Tank resr India 97 D5
also known as Khuria Tank
Manica Moz. 131 G3
Manica prov. Moz. 131 G3
Manicaland prov. Zimbabwe 131 G3
Manicoré Brazil 199 F6
Manicoré r. Brazil 199 F6
Manicouagan Canada 169 G3
Manicouagan r. Canada 169 G3
Manicouagan, Réservoir Canada 169 G3
Manic Trois, Réservoir Canada 169 G3
Maniema prov. Dem. Rep. Congo 126 E5
Manīfah Saudi Arabia 105 E2
Maniganggo China 86 A2
Manigotagan Canada 167 L5
Manihari India 97 E4
Manihiki atoll Cook Is 221 H6
formerly known as Great Ganges or Humphrey Island
Maniitsoq Greenland 165 N3
also known as Sukkertoppen
Manji r. Pak. 101 F5
Manikchhari Bangl. 97 G5
Manikganj Bangl. 97 F5
Manikgarh India see Rajura
Manikpur India 96 D4

▶Manila Phil. 74 B3
Capital of the Philippines.
world [cities] ▶ 24–25

Manila U.S.A. 180 E4
Manila Bay Phil. 74 B3
Manilaid i. Estonia 42 F3
Manilla Australia 147 F2
Manily Rus. Fed. 39 Q3
Manimbaya, Tanjung pt Indon. 75 A3
Maningrida Australia 148 B2
Maninjau, Danau l. Indon. 76 C3
Manipa i. Indon. 75 C3
Manipa, Selat sea chan. Indon. 75 C3
Manipur India see Imphal
Manipur state India 97 G4
Manipur r. India/Myanmar 97 G5
Manisa Turkey 106 A3
Manisa prov. Turkey 59 J10
Manises Spain 55 K5
Manissauá Missu r. Brazil 202 A4
Manistee U.S.A. 172 G6
Manistee r. U.S.A. 172 G6
Manistique U.S.A. 172 G5
Manistique Lake U.S.A. 172 H4
Manitoba prov. Canada 167 L4
Manitoba, Lake Canada 167 L5
Manito Lake Canada 167 I4
Manitou Canada 167 L5
Manitou r. Canada 169 H3
Manitou, Lake Canada 168 D4
Manitou Beach U.S.A. 176 H2
Manitou Falls Canada 168 A3
Manitou Island U.S.A. 172 F3
Manitou Islands U.S.A. 172 G5
Manitoulin Island Canada 168 D4
Manitouwadge Canada 168 C3
Manitowaning Canada 173 L5
Manitowik Lake Canada 173 I2
Manitowish Waters U.S.A. 172 D4
Manitowoc U.S.A. 172 F6
Maniwaki Canada 168 F4
Manizales Col. 198 C3
Manja Madag. 131 [inset] J4
Manjacaze Moz. 131 G5
Manjak Madag. 131 [inset] J3
Manjam Umm Qurayyāt waterhole Egypt 104 A3
Manjarabad India 94 B3
Manjeri India 94 C4
Manjhand Pak. 101 G5
Man Jiang r. China 82 B4
Manjil Iran 100 B2
Manjimup Australia 151 B7
Manjo Cameroon 125 H5
Manjra r. India 94 C2
Man Kabat Myanmar 78 B2
Mankachar India 97 F4
Mankanza Dem. Rep. Congo see Makanza
Mankato KS U.S.A. 178 C4
Mankato MN U.S.A. 178 D2
Mankono Côte d'Ivoire 124 D4
Mankota Canada 167 J5
Manlleu Spain 55 N3
Manly U.S.A. 174 A3
Manmad India 94 B1
Mann r. Australia 148 B2
Mann, Mount Australia 148 A5
Manna Indon. 76 C4
Mannahill Australia 146 C3
Mannar Sri Lanka 94 C4
Mannar, Gulf of India/Sri Lanka 94 C4
Mannargudi India 94 C4
Manneru r. India 94 D3
Mannheim Germany 48 F6
Mannicolo Islands Solomon Is see Vanikoro Islands
Männikuste Estonia 42 F3
Manning Canada 167 G3
Manning ND U.S.A. 178 B2
Manning SC U.S.A. 175 D5
Manning Provincial Park Canada 166 F5
Mannington U.S.A. 176 E6
Männlifluh mt. Switz. 51 N6
Mann Ranges mts Australia 148 A5
Mannsville U.S.A. 177 I2
Mannu r. Sardegna Italy 57 A8
Mannu r. Sardegna Italy 57 A9
Mannu r. Sardegna Italy 57 B9
Mannu, Capo c. Sardegna Italy 57 A8
Mannville Canada 167 I4
Mano r. Liberia/Sierra Leone 124 C5
Manoa Bol. 200 D2
Man-of-War Rocks is U.S.A. see Gardner Pinnacles
Manoharpur India 89 B7
Manohar Thana India 96 C4
Manokotak U.S.A. 164 D4
Manokwari Indon. 73 H7
Manombo Atsimo Madag. 131 [inset] I4
Manompana Madag. 131 [inset] K3
Manono Dem. Rep. Congo 127 E6
Manora Head Pak. 101 F5
Mano River Liberia 124 C5
Manosque France 51 L9
Manouane, Lac l. Canada 169 G3
Mano-wan b. Japan 90 F6
Man Pan Myanmar 78 B3
Manp'o N. Korea 83 B4
Manpur India 96 B5
Manra i. Kiribati 145 H2
formerly known as Sydney Island
Manresa Spain 55 M3
Mansa Gujarat India 96 B5
Mansa Punjab India 96 B3
Mansa Zambia 127 F7
formerly known as Fort Rosebery
Mansabá Guinea-Bissau 124 B3
Mansa Konko Gambia 124 B3
Man Sam Myanmar 78 B3
Mansehra Pak. 101 H3
Mansel Island Canada 165 L3
Mansel'kya ridge Fin./Rus. Fed. 44 O2
Mansfield Australia 147 E4
Mansfield U.K. 47 K10
Mansfield AR U.S.A. 179 D5
Mansfield LA U.S.A. 179 D5
Mansfield MA U.S.A. 177 N3
Mansfield OH U.S.A. 176 C5
Mansfield PA U.S.A. 177 H4
Mansfield, Mount U.S.A. 177 M1
Man Si Myanmar 78 B2
Mansi Myanmar 78 A2
Mansidão Brazil 202 D4
Manso r. Brazil see Mortes, Rio das
Manso-Nkwanta Ghana 125 E5
Mansuela Indon. 75 D3
Mansurlu Turkey 106 C3
also known as Tapan
Manta Ecuador 198 A5
long form San Pablo de Manta
Mantalingajan, Mount Phil. 74 A4
Mantantale Dem. Rep. Congo 126 D5
Mantaro r. Peru 200 B3
Manteca U.S.A. 182 C4
Mantecal Venez. 198 D3
Mantehage i. Indon. 75 C2
Manteigas Port. 54 D4
Mantena Brazil 203 D6
Manteo U.S.A. 174 F5
Mantes-la-Jolie France 50 H4
Manthani India 94 C2
Manti U.S.A. 183 M2
Mantiqueira, Serra da mts Brazil 203 C7
Manto Hond. 186 B4
Manton U.S.A. 172 H6
Mantorville U.S.A. 168 A4
Mantos Blancos Chile 200 C5
Mantoudi Greece 59 E10
also known as Mandhoúdhion
Mantova Italy see Mantua
Mäntsälä Fin. 45 N3
Mänttä Fin. 45 N3
Mantua Cuba 186 B2
Mantua Italy 56 C3
also spelt Mantova
Mantua U.S.A. 176 D4
Mantuan Downs Australia 149 E5
Manturovo Rus. Fed. 40 H4
Mäntyharju Fin. 45 N3
Mäntyjärvi Fin. 44 N2
Manu r. Bol. see Mapiri
Manú r. Peru 200 C3
Manu, Parque Nacional nat. park Peru 200 B3
Manuae atoll Fr. Polynesia 221 H7
also known as Fenua Ura; formerly known as Scilly, Île
Manua Islands American Samoa 145 I3
Manubi S. Africa 133 M9
Manuel Alves r. Brazil 202 B4
Manuel J. Cobo Arg. 204 F4
Manuel Rodriguez, Isla i. Chile 205 B9
Manuel Urbano Brazil 200 C2
Manuel Vitorino Brazil 202 D5
Manuelzinho Brazil 202 A3
Manui i. Indon. 75 B3
Manūjān Iran 100 D5
Manukan Phil. 74 B4
Manukau N.Z. 152 I4
Manukau Harbour N.Z. 152 I5
Manuk Manka i. Phil. 74 A5
Manunda watercourse Australia 146 C3
Manupari r. Bol. 200 D2
Manurimi r. Bol. 200 D2
Manuripi r. Bol. 200 D2
Manusela National Park Indon. 75 D3
Manus Island P.N.G. 73 K7
Manutuke N.Z. 152 L6
Manvi India 94 C3
Manwat India 94 C2
Many U.S.A. 179 D6
Manyallaluk Aboriginal reserve res. Australia 148 B2
Manyame r. Moz./Zimbabwe 131 F2
formerly known as Hunyani
Manyara, Lake salt l. Tanz. 129 B5
Manyas Turkey 59 I8
Manyas Gölü l. Turkey see Kuş Gölü
Manyatseng S. Africa 133 L6
Manyberries Canada 167 I5
Manych-Gudilo, Ozero l. Rus. Fed. 41 G7
Many Farms U.S.A. 183 O5
Manyinga Zambia 127 E8
Many Island Lake Canada 167 I5
Manyoni Tanz. 129 B6
Many Peaks, Mount hill Australia 151 B7
Manzala, Bahra el lag. Egypt see Manzala, Lake
Manzala, Lake lag. Egypt 108 D6
also known as Manzala, Bahra el
Manzanal, Puerto del pass Spain 54 E2
Manzanares Spain 55 H5
Manzaneda, Cabeza de mt. Spain 54 D2
Manzanillo Cuba 186 D2
Manzanillo Mex. 184 D5
Manzanillo, Punta pt Panama 186 D5
Manzanza Dem. Rep. Congo 126 F6
Manzariyeh Iran 100 B3
Manzengele Dem. Rep. Congo 127 C6
Manzhouli China 85 H1
Manzini Swaziland 133 P3
formerly known as Bremersdorp
Manzini admin. dist. Swaziland 133 P3
Manzovka Rus. Fed. see Sibirtsevo
Mao Chad 120 B6
Mao Dom. Rep. 187 F3
formerly known as Valverde
Maó Spain see Mahón
Mao, Nam r. Myanmar see Shweli
Maoba Guizhou China 86 C3
Maoba Hubei China 87 D2
Maocifan China 87 E2
Mao'ergai China 86 B1
Maoke, Pegunungan mts Indon. 73 I7
Maokeng S. Africa 133 L4
Maokui Shan mt. China 83 A4
Maomao Shan mt. China 84 D4
Maoming China 87 D4
Ma On Shan hill Hong Kong China 87 [inset]
Maopi Cape Taiwan see Maopi T'ou
Maopi T'ou c. Taiwan 87 G4
English form Maopi Cape
Maopora i. Indon. 75 C4
Maotou Shan mt. China 86 B3
Maowen China see Maoxian
Maoxian China 86 B2
also known as Fengyi; formerly known as Maowen
Mapai Moz. 131 F4
Mapam Yumco l. China 89 C6
Mapane Indon. 75 B3
Mapanza Zambia 127 E9
Mapastepec Mex. 185 G6
Maphodi S. Africa 133 J7
Mapi r. Indon. 73 I8
Mapiche, Serranía mts Venez. 199 E3
Mapimí Mex. 184 E3
Mapimí, Bolsón de des. Mex. 184 D3
Mapin i. Phil. 74 A5
Mapinhane Moz. 131 G4
Mapire Venez. 199 E3
Mapireme Brazil 199 H4
Mapiri Bol. 200 C3
Mapiri r. Bol. 200 D2
also known as Manu
Mapirpán Col. 198 C4
Mapiu N.Z. 152 J6
Maple r. IA U.S.A. 178 D3
Maple r. MI U.S.A. 173 I8
Maple r. ND U.S.A. 178 C2
Maple r. ND U.S.A. 178 C2
Maple Creek Canada 167 I5
Maple Peak U.S.A. 183 O8
Mapleton IA U.S.A. 178 D3
Mapleton UT U.S.A. 183 M1
Maplewood U.S.A. 172 F6
Mapoon Australia 149 D1
Mapoon Aboriginal Reserve Australia 149 D2
Mapor i. Indon. 76 D2
Mapoteng Lesotho 133 L6
Maprik P.N.G. 73 J7
Mapuca India 94 B3
Mapuera r. Brazil 199 G5
Mapulanguene Moz. 131 G5
Mapunda Dem. Rep. Congo 127 E7

▶Maputo Moz. 131 G5
Capital of Mozambique. Formerly known as Lourenço Marques.

Maputo prov. Moz. 131 G5
Maputo r. Moz./S. Africa 133 Q3
Maputo, Baía de b. Moz. 133 Q3
Maputo Elephant Reserve nature res. Moz. 133 Q3
Maputsoe Lesotho 133 L5
Maqanshy Kazakh. see Makanchi
Maqar an Na'am well Iraq 107 E5
Maqat Kazakh. see Makat
Maqên China 86 B1
also known as Dawu
Maqên Gangri mt. China 86 A1
Maqla, Jabal al mt. Saudi Arabia 108 G9

index

M

Maqnā Saudi Arabia **108** F9
Maqrat Yemen **105** E5
Maqteïr *reg.* Mauritania **122** C5
Maqu China **86** B1
also known as Nyinma
Ma Qu *r.* China *see* **Yellow River**
Maquan He *r.* China **89** D6
also known as Damqog Zangbo
Maqueda Channel Phil. **74** B3
Maquela do Zombo Angola **127** B6
Maquinchao Arg. **204** C6
Maquoketa U.S.A. **174** B3
Maquoketa *r.* U.S.A. **174** B3
Maquon U.S.A. **172** C10
Mar *r.* Pak. **101** F5
Mar, Serra do *mts Rio de Janeiro/São Paulo* Brazil **203** C7
Mar, Serra do *mts Rio Grande do Sul/Santa Catarina* Brazil **203** B9
Mar, Serra do *mts* Brazil **207** J9
Mara *r.* Canada **167** I1
Mara Guyana **199** G3
Mara India **97** D5
Mara *admin. reg.* Tanz. **128** B5
Maraã Brazil **199** E5
Maraba Brazil **202** B3
Marabahan Indon. **77** F3
Marabatua *i.* Indon. **77** F4
Marabitanas Brazil **199** E4
Maraboon, Lake *resr* Australia **149** F4
Maracá *r.* Brazil **199** I5
Maracá, Ilha *i.* Brazil **199** F4
Maracaí Brazil **206** C9
Maracaibo Venez. **198** D2
Maracaibo, Lago de *l.* Venez. *see* **Maracaibo, Lake**
Maracaibo, Lake Venez. **198** D2
also known as Maracaibo, Lago de
Maracaju Brazil **201** G5
Maracaju, Serra de *hills* Brazil **201** G5
Maracanã Brazil **202** C2
Maracanaquará, Planalto *plat.* Brazil **199** H5
Maracanda Uzbek. *see* **Samarkand**
Maracás Brazil **202** D5
Maracás, Chapada de *hills* Brazil **202** D5
Maracay Venez. **199** E2
Marachkova Belarus **43** J6
Marādah Libya **120** C2
Maradi Niger **125** G3
Maradi *dept* Niger **125** G3
Marāgheh Iran **100** A2
Maragogi Brazil **202** F4
Maragondon Phil. **74** B3
Marah Saudi Arabia **105** D2
Marahuaca, Cerro *mt.* Venez. **199** E4
Marais des Cygnes *r.* U.S.A. **178** D4
Marais du Cotentin et du Bessin, Parc Naturel Régional des *nature res.* France **50** E3
Marais Poitevin, Val de Sèvre et Vendée, Parc Naturel Régional *nature res.* France **50** F6
Marajó, Baía de *est.* Brazil **202** B2
Marajó, Ilha de *i.* Brazil **202** B2
Marakei *atoll* Kiribati **145** G1
also spelt Maraki; formerly known as Matthew
Maraki *atoll* Kiribati *see* **Marakei**
Marakkanam India **94** C3
Maralal Kenya **128** C4
Maralbashi China *see* **Bachu**
Maraldy Kazakh. **103** I1
Maraldy, Ozero *salt l.* Kazakh. **103** I1
Maralinga Australia **146** A2
Maralinga-Tjarutja Aboriginal Lands *res.* Australia **146** A2
Maralwexi China *see* **Bachu**
Maramasike *i.* Solomon Is **145** F2
Maramba Zambia *see* **Livingstone**
Marambio *research station* Antarctica **222** U2
long form Vicecomodoro Marambio
Marampit *i.* Indon. **75** C1
Maran *mt.* Pak. **101** F4
Marana U.S.A. **183** M9
Marand Iran **100** A2
Marandellas Zimbabwe *see* **Marondera**
Marang Myanmar **79** B6
Maranguape Brazil **202** E2
Maranhão *r.* Brazil **206** E1
Maranhão *state* Brazil **202** C3
Maranoa *r.* Australia **147** F1
Marañón *r.* Peru **198** C6
Marans France **50** E6
Marão Moz. **131** G5
formerly known as Mau-é-ele
Marão *mt.* Port. **54** D3
Maraoué *r.* Côte d'Ivoire **124** D5
Marapanim Brazil **202** C2
Marape Brazil **201** F3
Marapi, Gunung *vol.* Indon. **76** C3
Marari Brazil **199** E5
Mararoa *r.* N.Z. **153** B13
Mara Rosa Brazil **202** B5
Maraş Cyprus *see* **Varosia**
Maraş Turkey *see* **Kahramanmaraş**
Marasende *i.* Indon. **77** G4
Mărășești Romania **58** I3
Mărașu Romania **58** I4
Maratea Italy **57** H9
Marathia, Akra *pt* Greece **59** B11
Marathokampos Greece **59** H11
Marathon Canada **168** C3
Marathón Greece *see* **Marathonas**
Marathon *FL* U.S.A. **175** D7
Marathon *TX* U.S.A. **179** B6
Marathon *WI* U.S.A. **172** D6
Marathonas Greece **59** E10
also known as Marathón
Maratua *i.* Indon. **77** G2
Marauá Brazil **199** E5
Marauiá *r.* Brazil **199** E5
Maravatío Mex. **185** E5
Maravillas Creek *watercourse* U.S.A. **179** B6
Marāwah Libya **120** D1
Marawi Phil. **74** C4
Marayes Arg. **204** D3
Maray Lake Pak. **101** G4
Mar'ayt Yemen **105** E4
Mărăză Azer. **107** G2
Marbella Spain **54** G8
Marble Bar Australia **150** B4
Marble Canyon U.S.A. **183** M5
Marble Canyon *gorge* U.S.A. **183** M5
Marble Hall S. Africa **133** N1
Marble Hill U.S.A. **174** B4
Marble Island Canada **167** N2
Marbul Pass Jammu and Kashmir **96** B2
Marburg S. Africa **133** O7
Marburg Slovenia *see* **Maribor**
Marburg an der Lahn Germany **48** F5
Marca Peru **200** A2
Marca, Ponta do *pt* Angola **127** A9
Marcal *r.* Hungary **49** O8
Marcali Hungary **49** O9
Marcapata Peru **200** C3
Marcelino Brazil **199** E5
Marcellus *MI* U.S.A. **172** H8
Marcellus *NY* U.S.A. **177** I3
March *r.* Austria/Slovakia *see* **Morava**
March U.K. **47** M11
Marchant Hill *hill* Australia **146** C3
Marche *reg.* France **50** H6
Marche *admin. reg.* Italy **56** E5
Marche-en-Famenne Belgium **51** L2
Marchena Spain **54** F7
Mar Chiquita, Lago *l.* Arg. **204** E3
Marchtrenk Austria **49** L7
Marciena Latvia **42** H5
Marcona Peru **200** B3
Marcopeet Islands Canada **168** E1
Marcos Juárez Arg. **204** E4
Marcy, Mount U.S.A. **177** L1
Mardan Pak. **101** H3
Mar de Ajó Arg. **204** F5
Mar del Plata Arg. **204** F5
Mardiān Afgh. **101** F2
Mardin Turkey **107** E3
Mardudden Sweden **44** M2
Mardzad Mongolia **84** D2
Maré *i.* New Caledonia **145** F4
formerly known as Britannia Island
Mare de Déu del Toro *hill* Spain **55** P5
Maree, Loch *l.* U.K. **46** G6
Mareeba Australia **149** E3
Mareh Iran **101** D5
Maréna Mali **124** C3
Marendet Niger **125** G2
Marengo *IA* U.S.A. **174** A3
Marengo *IL* U.S.A. **172** E8
Marengo *WI* U.S.A. **172** C4
Marenisco U.S.A. **172** D4
Marennes France **50** E7
Marerano Madag. **131** [inset] J4
Maret Islands Australia **150** D2
Marettimo, Isola *i. Sicilia* Italy **57** E11
Mareuil France **50** G7
Mareuil-sur-Lay-Dissais France **50** E6
Marevo Rus. Fed. **43** N4
Marfa U.S.A. **181** F7
Margam Ri *mts* China **89** D5
Marganets Kazakh. *see* **Zhezdy**
Marganets Ukr. *see* **Marhanets'**
Margao India *see* **Madgaon**
Margaret *r.* Australia **150** D3
Margaret *watercourse* Australia **146** C2
Margaret, Mount *hill* Australia **150** B4
Margaret Lake *Alta* Canada **167** H3
Margaret Lake *N.W.T.* Canada **167** G1
Margaret River Australia **151** A7
Margaretville U.S.A. **177** K3
Margarita Arg. **204** E3
Margarita, Isla de *i.* Venez. **199** F2
Margaritovo Rus. Fed. **90** D3
Margate S. Africa **133** O7
Margate U.K. **47** N12
Margate City U.S.A. **177** K6
Mărgău Romania **58** D2
Margherita India **97** G4
Margherita, Lake Eth. *see* **Abaya, Lake**
Margherita di Savoia Italy **56** I7

Margherita Peak
Dem. Rep. Congo/Uganda **126** F4
3rd highest mountain in Africa. Also known as Stanley, Mount or Marguerite, Pic.
africa [landscapes] 112–113

Marghilon Uzbek. *see* **Margilan**
Marghita Romania **58** D1
Margilan Uzbek. **103** G4
also spelt Marghilon
Margionys Lith. **42** F8
Margo, Dasht-i *des.* Afgh. **101** E4
Margog Caka *l.* China **89** D5
Margos Peru **200** A2
Margosatubig Phil. **74** B5
Marguerite Canada **166** F4
Marguerite, Pic *mt.*
Dem. Rep. Congo/Uganda *see* **Margherita Peak**
Marguerite Bay Antarctica **222** T2
Margyang China **89** E6
Marhaj Khalīl Iraq **107** F4
Marhān Dāgh *hill* Iraq **107** E3
Marhanets' Ukr. **41** E7
also spelt Marganets; formerly known as Komintern
Marhoum Alg. **123** E2
Mari *r.* Brazil **201** D1
Mari Myanmar **78** B2
Mari P.N.G. **73** J8
Maria *r.* Brazil **203** A7
Maria *atoll* Fr. Polynesia **221** H7
María Cleofas, Isla *i.* Mex. **184** D4
María Elena Chile **200** C5
Mariager Denmark **45** J4
María Ignacia Arg. **204** F5
Maria Island *N.T.* Australia **148** B2
Maria Island *Tas.* Australia **147** F5
Mariala National Park Australia **149** E5
María Madre, Isla *i.* Mex. **184** D4
María Magdelena, Isla *i.* Mex. **184** D4
Marian Australia **149** F4
Mariana Brazil **207** J7
Marianao Cuba **186** C2

Mariana Trench *sea feature*
N. Pacific Ocean **220** D5
Deepest trench in the world.

Mariani India **97** G4
Mariánica, Cordillera *mts* Spain *see* **Morena, Sierra**
Marian Lake Canada **167** G2
Marianna *AR* U.S.A. **174** B5
Marianna *FL* U.S.A. **175** C6
Mariannelund Sweden **45** K4
Mariano Loza Arg. **204** F3
Mariano Machado Angola *see* **Ganda**
Mariánské Lázně Czech Rep. **49** J6
historically known as Marienbad
Mariapiri, Mesa de *hills* Col. **198** D4
Mariápolis Brazil **206** B8
Marias *r.* U.S.A. **180** E3
Marías, Islas *is* Mex. **184** D4

Mariato, Punta *pt* Panama **186** C6
Most southerly point of North America.

Maria van Diemen, Cape N.Z. **152** G2
Mariazell Austria **49** M8
Ma'rib Yemen **105** D5
Ma'rib *governorate* Yemen **105** D5
Maribel U.S.A. **172** F6
Maribo Denmark **48** I1
Maribor Slovenia **56** H2
historically known as Marburg
Maricá Brazil **207** K9
Marica *r.* Bulg. *see* **Maritsa**
Marico *r.* S. Africa **133** K1
Marico Bosveld Nature Reserve S. Africa **133** K2
Maricopa *AZ* U.S.A. **183** L8
Maricopa *CA* U.S.A. **182** E6
Maricopa Mountains U.S.A. **183** L8
Maricourt Canada *see* **Kangiqsujuaq**
Maridi Sudan **126** F3
Maridi *watercourse* Sudan **126** F3
Marié *r.* Brazil **199** E5
Marie Byrd Land *reg.* Antarctica **222** P1
Marie-Galante *i.* Guadeloupe **187** H4
Mariehamn Fin. **45** L3
also spelt Maarianhamina
Mari El *aut. rep.* Rus. Fed. *see* **Mariy El, Respublika**
Mariembero *r.* Brazil **202** B5
also known as Cristalino
Marienbad Czech Rep. *see* **Mariánské Lázně**
Marienburg Poland *see* **Malbork**
Mariental Namibia **130** C5
Marienville U.S.A. **176** F4
Marienwerder Poland *see* **Kwidzyn**
Mariestad Sweden **45** K4
Marietⅇ *r.* Canada **168** E1
Marietta *GA* U.S.A. **175** C5
Marietta *OH* U.S.A. **176** D6
Marietta *OK* U.S.A. **179** C5
Mariga *r.* Nigeria **125** G4
Marigliano Italy **56** G8
Marignane France **51** L9
Marigot Dominica **187** H4
Marigot West Indies **187** H3
Marii, Mys *pt* Rus. Fed. **82** F1
Mariinsk Rus. Fed. **80** D1
Mariinskoye Rus. Fed. **103** E1
Marijampolė Lith. **42** E7
formerly known as Kapsukas
Marikostinovo Bulg. **58** E7
Marília Brazil **206** D9
Marillana Australia **150** B4
Marimba Angola **127** C7
Marín Spain **54** C2
Marina U.S.A. **182** C5
Marina di Gioiosa Ionica Italy **57** I10
Mar'ina Gorka Belarus *see* **Mar"ina Horka**
Mar"ina Horka Belarus **42** J8
also spelt Mar'ina Gorka
Marinduque *i.* Phil. **74** B3
Marine City U.S.A. **173** K8
Marinella, Golfo di *b. Sardegna* Italy **56** B7
Mariner Glacier Antarctica **223** L2
Marinette U.S.A. **172** F5
Maringá Brazil **206** B10
Maringa *r.* Dem. Rep. Congo **126** C4
Maringo U.S.A. **176** C5
Maringué Moz. **131** G3
Marinha Grande Port. **54** C5
Marinjab Iran **100** B3
Mar'insko Rus. Fed. **43** J3
Marion *AL* U.S.A. **175** C5
Marion *AR* U.S.A. **174** B5
Marion *IA* U.S.A. **172** B8
Marion *IL* U.S.A. **174** B4
Marion *IN* U.S.A. **174** C3
Marion *KS* U.S.A. **178** C4
Marion *KY* U.S.A. **174** B4
Marion *NC* U.S.A. **174** D5
Marion *OH* U.S.A. **176** B5
Marion *SC* U.S.A. **175** E5
Marion *VA* U.S.A. **176** D9
Marion *WI* U.S.A. **172** E6
Marion, Lake U.S.A. **175** D5
Marion Bay Australia **146** C3
Marion Lake U.S.A. **178** C4
Marion Reef Australia **149** G3
Mariou, Adrar *mt.* Alg. **123** H5
Maripa Venez. **199** E3
Maripasoula Fr. Guiana **199** H4
Maripipi *i.* Phil. **74** C4
Mariposa U.S.A. **182** E4
Mariposa *r.* U.S.A. **182** D4
Mariquita Col. **198** C3
Marir, Gezîret *i.* Egypt **104** A3
English form Mirear Island
Marisa Indon. **75** B2
Mariscal Estigarribia Para. **201** E5
Mărișel Romania **58** E2
Mărișelu Romania **58** F1
Marite S. Africa **133** P1
Maritime Alps *mts* France/Italy **51** M8
also known as Maritimes, Alpes or Marittime, Alpi
Maritime Kray *admin. div.* Rus. Fed. *see* **Primorskiy Kray**
Maritimes, Alpes *mts* France/Italy *see* **Maritime Alps**
Maritsa Bulg. *see* **Simeonovgrad**
Maritsa *r.* Bulg. **58** H7
also spelt Marica
Marittime, Alpi *mts* France/Italy *see* **Maritime Alps**
Mari-Turek Rus. Fed. **40** I4
Mariupol' Ukr. **41** F7
formerly known as Zhdanov
Mariusa *nat. park* Venez. **199** F2
Mariusa, Isla *i.* Venez. **199** F2
Marīvān Iran **107** F4
formerly known as Dezh Shāhpūr
Mariy El, Respublika *aut. rep.* Rus. Fed. **40** I4
English form Mari El; formerly known as Mariyskaya A.S.S.R. or Mary A.S.S.R.
Mariyskaya A.S.S.R. *aut. rep.* Rus. Fed. *see* **Mariy El, Respublika**
Märjamaa Estonia **42** F3
Marjan Afgh. *see* **Wazi Khwa**
Marjayoûn Lebanon **108** G4
Marka *i.* Saudi Arabia **104** C4
Marka Somalia **128** E4
formerly spelt Merca
Markakol', Ozero *l.* Kazakh. **88** D1
also known as Marqaköl
Markala Mali **124** D3
Markam China **86** A2
also known as Gartog
Markapur India **94** C3
Markaryd Sweden **45** K4
Markawene *well* Eth. **128** E3
Markaz, Ra's c. Oman **105** G4
Markazī *prov.* Iran **100** B3
Markdale Canada **173** M6
Marken S. Africa **131** F4
Markermeer *l.* Neth. **48** C3
Market Harborough U.K. **47** L11
Market Rasen U.K. **47** L10
Market Weighton U.K. **47** L10
Markha *r.* Rus. Fed. **39** L3
Markham Canada **168** E5
Markham, Mount Antarctica **223** K1
Markhamet Uzbek. **103** H4
Markit China **88** B4
Markitta Sweden **44** M2
Markleeville U.S.A. **182** E3
Markleysburg U.S.A. **176** F6
Markounda Cent. Afr. Rep. **126** C3
Markovo *Chukotskiy Avtonomnyy Okrug* Rus. Fed. **39** R3
Markovo *Ivanovskaya Oblast'* Rus. Fed. **43** V4
Markoye Burkina **125** F3
Marks Rus. Fed. **102** A2
Marks U.S.A. **174** B5
Marksville U.S.A. **175** A6
Marktheidenfeld Germany **48** G6
Marktoberdorf Germany **48** H8
Marktosis Canada **166** E5
Marktredwitz Germany **48** J5
Marl Germany **48** E4
Marla Australia **146** B1
Marlboro U.S.A. **177** L4
Marlborough Australia **149** F4
Marlborough *admin. reg.* N.Z. **153** H9
Marlborough *MA* U.S.A. **177** N3
Marlborough *NH* U.S.A. **177** M3
Marle France **51** J3
Marlin U.S.A. **179** C6
Marlinton U.S.A. **176** E7
Marlo Australia **147** F4
Marloth Nature Reserve S. Africa **132** E11
Marlton U.S.A. **177** K6
Marmagao India **94** B3
formerly spelt Mormugao
Marmande France **50** G8
Marmara Turkey **58** I8
Marmara, Sea of *g.* Turkey **106** B2
also known as Marmara Denizi
Marmara Adası *i.* Turkey **58** I8
Marmara Denizi *g.* Turkey *see* **Marmara, Sea of**
Marmaraereğlisi Turkey **58** I8
Marmara Gölü *l.* Turkey **59** J10
Marmarica *reg.* Libya **120** E2
Marmaris Turkey **106** B3
Marmaro Greece **59** H10
Marmelos *r.* Brazil **201** E1
Marmet U.S.A. **176** D7
Marmion, Lake *salt l.* Australia **151** C6
Marmion Lake Canada **168** B3
Marmolada *mt.* Italy **56** D2
Marmolejo Spain **54** G6
Marne *r.* France **51** I4
Marne Germany **48** G2
Marne, Source de la *tourist site* France **48** C8
Marne-la-Vallée France **51** I4
Marneuli Georgia **107** F2
formerly known as Borchalo or Sarvani
Maro Chad **126** C2
Maroambihy Madag. **131** [inset] K2
Maroantsetra Madag. **131** [inset] K2
Maroba *r.* Brazil **207** N4
Marofandilia Madag. **131** [inset] J4
Marokopa N.Z. **152** I6
Marol Jammu and Kashmir **96** C2
Marolambo Madag. **131** [inset] K4
Maroldsweisach Germany **48** H5
Marolles-les-Braults France **50** G4
Maromokotro *mt.* Madag. **131** [inset] K2
Marondera Zimbabwe **131** F3
formerly spelt Marandellas
Maroni *r.* Fr. Guiana **199** H3
Maronne *r.* France **51** H7
Maroochydore Australia **149** G5
Maroonah Australia **150** A4
Maroon Peak U.S.A. **180** F5
Maros Indon. **75** A4
Maros *r.* Romania **58** B2
Maroseranana Madag. **131** [inset] K3
Maros-Körös Köze *plain* Hungary **49** R9
Marosleie Hungary **49** R9
Marosvásárhely Romania *see* **Târgu Mureș**
Marotandrano Madag. **131** [inset] K3
Marotolana Madag. **131** [inset] K2
Maroua Cameroon **125** I4
Marova Brazil **199** F5
Marovato *Antsirañana* Madag. **131** [inset] K2
Marovato *Toliara* Madag. **131** [inset] J5
Marovoay *Mahajanga* Madag. **131** [inset] J3
Marovoay *Toamasina* Madag. **131** [inset] K3
Marovoay Atsimo Madag. **131** [inset] J3
Marowali Indon. **75** B3
Marowijne *r.* Suriname **199** H3
Marqab al Khubbāz *hill* Iraq **109** N4
Marqādah Syria **109** L2
Marqaköl *l.* Kazakh. *see* **Markakol', Ozero**
Mar Qu *r.* China **86** B1
Marquard S. Africa **133** L5
Marquesas Islands Fr. Polynesia **221** I6
also known as Marquises, Îles
Marquesas Keys *is* U.S.A. **175** D7
Marquês de Valença Brazil **207** J9
Marquette U.S.A. **172** F4
Marquise France **50** H2
Marquises, Îles *is* Fr. Polynesia *see* **Marquesas Islands**
Marra *r.* Australia **147** E2
Marra, Jebel *mt.* Sudan **120** E6
Marra, Wādi *watercourse* Egypt **108** F9
Marra Aboriginal Land *res.* Australia **148** B2
Marracuene Moz. **133** Q2
formerly known as Vila Luísa
Marradi Italy **56** D4
Marrāk *i.* Saudi Arabia **104** C4
Marrakech Morocco **122** D3
English form Marrakesh
Marrakesh Morocco *see* **Marrakech**
Marra Plateau Sudan **120** E6
Marrawah Australia **147** E5
Marree Australia **146** C2
Marrero U.S.A. **175** B6
Marresale Rus. Fed. **40** M1
Marromeu Moz. **131** G3
Marromeu, Reserva de *nature res.* Moz. **131** G3
Marrupa Moz. **129** C8
Marryat Australia **148** B5
Mars *r.* France **51** I7
Mars U.S.A. **176** E5
Marsa Alam Egypt **121** G3
Marsa al Burayqah Libya **120** C2
Marsabit Kenya **128** C4
Marsabit National Reserve *nature res.* Kenya **128** C4
Marsa Darur Sudan **121** H5
Marsa Delwein Sudan **121** H4
Marsa 'Igli Egypt **104** A2
Marsala *Sicilia* Italy **57** E11
Marsa Mar'ob Sudan **104** B3
Marsa Matrûh Egypt **121** E2
historically known as Paraetonium
Marsa Oseif Sudan **104** B3
Marsa Salak Sudan **104** B3
Marsa Shin'ab Sudan **104** B3
Marsa Tundaba Egypt **104** A2
Mars Bay Bahamas **186** D2
Marsberg Germany **48** F4
Marsciano Italy **56** E6
Marsden Australia **147** E3
Marsden Canada **167** I4
Marseille France **51** L9
English form Marseilles; historically known as Massilia
Marseilles France *see* **Marseille**
Marseilles U.S.A. **172** E9
Marsella Bol. **200** D3
Marsfjället *mt.* Sweden **44** K2
Marshah, Jabal *mt.* Saudi Arabia **108** F9
Marshall *watercourse* Australia **148** C4
Marshall Canada **167** I4
Marshall *AR* U.S.A. **179** D5
Marshall *IL* U.S.A. **174** C4
Marshall *MI* U.S.A. **173** I8
Marshall *MN* U.S.A. **178** D2
Marshall *MO* U.S.A. **178** D4
Marshall *TX* U.S.A. **179** D5
Marshall *VA* U.S.A. **176** H7

Marshall Islands *country*
N. Pacific Ocean **220** G5
also known as Majōl
oceania [countries] 138–139

Marshalltown U.S.A. **174** A3
Marshfield *MO* U.S.A. **178** D4
Marshfield *WI* U.S.A. **172** C6
Marsh Harbour Bahamas **186** D1
Mars Hill U.S.A. **174** H2
Marsh Island U.S.A. **175** B6
Marsh Lake Canada **166** C2
Marsh Lake *l.* Canada **166** C2
Marsh Peak U.S.A. **183** O1
Marshūn Iran **100** B2
Marsing U.S.A. **180** C4
Märsta Sweden **45** L4
Marsyangdi *r.* Nepal **97** E4
Marta Italy **56** D6
Marta *r.* Italy **56** D6
Martaban Myanmar **78** B4
also known as Mōktama
Martaban, Gulf of Myanmar **78** B4
Martanai Besar *i. Sabah* Malaysia **77** G1
Martapura *Kalimantan Selatan* Indon. **77** F3
Martapura *Sumatra* Indon. **76** D4
Martel France **50** H8
Marten River Canada **168** E4
Marte R. Gómez, Presa *resr* Mex. **185** F3
Martés *mt.* Spain **55** K5
Martés, Serra *mts* Spain **55** J5
Martha's Vineyard *i.* U.S.A. **177** O4
Martí Cuba **186** D2
Martigny Switz. **51** N6
Martim Vaz, Ilhas *is* S. Atlantic Ocean *see* **Martin Vas, Ilhas**
Martin *r.* Canada **166** F2
Martin Slovakia **49** P6
Martín *r.* Spain **55** K3
Martin U.S.A. **178** B3
Martin, Lake U.S.A. **175** C5
Martina Franca Italy **57** J8
Martinborough N.Z. **152** J9
Martinet Spain **55** M2
Martínez Mex. **185** F4
Martinez *CA* U.S.A. **182** B3
Martinez *GA* U.S.A. **175** D5
Martinez Lake U.S.A. **183** J9
Martinho Campos Brazil **203** C6

Martinique *terr.* West Indies **187** H4
French Overseas Department.
oceania [countries] 138–139

Martinique Passage Dominica/Martinique **187** H4
Martino Greece **59** E10
Martinópolis Brazil **206** B9
Martin Peninsula Antarctica **222** Q2
Martins Bay N.Z. **153** B12
Martinsburg *OH* U.S.A. **176** C5
Martinsburg *PA* U.S.A. **176** G5
Martinsburg *WV* U.S.A. **176** H6
Martinsville *IN* U.S.A. **174** C4
Martinsville *VA* U.S.A. **176** F9

Martin Vas, Ilhas *is* S. Atlantic Ocean **217** M7
Most easterly point of South America. English form Martin Vaz Islands; also spelt Martim Vaz, Ilhas.

Martin Vaz Islands S. Atlantic Ocean *see* **Martin Vas, Ilhas**
Martök Kazakh. *see* **Martuk**
Marton N.Z. **152** J8
Martorell Spain **55** M3
Martos Spain **54** H7
Martuk Kazakh. **102** D2
also spelt Martök
Martuni Armenia **107** F2
Maru Nigeria **125** G3
Maruchak Afgh. **101** E3
Marudi *Sarawak* Malaysia **77** F1
Marudu, Teluk *b. Sabah* Malaysia **77** G1
Marugame Japan **91** C7
Maruia *r.* N.Z. **153** G9
Maruim Brazil **202** E4
Marukhis Ugheltekhili *pass* Georgia/Rus. Fed. **107** E2
Marum, Mount *vol.* Vanuatu **145** F3
Marūn *r.* Iran **100** B4
Marunga Angola **127** D9
Marusthali *reg.* India **96** A4
Maruwa Aboriginal Reserve Australia **150** D4
Maruwa Hills Sudan **128** B3
Marvast Iran **100** C4
Marv Dasht Iran **100** C4
Marvejols France **51** J8
Marvine, Mount U.S.A. **183** M3
Marwar Junction India **96** B4
Marwayne Canada **167** I4
Mary *r. N.T.* Australia **148** A2
Mary *r. Qld* Australia **149** G5
Mary *r. W.A.* Australia **150** D3
Mary Turkm. **103** E5
historically known as Alexandria or Merv
Mary A.S.S.R. *aut. rep.* Rus. Fed. *see* **Mariy El, Respublika**
Maryborough *Qld* Australia **149** G5
Maryborough *Vic.* Australia **147** D4
Marydale S. Africa **132** G6
Mar'yevka Rus. Fed. **102** B1
Mary Frances Lake Canada **167** J2
Maryland *state* U.S.A. **177** I7
Mary Oblast *admin. div.* Turkm. *see* **Maryyskaya Oblast'**
Mary's Harbour Canada **169** K2
Marystown Canada **169** K4
Marysvale U.S.A. **183** L3
Marysville *CA* U.S.A. **182** C2
Marysville *KS* U.S.A. **178** C4
Marysville *MI* U.S.A. **173** K8
Marysville *OH* U.S.A. **176** B5
Marysville *WA* U.S.A. **180** B2
Maryvale *N.T.* Australia **148** B5
Maryvale *Qld* Australia **149** E3
Maryville *MO* U.S.A. **178** D3
Maryville *TN* U.S.A. **174** D5
Maryyskaya Oblast' *admin. div.* Turkm. **103** E5
English form Mary Oblast
Marzagão Brazil **206** E4
Marzo, Cabo *c.* Col. **198** B3
Masachapa Nicaragua **186** B5
Masada *tourist site* Israel **108** G6
also spelt Metsada or Mezada
Maşaff, Wādī *watercourse* Syria/Turkey **109** L1
Masaguro Tanz. **129** C7
Masāhūn, Kūh-e *mt.* Iran **100** C4
Masai Mara National Reserve *nature res.* Kenya **128** B5
Masai Steppe *plain* Tanz. **129** C6
Masaka Uganda **128** A5
Masakhane S. Africa **133** K8
Masalanyane Pan *salt pan* Botswana **130** D4
Masalembu Besar *i.* Indon. **77** F4
Masalembu Kecil *i.* Indon. **77** F4
Masallı Azer. **107** G3
Masamba Indon. **75** B3
Masamba *mt.* Indon. **75** B3
Masan S. Korea **83** C6
Masāqif *i.* Saudi Arabia **104** C4
Masasi Tanz. **129** C7
Masavi Bol. **201** E4
Masaya Nicaragua **186** B5
Masaya, Volcán *vol.* Nicaragua **186** B5
Masbate Phil. **74** B3
Masbate *i.* Phil. **74** B3
Mascara Alg. **123** F2
also spelt Mouaskar
Mascot U.S.A. **176** B9
Mascota Mex. **184** D4
Mascote Brazil **207** N2
Mascouche Canada **169** F4
Masein Myanmar **78** A3
Ma Sekatok *b.* Indon. **77** G2
Masela Indon. **75** D5
Masela *i.* Indon. **75** D5
Maseno Kenya **128** B4
Masères, Lac *l.* Canada **173** Q2

Maseru Lesotho **133** L6
Capital of Lesotho.

Masfjorden Norway **45** I3
Mashaba Zimbabwe *see* **Mashava**
Mashābih *i.* Saudi Arabia **104** B2
Mashai Lesotho **133** M6
Mashala Dem. Rep. Congo **126** D6
Mashan China **87** D4
also known as Baishan
Mashava Zimbabwe **131** F4
formerly spelt Mashaba
Masherbrum *mt.* Jammu and Kashmir **96** C2
Masheve Ukr. **43** N9
Mashhad Iran **101** D2
English form Meshed
Mashi *r.* India **96** B4
Mashike Japan **90** G3
Mashket *r.* Pak. **101** E5
Mashki Chah Pak. **101** E4
Māshkīd *r.* Iran **101** E5
Mashonaland Central *prov.* Zimbabwe **131** F3
Mashonaland East *prov.* Zimbabwe **131** F3
Mashonaland West *prov.* Zimbabwe **131** F3
Mashtagi Azer. *see* **Maştağa**
Masiáca Mex. **184** C3
Masia-Mbia Dem. Rep. Congo **126** C5
Masibambane S. Africa **133** L8
Masif Baltîm Egypt **108** C6
Masīlah, Wādī al *watercourse* Yemen **105** E5
Masilo S. Africa **133** K5
Masi-Manimba Dem. Rep. Congo **126** C6
Masindi Uganda **128** A4
Masinloc Phil. **74** A3
Masinyusane S. Africa **132** H8
Masira, Gulf of Oman *see* **Maşīrah, Khalīj**
Masira Channel Oman *see* **Maşīrah, Tur'at**
Maşīrah, Jazīrat *i.* Oman **105** G3
English form Masira Island
Maşīrah, Khalīj *b.* Oman **105** G4
English form Masira, Gulf of
Maşīrah, Tur'at *sea chan.* Oman **105** G3
English form Masira Channel
Masira Island Oman *see* **Maşīrah, Jazīrat**
Masis Armenia **107** F2
Masisea Peru **200** B2
Masjaing S. Africa **133** M5
Masjed Soleymān Iran **100** B4
Mask, Lough *l.* Rep. of Ireland **47** C10
Maskanah Syria **109** J1
Maskūtān Iran **101** D5
Maslti Pak. **101** F4
Masna'ah Yemen **105** E5
Masoala, Parc National *nat. park* Madag. **131** [inset] K2
Masoala, Tanjona *c.* Madag. **131** [inset] K2
Masohi Indon. **75** D3
Mason *KY* U.S.A. **176** A7
Mason *MI* U.S.A. **173** I8
Mason *OH* U.S.A. **176** A6
Mason *TX* U.S.A. **179** C6
Mason *WI* U.S.A. **172** B4
Mason *WV* U.S.A. **176** C6
Mason, Lake *salt flat* Australia **151** B5
Mason Bay N.Z. **153** B14
Mason City U.S.A. **174** A3
Masoni *i.* Indon. **75** C3
Masontown *PA* U.S.A. **176** F6
Masontown *WV* U.S.A. **176** F6
Masqaţ Oman *see* **Muscat**
Masqaţ *governorate* Oman **105** G3
Masqaţ *reg.* Oman *see* **Muscat**
Massa Italy **56** C4
Massachusetts *state* U.S.A. **177** M3
Massachusetts Bay U.S.A. **177** O3
Massadona U.S.A. **183** P1
Massafra Italy **57** J8
Massaguet Chad **120** B6
Massakory Chad **120** B6
Massalassef Chad **126** C2
Massa Marittimo Italy **56** C5
Massambará Brazil **204** G3
Massana Gabon **126** A5
Massangena Moz. **131** G4
Massango Angola **127** C7
Massaroca Brazil **202** D4
Massarosa Italy **56** C5
Massau Angola **127** C6
Massawa Eritrea **121** H6
also spelt Mits'iwa
Massawa Channel Eritrea **121** H5
Massena U.S.A. **177** K1
Massenya Chad **126** C2
Masset Canada **166** C4
Masset Inlet Canada **166** C4
Masseube France **50** G9
Massey Canada **168** D4
Massiac France **51** J7
Massieville U.S.A. **176** C6
Massif Central *mts* France **51** J7
Massigui Mali **124** D4
Massilia France *see* **Marseille**
Massina Mali **124** D3
formerly spelt Ke Macina
Massinga Moz. **131** G4
Massingir Moz. **131** G4
Massintonto *r.* Moz./S. Africa **133** Q2
Masson Canada **173** R5
Masson Island Antarctica **223** G2
Maştağa Azer. **107** G2
also spelt Mashtagi
Mastchoh Tajik. **101** G2
also known as Matcha
Masterton N.Z. **152** J8
Mastichо, Akra *pt* Greece **59** H10
Mastic Point Bahamas **186** D1
Mastigouche, Réserve Faunique de *nature res.* Canada **169** F4
Mastrevik Norway **46** Q3
Mastuj Pak. **101** H2
Mastung Pak. **101** F4
Mastūrah Saudi Arabia **104** B3
Masty Belarus **42** F8
also spelt Mosty
Masuda Japan **91** B7
Masuika Dem. Rep. Congo **127** D6
Masuku Gabon *see* **Franceville**
Masuleh Iran **100** B2
Masulipatam India *see* **Machilipatnam**
Masuna *i.* American Samoa *see* **Tutuila**
Masurai, Bukit *mt.* Indon. **76** C3
Masvingo Zimbabwe **131** F4
formerly known as Fort Victoria or Nyande
Masvingo *prov.* Zimbabwe **131** F4
Maswe Tanz. **128** B5
Maswe Game Reserve *nature res.* Tanz. **128** B5
Maşyāf Syria **109** H2
Mat *r.* Albania **58** A7
Mata *r.* N.Z. **152** M5
Mata, Serranía de *mts* Venez. **199** E3
Mata Amarilla Arg. **205** C8
Matabaa Zambia **127** D8
Matabaan Somalia **128** E3
Matabeleland North *prov.* Zimbabwe **131** E3
Matabeleland South *prov.* Zimbabwe **131** F4
Matabhanga India **97** F4
Matachewan Canada **168** D4
Matachic Mex. **184** D2
Matadi Dem. Rep. Congo **127** B6
Matador U.S.A. **179** B5
Matagalpa Nicaragua **186** B4
Matagami Canada **168** E3
Matagami, Lac *l.* Canada **168** E3
Matagorda Island U.S.A. **179** C6
Mata Grande Brazil **202** E4
Matahiwi N.Z. **152** J7

Mataigou China *see* **Taole**
Matak *i.* Indon. **77** D2
Matak Kazakh. **103** H2
Matakana Island N.Z. **152** K5
Matakaoa Point N.Z. **152** M5
Matakitaki N.Z. **153** G9
Matala Angola **127** B8
Matale Sri Lanka **94** D5
Mataleng S. Africa **133** I5
Maṭālī', Jabal *hill* Saudi Arabia **104** C2
Matam Senegal **124** B3
Matamata N.Z. **152** J5
Mata-Mata S. Africa **132** E2
Matamau N.Z. **152** K8
Matamey Niger **125** H3
Matamoras U.S.A. **177** K4
Matamoros *Campeche* Mex. **185** H5
Matamoros *Coahuila* Mex. **185** E3
Matamoros *Tamaulipas* Mex. **185** F3
Ma'ta Moûlana *well* Mauritania **124** B2
Matana, Danau *l.* Indon. **75** B3
Matanal Point Phil. **74** B5
Ma'ṭan as Sārah *well* Libya **120** D4
Ma'ṭan Bishrah *well* Libya **120** D4
Matandu *r.* Tanz. **129** C7
Matane Canada **169** H3
Matane, Réserve Faunique de *nature res.* Canada **169** H3
Mata Negra Venez. **199** F2
Matanga Madag. **131** [inset] J4
Matangi N.Z. **152** J5
Matanzas Cuba **186** C2
Matão Brazil **206** E8
Matão, Serra do *hills* Brazil **202** B4
Matapalo, Cabo *c.* Costa Rica **186** C5
Matapan, Cape *pt* Greece *see* **Tainaro, Akra**
Mata Panew *r.* Poland **49** P5
Matapédia, Lac *l.* Canada **169** H3
Mataporquera Spain **54** G2
Maṭār *well* Saudi Arabia **105** D2
Matará Arg. **204** E3
Matara Sri Lanka **94** D5
also known as Matturai
Mataragka Greece **59** C10
also spelt Matarángа
Mataram Indon. **77** G5
Mataránga Greece *see* **Mataragka**
Mataranka Australia **148** B2
Matarinao Bay Phil. **74** C4
Matarka Morocco **123** E2
Matarma, Râs *pt* Egypt **108** D8
Mataró Spain **55** N3
Mataroa N.Z. **152** J7
Matarombea *r.* Indon. **75** B3
Matarraña *r.* Spain **55** L3
Mataruška Banja *Srbija* Yugo. **58** B5
Matasiri *i.* Indon. **77** F4
Matassi *well* Sudan **121** F5
Matassi Tanz. **129** C6
Matatiele S. Africa **133** M7
Matatila Dam India **96** C4
Matau N.Z. **152** I7
Mataura N.Z. **153** C14
Mataura *r.* N.Z. **153** C14

▶**Matā'utu** Wallis and Futuna Is **145** H3
Capital of Wallis and Futuna.

Matawai N.Z. **152** L6
Matawaia N.Z. **152** H3
Matawin *r.* Canada **169** F4
Matay Kazakh. **103** I3
Maṭbakh, Ra's al *pt* Qatar **105** E2
Matcha Tajik. *see* **Mastchoh**
Matchi-Manitou, Lac *l.* Canada **173** P2
Mategua Bol. **201** E3
Matehuala Mex. **185** E4
Matei Romania **58** F2
Mateke Hills Zimbabwe **131** F4
Matelica Italy **56** F5
Matelot Trin. and Tob. **187** H5
Matemanga Tanz. **129** C7
Matende Angola **127** C9
Matera Italy **57** I8
Matese, Monti del *mts* Italy **56** G7
Mátészalka Hungary **49** T8
Matetsi Zimbabwe **131** E3
Mateur Tunisia **57** B11
Mateus Leme Brazil **207** I6
Matewan U.S.A. **176** C8
Matha France **50** F7
Matheson Canada **168** D3
Mathews U.S.A. **177** I8
Mathias U.S.A. **176** G7
Mathis U.S.A. **179** C6
Mathraki *i.* Greece **59** A9
Mathura India **96** C4
Mati Phil. **74** C5
Matiacoali Burkina **125** F3
Matianxu China **87** E3
Matiari Pak. **101** G5
Matias Barbosa Brazil **207** J8
Matias Cardoso Brazil **202** D5
Matías Romero Mex. **185** G5
Matibane Moz. **131** I2
Matimekosh Canada **169** H2
Matina Costa Rica **186** C5
Matinicus Island U.S.A. **177** Q2
Matizi China **86** B1
Matjiesfontein S. Africa **132** E10
Matla *r.* India **97** F5
Matli Pak. **101** G5
Matlock U.K. **47** K10
Matlwangtlwang S. Africa **133** L4
Matna Sudan **104** A5
Mato *r.* Venez. **199** E3
Mato, Cerro *mt.* Venez. **199** E3
Matoaka U.S.A. **176** D8
Matobo Hills Zimbabwe **131** F4
also spelt Matopo Hills
Matobo National Park Zimbabwe **131** F4
formerly known as Rhodes Matopos National Park
Matogrossense, Pantanal *marsh* Brazil **201** G4
Mato Grosso Brazil **201** F3
▶**Mato Grosso** *state* Brazil **206** A2
southamerica [contrasts] ▶▶ 194–195
Mato Grosso, Planalto do *plat.* Brazil **202** A5
Mato Grosso do Sul *state* Brazil **206** A6
Matola Moz. **131** G5
Matondo Moz. **131** G3
Matope Malawi **129** B8
Matopo Hills Zimbabwe *see* **Matobo Hills**
Matos *r.* Bol. **200** D3
Matosinhos Port. **54** C3
Matou China *see* **Pingguo**
Mato Verde Brazil **207** K2
Matozinhos Brazil **207** I6
Mátra *mts* Hungary **49** Q8
Maṭraḥ Oman **105** G3
Matrai *park* Hungary **49** R8
Matrei in Osttirol Austria **49** J9
Matroosberg S. Africa **132** D10
Matroosberg *mt.* S. Africa **132** D10
Matrooster S. Africa **133** K2
Maṭrûh *governorate* Egypt **108** A8
Matsalu riiklik looduskaitseala *nature res.* Estonia **42** E3
Matsap S. Africa **132** G5
Matsesta Rus. Fed. **107** D2
Matsitama Botswana **131** E4
Matsudo Japan **91** F7
Matsue Japan **91** C7
Matsumae Japan **90** G4
Matsumoto Japan **91** E6
Matsusaka Japan **91** E7
Matsu Tao *i.* Taiwan **87** G3
Matsuura Japan **91** A8
Matsuyama Japan **91** C8
Matsuzaki Japan **91** F7
Mattagami *r.* Canada **168** D3
Mattamuskeet, Lake U.S.A. **174** E5
Mattawa Canada **168** E4
Matterhorn *mt.* Italy/Switz. **51** N7
Matterhorn *mt.* U.S.A. **180** D4
Mattersburg Austria **49** N8
Matthew *atoll* Kiribati *see* **Marakei**
Matthew U.S.A. **174** D5
Matthews Peak Kenya **128** C4
Matthews Ridge Guyana **199** F3
Matthew Town Bahamas **187** E2
Maṭṭī, Sabkhat *salt pan* Saudi Arabia **105** F3
Mattituck U.S.A. **177** M5
Mattmar Sweden **44** K3
Mattò Japan **91** E6
Mattoon U.S.A. **174** B4
Måttsund Sweden **44** M2
Matturai Sri Lanka *see* **Matara**
Matu *Sarawak* Malaysia **77** E2
Matua, Ostrov *i.* Rus. Fed. **81** Q3
Matucana Peru **200** A2
Matugama Sri Lanka **94** D5
Matuku *i.* Fiji **145** G3
Matumbo Angola **127** C8
Matun Afgh. *see* **Khowst**
Maturín Venez. **199** F2
Maturuca Brazil **199** F3
Matusadona National Park Zimbabwe **131** F3
Matutuang *i.* Indon. **75** C1
Matveyev, Ostrov *i.* Rus. Fed. **40** K1
Matveyevka Rus. Fed. **102** C1
Matwabeng S. Africa **133** L5
Matxitxako, Cabo *c.* Spain **55** I1
Maty Island P.N.G. *see* **Wuvulu Island**
Matyrskiy Rus. Fed. **43** U9
Mau *Madhya Pradesh* India **96** C4
Mau *Uttar Pradesh* India **97** D4
Mau *Uttar Pradesh* India **97** D4
Mau Aimma India **97** D4
Maubermé, Pic de *mt.* France/Spain **55** L2
Maubeuge France **51** J2
Maubin Myanmar **78** A4
Ma-ubin Myanmar **78** B2
Maubourguet France **50** G9
Mauchsberg S. Africa **133** O2
Maudaha India **96** D4
Maude Australia **147** E3
Mau-é-ele Moz. *see* **Marão**
Maués Brazil **199** G5
Maués *r.* Brazil **199** G5
Mauganj India **97** D4
Maug Islands N. Mariana Is **73** K2
Mauguio France **51** K9
Maui *i.* U.S.A. **181** [inset] Z1
Maukkadaw Myanmar **78** A3
Maule *admin. reg.* Chile **204** B4
Maule *r.* Chile **204** B4
Mauléon France **50** F6
Mauléon-Licharre France **50** F9
Maullín Chile **205** B6
Maulvi Bazar Bangl. **97** F4
also spelt Moulavibazar
Maumaupaki *hill* N.Z. **152** J5
Maumee U.S.A. **176** B4
Maumee *r.* U.S.A. **176** B4
Maumee Bay U.S.A. **176** B4
Maumere Indon. **75** B5
Maun Botswana **130** D3
Mauna Kea *vol.* U.S.A. **181** [inset] Z2
Mauna Loa *vol.* U.S.A. **181** [inset] Z2
Maun Game Sanctuary *nature res.* Botswana **130** D3
Maungataniwha *mt.* N.Z. **152** K6
Maungatapere N.Z. **152** I3
Maungaturoto N.Z. **152** I4
Maungdaw Myanmar **78** A3
Maungmagan Islands Myanmar **79** B5
Maungmagon Myanmar **79** B5
Maupin U.S.A. **180** B3
Mau Rampur India **96** C4
Maurawan India **96** D4
Maurepas, Lake U.S.A. **175** B6
Maures, Massif des *hills* France **51** M9
Mauri *r.* Bol. **200** C4
Mauriac France **51** I7
Maurice *country* Indian Ocean *see* **Mauritius**
Maurice, Lake *salt flat* Australia **146** A2
▶**Mauritania** *country* Africa **122** B6
spelt Al Mūrītāniyah *in Arabic or* Mauritanie *in French*
world [countries] ▶▶ 10–11
africa [countries] ▶▶ 114–117
Mauritanie *country* Africa *see* **Mauritania**
▶**Mauritius** *country* Indian Ocean **218** K7
also known as Maurice
africa [countries] ▶▶ 114–117
Mauro, Monte *mt.* Italy **56** G7
Mauron France **50** D4
Mauros *mt.* Spain **54** D3
Maurs France **51** I8
Mauston U.S.A. **172** C7
Mauvezin France **50** G9
Mauzé-sur-le-Mignon France **50** F6
Mava Dem. Rep. Congo **126** E4
Mavaca *r.* Venez. **199** E4
Mavago Moz. **129** C8
Mavasjaure *l.* Sweden **44** L2
Mavengue Angola **127** C9
Mavinga Angola **127** D8
Mavisdale U.S.A. **176** C8
Mavita Moz. **131** G3
Mavra *i.* Greece **59** H12
Mavrothalassa Greece **58** E8
Mavrovo *nat. park* Macedonia **58** B7
Mavume Moz. **131** G4
Mavuya S. Africa **133** L8
Mawa, Bukit *mt.* Indon. **77** F2
Ma Wan *i. Hong Kong* China **87** [inset]
Māwān, Khashm *hill* Saudi Arabia **105** D3
Mawana India **96** C3
Mawanga Dem. Rep. Congo **127** C6
Mawasangka Indon. **75** B4
Mawdaung Pass Myanmar/Thai. **79** B6
Mawei China **87** F3
Mawhai Point N.Z. **152** M6
Mawheraiti N.Z. **153** F10
Māwheranui *r.* N.Z. *see* **Grey**
Māwiyah Yemen **104** D5
Mawjib, Wādī al *r.* Jordan **108** G6
also known as Arnon
Mawkhi Myanmar **78** B4
Mawkmai Myanmar **78** B3
Mawlaik Myanmar **78** A3
also known as Upper Chindwin
Mawlamyaing Myanmar *see* **Moulmein**
Mawlamyine Myanmar *see* **Moulmein**
Mawphlang India **97** F4
Mawqaq Saudi Arabia **104** C2
Mawshij Yemen **104** C5
Mawson *research station* Antarctica **223** E2
Mawson Coast Antarctica **223** E2
Mawson Escarpment Antarctica **223** E2
Mawson Peninsula Antarctica **223** K2
Maw Taung *mt.* Myanmar **79** B6
Mawza Yemen **104** C5
Maxaas Somalia **128** E3
Maxán Arg. **204** D3
Maxcanú Mex. **185** H4
Maxhamish Lake Canada **166** F3
Maxia, Punta *mt. Sardegna* Italy **57** A9
Măxineni Romania **58** I3
Maxixe Moz. **131** G4
Maxmo Fin. **44** M3
Maxwell N.Z. **152** I7
Maxwelton Australia **149** D4
Maya Chad **126** C3
Maya *i.* Indon. **77** E3
Maya *r.* Rus. Fed. **39** N3
Mayaguana *i.* Bahamas **187** E2
Mayaguana Passage Bahamas **187** E2
Mayagüez Puerto Rico **187** G3
Mayahi Niger **125** G3
Mayak Rus. Fed. **102** C2
Mayakovskogo *mt.* Tajik. **101** G2
also known as Mayakovskogo, Pik
Mayakovskogo, Pik *mt.* Tajik. *see* **Mayakovskogo**
Mayakum Kazakh. **103** G4
also spelt Mayaqum
Mayala Dem. Rep. Congo **127** C6
Mayama Congo **126** B5
Mayamba Dem. Rep. Congo **126** C6
Mayamey Iran **100** C2
Maya Mountains Belize/Guat. **185** H5
Mayan China *see* **Mayanhe**
Mayang China **87** D3
also known as Gaocun
Mayanhe China **86** C1
formerly known as Mayan
Mayaqum Kazakh. *see* **Mayakum**
Mayarí Cuba **186** E2
Maya-san *mt.* Japan **90** F5
Maybeury U.S.A. **176** D8
Maybole U.K. **46** H8
Maych'ew Eth. **128** C1
Maydā Shahr Afgh. **101** G3
Maydh Somalia **128** E2
Maydos Turkey *see* **Eceabat**
Mayen Germany **48** E5
Mayenne France **50** F4
Mayenne *r.* France **50** F5
Mayer U.S.A. **183** L7
Mayêr Kangri *mt.* China **89** D5
Mayersville U.S.A. **175** B5
Mayerthorpe Canada **167** H4
Mayet France **50** G5
Mayfa'ah Yemen **105** D5
Mayfield N.Z. **153** F11
Mayfield *KY* U.S.A. **174** B4
Mayfield *UT* U.S.A. **183** M2
Mayhan Mongolia **84** D2
Mayi *r.* China **82** C3
Maykain Kazakh. **103** H2
also spelt Mayqayyng
Maykamys Kazakh. **103** I3
Maykop Rus. Fed. **41** G7
Mayluu-Suu Kyrg. **103** H4
formerly known as Mayly-Say
Mayly-Say Kyrg. *see* **Mayluu-Suu**
Maymak Kazakh. **103** G4
Maymyo Myanmar **78** B3
Mayna Rus. Fed. **80** E2
Mayna Rus. Fed. **41** H5
Maynardville U.S.A. **174** D4
Mayne *watercourse* Australia **149** D4
Mayni India **94** B2
Maynooth Canada **173** P5
Mayo Canada **166** C2
formerly known as Mayo Landing
Mayo *r.* Mex. **181** E8
Mayo *r.* Peru **198** B6
Mayo U.S.A. **175** D6
Mayo Alim Cameroon **125** I4
Mayo-Belwa Nigeria **125** I4
Mayo Darlé Cameroon **125** H5
Mayo-Kébbi *pref.* Chad **126** B2
Mayoko Congo **126** B5
Mayo Lake Canada **166** C2
Mayo Landing Canada *see* **Mayo**
Mayo Lara Cent. Afr. Rep. **126** B3
Mayon *vol.* Phil. **74** B3
Mayor, Puig *mt.* Spain *see* **Major, Puig**
Mayor Buratovich Arg. **204** E5
Mayor Island N.Z. **152** K5
Mayor Pablo Lagerenza Para. **201** E4

▶**Mayotte** *terr.* Africa **129** E8
French Territorial Collectivity.
africa [countries] ▶▶ 114–117

May Pen Jamaica **186** D3
Mayqayyng Kazakh. *see* **Maykain**
Mayraira Point Phil. **74** B2
Maysah, Tall al *mt.* Jordan **108** G6
Maysān *governorate* Iraq **107** F5
Mayskiy *Amurskaya Oblast'* Rus. Fed. **82** C1
Mayskiy *Kabardino-Balkarskaya Respublika* Rus. Fed. **41** H8
Mayskiy *Permskaya Oblast'* Rus. Fed. **40** J4
Mayskiy, Khrebet *mts* Rus. Fed. **82** D1
Mayskoye Kazakh. **103** I2
Mays Landing U.S.A. **177** K6
Mayson Lake Canada **167** J3
Maysville *KY* U.S.A. **176** B7
Maysville *MO* U.S.A. **178** D4
Maytag China *see* **Dushanzi**
Mayu *i.* Indon. **75** C2
Mayu *r.* Myanmar **78** A3
Mayumba Gabon **126** A5
Mayum La *pass* China **89** C6
Mayuram India **94** C4
Mayville *MI* U.S.A. **173** J7
Mayville *ND* U.S.A. **178** C2
Mayville *NY* U.S.A. **176** F3
Maywood U.S.A. **178** B3
Mayya Rus. Fed. **39** N3
Maza Arg. **204** E5
Maza Rus. Fed. **43** R2
Mazabuka Zambia **127** E8
Mazaca Turkey *see* **Kayseri**
Mazagan Morocco *see* **El Jadida**
Mazagão Brazil **199** I5
Ma'zah, Jabal *hill* Syria **109** L2
Maza Jugla *r.* Latvia **42** F5
Mazamet France **51** I9
Mazán Peru **198** C5
Māzandarān *prov.* Iran **100** B2
Mazao Dem. Rep. Congo **127** D7
Mazapil Mex. **185** E3
Mazar China **89** B4
Mazar, Koh-i- *mt.* Afgh. **101** F3
Mazāra Oman **105** G3
Mazara, Val di *valley Sicilia* Italy **57** E11
Mazara del Vallo *Sicilia* Italy **57** E11
Mazār-e Sharīf Afgh. **101** F2
Mazarrón Spain **55** J7
Mazartag *mt.* China **88** B4
Mazaruni *r.* Guyana **199** G3
Mazatán Mex. **184** C2
Mazatenango Guat. **185** H6
Mazatlán Mex. **184** D4
Mazatzal Peak U.S.A. **183** M7
Mazāvī *watercourse* Iran **100** D5
Mazeepa Bay S. Africa **133** M9
Mažeikiai Lith. **42** D5
Mazelet *well* Niger **125** H2
Mazı Turkey **59** I11
Mazie U.S.A. **176** C7
Mazirbe Latvia **42** D4
Mazocahui Mex. **184** C2
Mazocruz Peru **200** C4
Mazomanie U.S.A. **172** D7
Mazomeno Dem. Rep. Congo **126** E6
Mazomora Tanz. **129** C6
Mazong Shan *mt.* China **84** C3
Mazong Shan *mts* China **84** B3
Mazowe *r.* Zimbabwe **131** G3
Mazrub *well* Sudan **121** F6
Mazsalaca Latvia **42** G4
Mazu Iran **100** B3
Mazunga Zimbabwe **131** F4
Mazurskie, Pojezierze *reg.* Poland **49** R2
Mazyr Belarus **43** K9
also spelt Mozyr'
Mazzouna Tunisia **123** H2
Mba Cameroon **125** H5

▶**Mbabane** Swaziland **133** P3
Capital of Swaziland.

Mbacké Senegal **124** B3
Mbaéré *r.* Cent. Afr. Rep. **126** C4
Mbagne Mauritania **124** B2
Mbahiakro Côte d'Ivoire **124** D5
Mbaïki Cent. Afr. Rep. **126** C4
Mbakaou Cameroon **125** I5
Mbakaou, Lac de *l.* Cameroon **125** I5
Mbala Zambia **127** F7
formerly known as Abercorn
Mbalabala Zimbabwe **131** F4
formerly spelt Balla Balla
Mbalam Cameroon **125** I6
Mbale Uganda **128** B4
Mbalmayo Cameroon **125** H6
Mbam *r.* Cameroon **125** H5
Mbamba Bay Tanz. **129** B7
Mbandaka Dem. Rep. Congo **126** C5
formerly known as Coquilhatville
Mbandjok Cameroon **125** H5
Mbang Cameroon **125** I6
Mbanga Cameroon **125** H5
M'banza Congo Angola **127** B6
formerly known as São Salvador *or* São Salvador do Congo
Mbanza-Ngungu Dem. Rep. Congo **127** B6
formerly known as Songololo *or* Thysville
Mbar Senegal **124** B3
Mbarangandu Tanz. **129** C7
Mbarara Uganda **128** A5
Mbari *r.* Cent. Afr. Rep. **126** D3
Mbarika Mountains Tanz. **129** C7
Mbaswana S. Africa **133** Q4
Mbata Cent. Afr. Rep. **126** C4
Mbati Zambia **127** F7
Mbé Cameroon **125** I5
Mbé Congo **126** B5
Mbemba Moz. **129** B8
Mbembesi Zimbabwe **131** F3
Mbemkuru *r.* Tanz. **129** C7
Mbéni Comoros **129** D7
Mbènqué Côte d'Ivoire **124** D4
Mberengwa Zimbabwe **131** F4
formerly known as Belingwe
Mbereshi Zambia **127** F7
Mbeya Tanz. **129** B7
Mbeya *admin. reg.* Tanz. **129** B7
Mbi *r.* Cameroon **125** I5
Mbi *r.* Cent. Afr. Rep. **126** C3
Mbigou Gabon **126** A5
Mbinda Congo **126** B5
Mbinga Tanz. **129** B7
Mbini Equat. Guinea **125** H6
Mbini *r.* Equat. Guinea **125** H6
formerly known as Benito
Mbizi Zimbabwe **131** F4
Mbizi Mountains Tanz. **129** A7
Mbo Cent. Afr. Rep. **126** C2
Mboki Cent. Afr. Rep. **126** E3
Mbomo Congo **126** B4
Mbomou *pref.* Cent. Afr. Rep. **126** D3
Mbomou *r.* Cent. Afr. Rep./Dem. Rep. Congo **126** D3
Mbon Congo **126** B5
Mbouda Cameroon **125** H5
Mbour Senegal **124** A3
Mbout Mauritania **124** B2
Mbowela Zambia **127** E8
Mbozi Tanz. **129** B7
Mbrès Cent. Afr. Rep. **126** C3
Mbrostar Albania **58** A8
Mbuji-Mayi Dem. Rep. Congo **127** D6
Mbulu Tanz. **129** B5
Mbuluzi *r.* Swaziland **133** Q3
Mburucuyá Arg. **204** F3
Mbutini Hills Swaziland **133** P3
Mbuyuni Tanz. **129** C6
Mbwewe Tanz. **129** C6
McAdam Canada **169** H4
McAdoo U.S.A. **177** J5
McAlester U.S.A. **179** D5
McAllen U.S.A. **179** C7
McAllister U.S.A. **172** F5
McArthur *r.* Australia **148** C2
McArthur U.S.A. **176** C6
McArthur Mills Canada **173** P5
McArthur Wildlife Sanctuary *nature res.* Canada **166** C2
McBain U.S.A. **173** H6
McBride Canada **166** F4
McCall U.S.A. **180** C3
McCamey U.S.A. **179** B6
McCammon U.S.A. **180** D4
McCaslin Mountain *hill* U.S.A. **172** E5
McCauley Island Canada **166** D4
McClintock, Mount Antarctica **223** K1
McClintock Channel Canada **165** I2
McClintock Range *hills* Australia **150** D3
McClure, Lake U.S.A. **182** D4
McClure Strait Canada **165** H2
McClusky U.S.A. **178** B2
McComb *MS* U.S.A. **175** B6
McComb *OH* U.S.A. **176** B4
McConaughy, Lake U.S.A. **178** B3
McConnellsburg U.S.A. **176** H6
McConnelsville U.S.A. **176** D6
McCook U.S.A. **178** B3
McCormick U.S.A. **175** D5
McCoy U.S.A. **176** E8
McCrea *r.* Canada **167** H2
McCreary Canada **167** L5
McCullough Range *mts* U.S.A. **183** I6
McCullum, Mount Canada **166** B1
McCutchenville U.S.A. **176** B5
McDame Canada **166** D3
McDonald Islands Indian Ocean **219** L9
McDonald Peak U.S.A. **180** D3
McDouall Range *hills* Australia **148** B3
McDowell Peak U.S.A. **183** M8
McFarland *CA* U.S.A. **182** E6
McFarland *WI* U.S.A. **172** D7
McFarlane *r.* Canada **167** I3
McFarlane, Mount N.Z. **153** D11
McGill U.S.A. **183** J2
McGivney Canada **169** H4
McGrath *AK* U.S.A. **164** D3
McGrath *MN* U.S.A. **174** A2
McGregor *r.* Canada **166** F4
McGregor, Lake Canada **167** H5
McGregor Bay Canada **173** L4
McGregor Range *hills* Australia **147** D1
McGuire, Mount U.S.A. **180** D3
Mchinga Tanz. **129** C7
Mchinji Malawi **129** B8
formerly known as Fort Manning
McIlwraith Range *hills* Australia **149** D2
McInnes Lake Canada **167** M4
McIntosh U.S.A. **178** B2
McKay Range *hills* Australia **150** C4
McKean *i.* Kiribati **145** H2
formerly known as Drummond Island
McKee U.S.A. **176** A8
McKeesport U.S.A. **176** F5
McKees Rocks U.S.A. **176** E5
McKenney U.S.A. **176** H9
McKenzie U.S.A. **174** B4
McKenzie *r.* U.S.A. **180** B3
McKinlay Australia **149** D4
McKinlay *r.* Australia **149** D4

▶**McKinley, Mount** U.S.A. **164** D3
Highest mountain in North America.
northamerica [landscapes] ▶▶ 156–157

McKinney U.S.A. **179** C5
McKittrick U.S.A. **182** E6
McLeansboro U.S.A. **174** B4
McLennan Canada **167** G4
McLeod *r.* Canada **167** H4
McLeod Bay Canada **167** I2
McLeod Lake Canada **166** F4
McLeods Island Myanmar **79** B6
McMinns Creek *watercourse* Australia **148** B5
McMinnville *OR* U.S.A. **180** B3
McMinnville *TN* U.S.A. **174** C5
McMurdo *research station* Antarctica **223** L1
McMurdo Sound *b.* Antarctica **223** L1
McNary U.S.A. **183** O7
McNaughton U.S.A. **172** D5
McNaughton Lake Canada *see* **Kinbasket Lake**
McPhadyen *r.* Canada **169** H2
McPherson U.S.A. **178** C4
McPherson Range *mts* Australia **147** G2
McQuesten *r.* Canada **166** B2
McRae U.S.A. **175** D5
McTavish Arm *b.* Canada **167** G1
McVeytown U.S.A. **176** H5
McVicar Arm *b.* Canada **166** F1
McWhorter U.S.A. **176** E6
Mda *r.* Rus. Fed. **43** N3
Mdantsane S. Africa **133** L9
M'Daourouch Alg. **123** G1
Mdiq Morocco **54** F9
also known as Rincon
Mead, Lake *resr* U.S.A. **183** J5
Meade U.S.A. **178** B4
Meade *r.* U.S.A. **164** D2
Meadow Australia **151** A5
Meadow U.S.A. **183** L3
Meadowbank *r.* Canada **167** L1
Meadow Bridge U.S.A. **176** E8
Meadow Lake Canada **167** I4
Meadow Lake Provincial Park Canada **167** I4
Meadow Valley Wash *r.* U.S.A. **183** J5
Meadowview U.S.A. **176** D9
Meadville *MS* U.S.A. **175** B6
Meadville *PA* U.S.A. **176** E4
Meaford Canada **173** M6
Meaken-dake *vol.* Japan **90** I3
Mealhada Port. **54** C4
Mealy Mountains Canada **169** J2
Meandarra Australia **147** F1
Meander River Canada **167** G3
Meares *i.* Indon. **75** C1
Mearim *r.* Brazil **202** C2
Meaux France **51** I4
Mebridege *r.* Angola **127** B6
Mebtoun, Oued El *watercourse* Alg. **55** K9
Mebu India **97** G3
Mebulu, Tanjung *pt* Indon. **77** F5
Mecanhelas Moz. **131** G2
Mecca Saudi Arabia **104** B3
also spelt Makkah
Mecca U.S.A. **181** C6
Mechanic Falls U.S.A. **177** O1
Mechanicsburg *OH* U.S.A. **176** B5
Mechanicsburg *VA* U.S.A. **176** E8
Mechanicsville U.S.A. **176** H8
Mechanicville U.S.A. **177** L3
Mechelen Belgium **51** K1
also known as Malines
Mecherchar *i.* Palau *see* **Eil Malk**
Mecheria Alg. **123** E2
Mechernich Germany **48** D5
Mechiméré Chad **120** B6
Mechka *r.* Bulg. **58** G6
Mecidiye *Edirne* Turkey **58** H8
Mecidiye *Manisa* Turkey **59** I10
Mecitözü Turkey **106** C2
Meckenheim Germany **48** E5
Mecklenburger Bucht *b.* Germany **48** I1
Mecklenburg-Vorpommern *land* Germany **49** J2
English form Mecklenburg - West Pomerania
Mecklenburg - West Pomerania *land* Germany *see* **Mecklenburg-Vorpommern**
Meconta Moz. **131** H2
Mecubúri Moz. **131** H2
Mecubúri *r.* Moz. **131** I2
Mecúfi Moz. **131** I2
Mecula Moz. **129** C8
Meda *r.* Australia **150** C3
Meda Port. **54** D4
Meda *mt.* Spain **54** D2
Medak India **94** C2
Medan Indon. **76** B2
Medang *i.* Indon. **77** G5
Médanos *Buenos Aires* Arg. **204** E5
Médanos *Entre Ríos* Arg. **204** F4
Médanosa, Punta *pt* Arg. **205** D8
Médanos de Coro, Parque Nacional *nat. park* Venez. **198** D2
Medaryville U.S.A. **172** G9
Medchal India **94** C2
Médéa Alg. **123** F1
also known as Lemdiyya
Medeiros Neto Brazil **207** M4
Medellín Col. **198** C3
Medenine Tunisia **123** H2
Meder Eritrea **104** C5
Mederdra Mauritania **124** B2
Medford *NY* U.S.A. **177** M5
Medford *OK* U.S.A. **178** C4
Medford *OR* U.S.A. **180** B4
Medford *WI* U.S.A. **172** C5
Medgidia Romania **58** J4
Mediadilet *well* Mali **125** E2
Media Luna Arg. **204** D4
Mediapolis U.S.A. **172** B9
Mediaş Romania **58** F2
Medicine Bow *r.* U.S.A. **180** F4
Medicine Bow Mountains U.S.A. **180** F4
Medicine Bow Peak U.S.A. **180** F4
Medicine Hat Canada **167** I5
Medicine Lake U.S.A. **180** F2
Medicine Lodge U.S.A. **178** C4
Medina Brazil **202** D6
Medina Col. **198** C3
Medina Saudi Arabia **104** B2
also spelt Al Madinah
Medina *NY* U.S.A. **176** G2
Medina *OH* U.S.A. **176** D4
Medina *r.* U.S.A. **179** C6
Medinaceli Spain **55** I3
Medina del Campo Spain **54** G3
Medina de Pomar Spain **55** H2
Medina de Rioseco Spain **54** F3
Médina Gounas Senegal **124** B3
Medina-Sidonia Spain **54** F8
Medinet 15 Mayo Egypt **108** C8
English form 15th of May City
Medinet el Amal Egypt **108** C8
Medinet el Obour Egypt **108** C7
Medinet el Sadat Egypt **108** B7
Medinipur India **97** E5
formerly spelt Midnapore
Mediolanum Italy *see* **Milan**
Mediterranean Sea **53** C4
Medje Dem. Rep. Congo **126** E4
Medjedel Alg. **55** O9
Mednogorsk Rus. Fed. **102** D2
Mednoye Rus. Fed. **43** Q5
Mednyy, Ostrov *i.* Rus. Fed. **220** F2
Médoc *reg.* France **50** E7
Mêdog China **97** G3
also known as Dongbo
Medora U.S.A. **178** B2
Médouneu Gabon **126** A4
Medstead Canada **167** I4
Medu Kongkar China *see* **Maizhokunggar**
Meduro *atoll* Marshall Is *see* **Majuro**
Medveđa *Srbija* Yugo. **58** C6
Medvedevo Rus. Fed. **40** H4
Medveditsa *r.* Rus. Fed. **41** G6
Medvednica *mts* Croatia **56** H3
Medvedok Rus. Fed. **40** I4
Medvėgalio kalnis *hill* Lith. **42** D6
Medvezh'i, Ostrova *is* Rus. Fed. **39** Q2
Medvezh'yegorsk Rus. Fed. **40** E3
Medyn' Rus. Fed. **43** Q7
Medzilaborce Slovakia **49** S6
Meeberrie Australia **151** A5
Meekatharra Australia **151** B5
Meeker *CO* U.S.A. **180** F4
Meeker *OH* U.S.A. **176** B5
Meeks Bay U.S.A. **182** D2
Meeladeen Somalia **128** F2
Meelberg *mt.* S. Africa **132** I9
Meelpaeg Reservoir Canada **169** J3
Meerane Germany **49** J5
Meerapalu Estonia **42** I3
Meerut India **96** C3
Mefta Sidi Boubekeur Alg. **55** K9
Mēga Eth. **128** C3
Mega *i.* Indon. **76** C3
Mega Escarpment Eth./Kenya **128** C3
Megali Panagia Greece **59** E8
Megalo Eth. **128** D3
Megalo Chorio Greece **59** I12
Megalopoli Greece **59** D11
Megalos Anthropofas *i.* Greece **59** H11
Meganisi *i.* Greece **59** B10
Mégantic, Lac *l.* Canada **169** G4
Megara Greece **59** E10
Megezez *mt.* Eth. **128** C2

▶**Meghalaya** *state* India **97** F4
Highest mean annual rainfall in the world.
world [climate and weather] ▶▶ 16–17

Meghasani *mt.* India **97** E5
Meghna *r.* Bangl. **97** F5
Meghri Armenia **107** F3
also spelt Megri
Megion Rus. Fed. **38** H3
Mégiscane, Lac *l.* Canada **173** R2
Megisti *i.* Greece **59** K12
formerly known as Kastellorizon
Megletsy Rus. Fed. **43** P3
Meglino, Ozero *l.* Rus. Fed. **43** Q3
Megra *r.* Rus. Fed. **43** Q1
Megrega Rus. Fed. **43** O1
Megri Armenia *see* **Meghri**
Megrozero Rus. Fed. **43** O1
Mehadica Romania **58** D3
Mehamn Norway **44** N1
Mehar Pak. **101** F5
Meharry, Mount Australia **150** B4
Mehdia Tunisia *see* **Mahdia**
Mehedeby Sweden **45** L3
Mehekar India **94** C1
Meherpur Bangl. **97** F5
Meherrin U.S.A. **176** G8
Meherrin *r.* U.S.A. **176** I9
Mehidpur India **96** B5
Mehlville U.S.A. **174** B4
Mehmadabad India **96** B5
Mehndawal India **97** D4
Mehrābān Iran **100** A2
Mehrān Iran **100** C5
Mehrān *watercourse* Iran **100** C5
Mehrān Iraq **107** F4
Mehtar Lām Afgh. **101** G3
Mehun-sur-Yèvre France **51** I5
Meia Ponte *r.* Brazil **206** D5
Meicheng China *see* **Qianshan**
Meicheng China *see* **Minqing**
Meichengzhen China **87** D2
Meidougou Cameroon **125** I5
Meiganga Cameroon **125** I5
Meighen Island Canada **165** J2
Meigu China **86** B2
also known as Bapu
Meihekou China **82** B4
formerly known as Hailong
Meijiang China *see* **Ningdu**
Mei Jiang *r.* China **87** E3
Meikeng China **87** E3
Meikle *r.* Canada **166** G3
Meiktila Myanmar **78** A3
Meilen Switz. **51** O5
Meilin China *see* **Ganxian**
Meilleur *r.* Canada **166** E2
Meilü China *see* **Wuchuan**
Meiningen Germany **48** H5
Meira Spain **54** D1
Meiringen Switz. **51** O6
Meiringspoort *pass* S. Africa **132** G10
Meishan China *see* **Jinzhai**
Meishan China **86** B2
also known as Dongpo
Meißen Germany **49** K4
Meißner-Kaufunger Wald, Naturpark *nature res.* Germany **48** G4
Meister *r.* Canada **166** D2
Meitan China **87** C3
also known as Yiquan
Meitingen Germany **48** H7
Meixi China **82** C3
Meixian China *see* **Meizhou**
Meixian China **87** C1
Meixing China *see* **Xiaojin**
Meizhou China **87** F3
formerly known as Meixian
Mej *r.* India **96** C4
Méjan, Sommet de *mt.* France **51** K8
Mejaouda *well* Mauritania **122** D5
Mejez el Bab Tunisia **57** B12
Mejicana *mt.* Arg. **204** D3
Mejillones Chile **200** C5
Mejillones del Sur, Bahía de *b.* Chile **200** C5
Mekadio *well* Sudan **121** G5
Mékambo Gabon **126** B4
Mek'elē Eth. **128** C1
Mekhbaza Rus. Fed. **43** O1
Mékhé Senegal **124** A3
Mekhtar Pak. **101** G4
Mekkaw Nigeria **125** F5
Meknès Morocco **122** D2
Mekong *r.* Asia **78** D4
also known as Lancang Jiang (China) *or* Mènam Khong (Laos/Thailand)
Mekong, Mouths of the Vietnam **79** D6
Méla, Mont *hill* Cent. Afr. Rep. **126** D2
Melaka Malaysia **76** C2
formerly spelt Malacca
Melaka *state* Malaysia **76** C2
formerly spelt Malacca
Melalo, Tanjung *pt* Indon. **77** D3
Melanesia *is* Oceania **220** E6
Melar Iceland **44** [inset] B2
Melawi *r.* Indon. **77** E2

▶**Melbourne** Australia **147** E4
State capital of Victoria. 2nd most populous city in Oceania.
world [cities] ▶▶ 24–25

Melbourne *AR* U.S.A. **174** B4
Melbourne *FL* U.S.A. **175** D6
Melbu Norway **44** K1
Melchor, Isla *i.* Chile **205** B7
Melchor de Mencos Guat. **185** H5
Melchor Ocampo Mex. **185** E3
Meldal Norway **44** J3
Meldola Italy **56** E4
Meldorf Germany **48** G1
Meldrum U.S.A. **176** B9
Meldrum Bay Canada **168** D4
Mele, Capo *c.* Italy **56** A5
Melech *r.* Rus. Fed. **43** R4
Melekess Rus. Fed. *see* **Dimitrovgrad**
Melenci *Vojvodina, Srbija* Yugo. **58** B3
Melendiz Dağı *mt.* Turkey **106** C3
Melenki Rus. Fed. **40** G5
Melet Turkey *see* **Mesudiye**
Meleuz Rus. Fed. **102** C1
Mélèzes, Rivière aux *r.* Canada **169** G1
Melfa U.S.A. **177** J8
Melfi Chad **126** C2
Melfi Italy **56** H8
Melfort Canada **167** J4
Melgaço Brazil **202** B2
Melgar de Fernamental Spain **54** G2

Melhus Norway 44 J3
Meliadine Lake Canada 167 M2
Meliau, Gunung mt. Sabah Malaysia 77 G1
  also known as Melta, Mount
Melide Spain 54 C2
  also spelt Mellid
Meligalas Greece 59 C11

▶ Melilla N. Africa 55 I9
Spanish North Africa. Formerly known as
Rusaddir.
africa [countries] ⟹ 114–117

Melilli Sicilia Italy 57 H11
Melimoyu, Monte mt. Chile 205 B7
Melina, Mount N.Z. 153 D12
Melintang, Danau l. Indon. 77 G3
Melita Canada 167 K5
Melitene Turkey see Malatya
Melito di Porto Salvo Italy 57 H11
Melitopol' Ukr. 41 E7
Melk Austria 49 N7
Melka Guba Eth. 128 C3
Mellakoski Fin. 44 N2
Mellansel Sweden 44 L3
Mellerud Sweden 45 K3
Mellanström Sweden 44 L2
Melle Germany 48 F3
Mellègue, Barrage dam Tunisia 57 A12
Mellerud Sweden 45 K4
Mellid Spain see Melide
Mellit Sudan 121 E6
Mellizo Sur, Cerro mt. Chile 205 B8
Mellor Glacier Antarctica 223 H2
Mellrichstadt Germany 48 H5
Mellum i. Germany 48 F2
Melmoth S. Africa 133 P5
Mel'nichoye Rus. Fed. 82 D3
Melnik Czech Rep. 49 L5
Mel'nikovo Rus. Fed. 43 K1
Melo Arg. 204 E4
Melo Uruguay 204 G4
Meloding S. Africa 133 K5
Melololo Indon. 75 B5
Mélong Cameroon 125 H5
Melovoye Ukr. see Milove
Melozitna r. U.S.A. 164 D3
Melrhir, Chott salt l. Alg. 123 G2
Melrose Australia 151 C6
Melrose U.K. 46 J8
Melrose U.S.A. 178 C4
Melsetter Zimbabwe see Chimanimani
Melsungen Germany 48 G4
Melta, Mount Sabah Malaysia see
  Meliau, Gunung
Meltaus Fin. 44 N2
Melton Australia 147 E4
Melton Mowbray U.K. 47 L11
Meluan Sarawak Malaysia 77 E2
Melun France 51 I4
Melur India 94 C4
Melut Sudan 128 B2
Melville Canada 167 K5
Melville, Cape U.S.A. 164 E2
Melville, Cape Phil. 74 A5
Melville, Lake Canada 169 J2
Melville Bay Australia 148 C1
Melville Bugt b. Greenland see
  Qimusseriarsuaq
Melville Island Australia 148 A1
Melville Island Canada 165 I2
Melville Peninsula Canada 165 K3
Melvin, Lough l. Rep. of Ireland/U.K. 47 D9
Meíykút Hungary 49 Q9
Memali China see Wenlan
Mêmar Co salt l. China 89 C5
Memba Moz. 131 D7
Memba, Baía de b. Moz. 131 L2
Memberamo r. Indon. 73 I7
Memboro Indon. 75 A5
Memel Lith. see Klaipėda
Memel S. Africa 133 N4
Memele r. Latvia 42 F5
Memiakalnis hill Lith. 42 H6
Memmingen Germany 48 H8
Mempakul Sabah Malaysia 77 F1
Memphis tourist site Egypt 121 F2
Memphis MI U.S.A. 173 K6
Memphis MO U.S.A. 174 A3
Memphis TN U.S.A. 174 B5
Memphis TX U.S.A. 179 B5
Memuro-dake mt. Japan 90 H3
Mena U.S.A. 128 C5
Mena Indon. 75 C5
Mena Ukr. 41 E6
Mena U.S.A. 179 C5
Menabe mts Madag. 131 [inset] J4
Ménaka Mali 125 F3
Mènam Khong r. Asia 78 D4 see Mekong
Menanga Indon. 75 C3
Menarandra r. Madag. 131 [inset] J5
Menard U.S.A. 177 N2
Menasha U.S.A. 172 E6
Mencal mt. Spain 55 H7
Mencué Arg. 204 C6
Mendanau i. Indon. 77 D2
Mendarda India 96 A5
Mendarik i. Indon. 77 D2
Mendawai Indon. 77 F3
Mendawai r. Indon. 77 F3
Mende France 51 J8
Mendebo Mountains Eth. 128 C3
Mendefera Eritrea 121 H6
  also known as Adi Ugri
Mendeleyevsk Rus. Fed. 40 J5
  formerly known as Bondyuzhskiy
Menden (Sauerland) Germany 48 F4
Mendenhall U.S.A. 175 B6
Mendenhall, Cape U.S.A. 164 C4
Mendenhall Glacier U.S.A. 166 C3
Menderes Turkey 59 I10
Méndez Mex. 185 F3
Méndez-Núñez Phil. 74 B3

Mendi P.N.G. 73 J8
Mendip Hills U.K. 47 J12
Mendocino U.S.A. 182 A2
Mendocino, Cape U.S.A. 180 A4
Mendocino, Lake U.S.A. 182 A2
Mendota CA U.S.A. 182 D5
Mendota IL U.S.A. 174 B3
Mendota, Lake U.S.A. 172 D7
Mendoza Arg. 204 C4
Mendoza prov. Arg. 204 C4
Mendoza Bol. 200 D4
Mene de Mauroa Venez. 198 D2
Menemen Turkey 59 I10
Menez Brê hill France 50 C4
Menfi Sicilia Italy 57 E11
Menga, Puerto de pass Spain 54 F4
Mengalum i. Malaysia 77 F1
Mengban China 86 B4
Mengcheng China 87 F1
Mengen Turkey 106 C2
Menggala Indon. 76 D4
Menghai China 86 B4
  also known as Xiangshan
Mengibar Spain 54 H7
Mengkiang r. Indon. 77 E2
Mengkoka, Gunung mt. Indon. 75 B3
Menglang China see Lancang
Menglie China see Jiangcheng
Mengmeng China see Shuangjiang
Mengong Cameroon 125 H6
Mengshan China 87 D3
Mengxian China see Mengzhou
Mengyang China see Mingshan
Mengyin China 85 H5
Mengzhou China 87 E1
  formerly known as Mengxian
Mengzi China 86 B4
  also known as Wenlan
Menihek Canada 169 H2
Menindee Australia 147 D3
Menindee Aboriginal Reserve Australia
  147 D3
Menindee Lake Australia 147 D3
Meningie Australia 146 C3
Menkere Rus. Fed. 39 M3
Menna r. Eth. 104 B5
Mennecy France 51 I4
Menominee U.S.A. 172 F5
Menominee r. U.S.A. 172 F5
Menominee Indian Reservation res. U.S.A.
  172 E5
Menomonee Falls U.S.A. 172 E7
Menomonie U.S.A. 172 C6
Menongue Angola 127 C8
  formerly known as Serpa Pinto
Menor, Mar lag. Spain 55 K7
Menorca i. Spain see Minorca
Menor, Mar lag. Spain see Minorca
Menshikova, Mys c. Rus. Fed. 40 K1
Mentakab Malaysia see Mentekab
Mentarang r. Indon. 77 F2
Mentawai, Kepulauan is Indon. 76 B3
Mentawai, Selat sea chan. Indon. 76 C3
Mentaya r. Indon. 77 F3
Mentekab Malaysia 76 C2
  formerly spelt Mentakab
Mentiras hill Port. 54 D6
Mentiras mts Spain 55 I6
Mentok Indon. 76 D3
Menton France 51 N9
Mentone U.S.A. 179 B6
Mentor U.S.A. 176 E4
Mentuba r. Indon. 77 F3

Menufia governorate Egypt see Minūfiya
Menukung Indon. 77 F3
Menunu Indon. 75 B3
Menyapa, Gunung mt. Indon. 77 G2
Menyuan China 84 D4
  also known as Haomen
Menza r. Rus. Fed. 85 F1
Menzel Bourguiba Tunisia 123 H1
  formerly known as Ferryville
Menzelet Baraji reservoir Turkey 107 D3
Menzelinsk Rus. Fed. 40 J5
Menzel Temime Tunisia 57 D12
Menzies Australia 151 C6
Menzies, Mount Antarctica 223 F2
Meobbaai b. Namibia 130 B5
Meoqui Mex. 184 D2
Mepala Angola 127 B6
Meponda Moz. 131 G1
Meppel Neth. 48 D3
Meppen Germany 48 E3
Meqheleng S. Africa 133 L5
Mequénz r. Brazil 201 F3
Mequinenza, Embalse de resr Spain 55 L3
Mequon U.S.A. 172 F7
Mer France 50 H5
Merah Indon. 77 G2
Merak Indon. 77 D4
Meráker Norway 44 J3
Meramangye, Lake salt flat Australia
  146 B2
Meramec r. U.S.A. 178 D4
Merano Italy 56 D2
Merapi, Gunung vol. Java Indon. 77 E4
Merapi, Gunung vol. Indon. 77 F5
Merari, Serra mt. Brazil 199 F3
Meratswe r. Botswana 131 E4
Meratus, Pegunungan mts Indon. 77 F3
Merauke Indon. 73 J8
Merawwah i. U.A.E. 105 F2
Merbau Indon. 76 C2
Merbein Australia 147 D3
Mercadal Spain 55 P5
Merced U.S.A. 182 D4
Merced r. U.S.A. 182 D4
Mercedario, Cerro mt. Arg. 204 C3
Mercedes Corrientes Arg. 204 F3
Mercedes San Luis Arg. 204 D4
Mercedes Uruguay 204 F4
Merceditas Chile 204 C3
Mercer ME U.S.A. 177 P1
Mercer OH U.S.A. 176 A5
Mercer PA U.S.A. 176 E5
Mercer WI U.S.A. 172 C4
Mercersburg U.S.A. 176 H6
Mercês Acre Brazil 200 C2
Mercês Minas Gerais Brazil 203 D7
Mercier Bol. 200 C2
Mercury U.S.A. 183 I6
Mercury Bay N.Z. 152 J4
Merdenik Turkey see Göle
Merdja Zerga, Réserve de nature res.
  Morocco 122 D2
Meredith U.S.A. 177 N2
Meredith, Cape Falkland Is 205 E9
Meredith, Lake U.S.A. 179 B5
Meredoua Alg. 123 F4
Mereeg Somalia 128 E4
Merefa Ukr. 41 F6
Meremãe Estonia 42 I4
Meremere N.Z. 152 I5
Merenkurkku strait Fin./Sweden 44 M3
Merepah Aboriginal Holding res. Australia
  149 D2
Merezha Rus. Fed. 43 P5
Merga Oasis Sudan 121 E5
Mergenevo Kazakh. 102 B2
Mergui Myanmar 79 B5
  also known as Myeik
Mergui Archipelago is Myanmar 79 B6
Merhei, Lacul r. Romania 58 K3
Meribah Australia 146 D3
Meriç r. Greece/Turkey see Evros
Meriç r. Greece/Turkey 58 H8
Meriç Turkey 58 H7
Merichas Greece 59 F11

Mérida Mex. 185 H4
Mérida Spain 54 E6
  historically known as Emerita Augusta
Mérida state Venez. 198 D2
Mérida Venez. 198 D2
Mérida, Cordillera de mts Venez. 198 D2
Meriden U.S.A. 177 M4
Meridian MS U.S.A. 175 B5
Meridian TX U.S.A. 179 C6
Mérignac France 50 F8
Merijärvi Fin. 44 N2
Merikarvia Fin. 45 M3
Merimbula Australia 147 F4
Meringur Australia 146 D3
Merin, Laguna l. Brazil/Uruguay see
  Mirim, Lagoa
Merinda Australia 149 F4
Meringur Australia 146 D3
Merir i. Palau 73 H5
  historically known as Warren Hastings Island
Merirumã Brazil 199 H4
Merivale r. Australia 149 E5
Merke Kazakh. 103 H4
Merkel U.S.A. 179 B5
Merkinė Lith. 42 F7
Merlimau, Pulau reg. Sing. 76 [inset]
Mermaid Reef Australia 150 B3
Merolia Australia 151 C6
Meron, Har mt. Israel 108 G5
Meroša Srbija Yugo. 58 C5
Merowe Sudan 121 F5
Merredin Australia 151 B6
Merrick hill U.K. 47 H6
Merrickville Canada 173 R6
Merrill MI U.S.A. 173 I7
Merrill WI U.S.A. 172 D5
Merrill, Mount Canada 166 E2
Merrillan U.S.A. 172 C6
Merrillville U.S.A. 172 F9
Merriman S. Africa 132 H8
Merriman U.S.A. 178 B3
Merritt Canada 166 F5
Merritt Island U.S.A. 175 D6
Merritt Island National Wildlife Refuge
  nature res. U.S.A. 175 D6
Merriwa Australia 147 F3
Merrygoen Australia 147 F2
Mersa Fatma Eritrea 121 I6
Mersa Gulbub Eritrea 121 H5
Mersa Teklay Eritrea 121 H5
Mersch Lux. 51 M3
Merse r. Italy 56 C6
Merseburg (Saale) Germany 48 I4
Mersin Turkey see Içel
Mersing Malaysia 76 C2
Mersing, Bukit mt. Sarawak Malaysia 77 F2
Mersin Galgalo Eth. 128 E3
Mērsrags Latvia 42 E4
Mērsrags pt Latvia 42 E4
Merta India 96 B4
Merta Road India 96 B4
Merthyr Tydfil U.K. 47 I12
Merti Kenya 128 C4
Merti Plateau Kenya 128 C4
Mértola Port. 54 D7
Mertoutek Alg. 123 G4
Mertz Glacier Antarctica 223 J2
Mertz Glacier Tongue Antarctica 223 J2
Mertzon U.S.A. 179 B6
Méru France 51 I3
Meru Kenya 128 C4

▶ Meru vol. Tanz. 128 C5
4th highest mountain in Africa.
africa [landscapes] ⟹ 112–113

Meru Betiri National Park Indon. 77 F5
Merui Pak. 101 E4
Meru National Park Kenya 128 C4
Merv Turkm. see Mary
Merweville S. Africa 132 F9
Merzifon Turkey 106 C2
Merzig Germany 48 D6
Merz Peninsula Antarctica 222 T2
Mesa S. Africa 133 K3
Mesa i. Spain 55 J3
Mesa U.S.A. 183 M8
Mesabi Range hills U.S.A. 174 A2
Mesa Bolívar Venez. 198 D2
Mesagne Italy 57 J8
Mesara, Ormos b. Greece 59 F13
Mesa Verde National Park U.S.A. 181 E5
Mescalero Apache Indian Reservation
  res. U.S.A. 181 F6
Meschede Germany 48 F4
Meselefors Sweden 44 L2
Mesfinto Eth. 128 C1
Mesgouez Lake Canada 169 F3
Mesha r. Rus. Fed. 40 I5
Meshchovsk Rus. Fed. 43 Q7
Meshed Iran see Mashhad
Meshekli Uzbek. 103 E4
Meshkān Iran 100 D2
Meshoppen U.S.A. 173 Q9
Mesimeri Greece 59 E9
Meslay-du-Maine France 50 F5
Mesola Italy 56 E4
Mesolongi Greece 59 C10
  English form Missolonghi; also known as
  Mesolóngion
Mesolóngion Greece see Mesolongi
Mesopotamia Brazil 203 D6
Mesquite NV U.S.A. 179 C5
Mesquite TX U.S.A. 183 K6
Mesquite Lake U.S.A. 183 I6
Messaad Alg. 123 F2
Messak Mellet hills Libya 120 A3
Messalo r. Moz. 129 D7
Messana Sicilia Italy see Messina
Messaoud, Oued watercourse Alg. 123 E4
Messier, Canal sea chan. Chile 205 B8
Messina Sicilia Italy 57 H10
  historically known as Messana or Zancle
Messina S. Africa 131 F4
Messina, Strait of Italy 57 H10
  also known as Stretta di Messina
Messines Canada 173 Q4
Messini Greece 59 D11
Messiniakos Kolpos b. Greece 59 D12
Mesta r. Greece see Nestos
Mestghanem Alg. see Mostaganem
Meston, Akra pt Greece 59 G10
Mesudiye Turkey 107 D2
  also known as Melet
Mesuji r. Indon. 77 D4
Meta dept Col. 198 C4
Meta r. Col./Venez. 198 D3
Metairie U.S.A. 179 E6
Metaliferi, Munţii mts Romania 58 D2
Metallifere, Colline mts Italy 56 C5
Metallostroy Rus. Fed. 43 L2
Metamora U.S.A. 172 D10
Metán Arg. 204 D2
Metangula Moz. 129 B8
Metanara Eth. 128 D3
Metapan El Salvador 185 H6
Metauro r. Italy 56 F5
Meteghan Canada 169 H4
Metelys l. Lith. 42 E7
Metema Eth. 128 C1
Metengobalame Moz. 131 G2
Meteor Creek r. Australia 149 F5
Methoni Greece 59 C12
Methuen U.S.A. 177 N3
Methven N.Z. 153 F11
Metionga Lake Canada 168 B3
Metković Croatia 56 J5
Metlakatla U.S.A. 166 D4

Metlaoui Tunisia 123 H2
Metlika Slovenia 56 H3
Metoro Moz. 131 H2
Metu Indon. 76 D4
Metropolis U.S.A. 174 B4
Metsäda tourist site Israel see Masada
Metsäkylä Fin. 44 O2
Metsovo Greece 59 C9
Metter U.S.A. 175 D5
Mettler U.S.A. 182 F6
Mettuppalaiyam India 94 C4
Mettur India 94 C4
Metu Eth. 128 B2
Metundo, Ilha i. Moz. 129 D7
Metz France 51 M3
Metzingen Germany 48 G7
Meu r. France 50 E5
Meulaboh Indon. 76 B1
Meung-sur-Loire France 50 H5
Meurthe r. France 51 M4
Meuse r. Belgium/France 51 L1
  also spelt Maas (Netherlands)
Mêwa China 86 B1
Mexcala Mex. 185 F5
Mexia U.S.A. 179 C6
Mexiana, Ilha i. Brazil 202 B1
Mexicali Mex. 184 B1
Mexican Hat U.S.A. 183 O4
Mexican Water U.S.A. 183 O5

▶ Mexico country Central America 184 D4
2nd most populous and 4th largest country
in North America.
northamerica [countries] ⟹ 158–159

México Mex. see Mexico City
México state Mex. 185 F5
Mexico ME U.S.A. 177 O1
Mexico MO U.S.A. 174 A4
Mexico NY U.S.A. 177 I2
Mexico, Gulf of Mex./U.S.A. 171 G7

▶ Mexico City Mex. 185 F5
Capital of Mexico. Most populous city in
North America and 2nd in the world. Also
known as México.
world [cities] ⟹ 24–25

Meybod Iran 100 C3
Meydani, Ra's-e pt Iran 100 D5
Meyenburg Germany 49 J2
Meyersdale U.S.A. 176 F6
Meyerton S. Africa 133 M3
Meylan France 51 L7
Meymac France 51 I7
Meymaneh Afgh. 101 F3
Meymeh Iran 100 B3
Meynypil'gyno Rus. Fed. 39 R3
Meyo Centre Cameroon 125 H6
Meyssac France 50 H7
Meza r. Rus. Fed. 43 V3
Mezada tourist site Israel see Masada
Mezcalapa r. Mex. 185 G5
Mezdra Bulg. 58 E5
Mèze France 51 J9
Mezen' Rus. Fed. 40 H2
Mezen' r. Rus. Fed. 40 H2
Mézenc, Mont mt. France 51 K8
Mezhdurechensk Rus. Fed. 80 D2
  formerly known as Olzheras
Mezhdurechensk Rus. Fed. 40 I3
Mezhdurechenskiy Rus. Fed. 38 G4
Mezhdurechnye Rus. Fed. see Shali
Mezhdusharskiy, Ostrov i. Rus. Fed. 40 J1
Mézidon-Canon France 50 F3
Mézin France 50 G8
Mezinovskiy Rus. Fed. 43 V6
Mezitli Turkey 108 E1
Mezőberény Hungary 49 S9
Mezőhegyes Hungary 49 R9
Mezőkovácsháza Hungary 49 R9
Mezőkövesd Hungary 49 R8
Mezőtúr Hungary 49 R9
Mezquital Mex. 184 D4
Mezquital r. Mex. 184 D4
Mezquitic Mex. 184 E4
Mežvidi Latvia 42 I5
Mezzolombardo Italy 56 D2
Mfouati Congo 126 B5
Mfuwe Zambia 127 F8
Mgachi Rus. Fed. 82 F2
Mgbidi Nigeria 125 G5
Mglin Rus. Fed. 43 N8
Mgwali r. S. Africa 133 M8
Mhail, Rubh' a' pt U.K. 46 F8
Mhangura Zimbabwe 131 F3
  formerly spelt Mangula
Mhasvad India 94 B2
Mhlambanyatsi Swaziland 133 P3
Mhlume Swaziland 133 P3
Mhluzi S. Africa 133 N2
Mhow India 96 B5
Mi r. China 87 D3
Mi r. Myanmar 78 A3
Miahuatlán Mex. 185 F5
Miajadas Spain 54 F5
Miaméré Cent. Afr. Rep. 126 C2
Miami FL U.S.A. 175 D7
Miami OK U.S.A. 178 D4
Miami TX U.S.A. 179 B5
Miami Beach U.S.A. 175 D7
Miamisburg U.S.A. 176 A6
Miamitown U.S.A. 176 A6
Miānāb Iran 100 B4
Mianaz Pak. 101 E5
Miancaowan China 84 C5
Mian Chanmun Pak. 101 H4
Mianchi China 87 D1
Miāndasht Iran 100 D2
Miandowāb Iran 100 A2
Miandrivazo Madag. 131 [inset] J3
Miandur China 85 I1
Miāneh Iran 100 A2
Miangas i. Phil. 74 C5
Miani Hor b. Pak. 101 F5
Mianmar see Myanmar
Mianning China 86 B3
  also known as Chengxiang
Mianwali Pak. 101 G3
Mianxian China see Xiantao
Mianyang China 86 B2
Mianzhu China 86 C2
Miaodao Qundao is China 85 I4
Miao'ergou China 88 D2
  also known as Utu
Miaogao China see Suichang
Miaoli Taiwan 87 G3
Miaomiao Eth. 128 C2
Miass Germany 48 I8
Mi'eso Eth. 128 D2
Miarinarivo Antananarivo Madag.
  131 [inset] J3
Miarinarivo Toamasina Madag.
  131 [inset] J3
Miʼfin Saudi Arabia 104 C4
Miass Rus. Fed. 38 G4
Miastko Poland 49 N1
Miastkowce Chiu Romania 58 G2
Mica Creek Canada 166 G4
Mica Mountain U.S.A. 183 N9
Micang Shan mts China 86 C1
Micaune Moz. 131 H3
Michalovce Slovakia 49 S7
Michel Canada 167 I4
Michelson, Mount U.S.A. 164 E3
Micheng China see Midu
Miches Dom. Rep. 187 F3
Michigamme Lake U.S.A. 172 E4
Michigamme Reservoir U.S.A. 172 E4
Michigan state U.S.A. 173 E4

▶ Michigan, Lake U.S.A. 172 F7
3rd largest lake in North America and 5th in
the world.
northamerica [landscapes] ⟹ 156–157

Michigan City U.S.A. 174 C3
Michipicoten Bay Canada 168 C4
Michipicoten Island Canada 168 C4
Michipicoten River Canada 168 C4
Michoacán state Mex. 185 E5
Michurin Bulg. see Tsarevo
Michurinsk Rus. Fed. 41 G5
Micos Mex. 185 F4
Micoud St Lucia 187 H4
Micronesia, Federated States of country
  N. Pacific Ocean 220 F5

▶ Micronesia, Federated States of country
N. Pacific Ocean 220 F5
oceania [countries] ⟹ 138–139

Midai i. Indon. 77 D2
Midal well Niger 125 G2
Midale Canada 167 K5
Middelberg Pass S. Africa 132 D9
Middelburg Neth. 48 A4
Middelburg E. Cape S. Africa 132 H7
Middelburg Mpumalanga S. Africa 133 N2
Middelfart Denmark 45 J5
Middelharnis Neth. 48 B4
Middelpos S. Africa 132 E8
Middelwit S. Africa 133 L1
Middle Alkali Lake U.S.A. 180 B4
Middle Andaman i. India 95 G3
Middle Atlas mts Morocco see Moyen Atlas
Middle Bay Canada 169 J3
Middleboro U.S.A. 177 O4
Middleburg PA U.S.A. 177 H5
Middleburg VA U.S.A. 176 H7
Middleburg IN U.S.A. 172 H9
Middleburg VT U.S.A. 177 L1
Middle Concho r. U.S.A. 179 B6
Middle Congo country Africa see Congo
Middle Creek r. Canada 149 D3
Middle Island U.S.A. 177 M5
Middle Loup r. U.S.A. 178 C3
Middlemount Australia 149 F4
Middleport OH U.S.A. 176 C6
Middle Raccoon r. U.S.A. 178 D3
Middle Ridge Wildlife Reserve nature res.
  Canada 169 K3
Middle River U.S.A. 177 I6
Middlesboro U.S.A. 176 B9
Middlesbrough U.K. 47 K9
Middlesex U.S.A. 177 H3
Middle Strait India see Andaman Strait
Middleton Australia 149 D4
Middleton Canada 169 H4
Middleton S. Africa 133 J9
Middleton U.S.A. 172 D7
Middleton Reef Australia 145 E4
Middletown CA U.S.A. 182 B3
Middletown CT U.S.A. 177 M4
Middletown DE U.S.A. 177 J6
Middletown MD U.S.A. 176 H6
Middletown NY U.S.A. 177 K3
Middletown OH U.S.A. 176 A6
Middletown PA U.S.A. 177 I5
Middletown VA U.S.A. 176 G7
Middleville NY U.S.A. 177 K2
Middleville MI U.S.A. 172 H8
Midi r. Morocco 122 D2
Midi, Canal du France 50 I9
Midi de Bigorre, Pic du mt. France 50 G10
Midi-Pyrénées admin. reg. France 50 I8
Midland Canada 168 E4
Midland CA U.S.A. 183 J8
Midland MI U.S.A. 173 I7
Midland TX U.S.A. 179 B5
Midland Junction Australia 151 A6
Midlands prov. Zimbabwe 131 F3
Midleton Rep. of Ireland 47 D12
Midlothian TX U.S.A. 179 C5
Midlothian VA U.S.A. 176 H8
Midmar Nature Reserve S. Africa 133 O6
Midnapore India see Medinipur
Midongy Atsimo Madag. 131 [inset] J4
Midou r. France 50 F9
Midouze r. France 50 F9
Midsayap Phil. 74 C5
Midu China 86 B3
  also known as Micheng
Midvale U.S.A. 183 M1
Midway Oman see Thamarīt
Midway KY U.S.A. 176 A7
Midway UT U.S.A. 183 M1

▶ Midway Islands N. Pacific Ocean 220 G4
United States Unincorporated Territory.
oceania [countries] ⟹ 138–139

Midway Well Australia 150 C4
Midwest U.S.A. 180 F4
Midwest City U.S.A. 179 C5
Midyah Saudi Arabia 104 A2
Midyat Turkey 107 E3
Midye Turkey see Kıyıköy
Midzhur mt. Bulg./Yugo. 58 D5
Mie Japan 91 N3
Miechów Poland 49 R5
Miedwie, Jezioro l. Poland 49 L2
Międzychód Poland 49 M3
Międzylesie Poland 49 N5
Międzyrzec Podlaski Poland 49 T3
Międzyrzecz Poland 49 M3
Międzyzdroje Poland 49 L2
Miehikkälä Fin. 42 N2
Miekojärvi l. Fin. 44 N2
Mielec Poland 49 S5
Miembwe Tanz. 129 C7
Mienga Angola 127 C9
Mien r. Poland 49 P3
Mienga Zambia 127 F8
Mienhua Yü i. Taiwan 87 G3
Miangas i. Phil. 74 C5
Mieraslompolo Fin. 44 N1
  also known as Mieräšluoppal
Mieräšluoppal Fin. see Mieraslompolo
Miercurea-Ciuc Romania 58 F2
Mieres Spain 54 F1
  long form Mieres del Camín or Mieres del
  Camino
Mieres del Camín Spain see Mieres
Mieres del Camino Spain see Mieres
Mieron Norway 44 M1
Mierzeja Helska pen. Poland 49 P1
Mierzeja Wiślana spit Poland 49 Q1
Miesbach Germany 48 I8
Mi'eso Eth. 128 D2
Mieste Germany 48 I3
Mikono China 86 B3
  also known as Miyang
Milê Eth. 128 C2
Miles Australia 149 F5
Milesburg U.S.A. 176 H5
Miles City U.S.A. 180 F3
Milê Serdo Reserve nature res. Eth.
  128 C2
Miletin r. Romania 58 I1
Mileura Australia 151 B5
Milevsko Czech Rep. 49 L6
Mileyevo Rus. Fed. 43 Q8
Milford CT U.S.A. 177 L4
Milford DE U.S.A. 177 J7
Milford IL U.S.A. 172 F10
Milford MA U.S.A. 177 N3
Milford NE U.S.A. 178 C3
Milford NH U.S.A. 177 N3
Milford PA U.S.A. 177 K4
Milford UT U.S.A. 183 K3
Milford VA U.S.A. 176 H7
Milford Haven U.K. 47 G12
  also known as Aberdaugleddau
Milford Lake U.S.A. 178 C4
Milford Sound N.Z. 153 B12
Milford Sound inlet N.Z. 153 B12
  also known as Piopiotahi
Milgarra Australia 149 D3
Milgun Australia 151 B5
Milḩ, Baḩr al l. Iraq see
  Razāzah, Buḩayrat ar
Milḩ, Wādi al watercourse Iraq 109 P5
Milḩ Ashqar salt l. Iraq 109 N2
Miliana Alg. 55 N8
Milicz Poland 49 O4
Milikapiti Australia 148 A1
Miling Australia 151 B6
Milingimbi Australia 148 B2
Milip Vanuatu 145 F3
Milk r. U.S.A. 180 D2
Milk, Wadi el watercourse Sudan
  121 F5
Mil'kovo Rus. Fed. 39 P4
Milk River Canada 167 H5
Millaa Millaa Australia 149 E3
Millárs r. Spain 55 K4
Millau France 51 I8
Millboro U.S.A. 176 F8
Millbrook Canada 173 O6
Millbrook U.S.A. 177 L4
Mill City U.S.A. 180 B3
Mill Creek r. Australia 149 D4
Milledgeville GA U.S.A. 175 D5
Milledgeville IL U.S.A. 172 D9
Millen U.S.A. 175 D5
Mille Lacs lakes U.S.A. 174 A2
Mille Lacs, Lac des l. Canada 168 B4
Millennium Island Kiribati see
  Caroline Island
Miller S. Africa 132 H10
Miller U.S.A. 178 C2
Miller Dam Flowage resr U.S.A. 172 C4
Miller Lake Canada 173 L5
Millerovo Rus. Fed. 41 G6
Millersburg MI U.S.A. 173 I5
Millersburg OH U.S.A. 176 D5
Millers Creek Australia 146 C2
Millers Creek U.S.A. 176 B8
Millers Falls U.S.A. 177 M3
Millers Flat N.Z. 153 D13
Millerton U.S.A. 177 L4
Millerton Lake U.S.A. 182 E4
Miller Point U.S.A. 47 G8
Mill Glacier Antarctica 223 L1
Mill Hall U.S.A. 176 H4
Millicent Australia 146 D4

Millijiddie Aboriginal Reserve Australia **150** D3
Millington *MI* U.S.A. **173** J7
Millington *TN* U.S.A. **174** B5
Mill Inlet Antarctica **222** T2
Millinocket U.S.A. **174** G2
Milliri, Cerro *mt.* Bol. **200** C5
Mill Island Antarctica **223** G2
Mill Island Canada **165** L3
Millmerran Australia **147** F1
Millom U.K. **47** I9
Millsboro U.S.A. **177** J7
Mills Creek *watercourse* Australia **149** D4
Mills Lake Canada **167** G2
Millston U.S.A. **172** C6
Millstone U.S.A. **176** D7
Millstream Australia **150** B4
Millstream-Chichester National Park Australia **150** B4
Milltown U.S.A. **172** A5
Millungera Australia **149** D3
Millvale S. Africa **133** K2
Mill Valley U.S.A. **182** B4
Millville *CA* U.S.A. **182** B1
Millville *NJ* U.S.A. **177** J6
Millwood Lake U.S.A. **179** D5
Milly-la-Forêt France **51** I4
Milly Milly Australia **151** B5
Milne Bay P.N.G. **149** F1
Milne Land *i.* Greenland *see* **Ilimananngip Nunaa**
Milo *r.* Guinea **124** C4
Milo U.S.A. **174** G2
Milogradovo Rus. Fed. **82** D4
Milolii U.S.A. **181** [inset] Z2
Milos *i.* Greece **59** F12
Miloslavskoye Rus. Fed. **43** U8
Miłosław Poland **49** O3
Miloud *well* Alg. **122** D4
Milove Ukr. **41** G6
also spelt Melovoye
Milparinka Australia **146** D2
Milpitas U.S.A. **182** C4
Milroy U.S.A. **176** H5
Milton Canada **173** N7
Milton N.Z. **153** D14
Milton *DE* U.S.A. **177** J7
Milton *FL* U.S.A. **175** C6
Milton *VT* U.S.A. **177** L1
Milton *WV* U.S.A. **176** C7
Milton-Freewater U.S.A. **180** C3
Milton Keynes U.K. **47** L11
Miluo China **87** E2
Milverton Canada **173** M7
Milwaukee U.S.A. **172** F7

▶ **Milwaukee Deep** *sea feature* Caribbean Sea **216** J4
Deepest point in the Atlantic Ocean (Puerto Rico Trench).
oceans [features] ▶ 210–211

Mily Kazakh. **103** E2
Milybulabk Kazakh. **103** H2
formerly spelt Myylybulak
Milyushino Rus. Fed. **43** T3
Milyutinskaya Rus. Fed. **41** G6
Mimbelly Congo **126** C4
Mimbres *watercourse* U.S.A. **181** F6
Mimili Australia **146** B1
Mimisal India **94** C4
Mimizan France **50** E8
Mimoň Czech Rep. **49** L5
Mimongo Gabon **126** A5
Mimosa Rocks National Park Australia **147** F4
Mimoso Brazil **206** E2
Mimoso do Sul Brazil **207** L8
Mina Mex. **185** E3
Mina U.S.A. **182** F3
Mina, Nevado *mt.* Peru **200** C3
Mina, Oued *watercourse* Alg. **55** L9
Mīnāb Iran **100** D5
Mīnāb *r.* Iran **100** D5
Minabe Japan **91** D8
Mina Clavero Arg. **204** D3
Minaçu Brazil **202** B5
Minago *r.* Canada **167** L4
Minahasa, Semenanjung *pen.* Indon. **75** B2
English form Minahassa Peninsula
Minahassa Peninsula Indon. *see* **Minahasa, Semenanjung**
Mina Jebel Ali U.A.E. **105** F2
short form Jebel Ali
Minaker Canada *see* **Prophet River**
Minaki Canada **167** M5
Minamata Japan **91** B8
Minamia Australia **148** B2
Minami Alps National Park Japan **91** F7
Minami-Daitō-jima *i.* Japan **81** M7
Minami-Iō-jima *vol.* Japan **73** J2
Min'an China *see* **Longshan**
Minaret Peaks N.Z. **153** D12
Minas Cuba **186** D2
Minas Indon. **76** C2
Minas Uruguay **204** G4
Mīnā' Sa'ūd Kuwait **107** G5
Minas Basin *b.* Canada **169** H4
Minas Channel Canada **169** H4
Minas de Matahambre Cuba **186** C2
Minas Gerais *state* Brazil **207** I5
Minas Novas Brazil **207** K4
Minatitlán Mex. **185** G5
Minbu Myanmar **78** A3
Minbya Myanmar **78** A3
Minchinabad Pak. **101** H4
Minchinmávida *vol.* Chile **205** B6
Mincio *r.* Italy **56** C3
Mincivan Azer. **107** F3
also spelt Mindzhivan
Mindanao *i.* Phil. **74** C5
Mindanao *r.* Phil. **74** C5
Mindat Sakan Myanmar **78** A3
Mindelheim Germany **48** H7
Mindelo Cape Verde **124** [inset]
Minden Germany **48** F3
Minden *LA* U.S.A. **179** D5
Minden *NE* U.S.A. **178** C3
Minden *NV* U.S.A. **182** E3
Minden City U.S.A. **173** K7
Minderoo Australia **150** A4
Mindon Myanmar **78** A4
Mindona Lake *imp. l.* Australia **147** D3
Mindoro *i.* Phil. **74** B3
Mindoro Strait Phil. **74** A3
Mindouli Congo **126** B6
Mindszent Hungary **49** R9
Minduri Brazil **207** I8
Mindzhivan Azer. *see* **Mincivan**
Mine Japan **91** B7
Mine Centre Canada **172** A2
Minehead U.K. **47** I12
Mineiga, Gebel *mts* Egypt/Sudan **104** A3
Mineiros Brazil **206** A4
Mineola U.S.A. **179** D5
Mineral U.S.A. **176** H7
Mineral'nyye Vody Rus. Fed. **41** G7
Mineral Point U.S.A. **172** C8
Mineral Wells U.S.A. **179** C5
Mineralwells U.S.A. **176** D6
Minersville U.S.A. **183** L3
Minerva Reefs Fiji **145** H4
Minervino Murge Italy **56** I7
Minfeng China **89** C4
also known as Niya
Minga Dem. Rep. Congo **127** E7
Mingäçevir Azer. **107** F2
also spelt Mingechaur
Mingäçevir Su Anbarı *resr* Azer. **107** F2
also known as Mingechaurskoye Vodokhranilishche
Mingala Cent. Afr. Rep. **126** D3
Mingan Canada **169** H3
Mingan, Îles de *is* Canada **169** I3
Mingbulak Uzbek. **103** E4
Mingechaur Azer. *see* **Mingäçevir**
Mingechaurskoye Vodokhranilishche *resr* Azer. *see* **Mingäçevir Su Anbarı**
Mingela Australia **149** E3
Mingenew Australia **151** A6
Mingera Creek *watercourse* Australia **148** C4
Mingfeng China *see* **Yuan'an**
Minggang China **87** E1
Mingguang China **87** F1
formerly known as Jiashan
Mingin Myanmar **78** A3
Mingin Range *mts* Myanmar **78** A3
Ming-Kush Kyrg. **103** H4
also spelt Min-Kush
Minglanilla Spain **55** J5
Mingo Junction U.S.A. **176** E5
Mingoyo Tanz. **129** C7
Mingshan China *see* **Fengdu**
Mingshan China **86** B2
also known as Mengyang
Mingshui *Gansu* China **84** C3
Mingshui *Heilong.* China **82** B3
Mingteke China **89** A4
Minguez, Puerto de *pass* Spain **55** J4
Mingulay *i.* U.K. **46** E7
also spelt Miughalaigh
Mingxi China **87** F3
also known as Xuefeng
Mingzhou China *see* **Weixian**
Mingzhou China *see* **Suide**
Minhe China *see* **Jinxian**
Minhe China **80** G5
also known as Shangchuankou
Minhla *Magwe* Myanmar **78** A4
Minhla *Pegu* Myanmar **78** A4
Minho *reg.* Port. **54** C3
Minhou China **87** F3
also known as Ganzhe
Minicoy *i.* India **94** B4
Minigwal, Lake *salt flat* Australia **151** C6
Minija *r.* Lith. **42** C6
Minilya Australia **150** A4
Minilya *r.* Australia **150** A4
Miñimiñe Chile **200** C4
Mininian Côte d'Ivoire **124** D4
Minipi Lake Canada **169** I2
Ministra, Sierra *mts* Spain **55** I3
Minitonas Canada **167** K4
Minitskaya Rus. Fed. **43** P1
Minjian China *see* **Mabian**
Min Jiang *r. Sichuan* China **86** C2
Min Jiang *r.* China **87** F3
Minjilang Australia **148** B1
Min-Kush Kyrg. *see* **Ming-Kush**
Minlaton Australia **146** C3
Minle China **84** D4
Minna Nigeria **125** G4
Minna Bluff *pt* Antarctica **223** L1
Minne Sweden **45** K3
Minneapolis *KS* U.S.A. **178** C4
Minneapolis *MN* U.S.A. **174** A2
Minnedosa Canada **167** L5
Minnehaha Springs U.S.A. **176** F7
Minnesota *r.* U.S.A. **178** D2
Minnesota *state* U.S.A. **174** A2
Minnesota City U.S.A. **172** B6
Minnewaukan U.S.A. **178** C1
Min-ngaw Myanmar **79** B5
Minnie Creek Australia **150** A4
Minnipa Australia **146** B3
Minnitaki Lake Canada **168** B3
Miño *r.* Port./Spain **54** C3
Minokamo Japan **91** E7
Minonk U.S.A. **172** D10
Minorca *i.* Spain **55** O4
also spelt Menorca
Minot U.S.A. **178** B1
Minqār, Ghadīr *imp. l.* Syria **109** I5
Minqār Khurayif *hill* Egypt **108** B9
Minqin China **84** D4
Minqing China **87** F3
also known as Meicheng
Minquan China **87** E1
Min Shan *mts* China **86** B1
Minsin Myanmar **78** A2

▶ **Minsk** Belarus **42** I8
Capital of Belarus.

Minskaya Oblast' *admin. div.* Belarus *see* **Minskaya Voblasts'**
Minskaya Voblasts' *admin. div.* Belarus **42** I8
English form Minsk Oblast; *also known as* Minskaya Oblast'
Minsk Mazowiecki Poland **49** S3
Minsk Oblast *admin. div.* Belarus *see* **Minskaya Voblasts'**
Minster U.S.A. **176** A5
Mintaka Pass China/Jammu and Kashmir **89** A4
Mintang China **86** B1
Mintlaw U.K. **46** K6
Minto *N.B.* Canada **169** H4
Minto *Y.T.* Canada **166** B2
Minto, Lac *l.* Canada **169** F1
Minto, Mount Antarctica **223** L2
Minto Inlet Canada **165** H2
Mintom Cameroon **125** I6
Minton Canada **167** J5
Minturn U.S.A. **180** F5
Minturnae Italy *see* **Minturno**
Minturno Italy **56** F7
historically known as Minturnae
Minudasht Iran **100** C2
Minûf Egypt **108** B7
Minûfiya *governorate* Egypt **108** B7
also spelt Menufia
Minusinsk Rus. Fed. **80** E2
Minutang India **86** A2
Minvoul Gabon **126** B4
Minxian China **86** C1
Minya Konka *mt.* China *see* **Gongga Shan**
Minyar Rus. Fed. **40** K5
Minywa Myanmar **78** A3
Minzong India **97** H4
Mio *well* Niger **125** H2
Mio U.S.A. **173** I6
Mionica *Srbija* Yugo. **58** B4
Mipia, Lake *salt flat* Australia **148** C5
Miquan China **88** D3
Miquelon Canada **168** E3
Miquelon *i.* St Pierre and Miquelon **169** J4
Mir Belarus **42** H8
Mi'r, Wâdi el *watercourse* Egypt **108** E9
Mira *r.* Col. **198** B4
Mira Port. **54** C4
Mira *r.* Port. **54** C7
Mira, Sierra de *mts* Spain **55** J5
Mirabela Brazil **202** C6
Miracema Brazil **207** K8
Miracema do Norte Brazil *see* **Miracema do Tocantins**
Miracema do Tocantins Brazil **202** B4
formerly known as Miracema do Norte
Mirada Hills U.S.A. *see* **La Mirada**
Mirador Brazil **206** A10
Mirador, Parque Nacional de *nat. park* Brazil **202** C3
Mirador-Dos Lagunos-Río Azul, Parque Nacional *nat. park* Guat. **185** H5
Miradouro Brazil **207** K7
Miraflores *Boyaca* Col. **198** C3
Miraflores *Guaviare* Col. **198** C4
Mirah, Wādī al *watercourse* Iraq/Saudi Arabia **107** E4
Miraí Brazil **207** K8
Miraj India **94** B2
Miralta Brazil **207** J3
Miramar Arg. **204** F5
Miramar, Canal *sea chan.* Chile **205** B8
Miramas France **51** L9
Miramichi Bay Canada **169** H4
Miram Shah Pak. **101** G3
Miran China **88** E4
Miraña Col. **198** D5
Miranda Brazil **201** F5
Miranda *r.* Brazil **201** F4
Miranda Moz. *see* **Macaloge**
Miranda U.S.A. **182** A1
Miranda *state* Venez. **199** E2
Miranda, Lake *salt flat* Australia **151** C5
Miranda de Ebro Spain **55** I2
Miranda do Douro Port. **54** E3
Mirande France **50** G9
Mirandela Port. **54** D3
Mirandola Italy **56** D4
Miranta, Serra do *hills* Brazil **206** C9
Mirante do Paranapanema Brazil **206** B9
Mirapinima Brazil **199** F5
Miras Albania **58** B8
Mirassol Brazil **206** D7
Mir Bacheh Kowt Afgh. **101** G3
Mir-Bashir Azer. *see* **Tärtär**
Mirbāţ Oman **105** F4
Mirbāţ, Ra's *c.* Oman **105** F4
Mirear Island Egypt *see* **Marir, Gezîret**
Mirebalais Haiti **187** E3
Mirebeau France **50** G6
Mirecourt France **51** M4
Miréméné Chad **120** B6
Mirepoix France **50** H9
Mirganj India **97** E4
Mirgorod Ukr. *see* **Myrhorod**
Miri *Sarawak* Malaysia **77** F1
Miri *mt.* Pak. **101** E4
Miria Niger **125** H3
Mirialguda India **94** C2
formerly spelt Miryalaguda
Miriam Vale Australia **149** F5
Miri Hills India **97** G4
Mirim, Lagoa *l.* Brazil/Uruguay **204** G4
also known as Merín, Laguna
Mirim, Lagoa do *l.* Brazil **203** B9
Mirimire Venez. **198** D2
Mirina Greece *see* **Myrina**
Mirjan India **94** B3
Mirjāveh Iran **101** E4
Mirkovo Bulg. **58** F6
Mirna *r.* Croatia **56** F3
Mirny *research station* Antarctica **223** G2
Mirnyy *Arkhangel'skaya Oblast'* Rus. Fed. **40** G3
Mirnyy *Bryanskaya Oblast'* Rus. Fed. **43** M9
Mirnyy *Respublika Sakha (Yakutiya)* Rus. Fed. **39** L3
Miroč *hills* Yugo. **58** D4
Miromiro *mt.* N.Z. **153** G10
Mirond Lake Canada **167** K4
Mironovka Ukr. *see* **Myronivka**
Mirosławiec Poland **49** N2
Mirow Germany **49** J2
Mirpur Pak. **101** H3
Mirpur Batoro Pak. **101** G5
Mirpur Khas Pak. **101** G5
Mirpur Sakro Pak. **101** F5
Mirsale Somalia **128** E3
Mirsali China **88** D3
Mirs Bay *Hong Kong* China **87** [inset]
also known as Tai Pang Wan
Mirtoan Sea Greece *see* **Mirtoö Pelagos**
Mirtoö Pelagos *sea* Greece **59** E12
English form Mirtoan Sea
Miruro Moz. **129** A8
Miryalaguda India *see* **Mirialguda**
Miryang S. Korea **83** C6
Mirzachirla Turkm. *see* **Murzechirla**
Mirzachul Uzbek. *see* **Gulistan**
Mirzapur India **97** D4
Misaki Japan **91** C8
Misakubo Japan **91** E7
Misantla Mex. **185** F5
Misau Nigeria **125** H4
Misawa Japan **90** G4
Miscou Island Canada **169** H4
Misehkow *r.* Canada **168** B3
Misery, Mount St Kitts and Nevis **187** H3
Misgar Jammu and Kashmir **96** B1
Mish, Kūh-e *hill* Iran **100** D3
Misha India **95** G5
Mişhaf, Rujm al *hill* Iraq **109** O6
Mishamattawa *r.* Canada **168** C2
Mishan China **82** C3
Mishāsh al Ashāwī *well* Saudi Arabia **105** E2
Mishāsh al Hādī *well* Saudi Arabia **105** E2
Mishāsh az Zuayyinī *well* Saudi Arabia **105** E2
Mishawaka U.S.A. **172** G9
Misheronskiy Rus. Fed. **43** U6
Mishibishu Lake Canada **172** H2
Mishima Japan **91** F7
Mi-shima *i.* Japan **91** B7
Mishlah, Khashm *hill* Saudi Arabia **105** D3
Mishmi Hills India **97** G3
Mishutki Belarus **43** L6
Misilmeri *Sicilia* Italy **57** F10
Misima Island P.N.G. **149** G1
Misiones *prov.* Arg. **204** G2
Misis Dağ *hills* Turkey **108** G1
Miskah Saudi Arabia **104** C2
Miskitos, Cayos *is* Nicaragua **186** C4
Miskitos, Costa de *coastal area* Nicaragua *see* **Mosquitos, Costa de**
Miskolc Hungary **49** R7
Mislinja *r.* Slovenia **56** H2
Mismā, Jibāl al *mts* Saudi Arabia **104** C2
Mismā, Tall al *hill* Jordan **109** I5
Misoöl *i.* Indon. **75** D3
Misquah Hills U.S.A. **174** B2
Misr *country* Africa *see* **Egypt**
Misrac Turkey *see* **Kurtalan**
Mişrātah Libya **120** B1
also spelt Misuratah
Misrikh India **96** D4
Missanabie Canada **173** I2
Missinaibi *r.* Canada **168** D3
Missinaibi Lake Canada **168** D3
Missinipe Canada **167** J4
Mission *r.* Australia **149** D2
Mission *SD* U.S.A. **180** G4
Mission *TX* U.S.A. **179** C7
Mission Beach Australia **149** E3
Mission Viejo U.S.A. **182** G8
Missisa *r.* Canada **168** C2
Missisa Lake Canada **168** C2
Missisicabi *r.* Canada **168** E3
Missisagi *r.* Canada **168** D4
Mississauga Canada **168** E5
Mississinewa Lake U.S.A. **172** H10

▶ **Mississippi** *r.* Canada **173** Q5
world [changes] ▶ 20–21

▶ **Mississippi** *r.* U.S.A. **179** E6
4th longest river in North America. Part of the longest (Mississippi-Missouri).
northamerica [landscapes] ▶ 156–157

Mississippi *state* U.S.A. **175** B5
Mississippi Delta U.S.A. **175** B6
Mississippi Lake Canada **173** Q5

▶ **Mississippi-Missouri** *r.* U.S.A. **179** E6
Longest river in North America and 4th in world.
northamerica [landscapes] ▶ 156–157

Mississippi Sound *sea chan.* U.S.A. **175** B6
Missolonghi Greece *see* **Mesolongi**
Missoula U.S.A. **180** D3
Missour Morocco **122** E2

▶ **Missouri** *r.* U.S.A. **178** E4
3rd longest river in North America. Part of the longest (Mississippi-Missouri).
northamerica [landscapes] ▶ 156–157

Missouri *state* U.S.A. **174** A4
Missouri Valley U.S.A. **178** D3
Mistake Creek *r.* Australia **149** E4
Mistanipisipou *r.* Canada **169** I3
Mistassibi *r.* Canada **169** F3
Mistassini Canada **169** F3
Mistassini *r.* Canada **169** F3
Mistassini, Lac *l.* Canada **169** F3
Mistastin Lake Canada **169** I2
Mistelbach Austria **49** N7
Misterbianco *Sicilia* Italy **57** H11
Mistissini Canada **169** F3
formerly known as Baie-du-Poste
Mistras *tourist site* Greece **59** D11
Misty Fiords National Monument Wilderness *nat. park* U.S.A. **164** F4
Misuratah Libya *see* **Mişrātah**
Misvær Norway **44** K2
Mita, Punta de *pt* Mex. **184** D4
Mitande Moz. **131** G2
Mitaraca *hill* Suriname **199** H4
Mitatib Sudan **121** H6
Mitchell Australia **149** E5
Mitchell *r. N.S.W.* Australia **147** G2
Mitchell *r. Qld* Australia **149** D2
Mitchell *r. Vic.* Australia **147** E4
Mitchell Canada **173** L7
Mitchell *OR* U.S.A. **180** B3
Mitchell *SD* U.S.A. **178** C3
Mitchell, Lake Australia **149** E3
Mitchell, Lake U.S.A. **172** H6
Mitchell, Mount U.S.A. **174** D5
Mitchell and Alice Rivers National Park Australia **149** D2
Mitchell Island Cook Is *see* **Nassau**
Mitchell Island Tuvalu *see* **Nukulaelae**
Mitchell Point Australia **148** A1
Mitchell Range *hills* Australia **148** B2
Mitchells Pass S. Africa **132** D10
Mitchelstown Rep. of Ireland **47** D11
Mitchinamécus, Lake Canada **173** R3
Mît Fâris Egypt **108** C6
Mît Ghamr Egypt **108** C7
Mithapur India **96** A5
Mitha Tiwana Pak. **101** H3
Mithi Pak. **101** G5
Mithimna Greece *see* **Mithymna**
Mithrani Can *canal* Pak. **101** G5
Mithymna Greece **59** H9
also spelt Mithimna
Mitig, Gebel *mts* Egypt **104** A2
Mitilini Greece *see* **Mytilini**
Mitishkino Rus. Fed. **43** O7
Mitkof Island U.S.A. **166** C3
Mito Japan **91** G6
Mitomoni Tanz. **129** B7
Mitre *mt.* N.Z. **152** J8
Mitre, Peninsula *pen.* Arg. **205** D9
Mitre Island Solomon Is **145** G3
Mitrofanovka Rus. Fed. **41** F6
Mitrovica *Kosovo, Srbija* Yugo. *see* **Kosovska Mitrovica**
Mitsamiouli Comoros **129** D7
Mitsikeli *mt.* Greece **59** B9
Mitsinjo Madag. **131** [inset] J3
Mits'iwa Eritrea *see* **Massawa**
Mitsuke Japan **90** F6
Mitsushima Japan **91** A7
Mittagong Australia **147** F3
Mittelelbe *park* Germany **49** I4
Mittenwald Germany **48** I8
Mittersill Austria **49** J8
Mitterteich Germany **49** J6
Mittet Norway **44** I3
Mittimatalik Canada *see* **Pond Inlet**
Mittleres Saaletal *park* Germany **48** I5
Mitú Col. **198** D4
Mituas Col. **198** D4
Mitumba, Chaîne des *mts* Dem. Rep. Congo **127** E7
Mitumba, Monts *mts* Dem. Rep. Congo **126** F5
Mitwaba Dem. Rep. Congo **127** E7
Mît Yazîd Egypt **108** C7
Mitzic Gabon **126** A4
Miughalaigh *i.* U.K. *see* **Mingulay**
Miura Japan **91** F7
Mius *r.* Rus. Fed. **41** F7
Mixian China *see* **Xinmi**
Miya-gawa *r.* Japan **91** E7
Miyagi *pref.* Japan **90** G5
Miyah, Wādī al *watercourse* Saudi Arabia **104** C2
Miyāh, Wādī al *watercourse* Syria **109** K3
Miyake-jima *i.* Japan **91** F7
Miyako Japan **90** G5
Miyakoji Japan **90** G6
Miyakonojō Japan **91** B9
Miyako-rettō *is* Japan **81** K8
Miyaluo China **86** B2
Miyaly Kazakh. **102** C2
Miyang China *see* **Mile**
Miyani India **96** A5
Miyanojō Japan **91** B9
Miyanoura-dake *mt.* Japan **91** B9
Miyazaki Japan **91** B9
Miyazaki *pref.* Japan **91** B8
Miyazu Japan **91** D7
Miyi China **86** B3
also known as Panlian
Miyoshi Japan **91** C7
Miyun China **85** H3
Miyun Shuiku *resr* China **85** H3
Mīzānī Afgh. **101** F3
Mīzan Teferī Eth. **128** B3
Mizar Turkey *see* **Karakeçi**
Mizdah Libya **120** B2
Mizen Head Rep. of Ireland **47** C12
Mizhevichy Belarus **42** G9
Mizhhir"ya Ukr. **53** G2
Mizhi China **85** F4
Mizil Romania **58** H3
Miziya Bulg. **58** E5
Mizo Hills *state* India *see* **Mizoram**
Mizoram *state* India **97** G5
formerly known as Mizo Hills
Mizque Bol. **200** D4
Mizque *r.* Bol. **200** D4
Mizusawa Japan **90** G5
Mjelde Norway **44** K2
Mjølby Sweden **45** K4
Mjølfell Norway **45** I3
Mjøsa *l.* Norway **45** J3
Mkambati S. Africa **133** N8
Mkambati Nature Reserve S. Africa **133** O8
Mkata Tanz. **129** C6
Mkhaya Nature Reserve Swaziland **133** P3
Mkhondvo *r.* Swaziland **133** P3
Mkoani Tanz. **129** C6
Mkokotoni Tanz. **129** C6
Mkomazi Game Reserve *nature res.* Tanz. **129** C5
Mkujani Tanz. **129** C6
Mkumvura Zimbabwe *see* **Mukumbura**
Mkunja Tanz. **129** C7
Mkurusi Tanz. **129** B6
Mkushi Zambia **127** F8
Mkuze S. Africa **133** Q4
Mkuze *r.* S. Africa **133** Q4
Mkuzi Game Reserve *nature res.* S. Africa **133** Q4
Mladá Boleslav Czech Rep. **49** L5
Mladenovac *Srbija* Yugo. **58** B4
Mlala Hills Tanz. **129** A6
Mlandizi Tanz. **129** C6
Mlaula *r.* Swaziland **133** Q3
Mlava *r.* Yugo. **58** C4
Mława Poland **49** R2
Mlawula Nature Reserve Swaziland **133** Q3
Mlilwane Nature Reserve Swaziland **133** P3
Mljet *i.* Croatia **56** J6
Mljet *nat. park* Croatia **56** J6
Mljetski Kanal *sea chan.* Croatia **56** J6
Mlowoka Tanz. **129** C7
Mlumati *r.* S. Africa **133** P2
also known as Lomati
Mlungisi S. Africa **133** K8
Mmabatho S. Africa **133** J2
Mmadinare Botswana **131** E4
Mmashoro Botswana **131** E4
Mmathethe Botswana **131** E5
Mnjoli Dam Swaziland **133** P3
Mnogovershinnyy Rus. Fed. **82** E1
Mo Norway **45** I3
Moa *r.* Brazil **200** B1
Moa Cuba **187** E2
Moa *i.* Indon. **75** D5
Moab *reg.* Jordan **108** G6
also known as Mu'āb, Jibāl
Moab U.S.A. **183** O3
Moabi Gabon **126** A5
Moaco *r.* Brazil **200** C1
Moa Island Australia **73** J9
Moala *i.* Fiji **145** G3
Moamba Moz. **131** G5
Moana N.Z. **153** F10
Moanda Gabon **126** B5
Moate Rep. of Ireland **47** E10
Moatize Moz. **131** G3
Moba Dem. Rep. Congo **127** F6
formerly known as Baudouinville
Mobara Japan **91** G7
Mobārakābād Iran **100** C4
Mobārakeh Iran **100** B3
Mobaye Cent. Afr. Rep. **126** D3
Mobayembongo Dem. Rep. Congo *see* **Mobayi-Mbongo**
Mobayi-Mbongo Dem. Rep. Congo **126** D3
also spelt Mobayembongo; *formerly known as* Banzyville
Mobeka Dem. Rep. Congo **126** C4
Moberly U.S.A. **178** D4
Moberly Lake Canada **166** F4
Mobert Canada **172** H2
Mobile *AL* U.S.A. **175** B6
Mobile *AZ* U.S.A. **183** L8
Mobile Bay U.S.A. **175** B6
Mobile Point U.S.A. **175** C6
Moble *watercourse* Australia **147** E1
Mobo Phil. **74** B3
Mobridge U.S.A. **178** B2
Mobutu, Lake Dem. Rep. Congo/Uganda *see* **Albert, Lake**
Mobutu Sese Seko, Lake Dem. Rep. Congo/Uganda *see* **Albert, Lake**
Moca Geçidi *pass* Turkey **108** E1
Mocajuba Brazil **202** B2
Moçambicano, Planalto *plat.* Moz. **131** H2
Moçambique *country* Africa *see* **Mozambique**
Moçambique Moz. **131** I2
Mocambo, Porto *b.* Moz. **131** I2
Moçâmedes Angola *see* **Namibe**
Moccasin U.S.A. **182** D4
Moccasin Gap U.S.A. **176** C9
Mộc Châu Vietnam **78** D3
Mocha *r.* Rus. Fed. **43** S6
Mocha Yemen **104** C5
also spelt Al Mukhā
Mocha, Isla *i.* Chile **204** B5
Mochily Rus. Fed. **43** T7
Mochirma, Parque Nacional *nat. park* Venez. **199** E2
Mochudi Botswana **131** E5
Mocimboa da Praia Moz. **129** D7
Mocimboa do Rovuma Moz. **129** C7
Mociu Romania **58** F2
Möckeln *l.* Sweden **45** K4
Möckern-Magdeburger Forst *park* Germany **49** J3
Mocksville U.S.A. **174** D5
Mocó *r.* Brazil **199** E5
Mocoa Col. **198** B4
Mococa Brazil **206** G8
Mocorito Mex. **184** D3
Moctezuma *Chihuahua* Mex. **184** D2
Moctezuma *San Luis Potosí* Mex. **185** E4
Moctezuma *Sonora* Mex. **184** C2
Moctezuma *r.* Mex. **181** E7
Mocuba Moz. **131** H3
Mocun China **87** E4
Modane France **51** M7
Modasa India **96** B5
Modder *r.* S. Africa **133** I6
Modena Italy **56** C4
historically known as Mutina
Modena U.S.A. **183** K4
Modesto U.S.A. **182** D4
Modica *Sicilia* Italy **57** G12
Mödling Austria **49** N7
Modot Mongolia **85** F2
Modriča Bos.-Herz. **56** K4
Modugno Italy **56** I7
Moe Australia **147** E4
Moebase Moz. **131** H3
Moel Sych *hill* U.K. **47** I11
Moelv Norway **45** J3
Moemaneng S. Africa **133** L5
Moen Norway **44** L1
Moengo Suriname **199** H3
Moenkopi U.S.A. **183** M5
Moenkopi Wash *r.* U.S.A. **183** M6
Moeraki Point N.Z. **153** E13
Moerewa N.Z. **152** I3
Moergestel Neth. **48** C4
Moero, Lake Dem. Rep. Congo/Zambia *see* **Mweru, Lake**
Moers Germany **48** D4
Moeswal S. Africa **132** G4
Moffat U.K. **46** I8
Moga India **96** B3

▶ **Mogadishu** Somalia **128** E4
Capital of Somalia. Also spelt Muqdisho.

Mogador Morocco *see* **Essaouira**
Mogadouro Port. **54** E3
Mogadouro, Serra de *mts* Port. **54** E3
Mogalo Dem. Rep. Congo **126** C4
Mogalturra India **94** D2
Mogami-gawa *r.* Japan **90** F5
Mogandjo Dem. Rep. Congo **126** E4
Moganyaka S. Africa **133** N1
Mogareb *watercourse* Eritrea **104** B5
Mogaung Myanmar **78** B2
Mogdy Rus. Fed. **82** D2
Mogear Alg. **123** G2
Moghrar-Foukani Alg. **123** E2
Mogi-Guaçu Brazil **206** G9
Mogilev Belarus *see* **Mahilyow**
Mogilev Oblast *admin. div.* Belarus *see* **Mahilyowskaya Voblasts'**
Mogilev Podol'skiy Ukr. *see* **Mohyliv Podil's'kyy**
Mogilevskaya Oblast' *admin. div.* Belarus *see* **Mahilyowskaya Voblasts'**
Mogilno Poland **49** O3
Mogi-Mirim Brazil **206** G9
Mogiquiçaba Brazil **207** O3
Mogocha Rus. Fed. **81** J2
Mogocha *r.* Rus. Fed. **43** R4
Mogod *mts* Tunisia **123** H1
Mogoditshane Botswana **131** E5
Mogogh Sudan **128** A2
Mogok Myanmar **78** B3
Mogollon Plateau U.S.A. **183** M7
Mogontiacum Germany *see* **Mainz**
Mogor Eth. **128** D3
Mogoro *r. Sardegna* Italy **57** A9
Mogoşeşti Romania **58** I1
Mogoytuy Rus. Fed. **85** G1
Mogroum Chad **126** B2
Moguer Spain **54** E7
Moguqi China **85** I2
Mogwase S. Africa **133** L2
Mogzón Rus. Fed. **85** G1
Mohács Hungary **49** P9
Mohaka *r.* N.Z. **152** K7
Mohala India **94** D1
Mohale's Hoek Lesotho **133** L7
Mohall U.S.A. **178** B1
Mohammad Iran **100** D3
Moḩammadābād Iran *see* **Darreh Gaz**
Mohammadia Alg. **123** F2
formerly known as Perrégaux
Mohammad Reza Shah Pahlavi Dam *resr* Iran *see* **Dez, Sadd-e**
Mohan *r.* India/Nepal **96** D3
Mohana India **96** C4
Mohanganj Bangl. **97** F4
Mohave, Lake U.S.A. **183** J6
Mohave Mountains U.S.A. **183** J7
Mohawk U.S.A. **172** E3
Mohawk *r.* U.S.A. **177** L3
Mohawk Mountains U.S.A. **183** K9
Mohe China **82** A1
also known as Xilinji
Mohed Sweden **45** L3
Moheda Sweden **45** K4
Mohéli *i.* Comoros *see* **Mwali**
Mohembo Botswana **130** D3
Mohenjo Daro *tourist site* Pak. **101** G5
Möhkö Fin. **44** O3
Möhne *r.* Germany **48** E4
Mohnyin Myanmar **78** B2
Moho Peru **200** C3
Mohol India **94** B2
Mohon Peak U.S.A. **183** K7
Mohoro Tanz. **129** C7
Mohyliv Podil's'kyy Ukr. **41** C6
also spelt Mogilev Podol'skiy
Moi *Rogaland* Norway **45** I4
Moi *Vest-Agder* Norway **45** I4
Moijabana Botswana **131** E4
Moincêr China **89** C6
Moinda China **89** E6
also known as Zara
Moine Moz. **133** Q1
Moineşti Romania **58** H2
Moinkum *des.* Kazakh. *see* **Moyynkum, Peski**
Mointy Kazakh. *see* **Moyynty**
Moirai Greece *see* **Moires**
Mo i Rana Norway **44** K2
Moirang India **97** G4
Moires Greece **59** F13
also known as Moirai
Mõisaküla Estonia **42** G3
Moisie Canada **169** H3
Moisie *r.* Canada **169** H3
Moissac France **50** H8
Moïssala Chad **126** C2
Moitaco Venez. **199** E3
Mojácar Spain **55** J7
Mojados Spain **54** G3
Mojave U.S.A. **182** F6
Mojave *r.* U.S.A. **183** G7
Mojave Desert U.S.A. **183** G6
Mojerda *r.* Tunisia **57** C11
Mojiang China **86** B4
also known as Jiulian
Moji das Cruzes Brazil **207** G10
Moji-Guaçu *r.* Brazil **206** E7
Mojikō Japan **91** B8
Mojkovac *Crna Gora* Yugo. **58** A6
Mojo Bol. **200** D5
Mojo Eth. **128** C3
Mojokerto Indon. **77** F4
Mojones, Cerro *mt.* Arg. **204** D2
Mojos, Llanos de *plain* Bol. **200** D3
Mojo Shet' *r.* Eth. **128** D3
Mojotoro Bol. **200** D4
Moju Brazil **202** B2
Mōka Japan **91** G6
Mokai N.Z. **152** J6
Mokama India **97** E4
Mokambo Dem. Rep. Congo **127** F8
Mokaria Dem. Rep. Congo **126** D4
Mokau N.Z. **152** I6
Mokau *r.* N.Z. **152** I6
Mokéko Congo **126** B4
Mokelumne *r.* U.S.A. **182** C3
Mokelumne Aqueduct *canal* U.S.A. **182** C3
Mokhoabong Pass Lesotho **133** M6
Mokhotlong Lesotho **133** N6
Mokhovoye Rus. Fed. **43** R9
Mokhsogollokh Rus. Fed. **39** M3
Mokimbo Dem. Rep. Congo **127** F6
Mokhnine Tunisia **57** C13
Mokohinau Islands N.Z. **152** J3
Mokokchung India **97** G4
Mokolo Cameroon **125** I4
Mokolo *r.* S. Africa **131** E4
Mokoreta N.Z. **153** D14
Mokotua N.Z. **153** C14
Mokp'o S. Korea **83** B6
Mokra Gora *mts* Yugo. **58** B6
Mokrin *Vojvodina, Srbija* Yugo. **58** B3
Mokrous Rus. Fed. **102** A2
Moksha *r.* Rus. Fed. **40** G5
Mokshan Rus. Fed. **41** H5
Möktama Myanmar *see* **Martaban**
Mokundurra India *see* **Mukandwara**
Mokwa Nigeria **125** G4
Mokwallo S. Africa **133** L4
Mola di Bari Italy **56** J7
Molaly Kazakh. *see* **Mulaly**
Molango Mex. **185** F4
Molaoi Greece **59** D12
Molat *i.* Croatia **56** G4
Molatón *mt.* Spain **55** J6
Moldary Kazakh. **103** J2
Moldava nad Bodvou Slovakia **49** R7
Moldavia *country* Europe *see* **Moldova**
Moldavskaya S.S.R. *country* Europe *see* **Moldova**
Molde Norway **44** I3
Moldefjorden *inlet* Norway **44** I3
Moldjord Norway **44** K2

▶ **Moldova** *country* Europe **41** C6
formerly known as Moldavia or Moldavskaya S.S.R.
europe [countries] ▶ 32–35

Moldova *r.* Romania **58** H1
Moldova Nouă Romania **58** C4
Moldoveanu, Vârful *mt.* Romania **58** F3
Moldovei, Podişul *plat.* Romania **58** H1
Moldovei Centrale, Podişul *plat.* Moldova **58** I1
Moldovei de Sud, Cîmpia *plain* Moldova **58** J2
Molega Lake Canada **169** H4
Molegbe Dem. Rep. Congo **126** D3
Molen *r.* S. Africa **133** M4
Mole National Park Ghana **125** E4
Molepolole Botswana **131** E5
Molėtai Lith. **42** G6
Molfetta Italy **56** I7
Molières France **50** H8
Molina Arg. **204** C4
Molina de Aragón Spain **55** J4
Molina de Segura Spain **55** J6
Moline U.S.A. **174** B3
Molinella Italy **56** D4
Molinos Arg. **204** D2
Molins de Rei Spain **55** N3
Moliro Dem. Rep. Congo **127** F7

index M

Molise admin. reg. Italy 56 G7
Molkom Sweden 45 K4
Molledo Spain 54 G1
Mol Len mt. India 97 G4
Mollendo Peru 200 C4
Mollerin, Lake salt flat Australia 151 B6
Mollerussa Spain 55 L3
Mölln Germany 48 H2
Mölnlycke Sweden 45 K4
Molochnoye Rus. Fed. 43 U2
Molodechno Belarus see Maladzyechna
Molodezhnaya research station Antarctica 223 D2
Molod'kovo Rus. Fed. 43 N8
Molodoy Tud Rus. Fed. 43 O5
Mologa r. Rus. Fed. 43 S3
Molokai i. U.S.A. 181 [inset] Z1
Molokovo Rus. Fed. 43 R3
Moloma r. Rus. Fed. 40 I4
Molong Australia 147 F3
Molopo watercourse Botswana/S. Africa 132 E5
Moloporivier Botswana 133 I2
Molos Greece 59 D10
Molotov Rus. Fed. see Perm'
Molotovsk Kyrg. see Kayyngdy
Molotovsk Rus. Fed. see Severodvinsk
Molotovsk Rus. Fed. see Nolinsk
Molotovskaya Oblast' admin. div. Rus. Fed. see Permskaya Oblast'
Moloundou Cameroon 125 I6
Molowaie Dem. Rep. Congo 127 D6
Molsheim France 51 N4
Molson Lake Canada 167 L4
Molteno S. Africa 133 K8
Moltenopass pass S. Africa 132 G9
Molu i. Indon. 73 H8
Moluccas is Indon. 75 C3
also known as Malukken or Maluku; historically known as Spice Islands
Molucca Sea Indon. 75 C3
Moluengo mt. Spain 55 J5
Molumbo Moz. 131 H2
Molvotitsy Rus. Fed. 43 N4
Molwe Dem. Rep. Congo 127 E7
Moma Moz. 131 H3
Momba Australia 147 D2
Mombaça Brazil 202 E3
Mombasa Kenya 129 C5
Mombenzélé Dem. Rep. Congo 126 C4
Mombetsu Japan see Monbetsu
Mombetsu Japan see Monbetsu
Momboyo r. Dem. Rep. Congo 126 C5
Mombuca, Serra da hills Brazil 206 A5
Momchilgrad Bulg. 58 G7
Momeik Myanmar see Mông Mit
Momence U.S.A. 172 F9
Momi, Ra's pt Yemen 105 F5
Momotombo, Volcán vol. Nicaragua 186 B4
Mompog Passage Phil. 74 B3
Mompono Dem. Rep. Congo 126 D4
Mompós Col. 198 C2
Momskiy Khrebet mts Rus. Fed. 39 O3
Møn i. Denmark 45 K5
Mon India 97 G4
Mon state Myanmar 78 B4
Mona U.S.A. 183 M2
Mona, Isla i. Puerto Rico 187 G3
Monaca U.S.A. 176 E5
Monach Islands U.K. 46 E6
also known as Heisker Islands
▶Monaco country Europe 51 N9
historically known as Portus Herculis Monoeci
europe [countries] ▶ 32–35
Monadhliath Mountains U.K. 46 H6
Monagas state Venez. 199 E2
Monaghan Rep. of Ireland 47 F9
also spelt Muineachán
Monahans U.S.A. 179 B6
Mona Passage Dom. Rep./Puerto Rico 187 F3
Monapo Moz. 131 I2
Mona Quimbundo Angola 127 C7
Monar, Loch l. U.K. 46 G6
Monarch Mountain Canada 166 E5
Monarch Pass U.S.A. 181 F5
Monashee Mountains Canada 166 G5
Monasterio del Suso tourist site Spain 55 I2
Monastery of St Catherine tourist site Egypt 108 E9
Monastery of St Anthony tourist site Egypt 108 D9
Monastery of St Paul tourist site Egypt 108 D9
Monastir Macedonia see Bitola
Monastir Tunisia 123 H2
Monastyrishche Ukr. see Monastyrshche
Monastyrshchina Rus. Fed. 43 M7
Monastyrshche Ukr. 41 D6
also spelt Monastyrishche
Monavale N.Z. 153 E12
Monbetsu Hokkaidō Japan 90 H2
also spelt Mombetsu
Monbetsu Hokkaidō Japan 90 H3
also spelt Mombetsu
Monboré Cameroon 125 I4
Moncalieri Italy 51 N7
Moncalvo mt. Spain 54 E2
Monchegorsk Rus. Fed. 44 P2
Mönchengladbach Germany 48 D4
formerly spelt München-Gladbach
Monchique Port. 54 C7
Monchique, Serra de mts Port. 54 C7
Moncks Corner U.S.A. 175 D5
Monclova Mex. 185 E3
Moncton Canada 169 H4
Mondai Brazil 203 A8
Mondego r. Port. 54 C4
Mondego, Cabo c. Port. 54 C4
Mondimbi Dem. Rep. Congo 126 D4
Mondim de Basto Port. 54 D3
Mondjamboli Dem. Rep. Congo 126 D4
Mondlo S. Africa 133 O4
Mondo Chad 120 B6
Mondolfo Italy 56 F5
Mondoñedo Spain 54 D1
Mondovì Italy 51 N8
Mondovi U.S.A. 172 B6
Mondragón Spain see Arrasate
Mondragone Italy 56 F7
Mondsee l. Austria 49 K8
Mondúver hill Spain 55 K5
Monee U.S.A. 172 F9
Monemvasia Greece 59 E12
also known as Malvasia
Moneron, Ostrov i. Rus. Fed. 82 F3
Monessen U.S.A. 176 F5
Monesterio Spain 54 E6
Monet Canada 173 R2
Moneta U.S.A. 176 F8
Monéteau France 51 J5
Monfalcone Italy 56 F3
Monflanquin France 50 G8
Monfort Col. 198 D4
Monforte Port. 54 D5
Monforte Spain 54 D2
Monfurado hill Port. 54 C6
Monga Katanga Dem. Rep. Congo 127 E7
Monga Orientale Dem. Rep. Congo 126 D3
Mongaguá Brazil 206 G11
Mongala r. Dem. Rep. Congo 126 C4
Mongar Bhutan 97 F4
Mongbwalu Dem. Rep. Congo 126 F4
Mông Cai Vietnam 78 D3
Mongemputu Dem. Rep. Congo 126 D5
Mongers Lake salt flat Australia 151 B6
Mong Hang Myanmar 78 B3
Monghidoro Italy 56 D4
Mong Hpayak Myanmar 78 B3
Mong Hsat Myanmar 78 B3
Mong Hsu Myanmar 78 B3
Monghyr India see Munger
Mong Kung Myanmar 78 B3
Mong Kyawt Myanmar 78 B4
Mong La Myanmar 78 C3
Mong Lin Myanmar 78 C3
Mong Loi Myanmar 78 C3
Mong Long Myanmar 78 B3
Mông Mir Myanmar 78 B3
also known as Momeik
Mong Nai Myanmar 78 B3
Mong Nawng Myanmar 78 B3
Mongo Chad 120 C6
▶Mongolia country Asia 84 C2
known as Mongol Uls in Mongolian; formerly known as Outer Mongolia
asia [countries] ▶ 64–67
Mongolküre China see Zhaosu
Mongol Uls country Asia see Mongolia
Mongomo Equat. Guinea 125 H6
Mongonu Nigeria 125 I3
Mongora Pak. 101 H3
Mongororo Chad 120 D6
Mongoumba Cent. Afr. Rep. 126 C4
Mong Pan Myanmar 78 B3
Mong Pat Myanmar 78 B3
Mong Ping Myanmar 78 B3
Mongu Zambia 127 D8
Mongua Angola 127 B9
Mong Un Myanmar 78 C3
Mong Yai Myanmar 78 B3
Mong Yang Myanmar 78 B3
Mong Yawng Myanmar 78 C3
Mong Yu Myanmar 78 B3
Mönhbulag Mongolia 84 D2
Monhegan Island U.S.A. 177 P2
Mönh Hayrhan Uul mt. Mongolia 84 A2
Monico U.S.A. 172 D5
Moniquirá Col. 198 C3
Monistrol-sur-Loire France 51 K7
Monitor Mountain U.S.A. 183 H3
Monitor Range mts U.S.A. 183 H3
Moñitos Col. 198 B2
Monjolos Brazil 207 I5
Monkey Bay Malawi 129 B8
Monkey Mia Australia 151 A5
Mońki Poland 49 T2
Monkira Australia 149 D5
Monkoto Dem. Rep. Congo 126 D5
Monkton Canada 173 L7
Monmouth U.K. 47 J12
also known as Trefynwy
Monmouth CA U.S.A. 182 E5
Monmouth IL U.S.A. 174 B3
Monmouth Mountain Canada 166 F5
Monnett U.S.A. 176 B5
Mono r. Togo 125 F5
Mono, Punta del pt Nicaragua 186 C5
Mono Lake U.S.A. 182 F3
Monolithos Greece 59 I12
Monon U.S.A. 172 G10
Monona U.S.A. 172 B7
Monopoli Italy 56 J8
Monor Hungary 49 Q8
Monongahela r. U.S.A. 176 F5
Monou Chad 120 D5
Monóvar Spain 55 K6
Monowai, Lake N.Z. 153 B13
Monreal del Campo Spain 55 J4
Monreale Sicilia Italy 57 F10
Monroe GA U.S.A. 175 D5
Monroe IA U.S.A. 174 A3
Monroe LA U.S.A. 179 D5
Monroe MI U.S.A. 173 J9
Monroe NC U.S.A. 174 D5
Monroe NY U.S.A. 177 K4
Monroe UT U.S.A. 183 L3
Monroe VA U.S.A. 176 F8
Monroe WA U.S.A. 180 B3
Monroe WI U.S.A. 172 D8
Monroe Center U.S.A. 172 D6
Monroe City U.S.A. 174 B4
Monroe Lake U.S.A. 174 C4
Monroeton U.S.A. 177 I4
Monroeville AL U.S.A. 175 C6
Monroeville IN U.S.A. 176 A5
Monroeville OH U.S.A. 176 C4
▶Monrovia Liberia 124 C5
Capital of Liberia.
Mons Belgium 51 J2
Monsarás, Ponta de pt Brazil 207 N6
Monselice Italy 56 D3
Mons Klint cliff Denmark 49 J1
Mönsterås Sweden 45 L4
Montabaur Germany 48 E5
Montagu S. Africa 132 E10
Montague Canada 169 I4
Montague U.S.A. 176 C3
Montague Island U.S.A. 164 E3
Montague Range hills Australia 151 B5
Montague Sound b. Australia 150 D2
Montaigu France 50 E6
Montaigu-de-Quercy France 50 H8
Montalat r. Indon. 77 F3
Montalto mt. Italy 57 H10
Montalto di Castro Italy 56 D6
Montalto Uffugo Italy 57 I9
Montalvo Ecuador 198 B5
Montana Bulg. 58 E5
formerly known as Mikhaylovgrad
▶Montana state U.S.A. 180 E3
northamerica [environments] ▶ 162–163
Montaña de Comayagua, Parque Nacional nat. park Hond. 186 B4
Montaña de Cusuco, Parque Nacional nat. park Hond. 186 A4
Montaña de Yoro nat. park Hond. 186 B4
Montánchez hill Spain 54 E5
Montánchez, Sierra de mts Spain 54 E5
Montanha Brazil 207 M5
Montargis France 51 I5
Montauban France 50 H8
Montauk U.S.A. 177 N4
Montauk Point U.S.A. 177 N4
Mont-aux-Sources mt. Lesotho 133 M5
Montbard France 51 K5
Montbéliard France 51 M5
▶Mont Blanc mt. France/Italy 51 M7
5th highest mountain in Europe.
europe [landscapes] ▶ 30–31
Montblanc Spain 55 M3
also spelt Montblanch
Montblanch Spain see Montblanc
Montbrison France 51 K7
Montcalm U.S.A. 176 D8
Montceau-les-Mines France 51 K6
Montchanin France 51 K6
Montcuq France 50 H8
Mont-de-Marsan France 50 F9
Montdidier France 51 I3
Monte, Lago del l. Arg. 204 E5
Monteagudo Bol. 201 D4
Monte Alban tourist site Mex. 185 F5
Monte Alegre Brazil 199 H5
Monte Alegre r. Brazil 206 C4
Monte Alegre de Goiás Brazil 202 C5
Montealegre del Castillo Spain 55 J6
Monte Alegre de Minas Brazil 206 E5
Monte Aprazível Brazil 206 D7
Monte Azul Paulista Brazil 206 E7
Montebello Canada 169 F4
Montebello Islands Australia 150 A4
Montebelluna Italy 56 E3
Monte Buey Arg. 204 E4
Monte-Carlo Monaco 51 N9
English form Monte Carlo
Monte Carlo Monaco see Monte-Carlo
Monte Carmelo Brazil 206 F5
Monte Caseros Arg. 204 F3
Montecatini Terme Italy 56 C5
Montecchio Maggiore Italy 56 D3
Montech France 50 H9
Monte Christo S. Africa 131 E4
Montecito U.S.A. 182 E7
Monte Cotugna, Lago di l. Italy 57 I8
Monte Cristi Dom. Rep. 187 F3
Monte Cristi nat. park Dom. Rep. 187 F3
Montecristi Ecuador 198 A5
Monte Cristo Bol. 201 E3
Montecristo, Isola di i. Italy 56 C6
Monte da Rocha, Barragem do resr Port. 54 C7
Monte Dinero Arg. 205 C9
Monte Dourado Brazil 199 H5
Monte Escobedo Mex. 184 E4
Monte Falterona, Campigna e delle Foreste Casentinesi, Parco Nazionale del nat. park Italy 56 D5
Montefiascone Italy 56 E6
Montegiorgio Italy 56 F5
Montego Bay Jamaica 186 D3
Monte Hermoso Arg. 204 E5
Montehermoso Spain 54 E4
Monteiro Brazil 202 E3
Montejinnie Australia 148 A3
Montejunto, Serra de hill Port. 54 B5
Monte León Arg. 205 C8
Monte Líbano Col. 198 C2
Montélimar France 51 K8
historically known as Acunum Acusio
Monte Lindo r. Para. 201 F5
Montellano Spain 54 F7
Montello U.S.A. 172 D7
Montemayor, Meseta de plat. Arg. 205 D7
Montemorelos Mex. 185 F3
Montemor-o-Novo Port. 54 C6
Montendre France 50 F7
Montenegro aut. rep. Yugo. see Crna Gora
Monte Patria Chile 204 C3
Montepuez Moz. 131 H1
Montepuez r. Moz. 129 D8
Monte Quemado Arg. 204 E2
Montereau-faut-Yonne France 51 I4
Monterey Mex. see Monterrey
Monterey CA U.S.A. 182 C5
Monterey KY U.S.A. 176 A7
Monterey VA U.S.A. 176 F7
Monterey Bay U.S.A. 182 B5
Monterey Bay National Marine Sanctuary nature res. U.S.A. 182 B5
Montería Col. 198 C2
Monteriggioni Italy 56 D5
Montero Bol. 201 E4
Monteros Arg. 204 D2
Monterotondo Italy 56 E6
Monterrey Baja California Norte Mex. 183 I9
Monterrey Nuevo León Mex. 185 E3
also spelt Monterey
Montes Altos Brazil 202 C3
Montesano U.S.A. 180 B3
Montesano sulla Marcellana Italy 57 H8
Monte Sant'Angelo Italy 56 H7
Monte Santo Brazil 202 E4
Monte Santo de Minas Brazil 206 G8
Monte Santu, Capo di c. Sardegna Italy 57 B8
Montes Claros Brazil 202 D6
Montesilvano Italy 56 G6
Montesquieu-Volvestre France 50 H9
▶Montevideo Uruguay 204 F4
Capital of Uruguay.
Montevideo U.S.A. 178 D2
Monte Vista U.S.A. 181 F5
Montezinho, Parque Natural de nature res. Port. 54 E3
Montezuma U.S.A. 174 A3
Montezuma Creek U.S.A. 183 O4
Montezuma Creek r. U.S.A. 183 O4
Montezuma Peak U.S.A. 183 G4
Montfort-le-Gesnois France 50 G4
Montfragüe, Parque Natural de nature res. Spain 54 F5
Montgomery U.K. 47 I11
also known as Trefaldwyn
▶Montgomery AL U.S.A. 175 C5
State capital of Alabama.
Montgomery PA U.S.A. 177 I4
Montgomery WV U.S.A. 176 D7
Montgomery City U.S.A. 174 B4
Montgomery Islands Australia 150 C2
Monthey Switz. 51 M6
Monti Sardegna Italy 57 B8
Monticello AR U.S.A. 175 B5
Monticello FL U.S.A. 175 D6
Monticello GA U.S.A. 175 D5
Monticello IA U.S.A. 172 B8
Monticello IL U.S.A. 174 B3
Monticello IN U.S.A. 174 C3
Monticello KY U.S.A. 176 A9
Monticello MO U.S.A. 174 B3
Monticello MS U.S.A. 175 B6
Monticello NY U.S.A. 177 K4
Monticello UT U.S.A. 183 O4
Monticello WI U.S.A. 172 D8
Montichiari Italy 56 C3
Montiel, Cuchilla de hills Arg. 204 F3
Montier-en-Der France 51 K4
Montignac France 50 H7
Montigny, Lac de l. Canada 173 P2
Montijo Port. 54 C6
Montijo Spain 54 E6
Montilla Spain 54 G7
Monti Sibillini, Parco Nazionale dei nat. park Italy 56 F6
Montivilliers France 50 G3
Mont-Joli Canada 169 G3
Mont-Laurier Canada 168 F4
Mont Louis Canada 169 H3
Montluçon France 51 I6
Montmagny Canada 169 G4
Montmélian France 51 M7
Montmirail France 51 J4
Montmoreau-St-Cybard France 50 G7
Montmorillon France 50 G6
Monto Australia 149 F5
Montoire-sur-le-Loir France 50 G5
Montoro Spain 54 G6
Montour Falls U.S.A. 177 I3
Montoursville U.S.A. 177 I4
Mont Peko, Parc National du nat. park Côte d'Ivoire 124 D5
Montpelier ID U.S.A. 180 E4
Montpelier IN U.S.A. 172 H10
Montpelier OH U.S.A. 176 A4
▶Montpelier VT U.S.A. 177 M1
State capital of Vermont.
Montpellier France 51 J9
Montpezat-de-Quercy France 50 H8
Montpon-Ménestérol France 50 G7
Montréal Canada 169 F4
English form Montreal; historically known as Ville-Marie
Montreal Canada see Montréal
Montreal r. Ont. Canada 168 C4
Montreal r. Ont. Canada 168 E4
Montreal U.S.A. 172 C4
Montréal-Dorval airport Canada 169 F4
Montreal Island Canada 173 I3
Montreal Lake Canada 167 J4
Montreal Lake l. Canada 167 J4
Montréal-Mirabel airport Canada 169 F4
Montreal River Canada 168 C4
Montreuil France 50 H2
Montreux Switz. 51 M6
Montrose well S. Africa 132 E3
Montrose U.K. 46 J7
Montrose CO U.S.A. 181 F5
Montrose MI U.S.A. 173 J7
Montrose PA U.S.A. 177 J4
Montrose WV U.S.A. 176 F6
Monts France 50 G5
Mont-St-Aignan France 50 H3
Mont-St-Michel, Baie du b. France 50 E4
Montsalvy France 51 I8
Mont Sangbé, Parc National du nat. park Côte d'Ivoire 124 D5
Montseny, Parque Natural del nature res. Spain 55 N3
▶Montserrat terr. West Indies 187 H3
United Kingdom Overseas Territory.
oceania [countries] ▶ 138–139
Mont St Michel tourist site France see Le Mont-St-Michel
Montuosa, Isla i. Panama 186 C6
Montvale U.S.A. 176 F8
Montviel, Lac l. Canada 169 G2
Monument Draw watercourse U.S.A. 179 B5
Monument Valley reg. U.S.A. 183 N5
Monveda Dem. Rep. Congo 126 D4
Monyakeng S. Africa 133 K4
Monywa Myanmar 78 A3
Monza Italy 56 B3
Monza r. Rus. Fed. 43 V3
Monze Zambia 127 E9
Monze, Cape pt Pak. see Muari, Ras
Monzhukly Turkm. 102 C5
Monzón Peru 200 A2
Monzón Spain 55 L3
Mooi r. Kwazulu-Natal S. Africa 133 O5
Mooi r. North West S. Africa 133 K3
Mooifontein Namibia 132 A3
Mooirivier S. Africa 133 O6
Mookane Botswana 131 E4
Moolawatana Australia 146 C2
Moomba Australia 146 D2
Moomin Creek r. Australia 147 F2
Moonbi Range mts Australia 147 F2
Moonda Lake salt flat Australia 149 D5
Moonie Australia 147 F1
Moonie r. Australia 147 F2
Moonta Australia 146 C3
Moora Australia 151 B6
Mooraberree Australia 149 D5
Moorcroft U.S.A. 180 F3
Moordenaarsnek pass S. Africa 133 M7
Moordorf (Südbrookmerland) Germany 48 E2
Moore r. Australia 151 A6
Moore U.S.A. 180 E3
Moore, Lake salt flat Australia 151 B6
Moore Embayment b. Antarctica 223 K1
Moorefield U.S.A. 176 G6
Moore Haven U.S.A. 175 D7
Moore Reef Australia 149 F3
Moore Reservoir U.S.A. 177 N1
Moore River National Park Australia 151 A6
Moorfoot Hills U.K. 46 I8
Moorhead U.S.A. 178 C2
Moornanyah Lake imp. l. Australia 147 D3
Mooroopna Australia 147 E4
Moorpark U.S.A. 182 F7
Moorreesburg S. Africa 132 C10
Moorrinya National Park Australia 149 E4
Moosburg an der Isar Germany 48 I7
Moose r. Canada 168 D3
Moose Factory Canada 168 D3
Moosehead Lake U.S.A. 174 G2
Moose Jaw Canada 167 J5
Moose Jaw r. Canada 167 J5
Moose Lake U.S.A. 174 A2
Moose Mountain Creek r. Canada 167 K5
Moose River Canada 168 D3
Moosilauke, Mount U.S.A. 177 N1
Moosomin Canada 167 K5
Moosonee Canada 168 D3
Mootwingee National Park Australia 147 D2
Mopane S. Africa 131 F4
Mopeia Moz. 131 G3
Mopipi Botswana 131 E4
Mopti Mali 124 D3
Mopti admin. reg. Mali 124 E3
Moqatta Sudan 104 A5
Moquegua Peru 200 C4
Moquegua dept Peru 200 C4
Mór Hungary 49 P8
Mora Cameroon 125 I4
Mora Port. 54 C6
Mora Spain 54 H5
Mora Sweden 45 K3
Mora MN U.S.A. 174 A2
Mora NM U.S.A. 181 F6
Mora r. U.S.A. 181 F6
Mora, Cerro mt. Arg./Chile 204 C4
Morača r. Yugo. 58 A6
Morach r. Belarus 42 I9
Morad r. Pak. 101 F4
Moradabad India 96 C3
Morada Nova Amazonas Brazil 200 C1
Morada Nova Ceará Brazil 202 E3
Morada Nova de Minas Brazil 207 H5
Morafenobe Madag. 131 [inset] J3
Morąg Poland 49 Q2
Mórahalom Hungary 49 Q9
formerly known as Aslóközpont
Moraine Lake Canada 167 J1
Moraleda, Canal sea chan. Chile 205 B7
Moraleja Spain 54 E4
Morales Guat. 185 H6
Moram India 94 C2
Moramanga Madag. 131 [inset] K3
Moran MI U.S.A. 173 I5
Moran WY U.S.A. 180 E4
Moranbah Australia 149 F4
Morang Nepal see Biratnagar
Morangas Brazil 206 A6
Moranhat India 97 G4
Morant Cays is Jamaica 186 E3
Morant Point Jamaica 186 D3
Morappur India 94 C3
Morar, Loch l. U.K. 46 G7
Moratalla Spain 55 J6
Moratuwa Sri Lanka 94 C5
Morava reg. Czech Rep. see Moravia
Morava r. Europe 49 N7
also known as March
Moravato Madag. 131 [inset] K2
Moraveh Tappeh Iran 100 C2
Moravia reg. Czech Rep. 49 O6
also known as Morava; formerly known as Mähren
Moravia U.S.A. 177 I3
Moravian Falls U.S.A. 176 D9
Moravica r. Yugo. 58 B5
Moravica r. Yugo. 58 C5
Moravice r. Czech Rep. 49 O6
Moravská Třebová Czech Rep. 49 N6
Moravské Budějovice Czech Rep. 49 M6
Moravskoslezské Beskydy mts Czech Rep. 49 P6
Morawa Australia 151 A6
Morawhanna Guyana 199 G2
Moray Firth b. U.K. 46 H6
Moray Range hills Australia 148 A2
Morbach Germany 48 E6
Morbegno Italy 56 B2
Morbi India 96 A5
formerly spelt Morvi
Mörbylånga Sweden 45 L4
Morcenx France 50 F8
Morcillo Mex. 184 D3
Mordaga China 85 I1
Mor Dağı mt. Turkey 107 F3
Mordelles France 50 E4
Morden Canada 167 L5
Mordovia aut. rep. Rus. Fed. see Mordoviya, Respublika
Mordoviya, Respublika aut. rep. Rus. Fed. 41 H5
English form Mordovia or Mordvinia; formerly known as Mordovskaya A.S.S.R.
Mordovo Rus. Fed. 41 G5
Mordovskaya A.S.S.R. aut. rep. Rus. Fed. see Mordoviya, Respublika
Mordves Rus. Fed. 43 T7
Mordvinia aut. rep. Rus. Fed. see Mordoviya, Respublika
Mordy Poland 49 T3
Moreau r. U.S.A. 178 B2
Moreau, South Fork r. U.S.A. 178 B2
Morecambe U.K. 47 J9
Morecambe Bay U.K. 47 I9
Moree Australia 147 F2
Morehead P.N.G. 73 J8
Morehead U.S.A. 176 B7
Morehead City U.S.A. 174 E5
Moreira Brazil 199 F5
More-Iz, Gora hill Rus. Fed. 40 L1
Morel r. India 96 C4
Moreland U.S.A. 176 A8
Morelia Col. 198 C4
Morelia Mex. 185 E5
Morella Australia 149 D4
Morella Spain 55 K4
Morelos state Mex. 185 F5
Moremi Wildlife Reserve nature res. Botswana 130 D3
Morena India 96 C4
Morena, Sierra mts Spain 54 E7
formerly known as Mariánica, Cordillera
Morenci U.S.A. 183 O8
Moreni Romania 58 G4
Moreno Mex. 184 C2
Moreno Valley U.S.A. 183 G8
Møre og Romsdal county Norway 44 I3
Moreru r. Brazil 201 F2
Mores Sardegna Italy 57 A8
Moresby, Mount Canada 166 D4
Moresby Island Canada 166 D4
Moreton Bay Australia 147 G1
Moreton Island Australia 147 G1
Moreuil France 51 I3
Moreyu r. Rus. Fed. 40 K1
Morez France 51 M6
Morfou Cyprus 108 D2
also known as Güzelyurt; also spelt Morphou
Morfou Bay Cyprus 108 D2
Morgam-Viibus hill Fin. 44 N1
Morgan Australia 146 C3
Morgan U.S.A. 176 A7
Morgan, Mount U.S.A. 182 F4
Morgan City U.S.A. 175 B6
Morgan Hill U.S.A. 182 C4
Morgans Corner U.S.A. 177 I9
Morganton U.S.A. 174 D5
Morgantown KY U.S.A. 174 C4
Morgantown WV U.S.A. 176 F6
Morgenzon S. Africa 133 N3
Morges Switz. 51 M6
Morgex Italy 51 N7
Morhar r. India 97 E4
Mori China 88 E3
Mori Japan 90 G3
Moriah, Mount U.S.A. 183 J2
Moriarty U.S.A. 181 F6
Moriarty's Range hills Australia 147 E2
Moribaya Guinea 124 C4
Morice Lake Canada 166 E4
Moricetown Canada 166 E4
Morichal Col. 198 D4
Moricsalas rezervāts nature res. Latvia 42 D4
Morija Lesotho 133 L6
Moriki Nigeria 125 G3
Morin Dawa China see Nirji
Morine pass Bos.-Herz. 56 K5
Morioka Japan 90 G5
Morire Moz. 131 G3
Morisset Australia 147 F3
Moriyama Japan 91 E7
Moriyoshi Japan 90 G4
Moriyoshi-zan vol. Japan 90 G5
Morjärv Sweden 44 M2
Morjen r. Pak. 101 E4
Morki Rus. Fed. 40 I4
Morkiny Gory Rus. Fed. 43 R4
Morlaix France 50 C4
Morley Canada 167 H5
Mormal' Belarus 43 K9
Mormant France 51 I4
Mormon Lake U.S.A. 183 M7
Mormugao India see Marmagao
Morney watercourse Australia 149 D5
Mornington, Isla i. Chile 205 B8
Mornington Island Australia 148 C3
Mornos r. Greece 59 C10
Moro Pak. 101 F5
Moro U.S.A. 180 B3
Morobe P.N.G. 73 K8
▶Morocco country Africa 122 C3
africa [countries] ▶ 114–117
Morocco U.S.A. 172 F10
Moro Creek r. U.S.A. 179 D5
Morogoro Tanz. 129 C6
Morogoro admin. reg. Tanz. 129 C7
Moro Gulf Phil. 74 B5
Morojaneng S. Africa 133 K6
Morokweng S. Africa 132 H3
Moroleón Mex. 185 E4
Moromaho i. Indon. 75 C4
Morombe Madag. 131 [inset] I4
Moromoro Bol. 201 D4
Morón Arg. 204 E4
Morón Cuba 186 D2
Mörön Mongolia 84 D1
Morona Ecuador 198 B5
Morona r. Peru 198 B6
Morona-Santiago prov. Ecuador 198 B5
Morondava Madag. 131 [inset] J4
Morón de la Frontera Spain 54 F7
Morondo Côte d'Ivoire 124 D4
Morongo Valley U.S.A. 183 H7
▶Moroni Comoros 129 D7
Capital of the Comoros.
Moroni U.S.A. 183 M2
Moron Us He r. China 84 B5
Moros r. Spain 54 G3
Morotai i. Indon. 75 D2
Morotai, Selat sea chan. Indon. 75 C2
Moroto Uganda 128 B4
Moroto, Mount Uganda 128 B4
Morotsuka Japan 91 B8
Morowai N.Z. 153 B13
Morowali Reserve nature res. Indon. 75 B3
Morozova Rus. Fed. 43 L2
Morozovo Rus. Fed. 43 V5
Morozovsk Rus. Fed. 41 G6
Morpara Brazil 202 D4
Morpeth Canada 173 L8
Morpeth U.K. 47 K8
Morphou Cyprus see Morfou
Morretes Brazil 203 B8
Morrill U.S.A. 176 A8
Morrilton U.S.A. 179 D5
Morrin Canada 167 H5
Morrinhos Brazil 206 D4
Morrinsville N.Z. 152 J5
Morris Canada 167 L5
Morris IL U.S.A. 174 B3
Morris MN U.S.A. 178 D2
Morris PA U.S.A. 177 H4
Morrisburg Canada 177 J1
▶Morris Jesup, Kap c. Greenland 165 P1
Most northerly point of North America.
Morrison U.S.A. 174 B3
Morrisons N.Z. 153 E13
Morristown AZ U.S.A. 183 L8
Morristown NJ U.S.A. 177 K5
Morristown NY U.S.A. 177 J1
Morristown TN U.S.A. 176 B9
Morrisville NY U.S.A. 177 J3
Morrisville VT U.S.A. 177 M1
Morr Morr Aboriginal Holding res. Australia 149 D3
Morro Brazil 207 I3
Morro, Punta pt Chile 204 C2
Morro Agudo Brazil 206 E7
Morro Bay U.S.A. 182 D6
Morro d'Anta Brazil 203 E6
Morro de Papanoa hd Mex. 185 E5
Morro de Petatlán hd Mex. 185 E5
Morro do Chapéu Brazil 202 D4
Morro do Coco Brazil 207 L8
Morro do Sinal hills Brazil 201 G2
Morros Brazil 202 C2
Morrosquillo, Golfo de b. Col. 198 C2
Morrumbala Moz. 131 G3
Morrumbene Moz. 131 G4
Mors reg. Denmark 45 J4
Morse Canada 167 J5
Morse U.S.A. 172 C4
Morse, Cape Antarctica 223 I2
Morshanka Rus. Fed. 41 G5
formerly known as Morshansk
Morshansk Rus. Fed. see Morshanka
Morsi India 96 C5
Morsott Alg. 57 A13
Morsvikbotn Norway 44 K2
Mort watercourse Australia 149 D4
Mortagne-au-Perche France 50 G4
Mortagne-sur-Sèvre France 50 F5
Mortain France 50 F4
Mortara Italy 56 A3
Morteau France 51 M5
Morteros Arg. 204 E3
Mortes, Rio das r. Minas Gerais Brazil 207 I8
Mortes, Rio das r. Tocantins Brazil 202 B4
also known as Manso
Mortimer's Bahamas 187 E2
Mortlach Canada 167 J5
Mortlake Australia 147 D4
Mortlock Islands Micronesia 220 E5
also known as Nomoi Islands
Mortlock Islands P.N.G. see Tauu Islands
Morton IL U.S.A. 174 B3
Morton TX U.S.A. 179 B5
Morton WA U.S.A. 180 B3
Morton National Park Australia 147 F3
Mortugaba Brazil 207 K1
Morundah Australia 147 E3
Moruroa atoll Fr. Polynesia see Mururoa
Moruya Australia 147 F3
Morvan, Parc Naturel Régional du nature res. France 51 K5
Morven Australia 149 E5
Morven N.Z. 153 F12
Morven hill U.K. 46 I5
Morvern reg. U.K. 46 G7
Morvi India see Morbi
Morwell Australia 147 E4
Mor'ye Rus. Fed. 43 M1
Morzhovets, Ostrov i. Rus. Fed. 40 G2
Mosal'sk Rus. Fed. 43 P7
Mosbach Germany 48 G6
Mosby U.S.A. 180 F3
Moscarter, Punta des pt Spain 55 M5
▶Moscow Rus. Fed. 43 S6
Capital of the Russian Federation and 2nd most populous city in Europe. Also known as Moskva.
world [cities] ▶ 24–25
Moscow IA U.S.A. 172 B9
Moscow ID U.S.A. 180 C3
Moscow PA U.S.A. 177 J4
Moscow Oblast admin. div. Rus. Fed. see Moskovskaya Oblast'
Moscow University Ice Shelf Antarctica 223 I2
Mosel r. Germany 48 E5
Moselebe watercourse Botswana 130 D5
Moseley U.S.A. 176 H8
Moselle r. France 51 M3
Moses, Mount U.S.A. 183 G1
Moses Lake U.S.A. 180 C3
Mosgiel N.Z. 153 E13
Moshannon U.S.A. 176 G4
Moshaweng watercourse S. Africa 132 G3
Moshchnyy, Ostrov i. Rus. Fed. 42 I2
Moshenskoye Rus. Fed. 43 P3
Mosher Canada 173 I2
Moshi r. Nigeria 125 G4
Moshi Tanz. 128 C5
Mosina Poland 49 N3
Mosinee U.S.A. 172 D6
Mosi-oa-Tunya National Park Zimbabwe see Victoria Falls National Park
Mosita S. Africa 133 I3
Mosjøen Norway 44 K2
Moskal'vo Rus. Fed. 82 F1
Moskenesøy i. Norway 44 K2
Moskenestraumen sea chan. Norway 44 K2
Moskkugáisi mt. Norway 44 M1
Moskosel Sweden 44 L2
Moskovskaya Oblast' admin. div. Rus. Fed. 43 T6
English form Moscow Oblast
Moskovskiy Uzbek. see Shakhrikhan
Moskva Rus. Fed. see Moscow
Moskva r. Rus. Fed. 43 T6
Moskva Tajik. 101 G2
Moskvy, Kanal imeni canal Rus. Fed. 43 S5
Moșna Romania 58 I2
Mosonmagyaróvár Hungary 49 O8

Mosopo Botswana 133 J1
Mosor mts Croatia 56 I5
Mosquera Col. 198 B4
Mosquero U.S.A. 181 F6
Mosquitia reg. Hond. 186 C4
Mosquito Creek Lake U.S.A. 176 E4
Mosquito Lake Canada 167 K2
Mosquitos, Costa de coastal area Nicaragua 186 C4
also spelt Miskitos, Costa de
Moss Norway 45 J4
Mossaka Congo 126 C5
Mossâmedes Angola see Namibe
Mossâmedes Brazil 206 C3
Mossburn N.Z. 153 C13
Mosselbaai S. Africa see Mossel Bay
Mossel Bay S. Africa 132 G11
also spelt Mosselbaai
Mossel Bay b. S. Africa 132 G11
Mossendjo Congo 126 B5
Mossgiel Australia 147 E3
Mossman Australia 149 E3
Mossoró Brazil 202 E3
Moss Vale Australia 147 F3
Mossy r. Canada 167 K4
Most Bulg. 58 G7
Most Czech Rep. 49 K5
Mostaganem Alg. 123 F2
also spelt Mestghanem
Mostar Bos.-Herz. 56 J5
Mostardas Brazil 204 H3
Moşteni Romania 58 G4
Moştiştea r. Romania 58 H4
Móstoles Spain 54 H4
Mostoos Hills Canada 167 I4
Mostovskoy Rus. Fed. 41 G7
Mosty Belarus see Masty
Mosul Iraq 107 E3
also spelt Al Mawşil
Møsvatn Austfjell park Norway 45 J4
Møsvatnet l. Norway 45 J4
Mosvik Norway 44 J3
Mot'a Eth. 128 C2
Motaba r. Congo 126 C4
Mota del Cuervo Spain 55 I5
Motagua r. Guat. 185 H6
Motal' Belarus 42 G9
Motala Sweden 45 K4
Mota Lava i. Vanuatu 145 F3
also known as Saddle Island or Valua
Motaze Moz. 131 G5
Moţca Romania 58 H1
Motenge-Boma Dem. Rep. Congo 126 C4
Moteng Pass Lesotho 133 M5
Moth India 96 C4
Motherwell U.K. 46 I8
Mothibistat S. Africa 132 H4
Mothonaio, Akra pt Greece 59 E12
Motihari India 97 E4
Motilla hill Spain 54 F6
Motilla del Palancar Spain 55 J5
Motiti Island N.Z. 152 K5
Motlan Ling hill China 83 A4
Motloutse r. Botswana 131 F4
Motokwe Botswana 130 D5
Motovskiy Zaliv sea chan. Rus. Fed. 44 P1
Motoyoshi Japan 90 G5
Motozintla Mex. 185 G6
Motril Spain 55 H8
Motru Romania 58 D4
Motru r. Romania 58 E4
Motshikiri S. Africa 133 L2
Mott U.S.A. 178 B2
Motueka N.Z. 152 H9
Motuhora Island N.Z. 152 K5
also known as Whale Island; formerly known as Moutohora Island
Motu Ihupuku i. N.Z. see Campbell Island
Motukarara N.Z. 153 G11
Motul Mex. 185 H4
Motupipi N.Z. 152 G8
Mouali Gbangba Congo 126 C4
Mouan, Nam r. Laos 78 D4
Mouaskar Alg. see Mascara
Moubray Bay Antarctica 223 L2
Mouchalagane r. Canada 169 G3
Mouchet, Mont mt. France 51 J8
Mouchoir Bank sea feature Turks and Caicos Is 187 F2
Mouchoir Passage Turks and Caicos Is 187 F2
Mouding China 86 B3
also known as Gonghe
Moudjéria Mauritania 124 B2
Moudon Switz. 51 M6
Moudros Greece 59 G9
Mougri well Mauritania 124 B2
Mouhijärvi Fin. 45 M3
Mouhoun r. Africa 124 E4 see Black Volta
Mouila Gabon 126 A5
Moul well Niger 125 I3
Moulamein Australia 147 E3
Moulamein Creek r. Australia 147 D3
also known as Billabong Creek
Moulavibazar Bangl. see Maulvi Bazar
Moule Guadeloupe 187 H3
Moulèngui Binza Gabon 126 A5
Moulentâr well Mali 124 D2
Moulhoulé Djibouti 128 D1
Moulins France 51 J6
Moulins-Engilbert France 51 J6
Moulle de Jaut, Pic du mt. France 50 F9
Moulmein Myanmar 78 B4
also known as Mawlamyaing or Mawlamyine
Moulmeingyun Myanmar 78 A4
Mouloüya, Oued r. Morocco 122 E2
Moulton U.S.A. 174 C5
Moulton, Mount Antarctica 222 P1
Moultonborough U.S.A. 177 N2
Moultrie U.S.A. 175 D6
Moultrie, Lake U.S.A. 175 E5
Mounana Gabon 126 B5
Mound City KS U.S.A. 178 D4
Mound City MO U.S.A. 178 D3
Mound City SD U.S.A. 178 B2
Moundou Chad 126 C2
Moundsville U.S.A. 176 E6
Mounta, Akra pt Greece 59 B10
Mount Abu India 96 B4
Mountainair U.S.A. 181 F6
Mountain Brook U.S.A. 175 C5
Mountain City U.S.A. 176 D9
Mountain Grove U.S.A. 178 D4
Mountain Home AR U.S.A. 179 D4
Mountain Home ID U.S.A. 180 D4
Mountain Home UT U.S.A. 183 N1
Mountain Iron U.S.A. 172 A3
Mountain Lake Park U.S.A. 176 F6
Mountain Pass U.S.A. 183 I6
Mountain View AR U.S.A. 179 D5
Mountain View CA U.S.A. 182 B4
Mountain View HI U.S.A. 181 [inset] Z2
Mountain Village U.S.A. 164 C3
Mountain Zebra National Park S. Africa 133 J9
Mount Airy MD U.S.A. 177 H6
Mount Airy NC U.S.A. 176 E9
Mount Anderson Aboriginal Reserve Australia 150 C3
Mount Arapiles-Tooan State Park nature res. Australia 146 D4
Mount Aspiring National Park N.Z. 153 C12
Mount Assiniboine Provincial Park Canada 167 H5
Mount Augustus Australia 150 B5
Mount Ayliff S. Africa 133 N7
Mount Ayr U.S.A. 178 D3
Mount Baldy U.S.A. 182 G7
Mount Barker S.A. Australia 146 C3
Mount Barker W.A. Australia 151 B7
Mount Barnett Australia 150 D3
Mount Barnett Aboriginal Reserve Australia 150 D3
Mount Beauty Australia 147 E4
Mount Bellew Rep. of Ireland 47 D10
Mount Bruce N.Z. 152 J8
Mount Brydges Canada 173 L8
Mount Buffalo National Park Australia 147 E4
Mount Carmel IL U.S.A. 174 C4
Mount Carmel TN U.S.A. 176 C9
Mount Carmel Junction U.S.A. 183 L4
Mount Carroll U.S.A. 174 B3
Mount Clere Australia 151 B5
Mount Cook N.Z. 153 E11
also known as Aoraki
Mount Cook National Park N.Z. 153 E11
Mount Coolon Australia 149 E4
Mount Currie Nature Reserve S. Africa 133 N7
Mount Darwin Zimbabwe 131 F3
Mount Denison Australia 148 B4
Mount Desert Island U.S.A. 177 Q1
Mount Eba Australia 146 B2
Mount Eccles National Park Australia 146 D4
Mount Edziza Provincial Park Canada 166 D3
Mount Etna U.S.A. 172 H10
Mount Field National Park Australia 147 E5
Mount Fletcher S. Africa 133 M7
Mount Forest Canada 168 D5
Mount Frankland National Park Australia 151 B7
Mount Frere S. Africa 133 M7
also known as Kwabhaca
Mount Gambier Australia 146 D4
Mount Garnet Australia 149 E3
Mount Hagen P.N.G. 73 J8
Mount Holly U.S.A. 177 K6
Mount Holly Springs U.S.A. 177 H5
Mount Hope N.S.W. Australia 147 E3
Mount Hope S.A. Australia 146 B3
Mount Hope U.S.A. 176 D8
Mount Horeb U.S.A. 172 D7
Mount House Australia 150 D3
Mount Howitt Australia 149 D5
Mount Hutt N.Z. 153 F11
Mount Ida U.S.A. 179 D5
Mount Isa Australia 148 C4
Mount Jackson U.S.A. 176 G7
Mount James Aboriginal Reserve Australia 151 B5
Mount Jewett U.S.A. 176 G4
Mount Kaputar National Park Australia 147 F2
Mount Keith Australia 151 C5
Mount Kenya National Park Kenya 128 C5
Mount Lebanon U.S.A. 176 E5
Mount Lofty Range mts Australia 146 C3
Mount MacDonald Canada 173 M3
Mount Magnet Australia 151 B6
Mount Manara Australia 147 D3
Mount Manning Nature Reserve Australia 151 B6
Mount Maunganui N.Z. 152 K5
Mount McKinley National Park U.S.A. see Denali National Park and Preserve
Mount Meadows Reservoir U.S.A. 182 D1
Mount Molloy Australia 149 E3
Mount Moorosi Lesotho 133 L7
Mount Morgan Australia 149 F4
Mount Morris IL U.S.A. 172 D8
Mount Morris MI U.S.A. 173 J7
Mount Morris NY U.S.A. 176 H3
Mount Nebo U.S.A. 176 E7
Mount Olivet U.S.A. 176 A7
Mount Orab U.S.A. 176 B6
Mount Pearl Canada 169 K4
Mount Perry Australia 149 F5
Mount Pierre Aboriginal Reserve Australia 150 D3
Mount Pleasant Canada 169 H4
Mount Pleasant IA U.S.A. 174 B3
Mount Pleasant MI U.S.A. 173 I7
Mount Pleasant PA U.S.A. 176 F5
Mount Pleasant SC U.S.A. 175 E5
Mount Pleasant TX U.S.A. 179 D5
Mount Pleasant UT U.S.A. 183 M2
Mount Rainier National Park U.S.A. 180 B3
Mount Remarkable National Park Australia 146 C3
Mount Revelstoke National Park Canada 166 G5
Mount Richmond Forest Park nature res. N.Z. 152 H9
Mount Robson Provincial Park Canada 166 G4
Mount Rogers National Recreation Area park U.S.A. 176 D9
Mount Rupert S. Africa 133 I5
Mount St Helens National Volcanic Monument nat. park U.S.A. 180 B3
Mount Sanford Australia 148 A3
Mount's Bay U.K. 47 G13
Mount Shasta U.S.A. 180 B4
Mount Somers N.Z. 153 F11
Mount Sterling IL U.S.A. 174 B4
Mount Sterling KY U.S.A. 176 B7
Mount Sterling OH U.S.A. 176 B6
Mount Stewart S. Africa 133 I10
Mount Storm U.S.A. 176 F6
Mount Surprise Australia 149 E3
Mount Upton U.S.A. 177 J3
Mount Vernon Australia 150 B5
Mount Vernon GA U.S.A. 175 D5
Mount Vernon IA U.S.A. 172 B9
Mount Vernon IL U.S.A. 174 B4
Mount Vernon IN U.S.A. 174 C4
Mount Vernon KY U.S.A. 176 A8
Mount Vernon MO U.S.A. 178 D4
Mount Vernon OH U.S.A. 176 C5
Mount Vernon TX U.S.A. 179 D5
Mount Vernon WA U.S.A. 180 B2
Mount Wedge Australia 148 B4
Mount Welcome Aboriginal Reserve Australia 150 B4
Mount William National Park Australia 147 F5
Mount Willoughby Australia 146 B1
Moura Australia 149 F5
Moura Brazil 199 F5
Moura r. Brazil 200 B1
Moura Portugal 54 D6
Mourão Port. 54 D6
Mouraya Chad 126 D2
Mourdi, Dépression du depr. Chad 120 D5
Mourdiah Mali 124 D3
Mourenx France 50 F9
Mourne Mountains hills U.K. 47 F9
Mourre de Chanier mt. France 51 M9
Mourtzeflos, Akra pt Greece 59 G9
Mousa i. U.K. 46 K3
Mouscron Belgium 51 J2
Mousgougou Chad 126 C2
Mousie U.S.A. 176 C8
Moussafoyo Chad 126 C2
Moussoro Chad 120 C6
Moutamba Congo 126 B5
Mouth of Wilson U.S.A. 176 D9
Moûtiers France 51 M7
Moutohora Island N.Z. see Motuhora Island
Moutong Indon. 75 B2
Moutourwa Cameroon 125 I4
Mouydir, Monts du plat. Alg. 123 F4
Mouyondzi Congo 126 B5
Mouzaki Greece 59 C9
Mouzarak Chad 120 B6
Mouzon France 51 L3
Movas Mex. 184 C2
Movila Miresii Romania 58 I3
Movileni Romania 58 F4
Mowanjum Aboriginal Reserve Australia 150 C3
Mowbullan, Mount Australia 149 F5
Mowchadz' Belarus 42 G8
Moxahala U.S.A. 176 C6
Moxey Town Bahamas 186 D1
Moxico prov. Angola 127 C8
Moy r. Rep. of Ireland 47 C9
Moyahua Mex. 185 E4
Moyale Eth. 128 C4
Moyamba Sierra Leone 124 B4
Moyen Atlas mts Morocco 122 D2
English form Middle Atlas
Moyen-Chari pref. Chad 126 C2
Moyen Congo country Africa see Congo
Moyeni Lesotho 133 L7
also known as Quthing
Moyenne-Guinée admin. reg. Guinea 124 B4
Moyen-Ogooué prov. Gabon 126 A5
Moynalyk Rus. Fed. 88 F1
Moynaq Uzbek. see Muynak
Moyo i. Indon. 77 G5
Moyo Uganda 128 A4
Moyobamba Peru 198 B6
Moyowosi r. Tanz. 129 A6
Moysalen mt. Norway 44 K1
Moyto Chad 120 C6
Moyu China 89 B4
formerly known as Karakax
Moyum waterhole Kenya 128 C4
Moyynkum Kazakh. 103 H3
formerly known as Furmanovka
Moyynkum, Peski des. Kazakh. 103 F3
also known as Moinkum
Moyynty Kazakh. 103 H3
formerly spelt Mointy
Mozambique country Africa 131 G4
spelt Moçambique in Portuguese; historically known as Portuguese East Africa
africa [countries] 114–117
Mozambique Channel Africa 131 I4
Mozarlândia Brazil 206 C1
Mozdok Rus. Fed. 41 H8
Mozdūrān Iran 101 E2
Mozelle U.S.A. 176 B8
Mozhaysk Rus. Fed. 43 R6
Mozhga Rus. Fed. 40 J4
Mozhong China 86 A1
Mozo Myanmar 78 A3
Mozyr' Belarus see Mazyr
Mpal Senegal 124 A3
formerly spelt Pal
Mpanda Tanz. 129 A6
Mpandamatenga Botswana 131 E3
Mpande Zambia 127 F7
Mpé Congo 126 B5
Mpemvana S. Africa 133 O4
Mpessoba Mali 124 D3
Mpigi Uganda 128 B4
Mpika Zambia 127 F7
Mpoko r. Cent. Afr. Rep. 126 C3
Mpolweni S. Africa 133 O6
Mpongwe Zambia 127 F8
Mporokoso Zambia 127 F7
Mposa S. Africa 133 Q5
Mpouya Congo 126 C5
Mpui Tanz. 129 A7
Mpulungu Zambia 127 F7
Mpumalanga S. Africa 133 O6
Mpumalanga prov. S. Africa 133 N3
formerly known as Eastern Transvaal
Mpwapwa Tanz. 129 C6
Mqanduli S. Africa 133 M8
Mqinvartsveri mt. Georgia/Rus. Fed. see Kazbek
Mrągowo Poland 49 S2
Mrewa Zimbabwe see Murehwa
Mrežnica r. Croatia 56 H3
Mrkonjić-Grad Bos.-Herz. 56 J4
Mrocza Poland 49 O2
Mroga r. Poland 49 Q4
M'Saken Tunisia 57 C13
Msambweni Kenya 129 C6
Msata Tanz. 129 C6
Mshinskaya Rus. Fed. 43 K2
M'Sila Alg. 123 G2
Msta r. Rus. Fed. 43 P4
Msta r. Rus. Fed. 43 M3
Mstinskiy Most Rus. Fed. 43 N3
Mstislavl' Belarus see Mstsislaw
Mstsislaw Belarus 43 M7
also spelt Mstislavl'
Msunduze r. S. Africa 133 Q4
Mszana Dolna Poland 49 R6
Mtama Tanz. 129 C7
Mt'at'ushet'is Nakrdzali nature res. Georgia 107 F2
Mtelo Kenya 128 B4
Mtera Reservoir Tanz. 129 B6
Mtoko Zimbabwe see Mutoko
Mtonjaneni S. Africa 133 P5
Mtorashanga Zimbabwe see Mutorashanga
Mtsensk Rus. Fed. 43 R8
Mts'khet'a Georgia 107 F2
Mtukula Tanz. 129 A5
Mtunzini S. Africa 133 P5
Mtwara Tanz. 129 D7
Mtwara admin. reg. Tanz. 129 C7
Mu r. Myanmar 78 A3
Mu hill Port. 54 C7
Mu'āb, Jibāl reg. Jordan see Moab
Muaguide Moz. 129 C8
Mualama Moz. 131 H3
Muana Brazil 202 B2
Muanda Dem. Rep. Congo 127 B6
Muang Khammouan Laos 78 D4
Muang Không Laos 79 D5
Muang Khôngxédôn Laos 79 D5
Muang Luang r. Thai. 79 B6
Muang Pakbeng Laos 78 C4
Muang Pakxan Laos 78 C4
Muang Phin Laos 78 D4
Muang Phôn-Hông Laos 78 C4
Muang Sam Sip Thai. 79 D5
Muang Sing Laos 78 C3
Muang Thai country Asia see Thailand
Muang Vangviang Laos 78 C4
Muang Xaignabouri Laos 78 C4
also known as Sayabouri
Muanza Moz. 131 G3
Muar Malaysia 76 C2
Muar r. Malaysia 76 C2
Muara Brunei 77 F1
Muaraancalong Indon. 77 G2
Muaraatap Indon. 77 G2
Muarabeliti Indon. 76 C3
Muarabungo Indon. 76 C3
Muaradua Indon. 76 D4
Muaraenim Indon. 76 C3
Muarainu Indon. 77 F3
Muarakaman Indon. 77 G3
Muaralesan Indon. 77 G2
Muararupit Indon. 76 C3
Muarasoma Indon. 76 B2
Muaras Reef Indon. 75 A2
Muaratebo Indon. 76 C3
Muaratembesi Indon. 76 C3
Muaratewe Indon. 77 F3
Muara Tuang Sarawak Malaysia see Kota Samarahan
Muarawahau Indon. 77 G2
Muari, Ras pt Pak. 101 F5
Mu'aylā, Wādī al watercourse Iraq 109 M5
Muazzam India 96 B3
Mubārak, Jabal mt. Jordan/Saudi Arabia 108 G8
Mubarakpur India 97 D4
Mubarek Uzbek. 103 F5
also spelt Muborak
Mubarraz well Saudi Arabia 107 E5
Mubende Uganda 128 A4
Mubi Nigeria 125 I4
Muborak Uzbek. see Mubarek
Mubur i. Indon. 77 D2
Mucaba Angola 127 B6
Mucajá Brazil 199 G5
Mucajaí r. Brazil 199 F4
Mucajaí, Serra do mts Brazil 199 F4
Mucalic r. Canada 169 H1
Mučanj mt. Yugo. 58 B5
Mucheng China see Wuzhi
Muchinga Escarpment Zambia 127 F8
Muchiri Bol. 201 E4
Muchuan China 86 B2
also known as Muxi
Muck i. U.K. 46 F7
Muckadilla Australia 149 F5
Muckaty Aboriginal Land res. Australia 148 B3
Muco r. Col. 198 D3
Mucojo Moz. 129 D8
Muconda Angola 127 D7
formerly known as Nova Chaves
Mucope Angola 127 B9
Mucubela Moz. 131 H3
Mucucuaú r. Brazil 199 F5
Mucuim r. Brazil 199 E6
Mucumbura Moz. 131 F3
Mucundi Angola 127 C9
Mucunha Angola 127 C8
Mucupia Moz. 131 H3
Mucur Turkey 106 C3
Mucura Brazil 199 F5
Mucuri Brazil 203 E6
Mucuri r. Brazil 207 N5
Mucurici Brazil 207 M5
Mucuripe Brazil 198 D5
Mucuripe, Ponta de pt Brazil 202 E2
Mucusso, Coutada Pública do nature res. Angola 127 D9
Mucussueje Angola 127 D7
Muda r. Malaysia 76 C1
Mudabidri India 94 B3
Mudanjiang China 82 C3
Mudan Jiang r. China 82 C3
Mudan Ling mts China 82 B4
Mudanya Turkey 106 B2
Mudayrah Kuwait 107 F5
Mudaysīsāt, Jabal al hill Jordan 108 H6
Muddebihal India 94 C2
Muddus nationalpark nat. park Sweden 44 L2
Muddy r. U.S.A. 183 J5
Muddy Boggy Creek r. U.S.A. 179 D5
Muddy Creek r. U.S.A. 183 N3
Muddy Gap Pass U.S.A. 180 F4
Muddy Peak U.S.A. 183 J5
Mūd-e-Dahanāb Iran 101 D3
Muden S. Africa 133 O5
Mudgal India 94 C3
Mudgee Australia 147 F3
Mudhol India 94 B2
Mudigere India 94 B3
Mudjatik r. Canada 167 J3
Mudkhed India 94 C2
Mudki India 96 B3
Mud Lake U.S.A. 183 G4
Mudon Myanmar 78 B4
Mudraya country Africa see Egypt
Mudug admin. reg. Somalia 128 E3
Mudukani Tanz. 129 B5
Mudumu National Park Namibia 130 D3
Mudurnu Turkey 106 B2
Mud'yuga Rus. Fed. 40 F3
Muecate Moz. 131 H2
Mueda Moz. 129 C7
Muela de Arés mt. Spain 55 K4
Mueller Range hills Australia 150 D3
Muende Moz. 131 G2
formerly known as Vila Caldas Xavier
Muerto, Mar lag. Mex. 185 G5
Muertos Cays is Bahamas 186 C1
Muftah well Sudan 121 G4
Muftyuga Rus. Fed. 40 H2
Mufulira Zambia 127 F8
Mufumbwe Zambia 127 E8
Mufu Shan mts China 87 E2
Muğan Düzü lowland Azer. 107 G3
Muge r. Port. 54 C5
Mugeba Moz. 131 H3
Mughalbhin Pak. see Jati
Mughal Sarai India 97 D4
Mūghār Iran 100 C3
Mughayrā' Saudi Arabia 107 D5
Mughayrā' well Saudi Arabia 105 D2
Mughshin Oman 105 F4
Mughsu r. Tajik. 101 G2
also spelt Muksu
Mugia Spain see Muxía
Mugila, Monts mts Dem. Rep. Congo 127 F6
Muğla Turkey 106 B3
Muğla prov. Turkey 59 J11
Mugodzharskaya Kazakh. 102 D2
Mugodzhary, Gory mts Kazakh. 102 D3
Mug Qu r. China 80 E6
Muguia Moz. 129 C8
Mugu Karnali r. Nepal 97 D3
Mugur-Aksy Rus. Fed. 84 A1
Mugxung China 89 F5
Mūḩ, Sabkhat imp. l. Syria 109 J3
Muhagiriya Sudan 126 E2
Muhala Dem. Rep. Congo 127 F6
Muhammad, Râs pt Egypt 121 G3
Muhammadabad India 97 D4
Muhammad Qol Sudan 121 H4
Muhammarah Iran see Khorramshahr
Muḩayriqah Saudi Arabia 105 D3
Muḩaysh, Wādī al watercourse Jordan 108 H8
Muḩaywīr tourist site Iraq 109 M4
Muheza Tanz. 129 C6
Mühlacker Germany 48 F7
Mühlberg Germany 49 K4
Mühldorf am Inn Germany 49 J7
Mühlhausen (Thüringen) Germany 48 H4
Mühlig-Hofmann Mountains Antarctica 223 A2
Muhos Fin. 44 N2
Muḩradah Syria 109 H2
Muhu i. Estonia 42 E3
Muhukuru Tanz. 129 B7
Muhulu Moz. 131 H2
Muhulu Dem. Rep. Congo 126 E5
Mui Eth. 128 B3
Mui Bai Bung c. Vietnam see Mui Ca Mau
Mui Ca Mau c. Vietnam 79 D6
also known as Mui Bai Bung
Mui Dinh hd Vietnam 79 E6
Mui Đôc pt Vietnam 78 D4
Muidumbe Moz. 129 C7
Muié Angola 127 D8
Muiliyk i. Indon. 75 D3
Muineachán Rep. of Ireland see Monaghan
Muine Bheag Rep. of Ireland 47 F11
Muir U.S.A. 173 I8
Muir Glacier Canada/U.S.A. 166 B3
Muirkirk U.K. 46 H8
Mui Ron hd Vietnam 78 D4
Muisne Ecuador 198 B4
Muite Moz. 131 H2
Mujeres, Isla i. Mex. 186 B2
Muji China 88 B4
Mujong r. Sarawak Malaysia 77 F2
Muju S. Korea 83 B5
Mujuí Joboti Brazil 199 H5
Mukačevo Ukr. see Mukacheve
Mukacheve Ukr. 49 T7
also spelt Mukachevo or Mukačevo; historically known as Munkács
Mukachevo Ukr. see Mukacheve
Mukah Sarawak Malaysia 77 F2
Mukah r. Sarawak Malaysia 77 F2
Mukalla Yemen 105 E5
also spelt Al Mukallā
Mukandgarh India 96 B4
Mukandwara India 96 C4
also spelt Mokundurra
Mukanga Dem. Rep. Congo 127 D6
Mukawa Japan 90 G3
Mu-kawa r. Japan 90 G3
Mukawwar, Gezirat i. Sudan 121 H4
Mukdahan Thai. 78 D4
Mukden China see Shenyang
Mukerian India 96 B3
Muketei r. Canada 168 C2
Mukhen Rus. Fed. 82 E2
Mukhino Rus. Fed. 82 B1
Mukhorshibir' Rus. Fed. 85 F1
Mukhtuya Rus. Fed. see Lensk
Mukinbudin Australia 151 B6
Mu Ko Chang National Park Thai. 79 C6
Mukomuko Indon. 76 C3
Mukono Uganda 128 B4
Mukoshi Zambia 127 F7
Mukry Turkm. 103 F5
Muksu r. Tajik. see Mughsu
Muktinath Nepal 97 D3
Muktsar India 96 B3
Mukuku Zambia 127 F8
Mukumbura Zimbabwe 131 F3
formerly spelt Mkumvura
Mukunsa Zambia 127 F7
Mukur Atyrauskaya Oblast' Kazakh. 102 C3
also spelt Muqyr
Mukur Vostochnyy Kazakhstan Kazakh. 103 J2
Mukutawa r. Canada 167 L4
Mukwonago U.S.A. 172 E8
Mul India 94 C1
Mula r. India 94 B2
Mula r. Pak. 101 F4
Mula Spain 55 J6
Mulakatholhu Maldives 93 D10
formerly known as Mulaku
Mulaku atoll Maldives see Mulakatholhu
Mulaly Kazakh. 103 I3
Mulan China 82 C3
Mulanay Phil. 74 B3
Mulanje Malawi 129 B9
Mulapula, Lake salt flat Australia 146 C2
Mula-tupo Panama 186 D5
Mulayḩ salt pan Saudi Arabia 109 J8
Mulayjah Saudi Arabia 105 E2
Mulbagal India 94 C3
Mulbekh Jammu and Kashmir 96 C2
Mulberry AR U.S.A. 179 D5
Mulberry NC U.S.A. 176 D9
Mulchatna r. U.S.A. 164 D3
Mulchén Chile 204 B5
Mulde r. Germany 49 J4
Muleba Tanz. 128 A5
Mule Creek U.S.A. 180 F4
Mulegé Mex. 184 B3
Mulekatembo Zambia 129 B7
Mules i. Indon. 75 B5
Muleshoe U.S.A. 179 B5
Mulevala Moz. 131 H3
Mulga Park Australia 148 A5
Mulgathing Australia 146 B2
Mulhacén mt. Spain 55 H7
Mülhausen France see Mulhouse
Mülheim an der Ruhr Germany 48 D4
Mulhouse France 51 N5
also known as Mülhausen
Muli China 86 B3
also known as Qiaowa; formerly known as Bowa
Muli Rus. Fed. see Vysokogorniy
Mulilansolo Zambia 129 B7
Muling Heilong. China 82 C3
formerly known as Bamiantong
Muling Heilong. China 82 C3
Muling r. China 82 D3
Mull i. U.K. 46 G7
Mulla Ali Iran 100 B2
Mullaaxe Beyle Somalia 128 E2
Mullaittivu Sri Lanka 94 D4
Muller watercourse Australia 148 B4
Muller, Pegunungan mts Indon. 77 F2
Mullett Lake U.S.A. 173 I5
Mullewa Australia 151 A6
Müllheim Germany 48 E8
Mullica r. U.S.A. 177 K6
Mulligan watercourse Australia 148 C5
Mullingar Rep. of Ireland 47 E10
also known as An Muileann gCearr
Mullins U.S.A. 175 E5
Mull of Galloway c. U.K. 47 H9
Mull of Kintyre hd U.K. 47 G8
Mull of Oa hd U.K. 46 F8
Müllrose Germany 49 L3
Mullsjö Sweden 45 K4
Mullutu laht l. Estonia 42 D3
Mulobezi Zambia 127 E9
Mulondo Angola 127 B8
Mulonga Plain Zambia 127 D9
Mulongo Dem. Rep. Congo 127 E6
Mulsanne France 50 G5
Mulshi Lake India 94 B2
Multai India 96 C5
Multan Iran 101 E5
Multan Pak. 101 G4
Multia Fin. 44 N3
Mulu, Gunung mt. Sarawak Malaysia 77 F1
Mulug India 94 C2
Mulumbe, Monts mts Dem. Rep. Congo 127 E7
Mulurulu Lake Australia 147 D3
Mulūşī, Wādī al watercourse Iraq 109 K4
Muma Dem. Rep. Congo 126 D4
Mūmān Iran 101 E5
Mumbai India 94 B2
2nd most populous city in Asia and 3rd in the world. Formerly known as Bombay.
world [cities] 24–25
Mumbeji Zambia 127 D8
Mumbondo Angola 127 B7
Mumbwa Zambia 127 E8
Mumbwi Tanz. 129 C6
Mume Dem. Rep. Congo 127 E7
Muminabad Tajik. see Leningrad
Mu'minobod Tajik. see Leningrad
Mumoma Dem. Rep. Congo 127 D6
Mumra Rus. Fed. 102 A3
Mun, Mae Nam r. Thai. 79 D5
Muna i. Indon. 75 B4
Muna Mex. 185 H4
Muna r. Rus. Fed. 39 M3
Munabao Pak. 101 G5
Munaðarnes Iceland 44 [inset] B2
Munagala India 94 C2
Munakata Japan 91 B8
Munayly Kazakh. 102 C3
Munayshy Kazakh. 102 C4
Münchberg Germany 48 I5
München Germany see Munich
München-Gladbach Germany see Mönchengladbach
Munchique, Parque Nacional nat. park Col. 198 B4
Muncho Lake Canada 166 E3
Muncho Lake Provincial Park Canada 166 E3
Munch'ŏn N. Korea 83 B5
Muncie U.S.A. 174 C3
Muncoonie West, Lake salt flat Australia 148 C5
Muncy U.S.A. 177 I4
Munda Solomon Is 145 E2
Mundel Lake Sri Lanka 94 C5
Mundemba Cameroon 125 H5
Mundiwindi Australia 150 C4
Mundjura Creek r. Australia 149 D3
Mundo r. Spain 55 J6
Mundo Novo Brazil 202 D4
Mundra India 96 A5
Mundrabilla Australia 151 D6
Munds Park U.S.A. 183 M7
Mundubbera Australia 149 F5
Mundwa India 96 B4
Muneru r. India 94 D2
Munfordville U.S.A. 174 C4
Mungallala Australia 149 F5
Mungallala Creek r. Australia 147 E2
Mungana Australia 149 E3
Mungaoli India 96 C4
Mungári Moz. 131 G3
Mungaroona Range Nature Reserve Australia 150 B4
Mungbere Dem. Rep. Congo 126 F4
Mungeli India 97 D5
Munger India 97 E4
formerly spelt Monghyr
Munger U.S.A. 173 J7
Mungerannie Australia 146 C2
Mū Nggava i. Solomon Is see Rennell
Mungguresak, Tanjung pt Indon. 77 E2
Mungilli Aboriginal Reserve Australia 151 D5
Mungindi Australia 147 F2
Mungkarta Aboriginal Land res. Australia 148 B4
Mungla Bangl. 97 F5
Mungo Angola 127 C7
Mungo, Lake Australia 147 D3
Mungo National Park Australia 147 D3
Mungwi Zambia 127 F7
Mun'gyŏng S. Korea 83 B5
Munhango Angola 127 C8
Munhino Angola 127 B8
Munich Germany 48 I7
also known as München
Munising U.S.A. 172 G4
Muniz Freire Brazil 207 L7
Munkács Ukr. see Mukacheve
Munkedal Sweden 45 J4
Munkflohögen Sweden 44 K3
Munku-Sardyk, Gora mt. Mongolia/Rus. Fed. 84 D1
Munro, Mount Australia 147 F5
Munse Indon. 75 B4
Munshiganj Bangl. 97 F5
Münsingen Switz. 51 N6
Münster Niedersachsen Germany 48 H3
Münster Nordrhein-Westfalen Germany 48 E4
Munster reg. Rep. of Ireland 47 D11
Münsterland reg. Germany 48 E4
Münster-Osnabrück airport Germany 48 E3
Muntadgin Australia 151 B6
Munte Indon. 75 A2
Muntele Mare, Vârful mt. Romania 58 E2
Munteni Romania 58 I3
Mununga Zambia 127 F7
Munyal-Par sea feature India see Bassas de Pedro Padua Bank
Munyati r. Zimbabwe 131 F3
Munyu S. Africa 133 M8
Munzur Vadisi Milli Parkı nat. park Turkey 107 D3
Muodoslompolo Sweden 44 M2
Muojärvi l. Fin. 44 O2
Muonio Fin. 44 M2
Muonioälven r. Fin./Sweden 44 M2
also known as Muonionjoki
Muonionjoki r. Fin./Sweden see Muonioälven
Mupa Angola 127 B9
Mupa, Parque Nacional da nat. park Angola 127 B8
Mupfure r. Zimbabwe 131 F3
formerly known as Umfuli
Muping China 85 I4
Muqaddam watercourse Sudan 121 F5
Muqaybirah Yemen 105 D5
Muqaynimah well Saudi Arabia 105 E3
Muqdisho Somalia see Mogadishu
Muqniyāt Oman 105 G3
Muqshin, Wādī r. Oman 105 F4
Muquem Brazil 202 B5
Muqui Brazil 203 D7
Muqyr Kazakh. see Mukur
Mur r. Austria 49 N9
also spelt Mura
Mura r. Croatia/Slovenia 49 N9
also spelt Mur
Muradiye Turkey 59 I10
Muradiye Turkey 107 E3
also known as Bargiri
Murai, Tanjong pt Sing. 76 [inset]
Murai Reservoir Sing. 76 [inset]
Murakami Japan 90 F5
Murallón, Cerro mt. Chile 205 B8
Muramvya Burundi 126 F5
Murāḩ r. Slovakia 49 P7
Muranga Kenya 128 C5
formerly known as Fort Hall
Muras Spain 54 D1
Murashi Rus. Fed. 40 I4
Murat France 51 I7
Murat r. Turkey 107 D3
Muratlı Turkey 106 A2
Murayama Japan 90 G5
Murayr, Jabal hill Saudi Arabia 104 C2
Muraysah, Ra's al pt Libya 120 E2
Murça Port. 54 D3
Murcheh Khvort Iran 100 B3
Murchison Australia 147 E4
Murchison watercourse Australia 151 A5
Murchison N.Z. 153 G9
Murchison, Mount Antarctica 223 L2
Murchison, Mount hill Australia 151 B5
Murchison Falls Uganda 128 A4
Murchison Falls National Park Uganda 128 A4
also known as Kabalega Falls National Park or Kabarega National Park
Murchison Island Canada 168 B3
Murchison Mountains N.Z. 153 B13
Murchison Range hills Australia 148 B4
Murcia Spain 55 J7
Murcia aut. comm. Spain 55 J7
Murcielagos Bay Phil. 74 B4
Mûr-de-Bretagne France 50 D4
Murdo U.S.A. 178 B3
Murdochville Canada 169 H3
Mürefte Turkey 106 A2
Muregi Nigeria 125 G4
Murehwa Zimbabwe 131 F3
formerly spelt Mrewa or Murewa
Mureş r. Romania 58 B2
Muret France 50 H9
Murewa Zimbabwe see Murehwa
Murfjället mt. Norway 44 K2
Murfreesboro AR U.S.A. 179 D5
Murfreesboro NC U.S.A. 177 H9
Murfreesboro TN U.S.A. 174 C5
Murgab Tajik. see Murghob
Murgab r. Tajik. 101 H2
Murgab Turkm. see Murgap
Murgab r. Turkm. see Murgap
Murgap Turkm. 103 E5
also spelt Murgab
Murgap r. Turkm. 103 E5
formerly spelt Murgab
Murgeni Romania 58 J2
Murge Tarantine hills Italy 57 J8
Murghab r. Afgh. 101 E3
Murghab reg. Afgh. 101 E3
Murgha Kibzai Pak. 101 G4

index M N

Murghob Tajik. **101** H2
also spelt Murgab
Murgh Pass Afgh. **101** G3
Murgon Australia **149** F5
Murgoo Australia **151** B5
Muri *Qinghai* China **84** C4
Muri *Qinghai* China **84** D4
Muri India **97** E5
Mūrī Iran **100** D2
Muria, Gunung *mt.* Indon. **77** E4
Murici Brazil **203** D7
Muriege Angola **127** D7
Murii-dake *mt.* Japan **90** H3
Murillo Canada **172** D2
Müritz *l.* Germany **49** J2
Müritz, Nationalpark *nat. park* Germany **49** K2
Muriwai N.Z. **152** L6
Murjek Sweden **44** M2
Murkong Selek India **97** G4
Murmansk Rus. Fed. **44** P1
Murmanskaya Oblast' *admin. div.* Rus. Fed. **44** P1
English form Murmansk Oblast
Murmanskiy Bereg *coastal area* Rus. Fed. **40** E1
Murmansk Oblast *admin. div.* Rus. Fed. *see* **Murmanskaya Oblast'**
Murmashi Rus. Fed. **44** P1
Murmino Rus. Fed. **43** V7
Muro, Capo di *c. Corse* France **56** A7
Muro Lucano Italy **57** H8
Murom Rus. Fed. **40** G5
Murongo Tanz. **128** A5
Muroran Japan **90** G3
Muros Spain **54** B2
Muros e Noia, Ría de *est.* Spain **54** B2
Muroto Japan **91** D8
Muroto-zaki *pt* Japan **91** D8
Murowana-Goślina Poland **49** O3
Murphy *ID* U.S.A. **180** C4
Murphy *NC* U.S.A. **174** D5
Murphys U.S.A. **182** D3
Murrah *reg.* Saudi Arabia **105** E3
Murra Murra Australia **147** E2
Murranji Aboriginal Land *res.* Australia **148** B3
Murrat el Kubra, Buheirat *l.* Egypt *see* **Great Bitter Lake**
Murrat el Sughra, Buheirat *l.* Egypt *see* **Little Bitter Lake**

▶**Murray** *r. S.A.* Australia **147** C3
3rd longest river in Oceania. Part of the longest (Murray-Darling).
oceania [landscapes] ▶ 136–137

Murray *r. W.A.* Australia **151** A7
Murray *r.* Canada **166** F3
Murray *KY* U.S.A. **174** B4
Murray *UT* U.S.A. **183** M1
Murray, Lake P.N.G. **73** J8
Murray, Lake U.S.A. **175** D5
Murray, Mount Canada **166** D2
Murray Bridge Australia **146** C3
Murray City U.S.A. **176** C6

▶**Murray-Darling** *r.* Australia **144** D5
Longest river in Oceania.
oceania [landscapes] ▶ 136–137

Murray Downs Australia **148** B4
Murray Harbour Canada **169** I4
Murray Range *hills* Australia **151** E5
Murraysburg S. Africa **132** H8
Murray Sunset National Park Australia **146** D3
Murrayville Australia **146** D3
Murree Pak. **101** H3
Murrieta U.S.A. **183** G8
Murroa Moz. **131** H3

▶**Murrumbidgee** *r.* Australia **147** D3
4th longest river in Oceania.
oceania [landscapes] ▶ 136–137

Murrupula Moz. **131** H2
Murrurundi Australia **147** F2
Murshidabad India **97** F4
Murska Sobota Slovenia **56** I2
Murtajapur India **94** C1
Murten Switz. **51** N6
Murter Croatia **56** H5
Murter *i.* Croatia **56** H5
Murtoa Australia **147** D4
Murtovaara Fin. **44** O2
Muru *r.* Brazil **200** C2
Murua *i.* P.N.G. *see* **Woodlark Island**
Murud India **94** B2
Murud, Gunung *mt.* Indon. **77** F2
Murui *r.* Indon. **77** F3
Murui Sum Shuiku *resr* China **85** I3
Murung *r.* Indon. **77** F3
Murung *r.* Indon. **77** F3
Muruntau Uzbek. **103** F4
Murupara N.Z. **152** K6
Mururoa *atoll* Fr. Polynesia **221** I7
also spelt Moruroa; *historically known as* Osnaburg
Muruti, Ilha *i.* Brazil **199** I5
Murviedro Spain *see* **Sagunto**
Murwāni, Wādī *watercourse* Saudi Arabia **104** B3
Murwara India **96** D5
Murwillumbah Australia **147** G2
Murygino *Kirovskaya Oblast'* Rus. Fed. **40** I4
Murygino *Smolenskaya Oblast'* Rus. Fed. **43** N7
Mürz *r.* Austria **49** M8
Murzechirla Turkm. **102** E5
formerly spelt Mirzachirla
Murzuq Libya **120** B3
Mürzzuschlag Austria **49** M8
Muş Turkey **107** E3
Musa Dem. Rep. Congo **126** C4
Mūsa *r.* Latvia/Lith. **42** F5
Mūša *r.* Latvia/Lith. **42** F5
Mûsa, Gebel *mt.* Egypt *see* **Sinai, Mount**
Mūsā, Khowr-e *b.* Iran **100** B4
Musa Ali Terara *vol.* Africa **128** D1
Musabani India **97** E5
Musabeyli Turkey **109** H1
Muşabih Saudi Arabia **104** C4
Musa Khel Bazar Pak. **101** G4
Musala *mt.* Bulg. **58** E6
Musala *i.* Indon. **76** B2
Musalı Turkey **108** F1
Musan N. Korea **82** C4
Musandam *admin. reg.* Oman **105** G2
Musandam Peninsula Oman/U.A.E. **105** G2
Musa Qala, Rūd-i *r.* Afgh. **101** F3
Musay'īd Qatar *see* **Umm Sa'id**
Musaymir Yemen **104** D5
Musbat *well* Sudan **120** E6

▶**Muscat** Oman **105** G3
Capital of Oman. Also spelt Masqaţ.

Muscat *reg.* Oman **105** G2
also spelt Masqaţ
Muscat and Oman *country* Asia *see* **Oman**
Muscatine U.S.A. **174** B3
Muscoda U.S.A. **172** C7
Muscongus Bay U.S.A. **177** P2
Musė *r.* Lith. **42** F7
Musgrave Australia **149** D2
Musgrave, Mount N.Z. **153** E11
Musgrave Harbour Canada **169** K3
Musgrave Ranges *mts* Australia **148** A5
Mūshakī Afgh. **101** G3
Mushandike Sanctuary *nature res.* Zimbabwe **127** F10
Mushāsh al Kabid *well* Jordan **109** H8
Mushash Dabl *well* Saudi Arabia **109** H9
Mushāsh Muḍayyān *well* Saudi Arabia **109** J9
Mushaynīqah *well* Yemen **105** D4
Mushayyish, Wādī al *watercourse* Jordan **108** H7
Mushenge Dem. Rep. Congo **126** D6
Mushie Dem. Rep. Congo **126** C5
Mushin Nigeria **125** F5
Musi *r.* India **94** C2
Musi *r.* Indon. **76** D3
Musica *mt.* Macedonia **58** C7
Music Mountain U.S.A. **183** K6
Musikot Nepal **97** D3
Musinia Peak U.S.A. **183** M2
Muskeg *r.* Canada **166** F2
Muskeget Channel U.S.A. **177** O4
Muskegon U.S.A. **172** G7
Muskegon *r.* U.S.A. **172** G7
Muskegon Heights U.S.A. **172** G7
Muskeg River Canada **166** G4
Muskingum *r.* U.S.A. **176** D6
Muskogee U.S.A. **179** D5
Muskoka Canada **173** N6
Muskoka, Lake Canada **168** E4
Muskrat Dam Lake Canada **168** B2
Muskwa *r.* Canada **166** F3
Muslimbagh Pak. **101** F4
Muslim-Croat Federation *aut. div.* Bos.-Herz. *see* **Federacija Bosna i Hercegovina**
Musmar Sudan **121** G5
Musoma Tanz. **128** B5
Musombe Tanz. **129** B6
Musquanousse, Lac *l.* Canada **169** I3
Musquaro Canada **169** I3
Musquaro, Lac *l.* Canada **169** I3
Mussau Island P.N.G. **145** D2
Musselburgh U.K. **46** I8
Musselshell *r.* U.S.A. **180** F3
Mussende Angola **127** C7
Musserra Angola **127** B6
Mussidan France **50** G7
Mussolo Angola **127** C7
Mussoorie India **96** C3
Mussuma Angola **127** D8
Mussuma *r.* Angola **127** D8
Mustafabad India **97** D4
Mustafakemalpaşa Turkey **106** B2
Mustahīl Eth. **128** E3
Mustamaa *i.* Fin. **42** I1
Mustang Draw *watercourse* U.S.A. **179** B6
Mustau, Gora *mt.* China **88** D2
Mustayevo Rus. Fed. **102** C2
Musters, Lago *l.* Arg. **205** C7
Mustique *i.* St Vincent **187** H4
Mustjala Estonia **42** D3
Mustjõgi *r.* Estonia **42** H4
Mustla Estonia **42** G3
Mustvee Estonia **42** H3
Musu-dan *pt* N. Korea **83** C4
Muswellbrook Australia **147** F3
Mut Egypt **121** F3
Mut Turkey **106** C3
Mutá, Ponta do *pt* Brazil **202** E5
Mutanda Zambia **127** E8
Mutare Zimbabwe **131** G3
formerly spelt Umtali
Mutarjim, Khashm *hill* Saudi Arabia **105** D3
Mutayr *reg.* Saudi Arabia **105** D2
Mutina Italy *see* **Modena**
Mutis Col. **198** B3
Mutis, Gunung *mt.* Indon. **75** C5
Mutnyy Materik Rus. Fed. **40** J2
Mutoko Zimbabwe **131** G3
formerly spelt Mtoko
Mutombo Dem. Rep. Congo **127** D6
Mutooroo Australia **146** D3
Mutorashanga Zimbabwe **131** F3
formerly spelt Mtorashanga
Mutsamudu Comoros **129** E8
Mutshatsha Dem. Rep. Congo **127** E7
Mutsu Japan **90** G4
Mutsu-wan *b.* Japan **90** G4
Muttaburra Australia **149** E4
Muttonbird Islands N.Z. **153** B15
Muttukuru India **94** D3
Muttupet India **94** C4
Mutuali Moz. **131** H2
Mutum Brazil **207** L6
Mutum *r.* Brazil **198** D6
Mutum Biyu Nigeria **125** H4
Mutumparaná Brazil **200** D2
Mutungu-Tari Dem. Rep. Congo **127** C6
Mutunópolis Brazil **202** B5
Mutur Sri Lanka **94** D4
Muuga Estonia **42** H2
Muurame Fin. **45** N3
Muurla Fin. **42** E1
Muurola Fin. **44** N2
Mu Us Shamo *des.* China **85** F4
Muxaluando Angola **127** B7
Muxi China *see* **Muchuan**
formerly known as General Freire
Muxía Spain **54** B1
also spelt Mugía
Muxima Angola **127** B7
Muyezerskiy Rus. Fed. **44** P3
Muyinga Burundi **126** F5
Muynak Uzbek. **102** D4
also spelt Moynaq *or* Muynoq
Muynoq Uzbek. *see* **Muynak**
Muyombe Zambia **129** B7
Muyuka Cameroon **125** H5
Muyumba Dem. Rep. Congo **127** E6
Muyunkum, Peski *des.* Kazakh. **103** G3
Muyunkym Kazakh. **103** H4
Muyuping China **87** D2
Muzaffarabad Pak. **101** H3
Muzaffargarh Pak. **101** G4
Muzaffarnagar India **96** C3
Muzaffarpur India **97** E4
Muzamane Moz. **131** G4
Muzambinho Brazil **206** G8
Muzat He *r.* China **88** C3
Muze Moz. **131** F2
Muzillac France **50** D5
Mūzīn Iran **101** E5
Muzon, Cape U.S.A. **166** C4
Múzquiz Mex. **185** E3
Muztag *mt. Xinjiang* China **89** C5
Muztag *mt. Xinjiang* China **89** D4
Muztagata *mt.* China **88** A4
Muztor Kyrg. *see* **Toktogul**
Mvadi Gabon **126** B4
Mvangan Cameroon **125** H6
Mvolo Sudan **126** F3
Mvomero Tanz. **129** C6
Mvoung *r.* Gabon **126** B4
Mvouti Congo **126** B6
Mvuma Zimbabwe **131** F3
formerly spelt Umvuma
Mwali *i.* Comoros **129** D8
also spelt Mohéli
Mwanisenga Tanz. **129** B6
Mwanya Zambia **129** B8
Mwanza Malawi **129** B8
Mwanza Tanz. **128** B5
Mwanza *admin. reg.* Tanz. **128** B5
Mwape Zambia **127** F8
Mweho Dem. Rep. Congo **126** E6
Mweka Dem. Rep. Congo **126** D6
Mwenda Zambia **127** F7
Mwene-Biji Dem. Rep. Congo **127** D7
Mwene-Ditu Dem. Rep. Congo **127** D6
Mwenezi Zimbabwe **131** F4
Mwenezi *r.* Zimbabwe **131** F4
formerly known as Nuanetsi
Mwenga Dem. Rep. Congo **126** F5
Mwereni Kenya **129** C6
Mweru, Lake Dem. Rep. Congo/Zambia **127** F7
formerly spelt Moero, Lake
Mweru Plateau Tanz. **129** C7
Mweru Wantipa, Lake Zambia **127** F7
Mweru Wantipa National Park Zambia **127** F7
Mwewa Zambia **129** A7
Mwimba Dem. Rep. Congo **127** D7
Mwingi Kenya **128** C5
Mwinilunga Zambia **127** E7
Mya, Oued *watercourse* Alg. **123** G3
Myadzyel Belarus **42** H7
Myadzyel, Vozyera *l.* Belarus **42** H7
Myaing Myanmar **78** A3
Myajlar India **96** A4
Myakishevo Rus. Fed. **43** J5
Myakit Rus. Fed. **39** P3
Myaksa Rus. Fed. **43** T3
Myall Lakes National Park Australia **147** G3
Myamoura-dake *mt.* Japan **91** B9
Myanaung Myanmar **78** A4

▶**Myanmar** *country* Asia **78** A3
also known as Burma
asia [countries] ▶ 64–67

Myaretskiya Belarus **42** I6
Myatlevo Rus. Fed. **43** Q7
Myaundzha Rus. Fed. **39** O3
Myaungmya Myanmar **78** A4
Myawadi Thai. **78** B4
Mycenae *tourist site* Greece **59** D11
also known as Mikines *or* Mykines
Myeik Myanmar *see* **Mergui**
Myerkulavichy Belarus **43** L9
Myers U.S.A. **176** B7
Myingyan Myanmar **78** A3
Myinmoletkat *mt.* Myanmar **79** B5
Myinmu Myanmar **78** A3
Myitkyina Myanmar **78** B2
Myitson Myanmar **78** B3
Myitta Myanmar **79** B5
Myittha Myanmar **78** B3
Myittha *r.* Myanmar **95** G1
Myjava Slovakia **49** O7
Mykines *i.* Faroe Is **46** E1
Mykines *tourist site* Greece *see* **Mycenae**
Myklebostad Norway **44** K2
Mykolayiv Ukr. **41** E7
formerly spelt Nikolayev
Mykolayivka *Chernihivs'ka Oblast'* Ukr. **43** N9
Mykolayivka *Odes'ka Oblast'* Ukr. **58** L3
Mykolayivka-Novorosiys'ka Ukr. **58** K2
Mykonos Greece **59** G11
Mykonos *i.* Greece **59** G11
also spelt Míkonos
Myla Rus. Fed. **40** I2
Myla *r.* Rus. Fed. **40** I2
Mylae *Sicilia* Italy *see* **Milazzo**
Mylasa Turkey *see* **Milas**
Myllykoski Fin. **42** H1
Mymensing Bangl. *see* **Mymensingh**
Mymensingh Bangl. **97** F4
also spelt Mymensing; *formerly known as* Nasirabad
Mynäjoki *r.* Fin. **42** C1
Mynämäki Fin. **45** M3
Mynaral Kazakh. **103** H3
also spelt Myngaral
Mynfontein S. Africa **132** H7
Myngaral Kazakh. *see* **Mynaral**
Myohaung Myanmar **78** A3
Myŏnggan N. Korea **82** C4
Myory Belarus **42** I6
Myotha Myanmar **78** A3
Myōzin-sho *i.* Japan **91** G9
Mýrdalsjökull *ice cap* Iceland **44** [inset] C3
Myrdalssandur *sand area* Iceland **44** [inset] C3
Myre Norway **44** K1
Myrheden Sweden **44** M2
Myrhorod Ukr. **41** E6
also spelt Mirgorod
Myrina Greece **59** G9
also spelt Mírina
Myrlandshaugen Norway **44** L1
Myrnam Canada **167** I4
Myronivka Ukr. **58** K2
Myronivka Ukr. **41** D6
also spelt Mironovka
Myrskylä Fin. **45** N3
Myrtle Beach U.S.A. **175** E5
Myrtle Creek U.S.A. **180** B4
Myrtleford Australia **147** E4
Myrtle Point U.S.A. **180** A4
Myrzakent Kazakh. **103** G4
formerly known as Slavyanka
Mysen Norway **45** J4
Myshanka *r.* Belarus **42** G9
Myshkin Rus. Fed. **43** T4
formerly known as Myshkino
Myshkino Rus. Fed. *see* **Myshkin**
Mys Lazareva Rus. Fed. *see* **Lazarev**
Myślenice Poland **49** Q6
Myślibórz Poland **49** L3
My Son *tourist site* Vietnam **78** E5
Mysore India **94** C3
Mysore *state* India *see* **Karnataka**
Mysovsk Rus. Fed. *see* **Babushkin**
Mys Shmidta Rus. Fed. **39** S3
Myszków Poland **49** Q5
Myszyniec Poland **49** S2
Myt Rus. Fed. **40** G4
My Tho Vietnam **79** D6
Mytilene *i.* Greece *see* **Lesbos**
Mytilini Greece **59** H9
also spelt Mitilíni
Mytiliniol Greece **59** H11
Mytilini Strait Greece/Turkey **59** H9
Mytishchi Rus. Fed. **43** S6
Myton U.S.A. **183** N1
Mývatn *l.* Iceland **44** [inset] C2
Mývatn-Laxá *nature res.* Iceland **44** [inset] C2
Mývatnsöræfi *lava field* Iceland **44** [inset] C2
Myylybulak Kazakh. *see* **Milybulabk**
M'Zab Valley *tourist site* Alg. **123** F2
Mže *r.* Czech Rep. **49** J6
Mziha Tanz. **129** C6
Mzimba Malawi **129** B7
Mzingwani *r.* Zimbabwe **131** F4
also spelt Umzingwani
Mzuzu Malawi **129** B7

↓ N

Na, Nam *r.* China/Vietnam **86** B4
Naab *r.* Germany **48** J6
Naalehu U.S.A. **181** [inset] Z2
Naam Sudan **126** F2
Naama Alg. **123** E2
Naantali Fin. **45** M3
also known as Nådendal
Naas Rep. of Ireland **47** F10
also spelt An Nás
Näätämö Fin. **44** O1
Naba Myanmar **78** B2
Nababeep S. Africa **132** B6
Nabadwip India *see* **Navadwip**
Nabão *r.* Port. **54** C5
Nabarangapur India **95** D2
Nabas Phil. **74** B4
Nabatiyet et Tahta Lebanon **108** G4
Nabberu, Lake *salt flat* Australia **151** C5
Nabéré, Réserve Partielle de *nature res.* Burkina **124** E4
Naberera Tanz. **129** C6
Naberezhnyye Chelny Rus. Fed. **40** J5
formerly known as Brezhnev
Nabeul Tunisia **123** H1
Nabha India **96** C3
Nabileque *r.* Brazil **201** F5
Nabinagar India **97** E4
Nabire Indon. **73** I7
Nabi Younés, Ras en *pt* Lebanon **108** G4
Nāblus West Bank **108** G5
English form Nablus; *also known as* Shekhem; *also spelt* Nābulus
Nablus West Bank *see* **Nāblus**
Nabolo Ghana **125** E4
Naboomspruit S. Africa **131** F5
Nabra *r.* India **96** C2
Nabule Myanmar **79** B5
Nābulus West Bank *see* **Nāblus**
Nacajuca Mex. **185** G5
Nacala Moz. **131** I2
formerly known as Maiaia
Nacaome Hond. **186** B4
Nacaroa Moz. **131** H2
Nacebe Bol. **200** D2
Nacha Belarus **42** F7
Nacha *r.* Belarus **43** J7
Nachalovo Rus. Fed. **102** B3
Nachingwea Tanz. **129** C7
Nachna India **96** A4
Náchod Czech Rep. **49** N5
Nachuge India **95** G4
Nacimiento Chile **204** B5
Nacimiento Reservoir U.S.A. **182** D6
Nacogdoches U.S.A. **179** D6
Nacozari de García Mex. **184** C2
Nada China *see* **Danzhou**
Nadaleen *r.* Canada **166** C2
Nadbai India **96** C4
Nådendal Fin. *see* **Naantali**
Nadezhdinka Kazakh. **103** E1
formerly known as Nadezhdinskiy
Nadezhdinskiy Kazakh. *see* **Nadezhdinka**
Nadi Fiji **145** G3
Nadiad India **96** B5
Nădlac Romania **58** B2
Nador Morocco **123** E2
Nadorozh'ye Rus. Fed. **43** P1
Nădrag Romania **58** D3
Nadūshan Iran **100** C3
Nadvirna Ukr. **41** C6
also spelt Nadvornaya
Nadvornaya Ukr. *see* **Nadvirna**
Nadym Rus. Fed. **38** H3
Naenwa India **96** B4
Næstved Denmark **45** J5
Naf *r.* Bangl./Myanmar **97** G5
Nafas, Râs el *mt.* Egypt **108** F8
Nafha, Har *hill* Israel **108** F7
Nafpaktos Greece **59** C10
also spelt Návpaktos
Nafplio Greece **59** D11
also known as Návplion
Naft *r.* Iraq *see* **Āb Naft**
Naftalan Azer. **100** A1
Naft-e Safīd Iran **100** B4
Naft-e Shāh Iran *see* **Naft Shahr**
Naft Shahr Iran **107** F4
formerly known as Naft-e Shāh
Nafūd ad Daḥl *des.* Saudi Arabia **105** D3
Nafūd al Ghuwayṭah *des.* Saudi Arabia **109** J8
Nafūd al Jur'ā *des.* Saudi Arabia **105** D2
Nafūd al 'Urayq *des.* Saudi Arabia **104** C2
Nafūd as Sirr *des.* Saudi Arabia **104** D2
Nafūd as Surrah *des.* Saudi Arabia **104** C3
Nafūd Qunayfidhah *des.* Saudi Arabia **105** D2
Nafūsah, Jabal *hills* Libya **120** A2
Nafy Saudi Arabia **104** C2
Nag, Co *l.* China **89** E5
Naga Phil. **74** B3
Nagagami *r.* Canada **168** C3
Nagagami Lake Canada **168** C3
Nagahama *Ehime* Japan **91** C8
Nagahama *Shiga* Japan **91** E7
Naga Hills India **97** G4
Naga Hills *state* India *see* **Nagaland**
Nagai Japan **90** G5
Nagaland *state* India **97** G4
formerly known as Naga Hills
Nagambie Australia **147** E4
Nagano Japan **91** F6
Nagano *pref.* Japan **91** E6
Nagaoka Japan **90** F6
Nagaon India **97** G4
also spelt Nowgong
Nagapatam India *see* **Nagappattinam**
Nagappattinam India **94** C4
formerly spelt Nagapatam
Nagar *r.* Bangl./India **97** F4
Nagar *Himachal Pradesh* India **96** C2
Nagar *Karnataka* India **94** B3
Nagar *Rajasthan* India **96** C4
Nagaram India **94** D2
Nagarjuna Sagar Reservoir India **94** C2
Nagar Karnul India **94** C2
Nagarote Nicaragua **186** B4
Nagarzê China **89** E6
Nagasaki Japan **91** A8
Nagasaki *pref.* Japan **91** A8
Naga-shima *i.* Japan **91** B8
Naga-shima *i.* Japan **91** C8
Nagato Japan **91** B7
Nagaur India **96** B4
Nagavali *r.* India **95** D2
Nagda India **96** B5
Nagercoil India **94** C4
Nagha Kalat Pak. **101** F5
Nagina India **96** C3
Nagineh Iran **100** D3
Nagma Nepal **97** D3
Nagod India **96** D4
Nagold Germany **48** F7
Nagong Chu *r.* China *see* **Parlung Zangbo**
Nagorno-Karabakh *aut. reg.* Azer. *see* **Dağlıq Qarabağ**
Nagornyy Rus. Fed. **81** K1
Nagornyy Karabakh *aut. reg.* Azer. *see* **Dağlıq Qarabağ**
Nagorsk Rus. Fed. **40** I4
Nagor'ye Rus. Fed. **43** T5
Nagoya Japan **91** E7
Nagpur India **96** C5
Nagqu China **89** F6
Nag Qu *r.* China **89** F6
Nagu Fin. **45** M3
also known as Hauvo
Nagua Dom. Rep. **187** F3
Naguma Rus. Fed. **38** E1
Nagyatád Hungary **49** O9
Nagybecskerek *Vojvodina, Srbija* Yugo. *see* **Zrenjanin**
Nagyecsed Hungary **49** T8
Nagyenyed Romania *see* **Aiud**
Nagyhalász Hungary **49** S7
Nagykálló Hungary **49** S8
Nagykanizsa Hungary **49** N9
Nagykáta Hungary **49** Q8
Nagykőrös Hungary **49** Q8
Nagyszalonta Romania **49** R9
Nagyvárad Romania *see* **Oradea**
Naha Estonia **42** I3
Naha Japan **81** L7
Nahan India **96** C3
Nahang *r.* Iran/Pak. **101** E5
Nahanni Butte Canada **166** F2
also known as Tthenaagoo
Nahanni National Park Canada **166** E2
Nahanni Range *mts* Canada **166** F2
Nahari Japan **91** D8
Nahariyya Israel **108** G4
Nahāvand Iran **100** B3
N'Ahnet, Adrar *mts* Alg. **123** F4
Nahr, Jabal *hill* Saudi Arabia **104** B2
Nahr Ouassel, Oued *watercourse* Alg. **55** N9
Nahr 'Umr Iraq **100** A4
Nahuel Huapí Arg. **204** C6
Nahuel Huapí, Parque Nacional *nat. park* Arg. **204** C6
Nahuel Mapá Arg. **204** D4
Nahuel Niyeu Arg. **204** D6
Nahunta U.S.A. **175** D6
Naic Phil. **74** B3
Naica Mex. **184** D3
Naidor *well* Tanz. **129** C6
Naikliu Indon. **75** B5
Naik Murad Bangl. **97** F4
Nailung China **89** F6
Na'ima Sudan **121** G6
Naiman Qi China *see* **Daqin Tal**
Naimin Bulak *well* China **84** A2
Nain Canada **169** I1
Nā'īn Iran **100** C3
Naina India **97** D4
Naini Tal India **96** C3
Nainpur India **96** D5
Naiopué Moz. **131** H3
Nairn U.K. **46** I6
Nairn Centre Canada **173** L4

▶**Nairobi** Kenya **128** C5
Capital of Kenya.

Naissaar *i.* Estonia **42** F2
Naissus *Srbija* Yugo. *see* **Niš**
Naivasha Kenya **128** C5
Naizishan China **82** B4
Najafābād Iran **100** B3
Najasa *r.* Cuba **186** D2
Najd *reg.* Saudi Arabia **104** C2
English form Nejd
Nájera Spain **55** I2
Najerilla *r.* Spain **55** I2
Naji China **85** I1
also known as Arun Qi; *formerly known as* Najitun
Najibabad India **96** C3
Najin N. Korea **82** C4
Najitun China *see* **Naji**
Najmah Saudi Arabia **105** E2
Najrān Saudi Arabia **104** D4
Najrān *prov.* Saudi Arabia **105** D4
Najrān, Wādī *watercourse* Saudi Arabia **104** D4
Nakadōri-shima *i.* Japan **91** A8
Naka-gawa *r.* Japan **91** D8
Nakalele Point U.S.A. **181** [inset] Z1
Nakama Japan **91** B8
Nakambé *watercourse* Burkina/Ghana **125** E3 *see* **White Volta**
Nakamura Japan **91** C8
Nakanbe *watercourse* Burkina/Ghana **125** E3 *see* **White Volta**
Nakanno Rus. Fed. **39** K3
Nakano Japan **91** F6
Nakanojō Japan **91** F6
Nakano-shima *i.* Japan **83** C7
Nakapanya Tanz. **129** C7
Nakasatsunai Japan **90** H3
Nakashibetsu Japan **90** I3
Nakasongola Uganda **128** B4
Nakatonbetsu-chō *hill* Japan **90** H2
Nakatsu Japan **91** B8
Nakatsugawa Japan **91** E7
Nakfa Eritrea **121** H5
Nakfa Wildlife Reserve *nature res.* Eritrea **121** H5
Nakhichevan' Azer. *see* **Naxçıvan**
Nakhl Egypt **121** G2
Nakhl-e Taqī Iran **100** C5
Nakhodka Rus. Fed. **82** D4
Nakhola India **97** G4
Nakhon Nayok Thai. **79** C5
Nakhon Pathom Thai. **79** C5
Nakhon Phanom Thai. **78** D4
Nakhon Ratchasima Thai. **79** C5
also known as Korat
Nakhon Sawan Thai. **79** C5
also known as Paknampho
Nakhon Si Thammarat Thai. **79** B6
Nakhrachi Rus. Fed. *see* **Kondinskoye**
Nakhtarana India **96** A5
Nakina *r.* Canada **166** C3
Nakło nad Notecią Poland **49** O2
Naknek U.S.A. **164** D4
Nakodar India **96** B3
Nakonde Zambia **129** B7
Nakop Namibia **132** D5
Nākotne Latvia **42** E5
Nakpanduri Ghana **125** E4
Nakskov Denmark **45** J5
Näkten *l.* Sweden **44** K3
Naktong-gang *r.* S. Korea **83** C6
Nakuru Kenya **128** C5
Nakusp Canada **166** G5
Na-lang Myanmar **78** B3
Nalayh Mongolia **85** E2
Nalázi Moz. **131** G5
Nalbari India **97** F4
Nal'chik Rus. Fed. **41** G8
Naldurg India **94** C2
Nałęczów Poland **49** T4
Nalerigu Ghana **125** E4
Nalgonda India **94** C2
Nalhati India **97** E4
Nalitabari Bangl. **97** F4
Nalkhera India **96** C5
Nallamala Hills India **94** C3
Nallıhan Turkey **106** B2
Nalolo Zambia **127** D8
Nalón *r.* Spain **50** A9
Nālūt Libya **120** A2
Namaa, Tanjung *pt* Indon. **75** D3
Namaacha Moz. **131** G5
Namacala Moz. **131** H2
Namacunde Angola **127** B9
Namacurra Moz. **131** H3
Namadgi National Park Australia **147** F3
Namahadi S. Africa **133** M4
Namak, Daryācheh-ye *salt flat* Iran **100** B3
Namak-e Mīqhān, Kavīr-e *salt flat* Iran **100** B3
Nāmakī *watercourse* Iran **100** C4
Namakkal India **94** C4
Namakzar-e Shadad *salt flat* Iran **100** D4
Namanga Kenya **128** C5
Namangan Uzbek. **103** G4
Namangan Oblast *admin. div.* Uzbek. *see* **Namanganskaya Oblast'**
Namanganskaya Oblast' *admin. div.* Uzbek. **103** G4
English form Namangan Oblast; *also known as* Namangan Wiloyati
Namangan Wiloyati *admin. div.* Uzbek. *see* **Namanganskaya Oblast'**
Namanyere Tanz. **129** A6
Namapa Moz. **131** H2
Namaponda Moz. **131** H2
Namaqualand *reg.* S. Africa **132** A6
Namarrói Moz. **131** H2
Namasale Uganda **128** B4
Namatanai P.N.G. **145** E2
Namba Angola **127** B7
Nambol India **97** G4
Nambour Australia **149** G5
Nambucca Heads Australia **147** G2
Nambung National Park Australia **151** A6
Năm Căn Vietnam **79** D6
Namcha Barwa *mt.* China *see* **Namjagbarwa Feng**
Namche Bazar Nepal **97** E4
Namch'ŏn N. Korea **83** B5
Namco China **89** E6
Nam Co *salt l.* China **89** E6
Namdalen *valley* Norway **44** K2
Namdalseid Norway **44** J2
Nam Đinh Vietnam **78** D3
Namekagon *r.* U.S.A. **172** B5
Namen Belgium *see* **Namur**
Náměstovo Slovakia **49** Q6
Nametil Moz. **131** H2
Namew Lake Canada **167** K4
Nam-gang *r.* N. Korea **83** B5
Namhkam Myanmar **78** B3
Namhsan Myanmar **78** B3
Namialo Moz. **131** H2

▶**Namib Desert** Namibia **130** B5
world [land images] ▶ 12–13

Namibe Angola **127** B8
formerly known as Moçâmedes *or* Mossâmedes
Namibe *prov.* Angola **127** B8
Namibe, Reserva de *nature res.* Angola **127** B8

▶**Namibia** *country* Africa **130** B4
formerly known as South-West Africa; *historically known as* German South-West Africa
africa [countries] ▶ 114–117

Namib-Naukluft Game Park *nature res.* Namibia **130** B5
Namichiga Tanz. **129** C7
Namicunde Moz. **131** H2
Namidobe Moz. **131** H3
Namie Japan **90** G6
Namies S. Africa **132** D6
Namīn Iran **100** B2
Namina Moz. **131** H2
Namitete Malawi **129** B8
Namjagbarwa Feng *mt.* China **80** E7
also known as Namcha Barwa
Namji S. Korea **91** A7
Namka China *see* **Doilungdêqên**
Namlan Myanmar **78** B3
Namlang *r.* Myanmar **78** B3
Namlea Indon. **75** C3
Namling China **89** E6
also known as Namnulingzue
Nam Nao National Park Thai. **78** C4
Nam Ngum Reservoir Laos **78** C4
Namoi *r.* Australia **147** F2
Nampa Canada **167** G3
Nampa *mt.* Nepal **96** D3
Nampa U.S.A. **180** C4
Nampala Mali **124** D3
Namp'o N. Korea **83** B5
formerly known as Chinnamp'o
Nampuecha Moz. **131** I2
Nampula Moz. **131** H2
Nampula *prov.* Moz. **131** H2
Nam Pung Reservoir Thai. **78** C4
Namrole Indon. **75** C3
Namrup India **97** G4
Namsai Myanmar **78** B2
Namsang Myanmar **78** B3
Nam She Tsim *hill* Hong Kong China *see* **Sharp Peak**
Namsos Norway **44** J2
Namsskogan Norway **44** K2
Namtari Nigeria **125** I4
Namtok Myanmar **78** B4
Nam Tok Thai. **79** B5
Namtok Chattakan National Park Thai. **78** C4
Namtok Mae Surin National Park Thai. **78** B4
Namton Myanmar **78** B3
Namtsy Rus. Fed. **39** M3
Namtu Myanmar **78** B3
Namu Canada **166** E5
Namuli, Monte *mt.* Moz. **131** H2
Namuno Moz. **131** H2
Namur Belgium **51** K2
also known as Namen
Namutoni Namibia **130** C3
Namwala Zambia **127** E8
Namwera Malawi **129** B8
Namwŏn S. Korea **83** B6
Namya Ra Myanmar **78** B2
Namyit Island S. China Sea **72** D4
Namysłów Poland **49** O4
Nan Thai. **78** C4
Nan, Mae Nam *r.* Thai. **78** C5
Nana *r.* Cent. Afr. Rep. **126** B3
Nana Bakassa Cent. Afr. Rep. **126** C3
Nana Barya *r.* Cent. Afr. Rep./Chad **126** C3
Nana-Grébizi *pref.* Cent. Afr. Rep. **126** C3
Nanaimo Canada **166** F5
Nana-Mambéré *pref.* Cent. Afr. Rep. **126** B3
Nan'an China **87** F3
Nanango Australia **149** G5
Nananib Plateau Namibia **130** C5
Nan'ao China **87** F4
also known as Houzhai
Nan'ao China *see* **Dayu**
Nanao Japan **91** E6
Nanatsu-shima *i.* Japan **90** E6
Nanay *r.* Peru **198** C5
Nanbai China *see* **Zunyi**
Nanbaxian China **84** B4
Nanbin China *see* **Shizhu**
Nanbu China **86** C2
also known as Nanlong
Nancha China **82** C3
Nanchang *Jiangxi* China **87** E2
also known as Liantang
Nanchang *Jiangxi* China **87** E2
Nanchangshan China *see* **Changdao**
Nancheng China **87** F3
also known as Jianchang
Nanchong China **86** C2
Nanchuan China **86** C2

Ñancorainza Bol. 201 E5
Nancowry i. India 95 G5
Nancut Canada 166 E4
Nancy France 51 M4
Nancy U.S.A. 176 A8
Nanda Devi mt. India 96 D3
Nanda Kot mt. India 96 D3
Nandan China 87 C3
Nanded India 94 C2
formerly known as Nander
Nander India see Nanded
Nandewar Range mts Australia 147 F2
Nandgaon India 94 B1
Nandi Zimbabwe 131 F4
Nandigama India 94 D2
Nandikotkur India 94 C3
Nanding He r. China 86 A4
Nandod India 96 B5
Nandu Jiang r. China 87 D4
Nandura India 94 C1
Nandurbar India 96 B5
Nandyal India 94 C3
Nănești Romania 58 I3
Nanfeng Guangdong China 87 D4
Nanfeng Jiangxi China 87 F3
also known as Qinceng
Nang China 89 F6
Nangade Moz. 129 C7
Nanga Eboko Cameroon 125 I5
Nangah Dedai Indon. 77 E3
Nangahembaloh Indon. 77 F2
Nangahkemangai Indon. 77 F3
Nangahmau Indon. 77 E3
Nangahpinoh Indon. 77 E3
Nangahsuruk Indon. 77 F2
Nangahtempuai Indon. 77 F2
Nangalala Australia 148 B2
Nanganga Tanz. 129 C7
Nangang Shan mts China 82 C4

Nanga Parbat mt. Jammu and Kashmir 96 B2
9th highest mountain in the world and in Asia.
world [physical features] 8–9

Nangarhār prov. Afgh. 101 G3
Nangatayap Indon. 77 E3
Nangbéto, Retenue de resr Togo 125 F5
Nangin Myanmar 79 B6
Nangis France 51 J4
Nangnim N. Korea 83 B4
Nangnim-sanmaek mts N. Korea 83 B4
Nangō Japan 90 F6
Nangong China 85 G4
Nangqên China 86 A1
also known as Xangda
Nangulangwa Tanz. 129 C7
Nanguneri India 94 C4
Nanhe China 85 G4
also known as Heyang
Nanhu China 84 B4
Nanhua Gansu China 84 C4
Nanhua Yunnan China 86 B3
also known as Longchuan
Nanhui China 87 G2
also known as Huinan
Nani Afgh. 101 G3
Nanisivik Canada 165 K2
Nanjangud India 94 C3
Nanjian China 86 B3
Nanjiang China 86 C1
Nanjie China see Guangning
Nanjing Fujian China 87 F3
also known as Shancheng
Nanjing Jiangsu China 87 F1
formerly spelt Nanking
Nanji Shan i. China 87 G3
Nanka Jiang r. China 86 A4
Nankang China 87 E3
formerly known as Rongjiang
Nankang China see Xingzi
Nanking China see Nanjing
Nankoku Japan 91 C8
Nankova Angola 127 C9
Nanlan He r. China 86 A4
Nanle China 85 G4
Nanling China 87 F2
Nan Ling mts China 87 D3
Nanliu Jiang r. China 87 D4
Nanlong China see Nanbu
Nanma China see Yiyuan
Nanmulingzue China see Namling
Nannine Australia 151 B5
Nanning China 87 D4
Nannup Australia 151 A7
Na Noi Thai. 78 C4
Nanortalik Greenland 165 O3
Nanouki atoll Kiribati see Nonouti
Nanouti atoll Kiribati see Nonouti
Nanpan Jiang r. China 86 C3
Nanpara India 97 D4
Nanpi China 85 H4
Nanpiao China 85 I3
Nanping Fujian China 87 F3
Nanping Sichuan China 86 C1
also known as Yongle
Nanpu China see Pucheng
Nanpu Xi r. China 87 F3
Nanqiao China see Fengxian
Nanri Dao i. China 87 F3
Nansa r. Spain 54 G1
Nansebo Eth. 128 C3
Nansei-shotō is Japan see Ryukyu Islands
Nansenga Zambia 127 E8
Nansen Land reg. Greenland 165 O1
Nansen Sound sea chan. Canada 165 J1
Nanshan Island S. China Sea 72 E4
Nanshankou China 84 B3
Nansha Qundao is S. China Sea see Spratly Islands
Nansio Tanz. 128 B5
Nantawarrina Aboriginal Land res. Australia 146 C2
Nantes France 50 E5
Nantes à Brest, Canal de France 50 D5
Nanthi Kadal lag. Sri Lanka 94 D4
Nantiat France 50 H6
Nanticoke Canada 168 D5
Nanticoke MD U.S.A. 177 J7
Nanticoke PA U.S.A. 177 I4
Nanticoke r. U.S.A. 177 J7
Nanton Canada 167 H5
Nantong Jiangsu China 87 G1
Nantong Jiangsu China 87 G2
Nantou China 87 [inset]
Nant'ou Taiwan 87 G4
Nantucket U.S.A. 177 O4
Nantucket Island U.S.A. 177 P4
Nantucket Sound g. U.S.A. 177 O4
Nantulo Moz. 129 C8
Nanty Glo U.S.A. 176 G5
Nanumaga i. Tuvalu see Nanumanga
Nanumanga i. Tuvalu 145 G2
also spelt Nanumaga; formerly known as Hudson Island
Nanumea i. Tuvalu 145 G2
Nanuque Brazil 203 D6
Nanusa, Kepulauan is Indon. 75 C1
Nanutarra Roadhouse Australia 150 A4
Nanxi China 86 C2
Nanxian China 87 E2
also known as Nanzhou
Nanxiong China 87 E3
formerly known as Xiongzhou
Nanyandang Shan mt. China 87 G3
Nanyang China 87 E1
Nanyō Japan 90 G5
Nanyuki Kenya 128 C5
Nanzamu China 82 B4
Nanzhang China 87 D2
Nanzhao China see Zhao'an
Nanzhao China 87 E1
Nanzheng China 86 C1
also known as Zhoujiaping
Nanzhou China see Nanxian
Naogaon Bangl. 97 F4
Naokot Pak. 101 G5
Naoli r. China 82 D3
Naomid, Dasht-e des. Afgh./Iran 101 E3
Naousa Greece 58 D8
Napa U.S.A. 182 B3
Napak mt. Uganda 128 B4
Napaktulik Lake Canada 167 H1
also known as Takijuq Lake
Napanee Canada 168 E4
Napasar India 96 B4
Napasoq Greenland 165 N3
Naperville U.S.A. 174 B3
Napier N.Z. 152 K7
Napier S. Africa 132 D11
Napier Broome Bay Australia 150 D2
Napier Mountains Antarctica 223 D2
Napier Peninsula Australia 148 B2
Napier Range hills Australia 150 D3
Naples Italy 57 G8
also known as Napoli; historically known as Neapolis
Naples FL U.S.A. 175 D7
Naples ME U.S.A. 177 O2
Naples NY U.S.A. 177 H3
Naples UT U.S.A. 183 O1
Napo China 86 C4
Napo prov. Ecuador 198 B5
Napo r. Ecuador 198 C5
Napoleon ND U.S.A. 178 C2
Napoleon OH U.S.A. 176 A4
Napoleonville U.S.A. 175 B6
Napoli Italy see Naples
Napoli, Golfo di b. Italy 57 G8
Naposta Arg. 204 E5
Nappanee U.S.A. 172 H9
Napperby Australia 148 B4
Naqadeh Iran 100 A2
Naqb Malha mt. Egypt 108 D8
Naqūb Yemen 105 D5
Nara Japan 91 D7
Nara pref. Japan 90 D7
Nara Mali 124 D3
Nara r. Rus. Fed. 43 S7
Narach Belarus 42 H7
Narach r. Belarus 42 H7
Narach, Vozyera l. Belarus 42 H7
Naracoorte Australia 146 D4
Naradhan Australia 147 E3
Narail Bangl. 97 F5
Naraina India 96 B4
Naranbulag Dornod Mongolia 85 G1
Naranbulag Uvs Mongolia 84 B1
Narang Afgh. 101 G3
Naranjal Ecuador 198 B5
Naranjal Peru 198 C6
Naranjos Mex. 185 F4
Naran Sebstein Bulag spring China 84 C3
Narao Japan 91 A8
Naraq Iran 100 B3
Narasannapeta India 95 E2
Narasapatnam, Point India 94 D2
Narasapur India 94 D2
Narasaraopet India 94 D2
Narasinghapur India 95 E1
Narasun Rus. Fed. 85 G1
Narat China 88 D3
Narathiwat Thai. 79 C7
Narat Shan mts China 88 C3
Nara Visa U.S.A. 179 B5
Narayanganj Bangl. 97 F5
Narayanganj India 96 D5
Narayangaon India 94 B2
Narayanpet India 94 C2
Naray Kelay Afgh. 101 G3
Narbada r. India see Narmada
Narbo France see Narbonne
Narbonne France 51 J9
historically known as Narbo
Narbuvoll Norway 44 J3
Narcea r. Spain 54 E1
Narcondam Island India 95 G3
Nardin Iran 100 C2
Nardò Italy 57 K8
Nare Arg. 204 E3
Narechi r. Pak. 101 G4
Naregal India 94 B3
Narembeen Australia 151 B7
Nares Strait Canada/Greenland 165 L2
Naretha Australia 151 D6
Narew r. Poland 49 R3
Narewka r. Poland 42 E9
Nari r. Pak. 101 F4
Naria Bangl. 97 F5
Narib Namibia 130 C5
Narie, Jezioro l. Poland 49 R2
Nariep S. Africa 132 B7
Narimanov Rus. Fed. 102 A3
formerly known as Nizhnevolzhsk
Narimskiy Khrebet mts Kazakh. 88 D1
Narin Afgh. 101 G2
Narin reg. Afgh. 101 G2
Narin China 85 F4
Narince Turkey 107 D3
Narin Gol watercourse China 84 B4
Nariño dept Col. 198 B4
Narita Japan 91 G7
Nariu-misaki pt Japan 91 D7
Nariwa Japan 91 C7
Narizon, Punta pt Mex. 184 C3
Narkaus Fin. 44 N2
Narken Sweden 44 M2
Narmada r. India 96 B5
also known as Narbada
Narnaul India 96 C3
Narni Italy 56 E6
historically known as Narnia
Narnia Italy see Narni
Narodnaya, Gora mt. Rus. Fed. 40 L2
Naro-Fominsk Rus. Fed. 43 R6
Narok Kenya 128 B5
Narooma Australia 147 F4
Narowlya Belarus 41 D6
Närpes Fin. 44 M3
Narrabri Australia 147 F2
Narragansett Bay U.S.A. 177 N4
Narran r. Australia 147 E2
Narrandera Australia 147 E3
Narran Lake Australia 147 E2
Narrogin Australia 151 B7
Narromine Australia 147 F3
Narrow Hills Provincial Park Canada 167 J4
Narrows U.S.A. 176 E8
Narrowsburg U.S.A. 177 J4
Narsalik Greenland 165 O3
Narsapur India 94 C2
Narsaq Greenland 165 O3
Narsarsuaq Greenland 165 O3
Narsimhapur India 96 C5
Narsingdi Bangl. 97 F5
Narsinghgarh India 96 C5
Narsipatnam India 95 D2
Nart China 85 G3
Nart Mongolia 85 E1
Nartë Albania 58 A8
Nartkala Rus. Fed. 107 E2
formerly known as Dokshukino
Naruko Japan 90 G5
Naruto Japan 91 D7
Narva Estonia 43 J2
Narva r. Estonia/Rus. Fed. 42 J2
Narva Bay Estonia/Rus. Fed. 42 I2
also known as Narva laht or Narvskiy Zaliv
Narvacan Phil. 74 B2
Narva-Jõesuu Estonia 43 J2
Narva laht b. Estonia/Rus. Fed. see Narva Bay
Narva Reservoir Estonia/Rus. Fed. see Narvskoye Vodokhranilishche
Narva veehoidla resr Estonia/Rus. Fed. see Narvskoye Vodokhranilishche
Narvik Norway 44 L1
Narvskiy Zaliv b. Estonia/Rus. Fed. see Narva Bay
Narvskoye Vodokhranilishche resr Estonia/Rus. Fed. 43 J2
English form Narva Reservoir; also known as Narva veehoidla
Narwana India 96 C3
Narwar India 96 C4
Narwinbi Aboriginal Land res. Australia 148 C3
Nar'yan-Mar Rus. Fed. 40 J2
Naryn Kyrg. 103 H4
Naryn admin. div. Kyrg. 103 H4
English form Naryn Oblast; also known as Narynskaya Oblast'; formerly known as Tien Shan Oblast or Tyanshanskaya Oblast'
Naryn r. Kyrg./Uzbek. 103 H4
Naryn Rus. Fed. 84 B1
Narynkol Kazakh. 88 C3
also spelt Naryngol
Naryn Oblast admin. div. Kyrg. see Naryn
Narynqol Kazakh. see Narynkol
Narynskaya Oblast' admin. div. Kyrg. see Naryn
Naryshkino Rus. Fed. 43 Q9
Năsăud Romania 58 F1
Näsby Sweden 45 L4
Naseby N.Z. 153 E13
Nashik India 94 B1
also spelt Nasik
Nashua U.S.A. 177 N3
Nashville AR U.S.A. 179 D5
Nashville GA U.S.A. 175 D6
Nashville IL U.S.A. 174 B4
Nashville NC U.S.A. 174 E5
Nashville OH U.S.A. 176 C5

Nashville TN U.S.A. 174 C4
State capital of Tennessee.

Našice Croatia 56 K3
Nasielsk Poland 49 R3
Näsijärvi l. Fin. 45 M3
Nasik India see Nashik
Nasir Sudan 128 B2
Nasirabad Bangl. see Mymensingh
Nasirabad India 96 B4
Nasirabad Pak. 101 G4
Naskaupi r. Canada 169 I2
Nasmganj India 97 E4
Nasondoye Dem. Rep. Congo 127 E7
Nasonville U.S.A. 172 C6
Nasosnyy Azer. see Hacı Zeynalabdin
Nasr Egypt 108 B7
Naṣrābād Eşfahan Iran 100 B3
Naṣrābād Khorāsan Iran 101 D3
Naṣrānī, Jabal an mts Syria 109 I4
Nasratabad Iran see Zābol
Naṣrīān-e Pā'īn Iran 100 A3
Nass r. Canada 166 D4
Nassarawa Nigeria 125 G4
Nassarawa state Nigeria 125 H4
Nassau r. Australia 149 D2

Nassau Bahamas 186 D1
Capital of The Bahamas.

Nassau i. Cook Is 221 G6
formerly known as Mitchell Island
Nassau U.S.A. 177 L3
Nassau, Naturpark nature res. Germany 48 E5
Nassawadox U.S.A. 177 J8
Nasser, Lake resr Egypt 121 G4
Nassian Côte d'Ivoire 124 E4
Nässjö Sweden 45 K4
Nassuttooq inlet Greenland 165 N3
also known as Nordre Strømfjord
Nastapoca r. Canada 169 E1
Nastapoka Islands Canada 168 E1
Nastola Fin. 42 G1
Nasu-dake vol. Japan 90 F6
Nasugbu Phil. 74 B3
Nasva Rus. Fed. 43 L5
Nasva r. Rus. Fed. 43 L5
Nata Botswana 131 E4
Nata watercourse Botswana/Zimbabwe 131 E4
Nataboti Indon. 75 C3
Natal Amazonas Brazil 201 E1
Natal Rio Grande do Norte Brazil 202 F3
Natal Indon. 76 B2
Natal prov. S. Africa see Kwazulu-Natal
Natal Drakensberg National Park S. Africa 133 N6
Naṭanz Iran 100 B3
Natashquan Canada 169 I3
Natashquan r. Canada 169 I3
Natchez U.S.A. 175 B6
Natchitoches U.S.A. 179 D6
Nathalia Australia 147 E4
Nathana India 96 B3
Nathdwara India 96 B4
Nati, Punta pt Spain 55 O4
Natiaboani Burkina 125 F4
National City U.S.A. 183 G9
National Park N.Z. 152 J7
National West Coast Tourist Recreation Area park Namibia 130 B4
Natitingou Benin 125 F4
Natividad, Isla i. Mex. 184 B3
Natividade Rio de Janeiro Brazil 207 L8
Natividade Tocantins Brazil 202 C4
Natla r. Canada 166 D2
Natmauk Myanmar 78 A3
Natogyi Myanmar 78 A3
Nator Bangl. 97 F4
Natora Mex. 181 E7
Natori Japan 90 G5
Natron, Lake salt l. Tanz. 128 C5
Nattai National Park Australia 147 F3
Nattalin Myanmar 78 A4
Nattam India 94 C4
Nattaung mt. Myanmar 78 B4
Nattavaara Sweden 44 M2
Na'tū Iran 101 E3
Natuna, Kepulauan is Indon. 77 D1
also known as Bunguran, Kepulauan
Natuna Besar i. Indon. 77 E1
also known as Bunguran, Pulau
Natural Bridge U.S.A. 176 F8
Natural Bridges National Monument nat. park U.S.A. 183 N4
Naturaliste, Cape Australia 151 A7
Naturaliste Channel Australia 151 A5
Nature's Valley S. Africa 132 H10
Nau Tajik. see Nov
Naubinway U.S.A. 172 H4
Naucelle France 51 I8
Nauchas Namibia 130 C4
Nau Co l. China 89 C5
Naudesberg Pass S. Africa 133 I9
Nauen Germany 49 J3
Naugatuck U.S.A. 177 L4
Nau Hissar Pak. 101 F4
Naujan Phil. 74 B3
Naujoji Akmenė Lith. 42 D5
Naukh India 96 B4
Naulila Angola 127 B9
Naumburg (Saale) Germany 48 I4
Naungpale Myanmar 78 B4
Na'ūr Jordan 106 C5
Naurskaya Rus. Fed. 107 F2
Nauru i. Nauru 145 F2

Nauru country S. Pacific Ocean 145 F2
oceania [countries] 138–139

Naushahro Firoz Pak. 101 G5
Naushara Pak. 101 G5
Naushki Rus. Fed. 85 E1
Naustdal Norway 45 I3
Nauta Peru 198 C6
Nautaca Uzbek. see Karshi
Naute Dam Namibia 132 B3
Nautla Mex. 185 F4
Nautonwa India 97 D4
Nautsi Rus. Fed. 44 O1
Nauvoo U.S.A. 172 B10
Nava r. Dem. Rep. Congo 126 E4
Navabad Tajik. see Novobod
Navacerrada, Puerto de pass Spain 54 H4
Navachica mt. Spain 54 H8
Navadrutsk Belarus 42 I6
Navadwip India 97 F5
formerly spelt Nabadwip
Navahermosa Spain 54 G5
Navahrudak Belarus 42 G8
also spelt Novogrudok
Navahrudskaye Wzvyshsha hills Belarus 42 G8
Navajo r. U.S.A. 181 F5
Navajo Indian Reservation res. U.S.A. 183 O6
Navajo Lake U.S.A. 181 F5
Navajo Mountain U.S.A. 183 N4
Naval Phil. 74 C4
Navalmoral de la Mata Spain 54 F5
Navalvillar de Pela Spain 54 F5
Navan Rep. of Ireland 47 F10
also known as An Uaimh
Navangar India see Jamnagar
Navapolatsk Belarus 43 J6
also spelt Novopolotsk
Navarin, Mys c. Rus. Fed. 39 R3
Navarino, Isla i. Chile 205 D9
Navarra aut. comm. Spain 55 J2
English form Navarre
Navarre aut. comm. Spain see Navarra
Navarrenx France 50 F9
Navarro Peru 198 C6
Navarro r. U.S.A. 182 A2
Navashino Rus. Fed. 40 G5
Navasota U.S.A. 179 C6
Navasota r. U.S.A. 179 C6

Navassa Island terr. West Indies 187 E3
United States Unincorporated Territory.
oceania [countries] 138–139

Navasyolki Belarus 43 J9
Navayel'nya Belarus 42 G8
Naver r. U.K. 46 H5
Navesnoye Rus. Fed. 43 S9
Navesti r. Estonia 42 F3
Navia Spain 54 E1
Navia r. Spain 54 E1
Navidad Chile 204 C4
Navidad r. U.S.A. 179 C6
Naviraí Brazil 203 A7
Navlakhi India 96 A5
Navlya Rus. Fed. 43 P9
Navlya r. Rus. Fed. 43 P9
Năvodari Romania 58 J4
Navoi Uzbek. 103 F4
also spelt Nawoiy; formerly known as Kermine
Navoiyskaya Oblast' admin. div. Uzbek. 103 E4
English form Navoy Oblast; also known as Nawoiy Wiloyati
Navojoa Mex. 184 C3
Navolato Mex. 184 D3
Navoy Oblast admin. div. Uzbek. see Navoiyskaya Oblast'
Návpaktos Greece see Nafpaktos
Návplion Greece see Nafplio
Nävragöl Sweden 45 K4
Navrongo Ghana 125 E4
Navşar Turkey see Şemdinli
Navsari India 94 B1
Navua Fiji 145 G3
Nawa India 96 B4
Nawá Syria 108 H5
Nawabganj Bangl. 97 F4
Nawabganj India 97 D4
Nawabshah Pak. 101 G5
Nawada India 97 E4
Nāwah Afgh. 101 F3
Nawakot Nepal 97 E4
Nawalgarh India 96 B4
Nawar, Dasht-i imp. l. Afgh. 101 F3
Nawashahr India 89 B6
Nawāşīf, Ḩarrāt lava field Saudi Arabia 104 C3
Nawnghkio Myanmar 78 B3
Nawngleng Myanmar 78 B3
Nawoiy Uzbek. see Navoi
Nawoiy Wiloyati admin. div. Uzbek. see Navoiyskaya Oblast'
Naws, Ra's c. Oman 105 F4
Naxçıvan Azer. 107 F3
also spelt Nakhichevan'
Naxi China 86 C2
Naxos Greece 59 G11
Naxos i. Greece 59 G11
Naya Col. 198 B4
Nayagarh India 95 E1
Nayak Afgh. 101 F3
Nayarit state Mex. 184 D4
Nāy Band, Kūh-e mt. Iran 100 D3
Nayfah oasis Saudi Arabia 105 E4
Nayong China 86 C3
also known as Yongxi
Nayoro Japan 90 H2
Nayt Yemen 105 F5
Nayuchi Malawi 129 B8
Nayudupeta India 94 C3
Nayyāl, Wādī watercourse Saudi Arabia 104 B1
Nazaré Brazil 199 E4
Nazaré Brazil 202 E5
Nazareno Mex. 184 E3
Nazareth India 94 C4
Nazareth Israel 108 G5
Nazareth U.S.A. 177 J5
Nazário Brazil 206 D3
Nazas Mex. 184 D3
Nazas r. Mex. 184 D3
Nazca Peru 200 B3
Nāzīk Iran 100 A2
Nazilli Turkey 106 B3
Nazımiye Turkey 107 D3
Nazinon r. Burkina/Ghana 125 E4 see Red Volta
Nazira India 97 G4
Nazir Hat Bangl. 97 F5
Naziya Rus. Fed. 43 M2
Nazko Canada 166 F4
Nazko r. Canada 166 F4
Nazran' Rus. Fed. 41 H8
formerly known as Kosta-Khetagurovo
Nazrēt Eth. 128 C2
Nazwá Oman 105 G3
also spelt Nizwā
Nazyvayevsk Rus. Fed. 38 H4
formerly known as Novonazyvayevka
Nbâk Mauritania 124 B2
Ncanaha S. Africa 133 J10
Nchelenge Zambia 127 F7
Ncheu Malawi see Ntcheu
Ncora S. Africa 133 L8
Ncue Equat. Guinea 125 H6
Ndala Tanz. 129 B6
N'dalatando Angola 127 B7
formerly known as Salazar or Vila Salazar; formerly spelt Dalatando
Ndali Benin 125 F4
Ndanda Cent. Afr. Rep. 126 D3
Ndao i. Indon. 75 B5
Ndareda Tanz. 129 B6
Ndélé Cent. Afr. Rep. 126 D2
Ndélélé Cameroon 125 I5
Ndendé Gabon 126 A5
Ndende i. Solomon Is see Ndeni
Ndeni i. Solomon Is 145 F3
also spelt Ndende or Nitendi
Ndiael, Réserve de Faune du nature res. Senegal 124 A3
Ndikiniméki Cameroon 125 H5
Ndim Cent. Afr. Rep. 126 B3
N'Djamena Chad see Ndjamena

Ndjamena Chad 120 B6
Capital of Chad. Also spelt N'Djamena; formerly known as Fort Lamy.

Ndji r. Cent. Afr. Rep. 126 D3
Ndjim r. Cameroon 125 H5
Ndjolé Gabon 126 A5
Ndjouani i. Comoros see Nzwani
Ndjounou Gabon 126 B5
Ndofane Senegal 124 B3
Ndogo, Lagune lag. Gabon 126 A5
Ndoi i. Fiji see Doi
Ndok Cameroon 125 I5
Ndola Zambia 127 F8
Ndoto mt. Kenya 128 C4
Ndougou Gabon 126 A5
Nduke i. Solomon Is see Kolombangara
Ndumbwe Tanz. 129 C7
Ndumu S. Africa 133 Q3
Ndumu Game Reserve nature res. Moz. 133 Q3
Nduye Dem. Rep. Congo 126 F4
Ndwedwe S. Africa 133 O6
Nea Anchialos Greece 59 D9
Nea Apollonia Greece 58 E8
Nea Artaki Greece 59 E10
Neabul Creek r. Australia 147 E1
Neagh, Lough l. U.K. 47 F9
Neah Bay U.S.A. 180 A2
Neajlov r. Romania 58 G4
Nea Karvali Greece 58 F8
Neale, Lake salt flat Australia 148 A5
Neale Junction Nature Reserve Australia 151 D6
Neales watercourse Australia 146 C2
Nea Liosia Greece 59 E10
Nea Makri Greece 59 E10
Nea Moudania Greece 59 E8
Neamț r. Romania 58 H1
Nea Peramos Greece 58 F8
Neapoli Kriti Greece 59 G13
Neapoli Peloponnisos Greece 59 E12
Neapolis Italy see Naples
Nea Roda Greece 59 E8
Nea Santa Greece 58 D8
Neath U.K. 47 I12
also known as Castell-nedd
Nea Zichni Greece 58 E7
Nebbi Uganda 128 A4
Nebbou Burkina 125 E4
Nebesnaya, Gora mt. China 88 C3
Nebine Creek r. Australia 147 E2
Nebitdag Turkm. 102 C5
Nebo Australia 149 F4
Nebo, Mount U.S.A. 183 M2
Nebolchi Rus. Fed. 43 O2
Nebraska state U.S.A. 178 B3
Nebraska City U.S.A. 178 D3
Nebrodi, Monti mts Sicilia Italy 57 G11
Nebylnoye Rus. Fed. 43 U5
Necedah U.S.A. 172 C6
Necedah National Wildlife Refuge nature res. U.S.A. 172 C6
Neches r. U.S.A. 179 D6
Nechí r. Col. 198 C2
Nechisar National Park Eth. 128 C3
Neckarsulm Germany 48 G6
Neckartal-Odenwald, Naturpark nature res. Germany 48 G6
Necker Island U.S.A. 221 H4
Necochea Arg. 204 F5
Necoclí Col. 198 B2
Nedelino Bulg. 58 G7
Nedelišće Croatia 56 I2
Nedel'noye Rus. Fed. 43 R7
Nederland country Europe see Netherlands
Nederlandse Antillen terr. West Indies see Netherlands Antilles
Neder Rijn r. Neth. 48 C4
Nedlouc, Lac l. Canada 169 F1
also known as Nedluk Lake
Nedluk Lake Canada see Nedlouc, Lac
Nēdong China 89 E6
Nedre Soppero Sweden 44 M1
Nédroma Alg. 55 J9
Nedstrand Norway 45 I4
Needham U.S.A. 177 N3
Needles U.S.A. 183 J7
Needmore U.S.A. 176 G6
Neemuch India see Nimach
Neenah U.S.A. 172 E6
Neepawa Canada 167 L5
Neergaard Lake Canada 165 K2
Nefta Tunisia 123 G2
Neftçala Azer. 107 G3
also spelt Neftechala
Neftechala Azer. see 26 Bakı Komissarı
Neftechala Azer. see Neftçala
Neftegorsk Sakhalin Rus. Fed. 82 F1
formerly known as Vostok
Neftegorsk Samarskaya Oblast' Rus. Fed. 102 B1
also known as Kasevo
Neftekamsk Rus. Fed. 40 J4
formerly known as Kasevo
Neftekumsk Rus. Fed. 41 H7
Nefteyugansk Rus. Fed. 38 H3
formerly known as Ust'-Balyk
Neftezavodsk Turkm. see Seydi
Nefza Tunisia 57 B11
Negade Weyn well Eth. 128 E3
Negage Angola 127 B6
Négala Mali 124 C3
Negār Iran 100 D4
Negara Bali Indon. 77 F5
Negara Kalimantan Selatan Indon. 77 F3
Negara r. Indon. 77 F3
Negaunee U.S.A. 172 F4
Negēlē Oromia Eth. 128 C3
Negēlē Oromia Eth. 128 C3
Negeri Sembilan state Malaysia 76 C2
formerly spelt Negri Sembilan
Negev des. Israel 108 G7
also spelt HaNegev
Negomane Moz. 129 C7
Negombo Sri Lanka 94 C5
Negotin Srbija Yugo. 58 D4
Negotino Macedonia 58 D7
Negra, Cordillera mts Peru 200 A2
Negra, Lago l. Uruguay 204 G4
also known as Los Difuntios, Lago de
Negra, Punta pt Peru 198 A6
Negra, Serra mts Brazil 203 D6
Negra, Serranía de mts Bol. 201 E3
Negrais, Cape Myanmar 78 A5
Negratín, Embalse de resr Spain 55 I7
Negreira Spain 54 C2
Negreiros Chile 200 C4
Nègrepelisse France 50 H8
Negrești Romania 58 I2
Negri r. Australia 148 A3
Negri Romania 58 H2
Négrine Alg. 123 G2
Negri Sembilan state Malaysia see Negeri Sembilan
Negritos Peru 198 A6
Negro r. Arg. 204 E6
Negro r. Brazil 201 F4
Negro r. Para. 201 F6
Negro r. S. America 199 G5
Negro r. Uruguay 204 G4
Negro, Cabo c. Morocco 54 F9
Negroponte i. Greece see Evvoia
Negros i. Phil. 74 B4
Negru Vodă Romania 58 J5
Nehalem r. U.S.A. 180 B3
Nehavand Iran 100 B3
Nehbandān Iran 101 E4
Nehe China 85 J1
Nehoiu Romania 58 H3
Nehone Angola 127 C9
Neiafu Tonga 145 H3
Neiba Dom. Rep. 187 F3
Neijiang China 86 C2
Neilersdrif S. Africa 132 E5
Neill Island India 95 G4
Neillsville U.S.A. 172 C6
Nei Mongol Zizhiqu aut. reg. China 85 D3
English form Inner Mongolia
Neiqiu China 85 G4
Neiße r. Germany/Poland 49 L3
also known as Nysa Łużycka
Neiva Col. 198 C4
Neixiang China 87 D1
Nejanilini Lake Canada 167 L3
Nejapa Mex. 185 G5
Nejd reg. Saudi Arabia see Najd
Neka Iran 100 C2
Neka r. Iran 100 C2
Nek'emtē Eth. 128 C2
Nekhayevskaya Rus. Fed. 41 G6
formerly known as Nekhayevskiy
Nekhayevskiy Rus. Fed. see Nekhayevskaya
Neklyudovo Rus. Fed. 43 V6
Nekrasovskiy Rus. Fed. 43 S5
Nekrasovskoye Rus. Fed. 43 V4
Nekso Denmark 45 K5
Nela r. Spain 54 H2
Nelamangala India 94 C3
Nelas Port. 54 D4
Nelazskoye Rus. Fed. 43 S2
Nelia Australia 149 D4
Nelidovo Rus. Fed. 43 N5
Neligh U.S.A. 178 C3
Nel'kan Khabarovskiy Kray Rus. Fed. 39 N4
Nel'kan Respublika Sakha (Yakutiya) Rus. Fed. 39 O3
Nellie Lake Canada 173 M2
Nellim Fin. 44 O1
also spelt Njellim
Nellore India 94 C3
Nelluz watercourse Turkey 109 K1
Nelshoogte pass S. Africa 133 O2
Nelson Arg. 204 E3
Nelson Canada 166 G5
Nelson r. Canada 167 M3
Nelson N.Z. 152 H9
Nelson admin. reg. N.Z. 152 H9
Nelson AZ U.S.A. 183 K6
Nelson NE U.S.A. 178 C3
Nelson NV U.S.A. 183 J6
Nelson, Cape Australia 146 D4
Nelson, Estrecho strait Chile 205 B8
Nelson Bay Australia 147 G3
Nelson Creek N.Z. 153 F10
Nelson Forks Canada 166 F3
Nelson House Canada 167 L4
Nelson Lakes National Park N.Z. 153 G10
Nelspoort S. Africa 132 H9
Nelspruit S. Africa 133 O2
Nem r. Rus. Fed. 40 J3
Néma Mauritania 124 D2
Nema Rus. Fed. 40 I4
Nemadji r. U.S.A. 172 A4
Neman r. Belarus/Lith. see Nyoman
Neman Rus. Fed. 42 D6
Neman r. Rus. Fed. 42 D6
Ne'matābād Iran 100 D4
Nemausus France see Nîmes
Nembe Nigeria 125 G5
Nemda r. Rus. Fed. 40 G4
Nemea Greece 59 D11
Nemed Rus. Fed. 40 J3
Nemegos Canada 173 J3
Nemegosenda Lake Canada 173 J2
Nemenčinė Lith. 42 G7
Nemetocenna France see Arras
Nemetskiy, Mys c. Rus. Fed. 44 O1
Nemirov Ukr. see Nemyriv
Némiscau r. Canada 168 E3
Nemor r. China 85 J1
Nemours Alg. see Ghazaouet
Nemours France 51 I4
Nemrut Dağı mt. Turkey 107 E3
Nemta r. Rus. Fed. 82 D2
Nemunas r. Lith. 42 C6
Nemunėlio Radviliškis Lith. 42 F5
Nemunėlis r. Lith. 42 G5
Nemuro Japan 90 I3
Nemuro-hantō pen. Japan 90 I3
Nemuro-kaikyō sea chan. Japan/Rus. Fed. 90 I3
also known as Kunashirskiy Proliv
Nemuro-wan b. Japan 90 I3
Nemyriv Ukr. 41 D6
also spelt Nemirov
Nenagh Rep. of Ireland 47 D11
also known as An tAonach
Nenana U.S.A. 164 E3
Nenashevo Rus. Fed. 43 S7
Nene r. U.K. 47 M11
Nenets Autonomous Okrug admin. div. Rus. Fed. see Nenetskiy Avtonomnyy Okrug
Nenetskiy Avtonomnyy Okrug admin. div. Rus. Fed. 40 J2
English form Nenets Autonomous Okrug
Nenjiang China 85 J1
Nen Jiang r. China 85 J2
also known as Nonni
Neo Japan 91 E7
Neochori Greece 59 C9
also known as Neokhórion
Neo Karlovasi Greece 59 H11
also known as Néon Karlovásion
Neokhórion Greece see Neochori
Neola U.S.A. 183 N1
Neo Monastiri Greece 59 D9
Néon Karlovásion Greece see Neo Karlovasi
Neopit U.S.A. 172 E6
Neosho U.S.A. 178 D4
Neosho r. U.S.A. 178 D4
Neos Marmaras Greece 59 E8

Nepal country Asia 97 D3
asia [countries] 64–67

Nepalganj Nepal 97 D3
Nepanagar India 96 C5
Nepean Canada 168 F4
Nephi U.S.A. 183 M2
Nephin hill Rep. of Ireland 47 C9
Nephin Beg Range hills Rep. of Ireland 47 C9
Nepisiguit r. Canada 169 H4
Nepryadva r. Rus. Fed. 43 T8
Neptune U.S.A. 177 K5
Ner r. Poland 49 P3
Nera r. Italy 56 E6
Nérac France 50 G8
Neral India 94 B2
Nerang Australia 147 G1
Nera Tso l. Xizang China 89 F6
Neravai Lith. 42 F7
Nerchinsk Rus. Fed. 85 H1
Nerchinskiy Zavod Rus. Fed. 85 H1
Nereju Romania 58 H3
Nerekhta Rus. Fed. 43 V4
Nereta Latvia 42 G5
Neretva r. Bos.-Herz./Croatia 56 J5
Neretvanski Kanal sea chan. Croatia 56 J5
Neri India 94 C1
Nêri Pünco l. China 89 E6
Neriquinha Angola 127 D8
Neris r. Lith. 42 E7

index N

Nerka, Lake U.S.A. **164** D4
Nerl' *Ivanovskaya Oblast'* Rus. Fed. **43** V5
Nerl' *Tverskaya Oblast'* Rus. Fed. **43** T4
Nerl' *r.* Rus. Fed. **43** S4
Nero, Ozero *l.* Rus. Fed. **43** U4
Nerópolis Brazil **206** D3
Neroyka, Gora *mt.* Rus. Fed. **40** K2
Ner Pinglai India **96** C5
Neruch' *r.* Rus. Fed. **43** R9
Nerussa *r.* Rus. Fed. **43** O9
Neryungri Rus. Fed. **39** M4
Nes Norway **45** J3
Nes' Rus. Fed. **40** H2
Nes' *r.* Rus. Fed. **40** H2
Nesa' Iran **100** B2
Nesbyen Norway **45** J3
Nesebŭr Bulg. **58** I6
Neskaupstaður Iceland **44** [inset] D2
Nesna Norway **44** K2
Nesque *r.* France **51** K8
Nesri India **94** B2
Ness, Loch *l.* U.K. **46** H6
Ness City U.S.A. **178** C4
Nesse *r.* Germany **48** H5
Nesselrode, Mount Canada/U.S.A. **166** C3
Nesselwang Germany **48** H8
Neste *r.* France **50** G9
Nesterov Rus. Fed. **42** D7
Nesterovo Rus. Fed. **43** T2
Nestery Rus. Fed. **43** O7
Nestore *r.* Italy **56** E6
Nestor Falls Canada **168** A3
Nestoria U.S.A. **172** E4
Nestos *r.* Greece **58** F8
also known as Mesta
Nesvizh Belarus *see* **Nyasvizh**
Netanya Israel **108** F5
Netarhat India **97** E5
Netcong U.S.A. **177** K5
▶ **Netherlands** *country* Europe **48** B3
also known as Holland; *known as* Nederland in Dutch
europe [countries] ▶ 32–35

▶ **Netherlands Antilles** *terr.* West Indies **187** F4
Self-governing Netherlands Territory. Also known as Nederlandse Antillen; formerly known as Dutch West Indies.
oceania [countries] ▶ 138–139

Neto *r.* Italy **57** J9
Netrakona Bangl. **97** F4
Netrang India **96** B5
Nettilling Lake Canada **165** L3
Nettuno Italy **56** E7
Neubari *r.* Sudan **128** B3
Neubrandenburg Germany **49** K2
Neubukow Germany **48** I1
Neuburg an der Donau Germany **48** I7
Neuchâtel Switz. **51** M6
Neuchâtel, Lac de *l.* Switz. **51** M6
Neuenhagen Berlin Germany **49** K3
Neuenkirchen Germany **48** F2
Neuenkirchen-Seelscheid Germany **48** E5
Neufchâteau Belgium **51** L3
Neufchâteau France **51** L4
Neufchâtel-en-Bray France **50** H3
Neuhausen Rus. Fed. *see* **Gur'yevsk**
Neuhof Germany **48** G5
Neuillé-Pont-Pierre France **50** G5
Neukuhren Rus. Fed. *see* **Pionerskiy**
Neumarkt in der Oberpfalz Germany **48** I6
Neumayer *research station* Antarctica **223** X2
long form Georg von Neumayer
Neumünster Germany **48** G1
Neun, Nam *r.* Laos **78** D4
Neunkirchen Austria **49** N8
Neunkirchen Germany **48** E6
Neuquén Arg. **204** C5
Neuquén *prov.* Arg. **204** C5
Neuquén *r.* Arg. **204** D5
Neuruppin Germany **49** J3
Neu Sandez Poland *see* **Nowy Sącz**
Neuse *r.* U.S.A. **174** E5
Neusiedl am See Austria **49** N8
Neusiedler See *l.* Austria/Hungary **49** N8
Neusiedler See Seewinkel, Nationalpark *nat. park* Austria **49** N8
Neuss Germany **48** D4
Neustadt (Wied) Germany **48** E5
Neustadt am Rübenberge Germany **48** G3
Neustadt an der Aisch Germany **48** H6
Neustadt an der Hardt Germany *see* **Neustadt an der Weinstraße**
Neustadt an der Weinstraße Germany **48** F6
formerly known as Neustadt an der Hardt
Neustadt in Holstein Germany **48** H1
Neustadt in Sachsen Germany **49** L4
Neustift im Stubaital Austria **56** D1
Neustrelitz Germany **49** K2
Neuves-Maisons France **51** M4
Neuville-aux-Bois France **51** I4
Neuville-lès-Dieppe France **50** H3
Neuwerk *i.* Germany **48** F2
Neuwied Germany **48** E5
Nevada *IA* U.S.A. **174** A3
Nevada *MO* U.S.A. **178** D4
Nevada *state* U.S.A. **183** G2
Nevada, Sierra *mt.* Arg. **204** C2
Nevada, Sierra *mts* Spain **55** H7
Nevada, Sierra *nature res.* Spain **55** H7
Nevada, Sierra *mts* U.S.A. **182** C1
Nevada City U.S.A. **182** C2
Nevado, Cerro *mt.* Arg. **204** C4
Nevado, Sierra del *mts* Arg. **204** C5
Nevado de Colima, Parque Nacional *nat. park* Mex. **184** E5
Nevado de Toluca, Parque Nacional *nat. park* Mex. **185** F5
Nevasa India **94** B2
Nevdol'sk Rus. Fed. **43** P9
Nevdubstroy Rus. Fed. *see* **Kirovsk**
Neve, Serra da *mts* Angola **127** B8
Nevel' Rus. Fed. **43** K5
Nevel', Ozero *l.* Rus. Fed. **43** K6
Nevel'sk Rus. Fed. **82** F3
Neverkino Rus. Fed. **41** H5
Neveronys Lith. **42** F7
Nevers France **51** J5
Nevertire Australia **147** E2
Neves Brazil **207** J9
Nevesinje Bos.-Herz. **56** K5
Nevėžis *r.* Lith. **42** E7
Nevinnomyssk Rus. Fed. **41** G7
Nevis *i.* St Kitts and Nevis **187** H3
Nevşehir Turkey **106** C3
Nevskoye Rus. Fed. **90** C2
New *r.* *CA* U.S.A. **183** I8
New *r.* *WV* U.S.A. **176** D8
New Aiyansh Canada **166** D4
Newala Tanz. **129** C7
New Albany *IN* U.S.A. **174** C4
New Albany *MS* U.S.A. **174** B5
Newald U.S.A. **172** E5
New Amsterdam Guyana **199** G3
New Angledool Australia **147** E2
Newark *CA* U.S.A. **182** B4
Newark *DE* U.S.A. **177** J6
Newark *NJ* U.S.A. **177** K5
Newark *NY* U.S.A. **177** H2
Newark *OH* U.S.A. **176** C5
Newark *airport* U.S.A. **177** K5
Newark Lake U.S.A. **183** I2
Newark-on-Trent U.K. **47** L10
Newark Valley U.S.A. **177** I3
New Augusta U.S.A. **175** B6
Newaygo U.S.A. **172** H7
New Bedford U.S.A. **177** O4
Newberg U.S.A. **180** B3
New Berlin U.S.A. **177** J3
New Bern U.S.A. **174** E5
Newberry *MI* U.S.A. **172** H4
Newberry *SC* U.S.A. **175** D5
Newberry National Volcanic Monument *nat. park* U.S.A. **180** B4
Newberry Springs U.S.A. **183** H7
New Bethlehem U.S.A. **176** F4
New Bight Bahamas **187** E1
New Bloomfield U.S.A. **177** H5
Newboro Canada **168** E4
New Boston *IL* U.S.A. **172** C9
New Boston *OH* U.S.A. **176** C7
New Boston *TX* U.S.A. **179** D5
New Braunfels U.S.A. **179** C6
New Brighton U.S.A. **176** E5
New Britain *i.* P.N.G. **145** D2
New Brunswick *prov.* Canada **169** H4
New Brunswick U.S.A. **177** K5
New Buffalo U.S.A. **172** G9
Newburg U.S.A. **176** H5
Newburgh Canada **173** Q6
Newburgh U.K. **46** J6
Newburgh U.S.A. **177** K4
Newbury U.K. **47** K12
Newburyport U.S.A. **177** O3
New Caledonia *i.* S. Pacific Ocean *see* **Nouvelle Calédonie**

▶ **New Caledonia** *terr.* S. Pacific Ocean **145** F4
French Overseas Territory. Also known as Nouvelle Calédonie.
oceania [countries] ▶ 138–139
oceania [features] ▶ 142–143

New Carlisle Canada **169** H3
Newcastle Australia **147** F3
Newcastle *N.B.* Canada **169** H4
Newcastle *Ont.* Canada **168** E5
Newcastle S. Africa **133** N4
Newcastle U.K. **47** G9
Newcastle *CA* U.S.A. **182** C3
New Castle *DE* U.S.A. **177** J6
New Castle *IN* U.S.A. **174** C4
New Castle *KY* U.S.A. **174** C4
Newcastle *ME* U.S.A. **177** P1
New Castle *PA* U.S.A. **176** E4
Newcastle *UT* U.S.A. **183** K4
New Castle *VA* U.S.A. **176** E8
Newcastle *WY* U.S.A. **180** F4
Newcastle Creek *r.* Australia **148** B3
Newcastle Emlyn U.K. **47** H11
also known as Castell Newydd Emlyn
Newcastle Range *hills* Australia **149** D3
Newcastle-under-Lyme U.K. **47** J10
Newcastle upon Tyne U.K. **47** K9
New Church U.S.A. **177** J8
Newchwang China *see* **Yingkou**
New City U.S.A. **177** L4
Newcomerstown U.S.A. **176** D5
New Concord U.S.A. **176** D6
Newdegate Australia **151** B7

▶ **New Delhi** India **96** C3
Capital of India.

New Don Pedro Reservoir U.S.A. **182** D4
Newell, Lake *salt flat* Australia **151** D5
Newell, Lake Canada **167** I5
New England Range *mts* Australia **147** F2
Newenham, Cape U.S.A. **164** C4
New Era U.S.A. **172** G7
Newfane U.S.A. **176** G2
Newfound Lake U.S.A. **177** N2
Newfoundland *i.* Canada **169** J3
historically known as Vinland
Newfoundland *prov.* Canada **165** N4
Newfoundland U.S.A. **177** J4
Newfoundland Evaporation Basin *salt l.* U.S.A. **183** K1
New Freedom U.S.A. **177** I6
New Galloway U.K. **47** H8
New Georgia *i.* Solomon Is **145** E2
New Georgia Islands Solomon Is **145** E2
New Georgia Sound *sea chan.* Solomon Is **145** E2
also known as The Slot
New Glarus U.S.A. **172** D8
New Glasgow Canada **169** I4
Newgrange Tomb *tourist site* Rep. of Ireland **47** F10

▶ **New Guinea** *i.* Indon./P.N.G. **73** J8
Largest island in Oceania and 2nd in the world.
oceania [landscapes] ▶ 136–137

New Halfa Sudan **121** G6
Newhall U.S.A. **182** F7
New Hampshire *state* U.S.A. **177** N1
New Hanover *i.* P.N.G. **145** E2
also known as Lavongai
New Hanover S. Africa **133** O6
New Hartford U.S.A. **177** J2
Newhaven U.K. **47** M13
New Haven *CT* U.S.A. **177** M4
New Haven *IN* U.S.A. **173** H9
New Haven *MI* U.S.A. **173** K8
New Haven *WV* U.S.A. **176** D7
New Hazelton Canada **166** E4
New Hebrides *country* S. Pacific Ocean *see* **Vanuatu**
New Hogan Reservoir U.S.A. **182** D3
New Holland *country* Oceania *see* **Australia**
New Holland U.S.A. **177** I5
New Holstein U.S.A. **172** E7
New Iberia U.S.A. **175** B6
Newington S. Africa **133** P1
New Ireland *i.* P.N.G. **145** E2
New Jersey *state* U.S.A. **177** K6
New Kandla India **96** A5
New Kensington U.S.A. **176** F5
New Kent U.S.A. **177** H8
Newkirk U.S.A. **178** C4
New Lanark *tourist site* U.K. **46** I8
Newland Range *hills* Australia **151** C6
New Lexington U.S.A. **176** C6
New Lisbon U.S.A. **172** C7
New Liskeard Canada **168** E4
New London *CT* U.S.A. **177** M4
New London *IA* U.S.A. **172** B10
New London *OH* U.S.A. **176** C4
New London *WI* U.S.A. **172** E6
New Madrid U.S.A. **174** B4
Newman Australia **150** B4
Newman U.S.A. **182** C4
Newman, Mount Australia **150** B4
Newman Island Antarctica **222** O1
Newmarket Canada **168** E4
Newmarket Rep. of Ireland **47** C11
Newmarket U.K. **47** M11
Newmarket U.S.A. **177** O2
New Market *TN* U.S.A. **176** B9
New Market *VA* U.S.A. **176** G7
Newmarket-on-Fergus Rep. of Ireland **47** D11
New Martinsville U.S.A. **176** E6
New Meadows U.S.A. **180** C3
New Mexico *state* U.S.A. **181** F6
New Miami U.S.A. **176** A6
New Milford *CT* U.S.A. **177** L4
New Milford *PA* U.S.A. **177** J4
Newnan U.S.A. **175** C5
New Norcia Australia **151** B6
New Norfolk Australia **147** E5
New Orleans U.S.A. **175** B6
New Oxford U.S.A. **177** H6
New Paltz U.S.A. **177** K4
New Paris *IN* U.S.A. **172** H9
New Paris *OH* U.S.A. **176** A6
New Philadelphia U.S.A. **176** D5
New Plymouth N.Z. **152** I7
Newport *Isle of Wight, England* U.K. **47** K13
Newport *Newport, Wales* U.K. **47** I12
also known as Casnewydd
Newport *AR* U.S.A. **174** B5
Newport *DE* U.S.A. **177** J6
Newport *IN* U.S.A. **174** C4
Newport *ME* U.S.A. **177** P1
Newport *NH* U.S.A. **177** M2
Newport *NJ* U.S.A. **177** J6
Newport *OR* U.S.A. **180** A3
Newport *PA* U.S.A. **177** H5
Newport *RI* U.S.A. **177** N4
Newport *TN* U.S.A. **174** D5
Newport *VT* U.S.A. **177** M1
Newport *WA* U.S.A. **180** C2
Newport Beach U.S.A. **182** G8
Newport News U.S.A. **177** I8
New Port Richey U.S.A. **175** D6
New Providence *i.* Bahamas **186** D1
Newquay U.K. **47** G13
New Richmond Canada **169** H3
New Richmond U.S.A. **172** A5
New River U.S.A. **183** L8
New Roads U.S.A. **175** B6
New Rockford U.S.A. **178** C2
New Ross Canada **169** H4
New Ross Rep. of Ireland **47** F11
Newry Australia **148** A3
Newry U.K. **47** F9
Newry U.S.A. **172** C7
New Sharon U.S.A. **174** A3
New Siberia Islands Rus. Fed. **39** O2
also known as Novosibirskiye Ostrova
New Smyrna Beach U.S.A. **175** D6
New South Wales *state* Australia **147** E3
New Stanton U.S.A. **176** F5
New Tazewell U.S.A. **176** B9
Newton *GA* U.S.A. **175** C6
Newton *IA* U.S.A. **174** A3
Newton *IL* U.S.A. **174** B4
Newton *KS* U.S.A. **178** C4
Newton *MA* U.S.A. **177** N3
Newton *MS* U.S.A. **175** B5
Newton *NJ* U.S.A. **177** K4
Newton *TX* U.S.A. **179** D6
Newton Abbot U.K. **47** I13
Newton Falls U.S.A. **177** K1
Newton Stewart U.K. **47** H9
Newtontoppen *mt.* Svalbard **38** B2
Newtown U.K. **47** I11
also known as Y Drenewydd
New Town U.S.A. **178** B1
Newtown U.S.A. **177** K5
Newtownabbey U.K. **47** G9
Newtownards U.K. **47** G9
Newtownbarry Rep. of Ireland *see* **Bunclody**
Newtownbutler U.K. **47** E9
Newtown St Boswells U.K. **46** J8
Newtownstewart U.K. **47** E9
New Ulm U.S.A. **178** D2
New Vienna U.S.A. **176** B6
Newville U.S.A. **176** H5
New Vineyard U.S.A. **177** O1
New Woodstock U.S.A. **177** J3

▶ **New York** U.S.A. **177** L5
2nd most populous city in North America and 5th in the world.
world [land cover] ▶ 18–19
world [cities] ▶ 24–25

New York *state* U.S.A. **177** J3
New York Mountains U.S.A. **183** I6

▶ **New Zealand** *country* Oceania **152** E7
3rd largest and 3rd most populous country in Oceania. Known as Aotearoa in Maori.
oceania [countries] ▶ 138–139

Neya Rus. Fed. **40** G4
Neya *r.* Rus. Fed. **40** G4
Ney Bid Iran **100** D4
Neyestānak Iran **100** C3
Neyrīz Iran **100** C4
Neyshābūr Iran **100** D2
also spelt Nīshāpūr; *historically known as* Abarshahr
Neyyattinkara India **94** C4
Nezahualcóyotl, Presa *resr* Mex. **185** G5
Nezhin Ukr. *see* **Nizhyn**
Nezperce U.S.A. **180** C3
Nez Perce Indian Reservation *res.* U.S.A. **180** C3
Ngabang Indon. **77** E2
Ngabé Congo **126** C5
Nga Chong, Khao *mt.* Myanmar/Thai. **79** B5
Ngadda *watercourse* Nigeria **125** I3
Ngagahtawng Myanmar **78** B2
Ngagli Rus. Fed. **82** B1
Ngaiotonga N.Z. **152** I3
Ngajira Tanz. **129** B6
Ngala Nigeria **125** I3
Ngalipaëng Indon. **75** C2
Ngalu Indon. **75** B5
Ngam Chad **126** C2
Ngama Chad **126** C2
Ngamaseri *watercourse* Botswana **130** D3
Ngamatapouri N.Z. **152** I7
Ngambé Cameroon **125** H5
Ngamda China **86** A2
Ngamiland *admin. dist.* Botswana **130** D3
Ngamring China **89** D6
Ngangala Sudan **128** A3
Ngangla Ringco *salt l.* China **89** C6
Nganglong Kangri *mt.* China **89** C5
Nganglong Kangri *mts* China **89** C5
N'gangula Angola **127** B7
Ngangzê Co *salt l.* China **89** D6
Ngangzê Shan *mts* China **89** D6
Ngan Hei Shui Tong *resr Hong Kong* China *see* **Shing Mun Reservoir**
Nganjuk Indon. **77** E4
Ngan Sau, Sông *r.* Vietnam **86** C5
Ngao Thai. **78** B4
Ngaoundal Cameroon **125** I5
Ngaoundéré Cameroon **125** I5
Ngapuke N.Z. **152** J6
Ngara Malawi **129** B7
Ngara Tanz. **128** A5
Ngarkat Conservation Park *nature res.* Australia **146** D3
Ngarrab China *see* **Gyaca**
Ngaruawahia N.Z. **152** J5
Ngaruroro *r.* N.Z. **152** K7
Ngatapa N.Z. **152** L6
Ngathainggyaung Myanmar **78** A4
Ngau Mei Hoi *b. Hong Kong* China *see* **Port Shelter**
Ngawa China *see* **Aba**
Ngawan Chaung *r.* Myanmar **79** B5
Ngawi Indon. **77** E4
Ngayok Bay Myanmar **78** A4
Ngcheangel *atoll* Palau *see* **Kayangel**
Ngeaur *i.* Palau *see* **Angaur**
Ngegera Tanz. **129** A6
Ngeruangel *i.* Palau **73** H5
Ngezi Zimbabwe **131** F4
formerly spelt Ingezi
Nggelelevu *i.* Fiji *see* **Qelelevu**
Nghabe *r.* Botswana **130** D4
Ngiap *r.* Laos **78** C4
Ngilmina Indon. **75** C5
Ngimbang Indon. **77** F4
Ngiva Angola *see* **Ondjiva**
Ngo Congo **126** B5
Ngoc Linh *mt.* Vietnam **79** D5
Ngofakiaha Indon. **75** C2
Ngoïla Cameroon **125** I6
Ngoin, Co *salt l.* China **89** E6
Ngoko *r.* Cameroon/Congo **125** J6
Ngola Shankou *pass* China **84** C5
Ngol Bembo Nigeria **125** H4
Ngoma Zambia **127** E8
Ngoma Bridge Botswana **131** E3
Ngoma Tsé-Tsé Congo **126** B6
Ngomba Tanz. **129** B7
Ngome S. Africa **133** P4
Ngom Qu *r.* China **80** F6
Ngong Cameroon **125** I4
Ngongola Angola **127** C8
Ngongotaha N.Z. **152** K6
Ngong Shuen Chau *pen. Hong Kong* China *see* **Stonecutters' Island**
Ngoqumaima China **89** D5
Ngoring China **86** A1
Ngoring Hu *l.* China **86** A1
▶ **Ngorongoro Conservation Area** *nature res.* Tanz. **128** B5
world [land cover] ▶ 18–19
Ngorongoro Crater Tanz. **128** B5
Ngoumou Cameroon **125** H6
Ngounié *prov.* Gabon **126** A5
Ngounié *r.* Gabon **126** A5
Ngouoni Gabon **126** B5
Ngoura Chad **120** C6
Ngouri Chad **120** B6
Ngourti Niger **125** I3
Ngoutchey *well* Chad **120** C5
Ngozi Burundi **126** F5
Ngqeleni S. Africa **133** N8
Nguigmi Niger **125** I3
Nguini *well* Niger **125** H3
Nguiu Australia **148** A1
Ngukurr Australia **148** B2
Ngulu *atoll* Micronesia **73** I5
also spelt Goulou
Ngum, Nam *r.* Laos **78** C4
Ngundu Zimbabwe **131** F4
Ngunguru Bay N.Z. **152** I3
Ngunju, Tanjung *pt* Indon. **75** B5
Ngunza Angola *see* **Sumbe**
Ngunza-Kabolu Angola *see* **Sumbe**
Nguru Nigeria **125** H3
Nguru Mountains Tanz. **129** C6
Nguyên Binh Vietnam **78** D3
Ngwaketse *admin. dist.* Botswana **131** E5
Ngwako Pan *salt pan* Botswana **130** D4
Ngwane *country* Africa *see* **Swaziland**
Ngwathe S. Africa **133** L4
Ngwavuma *r.* Swaziland **133** Q3
also spelt Ingwavuma
Ngwelezana S. Africa **133** P5
Ngwempisi *r.* S. Africa **133** P3
Ngwezi *r.* Zambia **127** E9
Nhamatanda Moz. **131** G3
Nhamundá Brazil **199** G5
Nhamundá *r.* Brazil **199** G5
Nhandeara Brazil **206** C7
N'harea Angola **127** C7
Nha Trang Vietnam **79** E5
Nhecolândia Brazil **201** F4
Nhill Australia **146** D4
Nhlangano Swaziland **133** P4
formerly known as Goedgegun
Nhlazatshe S. Africa **133** P5
Nhoma Namibia **130** D3
Nho Quan Vietnam **78** D3
Nhulunbuy Australia **148** C2
Nhu Pora Brazil **203** A9
Niabembe Dem. Rep. Congo **126** E5
Niablé Ghana **124** E5
Niacam Canada **167** J4
Niafounké Mali **124** E3
Niagara U.S.A. **172** F5
Niagara Falls Canada **168** E5
Niagara Falls *waterfall* Canada/U.S.A. **176** G2
Niagara Falls U.S.A. **176** F2
Niagara-on-the-Lake Canada **173** N7
Niagassola Guinea **124** C3
Niagouelé, Mont du *hill* Guinea **124** C4
Niagzu Aksai Chin **89** B5
Niah *Sarawak* Malaysia **77** F2
Niak Nepal **97** E3
Niakaramandougou Côte d'Ivoire **124** D4

▶ **Niamey** Niger **125** F3
Capital of Niger.

Niamina Mali **124** D3
Nianbai China *see* **Ledu**
Niandan *r.* Guinea **124** C4
Niandankoro Guinea **124** C4
Niangandu Tanz. **129** C6
Niangara Dem. Rep. Congo **126** E4
Niangay, Lac *l.* Mali **124** E3
Niangoloko Burkina **124** D4
Niangua *r.* U.S.A. **178** D4
Niangxi China *see* **Xinshao**
Nia-Nia Dem. Rep. Congo **126** E4
Niankorodougou Burkina **124** D4
Niantic U.S.A. **177** M4
Nianzishan China **85** I2
Niari *admin. reg.* Congo **126** B5
Nias *i.* Indon. **76** B2
Niassa *prov.* Moz. **131** H2
formerly known as Lago
Niassa, Lago *l.* Africa *see* **Nyasa, Lake**
Niassa, Reserva do *nature res.* Moz. **129** C8
Niaur *i.* Palau *see* **Angaur**
Nibil Well Australia **150** D4
Nīca Latvia **42** C5
Nicaea Turkey *see* **İznik**

▶ **Nicaragua** *country* Central America **186** B4
5th largest country in North America.
northamerica [countries] ▶ 158–159

Nicaragua, Lago de *l.* Nicaragua *see* **Nicaragua, Lake**
Nicaragua, Lake Nicaragua **186** B5
also known as Nicaragua, Lago de
Nicaro Cuba **187** E2
Nicastro Italy **57** I10
Nice France **51** N9
also known as Nizza
Nice U.S.A. **182** B2
Nicephorium Syria *see* **Ar Raqqah**
Niceville U.S.A. **175** C6
Nichicun, Lac *l.* Canada **169** G2
Nichihara Japan **91** B7
Nichinan Japan **91** B9
Nichlaul India **97** D4
Nicholas Channel Bahamas/Cuba **186** C2
Nicholasville U.S.A. **176** A8
Nicholl's Town Bahamas **186** D1
Nichols *IA* U.S.A. **172** B9
Nichols *NY* U.S.A. **177** I3
Nicholson Australia **150** E3
Nicholson *r.* Australia **148** C3
Nicholson Canada **173** J3
Nicholson U.S.A. **177** J4
Nicholson Lake Canada **167** K2
Nicholson Range *hills* Australia **151** B5
Nicholville U.S.A. **177** K1
Nickol Bay Australia **150** B4
Nicobar Islands India **95** G4
Nicolae Bălcescu Romania **58** J4
Nicolás Bravo Mex. **185** H5
Nicolaus U.S.A. **182** C3
Nicomedia Turkey *see* **Kocaeli**
Nico Pérez Uruguay **204** G4
Nicopolis Bulg. *see* **Nikopol**

▶ **Nicosia** Cyprus **108** E2
Capital of Cyprus. Also known as Lefkosia or Lefkoşa.

Nicosia *Sicilia* Italy **57** G11
Nicotera Italy **57** H10
Nicoya Costa Rica **186** B5
Nicoya, Golfo de *b.* Costa Rica **186** B5
Nicoya, Península de *pen.* Costa Rica **186** B5
Nicuadala Moz. **131** H3
Niculițel Romania **58** J3
Nida Lith. **42** B6
Nida *r.* Poland **49** R5
Nidadavole India **94** D2
Nidagunda India **94** C2
Nidym Rus. Fed. **39** J3
Nidže *mt.* Greece/Macedonia **58** C8
Nidzica Poland **49** R2

longest rivers

	river	length	location	page#
1	Nile	6 695km / 4 160miles	Africa	121 F2
2	Amazon	6 516km / 4 049miles	South America	202 B1
3	Yangtze	6 380km / 3 964miles	Asia	87 G2
4	Mississippi-Missouri	5 969km / 3 709miles	North America	179 E6
5	Ob'-Irtysh	5 568km / 3 459miles	Asia	38 G3
6	Yenisey-Angara-Selenga	5 550km / 3 448miles	Asia	39 I2
7	Yellow	5 464km / 3 395miles	Asia	85 H4
8	Congo	4 667km / 2 900miles	Africa	127 B6
9	Río de la Plata-Paraná	4 500km / 2 796miles	South America	204 F4
10	Irtysh	4 440km / 2 759miles	Asia	38 G3

Nidzkie, Jezioro *l.* Poland **49** S2
Niebüll Germany **48** F1
Nied *r.* France **51** M3
Niederaula Germany **48** G5
Niederer Fläming *park* Germany **49** J3
Niedere Tauern *mts* Austria **49** K8
Niederlausitz *reg.* Germany **49** K4
Niedersachsen *land* Germany **48** F3
English form Lower Saxony
Niedersächsisches Wattenmeer, Nationalpark *nat. park* Germany **48** D2
Niefang Equat. Guinea **125** H6
Niekerkshoop S. Africa **132** G6
Niellé Côte d'Ivoire **124** D4
Niem Cent. Afr. Rep. **126** B3
Niemba Dem. Rep. Congo **127** F6
Niemegk Germany **49** J3
Niemisel Sweden **44** M2
Niéna Mali **124** D4
Nienburg (Weser) Germany **48** G3
Niéri Ko *watercourse* Senegal **124** B3
Niers *r.* Germany **48** C4
Niesky Germany **49** L4
Nietverdiend S. Africa **133** K2
Nieuw Amsterdam Suriname **199** H3
Nieuw Nickerie Suriname **199** G3
Nieuwoudtville S. Africa **132** D8
Nieuwpoort Belgium **51** I1
Nieves Spain *see* **As Neves**
Niğde Turkey **106** C3
Nigel S. Africa **133** M3
▶ **Niger** *country* Africa **125** G2
africa [countries] ▶ 114–117

▶ **Niger** *r.* Africa **124** G5
3rd longest river in Africa.
africa [landscapes] ▶ 112–113

Niger *state* Nigeria **125** G4
Niger, Mouths of the Nigeria **125** G5
Niger, Source of the *tourist site* Guinea **124** C4

▶ **Nigeria** *country* Africa **125** G4
Most populous country in Africa and 10th in the world.
world [population] ▶ 22–23
africa [countries] ▶ 114–117

Nighasan India **96** D3
Nightcaps N.Z. **153** C13
Nighthawk Lake Canada **168** D3
Nigrande Latvia **42** D5
Nigrita Greece **58** E8
Nihing Pak. **101** F4
Nihommatsu Japan *see* **Nihonmatsu**
Nihon *country* Asia *see* **Japan**
Nihonmatsu Japan **90** G6
also spelt Nihommatsu
Niigata Japan **90** F6
Niigata *pref.* Japan **90** F6
Niigata-yake-yama *vol.* Japan **91** F6
Niihama Japan **91** C8
Niihau *i.* U.S.A. **181** [inset] Y1
Nii-jima *i.* Japan **91** F7
Niikappu Japan **90** H3
Niimi Japan **91** C7
Niitsu Japan **90** F6
Nijar Spain **55** I8
Nijerāne *well* Mauritania **124** C2
Nijil, Wādī *watercourse* Jordan **108** G7
Nijmegen Neth. **48** C4
formerly spelt Nimwegen
Nijverdal Neth. **48** D3
Nikaia Greece **59** D9
Nikel' Rus. Fed. **44** O1
Nikel'tau Kazakh. **102** D2
Nikiniki Indon. **75** C5
Nikitinka Kazakh. **88** C1
Nikkaluokta Sweden **44** L2
Nikki Benin **125** F4
Nikkō Japan **91** F6
Nikkō National Park Japan **90** F6
Nikola Rus. Fed. **40** H4
Nikolaevo Bulg. **58** G6
Nikolayev Ukr. *see* **Mykolayiv**
Nikolayevka *Chelyabinskaya Oblast'* Rus. Fed. **103** E1
Nikolayevka *Khabarovskiy Kray* Rus. Fed. **82** D2
Nikolayevka *Ul'yanovskaya Oblast'* Rus. Fed. **41** H5
Nikolayevo Rus. Fed. **43** K3
Nikolayevsk Rus. Fed. **41** H6
formerly known as Nikolayevskiy
Nikolayevskiy Rus. Fed. *see* **Nikolayevsk**
Nikolayevsk-na-Amure Rus. Fed. **82** F1
Nikol'sk *Penzenskaya Oblast'* Rus. Fed. **41** H5
formerly known as Nikol'skaya Pestravka
Nikol'sk *Vologod. Obl.* Rus. Fed. **40** H4
Nikol'skaya Pestravka Rus. Fed. *see* **Nikol'sk**
Nikol'skiy Kazakh. *see* **Satpayev**
Nikol'skiy Rus. Fed. **43** P1
Nikol'skiy Torzhok Rus. Fed. **43** T2
Nikol'skoye *Kamchatskaya Oblast'* Rus. Fed. **39** Q4
Nikol'skoye *Lipetskaya Oblast'* Rus. Fed. **43** U9
Nikol'skoye *Orenburgskaya Oblast'* Rus. Fed. **102** C1
Nikol'skoye *Vologod. Obl.* Rus. Fed. **43** S2
Nikol'skoye Rus. Fed. *see* **Sheksna**
Nikopol Bulg. **58** F5
historically known as Nicopolis
Nikopol' Ukr. **41** E7
Nik Pey Iran **100** B2
Niksar Turkey **107** D2
Nīkshahr Iran **101** E5
also known as Gey
Nikšić *Crna Gora* Yugo. **56** K6
Nikumaroro *i.* Kiribati **145** H2
formerly known as Gardner Island
Nikunau *i.* Kiribati **145** G2
also spelt Nukunau; *formerly known as* Byron Island
Nīl, Bahr el *r.* Africa *see* **Nile**
Nila *vol.* Indon. **75** D4
Nilagiri India **97** E5
Nilakka *l.* Fin. **44** N3
Nilakkottai India **94** C4
Nilambur India **94** C4
Niland U.S.A. **183** I8
Nilandhoo Atoll Maldives **93** D10
Nilanga India **94** C2
Nilaveli Sri Lanka **94** D4

▶ **Nile** *r.* Africa **121** F2
Longest river in the world and in Africa. Also known as Nîl, Bahr el.
world [physical features] ▶ 8–9
africa [issues] ▶ 116–117

Nile *state* Sudan **121** G5
▶ **Nile Delta** Egypt **108** C6
world [physical features] ▶ 8–9
africa [issues] ▶ 116–117
Niles *MI* U.S.A. **172** G9
Niles *OH* U.S.A. **176** E4
Nileswaram India **94** B3
Nilgiri Hills India **94** C4
Nīlī *r.* Eth. **104** B5
Nilka China **88** C3
Nilópolis Brazil **207** J9
Nil Pass Afgh. **101** F3
Nilphamari Bangl. **97** F4
Nilsiä Fin. **44** O3
Niltepec Mex. **185** G5
Nilüfer *r.* Turkey **59** J8
Nimach India **96** B4
formerly spelt Neemuch
Nimaj India **96** B4
Niman *r.* Rus. Fed. **82** D2
Nimba, Monts *mts* Africa *see* **Nimba Mountains**
Nimbahera India **96** B4
also spelt Nimbhera
Nimbal India **94** B2
Nimba Mountains Africa **124** C5
also known as Nimba, Monts
Nimberra Well Australia **150** C4
Nimbhera India *see* **Nimbahera**
Nimelen *r.* Rus. Fed. **82** E1
Nîmes France **51** K9
historically known as Nemausus
Nimka Thana India **96** B4
Nimmitabel Australia **147** F4
Nimos *i.* Greece **59** I12
Nimpkish *r.* Canada **166** E5
Nimrod Glacier Antarctica **223** K1
Nīmrūz *prov.* Afgh. **101** E4
Nimu Jammu and Kashmir **96** C2
Nimule Sudan **128** B4
Nimwegen Neth. *see* **Nijmegen**
Nina Estonia **42** I3
Ninawá *governorate* Iraq **107** E4
Ninawá *tourist site* Iraq *see* **Nineveh**
Ninda Angola **127** D8
Nindai Tanz. **129** B7
Nindigully Australia **147** F2
Nine Degree Channel India **94** B4
Nine Islands P.N.G. *see* **Kilinailau Islands**
Nine Mile Lake *salt flat* Australia **147** D2
Ninemile Peak U.S.A. **183** H2
Ninepin Group *is Hong Kong* China **87** [inset]
also known as Kwo Chau Kwan To
Ninety Mile Beach Australia **147** E4
Ninety Mile Beach N.Z. **152** G2
Nineveh *tourist site* Iraq **107** E3
also spelt Ninawá
Ninfas, Punta *pt* Arg. **205** D6
Ningaloo Marine Park *nature res.* Australia **150** A4
Ning'an China **82** C3
Ningbo China **87** G2
also known as Yinxian
Ningcheng China **85** H3
also known as Tianyi
Ningde China **87** F3
Ningdu China **87** E3
also known as Meijiang
Ning'er China *see* **Pu'er**
Ningguo China **87** F2
also known as Helixi
Ninghai China **87** G2
Ninghe China **85** H4
also known as Lutai
Ninghsia *aut. reg.* China *see* **Ningxia Huizu Zizhiqu**
Ninghsia Hui Autonomous Region *aut. reg.* China *see* **Ningxia Huizu Zizhiqu**
Ninghua China **87** F3
also known as Cuijiang
Ningi Nigeria **125** H4
Ninging India **97** G3
Ningjiang China *see* **Songyuan**
Ningjing Shan *mts* China **86** A2
Ninglang China **86** B3
also known as Daxing
Ningling China **87** E1
Ningming China **86** C4
also known as Chengzhong
Ningnan China **86** B3
also known as Pisha
Ningqiang China **86** C1
Ningshan China **87** D1
Ningwu China **85** G4
Ningxia *aut. reg.* China *see* **Ningxia Huizu Zizhiqu**
Ningxia Huizu Zizhiqu *aut. reg.* China **85** E4
short form Ningxia; *English form* Ningsia *or* Ninghsia Hui Autonomous Region

Ningxian China **85** E5
also known as Xinning
Ningxiang China **87** E2
Ningyang China **85** H5
Ningyuan China **87** D3
Ningzhou China *see* **Huaning**
Ninh Binh Vietnam **78** D3
Ninh Hoa Vietnam **79** E5
Ninigo Group *is* P.N.G. **73** J7
Ninnis Glacier Antarctica **223** J2
Ninnis Glacier Tongue Antarctica **223** K2
Ninohe Japan **90** G4
Ninualac, Canal *sea chan.* Chile **205** B7
Nioaque Brazil **201** G5
Niobrara *r.* U.S.A. **178** C3
Nioghalvfjerdsfjorden *inlet* Greenland **165** R2
Nioki Dem. Rep. Congo **126** C5
Niokolo Koba, Parc National du *nat. park* Senegal **124** B3
Niono Mali **124** D3
Nioro Mali **124** C3
Niort France **50** F6
Nioût *well* Mauritania **124** D3
Nipa P.N.G. **73** J8
Nipani India **94** B2
Nipanipa, Tanjung *pt* Indon. **75** B3
Nipawin Canada **167** J4
Niphad India **94** B1
Nipigon Canada **168** B3
Nipigon, Lake Canada **168** B3
Nipigon Bay Canada **172** F2
Nipiodi Moz. **131** H3
Nipishish Lake Canada **169** I2
Nipissing Canada **173** N4
Nipissing, Lake Canada **168** E4
Nipomo U.S.A. **182** D6
Nippon *country* Asia *see* **Japan**
Nippon Hai *sea* N. Pacific Ocean *see* **Japan, Sea of**
Nippur *tourist site* Iraq **107** F4
Niquelândia Brazil **202** B5
Niquero Cuba **186** D2
Nir *Ardabīl* Iran **100** A2
Nir *Yazd* Iran **100** C4
Nīr, Jabal an *hills* Saudi Arabia **104** C2
Nira *r.* India **94** B2
Nirasaki Japan **91** F7
Nirji China **85** J1
also known as Morin Dawa
Nirmal India **94** C2
Nirmali India **97** E4
Nirmal Range *hills* India **94** C2
Nirzas *l.* Latvia **42** I5
Niš *Srbija* Yugo. **58** C5
historically known as Naissus
Nisa Port. **54** D5
Nişāb Yemen **105** D5
Nisah, Wādī *watercourse* Saudi Arabia **105** D2
Nišava *r.* Yugo. **58** C5
Niscemi *Sicilia* Italy **57** G11
Niseko Japan **90** G3
Nīshāpūr Iran *see* **Neyshābūr**
Nishcha *r.* Belarus **43** J6
Nishibetsu-gawa *r.* Japan **90** I3
Nishikawa Japan **90** G5
Nishinomiya Japan **91** D7
Nishino-omote Japan **91** B9
Nishino-shima *i.* Japan **91** C6
Nishino-shima *vol.* Japan **81** O7
Nishi-Sonogi-hantō *pen.* Japan **91** A8
Nishi-suidō *sea chan.* Japan/S. Korea **91** A7
also known as Chōsen-kaikyō
Nishiwaki Japan **91** D7
Nísia Floresta Brazil **202** F3
Nisibis Turkey *see* **Nusaybin**
Nisi-mera Japan **81** B8
Nísiros *i.* Greece *see* **Nisyros**
Niskanselkä *l.* Fin. **44** N2
Niskayuna U.S.A. **177** L3
Niskibi *r.* Canada **168** B1
Nisko Poland **49** T5
Nisling *r.* Canada **166** B2
Nisporeni Moldova **58** J1
Nissan *r.* Sweden **45** K4
Nisser *l.* Norway **45** J4
Nissum Bredning *b.* Denmark **45** J4
Nistru *r.* Moldova *see* **Dniester**
Nistrului Inferior, Cîmpia *lowland* Moldova **58** K1
Nisutlin *r.* Canada **166** C2
Nisyros *i.* Greece **59** I12
also spelt Nísiros
Nita Japan **91** C7
Nitchequon Canada **169** G2
Nitendi *i.* Solomon Is *see* **Ndeni**
Niterói Brazil **203** D7
Nith *r.* U.K. **47** I8
Niti Pass China **96** C3
Nitmiluk National Park Australia **148** B2
formerly known as Katherine Gorge National Park
Nitra Slovakia **49** P7
Nitra *r.* Slovakia **49** P8
Nitro U.S.A. **176** D7
Nittedal Norway **45** J3
Niuafo'ou *i.* Tonga **145** H3
also spelt Niuafu
Niuafu *i.* Tonga *see* **Niuafo'ou**
Niuatoputopu *i.* Tonga **145** H3
formerly known as Boscawen Island
Niubiziliang China **84** B4

Niue *terr.* S. Pacific Ocean **145** I3
Self-governing New Zealand Overseas Territory.
oceania [countries] 138–139

Niujing China *see* **Binchuan**
Niulakita *i.* Tuvalu **145** G3
formerly spelt Nurakita
Niulan Jiang *r.* China **86** B3
Niur, Pulau *i.* Indon. **76** C3
Niushan China *see* **Donghai**
Niutao *i.* Tuvalu **145** G2
Niutoushan China **87** F2
Niuzhuang China **85** I3
Nivala Fin. **44** N3
Nivastroy Rus. Fed. **44** P2
Nive *watercourse* Australia **149** E5
Nive *r.* France **50** E9
Nive Downs Australia **149** E5
Nivelles Belgium **51** K2
Nivnoye Rus. Fed. **43** N8
Nivskiy Rus. Fed. **44** P2
Niwai India **96** B4
Niwari India **96** C4
Niwas India **96** D5
Nixia China *see* **Sêrxu**
Nixon U.S.A. **182** E2
Niya China *see* **Minfeng**
Niya He *r.* China **89** C4
Niyut, Gunung *mt.* Indon. **77** E2
Niz Rus. Fed. **43** Q2
Nizamabad India **94** C2
also known as Indur
Nizampatnam India **94** D3
Nizam Sagar *l.* India **94** C2
Nizh Aydere Turkm. **102** D5
Nizhegorodskaya Oblast' *admin. div.* Rus. Fed. **40** H4
English form Nizhniy Novgorod Oblast; formerly known as Gor'kovskaya Oblast'
Nizhneangarsk Rus. Fed. **81** H1
Nizhnedevitsk Rus. Fed. **41** F6
Nizhnekamsk Rus. Fed. **40** I5
Nizhnekamskoye Vodokhranilishche *resr* Rus. Fed. **40** J5
Nizhnekolymsk Rus. Fed. **39** Q3
Nizhne-Svirskiy Zapovednik *nature res.* Rus. Fed. **43** O1
Nizhneudinsk Rus. Fed. **80** F2
Nizhnevartovsk Rus. Fed. **38** H3
Nizhnevolzhsk Rus. Fed. *see* **Narimanov**
Nizhneyansk Rus. Fed. **39** N2
Nizhneye Kuyto, Ozero *l.* Rus. Fed. **44** O2
Nizhni Irginski Rus. Fed. **40** K4
Nizhniy Baskunchak Rus. Fed. **102** A2
Nizhniy Chir Rus. Fed. **41** G6
Nizhniye Kresty Rus. Fed. *see* **Cherskiy**
Nizhniye Ustriki Poland *see* **Ustrzyki Dolne**
Nizhniy Lomov Rus. Fed. **41** G5
Nizhniy Novgorod Rus. Fed. **40** G4
formerly known as Gor'kiy
Nizhniy Novgorod Oblast *admin. div.* Rus. Fed. *see* **Nizhegorodskaya Oblast'**
Nizhniy Odes Rus. Fed. **40** J3
Nizhniy Pyandzh Tajik. *see* **Panji Poyon**
Nizhniy Tagil Rus. Fed. **38** F4
Nizhniy Yenangsk Rus. Fed. **40** H4
Nizhnyaya Mola Rus. Fed. **40** H2
Nizhnyaya Omra Rus. Fed. **40** J3
Nizhnyaya Pesha Rus. Fed. **40** H2
Nizhnyaya Pirenga, Ozero *l.* Rus. Fed. **44** P2
Nizhnyaya Poyma Rus. Fed. **80** F1
Nizhnyaya Suyetka Rus. Fed. **103** I1
Nizhnyaya Tunguska *r.* Rus. Fed. **39** I3
English form Lower Tunguska
Nizhnyaya Tura Rus. Fed. **38** F4
Nizhnyaya Zolotitsa Rus. Fed. **40** G2
Nizhyn Ukr. **41** D6
also spelt Nezhin
Nizina Mazowiecka *reg.* Poland **49** R3
Nizip Turkey **107** D3
Nizkabor"ye Belarus **43** L6
Nízke Beskydy *hills* Slovakia **49** S6
Nízke Tatry *mts* Slovakia **49** Q7
Nízke Tatry *nat. park* Slovakia **49** Q7
Nizmennyy, Mys *pt* Rus. Fed. **90** D3
Nizwā Oman *see* **Nazwá**
Nizza France *see* **Nice**
Nizza Monferrato Italy **56** A4
Njavve Sweden **44** L2
Njazidja *i.* Comoros **129** D7
also known as Grande Comore
Njegoš *mts* Yugo. **56** K6
Njellim Fin. *see* **Nellim**
Njinjo Tanz. **129** C7
Njombe Tanz. **129** B7
Njombe *r.* Tanz. **129** B6
Njutånger Sweden **45** L3
Nkai Zimbabwe *see* **Nkayi**
Nkambe Cameroon **125** H5
Nkandla S. Africa **133** P5
Nkasi Tanz. **129** A6
Nkawkaw Ghana **125** E5
Nkayi Zimbabwe **131** F3
formerly spelt Nkai
Nkhaïlé *well* Mauritania **124** D2
Nkhata Bay Malawi **129** B7
Nkhotakota Malawi **129** B8
Nkhotakota Game Reserve *nature res.* Malawi **129** B8
Nkomfap Nigeria **125** H5
Nkomi, Lagune *lag.* Gabon **126** A5
Nkondwe Tanz. **129** A6
Nkongsamba Cameroon **125** H5
Nkoranza Ghana **125** E5
Nkoteng Cameroon **125** I5
Nkululeko S. Africa **133** L7
Nkundi Tanz. **129** A6
Nkungwi Tanz. **129** A6
Nkurenkuru Namibia **130** C3
Nkwalini S. Africa **133** P5
Nkwanta Ghana **125** F4
Nkwenkwezi S. Africa **133** K10
Nmai Hka *r.* Myanmar **78** B2
Noa Dihing *r.* India **97** H4
Noakhali Bangl. **97** F5
Noamundi India **97** E5
Noatak *r.* U.S.A. **164** C3
Noatak National Preserve *nature res.* U.S.A. **164** D3
Nobeoka Japan **91** B8
Noblesville U.S.A. **174** C3
Nobokwe S. Africa **133** L8
Noboribetsu Japan **90** G3
Nobres Brazil **201** F3
Noccundra Australia **147** D1
Noce *r.* Italy **56** D2
Nocera Terinese Italy **57** I9
Nochistlán Mex. **185** E4
Nochixtlán Mex. **185** F5
Noci Italy **57** J8
Nockatunga Australia **147** D1
Nocoleche Nature Reserve Australia **147** E2
Nocona U.S.A. **179** C5
Noda Japan **91** F7
Nodaway *r.* U.S.A. **178** D4
Nodeland Norway **45** I4
Noel Kempff Mercado, Parque Nacional *nat. park* Bol. **201** E3
Noelville Canada **173** M4
Noenieput S. Africa **132** E4
Nogales Mex. **184** C2
also known as Heroica Nogales
Nogales U.S.A. **181** E7
Nogaro France **50** F9
Nogat *r.* Poland **49** Q1
Nōgata Japan **91** B8
Nogayty Kazakh. **102** C2
Nogent-le-Rotrou France **50** G4
Nogent-sur-Oise France **51** I3
Nogent-sur-Seine France **51** J4
Noginsk *Evenkiyskiy Avtonomnyy Okrug* Rus. Fed. **39** J3
Noginsk *Moskovskaya Oblast'* Rus. Fed. **43** T6
Nogliki Rus. Fed. **82** F2
Nogo *r.* Australia **149** F5
Nogoa *r.* Australia **149** F4
Nōgōhaku-san *mt.* Japan **91** E7
Nogoyá Arg. **204** F4
Nohar India **96** B3
Noheji Japan **90** G4
Nohfelden Germany **48** E6
Nohili Point U.S.A. **181** [inset] Y1
Nohur Turkm. *see* **Nokhur**
Noia Spain **54** C2
also spelt Noya
Noidore *r.* Brazil **206** A1
Noire *r.* Canada **173** Q5
Noire, Montagne *mts* France **51** I9
Noires, Pointe *pt* Morocco **55** H9
Noires, Montagnes *hills* France **50** C4
Noirmoutier, Île de *i.* France **50** D6
Noirmoutier-en-l'Île France **50** D5
Nojima-zaki *c.* Japan **91** F7
Nokesville U.S.A. **176** H7
Nokha India **96** B4
Nokhowch, Kūh-e *mt.* Iran **101** E5
Nokhur Turkm. **102** D5
also spelt Nohur
Nokia Fin. **45** M3
Nōkis Uzbek. *see* **Nukus**
Nok Kundi Pak. **101** E4
Nokomis Canada **167** J5
Nokomis Lake Canada **167** K3
Nokou Chad **120** B6
Nokrek Peak India **97** F4
Nola Cent. Afr. Rep. **126** C4
Nolichuky *r.* U.S.A. **176** B9
Nolinsk Rus. Fed. **40** I4
formerly known as Molotovsk
Noll S. Africa **132** G10
Nólsoy *i.* Faroe Is **46** F1
Noma-misaki *pt* Japan **91** B9
Nome U.S.A. **164** C3
Nomgon Mongolia **85** E3
Nomhon China **84** C4
Nomoi Islands Micronesia *see* **Mortlock Islands**
Nomonde S. Africa **133** K8
Nomo-zaki *pt* Japan **91** A8
Nomto Rus. Fed. **84** E1
Nomuka Tonga **145** H4
Nomzha Rus. Fed. **40** G4
Nonacho Lake Canada **167** I2
Nong'an China **82** B3
Nong Hong Thai. **79** C5
Nonghui China *see* **Guang'an**
Nong Khai Thai. **78** C4
Nongoma S. Africa **133** P4
Nongstoin India **97** F4
Nonni *r.* China *see* **Nen Jiang**
Nonoai Brazil **203** A8
Nonoava Mex. **184** D3
Nonouti *atoll* Kiribati **145** G2
also spelt Nanouki or Nanouti; formerly known as Sydenham
Nonsan S. Korea **83** B5
Nonthaburi Thai. **79** C5
Nontron France **50** G7
Nonzwakazi S. Africa **132** I7
Nōo Estonia **42** I3
Nookawarra Australia **151** B5
Noolyeanna Lake *salt flat* Australia **146** C1
Noonamah Australia **148** A2
Noondie, Lake *salt flat* Australia **151** B6
Noonkanbah Australia **150** D3
Noonkanbah Aboriginal Reserve Australia **150** D3
Noonthorangee Range *hills* Australia **147** D2
Noorama Creek *watercourse* Australia **147** E1
Noordbeveland *i.* Neth. **48** A4
Noorderhaaks *i.* Neth. **48** B3
Noordkaap S. Africa **133** P2
Noordkuil S. Africa **132** C9
Noordoewer Namibia **132** B5
Noordoost Polder Neth. **48** C3
Noordpunt *pt* Neth. Antilles **187** F4
Noormarkku Fin. **45** M3
Noorvik U.S.A. **164** C3
Nootka Island Canada **166** E5
Nóqui Angola **127** B6
Nora *r.* Rus. Fed. **82** C2
Norak Tajik. **101** G2
also spelt Nurek
Norala Phil. **74** C5
Noranda Canada **168** E3
Nor-Bayazet Armenia *see* **Kamo**
Norberg Sweden **45** K3
Nord *prov.* Cameroon **125** I4
Nord Greenland *see* **Station Nord**
Nord, Canal du France **48** A5
Nordaustlandet *i.* Svalbard **38** C2
Nordborg Denmark **48** G1
Nordbotn Norway **44** M1
Nordegg Canada **167** G4
Norden Germany **48** E2
Nordenshel'da, Arkhipelag *is* Rus. Fed. **39** J2
English form Nordenskjold Archipelago
Nordenskiold *r.* Canada **166** B2
Nordenskjold Archipelago *is* Rus. Fed. *see* **Nordenshel'da, Arkhipelag**
Norder Hever *sea chan.* Germany **48** F1
Norderney Germany **48** E2
Norderney *i.* Germany **48** E2
Norderstedt Germany **48** H2
Nordfjord Norway **44** O1
Nordfjord *inlet* Norway **44** I3
Nordfjordeid Norway **45** I3
Nordfold Norway **44** K2
Nordfriesische Inseln *is* Germany *see* **North Frisian Islands**
Nordhausen Germany **48** H4
Nordholz Germany **48** F2
Nordhorn Germany **48** E3
Nordhuglo Norway **45** I4
Nordingrå naturreservat *nature res.* Sweden **44** L3
Nord Kap *c.* Iceland *see* **Horn**
Nordkapp *c.* Norway *see* **North Cape**
Nord-Kivu *prov.* Dem. Rep. Congo **126** F5
Nord-Kvaløy *i.* Norway **44** L1
Nordkynhalvøya *i.* Norway **44** N1
Nordland *county* Norway **44** K2
Nordli Norway **44** K2
Nördliches Harzvorland *park* Germany **48** H4
Nördlingen Germany **48** H7
Nordmaling Sweden **44** L3
Nordmannvik Norway **44** M1
Nord- og Østgrønland, Nationalparken i *nat. park* Greenland **165** P2
Nordostrundingen *c.* Greenland *see* **Northeast Foreland**
Nord-Ostsee-Kanal *canal* Germany *see* **Kiel Canal**
Nord-Ouest *prov.* Cameroon **125** H5
Nord - Pas-de-Calais *admin. reg.* France **51** I2
Nord-Pas-de-Calais, Parc Naturel Régional du *nature res.* France **51** J2
Nordre Strømfjord *inlet* Greenland *see* **Nassuttooq**
Nordrhein-Westfalen *land* Germany **48** E4
English form North Rhine - Westphalia
Nordstrand *i.* Germany **48** F1
Nord-Trøndelag *county* Norway **44** K2
Norðurland eystra *constituency* Iceland **44** [inset] C2
Norðurland vestra *constituency* Iceland **44** [inset] B2
Nordvik Rus. Fed. **39** L2
Nordvika Norway **44** J3
Nore *r.* Rep. of Ireland **47** F11
Nore, Pic de *mt.* France **51** I9
Noreg *country* Europe *see* **Norway**
Noreikiškės Lith. **42** F7
Noresund Norway **45** J3
Norfolk *NE* U.S.A. **178** C3
Norfolk *NY* U.S.A. **177** K1
Norfolk *VA* U.S.A. **177** I9

Norfolk Island *terr.* S. Pacific Ocean **145** F4
Australian External Territory.
oceania [countries] 138–139

Norfork Lake U.S.A. **179** D4
Norge *country* Europe *see* **Norway**
Norheimsund Norway **45** I3
Noria Chile **200** C5
Norikura-dake *vol.* Japan **91** E6
Noril'sk Rus. Fed. **39** I3
Norkyung China *see* **Bainang**
Norland Canada **173** O6
Norlina U.S.A. **176** G9
Normal U.S.A. **174** B3
Norman *r.* Australia **149** D3
Norman U.S.A. **179** C5
Norman, Lake *resr* U.S.A. **174** D5
Normanby *r.* Australia **149** E2
Normanby N.Z. **152** I7
Normanby Island P.N.G. **145** E2
Normanby Range *hills* Australia **149** F4
Normandes, Îles *is* English Chan. *see* **Channel Islands**
Normandia Brazil **199** G4
Normandie *reg.* France *see* **Normandy**
Normandie, Collines de *hills* France **50** F4
Normandie-Maine, Parc Naturel Régional *nature res.* France **50** F4
Normandien S. Africa **133** N4
Normandy *reg.* France **50** F4
also spelt Normandie
Normanton Australia **149** D3
Norman Wells Canada **166** E1
Normétal Canada **173** N2
Norogachic Mex. **184** D3
Noroquay Canada **167** K5
Ñorquinco Arg. **205** C6
Norråker Sweden **44** K2
Norra Kvarken *strait* Fin./Sweden **44** M3
Norrbotten *county* Sweden **44** L2
Nørre Nebel Denmark **45** J5
Norrent-Fontes France **51** I2
Norrfjärden Sweden **44** M2
Norrhult-Klavreström Sweden **45** K4
Norris U.S.A. **176** A9
Norris Lake U.S.A. **176** B9
Norristown U.S.A. **177** J5
Norrköping Sweden **45** L4
Norrsundet Sweden **45** L3
Norrtälje Sweden **45** L4
Norseman Australia **151** C7
Norsewood N.Z. **152** K8
Norsjö Sweden **44** L2
Norsk Rus. Fed. **82** C1
Norske Øer *is* Greenland **165** R2
Norsup Vanuatu **145** F3
Norte, Punta *pt Buenos Aires* Arg. **204** F5
Norte, Punta *pt* Arg. **205** C8
Norte, Punta *pt* Arg. **205** E6
Norte, Serra do *hills* Brazil **201** F2
Norte de Santander *dept* Col. **198** C2
Nortelândia Brazil **201** F3
North, Cape Antarctica **223** L2
North, Cape Canada **169** I4
North Adams U.S.A. **177** L3
Northallerton U.K. **47** K9
Northam Australia **151** B6
Northam S. Africa **133** L1
Northampton Australia **151** A6
Northampton U.K. **47** L11
Northampton *MA* U.S.A. **177** M3
Northampton *PA* U.S.A. **177** J5
Northampton Downs Australia **149** E5
North Andaman *i.* India **95** G3
North Anna *r.* U.S.A. **176** H8
North Anson U.S.A. **177** P1
North Arm *b.* Canada **167** H2
North Balabac Strait Phil. **74** A4
North Baltimore U.S.A. **176** B4
North Battleford Canada **167** I4
North Bay Canada **168** E4
North Bend *OR* U.S.A. **180** A4
North Bend *PA* U.S.A. **176** H4
North Bennington U.S.A. **177** L3
North Berwick U.K. **46** J7
North Berwick U.S.A. **177** O2
North Borneo *state* Malaysia *see* **Sabah**
North Bosque *r.* U.S.A. **179** C6
North Branch *MI* U.S.A. **173** J7
North Branch *MN* U.S.A. **172** A5
North Caicos *i.* Turks and Caicos Is **187** F2
North Canadian *r.* U.S.A. **179** D5
North Cape Canada **169** H4
North Cape Norway **44** N1
also known as Nordkapp
North Cape N.Z. **152** H2
North Cape S. Georgia **205** [inset]
North Caribou Lake Canada **168** B2
North Carolina *state* U.S.A. **176** F9
North Cascades National Park U.S.A. **180** B2
North Central Aboriginal Reserve Australia **150** D4
North Channel *lake channel* Canada **168** D4
North Channel *str.* Northern Ireland/Scotland U.K. **47** G9
North Charleston U.S.A. **175** E5
North Cheyenne Indian Reservation *res.* U.S.A. **180** F3
Northcliffe Australia **151** B7
Northcliffe Glacier Antarctica **223** G2
North Collins U.S.A. **176** G3
North Concho *r.* U.S.A. **179** B6
North Conway U.S.A. **177** N1
North Cowichan Canada **166** F5
North Creek U.S.A. **177** L2
North Dakota *state* U.S.A. **178** B2
North Downs *hills* U.K. **47** L12
North East *admin. dist.* Botswana **131** E4
North East *MD* U.S.A. **177** J6
North East *PA* U.S.A. **176** F3
North East Cay *reef* Australia **149** G4
North-Eastern *prov.* Kenya **128** D4

Northeast Foreland *c.* Greenland **165** R1
Most easterly point of North America. Also known as Nordostrundingen.

North-East Frontier Agency *state* India *see* **Arunachal Pradesh**
Northeast Point Bahamas **175** F8
Northeast Providence Channel Bahamas **186** D1
North Edwards U.S.A. **182** G6
Northeim Germany **48** G4
North End Point Bahamas **175** F7
Northern *admin. reg.* Ghana **125** E4
Northern *admin. reg.* Malawi **129** B7
Northern *prov.* S. Africa **133** M1
formerly known as Northern Transvaal
Northern *prov.* Sierra Leone **124** C4
Northern *state* Sudan **121** F4
Northern *prov.* Zambia **127** F7
Northern Aegean *admin. reg.* Greece *see* **Voreio Aigaio**
Northern Areas *admin. div.* Pak. **101** H2
Northern Bahr el Ghazal *state* Sudan **126** E2
Northern Cape *prov.* S. Africa **132** D6
Northern Darfur *state* Sudan **121** E5
Northern Donets *r.* Rus. Fed./Ukr. *see* **Severskiy Donets**
Northern Dvina *r.* Rus. Fed. *see* **Severnaya Dvina**
Northern Indian Lake Canada **167** L3
Northern Ireland *prov.* U.K. **47** F9
Northern Kordofan *state* Sudan **121** F6
Northern Lau Group *is* Fiji **145** H3
Northern Light Lake Canada **168** B3

Northern Mariana Islands *terr.* N. Pacific Ocean **73** J3
United States Commonwealth. Historically known as Ladrones.
oceania [countries] 138–139

Northern Rhodesia *country* Africa *see* **Zambia**
Northern Sporades *is* Greece *see* **Voreioi Sporades**
Northern Territory *admin. div.* Australia **148** B3
Northern Transvaal *prov.* S. Africa *see* **Northern**
Northfield *IL* U.S.A. **174** B4
Northfield *MA* U.S.A. **177** M3
Northfield *MN* U.S.A. **174** A2
Northfield *NJ* U.S.A. **171** H3
Northfield *VT* U.S.A. **177** M1
Northfield *WI* U.S.A. **172** B6
North Foreland *c.* U.K. **47** N12
North Fork U.S.A. **182** E4
North Fork Pass Canada **166** B1
North Fox Island U.S.A. **172** H5
North French *r.* Canada **168** D3
North Frisian Islands Germany **48** F1
also known as Nordfriesische Inseln
North Geomagnetic Pole Arctic Ocean **224** T1
North Haven U.S.A. **177** M4
North Head N.Z. **152** I4
North Henik Lake Canada **167** L2
North Horr Kenya **128** C4
North Hero U.S.A. **177** L1
North Highlands U.S.A. **182** C3
North Hudson U.S.A. **177** L2
North Island India **94** B4

North Island N.Z. **152** H6
3rd largest island in Oceania.
oceania [landscapes] 136–137

North Island Phil. **74** B1
North Islet *reef* Phil. **74** B4
North Jadito Canyon *gorge* U.S.A. **183** N6
North Judson U.S.A. **172** G9
North Kazakhstan Oblast *admin. div.* Kazakh. *see* **Severnyy Kazakhstan**
North Kingsville U.S.A. **176** E4
North Knife *r.* Canada **167** M3
North Knife Lake Canada **167** L3
North Koel *r.* India **97** D4
North Komelik U.S.A. **183** M9

North Korea *country* Asia **83** B4
asia [countries] 64–67

North Lakhimpur India **97** G4
North Land *is* Rus. Fed. *see* **Severnaya Zemlya**
Northland Forest Park *nature res.* N.Z. **152** H3
North Las Vegas U.S.A. **183** I5
North Liberty U.S.A. **172** G9
North Little Rock U.S.A. **179** D5
North Loup *r.* U.S.A. **178** C3
North Luangwa National Park Zambia **129** B7
North Maalhosmadulu Atoll Maldives **94** B5
North Macmillan *r.* Canada **166** C2
North Magnetic Pole Canada **224** R1
North Mam Peak U.S.A. **180** F5
North Manchester U.S.A. **172** H10
North Middletown U.S.A. **176** A7
North Moose Lake Canada **167** K4
North Muiron Island Australia **150** A4
North Nahanni *r.* Canada **166** F2
North Ossetia *aut. rep.* Rus. Fed. *see* **Severnaya Osetiya-Alaniya, Respublika**
North Palisade *mt.* U.S.A. **182** F4
North Platte U.S.A. **178** B3
North Platte *r.* U.S.A. **178** B3
North Point Australia **151** A6
North Point *Hong Kong* China **87** [inset]
also known as Tsat Tsze Mui
North Pole Arctic Ocean **224** A1
Northport U.S.A. **175** C5
North Port U.S.A. **175** D7
North Reef Island India **95** G3
North Rhine - Westphalia *land* Germany *see* **Nordrhein-Westfalen**
North River Bridge Canada **169** I4
North Rona *i.* U.K. *see* **Rona**
North Ronaldsay *i.* U.K. **46** J4
North Saskatchewan *r.* Canada **167** J4
North Schell Peak U.S.A. **183** J2
North Sea Europe **46** N6
North Seal *r.* Canada **167** L3
North Sentinel Island India **95** G4
North Shoal Lake Canada **167** L5
North Shoshone Peak U.S.A. **183** G2
North Siberian Lowland Rus. Fed. **39** K2
also known as Severo-Sibirskaya Nizmennost'
North Simlipal National Park India **97** E5
North Sinai *governorate* Egypt *see* **Shamāl Sīnā'**
North Slope *plain* U.S.A. **164** E3
North Spirit Lake Canada **167** M4
North Stradbroke Island Australia **147** G1
North Stratford U.S.A. **177** N1
North Taranaki Bight *b.* N.Z. **152** I6
North Thompson *r.* Canada **166** F5
North Tonawanda U.S.A. **176** G2
North Trap *reef* N.Z. **153** B15
North Troy U.S.A. **177** M1
North Truro U.S.A. **177** O3
North Tuas Basin *dock* Sing. **76** [inset]
North Twin Island Canada **168** E2
North Twin Lake Canada **169** K3
North Ubian *i.* Phil. **74** B5
North Uist *i.* U.K. **46** E6
also known as Uibhist a' Tuath
Northumberland Isles Australia **149** F4
Northumberland National Park U.K. **46** J8
Northumberland Strait Canada **169** H4
North Umpqua *r.* U.S.A. **180** B4
North Vancouver Canada **166** F5
Northville U.S.A. **177** K2
North Wabasca Lake Canada **167** H3
North Walsham U.K. **47** N11
North Waterford U.S.A. **177** O1
Northway U.S.A. **166** A2
Northway Junction U.S.A. **166** A2
North West *prov.* S. Africa **133** J3
North West Cape Australia **150** A4
North-Western *prov.* Zambia **127** D8
North West Frontier *prov.* Pak. **101** G3
North West Nelson Forest Park *nat. park* N.Z. *see* **Kahurangi National Park**
Northwest Providence Channel Bahamas **186** D1
North West River Canada **169** J2
Northwest Territories *admin. div.* Canada **167** J2
North Wilkesboro U.S.A. **176** D9
North Windham U.S.A. **177** O2
Northwood *IA* U.S.A. **174** A3
Northwood *ND* U.S.A. **178** C2
Northwood *NH* U.S.A. **177** N2
Northwoods Beach U.S.A. **172** B5
North York Canada **173** N7
North York Moors *moorland* U.K. **47** L9
North York Moors National Park U.K. **47** L9
Norton Canada **169** H4
Norton *KS* U.S.A. **178** C4
Norton *VT* U.S.A. **174** G2
Norton de Matos Angola *see* **Balombo**
Norton Shores U.S.A. **172** G7
Norton Sound *sea chan.* U.S.A. **164** C3
Nortorf Germany **48** G1
Nort-sur-Erdre France **50** E5
Norvegia, Cape Antarctica **223** X2
Norwalk *OH* U.S.A. **176** C4
Norwalk *WI* U.S.A. **172** C7

Norway *country* Europe **45** J3
known as Norge or Noreg in Norwegian
europe [countries] 32–35

Norway U.S.A. **177** O1
Norway Bay Canada **173** Q5
Norway House Canada **167** L4
Norwegian Bay Canada **165** J2
Norwegian Sea N. Atlantic Ocean **224** A2
Norwich Canada **173** M8
Norwich U.K. **47** N11
Norwich *CT* U.S.A. **177** M4
Norwich *NY* U.S.A. **177** J3
Norwood *MA* U.S.A. **177** N3
Norwood *NY* U.S.A. **177** K1
Norwood *OH* U.S.A. **176** A6
Norzagaray Phil. **74** B3
Nose Lake Canada **167** I1
Noshappu-misaki *hd* Japan **90** G2
Noshiro Japan **90** G4
Noshul' Rus. Fed. **40** I3
Nosivka Ukr. **41** D6
also spelt Nosovka
Nosop *watercourse* Africa *see* **Nossob**
Nosovaya Rus. Fed. **40** J1
Nosovka Ukr. *see* **Nosivka**
Noşratābād Iran **101** D4
Nossa Senhora da Glória Brazil **200** B1
Nossa Senhora do Livramento Brazil **201** F3
Nossen Germany **49** K4
Nossob *watercourse* Africa **132** E3
also spelt Nosop
Nossob Camp S. Africa **132** E2
Nosy Varika Madag. **131** [inset] K4
Nota *r.* Fin./Rus. Fed. **44** O1
Notakwanon *r.* Canada **169** I1
Notch Peak U.S.A. **183** K2
Noteć *r.* Poland **49** M3
Notikewin *r.* Canada **166** G3
Notio Aigaio *admin. reg.* Greece **59** H12
English form Southern Aegean; also spelt Nótion Aiyaíon
Nótion Aiyaíon *admin. reg.* Greece *see* **Notio Aigaio**
Notios Evvoïkos Kolpos *sea chan.* Greece **59** E10
Notio Steno Kerkyras *sea chan.* Greece **59** B9
Noto *Sicilia* Italy **57** H12
Noto Japan **90** E6
Noto, Golfo di *g. Sicilia* Italy **57** H12
Notodden Norway **45** J4
Noto-hantō *pen.* Japan **90** E6
Notre Dame, Monts *mts* Canada **169** G4
Notre Dame Bay Canada **169** K3
Notre-Dame-de-Koartac Canada *see* **Quaqtaq**
Notre-Dame-de-la-Salette Canada **173** R5
Notre-Dame-du-Laus Canada **173** R4
Notre-Dame-du-Nord Canada **173** N3
Notsé Togo **125** F5
Notsu Japan **91** B8
Notsuke-saki *pt* Japan **90** I3
Notsuke-suidō *sea chan.* Japan/Rus. Fed. **90** I3
also known as Izmeny, Proliv
Nottawasaga Bay Canada **173** M6
Nottaway *r.* Canada **168** E3
Nottingham U.K. **47** K11
Nottingham Island Canada **165** L3
Nottingham Road S. Africa **133** O6
Nottoway U.S.A. **176** G8
Nottoway *r.* U.S.A. **176** I9
Notukeu Creek *r.* Canada **167** J5
Nouâdhibou Mauritania **122** A5
formerly known as Port Étienne
Nouâdhibou, Râs *c.* Mauritania **122** A5

Nouakchott Mauritania **124** B2
Capital of Mauritania.

Noual *well* Mauritania **124** D2
Nouâmghâr Mauritania **124** A2
Nouei Vietnam **79** D5

Nouméa New Caledonia **145** F4
Capital of New Caledonia.

Noun *r.* Cameroon **125** H5
Nouna Burkina **124** E3
Noupoort S. Africa **133** I8
Noupoortsnek *pass* S. Africa **133** M5
Nousu Fin. **44** O2
Nouveau-Comptoir Canada *see* **Wemindji**
Nouvelle Anvers Dem. Rep. Congo *see* **Makanza**
Nouvelle Calédonie *i.* S. Pacific Ocean **145** F4
also known as New Caledonia
Nouvelle Calédonie *terr.* S. Pacific Ocean *see* **New Caledonia**
Nouvelles Hébrides *country* S. Pacific Ocean *see* **Vanuatu**
Nov Tajik. **101** G1
also spelt Nau
Nõva Estonia **42** E2
Nova Almeida Brazil **207** M7
Nova América Brazil **206** D2
Nova Aurora Brazil **206** E5
Novabad Tajik. *see* **Novobod**
Nova Baña Slovakia **49** P7
Nova Chaves Angola *see* **Muconda**
Novaci Romania **58** E3
Nova Crnja *Vojvodina, Srbija* Yugo. **58** B3
Nova Cruz Brazil **202** F3
Nova Era Brazil **207** J6
Nova Esperança Angola *see* **Buengas**
Nova Esperança Brazil **206** A10
Nova Freixa Moz. *see* **Cuamba**
Nova Friburgo Brazil **203** D7
Nova Gaia Angola *see* **Cambundi-Catembo**
Nova Goa India *see* **Panaji**
Nova Gorica Slovenia **56** F3
Nova Gradiška Croatia **56** J3
Nova Granada Brazil **206** D7
Nova Iguaçu Brazil **203** D7
Nova Kakhovka Ukr. **41** E7
also spelt Novaya Kakhovka
Nova Lima Brazil **203** D6
Nova Lisboa Angola *see* **Huambo**
Nova Londrina Brazil **206** A9
Novalukoml' Belarus **43** K7
also spelt Novolukoml'
Nova Mambone Moz. **131** G4
Nova Nabúri Moz. **131** H3
Nova Odesa Ukr. **41** D7
also spelt Novaya Odessa
Nová Paka Czech Rep. **49** M5
Nova Paraiso Brazil **199** F4
Nova Pazova *Vojvodina, Srbija* Yugo. **58** B4
Nova Pilão Arcado Brazil **202** D4
Nova Ponte Brazil **206** F6
Nova Ponte, Represa *resr Minas Gerais* Brazil **206** F6
Nova Ponte, Represa *resr* Brazil **203** C6
Novara Italy **56** A3
Nova Remanso Brazil **202** D4
Nova Resende Brazil **206** G8
Nova Russas Brazil **202** D3
Nova Scotia *prov.* Canada **169** H5
historically known as Acadia
Nova Senna Sé Brazil **202** D4
Nova Serrana Brazil **207** I6
Nova Sintra Angola *see* **Catabola**
Nova Soure Brazil **202** E4
Novate Mezzola Italy **56** B2
Novato U.S.A. **182** B3
Nova Topola Bos.-Herz. **56** J3
Novator Rus. Fed. **40** H3
Nova Vandúzi Moz. **131** G3
Nova Varoš *Srbija* Yugo. **58** A5
Nova Venécia Brazil **203** D6
Nova Viçosa Brazil **207** N4
Nova Vida *Amazonas* Brazil **199** E5
Nova Vida *Rondônia* Brazil **201** E2
Nova Xavantino Brazil **206** A1
Novaya Kakhovka Ukr. *see* **Nova Kakhovka**
Novaya Kazanka Kazakh. **102** B2
also known as Zhanga Qazan
Novaya Ladoga Rus. Fed. **43** N1
Novaya Odessa Ukr. *see* **Nova Odesa**
Novaya Pismyanka Rus. Fed. *see* **Leninogorsk**
Novaya Sibir', Ostrov *i.* Rus. Fed. **39** O2

Novaya Zemlya *is* Rus. Fed. **40** J1
3rd largest island in Europe.
europe [landscapes] 30–31
arctic [features] 214–215

Novaya Zhizn Rus. Fed. *see* **Kazinka**
Nova Zagora Bulg. **58** H6
Novelda Spain **55** K6
Novellara Italy **56** C4
Nové Město nad Metují Czech Rep. **49** N5
Nové Mlýny, Vodní nádrž *resr* Czech Rep. **49** N7
Nové Zámky Slovakia **49** P8
Novgorod Rus. Fed. *see* **Velikiy Novgorod**
Novgorodka Rus. Fed. **43** J4
Novgorod Oblast *admin. div.* Rus. Fed. *see* **Novgorodskaya Oblast'**
Novgorod-Severskiy Ukr. *see* **Novhorod-Sivers'kyy**
Novgorodskaya Oblast' *admin. div.* Rus. Fed. **43** N3
English form Novgorod Oblast
Novgorod-Volynskiy Ukr. *see* **Novohrad-Volyns'kyy**
Novgradets Bulg. *see* **Suvorovo**

index

N O

Novhorod-Sivers'kyy Ukr. 41 E6
also spelt Novgorod-Severskiy
Novi U.S.A. 173 J8
Novi Bečej Vojvodina, Srbija Yugo. 58 B3
Novichikha Rus. Fed. 103 J1
Novi Grad Bos.-Herz. see Bosanski Novi
Novi Iskŭr Bulg. 58 E6
Novikovo Rus. Fed. 82 F3
Novi Kozarci Vojvodina, Srbija Yugo. 58 B3
Novi Kritsim Bulg. see Stamboliyski
Novi Ligure Italy 56 A4
Novillero Mex. 184 D4
Novi Marof Croatia 56 I2
Novi Pazar Bulg. 58 I5
Novi Pazar Srbija Yugo. 58 B5
Novi Sad Vojvodina, Srbija Yugo. 58 A3
also known as Újvidék
Novi Travnik Bos.-Herz. 56 J4
formerly known as Pucarevo
Novi Vinodolski Croatia 56 G3
Novlenskoye Rus. Fed. 43 U2
Novoaleksandrovsk Rus. Fed. 82 F3
Novoaleksandrovsk Rus. Fed. 41 G7
Novoaleksandrovskiy Rus. Fed. 43 P7
Novoalekseyevka Kazakh. see Khobda
Novoaltaysk Rus. Fed. 80 C2
formerly known as Chesnokovka
Novoanninskiy Rus. Fed. 41 G6
Novo Aripuanã Brazil 199 F6
Novoazovs'k Ukr. 41 F7
Novo Beograd Srbija Yugo. 58 B4
Novobod Tajik. 101 G2
also spelt Novabad
Novobod Tajik. 101 G2
also spelt Navabad; formerly known as Shul'mak; formerly spelt Novabad
Novobogatinsk Kazakh. see Novobogatinskoye
Novobogatinskoye Kazakh. 102 B3
also known as Novobogatinsk
Novobureyskiy Rus. Fed. 82 C2
formerly known as Bureya-Pristan'
Novocheboksarsk Rus. Fed. 40 H4
Novocherkassk Rus. Fed. 41 G7
Novo Cruzeiro Brazil 203 D6
Novodolinka Kazakh. 103 H2
Novodugino Rus. Fed. 43 P6
Novodvinsk Rus. Fed. 40 G2
formerly known as Pervomayskiy
Novogeorgiyevka Rus. Fed. 82 B2
Novognezdilovo Rus. Fed. 43 Q9
Novogrudok Belarus see Navahrudak
Novogurovskiy Rus. Fed. 43 S7
Novo Hamburgo Brazil 203 B9
Novo Horizonte Brazil 206 D8
Novohrad-Volyns'kyy Ukr. 41 C6
also spelt Novograd-Volynskiy
Novoil'insk Rus. Fed. 85 F1
Novokazalinsk Kazakh. see Ayteke Bi
Novokhopersk Rus. Fed. 41 G6
Novokhovansk Rus. Fed. 43 K6
Novokiyevskiy Uval Rus. Fed. 82 C2
Novokizhinginsk Rus. Fed. 85 F1
Novokubansk Rus. Fed. 107 E1
formerly known as Novokubanskiy
Novokubanskiy Rus. Fed. see Novokubansk
Novokuybyshevsk Rus. Fed. 102 B1
Novokuznetsk Rus. Fed. 80 D2
formerly known as Stalinsk
Novolazarevskaya research station Antarctica 223 A2
Novolukoml' Belarus see Novalukoml'
Novol'vovsk Rus. Fed. 43 T8
Novo Marapi Brazil 199 E5
Novomarkovka Kazakh. 103 H2
Novo Mesto Slovenia 56 H3
Novomichurinsk Rus. Fed. 43 U7
Novomikhaylovskiy Rus. Fed. 41 F7
Novo Miloševo Vojvodina, Srbija Yugo. 58 B3
Novomirgorod Ukr. see Novomyrhorod
Novomoskovsk Rus. Fed. 43 T7
formerly known as Bobriki or Stalinogorsk
Novomoskovs'k Ukr. 41 E6
Novomyrhorod Ukr. 41 D6
also spelt Novomirgorod
Novonazyvayevka Rus. Fed. see Nazyvayevsk
Novonikolayevka Kazakh. 103 G4
Novonikolayevsk Rus. Fed. see Novosibirsk
Novonikolayevskiy Rus. Fed. 41 G6
Novooleksiyivka Ukr. 41 E7
Novo Olinda do Norte Brazil 199 G5
Novo Oriente Brazil 202 D3
Novoorsk Rus. Fed. 102 D2
Novo Parnarama Brazil 202 D3
Novopashiyskiy Rus. Fed. see Gornozavodsk
Novopavlovka Rus. Fed. 85 F1
Novopokrovka Kustanayskaya Oblast' Kazakh. 103 F1
Novopokrovka Severnyy Kazakhstan Kazakh. 103 F1
Novopokrovka Vostochnyy Kazakhstan Kazakh. 103 J2
Novopokrovka Rus. Fed. 82 D3
Novopokrovskaya Rus. Fed. 41 G7
Novopolotsk Belarus see Navapolatsk
Novopolyan'ye Rus. Fed. 43 U8
Novopskov Ukr. 41 F6
Novo Redondo Angola see Sumbe
Novorepnoye Rus. Fed. 102 B2
Novorossiysk Rus. Fed. 41 F7
Novorossiyskiy Kazakh. see Novorossiyskoye
Novorossiyskoye Kazakh. 102 D2
formerly known as Novorossiyskiy
Novorybnaya Rus. Fed. 39 K2
Novorzhev Rus. Fed. 43 K4
Novoselki Moskovskaya Oblast' Rus. Fed. 43 T7
Novoselki Tverskaya Oblast' Rus. Fed. 43 M6
Novoselovo Rus. Fed. 43 U5
Novosel'skoye Rus. Fed. see Achkhoy-Martan
Novosel'ye Rus. Fed. 43 J3
Novosergiyevka Rus. Fed. 102 C1
Novoshakhtinsk Rus. Fed. 41 F7
Novoshakhtinskiy Rus. Fed. 82 D3
Novosheshminsk Rus. Fed. 40 I5
Novosibirsk Rus. Fed. 80 C1
formerly known as Novonikolayevsk
Novosibirskaya Oblast' admin. div. Rus. Fed. 80 C1
English form Novosibirsk Oblast
Novosibirskiye Ostrova is Rus. Fed. see New Siberia Islands
Novosibirsk Oblast admin. div. Rus. Fed. see Novosibirskaya Oblast'
Novosil' Rus. Fed. 43 S9
Novosokol'niki Rus. Fed. 43 L5
Novospasskoye Rus. Fed. 41 H5
Novotroitsk Rus. Fed. 102 D2
Novotroitskoye Kazakh. see Tole Bi
Novotroitskoye Rus. Fed. 43 O8
Novotroyits'ke Ukr. 41 E7
Novoukrainka Ukr. see Novoukrayinka
Novoukrayinka Ukr. 41 D6
also spelt Novoukrainka
Novoural'sk Rus. Fed. 102 D2
Novouzensk Rus. Fed. 102 B2
Novovasylivka Ukr. 43 O9
Novovolyns'k Ukr. 41 C6
Novovoronezh Rus. Fed. 41 F6
formerly known as Novovoronezhskiy
Novovoronezhskiy Rus. Fed. see Novovoronezh
Novo-Voskresenovka Rus. Fed. 82 B1
Novovoznesenovka Kyrg. 103 I4
Novoyamskoye Rus. Fed. 43 P9
Novoye Dubovoye Rus. Fed. 43 U9
Novoyegor'yevskoye Rus. Fed. 103 J2
Novoye Leushino Rus. Fed. 43 V5
Novozavidovskiy Rus. Fed. 43 R5
Novozhilovskaya Rus. Fed. 40 I2
Novozybkov Rus. Fed. 43 M9
Novska Croatia 56 I3
Novy Boletsk Belarus 43 L6
Nový Bor Czech Rep. 49 L5
Novy Bykhaw Belarus 43 L8
Novy Dvor Belarus 42 F9
Nový Jičín Czech Rep. 49 O6
Novyya Kruki Belarus 42 I6
Novyya Zhuravichy Belarus 43 L8
Novyy Bor Rus. Fed. 40 J2
Novyye Burasy Rus. Fed. 102 A1
Novyye Ivaytenki Rus. Fed. 43 O9
Novyye Petushki Rus. Fed. see Petushki
Novyy Izborsk Rus. Fed. 42 I4
Novyy Kholmogory Rus. Fed. see Archangel
Novyy Margelan Uzbek. see Fergana
Novyy Nekouz Rus. Fed. 43 T4
Novyy Oskol Rus. Fed. 41 F6
Novyy Port Rus. Fed. 38 H3
Novyy Ropsk Rus. Fed. 43 N9
Novyy Sinets Rus. Fed. 43 R8
Novyy Urengoy Rus. Fed. 38 H3
Novyy Urgal Rus. Fed. 82 D2
formerly known as Raz"yezd 3km
Novyy Uzen' Kazakh. see Zhanaozen
Novyy Zay Rus. Fed. 40 J5
Now Iran 100 C4
Nowa Dęba Poland 49 S5
Nowa Ruda Poland 49 N5
Nowa Sarzyna Poland 49 T5
Nowa Sól Poland 49 M4
Nowata U.S.A. 178 D4
Now Dezh Iran 100 B3
Nowdī Iran 100 B2
Nowe Poland 49 P2
Nowe Miasteczko Poland 49 M4
Nowe Miasto Lubawskie Poland 49 Q2
Nowe Miasto nad Pilicą Poland 49 R4
Nowe Skalmierzyce Poland 49 O4
Now Gombad Iran 100 C3
Nowgong India see Nagaon
Nowgong India 96 C4
Now Kharegan Iran 100 C2
Nowleye Lake Canada 167 K2
Nowogard Poland 49 M2
Nowogród Poland 49 S2
Nowogród Bobrzański Poland 49 M4
Nowood r. U.S.A. 180 F3
Noworadomsk Poland see Radomsko
Nowra Australia 147 F3
Nowshahr Iran 100 B2
Now Shahr Iran 100 B2
Nowshera Pak. 101 H3
Nowsūd Iran 100 A3
Nowy Dwór Gdański Poland 49 Q1
Nowy Dwór Mazowiecki Poland 49 R3
Nowy Sącz Poland 49 R6
historically known as Neu Sandez
Nowy Staw Poland 49 Q1
Nowy Targ Poland 49 R6
Nowy Tomyśl Poland 49 N3
Noxen U.S.A. 177 I4
Noxubee National Wildlife Refuge nature res. U.S.A. 175 B5
Noy, Xé r. Laos 78 D4
Noy, Xé r. Laos 78 D4
Noya Spain see Noia
Noyabr'sk Rus. Fed. 38 H3
Noyant France 50 G5
Noyes Island U.S.A. 166 C4
Noyil r. India 94 C4
Noyon France 51 I3
Nozay France 50 E5
Nozizwe S. Africa 133 J7
Npitamaiong mt. Kenya 128 B4
Nqabeni S. Africa 133 O7
Nqamakwe S. Africa 133 L9
Nqutu S. Africa 133 O5
Nsalamu Zambia 127 F8
Nsambi Dem. Rep. Congo 126 C5
Nsanje Malawi 129 B9
formerly known as Port Herald
Nsawam Ghana 125 E5
Nseluka Zambia 127 F7
Nsoc Equat. Guinea 125 H6
Nsoko Swaziland 133 P4
Nsombo Zambia 127 F7
Nsukka Nigeria 125 G5
Nsumbu National Park Zambia see Sumbu National Park
Ntalfa well Mauritania 122 B5
Ntambu Zambia 127 E8
Ntandembele Dem. Rep. Congo 126 C5
Ntcheu Malawi 129 B8
formerly spelt Ncheu
Ntchisi Malawi 129 B8
Ntem r. Cameroon 125 H6
formerly known as Campo
Ntha S. Africa 133 L4
Ntibane S. Africa 133 M8
Ntiona Chad 120 B6
Ntomba, Lac l. Dem. Rep. Congo 126 C5
Ntoroko Uganda 128 A4
Ntoum Gabon 126 A4
Ntui Cameroon 125 H5
Ntungamo Uganda 128 A5
Ntwetwe Pan salt pan Botswana 131 E4
Ntywenka S. Africa 133 M8
Nuakata Island P.N.G. 149 F1
Nuanetsi r. Zimbabwe see Mwenezi
Nuangan Indon. 75 C2
Nu'aym reg. Oman 105 F3
Nuba, Lake resr Sudan 121 F4
Nuba Mountains Sudan 128 A2
Nubian Desert Sudan 121 G4
Nubivarri hill Norway 44 M1
Nucet Romania 58 D2
Nūden Mongolia 85 F3
Nudol' Rus. Fed. 43 R5
Nueces r. U.S.A. 179 C7
Nueltin Lake Canada 167 L2
Nueva, Isla i. Chile 205 D9
Nueva Alejandría Peru 198 C6
Nueva Arcadia Hond. 186 A4
Nueva Ciudad Guerrero Mex. 179 C7
Nueva Esparta state Venez. 199 E2
Nueva Florida Venez. 198 D2
Nueva Germania Para. 201 F5
Nueva Gerona Cuba 186 C2
Nueva Harberton Arg. 205 D9
Nueva Loja Ecuador 198 B4
Nueva Lubecka Arg. 205 C7
Nueva Ocotepeque Hond. 186 A4
Nueva Palmira Uruguay 204 F4
Nueva Rosita Mex. 185 E3
Nueva San Salvador El Salvador 185 H6
Nueva Villa de Padilla Mex. 185 F3
Nueve de Julio Arg. see 9 de Julio
Nuevitas Cuba 186 D2
Nuevo, Cayo i. Mex. 185 H4
Nuevo, Golfo g. Arg. 205 D6
Nuevo Casas Grandes Mex. 184 D2
Nuevo Ideal Mex. 184 D3
Nuevo Laredo Mex. 185 F3
Nuevo León Mex. 183 I9
Nuevo León state Mex. 185 F3
Nuevo Mamo Venez. 187 H5
Nufayyid Şabḩah des. Saudi Arabia 104 D3
Nuga Mongolia 84 B1
Nugaal admin. reg. Somalia 128 F2
Nugaal watercourse Somalia 128 F3
Nuga Nuga, Lake Australia 149 F5
Nugget Point N.Z. 153 D14
Nugr' r. Rus. Fed. 43 R8
Nugrus, Gebel mt. Egypt 121 G3
Nugu r. India 94 C3
Nuguria Islands P.N.G. 145 E2
also known as Fead Group
Nuh, Ras pt Pak. 101 E5
Nuhaka N.Z. 152 L7
Nui i. Tuvalu 145 G2
Nui Con Voi r. Vietnam see Red River
Nuijamaa Fin. 43 J1
Nui Ti On mt. Vietnam 79 D5
Nuits-St-Georges France 51 K5
Nu Jiang r. China 86 A3 see Salween
Nukey Bluff hill Australia 146 B3
Nukha Azer. see Şäki

Nuku'alofa Tonga 145 H4
Capital of Tonga.
world [countries] 10–11

Nukufetau i. Tuvalu 145 G2
Nukulaelae i. Tuvalu 145 G2
also spelt Nukulailai; formerly known as Mitchell Island
Nukulailai i. Tuvalu see Nukulaelae
Nukumanu Islands P.N.G. 145 E2
Nukunau i. Kiribati see Nikunau
Nukunonu atoll Tokelau see Nukunonu
Nukunonu atoll Tokelau 145 H2
also spelt Nukunono; formerly known as Duke of Clarence
Nukus Uzbek. 102 D4
also spelt Nökis
Nulato U.S.A. 164 D3
Nules Spain 55 K5
Nullagine Australia 150 C4
Nullagine r. Australia 150 C4
Nullarbor Australia 146 A2
Nullarbor National Park Australia 146 A2
Nullarbor Plain Australia 146 A2
Nullarbor Regional Reserve park Australia 146 A2
Nuluarniavik, Lac l. Canada 168 E1
Nulu'erhu Shan mts China 85 H3
Num i. Indon. 73 I7
Num Nepal 97 E4
Numalla, Lake salt flat Australia 147 E2
Numan Nigeria 125 I4
Nu'mān i. Saudi Arabia 104 A2
Numata Gumma Japan 91 F6
Numata Hokkaidō Japan 90 G3
Numazu Japan 91 F7
Numbi Gate S. Africa 133 P2
Numbulwar Australia 148 B2
Numfoor i. Indon. 73 H7
Numin r. China 82 B3
Numkaub Namibia 130 C3
Nummi Fin. 45 M3
Numurkah Australia 147 E4
Nunaksaluk Island Canada 169 I2
Nunakuluut i. Greenland 165 O3
also known as Nunarsuit
Nunap Isua c. Greenland see Farewell, Cape
Nunarsuit i. Greenland see Nunakuluut
Nunavik reg. Canada 169 E1
Nunavut admin. div. Canada 167 L2
Nunda U.S.A. 176 H3
Nuneaton U.K. 47 K11
Nungatta National Park Australia 147 F4
Nungesser Lake Canada 167 M5
Nungnain Sum China 85 H2
Nungo Moz. 131 H2
Nunivak Island U.S.A. 164 C4
Nunkapasi India 95 E1
Nunkun mt. Jammu and Kashmir 96 C2
Nunligran Rus. Fed. 39 S3
Nuñoa Peru 200 C3
Nuñomoral Spain 54 E4
Nunukan i. Indon. 77 G2
Nuojiang China see Tongjiang
Nuomin r. China 85 J1
Nuoro Sardegna Italy 57 B8
Nupani i. Solomon Is 145 F3
Nuqayy, Jabal mts Libya 120 C4
Nuqrah Saudi Arabia 104 C2
Nuquí Col. 198 B3
Nūr r. Iran 100 C2
Nura r. Kazakh. 103 G2
Nūrābād Iran 100 B4
Nurakita i. Tuvalu see Niulakita
Nurata Uzbek. 103 F4
also spelt Nurota
Nuratau, Khrebet mts Uzbek. 103 F4
Nur Dağları mts Turkey 107 C3
Nure r. Italy 56 B3
Nurek Tajik. see Norak
Nuremberg Germany 48 I6
also spelt Nürnberg
Nür Gal Afgh. 101 G3
Nuri Mex. 184 C2
Nuri Sudan 121 G5
Nuri, Teluk b. Indon. 77 E3
Nuristan reg. Afgh. 101 G3
Nurla Jammu and Kashmir 96 C2
Nurlat Rus. Fed. 40 I5
Nurmes Fin. 44 O3
Nurmijärvi Fin. 45 N3
Nurmo Fin. 44 M3
Nürnberg Germany see Nuremberg
Nurota Uzbek. see Nurata
Nurpur Pak. 101 G4
Nurrai Lakes salt flat Australia 146 A2
Nurri, Mount hill Australia 147 E2
Nursfjellet mt. Norway 44 K2
Nurste Estonia 42 D3
Nürtingen Germany 48 G7
Nurzec r. Poland 49 T3
Nusa Tenggara Barat prov. Indon. 77 G5
English form Western Lesser Sunda Islands
Nusa Tenggara Timur prov. Indon. 75 B5
English form Eastern Lesser Sunda Islands
Nusaybin Turkey 107 E3
historically known as Nisibis
Nusela, Kepulauan is Indon. 75 D3
Nuşfalău Romania 58 D1
Nu Shan mts China 86 A3
Nushki Pak. 101 F4
Nutak Canada 169 I1
Nutarawit Lake Canada 167 L2
Nutrioso U.S.A. 183 O8
Nutwood Downs Australia 148 B2
Nuugaatsiaap Imaa inlet Greenland 165 N2
also known as Karrats Fjord
Nuugaatsiaq Greenland 165 N2

Nuuk Greenland 165 N3
Capital of Greenland. Also known as Godthåb.
world [countries] 10–11

Nuuksion kansallispuisto nat. park Fin. 42 F1
Nuupas Fin. 44 N2
Nuussuaq Greenland 165 N2
also known as Kraulshavn
Nuussuaq pen. Greenland 165 N2
Nuwakot Nepal 97 D3
Nuweiba el Muzeina Egypt 121 G2
Nuwekloof pass S. Africa 132 H10
Nuwerus S. Africa 132 C8
Nuweveldberge mts S. Africa 132 F9
Nuyts, Point Australia 151 B7
Nuyts Archipelago is Australia 146 B3
Nuyts Archipelago Conservation Park nature res. Australia 146 B3
Nuytsland Nature Reserve Australia 151 D7
Nuzvid India 94 D2
Nxai Pan National Park Botswana 131 E3
Nxaunxau Botswana 130 D3
Nyaān, Bukit hill Indon. 77 F2
Nyabessan Cameroon 125 H6
Nyabing Australia 151 B7
Nyack U.S.A. 177 L4
Nyagan' Rus. Fed. 38 G3
formerly known as Nyakh
Nyagquka China see Yajiang
Nyagrong China see Xinlong
Nyahua Tanz. 129 B6
Nyahururu Kenya 128 C4
formerly known as Thompson's Falls
Nyainqêntanglha Feng mt. China 89 E6
Nyainqêntanglha Shan mts China 89 E6
English form Nyenchen Tanglha Range
Nyainrong China 89 F5
also known as Sêrkang
Nyakahura Kagera Tanz. 128 A5
Nyakahura Kagera Tanz. 128 A5
Nyakaliro Tanz. 128 B5
Nyakallong S. Africa 133 K4
Nyakanazi Tanz. 128 A5
Nyåker Sweden 44 L3
Nyakh Rus. Fed. see Nyagan'
Nyakhachava Belarus 42 G9
Nyakrom Ghana 125 E5
Nyala Sudan 120 E6
Nyalam China 89 D6
also known as Congdü
Nyamandhlovu Zimbabwe 131 F3
Nyamapanda Zimbabwe 131 G3
Nyambiti Tanz. 128 B5
Nyamlell Sudan 126 E2
Nyamtumbo Tanz. 129 C7
Nyande Zimbabwe see Masvingo
Nyandoma Rus. Fed. 40 G3
Nyandomskiy Vozvyshennost' hills Rus. Fed. 40 F3
Nyanga Congo 126 A5
Nyanga Gabon 126 A5
Nyanga prov. Gabon 126 A5
Nyanga Zimbabwe 131 G3
formerly spelt Inyanga
Nyanga National Park Zimbabwe 131 G3
formerly known as Rhodes Inyanga National Park; formerly spelt Inyanga National Park
Nyang Qu r. China 89 E6
Nyang Qu r. China 89 F6
Nyankpala Ghana 125 E4
Nyanza prov. Kenya 128 B5
Nyapa, Gunung mt. Indon. 77 G2
Nyapongeth Sudan 128 B3
Nyar r. India 96 C3
Nyarling r. Canada 167 H2

Nyasa, Lake Africa 129 B7
3rd largest lake in Africa and 10th in the world. Also known as Malawi, Lake or Niassa, Lago.
africa [landscapes] 112–113

Nyasaland country Africa see Malawi
Nyashabozh Rus. Fed. 40 J2
Nyasvizh Belarus 42 H8
also spelt Nesvizh
Nyathi Zimbabwe 131 F3
formerly spelt Inyati
Nyaunglebin Myanmar 78 B4
Nyaungu Myanmar 78 A3
Nyays r. Rus. Fed. 40 L3
Nyazura Zimbabwe 131 G3
formerly spelt Inyazura
Nyborg Denmark 45 J5
Nyborg Norway 44 O1
Nyborg Sweden 44 M2
Nybro Sweden 45 K4
Nyeboe Land reg. Greenland 165 N1
Nyeharelaye Belarus 42 I8
Nyémo China 89 E6
also known as Tarrong
Nyenchen Tanglha Range mts China see Nyainqêntanglha Shan
Nyeri Kenya 128 C5
Nyeshcharda, Vozyera l. Belarus 43 K6
Nyhammar Sweden 45 K3
Nyi, Co l. China 89 D5
Nyika National Park Zambia 129 B7
also known as Malawi National Park
Nyika Plateau Malawi 129 B7
Nyima China 89 D6
Nyimba Zambia 127 F8
Nyingchi China 89 F6
also known as Pula
Nyinma China see Maqu
Nyíradony Hungary 49 S8
Nyírbátor Hungary 49 T8
Nyírbéltek Hungary 49 T8
Nyíregyháza Hungary 49 S8
Nyiri Desert Kenya 128 C5
Nyiru, Mount Kenya 128 C4
Nykarleby Fin. 44 M3
also known as Uusikaarlepyy
Nykøbing Denmark 45 J5
Nykøbing Mors Denmark 45 J4
Nykøbing Sjælland Denmark 45 J5
Nyköping Sweden 45 L4
Nykvarn Sweden 45 L4
Nylstroom S. Africa 133 M1
Nylsvley nature res. S. Africa 133 M1
Nymagee Australia 147 E3
Nymboida National Park Australia 147 G2
Nymburk Czech Rep. 49 M5
Nynäshamn Sweden 45 L4
Nyngan Australia 147 E2
Nyogzê China 89 C6
Nyoman r. Belarus/Lith. 42 E8
also spelt Neman
Nyomanskaya Nizina lowland Belarus 42 G8
Nyon Switz. 51 M6
Nyong r. Cameroon 125 H6
Nyons France 51 L8
Nýřany Czech Rep. 49 K6
Nyrob Rus. Fed. 40 K3
Nyrud Norway 44 O1
Nysa Poland 49 O5
Nysa Kłodzka r. Poland 49 O5
Nysa Łużycka r. Germany/Poland see Neiße
Nysäter Sweden 45 K4
Nysätern Sweden 44 K3
Nysh Rus. Fed. 82 F2
Nyssa U.S.A. 180 C4
Nystad Fin. see Uusikaupunki
Nyūdō-zaki pt Japan 90 F5
Nyuk, Ozero l. Rus. Fed. 44 O2
Nyuksenitsa Rus. Fed. 40 H3
Nyunzu Dem. Rep. Congo 127 F6
Nyurba Rus. Fed. 39 L3
Nyuvchim Rus. Fed. 40 I3
Nyuya Rus. Fed. 39 L3
Nyuya r. Rus. Fed. 39 L3
Nyyskiy Zaliv lag. Rus. Fed. 82 F1
Nyzhn'ohirs'kyy Ukr. 41 E7
Nzambi Congo 126 A5
Nzara Sudan 126 F3
Nzébéla Guinea 124 C4
Nzega Tanz. 129 B6
Nzérékoré Guinea 124 C5
N'zeto Angola 127 B6
formerly known as Ambrizete
Nzi r. Côte d'Ivoire 124 D5
Nzilo, Lac l. Dem. Rep. Congo 127 E7
Nzingu Dem. Rep. Congo 126 E5
Nzo r. Côte d'Ivoire 124 D5
N'Zo, Réserve de Faune du nature res. Côte d'Ivoire 124 D5
Nzobe Dem. Rep. Congo 127 B6
Nzoia r. Kenya 128 B4
Nzoro r. Dem. Rep. Congo 126 F4
Nzwani i. Comoros 129 E8
also known as Anjouan; also spelt Ndjouani

↓ O

Oahe, Lake U.S.A. 178 B2
Oahu i. U.S.A. 181 [inset] Y1
northamerica [environments] 162–163
Oaitupu i. Tuvalu see Vaitupu
Oakbank Australia 146 D3
Oak Bluffs U.S.A. 177 O4
Oak City U.S.A. 183 L2
Oak Creek U.S.A. 172 F8
Oakdale CA U.S.A. 182 D4
Oakdale LA U.S.A. 179 D6
Oakes U.S.A. 178 C2
Oakey Australia 147 F1
Oakfield U.S.A. 176 G2
Oak Grove LA U.S.A. 175 B5
Oak Grove MI U.S.A. 173 I6
Oakham U.K. 47 L11
Oak Harbor OH U.S.A. 176 B4
Oak Harbor WA U.S.A. 180 B2
Oak Hill OH U.S.A. 176 C7
Oak Hill WV U.S.A. 176 D8
Oakhurst U.S.A. 182 E4
Oak Island U.S.A. 172 C4
Oak Knolls U.S.A. 182 D7
Oak Lake Canada 167 K5
Oakland CA U.S.A. 182 B4
Oakland MD U.S.A. 176 F6
Oakland ME U.S.A. 177 P1
Oakland NE U.S.A. 178 C3
Oakland airport U.S.A. 182 B4
Oakland City U.S.A. 174 C4
Oaklands Australia 147 E3
Oak Lawn U.S.A. 174 C3
Oakley KS U.S.A. 178 B4
Oakley MI U.S.A. 173 I7
Oakover r. Australia 150 C4
Oak Park U.S.A. 172 F9
Oakridge U.S.A. 180 B4
Oak Ridge U.S.A. 176 A9
Oakura N.Z. 152 H7
Oak View U.S.A. 182 E7
Oakville Canada 168 E5
Oamaru N.Z. 153 E13
Oaonui N.Z. 152 H7
Oaro N.Z. 153 H10
Oasis U.S.A. 182 G4
Oates Coast reg. Antarctica see Oates Land
Oates Land reg. Antarctica 223 K2
also known as Oates Coast
Oatlands Australia 147 E5
Oatlands S. Africa 133 I9
Oaxaca Mex. 185 F5
Oaxaca state Mex. 185 F5
Ob' r. Rus. Fed. 38 G3
Ob, Gulf of sea chan. Rus. Fed. see Obskaya Guba
Oba Canada 168 C3
Oba i. Vanuatu see Aoba
Obaghan r. Kazakh. see Ubagan
Obal' Belarus 43 K6
Obal' canal Belarus 43 K6
Obala Cameroon 125 H5
Oba Lake Canada 173 I2
Obama Japan 91 D7
Oban Nigeria 125 H5
Oban U.K. 46 G7
Obanazawa Japan 90 G5
Obanbori Qayroqqum resr Tajik. 101 G1
also known as Kayrakkumskoye Vodokhranilishche
Oban Hills mt. Nigeria 125 H5
O Barco Spain 54 E2
also known as El Barco de Valdeorras
Obbia Somalia see Hobyo
Obbola Sweden 44 M3
Obdorsk Rus. Fed. see Salekhard
Óbecse Vojvodina, Srbija Yugo. see Bečej
Obed Canada 167 G4
Obeliai Lith. 42 G6
Obelisk mt. N.Z. 153 D13
Oberá Arg. 204 G2
Oberau Germany 48 I8
Obere Donau park Germany 48 F7
Obere Saale park Germany 48 I5
Oberes Westerzgebirge park Germany 49 J5
Oberlausitzer Bergland park Germany 49 L4
Oberlin KS U.S.A. 178 B4
Oberlin LA U.S.A. 179 D6
Obernai France 51 N4
Oberndorf am Neckar Germany 48 F7
Oberon Australia 147 F3
Oberpfälzer Wald mts Germany 49 J6
Oberpullendorf Austria 49 N8
Oberstdorf Germany 48 H8
Oberviechtach Germany 49 J6
Oberwart Austria 49 N8
Obi i. Indon. 75 C3
Obi, Kepulauan is Indon. 75 C3
Obi, Selat sea chan. Indon. 75 C3
Óbidos Brazil 199 H5
Obigarm Tajik. 101 G2
Obihiro Japan 90 H3
Obilatu i. Indon. 75 C3
Obilić Kosovo, Srbija Yugo. 58 C6
Obil'noye Rus. Fed. 41 H7
Obion r. U.S.A. 174 B4
Obira Japan 90 G2

Ob'-Irtysh r. Asia 38 G3
2nd longest river in Asia and 5th in the world.
asia [landscapes] 62–63

Obispos Venez. 198 D2
Obluch'ye Rus. Fed. 82 C2
Obninsk Rus. Fed. 43 R6
Obnora r. Rus. Fed. 43 V3
Obo Cent. Afr. Rep. 126 E3
Obo China 84 D4
Obobogorap S. Africa 132 E4
Obock Djibouti 128 D2
Obokote Dem. Rep. Congo 126 E5
Obolo Nigeria 125 G5
Obong, Gunung mt. Sarawak Malaysia 77 F1
Oborniki Poland 49 N3
Obouya Congo 126 B5
Oboyan' Rus. Fed. 41 F6
Obozerskiy Rus. Fed. 40 G3
Obra India 97 D4
Obra r. Poland 49 M3
Obrage Arg. 204 F3
Obregón, Presa resr Mex. 184 C3
Obrenovac Srbija Yugo. 58 B4
O'Brien U.S.A. 180 B4
Obrochishte Bulg. 58 J5
Obruk Turkey 106 C3
Obrzycko Poland 49 N3
Observatory Hill hill Australia 146 B2
Observatory Inlet Canada 166 D4
Obsha r. Rus. Fed. 43 N6
Obshchiy Syrt hills Rus. Fed. 102 B2
Obskaya Guba sea chan. Rus. Fed. 38 H3
English form Ob, Gulf of
Obuasi Ghana 125 E5
Obubra Nigeria 125 H5
Obudovac Bos.-Herz. 56 K4
Obudu Nigeria 125 H5
Obukhovo Rus. Fed. 43 T6
Obva r. Rus. Fed. 40 J4
Ob"yachevo Rus. Fed. 40 I3
Ocala U.S.A. 175 D6
Ocampo Mex. 185 E3
Ocaña Col. 198 C2
Ocaña Peru 200 B3
Ocaña Spain 55 H5
Occidental, Cordillera mts Chile 200 C4
Occidental, Cordillera mts Col. 198 B4
Occidental, Cordillera mts Peru 200 C4
Oceana U.S.A. 176 D8
Ocean Beach U.S.A. 177 L5
Ocean Cape U.S.A. 166 B3
Ocean City MD U.S.A. 177 J7
Ocean City NJ U.S.A. 177 K6
Ocean Falls Canada 166 E4
Ocean Island Kiribati see Banaba
Ocean Island atoll U.S.A. see Kure Atoll
Oceano U.S.A. 182 D6
Oceans Cay i. Bahamas 186 D1
Oceanside U.S.A. 183 G8
Ocean Springs U.S.A. 175 B6
Ochakiv Ukr. 41 D7
Och'amch'ire Georgia 107 E2
Ocher Rus. Fed. 40 J4
Ochi mt. Greece 59 F10
also known as Ókhi Óros
Ōchi Japan 91 C7
Ochiishi-misaki pt Japan 90 I3
Ochil Hills U.K. 46 I7
Ochkyne Ukr. 43 O9
Ochlockonee r. U.S.A. 175 C6
Ochrida, Lake Albania/Macedonia see Ohrid, Lake
Ochsenfurt Germany 48 H6
Ochthonia Greece 59 F10
also spelt Okhthonia
Ochthonia, Akra pt Greece 59 F10
Ocilla U.S.A. 175 D6
Ockelbo Sweden 45 L3
Ocland Romania 58 G2
Ocmulgee r. U.S.A. 175 D6
Ocna Mureş Romania 58 E2
Ocna Sibiului Romania 58 F3
Ocolaşul Mare, Vârful mt. Romania 58 G2
Ocoña Peru 200 B4
O'Connell Creek r. Australia 149 D4
Oconomowoc U.S.A. 172 E7
Oconto U.S.A. 172 F6
Oconto Falls U.S.A. 172 E6
O Corgo Spain 54 D2
Ocoruro Peru 200 C3
Ocos Guat. 185 G6
Ocosingo Mex. 185 G5
Ocotal Nicaragua 186 B4
Ocotlán Mex. 185 F5
Ocozocoautla Mex. 185 G5
October Revolution Island Rus. Fed. see Oktyabr'skoy Revolyutsii, Ostrov
Ocuri Bol. 200 D4
Ocussi East Timor see Pantemakassar
Ocussi enclave East Timor 75 C5
Oda Ghana 125 E5
Oda Japan 91 C7
Oda, Jebel mt. Sudan 121 H4
Ódáðahraun lava field Iceland 44 [inset] C2
Ŏdaejin N. Korea 82 C4
Odae-san National Park S. Korea 83 C5
Ōdaigahara-zan mt. Japan 91 E7
Odanah U.S.A. 172 C4
Ōdate Japan 90 G4
Odawara Japan 91 F7
Odda Norway 45 I3
Odder Denmark 45 J5
Odei r. Canada 167 L3
Odell U.S.A. 172 E9
Odem U.S.A. 179 C7
Odemira Port. 54 C7
Ödemiş Turkey 106 A3
Ödenburg Hungary see Sopron
Odendaalsrus S. Africa 133 K4
Odensbacken Sweden 45 K4
Odense Denmark 45 J5
Oder r. Germany 48 G4
also spelt Odra (Poland)
Oderbucht b. Germany 49 L1
Oderhaff b. Germany 49 L2
also known as Stettiner Haff
Oderzo Italy 56 E3
Odesa Ukr. 41 D7
also spelt Odessa
Ödeshog Sweden 45 K4
Odes'ka Oblast' admin. div. Ukr. 58 K1
English form Odessa Oblast; also spelt Odesskaya Oblast'
Odessa Ukr. see Odesa
Odessa U.S.A. 179 B6
Odessa Oblast admin. div. Ukr. see Odes'ka Oblast'
Odesskaya Oblast' admin. div. Ukr. see Odes'ka Oblast'
Odessus Bulg. see Varna
Odi watercourse Sudan 121 H5
Odiel r. Spain 54 E7
Odienné Côte d'Ivoire 124 D4
Odintsovo Rus. Fed. 43 S6
Odobeşti Romania 58 I3
Odobeştilor, Măgura hill Romania 58 H3
Odolanów Poland 49 O4
Odom Inlet Antarctica 222 T2
Odorheiu Secuiesc Romania 58 G2
Odoyev Rus. Fed. 43 R8
Odra r. Poland 49 P6
also spelt Oder (Germany)
Odra r. Spain 54 G2
Odžaci Vojvodina, Srbija Yugo. 58 A3
Odzala, Parc National d' nat. park Congo 126 B4
Odzi Zimbabwe 131 G3
Odzi r. Zimbabwe 131 G3
Oea Libya see Tripoli
Oedong S. Korea 91 A7
Oeiras Brazil 202 D3
Oelde Germany 48 F4
Oelixdorf Germany 48 G2
Oelrichs U.S.A. 178 B3
Oelsnitz Germany 49 J5
Oelwein U.S.A. 174 B3
Oenpelli Australia 148 B2

Oesel i. Estonia see Hiiumaa
Oeufs, Lac des l. Canada 169 F2
Oeversee Germany 48 G1
Of Turkey 107 E2
O'Fallon r. U.S.A. 180 F3
Ofanto r. Italy 57 I7
Offa Nigeria 125 G4
Offenbach am Main Germany 48 F5
Offenburg Germany 48 E7
Offerdal Sweden 44 K3
Ofidoussa i. Greece 59 H12
Ofotfjorden sea chan. Norway 44 L1
Ōfunato Japan 90 G5
Oga r. Indon. 77 F2
Oga Japan 90 F5
Ogachi Japan 90 G5
Ogadēn reg. Eth. 128 E3
Oga-hantō pen. Japan 90 F5
Ōgaki Japan 91 E7
Ogallala U.S.A. 178 B3
Ogan r. Indon. 76 D3
Ogasawara-shotō is N. Pacific Ocean see Bonin Islands
Ogascanane, Lac l. Canada 173 O3
Ogawa Japan 90 G6
Ogawara-ko l. Japan 90 G4
Ogbomosho Nigeria see Ogbomoso
Ogbomoso Nigeria 125 G4
also spelt Ogbomosho
Ogden IA U.S.A. 178 D3
Ogden UT U.S.A. 180 E4
Ogden, Mount Canada 166 C3
Ogdensburg U.S.A. 177 J1
Ogeechee r. U.S.A. 175 D6
Ogema U.S.A. 172 C5
Ogi Japan 90 F6
Ogidaki Canada 168 C4
Ogilvie r. Canada 164 F3
Ogilvie Mountains Canada 166 A1
'Oglât el Khnâchîch well Mali 122 E5
Oglat Sbot well Alg. 122 D4
Oglio r. Italy 56 C3
Ogmore Australia 149 F4
Ognon r. France 51 L5
Ognut Turkey see Göynük
Ogoamas, Gunung mt. Indon. 75 B2
Ogoja Nigeria 125 H5
Ogoki r. Canada 168 C3
Ogoki Lake Canada 168 C3
Ogoki Reservoir Canada 168 B3
Ogooué r. Gabon 126 A5
Ogooué-Ivindo prov. Gabon 126 B5
Ogooué-Lolo prov. Gabon 126 B5
Ogooué-Maritime prov. Gabon 126 A5
Ogoron Rus. Fed. 82 C1
Ogosta r. Bulg. 58 E5
Ogou r. Togo 125 F5
O'Grady, Lake salt flat Australia 151 B6
Ograzhden mts Bulg./Macedonia 58 D7
also spelt Ogražden
Ograzhden mts Bulg./Macedonia see Ograzhden
Ogre Latvia 42 F5
Ogre r. Latvia 42 F5
Ogudnevo Rus. Fed. 43 T5
Ogulin Croatia 56 H3
Ogun state Nigeria 125 F5
Ogurchinskiy, Ostrov i. Turkm. 102 C5
also known as Ogurjaly Adasy or Turkmen Adasy
Ogurjaly Adasy i. Turkm. see Ogurchinskiy, Ostrov
Oğuz Azer. 107 F2
formerly known as Vartashen
Ohafia Nigeria 125 G5
Ohai N.Z. 153 B13
Ohakune N.Z. 152 J7
Ohanet Alg. 123 H3
Ohangwena admin. reg. Namibia 130 C3
Ōhara Japan 91 G7
O'Hare airport U.S.A. 172 F9
Ōhata Japan 90 G4
Ohau N.Z. 152 J8
Ohau, Lake N.Z. 153 D12
Ohcejohka Fin. see Utsjoki
O'Higgins Chile 200 C5
O'Higgins admin. reg. Chile 204 C4
O'Higgins, Lago l. Chile 205 B8
Ohio U.S.A. 172 D9
Ohio r. U.S.A. 178 E4
Ohio state U.S.A. 176 C5
Ohio Range mts Antarctica 223 Q1
Ohm r. Germany 51 O2
Ōhne r. Estonia 42 H3
'Ohonua Tonga 145 H4
Ohope N.Z. 152 L5
Ohrdruf Germany 48 H5
Ohře r. Czech Rep. 49 L5
Ohre r. Germany 48 I3
Ohrid Macedonia 58 B7
Ohrid, Lake Albania/Macedonia 58 B7
also known as Ochrida, Lake or Ohridsko Ezero or Ohrit, Liqeni i
Ohridsko Ezero l. Albania/Macedonia see Ohrid, Lake
Ohrigstad S. Africa 133 O1
Ohrigstad Dam Nature Reserve S. Africa 133 O1
Öhringen Germany 48 G6
Ohrit, Liqeni i l. Albania/Macedonia see Ohrid, Lake
Ohura N.Z. 152 I6
Oiapoque Brazil 199 I4
Oiapoque r. Brazil/Fr. Guiana 199 I3
Oiba Col. 198 C3
Oich r. U.K. 46 H6
Oik Kazakh. see Uyuk
Oil City U.S.A. 176 F4
Oildale U.S.A. 182 E6
Oi Qu r. China 86 A2
Oirase-gawa r. Japan 90 G4
Oise r. France 51 I3
Oiseaux du Djoudj, Parc National des nat. park Senegal 124 A2
Ōita Japan 91 B8
Ōita pref. Japan 91 B8
Oiti mt. Greece 59 D10
Oiti nat. park Greece 59 D10
Oituz r. Romania 58 H2
Oiuru well Libya 120 C4
Oiwake Japan 90 G3
Ojai U.S.A. 182 E7
Ojailén r. Spain 54 H6
Ojalava i. Samoa see Upolu
Ojamaa r. Estonia 42 I2
Ojcowski Park Narodowy nat. park Poland 49 Q5
Öje Sweden 45 K3
Ojika-jima i. Japan 91 A8
Ojinaga Mex. 184 D2
Ojitlán Mex. 185 F5
Ojiya Japan 90 F6
Ojobo Nigeria 125 G5
Ojo de Laguna Mex. 184 D2
Ojo de Liebre, Lago b. Mex. 184 B3
Ojos del Salado, Nevado mt. Arg./Chile 204 C2
2nd highest mountain in South America.
southamerica [landscapes] 190–191
Ojuelos de Jalisco Mex. 185 E4
Öjung Sweden 45 K3
Oka Nigeria 125 G5
Oka r. Rus. Fed. 43 R9
Okahandja Namibia 130 C4
Okahu b. N.Z. see Jackson Bay
Okahukura N.Z. 152 J6
Okaihau N.Z. 152 H3
Okains Bay N.Z. 153 H11
Okains Bay b. N.Z. 153 H11
Okaka Nigeria 125 F4
Okakarara Namibia 130 C4
Okak Islands Canada 169 I1
Okanagan Falls Canada 166 G5
Okanagan Lake Canada 166 G5
Okanogan U.S.A. 180 C2
Okanogan r. U.S.A. 180 C2
Okanogan Range mts U.S.A. 180 B2
Okaputa Namibia 130 C4
Okara Pak. 101 H4
Okarem Turkm. 100 C2
also spelt Ekerem
Okarito Lagoon N.Z. 153 E11
Okaukuejo Namibia 130 B3
Okavango r. Botswana/Namibia 130 D3
world [land cover] 18–19
africa [issues] 116–117
Okavango admin. reg. Namibia 130 C3
Okavango Delta swamp Botswana 130 D3
Largest oasis in the world.
Ōkawa Japan 91 B8
Okaya Japan 91 F6
Okayama Japan 91 C7
Okayama pref. Japan 91 C7
Okazaki Japan 91 E7
Okeechobee U.S.A. 175 D7
Okeechobee, Lake U.S.A. 175 D7
Okeene U.S.A. 179 C4
Okefenokee National Wildlife Refuge and Wilderness nature res. U.S.A. 175 D6
Okefenokee Swamp U.S.A. 175 D6
Okemah U.S.A. 179 C5
Okene Nigeria 125 G5
Oker r. Germany 48 H3
Oketo Japan 90 H3
Okha India 96 A5
Okha Rus. Fed. 82 F1
Okhadunga Nepal see Okhaldhunga
Okhaldhunga Nepal 97 E4
also spelt Okhadunga
Okhansk Rus. Fed. 40 J4
Ókhi Óros mt. Greece see Ochi
Okhotino Rus. Fed. 43 T4
Okhotka r. Rus. Fed. 39 O4
Okhotsk Rus. Fed. 39 O4
Okhotsk, Sea of Japan/Rus. Fed. 90 I2
also known as Okhotskoye More
Okhotskoye More sea Japan/Rus. Fed. see Okhotsk, Sea of
Okhthoniá Greece see Ochthonia
Okhtyrka Ukr. 41 E6
also spelt Akhtyrka
Okhvat Rus. Fed. 43 N5
Okiep S. Africa 132 B6
Okinawa i. Japan 81 L7
Okinawa-guntō is Japan see Okinawa-shotō
Okinawa-shotō is Japan 81 L7
also known as Okinawa-guntō
Okino-Daitō-jima i. Japan 81 M8
Okino-shima i. Japan 91 B7
Okino-shima i. Japan 91 C8
Okino-Tori-shima i. Japan 81 N8
also known as Parece Vela; formerly known as Douglas Reef
Oki-shotō is Japan 91 C6
Okitipupa Nigeria 125 G5
Okkan Myanmar 78 A4
Oklahoma state U.S.A. 179 C5
Oklahoma City U.S.A. 179 C5
State capital of Oklahoma.
Oklawaha r. U.S.A. 175 D6
Okmulgee U.S.A. 179 C5
Oko, Wadi watercourse Sudan 121 H4
Okoia Cameroon 125 H5
Okolona MS U.S.A. 174 B5
Okolona OH U.S.A. 176 A4
Okondja Gabon 126 B5
Okonek Poland 49 N2
Okor r. Hungary 56 J3
Okotoks Canada 167 H5
Okotusu well Namibia 130 A3
Okovskiy Les for. Rus. Fed. 43 N7
Okoyo Congo 126 B5
Okpety, Gora mt. Kazakh. 88 C2
Øksbøl Denmark 45 J5
Øksfjord Norway 44 M1
Oksovskiy Rus. Fed. 40 F3
Øksskolten mt. Norway 44 K2
Oksu r. Tajik. 101 H2
also spelt Aksu
Oktemberyan Armenia see Hoktemberyan
Oktumkum, Peski des. Turkm. 102 C4
Oktwin Myanmar 78 B4
Oktyabr' Kazakh. see Kandyagash
Oktyabr' Kazakh. 103 I4
Oktyabr' Rus. Fed. 43 S4
Oktyabr'sk Kazakh. see Kandyagash
Oktyabr'sk Rus. Fed. 41 I5
Oktyabr'skaya Belarus see Aktsyabrskaya
Oktyabr'skiy Belarus see Aktsyabrski
Oktyabr'skiy Belarus see Aktsyabrski
Oktyabr'skiy Kazakh. 103 E1
Oktyabr'skiy Amurskaya Oblast' Rus. Fed. 82 C1
Oktyabr'skiy Arkhangel'skaya Oblast' Rus. Fed. 40 G3
Oktyabr'skiy Ivanovskaya Oblast' Rus. Fed. 43 V4
Oktyabr'skiy Kaluzhskaya Oblast' Rus. Fed. 43 R7
Oktyabr'skiy Kamchatskaya Oblast' Rus. Fed. 39 P4
Oktyabr'skiy Murmanskaya Oblast' Rus. Fed. 44 P2
Oktyabr'skiy Respublika Bashkortostan Rus. Fed. 40 J5
Oktyabr'skiy Ryazanskaya Oblast' Rus. Fed. 43 T7
Oktyabr'skiy Ryazanskaya Oblast' Rus. Fed. 43 U8
Oktyabr'skiy Sverdlovskaya Oblast' Rus. Fed. 40 K4
Oktyabr'skiy Volgogradskaya Oblast' Rus. Fed. 41 G7
formerly known as Kruglyakov
Oktyabr'skoye Kazakh. 103 F1
Oktyabr'skoye Rus. Fed. 38 G3
formerly known as Kondinskoye
Oktyabr'skoye Rus. Fed. 102 C1
Oktyabr'skoy Revolyutsii, Ostrov i. Rus. Fed. 39 J2
English form October Revolution Island
Oktyab'sk Turkm. 102 D4
Okučani Croatia 56 J3
Ōkuchi Japan 91 B8
Okulovka Rus. Fed. 43 O3
Okuru N.Z. 153 C11
Okushiri-kaikyō sea chan. Japan 90 F3
Okushiri-tō i. Japan 90 F3
Okutango-hantō pen. Japan 91 D7
Okwa watercourse Botswana 130 E4
Ola Rus. Fed. 39 P4
Ola U.S.A. 179 D5
Ólafsvík Iceland 44 [inset] B2
Olaine Latvia 42 E5
Olan, Pic d' mt. France 51 M8
Olancha Peak U.S.A. 182 F5
Olanchito Hond. 186 B4
Öland i. Sweden 45 L4
Olanga Rus. Fed. 44 O2
Olary Australia 146 D3
Olary watercourse Australia 146 D3
Olathe U.S.A. 178 D4
Olavakod India 94 C4
Olavarría Arg. 204 E5
Oława Poland 49 O5
Olbernhau Germany 49 K5
Olbia Sardegna Italy 56 B8
Olbia, Golfo di b. Sardegna Italy 56 B8
Ol'chan Rus. Fed. 39 O3
Olcott U.S.A. 176 G2
Old Bahama Channel Bahamas/Cuba 186 D2
Old Bastar India 94 D2
Old Cherrabun Australia 150 D3
Old Cork Australia 149 D4
Old Crow Canada 164 F3
Oldeide Norway 45 I3
Oldenburg Germany 48 F2
Oldenburg in Holstein Germany 48 H1
Oldenzaal Neth. 48 D3
Olderdalen Norway 44 M1
Oldfield r. Australia 151 C7
Old Forge U.S.A. 177 K2
Old Gidgee Australia 151 B5
Oldham U.K. 47 J10
Old Head of Kinsale Rep. of Ireland 47 D12
Oldmeldrum U.K. 46 J6
Old Mkushi Zambia 127 F8
Old Morley S. Africa 133 N8
Old Orchard Beach U.S.A. 177 O2
Old Perlican Canada 169 K4
Old River U.S.A. 182 E6
Olds Canada 167 H5
Old Saybrook U.S.A. 177 M4
Old Speck Mountain U.S.A. 177 O1
Old Station U.S.A. 182 C1
Oldtown U.S.A. 176 C7
Old Town U.S.A. 174 G2
Olduvai Gorge tourist site Tanz. 128 B5
Old Washington U.S.A. 176 D5
Old Wives Lake Canada 167 J5
formerly known as Johnstone Lake
Old Woman Mountains U.S.A. 183 I7
Öldziyt Arhangay Mongolia 84 D1
Öldziyt Dornogovĭ Mongolia 85 F2
Olean U.S.A. 176 G3
Olecko Poland 49 T1
Oleggio Italy 56 A3
Olekma r. Rus. Fed. 39 M3
Olekminsk Rus. Fed. 39 M3
Oleksandrivs'k Ukr. see Zaporizhzhya
Oleksandriya Ukr. 41 E6
also spelt Aleksandriya
Ølen Norway 45 I4
Olenegorsk Rus. Fed. 44 P1
formerly known as Olenya
Olenek Rus. Fed. 39 L3
Olenek r. Rus. Fed. 39 L2
Olenek Bay Rus. Fed. see Olenekskiy Zaliv
Olenekskiy Zaliv b. Rus. Fed. 39 M2
English form Olenek Bay
Olengti r. Kazakh. see Olenti
Olenino Rus. Fed. 43 O5
Olenitsa Rus. Fed. 40 E2
Olenivs'ki Kar"yery Ukr. see Dokuchayevs'k
Oleniy, Ostrov i. Rus. Fed. 39 H2
Olenti r. Kazakh. 102 C2
also spelt Ölengti
Olenti r. Kazakh. 103 H1
Olentuy Rus. Fed. 85 G1
Olenya Rus. Fed. see Olenegorsk
Oléron, Île d' i. France 50 E7
Oleshky Ukr. see Tsyurupyns'k
Oleśnica Poland 49 O4
Olesno Poland 49 P5
Olet Tongo mt. Indon. 77 G5
Olevs'k Ukr. 41 C6
Ølfjellet mt. Norway 44 K2
Ol'ga Rus. Fed. 82 D4
Olga, Lac l. Canada 168 E3
Olga, Mount Australia 148 A5
Ölgiy Mongolia 84 A1
Olhão Port. 54 D7
Olhava Fin. 44 N2
Olhos d'Água Brazil 207 J4
Olia Chain mts Australia 148 A5
Oliana Spain 55 M2
Olib i. Croatia 56 G4
Oliena Sardegna Italy 57 B8
Olifants watercourse Namibia 130 C5
Olifants r. W. Cape S. Africa 132 C8
Olifants r. W. Cape S. Africa 132 F10
Olifants r. S. Africa 131 F4
Olifantshoek S. Africa 132 G4
Olifantsrivierberge mts S. Africa 132 C9
Olimarao atoll Micronesia 73 K5
Olimbos hill Cyprus see Olympos
Olimbos mt. Greece see Olympus, Mount
Olímpia Brazil 206 E7
Olimpos Beydağları Milli Parkı nat. park Turkey 106 B3
Olinalá Mex. 185 F5
Olinda Entrance sea chan. Australia 149 E1
Olinga Moz. 131 H3
Olio Australia 149 D4
Öli Qoltyq Sory dry lake Kazakh. see Sor Mertvyy Kultuk
Olisipo Port. see Lisbon
Olite Spain 55 J2
Oliva Arg. 204 E4
Oliva Spain 55 K6
Oliva hill Spain 54 E6
Oliva, Cordillera de mts Arg./Chile 204 C3
Oliva de la Frontera Spain 54 E6
Olivares, Cerro de mt. Arg./Chile 204 C3
Olive Hill U.S.A. 176 B7
Olivehurst U.S.A. 182 C2
Oliveira Brazil 203 C7
Oliveira do Douro Port. 54 C3
Oliveira dos Brejinhos Brazil 202 D5
Olivença Moz. see Lupilichi
Olivença-a-Nova Angola see Capunda Cavilongo
Olivenza r. Port./Spain 54 D6
Olivenza Spain 54 D6
Oliver Canada 166 G5
Oliver Lake Canada 167 K3
Oliver Springs U.S.A. 176 A9
Olivet France 51 H5
Olivet U.S.A. 178 C3
Olivia U.S.A. 178 D2
Oljoro Wells Tanz. 129 C6
Ölkeyek r. Kazakh. see Ul'kayak
Ol'khovatka Rus. Fed. 41 F6
Ol'khovets Rus. Fed. 43 U8
Olkusz Poland 49 Q5
Ollachea Peru 200 C3
Ollagüe Chile 200 C5
Olliouiles France 51 L9
Ollita, Cordillera de mts Arg./Chile 204 C3
Ollitas mt. Arg. 204 C3
Ölölä Fin. 44 O3
Olombo Congo 126 B5
Olmaliq Uzbek. see Almalyk
Olmedo Spain 54 G3
Olmeto Corse France 56 A7
Olmos Peru 198 B6
Olmütz Czech Rep. see Olomouc
Olney IL U.S.A. 174 B4
Olney MD U.S.A. 177 H6
Olney TX U.S.A. 179 C5
Olochi Rus. Fed. 85 H1
Olofström Sweden 45 K4
Ol'oinka Kazakh. 103 F1
Olomane r. Canada 169 I3
Olomouc Czech Rep. 49 O6
also known as Olmütz
Olonets Rus. Fed. 43 N1
Olonetskaya Vozvyshennost' hills Rus. Fed. 43 O1
Olongapo Phil. 74 B3
Olongliko Indon. 77 F3
Olonne-sur-Mer France 50 E6
Oloron-Ste-Marie France 50 F9
Olosenga i. American Samoa see Swains Island
Olot Spain 55 N2
Olot Uzbek. see Alat
Olovo Bos.-Herz. 56 K4
Olovyannaya Rus. Fed. 85 G1
Oloy, Qatorkŭhi mts Asia see Alai Range
Olpad India 96 B5
Olpe Germany 48 E4
Ol'sa r. Belarus 43 K8
Olše r. Czech Rep. 49 P6
Ol'sha Rus. Fed. 43 M7
Olsztyn Poland 49 R2
historically known as Allenstein
Olsztynek Poland 49 R2
Olt r. Romania 58 F5
Olta Arg. 204 D3
Olte, Sierra de mts Arg. 205 C6
Olten Switz. 51 N5
Olteniţa Romania 58 H4
Olteţ r. Romania 58 F4
Oltina Romania 58 I4
Oltinkŭl Uzbek. see Altynkul'
Oltintopkan Tajik. 101 G1
also spelt Altyn-Topkan
Oltu Turkey 107 E2
Oluan Cape Taiwan see Oluan Pi
Oluan Pi c. Taiwan 87 G4
English form Oluan Cape
Olutanga i. Phil. 74 B5
Ólvega Spain 55 J3
Olvera Spain 54 F8
Ol'viopol' Ukr. see Pervomays'k
Olym r. Rus. Fed. 43 T9
Olymbos hill Cyprus see Olympos
Olymbos tourist site Greece 59 C11
Olympia U.S.A. 180 B3
State capital of Washington.
Olympic National Park U.S.A. 180 B3
Olympos hill Cyprus 108 E2
also spelt Olimbos or Olymbos
Olympos mt. Greece see Olympus, Mount
Olympos nat. park Greece 59 D8
Olympus, Mount Greece 59 D8
also spelt Ólimbos or Olympos
Olympus, Mount U.S.A. 180 B3
Olyutorskiy Rus. Fed. 39 Q3
Olyutorskiy, Mys c. Rus. Fed. 39 R4
Olyutorskiy Zaliv b. Rus. Fed. 39 Q4
Olzheras Rus. Fed. see Mezhdurechensk
Oma China 89 C5
Ōma Japan 90 G4
Oma r. Rus. Fed. 40 H2
Ōmachi Japan 91 E6
Ōmae-zaki pt Japan 91 F7
Ōmagari Japan 90 G5
Omagh U.K. 47 E9
Omaguas Peru 198 C6
Omaha U.S.A. 178 D3
Omaha Indian Reservation res. U.S.A. 178 C3
Omaheke admin. reg. Namibia 130 C4
Omakere N.Z. 152 K8
Omal'skiy Khrebet mts Rus. Fed. 82 E1
Omalur India 94 C4
Oman country Asia 105 F4
spelt 'Umān in Arabic; formerly known as Muscat and Oman
asia [countries] 64–67
Oman, Gulf of Asia 105 G2
Omangambo Namibia 130 B4
Omarama N.Z. 153 D12
Omarchevo Bulg. 58 H6
Omarska Bos.-Herz. 56 I4
Omaruru Namibia 130 B4
Omas Peru 200 A3
Omatako watercourse Namibia 130 D3
Omate Peru 200 C4
Omatjette Namibia 130 B4
Omaweneno Botswana 132 G2
Ōma-zaki c. Japan 90 G4
Omba i. Vanuatu see Aoba
Ombai, Selat sea chan. Indon. 75 C5
Ombalantu Namibia see Uutapi
Ombella-Mpoko pref. Cent. Afr. Rep. 126 C3
Ombika waterhole Namibia 130 B3
Omboué Gabon 126 A5
Ombrone r. Italy 56 D6
Ombu China 89 D6
Omdraaisvlei S. Africa 132 H7
Omdurman Sudan 121 G6
Ōme Japan 91 F7
Omedu Estonia 42 I3
Omegna Italy 56 A3
Omeo Australia 147 E4
Ömerler Turkey 59 K9
Ometepe, Isla de i. Nicaragua 186 B5
Ometepec Mex. 185 F5
Omgoy Wildlife Reserve nature res. Thai. 78 B4
Om Hajēr Eritrea 121 H6
Omīdīyeh Iran 100 B4
Ōmihachiman Japan 91 E7
Omihi N.Z. 153 G11
Omineca Mountains Canada 166 E3
Omiš Croatia 56 I5
Omitara Namibia 130 C4
Ōmiya Japan 91 F7
Ommaney, Cape U.S.A. 166 C3
Ommen Neth. 48 D3
Ömnögovĭ prov. Mongolia 84 E3
Omodeo, Lago l. Sardegna Italy 57 B8
Omoku Nigeria 125 G5
Omolon Rus. Fed. 39 Q3
Omolon r. Rus. Fed. 39 P3
Omo National Park Eth. 128 B3
Omono-gawa r. Japan 90 G5
Omo Wenz r. Eth. 128 C3
Omro U.S.A. 172 E6
Omsk Rus. Fed. 80 A1
Omskaya Oblast' admin. div. Rus. Fed. 80 A1
English form Omsk Oblast
Omsk Oblast admin. div. Rus. Fed. see Omskaya Oblast'
Omsukchan Rus. Fed. 39 P3
Ōmū Japan 90 H2
Omu, Vârful mt. Romania 58 G3
Omu-Aran Nigeria 125 G4
Omulew r. Poland 49 S2
Ōmura Japan 91 A8
Ōmura-wan b. Japan 91 A8
Omurtag Bulg. 58 H5
Omusati admin. reg. Namibia 130 B3
Omutninsk Rus. Fed. 40 J4
Onalaska U.S.A. 172 B7
Onaman Lake Canada 168 C3
Onancock U.S.A. 177 J8
Onang Indon. 75 A3
Onangué, Lac l. Gabon 126 A5
Onarga U.S.A. 172 E10
Onavas Mex. 184 C2
Onawa U.S.A. 178 C3
Onaway U.S.A. 173 I5
Onbingwin Myanmar 79 B5
Oncativo Arg. 204 E3
Oncócua Angola 127 B9
Öncül Turkey 109 K1
Onda Spain 55 K5
Ondal India see Andal
Ondangwa Namibia 130 B3
Ondarroa Spain 55 I1
Ondava r. Slovakia 49 S7
Onderstedorings S. Africa 132 E7
Ondjiva Angola 127 B9
also spelt Onjiva; formerly known as Pereira de Eça; formerly spelt Ngiva
Ondo Nigeria 125 G5
Ondo state Nigeria 125 G5
Öndörhaan Mongolia 85 F2
Öndörhushuu Mongolia 85 G1
Ondor Mod China 84 E3
Ondor Sum China 85 G3
One Botswana 130 D4
One and a Half Degree Channel Maldives 93 D10
One and a Half Mile Opening sea chan. Australia 149 E2
Onega Rus. Fed. 40 F3
Onega r. Rus. Fed. 40 F3
Onega, Lake Rus. Fed. 43 Q1
3rd largest lake in Europe. Also known as Onezhskoye Ozero.
europe [landscapes] 30–31
Onega Bay g. Rus. Fed. see Onezhskaya Guba
One Hundred and Fifty Mile House Canada see 150 Mile House
One Hundred Mile House Canada see 100 Mile House
Oneida IL U.S.A. 172 C9
Oneida NY U.S.A. 177 J2
Oneida TN U.S.A. 176 A9
Oneida Lake U.S.A. 177 J2
O'Neill U.S.A. 178 C3
Onekaka N.Z. 152 G8
Onekama U.S.A. 172 G6
Onekotan, Ostrov i. Rus. Fed. 39 P5
Oneonta AL U.S.A. 175 C5
Oneonta NY U.S.A. 177 J3
Oneroa N.Z. 152 J4
Oneşti Romania 58 H2
formerly known as Gheorghe Gheorghiu-Dej
Onet-le-Château France 51 I8
Onezhskaya Guba g. Rus. Fed. 40 E2
English form Onega Bay
Onezhskiy Kanal canal Rus. Fed. 43 Q1
Onezhskoye Ozero l. Rus. Fed. see Onega, Lake
Ong r. India 95 D1
Onga Gabon 126 B5
Ongaonga N.Z. 152 K7
Ông Đôc, Sông r. Vietnam 79 D6
Ongeri Dem. Rep. Congo 126 E6
Ongers watercourse S. Africa 132 H6
Ongerup Australia 151 B7
Ongi Dundgovĭ Mongolia 84 D2
Ongi Övörhangay Mongolia 84 D2
Ongiyn Gol r. Mongolia 84 D2
Ongjin N. Korea 83 B5
Ongniud Qi China see Wudan
Ongole India 94 D3
Ongon Mongolia 84 D2
Ongtüstik Qazaqstan Oblysy admin. div. Kazakh. see Yuzhnyy Kazakhstan
Onguday Rus. Fed. 88 D1
Oni Georgia 107 E2
Onida U.S.A. 178 B2
Onilahy r. Madag. 131 [inset] I4
Onistagane, Lac l. Canada 169 G3
Onitsha Nigeria 125 G5
Onjati Mountain Namibia 130 C4
Onjiva Angola see Ondjiva
Onkamo Fin. 44 O3
Onkivesi l. Fin. 44 N3
Onnes Rus. Fed. 39 N3
Ōno Fukui Japan 91 E7
Ōno Hokkaidō Japan 90 G4
Onoda Japan 91 B8
Ono-i-Lau i. Fiji 145 H4
Ōnojō Japan 91 B8
Ōnomichi Japan 91 C7
Onon Mongolia 85 F1
Onon r. Rus. Fed. 85 G1
Onon Gol r. Mongolia 85 G1
Onor, Gora mt. Rus. Fed. 82 F2
Onotoa atoll Kiribati 145 G2
also spelt Onutu
Ons, Illa de i. Spain 54 C2
Onsan S. Korea 91 A7
Onseepkans S. Africa 132 D5
Onslow Australia 150 A4
Onslow Bay U.S.A. 174 E5
Onsŏng N. Korea 82 C4
Ontake-san vol. Japan 83 E6
Ontaratue r. Canada 166 D1
Ontario prov. Canada 167 N5
Ontario CA U.S.A. 182 G7
Ontario OR U.S.A. 180 C3
Ontario WI U.S.A. 172 C7
Ontario, Lake Canada/U.S.A. 173 P7
Onteniente Spain see Ontinyent
Ontinyent Spain 55 K6
also spelt Onteniente
Ontojärvi l. Fin. 44 O2
Ontong Java Atoll Solomon Is 145 E2
formerly known as Lord Howe Atoll
Ontur Spain 55 J6
Onutu atoll Kiribati see Onotoa
Onverwacht Suriname 199 H3
Onyx U.S.A. 182 F6
Oodnadatta Australia 146 B1
Oodweyne Somalia 128 E2
Ooldea Australia 146 A2
Ooldea Range hills Australia 146 A2
Oologah Lake resr U.S.A. 178 D4
Oombulg Aboriginal Reserve Australia 150 D2
Oorindi Australia 149 D4
Oos-Londen S. Africa see East London
Oostanaula r. U.S.A. 174 C5
Oostende Belgium see Ostend
Oosterhout Neth. 48 B4
Oosterschelde est. Neth. 48 A4
Oostvleteren Belgium 51 I2
Ootacamund India see Udagamandalam
Ootsa Lake Canada 166 E4
Ootsa Lake l. Canada 166 E4
Opalenica Poland 49 N3
Oparau N.Z. 152 I6
Opari N.Z. 152 J8
Opari Sudan 128 B4
Oparino Rus. Fed. 40 I4
Oparo i. Fr. Polynesia see Rapa
Opasatika r. Canada 168 D3
Opasatika Lake Canada 168 D3
Opasquia Canada 167 M4
Opasquia Provincial Park Canada 167 M4
Opataca, Lac l. Canada 169 F3
Opatija Croatia 56 G3
Opatów Poland 49 S5
Opava Czech Rep. 49 O6
Opava r. Czech Rep. 49 O5
Opechenskiy Posad Rus. Fed. 43 P3
Opelika U.S.A. 175 C5
Opelousas U.S.A. 179 D6
Opeongo Lake Canada 168 E4
Opheim U.S.A. 180 F2
Ophir Canada 173 J4
Ophir N.Z. 153 D13
Ophir, Gunung vol. Indon. 76 C2
Opihikao U.S.A. 181 [inset] Z2
Opinaca r. Canada 169 E2
Opinaca, Réservoir Canada 168 E2
Opinnagau r. Canada 168 D2
Opis tourist site Iraq 107 F4
Opiscotéo, Lac l. Canada 169 G2
Opobo Nigeria 125 G5
Opochka Rus. Fed. 43 J5
Opoco Bol. 200 D4
Opoczno Poland 49 R4
Opodepe Mex. 184 C2
Opole Poland 49 O5
historically known as Oppeln
Opole Lubelskie Poland 49 S4
Opononi N.Z. 152 H3
Opornyy Kazakh. 102 C3
Oporto Port. 54 C3
also known as Porto
Opotiki N.Z. 152 L6
Opovo Vojvodina, Srbija Yugo. 58 B3
Opp U.S.A. 175 C6
Oppdal Norway 44 J3
Oppedal Norway 45 I3
Oppeln Poland see Opole
Oppido Lucano Italy 57 H8
Oppland county Norway 45 J3
Opportunity U.S.A. 180 C3
Oprişor Romania 58 E4
Optaşi-Măgura Romania 58 F4
Opuatia N.Z. 152 I5
Opunake N.Z. 152 H7
Opuwo Namibia 130 B3
Opytnoye Kazakh. 102 B3
Oqqal"a Uzbek. see Akkala
Oqtosh Uzbek. see Aktash
Oquawka U.S.A. 174 B3
Or' r. Rus. Fed. 102 D2
Øra Norway 44 M1
Oracle U.S.A. 183 N9
Oradea Romania 58 C1
also known as Nagyvárad
Orahovac Kosovo, Srbija Yugo. 58 B6
Orahovica Croatia 56 J3
Orai India 96 C4
Oraibi U.S.A. 183 N6
Oraibi Wash watercourse U.S.A. 183 N6
Orain r. France 51 L6
Orajärvi Fin. 44 N2
Oral Kazakh. see Ural'sk
Oran Alg. 123 E2
also spelt Ouahran or Wahran
Orán Arg. 201 D5
Oran, Sebkha d' salt pan Alg. 55 K9
Ŏrang N. Korea 82 C4
Orange Australia 147 F3
Orange France 51 K8
Orange r. Namibia/S. Africa 132 A5
also spelt Oranje
Orange CA U.S.A. 182 G8
Orange TX U.S.A. 179 D6
Orange VA U.S.A. 176 G7
Orange, Cabo c. Brazil 199 I3
Orangeburg U.S.A. 175 D5
Orange Cay i. Bahamas 186 D1
Orange City U.S.A. 178 C3
Orange Cove U.S.A. 182 E5
Orange Free State prov. S. Africa see Free State
Orange Park U.S.A. 175 D6
Orangerie Bay P.N.G. 149 F1
Orangevale U.S.A. 182 C3
Orangeville Canada 168 D5
Orangeville U.S.A. 183 M2
Orange Walk Belize 185 H5
Orani Sardegna Italy 57 B8
Orani Phil. 74 B3
Oranienburg Germany 49 K3
Oranje r. Namibia/S. Africa see Orange
Oranje Gebergte hills Suriname 199 H4
Oranjemund Namibia 130 C6
Oranjerivier S. Africa 133 I6
Oranjestad Aruba 187 F4
Capital of Aruba.
Oranjestad Neth. Antilles 187 H3
Oranjeville S. Africa 133 M3
Orantjugurr, Lake salt flat Australia 150 E4
Oranzherei Rus. Fed. 102 A3
Orapa Botswana 131 E4
Oras Phil. 74 C3
Orašac Bos.-Herz. 56 I4
Oras Bay Phil. 74 C3
Orăştie Romania 58 E3
Oraşul Stalin Romania see Braşov
Orava r. Slovakia 49 Q6
Orava, Vodná nádrž resr Slovakia 49 Q6
Oravais Fin. 44 M3
Oraviţa Romania 58 C3
Oravská Magura mts Slovakia 49 Q6
Orawia N.Z. 153 B14
Orba Co l. China 89 C5
Orbassano Italy 51 N7
Orbeasca Romania 58 G4
Orbec France 50 G3
Orbetello Italy 56 D6
Orbieu r. France 51 I9
Orbigo r. Spain 54 F3
Orbi Gorge Nature Reserve S. Africa 133 O7
Orbisonia U.S.A. 176 H5
Orbost Australia 147 F4
Orcadas research station S. Atlantic Ocean 222 V2
Orcera Spain 55 I6
Orchard Mesa U.S.A. 183 P2
Orchha India 96 C4
Orchila, Isla i. Venez. 199 E2
Orchomenos Greece 59 D10
also spelt Orkhomenós
Orchy r. U.K. 46 G7
Orcia r. Italy 56 D6
Orco r. Italy 51 N7
Orcotuna Peru 200 B2
Orcutt U.S.A. 182 D7
Ord r. Australia 150 E2
Ord U.S.A. 178 C3
Ord, Mount hill Australia 150 D3
Orda Rus. Fed. 40 K4
Órdenes Spain see Ordes
Ordes Spain 54 C1
also known as Órdenes
Ordesa - Monte Perdido, Parque Nacional de nat. park Spain 55 L2
Ord Mountain U.S.A. 183 H7
Ord River Dam Australia 150 E3
Ord River Nature Reserve Australia 150 E2
Ordu Turkey see Yayladağı
Ordu Turkey 107 D2
Ordubad Azer. 107 F3
Ordway U.S.A. 178 B4
Ordzhonikidze Kazakh. 103 E1
formerly known as Denisovka
Ordzhonikidze Rus. Fed. see Vladikavkaz
Ordzhonikidze Ukr. 41 E7
Ordzhonikidzeabad Tajik. see Kofarnihon
Ordzhonikidzevskaya Rus. Fed. see Sleptsovskaya
Ore Nigeria 125 G5
Öreälven r. Sweden 44 L3
Oreälven r. Sweden 45 K3
Oreana U.S.A. 182 F1
Örebro Sweden 45 K4
Örebro county Sweden 45 K4
Oredezh r. Rus. Fed. 43 K3
Oregon IL U.S.A. 174 B3
Oregon OH U.S.A. 176 B4
Oregon WI U.S.A. 172 D8
Oregon state U.S.A. 180 B4
Oregon City U.S.A. 180 B3
Öregrund Sweden 45 L3
Orekhi-Vydritsa Belarus see Arekhawsk
Orekhov Ukr. see Orikhiv
Orekhovo-Zuyevo Rus. Fed. 43 T6
Orekhovsk Belarus see Arekhawsk
Orel Orlovskaya Oblast' Rus. Fed. 43 R9
also spelt Oryol
Orel Permskaya Oblast' Rus. Fed. 40 K4
Orel, Gora mt. Rus. Fed. 82 E1
Orel', Ozero l. Rus. Fed. 82 E1
Orelek mt. Bulg. 58 E7
Orellana prov. Ecuador 198 B5
Orellana Peru 198 C6
Orellana, Embalse de resr Spain 54 F5
Orel Oblast admin. div. Rus. Fed. see Orlovskaya Oblast'
Orem U.S.A. 183 M1
Ore Mountains Czech Rep./Germany see Erzgebirge
Ören Turkey 59 K12
Ören Turkey 106 A3
Orenburg Rus. Fed. 102 C2
formerly known as Chkalov

Orenburg Oblast admin. div. Rus. Fed. see Orenburgskaya Oblast'
Orenburgskaya Oblast' admin. div. Rus. Fed. 102 B2
English form Orenburg Oblast; formerly known as Chkalovskaya Oblast'
Orense Arg. 204 F5
Orense Spain see Ourense
Oreón, Dhíavlos sea chan. Greece see Oreon, Diavlos
Oreon, Diavlos sea chan. Greece 59 D10
also spelt Oreón, Dhíavlos
Oreor Palau see Koror
Orepuki N.Z. 153 B14
Oresh Bulg. 58 G5
Öreskilsälven r. Sweden 45 J4
Orestiada Greece 58 H7
also known as Orestiás
Orestiás Greece see Orestiada
Öresund strait Denmark/Sweden 45 K5
Oretana, Cordillera mts Spain see Toledo, Montes de
Oreti r. N.Z. 153 C14
Orewa N.Z. 152 I4
Orfane well Niger 125 G2
Orfanou, Kolpos b. Greece 58 E8
Orford Bay Australia 149 D1
Orford Ness hd U.K. 47 N11
Organabo Fr. Guiana 199 H3
Organ Pipe Cactus National Monument nat. park U.S.A. 183 L9
Orgeyev Moldova see Orhei
Orgil Mongolia 84 C1
Orgiva Spain 55 H8
Orgon Tal China 85 G3
Orgtrud Rus. Fed. 43 V5
Orgūn Afgh. 101 G3
Orhaneli Turkey 106 B3
also known as Beyce
Orhangazi Turkey 58 K8
Orhei Moldova 58 J1
formerly spelt Orgeyev or Orkhey
Orhei prov. Moldova 53 H2
Orhon Gol r. Mongolia 84 E1
Orhontuul Mongolia 84 E1
Orhy, Pic d' mt. France/Spain 55 J2
Oria Spain 55 I7
Orichi Rus. Fed. 40 I4
Oriental, Cordillera mts Bol. 200 D4
Oriental, Cordillera mts Col. 198 C3
Oriental, Cordillera mts Peru 200 C3
Orientale prov. Dem. Rep. Congo 126 E4
formerly known as Haut-Congo or Haut-Zaïre
Oriente Brazil 201 D2
Orient Island U.S.A. 177 M4
Orihuela Spain 55 K6
Orikhiv Ukr. 41 E7
also spelt Orekhov
Orikum Albania 59 A8
Orillia Canada 168 E4
Orimattila Fin. 45 N3
Orin U.S.A. 180 F4
Orinoco r. Col./Venez. 199 F2
world [land images] 12–13
Orinoco Delta Venez. 199 F2
Orion U.S.A. 172 C9
Oripää Fin. 45 M3
Oriskany U.S.A. 177 J2
Orissa state India 95 E1
formerly known as Jajnagar
Orissaare Estonia 42 E3
Oristano Sardegna Italy 57 A9
Oristano, Golfo di b. Sardegna Italy 57 A9
Orivesi Fin. 45 N3
Orivesi l. Fin. 44 O3
Oriximiná Brazil 199 H5
Orizaba Mex. 185 F5
Orizaba, Pico de vol. Mex. 185 F5
3rd highest mountain in North America. Also known as Citlaltépetl. northamerica [landscapes] 156–157
Orizona Brazil 206 E4
Orjonikidzeobod Tajik. see Kofarnihon
Orkelljunga Sweden 45 K4
Orkhey Moldova see Orhei
Orkhomenós Greece see Orchomenos
Orkney S. Africa 133 K3
Orkney is U.K. 46 I4
Orla r. Poland 49 N4
Orla r. Poland 49 O2
Orland U.S.A. 182 B2
Orlândia Brazil 206 F7
Orlando U.S.A. 175 D6
Orleans Brazil 203 B9
Orléans France 51 H5
Orleans MA U.S.A. 177 P4
Orleans VT U.S.A. 177 M1
Orléans, Île d' i. Canada 169 G4
Orléansville Alg. see Ech Chélif
Orlické Hory mts Czech Rep. 49 N5
Orlik Rus. Fed. 80 F2
Orlík, Vodní nádrž resr Czech Rep. 49 L6
Orljava r. Croatia 56 J3
Orlov Rus. Fed. 40 I4
formerly known as Khalturin
Orlov Gay Rus. Fed. 102 B2
Orlovo Rus. Fed. 41 F6
Orlovskaya Oblast' admin. div. Rus. Fed. 43 R9
English form Orel Oblast
Orlovskiy Rus. Fed. 41 G7
Orly airport France 51 I4
Ormankalns hill Latvia 42 G5
Ormara Pak. 101 F5
Ormara, Ras hd Pak. 101 F5
Ormilia Greece see Ormylia
Ormoc Phil. 74 C4
Ormond N.Z. 152 L6
Ormond Beach U.S.A. 175 D6
Ormskirk U.K. 47 J10
Ormylia Greece 59 E8
also spelt Ormília
Ornans France 51 M5
Orne r. France 50 F3
Orne r. France 50 G4
Ørnes Norway 44 K2
Orneta Poland 49 R1
Ornö i. Sweden 45 L4
Örnsköldsvik Sweden 44 L3
Örö i. Fin. 42 D2
Oro N. Korea 83 B4
Oro, Lac l. Mali 124 E2
Orobayaya Bol. 201 E3
Orobie, Alpi mts Italy 56 B2
Orocó Brazil 202 E4
Orocué Col. 198 D3
Orodara Burkina 124 D4
Orofino U.S.A. 180 C3
Orog Nuur salt l. Mongolia 84 D2
Oro Grande U.S.A. 183 G7
Orol Dengizi salt l. Kazakh./Uzbek. see Aral Sea
Oromia admin. reg. Eth. 128 C2
Oromocto Canada 169 H4
Oromocto Lake Canada 169 H4
Oron Israel 108 G7
Oron Nigeria 125 H5
Orona i. Kiribati 145 H2
formerly known as Hull Island
Orono U.S.A. 174 G2
Oronoque Guyana 199 G4
Oronoque r. Guyana 199 G4
Orontes r. Lebanon/Syria 109 H3
also known as 'Āṣī or 'Āṣī, Nahr al
Orope Venez. 198 C2
Oropesa, Cabo de c. Spain 55 L4
Oroqen Zizhiqi China see Alihe
Oroquieta Phil. 74 B4
Ororbia Spain 55 J2
Orós Brazil 202 E3
Orós, Açude resr Brazil 202 E3
Orosei Sardegna Italy 57 B8
Orosei, Golfo di b. Sardegna Italy 57 B8
Orosháza Hungary 49 R9
Oroszlány Hungary 49 P8
Orotukan Rus. Fed. 39 P3
Oro Valley U.S.A. 183 N9
Oroville CA U.S.A. 182 C2
Oroville WA U.S.A. 180 C2
Oroville, Lake resr U.S.A. 182 C2
Orqohan China 85 I1
Orri, Monte hill Sardegna Italy 57 A9
Orrkjølen hill Norway 45 J3
Orroroo Australia 146 C3
Orsa Sweden 45 K3
Orségi Tájvédelmi Körzet nature res. Hungary 49 N9
Orsha Belarus 43 L7
Orsha Rus. Fed. 43 R5
Orshanka Rus. Fed. 40 H4
Orsjön l. Sweden 45 L3
Orsk Rus. Fed. 102 D2
Orşova Romania 58 D4
Ørsta Norway 44 I3
Örsundsbro Sweden 45 L4
Ortaca Turkey 59 J12
Orta Nova Italy 56 H7
Orta Toroslar plat. Turkey 108 E1
Orte Italy 56 E6
Ortegal, Cabo c. Spain 54 D1
Orteguaza r. Col. 198 C4
Orthez France 50 F9
Ortholmen Sweden 45 K3
Ortigueira Brazil 206 C11
Ortigueira Spain 54 D1
Ortişoara Romania 58 C3
Ortiz Mex. 184 C2
Ortíz Venez. 199 E2
Ortles mt. Italy 56 C2
Ortona Italy 56 G6
Ortonville MI U.S.A. 173 J8
Ortonville MN U.S.A. 178 C2
Ortospana Afgh. see Kābul
Orträsk Sweden 44 L2
Örtülü Turkey see Şenkaya
Oru Estonia 42 I2
Orulgan, Khrebet mts Rus. Fed. 39 M3
Orumbo Namibia 130 C4
Orumbo Boka hill Côte d'Ivoire 124 D5
Orūmīyeh Iran see Urmia
Orūmīyeh, Daryācheh-ye salt l. Iran see Urmia, Lake
Oruro Bol. 200 D4
Oruro dept Bol. 200 D4
Orūzgān prov. Afgh. 101 F3
Orvault France 50 E5
Orvieto Italy 56 E6
historically known as Urbs Vetus or Velsuna or Volsinii
Orville Coast Antarctica 222 T1
Orwell OH U.S.A. 176 E4
Orwell VT U.S.A. 177 L2
Orxon Gol r. China 85 H1
Oryakhovo Bulg. 58 E5
Oryol Rus. Fed. see Orel
Orzinuovi Italy 56 B3
Orzyc r. Poland 49 S3
Orzysz Poland 49 S2
Orzysz, Jezioro l. Poland 49 T2
Os Norway 44 J3
Oša r. Latvia 42 H5
Osa r. Poland 49 P2
Osa Rus. Fed. 40 J4
Osa, Península de pen. Costa Rica 186 C5
Osage IA U.S.A. 174 A3
Osage WV U.S.A. 176 E6
Osage r. U.S.A. 178 D4
Osage City U.S.A. 178 D4
Ōsaka Japan 91 D7
world [cities] 24–25
Ōsaka pref. Japan 90 D7
Osakarovka Kazakh. 103 H2
Ōsaka-wan b. Japan 91 D7
Osasco Brazil 206 G10
Osawatomie U.S.A. 178 D4
Osborn S. Africa 133 P5
Osborne U.S.A. 178 C4
Oscar Fr. Guiana 199 H4
Oscar Range hills Australia 150 D3
Osceola AR U.S.A. 174 B5
Osceola IA U.S.A. 174 A3
Osceola MO U.S.A. 178 D4
Osceola NE U.S.A. 178 C3
Osceola WI U.S.A. 172 A5
Oschersleben (Bode) Germany 48 I3
Oschiri Sardegna Italy 57 B8
Oscoda U.S.A. 173 J6
Osečina Srbija Yugo. 58 A4
O Seixo Spain 54 C3
Ösel i. Estonia see Hiiumaa
Osensjøen l. Norway 45 J3
Osetr r. Rus. Fed. 43 T7
Ōse-zaki pt Japan 91 A8
Osgoode Canada 168 F4
Osgood Mountains U.S.A. 180 C4
Osh Kyrg. 103 H4
Osh admin. div. Kyrg. 103 H4
English form Osh Oblast; also known as Oshskaya Oblast'
Oshakati Namibia 130 B3
Oshamambe Japan see Oshamanbe
Oshamanbe Japan 90 G3
also spelt Oshamambe
Oshana admin. reg. Namibia 130 B3
Oshawa Canada 168 E5
Oshika Japan 90 G5
Oshika-hantō pen. Japan 90 G5
Oshikango Namibia 130 B3
Oshikoto admin. reg. Namibia 130 C3
Oshikuku Namibia 130 B3
Ō-shima i. Japan 90 F4
Ō-shima i. Japan 91 D8
Ō-shima i. Japan 91 F7
Oshima-hantō pen. Japan 90 F3
Oshin r. Nigeria 125 G4
Oshivelo Namibia 130 C3
Oshkosh NE U.S.A. 178 B3
Oshkosh WI U.S.A. 172 E6
Oshmyany Belarus see Ashmyany
Oshnovīyeh Iran 100 A2
Osh Oblast admin. div. Kyrg. see Osh
Oshogbo Nigeria 125 G5
also spelt Osogbo
Oshper Rus. Fed. 40 L2
Oshskaya Oblast' admin. div. Kyrg. see Osh
Oshtorān Kūh mt. Iran 100 B3
Oshun state Nigeria see Osun
Oshwe Dem. Rep. Congo 126 C5
Osica de Sus Romania 58 F4
Osijek Croatia 56 K3
Osikovitsa Bulg. 58 F6
Osilinka r. B.C. Canada 166 E3
Osimo Italy 56 F5
Osipaonica Srbija Yugo. 58 C4
Osipenko Ukr. see Berdyans'k
Osipovichi Belarus see Asipovichy
Osire Namibia 130 C4
Osiyan India 96 B4
Osizweni S. Africa 133 O4
Osječenica mts Bos.-Herz. 56 I4
Oskaloosa IA U.S.A. 174 A3
Oskaloosa KS U.S.A. 178 D4
Oskarshamn Sweden 45 L4
Oskarström Sweden 45 K4
Oskélanéo Canada 173 R2
Öskemen Kazakh. see Ust'-Kamenogorsk
Oskil r. Ukr. see Oskol
Oskol r. Rus. Fed. 41 F6
also known as Oskil
Oskuya r. Rus. Fed. 43 M2
Oslava r. Czech Rep. 49 N6
Osława r. Poland 49 T6
Oslo Norway 45 J4
Capital of Norway. Historically known as Christiania or Kristiania.
Oslo airport Norway see Gardermoen
Oslob Phil. 74 B4
Oslofjorden sea chan. Norway 45 J4
Osmanabad India 94 C2
Osmancık Turkey 106 C2
Osmaneli Turkey 106 B2
Osmaniye Turkey 106 D3
Osmannagar India 94 C2
also known as Sultanabad
Os'mino Rus. Fed. 43 K2
Ösmo Sweden 45 L4
Osmussaar i. Estonia 42 E2
Osnabrück Germany 48 F3
Osnaburg atoll Fr. Polynesia see Mururoa
Osno Lubuskie Poland 49 L3
Oso r. Dem. Rep. Congo 126 E5
Osogbo Nigeria see Oshogbo
Osogovske Planine mts Bulg./Macedonia 58 D6
Osor hill Croatia 56 G4
Osório Brazil 203 B9
Osorno Chile 204 B6
Osorno Spain 54 G2
Osoyoos Canada 166 G5
Osøyri Hordaland Norway 46 P3
Ospino Venez. 198 D2
Osprey Reef Australia 149 E2
Oss Neth. 48 C4
Ossa hill Port. 54 D6
Ossa, Mount Australia 147 E5
Osse r. Nigeria 125 G5
Osseo U.S.A. 172 B6
Ossi Sardegna Italy 57 A8
Ossineke U.S.A. 173 J6
Ossining U.S.A. 177 L4
Ossipee Lake U.S.A. 177 N2
Ossokmanuan Lake Canada 169 H2
Ossora Rus. Fed. 39 Q4
Ossu East Timor 75 C5
Ostashevo Rus. Fed. 43 Q6
Ostashkov Rus. Fed. 43 O4
Oste r. Germany 48 G2
Osten Germany 48 G2
Ostend Belgium 51 I1
also spelt Oostende or Ostende
Ostende Belgium see Ostend
Oster Rus. Fed. 43 N7
Oster r. Rus. Fed. 43 N8
Oster Ukr. 41 D6
Osterburg (Altmark) Germany 48 I3
Österbybruk Sweden 45 L3
Österbymo Sweden 45 K4
Österdalälven l. Sweden 45 K3
Osterfärnebo Sweden 45 L3
Östergotland county Sweden 45 K4
Osterholz-Scharmbeck Germany 48 F2
Ostermundigen Switz. 51 N6
Osterode am Harz Germany 48 H4
Österreich country Europe see Austria
Östersund Sweden 44 K3
Östervåla Sweden 45 L3
Ostfildern Germany 49 K5
Østfold county Norway 45 J4
Ostfriesische Inseln is Germany see East Frisian Islands
Ostfriesland reg. Germany 48 E2
Östhammar Sweden 45 L3
Östra Kvarken strait Fin./Sweden 44 M3
Ostrava Czech Rep. 49 P6
Ostróda Poland 49 Q2
Ostrogozhsk Rus. Fed. 41 F6
Oštro Koplje mt. Yugo. 58 C5
Ostrołęka Poland 49 S3
Ostrov Czech Rep. 49 J5
Ostrov Romania 58 I4
Ostrov Romania 58 J4
Ostrov Rus. Fed. 43 J4
Ostrovets Poland see Ostrowiec Świętokrzyski
Ostrovskoye Rus. Fed. 40 G4
formerly known as Semyonovskoye
Ostrow Poland see Ostrów Wielkopolski
Ostrowiec Poland see Ostrowiec Świętokrzyski
Ostrowiec Świętokrzyski Poland 49 S5
formerly known as Ostrovets; short form Ostrowiec
Ostrów Lubelski Poland 49 T4
Ostrów Mazowiecka Poland 49 S3
Ostrowo Poland see Ostrów Wielkopolski
Ostrów Wielkopolski Poland 49 O4
formerly known as Ostrowo; short form Ostrow
Ostrzeszów Poland 49 O4
Ostseebad Binz Germany 49 K1
Ostseebad Kühlungsborn Germany 48 I1
Ostuni Italy 57 J8
Osuga r. Rus. Fed. 43 P4
Osuga r. Rus. Fed. 43 P5
O'Sullivan, Lac l. Canada 173 R3
Osum r. Albania 59 A8
Osūm r. Bulg. 58 F5
Ōsumi-hantō pen. Japan 91 B9
Ōsumi-kaikyō sea chan. Japan 91 B9
Ōsumi-shotō is Japan 91 B9
Osun state Nigeria 125 G5
also spelt Oshun
Osuna Spain 54 F7
Osvaldo Cruz Brazil 206 C8
Oswego IL U.S.A. 172 E9
Oswego KS U.S.A. 178 D4
Oswego NY U.S.A. 177 I2
Oswego r. U.S.A. 177 I2
Oswestry U.K. 47 I11
Oświęcim Poland 49 Q5
historically known as Auschwitz
Osyno Rus. Fed. 43 J5
Ōta Japan 91 F6
Otago admin. reg. N.Z. 153 D13
Otago Peninsula N.Z. 153 E13
Otahiti i. Fr. Polynesia see Tahiti
Otairi N.Z. 152 J7
Otaki N.Z. 152 J8
Otama N.Z. 153 C13
Otamauri N.Z. 152 K7
Otar Kazakh. 103 H4
Otaru Japan 90 G3
Otatara N.Z. 153 C14
Otautau N.Z. 153 B14
Otava r. Czech Rep. 49 L6
Otava Fin. 45 N3
Otavalo Ecuador 198 B4
Otavi Namibia 130 C3
Ōtawara Japan 90 G6
Otchinjau Angola 127 B9
Otdia atoll Marshall Is see Wotje
Otekaieke N.Z. 153 E12
Otelnuc, Lac l. Canada 169 G1
Oțelu Roșu Romania 58 D3
Otematata N.Z. 153 E12
Otepää Estonia 42 H3
Otepää kõrgustik hills Estonia 42 H3
Oteren Norway 44 L1
Oteros r. Mex. 181 E8
Otgon Tenger Uul mt. Mongolia 84 C2
Othe, Forêt d' for. France 51 J4
Othello U.S.A. 180 C3
Othonoi i. Greece 59 A9
Oti r. Ghana/Togo 125 F4
Oti Indon. 75 A3
Otimati S. Africa 133 P6
Otinapa Mex. 184 D3
Otira N.Z. 153 F10
Otisco Lake U.S.A. 177 I3
Otish, Monts hills Canada 169 G3
Otjikondo Namibia 130 B2
Otjinene Namibia 130 C4
Otjitambi Namibia 130 B3
Otjiwarongo Namibia 130 C4
Otjovasandu waterhole Namibia 130 B3
Otjozondjupa admin. reg. Namibia 130 C4
Otobe Japan 90 G4
Otobe-dake mt. Japan 90 G3
Otočac Croatia 56 H4
Otofuke Japan 90 H3
Otog Qi China see Ulan
Otoineppu Japan 90 H2
Otok Croatia 56 K3
Otoka Bos.-Herz. 56 I4
Otoko N.Z. 152 L6
Otonga N.Z. 152 I3
Otoro, Jebel mt. Sudan 121 F7
Otorohanga N.Z. 152 J6
also known as Harrodsville
Otoskwin r. Canada 168 B3
Ōtoyo Japan 91 C8
Otpan, Gora hill Kazakh. 102 B3
Otpor Rus. Fed. see Zabaykal'sk
Otradinskiy Rus. Fed. 43 R8
Otradnoye Rus. Fed. 43 L2
Otradnoye Rus. Fed. see Otradnyy
Otradnoye, Ozero l. Rus. Fed. 43 L1
Otradnyy Rus. Fed. 41 I5
formerly known as Otradnoye
Otranto Italy 57 K8
Otranto, Strait of Albania/Italy 56 K7
Otrogovo Rus. Fed. see Stepnoye
Otrokovice Czech Rep. 49 O6
Otrozhnyy Rus. Fed. 39 R3
Ötscher-Tormäuer nature res. Austria 49 M8
Otsego U.S.A. 172 H8
Otsego Lake U.S.A. 177 K3
Ōtsu Japan 91 D7
Otta Norway 45 J3
Ottawa Canada 168 F4
Capital of Canada.
Ottawa r. Canada 168 F4
also known as Outaouais, Rivière des
Ottawa IL U.S.A. 174 B3
Ottawa KS U.S.A. 178 D4
Ottawa OH U.S.A. 176 A4
Ottawa Islands Canada 168 D1
Otter r. U.K. 47 I13
Otterburn U.K. 47 J8
Otter Creek U.S.A. 172 C8
Otterstad Sweden 45 K4
Ottignies Belgium 51 K2
Ottosdal S. Africa 133 J3
Ottoshoop S. Africa 133 J2
Ottumwa U.S.A. 174 A3
Otukpa Nigeria 125 G5
Otukpo Nigeria 125 H5
Otuyo Bol. 200 D4
Otway U.S.A. 176 B7
Otway, Bahía b. Chile 205 B9
Otway, Cape Australia 147 D4
Otway, Seno b. Chile 205 C9
Otway National Park Australia 147 D4
Otway Range mts Australia 147 D4
Otwock Poland 49 S3
Ötztaler Alpen mts Austria 48 H9
Ou, Nam r. Laos 78 C3
Ouacha Niger 125 H3
Ouachita r. U.S.A. 179 E6
Ouachita, Lake U.S.A. 179 D5
Ouachita Mountains U.S.A. 179 D5
Ouadâne Mauritania 122 C5
Ouadda Cent. Afr. Rep. 126 D2
Ouaddaï pref. Chad 120 D6
Ouadjinkarem well Niger 125 G1
Ouâd Nâga Mauritania 124 B2
Ouadou watercourse Mauritania 124 C3
Ouagadougou Burkina 125 E3
Capital of Burkina.
Ouahigouya Burkina 124 E3
Ouahran Alg. see Oran
Ouaka pref. Cent. Afr. Rep. 126 D3
Ouaka r. Cent. Afr. Rep. 126 C3
Oualâta Mauritania 124 D2
Oualé r. Burkina 125 F4
Oualia Mali 124 C3
Ouallam Niger 125 F3
Ouallene Alg. 123 F4
Ouanary Fr. Guiana 199 I3
Ouanazein well Chad 120 C5
Ouanda-Djailé Cent. Afr. Rep. 126 D2
Ouandago Cent. Afr. Rep. 126 C3
Ouandja Haute-Kotto Cent. Afr. Rep. 126 D2
Ouandja Vakaga Cent. Afr. Rep. 126 D2
Ouando Cent. Afr. Rep. 126 E3
Ouango Cent. Afr. Rep. 126 D3
Ouangolodougou Côte d'Ivoire 124 D4
formerly spelt Wangolodougou
Ouani Kalaoua well Niger 125 G3
Ouanne r. France 51 I5
Ouaqui Fr. Guiana 199 H4
Ouara r. Cent. Afr. Rep. 126 E3
Ouarâne reg. Mauritania 122 C5
Ouargaye Burkina 125 F4
also known as Ouaragou
Ouargla Alg. 123 G3
also spelt Wargla
Ouarissibitil well Mali 125 F2
Ouaritoufoulout well Mali 125 F2
Ouarkziz, Jbel ridge Alg./Morocco 122 C3
Ouarogou Burkina see Ouargaye
Ouarsenis, Massif de l' Alg. 55 M9
Ouarzazate Morocco 122 D3
Ouatagouna Mali 125 F3
Oubangui r. Cent. Afr. Rep./Dem. Rep. Congo see Ubangi
Oubergpas pass S. Africa 133 I9
Oudenaarde Belgium 51 J2
also spelt Audenarde
Oudon r. France 50 F5
Oudtshoorn S. Africa 132 G10
Oued Laou Morocco 54 F9
Oued Rhiou Alg. 55 L9
Oued Tlélat Alg. 55 K9
Oued Zem Morocco 122 D2
Ouéléssébougou Mali 124 D4
Ouémé r. Benin 125 F5
Ouessa Burkina 124 E4
Ouessant, Île d' i. France 50 A4
historically known as Ushant
Ouésso Congo 126 C4
Ouest prov. Cameroon 125 H5
Ouezzane Morocco 122 D2
Oughterard Rep. of Ireland 47 C10
Ougnat, Jbel mt. Morocco 122 D3
Ouham pref. Cent. Afr. Rep. 126 C3
Ouham r. Cent. Afr. Rep./Chad 126 C2
Ouham Pendé pref. Cent. Afr. Rep. 126 C3
Ouidah Benin 125 F5
historically known as Whydah
Ouinardene Mali 125 E2
Ouiriego Mex. 184 C3
Ouistreham France 50 F3
Oujâf well Mauritania 124 D2
Oujda Morocco 123 E2
Oujeft Mauritania 124 B2
Oulad Teïma Morocco 122 C3
Oulainen Fin. 44 N2
Oulangan kansallispuisto nat. park Fin. 44 O2
Ould Yenjé Mauritania 124 C3
Ouled Djellal Alg. 123 G2
Ouled Farès Alg. 55 M8
Ouled Naïl, Monts des mts Alg. 123 F2
Ouled Saïd well Alg. 123 F3
Ouli Cameroon 125 I5
Oullins France 51 K7
Oulu Fin. 44 N2
also known as Uleåborg
Oulu prov. Fin. 44 N2
Oulujärvi l. Fin. 44 N2
Oulujoki r. Fin. 44 N2
Oulunsalo Fin. 44 N2
Oulx Italy 51 M7
Oum-Chalouba Chad 120 D6
Oumé Côte d'Ivoire 124 D5
Oum el Bouaghi Alg. 123 G2
Oum-Hadjer Chad 120 C6
Oumm ed Droûs Guebli, Sebkhet salt flat Mauritania 122 C5
Oumm ed Droûs Telli, Sebkha salt flat Mauritania 122 C4
Oumm el A'sel well Mali 122 D5
Ounara Morocco 122 C3
Ounasjoki r. Fin. 44 N2
Oungre Canada 167 K5
Ounianga Kébir Chad 120 D5
Ounianga Sérir Chad 120 D5
Ounissoui well Niger 125 I2
Oupeye Belgium 51 L2
Our r. Lux. 51 M3
Ouray U.S.A. 181 F5
Ourcq r. France 51 J3
Ouré Kaba Guinea 124 C4
Ourém Brazil 202 C2
Ourense Spain 54 D2
also spelt Orense
Ouricuri Brazil 202 D3
Ourinhos Brazil 206 D9
Ourini Chad 120 D5
Ourique Port. 54 C7
Ouro Brazil 202 C4
Ouro Branco Brazil 207 J7
Ouro Fino Brazil 206 G9
Ouro Preto Brazil 203 D7
Ourthe r. Belgium 51 L2
Ouse r. U.K. 47 L10
Oust r. France 50 D5
Outamba Kilimi National Park Sierra Leone 124 B4
Outaouais, Rivière des r. Canada see Ottawa
Outardes r. Canada 169 G3
Outardes Quatre, Réservoir Canada 169 G3
Outat Oulad el Haj Morocco 122 E2
Outeniekwaberge mts S. Africa 132 G10
Outer Hebrides is U.K. 46 E6
Outer Island U.S.A. 172 C3
Outer Mongolia country Asia see Mongolia
Outer Santa Barbara Channel U.S.A. 182 F8
Outjo Namibia 130 C4
Outlook Canada 167 J5
Outokumpu Fin. 40 D3
Outoul Alg. 123 G5
Outram N.Z. 153 E13
Out Skerries is U.K. 46 L3
Ouvéa i. New Caledonia 145 F4
also spelt Uéa or Uvéa
Ouyanghai Skuiku resr China 87 E3
Ouyen Australia 147 D3
Ova r. Turkey 58 I7
Ovace, Punta d' mt. Corse France 56 B7
Ovacık Turkey 107 D3
Ovada Italy 56 A4
Ovaeymiri Turkey 59 I11
Ovalle Chile 204 C3
Ovamboland reg. Namibia 130 B3
Ovan Gabon 126 B4
Ovar Port. 54 C4
Ovejas Col. 187 E5
Oveng Cameroon 125 I6
Ovens r. Australia 147 E4
Øvergard Norway 44 L1
Överhalla Norway 44 J2
Överkalix Sweden 44 M2
Overlander Roadhouse Australia 151 A5
Overland Park U.S.A. 178 D4
Övermark Fin. 44 M3
Overo, Volcán vol. Arg. 204 C4
Overton NV U.S.A. 183 J5
Overton TX U.S.A. 179 D5
Övertorneå Sweden 44 M2
Överum Sweden 45 L4
Överuman l. Sweden 44 K2
Ovid MI U.S.A. 173 I7
Ovid NY U.S.A. 177 I3
Ovidiopol' Ukr. 58 L2
Ovidiu Romania 58 J4
Oviedo Spain 54 F1
Ovinishchenskaya Vozvyshennost' hills Rus. Fed. 43 R3
Ovišrags hd Latvia 42 C4
Oviston Nature Reserve S. Africa 133 J7
Övögdiy Mongolia 84 C2
Ovoot Mongolia 85 G2
Övörhangay prov. Mongolia 84 D2
Øvre Anarjokka Nasjonalpark nat. park Norway 44 N1
Øvre Årdal Norway 45 I3
Øvre Dividal Nasjonalpark nat. park Norway 44 L1
Øvre Forra nature res. Norway 44 J3
Øvre Pasvik Nasjonalpark nat. park Norway 44 O1
Øvre Rendal Norway 45 J3
Övre Soppero Sweden 44 M1
Ovruch Ukr. 41 D6
Övt Mongolia 84 D2
Owahanga N.Z. 152 K8
Owaka N.Z. 153 D14
Owakonze Canada 172 C2
Owando Congo 126 B5
formerly known as Fort Rousset
Owasco Lake U.S.A. 177 I3
Owase Japan 91 E7
Owasso U.S.A. 179 D4
Owatonna U.S.A. 174 A2
Owbeh Afgh. 101 E3
Owego U.S.A. 177 I3
Owen, Mount N.Z. 153 G9
Owendale S. Africa 132 H5
Owen Falls Dam Uganda 128 B4
Owen Island Myanmar 79 B6
Owen River N.Z. 153 G9
Owens r. U.S.A. 182 G5
Owensboro U.S.A. 174 C4
Owens Lake U.S.A. 182 G5
Owen Sound Canada 168 D4
Owen Sound inlet Canada 173 M6
Owen Stanley Range mts P.N.G. 145 D2
Owensville MO U.S.A. 174 B4
Owensville OH U.S.A. 176 A6
Owenton U.S.A. 176 A7
Owerri Nigeria 125 G5
Owhango N.Z. 152 J7
Owikeno Lake Canada 166 E5
Owings U.S.A. 177 I7
Owingsville U.S.A. 176 B7
Owl r. Canada 167 M3
Owl Creek r. U.S.A. 180 E4
Owminzatow Toghi hills Uzbek. see Auminzatau, Gory
Owo Nigeria 125 G5
Owosso U.S.A. 173 I8
Owyhee r. U.S.A. 180 C4
Owyhee Mountains U.S.A. 180 C4
Owyhee North Fork r. U.S.A. 180 C4
Owyhee South Fork r. U.S.A. 180 C4
Oxapampa Peru 200 B2
Öxarfjörður b. Iceland 44 [inset] C2
Oxbow Canada 167 K5
Ox Creek r. U.S.A. 178 B1
Oxelösund Sweden 45 L4
Oxford N.Z. 153 G11
Oxford U.K. 47 K12
Oxford IA U.S.A. 172 B9
Oxford MA U.S.A. 177 N3
Oxford ME U.S.A. 177 O1
Oxford MI U.S.A. 173 J8
Oxford MS U.S.A. 174 B5
Oxford NC U.S.A. 176 G9
Oxford NY U.S.A. 177 J3
Oxford OH U.S.A. 176 A6
Oxford PA U.S.A. 177 J6
Oxford WI U.S.A. 172 D7
Oxford House Canada 167 M4
Oxford Junction U.S.A. 172 C9
Oxford Lake Canada 167 M4
Oxkutzcab Mex. 185 H4
Oxley Australia 147 E3
Oxleys Peak Australia 147 F2
Oxley Wild Rivers National Park Australia 147 G2
Ox Mountains hills Rep. of Ireland see Slieve Gamph
Oxnard U.S.A. 182 E7
Oxtongue Lake Canada 173 O5
Oxus r. Asia see Amudar'ya
Oxylithos Greece 59 F10
Oya r. Sarawak Malaysia 77 E2
Øya Norway 44 K2
Oyabe Japan 91 E6
Oyama Japan 91 F6
Ō-yama mt. Japan 91 F7
Ō-yama vol. Japan 91 F7
Oyapock r. Brazil/Fr. Guiana 199 I3
Oyapock, Baie d' b. Fr. Guiana 199 I3
Oyem Gabon 126 A4
Oyen Canada 167 I5
Øyeren l. Norway 45 J4
Oygon Mongolia 84 C1
Oykel r. U.K. 46 H6
Oymapınar Turkey 108 C1
Oymyakon Rus. Fed. 39 O3
Oyo Congo 126 B5
Oyo Nigeria 125 F5
Oyo state Nigeria 125 F4
Oyo Sudan 121 H4
Oyón Peru 200 A2
Oyonnax France 51 L6
Oyoqquduq Uzbek. see Ayakkuduk
Oyster Bay S. Africa 133 I11
Oytal Kazakh. 103 H4
Oy-Tal Kyrg. 103 H4
Oytograk China 89 C4
Oyukludağı mt. Turkey 108 D1
Oyyl Kazakh. see Uil
Oyyq Kazakh. see Uyuk
Özalp Turkey 107 F3
formerly known as Karakalli
Ozamiz Phil. 74 B4
Ozark AL U.S.A. 175 C6
Ozark AR U.S.A. 179 D5
Ozark MO U.S.A. 178 D4
Ozark Plateau U.S.A. 178 D4
Ozarks, Lake of the U.S.A. 178 D4
Ożarów Poland 49 S5
Özbaşı Turkey 59 I11
Ozbekiston country Asia see Uzbekistan
Ózd Hungary 49 R7
Özdere Turkey 59 I11
Ozen Kazakh. see Kyzylsay
Ozerevo Rus. Fed. 43 P2
Ozerishche Rus. Fed. 43 O7
Ozerne Ukr. 58 J3
Ozerninskoye Vodokhranilishche resr Rus. Fed. 43 R6
Ozernovskiy Rus. Fed. 39 P4
Ozernoye Kazakh. 103 E1
formerly known as Ozernyy
Ozernoye Rus. Fed. 102 B2
Ozerny Kazakh. see Shashubay
Ozernyy Kazakh. see Ozernoye
Ozernyy Ivanovskaya Oblast' Rus. Fed. 43 V4
Ozernyy Orenburgskaya Oblast' Rus. Fed. 103 E2
Ozernyy Smolenskaya Oblast' Rus. Fed. 43 N6
Ozerpakh Rus. Fed. 82 F1
Ozersk Rus. Fed. 42 D7
Ozerskiy Rus. Fed. 82 F3
Ozery Rus. Fed. 43 T7
Ozeryane Rus. Fed. 82 C2
Özgön Kyrg. 103 H4
also spelt Uzgen
Ozherel'ye Rus. Fed. 43 T7
Ozhogina r. Rus. Fed. 39 P3
Ozieri Sardegna Italy 57 B8
Ozimek Poland 49 P5
Ozinki Rus. Fed. 102 B2
Ozolnieki Latvia 42 E5
Ozona U.S.A. 179 B6
Ozorków Poland 49 Q4
Ōzu Ehime Japan 91 C8
Ōzu Kumamoto Japan 91 B8
Ozuki Japan 91 B7
Ozuluama Mex. 185 F4
Ozurget'i Georgia 107 E2
formerly known as Makharadze

↓ P

Pâ Burkina 124 E4
Paakkola Fin. 44 N2
Paamiut Greenland 165 O3
also known as Frederikshåb
Pa-an Myanmar 78 B4
also spelt Hpa-an
Paanopa i. Kiribati see Banaba

Paarl S. Africa 132 C10
Paasvere Estonia 42 H2
Paatsjoki r. Europe see Patsoyoki
Paauilo U.S.A. 181 [inset] Z1
Pabaigh i. U.K. see Pabbay
Paballelo S. Africa 132 F5
P'abal-li N. Korea 83 C4
Pabbay i. Western Isles, Scotland U.K. 46 E6
Pabbay i. Western Isles, Scotland U.K. 46 E7
also spelt Pabaigh
Pabianice Poland 49 Q4
historically known as Pabianitz
Pabianitz Poland see Pabianice
Pabna Bangl. 97 F4
Pabradė Lith. 42 G7
Pab Range mts Pak. 101 F5
Pacaás, Serra dos hills Brazil 201 D2
Pacaás Novos, Parque Nacional nat. park Brazil 201 E2
Pacaembu Brazil 206 B8
Pacahuaras r. Bol. 200 D2
Pacajus Brazil 202 E3
Pacaraimã, Serra mts S. America see Pakaraima Mountains
Pacaraima Mountains S. America see Pakaraima Mountains
Pacarán Peru 200 B3
Pacasmayo Peru 200 A1
Pacatuba Brazil 202 E2
Pacaya r. Peru 198 C6
Pacaya, Volcán de vol. Guat. 185 H6
Pacaya Samiria, Reserva Nacional nature res. Peru 198 C6
Paceco Sicilia Italy 57 E11
Pacheco Chihuahua Mex. 184 C2
Pacheco Zacatecas Mex. 185 E3
Pachia i. Greece 59 G12
also spelt Pakhiá
Pachía Peru 200 C4
Pachino Sicilia Italy 57 H12
Pachitea r. Peru 200 B2
Pachiza Peru 200 A1
Pachmarhi India 96 C5
Pachor India 96 C5
Pachora India 94 B1
Pachpadra India 96 B4
Pachuca Mex. 185 F4
Pacifica U.S.A. 182 B4
Pacific Grove U.S.A. 182 C5

▶Pacific Ocean 220
Largest ocean in the world.
oceans [features] ▶ 210–211

oceans	ocean	area sq km	area sq miles	greatest depth	page#
1	Pacific	166 241 000	64 186 000	10 920m / 35 826ft	220–221
2	Atlantic	86 557 000	33 420 000	8 605m / 28 231ft	216–217
3	Indian	73 427 000	28 350 000	7 125m / 23 376ft	218–219
4	Arctic	9 485 000	3 662 000	5 450m / 17 880ft	224

Pacific Rim National Park Canada 166 E5
Pacijan i. Phil. 74 C4
Pacinan, Tanjung pt Indon. 77 F4
Pačir Vojvodina, Srbija Yugo. 58 A3
Pacitan Indon. 77 E5
Packsattel pass Austria 49 L9
Pacov Czech Rep. 49 M6
Pacoval Brazil 199 H5
Pacuí r. Brazil 207 I3
Paczków Poland 49 O5
Padada Phil. 74 C5
Padalere Indon. 75 B3
Padali Rus. Fed. see Amursk
Padamarang i. Indon. 75 B4
Padampur India 96 B3
Padang Kalimantan Barat Indon. 77 E3
Padang Sumatra Indon. 76 C3
Padang i. Indon. 76 C2
Padangpanjang Indon. 76 C3
Padangsidimpuan Indon. 76 B2
Padangtikar Indon. 77 E3
Padangtikar i. Indon. 77 E3
Padany Rus. Fed. 40 E3
Padarosk Belarus 42 F9
Padas r. Sabah Malaysia 77 F1
Padasjoki Fin. 45 N3
Padatha, Kūh-e mt. Iran 100 B3
Padauiri r. Brazil 199 E5
Padaung Myanmar 78 A4
Padcaya Bol. 201 D5
Paddington Australia 147 E3
Paden City U.S.A. 176 E6
Paderborn Germany 48 F4
Padeşu, Vârful mt. Romania 58 D3
Padilla Bol. 201 D4
Padina Romania 58 I4
Padina Vojvodina, Srbija Yugo. 58 B3
Padinska Skela Srbija Yugo. 58 B4
Padjelanta nationalpark nat. park Sweden 44 L2
Padluzhzha Belarus 43 M8
Padma r. Bangl. see Ganges
Padmanabhapuram India 94 C4
Padmapur India 96 D5
Padova Italy see Padua
Padra India 96 B5
Padrão, Ponta pt Angola 127 B6
Padrauna India 97 E4
Padre Bernardo Brazil 206 E2
Padre Caro hill Spain 54 F7
Padre Island U.S.A. 179 C7
Padre Island National Seashore nature res. U.S.A. 179 C7
Padre Paraíso Brazil 207 L4
Padrón Spain 54 C2
Padrone, Cape S. Africa 133 K10
Padsvillye Belarus 42 I6
Padua India 95 D2
Padua Italy 56 D3
also spelt Padova; historically known as Patavium
Paducah KY U.S.A. 174 B4
Paducah TX U.S.A. 179 B5
Padul Spain 55 H7
Padum Jammu and Kashmir 96 C2
Pădurea Craiului, Munţii mts Romania 58 D2
Paekakariki N.Z. 152 I8
Paekdu-san mt. China/N. Korea 82 C4
Paengnyŏng-do i. S. Korea 83 B5
Paerau N.Z. 153 D13
Paeroa N.Z. 152 J5
Paese Italy 56 E3
Paestum tourist site Italy 57 G8
historically known as Poseidonia
Paete Phil. 74 B3
Pafos Cyprus see Paphos
Pafúri Moz. 131 F4
Pag Croatia 56 H4
Pag i. Croatia 56 G4
Paga r. Rus. Fed. 40 L2
Paga Conta Brazil 199 H6
Pagadenbaru Indon. 77 D4
Pagadian Phil. 74 B5
Pagai Selatan i. Indon. 76 C3
Pagai Utara i. Indon. 76 C3
Pagalu i. Equat. Guinea see Annobón
Pagan i. N. Mariana Is 73 K3
also spelt Pagon
Pagaralam Indon. 76 C3
Pagasitikos Kolpos b. Greece 59 D9
Pagatan Kalimantan Selatan Indon. 77 F3
Pagatan Kalimantan Tengah Indon. 77 F3
Page U.S.A. 183 M5
Pagėgiai Lith. 42 C6
Pagerdewa Indon. 76 D3
Paget, Mount S. Georgia 205 [inset]
Paget Cay reef Australia 149 G3
Paghman mt. Afgh. 101 G3
Pagirial Lith. 42 F6
Pagiriai Lith. 42 G7
Pagon i. N. Mariana Is see Pagan
Pagosa Springs U.S.A. 181 F5
Pagouda Togo 125 F4
Pagqên China see Gadê
Pagri China 89 E7
Pagwachuan r. Canada 168 C3
Pagwi P.N.G. 73 J7
Pahala U.S.A. 181 [inset] Z2
Pahang r. Malaysia 76 C2
Pahang state Malaysia 76 C2
Paharpur tourist site Bangl. 97 F4
Paharpur Pak. 101 G3
Pahauman Indon. 77 E2
Pahia Point N.Z. 153 B14
Pahiatua N.Z. 152 J8
Pahlavī Dezh Iran see Āq Qal'eh
Pahlgam Jammu and Kashmir 96 B2
Pahokee U.S.A. 175 D7
Pahost Vodaskhovishcha resr Belarus 42 H9
Pahra Kariz Afgh. 101 E3
Pahranagat Range mts U.S.A. 183 I4
Pahranichny Belarus 42 E8
formerly known as Byerastavitsa
Pahrump U.S.A. 183 I5
Pahuj r. India 96 C4
Pahute Mesa plat. U.S.A. 183 H4
Paiaguás Brazil 201 F4
Paicines U.S.A. 182 C5
Paide Estonia 42 G3
Paignton U.K. 47 I13
Paihia N.Z. 152 I3
Paiján Peru 200 A1
Päijänne l. Fin. 45 N3
Paikü Co l. China 89 D6
Paila r. Bol. 201 D4
Pailing China see Chun'an
Paillaco Chile 204 B6
Paimio Fin. 45 M3
Paimpol France 50 C4
Painan Indon. 76 C3
Painavu India 94 C4
Paine Chile 204 C4
Paine, Cerro mt. Chile 205 B8
Paineiras Brazil 207 H5
Painesdale U.S.A. 172 E3
Painesville U.S.A. 176 D4
Pains Brazil 207 H7
Painted Desert U.S.A. 183 M5
Painted Rock Dam U.S.A. 183 K8
Paint Hills Canada see Wemindji
Paint Lake Canada 167 L4
Paint Lake Provincial Recreation Park Canada 167 L4
Paint Lick U.S.A. 176 A8
Paint Rock U.S.A. 179 C6
Paintsville U.S.A. 176 C8
Paipa Col. 198 C3
Pairi r. India 94 D1
Paisley Canada 173 L6
Paisley U.K. 46 H8
País Vasco aut. comm. Spain 55 I1
English form Basque Country
Paita Peru 198 A6
Paitan, Teluk b. Sabah Malaysia 77 G1
Paithan India 94 B2
Paitou China 87 G2
Paiva r. Port. 54 C3
Paiva Couceiro Angola see Quipungo
Paixban Mex. 185 H5
Paizhou China 87 E2
Pajala Sweden 44 M2
Pajan Ecuador 198 A5
Pajarito Col. 198 C3
Pájaros, Islotes Chile 204 C3
Pajęczno Poland 49 P4
Pakala India 94 C3
Pakanbaru Indon. see Pekanbaru
Pakapė Lith. 42 E6
Pakaraima Mountains S. America 199 F4
English form Pacaraima Mountains; also known as Pacaraimã, Serra or Paracaima, Sierra
Pakashkan Lake Canada 168 B3
Pakaur India 97 E4
Pakawau N.Z. 152 G8
Pakch'ŏn N. Korea 83 B5
Pakesley Canada 168 D4
Pakhachi Rus. Fed. 39 Q3
Pakhar' Kazakh. 102 D2
Pakhiá i. Greece see Pachia
Pakhoi China see Beihai
Pakhomovo Rus. Fed. 43 S7
Pakhtaabad Uzbek. 103 H4
formerly known as Kokankishlak

▶Pakistan country Asia 101 F4
5th most populous country in Asia and 7th in the world.
world [population] ▶ 22–23
asia [countries] ▶ 64–67

Pak Ka Shan hill Hong Kong China see Parker, Mount
Pakkat Indon. 76 B2
Paklenica nat. park Croatia 56 H4
Paknampho Thai. see Nakhon Sawan
Pakokku Myanmar 78 A3
Pakoštane Croatia 56 H5
Pakotai N.Z. 152 H3
Pakowki Lake imp. l. Canada 167 I5
Pakpattan Pak. 101 H4
Pak Phanang Thai. 79 C6
Pak Phayun Thai. 79 C7
Pakra r. Croatia 56 I3
Pakrac Croatia 56 J3
Pakruojis Lith. 42 E6
Paks Hungary 49 P9
Pakse Laos see Pakxé
Pak Tam Chung Hong Kong China 87 [inset]
Pak Thong Chai Thai. 79 C5
Paktīā prov. Afgh. 101 G3
Paktīkā prov. Afgh. 101 G3
Paku r. Sarawak Malaysia 77 F2
Pakue Indon. 75 B3
Pakwash Lake Canada 167 M5
Pakxé Laos 79 D5
also spelt Pakse
Pal Senegal see Mpal
Pala Chad 126 B2
Pala Myanmar 79 B5
Palabuhanratu Indon. 77 D4
Palabuhanratu, Teluk b. Indon. 77 D4
Palacios Bol. 200 D3
Palaestinia reg. Asia see Palestine
Palafrugell Spain 55 O3
Palagiano Italy 57 J8
Palagruža i. Croatia 56 I6
Palaia Fokaia Greece 59 E11
Palaikastro Greece 59 H13
also known as Palaiókastron
Palaiochora Greece 59 E13
Palaiókastron Greece see Palaikastro
Palairos Greece 59 B10
Palaiseau France 51 I4
Palakkat India see Palghat
Palamakoloi Botswana 130 D4
Palamas Greece 59 D9
Palamós Spain 55 O3
Palam Pur India 96 C2
Palana India 96 B4
Palana Rus. Fed. 39 P4
Palanan Phil. 74 B2
Palanan Point Phil. 74 B2
Palancia r. Spain 55 K5
Palandur India 94 D1
Palanga Lith. 42 C6
Palangān, Kūh-e mts Iran 101 E4
Palangkaraya Indon. 77 F3
Palani India 94 C4
Palanpur India 96 B4
Palanro Indon. 75 A4
Palantak Pak. 101 F5
Palapag Phil. 74 C3
Palapye Botswana 131 E4
Palar r. India 94 D3
Palasa Indon. 75 B2
Palasbari India 97 F4
Palas de Rei Spain 54 D2
Palata r. Belarus 43 J6
Palatka Rus. Fed. 39 P3
Palatka U.S.A. 175 D6
Palau Sardegna Italy 56 B7
▶Palau country N. Pacific Ocean 73 H5
also spelt Belau
asia [countries] ▶ 64–67
Palaui i. Phil. 74 B2
Palauig Phil. 74 A3
Palau Islands Palau 73 H5
Palauk Myanmar 79 B5
Palaw Myanmar 79 B5
Palawan i. Phil. 74 A4
historically known as Paragua
Palawan Passage strait Phil. 74 A4
Palayan Phil. 74 B3
Palayankottai India 94 C4
Palazzo, Punta pt Corse France 51 O10
Paldiski Estonia 42 F2
Pale Bos.-Herz. 56 K5
Paleleh Indon. 75 B2
Palembang Indon. 76 D3
Palena Aisén Chile 205 B6
Palena Los Lagos Chile 205 C6
Palencia Spain 54 G2
Palenque Mex. 185 G5
Palermo Arg. 201 D6
Palermo Sicilia Italy 57 F10
historically known as Panormus
Palermo Punta Raisi airport Sicilia Italy 57 F10
Palestine reg. Asia 108 G5
historically known as Palaestinia
Palestine U.S.A. 179 D6
Paletwa Myanmar 78 A3
Palghar India 94 B2
Palghat India 94 C4
also spelt Palakkat
Palgrave, Mount hill Australia 150 A4
Palhoca Brazil 203 B8
Pali Madhya Pradesh India 96 D5
Pali Maharashtra India 94 B2
Pali Rajasthan India 96 B4
Palik Belarus 43 J7

▶Palikir Micronesia 220 E5
Capital of Micronesia.

Palimbang Phil. 74 C5
Palinuro, Capo c. Italy 57 H8
Paliouri Greece 59 E9
Paliouri, Akra pt Greece 59 E9
Palisade U.S.A. 180 E5
Palitana India 96 A5
Palivere Estonia 42 E3
Palja hill Sweden 44 L2
Paljakka hill Fin. 44 O2
Pälkäne Fin. 45 N3
Palk Bay Sri Lanka 94 C4
Palkino Rus. Fed. 42 J4
Palkohda India 95 D2
Palkonda Range mts India 94 C3
Palkot India 97 E5
Palk Strait India/Sri Lanka 94 C4
Palladani India 94 C4
Pallapalla mt. Peru 200 B3
Pallas ja Ounastunturin kansallispuisto nat. park Fin. 44 M1
Pallasovka Rus. Fed. 102 A2
Pallavaram India 94 D3
Palleru r. India 94 D2
Pallinup r. Australia 151 B7
Pallisa Uganda 128 B4
Palliser, Cape N.Z. 152 J9
Palliser, Îles is Fr. Polynesia 221 I7
Palliser Bay N.Z. 152 J9
Pallu India 96 B3
Palma r. Brazil 202 C5
Palma Moz. 129 D7
Palma del Río Spain 54 F7
Palma de Mallorca Spain 55 N5
Palma di Montechiaro Sicilia Italy 57 F11
Palmaner India 94 C3
Palmanova Italy 56 F3
Palmares Acre Brazil 200 D2
Palmares Pernambuco Brazil 202 F4
Palmares do Sul Brazil 203 B9
Palmarito Venez. 198 D3
Palmarola, Isola i. Italy 57 E8
Palmarolle Canada 173 N2
Palmar Sur Costa Rica 186 C5
Palmas Paraná Brazil 203 B8
Palmas Tocantins Brazil 202 B4
Palmas, Cape Liberia 124 D5
Palmas, Golfo di b. Sardegna Italy 57 A10
Palma Soriano Cuba 186 E2
Palm Bay U.S.A. 175 D7
Palmdale U.S.A. 182 F7
Palm Desert U.S.A. 183 H8
Palmeira Brazil 203 B8
Palmeira das Missões Brazil 203 A8
Palmeira dos Índios Brazil 202 E4
Palmeirais Brazil 202 D3
Palmeiras r. Brazil 202 C5
Palmeiras de Goiás Brazil 206 D3
Palmeirinhas, Ponta das pt Angola 127 B7
Palmer research station Antarctica 222 T2
Palmer r. Australia 149 D3
Palmer watercourse Australia 148 B5
Palmer U.S.A. 164 E3
Palmer Land reg. Antarctica 222 T2
Palmerston Australia see Darwin
Palmerston Australia 148 A2
Palmerston Canada 173 M7
Palmerston atoll Cook Is 221 H7
also known as Avarau
Palmerston N.Z. 153 E13
Palmerston, Cape Australia 149 F4
Palmerston North N.Z. 152 J8
Palmerton U.S.A. 177 J5
Palmerville Australia 149 E2
Palmetto U.S.A. 175 D7
Palmi Italy 57 H10
Palmillas Mex. 185 F4
Palmira Col. 198 B4
Palmira Cuba 186 C2
Palmital Brazil 206 C9
Palmnicken Rus. Fed. see Yantarnyy
Palm Springs U.S.A. 183 H8
Palm Tree Creek r. Australia 149 F5
▶Palm Valley Australia 148 B5
oceania [features] ▶ 142–143
Palmyra Syria see Tadmur
Palmyra NY U.S.A. 177 H2
Palmyra PA U.S.A. 177 I5
Palmyra VA U.S.A. 176 G8

▶Palmyra Atoll N. Pacific Ocean 221 H5
United States Unincorporated Territory.
oceania [countries] ▶ 138–139

Palmyras Point India 95 E1
Palni Hills India 94 C4
Palo Phil. 74 C4
Palo Alto U.S.A. 182 B4
Palo Blanco Arg. 204 D2
Palo Blanco Mex. 185 E3
Palo Chino watercourse Mex. 181 D7
Palo de las Letras Col. 198 B3
Palo Duro watercourse U.S.A. 179 B5
Paloh Sarawak Malaysia 77 E2
Paloich Sudan 128 B2
Palojoensuu Fin. 44 M1
Palomaa Fin. 44 N1
Palomani mt. Peru 200 C3
Palomares Mex. 185 G5
Palomar Mountain U.S.A. 183 H8
Palomera, Sierra mts Spain 55 J4
Palomitas Arg. 200 D6
Paloncha India 94 D2
also known as Palwancha
Palo Pinto U.S.A. 179 C5
Palopo Indon. 75 B3
Palos, Cabo de c. Spain 55 K7
Palo Santo Arg. 204 F2
Palouse r. U.S.A. 180 C3
Palo Verde U.S.A. 183 J8
Palo Verde, Parque Nacional nat. park Costa Rica 186 B5
Palovesi l. Fin. 45 M3
Palpa Ica Peru 200 B3
Palpa Lima Peru 200 A2
Palpetu, Tanjung pt Indon. 75 C3
Palsana India 96 B5
Paltamo Fin. 44 N2
Paltaselkä l. Fin. 44 N2
Pal'tsevo Rus. Fed. 43 J1
Pal'tso Rus. Fed. 43 P8
Palu Indon. 75 A3
Palu i. Indon. 75 B5
Palu r. Indon. 75 A3
Palu Turkey 107 D3
Paluan Phil. 74 B3
Paluan Bay Phil. 74 B3
Pal'vart Turkm. 103 F5
Palwal India 96 C3
Palwancha India see Paloncha
Pal'yanovo Rus. Fed. 38 G3
Palyatskishki Belarus 42 G7
Palyavaam r. Rus. Fed. 39 R3
Palyeskaya Nizina marsh Belarus/Ukr. see Pripet Marshes
Palyessye Belarus 43 K9
Palyessye Belarus 43 M8
Pama Austria 49 O7
Pama Burkina 125 F4
Pama r. Cent. Afr. Rep. 126 C3
Pama, Réserve Partielle de nature res. Burkina 125 F4
Pamamaroo Lake Australia 147 D3

▶Pamana i. Indon. 75 B5
Most southerly point of Asia.

Pamanukan Indon. 77 D4
Pamar Col. 198 D5
Pamban Channel India 94 C4
Pambarra Moz. 131 G4
Pambula Australia 147 F4
Pamekasan Indon. 77 F4
Pameungpeuk Indon. 77 D4
Pamfylla Greece 59 H9
Pamidi India 94 C3
Pamiers France 50 H9
Pamir r. Afgh./Tajik. 101 H2
Pamir mts Asia 99 I2
Pamlico r. U.S.A. 174 E5
Pamlico Sound sea chan. U.S.A. 174 E5
Pampa Chile 200 C5
Pampa U.S.A. 179 B5
Pampa Chica Arg. 205 C7
Pampachiri Peru 200 B3
Pampa de Infierno Arg. 204 E2
Pampa Grande Bol. 201 D4
Pampanua Indon. 75 B4
▶Pampas reg. Arg. 204 D5
southamerica [landscapes] ▶ 190–191
Pampas Peru 200 B3
Pampas r. Peru 200 B3
Pampeluna Spain see Pamplona
Pampierstad S. Africa 133 I4
Pamplin U.S.A. 176 G8
Pamplona Col. 198 C3
Pamplona Phil. 74 B4
Pamplona Spain 55 J2
also known as Iruña; historically known as Pampeluna
Pamukan, Teluk b. Indon. 77 G3
Pamukçu Turkey 59 I9
Pamukkale Turkey 59 K11
Pamukova Turkey 106 B2
Pamunkey r. U.S.A. 177 I8
Pamzal Jammu and Kashmir 96 C2
Pana Gabon 126 B5
Pana U.S.A. 174 B4
Panabá Mex. 185 H4
Panabo Phil. 74 C5
Panabutan Bay Phil. 74 B5
Panaca U.S.A. 183 J4
Panache, Lake Canada 168 D4
Panaci Romania 58 G1
Panaeati Island P.N.G. 149 G1
Panagar India 96 D5
Panagia i. Greece 58 F8
also spelt Panayía
Panagiri India 94 C2
Panagtaran Point Phil. 74 A4
Panagyurishte Bulg. 58 F6
Panaitan i. Indon. 76 D4
Panaitolio Greece 59 C10
Panaji India 94 B3
formerly known as Panjim; historically known as Nova Goa
▶Panama country Central America 186 C5
northamerica [countries] ▶ 158–159
Panamá Panama see Panama City
Panamá, Bahía de b. Panama 186 D5
Panamá, Golfo de g. Panama see Panama, Gulf of
Panama, Gulf of Panama 186 D6
also known as Panamá, Golfo de
Panama Canal Panama 186 D5

▶Panama City Panama 186 D5
Capital of Panama. Also known as Panamá.

Panama City U.S.A. 175 C6
Panamint Range mts U.S.A. 183 G5
Panamint Valley U.S.A. 183 G5
Panao Peru 200 A2
Panaon i. Phil. 74 C4
Panapompom Island P.N.G. 149 G1
Panar r. India 97 F4
Panarea, Isola i. Isole Lipari Italy 57 H10
Panarik Indon. 77 E2
Panaro r. Italy 56 D4
Panarukan Indon. 77 F4
Panatinane Island P.N.G. 149 G1
Panay i. Phil. 74 B4
Panayarvi Natsional'nyy Park nat. park Rus. Fed. 44 O2
Panay Gulf Phil. 74 B4
Panayía i. Greece see Panagia
Panbult S. Africa 133 O3
Pancake Range mts U.S.A. 183 I3
Pancas Brazil 207 M6
Pančevo Vojvodina, Srbija Yugo. 58 B4
also spelt Pancsova
Panchagarh Bangl. 97 F4
Panch'iao Taiwan 87 G3
Pancingapan, Bukit mt. Indon. 77 F2
Panciu Romania 58 I3
Pâncota Romania 58 C2
formerly spelt Pîncota
Pancsova Vojvodina, Srbija Yugo. see Pančevo
Panda Moz. 131 G5
Pandan Panay Phil. 74 B4
Pandan Phil. 74 C3
Pandan, Selat strait Sing. 76 [inset]
Pandan Bay Phil. 74 B4
Pandan Reservoir Sing. 76 [inset]
Pandaria India 97 D5
Pandavapura India 94 C3
Pan de Azúcar Chile 204 C2
Pan de Azúcar, Parque Nacional nat. park Chile 204 C2
Pandeglang Indon. 77 D4
Pandeiros r. Brazil 207 I2
Pandėlys Lith. 42 G5
Pandhana India 96 C5
Pandharpur India 94 B2
Pandhurna India 96 C5
Pando dept Bol. 200 D2
Pando Uruguay 204 G4
Pandokrátor hill Greece see Pantokratoras
Pandora Costa Rica 186 C5
Pandora Entrance sea chan. Australia 149 E1
Pandrup Denmark 45 J4
Paneas Syria see Bāniyās
Panelas Brazil 201 E2
Panevėžys Lith. 42 F6
Panfilov Kazakh. see Zharkent
Pang r. China 82 B1
Pang, Nam r. Myanmar 78 B3
Panga Dem. Rep. Congo 126 E4
Panga Estonia 42 D3
Pangai Tonga 145 H3
Pangal Andhra Pradesh India 94 C2
Pangal Andhra Pradesh India 94 C2
Pangandaran Indon. 77 E4
Pangani Tanz. 129 C6
also known as Ruvu
Pangani r. Tanz. 129 C6
Pañganiban Phil. 74 C3
Pangar Djerem, Réserve du nature res. Cameroon 125 I5
Pangean Indon. 75 A3
Panghsang Myanmar 78 B3
Pangi Dem. Rep. Congo 126 E5
Pangi Range mts Pak. 101 H3
Pangjiabu China 85 G3
Pangkah, Tanjung pt Indon. 77 F4
Pangkajene Indon. 75 A4
Pangkalanbuun Indon. 77 E3
Pangkalanlunang Indon. 76 B2
Pangkalansusu Indon. 76 B1
Pangkal Kalong Malaysia 76 C1
Pangkalpinang Indon. 77 D3
Pangkalsiang, Tanjung pt Indon. 75 B3
Panglang Myanmar 78 B2
Panglao i. Phil. 74 B4
Pangman Canada 167 J5
Pangnirtung Canada 165 M3
Pango Aluquém Angola 127 B7
Pangody Rus. Fed. 38 H3
Pangonda Cent. Afr. Rep. 126 D3
Pangong Tso salt l. China/Jammu and Kashmir see Bangong Co
Pangrango vol. Indon. 77 D4
Pang Sida National Park Thai. 79 C5
Pang Sua, Sungai r. Sing. 76 [inset]
Pangtara Myanmar 78 B3
Panguipulli Chile 204 B5
Panguitch U.S.A. 183 L4
Panguru N.Z. 152 H3
Pangururan Indon. 76 B2
Pangutaran i. Phil. 74 B5
Pangutaran Group is Phil. 74 B5
Panhandle U.S.A. 179 B5
Pania-Mwanga Dem. Rep. Congo 127 F6
Pani Mines India 96 B5
Panino Tverskaya Oblast' Rus. Fed. 43 P5
Panino Voronezhskaya Oblast' Rus. Fed. 41 G6
Paninskaya Rus. Fed. 43 R1
Panipat India 96 C3
Panitan Phil. 74 A4
Panizowye Belarus 43 L7
Panj r. Afgh./Tajik. see Pyandzh
Panj Tajik. 101 G2
also spelt Pyandzh; formerly known as Kirovabad
Panjāb Afgh. 101 F3
Panjakent Tajik. 101 F2
also spelt Pendzhikent
Panjang Indon. 76 D4
Panjang i. Indon. 77 E2
Panjang i. Indon. 77 G2
Panjang, Bukit Sing. 76 [inset]
Panjang, Selat sea chan. Indon. 76 C2
Panjgur Pak. 101 F5
Panjhra r. India 96 B5
Panjim India see Panaji
Panjin China 85 I3
also known as Panshan
Panji Poyon Tajik. 101 G2
also known as Nizhniy Pyandzh
Panjkora r. Pak. 101 G3
Panjnad r. Pak. 101 G4
Pankakoski Fin. 44 O3
Pankovka Rus. Fed. 43 M3
Panlian China see Miyi
Pan Ling mts China 82 C4
Panlong China see Queshan
Panna India 96 D4
Pannawonica Australia 150 B4
Pannonhalma Hungary 49 O8
formerly known as Győrszentmárton
Pano Aqil Pak. 101 G5
Panopah Indon. 77 E3
Panoplis Egypt see Akhmîm
Panorama Brazil 206 B8
Panormus Sicilia Italy see Palermo
Panruti India 94 C4
Panshan China see Panjin
Panshi China 82 B4
Panshui China see Pu'an
Pantaicermin, Gunung mt. Indon. 76 C3

▶Pantanal marsh S. America 201 F4
Largest area of wetlands in the world.

Pantanal de São Lourenço marsh Brazil 201 F4
Pantanal do Taquarí marsh Brazil 201 F4
Pantanal Matogrossense, Parque Nacional do nat. park Brazil 201 F4
Pantar i. Indon. 75 C5
Pantelaria Sicilia Italy see Pantelleria
Pantelleria Sicilia Italy 57 D12
historically known as Pantelaria
Pantelleria, Isola di i. Sicilia Italy 57 E12
Pantemakassar East Timor 75 C5
formerly known as Ocussi
Pantha Myanmar 78 A3
Panticapaeum Ukr. see Kerch
Pantijan Aboriginal Reserve Australia 150 D3
Pantokratoras hill Greece 59 A9
also known as Pandokrátor
Pantoowarinna, Lake salt flat Australia 146 C1
Pantukan Phil. 74 C5
Panu Dem. Rep. Congo 126 C5
Pánuco Mex. 185 F4
Pánuco r. Mex. 185 F4
Panvel India 94 B2
Panwari India 96 C4
Panxian China 86 C3
Panyu China 87 E4
also known as Shiqiao
Panzhihua China 86 B3
also known as Dukou
Panzi Dem. Rep. Congo 127 C6
Panzos Guat. 185 H6
Pao r. Venez. 199 E2
Pão de Açúcar Brazil 202 E4
Paola Italy 57 I9
Paola U.S.A. 178 D4
Paoli U.S.A. 174 C4
Paoni Indon. 75 D3
Paonia U.S.A. 180 F5
Paoua Cent. Afr. Rep. 126 C3
Paôy Pêt Cambodia 79 C5
Pap Uzbek. 103 G4
also spelt Pop
Pápa Hungary 49 O8
Papa, Monte del mt. Italy 57 H8
Papadianika Greece 59 D12
Papagaio r. Brazil see Sauêruiná
Papagaios Minas Gerais Brazil 207 I6
Papagaios Rondônia Brazil 201 E2
Papagni r. India 94 C3
Papakura N.Z. 152 I5
Papallacta Ecuador 198 B5
Papamoa Beach N.Z. 152 K5
Papanasam Tamil Nadu India 94 C4
Papanasam Tamil Nadu India 94 C4
Papantla Mex. 185 F4
Paparhahandi India 95 D2
Paparoa N.Z. 152 I4
Paparoa National Park N.Z. 153 F10
Paparoa Range mts N.Z. 153 F10
Papas, Akra pt Greece 59 G11
Papa Stour i. U.K. 46 K3
Pápateszér Hungary 49 O8
Papatoetoe N.Z. 152 I4
Papatowai N.Z. 153 D14
Papa Westray i. U.K. 46 J4
also known as Papay
Papay i. U.K. see Papa Westray

▶Papeete Fr. Polynesia 221 I7
Capital of French Polynesia.

Papenburg Germany 48 E2
Papendorp S. Africa 132 C8
Paphos Cyprus 108 D3
also spelt Pafos; historically known as Paphus
Paphus Cyprus see Paphos
Papigochic r. Mex. 181 F7
Papikio mt. Bulg./Greece 58 G7
Papilė Lith. 42 D5
Papillion U.S.A. 178 C3
Papineau-Labelle, Réserve Faunique de nature res. Canada 168 F4
Papiya hill Bulg. 58 I6
Papoose Lake U.S.A. 183 I4
Paposo Chile 204 C2
Papua, Gulf of P.N.G. 73 J8

▶Papua New Guinea country Oceania 144 D2
2nd largest and 2nd most populous country in Oceania.
oceania [countries] ▶ 138–139

Papun Myanmar 78 B4
Papunya Australia 148 A4
Pará r. Brazil 203 C6
Pará state Brazil 199 I5
Para i. Indon. 75 C2
Para r. Rus. Fed. 41 G5
Pará, Rio do r. Brazil 202 B2
Paraburdoo Australia 150 B4
Paracaima, Sierra mts S. America see Pakaraima Mountains
Paracale Phil. 74 B3
Paracambi Brazil 207 J9
Paracas Peru 200 A3
Paracas, Península pen. Peru 200 A3
Paracatu Brazil 206 G4
Paracatu r. Minas Gerais Brazil 206 H3
Paracel Islands S. China Sea 72 D3
also known as Dao Tay Sa or Hoang Sa or Hsi-sha Ch'un-tao or Quan Dao Hoang Sa or Xisha Qundao
Parachilna Australia 146 C2
Parachinar Pak. 101 G3
Paraćin Srbija Yugo. 58 C5
Parada, Punta pt Peru 200 B3
Pará de Minas Brazil 203 C6
Paradis Canada 168 E3
Paradise r. Canada 169 J2
Paradise Guyana 199 G3
Paradise CA U.S.A. 182 C2
Paradise MI U.S.A. 173 H4
Paradise NV U.S.A. 183 I5
Paradise Gardens Canada 167 H2
Paradise Hill Canada 167 I4
Paradise Peak U.S.A. 182 G3
Paradise River Canada 169 J2
Paradise Valley U.S.A. 183 M8
Parado Indon. 77 G5
Paradwip India 95 E1
Paraetonium Egypt see Marsa Matrûh
Paraf"yanava Belarus 42 I7
Paragominas Brazil 202 C2
Paragould U.S.A. 174 B4
Paragua r. Bol. 201 E3
Paragua i. Phil. see Palawan
Paragua r. Venez. 199 F3
Paraguaçu Brazil 207 H8
Paraguai r. Brazil 201 F5
Paraguáipoa Venez. 198 D2
Paraguarí Para. 201 F6
Paraguay r. Arg./Para. 201 F6
▶Paraguay country S. America 201 F5
southamerica [countries] ▶ 192–193
Paraíba r. Brazil 202 F3
Paraíba state Brazil 202 E3
Paraíba do Sul Brazil 207 J9
Paraíba do Sul r. Brazil 203 D7
Paraibuna Brazil 207 H10
Parainen Fin. see Pargas
Paraíso Brazil 206 A6
Paraíso Mex. 185 G5
Paraíso do Norte Brazil 202 B4
Paraisópolis Brazil 207 H9
Parakka Sweden 44 M2
Parakou Benin 125 F4
Parakylia Australia 146 C2
Paralakhemundi India 95 E2
formerly spelt Parlakimedi
Paralia Greece 59 D10
Paramagudi India see Paramakkudi
Paramakkudi India 94 C4
formerly spelt Paramagudi

▶Paramaribo Suriname 199 H3
Capital of Suriname.

Paramillo mt. Col. 198 C3
Paramillo, Parque Nacional nat. park Col. 198 B3
Paramirim Brazil 202 D5
Paramirim r. Brazil 202 D4
Páramo hill Spain 54 D2
Páramo de Masa, Puerto del pass Spain 54 H2
Paramonga Peru 200 A2
Paramushir, Ostrov i. Rus. Fed. 39 P4
Paramythia Greece 59 B9
Paran watercourse Israel 108 G7
Paraná Arg. 204 E3
Paranã Brazil 202 C5
Paraná r. Brazil 202 B5
Paraná state Brazil 206 B11

index P

Park City U.S.A. 183 M1
Parke Lake Canada 169 J2
Parkent Uzbek. 103 G4
Parker U.S.A. 183 J7
Parker, Mount hill Hong Kong China 87 [inset]
also known as Pak Ka Shan
Parker Dam U.S.A. 183 J7
Parker Lake Canada 167 M2
Parker Range hills Australia 151 B7
Parkersburg U.S.A. 176 D6
Parkers Lake U.S.A. 176 A9
Parkes Australia 147 F3
Park Falls U.S.A. 172 C5
Park Forest U.S.A. 172 F9
Parkhar Tajik. see Farkhor
Parkhill Canada 173 L7
Parkinson Canada 173 J4
Parkman U.S.A. 176 D4
Park Rapids U.S.A. 178 D2
Parksley U.S.A. 177 J8
Parkston U.S.A. 178 C3
Parksville Canada 166 E5
Parkutta Jammu and Kashmir 96 C2
Parla Spain 54 H4
Parlakimedi India see Paralakhemundi
Parla Kimedi India 95 E2
Parli Vaijnath India 94 C2
Parlung Zangbo r. China 86 A2
also known as Nagong Chu
Parma Italy 56 C4
Parma r. Italy 56 C4
Parma Rus. Fed. 40 K2
Parma ID U.S.A. 180 C4
Parma MI U.S.A. 173 I8
Parma OH U.S.A. 176 D4
Parmana Venez. 199 E3
Parnaguá Brazil 202 C4
Parnaíba Brazil 202 D2

Paraná r. S. America 206 B7
Part of the Río de la Plata - Paraná, 2nd longest river in South America.
southamerica [landscapes] 190–191

Paranaguá Brazil 203 B8
Paranaíba Brazil 206 B6
Paranaíba r. Brazil 206 B7
Paraná Ibicuy r. Arg. 204 F4
Paranaiguara Brazil 206 C5
Paranaíta r. Brazil 201 F2
Paranapanema r. Brazil 206 B9
Paranapiacaba, Serra mts Brazil 203 B8
Paranapura Peru 198 B6
Paranari Brazil 199 E5
Paranavaí Brazil 206 A10
Parandak Iran 100 B3
Parang i. Indon. 77 E4
Parang Phil. 74 B5
Parangi Aru r. Sri Lanka 94 D4
Parangipettai India 94 C4
historically known as Porto Novo
Parang Pass India 96 C2
Parângul Mare, Vârful mt. Romania 58 E3
Parantij India 96 B5
Paroreang, Bukit mt. Indon. 75 A3
Paraopeba Brazil 203 C6
Paraopeba r. Brazil 203 C6
Parapanda mt. Spain 54 H7
Parapara Indon. 75 C2
Pārapāra Iraq 107 F4
Paraparaumu N.Z. 152 I8
Parapuã Brazil 206 C8
Paraque, Cerro mt. Venez. 199 E3
Paras Norway 44 M1
Paraspori, Akra pt Greece 59 I13
Parati Brazil 203 C7
Paratinga Brazil 202 D5
Paratoo Australia 146 C3
Parāū, Kūh-e mt. Iraq 107 F4
Parauapebas r. Brazil 202 B3
Parauaquara, Serra hill Brazil 199 H5
Parauari r. Brazil 199 G6
Paraúna Brazil 206 C4
Paray-le-Monial France 51 K6
Parbati r. India 96 C4
Parbatipur Bangl. 97 F4
Parbhani India 94 C2
Parchim Germany 48 I2
Parchment U.S.A. 172 H8
Parczew Poland 49 T4
Pardee Reservoir U.S.A. 182 D3
Pardeeville U.S.A. 172 D7
Pardina Romania 58 J3
Pardo Arg. 204 F5
Pardo r. Bahia Brazil 207 O2
Pardo r. Mato Grosso do Sul Brazil 206 A8
Pardo r. Minas Gerais Brazil 207 I2
Pardo r. São Paulo Brazil 206 F7
Pardoo Australia 150 B4
Pardubice Czech Rep. 49 M5
Pare Indon. 77 F4
Parece Vela i. Japan see Okino-Tori-shima
Parechcha Belarus 42 F8
Pare Chu r. China 89 B5
Parecis Brazil 201 F3
Parecis r. Brazil 201 F3
Parecis, Serra dos hills Brazil 201 E2
Paredes de Nava Spain 54 G2
Paredón Mex. 185 E3
Paremata N.Z. 152 I9
Parenda India 94 B2
Parent Canada 169 F4
Parentis-en-Born France 50 E8
Pareora N.Z. 153 F12
Parepare Indon. 75 A4
Parfino Rus. Fed. 43 M4
Parga Greece 59 B9
Pargas Fin. 45 M3
also known as Parainen
Parghelia Italy 57 H10
Pargi India 94 C2
Pargolovo Rus. Fed. 43 L1
Paria Bol. 200 D4
Paria r. U.S.A. 183 M5
Paria, Gulf of Trin. and Tob./Venez. 187 H5
Paria, Peninsula de pen. Venez. 199 F2
Pariaman Indon. 76 C3
Paria Plateau U.S.A. 183 L5
Paricatuba Brazil 199 F6
Parida, Isla i. Panama 186 C5
Parigi Indon. 75 B3
Parikkala Fin. 45 O3
Parikud Islands India 95 E2
Parima r. Brazil see Uatatás
Parima, Serra mts Brazil 199 E4
Parima-Tapirapecó, Parque Nacional nat. park Venez. 199 E4
Parinari Peru 198 C6
Pariñas, Punta pt Peru 198 A6
Parintins Brazil 199 G5
Paris Canada 173 M7

Paris France 51 I4
Capital of France and most populous city in Europe. Historically known as Lutetia.
world [cities] 24–25

Paris ID U.S.A. 180 E4
Paris IL U.S.A. 174 C4
Paris KY U.S.A. 176 A7
Paris ME U.S.A. 177 O1
Paris MO U.S.A. 178 D4
Paris TN U.S.A. 174 B4
Paris TX U.S.A. 179 D5
Parish U.S.A. 177 I2
Parisienne, Île i. Canada 173 I4
Pāriz Iran 100 C4
Parizh Rus. Fed. 103 E1
Pärk Iran 101 E5
Park r. U.S.A. 178 C1
Parka Dem. Rep. Congo 126 E3
Parkajoki Sweden 44 M2
Parkal India 94 C2
Parkano Fin. 45 M3

Parnaíba r. Brazil 202 A4
Parnaíba r. Brazil 202 D2
Parnaibinha r. Brazil 202 C4
Parnarama Brazil 202 D3
Parnassos mt. Greece 59 D10
Parnassou nat. park Greece 59 D10
Parnassus N.Z. 153 H10
Parndana Australia 146 C3
Parner India 94 B2
Parnitha nat. park Greece 59 E10
Parnon mts Greece 59 D11
Pärnu Estonia 42 F3
formerly known as Pernov
Pärnu r. Estonia 42 F3
Pärnu-Jaagupi Estonia 42 F3
Pärnu laht b. Estonia 42 F3
Paro Bhutan 97 F4
Paroa N.Z. 153 F10
Parona Turkey see Fındık
Paroo watercourse Australia 147 D2
Paroo Channel watercourse Australia 147 D2
Paropamisus mts Afgh. 101 E3
also known as Safid Kūh
Paros Greece 59 G11
Paros i. Greece 59 G11
Parow S. Africa 132 C10
Parowan U.S.A. 183 L4
Parral Chile 204 C5
Parral r. Mex. 181 F8
Parramatta Australia 147 F3
Parramore Island U.S.A. 177 J8
Parras Mex. 185 E3
Parrish U.S.A. 172 D5
Parrita Costa Rica 186 B5
Parrsboro Canada 169 H4
Parry, Kap c. Greenland see Kangaarsussuaq
Parry Bay Canada 165 K3
Parry Channel Canada 165 H2
Parry Islands Canada 165 H2
Parry Lagoons Nature Reserve Australia 150 E2
Parry Range hills Australia 150 A4
Parry Sound Canada 168 D4
Pars prov. Iran see Fārs
Parsa India 97 E4
Parsa prov. Iran see Fārs
Parseta r. Poland 49 M1
Parsnip Peak U.S.A. 183 J3
Parsons KS U.S.A. 178 D4
Parsons WV U.S.A. 176 F6
Parsons Range hills Australia 148 B2
Partabgarh India 94 B2
Partabpur Chhattisgarh India 94 D2
Partabpur Chhattisgarh India 97 D5
Partakko Fin. 44 N1
Partanna Sicilia Italy 57 E11
Pärte mt. Sweden 44 L2
Partenstein Germany 48 G5
Parthenay France 50 F6
Partida, Isla i. Mex. 184 C3
Partinico Sicilia Italy 57 F10
Partizansk Rus. Fed. 82 D4
formerly known as Suchan
Partizánske Slovakia 49 P7
Partridge r. Canada 168 D3
Paru r. Brazil 199 H5
Parú, Serranía mts Venez. 199 E3
Parūd Iran 101 E5
Paru de Oeste r. Brazil 199 G5
Parur India 94 C4
Parvān prov. Afgh. 101 G3
Parvāreh Iran 100 D3
Parvatipuram India 95 D2
Parvatsar India 96 B4
Paryang China 89 C6
Parychy Belarus 43 K9
Parygino Kazakh. 88 D1
Parys S. Africa 133 L3
Pas r. Spain 54 H1
Pasa Dağı mt. Turkey 106 C3
Pasadena CA U.S.A. 182 F7
Pasadena TX U.S.A. 179 D6
Pasado, Cabo c. Ecuador 198 A5
Pasaje Ecuador 198 B5
Pa Sak, Mae Nam r. Thai. 79 C5
Paşalimanı Adası i. Turkey 58 I8
Pasan India 97 D5
Pasarwajo Indon. 75 B4
Pasawng Myanmar 78 B4
Pascagama r. Canada 168 F3
Pascagoula U.S.A. 175 B6
Pascagoula r. U.S.A. 175 B6
Paşcani Romania 58 H1
Pascalis Canada 173 P2
Pasco dept Peru 200 B2
Pasco U.S.A. 180 C3
Pascoag U.S.A. 177 N4
Pascoal, Monte hill Brazil 203 E6
Pascoe r. Australia 149 D2
Pascua, Isla de i. S. Pacific Ocean see Easter Island
Pascual Phil. 74 B3
Pas de Calais strait France/U.K. see Dover, Strait of
Pasewalk Germany 49 L2
Pasfield Lake Canada 167 J3
Pasha Rus. Fed. 43 O1
Pasha r. Rus. Fed. 43 N1
Pashkovo Rus. Fed. 82 C2
Pashozero Rus. Fed. 43 P1
Pashtun Zarghun Afgh. 101 E3
Pasig Phil. 74 B3
Pasi Ga Myanmar 78 B2
Pasighat India 97 G3
Pasinler Turkey 107 E3
Pasir Gudang Malaysia 76 [inset]
Pasirian Indon. 77 F5
Pasir Laba, Tanjong pt Sing. 76 [inset]
Pasir Mas Malaysia 76 C1
Pasirpangarayan Indon. 76 C2
Pasir Panjang Sing. 76 [inset]

Pasir Panjang hill Sing. 76 [inset]
Pasir Putih Malaysia 76 C1
Pasitelu, Pulau-pulau is Indon. 75 B4
Paskevicha, Zaliv l. Kazakh. see Shevchenko, Zaliv
Paskūh Iran 101 E5
Pasłęk Poland 49 Q1
Pasłęka r. Poland 49 Q1
Pasley, Cape Australia 151 C7
Paslıkaya Turkey 108 H1
Pašman i. Croatia 56 H5
Pasmore watercourse Australia 146 C2
Pasni Pak. 101 E5
Paso de Caballo Venez. 199 E2
Paso de Indios Arg. 205 C6
Paso del Limay Arg. 204 C6
Paso de los Libres Arg. 204 F3
Paso de los Toros Uruguay 204 F4
Paso del Sapo Arg. 205 C6
Paso de Patria Para. 201 F6
Paso de San Antonio Mex. 179 B6
Paso Real Hond. 186 B4
Paso Río Mayo Arg. 205 C7
Paso Robles U.S.A. 182 D6
Pasquia Hills Canada 167 K4
Pasrur Pak. 101 H3
Passage Island U.S.A. 172 E2
Passagem Franca Brazil 202 D3
Passaic U.S.A. 177 K5
Passa Quatro Brazil 207 I9
Passa Tempo Brazil 207 I7
Passau Germany 49 K7
Passi Phil. 74 B4
Passo Fundo Brazil 203 A9
Passo Real, Barragem resr Brazil 203 A9
Passos Brazil 206 G7
Pastavy Belarus 42 H6
also spelt Postavy
Pastaza prov. Ecuador 198 B5
Pastaza r. Peru 198 B6
Pasteur Arg. 204 E4
Pasto Col. 198 B4
Pasto Grande Brazil 201 E1
Pastora Peak U.S.A. 183 O5
Pastos Bons Brazil 202 C3
Pasu Jammu and Kashmir 96 B1
Pasuquin Phil. 74 B2
Pasur Turkey see Kulp
Pasuruan Indon. 77 F4
Pasvalys Lith. 42 F5
Pasvikelva r. Europe see Patsoyoki
Pásztó Hungary 49 Q8
Patache, Punta pt Chile 200 C5
Pata Bol. 200 C3
Pata i. Phil. 74 B5
Pata Senegal 124 B3

Patagonia reg. Arg. 205 C8
southamerica [contrasts] 194–195

Pataliputra India see Patna
Patan India see Somnath
Patan Gujarat India 96 B5
Patan Madhya Pradesh India 96 C5
Patan Maharashtra India 94 B2
Patan Nepal 97 E4
also known as Lalitpur
Patancheru India 94 C2
Patandar, Koh-i- mt. Pak. 101 F5
Patani Indon. 75 D2
Patani Nigeria 125 G5
Patan Saongi India 96 C5
Pataudi India 96 C3
Patavium Italy see Padua
Patay Arg. 204 E2
Patchewollock Australia 147 D3
Patch Grove U.S.A. 172 C8
Patchogue U.S.A. 177 L5
Patea N.Z. 152 I7
Patea r. N.Z. 152 I7
Pate Island Kenya 128 D5
Patensie S. Africa 133 I10
Paternion Austria 49 K9
Paternò Sicilia Italy 57 G11
Paterson r. Australia 147 E2
Paterson S. Africa 133 J10
Paterson U.S.A. 177 K5
Paterson Inlet N.Z. 153 B14
also known as Whaka a Te Wera
Paterson Range hills Australia 150 C4
Pathalgaon India 97 D5
Pathanamthitta India 94 C4
Pathankot India 96 B2
Patharia India 96 C5
Pathein Myanmar see Bassein
Pathfinder Reservoir U.S.A. 180 F4
Pathiu Thai. 79 B6
Pathri India 94 C2
Pathum Thani Thai. 79 C5
Pati Indon. 77 E4
Pati India 96 B5
Patía r. Col. 198 B4
Patiala India 96 C3
Patinti, Selat sea chan. Indon. 75 C3
Patitiri Greece 59 E9
Patívilca r. Peru 200 A2
Pātkai Bum mts India/Myanmar 78 A2
Patkaklik China 89 D4
Patlangıç Turkey 59 K12
Patmos i. Greece 59 H11
Patna India 97 E4
historically known as Pataliputra
Patnagarh India 95 D1
Patnanongan i. Phil. 74 B3
Patnos Turkey 107 E3
Pato, Cerro mt. Chile 205 B7
Pato Branco Brazil 203 A8
Patoda India 94 B2
Patoka r. U.S.A. 174 C4
Patomskoye Nagor'ye mts Rus. Fed. 39 L4
Patoniva Fin. 44 N1
also known as Buoddobohki
Patos Albania 58 A8
Patos Brazil 202 E3
Patos, Lagoa dos l. Brazil 203 B9
Patos, Rio dos r. Brazil 206 E1
Patos de Minas Brazil 206 G5
Patquía Arg. 204 D3
Patra Greece see Patras
Patrae Greece see Patras
Pátrai Greece see Patras
Patraïkos Kolpos b. Greece 59 C10
Patras Greece 59 C10
also known as Patra or Pátrai; historically known as Patrae
Patrasaer India 97 E5
Patratu India 97 E5
Patreksfjörður Iceland 44 [inset] B2
Patri India 96 A5
Patricio Lynch, Isla i. Chile 205 B8
Patrick Creek watercourse Australia 149 E4
Patrick Springs U.S.A. 176 E9
Patrimônio Brazil 206 E6
Patrocínio Brazil 206 F5
Patsoyoki r. Europe 40 D1
also known as Pasvikelva; also spelt Paatsjoki
Pattadakal tourist site India 94 B2
Pattanapuram India 94 C4
Pattani Thai. 79 C7
Pattani r. Thai. 79 C7
Pattaya Thai. 79 C5
Patten U.S.A. 174 G2
Patterson CA U.S.A. 182 C4
Patterson LA U.S.A. 175 B6
Patterson r. U.S.A. 176 G6
Patterson, Mount Canada 166 C1
Patterson, Point U.S.A. 172 H5
Patterson Mountain U.S.A. 182 E5
Patti India 97 D4
Patti Indon. 75 C5
Patti Sicilia Italy 57 G10
Pattijoki Fin. 44 N2
Pättikkä Fin. 44 M1
Pattikonda India 94 C3
Pattukkottai India 94 C4

Pattullo, Mount Canada 166 D3
Patu Brazil 202 E3
Patuakhali Bangl. 97 F5
Patuanak Canada 167 J4
Patuca, Parque Nacional nat. park Hond. 186 B4
Patuca, Punta pt Hond. 186 B4
Pătulele Romania 58 D4
Patur India 94 C1
Patutu mt. N.Z. 152 J7
Patuxent r. U.S.A. 177 I7
Patuxent Range mts Antarctica 223 S1
Patvinsuon kansallispuisto nat. park Fin. 44 O3
Pátzcuaro Mex. 185 E5
Pau France 50 F9
Pau-Brasil Brazil 207 N2
Paucartambo Peru 200 B2
Paucartambo r. Peru see Yavero
Pau d'Arco Brazil 202 B3
Pau d'Arco r. Brazil 201 H1
Pauhunri mt. China/India 89 E7
Pauillac France 50 F7
Pauini Brazil 200 D1
Pauini r. Brazil 199 F5
Pauini r. Brazil 200 D1
Pauk Myanmar 78 A3
Paukkaung Myanmar 78 A4
Paulatuk Canada 164 G3
Paulden U.S.A. 183 L7
Paulding Bay Antarctica 223 I2
Paulicéia Brazil 206 B8
Paulis Dem. Rep. Congo see Isiro
Păuliș Romania 58 C2
Paul Island Canada 169 I1
Paulista Brazil 202 F3
Paulistana Brazil 202 D4
Paulo Afonso Brazil 202 E4
Paulo de Faria Brazil 206 D7
Paulpietersburg S. Africa 133 O4
Pauls Valley U.S.A. 179 C5
Paumotu, Îles is Fr. Polynesia see Tuamotu Islands
Păunești Romania 58 I2
Paung Myanmar 78 B4
Paungbyin Myanmar 78 A2
Paungde Myanmar 78 A4
Pauni India 94 C1
Pauri India 96 C3
Pausa Peru 200 B3
Pauto r. Col. 198 D3
Pautrăsk Sweden 44 L2
Pauwela U.S.A. 181 [inset] Z1
Pavagada India 94 C3
Pavão Brazil 203 D6
Pavarandocito Col. 198 B3
Pāveh Iran 100 A3
Pavelets Rus. Fed. 43 U8
Pavia Italy 56 B3
historically known as Ticinum
Pavillon U.S.A. 176 G3
Pāvilosta Latvia 42 C5
Pavino Rus. Fed. 40 H4
Pavištyčio kalnas hill Lith. 42 D7
Pavlikeni Bulg. 58 G5
Pavlinovo Rus. Fed. 43 O7
Pavlivka Ukr. 58 K1
Pavlodar Kazakh. 103 I1
Pavlodar Oblast admin. div. Kazakh. see Pavlodarskaya Oblast'
Pavlodar Oblysy admin. div. Kazakh. see Pavlodarskaya Oblast'
Pavlodarskaya Oblast' admin. div. Kazakh. 103 I1
English form Pavlodar Oblast; also known as Pavlodar Oblysy
Pavlof Volcano U.S.A. 164 C4
Pavlograd Ukr. see Pavlohrad
Pavlohrad Ukr. 41 E6
also spelt Pavlograd
Pavlovka Akmolinskaya Oblast' Kazakh. 103 H2
Pavlovka Kustanayskaya Oblast' Kazakh. 103 E1
Pavlovka Respublika Bashkortostan Rus. Fed. 40 K5
Pavlovka Ul'yanovskaya Oblast' Rus. Fed. 41 H5
Pavlovo Rus. Fed. 40 G5
Pavlovsk Leningradskaya Oblast' Rus. Fed. 43 L2
Pavlovsk Voronezhskaya Oblast' Rus. Fed. 41 G6
Pavlovskaya Rus. Fed. 41 F7
Pavlovskiy Kazakh. 103 E1
Pavlovskiy Posad Rus. Fed. 43 T6
Pavlovskoye Rus. Fed. 43 V5
Pavlovskoye Vodokhranilishche resr Rus. Fed. 40 K5
Pavullo nel Frignano Italy 56 C4
Pavy Rus. Fed. 43 K3
Pawai India 96 D4
Pawan r. Indon. 77 E3
Pawarenga N.Z. 152 H3
Pawayan India 96 D3
Pawhuska U.S.A. 178 C4
Pawling U.S.A. 177 L4
Pawn r. Myanmar 78 B4
Pawnee U.S.A. 179 C4
Pawnee r. U.S.A. 178 C4
Pawnee City U.S.A. 178 C3
Paw Paw MI U.S.A. 172 H8
Paw Paw WV U.S.A. 176 G6
Pawu Aboriginal Land res. Australia 148 B4
Paxaro mt. Spain 54 D2
Paximada i. Greece 59 H13
Paximadia i. Greece 59 F13
Paxoi i. Greece 59 B9
Paxson U.S.A. 164 E3
Paxton U.S.A. 174 B3
Payahe Indon. 75 C2
Payakumbuh Indon. 76 C3
Paya Lebar Sing. 76 [inset]
Payerne Switz. 51 M6
Payette U.S.A. 180 C3
Payette r. U.S.A. 180 C3
Pay-Khoy, Khrebet hills Rus. Fed. 40 L1
Payne Canada see Kangirsuk
Payne U.S.A. 176 A4
Payne, Lac l. Canada 169 F1
Paynes Creek U.S.A. 182 C1
Payne's Find Australia 151 B6
Paynesville Australia 147 E4
Paynesville U.S.A. 178 D2
Paysandú Uruguay 204 F4
Pays de la Loire admin. reg. France 50 E5
Pays de Léon reg. France 50 B4
Payshanba Uzbek. 103 F4
formerly known as Kara-Dar'ya
Payson U.S.A. 183 M7
Payún, Cerro vol. Arg. 204 C5
Payyer, Gora mt. Rus. Fed. 40 M2
Payzawat China see Jiashi
Paz, Rio da r. Brazil 202 B4
Pazar Turkey 107 E2
Pazarcık Turkey 107 D3
Pazardzhik Bulg. 58 F6
Pazarköy Turkey 59 I9
Pazarlar Turkey 59 K10
Pazaryeri Turkey 59 K9
Paz de Ariporo Col. 198 D3
Paz de Rio Col. 198 C3
Pazin Croatia 56 F3
Pazña Bol. 200 D4
Pchevzha r. Rus. Fed. 43 M2
Pčinja r. Macedonia 58 C7
Pe Myanmar 79 B5
Peabiru Brazil 206 A10
Peabody KS U.S.A. 178 C4
Peabody MA U.S.A. 177 O3
Peace r. Canada 167 I3
Peace r. U.S.A. 175 D7

Peace Point Canada 167 H3
Peace River Canada 167 G3
Peach Creek U.S.A. 176 D8
Peachland Canada 166 G5
Peach Springs U.S.A. 183 K6
Peacock Hills Canada 167 I1
Peaima Falls Guyana 199 F3
Pea Island National Wildlife Refuge nature res. U.S.A. 174 F5
Peak Charles hill Australia 151 C7
Peak Charles National Park Australia 151 C7
Peak District National Park U.K. 47 K10
Peake watercourse Australia 146 C2
Peaked Mountain hill U.S.A. 174 G2
Peak Hill N.S.W. Australia 147 F3
Peak Hill W.A. Australia 151 B5
Peak Mountain U.S.A. 182 E7
Peak Range hills Australia 149 F4
Peaks Mill U.S.A. 176 A7
Peale, Mount U.S.A. 183 O3
Peanut U.S.A. 182 A1
Pearce Point Australia 148 A2
Pearisburg U.S.A. 176 E8
Pearl Canada 172 E2
Pearl r. U.S.A. 175 B6
Pearsall U.S.A. 179 C6
Pearson U.S.A. 175 D6
Pearson Islands Australia 146 B3
Pearston S. Africa 133 J9
Peary Channel Canada 165 J2
Peary Land reg. Greenland 165 P1
Pease r. U.S.A. 179 C5
Peawah r. Australia 150 B4
Peawanuck Canada 168 C2
Pebane Moz. 131 H3
Pebas Peru 198 D5
Pebble Island Falkland Is 205 F8
Pebengko Indon. 75 B3
Peć Kosovo, Srbija Yugo. 58 B6
also known as Peje
Pecan Bayou r. U.S.A. 179 C6
Peçanha Brazil 207 K5
Pecatonica U.S.A. 172 D8
Pécel Hungary 49 Q8
Pechea Romania 58 I3
Pechenga r. Rus. Fed. 44 O1
Pechenga Rus. Fed. 44 O1
formerly known as Petsamo
Pechenga r. Rus. Fed. 44 O1
Pechenitsy Rus. Fed. 43 P1
Pechenik Rus. Fed. 43 U7
Pechersk Rus. Fed. 43 N7
Pechora Rus. Fed. 40 K2
Pechora r. Rus. Fed. 40 J1
Pechora Sea Rus. Fed. see Pechorskoye More
Pechoro-Ilyskiy Zapovednik nature res. Rus. Fed. 40 K3
Pechorskaya Guba b. Rus. Fed. 40 J1
Pechorskoye More sea Rus. Fed. 40 J1
English form Pechora Sea
Pechory Rus. Fed. 42 I4
Pecica Romania 58 C2
Pecineaga Romania 58 J5
Peck U.S.A. 173 K7
Pecora, Capo c. Sardegna Italy 57 A9
Pecos U.S.A. 179 B6
Pecos r. U.S.A. 179 B6
Pécs Hungary 49 P9
formerly known as Fünfkirchen
Pécsvárad Hungary 49 P9
Pedasí Panama 186 C6
Peddavagu r. India 94 C2
Pedda Vagu r. India 94 C2
Pedder, Lake Australia 147 E5
Peddie S. Africa 133 L10
Pededze Latvia 42 I4
Pededze r. Latvia 42 H5
Pedernales Ecuador 198 A4
Pedernales Haiti 187 F3
Pedernales Mex. 181 F7
Pedernales r. U.S.A. 179 C6
Pedernales Venez. 199 F2
Pedernales, Salar de salt flat Chile 204 C2
Pederneiras Brazil 206 E9
Pedersöre Fin. 44 M3
Pediva Angola 127 B9
Pedra Azul Brazil 202 D5
Pedra Badejo Cape Verde 124 [inset]
Pedrada mt. Port. 54 C3
Pedrafita do Cebreiro Spain 54 D2
also known as Piedrafita
Pedra Lume Cape Verde 124 [inset]
Pedra Preta, Serra da mts Brazil 202 B5
Pedras r. Brazil 202 C5
Pedras de Maria da Cruz Brazil 207 I2
Pedras Negras Brazil 201 E3
Pedregal Panama 186 C5
Pedregal Venez. 198 D2
Pedregulho Brazil 206 F7
Pedreiras Maranhão Brazil 202 C3
Pedreiras São Paulo Brazil 206 G9
Pedriceña Mex. 184 E3
Pedro, Point Sri Lanka 94 D4
Pedro Afonso Brazil 202 B4
Pedro Avelino Brazil 202 E3
Pedro Bank sea feature Jamaica 186 D3
Pedro Barros Brazil 206 F11
Pedro Betancourt Cuba 175 D8
Pedro Cays is Jamaica 186 D3
Pedro Chico Col. 198 D4
Pedro Gomes Brazil 203 A6
Pedro Gómez mt. Spain 54 F5
Pedro II, Ilha reg. Brazil/Venez. 199 E4
Pedro Juan Caballero Para. 201 G5
Pedro Leopoldo Brazil 203 C6
Pedro Luro Arg. 204 E5
Pedro Muñoz Spain 55 I5
Pedro Osório Brazil 204 G3
Pedroso Port. 54 C3
Pedro Toledo Brazil 206 F11
Peebinga Australia 146 D3
Peebles U.K. 46 I8
Peebles U.S.A. 176 B7
Peedamulla Aboriginal Reserve Australia 150 A4
Pee Dee r. U.S.A. 175 E5
Peekskill U.S.A. 177 L4
Peel r. Canada 166 C1
Peel Isle of Man 47 H9
Peene r. Germany 49 K2
Peera Fin. 44 M1
Peera Peera Poolanna Lake salt flat Australia 148 C5
Peerless Lake Canada 167 H3
Peers Canada 167 G4
Peery Lake salt flat Australia 147 D2
Pegasus Bay N.Z. 153 G11
Pegnitz Germany 48 I6
Pego Spain 55 K6
Pegu Myanmar 78 B4
also spelt Bago
Pegu admin. div. Myanmar 78 A4
also spelt Bago
Pegu Yoma mts Myanmar 78 A4
Pehlivanköy Turkey 58 H7
Péhonko Benin 125 F4
Pehowa India 96 C3
Pehuajó Arg. 204 E4
Peikang Taiwan 87 G4
also spelt Beigang
Peine Chile 200 C5
Peine Germany 48 H3
Peineta, Cerro mt. Arg. 205 B8
Peint India 94 B1
Peipsi järv l. Estonia/Rus. Fed. see Peipus, Lake
Peipus, Lake Estonia/Rus. Fed. 42 I3
also known as Chudskoye, Ozero or Peipsi järv
Peiraias Greece see Piraeus

Pei Shan mts China see Bei Shan
Peitz Germany 49 L4
Peixe Brazil 202 B5
Peixe r. Goiás Brazil 206 C1
Peixe r. Goiás Brazil 206 E4
Peixe r. São Paulo Brazil 206 B8
Peixe, Rio do r. Brazil 206 A3
Peixes r. Brazil 201 F2
Peixes r. Brazil 207 J9
Peixes, Rio dos r. Brazil 206 B1
Peixian China see Pizhou
Peixian China 87 F1
Peixoto, Represa resr Brazil 206 G7
Peixoto de Azevedo Brazil 202 A4
Peixoto de Azevedo r. Brazil 201 G2
Pejantan i. Indon. 77 D2
Peje Kosovo, Srbija Yugo. see Peć
Pek r. Yugo. 58 C4
Pekabata Indon. 75 A3
Pekalongan Indon. 77 E4
Pekan Malaysia 76 C2
Pekanbaru Indon. 76 C2
also spelt Pakanbaru
Pékans, Rivière aux r. Canada 169 H2
Peki Ghana 125 F5
Pekin U.S.A. 174 B3
Peking China see Beijing
Peklino Rus. Fed. 43 O8
Pelabuhan Kelang Malaysia 76 C2
formerly known as Port Klang or Port Swettenham
Pelabuhan Sandakan inlet Sabah Malaysia 77 G1
Pelada, Pampa hills Arg. 205 C7
Pelado mt. Spain 55 J5
Pelagie, Isole is Sicilia Italy 57 E13
Pelagonija plain Macedonia 58 C7
Pelagonisou, Diavlos sea chan. Greece 59 F9
Pelaihari Indon. 77 F3
Pelalawan Indon. 76 C2
Pelapis i. Indon. 77 E3
Pelasgia Greece 59 D10
also spelt Pelasyía
Pelasyía Greece see Pelasgia
Pelat, Mont mt. France 51 M8
Pelatsoeu mt. Lesotho 133 M5
Pelawanbesar Indon. 77 G2
Pełczyce Poland 49 M2
Peleaga, Vârful mt. Romania 58 D3
Pelechuco Bol. 200 C3
Pelēči Latvia 42 H5
Pelée, Montagne vol. Martinique 187 H4
Pelee Island Canada 168 D5
Pelee Point Canada 168 D5
Peleliu i. Palau 73 H5
also spelt Beliliou
Peleng i. Indon. 75 B3
Peleng, Selat sea chan. Indon. 75 B3
Peleng, Teluk b. Indon. 75 B3
Peles Rus. Fed. 40 I3
Pelhřimov Czech Rep. 49 M6
Pelican Creek r. Australia 149 D3
Pelican Lake l. Canada 167 K4
Pelican Lake U.S.A. 172 D5
Pelican Lake l. U.S.A. 178 D1
Pelican Narrows Canada 167 K4
Pelister mt. Macedonia 58 C8
Pelister nat. park Macedonia 58 C8
Pelješac pen. Croatia 56 J6
Pelkosenniemi Fin. 44 N2
Pella S. Africa 132 D6
Pellatt Lake Canada 167 I1
Pellegrue France 50 G8
Pelleluhu Islands P.N.G. 73 J7
Pello Fin. 44 M2
Pellworm i. Germany 48 F1
Pelly r. Canada 166 B2
Pelly Bay Canada 165 K3
Pelly Crossing Canada 166 B2
Pelly Lake Canada 167 K1
Pelly Mountains Canada 166 C2
Pelokang is Indon. 77 G4
Peloponnese admin. reg. Greece see Peloponnisos
Peloponnese reg. Greece 59 C11
also known as Peloponnisos; historically known as Peloponnesus
Peloponnesus reg. Greece see Peloponnese
Peloponnisos admin. reg. Greece 59 D11
English form Peloponnese; historically known as Peloponnesus
Peloponnisos reg. Greece see Peloponnese
Peloritani, Monti mts Sicilia Italy 57 G11
Pelotas Brazil 204 G3
Pelotas, Rio das r. Brazil 203 B8
Pelovo Bulg. 58 F5
Pelplin Poland 49 P2
Pelsart Group is Australia 151 A6
Peltovuoma Fin. 44 N1
Pelusium tourist site Egypt 108 D6
Pelusium, Bay of Egypt see Tîna, Khalîg el
Pelvoux, Massif du mts France 51 M8
Pemache r. Canada 173 J3
Pemadumcook Lake U.S.A. 174 G2
Pemalang Indon. 77 E4
Pemangkat Indon. 77 E2
Pemarung, Pulau i. Indon. 77 G3
Pematangsiantar Indon. 76 B2
Pemba Moz. 131 I2
formerly known as Porto Amélia
Pemba Zambia 127 E9
Pemba, Baía de b. Moz. 129 D8
Pemba Channel Tanz. 129 C6
Pemba Island Tanz. 129 C6
Pemba North admin. reg. Tanz. 129 C6
Pemba South admin. reg. Tanz. 129 C6
Pemberton Australia 151 A7
Pemberton Canada 166 F5
Pemberton U.S.A. 177 K6
Pembina r. Canada 167 H4
Pembina r. U.S.A. 178 C1
Pembroke Canada 168 E4
Pembroke U.K. 47 H12
also known as Penfro
Pembroke U.S.A. 175 D5
Pembroke, Cape Falkland Is 205 F8
Pembroke, Mount N.Z. 153 B12
Pembroke Pines U.S.A. 175 D7
Pembrokeshire Coast National Park U.K. 47 G12
Pembuanghulu Indon. 77 F3
Pemuco Chile 204 B5
Pen India 94 B2
Pen r. Myanmar 78 A3
Pena Barrosa Bol. 200 D5
Peña Cabollera mt. Spain 55 H3
Peña de Francia mt. Spain 54 E4
Peña de Izaga mt. Spain 55 J2
Peña de Oroel mt. Spain 55 K2
Peñafiel Spain 54 G3
Peñaflor Spain 54 F7
Peñagolosa mt. Spain 55 K4
Peñalara mt. Spain 54 H4
Peñalba de Santiago tourist site Spain 54 E2
Peñalsordo Spain 54 F6
Penamacor Port. 54 D4
Penambo Range mts Sarawak Malaysia see Tama Abu, Banjaran
Peña Mira mt. Spain 54 E3
Peña Nevada, Cerro mt. Mex. 185 F4
Penang state Malaysia see Pinang
Peñaranda de Bracamonte Spain 54 F4
Pen Argyl U.S.A. 177 J5
Penarie Australia 147 D3
Peñarroya mt. Spain 55 K4
Peñarroya-Pueblonuevo Spain 54 F6
Peñas, Cabo de c. Spain 54 F1
Penas, Golfo de g. Chile 205 B7
Peñas Blancas Nicaragua 186 B5
Peñasco watercourse U.S.A. 181 F6

Penasi, Pulau i. Indon. 76 A1
also known as Dedap
Peña Ubiña mt. Spain 54 F1
Peña Utrera hill Spain 54 E6
Pench r. India 96 C5
Pencheng China see Ruichang
Pench National Park India 96 C5
Penck, Cape Antarctica 223 F2
Pendé r. Cent. Afr. Rep. 126 C3
Pendembu Sierra Leone 124 B4
Pender U.S.A. 178 C3
Pender Bay Australia 150 C3
Pender Bay Aboriginal Reserve Australia 150 C3
Pendik Turkey 58 K8
Pendleton U.S.A. 180 C3
Pendleton Bay Canada 166 E4
Pendopo Indon. 76 C3
Pend Oreille r. U.S.A. 180 C2
Pend Oreille Lake U.S.A. 180 C2
Pendra India 97 D5
Penduv India 94 B2
Pendzhikent Tajik. see Panjakent
Penebangan i. Indon. 77 E3
Peneda Gerês, Parque Nacional da nat. park Port. 54 C3
Pene-Mende Dem. Rep. Congo 126 F6
Pénessoulou Benin 125 F4
Penetanguishene Canada 173 N6
Penfield U.S.A. 176 G4
Penfro U.K. see Pembroke
Peng'an China 86 C2
also known as Zhoukou
Penganga r. India 94 C2
Peng Chau i. Hong Kong China 87 [inset]
P'engchia Yü i. Taiwan 87 G3
Penge Dem. Rep. Congo 127 E6
P'enghu Ch'üntao is Taiwan 87 F4
English form Pescadores; also known as P'enghu Liehtao
P'enghu Liehtao is Taiwan see P'enghu Ch'üntao
P'enghu Tao i. Taiwan 87 F4
Pengiki i. Indon. 77 E2
Peng Kang hill Sing. 76 [inset]
Penglai China 85 I4
formerly known as Dengzhou
Pengshan China 86 B2
Pengshui China 87 D2
also known as Hanjia
Peng Siang, Sungai r. Sing. 76 [inset]
Pengwa Myanmar 78 A3
Pengxi China 86 C2
also known as Chicheng
Pengxian China see Pengzhou
Pengze China 87 F2
also known as Longcheng
Pengzhou China 86 B2
formerly known as Pengxian
Penhalonga Zimbabwe 131 G3
Penhoek Pass S. Africa 133 K8
Penhook U.S.A. 176 F9
Peniche Port. 54 B5
Penicuik U.K. 46 I8
Penida i. Indon. 77 F5
Peninga Rus. Fed. 40 E3
Peninsular Malaysia Malaysia 76 C2
also known as Malaya or Semenanjung Malaysia; formerly known as West Malaysia
Penitente, Serra do hills Brazil 202 C4
Pēnjwīn Iraq 107 F4
Penmarch France 50 B5
Penmarch, Pointe de pt France 50 B5
Penn U.S.A. see Penn Hills
Penna, Punta della pt Italy 56 G6
Penne Italy 56 F6
Pennell Coast Antarctica 223 L2
Penner r. India 94 D3
Penneshaw Australia 146 C3
Penn Hills U.S.A. 176 F5
formerly known as Penn
Pennine, Alpi mts Italy/Switz. 51 N7
English form Pennine Alps
Pennine Alps mts Italy/Switz. see Pennine, Alpi
Pennines hills U.K. 47 J9
Pennington S. Africa 133 O7
Pennington Gap U.S.A. 176 B9
Pennsboro U.S.A. 176 E6
Penns Grove U.S.A. 177 J6
Pennsville U.S.A. 177 J6
Pennsylvania state U.S.A. 176 G4
Penny Icecap Canada 165 M3
Penny Point Antarctica 223 K1
Peno Rus. Fed. 43 N5
Penobscot r. U.S.A. 177 Q1
Penobscot Bay U.S.A. 177 Q1
Penola Australia 146 D4
Peñón Blanco Mex. 184 D3
Penong Australia 146 B2
Penonomé Panama 186 C5
Penrhyn atoll Cook Is 221 H6
also known as Tongareva
Penrith Australia 147 F3
Penrith U.K. 47 J9
Pensacola U.S.A. 175 C6
Pensacola Bay i. U.S.A. 175 C6
Pensacola Mountains Antarctica 223 T1
Pensamiento Bol. 201 E3
Pensaukee U.S.A. 172 F6
Pentadaktylos Range mts Cyprus 108 E2
also known as Kyrenia Mountains or Beşparmak Dağları
Pentakota India 95 D2
Pentecost Island Vanuatu 145 F3
also known as Pentecôte, Île; formerly known as Whitsun Island
Pentecôte r. Canada 169 H3
Pentecôte, Île i. Vanuatu see Pentecost Island
Penteleu, Vârful mt. Romania 58 H3
Penticton Canada 166 G5
Pentire Point U.K. 47 G13
Pentland Australia 149 E4
Pentland Firth sea chan. U.K. 46 I5
Pentland Hills U.K. 46 I8
Pentwater U.S.A. 172 G7
Penukonda India 94 C3
Penunjok, Tanjong pt Malaysia 76 C1
Penwegon Myanmar 78 B4
Pen-y-Bont ar Ogwr U.K. see Bridgend
Penygadair hill U.K. 47 I11
Penylan Lake Canada 167 J2
Penyu, Kepulauan is Indon. 75 C4
Penza Rus. Fed. 41 H5
Penzance U.K. 47 G13
Penza Oblast admin. div. Rus. Fed. see Penzenskaya Oblast'
Penzenskaya Oblast' admin. div. Rus. Fed. 41 H5
English form Penza Oblast
Penzhinskaya Guba b. Rus. Fed. 39 Q3
Peoples Creek r. U.S.A. 180 E2
Peoria AZ U.S.A. 183 L8
Peoria IL U.S.A. 174 B3
Peoria Heights U.S.A. 172 D10
Pepeekeo U.S.A. 181 [inset] Z2
Pepel Sierra Leone 124 B4
Peper Sudan 128 B3
Pepworth S. Africa 133 N5
Peqin Albania 58 A7
Pequi Brazil 207 I6
Pequop Mountains U.S.A. 183 J1
Pera Head Australia 149 D2
Peraitepuy Venez. 199 F3
Perak i. Malaysia 76 B1
Perak r. Malaysia 76 C1
Perak state Malaysia 76 C1
Perama Greece 59 F13
Perambalur India 94 C4
Perämeren kansallispuisto nat. park Fin. 44 N2
Perä-Posio Fin. 44 N2
Percé Canada 169 H3
Perche, Collines du hills France 50 G4
Percival Lakes salt flat Australia 150 D4
Percy France 50 E4
Percy U.S.A. 177 N1
Percy Isles Australia 149 F4
Percy Reach l. Canada 173 P6
Perdekop S. Africa 133 N4
Perdepoort pass S. Africa 132 H10
Perdida r. Brazil 202 C4
Perdido r. Brazil 201 F5
Perdido, Monte mt. Spain 55 L2
Perdiguère, Pic mt. France/Spain 55 L2
Perdika Greece 59 B9
Perdizes Brazil 206 F6
Perdões Brazil 207 H8
Perdu, Lac l. Canada 169 G3
Perechyn Ukr. 49 T7
Peregrebnoye Rus. Fed. 38 G3
Pereira Col. 198 C3
Pereira Barreto Brazil 206 B7
Pereira de Eça Angola see Ondjiva
Pereiro Brazil 202 E3
Perekhoda r. Rus. Fed. 43 M3
Perelyub Rus. Fed. 102 B2
Pere Marquette r. U.S.A. 172 G7
Peremetnoye Kazakh. 102 B2
Peremul Par reef India 94 B4
Peremyshl' Rus. Fed. 43 R7
Peremyshlyany Ukr. 41 C6
Perené r. Peru 200 B2
Perenjori Australia 151 B6
Pereshnoye, Ozero l. Rus. Fed. 43 T1
Pereslavl'-Zalesskiy Rus. Fed. 43 T5
Pereslavskiy Natsional'nyy Park nat. park Rus. Fed. 43 T5
Peretu Romania 58 G4
Perevolotskiy Rus. Fed. 102 C2
Pereyaslavka Rus. Fed. 82 D3
Pereyaslav-Khmel'nitskiy Ukr. see Pereyaslav-Khmel'nyts'kyy
Pereyaslav-Khmel'nyts'kyy Ukr. 41 D6
also spelt Pereyaslav-Khmel'nitskiy
Pérez Chile 204 C2
Perg Austria 49 L7
Pergamino Arg. 204 E4
Perge tourist site Turkey 108 B1
Pergine Valsugana Italy 56 D2
Pergola Italy 56 E5
Perhentian Besar i. Malaysia 76 C1
Perho Fin. 44 N3
Periam Romania 58 B2
Péribonca r. Canada 169 F3
Perico Arg. 200 D6
Pericos Mex. 184 D3
Peridot U.S.A. 183 N8
Perieni Romania 58 I2
Périers France 50 E3
Perigoso, Canal sea chan. Brazil 202 B2
Périgueux France 50 G7
Perijá, Parque Nacional nat. park Venez. 198 C2
Perija, Sierra de mts Venez. 198 C2
Perim Island Yemen see Barīm
Peringat Malaysia 79 C1
Periprava Romania 58 K3
Perişoru Romania 58 I4
Peristera i. Greece 59 E9
Peristerio Greece 59 E10
Periteasca-Gura Portiţei nature res. Romania 58 K4
Perito Moreno Arg. 205 C7
Perito Moreno, Parque Nacional nat. park Arg. 205 B7
Periyar r. India 94 C4
Perlas, Laguna de lag. Nicaragua 186 C4
Perlas, Punta de pt Nicaragua 186 C4
Perleberg Germany 48 I2
Perlis state Malaysia 76 C1
Perm' Rus. Fed. 40 K4
formerly known as Molotov
Permas Rus. Fed. 40 H4
Përmet Albania 59 B8
Perm Oblast admin. div. Rus. Fed. see Permskaya Oblast'
Permskaya Oblast' admin. div. Rus. Fed. 40 K4
English form Perm Oblast; formerly known as Molotovskaya Oblast'
Permuda i. Croatia 56 G4
Pernå Fin. 42 H1
Pernambuco Brazil see Recife
Pernambuco state Brazil 202 E4
Pernatty Lagoon salt flat Australia 146 C2
Pernem India 94 B3
Pernik Bulg. 58 E6
formerly known as Dimitrovo
Perniö Fin. 45 M3
Pernov Estonia see Pärnu
Perolândia Brazil 206 A4
Peron, Cape Australia 151 A5
Peron Islands Australia 148 A2
Péronnas France 51 L6
Péronne France 51 I3
Peron Peninsula Australia 151 A5
Perote Mex. 185 F5
Perpignan France 51 I10
Perrégaux Alg. see Mohammadia
Perris U.S.A. 183 G8
Perros-Guirec France 50 C4
Perry Canada 173 I3
Perry r. Canada 167 K1
Perry FL U.S.A. 175 D6
Perry GA U.S.A. 175 D5
Perry IA U.S.A. 178 D3
Perry MI U.S.A. 173 I8
Perry OK U.S.A. 179 C4
Perry Hall U.S.A. 177 I6
Perrymennyy, Cape Antarctica 223 G2
Perrysburg U.S.A. 176 B4
Perryton U.S.A. 179 B4
Perryville AR U.S.A. 179 D5
Perryville KY U.S.A. 176 A8
Persepolis tourist site Iran 100 C4
Persia country Asia see Iran
Persian Gulf Asia see The Gulf
Persis prov. Iran see Fārs
Pertek Turkey 107 D3
Perth Tas. Australia 147 E5

▶Perth W.A. Australia 151 A6
State capital of Western Australia. 4th most populous city in Oceania.
world [cities] ▶▶▶ 24–25

Perth Canada 168 E4
Perth U.K. 46 I7
Perth-Andover Canada 169 H4
Pertominsk Rus. Fed. 40 F2
Pertteli Fin. 42 E1
Pertuis France 51 L9
Pertuis Breton sea chan. France 50 E6
Pertuis d'Antioche sea chan. France 50 E6
Pertunmaa Fin. 45 N3
Pertusato, Capo c. Corse France 56 B7
Peru Bol. 200 D3
Peru atoll Kiribati see Beru

▶Peru country S. America 200 B2
3rd largest and 4th most populous country in South America.
southamerica [countries] ▶▶▶ 192–193

Peru IL U.S.A. 172 D9
Peru IN U.S.A. 174 C3
Peru NY U.S.A. 177 L1
Perućko Jezero l. Croatia 56 I5
Perugia Italy 56 E5
historically known as Perusia
Perugorría Arg. 204 F3
Peruhumpenai Mountains Reserve nature res. Indon. 75 B3
Peruíbe Brazil 206 G11
Peruru India 94 C3
Perushtitsa Bulg. 58 F6
Perusia Italy see Perugia
Péruwelz Belgium 51 J2
Pervoavgustovskiy Rus. Fed. 43 Q9
Pervomaisc Moldova 58 K2
Pervomay Kyrg. 103 H4
also known as Pervomayskoye; formerly known as Pervomayskiy
Pervomaysk Rus. Fed. 40 G5
formerly known as Tashino
Pervomays'k Ukr. 41 D6
formerly known as Ol'viopol'
Pervomayskiy Kazakh. 103 J2
Pervomayskiy Kyrg. see Pervomay
Pervomayskiy Rus. Fed. see Novodvinsk
Pervomayskiy Chitinskaya Oblast' Rus. Fed. 85 G1
Pervomayskiy Orenburgskaya Oblast' Rus. Fed. 102 C2
Pervomayskiy Smolenskaya Oblast' Rus. Fed. 43 N7
Pervomayskiy Tambovskaya Oblast' Rus. Fed. 41 G5
formerly known as Bogoyavlenskoye
Pervomayskiy Tul'skaya Oblast' Rus. Fed. 43 S7
Pervomayskoye Kyrg. see Pervomay
Pervomayskoye Rus. Fed. 82 B1
Pervomayskoye Rus. Fed. 43 K1
Pervomays'kyy Ukr. 41 F6
formerly known as Likhachevo or Likhachyovo
Pervorechenskiy Rus. Fed. 39 Q3
Per'yevo Rus. Fed. 43 U2
Pes' Rus. Fed. 43 P3
Pes' r. Rus. Fed. 43 Q2
Pesa r. Italy 56 D5
Pesaguan r. Indon. 77 E3
Pesaro Italy 56 E5
historically known as Pisaurum
Pescadero U.S.A. 182 B4
Pescadores is Taiwan see P'enghu Ch'üntao
Pescadores, Punta pt Peru 200 B4
Pescara Italy 56 G6
Pescara r. Italy 56 G6
Pescari Romania 58 C4
Peschanokopskoye Rus. Fed. 41 G7
Peschanoye Rus. Fed. see Yashkul'
Peschanyy, Mys pt Kazakh. 102 B4
Peschici Italy 56 I7
Pescia Italy 56 C5
Pesebre, Punta pt Canary Is 122 B3
Pesha r. Rus. Fed. 40 H2
Peshanjan Afgh. 101 E3
Peshawar Pak. 101 G3
Peshkopi Albania 58 B7
Peshnyye, Ostrova is Kazakh. see Bol'shiye Peshnyye, Ostrova
Peshtera Bulg. 58 F6
Peshtigo U.S.A. 172 F5
Peshtigo r. U.S.A. 172 F6
Peski Kazakh. 103 F1
Peski Moskovskaya Oblast' Rus. Fed. 43 T6
Peski Voronezhskaya Oblast' Rus. Fed. 41 G6
Peski Turkm. 103 E5
Peski Karakum des. Kazakh. see Karakum Desert
Peski Karakumy des. Turkm. see Karakum Desert
Peskovka Rus. Fed. 40 J4
Pesnica Slovenia 56 H2
Pesochnoye Rus. Fed. 43 U3
Pesochnya Rus. Fed. 43 O8
Peso da Régua Port. 54 D3
Pespire Hond. 186 B4
Pesqueira Brazil 202 E4
Pesqueira Mex. 184 C2
Pessac France 50 F8
Pessinki naturreservat nature res. Sweden 40 B2
Pestovo Rus. Fed. 43 Q3
Pestravka Rus. Fed. 102 B1
Pestyaki Rus. Fed. 40 G4
Petah Tiqwa Israel 108 F5
Petaihari Martapura Reserve nature res. Indon. 77 F3
Petäjävesi Fin. 44 N3
Petalidi Greece 59 C12
Petalioi i. Greece 59 F10
Petaluma U.S.A. 182 B3
Pétange Lux. 51 L3
Petangis Indon. 77 F3
Petare Venez. 199 E2
Petas Greece 59 C9
Petatlán Mex. 185 E5
Petauke Zambia 127 F8
Petawaga, Lac l. Canada 173 R4
Petawawa Canada 173 P5
Petén Itzá, Lago l. Guat. 185 H5
Petenwell Lake U.S.A. 172 D6
Peterbell Canada 168 D3
Peterborough S.A. Australia 146 C3
Peterborough Vic. Australia 147 D4
Peterborough Canada 168 E4
Peterborough U.K. 47 L11
Peterborough U.S.A. 177 N3
Peterhead U.K. 46 K6
Peter I Island Antarctica 222 R2
also known as Peter I Øy
Peter I Øy i. Antarctica see Peter I Island
Peter Lougheed Provincial Park Canada 167 H5
Petermann Aboriginal Land res. Australia 148 A5
Petermann Bjerg nunatak Greenland 165 Q2
Petermann Ranges mts Australia 148 A5
Peter Pond Lake Canada 167 I4
Petersburg S. Africa 133 I9
Petersburg AK U.S.A. 164 F4
Petersburg IL U.S.A. 174 B4
Petersburg IN U.S.A. 174 C4
Petersburg NY U.S.A. 177 L3
Petersburg OH U.S.A. 176 E5
Petersburg VA U.S.A. 176 H8
Petersburg WV U.S.A. 176 F7
Petershagen Germany 48 F3
Peters Mine Guyana 199 G3
Peterstown U.S.A. 176 E8
Petersville U.S.A. 164 D3
Peter the Great Bay Rus. Fed. see Petra Velikogo, Zaliv
Pétervárad Vojvodina, Srbija Yugo. see Petrovaradin
Peterwardein Vojvodina, Srbija Yugo. see Petrovaradin
Peth India 94 B2
Petilia Policastro Italy 57 I9
Petit Atlas mts Morocco see Anti Atlas
Petitcodiac Canada 169 H4
Petite Creuse r. France 51 H6
Petit-Goâve Haiti 187 E3
Petitjean Morocco see Sidi Kacem
Petit Lac Manicouagan l. Canada 169 H2
Petit-Loango, Réserve de nature res. Gabon 126 A5
Petit Maine r. France 50 E5
Petit Mécatina r. Canada see Little Mecatina
Petit Mécatina r. Canada 169 J3
Petit Mécatina, Île du i. Canada 169 J3
also known as Little Mecatina Island
Petit Morin r. France 51 J4
Petitot r. Canada 166 F2
Petit St-Bernard, Col du pass France 51 M7
Petkino Rus. Fed. 43 U7
Petkula Fin. 44 N2
Petlad India 96 B5
Petlawad India 96 B5
Peto Mex. 185 H4
Petoskey U.S.A. 173 I5
Petra tourist site Jordan 108 G7
also spelt Batrā'
Petras, Mount Antarctica 222 P1
Petra tou Romiou tourist site Cyprus see Aphrodite's Birthplace
Petra Velikogo, Zaliv b. Rus. Fed. 82 C4
English form Peter the Great Bay
Petre, Point Canada 173 P7
Petrich Bulg. 58 E7
Petrified Forest National Park U.S.A. 183 O6
Petrijevci Croatia 56 K3
Petrikau Poland see Piotrków Trybunalski
Petrikov Belarus see Pyetrykaw
Petrila Romania 58 E3
Petrinja Croatia 56 I3
Petro, Cerro de mt. Chile 204 C3
Petroaleksandrovsk Uzbek. see Turtkul'
Petrodvorets Rus. Fed. 43 K2
Petrograd Rus. Fed. see St Petersburg
Petrokov Poland see Piotrków Trybunalski
Petrokrepost' Rus. Fed. see Shlissel'burg
Petrokrepost', Bukhta b. Rus. Fed. 43 M1
Petrolândia Brazil 202 E4
Petrolia Canada 173 K8
Petrolina Amazonas Brazil 199 E5
Petrolina Pernambuco Brazil 202 D4
Petrolina de Goiás Brazil 206 D3
Petron, Limni l. Greece 58 C8
Petropavl Kazakh. see Petropavlovsk
Petropavlovka Kazakh. 103 J3
Petropavlovka Rus. Fed. 85 E1
Petropavlovka Rus. Fed. 41 G6
Petropavlovsk Kazakh. 38 G4
also known as Petropavl
Petropavlovsk Rus. Fed. see Petropavlovsk-Kamchatskiy
Petropavlovsk-Kamchatskiy Rus. Fed. 39 P4
historically known as Petropavlovsk
Petrópolis Brazil 207 J9
Petroșani Romania 58 E3
Petrovac Bos.-Herz. see Bosanski Petrovac
Petrovac Srbija Yugo. 58 C4
Petrovaradin Vojvodina, Srbija Yugo. 58 A3
also known as Pétervárad; historically known as Peterwardein
Petrovichi Rus. Fed. 43 N8
Petrovsk Rus. Fed. 41 H5
Petrovsk Rus. Fed. 43 V5
Petrovskoye Moskovskaya Oblast' Rus. Fed. 43 R5
Petrovskoye Rus. Fed. see Svetlograd
Petrovskoye Yaroslavskaya Oblast' Rus. Fed. 43 U4
Petrovsk-Zabaykal'skiy Rus. Fed. 85 F1
Petrov Val Rus. Fed. 41 H6
Petrozavodsk Rus. Fed. 40 E3
Petru Rareș Romania 58 F1
Petrusburg S. Africa 133 J6
Petrus Steyn S. Africa 133 M4
Petrusville S. Africa 133 I7
Petsamo Rus. Fed. see Pechenga
Petsana S. Africa 133 M4
Pettau Slovenia see Ptuj
Petukhovo Rus. Fed. 38 G4
Petushki Rus. Fed. 43 U6
formerly known as Novyye Petushki
Peuetsagu, Gunung vol. Indon. 76 B1
Peurasuvanto Fin. 44 N2
Peureula Indon. 76 B1
Pevek Rus. Fed. 39 R3
Pêxung China 89 F5
Peza r. Rus. Fed. 40 H2
Pézenas France 51 J9
Pezinok Slovakia 49 O7
Pfaffenhofen an der Ilm Germany 48 I7
Pfälzer Wald hills Germany 48 E6
Pfälzer Wald park Germany 48 E6
Pfarrkirchen Germany 49 J7
Pforzheim Germany 48 F7
Pfullendorf Germany 48 G8
Pfungstadt Germany 48 F6
Phagwara India 96 B3
Phahameng S. Africa 133 K5
Phalaborwa S. Africa 131 F4
Phalia Pak. 101 H3
Phalodi India 96 B4
Phalsbourg France 51 N4
Phalsund India 96 A4
Phaltan India 94 B2
Phalut Peak India/Nepal 97 F4
Phangan, Ko i. Thai. 79 C6
Phangnga Thai. 79 B6
Phan Rang Vietnam 79 E6
Phan Ri Vietnam 79 E6
Phan Thiêt Vietnam 79 E6
Phan Thiêt, Vinh b. Vietnam 79 E6
Phaphund India 96 C4
Phaplu Nepal 97 E4
Phat Diêm Vietnam 78 D3
Phatthalung Thai. 79 C7
Phayao Thai. 78 B4
Phek India 97 G4
Phelp r. Australia 148 B2
Phelps NY U.S.A. 177 H3
Phelps WI U.S.A. 172 D4
Phen Thai. 78 C4
Phenix U.S.A. 176 G8
Phenix City U.S.A. 175 C5
Phephane watercourse S. Africa 132 G2
Phet Buri Thai. 79 B5
Phetchabun Thai. 78 C4
Phichit Thai. 78 C4
Philadelphia Jordan see 'Ammān
Philadelphia S. Africa 132 C10
Philadelphia Turkey see Alaşehir
Philadelphia MS U.S.A. 175 B5
Philadelphia NY U.S.A. 177 J1
Philadelphia PA U.S.A. 177 J6
Philae tourist site Egypt 121 G4
Philip U.S.A. 178 B2
Philip Atoll Micronesia see Sorol
Philippeville Alg. see Skikda
Philippeville Belgium 51 K2
Philippi U.S.A. 176 E6
Philippi, Lake salt flat Australia 148 C5
▶Philippines country Asia 74 A3
spelt Filipinas or Pilipinas in Filipino
asia [countries] ▶▶▶ 64–67
Philippine Sea N. Pacific Ocean 74 B2

▶Philippine Trench sea feature N. Pacific Ocean 220 C5
3rd deepest trench in the world.

Philippolis S. Africa 133 J7
Philippolis Road S. Africa 133 J7
Philippopolis Bulg. see Plovdiv
Philipsburg Neth. Antilles 187 H3
Philipsburg U.S.A. 180 D3
Philip Smith Mountains U.S.A. 164 E3
Philipstown S. Africa 133 I7
Phillip Island Australia 147 E4
Phillips r. Australia 151 C7
Phillips ME U.S.A. 177 O1
Phillips WI U.S.A. 172 C5
Phillips Arm Canada 166 E5
Phillipsburg KS U.S.A. 178 C4
Phillipsburg NJ U.S.A. 177 J5
Phillips Inlet Canada 165 K1
Phillips Range hills Australia 150 D3
Phillipston U.S.A. 177 M3
Philmont U.S.A. 177 L3
Philomelium Turkey see Akşehir
Philpott Reservoir U.S.A. 176 E9
Phimun Mangsahan Thai. 79 D5
Phiritona S. Africa 133 L4
Phitsanulok Thai. 78 C4
Phlox U.S.A. 172 D5

▶Phnom Penh Cambodia 79 D6
Capital of Cambodia. Also spelt Phnum Pénh.

Phnum Pénh Cambodia see Phnom Penh
Pho, Laem pt Thai. 79 C7
Phoenicia U.S.A. 177 K3

▶Phoenix AZ U.S.A. 183 L8
State capital of Arizona.

Phoenix NY U.S.A. 177 I2
Phoenix Island Kiribati see Rawaki
Phoenix Islands Kiribati 145 H2
Phoenixville U.S.A. 177 J5
Phokwane S. Africa 133 N1
Phola S. Africa 133 N3
Phomolong S. Africa 133 L4
Phon Thai. 78 C5
Phong Nha Vietnam 78 D4
Phôngsali Laos 78 C3
also spelt Phong Saly
Phong Saly Laos see Phôngsali
Phong Thô Vietnam 78 C3
Phosphate Hill Australia 149 D4
Phrae Thai. 78 C4
Phra Nakhon Si Ayutthaya Thai. see Ayutthaya
Phrao Thai. 78 B4
Phra Saeng Thai. 79 B6
Phra Thong, Ko i. Thai. 79 B6
Phuchong-Nayoi National Park Thai. 79 D5
Phu Cuong Vietnam see Thu Dâu Môt
Phuduhudu Botswana 131 E4
Phuentsholing Bhutan 97 F4
also spelt Phuntsholing
Phuket Thai. 79 B7
Phuket, Ko i. Thai. 79 B7
Phu-khieo Wildlife Reserve nature res. Thai. 78 C4
Phulabani India 95 E1
Phulpur India 97 D4
Phu Luang Wildlife Reserve nat. park Thai. 78 C4
Phu Ly Vietnam 78 D3
Phumi Chhuk Cambodia 79 D6
also known as Chhuk
Phumĭ Kâmpóng Trâlach Cambodia 79 D5
Phumĭ Mlu Prey Cambodia 79 D5
Phumĭ Prâmaôy Cambodia 79 C5
Phumĭ Sâmraông Cambodia 79 C5
also known as Samrong
Phuntsholing Bhutan see Phuentsholing
Phu Phac Mo mt. Vietnam 78 C3
Phu Phan National Park Thai. 78 C4
Phu Quôc, Đao i. Vietnam 79 C6
formerly known as Quan Phu Quoc
Phuthaditjhaba S. Africa 133 M5
Phu Tho Vietnam 78 D3
Phu Vinh Vietnam see Tra Vinh
Pia Aboriginal Reserve Australia 151 B5
Piabung, Gunung mt. Indon. 77 F2
Piaca Brazil 202 C3
Piacatu Brazil 206 C8
Piacenza Italy 56 B3
historically known as Placentia
Piacouadie, Lac l. Canada 169 G3
Piadena Italy 56 C3
Piagochioui r. Canada 168 E2
Pian r. Australia 147 F2
Piana di Catania plain Sicilia Italy 57 G11
Piangil Australia 147 D3
Pianguan China 85 F4
Pianoro Italy 56 D4
Pianosa, Isola i. Italy 56 C6
Piaseczno Poland 49 S3
Piaski Poland 49 T4
Piassabussu Brazil 202 E4
Piatã Brazil 202 D5
Piatra Romania 58 G5
Piatra Neamț Romania 58 H2
Piatra Olt Romania 58 F4
Piatra Şoimului Romania 58 H2
Piauí r. Brazil 202 D3
Piauí state Brazil 202 D3
Piauí, Serra de hills Brazil 202 D4
Piave r. Italy 56 E3
Piazza Armerina Sicilia Italy 57 G11
Piazzi, Cima de' mt. Italy 56 C2
Piazzi, Isla i. Chile 205 B8
Pibor r. Sudan 128 B2
Pibor Post Sudan 128 B3
Pica Chile 200 C5
Picacho U.S.A. 183 M9
Picachos, Cerro dos mt. Mex. 184 B2
Picardie admin. reg. France 51 I3
Picardie reg. France see Picardy
Picardy reg. France 50 H3
also spelt Picardie
Picassent Spain 55 K5
Picayune U.S.A. 175 B6
Picháchic Mex. 184 D2
Pichanal Arg. 201 D5
Pichilemu Chile 204 B4
Pichilingue Mex. 184 C3
Pichi Mahuida Arg. 204 D5
Pichincha prov. Ecuador 198 B5
Pichor India 96 C4
Pichucalco Mex. 185 G5
Pic Island Canada 172 G2
Pickens U.S.A. 176 E7
Pickerel Lake Canada 172 B2
Pickering Canada 173 N7
Pickering U.K. 47 L9
Pickford U.S.A. 173 I4
Pickle Lake Canada 168 B3
Pico Bonito, Parque Nacional nat. park Hond. 186 B4
Pico da Neblina, Parque Nacional do nat. park Brazil 199 E4
Pico de Orizaba, Parque Nacional nat. park Mex. 185 F5
Pico de Tancítaro, Parque Nacional nat. park Mex. 185 E5
Picos Brazil 202 D3
Picos, Punta dos pt Spain 54 C3
Picota Peru 198 B6
Pico Truncado Arg. 205 D7
Pic River Canada 172 G2
Picton Australia 147 F3
Picton Canada 168 E5
Picton N.Z. 152 I9
Picton, Mount Australia 147 E5
Pictou Canada 169 I4
Picture Butte Canada 167 H5
Pictured Rocks National Lakeshore nature res. U.S.A. 172 G4
Picuí Brazil 202 E3
Picún Leufú Arg. 204 C5
Pidarak Pak. 101 E5
Pidurutalagala mt. Sri Lanka 94 D5
Piedade Brazil 206 F10
Pie de Palo, Sierra mts Arg. 204 C3
Piedimonte Matese Italy 56 G7
Piedmont admin. reg. Italy see Piemonte
Piedmont AL U.S.A. 175 C5
Piedmont MO U.S.A. 174 B4
Piedmont OH U.S.A. 176 D5
Piedmont Lake U.S.A. 176 D5
Piedra r. Spain 55 J3
Piedrabuena Spain 54 G5
Piedra de Aguila Arg. 204 C6
Piedrafita Spain see Pedrafita do Cebreiro
Piedrahita Spain 54 F4
Piedralaves Spain 54 G4
Piedras, Punta pt Arg. 204 F4
Piedras Blancas Spain 54 F1
Piedras Blancas Point U.S.A. 182 C6
Piedras Negras Guat. 185 H5
Piedras Negras Coahuila Mex. 185 E2
Piedras Negras Veracruz Mex. 185 F5
Pie Island Canada 172 D2
Pieksämäki Fin. 44 N3
Pielavesi Fin. 44 N3
Pielavesi l. Fin. 44 N3
Pielinen l. Fin. 44 O3
Pieljekaise nationalpark nat. park Sweden 44 L2
Piemonte admin. reg. Italy 56 A4
English form Piedmont
Pienaarsrivier S. Africa 133 M2
Pieniężno Poland 49 R1
Pieniński Park Narodowy nat. park Poland 49 R6
Pieninský nat. park Slovakia 49 R6
Pieńsk Poland 49 M4
Pierce U.S.A. 178 C3
Pierce Lake Canada 167 M4
Pierceland Canada 167 I4
Pierceton U.S.A. 172 H9
Pieria mts Greece 59 D8

▶Pierre U.S.A. 178 B2
State capital of South Dakota.

Pierre, Bayou r. U.S.A. 175 B6
Pierre Bayou r. U.S.A. 179 D6
Pierrelatte France 51 K8
Pieskehaure l. Sweden 44 L2
Piešťany Slovakia 49 O7
Pietermaritzburg S. Africa 133 O6
Pietersaari Fin. see Jakobstad
Pietersburg S. Africa 131 F4
also known as Polokwane
Piet Plessis S. Africa 133 I3
Pietraperzia Sicilia Italy 57 G11
Pietrasanta Italy 56 C5
Pietra Spada, Passo di pass Italy 57 I10
Piet Retief S. Africa 133 O4
Pietrosu, Vârful mt. Romania 58 G1
Pieve di Cadore Italy 56 E2
Pievepelago Italy 56 C4
Pigeon r. Canada/U.S.A. 174 B1
Pigeon Bay Canada 173 K9
Pigeon Lake Canada 167 H4
Pigeon River U.S.A. 172 D2
Pigg r. U.S.A. 176 F8
Piggott U.S.A. 174 B4
Pigg's Peak Swaziland 133 P2
Pigon, Limni l. Greece 59 C9
Pigs, Bay of Cuba 186 C2
also known as Cochinos, Bahía de
Pigüé Arg. 204 E5
Piguicas mt. Mex. 185 F4
Piha N.Z. 152 I4
Pihama N.Z. 152 H7
Pihani India 96 D4
Pi He r. China 87 F1
Pihkva järv l. Estonia/Rus. Fed. see Pskov, Lake
Pihlajavesi l. Fin. 45 O3
Pihlava Fin. 45 M3
Pihtipudas Fin. 44 N3
Piikkiö Fin. 42 D1
Piippola Fin. 44 N2
Piirissaar i. Estonia 42 I3
Piirsalu Estonia 42 F2
Piispajärvi Fin. 44 O2
Piji China see Puge
Pijijiapan Mex. 185 G6
Pikalevo Rus. Fed. 43 P2
Pike NY U.S.A. 176 G3
Pike WV U.S.A. 176 D6
Pikelot i. Micronesia 73 K5
formerly known as Coquille
Pikes Peak U.S.A. 180 F5
Piketberg S. Africa 132 C9
Piketon U.S.A. 176 B6
Pikeville KY U.S.A. 176 C8
Pikeville TN U.S.A. 174 C5
Pikihatiti b. N.Z. see Port Pegasus
Pikirakatahi mt. N.Z. see Earnslaw, Mount
Pikou China 85 I4
Pikounda Congo 126 C4
Pila Arg. 204 F5
Piła Poland 49 N2
historically known as Schneidemühl
Pila mt. Spain 55 J6
Pilagá r. Arg. 204 F2
Pilanesberg National Park S. Africa 133 L2
Pilani India 96 B3
Pilar Buenos Aires Arg. 204 F4
Pilar Córdoba Arg. 204 E3
Pilar Para. 201 F6
Pilar Phil. 74 C4
Pilar, Cabo c. Chile 205 B9
Pilar do Sul Brazil 206 F10
Pilas i. Phil. 74 B5
Pilas Spain 54 E7
Pilas Channel Phil. 74 B5
Pilat, Mont mt. France 51 K7
Pilat, Parc Naturel Régional du nature res. France 51 K7
Pilaya r. Bol. 201 D5
Pilcaniyeu Arg. 204 C6
Pilcomayo r. Bol./Para. 201 F6
Pilenkovo Georgia see Gant'iadi
Piler India 94 C3
Pili Greece see Pyli
Pili Phil. 74 B3
Pili, Cerro mt. Chile 200 D5
also known as Acamarachi
Piliakalnis hill Lith. 42 F7
Pilibangan India 96 B3
Pilibhit India 96 C3
Pilica r. Poland 49 S4
Piliga Nature Reserve Australia 147 F2
Pilipinas country Asia see Philippines
Pilisi park Hungary 49 P8
Pillau Rus. Fed. see Baltiysk
Pillcopata Peru 200 C3
Pilliga Australia 147 F2
Pillo, Isla del i. Arg. 204 E4
Pillsbury, Lake U.S.A. 182 B2
Pil'na Rus. Fed. 40 H5
Pil'nya, Ozero l. Rus. Fed. 40 K1
Pilões, Serra dos mts Brazil 206 F4
Pilón Cuba 186 D3
Pilón r. Mex. 179 C7
Pilos Greece see Pylos
Pilot Mountain hill U.S.A. 176 E9
Pilot Peak U.S.A. 182 G3
Pilot Point U.S.A. 164 D4
Pilot Rock U.S.A. 180 C3
Pilot Station U.S.A. 164 C3
Pilsen Czech Rep. see Plzeň
Pilsen U.S.A. 172 F6
Piltene Latvia 42 C4
Pilu, Nam r. Myanmar 78 B4
Pilvė r. Lith. 42 E7
Pilviškiai Lith. 42 E7
Pima U.S.A. 183 O9
Pimenta Bueno Brazil 201 E2
Pimpalner India 94 B1
Pimpri India 94 B1
Pimu Dem. Rep. Congo 126 D4
Pin r. Myanmar 78 A3
Pina r. Belarus 42 H9
Pinahat India 96 C4
Pinaleno Mountains U.S.A. 183 N9
Pinamalayan Phil. 74 B3
Pinamar Arg. 204 F5
Pinang Malaysia see George Town
Pinang i. Malaysia 76 C1
Pinang state Malaysia 76 C1
also known as Pulau Pinang; formerly spelt Penang
Pinar mt. Spain 54 F8
Pinar, Puerto del pass Spain 55 I6
Pınarbaşı Turkey 107 D3
also known as Aziziye
Pinar del Río Cuba 186 C2
Pinarhisar Turkey 106 A2

index P

Piñas Ecuador **198** B5
Pinatubo, Mt *vol.* Phil. **73** F3
Pincher Creek Canada **167** H5
Pinckneyville U.S.A. **174** B4
Pinconning U.S.A. **173** J7
Pincota Romania *see* **Pâncota**
Pińczów Poland **49** R5
Pindaíba Brazil **206** A1
Pindamonhangaba Brazil **207** H9
Pindar Australia **151** A6
Pindar *r.* India **96** C3
Pindaré *r.* Brazil **202** C2
Pind Dadan Khan Pak. **101** H3
Pindhos Óros *mts* Greece *see* **Pindus Mountains**
Pindi Batiau Pak. **101** H4
Pindi Gheb Pak. **101** H3
Pindobal Brazil **202** B2
Pindos *mts* Greece *see* **Pindus Mountains**
Pindos *nat. park* Greece **59** C9
Pindus Mountains Greece **59** B9
also known as Píndhos Óros; *also spelt* Píndos
Pindwara India **96** B4
Pine *watercourse* Australia **146** D3
Pine *r. MI* U.S.A. **172** H6
Pine *r. MI* U.S.A. **173** I7
Pine *r. WI* U.S.A. **172** C7
Pine *r. WI* U.S.A. **172** E5
Pine, Cape Canada **169** K4
Pine Bluff U.S.A. **174** A5
Pine Bluffs U.S.A. **180** F4
Pine City U.S.A. **178** D2
Pine Creek Australia **148** A2
Pine Creek *r.* U.S.A. **176** H4
Pine Creek *watercourse* U.S.A. **183** H1
Pinecrest U.S.A. **182** D3
Pinedale U.S.A. **180** E4
Pine Dock Canada **167** L5
Pine Falls Canada **167** L5
Pinega Rus. Fed. **40** G2
Pinega *r.* Rus. Fed. **40** G2
Pinegrove Australia **151** A5
Pine Grove *KY* U.S.A. **176** A7
Pine Grove *PA* U.S.A. **177** I5
Pine Grove *WV* U.S.A. **176** E6
Pine Hills *CA* U.S.A. **182** G7
Pine Hills *FL* U.S.A. **175** D6
Pinehouse Lake Canada **167** J4
Pinehouse Lake *l.* Canada **167** J4
Pineimuta *r.* Canada **168** B2
Pineios *r.* Greece **59** D9
also spelt Piniós
Pineiou, Techniti Limni *resr* Greece **59** C11
Pine Island Bay Antarctica **222** R2
Pine Island Glacier Antarctica **222** R1
Pine Islands *FL* U.S.A. **175** D7
Pine Islands *FL* U.S.A. **175** D7
Pine Knot U.S.A. **176** A9
Pinellas Park U.S.A. **175** D7
Pine Mountain U.S.A. **182** C6
Pine Peak U.S.A. **183** K7
Pine Point Canada **167** H2
Pine Point *pt* Canada **167** H2
Pineridge U.S.A. **182** E4
Pine Ridge U.S.A. **178** B3
Pine Ridge Indian Reservation *res.* U.S.A. **178** B3
Pinerolo Italy **51** N8
Pines, Isle of *i.* Cuba *see* **La Juventud, Isla de**
Pines, Isle of *i.* New Caledonia *see* **Pins, Île des**
Pines, Lake o' the U.S.A. **179** D5
Pineto Italy **56** G6
Pinetop U.S.A. **183** O7
Pinetown S. Africa **133** O6
Pine Valley U.S.A. **177** I3
Pineville *KY* U.S.A. **176** B9
Pineville *LA* U.S.A. **179** D6
Pineville *WV* U.S.A. **176** D8
Ping, Mae Nam *r.* Thai. **78** C5
Pingal Jammu and Kashmir **96** B1
Ping'an China **84** D4
formerly known as Ping'anyi
Ping'anyi China *see* **Ping'an**
Pingba China **86** C3
Pingbian China **86** B4
also known as Yupin
Pingchang China **86** C2
also known as Jiangkou
Ping Dao *i.* China **85** H5
Pingding China **85** G4
Pingdingbu China *see* **Guyuan**
Pingdingshan China **87** E1
Pingdong Taiwan *see* **P'ingtung**
Pingdu China *see* **Anfu**
Pingdu China **85** H4
Pinggu China **85** H3
Pingguo China **87** C4
also known as Matou
Pinghai China **87** E4
Pinghe China **87** F3
also known as Xiaoxi
Pinghu China **87** G2
Pingjiang China **87** E2
Pingle China **87** D3
Pingli China **87** D1
Pingliang China **85** E5
Pinglu China **87** D1
formerly known as Shengrenjian
Pingluo China **85** E4
Pingma China *see* **Tiandong**
Pingnan *Fujian* China **87** F3
also known as Gufeng
Pingnan *Guangxi* China **87** D4
Pingquan China **85** H3
Pingshan China *see* **Huidong**
Pingshan *Hebei* China **85** G4
Pingshan *Sichuan* China **86** C2
Pingshan China *see* **Luquan**
Pingshi China **87** E3
Pingshu China *see* **Daicheng**
Pingtan China **87** F3
also known as Tancheng
Pingtan Dao *i.* China *see* **Haitan Dao**
P'ingtung Taiwan **87** G4
also spelt Pingdong
Pingwu China **86** C1
also known as Long'an
Pingxi China *see* **Yuping**
Pingxiang China *see* **Tongwei**
Pingxiang *Guangxi* China **86** C4
Pingxiang *Jiangxi* China **87** E3
Pingyang *Heilong.* China **85** J1
Pingyang *Zhejiang* China **87** G3
also known as Kunyang
Pingyao China **85** G4
Pingyi China **85** H5
Pingyin China **85** H4
Pingyu China **87** E1
also known as Guhuai
Pingyuan *Guangdong* China **87** E3
also known as Dazhe
Pingyuan *Shandong* China **85** H4
Pingyuanjie China **86** B4
Pingzhai China **87** D3
Pinhal Brazil **206** G9
Pinhal Novo Port. **54** C6
Pinheiro Brazil **202** C2
Pinheiro Machado Brazil **204** G3
Pinheiros Brazil **207** M5
Pinhel Port. **54** D4
Pinhuã *r.* Brazil **199** E6
Pini *i.* Indon. **76** B2
Pinilla *r.* Spain **55** I6
Piniós *r.* Greece *see* **Pineios**
Pinjarra Australia **151** A7
Pinjin Aboriginal Reserve Australia **151** C6
Pinkafeld Austria **49** N8
Pinkawilinie Conservation Park *nature res.* Australia **146** B3
Pinkerton Range *hills* Australia **148** A2
Pink Mountain Canada **166** F3
Pinlaung Myanmar **78** B3
Pinlebu Myanmar **78** A2
Pinnacle U.S.A. **176** E9
Pinnacle *hill* U.S.A. **176** G6
Pinnacles National Monument *nat. park* U.S.A. **182** C5
Pinnaroo Australia **146** D3
Pinneberg Germany **48** G2
Pinnes, Akra *pt* Greece **59** F8
Pinofranqueado Spain **54** E4
Pinoh *r.* Indon. **77** E3
Pinos, Isla de *i.* Cuba *see* **La Juventud, Isla de**
Pinos, Mount U.S.A. **182** E7
Pinoso Spain **55** J6
Pinoso *mt.* Spain **55** I4
Pinos-Puente Spain **54** H7
Pinotepa Nacional Mex. **185** F5
Pinrang Indon. **75** A3
Pins, Île des *i.* New Caledonia **145** F4
English form Pines, Isle of; *also known as* Kunié
Pins, Pointe aux *pt* Canada **173** L8
Pinsk Belarus **42** H9
Pinta, Sierra *hill* U.S.A. **183** K9
Pintados Chile **200** C5
Pintasan *Sabah* Malaysia **77** G1
Pinto Spain **55** H4
Pintura U.S.A. **183** K4
Pinzolo Italy **56** C2
Pioche U.S.A. **183** J4
Pio IX Brazil **202** D3
Piombino Italy **56** C6
Pioneer *OH* U.S.A. **176** A4
Pioneer *TN* U.S.A. **176** A9
Pioneer Mountains U.S.A. **180** D3
Pioner, Ostrov *i.* Rus. Fed. **39** J2
Pionerskiy *Kaliningradskaya Oblast'* Rus. Fed. **42** B7
historically known as Neukuhren
Pionerskiy *Khanty-Mansiyskiy Avtonomnyy Okrug* Rus. Fed. **38** G3
Pionki Poland **49** S4
Piopio N.Z. **152** J6
Piopiotahi *inlet* N.Z. *see* **Milford Sound**
Piorini *r.* Brazil **199** F5
Piorini, Lago *l.* Brazil **199** F5
Piotrków Trybunalski Poland **49** Q4
formerly known as Petrokov; *historically known as* Petrikau
Piove di Sacco Italy **56** E3
Pīp Iran **101** E5
Pipa Dingzi *mt.* China **82** C4
Pipanaco, Salar de *salt flat* Arg. **204** D3
Pipar India **96** B4
Pipar Road India **96** B4
Piperi *i.* Greece **59** F9
Piper Peak U.S.A. **182** G4
Pipestone Canada **167** K5
Pipestone *r.* Canada **168** B2
Pipestone U.S.A. **178** C3
Pipirig Romania **58** H1
Pipiriki N.Z. **152** J7
Pipli India **96** B3
Pipmuacan, Réservoir Canada **169** G3
Pippingarra Aboriginal Reserve Australia **150** B4
Pipriac France **50** E5
Piqan China *see* **Shanshan**
Piqanlik China **88** C3
Piqua U.S.A. **176** A5
Piqueras, Puerto de *pass* Spain **55** I2
Piquet Carneiro Brazil **202** E3
Piquete Brazil **207** H9
Piquiri *r. Mato Grosso do Sul* Brazil **201** G4
Piquiri *r. Paraná* Brazil **203** A8
Piracaia Brazil **206** G10
Piracanjuba Brazil **206** D4
Piracanjuba *r.* Brazil **206** E5
Piracicaba Brazil **206** F9
Piracicaba *r. Minas Gerais* Brazil **203** D6
Piracicaba *r. São Paulo* Brazil **206** E9
Piraçununga Brazil **206** F8
Piracuruca Brazil **202** D2
Piraeus Greece **59** E11
also spelt Peiraias *or* Piráievs
Pirai do Sul Brazil **203** B8
Piráievs Greece *see* **Piraeus**
Piraju Brazil **206** D10
Pirajuba Brazil **206** E6
Pirajuí Brazil **206** D8
Pirallahı Adası Azer. **107** G2
Pirané Arg. **204** F2
Piranga Brazil **207** J7
Piranga *r.* Brazil **207** K7
Piranhas *Alagoas* Brazil **202** E4
Piranhas *Amazonas* Brazil **199** F6
Piranhas *Goiás* Brazil **206** B3
Piranhas *r. Goiás* Brazil **206** B3
Piranhas *r. Rio Grande do Norte* Brazil **202** E3
Pirapemas Brazil **202** C2
Pirapetinga *Amazonas* Brazil **201** E1
Pirapetinga *Minas Gerais* Brazil **207** K8
Pirapó *r.* Brazil **206** A9
Pirapora Brazil **203** C6
Pirapozinho Brazil **206** B9
Piraputangas Brazil **201** F4
Pirara Guyana **199** G4
Pirarajá Uruguay **204** G4
Pirari Nepal **97** E4
Piratini Brazil **204** G3
Piratininga Brazil **206** D9
Piratininga *r.* Brazil **207** G2
Pirawa India **96** C4
Pirchevan Azer. *see* **Zängilan**
Pire Mahuida, Sierra *mts* Arg. **205** C6
Pirenópolis Brazil **206** E2
Pires do Rio Brazil **206** E4
Piriganj Bangl. **97** F4
Pirgos Greece *see* **Pyrgos**
Pirgovo Bulg. **58** G5
Piriaka N.Z. **152** J6
Piriápolis Uruguay **204** G4
Pirin *mts* Bulg. **58** E7
Pirin *nat. park* Bulg. **58** E7
Pirineos *mts* Europe *see* **Pyrenees**
Piripá Brazil **207** L1
Piripiri Brazil **202** D3
Pirita *r.* Estonia **42** F2
Píritu *Falcón* Venez. **198** D2
Píritu *Portuguesa* Venez. **198** D2
Pirmasens Germany **48** E6
Pirmed India **94** C4
Pirna Germany **49** K5
Pirojpur Bangl. **97** F5
Pirón *r.* Spain **54** G3
Pirongia N.Z. **152** J5
Pirongia *vol.* N.Z. **152** J5
Pirongia Forest Park *nature res.* N.Z. **152** J5
Piros, Ozero *l.* Rus. Fed. **43** O3
Pirot *Srbija* Yugo. **58** D5
Pirpainti India **97** E4
Pir Panjal Pass Jammu and Kashmir **96** B2
Pir Panjal Range *mts* India/Pak. **96** B2
Pirrasit Dağ *hill* Turkey **107** E3
Pirsaat Azer. **100** B2
Pirsaatçay *r.* Azer. **107** G2
Piru Indon. **75** D3
Piru, Teluk *b.* Indon. **75** D3
Pir'yakh, Gora *mt.* Tajik. **101** G2
also known as Piryakh, Kūhi
Piryakh, Kūhi *mt.* Tajik. *see* **Pir'yakh, Gora**
Piryatin Ukr. *see* **Pyryatyn**
Piryetós Greece *see* **Pyrgetos**
Piryi Greece *see* **Pyrgi**
Pirzada Afgh. **101** F4
also known as Khugiana
Pisa Italy **56** C5
historically known as Pisae
Pisa *r.* Poland **49** S2
Pisac Peru **200** C3
Pisae Italy *see* **Pisa**
Pisagua Chile **200** C4
Pisang *i.* Indon. **75** D3
Pisa Range *mts* N.Z. **153** D12
Pisau, Tanjong *pt* Malaysia **77** G1
Pisaurum Italy *see* **Pesaro**
Pisba, Parque Nacional *nat. park* Col. **198** C3
Pisco Peru **200** A3
Pisco *r.* Peru **200** A3
Piseco Lake U.S.A. **177** K2
Písek Czech Rep. **49** L6
Pisha China *see* **Ningnan**
Pishan China **88** B4
also known as Guma
Pīshīn Iran **101** E5
Pishin Pak. **101** F4
Pishin Lora *r.* Pak. **101** F4
Pishkan, Ras *pt* Pak. **101** E5
Pishpek Kyrg. *see* **Bishkek**
Pisidia *reg.* Turkey **106** B3
Pising Indon. **75** B4
Pisinimo U.S.A. **183** L9
Piskent Uzbek. *see* **Pskent**
Pismo Beach U.S.A. **182** D6
Piso Firme Bol. **201** E3
Pisogne Italy **56** C3
Pissa *r.* Rus. Fed. **42** C7

▶**Pissis, Cerro** *mt.* Arg. **204** C2
4th highest mountain in South America.
south**america** [landscapes] 190–191

Pista *r.* Rus. Fed. **44** O2
Pisté Mex. **185** H4
Pisticci Italy **57** I8
Pistoia Italy **56** C5
historically known as Pistoriae
Pistoriae Italy *see* **Pistoia**
Pistsovo Rus. Fed. **43** V4
Pisuerga *r.* Spain **54** G3
Pisz Poland **49** S2
Pit *r.* U.S.A. **180** B4
Pita Guinea **124** B4
Pitaga Canada **169** H2
Pital Mex. **185** H5
Pitalito Col. **198** B4
Pitanga Brazil **203** B8
Pitangueiras Brazil **206** E8
Pitangui Brazil **203** C6
Pitarpunga Lake *imp. l.* Australia **147** D3

▶**Pitcairn Islands** *terr.* S. Pacific Ocean **221** J7
United Kingdom Overseas Territory.
oceania [countries] 138–139

Piteå Sweden **44** M2
Piteälven *r.* Sweden **44** M2
Pitelino Rus. Fed. **41** G5
Piterka Rus. Fed. **102** A2
Pitești Romania **58** F4
Pithiviers France **51** I4
Pithoragarh India **96** D3
Pitiquito Mex. **184** B2
Pitkul' Rus. Fed. **44** P2
Pitkyaranta Rus. Fed. **40** D3
Pitlochry U.K. **46** I7
Pitoa Cameroon **125** I4
Pitomača Croatia **56** J3
Pitong China *see* **Pixian**
Pitrufquén Chile **204** B5
Pitsane Siding Botswana **133** J2
Pitseng Lesotho **133** M6
Pitsunda Georgia *see* **Bichvint'a**
Pitti *i.* India **94** B4
Pitt Island Canada **166** D4
Pitt Island S. Pacific Ocean **145** H6
also known as Rangiauria
Pitt Islands Solomon Is *see* **Vanikoro Islands**
Pittsboro U.S.A. **174** E5
Pittsburg *CA* U.S.A. **182** C3
Pittsburg *KS* U.S.A. **178** D4
Pittsburg *TX* U.S.A. **179** D5
Pittsburgh U.S.A. **176** F5
Pittsfield *IL* U.S.A. **174** B4
Pittsfield *MA* U.S.A. **177** L3
Pittsfield *ME* U.S.A. **177** P1
Pittsfield *NH* U.S.A. **177** N2
Pittsfield *VT* U.S.A. **177** M2
Pittsville U.S.A. **172** C6
Pittsworth Australia **147** F1
Pituri Creek *watercourse* Australia **148** C4
Pitz Lake Canada **167** L2
Pium Brazil **202** B4
Piumhí Brazil **207** H7
Piura Peru **198** A6
Piura *dept* Peru **198** A6
Piusa *r.* Estonia **42** I4
Piute Mountains U.S.A. **183** I7
Piute Peak U.S.A. **182** F6
Piuthan Nepal **97** D3
Pivabiska *r.* Canada **168** D3
Pivijay Col. **198** C2
Piwniczna Poland **49** R6
Pixariá *mt.* Greece *see* **Pyxaria**
Pixian China **86** B2
also known as Pitong
Pixley U.S.A. **182** E6
Pixoyal Mex. **185** H5
Pizacoma Peru **200** C4
Pizhanka Rus. Fed. **40** I4
Pizhi Nigeria **125** G4
Pizhma Rus. Fed. **40** H4
Pizhma *r.* Rus. Fed. **40** I4
Pizhma *r.* Rus. Fed. **40** J2
Pizhou China **87** F1
formerly known as Peixian *or* Yunhe
Piz Kesch *mt.* Switz. **51** P6
Pizol *mt.* Switz. **51** P6
Piz Pisoc *mt.* Switz. **51** Q6
Piz Platta *mt.* Switz. **51** P6
Pizzo Italy **57** I10
Pizzo Carbonara *mt. Sicilia* Italy **57** G11
Pizzuto, Monte *mt.* Italy **56** E6
Placentia Canada **169** K4
Placentia Italy *see* **Piacenza**
Placentia Bay Canada **169** K4
Placer *Masbate* Phil. **74** B4
Placer *Mindanao* Phil. **74** C4
Placerville *CA* U.S.A. **182** D3
Placerville *CO* U.S.A. **181** E5
Placetas Cuba **186** D2
Plácido de Castro Brazil **200** D2
Plain Dealing U.S.A. **179** D5
Plainfield *IN* U.S.A. **174** C4
Plainfield *NJ* U.S.A. **177** K5
Plainfield *VT* U.S.A. **177** M1
Plainfield *WI* U.S.A. **172** D6
Plains U.S.A. **179** B5
Plainview *NE* U.S.A. **178** C3
Plainview *NY* U.S.A. **177** L5
Plainview *TX* U.S.A. **179** B5
Plainville U.S.A. **178** C4
Plainwell U.S.A. **172** H8
Plaisance France **50** G9
Plaisance Haiti **187** E3
Plaistow U.S.A. **177** N3
Plaju Indon. **76** D3
Plaka, Akra *pt* Greece **59** H13
Plakoti, Cape Cyprus **108** F2
also known as Yassı Burnu
Plampang Indon. **77** G5
Plana Cays *is* Bahamas **187** E2
Planada U.S.A. **182** D4
Planaltina Brazil **206** F2
Planalto Brazil **207** M1
Plancoët France **50** D4
Plandište *Vojvodina, Srbija* Yugo. **58** C3
Plane *r.* Germany **49** J3
Plankinton U.S.A. **178** C3
Plano *IL* U.S.A. **172** E9
Plano *TX* U.S.A. **179** C5
Plant City U.S.A. **175** D7
Planura Brazil **206** E7
Plaquemine U.S.A. **175** B6
Plasencia Spain **54** E4
Plaški Croatia **56** H3
Plaster City U.S.A. **183** I9
Plaster Rock Canada **169** H4
Plaston S. Africa **133** P2
Plastun Rus. Fed. **82** E3
Platamon, Rt *pt* Yugo. **56** K6
Platamonas Greece **59** D9
Platanal Peru **200** C4
Platani *r. Sicilia* Italy **57** F11
Platanistos Greece **59** F10
Platanos Greece **59** C11
Platbakkies S. Africa **132** C7
Platberg *mt.* S. Africa **133** N5

▶**Plateau** *research station* Antarctica
Lowest recorded annual mean temperature in the world.
world [climate and weather] 16–17

Plateau *state* Nigeria **125** G4
Plateaux *admin. reg.* Congo **126** B5
Plateliai Lith. **42** C5
Plateros Mex. **185** E4
Plathuis S. Africa **132** E10
Platičevo *Vojvodina, Srbija* Yugo. **58** A4
Platina U.S.A. **182** B1
Platinum U.S.A. **164** C4
Plato Col. **198** C2
Plato de Sopa Chile **204** C2
Platrand S. Africa **133** N4
Platte *r. MO* U.S.A. **178** D4
Platte *r. NE* U.S.A. **178** D3
Platte City U.S.A. **178** D4
Plattenberg *hill* Austria **49** L7
Platteville *CO* U.S.A. **180** F4
Platteville *WI* U.S.A. **172** C8
Plattling Germany **49** J7
Plattsburgh U.S.A. **177** L1
Plattsmouth U.S.A. **178** D3
Platy Greece **58** D8
Plau Germany **49** J2
Plauen Germany **48** J5
Plauer See *l.* Germany **49** J2
Plav *Crna Gora* Yugo. **58** A6
Plava *r.* Rus. Fed. **43** S8
Plaviņas Latvia **42** G5
Plavnik *i.* Croatia **56** G4
Plavsk Rus. Fed. **43** S8
Playa de Castilla *coastal area* Spain **54** E7
Playa del Carmen Mex. **185** I4
Playas Ecuador **198** A5
Plây Cu Vietnam **79** E5
Playgreen Lake Canada **167** L4
Playón Mex. **184** C3
Playones de Santa Ana *l.* Col. **198** C2
Plaza del Judío *mt.* Spain **54** G6
Plaza Huincul Arg. **204** C5
Pleasant, Lake U.S.A. **183** L8
Pleasant Bay U.S.A. **177** P4
Pleasant Grove U.S.A. **183** M1
Pleasanton *CA* U.S.A. **182** C4
Pleasanton *TX* U.S.A. **179** C6
Pleasant Point N.Z. **153** F12
Pleasantville U.S.A. **177** K6
Pleaux France **51** I7
Plechý *mt.* Czech Rep. **49** K7
Plei Doch Vietnam **79** D5
Pleiße *r.* Germany **51** S1
Plenty *watercourse* Australia **148** C5
Plenty, Bay of *g.* N.Z. **152** K5
Plentywood U.S.A. **180** F2
Plesetsk Rus. Fed. **40** G3
Pleshanovo Rus. Fed. **102** C1
Pleshchenitsy Belarus *see* **Plyeshchanitsy**
Pleshcheyevo, Ozero *l.* Rus. Fed. **43** T5
Pleso Rus. Fed. **43** Q2
Pleszew Poland **49** O4
Pleternica Croatia **56** J3
Pletipi, Lac *l.* Canada **169** G3
Plettenberg Germany **48** E4
Plettenberg Bay S. Africa **132** H11
Pleven Bulg. **58** F5
formerly spelt Plevna
Plevna Bulg. *see* **Pleven**
Pleyben France **50** C4
Plieran *r. Sarawak* Malaysia **77** F2
Plinkšių ežeras *l.* Lith. **42** D5
Pliszka *r.* Poland **49** L3
Plješevica *mts* Croatia **56** H4
Pljevlja *Crna Gora* Yugo. **58** A5
Ploaghe *Sardegna* Italy **57** A8
Ploče Croatia **56** J5
formerly known as Kardeljevo
Płock Poland **49** Q3
formerly spelt Plozk; *historically known as* Schröttersburg
Plöckenpass *pass* Austria/Italy **49** J9
Pločno *mt.* Bos.-Herz. **56** J5
Plodovoye Rus. Fed. **43** L1
Ploemeur France **50** C5
Ploërmel France **50** D5
Ploesti Romania *see* **Ploiești**
Ploeuc-sur-Lié France **50** D4
Ploiești Romania **58** H4
formerly spelt Ploești
Plomari Greece **59** H10
Plomb du Cantal *mt.* France **51** I7
Plombières-les-Bains France **51** M5
Plön Germany **48** H1
Płońsk Poland **49** R3
Plopiș Romania **58** D1
Ploskosh' Rus. Fed. **43** M5
Ploskoye Rus. Fed. *see* **Stanovoye**
Ploskoye Rus. Fed. **43** V3
Plotnitsa Belarus **42** H9
Płoty Poland **49** M2
Ploudalmézeau France **50** B4
Ploufragan France **50** D4
Plouguerneau France **50** B4
Plouha France **50** D4
Plouzané France **50** B4
Plouzévédé France **50** B4
Plovdiv Bulg. **58** F6
also known as Filibe; *historically known as* Philippopolis
Plover U.S.A. **172** D6
Plover *r.* U.S.A. **172** D6
Plover Cove Reservoir *Hong Kong* China **87** [inset]
Plozk Poland *see* **Płock**
Pluckemin U.S.A. **177** K5
Plum U.S.A. **176** F5
Plum Coulee Canada **167** L5
Plummer U.S.A. **180** C3
Plumridge Lakes *salt flat* Australia **151** D6
Plumridge Lakes Nature Reserve Australia **151** D6
Plumtree Zimbabwe **131** E4
Plungė Lith. **42** C6
Plutarco Elías Calles, Presa *resr* Mex. **181** E7
Plutarco Elís Calles, Presa *resr* Mex. **184** C2
Pluto, Lac *l.* Canada **169** G2
Plužine *Crna Gora* Yugo. **56** K5
Plyeshchanitsy Belarus **42** I7
also spelt Pleshchenitsy
Ply Huey Wati, Khao *mt.* Myanmar/Thai. **78** B4

▶**Plymouth** Montserrat **187** H3
Capital of Montserrat, largely abandoned in 1997 owing to volcanic activity.

Plymouth Trin. and Tob. **187** H5
Plymouth U.K. **47** H13
Plymouth *CA* U.S.A. **182** D3
Plymouth *IN* U.S.A. **172** G9
Plymouth *MA* U.S.A. **177** O4
Plymouth *NC* U.S.A. **174** E5
Plymouth *NH* U.S.A. **177** N2
Plymouth *PA* U.S.A. **177** J4
Plymouth *WI* U.S.A. **172** F7
Plymouth Bay U.S.A. **177** O4
Plynlimon *hill* U.K. **47** I11
Plyussa Rus. Fed. **43** K3
Plyussa *r.* Rus. Fed. **43** J2
Plzeň Czech Rep. **49** K6
historically known as Pilsen
Pmere Nyente Aboriginal Land *res.* Australia **148** B5
Pniewy Poland **49** N3
Pô Burkina **125** E4
Po *r.* Italy **56** E3
Pô, Parc National de *nat. park* Burkina **125** E4
Po, Tanjong *pt Sarawak* Malaysia **77** E2
Poás, Volcán *vol.* Costa Rica **186** B5
Poat *i.* Indon. **75** B3
Pobeda, Gora *mt.* Rus. Fed. **39** O3
Pobeda Peak China/Kyrg. **88** B3
also known as Jengish Chokusu *or* Tomur Feng; *formerly known as* Pobedy, Pik *or* Shengli Feng
Pobedinskiy Rus. Fed. *see* **Zarechnyy**
Pobedy, Pik *mt.* China/Kyrg. *see* **Pobeda Peak**
Pobiedziska Poland **49** O3
Poca U.S.A. **176** D7
Pocahontas *IA* U.S.A. **178** D3
Pocatalico *r.* U.S.A. **176** D7
Pocatello U.S.A. **180** D4
Pochala Sudan **128** B3
Pochayiv Ukr. **41** C6
Pochep Rus. Fed. **43** O9
Pochinki Rus. Fed. **40** H5
Pochinok *Smolenskaya Oblast'* Rus. Fed. **43** N7
Pochinok *Tverskaya Oblast'* Rus. Fed. **43** P4
Pochutla Mex. **185** F6
Pock, Gunung *hill Sabah* Malaysia **77** G1
Pocking Germany **49** K7
Poções Brazil **202** D5
Poço Fundo Brazil **207** H8
Pocomoke City U.S.A. **177** J7
Pocomoke Sound *b.* U.S.A. **177** J8
Pocona Bol. **200** D4
Poconé Brazil **201** F4
Pocono Mountains *hills* U.S.A. **177** J4
Pocono Summit U.S.A. **177** J4
Poco Ranakah *vol.* Indon. **75** B5
Poços de Caldas Brazil **206** G8
Pocrane Brazil **207** L6
Podberez'ye Rus. Fed. **43** L5
Podbořany Czech Rep. **49** K5
Podborov'ye Rus. Fed. **43** J4
Podcher'ye Rus. Fed. **40** K3
Podcher'ye *r.* Rus. Fed. **40** K3
Poddębice Poland **49** P4
Poddor'ye Rus. Fed. **43** M4
Podensac France **50** F8
Podgorac *Srbija* Yugo. **58** C5
Podgorenskiy Rus. Fed. **41** F6
Podgorica *Crna Gora* Yugo. **58** A6
formerly known as Titograd
Podgorie Albania **58** B8
Podgornoye Rus. Fed. **39** I4
Podile India **94** C3
Podișul Transilvaniei *plat.* Romania *see* **Transylvanian Basin**
Podkamennaya Tunguska Rus. Fed. **39** J3
Podkamennaya Tunguska *r.* Rus. Fed. **39** J3
Podkhozheye Rus. Fed. **43** T7
Podlesnoye Rus. Fed. **102** A2
Podocarpus, Parque Nacional *nat. park* Ecuador **198** B6
Podoleni Romania **58** H2
Podol'sk Rus. Fed. **43** S6
Podor Senegal **124** B2
Podosinki Rus. Fed. **43** M6
Podozerskiy Rus. Fed. **43** V4
Podporozh'ye Rus. Fed. **43** P1
Podujevo *Kosovo, Srbija* Yugo. **58** C6
Podyuga Rus. Fed. **40** G3
Podyvot'ye Rus. Fed. **43** P9
Poel *i.* Germany **48** I1
Poeppel Corner *salt flat* Australia **148** C5
Poetovio Slovenia *see* **Ptuj**
Pofadder S. Africa **132** D6
Pogamasing Canada **173** L4
Pogar Rus. Fed. **43** O9
Poggibonsi Italy **56** D5
Poggio Ballone *hill* Italy **56** C6
Poggio di Montieri *mt.* Italy **56** D5
Poggio Rusco Italy **56** D4
Pogled *mt.* Yugo. **58** B6
Pogoreloye-Gorodishche Rus. Fed. **43** P5
Pogradec Albania **58** B8
Pogrebishche Ukr. *see* **Pohrebyshche**
Po Hai *g.* China *see* **Bo Hai**
P'ohang S. Korea **83** C5
Pohja Fin. **45** M3
Pohnpei *atoll* Micronesia **220** E5
formerly spelt Ponape; *historically known as* Ascension
Pohrebyshche Ukr. **41** D6
also spelt Pogrebishche
Pohri India **96** C4
Poiana Mare Romania **58** E5
Poiana Ruscă, Munții *mts* Romania **58** D3
Poiana Stampei Romania **58** G1
Poienești Romania **58** I2
Poienița, Vârful *mt.* Romania **58** E2
Poindimié New Caledonia **145** F4
Poinsett, Cape Antarctica **223** H2
Point au Fer Island U.S.A. **175** B6
Point-Comfort Canada **173** R4
Pointe a la Hache U.S.A. **175** B6
Pointe-à-Pitre Guadeloupe **187** H3
Pointe au Baril Station Canada **173** M5
Pointe Aux Pins U.S.A. **173** I5
Pointe-Noire Congo **126** A6
Pointe Noire Guadeloupe **187** H3
Point Hope U.S.A. **164** C3
Point Kenny Australia **146** B3
Point Lake Canada **167** H1
Point Nepean National Park Australia **147** E4
Point of Rocks *MD* U.S.A. **176** H6
Point of Rocks *WY* U.S.A. **180** E4
Point Pelee National Park Canada **173** K9
Point Pleasant U.S.A. **177** K5
Point Reyes National Seashore *nature res.* U.S.A. **182** B3
Point Salvation Aboriginal Reserve Australia **151** C6
Point Samson Australia **144** A4
Poisevo Rus. Fed. **40** J5
Poisson Blanc, Lac du *l.* Canada **173** R5
Poissonnier Point Australia **150** B3
Poitiers France **50** G6
historically known as Limonum
Poitou, Plaines et Seuil du *plain* France **50** G6
Poitou-Charentes *admin. reg.* France **50** F6
Poix-de-Picardie France **51** H3
Pojo Bol. **200** D4
Pojuca Brazil **202** E5
Pokaran India **96** A4
Pokataroo Australia **147** F2
Pokats' *r.* Belarus **43** L9
Pokcha Rus. Fed. **40** K3
Pokeno N.Z. **152** J5
Pokhara Nepal **97** D3
Pokhvistnevo Rus. Fed. **41** J5
Pokigron Suriname **199** H3
Pokka Fin. **44** N1
Pok Liu Chau *i. Hong Kong* China *see* **Lamma Island**
Poko Dem. Rep. Congo **126** E4
Pokrov *Smolenskaya Oblast'* Rus. Fed. **43** Q6
Pokrov *Vladimirskaya Oblast'* Rus. Fed. **43** U6
Pokrovka Kazakh. **103** G2
Pokrovka Kyrg. **103** G4
Pokrovka Kyrg. *see* **Kyzyl-Suu**
Pokrovka *Moskovskaya Oblast'* Rus. Fed. **43** R5
Pokrovka *Orenburgskaya Oblast'* Rus. Fed. **102** C2
Pokrovka *Primorskiy Kray* Rus. Fed. **82** C4
Pokrovka *Primorskiy Kray* Rus. Fed. **90** C2
Pokrovka Rus. Fed. *see* **Priamurskiy**
Pokrovsk Rus. Fed. **39** M3
Pokrovsk Rus. Fed. *see* **Engel's**
Pokrovskoye *Lipetskaya Oblast'* Rus. Fed. **43** T9
Pokrovskoye *Orlovskaya Oblast'* Rus. Fed. **43** R9
Pokrovskoye *Rostovskaya Oblast'* Rus. Fed. **41** F7
Pokrovsk-Ural'skiy Rus. Fed. **40** K3
Pokshen'ga *r.* Rus. Fed. **40** H3
Pol' *r.* Rus. Fed. **43** V6
Pola Croatia *see* **Pula**
Pola Phil. **74** B3
Pola Rus. Fed. **43** M4
Pola *r.* Rus. Fed. **43** M4
Polacca U.S.A. **183** N6
Polacca Wash *watercourse* U.S.A. **183** N6
Pola de Allande Spain **54** E1
Pola de Laviana Spain **54** F1
Pola de Lena Spain **54** F1
Pola de Siero Spain **54** F1
Pola de Somiedo Spain **54** E1
Polān Iran **101** E5
Polán Spain **54** G5
Poľana *mt.* Slovakia **49** Q7

▶**Poland** *country* Europe **49** N3
known as Polska in Polish
europe [countries] 32–35

Połaniec Poland **49** S5
Polanów Poland **49** N1
Polar Bear Provincial Park Canada **168** D2
Polar Plateau Antarctica **223** V1
Polar Times Glacier Antarctica **223** E2
Polatlı Turkey **106** C3
Polatsk Belarus **43** J6
also spelt Polotsk
Polatskaya Nizina *lowland* Belarus **42** J6
Polavaram India **94** D2
Polazna Rus. Fed. **40** K4
Polcirkeln Sweden **44** N2
Połczyn Zdrój Poland **49** N2
Poldarsa Rus. Fed. **40** H3
Pol-e Fāsā Iran **100** C4
Pole-Khatum Iran **101** E2
Pol-e Khomrī Afgh. **101** G3
Pol-e Safid Iran **100** C2
Polessk Rus. Fed. **42** C7
Poles'ye *marsh* Belarus/Ukr. *see* **Pripet Marshes**
Polewali Indon. **75** A3
Poli Cameroon **125** I4
Poli Cyprus *see* **Polis**
Poliaigos *i.* Greece *see* **Polyaigos**
Poliçan Albania **58** B8
Policastro, Golfo di *b.* Italy **57** H9
Police Poland **49** L2
Polichnitos Greece **59** H9
also spelt Polikhnitos
Policoro Italy **57** I8
Polidhrosos Greece *see* **Polydroso**
Polignano a Mare Italy **56** J8
Poligny France **51** L6
Polikastron Greece *see* **Polykastro**
Polikhnitos Greece *see* **Polichnitos**
Polikrayshte Bulg. **58** G5
Polillo *i.* Phil. **74** B3
Polillo Islands Phil. **74** B3
Polillo Strait Phil. **74** B3
Polis Cyprus **108** D2
also known as Poli
Polis'ke Ukr. **41** D6
formerly known as Kaganovichi Pervyye
Polis'kyy Zapovidnyk *nature res.* Ukr. **41** D6
Polist' *r.* Rus. Fed. **43** M3
Polistena Italy **57** I10
Polisto, Ozero *l.* Rus. Fed. **43** L4
Politovo Rus. Fed. **40** I2
Poliyiros Greece *see* **Polygyros**
Polk U.S.A. **176** F4
Polkorona Latvia **42** H5
Polkowice Poland **49** N4
Polla Italy **57** H8
Pollachi India **94** C4
Pollard Islands U.S.A. *see* **Gardner Pinnacles**
Pöllauer Tal *nature res.* Austria **49** M8
Pollença Spain **55** O5
also spelt Pollensa
Pollensa Spain *see* **Pollença**
Pollino, Monte *mt.* Italy **57** I9
Pollino, Parco Nazionale del *nat. park* Italy **57** I9
Polloc Harbour *b.* Phil. **74** B5
Pollock Pines U.S.A. **182** D3
Pollock Reef Australia **151** C7
Pollok N.Z. **152** I5
Polmak Norway **44** N1
Polnovat Rus. Fed. **38** G3
Polo Fin. **44** O2
Polo U.S.A. **172** D9
Pologi Ukr. *see* **Polohy**
Polohy Ukr. **41** F7
also spelt Pologi; *formerly known as* Chubarovka
Polokwane S. Africa *see* **Pietersburg**
Polomet' *r.* Rus. Fed. **43** M4
Polomoloc Phil. **74** C5
Polonnaruwa Sri Lanka **94** D5
Polonne Ukr. **41** C6
also spelt Polonnoye

Polonnoye Ukr. *see* **Polonne**
Polotnyanyy Zavod Rus. Fed. 43 Q7
Polotsk Belarus *see* **Polatsk**
Polovinka Rus. Fed. *see* **Ugleural'skiy**
Polovragi Romania 58 E3
Pöls *r.* Austria 49 L8
Polska *country* Europe *see* **Poland**
Polski Trŭmbesh Bulg. 58 G5
Polson U.S.A. 180 D3
Polta *r.* Rus. Fed. 40 G2
Poltár Slovakia 49 Q7
Poltava Ukr. 41 E6
Poltavka Rus. Fed. 82 C3
Poltavskaya Rus. Fed. 41 F7 *formerly known as* Krasnoarmeyskaya
Poltoratsk Turkm. *see* **Ashgabat**
Põltsamaa Estonia 42 G3
Põltsamaa *r.* Estonia 42 H3
Polur India 94 C3
Põlva Estonia 42 I3
Polvadera U.S.A. 181 F6
Polvijärvi Fin. 44 O3
Polya *r.* Rus. Fed. 43 U6
Polyaigos *i.* Greece 59 F12 *also spelt* Políaigos
Polyanovgrad Bulg. *see* **Karnobat**
Polyany Rus. Fed. 43 K1
Polyarnoye Rus. Fed. *see* **Russkoye Ust'ye**
Polyarnyy *Chukotskiy Avtonomnyy Okrug* Rus. Fed. 39 R3
Polyarnyy *Murmanskaya Oblast'* Rus. Fed. 44 P1
Polyarnyye Zori Rus. Fed. 44 P2
Polyarnyy Krug Rus. Fed. 44 P2
Polyarnyy Ural *mts* Rus. Fed. 40 L2
Polydroso Greece 59 D10 *also known as* Polídhrosos
Polygyros Greece 59 E8 *also spelt* Políyiros
Polyiagou-Folegandrou, Steno *sea chan.* Greece 59 F12
Polykastro Greece 58 D8 *also known as* Políkastron
Polynesia *is* Oceania 220 G5
Polynésie Française *terr.* S. Pacific Ocean *see* **French Polynesia**
Pomabamba Peru 200 A2
Pomahaka *r.* N.Z. 153 D14
Pomarance Italy 56 C5
Pomarkku Fin. 45 M3
Pomba *r.* Brazil 203 D7
Pombal *Pará* Brazil 199 H5
Pombal *Paraíba* Brazil 202 E3
Pombal Port. 54 C5
Pombas *r.* Brazil 199 F6
Pombas Cape Verde 124 [inset]
Pombo *r.* Brazil 206 A7
Pomene Moz. 131 G4
Pomeroy S. Africa 133 O5
Pomeroy *OH* U.S.A. 176 C6
Pomeroy *WA* U.S.A. 180 C3
Pomezia Italy 56 E7
Pomfret S. Africa 132 H2
Pomio P.N.G. 145 E2
Pomokaira *reg.* Fin. 44 N2
Pomona Namibia 130 B5
Pomona U.S.A. 182 G7
Pomorie Bulg. 58 I6
Pomorska, Zatoka *b.* Poland 49 L1
Pomorskie, Pojezierze *reg.* Poland 49 O2
Pomorskiy Bereg *coastal area* Rus. Fed. 40 E2
Pomorskiy Proliv *sea chan.* Rus. Fed. 40 I1
Pomos Point Cyprus 108 D2 *also known as* Pomou, Akra
Pomo Tso *l.* China *see* **Puma Yumco**
Pomou, Akra *pt* Cyprus *see* **Pomos Point**
Pompei Italy 57 G8 *historically known as* Pompeii
Pompéia Brazil 206 C9
Pompeii Italy *see* **Pompei**
Pompéu Brazil 203 C6
Pompton Lakes U.S.A. 177 K4
Ponape *atoll* Micronesia *see* **Pohnpei**
Ponask Lake Canada 167 M4
Ponazyrevo Rus. Fed. 40 H4
Ponca U.S.A. 178 C3
Ponca City U.S.A. 178 C4
Ponce Puerto Rico 187 G3
Ponce de Leon Bay U.S.A. 175 D7
Poncha Springs U.S.A. 181 F5
Ponda India 94 B3
Pondicherry India 94 C4 *also spelt* Pondichéry *or* Puduchcheri
Pondicherry *union terr.* India 95 C4
Pondichéry India *see* **Pondicherry**
Pond Inlet Canada 165 L2 *also known as* Mittimatalik; *formerly known as* Ponds Bay
Pondoland *reg.* S. Africa 133 N8
Ponds, Island of Canada 169 K2
Ponds Bay Canada *see* **Pond Inlet**
Poneloya Nicaragua 186 B4
Ponente, Riviera di *coastal area* Italy 56 A5
Ponferrada Spain 54 E2
Pongakawa N.Z. 152 K5
Pongara, Pointe *pt* Gabon 126 A4
Pongaroa N.Z. 152 K8
Pongo *watercourse* Sudan 126 E3
Pongo de Manseriche *gorge* Peru 198 B6
Pongola S. Africa 133 P4
Pongola *r.* S. Africa 133 Q3
Pongolapoort Dam *l.* S. Africa 133 P4
Pongolapoort Public Resort Nature Reserve S. Africa 133 P4
Poniatowa Poland 49 T4
Poniki, Gunung *mt.* Indon. 75 B2
Ponindilisa, Tanjung *pt* Indon. 75 B3
Ponizov'ye Rus. Fed. 43 M6
Ponnagyun Myanmar 78 A3
Ponnaivar *r.* India 94 C4
Ponnampet India 94 B3
Ponnani India 94 B4
Ponnani *r.* India 94 B4
Ponneri India 94 D3
Ponnyadaung Range *mts* Myanmar 78 A3
Ponoka Canada 167 H4
Ponomarevka Rus. Fed. 102 C1
Ponorogo Indon. 77 E4
Ponoy *r.* Rus. Fed. 40 G2
Pons *r.* Canada 169 G1
Pons France 50 F7
Pons Spain *see* **Ponts**
Ponsacco Italy 56 C5
Ponsul *r.* Port. 54 D5
Pontacq France 50 F9

▶ **Ponta Delgada** Azores 216 M3
Capital of the Azores.

Ponta de Pedras Brazil 202 B2
Ponta dos Índios Brazil 199 I3
Ponta do Sol Cape Verde 124 [inset]
Ponta Grossa Brazil 203 B8
Pontal do Ipiranga Brazil 207 N6
Pontalina Brazil 206 D4
Pont-à-Mousson France 51 M4
Pontant Arg. 204 E5
Pontão Brazil 202 B3
Ponta Porã Brazil 201 G5
Pontarlier France 51 M6
Pontassieve Italy 56 D5
Pont-Audemer France 50 G3
Pont-Aven France 50 C5
Pontax *r.* Canada 168 E3
Pontchartrain, Lake U.S.A. 175 B6
Pontchâteau France 50 D5
Pont-d'Ain France 51 L6
Pont-de-Roide France 51 M5
Pont de Suert Spain 55 L2
Ponte Alta do Norte Brazil 202 C4
Ponteareas Spain 54 C2 *also spelt* Puenteareas
Pontebba Italy 56 F2
Ponte Branca Brazil 206 A3
Ponte-Ceso Spain 54 C1
Pontecorvo Italy 56 F7
Ponte de Pedra Brazil 201 F3
Pontedera Italy 56 C5
Ponte de Sor Port. 54 C5
Ponte do Rio Verde Brazil 203 A6
Ponte Firme Brazil 206 G5
Ponteix Canada 167 J5
Ponteland U.K. 47 K8
Ponte Nova Brazil 203 D7
Pontes-e-Lacerda Brazil 201 F3
Pontevedra Spain 54 C2
Pontevedra, Ría de *est.* Spain 54 C2
Ponthierville Dem. Rep. Congo *see* **Ubundu**
Pontiac *IL* U.S.A. 174 B3
Pontiac *MI* U.S.A. 173 J8
Pontiae *is* Italy *see* **Ponziane, Isole**
Pontianak Indon. 77 E3
Pontine Islands *is* Italy *see* **Ponziane, Isole**
Pontivy France 50 D4
Pont-l'Abbé France 50 B5
Pontoetoe Suriname 199 H4
Pontoise France 51 I3
Ponton *watercourse* Australia 151 C6
Ponton Canada 167 L4
Pontotoc U.S.A. 174 B5
Pontremoli Italy 56 B4
Ponts Spain 55 M3 *also spelt* Pons
Pont-St-Esprit France 51 K8
Pont-sur-Yonne France 51 J4
Pontypool Canada 173 O6
Pontypool U.K. 47 I12
Pontypridd U.K. 47 I12
Ponui Island N.Z. 152 J4
Ponyatovka Rus. Fed. 43 N8
Ponyri Rus. Fed. 43 R9
Ponza Italy 57 E8
Ponza, Isola di *i.* Italy 56 E8
Ponziane, Isole *is* Italy 56 E8 *English form* Pontine Islands; *historically known as* Pontiae
Poochera Australia 146 B3
Pool *admin. reg.* Congo 126 B5
Poole U.K. 47 K13
Poolowanna Lake *salt flat* Australia 148 C5
Poona India *see* **Pune**
Pooncarie Australia 147 D3
Poopelloe Lake Australia 147 E2
Poopó Bol. 200 D4
Poopó, Lago de *l.* Bol. 200 D4
Poor Knights Islands N.Z. 152 I3
Pop Uzbek. *see* **Pap**
Popa Mountain Myanmar 78 A3
Popayán Col. 198 B4
Pope Latvia 42 C4
Popes Creek U.S.A. 177 I7
Popigay *r.* Rus. Fed. 39 K2
Popilta Lake *imp. l.* Australia 146 D3
Popio Lake Australia 146 D3
Poplar *r. Man.* Canada 167 L4
Poplar *r. N.W.T.* Canada 166 G2
Poplar U.S.A. 172 B4
Poplar *r.* U.S.A. 180 F2
Poplar, West Fork *r.* U.S.A. 180 F2
Poplar Bluff U.S.A. 174 B4
Poplar Camp U.S.A. 176 E9
Poplar Plains U.S.A. 176 B7
Poplarville U.S.A. 175 B6
Poplevinskiy Rus. Fed. 43 U8

▶ **Popocatépetl, Volcán** *vol.* Mex. 185 F5
5th highest mountain in North America.
northamerica [landscapes] ▶ 156–157
northamerica [threats] ▶ 160–161

Popoh Indon. 77 E5
Popokabaka Dem. Rep. Congo 127 C6
Popoli Italy 56 F6
Popondetta P.N.G. 145 D2
Popovača Croatia 56 I3
Popovichskaya Rus. Fed. *see* **Kalininskaya**
Popovka *Vologod. Obl.* Rus. Fed. 43 S2
Popovka *Vologod. Obl.* Rus. Fed. 43 U1
Popovo Bulg. 58 H5
Popovo Polje *plain* Bos.-Herz. 56 J6
Popovska Reka *r.* Bulg. 58 H6
Poppberg *hill* Germany 48 I6
Poppenberg *hill* Germany 48 H4
Poprad *r.* Poland 49 R6
Poprad Slovakia 49 R6
Poquis, Nevado de *mt.* Chile 200 D5
Poquoson U.S.A. 177 I8
Por *r.* Poland 49 U5
Porali *r.* Pak. 101 F5
Porangahau N.Z. 152 K8
Porangatu Brazil 202 B5
Porazava Belarus 42 F9
Porbandar India 96 A5
Porcher Island Canada 166 D4
Porciúncula Brazil 207 K7
Porco Bol. 200 D4
Porcsalma Hungary 49 T8
Porcuna Spain 54 G7
Porcupine *r.* Canada/U.S.A. 164 E3
Porcupine, Cape Canada 169 J2
Porcupine Creek *r.* U.S.A. 180 F2
Porcupine Gorge National Park Australia 149 E4
Porcupine Hills Canada 167 K4
Porcupine Mountains U.S.A. 172 D4
Porcupine Plain Canada 167 K4
Porcupine Provincial Forest *nature res.* Canada 167 K4
Pordenone Italy 56 E3
Pordim Bulg. 58 F5
Pore Col. 198 D3
Poreč Croatia 56 F3
Porecatu Brazil 206 B9
Porech'ye *Moskovskaya Oblast'* Rus. Fed. 43 Q6
Porech'ye *Pskovskaya Oblast'* Rus. Fed. 43 L5
Porech'ye *Tverskaya Oblast'* Rus. Fed. 43 R3
Porech'ye-Rybnoye Rus. Fed. 43 U4
Poretskoye Rus. Fed. 40 H5
Porga Benin 125 F4
Pori Fin. 45 M3 *also known as* Björneborg
Porirua N.Z. 152 I9
Porjus Sweden 44 L2
Porkhov Rus. Fed. 43 K4
Porkkalafjärden *b.* Fin. 42 F2
Porlamar Venez. 199 F2
Porma *r.* Spain 54 F2
Pormpuraaw Australia 149 D2
Pornainen Fin. 45 N3
Pornic France 50 D5
Poro *i.* Phil. 74 C4
Poro, Monte *hill* Italy 57 H10
Poronaysk Rus. Fed. 82 F2
Porong China *see* **Baingoin**
Pôrông, Stœng *r.* Cambodia 79 D5
Poros Greece 59 E11
Poros *i.* Greece 59 E11
Porosozero Rus. Fed. 40 E3
Porpoise Bay Antarctica 223 I2
Porquerolles, Île de *i.* France 51 M10
Porquis Junction Canada 173 M2
Porrentruy Switz. 51 N5
Porriño Spain 54 C2
Porsangen *sea chan.* Norway 44 N1
Porsangerhalvøya *pen.* Norway 44 N1
Porsgrunn Norway 45 J4
Porsuk *r.* Turkey 106 B3
Portadown U.K. 47 F9
Portaferry U.K. 47 G9
Portage *IN* U.S.A. 172 F9
Portage *MI* U.S.A. 172 H8
Portage *PA* U.S.A. 176 G5
Portage *WI* U.S.A. 172 D7
Portage Lakes U.S.A. 176 D5
Portage la Prairie Canada 167 L5
Portal U.S.A. 178 B1
Port Alberni Canada 166 E5
Port Albert Australia 147 E4
Portalegre Port. 54 D5
Portalegre *admin. dist.* Port. 54 D5
Portales U.S.A. 179 B5
Port-Alfred Canada *see* **La Baie**
Port Alfred S. Africa 133 K10
Port Alice Canada 166 E5
Port Allegany U.S.A. 176 G4
Port Alma Australia 149 F4
Port Angeles U.S.A. 180 B2
Port Antonio Jamaica 186 D3
Port-à-Piment Haiti 187 E3
Portarlington Rep. of Ireland 47 E10
Port Arthur Australia 147 E5
Port Arthur China *see* **Lüshun**
Port Arthur U.S.A. 179 D6
Port Askaig U.K. 46 F8
Port Augusta Australia 146 C3
Port-au-Port Bay Canada 169 J3

▶ **Port-au-Prince** Haiti 187 E3
Capital of Haiti.

Port aux Choix Canada 169 J3
Port Beaufort S. Africa 132 E11
Port Blair India 95 G4
Port Bolster Canada 173 N6
Portbou Spain 55 O2
Port Bradshaw *b.* Australia 148 C2
Port Broughton Australia 146 C3
Port Burwell Canada 173 M8
Port Campbell Australia 147 D4
Port Campbell National Park Australia 147 D4
Port Canning India 97 F5
Port Carling Canada 173 N5
Port-Cartier Canada 169 H3 *formerly known as* Shelter Bay
Port Chalmers N.Z. 153 E13
Port Charles N.Z. 152 J4
Port Charlotte U.S.A. 175 D7
Port Clements Canada 166 C4
Port Clinton *OH* U.S.A. 176 C4
Port Clyde U.S.A. 177 P2
Port Colborne Canada 168 E5
Port Credit Canada 173 N7
Port Darwin *b.* Australia 148 A2
Port Davey *b.* Australia 147 E5
Port-de-Paix Haiti 187 E3
Port de Pollença Spain 55 O5 *also spelt* Puerto de Pollensa
Port Dickson Malaysia 76 C2
Port Douglas Australia 149 E3
Port Dover Canada 173 M8
Port Easington *inlet* Australia 148 A1
Porte des Morts *lake channel* U.S.A. 172 G5
Port Edward Canada 166 D4
Port Edward S. Africa 133 O8
Port Edwards U.S.A. 172 D6
Porteira Brazil 199 G5
Porteirinha Brazil 202 D5
Portel Brazil 202 B2
Portel Port. 54 D6
Portelândia Brazil 206 A4
Port Elgin *N.B.* Canada 169 H4
Port Elgin *Ont.* Canada 168 D4
Port Elizabeth S. Africa 133 J10
Port Ellen U.K. 46 F8
Port Erin Isle of Man 47 H9
Porter Lake *N.W.T.* Canada 167 J2
Porter Lake *Sask.* Canada 167 J3
Porter Landing Canada 166 D3
Porterville S. Africa 132 C10
Porterville U.S.A. 182 E5
Portes-lès-Valence France 51 K8
Port Étienne Mauritania *see* **Nouâdhibou**
Port Everglades U.S.A. *see* **Fort Lauderdale**
Port Fairy Australia 147 D4
Port Fitzroy N.Z. 152 J4
Port Francqui Dem. Rep. Congo *see* **Ilebo**
Port-Gentil Gabon 126 A5
Port Gibson U.S.A. 175 B6
Port Grosvenor S. Africa 133 N8
Port Harcourt Nigeria 125 G5
Port Hardy Canada 166 E5
Port Harrison Canada *see* **Inukjuak**
Port Hawkesbury Canada 169 I4
Porthcawl U.K. 47 I12
Port Hedland Australia 150 B4
Port Henry U.S.A. 177 L1
Port Herald Malawi *see* **Nsanje**
Porthmos Zakynthou *sea chan.* Greece 59 B11
Port Hope Canada 173 O7
Port Hope U.S.A. 173 K7
Port Hope Simpson Canada 169 K2
Port Hueneme U.S.A. 182 E7
Port Huron U.S.A. 173 K8
Port-İliç Azer. 107 G3
Portillo Cuba 186 D3
Portimão Port. 54 C7
Port Island *Hong Kong* China 87 [inset] *also known as* Chek Chau
Port Jackson Australia *see* **Sydney**
Port Jackson *inlet* Australia 147 F3
Port Jefferson U.S.A. 177 L5
Port Kaituma Guyana 199 G3
Port Keats Australia *see* **Wadeye**
Port Kent U.S.A. 177 L1
Port Klang Malaysia *see* **Pelabuhan Kelang**
Port Láirge Rep. of Ireland *see* **Waterford**
Portland Australia 146 D4
Portland *IN* U.S.A. 176 A5
Portland *ME* U.S.A. 177 O2
Portland *MI* U.S.A. 173 I8
Portland *OR* U.S.A. 180 B3
Portland, Isle of *pen.* U.K. 47 J13
Portland Bay Australia 146 D4
Portland Bill *hd* U.K. *see* **Bill of Portland**
Portland Canal *inlet* Canada 166 D4
Portland Creek Pond *l.* Canada 169 J3
Portland Inlet Canada 166 D4
Portland Point Jamaica 186 D3
Portland Roads Australia 149 D2
Portlaoise Rep. of Ireland 47 E10
Port Lavaca U.S.A. 179 C6
Port Lincoln Australia 146 B3
Port Loko Sierra Leone 124 B4
Port Louis Guadeloupe 187 H3

▶ **Port Louis** Mauritius 219 K7
Capital of Mauritius.

Port-Lyautrey Morocco *see* **Kénitra**
Port MacDonnell Australia 146 D4
Port Macquarie Australia 147 G2
Port Manvers *inlet* Canada 169 I1
Port McArthur *b.* Australia 148 C2
Port McNeill Canada 166 E5
Port-Menier Canada 169 H3
Port Moller *b.* U.S.A. 164 C4
Port Morant Jamaica 186 D3

▶ **Port Moresby** P.N.G. 73 K8
Capital of Papua New Guinea.

Port Musgrave *b.* Australia 149 D1
Portnacroish U.K. 46 G7
Portnahaven U.K. 46 F8
Port Neches U.S.A. 179 D6
Port Neill Australia 146 C3
Port Nelson Bahamas 187 E2
Portneuf *r.* Canada 169 G3
Portneuf, Réserve Faunique de *nature res.* Canada 169 F4
Port Nis U.K. 46 F5
Port Nolloth S. Africa 132 A6
Port Norris U.S.A. 177 J6
Port-Nouveau-Québec Canada *see* **Kangiqsualujjuaq**
Porto Brazil 202 D2
Porto Port. *see* **Oporto**
Porto *admin. dist.* Port. 54 C3
Porto, Golfe de *b. Corse* France 51 O10
Porto Acre Brazil 200 D2
Porto Alegre *Amazonas* Brazil 200 D2
Porto Alegre *Mato Grosso do Sul* Brazil 203 A7
Porto Alegre *Pará* Brazil 199 H6
Porto Alegre *Rio Grande do Sul* Brazil 203 B9
Porto Alencastro Brazil 206 C6
Porto Alexandre Angola *see* **Tombua**
Porto Amarante Brazil 201 E3
Porto Amboim Angola 127 B7 *also known as* Gunza
Porto Amélia Moz. *see* **Pemba**
Porto Artur Brazil 201 G3
Porto Azzurro Italy 56 C6
Porto Belo Brazil 203 B8
Portobelo Panama 186 D5
Portobelo, Parque Nacional *nat. park* Panama 186 D5
Porto Camargo Brazil 203 A7
Porto Cavlo Brazil 202 F4
Porto da Fôlha Brazil 202 E4
Porto da Lontra Brazil 199 H6
Porto de Meinacos Brazil 202 A5
Porto de Moz Brazil 199 H5
Porto de Santa Cruz Brazil 207 L2
Porto do Barka Brazil 199 H6
Porto do Massacas Brazil 201 E3
Porto dos Gaúchos Óbidos Brazil 201 F2
Porto do Son Spain 54 B2 *also spelt* Puerto del Son
Porto Empedocle *Sicilia* Italy 57 F11
Porto Esperança Brazil 201 F4
Porto Esperidião Brazil 201 F3
Porto Estrêla Brazil 201 F3
Porto Feliz Brazil 206 F10
Portoferraio Italy 56 C6
Porto Ferreira Brazil 206 F8
Porto Firme Brazil 207 J7
Porto Franco Brazil 202 C3

▶ **Port of Spain** Trin. and Tob. 187 H5
Capital of Trinidad and Tobago.

Porto Grande Brazil 199 I4
Portogruaro Italy 56 E3
Porto Inglês Cape Verde 124 [inset]
Porto Jofre Brazil 201 F4
Portola U.S.A. 182 D2
Porto Luceno Brazil 203 A8
Portomaggiore Italy 56 D4
Porto Mauá Brazil 203 A8
Porto Murtinho Brazil 201 F5
Porto Nacional Brazil 202 B4

▶ **Porto-Novo** Benin 125 F5
Capital of Benin.

Porto Novo Cape Verde 124 [inset]
Porto Novo India *see* **Parangipettai**
Portopalo di Capo Passero *Sicilia* Italy 57 H12
Porto Primavera, Represa *resr* Brazil 206 A8
Port Orange U.S.A. 175 D6
Port Orchard U.S.A. 180 B3
Port Orford U.S.A. 180 A4
Porto Rincão Cape Verde 124 [inset]
Porto San Giorgio Italy 56 F5
Porto Santana Brazil 199 I5
Porto Sant'Elpidio Italy 56 F5
Porto Santo, Ilha de *i.* Madeira 122 A2
Portoscuso *Sardegna* Italy 57 A9
Porto Seguro Brazil 202 E6
Porto Tolle Italy 56 E4
Porto Torres *Sardegna* Italy 56 A8 *historically known as* Turris Libisonis
Porto Triunfo Brazil 201 E3
Porto União Brazil 203 B8
Porto-Vecchio *Corse* France 52 D3
Porto Velho Brazil 201 E2
Portoviejo Ecuador 198 A5
Porto Wálter Brazil 200 B2
Portpatrick U.K. 47 G9
Port Pegasus *b.* N.Z. 153 B15 *also known as* Pikihatiti
Port Perry Canada 173 O6
Port Phillip Bay Australia 147 E4
Port Pirie Australia 146 C3
Portree U.K. 46 F6
Port Renfrew Canada 166 E5
Port Rexton Canada 169 K3
Port Roper *b.* Australia 148 B2
Port Rowan Canada 173 M8
Port Royal U.S.A. 177 H7
Port Royal Sound *inlet* U.S.A. 175 D5
Port Said Egypt 121 G2 *also known as* Bûr Sa'îd
Port St Joe U.S.A. 175 C6
Port St Johns S. Africa 133 N8
Port St-Louis Madag. *see* **Antsohimbondrona**
Port-St-Louis-du-Rhône France 51 K9
Port Saint Lucie City U.S.A. 175 D7
Port Salvador Falkland Is 205 F8
Ports de Beseit *mts* Spain 55 L4 *also spelt* Puertos de Beceite
Port Severn Canada 173 N6
Port Shelter *b. Hong Kong* China 87 [inset] *also known as* Ngau Mei Hoi
Port Shepstone S. Africa 133 O7
Port Simpson Canada *see* **Lax Kw'alaams**
Portsmouth Dominica 187 H4
Portsmouth U.K. 47 K13
Portsmouth *NH* U.S.A. 177 O2
Portsmouth *OH* U.S.A. 176 C7
Portsmouth *VA* U.S.A. 177 I9
Port Stanley Falkland Is *see* **Stanley**
Port Stephens Falkland Is 205 E9
Port Sudan Sudan 121 H5 *also known as* Būr Sudan
Port Sulphur U.S.A. 175 B6
Port-sur-Saône France 51 M5
Port Swettenham Malaysia *see* **Pelabuhan Kelang**
Port Talbot U.K. 47 I12
Port Tambang *b.* Phil. 74 B3
Porttipahdan tekojärvi *l.* Fin. 44 N1
Port Townsend U.S.A. 180 B2

▶ **Portugal** *country* Europe 54 C7
europe [countries] ▶ 32–35

Portugalete Spain 55 H1
Portugália Angola *see* **Chitato**
Portuguesa *state* Venez. 198 D2
Portuguese East Africa *country* Africa *see* **Mozambique**
Portuguese Guinea *country* Africa *see* **Guinea-Bissau**
Portuguese Timor *terr.* Asia *see* **East Timor**
Portuguese West Africa *country* Africa *see* **Angola**
Portumna Rep. of Ireland 47 D10
Portus Herculis Monoeci *country* Europe *see* **Monaco**
Port-Vendres France 51 J10
Port Victoria Australia 146 C3

▶ **Port Vila** Vanuatu 145 F3
Capital of Vanuatu. Also known as Vila.

Portville U.S.A. 176 G3
Port Vladimir Rus. Fed. 44 P1
Port Waikato N.Z. 152 I5
Port Wakefield Australia 146 C3
Port Warrender Australia 150 D2
Port Washington U.S.A. 172 F7
Port Wing U.S.A. 172 B4
Porumamilla India 94 C3
Porus'ya *r.* Rus. Fed. 43 M4
Porvenir *Pando* Bol. 200 C2
Porvenir *Santa Cruz* Bol. 201 E3
Porvenir Chile 205 C9
Porvoo Fin. 45 N3 *also known as* Borgå
Porvoonjoki *r.* Fin. 42 G1
Por'ya Guba Rus. Fed. 44 P2
Poryŏng S. Korea 83 B5 *formerly known as* Taech'ŏn
Porzuna Spain 54 G5
Posada *Sardegna* Italy 57 B8
Posada *r. Sardegna* Italy 57 B8
Posada Spain 54 F1
Posadas Arg. 204 G2
Posadas Spain 54 F7
Posadowsky Bay Antarctica 223 G2
Posavina *reg.* Bos.-Herz./Croatia 56 I3
Poschiavo Switz. 51 Q6
Poseidonia Greece 59 F11
Poseidonia *tourist site* Italy *see* **Paestum**
Posen Poland *see* **Poznań**
Posen U.S.A. 173 J5
Poshekhon'ye Rus. Fed. 43 U3 *formerly known as* Poshekon'ye-Volodarsk
Poshekon'ye-Volodarsk Rus. Fed. *see* **Poshekhon'ye**
Posht *watercourse* Iran 100 D4
Posht-e Badam Iran 100 C3
Poshteh-ye Chaqvīr *hill* Iran 100 D4
Posht-e Kūh *mts* Iran 100 A3
Posht Kūh *hill* Iran 100 B2
Posio Fin. 44 O2
Poskam China *see* **Zepu**
Poso Indon. 75 B3
Poso *r.* Indon. 75 B3
Poso, Danau *l.* Indon. 75 B3
Poso, Teluk *b.* Indon. 75 B3
Posof Turkey 107 E2
Posorja Ecuador 198 A5
Pospelikha Rus. Fed. 103 J1
Posse Brazil 202 C5
Possession Islands Antarctica 223 L2
Pößneck Germany 48 I5
Post U.S.A. 179 B5
Poşta Câlnău Romania 58 H3 *formerly spelt* Poşta Cîlnău
Poşta Cîlnău Romania *see* **Poşta Câlnău**
Postavy Belarus *see* **Pastavy**
Poste-de-la-Baleine Canada *see* **Kuujjuarapik**
Postmasburg S. Africa 132 H5
Postojna Slovenia 56 G3
Poston U.S.A. 183 J7
Postville Canada 169 J2
Postville U.S.A. 174 B3
Post Weygand Alg. 123 F4
Postysheve Ukr. *see* **Krasnoarmiys'k**
Posušje Bos.-Herz. 56 J5
Pos'yet Rus. Fed. 82 C4
Pota Indon. 75 B5
Potamia Greece 58 F8
Potamos Greece 59 D12
Potanino Rus. Fed. 43 N1
Potchefstroom S. Africa 133 L3
Potcoava Romania 58 F4
Poté Brazil 203 D6
Poteau U.S.A. 179 D5
Potegaon India 94 D2
Potentia Italy *see* **Potenza**
Potenza Italy 57 H8 *historically known as* Potentia
Potenza *r.* Italy 56 F5
Poteriteri, Lake N.Z. 153 B14
Potfontein S. Africa 132 I7
Potgietersrus S. Africa 131 F5
Poti *r.* Brazil 202 D3
P'ot'i Georgia 107 E2
Potikal India 94 D2
Potiraguá Brazil 202 E5
Potiskum Nigeria 125 H4
Potnarvin Vanuatu 145 F3
Poto Peru 200 C3
Po Toi *i. Hong Kong* China 87 [inset] *also spelt* Putoi
Potomac *r.* U.S.A. 177 I7
Potomac, South Branch *r.* U.S.A. 176 G6
Potomac, South Fork South Branch *r.* U.S.A. 176 F7
Potomana, Gunung *mt.* Indon. 75 C5
Potoru Sierra Leone 124 C5
Potosí Bol. 200 D4
Potosí *dept* Bol. 200 D5
Potosi U.S.A. 174 B4
Potosi Mountain U.S.A. 183 I6
Pototan Phil. 74 B4
Potrerillos Chile 204 C2
Potrero del Llano Mex. 184 D2
Potro *r.* Peru 198 B6
Potsdam Germany 49 K3
Potsdam U.S.A. 177 K1
Potsdamer Havelseengebiet *park* Germany 49 J3
Pottangi India 95 D2
Pottendorf Austria 49 N8
Potter U.S.A. 178 B3
Potter Valley U.S.A. 182 A2
Potterville U.S.A. 176 A3
Pottsville U.S.A. 177 I5
Potwar *reg.* Pak. 101 H3
Pouancé France 50 E5
Pouce Coupe Canada 166 F4
Pouch Cove Canada 169 K4
Poughkeepsie U.S.A. 177 L4
Poultney U.S.A. 177 L2
Pouma Cameroon 125 H6
Pound U.S.A. 176 C8
Poupan S. Africa 132 I7
Pourerere N.Z. 152 K8
Pouso Alegre Brazil 207 H9
Pouso Alegre, Serra *mts* Brazil 206 D2
Pouso Alto Brazil 206 A3
Poutasi Samoa 145 H3
Poŭthĭsăt Cambodia 79 C5 *also spelt* Pursat
Pouto N.Z. 152 I4
Pouzauges France 50 F6
Povarovo Rus. Fed. 43 S5
Považská Bystrica Slovakia 49 P6
Poved' *r.* Rus. Fed. 43 P4
Povenets Rus. Fed. 40 E3
Povlen *mt.* Yugo. 58 A4
Povoação Brazil 207 N6
Póvoa de Varzim Port. 54 C3
Povorino Rus. Fed. 41 G6
Povorotnyy, Mys *hd* Rus. Fed. 82 D4
Poway U.S.A. 183 G9
Powder *r. MT* U.S.A. 180 F3
Powder *r. OR* U.S.A. 180 C3
Powder, South Fork *r.* U.S.A. 180 F4
Powder River U.S.A. 180 F4
Powell U.S.A. 180 E3
Powell *r.* U.S.A. 176 B9
Powell, Lake *resr* U.S.A. 183 N4
Powell Creek *watercourse* Australia 149 D5
Powell Mountain U.S.A. 182 F3
Powell River Canada 166 E5
Powellsville U.S.A. 177 I9
Powers U.S.A. 172 F5
Powhatan U.S.A. 176 H8
Powhatan Point U.S.A. 176 E6
Powidzkie, Jezioro *l.* Poland 49 O3
Powo China 86 A1
Poxoréu Brazil 202 A5
Poyan, Sungai *r.* Sing. 76 [inset]
Poyang China *see* **Boyang**
Poyang Hu *l.* China 87 F2
Poyan Reservoir Sing. 76 [inset]
Poyarkovo Rus. Fed. 82 C2
Poygan, Lake U.S.A. 172 E6
Poynette U.S.A. 172 D7
Poyo, Cerro *mt.* Spain 55 I7
Poysdorf Austria 49 N7
Pöytyä Fin. 45 M3
Pozantı Turkey 106 C3
Požarevac *Srbija* Yugo. 58 C4
Poza Rica Mex. 185 F4
Požega Croatia 56 J3 *formerly known as* Slavonska Požega
Požega *Srbija* Yugo. 58 B5
Pozharskoye Rus. Fed. 90 D1
Pozhnya Rus. Fed. 43 M5
Pozhva Rus. Fed. 40 K4
Poznań Poland 49 N3 *historically known as* Posen
Pozo Alcón Spain 55 I7
Pozo Betbeder Arg. 204 D2
Pozoblanco Spain 54 G6
Pozo Colorado Para. 201 F5
Pozo del Tigre Arg. 201 E6
Pozo Hondo Arg. 204 D2
Pozohondo Spain 55 J6
Pozo Nuevo Mex. 184 C2
Pozos, Punta *pt* Arg. 205 D7
Pozo San Martin Arg. 204 E2
Pozsony Slovakia *see* **Bratislava**
Pozuzo Peru 200 B2
Pozzallo *Sicilia* Italy 57 G12
Pozzuoli Italy 57 G8 *historically known as* Puteoli
Pra *r.* Ghana 125 E5
Prabumulih Indon. 76 D3
Prabuty Poland 49 Q2
Prachatice Czech Rep. 49 L6
Prachi *r.* India 95 E2
Prachin Buri Thai. 79 C5
Prachuap Khiri Khan Thai. 79 B6
Pradairo *mt.* Spain 54 D1
Praděd *mt.* Czech Rep. 49 O5
Pradera Col. 198 B4
Prades France 51 I10
Prado Brazil 203 E6
Pradópolis Brazil 206 E8

▶ **Prague** Czech Rep. 49 L5
Capital of the Czech Republic. Also known as Praha.

Praha Czech Rep. *see* **Prague**
Prahova *r.* Romania 58 H4

▶ **Praia** Cape Verde 124 [inset]
Capital of Cape Verde.

Praia a Mare Italy 57 H9
Praia do Bilene Moz. 131 G5
Praia Grande Brazil 206 G11
Praia Rica Brazil 201 G3
Prainha *Amazonas* Brazil 201 E1
Prainha *Pará* Brazil 199 H5
Prairie Australia 149 E4
Prairie *r.* U.S.A. 174 A2
Prairie City U.S.A. 180 C3
Prairie Dog Town Fork *r.* U.S.A. 179 B5
Prairie du Chien U.S.A. 172 B7
Prairie River Canada 167 K4
Prakhon Chai Thai. 79 C5
Pram *r.* Austria 49 K7
Pramanta Greece 59 C9
Pran *r.* Thai. 79 C5
Pran Buri Thai. 79 B5
Prangli *i.* Estonia 42 G2
Pranhita *r.* India 94 C2
Prapat Indon. 76 B2
Prasonisi, Akra *pt* Greece 59 I13
Praszka Poland 49 P4
Prat *i.* Chile 205 B8
Prata Brazil 206 E6
Prata *r. Goiás* Brazil 206 A5
Prata *r. Minas Gerais* Brazil 206 D5
Prata *r. Minas Gerais* Brazil 207 G4
Pratapgarh India 96 B4
Pratas Islands China *see* **Dongsha Qundao**
Prat de Llobregat Spain *see* **El Prat de Llobregat**
Prathes Thai *country* Asia *see* **Thailand**
Pratinha Brazil 206 G6
Prato Italy 56 D5
Pratt U.S.A. 178 C4
Prattville U.S.A. 175 C5
Pravara *r.* India 94 B2
Pravda Bulg. 58 I5
Pravdinsk Rus. Fed. 42 C7 *historically known as* Friedland
Pravia Spain 54 E1
Praya Indon. 77 G5
Prazaroki Belarus 45 O5
Preah, Prêk *r.* Cambodia 79 D5
Preăh Vihear Cambodia 79 D5
Prechistoye *Smolenskaya Oblast'* Rus. Fed. 43 N6
Prechistoye *Yaroslavskaya Oblast'* Rus. Fed. 43 V3
Precipice National Park Australia 149 F5
Predazzo Italy 56 D2
Predeal Romania 58 G3
Preeceville Canada 167 K5
Pré-en-Pail France 50 F4
Preetz Germany 48 H1
Pregolya *r.* Rus. Fed. 42 B7
Preiļi Latvia 42 H5
Preissac, Lac *l.* Canada 173 O2
Prekornica *mts* Yugo. 58 A6
Prelate Canada 167 I5
Prémery France 51 J5
Premnitz Germany 49 J3
Prenj *mts* Bos.-Herz. 56 J5
Prentiss U.S.A. 175 B6
Prenzlau Germany 49 K2
Preobrazheniye Rus. Fed. 82 D4
Preparis Island Cocos Is 79 A5
Preparis North Channel Cocos Is 79 A5
Preparis South Channel Cocos Is 79 A5
Přerov Czech Rep. 49 O6
Presa de la Amistad, Parque Natural *nature res.* Mex. 185 E2
Presanella, Cima *mt.* Italy 56 C2
Presa San Antonio Mex. 185 E3
Prescott Canada 168 F4
Prescott *AR* U.S.A. 179 D5
Prescott *AZ* U.S.A. 183 L7
Prescott Valley U.S.A. 183 L7
Preservation Inlet N.Z. 153 A14
Preševo *Srbija* Yugo. 58 C6
Presidencia Roca Arg. 204 F2
Presidencia Roque Sáenz Peña Arg. 204 E2
Presidente Bernardes Brazil 206 B9
Presidente de la Plaza Arg. 204 F2
Presidente Dutra Brazil 202 C3
Presidente Eduardo Frei *research station* Antarctica 222 U2
Presidente Epitácio Brazil 206 A8
Presidente Hermes Brazil 201 E2
Presidente Jânio Quadros Brazil 207 L1
Presidente Juan Perón *prov.* Arg. *see* **Chaco**
Presidente Juscelino Brazil 207 I5
Presidente Olegário Brazil 206 G5
Presidente Prudente Brazil 206 B9
Presidente Venceslau Brazil 206 B8
Presidio U.S.A. 181 F7
Preslav Bulg. *see* **Veliki Preslav**
Prešov Slovakia 49 S7
Prespa, Lake Europe 58 C8 *also known as* Prespansko Ezero *or* Prespës, Liqeni i
Prespansko Ezero *l.* Europe *see* **Prespa, Lake**

P Q index

Prespes nat. park Greece 58 C8
Prespës, Liqeni i l. Europe see Prespa, Lake
Presque Isle ME U.S.A. 174 G2
Presque Isle MI U.S.A. 173 J5
Presque Isle WI U.S.A. 172 D4
Presque Isle Point U.S.A. 172 F4
Pressbaum Austria 49 N7
Pressburg Slovakia see Bratislava
Prestea Ghana 125 E5
Presteigne U.K. 47 I11
Přeštice Czech Rep. 49 K6
Preston U.K. 47 J10
Preston GA U.S.A. 175 C5
Preston IA U.S.A. 172 C8
Preston ID U.S.A. 180 E4
Preston MD U.S.A. 177 J7
Preston MN U.S.A. 174 A3
Preston, Cape Australia 150 B4
Prestonsburg U.S.A. 176 C8
Prestrud Inlet Antarctica 223 N1
Prestwick U.K. 46 H8
Preto r. Amazonas Brazil 199 F5
Preto r. Bahia Brazil 202 D4
Preto r. Goiás Brazil 206 C5
Preto r. Minas Gerais Brazil 206 G3
Preto r. Rondônia Brazil 201 E2
Preto r. São Paulo Brazil 206 D7

Pretoria S. Africa 133 M2
Official capital of South Africa.
world [countries] 10–11

Pretoria-Witwatersrand-Vereeniging prov. S. Africa see Gauteng
Preussisch-Eylau Rus. Fed. see Bagrationovsk
Preußisch Stargard Poland see Starogard Gdański
Preveza Greece 59 B10
Prey Vêng Cambodia 79 D6
Priamurskiy Rus. Fed. 82 D2
formerly known as Pokrovka
Priaral'skiye Karakumy, Peski des. Kazakh. 103 E3
Priargunsk Rus. Fed. 85 H1
formerly known as Tsurukhaytuy
Pribinić Bos.-Herz. 56 J4
Priboj Srbija Yugo. 58 A5
Příbram Czech Rep. 49 L6
Price r. Australia 148 A2
Price Canada 169 G3
Price NC U.S.A. 176 F9
Price UT U.S.A. 183 N2
Price r. U.S.A. 183 N2
Price Island Canada 166 D4
Prichaly Rus. Fed. 42 C6
Prichard AL U.S.A. 175 B6
Prichard WV U.S.A. 176 C7
Priego de Córdoba Spain 54 G7
Priekule Latvia 42 C5
Priekulė Lith. 42 C6
Priekuļi Latvia 42 G4
Prienai Lith. 42 E7
Prienai Lith. 42 G7
Prieska S. Africa 132 G6
Prieskapoort pass S. Africa 132 G6
Priest Lake U.S.A. 180 C2
Prieto hill Spain 55 H6
Prievidza Slovakia 49 P7
Prigor'ye Rus. Fed. 43 O8
Prijedor Bos.-Herz. 56 I4
Prijepolje Srbija Yugo. 58 A5
Prikaspiyskaya Nizmennost' lowland Kazakh./Rus. Fed. see Caspian Lowland
Prikro Côte d'Ivoire 124 E5
Prilep Macedonia 58 C7
Priluki Rus. Fed. 43 U2
Priluki Ukr. see Pryluky
Primavera Bol. 200 D2
Primavera do Leste Brazil 202 A5
Primeira Cruz Brazil 202 D2
Primero de Enero Cuba 186 D2
also known as Violeta
Primghar U.S.A. 178 D3
Primorsk Leningradskaya Oblast' Rus. Fed. 43 J1
Primorsk Volgogradskaya Oblast' Rus. Fed. 41 H6
formerly known as Lugovaya Proleyka
Primorsk Ukr. see Prymors'k
Primorskiy Rus. Fed. 82 C4
formerly known as Ust'-Mongunay
Primorskiy Khrebet mts Rus. Fed. 85 E1
Primorskiy Kray admin. div. Rus. Fed. 82 D3
English form Maritime Kray
Primorsko-Akhtarsk Rus. Fed. 41 F7
Primrose r. Canada 166 B2
Primrose Lake Canada 167 I4
Prince Albert Canada 167 J4
Prince Albert S. Africa 132 G10
Prince Albert Mountains Antarctica 223 K1
Prince Albert National Park Canada 167 J4
Prince Albert Peninsula Canada 165 H2
Prince Albert Road S. Africa 132 F9
Prince Albert Sound sea chan. Canada 165 H2
Prince Alfred, Cape Canada 164 G2
Prince Charles Island Canada 165 L3
Prince Charles Mountains Antarctica 223 E2
Prince Edward Island prov. Canada 169 I4

Prince Edward Islands Indian Ocean 219 J9
Part of South Africa.

Prince Edward Point Canada 173 Q7
Prince Frederick U.S.A. 177 I7
Prince Frederick Harbour Australia 150 D2
Prince George Canada 166 F4
Prince Gustaf Adolf Sea Canada 165 I2
Prince Harald Coast Antarctica 223 C2
also known as Prins Harald Kyst
Prince Karl Foreland i. Svalbard see Prins Karls Forland
Prince of Wales, Cape U.S.A. 164 C3
Prince of Wales Island Australia 149 D1
Prince of Wales Island Canada 165 J2
Prince of Wales Island U.S.A. 164 F4
Prince of Wales Strait Canada 165 H2
Prince Patrick Island Canada 165 H2
Prince Regent r. Australia 150 D2
Prince Regent Inlet sea chan. Canada 165 J2
Prince Regent Nature Reserve Australia 150 D2
Prince Rupert Canada 166 D4
Princess Anne U.S.A. 177 J7
Princess Astrid Coast Antarctica 223 A2
Princess Charlotte Bay Australia 149 D2
Princess Elizabeth Land reg. Antarctica 223 F2
Princess Mary Lake Canada 167 L1
Princess May Range hills Australia 150 D2
Princess Mountains N.Z. 153 B13
Princess Ragnhild Coast Antarctica 223 B2
Princess Royal Island Canada 166 D4
Princeton Canada 166 F5
Princeton CA U.S.A. 182 B2
Princeton IL U.S.A. 174 B3
Princeton IN U.S.A. 174 C4
Princeton KY U.S.A. 174 C4
Princeton MO U.S.A. 174 A3
Princeton NJ U.S.A. 177 K5
Princeton WI U.S.A. 172 D7
Prince William Sound b. U.S.A. 164 E3
Príncipe i. São Tomé and Príncipe 125 G6
Prineville U.S.A. 180 B3
Prinos Greece 58 F8
Prins Harald Kyst coastal area Antarctica see Prince Harald Coast
Prins Karls Forland i. Svalbard 38 B2
English form Prince Karl Foreland
Prinzapolca Nicaragua 186 C4
Priolo Gargallo Sicilia Italy 57 H11
Prior, Cabo c. Spain 54 C1
Priozernyy Kazakh. see Tugyl
Priozersk Rus. Fed. 43 L1
also spelt Priozyorsk
Priozyorsk Rus. Fed. see Priozersk
Pripet r. Belarus/Ukr. 41 C5
also spelt Pryp"yat' (Ukraine) or Prypyats' (Belarus)
Pripet Marshes Belarus/Ukr. 41 C6
also known as Palyeskaya Nizina or Poles'ye
Pripolyarnyy Ural mts Rus. Fed. 40 K2
Priponești Romania 58 I2
Prirechnyy Rus. Fed. 44 O1
Prisăcani Romania 58 I1
Priseka hill Croatia 56 I3
Pristan' Przheval'sk Kyrg. see Przheval'sk Pristany
Priština Kosovo, Srbija Yugo. 58 C6
Prithvipur India 96 C4
Pritzwalk Germany 49 J2
Privas France 51 K8
Privlaka Croatia 56 H4
Privokzal'nyy Rus. Fed. 43 Q6
Privolzhsk Rus. Fed. 40 G4
Privolzhskaya Vozvyshennost' hills Rus. Fed. 41 H6
English form Volga Upland
Privolzhskiy Rus. Fed. 41 H6
Privolzh'ye Rus. Fed. 41 I5
Priyutnoye Rus. Fed. 41 G7
Prizren Kosovo, Srbija Yugo. 58 B6
Prizzi Sicilia Italy 57 F11
Prnjavor Bos.-Herz. 56 J4
Probištip Macedonia 58 D6
Probolinggo Indon. 77 F4
Prochowice Poland 49 N4
Proctor MN U.S.A. 172 A4
Proctor VT U.S.A. 177 L2
Proctorville U.S.A. 176 C7
Proddatur India 94 C3
Proença-a-Nova Port. 54 D5
Professor van Blommestein Meer resr Suriname 199 H3
also known as Brokopondo Stuwmeer
Progreso Hond. 186 B4
Progreso Coahuila Mex. 185 E3
Progreso Hidalgo Mex. 185 F4
Progreso Yucatán Mex. 185 H4
Progress Rus. Fed. 82 C2
Progresso Brazil 200 C2
Project City U.S.A. 182 B1
Prokhladnyy Rus. Fed. 41 H8
Prokletije mts Albania/Yugo. 58 A6
Prokop'yevsk Rus. Fed. 80 D2
Prokuplje Srbija Yugo. 58 C5
Proletariy Rus. Fed. 43 M3
Proletarsk Rus. Fed. 41 G7
formerly known as Proletarskaya
Proletarskaya Rus. Fed. see Proletarsk
Prome Myanmar see Pyè
Promissão Brazil 201 G4
Promissão, Represa resr Brazil 206 D8
Promontorio del Gargano plat. Italy 56 H7
Pronino Rus. Fed. 40 G4
Pronsk Rus. Fed. 43 U7
Pronya r. Belarus 43 M8
Prophet r. Canada 166 F3
Prophet River Canada 166 F3
formerly known as Minaker
Prophetstown U.S.A. 172 D9
Propriá Brazil 202 E4
Proserpine Australia 149 F4
Proshkava Belarus 42 J6
Proskurov Ukr. see Khmel'nyts'kyy
Prosna r. Poland 49 O3
Prosotsani Greece 58 E7
Prospect NY U.S.A. 177 J2
Prospect OH U.S.A. 176 B5
Prospect OR U.S.A. 180 B4
Prospect PA U.S.A. 176 E5
Prosperidad Phil. 74 C4
Prosser U.S.A. 180 C3
Prostějov Czech Rep. 49 O6
Proston Australia 149 F5
Proszowice Poland 49 R5
Protem S. Africa 132 E11
Proti i. Greece 59 C11
Protva Rus. Fed. 43 R6
Protva r. Rus. Fed. 43 S7
Protvino Rus. Fed. 43 S7
Provadiya Bulg. 58 I5
Prøven Greenland see Kangersuatsiaq
Provence-Alpes-Côte-d'Azur admin. reg. France 51 M9
Providence U.S.A. see Annapolis

Providence U.S.A. 177 N4
State capital of Rhode Island.

Providence, Cape N.Z. 153 A14
Providence Atoll Seychelles 129 F7
Providence Bay Canada 173 K5
Providencia Ecuador 198 B5
Providencia, Isla de i. Caribbean Sea 186 C4
Providência, Serra de hills Brazil 201 E2
Providenciales Island Turks and Caicos Is 187 E2
Provideniya Rus. Fed. 39 S3
Providential Channel Australia 149 D2
Provincetown U.S.A. 177 O3
Provincia Col. 198 C3
Provins France 51 J4
Provo U.S.A. 183 M1
Provost Canada 167 I4
Prozor Bos.-Herz. 56 J5
Prozorovo Rus. Fed. 43 S3
formerly known as Mikhaykovskiy
Prrenjas Albania 58 B7
Pru r. Ghana 125 E4
Prub r. Rus. Fed. 40 J3
Prudentópolis Brazil 203 B8
Prudhoe Bay U.S.A. 164 E2
Prudhoe Island Australia 149 F4
Prudki Rus. Fed. 43 N7
Prudnik Poland 49 O5
Prudzinki Belarus 43 J6
Prüm Germany 48 D5
Prundeni Romania 58 F4
Prundu Romania 58 H4
Prundu Bârgăului Romania 58 F1
formerly spelt Prundu Bîrgăului
Prundu Bîrgăului Romania see Prundu Bârgăului
Pruntytown U.S.A. 176 E6
Prusa Turkey see Bursa
Prushkov Poland see Pruszków
Pruszcz Gdański Poland 49 P1
Pruszków Poland 49 R3
historically known as Prushkov
Prut r. Europe 58 J3
Pruzhany Belarus 42 F9
Prvić i. Croatia 56 G4
Prydz Bay Antarctica 223 F2
Pryelbrusskiy Natsional'nyy Park nat. park Rus. Fed. 41 G8
Pryluky Ukr. 41 E6
also spelt Priluki
Prymors'k Ukr. 41 F7
also spelt Primorsk
Prymors'ke Ukr. see Sartana
Prymors'ke Ukr. 58 K3
Pryor U.S.A. 179 D4
Pryp"yat' r. Ukr. see Pripet
Prypyats' r. Belarus 41 C5 see Pripet
Przasnysz Poland 49 R2
Przedbórz Poland 49 Q4
Przemyśl Poland 49 T6
Przeworsk Poland 49 T5
Przheval'sk Kyrg. see Karakol
Przheval'skoye Rus. Fed. 43 M6
formerly known as Sloboda
Przheval'sk Pristany Kyrg. 103 I4
also known as Pristan' Przheval'sk
Przysucha Poland 49 R4
Psachna Greece 59 E10
also spelt Psakhná
Psakhná Greece see Psachna
Psalidis, Akra pt Greece 59 F12
Psara Greece 59 G10
Psara i. Greece 59 G10
Psathoura i. Greece 59 F9
Psebay Rus. Fed. 41 G7
Pserimos i. Greece 59 I12
Pskent Uzbek. 103 G4
also spelt Piskent
P'skhus Nakrdzali nature res. Georgia 107 E2
Pskov Rus. Fed. 43 J4
Pskov, Lake Estonia/Rus. Fed. 42 I3
also known as Pihkva järv or Pskovskoye Ozero
Pskova r. Rus. Fed. 43 J4
Pskov Oblast admin. div. Rus. Fed. see Pskovskaya Oblast'
Pskovskaya Oblast' admin. div. Rus. Fed. 43 K4
English form Pskov Oblast
Pskovskoye Ozero l. Estonia/Rus. Fed. see Pskov, Lake
Psunj mts Croatia 56 J3
Ptan' r. Rus. Fed. 43 T8
Ptich' Belarus see Ptsich
Ptolemaïda Greece 58 C8
Ptolemais Israel see 'Akko
Ptsich Belarus 43 J9
also spelt Ptich'
Ptsich r. Belarus 42 J9
Ptuj Slovenia 56 H2
also known as Pettau; historically known as Poetovio
Pu r. China 85 E5
Pu r. Indon. 76 C3
Puaka hill Sing. 76 [inset]
Pu'an China 86 C3
also known as Panshui
Pu'an China see Jiange
Pucacuro Peru 198 C5
Pucacuro r. Peru 198 C5
Pucalá Peru 198 B6
Pucallpa Peru 200 B2
Pucará Bol. 201 D4
Pucara Peru 200 C3
Pucarani Bol. 200 C4
Pucarevo Bos.-Herz. see Novi Travnik
Puca Urco Peru 198 D5
Pucheng Fujian China 87 F3
also known as Nanpu
Pucheng Shaanxi China 87 D1
Puchezh Rus. Fed. 40 G4
Puch'ŏn S. Korea 83 B5
Pucioasa Romania 58 G3
Pucio Point Phil. 74 B4
Puck Poland 49 P1
Pucka, Zatoka b. Poland 49 P1
Puckford, Mount hill Australia 151 B5
Puçol Spain 55 K5
also spelt Puzol
Pucón Chile 204 C5
Pudai watercourse Afgh. see Dor
Pūdanū Iran 100 C3
Pudasjärvi Fin. 44 N2
Pudimoe S. Africa 133 I4
Puding China 86 C3
Pudozh Rus. Fed. 40 F3
Puducheri India see Pondicherry
Pudukkottai India 94 C4
Puebla Baja California Norte Mex. 183 I9
Puebla Puebla Mex. 185 F5
long form Puebla de Zaragoza
Puebla state Mex. 185 F5
Puebla de Don Fadrique Spain 55 I7
Puebla de Obando Spain 54 E5
Puebla de Zaragoza Mex. see Puebla
Pueblo U.S.A. 181 F5
Pueblo Hundido Chile 204 C2
Pueblo Viejo Col. 199 E4
Pueblo Viejo, Laguna de lag. Mex. 185 F4
Pueblo Yaqui Mex. 184 C3
Puech de Rouet hill France 51 I8
Puelches Arg. 204 D5
Puelén Arg. 204 D5
Puenteareas Spain see Ponteareas
Puente de Ixtla Mex. 185 F5
Puente del Inca Arg. 204 C4
Puente-Genil Spain 54 G7
Puente la Reina Spain 55 J2
also known as Gares
Puentes de García Rodríguez Spain see As Pontes de García Rodríguez
Puente Torres Venez. 198 D2
Pu'er China 86 B4
also known as Ning'er
Puerco watercourse AZ U.S.A. 183 N7
Puerco watercourse NM U.S.A. 181 F6
Puerto Aisén Chile 205 B7
Puerto Alegre Bol. 201 E3
Puerto Alejandría Bol. 200 D3
Puerto Alfonso Col. 198 D5
Puerto America Peru 198 B6
Puerto Ángel Mex. 185 F6
Puerto Antequera Para. 201 F6
Puerto Arista Mex. 185 G6
Puerto Armuelles Panama 186 C5
Puerto Asís Col. 198 B4
Puerto Ayacucho Venez. 199 E3
Puerto Bajo Pisagua Chile 205 B7
Puerto Barrios Guat. 185 H6
Puerto Berrío Col. 198 C3
Puerto Boyaca Col. 198 C3
Puerto Cabello Venez. 199 D2
Puerto Cabezas Nicaragua 186 C4
Puerto Cabo Gracias á Dios Nicaragua 186 C4
Puerto Carreño Col. 199 E3
Puerto Casado Para. 201 F5
Puerto Cavinas Bol. 200 D3
Puerto Cerpera Peru 198 C5
Puerto Ceticayo Peru 200 C2
Puerto Chacabuco Chile 205 B7
Puerto Chicama Peru 200 A1
Puerto Cisnes Chile 205 B7
Puerto Coig Arg. 205 C8
Puerto Córdoba Col. 198 D5
Puerto Cortés Costa Rica 186 C5
Puerto Cortés Hond. 186 B4
Puerto Cortés Mex. 184 C3
Puerto Cuemaní Col. 198 C4
Puerto Cumarebo Venez. 198 D2
Puerto de Cabras Canary Is see Puerto del Rosario
Puerto de Cayo Ecuador 198 A5
Puerto Definitivo Peru 200 C3
Puerto de Hierro Venez. 187 H5
Puerto de los Ángeles, Parque Natural nature res. Mex. 184 D4
Puerto del Rosario Canary Is 122 B3
formerly known as Puerto de Cabras
Puerto del Son Spain see Porto do Son
Puerto de Morelos Mex. 185 I4
Puerto de Nutrias Venez. 198 D2
Puerto de Pollensa Spain see Port de Pollença
Puerto Escondido Mex. 185 F6
Puerto Estrella Col. 198 D1
Puerto Flamenco Chile 204 C2
Puerto Francisco de Orellana Ecuador 198 B5
also known as El Coca; short form Francisco de Orellana
Puerto Génova Bol. 200 D3
Puerto Grether Bol. 201 D4
Puerto Guarani Para. 201 F5
Puerto Harberton Arg. 205 D9
Puerto Heath Bol. 200 C3
Puerto Huitoto Col. 198 C4
Puerto Inca Peru 200 B2
Puerto Ingeniero Ibáñez Chile 205 B7
Puerto Inírida Col. 199 E4
Puerto Irigoyen Arg. 201 E5
Puerto Isabel Bol. 201 F4
Puerto Jesus Costa Rica 186 B5
Puerto Juáres Mex. 185 I4
Puerto La Paz Arg. 201 E5
Puerto Leguízamo Col. 198 C5
Puerto Lempira Hond. 186 C4
Puerto Libertad Mex. 184 B2
Puertollano Spain 54 G6
Puerto Lobos Arg. 205 D6
Puerto Lopez Col. 198 D2
Puerto Lopéz Col. 198 C3
Puerto López Ecuador 198 A5
Puerto Lumbreras Spain 55 J7
Puerto Madero Mex. 185 G6
Puerto Madryn Arg. 205 D6
Puerto Magdalena Mex. 184 B3
Puerto Maldonado Peru 200 C3
Puerto Mamoré Bol. 200 D4
Puerto Manatí Cuba 186 D2
Puerto Máncora Peru 198 A6
Puerto María Auxiliadora Para. 201 F5
Puerto Marquez Bol. 200 D3
Puerto Melinka Chile 205 B6
Puerto Mercedes Col. 198 C4
Puerto México Mex. see Coatzacoalcos
Puerto Mihanovich Para. 201 F5
Puerto Miranda Venez. 199 E3
Puerto Montt Chile 205 B6
Puerto Morazán Nicaragua 186 B4
Puerto Natáles Chile 205 B8
Puerto Nuevo Col. 198 D3
Puerto Olaya Col. 187 E6
Puerto Ordaz Venez. 199 F2
Puerto Ospina Col. 198 C4
Puerto Padre Cuba 186 D2
Puerto Páez Venez. 199 E3
Puerto Pando Bol. 200 D3
Puerto Pardo Peru 198 B5
Puerto Pariamanu Peru 200 C3
Puerto Peñasco Mex. 184 B2
Puerto Pinasco Para. 201 F5
Puerto Pirámides Arg. 205 D6
Puerto Piritu Venez. 199 E2
Puerto Pizarro Col. 198 C5
Puerto Plata Dom. Rep. 187 F3
Puerto Portillo Peru 200 B2
Puerto Prado Peru 200 B2
Puerto Presidente Stroessner Para. see Ciudad del Este
Puerto Princesa Phil. 74 A4
Puerto Quepos Costa Rica 186 B5
Puerto Quetzal Guat. 185 H6
Puerto Real Spain 54 E8
Puerto Rico Arg. 204 G2
Puerto Rico Bol. 200 D2
Puerto Rico Col. 198 C4

Puerto Rico terr. West Indies 187 G3
United States Commonwealth.
oceania [countries] 138–139

Puerto Rico Trench sea feature Caribbean Sea 216 J4
Deepest trench in the Atlantic Ocean.

Puerto Saavedra Chile 204 B5
Puerto Salgar Col. 198 C3
Puerto Sama Cuba see Samá
Puerto San Agustin Peru 198 D5
Puerto San Carlos Chile 205 B7
Puerto Sandino Nicaragua 186 B4
formerly known as Puerto Somoza
Puerto San José Guat. 185 H6
Puerto Santa Cruz Arg. 205 C8
Puerto Sastre Para. 201 F5
Puerto Saucedo Bol. 201 E3
Puertos de Beceite mts Spain see Ports de Beseit
Puerto Serrano Spain 54 F8
Puerto Siles Bol. 200 D3
Puerto Socorro Peru 198 D5
Puerto Somoza Nicaragua see Puerto Sandino
Puerto Suárez Bol. 201 F4
Puerto Supe Peru 200 A2
Puerto Tahuantisuyo Peru 200 C3
Puerto Tejado Col. 198 B4
Puerto Tunigrama Peru 198 B5
Puerto Valdés Arg. 205 E6
Puerto Vallarta Mex. 184 D4
Puerto Varas Chile 205 B6
Puerto Victoria Peru 200 B2
Puerto Villazon Bol. 201 E3
Puerto Visser Arg. 205 D7
Puerto Wilches Col. 198 C3
Puerto Yartou Chile 205 C9
Puesto Arturo Peru 198 C5
Puga Brazil 201 F4
Pugachev Rus. Fed. 102 B1
Pugachevo Rus. Fed. 40 J4
Pugal India 96 B3
Puga Puga, Ilha i. Moz. 131 H2
Puge China 86 B3
also known as Piji
Puger Indon. 77 F5
Puglia admin. reg. Italy 56 H7
Pugwash Canada 169 I4
Puha N.Z. 152 L6
Pūhāl-e Khamīr, Kūh-e mts Iran 100 C5
Puhiwaero c. N.Z. see South West Cape
Puhja Estonia 42 H3
Pui Romania 58 E3
Puiești Romania 58 I3
Puig de Comanegra mt. Spain 55 N2
Puig des Galatzó mt. Spain 55 N5
Puigmal mt. France/Spain 55 N2
Pui O Wan b. Hong Kong China 87 [inset]
Puiseaux France 51 I4
Puits 29 well Chad 120 C6
Puits 30 well Chad 120 C6
Pujada Bay Phil. 74 C5
Puji China see Wugong
Pujiang China 87 F2
also known as Puyang
Pukaki, Lake N.Z. 153 E12
Puk'an-san National Park S. Korea 83 B5
Pukapuka atoll Cook Is 221 G6
also known as Danger Islands
Pukaskwa r. Canada 172 H2
Pukaskwa National Park Canada 168 C3
Pukatawagan Canada 167 K4
Pukchin N. Korea 83 B4
Pukch'ŏng N. Korea 83 C4
Pukë Albania 58 A6
Pukearuhe N.Z. 152 I6
Pukehoi N.Z. 152 K7
Pukekohe N.Z. 152 I5
Pukenui N.Z. 152 H2
Pukeokahu N.Z. 152 J7
Pukerau N.Z. 153 D14
Pukerua Bay N.Z. 152 I9
Puketeraki Range mts N.Z. 153 G11
Puketitiri N.Z. 152 K7
Puketoi Range hills N.Z. 152 K8
Puketutu N.Z. 152 J6
Pukeuri Junction N.Z. 153 F13
Pukhnovo Rus. Fed. 43 M6
Pukkila Fin. 42 G1
Puksoozero Rus. Fed. 40 G3
Puksubaek-san mt. N. Korea 83 B4
Pula China see Nyingchi
Pula Croatia 56 F4
formerly spelt Pola
Pula Sardegna Italy 57 B9
Pulacayo Bol. 200 D5
Pulandian China 85 I4
formerly known as Xinjin
Pulandian Wan b. China 85 I4
Pulangi r. Phil. 74 C5
Pulangpisau Indon. 77 F3
Pular, Cerro mt. Chile 200 C6
Pulasi i. Indon. 75 B4
Pulaski NY U.S.A. 177 I2
Pulaski TN U.S.A. 174 C5
Pulaski VA U.S.A. 176 E8
Pulaski WI U.S.A. 172 E6
Pulau r. Indon. 73 I8
Pulau Pinang state Malaysia see Pinang
Puławy Poland 49 S4
Pulheim Germany 48 D4
Pulicat India 94 D3
Pulicat Lake inlet India 94 D3
Pulivendla India 94 C3
Pulkau r. Austria 49 N7
Pulkkila Fin. 44 N2
Pullman U.S.A. 180 C3
Pulo Anna i. Palau 73 H6
Pulog, Mount Phil. 74 B2
Pulozero Rus. Fed. 40 E1
Púlpito, Punta pt Mex. 184 C3
Pulsano Italy 57 J8
Pułtusk Poland 49 S3
Pulu China 89 C4
Pülümür Turkey 107 D3
Pulutan Indon. 75 C1
Pulyatin Rus. Fed. 90 C3
Puma Tanz. 129 B6
Puma Yumco l. China 89 E6
also spelt Pomo Tso
Pumiao China see Yongning
Pumpkin Creek r. U.S.A. 180 F3
Puna Arg. 204 E2
Puná, Isla i. Ecuador 198 A5
Puna de Atacama plat. Arg. 204 D2
Punakaiki N.Z. 153 F10
Punakha Bhutan 97 F4
Punaluu U.S.A. 181 [inset] Z2
Punata Bol. 200 D4
Punch Pak. 101 H3
Punchaw Canada 166 F4
Punda Maria S. Africa 131 F4
Pundri India 96 C3
Pune India 94 B2
formerly spelt Poona
Punganuru India 94 C3
Punggol Sing. 76 [inset]
Punggol, Sungai r. Sing. 76 [inset]
P'ungsan N. Korea 83 C4
Púnguè r. Moz. 131 G3
Punia Dem. Rep. Congo 126 E5
Puning China 87 F4
Punitaqui Chile 204 C3
Punjab state India 96 B3
Punjab prov. Pak. 101 G4
Punkaharju Fin. 45 O3
Punmah Glacier China/Jammu and Kashmir 89 B5
Puno Peru 200 C3
Puno dept Peru 200 C3
Punpun r. India 97 E4
Punta, Cerro de mt. Puerto Rico 187 G3
Punta Alta Arg. 204 E5
Punta Arenas Chile 205 C9
formerly known as Magallanes
Punta Balestrieri mt. Sardegna Italy 57 B8
Punta de Bombón Peru 200 C4
Punta de Diaz Chile 204 C3
Punta Delgada Arg. 205 E6
Punta de los Llanos Arg. 204 D3
Punta Gorda Belize 185 H5
Punta Gorda Nicaragua 186 C5
Punta Gorda U.S.A. 175 D7
Punta Negra, Salar salt flat Chile 200 C6
Punta Norte Arg. 205 E6
Punta Prieta Mex. 184 B2
Puntarenas Costa Rica 186 B5
Puntas Negras, Cerro mt. Chile 200 D5
Punta Umbría Spain 54 E7
Punto Fijo Venez. 198 D2
Puntón de Guara mt. Spain 55 K2
Punxsutawney U.S.A. 176 G5
Puokio Fin. 44 N2
Puolanka Fin. 44 N2
Puquio Peru 200 B3
Puquios Chile 200 C4
Pur r. Rus. Fed. 39 H3
Puracé, Parque Nacional nat. park Col. 198 B4
Puranpur India 96 D3
Purari r. P.N.G. 73 J8
Purbalingga Indon. 77 E4
Purcell U.S.A. 179 C5
Purcell Mountains Canada 167 G5
Purcellville U.S.A. 176 H6
Pureba Conservation Park nature res. Australia 146 B2
Purekkari neem pt Estonia 42 G2
Puren Chile 204 B5
Pureora Forest Park nature res. N.Z. 152 J6
Purgatoire r. U.S.A. 178 B4
Purgstall an der Erlauf Austria 49 M7
Puri Angola 127 B6
Puri India 95 E2
Purmerend Neth. 48 B3
Purna India 94 C2
Purna r. Maharashtra India 94 C2
Purna r. Maharashtra India 96 C5
Purnabhaba r. India 97 F4
Purndu Saltpan salt flat Australia 146 A1
Purnea India see Purnia
Purnia India 97 E4
formerly spelt Purnea
Purnululu National Park Australia 150 E3
formerly known as Bungle Bungle National Park
Purranque Chile 204 B6
Pursat Cambodia see Poŭthĭsăt
Purtuniq Canada 165 L3
formerly known as Asbestos Hill
Puruandíro Mex. 185 E4
Puruê r. Brazil 198 D5
Purukcahu Indon. 77 F3
Puruliya India 97 E5

Purus r. Peru 199 F5
3rd longest river in South America.
southamerica [landscapes] 190–191

Puruvesi l. Fin. 45 O3
Purvis U.S.A. 175 B6
Pŭrvomay Bulg. 58 G6
Purwa India 96 D4
Purwakarta Indon. 77 D4
Purwareja Indon. 77 E4
Purwodadi Indon. 77 E4
Purwokerto Indon. 77 E4
Puryŏng N. Korea 82 C4
Pus r. India 94 C2
Puša Latvia 42 I5
Pusa r. Spain 54 G5
Pusad India 94 C2
Pusan S. Korea 83 C6
also spelt Busan or Fusan
Pusan Point Phil. 74 C5
Pusatdamai Indon. 77 E2
Pusatlı Dağı mt. Turkey 108 E1
Pushchino Rus. Fed. 43 S7
Pushemskiy Rus. Fed. 40 H3
Pushkar India 96 B4
Pushkin Rus. Fed. 43 L2
Pushkino Azer. see Biläsuvar
Pushkino Rus. Fed. 102 A2
Pushkinskaya, Gora mt. Rus. Fed. 82 F3
Pushkinskiye Gory Rus. Fed. 43 J4
Pusht-i Āsmān spring Iran 100 D3
Pusht-i-Rud reg. Afgh. 101 E4
Püspökladány Hungary 49 S8
Püssi Estonia 42 I2
Pusti Lisac mt. Yugo. 56 K6
Pustoshka Rus. Fed. 43 K5
Pusula Fin. 42 E1
Pusur r. Bangl. 97 F5
Puszcza Augustowska for. Poland 49 U2
Puszcza Natecka for. Poland 49 M3
Pusztaszeri park Hungary 49 R9
Putahow Lake Canada 167 K3
Putao Myanmar 78 B2
formerly known as Fort Hertz
Putaruru N.Z. 152 J6
Putbus Germany 49 K1
Puteoli Italy see Pozzuoli
Puteran i. Indon. 77 F4
Putere N.Z. 152 L6
Puteyets Rus. Fed. 40 K2
Puthein Myanmar see Bassein
Putian China 87 F3
Putignano Italy 56 J8
Putilovo Rus. Fed. 40 H4
Putimets Rus. Fed. 43 R9
Putina Peru 200 C3
Puting China see De'an
Puting, Tanjung pt Indon. 77 E3
Putla Mex. 185 F5
Putlitz Germany 48 J2
Putna r. Romania 58 I3
Putnam U.S.A. 177 N4
Putney U.S.A. 177 M3
Putoi i. Hong Kong China see Po Toi
Putorana, Gory mts Rus. Fed. 39 J3
Putrajaya Malaysia 76 C2
Putre Chile 200 C4
Putsonderwater S. Africa 132 F6
Puttalam Sri Lanka 94 C4
Puttalam Lagoon Sri Lanka 94 C4
Puttgarden Germany 48 I1
Puttur India 94 B3
Putú Chile 204 B4
Putumbumba Dem. Rep. Congo 126 C6
Putumayo dept Col. 198 C4
Putumayo r. Col. 198 D5
Pütürge Turkey 107 D3
also known as İmrun
Putusibau Indon. 77 F2
Putyvl' Ukr. 41 E6
Puula l. Fin. 45 N3
Puumala Fin. 45 O3
Puuwai U.S.A. 181 [inset] Y1
Puvurnituq Canada 165 L3
Puxian China 85 F4
Puyallup U.S.A. 180 B3
Puyang China 85 G5
Puyang China see Pujiang
Puy de Dôme mt. France 51 I7
Puy de Montoncel mt. France 51 J7
Puy de Sancy mt. France 51 I7
Puyehue, Parque Nacional nat. park Chile 204 C6
Puyel Arg. 205 C6
Puy Gris mt. France 51 M7
Puylaurens France 51 I9
Puyo Ecuador 198 B5
Puysegur Point N.Z. 153 A14
Puzol Spain see Puçol
Pwani admin. reg. Tanz. 129 C6
also known as Coast
Pweto Dem. Rep. Congo 127 F7
Pwllheli U.K. 47 H11
Pyalitsa Rus. Fed. 40 F2
Pyal'ma Rus. Fed. 40 E3
Pyamalaw r. Myanmar 78 A5
Pyandzh r. Afgh./Tajik. 101 G2
also known as Ab-i-Panja; also spelt Panj
Pyandzh Tajik. see Dusti
Pyandzh Tajik. see Panj
Pyaozero, Ozero l. Rus. Fed. 44 O2
Pyaozerskiy Rus. Fed. 44 O2
Pyapon Myanmar 78 A4
Pyasina r. Rus. Fed. 39 I2
Pyasino, Ozero l. Rus. Fed. 39 I3
Pyasinskiy Zaliv b. Rus. Fed. 39 I2
Pyasǔchnik r. Bulg. 58 F6
Pyatigorsk Rus. Fed. 41 G7
Pyatikhatki Ukr. see P"yatykhatky
Pyatimar Kazakh. see Pyatimarskoye
Pyatimarskoye Kazakh. 102 B2
formerly known as Pyatimar
Pyatirech'ye Rus. Fed. 43 L1
Pyatovskiy Rus. Fed. 43 R7
P"yatykhatky Ukr. 41 E6
also spelt Pyatikhatki
Pyaunglaung r. Myanmar 78 B4
Pyawbwe Myanmar 78 B3
Pyazhelka Rus. Fed. 43 Q1
Pyazhozero, Ozero l. Rus. Fed. 43 Q1
Pyè Myanmar 78 A4
also known as Pyin; formerly known as Prome
Pyershamayski Belarus 42 G8
Pyeski Belarus 42 F8
Pyes Pa N.Z. 152 K5
Pyetrykaw Belarus 43 J9
also spelt Petrikov
Pygmalion Point India 95 G5
Pyhäjärvi l. Fin. 42 E1

Pyhäjärvi l. Fin. 44 N3
Pyhäjärvi l. Fin. 44 N3
Pyhäjärvi l. Fin. 44 O3
Pyhäjärvi l. Fin. 45 M3
Pyhäjoki Fin. 44 N2
Pyhäjoki r. Fin. 44 N2
Pyhältö Fin. 42 I1
Pyhäntä Fin. 44 N2
Pyhäranta Fin. 45 M3
Pyhäsalmi Fin. 44 N3
Pyhäselkä Fin. 44 O3
Pyhäselkä l. Fin. 44 O3
Pyhätunturin kansallispuisto nat. park Fin. 44 N2
Pyhtää Fin. 45 N3
Pyin Myanmar see Pyè
Pyingaing Myanmar 78 A3
Pyinmana Myanmar 78 B4
Pyli Greece 59 I12
also spelt Píli
Pyl'karamo Rus. Fed. 39 I3
Pylos Greece 59 C12
also spelt Pílos
Pymatuning Reservoir U.S.A. 176 E4
Pyŏksŏng N. Korea 83 B5
Pyŏktong N. Korea 83 B4
P'yŏnggang N. Korea 83 B5
P'yŏngsong N. Korea 83 B5
P'yŏngt'aek S. Korea 83 B5

P'yŏngyang N. Korea 83 B5
Capital of North Korea.

Pyŏnsan Bando National Park S. Korea 83 B6
Pyramid Lake U.S.A. 182 E1
Pyramid Lake Indian Reservation res. U.S.A. 182 E1
Pyramid Range mts U.S.A. 182 E2
Pyrenees mts Europe 55 N2
also spelt Pyrénées or Pirineos
Pyrénées mts Europe see Pyrenees
Pyrénées Occidentales, Parc National des nat. park France/Spain 55 K2
Pyrgetos Greece 59 D9
also spelt Piryetós
Pyrgi Greece 59 G10
also known as Piryíon
Pyrgos Greece 59 C11
also spelt Pírgos
Pyrton, Mount hill Australia 150 B4
Pyryatyn Ukr. 41 E6
also spelt Piryatin
Pyrzyce Poland 49 L2
Pyshchug Rus. Fed. 40 H4
Pyshna Belarus 43 J7
Pyszna r. Poland 49 P4
Pytalovo Rus. Fed. 42 I4
Pythonga, Lac l. Canada 173 Q4
Pyu Myanmar 78 B4
Pyxaria mt. Greece 59 E10
also spelt Pixariá

Q

Qā', Wādī al watercourse Saudi Arabia 104 B2
Qaa Lebanon 109 H3
formerly spelt El Kaa
Qaanaaq Greenland see Thule
Qabanbay Kazakh. see Kabanbay
Qabātiya West Bank 108 G5
Qābil Oman 105 F3
Qabka China see Xaitongmoin
Qabnag China 89 F6
Qabqa China see Gonghe
Qabr Bandar tourist site Iraq 107 E5
Qabr Hūd Oman 105 E4
Qabyrgha r. Kazakh. see Kabyrga
Qacentina Alg. see Constantine
Qacha's Nek Lesotho 133 M7
Qaḍā' Chāy watercourse Iraq 109 P3
Qadamgāli Iran 100 D2
Qādes Afgh. 101 E3
Qaḍīmah Saudi Arabia 104 B3
Qādir Karam Iraq 107 F4
Qādisīyah, Buḩayrat al resr Iraq 109 N3
Qādisīyah, Sadd dam Iraq 107 E4
English form Qadisiyah Dam
Qadisiyah Dam Iraq see Qādisīyah, Sadd
Qādub Yemen 105 F5
Qa'emabad Iran 101 E4
Qā'emiyeh Iran 100 B4
Qagan China 85 H1
Qagan Ders China 85 E3
Qagan Nur Nei Mongol China 85 F4
Qagan Nur Nei Mongol China 85 G3
also known as Xulun Hobot Qagan Qi or Zhengxiangbai Qi
Qagan Nur Nei Mongol China 85 G3
Qagan Nur Qinghai China 84 C4
Qagan Nur l. China 85 J2
Qagan Nur resr China 85 G3
Qagan Teg China 85 G3
Qagan Tohoi China 84 B5
Qagan Us China see Dulan
Qagan Us He r. China 84 C4
Qagca China 86 A1
formerly known as Cacagoin
Qagchêng China see Xiangcheng
Qahar Youyi Houqi China see Bayan Qagan
Qahar Youyi Qianqi China see Togrog Ul
Qahar Youyi Zhongqi China see Hobor
Qā' Ḥazawẓā' depr. Saudi Arabia 107 D5
Qahd, Wādī watercourse Saudi Arabia 104 C2
Qahr, Jibāl al hills Saudi Arabia 104 D4
Qahremānshahr Iran see Kermānshāh
Qaḩṭān reg. Saudi Arabia 104 C3
Qaidam He r. China 84 B4
Qaidam Pendi basin China 84 B4
English form Tsaidam Basin
Qaidar China see Cêtar
Qainaqangma China 89 E5
Qaisar Afgh. 101 F3
Qaisar r. Afgh. 101 F2
Qaisar, Koh-i- mt. Afgh. 101 F3
Qalabotjha S. Africa 133 M4
Qalā Diza Iraq 107 F3
Qala'en Nahl Sudan 121 G6
Qala-i-Fateh Afgh. 101 E4
Qala-i-Kang Afgh. 101 E4
Qal'aikhum Tajik. 101 G2
also spelt Kalaikhum; formerly spelt Kalai-Khumb
Qalamat Abū Shafrah Saudi Arabia 105 F3
Qalamat Al Juḩaysh oasis Saudi Arabia 105 E3
Qalamat ar Rakabah oasis Saudi Arabia 105 F3
Qalamat Fāris oasis Saudi Arabia 105 E4
Qalamat Nadqān well Saudi Arabia 105 E3
Qalamat Shutfah well Saudi Arabia 105 F3
Qalansīyah Yemen 105 F5
Qala Shinia Takht Afgh. 101 F3
Qalāt Afgh. 101 F3
Qal'at al Aẓlam Saudi Arabia 104 A2
Qal'at al Ḩiṣn tourist site Syria 109 H3
Qal'at al Marqab tourist site Syria 108 G2
Qal'at al Mu'aẓẓam Saudi Arabia 104 B2
Qal'at Bīshah Saudi Arabia 104 C3
Qal'at Muqaybirah, Jabal mt. Syria 109 J2
Qal'at Şāliḩ Iraq 107 F5
Qala Vali Afgh. 101 E3
Qalbī Zhotasy mts Kazakh. see Kalbinskiy Khrebet
Qal'eh Iran 100 C2
Qal'eh Dāgh mt. Iran 100 A2
Qal'eh Tirpul Afgh. 101 E3
Qal 'eh-ye Bost Afgh. 101 F4
Qal 'eh-ye Now Afgh. 101 E3
Qal'eh-ye Shūrak well Iran 100 D3
Qalhāt Oman 105 G3
Qalīb Bāqūr well Iraq 107 F5
Qalqīlya West Bank 108 F5
Qalqutan Kazakh. see Koluton
Qalti el Adusa well Sudan 121 E5
Qalyûb Egypt 121 F2
Qalyûbîya governorate Egypt 108 C7
Qamalung China 86 A1
Qamanirjuaq Lake Canada 167 M2
also known as Kaminuriak Lake
Qamanittuaq Canada see Baker Lake
Qamar, Ghubbat al b. Yemen 105 F4
English form Qamar Bay
Qamar, Jabal al mts Oman 105 F4
Qamar Bay Yemen see Qamar, Ghubbat al
Qamashi Uzbek. see Kamashi
Qamdo China 86 A2
also spelt Chamdo
Qam Hadīl Saudi Arabia 104 C4
Qamīnis Libya 120 C2
Qamruddin Karez Pak. 101 G4
Qamşar Iran 100 B3
Qamystybas Kazakh. see Kamyshlybash
Qanawt Oman 105 F4
Qandahar Afgh. see Kandahār
Qandala Somalia 128 F2
Qandaranbashi mt. Iran 100 A2
Qandyaghash Kazakh. see Kandyagash
Qangzê China 89 B6
Qanṭara, Gebel hill Egypt 108 B7
Qapal Kazakh. see Kapal
Qapan Iran 100 C2
Qapqal China 88 C3
Qapshagay Kazakh. see Kapchagay
Qapshagay Bögeni resr Kazakh. see Kapchagayskoye Vodokhranilishche
Qaq Köli salt l. Kazakh. see Kak, Ozero
Qaqortoq Greenland 165 O3
also known as Julianehåb
Qara Egypt 106 A5
Qarā', Jabal al mts Oman 105 F4
Qara Āghach r. Iran see Mand, Rūd-e
Qara Anjīr Iraq 109 P2
Qaraaoun Lebanon 108 G4
Qarabas Kazakh. see Karabas
Qarabulaq Kazakh. see Karabulak
Qarabutaq Kazakh. see Karabutak
Qaraçala Azer. 100 B2
Qarachōq, Jabal mts Iraq 107 E4
Qara Ertis r. China/Kazakh. see Ertix He
Qaraghandy Kazakh. see Karaganda
Qaraghandy Oblysy admin. div. Kazakh. see Karagandinskaya Oblast'
Qaraghayly Kazakh. see Karagayly
Qārah Saudi Arabia 107 E5
Qārah, Jabal al hill Saudi Arabia 104 D4
Qarah Bāgh Ghaznī Afgh. 101 G3
Qarah Bāgh Kābul Afgh. 101 G3
Qarak China 88 B4
Qaraköl Kazakh. see Karakol'
Qaranqu r. Iran 100 A2
Qaraoy Kazakh. see Karaoy
Qara Özek Uzbek. see Karauzyak
Qaraqalpaqstan Respublikasy aut. rep. Uzbek. see Karakalpakistan, Respublika
Qara Qōsh Iraq 109 O1
Qaraqoyyn Köli salt l. Kazakh. see Karakoyyn, Ozero
Qaraqozha Kazakh. see Karaguzhikha
Qaraqum des. Kazakh. see Karakum Desert
Qaraqum des. Turkm. see Karakum Desert
Qarasū Kazakh. see Karasu
Qara Şū Chāy r. Syria/Turkey see Karasu
Qara Tarai mt. Afgh. 101 F3
Qarataū Kazakh. see Karatau
Qarataū Zhotasy mts Kazakh. see Karatau, Khrebet
Qaratöbe Kazakh. see Karatobe
Qaratoghay Kazakh. see Karatogay
Qaratomar Bögeni resr Kazakh. see Karatomarskoye Vodokhranilishche
Qaraton Kazakh. see Karaton
Qaraūyl Kazakh. see Karaul
Qarazhal Kazakh. see Karazhal
Qardho Somalia 128 F2
Qardud Sudan 126 F2
Qareh Chāy r. Iran 100 B3
Qareh Dāgh mts Iran 100 A2
Qareh Qāch, Kūh-e mts Iran 100 C3
Qareh Sū r. Iran 100 A2
Qâret Gahannam hill Egypt 108 B8
Qarhan China 84 B4
Qarkilik China see Ruoqiang
Qarnayţ, Jabal hill Saudi Arabia 104 C3
Qarnein i. U.A.E. 105 F2
Qarn el Kabsh, Gebel mt. Egypt 121 G2
Qarokŭl l. Tajik. 101 H2
also known as Karakul', Ozero
Qarqan China see Qiemo
Qarqan He r. China 88 D4
Qarqaraly Kazakh. see Karkaralinsk
Qarqi Xinjiang China 88 C3
Qarqi Xinjiang China 88 D3
Qārqi Iran 102 C5
Qarqīn Afgh. 101 F2
Qarrit, Qafa e pass Albania 58 B8
Qarsaqbay Kazakh. see Karsakpay
Qarshi Uzbek. see Karshi
Qarshi Chŭli plain Uzbek. see Karshinskaya Step'
Qartaba Lebanon 108 G3
Qārūh, Jazīrat i. Kuwait 107 G5
Qârûn Egypt 108 B8
Qaryat al Ulyā Saudi Arabia 105 D2
Qaşab, Wādī al watercourse Iraq 109 O2
Qasamī Iran 100 D3
Qasa Murg mts Afgh. 101 E3
Qasba India 97 E4
Qaşbah, Ras al pt Saudi Arabia 108 F9
Qāsemābād Khorāsan Iran 100 D3
Qāsemābād Khorāsan Iran 101 D2
Qashqadaryo r. Uzbek. see Kashkadar'ya
Qashqadaryo Wiloyati admin. div. Uzbek. see Kashkadar'inskaya Oblast'
Qash Qai reg. Iran 100 B4
Qashqantengiz Kazakh. see Kashkanteniz
Qasigiannguit Greenland 165 N3
also known as Christianshåb
Qasīm reg. Saudi Arabia 104 C2
Qaskelen Kazakh. see Kaskelen
Qasq China 85 F3
also known as Tumd Zuoqi
Qaşr ad Dayr, Jabal mt. Jordan 108 G7
Qaşr al Azraq Jordan 109 H6
Qasr al Ḩayr tourist site Syria 109 I3
Qasr al Khubbāz Iraq 107 E4
Qaşr 'Āmij Iraq 109 M4
Qaşr 'Amrah tourist site Jordan 109 H6
Qaşr aş Şabīyah Kuwait 107 G5
Qaşr Burqu' tourist site Jordan 109 I5
Qaşr-e-Qand Iran 101 E5
Qaşr-e Shīrīn Iran 107 F4
Qasr Farafra Egypt 121 E3
Qaşr Ḩimām Saudi Arabia 105 D3
Qaşr Larocu Libya 120 B3
Qaşr Shaqrah tourist site Iraq 107 F5
Qassimiut Greenland 165 O3
Qa'tabah Yemen 104 D5
Qaţanā Syria 108 H4
Qatar country Asia 105 E2
asia [countries] 64–67
Qatlish Iran 100 D2
Qaṭrâni, Gebel esc. Egypt 121 F2
Qaţrūyeh Iran 100 C4
Qaţţāfī, Wādī al watercourse Jordan 109 I6
Qattâra, Râs esc. Egypt 121 E2
Qattâra Depression Egypt 121 E2
also known as Qaţţārah, Munkhafaḍ al
Qaţţārah, Munkhafaḍ al depr. Egypt see Qattâra Depression
Qaţţīnah, Buḩayrat resr Syria 109 H3
also known as Ḩimş, Baḩrat
Qavāmābād Iran 100 D4
Qax Azer. 107 F2
also spelt Kakhi
Qāyen Iran 100 D3
Qayghy Kazakh. see Kayga
Qaynar Kazakh. see Kaynar
Qayraqty Kazakh. see Kayrakty
Qayroqqum Tajik. 101 G1
formerly spelt Kayrakkum
Qaysīyah, Qa' al imp. l. Jordan 109 H6
Qayyārah Iraq 107 E4
Qazaly Kazakh. see Kazalinsk
Qazangödağ mt. Armenia/Azer. 107 F3
also known as Kapydzhik, Gora
Qazaq Shyghanaghy b. Kazakh. see Kazakhskiy Zaliv
Qazaqstan country Asia see Kazakhstan
Qazax Azer. 107 F2
also spelt Kazakh
Qazi Ahmad Pak. 101 G5
Qazımämmäd Azer. 107 G2
also spelt Kazi Magomed
Qazvīn Iran 100 B2
Qazvīn prov. Iran 100 B2
Qazyqurt Kazakh. see Kazygurt
Qedir China 88 D3
Qeh China 84 D3
Qeisûm, Gezâ'ir is Egypt 104 A2
English form Qeisûm Islands; also spelt Geisûm, Gezâ'ir
Qeisûm Islands Egypt see Qeisûm, Gezâ'ir
Qelelevu i. Fiji 145 H3
also spelt Nggelelevu
Qena Egypt 121 G3
also spelt Qinā
Qena governorate Egypt 104 A2
Qena, Wâdi watercourse Egypt 121 G3
Qeqertarsuaq Greenland 165 N3
also known as Godhavn
Qeqertarsuaq i. Greenland 165 N3
also known as Disko
Qeqertarsuatsiaat Greenland 165 N3
also known as Fiskenæsset
Qeqertarsuatsiaq i. Greenland 165 N2
also known as Hareøen
Qeqertarsuup Tunua b. Greenland 165 N3
also known as Disko Bugt
Qeshlāq Iran 100 A3
Qeshm Iran 100 D5
Qeshm i. Iran 100 D5
Qeydār Iran 100 B2
Qeys i. Iran 100 C5
Qezel Owzan, Rūdkhāneh-ye r. Iran 100 B2
Qeẓi'ot Israel 108 F7
Qi r. China 85 G5
Qian r. China 87 C1
Qian'an Hebei China 85 H4
Qian'an Jilin China 85 J2
Qiancheng China 87 D3
Qiang r. China 87 F1
Qian Gorlos China see Qianguozhen
Qianguozhen China 82 B3
also known as Qian Gorlos
Qianjiang Chongqing China 87 D2
also known as Lianhe
Qianjiang Hubei China 87 E2
Qianjin China 82 D3
formerly known as Weidongmen
Qianning China 86 B2
also known as Gartar
Qianqihao China 85 I2
Qianshan China 87 F2
also known as Meicheng
Qian Shan mts China 85 I3
Qianshanlaoba China 88 D2
Qianwei China 86 B2
also known as Yujin
Qianxi Guizhou China 86 C3
Qianxi Hebei China 85 H3
also known as Xingcheng
Qianxian China 87 D1
Qianyang Hunan China 87 D3
also known as Anjiang
Qianyang Shaanxi China 86 C1
Qianyang Zhejiang China 87 F2
Qianyou China see Zhashui
Qiaocun China 85 G4
Qiaojia China 86 B3
also known as Xinhua
Qiaoshan China see Huangling
Qiaotou China see Datong
Qiaotou China 86 B3
Qiaowa China see Muli
Qiaowan China 84 C3
Qiaozhuang China see Qingchuan
Qibā' Saudi Arabia 104 D2
Qibing S. Africa 133 L6
Qibray Uzbek. see Kibray
Qichun China 87 E2
also known as Caohe; formerly known as Caojiahe
Qidong Hunan China 87 E3
formerly known as Hongqiao
Qidong Jiangsu China 87 G2
also known as Huilongzhen
Qiemo China 88 D4
formerly known as Cherchen or Qarqan
Qihe China 85 H4
also known as Yancheng
Qijiang China 86 C2
also known as Gunan
Qijiaojing China 88 E3
Qikiqtarjuaq Canada 165 M3
formerly known as Broughton Island
Qiktim China 88 E3
Qila Ladgasht Pak. 101 E5
Qilaotu Shan mts China 85 H3
Qila Safed Pak. 101 E4
Qila Saifullah Pak. 101 G4
Qili China see Shitai
Qilian China 84 D4
also known as Babao
Qilian Shan mt. China 84 C4
Qilian Shan mts China 84 C4
Qillak i. Greenland 165 P3
also known as Dannebrog Ø
Qīma Kazakh. see Kiyma
Qiman el 'Arûs Egypt 108 C8
Qimantag mts China 89 E4
Qimen China 87 F2
also known as Qishan
Qimusseriarsuaq b. Greenland 165 M2
also known as Melville Bugt
Qin r. China 87 E1
Qinā Egypt see Qena
Qināb, Wādī r. Yemen 105 E4
Qin'an China 86 C1
also known as Xingguo
Qincheng China see Nanfeng
Qing r. China 82 A4
Qing'an China 82 B3
Qingcheng China see Qingyang
Qingchengzi China 83 A4
Qingchuan China 86 C1
also known as Qiaozhuang
Qingdao China 85 I4
formerly spelt Tsingtao
Qinggang China 82 B3
Qinggil China see Qinghe
Qingguandu China 87 D2
Qinghai prov. China 84 C4
English form Tsinghai; formerly known as Chinghai
Qinghai Hu salt l. China 84 D4
Qinghai Nanshan mts China 84 C4
Qinghe Hebei China 85 G4
also known as Gexianzhuang
Qinghe Xinjiang China 84 A2
also known as Qinggil
Qinghua China see Bo'ai
Qingjian China 85 F4
also known as Xiuyan
Qingjiang China see Huaiyin
Qingjiang China see Zhangshu
Qing Jiang r. China 87 D2
Qingkou China see Ganyu
Qingliu China 87 F3
also known as Longjin
Qinglong Guizhou China 86 C3
also known as Liancheng
Qinglong Hebei China 85 H3
Qinglong r. China 85 H4
Qingpu China 87 G2
Qingquan China see Xishui
Qingshan China see Dedu
Qingshizui China 84 D4
Qingshui China see Qingshuipu
Qingshui China 86 C1
also known as Yongqing
Qingshuihe Nei Mongol China 85 F4
Qingshuihe Qinghai China 86 A1
also known as Domda
Qingshuihezi China 88 C2
Qingshuilang Shan mts China 86 A3
Qingshuipu China 84 C4
formerly known as Qingshui
Qingtian China 87 G2
also known as Hecheng
Qingtongxia China 85 E4
also known as Xiaoba
Qingxian China 85 H4
also known as Qingzhou
Qingxu China 85 G4
also known as Qingyuan
Qingyang Anhui China 87 F2
also known as Rongcheng
Qingyang Gansu China 85 E4
also known as Qingcheng
Qingyang China see Sihong
Qingyuan China see Weiyuan
Qingyuan Guangdong China 87 E4
Qingyuan China see Yizhou
Qingyuan Liaoning China 82 B4
Qingyuan China see Qingxu
Qingyuan Zhejiang China 87 F3
Qingyun China 85 H4
formerly known as Xiejiaji
Qingzang Gaoyuan plat. China see Tibet, Plateau of
Qingzhen China 86 C3
Qingzhou China see Qingxian
Qingzhou Hubei China 87 D2
Qingzhou Shandong China 85 H4
formerly known as Yidu
Qinhuangdao China 85 H4
Qinjiang China see Shicheng
Qin Ling mts China 87 C1
Qinshui China 85 G5
Qinting China see Lianhua
Qinxian China 85 G4
Qinyang China 85 G5
Qinyuan China 85 G4
Qinzhou China 87 D4
Qinzhou Wan b. China 87 D4
Qionghai China 87 D5
Qiongjiexue China see Qonggyai
Qionglai China 86 B2
Qionglai Shan mts China 86 B2
Qiongshan China 87 D5
Qiongxi China see Hongyuan
Qiongzhou Haixia strait China see Hainan Strait
Qiqihar China 85 I2
formerly spelt Tsitsihar
Qiquanhu China 88 E3
Qīr Iran 100 C4
Qira China 89 C4
Qîraîya, Wâdi watercourse Egypt 108 F7
Qiryat Gat Israel 108 F6
Qiryat Shemona Israel 108 G4
Qishan China see Qimen
Qishan China 87 C1
also known as Fengming
Qishn Yemen 105 E5
Qishon r. Israel 108 G5
Qishrān Island Saudi Arabia 104 C3
Qitab ash Shāmah vol. crater Saudi Arabia 107 D5
Qitai China 88 E3
Qitaihe China 82 C3
Qitbīt, Wādī r. Oman 105 F4
Qiubei China 86 C3
also known as Jinping
Qiujin China 87 E2
Qixia China 85 I4
Qixian Henan China 85 G5
formerly known as Zhaoge
Qixian Henan China 87 E1
Qixian Shanxi China 85 G4
Qixing r. China 82 D3
Qiyang China 87 D3
Qiying China 85 E4
Qizhou Liedao i. China 87 D5
Qızılağac Körfäzi b. Azer. 100 B2
formerly known as Kirova, Zaliv
Qizil-Art, Aghbai pass Kyrg./Tajik. see Kyzylart Pass
Qizilrabot Tajik. 101 H2
also spelt Kyzylrabot
Qizqetkan Uzbek. see Kyzketken
Qoboqobo S. Africa 133 M9
Qoghaly Kazakh. see Kugaly
Qogir Feng mt. China/Jammu and Kashmir see K2
Qog Qi China 85 E3
Qojūr Iran 100 A2
Qolora Mouth S. Africa 133 M9
Qoltag mts China 88 E3
Qom Iran 100 B3
Qom prov. Iran 100 B3
Qomdo China see Qumdo
Qomishēh Iran 100 B3
formerly known as Shahrezā
Qomolangma Feng mt. China/Nepal see Everest, Mount
Qonaqkänd Azer. 107 G2
Qonggyai China 89 E6
also known as Qiongjiexue; also spelt Chonggye
Qongj China 85 F3
Qongkol China 88 D3
Qongrat Uzbek. see Kungrad
Qongyrat Kazakh. see Kounradskiy
Qongyrat Kazakh. see Konyrat
Qongyröleng Kazakh. see Konyrolen
Qonj China 84 C4
Qonystanū Kazakh. see Konystanu
Qooriga Neegro b. Somalia 128 F3
Qoornoq Greenland 165 N3
Qoqek China see Tacheng
Qoqodala S. Africa 133 K8
Qoradaryo r. Kyrg. see Kara-Darya
Qoraghaty Kazakh. see Kuragaty
Qoraqalpoghiston Uzbek. see Karakalpakiya
Qoraqalpoghiston Respublikasi aut. rep. Uzbek. see Karakalpakistan, Respublika
Qoraŭzak Uzbek. see Karauzyak
Qorday Kazakh. see Kurday
Qorghalzhyn Kazakh. see Kurgal'dzhinskiy
Qornet es Saouda mt. Lebanon 108 H3
Qorowulbozor Uzbek. see Karaulbazar
Qoroy, Gardaneh-ye pass Iran 100 B2
Qorveh Iran 100 A3
Qosh Tepe Iraq 107 E3
Qosshaghyl Kazakh. see Koschagyl
Qostanay Kazakh. see Kostanay
Qostanay Oblysy admin. div. Kazakh. see Kustanayskaya Oblast'
Qoţbābād Iran 100 D5
Qoţūr Iran 100 A2
Qozhaköl l. Kazakh. see Kozhakol', Ozero
Qozonketkan Uzbek. see Kazanketken
Qozoqdaryo Uzbek. see Kazakhdar'ya
Quabbin Reservoir U.S.A. 177 M3
Quadra Island Canada 166 E5
Quadros, Lago dos l. Brazil 203 B9
Quaggasfontein Poort pass S. Africa 132 E8
Quail Mountains U.S.A. 183 G6
Quairading Australia 151 B7
Quakenbrück Germany 48 E3
Quamby Australia 149 D4
Quanah U.S.A. 179 C5
Quanbao Shan mt. China 87 D1
Quân Đao Cô Tô is Vietnam 78 D3
Quan Dao Hoang Sa is S. China Sea see Paracel Islands
Quân Đao Nam Du i. Vietnam 79 D6
Quan Dao Truong Sa is S. China Sea see Spratly Islands
Quang Ngai Vietnam 79 E5
Quang Tri Vietnam 78 D4
Quang Yen Vietnam 78 D3
Quan He r. China 87 E1
Quanjiang China see Suichuan
Quan Long Vietnam see Ca Mau
Quannan China 87 E3
also known as Chengxiang
Quan Phu Quoc i. Vietnam see Phu Quôc, Đao
Quanshang China 87 F3
Quanwan Hong Kong China see Tsuen Wan
Quanzhou Fujian China 87 F3
Quanzhou Guangxi China 87 D3
Qu'Appelle r. Canada 167 K5
Quaqtaq Canada 165 M3
formerly known as Notre-Dame-de-Koartac; formerly spelt Koartac
Quaraí Brazil 204 F3
Quarry Bay Hong Kong China 87 [inset]
Quarryville U.S.A. 177 I6
Quarteira Port. 54 C7
Quartu Sant'Elena Sardegna Italy 57 B9
Quartzite Mountain U.S.A. 183 H4
Quartzsite U.S.A. 183 J8
Quaryat al Faw tourist site Saudi Arabia 105 D4
Quba Azer. 107 G2
also spelt Kuba
Quchan Iran 100 D2
Qudaysah well Oman 105 G4
Qudeni S. Africa 133 O5
Queanbeyan Australia 147 F3

Québec Canada 169 G4
Provincial capital of Québec.

Québec prov. Canada 169 F2
Quebra Anzol r. Brazil 206 F6
Quedas Moz. 131 G3
Quedlinburg Germany 48 I4
Queen Adelaide Islands Chile see La Reina Adelaida, Archipiélago de
Queen Alia airport Jordan 108 G6
Queen Anne U.S.A. 177 J7
Queen Bess, Mount Canada 166 E5
Queen Charlotte Canada 166 C4
Queen Charlotte Bay Falkland Is 205 E8
Queen Charlotte Islands Canada 166 C4
Queen Charlotte Sound sea chan. Canada 166 D5
Queen Charlotte Strait Canada 166 E5
Queen Creek U.S.A. 183 M8
Queen Elizabeth Islands Canada 165 I2
Queen Elizabeth National Park Uganda 128 A5
formerly known as Ruwenzori National Park
Queen Elizabeth Range mts Antarctica 223 K1
Queen Fabiola Mountains Antarctica 223 C2
Queen Mary Land reg. Antarctica 223 G2
Queen Maud Bird Sanctuary nature res. Canada 167 K1
Queen Maud Gulf Canada 165 I3
Queen Maud Land reg. Antarctica 223 A2
also known as Dronning Maud Land
Queen Maud Mountains Antarctica 223 O1
Queensburgh S. Africa 133 O6
Queens Channel Australia 148 A2
Queenscliff Australia 147 E4
Queensland state Australia 149 E4
Queenstown Australia 147 E5
Queenstown N.Z. 153 C13
Queenstown Rep. of Ireland see Cóbh
Queenstown S. Africa 133 K8
Queenstown Sing. 76 [inset]
Queenstown U.S.A. 177 I7
Queen Victoria Spring Nature Reserve Australia 151 C6
Quehua Bol. 200 D4
Quehué Arg. 204 D5
Queiba well Chad 120 D5
Queimada Brazil 201 E2
Queimada, Ilha i. Brazil 202 B2
also known as Serraria, Ilha
Queimadas Brazil 202 E4
Queiroz Brazil 206 C8
Quela Angola 127 C7
Quelimane Moz. 131 H3
Quelite Mex. 184 D4
Quellón Chile 205 B6
Quelpart Island S. Korea see Cheju-do
Queluz Brazil 207 I9
Quemada Grande, Ilha i. Brazil 206 G11
Quemado U.S.A. 181 E6
Quembo r. Angola 127 D8
Quemchi Chile 205 B6
Quemoy i. Taiwan see Chinmen Tao
Quemú-Quemú Arg. 204 E5
Quepem India 94 B3
Que Que Zimbabwe see Kwekwe
Quequén Arg. 204 F5
Querência Brazil 202 A5
Querétaro Mex. 185 E4
Querétaro state Mex. 185 F4
Querfurt Germany 48 I4
Querobabi Mex. 184 C2
Querpon Peru 198 B6
Quesada Spain 55 H7
Quesat watercourse W. Sahara 122 C4
Queshan China 87 E1
also known as Panlong
Quesnel Canada 166 F4
Quesnel r. Canada 166 F4
Quesnel Lake Canada 166 F4
Questembert France 50 D5
Quetena de Lipez r. Bol. 200 D5
Quetico Provincial Park Canada 172 B2
Quetta Pak. 101 F4
Queuco Chile 204 C5
Queulat, Parque Nacional nat. park Chile 205 B7
Queupán Arg. 204 D6
Queyras, Parc Naturel Régional du nature res. France 51 M8
Quezaltenango Guat. 185 H6
Quezaltepeque El Salvador 185 H6
Quezon Negros Phil. 74 B4
Quezon Palawan Phil. 74 A4

Quezon City Phil. 74 B3
Former capital of the Philippines.

Qufu China 85 H5
Qugayatang China 89 E6
Quibala Angola 127 B7
Quibaxe Angola 127 B7
Quibdó Col. 198 B3
Quiberon France 50 C5
Quiberon, Baie de b. France 50 C5
Quíbor Venez. 198 D2
Quicama, Parque Nacional do nat. park Angola 127 B7
also spelt Kisama, Parque Nacional de
Quiet Lake Canada 166 C2
Quihita Angola 127 B8
Quiindy Para. 201 F6
Quilá Mex. 184 D3
Quilalí Nicaragua 186 B4
Quilán, Cabo c. Chile 205 B6
Quilandi India 94 B4
Quilca Peru 200 B4
Quilenda Angola 127 B7
Quilengues Angola 127 B8
Quillacollo Bol. 200 D4
Quillan France 51 I10
Quill Lakes Canada 167 J5
Quillota Chile 204 C4
Quilmes Arg. 204 F4
Quilon India 94 C4
also known as Kollam
Quilpie Australia 149 E5
Quilpué Chile 204 C4
Quimbele Angola 127 C6
Quimilí Arg. 204 E2
Quimome Bol. 201 E4
Quimper France 50 B5
Quimperlé France 50 C5
Quinault r. U.S.A. 180 A3
Quinault Indian Reservation res. U.S.A. 180 A3
Quince Mil Peru 200 C3
Quincinetto Italy 51 N7
Quincy CA U.S.A. 182 D2
Quincy FL U.S.A. 175 C6
Quincy IL U.S.A. 174 B4
Quincy MI U.S.A. 173 I9
Quincy OH U.S.A. 176 B5
Quindio dept Col. 198 C3
Quines Arg. 204 D4
Quinga Moz. 131 I2
Quinhagak U.S.A. 164 C4
Quinhámel Guinea-Bissau 124 B4
Qui Nhon Vietnam 79 E5
Quinigua, Cerro mts Venez. 199 E3
Quiniluban i. Phil. 74 B4
Quinkan Aboriginal Holding res. Australia 149 E2
Quinn r. U.S.A. 180 C4
Quinn Canyon Range mts U.S.A. 183 I4
Quinnimont U.S.A. 176 D8
Quiñones Bol. 200 D2
Quintana Brazil 206 C9
Quintana de la Serena Spain 54 F6
Quintanar de la Orden Spain 55 H5
Quintanar del Rey Spain 55 J5
Quintana Roo state Mex. 185 H5
Quintin France 50 D4
Quinto r. Arg. 204 D4
Quinto Spain 55 K3
Quinzau Angola 127 B6
Quinze, Lac des l. Canada 173 N3
Quionga Moz. 129 D7
Quiotepec Mex. 185 F5
Quipapá Brazil 202 F4
Quipungo Angola 127 B8
formerly known as Paiva Couceiro; formerly spelt Kipungo
Quiquive r. Bol. 200 D3
Quiriguá tourist site Guat. 185 H6
Quirihue Chile 204 B5
Quirima Angola 127 C7
Quirindi Australia 147 F2
Quirinópolis Brazil 206 C5
Quirke Lake Canada 173 K4
Quiroga Bol. 200 D4
Quiroga Spain 54 D2
Quisiro Venez. 198 D2
Quissac France 51 K9
Quissamã Brazil 207 L9
Quitapa Angola 127 C7
Quita Sueño Bank sea feature Caribbean Sea 186 C4
Quiterajo Moz. 129 D7
Quitéria r. Brazil 206 B7
Quitexe Angola see Dange
Quitilipi Arg. 204 E2
Quitman GA U.S.A. 175 D6
Quitman MS U.S.A. 175 B5

Quito Ecuador 198 B5
Capital of Ecuador.

Quitovac Mex. 184 B2
Quitralco, Parque Nacional nat. park Chile 205 B7
Quixadá Brazil 202 E3
Quixeramobim Brazil 202 E3
Qujiang China see Quxian
Qu Jiang r. China 86 C2
Qujing China 86 B3
Quko S. Africa 133 M9
Qulaly Araly i. Kazakh. see Kulaly, Ostrov
Qul'ân, Gezâ'ir i. Egypt 104 A2
English form Gulân Islands
Qulandy Kazakh. see Kulandy
Qulanötpes watercourse Kazakh. see Kulanotpes
Qulbān Layyah well Iraq 107 F5
Quljuqtow Toghi hills Uzbek. see Kul'dzhuktau, Gory
Qulsary Kazakh. see Kul'sary
Qulûsana Egypt 106 B5
Qulzum, Baḩr el b. Egypt see Suez Bay
Qumar He r. China 84 B5
Qumarheyan China 84 B5
Qumarlêb China 84 B5
also known as Yiggêtang
Qumbu S. Africa 133 M8
Qumdo China 97 G3
formerly spelt Qomdo
Qumola watercourse Kazakh. see Kumola
Qumrha S. Africa 133 L9
Qunayy well Saudi Arabia 105 D3
Qunayyin, Sabkhat al salt marsh Libya 120 D2
Qunfudh Yemen 105 E4
Qŭnghirot Uzbek. see Kungrad
Qu'nyido China 86 A2
Quoich r. Canada 167 M1
Quoin Island Australia 148 A2
Quoin Point S. Africa 132 D11
Quong Muztag mt. China 89 C5
Quorn Australia 146 C3
Quoxo r. Botswana 131 E4
Quqên China see Jinchuan
Qŭqon Uzbek. see Kokand
Qurayat Oman 105 G3
Qurayyah tourist site Saudi Arabia 108 H9
Qurayyat al Milḩ l. Jordan 109 I6
Qŭrghonteppa Tajik. 101 G2
also spelt Kurgantyube
Qus Egypt 121 G3
Qusar Azer. 107 G2
also spelt Kusary
Quşay'ir Saudi Arabia 105 E5
Quseir Egypt 121 G3
Qushan China see Beichuan
Qūshchī Iran 100 A2
Qūsheh Dāgh mts Iran 100 A2
Qŭshkŭpir Uzbek. see Koshkupyr
Qŭshrabot Uzbek. see Koshrabad
Qusmuryn Kazakh. see Kushmurun
Qusmuryn Köli salt l. Kazakh. see Kushmurun, Ozero
Qusum Xizang China 89 B5
Qusum Xizang China 89 F6
also known as Xiajiang
Quthing Lesotho see Moyeni
Quthing r. Lesotho 133 L7
Quţn, Jabal hill Saudi Arabia 104 C2

index

Q R

Qutū' Island Saudi Arabia 104 C4
Quwayq, Nahr r. Syria/Turkey 109 I2
also known as Haleparki Deresi
Qū' Wishām reg. Oman 105 F4
Quwu Shan mts China 85 E4
Quxar China see Lhazê
Quxian China 86 C2
also known as Qujiang
Qūxū China 89 E6
also known as Xoi
Quyang China see Jingzhou
Quyghan Kazakh. see Kuygan
Quyon Canada 173 Q5
Qūyūn Eshek i. Iran 100 A2
Qūz Saudi Arabia 104 C4
Quzhou Hebei China 85 G4
Quzhou Zhejiang China 87 F2
Quzi China 85 E4
Qvareli Georgia 107 F2
also spelt Kvareli
Qypshaq Köli salt l. Kazakh. see Kypshak, Ozero
Qyteti Stalin Albania see Kuçovë
Qyzan Kazakh. see Kyzan
Qyzylaghash Kazakh. see Kyzylagash
Qyzylkesek Kazakh. see Kyzylkesek
Qyzylköl l. Kazakh. see Kyzylkol', Ozero
Qyzylorda Kazakh. see Kyzylorda
Qyzylorda Oblysy admin. div. Kazakh. see Kzyl-Ordinskaya Oblast'
Qyzyltaū Kazakh. see Kyzyltau
Qyzyltū Kazakh. see Kishkenekol'
Qyzylzhar Kazakh. see Kyzylzhar

↓ R

Raab r. Austria 49 N9
Raab Hungary see Győr
Raahe Fin. 44 N2
Rääkkylä Fin. 44 O3
Raalte Neth. 48 D3
Ra'an, Khashm ar hill Saudi Arabia 104 C2
Raanujärvi Fin. 44 N2
Raas i. Indon. 77 F4
Raasay i. U.K. 46 F6
Raasiku Estonia 42 G2
Rab i. Croatia 56 G4
Rába r. Hungary 49 O8
Raba Indon. 77 G5
Raba r. Poland 49 R5
Rabaale Somalia 128 F2
Rabak Sudan 121 G6
Rabang China 89 C5
Rabat Gozo Malta see Victoria
Rabat Malta 53 E4

Rabat Morocco 122 D2
Capital of Morocco.

Rabatakbaytal Tajik. see Akbaytal
Rabāt-e Kamah Iran 100 D3
Rabaul P.N.G. 145 E2
Rabaul vol. P.N.G. 145 E2
Rabbath Ammon Jordan see 'Ammān
Rabbi r. Italy 56 E4
Rabbit r. Canada 166 E3
Rabbit Flat Australia 148 A4
Rabbitskin r. Canada 166 F2
Rábca r. Hungary 49 O8
Rabezha Rus. Fed. 43 O4
Rabidine well Niger 125 G3
Rābigh Saudi Arabia 104 B3
Rabinal Guat. 185 H6
Rabka Poland 49 Q6
Rabkob India see Dharmjaygarh
Rabnabad Islands Bangl. 97 F5
Râbnița Moldova see Rîbnița
Rābor Iran 100 D4
Rabotoqbaytal Tajik. see Akbaytal
Rabt Sbayta des. W. Sahara 122 B5
Rabyānah oasis Libya 120 D3
Rača Srbija Yugo. 58 B4
Racalmuto Sicilia Italy 57 F11
Racconigi Italy 51 N8
Raccoon Cay i. Bahamas 186 E2
Raccoon Creek r. U.S.A. 176 C7
Raceland U.S.A. 175 B6
Race Point U.S.A. 177 O3
Rachaïya Lebanon 108 G4
Rachel U.S.A. 183 I4
Rachevo Rus. Fed. 43 S3
Rach Gia Vietnam 79 D6
Rach Gia, Vinh b. Vietnam 79 D6
Raciąż Poland 49 R3
Racibórz Poland 49 P5
historically known as Ratibor
Racine WI U.S.A. 172 F8
Racine WV U.S.A. 176 D7
Racine Lake Canada 173 J2
Răciu Romania 58 F2
Racoș Romania 58 G2
Racovița Romania 58 D3
Radā' Yemen 104 D5
Radashkovichy Belarus 42 I7
also spelt Radoshkovichi
Rădăuți Romania 41 C7
Radbuza r. Czech Rep. 49 K6
Radchenko Rus. Fed. 43 R5
Radcliff U.S.A. 174 C4
Radd, Wādī ar watercourse Syria 109 M1
Radde Rus. Fed. 82 C2
Rade Norway 45 J4
Radebeul Germany 49 K4
Radenthein Austria 49 K9
Radew r. Poland 49 M1
Radford U.S.A. 176 E8
Radford Point Australia 148 A1
Radhanpur India 96 A5
Radishchevo Rus. Fed. 102 A1
Radisson Que. Canada 168 E2
Radisson Sask. Canada 167 J4
Raditsa-Krylovka Rus. Fed. 43 P8
Radium S. Africa 133 M2
Radium Hot Springs Canada 167 G5
Radlinski, Mount Antarctica 222 R1
Radnevo Bulg. 58 G6
Rado de Tumaco inlet Col. 198 B4
Radogoshcha Rus. Fed. 43 P2
Radolfzell am Bodensee Germany 48 F8
Radom Poland 49 S4
Radom Sudan 126 E2
Radomir Bulg. 58 D6
Radomir mt. Bulg./Greece 58 E7
formerly known as Kalabak
Radomka r. Poland 49 S4
Radom National Park Sudan 126 D2
Radomsko Poland 49 Q4
formerly known as Noworadomsk
Radomyshl' Ukr. 41 D6
Radoshkovichi Belarus see Radashkovichy
Radovets Bulg. 58 H7
Radoviš Macedonia 58 D7
Radovitskiy Rus. Fed. 43 U6
formerly known as Tsentral'nyy
Radovljica Slovenia 56 G2
Radøy i. Norway 46 Q3
Radstock, Cape Australia 146 B3
Răducăneni Romania 58 I2
Radun' Belarus 42 F7
Radunia r. Poland 49 P1
Radviliškis Lith. 42 E6
Radwā, Jabal mt. Saudi Arabia 104 B2
Radymno Poland 49 T6
Radziejów Poland 49 P3
Radzyń Podlaski Poland 49 T4
Rae Bareli India 96 D4
Raecreek r. Canada 166 B1
Rae-Edzo Canada 167 G2
also known as Edzo
Raeford U.S.A. 174 E5
Rae Lakes Canada 167 G1
Raeside, Lake salt flat Australia 151 C6
Raetihi N.Z. 152 J7
Rāf hill Saudi Arabia 107 D5
Rafaela Arg. 204 E3
Rafah Gaza see Rafiah
Rafaï Cent. Afr. Rep. 126 D3
Raffadali Sicilia Italy 57 F11
Rafhā' Saudi Arabia 107 E5
Rafiah Gaza 108 F6
also spelt Rafah
Rafina Greece 59 F10
Rafsanjān Iran 100 C4
also known as Bahāmabād
Raft r. U.S.A. 180 D4
Raga Sudan 126 E2
Ragag Sudan 126 E2
Ragana Latvia 42 F4
Ragang, Mount vol. Phil. 74 C5
Ragay Gulf Phil. 74 B3
Ragged, Mount hill Australia 151 C7
Ragged Island Bahamas 186 E2
Ragged Island U.S.A. 177 Q2
Raghogarh India 96 C4
Raghwah waterhole Saudi Arabia 109 P9
Raghwān, Wādī watercourse Yemen 104 D5
Raglan N.Z. 152 I5
Rago Nasjonalpark nat. park Norway 44 L2
Ragueneau Canada 169 G3
Ragusa Croatia see Dubrovnik
Ragusa Sicilia Italy 57 G12
Raha India 97 G4
Raha Indon. 75 B4
Rahachow Belarus 43 L8
also spelt Rogachev
Rahad r. Sudan 121 G6
Rahad Canal Sudan 121 G6
Rahad el Berdi Sudan 126 D2
Rahad Wahal well Sudan 120 E6
Rahaeng Thai. see Tak
Rahaṭ, Ḥarrat lava field Saudi Arabia 104 C3
Rahatgaon India 96 C5
Rahimatpur India 94 B2
Rahimyar Khan Pak. 101 G4
Rāhjerd Iran 100 B3
Rahotu N.Z. 152 H7
Rahouia Alg. 55 M9
Rahumäe Estonia 42 I3
Rahuri India 94 B2
Rahzanak Afgh. 101 E3
Raiatea i. Fr. Polynesia 221 H7
also known as Uliatea
Raibu i. Indon. see Air
Raichur India 94 C2
Raiganj India 97 F4
Raigarh Chhattisgarh India 97 D5
Raigarh Orissa India 94 D2
Raijua i. Indon. 75 B5
Raikot India 96 B3
Railroad Valley U.S.A. 183 I3
Raimangal r. Bangl. 97 F5
Raimbault, Lac l. Canada 169 G2
Rainbow Lake Canada 166 G3
Raine Entrance sea chan. Australia 149 E1
Raine Island Australia 149 E1
Rainelle U.S.A. 176 E8
Raini r. Pak. 101 G4
Rainier, Mount vol. U.S.A. 180 B3
Rainy r. U.S.A. 174 A1
Rainy Lake Canada 168 A3
Raippaluoto i. Fin. 44 M3
Raipur Bangl. 97 F5
Raipur Chhattisgarh India 97 D5
Raipur Rajasthan India 96 B4
Raipur W. Bengal India 97 E5
Rairangpur India 97 E5
Raisen India 96 C5
Raisinghnagar India 96 B3
Raisio Fin. 45 M3
Raistakka Fin. 44 O2
Raitalai India 96 C5
Raith Canada 172 D2
Rai Valley N.Z. 152 H9
Raivavae i. Fr. Polynesia 221 I7
also known as Vavitao
Raiwind Pak. 101 H4
Raja Estonia 42 I3
Raja, Ujung pt Indon. 76 B2
Rajaampat, Kepulauan is Indon. 75 D3
Rajabasa, Gunung vol. Indon. 77 D4
Rajagangapur India 97 E5
Rajahmundry India 94 D2
Raja-Jooseppi Fin. 44 O1
also known as Rājijovsset
Rajaldesar India 96 B3
Rajamäki Fin. 42 F1
Rajampet India 94 C3
Rajang r. Sarawak Malaysia 77 E2
Rajanpur Pak. 101 G4
Rajapalaiyam India 94 C4
Rajapur India 94 B2
Rajasthan state India 96 B4
historically known as Rajputana Agency
Rajasthan Canal India 96 B3
Rajauli India 97 E4
Rajbari Bangl. 97 F5
Rajgarh Madhya Pradesh India 96 C4
Rajgarh Maharashtra India 94 B2
Rajgarh Rajasthan India 96 B3
Rajgarh Rajasthan India 96 C4
Rajgir India 97 E4
Rajgród Poland 49 T2
Rājijovsset Fin. see Raja-Jooseppi
Rajim India 94 D1
Rajince Srbija Yugo. 58 C6
Rajkot India 96 A5
Rajmahal India 97 E4
Rajmahal Hills India 97 E4
Raj Nandgaon India 96 D5
Rajpipla India 96 B5
Rajpur India 96 B5
Rajpura India 96 C3
Rajputana Agency state India see Rajasthan
Rajsamand India 96 B4
Rajshahi Bangl. 97 F4
also known as Rampur Boalia
Rajshahi admin. div. Bangl. 97 F4
Rājū Syria 109 H1
Rajula India 96 A5
Rajur India 94 C1
Rajura India 94 C2
also known as Manikgarh
Rajura India see Ahmadpur
Raka China 89 D6
Rakahuri r. N.Z. see Ashley
Rakai Uganda 128 A5
Rakaia N.Z. 153 G11
Rakaia r. N.Z. 153 G11
Rakan, Ra's pt Qatar 105 E2
Rakaposhi mt. Jammu and Kashmir 96 B1
Raka Zangbo r. China see Dogxung Zangbo
Rakeahua, Mount hill N.Z. 153 B14
Rakhaing state Myanmar see Arakan
Rakhine state Myanmar see Arakan
Rakhiv Ukr. 53 G2
Rakhshan r. Pak. 101 E5
Rakiraki Fiji 145 G3
Rakit i. Indon. 77 E4
Rakitnitsa r. Bulg. 58 G6
Rakitnoye Rus. Fed. 41 E6
Rakitnoye Rus. Fed. 82 D3
Rakitu Island N.Z. 152 J4
formerly known as Arid Island
Rakiura i. N.Z. see Stewart Island
Rakke Estonia 42 H3
Rakkestad Norway 45 J4
Rakmanovskie Klyuchi Kazakh. 88 D1
Rakni r. Pak. 101 G4
Rakoniewice Poland 49 N3
Rakops Botswana 131 E4
Rakovitsa Bulg. 58 D5
Rakovník Czech Rep. 49 K5
Rakovski Bulg. 58 F6
Rakushechnyy, Mys pt Kazakh. 102 B4
Rakvere Estonia 42 H2
Ralebona Lesotho 133 M7
Raleigh MS U.S.A. 175 B5

Raleigh NC U.S.A. 174 E5
State capital of North Carolina.

Raleighvallen Voltsberg, Natuurreservaat nature res. Suriname 199 G3
Ralla Indon. 75 A4
Ralph U.S.A. 172 F4
Ralston Canada 167 I5
Ralston U.S.A. 177 I4
Ram r. Canada 166 F2
Rama Israel 108 G5
Rama Nicaragua 186 B4
Ramacca Sicilia Italy 57 G11
Ramādī, Saddat ar dam Iraq 109 O4
Ramaditas Chile 200 C5
Ramah Canada 169 I1
Ramales de la Victoria Spain 55 H1
Ramalho, Serra do hills Brazil 202 C5
Ramallah West Bank 108 G6
Ramallo Arg. 204 E4
Ramanagaram India 94 C3
Ramanathapuram India 94 C4
also known as Ramnad
Ramanuj Ganj India 97 D5
Ramas, Cape India 94 B3
Ramasukha Rus. Fed. 43 O9
Ramatlabama watercourse Botswana/S. Africa 133 J2
Ramatlabama S. Africa 133 J2
Ramayampet India 94 C2
Ramberg Norway 44 K1
Rambervillers France 51 M4
Rambouillet France 50 H4
Rambutyo Island P.N.G. 73 K7
historically known as Jesu Maria Island
Ramdurg India 94 B3
Ramechhap Nepal 97 E4
Rame Head S. Africa 133 N8
Rame Head U.K. 47 H13
Ramenskoye Rus. Fed. 43 T6
Rameshki Rus. Fed. 43 R4
Rameswaram India 94 C4
Ramezān Kalak Iran 101 E5
Ramgarh Bangl. 97 F5
Ramgarh Jharkhand India 97 E5
Ramgarh Rajasthan India 96 A4
Ramgarh Rajasthan India 96 C4
Ramgul reg. Afgh. 101 G3
Rāmhormoz Iran 100 B4
Ramingining Australia 148 B2
Ramit Tajik. see Romit
Ramitan Uzbek. see Romitan
Ramla Israel 108 F6
Ramlat al Ghāfah des. Saudi Arabia 105 F3
Ramlat al Wahībah des. Oman 105 G3
Ramlat Amilhayt des. Oman 105 F4
Ramlat as Sab'atayn des. Yemen 105 D5
Ramlat Dahm des. Saudi Arabia/Yemen 105 D4
Ramlat Rabyānah des. Libya see Rebiana Sand Sea
Ramm, Jabal mts Jordan 108 G8
also spelt Rum, Jebel
Rammulotsi S. Africa 133 K4
Ramnad India see Ramanathapuram
Ramnagar Madhya Pradesh India 96 D4
Ramnagar Uttaranchal India 96 C3
Ramnagar Jammu and Kashmir 96 B2
Ramnäs Sweden 45 L4
Ramni Belarus 43 L6
Râmnicu Sărat r. Romania 58 I3
Râmnicu Sărat Romania 58 I3
formerly spelt Rîmnicu Sărat
Râmnicu Vâlcea Romania 58 F3
formerly spelt Rîmnicu Vîlcea
Ramo Eth. 128 D3
Ramokgwebane Botswana 131 E4
Ramona U.S.A. 183 H8
Ramón Lista Arg. 205 D7
Ramonville-St-Agne France 50 H9
Ramore Canada 173 M2
Ramos Arg. 201 D5
Ramos Arizpe Mex. 185 E3
Ramotswa Botswana 131 E5
Rampart of Genghis Khan tourist site Asia 85 G1
Ramparts r. Canada 166 D1
Rampur Himachal Pradesh India 89 B6
Rampur Uttar Pradesh India 96 C3
Rampur Uttar Pradesh India 96 C3
Rampura India 96 B4
Rampur Boalia Bangl. see Rajshahi
Rampur Hat India 97 E4
Ramree Myanmar 78 A4
Ramree Island Myanmar 78 A4
Ramsele Sweden 44 L3
Ramsey Canada 173 K3
Ramsey Isle of Man 47 H9
Ramsey Lake Canada 168 D4
Ramsgate S. Africa 133 O7
Ramsgate U.K. 47 N12
Ramshai Hat India 97 F4
Rāmshir Iran 100 B4
Ramsing mt. India 97 G3
Ramsjö Sweden 45 K3
Ramtek India 96 C5
Ramu Bangl. 97 G5
Ramu r. P.N.G. 73 J7
Ramundberget Sweden 44 K3
Ramusio, Lac l. Canada 169 I2
Ramvik Sweden 44 L3
Ramygala Lith. 42 F6
Rana, Cerro hill Col. 199 D4
Rañadoiro, Puerto de pass Spain 54 E2
Rañadoiro, Sierra de mts Spain 54 E1
Ranaghat India 97 F5
Ranai i. U.S.A. see Lanai
Rana Pratap Sagar resr India 96 B4
Ranapur India 96 B5
Rånåsfoss Norway 45 J3
Ranau Sabah Malaysia 77 G1
Ranau, Danau l. Indon. 76 C4
Rancagua Chile 204 C4
Rance r. France 50 D4
Rancharia Brazil 206 C9
Rancheria Canada 166 D2
Rancheria r. Canada 166 D2
Ranchester U.S.A. 180 F3
Ranchi India 97 E5
Rancho Cordova U.S.A. 182 C3
Rancho de Caçados Tapiúnas Brazil 201 F2
Ranchos de Taos U.S.A. 181 F5
Rancho Veloz Cuba 175 D8
Ranco, Lago l. Chile 204 B6
Randallstown U.S.A. 177 I6
Randangan Panua Reserve nature res. Indon. 75 B2
Randazzo Sicilia Italy 57 G11
Randburg S. Africa 133 L3
Randers Denmark 45 J4
Randfontein S. Africa 133 L3
Randijaure l. Sweden 44 L2
Randolph MA U.S.A. 177 N3
Randolph ME U.S.A. 177 P1
Randolph NY U.S.A. 176 G3
Randolph UT U.S.A. 180 E4
Randolph VT U.S.A. 177 M2
Randow r. Germany 49 L2
Randsburg U.S.A. 182 G6
Randsfjorden l. Norway 45 J3
Randsjö Sweden 45 K3
Randsverk Norway 45 J3
Randvaal S. Africa 133 M3
Råneå Sweden 44 M2
Ranfurly N.Z. 153 E13
Ranga r. India 78 A2
Rangae Thai. 79 C7
Rangamati Bangl. 97 G5
Rangapara North India 97 G4
Rangas, Tanjung pt Indon. 75 A3
Rangasa, Tanjung pt Indon. 75 A3
Rangaunu Bay N.Z. 152 H2
Rangeley Lake U.S.A. 177 O1
Rangely U.S.A. 183 P1
Ranger Lake Canada 168 D4
Ranger Lake l. Canada 173 J4
Rangi India 94 D1
Rangia Patharughat India 97 F4
Rangiauria i. S. Pacific Ocean see Pitt Island
Rangiora N.Z. 153 G11
Rangipoua mt. N.Z. 152 L5
also known as Hardy, Mount
Rangitaiki N.Z. 152 K6
Rangitata N.Z. 153 F12
Rangitata r. N.Z. 153 F12
Rangitikei r. N.Z. 152 J8
Rangitoto Islands N.Z. 152 H8
Rangiwaea Junction N.Z. 152 J7
Rangiwahia N.Z. 152 J7
Rangkasbitung Indon. 77 D4
Rangke China see Zamtang
Rangkŭl Tajik. 101 H2
Rangôn Myanmar see Rangoon
Rangôn admin. div. Myanmar see Yangôn

Rangoon Myanmar 78 B4
Capital of Myanmar. Also known as Yangôn; also spelt Rangôn; historically known as Dagon.

Rangoon admin. div. Myanmar see Yangôn
Rangoon r. Myanmar 78 B4
Rangpur Bangl. 97 F4
Rangsang i. Indon. 76 C2
Rangse Myanmar 78 A2
Rani India 96 B4
Rania India 96 B3
Ranibennur India 94 B3
Raniganj India 97 E5
Ranijula Peak India 97 D5
Ranikhet India 96 C3
Ranipur Pak. 101 G5
Raniwara India 96 B4
Ranken watercourse Australia 148 C4
Rankin U.S.A. 179 B6
Rankin Inlet Canada 167 M2
Rankin Inlet inlet Canada 167 M2
Rankin's Springs Australia 147 E3
Rankovićevo Srbija Yugo. see Kraljevo
Ranna Estonia 42 I3
Rannes Australia 149 F5
Ranneye Rus. Fed. 102 C2
Rannoch, Loch l. U.K. 46 H7
Rannu Estonia 42 H3
Rano Nigeria 125 H4
Ranobe r. Madag. 131 [inset] J3
Ranohira Madag. 131 [inset] J4
Ranomafana Madag. 131 [inset] K3
Ranomatana Madag. 131 [inset] J5
Ranong Thai. 79 B6
Ranongga i. Solomon Is 145 E2
Ranopiso Madag. 131 [inset] J5
Ranot Thai. 79 C7
Ranotsara Avaratra Madag. 131 [inset] J4
Ranova r. Rus. Fed. 43 V7
Ranpur India 96 A5
Ransiki Indon. 73 H7
Ransom U.S.A. 172 E9
Ranta Fin. 44 N1
Rantabe Madag. 131 [inset] K2
Rantasalmi Fin. 44 O3
Rantau Indon. 77 F3
Rantau i. Indon. 76 C2
Rantaukampar Indon. 76 C2
Rantaupanjang Kalimantan Tengah Indon. 77 F3
Rantaupanjang Kalimantan Timur Indon. 77 G2
Rantauprapat Indon. 76 B2
Rantaupulut Indon. 77 F3
Rantemario, Gunung mt. Indon. 75 B3
Rantepao Indon. 75 A3
Rantoul U.S.A. 174 B3
Rantsevo Rus. Fed. 43 P5
Rantsila Fin. 44 N2
Ranua Fin. 44 N2
Ranxë Albania 58 A7
Rānya Iraq 107 F3
Ranyah, Wādī watercourse Saudi Arabia 104 C3
Rao Go mt. Laos/Vietnam 78 D4
Raohe China 82 D3
Raon-l'Étape France 51 M4
Raoul Island N.Z. 145 H4
Rapa i. Fr. Polynesia 221 I7
also known as Oparo or Rapa-iti
Rapa-iti i. Fr. Polynesia see Rapa
Rapallo Italy 56 B4
Rapar Gujarat India 96 A5
Rapar Punjab India 96 C3
Rapch watercourse Iran 101 D5
Raper, Cape Canada 165 M3
Rapidan r. U.S.A. 176 H7
Rapid Bay Australia 146 C3
Rapid City U.S.A. 178 B2
Rapide-Deux Canada 173 O3
Rapide-Sept Canada 173 O3
Räpina Estonia 42 I3
Rapirrān r. Brazil 200 D2
Rapla Estonia 42 F3
Rappahannock r. U.S.A. 177 I8
Rappang Indon. 75 A3
Rapti r. India 97 D4
Rapulo r. Bol. 200 D3
Rapur Andhra Pradesh India 94 C3
Rapur Gujarat India 96 A5
Rapurapu i. Phil. 74 C3
Raqqa Syria see Ar Raqqah
Raquette r. U.S.A. 177 K1
Raquette Lake U.S.A. 177 K2
Rara National Park Nepal 97 D3
Raritan Bay U.S.A. 177 K5
Raroia atoll Fr. Polynesia 221 I7
formerly known as Barclay de Tolly
Rarotonga i. Cook Is 221 H7
historically known as Armstrong Island or Roxburgh Island
Ras India 96 B4
Raša r. Croatia 56 G3
Rasa i. Phil. 74 A4
Rasa, Punta pt Arg. 204 E6
Ra's ad Daqm Oman 105 G4
Ra's al 'Ayn Syria 109 L1
Ra's al Ḥadd Oman 105 G3
Ras al Khaimah U.A.E. see Ra's al Khaymah
Ra's al Khaymah U.A.E. 105 F2
English form Ras al Khaimah
Ra's al Mish'āb Saudi Arabia 105 E1
Raşan, Jabal hill Saudi Arabia 104 C3
Ra's an Naqb Jordan 108 G7
Ra's ash Shaykh Ḥumayd Saudi Arabia 104 A1

Ras Dashen mt. Eth. 128 C1
5th highest mountain in Africa.
africa [landscapes] 112–113

Raseiniai Lith. 42 E6
Ras el Ma Alg. 123 E2
formerly known as Bedeau
Râs el Mâ Mali 124 D2
Râs Ghârib Egypt 121 G2
Rashaant Bayan-Ölgiy Mongolia 84 A2
Rashaant Dundgovĭ Mongolia 85 E2
Rashad Sudan 128 A2
Rashīd Egypt 121 F2
historically known as Rosetta
Rāshid reg. Saudi Arabia 105 F3
Rashid Qala Afgh. 101 F4
Rashshah Yemen 105 D5
Rasht Iran 100 B2
Rasina Estonia 42 I3
Rasina r. Yugo. 58 C5
Råsjö Sweden 44 K3
Rāsk Iran 101 E5
also known as Firuzabad
Raška Srbija Yugo. 58 B5
Raskam mts China 89 A4
Ras Koh mt. Pak. 101 F4
Raskoh mts Pak. 101 F4
Râs Muhammad National Park Egypt 104 A2
Rasmussen Basin sea feature Canada 165 J3
Rasna Belarus 43 M7
Rasna Belarus 43 K7
Râşnov Romania 58 G3
formerly spelt Rîşnov
Raso i. Cape Verde 124 [inset]
Raso da Catarina hills Brazil 202 E4
Rason Lake salt flat Australia 151 D6
Rasony Belarus 43 J6
also spelt Rossony
Rasova Romania 58 I4
Rasovo Bulg. 58 E5
Rasra India 97 D4
Ra's Sāq, Jabal hill Saudi Arabia 104 B2
Ra's Sharwayn c. Yemen 105 E5
Rasshua, Ostrov i. Rus. Fed. 81 Q3
Ra's Şirāb Oman 105 G3
Rass Jebel Tunisia 57 C11
Rasskazovo Rus. Fed. 41 G5
Rast Romania 58 E5
Rasta r. Belarus 43 L8
Ras Tannūrah Saudi Arabia 105 E2
Rastatt Germany 48 F7
Rastede Germany 48 F2
Rästojaure l. Sweden 44 M1
Rastorguyevo Rus. Fed. see Vidnoye
Rata N.Z. 152 J7
Ratae U.K. see Leicester
Ratai, Gunung mt. Indon. 76 D4
Ratamka Belarus 42 I8
Ratanda S. Africa 133 M3
Ratangarh Madhya Pradesh India 96 B4
Ratangarh Rajasthan India 96 B3
Ratanpur Chhattisgarh India 97 D5
Ratanpur Gujarat India 96 B5
Rätansbyn Jämtland Sweden 44 K3
Rat Buri Thai. 79 B5
Ratchino Rus. Fed. 102 C1
Ratelfontein S. Africa 132 C8
Rath India 96 C4
Rathbun Lake U.S.A. 174 A3
Rathedaung Myanmar 78 A3
Rathenow Germany 49 J3
Rathenower Wald- und Seengebiet park Germany 49 J3
Rathlin Island U.K. 47 F8
Rathluirc Rep. of Ireland 47 D11
also known as Charleville
Ratibor Poland see Racibórz
Ratisbon Germany see Regensburg
Ratitovec mt. Slovenia 56 G2
Ratiya India 96 B3
Raṭiyah, Wādī ar watercourse Jordan 108 H8
Rat Lake Canada 167 L3
Ratlam India 96 B5
Ratnagiri India 94 B2
Ratnapura Sri Lanka 94 D5
Ratne Ukr. 41 C6
also spelt Ratno
Ratno Ukr. see Ratne
Rato Dero Pak. 101 G5
Raton U.S.A. 181 F5
Ratqah, Wādī ar watercourse Iraq 109 L3
Rattray Head U.K. 46 K6
Rättvik Sweden 45 K3
Ratz, Mount Canada 166 C3
Ratzeburg Germany 48 H2
Rau i. Indon. 75 D2
Raub Malaysia 76 C2
Rauch Arg. 204 F5
Raudamýri Iceland 44 [inset] B2
Raudanjoki r. Fin. 44 N2
Râu de Mori Romania 58 D3
Raudhatain Kuwait 107 F5
Raudna r. Estonia 42 G3
Raudondvaris Lith. 42 E7
Raufarhöfn Iceland 44 [inset] D2
Raukokore N.Z. 152 L5
Raukumara mt. N.Z. 152 M5
Raukumara Forest Park nature res. N.Z. 152 L5
Raukumara Range mts N.Z. 152 L6
Raul r. India 95 D1
Raul Soares Brazil 207 K7
Rauma Fin. 45 M3
Rauna Latvia 42 G4
Raurimu N.Z. 152 J7
Raurkela India 97 E5
Rauschen Rus. Fed. see Svetlogorsk
Rausu Japan 90 I2
Rausu-dake mt. Japan 90 I2
Rautalampi Fin. 44 N3
Rautavaara Fin. 44 O3
Rautjärvi Fin. 45 O3
Rauza India see Khuldabad
Ravalli U.S.A. 180 D3
Ravānsar Iran 100 A3
Ravanusa Sicilia Italy 57 F11
Rāvar Iran 100 D4
Ravat Kyrg. 101 G2
Ravena U.S.A. 177 L3
Ravenna Italy 56 E4
Ravenna NE U.S.A. 178 C3
Ravenna OH U.S.A. 176 D4
Ravensburg Germany 48 G8
Ravenshoe Australia 149 E3
Ravensthorpe Australia 151 C7
Ravenswood Australia 149 E4
Ravenswood U.S.A. 176 D7
Raver India 96 C5
Ravi r. Pak. 101 G4
Ravna Gora Croatia 56 G3
Ravna Gora hill Croatia 56 J3
Ravnina Turkm. 103 E5
also spelt Rawnina
Ravshan Uzbek. 102 D4
Rawa Aopa Watumohe National Park Indon. 75 B4
Rāwah Iraq 107 E4
Rawai well Sudan 104 A4
Rawaki i. Kiribati 145 H2
formerly known as Phoenix Island
Rawala Kot Pak. 101 H3
Rawalpindi Pak. 101 H3
Rawalpindi Lake Canada 167 H1
Rawa Mazowiecka Poland 49 R4
Rawāndiz Iraq 107 F3
Rawāndiz, Rūbār-i r. Iraq 109 P1
Rawas r. Indon. 76 C3
Rawatsar India 96 B3
Rawdah Yemen 104 D5
Rawdah, Sabkhat ar salt flat Syria 109 M2
Rawghah watercourse Saudi Arabia 109 I9
Rawhide Lake Canada 173 K4
Rawi i. Thai. 79 B7
Rawicz Poland 49 N4
Rawka r. Poland 49 R4
Rawlinna Australia 151 D6
Rawlins U.S.A. 180 F4
Rawlinson, Mount hill Australia 151 D5
Rawlinson Range hills Australia 151 E5
Rawnina Turkm. see Ravnina
Rawson Arg. 205 D6
Rawson Mountains Antarctica 223 N1
Rawu China 86 A2
Raxaul India 97 E4
Ray, Cape Canada 169 J4
Raya, Bukit mt. Kalimantan Indon. 77 E3
Raya, Bukit mt. Kalimantan Indon. 77 F3
Rayachoti India 94 C3
Rayadurg India 94 C3
Rayagarha India 95 D2
Rayak Lebanon 108 H4
Raychikhinsk Rus. Fed. 82 C2
Rayda Rus. Fed. 43 R3
Raydah Yemen 104 D5
Raydār Iraq 109 P2
Rāyen Iran 100 D4
Rayes Peak U.S.A. 182 E7
Rayevskiy Rus. Fed. 40 J5
Raymān i. Saudi Arabia 108 G9
Raymond Canada 167 H5
Raymond NH U.S.A. 177 N2
Raymond WA U.S.A. 180 B3
Raymond Terrace Australia 147 F3
Raymondville U.S.A. 179 C7
Raymore Canada 167 J5
Rayna India 97 E5
Rayner Glacier Antarctica 223 D2
Rayón Mex. 185 F4
Rayones Mex. 185 E3
Rayong Thai. 79 C5
Raystown Lake U.S.A. 176 G5
Raysūt Oman 105 F4
Rayth al Khayl watercourse Saudi Arabia 109 I9
Rayton S. Africa 133 M2
Rayville U.S.A. 175 B5
Rayyis Saudi Arabia 104 B3
Raz, Pointe du pt France 50 B4
Razam India 95 D2
Razan Iran 100 B3
Ražanj Srbija Yugo. 58 C5
Razāzah, Buhayrat ar l. Iraq 107 E4
formerly known as Milḥ, Baḥr al
Razdan Armenia see Hrazdan
Razdel'naya Ukr. see Rozdil'na
Razdol'noye Rus. Fed. 82 C4
Razdzyalavichy Belarus 42 H9
Razeh Iran 100 B3
Razgrad Bulg. 58 H5
Razhêng Zangbo r. China 89 E6
Razim, Lacul lag. Romania 58 J4
Razlog Bulg. 58 E7
Rāznas l. Latvia 42 I5
Raz"yezd 3km Rus. Fed. see Novyy Urgal
R. D. Bailey Lake U.S.A. 176 D8
Ré, Île de i. France 50 E6
Reading U.K. 47 L12
Reading MI U.S.A. 173 I9
Reading OH U.S.A. 176 A6
Reading PA U.S.A. 177 J5
Readsboro U.S.A. 177 M3
Readstown U.S.A. 172 C7
Reagile S. Africa 133 K2
Real r. Brazil 202 E4
Real Spain 54 C1
Reales mt. Spain 54 F8
Realicó Arg. 204 D4
Réalmont France 51 I9
Reăng Kesei Cambodia 79 C5
Reata Mex. 185 E3
Reate Italy see Rieti
Rebaa Alg. 123 H3
Rebbenesøy i. Norway 44 L1
Rebecca, Lake salt flat Australia 151 C6
Rebiana Sand Sea des. Libya 120 D3
also known as Ramlat Rabyānah
Rebollera mt. Spain 54 G6
Reboly Rus. Fed. 44 O3
Rebrebti Dhubo well Eth. 128 E3
Rebrikha Rus. Fed. 103 J1
Rebun-tō i. Japan 90 G2
Recanati Italy 56 F5
Recaș Romania 58 C3
Recco Italy 56 B4
Rechane Rus. Fed. 43 M5
Recherche, Archipelago of the is Australia 151 C7
Recherche Archipelago Nature Reserve Australia 151 C7
Rechitsa Belarus see Rechytsa
Rechna Doab lowland Pak. 101 H4
Rechytsa Belarus 43 L9
also spelt Rechitsa
Recife Brazil 202 F4
formerly known as Pernambuco
Recife, Cape S. Africa 133 J11
Recinto Chile 204 C5
Recklinghausen Germany 48 E4
Recknitz r. Germany 49 J1
Reconquista Arg. 204 F3
Recovery Glacier Antarctica 223 V1
Recreio Mato Grosso Brazil 201 F2
Recreio Minas Gerais Brazil 207 K8
Recreo Arg. 204 D3
Rectorville U.S.A. 176 B7
Recz Poland 49 M2
Red r. Australia 149 D3
Red r. Canada 166 E3
Red r. Canada/U.S.A. 167 L5
Red r. U.S.A. 179 E6
Red, North Fork r. U.S.A. 179 C5
Redang i. Malaysia 76 C1

Red Bank NJ U.S.A. 177 K5
Red Bank TN U.S.A. 174 C5
Red Basin China see Sichuan Pendi
Red Bay Canada 169 J3
Redberry Lake Canada 167 J4
Red Bluff hill Australia 151 B5
Red Bluff U.S.A. 182 B1
Red Bluff Lake U.S.A. 179 B6
Red Butte mt. U.S.A. 183 L6
Redcar U.K. 47 K9
Redcliff Canada 167 I5
Red Cliff U.S.A. 172 C4
Redcliff Zimbabwe 131 F3
Redcliffe, Mount hill Australia 151 C6
Red Cliffs Australia 147 D3
Red Cloud U.S.A. 178 C3
Red Deer Canada 167 H4
Red Deer r. Alta/Sask. Canada 167 I5
Red Deer r. Man./Sask. Canada 167 K4
Red Deer Lake Canada 167 K4
Reddersburg S. Africa 133 K6
Redding U.S.A. 182 B1
Redditch U.K. 47 K11
Red Earth Creek Canada 167 H3
Redelinghuys S. Africa 132 C9
Redenção Pará Brazil 202 B3
Redenção Piauí Brazil 202 C4
Redeyef Tunisia 123 H2
Redfield U.S.A. 178 C2
Red Granite Mountain Canada 166 B2
Redhill Australia 146 C3
Red Hills U.S.A. 178 C4
Red Hook U.S.A. 177 L4
Red Idol Gorge China 89 E6
Red Indian Lake Canada 169 J3
Redkino Rus. Fed. 43 R5
Redknife r. Canada 166 G2
Red Lake Canada 167 M5
Red Lake l. Canada 167 M5
Red Lake U.S.A. 183 L6
Red Lake r. U.S.A. 178 C2
Red Lake Falls U.S.A. 178 C2
Red Lake Indian Reservation res. U.S.A. 178 D1
Red Lakes U.S.A. 178 D1
Redlands U.S.A. 183 G7
Red Lion NJ U.S.A. 177 K6
Red Lion PA U.S.A. 177 I6
Red Lodge U.S.A. 180 E3
Red Mercury Island N.Z. 152 J4
Redmond OR U.S.A. 180 B3
Redmond UT U.S.A. 183 M2
Red Oak U.S.A. 178 D3
Redojari waterhole Kenya 128 C5
Redon France 50 D5
Redonda i. Antigua and Barbuda 187 H3
Redondela Spain 54 C2
Redondo Port. 54 D6
Redondo Beach U.S.A. 182 F8
Red Peak U.S.A. 180 D3
Red River r. Vietnam 78 D3
also known as Hông, Sông or Nui Con Voi
Red Rock Canada 168 B3
Red Rock AZ U.S.A. 183 M9
Red Rock PA U.S.A. 177 I4
Red Rock r. U.S.A. 180 D3
Red Sea Africa/Asia 104 A2
Red Sea state Sudan 121 G5
Redstone Canada 166 F4
Redstone r. N.W.T. Canada 166 E1
Redstone r. Ont. Canada 173 L2
Red Volta r. Burkina/Ghana 125 E4
also known as Nazinon (Burkina)
Redwater r. U.S.A. 180 F2
Redway U.S.A. 182 A1
Red Willow Creek r. U.S.A. 178 B3
Red Wine r. Canada 169 J2
Red Wing U.S.A. 174 A2
Redwood City U.S.A. 182 B4
Redwood Falls U.S.A. 178 D2
Redwood National Park U.S.A. 180 A4
Redwood Valley U.S.A. 182 A2
Ree, Lough l. Rep. of Ireland 47 E10
Reed City U.S.A. 172 H7
Reed Lake Canada 167 K4
Reedley U.S.A. 182 E5
Reedsburg U.S.A. 172 D7
Reedsport U.S.A. 180 A4
Reedsville OH U.S.A. 176 D6
Reedsville PA U.S.A. 176 H5
Reedville U.S.A. 177 I8
Reedy U.S.A. 176 D7
Reedy Creek watercourse Australia 149 E4
Reedy Glacier Antarctica 223 P1
Reefton N.Z. 153 F10
Reese U.S.A. 173 J7
Reese r. U.S.A. 183 H1
Refahiye Turkey 107 D3
Reform U.S.A. 175 B5
Reforma Mex. 185 G5
Refugio U.S.A. 179 C6
Rega r. Poland 49 M1
Regen Germany 49 K7
Regência Brazil 207 N6
Regensburg Germany 48 J6
historically known as Castra Regina or Ratisbon
Regenstauf Germany 49 J6
Regente Feijó Brazil 206 B9
Reggane Alg. 123 F4
Reggio Italy see Reggio di Calabria
Reggio Italy see Reggio nell'Emilia
Reggio di Calabria Italy 57 H10
historically known as Rhegium; short form Reggio
Reggio Emilia Italy see Reggio nell'Emilia
Reggio nell'Emilia Italy 56 C4
also known as Reggio Emilia; historically known as Regium Lepidum; short form Reggio
Reghin Romania 58 F2
Regi Afgh. 101 F3

► Regina Canada 167 J5
Provincial capital of Saskatchewan.

Régina Fr. Guiana 199 H3
Registan reg. Afgh. 101 F4
Registro Brazil 206 F11
Registro do Araguaia Brazil 206 B2
Regium Lepidum Italy see Reggio nell'Emilia
Regozero Rus. Fed. 44 O2
Rehli India 96 C5
Rehoboth Namibia 130 C4
Rehoboth Bay U.S.A. 177 J7
Rehoboth Beach U.S.A. 177 J7
Rehovot Israel 108 F6
Reibell Alg. see Ksar Chellala
Reichenbach Germany 49 J5
Reichshoffen France 51 N4
Reid Australia 151 E6
Reidsville GA U.S.A. 175 D5
Reidsville NC U.S.A. 176 F9
Reigate U.K. 47 L12
Reiley Peak U.S.A. 183 N9
Reims France 51 K3
English form Rheims; historically known as Durocortorum or Remi
Reinach Switz. 51 N5
Reinbek Germany 48 H2
Reindeer r. Canada 167 K4
Reindeer Island Canada 167 L4
Reindeer Lake Canada 167 K3
Reine Norway 44 K2
Reinersville U.S.A. 176 D6
Reineskarvet mt. Norway 45 J3
Reinga, Cape N.Z. 152 G2
Reinosa Spain 54 G2
Reinsfeld Germany 48 D6
Reiphólsfjöll hill Iceland 44 [inset] B2
Reisa Nasjonalpark nat. park Norway 44 M1
Reisjärvi Fin. 44 N3
Reisterstown U.S.A. 177 I6
Reitz S. Africa 133 M4
Reitzburg S. Africa 133 L4
Reiu r. Estonia 42 F3
Reivilo S. Africa 132 I4
Rejowiec Fabryczny Poland 49 U4
Rekapalle India 94 D2
Rekohua i. S. Pacific Ocean see Chatham Island
Rekovac Srbija Yugo. 58 C5
Rėkyvos ežeras l. Lith. 42 E6
Reliance Canada 167 I2
Relizane Alg. 123 F2
Rellano Mex. 184 D3
Relli India 95 D2
Remada Tunisia 123 H2
Remarkable, Mount hill Australia 146 C3
Rembang Indon. 77 E4
Remedios Cuba 186 D2
Remedios, Punta pt El Salvador 185 H6
Remel el Abiod des. Tunisia 123 H3
Remennikovo Rus. Fed. 43 J5
Remeshk Iran 100 D5
Remeskylä Fin. 44 N3
Remi France see Reims
Remington U.S.A. 176 H7
Rémire Fr. Guiana 199 H3
Remiremont France 51 M4
Remmel Mountain U.S.A. 180 B2
Remo Glacier Jammu and Kashmir 96 C2
Remontnoye Rus. Fed. 41 G7
Rempang i. Indon. 76 D2
Remscheid Germany 48 E4
Remus U.S.A. 173 H7
Rena Norway 45 J3
Rena r. Norway 45 J3
Renabie Canada 173 J2
Renaix Belgium see Ronse
Renapur India 94 C2
Renard Islands P.N.G. 149 G1
Rende Italy 57 I9
Rende China see Xundian
Rend Lake U.S.A. 174 B4
Rendsburg Germany 48 G1
Renedo Spain 54 H1
René-Levasseur, Île i. Canada 169 G3
Renens Switz. 51 M6
Renews Canada 169 K4
Renfrew Canada 168 E4
Rengat Indon. 76 C3
Rengo Chile 204 C4
Ren He r. China 87 D1
Renheji China 87 E2
Renhou China see Tangxian
Renhua China 87 E3
Renhuai China 86 C3
Reni Ukr. 41 D7
Renick U.S.A. 176 E8
Renigunta India 94 C3
Renko Fin. 42 F1
Renland reg. Greenland see Tuttut Nunaat
Renmark Australia 146 D3
Rennell i. Solomon Is 145 F3
also known as Mu Nggava
Rennell, Islas is Chile 205 B8
Rennerod Germany 48 F5
Renner Springs Australia 148 B3
Rennes France 50 E4
Rennes, Bassin de basin France 50 E4
Rennick Glacier Antarctica 223 K2
Rennie Canada 167 M5
Reno r. Italy 56 E4
Reno MN U.S.A. 172 B7
Reno NV U.S.A. 182 E2
Renoster r. S. Africa 133 K3
Renoster watercourse S. Africa 132 E8
Renosterkop S. Africa 132 G9
Renovo U.S.A. 176 H4
Renqiu China 85 H4
Renshou China 86 C2
also known as Wenlin
Rensselaer IN U.S.A. 174 C3
Rensselaer NY U.S.A. 177 L3
Rentjärn Sweden 44 L2
Renton U.S.A. 180 B3
Renukut India 97 D4
Renwick N.Z. 152 H9
Renya r. Rus. Fed. 43 S3
Réo Burkina 124 E3
Reo Indon. 75 B5
Repartimento Brazil 199 G5
Repembe r. Moz. 131 G4
Repetek Turkm. 103 E5
Repetekskiy Zapovednik nature res. Turkm. 103 E5
Repino Rus. Fed. 43 N6
Repokaira reg. Fin. 44 N1
Repolka Rus. Fed. 43 K2
Reporoa N.Z. 152 K6
Reposaari Fin. 45 M3
Republic OH U.S.A. 176 B4
Republic WA U.S.A. 180 C2
Republican r. U.S.A. 178 C4
Republican, South Fork r. U.S.A. 178 B3
Republika Srpska aut. div. Bos.-Herz. 56 J4
Repulse Bay b. Australia 149 F4
Repulse Bay Canada 165 K3
Repvåg Norway 44 N1
Requena Peru 198 C6
Requena Spain 55 J5
Réquista France 51 I8
Reriutaba Brazil 202 D3
Reşadiye Turkey 107 E3
also known as Sorp
Reşadiye Turkey 107 D2
Reşadiye Yarımadası pen. Turkey 59 I12
Resag, Gunung mt. Indon. 76 D4
Resava r. Yugo. 58 C4
Resavica Srbija Yugo. 58 C4
Resen Macedonia 58 C7
Resende Brazil 207 I9
Reserva Brazil 203 B8
Reserve U.S.A. 181 E6
Reshetnikovo Rus. Fed. 43 R5
Reshi China 87 D2
Resia, Passo di pass Austria/Italy 48 H9
Resistencia Arg. 204 F2
Reşiţa Romania 58 C3
Resko Poland 49 M2
Resolute Bay Canada 165 J2
Resolution Island Canada 165 M3
Resolution Island N.Z. 153 A13
Resplendor Brazil 207 L6
Ressa r. Rus. Fed. 43 Q7
Ressango Garcia S. Africa 133 P2
Resseta r. Rus. Fed. 43 Q8
Restefond, Col de pass France 51 M8
Restelica Kosovo, Srbija Yugo. 58 B7
Restinga de Marambaia coastal area Brazil 207 I10
Restinga Seca Brazil 203 A9
Restrepo Col. 198 C3
Resülayn Turkey see Ceylanpınar
Retalhuleu Guat. 185 H6
Retem, Oued er watercourse Alg. 123 G2
Retén Llico Chile 204 B4
Retezat, Parcul Naţional nat. park Romania 58 D3
Retford U.K. 47 L10
also known as East Retford
Rethel France 51 K3
Réthimnon Greece see Rethymno
Rethymno Greece 59 F13
also known as Réthimnon
Retiers France 50 E5
Retortillo tourist site Spain 54 G2
Rettikhovka Rus. Fed. 90 C2
Retuerta mt. Spain 55 J4

► Réunion terr. Indian Ocean 218 K7
French Overseas Department. Historically known as Bourbon.
africa [countries] ▶▶ 114–117

Reus Spain 55 M3
Reusam, Pulau i. Indon. 76 B2
Reutlingen Germany 48 G7
Reutov Rus. Fed. 43 S6
Reval Estonia see Tallinn
Revda Rus. Fed. 44 P2
Reveille Peak U.S.A. 183 H4
Revel Estonia see Tallinn
Revel France 51 I9
Revelganj India 97 E4
Revelstoke Canada 166 G5
Reventazón Peru 198 A6
Revermont reg. France 51 L7
Reviga Romania 58 I4
Reviga r. Romania 58 I4
Revigny-sur-Ornain France 51 K4
Revillagigedo, Islas is Mex. 184 B5
Revillagigedo Island U.S.A. 164 F4
Revna r. Rus. Fed. 43 P9
Revolyutsiya, Pik mt. Tajik. see Revolyutsiya, Qullai
Revolyutsiya, Qullai mt. Tajik. 101 H2
also known as Revolyutsii, Pik
Revsnes Norway 44 L1
Revúca Slovakia 49 R7
Revuè r. Moz. 131 G3
Revyakino Rus. Fed. 43 S7
Rewa India 96 D4
Rewari India 96 C3
Rex, Mount Antarctica 222 S2
Rexburg U.S.A. 180 E4
Rexton Canada 169 H4
Rey, Isla del i. Panama 186 D5
Reyes Bol. 200 D3
Reyes, Point U.S.A. 182 A3
Reyes, Punta pt Col. 198 B4
Reyhanlı Turkey 109 H1
Reykir Iceland 44 [inset] B2
Reykjanes constituency Iceland 44 [inset] B3
Reykjanestá pt Iceland 44 [inset] B3

► Reykjavík Iceland 44 [inset] B2
Capital of Iceland. English form Reykjavik.

Reykjavik Iceland see Reykjavík
Reynolds Range mts Australia 148 B4
Reynosa Mex. 185 F3
Reyssouze r. France 51 K6
Rezā, Kūh-e hill Iran 100 B3
Reẕā'īyeh Iran see Urmia
Reẕā'īyeh, Daryācheh-ye salt l. Iran see Urmia, Lake
Rēzekne Latvia 42 I5
Rēzekne r. Latvia 42 I5
Rezinjski vrh mt. Slovenia 56 G3
Rezovska Reka r. Bulg./Turkey 58 J7
Rezvāndeh Iran see Rezvānshahr
Rezvānshahr Iran 100 B2
formerly known as Rezvāndeh
R. F. Magón Mex. see Ricardo Flores Magón
Rgotina Srbija Yugo. 58 D4
Rharbi, Oued el watercourse Alg. 123 F3
Rhegium Italy see Reggio di Calabria
Rheims France see Reims
Rhein r. Germany 48 D4 see Rhine
Rheine Germany 48 E3
Rheinland-Pfalz land Germany 48 E6
English form Rhineland-Palatinate
Rheinsberg Germany 49 J2
Rhein-Taunus, Naturpark nature res. Germany 48 F5
Rheinwaldhorn mt. Switz. 51 P6
Rhemilès well Alg. 122 D3
Rheris, Oued watercourse Morocco 122 D3
Rhin r. France 51 N4 see Rhine
Rhine r. Europe 48 D4
also spelt Rhein (Germany) or Rhin (France)
Rhinebeck U.S.A. 177 L4
Rhinelander U.S.A. 172 D5
Rhineland-Palatinate land Germany see Rheinland-Pfalz
Rhinluch marsh Germany 49 J3
Rhino Camp Uganda 128 A4
Rhinow Germany 49 J3
Rhir, Cap c. Morocco 122 C3
Rho Italy 56 B3
Rhode Island state U.S.A. 177 N4
Rhodes Greece 59 J12
also spelt Rodos
Rhodes i. Greece 59 J12
also spelt Rodos or Ródhos; formerly known as Rodi; historically known as Rhodus
Rhodesia country Africa see Zimbabwe
Rhodes Inyanga National Park Zimbabwe see Nyanga National Park
Rhodes Matopos National Park Zimbabwe see Matobo National Park
Rhodes Peak U.S.A. 180 D3
Rhodope Mountains mts Bulg. 58 E7
Rhodope Mountains Bulg./Greece 58 E7
also known as Rodopi Planina
Rhodus i. Greece see Rhodes
Rhône r. France/Switz. 51 K9
Rhône-Alpes admin. reg. France 51 L7
Rhube, Oasis of Syria see Ruḩbah
Rhuthun U.K. see Ruthin
Rhyl U.K. 47 I10
Riaba Equat. Guinea 125 H6
Riachão Brazil 202 C3
Riachão das Neves Brazil 202 C4
Riacho de Santana Brazil 202 D5
Riacho dos Machados Brazil 207 J2
Ri'al Fuhah hill Saudi Arabia 108 H9
Rialma Brazil 206 D2
Rialp, Pantà de resr Spain 55 M3
Rialto U.S.A. 183 G7
Riangnom Sudan 126 F2
Riaño, Embalse de resr Spain 54 F2
Rianópolis Brazil 206 D2
Riansáres r. Spain 55 H5
Riasi Jammu and Kashmir 96 B2
Riau prov. Indon. 76 C2
Riau, Kepulauan is Indon. 76 D2
Riaza Spain 55 H3
Riaza r. Spain 55 H3
Ribadavia Spain 54 C2
Ribadeo Spain 54 D1
Ribadesella Spain 54 F1
Ribas de Fresser Spain see Ribes de Fresser
Ribas do Rio Pardo Brazil 203 A7
Ribat Afgh. 101 G2
Ribat-i-Shur waterhole Iran 100 D3
Ribáuè Moz. 131 H2
Ribble r. U.K. 47 J10
Ribe Denmark 45 J5
Ribeirão Branco Brazil 206 E11
Ribeirão das Neves Brazil 207 I6
Ribeirão do Pinhal Brazil 206 C10
Ribeirão Preto Brazil 206 F8
Ribera Sicilia Italy 57 F11
Ribérac France 50 G7
Riberalta Bol. 200 D2
Ribes de Fresser Spain 55 N2
also spelt Ribas de Fresser
Ribnica Slovenia 56 G3
Rîbniţa Moldova 41 D7
formerly spelt Râbniţa or Rybnitsa
Ribnitz-Damgarten Germany 49 J1
Ribnovo Bulg. 58 E7
Rica Aventura Chile 200 C5
Říčany Czech Rep. 49 L6
Ricardo Flores Magón Mex. 184 D2
short form R. F. Magón
Riccione Italy 56 E4
Rice CA U.S.A. 183 J7
Rice VA U.S.A. 176 G8
Rice Lake l. Ont. Canada 168 E4
Rice Lake l. Ont. Canada 173 K3
Rice Lake U.S.A. 172 B5
Riceville U.S.A. 176 C8
Richards Bay S. Africa 133 Q5
Richards Inlet Antarctica 223 L1
Richards Island Canada 164 F3
Richardson r. Canada 167 I3
Richardson Island Canada 167 G1
Richardson Lakes U.S.A. 177 O1
Richardson Mountains Canada 164 F3
Richardson Mountains N.Z. 153 C12
Richard Toll Senegal 124 B2
Richelieu France 50 G5
Richfield U.S.A. 183 L3
Richfield Springs U.S.A. 177 K3
Richford NY U.S.A. 177 I3
Richford VT U.S.A. 177 M1
Richgrove U.S.A. 182 E6
Richibucto Canada 169 H4
Rich Lake Canada 167 I4
Richland U.S.A. 180 C3
Richland Center U.S.A. 172 C7
Richlands U.S.A. 176 D8
Richmond N.S.W. Australia 147 F3
Richmond Qld Australia 149 D4
Richmond Ont. Canada 173 R5
Richmond Que. Canada 169 F4
Richmond N.Z. 152 H9
Richmond Kwazulu-Natal S. Africa 133 O6
Richmond N. Cape S. Africa 132 H8
Richmond U.K. 47 K9
Richmond CA U.S.A. 182 B4
Richmond IL U.S.A. 172 E8
Richmond IN U.S.A. 176 A6
Richmond KY U.S.A. 176 A8
Richmond ME U.S.A. 177 P1
Richmond MI U.S.A. 173 K8
Richmond TX U.S.A. 179 D6

► Richmond VA U.S.A. 176 H8
State capital of Virginia.

Richmond VT U.S.A. 177 M1
Richmond, Mount N.Z. 152 H9
Richmond Dale U.S.A. 176 C6
Richmond Hill Canada 168 E5
Richmond Hill U.S.A. 175 D6
Richmond Range hills Australia 147 G2
Richmond Range mts N.Z. 152 H9
Richmondville U.S.A. 177 K3
Rich Square U.S.A. 177 H9
Richtersveld National Park S. Africa 132 B5
Richvale U.S.A. 182 C2
Richwood OH U.S.A. 176 B5
Richwood WV U.S.A. 176 E7
Rickleån r. Sweden 44 M2
Ricobayo, Embalse de resr Spain 54 F3
also known as Esla, Embalse de
Ricomagus France see Riom
Riddell Nunataks Antarctica 223 E2
Ridder Kazakh. see Leninogorsk
Riddlesburg U.S.A. 176 G5
Rideau r. Canada 173 R5
Rideau Lakes Canada 168 E4
Ridge r. Canada 168 C3
Ridgecrest U.S.A. 182 G6
Ridgefield U.S.A. 177 L4
Ridgeland MS U.S.A. 175 B5
Ridgeland SC U.S.A. 175 D5
Ridgeland WI U.S.A. 172 B5
Ridgetown Canada 173 L8
Ridgeway U.S.A. 176 F9
Ridgway U.S.A. 176 G4
Riding Mountain National Park Canada 167 K5
Ridley r. Australia 150 B4
Riebeek-Kasteel S. Africa 132 C10
Riebeek-Oos S. Africa 133 K10
Riebeek Wes S. Africa 132 C10
Riecito Venez. 198 D2
Ried im Innkreis Austria 49 K7
Riedlingen Germany 48 G7
Riekertsdam S. Africa 133 K2
Rieppesgai'sa mt. Norway 44 M1
Riesa Germany 49 K4
Riesco, Isla i. Chile 205 B9
Riesi Sicilia Italy 57 G11
Rieste Germany 48 F3
Riet r. S. Africa 133 H6
Riet watercourse S. Africa 132 E8
Rietavas Lith. 42 C6
Rietberg Germany 48 F4
Rietbron S. Africa 132 H9
Rietfontein S. Africa 132 E3
Rietkuilskraal S. Africa 132 F11
Rieti Italy 56 E6
historically known as Reate
Rietpoort S. Africa 132 C7
Rietschen Germany 49 L4
Riet se Vloer salt pan S. Africa 132 E7
Rietvlei S. Africa 133 O6
Rieumes France 50 H9
Rīfā'ī, Tall mt. Jordan/Syria 109 H5
Rifaina Brazil 206 F7
Rifeng China see Lichuan
Rifle U.S.A. 180 F5
Rift Valley prov. Kenya 128 B4
Rift Valley Lakes National Park Eth. see Abijatta-Shalla National Park

► Rīga Latvia 42 F5
Capital of Latvia. English form Riga.

Riga Latvia see Rīga
Riga, Gulf of Estonia/Latvia 42 E4
also known as Liivi laht or Rīgas jūras līcis or Riia laht
Rigacikun Nigeria 125 G4
Rigaio Greece 59 D9
Rigān Iran 100 D4
Rīgas jūras līcis b. Estonia/Latvia see Riga, Gulf of
Rigby U.S.A. 180 E4
Rig-Rig Chad 120 B6
Riguel r. Spain 55 J2
Riia laht b. Estonia/Latvia see Riga, Gulf of
Riihimäki Fin. 45 N3
Riiser-Larsen Ice Shelf Antarctica 223 W2
Riisipere Estonia 42 F2
Riisitunturin kansallispuisto nat. park Fin. 44 O2
Riito Mex. 184 B1
Rijau Nigeria 125 G4
Rijećki Zaliv b. Croatia 56 G3
Rijeka Croatia 56 G3
formerly known as Fiume
Rijm al Mudhari hill Iraq 109 K5
Rikā, Wādī ar watercourse Saudi Arabia 104 D3
Rikubetsu Japan 90 H3
Rikuchū-kaigan National Park Japan 90 H5
Rikuzen-takata Japan 90 G5
Rila Bulg. 58 E6
Rila mts Bulg. 58 E6
Rila China 89 D6
Riley U.S.A. 180 C4
Rileyville U.S.A. 176 G7
Rillieux-la-Pape France 51 K7
Rillito U.S.A. 183 M9
Rima watercourse Niger/Nigeria 125 G3
Rimah, Wādī al watercourse Saudi Arabia 104 C2
Rimau, Pulau i. Indon. 76 D3
Rimava r. Slovakia 49 R7
Rimavská Sobota Slovakia 49 R7
Rimbey Canada 167 H4
Rimbo Sweden 45 L4
Rimersburg U.S.A. 176 F4
Rimetea Romania 58 E2
Rimforsa Sweden 45 K4
Rimini Italy 56 E4
historically known as Ariminum
Rîmnicu Sărat Romania see Râmnicu Sărat
Rîmnicu Vîlcea Romania see Râmnicu Vâlcea
Rimouski Canada 169 G3
Rimouski, Réserve Faunique de nature res. Canada 169 G3
Rimutaka Forest Park nature res. N.Z. 152 J9
Rinbung China 89 E6
also known as Deji
Rinca i. Indon. 75 A5
Rincão Brazil 206 E8
Rincon Morocco see Mdiq
Rincón, Cerro del mt. Chile 200 D6
Rinconada Arg. 200 D5
Rincón del Bonete, Lago Artificial de resr Uruguay 204 F4
Rincón de los Sauces Arg. 204 C5
Rincón de Romos Mex. 185 E4
Rind r. India 96 D4
Rinda r. Latvia 42 C4
Rindal Norway 44 J3
Rineia i. Greece 59 G11
also spelt Rinía
Riner U.S.A. 176 E8
Ringarooma Bay Australia 147 E5
Ringas India 96 B4
Ringe Denmark 45 J5
Ringebu Norway 45 J3
Ringgold U.S.A. 174 C5
Ringim Nigeria 125 H3
Ringkøbing Denmark 45 J4
Ringkøbing Fjord lag. Denmark 45 J5
Ringsted Denmark 45 J5
Ringvassøy i. Norway 44 L1
Ringwood U.K. 47 K13
Ringwood U.S.A. 177 K4
Rinía i. Greece see Rineia
Rinópolis Brazil 206 C8
Rinteln Germany 48 G3
Rinya r. Romania 49 O9
Rio IL U.S.A. 172 C9
Rio WI U.S.A. 172 D7
Rio Alegre Brazil 201 F4
Riobamba Ecuador 198 B5
Rio Bananal Brazil 207 M6
Rio Blanco U.S.A. 180 F5
Rio Bonito Brazil 207 K9
Rio Branco Brazil 200 D2
Rio Branco state Brazil see Roraima
Rio Branco, Parque Nacional do nat. park Brazil 199 F4
Río Bravo, Parque Internacional del nat. park Mex. 185 E2
Rio Brilhante Brazil 203 A7
Río Bueno Chile 204 B6
Río Caribe Venez. 199 F2
Rio Casca Brazil 203 D7
Río Chico Arg. 205 C8
Río Chico Venez. 199 E2
Rio Claro Rio de Janeiro Brazil 207 I9
Rio Claro São Paulo Brazil 206 F9
Rio Claro Trin. and Tob. 187 H5
Río Claro Venez. 187 F5
Rio Colorado Arg. 204 D5
Río Corrientes Ecuador 198 B5
Río Cuarto Arg. 204 D4
Rio das Almas r. Brazil 201 H3
Rio das Pedras Moz. 131 G4

► Rio de Janeiro Brazil 203 D7
3rd most populous city in South America. Former capital of Brazil.
world [cities] ▶▶ 24–25

Rio de Janeiro state Brazil 203 D7
Río de Jesús Panama 186 C6

► Río de la Plata - Paraná r. S. America 204 F4
2nd longest river in South America and 9th in the world.
southamerica [landscapes] ▶▶ 190–191

Rio Dell U.S.A. 180 A4
Rio do Sul Brazil 203 B8
Rio Formoso Brazil 202 F4
Río Frío Costa Rica 186 C5
Río Gallegos Arg. 205 C8
Río Grande Arg. 205 D9
Río Grande Bol. 200 D5
Rio Grande Brazil 204 G4
Río Grande Mex. 185 E4
Rio Grande r. Mex./U.S.A. 185 F3
also known as Bravo del Norte, Río
Río Grande, Salar de salt flat Arg. 204 C2
Rio Grande City U.S.A. 179 C7
Rio Grande do Norte state Brazil 202 E3
Rio Grande do Sul state Brazil 203 A9
Ríohacha Col. 198 C2
Río Hato Panama 186 C5
Río Hondo, Embalse resr Arg. 204 D2
Rioja Peru 198 B6
Río Lagartos Mex. 185 H4
Rio Largo Brazil 202 F4
Riom France 51 J7
historically known as Ricomagus
Rio Maior Port. 54 C5
Riom-ès-Montagnes France 51 I7
Río Muerto Arg. 204 E2
Río Mulatos Bol. 200 D4
Río Muni reg. Equat. Guinea 125 H6
Río Negro prov. Arg. 204 D5
Rio Negro Brazil 203 B8
Río Negro Chile 204 B6
Rionero in Vulture Italy 56 H8
Rioni r. Georgia 107 E2
Rio Novo Brazil 207 J8
Rio Novo do Sul Brazil 207 M7
Rio Pardo de Minas Brazil 202 D5
Río Plátano, Reserva Biósfero del nature res. Hond. 186 B4
Rio Pomba Brazil 207 J8
Rio Preto Brazil 207 J9
Rio Preto, Serra do hills Brazil 206 G3
Rio Rancho U.S.A. 181 F6
Ríos Spain 54 D3
Ríosucio Col. 198 B3
Río Tercero Arg. 204 D4
Río Tigre Ecuador 198 B5
Rio Tinto Brazil 202 F3
Río Tuba Phil. 74 A4
Riou, Oued watercourse Alg. 55 L9
Riou Lake Canada 167 J3
Rio Verde Brazil 206 C4
Río Verde Chile 205 C9
Rioverde Ecuador 198 B4
Río Verde Quintana Roo Mex. 185 H5
Río Verde San Luis Potosí Mex. 185 F4
Rio Verde de Mato Grosso Brazil 203 A6
Rio Vermelho Brazil 207 J5
Rio Vista U.S.A. 182 C3
Riozinho Brazil 200 D2
Riozinho r. Amazonas Brazil 199 E5
Riozinho r. Mato Grosso do Sul Brazil 201 F4
Ripanj Srbija Yugo. 58 B4
Ripats Sweden 44 M2
Ripky Ukr. 41 D6
Ripley MS U.S.A. 174 B5
Ripley NY U.S.A. 176 F3
Ripley OH U.S.A. 176 B7
Ripley TN U.S.A. 174 B5
Ripley WV U.S.A. 176 D7
Ripoll Spain 55 N2
Ripon U.K. 47 K9
Ripon CA U.S.A. 182 C4
Ripon WI U.S.A. 172 E7
Riposto Sicilia Italy 57 H11
Risalpur Pak. 101 H3
Risān 'Aneiza hill Egypt 108 E7
Risaralda dept Col. 198 C3
Risasi Dem. Rep. Congo 126 E5
Risbäck Sweden 44 K2
Riscle France 50 F9
Risco Plateado mt. Arg. 204 C4
Risha, Birket Umm salt l. Egypt 108 B7
Rishā', Wādī ar watercourse Saudi Arabia 104 D2
Rishikesh India 96 C3
Rishiri-Rebun-Sarobetsu National Park Japan 90 G2
Rishiri-tō i. Japan 90 G2
Rishiri-zan vol. Japan 82 F3
Rishon Le Ẕiyyon Israel 108 F6
Rising Sun IN U.S.A. 176 A7
Rising Sun MD U.S.A. 177 I6
Risle r. France 50 G3
Risnjak nat. park Croatia 56 G3
Rîşnov Romania see Râşnov
Rison U.S.A. 179 D5
Risør Norway 45 J4
Rissa Norway 44 J3
Rissington N.Z. 152 K7
Rişşu, Gebel hill Egypt 108 B8
Ristiina Fin. 45 N3
Ristijärvi Fin. 44 O2
Ristikent Rus. Fed. 44 O1
Risum China 89 B5
Ritan r. Indon. 77 F2
Rītausma Latvia 42 F5
Ritchie S. Africa 133 I6
Ritchie's Archipelago is India 95 G3
Ritch Island Canada 167 G1
Ritscher Upland mts Antarctica 223 X2
Ritsem Sweden 44 L2
Ritsis Nakrdzali nature res. Georgia 107 E2
Ritter, Mount U.S.A. 182 E4
Ritupe r. Latvia 42 I5
Ritzville U.S.A. 180 C3
Riu, Mount hill P.N.G. 149 G1
Riva r. Latvia 42 C5
Rivadavia Buenos Aires Arg. 204 E4
Rivadavia Mendoza Arg. 204 C4
Rivadavia Salta Arg. 201 E6
Rivadavia Chile 204 C3
Riva del Garda Italy 56 C3
Riva Palacio Mex. 181 F7
Rivarolo Canavese Italy 51 N7
Rivas Nicaragua 186 B5
Rivash Iran 100 D3
Rive-de-Gier France 51 K7
Rivera Arg. 204 E5
Rivera Uruguay 204 G3
River Cess Liberia 124 C5
Riverdale U.S.A. 182 E5
Riverhead U.S.A. 177 M5
Riverina Australia 151 C6
Riverina reg. Australia 147 E3
Rivero, Isla i. Chile 205 B7
Rivers state Nigeria 125 G5
Riversdale N.Z. 153 C13
Riversdale S. Africa 132 F11
Riversdale Beach N.Z. 152 K9
Riverside S. Africa 133 N7
Riverside CA U.S.A. 182 G8
Riverside IA U.S.A. 172 B9
Riversleigh Australia 148 C3
Riverton Canada 167 L5
Riverton N.Z. 153 C14
also known as Aparima
Riverton S. Africa 133 I5
Riverton UT U.S.A. 183 M1
Riverton VA U.S.A. 176 G7
Riverton WY U.S.A. 180 E4
Riverview Canada 169 H4
River View S. Africa 133 Q5
Rives France 51 L7
Rivesaltes France 51 I10
Riviera U.S.A. 176 E6
Rivière-au-Renard Canada 169 H3
Rivière Bleue Canada 169 G4
Rivière-du-Loup Canada 169 G4
Rivière-Pentecôte Canada 169 H3
Rivière-Pigou Canada 169 H3
Rivière-Pilote Martinique 187 H4
Riviersonderend S. Africa 132 D11
Riviersonderend Mountains S. Africa 132 D11
Rivne Ukr. 41 C6
also spelt Rovno; formerly spelt Równe
Rivoli Italy 51 N7
Rivulets S. Africa 133 O2
Rivungo Angola 127 D9
Riwaka N.Z. 152 G9
Riwoqê China 86 A2

► Riyadh Saudi Arabia 105 D2
Capital of Saudi Arabia. Also spelt Ar Riyāḑ.

Riyan Yemen 105 E5
Riyue Shankou pass China 84 D4
Riza well Iran 100 C3
Rizal Phil. 74 B3
Rize Turkey 107 E2
Rizhao Shandong China 85 H5
formerly known as Shijiusuo
Rizhao Shandong China 85 H5
Rizokarpaso Cyprus see Rizokarpason
Rizokarpason Cyprus 108 F2
also known as Dipkarpaz or Rizokarpaso
Rizū well Iran 100 C3
Rizū'īyeh Iran 100 D4
Rjukan Norway 45 J4
Rkîz, Lac l. Mauritania 124 B2
Roa Norway 45 J3
Roa Spain 54 H3
Roach Lake U.S.A. 183 I6
Roads U.S.A. 176 C6

► Road Town Virgin Is (U.K.) 187 G3
Capital of the British Virgin Islands.

Roan Norway 44 J2
Roan Cliffs ridge U.S.A. 183 O2
Roan Fell hill U.K. 47 J8
Roan Mountain U.S.A. 176 C9
Roanne France 51 K6
Roanoke AL U.S.A. 175 C5
Roanoke IL U.S.A. 172 D10
Roanoke VA U.S.A. 176 F8
Roanoke r. U.S.A. 176 I9
Roanoke Rapids U.S.A. 176 H9
Roan Plateau U.S.A. 183 O2
Roaringwater Bay Rep. of Ireland 47 C12
Roatán Hond. 186 B3
also known as Coxen Hole
Robat r. Afgh. 101 E4
Robāṭ Iran 100 D4
Robāṭ-e Khān Iran 100 D3
Robāṭ-e Shahr-e Bābak Iran 100 C4
Robāṭe Tork Iran 100 B3
Robāṭ-e Ţoroq Iran 101 D2
Robāṭ Karīm Iran 100 B3
Robāṭ-Sang Iran 101 D3
Robat Thana Pak. 101 E4
Robb Canada 167 G4
Robben Island S. Africa 132 C10
Robbins U.S.A. 176 A9
Robbins Island Australia 147 E5
Robbinsville U.S.A. 174 D5
Robe r. Australia 150 A4
Robe, Mount hill Australia 146 D2
Röbel Germany 49 J2
Robert Glacier Antarctica 223 D2
Robert Lee U.S.A. 179 B6
Roberts U.S.A. 180 D4
Roberts, Mount Australia 147 G2
Robertsburg U.S.A. 176 D7
Roberts Butte mt. Antarctica 223 K2
Roberts Creek Mountain U.S.A. 183 H2
Robertsfors Sweden 44 M2
Robertsganj India 97 D4

Robert S. Kerr Reservoir U.S.A. 179 D5
Robertson r. Australia 149 D3
Robertson S. Africa 132 D10
Robertson, Lac l. Canada 169 J3
Robertson Bay Antarctica 223 L2
Robertson Island Antarctica 222 U2
Robertson Point N.Z. 152 I9
Robertson Range hills Australia 150 C4
Robertsport Liberia 124 C5
Robertstown Australia 146 C3
Robert Williams Angola see Caála
Roberval Canada 169 F3
Robeson Channel Canada/Greenland 165 M1
Robhanais, Rubha hd U.K. see Butt of Lewis
Robin's Nest hill Hong Kong China 87 [inset] also known as Hung Fa Leng
Robinson r. N.T. Australia 148 C3
Robinson r. W.A. Australia 150 D3
Robinson Canada 166 C2
Robinson IL U.S.A. 174 C4
Robinson KY U.S.A. 176 A7
Robinson Creek r. Australia 149 F5
Robinson Range hills Australia 151 B5
Robinvale Australia 147 D3
Robles La Paz Col. 198 C2
Roblin Canada 167 K5
Robore Bol. 201 F4
Robsart Canada 167 I5
Robson, Mount Canada 166 G4
Robstown U.S.A. 179 C7
Roby U.S.A. 179 B5
Roçadas Angola see Xangongo
Roca Partida, Isla i. Mex. 184 B5
Rocas, Atol das atoll Brazil 202 F2
Rocas Alijos is Mex. 184 B3
Rocca Busambra mt. Sicilia Italy 57 F11
Rocca Imperiale Italy 57 I8
Roccastrada Italy 56 D5
Roc de Montalet mt. France 51 I9
Roc d'Enfer mt. France 51 M6
Rocha Uruguay 204 G4
Rochdale U.K. 47 J10
Rochechouart France 50 G7
Roche de Vic hill France 50 H7
Rochedo Brazil 203 A6
Rochefort Belgium 51 L2
Rochefort France 50 F7
Rochefort, Lac l. Canada 169 F1
Rochegda Rus. Fed. 40 G3
Rochelle U.S.A. 172 D9
Rochester IN U.S.A. 174 C3
Rochester MN U.S.A. 174 A2
Rochester NH U.S.A. 177 O2
Rochester NY U.S.A. 176 H2
Roc'h Trévezel hill France 50 C4
Rocina r. Spain 54 E8
Rock r. Canada 166 E2
Rock U.S.A. 172 F4
Rock r. IA U.S.A. 178 C3
Rock r. IL U.S.A. 174 B3
Rock and Pillar Range mts N.Z. 153 D13
Rock Bay Canada 166 E5
Rock Creek Canada 166 B1
Rock Creek r. U.S.A. 180 F2
Rockdale U.S.A. 179 C6
Rockefeller National Wildlife Refuge nature res. U.S.A. 179 D6
Rockefeller Plateau Antarctica 222 O1
Rockford AL U.S.A. 175 C5
Rockford IL U.S.A. 174 B3
Rockford NC U.S.A. 176 E9
Rockford OH U.S.A. 176 A5
Rockglen Canada 167 J5
Rock Hall U.S.A. 177 I6
Rockhampton Australia 149 F4
Rockhampton Downs Australia 148 B3
Rock Hill U.S.A. 174 D5
Rockingham Australia 151 A7
Rockingham U.S.A. 174 E5
Rockingham Bay Australia 149 E3
Rockinghorse Lake Canada 167 H1
Rock Island U.S.A. 174 B3
Rockland MA U.S.A. 177 O3
Rockland ME U.S.A. 177 P1
Rocklands Reservoir Australia 147 D4
Rocklea Australia 150 B4
Rocklin U.S.A. 182 C3
Rocknest Lake Canada 167 H1
Rock Point U.S.A. 183 O5
Rockport IN U.S.A. 174 C4
Rockport MA U.S.A. 177 O3
Rockport TX U.S.A. 179 C7
Rockport WV U.S.A. 176 D6
Rock Rapids U.S.A. 178 C3
Rock River U.S.A. 180 F4
Rock Sound Bahamas 186 D1
Rock Springs MT U.S.A. 180 F3
Rocksprings U.S.A. 179 B6
Rock Springs WY U.S.A. 180 E4
Rockstone Guyana 199 G3
Rockton U.S.A. 172 D8
Rockville IN U.S.A. 174 C4
Rockville MD U.S.A. 177 H6
Rockwall U.S.A. 179 C5
Rockwell City U.S.A. 178 D3
Rockwood U.S.A. 173 J8
Rocky Boy's Indian Reservation res. U.S.A. 180 E2
Rockyford Canada 167 H5
Rocky Ford U.S.A. 178 B4
Rocky Fork U.S.A. 176 C9
Rocky Fork Lake U.S.A. 176 B6
Rocky Harbour Canada 169 J3
Rocky Hill U.S.A. 176 C7
Rocky Lane Canada 167 G3
Rocky Mount NC U.S.A. 174 E5
Rocky Mount VA U.S.A. 176 F9
Rocky Mountain House Canada 167 H4
Rocky Mountain National Park U.S.A. 180 F4
Rocky Mountains U.S.A. 170 E3
Rocky Mountains Forest Reserve nature res. Canada 167 G4
Rocroi France 51 K3
Rodberg Norway 45 J3
Rødbyhavn Denmark 45 J5
Roddickton Canada 169 K3
Rode S. Africa 133 N7
Rödeby Sweden 45 K4
Rodeo Mex. 184 D3
Roderick r. Australia 151 B5
Rodez France 51 I8
Rodholívos Greece see Rodolivos
Rodhópolis Greece see Rodopoli
Ródhos i. Greece see Rhodes
Rodi i. Greece see Rhodes
Roding Germany 49 J6
Rodino Rus. Fed. 103 J1
Rødlia Norway 44 K2
Rodna Romania 58 F1
Rodney, Cape N.Z. 152 I4
Rodnichek Rus. Fed. see Rodnichok
Rodnichok Rus. Fed. 41 G6 also spelt Rodnichek
Rodnya Belarus 43 N8
Rodnykovka Kazakh. 102 D2
Rodolfo Sanchez Toboada Mex. 184 A2
Rodolivos Greece 58 E8 also spelt Rodholívos
Rodonit, Kepi i pt Albania 58 A7
Rodopi Planina mts Bulg./Greece see Rhodope Mountains
Rodopoli Greece 58 E7 also known as Rodhópolis
Rodopos Greece 59 E13
Rodos Greece see Rhodes
Rodos i. Greece see Rhodes
Rodosto Turkey see Tekirdağ
Rodovoye Rus. Fed. 42 I4
Rodøya i. Norway 44 K2
Rodrigues Peru 198 C6
Rodrigues Island Mauritius 218 L7
Rødsand Norway 44 O1
Roe r. Australia 150 D2
Roebourne Australia 150 B4
Roebuck Bay Australia 150 C3
Roedtan S. Africa 131 F5
Roe Plains Australia 151 D6
Roermond Neth. 48 C4
Roeselare Belgium 51 J2 also known as Roulers
Roes Welcome Sound sea chan. Canada 167 O2
Rogachev Belarus see Rahachow
Rogachevo Rus. Fed. 43 S5
Rogagua, Laguna l. Bol. 200 D3
Rogaland county Norway 45 I4
Rogaška Slatina Slovenia 49 M9
Rogatica Bos.-Herz. 56 L5
Roger, Lac l. Canada 173 O3
Rogers Canada 167 G5
Rogers U.S.A. 179 D4
Rogers, Mount U.S.A. 176 D9
Rogers City U.S.A. 173 J5
Rogers Lake U.S.A. 182 G7
Rogersville U.S.A. 176 B9
Roggan r. Canada 168 E2
Roggan, Lac l. Canada 168 E2
Roggeveld plat. S. Africa 132 E9
Roggeveldberge esc. S. Africa 132 E9
Rogliano Italy 57 I9
Rognan Norway 44 K2
Rognedino Rus. Fed. 43 O8
Rögnitz r. Germany 48 H2
Rogoźno Poland 49 O3
Rogue r. U.S.A. 180 A4
Roha India 94 B2
Rohnert Park U.S.A. 182 B3
Rohrbach in Oberösterreich Austria 49 K7
Rohri Pak. 101 G5
Rohtak India 96 C3
Rohuküla Estonia 42 E3
Roi Et Thai. 78 C4
Roi Georges, Îles du is Fr. Polynesia 221 I6 English form King George Islands
Roine l. Fin. 45 N3
Roing India 97 G3
Roja Latvia 42 D4
Rojas Arg. 204 E4
Röjdåfors Sweden 45 K3
Rojhan Pak. 101 G4
Rojo, Cabo c. Mex. 185 F4
Rojo, Cabo c. Puerto Rico 187 G3
Rojo Aguado, Laguna l. Bol. 200 D3
Rokan r. Indon. 76 C2
Rokeby Australia 149 D2
Rokeby National Park Australia 149 D2
Rokiškis Lith. 42 G6
Rokkasho Japan 90 G4
Rokkō-zaki pt Japan 90 E6
Røkland Norway 44 K2
Roknäs Sweden 44 M2
Rokycany Czech Rep. 49 K6
Rokytne Ukr. 41 C6
Rola Kangri mt. China 89 E5
Rolândia Brazil 206 B10
Rolas, Ilha das i. São Tomé and Príncipe 125 G7
Rolim de Moura Brazil 201 E2
Roll U.S.A. 183 K9
Rolla MO U.S.A. 174 B4
Rolla ND U.S.A. 178 C1
Rollag Norway 45 J3
Rolleston Australia 149 F5
Rolleston N.Z. 153 G11
Rollet Canada 173 N3
Rolleville Bahamas 186 E2
Rolling Fork U.S.A. 175 B5
Rollinsford U.S.A. 177 O2
Rolphton Canada 173 P4
Rolvsøya i. Norway 44 N1
Rom mt. Uganda 128 B4
Roma Australia 149 F5
Roma i. Indon. 75 C4
Roma Italy see Rome
Roma Lesotho 133 L6
Roma U.S.A. 179 C7
Romain, Cape U.S.A. 171 K5
Romaine r. Canada 169 I3
Roman Romania 58 H2
Română, Câmpia plain Romania 58 E4
Romanaţilor, Câmpia plain Romania 58 E4
Romanet, Lac l. Canada 169 H1
Români Egypt 108 D6
Romania country Europe 58 E3 also spelt Roumania or Rumania
europe [countries] 32–35
Roman-Kosh mt. Ukr. 41 E7
Romano, Cayo i. Cuba 186 D2
Romanovka Moldova see Basarabeasca
Romanovka Rus. Fed. 81 I2
Romanovka Rus. Fed. 41 G6
Romanovo Rus. Fed. 103 J1
Romans-sur-Isère France 51 L7
Romanzof, Cape U.S.A. 164 C3
Romão Brazil 199 F5
Rombas France 51 M3
Romblon Phil. 74 B3
Romblon i. Phil. 74 B3
Romblon Passage Phil. 74 B3
Rombo, Ilhéus do is Cape Verde see Secos, Ilhéus
Rome Italy 56 E7 Capital of Italy. Also spelt Roma.
Rome GA U.S.A. 179 F5
Rome ME U.S.A. 177 P1
Rome NY U.S.A. 177 J2
Romeo U.S.A. 173 J8
Romford U.K. 47 M12
Romilly-sur-Seine France 51 J4
Romit Tajik. 101 G2 also spelt Ramit
Romitan Uzbek. 103 F5 formerly spelt Ramitan
Romney U.S.A. 176 G6
Romny Ukr. 41 E6
Rømø i. Denmark 45 J5
Romorantin-Lanthenay France 50 H5
Rompin r. Malaysia 76 C2
Romppala Fin. 44 O3
Romsey U.K. 47 K13
Romu mt. Indon. 77 G5
Romulus U.S.A. 173 J8
Ron India 94 B3
Rona i. U.K. 46 G4 also known as North Rona
Ronas Hill hill U.K. 46 K3
Roncador, Serra do hills Brazil 202 A5
Roncador Cay i. Caribbean Sea 186 C4
Roncador Reef Solomon Is 145 E2
Ronceverte U.S.A. 176 E8
Ronciglione Italy 56 E6
Ronco r. Italy 56 E4
Ronda Spain 54 F8
Ronda, Serranía de mts Spain 54 F8
Ronda, Serranía de nature res. Spain 54 G8
Ronda das Salinas Brazil 201 E3
Rondane Nasjonalpark nat. park Norway 45 J3
Ronde i. Grenada 187 H4
Rondon Brazil 206 A10
Rondón Col. 198 D3
Rondônia state Brazil 201 E2 formerly known as Guaporé
Rondonópolis Brazil 202 A6
Rondout Reservoir U.S.A. 177 K4
Rong'an China 87 D3 also known as Chang'an
Rongbaca China 86 A2
Rongchang China 86 C2 also known as Changyuan
Rongcheng China see Qingyang
Rongcheng China see Rongxian
Rongcheng China see Jianli
Rongcheng China 85 I4 formerly known as Yatou
Rongcheng Wan b. China 85 I4
Rong Chu r. China 89 E6
Rongelap atoll Marshall Is 220 F6 also known as Kongelab; also spelt Rōnlap
Rongjiang China 87 D3 also known as Guzhou
Rongjiang China see Nankang
Rong Jiang r. China 87 D4
Rongjiawan China see Yueyang
Rongklang Range mts Myanmar 78 A3
Rongmei China see Hefeng
Rongshui China 87 D3
Rongwo China see Tongren
Rongxian Guangxi China 87 D4 also known as Rongcheng
Rongxian Sichuan China 86 C2 also known as Xuyang
Rongzhag China see Danba
Rōnlap atoll Marshall Is see Rongelap
Rønne Denmark 45 K5
Ronneby Sweden 45 K4
Ronne Entrance strait Antarctica 222 S2
Ronne Ice Shelf Antarctica 222 T1 formerly known as Edith Ronne Land
Ronnenberg Germany 48 G3
Ronse Belgium 51 J2 also known as Renaix
Ronuro r. Brazil 202 A5
Roodebank S. Africa 133 N3
Rooiberg mt. Free State S. Africa 133 M5
Rooiberg mt. W. Cape S. Africa 132 F10
Rooikloof pass S. Africa 132 E9
Rooikraal S. Africa 133 N2
Rooke Island P.N.G. see Umboi
Rookh Aboriginal Reserve Australia 150 B4
Roorkee India 96 C3
Roosboom S. Africa 133 N5
Roosendaal Neth. 48 B4
Roosevelt AZ U.S.A. 183 M8
Roosevelt UT U.S.A. 183 O1
Roosevelt, Mount Canada 166 E3
Roosevelt Island Antarctica 223 N1
Roosna-Alliku Estonia 42 G2
Roossenekal S. Africa 133 N2
Root r. Canada 166 F2
Root r. U.S.A. 174 B3
Ropa r. Poland 49 S6
Ropaži Latvia 42 F5
Ropczyce Poland 49 S5
Roper r. Australia 148 B2
Roper Bar Australia 148 B2
Roper Bar Aboriginal Land res. Australia 148 B2 also known as Yutpundji Djindiniwirritj
Roper Creek r. Australia 149 F4
Ropinsalmi Fin. 44 M1
Roquebrune-sur-Argens France 51 M9
Roquefort France 50 F8
Roquetas de Mar Spain 55 I8
Roraima state Brazil 199 F4 formerly known as Rio Branco
Roraima, Mount Guyana 199 F3
Rorey Lake Canada 166 D1
Rori India 96 B3
Røros Norway 44 J3
Rorschach Switz. 51 P5
Rørvik Norway 44 J2
Ros' r. Belarus 42 F8
Roś, Jezioro l. Poland 49 S2
Rosa, Lake Bahamas 187 E2
Rosa, Punta pt Mex. 184 C3
Rosal de la Frontera Spain 54 D7
Rosales Mex. 184 D2
Rosalia U.S.A. 180 C3
Rosalind Bank sea feature Caribbean Sea 186 C3
Rosamond U.S.A. 182 F7
Rosamond Lake U.S.A. 182 F7
Rosamorada Mex. 184 D4
Rosario Jujuy Arg. 200 D5
Rosario Santa Fé Arg. 204 E4
Rosário Brazil 202 C2
Rosario Baja California Norte Mex. 184 B2
Rosario Coahuila Mex. 185 E3
Rosario Sinaloa Mex. 184 D4
Rosario Sonora Mex. 184 C3
Rosario Para. 201 F6
Rosario Luzon Phil. 74 B2
Rosario Luzon Phil. 74 B3
Rosario Venez. 198 C2
Rosario, Cayo del i. Cuba 186 C2
Rosario, Sierra del hills Cuba 175 D8
Rosario de la Frontera Arg. 204 D2
Rosario de Lerma Arg. 200 D6
Rosário do Sul Brazil 203 A9
Rosário Oeste Brazil 201 F3
Rosarito Baja California Norte Mex. 184 A1
Rosarito Baja California Norte Mex. 184 B2
Rosarito Baja California Sur Mex. 184 C3
Rosarno Italy 57 H10
Rosas Spain see Roses
Rosas, Golfo de b. Spain see Roses, Golf de
Rosa Zárate Ecuador 198 B4
Roscoff France 50 C4
Roscommon Rep. of Ireland 47 D10
Roscommon U.S.A. 173 I6
Roscrea Rep. of Ireland 47 E11
Rose r. Australia 148 B2
Rose, Mount U.S.A. 182 E2
Roseau Dominica 187 H4 Capital of Dominica.
Roseau U.S.A. 178 D1
Roseau r. U.S.A. 178 C1
Roseberth Australia 148 C5
Rosebery Australia 147 E5
Rose Blanche Canada 169 J4
Rosebud r. Canada 167 H5
Rosebud Creek r. U.S.A. 180 F3
Rosebud Indian Reservation res. U.S.A. 178 B3
Roseburg U.S.A. 180 B4
Rose City U.S.A. 173 I6
Rosedale MS U.S.A. 174 B5
Rosedale TN U.S.A. 176 A9
Rosedene S. Africa 132 G9
Rosehall Guyana 199 G3
Roseires Reservoir Sudan 128 B2
Rosemary Island Australia 150 B4
Rosenberg U.S.A. 179 D6
Rosendal Norway 45 I4
Rosendal S. Africa 133 L5
Rosendale U.S.A. 172 E7
Rosengarten Germany 48 G2
Rosenheim Germany 48 J8
Rose Peak U.S.A. 183 O8
Rose Point Canada 166 D4
Roses Spain 55 O2 also spelt Rosas
Roses, Golf de b. Spain 55 O2 also spelt Rosas, Golfo de
Roseto degli Abruzzi Italy 56 G6
Rosetown Canada 167 J5
Rosetta Egypt see Rashîd
Rosetta Creek r. Australia 149 E4
Rose Valley Canada 167 K4
Roseville CA U.S.A. 182 C3
Roseville IL U.S.A. 174 B3
Roseville MI U.S.A. 173 K8
Roseville OH U.S.A. 176 C6
Roshal' Rus. Fed. 43 U6
Roshchino Rus. Fed. 43 K1
Roshchino Rus. Fed. 90 D2
Roshkhvār Iran 101 D3
Rosholt U.S.A. 172 D6
Rosh Pinah Namibia 130 C5
Roshtkala Tajik. see Roshtqal'a
Roshtqal'a Tajik. 96 A1 also spelt Roshtkala
Rosignano Marittimo Italy 56 C5
Rosily Island Australia 150 A4
Roşiori Romania 58 I4
Roşiori de Vede Romania 58 G4
Rositsa Bulg. 58 I5
Rositsa r. Bulg. 58 G5
Roskilde Denmark 45 K5
Roskovec Albania 58 A8
Roskruge Mountains U.S.A. 183 M9
Roslavl' Rus. Fed. 43 N8
Roslyakovo Rus. Fed. 44 P1
Roslyatino Rus. Fed. 40 H4
Rosmead S. Africa 133 J8
Rosolina Italy 56 E3
Rosolini Sicilia Italy 57 G12
Rosporden France 50 C5
Ross Australia 147 E5
Ross r. Canada 166 C2
Ross N.Z. 153 E10
Ross, Mount hill N.Z. 152 J9
Rossano Italy 57 I9
Rossan Point Rep. of Ireland 47 D9
Ross Barnett Reservoir U.S.A. 175 B5
Ross Bay Junction Canada 169 H2
Ross Dependency Antarctica 222 N2
Rosseau, Lake Canada 173 N5
Rossel Island P.N.G. 149 G1
Rossel Lagoon P.N.G. 149 G1
Ross Ice Shelf Antarctica 223 M1
Rossignol, Lac l. Canada 169 F2
Rössing Namibia 130 B4
Ross Island Antarctica 223 L1
Ross Island Myanmar see Daung Kyun
Rossiter Bay Australia 151 C7
Rossiyskaya Sovetskaya Federativnaya Sotsialisticheskaya Respublika country Asia/Europe see Russian Federation
Rossland Canada 166 G5
Rosslare Rep. of Ireland 47 F11
Rosslare Harbour Rep. of Ireland 47 F11
Rosso Mauritania 124 B2
Rossön Sweden 44 L3
Ross-on-Wye U.K. 47 J12
Rossony Belarus see Rasony
Rossosh' Rus. Fed. 41 F6
Rossouw S. Africa 133 L8
Rossport Canada 172 F2
Ross River Australia 148 B4
Ross River Canada 166 C2
Ross Sea Antarctica 223 L1
Røssvatnet l. Norway 44 K2
Rossville U.S.A. 172 B7
Rosswood Canada 166 D4
Rōst Iraq 107 F3
Røst Norway 44 K2
Rostāq Afgh. 101 G2
Rostāq Fārs Iran 100 C4
Rostāq Hormozgan Iran 100 C5
Røsthavet sea chan. Norway 44 K2
Rosthern Canada 167 J4
Rostock Germany 49 J1
Rostonsölkä ridge Sweden 44 M1
Rostov Rus. Fed. 43 U4
Rostov-na-Donu Rus. Fed. 41 F7 English form Rostov-on-Don
Rostov Oblast admin. div. Rus. Fed. see Rostovskaya Oblast'
Rostov-on-Don Rus. Fed. see Rostov-na-Donu
Rostovskaya Oblast' admin. div. Rus. Fed. 41 G7 English form Rostov Oblast
Rostrenen France 50 C4
Røsvik Norway 44 K2
Rosvik Sweden 44 M2
Roswell GA U.S.A. 175 C5
Roswell NM U.S.A. 181 F6
Rota i. N. Mariana Is 73 K4 formerly known as Sarpan
Rotch Island Kiribati see Tamana
Rote i. Indon. 75 B5 also spelt Roti
Rotenburg (Wümme) Germany 48 G2
Rote Wand mt. Austria 48 G8
Roth Germany 48 I6
Rothenburg ob der Tauber Germany 48 H6
Rothera research station Antarctica 222 T2
Rotherham N.Z. 153 G10
Rotherham U.K. 47 K10
Rothes U.K. 46 I6
Rothesay U.K. 46 G8
Rothschild U.S.A. 172 D6
Rothschild Island Antarctica 222 T2
Roti Indon. 75 B5
Roti i. Indon. see Rote
Roti, Selat sea chan. Indon. 75 B5
Roto Australia 147 E3
Rotoaira, Lake N.Z. 152 J7
Rotomagus France see Rouen
Rotomanu N.Z. 153 F10
Rotondo, Monte mt. Corse France 56 B6
Rotorua N.Z. 152 K6
Rotorua, Lake N.Z. 152 K6
Rott r. Germany 49 K7
Rottenburg am Neckar Germany 48 F7
Rottenmann Austria 49 L8
Rotterdam Neth. 48 B4
Rotterdam U.S.A. 177 L3
Rottnest Island Australia 151 A7
Rottweil Germany 48 F7
Rotuma i. Fiji 145 G3 formerly known as Grenville Island
Rotunda Romania 58 F5
Rötviken Sweden 44 K3
Rötz Germany 49 J6
Roubaix France 51 J2
Roudnice nad Labem Czech Rep. 49 L5
Rouen France 50 H3 historically known as Rotomagus
Rõuge Estonia 42 H4
Rouge-Matawin, Réserve Faunique nature res. Canada 169 F4
Rougemont U.S.A. 176 G9
Rough Ridge N.Z. 153 D13
Rouhia Tunisia 57 B13
Roui, Oued er watercourse Niger 125 H1
Roulers Belgium see Roeselare
Roulette U.S.A. 176 G4
Roulpmaulpma Aboriginal Land res. Australia 148 B4
Roumania country Europe see Romania
Roundeyed Lake Canada 169 G2
Roundhead U.S.A. 176 B5
Round Hill Nature Reserve Australia 147 E3
Round Lake Canada 168 E4
Round Mountain mt. Australia 147 G2
Round Mountain U.S.A. 183 G3
Round Rock AZ U.S.A. 183 O5
Round Rock TX U.S.A. 179 C6
Roundup U.S.A. 180 E3
Roura Fr. Guiana 199 H3
Rousay i. U.K. 46 I4
Rouses Point U.S.A. 177 L1
Roussillon France 51 K7
Routh Bank sea feature Phil. see Seahorse Bank
Rouxville S. Africa 133 K7
Rouyn Canada 168 E3
Rouyuan China see Huachi
Rouyuanchengzi China see Huachi
Rovaniemi Fin. 44 N2
Rovato Italy 56 C3
Roven'ki Rus. Fed. 41 F6
Rovereto Italy 56 D3
Roversi Arg. 204 E2
Rovigo Italy 56 D3
Rovinari Romania 58 E4
Rovinj Croatia 56 F3
Rovkul'skoye, Ozero l. Rus. Fed. 44 O3
Rovno Ukr. see Rivne
Rovnoye Rus. Fed. 102 A2
Rowlesburg U.S.A. 176 F6
Rowley Island Canada 165 L3
Rowley Shoals sea feature Australia 150 B3
Rownaye Belarus 43 K6
Równe Ukr. see Rivne
Rów Polski r. Poland 49 N4
Rowsburg U.S.A. 176 C5
Roxas Luzon Phil. 74 B2
Roxas Mindanao Phil. 74 B4
Roxas Mindoro Phil. 74 B3
Roxas Palawan Phil. 74 A4
Roxas Panay Phil. 74 B4
Roxboro U.S.A. 176 G9
Roxborough Downs Australia 148 C4
Roxburgh Island Cook Is see Rarotonga
Roxby Downs Australia 146 C2
Roxen l. Sweden 45 K4
Roxo r. Port. 54 C7
Roxo, Barragem do resr Port. 54 C7
Royal Canal Rep. of Ireland 47 E10
Royal Center U.S.A. 172 G10
Royal Chitwan National Park Nepal 97 E4
Royale, Île i. Canada see Cape Breton Island
Royale, Isle i. U.S.A. 172 E2
Royal Natal National Park S. Africa 133 M5
Royal Oak U.S.A. 173 J8
Royal Society Range mts Antarctica 223 K1
Royalton U.S.A. 172 E6
Royan France 50 E7
Roye France 51 I3
Roy Hill Australia 150 B4
Royston U.K. 47 L11
Röyttä Fin. 44 N2
Rožaje Crna Gora Yugo. 58 B6
Różan Poland 49 S3
Rožanj hill Yugo. 58 A4
Rozdil'na Ukr. 41 D7 also known as Razdel'naya
Rozdol'ne Ukr. 41 E7
Rozhdestvenka Kazakh. 103 G2
Rozhdestveno Tverskaya Oblast' Rus. Fed. 43 R5
Rozhdestveno Yaroslavskaya Oblast' Rus. Fed. 43 S4
Rozhdestvenskoye Rus. Fed. 40 H4
Rozhdestvo Rus. Fed. 43 O4
Rozhkovychi Rus. Fed. 43 P9
Rozino Bulg. 58 F6
Rozivka Ukr. 41 F7
Rožňava Slovakia 49 R7
Rozoy-sur-Serre France 51 K3
Roztoczański Park Narodowy nat. park Poland 49 U5
Rozveh Iran 100 B3
Rozzano Italy 56 B3
Rrëshen Albania 58 A7
Rrogozhinë Albania 58 A7
Rtishchevo Rus. Fed. 41 G5
Ruacana Namibia 130 B3
Ruaha National Park Tanz. 129 B6
Ruahine Forest Park nature res. N.Z. 152 K7
Ruahine Range mts N.Z. 152 K8
Ruakaka N.Z. 152 I3
Ruanda country Africa see Rwanda
Ruapehu, Mount vol. N.Z. 152 J7
Ruapuke Island N.Z. 153 C14
Ruarwe Malawi 129 B7
Ruatangata N.Z. 152 I3
Ruatapu N.Z. 153 E10
Ruatoria N.Z. 152 M5
Ruba Belarus 43 L6 formerly known as Vyarkhowye
Rub' al Khālī des. Saudi Arabia 105 D4 Largest uninterrupted stretch of sand in the world. English form Empty Quarter.
Rubaydā reg. Saudi Arabia 105 E2
Rubeho Mountains Tanz. 129 C6
Rubelita Brazil 207 K3
Rubeshibe Japan 90 H3
Rubezhnoye Ukr. see Rubizhne
Rubi r. Dem. Rep. Congo 126 E4
Rubiácea Brazil 206 C8
Rubiataba Brazil 206 D2
Rubicon r. U.S.A. 182 C3
Rubim Brazil 207 M3
Rubinéia Brazil 206 C7
Rubio U.S.A. 172 B9
Rubizhne Ukr. 41 F6 also spelt Rubezhnoye
Rubondo National Park Tanz. 128 A5
Rubtsovsk Rus. Fed. 88 C1
Rubuga Tanz. 129 B6
Rubūţ, Jabal ar hill Saudi Arabia 104 C4
Ruby U.S.A. 164 D3
Ruby Dome mt. U.S.A. 183 I1
Ruby Lake U.S.A. 183 I1
Ruby Lake National Wildlife Refuge nature res. U.S.A. 180 D4
Ruby Mountains U.S.A. 183 I1
Rubys Inn U.S.A. 183 L4
Ruby Valley U.S.A. 183 I1
Rucăr Romania 58 G3
Ruchay Belarus 42 I6
Rucheng China see Ruyuan
Rucheng China 87 E3
Ruciane-Nida Poland 49 S2
Ruckersville U.S.A. 176 G7
Rudall watercourse Australia 150 C4
Rudall River National Park Australia 150 C4
Rudarpur India 97 D4
Ruda Śląska Poland 49 P5
Rudauli India 97 D4
Rudbar Afgh. 101 E4
Rūdbār Iran 100 B2
Rūd-e Kor watercourse Iran 100 C4
Rüdersdorf Berlin Germany 49 K3
Rudhumatal Hiri hill Iraq 109 K4
Rudina pass Yugo. 58 A5
Rūd-i-Shur watercourse Iran 100 D4
Rūdiškės Lith. 42 F7
Rudka r. Poland 49 U4
Rudkøbing Denmark 45 J5
Rudna Glava Srbija Yugo. 58 D4
Rudnaya Pristan' Primorskiy Kray Rus. Fed. 82 D3 formerly known as Tetyukhe-Pristan'
Rudnaya Pristan' Primorskiy Kray Rus. Fed. 82 D4
Rudnichnyy Kazakh. 103 I3
Rudnichnyy Rus. Fed. 40 J4
Rudnik Poland 49 T5
Rudnik Ingichka Uzbek. see Ingichka
Rudnya Smolenskaya Oblast' Rus. Fed. 43 M7
Rudnya Tverskaya Oblast' Rus. Fed. 43 M5
Rudnya Volgogradskaya Oblast' Rus. Fed. 41 H6
Rudnyy Kazakh. 103 E1
Rudnyy Rus. Fed. 82 D3 formerly known as Lifudzin
Rudolf, Lake salt l. Eth./Kenya see Turkana, Lake
Rudol'fa, Ostrov i. Rus. Fed. 38 F1 Most northerly point of Europe. English form Rudolph Island.
Rudolph Island Rus. Fed. see Rudol'fa, Ostrov
Rudolstadt Germany 48 I5
Rudong China 87 G1 also known as Juegang
Rudozem Bulg. 58 F7
Rūdsar Iran 100 B2
Rudzyensk Belarus 42 I8
Rue France 50 H2
Ruecas r. Spain 54 F5
Ruel Canada 173 L3
Ruen mt. Macedonia see Rujen
Ruenya r. Zimbabwe 131 G3
Rufa'a Sudan 121 G6
Ruffec France 50 G6
Rufiji r. Tanz. 129 C7
Rufino Arg. 204 E4
Rufisque Senegal 124 A3
Rufunsa Zambia 127 F8
Rugāji Latvia 42 I4
Rugao China 87 G1
Rugby U.K. 47 K11
Rugby ND U.S.A. 178 B1
Rugby TN U.S.A. 176 A9
Rügen i. Germany 49 K1
Rügen, Naturpark park Germany 49 K1
Rugged Mountain Canada 166 E5
Rugheiwa well Sudan 121 F5
Rugles France 50 G4
Ruhangino Tanz. 129 C7
Ruḩayyat al Ḩamr'ā' waterhole Saudi Arabia 105 D2
Ruḩbah oasis Syria 109 I5 English form Rhube, Oasis of
Ruhengeri Rwanda 126 F5
Ruhla Germany 48 H5
Ruhnu i. Estonia 42 E4
Ruhpolding Germany 49 J8
Ruhr r. Germany 48 D4
Ruhudji r. Tanz. 129 B7
Ruhuna National Park Sri Lanka 94 D5 also known as Yala National Park
Rui'an China 87 G3
Ruichang China 87 E2 formerly known as Pencheng
Ruidoso U.S.A. 181 F6
Ruijin China 87 E3
Ruiz Mex. 184 D4
Ruiz, Nevado del vol. Col. 198 C3
Ruj mt. Bulg. 58 D6
Rūja r. Latvia 42 G4
Rujaylah, Ḩarrat ar lava field Jordan 109 I5
Rujen mt. Macedonia 58 D6 also spelt Ruen
Rūjiena Latvia 42 G4
Ruki r. Dem. Rep. Congo 126 C4
Rukumkot Nepal 97 D3
Rukungiri Uganda 128 A5
Rukuwa Indon. 75 C4
Rukwa admin. reg. Tanz. 129 A6
Rukwa, Lake Tanz. 129 B7
Rūl Ḑadnah U.A.E. 105 G2
Ruleville U.S.A. 175 B5
Rulin China see Chengbu
Rulong China see Xinlong
Rūm Iran 101 D3
Rum i. U.K. 46 F7
Rum r. U.S.A. 174 A2
Rum, Jebel mts Jordan see Ramm, Jabal
Ruma Nigeria 125 G3
Ruma Vojvodina, Srbija Yugo. 58 A3
Rumādah Yemen 104 C5
Rumāh Saudi Arabia 105 D2
Ruma National Park Kenya 128 B5
Rumania country Europe see Romania
Rumaylah waterhole Iraq 109 O4
Rumaylah, Wādī watercourse Syria 109 M1
Rumayn i. Saudi Arabia 104 C4
Rumbek Sudan 126 F3
Rumblar r. Spain 54 H6
Rumburk Czech Rep. 49 L5
Rum Cay i. Bahamas 187 E2
Rumford U.S.A. 177 O1
Rumia Poland 49 P1
Rumilly France 51 L7
Rummān, Jabal ar mts Saudi Arabia 104 C2
Rummānā hill Syria 109 J4
Rumoi Japan 90 G3
Rumphi Malawi 129 B7
Runan China 87 E1 also known as Runing
Runanga N.Z. 153 F10
Runaway, Cape N.Z. 152 L5
Runcorn U.K. 47 J10
Runcu Romania 58 E3
Runde r. Zimbabwe 131 G4 formerly spelt Lundi
Rundu Namibia 130 C3
Rundvik Sweden 44 L3
Rŭng, Kaôh i. Cambodia 79 C6
Rungan r. Indon. 77 F3
Rungu Dem. Rep. Congo 126 E4
Rungwa Rukwa Tanz. 129 A6
Rungwa Singida Tanz. 129 B6
Rungwa r. Tanz. 129 A6
Rungwa Game Reserve nature res. Tanz. 129 B6
Runing China see Runan
Rūnīz-e Bālā Iran 100 C4
Runn l. Sweden 45 K3
Running Springs U.S.A. 183 G7
Running Water watercourse U.S.A. 179 B5
Runton Range hills Australia 150 C4
Ruokolahti Fin. 45 O3
Ruoqiang China 88 E4 formerly known as Charkhlik or Qarkilik

Ruoqiang He r. China 88 E4
Ruo Shui watercourse China 84 D3
Ruotsinpyhtää Fin. 42 H1
Ruovesi Fin. 45 N3
Rupa India 97 G4
Rupat i. Indon. 76 C2
Rupea Romania 58 G2
Rupert r. Canada 168 E3
Rupert ID U.S.A. 180 D4
Rupert WV U.S.A. 176 E8
Rupert Bay Canada 168 E3
Rupert Coast Antarctica 222 O1
Rupert Creek r. Australia 149 D4
Rupnagar India 96 B4
Rupshu reg. Jammu and Kashmir 96 C2
Ruqayṭah Saudi Arabia 104 C3
Ruqqād, Wādī ar watercourse Israel 108 G5
Rural Hall U.S.A. 176 E9
Rural Retreat U.S.A. 176 D9
Rurrenabaque Bol. 200 D3
Rus Romania 58 E1
Rusaddir N. Africa see Melilla
Rusape Zimbabwe 131 G3
Rusca Montană Romania 58 D3
Ruschuk Bulg. see Ruse
Ruse Bulg. 58 G5
historically known as Ruschuk
Rusenski Lom nat. park Bulg. 58 H5
Rusera India 97 E4
Ruşeţu Romania 58 I4
Rushan China 85 I4
formerly known as Xiacun
Rushan Tajik. see Rushon
Rushanskiy Khrebet mts Tajik. see Rushon, Qatorkŭhi
Rush Creek r. U.S.A. 178 B4
Rushford U.S.A. 174 B3
Rush Lake U.S.A. 172 E7
Rushmere U.S.A. 177 I8
Rushon Tajik. 101 G2
also spelt Rushan
Rushon, Qatorkŭhi mts Tajik. 101 G2
also known as Rushanskiy Khrebet
Rushui r. China 85 E5
Rushville IL U.S.A. 174 B3
Rushville IN U.S.A. 174 C4
Rushville NE U.S.A. 178 B3
Rushville OH U.S.A. 176 C6
Rushworth Australia 147 E4
Rusk U.S.A. 179 D6
Ruskele Sweden 44 L2
Ruskin U.S.A. 175 D7
Rusnė Lith. 42 C6
Rusokastro Bulg. 58 I6
Rušona Latvia 42 H5
Rušonu ezers l. Latvia 42 H5
Russarö i. Fin. 42 D2
Russas Brazil 202 E3
Russell Man. Canada 167 K5
Russell Ont. Canada 173 R5
Russell N.Z. 152 I3
Russell KS U.S.A. 178 C4
Russell PA U.S.A. 176 F4
Russell Bay Antarctica 222 P2
Russell Island Canada 165 J2
Russell Lake Man. Canada 167 K3
Russell Lake N.W.T. Canada 167 H2
Russellville AL U.S.A. 174 C5
Russellville AR U.S.A. 179 D5
Russellville KY U.S.A. 174 C4
Russellville OH U.S.A. 176 B7
Rüsselsheim Germany 48 F5
Russi Italy 56 E4
Russia country Asia/Europe see Russian Federation

▶ Russian Federation country Asia/Europe 38 F3
Largest country in the world, Europe and Asia. Most populous country in Europe, 3rd in Asia and 6th in the world. Formerly known as Russian Soviet Federal Socialist Republic or Rossiyskaya Sovetskaya Federativnaya Sotsialisticheskaya Respublika; short form Russia.
world [countries] ▶ 10–11
world [population] ▶ 22–23
europe [countries] ▶ 32–35
asia [countries] ▶ 64–67

largest countries

	country	area sq km	area sq miles	location	page#
1 ▶	Russian Federation	17 075 400	6 592 849	Asia/Europe	38 F3
2 ▶	Canada	9 970 610	3 849 674	North America	164 G3
3 ▶	USA	9 809 378	3 787 422	North America	170 E3
4 ▶	China	9 584 492	3 700 593	Asia	80 D5
5 ▶	Brazil	8 547 379	3 300 161	South America	202 B4
6 ▶	Australia	7 682 395	2 966 189	Oceania	144 A4
7 ▶	India	3 065 027	1 183 414	Asia	93 E6
8 ▶	Argentina	2 766 889	1 068 302	South America	204 C4
9 ▶	Kazakhstan	2 717 300	1 049 155	Asia	102 C2
10 ▶	Sudan	2 505 813	967 500	Africa	121 E5

Russian Soviet Federal Socialist Republic country Asia/Europe see Russian Federation
Russkaya-Polyana Rus. Fed. 103 H1
Russkiy, Ostrov i. Rus. Fed. 90 B3
Russkiy Brod Rus. Fed. 43 S9
Russkiy Kameshkir Rus. Fed. 41 H5
Russkiy Zavorot, Poluostrov pen. Rus. Fed. 40 J1
Russkoye Rus. Fed. 43 N8
Russkoye Ust'ye Rus. Fed. 39 O2
formerly known as Polyarnoye
Rust'avi Georgia 107 F2
Rustburg U.S.A. 176 F8
Rust de Winter S. Africa 133 M2
Rust de Winter Nature Reserve S. Africa 133 M2
Rustenburg S. Africa 133 L2
Rustenburg Nature Reserve S. Africa 133 L2
Rustfontein Dam l. S. Africa 133 K6
Rustig S. Africa 133 L4
Ruston U.S.A. 179 D5
Rut' r. Rus. Fed. 43 R6
Ruta Indon. 75 C3
Rutana Burundi 126 F5
Rutanzige, Lake Dem. Rep. Congo/Uganda see Edward, Lake
Rute Spain 54 G7
Ruteng Indon. 75 B5
Rutenga Zimbabwe 131 F4
Rutherfordton U.S.A. 174 D5
Rutherglen Canada 173 N4
Ruther Glen U.S.A. 176 H8
Ruthin U.K. 47 I10
also spelt Rhuthun
Rutland U.S.A. 177 M2
Rutland Island India 95 G4
Rutland Plains Australia 149 D2
Rutledge U.S.A. 176 B9
Rutledge Lake Canada 167 I2
Rutog Xizang China 89 B5
also known as Dêrub
Rutog Xizang China 89 D6
Rutog Xizang China 89 F6
Rutshuru Dem. Rep. Congo 126 F5
Rutter Canada 173 M4
Rutul Rus. Fed. 102 A4
Ruukki Fin. 44 N2
Ruusa Estonia 42 I3
Ruvaslahti Fin. 44 O3
Ruvo di Puglia Italy 56 I7
Ruvozero Rus. Fed. 44 O2
Ruvozero, Ozero l. Rus. Fed. 44 O2
Ruvu Tanz. see Pangani
Ruvuma r. Moz./Tanz. 129 D7
Ruvuma admin. reg. Tanz. 129 C7
Ruwaydah Saudi Arabia 105 D2
Ruwayshid, Wādī watercourse Jordan 109 I5
Ruwayṭah, Wādī watercourse Jordan 108 H8
Ruweijil pt Saudi Arabia 108 F8
Ruweis U.A.E. 105 F2
Ruwenzori mts Dem. Rep. Congo/Uganda 126 F5
Ruwenzori National Park Uganda see Queen Elizabeth National Park
Ruya r. Zimbabwe 131 G3
Ruyigi Burundi 126 F5
Ruyuan China 87 E3
also known as Rucheng
Ruza Rus. Fed. 43 R6
Ruzayevka Kazakh. 103 F1
Ruzayevka Rus. Fed. 41 H5
Ruzbugino Rus. Fed. 43 V3
Ruzhany Belarus 42 F9
Ruzhou China 87 E1
formerly known as Linru
Ružomberok Slovakia 49 Q6
▶ Rwanda country Africa 126 F5
formerly spelt Ruanda
africa [countries] ▶ 114–117
Ryābād Iran 100 C2
Ryabovo Rus. Fed. 43 J1
Ryal Bush N.Z. 153 C14
Ryall, Mount N.Z. 153 F10
Ryan, Loch b. U.K. 47 G8
Ryazan' Rus. Fed. 43 U7
Ryazan Oblast admin. div. Rus. Fed. see Ryazanskaya Oblast'
Ryazanovskiy Rus. Fed. 43 U6
Ryazanskaya Oblast' admin. div. Rus. Fed. 43 V7
English form Ryazan Oblast
Ryazantsevo Rus. Fed. 43 U5
Ryazhsk Rus. Fed. 41 G5
Rybache Kazakh. 88 C2
Rybachiy, Poluostrov pen. Rus. Fed. 44 P1
Rybachiy Poselok Uzbek. 102 D3
Rybach'ye Kyrg. see Balykchy
Rybinsk Rus. Fed. 43 T3
formerly known as Andropov or Shcherbakov
Rybinskoye Vodokhranilishche resr Rus. Fed. 43 T3
Rybnik Poland 49 P5
Rybnitsa Moldova see Rîbniţa
Rybnoye Rus. Fed. 43 U7
Rybreka Rus. Fed. 40 E3
Rychnov nad Kněžnou Czech Rep. 49 N5
Rycroft Canada 166 G4
Ryd Sweden 45 K4
Rydberg Peninsula Antarctica 222 S2
Ryde U.K. 47 K13
Rye Beach U.S.A. 177 O3
Ryegate U.S.A. 180 E3
Rye Patch Dam U.S.A. 182 F1
Rye Patch Reservoir U.S.A. 182 F1
Ryki Poland 49 S4
Rykovo Ukr. see Yenakiyeve
Ryl'sk Rus. Fed. 41 E6
Rymanów Poland 49 S6
Rýmařov Czech Rep. 49 O6
Rymättylä Fin. 45 M3
Ryn Poland 49 S2
Ryn-Peski des. Kazakh. 102 B3
Ryńskie, Jezioro l. Poland 49 S2
Ryojun China see Lüshun
Ryōtsu Japan 90 F5
Rypin Poland 49 Q2
Rysjedal Norway 45 I3
Rytterknægten hill Denmark 45 K5
Ryttylä Fin. 42 F1
Ryukhovo Rus. Fed. 43 N9
Ryukyu Islands Japan 81 K8
also known as Ryūkyū-rettō or Nansei-shotō; historically known as Loochoo Islands
Ryūkyū-rettō is Japan see Ryukyu Islands
Ryzhikovo Rus. Fed. 43 M7
Ryzhkawka Belarus 43 L8
Rządza r. Poland 49 S3
Rzav r. Bos.-Herz. 56 L5
Rzepin Poland 49 L3
Rzeszów Poland 49 T5
Rzhaksa Rus. Fed. 41 G5
Rzhanitsa Rus. Fed. 43 O8
Rzhawka r. Belarus 43 L9
Rzhev Rus. Fed. 43 P5

↓ S

Sa'ābād Iran 100 D3
Saacow Somalia 128 D4
Sa'ādah al Barṣā' pass Saudi Arabia 109 H8
Sa'ādatābād Fārs Iran 100 C4
Sa'ādatābād Hormozgan Iran 100 C4
Saaifontein S. Africa 132 F8
Saalach r. Germany 49 K8
Saale park Germany 48 I4
Saale r. Germany 48 I4
Saalfeld Germany 48 I5
Saalfelden am Steinernen Meer Austria 49 J8
Saanen Switz. 51 N6
Saanich Canada 166 F5
Saar land Germany see Saarland
Saar r. Germany 48 D6
Saarbrücken Germany 48 D6
Saare Estonia 42 H3
Sääre Estonia 42 D4
Saaremaa i. Estonia 42 D3
Saarenkylä Fin. 44 N2
Saar-Hunsrück, Naturpark nature res. Germany 48 D6
Saari Fin. 45 O3
Saarijärvi Fin. 44 N3
Saari-Kämä Fin. 44 N2
Saarikoski Fin. 44 M1
Saariselkä Fin. 44 N1
also known as Suoločielgi
Saaristomeren Kansallispuisto nat. park Fin. see Skärgårdshavets Nationalpark
Saarland land Germany 48 D6
English form Saar
Saarlouis Germany 48 D6
Saatlı Azer. 107 G3
also spelt Saatly
Saatly Azer. see Saatlı
Saatse Estonia 42 I4
Saba i. Neth. Antilles 187 H3
Saba, Wādī watercourse Saudi Arabia 104 B1
Sab' Ābār Syria 109 I4
Šabac Srbija Yugo. 58 A4
Sabadell Spain 55 N3
Sabae Japan 91 E7
Sabah state Malaysia 77 G1
formerly known as North Borneo
Sabak Malaysia 76 C2
Sabaki r. Kenya 128 D5
Sabalan, Kūhhā-ye mts Iran 100 A2
Sabalana i. Indon. 75 A4
Sabalana, Kepulauan is Indon. 75 A4
Sabalgarh India 96 C4
Sabamagrande Hond. 186 B4
Saban Venez. 199 E2
Sabana, Archipiélago de is Cuba 186 C2
Sabana de la Mar Dom. Rep. 187 F3
Sabanalarga Col. 198 C2
Sabaneta Dom. Rep. 187 E3
Sabang Sulawesi Selatan Indon. 75 B3
Sabang Sulawesi Tengah Indon. 75 A2
Sabang Indon. 76 A1
Sabano Col. 198 C5
Şabanözü Turkey 106 C2
Săbăoani Romania 58 H1
Sabará Brazil 203 D6
Sabari r. India 94 D2
also known as Kolab
Sabarmati r. India 96 B5
Sabaru i. Indon. 75 A4
Sabastiya West Bank 108 G5
Sabaudia Italy 56 F7
Sabaya Bol. 200 C4
Şabāyā Island Saudi Arabia 104 C4
Sabelo S. Africa 132 H8
Sabena Desert Kenya 128 C4
Sabhā Libya 120 B3
Şabḩā' Saudi Arabia 104 D3
Sabhrai India 96 A5
Sabi r. India 96 C3
Sabi r. Moz./Zimbabwe see Save
Sabie Moz. 131 G5
Sabie r. Moz./S. Africa 133 Q2
Sabie S. Africa 133 O2
Sabile Latvia 42 D4
Sabina U.S.A. 176 B6
Sabinal Mex. 184 D2
Sabinal, Cayo i. Cuba 186 D2
Sabiñánigo Spain 55 K2
Sabinar, Punta del mt. Spain 55 I8
Sabinas Mex. 185 E3
Sabinas r. Coahuila Mex. 179 B7
Sabinas r. Nuevo León Mex. 179 C7
Sabinas Hidalgo Mex. 185 E3
Sabine r. U.S.A. 179 D6
Sabine Lake U.S.A. 179 D6
Sabine National Wildlife Refuge nature res. U.S.A. 179 D6
Sabinópolis Brazil 207 J5
Sabinov Slovakia 49 S6
Sabirabad Azer. 107 G2
Sablayan Phil. 74 B3
Sable, Cape Canada 169 H5
Sable, Cape U.S.A. 175 D7
Sable, Lac du l. Canada 169 H2
Sable, Rivière du r. Canada 169 G2
Sable Island Canada 169 J5
Sables, River aux r. Canada 173 K4
Sablé-sur-Sarthe France 50 F5
Sablon, Pointe du pt France 51 K9
Saboeiro Brazil 202 E3
Sabon Kafi Niger 125 H3
Sabou Burkina 125 E3
Sabourin, Lac l. Canada 173 P3
Sabres France 50 F8
Sabrina Coast Antarctica 223 H2
Sabtang i. Phil. 74 B1
Sabugal Port. 54 D4
Sabula U.S.A. 172 C8
Sabulu Indon. 75 B3
Sabunten i. Indon. 77 F4
Şabyā Saudi Arabia 104 C4
Sabzawar Afgh. see Shīndand
Sabzevār Iran 100 D2
Sabzvārān Iran see Jīroft
Saca, Vârful mt. Romania 58 G2
Sacaba Bol. 200 D4
Sa Cabaneta Spain 55 N5
Sacaca Bol. 200 D4
Sacalinul Mare, Insula i. Romania 58 K4
Sacandaga r. U.S.A. 177 K2
Sacaton U.S.A. 183 M8
Saccarel, Mont mt. France/Italy 51 N8
Sac City U.S.A. 178 D3
Sacco r. Italy 56 F7
Săcele Romania 58 G3
Săcele Romania 58 J4
Săceni Romania 58 G4
Sachanga Angola 127 C8
Sachigo r. Canada 168 B2
Sachigo Lake Canada 167 M4
Sachin India 96 B5
Sach'on S. Korea 83 C6
formerly known as Samch'ŏnp'o
Sach'ŏn S. Korea 91 A7
Sach Pass India 96 C2
Sachsen land Germany 49 K4
English form Saxony
Sachsen-Anhalt land Germany 48 I3
English form Saxony-Anhalt
Sachs Harbour Canada 164 G2
also known as Ikaahuk
Sächsische Schweiz park Germany 49 L5
Sacirsuyu r. Syria/Turkey see Sājūr, Nahr
Sackpfeife hill Germany 48 F5
Sackville Canada 169 H4
Saco U.S.A. 177 O2
Sacol i. Phil. 74 B5
Sacramento Brazil 206 F6

▶ Sacramento U.S.A. 182 C3
State capital of California.

Sacramento r. U.S.A. 182 C3
Sacramento, Pampa del plain Peru 200 A1
Sacramento Mountains U.S.A. 181 F6
Sacramento Valley U.S.A. 182 B1
Sacratif, Cabo c. Spain 55 H8
Săcueni Romania 58 D1
Sacuriuiná r. Brazil 201 F3
Sacxán Mex. 185 H5
Sada S. Africa 133 K9
Sádaba Spain 55 J2
Sa'dābād Iran 100 B4
Sá da Bandeira Angola see Lubango
Sadad Syria 109 H3
Şa'dah Yemen 104 C4
Şa'dah governorate Yemen 104 C4
Sada-misaki pt Japan 91 C8
Sadang r. Indon. 75 A3
Sadani Tanz. 129 C6
Sadao Thai. 79 C7
Şadārah Yemen 105 E5
Sadaseopet India 94 C2
Saddat al Hindīyah Iraq 107 F4
Saddleback pass S. Africa 133 P2
Saddleback Mesa mt. U.S.A. 179 B5
Saddle Hill hill Australia 149 E2
Saddle Island Vanuatu see Mota Lava
Saddle Peak hill India 95 G3
Sa Đec Vietnam 79 D6
Sadḩ Oman 105 F4
Sadhaura India 96 C3
Sadi Eth. 128 B2
Sadieville U.S.A. 176 A7
Sadīj watercourse Iran 100 D5
Sadiqabad Pak. 101 G4
Sadiya India 80 F7
Sa'diya Saudi Arabia 104 B3
Sa'dīyah, Hawr as imp. l. Iraq 107 F4
Sa'diyyat i. U.A.E. 105 F2
Sadjoavato Madag. 131 [inset] K2
Sad-Kharv Iran 100 D2
Sado r. Port. 54 C6
Sadoga-shima i. Japan 90 F6
Sadon Rus. Fed. 41 H8
Sadong r. Sarawak Malaysia 77 E2
Sadovoye Rus. Fed. 41 H7
Sa Dragonera i. Spain 55 N5
also known as Dragonera, Isla
Sadri India 96 B4
Sadulshahar India 96 B3
Sādūs Saudi Arabia 105 D2
Sæby Denmark 45 J4
Saegertown U.S.A. 176 E4
Saena Julia Italy see Siena
Safad Israel see Zefat
Safâga, Gezîret i. Egypt 104 A2
English form Safâga Island
Safâga Island Egypt see Safâga, Gezîret
Safané Burkina 124 E3
Šafárikovo Slovakia see Tornaľa
Safayal Maqūf well Iraq 107 F5
Safed Khirs mts Afgh. 101 G2
Safed Koh mts Afgh. 101 F3
Safed Koh mts Afgh./Pak. 101 G3
Säffle Sweden 45 K4
Safford U.S.A. 183 O9
Safi Jordan see Aş Şāfī
Safi Morocco 122 C2
Safīabad Iran 100 D2
Safīd r. Iran 100 B2
Safīdabeh Iran 101 E4
Safīdār, Kūh-e mt. Iran 100 C4
Safīd Dasht Iran 100 B3
Safīd Kūh mts Afgh. see Paropamisus
Safīd Sagak Iran 101 E3
Säfir Yemen 105 D5
Safiras, Serra das mts Brazil 203 D6
Şāfītā Syria 108 H3
Safonovo Arkhangel'skaya Oblast' Rus. Fed. 40 I2
Safonovo Smolenskaya Oblast' Rus. Fed. 43 O6
Safotu Samoa 145 H3
Safrā' al Asyāḩ esc. Saudi Arabia 104 C2
Safrā' as Sark esc. Saudi Arabia 104 D2
Safranbolu Turkey 106 C2
Safwān Iraq 107 F5
Şag Romania 58 C3
Saga China 89 D6
also known as Gya'gya
Saga Japan 91 B8
Saga pref. Japan 91 B8
Saga Kazakh. 103 F2
Sagae Japan 90 G5
Sagaing Myanmar 78 A3
Sagaing admin. div. Myanmar 78 A3
Sagala Mali see Ségala
Sagamihara Japan 91 F7
Sagami-nada g. Japan 91 F7
Sagami-wan b. Japan 91 F7
Sagamu Nigeria 125 F5
also spelt Shagamu
Saganash Lake Canada 173 K1
Saganoseki Japan 91 B8
Saganthit Kyun i. Myanmar 79 B5
also known as Sellore Island
Sagar Karnataka India 94 B3
Sagar Karnataka India 94 C2
Sagar Madhya Pradesh India 96 C5
Sagaredzho Georgia see Sagarejo
Sagarejo Georgia 107 F2
also spelt Sagaredzho
Sagaria Bangl. 97 F5
Sagar Island India 97 F5
Sagarmatha mt. China/Nepal see Everest, Mount
Sagarmatha National Park Nepal 97 E4
Sagastyr Rus. Fed. 39 M2
Sagauli India 97 E4
Sagavanirktok r. U.S.A. 164 E2
Sage U.S.A. 180 E4
Sage Creek r. U.S.A. 180 E2
Saggi, Har mt. Israel 108 F7
Saghand Iran 100 C3
Saghyz Kazakh. see Sagiz
Sagileru r. India 94 C3
Saginaw MI U.S.A. 173 J7
Saginaw MN U.S.A. 172 A4
Saginaw Bay U.S.A. 173 J7
Sağırlar Turkey 59 J9
Sagiz Atyrauskaya Oblast' Kazakh. 102 C2
also spelt Saghyz
Sagiz Atyrauskaya Oblast' Kazakh. 102 C3
Sagiz r. Kazakh. see Sagyz
Sağlamtaş Turkey 58 I8
Saglelpie Liberia 124 C5
Saglek Bay Canada 169 I1
Saglouc Canada see Salluit
Sagly Rus. Fed. 88 E1
Sagone, Golfe de b. Corse France 56 A6
Sagra mt. Spain 55 I7
Sagres Port. 54 C7
Sagres, Ponta de pt Port. 54 C8
Sagsay watercourse Mongolia 84 C2
Sagu Indon. 75 B5
Sagu Myanmar 78 A3
Saguache U.S.A. 181 F5
Saguache Creek r. U.S.A. 181 F5
Sagua de Tánamo Cuba 187 E2
Sagua la Grande Cuba 186 C2
Saguaro National Park U.S.A. 183 N9
Saguenay r. Canada 169 G3
Sagunt Spain see Sagunto
Sagunto Spain 55 K5
also spelt Sagunt; historically known as Murviedro or Saguntum
Saguntum Spain see Sagunto
Sagwara India 96 B5
Sagyndyk, Mys pt Kazakh. 102 B3
Sagyz r. Kazakh. 102 C3
formerly spelt Sagiz
Saḩāb Jordan 108 H6
Sahabab India 96 C3
Sahagún Spain 54 F2
Sahand, Kūh-e mt. Iran 100 A2
▶ Sahara des. Africa 123 F4
africa [landscapes] ▶ 112–113
africa [locations] ▶ 118–119
Sahara, Gebel mt. Egypt 108 F9
Şahara el Gharbîya des. Egypt see Western Desert
Şahara el Sharqîya des. Egypt see Eastern Desert
Saharan Atlas mts Alg. see Atlas Saharien
Saharanpur India 96 C3
Sahara Well Australia 150 C4
Saharsa India 97 E4
Sahaswan India 96 C3
Sahat, Kūh-e hill Iran 100 C3
Sahatwar India 97 E4
Sahavato Madag. 131 [inset] K4
Sahbā', Wādī as watercourse Saudi Arabia 105 E3
Şahbuz Azer. 107 F3
also spelt Shakhbuz
Saheira, Wâdi el watercourse Egypt 108 E7
Sahel reg. Africa 124 C3
Sahel prov. Eritrea 104 B4
Sahel, Réserve Partielle du nature res. Burkina 125 E3
Sahibganj India 97 E4
Sahiwal Punjab Pak. 101 H4
Sahiwal Punjab Pak. 101 H4
Sahlābād Iran 101 D3
Sahl al Maṭrān Saudi Arabia 104 B2
Sahl Rakbah plain Saudi Arabia 104 C3
Şaḩneh Iran 100 A3
Şaḩrā al Ḩijārah reg. Iraq 107 F5
Şahragt el-Kubra Egypt 108 C7
Sahu China see Zadoi
Sahuaripa Mex. 184 C2
Sahuayo Mex. 185 E4
Şāḩūq reg. Saudi Arabia 104 C2
Şāḩūq, Wādī watercourse Saudi Arabia 104 C2
Šahy Slovakia 49 P7
Sahyadri mts India see Western Ghats
Sahyadriparvat Range hills India 94 B1
also known as Ajanta Range
Şahyūn tourist site Syria 108 H2
Sai r. India 96 D4
Saibai Island Australia 73 J8
Sai Buri Thai. 79 C7
Sai Buri r. Thai. 79 C7
Saïda Alg. 123 F2
Saïda Lebanon see Sidon
Saïda, Monts de mts Alg. 55 L9
Sai Dao Tai, Khao mt. Thai. 79 C5
Sa'id Bin Sahrān Oman 105 G3
Saïdia Morocco 55 I9
Saidpur Bangl. 97 F4
Saidpur India 97 D4
Saidu Pak. 101 H3
Saigō Japan 91 C6
Saigon Vietnam see Ho Chi Minh City
Saiha India 97 G5
Saihan Tal China 85 G3
also known as Sonid Youqi
Saihan Toroi China 84 D3
Saija Fin. 44 O2
Saijō Japan 91 C8
Saikai National Park Japan 91 A8
Saikanosy Masoala pen. Madag. 131 [inset] K2
Saiki Japan 91 B8
Sai Kung Hong Kong China 87 [inset]
Sailana India 96 B5
Sailyugem Mountains Rus. Fed. 84 A1
Saimaa l. Fin. 45 O3
Saimaankanava r. Fin. 45 O3
Saimbeyli Turkey 106 D3
Sain Alto Mex. 185 E4
Saindak Pak. 101 E4
Sa'īndezh Iran 100 A2
also known as Sa'īn Qal'eh; formerly known as Shāhīn Dezh
Sa'īn Qal'eh Iran see Sa'īndezh
Saïnsoubou Senegal 124 C3
Saint r. U.S.A. 178 E4
St Abb's Head U.K. 46 J8
St-Affrique France 51 I9
St-Aignan France 50 H5
St Alban's Canada 169 K4
St Albans U.K. 47 L12
historically known as Verulamium
St Albans VT U.S.A. 177 L1
St Albans WV U.S.A. 176 D7
St Alban's Head U.K. 47 J13
also known as St Aldhelm's Head
St Albert Canada 167 H4
St Aldhelm's Head U.K. see St Alban's Head
St-Amand-les-Eaux France 51 J2
St-Amand-Montrond France 51 I6
St-Ambroise Canada 169 G3
St-Amour France 51 L6
St-André, Cap pt Madag. see Vilanandro, Tanjona
St-André-de-Cubzac France 50 F8
St Andrews N.Z. 153 F12
St Andrews U.K. 46 J7
St Andrew Sound inlet U.S.A. 175 D6
Saint Anne U.S.A. 172 F9
St Ann's Bay Jamaica 186 D3
St Anthony Canada 169 K3
Saint Anthony U.S.A. 180 E4
St Arnaud Australia 147 D4
St Arnaud N.Z. 153 G9
St-Arnoult-en-Yvelines France 51 H4
St Asaph Bay Australia 148 A1
St-Astier France 50 G7
St-Aubin-du-Cormier France 50 E4
St-Augustin Canada 169 J3
St Augustin r. Canada 169 J3
St Augustine U.S.A. 175 D6
historically known as San Agostín
St-Aulaye France 50 G7
St Austell U.K. 47 H13
St-Avé France 50 D5
St Barbe Canada 169 J3
St-Barthélemi Canada 169 F4
St-Barthélemy i. West Indies 187 H3
St-Barthélemy, Pic de mt. France 50 H10
St Bathans N.Z. 153 D12
St Bees Head U.K. 47 I9
St Bernard mt. N.Z. 153 H10
St-Blaise Switz. 51 M5
St-Brice-en-Coglès France 50 E4
St Bride's Bay U.K. 47 G12
St-Brieuc France 50 D4
St-Brieuc, Baie de b. France 50 D4
St-Calais France 50 G5
St Catharines Canada 168 E5
St Catherine's Canada 169 K4
St Catherine's Point U.K. 47 K13
St-Céré France 50 H8
St-Chamond France 51 K7
St Charles Canada 173 M4
Saint Charles U.S.A. 173 I7
St Charles MD U.S.A. 177 I7
St Charles MO U.S.A. 174 B4
St-Chély-d'Apcher France 51 J8
St-Christol-lès-Alès France 51 K8
St Christopher i. St Kitts and Nevis see St Kitts
St Christopher and Nevis country West Indies see St Kitts and Nevis
St-Ciers-sur-Gironde France 50 F7
St Clair r. Canada/U.S.A. 174 D3
St Clair U.S.A. 173 K8
St Clair, Lake Canada/U.S.A. 173 K8
St Clairsville U.S.A. 176 E5
St-Claude France 51 L6
Saint Cloud U.S.A. 175 D6
St Cloud U.S.A. 178 D2
St-Coeur-de-Marie Canada 169 G3
St Croix r. Canada/U.S.A. 165 M5
St Croix r. U.S.A. 172 A5
St Croix Falls U.S.A. 172 A5
St Croix Island Virgin Is (U.S.A.) 187 G3
St-Cyr-sur-Loire France 50 G5
St David's U.K. 47 G12
also known as Tyddewi
St David's Head U.K. 47 G12
St-Denis France 51 I4

▶ St-Denis Réunion 219 K7
Capital of Réunion.

St-Denis-du-Sig Alg. see Sig
St-Dié France 51 M4
St-Dizier France 51 K4
St-Domingue country West Indies see Haiti
Sainte Anne Canada 167 L5
Sainte Anne, Lac l. Alta Canada 167 H4
Sainte Anne, Lac l. Que. Canada 169 H3
Ste-Anne-de-Beaupré Canada 169 G4
Ste-Anne-de-Portneuf Canada 169 G3
Ste-Anne-des-Monts Canada 169 H3
Ste-Anne-du-Lac Canada 173 R4
Ste-Émélie-de-l'Énergie Canada 169 F4
Ste-Foy-la-Grande France 50 G8
Sainte Genevieve U.S.A. 174 B4
St-Égrève France 51 L7
Ste-Hermine France 50 E6
St Elias, Cape U.S.A. 164 E4

▶ St Elias, Mount U.S.A. 166 A2
4th highest mountain in North America.
northamerica [landscapes] ▶ 156–157

St Elias Mountains Canada 166 A2
St Élie Fr. Guiana 199 H3
St-Éloy-les-Mines France 51 I6
Sainte Marguerite r. Canada 169 H3
Ste-Marie Canada 169 G4
Ste-Marie Martinique 187 H4
Ste-Marie, Cap c. Madag. see Vohimena, Tanjona
Ste-Maure-de-Touraine France 50 G5
Ste-Maxime France 51 M9
Ste-Rose Guadeloupe 187 H3
Ste-Rose-du-Dégelé Canada see Dégelis
Sainte Rose du Lac Canada 167 L5
Saintes France 50 F7
Saintes, Îles des is Guadeloupe 187 H4
Sainte Thérèse, Lac l. Canada 166 F1
St-Étienne France 51 K7
St-Étienne-de-Tinée France 51 M8
St-Étienne-du-Rouvray France 50 H3
St Eustatius i. Neth. Antilles 187 H3
St-Fabien Canada 169 G3
St Faith's S. Africa 133 O7
St-Félicien Canada 169 F3
St-Félix-de-Dalquier Canada 173 O2
St-Florentin France 51 J4
St-Florent-sur-Cher France 51 I6
St Floris, Parc National nat. park Cent. Afr. Rep. 126 D2
St-Flour France 51 J7
St Francesville U.S.A. 175 B6
St Francis r. Canada/U.S.A. 174 G2
St Francis r. U.S.A. 174 B5
St Francis, Cape S. Africa 133 I11
St Francis Bay S. Africa 133 J11
St Francis Isles Australia 146 B3
St-François r. Canada 169 F4
St-François, Lac l. Canada 169 G4
St-Gaudens France 50 G9
St-Gaultier France 50 H6
St-Gély-du-Fesc France 51 J9
St-Geniez-d'Olt France 51 I8
St George Australia 147 F2
St George r. Australia 149 E3
St George Canada 169 H4
St George AK U.S.A. 164 C4
St George SC U.S.A. 175 D5
St George UT U.S.A. 183 K4
St George, Cape P.N.G. 145 E2
St George, Point U.S.A. 180 A4
St George Head Australia 147 F3
St George Island AK U.S.A. 164 C4
St George Island FL U.S.A. 175 C6
St George Range hills Australia 150 D3
St George's Canada 169 J3
St-Georges Canada 169 G4
St Georges Fr. Guiana 199 I4

▶ St George's Grenada 187 H4
Capital of Grenada.

St George's Bay Nfld. Canada 169 J3
St George's Bay N.S. Canada 169 I4
St George's Cay i. Belize 185 I5
St George's Channel India 95 G5
St George's Channel P.N.G. 145 E2
St George's Channel Rep. of Ireland/U.K. 47 F12
St Germain U.S.A. 172 D5
St-Germain-du-Puy France 51 I5
St-Germain-les-Belles France 50 H7
St-Gildas, Pointe de pt France 50 D5
St-Gildas-des-Bois France 50 D5
St-Gilles France 51 K9
St-Gilles-Croix-de-Vie France 50 E6
St Govan's Head U.K. 47 H12
St Helen U.S.A. 173 I6

▶ St Helena terr. S. Atlantic Ocean 216 N7
United Kingdom Overseas Territory.

St Helena U.S.A. 182 B3
St Helena Bay S. Africa 132 C9
St Helena Bay b. S. Africa 132 C9
St Helena Sound inlet U.S.A. 175 D5
St Helens Australia 147 F5
St Helens U.K. 47 J10
St Helens U.S.A. 180 B3
▶ St Helens, Mount vol. U.S.A. 180 B3
northamerica [threats] ▶ 160–161
St Helens Point Australia 147 F5

▶ St Helier Channel Is 50 D3
Capital of Jersey.

St-Hilaire-du-Harcouët France 50 E4
Sainthiya India 97 E5
St-Hubert Belgium 51 L2
St-Hyacinthe Canada 169 F4
St Ignace U.S.A. 173 I5
St Ignace Island Canada 168 C3
St Ignatius Guyana 199 G4
St Ives U.K. 47 G13
St Jacques, Cap Vietnam see Vung Tau
St-Jacques-de-Dupuy Canada 168 E3
St-Jacques-de-la-Lande France 50 E4
St-James France 50 E4
St James MI U.S.A. 172 H5
St James MN U.S.A. 178 D3
St James MO U.S.A. 174 B4
St James NY U.S.A. 177 L5
St James, Cape Canada 166 D5
St-Jean r. Que. Canada 169 H3
St-Jean r. Que. Canada 169 H3
St Jean Fr. Guiana 199 H3
St-Jean, Lac l. Canada 169 F3
St-Jean-d'Acre Israel see 'Akko
St-Jean-d'Angély France 50 F7
St-Jean-de-la-Ruelle France 50 H5
St-Jean-de-Luz France 50 E9
St-Jean-de-Maurienne France 51 M7
St-Jean-de-Monts France 50 D6
St-Jean-de-Port-Joli Canada 169 G4
St-Jean-sur-Richelieu Canada 169 F4
St-Jérôme Canada 169 F4
St Joe r. U.S.A. 180 C3
Saint John Canada 169 H4
St John r. Liberia 124 C5
St John U.S.A. 178 C4
St John r. U.S.A. 174 H2
St John, Cape Canada 169 K3
St John Bay Canada 169 J3
St John Island Canada 169 J3
St John Island Virgin Is (U.S.A.) 187 G3

▶ St John's Antigua and Barbuda 187 H3
Capital of Antigua and Barbuda.

▶ St John's Canada 169 K4
Provincial capital of Newfoundland.

St Johns AZ U.S.A. 183 O7
St Johns MI U.S.A. 173 I7
St Johns OH U.S.A. 176 A5
St Johns r. U.S.A. 175 D6
St Johnsbury U.S.A. 177 M1
St Johnsville U.S.A. 177 K3
St Joseph LA U.S.A. 175 B6
St Joseph MI U.S.A. 172 G8
St Joseph MO U.S.A. 178 D4
St Joseph r. MI U.S.A. 172 G8
St Joseph r. MI U.S.A. 173 H9
St Joseph, Lake Canada 168 B3
St-Joseph-d'Alma Canada see Alma
St Joseph Island Canada 168 D4
St Joseph Island U.S.A. 179 C7
St Jovité Canada 169 F4
St-Juéry France 51 I9
St-Julien-de-Concelles France 50 E5
St-Julien-en-Genevois France 51 M6
St Junien France 50 G7
St-Just-en-Chaussée France 51 I3

S index

St-Just-St-Rambert France **51** K7
St Kilda *i.* U.K. **46** D6
St Kitts *i.* St Kitts and Nevis **187** H3
also known as St Christopher
St Kitts and Nevis *country* West Indies **187** H3
also known as St Christopher and Nevis
northamerica [countries] 158–159
St-Laurent, Golfe du *g.* Canada *see* **St Lawrence, Gulf of**
St-Laurent-du-Maroni Fr. Guiana **199** H3
St Lawrence Australia **149** F4
St Lawrence Canada **169** K4
St Lawrence *inlet* Canada **169** G3
St Lawrence, Cape Canada **169** I4
St Lawrence, Gulf of Canada **169** I3
also known as St-Laurent, Golfe du
St Lawrence Island U.S.A. **164** C3
St Lawrence Islands National Park Canada **173** R6
St Lawrence Seaway *sea chan.* Canada/U.S.A. **174** F2
St Lazare Canada **167** K5
St-Léonard *N.B.* Canada **169** H4
St-Léonard *Que.* Canada **169** F4
St Leonard U.S.A. **177** I7
St-Léonard-de-Noblat France **50** H7
St Lewis Canada **169** K2
St Lewis *r.* Canada **169** J2
St-Lô France **50** E3
St-Louis France **51** N5
St-Louis Senegal **124** A2
St Louis *MI* U.S.A. **173** I7
St Louis *MO* U.S.A. **174** B4
St Louis *r.* U.S.A. **174** A2
St-Louis du Nord Haiti **187** E3
St-Loup-sur-Semouse France **51** M5
St Lucia *country* West Indies **187** H4
northamerica [countries] 158–159
St Lucia, Lake S. Africa **133** Q5
St Lucia Channel Martinique/St Lucia **187** H4
St Lucia Estuary S. Africa **133** Q5
St Lucia Game Reserve *nature res.* S. Africa **133** Q5
St Lucia Park *nature res.* S. Africa **133** Q5
St Luke's Island Myanmar *see* **Zadetkale Kyun**
St-Macaire-en-Mauges France **50** F5
St Magnus Bay U.K. **46** K3
St-Maixent-l'École France **50** F6
St-Malo France **50** D4
St-Malo, Golfe de *g.* France **50** D4
St-Mandrier-sur-Mer France **51** L9
St Marc Haiti **187** E3
St-Marc, Canal de *sea chan.* Haiti **187** E3
St-Marcellin France **51** L7
St Margaret's Hope U.K. **46** J5
Saint Maries U.S.A. **180** C3
St Marks S. Africa **133** L9
St Mark's S. Africa *see* **Cofimvaba**
St Marks National Wildlife Refuge *nature res.* U.S.A. **175** C6

St Martin *i.* West Indies **187** H3
Dependency of Guadeloupe (France). The southern part of the island is the Dutch territory of Sint Maarten.

St Martin, Lake Canada **167** L5
St-Martin-de-Crau France **51** K9
St-Martin-de-Ré France **50** E6
St-Martin-d'Hères France **51** L7
St Mary *r.* Canada **167** H5
St Mary, Mount N.Z. **153** D12
St Mary Peak Australia **146** C2
St Marys Australia **147** F5
St Mary's Canada **173** L6
St Mary's *i.* U.K. **47** F14
Saint Marys U.S.A. **178** C4
St Marys *OH* U.S.A. **176** A5
St Marys *PA* U.S.A. **176** G4
St Marys *WV* U.S.A. **176** D6
St Marys *r.* U.S.A. **176** A5
St Mary's, Cape Canada **169** K4
St Mary's Bay Canada **169** K4
St Marys City U.S.A. **177** I7
St-Mathieu Canada **173** O2
St-Mathieu, Pointe de *pt* France **50** B4
St Matthew Island U.S.A. **164** B3
Saint Matthews U.S.A. **175** D5
St Matthew's Island Myanmar *see* **Zadetkyi Kyun**
St Matthias Group *is* P.N.G. **145** D2
St Maurice *r.* Canada **169** F4
St-Maurice, Réserve Faunique du *nature res.* Canada **169** F4
St-Maximin-la-Ste-Baume France **51** L9
St-Médard-en-Jalles France **50** F8
St Michaels U.S.A. **177** I7
St Michael's Bay Canada **169** K2
St Michael's Mount *tourist site* U.K. **47** G13
St-Michel-de-Maurienne France **51** M7
St-Michel-des-Saints Canada **169** F4
St-Mihiel France **51** L4
St-Nazaire France **50** D5
St Nicolas Belgium *see* **Sint-Niklaas**
St-Nicolas-de-Port France **51** M4
St Niklaus Switz. **51** N6
St-Omer France **51** I2
Saintonge *reg.* France **50** F7
St-Pacôme Canada **169** G4
St-Palais France **50** E9
St Paris U.S.A. **176** B5
St Pascal Canada **169** G4
St-Patrice, Lac *l.* Canada **173** P4
St Paul Canada **167** I4
St Paul *r.* Canada **169** J3
St Paul *r.* Liberia **124** C5
St Paul *IA* U.S.A. **172** B10

St Paul *MN* U.S.A. **174** A2
State capital of Minnesota.

St Paul *NE* U.S.A. **178** C3
St Paul *VA* U.S.A. **176** C9
St Paul, Île *i.* Indian Ocean **219** M8
English form St Paul Island
St-Paul-de-Fenouillet France **51** I10
St Paul Island Canada **169** I4
St Paul Island Indian Ocean *see* **St Paul, Île**
St-Paul-lès-Dax France **50** E9
St Paul Subterranean River National Park Phil. **74** A4
St Peter U.S.A. **174** A2
St Peter and St Paul Rocks *is* N. Atlantic Ocean *see* **São Pedro e São Paulo**

St Peter Port Channel Is **50** D3
Capital of Guernsey.

St Peter's Canada **169** I4
St Peters Canada **169** I4

St Petersburg Rus. Fed. **43** L2
5th most populous city in Europe. Also known as Sankt-Peterburg; formerly known as Leningrad; historically known as Petrograd.
world [cities] 24–25

St Petersburg U.S.A. **175** D7
St Petrus *i.* Indon. **77** E2
St-Philbert-de-Grand-Lieu France **50** E5
St-Pierre *mt.* France **51** L9
St Pierre Mauritius **129** F7

St-Pierre St Pierre and Miquelon **169** K4
Capital of St Pierre and Miquelon.

St-Pierre, Lac *l.* Canada **169** F4

St Pierre and Miquelon *terr.* N. America **169** J4
French Territorial Collectivity.
oceania [countries] 138–139

St-Pierre-des-Corps France **50** G5
St-Pierre-d'Oléron France **50** E7
St-Pierre-le-Moûtier France **51** J6
St-Pol-sur-Ternoise France **51** I2
St-Pons-de-Thomières France **51** I9
St-Pourçain-sur-Sioule France **51** J6
St Quentin Canada **169** H4
St-Quentin France **51** J3
St-Raphaël France **51** M9
St Regis *r.* U.S.A. **177** K1
St Regis Falls U.S.A. **177** K1
St-Renan France **50** B4
St-Rigaud, Mont *mt.* France **51** K6
St-Sauveur-des-Monts Canada **169** F4
St-Savin France **50** F7
St-Savinien France **50** F7
St-Sébastien-sur-Loire France **50** E5
St Siméon Canada **169** G4
St-Sorlin, Mont de *mt.* France **51** M6
St Stephen U.S.A. **175** E5
St-Symphorien France **50** F8
St Terese U.S.A. **166** C3
St Theresa Point Canada **167** M4
St Thomas Canada **168** D5
St Thomas Island Virgin Is (U.S.A.) **187** G3
St-Tite-des-Caps Canada **169** G4
St-Tropez France **51** M9
St-Tropez, Cap de *c.* France **51** M9
St-Valery-en-Caux France **50** G3
St-Valery-sur-Somme France **51** H2
St-Vallier *Bourgogne* France **51** K6
St-Vallier *Rhône-Alpes* France **51** K7
St-Vaury France **50** H6
St-Vincent Italy **51** N7
St Vincent *i.* West Indies **199** F1
St-Vincent, Cap *pt* Madag. *see* **Ankaboa, Tanjona**
St Vincent, Cape Australia **147** E5
St Vincent, Cape Port. *see* **São Vicente, Cabo de**
St Vincent, Gulf Australia **146** C3
St Vincent and the Grenadines *i.* West Indies **187** H4
northamerica [countries] 158–159
St-Vincent-de-Tyrosse France **50** E9
St Vincent Island U.S.A. **175** C6
St Vincent Passage St Lucia/St Vincent **187** H4
St Walburg Canada **167** I4
St-Yrieix-la-Perche France **50** H7
Saipal *mt.* Nepal **97** D3
Saipan *i.* N. Mariana Is **73** K3
also spelt Seypan
Saison *r.* France **50** F9
Saitama *pref.* Japan **90** F7
Saiteli Turkey *see* **Kadınhanı**
Saito Japan **91** B8
Saittanulkki *hill* Fin. **40** C2
Saivomuotka Sweden **44** M1
Sai Yok National Park Thai. **79** B5
Sajama, Nevado *mt.* Bol. **200** C4
Sājid Saudi Arabia **104** C4
Sājir Saudi Arabia **104** D2
Sājir, Ra's *c.* Oman **105** F4
Sajó *r.* Hungary **49** R8
Sajóhidvég Hungary **49** R7
Sājūr, Nahr *r.* Syria/Turkey **109** J1
also known as Bağırsak Deresi *or* Sacirsuyu
Sajzī Iran **100** C3
Sak *watercourse* S. Africa **132** F6
Saka Eth. **128** C2
Sakai Japan **91** D7
Sakaide Japan **91** C7
Sakaiminato Japan **91** C7
Sakākah Saudi Arabia **107** E5
also known as Sikaka
Sakakawea, Lake U.S.A. **178** B2
Sakala *i.* Indon. **77** G4
Sakalile Tanz. **129** A7
Sakami Canada **168** F2
Sakami *r.* Canada **169** E2
Sakami Lake Canada **168** E2
Sakania Dem. Rep. Congo **127** F8
Sakar *mts* Bulg. **58** H7
Sakar Turkm. **103** E5
Sakaraha Madag. **131** [inset] J4
Sakar-Chaga Turkm. **103** E5
Sakartvelo *country* Asia *see* **Georgia**
Sakarya Turkey **106** B2
also known as Adapazari; *formerly known as* Adabazar
Sakarya *r.* Turkey **106** B2
Sakassou Côte d'Ivoire **124** D5
Sakata Japan **90** F5
Sakawa Japan **91** C8
Sakchu N. Korea **83** B4
Saken Seyfullin Kazakh. **103** H2
formerly known as Zharyk
Sa Keo *r.* Thai. **79** C5
Sakété Benin **125** F5
Sakhalin *i.* Rus. Fed. **82** F2
Sakhalin Oblast *admin. div.* Rus. Fed. *see* **Sakhalinskaya Oblast'**
Sakhalinskaya Oblast' *admin. div.* Rus. Fed. **82** F2
English form Sakhalin Oblast
Sakhalinskiy Zaliv *b.* Rus. Fed. **82** F1
Sakhanina, Mys *c.* Rus. Fed. **40** J1
Sakharovo Rus. Fed. **43** R5
Sakhelwe S. Africa **133** O2
Sakhile S. Africa **133** N3
Sakhra Turkm. **102** D5
formerly known as Gyaurs
Sakht-Sar Iran **100** B2
Şäki Azer. **107** F2
also spelt Sheki; *formerly known as* Nukha
Saki Nigeria **125** F4
also spelt Shaki
Saki Ukr. *see* **Saky**
Šakiai Lith. **42** E7
Sakiet Sidi Youssef Tunisia **57** A12
Sakir *mt.* Pak. **101** F4
Sakishima-shotō *is* Japan **81** K8
Sakleshpur India **94** B3
Sakmara Rus. Fed. **102** C2
Sa-koi Myanmar **78** B4
Sakoli India **96** C5
Sakon Nakhon Thai. **78** D4
Sakra, Pulau *reg.* Sing. **76** [inset]
Sakrand Pak. **101** G5
Sakrivier S. Africa **132** E7
Saksaul'skiy Kazakh. **103** E3
also known as Sekseüil; *formerly known as* Saksaul'skoye
Saksaul'skoye Kazakh. *see* **Saksaul'skiy**
Sakshaug Norway **44** J3
Sakti India **97** D5
Saku Estonia **42** F2
Saku Japan **91** F6
Sakura Japan **91** G7
Sakura-jima *vol.* Japan **91** B9
Saky Ukr. **41** E7
also spelt Saki
Säkylä Fin. **45** M3
Sal *i.* Cape Verde **124** [inset]
Sal *r.* Rus. Fed. **53** K2
Sal, Punta *pt* Hond. **186** B4
Sala Latvia **42** G5
Sala Latvia **42** E5
Šaľa Slovakia **49** O7
Sala Sweden **45** L4
Salabangka, Kepulauan *is* Indon. **75** B3
Salaberry-de-Valleyfield Canada **169** F4
Salaca *r.* Latvia **42** F4
Sălacea Romania **58** D1
Salacgrīva Latvia **42** F4
Sala Consilina Italy **57** H8
Salada, Bahía *b.* Chile **204** C2
Salada, Laguna *salt l.* Mex. **184** B1
Saladas Arg. **204** F3
Saladīh, Wādī *watercourse* Jordan **108** G8
Saladillo Arg. **204** F4
Saladillo *r.* Córdoba Arg. **204** E4
Saladillo *r.* Santiago del Estero Arg. **204** E3
Salado Ecuador **198** B5
Salado *r.* Buenos Aires Arg. **204** F4
Salado *r.* Formosa Arg. **204** F2
Salado *r.* La Rioja Arg. **204** C3
Salado *r.* Río Negro Arg. **204** D6
Salado *r.* Santa Fé Arg. **204** E4
Salado *r.* Arg. **204** D5
Salado *r.* Cuba **186** D2
Salado *r.* Ecuador **198** B5
Salado *r.* Mex. **185** F3
Salado *r.* Spain **54** F8
Salado *watercourse* U.S.A. **181** F6
Saladou Guinea **124** C4
Salaga Ghana **125** E4
Şalāḩ Saudi Arabia **104** C3
Şalāḩ, Tall *hill* Jordan **109** J4
Şalāḩ ad Dīn *governorate* Iraq **107** E4
Salahuddin Iraq **107** F3
Salajwe Botswana **131** E4
Salakh, Jabal *mt.* Oman **105** G3
Salal Chad **120** C6
Salâla Sudan **121** H4
Şalālah Oman **105** F4
Salalé *well* Niger **125** I3
Salamá Guat. **185** H6
Salamá Hond. **186** B4
Salamajärven kansallispuisto *nat. park* Fin. **44** N3
Salamanca Chile **204** C3
Salamanca Mex. **185** E4
Salamanca Spain **54** F4
historically known as Helmantica *or* Salamantica
Salamanca U.S.A. **176** G3
Salamanga Moz. **131** G5
Salamantica Spain *see* **Salamanca**
Salamat *pref.* Chad **126** D2
Salamat, Bahr *r.* Chad **126** C2
Salāmatābād Iran **100** A3
Salamban Indon. **77** F3
Salamina Greece **59** E11
Salamina *i.* Greece **59** E11
also known as Salamís
Salamis *tourist site* Cyprus **108** E2
also known as Constantia
Salamís *i.* Greece *see* **Salamina**
Salamīyah Syria **109** I2
Salamonie *r.* U.S.A. **172** H10
Salamonie Lake U.S.A. **172** H10
Salandi *r.* India **95** E1
Salantai Lith. **42** C5
Salaqi China **85** F3
also known as Tumd Youqi
Sălard Romania **58** D1
Salar de Pocitos Arg. **200** D6
Salas Spain **54** E1
Salas de los Infantes Spain **55** H2
Salaspils Latvia **42** F5
Salat *r.* France **50** G9
Salatiga Indon. **77** E4
Sălăuța *r.* Romania **58** F1
Salavat Rus. Fed. **102** C1
Salaverry Peru **200** A2
Salawati *i.* Indon. **73** H7
Salawin Wildlife Reserve *nature res.* Thai. **78** B4
Salay Phil. **74** C4
Salaya India **96** A5
Salayar *i.* Indon. **75** B4
Salayar, Selat *sea chan.* Indon. **75** B4
Sala y Gómez, Isla *i.* S. Pacific Ocean **221** K7
Salazar Angola *see* **N'dalatando**
Salazar Arg. **204** E5
Salbris France **51** I5
Salcantay, Cerro *mt.* Peru **200** B3
Salcedo Dom. Rep. **187** F3
Šalčiai *r.* Lith. **42** F7
Šalčininkai Lith. **42** G7
Sălciua Romania **58** E2
Salcoa Romania **58** H4
Saldae Alg. *see* **Bejaïa**
Salda Gölü *l.* Turkey **59** K11
Saldaña Col. **198** C4
Saldaña Spain **54** G2
Saldanha S. Africa **132** B10
Saldanha Bay S. Africa **132** B10
Saldus Latvia **42** D5
Sale Australia **147** E4
Sale Myanmar **78** A3
Salea Indon. **75** B3
Saleh, Teluk *b.* Indon. **77** G5
Şāleḩābād *Hamadān* Iran **100** B3
Şāleḩābād *Khorāsan* Iran **101** E3
Salekhard Rus. Fed. **38** G3
historically known as Obdorsk
Salem India **94** C4
Salem S. Africa **133** K10
Salem *AR* U.S.A. **174** B4
Salem *IA* U.S.A. **172** B10
Salem *IL* U.S.A. **174** B4
Salem *IN* U.S.A. **174** C4
Salem *MA* U.S.A. **177** O3
Salem *MO* U.S.A. **174** B4
Salem *NJ* U.S.A. **177** J6
Salem *NY* U.S.A. **177** L2

Salem *OR* U.S.A. **180** B3
State capital of Oregon.

Salem *SD* U.S.A. **178** C3
Salem *UT* U.S.A. **183** M1
Salem *VA* U.S.A. **176** E8
Salem *WV* U.S.A. **176** E6
Salemi *Sicilia* Italy **57** E11
Sälen Sweden **45** K3
Salerno Italy **57** G8
historically known as Salernum
Salerno, Golfo di *g.* Italy **57** G8
Salernum Italy *see* **Salerno**
Sales Oliveira Brazil **206** F7
Salesópolis Brazil **207** H10
Salford U.K. **47** J10
Salgada Brazil **199** F5
Salgado Brazil **202** E4
Salgótarján Hungary **49** Q7
Salgueiro Brazil **202** E4
Sali Alg. **123** E4
Salian Afgh. **101** E4
Salibabu *i.* Indon. **75** C2
Salida U.S.A. **181** F5
Saliena Latvia **42** E5
Salignac-Eyvignes France **50** H8
Salihli Turkey **106** B3
Salihorsk Belarus **42** I9
also spelt Soligorsk
Salihorskaye Vodaskhovishcha *resr* Belarus **42** I9
Salikéné Senegal **124** B3
Salimbatu Indon. **77** G2
Salimi Dem. Rep. Congo **127** D7
Salimo Moz. **129** C8
Salina *KS* U.S.A. **178** C4
Salina *UT* U.S.A. **183** M3
Salina, Isola *i.* Isole Lipari Italy **57** G10
Salina Cruz Mex. **185** G5
Salinas Brazil **202** D6
Salinas Ecuador **198** A5
Salinas Mex. **185** E4
Salinas *r.* Mex. **179** C7
Salinas U.S.A. **182** C5
Salinas *r.* U.S.A. **182** C5
Salinas, Cabo de *c.* Spain *see* **Ses Salines, Cap de**
Salinas India **96** A4
Salinas, Ponta das *pt* Angola **127** B8
Salinas, Punta *pt* Dom. Rep. **187** F3
Salinas de Garci Mendoza Bol. **200** D4
Salinas Peak U.S.A. **181** F6
Saline U.S.A. **173** J8
Saline *r. AR* U.S.A. **179** D5
Saline *r. KS* U.S.A. **178** C4
Saline Valley *depr.* U.S.A. **182** G5
Salinéville U.S.A. **176** E5
Salingyi Myanmar **78** A3
Salinópolis Brazil **202** C2
Salinosó Lachay, Punta *pt* Peru **200** A2
Salisbury U.K. **47** K12
Salisbury *MD* U.S.A. **177** J7
Salisbury *NC* U.S.A. **174** D5
Salisbury *PA* U.S.A. **176** F6
Salisbury Zimbabwe *see* **Harare**
Salisbury Island Canada **165** L3
Salisbury Plain U.K. **47** J12
Săliște Romania **58** E3
Salitre *r.* Brazil **202** D4
Şalkhad Syria **109** H5
Salki *r.* India **95** E1
Salla Fin. **44** O2
Salliqueló Arg. **204** E5
Sallisaw U.S.A. **179** D5
Sallom Sudan **104** B4
Salluit Canada **165** L3
formerly known as Saglouc
Sallyana Nepal **97** D3
Salmá Syria **108** H2
Salmās Iran **100** A2
also known as Shāhpūr
Salmi Rus. Fed. **40** D3
Salmivaara Fin. **44** O2
Salmo Canada **167** G5
Salmon U.S.A. **180** D3
Salmon *r.* U.S.A. **180** C3
Salmon, Middle Fork *r.* U.S.A. **180** D3
Salmon Arm Canada **166** G5
Salmon Falls Creek *r.* U.S.A. **180** D4
Salmon Gums Australia **151** C7
Salmon Reservoir U.S.A. **177** J2
Salmon River Mountains U.S.A. **180** D3
Salmonsdam Nature Reserve S. Africa **132** D11
Salmtal Germany **48** D6
Sal'nyye Tundry, Khrebet *mts* Rus. Fed. **44** O1
Salo Cent. Afr. Rep. **126** C4
Salo Fin. **45** M3
Salò Italy **56** C3
Saloinen Fin. **44** N2
Salome U.S.A. **183** K8
Salon India **97** D4
Salon-de-Provence France **51** L9
Salonga *r.* Dem. Rep. Congo **126** D5
Salonica Greece *see* **Thessaloniki**
Salonika Greece *see* **Thessaloniki**
Salonta Romania **58** C2
Salor *r.* Spain **54** D5
Salou Spain **55** M3
Salou, Cap de *c.* Spain **55** M3
Saloum *watercourse* Senegal **124** A3
Salpausselkä *reg.* Fin. **45** N3
Salsacate Arg. **204** D3
Salsbruket Norway **44** J2
Salses, Étang de *l.* France *see* **Leucate, Étang de**
Sal'sk Rus. Fed. **41** G7
Salso *r. Sicilia* Italy **57** F11
Salso *r. Sicilia* Italy **57** G11
Salsomaggiore Terme Italy **56** B4
Salt Jordan *see* **As Salt**
Salt *watercourse* S. Africa **132** H10
Salt Spain **55** N3
Salt *r. AZ* U.S.A. **183** L8
Salt *r. MO* U.S.A. **178** E4
Salt *r. WY* U.S.A. **180** E4
Salta Arg. **200** D6
Salta *prov.* Arg. **204** D2
Saltaнovka Rus. Fed. **43** P9
Saltash U.K. **47** H13
Salt Creek *r.* U.S.A. **176** C6
Saltee Islands Rep. of Ireland **47** F11
Saltery Bay Canada **166** E5
Saltfjellet Svartisen Nasjonalpark *nat. park* Norway **44** K2
Salt Fork *r.* U.S.A. **178** C4
Salt Fork Arkansas *r.* U.S.A. **178** C4
Salt Fork Brazos *r.* U.S.A. **179** B5
Salt Fork Lake U.S.A. **176** D5
Salt Fork Red *r.* U.S.A. **179** C5
Saltillo Mex. **185** E3
Salt Lake *salt l.* India **89** A7
Salt Lake S. Africa **132** I6

Salt Lake City U.S.A. **183** M1
State capital of Utah.

Salt Lick U.S.A. **176** B7
Salt Marsh Lake *salt l.* U.S.A. **183** K2
Salto Arg. **204** E4
Salto Brazil **206** F10
Salto *r.* Italy **56** E6
Salto Uruguay **204** F3
Salto da Divisa Brazil **202** E6
Salto de Agua Mex. **185** G5
Salto del Guairá Para. **201** G6
Salto Grande Brazil **206** D9
Salto Grande, Embalse de *resr* Uruguay **204** F3
Salton City U.S.A. **183** H8
Salton Sea *salt l.* U.S.A. **183** I8
Saltpond Ghana **125** E5
Salt River Canada **167** H2
Saltrou Haiti *see* **Belle-Anse**
Saltvik Fin. **45** L3
Saltykí Rus. Fed. **43** U8
Saltville U.S.A. **176** D9
Saluda *SC* U.S.A. **175** D5
Saluda *VA* U.S.A. **177** I8
Saluda *r.* U.S.A. **174** D5
Saluebesar *i.* Indon. **75** B3
Salue Timpaus, Selat *sea chan.* Indon. **75** B3
Salûm Egypt **106** A5
Salûm, Gulf of Egypt **121** E2
Salumbar India **96** B4
Saluq, Kūh-e *mt.* Iran **100** D2
Salur India **95** D2
Saluzzo Italy **51** N8
Salvador Brazil **202** E5
formerly known as Bahia
Salvador *country* Central America *see* **El Salvador**
Salvador, Lake U.S.A. **175** B6
Salvador Mazza Arg. **201** E5
Salvaterra Brazil **202** B2
Salvatierra Mex. **185** E4
Salvation Creek *r.* U.S.A. **183** N3
Salviac France **50** H8
Salwah Saudi Arabia **105** E2
Salwah, Dawhat *b.* Qatar/Saudi Arabia **105** E2
Salween *r.* China/Myanmar **78** B4
also known as Mae Nam Khong *or* Thanlwin (Myanmar) *or* Nu Jiang (China)
Salyan Azer. **107** G3
also spelt Sal'yany
Sal'yany Azer. *see* **Salyan**
Salyersville U.S.A. **176** B8
Salza *r.* Austria **49** L8
Salzach *r.* Austria/Germany **49** J7
Salzbrunn Namibia **130** C5
Salzburg Austria **49** K8
Salzgitter Germany **48** H3
formerly known as Watenstadt-Salzgitter
Salzkotten Germany **48** F4
Salzwedel Germany **48** I3
Salzwedel-Diesdorf *park* Germany **48** H3
Sam Gabon **126** A4
Sam India **96** A4
Sam, Nam *r.* Laos/Vietnam **78** D4
Samá Cuba **186** E2
also known as Puerto Sama
Šamac Bos.-Herz. *see* **Bosanski Šamac**
Şamad Oman **105** G3
Samae San, Laem *pt* Thai. **79** C5
English form Liant, Cape
Samagaltay Rus. Fed. **84** B1
Samāh *well* Saudi Arabia **105** D1
Samaida Iran *see* **Someydeh**
Samaipata Bol. **201** E4
Samak, Tanjung *pt* Indon. **77** D3
Samakoulou Mali **124** C3
Samal *i.* Phil. **74** C5
Samalayuca Mex. **184** D2
Samales Group *is* Phil. **74** B5
Samalkot India **95** D2
Samâlût Egypt **121** F2
Samaná Dom. Rep. **187** F3
Samana India **96** C3
Samaná, Cabo *c.* Dom. Rep. **187** F3
Samana Cay *i.* Bahamas **187** E2
Samanala *mt.* Sri Lanka *see* **Adam's Peak**
Samandağı Turkey **106** C3
also known as Alevişik; *historically known as* Seleucia Pieria
Samangān *prov.* Afgh. **101** F2
Samangān Iran **101** E3
Samani Japan **90** H3
Samaniego Col. **198** B4
Samanlı Dağları *mts* Turkey **58** J8
Samannûd Egypt **108** C7
also spelt Sebennytos
Samaqua *r.* Canada **169** F3
Samar Kazakh. *see* **Samarskoye**
Samar *i.* Phil. **74** C4
Samara Rus. Fed. **102** B1
formerly known as Kuybyshev
Samara *r.* Rus. Fed. **102** B1
Samarahan *Sarawak* Malaysia *see* **Sri Aman**
Samarai P.N.G. **149** F1
Samara Oblast *admin. div.* Rus. Fed. *see* **Samarskaya Oblast'**
Samarga Rus. Fed. **82** E3
Samaria *nat. park* Greece **59** E13
Samariapo Venez. **199** E3
Samarinda Indon. **77** G3
Samarka Rus. Fed. **82** D3
Samarkand Uzbek. **103** F5
also spelt Samarqand; *historically known as* Maracanda
Samarkand, Pik *mt.* Tajik. **101** G2
also known as Samarqand, Qullai
Samarkand Oblast *admin. div.* Uzbek. *see* **Samarkandskaya Oblast'**
Samarkandskaya Oblast' *admin. div.* Uzbek. **103** F5
English form Samarkand Oblast; *also known as* Samarqand Wiloyati
Samarobriva France *see* **Amiens**
Samarqand Uzbek. *see* **Samarkand**
Samarqand, Qullai *mt.* Tajik. *see* **Samarkand, Pik**
Samarqand Wiloyati *admin. div.* Uzbek. *see* **Samarkandskaya Oblast'**
Sāmarrā' Iraq **107** E4
Sāmarrā', Saddat dam Iraq **109** O3
Samar Sea *g.* Phil. **74** C4
Samarskaya Oblast' *admin. div.* Rus. Fed. **102** B1
English form Samara Oblast; *formerly known as* Kuybyshevskaya Oblast'
Samarskoye Kazakh. **88** C1
also known as Samar
Samasata Pak. **101** G4
Samassi *Sardegna* Italy **57** A9
Samastipur India **97** E4
Samaúma Brazil **199** F6
Şamaxı Azer. **107** G2
also spelt Shemakha
Samba Dem. Rep. Congo **126** E6
Samba *r.* Indon. **77** F3
Samba Jammu and Kashmir **96** B2
Samba Cajú Angola **127** B7
Sambaliung *mts* Indon. **77** G2
Sambalpur India **97** D5
Sambar, Tanjung *pt* Indon. **77** E3
Sambas Indon. **77** E2
Sambat Ukr. *see* **Kiev**
Sambava Madag. **131** [inset] K2
Sambhal India **96** C3
Sambhar India **96** B4
Sambhar Lake India **96** B4
Sambir Ukr. **53** G2
also spelt Sambor
Sambit *i.* Indon. **77** G2
Sambo Angola **127** C8
Sambo Indon. **75** A3
Sambogja Indon. **77** G3
Sambor Ukr. *see* **Sambir**
Sâmbor Dam Cambodia **79** D5
Samborombón, Bahía *b.* Arg. **204** F4
Samch'ŏk S. Korea **83** C5
Samch'ŏnp'o S. Korea *see* **Sach'on**
Sameikkon Myanmar **78** A3
Samer France **50** H2
Samet' Rus. Fed. **43** V4
Samet, Ko *i.* Thai. **79** C5
Samfya Zambia **127** F7
Samḩah *i.* Yemen **105** F5
Samḩān, Jabal *mts* Oman **105** F4
Sami India **96** A5
Sami Pak. **101** E5
Samīrah Saudi Arabia **104** C2
Samiria *r.* Peru **198** C6
Samirum Iran *see* **Yazd-e Khvāst**
Samka Myanmar **78** B3
Şämkir Azer. **107** F2
also spelt Shamkhor
Samnah *oasis* Saudi Arabia **104** B2
Samnan va Damghan *reg.* Iran **100** C3
Sam Neua Laos *see* **Xam Hua**
Samnū Libya **120** B3
Samoa *country* S. Pacific Ocean **145** H3
formerly known as Western Samoa *or* Samoa i Sisifo
oceania [countries] 138–139
Samoa i Sisifo *country* S. Pacific Ocean *see* **Samoa**
Samobor Croatia **56** H3
Samoded Rus. Fed. **40** G3
Samokov Bulg. **58** E6
Šamorín Slovakia **49** O7
Samos Greece **59** H11
Samos *i.* Greece **59** H11
Samosir *i.* Indon. **76** B2
Samothrace *i.* Greece *see* **Samothraki**
Samothraki Greece **58** G8
Samothraki *i.* Greece **59** G8
English form Samothrace
Samovodene Bulg. **58** G5
Samoylovka Rus. Fed. **41** G6
Sampa Côte d'Ivoire **124** E5
Sampacho Arg. **204** D4
Sampaga Indon. **75** A3
Sampang Indon. **77** F4
Sampit Indon. **77** F3
Sampit *r.* Indon. **77** F3
Sampit, Teluk *b.* Indon. **77** F3
Sampolawa Indon. **75** B4
Sampur Rus. Fed. **41** G5
Sampwe Dem. Rep. Congo **127** E7
Sam Rayburn Reservoir U.S.A. **179** D6
Samreboe Ghana **124** E5
Samr el 'Abd, Gebel *mt.* Egypt **108** D9
Samro, Ozero *l.* Rus. Fed. **43** J3
Samrong Cambodia *see* **Phumĭ Sâmraông**
Samsang China **89** C6
Sam Sao, Phou *mts* Laos/Vietnam **78** C3
Samsø *i.* Denmark **45** J5
Samsø Bælt *sea chan.* Denmark **45** J5
Sâm Sơn Vietnam **78** D4
Samsun Turkey **107** D2
historically known as Amisus
Samsy Kazakh. **103** I4
Samtens Germany **49** K1
Samthar India **96** C4
Samtredia Georgia **107** E2
Samui, Ko *i.* Thai. **79** C6
Samulun, Pulau *i.* Sing. **76** [inset]
Samundri Pak. **101** H4
Samur *r.* Azer./Rus. Fed. **107** G2
Samutlu Turkey *see* **Temelli**
Samut Prakan Thai. **79** C5
Samut Sakhon Thai. **79** C5
Samut Songkhram Thai. **79** C5
San Mali **124** D3
San *r.* Poland **49** S5
San, Phou *mt.* Laos **78** C4
San, Tônlé *r.* Cambodia **79** D5
Sana *r.* Bos.-Herz. **56** I3

Ṣan'ā' Yemen **104** D5
Capital of Yemen.

Ṣan'ā' *governorate* Yemen **104** D5
Sanaag *admin. reg.* Somalia **128** E2
San Adrián, Cabo de *c.* Spain **54** C1
Sanae *research station* Antarctica **223** X2
Sanaga *r.* Cameroon **125** H6
San Agostín U.S.A. *see* **St Augustine**
San Agustín Col. **198** B4
San Agustín, Cape Phil. **74** C5
Sanak Island U.S.A. **164** C4
Sanām Saudi Arabia **104** D3
San Ambrosio *i.* S. Pacific Ocean **200** A6
Sanana Indon. **75** C3
Sanandaj Iran **100** A3
also known as Sinneh
Sanando Mali **124** D3
San Andreas U.S.A. **182** D3
San Andrés Bol. **201** D3
San Andrés Col. **198** C3
San Andres Phil. **74** C3
San Andrés, Isla de *i.* Caribbean Sea **186** C4
San Andrés del Rabanedo Spain **54** F2
San Andres Mountains U.S.A. **181** F6
San Andrés Tuxtla Mex. **185** G5
San Angelo U.S.A. **179** B6
Sanankoroba Mali **124** D3
San Antolín de Ibias Spain **54** E1
San Antonio Arg. **204** D3
San Antonio Belize **185** H5
San Antonio Bol. **201** D3
San Antonio Chile **204** C2
San Antonio Hond. **186** B4
San Antonio Peru **198** C5
San Antonio Phil. **74** B3
San Antonio *NM* U.S.A. **181** F6
San Antonio *TX* U.S.A. **179** C6
San Antonio *r. CA* U.S.A. **182** D6
San Antonio *r. TX* U.S.A. **179** C6
San Antonio Venez. **187** F5
San Antonio, Cabo *c.* Arg. **204** F5
San Antonio, Cabo *c.* Cuba **186** B2
San Antonio, Mount U.S.A. **182** G7
San Antonio Abad Spain **55** M6
San Antonio Bay Phil. **74** A4
San Antonio de Caparo Venez. **198** D3
San Antonio del Mar Mex. **184** A2
San Antonio de los Cobres Arg. **200** D6
San Antonio de Palé Equat. Guinea **125** G7
San Antonio de Tamanaco Venez. **199** E2
San Antonio Este Arg. **204** D6
San Antonio Oeste Arg. **204** D6
San Antonio Reservoir U.S.A. **182** D6
San Augustín Arg. **204** F5
San Augustín de Valle Fértil Arg. **204** D3
San Augustine U.S.A. **179** D6
Sanaw Yemen **105** E4
Sanawad India **96** C5
San Bartolo Mex. **185** E4
San Bartolomeo in Galdo Italy **56** H7
San Benedetto del Tronto Italy **56** F6
San Benedicto, Isla *i.* Mex. **184** C5
San Benito Guat. **185** H5
San Benito U.S.A. **179** C7
San Benito *r.* U.S.A. **182** C5
San Benito Mountain U.S.A. **182** D5
San Bernardino U.S.A. **183** G7
San Bernardino, Passo di *pass* Switz. **51** P6
San Bernardino Mountains U.S.A. **183** G7
San Bernardino Strait Phil. **74** C3
San Bernardo Chile **204** C4
San Bernardo Mex. **184** D3
San Blas Arg. **204** E5
San Blas *Nayarit* Mex. **184** D4
San Blas *Sinaloa* Mex. **184** C3
San Blas, Archipiélago de *is* Panama **186** D5
formerly known as Las Mulatas
San Blas, Cape U.S.A. **175** C6
San Blas, Cordillera de *mts* Panama **186** D5
San Borja Bol. **200** D3
Sanborn U.S.A. **178** D3
Sanbornville U.S.A. **177** N2
San Buenaventura Mex. **185** E3
Sança Moz. **131** G3
San Candido Italy **56** E2
historically known as Aguntum
San Caprasio *hill* Spain **55** K3
San Carlos *Mendoza* Arg. **204** C4
San Carlos *Salta* Arg. **204** D2
San Carlos Chile **204** C5
San Carlos Equat. Guinea *see* **Luba**
San Carlos *Coahuila* Mex. **185** E2
San Carlos *Tamaulipas* Mex. **185** F3
San Carlos Nicaragua **186** B5
San Carlos Para. **201** F5
San Carlos *r.* Para. **201** F5
San Carlos *Luzon* Phil. **74** B3
San Carlos *Negros* Phil. **74** B4
San Carlos Uruguay **204** G4
San Carlos U.S.A. **183** N8
San Carlos *Amazonas* Venez. **199** E4
San Carlos *Apure* Venez. **199** E3
San Carlos *Cojedes* Venez. **198** D2
San Carlos de Bariloche Arg. **204** C6
San Carlos de Bolívar Arg. **204** E5

San Carlos de la Rápita Spain see Sant Carles de la Ràpita
San Carlos del Zulia Venez. 198 D2
San Carlos Indian Reservation res. U.S.A. 183 N8
San Carlos Lake U.S.A. 183 N8
San Cataldo Sicilia Italy 57 F11
San Cayetano Arg. 204 F5
San Celoni Spain see Sant Celoni
Sancerre France 51 I5
Sancerrois, Collines du hills France 51 I5
San Cesario di Lecce Italy 57 K8
Sancha Gansu China 86 C1
Sancha Shanxi China 85 F4
Sanchahe China see Fuyu
Sancha He r. China 86 C3
Sanchakou China 88 B4
Sanchi India 96 C5
San Chien Pau mt. Laos 78 C3
Sanchor India 96 A4
Sanchuan r. China 85 F4
Sanchursk Rus. Fed. 40 H4
San Ciro de Acosta Mex. 185 F4
San Clemente Chile 204 C4
San Clemente Spain 55 I5
San Clemente U.S.A. 182 G8
San Clemente del Tuyú Arg. 204 F5
San Clemente Island U.S.A. 182 F9
Sancoins France 51 I6
Sanco Point Phil. 74 C4
San Cristóbal Arg. 204 E3
San Cristóbal Potosí Bol. 200 D5
San Cristóbal Santa Cruz Bol. 201 E3
San Cristóbal Col. 198 C5
San Cristóbal Dom. Rep. 187 F3
San Cristobal i. Solomon Is 145 F3
also known as Arossi, or Makira
San Cristóbal Venez. 198 C3
San Cristóbal, Volcán vol. Nicaragua 186 B4
San Cristóbal de las Casas Mex. 185 G5
San Cristobal Wash watercourse U.S.A. 183 K9
Sancti Spíritus Cuba 186 D2
Sand Norway 45 I4
Sand r. Free State S. Africa 133 K5
Sand r. Northern S. Africa 131 F4
Sanda Japan 91 D7
Sandagou Rus. Fed. 90 D3
Sandai Indon. 77 E3
Sandakan Sabah Malaysia 77 G1
Sandakphu Peak India 97 F4
Sandane Norway 45 I3
Sandanski Bulg. 58 E7
Sandaohezi China see Shawan
Sandaré Mali 124 C3
Sanday i. U.K. 46 J4
Sandberg S. Africa 132 C9
Sandbukt Norway 44 M1
Sand Cay reef India 94 B4
Sande Sogn og Fjordane Norway 45 I3
Sande Vestfold Norway 45 J4
Sandefjord Norway 45 J4
Sandefjord (Torp) airport Norway 45 J4
Sandercock Nunataks Antarctica 223 D2
Sanders U.S.A. 183 O6
Sanderson U.S.A. 179 B6
Sandersville U.S.A. 175 D5
Sandfire Roadhouse Australia 150 C3
Sandfloeggi mt. Norway 45 I4
Sand Hill r. U.S.A. 178 C2
Sand Hills U.S.A. 178 B3
Sandhornøy i. Norway 44 K2
Sandi India 96 D4
Sandia Peru 200 C3
San Diego Mex. 181 E7
San Diego CA U.S.A. 183 G9
San Diego TX U.S.A. 179 C7
San Diego, Cabo c. Arg. 205 D9
San Diego, Sierra mts Mex. 184 C2
San Diego de Cabrutica Venez. 199 E2
Sandıklı Turkey 106 B3
Sandila India 96 D4
Sanding i. Indon. 76 C3
Sand Island U.S.A. 172 C4
Sandivey r. Rus. Fed. 40 K2
Sand Lake Canada 168 C4
Sand Lake l. Canada 167 M5
Sandnes Norway 45 I4
Sandnessjøen Norway 44 K2
Sando i. Faroe Is see Sandoy
Sandoa Dem. Rep. Congo 127 D7
Sandomierz Poland 49 S5
Sândominic Romania 58 G2
formerly spelt Sîndominic
San Domino, Isole i. Italy 56 H6
Sandoná Col. 198 B4
San Donà di Piave Italy 56 E3
Sandover watercourse Australia 148 C4
Sandovo Rus. Fed. 43 R3
Sandow, Mount Antarctica 223 G2
Sandoway Myanmar 78 A4
also known as Thandwè
Sandoy i. Faroe Is 46 F2
also spelt Sandø
Sandpoint U.S.A. 180 C2
Sandray i. U.K. 46 E7
also spelt Sanndraigh
Sandringham Australia 148 C5
Sand River Reservoir Swaziland 133 P3
Sandsele Sweden 44 L2
Sandspit Canada 166 D4
Sand Springs IA U.S.A. 172 B8
Sand Springs OK U.S.A. 179 C4
Sand Springs Salt Flat U.S.A. 182 F2
Sandspruit r. S. Africa 133 K4
Sandstone Australia 151 B5
Sandstone U.S.A. 174 A2
Sand Tank Mountains U.S.A. 183 L9
Sandton S. Africa 133 M3
Sandu Guizhou China 87 C3
also known as Sanhe
Sandu Hunan China 87 E3
Sandur India 94 C3
Sandusky MI U.S.A. 173 K7
Sandusky OH U.S.A. 176 C4
Sandusky Bay U.S.A. 176 C4
Sandveld mts S. Africa 132 C8
Sandveld Nature Reserve S. Africa 133 J4
Sandverhaar Namibia 132 B3
Sandvika Akershus Norway 45 J4
Sandvika Nord-Trøndelag Norway 44 K3
Sandviken Sweden 45 L3
Sandvlakte S. Africa 133 I10
Sandwich U.S.A. 177 O4
Sandwich Bay Canada 169 J2
Sandwich Island Vanuatu see Éfaté
Sandwip Bangl. 97 F5
Sandwip Channel Bangl. 97 F5
Sandy U.S.A. 183 M1
Sandy r. U.S.A. 177 P1
Sandy Bay Canada 167 K4
Sandy Bight b. Australia 151 C7
Sandy Cape Qld Australia 149 G5
Sandy Cape Tas. Australia 147 E5
Sandy Creek r. Australia 148 C3
Sandy Island Australia 150 C2
Sandykachi Turkm. 103 E5
Sandykly Gumy des. Turkm. see Sundukli, Peski
Sandy Lake Alta Canada 167 H4
Sandy Lake Ont. Canada 167 M4
Sandy Lake l. Canada 167 M4
Sandy Springs U.S.A. 175 C5
Sandyville U.S.A. 176 D7
Sân el Hagar Egypt 108 C7
San Estanislao Para. 201 F6
San Esteban Hond. 186 B4
San Esteban, Isla i. Mex. 184 B2
San Fabián de Alico Chile 204 C5
San Felipe Chile 204 C4
San Felipe Baja California Norte Mex. 184 B2
San Felipe Chihuahua Mex. 184 D3
San Felipe Guanajuato Mex. 185 E4
San Felipe mt. Spain 55 J4
San Felipe Venez. 198 D2
San Felipe, Cayos de is Cuba 186 C2
San Feliú de Guíxols Spain see Sant Feliu de Guíxols
San Félix, Isla i. S. Pacific Ocean 221 M7
San Fernando Arg. 204 F4
San Fernando Chile 204 C4
San Fernando Baja California Norte Mex. 184 B2
San Fernando Tamaulipas Mex. 185 F3
San Fernando Luzon Phil. 74 B2
San Fernando Luzon Phil. 74 B3
San Fernando Spain 54 E8
San Fernando Trin. and Tob. 187 H5
San Fernando U.S.A. 182 F7
San Fernando de Apure Venez. 199 E3
San Fernando de Atabapo Venez. 199 E3
San Filipe Creek watercourse U.S.A. 183 I8
Sånfjället nationalpark nat. park Sweden 45 K3
Sanford r. Australia 151 A5
Sanford FL U.S.A. 175 D6
Sanford ME U.S.A. 177 O2
Sanford MI U.S.A. 173 I7
Sanford NC U.S.A. 174 E5
San Francisco Arg. 204 E3
San Francisco Bol. 200 D3
San Francisco Mex. 184 B2
San Francisco U.S.A. 182 B4
world [cities] 24–25
world [communications] 26–27
San Francisco r. U.S.A. 181 E6
San Francisco, Paso de pass Arg. 204 C2
San Francisco, Sierra mts Mex. 184 B3
San Francisco Bay inlet U.S.A. 182 B4
San Francisco del Oro Mex. 184 D3
San Francisco de Macorís Dom. Rep. 187 F3
San Francisco de Paula, Cabo c. Arg. 205 D8
San Francisco Gotera El Salvador 185 H6
San Francisco Javier Spain 55 M6
Sanga Dem. Rep. Congo 127 F6
San Gabriel Ecuador 198 B4
San Gabriel, Punta pt Mex. 184 B2
San Gabriel Mountains U.S.A. 182 F7
Sangachaly Azer. see Sanqaçal
Sangai, Parque Nacional nat. park Ecuador 198 B5
Sangaigerong Indon. 76 D3
Sa'ngain China 86 A2
San Gallan, Isla i. Peru 200 A3
Sangam India 94 C3
Sangameshwar India 94 B2
Sangamner India 94 B2
Sangamon r. U.S.A. 174 B3
Sangān Iran 101 D3
Sangan, Koh-i- mt. Afgh. 101 F3
Sangar r. Pak. 101 G4
Sangar Rus. Fed. 39 M3
Sangaréa Guinea 124 B4
Sangareddi India 94 C2
Sangarédi Guinea 124 B4
Sangaria India 96 B3
Sangasanga Indon. 77 G3
Sanga Sanga i. Phil. 74 A5
Sangasso Mali see Zangasso
Sangaste Estonia 42 H4
San Gavino Monreale Sardegna Italy 57 A9
Sangay, Volcán vol. Ecuador 198 B5
Sang Bast Iran 101 D3
Sangbé Cameroon 125 I5
Sangboy Islands Phil. 74 B5
Sangbur Afgh. 101 E3
Sangeang i. Indon. 77 G5
Sangejing China 85 E3
Sângeorgiu de Pădure Romania 58 F2
formerly spelt Sîngeorgiu de Pădure
Sângeorz-Băi Romania 58 F1
formerly spelt Sîngeorz-Băi
Sangequanzi China 88 E3
Sânger Romania 58 F2
Sanger U.S.A. 182 E5
Sângera Moldova see Sîngera
Sangerfield U.S.A. 177 J3
Sangerhausen Germany 48 I4
San Germán Puerto Rico 187 G3
Sanggan r. China 85 G3
Sanggar, Teluk b. Indon. 77 G5
Sanggarmai China 86 B1
Sanggau Indon. 77 E2
Sanggou Wan b. China 85 I4
Sangha admin. reg. Congo 126 B4
Sangha r. Congo 126 C5
Sangha-Mbaéré pref. Cent. Afr. Rep. 126 C4
Sanghar Pak. 101 G5
San Gil Col. 198 C3
Sangilen, Nagor'ye mts Rus. Fed. 84 B1
San Giovanni in Fiore Italy 57 I9
San Giovanni Rotondo Italy 56 H7
San Giovanni Suergiu Sardegna Italy 57 A9
Sangir India 96 B5
Sangir i. Indon. 75 C2
Sangir, Kepulauan is Indon. 75 C2
Sangiran tourist site Indon. 77 E4
San Giuliano Terme Italy 56 C5
San Giustino Italy 56 E5
Sangiyn Dalay Mongolia 84 E2
Sangiyn Dalay Nuur salt l. Mongolia 84 C1
Sangju S. Korea 83 C5
Sangkapura Indon. 77 F4
Sangkarang, Kepulauan is Indon. 75 A4
Sângke, Stœng r. Cambodia 79 C5
Sangkulirang Indon. 77 G2
Sangkulirang, Teluk b. Indon. 77 G2
Sangla Pak. 101 H4
Sangli India 94 B2
San Glorio, Puerto de pass Spain 54 G1
Sangmélima Cameroon 125 H6
Sango Zimbabwe 131 F4
formerly known as Vila Salazar or Villasalazar
Sangod India 96 C4
Sangole India 94 B2
San Gorgonio Mountain U.S.A. 183 H7
Sangowo Indon. 75 D2
Sangpi China see Xiangcheng
Sang Qu r. China 86 A2
Sangre de Cristo Range mts U.S.A. 181 F5
San Gregorio de Polanco Uruguay 204 G4
Sangre Grande Trin. and Tob. 187 H5
Sangri China 89 F6
also known as Xueba
Sangro r. Italy 56 G6
Sangrur India 96 B3
Sangsang China 89 D6
Sangu r. Bangl. 97 F5
Sangue r. Brazil 201 F2
Sangüesa Spain 55 J2
San Guiliano Milanese Italy 56 B3
Sangū'īyeh Iran 100 D4
also known as Isfandaqeh
Sangyuan China see Wuqiao
Sangzhi China 87 D2
also known as Liyuan
Sanhe China see Sandu
Sanhe China 85 I1
Sanhezhen China 87 F2
San Hilario Mex. 184 C3
San Hipólito, Punta pt Mex. 184 B3
Sanhûr Egypt 121 F2
San Ignacio Belize 185 H5
San Ignacio Beni Bol. 200 D3
San Ignacio Santa Cruz Bol. 201 E4
San Ignacio Santa Cruz Bol. 201 E4
San Ignacio Baja California Sur Mex. 184 B3
San Ignacio Sonora Mex. 184 C2
San Ignacio Para. 201 F6
San Ignacio Peru 198 B6
San Ignacio, Laguna l. Mex. 184 B3
Sanikiluaq Canada 168 E1
San Ildefonso Peninsula Phil. 74 B2
Sanin-kaigan National Park Japan 91 D7
Sanipas pass S. Africa 133 N6
Sanislău Romania 49 T8
Sanitz Germany 49 J1
Sāniyat al Fawākhir well Libya 120 C3
San Jacinto Col. 198 C2
San Jacinto Phil. 74 B3
San Jacinto U.S.A. 183 H8
San Jacinto Peak U.S.A. 183 H8
Sanjai r. India 97 E5
San Jaime Arg. 204 F3
San Javier Arg. 204 F3
San Javier Beni Bol. 200 D3
San Javier Santa Cruz Bol. 201 E4
San Javier Spain 55 K7
San Javier de Loncomilla Chile 204 C4
Sanjawi Pak. 101 G4
Sanjbod Iran 100 B2
San Jerónimo Mex. 185 E5
San Jerónimo Peru 200 B1
Sanjiang China see Liannan
Sanjiang China 87 D3
also known as Guyi
Sanjiang China see Jinping
Sanjiaocheng China see Haiyan
Sanjiaoping China 87 D2
Sanjie China 87 G2
Sanjō Japan 90 F6
San Joaquín Bol. 200 D3
San Joaquín Para. 201 F6
San Joaquin U.S.A. 182 D5
San Joaquin r. U.S.A. 182 C3
San Joaquin Valley U.S.A. 182 D4
San Jon U.S.A. 178 B5
San Jorge Arg. 204 E3
San Jorge, Golfo de g. Arg. 205 D7
San Jorge, Golfo de g. Spain see Sant Jordi, Golf de
San José Col. 199 D4
San José Costa Rica 186 B5
Capital of Costa Rica.
San José watercourse Mex. 181 D8
San Jose Luzon Phil. 74 B3
San Jose Mindoro Phil. 74 B3
San Jose Mindoro Phil. 74 B3
San Jose CA U.S.A. 182 C4
San Jose NM U.S.A. 181 F6
San Jose watercourse U.S.A. 181 F6
San José Venez. 199 E2
San José, Cabo c. Arg. 205 D7
San José, Cuchilla de hills Uruguay 204 F3
San José, Golfo g. Arg. 205 D6
San José, Isla i. Mex. 184 C3
San José, Volcán vol. Chile 204 C4
San José de Amacuro Venez. 199 F2
San José de Bavicora Mex. 184 D2
San José de Buenavista Phil. 74 B4
San José de Chiquitos Bol. 201 E4
San José de Comondú Mex. 184 C3
San José de Gracia Baja California Sur Mex. 184 B3
San José de Gracia Sonora Mex. 184 C2
San José de Guaribe Venez. 187 G5
San Jose de Jáchal Arg. 204 C3
San José de la Brecha Mex. 184 C3
San José de la Dormida Arg. 204 E3
San José de la Mariquina Chile 204 B5
San José del Boquerón Arg. 204 E2
San José del Cabo Mex. 184 C4
San José del Guaviare Col. 198 C4
San José de Mayo Uruguay 204 F4
San José de Ocuné Col. 198 D3
San José de Primas Mex. 181 E7
San José de Raíces Mex. 185 E3
San Juan Arg. 204 C3
San Juan prov. Arg. 204 C3
San Juan Bol. 201 E4
San Juan Col. 198 B2
San Juan r. Col. 198 B3
San Juan r. Costa Rica/Nicaragua 186 C5
San Juan mt. Cuba 186 C2
San Juan Dom. Rep. 187 F3
San Juan Chihuahua Mex. 184 D3
San Juan Coahuila Mex. 185 E3
San Juan Peru 200 B3
San Juan Phil. 74 C4
San Juan Puerto Rico 187 G3
Capital of Puerto Rico.
San Juan r. CA U.S.A. 182 D6
San Juan r. UT U.S.A. 183 N4
San Juan Venez. 199 E3
San Juan, Cabo c. Arg. 205 E9
San Juan, Cabo c. Equat. Guinea 125 H6
San Juan, Punta pt El Salvador 186 A4
San Juan Bautista Para. 201 F6
San Juan Bautista Spain 55 M5
San Juan Bautista U.S.A. 182 C5
San Juan Bautista Tuxtepec Mex. 185 F5
San Juan Capistrano U.S.A. 182 G8
San Juancito Hond. 186 B4
San Juan de César Col. 198 C2
San Juan de Guadalupe Mex. 185 E3
San Juan dela Costa Chile 204 B6
San Juan de la Peña, Sierra de mts Spain 55 K2
San Juan del Norte Nicaragua 186 C5
San Juan del Norte, Bahía de b. Nicaragua 186 C5
San Juan de los Cayos Venez. 198 D2
San Juan de los Morros Venez. 199 E2
San Juan del Río Durango Mex. 184 D3
San Juan del Río Querétaro Mex. 185 F4
San Juan del Sur Nicaragua 186 B5
San Juan de Salvamento Arg. 205 E9
San Juan Evangelista Mex. 185 G5
San Juan Islands U.S.A. 180 B2
San Juanito Mex. 184 D3
San Juanito, Isla i. Mex. 184 D4
San Juan Mountains U.S.A. 181 F5
San Juan y Martínez Cuba 186 C2
San Julián Arg. 205 D8
San Just mt. Spain 55 K4
San Justo Arg. 204 E3
Sankarani r. Côte d'Ivoire/Guinea 124 C4
Sankarankovil India 94 C4
Sankeshwar India 94 B2
Sankh r. India 97 E5
Sankosh r. Bhutan see Sunkosh
Sankra Chhattisgarh India 94 D1
Sankra Rajasthan India 96 A4
Sankt Andrä Austria 49 L9
Sankt Gallen Switz. 51 P5
Sankt Gotthard Hungary see Szentgotthárd
Sankt Johann im Pongau Austria 49 K8
Sankt Moritz Switz. 51 P6
Sankt-Peterburg Rus. Fed. see St Petersburg
Sankt Peter-Ording Germany 48 F1
Sankt Pölten Austria 49 M7
Sankt Veit an der Glan Austria 49 L9
Sankt Wendel Germany 48 E6
Sankuru r. Dem. Rep. Congo 126 D6
San Lázaro Para. 201 F5
San Lázaro, Cabo c. Mex. 184 B3
San Leandro U.S.A. 182 B4
San Leonardo in Passiria Italy 56 D2
Şanlıurfa Turkey 107 D3
formerly known as Urfa; historically known as Edessa
Şanlıurfa prov. Turkey 109 J1
San Lorenzo Corrientes Arg. 204 F3
San Lorenzo Santa Fé Arg. 204 E4
San Lorenzo Beni Bol. 200 D3
San Lorenzo Pando Bol. 200 D2
San Lorenzo Tarija Bol. 200 D5
San Lorenzo Ecuador 198 B4
San Lorenzo Hond. 186 B4
San Lorenzo Mex. 184 D2
San Lorenzo Peru 200 C2
San Lorenzo mt. Spain 55 I2
San Lorenzo, Cabo c. Ecuador 198 A5
San Lorenzo, Cerro mt. Arg./Chile 205 B7
San Lorenzo, Isla i. Mex. 184 B2
San Lorenzo, Isla i. Peru 200 A3
Sanlúcar de Barrameda Spain 54 E8
San Lucas Bol. 200 D5
San Lucas Baja California Sur Mex. 184 B3
San Lucas Baja California Sur Mex. 184 C4
San Lucas, Cabo c. Mex. 184 C4
San Lucas, Serranía de mts Col. 198 C3
San Luis Arg. 204 D4
San Luis prov. Arg. 204 D4
San Luís Brazil 200 D2
San Luis Cuba 186 E2
San Luis Guat. 185 H5
San Luis Mex. 185 E5
San Luis Peru 198 C5
San Luis AZ U.S.A. 183 J9
San Luis AZ U.S.A. 183 M9
San Luis CO U.S.A. 181 F5
San Luis Venez. 198 D2
San Luis, Isla i. Mex. 184 B2
San Luis, Sierra de mts Arg. 204 D4
San Luis de la Paz Mex. 185 E4
San Luis del Palmar Arg. 204 F2
San Luis Gonzaga Mex. 184 C3
San Luisito Mex. 184 B2
San Luis Obispo U.S.A. 182 D6
San Luis Obispo Bay U.S.A. 182 D6
San Luis Potosí Mex. 185 E4
San Luis Potosí state Mex. 185 E4
San Luis Reservoir U.S.A. 182 C4
San Luis Río Colorado Mex. 184 B1
Sanluri Sardegna Italy 57 A9
San Manuel U.S.A. 183 N9
San Marcello Pistoiese Italy 56 C4
San Marcial, Punta pt Mex. 184 C3
San Marco, Capo c. Sardegna Italy 57 A9
San Marco, Capo c. Sicilia Italy 57 F11
San Marcos Chile 204 C3
San Marcos Col. 198 C2
San Marcos Guat. 185 H6
San Marcos Hond. 186 B4
San Marcos Mex. 185 F5
San Marcos Peru 200 A1
San Marcos U.S.A. 179 C6
San Marcos r. U.S.A. 179 C6
San Marcos, Isla i. Mex. 184 B3
San Marino country Europe 56 E5
europe [countries] 32–35
San Marino San Marino 56 E5
Capital of San Marino.
San Martín research station Antarctica 222 T2
long form General San Martín
San Martín Catamarca Arg. 204 D3
San Martín Mendoza Arg. 204 C4
San Martín r. Bol. 201 E3
San Martín dept Peru 200 A1
San Martín, Lago l. Arg./Chile 205 B8
San Martín, Volcán vol. Mex. 185 G5
San Martín de los Andes Arg. 204 C6
San Martín de Valdeiglesias Spain 54 G4
San-Martino-di-Lota Corse France 51 P10
San Mateo Peru 198 D5
San Mateo U.S.A. 182 B4
San Mateo Venez. 199 E2
San Matías Bol. 201 F4
San Matías, Golfo g. Arg. 204 D6
San Mauricio Venez. 199 E2
Sanmen China 87 G2
also known as Haiyou
Sanmen Wan b. China 87 G2
Sanmenxia China 87 D1
San Miguel Arg. 204 F3
San Miguel Bol. 201 E4
San Miguel r. Bol. 201 E3
San Miguel r. Col. 198 C4
San Miguel El Salvador 185 H6
San Miguel Panama 186 D5
San Miguel Peru 200 B3
San Miguel U.S.A. 182 D6
San Miguel r. U.S.A. 181 E5
San Miguel Bay Phil. 74 B3
San Miguel de Allende Mex. 185 E4
San Miguel de Cruces Mex. 184 D3
San Miguel de Horcasitas r. Mex. 184 C2
San Miguel de Huachi Bol. 200 D3
San Miguel del Monte Arg. 204 F4
San Miguel de Tucumán Arg. 204 D2
short form Tucumán
San Miguel do Araguaia Brazil 202 B5
San Miguel el Alto Mex. 185 E4
San Miguel Island U.S.A. 182 D7
San Miguel Islands Phil. 74 A5
San Miguelito Panama 186 D5
San Miguel Sola de Vega Mex. 185 F5
Sanming China 87 F3
San Miniato Italy 56 C5
Sanna r. Poland 49 S5
San Narciso Phil. 74 B3
Sannaspos S. Africa 133 K6
Sanndatti India 94 B3
Sanndraigh i. U.K. see Sandray
Sannicandro Garganico Italy 56 H7
San Nicolás Mex. 185 F3
San Nicolas Phil. 74 B2
San Nicolás, Bahía de b. Peru 200 B3
San Nicolás de los Arroyos Arg. 204 E4
San Nicolás del Presidio Mex. 184 D3
San Nicolas Island U.S.A. 182 E8
Sânnicolau Mare Romania 58 B2
formerly spelt Sînnicolau Mare
Sannieshof S. Africa 133 J3
Sanniquellie Liberia 124 C5
Sannohe Japan 90 G4
Sañogasta, Sierra de mts Arg. 204 D3
Sanok Poland 49 T6
San Onofre Col. 198 C2
San Pablo Arg. 205 D9
San Pablo Potosí Bol. 200 D5
San Pablo Santa Cruz Bol. 201 E3
San Pablo r. Bol. 201 E3
San Pablo Col. 198 D3
San Pablo Mex. 185 F4
San Pablo Phil. 74 B3
San Pablo U.S.A. 182 B4
San Pablo de Manta Ecuador see Manta
San Pedro Buenos Aires Arg. 204 F4
San Pedro Catamarca Arg. 204 D2
San Pedro Jujuy Arg. 200 D6
San Pedro Misiones Arg. 204 G2
San Pedro Belize 185 I5
San Pedro Beni Bol. 200 D3
San Pedro Santa Cruz Bol. 201 E4
San Pedro r. Bol. 200 D4
San-Pédro Côte d'Ivoire 124 D5
San Pedro r. Cuba 186 D2
San Pedro Mex. 184 C4
San Pedro r. Mex. 181 F7
San Pedro Peru 200 C2
San Pedro Phil. 74 B3
San Pedro watercourse U.S.A. 183 N9
San Pedro, Punta pt Costa Rica 186 C5
San Pedro, Sierra de mts Spain 54 D5
San Pedro Carchá Guat. 185 H6
San Pedro Channel U.S.A. 182 F8
San Pedro de Atacama Chile 200 C5
San Pedro de las Colonias Mex. 185 E3
San Pedro de Lloc Peru 200 A1
San Pedro del Pinatar Spain 55 K7
San Pedro de Macorís Dom. Rep. 187 F3
San Pedro de Ycuamandyyú Para. 201 F6
San Pedro el Saucito Mex. 184 C2
San Pedro Mártir, Parque Nacional nat. park Mex. 184 B2
San Pedro Sula Hond. 186 A4
San Pietro, Isola di i. Sardegna Italy 57 A9
San Pietro in Cariano Italy 56 C3
San Pitch r. U.S.A. 183 M2
Sanqaçal Azer. 107 G2
also spelt Sangachaly
Sanquhar U.K. 46 I8
Sanquianga, Parque Nacional nat. park Col. 198 B4
San Quintín, Cabo c. Mex. 184 A2
San Rafael Arg. 204 C4
San Rafael Bol. 201 E4
San Rafael U.S.A. 182 B4
San Rafael r. U.S.A. 183 N3
San Rafael Venez. 198 D2
also known as San Rafael del Moján
San Rafael del Moján Venez. see San Rafael
San Rafael del Norte Nicaragua 186 B4
San Rafael del Yuma Dom. Rep. 187 F3
San Rafael Knob mt. U.S.A. 183 N3
San Rafael Mountains U.S.A. 182 D7
San Ramón Beni Bol. 200 D3
San Ramón Santa Cruz Bol. 201 E4
San Remo Italy 51 N9
San Rodrigo watercourse Mex. 179 B6
San Román, Cabo c. Venez. 198 D1
San Roque Andalucía Spain 54 F8
San Roque Galicia Spain 54 C1
San Roque Galicia Spain 54 C2
San Roque, Punta pt Mex. 184 B3
San Saba U.S.A. 179 C6
San Saba r. U.S.A. 179 C6
Sansalé Guinea 124 B4
San Salvador Arg. 204 F3
San Salvador i. Bahamas 187 E1
formerly known as Watling Island
San Salvador El Salvador 185 H6
Capital of El Salvador.
San Salvador Peru 198 D5
San Salvador de Jujuy Arg. 200 D6
San Salvo Italy 56 G6
Sansané Haoussa Niger 125 F3
Sansanné-Mango Togo 125 F4
San Sebastián Arg. 205 C9
San Sebastián hill Spain 54 C2
San Sebastián, Bahía de b. Arg. 205 C9
San Sebastián de los Reyes Spain 55 H4
Sansepolcro Italy 56 E5
San Severino Marche Italy 56 F5
San Severo Italy 56 H7
Sansha China 87 G3
San Silvestre Bol. 200 C2
San Silvestre Venez. 198 D2
San Simon U.S.A. 183 O9
Sanski Most Bos.-Herz. 56 I4
Sanson N.Z. 152 J8
Sansoral Islands Palau see Sonsorol Islands
Sansui China 87 D3
also known as Bagong
Santa Peru 200 A2
Santa r. Peru 200 A2
Santa Adélia Brazil 206 E8
Santa Ana Arg. 204 D2
Santa Ana La Paz Bol. 200 D3
Santa Ana Santa Cruz Bol. 201 F4
Santa Ana El Salvador 185 H6
Santa Ana Mex. 184 C2
Santa Ana U.S.A. 182 G8
Santa Ana de Yacuma Bol. 200 D3
Santa Anita Mex. 184 C4
Santa Anna U.S.A. 179 C6
Santa Bárbara Brazil 201 F3
Santa Bárbara Cuba see La Demajagua
Santa Bárbara Hond. 186 A4
Santa Bárbara Mex. 184 D3
Santa Bárbara mt. Spain 55 I7
Santa Bárbara mt. Spain 55 J6
Santa Barbara U.S.A. 182 E7
Santa Bárbara Amazonas Venez. 199 E4
Santa Bárbara Barinas Venez. 198 D3
Santa Bárbara, Ilha i. Brazil 207 O4
Santa Barbara, Parque Nacional nat. park Hond. 186 A4
Santa Bárbara, Serra de hills Brazil 203 A7
Santa Barbara Channel U.S.A. 182 D7
Santa Bárbara d'Oeste Brazil 206 F9
Santa Barbara do Sul Brazil 203 A9
Santa Barbara Island U.S.A. 182 E8
Santa Catalina Chile 204 C2
Santa Catalina Panama 186 C5
Santa Catalina Venez. 199 F2
Santa Catalina, Gulf of U.S.A. 182 G8
Santa Catalina, Isla i. Mex. 184 C3
Santa Catalina de Armada Spain 54 C1
Santa Catalina Island U.S.A. 182 F8
Santa Catarina state Brazil 203 B8
Santa Catarina Baja California Norte Mex. 184 B2
Santa Catarina Nuevo León Mex. 185 E3
Santa Catarina Neth. Antilles 187 F4
also spelt Santa Catharina
Santa Catarina, Ilha de i. Brazil 203 B8
Santa Catharina Neth. Antilles see Santa Catarina
Santa Clara Col. 198 D5
Santa Clara Cuba 186 D2
Santa Clara r. Mex. 181 F7
Santa Clara CA U.S.A. 182 C4
Santa Clara UT U.S.A. 183 K4
Santa Clara r. U.S.A. 182 E7
Santa Clara, Barragem de resr Port. 54 C7
Santa Clarita U.S.A. 182 F7
Santa Clotilde Peru 198 C5
Santa Coloma de Farners Spain 55 N3
Santa Coloma de Gramanet Spain 55 N3
Santa Comba Angola see Waku-Kungo
Santa Comba Dão Port. 54 C4
Santa Croce Camerina Sicilia Italy 57 G12
Santa Cruz prov. Arg. 205 C8
Santa Cruz r. Arg. 205 C8
Santa Cruz Bol. 201 E4
Santa Cruz dept Bol. 201 E4
Santa Cruz Espírito Santo Brazil 207 M6
Santa Cruz Pará Brazil 199 H5
Santa Cruz Pará Brazil 202 B2
Santa Cruz Costa Rica 186 B5
Santa Cruz Mex. 184 C2
Santa Cruz Peru 198 C6
Santa Cruz Luzon Phil. 74 A3
Santa Cruz Luzon Phil. 74 B2
Santa Cruz Luzon Phil. 74 B3
Santa Cruz mt. Spain 55 J3
Santa Cruz U.S.A. 182 B5
Santa Cruz watercourse U.S.A. 183 L8
Santa Cruz, Isla i. Mex. 184 C3
Santa Cruz, Puerto inlet Arg. 205 C8
Santa Cruz Barillas Guat. 185 H6
Santa Cruz Cabrália Brazil 202 E6
Santa Cruz das Palmeiras Brazil 206 F8
Santa Cruz de Goiás Brazil 206 E4
Santa Cruz de la Palma Canary Is 122 A3
Santa Cruz del Quiché Guat. 185 H6
Santa Cruz del Sur Cuba 186 D2
Santa Cruz de Mudela Spain 55 H6
Santa Cruz de Tenerife Canary Is 122 A3
Joint capital of the Canary Islands.
Santa Cruz de Yojoa Hond. 186 B4
Santa Cruz do Rio Pardo Brazil 206 D9
Santa Cruz do Sul Brazil 203 A9
Santa Cruz Island U.S.A. 182 E7
Santa Cruz Islands Solomon Is 145 F3
Santa Efigênia de Minas Brazil 207 K5
Santa Elena Buenos Aires Arg. 204 E5
Santa Elena Entre Ríos Arg. 204 F3
Santa Elena Bol. 200 D5
Santa Elena Peru 198 C6
Santa Elena Venez. 199 F3
Santa Elena, Cabo c. Costa Rica 186 B5
Santa Elena, Punta pt Ecuador 198 A5
Santa Eufemia, Golfo di g. Italy 57 I10
Santa Eugenia Spain 54 C2
Santa Eulalia del Río Spain 55 M6
Santa Fé Arg. 204 E3
Santa Fé prov. Arg. 204 E3
Santa Fé Cuba 186 C2
Santa Fé Panama 186 C5
Santa Fe Phil. 74 B3
Santa Fe Spain 54 H7
Santa Fe U.S.A. 181 F6
State capital of New Mexico.
Santa Fé de Bogotá Col. see Bogotá
Santafé de Bogotá municipality Col. 198 C4
Santa Fé de Minas Brazil 202 C6
Santa Fé do Sul Brazil 206 C7
Santa Filomena Brazil 202 C4
Sant'Agata di Militello Sicilia Italy 57 G10
Santa Helena Brazil 202 C2
Santa Helena de Goiás Brazil 206 C4
Santai Sichuan China 86 C2
also known as Tongchuan
Santai Xinjiang China 88 C2
Santa Inês Bahia Brazil 202 E5
Santa Inês Maranhão Brazil 202 C2
Santa Inés, Isla i. Chile 205 B9
Santa Isabel Arg. 204 D5
Santa Isabel Bol. 200 D5
Santa Isabel Brazil 201 E3
Santa Isabel Equat. Guinea see Malabo
Santa Isabel i. Solomon Is 145 E2
formerly spelt Santa Ysabel
Santa Isabel, Ilha Grande de i. Brazil 202 D2
Santa Isabel, Sierra mts Mex. 184 B2
Santa Isabel de Sihuas Peru 200 B4
Santa Isabel do Araguaia Brazil 201 H1
Santa Juliana Brazil 206 F6
Santalpur India 96 A5
Santa Lucia Chile 200 C5
Santa Lucía Ecuador 198 B5
Santa Lucia Guat. 185 H6
Santa Lucía, Cerro de mt. Spain 54 G7
Santa Lucia Range mts U.S.A. 182 C5
Santa Luzia Maranhão Brazil 202 C3
Santa Luzia Paraíba Brazil 202 E3
Santa Luzia i. Cape Verde 124 [inset]
Santa Magdalena Arg. 204 E4
Santa Margarita Arg. 204 E3
Santa Margarita Spain 55 O5
Santa Margarita U.S.A. 182 D6
Santa Margarita, Isla i. Mex. 184 C3
Santa María Arg. 204 D2
Santa María Bol. 201 E3
Santa Maria Amazonas Brazil 199 F5
Santa Maria Amazonas Brazil 199 G5
Santa Maria Pará Brazil 199 H5
Santa Maria Rio Grande do Sul Brazil 203 A9
Santa Maria r. Brazil 203 A9
Santa Maria r. Brazil 206 G1
Santa Maria Cape Verde 124 [inset]
Santa María Mex. 185 H5
Santa María r. Mex. 184 D2
Santa Maria U.S.A. 182 D7
Santa María r. U.S.A. 183 K7
Santa María Venez. 199 E3
Santa Maria, Cabo de c. Moz. 131 G5
Santa Maria, Cabo de c. Port. 54 D8
Santa Maria, Cape Bahamas 175 F8
Santa María, Cayo i. Cuba 186 D2
Santa Maria, Chapadão de hills Brazil 202 C5
Santa María, Isla i. Chile 204 B5
Santa María, Punta pt Peru 200 B3
Santa Maria, Serra de hills Brazil 206 G1
Santa Maria Capua Vetere Italy 56 G7
Santa Maria da Boa Vista Brazil 202 E4
Santa Maria das Barreiras Brazil 202 B4
Santa Maria da Vitória Brazil 202 C5
Santa María de Ipire Venez. 199 E2
Santa María del Oro Mex. 184 D3
Santa María del Río Mex. 185 E4
Santa Maria di Leuca, Capo c. Italy 57 K9
Santa Maria do Salto Brazil 207 M3
Santa Maria do Suaçuí Brazil 203 D6
Santa Maria Island Vanuatu 145 F3
Santa Maria Mountains U.S.A. 183 L7
Santa Marina Salina Isole Lipari Italy 57 G10
Santa Marinella Italy 56 D6
Santa Marta Col. 198 C2
Santa Marta, Cabo de c. Angola 127 B8
Santa Marta, Serra de mts Brazil see Divisões, Serra das
Santa Marta Grande, Cabo de c. Brazil 203 B9
Santa Martha, Cerro mt. Mex. 185 G5
Santa Maura i. Greece see Lefkada
Santa Monica U.S.A. 182 F7
Santa Monica Bay U.S.A. 182 F8
Santan Indon. 77 G3
Santana Amazonas Brazil 199 E4
Santana Bahia Brazil 202 D5
Santana r. Brazil 206 B6
Sântana Romania 58 C2
Santana da Boa Vista Brazil 203 A9
Santana do Acarau Brazil 202 D2
Santana do Araguaia Brazil 202 B4
Santana do Cariri Brazil 202 E3
Santana do Livramento Brazil 204 G3
Santander Col. 198 B4
Santander dept Col. 198 C3
Santander Spain 54 H1
Santa Nella U.S.A. 182 C4
Sant'Angelo in Lizzola Italy 56 E5
Sant'Angelo Lodigiano Italy 56 B3
Santanghu China 84 B2
Santanilla, Islas is Caribbean Sea see Swan Islands
Santan Mountain hill U.S.A. 183 M8
Sant'Anna, Ilha de i. Brazil 207 L9
Sant'Antioco Sardegna Italy 57 A9
historically known as Sulci or Sulcis
Sant'Antioco, Isola di i. Sardegna Italy 57 A9
Santañy Spain see Santanyí
Santanyí Spain 55 O5
also spelt Santañy
Santa Paula U.S.A. 182 E7
Santapilly India 95 D2
Santa Pola Spain 55 K6
Santa Pola, Cabo de c. Spain 55 K6
Santaquin U.S.A. 183 M2
Santa Quitéria Brazil 202 D3
Sant Arcangelo Italy 57 I8
Santarém Brazil 199 H5
Santarém Port. 54 C5
Santarém admin. dist. Port. 54 C5
Santa Rita Mato Grosso Brazil 201 F1
Santa Rita Paraíba Brazil 202 F3
Santa Rita Col. 198 C4
Santa Rita Mex. 185 E3
Santa Rita Guárico Venez. 199 E2
Santa Rita Zulia Venez. 198 D2
Santa Rita de Cassia Brazil 202 C4
Santa Rita do Araguaia Brazil 203 A6
Santa Rita do Pardo Brazil 206 A8
Santa Rita do Sapucaí Brazil 207 H9
Santa Rita do Weil Brazil 198 D5
Santa Rosa Corrientes Arg. 204 F3
Santa Rosa La Pampa Arg. 204 D5
Santa Rosa Río Negro Arg. 204 D6
Santa Rosa Salta Arg. 200 D6
Santa Rosa Bol. 200 D3
Santa Rosa Acre Brazil 200 C2
Santa Rosa Rio Grande do Sul Brazil 203 A8
Santa Rosa Col. 198 D4

S index

Santa Rosa Ecuador 198 B5
Santa Rosa Mex. 185 H5
Santa Rosa Para. 201 F6
Santa Rosa *Loreto* Peru 198 C5
Santa Rosa *Puno* Peru 200 C3
Santa Rosa *CA* U.S.A. 182 B3
Santa Rosa *NM* U.S.A. 181 F6
Santa Rosa Venez. 199 E4
Santa Rosa de Copán Hond. 186 A4
Santa Rosa de la Roca Bol. 201 E4
Santa Rosa del Conlara Arg. 204 D4
Santa Rosa del Palmar Bol. 201 E4
Santa Rosa de Osos Col. 198 C3
Santa Rosa de Viterbo Brazil 206 F8
Santa Rosa Island U.S.A. 182 D8
Santa Rosalía Mex. 184 B3
Santa Rosa Mountains U.S.A. 183 H8
Santa Rosa Range *mts* U.S.A. 180 C4
Santa Rosa Wash *watercourse* U.S.A. 183 L8
Santa Sylvina Arg. 204 E2
Santa Teresa Australia 148 B5
Santa Teresa Brazil 207 M6
Santa Teresa *r.* Brazil 202 B4
Santa Teresa Mex. 185 F3
Santa Teresa, Embalse de *resr* Spain 54 F4
Santa Teresa Aboriginal Land *res.* Australia *see* Ltyentye Apurte Aboriginal Land
Santa Teresa di Gallura *Sardegna* Italy 56 B7
Santa Terezinha Brazil 202 B4
Santa Vitória Brazil 206 C5
Santa Vitória do Palmar Brazil 204 G4
Santa Vittoria, Monte *mt.* *Sardegna* Italy 57 B9
Santa Ynez *r.* U.S.A. 182 D7
Santa Ysabel *i.* Solomon Is *see* Santa Isabel
Sant Carles de la Ràpita Spain 55 L4
also spelt San Carlos de la Rápita
Sant Celoni Spain 55 N3
also spelt San Celoni
Santee U.S.A. 183 H9
Santee *r.* U.S.A. 175 E5
Santeramo in Colle Italy 57 I8
Santerno *r.* Italy 56 D4
Sant Feliu de Guíxols Spain 55 O3
also spelt San Feliú de Guíxols
Santiago Brazil 203 A9

▶Santiago Chile 204 C4
Capital of Chile.
southamerica [countries] ▶▶ 192–193

Santiago *admin. reg.* Chile 204 C4
Santiago Dom. Rep. 187 F3
long form Santiago de los Caballeros
Santiago *Baja California Sur* Mex. 184 C4
Santiago *Nuevo León* Mex. 185 E3
Santiago Panama 186 C5
Santiago Para. 201 F6
Santiago Peru 200 B3
Santiago *r.* Peru 198 B6
Santiago Phil. 74 B2
Santiago, Cabo *c.* Chile 205 B8
Santiago, Cerro *mt.* Panama 186 C5
Santiago, Río Grande de *r.* Mex. 184 D4
Santiago, Sierra de *hills* Bol. 201 F4
Santiago Astata Mex. 185 G5
Santiago de Cao Peru 200 A1
Santiago de Compostela Spain 54 C2
Santiago de Cuba Cuba 186 E2
Santiago de la Espada Spain 55 I6
Santiago del Estero Arg. 204 D2
Santiago del Estero *prov.* Arg. 204 E2
Santiago de los Caballeros Dom. Rep. *see* Santiago
Santiago de Mendez Ecuador 198 B5
Santiago de Pacaguaras Bol. 200 C3
Santiago do Cacém Port. 54 C6
Santiago Ixcuintla Mex. 184 D4
Santiago Peak U.S.A. 182 G8
Santiago Temple Arg. 204 E3
Santiago Vazquez Uruguay 204 F4
Santiaguillo, Laguna de *l.* Mex. 184 D3
Santillana Spain 54 G1
San Timoteo Venez. 198 D2
Santipur India *see* Shantipur
Santisteban del Puerto Spain 55 H6
Sant Jordi, Golf de *g.* Spain 55 L4
also spelt San Jorge, Golfo de
Sant Llorenç del Munt i de la Serra de L'Obac, Parque Natural de *nature res.* Spain 55 M3
Santo Amaro Brazil 202 E5
Santo Amaro de Campos Brazil 207 L8
Santo Anastácio *r.* Brazil 206 A8
Santo André Brazil 206 G10
Santo André Port. 54 C6
Santo Angelo Brazil 203 A9

▶Santo Antão *i.* Cape Verde 124 [inset]
Most westerly point of Africa.

Santo Antônio *Amazonas* Brazil 199 F5
Santo Antônio *Maranhão* Brazil 202 C3
Santo Antônio *Rio Grande do Norte* Brazil 202 F3
Santo Antônio *r.* Brazil 203 D6
Santo Antônio São Tomé and Príncipe 125 G6
Santo Antônio, Ponta *pt* Brazil 207 O3
Santo Antônio da Barra Brazil 206 C4
Santo Antônio da Cachoeira Brazil 199 H5
Santo Antônio da Platina Brazil 206 C10
Santo Antônio de Jesus Brazil 202 E5
Santo Antônio de Leverger Brazil 201 F3
Santo Antônio de Pádua Brazil 207 K8
Santo Antônio do Amparo Brazil 207 I7
Santo Antônio do Içá Brazil 199 E5
Santo Antônio do Jacinto Brazil 207 M3
Santo Antônio do Monte Brazil 207 H7
Santo Antônio do Rio Verde Brazil 206 F4
Santo Antônio dos Cavaleiros Port. 54 B6
Santo Antônio do Zaire Angola *see* Soyo
Santo Corazón Bol. 201 F4
Santo Domingo Cuba 186 C2

▶Santo Domingo Dom. Rep. 187 F3
Capital of the Dominican Republic. Formerly known as Ciudad Trujillo.

Santo Domingo *Baja California Norte* Mex. 184 B2
Santo Domingo *San Luis Potosí* Mex. 185 E4
Santo Domingo Nicaragua 186 B4
Santo Domingo Peru 200 C3
Santo Domingo *country* West Indies *see* Dominican Republic
Santo Domingo de la Calzada Spain 55 I2
Santo Domingo Pueblo U.S.A. 181 F6
Santo Domingo Tehuantepec Mex. 185 G5
Santo Eduardo Brazil 207 L8
Santo Hipólito Brazil 207 I5
Santo Inácio Brazil 206 B9
San Tomé Venez. 199 E2
Santoña Spain 55 H1
Santong *r.* China 82 B4
Santo Niño *i.* Phil. 74 C4
Santorini *i.* Greece *see* Thira
Santos Brazil 207 G10
Santos Dumont Brazil 207 J8
Santos Mercado Bol. 200 D2
Santo Stefano di Camastra *Sicilia* Italy 57 G10
Santo Tirso Port. 54 C3
Santo Tomás *Chihuahua* Mex. 181 F7
Santo Tomás *Sonora* Mex. 181 D7
Santo Tomás Nicaragua 186 B4
Santo Tomás Peru 200 B3
Santo Tomé Arg. 204 F3
Santrampur India 96 B5
Sanup Plateau U.S.A. 183 K5
San Valentín, Cerro *mt.* Chile 205 B7
San Vicente El Salvador 185 H6
San Vicente Mex. 184 A2
San Vicente Phil. 74 B2
San Vicente de Cañete Peru 200 A3
San Vicente de la Barquera Spain 54 G1
San Vicente del Caguán Col. 198 C4
San Vicente del Raspeig Spain 55 K6
San Vincenzo Italy 56 C5
San Vito, Capo *c.* *Sicilia* Italy 57 E10
San Vito al Tagliamento Italy 56 E3
San Vito Chietino Italy 56 G6
San Vito dei Normanni Italy 57 J8
San Vito lo Capo *Sicilia* Italy 57 E10
Sanwer India 96 B5
Sanya China 87 D5
formerly known as Yaxian
San Yanaro Col. 198 D4
Sanyati *r.* Zimbabwe 131 F3
Sanyuan China 87 D1
Sanza Pombo Angola 127 C6
Sao, Phou *mt.* Laos 78 C4
São Bartolomeu *r.* Brazil 206 F3
São Benedito Brazil 202 D3
São Bento *Amazonas* Brazil 200 D1
São Bento *Maranhão* Brazil 202 C2
São Bento *Roraima* Brazil 199 F4
São Bento do Norte Brazil 202 F3
São Bernardo Brazil 202 D2
São Bernardo do Campo Brazil 206 G10
São Borja Brazil 204 F3
São Carlos *Rondônia* Brazil 201 D2
São Carlos *Rondônia* Brazil 201 E2
São Carlos *São Paulo* Brazil 206 F9
São Desidério Brazil 202 C5
São Domingos Brazil 202 C5
São Domingos *r.* *Mato Grosso do Sul* Brazil 203 A7
São Domingos *r.* *Minas Gerais* Brazil 206 C6
São Domingos *r.* Brazil 206 G2
São Domingos do Norte Brazil 207 M6
São Felipe, Serra de *hills* Brazil 202 C5
São Félix *Bahia* Brazil 202 E5
São Félix *Mato Grosso* Brazil 202 B4
São Félix *Pará* Brazil 199 I6
São Fidélis Brazil 203 D7
São Filipe Cape Verde 124 [inset]
São Francisco *Acre* Brazil 200 C2
São Francisco *Amazonas* Brazil 199 F6
São Francisco *Minas Gerais* Brazil 202 C5
São Francisco *r.* Brazil 200 D2

▶São Francisco *r.* Brazil 207 H4
5th longest river in South America.
southamerica [landscapes] ▶▶ 190–191

São Francisco, Ilha de *i.* Brazil 203 B8
São Francisco de Assis Brazil 203 A9
São Francisco de Goiás Brazil 206 D2
São Francisco de Paula Brazil 203 B9
São Francisco de Sales Brazil 206 D6
São Francisco do Sul Brazil 203 B8
São Gabriel Brazil 203 A9
São Gabriel da Palha Brazil 207 M6
São Gabriel de Goiás Brazil 206 F2
São Gonçalo Brazil 203 D7
São Gonçalo do Abaeté Brazil 203 C6
São Gotardo Brazil 207 H6
Sao Hill Tanz. 129 B7
São Jerônimo da Serra Brazil 206 C10
São João Brazil 199 E5
São João, Ilhas de *is* Brazil 202 C2
São João, Serra de *hills* Brazil 201 E2
São João da Aliança Brazil 202 C5
São João da Barra Brazil 203 D7
São João da Boa Vista Brazil 206 G8
São João da Madeira Port. 54 C4
São João da Ponte Brazil 207 I2
São João das Duas Pontas Brazil 206 C7
São João del Rei Brazil 203 C7
São João de Meriti Brazil 207 J9
São João do Araguaia Brazil 202 B3
São João do Caiuá Brazil 206 A9
São João do Cariri Brazil 202 E3
São João do Paraíso Brazil 202 D5
São João do Piauí Brazil 202 D4
São João dos Patos Brazil 202 D3
São João do Sul Angola 127 B8
São João Evangelista Brazil 207 K5
São Joaquim *Amazonas* Brazil 199 E4
São Joaquim *Santa Catarina* Brazil 203 B9
São Jorge da Mina Ghana *see* Elmina
São José *Amazonas* Brazil 199 E5
São José *Santa Catarina* Brazil 203 B8
São José do Anauá Brazil 199 F4
São José do Belmonte Brazil 202 E3
São José do Divino Brazil 207 L5
São José do Egito Brazil 202 E3
São José do Jacuri Brazil 207 K5
São José do Norte Brazil 204 G4
São José do Peixe Brazil 202 D3
São José do Rio Pardo Brazil 206 G8
São José do Rio Preto Brazil 206 D7
São José dos Campos Brazil 207 H10
São José dos Dourados *r.* Brazil 206 B7
São José dos Pinhais Brazil 203 B8
São Lourenço Brazil 207 H9
São Lourenço *r.* Brazil 201 F4
São Lourenço do Sul Brazil 204 H3
São Lucas Angola 127 C7
São Luís Brazil 202 C2
São Luís Brazil 199 G6
São Luís de Montes Belos Brazil 206 C3
São Luís do Paraitinga Brazil 207 H10
São Luís do Quitunde Brazil 202 F4
São Luís Gonzaga Brazil 203 A9
São Manuel Brazil 206 E9
São Marcelino Brazil 199 E4
São Marcos *r.* Brazil 206 F5
São Marcos, Baía de *b.* Brazil 202 C2
São Martinho Brazil 199 G6
São Mateus Brazil 203 E6
São Mateus *r.* Brazil 207 N5
São Mateus do Sul Brazil 203 B8
São Miguel *i.* Azores 216 M3
São Miguel *r.* Brazil 206 G3
São Miguel Arcanjo Brazil 206 F10
São Miguel do Tapuio Brazil 202 D3
São Miguel Jesuit Missions *tourist site* Brazil 203 A9
Saona, Isla *i.* Dom. Rep. 187 F3
Saône *r.* France 51 K7
São Nicolau Angola *see* Bentiaba
São Nicolau *i.* Cape Verde 124 [inset]

▶São Paulo Brazil 206 G10
Most populous city in South America and 4th in the world.
world [cities] ▶▶ 24–25

São Paulo *state* Brazil 206 E9
São Paulo de Olivença Brazil 198 D5
São Pedro *Amazonas* Brazil 199 G6
São Pedro *Mato Grosso do Sul* Brazil 206 B6
São Pedro *Rondônia* Brazil 201 E2
São Pedro *São Paulo* Brazil 206 F9
São Pedro da Aldeia Brazil 203 D7
São Pedro do Desterro Brazil 200 D2
São Pedro do Ivaí Brazil 206 B10
São Pedro do Sul Brazil 203 A9
São Pedro do Sul Port. 54 C4
São Pedro e São Paulo *is* N. Atlantic Ocean 216 M5
English form St Peter and St Paul Rocks
São Pires *r.* Brazil *see* Teles Pires
São Raimundo das Mangabeiras Brazil 202 C3
São Raimundo Nonato Brazil 202 D4
São Romão *Amazonas* Brazil 199 E6
São Romão *Minas Gerais* Brazil 202 C6
São Roque Brazil 206 F10
São Roque de Minas Brazil 206 G7
São Salvador Angola *see* M'banza Congo
São Salvador do Congo Angola *see* M'banza Congo
São Sebastião *Amazonas* Brazil 200 C1
São Sebastião *Pará* Brazil 199 H6
São Sebastião *Rondônia* Brazil 201 E2
São Sebastião *São Paulo* Brazil 203 C7
São Sebastião, Ilha do *i.* Brazil 203 C7
São Sebastião da Amoreira Brazil 206 C10
São Sebastião da Boa Vista Brazil 202 B2
São Sebastião do Paraíso Brazil 206 G7
São Simão *Mato Grosso do Sul* Brazil 201 F5
São Simão *Minas Gerais* Brazil 206 C5
São Simão, Barragem de *resr* Brazil 206 C6
São Simão, Represa de *resr* Brazil 206 D5
Sao-Siu Indon. 75 C2
São Tiago Brazil 207 I7
São Tiago *i.* Cape Verde 124 [inset]

▶São Tomé São Tomé and Príncipe 125 G6
Capital of São Tomé and Príncipe.

São Tomé *i.* São Tomé and Príncipe 125 G6
São Tomé, Cabo de *c.* Brazil 203 D7
São Tomé, Pico de *mt.* São Tomé and Príncipe 125 G6
▶São Tomé and Príncipe *country* Africa 125 G6
africa [countries] ▶▶ 114–117
Saoura, Oued *watercourse* Alg. 123 E3
São Vicente Brazil 206 G10
São Vicente *i.* Cape Verde 124 [inset]
São Vicente, Cabo de *c.* Port. 54 C7
English form St Vincent, Cape
São Vicente Ferrer Brazil 202 C2
Sápai Greece *see* Sapes
Sapallanga Peru 200 B3
Sapanca Turkey 106 B2
Sapão *r.* Brazil 202 C4
Saparua Indon. 75 D3
Saparua *i.* Indon. 75 D3
Sape, Selat *sea chan.* Indon. 75 A5
Sape, Teluk *b.* Indon. 77 G5
Sapele Nigeria 125 G5
Sapes Greece 58 G7
also known as Sápai
Şaphane Turkey 59 K9
Sapientza *i.* Greece 59 C12
Sapo, Serranía del *mts* Panama 186 D6
Sa Pobla Spain 55 O5
also spelt La Puebla
Sapo National Park Liberia 124 C5
Sapopema Brazil 206 C10
Sapotskin Belarus 42 E8
Sapouy Burkina 125 E4
Sapozhok Rus. Fed. 41 G5
Sappa Creek *r.* U.S.A. 178 C3
Sapporo Japan 90 G3
Saptamukhi *r.* India 97 F5
Sapucaí *r.* *Minas Gerais* Brazil 207 H8
Sapucaí *r.* *São Paulo* Brazil 206 E7
Sapucaia Brazil 199 G5
Sapudi *i.* Indon. 77 F4
Sapulpa U.S.A. 179 C4
Sapulut *Sabah* Malaysia 77 G1
Sāq, Jabal *hill* Saudi Arabia 104 C2
Sāqi Iran 101 D3
Saqqaq Greenland 165 N2
Saqqez Iran 100 A2
Sara Bangl. 97 F4
Sarā Iran 100 A2
Sarāb Iran 100 A2
Sarabit el Khâdim *tourist site* Egypt 108 E8
Sara Buri Thai. 79 C5
Saracá, Lago *l.* Brazil 199 G5
Saraf Doungous Chad 120 C6
Saragossa Spain *see* Zaragoza
Saraguro Ecuador 198 B5
Saraikela India 97 E5
Sarai Sidhu Pak. 101 H4
Säräisniemi Fin. 44 N2

▶Sarajevo Bos.-Herz. 56 K5
Capital of Bosnia-Herzegovina. Historically known as Bosna Saray.

Sarakhs Turkm. 102 E5
Sarakiniko, Akra *pt* Greece 59 E10
Sarakino *i.* Greece 59 F10
Saraktash Rus. Fed. 102 D2
Saraland U.S.A. 175 B6
Saralzhin Kazakh. 102 C2
Saramati *mt.* India/Myanmar 97 G4
Sarameriza Peru 198 B6
Saran France 51 H5
Saran' Kazakh. 103 H2
Saran, Gunung *mt.* Indon. 77 E3
Saranac *r.* U.S.A. 177 L1
Saranac Lake U.S.A. 177 K1
Sarandë Albania 59 B9
Sarandi *Paraná* Brazil 206 B10
Sarandi *Rio Grande do Sul* Brazil 203 A8
Sarandib *country* Asia *see* Sri Lanka
Sarandí del Yí Uruguay 204 G4
Sarandí Grande Uruguay 204 F4
Sarangani *i.* Phil. 74 C5
Sarangani Bay Phil. 74 C5
Sarangani Islands Phil. 74 C5
Sarangani Strait Phil. 74 C5
Sarangarh India 97 D5
Sarangpur India 96 C5
Saransk Rus. Fed. 41 H5
Sara Peak Nigeria 125 H4
Sarapul Rus. Fed. 40 J4
Sarasota U.S.A. 175 D7
Saraswati *r.* India 96 A5
Sărata *r.* Moldova 58 J2
Sărata *r.* Romania 58 H4
Sarata Ukr. 41 D7
Sarata *r.* Ukr. 58 K3
Saratoga *CA* U.S.A. 182 B4
Saratoga *WY* U.S.A. 180 F4
Saratoga Springs U.S.A. 177 L2
Saratok *Sarawak* Malaysia 77 E2
Saratov Rus. Fed. 41 H6
Saratov Oblast *admin. div.* Rus. Fed. *see* Saratovskaya Oblast'
Saratovskaya Oblast' *admin. div.* Rus. Fed. 102 A2
English form Saratov Oblast
Saratovskoye Vodokhranilishche *resr* Rus. Fed. 102 A1
Saravan Iran 101 E5
Saravan Laos 79 D5
Sarawa *r.* Myanmar 79 B5
Sarawak *state* Malaysia 77 E2
Saray Turkey 106 A2
Saraya Guinea 124 C4
Saraya Senegal 124 C3
Saraya, Pulau *reg.* Sing. 76 [inset]
Sarayçık Turkey 59 K10
Sarayköy Turkey 106 B3
Saraylar Turkey 58 I8
Sarayönü Turkey 106 C3
Sarbāz Iran 101 E5
Sarbāz *r.* Iran 101 E5
Sarbāz *reg.* Iran 101 E5
Sârbeni Romania 58 G4
Sarbhang Bhutan 97 F4
Sarbīsheh Iran 101 D3
Sárbogárd Hungary 49 P9
Sarbulak China 84 A2
Sarcham Iran 100 B2
Sarco Chile 204 C3
Sarda *r.* India/Nepal 99 K4
Sardab Pass Afgh. 101 G2
Sardarpur India 96 B5
Sardarshahr India 96 B3
Sar Dasht Iran 100 A2
Sardasht *Būshehr* Iran 100 B4
Sardasht *Khūzestān* Iran 100 B3
Sardegna *admin. reg.* Italy 57 B8
Sardegna *i.* Italy *see* Sardinia
Sardica Bulg. *see* Sofia
Sardinata Col. 198 C2
Sardinia Costa Rica 186 B5
Sardinia *i.* Italy 57 A8
also spelt Sardegna
Sardis U.S.A. 174 B5
Sardis Lake *resr* U.S.A. 174 B5
Sardoal Port. 54 C5
Sareb, Rās-as- *pt* U.A.E. 105 E2
Sareks nationalpark *nat. park* Sweden 44 L2
Sarektjåkkå *mt.* Sweden 44 L2
Sarempaka, Gunung *mt.* Indon. 77 F3
Sar-e Pol Afgh. 101 F2
Sar-e Pol *prov.* Afgh. 101 F2
Sar Eskandar Iran *see* Hashtrud
Sare Yazd Iran 100 C4
Sarez, Kŭli *l.* Tajik. 101 H2
also known as Sarezskoye Ozero
Sarezskoye Ozero *l.* Tajik. *see* Sarez, Kŭli
Sargasso Sea Europe 216 J4
Sargentu Loros Peru 198 C5
Sargodha Pak. 101 H3
Sarh Chad 126 C2
formerly known as Fort Archambault
Sarhad *reg.* Iran 101 E4
Sarhro, Jbel *mt.* Morocco 122 D3
Sārī Iran 100 C2
Saria *i.* Greece 59 I13
Sar-i-Bum Afgh. 101 F3
Sáric Mex. 184 C2
Sarichioi Romania 58 J4
Sarigan *i.* N. Mariana Is 73 K3
Sarıgöl Turkey 106 B3
Sarıkamış Turkey 107 E2
Sarikei *Sarawak* Malaysia 77 E2
Sarıkemer Turkey 59 I11
Sarıköy Turkey 59 I8
Sarikŭl, Qatorkŭhi *mts* China/Tajik. *see* Sarykol Range
Sarila India 96 C4
Sarimbun Reservoir Sing. 76 [inset]
Sarina Australia 149 F4
Sariñena Spain 55 K3
Sarıoğlan Turkey *see* Belören
Sar-i Pīrān *mt.* Iraq 100 A2
Sar-i-Pul Afgh. 101 F3
Sārī Qamīsh Iran 100 C2
Sariqamish Kuli *salt l.* Turkm./Uzbek. *see* Sarykamyshkoye Ozero
Sarir Tibesti *des.* Libya 120 C4
Sarir Water Wells Field Libya 120 D3
Sarita U.S.A. 179 C7
Sarıveliler Turkey 108 D1
Sariwŏn N. Korea 83 B5
Sarıyer Turkey 106 B2
Sarız Turkey 107 D3
Sark *i.* Channel Is 50 D3
Sarkad Hungary 49 S9
Sarkand Kazakh. 103 I3
Sarkari Tala India 96 A4
Şarkikaraağaç Turkey 106 B3
Särkisalo Fin. 42 D1
Şarkışla Turkey 107 D3
Sarkŏr *watercourse* Iran 101 E5
Şarköy Turkey 106 A2
Sarlath Range *mts* Afgh./Pak. 101 F4
Sarlat-la-Canéda France 50 H8
Sarmanovo Rus. Fed. 40 J5
Sărmășag Romania 58 D1
Sărmașu Romania 58 F2
Sarmento *r.* Italy 57 I8
Sarmi Indon. 73 I7
Sarmiento Arg. 205 C7
Särna Sweden 45 K3
Sārnate Latvia 42 C4
Sarneh Iran 100 A3
Sarnen Switz. 51 O6
Sarni India *see* Amla
Sarnia Canada 168 D5
Sarny Ukr. 41 C6
Saroako Indon. 75 B3
Sarogozha *r.* Rus. Fed. 43 Q3
Sarolangun Indon. 76 C3
Saroma-ko *l.* Japan 90 H2
Sarona U.S.A. 172 B5
Saronikos Kolpos *g.* Greece 59 E11
Saros Körfezi *b.* Turkey 106 A2
Sárospatak Hungary 49 S7
Sarotra India 96 B4
Sarova Rus. Fed. 40 G5
Sarowbi Afgh. 101 G3
Sarpa, Ozero *l.* Rus. Fed. 41 H7
Sarpan *i.* N. Mariana Is *see* Rota
Šar Planina *mts* Macedonia/Yugo. 58 B7
Sarpsborg Norway 45 J4
Sarqant Kazakh. *see* Sarkand
Sarre *r.* France 51 N3
Sarrebourg France 51 N4
Sarreguemines France 51 N3
Sarre-Union France 51 N4
Sarria Spain 54 D2
Sarrión Spain 55 K4
Sarro Mali 124 D3
Sarroch *Sardegna* Italy 57 B9
Sars Rus. Fed. 40 K4
Sartana Ukr. 41 F7
formerly known as Prymors'ke
Sartène *Corse* France 56 A7
Sarthe *r.* France 50 F5
Sarti Greece 59 E8
Sartininkai Lith. 42 C6
Sartu China *see* Daqing
Sarud, Rūdkhāneh-ye *r.* Iran 100 B3
Saruhanlı Turkey 59 I10
Saruna *r.* Pak. 101 F5
Sarupsar India 96 B3
Şärur Azer. 107 F3
also spelt Sharur; *formerly known as* Il'ichevsk
Saru Tara *tourist site* Afgh. 101 E4
Sarvābād Iran 100 A3
Sarvani Georgia *see* Marneuli
Sárvár Hungary 49 N8
Sarvestān Iran 100 C4
Sárvíz *r.* Romania 49 P9
Sarwar India 96 B4
Sarya *r.* India 94 B2
Saryagach Kazakh. 103 G4
Sary-Bulak Kyrg. 103 H4
Sarydhaz *r.* Kyrg. *see* Sary-Jaz
Sarydzhas Kazakh. *see* Saryzhaz
Sarygamysh Köli *salt l.* Turkm./Uzbek. *see* Sarykamyshkoye Ozero
Sary-Ishikotrau, Peski *des.* Kazakh. *see* Saryyesik-Atyrau, Peski
Sary-Jaz *r.* Kyrg. 103 I4
also spelt Sarydhaz
Sarykamys Kazakh. 102 C3
also spelt Saryqamys
Sarykamyshkoye Ozero *salt l.* Turkm./Uzbek. 102 D4
also known as Sariqamish Kuli *or* Sarygamysh Köli
Sarykemer Kazakh. 103 G4
formerly known as Mikhaylovka
Sarykiyak Kazakh. 103 H2
Sarykol Range *mts* China/Tajik. 88 A4
also known as Sarikŭl, Qatorkŭhi
Sarymoyyn, Ozero *salt l.* Kazakh. 103 F2
Saryozek Kazakh. 103 I3
Saryqamys Kazakh. *see* Sarykamys
Saryshagan Kazakh. 103 H3
Sarysu *watercourse* Kazakh. 103 F3
formerly known as Zhaksy Sarysu
Sary-Tash Kyrg. 103 H5
Saryter, Gora *mt.* Kyrg. 103 I4
Saryumir Kazakh. 102 B2
Sary Yazikskoye Vodokhranilishche *resr* Turkm. 103 E5
Saryyesik-Atyrau, Peski *des.* Kazakh. 103 H3
formerly known as Sary-Ishikotrau, Peski
Saryzhal Kazakh. *see* Sarzhal
Saryzhaz Kazakh. 103 I4
also spelt Sarydzhas
Sarzana Italy 56 B4
Sarzeau France 50 D5
Sarzhal Kazakh. 103 I2
also spelt Saryzhal
Sasak Indon. 76 B2
Sasar, Tanjung *pt* Indon. 75 A5
Sasaram India 97 E4
Sásd Hungary 49 P9
Sasebo Japan 91 A8
Saskatchewan *prov.* Canada 167 J4
Saskatchewan *r.* Canada 167 K4
Saskatoon Canada 167 J4
Saskylakh Rus. Fed. 39 L2
Saslaya *mt.* Nicaragua 186 B4
Saslaya, Parque Nacional *nat. park* Nicaragua 186 B4
Sasnovy Bor Belarus 43 K9
also spelt Sosnovyy Bor; *formerly known as* Golyashi
Sasolburg S. Africa 133 L3
Sasovo Rus. Fed. 41 G5
Sass *r.* Canada 167 H2
Sassandra Côte d'Ivoire 124 D5
Sassandra *r.* Côte d'Ivoire 124 D5
Sassari *Sardegna* Italy 57 A8
Sassnitz Germany 49 K1
Sassoferrato Italy 56 E5
historically known as Sentinum
Sasso Marconi Italy 56 D4
Sass Rigais *mt.* Italy 56 D2
Sass Town Liberia 124 C5
Sassuolo Italy 56 C4
Sastobe Kazakh. 103 G4
also spelt Saztöbe
Sastre Arg. 204 E3
Sasvad India 94 B2
Sasykkol', Ozero *l.* Kazakh. 103 J3
also known as Sasyqköl
Sasyqköl *l.* Kazakh. *see* Sasykkol', Ozero
Satadougou Mali 124 C3
Satahual *i.* Micronesia *see* Satawal
Sata-misaki *c.* Japan 91 B9
Satana India 94 B1
Satara India 94 B2
Satara S. Africa 131 F5
Satawal *i.* Micronesia 73 K5
also spelt Satahual
Sätbaev Kazakh. *see* Satpayev
Satchinez Romania 58 C3
Satéma Cent. Afr. Rep. 126 D3
Satengar *i.* Indon. 77 G4
Säter Sweden 45 K3
Satevó Mex. 184 D3
Saticoy U.S.A. 182 E7
Satihaure *l.* Sweden 44 L2
Satilla *r.* U.S.A. 175 D6
Satipo Peru 200 B2
Satiri Burkina 124 D4
Satırlar Turkey *see* Yeşilova
Satka Rus. Fed. 38 F4
Satkania Bangl. 97 G5
Satkhira Bangl. 97 F5
Satluj *r.* India/Pak. *see* Sutlej
Satmala Range *hills* India 94 C2
Satna India 96 D4
Sátoraljaújhely Hungary 49 S7
Satorina *mt.* Croatia 56 H4
Satpayev Kazakh. 103 F3
also spelt Sätbaev; *formerly known as* Nikol'skiy
Satpura Range *mts* India 96 B5
Šatrijos kalnis *hill* Lith. 42 D6
Satsuma-hantō *pen.* Japan 91 B9
Satsunai-gawa *r.* Japan 90 H3
Sattahip Thai. 79 C5
Sattanen Fin. 44 N2
Sattenapalle India 94 D2
Satthwa Myanmar 78 A4
Satti Jammu and Kashmir 96 C2
Satu Mare Romania 53 G2
Satun Thai. 79 C7
Satwas India 96 C5
Saubi *i.* Indon. 77 F4
Sauce Arg. 204 F3
Sauceda Mountains U.S.A. 183 L9
Sauce de Luna Arg. 204 F3
Saucillo Mex. 184 D2
Sauda Norway 45 I4
Saudakent Kazakh. 103 G4
formerly known as Baykadam *or* Bayqadam
Sauðárkrókur Iceland 44 [inset] C2
▶Saudi Arabia *country* Asia 104 C3
known as Al 'Arabīyah as Sa'ūdīyah *in Arabic*
asia [landscapes] ▶▶ 62–63
asia [countries] ▶▶ 64–67
Saue Estonia 42 F2
Sauêruiná *r.* Brazil 201 F3
also known as Papagaio
Saug *r.* Phil. 74 C5
Sauga *r.* Estonia 42 F3
Saugeen *r.* Canada 168 D4
Saugerties U.S.A. 177 L3
Saugues France 51 J8
Sāūjbolāgh Iran *see* Mahābād
Saujil Arg. 204 D2
Saujon France 50 F7
Saukas ezers *l.* Latvia 42 G5
Sauk Center U.S.A. 178 D2
Sauk City U.S.A. 172 D7
Saul Fr. Guiana 199 H4
Sauland Norway 45 J4
Sauldre *r.* France 51 H5
Saulgau Germany 48 G7
Saulieu France 51 K5
Saulkrasti Latvia 42 F4
Sault Sainte Marie Canada 168 C4
Sault Ste Marie U.S.A. 173 I4
Saumalkol' Kazakh. 103 G1
formerly known as Volodarskoye
Saumarez Reef Australia 149 G4
Saumlakki Indon. 73 H8
Saumur France 50 F5
Saunavaara Fin. 44 N2
Saunders, Mount *hill* Australia 148 A2
Saunders Coast Antarctica 222 O1
Saunders Island Falkland Is 205 E8
Saunemin U.S.A. 172 E10
Saungka Myanmar 78 B2
Sauquoit U.S.A. 177 J2
Saur, Khrebet *mts* China/Kazakh. 88 D2
Saurieši Latvia 42 F5
Saurimo Angola 127 D7
formerly known as Henrique de Carvalho
Sausalito U.S.A. 182 B4
Sausar India 96 C5
Sautar Angola 127 C7
Sava *r.* Europe 49 M9
Savá Hond. 186 B4
Sava Italy 57 J8
Savage U.S.A. 177 I6
Savage River Australia 147 E5
Savai'i *i.* Samoa 145 H3
historically known as Chatham Island
Savala *r.* Rus. Fed. 41 G6
Savalou Benin 125 F5
Savanat Iran *see* Eşţahbān
Savane *r.* Canada 169 G3
Savane Moz. 131 G3
Savanna U.S.A. 174 B3
Savannah *GA* U.S.A. 175 D5
Savannah *MO* U.S.A. 178 D4
Savannah *OH* U.S.A. 176 C5
Savannah *TN* U.S.A. 174 B5
Savannah *r.* U.S.A. 175 D5
Savannah Sound Bahamas 186 D1
Savannakhét Laos 78 D4
Savanna-la-Mar Jamaica 186 D3
Savanne Canada 172 C2
Savant Lake Canada 168 B3
Savantvadi India *see* Vadi
Savanur India 94 B3
Sävar Sweden 44 M3
Săvârșin Romania 58 D2
Sävast Sweden 44 M2
Savaştepe Turkey 106 A3
Savè Benin 125 F4
Save *r.* France 50 H9
Save Moz. 131 G4
Save *r.* Moz./Zimbabwe 131 G4
formerly spelt Sabi
Sāveh Iran 100 B3
Savelugu Ghana 125 E4
Savenay France 50 E5
Saveretik Guyana 199 G3
Saverne France 51 N4
Savigliano Italy 51 N8
Săvinești Romania 58 H2
Savinja *r.* Slovenia 56 H2
Savino Rus. Fed. 40 G4
Savinskiy Rus. Fed. 40 G3
Savinskoye Rus. Fed. 43 U6
Savio *r.* Italy 56 E4
Savitaipale Fin. 45 N3
Savitri *r.* India 94 B2
Sävja Sweden 45 L4
Šavnik *Crna Gora* Yugo. 58 A6
Savoie *reg.* France *see* Savoy
Savona Italy 56 A4
Savonlinna Fin. 45 O3
Savonranta Fin. 44 O3
Savoonga U.S.A. 164 B3
Savoy *reg.* France 51 M6
also spelt Savoie
Savozero, Ozero *l.* Rus. Fed. 43 O1
Şavşat Turkey 107 E2
Sävsjö Sweden 45 K4
Savu *i.* Indon. 75 B5
also spelt Sawu
Savudrija, Rt *pt* Croatia 56 F3
Savukoski Fin. 44 O2
Savur Turkey 107 E3
Savute *r.* Botswana 130 E3
Savuti Botswana 131 E3
Saw Myanmar 78 A3
Şawab, Wādī aş *watercourse* Iraq 109 K4
Şawāb, Wādī aş *watercourse* Syria 109 L3
Sawahlunto Indon. 76 C3
Sawai, Teluk *b.* Indon. 75 D3
Sawai Madhopur India 96 C4
Sawan Indon. 77 F3
Sawan Myanmar 78 B2
Sawankhalok Thai. 78 B4
also known as Wang Mai Khon
Sawar India 96 B4
Sawara Japan 91 G7
Sawasaki-bana *pt* Japan 90 F6
Sawata Japan 90 F6
Sawatch Range *mts* U.S.A. 180 F5
Sawdā', Jabal as *hills* Libya 120 B2
Sawi, Ao *b.* Thai. 79 B6
Şawl Egypt 108 C8
Sawla Ghana 124 E4
Sawmills Zimbabwe 131 F3
Sawn China 86 A4
Şawqirah, Dawḩat *b.* Oman 105 G4
English form Şawqirah Bay
Şawqirah, Ra's *c.* Oman 105 G4
Şawqirah Bay Oman *see* Şawqirah, Dawḩat
Sawtell Australia 147 G2
Sawtooth Mountains *hills* U.S.A. 174 B2
Sawtooth Range *mts* *ID* U.S.A. 180 D3
Sawtooth Range *mts* *WA* U.S.A. 180 B2
Sawu Indon. 75 B5
Sawu *i.* Indon. *see* Savu
Sawu Sea Indon. 75 B5
Saxby *r.* Australia 149 D3
Saxnäs Sweden 44 K2
Saxony *land* Germany *see* Sachsen
Saxony-Anhalt *land* Germany *see* Sachsen-Anhalt
Saxton *KY* U.S.A. 176 A9
Saxton *PA* U.S.A. 176 G5
Say Mali 124 D3
Say Niger 125 F3
Sayabouri Laos *see* Muang Xaignabouri
Sayafi *i.* Indon. 75 D2
Sayak Kazakh. 103 I3
also spelt Sayaq
Sayalkudi India 94 C4
Sayam *well* Niger 125 I3
Sayán Peru 200 A2
Sayang *i.* Indon. 75 D2
Sayano-Shushenskoye Vodokhranilishche *resr* Rus. Fed. 80 E2
Sayaq Kazakh. *see* Sayak
Sayat Turkm. 103 E5
also spelt Sayot; *formerly spelt* Sayyod
Sayda Lebanon *see* Sidon
Sāyen Iran 100 C4
Sayer Island Thai. 79 B6
Sayghān Afgh. 101 F3
Şayḩ *well* Yemen 104 D4
Sayḩ al Aḩmar *reg.* Oman 105 G3
Sayḩūt Yemen 105 E5
Sayingpan China 86 B3
Saykhin Kazakh. 102 A2
also spelt Sayqyn
Sāylac Somalia 128 D2
Saylan *country* Asia *see* Sri Lanka
Saynshand Mongolia 85 F2
Sayn-Ust Mongolia 84 B2
Sayot Turkm. *see* Sayat
Say-Ötesh Kazakh. *see* Say-Utes
Şayqal, Baḩr *imp. l.* Syria 109 I4
Sayqyn Kazakh. *see* Saykhin
Sayram Hu *salt l.* China 88 C2

Sayramskiy, Pik mt. Uzbek. 103 G4
Sayre OK U.S.A. 179 C5
Sayre PA U.S.A. 177 I4
Sayreville U.S.A. 177 K5
Sayula Jalisco Mex. 184 E5
Sayula Veracruz Mex. 185 G5
Say'ūn Yemen 105 E4
Say-Utes Kazakh. 102 C3
also spelt Say-Ötesh
Sayward Canada 166 E5
Sayy well Oman 105 G4
Sayyod Turkm. see Sayat
Sazan i. Albania 58 A8
Sázava r. Czech Rep. 49 L6
Sazonovo Rus. Fed. 43 Q2
Saztöbe Kazakh. see Sastobe
Sbaa Alg. 123 E3
Sbeitla Tunisia 123 H2
Sbiba Tunisia 57 B13
Scaddan Australia 151 C7
Scaër France 50 C4
Scafell Pike hill U.K. 47 I9
Scalea Italy 57 H9
Scaletta Zanclea Sicilia Italy 57 H10
Scalloway U.K. 46 K3
Scalpaigh, Eilean i. U.K. see Scalpay
Scalpay i. U.K. 46 F6
also known as Scalpaigh, Eilean
Scandicci Italy 56 D5
Scansano Italy 56 D6
Scânteia Romania 58 I4
Scanzano Jonico Italy 57 I8
Scapa Flow inlet U.K. 46 I5
Scarba i. U.K. 46 G7
Scarborough Canada 168 E5
Scarborough Trin. and Tob. 187 H5
Scarborough U.K. 47 L9
Scarborough Shoal sea feature S. China Sea 73 E3
Scargill N.Z. 153 G10
Scarinish U.K. 46 F7
Scarp i. U.K. 46 E5
Scarpanto i. Greece see Karpathos
Scaterie Island Canada 169 J4
Scawfell Shoal sea feature S. China Sea 77 D1
Sceale Bay Australia 146 B3
Šćedro i. Croatia 56 I5
Schaale r. Germany 48 H2
Schaalsee l. Germany 48 H2
Schaalsee park Germany 48 H2
Schaffhausen Switz. 51 O5
Schagen Neth. 48 B3
Schakalskuppe Namibia 130 C5
Schao watercourse Afgh./Iran 101 E4
Scharbeutz Germany 48 H1
Schärding Austria 49 K7
Scharhörn sea feature Germany 48 F2
Schaumburg U.S.A. 172 E8
Scheeßel Germany 48 G2
Schefferville Canada 169 H2
formerly known as Knob Lake
Scheibbs Austria 49 M7
Schell Creek Range mts U.S.A. 183 J3
Schellsburg U.S.A. 176 G5
Schellville U.S.A. 182 B3
Schenectady U.S.A. 177 L3
Schenefeld Germany 48 G2
Schertz U.S.A. 179 C6
Schesaplana mt. Austria/Switz. 51 P5
Scheßlitz Germany 48 I6
Schierling Germany 48 J7
Schiermonnikoog i. Neth. 48 D2
Schiermonnikoog Nationaal Park nat. park Neth. 48 D2
Schiers Switz. 51 P6
Schimatari Greece 59 E10
also known as Skhimatárion
Schio Italy 56 D3
Schirmeck France 51 N4
Schitu Duca Romania 58 I1
Schiza i. Greece 59 C12
also spelt Skhiza
Schkeuditz Germany 49 J4
Schladen Germany 48 H3
Schladming Austria 49 K8
Schlei r. Germany 48 H1
Schleiz Germany 48 I5
Schleswig Germany 48 G1
Schleswig-Holstein land Germany 48 G1
Schleswig-Holsteinisches Wattenmeer, Nationalpark nat. park Germany 48 F1
Schlosshof tourist site Austria 49 N7
Schloß Holte-Stukenbrock Germany 48 F4
Schluchsee Germany 48 F8
Schlüchtern Germany 48 G5
Schlüsselburg Rus. Fed. see Shlissel'burg
Schmallenberg Germany 48 F4
Schmidt Island Rus. Fed. see Shmidta, Ostrov
Schmidt Peninsula Rus. Fed. see Shmidta, Poluostrov
Schmidtsdrif S. Africa 132 I5
Schneidemühl Poland see Piła
Schneverdingen Germany 48 G2
Schoemanskloof pass S. Africa 133 O2
Schoharie U.S.A. 177 K3
Schokland tourist site Neth. 48 C3
Schombee S. Africa 133 J8
Schönebeck (Elbe) Germany 48 I3
Schönefeld airport Germany 49 K3
Schöningen Germany 48 H3
Schoodic Point U.S.A. 177 R1
Schoolcraft U.S.A. 172 H8
Schoonhoven Neth. 48 B4
Schöpfl hill Austria 49 N7
Schorfheide reg. Germany 49 K3
Schouten Island Australia 147 F5
Schouten Islands P.N.G. 73 J7
Schrankogel mt. Austria 48 I8
Schreiber Canada 168 C3
Schrems Austria 49 M7
Schrobenhausen Germany 48 I7
Schroon Lake U.S.A. 177 L2
Schröttersburg Poland see Płock
Schulenburg U.S.A. 179 C6
Schull Rep. of Ireland 47 C12
Schultz Lake Canada 167 L1
Schuyler U.S.A. 178 C3
Schuyler Lake U.S.A. 177 J3
Schuylerville U.S.A. 177 L3
Schuylkill Haven U.S.A. 177 I5
Schwaan Germany 49 J2
Schwabach Germany 48 I6
Schwäbische Alb mts Germany 48 F8
Schwäbisch-Fränkischer Wald, Naturpark nature res. Germany 48 G7
Schwäbisch Hall Germany 48 G6
Schwabmünchen Germany 48 H7
Schwalm r. Germany 51 P1
Schwanden Switz. 51 P5
Schwandorf Germany 48 J6
Schwaner, Pegunungan mts Indon. 77 F3
Schwangau Germany 48 H8
Schwartz Range mts Antarctica 223 D2
Schwarzenbek Germany 48 H2
Schwarzenberg Germany 49 J5
Schwarzer Mann hill Germany 48 D5
Schwarzrand mts Namibia 130 C5
Schwarzwald mts Germany see Black Forest
Schwaz Austria 48 I8
Schwedeneck Germany 48 H1
Schwedt an der Oder Germany 49 L2
Schweinfurt Germany 48 H5
Schweiz country Europe see Switzerland
Schweizer-Reneke S. Africa 133 J4
Schwerin Germany 48 I2
Schweriner See l. Germany 48 I2
Schweriner Seenlandschaft park Germany 48 I2
Schwyz Switz. 51 O5
Sciacca Sicilia Italy 57 F11
Scicli Sicilia Italy 57 G12
Science Hill U.S.A. 176 A8
Scilla Italy 57 H10
Scilly, Île atoll Fr. Polynesia see Manuae
Scilly, Isles of U.K. 47 F14
Scio U.S.A. 176 D5
Scioto r. U.S.A. 176 C7
Scipio U.S.A. 183 L2
Scobey U.S.A. 180 F2
Scodra Albania see Shkodër
Scofield Reservoir U.S.A. 183 M2
Scone Australia 147 F3
Scordia Sicilia Italy 57 G11
Scoresby Land reg. Greenland 165 Q2
Scoresbysund Greenland see Ittoqqortoormiit
Scoresby Sund sea chan. Greenland see Kangertittivaq
Scorniceşti Romania 58 F4
Scorpion Bight b. Australia 151 D7
Scorzè Italy 56 E3
Scotia Sea S. Atlantic Ocean 217 K9
Scotland admin. div. U.K. 46 I6
historically known as Caledonia
europe [environments] 36–37
Scotland U.S.A. 177 I7
Scotstown Canada 169 G4
Scott, Cape Australia 148 A2
Scott, Cape Canada 166 D5
Scott, Mount hill U.S.A. 179 C5
Scott Base research station Antarctica 223 L1
Scottburgh S. Africa 133 O7
Scott City U.S.A. 178 B4
Scott Coast Antarctica 223 K1
Scott Glacier Antarctica 223 G2
Scott Glacier Antarctica 223 N1
Scott Inlet Canada 165 L2
Scott Island Antarctica 223 L2
Scott Islands Canada 166 D5
Scott Mountains Antarctica 223 D2
Scott Reef Australia 150 C2
Scottsbluff U.S.A. 178 B3
Scottsboro U.S.A. 174 C5
Scottsburg U.S.A. 174 C4
Scottsdale Australia 147 E5
Scotts Head Dominica 187 H4
Scottsville KY U.S.A. 174 C4
Scottsville VA U.S.A. 176 G8
Scottville U.S.A. 172 G7
Scourie U.K. 46 G5
Scranton U.S.A. 177 J4
Scugog, Lake Canada 168 E4
Scunthorpe U.K. 47 L10
Scuol Switz. 51 Q6
Scupi Macedonia see Skopje
Scutari Albania see Shkodër
Scutari, Lake Albania/Yugo. 58 A6
also known as Shkodrës, Liqeni i or Skadarsko Jezero
Seaboard U.S.A. 176 H9
Seabrook, Lake salt flat Australia 151 B6
Seaca Romania 58 F4
Seaford U.K. 47 M13
Seaford U.S.A. 177 J7
Seaforth Canada 173 L7
Seahorse Bank sea feature Phil. 74 A4
also known as Routh Bank
Seal r. Canada 167 M3
Seal, Cape S. Africa 132 H11
Sea Lake Australia 147 D3
Seal Bay Antarctica 223 X2
Seal Cove Canada 169 J3
Seal Island U.S.A. 177 Q2
Seal Lake Canada 169 I2
Sealy U.S.A. 179 C6
Seaman U.S.A. 176 B7
Seaman Range mts U.S.A. 183 I4
Searcy U.S.A. 174 B5
Searles Lake U.S.A. 183 G6
Searsport U.S.A. 177 Q1
Seascale U.K. 47 I9
Seaside CA U.S.A. 182 C5
Seaside OR U.S.A. 180 B3
Seaside Park U.S.A. 177 K6
Seaton Glacier Antarctica 223 D2
Seattle U.S.A. 180 B3
Sea View S. Africa 133 J11
Seaview Range mts Australia 149 E3
Seaville U.S.A. 177 K6
Seaward Kaikoura Range mts N.Z. 153 H10
Seba Indon. 75 B5
Sebaco Nicaragua 186 B4
Sebago Lake U.S.A. 177 O2
Sebakwe Recreational Park Zimbabwe 127 F9
Sebangan, Teluk b. Indon. 77 F3
Sebangka i. Indon. 76 D2
Sebastea Turkey see Sivas
Sebastian U.S.A. 175 D7
Sebastián Vizcaíno, Bahía b. Mex. 184 B2
Sebasticook r. U.S.A. 177 P1
Sebastopol Ukr. see Sevastopol'
Sebastopol U.S.A. 182 B3
Sebatik i. Indon. 77 G1
Sebauh Sarawak Malaysia 77 F2
Sebayan, Bukit mt. Indon. 77 E3
Sebba Burkina 125 F3
Sebderat Eritrea 121 H6
Sebdou Alg. 123 E2
Sébékoro Mali 124 C3
Seben Turkey 106 B2
Sebenico Croatia see Šibenik
Sebennytos Egypt see Samannûd
Sebeş Romania 58 E3
Sebeş r. Romania 58 E2
Sebewaing U.S.A. 173 J7
Sebezh Rus. Fed. 43 J5
Şebinkarahisar Turkey 107 D2
Sebiş Romania 58 D2
Sebisseb, Oued r. Alg. 55 O9
Sebla r. Rus. Fed. 43 S3
Seblat, Gunung mt. Indon. 76 C3
Sebrell U.S.A. 177 H9
Sebring U.S.A. 175 D7
Sebuku i. Indon. 77 G3
Sebuku r. Indon. 77 G1
Sebuku, Teluk b. Indon. 77 G2
Sečanj Vojvodina, Srbija Yugo. 58 B3
Secaş r. Romania 58 E2
Secas, Islas is Panama 186 C6
Secchia r. Italy 56 D3
Seccia Mountains Eth. 128 C3
Sechelt Canada 166 F5
Sechenovo Rus. Fed. 40 H5
Sechura Peru 198 A6
Sechura, Bahía de b. Peru 198 A6
Second Cataract rapids Sudan see 2nd Cataract
Second Mesa U.S.A. 183 N6
Second Three Mile Opening sea chan. Australia 149 D2
Secos, Ilhéus is Cape Verde 124 [inset]
also known as Rombo, Ilhéus do
Sečovce Slovakia 49 S7
Secretary Island N.Z. 153 A13
Secunda S. Africa 133 N3
Secunderabad India 94 C2
Sécure r. Bol. 200 D3
Seda Latvia 42 G4
Seda r. Latvia 42 G4
Seda Lith. 42 D5
Seda r. Port. 54 C6
Sedalia U.S.A. 178 D4
Sedam India 94 C2
Sedan France 51 K3
Sedan U.S.A. 178 C4
Sedan Dip Australia 149 D3
Seddon N.Z. 153 I9
Seddonville N.Z. 153 F9
Sedeh Fārs Iran 100 C4
Sedeh Khorāsan Iran 101 D3
Sedgefield U.S.A. 176 F9
Sedgewick Canada 167 I4
Sedgwick U.S.A. 177 Q1
Sédhiou Senegal 124 B3
Sedico Italy 56 E2
Sedlčany Czech Rep. 49 L6
Sedlets Poland see Siedlce
Sedom Israel 108 G6
Sedona U.S.A. 183 M7
Sédrata Alg. 123 G1
Šeduva Lith. 42 E6
Sędziszów Poland 49 R5
Seebad Heringsdorf Germany 49 L2
Seeberg pass Austria/Slovenia 49 L9
Seehausen (Altmark) Germany 48 I3
Seeheim Namibia 130 C5
Seeheim-Jugenheim Germany 48 F6
Seekoegat S. Africa 132 G10
Seekoei r. S. Africa 133 I7
Seekoevlei Nature Reserve S. Africa 133 N4
Seela Pass Canada 166 B1
Seeley U.S.A. 183 I9
Seelig, Mount Antarctica 222 R1
Seelow Germany 49 L3
Seenu Atoll Maldives see Addu Atoll
Sées France 50 G4
Seesen Germany 48 H4
Seevetal Germany 48 H2
Sefadu Sierra Leone 124 C4
also known as Koidu
Seferihisar Turkey 59 H10
Sefid, Kūh-e mt. Iran 100 B3
Sefid, Kūh-e mts Iran 100 B4
Sefophe Botswana 131 E4
Ségala Mali 124 C3
Segalstad Norway 45 J3
Segama r. Sabah Malaysia 77 G1
Segamat Malaysia 76 C2
Segangane Morocco 55 H9
Şegarcea Romania 58 E4
Ségbana Benin 125 F4
Segen Wenz watercourse Eth. 128 C3
Segera Tanz. 129 C6
Segezha Rus. Fed. 40 E3
Seggeur, Oued watercourse Alg. 123 F2
Seghnān Afgh. 101 G2
Séghouane Alg. 55 N8
Segiz, Ozero salt l. Kazakh. 103 F3
Segontia U.K. see Caernarfon
Segontium U.K. see Caernarfon
Segonzac France 50 F7
Segorbe Spain 55 K5
Ségou Mali 124 D3
Ségou admin. reg. Mali 124 D3
Segovia Col. 198 C3
Segovia r. Hond./Nicaragua see Coco
Segovia Spain 54 G4
Segozerskoye, Ozero resr Rus. Fed. 40 E3
Segré France 50 F5
Segre r. Spain 55 L3
Séguédine Niger 125 I1
Séguéla Côte d'Ivoire 124 D5
Séguéla Mali 124 D3
formerly spelt Sagala
Séguénéga Burkina 125 E3
Seguin U.S.A. 179 C6
Segura r. Spain 55 K6
Segura, Sierra de mts Spain 55 I7
Sehithwa Botswana 130 D4
Sehlabathebe Lesotho 133 N6
Sehlabathebe National Park Lesotho 133 N6
Seho i. Indon. 75 C3
Sehore India 96 C5
Sehwan Pak. 101 F5
Seiche r. France 50 E5
Seignelay r. Canada 169 G3
Seikpyu Myanmar 78 A3
Seiland i. Norway 44 M1
Seiling U.S.A. 179 C4
Seille r. France 51 K6
Seille r. France 51 M3
Šeimena r. Lith. 42 D7
Sein, Île de i. France 50 B4
Seinäjoki Fin. 44 M3
Seine r. Canada 168 B3
Seine r. France 51 G3
Seine, Baie de b. France 50 F3
Seine, Sources de la tourist site France 51 K5
Seine, Val de valley France 51 J4
Sejipinang Indon. 77 F3
Seistan reg. Iran see Sīstan
Seitsemisen kansallispuisto nat. park Fin. 45 M3
Seival Brazil 204 G3
Sejny Poland 49 U1
Sekadau Indon. 77 E2
Sekanak, Teluk b. Indon. 76 D3
Sekatak Bengara Indon. 77 G2
Sekayu Indon. 76 C3
Sekčov r. Slovakia 49 S7
Seke China see Sêrtar
Seke-Banza Dem. Rep. Congo 127 B6
Sekhukhune S. Africa 133 O1
Seki Japan 91 E7
Seki Turkey 108 A1
Seki r. Turkey 108 A1
Sekicau, Gunung vol. Indon. 76 D4
Sekoma Botswana 131 D5
Sekondi Ghana 125 E5
Sek'ot'a Eth. 128 C1
Sekseŭil Kazakh. see Saksaul'skiy
Sekūheh Iran 101 E4
Sel r. Rus. Fed. see Shali
Selagan r. Indon. 76 C3
Selah U.S.A. 180 B3
Selangor state Malaysia 76 C2
Selargius Sardegna Italy 57 B9
Selaru i. Indon. 73 H8
Selatan, Tanjung pt Indon. 77 F4
Selatpanjang Indon. 76 C2
Selawik U.S.A. 164 C3
Selbjørnsfjorden sea chan. Norway 46 Q4
Selbu Norway 44 J3
Selby U.K. 47 K10
Selby U.S.A. 178 B2
Selbyville U.S.A. 177 J7
Selçuk Turkey 59 I11
also known as Akıncılar
Sele r. Italy 57 G8
Selebi-Phikwe Botswana 131 E4
formerly spelt Selebi-Pikwe
Selebi-Pikwe Botswana see Selebi-Phikwe
Selečka Planina mts Macedonia 58 C7
Selemdzha r. Rus. Fed. 82 C1
Selemdzhinskiy Khrebet mts Rus. Fed. 82 D1
Selendi Turkey 59 J10
Selenduma Rus. Fed. 85 E1

Selenga r. Rus. Fed. 85 E1
Part of the Yenisey-Angara-Selenga, 3rd longest river in Asia.
asia [landscapes] 62–63

Selenge Dem. Rep. Congo 126 C5
Selenge Mongolia 84 D1
Selenge prov. Mongolia 85 E1
Selenge Mörön r. Mongolia 85 E1
Selenginsk Rus. Fed. 85 E1
Selenicë Albania 58 A8
Sélestat France 51 N4
Seletar Sing. 76 [inset]
Seletar, Pulau i. Sing. 76 [inset]
Seletar Reservoir Sing. 76 [inset]
Seletinskoye Kazakh. 103 H1
also known as Sileti
Selety r. Kazakh. see Sileti
Seletyteniz, Ozero salt l. Kazakh. see Siletiteniz, Ozero
Seleucia Turkey see Silifke
Seleucia Pieria Turkey see Samandağı
Seleznevo Rus. Fed. 43 J1
Selezni Rus. Fed. 43 M6
Selfoss Iceland 44 [inset] B3
Sel'gon Stantsiya Rus. Fed. 82 D2
Selib Rus. Fed. 40 I3
Sélibabi Mauritania 124 B3
Seligenstadt Germany 48 F5
Seliger, Ozero l. Rus. Fed. 43 O4
Seligman U.S.A. 183 L6
Selikhino Rus. Fed. 82 E2
Selima Oasis Sudan 121 F4
Selimiye Turkey 59 I11
Sélingué, Lac de l. Mali 124 C4
Selinnkegni Mali 124 C3
Selinous r. Greece 59 D10
Selinsgrove U.S.A. 177 I5
Selinunte tourist site Sicilia Italy 57 E11
Selishche Rus. Fed. 43 O5
Selishchi Rus. Fed. 41 G5
Selitrennoye Rus. Fed. 102 A3
Seliu i. Indon. 77 D3
Selizharovo Rus. Fed. 43 O5
Selje Norway 44 I3
Seljord Norway 45 J4
Selkirk Canada 167 L5
Selkirk U.K. 46 J8
Selkirk Mountains Canada 167 G4
Selkopp Norway 44 N1
Sellia Marina Italy 57 I10
Sellore Island Myanmar see Saganthit Kyun
Selma AL U.S.A. 175 C5
Selma CA U.S.A. 182 E5
Selmer U.S.A. 174 B5
Selmeţ Wielki, Jezioro l. Poland 49 T2
Selong Indon. 77 G5
Selongey France 51 L5
Selonsrivier S. Africa 133 N2
Sélouma Guinea 124 C4
Selous, Mount Canada 166 C2
Selous Game Reserve nature res. Tanz. 129 C7
Selseleh-ye Pīr Shūrān mts Iran 101 E4
Selsey Bill hd U.K. 47 L13
Sel'tso Bryanskaya Oblast' Rus. Fed. 43 P8
Sel'tso Bryanskaya Oblast' Rus. Fed. 43 P8
Selty Rus. Fed. 40 J4
Seluan i. Indon. 77 D1
Selukwe Zimbabwe see Shurugwi
Selvagens, Ilhas is Madeira 122 B3
Selvānā Iran 100 A2
Selvas reg. Brazil 199 D6
Selviria Brazil 206 B7
Selway r. U.S.A. 180 D3
Selwyn Lake Canada 167 J2
Selwyn Mountains Canada 166 D1
Selwyn Range hills Australia 149 C4
Seman r. Albania 58 A8
Semangka, Teluk b. Indon. 76 D4
Semarang Indon. 77 E4
Sematan Sarawak Malaysia 77 E2
Semau i. Indon. 75 B5
Semayang, Danau l. Indon. 77 G3
Sembakung r. Indon. 77 G2
Sembawang Sing. 76 [inset]
Sembawang, Sungai r. Sing. 76 [inset]
Sembé Congo 126 B4
Şemdinli Turkey 107 F3
also known as Navşar
Semendire Srbija Yugo. see Smederevo
Semendua Dem. Rep. Congo 126 C5
Semendyayevo Rus. Fed. 43 T4
Semenic, Vârful mt. Romania 58 D3
Semenivka Ukr. 41 E5
also spelt Semenovka
Semenov Rus. Fed. 40 H4
Semenovka Ukr. see Semenivka
Semenovskoye Rus. Fed. 43 U3
Semeru, Gunung vol. Indon. 77 F5
Semey Kazakh. see Semipalatinsk
Semhar prov. Eritrea 104 B5
Semibratovo Rus. Fed. 43 U4
Semidi Islands U.S.A. 164 D4
Semigorodnyaya Rus. Fed. 43 V2
Semikarakorsk Rus. Fed. 41 G7
Semiluki Rus. Fed. 41 F6
Semily Czech Rep. 49 M5
Seminoe Reservoir U.S.A. 180 F4
Seminole U.S.A. 179 B5
Seminole, Lake U.S.A. 175 C6
Semiozernoye Kazakh. 103 F1
Semipalatinsk Kazakh. 103 J2
also known as Semey
Semirara i. Phil. 74 B3
Semirara Islands Phil. 74 B4
Semīrom Iran 100 B4
Semitau Indon. 77 E2
Semiyarka Kazakh. 103 I2
Semizbuga Kazakh. 103 H2
also known as Semizbughy
Semizbughy Kazakh. see Semizbuga
Semkhoz Rus. Fed. 43 T5
Sem Kolodezey Ukr. see Lenine
Semlac Romania 58 B2
Semlevo Smolenskaya Oblast' Rus. Fed. 43 O6
Semlevo Smolenskaya Oblast' Rus. Fed. 43 O6
Semnān Iran 100 C3
Semnān prov. Iran 100 B3
Sêmnyi China 84 D4
Semois r. Belgium 51 K3
Semonkong Lesotho 133 M6
Sempach Switz. 51 O5
Semporna Sabah Malaysia 77 G1
Sempu i. Indon. 77 F5
Sem Tripa Brazil 199 H6
Semtsy Rus. Fed. 43 O9
Semyonovskoye Rus. Fed. see Bereznik
Semyonovskoye Rus. Fed. see Ostrovskoye
Sên, Stœng r. Cambodia 79 D5
Sena Bol. 200 D2
Senador Canedo Brazil 206 D3
Senador Pompeu Brazil 202 E3
Senafe Eritrea 104 B5
Senaki Georgia 107 E2
formerly known as Mikha Tskhakaia or Tskhakaia
Sena Madureira Brazil 200 C2
Senanayake Samudra l. Sri Lanka 94 D5
Senanga Zambia 127 D9
Sénas France 51 L9
Senatobia U.S.A. 174 B5
Sendai Kagoshima Japan 91 B9
Sendai Miyagi Japan 90 G5
Sendai-wan b. Japan 90 G5
Sendelingsfontein S. Africa 133 K3
Senden Germany 48 H7
Şendreni Romania 58 I3
Sene r. Ghana 125 E5
Senebui, Tanjung pt Indon. 76 C2
Seneca IL U.S.A. 172 E9
Seneca KS U.S.A. 178 C4
Seneca OR U.S.A. 180 C3
Seneca PA U.S.A. 176 F4
Seneca Lake U.S.A. 177 I3
Seneca Rocks U.S.A. 176 F7
Senecaville Lake U.S.A. 176 D6
Senegal country Africa 124 B3
world [countries] 10–11
africa [countries] 114–117
Sénégal r. Mauritania/Senegal 124 A2
Seneka, Mys hd Rus. Fed. 82 E1
Senekal S. Africa 133 L5
Seney National Wildlife Refuge nature res. U.S.A. 172 G4
Senftenberg Germany 49 L4
Senga Malawi 129 B8
Senga Hill Zambia 127 F7
Sengar r. India 96 C4
Sengata Indon. 77 G2
Sengerema Tanz. 128 B5
Sengés Brazil 206 D11
Sengeyskiy, Ostrov i. Rus. Fed. 40 I1
Sengiley Rus. Fed. 41 I5
Sengirli, Mys pt Kazakh. see Syngyrli, Mys
Sengirli, Mys pt Kazakh. 102 C4
also spelt Syngyrli, Mys
Sêngli Co l. China 89 D6
Senguerr r. Arg. 205 C7
Sengwa r. Zimbabwe 131 F3
Senhit prov. Eritrea 104 B5
Senhor do Bonfim Brazil 202 D4
Senica Slovakia 49 O7
Senigallia Italy 56 F5
Senj Croatia 56 G4
Senja i. Norway 44 L1
Senjehopen Norway 44 L1
Şenkaya Turkey 107 E2
also known as Örtülü
Senko Guinea 124 C4
Senkobo Zambia 127 E9
Sen'kove Ukr. 41 F6
Sen'kovo Rus. Fed. 43 L6
Şenköy Turkey 108 H1
Senku Jammu and Kashmir 96 C2
Senlac S. Africa 132 H2
Senlin Shan mt. China 82 C4
Senlis France 51 I3
Senmonorom Cambodia 79 D5
Sennar Sudan 121 G6
Sennar state Sudan 121 G6
Senneterre Canada 168 E3
Senno Belarus see Syanno
Senonches France 50 H4
Senorbì Sardegna Italy 57 B9
Senqu r. Lesotho 133 L7
Sens France 51 J4
Sensuntepeque El Salvador 185 H6
Senta Vojvodina, Srbija Yugo. 58 B3
also spelt Zenta
Sentinel Peak Canada 166 F4
Sentinel Range mts Antarctica 222 S1
Sentinum Italy see Sassoferrato
Sentosa i. Sing. 76 [inset]
formerly known as Blakang Mati, Pulau
Şenyurt Turkey 107 E3
also known as Derbesiye
Seo de Urgell Spain see La Seu d'Urgell
Seonath r. India 97 D5
Seondha India 96 C4
Seoni India 96 C5
Seoni Chhapara India 96 C5
Seoni-Malwa India 96 C5

Seoul S. Korea 83 B5
Capital of South Korea. Also spelt Sŏul.
world [cities] 24–25

Séoune r. France 50 G8
Sepanjang i. Indon. 77 F4
Separation Point N.Z. 152 G8
Separation Well Australia 150 C4
Separ Shāhābād Iran 100 A3
Sepasu Indon. 77 G2
Sepatini r. Brazil 200 D1
Sepetiba, Baía de b. Brazil 207 I10
Sepik r. P.N.G. 73 J7
Sepinang Indon. 77 G2
Sepino Italy 56 G7
Sep'o N. Korea 83 B5
Sępólno Krajeńskie Poland 49 O2
Sepotuba r. Brazil 201 F3
Seppa India 97 G4
Şepreuş Romania 58 C2
Septèmes-les-Vallons France 51 L9
Sept-Îles Canada 169 H3
also known as Seven Islands
Sept-Îles-Port-Cartier, Réserve Faunique de nature res. Canada 169 H3
Sepupa Botswana 130 D3
Seputih r. Indon. 77 D4
Sequillo r. Spain 54 F3
Sequoia National Park U.S.A. 182 F5
Serae prov. Eritrea 104 B5
Serafimovich Rus. Fed. 41 G6
Sêraitang China see Baima
Seram i. Indon. 75 D3
English form Ceram
Seram, Laut sea Indon. 75 D3
English form Ceram Sea
Serang Indon. 77 D4
Serangoon, Pulau i. Sing. 76 [inset]
also known as Coney Island
Serangoon, Sungai r. Sing. 76 [inset]
Serangoon Harbour b. Sing. 76 [inset]
Serapeum Egypt 108 D7
Serapong, Mount hill Sing. 76 [inset]
Serasan i. Indon. 77 E2
Serasan, Selat sea chan. Indon. 77 E2
Seraya i. Indon. 77 E2
Serbāl, Gebel mt. Egypt 108 E9
Serbia aut. rep. Yugo. see Srbija
Sêrbug Co l. China 89 E5
Sêrca China 97 G3
Serdica Bulg. see Sofia
Serdo Eth. 128 D2
Serdoba r. Rus. Fed. 41 H5
Serdobsk Rus. Fed. 41 H5
Serebryanka Rus. Fed. 40 J3
Serebryansk Kazakh. 88 C1
Serebryanyye Prudy Rus. Fed. 43 T7
Sered' Slovakia 49 O7
Sereda Moskovskaya Oblast' Rus. Fed. 43 Q6
Sereda Yaroslavskaya Oblast' Rus. Fed. 43 V4
Seredeyskiy Rus. Fed. 43 Q7
Seredka Rus. Fed. 43 J3
Serednikovo Rus. Fed. 43 U6
Seredniy Kuyal'nyk r. Ukr. 58 L2
Seredyna-Buda Rus. Fed. 43 P9
Seredyne Ukr. 49 T7
Şereflikoçhisar Turkey 106 C3
Serein r. France 51 J5
Seremban Malaysia 76 C2
Serengeti National Park Tanz. 128 B5
Serengeti Plain Tanz. 128 B5
Serenje Zambia 127 F8
Serere Uganda 128 B4
Serezha r. Rus. Fed. 40 G5
Serezha r. Rus. Fed. 43 L5
Sergach Rus. Fed. 40 H5
Sergeikha Rus. Fed. 43 V5
Sergelen Dornod Mongolia 85 G1
Sergelen Sühbaatar Mongolia 85 F2
Sergen Turkey 58 I7
Sergeyevka Rus. Fed. 90 C3
Sergeyevka Akmolinskaya Oblast' Kazakh. 103 G2
Sergeyevka Severnyy Kazakhstan Kazakh. 103 F1
Sergino Rus. Fed. 38 G3
Sergipe state Brazil 202 E4
Sergiyev Posad Rus. Fed. 43 T5
formerly known as Zagorsk
Sergiyevskiy Rus. Fed. see Fakel
Sergiyevskoye Rus. Fed. 43 S9
Sergo Ukr. see Stakhanov
Serhiyivka Ukr. 58 L2
Seria Brunei 77 F1
Serian Sarawak Malaysia 77 E2
Seribu, Kepulauan is Indon. 77 D4
Seribudolok Indon. 76 B2
Serifos Greece 59 F11
Serifos i. Greece 59 F11
Serifou, Steno sea chan. Greece 59 F11
Sérignan France 51 J9
Sérigny r. Canada 169 G2
Sérigny, Lac l. Canada 169 G2
Serik Turkey 106 B3
Serikbuya China 88 B4
Serikkembelo Indon. 75 C3
Sèrinama Madag. 131 [inset] J3
Seringa, Serra da hills Brazil 199 I6
Seringapatam Reef Australia 150 C2
Serinhisar Turkey 59 K11
Serio r. Italy 56 B3
Serio, Parco del park Italy 56 B3
Sêrkang China see Nyainrong
Sermata i. Indon. 75 D5
Sermata, Kepulauan is Indon. 75 D5
Sermersuaq glacier Greenland 165 M2
also known as Humboldt Gletscher
Sermersuaq glacier Greenland 165 N2
also known as Steenstrup Gletscher
Sērmūkši Latvia 42 G4
Sernovodsk Rus. Fed. 41 I5
Sernur Rus. Fed. 40 I4
Sernyy Zavod Turkm. see Kukurtli
Serón Spain 55 I7
Seronga Botswana 130 D3
Serouenout well Alg. 123 G4
Serov Rus. Fed. 38 G4
Serowe Botswana 131 E4
Serpa Port. 54 D7
Serpa Pinto Angola see Menongue
Serpent r. Canada 169 G3
Serpent, Vallée du watercourse Mali 124 C3
Serpentine r. Australia 151 A7
Serpentine Lakes salt flat Australia 146 A2
Serpent's Mouth sea chan. Trin. and Tob./Venez. 187 H5
Serpeysk Rus. Fed. 43 Q7
Serpis r. Spain 55 K6
Serpneve Ukr. 58 K2
Serpukhov Rus. Fed. 43 S7
Serra Brazil 203 D7
Serra Bonita Brazil 206 G2
Serra da Bocaina, Parque Nacional da nat. park Brazil 203 C7
Serra da Canastra, Parque Nacional da nat. park Brazil 206 G7
Serra da Capivara, Parque Nacional da nat. park Brazil 202 D4
Serra da Estrela, Parque Natural da nature res. Port. 54 D4
Serra da Mesa, Represa resr Brazil 202 B5
Serra das Araras Brazil 207 H2
Serra de Outes Spain 54 C2
Serradilla Spain 54 E5
Serra do Divisor, Parque Nacional da nat. park Brazil 200 B2
Serra do Navio Brazil 199 H4
Serra dos Aimorés Brazil 207 M4
Serra do Salitre Brazil 206 G6
Sérrai Greece see Serres
Serramanna Sardegna Italy 57 A9
Serrana Brazil 206 F8
Serrana Bank sea feature Caribbean Sea 186 C4
Serranía de la Neblina, Parque Nacional nat. park Venez. 199 E4
Serranilla Bank sea feature Caribbean Sea 186 D4
Serrano i. Chile 205 B8
Serranópolis Brazil 206 A5
Serraria, Ilha i. Brazil see Queimada, Ilha
Serra San Bruno Italy 57 I10
Serras de Aire e Candeeiros, Parque Natural das nature res. Port. 54 C5
Serra Talhada Brazil 202 E3
Serravalle Scrivia Italy 56 A4
Serre r. France 51 J3
Serres Greece 58 E7
also known as Sérrai
Serrezuela Arg. 204 D3
Serrinha Brazil 202 E4
Serrita Brazil 202 E3
Sêrro Brazil 203 D6
Serrota mt. Spain 54 F4
Sers Tunisia 57 A12
Sersou, Plateau du Alg. 55 M9
Sertã Port. 54 C5
Sertânia Brazil 202 E4
Sertanópolis Brazil 206 B10
Sertão de Camapuã reg. Brazil 206 A6
Sertãozinho Brazil 206 F8
Sêrtar China 86 B1
also known as Seke
Sertavul Geçidi pass Turkey 108 E1
Sertolovo Rus. Fed. 43 L1
Serua vol. Indon. 75 D4
Serui Indon. 73 I7
Serule Botswana 131 E4
Serutu i. Indon. 77 E3
Seruyan r. Indon. 77 F3
Servach r. Belarus 42 I7
Servia Greece 59 D8
Servol r. Spain 55 L4
also spelt Cerbol
Serwaru Indon. 75 C5
Sêrxu China 86 A1
also known as Nixia
Sesayap Indon. 77 G2
Sesayap r. Indon. 77 G2
Sese Dem. Rep. Congo 126 E4
Sesekinika Canada 173 M2
Sesel country Indian Ocean see Seychelles
Sesepe Indon. 75 C3
Sesfontein Namibia 130 B3
Seshachalam Hills India 94 C3
Seshcha Rus. Fed. 43 O8
Sesheke Zambia 127 E9
Sesia r. Italy 56 A3
Seskar Furö i. Sweden 44 M2
Seskilo i. Greece 59 I12
Sesostris Bank sea feature India 94 A3
S'Espalmador i. Spain 55 M6
also known as Espalmador, Isla
Sessa Angola 127 D8
Ses Salines, Cap de c. Spain 55 O5
also spelt Salinas, Cabo de
Sestra r. Rus. Fed. 43 S5
Sestri Levante Italy 56 B4
Sestroretsk Rus. Fed. 43 K1
Sestrunj i. Croatia 56 G4
Sestu Sardegna Italy 57 B9
Šešupė r. Lith./Rus. Fed. 42 D6
Sesvete Croatia 56 I3
Set r. Spain 55 L3
Set, Phou mt. Laos 79 D5
Sète France 51 J9
Sete Barras Brazil 206 F11
Šetekšna r. Lith. 42 G6
Sete Lagoas Brazil 203 C6
Setermoen Norway 44 L1
Setesdal valley Norway 45 I4
Seti r. Nepal 97 D3
Seti r. Nepal 97 E4
Setia Italy see Sezze
Sétif Alg. 123 G1
also spelt Stif
Setit r. Africa 121 H6
Seto Japan 91 E7
Seto-naikai sea Japan 91 C8
English form Inland Sea
Seto-naikai National Park Japan 91 C7
Setsan Myanmar 78 A4
Settat Morocco 122 D2
Setté Cama Gabon 126 A5
Settepani, Monte mt. Italy 56 A4
Settimo Torinese Italy 51 N7
Settle U.K. 47 J9
Settlement Creek r. Australia 148 C3
Settlers S. Africa 133 M1
Setúbal r. Brazil 207 K3
Setúbal Port. 54 C6
Setúbal admin. dist. Port. 54 C6
Setúbal, Baía de b. Port. 54 B6
Setubinha Brazil 207 K4
Seugne r. France 50 F7
Seul, Lac l. Canada 168 A3
Seurre France 51 L5
Sev r. Rus. Fed. 43 P9

S index

Sevan Armenia 107 F2
Sevan, Lake Armenia 107 F2
also known as Sevan, Ozero or Sevana Lich
Sevan, Ozero l. Armenia see Sevan, Lake
Sevana Lich l. Armenia see Sevan, Lake
Sevaruyo Bol. 200 D4
Sevastopol' Ukr. 41 E7
English form Sebastopol
Seven Islands Canada see Sept-Îles
Sevenoaks S. Africa 133 O6
Sevenoaks U.K. 47 M12
Seventeen Seventy Australia 149 F5
Seventy Mile House Canada see 70 Mile House
Sévérac-le-Château France 51 J8
Severino Ribeiro Brazil 204 G3
Severka r. Rus. Fed. 43 T6
Severn r. Australia 147 F2
Severn r. Canada 168 C2
Severn mt. N.Z. 153 H10
Severn S. Africa 132 G3
Severn r. U.K. 47 J12
Severn U.S.A. 177 H9
Severnaya Dvina r. Rus. Fed. 40 G2
English form Northern Dvina
Severnaya Mylva r. Rus. Fed. 40 K3
Severnaya Osetiya-Alaniya, Respublika aut. rep. Rus. Fed. 41 H8
English form North Ossetia; formerly known as Severo-Osetinskaya A.S.S.R.
Severnaya Sos'va r. Rus. Fed. 38 G3
Severnaya Zemlya is Rus. Fed. 39 K1
English form North Land
Severn Lake Canada 168 B2
Severnoye Rus. Fed. 41 J5
formerly known as Sol-Karmala
Severnyy Moskovskaya Oblast' Rus. Fed. 43 S5
Severnyy Nenetskiy Avtonomnyy Okrug Rus. Fed. 40 I1
Severnyy Respublika Komi Rus. Fed. 40 M2
Severnyy Anyuyskiy Khrebet mts Rus. Fed. 39 R3
Severnyy Berezovyy, Ostrov i. Rus. Fed. 43 J1
Severnyy Chink Ustyurta esc. Kazakh. 102 D3
Severnyy Kazakhstan admin. div. Kazakh. 103 G1
English form North Kazakhstan Oblast; also known as Soltüstik Qazaqstan Oblysy; long form Severo-Kazakhstanskaya Oblast'
Severnyy Kommunar Rus. Fed. 40 J4
Severnyy Suchan Rus. Fed. see Uglekamensk
Severnyy Ural mts Rus. Fed. 40 K3
Severobaykal'sk Rus. Fed. 81 H1
Severo-Baykalskoye Nagor'ye mts Rus. Fed. 81 I1
Severodonetsk Ukr. see Syeverodonets'k
Severodvinsk Rus. Fed. 40 F2
formerly known as Molotovsk
Severo-Kazakhstanskaya Oblast' admin. div. Kazakh. see Severnyy Kazakhstan
Severo-Kuril'sk Rus. Fed. 39 P4
Severomorsk Rus. Fed. 44 P1
formerly known as Vayenga
Severoonezhsk Rus. Fed. 40 F3
Severo-Osetinskaya A.S.S.R. aut. rep. Rus. Fed. see Severnaya Osetiya-Alaniya, Respublika
Severo-Sibirskaya Nizmennost' lowland Rus. Fed. see North Siberian Lowland
Severoural'sk Rus. Fed. 40 K3
Severo-Yeniseyskiy Rus. Fed. 39 J3
Severo-Zadonsk Rus. Fed. 43 T7
Severskaya Rus. Fed. 107 D1
Severskiy Donets r. Rus. Fed./Ukr. 41 G7
English form Northern Donets; also spelt Sivers'kyy Donets'
Seveso Italy 56 B3
Sevettijärvi Fin. 44 O1
also spelt Čevetjävri
Sevier U.S.A. 183 L3
Sevier r. U.S.A. 183 L2
Sevier Bridge Reservoir U.S.A. 183 M2
Sevier Desert U.S.A. 183 L2
Sevier Lake U.S.A. 183 K3
Sevierville U.S.A. 174 D5
Sevilla Col. 198 C3
Sevilla Spain see Seville
Seville Spain 54 F7
also spelt Sevilla; historically known as Hispalis
Sevlievo Bulg. 58 G5
Sevnica Slovenia 56 H2
Sevojno Srbija Yugo. 58 A5
Sèvre Nantaise r. France 50 E5
Sevsk Rus. Fed. 43 P9
Sewand r. India 94 B2
Sewani India 96 B3
Seward AK U.S.A. 164 E3
Seward IL U.S.A. 172 D8
Seward NE U.S.A. 178 C3
Seward PA U.S.A. 176 F5
Seward Mountains Antarctica 222 T2
Seward Peninsula U.S.A. 164 C3
Sewell Chile 204 C4
Sewell Inlet Canada 166 C4
Sexi Spain see Almuñécar
Sexsmith Canada 166 G4
Sextín Mex. 184 D3
Sextín r. Mex. 184 D3
Seyah Band Koh mts Afgh. 101 E3
Seyakha Rus. Fed. 38 H2
Seybaplaya Mex. 185 H5
▶Seychelles country Indian Ocean 218 K6
also spelt Sesel
africa [countries] ▶ 114–117
Seydi Turkm. 103 E5
formerly known as Neftezavodsk
Seydişehir Turkey 106 B3
Seyðisfjörður Iceland 44 [inset] D2
Seyfe Gölü salt flat Turkey 106 C3
Seyhan Turkey see Adana
Seyhan r. Turkey 106 C3
Seyitgazi Turkey 106 B3
Seyitömer Turkey 59 K9
Seym r. Rus. Fed./Ukr. 41 E6
Seymchan Rus. Fed. 39 P3
Seymour Australia 147 E4
Seymour S. Africa 133 K9
Seymour IN U.S.A. 174 C4
Seymour TX U.S.A. 179 C5
Seymour Inlet Canada 166 E5
Seymour Range mts Australia 148 B5
Seynod France 51 M7
Seypan i. N. Mariana Is see Saipan
Seytan r. Turkey 58 I7
Seyyedābād Afgh. 101 G3
Sežana Slovenia 56 F3
Sézanne France 51 J4
Sezela S. Africa 133 O7
Sezha r. Rus. Fed. 43 P6
Sezze Italy 56 F7
historically known as Setia
Sfakia Greece 59 F13
Sfântu Gheorghe Romania 58 G3
formerly spelt Sfîntu Gheorghe
Sfântu Gheorghe Romania 58 K4
Sfântu Gheorghe, Braţul watercourse Romania 58 K3
Sfântu Gheorghe-Palade-Perişor nature res. Romania 58 K4
Sfax Tunisia 123 H2
also spelt Aş Şafāqīs
Sfendami Greece 59 D8
Sfîntu Gheorghe Romania see Sfântu Gheorghe
Sfizef Alg. 55 K9
Sgiersch Poland see Zgierz
's-Gravenhage Neth. see The Hague
Sgurr Alasdair hill U.K. 46 F6
Sgurr Mor mt. U.K. 46 G6
Sgurr na Ciche mt. U.K. 46 G6
Sha r. China 85 G4
Shaanxi prov. China 87 D1
English form Shensi
Shaartuz Tajik. see Shahrtuz
Shaba prov. Dem. Rep. Congo see Katanga
Shâba Egypt 108 B6
Shabani Zimbabwe see Zvishavane
Shabbaz Uzbek. see Beruni
Shabeellaha Dhexe admin. reg. Somalia 128 E4
Shabeellaha Hoose admin. reg. Somalia 128 D4
Shabestar Iran 100 A2
Shabla Bulg. 58 J5
Shabla, Nos pt Bulg. 58 J5
Shablykino Rus. Fed. 43 Q9
Shabogamo Lake Canada 169 H2
Shabunda Dem. Rep. Congo 126 E5
Shabwah Yemen 105 D5
Shabwah governorate Yemen 105 D5
Shacha r. Rus. Fed. 43 V3
Shache China 88 B4
formerly known as Yarkand or Yarkant
Shacheng China see Huailai
Shackleton Coast Antarctica 223 L1
Shackleton Glacier Antarctica 223 M1
Shackleton Ice Shelf Antarctica 223 G2
Shackleton Range mts Antarctica 223 V1
Shadād Saudi Arabia 104 C3
Shadadkot Pak. 101 F5
Shadaogou China 87 D2
Shade U.S.A. 176 C6
Shādegān Iran 100 B4
Shādkām watercourse Iran 100 C4
Shadrinsk Rus. Fed. 38 G4
Shadwân Island Egypt see Shâkir, Gezîret
Shadwell U.S.A. 176 G7
Shady Grove U.S.A. 180 B4
Shady Spring U.S.A. 176 D8
Sha'fāt al Bashīr hill Syria 109 K2
Shafer, Lake U.S.A. 172 G10
Shafer Peak Antarctica 223 K2
Shafi'abad Iran 100 D2
Shafirkan Uzbek. 103 F4
also spelt Shofirkon; formerly spelt Shafrikan
Shafranovo Rus. Fed. 40 J5
Shafrikan Uzbek. see Shafirkan
Shafter U.S.A. 182 E6
Shaftesbury U.K. 47 J12
Shag r. N.Z. 153 E13
Shagamu r. Canada 168 C2
Shagamu Nigeria see Sagamu
Shagan watercourse Kazakh. 102 D3
Shagan watercourse Kazakh. 103 I2
Shagedu China 85 F4
also known as Jungar Qi
Shaghab oasis Saudi Arabia 104 B2
Shaghan Kazakh. see Chagan
Shaghyray Üstirti plat. Kazakh. see Shagyray, Plato
Shagonar Respublika Tyva Rus. Fed. 84 B1
Shagonar Respublika Tyva Rus. Fed. 84 B1
Shag Point N.Z. 153 E13
Shag Rocks is S. Georgia 217 L9
Shagyray, Plato plat. Kazakh. 102 D3
also known as Shaghyray Üstirti; formerly known as Chagrayskoye Plato
Shagyrlyk Uzbek. 102 D4
Shahabad Andhra Pradesh India 94 C2
Shahabad Haryana India 96 C3
Shahabad Karnataka India 94 C2
Shahabad Rajasthan India 96 C4
Shahabad Uttar Pradesh India 96 D4
Shāhābād Iran see Eslāmābād-e Gharb
Shahada India 96 B5
Shah Alam Malaysia 76 C2
Şhahana Pak. 101 E5
Şhahapur Karnataka India 94 B3
Shahapur Maharashtra India 94 B2
Shahbā' Syria 109 H5
Shahbazpur sea chan. Bangl. 97 F5
Shahdād Iran 100 D4
also known as Khabis
Shahdadpur Pak. 101 G5
Shahdol India 97 D5
Shahe Chongqing China 87 D2
Shahe Shandong China 85 H4
Shahe Shanxi China 85 G4
Shahejie China see Jiujiang
Shahepu China see Linze
Shahezhen China see Linze
Shahezhen China see Jiujiang
Shah Fuladi mt. Afgh. 101 F3
Shahganj India 97 D4
Shahgarh Madhya Pradesh India 96 C4
Shahgarh Rajasthan India 96 A4
Shaḥḥāt Libya 120 D1
Shāhīn Dezh Iran see Sa'īndezh
Shah Ismail Afgh. 101 F4
Shahjahanpur Uttar Pradesh India 96 C4
Shāh Jehān, Kūh-e mts Iran 100 D2
Shāh Jūy Afgh. 101 F3
Shāh Kūh mt. Iran 101 D4
Shahpur Karnataka India 94 C2
Shahpur Madhya Pradesh India 96 C5
Shahpur Madhya Pradesh India 96 C5
Shahpur Madhya Pradesh India 96 C5
Shāhpūr Iran see Salmās
Shahpur Balochistān Pak. 101 G4
Shahpur Punjab Pak. 101 H3
Shahpur Sindh Pak. 101 G5
Shahpura Madhya Pradesh India 96 C5
Shahpura Madhya Pradesh India 96 D5
Shahpura Rajasthan India 96 B4
Shahr oasis Saudi Arabia 105 E4
Shahrak Afgh. 101 F3
Shāhrakht Iran 101 E3
Shahran reg. Saudi Arabia 104 C4
Shahr-e Bābak Iran 100 C4
Shahr-e Kord Iran 100 B3
Shahr-e-Now Iran 101 E3
Shahrezā Iran see Qomishēh
Shahrisabz Uzbek. see Shakhrisabz
Shahriston Tajik. 101 G2
also spelt Shakhristan
Shahr Rey Iran 100 B3
Shahr Sultan Pak. 101 G4
Shahrtuz Tajik. 101 G2
also spelt Shaartuz
Shāhrūd Iran see Emāmrūd
Shāhrūd, Rūdkhāneh-ye r. Iran 100 B2
Shahrud Bustam reg. Iran 100 C3
Shāh Savārān, Kūh-e mts Iran 100 D4
Shāh Taqī Iran see Emām Taqī
Sha'ibān el Jiraniyat watercourse Saudi Arabia 109 J6
Shaidara, Step' plain Kazakh. 103 F4
Shaikh Husain mt. Pak. 101 F4
Shā'īr, Jabal mts Syria 109 I3
Sha'îra, Gebel mt. Egypt 108 F8
Shaistaganj Bangl. 97 F4
Shaj'ah, Jabal hill Saudi Arabia 105 E2
Shajapur India 96 C5
Shakar Bolāghī Iran 100 A2
Shakaskraal S. Africa 133 P6
Shakaville S. Africa 133 P6
Shakawe Botswana 130 D3
Shakespeare Island Canada 168 B3
Shakh Tajik. 101 G2
also known as Shoh
Shakhbuz Azer. see Şahbuz
Shakhovskaya Rus. Fed. 43 Q5
Shakhrikhan Uzbek. 103 H4
formerly known as Moskovskiy or Stalino
Shakhrisabz Uzbek. 103 F5
also spelt Shahrisabz
Shakhristan Tajik. see Shahriston
Shakhtars'k Ukr. 41 F6
also spelt Shakhtersk or Shakhtyorsk; formerly known as Katyk
Shakhtersk Ukr. see Shakhtars'k
Shakhtinsk Kazakh. 103 H2
Shakhty Rus. Fed. see Gusinoozersk
Shakhty Rus. Fed. 41 G7
Shakhtyorsk Ukr. see Shakhtars'k
Shakhun'ya Rus. Fed. 40 H4
Shaki Nigeria see Saki
Shâkir, Gezîret i. Egypt 121 G3
English form Shadwân Island
Shakopee U.S.A. 178 D2
Shakotan-hantō pen. Japan 90 G3
Shakotan-misaki c. Japan 90 G3
Shakou China 87 E3
Shala Hāyk' l. Eth. 128 C3
Shalakusha Rus. Fed. 40 G3
Shālamzār Iran 100 B3
Shalday Kazakh. 103 I2
Shalginskiy Kazakh. 103 G3
also known as Shalqīya; formerly known as Shalgiya
Shalgiya Kazakh. see Shalginskiy
Shali Rus. Fed. 41 H8
also known as Şela; formerly known as Mezhdurechnye
Shalim Oman 105 F4
Shaliuhe China see Gangca
Shalkar, Ozero salt l. Kazakh. 102 B2
also known as Shalqar Köli; formerly spelt Chalkar, Ozero
Shalkar Karashatau salt l. Kazakh. 103 E2
Shalkar-Yega-Kara, Ozero l. Rus. Fed. 103 E2
Shâlma Egypt 108 B6
Shalqar Kazakh. see Chelkar
Shalqar Köli salt l. Kazakh. see Shalkar, Ozero
Shalqīya Kazakh. see Shalginskiy
Shaluli Shan mts China 86 A2
Shaluni mt. India 97 H3
Shama r. Tanz. 129 B6
Shamâl Sînâ' governorate Egypt 108 D7
English form North Sinai; also known as Sinai ash Shamâlîya
Shamalzā'ī Afgh. 101 F4
Shamary Rus. Fed. 40 K4
Shāmat al Akbād des. Saudi Arabia 104 C1
Shamattawa Canada 167 M3
Shamattawa r. Canada 168 C2
Shamava Belarus 43 M7
Shambār Iran 100 B3
Shambe Sudan 128 A3
Shambu Eth. 128 C2
Shambuanda Dem. Rep. Congo 127 D6
Sham Chun r. China 87 [inset]
Shamgarh India 96 B4
Shamgong Bhutan see Zhemgang
Shamis U.A.E. 105 F3
Shamkhal Rus. Fed. 102 A4
Shamkhor Azer. see Şämkir
Shammar, Jabal reg. Saudi Arabia 104 C2
Shamoksha Rus. Fed. 43 O1
Shamrock U.S.A. 179 B5
Shamva Zimbabwe 131 F3
Shan state Myanmar 78 B3
Shancheng China see Nanjing
Shancheng China see Shanxian
Shand Afgh. 101 E4
Shandan China 84 D4
Shandian r. China 85 H3
Shandiz Iran 101 D2
Shandong prov. China 85 H4
English form Shantung
Shandong Bandao pen. China 85 I4
Shandrūkh Iraq 107 F4
Shandur Pass Pak. 101 H2
Shangani r. Zimbabwe 131 E3
Shangcai China 87 E1
also known as Caidu
Shangcheng China 87 E2
Shang Chu r. China 89 E6
Shangchuan Dao i. China 87 E4
Shangchuankou China see Minhe
Shangdu China 85 G3
Shangganling China 82 C3
Shanggao China 87 E2
also known as Aoyang
▶Shanghai China 87 G2
4th most populous city in Asia and 9th in the world.
world [cities] ▶ 24–25
Shanghai municipality China 87 G2
Shanghang China 87 F3
also known as Linjiang
Shanghe China 85 H4
Shanghekou China 83 B4
Shangji China see Xichuan
Shangjie China see Yangbi
Shangjin China 87 D1
Shangkuli China 85 I1
Shangnan China 87 D1
Shangombo Zambia 127 D9
Shangpai China see Feixi
Shangpaihe China see Feixi
Shangqiu Henan China 87 E1
Shangqiu Henan China 87 E1
also known as Zhuji
Shangrao China 87 F2
Shangshui China 87 E1
Shangsi China 87 D4
also known as Siyang
Shangtang China see Yongjia
Shangyou China 87 E3
also known as Dongshan
Shangyou Shuiku salt flat China 88 C3
Shangyu China 87 G2
also known as Baiguan
Shangzhi China 82 B3
Shangzhou China 87 D1
Shanhaiguan China 85 H3
Shanhe China see Zhengning
Shanhetun China 82 B3
Shani Nigeria 125 I4
Shankou China 84 B3
Shannon N.Z. 152 J8
Shannon airport Rep. of Ireland 47 D11
Shannon est. Rep. of Ireland 47 D11
Shannon r. Rep. of Ireland 47 D11
Shannon S. Africa 133 K6
Shannon U.S.A. 172 D8
Shannon, Mouth of the Rep. of Ireland 47 C11
Shannon National Park Australia 151 B7
Shannon Ø i. Greenland 165 R2
Shan Plateau Myanmar 78 B3
Shanshan China 88 E3
also known as Piqan
Shanshanzhan China 88 E3
Shansi prov. China see Shanxi
Shantarskiye Ostrova is Rus. Fed. 39 N4
Shan Tei Tong hill Hong Kong China see Stenhouse, Mount
Shan Teng hill Hong Kong China see Victoria Peak
Shantipur India 97 F5
also spelt Santipur
Shantou China 87 F4
formerly known as Swatow
Shantung prov. China see Shandong
Shanwei China 87 E4
Shanxi prov. China 85 F4
English form Shansi
Shanxian China 87 F1
also known as Shancheng
Shanya r. Rus. Fed. 43 Q7
Shanyang China 87 D1
Shanyin China 85 G4
also known as Daiyue
Shaodong China 87 D3
also known as Liangshi
Shaoguan China 87 E3
Shaoshan China 87 E3
Shaowu China 87 F3
Shaoxing China 87 G2
Shaoyang China 87 D3
Shapa China 87 D4
Shapembe Dem. Rep. Congo 126 D6
Shaping China see Ebian
Shapinsay i. U.K. 46 J4
Shapki Rus. Fed. 43 M2
Shapkina r. Rus. Fed. 40 J2
Shapsha Rus. Fed. 43 P1
Shapyalyevichy Belarus 43 K7
Shaqlāwa Iraq 109 P1
Shaqq el Giefer, Wadi watercourse Sudan 121 E6
Shaqq el Khadir Sudan 121 E6
Shaqrā' Saudi Arabia 105 D2
Shar Kazakh. 103 J2
formerly known as Charsk
Shār, Jabal mt. Saudi Arabia 104 A2
Sharaf well Iraq 107 E5
Sharafa Sudan 121 E6
Sharāh, Jibāl ash mts Jordan 108 G7
Sharalday Rus. Fed. 85 E1
Sharanga Rus. Fed. 40 H4
Sharan Jogizai Pak. 101 G4
Sharashova Belarus 42 F9
Sharâtîb, Râs pt Egypt 108 E9
Sharawrā, Jabal hills Saudi Arabia 109 H9
Sharawrā', Qa' salt pan Saudi Arabia 109 H9
Sharbaqty Kazakh. see Shcherbakty
Sharbithāt, Ra's c. Oman 105 G4
Sharbulag Mongolia 84 B1
Sharchino Rus. Fed. 103 J1
Shardara Kazakh. 103 F4
formerly spelt Chardara
Shardara Bögeni resr Kazakh./Uzbek. see Chardarinskoye Vodokhranilishche
Shardi Pak. 101 H3
Sharga Govĭ-Altay Mongolia 84 B2
Sharga Hövsgöl Mongolia 84 C1
formerly known as Tsagaan-Uul
Shargorod Ukr. see Sharhorod
Shargun' Uzbek. 103 F5
also spelt Shorghun
Sharhorod Ukr. 41 D6
also spelt Shargorod
Sharhulsan Mongolia 84 E2
Shari r. Cameroon/Chad see Chari
Shari Japan 90 I3
Shārī, Buḥayrat imp. l. Iraq 107 F4
Shari-dake vol. Japan 90 I3
Sharira Pass Egypt 108 F9
Sharjah U.A.E. 105 F2
also known as Ash Shāriqah
Sharka-leb La pass China 89 E6
Sharkawshchyna Belarus 42 I6
Shark Bay Australia 151 A5
Shark Fin Bay Phil. 74 A4
Sharkhāt Yemen 105 E5
Shark Reef Australia 149 E2
Sharlawuk Turkm. see Sharlouk
Sharlouk Turkm. 102 C5
also spelt Sharlawuk
Sharlyk Rus. Fed. 102 C1
Sharmah Saudi Arabia 104 A1
Sharm el Sheikh Egypt 121 G3
Sharon PA U.S.A. 176 E4
Sharon WI U.S.A. 172 E8
Sharon, Plain of Israel 108 F5
also known as HaSharon
Sharon Springs U.S.A. 178 B4
Sharonville U.S.A. 176 A6
Sharpe, Lake salt flat Australia 151 C7
Sharpe Lake Canada 167 M4
Sharp Peak hill Hong Kong China 87 [inset]
also known as Nam She Tsim
Sharpsburg U.S.A. 176 D6
Sharqat Iraq see Ash Sharqāţ
Sharqī, Jabal ash mts Lebanon/Syria 108 G4
English form Anti Lebanon
Sharqīya governorate Egypt 108 C7
Sharqpur Pak. 101 H4
Sharur Azer. see Şărur
Shar Us Gol r. Mongolia 84 C2
Shary well Saudi Arabia 104 C2
Shar'ya Rus. Fed. 40 H4
Shar'ya r. Rus. Fed. 43 N2
Sharyn Kazakh. see Charyn
Shashe r. Botswana/Zimbabwe 131 F4
Shashemenē Eth. 128 C3
Shashi China see Jingzhou
Shashubay Kazakh. 103 H3
formerly known as Ozernyy
Shasta U.S.A. 182 B1
Shasta, Mount vol. U.S.A. 180 B4
Shasta Dam U.S.A. 182 B1
Shasta Lake U.S.A. 182 B1
Shatalovo Rus. Fed. 43 N7
Sha Tau Kok Hoi inlet Hong Kong China see Starling Inlet
Shāţi', Wādī ash watercourse Libya 120 B3
Shatilki Belarus see Svyetlahorsk
Sha Tin Hong Kong China 87 [inset]
Shatki Rus. Fed. 40 H5
Shaţnat as Salmās, Wādī watercourse Syria 109 J2
Sha Tong Hau Shan i. Hong Kong China see Bluff Island
Shatoy Rus. Fed. 41 H8
formerly known as Sovetskoye
Shatsk Rus. Fed. 41 G5
Shats'k nat. park Ukr. 41 B6
Shaţţ, Ra's osh pt Iran 100 B4
Shaţţ al 'Arab r. Iran/Iraq 107 G5
Shaţţ al Gharrāf r. Iraq 107 F5
Shattuck U.S.A. 179 C4
Shatura Rus. Fed. 43 U6
Shaturtorf Rus. Fed. 43 U6
Shaubak Jordan see Ash Shawbak
Shäūildir Kazakh. see Shaul'der
Shaul'der Kazakh. 103 G4
also spelt Shäūildir
Shaunavon Canada 167 I5
Shaverki Rus. Fed. 44 O3
Shaver Lake U.S.A. 182 E4
Shavers Fork r. U.S.A. 176 F7
Shaw r. Australia 150 B4
Shawan China 88 D2
also known as Sandaohezi
Shawangunk Mountains hills U.S.A. 177 K4
Shawano U.S.A. 172 E6
Shawano Lake U.S.A. 172 E6
Shawāq well Saudi Arabia 104 B2
Shawnee U.S.A. 179 C5
Shawsville U.S.A. 176 E8
Sha Xi r. China 87 F3
Shaxian China 87 F3
also known as Fenggang
Shayan Kazakh. 103 G4
formerly spelt Chayan
Shayang China 87 E2
Shaybārā i. Saudi Arabia 104 B2
Shayboveyem r. Rus. Fed. 39 Q3
Shay Gap Australia 150 C4
Shaykh, Sha'īb ash watercourse Iraq 109 N5
Shaykh Jūwī Iraq 107 F4
Shaykh Sa'd Iraq 107 F4
Shaykovka Rus. Fed. 43 P7
Shāzand Iran 100 B3
Shazaoyuan China 84 B4
Shaẓāẓ, Jabal mt. Saudi Arabia 104 C2
Shāẓī Ḥāmīr, Wādī watercourse Saudi Arabia 109 M6
Shazud Tajik. 101 H2
Shchara r. Belarus 42 F8
Shchekino Rus. Fed. 43 S7
Shchelkanovo Rus. Fed. 43 Q7
Shchelkovo Rus. Fed. 43 T6
Shchel'yayur Rus. Fed. 40 J2
Shcherbakov Rus. Fed. see Rybinsk
Shcherbakty Kazakh. 103 I1
also spelt Sharbaqty
Shchetinskoye Rus. Fed. 43 T3
Shchichengskoye, Ozero l. Rus. Fed. 43 V2
Shchigry Rus. Fed. 41 F6
Shcholkine Ukr. 41 E7
Shchomyslitsa Belarus 42 I8
Shchors Ukr. 41 D6
formerly known as Snovsk
Shchuchin Belarus see Shchuchyn
Shchuchinsk Kazakh. 103 G1
Shchuchyn Belarus 42 F8
also spelt Shchuchin
Shchuger r. Rus. Fed. 40 K2
Shchytkavichy Belarus 42 J8
Shea Guyana 199 G4
Shebalino Rus. Fed. 88 D1
Shebandowan Lakes Canada 172 C2
Shebekino Rus. Fed. 41 F6
Sheberghān Afgh. 101 F2
Sheboygan U.S.A. 172 F7
Shebshi Mountains Nigeria 125 H4
Shebunino Rus. Fed. 82 F3
Shecheng China see Shexian
Shediac Canada 169 H4
Shedin Peak Canada 166 E4
Shedok Rus. Fed. 107 E1
Sheelin, Lough l. Rep. of Ireland 47 E10
Sheepmoor S. Africa 133 O3
Sheep Peak U.S.A. 183 I5
Sheerness U.K. 47 M12
Sheet Harbour Canada 169 I4
Shefar'am Israel 108 G5
Sheffield N.Z. 153 G11
Sheffield U.K. 47 K10
Sheffield AL U.S.A. 174 C5
Sheffield IL U.S.A. 172 D9
Sheffield PA U.S.A. 176 F4
Sheffield TX U.S.A. 179 B6
Sheffield Lake Canada 169 J3
Shegaon India 94 C1
Sheguiandah Canada 173 L5
Shēh Husēn Eth. 128 D3
Shehong China 86 C2
also known as Taihe; formerly known as Taihezhen
Sheikh, Jebel esh mt. Lebanon/Syria see Hermon, Mount
Sheikh, Wâdi es watercourse Egypt 108 E9
Sheikh Othman Yemen see Ash Shaykh 'Uthman
Shekak r. Canada 168 C3
Shekhawati reg. India 96 B4
Shekhem West Bank see Nāblus
Shekhupura Pak. 101 H4
Sheki Azer. see Şäki
Shekka Ch'ün-Tao is Hong Kong China see Soko Islands
Shek Kwu Chau i. Hong Kong China 87 [inset]
Shekou China 87 [inset]
Shek Pik resr Hong Kong China see Shek Pik Reservoir
Shek Pik Reservoir Hong Kong China 87 [inset]
also known as Shek Pik
Sheksna Rus. Fed. 43 T2
formerly known as Nikol'skoye
Sheksna r. Rus. Fed. 43 T2
Sheksninskoye Vodokhranilishche resr Rus. Fed. 43 T2
Shek Uk Shan mt. Hong Kong China 87 [inset]
Shela China 89 F6
Shelag watercourse Afgh./Iran 101 E4
Shelagskiy, Mys pt Rus. Fed. 39 R2
Shelbiana U.S.A. 176 C8
Shelbina U.S.A. 178 D4
Shelburn U.S.A. 174 C4
Shelburne N.S. Canada 169 H5
Shelburne Ont. Canada 173 M6
Shelburne Bay Australia 149 D1
Shelburne Falls U.S.A. 177 M3
Shelby MS U.S.A. 174 B5
Shelby MT U.S.A. 180 E2
Shelby NC U.S.A. 174 D5
Shelby OH U.S.A. 176 C5
Shelbyville IL U.S.A. 174 B4
Shelbyville IN U.S.A. 174 C4
Shelbyville MO U.S.A. 178 D4
Shelbyville TN U.S.A. 174 C5
Shelbyville, Lake U.S.A. 174 B4
Sheldon S. Africa 133 J10
Sheldon IA U.S.A. 178 D3
Sheldon IL U.S.A. 172 F10
Sheldon WI U.S.A. 172 C5
Sheldon National Wildlife Refuge nature res. U.S.A. 180 C4
Sheldon Springs U.S.A. 177 M1
Sheldrake Canada 169 H3
Shelek Kazakh. see Chilik
Shelekhov Rus. Fed. 84 D1
Shelikhova, Zaliv g. Rus. Fed. 39 P3
Shelikof Strait U.S.A. 164 D4
Shellbrook Canada 167 J4
Shelley U.S.A. 180 D4
Shell Lake Canada 167 J4
Shell Lake U.S.A. 172 B5
Shell Lakes salt flat Australia 151 D6
Shell Mountain U.S.A. 182 A1
Shellsburg U.S.A. 172 B8
Shelon' r. Rus. Fed. 43 L3
Shelopugino Rus. Fed. 85 H1
Shelter Bay Canada see Port-Cartier
Shelter Island U.S.A. 177 M4
Shelter Point N.Z. 153 C15
Shelton U.S.A. 180 B3
Sheltozero Rus. Fed. 40 E3
Shemakha Azer. see Şamaxı
Shemankar r. Nigeria 125 H4
Shemenichi Rus. Fed. 43 P1
Shemonaikha Kazakh. 103 J2
Shemordan Rus. Fed. 40 I4
Shemursha Rus. Fed. 40 H5
Shenandoah IA U.S.A. 178 D3
Shenandoah PA U.S.A. 177 I5
Shenandoah VA U.S.A. 176 G7
Shenandoah r. U.S.A. 176 H6
Shenandoah Mountains U.S.A. 176 F7
Shenandoah National Park U.S.A. 176 G7
Shenbertal Kazakh. 103 E2
Shenchi China 85 G4
Shendam Nigeria 125 H4
Shendi Sudan 121 G5
Shending Shan hill China 82 D3
Shenge Sierra Leone 124 B5
Shengel'di Kazakh. 103 G4
Shengel'dy Kazakh. 103 E3
formerly spelt Chengel'dy
Shëngjin Albania 58 A7
Shengli China 87 E2
Shengli Daban pass China 88 D3
Shengli Feng mt. China/Kyrg. see Pobeda Peak
Shengrenjian China see Pinglu
Shengsi China 87 G2
also known as Caiyuanzhen
Shengsi Liedao is China 87 G2
Shengxian China see Shengzhou
Shengzhou China 87 G2
formerly known as Shengxian
Shënkoll Albania 58 A7
Shenkursk Rus. Fed. 40 G3
Shenmu China 85 F4
Shennongjia China 87 D2
also known as Songbai
Shenqiu China 87 E1
also known as Huaidian
Shenshu China 82 C3
Shensi prov. China see Shaanxi
Shentala Rus. Fed. 40 I5
Shenton, Mount hill Australia 151 C6
Shenxian China see Shenzhou
Shenxian China 85 G4
Shenyang China 85 I3
formerly known as Mukden
▶Shenzhen China 87 [inset]
also known as Bao'an
world [changes] ▶ 20–21
Shenzhen Wan b. Hong Kong China see Deep Bay
Shenzhou China 85 G4
formerly known as Shenxian
Sheoganj India 96 B4
Sheopur India 96 C4
Shepard Island Antarctica 222 P2
Shepetivka Ukr. 41 C6
also spelt Shepetovka
Shepetovka Ukr. see Shepetivka
Shepherd Islands Vanuatu 145 F3
Shepparton Australia 147 E4
Sheptaky Ukr. 43 O9
Sheqi China 87 E1
Sherabad Uzbek. 103 F5
also spelt Sherobod
Sherard, Cape Canada 165 K2
Sherborne S. Africa 133 I8
Sherborne U.K. 47 J13
Sherbro Island Sierra Leone 124 B5
Sherbrooke N.S. Canada 169 I4
Sherbrooke Que. Canada 169 G4
Sherburne U.S.A. 177 J3
Shercock Rep. of Ireland 47 F10
Sherda well Chad 120 C4
Sherdoyak Kazakh. 88 C1
Shereiq Sudan 121 G5
Shergarh India 96 B4
Sherghati India 97 E4
Sheridan AR U.S.A. 179 D5
Sheridan WY U.S.A. 180 F3
Sherkaly Rus. Fed. 38 G3
Sherlock r. Australia 150 B4
Sherlovaya Gora Rus. Fed. 85 H1
Sherman NY U.S.A. 176 F3
Sherman TX U.S.A. 179 C5
Sherman Mountain U.S.A. 183 I1
Sherobod Uzbek. see Sherabad
Sherovichi Rus. Fed. 43 M7
Sherpur Dhaka Bangl. 97 F4
Sherpur Rajshahi Bangl. 97 F4
Sherridon Canada 167 K4
Shertally India 94 C4
also known as Cherthala
's-Hertogenbosch Neth. 48 C4
also known as Den Bosch
Sherwood U.S.A. 176 A4
Sherwood Downs N.Z. 153 E11
Sherwood Lake Canada 167 K2
Sheryshevo Rus. Fed. 82 C2
Sheshegwaning Canada 173 K5
Sheshtamad Iran 100 D2
Sheslay Canada 166 D3
Sheslay r. Canada 166 C3
Shestikhino Rus. Fed. 43 T4
Shethanei Lake Canada 167 L3
Shetland admin. div. U.K. 46 L3
Shetpe Kazakh. 102 C3
Sheung Shui Hong Kong China 87 [inset]
Sheung Sze Mun sea chan. Hong Kong China 87 [inset]
Sheung Yue Ho r. Hong Kong China 87 [inset]
Shevaroy Hills India 94 C4
Shevchenko Kazakh. see Aktau
Shevchenko, Zaliv l. Kazakh. 102 E3
formerly known as Paskevicha, Zaliv
Shevgaon India 94 B2
Shevli r. Rus. Fed. 82 D1
Shexian Anhui China 87 F2
also known as Huicheng
Shexian Hebei China 85 G4
also known as Shecheng
Sheya Rus. Fed. 39 L3
Sheyang China 87 G1
also known as Hede
Sheybukhta Rus. Fed. 43 V2
Sheyenne r. U.S.A. 178 C2
Sheykh Sho'eyb i. Iran 100 C5
Sheykino Rus. Fed. 43 M5
Shey Phoksundo National Park Nepal 97 D3
Shiant Islands U.K. 46 F6
Shiashkotan, Ostrov i. Rus. Fed. 81 Q3
Shiawassee r. U.S.A. 173 J7
Shibām Yemen 105 E5
Shibar Pass Afgh. 101 G3
Shibata Japan 90 F6
Shibazhan China 82 B1
Shibetsu Hokkaidō Japan 90 H2
Shibetsu Hokkaidō Japan 90 I3
Shibîn el Kôm Egypt 121 F2
Shibing China 87 D3
Shibogama Lake Canada 168 B2
Shibotsu-jima i. Rus. Fed. see Zelenyy, Ostrov
Shibukawa Japan 91 F6
Shibushi Japan 91 B9
Shibushi-wan b. Japan 91 B9
Shicheng China see Zhouning
Shicheng China 87 F3
also known as Qinjiang
Shicheng Dao i. China 85 I4
Shichinohe Japan 90 G4
Shickshinny U.S.A. 177 I4
Shicun China see Xiangfen
Shidād al Mismā' hill Saudi Arabia 109 J6
Shidao China 85 I4
Shiderti r. Kazakh. 103 H1
Shidongsi China see Gaolan
Shiel, Loch l. U.K. 46 G7
Shield, Cape Australia 148 C2
Shīeli Kazakh. see Chiili
Shifa, Jabal ash mts Saudi Arabia 104 A1
Shifang China 86 C2
Shiga pref. Japan 91 D7
Shigatse China see Xigazê

Shiggaon India 94 B3
Shigong China 88 F3
Shigony Rus. Fed. 41 I5
Shiguai China 85 F3
formerly known as Shiguaigou
Shiguaigou China see Shiguai
Shihan Yemen 105 F4
Shihan, Wādī r. Oman 105 F4
Shihezi China 88 D2
Shihkiachwang China see Shijiazhuang
Shiikh Somalia 128 E2
Shijak Albania 58 A7
Shijiao China see Fogang
Shijiazhuang China 85 G4
formerly spelt Shihkiachwang
Shijiu Hu l. China 87 F2
Shijiusuo China see Rizhao
Shikabe Japan 90 G3
Shikag Lake Canada 168 B3
Shikar r. Pak. 101 E4
Shikarpur India 94 B3
Shikarpur Pak. 101 G5
Shikengkong mt. China 87 E3
Shikhany Rus. Fed. 102 A1
Shikohabad India 96 C4
Shikoku i. Japan 91 C8
Shikoku-sanchi mts Japan 91 C8
Shikotan, Ostrov i. Rus. Fed. 82 G4
also known as Shikotan-tō
Shikotan-tō i. Rus. Fed. see Shikotan, Ostrov
Shikotsu vol. Japan 90 G3
also known as Tarumae-san
Shikotsu-Tōya National Park Japan 90 G3
Shil'da Rus. Fed. 102 D2
Shilega Rus. Fed. 40 H2
Shiliguri India 97 F4
also spelt Siliguri
Shilipu China 87 E2
Shiliu China see Changjiang
Shilka Rus. Fed. 85 H1
Shilla mt. Jammu and Kashmir 96 C2
Shillelagh Rep. of Ireland 47 F11
Shillington Canada 173 M2
Shillo r. Israel 108 F5
Shillong India 97 F4
Shilou China 85 F4
Shilovo Ryazanskaya Oblast' Rus. Fed. 41 G5
Shilovo Tul'skaya Oblast' Rus. Fed. 43 T8
Shilüüstey Mongolia see Balgatay
Shimabara Japan 91 B8
Shimabara-wan b. Japan 91 B8
Shimada Japan 91 F7
Shimamaki Japan 90 G3
Shimane pref. Japan 91 C7
Shimane-hantō pen. Japan 91 C7
Shimanovsk Rus. Fed. 82 B1
Shimbiris mt. Somalia 128 E2
also known as Surud Ad
Shimbirre waterhole Kenya 128 D4
Shimen China 87 D2
Shimian China 86 B2
also known as Xinmian
Shimizu Hokkaidō Japan 90 H3
Shimizu Shizuoka Japan 91 F7
Shimla India 96 C3
formerly spelt Simla
Shimminato Japan see Shinminato
Shimoda Japan 91 F7
Shimodate Japan 91 F6
Shimoga India 94 B3
Shimokawa Japan 90 H2
Shimokita-hantō pen. Japan 90 G4
Shimoni Kenya 129 C6
Shimonoseki Japan 91 B8
formerly known as Akamagaseki
Shimotsuma Japan 91 F6
Shimsha r. India 94 C3
Shimshal Jammu and Kashmir 96 B1
Shimsk Rus. Fed. 43 L3
Shin, Loch l. U.K. 46 H5
Shināfiyah Iraq see Ash Shanāfiyah
Shinan China 87 D4
Shindand Afgh. 101 E3
also known as Sabzawar
Shingbwiyang Myanmar 78 B2
Shingshal Pass Pak. 101 H2
Shinglehouse U.S.A. 176 G4
Shingleton U.S.A. 172 G4
Shingletown U.S.A. 182 C1
Shing Mun Reservoir Hong Kong China 87 [inset]
also known as Ngan Hei Shui Tong
Shingozha Kazakh. 103 J3
also spelt Shyngqozha
Shingū Japan 91 E8
Shingwedzi S. Africa 131 F4
Shining Tree Canada 173 L3
Shinjō Japan 90 G5
Shinkai Hills Afgh. 101 G3
Shīnkāy Afgh. 101 F4
Shinminato Japan 91 E6
also spelt Shimminato
Shinnan-yō Japan 91 B7
Shinnston U.S.A. 176 E6
Shinshiro Japan 91 E7
Shintoku Japan 90 H3
Shinyanga Tanz. 128 B5
Shinyanga admin. reg. Tanz. 129 B5
Shiogama Japan 90 G5
Shiojiri Japan 91 E6
Shiono-misaki c. Japan 91 D8
Shioya-zaki pt Japan 90 G6
Shipai China see Huaining
Ship Chan Cay i. Bahamas 175 E7
Shipchenski Prokhod pass Bulg. 58 G6
Shipilovo Rus. Fed. 43 T4
Shiping China 86 B4
also known as Yilong
Shipki Pass China/India 89 B6
Shipman U.S.A. 176 G8
Shippegan Canada 169 H4
Shippegan Island Canada 169 H4
Shippensburg U.S.A. 176 H5
Shippenville U.S.A. 176 F4
Shiprock U.S.A. 183 P5
Shiprock Peak U.S.A. 183 P5
Shipu China see Huanglong
Shipu China 87 G2
Shipunskiy, Mys hd Rus. Fed. 39 Q4
Shiqian China 87 D3
Shiqiao China see Panyu
Shiqizhen China see Zhongshan
Shiqqat al Kharītah des. Saudi Arabia 105 D4
Shiquan China 87 D1
Shiquanhe China see Ali
Shiquanhe China see Gar
Shiquanh He r. China see Indus
Shi'r, Jabal hill Saudi Arabia 104 C2
Shirā'awh i. Qatar 105 F2
Shīrābād Iran 100 B2
Shirakami-misaki pt Japan 90 G4
Shirakawa Fukushima Japan 90 G6
Shirakawa Gifu Japan 91 E6
Shirane-san mt. Japan 91 F7
Shirane-san vol. Japan 90 F6
Shiranuka Japan 90 I3
Shiraoi Japan 90 G3
Shirase Coast Antarctica 223 O1
Shirase Glacier Antarctica 223 C2
Shirataki Japan 90 H3
Shirati Tanz. 128 B5
Shīrāz Iran 100 C4
Shirbīn Egypt 108 C6
Shire r. Malawi 129 B9
Shireet Mongolia 85 G2
Shirega Rus. Fed. 43 V1
Shiretoko-hantō pen. Japan 90 I3
Shiretoko-misaki c. Japan 90 I2
Shiretoko National Park Japan 90 I2
Shirin Uzbek. 103 G4
Shirinab r. Pak. 101 F4
Shīrīn Tagāb Afgh. 101 F2
Shiriya-zaki c. Japan 90 G4
Shirkala reg. Kazakh. 102 D3
Shīr Kūh mt. Iran 100 C4
Shiroishi Japan 90 G6
Shirone Japan 90 F6
Shiroro Reservoir Nigeria 125 G4
Shirotori Japan 91 E7
Shirpur India 96 B5
Shirten Holoy Gobi des. China 84 C3
Shirvān Iran 100 D2
Shisanjianfang China 88 E3
Shisanzhan China 82 B2
Shiselweni admin. dist. Swaziland 133 P4
Shishaldin Volcano U.S.A. 164 C4
Shisha Pangma mt. China see Xixabangma Feng
Shishou China 87 E2
Shishovka Rus. Fed. 43 T3
Shitai China 87 F2
also known as Qili
Shitan China 87 E3
Shitang China 87 G2
Shitanjing China 85 E4
Shithāthah Iraq 109 O5
Shiv India 96 A4
Shiveluch, Sopka vol. Rus. Fed. 39 Q4
Shivpuri India 96 C4
Shivta tourist site Israel 108 F7
also known as Subeita
Shivwits U.S.A. 183 K4
Shivwits Plateau U.S.A. 183 K5
Shiwan Dashan mts China 87 C4
Shiwa Ngandu Zambia 127 F7
Shixing China 87 E3
also known as Taiping
Shiyan China 87 D1
Shizhu China 87 D2
also known as Nanbin
Shizilu China see Junan
Shizipu China 87 F2
Shizong China 86 B3
also known as Danfeng
Shizugawa Japan 90 G5
Shizuishan China 85 E4
also known as Dawukou
Shizukuishi Japan 90 G5
Shizuoka Japan 91 F7
historically known as Sumpu
Shizuoka pref. Japan 91 F7
Shkhara mt. Georgia/Rus. Fed. 107 E2
3rd highest mountain in Europe.
europe [landscapes] 30–31
Shklov Belarus see Shklow
Shklow Belarus 43 L7
also spelt Shklov
Shkodër Albania 58 A6
formerly known as Scutari; historically known as Scodra
Shkodrës, Liqeni i l. Albania/Yugo. see Scutari, Lake
Shkotovo Rus. Fed. 90 C3
Shkumbin r. Albania 58 A7
Shlina r. Rus. Fed. 43 P4
Shlino, Ozero l. Rus. Fed. 43 O4
Shlissel'burg Rus. Fed. 43 M2
also spelt Schlüsselburg; formerly known as Petrokrepost'
Shmidta, Ostrov i. Rus. Fed. 39 J1
English form Schmidt Island
Shmidta, Poluostrov pen. Rus. Fed. 82 F1
English form Schmidt Peninsula
Shmoylovo Rus. Fed. 43 J4
Shoalhaven r. Australia 147 F3
Shoal Lake Man. Canada 167 K5
Shoal Lake Sask. Canada 167 K4
Shoals U.S.A. 174 C4
Shoalwater Bay Australia 149 F4
Shōbara Japan 91 C7
Shōdo-shima i. Japan 91 D7
Shoemakersville U.S.A. 177 J5
Shofirkon Uzbek. see Shafirkan
Shoghlābād Iran 100 D2
Shoh Tajik. see Shakh
Shohi Pass Pak. see Tal Pass
Shokanbetsu-dake mt. Japan 90 G3
Shokotsu-gawa r. Japan 90 H2
Shokpar Kazakh. see Chokpar
Shola r. Rus. Fed. 43 S1
Sholakkorgan Kazakh. 103 F2
also spelt Sholaqsay
Sholapur India see Solapur
Sholaqorghan Kazakh. see Shollakorgan
Sholaqsay Kazakh. see Sholaksay
Shollakorgan Kazakh. 103 G4
also spelt Sholaqorghan; formerly spelt Chulakkurgan
Shomba r. Rus. Fed. 40 E2
Shongar Bhutan 97 F4
Shonzha Kazakh. see Chundzha
Shopsha Rus. Fed. 43 U4
Shoptykol' Kazakh. 103 H2
Shoqpar Kazakh. see Chokpar
Shoranur India 94 C4
Shorap Pak. 101 F5
Shorapur India 94 C2
Shorawak reg. Afgh. 101 F4
Shor Barsa-Kel'mes salt marsh Uzbek. 102 D4
Shorghun Uzbek. see Shargun'
Shorkot Pak. 101 H4
Shorkozakhly, Solonchak depr. Turkm. 102 D4
Shornaq Kazakh. see Chernak
Shorobe Botswana 130 D3
Shortandy Kazakh. 103 G2
Shortsville U.S.A. 177 H3
Shosambetsu Japan see Shosanbetsu
Shosanbetsu Japan 90 G2
also spelt Shosambetsu
Shosha r. Rus. Fed. 43 R5
Shoshone CA U.S.A. 183 H6
Shoshone ID U.S.A. 180 D4
Shoshone r. U.S.A. 180 E3
Shoshone Mountains U.S.A. 183 G2
Shoshone Peak U.S.A. 183 H5
Shoshong Botswana 131 E4
Shoshoni U.S.A. 180 E4
Shostka Ukr. 41 E6
Shouguang China 85 H4
Shouxian China 87 F1
Shouyang China 85 G4
Shouyang Shan mt. China 87 D1
Showak Sudan 121 G6
Show Low U.S.A. 183 N7
Shoyna Rus. Fed. 40 H2
Shpakovskoye Rus. Fed. 41 G7
formerly known as Mikhaylovskoye
Shpola Ukr. 41 D6
Shqipërisë, Republika e country Europe see Albania
Shreve U.S.A. 176 C5
Shreveport U.S.A. 179 D5
Shrewsbury U.K. 47 J11
Shrigonda India 94 B2
Shri Lanka country Asia see Sri Lanka
Shri Mohangarh India 96 A4
Shrirampur India 97 F5
Shrirangapattana India 94 C3
Shtefan-Vode Moldova see Ştefan Vodă
Shtërmen Albania 58 B8
Shtiqën Albania 58 B6
Shu r. China 87 F1
Shu Kazakh. 103 H4
formerly spelt Chu
Shu'ab, Ghubbat b. Yemen 105 F5
Shu'ab, Ra's pt Yemen 105 F5
Shu'aiba Iraq 107 F5
Shuajingsi China 86 B1
Shuangbai China 86 B3
also known as Tuodian
Shuangcheng China see Zherong
Shuangcheng China 82 B3
Shuanghe China 87 E2
Shuanghechang China 87 C2
Shuanghedagang China 82 C2
Shuanghuyu China see Zizhou
Shuangjiang China see Jiangkou
Shuangjiang China see Tongdao
Shuangjiang China 86 A4
also known as Mengmeng
Shuangjiang China see Eshan
Shuangliao China 85 I3
formerly known as Zhengjiatun
Shuangpai China 87 D3
Shuangshipu China see Fengxian
Shuangyang China 82 B4
Shuangyashan China 82 C3
Shuangzhong China see Hukou
Shu'ayt, Wādī r. Yemen 105 E4
Shubarkuduk Kazakh. 102 D2
Shubarshi Kazakh. 102 D2
Shubayh well Saudi Arabia 109 J7
Shubrâ el Kheima Egypt 121 F2
Shubrāmīyah well Saudi Arabia 104 C3
Shucheng China 87 F2
Shucushuyacu Peru 198 C6
Shufu China 88 A4
Shuganu India 97 G4
Shughnon, Qatorkŭhi mts Tajik. 101 G2
also known as Shugnanskiy Khrebet
Shugnanskiy Khrebet mts Tajik. see Shughnon, Qatorkŭhi
Shugozero Rus. Fed. 43 P2
Shugur Rus. Fed. 38 G3
Shuicheng China see Lupanshui
Shuiding China see Huocheng
Shuidong China see Dianbai
Shuihu China see Changfeng
Shuiji China 87 F3
Shuiji China see Laixi
Shuijing China 86 C1
Shuikou Guangdong China 87 E4
Shuikou Hunan China 87 D3
also known as Tuojiang
Shuikuguan China 86 C4
Shuikoushan China 87 E3
Shuiluocheng China see Zhuanglang
Shuiquanzi China 84 D4
Shuituo He r. China 86 B3
Shuizhai China see Wuhua
Shujaabad Pak. 101 G4
Shulan China 82 B3
Shule China 88 B4
Shule He r. China 84 B3
Shule Nanshan mts China 84 C4
Shulinzhao China 85 F3
also known as Dalad Qi
Shul'mak Tajik. see Novobod
Shulu China see Xinji
Shum Rus. Fed. 43 M2
Shumagin Islands U.S.A. 164 C4
Shumanay Uzbek. 102 D4
formerly known as Taza-Bazar
Shumarinai-ko l. Japan 90 H2
Shumen Bulg. 58 H5
formerly known as Kolarovgrad
Shumensko Plato nat. park Bulg. 58 H5
Shumerlya Rus. Fed. 40 H5
Shumikha Rus. Fed. 38 G4
Shumilina Belarus 43 K6
Shumshu, Ostrov i. Rus. Fed. 39 P4
Shumyachi Rus. Fed. 43 N8
Shunak, Gora mt. Kazakh. 103 H3
Shūnat Nimrīn Jordan 108 G6
Shunde China 87 E4
also known as Daliang
Shunga Rus. Fed. 43 V4
Shunyi China 85 H3
Shuolong China 86 C4
Shuoxian China see Shuozhou
Shuozhou China 85 G4
formerly known as Shuoxian
Shupiyan Jammu and Kashmir 89 A5
Shuqqat Najrān depr. Saudi Arabia 105 D4
Shuqrah Yemen 105 D5
Shūr r. Iran 100 C4
Shūr r. Iran 100 C3
Shūr r. Iran 101 E3
Shūr r. Iran 101 E4
Shūr watercourse Iran 100 C4
Shūr watercourse Iran 100 C4
Shūr watercourse Iran 100 C5
Shur watercourse Iran 100 D3
Shūrāb Chahār Maḩāll va Bakhtīārī Iran 100 B3
Shūr Āb Iran 100 B3
Shūrāb Khorāsan Iran 100 D3
Shūrāb Yazd Iran 100 C3
Shūr Āb watercourse Iran 100 C4
Shurab Tajik. see Shŭrob
Shurchi Uzbek. 103 F5
Shureghestan Iran 100 C3
Shūr Gaz Iran 101 D4
Shūrjestān Iran 100 C4
Shurma Rus. Fed. 40 I4
Shŭrob Tajik. 101 G1
also spelt Shurab
Shūrū Iran 101 E4
Shurugwi Zimbabwe 131 F3
formerly spelt Selukwe
Shuruppak tourist site Iraq 107 F5
Shusf Iran 101 E4
Shūsh Iran 100 B3
Shusha Azer. see Şuşa
Shushicë r. Albania 59 A8
Shushkodom Rus. Fed. 43 V3
Shushtar Iran 100 B3
Shuswap Lake Canada 166 G5
Shutar Khun Pass Afgh. 101 F3
Shuwaysh, Tall ash hill Jordan 109 I6
Shuya Ivanovskaya Oblast' Rus. Fed. 40 G4
Shuya Respublika Kareliya Rus. Fed. 40 E3
Shuyak Island U.S.A. 164 D4
Shuyang China 87 F1
Shuyskoye Rus. Fed. 43 V2
Shvartsevskiy Rus. Fed. 43 S7
Shwebandaw Myanmar 78 A4
Shwebo Myanmar 78 A3
Shwedaung Myanmar 78 A4
Shwedwin Myanmar 78 A2
Shwegun Myanmar 78 B4
Shwegyin Myanmar 78 B4
Shwelaung r. Myanmar 78 A4
Shweli r. Myanmar 78 B3
also known as Mao, Nam
Shwenyaung Myanmar 78 B3
Shweudaung mt. Myanmar 78 B3
Shyganaq Kazakh. see Chiganak
Shyghys Qazaqstan Oblysy admin. div. Kazakh. see Vostochnyy Kazakhstan
Shyghys-Qongyrat Kazakh. see Shygys Konyrat
Shygys Konyrat Kazakh. 103 H3
also spelt Shyghys-Qongyrat; formerly known as Vostochno-Kounradskiy
Shymkent Kazakh. 103 G4
formerly spelt Chimkent
Shyngghyrlau Kazakh. see Chingirlau
Shyngqozha Kazakh. see Shingozha
Shyok r. India 96 B2
Shyok Jammu and Kashmir 96 C2
Shypuvate Ukr. 41 F6
Shyshchytsy Belarus 42 I8
Si, Laem pt Thai. 79 B6
Sia Indon. 73 H8
Siabu Indon. 76 B2
Siachen Glacier Jammu and Kashmir 96 C2
Siahan Range mts Pak. 101 E5
Sīah Chashmeh Iran 100 A2
Siahgird Afgh. 101 F2
Siah Koh mts Afgh. 101 F3
Sīāh Kūh mts Iran 100 C3
Siak r. Indon. 76 C2
Siak Sri Inderapura Indon. 76 C2
Sialkot Pak. 101 H3
Siam country Asia see Thailand
Sian China see Xi'an
Sianów Poland 49 N1
Siantan i. Indon. 77 D2
Siapa r. Venez. 199 E4
Siargao i. Phil. 74 C4
Siasconset U.S.A. 177 P4
Siasi Phil. 74 B5
Siasi i. Phil. 74 B5
Siatista Greece 59 C8
Siaton Phil. 74 B4
Siau i. Indon. 75 C2
Šiauliai Lith. 42 E6
Siavonga Zambia 127 F9
Siayan i. Phil. 74 B1
Siazan' Azer. see Siyäzän
Sib Iran 101 E5
Sīb Oman 105 G3
Sibanicú Cuba 186 D2
Sibati China see Xibet
Sibay i. Phil. 74 B4
Sibay Rus. Fed. 102 D1
Sibayi, Lake S. Africa 133 Q4
Sibbald, Cape Antarctica 223 L2
Sibbo Fin. 45 N3
Sibbofjärden b. Fin. 42 G1
Šibenik Croatia 56 H5
formerly spelt Sebenico
Siberia Rus. Fed. see Central Siberian Plateau
Siberut i. Indon. 76 B3
Siberut, Selat sea chan. Indon. 76 B3
Siberut National Park Indon. 76 B3
Sibi Pak. 101 F4
Sibidiri P.N.G. 73 J8
Sibigo Indon. 76 A2
Sibiloi National Park Kenya 128 C4
Sibirtsevo Rus. Fed. 82 D3
formerly known as Manzovka
Sibiryakova, Ostrov i. Rus. Fed. 39 H2
Sibiti Congo 126 B5
Sibiu Romania 58 F3
Sibley U.S.A. 178 D3
Siboa Indon. 75 B2
Sibolga Indon. 76 B2
Siborongborong Indon. 76 B2
Sibowe r. Swaziland 133 P3
Sibsagar India 97 G4
Sibu Sarawak Malaysia 77 E2
Sibuco Phil. 74 B5
Sibuco Bay Phil. 74 B5
Sibuguey r. Phil. 74 B5
Sibuguey Bay Phil. 74 B5
Sibut Cent. Afr. Rep. 126 C3
Sibutu i. Phil. 74 A5
Sibutu Passage Phil. 74 A5
Sibuyan i. Phil. 74 B3
Sibuyan Sea Phil. 74 B3
Sic Romania 58 E2
Sicamous Canada 166 G5
Sicapoo mt. Phil. 74 B2
Sicca Veneria Tunisia see Le Kef
Siccus watercourse Australia 146 C2
Sicheng China see Lingyun
Sichon Thai. 79 B6
Sichuan prov. China 86 B2
English form Szechwan
Sichuan Pendi basin China 86 C2
English form Red Basin
Sicié, Cap c. France 51 L9
Sicilia admin. reg. Italy 57 G11
Sicilia i. Italy see Sicily
Sicilian Channel Italy/Tunisia 57 E11
Sicily i. Italy 57 G10
also known as Sicilia
Sicuani Peru 200 C3
Šid Vojvodina, Srbija Yugo. 58 A3
Sidangoli Indon. 75 C2
Sidareja Indon. 77 E4
Siddhapur India 96 B5
also spelt Sidhpur
Siddharthanagar Nepal see Bhairawa
Siddipet India 94 C2
Sideby Fin. 45 M3
also known as Siipyy
Sideia Island P.N.G. 149 F1
Sidi el Na'âm, Gebel hill Egypt 108 C8
Sidenreng, Danau l. Indon. 75 A3
Sidensjö Sweden 44 L3
Sidéradougou Burkina 124 D4
Sideros, Akra pt Greece 59 H13
Sidesaviwa S. Africa 132 G9
Sidhauli India 96 D4
Sidhi India 97 D4
Sidhirókastron Greece see Sidirokastro
Sidhpur India see Siddhapur
Sidi Aïssa Alg. 55 O9
Sidi Ali Alg. 55 L8
Sidi Ameur Alg. 55 O9
Sidi Barrani Egypt 121 E2
Sidi Bel Abbès Alg. 123 E2
Sidi Bennour Morocco 122 C2
Sidi Bou Sa'id Tunisia see Sidi Bouzid
Sidi Bouzid Tunisia 123 H2
also known as Sīdī Bou Sa'īd
Sidi El Hani, Sebkhet de salt pan Tunisia 123 H2
Sidi el Mokhtâr well Mali 124 E2
Sidi Ifni Morocco 122 C3
Sidi Kacem Morocco 122 D2
formerly known as Petitjean
Sidikalang Indon. 76 B2
Sidi Khaled Alg. 123 G2
Sidi Ladjel Alg. 55 N9
Sidi Mannsour well Alg. 123 G3
Sidi Mhamed well W. Sahara 122 B5
Sidi Okba Alg. 123 G2
Sidirokastro Greece 58 E7
also known as Sidhirókastron
Sidi Saâd, Barrage dam Tunisia 57 B13
Sidi Sâlim Egypt 108 B6
Sidi-Smaïl Morocco 122 C2
Sid Lake Canada 167 J2
Sidlaw Hills U.K. 46 I7
Sidley, Mount Antarctica 222 P1
Sidmouth U.K. 47 I13
Sidmouth, Cape Australia 149 D2
Sidnaw U.S.A. 172 E4
Sidney Canada 166 F5
Sidney IA U.S.A. 178 D3
Sidney MT U.S.A. 180 F3
Sidney NE U.S.A. 178 B3
Sidney NY U.S.A. 177 J3
Sidney OH U.S.A. 176 A5
Sidney Lanier, Lake U.S.A. 174 D5
Sido Mali 124 D4
Sidoan Indon. 75 B2
Sidoarjo Indon. 77 F4
Sidoktaya Myanmar 78 A3
Sidon Lebanon 108 G4
also spelt Saïda or Sayda
Sidorovo Rus. Fed. 43 V3
Sidra r. Poland 49 U2
Sidrī, Wādī watercourse Egypt 108 E9
Sidrolândia Brazil 203 A7
Sidvokodvo Swaziland 133 P3
Sidwadweni S. Africa 133 M8
Sidzhak Uzbek. 103 G4
also spelt Sijjak; formerly spelt Sydzhak
Siebe Norway 44 M1
Siedlce Poland 49 T3
historically known as Sedlets
Sieg r. Germany 48 E5
Siegen Germany 48 F5
Siemianówka, Jezioro l. Poland 49 T3
Siemiatycze Poland 49 T3
Siĕmréab Cambodia 79 C5
also spelt Siem Reap
Siem Reap Cambodia see Siĕmréab
Si'en China see Huanjiang
Siena Italy 56 D5
historically known as Saena Julia
Sieniawa Poland 49 T5
Sieppijärvi Fin. 44 M2
Sieradz Poland 49 P4
Sieraków Poland 49 N3
Sierpc Poland 49 Q3
Sierpienica r. Poland 49 Q3
Sierra Bahoruco nat. park Dom. Rep. 187 F3
Sierra Blanca U.S.A. 181 F7
Sierra Chica Arg. 204 E5
Sierra Colorada Arg. 204 D6
Sierra de Cazorla Segura y las Villas park Spain 55 I6
Sierra del Gistral mts Spain see Xistral, Serra do
Sierra Grande Arg. 205 D6
Sierra Leone country Africa 124 B4
africa [countries] 114–117
Sierra Madre Mountains U.S.A. 182 D6
Sierra Mojada Mex. 184 E3
Sierra Nevada, Parque Nacional nat. park Venez. 198 D2
Sierra Nevada de Santa Marta, Parque Nacional nat. park Col. 198 C2
Sierraville U.S.A. 182 D2
Sierra Vista U.S.A. 181 E7
Sierre Switz. 51 N6
Siesartis r. Lith. 42 D7
Siesartis r. Lith. 42 F6
Şieu Romania 58 F1
Şieu r. Romania 58 F1
Sieve r. Italy 56 D5
Sievi Fin. 44 N3
Sifang Ling mts China 87 C4
Sīfenī Eth. 128 D1
Sifié Côte d'Ivoire 124 D5
Sifnos i. Greece 59 F11
Sifnou, Steno sea chan. Greece 59 F11
Sig Alg. 123 E2
Sig Rus. Fed. see Saint-Denis-du-Sig
Sig, Ozero l. Rus. Fed. 43 O4
Sigani well Saudi Arabia 105 F4
Sigatoka Fiji 145 G3
also spelt Singatoka
Sigave Wallis and Futuna Is 145 H3
also known as Leava; also spelt Singave
Sigean France 51 I9
Sigep, Tanjung pt Indon. 76 B3
Siggiuup Nunaa pen. Greenland 165 N2
also known as Svartenhuk Halvø
Sighişoara Romania 58 F2
Sigiriya Sri Lanka 94 D5
Siglap Sing. 76 [inset]
Sigli Indon. 76 A1
Siglufjörður Iceland 44 [inset] C2
Sigma Phil. 74 B4
Sigmaringen Germany 48 G7
Signal de Mailhebiau mt. France 51 J8
Signal de Randon mt. France 51 J8
Signal du Pic hill France 50 H7
Signal Peak U.S.A. 183 J8
Signy-l'Abbaye France 51 K3
Sigoga S. Africa 133 M7
Sigoisooinan Indon. 76 B3
Sigourney U.S.A. 174 A3
Sigri, Akra pt Greece 59 G9
Siguatepeque Hond. 186 B4
Sigüeiro Spain 54 C2
Sigüenza Spain 55 I3
Siguiri Guinea 124 C4
Sigulda Latvia 42 F4
Sigurd U.S.A. 183 M3
Sihanoukville Cambodia 79 C6
formerly known as Kâmpóng Saôm or Kompong Som
Sihanoukville, Chhâk b. Cambodia 79 C6
formerly known as Kompong Som Bay
Sihaung Myauk Myanmar 78 A3
Sihawa India 94 D1
Sihhoya Swaziland 133 P2
Sihong China 87 F1
also known as Qingyang
Sihora Madhya Pradesh India 96 D5
Sihora Maharashtra India 96 C5
Sihou China see Changdao
Sihuas Peru 200 A2
Sihui China 87 E4
Siikainen Fin. 45 M3
Siikajoki Fin. 44 N2
Siikajoki r. Fin. 44 N2
Siilinjärvi Fin. 44 N3
Siipyy Fin. see Sideby
Siirt Turkey 107 E3
historically known as Tigranocerta
Sijjak Uzbek. see Sidzhak
Sijunjung Indon. 76 C3
Sika India 96 A5
Sikaka Saudi Arabia see Sakākah
Sikandra Rao India 96 C4
Sikanni Chief Canada 166 F3
Sikanni Chief r. Canada 166 F3
Sikar India 96 B4
Sikaram mt. Afgh. 101 G3
Sikasso Mali 124 D4
Sikasso admin. reg. Mali 124 D4
Sikaw Myanmar 78 B3
Sikea Greece 59 E8
Sikeli Indon. 75 B4
Sikeston U.S.A. 174 B4
Sikhote-Alin' mts Rus. Fed. 82 D4
Sikhote-Alinskiy Zapovednik nature res. Rus. Fed. 82 E3
Sikinos Greece 59 G12
Sikinos i. Greece 59 G12
Sikirevci Croatia 56 K3
Sikkim state India 97 F4
Siklós Hungary 56 K3
Sikongo Zambia 127 D8
Siksjö Sweden 44 L2
Sikta India 97 E4
Sikuaishi China see Changhai
Sikuati Sabah Malaysia 77 G1
Sila' i. Saudi Arabia 104 A2
Silago Phil. 74 C4
Šilalė Lith. 42 D6
Silandro Italy 56 C2
Si Lanna National Park Thai. 78 B4
Silao Mex. 185 E4
Sila Point Phil. 74 C3
Silawaih Agam vol. Indon. 76 A1
Silay Phil. 74 B4
Silba i. Croatia 56 G4
Silchar India 97 G4
Sile Turkey 58 K7
Silene Latvia 42 H6
Siler City U.S.A. 174 E5
Sileru r. India 94 D2
Silesia reg. Czech Rep./Poland 49 N5
Silet Alg. 123 G5
Sileti Kazakh. see Seletinskoye
Sileti r. Kazakh. 103 H1
formerly spelt Selety
Siletitengiz, Ozero salt l. Kazakh. 103 H1
formerly spelt Seletyteniz, Ozero
Silgadi Nepal see Silgarhi
Silgarhi Nepal 96 D3
also spelt Silgadi
Silghat India 97 G4
Siliana Tunisia 123 H1
Silifke Turkey 106 C3
historically known as Seleucia
Siliguri India see Shiliguri
Silino Zambia 127 E9
Siling Co salt l. China 89 E6
Silipur India 96 C4
Silisili, Mount Samoa 145 H3
Silistat Turkey 106 B3
Siliştea Romania 58 G4
Siliştea Nouă Romania 58 F4
Silistra Bulg. 58 I4
historically known as Dorostol or Durostorum or Silistria
Silistria Bulg. see Silistra
Silivri Turkey 106 B2
Siljan Norway 45 J4
Siljan l. Sweden 45 K3
Silkaatskop S. Africa 133 K2
Silkeborg Denmark 45 J4
Silla Spain 55 K5
Sillamäe Estonia 42 I2
Sillaro r. Italy 56 D4
Sille Turkey 106 C3
Silleda Spain 54 C2
Silleiro, Cabo c. Spain 54 C2
Sillé-le-Guillaume France 50 F4
Silli India 97 E5
Sillod India 94 B1
Sillon de Talbert pen. France 50 C4
Siloam Springs U.S.A. 179 D4
Silobela S. Africa 133 O3
Silovayakha r. Rus. Fed. 40 L2
Silsbee U.S.A. 179 D6
Silsby Lake Canada 167 M4
Siltaharju Fin. 44 N2
Siltakylä Fin. 42 H1
Siltou well Chad 120 B5
Siluas Indon. 77 E2
Silūp r. Iran 101 E5
Šilutė Lith. 42 C6
Silutshana S. Africa 133 O5
Šiluva Lith. 42 E6
Silva Jardim Brazil 207 K9
Silvan Turkey 107 E3
Silvânia Brazil 206 E3
Silvassa India 94 B1
Silver Bank sea feature Turks and Caicos Is 187 F2
Silver Bank Passage Turks and Caicos Is 187 F2
Silver Bay U.S.A. 174 B2
Silver City Canada 166 B2
Silver City U.S.A. 181 E6
Silver Creek U.S.A. 176 F3
Silver Creek r. U.S.A. 183 N7
Silverdale N.Z. 152 I4
Silver Islet Canada 172 E2
Silver Lake U.S.A. 172 D6
Silver Lake l. CA U.S.A. 183 H6
Silver Lake l. MI U.S.A. 172 D5
Silvermine Mountains hills Rep. of Ireland 47 D11
Silver Peak Range mts U.S.A. 182 G4
Silver Spring U.S.A. 177 I7
Silver Springs U.S.A. 182 E2
Silverthrone Mountain Canada 166 E5
Silvertip Mountain Canada 180 B2
Silverton Australia 146 D2
Silverton Canada 166 G5
Silverton CO U.S.A. 181 F5
Silverton TX U.S.A. 179 B5
Silver Water Canada 173 K5
Silves Brazil 199 G5
Silves Port. 54 C7
Silvia Col. 198 B4
Silvies r. U.S.A. 180 C4
Silvituc Mex. 185 H5
Silvretta Gruppe mts Switz. 51 Q6
Sim r. Rus. Fed. 40 K5
Sima Comoros 129 E8
Sima Rus. Fed. 43 U5
Simao China 86 B4
Simão Dias Brazil 202 E4
Simarana Venez. 199 F3
Simàrd, Lac l. Canada 173 O3
Simaria Jharkhand India 97 E4
Simaria Madhya Pradesh India 96 D4
Simatang i. Indon. 75 B2
Simav Turkey 106 B3
Simav Dağları mts Turkey 106 B3
Simayr i. Saudi Arabia 104 C4
Simba Dem. Rep. Congo 126 D4
Simbirsk Rus. Fed. see Ul'yanovsk
Simbruini, Monti mts Italy 56 F7
Simbukhovo Rus. Fed. 43 R6
Simcoe Canada 168 D5
Simcoe, Lake Canada 168 E4
Simdega India 97 E5
Simeå Sweden 45 L3
Simēn Mountain National Park Eth. 128 C1
Simēn Mountains Eth. 128 C1
Simeonovgrad Bulg. 58 G6
formerly known as Maritsa
Simeria Romania 58 E3
Simeto r. Sicilia Italy 57 H11
Simeulue i. Indon. 76 B2
Simferopol' Ukr. 41 E7
Simi i. Greece see Symi
Simikot Nepal 97 D3
Simindou Cent. Afr. Rep. 126 D3
Siminy mt. Slovakia 49 R6
Simitli Bulg. 58 E7
Simi Valley U.S.A. 182 F7
Simla India see Shimla
Şimleu Silvaniei Romania 58 D1
Simmern (Hunsrück) Germany 48 E6
Simmesport U.S.A. 175 B6
Simm's Bahamas 187 E2
Simnas Lith. 42 E7
Simo Fin. 44 N2
Simojärvi l. Fin. 44 N2
Simonette r. Canada 166 G4
Simonhouse Canada 167 K4
Šimonka mt. Slovakia 49 S7
Simons U.S.A. 176 E4
Simon's Town S. Africa 132 C11
Simontornya Hungary 49 P9
Simon Wash watercourse U.S.A. 183 O9
Simpang Indon. 76 D3
Simpang Mangayau, Tanjong pt Sabah Malaysia 77 G1
Simplício Mendes Brazil 202 D3
Simplon Pass Switz. 51 O6
Simpson Canada 167 J5
Simpson Desert Australia 148 C5
Simpson Desert Conservation Park nature res. Australia 146 C5
Simpson Desert National Park Australia 148 C5
Simpson Desert Regional Reserve nature res. Australia 146 C1
Simpson Hill hill Australia 151 D5
Simpson Island Canada 172 F2
Simpson Islands Canada 167 H2
Simpson Park Mountains U.S.A. 183 H2
Simpson Peninsula Canada 165 K3
Simpsonville U.S.A. 174 D5
Simra Nepal 97 E4
Simrishamn Sweden 45 K5
Simuk i. Indon. 76 B3
Simulubek Indon. 76 B3
Simunjan Sarawak Malaysia 77 E2
Simunul i. Phil. 74 A5
Simushir, Ostrov i. Rus. Fed. 81 Q3
Sina r. India 94 B2
Sīnā', Shibh Jazīrat pen. Egypt see Sinai
Sinabang Indon. 76 B2
Sinabung vol. Indon. 76 B2
Sina Dhaqa Somalia 128 E3
Sinai pen. Egypt 121 G2
also known as Sīnā', Shibh Jazīrat
world [physical features] 8–9
Sinai, Mont hill France 51 K3
Sinai, Mount Egypt 108 E9
also known as Mūsa, Gebel
Sinaia Romania 58 G3
Sinai al Janūbīya governorate Egypt see Janūb Sīnā'
Sinai ash Shamālīya governorate Egypt see Shamāl Sīnā'
Si Nakarin Reservoir Thai. 79 B5

S index

Sinaloa state Mex. 184 C3
Sinamaica Venez. 198 D2
Sinan China 87 D3
Sinancha Rus. Fed. see Cheremshany
Sinanju N. Korea 83 B5
Sinarades Greece 59 A9
Sināwin Libya 120 A2
Sinazongwe Zambia 127 E9
Sinbaungwe Myanmar 78 A4
Sinbo Myanmar 78 B2
Sinbyugyun Myanmar 78 A3
Sincan Turkey 107 D3
Sincé Col. 198 C2
Sincelejo Col. 198 C2
Sinchu Taiwan see T'aoyüan
Sinclair, Lake U.S.A. 175 D5
Sinclair Mills Canada 166 F4
Sincora, Serra do hills Brazil 202 D5
Sind r. India 96 C4
Sind prov. Pak. see Sindh
Sinda Rus. Fed. 82 E2
Sinda Zambia 127 F8
Sindal Denmark 45 J4
Sindañgan Phil. 74 B4
Sindangan Bay Phil. 74 B4
Sindangbarang Indon. 77 D4
Sindara Gabon 126 A5
Sindari India 96 A4
Sindeh, Teluk b. Indon. 75 B5
Sindelfingen Germany 48 F7
Sindgi India 94 C2
Sindh prov. Pak. 101 G5
formerly spelt Sind
Sindhnur India 94 C3
Sindhuli Garhi Nepal 97 E4
also known as Sindhulimadi
Sindhulimadi Nepal see Sindhuli Garhi
Sindi Estonia 42 F3
Sindi India 94 C1
Sındırgı Turkey 106 B3
Sindkhed India 94 C2
Sindkheda India 96 B5
Sindominic Romania see Sândominic
Sindor Rus. Fed. 40 I3
Sindou Burkina 124 D4
Sindphana r. India 94 C2
Sindri India 97 E5
Sind Sagar Doab lowland Pak. 101 G4
Sinegor'ye Rus. Fed. 40 I4
Sinekçi Turkey 59 I8
Sinel'nikovo Ukr. see Synel'nykove
Sinendé Benin 125 F4
Sines Port. 54 C7
Sines, Cabo de c. Port. 54 C7
Sinettä Fin. 44 N2
Sinezerki Rus. Fed. 43 P8
Sinfra Côte d'Ivoire 124 D5
Sing Myanmar 78 B3
Singa Sudan 121 G6
Singahi India 96 D3
Singaingmyo Myanmar 78 B3
Singapore country Asia 76 C2
known as Hsin-chia-p'o in Chinese; spelt Singapura in Malay
asia [countries] 64–67
Singapore Sing. 76 C2
Capital of Singapore. Also known as Hsin-chia-p'o; also spelt Singapura; historically known as Tumasik.
Singapore r. Sing. 76 [inset]
Singapore, Strait of Indon./Sing. 76 C2
Singapura country Asia see Singapore
Singapura Sing. see Singapore
Singaraja Indon. 77 F5
Singareni India 94 D2
Singatoka Fiji see Sigatoka
Singave Wallis and Futuna Is see Sigave
Sing Buri Thai. 79 C5
Singen (Hohentwiel) Germany 48 F8
Singeorgiu de Pădure Romania see Sângeorgiu de Pădure
Singeorz-Băi Romania see Sângeorz-Băi
Singera Moldova 58 J2
formerly spelt Sîngera
Singgimtay China 88 E3
formerly known as Singim
Singh India 89 A6
Singhampton Canada 173 M6
Singida Tanz. 129 B6
Singida admin. reg. Tanz. 129 B6
Singidunum Srbija Yugo. see Beograd
Singim China see Singgimtay
Singkaling Hkamti Myanmar 78 A2
Singkang Indon. 75 B4
Singkawang Indon. 77 E2
Singkep i. Indon. 76 D3
Singkil Indon. 76 B2
Singkuang Indon. 76 B2
Singleton Australia 147 F3
Singleton, Mount hill N.T. Australia 148 A4
Singleton, Mount hill W.A. Australia 151 B6
Singoli India 96 B4
Singon Myanmar 78 A3
Singora Thai. see Songkhla
Sin'gosan N. Korea see Kosan
Singou, Réserve Totale du nature res. Burkina 125 F4
Singra India 97 F4
Singu Myanmar 78 A3
Singureni Romania 58 G4
Sin'gye N. Korea 83 B5
Sinhala country Asia see Sri Lanka
Sinharaja Forest Reserve nature res. Sri Lanka 94 D5
Sinhŭng N. Korea 83 B4
Siniloan Phil. 74 B3
Sining China see Xining
Sinio, Gunung mt. Indon. 75 A3
Siniscola Sardegna Italy 57 B8
Sini Vrŭkh mt. Bulg. 58 G7
Siniy-Shikhan Rus. Fed. 103 E2
Sinj Croatia 56 I5
Sinjai Indon. 75 B4
Sinjār Iraq 107 E3
Sinjār, Jabal mt. Iraq 107 E3
Sinkat Sudan 121 H5
Sinkiang aut. reg. China see Xinjiang Uygur Zizhiqu
Sinkiang Uighur Autonomous Region aut. reg. China see Xinjiang Uygur Zizhiqu
Sinking Spring U.S.A. 176 B6
Sinkyevichy Belarus 42 I9
Sinmi-do i. N. Korea 83 B5
Sinnamary Fr. Guiana 199 H3
Sinnar India 94 B2
Şinnār, Khashm hill Saudi Arabia 109 O8
Sinn Bishr, Gebel hill Egypt 108 D8
Sinneh Iran see Sanandaj
Sinn el Kaddâb esc. Egypt 121 F4
Sinnemahoning U.S.A. 176 G4
Sinni r. Italy 57 I8
Sinnicolau Mare Romania see Sânnicolau Mare
Sinnûris Egypt 108 B8
Sinoia Zimbabwe see Chinhoyi
Sinoie, Lacul lag. Romania 58 J4
Sinole Latvia 42 H4
Sinop Brazil 201 G2
Sinop Turkey 106 C2
historically known as Sinope
Sinope Turkey see Sinop
Sinoquipe Mex. 184 C2
Sinp'a N. Korea 82 B4
Sinp'o N. Korea 83 C4
Sinp'yŏng N. Korea 83 B5
Sinsang N. Korea 83 B5
Sinsheim Germany 48 F6
Sintang Indon. 77 E2
Sint-Laureins Belgium 51 J1
Sint Maarten i. Neth. Antilles 187 H3
Part of the Netherlands Antilles. The northern part of the island is the French territory of St Martin.
Sint Nicolaas Aruba 187 F4
Sint-Niklaas Belgium 51 K1
also spelt St Nicolas
Sinton U.S.A. 179 C6
Sintsovo Rus. Fed. 43 R5
Sint-Vith Belgium 51 M2
Sinú r. Col. 198 C2
Sinŭiju N. Korea 83 B4
Sinujiif Somalia 128 F2
Sinyaya r. Rus. Fed. 43 J4
Siocon Phil. 74 B5
Siófok Hungary 49 P9
Sioma Zambia 127 D9
Sioma Ngwezi National Park Zambia 127 D9
Sion Switz. 51 N6
Siorapaluk Greenland 165 L2
Sioule r. France 51 J6
Sioux Center U.S.A. 178 C3
Sioux City U.S.A. 178 C3
Sioux Falls U.S.A. 178 C3
Sioux Lookout Canada 168 B3
Sipacate Guat. 185 H6
Sipalay Phil. 74 B4
Šipan i. Croatia 56 J6
Sipang, Tanjong pt Sarawak Malaysia 77 E2
Siphaqeni S. Africa see Flagstaff
Siping China 82 B4
Sipiwesk Canada 167 L4
Sipiwesk Lake Canada 167 L4
Siple, Mount Antarctica 222 P2
Siple Coast Antarctica 223 N1
Siple Island Antarctica 222 P2
Sipolilo Zimbabwe see Guruve
Šipovo Bos.-Herz. 56 J4
Sipsey r. U.S.A. 175 B5
Sipura i. Indon. 76 B3
Sipura, Selat sea chan. Indon. 76 B3
Siq, Wādī el watercourse Egypt 108 D8
Siqirah Yemen 105 F5
Siqueira Campos Brazil 206 D10
Siquijor Phil. 74 B4
Siquijor i. Phil. 74 B4
Siquisique Venez. 198 D2
Sir r. Pak. 101 G6
Sira India 94 C3
Sira Norway 45 I4
Şīr Abū Nu'āyr i. U.A.E. 105 F2
Si Racha Thai. 79 C5
Siracusa Sicilia Italy see Syracuse
Sirajganj Bangl. 97 F4
Sirha Nepal see Sirha
Sir Alexander, Mount Canada 166 F4
Şiran Turkey 107 D2
Sirathu India 97 D4
Sirba r. Burkina/Niger 125 F3
Şir Banī Yās i. U.A.E. 105 F2
Sircilla India see Sirsilla
Sirdaryo r. Asia see Syrdar'ya
Sirdaryo Uzbek. see Syrdar'ya
Sirdaryo Wiloyati admin. div. Uzbek. see Syrdar'inskaya Oblast'
Sirdingka China see Lhari
Sire Tanz. 129 A6
Sir Edward Pellew Group is Australia 148 C2
Siren U.S.A. 172 A5
Siret r. Romania 58 J3
Sir Graham Moore Islands Australia 150 D2
Sirha Nepal 97 E4
also spelt Siraha
Sirḥān, Wādī as watercourse Jordan/Saudi Arabia 109 I6
Sirhind India 96 C3
Siri, Cape P.N.G. 149 G1
Şiria Romania 58 C2
Sīrīk Iran 100 D5
Sirik, Tanjong pt Sarawak Malaysia 77 E2
Sirikit Reservoir Thai. 78 C4
Sirina i. Greece see Syrna
Siritoi r. Pak. 101 G4
Sirjā Iran 101 E5
Sir James MacBrien, Mount Canada 166 E2
Sirjān Iran 100 C4
Sirjān salt flat Iran 100 C4
Sir Joseph Banks Group Conservation Park nature res. Australia 146 C3
Sirkka Fin. 44 N2
Sirmaur India 96 C3
formerly spelt Sirmur
Sirmium Vojvodina, Srbija Yugo. see Sremska Mitrovica
Sirmour India 97 D4
Sirmur India see Sirmaur
Şırnak Turkey 107 E3
Sirniö Fin. 44 O2
Sirohi India 96 B4
Sironcha India 94 D2
Sironj India 96 C4
Síros i. Greece see Syros
Sirotsina Belarus 43 K6
Sirouа, Jbel mt. Morocco 122 D3
Sirpur India 94 C2
Sirrayn Island Saudi Arabia 104 C4
Sirrei Eth. 128 D3
Sirretta Peak U.S.A. 182 F6
Sīrrī, Jazīreh-ye i. Iran 100 C5
Sirsa India 96 B3
Sir Sandford, Mount Canada 166 G5
Sirs el Laiyâna Egypt 108 B7
Sirsi Karnataka India 94 B3
Sirsi Uttar Pradesh India 96 C3
Sirsilla India 94 C2
formerly spelt Sircilla
Sirte Libya 120 C2
also spelt Surt
Sirte, Gulf of Libya 120 C2
also known as Surt, Khalīj
Sir Thomas, Mount hill Australia 146 A1
Siruguppa India 94 C3
Sirupa r. Mex. 181 E7
Sirur Karnataka India 94 B2
Sirur Maharashtra India 94 B2
Širutiškis Lith. 42 E6
Şirvan Turkey 107 E3
Sirvel India 94 C3
Širvintos Lith. 42 F6
Şirwāḥ Yemen 104 D5
Sīrwān r. Iraq 107 F4
Sir Wilfrid Laurier, Mount Canada 166 G4
Sir William Thompson Range hills Australia 149 D2
Siryan Iran 100 D3
Sis Turkey see Kozan
Sisak Croatia 56 I3
historically known as Siscia
Sisaket Thai. 79 D5
Sisal Mex. 185 H4
Sisante Spain 55 I5
Siscia Croatia see Sisak
Sishen S. Africa 132 H4
Sishilipu China 85 E5
Sisian Armenia 107 F3
Sisimiut Greenland 165 N3
also known as Holsteinsborg
Sisipuk Lake Canada 167 K4
Siskiwit Bay U.S.A. 172 E3
Sisogúichic Mex. 184 D3
Sisŏphŏn Cambodia 79 C5
Sisquoc r. U.S.A. 182 D7
Sissach Switz. 51 N5
Sisseton U.S.A. 178 C2
Sissili r. Burkina 125 E4
Sissonville U.S.A. 176 D7
Sistān reg. Iran 101 E4
also spelt Seistan
Sīstan, Daryācheh-ye marsh Afgh. 101 E4
Sister Bay U.S.A. 172 F5
Sisteron France 51 L8
Sisters U.S.A. 180 B3
Sistersville U.S.A. 176 E6
Sisto r. Italy 56 F7
Sit' r. Rus. Fed. 43 S3
Sitalike Tanz. 129 A6
Sitamarhi India 97 E4
Sitamau India 96 B5
Sitampiky Madag. 131 [inset] J3
Sitapur India 96 D4
Siteia Greece 59 H13
also spelt Sitía
Siteki Swaziland 133 P3
formerly spelt Stegi
Sithonia pen. Greece 59 E8
Sitía Greece see Siteia
Sitian China 84 B3
Sitila Moz. 131 G4
Siting China 87 C3
Sítio da Abadia Brazil 202 C5
Sítio do Mato Brazil 202 D5
Sitka India 89 D7
Sitka U.S.A. 164 F4
Sitnica r. Yugo. 58 B6
Sitno mt. Slovakia 49 P7
Sitnya r. Rus. Fed. 43 K4
Sitra oasis Egypt 121 E2
Sitsyenyets Belarus 43 K6
Sittang r. Myanmar 78 B4
also spelt Sittaung or Sittoung
Sittard Neth. 48 C5
Sittaung Myanmar 78 A2
Sittaung r. Myanmar see Sittang
Sittoung r. Myanmar see Sittang
Sittwe Myanmar 78 A3
formerly known as Akyab
Situbondo Indon. 77 F4
Siu A Chau i. Hong Kong China 87 [inset]
Siumpain, Rubha an t- hd U.K. see Tiumpan Head
Siumpu i. Indon. 75 B4
Siuna Nicaragua 186 B4
Siuntio Fin. 42 F1
Siuri India 97 E5
formerly spelt Suri
Siva Rus. Fed. 40 J4
Sivaganga India 94 C4
Sivakasi India 94 C4
Sivaki Rus. Fed. 82 B1
Sivand Iran 100 C4
Sivas Turkey 107 D3
historically known as Sebastea
Sivaslı Turkey 106 B3
Siverek Turkey 107 D3
Sīvers i. Latvia 42 I5
Siverskiy Rus. Fed. 43 L2
Sivers'kyy Donets' r. Rus. Fed./Ukr. see Severskiy Donets
Sivomaskinskiy Rus. Fed. 40 L2
Sivrice Turkey 107 D3
Sivrihisar Turkey 106 B3
Sivukile S. Africa 133 N3
Siwa Egypt 121 E2
Siwa Indon. 75 B3
Siwalik Range mts India/Nepal 96 C3
Siwan India 97 E4
Siwana India 96 B4
Siwa Oasis Egypt 121 E2
Six Cross Roads Barbados 187 I4
Six-Fours-les-Plages France 51 L9
Sixian China 87 F1
Six Lakes U.S.A. 173 H7
Sixtymile Canada 166 A1
Siyabuswa S. Africa 133 N2
Siyang China see Shangsi
Siyang China 87 F1
also known as Zhongxing
Siyathemba S. Africa 133 M3
Siyathuthuka S. Africa 133 O2
Siyäzän Azer. 107 G2
also spelt Siazan'; formerly known as Kyzyl-Burun
Siyitang China 85 F3
Siyom r. India 78 A1
Sīyunī Iran 100 C3
Siziwang Qi China see Ulan Hua
Sizyabsk Rus. Fed. 40 J2
Sjælland i. Denmark see Zealand
Sjaunja naturreservat nature res. Sweden 44 L2
Sjenica Srbija Yugo. 58 B5
Sjoa Norway 45 J3
Sjöbo Sweden 45 K5
Sjøholt Norway 44 I3
Sjona sea chan. Norway 44 K2
Sjoutnäset Sweden 44 K2
Sjøvegan Norway 44 L1
Sjulsmark Sweden 44 M2
Sjuøyane is Svalbard 38 C1
Skäckerfjällen mts Sweden 44 K3
Skadarsko Jezero nat. park Yugo. 58 A6
Skadovs'k Ukr. 41 E7
Skælsør Denmark 45 J5
Skærbæk Denmark 45 J5
Skærfjorden inlet Greenland 165 R2
Skaftafell nat. park Iceland 44 [inset] C2
Skaftárós r. mouth Iceland 44 [inset] C3
Skagafjörður inlet Iceland 44 [inset] B2
Skagaheiði reg. Iceland 44 [inset] B2
Skagen Denmark 45 J4
Skagern l. Sweden 45 K4
Skagerrak strait Denmark/Norway 45 J4
Skagit r. U.S.A. 180 B2
Skagit Mountain Canada 166 F5
Skagway U.S.A. 164 F4
Skaidi Norway 44 N1
Skaidiškės Lith. 42 G7
Skala Notio Aigaio Greece 59 H11
Skala Peloponnisos Greece 59 D12
Skala Kallonis Greece 59 H9
Skaland Norway 44 L1
Skalino Rus. Fed. 43 V3
Skallelv Norway 44 O1
Skalmodal Sweden 44 K2
Skanderborg Denmark 45 J4
Skåne county Sweden 45 K5
Skaneateles U.S.A. 177 I3
Skaneateles Lake U.S.A. 177 I3
Skånevik Norway 45 I4
Skanshelm Sweden 44 L2
Skantzoura i. Greece 59 F9
Skara Sweden 45 K4
Skara Brae tourist site U.K. 46 I4
Skarberget Norway 44 L1
Skardarsko Jezero l. Albania/Yugo. see Scutari, Lake
Skardu Jammu and Kashmir 96 B2
Skare Norway 45 I4
Skärgårdshavets Nationalpark nat. park Fin. 45 M4
also known as Saaristomeren Kansallispuisto
Skarnes Norway 45 J3
Skärplinge Sweden 45 L3
Skärsjövålen Sweden 45 K3
Skarstind mt. Norway 45 J3
Skarszewy Poland 49 P1
Skarvedalseggen mt. Norway 45 J3
Skarvsjöby Sweden 44 L2
Skaryszew Poland 49 S4
Skarżysko-Kamienna Poland 49 R4
Skaudvilė Lith. 42 D6
Skaulo Sweden 44 M2
Skaune Belarus 45 N4
Skaupsjøen-Hardangerjøkulen park Norway 45 I3
Skawa r. Poland 49 Q5
Skawina Poland 49 Q6
Skaymat W. Sahara 122 B4
Skeena r. Canada 166 D4
Skeena Mountains Canada 166 D3
Skegness U.K. 47 M10
Skeiðarársandur sand area Iceland 44 [inset] C3
Skeleton Coast Game Park nature res. Namibia 130 B3
Skellefteå Sweden 44 M2
Skellefteälven r. Sweden 44 M2
Skelleftebukten b. Sweden 44 M2
Skelleftehamn Sweden 44 M2
Skeppshamn Sweden 44 L3
Skerries Rep. of Ireland 47 F10
Skhimatárion Greece see Schimatari
Skhira Tunisia 123 H2
Skhíza i. Greece see Schiza
Ski Norway 45 J4
Skiathos Greece 59 E9
Skiathos i. Greece 59 E9
Skibbereen Rep. of Ireland 47 C12
Skibotn Norway 44 M1
Skidal' Belarus 42 F8
also spelt Skidel'
Skiddaw hill U.K. 47 I9
Skidegate Mission Canada 166 D4
Skidel' Belarus see Skidal'
Skiemonys Lith. 42 G6
Skien Norway 45 J4
Skierniewice Poland 49 R4
Skikda Alg. 123 G1
formerly known as Philippeville
Šķilbēni Latvia 42 I4
Skinari, Akra pt Greece 59 B11
Skinnskatteberg Sweden 45 K4
Skio Jammu and Kashmir 96 C2
Skipskop S. Africa 132 E11
Skipton Australia 147 D4
Skipton U.K. 47 J10
Skiropoúla i. Greece see Skyropoula
Skíros i. Greece see Skyros
Skive Denmark 45 J4
Skjálfandafljót r. Iceland 44 [inset] C2
Skjálfandi b. Iceland 44 [inset] C2
Skjelatinden mt. Norway 44 K2
Skjellbreid Norway 44 K2
Skjellinhovde hill Norway 45 J3
Skjerkeknuten hill Norway 45 I4
Skjern Denmark 45 J5
Skjern Norway 44 J2
Skjerstadejorden inlet Norway 44 K2
Skjervøy Norway 44 M1
Skjolden Norway 45 I3
Skoby Sweden 45 L3
Skobelev Uzbek. see Fergana
Skobeleva, Pik mt. Kyrg. 103 H5
Skocjanske Jame tourist site Slovenia 56 F3
Skoenmakerskop S. Africa 133 J11
Škofja Loka Slovenia 56 G2
Skog Sweden 45 L3
Skoganvarre Norway 44 N1
Skogfoss Norway 44 O1
Skoki Poland 49 O3
Skokie U.S.A. 172 F8
Skol' Kazakh. 103 E2
Skomvær is Norway 44 J2
Skoonspruit r. S. Africa 133 K4
Skopelos Greece 59 E9
Skopelos i. Greece 59 E9
Skopia hill Greece 59 G9
Skopin Rus. Fed. 43 U8
Skopje Macedonia 58 C7
Capital of Macedonia. Also spelt Skoplje; historically known as Scupi.
Skoplje Macedonia see Skopje
Skopunarfjørður sea chan. Faroe Is 46 F2
Skórcz Poland 49 P2
Skorodnoye Rus. Fed. 41 F6
Skørping Denmark 45 J4
Skotoussa Greece 58 E7
Skotterud Norway 45 K4
Skoutari Greece 58 E7
Skoutaros Greece 59 H9
Skövde Sweden 45 K4
Skovorodino Rus. Fed. 82 A1
Skowhegan U.S.A. 177 P1
Skriveri Latvia 42 G5
Škrlatica mt. Slovenia 56 F2
Skröven Sweden 44 M2
Skrunda Latvia 42 D5
Skrwa r. Poland 49 Q3
Skrydlyeva Belarus 43 L6
Skúgvoy i. Faroe Is 46 F2
Skukum, Mount Canada 166 C2
Skukuza S. Africa 133 P1
Skuleskogens nationalpark nat. park Sweden 44 L3
Skull Peak U.S.A. 183 H5
Skull Valley U.S.A. 183 L7
Skultuna Sweden 45 L4
Skunk r. U.S.A. 174 B3
Skuodas Lith. 42 C5
Skuratovskiy Rus. Fed. 43 S7
Skurup Sweden 45 K5
Skŭt r. Bulg. 58 E5
Skutskär Sweden 45 L3
Skvyra Ukr. 41 D6
Skwierzyna Poland 49 M3
Skye i. U.K. 46 F6
Skykula hill Norway 45 I4
Skyring, Seno b. Chile 205 B9
Skyropoula i. Greece 59 F10
also spelt Skiropoúla
Skyros Greece 59 F10
Skyros i. Greece 59 F10
also spelt Skíros
Skytrain Ice Rise Antarctica 222 S1
Slabodka Belarus 42 I6
Slættaratindur hill Faroe Is 46 E1
Slagelse Denmark 45 J5
Slagnäs Sweden 44 L2
Slamet, Gunung vol. Indon. 77 E4
Slaná r. Slovakia 49 R7
Slaney r. Rep. of Ireland 47 F11
Slănic Romania 58 G3
Slănic r. Romania 58 H3
Slănic Moldova Romania 58 H2
Slanské Vrchy mts Slovakia 49 S7
Slantsy Rus. Fed. 43 J2
Slaný Czech Rep. 49 L5
Šlapaberžė Lith. 42 E6
Slapovi Krke nat. park Croatia 56 H5
Slashers Reefs Australia 149 E3
Śląska, Wyżyna hills Poland 49 P5
Slate Islands Canada 168 C3
Slatina Croatia 56 J3
Slatina Romania 58 F4
Slatina r. Slovakia 49 Q7
Slatina-Timiș Romania 58 D3
Slaty Fork U.S.A. 176 E7
Slautnoye Rus. Fed. 39 Q3
Slave r. Canada 167 H2
Slave Coast Africa 125 F5
Slave Lake Canada 167 H4
Slave Point Canada 167 H2
Slavgorod Belarus see Slawharad
Slavgorod Rus. Fed. 103 I1
Slavkovichi Rus. Fed. 43 K4
Slavnoye Rus. Fed. 43 R5
Slavonia reg. Croatia 56 J3
also spelt Slavonija
Slavonija reg. Croatia see Slavonia
Slavonska Požega Croatia see Požega
Slavonski Brod Croatia 56 K3
Slavsk Rus. Fed. 42 C6
historically known as Heinrichswalde
Slavuta Ukr. 41 C6
Slavutych Ukr. 41 D6
Slavyanka Kazakh. see Myrzakent
Slavyanka Rus. Fed. 82 C4
Slavyanovo Bulg. 58 F5
Slavyansk Ukr. see Slov"yans'k
Slavyanskaya Rus. Fed. see Slavyansk-na-Kubani
Slavyansk-na-Kubani Rus. Fed. 41 F7
formerly known as Slavyanskaya
Sława Poland 49 N4
Slawharad Belarus 43 M8
also spelt Slavgorod
Sławno Poland 49 N1
Slayton U.S.A. 178 D3
Sleaford U.K. 47 L10
Sleaford Bay Australia 146 B3
Slea Head Rep. of Ireland 47 B11
Sleat, Sound of sea chan. U.K. 46 G6
Sled Lake Canada 167 J4
Sleeper Islands Canada 168 E1
Sleeping Bear Dunes National Lakeshore nature res. U.S.A. 172 G6
Sleeping Bear Point U.S.A. 172 G6
Sleep Island Hong Kong China 87 [inset]
Sleman Indon. 77 E4
Sleptsovskaya Rus. Fed. 41 H8
formerly known as Ordzhonikidzevskaya
Slessor Glacier Antarctica 223 W1
Ślęża hill Poland 49 N5
Slick Rock U.S.A. 183 P3
Slidell U.S.A. 175 B6
Slide Mountain U.S.A. 177 K4
Slidre Norway 45 J3
Slieve Car hill Rep. of Ireland 47 C9
Slieve Donard hill U.K. 47 G9
Slieve Gamph hills Rep. of Ireland 47 C10
also known as Ox Mountains
Slieve Mish Mountains hills Rep. of Ireland 47 B11
Sligachan U.K. 46 F6
Sligeach Rep. of Ireland see Sligo
Sligo Rep. of Ireland 47 D9
also spelt Sligeach
Sligo U.S.A. 176 F4
Sligo Bay Rep. of Ireland 47 D9
Slipper Island N.Z. 152 J5
Slippery Rock U.S.A. 176 E4
Slīteres rezervāts nature res. Latvia 42 D4
Sliven Bulg. 58 H6
Slivnitsa Bulg. 58 E6
Slivo Pole Bulg. 58 H5
Sljeme mt. Croatia 56 H3
Sloan r. Canada 167 G1
Sloan U.S.A. 183 I6
Sloat U.S.A. 182 D2
Sloboda Rus. Fed. see Ezhva
Sloboda Rus. Fed. see Przheval'skoye
Sloboda Rus. Fed. 41 G6
Slobodchikovo Rus. Fed. 40 I3
Slobodka Rus. Fed. 43 P7
Slobodskoy Rus. Fed. 40 I4
Slobodzeya Moldova see Slobozia
Slobozia Moldova 58 K2
formerly spelt Slobodzeya
Slobozia Romania 58 I4
Slobozia Bradului Romania 58 I3
Słomniki Poland 49 R5
Slonim Belarus 42 G8
Slough U.K. 47 L12
Slovakia country Europe 49 P7
known as Slovensko in Slovakian
europe [countries] 32–35
Slovenia country Europe 56 G2
spelt Slovenija in Slovenian
europe [countries] 32–35
Slovenija country Europe see Slovenia
Slovenj Gradec Slovenia 56 H2
Slovenska Bistrica Slovenia 56 H2
Slovenske Gorice hills Slovenia 56 H2
Slovenské Rudohorie mts Slovakia 49 Q7
Slovensko country Europe see Slovakia
Slovenský kras mts Slovakia 49 R7
Slovenský raj nat. park Slovakia 49 R7
Slov"yans'k Ukr. 41 F6
also spelt Slavyansk
Słowiński Park Narodowy nat. park Poland 49 O1
Słubice Poland 49 L3
Sluch r. Belarus 42 I9
Sluch r. Ukr. 53 H1
Sludka Rus. Fed. 40 I4
Slunj Croatia 56 H3
Słupca Poland 49 O3
Słupia r. Poland 49 N1
Słupsk Poland 49 O1
Slussfors Sweden 44 L2
Slutsk Belarus 42 I8
Šlyna r. Lith. 42 D6
Slyne Head Rep. of Ireland 47 B10
Slyudyanka Rus. Fed. 84 D1
Smackover U.S.A. 179 D5
Smålandsstenar Sweden 45 K4
Small Point U.S.A. 177 P2
Smallwood Reservoir Canada 169 H2
Smalowka Belarus 43 L6
Smalyavichy Belarus 42 J7
also spelt Smolevichi
Smarhon' Belarus 42 H7
also spelt Smorgon'
Smartt Syndicate Dam resr S. Africa 132 H7
Smeaton Canada 167 J4
Smederevo Srbija Yugo. 58 B4
historically known as Semendire
Smederevska Palanka Srbija Yugo. 58 B4
Smeeni Romania 58 H3
Smela Ukr. see Smila
Smelror Norway 44 O1
Smethport U.S.A. 176 G4
Śmigiel Poland 49 N3
Smila Ukr. 41 D6
also spelt Smela
Smilavichy Belarus 42 J8
Smiltene Latvia 42 G4
Smiltiņu kalns hill Latvia 42 D5
Smines Norway 44 K1
Smirnykh Rus. Fed. 82 F2
Smith Canada 167 H4
Smith r. MT U.S.A. 180 E3
Smith r. VA U.S.A. 176 F9
Smith Arm b. Canada 166 F1
Smith Bay U.S.A. 164 D2
Smith Center U.S.A. 178 C4
Smithers Canada 166 E4
Smithers Landing Canada 166 E4
Smithfield S. Africa 133 K7
Smithfield NC U.S.A. 174 E5
Smithfield UT U.S.A. 180 E4
Smithfield VA U.S.A. 177 I9
Smith Glacier Antarctica 222 Q1
Smith Island Antarctica 222 T2
Smith Island India 95 G3
Smith Island MD U.S.A. 177 I7
Smith Island VA U.S.A. 177 J8
Smithland U.S.A. 174 B4
Smith Mountain Lake U.S.A. 176 F8
Smith River Canada 166 E3
Smithsburg U.S.A. 176 H6
Smiths Falls Canada 168 E4
Smith Sound sea chan. Canada/Greenland 165 L2
Smithton Australia 147 E5
Smithville TN U.S.A. 174 C5
Smithville WV U.S.A. 176 D6
Smitskraal S. Africa 133 I10
Smjörfjöll mts Iceland 44 [inset] D2
Smoke Creek Desert U.S.A. 182 E1
Smoky r. Canada 166 G3
Smoky Bay Australia 146 B3
Smoky Cape Australia 147 G2
Smoky Falls Canada 168 D3
Smoky Hill r. U.S.A. 178 B4
Smoky Hill, North Fork r. U.S.A. 178 B4
Smoky Hills KS U.S.A. 178 C4
Smoky Lake Canada 167 H4
Smoky Mountains U.S.A. 180 D4
Smøla i. Norway 44 I3
Smolenka Rus. Fed. 102 B2
Smolensk Rus. Fed. 43 N7
Smolenskaya Oblast' admin. div. Rus. Fed. 43 O7
English form Smolensk Oblast
Smolensk Oblast admin. div. Rus. Fed. see Smolenskaya Oblast'
Smolensko-Moskovskaya Vozvyshennost' hills Rus. Fed. 43 N7
Smolevichi Belarus see Smalyavichy
Smolikas mt. Greece 59 B8
Smolyan Bulg. 58 F7
Smolyoninovo Rus. Fed. 82 D4
Smooth Rock Falls Canada 168 D3
Smoothrock Lake Canada 168 B3
Smoothstone Lake Canada 167 J4
Smørfjord Norway 44 N1
Smorgon' Belarus see Smarhon'
Smotrova Buda Rus. Fed. 43 N9
Smyadovo Bulg. 58 I5
Smyley Island Antarctica 222 S2
Smyrna Turkey see İzmir
Smyrna DE U.S.A. 177 J6
Smyrna GA U.S.A. 175 C5
Smyrna TN U.S.A. 174 C5
Smyth, Canal sea chan. Chile 205 B8
Snæfell mt. Iceland 44 [inset] D2
Snaefell hill Isle of Man 47 H9
Snæfellsjökull ice cap Iceland 44 [inset] B2
Snæfellsnes pen. Iceland 44 [inset] B2
Snake r. Canada 166 C1
Snake r. NE U.S.A. 178 B3
Snake r. U.S.A. 180 C3
Snake Range mts U.S.A. 183 J2
Snake River Canada 166 F3
Snake River Plain U.S.A. 180 D4
Snare r. Canada 167 G2
Snare Lake Canada 167 J3
Snare Lakes Canada see Wekweti
Snares Islands N.Z. 145 F6
also known as Tini Heke
Snåsa Norway 44 K2
Snåsvatn l. Norway 44 K2
Sneedville U.S.A. 176 B9
Sneek Neth. 48 C2
Sneem Rep. of Ireland 47 C12
Sneeuberg mts S. Africa 132 D9
Sneeuberge mts S. Africa 133 I8
Snegamook Lake Canada 169 I2
Snegurovka Ukr. see Tetiyiv
Snelling U.S.A. 182 D4
Snēpele Latvia 42 C5
Snezhed' r. Rus. Fed. 43 R8
Snezhnogorsk Rus. Fed. 39 I3
Sněžka mt. Czech Rep. 49 M5
also spelt Śnieżka
Snežnik mt. Slovenia 56 G3
Śniardwy, Jezioro l. Poland 49 S2
Sniečkus Lith. see Visaginas
Śnieżka mt. Czech Rep. see Sněžka
Śnieżnik mt. Poland 49 N5
Snihurivka Ukr. 41 E7
Snina Slovakia 49 T7
Snøhetta mt. Norway 44 J3
Snohomish U.S.A. 180 B3
Snønuten mt. Norway 45 I4
Snopot' r. Rus. Fed. 43 O8
Snov r. Ukr. 43 N9
Snova r. Rus. Fed. 43 R9
Snova r. Rus. Fed. 43 T9
Snovsk Ukr. see Shchors
Snow Belarus 42 H8
Snowbird Lake Canada 167 K2
Snowcrest Mountain Canada 167 G5
Snowdon mt. U.K. 47 H10
also known as Yr Wyddfa
Snowdonia National Park U.K. 47 I11
Snowdrift Canada see Łutselk'e
Snowdrift r. Canada 167 I2
Snowflake U.S.A. 183 N7
Snow Hill MD U.S.A. 177 J7
Snow Hill NC U.S.A. 174 E5
Snow Lake Canada 167 K4
Snowtown Australia 146 C3
Snow Water Lake U.S.A. 183 J1
Snowy r. Australia 147 F4
Snowy Mountain U.S.A. 177 K2
Snowy Mountains Australia 147 E4
Snudy, Vozyera l. Belarus 42 I6
Snug Corner Bahamas 187 E2
Snug Harbour Nfld. Canada 169 K2
Snug Harbour Ont. Canada 173 M5
Snyder OK U.S.A. 179 C5
Snyder TX U.S.A. 179 B5
Snyderspoort pass S. Africa 132 E8
Snykhovo Rus. Fed. 43 R8
Soahany Madag. 131 [inset] J3
Soaigh i. U.K. see Soay
Soalala Madag. 131 [inset] J3
Soamanonga Madag. 131 [inset] J4
Soanierana-Ivongo Madag. 131 [inset] K3
Soan-kundo is S. Korea 83 B6
Soata Col. 198 C3
Soavinandriana Madag. 131 [inset] J3
Soay i. U.K. 46 D6
also spelt Soaigh
Sobaek-sanmaek mts S. Korea 83 B6
Sobaek-san National Park S. Korea 83 C5
Sobat r. Sudan 128 A2
Soběslav Czech Rep. 49 L6
Sobger r. Indon. 73 J7
Sobinka Rus. Fed. 43 V6
Sobolevo Rus. Fed. 43 T6
Sobo-san mt. Japan 91 B8
Sobradinho Brazil 206 F2
Sobradinho, Barragem de resr Brazil 202 D4
Sobrado Bahia Brazil 202 D4
Sobrado Pará Brazil 199 H6
Sobral Brazil 202 D2
Sobrance Slovakia 49 T7
Soča r. Italy see Isonzo

Soča r. Slovenia 56 F3
Sochaczew Poland 49 R3
Sochi Rus. Fed. 41 F8
Sŏch'ŏn S. Korea 83 B5
Sochos Greece 58 E8
also spelt Sokhós
Société, Archipel de la is Fr. Polynesia see Society Islands
▶Society Islands Fr. Polynesia 221 H7
also known as Société, Archipel de la
oceania [issues] 140–141
Socol Romania 58 C4
Socompa Chile 200 C6
Soconusco, Sierra de mts Mex. see Madre, Sierra
Socorro Brazil 206 G9
Socorro Col. 198 C3
Socorro U.S.A. 181 F6
Socorro, Isla i. Mex. 184 C5
Socota Peru 198 B6
Socotra i. Yemen 105 F5
also spelt Suquṭrā
Socovos Spain 55 J6
Soc Trăng Vietnam 79 D6
formerly known as Khan Hung
Socuéllamos Spain 55 I5
Soda Lake CA U.S.A. 182 E6
Soda Lake CA U.S.A. 183 H6
Sodankylä Fin. 44 N2
Soda Plains Aksai Chin 89 B5
Soda Springs U.S.A. 180 E4
Söderhamn Sweden 45 L3
Söderköping Sweden 45 L4
Södermanland county Sweden 45 L4
Södertälje Sweden 45 L4
Sodiri Sudan 121 F6
Sodium S. Africa 132 H7
Sodo Eth. 128 C3
Södra Kvarken strait Fin./Sweden 45 L3
Sodus U.S.A. 177 H2
Sodwana Bay National Park S. Africa 133 Q4
Soë Indon. 75 C5
Soekmekaar S. Africa 131 F4
Soela väin sea chan. Estonia 42 D3
Soerabaia Indon. see Surabaya
Soest Germany 48 F4
Soetdoring Nature Reserve S. Africa 133 K5
Soetendalsvlei l. S. Africa 132 D11
Sofades Greece 59 D9
Sofala Moz. 131 G4
Sofala prov. Moz. 131 G3
formerly known as Beira
Sofala, Baía de b. Moz. 131 G4

▶Sofia Bulg. 58 E6
Capital of Bulgaria. Also spelt Sofiya; historically known as Sardica or Serdica or Sredets.

Sofia r. Madag. 131 [inset] J2
Sofiko Greece 59 E11
Sofiya Bulg. see Sofia
Sofiyevka Ukr. see Vil'nyans'k
Sofiysk Khabarovskiy Kray Rus. Fed. 82 D1
Sofiysk Khabarovskiy Kray Rus. Fed. 82 E2
Sofporog Rus. Fed. 44 O2
Sofrino Rus. Fed. 43 S5
Softa Kalesi tourist site Turkey 108 D1
Sōfu-gan i. Japan 81 O7
English form Lot's Wife
Sog China 89 F6
also known as Garqêntang
Sogamoso Col. 198 C3
Sogat China 88 D3
formerly spelt Süget
Sogda Rus. Fed. 82 D2
Sogma China 89 C5
Søgne Norway 45 I4
Sognefjorden inlet Norway 45 I3
Sogn og Fjordane county Norway 45 I3
Sogo Rus. Fed. 39 M2
Sogod Phil. 74 C4
Sogod Bay Phil. 74 C4
Sogo Hills Kenya 128 C4
Sogolle well Chad 120 B6
Sogo Nur l. China 84 D3
Sogozha r. Rus. Fed. 43 U3
Söğüt Turkey 106 B2
Söğüt Dağı mts Turkey 106 B3
Sŏgwip'o S. Korea 83 B6
Sohâg Egypt 121 F3
also spelt Sūhāj
Sohagpur India 96 C5
Sohalinskiy Kazakh. 103 G2
Sohan r. Pak. 101 G3
Sohano P.N.G. 145 E2
Sohar Oman see Şuḩār
Sohela India 97 D5
Sohna India 96 C3
Sohng Gwe, Khao hill Myanmar/Thai. 79 B5
Soignies Belgium 51 K2
Soila China 86 A2
Soini Fin. 44 N3
Soissons France 51 J3
Sōja Japan 91 C7
Sojat India 96 B4
Sojat Road India 96 B4
Sojoton Point Phil. 74 B4
Sok r. Rus. Fed. 41 I5
Sokch'o S. Korea 83 C5
Söke Turkey 106 A3
Sokele Dem. Rep. Congo 127 E7
Sokhondo, Gora mt. Rus. Fed. 85 F1
Sokhor, Gora mt. Rus. Fed. 85 E1
Sokhós Greece see Sochos
Sokhumi Georgia 107 E2
also known as Aq"a; also spelt Sukhumi; historically known as Dioscurias or Sukhum-Kale
Sokiryany Ukr. see Sokyryany
Sokkuram Grotto tourist site S. Korea 90 A7
Soknedal Norway 44 J3
Sokobanja Srbija Yugo. 58 C5
Sokodé Togo 125 F4
Soko Islands Hong Kong China 87 [inset]
also known as Shekka Ch'ün-Tao
Sokol Rus. Fed. 82 F3
Sokol Rus. Fed. 43 V2
Sokolac Bos.-Herz. 56 K5
Sokółka Poland 49 U2
Sokol'niki Tul'skaya Oblast' Rus. Fed. 43 T7
Sokol'niki Tverskaya Oblast' Rus. Fed. 43 P5
Sokolo Mali 124 D3
Sokolov Czech Rep. 49 J5
Sokolovka Rus. Fed. 90 C3
Sokołów Małopolski Poland 49 T5
Sokołów Podlaski Poland 49 T3
Sokolozero, Ozero l. Rus. Fed. 44 O2
Sokone Senegal 124 A3
Sokosti hill Fin. 44 O1
Sokoto Nigeria 125 G3
Sokoto r. Nigeria 125 G4
Sokoto state Nigeria 125 G3
Sokourala Guinea 124 C4
Sokyryany Ukr. 41 C6
also spelt Sokiryany
Sola Cuba 186 D2
Sola r. Poland 49 Q6
Sola i. Tonga see Ata
Solan India 96 C3
Solana Beach U.S.A. 183 G9
Solander Island N.Z. 153 A14
Solanet Arg. 204 F5
Solano Phil. 74 B2
Solano Venez. 199 E4
Solapur India 94 B2
formerly spelt Sholapur
Soldado Bartra Peru 198 C5
Soldotna U.S.A. 164 D3
Solec Kujawski Poland 49 P2
Soledad Arg. 204 E3
Soledad U.S.A. 182 C5
Soledad Venez. 199 F2
Soledad de Doblado Mex. 185 F5
Soledade Brazil 198 D6
Solen mt. Norway 45 J3
Solenoye Rus. Fed. 41 G7
Solenzo Burkina 124 D3
Solfjellsjøen Norway 44 K2
Solginskiy Rus. Fed. 40 G3
Solhan Turkey 107 E3
Soligalich Rus. Fed. 40 G4
Soligorsk Belarus see Salihorsk
Solihull U.K. 47 K11
Solikamsk Rus. Fed. 40 K4
Sol'-Iletsk Rus. Fed. 102 C2
Soliman Tunisia 57 C12
Solimón, Punta pt Mex. 185 I5
Solingen Germany 48 E4
Solita Col. 198 C4
Solita Venez. 187 F5
Sol-Karmala Rus. Fed. see Severnoye
Sölktäler nature res. Austria 49 K8
Sollefteå Sweden 44 L3
Sollentuna Sweden 45 L4
Sóller Spain 55 N5
Sollerön Sweden 45 K3
Solling hills Germany 48 G4
Solnechnogorsk Rus. Fed. 43 R5
Solnechnyy Rus. Fed. 82 E2
Solnechnyy Rus. Fed. see Gornyy
Solo r. Java Indon. 77 F4
Solo r. Sulawesi Indon. 75 B3
Solofra Italy 57 G8
Solok Indon. 76 C3
Sololá Guat. 185 H6
Solomon U.S.A. 183 O9
Solomon r. U.S.A. 178 C4
Solomon, North Fork r. U.S.A. 178 C4
Solomon, South Fork r. U.S.A. 178 C4

▶Solomon Islands country S. Pacific Ocean 145 F2
4th largest and 5th most populous country in Oceania. Formerly known as British Solomon Islands.
oceania [countries] 138–139

Solomon Sea P.N.G./Solomon Is 145 E2
Solon China 85 I2
Solon U.S.A. 172 B9
Solor i. Indon. 75 B5
Solor, Kepulauan is Indon. 75 B5
Solotcha Rus. Fed. 43 U7
Solothurn Switz. 51 N5
Solovetskiy Rus. Fed. 40 E2
formerly known as Kreml'
Solovetskiye Ostrova is Rus. Fed. 40 E2
Solovetskoye Rus. Fed. 40 H4
Solov'yevo Rus. Fed. 43 N7
Solov'yevsk Mongolia 85 G1
Solov'yevsk Rus. Fed. 82 B1
Solsona Spain 55 M3
Solt Hungary 49 Q9
Šolta i. Croatia 56 I5
Solṭānābād Khorāsan Iran 100 D2
Solṭānābād Iran 101 D3
Solṭānābād Tehrān Iran 100 B3
Soltān-e Bakva Afgh. 101 E3
Solṭānī, Khowr-e b. Iran 100 B4
Solṭanqoli Iran 100 A3
Soltau Germany 48 G3
Sol'tsy Rus. Fed. 43 L3
Soltüstik Qazaqstan Oblysy admin. div. Kazakh. see Severnyy Kazakhstan
Soltvadkert Hungary 49 Q9
Solunska Glava mt. Macedonia 58 C7
Solvang U.S.A. 182 D7
Solvay U.S.A. 177 I2
Sölvesborg Sweden 45 K4
Sol'vychegodsk Rus. Fed. 40 H3
Solway Firth est. U.K. 47 I9
Solwezi Zambia 127 E8
Sōma Japan 90 G6
Soma Turkey 106 A3
Somabhula Zimbabwe 131 F3
formerly spelt Somabula
Somabula Zimbabwe see Somabhula
Somali admin. reg. Eth. 128 D3
▶Somalia country Africa 128 E4
spelt Soomaaliya in Somali; long form Somali Republic
africa [countries] 114–117
Somali Republic country Africa see Somalia
Somanga Tanz. 129 C7
Somanya Ghana 125 E5
Sombang, Gunung mt. Indon. 77 G2
Sombo Angola 127 D7
Sombor Vojvodina, Srbija Yugo. 58 A3
also spelt Zombor
Sombrerete Mex. 184 E4
Sombrero i. Anguilla 187 H3
Sombrero Chile 205 C9
Sombrero Channel India 95 G5
Somdari India 96 B4
Somero Fin. 45 M3
Somerset KY U.S.A. 176 A8
Somerset MA U.S.A. 177 N4
Somerset MI U.S.A. 173 I8
Somerset OH U.S.A. 176 C6
Somerset PA U.S.A. 176 F6
Somerset East S. Africa 133 J9
Somerset Island Canada 165 J2
Somerset West S. Africa 132 C11
Somersworth U.S.A. 177 O2
Somerton U.S.A. 183 J9
Sōmeru Estonia 42 H2
Somerville NJ U.S.A. 177 K5
Somerville TN U.S.A. 174 B5
Somerville Reservoir U.S.A. 179 C6
Someșan, Podișul plat. Romania 58 E2
Someșu Cald r. Romania 58 E2
Someșul Mare r. Romania 58 E1
Someșu Mic r. Romania 58 E1
Somesville U.S.A. 177 Q1
Someydeh Iran 100 A3
also spelt Samaida
Somino Rus. Fed. 43 P2
Somkele S. Africa 133 Q5
Sømmarøy Norway 44 L1
Somme r. France 50 H2
Sommen l. Sweden 45 K4
Sömmerda Germany 48 I4
Sommet, Lac du l. Canada 169 G2
Somnath India 94 A1
also known as Patan
Somogyszob Hungary 49 O9
Somosomo Fiji 145 H3
Somotillo Nicaragua 186 B4
Somoto Nicaragua 186 B4
Somovo Orlovskaya Oblast' Rus. Fed. 43 Q9
Somovo Tul'skaya Oblast' Rus. Fed. 43 R8
Sompeta India 95 E2
Sompolno Poland 49 P3
Somport, Col du pass France/Spain 55 K2
Šomrda hill Yugo. 58 C4
Somuncurá, Mesa Volcánica de plat. Arg. 204 D6
Somvarpet India 94 B3
Son r. India 96 E4
Soná Panama 186 C6
Sonag China see Zêkog
Sonai r. India 97 G4
Sonai r. India 97 G4
Sonakhan India 97 D5
Sonala India 94 C1
Sonaly Kazakh. 103 G2
Sonamukhi India 97 E5
Sonapur India 95 D1
Sonari India 97 G4
Sŏnch'ŏn N. Korea 83 B5
Sondalo Italy 56 C2
Sønderå r. Denmark 48 F1
Sønderborg Denmark 45 J5
Sondershausen Germany 48 H4
Sønderup Denmark 45 J4
Søndre Strømfjord Greenland see Kangerlussuaq
Søndre Strømfjord inlet Greenland see Kangerlussuaq
Søndre Upernavik Greenland see Upernavik Kujalleq
Sondrio Italy 56 B2
Sonepat India 94 C2
Song Nigeria 125 I4
Songa Indon. 75 C3
Songad India 96 A5
Songbai China see Shennongjia
Songbu China 87 E2
Sông Cau Vietnam 79 E5
Songcheng China see Xiapu
Sông Da, Hô resr Vietnam 78 D3
Songea Tanz. 129 B7
Sŏnggan N. Korea 83 B4
Songhua Hu resr China 82 B4
Songhua Jiang r. China 82 D3
English form Sungari
Songjiachuan China see Wubu
Songjiang Jilin China 82 C4
formerly known as Antu
Songjiang Shanghai China 87 G2
formerly known as Sungkiang
Songjianghe China 82 B4
Sŏngjin N. Korea see Kimch'aek
Sŏngju S. Korea 91 A7
Songkan China 86 C2
Songkhla Thai. 79 C7
also known as Singora
Song Khram, Mae Nam r. Thai. 78 D4
Songköl l. Kyrg. 103 H4
also known as Sonkël', Ozero
Songling China 85 I2
Song Ling mts China 85 H3
Songmai China see Dêrong
Songming China 86 B3
also known as Songyang
Songnam S. Korea 83 B5
Songnim N. Korea 83 B5
Songni-san National Park S. Korea 83 B5
Songo Angola 127 B6
Songo Moz. 131 G2
Songololo Dem. Rep. Congo 127 B6
Songololo Dem. Rep. Congo see Mbanza-Ngungu
Songpan China 86 B1
also known as Jin'an or Sungqu
Songsak India 97 F4
Sŏngsan S. Korea 83 B6
Songshan China see Ziyun
Song Shan mt. China 87 E1
Songtao China 87 D2
Songxi China 87 F3
also known as Songyuan
Songxian China 87 E1
Songyang China see Songming
Songyuan China see Songxi
Songyuan China 82 B3
also known as Ningjiang; formerly known as Fuyu
Songzi China 87 D2
formerly known as Xinjiangkou
Sonhat India 97 D5
Sonid Youqi China see Saihan Tal
Sonid Zuoqi China see Mandalt
Sonipat India 96 C3
Sonkajärvi Fin. 44 N3
Sonkël', Ozero l. Kyrg. see Songköl
Sonkovo Rus. Fed. 43 S4
Son La Vietnam 78 C3
Sonmiani Bay Pak. 101 F5
Sonneberg Germany 48 I5
Sonnenjoch mt. Austria 48 J8
Sono r. Minas Gerais Brazil 203 C6
Sono r. Tocantins Brazil 202 B4
Sonoita watercourse Mex. 181 D7
Sonoma U.S.A. 182 B3
Sonoma Peak U.S.A. 182 G1
Sonora r. Mex. 184 C2
Sonora state Mex. 184 C2
Sonora CA U.S.A. 182 D4
Sonora TX U.S.A. 179 B6
Sonora Peak U.S.A. 182 E3
Sonqor Iran 100 A3
Sonseca Spain 54 H5
Son Servera Spain 55 O5
Sonsón Col. 198 C3
Sonsonate El Salvador 185 H6
Sonsorol Islands Palau 73 H5
also spelt Sansoral Islands
Sonstraal S. Africa 132 G4
Son Tây Vietnam 78 D3
Sonthofen Germany 48 H8
Sonwabile S. Africa 133 M8
Soochow China see Suzhou
Soodla r. Estonia 42 G2
Soomaaliya country Africa see Somalia
Soperton U.S.A. 175 D5
Sopi, Tanjung pt Indon. 75 D2
Sopo watercourse Sudan 126 E2
Sopot Bulg. 58 F6
Sopot Poland 49 P1
Sopot Srbija Yugo. 58 B4
Sopron Hungary 49 N8
historically known as Ödenburg
Sopu-Korgon Kyrg. 88 A4
also known as Sufi-Kurgan
Sopur Jammu and Kashmir 96 B2
Soputan, Gunung vol. Indon. 75 C2
Sor r. France 51 I9
Sor r. Port. 54 C6
Sor r. Spain 54 D1
Sora Italy 56 F7
Sorab India 94 B3
Soråker Sweden 44 L3
Sŏrak-san mt. S. Korea 83 C5
Sorak-san National Park S. Korea 83 C5
Sorata Bol. 200 C3
Sør-Audnedal Norway 45 I4
Sorbas Spain 55 I7
Sorbe r. Spain 55 H4
Sor Donyztau dry lake Kazakh. 102 D3
Sorel Canada 169 F4
Sorell Australia 147 E5
Soreq r. Israel 108 F6
Sørfjorden inlet Norway 45 I3
Sorgono Sardegna Italy 57 B8
Sorgues France 51 K8
Sorgues r. France 51 I9
Sorgun Yozgat Turkey 106 C3
also known as Yeşilova
Sorgun r. Turkey 108 F1
Soria Spain 55 I3
Sorikmarapi vol. Indon. 76 B2
Sørkappøya i. Svalbard 38 C2
Sor Kaydak dry lake Kazakh. 102 C3
Sorkh, Kūh-e mts Iran 100 C3
Sorkheh Iran 100 C3
Sørland Norway 44 K2
Sørli Norway 44 K2
Sor Mertvyy Kultuk dry lake Kazakh. 102 C3
also known as Öli Qoltyq Sory
Sörmjöle Sweden 44 M3
Sorø Denmark 45 J5
Soro India 97 E5
Soro, Monte mt. Sicilia Italy 57 G11
Soroca Moldova 41 D6
formerly spelt Soroki
Sorocaba Brazil 206 F10
Sorochinsk Rus. Fed. 102 C1
Soroki Moldova see Soroca
Sorokino Rus. Fed. 43 K4
Sorol atoll Micronesia 73 J5
formerly known as Philip Atoll
Sorong Indon. 73 H7
Sororó r. Brazil 202 B3
Sororoca Brazil 199 F4
Sorot' r. Rus. Fed. 43 J4
Soroti Uganda 128 B4
Sørøya i. Norway 44 M1
Sørøysundet sea chan. Norway 44 M1
Sorraia r. Port. 54 C5
Sorreisa Norway 44 L1
Sorrento Italy 56 G8
Sorsakoski Fin. 44 N3
Sorsatunturi hill Fin. 44 O2
Sorsele Sweden 44 L2
Sorso Sardegna Italy 57 A8
Sorsogon Phil. 74 C3
Sortavala Rus. Fed. 45 O3
Sortland Norway 44 K1
Sortot Sudan 121 F5
Sør-Trøndelag county Norway 44 J3
Sørvær Norway 44 M1
Sørvågen Norway 44 K2
Sõrve väin sea chan. Estonia/Latvia see Irbe Strait
Sŏsan S. Korea 83 B5
Sosedno Rus. Fed. 43 J3
Sosenskiy Rus. Fed. 43 Q7
Soshanguve S. Africa 133 M2
Soskovo Rus. Fed. 43 Q9
Sosna r. Rus. Fed. 43 T9
Sosnogorsk Rus. Fed. 40 J3
formerly known as Izhma
Sosnovka Kazakh. 103 I2
Sosnovka Arkhangel'skaya Oblast' Rus. Fed. 40 H3
Sosnovka Murmanskaya Oblast' Rus. Fed. 40 G2
Sosnovka Tambovskaya Oblast' Rus. Fed. 41 G5
Sosnovka Vologod. Obl. Rus. Fed. 43 S3
Sosnovka Vologod. Obl. Rus. Fed. 43 U2
Sosnovo Rus. Fed. 43 L1
Sosnovoborsk Rus. Fed. 41 H5
Sosnovo-Ozerskoye Rus. Fed. 81 I2
Sosnovyy Rus. Fed. 44 P2
Sosnovyy Bor Belarus see Sasnovy Bor
Sosnovyy Bor Rus. Fed. 43 K2
Sosnowiec Poland 49 Q5
historically known as Sosnowitz
Sosnowitz Poland see Sosnowiec
Sosny Belarus 42 I9
Sosso Cent. Afr. Rep. 126 B4
Sos'va Rus. Fed. 38 G4
Sot' r. Rus. Fed. 43 V4
Sota r. Benin 125 F4
Sotang China 97 G3
Sotério r. Brazil 201 D2
Sotillo r. Spain 54 F6
Sotkamo Fin. 44 O2
Soto Arg. 204 D3
Soto la Marina Mex. 185 F4
Sotouboua Togo 125 F4
Sotteville-lès-Rouen France 50 H3
Sottunga Fin. 45 M3
Sotuta Mex. 185 H4
Souanké Congo 126 B4
Soubré Côte d'Ivoire 124 D5
Soucis, Cape N.Z. 152 H9
Souda Greece 59 F13
also spelt Soúdha
Soudan Australia 148 C4
Soudas, Ormos b. Greece 59 F13
Soúdha Greece see Souda
Souflí Greece 58 H7
Soufrière vol. Guadeloupe 187 H3
Soufrière St Lucia 187 H4
Soufrière vol. St Vincent 199 F1
Soufrière Hills Montserrat 187 H3
Souguéta Guinea 124 B4
Sougueur Alg. 55 M9
Souillac France 50 H8
Souk Ahras Alg. 123 G1
Souk el Arbaâ du Rharb Morocco 122 D2
Souk el Had el Rharbia Morocco 54 F9
Souk el Kella Morocco 54 F9
Souk Khemis du Sahel Morocco 54 E9
Soukoukoutane Niger 125 F3
Souk Tleta Taghramet Morocco 54 F9
Souk-Tnine-de-Sidi-el-Yamani Morocco 54 F9
Sŏul S. Korea see Seoul
Soulac-sur-Mer France 50 E7
Sounding Creek r. Canada 167 I4
Sounfat well Mali see Tessoûnfat
Souniou nat. park Greece 59 F11
Soûr Lebanon see Tyre
Sourdeval France 50 F4
Soure Brazil 202 B2
Sour el Ghozlane Alg. 55 O8
Souris Man. Canada 167 K5
Souris P.E.I. Canada 169 I4
Souris r. Canada 167 L5
Souriya country Asia see Syria
Souroumelli well Mauritania 124 C2
Sous, Oued watercourse Morocco 122 C3
Sousa Brazil 202 E3
Sousa Lara Angola see Bocoio
Sousel Port. 54 D6
Sousse Tunisia 123 H2
also spelt Susah; historically known as Hadrumetum
Soussellem, Oued watercourse Alg. 55 N9
Soustons France 50 E9
Sout r. S. Africa 132 C8
Sout watercourse S. Africa 132 E5
South Africa country Africa see South Africa, Republic of
▶South Africa, Republic of country Africa 130 D6
known as Suid-Afrika in Afrikaans; short form South Africa
africa [countries] 114–117
South Alligator r. Australia 148 B2
Southampton Canada 168 D4
Southampton U.K. 47 K13
historically known as Hamwic
Southampton U.S.A. 177 M5
Southampton Island Canada 167 O1
South Andaman i. India 95 G4
South Anna r. U.S.A. 176 H8
South Aulatsivik Island Canada 169 I1
South Australia state Australia 146 B2
Southaven U.S.A. 174 B5
South Baldy mt. U.S.A. 181 F6
South Bay U.S.A. 175 D7
South Bend IN U.S.A. 174 C3
South Bend WA U.S.A. 180 B3
South Bight pt Bahamas 187 E2
South Boston U.S.A. 176 G9
Southbridge N.Z. 153 G11
Southbridge U.S.A. 177 M3
South Brook Canada 169 J3
South Burlington U.S.A. 177 L1
Southburn N.Z. 153 F12
South Carolina state U.S.A. 175 D5
South Charleston OH U.S.A. 176 B6
South Charleston WV U.S.A. 176 D7
South China Sea N. Pacific Ocean 72 E4
South Coast Town Australia see Gold Coast
South Dakota state U.S.A. 178 B2
South Deerfield U.S.A. 177 M3
South Downs hills U.K. 47 L13
South East admin. dist. Botswana 133 J2
South East Cape Australia 147 E5
South East Isles Australia 151 C7
Southend Canada 167 K3
Southend-on-Sea U.K. 47 M12
Southern admin. reg. Eth. 128 C3
Southern admin. reg. Malawi 129 B8
Southern prov. Sierra Leone 124 B5
Southern prov. Zambia 127 E9
Southern Aegean admin. reg. Greece see Notio Aigaio
Southern Alps mts N.Z. 153 E11
also known as Kā Tiritiri o te Moana
Southern Central Aboriginal Reserve Australia 151 D5
Southern Cross Australia 151 B6
Southern Darfur state Sudan 126 E2
Southern Indian Lake Canada 167 L3
Southern Kordofan state Sudan 128 A2
Southern Lau Group is Fiji 145 H3
Southern National Park Sudan 126 F3
Southern Ocean 222 F3
Southern Pines U.S.A. 174 E5
Southern Rhodesia country Africa see Zimbabwe
Southern Uplands hills U.K. 46 H8
Southern Urals mts Rus. Fed. see Yuzhnyy Ural
Southern Ute Indian Reservation res. U.S.A. 181 F5
South Esk Tableland reg. Australia 150 D3
Southey Canada 167 J5
Southeyville S. Africa 133 L8
South Fabius r. U.S.A. 178 E4
Southfield U.S.A. 173 J8
Southfields U.S.A. 177 K4
South Fork CA U.S.A. 182 A1
South Fork CO U.S.A. 181 F5
South Fork PA U.S.A. 176 G5
South Fox Island U.S.A. 172 H5
Southgate r. Canada 166 E5
South Geomagnetic Pole (2000) Antarctica 223 H1

▶South Georgia and South Sandwich Islands terr. S. Atlantic Ocean 217 L9
United Kingdom Overseas Territory.
southamerica [countries] 192–193

South Gillies Canada 172 D2
South Grand r. U.S.A. 178 D4
South Hatia Island Bangl. 97 F5
South Haven U.S.A. 172 G8
South Head N.Z. 152 I4
South Head N.Z. 152 I4
South Henik Lake Canada 167 L2
South Hero U.S.A. 177 L1
South Hill U.S.A. 176 G9
South Horr Kenya 128 C4
South Indian Lake Canada 167 L3
South Island India 94 B4

▶South Island N.Z. 153 G12
2nd largest island in Oceania. Also known as Te Waipounamu.
oceania [landscapes] 136–137

South Islet reef Phil. 74 A4
South Junction Canada 167 M5
South Kazakhstan Oblast admin. div. Kazakh. see Yuzhnyy Kazakhstan
South Kitui National Reserve nature res. Kenya 128 C5
South Koel r. India 97 E5
▶South Korea country Asia 83 B5
asia [countries] 64–67
South Lake Tahoe U.S.A. 182 D3
Southland admin. reg. N.Z. 153 B13
South Loup r. U.S.A. 178 C3
South Luangwa National Park Zambia 127 F8
South Macmillan r. Canada 166 C2
South Magnetic Pole (2000) Antarctica 223 J2
South Manitou Island U.S.A. 173 G5
South Mills U.S.A. 177 I9
Southminster U.K. 47 M12
South Moose Lake Canada 167 K4
South Mountains hills U.S.A. 177 H6
South Muiron Island Australia 150 A4
South Nahanni r. Canada 166 D1
South Negril Point Jamaica 186 D3
South New Berlin U.S.A. 177 J3
South Orkney Islands S. Atlantic Ocean 222 V2
South Paris U.S.A. 177 O1
South Passage Australia 151 A5
South Patrick Shores U.S.A. 175 D6
South Platte r. U.S.A. 178 B3
South Point pt U.S.A. 181 [inset] Z2
South Pole Antarctica 223 T1
South Porcupine Canada 173 L2
Southport Australia 147 E5
Southport U.K. 47 I10
Southport NC U.S.A. 175 E5
Southport NY U.S.A. 177 I3
South Portland U.S.A. 177 O2
South River Canada 173 N5
South Ronaldsay i. U.K. 46 J5
South Royalton U.S.A. 177 M2
South Salt Lake U.S.A. 183 M1
South San Francisco U.S.A. 182 B4
South Saskatchewan r. Canada 167 J4
South Seal r. Canada 167 L3
South Shetland Islands Antarctica 222 U2
South Shields U.K. 47 K8
South Sinai governorate Egypt see Janūb Sīnā'
South Skunk r. U.S.A. 174 A3
South Taranaki Bight b. N.Z. 152 I7
South Tent mt. U.S.A. 183 M2
South Tons r. India 97 D4
South Tucson U.S.A. 183 N9
South Turkana Nature Reserve Kenya 128 B4
South Twin Island Canada 168 E2
South Twin Lake Canada 169 K3
South Uist i. U.K. 46 E6
also known as Uibhist a' Deas
South Umpqua r. U.S.A. 180 B4
South Wellesley Islands Australia 148 C3
South-West Africa country Africa see Namibia
South West Cape Australia 147 E5
South West Cape N.Z. 153 B15
also known as Puhiwaero
South West Cay reef Australia 149 G4
Southwest Conservation Area nature res. Australia 147 E5
South West Entrance sea chan. P.N.G. 149 F1
Southwest Harbor U.S.A. 177 Q1
South West Island Australia 149 F3
South West National Park Australia 147 E5
South West Rocks Australia 147 G2
South Whitley U.S.A. 172 H9
South Williamson U.S.A. 176 C8
South Williamsport U.S.A. 177 I4
South Windham U.S.A. 177 O2
Southwold U.K. 47 N11
Southwood National Park Australia 147 F1
South Zanesville U.S.A. 176 C6
Soutpansberg mts S. Africa 131 F4
Souttouf, Adrar mts W. Sahara 122 B5
Souvigny France 51 J6
Sovata Romania 58 G2
Soveja Romania 58 H2
Soverato Italy 57 I10
Sovet Tajik. 101 G2
also known as Sovetskiy
Sovetabad Uzbek. see Khanabad
Sovetsk Kaliningradskaya Oblast' Rus. Fed. 42 C6
historically known as Tilsit
Sovetsk Kirovskaya Oblast' Rus. Fed. 40 I4
Sovetsk Tul'skaya Oblast' Rus. Fed. 43 S8
Sovetskaya Rus. Fed. 107 F1
Sovetskaya Gavan' Rus. Fed. 82 F2
Sovetskiy Khanty-Mansiyskiy Avtonomnyy Okrug Rus. Fed. 38 G3
Sovetskiy Leningradskaya Oblast' Rus. Fed. 43 J1
Sovetskiy Respublika Mariy El Rus. Fed. 40 I4
Sovetskiy Tajik. see Sovet
Sovetskoye Rus. Fed. see Shatoy
Sovetskoye Rus. Fed. 102 A2
Sovetskoye Rus. Fed. see Zelenokumsk
Sovići Bos.-Herz. 56 J5
Sowa Botswana 131 E4
Sowa China 86 A2
formerly known as Dagxoi
Sowa Pan salt pan Botswana 131 E4
Soweto S. Africa 133 L3
Sōya-kaikyō strait Japan/Rus. Fed. see La Pérouse Strait
Soyaló Mex. 185 G5
Sōya-misaki c. Japan 90 G2
Soyana r. Rus. Fed. 40 G2
Soyang-ho l. S. Korea 83 B5
Soyaux France 50 G7
Sōya-wan b. Japan 90 G2
Soylan Armenia see Vayk'
Soyma r. Rus. Fed. 40 I2
Soyo Angola 127 B6
formerly known as Santo António do Zaire
Sozaq Kazakh. see Suzak
Sozh r. Europe 43 L9
Sozimskiy Rus. Fed. 40 J4
Sozopol Bulg. 58 I6
historically known as Apollonia
Spaatz Island Antarctica 222 T2
Spadafora Sicilia Italy 57 H10

▶Spain country Europe 54 F4
4th largest country in Europe. Known as España in Spanish; historically known as Hispania.
europe [countries] 32–35

Spalato Croatia see Split
Spalatum Croatia see Split
Spalding Australia 146 C3
Spalding U.K. 47 L11
Spaniard's Bay Canada 169 K4
Spanish Canada 168 D4
Spanish r. Canada 168 D4
Spanish Fork U.S.A. 183 M1
Spanish Guinea country Africa see Equatorial Guinea
Spanish Netherlands country Europe see Belgium
Spanish Point Rep. of Ireland 47 C11
Spanish Sahara terr. Africa see Western Sahara
Spanish Town Jamaica 186 D3
Spanish Wells Bahamas 175 E7
Sparagio, Monte mt. Sicilia Italy 57 E10
Sparks U.S.A. 182 E2
Sparta Greece see Sparti
Sparta GA U.S.A. 175 D5
Sparta MI U.S.A. 172 H7
Sparta NC U.S.A. 176 D9
Sparta TN U.S.A. 174 C5
Sparta WI U.S.A. 172 C7
Spartanburg U.S.A. 174 D5
Spartansburg U.S.A. 176 F4
Spartel, Cap c. Morocco 54 F9
Sparti Greece 59 D11
historically known as Lacedaemon or Sparta
Spartivento, Capo c. Sardegna Italy 57 A10
Spartivento, Capo c. Italy 57 I11
Sparwood Canada 167 H5
Spas-Demensk Rus. Fed. 43 P7
Spas-Klepiki Rus. Fed. 43 V6
Spass Rus. Fed. 43 Q6
Spasskaya Polist' Rus. Fed. 43 M3
Spassk-Dal'niy Rus. Fed. 82 D3
Spasskoye Kazakh. 103 G1
Spasskoye-Lutovinovo Rus. Fed. 43 R8
Spas-Ugol Rus. Fed. 43 S5
Spatha, Akra pt Greece 59 E13
Spatsizi Plateau Wilderness Provincial Park Canada 166 D3
Spean Bridge U.K. 46 H7
Spearfish U.S.A. 178 B2
Spearman U.S.A. 179 B4
Speers Canada 167 J4
Speightstown Barbados 187 I4
Speikkogel mt. Austria 49 M8
Speke Gulf Tanz. 128 B5
Spence Bay Canada see Taloyoak
Spencer IA U.S.A. 178 D3
Spencer ID U.S.A. 180 D3
Spencer IN U.S.A. 174 C4
Spencer MA U.S.A. 177 N3
Spencer NY U.S.A. 177 I3
Spencer VA U.S.A. 176 E9
Spencer, Cape Australia 146 C3
Spencer, Cape U.S.A. 166 B3
Spencer, Point U.S.A. 39 T3
Spencer Gulf est. Australia 146 C3
Spencer Range hills N.T. Australia 148 A2
Spencer Range hills N.T. Australia 148 B2
Spences Bridge Canada 166 F5
Spenser Mountains N.Z. 153 G10
Sperchoeios r. Greece 59 D10
also spelt Sperkhiós
Sperkhiós r. Greece see Spercheios
Spermezeu Romania 58 F1
Sperrin Mountains hills U.K. 47 E9
Sperryville U.S.A. 176 G7
Spétsai i. Greece see Spetses
Spetses Greece 59 E11
Spetses i. Greece 59 E11
also known as Spétsai
Spey r. U.K. 46 I6
Speyer Germany 48 F6
Spezand Pak. 101 F4
Spice Islands Indon. see Moluccas
Spiekeroog i. Germany 48 E2
Spiez Switz. 51 N6
Spijkenisse Neth. 48 B4
Spil Dağı Milli Parkı nat. park Turkey 59 I10
Spilimbergo Italy 56 E2
Spīn Būldak Afgh. 101 F4
Spioenkop Dam Nature Reserve S. Africa 133 N5
Spirit Lake U.S.A. 178 D3
Spiritwood Canada 167 J4
Spirovo Rus. Fed. 43 P4
Spišská Nová Ves Slovakia 49 R7
Spitak Armenia 107 F2
Spiti r. India 96 C3
Spit Point Australia 150 B4

▶Spitsbergen i. Svalbard 38 B2
5th largest island in Europe. Also spelt Spitzbergen.
europe [landscapes] 30–31

Spitskop mt. S. Africa 132 G10
Spitskopvlei S. Africa 133 J8
Spitsyno Rus. Fed. 42 I3
Spittal an der Drau Austria 49 K9
Spitzbergen i. Svalbard see Spitsbergen
Split Croatia 56 I5
formerly known as Spalato; historically known as Spalatum
Split Lake Canada 167 L3
Split Lake l. Canada 167 L3
Spokane U.S.A. 180 C3
Spokane r. U.S.A. 180 C3
Spokane Indian Reservation res. U.S.A. 180 C3
Spoon r. U.S.A. 174 B3
Spooner U.S.A. 172 B5
Spot Bay Cayman Is 186 D3
Spotsylvania U.S.A. 176 H7
Spragge Canada 173 K4
Sprague r. U.S.A. 180 B4
Spranger, Mount Canada 166 F4
Spratly Island S. China Sea 72 D5
Spratly Islands S. China Sea 72 D5
also known as Nansha Qundao or Quan Dao Truong Sa or Truong Sa

S index

Spread Eagle U.S.A. 172 E5
Spreča r. Bos.-Herz. 56 K4
Spree r. Germany 49 K3
Spreewald park Germany 49 L4
Spremberg Germany 49 L4
Spring r. U.S.A. 178 D4
Spring Bay Canada 173 K5
Springbok S. Africa 132 B6
Spring City U.S.A. 183 M2
Spring Creek r. Australia 148 C3
Spring Creek U.S.A. 183 I1
Springdale Canada 169 K3
Springdale U.S.A. 179 D4
Springe Germany 48 G3
Springer U.S.A. 181 F5
Springerville U.S.A. 183 O7
Springfield N.Z. 153 F11
Springfield CO U.S.A. 178 B4
Springfield GA U.S.A. 175 D5

Springfield IL U.S.A. 174 B4
State capital of Illinois.

Springfield KY U.S.A. 174 C4
Springfield MA U.S.A. 177 M3
Springfield MN U.S.A. 178 D2
Springfield MO U.S.A. 178 D4
Springfield OH U.S.A. 176 B6
Springfield OR U.S.A. 180 B3
Springfield TN U.S.A. 174 C4
Springfield VT U.S.A. 177 M2
Springfield WV U.S.A. 176 G6
Springfontein S. Africa 133 J7
Spring Garden Guyana 199 G3
Spring Glen U.S.A. 183 N2
Spring Green U.S.A. 172 C7
Spring Grove MN U.S.A. 172 B7
Spring Grove VA U.S.A. 177 I8
Springhill Canada 169 H4
Spring Hill U.S.A. 175 D6
Springhouse Canada 166 F5
Spring Mountains U.S.A. 183 I5
Springport U.S.A. 173 I8
Springs S. Africa 133 M3
Springs Junction N.Z. 153 G10
Springsure Australia 149 F5
Spring Valley S. Africa 133 K9
Spring Valley U.S.A. 183 H9
Springview U.S.A. 178 C3
Springville CA U.S.A. 182 F5
Springville NY U.S.A. 176 G3
Springville PA U.S.A. 177 J4
Springville UT U.S.A. 183 M1
Springwater U.S.A. 176 H3
Spruce Grove Canada 167 H4
Spruce Knob mt. U.S.A. 176 F7
Spruce Mountain CO U.S.A. 183 P3
Spruce Mountain NV U.S.A. 183 J1
Spulico, Capo c. Italy 57 I9
Spurn Head U.K. 47 M10
Spurr, Mount vol. U.S.A. 164 D3
Spuzzum Canada 166 F5
Squamish Canada 166 F5
Squamish r. Canada 166 F5
Squam Lake U.S.A. 177 N2
Square Lake U.S.A. 174 G2
Squillace Italy 57 I10
Squillace, Golfo di g. Italy 57 I10
Squinzano Italy 57 K8
Squire U.S.A. 176 D8
Squires, Mount hill Australia 151 D5
Sragen Indon. 77 E4
Srbica Kosovo, Srbija Yugo. 58 B6
Srbija aut. rep. Yugo. 58 B5
English form Serbia
Srbinje Bos.-Herz. see Foča
Srbobran Bos.-Herz. see Donji Vakuf
Srbobran Vojvodina, Srbija Yugo. 58 A3
Srebărna tourist site Bulg. 58 I4
Srebrenica Bos.-Herz. 56 L4
Sredets Bulg. 58 I6
formerly known as Grudovo
Sredets Bulg. see Sofia
Sredetska Reka r. Bulg. 58 I6
formerly known as Mandrenska
Sredinnyy Khrebet mts Rus. Fed. 39 P4
Sredishte Bulg. 58 I5
Sredna Gora mts Bulg. 58 E6
Srednebelaya Rus. Fed. 82 B2
Srednekolymsk Rus. Fed. 39 P3
Sredne-Russkaya Vozvyshennost' hills Rus. Fed. see Central Russian Upland
Sredne-Sibirskoye Ploskogor'ye plat. Rus. Fed. see Central Siberian Plateau
Sredneye Kuyto, Ozero l. Rus. Fed. 44 O2
Srednogorie Bulg. 58 F6
Srednyaya Akhtuba Rus. Fed. 41 H6
Śrem Poland 49 O3
Srem reg. Yugo. 58 A3
Sremska Mitrovica Vojvodina, Srbija Yugo. 58 A4
historically known as Sirmium
Srêpok, Tônlé r. Cambodia 79 D5
Sretensk Rus. Fed. 81 J2
Sri Aman Sarawak Malaysia 77 E2
formerly known as Samarahan
Sriharikota Island India 94 D3

Sri Jayewardenepura Kotte Sri Lanka 94 C5
Capital of Sri Lanka. Short form Kotte.

Srikakulam India 95 E2
also known as Chicacole
Sri Kalahasti India 94 C3
Sri Lanka country Asia 94 D5
also known as Sarandib or Saylan; also spelt Shri Lanka; formerly known as Ceylon; historically known as Lanka or Sinhala or Taprobane
asia [countries] 64–67
Sri Madhopur India 96 B4
Srimangal Bangl. 97 F4
Srinagar India 96 C3
Srinagar Jammu and Kashmir 96 B2

Sringeri India 94 B3
Sri Pada mt. Sri Lanka see Adam's Peak
Srirangam India 94 C4
Srisailam India 94 C2
Srivaikuntam India 94 C4
Srivardhan India 94 B2
Srivilliputtur India 94 C4
Srnetica mts Bos.-Herz. 56 I4
Srnice Bos.-Herz. 56 K4
also known as Hasić
Środa Śląska Poland 49 N4
Środa Wielkopolska Poland 49 O3
Srpska Crnja Vojvodina, Srbija Yugo. 58 B3
Srpska Kostajnica Bos.-Herz. see Bosanska Kostajnica
Srpski Brod Bos.-Herz. see Bosanski Brod
Srpski Itebej Vojvodina, Srbija Yugo. 58 B3
Srungavarapukota India 95 D2
Sselki Rus. Fed. 43 U9
Staansaam S. Africa 132 E4
Staaten r. Australia 149 D3
Staaten River National Park Australia 149 D3
Stabbursdalen Nasjonalpark nat. park Norway 44 N1
Staberhuk c. Germany 48 I1
Stabroek Guyana see Georgetown
Stade Germany 48 G2
Städjan-Nipfjällets naturreservat nature res. Sweden 45 K3
Stadskanaal Neth. 48 D3
Stadtallendorf Germany 48 G5
Stadthagen Germany 48 G3
Staffa i. U.K. 46 F7
Staffelstein Germany 48 H5
Stafford U.K. 47 J11
Stafford Creek Bahamas 186 D1
Stafford's Post S. Africa 133 N7
Stafford Springs U.S.A. 177 M4
Stagen Indon. 77 G3
Stagg Lake Canada 167 H2
Stahlstown U.S.A. 176 F5
Staicele Latvia 42 F4
Stakhanov Ukr. 41 F6
formerly known as Kadiyevka or Sergo
Stakhanovo Rus. Fed. see Zhukovskiy
Stalin Bulg. see Varna
Stalin, Mount Canada 166 E3
Stalinabad Tajik. see Dushanbe
Stalingrad Rus. Fed. see Volgograd
Stalingradskaya Oblast' admin. div. Rus. Fed. see Volgogradskaya Oblast'
Staliniri Georgia see Ts'khinvali
Stalino Ukr. see Donets'k
Stalino Uzbek. see Shakhrikhan
Stalinogorsk Rus. Fed. see Novomoskovsk
Stalinogród Poland see Katowice
Stalinsk Rus. Fed. see Novokuznetsk
Stalowa Wola Poland 49 T5
Stâlpu Romania 58 H3
Stalwart Point S. Africa 133 L10
Stamboliyski Bulg. 58 F6
formerly known as Novi Kritsim
Stamford Australia 149 D4
Stamford U.K. 47 L11
Stamford CT U.S.A. 177 L4
Stamford NY U.S.A. 177 K3
Stamford TX U.S.A. 179 C5
Stampalia i. Greece see Astypalaia
Stampriet Namibia 130 C5
Stamsund Norway 44 K1
Stanardsville U.S.A. 176 G7
Stancomb-Wills Glacier Antarctica 223 W1
Standerton S. Africa 133 N3
Standing Rock Indian Reservation res. U.S.A. 178 B2
Standish U.S.A. 173 J7
Stănești Romania 58 F4
Stanfield U.S.A. 183 M9
Stanford S. Africa 132 D11
Stanford KY U.S.A. 176 A8
Stanford MT U.S.A. 180 E3
Stangenestind hill Norway 44 O1
Stanger S. Africa 133 P6
Stănilești Romania 58 J2
Stanišić Vojvodina, Srbija Yugo. 58 A3
Stanislav Ukr. see Ivano-Frankivs'k
Stânișoarei, Munții mts Romania 58 G1
Stanke Dimitrov Bulg. see Dupnitsa
Stanley Australia 147 E5
Stanley Hong Kong China 87 [inset]
also known as Chek Chue

Stanley Falkland Is 205 F8
Capital of the Falkland Islands. Long form Port Stanley.

Stanley ID U.S.A. 180 D3
Stanley ND U.S.A. 178 B1
Stanley VA U.S.A. 176 G7
Stanley WI U.S.A. 172 C6
Stanley, Chutes waterfall Dem. Rep. Congo see Boyoma Falls
Stanley, Mount hill N.T. Australia 148 A4
Stanley, Mount hill Tas. Australia 147 E5
Stanley, Mount Dem. Rep. Congo/Uganda see Margherita Peak
Stanley Reservoir India 94 C4
Stanleyville Dem. Rep. Congo see Kisangani
Stanmore Zimbabwe 131 F4
Stann Creek Belize see Dangriga
Stanos Greece 59 C10
Stanovaya Rus. Fed. 43 T9
Stanovoye Rus. Fed. 43 T9
formerly known as Ploskoye
Stanovoye Nagor'ye mts Rus. Fed. 81 J1
Stanovoy Khrebet mts Rus. Fed. 81 K1
Stanovoy Kolodez' Rus. Fed. 43 R9
Stans Switz. 51 O6
Stansmore Range hills Australia 150 E4
Stansted airport U.K. 47 M12
Stanthorpe Australia 147 F2
Stanton KY U.S.A. 176 B8
Stanton MI U.S.A. 173 H7
Stanton ND U.S.A. 178 B2
Stanton NE U.S.A. 178 C3
Stanton TX U.S.A. 179 B5
Stantsiya Babayurkino Rus. Fed. 43 T9
Stantsiya Skuratovo Rus. Fed. 43 S8
Stantsiya-Yakkabag Uzbek. see Yakkabag
Staples U.S.A. 178 D2
Stapleton U.S.A. 178 B3
Stąporków Poland 49 R4
Star' Rus. Fed. 43 P8
Starachowice Poland 49 S4
Stara Huta Ukr. 43 O9
Stará Ľubovňa Slovakia 49 R6
Stara Pazova Vojvodina, Srbija Yugo. 58 B4
Stara Planina mts Bulg./Yugo. see Balkan Mountains
Staraya Kulatka Rus. Fed. 102 A1
Staraya Poltavka Rus. Fed. 102 A2
Staraya Russa Rus. Fed. 43 M4
Staraya Toropa Rus. Fed. 43 M5
Stara Zagora Bulg. 58 G6
Starbuck Island Kiribati 221 H6
formerly known as Barren Island or Low Island or Starve Island
Starchiojd Romania 58 H3
Star City AR U.S.A. 174 B5
Star City IN U.S.A. 172 G10
Starcke National Park Australia 149 E2
Stargard in Pommern Poland see Stargard Szczeciński
Stargard Szczeciński Poland 49 M2
historically known as Stargard in Pommern
Stari Ras and Sopoćani tourist site Yugo. 58 B5
Staritsa Rus. Fed. 43 P5
Starke U.S.A. 175 D6
Starkey U.S.A. 176 F8

Starkovo Rus. Fed. 43 V6
Starkville U.S.A. 175 B5
Star Lake U.S.A. 177 J1
Starling Inlet Hong Kong China 87 [inset]
also known as Sha Tau Kok Hoi
Starnberg Germany 48 I8
Starnberger See l. Germany 48 I8
Starobaleyskoye Rus. Fed. 88 C1
Starobel'sk Ukr. see Starobil's'k
Starobil's'k Ukr. 41 F6
also spelt Starobel'sk
Starobyn Belarus 42 I9
Starodub Rus. Fed. 43 N9
Starogard Gdański Poland 49 P2
historically known as Preußisch Stargard
Starokonstantinov Ukr. see Starokostyantyniv
Starokostyantyniv Ukr. 41 C6
also spelt Starokonstantinov
Starokozache Ukr. 58 K2
Staroletovo Rus. Fed. 43 U7
Starominskaya Rus. Fed. 41 F7
Staro Oryakhovo Bulg. 58 I6
Starosel Bulg. 58 F6
Staro Selo Bulg. 58 H5
Staroshcherbinovskaya Rus. Fed. 41 F7
Starosubkhangulovo Rus. Fed. 102 D1
Staroye Rus. Fed. 43 V2
Staroye Istomino Rus. Fed. 43 O6
Staroye Melkovo Rus. Fed. 43 R5
Staroye Sandovo Rus. Fed. 43 R3
Staroye Syalo Belarus 43 K6
Staroyur'yevo Rus. Fed. 41 G5
Starozhilovo Rus. Fed. 43 U7
Star Peak U.S.A. 182 F1
Start Point U.K. 47 I13
Starve Island Kiribati see Starbuck Island
Starynki Belarus 42 I7
Staryya Darohi Belarus 43 J8
also spelt Staryye Dorogi
Staryy Dvor Rus. Fed. 43 V5
Staryye Dorogi Belarus see Staryya Darohi
Staryye Yurkovichi Rus. Fed. 43 M9
Staryy Kayak Rus. Fed. 39 K2
Staryy Nadym Rus. Fed. 38 H3
Staryy Oskol Rus. Fed. 41 F6
Staryy Sambir Ukr. 49 T6
also spelt Staryy Sambor
Staryy Sambor Ukr. see Staryy Sambir
Staßfurt Germany 48 I4
Staszów Poland 49 S5
State College U.S.A. 176 H5
Staten Island Arg. see Los Estados, Isla de
Statenville U.S.A. 175 D6
State Road U.S.A. 176 E9
Statesboro U.S.A. 175 D5
Statesville U.S.A. 174 D5
Stathelle Norway 45 J4
Station U.S.A. 176 A7
Station No. 6 Sudan 121 G4
Station No. 10 Sudan 121 G5
Station Nord Greenland 165 R1
also known as Nord
Statzberg hill Austria 49 M7
Stăuceni Moldova 58 J1
Staunton U.S.A. 176 F7
Stavanger Norway 45 I4
Staveley U.K. 47 K10
Stavertsi Bulg. 58 F5
Stavropol' Rus. Fed. 41 G7
formerly known as Voroshilovsk
Stavropolka Kazakh. 103 F1
Stavropol Kray admin. div. Rus. Fed. see Stavropol'skiy Kray
Stavropol'-na-Volge Rus. Fed. see Tol'yatti
Stavropol'skaya Vozvyshennost' hills Rus. Fed. 41 G7
Stavropol'skiy Kray admin. div. Rus. Fed. 41 G7
English form Stavropol Kray
Stavros Greece 58 E8
Stavros, Akra pt Kriti Greece 59 F13
Stavros, Akra pt Naxos Greece 59 G11
Stawbun Belarus 43 M9
Stawell Australia 147 D4
Stawell r. Australia 149 D4
Stawiski Poland 49 T2
Stawiszyn Poland 49 P4
Stawki, Park Krajobrazowy Poland 49 Q5
Stayki Rus. Fed. 43 Q8
Stayner Canada 173 M6
Stayton U.S.A. 180 B3
Steamboat U.S.A. 182 E2
Steamboat Springs U.S.A. 180 F4
Stearns U.S.A. 176 A9
Stebbins U.S.A. 164 C3
Steekdorings S. Africa 133 I4
Steel r. Canada 168 C3
Steele Island Antarctica 222 T2
Steelpoort S. Africa 133 O1
Steelton U.S.A. 177 I5
Steelville U.S.A. 174 B4
Steen r. Canada 167 G3
Steenkampsberge mts S. Africa 133 O2
Steen River Canada 167 G3
Steens Mountain U.S.A. 180 C4
Steenstrup Gletscher glacier Greenland see Sermersuaq
Steenvoorde France 51 I2
Steenwijk Neth. 48 D3
Steep Point Australia 151 A5
Stefanoviki Greece 59 D9
Stefansson Bay Antarctica 223 D2
Stefansson Island Canada 165 I2
Ștefan Vodă Moldova 58 K2
formerly known as Biruintsa or Kyzyl or Suvorovo; formerly spelt Shtefan-Vode
Ștefan Vodă Romania 58 I4
Stegalovka Rus. Fed. 43 T9
Stege Denmark 45 K5
Stegi Swaziland see Siteki
Stegrimovo Rus. Fed. 43 M7
Ștei Romania 58 D2
formerly known as Doctor Petru Groza
Steigerwald mts Germany 48 H6
Steigerwald park Germany 48 H6
Steilrand S. Africa 133 P4
Steinar Iceland 44 [inset] C3
Steinbach Canada 167 L5
Steinfurt Germany 48 E3
Steinhausen Namibia 130 C4
Steinhuder Meer, Naturpark nature res. Germany 48 G3
Steinkjer Norway 44 J2
Steinkopf S. Africa 132 B6
Steinsland Norway 46 R3
Stekaar S. Africa 132 H8
Stella S. Africa 133 I3
Stella Maris Bahamas 187 E2
Stellenbosch S. Africa 132 C10
Stello, Monte mt. Corse France 51 P10
Stelvio, Parco Nazionale dello nat. park Italy 56 C2
Stelvio, Passo dello pass Italy 56 C2
Stenay France 51 L3
Stendal Germany 48 I3
Stende Latvia 42 D4
Stenhouse, Mount hill Hong Kong China 87 [inset]
also known as Shan Tei Tong
Stenudden Sweden 44 L2
Stenungsund Sweden 45 J4
Steornabhagh U.K. see Stornoway
Stepanakert Azer. see Xankändi
Stepanovka Kazakh. 102 D2
Stepantsevo Rus. Fed. 43 V5
Stephens watercourse Australia 146 D3
Stephens, Cape N.Z. 152 H8
Stephens City U.S.A. 176 G6
Stephens Lake Canada 167 M3
Stephenson, Mount Antarctica 222 T2
Stephenville Canada 169 J3

Stephenville U.S.A. 179 C5
Stepne Ukr. 43 O9
Stepnogorsk Kazakh. 103 H1
Stepnoy Rus. Fed. see Elista
Stepnoye Saratovskaya Oblast' Rus. Fed. 102 A2
formerly known as Otrogovo
Stepnoye Stavropol'skiy Kray Rus. Fed. 107 F1
Stepnyak Kazakh. 103 G1
Stepojevac Srbija Yugo. 58 B4
Stepurino Rus. Fed. 43 Q5
Sterea Ellas admin. reg. Greece 59 E10
Sterkfontein Dam resr S. Africa 133 N5
Sterkspruit S. Africa 133 L7
Sterkstroom S. Africa 133 K8
Sterlet Lake Canada 167 I1
Sterlibashevo Rus. Fed. 102 C1
Sterling S. Africa 132 F8
Sterling CO U.S.A. 178 B3
Sterling IL U.S.A. 174 B3
Sterling KS U.S.A. 178 C4
Sterling MI U.S.A. 173 I6
Sterling UT U.S.A. 183 M2
Sterling City U.S.A. 179 B6
Sterling Heights U.S.A. 173 J8
Sterlitamak Rus. Fed. 102 C1
Šternberg Germany 48 I2
Šternberk Czech Rep. 49 O6
Stes-Maries-de-la-Mer France 51 K9
Stęszew Poland 49 N3
Stettin Poland see Szczecin
Stettiner Haff b. Germany see Oderhaff
Stettler Canada 180 D1
Steubenville KY U.S.A. 176 A9
Steubenville OH U.S.A. 176 E5
Stevenage U.K. 47 L12
Stevens, Mount N.Z. 152 G8
Stevenson U.S.A. 180 B3
Stevenson Lake Canada 167 L4
Stevens Point U.S.A. 172 D6
Stevensville MD U.S.A. 177 I7
Stevensville MI U.S.A. 172 G8
Stevensville PA U.S.A. 177 I4
Steventon Island Antarctica 222 O1
Stewart r. Australia 149 D2
Stewart Canada 166 D4
Stewart r. Canada 166 B2
Stewart, Cape Australia 148 B1
Stewart, Isla i. Chile 205 C9
Stewart Crossing Canada 166 B2
Stewart Island N.Z. 153 B15
also known as Rakiura
Stewart Island nature res. N.Z. 153 B15
Stewart Islands Solomon Is 145 F2
Stewarts Point U.S.A. 182 A3
Stewart Valley Canada 167 J5
Stewiacke Canada 169 I4
Steynrus S. Africa 133 L4
Steynsburg S. Africa 133 J8
Steyr Austria 49 L7
Steytlerville S. Africa 133 I10

St Helena and Dependencies terr. S. Atlantic Ocean 216
Consists of St Helena, Ascension, Tristan da Cunha and Gough Island.
africa [countries] 114–117

Stif Alg. see Sétif
Stigler U.S.A. 179 D5
Stigliano Italy 57 I8
Stigtomta Sweden 45 L4
Stikine r. Canada 166 C3
Stikine Plateau Canada 166 D3
Stilbaai S. Africa 132 F11
Stilfontein S. Africa 133 K3
Stilís Greece see Stylida
Stillwater MN U.S.A. 172 A5
Stillwater OK U.S.A. 179 C4
Stillwater r. U.S.A. 180 E3
Stillwater National Wildlife Refuge nature res. U.S.A. 182 F2
Stillwater Range mts U.S.A. 182 F2
Stilo Italy 57 I10
Stilo, Punta pt Italy 57 I10
Štilt mt. Bos.-Herz. 56 J4
Stilwell U.S.A. 179 D5
Štimlje Kosovo, Srbija Yugo. 58 C6
Stinear, Mount Antarctica 223 E2
Stinnett U.S.A. 179 B5
Štip Macedonia 58 D7
Stipanov Grič mt. Croatia 56 H4
Stirling Australia 148 B4
Stirling Canada 173 P6
Stirling U.K. 46 I7
Stirling Creek r. Australia 148 A3
Stirling Range mts Australia 151 B7
Stirling Range National Park Australia 151 B7
Stirrat U.S.A. 176 C8
Stittsville Canada 173 R5
Stjernøya i. Norway 44 M1
Stjørdalshalsen Norway 44 J3
Stockach Germany 48 G8
Stockbridge U.S.A. 173 I8
Stockerau Austria 49 N7

Stockholm Sweden 45 L4
Capital of Sweden.

Stockholm county Sweden 45 L4
Stockinbingal Australia 147 E3
Stockport U.K. 47 J10
Stocksbridge U.K. 47 K10
Stockton CA U.S.A. 182 C4
Stockton IL U.S.A. 172 C8
Stockton KS U.S.A. 178 C4
Stockton MO U.S.A. 178 D4
Stockton UT U.S.A. 183 L1
Stockton Island U.S.A. 172 C4
Stockton Lake U.S.A. 178 D4
Stockton-on-Tees U.K. 47 K9
Stockton Plateau U.S.A. 179 B6
Stockton Springs U.S.A. 177 Q1
Stockville U.S.A. 178 B3
Stoczek Łukowski Poland 49 S4
Stöde Sweden 44 L3
Stodolishche Rus. Fed. 43 N7
Stœng Trêng Cambodia 79 D5
also spelt Stung Treng
Stoffberg S. Africa 133 N2
Stogovo Planina mts Macedonia 58 B7
Stoke-on-Trent U.K. 47 J10
Stokes, Mount N.Z. 152 I9
Stokes Inlet Australia 151 C7
Stokes Point Australia 147 D5
Stokes Range hills Australia 148 A3
Stokkseyri Iceland 44 [inset] B3
Stokkvågen Norway 44 K2
Stokmarknes Norway 44 K1
Stol mt. Yugo. 58 D4
Stolac Bos.-Herz. 56 J5
Stolberg (Rheinland) Germany 48 D5
Stolbovoy Rus. Fed. 38 F2
Stolbovoy, Ostrov i. Rus. Fed. 39 N2
Stolbtsy Belarus see Stowbtsy
Stolice hill Bos.-Herz. 56 K4
Stolin Belarus 41 C6
Stollberg Germany 49 J5
Stolp Poland see Słupsk
Stolsheimen park Norway 45 I3
Stolzenau Germany 48 G3
Stompneusbaai S. Africa 132 B9
Stone U.K. 47 J11
Stoneboro U.S.A. 176 E4
Stonecliffe Canada 168 E4
Stonecutters' Island pen. Hong Kong China 87 [inset]
also known as Ngong Shuen Chau
Stoneham U.S.A. 180 G4
Stone Harbor U.S.A. 177 K6

Stonehaven U.K. 46 J7
Stonehenge Australia 149 D5
Stonehenge tourist site U.K. 47 K12
Stone Lake U.S.A. 172 B5
Stone Mountain Provincial Park Canada 166 E3
Stone Ridge U.S.A. 177 K4
Stoner U.S.A. 176 F9
Stonewall Canada 167 L5
Stoney Creek Canada 173 N7
Stoney Point Canada 173 K8
Stongfjorden Norway 46 R2
Stonington U.S.A. 177 Q1
Stony Creek U.S.A. 176 H9
Stony Gorge Reservoir U.S.A. 182 B2
Stony Lake Canada 167 L3
Stony Point U.S.A. 177 I2
Stony Rapids Canada 167 J3
Stooping r. Canada 168 D2
Stör r. Germany 48 G2
Stora Le l. Sweden 45 J4
Stora Lulevatten l. Sweden 44 L2
Stora Sjöfallets nationalpark nat. park Sweden 44 L2
Storavan l. Sweden 44 L2
Storbäcken Sweden 45 K3
Storbekkfjellet mt. Norway 45 J3
Storbo Sweden 45 K3
Stord i. Norway 45 I4
Stordal Norway 44 I3
Store mt. Norway 45 I4
Store Bælt sea chan. Denmark see Great Belt
Storebø Norway 46 R3
Store Heddinge Denmark 45 K5
Store Jukleeggi mt. Norway 45 J3
Store Koldewey i. Greenland 165 R2
Store Lenangstind mt. Norway 44 M1
Store Moss nationalpark nat. park Sweden 45 K4
Støren Norway 44 J3
Store Sotra i. Norway 45 I3
Storfjärden l. Sweden 45 L3
Storfjorden sea chan. Svalbard 38 B2
Storforshei Norway 44 K2
Storjola Sweden 44 K2
Storjord Norway 44 K2
Storjuktan l. Sweden 44 L2
Storkerson Peninsula Canada 165 I2
Storm Bay Australia 147 E5
Stormberg S. Africa 133 K8
Stormberg mt. S. Africa 133 K7
Stormberg r. S. Africa 133 K7
Stormberge mts S. Africa 133 K8
Storm Lake U.S.A. 178 D3
Stormsrivier S. Africa 132 H10
Stornoway U.K. 46 F5
also spelt Steornabhagh
Storo Italy 56 C3
Storøya i. Svalbard 38 C2
Storozhenskiy, Mys pt Rus. Fed. 43 N1
Storozhevsk Rus. Fed. 40 J3
Storozhno Rus. Fed. 43 N1
Storozhynets' Ukr. 41 C6
Storseleby Sweden 44 L2
Storsjøen l. Norway 45 J3
Storsjön l. Sweden 44 K3
Storsjön l. Sweden 45 L3
Storskarhø mt. Norway 44 J3
Storskog Sweden 44 K2
Storslett Norway 44 M1
Storstrømmen sea chan. Denmark 45 J5
Stortemelk sea chan. Neth. 48 C2
Storuman Sweden 44 L2
Storuman l. Sweden 44 L2
Storvigelen mt. Norway 44 K3
Storvik Sweden 45 L3
Storvorde Denmark 45 J4
Storvreta Sweden 45 L4
Stosch, Isla i. Chile 205 B8
Stoughton Canada 167 K5
Stoŭng, Stœng r. Cambodia 79 D5
Stour r. Dorset, England U.K. 47 K13
Stour r. Essex/Suffolk, England U.K. 47 N12
Stour r. Kent, England U.K. 47 N12
Stout Lake Canada 168 A2
Stovall U.S.A. 176 G9
Stowbtsy Belarus 42 H8
also known as Stolbtsy
Stowmarket U.K. 47 M11
Stoyba Rus. Fed. 82 C1
Straatsdrif S. Africa 133 K2
Strabane U.K. 47 E9
Stradella Italy 56 B3
Strahan Australia 147 E5
Straight Cliffs ridge U.S.A. 183 M4
Strakonice Czech Rep. 49 K6
Straldzha Bulg. 58 H6
Stralsund Germany 49 K1
Strand S. Africa 132 C11
Stranda Norway 44 I3
Strangford Lough inlet U.K. 47 G9
Strängnäs Sweden 45 L4
Strangways r. Australia 148 B2
Strangways Range mts Australia 148 B4
Stranraer U.K. 47 G9
Strasbourg France 51 N4
historically known as Argentoratum, or Strassburg
Strasburg Germany 49 K2
Strasburg OH U.S.A. 176 D5
Strasburg PA U.S.A. 177 I6
Strasburg VA U.S.A. 176 G7
Strășeni Moldova 58 J1
formerly spelt Strasheny
Strasheny Moldova see Strășeni
Strassburg France see Strasbourg
Straßwalchen Austria 49 K8
Stratford Canada 168 D5
Stratford N.Z. 152 I7
Stratford CA U.S.A. 182 E5
Stratford CT U.S.A. 177 L4
Stratford TX U.S.A. 178 B4
Stratford WI U.S.A. 172 C6
Stratford-upon-Avon U.K. 47 K11
Strathalbyn Australia 146 C3
Strathcona, Mount Antarctica 223 G2
Strathcona Provincial Park Canada 166 E5
Strathgordon Australia 147 E5
Strathmore Canada 167 H5
Strathmore r. U.K. 46 H5
Strathmore U.S.A. 182 E5
Strathnaver Canada 166 F4
Strathord Island P.N.G. 73 J8
Strathpeffer U.K. 46 H6
Strathroy Canada 173 L8
Strathspey valley U.K. 46 I6
Stratton Mountain U.S.A. 177 M2
Straubing Germany 49 J7
Straume Norway 44 K1
Straumen Nordland Norway 44 K2
Straumen Nordland Norway 44 K2
Straumnes pt Iceland 44 [inset] B2
Strausberg Germany 49 K3
Strawberry U.S.A. 183 M7
Strawberry Mountain U.S.A. 180 C3
Strawberry Point U.S.A. 172 B8
Strawberry Reservoir U.S.A. 183 M1
Strawn U.S.A. 172 E10
Straža mt. Macedonia 58 D6
Strazhitsa Bulg. 58 G5
Streaky Bay Australia 146 B3
Streaky Bay b. Australia 146 B3
Streator U.S.A. 174 B3
Strehaia Romania 58 E4
Strei r. Romania 58 E3
Střela r. Czech Rep. 49 K6
Strelcha Bulg. 58 F6
Strelka Rus. Fed. 39 P3
Strelkovo Rus. Fed. 43 P1
Strelley Australia 150 B4
Strelley r. Australia 150 B4

Strelley Aboriginal Reserve Australia 150 B4
Strel'na r. Rus. Fed. 40 F2
Strenči Latvia 42 G4
Stretta di Messina strait Italy see Messina, Strait of
Streymoy i. Faroe Is 46 E1
Strezhevoy Rus. Fed. 38 H3
Stříbro Czech Rep. 49 J6
Strickland r. P.N.G. 73 J8
Strimonas r. Greece 58 E8
Strizivojna Croatia 56 K3
Stroeder Arg. 204 E6
Strofades i. Greece 59 C11
Ströhen Germany 48 F3
Stromboli, Isola i. Isole Lipari Italy 57 H10
Stromeferry U.K. 46 G6
Stromness S. Georgia 205 [inset]
Stromness U.K. 46 I5
Stromsburg U.S.A. 178 C3
Strømsmo Norway 44 L1
Strömstad Sweden 45 J4
Strömsund Sweden 44 K3
Strongoli Italy 57 J9
Strongsville U.S.A. 176 D4
Stronsay i. U.K. 46 J4
Stropkov Slovakia 49 S6
Stroud U.K. 47 J12
Strücklingen (Saterland) Germany 48 E2
Struer Denmark 45 J4
Struga Macedonia 58 B7
Strugi-Krasnyye Rus. Fed. 43 K3
Struis Bay S. Africa 132 E11
Struis Bay b. S. Africa 132 E11
Struma r. Bulg. 58 E7
Strumica Macedonia 58 D7
Strumica r. Macedonia 58 D7
Strunino Rus. Fed. 43 T5
Struthers U.S.A. 176 E4
Stryama r. Bulg. 58 F6
Strydenburg S. Africa 132 H6
Stryn Norway 45 I3
Stryy Ukr. 53 G2
Strzegomka r. Poland 49 N5
Strzelce Krajeńskie Poland 49 M3
Strzelce Opolskie Poland 49 P5
Strzelecki, Mount hill Australia 148 B4
Strzelecki Creek watercourse Australia 146 C2
Strzelecki Regional Reserve nature res. Australia 146 C2
Strzelin Poland 49 O5
Strzelno Poland 49 P3
Strzyżów Poland 49 S6
Stuart r. Australia 149 F5
Stuart FL U.S.A. 175 D7
Stuart IA U.S.A. 178 D3
Stuart VA U.S.A. 176 E9
Stuart Bluff Range mts Australia 148 B4
Stuart Lake Canada 166 E4
Stuart Mountains N.Z. 153 B13
Stuart Range hills Australia 146 B2
Stuarts Draft U.S.A. 176 F7
Stubaier Alpen mts Austria 48 I8
Stubbenkammer hd Germany 49 K1
Stubica Srbija Yugo. 58 C5
Stubline Srbija Yugo. 58 B4
Stuchka Latvia see Aizkraukle
Stučka Latvia see Aizkraukle
Studenica tourist site Yugo. 58 B5
Studen Kladenets, Yazovir resr Bulg. 58 G7
Studenoye Rus. Fed. 43 S9
Studholme Junction N.Z. 153 F12
Studis S. Africa 132 I10
Stugun Sweden 44 K3
Stulpicani Romania 58 G1
Stung Treng Cambodia see Stœng Trêng
Stupart r. Canada 167 M4
Stupino Rus. Fed. 43 T7
Stura di Demonte r. Italy 51 N8
Sturge Island Antarctica 223 K2
Sturgeon r. Ont. Canada 168 E4
Sturgeon r. Sask. Canada 167 J4
Sturgeon r. U.S.A. 172 G5
Sturgeon, Lake Canada 172 B2
Sturgeon Bay b. Canada 167 L4
Sturgeon Bay U.S.A. 172 F6
Sturgeon Bay b. U.S.A. 173 I5
Sturgeon Bay Canal lake channel U.S.A. 172 F6
Sturgeon Falls Canada 168 E4
Sturgeon Lake Canada 173 O6
Sturgis KY U.S.A. 174 C4
Sturgis MI U.S.A. 172 H9
Sturgis SD U.S.A. 178 B2
Šturlić Bos.-Herz. 56 H3
Sturt, Mount hill Australia 146 D2
Sturt Bay Australia 146 C3
Sturt Creek Australia 150 E3
Sturt Creek watercourse Australia 150 D3
Sturtevant U.S.A. 172 F8
Sturt National Park Australia 146 D2
Sturt Plain Australia 148 B3
Sturt Stony Desert Australia 146 D2
Stutterheim S. Africa 133 L9
Stuttgart Germany 48 G7
Stuttgart U.S.A. 174 B5
Stykkishólmur Iceland 44 [inset] B2
Stylida Greece 59 D10
also known as Stilís
Styr r. Belarus/Ukr. 38 C4
Suaçuí Grande r. Brazil 203 D6
Suai East Timor 75 C5
Suaita Col. 198 C3
Suakin Sudan 121 H5
Suakin Archipelago is Sudan 121 H5
Suana Dem. Rep. Congo 127 D6
Suao Taiwan 87 G3
Suaqui Grande Mex. 184 C2
Suara, Mount Eritrea 121 H5
Suardi Arg. 204 E3
Suárez Col. 198 B4
Suata Venez. 199 E2
Suau P.N.G. 149 F1
Subačius Lith. 42 F6
Subang Indon. 77 D4
Subansiri r. India 78 A2
Subarnarekha r. India 97 E5
Sūbāshī Iran 100 B3
Subaşı Turkey 58 J7
Subate Latvia 42 G5
Subay reg. Saudi Arabia 105 D2
Şubayḩah Saudi Arabia 109 J7
Şubayḩī reg. Yemen 104 D5
Subcetate Romania 58 G2
Subei China 84 B4
also known as Dangchengwan
Subeita tourist site Israel see Shivta
Subiaco Italy 56 F7
Subi Besar i. Indon. 77 E2
Subi Kecil i. Indon. 77 E2
Sublette U.S.A. 178 B4
Subotica Vojvodina, Srbija Yugo. 58 A2
also known as Szabadka
Subucle mt. Eritrea 121 I6
Success, Lake U.S.A. 182 F5
Suceava Romania 53 H2
formerly spelt Suczawa
Sucha Beskidzka Poland 49 Q6
Suchan Rus. Fed. see Partizansk
Suchan r. Rus. Fed. 82 D4
Suchedniów Poland 49 R4
Suchixtepec Mex. 185 F5
Sucio r. Col. 198 B3
Suciu de Sus Romania 58 F1
Suck r. Rep. of Ireland 47 D10
Sucker Creek Landing Canada 173 M4

Sucre Bol. 200 D4
Legislative capital of Bolivia.
world [countries] 10–11

Sucre dept Col. 198 C2

Sucre *state* Venez. **199** F2
Sucuaro Col. **198** D3
Sucumbíos *prov.* Ecuador **198** B5
Sucunduri *r.* Brazil **199** G6
Sucuriú *r.* Brazil **206** B7
Suczawa Romania *see* **Suceava**
Sud *prov.* Cameroon **125** H6
Sud, Rivière du *r.* Canada **177** L1
Suda Rus. Fed. **43** S2
Suda *r.* Rus. Fed. **43** S2
Sudak Ukr. **41** E7

▶ **Sudan** *country* Africa **121** E5
Largest country in Africa and 10th largest in the world. Historically known as Anglo-Egyptian Sudan.
world [countries] ▶ 10–11
africa [countries] ▶ 114–117

Suday Rus. Fed. **40** G4
Sudayr *reg.* Saudi Arabia **105** D2
Sudayr, Sha'īb *watercourse* Iraq **107** F5
Sudbishchi Rus. Fed. **43** S9
Sud'bodarovka Rus. Fed. **102** C1
Sudbury Canada **168** D4
Sudbury U.K. **47** M11
Sudd *swamp* Sudan **126** F3
Suddie Guyana **199** G3
Sude *r.* Germany **48** H2
Sudest Island P.N.G. *see* **Tagula Island**
Sudetenland *mts* Czech Rep./Poland *see* **Sudety**
Sudety *mts* Czech Rep./Poland **49** M5
historically known as Sudetenland
Sudimir Rus. Fed. **43** P8
Sudislavl' Rus. Fed. **40** G4
Sud-Kivu *prov.* Dem. Rep. Congo **126** F5
Sudlersville U.S.A. **177** J6
Sudogda Rus. Fed. **40** G5
Sudomskiye Vysoty *hills* Rus. Fed. **43** K4
Sudost' *r.* Rus. Fed. **43** O9
Sud-Ouest *prov.* Cameroon **125** H5
Sudr Egypt **121** G2
Sudr, Râs el *pt* Egypt **108** D8
Suðurland *constituency* Iceland **44** [inset] B2
Suðuroy *i.* Faroe Is **46** F2
Suðuroyarfjørður *sea chan.* Faroe Is **46** F2
Sue *watercourse* Sudan **126** F3
Sueca Spain **55** K5
Süedinenie Bulg. **58** F6
Suez Egypt **121** G2
also spelt El Suweis *or* As Suways
Suez, Gulf of Egypt **121** G2
also known as Suweis, Khalîg el *or* Suways, Khalīj as
Suez Bay Egypt **108** D8
also known as Qulzum, Baḥr el
Suez Canal Egypt **121** G2
also known as Suweis, Qanâ el
Şufaynah Saudi Arabia **104** C3
Suffolk U.S.A. **177** I9
Sūfīān Iran **100** A2
Sufi-Kurgan Kyrg. *see* **Sopu-Korgon**
Sug-Aksy Rus. Fed. **88** E1
Sugar *r.* U.S.A. **172** D8
Sugarbush Hill *hill* U.S.A. **172** E5
Sugar Grove *NC* U.S.A. **176** D9
Sugar Grove *OH* U.S.A. **176** C6
Sugarloaf Mountain U.S.A. **174** G2
Sugarloaf Point Australia **147** G3
Sugar Notch U.S.A. **173** R9
Sugbuhan Point Phil. **74** C4
Süget China *see* **Sogat**
Sugi *i.* Indon. **76** C2
Sugun China **88** B4
Sugut *r. Sabah* Malaysia **77** G1
Sugut, Tanjong *pt Sabah* Malaysia **77** G1
Suhaia Romania **58** G5
Suhai Hu *l.* China **84** B4
Suhait China **84** E4
Sūhāj Egypt *see* **Sohâg**
Şuḥār Oman **105** G2
English form Sohar
Sühbaatar Mongolia **85** E1
Sühbaatar *prov.* Mongolia **85** G2
Suheli Par *i.* India **94** B4
Suhl Germany **48** H5
Suhopolje Croatia **56** J3
Suhul *reg.* Saudi Arabia **105** D3
Suhūl al Kidan *plain* Saudi Arabia **105** F3
Suhum Ghana **125** E5
Şuhut Turkey **106** B3
Suiá Missur *r.* Brazil **202** A4
Sui'an China *see* **Zhangpu**
Suibin China **82** C3
Suichang China **87** F2
also known as Miaogao
Suicheng China *see* **Jianning**
Suicheng China *see* **Suixi**
Suichuan China **87** E3
also known as Quanjiang
Suid-Afrika *country* Africa *see* **South Africa, Republic of**
Suide China **85** F4
also known as Mingzhou
Suidzhikurmsy Turkm. *see* **Madau**
Suifen *r.* China **82** C4
Suifenhe China **82** C3
Suigam India **96** A4
Suihua China **82** B3
Suijiang China **86** B2
also known as Zhongcheng
Suileng China **82** B3
Suining *Hunan* China **87** D3
also known as Changpu
Suining *Jiangsu* China **87** F1
Suining *Sichuan* China **86** C2
Suiping China **87** E1
also known as Zhuoyang
Suippes France **51** K3
Suir *r.* Rep. of Ireland **47** E11
Suisse *country* Europe *see* **Switzerland**
Suixi *Anhui* China **87** F1
Suixi *Guangdong* China **87** D4
also known as Suicheng
Suixian China **87** E1
Suixian China *see* **Suizhou**
Suiyang China **87** C3
also known as Yangchuan
Suizhai China *see* **Xiancheng**
Suizhong China **85** I3
Suizhou China **87** E2
formerly known as Suixian
Sujangarh India **96** B4
Sujawal Pak. **101** G5
Sukabumi Indon. **77** D4
Sukadana *Kalimantan Barat* Indon. **77** E3
Sukadana *Sumatra* Indon. **77** D4
Sukadana, Teluk *b.* Indon. **77** E3
Sukagawa Japan **90** G6
Sukaramai Indon. **77** E3
Sukarnapura Indon. *see* **Jayapura**
Sukarno, Puntjak *mt.* Indon. *see* **Jaya, Puncak**
Suket India **96** C4
Sukeva Fin. **44** N3
Sukhanovka Rus. Fed. **90** C1
Sukhary Belarus **43** L8
Sukhinichi Rus. Fed. **43** Q7
Sukhodol'skoye, Ozero *l.* Rus. Fed. **43** L1
Sukhodrev *r.* Rus. Fed. **43** Q7
Sukhona *r.* Rus. Fed. **43** V2
Sukhothai Thai. **78** B4
Sukhoverkovo Rus. Fed. **43** Q5
Sukhumi Georgia *see* **Sokhumi**
Sukhum-Kale Georgia *see* **Sokhumi**
Sukkertoppen Greenland *see* **Maniitsoq**
Sukkozero Rus. Fed. **40** E3
Sukkur Pak. **101** G5
Sukkur Barrage Pak. **101** G5
Sukma India **94** D2
Sukpay Rus. Fed. **82** E3
Sukpay *r.* Rus. Fed. **82** E3
Sukri *r.* India **96** B4
Sukromlya Rus. Fed. **43** P5
Sukromny Rus. Fed. **43** R4
Sukses Namibia **130** C4
Suktel *r.* India **95** D1
Sukumo Japan **91** C8
Sukun *i.* Indon. **75** B5
Sul, Canal do *sea chan.* Brazil **202** B2
Sul, Pico do *mt.* Brazil **207** J7
Sula *i.* Norway **46** Q2
Sula *r.* Rus. Fed. **40** I2
Sula, Kepulauan *is* Indon. **75** C3
Sula, Ozero *l.* Rus. Fed. **44** O3
Sulabesi *i.* Indon. **75** C3
Sulaiman Ranges *mts* Pak. **101** G4
Sulak Rus. Fed. **102** A4
Sulak *r.* Rus. Fed. **102** A4
Sūlār Iran **100** B4
Sula Sgeir *i.* U.K. **46** F4
Sulasih, Gunung *vol.* Indon. **76** C3
Sulat Phil. **74** C4
Sulawesi *i.* Indon. *see* **Celebes**
Sulawesi Selatan *prov.* Indon. **75** A3
Sulawesi Tengah *prov.* Indon. **75** B3
Sulawesi Tenggara *prov.* Indon. **75** B4
Sulawesi Utara *prov.* Indon. **75** C2
Sulaymān Beg Iraq **107** F4
Sulayyimah Saudi Arabia **105** D3
Sulci *Sardegna* Italy *see* **Sant'Antioco**
Sulcis *Sardegna* Italy *see* **Sant'Antioco**
Sulechów Poland **49** M3
Sulęcin Poland **49** M3
Suledeh Iran **100** B2
Sulejów Poland **49** Q4
Sulejowskie, Jezioro *l.* Poland **49** Q4
Suleman, Teluk *b.* Indon. **75** A2
Sule Skerry *i.* U.K. **46** H4
Sule Stack *i.* U.K. **46** H4
Süleymanlı Turkey **107** D3
Suliki Indon. **76** C3
Sulima Sierra Leone **124** C5
Sulina Romania **58** K3
Sulina, Braţul *watercourse* Romania **58** K3
Suliskongen *mt.* Norway **44** L2
Sulitjelma Norway **44** L2
Sulkava Fin. **45** O3
Sullana Peru **198** A6
Süller Turkey **59** K10
Sullivan *IL* U.S.A. **174** B4
Sullivan *IN* U.S.A. **174** C4
Sullivan Bay Canada **166** E5
Sullivan Island Myanmar *see* **Lanbi Kyun**
Sullivan Lake Canada **167** I5
Sully-sur-Loire France **51** I5
Sulmo Italy *see* **Sulmona**
Sulmona Italy **56** F6
historically known as Sulmo
Süloğlu Turkey **58** H7
Sulphur *LA* U.S.A. **179** D6
Sulphur *OK* U.S.A. **179** C5
Sulphur *r.* U.S.A. **179** D5
Sulphur Draw *watercourse* U.S.A. **179** B5
Sulphur Springs U.S.A. **179** D5
Sulphur Springs Draw *watercourse* U.S.A. **179** B5
Sultan Canada **168** D4
Sultan Libya **120** D2
Sultan, Koh-i- *mts* Pak. **101** E4
Sultanabad India *see* **Osmannagar**
Sultanabad Iran *see* **Arāk**
Sultanbeyli Turkey **58** K8
Sultanhanı Turkey **106** C3
Sultanhisar Turkey **59** J11
Sultaniça Turkey **58** H8
Sultanıye Turkey *see* **Karapınar**
Sultanpur India **97** D4
Sultansandzharskoye Vodokhranilische *resr* Turkm. **103** E4
Sulu Dem. Rep. Congo **126** E6
Suluan *i.* Phil. **74** C4
Sulu Archipelago *is* Phil. **74** B5
Sülüklü Turkey **106** C3
Sülüktü Kyrg. **103** G5
also spelt Sulyukta
Suluntah Libya **120** D1
Sulūq Libya **120** D2
Suluru India **94** D3
Sulu Sea N. Pacific Ocean **74** A4
Sulyukta Kyrg. *see* **Sülüktü**
Sulzbach-Rosenberg Germany **48** I6
Sulzberger Bay Antarctica **222** N1
Sumaco, Volcán *vol.* Ecuador **198** B5
Šumadija *reg.* Yugo. **58** B4
Şumāil Oman **105** G3
Sumalata Indon. **75** B2
Sumampa Arg. **204** E3
Sumangat, Tanjong *pt Sabah* Malaysia **74** A5
Sumapaz, Parque Nacional *nat. park* Col. **198** C4
Sumatera *i.* Indon. *see* **Sumatra**
Sumatera Barat *prov.* Indon. **76** C3
Sumatera Selatan *prov.* Indon. **76** C3
Sumatera Utara *prov.* Indon. **76** B2

▶ **Sumatra** *i.* Indon. **76** B2
2nd largest island in Asia and 6th in the world. Also spelt Sumatera.
asia [landscapes] ▶ 62–63

Sumaúma Brazil **201** E1
Šumava *mts* Czech Rep. **49** K6
Šumava *nat. park* Czech Rep. **49** K6
Sumba *i.* Indon. **75** B5
Sumba, Île *i.* Dem. Rep. Congo **126** C4
Sumba, Selat *sea chan.* Indon. **75** A5
Sumbar *r.* Turkm. **102** C5
Sumbawa *i.* Indon. **77** G5
Sumbawabesar Indon. **77** G5
Sumbawanga Tanz. **129** A6
Sumbay Peru **200** C3
Sumbe Angola **127** B7
formerly known as Ngunza *or* Ngunza-Kabolu *or* Novo Redondo
Sumbing, Gunung *vol.* Indon. **76** C3
Sumbu Zambia **127** F7
Sumbu National Park Zambia **127** F7
also spelt Nsumbu National Park
Sumburgh U.K. **46** K4
Sumburgh Head U.K. **46** K4
Sumbuya Sierra Leone **124** C5
Sumdo Aksai Chin **89** B5
Sumdo China **86** B2
Sumdum, Mount U.S.A. **166** C3
Sumé Brazil **202** E3
Sumedang Indon. **77** D4
Sume'eh Sarā Iran **100** B2
Sümeg Hungary **49** O9
Sumeih Sudan **126** E2
Sumenep Indon. **77** F4
Sumerpur India **96** B4
Sumgait Azer. *see* **Sumqayıt**
Sumisu-jima *i.* Japan **91** G9
Sümiyn Bulag Mongolia **85** G1
Summēl Iraq **107** E3
Summer Beaver Canada **168** B2
Summerdown Namibia **130** C4
Summerford Canada **169** K3
Summer Island U.S.A. **172** G5
Summerland Canada **166** G5
Summerside Canada **169** I4
Summersville U.S.A. **176** E7
Summersville Lake U.S.A. **176** E7
Summerville *GA* U.S.A. **174** C5
Summerville *SC* U.S.A. **175** D5
Summit Lake *B.C.* Canada **166** E3
Summit Lake *B.C.* Canada **166** F4
Summit Mountain U.S.A. **183** H2
Summit Peak U.S.A. **181** F5
Sumnal Aksai Chin **89** B5
Sumner U.S.A. **174** B5
Sumner, Lake N.Z. **153** G10
Sumner Strait U.S.A. **166** C3
Sumon-dake *mt.* Japan **90** F6
Sumoto Japan **91** D7
Sumpangbinangae Indon. **75** A4
Šumperk Czech Rep. **49** N6
Sumprabum Myanmar **78** B2
Sumpu Japan *see* **Shizuoka**
Sumqayıt Azer. **107** G2
also spelt Sumgait
Sumqayıt *r.* Azer. **107** G2
Sumsar Kyrg. **103** G4
Sumskiy Posad Rus. Fed. **40** E2
Sumter U.S.A. **175** D5
Sumur Jammu and Kashmir **96** C2
Sumy Ukr. **41** E6
Sun *r.* U.S.A. **180** E3
Suna Rus. Fed. **40** I4
Sunagawa Japan **90** G3
Sunam India **96** B3
Sunamganj Bangl. **97** F4
Sunan China **84** C4
also known as Hongwansi
Sunan N. Korea **83** B5
Şunaynah Oman **105** F3
Sunaysilah *salt l.* Iraq **109** M2
Sunbright U.S.A. **176** A9
Sunbula Kuh *mts* Iran **100** A3
Sunbury Australia **147** E4
Sunbury *NC* U.S.A. **177** I9
Sunbury *OH* U.S.A. **176** C5
Sunbury *PA* U.S.A. **177** I5
Sunchales Arg. **204** E3
Suncho Corral Arg. **204** E2
Sunch'ŏn N. Korea **83** B5
Sunch'ŏn S. Korea **83** B6
Sun City S. Africa **133** L2
Sun City U.S.A. **183** L8
Suncook U.S.A. **177** N2
Sund Fin. **42** B1
Sunda, Selat *strait* Indon. **77** D4
English form Sunda Strait
Sunda Kalapa Indon. *see* **Jakarta**
Sundance U.S.A. **180** F3
Sundarbans *reg.* Bangl./India **97** F5
Sundarbans National Park Bangl./India **97** F5
Sundargarh India **97** E5
Sundarnagar India **96** C3
Sunda Strait Indon. *see* **Sunda, Selat**
Sundays *r. E. Cape* S. Africa **133** J10
Sundays *r. Kwazulu-Natal* S. Africa **133** O5
Sunday Strait Australia **150** C3
Sunderland U.K. **47** K9
Sündiken Dağları *mts* Turkey **106** B3
Sundre Canada **167** H5
Sundridge Canada **168** E4
Sundsvall Sweden **45** L3
Sundukli, Peski *des.* Turkm. **103** E5
also known as Sandykly Gumy
Sundumbili S. Africa **133** P6
Sunel India **96** C4
Sunga Tanz. **129** C6
Sungaiapit Indon. **76** C2
Sungaiguntung Indon. **76** C2
Sungailiat Indon. **77** D3
Sungaipenuh Indon. **76** C3
Sungaipinyuh Indon. **77** E2
Sungai Tuas Basin *dock* Sing. **76** [inset]
Sungari *r.* China *see* **Songhua Jiang**
Sungei Petani Malaysia **76** C1
Sungei Seletar Reservoir Sing. **76** [inset]
Sungguminasa Indon. **75** A4
Sungikai Sudan **121** F6
Sungkiang China *see* **Songjiang**
Sung Kong *i. Hong Kong* China **87** [inset]
Sungo Moz. **131** G3
Sungqu China *see* **Songpan**
Sungurlare Bulg. **58** H6
Sungurlu Turkey **106** C2
Sunja Croatia **56** I3
Sunkar, Gora *mt.* Kazakh. **103** H3
Sunkosh *r.* Bhutan **97** F4
also spelt Sankosh
Sun Kosi *r.* Nepal **97** E4
Sunndal Norway **45** I3
Sunndalsøra Norway **44** J3
Sunne Sweden **45** K4
Sunnyside *UT* U.S.A. **183** N2
Sunnyside *WA* U.S.A. **180** C3
Sunnyvale U.S.A. **182** B4
Sun Prairie U.S.A. **172** D7
Sunsas, Sierra de *hills* Bol. **201** F4
Sunset House Canada **167** G4
Sunset Peak *hill Hong Kong* China **87** [inset]
also known as Tai Tung Shan
Sunshine Island *Hong Kong* China **87** [inset]
also known as Chau Kung To
Suntar Rus. Fed. **39** L3
Suntsar Pak. **101** E5
Suntu Eth. **128** C2
Sunwi-do *i.* N. Korea **83** B5
Sunwu China **82** B2
Sunyani Ghana **124** E5
Suojanperä Fin. **44** O1
Suolahti Fin. **44** N3
Suolijärvet *l.* Fin. **40** D2
Suolocielgi Fin. *see* **Saariselkä**
Suoluvuobmi Norway **44** M1
Suomenniemi Fin. **45** N3
Suomi Canada **172** D2
Suomi *country* Europe *see* **Finland**
Suomusjärvi Fin. **42** E1
Suomussalmi Fin. **44** O2
Suō-nada *b.* Japan **91** B8
Suonenjoki Fin. **44** N3
Suŏng Cambodia **79** D6
Suong *r.* Laos **78** C4
Suontee Fin. **44** N3
Suontienselkä *l.* Fin. **44** N3
Suoyarvi Rus. Fed. **40** E3
Suozhen China *see* **Huantai**
Supa India **94** B3
Supai U.S.A. **183** L5
Supaul India **97** E4
Superfosfatnyy Uzbek. **103** F5
Superior *AZ* U.S.A. **183** M8
Superior *MT* U.S.A. **180** D3
Superior *NE* U.S.A. **178** C3
Superior *WI* U.S.A. **172** A4
Superior, Laguna *lag.* Mex. **185** G5

▶ **Superior, Lake** Canada/U.S.A. **172** F3
Largest lake in North America and 2nd in the world.
northamerica [landscapes] ▶ 156–157

Supetar Croatia **56** I5
Suphan Buri Thai. **79** C5
Süphan Dağı *mt.* Turkey **107** E3
Supiori *i.* Indon. **73** I7
Suponevo Rus. Fed. **43** P8
Support Force Glacier Antarctica **223** V1
Supraśl Poland **49** U2
Supraśl *r.* Poland **49** U2
Sup'sa *r.* Georgia **107** E2
Supung N. Korea **83** B4
Sūq al Inān Yemen **104** D4
Sūq ar Rubū' Saudi Arabia **104** C3
Sūq ash Shuyūkh Iraq **107** F5
Suqian China **87** F1
Sūq Suwayq Saudi Arabia **104** B2
Suquṭrā *i.* Yemen *see* **Socotra**
Sur *r.* Ghana **125** E4
Sūr Hungary **49** P8
Şūr Oman **105** G3
Sur, Point U.S.A. **182** C5
Sur, Punta *pt* Arg. **204** F5
Sura Rus. Fed. **41** H5
Sura *r.* Rus. Fed. **41** H4
Şuraabad Azer. **107** G2
Surab Pak. **101** F4
Surabaya Indon. **77** F4
formerly spelt Soerabaia
Surajpur India **97** D5
Sūrak Iran **100** D5
Surakarta Indon. **77** E4
Suramana Indon. **75** A3
Şura Mare Romania **58** F3
Sūrān Iran **101** E5
Şūrān Syria **109** H2
Surára Brazil **199** F6
Surat Australia **147** F1
Surat India **96** B5
Suratgarh India **96** B3
Surat Thani Thai. **79** B6
also known as Ban Don
Suraż Poland **49** T3
Surazh Belarus **43** L6
Surazh Rus. Fed. **43** N8
Surbiton Australia **149** E4
Surdâsh Iraq **107** F4
Surdila-Greci Romania **58** I3
Surduc Romania **58** E1
Surdulica *Srbija* Yugo. **58** D6
Sûre *r.* Germany/Lux. **51** M3
Surendranagar India **96** A5
formerly known as Wadhwan
Suretka Costa Rica **186** C5
Surf U.S.A. **182** D7
Surgana India **94** B1
Surgères France **50** F6
Surgidero de Batabanó Cuba **186** C2
Surgut Rus. Fed. **38** H3
Suri India *see* **Siuri**
Suriapet India **94** C2
also spelt Suryapet
Surigao Phil. **74** C4
Surigao Strait Phil. **74** C4
Surimena Col. **198** C4
Surin Thai. **79** C5
Surinam *country* S. America *see* **Suriname**
▶ **Suriname** *country* S. America **199** G3
also spelt Surinam; *formerly known as* Dutch Guiana
southamerica [countries] ▶ 192–193
Suriname *r.* Suriname **199** H3
Suripá Venez. **198** D3
Suriyān Iran **100** C4
Surkhābād Iran **100** C3
Surkhandar'inskaya Oblast' *admin. div.* Uzbek. **103** F5
English form Surkhandarya Oblast; *also known as* Surkhondaryo Wiloyati
Surkhandar'ya *r.* Uzbek. **103** F5
also spelt Surkhondaryo
Surkhandarya Oblast *admin. div.* Uzbek. *see* **Surkhandar'inskaya Oblast'**
Surkhet Nepal **97** D3
also known as Birendranagar
Surkhob *r.* Tajik. **101** G2
Surkhondaryo *r.* Uzbek. *see* **Surkhandar'ya**
Surkhondaryo Wiloyati *admin. div.* Uzbek. *see* **Surkhandar'inskaya Oblast'**
Surmāq Iran **100** C4
Sürmene Turkey **107** E2
Surnadalsøra Norway **44** J3
Sŭrnevo Bulg. **58** G6
Surovikino Rus. Fed. **41** G6
Surprise Canada **166** C3
Surprise Lake Canada **166** C3
Surrey Canada **166** F5
Surskoye Rus. Fed. **41** H5
Surt Libya *see* **Sirte**
Surt, Khalīj *g.* Libya *see* **Sirte, Gulf of**
Surtsey *i.* Iceland **44** [inset] B3
Sūrū Iran **100** D5
Suru, Vârful *mt.* Romania **58** F3
Surubiú *r.* Brazil **202** B2
Sürüç Turkey **107** D3
Surud, Raas *pt* Somalia **128** E2
Surud Ad *mt.* Somalia *see* **Shimbiris**
Suruga-wan *b.* Japan **91** F7
Surulangun Indon. **76** C3
Surumú *r.* Brazil **199** F4
Surup Phil. **74** C5
Suryapet India *see* **Suriapet**
Şuşa Azer. **107** F3
also spelt Shusha
Susa Italy **51** N7
Susa Japan **91** B7
Sušac *i.* Croatia **56** I6
Susah Tunisia *see* **Sousse**
Susak *i.* Croatia **56** G4
Susaki Japan **91** C8
Susami Japan **91** D8
Susan U.S.A. **177** I8
Sūsangerd Iran **100** B4
Susanville U.S.A. **182** D1
Suşehri Turkey **107** D2
Sushitsa Bulg. **58** G5
Sushui *r.* China **87** D1
Sušice Czech Rep. **49** K6
Šuškova Latvia **43** J5
Susner India **96** C5
Susong China **87** F2
Susquehanna U.S.A. **177** J4
Susquehanna *r.* U.S.A. **177** I6
Susquehanna, West Branch *r.* U.S.A. **176** I5
Susques Arg. **200** D5
Sussex Canada **169** H4
Sussex U.S.A. **177** K4
Susua Indon. **75** B3
Susuman Rus. Fed. **39** O3
Susupu Indon. **75** C2
Susurluk Turkey **106** B3
Sušvė *r.* Lith. **42** E6
Suswa, Mount Kenya **128** B5
Susz Poland **49** Q2
Sutak Jammu and Kashmir **96** C2
Sutaşı Turkey **108** G1
Sutay Uul *mt.* Mongolia **84** B2
Sutherland Australia **147** F3
Sutherland S. Africa **132** E9
Sutherland *NE* U.S.A. **178** B3
Sutherland *VA* U.S.A. **176** H8
Sutherland Range *hills* Australia **151** D5
Sutjeska *nat. park* Bos.-Herz. **56** K5
Sutlej *r.* India/Pak. **96** A3
also spelt Satluj
Sutlepa meri *l.* Estonia **42** E2
Sütlüce Turkey **108** F1
Sütlüce Turkey **58** I7
Sutter U.S.A. **182** C2
Sutter Creek U.S.A. **182** D3
Sutton Canada **168** D2
Sutton N.Z. **153** E13
Sutton *NE* U.S.A. **178** C3
Sutton *WV* U.S.A. **176** E7
Sutton Coldfield U.K. **47** K11
Sutton Lake Canada **168** C2
Sutton Lake U.S.A. **176** E7
Suttor *r.* Australia **149** E4
Suttsu Japan **90** G3
Sutwik Island U.S.A. **164** D4
Sutyr' *r.* Rus. Fed. **82** D2
Suugant Mongolia **85** E2
Suurberg *mt.* S. Africa **133** J8
Suurberg *mts* S. Africa **133** J10
Suurbraak S. Africa **132** E11
Suure-Jaani Estonia **42** G3
Suuremõisa Estonia **42** D3
Suur katel *b.* Estonia **42** D3
Suur-Pakri *i.* Estonia **42** E2
Suurpea Estonia **42** G2
Suur väin *sea chan.* Estonia **42** E3

▶ **Suva** Fiji **145** G3
Capital of Fiji.

Suvalki Poland *see* **Suwałki**
Suva Reka *Kosovo, Srbija* Yugo. **58** B6
Suvarov *atoll* Cook Is *see* **Suwarrow**
Suvorov Rus. Fed. **43** R7
Suvorove Ukr. **58** J3
Suvorovo Bulg. **58** I5
formerly known as Novgradets
Suvorovo Moldova *see* **Ştefan Vodă**
Suwa Japan **91** F6
Suwakong Indon. **77** F3
Suwałki Poland **49** T1
formerly spelt Suvalki
Suwannaphum Thai. **79** C5
Suwannee *r.* U.S.A. **175** D6
Suwanose-jima *i.* Japan **83** C7
Suwaran, Gunung *mt.* Indon. **77** G2
Suwarrow *atoll* Cook Is **221** H6
also known as Anchorage Island; *also spelt* Suvorov
Suwaylih Jordan **108** G5
also spelt Suweilih
Suwayqiyah, Hawr as *imp. l.* Iraq **107** F4
Suwayr *well* Saudi Arabia **107** E5
Suways, Khalīj as *g.* Egypt *see* **Suez, Gulf of**
Suweilih Jordan *see* **Suwaylih**
Suweis, Khalîg el *g.* Egypt *see* **Suez, Gulf of**
Suweis, Qanâ el *canal* Egypt *see* **Suez Canal**
Suwŏn S. Korea **83** B5
Suxu China **87** D4
Suykbulak Kazakh. **103** J2
also spelt Süyqbulaq
Suyo Peru **198** A6
Süyqbulaq Kazakh. *see* **Suykbulak**
Suz, Mys *pt* Kazakh. **102** C4
Sūzā Iran **100** D5
Suzak Kazakh. **103** G3
also spelt Sozaq
Suzaka Japan **91** F6
Suzdal' Rus. Fed. **43** V5
Suzemka Rus. Fed. **43** P9
Suzhou *Anhui* China **87** F1
Suzhou China *see* **Jiuquan**
Suzhou *Jiangsu* China **87** G2
formerly spelt Soochow
Suzi *r.* China **82** B4
Suzu Japan **90** E6
Suzuka Japan **91** E7
Suzu-misaki *pt* Japan **83** E5
Suzzara Italy **56** C4
Sværholthalvøya *pen.* Norway **44** N1

▶ **Svalbard** *terr.* Arctic Ocean **38** A2
Part of Norway.

Svalenik Bulg. **58** H5
Svanstein Sweden **44** M2
Svapa *r.* Rus. Fed. **43** Q9
Svappavaara Sweden **44** M2
also known as Veaikevárri
Svapushcha Rus. Fed. **43** N4
Svärdsjö Sweden **45** K3
Svarta *r.* Fin. **42** G1
Svartälven *r.* Sweden **45** K4
Svartbyn Sweden **44** M2
Svartenhuk Halvø *pen.* Greenland *see* **Sigguup Nunaa**
Svartlå Sweden **44** M2
Svatove Ukr. **41** F6
Svay Riĕng Cambodia **79** D6
Svecha Rus. Fed. **40** H4
Švėdasai Lith. **42** G6
Sveg Sweden **45** K3
Svegsjön *l.* Sweden **45** K3
Sveio Norway **45** I4
Sveki Latvia **42** H4
Švėkšna Lith. **42** C6
Svelgen Norway **45** I3
Svellingen Norway **44** J3
Švenčionėliai Lith. **42** G6
Švenčionys Lith. **42** H6
Svendborg Denmark **45** J5
Svenljunga Sweden **45** K4
Svenstavik Sweden **44** K3
Šventoji *r.* Lith. **42** F6
Sverchkovo Rus. Fed. **43** Q6
Sverdlovsk Rus. Fed. *see* **Yekaterinburg**
Sverdlovs'k Ukr. **41** F6
Sverdlovsk Uzbek. **103** F5
Sverdlovskaya Oblast' *admin. div.* Rus. Fed. **40** L4
English form Sverdlovsk Oblast
Sverdlovsk Oblast *admin. div.* Rus. Fed. *see* **Sverdlovskaya Oblast'**
Sverdrup Channel Canada **165** J2
Sverdrup Islands Canada **165** J2
Sverige *country* Europe *see* **Sweden**
Sveta Andrija *i.* Croatia **56** H5
Švėtė *r.* Lith. **42** E5
Sveti Ivan Zelina Croatia *see* **Zelina**
Sveti Jure *mt.* Croatia **56** J5
Sveti Nikole Macedonia **58** C7
Svetlaya Rus. Fed. **82** E3
Svetlodarskoye Rus. Fed. **82** F2
Svetlogorsk Belarus *see* **Svyetlahorsk**
Svetlogorsk *Kaliningradskaya Oblast'* Rus. Fed. **42** B7
historically known as Rauschen
Svetlogorsk *Krasnoyarskiy Kray* Rus. Fed. **39** I3
Svetlograd Rus. Fed. **41** G7
formerly known as Petrovskoye
Svetlopolyansk Rus. Fed. **40** J3
Svetlovodsk Ukr. *see* **Svitlovods'k**
Svetlyy Rus. Fed. **42** B7
historically known as Zimmerbude
Svetlyy Rus. Fed. **103** E2
Svetlyy Yar Rus. Fed. **41** H6
Svetogorsk Rus. Fed. **43** J1
Svetozarevo *Srbija* Yugo. *see* **Jagodina**
Svētupe *r.* Latvia **42** F4
Svíahnúkar *vol.* Iceland **44** [inset] C2
Svidník Slovakia **49** S6
Svilaja *mts* Croatia **56** I5
Svilajnac *Srbija* Yugo. **58** C4
Svilengrad Bulg. **58** H7
Svinecea Mare, Vârful *mt.* Romania **58** D4
Svinø *i.* Faroe Is *see* **Svínoy**
Svínoy *i.* Faroe Is **46** F1
also spelt Svinø
Svintsovyy Rudnik Turkm. **103** F5
Svir Belarus **42** H7
Svir' *r.* Rus. Fed. **43** P1
Svir, Vozyera *l.* Belarus **42** H7
Sviritsa Rus. Fed. **43** N1
Svirskaya Guba *b.* Rus. Fed. **43** N1
Svir'stroy Rus. Fed. **43** O1
Svishtov Bulg. **58** G5
Svislach *Hrodzyenskaya Voblasts'* Belarus **42** F8
Svislach *Minskaya Voblasts'* Belarus **42** I8
Svislach *r.* Belarus/Poland **42** F8
also spelt Svisloch *or* Świsłocz
Svislach *r.* Belarus **42** J8
also spelt Svisloch
Svisloch Belarus *see* **Svislach**
Svisloch *r.* Belarus *see* **Svislach**
Svit Slovakia **49** R6
Svitava *r.* Czech Rep. **49** N7
Svitavy Czech Rep. **49** N6
Svitlovods'k Ukr. **41** E6
also spelt Svetlovodsk; *formerly known as* Khrushchev *or* Kremges
Svizzera *country* Europe *see* **Switzerland**
Svoboda Rus. Fed. **42** C7
Svobodnyy Rus. Fed. **82** C2
Svoge Bulg. **58** E6
Svol'nya *r.* Belarus **43** J6
Svolvær Norway **44** K1
Svratka *r.* Czech Rep. **49** N6
Svrljig *Srbija* Yugo. **58** D5
Svrljiške Planine *mts* Yugo. **58** D5
Svyantsyanskiya Hrady *hills* Belarus **42** H7
Svyatoy Nos, Mys *c.* Rus. Fed. **40** I2
Svyatsk Rus. Fed. **43** M9
Svyetlahorsk Belarus **43** K9
also spelt Svetlogorsk; *formerly known as* Shatilki
Svyha *r.* Ukr. **43** O9
Swabi Pak. **101** H3
Swaershoek S. Africa **133** J9
Swaershoekpas *pass* S. Africa **133** J9
Swain Reefs Australia **149** G4
Swainsboro U.S.A. **175** D5
Swains Island American Samoa **145** H3
also known as Olosenga
Swakop *watercourse* Namibia **130** B4
Swakopmund Namibia **130** B4
Swale *r.* U.K. **47** K9
Swallow Islands Solomon Is **145** F3
Swampy *r.* Canada **169** G1
Swan *r.* Australia **151** A6
Swan *r. Man./Sask.* Canada **167** K4
Swan *r. Ont.* Canada **168** D2
Swanage U.K. **47** K13
Swana-Mume Dem. Rep. Congo **127** E7
Swandale U.S.A. **176** E7
Swanepoelspoort *mt.* S. Africa **132** H10
Swan Hill Australia **147** D3
Swan Hills Canada **167** H4
Swan Islands *is* Caribbean Sea **186** C3
also known as Santanilla, Islas
Swan Lake *B.C.* Canada **166** D4
Swan Lake *Man.* Canada **167** K4
Swan Lake U.S.A. **178** D2
Swanlinbar Rep. of Ireland **47** E9
Swanquarter U.S.A. **174** E5
Swanquarter National Wildlife Refuge *nature res.* U.S.A. **174** E5
Swan Reach Australia **146** C3
Swan River Canada **167** K4
Swansea Australia **147** F5
Swansea U.K. **47** I12
also known as Abertawe
Swansea Bay U.K. **47** I12
Swans Island U.S.A. **177** Q1
Swanton *CA* U.S.A. **182** B4
Swanton *VT* U.S.A. **177** L1
Swartberg S. Africa **133** N7
Swartberg *mt.* S. Africa **132** D11
Swartbergpas *pass* S. Africa **132** F10
Swartdoorn *r.* S. Africa **132** B7
Swart Kei *r.* S. Africa **133** L9
Swartkolkvloer *salt pan* S. Africa **132** E7
Swartkops *r.* S. Africa **133** J10
Swart Nossob *watercourse* Namibia *see* **Black Nossob**
Swartplaas S. Africa **133** K3
Swartputs S. Africa **132** H5
Swartput se Pan *salt pan* Namibia **132** D3
Swartruggens S. Africa **133** K2
Swartruggens *mts* S. Africa **133** K2
Swartz Creek U.S.A. **173** J8
Swarzędz Poland **49** O3
Swasey Peak U.S.A. **183** K2
Swastika Canada **173** M2
Swat *r.* Pak. **101** G3
Swat Kohistan *reg.* Pak. **101** H3
Swatow China *see* **Shantou**
▶ **Swaziland** *country* Africa **133** P3
known as Ngwane in Swazi
africa [countries] ▶ 114–117

▶ **Sweden** *country* Europe **45** K4
5th largest country in Europe. Known as Sverige in Swedish.
europe [countries] ▶ 32–35

Swedesburg U.S.A. **172** B9
Sweet Briar U.S.A. **176** F8
Sweet Home U.S.A. **180** B3
Sweet Springs U.S.A. **176** E8
Sweetwater U.S.A. **179** B5
Sweetwater *r.* U.S.A. **180** F4
Swellendam S. Africa **132** E11
Swempoort S. Africa **133** L8
Świder *r.* Poland **49** S3
Świdnica Poland **49** N5
Świdnik Poland **49** T4
Świdwin Poland **49** M2
Świebodzice Poland **49** N5
Świebodzin Poland **49** M3
Świecie Poland **49** P2
Świętokrzyskie, Góry *hills* Poland **49** R5
Świętokrzyski Park Narodowy *nat. park* Poland **49** R5
Swift *r.* U.S.A. **177** O1
Swift Current Canada **167** J5
Swiftcurrent Creek *r.* Canada **167** J5
Swilly, Lough *inlet* Rep. of Ireland **47** E8
Swindon U.K. **47** K12
Swinkpan *imp. l.* S. Africa **133** J5
Świnoujście Poland **49** L2
Swiss Confederation *country* Europe *see* **Switzerland**
Swiss National Park Switz. **51** Q6
Świsłocz *r.* Belarus *see* **Svislach**
▶ **Switzerland** *country* Europe **51** N6
known as Schweiz *in German or* Suisse *in French or* Svizzera *in Italian; also known as* Swiss Confederation; *long form* Confoederatio Helvetica
europe [countries] ▶ 32–35
Swords Rep. of Ireland **47** F10
Swords Range *hills* Australia **149** D4
Syalyets Belarus **43** L8
Syalyets Vodaskhovishcha *resr* Belarus **42** F9
Syamozero, Ozero *l.* Rus. Fed. **40** E3
Syamzha Rus. Fed. **43** V2
Syang Nepal **97** D3
Syanno Belarus **43** K7
also spelt Senno
Syarednenemanskaya Nizina *lowland* Belarus/Lith. **42** F8
Syas' *r.* Rus. Fed. **43** N1
Syas'troy Rus. Fed. **43** N1
Sybrandskraal S. Africa **133** M2
Sycamore U.S.A. **172** E9
Sychevka Rus. Fed. **43** P6
Sychevo Rus. Fed. **43** R6
Syców Poland **49** O4
Sydenham *atoll* Kiribati *see* **Nonouti**

▶ **Sydney** Australia **147** F3
State capital of New South Wales. Most populous city in Oceania. Historically known as Port Jackson.
world [cities] ▶ 24–25
oceania [features] ▶ 142–143

Sydney Canada **169** I4
Sydney Island Kiribati *see* **Manra**
Sydney Lake Canada **167** M5
Sydney Mines Canada **169** I4
Sydzhak Uzbek. *see* **Sidzhak**
Syedra *tourist site* Turkey **108** D1
Syeverodonets'k Ukr. **41** F6
also spelt Severodonetsk; *formerly known as* Leskhimstroy
Sykesville U.S.A. **176** G4
Sykkylven Norway **44** I3
Syktyvkar Rus. Fed. **40** I3
Sylacauga U.S.A. **175** C5
Sylhet Bangl. **97** F4
Sylhet *admin. div.* Bangl. **97** F4
Sylt *i.* Germany **48** F1
Sylva *r.* Rus. Fed. **40** K4
Sylva U.S.A. **174** D5
Sylvania *GA* U.S.A. **175** D5
Sylvania *OH* U.S.A. **176** B4
Sylvan Lake Canada **167** H4
Sylvester U.S.A. **175** D6
Sylvester, Lake *salt flat* Australia **148** B3
Sylvia, Mount Canada **166** E3

index S T

Symi Greece 59 I12
Symi i. Greece 59 I12
also spelt Simi
Syndicate Phil. 74 B3
Synel'nykove Ukr. 41 E6
also spelt Sinel'nikovo
Syngyrli, Mys pt Kazakh. 41 J8
also spelt Sengirli, Mys
Syngyrli, Mys pt Kazakh. see Sengirli, Mys
Synnagyn, Khrebet mts Rus. Fed. 39 M4
Synnfjell mt. Norway 45 J3
Synnott Range hills Australia 150 D3
Synya Rus. Fed. 40 K2
Synya r. Rus. Fed. 40 M2
Syowa research station Antarctica 223 C2
Syracuse Sicilia Italy see Syracuse
Syracuse Sicilia Italy 57 H11
also spelt Siracusa; historically known as Syracusae
Syracuse KS U.S.A. 178 B4
Syracuse NY U.S.A. 177 I2
Syrdar'inskaya Oblast' admin. div. Uzbek. 103 G4
English form Syr Darya Oblast; also known as Sirdaryo Wiloyati
Syr Darya r. Asia see Syrdar'ya
Syrdar'ya r. Asia 99 H1
English form Syr Darya; also known as Dar"yoi Sir; also spelt Sirdaryo
Syrdar'ya Uzbek. 103 G4
also spelt Sirdaryo; formerly known as Syrdaryinskiy
Syrdarya Oblast admin. div. Uzbek. see Syrdar'inskaya Oblast'
Syrdaryinskiy Uzbek. see Syrdar'ya
Syria country Asia 109 I2
spelt As Sūrīyah or Souriya in Arabic
asia [countries] 64–67
Syriam Myanmar 78 B4
Syrian Desert Asia 107 D4
also known as Bādiyat ash Shām
Syrna i. Greece 59 H12
also spelt Sirina
Syrokvashino Rus. Fed. 43 L5
Syros i. Greece 59 F11
also spelt Síros
Syrskiy Rus. Fed. 43 U9
Sysmä Fin. 45 N3
Sysola r. Rus. Fed. 40 I3
Sysoyevo Rus. Fed. 43 R2
Syumsi Rus. Fed. 40 I4
Syun r. Rus. Fed. 40 J5
Syurkum Rus. Fed. 82 F2
Syurkum, Mys pt Rus. Fed. 82 F2
Syzran' Rus. Fed. 41 I5
Szabadka Vojvodina, Srbija Yugo. see Subotica
Szabadszállás Hungary 49 Q9
Szadek Poland 49 P4
Szamocin Poland 49 O2
Szamos r. Hungary 49 T7
Szamotuły Poland 49 N3
Szany Hungary 49 O8
Szarvas Hungary 49 R9
Szatmár-Beregi park Hungary 49 T7
Szazhalombatta Hungary 49 P8
Szczebrzeszyn Poland 49 T5
Szczecin Poland 49 L2
historically known as Stettin
Szczecinek Poland 49 N2
Szczekociny Poland 49 Q5
Szczuczyn Poland 49 T2
Szczytno Poland 49 R2
Szechwan prov. China see Sichuan
Szeged Hungary 49 R9
Szeghalom Hungary 49 S8
Székesfehérvár Hungary 49 P8
Szekszárd Hungary 49 P9
Szentes Hungary 49 R9
Szentgotthárd Hungary 49 N9
historically known as Sankt Gotthard
Szentőrinc Hungary 49 O9
Szerencs Hungary 49 S7
Szeska Góra hill Poland 49 T1
Szigetszentmiklós Hungary 49 Q8
Szigetvár Hungary 49 O9
Szkwa r. Poland 49 S2
Szlichtyngowa Poland 49 N4
Szolnok Hungary 49 R8
Szombathely Hungary 49 N8
Szprotawa Poland 49 M4
Sztálinváros Hungary see Dunaújváros
Sztum Poland 49 Q2
Szubin Poland 49 O2
Szűcsi Hungary 49 Q8
Szydłowiec Poland 49 R4
Szypliszki Poland 49 T1

↓ T

Taabo, Lac de l. Côte d'Ivoire 124 D5
Taagga Duudka reg. Somalia 128 D2
Taal, Lake Phil. 74 B3
Tab Hungary 49 P9
Tabaco Phil. 74 B3
Tābah Saudi Arabia 104 C2
Tabajara Brazil 201 E2
Tabakat well Mali 123 E5
Tabanan Indon. 77 F5
Tabang Indon. 77 G2
Tabang r. Indon. 77 F2
Tabankulu S. Africa 133 N7
Ţabaqah Syria 109 J2
Ţabaqah Syria see Madīnat ath Thawrah
Tabar Islands P.N.G. 145 E2
Tabarka Tunisia 57 A12
Ţabas Khorāsan Iran 100 D3
Ţabas Khorāsan Iran 101 E3
Tabasalu Estonia 42 F2
Tabasco state Mex. 185 G5
Tabāsin Iran 100 D4
Tābask, Kūh-e mt. Iran 100 B4
Tabatinga Brazil 198 D6
Tabatinga, Serra da hills Brazil 202 C4
Tabayoo, Mount Phil. 74 B2
Tabédé well Chad 120 B6
Tabelbala Alg. 123 E3
Taber Canada 167 H5
Taberdga Alg. 123 G2
Tabernas Spain 55 I7
Tabernes de Valldigna Spain see Tavernes de la Valldigna
Tabet, Nam r. Myanmar 78 B2
Tabia Tsaka salt l. China 89 D6
Tabin Wildlife Reserve nature res. Sabah Malaysia 77 G1
Tabir r. Indon. 76 C3
Tabiteuea atoll Kiribati 145 G2
also spelt Taputeouea; formerly known as Drummond
Tabivere Estonia 42 H3
Tablas i. Phil. 74 B3
Tablas Strait Phil. 74 B3
Table Bay S. Africa 132 C10
Table Cape N.Z. 152 L7
Table Islands India 79 A5
Table Mountain hill S. Africa 132 C10
Table Point Phil. 74 A4
Table Rock Reservoir U.S.A. 178 D4
Tabligbo Togo 125 F5
Taboca Brazil 199 F5
Tabocal r. Brazil 199 F6
Tabocó r. Brazil 201 G4
Tabong Myanmar 78 B2
Tábor Czech Rep. 49 L6
Tabora Tanz. 129 B6
Tabora admin. reg. Tanz. 129 B6
Taboshar Tajik. 101 G1
Tabou Côte d'Ivoire 124 D5
Tabrichat well Mali 125 F2
Tabrīz Iran 100 A2
Tabuaeran i. Kiribati 221 H5
Tabūk Saudi Arabia 104 B1
Tabūk prov. Saudi Arabia 104 B1
Tabulam Australia 147 G2
Tabulan Indon. 75 B3
Tabuny Rus. Fed. 103 I1
Tabuyung Indon. 76 B2
Täby Sweden 45 L4
Tacaipu, Serra hills Brazil 199 H5
Tacalé Brazil 199 H4
Tacámbaro Mex. 185 E5
Tacaná, Volcán de vol. Mex. 185 G6
Tacarcuna, Cerro mt. Panama 186 D5
Tachdaït well Mali 125 F2
Tacheng China 88 C2
also known as Qoqek; formerly known as Chuguchak
Tachibana-wan b. Japan 91 A8
Tachie Canada 166 E4
Tachikawa Tōkyō Japan 91 F7
Tachikawa Yamagata Japan 90 F5
Táchira state Venez. 198 C2
Tachiumet well Libya 120 A3
Tachov Czech Rep. 49 J6
Tacina r. Italy 57 I10
Taciuã, Lago l. Brazil 199 F6
Tacloban Phil. 74 C4
Tacna Col. 198 D5
Tacna Peru 200 C4
Tacna dept Peru 200 C4
Tacoma U.S.A. 180 B3
Taconite Harbor U.S.A. 172 C3
Taco Pozo Arg. 204 E2
Tacuarembó Uruguay 204 G3
Tacupeto Mex. 184 C2
Tadami Japan 90 F6
Tadami-gawa r. Japan 90 F6
Tadélaka well Niger 125 G3
Tademaït, Plateau du Alg. 123 F3
English form Tademaït Plateau
Tademaït Plateau Alg. see Tademaït, Plateau du
Tadine New Caledonia 145 F4
Tadjentourt hill Alg. 123 H4
Tadjeraout, Oued watercourse Alg. 123 F5
Tadjikistan country Asia see Tajikistan
Tadjoura Djibouti 128 D2
Tadjoura, Golfe de g. Djibouti 128 D2
Tadjrouna Alg. 123 F2
Tadmur Syria 109 J3
also known as Tamar; historically known as Palmyra
Tadó Col. 198 B3
Tadohae Haesang National Park S. Korea 83 B6
Tadoule Lake Canada 167 L3
Tadoussac Canada 169 G3
Tadpatri India 94 C3
Tadrart Acacus tourist site Libya 120 A3
Tadwale India 94 C2
Tadzhikabad Tajik. see Tojikobod
Tadzhikskaya S.S.R. country Asia see Tajikistan
T'aean Haean National Park S. Korea 83 B5
T'aebaek-sanmaek mts N. Korea/S. Korea 83 B5
Taebla Estonia 42 E3
Taech'ŏn S. Korea see Poryŏng
Taech'ŏng-do i. S. Korea 83 B5
Taedong-gang r. N. Korea 83 B5
formerly known as Daido
Taedong-man b. N. Korea 83 B5
Taegu S. Korea 83 C6
Taehŭksan-kundo is S. Korea 83 B6
Taejŏn S. Korea 83 B5
Taejŏng S. Korea 83 B6
T'aepaek S. Korea 83 C5
Taevaskoja Estonia 42 I3
Tafahi i. Tonga 145 H3
formerly known as Keppel Island
Tafalla Spain 55 J2
Tafassasset, Oued watercourse Alg./Niger 123 H5
Tafelberg S. Africa 133 J8
Tafelberg mt. S. Africa 132 F9
Tafelberg mt. Suriname 199 G4
Tafelberg, Natuurreservaat nature res. Suriname 199 G4
Tafila Jordan see Aţ Ţafilah
Tafiré Côte d'Ivoire 124 D4
Tafi Viejo Arg. 204 D2
Tafjord Norway 44 I3
Tafraoute Morocco 122 C3
Tafresh Iran 100 B3
Taft Iran 100 C4
Taft U.S.A. 182 E6
Taftān, Kūh-e mt. Iran 101 E4
Taftanāz Syria 109 H2
Tagab Sudan 121 F5
Tagajō Japan 90 G5
Tagânet Keyna well Mali 124 E2
Taganrog Rus. Fed. 41 F7
Taganrog, Gulf of Rus. Fed./Ukr. 41 F7
also known as Taganrogskiy Zaliv or Tahanroz'ka Zatoka
Taganrogskiy Zaliv b. Rus. Fed./Ukr. see Taganrog, Gulf of
Tagant admin. reg. Mauritania 124 C2
Tagarev, Gora mt. Iran/Turkm. 100 D2
Tagawa Japan 91 B8
Tagay Rus. Fed. 41 H5
Tagaza well Niger 125 G2
Tagbilaran Phil. 74 B4
Tagchagpu Ri mt. China 89 C5
Tagdempt Alg. see Tiaret
Taggia Italy 51 N9
Taghmanant well Mali 122 D4
also spelt Tarhmanant
Tagish Canada 166 C2
Tagish Lake Canada 166 C3
Tagliacozzo Italy 56 F6
Tagliamento r. Italy 56 F3
Tagnout Chaggueret well Mali 123 E5
also spelt Taguenout Haggueret
Tagoloan r. Phil. 74 C4
Tagomago i. Spain 55 M5
Tagourâret well Mauritania 124 D2
Tagta Turkm. 102 D4
formerly spelt Takhta
Tagtabazar Turkm. 101 E3
formerly spelt Takhta-Bazar
Taguatinga Minas Gerais Brazil 206 E2
Taguatinga Tocantins Brazil 202 C5
Tagudin Phil. 74 B2
Taguenout Haggueret well Mali see Tagnout Chaggueret
Tagula P.N.G. 149 G1
Tagula Island P.N.G. 149 G1
Tagum Phil. 74 C5
Tagus r. Port./Spain 54 D5
also known as Tajo (Spain) or Tejo (Portugal)
Tah, Sabkhat salt pan Morocco 122 B4
Taha China 85 J2
Tahaetkun Mountain Canada 166 G5
Tahalra reg. Alg. 123 G5
Tahan, Gunung mt. Malaysia 76 C1
Tahanroz'ka Zatoka b. Rus. Fed./Ukr. see Taganrog, Gulf of
Tahat, Mont mt. Alg. 123 G5
Tahaurawe i. U.S.A. see Kahoolawe
Tahe China 82 B1
Taheke N.Z. 152 H3
Tähemaa Estonia 42 I3
Tahifet Alg. 123 G5
Tahilt Mongolia 84 C2
Tahiti i. Fr. Polynesia 221 I7
also spelt Otahiti
Tahkuna nina pt Estonia 42 D2
Tahlab r. Iran/Pak. 101 E4
Tahlab, Dasht-i plain Pak. 101 E4
Tahlequah U.S.A. 179 D5
Tahltan Canada 166 D3
Tahoe, Lake U.S.A. 182 D2
Tahoe City U.S.A. 182 D2
Tahoe Vista U.S.A. 182 D2
Tahoka U.S.A. 179 B5
Tahora N.Z. 152 I7
Tahorakuri N.Z. 152 K6
Tahoua Niger 125 G3
Tahoua dept Niger 125 G3
Tahrūd Iran 100 D4
Tahrūd r. Iran 100 D4
Taht, Oued El watercourse Alg. 55 L9
Tahta Egypt 121 F3
Tahtalı Dağ mt. Turkey 108 B1
Tahtsa Peak Canada 166 E4
Tahua Bol. 200 D4
Tahuamanú r. Bol. 200 D2
Tahuamanú Peru 200 C2
Tahulandang i. Indon. 75 C2
Tahuna Indon. 75 C2
Taï Côte d'Ivoire 124 D5
Taï, Parc National de nat. park Côte d'Ivoire 124 D5
Tai A Chau i. Hong Kong China 87 [inset]
Tai'an Liaoning China 85 I3
Tai'an Shandong China 85 H4
Taibai China 87 C1
also known as Zuitou
Taibai Shan mt. China 87 C1
Taibei Taiwan see T'aipei
Taïbet Alg. 123 G2
Tabilla r. Spain 55 I6
Taibilla, Sierra de mts Spain 55 I6
Taibus Qi China see Baochang
T'aichung Taiwan 87 G3
also spelt Taizhong
Taidong Taiwan see T'aitung
Taieri r. N.Z. 153 E14
Taigu China 85 G4
Taihang Shan mts China 85 G4
Taihang Shan mts China 85 G4
Taihape N.Z. 152 J7
Taihe Anhui China 87 E1
Taihe Jiangxi China 87 E3
also known as Chengjiang
Taihe China see Shehong
Taihezhen China see Shehong
Tai Ho Wan Hong Kong China 87 [inset]
Taihu China 87 F2
Tai Hu l. China 87 G2
Taikang Heilong. China 85 J2
formerly known as Dorbod
Taikang Henan China 87 E1
Taikkyi Myanmar 78 A4
Tailai China 85 I2
Tailako East Timor 75 C5
Tai Lam Chung Reservoir Hong Kong China 87 [inset]
Taileleo Indon. 76 B3
Tailem Bend Australia 146 C3
Tai Long Wan b. Hong Kong China 87 [inset]
Tailuge Taiwan see T'ailuko
T'ailuko Taiwan 87 G3
also spelt Tailuge
Taim Brazil 204 G4
Taimani reg. Afgh. 101 E3
Tai Mo Shan hill Hong Kong China 87 [inset]
Tain r. Ghana 124 E4
Tain U.K. 46 H6
T'ainan Taiwan 87 G4
Tainaro, Akra pt Greece 59 D12
English form Matapan, Cape
Tai O Hong Kong China 87 [inset]
Taiobeiras Brazil 202 D5
Taipa Indon. 75 B3
Taipa N.Z. 152 H3
Tai Pak Wan b. Hong Kong China see Discovery Bay
Taipalsaari Fin. 45 O3
Tai Pang Wan b. Hong Kong China see Mirs Bay
Taipei Taiwan see T'aipei
T'aipei Taiwan 87 G3
Capital of Taiwan. English form Taipei; also spelt Taibei.
Taiping China see Shixing
Taiping Guangdong China 87 E4
Taiping China see Chongzuo
Taiping Guangxi China 87 D4
Taiping Malaysia 76 C1
Taiping Ling mt. China 85 I2
Tai Po Hong Kong China 87 [inset]
Tai Po Hoi b. Hong Kong China see Tolo Harbour
Tai Poutini National Park N.Z. see Westland National Park
Taipu Brazil 202 F3
Taipudia India 97 G4
Taiqian China 85 G5
Tairadate-kaikyō sea chan. Japan 90 G4
Tairbeart U.K. see Tarbert
Tai Rom Yen National Park Thai. 79 B6
Tairua N.Z. 152 J5
Tairuq Iran 100 A3
Tais Indon. 76 C4
Taisetsu-zan mts Japan 90 H3
Taishan China 87 E4
Tai Shek Mo hill Hong Kong China see Crest Hill
Taishun China 87 F3
also known as Luoyang
Tai Siu Mo To is Hong Kong China see The Brothers
Taitaitanopo i. Indon. 76 C3
Tai Tan Hoi Hap inlet Hong Kong China see Long Harbour
Taitanu N.Z. 153 G11
Taitao, Peninsula de pen. Chile 205 B7
Taitao, Punta pt Chile 205 B7
Taiti mt. Kenya 128 B4
Tai To Yan mt. Hong Kong China 87 [inset]
T'aitung Taiwan 87 G4
also spelt Taidong
Tai Tung Shan hill Hong Kong China see Sunset Peak
T'aitung Shan mts Taiwan 87 G4
also known as Haian Shanmo
Taivalkoski Fin. 44 O2
Taivaskero hill Fin. 44 N1
Taivassalo Fin. 45 M3
Taiwan country Asia 87 G4
also known as China, Republic of or Chung-hua Min-kuo; formerly known as Formosa
asia [countries] 64–67
Taiwan Haixia strait China/Taiwan see Taiwan Strait
Taiwan Shan mts Taiwan see Chungyang Shanmo
Taiwan Strait China/Taiwan 87 F4
also known as Taiwan Haixia; formerly known as Formosa Strait
Taixian China see Jiangyan
Taixing China 87 G1
Taïyetos Óros mts Greece see Tavgetos
Taiyuan China 85 G4
Tai Yue Shan i. Hong Kong China see Lantau Island
Taiyue Shan mts China 85 F4
Taizhao China 89 F6
Taizhong Taiwan see T'aichung
Taizhou Jiangsu China 87 F1
Taizhou Zhejiang China 87 G2
also known as Jiaojiang
Taizhou Liedao i. China 87 G2
Taizhou Wan b. China 87 G2
Taizi r. China 83 B4
Ta'izz Yemen 104 C5
Ta'izz governorate Yemen 104 C5
Tajam, Tanjong pt Sing. 76 [inset]
Tajamulco, Volcán de vol. Guat. 185 H6
Tajarḥī Libya 120 B3
Tajem, Gunung hill Indon. 77 D3
Tāj-e Malekī Iran 100 B4
Tajerouine Tunisia 123 H2
Tajikistan country Asia 101 G2
spelt Tojikiston in Tajik; formerly known as Tadzhikskaya S.S.R.; formerly spelt Tadjikistan
asia [countries] 64–67
Tajima Japan 90 F6
Tajitos Mex. 184 B2
Taj Mahal tourist site India 96 C4
Tajo r. Spain 54 D5 see Tagus
Tajobum India 86 A2
Tajsara, Cordillera de mts Bol. 200 D5
Tajuña r. Spain 55 H4
Tak Thai. 78 B4
also known as Rahaeng
Takāb Iran 100 A2
Takabba Kenya 128 D4
Taka'Bonerate, Kepulauan atolls Indon. 75 B4
also known as Macan, Kepulauan
Takadja Cent. Afr. Rep. 126 D2
Takahagi Japan 90 G6
Takahashi Japan 91 C7
Takahe, Mount Antarctica 222 Q1
Takaka N.Z. 152 G8
Takal India 96 C5
Takalaou Chad 126 C2
Takalous, Oued watercourse Alg. 123 G5
Takama Guyana 199 G3
Takamatsu Japan 91 D7
Takamori Japan 91 B8
Takanabe Japan 91 B8
Takanosu Japan 90 G4
Takaoka Japan 91 E6
Takapau N.Z. 152 K8
Takapuna N.Z. 152 I4
Takara-jima i. Japan 83 C7
Takasaki Japan 91 F6
Takatokwane Botswana 131 E5
Takatshwaane Botswana 130 D4
Takatsuki Japan 91 D7
Takatsuki-yama mt. Japan 91 C8
Takatu r. Brazil/Guyana 199 G4
Ta-Kaw Myanmar 78 B3
Takayama Japan 91 E6
Tak Bai Thai. 79 C7
Takefu Japan 91 E7
Takehara Japan 91 C7
Takengon Indon. 76 B1
Takeo Cambodia see Takêv
Takeo Japan 91 B8
Take-shima i. N. Pacific Ocean see Liancourt Rocks
Takestān Iran 100 B2
Taketa Japan 91 B8
Takêv Cambodia 79 D6
also spelt Takeo
Takfon Tajik. 101 G2
Takhādīd well Iraq 107 F5
Takhar prov. Afgh. 101 G2
Takhatpur India 97 D5
Takhemaret Alg. 55 L9
Takhiatash Uzbek. see Gulabie
Takhini r. Canada 166 C2
Takhini Hotspring Canada 166 C2
Ta Khli Thai. 79 C5
Ta Khmau Cambodia 79 D6
Takhta Turkm. see Tagta
Takhta-Bazar Turkm. see Tagtabazar
Takhtabrod Kazakh. 103 F1
Takhtakupyr Uzbek. 102 E4
Takht Apān, Kūh-e mt. Iran 100 B3
Takhteh Iran 100 C4
Takht-i-Sulaiman mt. Pak. 101 G4
Takht-i-Suleiman mt. Iran 100 B2
Takiéta Niger 125 H3
Takijuq Lake Canada see Napaktulik Lake
Takikawa Japan 90 G3
Takinoue Japan 90 H2
Takisset, Oued watercourse Alg./Libya 123 H4
Takisung Indon. 77 F3
Takitimu Mountains N.Z. 153 B13
Takla Lake Canada 166 E4
Takla Landing Canada 166 E4
Takla Makan des. China see Taklimakan Desert
Taklimakan Desert China 88 C4
also known as Takla Makan or Taklimakan Shamo
world [land images] 12–13
Taklimakan Shamo des. China see Taklimakan Desert
Takob Tajik. 101 G2
Takoradi Ghana 125 E5
Takpa Shiri mt. China 89 F6
Taku Canada 166 C3
Taku r. Canada/U.S.A. 164 F4
Taku Japan 91 B8
Takua Pa Thai. 79 B6
Takua Thung Thai. 79 B6
Takum Nigeria 125 H5
Takundi Dem. Rep. Congo 126 C6
Tal India 96 B5
Tala Egypt 108 B7
Tala Uruguay 204 G4
Talachyn Belarus 43 K7
also spelt Tolochin
Talagang Pak. 101 H3
Talaiassa, Serra hill Spain 55 M6
Talaja India 96 B5
Talakan Amurskaya Oblast' Rus. Fed. 82 C2
Talakan Khabarovskiy Kray Rus. Fed. 82 D2
Talala India 94 A1
Talandzha Rus. Fed. 82 C2
Talang, Gunung vol. Indon. 76 C3
Talangbatu Indon. 77 D3
Talangbetutu Indon. 76 D3
Talara Peru 198 A6
Talar-i-Band mts Pak. 101 E5
also known as Makran Coast Range
Talas r. Kazakh./Kyrg. 103 G3
Talas Kyrg. 103 H4
Talas admin. div. Kyrg. 103 G4
English form Talas Oblast; also known as Talasskaya Oblast'
Talas Ala-Too mts Kyrg. 103 G4
English form Talas Range; also known as Talasskiy Alatau, Khrebet
Talashkino Rus. Fed. 43 N7
Talas Oblast admin. div. Kyrg. see Talas
Talas Range mts Kyrg. see Talas Ala-Too
Talasskaya Oblast' admin. div. Kyrg. see Talas
Talasskiy Alatau, Khrebet mts Kyrg. see Talas Ala-Too
Tal'at al Jamā'ah, Rujm mt. Jordan 108 G7
Talata-Mafara Nigeria 125 G3
Ţal 'at Mūsá mt. Lebanon/Syria 109 H3
Talaud, Kepulauan is Indon. 75 C1
Talavera de la Reina Spain 54 G5
Talawanta Australia 149 D3
Talawgyi Myanmar 78 B2
Talaya Rus. Fed. 39 P3
Talayan Phil. 74 C5
Talayuela Spain 54 F5
Talayuelo mt. Spain 55 I5
Talbehat India 96 C4
Talbot, Mount hill Australia 151 D5
Talbot Inlet Canada 165 L2
Talbot Lake Canada 167 L4
Talbotton U.S.A. 175 C5
Talbragar r. Australia 147 F3
Talca Chile 204 C4
Talca, Punta pt Chile 204 C4
Talcahuano Chile 204 B5
Talcher India 95 E1
Taldan Rus. Fed. 82 B1
Taldom Rus. Fed. 43 S5
Taldyk Uzbek. 102 D4
Taldyk, Pereval pass Kyrg. 103 H5
Taldykorgan Kazakh. 103 I3
also spelt Taldyqorghan; formerly spelt Taldy-Kurgan
Taldy-Kurgan Kazakh. see Taldykorgan
Taldyqorghan Kazakh. see Taldykorgan
Taldysu Kyrg. see Taldy-Suu
Taldy-Suu Kyrg. 103 I4
also spelt Taldysu
Talegaon Maharashtra India 94 B2
Talegaon Maharashtra India 94 C1
Talen India 96 C5
Taleni S. Africa 133 M9
Tālesh Iran see Hashtpar
Talets, Ozero l. Rus. Fed. 43 R2
Talga r. Australia 150 B4
Talgar Kazakh. 103 I4
Talgar, Pik mt. Kazakh. 103 I4
Talguharai Sudan 121 G5
Talḥah Saudi Arabia 104 C4
Taliabu i. Indon. 75 C3
Talibon Phil. 74 C4
Talikota India 94 C2
Talikud i. Phil. 74 C5
Talimardzhan Uzbek. 103 F5
also spelt Tallymerjen or Tollimarjon
Taliouine Morocco 122 D3
Taliparamba India 94 B3
also spelt Thaliparamba
Tali Post Sudan 128 A3
Talisay Phil. 74 B4
Talisayan Indon. 77 G2
Talisayan Phil. 74 C4
Talış Dağları mts Azer./Iran 107 G3
also known as Talyshskiye Gory
Taliseí i. Indon. 75 C2
Talitsa Kostromskaya Oblast' Rus. Fed. 40 H4
Talitsa Lipetskaya Oblast' Rus. Fed. 43 T9
Taliwang Indon. 77 G5
Tal'ka Belarus 43 J8
Tallacootra, Lake salt flat Australia 146 B2
Talladega U.S.A. 175 C5
Tall 'Afar Iraq 107 E3
Tallahassee U.S.A. 175 C6
State capital of Florida.
Tallangatta Australia 147 E4
Tallapoosa r. U.S.A. 175 C5
Tallaringa Conservation Park nature res. Australia 146 B2
Talla Talla Seghir Island Sudan 104 B4
Tall Baydar Syria 109 L1
Tallinn Estonia 42 F2
Capital of Estonia. Historically known as Reval or Revel.
Tallinna laht b. Estonia 42 F2
Tall Kalakh Syria 108 H3
Tall Kayf Iraq 107 E3
Tall Küjik Syria 109 N1
Tallmadge U.S.A. 176 D4
Tall Tamir Syria 109 L1
Tallulah U.S.A. 175 B5
Tall 'Uwaynāt Iraq 107 E3
Tallymerjen Uzbek. see Talimardzhan
Tălmaciu Romania 58 F3
Talmiã Brazil 199 H4
Talmont-St-Hilaire France 50 E6
Tal'ne Ukr. 41 D6
also spelt Tal'noye
Tal'noye Ukr. see Tal'ne
Talod India 96 B5
Taloda India 96 B5
Talodi Sudan 128 A2
Taloga U.S.A. 179 C4
Taloi Range mts Pak. 101 F5
Talon, Lac l. Canada 169 H2
Tāloqān Afgh. 101 G2
Talos Dome ice feature Antarctica 223 K2
Ta Loung San mt. Laos 78 C3
Taloyoak Canada 165 J3
formerly known as Spence Bay
Talpa Mex. 184 D4
Tal Pass Pak. 101 H3
also known as Shohi Pass
Talras well Niger 125 H3
Talshand Mongolia 84 C2
Talsi Latvia 42 D4
Tal Siyāh Iran 101 E4
Taltal Chile 204 C2
Taltson r. Canada 167 H2
Talu China 89 F6
Talu Indon. 76 C2
Taludaa Indon. 75 B2
Taluti, Teluk b. Indon. 75 D3
Talvik Norway 44 M1
Talwood Australia 147 F2
Taly Rus. Fed. 41 G6
Talyawalka r. Australia 147 D3
Talyshskiye Gory mts Azer./Iran see Talış Dağları
Talyy Rus. Fed. 40 J2
Tama Abu, Banjaran mts Sarawak Malaysia 77 F2
also known as Penambo Range or Tamabo Range
Tamabo Range mts Sarawak Malaysia see Tama Abu, Banjaran
Tamadaw Myanmar 78 A3
Tamai, Nam r. Myanmar 78 B2
Tamaki Strait N.Z. 152 I4
Tamala Australia 151 A5
Tamala Rus. Fed. 41 G5
Tamalameque Col. 187 E5
Tamale Ghana 125 E4
Tamalelt well Mali 125 F3
Tamalung Indon. 77 F3
Tamana Japan 91 B8
Tamana i. Kiribati 145 G2
formerly known as Rotch Island
Tamanar Morocco 122 C3
Tamanco Peru 198 C6
Tamanhint Libya 120 B3
Tamani Mali 124 D3
Taman Negara National Park Malaysia 76 C1
Tamano Japan 91 C7
Tamanrasset Alg. 123 G5
also known as Tamenghest; formerly known as Fort Laperrine
Tamanrasset, Oued watercourse Alg. 123 F5
Tamanthi Myanmar 78 A2
Tamaqua U.S.A. 177 J5
Tamar India 97 E5
Tamar Syria see Tadmur
Tamar r. U.K. 47 H13
Tamaradant well Mali 125 F2
Tamarai Japan 91 B8
Tamarugal, Pampa de plain Chile 200 C4
Tamasane Botswana 131 E4
Tamási Hungary 49 P9
Tamași Romania 58 I2
Tamatave Madag. see Toamasina
Tamaulipas state Mex. 185 F4
Tamaulipas, Sierra de mts Mex. 185 F4
Tama Wildlife Reserve nature res. Eth. 128 C3
Tamayama Japan 90 G5
Tamazula Durango Mex. 184 D3
Tamazula Jalisco Mex. 185 E5
Tamazulápam Mex. 185 F5
Tamazunchale Mex. 185 F4
Tambach Kenya 128 B4
Tambacounda Senegal 124 B3
Tambangsawah Indon. 76 C3
Tambankulu Swaziland 133 P3
Tambaoura, Falaise de esc. Mali 124 C3
Tambaqui Brazil 199 F6
Tambara Moz. 131 G3
Tambau Brazil 206 F8
Tambawel Nigeria 125 G3
Tambelan, Kepulauan is Indon. 77 D2
Tambelan Besar i. Indon. 77 D2
Tambellup Australia 151 B7
Tamberu Indon. 77 F4
Tambisan Sabah Malaysia 77 G1
Tambo Australia 149 E5
Tambo r. Australia 147 E4
Tambo r. Peru 200 C4
Tambobamba Peru 200 B3
Tambo Grande Peru 198 A6
Tambohorano Madag. 131 [inset] I3
Tambopata r. Peru 200 C3
Tambor Angola 127 B9
Tambora, Gunung vol. Indon. 77 G5
Tamboril Brazil 202 D3
Tamboryacu r. Peru 198 C5
Tamboura Cent. Afr. Rep. 126 E3
Tambov Rus. Fed. 41 G5
Tambovka Rus. Fed. 82 C2
Tambov Oblast admin. div. Rus. Fed. see Tambovskaya Oblast'
Tambovskaya Oblast' admin. div. Rus. Fed. 41 G5
English form Tambov Oblast
Tambre r. Spain 54 C2
Tambu, Teluk b. Indon. 75 A2
Tambunan Sabah Malaysia 77 G1
formerly known as Tibabar
Tambunan, Bukit hill Sabah Malaysia 77 G1
Tambura Sudan 126 E3
Tambuyukon, Gunung mt. Sabah Malaysia 77 G1
Tâmchekket Mauritania 124 C2
Tamdy Kazakh. 102 F4
Tamdybulak Uzbek. 103 F4
also spelt Tomdibuloq
Tamdytau, Gory hills Uzbek. 103 F4
also known as Tomditow Toghi
Tame Col. 198 D3
Tâmega r. Port. 54 C3
Tamel Aike Arg. 205 C8
Tamelos, Akra pt Greece 59 F11
Tamenghest Alg. see Tamanrasset
Tamenglong India 97 G4
Tamerlanovka Kazakh. see Temirlanovka
Tamesna reg. Niger 125 G2
Tamgak, Adrar mt. Niger 125 H2
Tamgout de Lalla Khedidja mt. Alg. 55 P8
Tamgué, Massif du mt. Guinea 124 B3
Tamia India 96 C5
Tamiahua Mex. 185 F4
Tamiahua, Laguna de lag. Mex. 185 F4
Tamiami Canal U.S.A. 175 D7
Tamiang r. Indon. 76 B1
Tamiang, Ujung pt Indon. 76 B1
Tamil Nadu state India 94 C4
formerly known as Madras
Tamirin Gol r. Mongolia 84 D2
Tamiš r. Yugo. 58 B4
Tamitsa Rus. Fed. 40 F2
Tāmīya Egypt 121 F2
Tamiyah, Jabal hill Saudi Arabia 104 C2
Tamjit well Niger 125 H1
Tamlelt, Plaine de plain Morocco 123 E2
Tamluk India 97 E5
Tammaro r. Italy 56 G7
Tammarvi r. Canada 167 K1
Tammela Etelä-Suomi Fin. 42 E1
Tammela Oulu Fin. 44 O2
Tammerfors Fin. see Tampere
Tammio i. Fin. 42 I1
Tammisaaren Saariston Kansallispuisto nat. park Fin. see Ekenäs skärgårds Nationalpark
Tammisaari Fin. see Ekenäs
Tammispää Estonia 42 I3
Tamnava r. Yugo. 58 B4
Tamou Niger 125 F3
Tamou, Réserve Totale de Faune de nature res. Niger 125 F3
Tampa U.S.A. 175 D7
Tampa Bay U.S.A. 175 D7
Tampang Indon. 76 D4
Tampere Fin. 45 M3
also known as Tammerfors
Tampico Mex. 185 F4
Tampines Sing. 76 [inset]
Tampines, Sungai r. Sing. 76 [inset]
Tampo Indon. 75 B4
Tamrah Saudi Arabia 105 D3
Tamsagbulag Mongolia 85 H2
Tamsalu Estonia 42 H2
Tamshiyacu Peru 198 C6
Tamsweg Austria 49 K8
Tamu Myanmar 78 A2
Tamuín Mex. 185 F4
Tamur r. Nepal 97 E4
Tamworth Australia 147 F2
Tamworth U.K. 47 K11
Tan Kazakh. 103 I2
Tana r. Fin./Norway see Tenojoki
Tana r. Kenya 128 D5
Tana Madag. see Antananarivo
Tana i. Vanuatu see Tanna
Tana, Lake Eth. 128 C2
also known as T'ana Hāyk'
Tanabe Japan 91 D8
Tanabi Brazil 206 D7
Tana Bru Norway 44 O1

Tanafjorden inlet Norway 44 O1
also known as Deanuvuotna
Tanagro r. Italy 57 H8
Tanah, Tanjung pt Indon. 77 E4
T'ana Hāyk' l. Eth. see Tana, Lake
Tanahbala i. Indon. 76 B3
Tanahgrogot Indon. 77 G3
Tanahjampea i. Indon. 75 B4
Tanahmasa i. Indon. 76 B3
Tanahmerah Indon. 77 G2
Tanahputih Indon. 76 C2
Tanakeke i. Indon. 75 A4
Tanakpur India 96 D3
Tanambung Indon. 75 A3
Tanami Australia 148 A3
Tanami Desert Australia 148 A3
Tanami Downs Aboriginal Land res. Australia 148 A4
Tân An Vietnam 79 D6
Tananarive Madag. see Antananarivo
Tanandava Madag. 131 [inset] I4
Tanāqib, Ra's pt Saudi Arabia 105 E2
Tanaro r. Italy 56 A3
Tanauan Phil. 74 C4
Tanbar Australia 149 D5
Tancheng China see Pingtan
Tancheng China 87 F1
Tanch'ŏn N. Korea 83 C4
Tanda Côte d'Ivoire 124 E5
Tanda Uttar Pradesh India 96 C3
Tanda Uttar Pradesh India 97 D4
Tandag Phil. 74 C4
Tăndărei Romania 58 I4
Tandaué Angola 127 C9
Tandek Sabah Malaysia 77 G1
formerly known as Taritipan
Tandi India 96 C2
Tandil Arg. 204 F5
Tandjilé pref. Chad 126 C2
Tando Adam Pak. 101 G5
Tando Alahyar Pak. 101 G5
Tando Bago Pak. 101 G5
Tando Muhammmad Khan Pak. 101 G5
Tandou Lake imp. l. Australia 147 D3
Tandsjöborg Sweden 45 K3
Tandubatu i. Phil. 74 B5
Tandula r. India 96 D5
Tandur Andhra Pradesh India 94 C2
Tandur Andhra Pradesh India 94 C2
Taneatua N.Z. 152 K6
Tanega-shima i. Japan 91 B9
Taneichi Japan 90 G4
Tanen Taunggyi mts Thai. 78 B4
Taneti i. Indon. 75 C3
Tanew r. Poland 49 T5
Taneytown U.S.A. 177 H6
Tanezrouft reg. Alg./Mali 123 E5
Tanezrouft Tan-Ahenet reg. Alg. 123 E5
Ṭanf, Jabal aṭ hill Syria 109 J4
Tang, Ra's-e pt Iran 101 D5
Tanga Rus. Fed. 85 F1
Tanga Tanz. 129 C6
Tanga admin. reg. Tanz. 129 C6
Tangahe N.Z. 152 I4
Tangail Bangl. 97 F4
Tanga Islands P.N.G. 145 E2
Tangalla Sri Lanka 94 D5
Tanganyika country Africa see Tanzania

▶ **Tanganyika, Lake** Africa 127 F6
Deepest and 2nd largest lake in Africa and 7th largest in the world.
africa [landscapes] ▶ 112–113

Tangar Iran 100 C2
Tangasseri India 94 C4
Tangdan China 86 B3
formerly known as Dongshuan
Tangeli Iran 100 C2
Tange Promontory hd Antarctica 223 D2
Tanger Morocco see Tangier
Tangerang Indon. 77 D4
Tangermünde Germany 48 I3
Tang-e Sarkheh Iran 101 D5
Tanggor China 86 B1
Tanggu China 85 H4
Tanggulashan China see Tuotuoheyan
Tanggula Shan mt. China 89 E5
Tanggula Shan mts China 89 E5
also known as Dangla Shan
Tanggula Shankou pass China 89 E5
Tangguo China 89 D6
Tanghe China 87 E1
Tang He r. China 87 E1
Tangi Pak. 101 G3
Tangier Morocco 122 D2
also spelt Tanger or Tanjah; historically known as Tingis
Tangimoana N.Z. 152 J8
Tangkittebak, Gunung mt. Indon. 76 D4
Tang La pass China 89 E7
Tanglag China 86 A1
Tanglin Sing. 76 [inset]
Tangmai China 97 G3
Tango Japan 91 D7
Tangorin Australia 149 E4
Tangra Yumco salt l. China 89 D6
Tangse Indon. 76 A1
Tangshan China 85 H4
Tangsyq Kazakh. see Tansyk
Tangte mt. Myanmar 78 B3
Tangub Mindanao Phil. 74 B4
Tangub Negros Phil. 74 B4
Tanguieta Benin 125 F4
Tangwan China 87 D3
Tangwang r. China 82 C3
Tangwanghe China 82 C2
Tangxian China 85 G4
also known as Renhou
Tangxianzhen China 87 E2
Tang-yan Myanmar 78 B3
Tangyan He r. China 87 D2
Tangyin China 85 G5
Tangyuan China 82 C3
Tanhaçu Brazil 202 D5
Tanhua Fin. 44 N2
Taniantaweng Shan mts China 86 A2
Tanimbar, Kepulauan is Indon. 73 H8
Tanintharyi Myanmar see Tenasserim
Tanintharyi Myanmar see Tenasserim
Tanintharyi admin. div. Myanmar see Tenasserim
Taninthayi Myanmar see Tenasserim
Taniwel Indon. 75 D3
Tanjah Morocco see Tangier
Tanjay Phil. 74 B4
Tanjore India see Thanjavur
Tanjung Kalimantan Selatan Indon. 77 F3
Tanjung Sumatra Indon. 76 D3
Tanjungbalai Sumatra Indon. 76 B2
Tanjungbalai Sumatra Indon. 76 C2
Tanjungbaliha Indon. 75 C3
Tanjungbatu Kalimantan Timur Indon. 77 G2
Tanjungbatu Sumatra Indon. 76 C2
Tanjungbuayabuaya, Pulau i. Indon. 77 G2
Tanjunggaru Indon. 77 G3
Tanjungkarang-Telukbetung Indon. 76 D4
also known as Telukbetung; formerly known as Bandar Lampung
Tanjungpandan Indon. 77 D3
Tanjungpinang Indon. 76 D2
Tanjungpura Indon. 76 B2
Tanjung Puting National Park Indon. 77 F3
Tanjungraja Indon. 76 D3
Tanjungredeb Indon. 77 G2
Tanjungsaleh i. Indon. 77 E3
Tanjungsatai Indon. 77 E3
Tanjungselor Indon. 77 G2
Tank Pak. 101 G3
Tankara India 96 A5
Tankavaara Fin. 44 N1
Tankhala India 96 B5
Tankhoy Rus. Fed. 85 E1
Tankse Jammu and Kashmir 96 C2
Tankuhi India 97 E4
Tankwa r. S. Africa 132 D9
Tankwa-Karoo National Park S. Africa 132 D9
Tanlwe r. Myanmar 78 A4
Tanna i. Vanuatu 145 F3
also spelt Tana
Tännäs Sweden 44 K3
Tanner, Mount Canada 166 G5
Tannila Fin. 44 N2
Tannu-Ola, Khrebet mts Rus. Fed. 84 A1
Tannu Tuva aut. rep. Rus. Fed. see Tyva, Respublika
Tano Japan 91 B9
Tañon Strait Phil. 74 B4
Tanot India 96 A4
Tanout Niger 125 H3
Tanquian Mex. 185 F4
Tansen Nepal 97 D4
Tanshui Taiwan 87 G3
also spelt Danshui
Tansilla Burkina 124 D3
Tansyk Kazakh. 103 I3
also spelt Tangsyq
Tanta Egypt 121 F2
Tantabin Pegu Myanmar 78 B4
Tantabin Sagaing Myanmar 78 A3
Tan-Tan Morocco 122 C3
Tantoyuca Mex. 185 F4
Tantpur India 96 C4
Tantu China 85 I2
Tantura Israel 108 F5
Tanuku India 94 D2
Tanumshede Sweden 45 J4
Tanwakka, Sabkhat well W. Sahara 122 B5
▶ **Tanzania** country Africa 129 B6
formerly known as Tanganyika
africa [countries] ▶ 114–117
Tanzilla r. Canada 166 D3
Tao, Ko i. Thai. 79 B6
Tao'an China see Taonan
Taocheng China see Yongchun
Taocheng China see Daxin
Taodeni Mali see Taoudenni
Tao'er r. China 85 I2
Tao He r. China 84 D5
also known as Lu Qu
Taohong China see Longhui
Taohuaping China see Longhui
Taojiang China 87 E2
Taolanaro Madag. see Tôlañaro
Taole China 85 E4
also known as Mataigou
Taonan China 85 I2
formerly known as Tao'an
Taongi atoll Marshall Is 220 F5
Taormina Sicilia Italy 57 H11
Taos U.S.A. 181 F5
Taouârdeï well Mali 125 F2
Taoudenni Mali 122 E5
also spelt Taodeni
Taounate Morocco 122 D2
Taounnant well Mali 123 E5
formerly known as Tin Tounnant
Taourirt Morocco 123 E2
Taoxi China 87 F3
Taoyang China see Lintao
Taoyuan China 87 D2
T'aoyüan Taiwan 87 G3
also known as Sinchu
Taozhou China see Guangde
Tapa Estonia 42 G2
Tapaan Passage Phil. 74 B5
Tapachula Mex. 185 G6
Tapajós r. Brazil 199 H5
Tapaktuan Indon. 76 B2
Tapalqué Arg. 204 E5
Tapan Indon. 76 C3
Tapan Turkey see Mansurlu
Tapanahoni r. Suriname 199 H3
Tapanatepec Mex. 185 G5
Tapanuli, Teluk b. Indon. 76 B2
Tapará, Ilha Grande do i. Brazil 199 H5
Tapara, Serra do hills Brazil 199 H5
Tapat i. Indon. 75 C3
Tapauá Brazil 199 E6
Tapauá r. Brazil 199 E6
Tapawera N.Z. 152 G9
Tapera Rio Grande do Sul Brazil 203 A9
Tapera Roraima Brazil 199 F5
Tapera Chile 205 C7
Taperoá Brazil 202 E5
Tapes Brazil 203 B9
Tapeta Liberia 124 C5
Tapi r. India 96 B5
Tapia, Sierra de hills Bol. 201 F4
Tapi Aike Arg. 205 C8
Tapiantana i. Phil. 74 B5
Tapiau Rus. Fed. see Gvardeysk
Tapiche r. Peru 198 C6
Tápió r. Hungary 49 R8
Tapiocanga, Chapada do hills Brazil 206 F3
Tápiószecső Hungary 49 Q8
Tapira Brazil 206 G6
Tapiracanga Brazil 202 C5
Tapiraí Brazil 206 F10
Tapirapé r. Brazil 202 B4
Tapirapecó, Sierra mts Brazil/Venez. 199 E4
Tapirapuã Brazil 201 F3
Tapis mt. Malaysia 76 C1
Tapisuelas Mex. 184 C3
Taplejung Nepal 97 E4
Tap Mun Chau i. Hong Kong China 87 [inset]
Tapoa watercourse Burkina 125 F3
Tapol Chad 126 B2
Tapolca Hungary 49 O9
Ta-pom Myanmar 78 B3
Tappahannock U.S.A. 177 I8
Tappal India 96 C3
Tappeh, Kūh-e hill Iran 100 B3
Tappi-zaki pt Japan 90 G4
Taprobane country Asia see Sri Lanka
Tapuaenuku mt. N.Z. 153 H9
Tapul Phil. 74 B5
Tapul Group is Phil. 74 B5
Tapulonanjing mt. Indon. 76 B2
Tapung r. Indon. 76 C2
Tapurú Brazil 199 F6
Tapurucuara Brazil 199 E5
Taputeouea atoll Kiribati see Tabiteuea
Taqar mt. Yemen 104 D5
Ṭaqṭaq Iraq 107 F4
Taquara Brazil 203 B9
Taquaral, Serra do hills Brazil 206 A2
Taquarí Brazil 203 A6
Taquari r. Brazil 201 F4
Taquaritinga Brazil 206 E8
Taquarituba Brazil 206 D10
Taquaruçu r. Brazil 206 A8
Tara Australia 147 F1
Tara r. Bos.-Herz./Yugo. 56 K5
Tara nat. park Yugo. 58 A5
Taraba r. Nigeria 125 H4
Taraba state Nigeria 125 H4
Tarabaí Brazil 206 B9
Tarabuco Bol. 200 D4
Țarābulus Libya see Tripoli
Taraclia Moldova 58 J3
formerly spelt Tarakliya
Taraco Peru 200 C3
Taracua Brazil 198 D4
Taradale N.Z. 152 K7
Tarāghin Libya 120 B3
Tarai reg. India 97 E4
Taraira r. Brazil see Traíra
Tarairi Bol. 201 E5
Tarakan Indon. 77 G2
Tarakan i. Indon. 77 G2
Tarakki reg. Afgh. 101 F3
Taraklı Turkey 106 B2
Tarakliya Moldova see Taraclia
Tarakua Fiji 145 H3
Taran, Mys pt Rus. Fed. 42 A7
Tarana India 96 C5
Taranagar India 96 B3
Taranaki admin. reg. N.Z. 152 H7
Taranaki, Mount vol. N.Z. 152 I7
also known as Egmont, Mount
Tarancón Spain 55 H4
Tarangambadi India 94 C4
Tarangara Chad 126 C2
Tarangire National Park Tanz. 129 C6
Tarangul l. Kazakh. see Tarankol', Ozero
Tarankol', Ozero l. Kazakh. 103 G1
formerly known as Tarangul
Taranovskoye Kazakh. 103 E1
formerly known as Viktorovka
Taranto Italy 57 J8
historically known as Tarentum
Taranto, Golfo di g. Italy 57 J8
Tarapacá admin. reg. Chile 200 C4
Tarapacá Col. 198 D5
Tarapoto Peru 198 B6
Ṭaraq an Na'jah reg. Syria 109 K3
Tarare France 51 K7
Tararua Forest Park nature res. N.Z. 152 J8
Tararua Range mts N.Z. 152 J8
Tarascon-sur-Ariège France 50 H10
Tarashcha Ukr. 41 D6
Tarasht Iran 100 D3
Tarasovskiy Rus. Fed. 41 G6
Tarat Alg. 123 H4
Tarata Peru 200 C4
Tarauacá Brazil 200 C2
Tarauacá r. Brazil 198 D6
Taravo r. Corse France 56 A7
Tarawa atoll Kiribati 145 G1
also known as Cook Atoll or Knox Atoll
Tarawera N.Z. 152 K7
Tarawera, Lake N.Z. 152 K6
Tarawera, Mount N.Z. 152 K6
Taraz Kazakh. 103 G4
formerly known as Dzhambul or Zhambyl; historically known as Auliye Ata
Tarazona Spain 55 J3
Tarazona de la Mancha Spain 55 J5
Tarbagatay Kazakh. 103 J3
Tarbagatay Rus. Fed. 85 E1
Tarbagatay, Khrebet mts Kazakh. 88 C2
Tarbat Ness pt U.K. 46 I6
Tarbert Rep. of Ireland 47 C11
Tarbert Argyll and Bute, Scotland U.K. 46 G8
Tarbert Western Isles, Scotland U.K. 46 F6
also spelt Tairbeart
Tarbes France 50 G9
Tarbet U.K. 46 H7
Tarboro U.S.A. 174 E5
Tarcoola Australia 146 B2
Tarcoon Australia 147 E2
Tarcoonyinna watercourse Australia 146 B1
Tarcului, Munții mts Romania 58 D3
Tardes r. France 51 I6
Tardoire r. France 50 G7
Tardoki-Yani, Gora mt. Rus. Fed. 82 E2
Taree Australia 147 G2
Tareifing Sudan 128 B2
Tärendö Sweden 44 M2
Tarentum Italy see Taranto
Tareya Rus. Fed. 39 J2
Ṭarfā, Ra's aṭ pt Saudi Arabia 104 C4
Tarfaya Morocco 122 B4
formerly known as Cabo Yubi or Cape Juby or Villa Bens
Targa well Niger 125 G2
Targan Kazakh. see Targyn
Targhee Pass U.S.A. 180 E3
Târgovişte Romania 58 G4
formerly spelt Tîrgovişte
Târgu Bujor Romania 58 I3
formerly spelt Tîrgu Bujor
Târgu Cărbuneşti Romania 58 E4
formerly spelt Tîrgu Cărbuneşti
Târgu Frumos Romania 58 H1
formerly spelt Tîrgu Frumos
Targuist Morocco 122 D2
Târgu Jiu Romania 58 E3
formerly spelt Tîrgu Jiu
Târgu Lăpuş Romania 58 E1
formerly spelt Tîrgu Lăpuş
Târgu Mureş Romania 58 F2
also known as Marosvásárhely; formerly spelt Tîrgu Mureş
Târgu Neamţ Romania 58 H1
formerly spelt Tîrgu Neamţ
Târgu Ocna Romania 58 H2
formerly spelt Tîrgu Ocna
Târgu Secuiesc Romania 58 H2
formerly spelt Tîrgu Secuiesc
Targyailing China 89 D6
Targyn Kazakh. 88 C1
formerly spelt Targan
Tarhān Iran 100 A3
Tarhmanant well Mali see Taghmanant
Tarhūnah Libya 120 B1
Tari P.N.G. 73 J8
Tarian Gol China 85 F4
Tarib, Wādī watercourse Saudi Arabia 104 C4
Tarif U.A.E. 105 F2
Tarifa Spain 54 F8
Tarifa, Punta de pt Spain 54 F8
Tarigtig Point Phil. 74 B2
Tarija Bol. 201 D5
Tarija dept Bol. 201 D5
Tarikere India 94 B3
Tariku r. Indon. 73 I7
Tarim Yemen 105 E4
Tarim Basin China 88 C4
also known as Tarim Pendi
Tarime Tanz. 128 B5
Tarim He r. China 88 D3
Tarim Liuchang China 88 D3
Tarim Pendi basin China see Tarim Basin
Taringuiti Bol. 201 E5
Tarin Kowt Afgh. 101 F3
Taritatu r. Indon. 73 I7
Taritipan Sabah Malaysia see Tandek
Tarjil Iraq 109 P2
Tarka r. S. Africa 133 J9
Tarka, Vallée de watercourse Niger 125 G3
Tarkastad S. Africa 133 K9
Tarkio U.S.A. 178 D3
Tarko-Sale Rus. Fed. 39 H3
Tarkwa Ghana 125 E5
Tarlac Phil. 74 B3
Tarlac r. Phil. 74 B2
Tarlo River National Park Australia 147 F3
Tarlton U.S.A. 176 C6
Tarma Junín Peru 200 B2
Tarma Loreto Peru 198 D5
Tarn r. France 51 H8
Tarna r. Hungary 49 Q8
Tärnaby Sweden 44 K2
Tarnak r. Afgh. 101 F4
Târnava Mare r. Romania 58 E2
Târnava Mică r. Romania 58 E2
Târnăveni Romania 58 F2
formerly spelt Tîrnăveni
Tarnica mt. Poland 49 T6
Tarnobrzeg Poland 49 S5
Tarnogród Poland 49 T5
Tarnogskiy Gorodok Rus. Fed. 40 G3
Tarnopol Ukr. see Ternopil'
Tarnos France 50 E9
Tărnova Romania 58 D3
Tarnów Poland 49 R5
Tarnowitz Poland see Tarnowskie Góry
Tarnowskie Góry Poland 49 P5
historically known as Tarnowitz
Tärnvik Norway 44 K2
Taro r. Italy 56 C4
Tarō Japan 90 G5
Taro Co salt l. China 89 C6
Ṭarom Iran 100 C4
Taroom Australia 149 F5
Taroudannt Morocco 122 C3
Tarpasa Bangl. 97 F5
Tarpaulin Swamp Australia 148 C3
Tarpon Springs U.S.A. 175 D6
Tarpum Bay Bahamas 175 E7
Tarq Iran 100 B3
Tarquinia Italy 56 D6
historically known as Corneto or Tarquinii
Tarquinii Italy see Tarquinia
Tarrabool Lake salt flat Australia 148 B3
Tarracina Italy see Terracina
Tarraco Spain see Tarragona
Tarragona Spain 55 M3
historically known as Tarraco
Tårrajaur Sweden 44 L2
Tarraleah Australia 147 E5
Tarrant Point Australia 148 C3
Tarras N.Z. 153 D12
Tarrasa Spain see Terrassa
Tàrrega Spain 55 M3
Tarrong China see Nyêmo
Tarso Ahon mt. Chad 120 C4
Tarso Emissi mt. Chad 120 C4
Tarso Kobour mt. Chad 120 C4
Tarsus Turkey 106 C3
Tarta Turkm. see Darta
Tartagal Salta Arg. 201 E5
Tartagal Santa Fé Arg. 204 F3
Tärtär Azer. 107 F2
also spelt Terter; formerly known as Mir-Bashir
Tartas France 50 F9
Tartu Estonia 42 H3
formerly known as Yur'yev; historically known as Dorpat
Ṭarṭūs Syria 108 G3
Ṭarṭūs governorate Syria 108 H2
Tarumae-san vol. Japan see Shikotsu
Tarumirim Brazil 207 L6
Tarumizu Japan 91 B9
Tarumovka Rus. Fed. 102 A3
Tarung Hka r. Myanmar 78 B2
Tarusa Rus. Fed. 43 S7
Tarusa r. Rus. Fed. 43 S7
Tarūt Saudi Arabia 105 E2
Tarutung Indon. 76 B2
Tarutyne Ukr. 58 K2
Tarvisio Italy 56 F2
Tarvisium Italy see Treviso
Tarvo Bol. 201 E3
Tarz Iran 100 D4
Tasaral Kazakh. 88 A2
Tasbuget Kazakh. 103 F3
Taschereau Canada 173 O2
Taseko Mountain Canada 166 F5
Tasendjanet, Oued watercourse Alg. 123 F4
Tasgaon India 94 B2
Tashauz Turkm. see Dashkhovuz
Tashauzskaya Oblast' admin. div. Turkm. see Dashkhovuzskaya Oblast'
Tashbunar r. Ukr. 58 J3
Tashi China 84 B3
Tashi Chho Bhutan see Thimphu
Tashigang Bhutan see Trashigang
Tashino Rus. Fed. see Pervomaysk
Tashir Armenia 107 F2
formerly known as Kalinino
Tashk, Daryācheh-ye l. Iran 100 C4

▶ **Tashkent** Uzbek. 103 G4
Capital of Uzbekistan. Also spelt Toshkent.

Tashkent Oblast admin. div. Uzbek. see Tashkentskaya Oblast'
Tashkentskaya Oblast' admin. div. Uzbek. 103 G4
English form Tashkent Oblast; also known as Toshkent Wiloyati
Tashkepri Turkm. 103 E5
also spelt Dashköpri
Tash-Kömür Kyrg. 103 H4
also spelt Tash-Kumyr
Tash-Kumyr Kyrg. see Tash-Kömür
Tashla Rus. Fed. 102 C2
Tāshqurghan Afgh. see Kholm
Tasialujjuaq, Lac l. Canada 169 F1
Tasiat, Lac l. Canada 169 F1
Tasiilap Karra c. Greenland 165 P3
also known as Gustav Holm, Kap
Tasiilaq Greenland see Ammassalik
Tasikmalaya Indon. 77 E4
Tasiujaq Canada 169 G1
formerly known as Baie-aux-Feuilles or Leaf Bay
Tasiusaq Greenland 165 N2
Tåsjö Sweden 44 K2
Task well Niger 125 H3
Tasker Niger 125 H3
Taskesken Kazakh. 103 J3
Taşköprü Turkey 106 C2
Taşlıçay Turkey 107 E3
Tasman N.Z. 152 H9
Tasman admin. reg. N.Z. 152 G9
Tasman r. N.Z. 153 E12
Tasman, Mount N.Z. 153 E11
Tasman Bay N.Z. 152 H9

▶ **Tasmania** state Australia 147 E5
4th largest island in Oceania. Historically known as Van Diemen's Land.
oceania [landscapes] ▶ 136–137

Tasman Mountains N.Z. 152 G9
Tasman Peninsula Australia 147 F5
Tasman Sea S. Pacific Ocean 145 G6
Tăşnad Romania 58 D1
Taşova Turkey 107 D2
also known as Yemişenbükü
Tassara Niger 125 G2
Tasselot, Mont hill France 51 K5
Tassi Gabon 126 A5
Tassialouc, Lac l. Canada 169 F1
Tassili du Hoggar plat. Alg. 123 G5
Tassili n'Ajjer plat. Alg. 123 G4
Tassin-la-Demi-Lune France 51 K7
Tåstrup Denmark 45 K5
Tas-Tumus Rus. Fed. 39 M3
Tasty Kazakh. 103 G3
Tasty-Taldy Kazakh. 103 F2
Tasu Canada 166 C4
Taşucu Turkey 108 E1
Tas-Yuryakh Rus. Fed. 39 L3
Tata Hungary 49 P8
Tata Morocco 122 C3
Tataba Indon. 75 B3
Tatabánya Hungary 49 P8
Tatamagouche Canada 169 I4
Tata Mailau, Gunung mt. East Timor 75 C5
Tatanagar India 97 E5
Tataouine Tunisia 123 H2
Tatarbunary Ukr. 41 D7
Tatarka Belarus 43 J8
Tatarpur India 96 C4
Tatarsk Rus. Fed. 80 B1
Tatarsk Rus. Fed. 43 M7
Tatarskaya A.S.S.R. aut. rep. Rus. Fed. see Tatarstan, Respublika
Tatarskiy Proliv strait Rus. Fed. 82 F2
English form Tatar Strait
Tatarstan, Respublika aut. rep. Rus. Fed. 40 I5
formerly known as Tatarskaya A.S.S.R.
Tatar Strait Rus. Fed. see Tatarskiy Proliv
Tătăruşi Romania 58 H1
Tatau Sarawak Malaysia 77 F2
Tatavi r. Iran 100 A2
Tate r. Australia 149 D3
Tatebayashi Japan 91 F6
Tateyama Japan 91 F7
Tate-yama vol. Japan 91 E6
Tathlina Lake Canada 167 G2
Tathlīth Saudi Arabia 104 C4
Tathlīth, Wādī watercourse Saudi Arabia 104 D3
Tathra Australia 147 F4
Tati Botswana 131 E4
Tātilt well Mauritania 124 B2
Tatishchevo Rus. Fed. 41 H6
Tatkon Myanmar 78 B3
Tatla Lake Canada 166 E5
Tatlatui Provincial Park Canada 166 E3
Tatlayoko Lake Canada 166 E5
Tatlikbulak China 88 D4
Tatnam, Cape Canada 167 N3
Tatra Mountains Poland/Slovakia 49 Q6
also known as High Tatras or Tatry
Tatrang China 88 D4
Tatranský nat. park Slovakia 49 R6
Tatry mts Poland/Slovakia see Tatra Mountains
Tatrzański Park Narodowy nat. park Poland 49 Q6
Tatshenshini r. Canada 166 B3
Tatshenshini-Alsek Provincial Wilderness Park Canada 166 B3
Tatsuno Japan 91 D7
Tatta Pak. 101 F5
Tatti Kazakh. 103 H4
formerly spelt Tatty
Tatty Kazakh. see Tatti
Tatuí Brazil 206 F10
Tatuk Mountain Canada 166 E4
Tatula r. Lith. 42 F5
Tatum NM U.S.A. 178 B5
Tatum TX U.S.A. 179 D5
Tatvan Turkey 107 E3
Ta'ū i. American Samoa 145 I3
Taua Brazil 202 D3
Tauapeçaçu Brazil 199 F5
Tauariã Brazil 199 F6
Taubaté Brazil 203 C7
Tauber r. Germany 48 G6
Tauberbischofsheim Germany 48 G6
Tauchik Kazakh. 102 B3
also spelt Taūshyq
Taufkirchen (Vils) Germany 48 J7
Tauhara mt. N.Z. 152 K6
Tauhoa N.Z. 152 I4
Tauini r. Brazil 199 G4
Taukum, Peski des. Kazakh. 103 H3
Taumarunui N.Z. 152 J6
Taumaturgo Brazil 200 B2
Taunay Brazil 201 G5
Taung S. Africa 133 I4
Taungbon Myanmar 79 B5
Taungdwingyi Myanmar 78 A3
Taunggyi Myanmar 78 B3
Taunglau Myanmar 78 B3
Taungnyo Range mts Myanmar 78 B4
Taungtha Myanmar 78 A3
Taunqup Myanmar 78 A4
Taunsa Pak. 101 G4
Taunton U.K. 47 I12
Taunton U.S.A. 177 N4
Taunus hills Germany 48 E5
Taupiri N.Z. 152 J5
Taupo N.Z. 152 K6
Taupo, Lake N.Z. 152 J6
Tauragė Lith. 42 D6
Tauralaukis Lith. 42 C6
Tauramena Col. 198 C3
Tauranga N.Z. 152 K5
Taurasia Italy see Turin
Taureau, Réservoir Canada 169 F4
Taurianova Italy 57 I10
Taurikura N.Z. 152 I3
Taurion r. France 50 H7
Tauroa Point N.Z. 152 H3
Taurus Mountains Turkey 106 C3
also known as Toros Dağları
Taūshyq Kazakh. see Tauchik
Tauste Spain 55 J3
Tautira Fr. Polynesia 221 I7
Tauu Islands P.N.G. 145 E2
formerly known as Mortlock Islands
Tauwhareparae N.Z. 152 M6
Tauyskaya Guba g. Rus. Fed. 39 P4
Tauz Azer. see Tovuz
Tavagnacco Italy 56 F2
Tavankut Vojvodina, Srbija Yugo. 58 A2
Tavares U.S.A. 175 D6
Tavas Turkey 106 B3
also known as Yarangüme
Tavastehus Fin. see Hämeenlinna
Tavda Rus. Fed. 38 G4
Tavelsjö Sweden 44 M2
Tavernes de la Valldigna Spain 55 K5
also spelt Tabernes de Valldigna
Taveuni i. Fiji 145 H3
Tavgetos mts Greece 59 D11
also known as Taÿetos Óros
Taviano Italy 57 K9
Tavignano r. Corse France 56 B6
Tavil'dara Tajik. 101 G2
also spelt Tovil'-Dora
Tavira Port. 54 D7
Tavistock Canada 173 M7
Tavistock U.K. 47 H13
Tavolara, Isola i. Sardegna Italy 56 B8
Tavoliere reg. Italy 56 H7
Tavolzhan Kazakh. 103 I1
also spelt Tobylzhan
Távora r. Spain 54 D3
Tavoy Myanmar 79 B5
also known as Dawei; also spelt Tawè
Tavoy r. Myanmar 79 B5
also known as Dawei
Tavoy Island Myanmar see Mali Kyun
Tavoy Point Myanmar 79 B5
Tavrichanka Rus. Fed. 90 B3
Tavricheskoye Kazakh. 103 J2
also known as Tavrīl
Tavrīl Kazakh. see Tavricheskoye
Tavşanlı Turkey 106 B3
Tavua Fiji 145 G3
Taw r. U.K. 47 H12
Tawakoni, Lake U.S.A. 179 D5
Tawallah Range hills Australia 148 B2
Tawang India 97 F4
Tawas Bay U.S.A. 173 J6
Tawas City U.S.A. 173 J6
Tawau Sabah Malaysia 77 G1
Tawau, Telukan b. Sabah Malaysia 77 G1
Tawè Myanmar see Tavoy
Taweisha Sudan 121 E6
Tawi r. India 96 B2
Ṭawi Ḥafir well U.A.E. 105 F2
Tawila Sudan 120 E6
Tawīla, Gezâ'ir is Egypt 104 A2
English form Tawila Islands
Tawila Islands Egypt see Tawīla, Gezâ'ir
Ṭawī Murra well U.A.E. 105 F2
Tawitawi i. Phil. 74 A5
Tawmaw Myanmar 78 B2
Tawu Taiwan 87 G4
also spelt Dawu
Taxco Mex. 185 F5
Taxkorgan China 88 A4
Tay r. Canada 166 C2
Tay r. U.K. 46 I7
Tay, Firth of est. U.K. 46 I7
Tay, Lake salt flat Australia 151 C7
Tay, Loch l. U.K. 46 H7
Tayabamba Peru 200 A2
Tayabas Bay Phil. 74 B3
Tayan Indon. 77 E2
Tayeeglow Somalia 128 E3
Tayga Rus. Fed. 80 D1
Taygan Mongolia 84 C2
Taygonos, Mys c. Rus. Fed. 39 Q3
Taykanskiy Khrebet mts Rus. Fed. 82 D1
Taylor Canada 166 F3
Taylor AZ U.S.A. 183 N7
Taylor NE U.S.A. 178 C3
Taylor TX U.S.A. 179 C6
Taylor, Mount N.Z. 153 F11
Taylor, Mount U.S.A. 181 F6
Taylorsville U.S.A. 174 C4
Taylorville U.S.A. 174 B4
Taymā' Saudi Arabia 104 B2
Taymura r. Rus. Fed. 39 J3
Taymyr, Ozero l. Rus. Fed. 39 K2
Taymyr, Poluostrov pen. Rus. Fed. see Taymyr Peninsula
Taymyr Peninsula Rus. Fed. 39 I2
also known as Taymyr, Poluostrov
Tây Ninh Vietnam 79 D6
Taypak Kazakh. 102 B2
also spelt Taypaq; formerly known as Kalmykovo
Taypaq Kazakh. see Taypak
Tayport U.K. 46 J7
Tayshet Rus. Fed. 80 F1
Taysoygan, Peski des. Kazakh. 102 C2
Tayspun tourist site Iraq see Ctesiphon
Taytan Turkey 59 J10
Taytay Luzon Phil. 74 B3
Taytay Palawan Phil. 74 A4
Taytay Bay Phil. 74 A4
Tayu Indon. 77 E4
Tayuan China 82 B2
Tayyebād Iran 101 E3
Tayynsha Kazakh. 103 G1
formerly known as Krasnoarmeysk
Taz r. Rus. Fed. 39 H3
Taza Morocco 122 E2
Taza-Bazar Uzbek. see Shumanay
Tāza Khurmātū Iraq 107 F4
Taze Myanmar 78 A3
Tazeh Kand Azer. 107 F3
Tazenakht Morocco 122 D3
Tazewell TN U.S.A. 176 B9
Tazewell VA U.S.A. 176 D8
Tazin r. Canada 167 I2
Tāzirbū Libya 120 D3
Tazirbu Water Wells Field Libya 120 D3
Tazizilet well Niger 125 H2
Tazlău Romania 58 H2
Tazlău r. Romania 58 H2
Tazmalt Alg. 55 P8
Tazoghrane Tunisia 57 C12
Tazouikert hill Mali 123 E5
Tazovskaya Guba sea chan. Rus. Fed. 39 H3
Tazovskiy Rus. Fed. 39 H3
Tazrouk Alg. 123 G5
Tazzarine Morocco 122 D3
Tazzouguert Morocco 122 E2
Tbessa Alg. see Tébessa

▶ **T'bilisi** Georgia 107 F2
Capital of Georgia. English form Tbilisi; historically known as Tiflis.

Tbilisi Georgia see T'bilisi
Tchabal Mbabo mt. Cameroon 125 I5
Tchad country Africa see Chad
Tchamba Togo 125 F4
Tchaourou Benin 125 F4
Tchetti Benin 125 F5
Tchibanga Gabon 126 A5
Tchidoutene watercourse Niger 125 G2
Tchié well Chad 120 C5
Tchigaï, Plateau du Niger 123 I5
Tchikala-Tcholohanga Angola 127 C8
formerly known as Vila Nova
Tchin-Tabaradene Niger 125 G3
Tcholliré Cameroon 125 I4
Tczew Poland 49 P1
historically known as Dirschau
Te, Prêk r. Cambodia 79 D5
Tea r. Brazil 199 E5
Teacapán Mex. 184 D4
Teague, Lake salt flat Australia 151 C5
Te Anau N.Z. 153 B13
Te Anau, Lake N.Z. 153 B13
Te Anga N.Z. 152 I6
Teano Italy 56 G7
historically known as Teanum Sidicinum
Teano Range mts Australia 150 B5
Teanum Sidicinum Italy see Teano
Teapa Mex. 185 G5
Te Araroa N.Z. 152 M5
Te Aroha N.Z. 152 J5
Te Aroha, Mount hill N.Z. 152 J5
Teate Italy see Chieti
Te Awamutu N.Z. 152 J6
Tébarat Niger 125 G3
Tebedu Sarawak Malaysia 77 E2
Teberda Rus. Fed. 41 G8
Teberdinskiy Zapovednik nature res. Rus. Fed. 107 E2
Tebesjuak Lake Canada 167 L2
Tébessa Alg. 123 H2
also spelt Tbessa; historically known as Theveste
Tébessa, Monts de mts Alg. 123 H2
Tebicuary Para. 201 F6
Tebicuary r. Para. 201 F6
Tebingtinggi Sumatra Indon. 76 B2
Tebingtinggi Sumatra Indon. 76 C3
Tebo r. Indon. 76 C3
Téboursouk Tunisia 57 B12
Téboursouk Tunisia 57 B12
Tebulos Mt'a Georgia/Rus. Fed. 41 H8
Tecalitlán Mex. 185 E5
Tecate Mex. 184 A1
Tece Turkey 108 F1
Tech r. France 51 J10
Techiman Ghana 125 E5
Techirghiol Romania 58 J4
Tecka Arg. 205 C6
Tecka r. Arg. 205 C6
Tecoh Mex. 185 H4
Tecolutla Mex. 185 F4
Tecomán Mex. 184 E5
Tecopa U.S.A. 183 H6
Tecoripa Mex. 184 C2
Técpan Mex. 185 E5
Tecuala Mex. 184 D4
Tecuci Romania 58 I3
Tecumseh MI U.S.A. 173 J9
Tecumseh NE U.S.A. 178 C3
Ted Somalia 128 D3
Tedzhen Turkm. 102 E5
also spelt Tejen
Tedzhen r. Turkm. 102 E5
Tedzhenstroy Turkm. 102 E5
Teec Nos Pos U.S.A. 183 O5
Teekloof Pass S. Africa 132 F9
Teel Mongolia 84 D1
Teeli Rus. Fed. 84 A1
Teeli Rus. Fed. 47 K9
Teeswater Canada 173 L6
Tefé Brazil 199 E5
Tefé r. Brazil 199 E5
Tefé, Lago l. Brazil 199 E5
Tefedest mts Alg. 123 G4
Téfoûlet well Mali 125 F2
Tegal Indon. 77 E4
Tegel airport Germany 49 K3
Tegina Nigeria 125 G4

▶ **Tegucigalpa** Hond. 186 B4
Capital of Honduras.

Teguidda-n-Tessoumt Niger 125 G2
Tehachapi U.S.A. 182 F6
Tehachapi Mountains U.S.A. 182 E7
Tehachapi Pass U.S.A. 182 F6
Te Hana N.Z. 152 I4
Te Hauke N.Z. 152 K7
Tehek Lake Canada 167 M1
Teheran Iran see Tehrān
Tehery Lake Canada 167 M1
Téhini Côte d'Ivoire 124 E4
Tehran Iran see Tehrān

index T

Tehrān Iran 100 B3
Capital of Iran. Also spelt Teheran.

Tehrān prov. Iran 100 B3
Tehri India see Tikamgarh
Tehri India 96 C3
Tehuacán Mex. 185 F5
Tehuantepec, Gulf of Mex. 185 G6
also known as Tehuantepec, Golfo de
Tehuantepec, Istmo de isthmus Mex. 185 G5
Tehuitzingo Mex. 185 F5
Teiču rezervāts nature res. Latvia 42 H5
Teide, Pico del vol. Canary Is 122 A3
Teifi r. U.K. 47 H11
Teignmouth U.K. 47 I13
Teiskot well Mali 125 F2
Teita Hills Kenya 128 C5
Teiu Romania 58 G4
Teiuş Romania 58 E2
Teixeira Brazil 202 E3
Teixeira da Silva Angola see Bailundo
Teixeira de Freitas Brazil 207 N4
Teixeira de Sousa Angola see Luau
Teixeiras Brazil 207 K7
Tejakula Indon. 77 F5
Tejeda y Almijara, Sierra de nature res. Spain 54 H8
Tejen Turkm. see Tedzhen
Tejgaon Bangl. 97 F5
Tejira well Niger 125 H3
Tejo r. Port. 54 C5 see Tagus
Tejupan, Punta pt Mex. 184 E5
Te Kaha N.Z. 152 L5
Te Kao N.Z. 152 G2
Tekapo r. N.Z. 153 E12
Tekapo, Lake N.Z. 153 E11
Tekari India 97 E4
Te Kauwhata N.Z. 152 J5
Tekax Mex. 185 H4
Teke Kazakh. 103 G4
Teke r. Turkey 58 H7
Teke, Ozero salt l. Kazakh. 103 H1
Tekeli Aktyubinskaya Oblast' Kazakh. 102 E2
Tekeli Almatinskaya Oblast' Kazakh. 103 I3
Tekes China 88 C3
Tekes Kazakh. 103 J4
Tekes He r. China 88 C3
Tekezē Wenz r. Eritrea/Eth. 121 H6
Tekiliktag mt. China 89 C4
Tekin Rus. Fed. 82 D2
Tekirdağ Turkey 106 A2
formerly known as Rodosto
Tekirdağ prov. Turkey 58 I7
Tekirova Turkey 108 B1
Tekkali India 95 E2
Tekman Turkey 107 E3
Teknaf Bangl. 97 G5
Tekoa, Mount N.Z. 153 G10
Tekong Kechil, Pulau i. Sing. 76 [inset]
Te Kopuru N.Z. 152 H4
Tekouiat, Oued watercourse Alg. 123 F5
Te Kowhai N.Z. 152 J5
Tékro well Chad 120 D5
Tektek Dağları hills Turkey 109 K1
Teku Indon. 75 B3
Te Kuiti N.Z. 152 J6
Tel r. India 95 D1
Tela Dem. Rep. Congo 127 F8
Tela Hond. 186 B4
Telanaipura Indon. see Jambi
Télataï Mali 125 F2
T'elavi Georgia 107 F2
Tel Aviv-Yafo Israel 108 F5
English form Jaffa; also known as Yafa; historically known as Joppa
Telč Czech Rep. 49 M6
Telchac Puerto Mex. 185 H4
Tel'ch'ye Rus. Fed. 43 R8
Telciu Romania 58 F1
Tele r. Dem. Rep. Congo 126 D4
Télé, Lac l. Mali 124 E2
Teleajen r. Romania 58 G3
Telegapulang Indon. 77 F3
Telegraph Creek Canada 166 D3
Telekhany Belarus see Tsyelyakhany
Telêmaco Borba Brazil 203 B8
Telemark county Norway 45 J4
Telén Arg. 204 D5
Telen r. Indon. 77 G2
Teleorman r. Romania 58 G5
Telertheba, Djebel mt. Alg. 123 G4
Telescope Peak U.S.A. 183 G5
Teles Pires r. Brazil 201 F1
also known as São Pires
Teletskoye, Ozero l. Rus. Fed. 88 D1
Telfer Mining Centre Australia 150 C4
Telford U.K. 47 J11
Telfs Austria 48 I8
Telîmélé well Mali 122 E5
Télimélé Guinea 124 B4
Télissour well Chad 120 D5
Teljo, Jebel mt. Sudan 121 E6
Telkwa Canada 166 E4
Tellaro r. Sicilia Italy 57 H12
Tell Atlas mts Alg. see Atlas Tellien
Teller U.S.A. 164 C3
Tell es-Sultan West Bank see Jericho
Tellicherry India 94 B4
also known as Thalassery
Tellodar Ukr. 58 L2
Telloh Iraq 107 F5
Tell Râk Egypt 108 C7
Telluride U.S.A. 181 F5
Tel'mansk Turkm. see Gubadag
Tel Megiddo tourist site Israel 108 G5
historically known as Armageddon
Telmen Nuur salt l. Mongolia 84 C1
Telo Indon. 76 B3
Teloloapán Mex. 185 F5
Telo Martius France see Toulon
Tel'pos-Iz, Gora mt. Rus. Fed. 40 K3
Telsen Arg. 205 D6
Telšiai Lith. 42 D6
Teluk Anson Malaysia 76 C1
also known as Teluk Intan
Telukbajur Indon. see Telukbayur
Telukbatang Indon. 77 E3
Telukbayur Indon. 76 C3
formerly known as Emmahaven; formerly spelt Telukbajur
Telukbetung Indon. see Tanjungkarang-Telukbetung
Telukdalam Indon. 76 B2
Teluk Intan Malaysia see Teluk Anson
Telukkuantan Indon. 76 C3
Teluknaga Indon. 77 D4
Telukpakedai Indon. 77 E3
Telyazh'ye Rus. Fed. 43 S9
Tema Ghana 125 F5
Temagami Canada 173 N3
Temagami Lake Canada 168 E4
Temaju i. Indon. 77 E2
Temanggung Indon. 77 E4
Temapache Mex. 185 F4
Te Mapou hill N.Z. 152 I7
Temax Mex. 185 H4
Temba S. Africa 133 M2
Tembagapura Indon. 73 I7
Tembe r. Moz. 133 Q3
Tembe Elephant Park nature res. S. Africa 133 Q3
Tembenchi r. Rus. Fed. 39 J3
Tembesi r. Indon. 76 C3
Tembilahan Indon. 76 C3
Tembisa S. Africa 133 M3
Tembo Aluma Angola 127 C6
Tembué Moz. see Chifunde
Tembuland reg. S. Africa 133 M8
Tembwe Zambia 129 B7
Teme r. U.K. 47 J11
Temecula U.S.A. 183 G8
Temelli Turkey 106 C3
also known as Samutlu
Temenchula, Gora mt. Rus. Fed. 84 C1
Temengor, Tasik resr Malaysia 76 C1
Téméra Mali 125 E2
Temerin Vojvodina, Srbija Yugo. 58 A3
Temerloh Malaysia 76 C2
Teminabuan Indon. 73 H7
Temir Kazakh. 102 D2
Temir Kazakh. see Tumur
Temirlan Kazakh. see Temirlanovka
Temirlanovka Kazakh. 103 G4
also known as Temirlan; also spelt Tamerlanovka
Temirtau Kazakh. 103 H2
Témiscamie r. Canada 169 F3
Témiscaming Canada 168 E4
Témiscamingue, Lac l. Canada 173 N3
also known as Timiskaming, Lake
Témiscouata, Lac l. Canada 169 G4
Temiyang i. Indon. 76 D2
Temkino Rus. Fed. 43 P6
Temmes Fin. 44 N2
Temnikov Rus. Fed. 41 G5
Temo r. Sardegna Italy 57 A8
Temora Australia 147 E3
Temósachic Mex. 184 D2
Tempe U.S.A. 183 M8
Tempe, Danau l. Indon. 75 A4
Tempe Downs Australia 148 B5
Tempelhof airport Germany 49 K3
Tempio Pausania Sardegna Italy 56 B8
Temple MI U.S.A. 173 H6
Temple TX U.S.A. 179 C6
Temple Bay Australia 149 D2
Templemore Rep. of Ireland 47 E11
Templer Bank sea feature Phil. 74 A4
Templeton watercourse Australia 148 C4
Templeton N.Z. 153 G11
Templeton U.S.A. 182 D6
Templin Germany 49 K2
Tempoal Mex. 185 F4
Tempué Angola 127 C8
Tëmpung China 84 C4
Temryuk Rus. Fed. 41 F7
Temryukskiy Zaliv b. Rus. Fed. 41 F7
Temuco Chile 204 B5
Temuka N.Z. 153 F12
Temuli China see Butuo
Temyasovo Rus. Fed. 102 D1
Tena Ecuador 198 B5
Tenabo Mex. 185 H4
Tenabo, Mount U.S.A. 183 H1
Tenala Fin. 42 E1
Tenali India 94 D2
Tenango Mex. 185 F5
Tenasserim Myanmar 79 B5
also known as Taninthari or Tanintharyi or Taninthayi
Tenasserim admin. div. Myanmar 79 B5
also known as Tanintharyi
Tenasserim r. Myanmar 79 B5
Tenby U.K. 47 H12
also known as Dinbych-y-Pysgod
Tenby Bay Canada 173 J4
Tence France 51 K7
Tendaho Eth. 128 D2
Tende France 51 N8
Tende, Col de pass France/Italy 51 N8
Ten Degree Channel India 95 G4
Tendelti Sudan 121 F6
Te-n-Dghâmcha, Sebkhet salt marsh Mauritania 124 B2
Tendō Japan 90 G5
Tendrara Morocco 123 E2
Tendre, Mont mt. Switz. 51 M6
Tendukheda India 96 C5
Téné r. Guinea 124 C4
Tenedos i. Turkey see Bozcaada
Ténenkou Mali 124 D3
Tenenys r. Lith. 42 C6
Ténéré du Tafassâsset des. Niger 125 H1
Tenerife i. Canary Is 122 A3
Ténès Alg. 123 F1
Ténès, Cap c. Alg. 55 M8
Tenevo Bulg. 58 H6
Teng, Nam r. Myanmar 78 B4
Tengah, Kepulauan is Indon. 77 G4
Tengah, Sungai r. Sing. 76 [inset]
Tengcheng China see Tengxian
Tengchong China 86 A3
Tenge Kazakh. 102 C4
Tengeh Reservoir Sing. 76 [inset]
Tenggarong Indon. 77 G3
Tengger Shamo des. China 84 E4
Tengiz, Ozero salt l. Kazakh. 103 G2
Tengréla Côte d'Ivoire 124 D4
formerly spelt Tingrela
Ten'gushevo Rus. Fed. 40 G5
Tengxian China 87 D4
also known as Tengcheng
Tengxian China see Tengzhou
Tengzhou China 85 H5
formerly known as Tengxian
Teniente Enciso, Parque Nacional nat. park Para. 201 E5
Teniente Jubany research station Antarctica see Jubany
Te-n-Ioubrar, Sebkhet salt marsh Mauritania 124 A2
Tenkasi India 94 C4
Tenke Dem. Rep. Congo 127 E7
Tenkeli Rus. Fed. 39 O2
Tenkodogo Burkina 125 E4
Ten Mile Lake salt flat Australia 151 C5
Ten Mile Lake Canada 169 J3
Tenna r. Italy 56 F5
Tennant Creek Australia 148 B3
Tennessee r. U.S.A. 174 B4
Tennessee state U.S.A. 176 B9
Tennessee Pass U.S.A. 180 F5
Tennevoll Norway 44 L1
Tennholmfjorden sea chan. Norway 44 K2
Tenniöjoki r. Fin./Rus. Fed. 44 O2
Tennyson U.S.A. 172 C8
Teno Chile 204 C4
Tenojoki r. Fin./Norway 44 O1
also known as Tana
Tenom Sabah Malaysia 77 F1
Tenosique Mex. 185 H5
Tenryū Japan 91 E7
Tenryū-gawa r. Japan 91 E7
Tenteno Indon. 75 B3
Tenterfield Australia 147 G2
Ten Thousand Islands U.S.A. 175 D7
Tentolomatinan, Gunung mt. Indon. 75 B2
Tentudia mt. Spain 54 E6
Tenu r. France 50 E5
Teocaltiche Mex. 185 E4
Teocelo Mex. 185 F5
Teodoro Sampaio Brazil 206 A9
Teófilo Otôni Brazil 203 D6
Teomabal i. Phil. 74 B5
Teonthar India 97 D4
Teopisca Mex. 185 G5
Teotihuacán tourist site Mex. 185 F5
Tepa Ghana 125 E5
Tepa Indon. 75 D4
Tepache Mex. 184 C2
Te Paki N.Z. 152 G2
Tepasto Fin. 44 N2
Tepatitlán Mex. 185 E4
Tepecik Turkey 58 J7
Tepehuanes Mex. 184 D3
Tepeji Mex. 185 F5
Tepeköy Turkey see Karakoçan
Tepelenë Albania 59 B8
Tepelmeme de Morelos Mex. 185 F5
Tepelská Vrchovina hills Czech Rep. 49 J6
Tepequem, Serra mts Brazil 199 F4
Tepianlangsat Indon. 77 G2
Tepic Mex. 184 D4
Teplá r. Czech Rep. 49 J5
Teplaya Gora Rus. Fed. 40 K4
Teplice Czech Rep. 49 K5
Teploye Lipetskaya Oblast' Rus. Fed. 43 T8
Teploye Tul'skaya Oblast' Rus. Fed. 43 S8
Tepopa, Punta pt Mex. 184 B2
Te Puke N.Z. 152 K5
Te Puna N.Z. 152 K5
Tequila Mex. 184 E4
Tequisistlán Mex. 185 G5
Tequisquiapán Mex. 185 F4
Ter r. Spain 55 O2
Téra Niger 125 F3
Tera r. Port. 54 C6
Tera r. Spain 54 F3
Terakeka Sudan 128 A3
Teram Kangri mt. China/Jammu and Kashmir 89 B5
Teramo Italy 56 F6
historically known as Interamna
Terang Australia 147 D4
Teratani r. Pak. 101 G4
Terbuny Rus. Fed. 43 T9
Tercan Turkey 107 E3
Tereben' Rus. Fed. 43 Q8
Terebovlya Ukr. 41 C6
Terebush Rus. Fed. 43 T7
Teregova Romania 58 D3
Terek Rus. Fed. 107 F2
Terek r. Rus. Fed. 41 H8
Tere-Khol' Rus. Fed. 84 B1
Tere-Khol', Ozero l. Rus. Fed. 84 C1
Terek-Say Kyrg. 103 G4
Terektinskiy Khrebet mts Rus. Fed. 88 D1
Terekty Karagandinskaya Oblast' Kazakh. 103 G2
Terekty Vostochnyy Kazakhstan Kazakh. 88 D1
formerly known as Alekseyevka
Teren'ga Rus. Fed. 41 I5
Terengganu state Malaysia 76 C1
formerly spelt Trengganu
Terengözek Kazakh. see Terenozek
Terenos Brazil 203 A7
Terenozek Kazakh. 103 F3
also spelt Terengözek or Teren-Uzyak
Terensay Rus. Fed. 102 D2
Terentang Indon. 77 E3
Terentang, Pulau i. Indon. 77 G3
Teren-Uzyak Kazakh. see Terenozek
Tereshka r. Rus. Fed. 102 A2
Teresina Brazil 202 D3
Teresina de Goias Brazil 202 C5
Teresita Col. 198 D4
Teresópolis Brazil 207 K9
Terespol Poland 42 E9
Teressa Island India 95 G4
Terezinha Brazil 199 H4
Terges r. Port. 54 D7
Tergeste Italy see Trieste
Tergnier France 51 J3
Terhiyn Tsagaan Nuur l. Mongolia 84 C1
Teriberka Rus. Fed. 44 P1
Teriberka r. Rus. Fed. 44 P1
Teriberskiy, Mys pt Rus. Fed. 44 P1
Terisakkan r. Kazakh. 103 F2
formerly spelt Tersakkan
Terjît well Mauritania 122 B5
Terka Reba Eth. 128 D3
Terkezi well Chad 120 D5
Terlingua Creek r. U.S.A. 179 B6
Terma, Ras pt Eritrea 104 C5
Termas de Socos Chile 204 C3
Terme Turkey 107 D2
Termessos Milli Parkı nat. park Turkey 108 B1
Termez Uzbek. 103 F5
also spelt Termiz
Termination Island Australia 151 C7
Termini Imerese Sicilia Italy 57 F11
Termini Imerese, Golfo di b. Sicilia Italy 57 F10
Términos, Laguna de lag. Mex. 185 H5
Termit well Niger 120 A5
Termit, Massif de hill Niger 125 H2
Termit-Kaoboul Niger 125 H3
Termiz Uzbek. see Termez
Termo U.S.A. 182 D1
Termoli Italy 56 G7
Termonde Belgium see Dendermonde
Tern r. U.K. 47 J11
Ternate Indon. 75 C2
Ternate i. Indon. 75 C2
Terneuzen Neth. 48 A4
Terney Rus. Fed. 82 E3
Terni Italy 56 E6
Ternitz Austria 49 N8
Ternopil' Ukr. 41 C6
also spelt Ternopol'; formerly spelt Tarnopol
Ternopol' Ukr. see Ternopil'
Terowie Australia 146 C3
Terpeniya, Mys c. Rus. Fed. 82 G2
Terpeniya, Zaliv g. Rus. Fed. 82 F2
Terra Alta U.S.A. 176 F6
Terra Bella U.S.A. 182 E6
Terra Boa Brazil 206 A10
Terra Branca Brazil 207 J4
Terrace Canada 166 D4
Terrace Bay Canada 168 C3
Terracina Italy 56 F7
formerly spelt Tarracina; historically known as Anxur
Terra Firma S. Africa 132 H2
Terråk Norway 44 K2
Terralba Sardegna Italy 57 A9
Terra Nova Bay Antarctica 223 K1
Terra Nova National Park Canada 169 K3
Terranuova Bracciolini Italy 56 D5
Terra Preta Brazil 199 G6
Terra Rica Brazil 206 A9
Terrasini Sicilia Italy 57 F10
Terrassa Spain 55 N3
also spelt Tarrasa
Terrasson-la-Villedieu France 50 H7
Terrazas Mex. 184 D2
Terre Adélie reg. Antarctica see Adélie Land
Terrebonne Bay U.S.A. 175 B6
Terre Haute U.S.A. 174 C4
Terrell U.S.A. 179 C5
Terre Plaine plain France 51 K5
Terrero Mex. 184 D2
Terres Australes et Antarctiques Françaises terr. Indian Ocean see French Southern and Antarctic Lands
Terril mt. Spain 54 F8
Terry U.S.A. 180 F3
Tersakkan r. Kazakh. see Terisakkan
Terschelling i. Neth. 48 C2
Terskey Alatau, Khrebet mts Kyrg. see Terskey Ala-Too
Terskey Ala-Too mts Kyrg. 103 I4
also known as Terskey Alatau, Khrebet
Terskiy Bereg coastal area Rus. Fed. 40 F2
Tersko-Kumskiy Kanal canal Rus. Fed. 107 F1
Tertenia Sardegna Italy 57 B9
Terter Azer. see Tärtär
Teruel Spain 55 J4
Terutao i. Thai. 79 B7
Terutao National Park Thai. 79 B7
Tervakoski Fin. 42 F1
Tervel Bulg. 58 I5
Tervo Fin. 44 N3
Tervola Fin. 44 N2
Teryayevo Rus. Fed. 43 R5
Tešanj Bos.-Herz. 56 J4
Teseney Eritrea 121 H6
Tesha r. Rus. Fed. 40 G5
Teshekpuk Lake U.S.A. 164 D2
Teshikaga Japan 90 I3
Teshio Japan 90 G2
Teshio-dake mt. Japan 90 H3
Teshio-gawa r. Japan 90 G2
Teshio-sanchi mts Japan 90 G2
Tešica Srbija Yugo. 58 C5
Tesiyn Gol r. Mongolia 84 B1
Teslić Bos.-Herz. 56 J4
Teslin Canada 166 C2
Teslin r. Canada 166 C2
Teslin Lake Canada 166 C2
Teslui r. Romania 58 F4
Teso Santo hill Spain 54 F3
Tesouras r. Brazil 206 C1
Tesouro Brazil 202 A6
Tesovo-Netyl'skiy Rus. Fed. 43 M3
Tesovskiy Rus. Fed. 43 L3
Tessala, Monts du mts Alg. 55 K9
Tessalit Mali 123 F5
Tessaoua Niger 125 G3
Tesséroukane well Niger 125 G2
Tessolo Moz. 131 G4
Tessoûnfat well Mali 123 F5
formerly spelt Sounfat
Test r. U.K. 47 K13
Testour Tunisia 123 H1
Têt r. France 51 J10
Tetachuck Lake Canada 166 E4
Tetagouche r. Canada 169 H4
Tetas, Punta pt Chile 200 C5
Tete Moz. 131 G3
Tete prov. Moz. 131 G2
Tetehosi Indon. 76 B2
Tête Jaune Cache Canada 166 G4
Te Teko N.Z. 152 K6
Teterino Rus. Fed. 43 V3
Teteriv r. Ukr. 41 D6
Teterow Germany 49 J2
Teteven Bulg. 58 F6
Tetiyev Ukr. see Tetiyiv
Tetiyiv Ukr. 41 D6
also spelt Tetiyev; formerly known as Snegurovka
Teton r. U.S.A. 180 E3
Teton Range mts U.S.A. 180 E4
Tétouan Morocco 122 D2
also spelt Tetuán; historically known as Titawin
Tetovo Macedonia 58 B6
Tetpur India 96 A5
Tetuán Morocco see Tétouan
Tetulia sea chan. Bangl. 97 F5
Tetyukhe Rus. Fed. see Dal'negorsk
Tetyukhe-Pristan' Rus. Fed. see Rudnaya Pristan'
Tetyushi Rus. Fed. 40 I5
Teuchezhsk Rus. Fed. see Adygeysk
Teuchi Japan 91 A9
Teuco r. Arg. 204 E2
Teulada Sardegna Italy 57 A10
Teulada, Capo c. Sardegna Italy 57 A10
Teul de González Ortega Mex. 184 E4
Teun vol. Indon. 75 D4
Teunom Indon. 76 A1
Teunom r. Indon. 76 A1
Teupitz-Köriser Seengebiet park Germany 49 K3
Teuri-tō i. Japan 90 G2
Teustepe Nicaragua 186 B4
Teutoburger Wald hills Germany 48 F3
Teuva Fin. 44 M3
Tevere r. Italy see Tiber
Teverya Israel see Tiberias
Teviot N.Z. 153 D13
Teviot r. U.K. 46 J8
Teviothead U.K. 46 J8
Te Waewae N.Z. 153 B14
Te Waewae Bay N.Z. 153 B14
Te Waiponamu i. N.Z. see South Island
Tewane Botswana 131 E4
Tewantin Australia 149 G5
Teweh r. Indon. 77 F3
Te Wera North I. N.Z. 152 I7
Te Wera North I. N.Z. 152 L6
Te Wharau N.Z. 152 J9
Tewli Belarus 42 F9
Têwo China 86 B1
also known as Dêngka; formerly known as Dêngkagoin
Texarkana AR U.S.A. 179 D5
Texarkana TX U.S.A. 179 D5
Texas Australia 147 F2
Texas state U.S.A. 179 C6
Texas City U.S.A. 179 D6
Texcoco Mex. 185 F5
Texel i. Neth. 48 B2
Texoma, Lake U.S.A. 179 C5
Teyateyaneng Lesotho 133 L6
Teykovo Rus. Fed. 43 V5
Teyvareh Afgh. 101 F3
Teza r. Rus. Fed. 40 G4
Teza S. Africa 133 Q5
Teziutlán Mex. 185 F5
Tezpur India 97 G4
Tezu India 97 H4
Tfaritiy W. Sahara 122 C4
Tha, Nam r. Laos 78 C3
Tha-anne r. Canada 167 M2
Thabana-Ntlenyana mt. Lesotho 133 N6
Thaba Nchu S. Africa 133 K6
Thabankulu mt. S. Africa 133 O4
Thaba Putsoa mt. Lesotho 131 E6
Thaba Putsoa mts S. Africa 133 L7
Thaba-Tseka Lesotho 133 M6
Thabazimbi S. Africa 131 E5
Thabeikkyin Myanmar 78 B3
Thab Lan National Park Thai. 79 C5
Tha Bo Laos 78 C4
Thabong S. Africa 133 K4
Thabt, Gebel el mt. Egypt 108 F9
Thabyedaung Myanmar 78 B3
Thac Ba, Hô l. Vietnam 78 D3
Thade r. Myanmar 78 A4
Thādiq Saudi Arabia 105 D2
Thagyettaw Myanmar 79 B5
Tha Hin Thai. see Lop Buri
Thai Binh Vietnam 78 D3
Thailand country Asia 78 C4
known in Thai as Muang Thai or Prathes Thai; formerly known as Siam
asia [countries] 64–67
Thailand, Gulf of Asia 79 C6
Thai Muang Thai. 79 B6
Thai Nguyên Vietnam 78 D3
Thaj Saudi Arabia 105 E2
Thakurgaon Bangl. 97 F4
Thakurtola India 96 D5
Thal Pak. 101 G3
Thala Tunisia 123 H2
Thalang Thai. 79 B6
Thalassery India see Tellicherry
Thal Desert Pak. 101 G4
Thale (Harz) Germany 48 I4
Thale Luang lag. Thai. 79 C7
Thalgau Austria 49 K8
Tha Li Thai. 78 C4
Thaliparamba India see Taliparamba
Thallon Australia 147 F2
Thamad Bū Hashishah well Libya 120 C3
Thamaga Botswana 131 E5
Thamar, Jabal mt. Yemen 105 D5
Thamarīt Oman 105 F4
English form Midway
Thames r. Canada 173 K8
Thames N.Z. 152 J5
Thames est. U.K. 47 M12
Thames r. U.K. 47 M12
Thames, Firth of b. N.Z. 152 J4
Thamesford Canada 173 M7
Thamesville Canada 173 L8
Thamūd Yemen 105 E4
Thamugadi tourist site Alg. see Timgad
Thana India see Thane
Thana Ghazi India 96 C4
Thanatpin Myanmar 78 B4
Thanbyuzayat Myanmar 78 B5
Thandla India 96 B5
Thandwè Myanmar see Sandoway
Thane India 94 B2
formerly spelt Thana
Thangadh India 96 A5
Thangoo Australia 150 C3
Thanh Hoa Vietnam 78 D4
Thanjavur India 94 C4
also known as Tanjore
Than Kyun i. Myanmar 79 B6
also known as Davis
Thanlwin r. Myanmar see Salween
Thano Bula Khan Pak. 101 F5
Than Uyen Vietnam 86 B4
Thaoge r. Botswana 130 D3
Thaolintoa Lake Canada 167 L2
Thap Put Thai. 79 B6
Thap Sakae Thai. 79 B6
Thara India 96 A5
Tharad India 96 A4
Tharaka Kenya 128 C5
Thar Desert India/Pak. 96 A4
also known as Indian Desert
Thargomindah Australia 147 D1
Tharrawaddy Myanmar 78 A4
Tharrawaw Myanmar 78 A4
Tharthār, Buḩayrat ath l. Iraq 107 E4
Tharthār Canal Iraq see Dijlah - Ath Tharthār, Qanāt
Tharwāniyyah U.A.E. 105 F3
Thasos Greece 58 F8
Thasos i. Greece 58 F8
Thatcher U.S.A. 183 O9
Thatē, Mali i mt. Albania 58 B8
Thất Khê Vietnam 78 D3
Thaton Myanmar 78 B4
Thau, Bassin de lag. France 51 J9
Thaungdut Myanmar 78 A2
Thaungyin r. Myanmar/Thai. 78 B4
Tha Uthen Thai. 78 D4
Thawr, Jabal mt. Jordan 108 G8
Thayawthadangyi Kyun i. Myanmar 79 B5
also known as Elphinstone
Thayetmyo Myanmar 78 A4
Thazi Myanmar 78 B3
The Aldermen Islands N.Z. 152 K4
Theba U.S.A. 183 L9
Thebae tourist site Egypt see Thebes
The Bahamas country West Indies 186 D1
northamerica [countries] 158–159
Thebes tourist site Egypt 121 G3
historically known as Diospolis Magna or Thebae
Thebes Greece see Thiva
The Bluff Bahamas 186 D1
The Broads nat. park U.K. 47 N11
The Brothers is Hong Kong China 87 [inset]
also known as Tai Siu Mo To
The Brothers is Yemen see Al Ikhwān
The Calvados Chain is P.N.G. 149 G1
The Cheviot hill U.K. 46 J8
The Coorong inlet Australia 146 C3
The Dalles U.S.A. 180 B3
also known as Dalles City
Thedford U.S.A. 178 B3
The English Company's Islands Australia 148 C1
The Entrance Australia 147 F3
Theewaterskloof Dam resr S. Africa 132 D11
The Fens reg. U.K. 47 L11
The Gambia country Africa 124 A3
africa [countries] 114–117
The Great Oasis Egypt see Kharga Oasis
The Grenadines is St Vincent 187 H4
The Gulf Asia 105 E1
also known as Persian Gulf or Arabian Gulf

The Hague Neth. 48 B3
Seat of government of the Netherlands. Also known as Den Haag or 's-Gravenhage.
world [countries] 10–11

The Haven S. Africa 133 M9
The Horseshoe mt. S. Africa 132 H8
The Hunters Hills N.Z. 153 E12
Theinkun Myanmar 79 B6
Theinzeik Myanmar 78 B4
The Key N.Z. 153 B13
Thekulthili Lake Canada 167 I2
The Lakes National Park Australia 147 E4
Thelon r. Canada 167 L1
Thelon Game Sanctuary nature res. Canada 167 K1
The Lynd Junction Australia 149 E3
Themar Germany 48 H5
Thembalesizwe S. Africa 132 I9
Thembalihle S. Africa 133 N4
The Minch sea chan. U.K. 46 F5
The Mullet b. Rep. of Ireland 47 B9
The Needles stack U.K. 47 K13
Theni India 96 C5
Thenia Alg. 55 O8
Theniet El Had Alg. 55 N9
Thenon France 50 H7
Theodore Australia 149 F5
Theodore Canada 167 K5
Theodore Roosevelt r. Brazil 201 E1
Theodore Roosevelt Lake U.S.A. 183 M8
Theodore Roosevelt National Park U.S.A. 178 B2
Theodosia Ukr. see Feodosiya
The Officer Creek watercourse Australia 146 B1
The Paps hill Rep. of Ireland 47 C11
The Pas Canada 167 K4
Thera i. Greece see Thira
Thérain r. France 51 I3
The Remarkables mts N.Z. 153 C13
Theresa U.S.A. 177 J1
Theresa Creek r. Australia 149 F4
Therma Greece 58 G8
Thermaïkos Kolpos g. Greece 59 D8
Thermo Greece 59 C10
also known as Thérmon
Thérmon Greece see Thermo
Thermopolis U.S.A. 180 E4
The Salt Lake salt flat Australia 147 D2

The Settlement Christmas I. 220 B6
Capital of Christmas Island.

Thesiger Bay Canada 164 G2
The Skaw spit Denmark see Grenen
The Slot sea chan. Solomon Is see New Georgia Sound
The Solent strait U.K. 47 K13
Thesprotiko Greece 59 B9
Thessalia admin. reg. Greece 59 C9
English form Thessaly
Thessalon Canada 168 D4
Thessalonica Greece see Thessaloniki
Thessaloniki Greece 58 D8
also known as Salonika or Thessalonica; formerly known as Salonica
Thessaly admin. reg. Greece see Thessalia
The Storr hill U.K. 46 F6
The Teeth mt. Phil. 74 A4
The Terraces hills Australia 151 C6
Thetford U.K. 47 M11
Thetford Mines Canada 169 G4
The Thumbs mt. N.Z. 153 E11
Thetkethaung r. Myanmar 78 A5
The Triangle mts Myanmar 78 B2
The Twins Australia 146 B2
Theun r. Laos 78 D4
Theunissen S. Africa 133 K5
Theva-i-Ra reef Fiji see Ceva-i-Ra

The Valley Anguilla 187 H3
Capital of Anguilla.

Thevenard Australia 146 B3
Thevenard Island Australia 150 A4
Thévenet, Lac l. Canada 169 G1
Theveste Alg. see Tébessa
The Wash b. U.K. 47 M11
The Weald reg. U.K. 47 M12
The Woodlands U.S.A. 179 D6
Thíamis r. Greece see Thyamis
Thibodaux U.S.A. 179 E6
Thief River Falls U.S.A. 178 C1
Thiel Neth. see Tiel
Thiel Mountains Antarctica 223 R1
Thielsen, Mount U.S.A. 180 B4
Thielt Belgium see Tielt
Thiers France 51 J7
Thiès Senegal 124 A3
Thika Kenya 128 C5
Thikombia i. Fiji see Cikobia
Thiladhunmathee Atoll Maldives 94 B5
Thilogne Senegal 124 B3
also spelt Tilogne
Thimbu Bhutan see Thimphu

Thimphu Bhutan 97 F4
Capital of Bhutan. Also known as Tashi Chho; also spelt Thimbu.

Thingvallavatn (Þingvallavatn) l. Iceland 44 [inset] B2
Thingvellir (Þingvellir) Iceland 44 [inset] B2
Thionville France 51 M3
formerly known as Diedenhofen
Thira Greece 59 G12
Thira i. Greece 59 G12
also known as Santorini; historically known as Thera
Thirasia i. Greece 59 G12
Third Cataract rapids Sudan see 3rd Cataract
Thirsk U.K. 47 K9
Thirty Mile Lake Canada 167 L2
Thiruvananthapuram India see Trivandrum
Thiruvarur India 94 C4
Thiruvattiyur India see Tiruvottiyur
Thissavros, Techniti Limni resr Greece 58 F7
Thisted Denmark 45 J4
Thistilfjörður (Þistilfjörður) b. Iceland 44 [inset] D2
Thistle Creek Canada 166 B2
Thistle Island Australia 146 C3
Thistle Lake Canada 167 I1
Thityabin Myanmar 78 A3
Thiva Greece 59 E10
also known as Thívai; historically known as Thebes
Thívai Greece see Thiva
Thiviers France 50 G7
Thjórsá (Þjórsá) r. Iceland 44 [inset] B3
Thlewiaza r. Canada 167 M2
Thoa r. Canada 167 I2
Thô Chu, Đao i. Vietnam 79 C6
Thoen Thai. 78 B4
Thoeng Thai. 78 C4
Thohoyandou S. Africa 131 F4
Tholen i. Neth. 48 B4
Thomas r. Australia 151 B5
Thomas, Lake salt flat Australia 148 C5
Thomas Hill Reservoir U.S.A. 178 D4
Thomas Hubbard, Cape Canada 165 J1
Thomas Mountain U.S.A. 183 H8
Thomaston CT U.S.A. 177 L4
Thomaston GA U.S.A. 175 C5
Thomaston ME U.S.A. 177 P1
Thomastown Rep. of Ireland 47 E11
Thomasville AL U.S.A. 175 C6
Thomasville GA U.S.A. 175 D6
Thomasville NC U.S.A. 174 D5
Thomonde Haiti 187 F3
Thompson Canada 167 L4
Thompson r. Canada 166 F5
Thompson MI U.S.A. 172 G5
Thompson UT U.S.A. 183 O3
Thompson r. U.S.A. 174 A4
Thompson Falls U.S.A. 180 D3
Thompson Peak U.S.A. 181 F6
Thompson's Falls Kenya see Nyahururu
Thompson Sound Canada 166 E5
Thompson Sound inlet N.Z. 153 A13
Thompsonville U.S.A. 177 M4
Thomson watercourse Australia 149 D5
Thomson GA U.S.A. 175 D5
Thomson IL U.S.A. 172 C9
Thon Buri Thai. 79 C5
Thongwa Myanmar 78 B4
Thonon-les-Bains France 51 M6
Thoreau U.S.A. 181 E6
Thorhild Canada 167 H4
Thórisvatn (Þórisvatn) l. Iceland 44 [inset] C2
Thorn Poland see Toruń
Thornapple r. U.S.A. 173 H8
Thornbury N.Z. 153 C14
Thorne Canada 173 N4
Thorne U.K. 47 L10
Thorne U.S.A. 182 F3
Thornhill U.K. 47 I8
Thornton r. Australia 148 C3
Thornton U.S.A. 172 E6
Thorp U.S.A. 172 C6
Thorsby Canada 167 H4
Thorshavn Faroe Is see Tórshavn
Thorshavnfjella reg. Antarctica see Thorshavnheiane
Thorshavnheiane reg. Antarctica 223 B2
also known as Thorshavnfjella
Thórshöfn (Þórshöfn) Iceland 44 [inset] D2
Thorvaldsfell (Þorvaldsfell) vol. Iceland 44 [inset] C2
Thota-ea-Moli Lesotho 133 L6
Thouars France 50 F6
Thoubal India 97 G4
Thouet r. France 50 F5

largest cities

	city	population	location		page#
1	Tōkyō	26 444 000	Japan	Asia	91 F7
2	Mexico City	18 131 000	Mexico	North America	185 F5
3	Mumbai (Bombay)	18 066 000	India	Asia	94 B2
4	São Paulo	17 755 000	Brazil	South America	206 G10
5	New York	16 640 000	USA	North America	177 L5
6	Lagos	13 427 000	Nigeria	Africa	125 F5
7	Los Angeles	13 140 000	USA	North America	182 F7
8	Kolkata (Calcutta)	12 918 000	India	Asia	97 F5
9	Shanghai	12 887 000	China	Asia	87 G2
10	Buenos Aires	12 560 000	Argentina	South America	204 F4

index

T

Tōlañaro Madag. **131** [inset] J5
also known as Faradofay; *formerly known as* Fort-Dauphin; *formerly spelt* Taolanaro
Tolar, Cerro *mt.* Arg. **204** D2
Tolbazy Rus. Fed. **40** J5
Tolbo Mongolia **84** A1
Tolbukhin Bulg. *see* **Dobrich**
Tolbukhino Rus. Fed. **43** V4
formerly known as Davydkovo
Tolchin, Mount Antarctica **223** T1
Tolé Panama **186** C5
Tole Bi Kazakh. **103** H4
formerly known as Novotroitskoye
Toledo *Amazonas* Brazil **198** C6
Toledo *Paraná* Brazil **203** A8
Toledo Chile **204** C2
Toledo Spain **54** G5
historically known as Toletum
Toledo *IA* U.S.A. **174** A3
Toledo *OH* U.S.A. **176** B4
Toledo *OR* U.S.A. **180** B3
Toledo, Montes de *mts* Spain **54** G5
formerly known as Oretana, Cordillera
Toledo Bend Reservoir U.S.A. **179** D6
Tolentino Italy **56** F5
Toletum Spain *see* **Toledo**
Tolga Norway **44** J3
Toli China **88** C2
Toliara Madag. **131** [inset] I4
formerly spelt Tuléar
Toliara *prov.* Madag. **131** [inset] J4
Tolima *dept* Col. **198** C4
Toling China *see* **Zanda**
Tolitoli Indon. **75** B2
Tol'ka Rus. Fed. **39** I3
Tolkmicko Poland **49** Q1
Tollense *r.* Germany **49** K2
Tollensesee-Becken *park* Germany **49** K2
Tolleson U.S.A. **183** L8
Tollimarjon Uzbek. *see* **Talimardzhan**
Tolmachevo Rus. Fed. **43** K3
Tolmezzo Italy **56** F2
Tolmin Slovenia **56** F2
Tolna Hungary **49** P9
Tolo Dem. Rep. Congo **126** C5
Tolo Channel *Hong Kong* China **87** [inset]
also known as Chek Mun Hoi Hap
Tolochin Belarus *see* **Talachyn**
Tolo Harbour *b. Hong Kong* China **87** [inset]
also known as Tai Po Hoi
Tolonen Fin. **44** N1
Tolosa France *see* **Toulouse**
Tolosa Spain **55** I1
Tolsan-do *i.* S. Korea **83** B6
Tolsmaville Canada **173** J5
Tolstoy, Mys *c.* Rus. Fed. **39** P4
Toltén Chile **204** B5
Tolú Col. **198** C2
Toluca Mex. **185** F5
Tolvand, Ozero *l.* Rus. Fed. **44** O2
Tol'yatti Rus. Fed. **41** I5
English form Togliatti; *formerly known as* Stavropol'-na-Volge
Tolybay Kazakh. **103** E2
Tom' *r.* Rus. Fed. **82** E2
Toma Burkina **124** E3
Tomah U.S.A. **172** C7
Tomahawk U.S.A. **172** D5
Tomakomai Japan **90** G3
Tomales U.S.A. **182** B3
Tomamae Japan **90** G2
Tomani *Sabah* Malaysia **77** F1
Tomar Brazil **199** F5
Tomar Port. **54** C5
Tomari Japan **90** G3
Tomari Rus. Fed. **82** F3
Tomaros *mt.* Greece **59** B9
Tomarza Turkey **106** C3
Tomaszów Mazowiecki Poland **49** R4
Tomatlán Mex. **184** D5
Tomave Bol. **200** D5
Tomazina Brazil **206** D10
Tombador, Serra do *hills Bahia* Brazil **202** D4
Tombador, Serra do *hills Mato Grosso* Brazil **201** F3
Tombigbee *r.* U.S.A. **175** C6
Tombo S. Africa **133** N8
Tomboco Angola **127** B6
Tombos Brazil **207** K7
Tombouctou Mali *see* **Timbuktu**
Tombouctou *admin. reg.* Mali **124** E2
Tombstone U.S.A. **181** E7
Tombua Angola **127** A8
formerly known as Porto Alexandre
Tom Burke S. Africa **131** E4
Tomdibuloq Uzbek. *see* **Tamdybulak**
Tomditow Toghi *hills* Uzbek. *see* **Tamdytau, Gory**
Tomé Chile **204** B5
Tome Moz. 131 G4
Tomea *i.* Indon. **75** B4
Tomelilla Sweden **45** K5
Tomelloso Spain **55** H5
Tomenaryk Kazakh. **103** F4
formerly spelt Tyumen'-Aryk
Tomi Romania *see* **Constanța**
Tomiko Canada **173** N4
Tomina Bol. **201** D4
Tominé *r.* Guinea **124** B3
Tomingley Australia **147** F3
Tomini, Teluk *g.* Indon. **75** B3
Tominian Mali **124** D3
Tomioka *Fukushima* Japan **90** G6
Tomioka *Gumma* Japan **91** F6
Tomislavgrad Bos.-Herz. **56** J5
formerly known as Duvno
Tomkinson Ranges *mts* Australia **146** A1
Tømmerneset Norway **44** K2
Tommot Rus. Fed. **39** M4
Tomo Col. **199** E4
Tomo *r.* Col. **198** E3
Tomóchic Mex. **184** D2
Tomorit, Maja e *mt.* Albania **58** B8
Tomorlog China **88** E4
Tomortei China **85** G3
Tompa Hungary **49** Q9
Tompira Indon. **75** B3
Tompi Seleka S. Africa **133** N1
Tompo Indon. **75** A3
Tompo Rus. Fed. **39** N3
Tom Price Australia **150** B4
Tomra China **89** D6
Tomsk Rus. Fed. **80** D1
Toms River U.S.A. **177** K6
Tomtor Rus. Fed. **39** O3
Tömük Turkey **108** F1
also known as Elvanlı
Tomuraushi-yama *mt.* Japan **90** H3
Tomur Feng *mt.* China/Kyrg. *see* **Pobeda Peak**
Tomuzlovka *r.* Rus. Fed. **41** H7
Tom White, Mount U.S.A. **164** E3
Tonalá *Chiapas* Mex. **185** G5
Tonalá *Veracruz* Mex. **185** G5
Tonami Japan **91** E6
Tonantins Brazil **199** E5
Tonate Fr. Guiana **199** H3
Tonawanda U.S.A. **176** G2
Tonb-e Bozorg, Jazīreh-ye *i.* The Gulf *see* **Greater Tunb**
Tonb-e Kūchek, Jazīreh-ye *i.* The Gulf *see* **Lesser Tunb**
Tonbridge U.K. **47** M12
Tondano Indon. **75** C2
Tondela Port. **54** C4
Tønder Denmark **45** J5
Tondi India **94** C4
Toney Mount Antarctica **222** Q1
Tonga Cameroon **125** H5
▶**Tonga** *country* S. Pacific Ocean **145** H3
historically known as Friendly Islands
oceania [countries] ▶▶ 138–139
Tonga Sudan **128** A2
Tongaat S. Africa **133** P6
Tong'an China **87** F3
also known as Datong
Tonga Plateau Zambia **127** E9
Tongaporutu N.Z. **152** I6
Tongareva *atoll* Cook Is *see* **Penrhyn**
Tongariro *vol.* N.Z. **152** J7
Tongariro National Park N.Z. **152** J7
Tongatapu *i.* Tonga **145** H4
Tongatapu Group *is* Tonga **145** H4

▶**Tonga Trench** *sea feature* S. Pacific Ocean **220** G7
2nd deepest trench in the world.

Tongbai China **87** E1
Tongbai Shan *mts* China **87** E1
Tongcheng *Anhui* China **87** F2
Tongcheng *Hubei* China **87** E2
also known as Juanshui
Tongcheng China *see* **Dong'e**
T'ongch'ŏn N. Korea **83** B5
Tongchuan China **85** F5
Tongchuan China *see* **Santai**
Tongdao China **87** D3
also known as Shuangjiang
Tongde China **84** D5
also known as Gabasumdo
Tongduch'ŏn S. Korea **83** B5
Tongeren Belgium **51** L2
also spelt Tongres
Tonggu China **87** E2
also known as Yongning
Tongguan China **87** D1
Tonggu Jiao *pt* China **87** D5
Tonghae S. Korea **83** C5
Tonghai China **86** B3
also known as Xiushan
Tonghe China **82** C3
Tonghua *Jilin* China **82** B4
also known as Kuaidamao
Tonghua *Jilin* China **82** B4
Tongi Bangl. *see* **Tungi**
Tongjiang *Heilong.* China **82** D3
Tongjiang *Sichuan* China **87** C2
also known as Nuojiang
Tongken *r.* China **82** B3
Tongking, Gulf of China/Vietnam **78** E3
Tongle China *see* **Leye**
Tongliao China **85** I3
Tongling *Anhui* China **87** F2
Tongling *Anhui* China **87** F2
Tonglu China **87** F2
Tongnae S. Korea **91** A7
Tongo Australia **147** D2
Tongobory Madag. **131** [inset] J4
Tongo Lake *salt flat* Australia **147** D2
Tongquan China *see* **Malong**
Tongquil *i.* Phil. **74** B5
Tongren *Guizhou* China **87** D3
Tongren *Qinghai* China **84** D5
also known as Rongwo
Tongres Belgium *see* **Tongeren**
Tongsa Bhutan *see* **Trongsa**
Tongshan China **87** F1
also known as Xuzhou
Tongshi China **87** D5
formerly known as Hongqizhen
Tongta Myanmar **78** B3
Tongtian He *r.* China *see* **Yangtze**
Tongue U.K. **46** H5
Tongue *r.* U.S.A. **180** F3
Tongue of the Ocean *sea chan.* Bahamas **186** D1
Tongwei China **84** E5
also known as Pingxiang
Tongxian China *see* **Tongzhou**
Tongxiang China **87** G2
Tongxin China **85** E4
T'ongyŏng S. Korea **83** C6
formerly known as Ch'ungmu
Tongyu China **85** I2
also known as Kaitong
Tongzhou China **85** H4
formerly known as Tongxian
Tongzi China **86** C2
Tonhil Mongolia *see* **Dzüyl**
Tonica U.S.A. **172** D9
Tōnichi Mex. **184** C2
Tonila Mex. **184** E5
Tonj Sudan **126** F3
Tonj *watercourse* Sudan **126** F3
Tonk India **96** B4
Tonkābon Iran **100** B2
Tonkawa U.S.A. **178** C4
Tonkin *reg.* Vietnam **78** D3
Tônlé Repou *r.* Laos **79** D5
Tônlé Sab *l.* Cambodia *see* **Tonle Sap**

▶**Tonle Sap** *l.* Cambodia **79** C5
Largest lake in Southeast Asia. Also spelt Tônlé Sab.

Tonnay-Charente France **50** F7
Tonneins France **50** G8
Tonnerre France **51** J5
Tönning Germany **48** F1
Tōno Japan **90** G5
Tonopah *AZ* U.S.A. **183** L8
Tonopah *NV* U.S.A. **183** G3
Tonosí Panama **186** C6
Tons *r.* India **89** B6
Tønsberg Norway **45** J4
Tonshalovo Rus. Fed. **43** S2
Tonstad Norway **45** I4
Tonteiboş S. Africa **132** E7
Tonto Basin U.S.A. **183** M8
Tonto Creek *watercourse* U.S.A. **183** M8
Tonzang Myanmar **78** A3
Toobeah Australia **147** F2
Toobli Liberia **124** C5
Tooele U.S.A. **183** L1
Toolonga Nature Reserve Australia **151** A5
Toompine Australia **147** E1
Toorberg *mt.* S. Africa **132** I9
Toowoomba Australia **147** F1
Tooxin Somalia **128** F2
Top Afgh. **101** G3
Topalki Rus. Fed. **43** R3
Topana Romania **58** F4
Topaz Lake U.S.A. **182** E3

▶**Topeka** U.S.A. **178** D4
State capital of Kansas.

Topia Mex. **184** D3
Topkanovo Rus. Fed. **43** T7
Topki Rus. Fed. **80** D1
Topla *reg.* India **96** D5
Topľa *r.* Slovakia **49** S7
Toplana, Gunung *mt.* Indon. **75** D3
Topley Canada **166** E4
Topley Landing Canada **166** E4
Toplica *r.* Yugo. **58** C5
Toplița Romania **58** G2
Topocalma, Punta *pt* Chile **204** B4
Topock U.S.A. **183** J7
Topoľčany Slovakia **49** P7
Topolnitsa *r.* Bulg. **58** F6
Topolobampo Mex. **184** C3
Topolog Romania **58** J4
Topolog *r.* Romania **58** F3
Topoloveni Romania **58** G4
Topolovgrad Bulg. **58** H6
Topozero, Ozero *l.* Rus. Fed. **44** P2
Toppenish U.S.A. **180** B3
Topraisar Romania **58** J4
Topterek China *see* **Jeminay**
Topuni N.Z. **152** I4
Toqyraū *watercourse* Kazakh. *see* **Tokyrau**
Tor Eth. **128** B3
Tora Dem. Rep. Congo **126** F4
Torata Peru **200** C4
Tor Baldak *mt.* Afgh. **101** F4
Torbalı Turkey **106** A3
Torbat-e Heydarīyeh Iran **101** D3
Torbat-e Jām Iran **101** E3
Torbay Bay Australia **151** B7
Torbeyevo *Respublika Mordoviya* Rus. Fed. **41** G5
Torbeyevo *Smolenskaya Oblast'* Rus. Fed. **43** P6
Torch *r.* Canada **167** K4
Torchino Rus. Fed. **43** V5
Tordesillas Spain **54** G3
Tórdiga, Puerto de *pass* Spain **55** I5
Tordino *r.* Italy **56** F6
Töre Sweden **44** M2
Töreboda Sweden **45** K4
Torelló Spain **55** N2
Toreno Spain **54** E2
Toreo Indon. **75** B3
Torere N.Z. **152** L5
Toretam Kazakh. *see* **Baykonur**
Torey Rus. Fed. **84** E1
Torgau Germany **49** J4
Torgelow Germany **49** L2
Torghay Kazakh. *see* **Turgay**
Torgun *r.* Rus. Fed. **102** A2
Torhamn Sweden **45** K4
Torhout Belgium **51** J1
also spelt Thourout
Tori Estonia **42** F3
Tori India **97** E5
Tori *r.* Sudan **128** A3
Torigni-sur-Vire France **50** F3
Torine *pass* Bos.-Herz. **56** K5
Torino Italy *see* **Turin**
Tori-shima *i.* Japan **91** G9
Torit Sudan **128** B3
Torixoreu Brazil **206** A3
Torkamān Iran **100** A2
Torkovichi Rus. Fed. **43** L3
Torma Estonia **42** H3
Tormänen Fin. **44** N1
Torment, Point Australia **150** C3
Tormes *r.* Spain **54** E3
Tornado Mountain Canada **167** H5
Tornaľa Slovakia **49** R7
formerly known as Šafárikovo
Tornavacas, Puerto de *pass* Spain **54** F4
Torneå Fin. *see* **Tornio**
Torneälven *r.* Sweden **44** N2
Torneträsk Sweden **44** L1
Torneträsk *l.* Sweden **44** L1
Torngat, Monts *mts* Canada *see* **Torngat Mountains**
Torngat Mountains Canada **169** H1
also known as Torngat, Monts
Tornik *mt.* Yugo. **58** A5
Tornio Fin. **44** N2
also spelt Torneå
Tornquist Arg. **204** E5
Toro Nigeria **125** H4
Toro Spain **54** F3
Toro, Lago del *l.* Chile **205** B8
Toro, Pico del *mt.* Mex. **185** E3
Torobuku Indon. **75** B4
Torodi Niger **125** F3
Törökszentmiklós Hungary **49** R8

▶**Toronto** Canada **168** E5
Provincial capital of Ontario and 5th most populous city in North America.
world [cities] ▶▶ 24–25

Toronto U.S.A. **176** E5
Toropatsa Rus. Fed. **43** M5
Toro Peak U.S.A. **183** H8
Toropets Rus. Fed. **43** M5
Tororo Chad **120** C6
Tororo Uganda **128** B4
Toros Dağları *mts* Turkey *see* **Taurus Mountains**
Toroshino Rus. Fed. **43** J4
Torquato Severo Brazil **204** G3
Torquay Australia **147** E4
Torquay U.K. **47** I13
Torrance U.S.A. **182** F8
Torrão Port. **54** C6
Torre *mt.* Port. **54** D4
Torre Annunziata Italy **57** G8
Torreblanca Spain **55** L4
Torre Blanco, Cerro *mt.* Mex. **184** B1
Torrecerredo *mt.* Spain **54** G1
Torrecilla *mt.* Spain **54** G8
Torre del Greco Italy **57** G8
Torre de Moncorvo Port. **54** D3
Torredonjimeno Spain **54** H7
Torrejón de Ardoz Spain **55** H4
Torrejón-Tajo, Embalse de *resr* Spain **54** F5
Torrelaguna Spain **55** H4
Torrelavega Spain **54** G1
Torremaggiore Italy **56** H7
Torremolinos Spain **54** G8

▶**Torrens, Lake** *salt flat* Australia **146** C2
2nd largest lake in Oceania.
oceania [landscapes] ▶▶ 136–137

Torrens Creek Australia **149** E4
Torrent Arg. **204** F3
Torrent Spain **55** K5
also spelt Torrente
Torrente Spain *see* **Torrent**
Torreón Mex. **185** E3
Torre Orsaia Italy **57** H8
Torre-Pacheco Spain **55** K7
Torreparedones *hill* Spain **54** G7
Torres Brazil **203** B9
Torres del Paine, Parque Nacional *nat. park* Chile **205** B8
Torres Islands Vanuatu **145** F3
Torres Novas Port. **54** C5
Torres Strait Australia **144** D2
Torres Vedras Port. **54** B5
Torrevieja Spain **55** K7
Torrey U.S.A. **183** M3
Torridge *r.* U.K. **47** H13
Torriglia Italy **56** B4
Torrijos Spain **54** G5
Torrington U.S.A. **180** F4
Torroella de Montgrí Spain **55** O2
Torrön *l.* Sweden **44** K3
Torronsuon kansallispuisto *nat. park* Fin. **42** E1
Torrox Spain **54** H8
Torsa Chhu *r.* Bhutan **97** F4
Torsby Sweden **45** K3

▶**Tórshavn** Faroe Is **46** F1
Capital of the Faroe Islands. Also spelt Thorshavn.

Torsvåg Norway **44** L1
Tortilla Flat U.S.A. **183** M8
Törtköl Uzbek. *see* **Turtkul'**
Tortkuduk Kazakh. **103** H2
Tortola *i.* Virgin Is (U.K.) **187** G3
Tortoli *Sardegna* Italy **57** B9
Tortomanu Romania **58** J4
Tortona Italy **56** A4
Tortorici *Sicilia* Italy **57** G10
Tortosa Spain **55** L4
Tortuga, Laguna *l.* Mex. **185** F4
Tortuguero, Parque Nacional *nat. park* Costa Rica **186** C5
Tortum Turkey **107** E2
Ţorūd Iran **100** C3
Torugart, Pereval *pass* China/Kyrg. *see* **Turugart Pass**
Torul Turkey **107** D2
Toruń Poland **49** P2
historically known as Thorn
Tõrva Estonia **42** G3
Torvløysa *mt.* Norway **44** I3
Tory Island Rep. of Ireland **47** D8
Torysa *r.* Slovakia **49** S7
Tory Sound *sea chan.* Rep. of Ireland **47** D8
Torzhkovskaya Gryada *hills* Rus. Fed. **43** P5
Torzhok Rus. Fed. **43** P4
Tosa Japan **91** C8
Tosashimizu Japan **91** C8
Tosa-wan *b.* Japan **91** C8
Tosa-yamada Japan **91** C8
Tosbotn Norway **44** K2
Tosca S. Africa **132** H2
Tosca, Punta *pt* Mex. **184** C3
Toscana *admin. reg.* Italy **56** D5
English form Tuscany
Toscana *reg.* Italy *see* **Tuscany**
Toscano, Arcipelago *is* Italy **56** B5
Tosenfjorden *inlet* Norway **44** K2
To-shima *i.* Japan **91** F7
Tōshima-yama *mt.* Japan **90** G4
Toshkent Uzbek. *see* **Tashkent**
Toshkent Wiloyati *admin. div.* Uzbek. *see* **Tashkentskaya Oblast'**
Toshnya *r.* Rus. Fed. **43** U2
Tosno Rus. Fed. **43** L2
Toson Hu *l.* China **84** C4
Tosontsengel Mongolia **84** C1
Tossal de la Baltasana *mt.* Spain **55** M3
Tossal de l'Orri *mt.* Spain **55** M2
also spelt Tozal del Orri
Tostado Arg. **204** E3
Tõstamaa Estonia **42** E3
Tostedt Germany **48** G2
Tosya Turkey **106** C2
Toszek Poland **49** P5
Totana Spain **55** J7
Totapola *mt.* Sri Lanka **94** D5
Totaranui N.Z. **152** G8
Toteng Botswana **130** D4
Tôtes France **50** H3
Tot'ma Rus. Fed. **40** G4
Totness Suriname **199** G3
Totolapan Mex. **185** F5
Totonicapán Guat. **185** H6
Totora Bol. **200** D4
Totoral Chile **204** C2
Totoralejos Arg. **204** D3
Totoya *i.* Fiji **145** H3
Totskoye Rus. Fed. **102** C1
Tottori Japan **91** D7
Tottori *pref.* Japan **91** C7
Touârèt *well* Niger **125** G1
Touba Côte d'Ivoire **124** D4
Touba Senegal **124** B3
Toubkal, Parc National *nat. park* Morocco **122** D3
Touboro Cameroon **125** I5
Touchet *r.* U.S.A. **180** C3
Toucy France **51** J5
Toudaohu China **84** E4
Touefinna *well* Mauritania **122** B5
Touérât *well* Mali **124** E2
Toufourine *well* Mali **122** D4
Tougan Burkina **124** E3
Touggourt Alg. **123** G2
Tougouri Burkina **125** E3
Touil Mauritania **124** C3
Toukoto Mali **124** C3
Toul France **51** L4
Toulépleu Côte d'Ivoire **124** C5
Toulfé Burkina **125** E3
Touliu Taiwan **87** G4
also spelt Douliu
Toulnustouc *r.* Canada **169** G3
Toulon France **51** L9
historically known as Telo Martius
Toulon U.S.A. **174** B3
Toulouk *well* Niger **125** G2
Toulouse France **50** H9
historically known as Tolosa
Toumbélaga *well* Niger **125** G3
Toummo *well* Niger **123** I5
Toumodi Côte d'Ivoire **124** D5
Toungo Nigeria **125** I4
Toungoo Myanmar **78** B4
Toupai China **87** D3
Touques *r.* France **50** G3
Touraine *reg.* France **50** G5
Tourane Vietnam *see* **Đa Năng**
Tourassine *well* Mauritania **122** C4
Tourba Chad **120** B6
Tourgis Lake Canada **167** J1
Touriñán, Cabo *c.* Spain **54** B1
Tourlaville France **50** E3
Tour Matagrin *hill* France **51** K7
Tournai Belgium **51** J2
Tournavista Peru **200** B2
Tourndo, Oued *watercourse* Alg./Niger **123** H5
Tournon-sur-Rhône France **51** K7
Tournus France **51** K6
Touros Brazil **202** F3
Touroua Cameroon **125** I4
Tours France **50** G5
historically known as Caesarodunum *or* Turones
Tous, Embalse de *resr* Spain **55** K5
Toussiana Burkina **124** D4
Toussidé, Pic *mt.* Chad **120** C4
Toussoro, Mont *mt.* Cent. Afr. Rep. **126** D2
Toutai China **82** B3
Touws *r.* S. Africa **132** F10
Touwsrivier S. Africa **132** E10
Tõv *prov.* Mongolia **85** E2
Tovar Venez. **198** D2
Tovarkovo Rus. Fed. **43** Q7
Tovarkovskiy Rus. Fed. **43** T8
formerly known as Kaganovich
Tovarnik Croatia **56** L3
Tovil'-Dora Tajik. *see* **Tavil'dara**
Tovu Fiji **145** H3
Tovuz Azer. **107** F2
also spelt Tauz
Towada Japan **90** G4
Towada-Hachimantai National Park Japan **90** G5
Towada-ko *l.* Japan **90** G4
Towai N.Z. **152** I3
Towakaima Guyana **199** G3
Towak Mountain *hill* U.S.A. **164** C3
Towanda U.S.A. **177** I4
Towaoc U.S.A. **183** P4
Towari Indon. **75** B4
Tower U.S.A. **172** A3
Tower City U.S.A. **177** I5
Towerhill Creek *watercourse* Australia **149** E4
Towner U.S.A. **178** B1
Towns *r.* Australia **148** B2
Townsend *MA* U.S.A. **177** N3
Townsend *MT* U.S.A. **180** E3
Townshend Island Australia **149** F4
Townsville Australia **149** E3
Towori, Teluk *b.* Indon. **75** B3
Towot Sudan **128** B3
Towr Kham Afgh. **101** G3
Towson U.S.A. **177** I6
Towuti, Danau *l.* Indon. **75** B3
Toxkan He *r.* China **88** C3
Toy U.S.A. **182** F1
Toyah U.S.A. **179** B6
Tōya-ko *l.* Japan **90** G3
Toyama Japan **91** E6
Toyama *pref.* Japan **91** E6
Toyama-wan *b.* Japan **90** E6
Tōyo Japan **91** C8
Toyohashi Japan **91** E7
Toyokawa Japan **91** E7
Toyonaka Japan **83** D6
Toyooka Japan **91** D7
Toyosaka Japan **90** F6
Toyota Japan **91** E7
Toyotomi Japan **90** G2
Töysä Fin. **44** M3
Toytepa Uzbek. **103** G4
also spelt Tŭytepa
Tozal del Orri *mt.* Spain *see* **Tossal de l'Orri**
Tozanlı Turkey *see* **Almus**
Tozê Kangri *mt.* China **89** C5
Tozeur Tunisia **123** H2
Tqibuli Georgia **107** E2
also spelt Tkibuli
Tqvarch'eli Georgia **107** E2
also spelt Tkvarcheli
Trâblous Lebanon *see* **Tripoli**
Trabotivište Macedonia **58** D7
Trabzon Turkey **107** D2
English form Trebizond; *historically known as* Trapezus
Tracy *CA* U.S.A. **182** C4
Tracy *MN* U.S.A. **178** D2
Trade Lake U.S.A. **172** A5
Trading *r.* Canada **168** B3
Træna *i.* Norway **44** K2
Tranfjorden *sea chan.* Norway **44** K2
Traer U.S.A. **174** A3
Trafalgar, Cabo *c.* Spain **54** E8
Traffic Mountain Canada **166** D2
Traian Romania **58** G5
Traiguén Chile **204** B5
Trail Canada **166** G5
Traill Island Greenland *see* **Traill Ø**
Traill Ø *i.* Greenland **165** Q2
English form Traill Island
Traipu Brazil **202** E4
Traíra *r.* Brazil **198** D5
also spelt Taraíra
Trairas *r.* Brazil **206** G4
Trairi Brazil **202** E2
Traisen *r.* Austria **49** M7
Trajano de Morais Brazil **207** K9
Trajectum Neth. *see* **Utrecht**
Traka *r.* S. Africa **132** H10
Trakai Lith. **42** F7
Trakai *nat. park* Lith. **42** F7
Trakiya *reg.* Turkey *see* **Thrace**
Trakt Rus. Fed. **40** I3
Trakya *reg.* Turkey *see* **Thrace**
Tralee Rep. of Ireland **47** C11
also spelt Trá Lí
Trá Lí Rep. of Ireland *see* **Tralee**
Trá Mhór Rep. of Ireland *see* **Tramore**
Trammel U.S.A. **176** C8
Tramore Rep. of Ireland **47** E11
also spelt Trá Mhór
Tramuntana, Serra de *mts* Spain **55** N5
Tranås Sweden **45** K4
Trancas Arg. **204** D2
Trancoso Port. **54** D4
Tranebjerg Denmark **45** J5
Tranemo Sweden **45** K4
Trang Thai. **79** B7
Trangan *i.* Indon. **73** H8
Trangie Australia **147** E3
Trani Italy **56** I7
Tranoroa Madag. **131** [inset] J5
Tranqueras Uruguay **204** G3
Transantarctic Mountains Antarctica **223** K2
Trans Canada Highway Canada **167** H5
Transcona Canada **167** L5
Transtrand Sweden **45** K3
Transylvanian Alps *mts* Romania **58** D3
also known as Carpații Meridionali
Transylvanian Basin *plat.* Romania **58** F2
also known as Podișul Transilvaniei
Tra Ôn Vietnam **79** D6
Trapani *Sicilia* Italy **57** E10
Trapezus Turkey *see* **Trabzon**
Trapper Peak U.S.A. **180** D3
Trappes France **51** I4
Trapua *r.* Brazil **203** A9
Traralgon Australia **147** E4
Traras, Monts des *mts* Alg. **55** J9
Trarza *admin. reg.* Mauritania **124** B2
Trascăului, Munții *mts* Romania **58** E2
Trashigang Bhutan **97** F4
also spelt Tashigang
Trasimeno, Lago *l.* Italy **56** E5
Trás-os-Montes *reg.* Port. **54** D3
Trasvase, Canal de Spain **55** I5
Trasvase Tajo-Segura, Canal de Spain **55** I5
Trat Thai. **79** C5
Traun Austria **49** L7
Traun *r.* Austria **49** L7
Traunreut Germany **49** J8
Traunsee *l.* Austria **49** K8
Traunstein Germany **49** J8
Traupis Lith. **42** F6
Trave *r.* Germany **48** H2
Travellers Lake *imp. l.* Australia **147** D3
Traverse City U.S.A. **172** H6
Travesía Puntana *des.* Arg. **204** D4
Travesía Tunuyán *des.* Arg. **204** D4
Travessão Brazil **207** L8
Tra Vinh Vietnam **79** D6
formerly known as Phu Vinh
Travis, Lake U.S.A. **179** C6
Travnik Bos.-Herz. **56** J4
Trbovlje Slovenia **56** H2
Trebević *nat. park* Bos.-Herz. **56** K5
Trebel *r.* Germany **49** K2
Trèbes France **51** I9
Třebíč Czech Rep. **49** M6
Trebinje Bos.-Herz. **56** K6
Trebisacce Italy **57** I9
Trebišnjica *r.* Bos.-Herz. **56** J6
Trebišov Slovakia **49** S7
Trebižat *r.* Bos.-Herz. **56** J5
Trebizond Turkey *see* **Trabzon**
Trebnje Slovenia **56** H3
Třeboň Czech Rep. **49** L6
Tree *r.* Canada **167** I1
Tree Island India **94** B4
Treene *r.* Germany **48** G1
Trefaldwyn U.K. *see* **Montgomery**
Trefynwy U.K. *see* **Monmouth**
Tregosse Islets and Reefs Australia **149** F3
Tréguier France **50** H7
Treinta y Tres Uruguay **204** G4
Trelew Arg. **205** D6
Trelleborg Sweden **45** K5
Trélon France **51** K2
Trem *mt.* Yugo. **58** D5
Tremblant, Mont *hill* Canada **169** F4
Trembleur Lake Canada **166** E4
Tremiti, Isole *is* Italy **56** H6
Tremlya *r.* Belarus **43** K9
Tremont U.S.A. **177** I5
Tremonton U.S.A. **180** D4
Tremp Spain **55** L2
Trempealeau *r.* U.S.A. **172** B6
Trenche *r.* Canada **169** F4
Trenčín Slovakia **49** P7
Trenggalek Indon. **77** E5
Trengganu *state* Malaysia *see* **Terengganu**
Trenque Lauquén Arg. **204** E4
Trent Italy *see* **Trento**
Trent *r.* U.K. **47** L10
Trentino - Alto Adige *admin. reg.* Italy **56** D2
Trento Italy **56** D2
English form Trent; *historically known as* Tridentum
Trenton Canada **168** E4
Trenton *FL* U.S.A. **175** D6
Trenton *GA* U.S.A. **174** C5
Trenton *MO* U.S.A. **174** A3
Trenton *NC* U.S.A. **174** E5
Trenton *NE* U.S.A. **178** B3

▶**Trenton** *NJ* U.S.A. **177** K5
State capital of New Jersey.

Trenton *TN* U.S.A. **174** B5
Trepang Bay Australia **148** A1
Trepassey Canada **169** K4
Tres Arboles Uruguay **204** F4
Tres Arroyos Arg. **204** E5
Tres Cerros Arg. **205** D8
Três Corações Brazil **203** C7
Tres Cruces Arg. **200** D5
Tres Cruces Chile **204** C3
Tres Esquinas Col. **198** C4
Tres Forcas, Cabo *c.* Morocco *see* **Trois Fourches, Cap des**
Três Irmãos, Represa *resr* Brazil **206** C7
Tres Isletas Arg. **204** E2
Treska *r.* Macedonia **58** C6
Treski Estonia **42** I4
Três Lagoas Brazil **206** B7
Tres Lagos Arg. **205** C8
Tres Lomas Arg. **204** E5
Três Marias Brazil **207** H5
Três Marias, Represa *resr* Brazil **203** C6
Tres Matas Venez. **199** E2
Tres Montes, Península *pen.* Chile **205** B7
Tres Picachos, Sierra *mts* Mex. **181** F7
Tres Picos *mt.* Arg. **205** C6
Tres Picos Mex. **185** G6
Tres Picos, Cerro *mt.* Arg. **204** E5
Tres Picos, Cerro *mt.* Mex. **185** G5
Tres Piedras U.S.A. **181** F5
Tres Pinos U.S.A. **182** C5
Três Pontas Brazil **203** C7
Tres Puentes Chile **204** C2
Tres Puntas, Cabo *c.* Arg. **205** D7
Três Ranchos Brazil **206** F5
Três Rios Brazil **203** D7
Třešť Czech Rep. **49** M6
Trestino Rus. Fed. **43** O4
Trestna Rus. Fed. **43** R4
Três Unidos Brazil **198** D6
Tres Zapotes *tourist site* Mex. **185** G5
Tretten Norway **45** J3
Treuchtlingen Germany **48** H7
Treuenbrietzen Germany **49** J3
Treungen Norway **45** J4
Trevelín Arg. **205** C6
Treves Germany *see* **Trier**
Trevi Italy **56** E6
Treviglio Italy **56** B3
Treviso Italy **56** E3
historically known as Tarvisium
Trevose Head U.K. **47** G13
Trgovište *Srbija* Yugo. **58** D6
Triabunna Australia **147** E5
Tri An, Hồ *resr* Vietnam **79** D6
Triánda Greece *see* **Trianta**
Triangle U.S.A. **177** H7
Tria Nisia *i.* Greece **59** H12
Trianta Greece **59** J12
also spelt Triánda
Tribal Areas *admin. div.* Pak. **101** G3
Tribeč *mts* Slovakia **49** P7
Tri Brata, Gora *hill* Rus. Fed. **82** F1
Tribune U.S.A. **178** B4
Tricarico Italy **57** I8
Tricase Italy **57** K9
Trichinopoly India *see* **Tiruchchirappalli**
Trichonida, Limni *l.* Greece **59** C10
Trichur India **94** C4
also known as Thrissur
Trida Australia **147** E3
Tridentum Italy *see* **Trento**
Trier Germany **48** D6
historically known as Augusta Treverorum *or* Treves
Trieste Italy **56** F3
historically known as Tergeste
Trieste, Golfo di *g.* Europe *see* **Trieste, Gulf of**
Trieste, Gulf of Europe **56** F3
also known as Trieste, Golfo di
Trie-sur-Baïse France **50** G9
Trieux *r.* France **50** C4
Triggiano Italy **56** I7
Triglavski Narodni Park *nat. park* Slovenia **56** F2
Trigno *r.* Italy **56** G6
Trikala Greece **59** C9
also spelt Tríkkala
Tríkkala Greece *see* **Trikala**
Trikomo Cyprus *see* **Trikomon**
Trikomon Cyprus **108** E2
also known as Trikomo *or* İskele

▶**Trikora, Puncak** *mt.* Indon. **73** I7
2nd highest mountain in Oceania.
oceania [landscapes] ▶▶ 136–137

Trikorfa *mt.* Greece **59** D10
Trilj Croatia **56** I5
Trim Rep. of Ireland **47** F10
Trincheras Mex. **184** C2
Trincomalee Sri Lanka **94** D4
Trindade Brazil **206** D3
Trindade, Ilha da *i.* S. Atlantic Ocean **217** L7
Tringia *mt.* Greece **59** C9
Trinidad Bol. **200** D3
Trinidad Cuba **186** D2
Trinidad *i.* Trin. and Tob. **187** H5
Trinidad Uruguay **204** F4
Trinidad U.S.A. **181** F5
Trinidad, Golfo *b.* Chile **205** B8
▶**Trinidad and Tobago** *country* West Indies **187** H5
northamerica [countries] ▶▶ 158–159
Trinitapoli Italy **56** I7
Trinity U.S.A. **179** D6
Trinity *r. CA* U.S.A. **182** A1
Trinity *r. TX* U.S.A. **179** D6
Trinity, West Fork *r.* U.S.A. **179** C5

Trinity Bay Australia 149 E3
Trinity Bay Canada 169 K4
Trinity Dam U.S.A. 182 B1
Trinity Islands U.S.A. 164 D4
Trinity Range mts U.S.A. 182 E1
Trinkat Island India 95 G4
Trinkitat Sudan 104 B4
Trino Italy 56 A3
Trinway U.S.A. 176 C5
Trionto, Capo c. Italy 57 I9
Tripa r. Indon. 76 B2
Tripoli Greece 59 D11
also known as Tripolis
Tripoli Lebanon 108 G3
also known as Trâblous; historically known as Tripolis

Tripoli Libya 120 B1
Capital of Libya. Also known as Țarābulus; historically known as Oea.

Tripolis Greece see Tripoli
Tripolis Lebanon see Tripoli
Tripolitania reg. Libya 120 B2
Tripunittura India 94 C4
Tripura state India 97 F5
Trischen i. Germany 48 F1

Tristan da Cunha i. S. Atlantic Ocean 217 N8
Dependency of St Helena.

Tristao, Îles is Guinea 124 B4
Trisul mt. India 96 C3
Triton Canada 169 K3
Triton Island atoll Paracel Is 72 D3
Triunfo Pernambuco Brazil 202 E3
Triunfo Rondônia Brazil 200 D2
Triunfo Hond. 186 B4
Trivandrum India 94 C4
also spelt Thiruvananthapuram
Trivento Italy 56 G7
Trizina Greece 59 E11
Trnava Slovakia 49 O7
Trobriand Islands P.N.G. 145 E2
also known as Kiriwina Islands
Trofa Port. 54 C3
Trofaiach Austria 49 M8
Trofors Norway 44 K2
Trogir Croatia 56 I5
Troglav mt. Croatia 56 I5
Troina Sicilia Italy 57 G11
Troisdorf Germany 48 E5
Trois Fourches, Cap des c. Morocco 123 E2
also known as Tres Forcas, Cabo or Uarc, Ras
Trois-Pistoles Canada 169 G3
Trois-Rivières Canada 169 F4
Troitsa Rus. Fed. 38 G3
Troitsk Chelyabinskaya Oblast' Rus. Fed. 38 G4
Troitsk Moskovskaya Oblast' Rus. Fed. 43 S6
formerly known as Troitskiy
Troitskiy Rus. Fed. see Troitsk
Troitsko-Pechorsk Rus. Fed. 40 K3
Troitskoye Khabarovskiy Kray Rus. Fed. 82 E2
Troitskoye Orenburgskaya Oblast' Rus. Fed. 102 C1
Troitskoye Respublika Bashkortostan Rus. Fed. 102 D1
Troitskoye Respublika Kalmykiya - Khalm'g-Tangch Rus. Fed. 41 H7
Trolla well Chad 120 B6
Trollhättan Sweden 45 K4
Trollheimen park Norway 44 J3
Trombetas r. Brazil 199 G5
Tromelin, Île i. Indian Ocean 218 K7
English form Tromelin Island
Tromelin Island Indian Ocean see Tromelin, Île
Tromelin Island Micronesia see Fais
Tromen, Volcán vol. Arg. 204 C5
Trompsburg S. Africa 133 J7
Troms county Norway 44 L1
Tromsø Norway 44 L1
Trona U.S.A. 183 G6
Tronador, Monte mt. Arg. 204 C6
Tronçais, Forêt de for. France 51 I6
Trondheim Norway 44 J3
Trondheimsfjorden sea chan. Norway 44 J3
Trondheimsleia sea chan. Norway 44 J3
Trongsa Bhutan 97 F4
also spelt Tongsa
Trongsa Chhu r. Bhutan 97 F4
also known as Mangde Chhu
Tronto r. Italy 56 F6
Troödos, Mount Cyprus 108 D3
Troödos Mountains Cyprus 108 D3
Troon U.K. 46 H8
Tropaia Greece 59 C11
Troparevo Rus. Fed. 43 Q6
Tropas r. Brazil 199 G6
Tropea Italy 57 H10
Tropeiros, Serra dos hills Brazil 202 C5
Tropic U.S.A. 183 L4
Trosh Rus. Fed. 40 J2
Trosna Rus. Fed. 43 Q9
Trostan' Rus. Fed. 43 N9
Trostan hill U.K. 47 F8
Trostberg Germany 49 J7
Trotuș r. Romania 58 H2
Trout r. B.C. Canada 166 E3
Trout r. N.W.T. Canada 166 G2
Trout Creek Canada 173 N5
Trout Creek U.S.A. 172 D4
Trout Dale U.S.A. 176 D9
Trout Lake Alta Canada 167 H3
Trout Lake N.W.T. Canada 166 F2
Trout Lake l. N.W.T. Canada 166 F2
Trout Lake l. Ont. Canada 167 M5
Trout Lake U.S.A. 172 D4
Trout Lake l. U.S.A. 172 D4
Trout Run U.S.A. 177 H4
Troutville U.S.A. 176 F8
Trowbridge U.K. 47 J12
Trowutta Australia 147 E5
Troy tourist site Turkey 106 A3
also known as Truva; historically known as Ilium
Troy AL U.S.A. 175 C6
Troy KS U.S.A. 178 D4
Troy MI U.S.A. 173 J8
Troy MO U.S.A. 174 B4
Troy NC U.S.A. 174 E5
Troy NH U.S.A. 177 M3
Troy NY U.S.A. 177 L3
Troy OH U.S.A. 176 A5
Troy PA U.S.A. 177 I4
Troyan Bulg. 58 F6
Troyekurovo Lipetskaya Oblast' Rus. Fed. 43 T9
Troyekurovo Lipetskaya Oblast' Rus. Fed. 43 U8
Troyes France 51 K4
Troy Lake U.S.A. 183 H7
Troy Peak U.S.A. 183 I3
Trstenik Srbija Yugo. 58 C5
Trubchevsk Rus. Fed. 43 O9
Trubetchino Rus. Fed. 43 U9
Trubia r. Spain 54 F1
Truc Giang Vietnam see Bên Tre
Trucial Coast country Asia see United Arab Emirates
Trucial States country Asia see United Arab Emirates
Truckee U.S.A. 182 D2
Trud Rus. Fed. 43 O4
Trudovoy Kazakh. see Kuybyshevskiy
Trudovoy Rus. Fed. see Yusta
Trudovoye Rus. Fed. 82 D4
Trudy r. Rus. Fed. 43 S9
Truer Range hills Australia 148 A4
Trufanovo Rus. Fed. 40 H2
Trujillo Hond. 186 B4
Trujillo Peru 200 A2
Trujillo Spain 54 F5
Trujillo Venez. 198 D2
Trujillo state Venez. 198 D2
Trujillo, Monte mt. Dom. Rep. see Duarte, Pico
Trumann U.S.A. 174 B5
Trumansburg U.S.A. 177 I3
Trumbull U.S.A. 177 L4
Trumbull, Mount U.S.A. 183 K5
Trumon Indon. 76 B2
Trŭn Bulg. 58 D6
Trun France 50 G4
Trŭna mt. Bulg. 58 E6
Trung Khanh Vietnam 78 D3
Truong Sa is S. China Sea see Spratly Islands
Truro Canada 169 I4
Truro U.K. 47 G13
Trusan Sarawak Malaysia 77 F1
Trusan r. Sarawak Malaysia 77 F1
Truskmore hill Rep. of Ireland 47 D9
Trus Madi, Gunung mt. Sabah Malaysia 77 G1
Trŭstenik Bulg. 58 F5
Trutch Canada 166 F3
Trutch Creek r. Canada 166 F3
Truth or Consequences U.S.A. 181 F6
formerly known as Hot Springs
Trutnov Czech Rep. 49 M5
Truva tourist site Turkey see Troy
Truyère r. France 51 I8
Truzhenik Rus. Fed. 43 Q3
Tryavna Bulg. 58 G6
Tryon U.S.A. 178 B3
Trypiti, Akra pt Kriti Greece 59 F13
Trypiti, Akra pt Greece 59 F9
Trysil Norway 45 K3
Trysilelva r. Norway 45 K3
Trysilfjellet mt. Norway 45 K3
Tryškiai Lith. 42 D5
Tržac Bos.-Herz. 56 H4
Trzcianka Poland 49 N2
Trzebiatów Poland 49 M1
Trzebinia Poland 49 Q5
Trzebnica Poland 49 O4
Trzemeszno Poland 49 O3
Tržič Slovenia 56 G2
Trzrciński-Zdrój Poland 49 L3
Tsagaannuur Bayan-Ölgiy Mongolia 84 A1
Tsagaannuur Dornod Mongolia 85 H2
Tsagaan Nuur salt l. Mongolia 84 B2
Tsagaan-Olom Mongolia 84 C2
Tsagaan Ovoo Mongolia 85 G1
Tsagaan-Ovoo Mongolia 84 D2
Tsagaan-Uul Mongolia see Sharga
Tsagan Aman Rus. Fed. 102 A3
formerly known as Burunniy
Tsagan Khurtey, Khrebet mts Rus. Fed. 85 F1
Tsagan-Nur Rus. Fed. 41 H7
Tsaidam Basin China see Qaidam Pendi
Tsåktso mt. Sweden 44 M1
Tsalenjikha Georgia 107 E2
Tsama I Congo 126 B5
Tsangatjåkkå mt. Sweden 44 K2
Tsao Botswana 130 D4
Tsaratanana, Massif du mts Madag. 131 [inset] K2
Tsarevo Bulg. 58 I6
formerly known as Michurin
Tsarevo-Zaymishche Rus. Fed. 43 P6
Tsaribrod Srbija Yugo. see Dimitrovgrad
Tsarimir Bulg. 58 F6
Tsaritsyn Rus. Fed. see Volgograd
Tsatsana mt. S. Africa 133 M7
Tsat Tsze Mui pt Hong Kong China see North Point
Tsaukaib Namibia 130 B5
Tsavo East National Park Kenya 128 C5
Tsavo West National Park Kenya 129 C5
Tsazo S. Africa 133 L8
Tsebanana Botswana 131 E3
Tseel Mongolia 84 B2
Tsefat Israel see Zefat
Tselina Rus. Fed. 41 G7
Tselinnyy Rus. Fed. 103 E2
Tselinograd Kazakh. see Astana
Tselinogradskaya Oblast' admin. div. Kazakh. see Akmolinskaya Oblast'
Tsementnyy Rus. Fed. see Fokino
Tsengel Mongolia 84 D1
Tsenogora Rus. Fed. 40 H2
Tsentralen Balkan nat. park Bulg. 58 F6
Tsentral'nyy Kirovskaya Oblast' Rus. Fed. 40 I4
Tsentral'nyy Rus. Fed. see Radovitskiy
Tsentral'nyy Ryazanskaya Oblast' Rus. Fed. 43 U8
Tserkovishche Rus. Fed. 43 L6
Tserovo Bulg. 58 E5
Tses Namibia 130 C5
Tsetsegnuur Mongolia 84 B2
Tsetseng Botswana 130 D4
Tsetserleg Mongolia 84 D2
Tsetserleg Mongolia see Halban
Tsévié Togo 125 F5
Tshabong Botswana 130 D5
Tshad country Africa see Chad
Tshchikskoye Vodokhranilishche resr Rus. Fed. 41 F7
Tshela Dem. Rep. Congo 126 B6
Tshene Dem. Rep. Congo 126 C6
Tshibala Dem. Rep. Congo 127 D6
Tshibuka Dem. Rep. Congo 127 D6
Tshibwika Dem. Rep. Congo 127 D7
Tshidilamolomo Botswana 133 I2
Tshikapa Dem. Rep. Congo 127 D6
Tshikapa r. Dem. Rep. Congo 127 D6
Tshilenge Dem. Rep. Congo 127 D6
Tshimbulu Dem. Rep. Congo 127 D6
Tshing S. Africa 133 K3
Tshipise S. Africa 131 F4
Tshiumbe r. Angola/Dem. Rep. Congo 127 D6
Tshofa Dem. Rep. Congo 127 E6
Tshokwane S. Africa 133 P1
Tsholotsho Zimbabwe 131 E3
formerly spelt Tjolotjo
Tshootsha Botswana 130 D4
Tshuapa r. Dem. Rep. Congo 126 D5
Tshumbiri Dem. Rep. Congo 126 C5
Tsiazonano mt. Madag. 131 [inset] J3
Tsibritsa r. Bulg. 58 E5
Tsiigehtchic Canada 164 F3
formerly known as Arctic Red River
Tsil'ma r. Rus. Fed. 40 I2
Tsimkavichy Belarus 42 H8
also spelt Timkovichi
Tsimlyansk Rus. Fed. 41 G7
Tsimlyanskoye Vodokhranilishche resr Rus. Fed. 41 G7
Tsinan China see Jinan
Tsineng S. Africa 132 H4
Tsinghai prov. China see Qinghai
Tsing Shan hill Hong Kong China see Castle Peak
Tsing Shan Wan b. Hong Kong China see Castle Peak Bay
Tsing Shui Wan b. Hong Kong China see Clear Water Bay
Tsingtao China see Qingdao
Tsingy de Bemaraha, Réserve nature res. Madag. 131 [inset] J3
Tsing Yi i. Hong Kong China 87 [inset]
Tsining China see Jining
Tsinjomay mt. Madag. 131 [inset] J3
Tsintsabis Namibia 130 C3
Tsiombe Madag. 131 [inset] J5
Tsiroanomandidy Madag. 131 [inset] J3
Tsiteli Tskaro Georgia see Dedop'listsqaro
Tsitondroina Madag. 131 [inset] J4
Tsitsihar China see Qiqihar
Tsitsikamma Forest and Coastal National Park S. Africa 132 H11
Tsitsutl Peak Canada 166 E4
Tsivil'sk Rus. Fed. 40 H5
Tskhakaia Georgia see Senaki
Tskhaltubo Georgia see Tsqaltubo
Ts'khinvali Georgia 107 E2
formerly known as Staliniri
Tsna r. Belarus 42 I9
Tsna r. Rus. Fed. 41 G5
Tsna r. Rus. Fed. 43 P4
Tsna r. Rus. Fed. 43 U6
Tsnori Georgia 107 F2
Tsodilo Hills Botswana 130 D3
Tsolo S. Africa 133 M8
Tsomo S. Africa 133 L9
Tsomo r. S. Africa 133 L9
Tso Morari Lake Jammu and Kashmir 96 C2
Tson r. Rus. Fed. 43 R9
Tsona China see Cona
Tsopan hill Greece 58 G8
Tsqaltubo Georgia 107 E2
also spelt Tskhaltubo
Tsu Japan 91 E7
Tsubame Japan 90 F6
Tsubata Japan 91 E6
Tsubetsu Japan 90 I3
Tsuchiura Japan 91 G6
Tsuen Wan Hong Kong China 87 [inset]
also known as Quanwan
Tsugarū-kaikyō strait Japan 90 G4
English form Tsugaru Strait
Tsugaru Strait Japan see Tsugarū-kaikyō
Tsukigata Japan 90 G3
Tsukuba Japan 91 G6
Tsukumi Japan 91 B8
Tsul-Ulaan Mongolia 84 E2
Tsumeb Namibia 130 C3
Tsumis Park Namibia 130 C4
Tsumkwe Namibia 130 D3
Tsuno-shima i. Japan 91 B7
Tsuru Japan 91 F7
Tsuruga Japan 91 E7
Tsurugi-san mt. Japan 91 D8
Tsurukhaytuy Rus. Fed. see Priargunsk
Tsuruoka Japan 90 F5
Tsushima Japan 91 E7
Tsushima is Japan 91 A7
Tsushima-kaikyō strait Japan/S. Korea see Korea Strait
Tsuyama Japan 91 D7
Tsvetino Bulg. 58 E7
Tswaane Botswana 130 D4
Tswaraganang S. Africa 133 J5
Tswelelang S. Africa 133 J4
Tsyelyakhany Belarus 42 G9
also spelt Telekhany
Tsyerakhowka Belarus 43 M9
Ts'yl-os Provincial Park Canada 166 E5
Tsyomny Lyes Belarus 43 M7
Tsyp-Navolok Rus. Fed. 44 P1
Tsyurupyns'k Ukr. 41 E7
formerly known as Aleshki or Oleshky
Tthenaagoo Canada see Nahanni Butte
Tua r. Port. 54 D3
Tua, Tanjung pt Indon. 77 D4
Tuakau N.Z. 152 I5
Tual Indon. 73 H8
Tuam Rep. of Ireland 47 D10
Tuamarina N.Z. 152 H9
Tuamotu, Archipel des is Fr. Polynesia see Tuamotu Islands
Tuamotu Archipelago is Fr. Polynesia see Tuamotu Islands
Tuamotu Islands Fr. Polynesia 221 I6
English form Tuamotu Archipelago; also known as Tuamotu, Archipel des; formerly known as Paumotu, Îles
Tuân Giao Vietnam 78 C3
Tuangku i. Indon. 76 B2
Tuapeka Mouth N.Z. 153 D14
Tuapse Rus. Fed. 41 F7
Tuaran Sabah Malaysia 77 G1
Tuas Sing. 76 [inset]
Tuatapere N.Z. 153 B14
Tuath, Loch a' b. U.K. see Broad Bay
Tuba City U.S.A. 183 M5
Tubalai i. Indon. 75 D3
Tuban Indon. 77 F4
Tubarão Brazil 203 B9
Tūbās West Bank 108 G5
Tubau Sarawak Malaysia 77 F2
Tubbataha Reefs Phil. 74 A4
Tubeya Dem. Rep. Congo 127 D6
Tubigan i. Phil. 74 B5
Tübingen Germany 48 G7
Tubinskiy Rus. Fed. 102 D1
Tubmanburg Liberia 124 C5
Tubo r. Nigeria 125 G4
Tubod Phil. 74 B4
Tubou Fiji 145 H3
also spelt Tumbou
Tubruq Libya 120 D1
English form Tobruk
Tubu r. Indon. 77 G2
Tubuai i. Fr. Polynesia 221 I7
Tubuai Islands Fr. Polynesia 221 H7
also known as Australes, Îles
Tubutama Mex. 184 C2
Tucanderra Brazil 199 F5
Tucannon r. U.S.A. 180 C3
Tucano Brazil 202 E4
Tucavaca Bol. 201 F4
Tucavaca r. Bol. 201 F4
Tuchitua Canada 166 D2
Tuchkovo Rus. Fed. 43 R6
Tuchodi r. Canada 166 F3
Tuchola Poland 49 O2
Tuchów Poland 49 S6
Tuckanarra Australia 151 B5
Tucker Glacier Antarctica 223 L2
Tuckerton U.S.A. 177 K6
Tucson U.S.A. 183 N9
Tucson Mountains U.S.A. 183 M9
Tuctuc r. Canada 169 H1
Tucumán Arg. see San Miguel de Tucumán
Tucumán prov. Arg. 204 D2
Tucumcari U.S.A. 179 B5
Tucunuco Arg. 204 C3
Tucuparé Brazil 199 H6
Tucupita Venez. 199 F2
Tucuracas Col. 198 C2
Tucuruí Brazil 202 B2
Tucuruí, Represa resr Brazil 202 B3
Tuczno Poland 49 N2
Tudela Spain 55 J2
also spelt Tutera
Tudela de Duero Spain 54 G3
Tuder Italy see Todi
Tudor Vladimirescu Romania 58 I3
Tudovka r. Rus. Fed. 43 O5
Tudu Estonia 42 H2
Tudulinna Estonia 42 I2
Tuen Mun Hong Kong China 87 [inset]
Tuensang India 97 G4
Tueré r. Brazil 199 I5
Tuerto r. Spain 50 A10
Tufanovo Rus. Fed. 43 V3
Tufayh Saudi Arabia 105 E2
Tufi P.N.G. 145 D2
Tugela r. S. Africa 133 P6
Tugela Ferry S. Africa 133 O5
Tūghyl Kazakh. see Tugyl
Tuglung China 89 F6
Tugnug Point Phil. 74 C4
Tuguancun China 86 B3
Tuguegarao Phil. 74 B2
Tugur Rus. Fed. 82 E1
Tugurskiy Zaliv b. Rus. Fed. 82 E1
Tugwi r. Zimbabwe 131 F4
formerly spelt Tokwe
Tugyl Kazakh. 88 D2
also spelt Tūghyl; formerly known as Priozernyy
Tuhai r. China 85 H4
Tuhemberua Indon. 76 B2
Tui Spain 54 C2
also spelt Túy
Tuichi r. Bol. 200 D3
Tuilianpui r. Bangl./India 97 G5
Tuinplaas S. Africa 133 M1
Tuins watercourse S. Africa 132 E6
Tūja Latvia 42 F4
Tujiabu China see Yongxiu
Tujuh, Kepulauan is Indon. 77 D3
Tukan Rus. Fed. 102 D1
Tukangbesi, Kepulauan is Indon. 75 B4
Tukangbesi Marine Reserve nature res. Indon. 75 B4
Tukarak Island Canada 168 E1
Tukayel Eth. 128 E2
Tûkh Egypt 108 C7
Tukhavichy Belarus 42 G9
Tŭkhtamish Tajik. 101 H2
also spelt Tokhtamysh
Tukituki r. N.Z. 152 K7
Tūkrah Libya 120 D1
Tuktoyaktuk Canada 164 F3
formerly known as Fort Brabant
Tuktut Nogait National Park Canada 164 G3
Tukums Latvia 42 E5
Tukung, Bukit mt. Indon. 77 E3
Tukuringra, Khrebet mts Rus. Fed. 82 B1
Tukuyu Tanz. 129 B7
Tula watercourse Kenya 128 C5
Tula Mex. 185 F4
Tula Rus. Fed. 43 S7
Tulach Mhór Rep. of Ireland see Tullamore
Tulagt Ar Gol r. China 89 F4
Tulai China 84 C4
Tulai Nanshan mts China 84 C4
Tulai Shan mts China 84 C4
Tulak Afgh. 101 E3
Tula Mountains Antarctica 223 D2
Tulancingo Mex. 185 F4
Tulangbawang r. Indon. 76 D4
Tula Oblast admin. div. Rus. Fed. see Tul'skaya Oblast'
Tulare U.S.A. 182 E5
Tulare Lake Bed U.S.A. 182 E6
Tularosa U.S.A. 181 F6
Tulasi mt. India 94 D2
Tulcán Ecuador 198 B4
Tulcea Romania 58 J3
Tul'chin Ukr. see Tul'chyn
Tul'chyn Ukr. 41 D6
also spelt Tul'chin
Tule r. U.S.A. 182 E5
Tulé Venez. 187 E5
Tuléar Madag. see Toliara
Tulehu Indon. 75 D3
Tulelake U.S.A. 180 B4
Tule Mod China 85 I2
Tulghes Romania 58 G2
Tulia U.S.A. 179 B5
Tulihe China 85 I1
Tuliszków Poland 49 P3
Tulít'a Canada 166 E1
formerly known as Fort Norman
Tuljapur India 94 C2
Tulkarm West Bank see Ţūlkarm
Ţūlkarm West Bank 108 G5
English form Tulkarm
Tullahoma U.S.A. 174 C5
Tullamore Australia 147 E3
Tullamore Rep. of Ireland 47 E10
also spelt Tulach Mhór
Tulle France 50 H7
Tullibigeal Australia 147 E3
Tulln Austria 49 N7
Tullow Rep. of Ireland 47 F11
Tully Australia 149 E3
Tully Falls Australia 149 E3
Tulnici Romania 58 H3
Tuloma r. Rus. Fed. 44 P1
Tulos Rus. Fed. 44 O3
Tulppio Fin. 44 O2
Tulsa U.S.A. 179 D4
Tulsequah Canada 166 C3
Tulsipur Nepal 97 D3
Tul'skaya Oblast' admin. div. Rus. Fed. 43 S8
English form Tula Oblast
Tul'skiy Kazakh. 103 H1
Tuluá Col. 198 B3
Tulucești Romania 58 J3
Tuluksak U.S.A. 164 C3
Tulūl al Ashāqif hills Jordan 109 I5
Tulūl ar Ruḩayl hills Saudi Arabia 109 K6
Tulum tourist site Mex. 185 I4
Tulun Rus. Fed. 80 G2
Tulungagung Indon. 77 E5
Tulu-Tuloi, Serra hills Brazil 199 F4
Tulu Welel mt. Eth. 128 B2
Tulva r. Rus. Fed. 40 J4
Tuma Rus. Fed. 40 G5
Tumaco Col. 198 B4
Tumahole S. Africa 133 L3
Tumain China 89 E5
Tumak Rus. Fed. 102 B3
Tūmān Āqā Iran 101 E3
Tuman-gang r. Asia see Tumen Jiang
Tumannaya r. Asia see Tumen Jiang
Tumannyy Rus. Fed. 40 E1
Tumanovo Rus. Fed. 43 P6
Tumanskiy Rus. Fed. 39 R3
Tumasik Sing. see Singapore
Tumatumari Guyana 199 G3
Tumazy Rus. Fed. 43 P1
Tumba Sweden 45 L4
Tumbangmiri Indon. 77 F3
Tumbangsamba Indon. 77 F3
Tumbangtiti Indon. 77 E3
Tumbao Phil. 74 C5
Tumbarumba Australia 147 F3
Tumbes Peru 198 A5
Tumbes dept Peru 198 A5
Tumbiscatio Mex. 185 E5
Tumbler Ridge Canada 166 F4
Tumbou Fiji see Tubou
Tumby Bay Australia 146 C3
Tumcha r. Fin./Rus. Fed. 44 O2
Tumd Youqi China see Salaqi
Tumd Zuoqi China see Qasq
Tumen Jilin China 82 C4
Tumen Shaanxi China 87 D1
Tumen Jiang r. Asia 82 C4
also known as Tuman-gang or Tumannaya
Tumeremo Venez. 199 F3
Tumereng Guyana 199 F3
Tumindao i. Phil. 74 A5
Tumiritinga Brazil 203 D6
Tumkur India 94 C3
Tumlingtar Nepal 97 E4
Tummo, Mountains of Libya/Niger 120 B4
Tumnin r. Rus. Fed. 82 F2
Tump Pak. 101 E5
Tumpah Indon. 77 F3
Tumpôr, Phnum mt. Cambodia 79 C5
Tumpu, Gunung mt. Indon. 75 B3
Tumputiga, Gunung mt. Indon. 75 B3
Tumsar India 96 C5
Tumshuk Uzbek. 103 F5
Tumu Ghana 125 E4
Tumucumaque, Serra hills Brazil 199 G4
Tumudibandh India 95 D2
Tumupasa Bol. 200 D3
Tumur Kazakh. 103 G4
also spelt Temir; formerly spelt Timur
Tumusla Bol. 200 D5
Tumut Australia 147 F3
Tumutuk Rus. Fed. 40 J5
Tumxuk China 88 C3
Tuna Ghana 124 E4
Tunapuna Trin. and Tob. 187 H5
Tunas de Zaza Cuba 186 D2
Ţunb al Kubrá i. The Gulf see Greater Tunb
Ţunb aş Şughrá i. The Gulf see Lesser Tunb
Tunbridge Wells, Royal U.K. 47 M12
Tunçbilek Turkey 59 K9
Tunceli Turkey 107 D3
Tuncurry Australia 147 G3
Tundla India 89 B7
Tundubai well Sudan 121 F5
Tunduma Tanz. 129 B7
Tunduru Tanz. 129 C7
Tundzha r. Bulg. 58 H7
Tunes Tunisia see Tunis
Tunga Nigeria 125 H4
Tungabhadra r. India 94 C3
Tungabhadra Reservoir India 94 C3
Tungawan Phil. 74 B5
Tungdor China see Mainling
Tungi Bangl. 97 F5
also spelt Tongi
Tungku Sabah Malaysia 77 G1
Tungla Nicaragua 186 B4
Tung Lung Chau i. Hong Kong China see Tung Lung Island
Tung Lung Island Hong Kong China 87 [inset]
also known as Tung Lung Chau
Tungnaá r. Iceland 44 [inset] C2
Tungor Rus. Fed. 82 F1
Tungozero Rus. Fed. 44 O2
Tung Pok Liu Hoi Hap sea chan. Hong Kong China see East Lamma Channel
Tungsten Canada 166 D2
Tungun, Bukit mt. Indon. 77 F2
Tungurahua prov. Ecuador 198 B5
Tung Wan b. Hong Kong China 87 [inset]
Tuni India 95 D2
Tunica U.S.A. 174 B5
Tunis Canada 173 M2

Tunis Tunisia 123 H1
Capital of Tunisia. Historically known as Tunes.

Tunis, Golfe de g. Tunisia 123 H1
Tunisia country Africa 123 H2
spelt At Tūnisīyah in Arabic; historically known as Africa Nova
africa [countries] 114–117
Tunja Col. 198 C3
Tunkhannock U.S.A. 177 J4
Tunki Nicaragua 186 B4
Tunkinskiye Gol'tsy mts Rus. Fed. 84 D1
Tunliu China 85 G4
Tunnel City U.S.A. 172 C6
Tunnelton U.S.A. 176 F6
Tunnsjøen l. Norway 44 K2
Tunoshna Rus. Fed. 43 V4
Tuntsa Fin. 44 O2
Tunulic r. Canada 169 H1
Tununak U.S.A. 164 C3
Tunungayualok Island Canada 169 I1
Tunuyán Arg. 204 C4
Tunuyán r. Arg. 204 D4
Tunxi China see Huangshan
Tuodian China see Shuangbai
Tuo He r. China 87 F1
Tuojiang China see Fenghuang
Tuojiang China see Shuikou
Tuo Jiang r. China 86 C2
Tuolumne U.S.A. 182 D4
Tuolumne r. U.S.A. 182 C4
Tuolumne Meadows U.S.A. 182 E4
Tuoniang Jiang r. China 86 C3
Tuotuo He r. China 97 G2
Tuotuoheyan China 84 B5
also known as Tanggulashan
Tüp Kyrg. 103 I4
also spelt Tyup
Tupă Brazil 206 C8
Tupaciguara Brazil 206 E5
Tupanaóca Brazil 199 F5
Tupanciretã Brazil 203 A9
Tupelo U.S.A. 174 B5
Tupinambarama, Ilha i. Brazil 199 G5
Tupi Paulista Brazil 206 B8
Tupiza Bol. 200 D5
Tupper Canada 166 F4
Tupper Lake U.S.A. 177 K1
Tupper Lake l. U.S.A. 177 K1
Tüpqaraghan Tübegi pen. Kazakh. see Mangyshlak, Poluostrov
Tupungato Arg. 204 C4

Tupungato, Cerro mt. Arg./Chile 204 C4
5th highest mountain in South America.
southamerica [landscapes] 190–191

Tuqayyid well Iraq 107 F5
Tuquan China 85 I2
Túquerres Col. 198 B4
Tuqu Wan b. China 87 D5
Tura China 89 D4
Tura India 97 F4
Tura Rus. Fed. 39 K3
Turabah Ḩā'il Saudi Arabia 104 C1
Turabah Makkah Saudi Arabia 104 C3
Turabah, Wādī watercourse Saudi Arabia 104 C3
Turagua, Serranía mt. Venez. 199 E3
Turakina N.Z. 152 J8
Turakina r. N.Z. 152 J8
Turana, Khrebet mts Rus. Fed. 82 C2
Turangi N.Z. 152 J6
Turan Lowland Asia 101 D2
also known as Turanskaya Nizmennost'
Turanskaya Nizmennost' lowland Asia see Turan Lowland
Ţurāq al 'Ilab hills Syria 109 J4
Turar Ryskulov Kazakh. 103 G4
formerly known as Vannovka
Turaw Belarus 42 I9
Turayf Saudi Arabia 107 D5
Turayf well Saudi Arabia 105 E2
Ţurayf, Wādī watercourse Iraq 109 N4
Turba Estonia 42 F2
Turbaco Col. 198 C2
Turbacz mt. Poland 49 R6
Turbat Pak. 101 E5
Turbo Col. 198 B2
Turčianske Teplice Slovakia 49 P7
Turco Bol. 200 C4
Turda Romania 58 E2
Tureh Iran 100 B3
Turek Poland 49 P3
Turfan China see Turpan
Turfan Depression China see Turpan Pendi
Turgay Akmolinskaya Oblast' Kazakh. 103 H2
Turgay Kustanayskaya Oblast' Kazakh. 103 E2
also spelt Torghay
Turgay r. Kazakh. 103 E3
Turgayskaya Dolina valley Kazakh. 103 E2
Turgayskaya Stolovaya Strana reg. Kazakh. 103 E2
Türgen Uul mt. Mongolia 84 A1
Türgen Uul mts Mongolia 84 A1
Turgeon r. Canada 168 E3
Türgovishte Bulg. 58 H5
Turgut Turkey 106 B3
Turgut Turkey 59 J11
Turgutalp Turkey 59 I9
Turgutlu Turkey 106 A3
also known as Kasaba
Turgutreis Turkey 59 I12
Turhal Turkey 106 D2
Türi Estonia 42 G3
Turi Italy 56 J8
Turia r. Spain 55 K5
Turiaçu Brazil 202 C2
Turiaçu r. Brazil 202 C2
Turiaçu, Baía de b. Brazil 202 C2
Turiamo Venez. 199 E2
Turiec r. Slovakia 49 P6
Turin Canada 167 H5
Turin Italy 51 N7
also spelt Torino; historically known as Augusta Taurinorum or Taurasia
Turinsk Rus. Fed. 38 G4
Turiy Rog Rus. Fed. 82 C3
Türje Hungary 49 O9
Turka Rus. Fed. 81 H2
Turkana, Lake salt l. Eth./Kenya 128 B4
formerly known as Rudolf, Lake
Türkeli Turkey 58 I8
Türkeli Adası i. Turkey 58 I8
Turkestan Kazakh. 103 G4
also spelt Türkistan
Turkestan Range mts Asia 99 H2
Túrkeve Hungary 49 R8
Turkey country Asia 106 B3
asia [countries] 64–67
Turkey U.S.A. 176 B8
Turkey r. U.S.A. 174 B3
Turki Rus. Fed. 41 G6
Türkistan Kazakh. see Turkestan
Turkmenabat Turkm. see Chardzhev
Türkmen Adasy i. Turkm. see Ogurchinskiy, Ostrov
Türkmen Aylagy b. Turkm. see Turkmenskiy Zaliv
Türkmenbashi Turkm. 102 C4
formerly known as Krasnovodsk
Türkmen Dağı mt. Turkey 106 B3
Turkmengala Turkm. 103 E5
formerly spelt Turkmen-Kala
Turkmenistan country Asia 102 D5
spelt Türkmenostan in Turkmen; formerly known as Turkmeniya or Turkmenskaya S.S.R.
asia [countries] 64–67
Turkmeniya country Asia see Turkmenistan
Turkmen-Kala Turkm. see Turkmengala
Turkmenkarakul' Turkm. 101 E3
Türkmenostan country Asia see Turkmenistan
Turkmenskaya S.S.R. country Asia see Turkmenistan
Turkmenskiy Zaliv b. Turkm. 102 C5
also known as Türkmen Aylagy
Türkoğlu Turkey 107 D3
Turkova Belarus 42 J6

Turks and Caicos Islands terr. West Indies 187 F2
United Kingdom Overseas Territory.
oceania [countries] 138–139

Turks Island Passage Turks and Caicos Is 187 F2
Turks Islands Turks and Caicos Is 187 F2
Turku Fin. 45 M3
also known as Åbo
Turkwel watercourse Kenya 128 C4
Turlock U.S.A. 182 D4
Turlock Lake U.S.A. 182 D4
Turmalina Brazil 203 D6
Turmus, Wādī at watercourse Saudi Arabia 104 C2
Turnagain r. Canada 166 E3
Turnagain, Cape N.Z. 152 K8
Turnbull, Mount U.S.A. 183 N8
Turneffe Islands Belize 185 I5
Turner r. Australia 150 B4
Turner watercourse Australia 151 B5
Turner U.S.A. 173 J6
Turner River Australia 150 E3
Turner's Peninsula Sierra Leone 124 B5
Turner Valley Canada 167 H5
Turnhout Belgium 51 K1
Turnor Lake Canada 167 I3
Turnor Lake l. Canada 167 I3
Turnov Czech Rep. 49 M5
Tŭrnovo Bulg. see Veliko Tŭrnovo
Turnu Măgurele Romania 58 F5
Turnu Severin Romania see Drobeta - Turnu Severin
Turon r. Australia 147 F3
Turones France see Tours
Turopolje plain Croatia 56 H3
Turovets Rus. Fed. 40 G4
Turovo Rus. Fed. 43 S7
Turpan China 88 E3
also spelt Turfan

Turpan Pendi depr. China 88 E3
Lowest point in northern Asia. English form Turfan Depression.

Turpan Zhan China 88 E3
also known as Daheyan
Turrialba Costa Rica 186 C5
Turriff U.K. 46 J6
Turris Libisonis Sardegna Italy see Porto Torres
Tursāq Iraq 107 F4
Turtkul' Uzbek. 103 E4
also spelt Tŏrtkŏl; formerly known as Petroaleksandrovsk
Turtle Flambeau Flowage resr U.S.A. 172 C4
Turtleford Canada 167 I4
Turtle Island Australia 149 F3
Turtle Island Fiji see Vatoa
Turtle Islands Phil. 74 A5
Turtle Lake l. Canada 167 I4
Turtle Lake U.S.A. 172 A5
Turugart Pass China/Kyrg. 88 A3
also known as Torugart, Pereval or Turugart Shankou
Turugart Shankou pass China/Kyrg. see Turugart Pass
Turukhansk Rus. Fed. 39 I3
Turuna r. Brazil 199 G4
Turunçova Turkey 108 B1
Turush Kazakh. 102 D3
Turuvanur India 94 C3
Turvelândia Brazil 206 C4
Turvo Brazil 203 B9
Turvo r. Goiás Brazil 206 C4
Turvo r. São Paulo Brazil 206 D6
Turvo r. São Paulo Brazil 206 D9
Ţūs Iran 101 D2
Tusayan U.S.A. 183 L6
Tuscaloosa U.S.A. 175 C5
Tuscania Italy 56 D6
Tuscany admin. reg. Italy see Toscana
Tuscany reg. Italy 56 C5
also known as Toscana
Tuscarawas r. U.S.A. 176 D5
Tuscarora Mountains hills U.S.A. 176 H5
Tuscola U.S.A. 174 B4
Tuscumbia AL U.S.A. 174 C5
Tuscumbia MO U.S.A. 178 D4
Tuskegee U.S.A. 175 C5
Tussey Mountains hills U.S.A. 176 G5
Tustin U.S.A. 172 H6
Tuszyn Poland 49 Q4
Tutak Turkey 107 E3
Tutaul Rus. Fed. 82 B1
Tutayev Rus. Fed. 43 U4
Tutera Spain see Tudela
Tuticorin India 94 C4
Tutoh r. Sarawak Malaysia 77 F2
Tutong Brunei 77 F1
Tutova r. Romania 58 I2
Tutrakan Bulg. 58 H4
Tuttle Creek Reservoir U.S.A. 178 C4
Tuttlingen Germany 48 F8

Tuttut Nunaat reg. Greenland 165 Q2
also known as Renland
Tutuala East Timor 75 C5
Tutubu Tanz. 129 B6
Tutuila i. American Samoa 145 H3
formerly known as Masuna
Tutukaka N.Z. 152 I3
Tutume Botswana 131 E4
Tutūn Egypt 108 B8
Tutunendo Col. 198 B3
Tutupaca, Volcán vol. Peru 200 C4
Tuturumuri N.Z. 152 J9
Tututepec Mex. 185 F5
Tuul Gol r. Mongolia 85 E1
Tuun-bong mt. N. Korea 83 B4
Tuupovaara Fin. 44 O3
Tuusniemi Fin. 44 O3
Tuusula Fin. 45 N3
Tuva aut. rep. Rus. Fed. see Tyva, Respublika
▶Tuvalu country S. Pacific Ocean 145 G2
formerly known as Ellice Islands
oceania [countries] 138–139
Tuvana-i-Colo i. Fiji 145 H4
also spelt Tuvana-i-Tholo
Tuvana-i-Tholo i. Fiji see Tuvana-i-Colo
Tuve Sweden 45 J4
Tuve, Mount Antarctica 222 S2
Tuvinskaya A.S.S.R. aut. rep. Rus. Fed. see Tyva, Respublika
Tuvuk Kazakh. 103 I4
Tuwau r. Indon. 77 G2
Tuwayq, Jabal hills Saudi Arabia 105 D2
Tuwayq, Jabal mts Saudi Arabia 105 D3
Ţuwayyil al Ḩājj mt. Jordan 108 G8
Ţuwayyil ash Shihāq mt. Jordan 108 H7
Tuwwal Saudi Arabia 104 B3
Tuxer Gebirge mts Austria 48 I8
Tuxpan Jalisco Mex. 185 E5
Tuxpan Nayarit Mex. 184 D4
Tuxpan Veracruz Mex. 185 F4
Tuxtla Gutiérrez Mex. 185 G5
Túy Spain see Tui
Tuya Lake Canada 166 D3
Tuy Đuc Vietnam 79 D5
Tuyên Quang Vietnam 78 D3
Tuy Hoa Vietnam 79 E5
Tuymazy Rus. Fed. 40 J5
Tūysarkān Iran 100 B3
Tüytepa Uzbek. see Toytepa
Tuz, Lake salt l. Turkey 106 C3
also known as Tuz Gölü
Tuz Gölü salt l. Turkey see Tuz, Lake
Tŭzha Bulg. 58 G6
Tuzha Rus. Fed. 40 H4
Tuz Khurmātū Iraq 107 F4
Tuzla Bos.-Herz. 56 K4
Tuzla Romania 58 J4
Tuzla Turkey 106 C3
Tuzla r. Turkey 107 E3
Tuzlov r. Rus. Fed. 41 G7
Tuzu r. Myanmar 78 A2
Tuzugu well Libya 120 C4
Tvååker Sweden 45 K4
Tvärålund Sweden 44 L2
Tvedestrand Norway 45 J4
Tver' Rus. Fed. 43 Q5
formerly known as Kalinin
Tver Oblast admin. div. Rus. Fed. see Tverskaya Oblast'
Tverskaya Oblast' admin. div. Rus. Fed. 43 Q4
English form Tver Oblast; formerly known as Kalininskaya Oblast'
Tvertsa r. Rus. Fed. 43 Q5
Tveroyri Faroe Is 46 F2
Tvorozhkovo Rus. Fed. 43 J3
Tvŭrditsa Bulg. 58 G6
Twain Harte U.S.A. 182 D3
Twardogóra Poland 49 O4
Tweed Canada 173 P6
Tweed r. U.K. 46 J8
Tweed Heads Australia 147 G2
Tweedie Canada 167 I4
Tweedsmuir Provincial Park Canada 166 E4
Tweefontein S. Africa 132 D9
Tweeling S. Africa 133 M4
Twee Rivier Namibia 130 C5
Twee Rivieren Botswana 132 E3
Tweespruit S. Africa 133 L6
Twentynine Palms U.S.A. 183 H7
Twillingate Canada 169 K3
Twin Bridges U.S.A. 182 D3
Twin Buttes Reservoir U.S.A. 179 B6
Twin Falls Canada 169 H2
Twin Falls U.S.A. 180 D4
Twingi Zambia 127 F7
Twin Heads hill Australia 150 D4
Twin Mountain U.S.A. 177 N1
Twin Peak U.S.A. 182 D2
Twin Peaks hill Australia 151 B7
Twinsburg U.S.A. 176 D4
Twins Creek watercourse Australia 146 C2
Twisp U.S.A. 180 B2
Twitchen Reservoir U.S.A. 182 D6
Twitya r. Canada 166 D1
Twizel N.Z. 153 E12
Two Butte Creek r. U.S.A. 178 B4
Two Harbors U.S.A. 174 B2
Two Hills Canada 167 I4
Two Rivers U.S.A. 172 F6
Tyan' Shan' mts China/Kyrg. see Tien Shan
Tyanshanskaya Oblast' admin. div. Kyrg. see Naryn
Tyao r. India/Myanmar 97 G5
Tyatya, Vulkan vol. Rus. Fed. 82 G3
Tychy Poland 49 P5
historically known as Tichau
Tyczyn Poland 49 T6
Tydal Norway 44 J3
Tyddewi U.K. see St David's
Tygart Valley U.S.A. 176 F7
Tygda Rus. Fed. 82 B1
Tygda r. Rus. Fed. 82 B1
Tyinkrysset Norway 45 J3
Tykhero Greece 58 H7
also known as Tikherón
Tykocin Poland 49 T2
Tyler U.S.A. 179 D5
Tylertown U.S.A. 175 B6
Tylihul r. Ukr. 58 L1
Tyl'skiy Khrebet mts Rus. Fed. 82 D1
Tym' r. Rus. Fed. 82 F2
Tymonovychi Ukr. 43 N9
Tymovskoye Rus. Fed. 82 F2
Tympaki Greece 59 F13
also known as Timbákion
Tynda Rus. Fed. 81 K1
formerly known as Tyndinskiy
Tyndall U.S.A. 178 C3
Tyndinskiy Rus. Fed. see Tynda
Tyndrum U.K. 46 H7
Tyne r. U.K. 47 J7
Tyngsboro U.S.A. 177 N3
Tyngsjö Sweden 45 K3
Týn nad Vltavou Czech Rep. 49 L6
Tynset Norway 45 J3
Tyr Lebanon see Tyre
Tyras Ukr. see Bilhorod-Dnistrovs'kyy
Tyre Lebanon 108 G4
also known as Soûr; also spelt Tyr; historically known as Tyrus
Tyree, Mount Antarctica 222 S1
Tyrifjorden l. Norway 45 J3
Tyrma Rus. Fed. 82 D2
Tyrma r. Rus. Fed. 82 C2
Tyrnävä Fin. 44 N2
Tyrnavos Greece 59 D9
also spelt Tírnavos
Tyrnyauz Rus. Fed. 107 E2
Tyrone U.S.A. 176 G5
Tyrrell r. Australia 147 D3
Tyrrell, Lake dry lake Australia 147 D3
Tyrrell Lake Canada 167 J2
Tyrrhenian Sea France/Italy 57 C8
also known as Tirreno, Mare
Tyrus Lebanon see Tyre
Tysnesøy i. Norway 45 I4
Tyson Wash watercourse U.S.A. 183 J8
Tysse Norway 45 I3
Tytuvėnai Lith. 42 E6
Tyubelyakh Rus. Fed. 39 O3
Tyub-Karagan, Mys pt Kazakh. 102 B3
Tyukalinsk Rus. Fed. 38 H4
Tyulen'i, Ostrova is Kazakh. 102 B3
Tyul'gan Rus. Fed. 102 D1
Tyul'kino Rus. Fed. 40 K4
Tyumen' Rus. Fed. 38 G4
also spelt Tjumen'
Tyumen'-Aryk Kazakh. see Tomenaryk
Tyung r. Rus. Fed. 39 M3
Tyup Kyrg. see Tüp
Tyuratam Kazakh. see Baykonur
Tyuva-Guba Rus. Fed. 44 P1
Tyuyamuyunskoye Vodokhranilische resr Turkm./Uzbek. 103 E4
Tyva, Respublika aut. rep. Rus. Fed. 84 C1
formerly known as Tuva or Tuvinskaya A.S.S.R.; historically known as Tannu Tuva
Tywi r. U.K. 47 H12
Tzaneen S. Africa 131 F4
Tzucacab Mex. 185 H4

↓ U

Uacauyén Venez. 199 F3
Uaco Congo Angola see Waku-Kungo
Uainambi Brazil 198 D4
Ualan atoll Micronesia see Kosrae
Ūālīkhanov Kazakh. see Valikhanov
Uamanda Angola 127 D9
Uape Moz. 131 H3
Uara Brazil 199 E5
Uarc, Ras c. Morocco see Trois Fourches, Cap des
Uari Brazil 199 G6
Uarini Brazil 199 E5
Uaroo Australia 150 A4
Uaruma Brazil 198 D4
Uasadi-jidi, Sierra mts Venez. 199 E3
Uatatás r. Brazil 199 E4
also known as Parima
Uatumã r. Brazil 199 G5
Uauá Brazil 202 E4
Uaupés Brazil 199 E5
Uaupés r. Brazil 198 E4
Uaxactún Guat. 185 H5
U'ayfirah well Saudi Arabia 104 D3
U'aylī, Wādī al watercourse Saudi Arabia 109 J7
U'aywij well Saudi Arabia 104 D1
U'aywij, Sha'īb al watercourse Saudi Arabia 109 P8
U'aywij, Wādī al watercourse Saudi Arabia 107 E5
Ub Srbija Yugo. 58 B4
Ubá Brazil 203 D7
Uba r. Kazakh. 103 J2
Ubagan r. Kazakh. 103 F1
also spelt Obaghan
Ubaí Brazil 202 C6
Ubaid well Sudan 121 E6
Ubaitaba Brazil 202 E5
'Ubāl Yemen 104 C5
Ubal Karabaur hills Uzbek. 102 C4
Ubal Muzbel' hills Kazakh. 102 C4
Ubangi r. Cent. Afr. Rep./Dem. Rep. Congo 126 C5
also spelt Oubangui
Ubangi-Shari country Africa see Central African Republic
Ubaporanga Brazil 207 K6
Ubate Col. 198 C3
Ubatuba Brazil 207 H10
Ubauro Pak. 101 G4
'Ubaydāt, Sha'īb al watercourse Iraq 109 N6
Ubayyiḑ, Wādī al watercourse Iraq/Saudi Arabia 107 E4
Ube Japan 91 B8
Úbeda Spain 55 H6
Ubenazomozi Tanz. 129 C6
Uberaba Brazil 206 F6
Uberaba r. Brazil 206 E7
Uberlândia Brazil 206 E5
Überlingen Germany 48 G8
Ubin, Pulau i. Sing. 76 [inset]
Ubinskoye, Ozero l. Rus. Fed. 80 C1
Ubly U.S.A. 173 K7
Ubolratna Reservoir Thai. 78 C4
Ubombo S. Africa 133 Q4
Ubon Ratchathani Thai. 79 D5
Ubori Sudan 126 F3
Ubrique Spain 54 F8
Ubundu Dem. Rep. Congo 126 E5
formerly known as Ponthierville
Ucar Azer. 107 F2
also spelt Udzhary
Ucayali dept Peru 200 B2
Ucayali r. Peru 198 C6
Ucero r. Spain 55 H3
Uch Pak. 101 G4
Uch-Adzhi Turkm. 103 E5
also spelt Üçhajy
Üçhajy Turkm. see Uch-Adzhi
Ūchān Iran 100 B2
Ucharal Kazakh. 103 J3
also spelt Üsharal
Uchinoura Japan 91 B9
Uchiura Japan 90 E6
Uchiura-wan b. Japan 90 G3
English form Volcano Bay
Uchiza Peru 200 A2
Uchkuduk Uzbek. 103 E4
also spelt Uchquduq
Uchkyay Uzbek. 103 F5
Uchquduq Uzbek. see Uchkuduk
Uchsay Uzbek. 102 D4
also spelt Uchsoy
Uchsoy Uzbek. see Uchsay
Uchte r. Germany 48 I3
Uchto r. Pak. 101 F5
Uchur r. Rus. Fed. 39 N4
Uckermark reg. Germany 49 K2
Uckfield U.K. 47 M13
Ucluelet Canada 166 E5
Uda r. Rus. Fed. 82 D1
Uda r. Rus. Fed. 85 E1
Udachnoye Rus. Fed. 102 A3
Udachnyy Rus. Fed. 39 L3
Udagamandalam India 94 C4
also spelt Udhagamandalam; formerly known as Ootacamund
Udaipur Rajasthan India 96 B4
Udaipur Tripura India 97 F5
Udaipura India 96 C5
Udaipur Garhi Nepal 97 E4
Udalguri India 97 G4
Udanti r. India/Myanmar 95 D1
Uda Walawe Reservoir Sri Lanka 94 D5
Udayagiri India 94 C3
'Udaynān well Saudi Arabia 105 E3
Uddeholm Sweden 45 K3
Uddevalla Sweden 45 J4
Uddjaure l. Sweden 44 L2
'Udeid, Khōr al inlet Qatar 105 E2
Uden Neth. 48 C4
Udgir India 94 C2
Udhagamandalam India see Udagamandalam
Udhampur Jammu and Kashmir 96 B2
Udimskiy Rus. Fed. 40 H3
Udine Italy 56 F2
Udjuktok Bay Canada 169 I2
Udmalaippettai India see Udumalaippettai
Udmurtia aut. rep. Rus. Fed. see Udmurtskaya Respublika
Udmurtskaya A.S.S.R. aut. rep. Rus. Fed. see Udmurtskaya Respublika
Udmurtskaya Respublika aut. rep. Rus. Fed. 40 J4
English form Udmurtia; formerly known as Udmurtskaya A.S.S.R.
Udokan, Khrebet mts Rus. Fed. 81 J1
Udomlya Rus. Fed. 43 Q4
Udon Thani Thai. 78 C4
Udskoye Rus. Fed. 82 D1
Udumalaippettai India 94 C4
also known as Udmalaippettai
Udupi India 94 B3
Udyl', Ozero l. Rus. Fed. 82 E1
Udzhary Azer. see Ucar
Uea i. New Caledonia see Ouvéa
Uebonti Indon. 75 B3
Uecker r. Germany 49 L2
Ueckermünde Germany 49 L2
Ueda Japan 91 F6
Uekuli Indon. 75 B3
Uele r. Dem. Rep. Congo 126 D3
Uelen Rus. Fed. 39 T3
Uel'kal' Rus. Fed. 39 S3
Uelzen Germany 48 H3
Ueno Japan 91 E7
Uere r. Dem. Rep. Congo 126 E4
Ufa Rus. Fed. 40 J5
Ufa r. Rus. Fed. 40 K5
Uffing am Staffelsee Germany 48 I8
Uftyuga r. Rus. Fed. 40 H3
Uftyuga r. Rus. Fed. 43 U2
Ugab watercourse Namibia 130 B4
Ugāle Latvia 42 D4
Ugalla r. Tanz. 129 A6
Ugalla River Game Reserve nature res. Tanz. 129 A6
▶Uganda country Africa 128 A4
africa [countries] 114–117
Ugar r. Bos.-Herz. 56 J4
Ugento Italy 57 K9
Uggdal Norway 45 I3
Ughelli Nigeria 125 G5
Ugie S. Africa 133 M8
Ūgīnak Iran 101 E5
Ugine France 51 M7
Uglegorsk Rus. Fed. 82 F2
Uglekamensk Rus. Fed. 82 D4
formerly known as Severnyy Suchan
Ugleural'skiy Rus. Fed. 40 K4
formerly known as Polovinka
Uglich Rus. Fed. 43 T4
Ugljan i. Croatia 56 H4
Uglovka Rus. Fed. 43 O3
Uglovoye Amurskaya Oblast' Rus. Fed. 82 C2
Uglovoye Primorskiy Kray Rus. Fed. 82 D4
Uglovskoye Rus. Fed. 88 C1
Ugodskiy Zavod Rus. Fed. see Zhukovo
Ugol'noye Rus. Fed. 39 O3
Ugol'nyy Rus. Fed. see Beringovskiy
Ugol'nyye Kopi Rus. Fed. 39 R3
Ugra Rus. Fed. 43 P7
Ugra r. Rus. Fed. 43 R7
Ugŭrchin Bulg. 58 F5
Ugut Rus. Fed. 38 H3
Uher Hudag China 85 F3
Uherské Hradiště Czech Rep. 49 O6
Úhlava r. Czech Rep. 49 K6
Uibai Brazil 202 D4
Uibhist a' Deas i. U.K. see South Uist
Uibhist a' Tuath i. U.K. see North Uist
Uig U.K. 46 F6
Uige Angola 127 B6
formerly known as Carmona or Vila Marechal Carmona
Uige prov. Angola 127 B6
Ŭijŏngbu S. Korea 83 B5
Ŭiju N. Korea 83 B4
Uil Kazakh. 102 C2
also spelt Oyyl
Uil r. Kazakh. 102 C2
Uimaharju Fin. 44 O3
Uinkaret Plateau U.S.A. 183 K5
Uinskoye Rus. Fed. 40 K4
Uinta r. U.S.A. 183 O1
Uintah and Ouray Indian Reservation res. U.S.A. 183 O1
Uinta Mountains U.S.A. 183 N1
Uiryŏng S. Korea 91 A7
Uis Mine Namibia 130 B4
Uitenhage S. Africa 133 J10
Uithuizen Neth. 48 D2
Uitkyk S. Africa 132 C6
Uitsakpan salt pan S. Africa 132 E4
Uitspankraal S. Africa 132 D9
Újfehértó Hungary 49 S8
Ujhani India 96 C4
Uji Japan 91 D7
Uji-guntō is Japan 91 A9
Ujiyamada Japan see Ise
Ujjain India 96 B5
Újkígyós Hungary 49 S9
Ujohbilang Indon. 77 F2
Ujście Poland 49 N2
Ujung Kulon National Park Indon. 76 D4
Ujung Pandang Indon. 75 A4
formerly known as Macassar or Makassar
Újvidék Vojvodina, Srbija Yugo. see Novi Sad
Ukal Sagar l. India 96 B5
Ukata Nigeria 125 G4
'Ukayrishah well Saudi Arabia 104 D2
Ukerewe Island Tanz. 128 B5
Ukhaydir tourist site Iraq 107 E4
Ukhdūd tourist site Saudi Arabia 104 D4
Ukholovo Rus. Fed. 41 G5
Ukhra r. Rus. Fed. 43 U3
Ukhrul India 97 G4
Ukhta Rus. Fed. see Kalevala
Ukhta Rus. Fed. 40 J3
Ukhta r. Rus. Fed. 40 J3
Ukhtoma r. Rus. Fed. 43 U3
Ukhvala Belarus 43 K7
Ukiah U.S.A. 182 A2
Ukimbo Tanz. 129 B6
Ukkusissat Greenland 165 N2
Ukmergė Lith. 42 F6

▶Ukraine country Europe 41 D6
2nd largest country in Europe. Spelt Ukrayina in Ukrainian; formerly known as Ukrainskaya S.S.R.
europe [countries] 32–35

Ukrainka Kazakh. 88 C1
Ukrainskaya S.S.R. country Europe see Ukraine
Ukrayina country Europe see Ukraine
Ukrina r. Bos.-Herz. 56 J4
Uku Angola 127 B7
formerly known as Vila Nova do Seles
Uku-jima i. Japan 91 A8
Ukuma Angola 127 B8
Ukwi Botswana 130 D4
Ul r. India 89 B6
Ula Belarus 43 K6
Ula r. Belarus 43 K6
Ula Turkey 59 J11
also known as Gökova
Ulaanbaatar Mongolia see Ulan Bator
Ulaanbaatar municipality Mongolia 85 E2
Ulaan-Ereg Mongolia 85 F2
Ulaangom Mongolia 84 B1
Ulaanhudag Mongolia 84 E2
Ulaan Nuur salt l. Mongolia 84 D2
Ulaan-Uul Bayanhongor Mongolia 84 D2
Ulaan-Uul Dornogovĭ Mongolia 85 F2
Ulan Nei Mongol China 85 F4
also known as Otog Qi
Ulan Qinghai China 84 C4
also known as Xiligou

▶Ulan Bator Mongolia 85 E2
Capital of Mongolia. Also spelt Ulaanbaatar; historically known as Urga.

Ulanbel' Kazakh. 103 G3
Ulan Buh Shamo des. China 85 E3
Ulan Erge Rus. Fed. 41 H7
formerly known as Krasnoye
Ulanhad China see Chifeng
Ulanhot China 85 I2
also known as Horqin Youyi Qianqi
Ulan Hua China 85 F3
also known as Dorbod Qi or Siziwang Qi
Ulan-Khol Rus. Fed. 102 A3
Ulansuhai Nur l. China 85 F3
Ulan Tohoi China 84 D3
Ulan-Ude Rus. Fed. 85 E1
Ulan Ul Hu l. China 89 E5
Ulapes Arg. 204 D3
Ulaş Turkey 107 D3
Ulaş Turkey 58 I7
Ulastai China 88 D3
Ulaya Tanz. 129 C6
'Ulayam aẓ Ẓama' hill Saudi Arabia 109 L9
Ulayyah reg. Saudi Arabia 105 D3
Ul'ba Kazakh. 88 C1
also spelt Ülbi
Ul'banskiy Zaliv b. Rus. Fed. 82 E1
UL Bend National Wildlife Refuge nature res. U.S.A. 180 F3
Ülbi Kazakh. see Ul'ba
Ulbroka Latvia 42 F5
Ulchin S. Korea 83 C5
Ulcinj Crna Gora Yugo. 58 A7
Ulco S. Africa 133 I5
Uldz Mongolia 85 F1
Uldz r. Mongolia 85 G1
Uleåborg Fin. see Oulu
Ulefoss Norway 45 J4
Ulei Vanuatu 145 F3
Ülenurme Estonia 42 H3
Ulety Rus. Fed. 85 G1
Ulfborg Denmark 45 J4
Ulgain Gol r. China 85 H2
Ul'gili Kazakh. 103 F2
Ulhasnagar India 94 B2
Uliastai China 85 H2
also known as Dong Ujimqin Qi
Uliastay Mongolia 84 C2
Uliatea i. Fr. Polynesia see Raiatea
Ulie atoll Micronesia see Woleai
Ulindi r. Dem. Rep. Congo 126 E5
Ulithi atoll Micronesia 73 I4
formerly known as Mackenzie
Ul'kayak r. Kazakh. 103 E2
also spelt Ölkeyek
Ul'ken-Karoy, Ozero salt l. Kazakh. 103 G1
Ülkenözen r. Kazakh./Rus. Fed. see Bol'shoy Uzen'
Ul'ken Sulutar Kazakh. 103 H4
formerly known as Krasnogorka
Ülken Vladimirovka Kazakh. see Bol'shaya Vladimirovka
Ulla r. Spain 54 C2
Ulladulla Australia 147 F3
Ullapool U.K. 46 G6
Ullatti Sweden 44 M2
Ullawarra Aboriginal Reserve Australia 150 B4
Ulldecona Spain 55 L4
Ullmer, Mount Antarctica 222 S1
Ullsfjorden sea chan. Norway 44 L1
Ullung-do i. S. Korea 83 C5
Ulm Germany 48 G7
Ul'ma r. Rus. Fed. 82 C2
Ulmeni Romania 58 H4
Ulmeni Romania 58 E1
Ulongue Moz. 131 G2
formerly known as Coutinho or Vila Coutinho
Ulooowaranie, Lake salt flat Australia 148 C5
Ulricehamn Sweden 45 K4
Ulsan S. Korea 83 C6
Ulsberg Norway 44 J3
Ulsta U.K. 46 K3
Ulsteinvik Norway 44 I3
Ulster reg. Rep. of Ireland/U.K. 47 E9
Ulster U.S.A. 177 I4
Ultima Australia 147 D3
Ultraoriental, Cordillera mts Peru 200 B1
also known as Divisor, Sierra de
Ulu Indon. 75 C2
Ulu Sudan 128 B2
Ulua r. Hond. 185 I6
Ulubat Gölü l. Turkey 106 B2
Ulubey Turkey 106 B3
Uluborlu Turkey 106 B3
Uluçay r. Turkey 107 E3
Uludağ mt. Turkey 106 B2
Uludağ Milli Parkı nat. park Turkey 59 K8
Uluqqat China see Wuqia
Ulu Kali, Gunung mt. Malaysia 76 C2
Ulukışla Turkey 106 C3
Ulundi S. Africa 133 P5
Ulungur He r. China 84 A2
Ulungur Hu l. China 88 D2
Ulupalakua U.S.A. 181 [inset] Z1
Ulu Pandan Sing. 76 [inset]
Uluqsaqtuuq Canada see Holman
▶Uluru hill Australia 148 A5
also known as Ayers Rock
world [land cover] 18–19
oceania [features] 142–143
Uluru National Park Australia 148 A5
Ulus Dağı mt. Turkey 59 J9
Ulutau Kazakh. see Ulytau
Ulutau, Gory mts Kazakh. 103 F3
Ulverston U.K. 47 I9
Ulverstone Australia 147 E5
Ulvsjön Sweden 45 L3
Ul'yanikha Rus. Fed. 43 S3
Ul'yanino Rus. Fed. 43 T6
Ül'yanov Kazakh. see Ul'yanovskiy
Ul'yanovka Rus. Fed. 43 L2
Ul'yanovo Kaliningradskaya Oblast' Rus. Fed. 42 D7
Ul'yanovo Kaluzhskaya Oblast' Rus. Fed. 43 Q8
Ul'yanovo Uzbek. 103 G4
Ul'yanovsk Rus. Fed. 41 I5
also known as Simbirsk; also spelt Uljanovsk
Ul'yanovskaya Oblast' admin. div. Rus. Fed. 41 H5
English form Ulyanovsk Oblast
Ul'yanovskiy Kazakh. 103 H2
also known as Ül'yanov; formerly known as Ul'yanovskoye
Ulyanovsk Oblast admin. div. Rus. Fed. see Ul'yanovskaya Oblast'
Ul'yanovskoye Kazakh. see Ul'yanovskiy
Ulyatuy Rus. Fed. 85 H1
Ulysses KS U.S.A. 178 B4
Ulysses KY U.S.A. 176 C8
Ulytau Kazakh. 103 F2
formerly spelt Ulutau
Uly-Zhylanshyk r. Kazakh. 103 E2
Umag Croatia 56 F3
Umala Bol. 200 D4
'Umān country Asia see Oman
Umán Mex. 185 H4
Uman' Ukr. 41 D6
Umango, Cerro mt. Arg. 204 C3
'Umarī, Qa' al salt pan Jordan 109 H6
Umaria India 96 D5
Umarkhed India 94 C2
Umarkot India 95 D2
Umarkot Pak. 101 G5
Umaroona, Lake salt flat Australia 146 C1
Umarpada India 96 B5
Umatilla U.S.A. 180 C3
Umayan r. Phil. 74 C4
'Umayrī, Wādī watercourse Oman 105 G3
Umba Rus. Fed. 40 E2
formerly known as Lesnoy
Umba r. Rus. Fed. 44 P2
Umbagog Lake U.S.A. 177 N1
Umbakumba Australia 148 C2
Umbeara Australia 148 B5
Umbelasha watercourse Sudan 126 E2
Umbertide Italy 56 E5
Umboi i. P.N.G. 73 K8
formerly known as Rooke Island
Umbozero Rus. Fed. 44 P2
Umbrella Mountains N.Z. 153 D13
Umbria admin. reg. Italy 56 E6
Umeå Sweden 44 M3
Umeälven r. Sweden 44 M3
Umet Rus. Fed. 41 G5
Umfolozi r. S. Africa 133 Q5
Umfolozi Game Reserve nature res. S. Africa 133 P5
Umfreville Lake Canada 167 M5
Umfuli r. Zimbabwe see Mupfure
Umgeni r. S. Africa 133 P6
Umhlanga S. Africa 133 P6
Umhlatuzi Lagoon S. Africa 133 Q5
Umiiviip Kangertiva inlet Greenland 165 O3
also known as Gyldenløve Fjord
Umingmaktok Canada 165 I3
Umirzak Kazakh. 102 B4
Umiujaq Canada 168 E1
Umkomaas S. Africa 133 O7
Umkomaas r. S. Africa 133 O7
Umlazi S. Africa 133 P6
Umma tourist site Iraq 107 F5
Umm ad Daraj, Jabal mt. Jordan 108 G5
Umm al Birak Saudi Arabia 104 B3
Umm al Ghār, Khabrat waterhole Iraq 109 N5
Umm al Hashīm, Jabal mt. Jordan 108 G8
Umm al Jamājim well Saudi Arabia 105 D2
Umm al Qaiwain U.A.E. see Umm al Qaywayn
Umm al Qaywayn U.A.E. 105 F2
English form Umm al Qaiwain
Umm ar Raghībah waterhole Iraq 109 N3
Umm ar Raqabah, Khabrat imp. l. Saudi Arabia 109 I8
Umm as Samīm salt flat Oman 105 F3
Umm at Qalbān Saudi Arabia 104 C2
Umm az Zumūl well Oman 105 F3
Umm Bāb Qatar 105 E2
Umm Badr Sudan 121 E6
Umm Dam Sudan 121 F6
Umm Ḩarb Saudi Arabia 104 B2
Umm Jumayyiḩ waterhole Saudi Arabia 109 N9
Umm Keddada Sudan 121 E6
Umm Lajj Saudi Arabia 104 B2
Umm Mafrūd, Gebel mt. Egypt 108 F8
Umm Mukhbār, Jabal hill Saudi Arabia 104 B3
Umm Nukhaylah hill Saudi Arabia 109 J8
Umm Nukhaylah well Saudi Arabia 108 G9
Umm Qasr Iraq 107 F5
Umm Qurein well Sudan 121 F5
Umm Quşur i. Saudi Arabia 104 A2
Umm Raqm, Gebel hill Egypt 108 C7
Umm Rumeila well Sudan 121 G5
Umm Ruwaba Sudan 121 F6
Umm Sa'ad Libya 120 E2
Umm Sa'id Qatar 105 E2
also known as Musay'īd
Umm Saiyala Sudan 121 F6
Umm Şalāl 'Alī Qatar 105 E2
Umm Samā Saudi Arabia 104 B3
Umm Saysabān, Jabal mt. Jordan 108 G8
Umm Shaitiya well Jordan 108 H8
Umm Shomar, Gebel mt. Egypt 108 E9
Umm Shugeira Sudan 121 F6
Umm Sīlsh, Sha'īb watercourse Iraq 109 O5
Umm Tināşşib, Gebel mt. Egypt 108 D9
Umm Urūmah i. Saudi Arabia 104 B2
Umm Wa'āl hill Saudi Arabia 109 J6
Umm Wazīr well Saudi Arabia 105 D3
Umm Zanatir mt. Egypt 108 D9
Umnak Island U.S.A. 164 C4
Umphang Wildlife Reserve nature res. Thai. 78 B5
Umpilua Moz. 131 H2
Umpqua r. U.S.A. 180 A4
Umred India 94 C1
Umreth India 94 B1
Umtali Zimbabwe see Mutare
Umtamvuna r. S. Africa 133 O8
Umtata S. Africa 133 M8
Umtata r. S. Africa 133 N8
Umtata Dam resr S. Africa 133 M8
Umtentweni S. Africa 133 O7
Umuahia Nigeria 125 G5
Umuarama Brazil 203 A7
Umurbey Turkey 59 H8
Umurlar Turkey 59 J9
Umutoi N.Z. 152 J8
Umvoti r. S. Africa 133 P6
Umvuma Zimbabwe see Mvuma
Umzimhlava r. S. Africa 133 N8
Umzimkulu S. Africa 133 N7
Umzimkulu r. S. Africa 133 O7
Umzimvubu r. S. Africa 133 N8
Umzingwani r. Zimbabwe see Mzingwani
Umzinto S. Africa 133 O7
Una Belarus 43 L6
Una r. Bos.-Herz./Croatia 56 I3
Una Brazil 202 E5
Una r. Brazil 202 F4
Una India 96 C3
Una, Mount N.Z. 153 G10
'Unāb, Jabal al hill Jordan 109 H8
English form Black Rock
'Unāb, Wādī al watercourse Jordan 109 H7
Unac r. Bos.-Herz. 56 I4
Unadilla U.S.A. 177 J3
Unadilla r. U.S.A. 177 J3
Unaí Brazil 206 G3
Unai Pass Afgh. 101 G3
Unalakleet U.S.A. 164 C3
Unalaska Island U.S.A. 164 C4
Unango Moz. 129 B8
Unari Fin. 44 N2
Unauna i. Indon. 75 B3
'Unayzah Saudi Arabia 104 C2
'Unayzah, Jabal hill Iraq 107 D4
also spelt 'Aneiza, Jabal
Unchahra India 96 D4
Uncompahgre Plateau U.S.A. 183 P3
Unda r. Rus. Fed. 85 H1
Undara National Park Australia 149 E3
Unden l. Sweden 45 K4
Underberg S. Africa 133 N6
Underbool Australia 146 D3
Undersåker Sweden 44 K3
Undva Estonia 42 C3
Unecha Rus. Fed. 43 N9
Unecha r. Rus. Fed. 43 M9
Uneiuxi r. Brazil 199 E5
Unga Island U.S.A. 164 C4
Ungarie Australia 147 E3
Ungava, Baie d' b. Canada see Ungava Bay
Ungava, Péninsule d' pen. Canada 165 L3
also known as Ungava Peninsula
Ungava Bay Canada 169 H1
also known as Ungava, Baie d'
Ungava Peninsula Canada see Ungava, Péninsule d'
Ungeny Moldova see Ungheni
Unggi N. Korea 82 C4
Ungheni Moldova 58 I1
formerly spelt Ungeny
Ungheni Romania 58 F2
Unguana Moz. 131 G4
Unguja North admin. reg. Tanz. see Zanzibar North
Unguja South admin. reg. Tanz. see Zanzibar South
Unguja West admin. reg. Tanz. see Zanzibar West
Ungurași Romania 58 F1
Unguz, Solonchakovyye Vpadiny salt flat Turkm. 102 D5
Üngüz Angyrsyndaky Garagum des. Turkm. see Zaunguzskiye Karakumy
Ungvár Ukr. see Uzhhorod
Ungwana Bay Kenya 128 D5
Uni Rus. Fed. 40 I4
União Acre Brazil 200 C2
União Minas Gerais Brazil 206 C6
União da Vitória Brazil 203 B8
União do Marará Brazil 199 F5
União dos Palmares Brazil 202 F4
Uniara India 96 C4
Unicoi U.S.A. 176 C9
Uniejów Poland 49 P4
Unije i. Croatia 56 G4
Unimak Island U.S.A. 164 C4
Unini r. Brazil 199 F5
Unini Peru 200 B2
Unión Arg. 204 D4
Unión Para. 201 F6
Union ME U.S.A. 177 P1
Union MO U.S.A. 174 B4
Union OR U.S.A. 180 C3
Union WV U.S.A. 176 E8
Unión, Bahía b. Arg. 204 E5
Union, Mount U.S.A. 183 L7
Union City OH U.S.A. 176 A5
Union City PA U.S.A. 176 F4
Union City TN U.S.A. 174 B4
Uniondale S. Africa 132 H10
Unión de Reyes Cuba 186 C2

▶Union of Soviet Socialist Republics
Divided in 1991 into 15 independent nations: Armenia, Azerbaijan, Belarus, Estonia, Georgia, Kazakhstan, Kyrgyzstan, Latvia, Lithuania, Moldova, the Russian Federation, Tajikistan, Turkmenistan, Ukraine and Uzbekistan.

Union Springs AL U.S.A. 175 C5
Union Springs NY U.S.A. 177 I3
Uniontown U.S.A. 176 F6
Union Valley Reservoir U.S.A. 182 D3
Unionville MI U.S.A. 173 J7
Unionville MO U.S.A. 174 A3
Unionville NV U.S.A. 182 F1
Unionville VA U.S.A. 176 H7
▶United Arab Emirates country Asia 105 F3
known as Al Imārāt al 'Arabīyah at Muttaḩidah, in Arabic; formerly known as Trucial Coast or Trucial States
asia [countries] 64–67
United Arab Republic country Africa see Egypt

▶United Kingdom country Europe 47 L8
3rd most populous country in Europe.
europe [countries] 32–35

United Provinces state India see Uttar Pradesh

▶United States of America country N. America 170 E3
Most populous country in North America and 3rd in the world. 2nd largest country in North America and 3rd in the world.
world [countries] 10–11
world [changes] 20–21
world [population] 22–23
northamerica [countries] 158–159

United States Range mts Canada 165 M1
Unity Canada 167 I4
Unjab watercourse Namibia 130 B4
Unjha India 96 B5
Unnao India 96 D4
Ŭnp'a N. Korea 83 B5
Unsan N. Korea 83 B4
Ŭnsan N. Korea 83 B5
Unst i. U.K. 46 L3
Unstrut r. Germany 48 I4
Unstrut-Trias-Land park Germany 48 I4
Untari India 97 D4
Untere Havel park Germany 48 J3
Unteres Odertal nat. park Germany 49 L3
Unterschleißheim Germany 48 I7
Unturán, Sierra de mts Venez. 199 E4
Unuk r. Canada/U.S.A. 166 D3
Unuli Horog China 97 F2

Un'ya r. Rus. Fed. 40 K3
Unzen-Amakusa National Park Japan 91 B8
Unzen-dake vol. Japan 91 B8
Unzha Rus. Fed. 40 H4
Uozu Japan 91 E6
Úpa r. Czech Rep. 49 M5
Upa r. Rus. Fed. 43 R7
Upalco U.S.A. 183 N1
Upar Ghat reg. India 97 E5
Upata Venez. 199 F2
Upemba, Lac l. Dem. Rep. Congo 127 E7
Upernavik Greenland 165 N2
Upernavik Kujalleq Greenland 165 N2
also known as Søndre Upernavik
Upi Phil. 74 C5
Upía r. Col. 198 C3
Upington S. Africa 132 F5
Upinniemi Fin. 45 N3
Upland U.S.A. 182 G7
Upleta India 96 A5
Upokongaro N.Z. 152 J7
Upoloksha Rus. Fed. 44 O2
Upolu i. Samoa 145 H3
formerly known as Ojalava
Upolu Point U.S.A. 181 [inset] Z1
Upper Alkali Lake U.S.A. 180 B4
Upper Arlington U.S.A. 176 B5
Upper Arrow Lake Canada 166 G5
Upper Chindwin Myanmar see Mawlaik
Upper East admin. reg. Ghana 125 E4
Upper Fraser Canada 166 F4
Upper Garry Lake Canada 167 K1
Upper Hutt N.Z. 152 J9
Upper Iowa r. U.S.A. 174 B3
Upper Klamath Lake U.S.A. 180 B4
Upper Liard Canada 166 D2
Upper Lough Erne l. U.K. 47 E9
Upper Marlboro U.S.A. 177 I7
Upper Mazinaw Lake Canada 173 P6
Upper Nile state Sudan 128 B2
Upper Peirce Reservoir Sing. 76 [inset]
Upper Preoria Lake U.S.A. 172 D10
Upper Red Lake U.S.A. 178 D1
Upper Sandusky U.S.A. 176 B5
Upper Saranac Lake U.S.A. 177 K1
Upper Seal Lake Canada see Iberville, Lac d'
Upper Takaka N.Z. 152 G9
Upper Tunguska r. Rus. Fed. see Angara
Upper Volta country Africa see Burkina
Upper West admin. reg. Ghana 125 E4
Uppinangadi India 94 B3
Upplands-Väsby Sweden 45 L4
Uppsala Sweden 45 L4
Uppsala county Sweden 45 L3
Upsala Canada 168 B3
Upshi Jammu and Kashmir 96 C2
Upson U.S.A. 172 C4
Upstart, Cape Australia 149 E3
Upstart Bay Australia 149 E3
Upton U.S.A. 177 N3
'Uqayqah, Wādī watercourse Jordan 108 G7
'Uqayribāt Syria 109 I2
Uqlat al 'Udhaybah well Iraq 107 F5
'Uqlat aş Şuqūr Saudi Arabia 104 C2
Uqturpan China see Wushi
Urabá, Golfo de b. Col. 198 B2
Urad Qianqi China see Xishanzui
Urad Zhongqi China 85 F3
also known as Haliut
Ūrāf Iran 100 D4
Uraga-suidō sea chan. Japan 91 F7
Uragawara Japan 90 F6
Ura-Guba Rus. Fed. 44 P1
Urahoro Japan 90 H3
Urakam India 94 C4
Urakawa Japan 90 H3
Ural hill Australia 147 E3
Ural r. Kazakh./Rus. Fed. 102 B3
also known as Zhayyq
Uralla Australia 147 F2
Ural Mountains Rus. Fed. 40 K2
also known as Ural'skiye Gory or Ural'skiy Khrebet
Uralovka Rus. Fed. 82 C1
Ural'sk Kazakh. 102 B2
also known as Oral
Ural'skaya Oblast' admin. div. Kazakh. see Zapadnyy Kazakhstan
Ural'skiye Gory mts Rus. Fed. see Ural Mountains
Ural'skiy Khrebet mts Rus. Fed. see Ural Mountains
Urambo Tanz. 129 B6
Uran India 94 B2
Urana Australia 147 E3
Urana, Lake Australia 147 E3
Urandangi Australia 148 C4
Urandi Brazil 202 D5
Uranium City Canada 167 I3
Urapunga Australia 148 B2
Urapuntja Australia 148 B4
Uraricoera Brazil 199 F4
Uraricoera r. Brazil 199 F4
Urartu country Asia see Armenia
Uras Sardegna Italy 57 A9
Ura-Tyube Tajik. see Üroteppa
Uravakonda India 94 C3
Uravan U.S.A. 183 P3
Urawa Japan 91 F7
Uray Rus. Fed. 38 G3
Uray'irah Saudi Arabia 105 E2
'Urayq ad Duḩūl des. Saudi Arabia 105 D2
'Urayq Sāqān des. Saudi Arabia 105 D2
Urazovka Rus. Fed. 40 H5
Urazovo Rus. Fed. 41 F6
Urbana IA U.S.A. 172 B8
Urbana IL U.S.A. 174 B3
Urbana IN U.S.A. 172 H10
Urbana OH U.S.A. 176 B5
Urbania Italy 56 E5
Urbano Santos Brazil 202 D2
Urbel r. Spain 54 H2
Urbino Italy 56 E5
historically known as Urbinum
Urbinum Italy see Urbino
Urbión mt. Spain 55 I2
Urbs Vetus Italy see Orvieto
Urcos Peru 200 C3
Urda Spain 54 H5
Ur'devarri hill Fin./Norway see Urtivaara
Urdoma Rus. Fed. 40 I3
Urd Tamir Gol r. Mongolia 84 D2
Urdyuzhskoye, Ozero l. Rus. Fed. 40 I2
Urdzhar Kazakh. 88 C2
also spelt Ürzhar
Ure r. U.K. 47 K9
Urechcha Belarus 42 I9
Urecheşti Romania 58 I2
Urein Egypt 108 B7
Uren' Rus. Fed. 40 H4
Urengoy Rus. Fed. 39 H3
Urenosi mt. Norway 45 I4
Urenui N.Z. 152 I6
Uréparapara i. Vanuatu 145 F3
Urewera National Park N.Z. 152 L6
Urfa Turkey see Şanlıurfa
Urga Mongolia see Ulan Bator
Urgal r. Rus. Fed. 82 D2
Urganch Uzbek. see Urgench
Urganlı Turkey 59 I10
Urgench Uzbek. 102 E4
also spelt Urganch
Ürgüp Turkey 106 C3
Urgut Uzbek. 103 F5
Urho China 88 D2
Urho Kekkosen kansallispuisto nat. park Fin. 44 N1
Uri Jammu and Kashmir 96 B2
Uribia Col. 198 C2
Uripitijuata, Cerro mt. Mex. 185 E5
Urique r. Mex. 181 F8
Urisino Australia 147 D2
Uritskiy Kazakh. 103 F1
Uritskoye Rus. Fed. 43 T9
Uri Wenz r. Eth. 104 B5
Urjala Fin. 45 M3
Urk Neth. 48 C3
Urkan Rus. Fed. 82 B1
Urkan r. Rus. Fed. 82 B1
Urkut Somalia 128 D4
Urla Turkey 106 A3
Urlaţi Romania 58 H4
Urlui r. Romania 58 G5
Urluk Rus. Fed. 85 E1
Urmai China 89 D6
Urmary Rus. Fed. 40 H5
Urmetan Tajik. 101 G2
Urmi r. Rus. Fed. 82 D2
Urmia Iran 100 A2
also spelt Orūmīyeh; formerly known as Reẓā'īyeh
Urmia, Lake salt l. Iran 100 A2
also known as Orūmīyeh, Daryācheh-ye; formerly known as Reẓā'īyeh, Daryācheh-ye
Urmston Road sea chan. Hong Kong China 87 [inset]
Uromi Nigeria 125 G5
Uroševac Kosovo, Srbija Yugo. 58 C6
Urosozero Rus. Fed. 40 E3
Üroteppa Tajik. 101 G2
also spelt Ura-Tyube
Urru Co salt l. China 89 D6
also known as Jagok Tso
Ursat'yevskaya Uzbek. see Khavast
Urshel'skiy Rus. Fed. 43 V6
Urt Mongolia 84 D3
Urtivaara hill Fin./Norway 44 M1
also spelt Ur'devarri
Urt Moron China 84 B4
Uru r. Brazil 206 D2
Uruáchic Mex. 184 C3
Uruaçu Brazil 202 B5
Uruana Brazil 206 D2
Uruapan Baja California Norte Mex. 184 A2
Uruapan Michoacán Mex. 185 E5
Urubamba Peru 200 B3
Urubaxi r. Brazil 199 E5
Urubu r. Brazil 199 G5
Urubupungá, Salto do waterfall Brazil 206 B7
Urucara Brazil 199 G5
Uruch'ye Rus. Fed. 43 O9
Urucu r. Brazil 199 F6
Uruçuí Brazil 202 C3
Uruçuí, Serra do hills Brazil 202 C4
Urucuia Brazil 202 C6
Urucuia r. Brazil 202 C6
Uruçuí Preto r. Brazil 202 C3
Urucum Brazil 201 F4
Urucurituba Brazil 199 G5
Uruguai r. Brazil 203 A8
also spelt Uruguay
Uruguaiana Brazil 204 F3
Uruguay r. Arg./Uruguay 204 F4
also spelt Uruguai
▶ Uruguay country S. America 204 F4
southamerica [countries] ▶▶▶ 192–193
Urukthapel i. Palau 73 H5
Urumchi China see Ürümqi
Ürümqi China 88 D3
English form Urumchi
Urundi country Africa see Burundi
Urunga Australia 147 G2
Urup r. Rus. Fed. 41 G7
Urup, Ostrov i. Rus. Fed. 81 Q3
Urup, Proliv strait Rus. Fed. 81 Q3
Urupá r. Brazil 201 E2
Uru Pass China/Kyrg. 88 B3
'Urūq al Awārik des. Saudi Arabia 105 D4
'Urūq ash Shaybah des. Saudi Arabia 105 F3
Urusha Rus. Fed. 82 A1
Urusha r. Rus. Fed. 82 A1
Urussu Rus. Fed. 40 J5
Uruti N.Z. 152 I6
Uruwira Tanz. 129 A6
Uryl' Kazakh. 88 D1
Uryū Japan 90 G3
Uryupinsk Rus. Fed. 41 G6
Ürzhar Kazakh. see Urdzhar
Urzhum Rus. Fed. 40 I4
Urziceni Romania 58 H4
Usa r. Belarus 43 J8
Usa Japan 91 B8
Usa r. Rus. Fed. 40 K2
Usada i. Phil. 74 B5
Uşak Turkey 106 B3
Uşak prov. Turkey 59 K10
Usakos Namibia 130 B4
Usambara Mountains Tanz. 129 C6
Usangu Flats plain Tanz. 129 B7
Usarp Mountains Antarctica 223 K2
'Usaylān Yemen 105 D5
Usborne, Mount hill Falkland Is 205 F8
Usedom Germany 49 K2
Usedom i. Germany 49 L2
Useless Loop Australia 151 A5
Usengi Kenya 128 B5
Usfān Saudi Arabia 104 B3
Usha r. Belarus 42 G8
Usha r. Belarus 43 J8
Ushachi Belarus see Ushachy
Ushachy Belarus 43 J6
also spelt Ushachi
Ushakova, Ostrov i. Rus. Fed. 39 H1
Ushanovo Kazakh. 88 C1
Ushant i. France see Ouessant, Île d'
Usharal Kazakh. see Ucharal
Usharal Kazakh. 103 G4
Ushayqir Saudi Arabia 105 D2
'Ushayrah Saudi Arabia 104 C3
Ushcha r. Rus. Fed. 43 K6
Ushcherp'ye Rus. Fed. 43 M9
Ushibuka Japan 91 B8
Ushirombo Tanz. 128 A5
Ushtobe Kazakh. 103 I3
formerly spelt Ush-Tyube
Ush-Tyube Kazakh. see Ushtobe
Ushuaia Arg. 205 C9
Uši Latvia 42 D4
Usina Brazil 202 A3
Usinsk Rus. Fed. 40 K2
Usk r. U.K. 47 J12
Uska India 97 D4
Uskhodni Belarus 42 I8
Uskoplje Bos.-Herz. see Gornji Vakuf
Üsküdar Turkey 106 B2
Üsküp Turkey 58 I7
Usma Latvia 42 D4
Usman' Rus. Fed. 41 F5
Usmas ezers l. Latvia 42 D4
Usmat Uzbek. 103 F5
formerly spelt Usmet
Usmet Uzbek. see Usmat
Usmyn' Rus. Fed. 43 M6
Uso r. Spain 54 F5
Usogorsk Rus. Fed. 40 I3
Usoke Tanz. 129 B6
Usol'ye Rus. Fed. 40 K4
Usol'ye-Sibirskoye Rus. Fed. 80 G2
Usora r. Bos.-Herz. 56 K4
Usozha r. Rus. Fed. 43 P9
Usozha r. Rus. Fed. 43 Q9
Uspallata Arg. 204 C4
Uspenka Kazakh. 103 I1
Uspenskiy Kazakh. 103 H2
Uspenskoye Rus. Fed. 43 L5
Uspen'ye Rus. Fed. 40 G4
Ussel France 51 I7
Ussuri r. Rus. Fed. 82 D2
also known as Wusuli Jiang
Ussuriysk Rus. Fed. 82 C4
formerly known as Voroshilov
Ust'-Abakanskoye Rus. Fed. see Abakan
Ust'-Alekseyevo Rus. Fed. 40 H3
Usta Muhammad Pak. 101 G4
Ust'-Balyk Rus. Fed. see Nefteyugansk
Ust'-Barguzin Rus. Fed. 81 H2
Ust'-Dolyssy Rus. Fed. 43 K5
Ust'-Donetskiy Rus. Fed. 41 G7
Ust'-Dzheguta Rus. Fed. 41 G7
formerly known as Ust'-Dzhegutinskaya
Ust'-Dzhegutinskaya Rus. Fed. see Ust'-Dzheguta
Uster Switz. 51 O5
Ustica, Isola di i. Sicilia Italy 57 F10
Ust'-Ilimsk Rus. Fed. 39 K4
Ust'-Ilimskiy Vodokhranilishche resr Rus. Fed. 80 G1
Ust'-Ilya Rus. Fed. 85 G1
Ust'-Ilych Rus. Fed. 40 K3
Ústí nad Labem Czech Rep. 49 L5
Ústí nad Orlicí Czech Rep. 49 N6
Ustinov Rus. Fed. see Izhevsk
Ustirt plat. Kazakh./Uzbek. see Ustyurt Plateau
Ustka Poland 49 N1
Ust'-Kamchatsk Rus. Fed. 39 Q4
Ust'-Kamenogorsk Kazakh. 88 C1
also known as Öskemen
Ust'-Kan Rus. Fed. 88 D1
Ust'-Kara Rus. Fed. 40 M1
Ust'-Koksa Rus. Fed. 88 D1
Ust'-Kulom Rus. Fed. 40 J3
Ust'-Kut Rus. Fed. 80 H1
Ust'-Kuyga Rus. Fed. 39 N2
Ust'-Labinsk Rus. Fed. 41 F7
formerly known as Ust'-Labinskaya
Ust'-Labinskaya Rus. Fed. see Ust'-Labinsk
Ust'-Luga Rus. Fed. 43 J2
Ust'-Lyzha Rus. Fed. 40 K2
Ust'-Maya Rus. Fed. 39 N3
Ust'-Mongunay Rus. Fed. see Primorskiy
Ust'-Munduyka Rus. Fed. 39 I3
Ust'-Nem Rus. Fed. 40 J3
Ust'-Nera Rus. Fed. 39 O3
Ust'-Olenek Rus. Fed. 39 L2
Ust'-Omchug Rus. Fed. 39 O3
Ust'-Orda Buryat Autonomous Okrug admin. div. Rus. Fed. see Ust'-Ordynskiy Buryatskiy Avtonomnyy Okrug
Ust'-Ordynskiy Rus. Fed. 80 G2
Ust'-Ordynskiy Buryatskiy Avtonomnyy Okrug admin. div. Rus. Fed. 80 G2
English form Ust-Orda Buryat Autonomous Okrug
Ust'-Port Rus. Fed. 39 I3
Ustrem Bulg. 58 H6
Ustrzyki Dolne Poland 49 T6
formerly known as Nizhniye Ustriki
Ust'-Sara Rus. Fed. 43 Q1
Ust'-Shonosha Rus. Fed. 40 G3
Ust'-Tsil'ma Rus. Fed. 40 J2
Ust'-Ulagan Rus. Fed. 88 D1
Ust'-Umalta Rus. Fed. 82 D2
Ust'-Ura Rus. Fed. 40 H3
Ust'-Usa Rus. Fed. 40 K2
Ust'-Vayen'ga Rus. Fed. 40 G3
Ust'-Voya Rus. Fed. 40 K2
Ust'ya r. Rus. Fed. 40 G3
Ust'-Yansk Rus. Fed. 39 N2
Ust'ye Tverskaya Oblast' Rus. Fed. 43 M5
Ust'ye Vologod. Obl. Rus. Fed. 40 G4
Ust'ye Vologod. Obl. Rus. Fed. 43 U2
Ust'ye Yaroslavskaya Oblast' Rus. Fed. 43 U4
Ust'ye r. Rus. Fed. 43 U4
Ust'ye-Kirovskoye Rus. Fed. 43 Q3
Ustyurt, Plato plat. Kazakh./Uzbek. see Ustyurt Plateau
Ustyurt Plateau Kazakh./Uzbek. 102 D4
also known as Ustirt or Ustyurt, Plato or Ustyurt Platosi
Ustyurt Platosi plat. Kazakh./Uzbek. see Ustyurt Plateau
Ustyutskoye Rus. Fed. 43 Q3
Ustyuzhna Rus. Fed. 43 R3
Usu China 88 D2
Usuki Japan 91 B8
Usulután El Salvador 185 H6
Usumacinta r. Guat./Mex. 185 G5
Usumbura Burundi see Bujumbura
Usun Apau, Dataran Tinggi plat. Sarawak Malaysia 77 F2
Usutu r. Africa 133 Q3
also known as Great Usutu or Lusutufu
Usvyaty Rus. Fed. 43 L6
Usvyeyka r. Belarus 43 K7
Uta Indon. 73 I7
Utah state U.S.A. 183 M2
Utah Lake U.S.A. 183 M1
Utajärvi Fin. 44 N2
Utan Indon. 77 G5
Utashinai Rus. Fed. see Yuzhno-Kuril'sk
'Utaybah reg. Saudi Arabia 104 C3
'Utaybah, Buḩayrat al imp. l. Syria 109 H4
Utayyiq Saudi Arabia 105 E2
Utbjoa Norway 45 I4
Utebo Spain 55 K3
Ute Creek r. U.S.A. 179 B5
Utembo r. Angola 127 D9
Ute Mountain Indian Reservation res. U.S.A. 183 P4
Utena Lith. 42 G6
Utete Tanz. 129 C7
Uthai Thani Thai. 79 C5
Uthal Pak. 101 F5
Utiariti Brazil 201 F3
Utica NY U.S.A. 177 J2
Utica OH U.S.A. 176 C5
Utiel Spain 55 J5
Utikuma Lake Canada 167 H4
Utila Hond. 186 B3
Utinga r. Brazil 202 D5
Utladalen park Norway 45 I3
Utlwanang S. Africa 133 J4
Uto Japan 91 B8
Utrata r. Poland 49 R3
Utraula India 97 D4
Utrecht Neth. 48 C3
historically known as Trajectum
Utrecht S. Africa 133 O4
Utrera Spain 54 F7
Utroya r. Rus. Fed. 42 J4
Utsira Norway 46 Q4
Utsjoki Fin. 44 N1
also spelt Ohcejohka
Utsunomiya Japan 91 F6
Utta Rus. Fed. 102 A3
Uttaradit Thai. 78 C4
Uttaranchal state India 96 C3
Uttarkashi India 96 C3
Uttar Pradesh state India 96 C4
formerly known as United Provinces
Utu China see Miao'ergou
Utubulak China 88 D2
Utupua i. Solomon Is 145 F3
formerly known as Edgecumbe Island
Utva r. Kazakh. 102 C2
Uulu Estonia 42 F3
Uummannaq Greenland see Dundas
Uummannaq Greenland 165 N2
Uummannaq Fjord inlet Greenland 165 N2
Uummannarsuaq c. Greenland see Farewell, Cape
Uurainen Fin. 44 N3
Üüreg Nuur salt l. Mongolia 84 A1
Üür Gol r. Mongolia 84 D1
Uusikaarlepyy Fin. see Nykarleby
Uusikaupunki Fin. 45 M3
also known as Nystad
Uutapi Namibia 130 B3
also known as Ombalantu
Uva r. Col. 198 D4
Uva Rus. Fed. 40 J4
Uvac r. Bos.-Herz./Yugo. 58 A5
Uvalde U.S.A. 179 C6
Uvaravichy Belarus 43 L9
Uvarovka Rus. Fed. 43 Q6
Uvarovo Rus. Fed. 41 G6
Uvéa i. New Caledonia see Ouvéa
Uvel'r. Rus. Fed. 43 P3
Uvinza Tanz. 129 A6
Uvira Dem. Rep. Congo 126 F5
Uvod' r. Rus. Fed. 43 V4
Uvongo S. Africa 133 O7
Uvs prov. Mongolia 84 B1
Uvs Nuur salt l. Mongolia 84 B1
Uwa Japan 91 C8
Uwainid, Wādī al watercourse Saudi Arabia 109 H9
Uwajima Japan 91 C8
Uwa-kai b. Japan 91 C8
'Uwayfī Oman 105 G3
'Uwayja well Saudi Arabia 104 C2
'Uwaynāt Wannīn Libya 120 B2
'Uwayriḑ, Ḩarrat al lava field Saudi Arabia 104 B2
Uwaysiṭ well Saudi Arabia 109 J7
Uweinat, Jebel mt. Sudan 120 E4
Uwemba Tanz. 129 B7
Uwi i. Indon. 77 D2
Uxin Ju China 85 F4
Uxin Qi China see Dabqig
Uxmal tourist site Mex. 185 H4
Uxxaktal China 88 D3
Uyaly Kazakh. 103 E3
Uyaly, Ozero l. Kazakh. see Koshkarkol', Ozero
Uyar Rus. Fed. 80 E1
Üydzin Mongolia 85 E2
Uyo Nigeria 125 G5
Üyönch Mongolia 84 B2
Üyönch Gol r. China 84 A2
Uyu Chaung r. Myanmar 78 A2
Uyuk Kazakh. 103 G4
also spelt Oyyq; formerly spelt Oik
Uyun Saudi Arabia 105 E2
Uyuni Bol. 200 D5
Uyuni, Salar de salt flat Bol. 200 D5
Uza r. Rus. Fed. 41 H5
'Uzaym, Nahr al r. Iraq 107 F4
▶ Uzbekistan country Asia 102 D4
spelt O'zbekiston or Ŭzbekiston in Uzbek; formerly known as Uzbekskaya S.S.R. or Uzbek S.S.R.
asia [countries] ▶▶▶ 64–67
Ŭzbekiston country Asia see Uzbekistan
Uzbekskaya S.S.R. country Asia see Uzbekistan
Uzbek S.S.R. country Asia see Uzbekistan
Uzda Belarus 42 I8
Uzen' Kazakh. see Kyzylsay
Uzengyu-Kuush, Gora mt. China/Kyrg. 88 B3
Uzerche France 50 H7
Uzès France 51 K8
Uzgen Kyrg. see Özgön
Uzh r. Ukr. 49 T7
Uzh r. Ukr. 41 D6
Uzha r. Rus. Fed. 43 O7
Uzhgorod Ukr. see Uzhhorod
Uzhhorod Ukr. 49 T7
also spelt Uzhgorod; formerly spelt Užhorod; historically known as Ungvár
Uzhok Ukr. 49 T7
Užhorod Ukr. see Uzhhorod
Užice Srbija Yugo. 58 A5
formerly known as Titovo Užice
Uzlovaya Rus. Fed. 43 T8
Uzola r. Rus. Fed. 40 G4
Üzümlü Turkey 59 K12
Uzun Uzbek. 103 G5
Uzun Ada i. Turkey 59 H10
Uzunagach Almatinskaya Oblast' Kazakh. 103 I4
also spelt Uzynaghash
Uzunagach Almatinskaya Oblast' Kazakh. 103 I4
Uzunbulak China 88 D2
Uzuncaburç Turkey 108 E1
Uzunköprü Turkey 106 A2
Uzventis Lith. 42 D6
Uzvoz Rus. Fed. 43 M6
Uzyn Ukr. 41 D6
Uzynaghash Kazakh. see Uzunagach
Uzynkair Kazakh. 103 E3

↓ V

Vaajakoski Fin. 44 N3
Vaal r. S. Africa 132 H6
Vaala Fin. 44 N2
Vaalbos National Park S. Africa 133 I5
Vaal Dam S. Africa 133 M4
Vaal Dam Nature Reserve S. Africa 133 M3
Vaalplaas S. Africa 133 M2
Vaalwater S. Africa 131 F5
Vaartsi Estonia 42 I4
Vaasa Fin. 44 M3
also spelt Vasa
Vabalninkas Lith. 42 F6
Vabich r. Belarus 43 K8
Vabkent Uzbek. 103 F4
also spelt Wobkent
Vablya r. Rus. Fed. 43 O9
Vác Hungary 49 Q8
Vacaré r. Brazil 207 H8
Vacaria Brazil 203 B9
Vacaria r. Mato Grosso do Sul Brazil 203 A7
Vacaria r. Minas Gerais Brazil 202 D6
Vacaria, Campo da plain Brazil 203 B9
Vacaria, Serra hills Brazil 203 A7
Vacaville U.S.A. 182 C3
Vache, Île-à- i. Haiti 187 E3
Väckelsång Sweden 45 K4
Vad Rus. Fed. 40 H5
Vad r. Rus. Fed. 41 G5
Vada India 94 B2
Vadakste r. Latvia/Lith. 42 D5
Vădăstrița Romania 58 F5
Vadehavet nature res. Denmark 45 J5
Vădeni Romania 58 I3
Vadi India 94 B3
also known as Savantvadi
Vadodara India 96 B5
formerly known as Baroda
Vadsø Norway 44 O1
Vadstena Sweden 45 K4
Vadu Crişului Romania 58 D2
▶ Vaduz Liechtenstein 48 G8
Capital of Liechtenstein.
Værøy i. Norway 44 K2
Vaga r. Rus. Fed. 43 V1
Vågåmo Norway 45 J3
Vaganski Vrh mt. Croatia 56 H4
Vágar i. Faroe Is 46 E1
Vagavaram India 94 D2
Vagnhärad Sweden 45 L4
Vagos Port. 54 C4
Vägsele Sweden 44 L2
Vågsfjorden sea chan. Norway 44 L1
Váh r. Slovakia 49 P8
Vahhābī Iran 100 D4
Vahsel, Cape S. Georgia 205 [inset]
Vahto Fin. 45 M3
▶ Vaiaku Tuvalu 145 G2
Capital of Tuvalu, on Funafuti atoll.
world [countries] ▶▶▶ 10–11
Vaida Estonia 42 F2
Vaiden U.S.A. 175 B5
Vaigai r. India 94 C4
Vaijapur India 94 B2
Vaikam India 94 C4
Väike Emajõgi r. Estonia 42 H3
Väike-Maarja Estonia 42 H2
Väike-Pakri i. Estonia 42 E2
Vaikijaur Sweden 44 L2
Väimela Estonia 42 I4
Vainode Latvia 42 C5
Vaippar r. India 94 C4
Vair r. France 51 L4
Vairowal India 96 B3
Vaison-la-Romaine France 51 L8
Vaitupu i. Tuvalu 145 G2
also spelt Oaitupu
Vajrakarur India see Kanur
Vajszló Hungary 56 J3
Vakaga pref. Cent. Afr. Rep. 126 D2
Vakaga r. Cent. Afr. Rep. 126 D2
Vakhan Tajik. 96 B1
Vakhsh Tajik. 101 G2
formerly known as Vakhstroy
Vakhsh r. Tajik. 101 G2
Vakhstroy Tajik. see Vakhsh
Vakīlābād Iran 100 D4
Vaksdal Norway 45 I3
Vålådalen naturreservat nature res. Sweden 44 K3
Valamaz Rus. Fed. 40 J4
Valandovo Macedonia 58 D7
Valašské Klobouky Czech Rep. 49 P6
Valašské Meziříčí Czech Rep. 49 O6
Valaxa i. Greece 59 F10
Val-Barrette Canada 173 R4
Vâlcăneşti Romania 58 G3
Vâlcanului, Munţii mts Romania 58 D3
Valcheta Arg. 204 D6
Valdai Hills Rus. Fed. see Valdayskaya Vozvyshennost'
Valday Rus. Fed. 43 O4
Valdayskaya Vozvyshennost' hills Rus. Fed. 43 N5
English form Valdai Hills
Valdayskoye, Ozero l. Rus. Fed. 43 O3
Valdecañas, Embalse de resr Spain 54 F5
Val del Ticino, Parco della park Italy 56 A3
Valdemārpils Latvia 42 D4
Valdemarsvik Sweden 45 L4
Val-de-Meuse France 51 L4
Valdemoro Spain 54 H4
Valdepeñas Spain 55 H6
Valderaduey r. Spain 54 F3
Valderas Spain 54 F2
Val-de-Reuil France 50 H3
Valders U.S.A. 172 F6
▶ Valdés, Península pen. Arg. 205 E6
Lowest point in South America.
southamerica [landscapes] ▶▶▶ 190–191
Val-des-Bois Canada 173 R5
Valdez U.S.A. 164 E3
Valdivia Chile 204 B5
Valdivia Col. 198 C3
Valdobbiadene Italy 56 D3
Val-d'Or Canada 168 E3
Valdosa mt. Spain 55 H3
Valdosta U.S.A. 175 D6
Valdres valley Norway 45 J3
Vale Georgia 107 E2
Vale U.S.A. 180 C3
Valea lui Mihai Romania 49 T8
Valea Lungă Romania 58 F2
Valea Lungă Romania 58 G3
Valemount Canada 166 G4
Valença Brazil 202 E5
Valença do Piauí Brazil 202 D3
Valençay France 50 H5
Valence Midi-Pyrénées France 50 G8
Valence Rhône-Alpes France 51 K8
Valencia Spain 55 K5
historically known as Valentia
Valencia aut. comm. Spain 55 K5
also known as Valenciana, Comunidad
Valencia Venez. 199 E2
Valencia, Golfo de g. Spain 55 L5
Valencia de Alcántara Spain 54 D5
Valencia de Don Juan Spain 54 F2
Valencia Island Rep. of Ireland 47 B12
Valenciana, Comunidad aut. comm. Spain see Valencia
Valenciennes France 51 J2
Văleni de Munte Romania 58 H3
Valensole, Plateau de France 51 M9
Valentia Spain see Valencia
Valentin Rus. Fed. 82 D4
Valentine U.S.A. 178 B3
Valentine National Wildlife Refuge nature res. U.S.A. 178 B3
Valenza Italy 56 A3
Valenzuela Phil. 74 B3
Våler Norway 45 J3
Valera Venez. 198 D2
Vale Verde Brazil 207 N3
Valga Estonia 42 H4
Valgejõgi r. Estonia 42 G2
Valhalla Provincial Park Canada 166 G5
Valikhanovo Kazakh. 103 G1
also known as Uälikhanov
Valinco, Golfe de b. Corse France 56 A7
Valinhos Brazil 206 G9
Valjevo Srbija Yugo. 58 A4
Valka Latvia 42 H4
Valkeakoski Fin. 45 N3
Valkenswaard Neth. 48 C4
Valkla Estonia 42 G2
Valko Fin. 42 H1
also spelt Valkom
Valkom Fin. see Valko
Valky Ukr. 41 E6
Valkyrie Dome ice feature Antarctica 223 C1
Vallabhipur India 96 A5
Valladolid Mex. 185 H4
Valladolid Spain 54 G3
Vallard, Lac l. Canada 169 G2
Valldal Norway 44 I3
Vall de Uxó Spain 55 K5
Valle dept Col. 198 B4
Valle Norway 45 I4
Vallecito Arg. 204 D3
Valle d'Aosta admin. reg. Italy 51 N7
Valle de la Pascua Venez. 199 E2
Valle de Rosario Mex. 181 F8
Valle de Santiago Mex. 185 E4
Valle de Zaragoza Mex. 184 D3
Valledupar Col. 198 C2
Vallée-Jonction Canada 169 G4
Valle Fértil, Sierra de mts Arg. 204 C3
Valle Grande Bol. 201 D4
Valle Hermoso Mex. 185 F3
Vallejo U.S.A. 182 B3
Vallelunga Pratameno Sicilia Italy 57 F11
Valle Nacional Mex. 185 F5
Vallenar Chile 204 C3
Vallentuna Sweden 45 L4
▶ Valletta Malta 57 G13
Capital of Malta.
Valley r. Canada 167 L5
Valley Center U.S.A. 183 G8
Valley City U.S.A. 178 C2
Valley Falls U.S.A. 180 B4
Valley Head Phil. 74 B2
Valley Head U.S.A. 176 E7
Valley of The Kings tourist site Egypt 121 G3
Valley Springs U.S.A. 182 D3
Valley Station U.S.A. 174 C4
Valley Stream U.S.A. 177 L5
Valleyview Canada 167 G4
Valley View U.S.A. 176 A8
Vallo della Lucania Italy 57 H8
Valls Spain 55 M3
Vallsta Sweden 45 L3
Val Marie Canada 167 J5
Valmaseda Spain see Balmaseda
Valmiera Latvia 42 G4
Valmy U.S.A. 183 G1
Valnera mt. Spain 55 H1
Valognes France 50 E3
Valona Albania see Vlorë
Valozhyn Belarus 42 H7
also spelt Volozhin
Valpaços Port. 54 D3
Val-Paradis Canada 168 E3
Valparai India 94 C4
Valparaíso Brazil 206 C8
Valparaíso Chile 204 C4
Valparaíso admin. reg. Chile 204 C4
Valparaíso Mex. 184 E4
Valparaiso FL U.S.A. 185 I2
Valparaiso IN U.S.A. 174 C3
Valpelline valley Italy 51 N7
Valpoi India 94 B3
Valpovo Croatia 56 K3
Valronquillo hill Spain 54 G5
Vals r. S. Africa 133 K4
Vals, Tanjung c. Indon. 73 I8
Valsad India 94 B1
Valshui Wash watercourse U.S.A. 181 D7
Valspan S. Africa 131 E5
Valsrivier S. Africa 133 M5
Valtimo Fin. 44 O3
Valtou mts Greece 59 C9
Valua i. Vanuatu see Mota Lava
Valuyets Rus. Fed. 43 O9
Valuyevka Rus. Fed. 41 G7
Valuyki Rus. Fed. 41 F6
Valverde Dom. Rep. see Mao
Valverde del Camino Spain 54 E7
Valverde del Fresno Spain 54 E4
Vam Co Đông r. Vietnam 79 D6
Vam Co Tay r. Vietnam 79 D6
Vamizi, Ilha i. Moz. 129 D7
Vammala Fin. 45 M3
Vampula Fin. 45 M3
Vamsadhara r. India 95 E2
Vamvakas, Akra pt Greece 59 H10
Van Turkey 107 E3
Van, Lake salt l. Turkey 107 E3
also known as Van Gölü
Vanadzor Armenia 107 F2
formerly known as Karaklis or Kirovakan
Vanajavesi l. Fin. 45 N3
Vana-Koiola Estonia 42 I4
Vanån r. Sweden 45 K3
Vânători Romania 58 J3
Vânători Romania 58 F2
Vanavara Rus. Fed. 39 K3
Van Buren AR U.S.A. 179 D5
Van Buren IN U.S.A. 172 H10
Van Buren MO U.S.A. 174 B4
Van Buren U.S.A. see Kettering
Vanceburg U.S.A. 176 B7
Vanch Tajik. see Vanj
Vanchskiy Khrebet mts Tajik. see Vanj, Qatorkŭhi
Vancleve U.S.A. 176 B8
Vancouver Canada 166 F5
Vancouver U.S.A. 180 B3
Vancouver, Mount Canada/U.S.A. 166 B2
Vancouver Island Canada 166 E5
Vanda Fin. see Vantaa
Vandalia IL U.S.A. 174 B4
Vandalia OH U.S.A. 176 A6
Vandavasi India 94 C3
formerly spelt Wandiwash
Vandekerckhove Lake Canada 167 K3
Vandellós Spain 55 L3
Vanderbijlpark S. Africa 133 L3
Vanderbilt U.S.A. 173 I5
Vandergrift U.S.A. 176 F5
Vanderhoof Canada 166 E4
Vanderkloof Dam resr S. Africa 133 I7
Vanderlin Island Australia 148 C2
Van Diemen, Cape N.T. Australia 148 A1
Van Diemen, Cape Qld Australia 148 C3
Van Diemen Gulf Australia 148 B1
Van Diemen's Land state Australia see Tasmania
Vändra Estonia 42 G3
Vandyksdrif S. Africa 133 N3
Vandžiogala Lith. 42 E6
Vāne Latvia 42 D5
Väner, Lake Sweden see Vänern
▶ Vänern l. Sweden 45 K4
4th largest lake in Europe. English form Väner, Lake.
europe [landscapes] ▶▶▶ 30–31
Vänersborg Sweden 45 K4
Vaneteze r. Moz. 133 Q2
Vang, Mount Antarctica 222 T2
Vanga Kenya 129 C6
Vangaindrano Madag. 131 [inset] J4
Vangaži Latvia 42 F4
Van Gölü salt l. Turkey see Van, Lake
Vangsvik Norway 44 L1
Vanguard Canada 167 J5
Van Horn U.S.A. 181 F7
Vanier Canada 168 F4
formerly known as Eastview
Vanikoro Islands Solomon Is 145 F3
also known as Mannicolo Islands; formerly known as Pitt Islands
Vanil Noir mt. Switz. 51 N6
Vanimo P.N.G. 73 J7
Vanino Rus. Fed. 82 F2
Vanivilasa Sagara resr India 94 C3
Vaniyambadi India 94 C3
Vanj Tajik. 101 G2
also spelt Vanch
Vanj, Qatorkŭhi mts Tajik. 101 G2
also known as Vanchskiy Khrebet
Vänjaurträsk Sweden 44 L2
Vânju Mare Romania 58 D4
formerly spelt Vînju Mare
Vankarem Rus. Fed. 39 S3
Vankavesi l. Fin. 45 M3
Vanna i. Norway 44 L1
Vännäs Sweden 44 L3
Vanne r. France 51 J4
Vannes France 50 D5
Vannes, Lac l. Canada 169 H2
Vannovka Kazakh. see Tura-Ryskulova
Vanntindan mt. Norway 44 L1
Van Reenen S. Africa 133 N5
Van Rees, Pegunungan mts Indon. 73 I7
Vanrhynsdorp S. Africa 132 C8
Van Riebeeck Nature Reserve S. Africa 133 M2
Vanrook Australia 149 D3
Vanrook Creek r. Australia 149 D3
Vansada India 94 B1
Vansant U.S.A. 176 C8
Vansbro Sweden 45 K3
Vanse Norway 45 I4
Vansittart Bay Australia 150 D2
Vansittart Island Canada 165 K3
Vanstadensrus S. Africa 133 L6
Vantaa Fin. 45 N3
also spelt Vanda
Vantaa r. Fin. 42 F1
Van Truer Tableland reg. Australia 151 C5
Vant's Drift S. Africa 133 O5
Vanua Balavu i. Fiji 145 H3
also spelt Vanua Mbalavu or Vanua Valavo
Vanua Lava i. Vanuatu 145 F3
Vanua Levu i. Fiji 145 G3
Vanua Mbalavu i. Fiji see Vanua Balavu

index V

Vanuatu *country* S. Pacific Ocean **145** F3
formerly known as New Hebrides *or* Nouvelles Hébrides
oceania [countries] 138–139
oceania [features] 142–143
Vanua Valavo *i.* Fiji *see* **Vanua Balavu**
Van Wert U.S.A. **176** A5
Van Wyksdorp S. Africa **132** F10
Vanwyksvlei S. Africa **132** F7
Vanwyksvlei *l.* S. Africa **132** F7
Van Zylsrus S. Africa **132** G3
Vao, Embalse de *resr* Spain **54** D2
also spelt Bao, Embalse del
Var *r.* France **51** N9
Vara Estonia **42** H3
Vara Sweden **45** K4
Varada *r.* India **94** C3
Varadero Cuba **186** C2
Varahi India **96** A5
Varaita *r.* Italy **51** N8
Varakļāni Latvia **42** H5
Varalé Côte d'Ivoire **124** E4
Varallo Italy **56** A3
Varāmīn Iran **100** B3
Varanasi India **97** D4
formerly known as Benares; *historically known as* Kasi
Varandey Rus. Fed. **40** K1
Varangerfjorden *sea chan.* Norway **44** O1
Varangerhalvøya *pen.* Norway **44** O1
also known as Várnjárg
Varano, Lago di *lag.* Italy **56** H7
Varapayeva Belarus **42** I6
Varaždin Croatia **56** I2
Varazze Italy **56** A4
Varberg Sweden **45** K4
Varbla Estonia **42** E3
Varda Greece **59** C10
Vardak *prov.* Afgh. **101** G3
Vardannapet India **94** C2
Vardar *r.* Macedonia **58** D7
Varde Denmark **45** J5
Vardenis Armenia **107** F2
formerly known as Basargechar
Vårdö Fin. **42** B1
Vardø Norway **44** O1
Varduva *r.* Lith. **42** D5
Varegovo Rus. Fed. **43** U4
Varel Germany **48** F2
Varela Arg. **204** D4
Varėna Lith. **42** F7
Vareš Bos.-Herz. **56** K4
Varese Italy **56** A3
Varfolomeyevka Rus. Fed. **82** D3
Vårgårda Sweden **45** K4
Vargas Arg. **204** C4
Vargem *r.* Brazil **202** E4
Vargem Alta Brazil **207** L7
Vargem Grande Brazil **202** D2
Vargem Grande do Sul Brazil **206** G8
Varginha Brazil **203** C7
Varhaug Norway **45** I4
Varkana Iran *see* **Gorgān**
Varkaus Fin. **44** N3
Varkhi Belarus **43** K6
Varmahlíð Iceland **44** [inset] C2
Varmeln *l.* Sweden **45** K4
Värmland *county* Sweden **45** K4
Värmlandsnäs *i.* Sweden **45** K4
Varna Bulg. **58** I5
formerly known as Stalin; *historically known as* Odessus
Varna *r.* India **94** B2
Varna Rus. Fed. **103** E1
Värnamo Sweden **45** K4
Värnäs Sweden **45** K3
Varnavino Rus. Fed. **40** H4
Varnek Rus. Fed. **40** L1
Varniai Lith. **42** D6
Varnja Estonia **42** I3
Várnjárg *pen.* Norway *see* **Varangerhalvøya**
Varnyany Belarus **42** H7
Varosha Cyprus *see* **Varosia**
Varosia Cyprus **108** E2
also known as Maraş; *also spelt* Varosha
Varoška Rijeka Bos.-Herz. **56** I3
Varpaisjärvi Fin. **44** N3
Várpalota Hungary **49** P8
Värriön luonnonpuisto *nature res.* Fin. **44** O2
Vârşag Romania **58** G2
Varsaj Afgh. **101** G2
Vârşand Romania **58** C2
Varsh, Ozero *l.* Rus. Fed. **40** H2
Varsinais-Suomi *reg.* Fin. **45** M3
also known as Egentliga Finland
Värska Estonia **42** I4
Vartashen Azer. *see* **Oğuz**
Vartdalsfjorden *inlet* Norway **44** I3
Vartholomio Greece **59** C11
Varto Turkey **107** E3
also known as Gümgüm
Vârtop Romania **58** E4
Vârtop, Pasul *pass* Romania **58** D2
Värtsilä Fin. **44** O3
Var'yegan Rus. Fed. **38** H3
Varzaneh Iran **100** C3
Várzea Alegre Brazil **202** E3
Várzea da Palma Brazil **203** C6
Várzea Grande Brazil **202** D3
Varzelândia Brazil **207** I2
Varzo Italy **56** A2
Varzob Tajik. **101** G2
Varzuga Rus. Fed. **40** F2
Vasa Fin. *see* **Vaasa**
Vasa Barris *r.* Brazil **202** E4
Vasai India **94** B2
Vasalemma Estonia **42** F2
Vasalemma *r.* Estonia **42** F2
Vásárosnamény Hungary **49** T7
Vascão *r.* Port. **54** D7
Vaşcău Romania **58** D2
Vashka *r.* Rus. Fed. **40** H2
Vasht Iran *see* **Khāsh**
Vasilika Greece **58** E8
Vasilkov Ukr. *see* **Vasyl'kiv**
Vasilyevichy Belarus **43** K9
Vasil'yevo Rus. Fed. **42** I4
Vasil'yevskiy Mokh Rus. Fed. **43** Q4
Vas'kavichy Belarus **43** L8
Vaskivesi Fin. **45** M3
Vasknarva Estonia **42** I2
Vaslui Romania **58** I2
Vassar U.S.A. **173** J7
Vassenden Norway **45** I3
Vassfaret og Vidalen *park* Norway **45** J3
Vas-Soproni-síkság *hills* Hungary **49** N8
Vassouras Brazil **207** J9
Vastan Turkey *see* **Gevaş**
Västana Sweden **44** L3
Västanfjärd Fin. **42** D1
Västansjö Sweden **44** L2
Vastemõisa Estonia **42** G3
Vastenjaure *l.* Sweden **44** L2
Västerås Sweden **45** L4
Västerbotten *county* Sweden **44** K2
Västerdalälven *r.* Sweden **45** K3
Västerhaninge Sweden **45** L4
Västernorrland *county* Sweden **44** L3
Västervik Sweden **45** L4
Västmanland *county* Sweden **45** K4
Vasto Italy **56** G6
Västra Götaland *county* Sweden **45** K4
Västra Ormsjö Sweden **44** L2
Vastse-Kuuste Estonia **42** H3
Vasvár Hungary **49** N8
Vasyl'kiv Ukr. **41** D6
also spelt Vasilkov
Vatan France **50** H5
Väte Sweden **45** L4
Vaté *i.* Vanuatu *see* **Éfaté**
Vatersay *i.* U.K. **46** E7
Vathi Greece *see* **Ithaki**
Vathí Greece *see* **Vathy**
Vathia Greece **59** D12
Vathy *Notio Aigaio* Greece **59** H12
Vathy *Voreio Aigaio* Greece **59** H11
also spelt Vathí

Vatican City Europe **56** E7
Independent papal state, the smallest country in the world. English form Holy See; known as Città del Vaticano in Italian
world [countries] 10–11
europe [countries] 32–35

Vaticano, Capo *c.* Italy **57** H10
Vaticano, Città del Europe *see* **Vatican City**
Vatio Greece **59** I12
Vatnajökull *ice cap* Iceland **44** [inset] C2
Vatne Norway **44** I3
Vatoa *i.* Fiji **145** H3
also known as Turtle Island
Vatomandry Madag. **131** [inset] K3
Vatoussa Greece **59** H9
Vatra Dornei Romania **58** G1
Vätter, Lake Sweden *see* **Vättern**
Vättern *l.* Sweden **45** K4
also known as Vätter, Lake
Vattrång Sweden **45** L3
Vatulele *i.* Fiji **145** G3
Vaucluse, Monts de *mts* France **51** L9
Vaucouleurs France **51** L4
Vaughan Springs Australia **148** A4
Vaughn U.S.A. **181** F6
Vaulx-en-Velin France **51** K7
Vaupés *dept* Col. **198** D4
Vaupés *r.* Col. **198** D4
Vauquelin *r.* Canada **168** E2
Vauvert France **51** K9
Vauxhall Canada **167** H5
Vav India **96** A4
Vavatenina Madag. **131** [inset] K3
Vava'u *i.* Tonga **145** H3
Vava'u Group *is* Tonga **145** H3
Vavitao *i.* Fr. Polynesia *see* **Raivavae**
Vavoua Côte d'Ivoire **124** D5
Vavozh Rus. Fed. **40** I4
Vavuniya Sri Lanka **94** D4
Vawkalata Belarus **42** I7
Vawkavichy Belarus **43** L8
also known as Volkovichi
Vawkavysk Belarus **42** F8
also known as Volkovysk
Vawkavyskaye Wzvyshsha *hills* Belarus **42** F8
also known as Volkovyskiye Vysoty
Växjö Sweden **45** K4
Vây, Đao *i.* Vietnam **79** C6
Vayalpad India **94** C3
Vayenga Rus. Fed. *see* **Severomorsk**
Vaygach, Ostrov *i.* Rus. Fed. **40** K1
Vayittiri India **94** C4
Vayk' Armenia **107** F3
formerly known as Azizbekov *or* Soylan
Vazante Brazil **206** G4
Vazáš Sweden *see* **Vittangi**
Vazobe *mt.* Madag. **131** [inset] J3
Vazuza *r.* Rus. Fed. **43** P6
Vazuzskoye Vodokhranilishche *resr* Rus. Fed. **43** P6
Veaikevárri Sweden *see* **Svappavaara**
Vecht *r.* Neth. **48** D3
also known as Vechte (Germany)
Vechta Germany **48** F3
Vechte *r.* Germany **48** D3
also known as Vecht (Neth.)
Vecmikeļi Latvia **42** E5
Vecumnieki Latvia **42** F5
Vedana Rus. Fed. *see* **Vedeno**
Vedaranniyam India **94** C4
Vedasandur India **94** C4
Veddige Sweden **45** K4
Vedea Romania **58** F4
Vedea Romania **58** G5
Vedea *r.* Romania **58** G5
Vedeno Rus. Fed. **107** F2
also known as Vedana
Vedi Armenia **107** F3
Vedia Arg. **204** E4
Vedlozero Rus. Fed. **40** E3
Vedrych *r.* Belarus **43** L9
Veendam Neth. **48** D2
Veenendaal Neth. **48** C3
Vega *i.* Norway **44** J2
Vega U.S.A. **179** B5
Vegadeo Spain **54** D1
Vegarshei Norway **45** J4
Vegoritis, Limni *l.* Greece **58** C8
Vegreville Canada **167** H4
Végueta Peru **200** A2
Vehkalahti Fin. **42** I1
Vehmaa Fin. **45** M3
Vehoa *r.* Pak. **101** G4
Veidnes Norway **44** N1
Veinticinco de Mayo Arg. *see* **25 de Mayo**
Veinticinco de Mayo Arg. *see* **25 de Mayo**
Veinticinco de Mayo Arg. *see* **25 de Mayo**
Veiros Brazil **199** H5
Veisiejis Lith. **42** E7
Veitsiluoto Fin. **44** N2
Vejer de la Frontera Spain **54** F8
Vejle Denmark **45** J5
Velachha India **96** B5
Vela Luka Croatia **56** I6
Velardena Mex. **184** E3
Velas, Cabo *c.* Costa Rica **186** B5
Velasco, Sierra de *mts* Arg. **204** D3
Vela Vrata, Kanal *sea chan.* Croatia **56** G3
Velázquez Uruguay **204** G4
Velbŭzhdki Prokhod *pass* Macedonia **58** D6
also known as Deve Bair
Velddrif S. Africa **132** C9
Velden am Wörther See Austria **49** L9
Veldhoven Neth. **48** C4
Velduri India **94** C3
Velebit *mts* Croatia **56** G4
Velebitski Kanal *sea chan.* Croatia **56** G3
Veleka *r.* Bulg. **58** I6
Velen Germany **48** D4
Velenje Slovenia **56** H2
formerly known as Titovo Velenje
Veles Macedonia **58** C7
formerly known as Titov Veles
Velēs, Mali i *mt.* Albania **58** A7
Velež *mts* Bos.-Herz. **56** J5
Vélez Col. **198** C3
Vélez-Málaga Spain **54** G8
Vélez-Rubio Spain **55** I7
Velhas *r. Minas Gerais* Brazil **203** C6
Velhas *r. Minas Gerais* Brazil **206** F6
Velia *tourist site* Italy **57** H8
Velibaba Turkey *see* **Aras**
Velichayevskoye Rus. Fed. **41** H7
Velika Drenova *Srbija* Yugo. **58** C5
Velika Gorica Croatia **56** I3
Velika Kapela *mts* Croatia **56** G3
Velika Kladuša Bos.-Herz. **56** H3
Velika Mlaka Croatia **56** I3
Velika Morava *canal* Yugo. **58** C4
Velika Plana *Srbija* Yugo. **58** C4
Velikaya Rus. Fed. **40** I4
Velikaya *r.* Rus. Fed. **39** R3
Velikaya *r.* Rus. Fed. **40** I4
Velikaya *r.* Rus. Fed. **43** J4
Velikaya Guba Rus. Fed. **40** E3
Velikaya Kema Rus. Fed. **82** E3
Veliki Drvenik *i.* Croatia **56** I5
Veliki Jastrebac *mts* Yugo. **58** C5
Veliki Preslav Bulg. **58** H5
formerly known as Preslav
Veliki Risnjak *mt.* Croatia **56** G3
Veliki Šiljegovac *Srbija* Yugo. **58** C5
Veliki Šturac *mt.* Yugo. **58** B4
Velikiye Luki Rus. Fed. **43** L5
Velikiy Novgorod Rus. Fed. **43** M3
formerly known as Novgorod; *historically known as* Holmgard
Velikiy Ustyug Rus. Fed. **40** H3
Velikonda Range *hills* India **94** C3
Velikooktyabr'skiy Rus. Fed. **43** O4
Veliko Tŭrnovo Bulg. **58** G5
formerly known as Tŭrnovo
Velikoye *Vologod. Obl.* Rus. Fed. **43** R2
Velikoye *Yaroslavskaya Oblast'* Rus. Fed. **43** U4
Velikoye, Ozero *l.* Rus. Fed. **43** R4
Velikoye, Ozero *l.* Rus. Fed. **43** V6
Vélingara Senegal **124** B3
Vélingara Senegal **124** B3
Velingrad Bulg. **58** F6
Velino *r.* Italy **56** E6
Velino, Monte *mt.* Italy **56** F6
Veliuona Lith. **42** E6
Velizh Rus. Fed. **43** M6
Velká Bíteš Czech Rep. **49** N6
Veľká Domaša, Vodná nádrž *resr* Slovakia **49** S6
Veľká Fatra *mts* Slovakia **49** P7
Velká Javořina *hill* Czech Rep./Slovakia **49** O7
Veľké Kapušany Slovakia **49** T7
Velké Meziříčí Czech Rep. **49** N6
Velkua Fin. **42** C1
Veľký Krtíš Slovakia **49** Q7
Veľký Meder Slovakia **49** O8
formerly known as Čalovo
Vella Lavella *i.* Solomon Is **145** E2
Vellar *r.* India **94** C4
Velletri Italy **56** E7
Vellinge Sweden **45** K5
Vellore India **94** C3
Vel'mo *r.* Rus. Fed. **39** J3
Velopoula *i.* Greece **59** E12
Vel'sk Rus. Fed. **40** G3
Velsuna Italy *see* **Orvieto**
Vel't Rus. Fed. **40** I1
Velten Germany **49** K3
Veluwezoom, Nationaal Park *nat. park* Neth. **48** C3
Velvendos Greece **59** D8
Vel'ye, Ozero *l.* Rus. Fed. **43** N4
Velyka Mykhaylivka Ukr. **58** K1
Velykodolyns'ke Ukr. **58** L2
Velykyy Tokmak Ukr. *see* **Tokmak**
Vel'yu *r.* Rus. Fed. **40** J3
Vemalwada India **94** C2
Vembanad Lake India **94** C4
Vemor'ye Rus. Fed. **82** F3
Vempalle India **94** C3
Venado Tuerto Arg. **204** E4
Venafro Italy **56** G7
Venamo *r.* Guyana/Venez. **199** F3
Venamo, Cerro *mt.* Venez. **199** F3
Venarey-les-Laumes France **51** K5
Venaria Italy **51** N7
Vencedor Brazil **199** F6
Venceslau Bráz Brazil **206** D10
Venciūnai Lith. **42** F7
Venda Nova Brazil **207** L7
Vendenheim France **51** N4
Vendeuvre-sur-Barse France **51** K4
Vendinga Rus. Fed. **40** H3
Vendôme France **50** H5
Vendrell Spain *see* **El Vendrell**
Venecia Col. **198** C4
Venegas Mex. **185** E4
Veneta, Laguna *lag.* Italy **56** E3
Venetia Italy *see* **Venice**
Veneto *admin. reg.* Italy **56** D3
Venev Rus. Fed. **43** T7
Venezia Italy *see* **Venice**
Venezia, Golfo di *g.* Europe *see* **Venice, Gulf of**

Venezuela *country* S. America **199** E3
5th most populous country in South America.
southamerica [countries] 192–193

Venezuela, Golfo de *g.* Venez. **198** D2
Vengurla India **94** B3
Veniaminof Volcano U.S.A. **164** D4
Venice Italy **56** E3
also known as Venezia; *historically known as* Venetia
Venice *FL* U.S.A. **175** D7
Venice *LA* U.S.A. **175** B6
Venice, Gulf of Europe **56** E3
also known as Venezia, Golfo di
Vénissieux France **51** K7
Venjan Sweden **45** K3
Venkatagiri India **94** C3
Venkatapuram India **94** D2
Venlo Neth. **48** D4
Vennesla Norway **45** I4
Venosa Italy **56** H8
historically known as Venusia
Venosta, Val *valley* Italy **56** C2
Venray Neth. **48** C4
Venta *r.* Latvia/Lith. **42** D5
Venta Lith. **42** D5
Venta de Baños Spain **54** G3
Ventania Brazil **206** C11
Ventersburg S. Africa **133** L5
Ventersdorp S. Africa **133** K3
Venterstad S. Africa **133** J7
Ventimiglia Italy **51** N9
Ventisquero *mt.* Arg. **205** C6
Ventnor U.K. **47** K13
Ventotene, Isola *i.* Italy **57** F8
Ventoux, Mont *mt.* France **51** L8
Ventspils Latvia **42** C4
historically known as Windau
Ventuari *r.* Venez. **199** E3
Ventura U.S.A. **182** E7
Venus Bay Australia **147** E4
Venusia Italy *see* **Venosa**
Venustiano Carranza, Presa *resr* Mex. **185** E3
Venzone Italy **56** F2
Vepsovskaya Vozvyshennost' *hills* Rus. Fed. **43** P1
Vera Arg. **204** E3
Vera Spain **55** J7
Verá, Lago *l.* Para. **201** F6
Vera Cruz *Amazonas* Brazil **200** D2
Vera Cruz *São Paulo* Brazil **206** D9
Vera Cruz Mex. *see* **Veracruz**
Veracruz Mex. **185** F5
also spelt Vera Cruz
Veracruz *state* Mex. **185** F4
Vera de Bidasoa Spain **55** J1
Veranópolis Brazil **203** B9
Veraval India **94** A1
Verbania Italy **56** A3
Verbilki Rus. Fed. **43** S5
Verbovskiy Rus. Fed. **40** G5
Vercelli Italy **56** A3
Vercors *reg.* France **51** L8
Vercors, Parc Naturel Régional du *nature res.* France **51** L8
Vercovicium *tourist site* U.K. *see* **Housesteads**
Verda *r.* Rus. Fed. **43** V8
Verdalsøra Norway **44** J3
Verde *r.* Arg. **205** D6
Verde *r. Bahia* Brazil **202** D4
Verde *r. Goiás* Brazil **206** C5
Verde *r. Goiás/Minas Gerais* Brazil **206** F5
Verde *r. Mato Grosso* Brazil **202** A4
Verde *r. Mato Grosso do Sul* Brazil **206** B8
Verde *r. Minas Gerais* Brazil **206** C6
Verde *r. Minas Gerais* Brazil **206** D6
Verde *r. Minas Gerais* Brazil **207** H8
Verde *r.* Brazil **206** E2
Verde *r.* Mex. **184** D3
Verde *r.* Para. **201** F5
Verde *r.* U.S.A. **183** M8
Verde, Cabo *c.* Senegal *see* **Vert, Cap**
Verde, Península *pen.* Arg. **204** E5
Verde Grande *r.* Brazil **202** D5
Verde Island Passage Phil. **74** B3
Verden (Aller) Germany **48** G3
Verde Pequeno *r.* Brazil **202** D5
Verdi U.S.A. **182** E2
Verdigris *r.* U.S.A. **178** D5
Verdikoussa Greece **59** C9
Verdinho *r.* Brazil **206** C4
Verdinho, Serra do *mts* Brazil **206** B5
Verdon *r.* France **51** L9
Verdun France **51** L3
Verdun-sur-Garonne France **50** H9
Vereeniging S. Africa **133** L3
Verena S. Africa **133** N2
Vereshchagino Rus. Fed. **40** J4
Verestovo, Ozero *l.* Rus. Fed. **43** R4
Vereya Rus. Fed. **43** R6
Verfeil France **50** H9
Verga, Cap *c.* Guinea **124** B4
Vergara Uruguay **204** G4
Vergeleë S. Africa **133** I2
Vergennes U.S.A. **177** L1
Vergina Greece **58** D8
also spelt Veryína
Vería Greece *see* **Veroia**
Verigino Rus. Fed. **43** T5
Verín Spain **54** D3
Veriora Estonia **42** I3
Veríssimo Brazil **206** E6
Veríssimo Sarmento Angola *see* **Camissombo**
Verkeerdevlei S. Africa **133** K5
Verkhe-Avzyan Rus. Fed. **102** D1
Verkhe-berezovskiy Kazakh. **88** C1
Verkhnedneprovsk Ukr. *see* **Verkhn'odniprovs'k**
Verkhnedneprovskiy Rus. Fed. **43** O7
Verkhneimbatsk Rus. Fed. **39** I3
Verkhnekolvinsk Rus. Fed. **40** K2
Verkhneruzskoye Vodokhranilishche *resr* Rus. Fed. **43** Q6
Verkhnespasskoye Rus. Fed. **40** H4
Verkhnetulomskiy Rus. Fed. **44** O1
Verkhnetulomskoye Vodokhranilishche *resr* Rus. Fed. **44** O1
Verkhneural'sk Rus. Fed. **102** D1
Verkhnevilyuysk Rus. Fed. **39** M3
Verkhnevolzhskoye Vodokhranilishche *resr* Rus. Fed. **43** N4
Verkhneyarkeyevo Rus. Fed. **40** J5
Verkhneye Kuyto, Ozero *l.* Rus. Fed. **44** O2
Verkhnezeysk Rus. Fed. **82** C1
Verkhniy At-Uryakh Rus. Fed. **39** P3
Verkhniy Baskunchak Rus. Fed. **102** A2
Verkhniy Koshevichi Rus. Fed. **43** M6
Verkhniye Mokhovichi Rus. Fed. **43** M8
Verkhniy Lomovets Rus. Fed. **43** T9
Verkhniy Mamon Rus. Fed. **41** G6
Verkhniy Shergol'dzhin Rus. Fed. **85** F1
Verkhniy Tatyshly Rus. Fed. **40** J4
Verkhniy Vyalozerskiy Rus. Fed. **40** E2
Verkhn'odniprovs'k Ukr. **41** E6
also spelt Verkhnedneprovsk
Verkhnyaya Inta Rus. Fed. **40** L2
Verkhnyaya Pakhachi Rus. Fed. **39** Q3
Verkhnyaya Taymyra *r.* Rus. Fed. **39** J2
Verkhnyaya Toyma Rus. Fed. **40** H3
Verkhnyaya Troitsa Rus. Fed. **43** S4
Verkhnyaya Tunguska *r.* Rus. Fed. *see* **Angara**
Verkhnyaya Yelovka Kazakh. **88** D1
Verkhoshizhem'ye Rus. Fed. **40** I4
Verkhovazh'ye Rus. Fed. **40** G3
Verkhov'ye Rus. Fed. **43** S9
Verkhoyanskiy Khrebet *mts* Rus. Fed. **39** M2
Verkhuba Kazakh. **88** C1
Verknė *r.* Lith. **42** F7
Verkola Rus. Fed. **40** H3
Verkykerskop S. Africa **133** N4
Verlatekloof *pass* S. Africa **132** E9
Verma Norway **44** J3
Vermaaklikheid S. Africa **132** F11
Vermelha, Serra *hills* Brazil **206** C10
Vermelho *r. Mato Grosso* Brazil **206** B1
Vermelho *r. Pará* Brazil **202** B3
Vermelho *r. Tocantins* Brazil **202** C3
Vermenton France **51** J5
Vermeş Romania **58** C3
Vermilion Canada **167** I4
Vermilion *r.* U.S.A. **174** B3
Vermilion Bay U.S.A. **179** E6
Vermilion Cliffs *esc. AZ* U.S.A. **183** L5
Vermilion Cliffs *esc. UT* U.S.A. **183** L4
Vermilion Lake U.S.A. **174** A2
Vermilion Range *hills* U.S.A. **172** A3
Vermillion U.S.A. **178** C3
Vermillion *r.* U.S.A. **178** C3
Vermillion Bay Canada **168** A3
Vermillon *r.* Canada **174** F2
Vermont *state* U.S.A. **177** M1
Vernadsky *research station* Antarctica **222** T2
long form Academician Vernadskiy
Vernal U.S.A. **183** O1
Verner Canada **168** D4
Verneuil-sur-Avre France **50** G4
Verneuk Pan *salt pan* S. Africa **132** F6
Verneř Switz. **51** M6
Vernio Italy **56** D4
Vernon Canada **166** G5
Vernon France **50** H3
Vernon *AL* U.S.A. **175** B5
Vernon *TX* U.S.A. **179** C5
Vernon, Mount *hill* Australia **150** B5
Vernon Islands Australia **148** A2
Vernoye Rus. Fed. **82** C2
Vernyy Kazakh. *see* **Almaty**
Vero Beach U.S.A. **175** D7
Veroia Greece **58** D8
also spelt Véria; *historically known as* Beroea
Verona Italy **56** C3
Verona *VA* U.S.A. **176** F7
Verona *WI* U.S.A. **172** D8
Verres Italy **51** N7
Versailles France **51** I4
Versailles *IN* U.S.A. **174** C4
Versailles *KY* U.S.A. **176** A7
Versailles *MO* U.S.A. **178** D4
Versailles *OH* U.S.A. **176** A5
Versalles Bol. **201** E3
Versec *Vojvodina, Srbija* Yugo. *see* **Vršac**
Verseka *r.* Lith. **42** F7
Versmold Germany **48** F3
Versoix Switz. **51** M6
Vert, Cap *c.* Senegal **124** A3
also known as Verde, Cabo
Vert, Île *i.* Canada **169** G3
Vertentes *r.* Brazil **202** B4
Vertesi *park* Hungary **49** P8
Vertientes Cuba **186** D2
Vertou France **50** E5
Vertus France **51** K4
Verulam S. Africa **133** P6
Verulamium U.K. *see* **St Albans**
Verviers Belgium **51** L2
Vervins France **51** J3
Verwoerdburg S. Africa *see* **Centurion**
Verwood Canada **167** J5
Veryína Greece *see* **Vergina**
Vesanto Fin. **44** N3
Vescovato *Corse* France **51** P10
Vesele Ukr. **41** E7
Veselevo Rus. Fed. **43** R6
Veselina *r.* Bulg. **58** G5
Veselí nad Lužnicí Czech Rep. **49** L6
Veselí nad Moravou Czech Rep. **49** O7
Veselovskoye Vodokhranilishche *resr* Rus. Fed. **41** G7
Veseloyarsk Rus. Fed. **88** C1
Veselyy Rus. Fed. **41** G7
Veselyy Podol Kazakh. **103** F1
Veshenskaya Rus. Fed. **41** G6
Vesijärvi *l.* Fin. **45** N3
Vesle *r.* France **51** J3
Veslyana *r.* Rus. Fed. **40** J3
Vesontio France *see* **Besançon**
Vesoul France **51** M5
Vesselyy Yar Rus. Fed. **90** D3
Vest-Agder *county* Norway **45** I4
Vesterålen *is* Norway **44** K1
Vesterålsfjorden *sea chan.* Norway **44** K1
Vestfirðir *constituency* Iceland **44** [inset] B2
Vestfjorddalen *valley* Norway **45** J4
Vestfjorden *sea chan.* Norway **44** K2
Vestfold *county* Norway **45** J4
Vestfold Hills Antarctica **223** F2
Vestmanna Faroe Is **46** E1
Vestmannaeyjar *is* Iceland **44** [inset] B3
English form Westman Islands
Vestnes Norway **44** I3
Vestre Jakobselv Norway **44** O1
Veststraumen Glacier Antarctica **223** X2
Vesturland *constituency* Iceland **44** [inset] B2
Vestvågøy *i.* Norway **44** K1
Vesuvio *vol.* Italy *see* **Vesuvius**
Vesuvio, Parco Nazionale del *nat. park* Italy **57** G8
Vesuvius *vol.* Italy **57** G8
also spelt Vesuvio
Ves'yegonsk Rus. Fed. **43** S3
Veszprém Hungary **49** O8
Vésztő Hungary **49** S9
Vet *r.* S. Africa **133** J4
Vetauua *i.* Fiji **145** H3
Veteli Fin. **44** M3
Veteran Canada **167** I4
Veternik *Vojvodina, Srbija* Yugo. **58** A3
Vetlanda Sweden **45** K4
Vetlefjorden Norway **45** I3
Vetluga Rus. Fed. **40** H4
Vetluga *r.* Rus. Fed. **40** H4
Vetluzhskiy *Kostromskaya Oblast'* Rus. Fed. **38** E4
formerly known as Golyshi
Vetluzhskiy *Nizhegorodskaya Oblast'* Rus. Fed. **40** H4
Vet'ma *r.* Rus. Fed. **43** O8
Vetovo Bulg. **58** H5
Vetralla Italy **56** E6
Vetren Bulg. **58** I6
formerly known as Zhitarovo
Vetrişoaia Romania **58** J2
Vetsikko Fin. **44** N1
Vettasjärvi Sweden **44** M2
Vettore, Monte *mt.* Italy **56** F6
Veurne Belgium **51** I1
also known as Furnes
Vevay U.S.A. **174** C4
Veveno *r.* Sudan **128** B3
Vevey Switz. **51** M6
Veydelevka Rus. Fed. **41** F6
Veyle *r.* France **51** K6
Veynes France **51** L8
Veyo U.S.A. **183** K4
Veys Iran **100** B4
Vėžaičiai Lith. **42** C6
Vézère *r.* France **50** G8
Vezhen *mt.* Bulg. **58** F6
Vezirköprü Turkey **106** C2
Via *r.* Liberia **124** C5
Viacha Bol. **200** C4
Viadana Italy **56** C4
Vialar Alg. *see* **Tissemsilt**
Viamao Brazil **203** B9
Viamonte Arg. **205** D9
Viana Angola **127** B7
Viana *Espírito Santo* Brazil **207** M7
Viana *Maranhão* Brazil **202** C2
Viana del Bollo Spain *see* **Viana do Bolo**
Viana do Alentejo Port. **54** D6
Viana do Bolo Spain **54** D2
also spelt Viana del Bollo
Viana do Castelo Port. **54** C3
Viana do Castelo *admin. dist.* Port. **54** C3
Vianden Lux. **51** M3
Viangchan Laos *see* **Vientiane**
Viangphoukha Laos **78** C3
Viaño Pequeno Spain **54** C1
Vianópolis Brazil **206** E3
Viar *r.* Spain **54** F7
Viareggio Italy **56** C5
Viaur *r.* France **51** H8
Viborg Denmark **45** J4
Viborg Rus. Fed. *see* **Vyborg**
Vibo Valentia Italy **57** I10
historically known as Hipponium
Vic Spain **55** N3
also spelt Vich
Vicam Mex. **184** C3
Vicdessos *r.* France **50** H10
Vicecomodoro Marambio *research station* Antarctica *see* **Marambio**
Vic-en-Bigorre France **50** G9
Vicente, Point U.S.A. **182** F8
Vicente Guerrero Mex. **184** A2
Vicenza Italy **56** D3
Vic-Fezensac France **50** G9
Vich Spain *see* **Vic**
Vichada *dept* Col. **198** D3
Vichada *r.* Col. **198** C3
Vichadero Uruguay **204** G3
Vichuga Rus. Fed. **40** G4
Vichy France **51** J6
Vicksburg *AZ* U.S.A. **183** K8
Vicksburg *MI* U.S.A. **172** H8
Vicksburg *MS* U.S.A. **175** B5
Vic-le-Comte France **51** J7
Vico, Lago di *l.* Italy **56** E6
Viçosa *Alagoas* Brazil **202** E4
Viçosa *Minas Gerais* Brazil **203** D7
Vic-sur-Cère France **51** I8
Victor, Mount Antarctica **223** C2
Victor Harbor Australia **146** C3
Victoria Arg. **204** E4
Victoria *r.* Australia **148** A2
Victoria *state* Australia **147** E4
Victoria Cameroon *see* **Limbe**

Victoria Canada **166** F5
Provincial capital of British Columbia.

Victoria *La Araucania* Chile **204** B5
Victoria *Magallanes* Chile **205** C9
Victoria Hond. **186** B4
Victoria Malaysia *see* **Labuan**
Victoria Malta **57** G12
also known as Rabat
Victoria Phil. **74** B3
Victoria Romania **58** I4
Victoria Romania **58** F3

Victoria Seychelles **218** K6
Capital of the Seychelles.

Victoria *TX* U.S.A. **179** C6
Victoria *VA* U.S.A. **176** G9
Victoria, Isla *i.* Chile **205** B7

Victoria, Lake Africa **128** B5
Largest lake in Africa and 3rd in the world.
africa [landscapes] 112–113

Victoria, Lake Australia **146** D3
Victoria, Mount Myanmar **78** A3
Victoria, Mount N.Z. **153** G10
Victoria, Mount P.N.G. **73** K8
Victoria and Albert Mountains Canada **165** L2

Victoria Falls *waterfall* Zambia/Zimbabwe **127** E9
africa [locations] 118–119

Victoria Falls Zimbabwe **131** E3
Victoria Falls National Park Zimbabwe **131** E3
also known as Mosi-oa-Tunya National Park
Victoria Fjord *inlet* Greenland **165** O1
Victoria Forest Park *nature res.* N.Z. **153** G9
Victoria Harbour *sea chan.* Hong Kong China *see* **Hong Kong Harbour**

Victoria Island Canada **165** H2
3rd largest island in North America and 9th in the world.
northamerica [landscapes] 156–157

Victoria Lake Canada **169** J3
Victoria Land *coastal area* Antarctica **223** K2
Victoria Peak *hill* Hong Kong China **87** [inset]
also known as Shan Teng
Victoria Range *mts* N.Z. **153** G10
Victoria River Australia **148** A2
Victoria River Downs Australia **148** A3
Victoria Valley N.Z. **152** H3
Victoriaville Canada **169** G4
Victoria West S. Africa **132** H8
Victorica Arg. **204** D5
Victorino Venez. **199** E4
Víctor Rosales Mex. **185** E4
Victorville U.S.A. **183** G7
Victory U.S.A. **177** I2
Victory Downs Australia **148** B5
Vicuña Chile **204** C3
Vicuña Mackenna Arg. **204** D4
Vidal, Isla *i.* Chile **205** B8
Vidalia U.S.A. **175** B6
Vidal Junction U.S.A. **183** J7
Vidamlya Belarus **42** E9
Videle Romania **58** G4
Viden *mt.* Bulg. **58** D6
Vidigueira Port. **54** D6
Vidima *r.* Bulg. **58** G6
Vidin Bulg. **58** D5
Vidisha India **96** C5
Vidlitsa Rus. Fed. **40** E3
Vidnoye Rus. Fed. **43** S6
formerly known as Rastorguyevo
Vidourle *r.* France **51** K9
Vidova Gora *hill* Croatia **56** I5
Vidsel Sweden **44** M2
Vidukle Lith. **42** D6
Viduša *mts* Bos.-Herz. **56** K6
Vidzemes Centrālā Augstiene *hills* Latvia **42** G5
Vidzy Belarus **42** H6
Viechtach Germany **49** J6
Viedgesville S. Africa **133** M8
Viedma Arg. **204** E6
Viedma, Lago *l.* Arg. **205** B8
southamerica [landscapes] 190–191
Viehberg *mt.* Austria **49** L7
Viejo, Cerro *mt.* Mex. **184** B2
Viekšniai Lith. **42** D5
Vielha Spain **55** L2
also spelt Viella
Viella Spain *see* **Vielha**
Vielsalm Belgium **51** L2
Vienenburg Germany **48** H4

Vienna Austria **49** N7
Capital of Austria. Also known as Wien; historically known as Vindobona.

Vienna *GA* U.S.A. **175** D5
Vienna *IL* U.S.A. **174** B4
Vienna *MD* U.S.A. **177** J7
Vienna *MO* U.S.A. **174** B4
Vienna *WV* U.S.A. **176** D6
Vienne France **51** K7
Vienne *r.* France **50** G5

Vientiane Laos **78** C4
Capital of Laos. Also spelt Viangchan.

Vieques *i.* Puerto Rico **187** G3
Vieremä Fin. **44** N3
Viersen Germany **48** D4
Vierwaldstätter See *l.* Switz. **51** O5
Vierzon France **51** I5
Viesca Mex. **185** E3
Viesīte Latvia **42** G5
Vieste Italy **56** I7
Viešvilės rezervatas *nature res.* Lith. **42** D6
Vietas Sweden **44** L2
Vietnam *country* Asia **78** D4
also spelt Viet Nam
asia [countries] 64–67
Viet Nam *country* Asia *see* **Vietnam**
Việt Tri Vietnam **78** D3
Vieux Comptoir, Lac du *l.* Canada **168** E2
Vieux-Fort Canada **169** J3
Vieux Fort St Lucia **187** H4
Vieux Poste, Pointe du *pt* Canada **169** I3
Vievis Lith. **42** F7
Vigala *r.* Estonia **42** F3
Vigan Phil. **74** B2
Vigeois France **50** H7
Vigevano Italy **56** A3
Vigia Brazil **202** B2
Vigia *hill* Port. **54** C7
Vigía Chico Mex. **185** I5
Viglio, Monte *mt.* Italy **56** F7
Vignemale *mt.* France **50** F10
Vignola Italy **56** D4
Vigny France **51** H3
Vigo Spain **54** C2
Vigo, Ría de *est.* Spain **54** C2
Vigors, Mount Australia **150** B4
Vihanti Fin. **44** N2
Vihari Pak. **101** H4
Vihiers France **50** F5
Vihorlat *mt.* Slovakia **49** T7
Vihterpalu *r.* Estonia **42** E2
Vihti Fin. **45** N3
Viiala Fin. **45** M3
Viipuri Rus. Fed. *see* **Vyborg**

Viirinkylä Fin. 44 N2
Viitasaari Fin. 44 N3
Viitka Estonia 42 I4
Vijainagar India 96 B3
Vijapur India 96 B5
Vijayadurg India 94 B2
Vijayanagar India see Hampi
Vijayapati India 94 C4
Vijayawada India 94 D2 also known as Bezwada
Vík Iceland 44 [inset] C3
Vik Norway 44 K2
Vikajärvi Fin. 44 N2
Vikarabad India 94 C2
Vikedal Norway 45 I4
Vikeke East Timor 75 C5 also known as Viqueque
Vikersund Norway 45 J4
Vikhra r. Rus. Fed. 43 M7
Vikhren mt. Bulg. 58 E7
Viking Canada 167 I4
Vikna i. Norway 44 J2
Vikos-Aoos nat. park Greece 59 B9
Vikøyri Norway 45 I3
Vikran Norway 44 L1
Viktorovka Kazakh. see Taranovskoye
Vila Spain 54 C3
Vila Vanuatu see Port Vila
Vila Alferes Chamusca Moz. see Guija
Vila Arriaga Angola see Bibala
Vila Bittencourt Brazil 198 D5
Vila Braga Brazil 199 G6
Vila Bugaço Angola see Camanongue
Vila Cabral Moz. see Lichinga
Vila Caldas Xavier Moz. see Muende
Vilacaya Bol. 200 D4
Vila Coutinho Moz. see Ulongue
Vila da Ponte Angola see Kuvango
Vila da Ribeira Brava Cape Verde 124 [inset]
Vila de Aljustrel Angola see Cangamba
Vila de Almoster Angola see Chiange
Vila de João Belo Moz. see Xai-Xai
Vila de Junqueiro Moz. see Gurué
Vila de Sal Rei Cape Verde 124 [inset]
Vila de Sena Moz. 131 G3
Vila de Trego Morais Moz. see Chókwé
Vila do Conde Port. 54 C3
Vila do Tarrafal Cape Verde 124 [inset]
Vila Flor Port. 54 D3
Vila Fontes Moz. see Caia
Vilafranca del Penedès Spain 55 M3 also spelt Villafranca del Penedès
Vila Franca de Xira Port. 54 C6
Vilagarcía de Arousa Spain 54 C2 also spelt Villagarcía de Arosa
Vila Gomes da Costa Moz. 131 G5
Vila Gouveia Moz. see Catandica
Vilaine r. France 50 D5
Viļaka Latvia 42 I4
Vilalba Spain 54 D1
Vila Luísa Moz. see Marracuene
Vila Marechal Carmona Angola see Uíge
Vila Miranda Moz. see Macaloge
Vila Murtinho Brazil 200 D2
Vilanandro, Tanjona pt Madag. 131 [inset] J3 formerly known as St-André, Cap
Vilanculos Moz. 131 G4
Viļāni Latvia 42 H5
Vila Nova Angola see Tchikala-Tcholohanga
Vila Nova da Fronteira Moz. 131 G3
Vilanova de Arousa Spain 54 C2 also spelt Villanueva de Arosa
Vila Nova de Foz Coa Port. 54 D3
Vila Nova de Gaia Port. 54 C3
Vila Nova de Ourém Port. 54 C5
Vila Nova de Paiva Port. 54 D4
Vila Nova do Seles Angola see Uku
Vilanova i la Geltrú Spain 55 M3 also spelt Villanueva-y-Geltrú
Vila Nova Sintra Cape Verde 124 [inset]
Vila Paiva de Andrada Moz. see Gorongosa
Vila Pery Moz. see Chimoio
Vila Pouca de Aguiar Port. 54 D3
Vila Real Port. 54 D3
Vila Real admin. dist. Port. 54 D3
Vila-real de los Infantes Spain 55 K5 also spelt Villareal de los Infantes; formerly known as Villareal
Vilar Formoso Port. 54 E4
Vila Salazar Angola see N'dalatando
Vila Salazar Zimbabwe see Sango
Vila Teixeira de Sousa Angola see Luau
Vilavankod India 94 C4
Vila Velha Amapá Brazil 199 I4
Vila Velha Espírito Santo Brazil 203 D7 formerly known as Espirito Santo
Vila Velha de Ródão Port. 54 D5
Vila Verde Port. 54 C3
Vilcabamba, Cordillera mts Peru 200 B3
Vilcanota, Cordillera de mts Peru 200 C3
Vil'cheka, Zemlya i. Rus. Fed. 38 G1 English form Wilczek Land
Viled' r. Rus. Fed. 40 H3
Vileyka Belarus see Vilyeyka
Vil'gort Permskaya Oblast' Rus. Fed. 40 K3
Vil'gort Respublika Komi Rus. Fed. 40 I3
Vilhelmina Sweden 44 L2
Vilhena Brazil 201 E3
Viliya r. Belarus/Lith. 42 G7
Viljandi Estonia 42 G3
Viljoenskroon S. Africa 133 K4
Vilkaviškis Lith. 42 E7
Vilkija Lith. 42 E6
Vil'kitskogo, Ostrov i. Rus. Fed. 39 H2
Vil'kitskogo, Proliv strait Rus. Fed. 39 J2
Villa Abecia Bol. 200 D5
Villa Adriana tourist site Italy 56 E7
Villa Ahumada Mex. 184 D2
Villa Alba Arg. 204 E5
Villa Altagracia Dom. Rep. 187 F3
Villa Ana Arg. 204 F3
Villa Angela Arg. 204 E2
Villa Bella Bol. 200 D2
Villa Bens Morocco see Tarfaya
Villablino Spain 54 E2
Villacañas Spain 55 H5
Villacarrillo Spain 55 H6
Villach Austria 49 K9 also known as Beljak
Villacidro Sardegna Italy 57 A9
Villa Cisneros W. Sahara see Ad Dakhla
Villa Constitución Arg. 204 E4
Villa Constitución Mex. see Ciudad Constitución
Villa de Álvarez Mex. 184 E5
Villa de Cos Mex. 185 E4
Villa de Cura Venez. 199 E2
Villa de Guadalupe Mex. 185 H5
Villa del Rosario Arg. 204 E3
Villa del Totoral Arg. 204 D3
Villa Diego Arg. 204 E4
Villadiego Spain 54 G2
Villa Dolores Arg. 204 D3
Villadossola Italy 56 A2
Villa Flores Mex. 185 G5
Villafranca Spain 55 J2
Villafranca del Bierzo Spain 54 E2
Villafranca del Cid Spain 55 K4
Villafranca de los Barros Spain 54 E6
Villafranca del Penedès Spain see Vilafranca del Penedès
Villafranca di Verona Italy 56 C3
Villagarcía de Arosa Spain see Vilagarcía de Arousa
Villa Gesell Arg. 204 F5
Villagrán Mex. 185 F3
Villaguay Arg. 204 F3
Villa Guillermina Arg. 204 F3
Villa Hayes Para. 201 F6
Villahermosa Mex. 185 G5
Villa Hidalgo Mex. 181 E7
Villa Huidobro Arg. 204 D4
Villaines-la-Juhel France 50 F4
Villa Insurgentes Mex. 184 C3
Villa Iris Arg. 204 E5
Villajoyosa Spain 55 K6
Villa Juárez Mex. 181 E8
Villaldama Mex. 185 E3
Villálonga Arg. 204 E5
Villa María Arg. 204 E4
Villa María Grande Arg. 204 F3
Villa Martín Bol. 200 D5
Villamartín Spain 54 F8
Villa Matoque Arg. 204 E2
Villa Montes Bol. 201 E5
Villanova Monteleone Sardegna Italy 57 A8
Villa Nueva Arg. 204 E4
Villanueva Col. 198 C2
Villanueva Mex. 185 E4
Villanueva de Arosa Spain see Vilanova de Arousa
Villanueva de Córdoba Spain 54 G6
Villanueva de la Serena Spain 54 F6
Villanueva de los Castillejos Spain 54 D7
Villanueva de los Infantes Spain 55 I6 formerly known as Infantes
Villanueva-y-Geltrú Spain see Vilanova i la Geltrú
Villa Ocampo Arg. 204 F3
Villa Ocampo Mex. 184 D3
Villa O'Higgins Chile 205 B8
Villa Ojo de Agua Arg. 204 E3
Villa O. Pereyra Mex. see Villa Orestes Pereyra
Villa Orestes Pereyra Mex. 184 D3 short form Villa O. Pereyra
Villa Oropeza Bol. 200 D4
Villa Pesqueira Mex. 181 E7
Villaputzu Sardegna Italy 57 B9
Villar del Rey Spain 54 E5
Villareal Spain see Vila-real de los Infantes
Villareal de los Infantes Spain see Vila-real de los Infantes
Villa Regina Arg. 204 D5
Villarrica Chile 204 B5
Villarrica Para. 201 F6
Villarrica, Lago l. Chile 204 B5
Villarrica, Parque Nacional nat. park Chile 204 C5
Villarrobledo Spain 55 I5
Villarrubia de los Ojos Spain 55 H5
Villas U.S.A. 177 K6
Villasalazar Zimbabwe see Sango
Villasana de Mena Spain 55 H1
Villa San Giovanni Italy 57 H10
Villa Sanjurjo Morocco see Al Hoceima
Villa San Martín Arg. 204 D3
Villasboas Uruguay 204 F4
Villa Serrano Bol. 201 D4
Villasimius Sardegna Italy 57 B9
Villa Unión Arg. 204 C3
Villa Unión Coahuila Mex. 185 E2
Villa Unión Durango Mex. 184 D4
Villa Unión Sinaloa Mex. 184 D4
Villa Valeria Arg. 204 D4
Villa Vasquez Dom. Rep. 187 F3
Villavicencio Col. 198 C3
Villaviciosa Spain 54 F1
Villaviciosa de Córdoba Spain 54 F6
Villa Viscarra Bol. 200 D4
Villazon Bol. 200 D5
Villedieu-les-Poêles France 50 E4
Villefranche-de-Lauragais France 50 H9
Villefranche-de-Rouergue France 51 I8
Villefranche-sur-Saône France 51 K7
Ville-Marie Canada see Montréal
Ville-Marie Canada 173 N3
Villemontel Canada 173 O2
Villemur-sur-Tarn France 50 H9
Villena Spain 55 K6
Villenauxe-la-Grande France 51 J4
Villeneuve-de-Marsan France 50 F9
Villeneuve-sur-Lot France 50 G8
Villeneuve-sur-Yonne France 51 J4
Ville Platte U.S.A. 179 D6
Villers-Bocage France 50 F3
Villers-Cotterêts France 51 J3
Villeta Para. 201 F6
Villeurbanne France 51 K7
Villicun, Sierra mts Arg. 204 C3
Villiers S. Africa 133 M4
Villingen Germany 48 F7
Villupuram India see Viluppuram
Vilna Canada 167 I4
Vilna Lith. see Vilnius
Vilnius Lith. 42 G7
Capital of Lithuania. Formerly known as Wilno; historically known as Vilna.
Vil'nyans'k Ukr. 41 E7 also spelt Vol'nyansk; formerly known as Chervonoarmeyskoye or Sofiyevka
Vilppula Fin. 45 N3
Vils r. Germany 48 I6
Vils r. Germany 49 K7
Vilsandi i. Estonia 42 C3
Vilsandi nature res. Estonia 42 C3
Vilsbiburg Germany 49 J7
Vilshofen Germany 49 K7
Viluppuram India 94 C4 also spelt Villupuram
Vilvoorde Belgium 51 K2
Vilyeyka Belarus 42 H7 also spelt Vileyka
Vilyeyskaye, Vozyera l. Belarus 42 I7
Vilyuy r. Rus. Fed. 39 M3
Vilyuyskoye Vodokhranilishche resr Rus. Fed. 39 L3
Vimbe mt. Zambia 127 F8
Vimercate Italy 56 B3
Vimianzo Spain 54 B1
Vimioso Port. 54 E3
Vimmerby Sweden 45 K4
Vimoutiers France 50 G4
Vimpeli Fin. 44 M3
Vimperk Czech Rep. 49 K6
Vina r. Cameroon 125 I5 also spelt Wina
Vina U.S.A. 182 B2
Viña del Mar Chile 204 C4
Vinalhaven U.S.A. 177 Q1
Vinalopó r. Spain 55 K6
Vinanivao Madag. 131 [inset] K2
Vinaròs Spain 55 L4 also spelt Vinaroz
Vinaroz Spain see Vinaròs
Vincelotte, Lac l. Canada 169 F2
Vincennes U.S.A. 174 C4
Vincennes Bay Antarctica 223 H2
Vinces r. Ecuador 198 B5
Vinchina Arg. 204 C3
Vinchos Peru 200 B3
Vindelälven r. Sweden 44 L3
Vindelfjällens naturreservat nature res. Sweden 44 K2
Vindeln Sweden 44 L2
Vindhya Range hills India 96 B5
Vindobona Austria see Vienna
Vineland U.S.A. 177 J6
Vinga Romania 58 C2
Vingăi, Câmpia plain Romania 58 C2
Vingåker Sweden 45 K4
Vinh Vietnam 78 D4
Vinhais Port. 54 E3
Vinh Long Vietnam 79 D6
Vinh Thuc, Đao i. Vietnam 78 D3
Vinh Yên Vietnam 78 D3
Vinica Macedonia 58 D7
Vinita U.S.A. 178 D4
Vinjhan India 96 A5
Vînju Mare Romania see Vânju Mare
Vinkovci Croatia 56 K3
Vinland i. Canada see Newfoundland
Vinni Estonia 42 H2
Vinnitsa Ukr. see Vinnytsya
Vinnitsy Rus. Fed. 43 P1
Vinnytsya Ukr. 41 D6 also spelt Vinnitsa
Vinogradovo Rus. Fed. 43 T6
Vinson Massif mt. Antarctica 222 S1
Highest mountain in Antarctica.
antarctica [features] 212–213
Vinstra Norway 45 J3
Vintar Phil. 74 B2
Vinton U.S.A. 174 A3
Vinukonda India 94 C2
Vinza Congo 126 B5
Viola CA U.S.A. 182 C1
Viola IL U.S.A. 172 C9
Violeta Cuba see Primero de Enero
Violet Valley Aboriginal Reserve Australia 150 D3
Vioolsdrif S. Africa 132 B5
Viphya Mountains Malawi 129 B8
Vipiteno Italy 56 D2
Viqueque East Timor see Vikeke
Vir i. Croatia 56 H4
Virac Phil. 74 C3
Virac Point Phil. 74 C3
Viramgam India 96 B5
Viranşehir Turkey 107 D3
Virarajendrapet India 94 B3
Virawah Pak. 101 G5
Virawlya Belarus 43 K6
Vircava r. Latvia/Lith. 42 E5
Virchow, Mount hill Australia 150 B4
Virdáánjarga Fin. see Virtaniemi
Virden Canada 167 K5
Vire France 50 F4
Virei Angola 127 B8
Vîrful Highiş hill Romania 58 C2
Vírgenes, Cabo c. Arg. 205 C9
Virgilina U.S.A. 176 G9
Virgin r. U.S.A. 183 J5
Virginatown Canada 173 N2
Virgin Gorda i. Virgin Is (U.K.) 187 G3
Virginia S. Africa 133 K5
Virginia U.S.A. 174 A2
Virginia state U.S.A. 176 G8
Virginia Beach U.S.A. 177 J9
Virginia City MT U.S.A. 180 E3
Virginia City NV U.S.A. 182 E2
Virginia Falls Canada 166 E2
Virgin Islands (U.K.) terr. West Indies 187 G3
United Kingdom Overseas Territory.
oceania [countries] 138–139
Virgin Islands (U.S.A.) terr. West Indies 187 G3
United States Unincorporated Territory.
oceania [countries] 138–139
Virgin Mountains U.S.A. 183 J5
Virginópolis Brazil 203 D6
Virje Croatia 56 J2
Virkkala Fin. 45 N3
Virmasvesi l. Fin. 44 N3
Virôchey Cambodia 79 D5
Virolahti Fin. 45 N3
Viroqua U.S.A. 172 C7
Virovitica Croatia 56 J3
Virpe Latvia 42 D4
Virrat Fin. 44 M3
Virserum Sweden 45 K4
Virtaniemi Fin. 44 O1 also known as Virdáánjarga
Virton Belgium 51 L3
Virtsu Estonia 42 E3
Virú Peru 200 A2
Virudunagar India 94 C4
Virunga, Parc National des nat. park Dem. Rep. Congo 126 F5 formerly known as Albert, Parc National
Virvytė r. Lith. 42 D5
Vis Croatia 56 I5 also known as Issa or Lissa
Vis i. Croatia 56 I5
Visaginas Lith. 42 H6 formerly known as Sniečkus
Visakhapatnam India see Vishakhapatnam
Visalia U.S.A. 182 E5
Vişani Romania 58 I3
Visapur India 94 B2
Visavadar India 96 A5
Visayan Sea Phil. 74 B4
Visby Sweden 45 L4
Visconde do Rio Branco Brazil 207 K8
Viscount Melville Sound sea chan. Canada 165 H2
Vise, Ostrov i. Rus. Fed. 39 H2
Višegrad Bos.-Herz. 56 L5
Viseu Brazil 202 C2
Viseu Port. 54 D4
Viseu admin. dist. Port. 54 D4
Vishakhapatnam India 95 D2 also spelt Visakhapatnam; formerly spelt Vizagapatam
Vishegrad hill Bulg. 58 H7
Vishera r. Rus. Fed. 40 J3
Vishera r. Rus. Fed. 40 K4
Vishera r. Rus. Fed. 43 M3
Vishnevka Kazakh. 103 H2
Vishnyeva Belarus 42 H7
Vīsikums Latvia 42 I4
Vişina Romania 58 G4
Viški Latvia 42 H5
Viški Kanal sea chan. Croatia 56 I5
Visnagar India 96 B5
Viso, Monte mt. Italy 51 N8
Viso del Marqués Spain 55 H6
Visoko Bos.-Herz. 56 K5
Visp Switz. 51 N6
Visrivier S. Africa 133 J8
Vissannapeta India 94 D2
Vista U.S.A. 183 G8
Vista Alegre Amazonas Brazil 199 D4
Vista Alegre Amazonas Brazil 199 D6
Vista Alegre Amazonas Brazil 199 F6
Vista Alegre Mato Grosso do Sul Brazil 201 F4
Vista Alegre Roraima Brazil 199 F4
Vista Lake U.S.A. 182 E6
Vistonida, Limni lag. Greece 58 G7
Vistula r. Poland 49 P1 also spelt Wisła
Vištytis Lith. 42 D7
Vit r. Bulg. 58 F5
Vita r. Col. 198 E3
Vitao mt. Yugo. 56 K5
Vitebsk Belarus see Vitsyebsk
Vitebskaya Oblast' admin. div. Belarus see Vitsyebskaya Voblasts'
Vitebsk Oblast admin. div. Belarus see Vitsyebskaya Voblasts'
Viterbo Italy 56 E6
Vitez Bos.-Herz. 56 J4
Vitez pass Bos.-Herz. 56 K5
Vitigudino Spain 54 E3
Viti Levu i. Fiji 145 G3
Vitim r. Rus. Fed. 81 I1
Vitimskoye Ploskogor'ye plat. Rus. Fed. 81 I2
Vitina Kosovo, Srbija Yugo. 58 C6
Vitomirica Kosovo, Srbija Yugo. 58 B6
Vitor Peru 200 C4
Vitor r. Peru 200 B4
Vitória Espírito Santo Brazil 203 D7
Vitória Pará Brazil 199 H5
Vitoria Spain see Vitoria-Gasteiz
Vitória da Conquista Brazil 202 D5
Vitoria-Gasteiz Spain 55 I2 also known as Gasteiz or Vitoria
Vitosha nat. park Bulg. 58 E6
Vitré France 50 E4
Vitrolles France 51 L9
Vitry-en-Artois France 51 I2
Vitry-le-François France 51 K4
Vitsyebsk Belarus 43 L6 English form Vitebsk
Vitsyebskaya Voblasts' admin. div. Belarus 43 J6 English form Vitebsk Oblast; also known as Vitebskaya Oblast'
Vittangi Sweden 44 M2 also known as Vazáš
Vitteaux France 51 K5
Vittel France 51 L4
Vittoria Sicilia Italy 57 G12
Vittorio Veneto Italy 56 E3
Vivarais, Monts du mts France 51 K8
Viveiro Spain 54 D1 also spelt Vivero
Vivero Spain see Viveiro
Vivian U.S.A. 179 D5
Vivo S. Africa 131 F4
Vivonne France 50 G6
Vivoratá Arg. 204 F5
Vivorillo, Cayos is Hond. 186 C4
Vizagapatam India see Vishakhapatnam
Vizcaíno Mex. 181 D8
Vizcaíno, Desierto de des. Mex. 184 B3
Vizcaíno, Sierra mts Mex. 184 B3
Vize Turkey 106 A2
Vizhas r. Rus. Fed. 40 H2
Vizianagaram India 95 D2
Vizinga Rus. Fed. 40 I3
Viziru Romania 58 I3
Vizzini Sicilia Italy 57 G11
V. J. José Perez Bol. 200 C3
Vjosë r. Albania 59 A8
Vlaardingen Neth. 48 B4
Vlădeasa, Vârful mt. Romania 58 D2
Vladičin Han Srbija Yugo. 58 D6
Vladikavkaz Rus. Fed. 41 H8 also known as Dzaudzhikau; formerly known as Ordzhonikidze
Vladimir Rus. Fed. 90 D3
Vladimir Rus. Fed. 43 V5 historically known as Lodomeria
Vladimiro-Aleksandrovskoye Rus. Fed. 82 D4
Vladimir Oblast admin. div. Rus. Fed. see Vladimirskaya Oblast'
Vladimirovka Kazakh. 103 F1 formerly known as Vladimirovskiy
Vladimirovo Bulg. 58 E5
Vladimirovskiy Kazakh. see Vladimirovka
Vladimirskaya Oblast' admin. div. Rus. Fed. 43 V6 English form Vladimir Oblast
Vladimirskiy Tupik Rus. Fed. 43 O6
Vladimir-Volynskiy Ukr. see Volodymyr-Volyns'kyy
Vladivostok Rus. Fed. 82 C4
Vladychnoye Rus. Fed. 43 U3
Vlăhiţa Romania 58 G2
Vlajna mt. Yugo. 58 C6
Vlasenica Bos.-Herz. 56 K4
Vlašić Planina mts Yugo. 58 A4
Vlašim Czech Rep. 49 L6
Vlasotince Srbija Yugo. 58 D6
Vlasovo Rus. Fed. 43 U6
Vlas'yevo Rus. Fed. 82 F1
Vlazovichi Rus. Fed. 43 N8
Vleesbaai b. S. Africa 132 F11
Vlieland i. Neth. 48 B2
Vlissingen Neth. 48 A4 historically known as Flushing
Vlorë Albania 58 A8 also known as Aulon or Valona; historically known as Avlona
Vlorës, Gjiri i b. Albania 58 A8
Vlotslavsk Poland see Włocławek
Vltava r. Czech Rep. 49 L5
Vnina r. Rus. Fed. 43 R2
Vöcklabruck Austria 49 K7
Vodice Croatia 56 H5
Vodlozero, Ozero l. Rus. Fed. 40 F3
Vodňany Czech Rep. 49 L6
Vodnjan Croatia 56 F4
Vodopyanovo Rus. Fed. see Donskoye
Voël r. S. Africa 133 J10
Vogan Togo 125 F5
Vogelkop Peninsula Indon. see Doberai, Jazirah
Vogelsberg hills Germany 48 F5
Voghera Italy 56 B4
Vognill Norway 44 J3
Vogošća Bos.-Herz. 56 K5
Vohburg an der Donau Germany 48 I7
Vohémar Madag. see Iharaña
Vohibinany Madag. see Ampasimanolotra
Vohilava Fianarantsoa Madag. 131 [inset] J4
Vohilava Fianarantsoa Madag. 131 [inset] K4
Vohimarina Madag. see Iharaña
Vohimena, Tanjona c. Madag. 131 [inset] J5 formerly known as Ste-Marie, Cap
Vohipeno Madag. 131 [inset] J4
Võhma Estonia 42 G3
Voi Kenya 128 C5
Voikoski Fin. 45 N3
Voineasa Romania 58 E3
Voineşti Romania 58 I1
Voinjama Liberia 124 C4
Voin Pervyy Rus. Fed. 43 R8
Voiron France 51 L7
Voitsberg Austria 49 M8
Vojvodina prov. Yugo. 58 A3
Voka Estonia 42 I2
Vokhma Rus. Fed. 40 H4
Vokhtoga Rus. Fed. 43 V3
Voknavolok Rus. Fed. 44 O2
Voko Cameroon 125 I4
Vol' r. Rus. Fed. 40 J3
Volaterrae Italy see Volterra
Volcán Arg. 200 D5
Volcán, Cerro vol. Bol. 200 D5
Volcán Barú, Parque Nacional nat. park Panama 186 C5
Volcano Bay Japan see Uchiura-wan
Volcano Islands N. Pacific Ocean 220 D4
Part of Japan. Also known as Kazan-rettō.
Volcans d'Auvergne, Parc Naturel Régional des nature res. France 51 I7
Volchas r. Belarus 43 M8
Volchikha Rus. Fed. 103 J1
Volchina r. Rus. Fed. 43 Q4
Volchiy Nos, Mys pt Rus. Fed. 43 N1
Volda Norway 44 I3
Vol'dino Rus. Fed. 40 J3
Volens U.S.A. 176 F9
Volga Rus. Fed. 43 T4
Volga r. Rus. Fed. 43 Q5
Longest river in Europe.
europe [landscapes] 30–31
Volga r. U.S.A. 172 B8
Volga Upland hills Rus. Fed. see Privolzhskaya Vozvyshennost'
Volgodonsk Rus. Fed. 41 G7
Volgograd Rus. Fed. 41 H6 formerly known as Stalingrad; historically known as Tsaritsyn
Volgograd Oblast admin. div. Rus. Fed. see Volgogradskaya Oblast'
Volgogradskaya Oblast' admin. div. Rus. Fed. 41 H6 English form Volgograd Oblast; formerly known as Stalingradskaya Oblast'
Volgogradskoye Vodokhranilishche resr Rus. Fed. 41 H6
Volissos Greece 59 G10
Völkermarkt Austria 49 L9
Volkhov Rus. Fed. 43 N2
Volkhov r. Rus. Fed. 43 N1
Volkhovskaya Guba b. Rus. Fed. 43 N1
Volkhovskiy Rus. Fed. 43 M3
Völklingen Germany 48 D6
Volkovichi Belarus see Vawkavichy
Volkovo Rus. Fed. 43 L7
Volkovysk Belarus see Vawkavysk
Volkovyskiye Vysoty hills Belarus see Vawkavyskaye Wzvyshsha
Volksrust S. Africa 133 N4
Vol'no-Nadezhdinskoye Rus. Fed. 82 C4
Volnovakha Ukr. 41 F7
Vol'nyansk Ukr. see Vil'nyans'k
Volochanka Rus. Fed. 39 J2
Volochayevka-Vtoraya Rus. Fed. 82 D2
Volochisk Ukr. see Volochys'k
Volochys'k Ukr. 41 C6 also spelt Volochisk
Volodars'ke Ukr. 41 F7
Volodarskiy Rus. Fed. 102 B3
Volodarskoye Kazakh. see Saumalkol'
Volodymyr-Volyns'kyy Ukr. 41 C6 also spelt Vladimir-Volynskiy
Vologda Rus. Fed. 43 U2
Vologda r. Rus. Fed. 43 V2
Vologda Oblast admin. div. Rus. Fed. see Vologodskaya Oblast'
Vologodskaya Oblast' admin. div. Rus. Fed. 43 T1 English form Vologda Oblast
Volokolamsk Rus. Fed. 43 Q5
Volokonovka Rus. Fed. 41 F6
Volokoslavinskoye Rus. Fed. 43 T2
Volop S. Africa 132 G5
Volos Greece 59 D9
Voloshka Rus. Fed. 40 G3
Volosovo Rus. Fed. 43 K2
Volot Rus. Fed. 43 L4
Volovo Lipetskaya Oblast' Rus. Fed. 43 S9
Volovo Tul'skaya Oblast' Rus. Fed. 43 T8
Voloye Rus. Fed. 43 P7
Volozhin Belarus see Valozhyn
Volsini, Monti mts Italy 56 D6
Volsinii Italy see Orvieto
Vol'sk Rus. Fed. 102 A1
Volstruisleegte S. Africa 132 H10
Volstruispoort pass S. Africa 132 G7
Volta admin. reg. Ghana 125 F5
Volta r. Ghana 125 F5
Volta Blanche watercourse Burkina/Ghana see White Volta
Volta, Lake resr Ghana 125 F5
5th largest lake in Africa.
africa [landscapes] 112–113
Voltaire, Cape Australia 150 D2
Volta Noire r. Africa see Black Volta
Volta Redonda Brazil 203 C7
Volterra Italy 56 C5 historically known as Volaterrae
Voltoya r. Spain 54 G3
Volturino, Monte mt. Italy 57 H8
Volturno r. Italy 56 F7
Volubilis tourist site Morocco 122 D2
Voluntari Romania 58 H4
Volunteer Point Falkland Is 205 F8
Volvi, Limni l. Greece 58 E8
Vol'ya r. Rus. Fed. 40 L3
Volzhsk Rus. Fed. 40 I5
Volzhskiy Samarskaya Oblast' Rus. Fed. 41 I5 formerly known as Bol'shaya Tsarevshchina
Volzhskiy Volgogradskaya Oblast' Rus. Fed. 41 H6
Vomano r. Italy 56 G6
Vondanka Rus. Fed. 40 H4
Vondrozo Madag. 131 [inset] J4
Vonga Rus. Fed. 40 G2
Vonitsa Greece 59 B10
Võnnu Estonia 42 I3
Vonozero Rus. Fed. 43 P1
Vontimitta India 94 C3
Voorheesville U.S.A. 177 L3
Voosi kurk sea chan. Estonia 42 E2
Vop' r. Rus. Fed. 43 N7
Vopnafjörður Iceland 44 [inset] D2
Vopnafjörður b. Iceland 44 [inset] D2
Vörå Fin. 44 M3 also spelt Vöyri
Voran' Belarus 43 J6
Voranava Belarus 42 G7
Vordingborg Denmark 45 J5
Vordorf Germany 48 H3
Vorë Albania 58 A7
Voreio Aigaio admin. reg. Greece 59 G9 English form Northern Aegean
Voreioi Sporades is Greece 59 E9 English form Northern Sporades; also spelt Voríai Sporádhes
Voreios Evvoïkos Kolpos sea chan. Greece 59 E10
Vorga Rus. Fed. 43 N8
Vorgashor Rus. Fed. 40 L2
Voríai Sporádhes is Greece see Voreioi Sporades
Vorjing mt. India 97 G3
Vorkuta Rus. Fed. 40 M2
Vormedalsheia park Norway 45 I4
Vormsi i. Estonia 42 E2
Vorob'yevka Lipetskaya Oblast' Rus. Fed. 43 U9
Vorob'yevka Voronezhskaya Oblast' Rus. Fed. 41 G6
Vorob"yivka Ukr. 43 O9
Vorogovo Rus. Fed. 39 I3
Vorona r. Rus. Fed. 41 G6
Voronezh Rus. Fed. 41 F6
Voronezh r. Rus. Fed. 43 U9
Voronezh Oblast admin. div. Rus. Fed. see Voronezhskaya Oblast'
Voronezhskaya Oblast' admin. div. Rus. Fed. 41 G6 English form Voronezh Oblast
Voronov, Mys pt Rus. Fed. 40 G2
Voronov, Mys pt Rus. Fed. 43 N1
Voronovo Rus. Fed. 43 S6
Vorontsovka Kazakh. 103 J2
Vorontsovo Rus. Fed. 43 J4
Vorontsovo-Aleksandrovskoye Rus. Fed. see Zelenokumsk
Voron'ye Rus. Fed. 40 G4
Voroshilov Rus. Fed. see Ussuriysk
Voroshilovgrad Ukr. see Luhans'k
Voroshilovsk Rus. Fed. see Stavropol'
Voroshilovsk Ukr. see Alchevs'k
Vorot'kovo Rus. Fed. 43 O6
Vorotynets Rus. Fed. 40 H4
Vorotynsk Rus. Fed. 43 R7
Vorozhba Ukr. 41 E6
Vorpommersche Boddenlandschaft, Nationalpark nat. park Germany 49 J1
Vorposten Peak Antarctica 223 B2
Vorskla r. Rus. Fed. 41 E6
Vorstershoop S. Africa 132 H2
Vørterkaka Nunatak mt. Antarctica 223 B2
Võrtsjärv l. Estonia 42 G3
Võru Estonia 42 I4
Vorukh Tajik. 101 G2
Vorya r. Rus. Fed. 43 P7
Vosburg S. Africa 132 G7
Vose Tajik. 101 G2 formerly known as Aral
Vosges mts France 51 M5
Vosges du Nord, Parc Naturel Régional des nature res. France 51 N4
Voshchazhnikovo Rus. Fed. 43 U4
Voskresensk Rus. Fed. 43 T6
Voskresenskoye Lipetskaya Oblast' Rus. Fed. 43 T8
Voskresenskoye Respublika Bashkortostan Rus. Fed. 102 D1
Voskresenskoye Tul'skaya Oblast' Rus. Fed. 43 S7
Voskresenskoye Vologod. Obl. Rus. Fed. 43 S2
Voskresenskoye Yaroslavskaya Oblast' Rus. Fed. 43 S4
Voss Norway 45 I3
Vostochnaya Litsa Rus. Fed. 40 F1
Vostochno-Kazakhstanskaya Oblast' admin. div. Kazakh. see Vostochnyy Kazakhstan
Vostochno-Kounradskiy Kazakh. see Shygys Konyrat
Vostochno-Sakhalinskiy Gory mts Rus. Fed. 82 F2
Vostochno-Sibirskoye More sea Rus. Fed. see East Siberian Sea
Vostochnyy Rus. Fed. 40 J4
Vostochnyy Chink Ustyurta esc. Uzbek. 102 D4
Vostochnyy Kazakhstan admin. div. Kazakh. 103 I2 English form East Kazakhstan Oblast; also known as Shyghys Qazaqstan Oblysy; long form Vostochno-Kazakhstanskaya Oblast'
Vostochnyy Sayan mts Rus. Fed. 80 E2 English form Eastern Sayan Mountains
Vostok research station Antarctica
Lowest recorded screen temperature in the world.
world [climate and weather] 16–17
Vostok Rus. Fed. 82 D3
Vostok Rus. Fed. see Neftegorsk
Vostok Island Kiribati 221 H6
Vostretsovo Rus. Fed. 82 D3
Vostroye Rus. Fed. 40 H3
Võsu Estonia 42 G2
Votkinsk Rus. Fed. 40 J4
Votkinskoye Vodokhranilishche resr Rus. Fed. 40 J4
Votorantim Brazil 206 F10
Votrya r. Rus. Fed. 43 N6
Votuporanga Brazil 206 D7
Voudi, Akra pt Greece 59 J12
Vouga Angola see Cunhinga
Vouga r. Port. 54 C4
Vouillé France 50 G6
Voula Greece 59 E11
Vourinos mt. Greece 59 C8
Vouziers France 51 K3
Voves France 50 H4
Vovodo r. Cent. Afr. Rep. 126 E3
Voxna Sweden 45 K3
Voxnan r. Sweden 45 L3
Voya r. Rus. Fed. 40 I4
Voyageurs National Park U.S.A. 174 A1
Voykar r. Rus. Fed. 40 M2
Voynitsa Rus. Fed. 44 O2
Vöyri Fin. see Vörå
Voyvozh Respublika Komi Rus. Fed. 40 J2
Voyvozh Respublika Komi Rus. Fed. 40 J3
Vozdvizhenskoye Moskovskaya Oblast' Rus. Fed. 43 R5
Vozdvizhenskoye Moskovskaya Oblast' Rus. Fed. 43 T5
Vozha r. Rus. Fed. 43 U7
Vozhayel' Rus. Fed. 40 I3
Vozhd' Proletariata Rus. Fed. 43 U6
Vozhe, Ozero l. Rus. Fed. 43 T1
Vozhega Rus. Fed. 43 V1
Vozhega r. Rus. Fed. 43 U1
Vozhgora Rus. Fed. 40 I2
Voznesenka Kazakh. 103 G1
Voznesens'k Ukr. 41 D7
Voznesen'ye Rus. Fed. 43 Q1
Vozrovdenye Uzbek. 102 D3
Vozrozhdeniya, Ostrov i. Uzbek. 102 D3 also known as Wozrojdeniye Oroli
Vozzhayevka Rus. Fed. 82 C2
Vrå Denmark 45 J4
Vrabevo Bulg. 58 F6
Vrachionas hill Greece 59 B11 also known as Vrakhiónas Óros
Vrachnaiika Greece 59 C10 also spelt Vrakhnaíika
Vrådal Norway 45 J4
Vrakhiónas Óros hill Greece see Vrachionas
Vrakhnaíika Greece see Vrachnaiika
Vran mt. Bos.-Herz. 56 J5
Vrana r. Bulg. 58 H5
Vrangel' Rus. Fed. 82 D4
Vrangelya, Mys pt Rus. Fed. 82 E1
Vrangelya, Ostrov i. Rus. Fed. see Wrangel Island
Vranjak Bos.-Herz. 56 K4
Vranje Srbija Yugo. 58 C6
Vranjska Banja Srbija Yugo. 58 D6
Vranov, Vodní nádrž resr Czech Rep. 49 M7
Vranov nad Topľou Slovakia 49 S7
Vrapčište Macedonia 58 B7
Vrasidas, Akra pt Greece 58 F8
Vratnik pass Bulg. 58 H6
Vratsa Bulg. 58 E5
Vrbanja r. Bos.-Herz. 56 J4
Vrbas r. Bos.-Herz. 56 J3
Vrbas Vojvodina, Srbija Yugo. 58 A3 formerly known as Titov Vrbas
Vrbno pod Pradědem Czech Rep. 49 O5
Vrbovec Croatia 56 I3
Vrbovsko Croatia 56 H3
Vrchlabí Czech Rep. 49 M5
Vrede S. Africa 133 N4
Vredefort S. Africa 133 L3
Vredenburg S. Africa 132 B9
Vredendal S. Africa 132 C8
Vredeshoop Namibia 132 D4
Vreed-en-Hoop Guyana 199 G3
Vrela Kosovo, Srbija Yugo. 58 B6
Vrhnika Slovenia 56 G3
Vriddhachalam India 94 C4
Vrigstad Sweden 45 K4
Vrindavan India 89 B7
Vrnjačka Banja Srbija Yugo. 58 B5
Vrolijkheid Nature Reserve S. Africa 132 D10
Vrrin Albania 58 A7
Vršac Vojvodina, Srbija Yugo. 58 C3 also known as Versec
Vryburg S. Africa 133 I3
Vryheid S. Africa 133 O4
Vsetín Czech Rep. 49 O6
Vsevolozhsk Rus. Fed. 43 L1
Vskhody Rus. Fed. 43 P7
Vtáčnik mt. Slovakia 49 P7
Vtáčnik mts Slovakia 49 P7
Vůcha r. Bulg. 58 F7
Vučica r. Croatia 56 K3
Vučitrn Kosovo, Srbija Yugo. 58 B6
Vučje Srbija Yugo. 58 C6
Vuka r. Croatia 56 L3
Vukovar Croatia 56 L3
Vuktyl' Rus. Fed. 40 K3
Vukuzakhe S. Africa 133 N4
Vulcan Canada 167 H5
Vulcan Romania 58 E3
Vulcăneşti Moldova 58 J3 formerly spelt Vulkaneshty
Vulcan Island P.N.G. see Manam Island
Vulcano, Isola i. Isole Lipari Italy 57 G10
Vŭlchedrŭm Bulg. 58 E5
Vŭlchidol Bulg. 58 I5
Vulkaneshty Moldova see Vulcăneşti
Vulture Mountains U.S.A. 183 K8
Vung Dung Quat b. Vietnam 79 E5

index

V W

Vung Tau Vietnam 79 D6
formerly known as St Jacques, Cap
Vuohijärvi Fin. 42 H1
Vuohijärvi *l.* Fin. 45 N3
Vuokatti Fin. 44 O2
Vuoksa *r.* Rus. Fed. 43 L1
Vuoksa, Ozero *l.* Rus. Fed. 43 K1
Vuolijoki Fin. 44 N2
Vuollerim Sweden 44 M2
Vuolvojaure *l.* Sweden 44 L2
Vuostimo Fin. 44 N2
Vuotso Fin. 44 N1
Vŭrbitsa Bulg. 58 H6
Vurpăr Romania 58 F3
Vŭrshets Bulg. 58 E5
Vustsye Belarus 42 I6
Vutcani Romania 58 I2
Vuyyuru India 94 D2
Vuzlove Ukr. 49 T7
Vuzlyanka *r.* Belarus 42 H7
Vvedenka Kazakh. 103 E1
Vwaza Game Reserve *nature res.* Malawi 129 B7
Vyalikiya Bortniki Belarus 43 K8
Vyal'ye, Ozero *l.* Rus. Fed. 43 L2
Vyara India 96 B5
Vyarechcha Belarus 43 L6
Vyarkhovichy Belarus 42 E9
Vyarkhowye Belarus *see* Ruba
Vyatchyn Belarus 42 J9
Vyatka Rus. Fed. *see* Kirov
Vyatka *r.* Rus. Fed. 40 I5
Vyatskiye Polyany Rus. Fed. 40 I4
Vyatskoye Rus. Fed. 43 V4
Vyaz Rus. Fed. 43 K5
Vyazemskiy Rus. Fed. 82 D3
Vyaz'ma Rus. Fed. 43 P6
Vyaz'ma *r.* Rus. Fed. 43 O6
Vyazniki Rus. Fed. 40 G4
Vyazovka Rus. Fed. 102 A1
Vyazovka Rus. Fed. 41 G6
Vyazovo Rus. Fed. 43 U8
Vyborg Rus. Fed. 43 J1
formerly known as Viipuri; formerly spelt Viborg
Vyborgskiy Zaliv *b.* Rus. Fed. 43 J1
Vychegda *r.* Rus. Fed. 40 H3
Vychegodskiy Rus. Fed. 40 H3
Vydrino Rus. Fed. 85 E1
Vyeramyeyki Belarus 43 M8
Vyerkhnyadzvinsk Belarus 42 I6
formerly known as Drissa
Vyetka Belarus 43 M9
Vyetryna Belarus 43 J6
Vygonichi Rus. Fed. 43 P8
Vygozero, Ozero *l.* Rus. Fed. 40 E3
Vyksa Rus. Fed. 40 G5
Vylkove Ukr. 41 D7
Vym' *r.* Rus. Fed. 40 I3
Vypolzovo Rus. Fed. 43 O4
Vyritsa Rus. Fed. 43 L2
Vyselki Rus. Fed. 41 F7
Vyshgorod Rus. Fed. 43 V7
Vyshgorodok Rus. Fed. 42 I4
Vyshhorod Ukr. 41 D6
Vyshkov Rus. Fed. 43 M9
Vyshkovo Rus. Fed. 43 Q4
Vyshnevolotskaya Gryada *ridge* Rus. Fed. 43 P5
Vyshnevolotskoye Vodokhranilishche *resr* Rus. Fed. 43 P4
Vyshneye-Ol'shanoye Rus. Fed. 43 S9
Vyshniy-Volochek Rus. Fed. 43 P4
Vyskod' Rus. Fed. 43 L4
Vyškov Czech Rep. 49 O6
Vysoká *hill* Slovakia 49 O7
Vysokaye Belarus 42 E9
also spelt Vysokoye
Vysokaye Belarus 43 L7
Vysoké Mýto Czech Rep. 49 N6
Vysokinichi Rus. Fed. 43 R7
Vysokogorniy Rus. Fed. 82 E2
formerly known as Mulí
Vysokovo Rus. Fed. 43 T4
Vysokovsk Rus. Fed. 43 R5
Vysokoye Belarus *see* Vysokaye
Vysokoye Rus. Fed. 43 P5
Vysotsk Rus. Fed. 43 J1
Vystupovychi Ukr. 41 D6
Vytebet' *r.* Rus. Fed. 43 Q8
Vytegra Rus. Fed. 40 F3
Vyvenka Rus. Fed. 39 Q3
Vyya *r.* Rus. Fed. 40 H3
Vyžuona *r.* Lith. 42 G6

↓ W

Wa Ghana 124 E4
Waajid Somalia 128 D4
Waal *r.* Neth. 48 B4
Waalwijk Neth. 48 C4
Waanyi/Garawa Aboriginal Land *res.* Australia 148 C3
Waat Sudan 128 B2
Wabag P.N.G. 73 J8
Wabakimi Lake Canada 168 B3
Wabalı *well* Oman 105 G3
Wabamun Lake Canada 167 H4
Wabasca *r.* Canada 167 H3
Wabasca-Desmarais Canada 167 H4
Wabash *IN* U.S.A. 174 C3
Wabash *OH* U.S.A. 173 I10
Wabash *r.* U.S.A. 174 B4
Wabasha U.S.A. 174 A2
Wabassi *r.* Canada 168 C3
Wabatongushi Lake Canada 173 I2
Wabē Gestro *r.* Eth. 128 D3
Wabē Mena *r.* Eth. 128 D3
Wabeno U.S.A. 172 E5
Wabē Shebelē Wenz *r.* Eth. 128 E3
Wabigoon Lake Canada 168 A3
Wabowden Canada 167 L4
Wabrah *well* Saudi Arabia 105 D2
Wąbrzeźno Poland 49 P2
Wabu China 87 F1
Wabuk Point Canada 168 C2
Wabush Canada 169 H2
Wabush Lake Canada 169 H2
Waccamaw *r.* U.S.A. 175 E5
Waccamaw, Lake U.S.A. 175 E5
Waccasassa Bay U.S.A. 175 D6
Wachapreague U.S.A. 177 J8
Wächtersbach Germany 48 G5
Wachusett Reservoir U.S.A. 177 N3
Waco Canada 169 H3
Waco U.S.A. 179 C6
Waconda Lake U.S.A. 178 C4
Wad Pak. 101 F5
Wada'a Sudan 121 E6
Wada Wadalla Aboriginal Land *res.* Australia 148 C2
Wadayama Japan 91 D7
Wad Banda Sudan 121 E6
Wadbilliga National Park Australia 147 F4
Waddān Libya 120 C2
Waddān, Jabal *hills* Libya 120 B2
Waddell Dam U.S.A. 183 L8
Waddeneilanden *is* Neth. *see* West Frisian Islands
Wadden Islands Neth. *see* West Frisian Islands
Waddenzee *sea chan.* Neth. 48 B3
Waddikee Australia 146 C3
Waddington, Mount Canada 166 E5
Waddinxveen Neth. 48 B3
Wadena Canada 167 K5
Wadena U.S.A. 178 D2
Wad en Nail Sudan 121 G6
Wadesboro U.S.A. 174 D5
Wadeye Australia 148 A2
formerly known as Port Keats
Wadgaon *Maharashtra* India 94 B2
Wadgaon *Maharashtra* India 94 C1
Wad Hamid Sudan 121 G5
Wadhwan India 96 A5
Wadhwan India *see* Surendranagar
Wadi India 94 C2
Wadian China 87 E1
Wādī as Sīr Jordan 108 G6
Wādī Gimāl, Gezîret *i.* Egypt 104 A2
English form Wādī Gimāl Island
Wādī Gimāl Island Egypt *see* Wādī Gimāl, Gezîret
Wadi Halfa Sudan 121 F4
Wādī Ḩammah Saudi Arabia 104 C3
Wādī Mūsā Jordan 108 G7
Wad Medani Sudan 121 G6
Wadsworth *NV* U.S.A. 182 E2
Wadsworth *OH* U.S.A. 176 D4
Waegwan S. Korea 91 A7
Waenhuiskrans S. Africa 132 E11
Waesche, Mount Antarctica 222 P1
Wafangdian China 85 I4
formerly known as Fuxian
Wafra Kuwait *see* Al Wafrah
Wagah India 96 B3
Wagait Aboriginal Land *res.* Australia 148 A2
Wageningen Neth. 48 C4
Wageningen Suriname 199 G3
Wager Bay Canada 167 N1
Wagga Wagga Australia 147 E3
Wagiman Aboriginal Land *res.* Australia 148 A2
Wagin Australia 151 B7
Waglisla Canada 166 D4
Wagner Brazil 202 D5
Wagner U.S.A. 178 C3
Wagoner U.S.A. 179 D4
Wagon Mound U.S.A. 181 F5
Wągrowiec Poland 49 O3
Wah Pak. 101 H3
Wahai Indon. 75 D3
Wahda *state* Sudan 126 F2
Wahemen, Lac *l.* Canada 169 G2
Wahiawa U.S.A. 181 [inset] Y1
Wahoo U.S.A. 178 C3
Wahpeton U.S.A. 178 C2
Wahran Alg. *see* Oran
Wah Wah Mountains U.S.A. 183 K3
Wai India 94 B2
Waiapu *r.* N.Z. 152 M5
Waiau N.Z. 153 H10
Waiau *r.* *North I.* N.Z. 152 L6
Waiau *r.* *South I.* N.Z. 153 B14
Waiau *r.* *South I.* N.Z. 153 H10
Waidhofen an der Thaya Austria 49 M7
Waidhofen an der Ybbs Austria 49 L8
Waigama Indon. 75 D3
Waigeo *i.* Indon. 73 H7
Waihao Downs N.Z. 153 E12
Waiharara N.Z. 152 H2
Waiharoa N.Z. 152 J5
Waiheke Island N.Z. 152 J4
Waihi N.Z. 152 J5
Waihi Beach N.Z. 152 J5
Waihou *r.* N.Z. 152 J5
Waihua N.Z. 152 L7
Waikabubak Indon. 75 A5
Waikaia *r.* N.Z. 153 C13
Waikaia *r.* N.Z. 153 C13
Waikaka N.Z. 153 D13
Waikanae N.Z. 152 J8
Waikare, Lake N.Z. 152 J5
Waikaremoana, Lake N.Z. 152 K6
Waikaretu N.Z. 152 I5
Waikari N.Z. 153 G10
Waikato *admin. reg.* N.Z. 152 I5
Waikato *r.* N.Z. 152 I5
Waikawa N.Z. 153 D14
Waikeria N.Z. 152 J6
Waikerie Australia 146 C3
Waikiki U.S.A. 181 [inset] Z2
Waikirikiri N.Z. 152 K6
Waiklibang Indon. 75 B5
Waikoikoi N.Z. 153 D14
Waikokopu N.Z. 152 L7
Waikouaiti N.Z. 153 E13
Wailuku U.S.A. 181 [inset] Z1
Waimahaka N.Z. 153 C14
Waimakariri *r.* N.Z. 153 G11
Waimangaroa N.Z. 153 F9
Waimarama N.Z. 152 K7
Waimarie N.Z. 153 F9
Waimate N.Z. 153 F12
Waimatenui N.Z. 152 H3
Waimauku N.Z. 152 I4
Waimea U.S.A. 181 [inset] Z1
Wainganga *r.* India 94 C2
Waingapu Indon. 75 B5
Waingawa N.Z. 152 J8
Waini Point Guyana 199 G2
Wainwright Canada 167 I4
Wainwright U.S.A. 164 D2
Waiotira N.Z. 152 I3
Waiouru N.Z. 152 J7
Waipa *r.* N.Z. 152 J5
Waipahi N.Z. 153 D14
Waipahu U.S.A. 181 [inset] Y1
Waipaoa *r.* N.Z. 152 L6
Waipapa Point N.Z. 153 C14
Waipara N.Z. 153 G11
Waipawa N.Z. 152 K7
Waipipi N.Z. 152 I5
Waipu N.Z. 152 I3
Waipukurau N.Z. 152 K7
Wairakei N.Z. 152 K6
Wairarapa, Lake N.Z. 152 J9
Wairau *r.* N.Z. 153 I9
Wairau Valley N.Z. 152 H9
Wairoa N.Z. 152 L7
Wairoa *r.* *North I.* N.Z. 152 I4
Wairoa *r.* *North I.* N.Z. 152 L7
Waishe China 87 F2
Waitahanui N.Z. 152 K6
Waitahuna N.Z. 153 D13
Waitakaruru N.Z. 152 J5
Waitaki N.Z. 153 F12
Waitaki *r.* N.Z. 153 F12
Waitangi S. Pacific Ocean 145 H6
Waitangitaona *r.* N.Z. 153 E11
Waitara N.Z. 152 I6
Waitati N.Z. 153 E13
Waite River Australia 148 B4
Waitomo Caves N.Z. 152 J6
Waitotara N.Z. 152 I7
Waitotara *r.* N.Z. 152 I7
Waitsburg U.S.A. 180 C3
Waiuku N.Z. 152 I5
Waiwera South N.Z. 153 D14
Waiya Indon. 75 D3
Waiyang China 87 F3
Waiyevu Fiji 145 H3
Wajid, Jabal al *hills* Saudi Arabia 104 D4
Wajiki Japan 91 D8
Wajima Japan 90 E6
Wajir Kenya 128 D4
Waka Dem. Rep. Congo 126 D5
Waka, Tanjung *pt* Indon. 75 C3
Wakami Lake Canada 173 K3
Wakapuaka N.Z. 152 H9
Wakasa-wan *b.* Japan 91 D7
Wakatipu, Lake N.Z. 153 C13
Wakatoma Lake Canada 173 J4
Wakaw Canada 167 J4
Wakaya Aboriginal Land *res.* Australia 148 C3
Wakayama Japan 91 D7
Wakayama *pref.* Japan 91 D8

▶ Wake Atoll *terr.* N. Pacific Ocean 220 F4
United States Unincorporated Territory. Also known as Āneen-Kio or EnenKio; formerly known as Wake Island.
oceania [countries] ▶▶ 138–139

WaKeeney U.S.A. 178 C4
Wakefield Canada 173 R5
Wakefield N.Z. 152 H9
Wakefield U.K. 47 K10
Wakefield *MI* U.S.A. 172 D4
Wakefield *OH* U.S.A. 176 B7
Wakefield *RI* U.S.A. 177 N4
Wakefield *VA* U.S.A. 177 I9
Wakeham Canada *see* Kangiqsujuaq
Wake Island *terr.* N. Pacific Ocean *see* Wake Atoll
Wakema Myanmar 78 A4
Wakhan *reg.* Afgh. 101 H2
Waki Japan 91 D7
Wakinosawa Japan 90 G4
Wakiro *watercourse* Eritrea 104 B5
Wakkanai Japan 90 G2
Wakkerstroom S. Africa 133 O4
Wakool Australia 147 E3
Wakool *r.* Australia 147 D3
Wakuach, Lac *l.* Canada 169 H2
Waku-Kungo Angola 127 B7
formerly known as Santa Comba; formerly spelt Uaco Congo
Wakuya Japan 90 G5
Wakwayowkastic *r.* Canada 168 D3
Walagunya Aboriginal Reserve Australia 150 C4
Walajapet India 94 C3
Wałbrzych Poland 49 N5
historically known as Waldenburg
Walcha Australia 147 F2
Walcott U.S.A. 180 F4
Wałcz Poland 49 N2
Waldaist *r.* Austria 49 L7
Waldburg Range *mts* Australia 151 B5
Walden U.S.A. 177 K4
Waldenburg Poland *see* Wałbrzych
Waldkraiburg Germany 49 J7
Waldo U.S.A. 172 F7
Waldorf U.S.A. 177 I7
Waldport U.S.A. 180 A3
Waldron U.S.A. 179 D5
Waldron, Cape Antarctica 223 H2
Waldshut Germany 48 F8
Walea, Selat *sea chan.* Indon. 75 B3
Waleabahi *i.* Indon. 75 B3
Walêg China 86 B2
formerly known as Warli
Walej, Sha'ib al *watercourse* Iraq 109 K5
Wales *admin. div.* U.K. 47 I11
also known as Cymru; historically known as Cambria
Walewale Ghana 125 E4
Walford U.S.A. 172 B9
Walgett Australia 147 F2
Walgreen Coast Antarctica 222 Q1
Walhalla *MI* U.S.A. 172 G7
Walhalla *ND* U.S.A. 178 C1
Walhalla *SC* U.S.A. 174 D5
Walikale Dem. Rep. Congo 126 F5
Walker *r.* Australia 148 B2
Walker *watercourse* Australia 148 B5
Walker *IA* U.S.A. 172 B8
Walker *MI* U.S.A. 172 H7
Walker *MN* U.S.A. 178 D2
Walker *r.* U.S.A. 182 F3
Walker Bay S. Africa 132 D11
Walker Cay *i.* Bahamas 186 D1
Walker Creek *r.* Australia 149 D3
Walker Lake *l.* Canada 167 L4
Walker Lake U.S.A. 182 F3
Walker Lake *l.* U.S.A. 182 F3
Walker Mountains Antarctica 222 R2
Walker River Indian Reservation *res.* U.S.A. 182 F3
Walkersville *MD* U.S.A. 177 H6
Walkersville *WV* U.S.A. 176 E7
Walkerton U.S.A. 172 G9
Wall, Mount *hill* Australia 150 B4
Wallabi Group *is* Australia 151 A6
Wallaby Island Australia 149 D2
Wallace *ID* U.S.A. 180 C3
Wallace *NC* U.S.A. 174 E5
Wallace *VA* U.S.A. 176 C9
Wallaceburg Canada 168 D5
Wallal Downs Australia 150 C3
Wallambin, Lake *salt flat* Australia 151 B6
Wallangarra Australia 147 F2
Wallaroo Australia 146 C3
Walla Walla U.S.A. 180 C3
Walldürn Germany 48 G5
Wallekraal S. Africa 132 B7
Wallenpaupack, Lake U.S.A. 177 J4
Wallingford *CT* U.S.A. 177 M4
Wallingford *VT* U.S.A. 177 M2
Wallis, Îles *is* Wallis and Futuna Is *see* Wallis Islands

▶ Wallis and Futuna Islands *terr.* S. Pacific Ocean 145 H3
French Overseas Territory. Also known as Wallis et Futuna, Îles.
oceania [countries] ▶▶ 138–139

Wallis et Futuna, Îles *terr.* S. Pacific Ocean *see* Wallis and Futuna Islands
Wallis Islands Wallis and Futuna Is 145 H3
also known as Wallis, Îles
Wallis Lake *inlet* Australia 147 G3
Wallops Island U.S.A. 177 J8
Wallowa Mountains U.S.A. 180 C3
Walls U.K. 46 K3
Walls of Jerusalem National Park Australia 147 E5
Wallumbilla Australia 149 F5
Walmsley Lake Canada 167 I2
Walney, Isle of *i.* U.K. 47 I9
Walnut Bottom U.S.A. 176 H5
Walnut Cove U.S.A. 176 E9
Walnut Creek U.S.A. 182 B4
Walnut Creek *r.* U.S.A. 178 C4
Walnut Grove U.S.A. 182 C3
Walnut Ridge U.S.A. 174 B4
Walong India 97 H3
Walpole U.S.A. 177 M2
Walpole, Île *i.* New Caledonia 145 F4
Walsall U.K. 47 K11
Walsenburg U.S.A. 181 F5
Walsh *r.* Australia 149 D3
Walsrode Germany 48 G3
Waltair India 95 D2
Walterboro U.S.A. 175 D5
Walter F. George Reservoir U.S.A. 175 C6
Walters U.S.A. 179 C5
Walter's Range *hills* Australia 147 E2
Walthall U.S.A. 175 B5
Waltham Canada 173 Q5
Waltham *MA* U.S.A. 177 N3
Waltham *ME* U.S.A. 177 Q1
Walton *IN* U.S.A. 172 G10
Walton *KY* U.S.A. 176 A7
Walton *NY* U.S.A. 177 J3
Walton *WV* U.S.A. 176 D7
Walton-on-the-Naze U.K. 47 N12
Walvisbaai Namibia *see* Walvis Bay
Walvis Bay Namibia 130 B4
also spelt Walvisbaai
Walvis Bay *b.* Namibia 130 B4
Wamala, Lake Uganda 128 A4
Wamba Dem. Rep. Congo 126 E4
Wamba *r.* Dem. Rep. Congo 126 C5
Wamba Nigeria 125 H4
Wambardi Aboriginal Land *res.* Australia 148 A2
Wamena Indon. 73 I7
Wami *r.* Tanz. 129 C6
Wamlana Indon. 75 C3
Wampaya Aboriginal Land *res.* Australia 148 B3
Wampsville U.S.A. 173 R7
Wampusirpi Hond. 186 B4
Wanaaring Australia 147 E2
Wanaka N.Z. 153 D12
Wanaka, Lake N.Z. 153 D12
Wan'an China 87 E3
also known as Furong
Wanapitei Lake Canada 173 M4
Wanaque Reservoir U.S.A. 177 K4
Wanasabari Indon. 75 B4
Wanbi Australia 146 D3
Wanbi China 86 B3
Wanci Indon. 75 B4
Wanda Arg. 204 G2
Wandana Nature Reserve Australia 151 A6
Wanda Shan *mts* China 82 D3
Wandering River Canada 167 H4
Wanding China 86 A3
formerly known as Wandingzhen
Wandingzhen China *see* Wanding
Wandiwash India *see* Vandavasi
Wandle Downs N.Z. 153 H10
Wandlitz Germany 49 K3
Wandoan Australia 149 F5
Wang, Mae Nam *r.* Thai. 78 B4
Wanganui N.Z. 152 J7
Wanganui *r.* *North I.* N.Z. 152 I7
Wanganui *r.* *South I.* N.Z. 153 E11
Wangaratta Australia 147 E4
Wangary Australia 146 B3
Wangcang China 86 C1
also known as Hongjiang; formerly known as Fengjiaba
Wangcheng China 87 E2
formerly known as Gaotangling
Wangda China *see* Zogang
Wangdu China 85 G4
Wangdue Phodrang Bhutan 97 F4
Wangerooge *i.* Germany 48 E2
Wanggamet, Gunung *mt.* Indon. 75 B5
Wang Gaxun China 84 C4
Wanggezhuang China *see* Jiaonan
Wangiwangi *i.* Indon. 75 B4
Wangjiang China 87 F2
Wangkibila Hond. 186 B4
Wangkui China 82 B3
Wang Mai Khon Thai. *see* Sawankhalok
Wangmao China 87 D4
Wangmo China 86 C3
also known as Fuxing
Wangolodougou Côte d'Ivoire *see* Ouangolodougou
Wangqing China 82 C4
Wangying China *see* Huaiyin
Wangziguan China 86 C1
Wanham Canada 166 G4
Wanhatti Suriname 199 H3
Wan Hsa-la Myanmar 78 B3
Wanie-Rukula Dem. Rep. Congo 126 E4
Wanimiyn Aboriginal Land *res.* Australia 148 A2
Wanjarri Nature Reserve Australia 151 C5
Wankaner India 96 A5
Wankie Zimbabwe *see* Hwange
Wanlaweyn Somalia 128 E4
Wanna Lakes *salt flat* Australia 151 E6
Wannian China 87 F2
also known as Chenying
Wanning China 87 D5
Wanrong China 85 F5
Wanshan China 87 D3
Wanshan Qundao *is* China 87 E4
English form Lima Islands
Wanstead N.Z. 152 K8
Wantage U.K. 47 K12
Wanup Canada 173 M4
Wanxian China 87 D2
Wanyuan China 87 D1
Wanzai China 87 E2
also known as Kangle
Wanzhi China *see* Wuhu
Wapakoneta U.S.A. 176 A5
Wapawekka Lake Canada 167 J4
Wapello U.S.A. 172 B9
Wapikopa Lake Canada 168 B2
Wapiti *r.* Canada 166 G4
Wapotih Indon. 75 C3
Wappingers Falls U.S.A. 177 L4
Wapsipinicon *r.* U.S.A. 174 B3
Waqên China 86 B1
Waqf aş Şawwān, Jibāl *hills* Jordan 109 H6
Wāqişah *well* Iraq 107 E5
Waqr *well* Saudi Arabia 105 E3
Waqr Maryamah *well* Yemen 105 D4
War U.S.A. 176 D8
Wa'r, Wādī al *watercourse* Syria 109 L3
Warab Sudan 126 F2
Warab *state* Sudan 126 F2
Warah Pak. 101 F5
Warakurna-Wingellina-Irrunytju Aboriginal Reserve Australia 151 E5
Warandab Eth. 128 E3
Warangal India 94 C2
Waraseoni India 96 D5
Waratah Australia 147 E5
Warbreccan Australia 149 D5
Warburg Germany 48 G4
Warburton *Vic.* Australia 147 E4
Warburton *W.A.* Australia 151 D5
Warburton *watercourse* Australia 146 C1
Warburton S. Africa 133 O3
Warburton Aboriginal Reserve Australia 151 D5
Warburton Bay Canada 167 I2
Warburton Range *hills* Australia 151 D5
Warche *r.* Belgium 51 L2
Ward *watercourse* Australia 149 E5
Ward N.Z. 153 I9
Ward, Mount Antarctica 222 T2
Ward, Mount *South I.* N.Z. 153 B13
Ward, Mount *South I.* N.Z. 153 D11
Wardang Island Australia 146 C3
Wardeglo *waterhole* Kenya 128 D4
Warden S. Africa 133 M4
Wardha India 94 C1
Wardha *r.* India 94 C2
Ward Hill *hill* U.K. 46 I5
Ware Canada 166 E3
also known as Fort Ware
Ware U.S.A. 177 M3
Wareham U.K. 47 J13
Waremme Belgium 51 L2
Waren Germany 49 J2
Warendorf Germany 48 E4
Warginburra Peninsula Australia 149 F4
Wargla Alg. *see* Ouargla
War Gunbi *waterhole* Somalia 128 E2
Warialda Australia 147 F2
Wari Island P.N.G. 149 F1
Warin Chamrap Thai. 79 D5
Warka Poland 49 S4
Warkworth N.Z. 152 I4
War Idaad Somalia 128 E2
Warli China *see* Walêg
Warman Canada 167 J4
Warmbad Namibia 130 C6
Warmbad S. Africa 133 M1
Warmfontein Namibia 132 D4
Warmia *reg.* Poland 49 R1
Warm Springs *NV* U.S.A. 183 H3
Warm Springs *VA* U.S.A. 176 F7
Warm Springs Indian Reservation *res.* U.S.A. 180 B3
Warmwaterberg S. Africa 132 E10
Warmwaterberg *mts* S. Africa 132 E10
Warner Canada 167 H5
Warner Lakes U.S.A. 180 C4
Warner Mountains U.S.A. 180 B4
Warner Robins U.S.A. 175 D5
Warner Springs U.S.A. 183 H8
Warnes Bol. 201 E4
Warnow *r.* Germany 49 J1
Waronda India 94 C2
Waroona Australia 151 A7
Warora India 94 C1
Warra Australia 149 F5
Warrabri Aboriginal Land *res.* Australia 148 B4
Warracknabeal Australia 147 D4
Warragamba Reservoir Australia 147 F3
Warragul Australia 147 E4
Warrakalanna, Lake *salt flat* Australia 146 C2
Warrambool *hill* Australia 151 B6
Warrambool *r.* Australia 147 E2
Warrandirinna, Lake *salt flat* Australia 146 C1
Warrâq el-'Arab Egypt 108 C7
Warrawagine Australia 150 C4
Warrego *r.* Australia 147 E2
Warrego Range *hills* Australia 149 E5
Warren Australia 147 E2
Warren *r.* Australia 151 A7
Warren Canada 173 M4
Warren *AR* U.S.A. 179 D5
Warren *IL* U.S.A. 172 D8
Warren *IN* U.S.A. 172 H10
Warren *MI* U.S.A. 173 J8
Warren *MN* U.S.A. 178 C1
Warren *OH* U.S.A. 176 E4
Warren *PA* U.S.A. 176 F4
Warren Hastings Island Palau *see* Merir
Warren Island U.S.A. 166 C4
Warrenpoint U.K. 47 F9
Warrens U.S.A. 172 C6
Warrensburg *MO* U.S.A. 178 D4
Warrensburg *NY* U.S.A. 177 L2
Warrenton S. Africa 133 I5
Warrenton *GA* U.S.A. 175 D5
Warrenton *MO* U.S.A. 174 B4
Warrenton *NC* U.S.A. 176 G9
Warrenton *VA* U.S.A. 176 H7
Warri Nigeria 125 G5
Warriedar *hill* Australia 151 B6
Warriners Creek *watercourse* Australia 146 C2
Warrington N.Z. 153 E13
Warrington U.K. 47 J10
Warrington U.S.A. 175 C6
Warrnambool Australia 147 D4
Warroad U.S.A. 178 D1
Warrumbungle National Park Australia 147 F2
Warrumbungle Range *mts* Australia 147 F2
Warruwi Australia 148 B1
Warry Warry *watercourse* Australia 146 D2

▶ Warsaw Poland 49 S3
Capital of Poland. Also spelt Warszawa.

Warsaw *IN* U.S.A. 174 C3
Warsaw *KY* U.S.A. 176 A7
Warsaw *MO* U.S.A. 178 D4
Warsaw *NY* U.S.A. 176 G3
Warsaw *VA* U.S.A. 177 I8
Warsingsfehn Germany 48 E2
Warszawa Poland *see* Warsaw
Warta Poland 49 P4
Warta *r.* Poland 49 L3
Wartburg U.S.A. 176 A9
Wartburg, Schloß *tourist site* Germany 48 H4
Waru Indon. 77 G3
Warud India 96 C5
Warumungu Aboriginal Land *res.* Australia 148 B3
Warwick Australia 147 G2
Warwick U.K. 47 K11
Warwick *NY* U.S.A. 177 K4
Warwick *RI* U.S.A. 177 N4
Warwick Channel Australia 148 C2
Warzhong China 86 B2
Wasa Canada 167 H5
Wasagu Nigeria 125 G4
Wasaga Beach Canada 173 M6
Wasatch Range *mts* U.S.A. 183 M2
Wasbank S. Africa 133 O5
Wascana Creek *r.* Canada 167 J5
Wasco U.S.A. 182 E6
Wascott U.S.A. 172 B4
Waseca U.S.A. 174 A2
Wasekamio Lake Canada 167 I3
Washado Suriname 199 G3
Washap Pak. 101 E5
Washburn *IL* U.S.A. 172 D10
Washburn *ND* U.S.A. 178 B2
Washburn *TN* U.S.A. 176 B9
Washburn *WI* U.S.A. 172 C4
Washim India 94 C1
Washimeska *r.* Canada 169 F3

▶ Washington *DC* U.S.A. 177 H7
Capital of the United States of America.
world [countries] ▶▶ 10–11

Washington *GA* U.S.A. 175 D5
Washington *IA* U.S.A. 172 B9
Washington *IL* U.S.A. 172 D10
Washington *IN* U.S.A. 174 C4
Washington *KS* U.S.A. 178 C4
Washington *KY* U.S.A. 176 B7
Washington *NC* U.S.A. 174 E5
Washington *NH* U.S.A. 177 M2
Washington *NJ* U.S.A. 177 K5
Washington *PA* U.S.A. 176 E5
Washington *UT* U.S.A. 183 K4

▶ Washington *state* U.S.A. 180 B3
world [changes] ▶▶ 20–21

Washington, Cape Antarctica 223 L2
Washington, Mount U.S.A. 177 N1
Washington Court House U.S.A. 176 B6
Washington Island U.S.A. 172 G5
Washington Land *reg.* Greenland 165 M2
Washir Afgh. 101 E3
Washita *r.* U.S.A. 179 C5
Washpool National Park Australia 147 G2
Washtucna U.S.A. 180 C3
Wasī' Saudi Arabia 105 D2
Wasī' *well* Saudi Arabia 105 E3
Wasilków Poland 49 U2
Wasilla U.S.A. 164 E3
Wāsiţ *governorate* Iraq 107 F4
Wasit *tourist site* Iraq 107 F4
Wāsiţah Saudi Arabia 104 B3
Waskaganish Canada 168 E3
also known as Fort Rupert
Waskaiowaka Lake Canada 167 L3
Waskatenau Canada 167 H4
Wąsosz Poland 49 N4
Waspán Nicaragua 186 B4
Wassadou Senegal 124 B3
Wassamu Japan 90 H2
Wassenaar Neth. 48 B3
Wasser Namibia 130 C5
Wasserkuppe *hill* Germany 48 G5
Wassou Guinea 124 B4
Wassuk Range *mts* U.S.A. 182 F3
Wassy France 51 K4
Waswanipi, Lac *l.* Canada 168 E3
Watabeag Lake Canada 173 M2
Watambayoli Indon. 75 B3
Watampone Indon. 75 B4
Watansoppeng Indon. 75 A4
Watapi Lake Canada 167 I4
Watarrka National Park Australia 148 A5
Watauga *r.* U.S.A. 176 C9
Watauga Lake U.S.A. 176 C9
Watenstadt-Salzgitter Germany *see* Salzgitter
Waterberg Namibia 130 C4
Waterberg Plateau Game Park *nature res.* Namibia 130 C4
Waterbury *CT* U.S.A. 177 L4
Waterbury *VT* U.S.A. 177 M1
Water Cays *i.* Bahamas 186 D2
Waterdown Canada 173 N7
Wateree *r.* U.S.A. 175 D5
Waterford Rep. of Ireland 47 E11
also known as Port Láirge
Waterford S. Africa 133 J10
Waterford *CA* U.S.A. 182 D4
Waterford *PA* U.S.A. 176 F4
Waterford Harbour Rep. of Ireland 47 F11
Waterhen *r.* Canada 167 J4
Waterhen Lake Canada 167 L4
Waterhouse *r.* Australia 148 B2
Waterhouse Range *mts* Australia 148 B5
Waterloo Canada 168 D5
Waterloo Sierra Leone 124 B4
Waterloo *IA* U.S.A. 174 A3
Waterloo *IL* U.S.A. 174 B4
Waterloo *NY* U.S.A. 177 I3
Waterloo *WI* U.S.A. 172 E7
Waterlooville U.K. 47 K13
Waterman U.S.A. 172 E9
Waterpoort S. Africa 131 F4
Waterton Lakes National Park Canada 167 H5
Watertown Park Canada 167 H5
Watertown *NY* U.S.A. 177 J2
Watertown *SD* U.S.A. 178 C2
Watertown *WI* U.S.A. 172 E7
Waterval *r.* S. Africa 133 M3
Waterval-Boven S. Africa 133 O2
Water Valley U.S.A. 174 B5
Waterville Rep. of Ireland 47 B12
Waterville *ME* U.S.A. 177 P1
Waterville *WA* U.S.A. 180 B3
Watervliet U.S.A. 177 L3
Wates Indon. 77 E4
Watford Canada 173 L8
Watford U.K. 47 L12
Watford City U.S.A. 178 B2
Wathaman *r.* Canada 167 K3
Wathaman Lake Canada 167 K3
Watheroo Australia 151 B6
Watheroo National Park Australia 151 A6
Watino Canada 167 G4
Watīr, Wādī *watercourse* Egypt 108 F8
Watkins Glen U.S.A. 177 I3
Watkinsville U.S.A. 175 D5
Watling Island Bahamas *see* San Salvador
Watonga U.S.A. 179 C5
Watowato, Bukit *mt.* Indon. 75 D2
Watrous Canada 167 J5
Watrous U.S.A. 181 F6
Watsa Dem. Rep. Congo 126 F4
Watseka U.S.A. 174 C3
Watson *r.* Australia 149 D2
Watson Canada 167 J4
Watson Escarpment Antarctica 223 P1
Watson Lake Canada 166 D2
Watsonville U.S.A. 182 C5
Watt, Mount *hill* Australia 151 D5
Watterson Lake Canada 167 L2
Wattiwarriganna *watercourse* Australia 146 C2
Watts Bar Lake *resr* U.S.A. 174 C5
Wattsburg U.S.A. 176 F3
Watubela, Kepulauan *is* Indon. 73 H7
Wau P.N.G. 73 K8
Wau Sudan 126 E3
Wau *watercourse* Sudan 126 E3
Waubay Lake U.S.A. 178 C2
Wauchope *N.S.W.* Australia 147 G2
Wauchope *N.T.* Australia 148 B4
Wauchula U.S.A. 175 D7
Waukara, Gunung *mt.* Indon. 75 A3
Waukarlycarly, Lake *salt flat* Australia 150 C4
Waukau U.S.A. 172 E7
Waukegan U.S.A. 174 C3
Waukesha U.S.A. 172 E7
Waukon U.S.A. 174 B3
Waunakee U.S.A. 172 D7
Waupaca U.S.A. 172 E6
Waupun U.S.A. 172 E7
Waurika U.S.A. 179 C5
Wausau U.S.A. 172 D6
Wauseon U.S.A. 176 A4
Wautoma U.S.A. 172 D6
Wave Hill Australia 148 A3
Waverley N.Z. 152 I7
Waverly *IA* U.S.A. 174 A3
Waverly *NY* U.S.A. 177 I3
Waverly *OH* U.S.A. 176 C6
Waverly *TN* U.S.A. 174 C4
Waverly *VA* U.S.A. 177 H8
Wavre Belgium 51 K2
Waw Myanmar 78 B4
Wawa Canada 168 C4
formerly known as Jamestown
Wawa Nigeria 125 G4
Wawagosic *r.* Canada 168 E3
Wawalalindu Indon. 75 B3
Wāw al Kabīr Libya 120 C3
Wāw an Nāmūs *waterhole* Libya 120 C3
Wawasee, Lake U.S.A. 172 H9
Wawo Indon. 75 B3
Wawoi *r.* P.N.G. 73 J8
Wawotebi Indon. 75 B3
Waxahachie U.S.A. 179 C5

Waxü China **86** B1
Waxxari China **88** D4
Way, Lake *salt flat* Australia **151** C5
Wayabula Indon. **75** D2
Wayag *i.* Indon. **75** D2
Wayamli Indon. **75** D2
Wayaobu China *see* **Zichang**
Waycross U.S.A. **175** D6
Way Kambas National Park Indon. **77** D4
Waykilo Indon. **75** C3
Wayland *KY* U.S.A. **176** C8
Wayland *MI* U.S.A. **172** H8
Wayland *NY* U.S.A. **176** H3
Wayne *MI* U.S.A. **173** J8
Wayne *NE* U.S.A. **178** C3
Wayne *WV* U.S.A. **176** C7
Waynesboro *GA* U.S.A. **175** D5
Waynesboro *MS* U.S.A. **175** B6
Waynesboro *PA* U.S.A. **176** H6
Waynesboro *TN* U.S.A. **174** C5
Waynesboro *VA* U.S.A. **176** G7
Waynesburg U.S.A. **176** E6
Waynesville *MO* U.S.A. **178** D4
Waynesville *NC* U.S.A. **174** D5
Waza Myanmar **78** B2
Waza, Parc National de *nat. park* Cameroon **125** I4
Wazi Khwa Afgh. **101** G3
also known as Marjan
Wazirabad Pak. **101** H3
Wda *r.* Poland **49** P2
W du Niger, Parcs Nationaux du *nat. park* Niger **125** F4
We New Caledonia **145** F4
We, Pulau *i.* Indon. **76** A1
Weagamow Lake Canada **168** B2
Wear *r.* U.K. **47** K9
Weare U.S.A. **177** N2
Wearyan *r.* Australia **148** C3
Weatherford *OK* U.S.A. **179** C5
Weatherford *TX* U.S.A. **179** C5
Weatherly U.S.A. **177** J5
Weaver Lake Canada **167** L4
Weaverville U.S.A. **182** B1
Webequie Canada **168** C2
Weber N.Z. **152** K8
Weber *r.* U.S.A. **183** M1
Weber, Mount Canada **166** D4
Weber Basin *sea feature* Indon. **218** P6
Weber Inlet Antarctica **222** T2

▶**Webi Shabeelle** *r.* Somalia **128** D4
5th longest river in Africa.
africa [landscapes] ➤ 112–113

Webster *MA* U.S.A. **177** N3
Webster *SD* U.S.A. **178** C2
Webster *WI* U.S.A. **172** A5
Webster City U.S.A. **174** A3
Webster Springs U.S.A. **176** E7
Webuye Kenya **128** B4
formerly known as Broderick Falls
Wecho *r.* Canada **167** H2
Wecho Lake Canada **167** H2
Weda Indon. **75** C2
Weda, Teluk *b.* Indon. **75** D2
Weddell Island Falkland Is **205** E8
Weddell Sea Antarctica **222** V2
Wedderburn N.Z. **153** E13
Wedge Mountain Canada **166** F5
Weed U.S.A. **180** B4
Weedville U.S.A. **176** G4
Weenen S. Africa **133** O5
Weenen Nature Reserve S. Africa **133** O5
Weener Germany **48** E2
Weert Neth. **48** C4
Wee Waa Australia **147** F2
Wegberg Germany **48** D4
Węgliniec Poland **49** M4
Węgorzewo Poland **49** S1
Węgorzyno Poland **49** M2
Węgrów Poland **49** T3
Wehnī Eth. **104** B5
Wei *r. Henan* China **85** G4
Wei *r. Shaanxi* China **86** D1
Wei *r. Shandong* China **85** H4
Weichang China **85** H3
Weiden in der Oberpfalz Germany **48** J6
Weidongmen China *see* **Qianjin**
Weifang China **85** H4
Weihai China **85** I4
Weihui China **85** G5
formerly known as Jixian
Weihu Ling *mts* China **82** B4
Weilburg Germany **51** O2
Weilheim in Oberbayern Germany **48** I8
Weimar Germany **48** I5
Weinan China **87** D1
Weingarten Germany **48** G8
Weinheim Germany **48** F6
Weining China **86** C3
Weipa Australia **149** D2
Weipa Aboriginal Reserve Australia **149** D2
Weipa South Aboriginal Reserve Australia **149** D2
Weiqu China *see* **Chang'an**
Weir *r.* Australia **147** F2
Weiragoo Range *hills* Australia **151** B5
Weir River Canada **167** M3
Weiser U.S.A. **180** C3
Weiser *r.* U.S.A. **180** C3
Weishan *Shandong* China **87** F1
also known as Xiazhen
Weishan *Yunnan* China **86** B3
also known as Wenhua
Weishan Hu *l.* China **87** F1
Weishi China **87** E1
Weiße Elster *r.* Germany **51** R1
Weißenburg in Bayern Germany **48** H6
Weißenfels Germany **48** I4
Weisshorn *mt.* Switz. **51** N6
Weiss Lake U.S.A. **179** F5
Weissmies *mt.* Switz. **51** O6
Weissrand Mountains Namibia **130** C5
Weißwasser Germany **49** L4
Weixian China **85** G4
also known as Mingzhou
Weixin China **86** C3
also known as Zhaxi
Weiya China **84** B3
Weiyuan China **84** E5
also known as Qingyuan
Weiyuan China *see* **Huzhu**
Weiyuan China *see* **Jinggu**
Weiyuan Jiang *r.* China **86** B4
Weiz Austria **49** M8
Weizhou China *see* **Wenchuan**
Weizhou Dao *i.* China **87** D4
Weizi China **85** I3
Wejherowo Poland **49** P1
Wekusko Canada **167** L4
Wekusko Lake Canada **167** L4
Wekweti Canada **167** H1
formerly known as Snare Lakes
Wel *r.* Poland **49** Q2
Welatam Myanmar **78** B2
Welbedacht Dam S. Africa **133** K6
Welbourn Hill Australia **146** B1
Welch U.S.A. **176** D8
Weld U.S.A. **177** O1
Weld, Mount *hill* Australia **151** C6
Weldiya Eth. **128** C2
Weldon U.S.A. **176** H9
Weld Range *hills* Australia **151** B5
Welford National Park Australia **149** D5
formerly known as Barcoo National Park
Welk'īt'ē Eth. **128** C2
Welkom S. Africa **133** K4
Welland Canada **173** N8
Welland *r.* U.K. **47** L11
Welland Canal Canada **173** N7
Wellesley Canada **173** M7
Wellesley Islands Australia **148** C3
Wellesley Islands Aboriginal Reserve Australia **148** C3
Wellesley Lake Canada **166** B2
Wellfleet U.S.A. **177** O4
Wellingborough U.K. **47** L11
Wellington Australia **147** F3
Wellington Canada **173** P7

▶**Wellington** N.Z. **152** I9
Capital of New Zealand.
world [countries] ➤ 10–11

Wellington *admin. reg.* N.Z. **152** J9
Wellington S. Africa **132** C10
Wellington *CO* U.S.A. **180** F4
Wellington *KS* U.S.A. **178** C4
Wellington *NV* U.S.A. **182** E3
Wellington *OH* U.S.A. **176** C4
Wellington *TX* U.S.A. **179** B5
Wellington *UT* U.S.A. **183** N2
Wellington, Isla *i.* Chile **205** B8
Wellington Range *hills N.T.* Australia **148** B2
Wellington Range *hills W.A.* Australia **151** C5
Wells Canada **166** F4
Wells U.S.A. **180** D4
Wells, Lake *salt flat* Australia **151** C5
Wellsboro U.S.A. **177** H4
Wellsford N.Z. **152** I4
Wells Gray Provincial Park Canada **166** F4
Wells-next-the-Sea U.K. **47** M11
Wellston U.S.A. **172** H6
Wellsville *NY* U.S.A. **176** H3
Wellsville *OH* U.S.A. **176** E5
Wellton U.S.A. **183** J9
Wełna *r.* Poland **49** N3
Weloka U.S.A. **181** [inset] Z2
Wels Austria **49** L7
Welshpool U.K. **47** I11
also known as Y Trallwng
Welton U.S.A. **172** C9
Welwel Eth. **128** E3
Welwitschia Namibia *see* **Khorixas**
Wema Dem. Rep. Congo **126** D5
Wembere *r.* Tanz. **129** B6
Wembesi S. Africa **133** N6
Wembley Canada **166** G4
Wemindji Canada **168** E2
formerly known as Nouveau-Comptoir *or* Paint Hills
Wemyss Bight Bahamas **186** D1
Wen *r.* China **85** H5
Wenamu *r.* Guyana/Venez. **199** F3
Wenatchee U.S.A. **180** B3
Wenatchee Mountains U.S.A. **180** B3
Wenchang China **87** D5
Wenchang China *see* **Zitong**
Wencheng China **87** G3
also known as Daxue
Wenchi Ghana **125** E5
Wench'ït Shet' *r.* Eth. **128** C2
Wenchow China *see* **Wenzhou**
Wenchuan China **86** B2
also known as Weizhou
Wendelstein *mt.* Germany **48** J8
Wenden Latvia *see* **Cēsis**
Wenden U.S.A. **183** K8
Wendeng China **85** I4
Wendo Eth. **128** C3
Wéndou Mbôrou Guinea **124** B4
Wendover U.S.A. **183** J1
Wenebegon Lake Canada **173** J3
Wenfeng China *see* **Yongfeng**
Wengshui China **86** A2
Wengyuan China **87** E3
also known as Longxian
Wenhua China *see* **Weishan**
Wenjiang China *see* **Gaoxian**
Wenjiashi China **87** E3
Wenlan China *see* **Mengzi**
Wenlin China *see* **Renshou**
Wenling China **87** G2
Wenlock *r.* Australia **149** D2
Wenona *IL* U.S.A. **172** D9
Wenona *MD* U.S.A. **177** J7
Wenping China *see* **Ludian**
Wenquan *Chongqing* China **87** D2
Wenquan *Guizhou* China **87** C2
Wenquan China *see* **Yingshan**
Wenquan *Qinghai* China **84** C5

▶**Wenquan** *Qinghai* China **89** E5
Highest settlement in the world.

Wenquan *Xinjiang* China **88** C2
also known as Arixang
Wenquanzhen China **87** E2
Wenshan China **86** C4
also known as Kaihua
Wenshui China **86** C2
Wensu China **88** C3
Wensum *r.* U.K. **47** N11
Wentworth Australia **146** D3
Wentworth *NC* U.S.A. **176** F9
Wentworth *NH* U.S.A. **177** N2
Wenxi China **85** F5
Wenxian China **86** C1
Wenyu *r.* China **85** F4
Wenzhou China **87** G3
formerly spelt Wenchow
Wer India **96** C4
Werda Botswana **130** D5
Werdau Germany **49** J5
Werdër Eth. **128** E3
Werder Germany **49** J3
Wêreldend S. Africa **132** E1
Werinama Indon. **75** D3
Werl Germany **48** E4
Wermsdorfer Forst *park* Germany **49** J4
Wernberg-Köblitz Germany **49** J6
Wernecke Mountains Canada **166** B1
Wernigerode Germany **48** H4
Werota Eth. **128** C2
Werra *r.* Germany **48** G4
Werrimull Australia **146** D3
Werris Creek Australia **147** F2
Wertheim Germany **48** G6
Werwaru Indon. **75** D5
Wesel Germany **48** D4
Wesendorf Germany **48** H3
Weser *r.* Germany **48** F2
Weser *sea chan.* Germany **48** F2
Wesergebirge *hills* Germany **48** F3
Weska Weka Eth. **128** B3
Weslemkoon Lake Canada **173** P5
Wesley S. Africa **133** L10
Wesleyville Canada **169** K3
Wessel, Cape Australia **148** C1
Wessel Islands Australia **148** C1
Wesselsbron S. Africa **133** K4
Wesselsvlei S. Africa **132** H4
Wesselton S. Africa **133** N3
Wessington Springs U.S.A. **178** C2
West Alligator *r.* Australia **148** B2
West Allis U.S.A. **172** E7
West Antarctica *reg.* Antarctica **222** P1
West Baines *r.* Australia **148** A2
West Banas *r.* India **96** A5

▶**West Bank** *terr.* Asia **108** G6
Territory occupied by Israel.
asia [countries] ➤ 64–67

West Bay Canada **169** J2
West Bay Cayman Is **186** C3
West Bay *b.* U.S.A. **175** B6
West Bend U.S.A. **172** E7
West Bengal *state* India **97** E5
also known as Bangla
West Branch U.S.A. **173** I6
Westbrook U.S.A. **177** O2
West Burke U.S.A. **177** N1
Westby U.S.A. **172** C7
West Caicos *i.* Turks and Caicos Is **187** E2
West Cape N.Z. **153** A13
West Cape Howe Australia **151** B7
West Chester U.S.A. **177** J6
Westcliffe U.S.A. **181** F5
West Coast *admin. reg.* N.Z. **153** E10
West Coast National Park S. Africa **132** C10
West Dome *mt.* N.Z. **153** C13
West End Bahamas **175** E7
West End U.S.A. **177** J3
Westerburg Germany **48** E5
Westerholt Germany **48** E2
Westerland Germany **48** F1
Western *watercourse* Australia **149** D4
Western *r.* Canada **167** J1
Western *admin. reg.* Ghana **124** E5
Western *prov.* Kenya **128** B4
Western *prov.* Zambia **127** D8
Western Area *admin. div.* Sierra Leone **124** B4
Western Australia *state* Australia **146** A2
Western Bahr el Ghazal *state* Sudan **126** E3
Western Cape *prov.* S. Africa **132** E10
Western Darfur *state* Sudan **120** D6
Western Desert Egypt **121** F3
also known as Ṣaḥara el Gharbîya
Western Desert Aboriginal Land *res.* Australia **148** A3
Western Dvina *r.* Europe *see* **Zapadnaya Dvina**
Western Equatoria *state* Sudan **126** F3
Western Ghats *mts* India **94** B3
also known as Sahyadri
Western Kordofan *state* Sudan **126** F2
Western Lesser Sunda Islands *prov.* Indon. *see* **Nusa Tenggara Barat**
Western Port *b.* Australia **147** E4
Western Province *prov.* Zambia *see* **Copperbelt**

▶**Western Sahara** *terr.* Africa **122** B4
Disputed territory (Morocco). Formerly known as Spanish Sahara.
africa [countries] ➤ 114–117

Western Samoa *country* S. Pacific Ocean *see* **Samoa**
Western Sayan Mountains *reg.* Rus. Fed. *see* **Zapadnyy Sayan**
Westerschelde *est.* Neth. **48** A4
Westerstede Germany **48** E2
Westerville U.S.A. **176** C5
Westerwald *hills* Germany **48** E5
West Falkland *i.* Falkland Is **205** E8
West Fargo U.S.A. **178** C2
West Fayu *atoll* Micronesia **73** K5
Westfield *MA* U.S.A. **177** M3
Westfield *NY* U.S.A. **176** F3
Westfield *PA* U.S.A. **176** H4
Westfield *WI* U.S.A. **172** D7
West Frisian Islands Neth. **48** B2
also known as Wadden Islands *or* Waddeneilanden
Westgate Australia **149** E5
West Grand Lake U.S.A. **169** H4
West Hamlin U.S.A. **176** C7
West Hartford U.S.A. **177** M4
West Haven U.S.A. **177** M4
West Ice Shelf Antarctica **223** F2
West Indies N. America **171** L7
West Irian *prov.* Indon. *see* **Irian Jaya**
West Island India **95** G3
West Jordan U.S.A. **183** M1
West Kazakhstan Oblast *admin. div.* Kazakh. *see* **Zapadnyy Kazakhstan**
West Lafayette U.S.A. **174** C3
West Lamma Channel *Hong Kong* China **87** [inset]
Westland Australia **149** D4
Westland National Park N.Z. **153** E11
also known as Tai Poutini National Park
West Liberty *IA* U.S.A. **172** B9
West Liberty *KY* U.S.A. **176** B8
West Liberty *OH* U.S.A. **176** B5
Westlock Canada **167** H4
West Lorne Canada **168** D5
West Lunga *r.* Zambia **127** E8
West Lunga National Park Zambia **127** E8
West MacDonnell National Park Australia **148** B4
West Malaysia *pen.* Malaysia *see* **Peninsular Malaysia**
Westmalle Belgium **51** K1
Westman Islands Iceland *see* **Vestmannaeyjar**
Westmar Australia **147** F1
West Memphis U.S.A. **174** B5
West Milton U.S.A. **176** A6
Westminster U.S.A. **177** I6
West Monroe U.S.A. **179** D5
Westmoreland Australia **148** C3
Westmoreland U.S.A. **178** C4
Westmorland U.S.A. **183** I8
West Nicholson Zimbabwe **131** F4
West Nueces *r.* U.S.A. **179** C6
Westoe Dam S. Africa **133** O3
Weston *OH* U.S.A. **176** B4
Weston *WV* U.S.A. **176** E6
Westonaria S. Africa **133** L3
Weston-super-Mare U.K. **47** J12
Westover U.S.A. **177** J7
West Palm Beach U.S.A. **175** D7
West Papua *prov.* Indon. *see* **Irian Jaya**
West Plains U.S.A. **178** E4
West Point *pt* Australia **147** E5
West Point *CA* U.S.A. **182** D3
West Point *IA* U.S.A. **172** B10
West Point *MS* U.S.A. **175** B5
West Point *NE* U.S.A. **178** C3
West Point *NY* U.S.A. **177** L4
West Point *OH* U.S.A. **176** E5
West Point *VA* U.S.A. **177** I8
West Point Lake *resr* U.S.A. **175** C5
Westport Canada **173** Q6
Westport N.Z. **153** F9
Westport Rep. of Ireland **47** C10
Westport *CA* U.S.A. **182** A2
Westport *NY* U.S.A. **177** L1
Westray Canada **167** K4
Westray *i.* U.K. **46** I4
Westray Firth *sea chan.* U.K. **46** I4
Westree Canada **168** D4
West Road *r.* Canada **166** F4
West Rutland U.S.A. **177** L2
West Sacramento U.S.A. **182** C3
West Salem U.S.A. **176** C5
West Seneca U.S.A. **176** G3
West Siberian Plain Rus. Fed. **38** I3
also known as Zapadno-Sibirskaya Nizmennost' *or* Zapadno-Sibirskaya Ravnina
West Stewartstown U.S.A. **177** N1
West Topsham U.S.A. **177** M1
West Union *IA* U.S.A. **174** B3
West Union *OH* U.S.A. **176** B7
West Union *WV* U.S.A. **176** E6
West Valley City U.S.A. **183** M1
Westville *IN* U.S.A. **172** G9
Westville *OK* U.S.A. **179** D5
West Virginia *state* U.S.A. **176** E7
West Walker *r.* U.S.A. **182** E3
Westwood Australia **149** F4
Westwood U.S.A. **182** D1
West Wyalong Australia **147** E3
West York U.S.A. **177** I6
Wetan *i.* Indon. **75** D4
Wetar *i.* Indon. **75** C4
Wetar, Selat *sea chan.* Indon. **75** C5
Wetaskiwin Canada **167** H4
Wete Dem. Rep. Congo **126** E6
Wete Tanz. **129** C6
Wethersfield U.S.A. **177** M4
Wetmore U.S.A. **172** G4
Wetmore Glacier Antarctica **222** T2
Wetumpka U.S.A. **175** C5
Wetzlar Germany **48** F5
Wever U.S.A. **172** B10
Wewahitchka U.S.A. **175** C6
Wewak P.N.G. **73** J7
Wewoka U.S.A. **179** C5
Wexford Rep. of Ireland **47** F11
also known as Loch Garman
Wexford Harbour *b.* Rep. of Ireland **47** F11
Weyakwin Canada **167** J4
Weyauwega U.S.A. **172** E6
Weyburn Canada **167** K5
Weyer Markt Austria **49** L8
Weyhausen Germany **48** H3
Weyhe Germany **48** F3
Weymouth Canada **169** H4
Weymouth U.K. **47** J13
Weymouth U.S.A. **177** O3
Weymouth, Cape Australia **149** D2
Whakaari *i.* N.Z. **152** L5
also known as White Island
Whaka a Te Wera *inlet* N.Z. *see* **Paterson Inlet**
Whakaki N.Z. **152** L7
Whakamaru N.Z. **152** J6
Whakapunake *hill* N.Z. **152** L6
Whakarewarew Forest Park *nature res.* N.Z. **152** K6
Whakatane N.Z. **152** K5
Whalan Creek *r.* Australia **147** F2
Whale *r.* Canada *see* **La Baleine, Rivière à**
Whale Bay U.S.A. **166** C3
Whale Cay *i.* Bahamas **186** D1
Whale Cove Canada **167** M2
Whale Island N.Z. *see* **Motuhora Island**
Whaleyville U.S.A. **177** I9
Whalsay *i.* U.K. **46** L3
Whampoa, Sungai *r.* Sing. **76** [inset]
Whangaehu *r.* N.Z. **152** J8
Whangamata N.Z. **152** J5
Whangamoa N.Z. **152** H9
Whangamomona N.Z. **152** I7
Whanganui Inlet N.Z. **152** G8
Whanganui National Park N.Z. **152** I7
Whangaparaoa N.Z. **152** I4
Whangara N.Z. **152** M6
Whangarei N.Z. **152** I3
Whangaroa Bay N.Z. **152** H3
Whapmagoostui Canada **168** E2
Wharanui N.Z. **153** I9
Whareama N.Z. **152** K8
Wharfe *r.* U.K. **47** K10
Wharncliffe Canada **173** J4
Wharncliffe U.S.A. **176** D8
Wharton U.S.A. **179** C6
Wharton Lake Canada **167** L1
Whataroa N.Z. **153** E11
Wha Ti Canada **167** G2
formerly known as Lac la Martre
Wheatland *CA* U.S.A. **182** C2
Wheatland *IA* U.S.A. **172** C9
Wheatland *WY* U.S.A. **180** F4
Wheatley Canada **173** K8
Wheatley U.S.A. **176** A7
Wheaton *IL* U.S.A. **174** B3
Wheaton *MN* U.S.A. **178** C2
Wheaton-Glenmont U.S.A. **177** H6
Wheeler *TX* U.S.A. **179** B5
Wheeler *WI* U.S.A. **172** B5
Wheeler Lake Canada **167** H2
Wheeler Lake *resr* U.S.A. **174** C5
Wheeler Peak *NM* U.S.A. **181** F5
Wheeler Peak *NV* U.S.A. **183** J3
Wheelersburg U.S.A. **176** C7
Wheeler Springs U.S.A. **182** E7
Wheeling U.S.A. **176** E5
Wheelwright Arg. **204** E4
Whernside *hill* U.K. **47** J9
Whim Creek Australia **150** B4
Whinham, Mount Australia **148** A5
Whirihaki Forest Park *nature res.* N.Z. **152** K6
Whiskey Jack Lake Canada **167** K3
Whiskeytown Lake U.S.A. **182** B1
Whispering Pines U.S.A. **182** B3
Whistler Canada **166** F5
Whitbourne Canada **169** K4
Whitby Canada **173** O7
Whitby U.K. **47** L9
Whitchurch U.K. **47** J11
Whitchurch-Stouffville Canada **173** N7
Whitcombe, Mount N.Z. **153** E11
White *r.* Canada **168** C3
White *r.* Canada/U.S.A. **166** B2
White *r. AR* U.S.A. **174** B5
White *r. CO* U.S.A. **183** O1
White *r. IN* U.S.A. **174** C4
White *r. MI* U.S.A. **172** G7
White *r. NV* U.S.A. **183** J5
White *r. SD* U.S.A. **178** C3
White *r. VT* U.S.A. **177** M2
White *r. WI* U.S.A. **172** C4
White *watercourse AZ* U.S.A. **183** N8
White *watercourse TX* U.S.A. **179** B5
White, East Fork *r.* U.S.A. **174** C4
White, Lake *salt flat* Australia **148** A4
White, North Fork *r.* U.S.A. **178** D4
White Bay Canada **169** J3
White Butte *mt.* U.S.A. **178** B2
White Canyon U.S.A. **183** N4
White Cliffs Australia **147** D2
White Cloud U.S.A. **172** H7
Whitecourt Canada **167** H4
White Earth Indian Reservation *res.* U.S.A. **178** D2
Whiteface Lake U.S.A. **172** A3
Whiteface Mountain U.S.A. **177** L1
Whitefield U.S.A. **177** N1
Whitefish Canada **173** L4
Whitefish *r.* Canada **166** E1
Whitefish U.S.A. **180** D2
Whitefish *r.* U.S.A. **172** G5
Whitefish Bay U.S.A. **172** F6
Whitefish Lake *N.W.T.* Canada **167** J2
Whitefish Lake *Ont.* Canada **172** D2
Whitefish Point U.S.A. **173** I4
White Hall U.S.A. **174** B4
Whitehall *MI* U.S.A. **172** G7
Whitehall *MT* U.S.A. **180** D3
Whitehall *NY* U.S.A. **177** L2
Whitehall *OH* U.S.A. **176** C6
Whitehall *WI* U.S.A. **172** B6
Whitehaven U.K. **47** I9
White Haven U.S.A. **177** J4
White Hill *hill* Canada **169** I4

▶**Whitehorse** Canada **166** C2
Territorial capital of Yukon.

White Horse, Vale of *valley* U.K. **47** K12
White Island Antarctica **223** D2
White Island N.Z. *see* **Whakaari**
White Kei *r.* S. Africa **133** L9
White Lake *salt flat* Australia **151** C5
White Lake *Ont.* Canada **168** C3
White Lake *Ont.* Canada **168** E4
White Lake *LA* U.S.A. **179** D6
White Lake *MI* U.S.A. **172** G7
Whitemark Australia **147** F5
White Mountain Peak U.S.A. **182** F4
White Mountains U.S.A. **177** N1
White Mountains National Park Australia **149** E4
Whitemouth *r.* Canada **171** G1
Whitemouth Lake Canada **167** M5
White Nile *r.* Sudan/Uganda **126** G1
also known as Abiad, Bahr el *or* Jebel, Bahr el
White Nile Dam Sudan **121** G6
White Nossob *watercourse* Namibia **130** C4
White Oak U.S.A. **176** B8
White Otter Lake Canada **168** B3
White Pass Canada/U.S.A. **166** C3
White Pine *MI* U.S.A. **172** D4
White Pine *TN* U.S.A. **176** B9
White Pine Range *mts* U.S.A. **183** I3
White River Canada **168** C3
Whiteriver U.S.A. **183** O8
White River U.S.A. **178** B3
White River Junction U.S.A. **177** M2
White River National Wildlife Refuge *nature res.* U.S.A. **174** B5
White River Valley U.S.A. **183** I3
White Rock Peak U.S.A. **183** J3
White Russia *country* Europe *see* **Belarus**
Whitesail Lake Canada **166** E4
White Salmon U.S.A. **180** B3
Whitesand *r. Alta/N.W.T.* Canada **167** H2
Whitesand *r. Sask.* Canada **167** K5
White Sands National Monument *nat. park* U.S.A. **181** F6
Whitesboro U.S.A. **177** J2
Whitesburg U.S.A. **176** C8
White Sea Rus. Fed. **40** F2
also known as Beloe More *or* Beloye More
White Stone U.S.A. **177** I8
White Sulphur Springs *MT* U.S.A. **180** E3
White Sulphur Springs *WV* U.S.A. **176** E8
Whitesville U.S.A. **176** D8
White Umfolozi *r.* S. Africa **133** P5
Whiteville U.S.A. **174** E5
White Volta *watercourse* Burkina/Ghana **125** E3
also known as Nakambé *or* Nakanbe *or* Volta Blanche
White Water U.S.A. **183** H8
Whitewater *CO* U.S.A. **183** P3
Whitewater *WI* U.S.A. **172** E8
Whitewater Baldy *mt.* U.S.A. **181** E6
White Well Australia **146** A2
White Woman Creek *r.* U.S.A. **178** B4
Whitewood Australia **149** D4
Whitewood Canada **167** K5
Whithorn U.K. **47** H9
Whitianga N.Z. **152** J4
Whitley City U.S.A. **176** A9
Whitmire U.S.A. **174** D5
Whitmore S. Africa **133** M8
Whitmore Mountains Antarctica **222** Q1
Whitney Canada **173** O5
Whitney, Lake U.S.A. **179** C5
Whitney, Mount U.S.A. **182** F5
Whitstable U.K. **47** N12
Whitsunday Group *is* Australia **149** F4
Whitsunday Island Australia **149** F4
Whitsunday Island National Park Australia **149** F4
Whitsunday Passage Australia **149** F4
Whitsun Island Vanuatu *see* **Pentecost Island**
Whittemore U.S.A. **173** J6
Whittier U.S.A. **182** F8
Whittington Range *hills* Australia **148** B3
Whittlesea S. Africa **133** K9
Whittlesey U.K. **47** L11
Whittlesey U.S.A. **172** C5
Whittlesey, Mount *hill* U.S.A. **172** C4
Whitton Australia **147** E3
Whitula *watercourse* Australia **149** D5
Wholdaia Lake Canada **167** J2
Why U.S.A. **183** L9
Whyalla Australia **146** C3
Whydah Benin *see* **Ouidah**
Wiang Kosai National Park Thai. **78** B4
Wiang Pa Pao Thai. **78** B4
Wiang Phran Thai. **78** B3
Wiang Sa Thai. **78** C4
Wiarton Canada **168** D4
Wiasi Ghana **125** E4
Wibaux U.S.A. **180** F3
Wichelen Belgium **48** A4
Wichita U.S.A. **178** C4
Wichita *r.* U.S.A. **179** C5
Wichita Falls U.S.A. **179** C5
Wichita Mountains U.S.A. **179** C5
Wichita Mountains National Wildlife Refuge *nature res.* U.S.A. **179** C5
Wick U.K. **46** I5
Wickenburg U.S.A. **183** L8
Wickepin Australia **151** B7
Wickham Australia **150** B4
Wickham *r.* Australia **148** A3
Wickham, Cape Australia **147** D4
Wicklow Rep. of Ireland **47** F11
also known as Cill Mhantáin
Wicklow Head Rep. of Ireland **47** G11
Wicklow Mountains Rep. of Ireland **47** F11
Wicklow Mountains National Park Rep. of Ireland **47** F10
Wicko, Jezioro *lag.* Poland **49** N1
Widawa *r.* Poland **49** O4
Widawka *r.* Poland **49** P4
Wide Bay Australia **149** G5
Widerøe, Mount Antarctica **223** B2
Widgeegoara *watercourse* Australia **147** E1
Widgiemooltha Australia **151** C6
Widi, Kepulauan *is* Indon. **75** D3
Wi-do *i.* S. Korea **83** B6
Więcbork Poland **49** O2
Wied *r.* Germany **48** E5
Wiehengebirge *hills* Germany **48** F3
Wiehl Germany **48** E5
Wieleń Poland **49** N3
Wielka Sowa *mt.* Poland **49** N5
Wielkopolskie, Pojezierze *reg.* Poland **49** O3
Wielkopolski Park Narodowy *nat. park* Poland **49** N3
Wieluń Poland **49** P4
Wien Austria *see* **Vienna**
Wiener Neustadt Austria **49** N8
Wiensberg *mt.* Austria **49** M7
Wieprz *r.* Poland **49** S4
Wieprza *r.* Poland **49** N1
Wieprz-Krzna, Kanał *canal* Poland **49** U4
Wieringerwerf Neth. **48** C3
Wieruszów Poland **49** P4
Wierzyca *r.* Poland **49** P2
Wiesbaden Germany **48** F5
Wiesloch Germany **48** F6
Wiesmoor Germany **48** E2
Wieżyca *hill* Poland **49** P1
Wigan U.K. **47** J10
Wiggins U.S.A. **175** B6
Wight, Isle of *i.* U.K. **47** K13
Wigierski Park Narodowy *nat. park* Poland **49** U1
Wignes Lake Canada **167** J2
Wigry, Jezioro *l.* Poland **49** U1
Wigtown U.K. **47** H9
Wigtown Bay U.K. **47** H9
Wijchen Neth. **48** C4
Wikieup U.S.A. **183** K7
Wik'ro Eth. **128** C1
Wikwemikong Canada **173** L5
Wil Switz. **51** P5
Wilber U.S.A. **178** C3
Wilberforce *r.* N.Z. **153** F11
Wilberforce, Cape Australia **148** C1
Wilbur U.S.A. **180** C3
Wilburton U.S.A. **179** D5
Wilcannia Australia **147** D2
Wilcox U.S.A. **176** G4
Wilczek Land *i.* Rus. Fed. *see* **Vil'cheka, Zemlya**
Wildalpener Salzatal *nature res.* Austria **49** M8
Wildcat Hill Wilderness Area *nature res.* Canada **167** K4
Wildcat Peak U.S.A. **183** H3
Wild Coast S. Africa **133** N8
Wilderness S. Africa **132** G10
Wilderness U.S.A. **176** H7
Wilderness National Park S. Africa **132** G11
Wildeshausen Germany **48** F3
Wild Goose Canada **172** D2
Wildhay *r.* Canada **167** G4
Wildhorn *mt.* Switz. **51** N6
Wild Horse Draw *r.* U.S.A. **181** F7
Wild Horse Hill *mt.* U.S.A. **178** B3
Wildon Austria **49** M9
Wild Rice *r. MN* U.S.A. **178** C2
Wild Rice *r. ND* U.S.A. **178** C2
Wild Rice Lake U.S.A. **172** A4
Wildwood Canada **167** H4
Wildwood *FL* U.S.A. **175** D6
Wildwood *NJ* U.S.A. **177** K7
Wiley Ford U.S.A. **176** G6
Wilga *r.* Poland **49** S4
Wilge *r. Free State* S. Africa **133** M4
Wilge *r. Gauteng/Mpumalanga* S. Africa **133** N2
Wilgena Australia **146** B2

▶**Wilhelm, Mount** P.N.G. **73** J8
5th highest mountain in Oceania.
oceania [landscapes] ➤ 136–137

Wilhelmina Gebergte *mts* Suriname **199** G4
Wilhelm-Pieck-Stadt Germany *see* **Guben**
Wilhelmsburg Austria **49** M7
Wilhelmshaven Germany **48** F2
Wilhelmstal Namibia **130** C4
Wilkes-Barre U.S.A. **177** J4
Wilkesboro U.S.A. **176** D9
Wilkes Coast Antarctica **223** I2
Wilkes Land *reg.* Antarctica **223** I2
Wilkie Canada **167** I4
Wilkinsburg U.S.A. **176** F5
Wilkins Coast Antarctica **222** T2
Wilkins Ice Shelf Antarctica **222** T2
Wilkinson Lakes *salt flat* Australia **146** B2
Will, Mount Canada **166** D3
Willamette *r.* U.S.A. **180** B3
Willandra Billabong *watercourse* Australia **147** E3
Willandra National Park Australia **147** E3
Willapa Bay U.S.A. **180** A3
Willard Mex. **184** C2
Willard *NM* U.S.A. **181** F6
Willard *OH* U.S.A. **176** C4
Willards U.S.A. **177** J7
Willcox U.S.A. **183** O9
Willcox Playa *salt flat* U.S.A. **183** O9
Willebroek Belgium **51** K1
Willem Pretorius Game Reserve *nature res.* S. Africa **133** L5

▶**Willemstad** Neth. Antilles **187** F4
Capital of the Netherlands Antilles.

Willeroo Australia **148** A2
William *r.* Canada **167** I3
William, Mount Australia **147** D4
William Creek Australia **146** C2
William Lake Canada **167** L4
Williams Australia **151** B7
Williams *r. Qld* Australia **149** D4
Williams *r. W.A.* Australia **151** B7
Williams *AZ* U.S.A. **183** L6
Williams *CA* U.S.A. **182** B2
Williamsburg *IA* U.S.A. **174** A3
Williamsburg *KY* U.S.A. **176** A9
Williamsburg *MI* U.S.A. **172** H6
Williamsburg *OH* U.S.A. **176** A6
Williamsburg *PA* U.S.A. **176** G5
Williamsburg *VA* U.S.A. **177** I8
Williams Lake Canada **166** F4
Williamson *NY* U.S.A. **177** H2
Williamson *WV* U.S.A. **176** C8
Williamsport *IN* U.S.A. **174** C3
Williamsport *OH* U.S.A. **176** B6
Williamsport *PA* U.S.A. **177** H4
Williamston *MI* U.S.A. **173** I8
Williamston *NC* U.S.A. **174** E5
Williamstown *KY* U.S.A. **176** A7
Williamstown *MA* U.S.A. **177** L3
Williamstown *NY* U.S.A. **177** J2
Willimantic U.S.A. **177** M4
Willis Group *atolls* Australia **149** F3
Willis Islands S. Georgia **205** [inset]
Williston S. Africa **132** E8
Williston *FL* U.S.A. **175** D6
Williston *ND* U.S.A. **178** B1
Williston *SC* U.S.A. **175** D5
Williston Lake Canada **166** F4
Willits U.S.A. **182** A2
Willmar U.S.A. **178** D2
Willmore Wilderness Provincial Park Canada **166** G4
Willochra *watercourse* Australia **146** C2
Willoughby U.S.A. **176** D4
Willow *r.* Canada **166** F4
Willow Beach U.S.A. **183** J6
Willow Bunch Canada **167** J5
Willow Creek *r.* Canada **167** H5
Willow Creek U.S.A. **180** B4
Willow Creek *r. OR* U.S.A. **180** B3
Willow Creek *r. UT* U.S.A. **183** O1
Willow Hill U.S.A. **176** H5
Willow Lake Canada **167** G2
Willowlake *r.* Canada **166** F2
Willowmore S. Africa **132** H10
Willowra Australia **148** B4
Willowra Aboriginal Land Trust *res.* Australia *see* **Wirliyajarrayi Aboriginal Land Trust**
Willow Reservoir U.S.A. **172** D5
Willows U.S.A. **182** B2
Willow Springs U.S.A. **178** E4
Willowvale S. Africa **133** M9
Wills, Lake *salt flat* Australia **150** E4
Wills Creek *watercourse* Australia **148** D4
Willunga Australia **146** C3
Wilmington Australia **146** C3
Wilmington *DE* U.S.A. **177** J6
Wilmington *NC* U.S.A. **175** E5
Wilmington *OH* U.S.A. **176** B6
Wilmington *VT* U.S.A. **177** M3
Wilmington Island U.S.A. **175** D5
Wilmore U.S.A. **176** A8
Wilno Lith. *see* **Vilnius**
Wilnsdorf Germany **48** F5
Wilpattu National Park Sri Lanka **94** D4
Wilpena *watercourse* Australia **146** C2
Wilson *r.* Australia **150** E3
Wilson *watercourse* Australia **147** D1
Wilson *atoll* Micronesia *see* **Ifalik**
Wilson *MN* U.S.A. **172** B7
Wilson *NC* U.S.A. **174** E5
Wilson *NY* U.S.A. **176** G2
Wilson, Mount *CO* U.S.A. **181** F5
Wilson, Mount *NV* U.S.A. **183** J3
Wilson, Mount *OR* U.S.A. **180** B3
Wilson Hills Antarctica **223** K2
Wilsonia U.S.A. **182** F5
Wilson Lake *resr* U.S.A. **174** C5
Wilsons U.S.A. **176** H8
Wilson's Promontory *pen.* Australia **147** E4
Wilson's Promontory National Park Australia **147** E4
Wilton *r.* Australia **148** B2
Wilton *ME* U.S.A. **177** O1
Wilton *NH* U.S.A. **177** N3
Wiltz Lux. **51** L3
Wiluna Australia **151** C5
Wimbledon N.Z. **152** K8
Wimereux France **50** H2
Wimmera *r.* Australia **147** D4
Wina *r.* Cameroon *see* **Vina**
Winamac U.S.A. **174** C3
Winam Gulf Kenya **128** B5
formerly known as Kavirondo Gulf
Winbin *watercourse* Australia **149** E5

index W X Y

Winburg S. Africa **133** L5
Wincanton S. Africa **132** G4
Wincanton U.K. **47** J12
Winchendon U.S.A. **177** M3
Winchester N.Z. **153** F12
Winchester U.K. **47** K12
Winchester *IL* U.S.A. **174** B4
Winchester *IN* U.S.A. **176** A5
Winchester *KY* U.S.A. **176** A8
Winchester *NH* U.S.A. **177** M3
Winchester *TN* U.S.A. **174** C5
Winchester *VA* U.S.A. **176** G6
Wind *r.* Canada **166** C1
Wind *r.* U.S.A. **180** E4
Windabout, Lake *salt flat* Australia **146** C2
Windau Latvia *see* **Ventspils**
Windber U.S.A. **176** G5
Wind Cave National Park U.S.A. **178** B3
Winder U.S.A. **175** D5
Windermere U.K. **47** J9
Windham U.S.A. **176** D4

▶**Windhoek** Namibia **130** C4
Capital of Namibia.

Windidda Aboriginal Reserve Australia **151** C5
Windigo *r.* Canada **168** A2
Windigo Lake Canada **168** B2
Windischgarsten Austria **49** L8
Wind Mountain U.S.A. **181** F6
Windom U.S.A. **178** D3
Windorah Australia **149** D5
Window Rock U.S.A. **183** O6
Wind Point U.S.A. **172** F8
Wind Ridge U.S.A. **176** E6
Wind River Indian Reservation *res.* U.S.A. **180** E4
Wind River Range *mts* U.S.A. **180** E4
Winds, Bay of Antarctica **223** G2
Windsor Australia **147** F3
Windsor *Nfld.* Canada **169** K3
Windsor *N.S.* Canada **169** H4
Windsor *Ont.* Canada **168** D5
Windsor *Que.* Canada **169** F4
Windsor U.K. **47** L12
Windsor *NC* U.S.A. **174** E4
Windsor *NY* U.S.A. **177** J3
Windsor *VA* U.S.A. **177** I9
Windsor *VT* U.S.A. **177** M2
Windsor Dam U.S.A. **177** M3
Windsor Locks U.S.A. **177** M4
Windsorton S. Africa **133** I5
Windula *watercourse* Australia **149** D5
Windward Islands Caribbean Sea **187** H4
Windward Passage Cuba/Haiti **187** E3
Windy Harbour Australia **151** A7
Winefred Lake Canada **167** I4
Winfield *AL* U.S.A. **175** C5
Winfield *IA* U.S.A. **172** B9
Winfield *KS* U.S.A. **178** C4
Winfield *WV* U.S.A. **176** D7
Wingate Mountains *hills* Australia **148** A2
Wingene Belgium **51** J1
Wingham Canada **168** D5
Wini East Timor **75** C5
Winifred, Lake *salt flat* Australia **150** C4
Winifreda Arg. **204** D5
Winisk Canada **168** C2
Winisk *r.* Canada **168** C2
Winisk Lake Canada **168** C2
Winisk River Provincial Park Canada **168** C2
Winkana Myanmar **79** B5
Winkelhaaks *r.* S. Africa **132** D9
Winkelman U.S.A. **183** N9
Winkelpos S. Africa **133** K4
Winkler Canada **167** L5
Winlock U.S.A. **180** B3
Winnalls Ridge Australia **148** A5
Winneba Ghana **125** E5
Winnebago U.S.A. **178** D3
Winnebago, Lake U.S.A. **172** E6
Winnebago Indian Reservation *res.* U.S.A. **178** C3
Winnecke Creek *watercourse* Australia **148** A3
Winneconne U.S.A. **172** E6
Winnemucca U.S.A. **182** G1
Winnemucca Lake U.S.A. **182** E1
Winner U.S.A. **178** B3
Winnett U.S.A. **180** E3
Winnfield U.S.A. **179** D6
Winnibigoshish, Lake U.S.A. **178** D2
Winning Australia **150** A4

▶**Winnipeg** Canada **167** L5
Provincial capital of Manitoba.

Winnipeg *r.* Canada **167** L5
Winnipeg, Lake Canada **167** L5
Winnipegosis Canada **167** L5
Winnipegosis, Lake Canada **167** K4
Winnipesaukee, Lake U.S.A. **177** N2
Winnsboro *SC* U.S.A. **174** D5
Winnsboro *TX* U.S.A. **179** D5
Winona *AZ* U.S.A. **183** M6
Winona *MI* U.S.A. **172** E4
Winona *MN* U.S.A. **174** B2
Winona *MO* U.S.A. **174** B4
Winona *MS* U.S.A. **175** B5
Winooski U.S.A. **177** L1
Winooski *r.* U.S.A. **177** L1
Winschoten Neth. **48** E2
Winsen (Aller) Germany **48** G3
Winsen (Luhe) Germany **48** H2
Winslow *AZ* U.S.A. **183** N6
Winslow *ME* U.S.A. **177** P1
Winsted U.S.A. **177** L4
Winston-Salem U.S.A. **176** E9
Winter U.S.A. **172** B5
Winterberg Germany **48** F4
Winterberg *mts* S. Africa **133** K9
Winter Harbor U.S.A. **177** Q1
Winter Haven U.S.A. **175** D6
Winter Park U.S.A. **175** D6
Winterport U.S.A. **177** Q1
Winters *CA* U.S.A. **182** C3
Winters *TX* U.S.A. **179** C6
Winterset U.S.A. **178** D3
Winterswijk Neth. **48** D4
Winterthur Switz. **51** O5
Winterton S. Africa **133** N5
Winterveld S. Africa **133** M2
Winthrop U.S.A. **177** P1
Winton Australia **149** D4
Winton N.Z. **153** C14
Winton U.S.A. **177** I9
Wirliyajarrayi Aboriginal Land Trust *res.* Australia **148** B4
formerly known as Willowra Aboriginal Land Trust
Wirrabara Australia **146** C3
Wirraminna Australia **146** C2
Wirrida, Lake *salt flat* Australia **146** B2
Wirrulla Australia **146** B3
Wisbech U.K. **47** M11
Wiscasset U.S.A. **177** P1
Wisconsin *r.* U.S.A. **172** B7
Wisconsin *state* U.S.A. **174** B2
Wisconsin, Lake U.S.A. **172** D7
Wisconsin Dells U.S.A. **172** D7
Wisconsin Rapids U.S.A. **172** D6
Wise U.S.A. **176** C9
Wisil Dabarow Somalia **128** F3
Wisła *r.* Poland *see* **Vistula**
Wisłok *r.* Poland **49** T5
Wisłoka *r.* Poland **49** S5
Wismar Germany **48** I2
Wisner U.S.A. **175** B6
Wissota Lake U.S.A. **172** B6
Wistaria Canada **166** E4
Witbank S. Africa **133** N2
Witbooisvlei Namibia **130** C5
Witdraai S. Africa **132** E3
Witham *r.* U.K. **47** M11
Witherbee U.S.A. **177** L1
Withernsea U.K. **47** M10
Withlacoochee *r. FL* U.S.A. **175** D6
Withlacoochee *r. FL* U.S.A. **175** D6
Witjira National Park Australia **146** B1
Witkoppies *mt.* S. Africa **133** N4
Witkowo Poland **49** O3
Witkransnek *pass* S. Africa **133** J8
Witmos S. Africa **133** J9
Witnek S. Africa **133** M2
Witney U.K. **47** K12
Witnica Poland **49** L3
Witput S. Africa **133** I6
Witrivier S. Africa **133** P2
Witteberg *mt. E. Cape* S. Africa **132** G10
Witteberg *mt. Free State* S. Africa **133** M5
Witteberg *mts* S. Africa **133** L7
Witteberge *mts* S. Africa **132** E10
Wittenberg Germany *see* Lutherstadt Wittenberg
Wittenberg U.S.A. **172** D6
Wittenberge Germany **48** I3
Wittenburg Germany **48** I2
Wittenheim France **51** N5
Wittenoom Australia **150** B4
also known as Wittenoom Gorge
Wittenoom Gorge Australia *see* **Wittenoom**
Witti, Banjaran *mts Sabah* Malaysia **77** G1
Wittingen Germany **48** H3
Wittlich Germany **48** D5
Wittmund Germany **48** E2
Wittow *pen.* Germany **49** K1
Wittstock Germany **49** J2
Witu Kenya **128** D5
Witu Islands P.N.G. **145** D2
Witvlei Namibia **130** C4
Witwatersberg *mts* S. Africa **133** L3
Witwatersrand *mts* S. Africa **133** K3
Witzenhausen Germany **48** G4
Wivenhoe, Lake Australia **147** G1
Wkra *r.* Poland **49** R3
Władysławowo Poland **49** P1
Włocławek Poland **49** Q3
historically known as Vlotslavsk
Włoszczowa Poland **49** Q5
Wobkent Uzbek. *see* **Vabkent**
Wodonga Australia **147** E4
Wodzisław Śląski Poland **49** P5
historically known as Loslau
Wohko *watercourse* Sudan **126** F3
Wohlthat Mountains Antarctica **223** A2
Wōjjā *atoll* Marshall Is *see* **Wotje**
Wokam *i.* Indon. **73** H8
Woken *r.* China **82** C3
Wokha India **97** G4
Woking U.K. **47** L12
Wokingham *watercourse* Australia **149** D4
Woko National Park Australia **147** F2
Wolcott *IN* U.S.A. **172** F10
Wolcott *NY* U.S.A. **177** I2
Wolcott *VT* U.S.A. **177** M1
Wolcottville U.S.A. **172** H9
Wołczyn Poland **49** P4
Woldegk Germany **49** K2
Woleai *atoll* Micronesia *see* **Woleai**
Woleai *atoll* Micronesia **73** J5
also known as Uleei; *also spelt* Wolea
Woleu-Ntem *prov.* Gabon **126** A4
Wolf *r.* Canada **166** C2
Wolf *r.* U.S.A. **172** E6
Wolf Creek *MT* U.S.A. **180** D3
Wolf Creek *OR* U.S.A. **180** B4
Wolf Creek *r.* U.S.A. **179** C4
Wolf Creek Pass U.S.A. **181** F5
Wolfeboro U.S.A. **177** N2
Wolfen Germany **49** J4
Wolfenbüttel Germany **48** H3
Wolfhagen Germany **48** G4
Wolf Lake Canada **166** D2
Wolf Point U.S.A. **180** F2
Wolfsberg Austria **49** L9
Wolfsburg Germany **48** H3
Wolfstein Germany **48** E6
Wolfville Canada **169** H4
Wolgast Germany **49** K1
Wolhusen Switz. **51** O5
Wolin Poland **49** L2
Wolin *i.* Poland **49** L2
Woliński Park Narodowy *nat. park* Poland **49** L2
Wolkersdorf Austria **49** N7
Wollaston, Islas *is* Chile **205** D9
Wollaston Lake Canada **167** K3
Wollaston Lake *l.* Canada **167** K3
Wollaston Peninsula Canada **165** H3
Wollemi National Park Australia **147** F3
Wollerau Switz. **51** O5
Wollongong Australia **147** F3
Wolmaransstad S. Africa **133** J4
Wolmirstedt Germany **48** I3
Wołomin Poland **49** S3
Wolong Reserve *nature res.* China **86** B2
Wołów Poland **49** N4
Wolowaru Indon. **75** B5
Wolseley Australia **146** D4
Wolseley S. Africa **132** D10
Wolsztyn Poland **49** N3
Wolvega Neth. **48** D3
Wolverhampton U.K. **47** J11
Wolverine U.S.A. **173** I5
Wolwefontein S. Africa **133** I10
Wolwespruit S. Africa **133** J5
Wolya *r.* Indon. **76** A1
Wonarah Australia **148** C3
Wondai Australia **149** F5
Wonderfontein S. Africa **133** N2
Wonderkop *mt.* S. Africa **133** L5
Wondermere S. Africa **133** K2
Wongalarroo Lake *salt l.* Australia **147** E2
Wonga Wongué, Réserve de *nature res.* Gabon **126** A5
Wong Chhu *r.* Bhutan **97** F4
Wong Chuk Hang *Hong Kong* China **87** [inset]
Wong Leng *hill Hong Kong* China **87** [inset]
Wong Wan Chau *i. Hong Kong* China *see* **Double Island**
Wŏnju S. Korea **83** B5
Wonogiri Indon. **77** E4
Wonosari Indon. **77** E4
Wonosobo Indon. **77** E4
Wonowon Canada **166** F3
Wonreli Indon. **75** C5
Wŏnsan N. Korea **83** B5
Wonthaggi Australia **147** E4
Wonyulgunna, Mount *hill* Australia **151** B5
Woocalla Australia **146** C2
Wood, Mount Canada **166** A2
Woodbine U.S.A. **177** K6
Woodboro U.S.A. **172** D5
Woodbourne U.S.A. **177** K4
Woodbridge *NJ* U.S.A. **177** K5
Woodbridge *VA* U.S.A. **177** H7
Wood Buffalo National Park Canada **167** H3
Woodburn *IN* U.S.A. **176** A4
Woodburn *OR* U.S.A. **180** B3
Woodbury *CT* U.S.A. **177** L4
Woodbury *MI* U.S.A. **173** H8
Woodbury *NJ* U.S.A. **177** J6
Woodend Australia **147** E4
Woodfords U.S.A. **182** E3
Woodhall Spa U.K. **47** L10
Woodhull U.S.A. **172** C9
Wood Lake Canada **167** K4
Woodlake U.S.A. **182** E5
Woodland *CA* U.S.A. **182** C3
Woodland *NC* U.S.A. **177** H9
Woodland *WA* U.S.A. **180** B3
Woodland Park U.S.A. **180** F5
Woodlands Sing. **76** [inset]
Woodlark Island P.N.G. **145** E2
also known as Murua
Woodmurra Creek *watercourse* Australia **146** C1
Woodridge Canada **167** L5
Woodroffe *watercourse* Australia **148** C4
Woodroffe, Mount Australia **146** A1
Woodruff U.S.A. **172** D5
Woods, Lake *salt flat* Australia **148** B3
Woods, Lake of the Canada/U.S.A. **165** J5
Woodsfield U.S.A. **176** D6
Woods Hole U.S.A. **177** O4
Woodside Australia **149** E3
Woodstock *N.B.* Canada **169** H4
Woodstock *Ont.* Canada **168** D5
Woodstock *IL* U.S.A. **174** B3
Woodstock *VA* U.S.A. **176** G7
Woodstock *VT* U.S.A. **177** M2
Woodstock Dam *resr* S. Africa **133** N5
Woodstown U.S.A. **177** J6
Woodsville U.S.A. **177** M1
Woodville N.Z. **152** J8
Woodville *MS* U.S.A. **175** B6
Woodville *OH* U.S.A. **176** B4
Woodville *TX* U.S.A. **179** D6
Woodward U.S.A. **179** C4
Woody U.S.A. **182** F6
Wŏōl Indon. **73** I7
Wooler U.K. **46** J8
Woolgar *r.* Australia **149** D4
Woolgoolga Australia **147** G2
Woolla Downs Australia **148** B4
Woollard, Mount Antarctica **222** R1
Wooltana Australia **146** C2
Woolwine U.S.A. **176** E9
Woomera Australia **146** C2
Woomera Prohibited Area Australia **146** B2
Woonsocket U.S.A. **178** C2
Woorabinda Australia **149** F5
Wooramel *r.* Australia **151** A5
Wooster U.S.A. **176** D5
Woqooyi Galbeed *admin. reg.* Somalia **128** D2
Worak-san National Park S. Korea **83** C5
Worb Switz. **51** N6
Worbody Point Australia **149** D2
Worcester S. Africa **132** D10
Worcester U.K. **47** J11
Worcester *MA* U.S.A. **177** N3
Worcester *NY* U.S.A. **177** K3
Wörgl Austria **48** J8
Workai *i.* Indon. **73** H8
Workington U.K. **47** I9
Worland U.S.A. **180** F3
Worms Germany **48** F6
Worms Head U.K. **47** H12
Worofla Côte d'Ivoire **124** D4
Wörth am Rhein Germany **48** F6
Worthing U.K. **47** L13
Worthington *MN* U.S.A. **178** D3
Worthington *OH* U.S.A. **176** B5
Wosi Indon. **75** C3
Wotjalum Aboriginal Reserve Australia **150** C3
Wotje *atoll* Marshall Is **220** F6
also spelt Wōjjā; *formerly known as* Otdia
Wotu Indon. **75** B3
Wour Chad **120** B4
Wouri *r.* Cameroon **125** H5
Wowoni *i.* Indon. **75** B4
Wowoni, Selat *sea chan.* Indon. **75** B3
Wozrojdeniye Oroli *i.* Uzbek. *see* **Vozrozhdeniya, Ostrov**
Wrangel Island Rus. Fed. **39** S2
also known as Vrangelya, Ostrov
Wrangell U.S.A. **166** C3
Wrangell Island U.S.A. **166** C3
Wrangell Mountains U.S.A. **164** D4
Wrangell-St Elias National Park and Preserve *AK* U.S.A. **164** E3
Wrath, Cape U.K. **46** G5
Wray U.S.A. **178** B3
Wreck Reef Australia **149** G4
Wrecsam U.K. *see* **Wrexham**
Wrens U.S.A. **175** D5
Wrexham U.K. **47** J10
also spelt Wrecsam
Wriezen Germany **49** L3
Wright Phil. **74** C4
Wrightmyo India **95** G4
Wright Patman Lake U.S.A. **179** D5
Wrightson, Mount U.S.A. **181** E7
Wrightstown U.S.A. **172** E6
Wrightsville U.S.A. **175** D5
Wrightwood U.S.A. **182** G7
Wrigley Canada **166** F2
Wrigley U.S.A. **176** B7
Wrigley Gulf Antarctica **222** P2
Wrocław Poland **49** O4
historically known as Breslau
Wronki Poland **49** N3
Września Poland **49** O3
Wrześnica *r.* Poland **49** O3
Wschowa Poland **49** N4
Wu'an China *see* **Changtai**
Wu'an China **85** G4
Wubalawun *res.* Australia *see* **Larrimah Aboriginal Land**
Wubin Australia **151** B6
Wubu China **85** F4
also known as Songjiachuan
Wuchagou China **85** I2
Wuchang *Heilong.* China **82** B3
Wuchang *Hubei* China **87** E2
formerly known as Jiangxia
Wucheng China **87** F2
Wuchow China *see* **Wuzhou**
Wuchuan *Guangdong* China **87** D4
also known as Meilü
Wuchuan *Guizhou* China **87** C2
also known as Duru
Wuchuan *Nei Mongol* China **85** F3
also known as Hoh Ereg
Wuda China **85** E4
Wudan China **85** H3
also known as Ongniud Qi
Wudang Shan *mts* China **87** D1
Wudao China **85** I4
Wuday'ah *well* Saudi Arabia **105** D4
Wudi China **85** H4
Wudil Nigeria **125** H4
Wuding China **86** B3
also known as Jincheng
Wuding *r.* China **85** F4
Wudinna Australia **146** B3
Wudu China **86** C1
Wufeng China **87** D2
Wufeng China *see* **Zhenxiong**
Wugang China **87** D3
Wugong China **87** D1
also known as Puji
Wuhai China **85** E4
Wuhan China **87** E2
Wuhe China **87** F1
Wuhu *Anhui* China **87** F2
also known as Wanzhi
Wuhu *Anhui* China **87** F2
Wuhua China **87** E4
also known as Shuizhai
Wüjang China **89** B5
Wujiang China **87** G2
Wu Jiang *r.* China **87** C2
Wujin China *see* **Changzhou**
Wujin China *see* **Xinjin**
Wukari Nigeria **125** H5
Wuleidao Wan *l.* China **85** I4
Wulian Feng *mts* China **86** B2
Wuliang Shan *mts* China **86** B3
Wuliaru *i.* Indon. **73** H8
Wuling Shan *mts* China **87** D2
Wulong China **87** C2
also known as Xiangkou
Wulong *r.* China **85** I4
Wulongji China *see* **Huaibin**
Wulur Indon. **75** D4
Wum Cameroon **125** H5
Wumeng Shan *mts* China **86** B3
Wuming China **87** D4
Wümme *r.* Germany **48** F2
Wungda China **86** B2
Wuning China **87** E2
also known as Xinning
Wunnummin Lake Canada **168** B2
Wun Rog Sudan **126** F2
Wun Shwai Sudan **126** F2
Wunsiedel Germany **48** J5
Wunstorf Germany **48** G3
Wuntau Sudan **128** B2
Wuntho Myanmar **78** A3
Wupatki National Monument *nat. park* U.S.A. **183** M6
Wuping China **87** F3
Wuppertal Germany **48** E4
formerly known as Barmen-Elberfeld
Wuppertal S. Africa **132** D9
Wuqi China **85** F4
Wuqia *Xinjiang* China **88** A4
also known as Ulugqat
Wuqia *Xinjiang* China **88** A4
Wuqiang China **85** G4
also known as Xiaofan
Wuqiao China **85** H4
also known as Sangyuan
Wuqing China **85** H4
also known as Yangcun
Wuquan China *see* **Wuyang**
Wuqub, Wādī *watercourse* Saudi Arabia **108** F9
Wuranga Australia **151** B6
Würm *r.* Germany **48** I7
Wurno Nigeria **125** G3
Wurralibi Aboriginal Land *res.* Australia **148** C2
Wurzbach Germany **48** I5
Würzburg Germany **48** G6
Wurzen Germany **49** J4
Wushan *Chongqing* China **87** D2
also known as Wuxia
Wushan *Gansu* China **86** C1
Wu Shan *mts* China **87** D2
Wusheng *Sichuan* China **86** C2
also known as Yankou
Wusheng *Zhejiang* China **87** F2
Wushi China **88** B3
also known as Uqturpan
Wüstegarten *hill* Germany **48** G4
Wusuli Jiang *r.* Rus. Fed. *see* **Ussuri**
Wutai China **85** G4
Wutai Shan *mts* China **85** G4
Wutong *r.* China **82** C3
Wutonggou China **88** E3
Wutongwozi Quan *well* China **84** B3
Wuvulu Island P.N.G. **73** J7
also known as Maty Island
Wuwei *Anhui* China **87** F2
Wuwei *Gansu* China **84** D4
formerly known as Liangzhou
Wuxi *Chongqing* China **87** D2
also known as Chengxiang
Wuxi China *see* **Luxi**
Wuxi *Jiangsu* China **87** G2
Wuxia China *see* **Wushan**
Wuxiang China **85** G4
also known as Duancun
Wuxing China *see* **Huzhou**
Wuxu China **87** D4
Wuxuan China **87** D4
Wuxue China **87** E2
Wuyang China *see* **Zhenyuan**
Wuyang China **87** E1
also known as Wuquan
Wuyi China **87** F2
also known as Hushan
Wuyiling China **82** C2
Wuyishan China **87** F3
formerly known as Chong'an
Wuyi Shan *mts* China **87** F3
Wuyi Shan *tourist site* China **87** F3
Wuyuan *Jiangxi* China **87** F2
also known as Ziyang
Wuyuan *Nei Mongol* China **85** F3
Wuyuan China *see* **Haiyan**
Wuyun China *see* **Jinyun**
Wuzhai China **85** F4
Wuzhen China **87** D2
Wuzhi China **85** G5
also known as Mucheng
Wuzhi Shan *mts* China **87** D5
Wuzhong China **85** E4
Wuzhou China **87** D4
formerly spelt Wuchow
Wyaaba Creek *r.* Australia **149** D3
Wyalkatchem Australia **151** B6
Wyalusing *PA* U.S.A. **177** I4
Wyalusing *WI* U.S.A. **172** B8
Wyandra Australia **147** E1
Wyanet U.S.A. **172** D9
Wyangala Reservoir Australia **147** F3
Wyara, Lake *salt flat* Australia **147** E2
Wye *r.* U.K. **47** J12
Wyemandoo *hill* Australia **151** B6
Wye Mills U.S.A. **177** I7
Wyeville U.S.A. **172** C6
Wyk auf Föhr Germany **48** F1
Wylliesburg U.S.A. **176** G9
Wyloo Australia **150** B4
Wymondham U.K. **47** N11
Wymore U.S.A. **178** C3
Wynbring Australia **146** B2
Wyndham Australia **150** E2
Wyndham N.Z. **153** C14
Wyndham-Werribee Australia **147** E4
Wynne U.S.A. **174** B5
Wynniatt Bay Canada **165** H2
Wynyard Australia **147** E5
Wynyard Canada **167** J5
Wyocena U.S.A. **172** D7
Wyola Lake *salt flat* Australia **146** A2
Wyoming *DE* U.S.A. **177** J6
Wyoming *IA* U.S.A. **172** B8
Wyoming *IL* U.S.A. **172** D9
Wyoming *MI* U.S.A. **172** H8
▶**Wyoming** *state* U.S.A. **180** F4
northamerica [environments] ▶▶ 162–163
Wyoming Peak U.S.A. **180** E4
Wyoming Range *mts* U.S.A. **180** E4
Wyong Australia **147** F3
Wyperfeld National Park Australia **146** D3
Wysoka Poland **49** O2
Wysokie Mazowieckie Poland **49** T3
Wysox U.S.A. **177** I4
Wyszków Poland **49** S3
Wytheville U.S.A. **176** D9
Wyżnica *r.* Poland **49** S4

↓ X

▶**Xaafun, Raas** *pt* Somalia **128** F2
Most easterly point of Africa.

Xaafuun Somalia **128** F2
Xaçmaz Azer. **107** G2
also spelt Khachmas
Xade Botswana **130** D4
Xagnay China **89** C5
Xago China **89** E6
Xagquka China **89** F6
Xaidulla China **89** B4
Xainza China **89** E6
also known as Kangsangdobdê
Xaitongmoin China **89** E6
also known as Qabka
Xai-Xai Moz. **131** G5
formerly known as João Belo *or* Vila de João Belo
Xal, Cerro de *hill* Mex. **185** H4
Xalapa Mex. *see* **Jalapa Enríquez**
Xalin Somalia **128** F2
Xaltianguis Mex. **185** F5
Xamavera Angola **127** D9
Xamba China **85** E3
also known as Hanggin Houqi
Xambioá Brazil **202** B3
Xam Hua Laos **78** D3
formerly known as Sam Neua
Xá-Muteba Angola **127** C7
formerly known as Cinco de Outubro
Xan *r.* Laos **78** C4
Xan, Xê *r.* Vietnam **79** D5
Xangda China *see* **Nangqên**
Xangdin Hural China **85** F3
Xangdoring China *see* **Xungba**
Xangongo Angola **127** B9
formerly known as Roçadas
Xankändi Azer. **107** F3
also known as Stepanakert; *also spelt* Khankendi
Xanlar Azer. **107** F2
Xanthi Greece **58** F7
Xanxerê Brazil **203** A8
Xapuri Brazil **200** C2
Xarardheere Somalia **128** E3
Xarba La *pass* China **89** D6
Xar Burd China *see* **Bayan Nuru**
Xar Moron *r.* China **85** F3
Xar Moron *r.* China **85** I3
Xarrama *r.* Port. **54** C6
Xarrë Albania **59** B9
Xarsingma China *see* **Yadong**
Xassengue Angola **127** C7
Xátiva Spain **55** K6
also spelt Játiva
Xau, Lake Botswana **131** E4
also known as Dow, Lake
Xaudum *watercourse* Botswana/Namibia **130** D3
Xavantes, Represa de *resr* Brazil **206** D10
Xavantes, Serra dos *hills* Brazil **202** B5
Xa Vo Dat Vietnam **79** D6
Xayar China **88** C3
Xcalak Mex. **185** I5
X-Can Mex. **185** I4
Xekar China **88** B4
Xenia U.S.A. **176** B6
Xeriuini *r.* Brazil **199** F5
Xero Potamos *r.* Cyprus *see* **Xeros**
Xeros *r.* Cyprus **108** D3
also known as Xero Potamos
Xhora S. Africa *see* **Elliotdale**
Xhorodomo Pan *salt pan* Botswana **131** E4
Xi *r.* China **85** I3
Xiabancheng China **85** H3
Xiabole Shan *mt.* China **82** B2
Xiachengzi China **82** C3
Xiachuan Dao *i.* China **87** E4
Xiacun China *see* **Rushan**
Xiadong China **84** B3
Xiaguan China *see* **Dali**
Xiahe China **84** D5
also known as Labrang
Xiajiang China **87** E3
also known as Baqiu
Xiajiang China *see* **Qusum**
Xiajin China **85** H4
Xiamen China **87** F3
formerly known as Amoy
Xi'an China **87** D1
formerly spelt Sian
Xianchang China **87** E1
also known as Suizhai
Xianfeng China **87** D2
also known as Gaoleshan
Xiangcheng *Henan* China **87** E1
Xiangcheng *Sichuan* China **86** A2
also known as Qagchêng *or* Sangpi
Xiangcheng China *see* **Xiangyun**
Xiangfan China **87** E1
also known as Xiangyang
Xiangfen China **85** F5
also known as Shicun
Xiangfeng China *see* **Laifeng**
Xianggang *Hong Kong* China *see* **Hong Kong**
Xianggang Tebie Xingzhengqu *special admin. reg.* China *see* **Hong Kong**
Xianghuang Qi China *see* **Xin Bulag**
Xiangjiang China *see* **Huichang**
Xiang Jiang *r.* China **87** E2
Xiangkhoang Laos **78** C4
also known as Xieng Khouang
Xiangkhoang Plateau Laos **78** C4
Xiangkou China *see* **Wulong**
Xiangning China **85** F5
Xiangquan He *r.* China **89** B6
Xiangride China **84** C5
Xiangshan China *see* **Menghai**
Xiangshan China **87** G2
also known as Dancheng
Xiangshan Gang *b.* China **87** G2
Xiangshui China **87** F1
Xiangshuiba China **87** D3
Xiangtan China **87** E3
Xiangxiang China **87** E3
Xiangyang China *see* **Xiangfan**
Xiangyang Hu *l.* China **89** E5
Xiangyin China **87** E2
Xiangyun China **86** B3
also known as Xiangcheng
Xianju China **87** G2
Xianning China **87** E2
Xiannümiao China *see* **Jiangdu**
Xianshui China *see* **Dawu**
Xianshui He *r.* China **86** B2
Xiantao China **87** E2
formerly known as Mianyang
Xianxia Ling *mts* China **87** F3
Xianxian China **85** H4
also known as Leshou
Xianyang China **87** D1
Xianyou China **87** F3
also known as Licheng
Xiaoba China *see* **Qingtongxia**
Xiaochang China **87** E2
also known as Huayuan
Xiaodong China **87** D4
Xiao'ergou China **85** I1
Xiaofan China *see* **Wuqiang**
Xiaogan China **87** E2
Xiaoguai China **88** D2
Xiao Hinggan Ling *mts* China **82** B2
English form Lesser Khingan Mountains
Xiaojin China **86** B2
also known as Meixing *or* Zainlha
Xiaomei China **87** F3
Xiaonan China **84** D5
also known as Dongxiangzu
Xiaonanchuan China **84** B5
Xiao Qaidam China **84** B4
Xiaoqing *r.* China **85** H4
Xiaosanjiang China **87** E3
Xiaoshan China **87** G2
Xiao Surmang China **86** A1
Xiaotao China **87** F3
Xiaowutai Shan *mt.* China **85** G4
Xiaoxi China *see* **Pinghe**
Xiaoxian China **87** F1
also known as Longcheng
Xiaoxiang Ling *mts* China **86** B2
Xiaoyi China *see* **Gongyi**
Xiaoyi China **85** F4
Xiapu China **87** G3
also known as Songcheng
Xiaqiong China *see* **Batang**
Xiatil Mex. **185** H5
Xiaxian China **85** F5
Xiayanjing China *see* **Yanjing**
Xiayingpan China *see* **Luzhi**
Xiayingpan China *see* **Lupanshui**
Xiazhen China *see* **Weishan**
Xibdê China **86** A2
Xibet China **84** A2
formerly known as Sibati
Xibing China **87** F3
Xibu China *see* **Dongshan**
Xichang China **86** B3
Xicheng China *see* **Yangyuan**
Xichou China **86** C4
also known as Xisa
Xichuan China **87** D1
formerly known as Shangji
Xide China **86** B2
also known as Guangming
Xidu China *see* **Hengyang**
Xié *r.* Brazil **199** E4
Xiejiaji China *see* **Qingyun**
Xiemahe' China **87** D2
Xieng Khouang Laos *see* **Xiangkhoang**
Xieyang Dao *i.* China **87** D4
Xifei He *r.* China **87** F1
Xifeng *Gansu* China **85** E5
formerly known as Xifengzhen
Xifeng *Guizhou* China **86** C3
also known as Yongjing
Xifeng *Liaoning* China **82** B4
also known as Yongjing
Xifengzhen China *see* **Xifeng**
Xigazê China **89** E6
formerly spelt Shigatse
Xihan Shui *r.* China **86** C1
Xihe China **86** C1
also known as Hanyuan
Xi He *r.* China **86** C2
Xi He *watercourse* China **84** D3
Xihu China **84** B3
Xihua China **87** E1
Xihuachi China *see* **Heshui**
Xiji China **85** E5
Xi Jiang *r.* China **87** E4
Xijian Quan *well* China **84** C3
Xijir Ulan Hu *salt l.* China **97** F2
Xil China **85** G3
Xilagani Greece *see* **Xylagani**
Xilaotou Shan *mt.* China **85** I2
Xiliao *r.* China **85** I3
Xiligou China *see* **Ulan**
Xilin China **86** C3
also known as Bada
Xilinhot China **85** H3
formerly known as Abagnar Qi
Xilinji China *see* **Mohe**
Xilókastron Greece *see* **Xylokastro**
Xilópolis Greece *see* **Xylopoli**
Ximiao China **84** D3
Xin China **85** F4
also known as Hanggin Qi
Xin'an China *see* **Lai'an**
Xin'an China *see* **Anxin**
Xin'an China **87** E1
Xin'anjiang Shuiku *resr* China **87** F2
Xinavane Moz. **133** Q2
Xin Barag Youqi China *see* **Altan Emel**
Xin Barag Zuoqi China *see* **Amgalang**
Xinbin China **82** B4
Xin Bulag China **85** G3
also known as Hobot Xar Qi *or* Xianghuang Qi
Xincai China **87** E1
also known as Gulü
Xinchang China *see* **Yifeng**
Xinchang China **87** G2
Xincheng China *see* **Gutian**
Xincheng China *see* **Xinxing**
Xincheng *Guangxi* China **87** D3
Xincheng *Ningxia* China **85** E4
Xincheng China *see* **Yuanqu**
Xincheng China *see* **Zhaojue**
Xinchengbu China **85** F4
Xincun China *see* **Dongchuan**
Xindi China **87** D4
Xindi China *see* **Honghu**
Xindu *Guangxi* China **87** D4
Xindu China *see* **Luhuo**
Xindu *Sichuan* China **86** C2
Xinduqiao China **86** B2
Xinfeng *Guangdong* China **87** E3
also known as Fengcheng
Xinfeng *Jiangxi* China **87** E3
also known as Jiading
Xinfengjiang Shuiku *resr* China **87** E4
Xing'an China **87** D3

Xingan China 87 E3
also known as Jinchuan
Xingba China see Lhünzê
Xingcheng China see Qianxi
Xingcheng China 85 I3
Xingdi China 88 D3
Xinge Angola 127 C7
Xingguo China see Qin'an
Xingguo China 87 E3
also known as Lianjiang
Xinghai China 84 C5
also known as Ziketan
Xinghua China 87 F1
Xinghua Wan b. China 87 F3
Xingkai China 82 D3
Xingkai Hu l. China/Rus.Fed. see Khanka, Lake
Xinglong Hebei China 85 H3
Xinglong Heilong. China 82 B2
Xinglongzhen China 82 B3
Xingning China 87 E3
Xingou China 87 E2
Xingping China 87 D1
Xingren China 86 C3
Xingrenbu China 84 E4
Xingsagoinba China 86 B1
Xingshan China see Majiang
Xingshan China 87 D2
also known as Gufu
Xingtai China 85 G4
Xingtang China 85 G4
Xingu r. Brazil 199 H5
Xingu, Parque Indígena do res. Brazil 202 A4
Xinguara Brazil 202 B3
Xingxian China 85 F4
Xingxingxia China 84 B3
Xingyang China 87 E1
Xingyi China 86 C3
also known as Huangcaoba
Xingzi China 87 F2
also known as Nankang
Xinhe Hebei China 85 G4
Xinhe Xinjiang China 88 C3
also known as Toksu
Xin Hot China 85 G3
also known as Abag Qi
Xinhua China see Huadu
Xinhua China 87 D3
Xinhua China see Qiaojia
Xinhua China see Funing
Xinhuacun China 84 D4
Xinhuang China 87 D3
Xinhui China 85 H3
also known as Aohan Qi
Xining China 84 D4
formerly spelt Sining
Xinji China 85 G4
formerly known as Shulu
Xinji China see Xinxian
Xinjian China 87 E2
also known as Changleng
Xinjiang China 85 F5
Xinjiang aut. reg. China see Xinjiang Uygur Zizhiqu
Xin Jiang r. China 87 F2
Xinjiangkou China see Songzi
Xinjiang Uygur Autonomous Region aut. reg. China see Xinjiang Uygur Zizhiqu
Xinjiang Uygur Zizhiqu aut. reg. China 84 B3
English form Sinkiang Uighur Autonomous Region or Xinjiang Uygur Autonomous Region; short form Sinkiang or Xinjiang; formerly known as Chinese Turkestan
Xinjie China 85 F4
Xinjie China see Yuanyang
Xinjin China see Pulandian
Xinjin China 86 B2
also known as Wujin
Xinjing China see Jingxi
Xinkai r. China 85 I3
Xinling China see Badong
Xinlong China 86 B2
also known as Nyagrong or Rulong
Xinmi China 87 E1
formerly known as Mixian
Xinmian China see Shimian
Xinmin China 85 I3
Xinning China see Ningxian
Xinning China see Fusui
Xinning China 87 D3
also known as Jinshi
Xinning China see Wuning
Xinning China see Kaijiang
Xinping China 86 B3
also known as Guishan
Xinqing China 82 C2
Xinquan China 87 F3
Xinshan China see Anyuan
Xinshao China 87 D3
also known as Niangxi
Xinshi China see Jingshan
Xinshiba China see Ganluo
Xintai China 85 H5
Xintanpu China 87 E2
Xintian China 87 E3
Xinxian China 87 E2
also known as Xinji
Xinxiang China 85 G5
Xinxing China 87 E4
also known as Xincheng
Xinyang China 87 E1
Xinyang Gang r. China 87 G1
Xinye China 87 E1
Xinyi r. China 87 F1
Xinyi Guangdong China 87 D4
Xinyi Jiangsu China 87 F1
Xinying China 87 D5
Xinying Taiwan see Hsinying
Xinyu China 87 E3
Xinyuan China see Tianjun
Xinyuan China 88 C3
also known as Künes
Xinzhangfang China 85 I1
Xinzheng China 87 E1
Xinzhou China see Longlin
Xinzhou China see Huangping
Xinzhou Hubei China 87 E2
Xinzhou Shanxi China 85 G4
Xinzhu Taiwan see Hsinchu
Xinzo de Limia Spain 54 D2
also spelt Ginzo de Limia
Xiongshan China see Zhenghe
Xiongzhou China see Nanxiong
Xipamanu r. Bol./Brazil 200 D2
Xiping Henan China 87 D1
also known as Baicheng
Xiping Henan China 87 E1
Xiqing Shan mts China 86 B1
Xique Xique Brazil 202 D4
Xiro hill Greece 59 E10
Xirokampo Greece 59 H11
Xiruá r. Brazil 198 E6
Xisa China see Xichou
Xishanzui China 85 F3
also known as Urad Qianqi
Xisha Qundao is S. China Sea see Paracel Islands
Xishuangbanna reg. China 86 B4
Xishui Guizhou China 86 C2
Xishui Hubei China 87 E2
also known as Qingquan
Xistral, Serra do mts Spain 54 D1
also spelt Sierra del Gistral
Xi Taijnar Hu l. China 84 B4
Xitole Guinea-Bissau 124 B4
Xiucaiwan China see Fengdu
Xiugu China see Jinxi
Xi Ujimqin Qi China see Bayan Ul Hot
Xiuning China 87 F2
also known as Haiyang
Xiushan China 87 D2
also known as Zhonghe
Xiushan China see Tonghai
Xiushui China 87 E2
also known as Yining
Xiu Shui r. China 87 E2
Xiuwen China 86 C3
Xiuwu China 85 G5
Xiuyan China 85 I3
Xiuyan China see Qingjian
Xiuying China 87 D4
Xiwanzi China see Chongli
Xiwu China 86 A1
Xixabangma Feng mt. China 89 D6
also known as Shisha Pangma; formerly known as Gosainthan
Xixia China 87 D1
Xixian Henan China 87 E1
Xixian Shanxi China 85 F4
Xixiang China 87 C1
Xixón Spain see Gijón
Xiyang China 85 G4
Xiyang Dao i. China 87 G3
Xiyang Jiang r. China 86 C3
Xizang aut. reg. China see Xizang Zizhiqu
Xizang Gaoyuan plat. China see Tibet, Plateau of
Xizang Zizhiqu aut. reg. China 86 A2
English form Tibet or Tibet Autonomous Region; short form Xizang
Xizhong Dao i. China 85 I4
Xocavänd Azer. 107 F3
also spelt Khodzhavend
Xodoto, Akra pt Greece 59 H12
Xoi China see Qüxü
Xolobe S. Africa 133 L9
Xom An Lôc Vietnam 79 D6
Xom Duc Hanh Vietnam 79 D6
Xonxa Dam S. Africa 133 L8
Xorkol China 88 E4
Xuancheng China see Xuanzhou
Xuan'en China 87 D2
also known as Zhushan
Xuanhan China 87 C2
also known as Dongxiang
Xuanhua China 85 G3
Xuân Lôc Vietnam 79 D6
Xuanwei China 86 C3
Xuanzhou China 87 F2
formerly known as Xuancheng
Xuchang Henan China 87 E1
Xucheng China see Xuwen
Xudat Azer. 107 G2
also spelt Khudat
Xuddur Somalia 128 D3
Xudun Somalia 128 E2
Xueba China see Sangri
Xuefeng China see Mingxi
Xuefeng Shan mts China 87 D3
Xuehua Shan hill China 87 D1
Xue Shan mts China 86 A3
Xugou China 87 F1
Xugui China 84 B5
Xuguit Qi China see Yakeshi
Xujiang China see Guangchang
Xulun Hobot Qagan Qi China see Qagan Nur
Xulun Hoh Qi China see Dund Hot
Xümatang China 86 A1
Xun r. China 82 C2
Xundian China 86 B3
also known as Rende
Xungba China 89 C5
also known as Xangdoring
Xungmai China 89 E6
Xung Qu r. China 89 F6
Xungru China 89 D6
Xunhe China 82 B2
Xun He r. China 87 D1
Xunhua China 84 D5
also known as Jishi
Xun Jiang r. China 87 D4
Xunke China 82 C2
Xunwu China 87 E3
also known as Changning
Xunxian China 85 G5
Xunyang China 87 D1
Xunyi China 85 F5
Xupu China 87 D3
also known as Lufeng
Xuru Co salt l. China 89 D6
Xushui China 85 G4
also known as Ansu
Xuwen China 87 D4
also known as Xucheng
Xuyang China see Rongxian
Xuyi China 87 F1
Xuyong China 86 C2
also known as Yongning
Xuzhou China see Tongshan
Xylagani Greece 58 G8
also spelt Xilagani
Xylokastro Greece 59 D10
also known as Xilókastron
Xylopoli Greece 58 E8
also known as Xilópolis

↓ Y

Ya'an China 86 B2
Yaapeet Australia 147 D3
Yabanabat Turkey see Kızılcahamam
Yabassi Cameroon 125 H5
Yabēlo Eth. 128 C3
Yabēlo Wildlife Sanctuary nature res. Eth. 128 C3
Yablanitsa Bulg. 58 F5
Yablanovo Bulg. 58 H6
Yablonovyy Khrebet mts Rus. Fed. 85 F1
Yabo Nigeria 125 G3
Yabrai Shan mts China 84 D4
Yabrai Yanchang China 84 D4
Yabrīn reg. Saudi Arabia 105 E3
Yabrūd Syria 109 H4
Yabuli China 82 C3
Yabuyanos Peru 198 C5
Yacha China see Baisha
Yacheng China 87 D5
Yachi He r. China 86 C3
Yacireta, Isla i. Para. 201 F6
Yacireta Apipé, Embalse resr Para. 201 F6
Yacuiba Bol. 201 E5
Yacurai Venez. 199 E3
Yadé, Massif du mts Cent. Afr. Rep. 126 B3
Yadgir India 94 C2
Yadiki India 94 C3
Yadkin r. U.S.A. 174 D5
Yadkinville U.S.A. 176 E9
Yadong China 89 E7
also known as Xarsingma; formerly known as Chomo
Yadrin Rus. Fed. 40 H5
Yaeyama-rettō is Japan 81 K8
Yafa Israel see Tel Aviv-Yafo
Yafran Libya 120 B1
Yagaba Ghana 125 E4
Yagaing state Myanmar see Arakan
Yağcılı Turkey 59 I9
Yağda Turkey see Erdemli
Yagman Turkm. 102 C5
Yagmo China 89 D6
Yagnitsa Rus. Fed. 43 S3
Yago Mex. 184 D4
Yagoda Bulg. 58 G6
Yagodnaya Polyana Rus. Fed. 41 H6
Yagodnoye Kaluzhskaya Oblast' Rus. Fed. 43 Q8
Yagodnoye Magadanskaya Oblast' Rus. Fed. 39 O3
Yagodnyy Rus. Fed. 82 E2
Yagoua Cameroon 125 I4
Yagra China 89 C6
Yagradagzê Shan mt. China 84 B5
Yaguajay Cuba 186 D2
Yaguarón r. Brazil/Uruguay see Jaguarão
Yaguas r. Peru 198 D5
Yaha Thai. 79 C7
Yahk Canada 167 G5
Yahualica Mex. 185 E4
Yahyalı Turkey 98 B2
also known as Gazibenli
Yahya Wana Afgh. 96 A3
Yai, Khao hill Thai. 79 B5
Yaita Japan 90 F6
Yaizu Japan 91 F7
Yajiang China 86 B2
also known as Hekou or Nyagquka
Yakacık Turkey 108 H1
Yakapınar Turkey 108 G1
Yakeshi China 85 I1
formerly known as Xuguit Qi
Yakhab waterhole Iran 100 D3
Yakhehal Afgh. 101 F4
Yakhroma Rus. Fed. 43 S5
Yakima U.S.A. 180 B3
Yakima r. U.S.A. 180 C3
Yakima Indian Reservation res. U.S.A. 180 B3
Yakinish Iran 100 C3
Yakkabag Uzbek. 103 F5
formerly known as Stantsiya-Yakkabag
Yakmach Pak. 101 E4
Yako Burkina 125 E3
Yakobi Island U.S.A. 166 B3
Yakoma Dem. Rep. Congo 126 D3
Yakoruda Bulg. 58 E6
Yakovlevka Rus. Fed. 82 D3
Yakumo Japan 90 G3
Yaku-shima i. Japan 91 B9
Yakutat U.S.A. 166 B3
Yakutat Bay U.S.A. 164 E4
Yakutsk Rus. Fed. 39 M3
Yakymivka Ukr. 41 E7
Yala Ghana 125 E4
Yala Thai. 79 C7
Yalai China 89 D6
Yalakdere Turkey 58 K8
Yala National Park Sri Lanka see Ruhuna National Park
Yalan Dünya Mağarası tourist site Turkey 108 D1
Yalata Aboriginal Lands res. Australia 146 A2
Yale Canada 166 F5
Yale U.S.A. 173 K7
Yalgoo Australia 151 B6
Yalıkavak Turkey 59 I11
Yalıköy Turkey 58 J7
Yalinga Cent. Afr. Rep. 126 D3
Yalizava Belarus 43 K8
Yalkubul, Punta pt Mex. 185 H4
Yalleroi Australia 149 E5
Yallo Burkina 124 E3
Yallourn Australia 147 E4
Yaloké Cent. Afr. Rep. 126 C3
Yalong Jiang r. China 86 B3
Yalova Turkey 106 B2
Yalova prov. Turkey 58 K8
Yaloven' Moldova see Ialoveni
Yalpirakinu Aboriginal Land res. Australia 148 B4
Yalpuh, Ozero l. Ukr. 58 J3
Yalpukh r. Moldova see Ialpug
Yalta Ukr. 41 E7
Yaltins'kyy Zapovidnyk nature res. Ukr. 106 C1
Yalu Jiang r. China 85 I2
Yalu Jiang r. China/N. Korea 83 B4
also known as Amnok-kang
Yalutorovsk Rus. Fed. 38 G4
Yalvaç Turkey 106 B3
Yām reg. Saudi Arabia 105 D4
Yamada Japan 90 G5
Yamaga Japan 91 B8
Yamagata Iwate Japan 90 G4
Yamagata Yamagata Japan 90 G5
Yamagata pref. Japan 90 F5
Yamaguchi Japan 91 B7
Yamaguchi pref. Japan 91 B7
Yamal, Poluostrov pen. Rus. Fed. see Yamal Peninsula
Yam Alin', Khrebet mts Rus. Fed. 82 D1
Yamal Peninsula Rus. Fed. 38 G2
also known as Yamal, Poluostrov
Yamanashi pref. Japan 90 F7
Yamanie Falls National Park Australia 149 E3
Yamankhalinka Kazakh. see Makhambet
Yamarovka Rus. Fed. 85 F1
Yamasaki Japan 91 D7
Yamatsuri Japan 90 G6
Yamba Australia 147 G2
Yambacoona Australia 147 D4
Yambarran Range hills Australia 148 A2
Yambéring Guinea 124 B4
Yambi, Mesa de hills Col. 198 D4
Yambio Sudan 126 F3
Yambol Bulg. 58 H6
Yambrasbamba Peru 198 B6
Yamdena i. Indon. 73 H8
Yame Japan 91 B8
Yamethin Myanmar 78 B3
Y'ami i. Phil. 74 B1

▶Yamin, Puncak mt. Indon. 73 I7
4th highest mountain in Oceania.
oceania [landscapes] ▶▶ 136–137

Yamizo-san mt. Japan 90 G6
Yamkanmardi India 94 B2
Yamkhad Syria see Aleppo
Yamkino Rus. Fed. 43 K4
Yamm Rus. Fed. 43 J3
Yamma Yamma, Lake salt flat Australia 149 D5
also known as Mackillop, Lake

▶Yamoussoukro Côte d'Ivoire 124 D5
Capital of Côte d'Ivoire.

Yampil' Ukr. 41 D6
also spelt Yampol'
Yampol' Ukr. see Yampil'
Yamuna r. India 96 D4
English form Jumna
Yamunanagar India 96 C3
Yamzho Yumco l. China 89 E6
Yan r. China 85 F4
Yana r. Rus. Fed. 39 N2
Yanac Australia 146 D4
Yanachaga-Chemillen, Parque Nacional nat. park Peru 200 B2
Yanadani Japan 91 C8
Yanai Japan 91 C8
Yanam India 95 D2
formerly known as Yanaon
Yan'an China 85 F4
Yanaoca Peru 200 C3
Yanaon India see Yanam
Yanaul Rus. Fed. 40 J5
Yanavichy Belarus 43 L6
Yanayacu Peru 198 C5
Yanbian China 86 B3
also known as Dapingdi
Yanbu' al Baḩr Saudi Arabia 104 B2
Yanbu' an Nakhl reg. Saudi Arabia 104 B2
Yanceyville U.S.A. 176 F9
Yanchang China 85 F4
Yancheng China 87 G1
Yancheng China see Qihe
Yancheng China see Jingyan
Yanchep Australia 151 A6
Yanchi Ningxia China 85 E4
Yanchi Xinjiang China 84 B3
Yanchuan China 85 F4
Yanco Creek r. Australia 147 E3
Yanco Glen Australia 146 D2
Yanda watercourse Australia 147 E2
Yandama Creek watercourse Australia 146 D2
Yandang Shan mts China 87 G3
Yandao China see Yingjing
Yandaxkak China 88 E4
Yandeyarra Aboriginal Reserve Australia 150 B4
Yandil Australia 151 B5
Yandina Solomon Is 145 E2
Yandja Dem. Rep. Congo 126 C5
Yandoon Myanmar 78 A4
Yandun China 84 B3
Yanega Rus. Fed. 43 O1
Yanfolila Mali 124 C4
Yang r. China 85 G3
Yangalia Cent. Afr. Rep. 126 D3
Yangambi Dem. Rep. Congo 126 E4
Ya'ngamdo Xizang China 89 F6
Ya'ngamdo Xizang China 89 F6
Yangasso Mali 124 D3
Yangbajain China 89 E6
Yangbi China 86 A3
also known as Shangjie
Yangcheng China see Yangshan
Yangcheng China 85 G5
Yangchuan China see Suiyang
Yangchun China 87 D4
Yangcun China 87 E4
Yangcun China see Wuqing
Yangdok N. Korea 83 B5
Yanggao China 85 G3
Yanggu China 85 G4
Yanghe China see Yongning
Yang Hu l. China 89 D5
Yangiaryk Uzbek. 102 E4
Yangi Davan pass Aksai Chin/China 89 B5
Yangi-Nishan Uzbek. 103 F5
Yangi Qal'eh Afgh. 101 G2
Yangirabad Uzbek. 103 F4
Yangiyul' Uzbek. 103 G4
Yangjialing China 85 F4
Yangjiang China 87 D4
Yangjiaogou China 85 H4
Yangôn Myanmar see Rangoon
Yangôn admin. div. Myanmar 78 B4
English form Rangoon; also spelt Rangôn
Yangping China 87 D2
Yangquan China 85 G4
Yangshan China 87 E3
also known as Yangcheng
Yangshuo China 87 D3
Yang Talat Thai. 78 C4
Yangtouyan China 86 B3

▶Yangtze r. China 87 G2
Longest river in Asia and 3rd in the world. Also known as Yangtze Kiang or Chang Jiang or Jinsha Jiang or Tongtian He or Zhi Qu.
asia [landscapes] ▶▶ 62–63

Yangtze Kiang r. China 87 F2
also known as Yangtze
Yangtze, Mouth of the China 87 G2
also known as Changjiang Kou
Yangudi Rassa National Park Eth. 128 D2
Yangweigang China 87 F1
Yangxian China 87 C1
Yangyang S. Korea 83 C5
Yangyuan China 85 G3
also known as Xicheng
Yangzhou China see Hanjiang
Yanhe China 87 D2
also known as Heping
Yanhu China 88 E3
Yaninee, Lake salt flat Australia 146 B3
Yanishpole Rus. Fed. 40 E3
Yanis"yarvi, Ozero l. Rus. Fed. 44 O3
Yanji China 82 C4
Yanjin Henan China 85 G5
Yanjin Yunnan China 86 C2
Yanjing China see Yanyuan
Yanjing China 86 A2
also known as Xiayanjing; formerly known as Caka'lho
Yanjing China see Yanjin
Yankara National Park Nigeria 125 H4
Yankavichy Belarus 43 J6
Yankou China see Wusheng
Yankton U.S.A. 178 C3
Yankton Indian Reservation res. U.S.A. 178 C3
Yanling Henan China 87 E1
also known as Anling
Yanling Hunan China 87 E3
formerly known as Lingxian
Yannina Greece see Ioannina
Yano-Indigirskaya Nizmennost' lowland Rus. Fed. 39 O2
Yanovo Rus. Fed. 43 N7
Yanov-Stan Rus. Fed. 39 I3
Yan Oya r. Sri Lanka 94 D4
Yanqi China 88 D3
Yanqing China 85 G3
Yanqul Oman 105 G3
Yanrey r. Australia 150 A4
Yanshan Hebei China 85 H4
Yanshan Jiangxi China 87 F2
also known as Hekou
Yanshan Yunnan China 86 C4
also known as Jiangna
Yan Shan mts China 85 H3
Yanshi China 87 E1
Yanshiping China 97 G2
Yanshou China 82 C3
Yanskiy Zaliv g. Rus. Fed. 39 N2
Yantabulla Australia 147 E2
Yantai China 85 I4
formerly known as Chefoo
Yántales, Cerro mt. Chile 205 B6
Yantarnyy Rus. Fed. 42 A7
historically known as Palmnicken
Yanting China 86 C2
also known as Yunxi
Yantongshan China 82 B4
Yantou China 87 G2
Yantra r. Bulg. 58 G5
Yanūfi, Jabal al hill Saudi Arabia 104 C3
Yany-Kurgan Kazakh. see Zhanakorgan
Yanyuan China 86 B3
also known as Yanjing
Yanzhou China 85 H5
Yao'an China 86 B3
also known as Dongchuan
Yaodu China see Dongzhi
Yaojie China see Honggu
Yaoli China 87 F2

▶Yaoundé Cameroon 125 H6
Capital of Cameroon.

Yaoxian China 87 D1
Yao Yai, Ko i. Thai. 79 B6
Yaozhen China 85 F4
Yap i. Micronesia 73 I5
formerly spelt Eap
Yapacana, Parque Nacional nat. park Venez. 199 E4
Yapacani r. Bol. 201 D3
Yapen i. Indon. 73 I7
Yapen, Selat sea chan. Indon. 73 I7
Yappar r. Australia 149 D3
Yapukarri Guyana 199 G4
Yapuparra Aboriginal Reserve Australia 151 D5
Yaqui r. Mex. 184 C3
Yar Rus. Fed. 40 J4
Yara Cuba 186 D2
Yaracal Venez. 198 D2
Yaracuy state Venez. 198 D2
Yaradzha Turkm. see Yaradzhi
Yaradzhi Turkm. 102 D5
formerly spelt Yaradzha
Yaraka Australia 149 E5
Yarangüme Turkey see Tavas
Yaransk Rus. Fed. 40 H4
Yardan Uzbek. see Iordan
Yardea Australia 146 B3
Yardımcı Burnu pt Turkey 106 B3
also known as Gelidonya Burnu
Yardımlı Azer. 107 G3
also spelt Yardymly
Yardley U.S.A. 177 K5
Yardoi China 89 E6
Yardymly Azer. see Yardımlı
Yare r. U.K. 47 N11
Yarega Rus. Fed. 40 J3

▶Yaren Nauru 145 F2
Capital of Nauru.
world [countries] ▶▶ 10–11

Yarenga r. Rus. Fed. 40 I3
Yarensk Rus. Fed. 40 I3
Yargara Moldova see Iargara
Yarí r. Col. 198 C5
also known as Engaños, Río de los
Yariga-take mt. Japan 91 E6
Yarim Yemen 104 D5
Yarımca Turkey see Körfez
Yaringa watercourse Australia 148 C4
Yaripo Brazil 199 H4
Yaris well Niger 125 G3
Yaritagua Venez. 187 F5
Yarkand China see Shache
Yarkant China see Shache
Yarkant He r. China 88 B4
Yarker Canada 173 Q6
Yarkhun r. Pak. 101 H2
Yarlovo Bulg. 58 E6
Yarlung Zangbo r. China 89 D6 see Brahmaputra
Yarmouth Canada 169 H5
Yarmouth U.K. see Great Yarmouth
Yarmouth U.S.A. 177 O2
Yarmūk r. Asia 108 G5
Yarnell U.S.A. 183 L7
Yaroslavichi Rus. Fed. 43 P1
Yaroslavl' Rus. Fed. 43 U4
Yaroslavl Oblast admin. div. Rus. Fed. see Yaroslavskaya Oblast'
Yaroslavskaya Oblast' admin. div. Rus. Fed. 43 U4
English form Yaroslavl Oblast
Yaroslavskiy Rus. Fed. 82 D3
Yarqon r. Israel 108 F5
Yarrabah Aboriginal Reserve Australia 149 E3
Yarra Junction Australia 147 E4
Yarralin Aboriginal Land res. Australia 148 A3
Yarram Australia 147 E4
Yarraman Australia 149 F5
Yarrawonga Australia 147 E4
Yarra Yarra Lakes salt flat Australia 151 A6
Yarrie Australia 150 C4
Yarronvale Australia 149 E5
Yarrowmere Australia 149 E4
Yartsevo Krasnoyarskiy Kray Rus. Fed. 39 I3
Yartsevo Smolenskaya Oblast' Rus. Fed. 43 N6
Yaru r. China 89 D6
Yarumal Col. 198 C3
Yarwa China 86 A2
Yary Rus. Fed. 40 M1
Yarzhong China 86 A2
Yaş Romania see Iaşi
Yasa Dem. Rep. Congo 126 D5
Yasai r. India 95 E1
Yasawa Group is Fiji 145 G3
Yasenkovo Bulg. 58 H5
Yashi Nigeria 125 G3
Yashikera Nigeria 125 F4
Yashilkŭl l. Tajik. 101 H2
Yashkino Rus. Fed. 41 J5
Yashkul' Rus. Fed. 41 H7
formerly known as Peschanoye
Yasin Jammu and Kashmir 96 B1
Yaskavichy Belarus 42 I9
Yasna Polyana Bulg. 58 I6
Yasnogorsk Rus. Fed. 43 S7
formerly known as Laptevo
Yasnyy Amurskaya Oblast' Rus. Fed. 82 C1
Yasnyy Orenburgskaya Oblast' Rus. Fed. 102 D2
Yasothon Thai. 78 D5
Yass Australia 147 F3
Yass r. Australia 147 F3
Yassı Burnu c. Cyprus see Plakoti, Cape
Yasski Rus. Fed. 43 L4
Yasugi Japan 91 C7
Yāsūj Iran 100 B4
Yasuni nat. park Ecuador 198 C5
Yasur vol. Vanuatu 145 F3
Yat well Niger 125 I1
Yata r. Bol. 200 D2
Yata r. Cent. Afr. Rep. 126 D2
Yatağan Turkey 106 B3
Yatakala Niger 125 F3
Yata Plateau Kenya 128 C5
Yaté New Caledonia 145 F4
Yates r. Canada 167 H2
Yates Center U.S.A. 178 D4
Yathkyed Lake Canada 167 L2
Yathong Nature Reserve Australia 147 E3
Yatolema Dem. Rep. Congo 126 E4
Yatou China see Rongcheng
Yatsuga-take vol. Japan 91 F7
Yatsushiro Japan 91 B8
Yatsushiro-kai b. Japan 91 B8
Yatta West Bank 108 G6
also spelt Yuta
Yauca Peru 200 B3
Yauca r. Peru 200 B3
Yauco Puerto Rico 187 G3
Yauli Peru 200 A2
Yauna Maloca Col. 198 D5
Yauri Peru 200 C3
Yauricocha Peru 200 B3
Yau Tong b. Hong Kong China 87 [inset]
Yauyos Peru 200 B3
Yavan Tajik. see Yovon
Yavari r. Peru 198 D6
also spelt Javari
Yávaros Mex. 184 C3
Yavatmal India 94 C1
formerly spelt Yeotmal
Yavero r. Peru 200 B3
also known as Paucartambo
Yavi, Cerro mt. Venez. 199 E3
Yavr r. Fin./Rus. Fed. 44 O1
Yavuzlu Turkey 109 I1
Yawatahama Japan 91 C8
Yawatongguz He r. China 89 C4
Yawatongguzlangar China 89 C4
Yaw Chaung r. Myanmar 78 A3
Yawng-hwe Shan Myanmar 78 B3
Yaxchilan tourist site Guat. 185 H5
Yaxian China see Sanya
Yayladağı Turkey 108 H2
also known as Ordu
Yayva Rus. Fed. 40 K4
Yazagyo Myanmar 78 A3
Yazd Iran 100 C4
Yazd prov. Iran 100 C4
Yazdān Iran 101 E3
Yazd-e Khvāst Iran 100 C4
also known as Samirum
Yazgulemskiy Khrebet mts Tajik. see Yazgulom, Qatorkŭhi
Yazgulom, Qatorkŭhi mts Tajik. 101 G2
also known as Yazgulemskiy Khrebet
Yazhelbitsy Rus. Fed. 43 N3
Yazıhan Turkey 107 D3
also known as Fethiye
Yazıkent Turkey 59 J11
Yazoo r. U.S.A. 175 B5
Yazoo City U.S.A. 175 B5
Yaz'va r. Rus. Fed. 40 K3
Ybakoura well Chad 120 B4
Y Bala U.K. see Bala
Ybbs r. Austria 49 M7
Ybbs an der Donau Austria 49 M7
Ybycui Para. 201 F6
Yding Skovhøj hill Denmark 45 J5
Ydra Greece 59 E11
Ydra i. Greece 59 E11
English form Hydra; also spelt Ídhra or Ídra
Ydras, Kolpos sea chan. Greece 59 E11
also spelt Ídhras, Kólpos
Y Drenewydd U.K. see Newtown
Ye Myanmar 79 B5
Ye r. Myanmar 79 B5
Yebaishou China see Jianping
Yebawmi Myanmar 78 A2
Yebbi-Bou Chad 120 C4
Yebekshi Kazakh. 103 G4
Yecheng China 88 B4
formerly known as Karghalik or Kargilik
Yecla Spain 55 J6
Yécora Mex. 184 C2
Yedashe Myanmar 78 B4
Yedatore India 94 C3
Yedi Burun Başı pt Turkey 59 K12
Yedoma Rus. Fed. 40 H3
Yedri well Chad 120 C4
Yedrovo Rus. Fed. 43 O4
Yedy Belarus 42 I6
Yeed Eth. 128 D3
Yeeda River Australia 150 C3
Yeelanna Australia 146 B3
Yefimovskiy Rus. Fed. 43 P2
Yefremov Rus. Fed. 43 T8
Yêgainnyin China see Henan
Yeggueba well Niger 125 I2
Yeghegnadzor Armenia 107 F3
formerly known as Mikoyan; formerly spelt Yekhegnadzor
Yegindybulak Kazakh. 103 I2
also spelt Egindibulaq
Yegorlyk r. Rus. Fed. 41 G7
Yegorlykskaya Rus. Fed. 41 G7
Yegorova, Mys pt Rus. Fed. 82 E3
Yegor'ye Rus. Fed. 43 O6
Yegor'yevsk Rus. Fed. 43 U6
Yégué Togo 125 F4
Yei Sudan 128 A3
Yei r. Sudan 128 A3
Yeina Island P.N.G. 149 G1
Yeji China 87 E2
formerly known as Yejiaji
Yeji Ghana 125 E4
Yejiaji China see Yeji
Yekaterinburg Rus. Fed. 38 G4
formerly known as Sverdlovsk
Yekaterinodar Rus. Fed. see Krasnodar
Yekaterinoslav Ukr. see Dnipropetrovs'k
Yekaterinoslavka Rus. Fed. 82 C2
Yekaterinovka Lipetskaya Oblast' Rus. Fed. 43 T9
Yekaterinovka Saratovskaya Oblast' Rus. Fed. 41 H5
Yekhegnadzor Armenia see Yeghegnadzor
Yekimovichi Rus. Fed. 43 O7
Yekokora r. Dem. Rep. Congo 126 D4
Yelabuga Rus. Fed. 82 D2
Yelabuga Rus. Fed. 40 I5
Yelan' Rus. Fed. 41 G6
Yelbarsli Turkm. 102 E5
Yeleğen Turkey 59 J10
Yelenovskiye Kar'yery Ukr. see Dokuchayevs'k
Yelenskiy Rus. Fed. 43 Q8
Yelets Rus. Fed. 43 T9
Yeletskiy Rus. Fed. 40 M2
Yeligovo Rus. Fed. 43 O3
Yélimané Mali 124 C3
Yelino Rus. Fed. 43 U7
Yelizavetgrad Ukr. see Kirovohrad
Yelizovo Rus. Fed. 39 P4
Yelkhovka Rus. Fed. 41 I5
Yell i. U.K. 46 K3
Yellabina Regional Reserve nature res. Australia 146 B2
Yellandu India 94 D2
Yellapur India 94 B3
Yellareddi India 94 C2

▶Yellow r. China 85 H4
4th longest river in Asia and 7th in the world. Also known as Huang He or Ma Qu; formerly spelt Hwang Ho.
asia [landscapes] ▶▶ 62–63

Yellow r. U.S.A. 172 C7
Yellow Bluff hd Canada 167 O1
Yellowdine Australia 151 B6
Yellowhead Pass Canada 166 G4

▶Yellowknife Canada 167 H2
Capital of Northwest Territories.

Yellowknife r. Canada 167 H2
Yellow Mountain hill Australia 147 E3
Yellow Sea N. Pacific Ocean 83 B6
Yellow Springs U.S.A. 176 B6
Yellowstone r. U.S.A. 178 B2
Yellowstone Lake U.S.A. 180 E3
▶Yellowstone National Park U.S.A. 180 E3
northamerica [environments] ▶▶ 162–163
Yell Sound strait U.K. 46 K3
Yellville U.S.A. 179 D4
Yelm U.S.A. 180 B3
Yel'nya Rus. Fed. 43 O7
Yeloten Turkm. 103 E5
also spelt Yolöten; formerly spelt Iolotan'
Yelovo Rus. Fed. 40 J4
Yel'sk Belarus 41 D6
Yel'tsy Rus. Fed. 43 O5
Yelva r. Rus. Fed. 40 I3
Yelverton Bay Canada 165 K1
Yelwa Nigeria 125 H4
Yema Nanshan mts China 84 B4
Yema Shan mts China 84 B4
Yematan China 84 C4
Yembo Eth. 128 C2
▶Yemen country Asia 104 D5
asia [countries] ▶▶ 64–67
Yemetsk Rus. Fed. 40 G3
Yemişenbükü Turkey see Taşova
Yemmiganur India see Emmiganuru
Yemtsa Rus. Fed. 40 G3
Yemva Rus. Fed. 40 I3
formerly known as Zheleznodorozhnyy
Yena Rus. Fed. 44 O2
Yenagoa Nigeria 125 G5
Yenakiyeve Ukr. 41 F6
also spelt Yenakiyevo; formerly known as Rykovo
Yenakiyevo Ukr. see Yenakiyeve
Yenangyat Myanmar 78 A3
Yenangyaung Myanmar 78 A3
Yenanma Myanmar 78 A4
Yên Bai Vietnam 78 D3
Yendi Ghana 125 E4
Yêndum China see Zhag'yab
Yénéganou Congo 126 B5
Yenge r. Dem. Rep. Congo 126 D5
Yengejeh Iran 100 A2
Yengema Sierra Leone 124 C4

index

Y Z

Yengisar Xinjiang China **88** B4
Yengisar Xinjiang China **88** D3
Yengo Congo **126** B4
Yengo National Park Australia **147** F3
Yenice Turkey **59** I9
Yenice Turkey **108** G1
Yeniceoba Turkey **106** C3
Yeniçiftlik Turkey **58** I7
Yenidere r. Turkey **59** J11
Yenifoça Turkey **59** H10
Yenihan Turkey see **Yıldızeli**
Yenihisar Turkey **59** I11
Yenije-i-Vardar Greece see **Giannitsa**
Yeniköy Kütahya Turkey **59** J9
Yeniköy Kütahya Turkey **59** K10
Yenipazar Turkey **59** J11
Yenişakran Turkey **59** I10
Yeniséa Greece see **Genisea**
Yenişehir Greece see **Larisa**
Yenişehir Turkey **106** B2
Yenisey r. Rus. Fed. **84** B1

▶**Yenisey-Angara-Selenga** r. Rus. Fed. **39** I2
3rd longest river in Asia and 6th in the world.
asia [landscapes] ▶▶ 62–63

Yeniseysk Rus. Fed. **39** J4
Yeniseyskiy Kryazh ridge Rus. Fed. **39** J4
Yeniseyskiy Zaliv inlet Rus. Fed. **39** H2
Yeniugou China **86** A1
Yeniyol Turkey see **Borçka**
Yenotayevka Rus. Fed. **102** A3
Yeola India **94** B1
Yeo Lake salt flat Australia **151** D5
Yeo Lake Nature Reserve Australia **151** D6
Yeotmal India see **Yavatmal**
Yeovil U.K. **47** J13
Yeo Yeo r. Australia see **Bland**
Yepachi Mex. **184** C2
Yepifan' Rus. Fed. **43** T8
Yeppoon Australia **149** F4
Yerakaroú Greece see **Gerakarou**
Yerakhtur Rus. Fed. **41** G5
Yeráki, Ákra pt Greece see **Geraki, Akra**
Yerákion Greece see **Geraki**
Yeraliyev Kazakh. see **Kuryk**
Yerbent Turkm. **102** D5
Yerbogachen Rus. Fed. **39** K3
Yercaud India **94** C4
Yerementau, Gory hills Kazakh. **103** H2

▶**Yerevan** Armenia **107** F2
Capital of Armenia. Also spelt Erevan.

Yereymentau Kazakh. **103** H2
also spelt Ereymentaū; formerly spelt Yermentau
Yergara India **94** C2
Yergeni hills Rus. Fed. **41** H7
Yergoğu Romania see **Giurgiu**
Yeriho West Bank see **Jericho**
Yerilla Australia **151** C6
Yerington U.S.A. **182** E3
Yerköy Turkey **106** C3
Yerla r. India **94** B2
Yermak Kazakh. see **Aksu**
Yermakovo Rus. Fed. **43** T3
Yermentau Kazakh. see **Yereymentau**
Yermo Mex. **184** D3
Yermo U.S.A. **183** H7
Yerofey Pavlovich Rus. Fed. **81** K2
Yeroham Israel **108** F7
Yersa r. Rus. Fed. **40** J2
Yershi Rus. Fed. **43** P7
Yershichi Rus. Fed. **43** N8
Yershov Rus. Fed. **102** B2
Yershovo Rus. Fed. **43** J4
Yertsevo Rus. Fed. **40** G3
Yerupaja mt. Peru **200** A2
Yerushalayim Israel/West Bank see **Jerusalem**
Yeruslan r. Rus. Fed. **102** A2
Yerzhar Uzbek. see **Gagarin**
Yesenovichi Rus. Fed. **43** P4
Yesil' Kazakh. **103** F2
also spelt Esil
Yeşil Turkey **108** H1
Yeşildere Turkey **59** K11
Yeşildere Turkey **109** I1
Yeşilhisar Turkey **106** C3
Yeşilırmak r. Turkey **107** D2
Yeşilkent Turkey **109** I1
Yeşilova Turkey **106** B3
also known as Satırlar
Yeşilova Turkey see **Sorgun**
Yesiplevo Rus. Fed. **43** U5
Yessentuki Rus. Fed. **41** G7
Yessey Rus. Fed. **39** K3
Yeste Spain **55** I6
Yes Tor hill U.K. **47** H13
Yêtatang China see **Baqên**
Yeu Myanmar **78** A3
Yeu, Île d' i. France **50** D6
Yevdokimovskoye Rus. Fed. see **Krasnogvardeyskoye**
Yevlakh Azer. see **Yevlax**
Yevlax Azer. **107** F2
also spelt Yevlakh
Yevpatoriya Ukr. **41** E7
Yevreyskaya Avtonomnaya Oblast' admin. div. Rus. Fed. **82** D2
English form Jewish Autonomous Oblast
Yexian China **87** E1
also known as Kunyang
Yexian China see **Laizhou**
Yeygen'yevka Kazakh. **103** I4
Yeyik China **89** C4
Yeysk Rus. Fed. **41** F7
Yeyungou China **88** D3
Yezerishche, Ozero l. Belarus/Rus. Fed. **43** L6
Yezhou China see **Jianshi**
Yezhuga r. Rus. Fed. **40** H2
Yezo i. Japan see **Hokkaidō**
Yezyaryshcha Belarus **43** K6
Y Fenni U.K. see **Abergavenny**
Y Fflint U.K. see **Flint**
Yi r. Henan China **87** E1
Yi r. Shandong China **87** F1
Yí r. Uruguay **204** F4
Yialí i. Greece see **Gyali**
Yi'allaq, Gebel mt. Egypt **108** E7
Yialousa Cyprus see **Aigialousa**
Yi'an China **82** B3
Yianisádha i. Greece see **Gianysada**
Yiannitsá Greece see **Giannitsa**
Yibā, Wādī watercourse Saudi Arabia **104** C4
Yibin Sichuan China **86** C2
also known as Baixi
Yibin Sichuan China **86** C2
Yibug Caka salt l. China **89** D5
Yichang China **87** D2
Yicheng Hubei China **87** E2
Yicheng Shanxi China **85** F5
Yichuan Henan China **87** E1
Yichuan Shaanxi China **85** F5
also known as Danzhou
Yichun Heilong. China **82** C3
Yichun Jiangxi China **87** E3
Yidu China see **Qingzhou**
Yidun China **86** A2
also known as Dagxoi
Yifeng China **87** E2
also known as Xinchang
Yiggêtang China see **Qumarlêb**
Yihuang China **87** F3
also known as Fenggang
Yijiang China see **Yiyang**
Yijun China **85** F5
Yilaha China **85** J1
Yilan China **82** C3
Yilan Taiwan see **Ilan**
Yıldız Dağları mts Turkey **106** A2
Yıldızeli Turkey **107** D3
also known as Yenihan
Yilehuli Shan mts China **85** I1
Yiliang Yunnan China **86** B3
also known as Kuangyuan
Yiliang Yunnan China **86** C3
also known as Jiaokui
Yiliping China **84** B4
Yilliminning Australia **151** B7
Yilong Heilong. China **82** B3
Yilong Sichuan China **86** C2
also known as Jincheng
Yilong China see **Shiping**
Yilong Hu l. China **86** B4
Yimatu r. China **85** H3
Yimianpo China **82** C3
Yimin r. China **85** H1
Yinan China **85** H5
also known as Jiehu
Yincheng China see **Dexing**
Yinchuan China **85** E4
Yindarlgooda, Lake salt flat Australia **151** C6
Yingawunarri Aboriginal Land res. Australia **148** A3
Yingcheng China **87** E2
Yingde China **87** E3
Ying He r. China **87** F1
Yingjiang China **86** B2
also known as Yandao
Yingkou China **85** I3
historically known as Newchwang
Yingkou China see **Dashiqiao**
Yingpanshui China **84** E4
Yingshan Hubei China **87** E2
also known as Wenquan
Yingshan Sichuan China **86** C2
also known as Chengshou
Yingshang China **87** F1
Yingtan China **87** F2
Yingtaoyuan China see **Fanxian**
Yingxian China **85** G4
Yining China see **Xiushui**
Yining China **88** C3
also known as Gulja; formerly known as Kuldja
Yiningarra Aboriginal Land res. Australia **148** A4
Yinjiang China **87** D3
Yinkeng China **87** E3
Yinma r. China **82** B3
Yinmabin Myanmar **78** A3
Yinnyein Myanmar **78** B4
Yin Shan mts China **85** F3
Yinxian China see **Ningbo**
Yi'ong Zangbo r. China **89** F6
Yioúra i. Greece see **Gioura**
Yipinglang China **86** B3
Yiquan China see **Meitan**
Yíra Chapéu, Monte mt. Brazil **207** I9
Yirga Alem Eth. **128** C3
Yirol Sudan **128** A3
Yirrkala Australia **148** C2
Yirshi China see **Yirxie**
Yirxie China **85** H2
formerly known as Yirshi
Yisa China see **Honghe**
Yishan China see **Yizhou**
Yishan China see **Guanyun**
Yi Shan mt. China **85** H4
Yi Shan mts China **85** H4
Yishui China **85** H5
Yishun Sing. **76** [inset]
Yi Tchouma well Niger **125** I1
Yithion Greece see **Gytheio**
Yitiaoshan China see **Jingtai**
Yitong China **82** B4
Yitong r. China **82** B3
Yi Tu, Nam r. Myanmar **78** B3
Yituline China **85** I1
Yiwanquan China **84** B3
Yiwu China **84** B3
also known as Aratürük
Yiwulü Shan mts China **85** I3
Yixian Anhui China **87** F2
also known as Biyang
Yixian Hebei China **85** G4
also known as Yizhou
Yixian Liaoning China **85** I3
also known as Yizhou
Yixing China **87** F2
Yixun r. China **85** H3
Yiyang Hunan China **87** E2
Yiyang Jiangxi China **87** F2
Yiyuan China **85** H4
also known as Nanma
Yizhang China **87** E3
Yizheng China **87** F1
Yizhou China **87** D3
formerly known as Qingyuan or Yishan
Yizhou China see **Yixian**
Yizhou China see **Yixian**
Yizra'el country Asia see **Israel**
Ylä-Keitele l. Fin. **44** N3
Ylämaa Fin. **45** O3
Yläne Fin. **45** M3
Ylihärmä Fin. **44** M3
Yli-Ii Fin. **44** N2
Yli-Kärppä Fin. **44** N2
Ylikiiminki Fin. **44** N2
Yli-Kitka l. Fin. **44** O2
Ylistaro Fin. **44** M3
Ylitornio Fin. **44** M2
Ylivieska Fin. **44** N2
Ylläs hill Fin. **44** N2
Ylöjärvi Fin. **45** M3
Ymer Nunatak Greenland **165** Q2
Ymer Ø i. Greenland **165** Q2
Ynykchanskiy Rus. Fed. **39** N3
Ynys Môn i. U.K. see **Anglesey**
Yoakum U.S.A. **179** C6
Yobe state Nigeria **125** H4
Yobetsu-dake vol. Japan **90** G3
Yoboki Djibouti **128** D2
Yogan, Cerro mt. Chile **205** C9
Yogoum well Chad **120** C5
Yogyakarta Indon. **77** E4
formerly spelt Jogjakarta
Yogyakarta admin. dist. Indon. **77** E5
Yoho National Park Canada **167** G5
Yoichi Japan **90** G3
Yoichi-dake mt. Japan **90** G3
Yojoa, Lago de l. Hond. **186** B4
Yŏju S. Korea **83** B5
Yōka Japan **91** D7
Yokadouma Cameroon **125** I6
Yōkaichi Japan **91** E7
Yōkaichiba Japan **91** G7
Yokkaichi Japan **91** E7
Yoko Cameroon **125** I5
Yokohama Aomori Japan **90** G4
Yokohama Kanagawa Japan **91** F7
Yokosuka Japan **91** F7
Yokote Japan **90** G5
Yokotsu-dake mt. Japan **90** G4
Yola Nigeria **125** I4
Yolo U.S.A. **182** C3
Yolombo Dem. Rep. Congo **126** D5
Yolöten Turkm. see **Yeloten**
Yoluk Mex. **185** I4
Yom, Mae Nam r. Thai. **78** C5
Yomou Guinea **124** C5
Yonago Japan **91** C7
Yŏnan N. Korea **83** B5
Yoneshiro-gawa r. Japan **90** G4
Yonezawa Japan **90** G6
Yŏng-am S. Korea **83** B6
Yong'an China see **Fengjie**
Yong'an China **87** F3
Yongbei China see **Yongsheng**
Yongchang China **84** D4
Yongcheng China **87** F1
Yŏngch'ŏn S. Korea **83** C6
Yongchuan China **86** C2
Yongchun China **87** F3
also known as Taocheng
Yongdeng China **84** D4
Yongding China **87** F3
also known as Fengcheng
Yongding China see **Yongren**
Yongding China see **Fumin**
Yongding r. China **85** H4
Yongfeng China **87** E3
also known as Wenfeng; formerly known as Jishui
Yongfeng China see **Guangfeng**
Yongfengqu China **88** D3
Yongfu China **87** D3
Yŏnggwang S. Korea **83** B6
Yŏnghŭng N. Korea **83** B5
Yŏnghŭng-man b. N. Korea **83** B5
Yongji China **82** B4
also known as Kouqian
Yongjia China **87** G2
also known as Shangtang
Yongjing China **84** D5
also known as Liujiaxia
Yongjing China see **Xifeng**
Yongjing China see **Xifeng**
Yŏngju S. Korea **83** C5
Yongkang China **87** G2
Yongle China see **Zhen'an**
Yongle China see **Nanping**
Yongling China **82** B4
Yongnian China **85** G4
also known as Linmingguan
Yongning Guangxi China **87** D4
also known as Pumiao
Yongning China see **Tonggu**
Yongning Ningxia China **85** E4
also known as Yanghe
Yongning China see **Xuyong**
Yongqing China see **Qingshui**
Yongren China **86** B3
also known as Yongding
Yŏngsan-gang r. S. Korea **83** B6
Yongshan China **86** B2
also known as Jingxin
Yongsheng China **86** B3
also known as Yongbei
Yongshou China **87** D1
also known as Jianjun
Yongshun China **87** D2
also known as Lingxi
Yongtai China **87** F3
also known as Zhangcheng
Yŏngwol S. Korea **83** C5
Yongxi China see **Nayong**
Yongxing Hunan China **87** E3
Yongxing Jiangxi China **87** E3
also known as Hechuan
Yongxiu China **87** E2
also known as Tujiabu
Yongzhou China **87** D3
Yonkers U.S.A. **177** L5
Yonne r. France **51** I4
Yoo Baba well Niger **125** I2
Yopal Col. **198** C3
Yopurga China **88** B4
Yordon Uzbek. see **Iordan**
Yordu Jammu and Kashmir **96** B2
York Australia **151** B6
York Canada **173** N7
York r. Canada **167** M4
York U.K. **47** K10
historically known as Eburacum
York AL U.S.A. **175** B5
York NE U.S.A. **178** C3
York PA U.S.A. **177** I6
York, Cape Australia **149** D1
York, Kap c. Greenland see **Innaanganeq**
York Downs Australia **149** D2
Yorke Peninsula Australia **146** C3
Yorkshire Dales National Park U.K. **47** J9
Yorkshire Wolds hills U.K. **47** L10
York Springs U.S.A. **177** H5
Yorkton Canada **167** K5
Yorktown U.S.A. **177** I8
Yoro Hond. **186** B4
Yoronga i. Indon. **75** D3
Yŏrŏö Gol r. Mongolia **85** E1
Yosemite U.S.A. **176** A8
Yosemite National Park U.S.A. **182** E4
Yosemite Village U.S.A. **182** E4
Yoshino-gawa r. Japan **91** C7
Yoshino-Kumano National Park Japan **91** E8
Yoshkar-Ola Rus. Fed. **40** H4
Yos Sudarso i. Indon. see **Dolak, Pulau**
Yŏsu S. Korea **83** B6
Yotau Bol. **201** E4
Yōtei-zan mt. Japan **90** G3
Yotvata Israel **108** G8
Youbou Canada **166** E5
Youdunzi China **88** E4
Youghal Rep. of Ireland **47** E12
also spelt Eochaill
You Jiang r. China **87** D4
Youlin China **85** H4
Young Australia **147** F3
Young r. Australia **151** C7
Young Uruguay **204** F4
Young U.S.A. **183** N7
Younghusband, Lake salt flat Australia **146** C2
Younghusband Peninsula Australia **146** C3
Young Island Antarctica **223** K2
Young Nicks Head N.Z. **152** L6
Young Range mts N.Z. **153** D12
Youngstown Canada **167** I5
Youngstown U.S.A. **176** E4
Youngsville NC U.S.A. **176** G9
Youngsville PA U.S.A. **176** F4
Yountville U.S.A. **182** B3
Youshashan China **88** E4
You Shui r. China **87** D2
Youssoufia Morocco **122** C2
formerly known as Louis-Gentil
Youvarou Mali **124** D3
Youxi China **87** F3
Youxian China **87** E3
Youyang China **87** D2
also known as Zhongduo
Youyi China **82** C3
Youyi Feng mt. China/Rus. Fed. **88** D1
Youyu China **85** G4
also known as Liangjiayoufang
Yovon Tajik. **101** G2
also spelt Yavan
Yowah watercourse Australia **147** E2
Yowereena Hill hill Australia **151** B5
Yozgat Turkey **106** C3
Ypé-Jhú Para. **201** G5
Yppäri Fin. **44** N2
Ypres Belgium see **Ieper**
Ypsilanti U.S.A. **173** J8
Yreka U.S.A. **180** B4
Yrghyz Kazakh. see **Irgiz**
Yr Wyddfa mt. U.K. see **Snowdon**
Yser r. France **51** I2
also known as IJzer (Belgium)
Yssingeaux France **51** K7
Ystad Sweden **45** K5
Ysyk-Köl Kyrg. see **Balykchy**
Ysyk-Köl admin. div. Kyrg. **103** I4
English form Issyk-Kul Oblast; also known as Issyk-Kul'skaya Oblast'

▶**Ysyk-Köl** salt l. Kyrg. **103** I4
5th largest lake in Asia. Also known as Issyk-Kul', Ozero.
asia [landscapes] ▶▶ 62–63

Y Trallwng U.K. see **Welshpool**
Ytre Vinje Norway see **Åmot**
Ytyk-Kyuyel' Rus. Fed. **39** N3
Yu r. China **85** G4
Yu i. Indon. **75** D3
Yuan'an China **87** D2
also known as Mingfeng
Yuanbao Shan mt. China **87** D3
Yuanjiang Hunan China **87** E2
Yuanjiang Yunnan China **86** B4
also known as Lijiang
Yuan Jiang r. Hunan China **87** D2
Yuan Jiang r. Yunnan China **86** B4
Yuanjiazhuang China see **Foping**
Yüanli Taiwan **87** G3
Yuanlin China **85** I1
Yuanling China **87** D2
Yuanma China see **Yuanmou**
Yuanmou China **86** B3
also known as Yuanma
Yuanping China **85** G4
Yuanqu China **85** F5
also known as Xincheng; formerly known as Liuzhangzhen
Yuanquan China see **Anxi**
Yuanshan China see **Lianping**
Yuanshanzi China **84** C4
Yuanyang China **86** B4
also known as Xinjie
Yuba City U.S.A. **182** C2
Yūbari Japan **90** G3
Yūbari-dake mt. Japan **90** H3
Yūbari-sanchi mts Japan **90** H3
Yubei China **86** C2
formerly known as Jiangbei
Yūbetsu Japan **90** H2
Yūbetsu-gawa r. Japan **90** H2
Yubileynyy Kazakh. **103** J2
Yubu Sudan **126** E3
Yucaipa U.S.A. **183** G7
Yucatán pen. Mex. **185** H5
Yucatán state Mex. **185** H4
Yucatan Channel Cuba/Mex. **171** I7
Yucca U.S.A. **183** J7
Yucca Lake U.S.A. **183** H5
Yucca Valley U.S.A. **183** H7
Yucheng China see **Yunan**
Yucheng Henan China **87** E1
Yucheng Shandong China **85** H4
Yudino Moskovskaya Oblast' Rus. Fed. **43** S5
Yudino Yaroslavskaya Oblast' Rus. Fed. **43** U3
Yudoma r. Rus. Fed. **39** N4
Yudu China **87** E3
also known as Gongjiang
Yuecheng China see **Yuexi**
Yuechi China **86** C2
also known as Jiulong
Yuelai China see **Huachuan**
Yueliang Pao l. China **85** I2
Yuendumu Australia **148** A4
Yuendumu Aboriginal Land res. Australia **148** A4
Yuen Long Hong Kong China **87** [inset]
Yueqing China **87** G2
Yuexi Anhui China **87** F2
also known as Tiantang
Yuexi Sichuan China **86** B2
also known as Yuecheng
Yueyang Hunan China **87** E2
also known as Rongjiawan
Yueyang Hunan China **87** E2
Yueyang China see **Anyue**
Yug Rus. Fed. **40** K4
Yug r. Rus. Fed. **40** H3
Yugan China **87** F2
Yugo Dağı mts Turkey **108** E1
Yugo-Kamskiy Rus. Fed. **40** J4
Yugorsk Rus. Fed. **38** G3
formerly known as Komsomol'skiy
Yugorskiy Poluostrov pen. Rus. Fed. **40** L1
Yugorskiy Shar Rus. Fed. **40** L1
▶**Yugoslavia** country Europe **58** B5
spelt Jugoslavija in Serbian
europe [countries] ▶▶ 32–35

▶**Yugoslavia**
Up to 1993 included Bosnia-Herzegovina, Croatia, Macedonia and Slovenia.

Yuhang China **87** G2
Yuhu China see **Eryuan**
Yuhuan China **87** G2
also known as Huanshan
Yuhuang Ding mt. China **85** H4
Yuin Australia **151** B5
Yujiang China **87** F2
also known as Dengjiabu
Yu Jiang r. China **87** D4
Yujin China see **Qianwei**
Yukagirskoye Ploskogor'ye plat. Rus. Fed. **39** P3
Yukamenskoye Rus. Fed. **40** J4
Yukarı Sakarya Ovaları plain Turkey **106** B3
Yukarısarıkaya Turkey **106** C3
Yukhavichy Belarus **43** J5
Yukhmachi Rus. Fed. **40** I5
Yukhnov Rus. Fed. **43** Q7
Yukhovo Rus. Fed. **43** L5
Yuki Dem. Rep. Congo **126** C5
Yuki Japan **91** C7

▶**Yukon** r. Canada/U.S.A. **164** C3
5th longest river in North America.
northamerica [landscapes] ▶▶ 156–157

Yukon-Charley Rivers National Preserve nature res. U.S.A. **164** E3
Yukon Crossing Canada **166** B2
Yukon Territory admin. div. Canada **166** C2
Yüksekova Turkey **107** F3
also known as Dize
Yukuhashi Japan **91** B8
Yulara Australia **148** A5
Yuldybayevo Rus. Fed. **102** D1
Yule r. Australia **150** B4
Yuleba Australia **149** F5
Yuli China **88** D3
also known as Lopnur
Yüli Taiwan **87** G4
Yulin Guangxi China **87** D4
Yulin Shaanxi China **85** F4
Yulongxue Shan mt. China **86** B3
Yuma AZ U.S.A. **183** J9
Yuma CO U.S.A. **178** B3
Yuma Desert U.S.A. **183** J9
Yumaguzino Rus. Fed. **102** D1
Yumbarra Conservation Park nature res. Australia **146** B2
Yumbi Bandundu Dem. Rep. Congo **126** C5
Yumbi Maniema Dem. Rep. Congo **126** E5
Yumbo Col. **198** B4
Yumen China **84** C4
also known as Laojunmiao
Yumendongzhan China **84** C4
Yumenguan China **84** B3
Yumenzhen China **84** C3
Yumin China **88** C2
also known as Karabura
Yumt Uul mt. Mongolia **84** C2
Yumurtalık Turkey **108** G1
Yuna Australia **151** A6
Yuna r. Dom. Rep. **187** F3
Yunak Turkey **106** B3
Yunan China **87** D4
also known as Yucheng
Yunchara Bol. **200** D5
Yuncheng Shandong China **85** G5
Yuncheng Shanxi China **87** D1
Yundamindera Australia **151** C6
Yunfu China **87** E4
Yungas reg. Bol. **200** D4
Yungay Chile **200** C6
Yungayo Peru **200** C4
Yun Gui Gaoyuan plat. China **86** B3
Yunhe China see **Pizhou**
Yunhe China see **Heqing**
Yunhe China **87** F2
Yunjinghong China see **Jinghong**
Yunkai Dashan mts China **87** D4
Yunkanjini Aboriginal Land res. Australia **148** A4
Yunling China see **Yunxiao**
Yun Ling mts China **86** A3
Yunmeng China **87** E2
Yunmenling China **87** E3
Yunnan prov. China **86** B3
Yun Shui r. China **87** E2
Yunta Australia **146** C3
Yunt Dağı mt. Turkey **108** D1
Yuntut National Park Canada **164** F3
Yunuslar Turkey **59** K9
Yunwu Shan mts China **87** D4
Yunxi China **87** D1
Yunxi China see **Yanting**
Yunxian Hubei China **87** D1
Yunxian Yunnan China **86** B3
also known as Aihua
Yunxiao China **87** F4
also known as Yunling
Yun'yakha r. Rus. Fed. **40** L2
Yunyang Chongqing China **87** D2
Yunyang Henan China **87** E1
Yupin China see **Pingbian**
Yuping China see **Libo**
Yuping China **87** D3
also known as Pingxi
Yuqing China **87** C3
also known as Baini
Yura Bol. **200** D5
Yura r. Bol. **200** D5
Yura Peru **200** C4
Yuracyacu Peru **198** B6
Yura-gawa r. Japan **91** D7
Yūrappu-dake mt. Japan **90** G3
Yuratsishki Belarus **42** G7
Yuraygir National Park Australia **147** G2
Yurba Co l. China **89** D5
Yurga Rus. Fed. **80** C1
Yurimaguas Peru **198** B6
Yurino Rus. Fed. **40** H4
Yurla Rus. Fed. **40** J4
Yurungkax He r. China **89** C4
Yur'ya Rus. Fed. **40** I4
Yur'yakha r. Rus. Fed. **40** J2
Yuryev Estonia see **Tartu**
Yur'yevets Ivanovskaya Oblast' Rus. Fed. **40** G4
Yur'yevets Vladimirskaya Oblast' Rus. Fed. **43** V5
Yur'yev-Pol'skiy Rus. Fed. **43** U5
Yuscarán Hond. **186** B4
Yushan Fujian China **87** F3
Yushan Jiangxi China **87** F2
also known as Bingxi
Yü Shan mt. Taiwan **87** G4
Yushan Liedao is China **87** G2
Yushe China **85** G4
Yushino Rus. Fed. **40** J1
Yushkozero Rus. Fed. **40** E2
Yushu Jilin China **82** B3
Yushu Qinghai China **86** A1
also known as Gyêgu
Yushugou China **88** D3
Yushut r. Rus. Fed. **40** I4
Yushuwan China see **Huaihua**
Yusta Rus. Fed. **102** A3
formerly known as Trudovoy
Yusufeli Turkey **107** E2
Yusuhara Japan **91** C8
Yus'va Rus. Fed. **40** J4
Yuta West Bank see **Yaţţa**
Yutai China **87** F1
also known as Guting
Yutian Hebei China **85** H4
Yutian Xinjiang China **89** C4
also known as Keriya or Muhala
Yutpundji Djindiniwirritj res. Australia see **Roper Bar Aboriginal Land**
Yuty Para. **201** F6
Yuva Turkey **108** A1
Yuwang China **85** E4
Yuxi China see **Daozhen**
Yuxi Hubei China **87** D2
Yuxi Yunnan China **86** B3
Yuxiakou China **87** D2
Yuxian Hebei China **85** G4
also known as Yuzhou
Yuxian Shanxi China **85** G4
Yuxikou China **87** F2
Yuyangguan China **87** D2
Yuyao China **87** G2
Yuyue China see **Jiayu**
Yuza Japan **90** F5
Yuzawa Japan **90** G5
Yuzha Rus. Fed. **40** G4
Yuzhno-Alichurskiy, Khrebet mts Tajik. see **Alichuri Janubī, Qatorkŭhi**
Yuzhno-Kamyshovyy Khrebet ridge Rus. Fed. **82** F3
Yuzhno-Kazakhstanskaya Oblast' admin. div. Kazakh. see **Yuzhnyy Kazakhstan**
Yuzhno-Kuril'sk Rus. Fed. **82** G3
also known as Utashinai
Yuzhno-Muyskiy Khrebet mts Rus. Fed. **81** I1
Yuzhno-Sakhalinsk Rus. Fed. **82** F3
Yuzhno-Sukhokumsk Rus. Fed. **41** H7
Yuzhnoukrayinsk Ukr. **41** D7
also spelt Južnoukrajinsk
Yuzhnyy Rus. Fed. see **Adyk**
Yuzhnyy Rus. Fed. **41** G7
Yuzhnyy, Mys hd Rus. Fed. **39** P4
Yuzhnyy Altay, Khrebet mts Kazakh. **88** D1
Yuzhnyy Kazakhstan admin. div. Kazakh. **103** G4
English form South Kazakhstan Oblast; also known as Ongtüstik Qazaqstan Oblysy; formerly known as Chimkentskaya Oblast'; long form Yuzhno-Kazakhstanskaya Oblast'
Yuzhnyy Ural mts Rus. Fed. **102** D1
English form Southern Urals
Yuzhong China **84** E5
Yuzhou China see **Yuxian**
Yuzhou China **87** E1
Yuzkuduk Uzbek. **103** E4
also spelt Yuzquduq
Yuzovka Ukr. see **Donets'k**
Yuzquduq Uzbek. see **Yuzkuduk**
Yverdon Switz. **51** M6
Yvetot France **50** G3
Ywamun Myanmar **78** A3
Ywathit Myanmar **78** B4
Yylanly Turkm. **102** D4
formerly spelt Il'yaly
Yzerfonteinpunt pt S. Africa **132** C10
Yzeure France **51** J6

↓ Z

Za, Oued r. Morocco **123** E2
Zaaimansdal S. Africa **132** H10
Zaamin Uzbek. **103** G5
also spelt Zomin
Zaandam Neth. **48** B3
Zăbala r. Romania **58** H3
Žabalj Vojvodina, Srbija Yugo. **58** B3
Zāb al Kabīr, Nahr az r. Iraq **107** E3
English form Great Zab
Zabalova Latvia **42** I4
Zāb aş Şaghīr, Nahr az r. Iraq **107** E4
English form Little Zab
Zabaykal'sk Rus. Fed. **85** H1
formerly known as Otpor
Zab-e Kuchek r. Iran **100** A3
Zabia Dem. Rep. Congo **126** E4
Zabīd Yemen **104** C5
Zabīd, Wādī watercourse Yemen **104** C5
Ząbkowice Śląskie Poland **49** N5
Zabłudów Poland **49** U2
Żabno Poland **49** R5
Zabok Croatia **56** H2
Zābol prov. Afgh. **101** F3
Zābol Iran **101** E4
also known as Nasratabad
Zābolī Iran **101** E5
also known as Magas
Zabor'ye Rus. Fed. **43** Q2
Zabqung China see **Gyêwa**
Zăbrani Romania **58** C2
Zabré Burkina **125** E4
Zabrze Poland **49** P5
historically known as Hindenburg
Zaburun'ye Kazakh. **102** B3
Zacapa Guat. **185** H6
Zacapoaxtla Mex. **185** F5
Zacapu Mex. **185** E5
Zacatecas Mex. **185** E4
Zacatecas state Mex. **185** E4
Zacatecoluca El Salvador **185** H6
Zacatepec Morelos Mex. **185** F5
Zacatepec Oaxaca Mex. **185** F5
Zacatlán Mex. **185** F5
Zachagansk Kazakh. **102** B2
Zacharo Greece **59** C11
also spelt Zakháro
Zacoalco Mex. **184** E4
Zacualtipán Mex. **185** F4
Zacynthus i. Greece see **Zakynthos**
Zad, Col du pass Morocco **122** D2
Zadar Croatia **56** H4
formerly known as Zara; historically known as Iadera
Zadarski Kanal sea chan. Croatia **56** H4
Zadetkale Kyun i. Myanmar **79** B6
also known as St Luke's Island
Zadetkyi Kyun i. Myanmar **79** B6
also known as St Matthew's Island
Zadi Myanmar **79** B5
Zadoi China **97** G2
also known as Sahu
Zadonsk Rus. Fed. **43** T9
Zadran reg. Afgh. **101** G3
Za'farāna Egypt **121** G2
Za'farāna, Rās pt Egypt **108** D8
Zafarwal Pak. **101** H3
Zafer Adaları is Cyprus see **Kleides Islands**
Zafer Burnu c. Cyprus see **Apostolos Andreas, Cape**
Zafora i. Greece **59** H12
Zafra Spain **54** E6
Zag Morocco **122** C3
Żagań Poland **49** M4
Žagarė Lith. **42** E5
Zagazig Egypt **121** F2
also spelt Az Zaqāziq
Zaghdeh well Iran **100** D3
Zāgheh Iran **100** B3
Zāgheh-ye Bālā Iran **100** A3
Zaghouan Tunisia **123** H1
Zagon Romania **58** H3
Zagora Greece **59** E9
Zagora Morocco **122** D3
Zagorje ob Savi Slovenia **56** G2
Zagorsk Rus. Fed. see **Sergiyev Posad**
Zagórz Poland **49** T6
Zagrazhden Bulg. **58** F7

▶**Zagreb** Croatia **56** H3
Capital of Croatia. Historically known as Agram.

Zagros, Kūhhā-ye mts Iran see **Zagros Mountains**
Zagros Mountains Iran **100** A3
also known as Zagros, Kūhhā-ye
Žagubica Srbija Yugo. **58** C4
Zagunao China see **Lixian**
Za'gya Zangbo r. China **89** E6
Zahamena, Réserve de nature res. Madag. **131** [inset] K3
Zahawn, Wādī r. Yemen **105** E4
Zāhedān Balūchestān va Sīstān Iran **101** E4
also known as Duzdab
Zāhedān Fārs Iran **100** C4
Zahlé Lebanon **108** G4
Zähmet Turkm. see **Zakhmet**
Zahrān Saudi Arabia **104** C4
Zahrat al Baṭn des. Iraq **109** N6
Zahrez Chergui salt pan Alg. **55** O9
Zaiceva Latvia **42** I4
Žaiginys Lith. **42** E6
Zaigrayevo Rus. Fed. **85** F1
Zā'in, Jabal hill Saudi Arabia **104** D3
Zaindeh r. Iran **100** C3
Zainlha China see **Xiaojin**
Zair Uzbek. **102** D4
also spelt Zayyr or Zoir

Zaire country Africa see **Congo, Democratic Republic of**
Zaire prov. Angola **127** B6
Zaïre r. Congo/Dem. Rep. Congo see **Congo**
Zaječar Srbija Yugo. **58** D5
Zaka Zimbabwe **131** F4
Zakamensk Rus. Fed. **84** D1 formerly known as Gorodok
Zakataly Azer. see **Zaqatala**
Zakháro Greece see **Zacharo**
Zakharovka Kazakh. **103** G2
Zakharovo Rus. Fed. **43** U7
Zakhmet Turkm. **103** E5 also spelt Zähmet
Zākhō Iraq **107** E3
Zakhodnyaya Dzvina r. Europe see **Zapadnaya Dvina**
Zakhrebetnoye Rus. Fed. **40** F1
Zákinthos i. Greece see **Zakynthos**
Zakopane Poland **49** Q6
Zakouma Chad **126** C2
Zakouma, Parc National de nat. park Chad **126** C2
Zakros Greece **59** H13
Zakwaski, Mount Canada **166** F5
Zakynthos Greece **59** B11
Zakynthos i. Greece **59** B11 also spelt Zákinthos; historically known as Zacynthus
Zala Angola **127** B6
Zala r. Romania **49** O9
Zalābiyah tourist site Syria **109** K2
Zalaegerszeg Hungary **49** N9
Zalai-domsag hills Hungary **49** N9
Zalakomár Hungary **49** O9
Zalamea de la Serena Spain **54** F6
Zalanga Nigeria **125** H4
Zalantun China **85** I2 also known as Butha Qi
Zalaszentgrót Hungary **49** O9
Zalău Romania **58** E1
Zalavas Lith. **42** H7
Žalec Slovenia **56** H2
Zalegoshch' Rus. Fed. **43** R9
Zaleski U.S.A. **176** C6
Zales'ye Rus. Fed. **43** R3
Zalewo Poland **49** Q2
Zalew Szczeciński b. Poland **49** L2
Zalew Wiślany b. Poland **49** Q1
Zalim Saudi Arabia **104** C3
Zalingei Sudan **120** D6
Zalmā, Jabal az mt. Saudi Arabia **104** B2
Zaltan, Jabal hills Libya **120** C2
Zaluch'ye Rus. Fed. **43** M4
Zama Japan **91** F7
Zama Niger **125** F3
Zama City Canada **166** G3
Zamakh Saudi Arabia **105** D4
Zamani S. Africa **133** N4
Zamanti r. Turkey **106** C3
Zambales Mountains Phil. **74** B3
Zambeze r. Africa **131** G2 see **Zambezi**

▶**Zambezi** r. Africa **131** G2
4th longest river in Africa. Also spelt Zambeze.
africa [landscapes] ▶▶ 112–113

Zambezi Zambia **127** D8
Zambézia prov. Moz. **131** H3
Zambezi Escarpment Zambia/Zimbabwe **127** E9
Zambezi National Park Zimbabwe **131** E3
▶**Zambia** country Africa **127** E8 formerly known as Northern Rhodesia
africa [countries] ▶▶ 114–117
Zamboanga Phil. **74** B5
Zamboanga Peninsula Phil. **74** B5
Zamboanguita Phil. **74** B4
Zambrów Poland **49** T3
Zambue Moz. **131** F2
Zamfara state Nigeria **125** G3
Zamfara watercourse Nigeria **125** G3
Zamlat Amagraj hills W. Sahara **122** B4
Zamogil'ye Rus. Fed. **42** I3
Zamora Ecuador **198** B6
Zamora r. Ecuador **198** B5
Zamora Spain **54** F3
Zamora-Chinchipe prov. Ecuador **198** B5
Zamora de Hidalgo Mex. **185** E5
Zamość Poland **53** G1 formerly known as Zamost'ye
Zamost'ye Poland see **Zamość**
Zamtang China **86** B1 also known as Rangke; formerly known as Gamda
Zamuro, Punta pt Venez. **187** F5
Zamuro, Sierra del mts Venez. **199** F3
Zamzam, Wādī watercourse Libya **120** B2
Zanaga Congo **126** B5
Zanatepec Mex. **185** G5
Záncara r. Spain **55** H5
Zancle Sicilia Italy see **Messina**
Zanda China **89** B6 also known as Toling
Zandamela Moz. **131** G5
Zanderij Suriname **199** H3
Zandvliet Belgium **51** K1
Zanesville U.S.A. **176** C6
Zangasso Mali **124** D3 formerly spelt Sangasso
Zangelan Azer. see **Zängilan**
Zängilan Azer. **107** F3 also spelt Zangelan; formerly known as Pirchevan
Zangla Jammu and Kashmir **96** C2
Zangsêr Kangri mt. China **89** D5
Zanhuang China **85** G4
Zanjān Iran **100** B2
Zanjān prov. Iran **100** B2
Zanjān Rūd r. Iran **107** F3
Zannah, Jabal az hill U.A.E. **105** F2
Zanskar reg. Jammu and Kashmir see **Zaskar**
Zanthus Australia **151** C6
Zantiébougou Mali **124** D4
Zanzibar Tanz. **129** C6
Zanzibar Channel Tanz. **129** C6
Zanzibar Island Tanz. **129** C6
Zanzibar North admin. reg. Tanz. **129** C6 also known as Unguja North
Zanzibar South admin. reg. Tanz. **129** C6 also known as Unguja South
Zanzibar West admin. reg. Tanz. **129** C6 also known as Unguja West
Zaokskiy Rus. Fed. **43** S7
Zaonia Mornag Tunisia **57** C12
Zaoro-Songou Cent. Afr. Rep. **126** C3
Zaoshi Hubei China **87** E2
Zaoshi Hunan China **87** E3
Zaouatallaz Alg. **123** H4 formerly known as Fort Gardel
Zaouet el Kahla Alg. see **Bordj Omer Driss**
Zaouiet Kounta Alg. **123** E4
Zaoyang China **87** E1
Zaoyangzhan China **87** E1
Zaō-zan vol. Japan **90** G5
Zaozernyy Kazakh. **103** G1 formerly known as Aysarinskoye or Aysary
Zaozernyy Rus. Fed. **80** E1
Zaozer'ye Rus. Fed. **43** T4
Zaozhuang China **87** F1
Zap r. Turkey **107** E3
Zapadna Morava r. Yugo. **58** C5
Zapadnaya Dvina r. Europe **43** L6 English form Western Dvina; also spelt Zakhodnyaya Dzvina
Zapadnaya Dvina Rus. Fed. **43** N5
Zapadno-Kazakhstanskaya Oblast' admin. div. Kazakh. see **Zapadnyy Kazakhstan**
Zapadno-Sakhalinskiy Khrebet mts Rus. Fed. **82** F2
Zapadno-Sibirskaya Nizmennost' plain Rus. Fed. see **West Siberian Plain**
Zapadno-Sibirskaya Ravnina plain Rus. Fed. see **West Siberian Plain**
Zapadnyy Alamedin, Pik mt. Kyrg. **103** H4
Zapadnyy Berezovyy, Ostrov i. Rus. Fed. **43** J1
Zapadnyy Chink Ustyurta esc. Kazakh. **102** C4
Zapadnyy Kazakhstan admin. div. Kazakh. **102** B2 English form West Kazakhstan Oblast; also known as Batys Qazaqstan Oblysy; formerly known as Ural'skaya Oblast'; long form Zapadno-Kazakhstanskaya Oblast'
Zapadnyy Sayan reg. Rus. Fed. **80** D2 English form Western Sayan Mountains
Zapala Arg. **204** C5
Zapardiel r. Spain **54** F3
Zapata U.S.A. **179** C7
Zapata, Península de pen. Cuba **186** C2
Zapatoca Col. **198** C3
Zapatón r. Spain **54** E6
Zapatosa, Ciénaga de l. Col. **198** C2
Zapiga Chile **200** C4
Zaplyus'ye Rus. Fed. **43** K3
Zăpodeni Romania **58** I2
Zapolyarnyy Murmanskaya Oblast' Rus. Fed. **44** O1
Zapolyarnyy Respublika Komi Rus. Fed. **40** L2
Zapol'ye Pskovskaya Oblast' Rus. Fed. **43** K3
Zapol'ye Vologod. Obl. Rus. Fed. **43** R2
Zaporizhzhya Ukr. **41** E7 also spelt Zaporozh'ye; formerly known as Aleksandrovsk or Oleksandrivs'k
Zaporozhskoye Rus. Fed. **43** L1
Zaporozh'ye Ukr. see **Zaporizhzhya**
Zapponeta Italy **56** H7
Zaprešić Croatia **56** H3
Zaprudnya Rus. Fed. **43** S5
Zaprudy Belarus **42** F9
Zapug China **89** C5
Zaqatala Azer. **107** F2 also spelt Zakataly
Zaqên China **97** G2
Zaqqui Libya **120** C2
Za Qu r. China **86** A2
Zaqungngomar mt. China **89** E5
Zara China see **Moinda**
Zara Croatia see **Zadar**
Zara Turkey **107** D3
Zarafshan Uzbek. **103** F4 also spelt Zarafshon
Zarafshon Tajik. **101** G2 also spelt Zeravshan
Zarafshon r. Tajik. **101** G2 also spelt Zeravshan
Zarafshon Uzbek. see **Zarafshan**
Zarafshon r. Uzbek. see **Zeravshan**
Zarafshon, Qatorkŭhi mts Tajik. **101** F2 also known as Zeravshanskiy Khrebet
Zaragoza Col. **198** C3
Zaragoza Mex. **185** E2
Zaragoza Spain **55** K3 English form Saragossa; historically known as Caesaraugusta
Zarand Kermān Iran **100** D4
Zarand Markazī Iran **100** B3
Zarandului, Munţii hills Romania **58** D2
Zarang China **89** B6
Zaranj Afgh. **101** E4
Zarasai Lith. **42** H6
Zárate Arg. **204** F4
Zarautz Spain **55** I1
Zaraysk Rus. Fed. **43** T7
Zaraza Venez. **199** E2
Zarbdar Uzbek. **103** G4
Zardab Azer. **107** F2
Zardak Iran **100** D3
Zard Kuh mts Iran **100** B3
Zarechensk Rus. Fed. **40** D2
Zarechka Belarus **42** G9
Zarechnyy Rus. Fed. **85** E1
Zarechnyy Rus. Fed. **43** U8 formerly known as Pobedinskiy
Zāreh Iran **100** B3
Zarembo Island U.S.A. **166** C3
Žarėnai Lith. **42** D6
Zarghat Saudi Arabia **104** C2
Zarghūn Shahr Afgh. **101** G3
Zargun mt. Pak. **101** F4
Zari Afgh. **101** F3
Zaria Nigeria **125** G4
Zariaspa Afgh. see **Balkh**
Zarichne Ukr. **41** C6
Zarineh Rūd r. Iran **100** A2
Zaring China **89** E6
Zarmardan Afgh. **101** E3
Zărneşti Romania **58** G3
Żarnowieckie, Jezioro l. Poland **49** P1
Zarqā' Jordan see **Az Zarqā'**
Zarqā', Nahr az r. Jordan **108** G5
Zarqān Iran **100** C4
Zarubino Rus. Fed. **43** O3
Zarubino Rus. Fed. **82** C4
Żary Poland **49** M4
Zarzaïtine Alg. **123** H3
Zarzal Col. **198** B3
Zarzis Tunisia **123** H2
Zasa Latvia **42** G5
Zashchita Kazakh. **88** C1
Zasheyek Rus. Fed. **44** O2
Zaskar r. India **96** C2
Zaskar reg. Jammu and Kashmir **96** C2 also spelt Zanskar
Zaskarki Belarus **43** J6
▶**Zaskar Mountains** India **96** C2
world [land images] ▶▶ 12–13
Zaslawkaye Vodaskhovishcha resr Belarus **42** I8
Zaslawye Belarus **42** I7
Zastron S. Africa **133** L7
Za'tarī, Wādī az watercourse Jordan **109** H5
Žatec Czech Rep. **49** K5
Zaterechnyy Rus. Fed. **107** F1
Zatobol'sk Kazakh. **103** E1
Zatoka Ukr. **58** L2 formerly known as Bugaz
Zatyshshya Ukr. **58** K1
Zaunguzskiye Karakumy des. Turkm. **102** D4 also known as Üngüz Angyrsyndaky Garagum
Zautla Mex. **185** F5
Zavadovskiy Island Antarctica **223** F2
Zavareh Iran **100** C3
Zavety Il'icha Rus. Fed. **82** F2
Zavidovići Bos.-Herz. **56** K4
Zavidovskiy Zapovednik nature res. Rus. Fed. **43** R5
Zavitaya Rus. Fed. see **Zavitinsk**
Zavitinsk Rus. Fed. **82** C2 formerly known as Zavitaya
Zavodskoy Rus. Fed. see **Komsomol'skiy**
Zavolzhsk Rus. Fed. **40** G4 formerly known as Zavolzh'ye
Zavolzh'ye Rus. Fed. see **Zavolzhsk**
Závora, Ponta pt Moz. **131** G5
Zavutstsye Belarus **42** J6
Zavyachellye Belarus **43** J6
Zav'yalova, Ostrov i. Rus. Fed. **39** P4
Zav'yalovo Rus. Fed. **103** J1
Zawa Qinghai China **84** D4
Zawa Xinjiang China **96** C1
Zawadzkie Poland **49** P5
Zawgyi r. Myanmar **78** B3
Zawiercie Poland **49** Q5
Zawīlah Libya **120** B3
Zāwiyah, Jabal az hills Syria **109** H2
Zāwiyat Masūs Libya **120** D2
Zawlīyah, Jiddat az plain Oman **105** F3
Zawr, Ra's az pt Saudi Arabia **105** E2
Zâwyet Shammâs pt Egypt **106** A5
Zâwyet Sîdi Ghâzi Egypt **108** B6
Zay r. Rus. Fed. **40** I5
Zaydī, Wādī az watercourse Syria **109** H5
Zaysan Kazakh. **88** D2
Zaysan, Lake Kazakh. **88** C1 also known as Zaysan, Ozero
Zaysan, Ozero l. Kazakh. see **Zaysan, Lake**
Zaytsevo Rus. Fed. **43** J4
Zayü Xizang China **86** A2
Zayü Xizang China **86** A2 also known as Gyigang
Zayü Qu r. China/India **86** A2 also known as Lohil or Luhit
Zayyr Uzbek. see **Zair**
Zazafotsy Madag. **131** [inset] J4
Zazir, Oued watercourse Alg. **123** G6
Zbąszynek Poland **49** M3
Zborište mt. Yugo. **58** A5
Žďar nad Sázavou Czech Rep. **49** M6
Žďárské Vrchy hills Czech Rep. **49** M6
Zdolbuniv Ukr. **41** C6 also spelt Zdolbunov
Zdolbunov Ukr. see **Zdolbuniv**
Zduńska Wola Poland **49** P4
Zealand i. Denmark **45** J5 also spelt Sjælland
Zēbāk Afgh. **101** G2
Zeballos mt. Arg. **205** C7
Zeballos Canada **166** E5
Zēbār Iraq **107** F3
Zebargad, Gezîret i. Egypt **104** B3 English form Zebirget Island
Zebirget Island Egypt see **Zebargad, Gezîret**
Žebrák Czech Rep. **49** K6
Zebulon GA U.S.A. **175** C5
Zebulon KY U.S.A. **176** C8
Zebulon NC U.S.A. **174** E5
Zeebrugge Belgium **51** J1
Zeehan Australia **147** E5
Zeeland U.S.A. **172** G8
Zeerust S. Africa **133** K2
Ẓefat Israel **108** G5 also known as Safad; also spelt Tsefat
Zegrzyńskie, Jezioro l. Poland **49** S3
Zehdenick Germany **49** K3
Zeil, Mount Australia **148** B4 formerly spelt Ziel, Mount
Žeimelis Lith. **42** F5
Zeitz Germany **48** J4
Zêkog China **86** B1 also known as Sonag
Zela Turkey see **Zile**
Żelechów Poland **49** S4
Zelena Gora mt. Bos.-Herz. **56** J5
Zelenaya Roshcha Kazakh. **103** H1
Zelengora mts Bos.-Herz. **56** K5
Zelennik Rus. Fed. **40** H3
Zelenoborskiy Rus. Fed. **44** P2
Zelenodol'sk Rus. Fed. **40** I5
Zelenogorsk Rus. Fed. **43** K1
Zelenograd Rus. Fed. **43** S5
Zelenogradsk Rus. Fed. **42** B7 historically known as Cranz
Zelenokumsk Rus. Fed. **41** G7 formerly known as Sovetskoye or Vorontsovo-Aleksandrovskoye
Zelentsovo Rus. Fed. **40** H4
Zelenyy, Ostrov i. Rus. Fed. **82** G4 also known as Shibotsu-jima
Zelenyy Gay Kazakh. **103** G2
Železné Hory hills Czech Rep. **49** M6
Zelienople U.S.A. **176** E5
Želiezovce Slovakia **49** P7
Zelina Croatia **56** I3 formerly known as Sveti Ivan Zelina
Zelinggou China **84** C4
Želivka, Vodní nádrž resr Czech Rep. **49** L6
Željin mt. Yugo. **58** B5
Zell am See Austria **49** J8
Zellerrain pass Austria **49** M8
Zelów Poland **49** Q4
Zeltiņi Latvia **42** H4
Zel'va Belarus **42** F8
Žemaičių Naumiestis Lith. **42** C6
Žemaitijos nacionalinis parkas nat. park Lith. **42** C5
Zêmdasam China **86** B1
Zemen Bulg. **58** D6
Zemes Romania **58** H2
Zemetchino Rus. Fed. **41** G5
Zémio Cent. Afr. Rep. **126** E3
Zemmora Alg. **55** L9
Zemongo, Réserve de Faune de nature res. Cent. Afr. Rep. **126** E3
Zempleni park Hungary **49** S7
Zemplínska šírava l. Slovakia **49** T7
Zempoaltépetl, Nudo de mt. Mex. **185** G5
Zemtsy Rus. Fed. **43** N5
Zemun Srbija Yugo. **58** B4
Zênda China **86** A1
Zengcheng China **87** E4
Zengfeng Shan mt. China **82** C4
Zenica Bos.-Herz. **56** J4
Zenifim watercourse Israel **108** F7
Zenta Vojvodina, Srbija Yugo. see **Senta**
Zentsūji Japan **91** C7
Zenyeh Afgh. **101** G3
Zenzach Alg. **55** O9
Žepče Bos.-Herz. **56** K4
Zephyr Cove U.S.A. **182** E2
Zepu China **88** B4 formerly known as Poskam
Zeraf, Bahr el r. Sudan **128** A2
Zeravshan Tajik. see **Zarafshon**
Zeravshan r. Tajik. see **Zarafshon**
Zeravshan r. Uzbek. **103** E5 also spelt Zarafshon
Zeravshanskiy Khrebet mts Tajik. see **Zarafshon, Qatorkŭhi**
Zerenda Kazakh. **103** G1
Zeribet el Oued Alg. **123** G2
Żerków Poland **49** O3
Zermatt Switz. **51** N6
Zernograd Rus. Fed. **41** G7 formerly known as Zernovoy
Zernovoy Rus. Fed. see **Zernograd**
Zestafoni Georgia see **Zestap'oni**
Zestap'oni Georgia **107** E2 also spelt Zestafoni
Zeta r. Yugo. **58** A6
Zêtang China **89** E6
Zetea Romania **58** G2
Zeulenroda Germany **48** I5
Zeven Germany **48** G2
Zevenaar Neth. **48** D4
Zevgolatio Greece **59** D11
Zeya Rus. Fed. **82** B1
Zeya r. Rus. Fed. **82** B2
Zeydābād Iran **100** C4
Zeydar Iran **100** D2
Zeynalābād Iran **100** D4
Zeyskiy Zapovednik nature res. Rus. Fed. **82** B1
Zeysko-Bureinskaya Vpadina depr. Rus. Fed. **82** C2
Zeyskoye Vodokhranilishche resr Rus. Fed. **82** B1
Zeytin Burnu c. Cyprus see **Elaia, Cape**
Zeytindağ Turkey **59** I10
Zêzere r. Port. **54** C5
Zgharta Lebanon **108** G3
Zgierz Poland **49** Q4 historically known as Sgiersch
Zhabdün China **89** E6
Zhabinka Belarus **42** F9
Zhadove Ukr. **43** N9
Zhaggo China see **Luhuo**
Zhaglag China **86** A1
Zhag'yab China **86** A2 also known as Yêndum
Zhailma Kazakh. **103** E2 also spelt Zhayylma
Zhaksy Kazakh. **103** F2 also spelt Zhaqsy; formerly spelt Dzhaksy
Zhaksy-Kon watercourse Kazakh. **103** G2
Zhaksykylysh, Ozero salt l. Kazakh. **103** E3
Zhaksy Sarysu watercourse Kazakh. see **Sarysu**
Zhalaghash Kazakh. see **Dzhalagash**
Zhalanash Kazakh. **103** I4
Zhalanash Kazakh. see **Damdy**
Zhalgyztöbe Kazakh. see **Zhangiztobe**
Zhalpaktal Kazakh. **102** B2 also spelt Zhalpaqtal; formerly known as Furmanovo
Zhalpaqtal Kazakh. see **Zhalpaktal**
Zhaltyr Kazakh. **103** G2 formerly spelt Dzhaltyr
Zhaltyr, Ozero l. Kazakh. **102** B3
Zhaludok Belarus **42** F8
Zhamanakkol', Ozero salt l. Kazakh. **103** E2
Zhamansor Kazakh. **102** C3
Zhambyl Kazakh. **103** G3
Zhambyl Kazakh. see **Taraz**
Zhambyl Oblast admin. div. Kazakh. see **Zhambylskaya Oblast'**
Zhambylskaya Oblast' admin. div. Kazakh. **103** H3 English form Zhambyl Oblast; formerly known as Dzhambulskaya Oblast'
Zhameuka Kazakh. **103** J3
Zhamo China see **Bomi**
Zhan r. China **82** C2
Zhanakorgan Kazakh. **103** F4 also spelt Zhangaqorghan; formerly known as Yany-Kurgan
Zhanakurylys Kazakh. **103** E3
Zhanang China **89** E6 also known as Chatang
Zhanaortalyk Kazakh. **103** H3
Zhanaozen Kazakh. **102** C4 also spelt Zhangaözen; formerly known as Novyy Uzen'
Zhanatala Kazakh. **103** I4
Zhanatas Kazakh. **103** G4 also spelt Zhangatas
Zhanbay Kazakh. **102** B3
Zhanbei China **82** B2 formerly known as Zhanhe
Zhang r. China **85** G4
Zhangaözen Kazakh. see **Zhanaozen**
Zhangaqazaly Kazakh. see **Ayteke Bi**
Zhanga Qazan Kazakh. see **Novaya Kazanka**
Zhangaqorghan Kazakh. see **Zhanakorgan**
Zhangatas Kazakh. see **Zhanatas**
Zhangbei China **85** G3
Zhangcheng China see **Yongtai**
Zhangcunpu China **87** F1
Zhangde China see **Anyang**
Zhangdian China see **Zibo**
Zhanggu China see **Danba**
Zhangguangcai Ling mts China **82** C3
Zhanghua Taiwan see **Changhua**
Zhangiztobe Kazakh. **103** J2 also known as Zhalgyztöbe
Zhangjiajie China see **Dayong**
Zhangjiakou China **85** G3 also known as Kalgan
Zhangjiapan China see **Jingbian**
Zhangla China **86** B1
Zhanglou China **87** F1
Zhangping China **87** F3
Zhangpu China **87** F3 also known as Sui'an
Zhangqiu China **85** H4
Zhangshu China **87** E2 formerly known as Qingjiang
Zhangwei Xinhe r. China **85** H4
Zhangwu China **85** I3
Zhangxian China **86** C1
Zhangye China **84** D4
Zhangzhou China **87** F3 formerly spelt Changchow
Zhangzi China **85** G4
Zhanhe China see **Zhanbei**
Zhanhua China **85** H4 also known as Fuguo
Zhänibek Kazakh. see **Dzhanybek**
Zhanjiang China **87** D4 formerly spelt Changkiang
Zhansügirov Kazakh. see **Dzhansugurov**
Zhanterek Kazakh. **102** C3
Zhanyi China **86** B3
Zhao'an China **87** F4 also known as Nanzhao
Zhaodong China **82** B3
Zhaoge China see **Qixian**
Zhaojue China **86** B2 also known as Xincheng
Zhaoliqiao China **87** E2
Zhaoping China **87** D3
Zhaoqing China **87** E4
Zhaoren China see **Changwu**
Zhaosu China **88** C3 also known as Mongolküre
Zhaosutai r. China **85** I3
Zhaotong China **86** B3
Zhaoxian China **85** G4 also known as Zhaozhou
Zhaoyuan Heilong. China **82** B3
Zhaoyuan Shandong China **85** I4
Zhaozhen China see **Jintang**
Zhaozhou China see **Zhaoxian**
Zhaozhou China **82** B3
Zhapo China **87** D4
Zhaqsy Kazakh. see **Zhaksy**
Zharbulak Kazakh. see **Kabanbay**
Zharbulak Kazakh. **88** C2
Zhardzyazhzha Belarus **42** I7
Zhari Namco salt l. China **89** D6
Zharkamys Kazakh. **102** D3
Zharkent Kazakh. **103** J3 formerly known as Panfilov; formerly spelt Dzharkent
Zharkovskiy Rus. Fed. **43** N6
Zharma Kazakh. **103** J2
Zharmysh Kazakh. **102** C3
Zharsuat Kazakh. **103** J3
Zharyk Kazakh. see **Saken Seyfullin**
Zhashkiv Ukr. **41** D6 also spelt Zhashkov
Zhashkov Ukr. see **Zhashkiv**
Zhashui China **87** D1 also known as Qianyou
Zhaslyk Uzbek. **102** D4 also spelt Jasliq
Zhastkovo Rus. Fed. **43** N8
Zhaxi China see **Weixin**
Zhaxi Co salt l. China **89** D5
Zhaxigang China **89** B5
Zhaxizê China **86** A2
Zhayrem Kazakh. **103** G2
Zhayü China **86** A2
Zhayylma Kazakh. see **Zhailma**
Zhayyq r. Kazakh./Rus. Fed. see **Ural**
Zhdanov Ukr. see **Mariupol'**
Zhdanovo Kazakh. **103** G4
Zhdanovo Rus. Fed. **43** O4
Zhdanovsk Azer. see **Beyläqan**
Zhecheng China **87** E1
Zhedao China see **Lianghe**
Zhêhor China **86** B2
Zhejiang prov. China **87** G2 English form Chekiang
Zhelang China **87** E4
Zhelaniya, Mys c. Rus. Fed. **39** G2
Zhelcha r. Rus. Fed. **42** I3
Zhelezinka Kazakh. **103** H1
Zheleznodorozhnyy Rus. Fed. **42** C7 historically known as Gerdauen
Zheleznodorozhnyy Rus. Fed. see **Yemva**
Zheleznodorozhnyy Uzbek. see **Kungrad**
Zheleznogorsk Rus. Fed. **43** Q9
Zheleznya Rus. Fed. **43** S7
Zhelou China see **Ceheng**
Zheltorangy Kazakh. **103** H3
Zheltyye Vody Ukr. see **Zhovti Vody**
Zhelyu Voyvoda Bulg. **58** H6
Zhem Kazakh. see **Emba**
Zhemgang Bhutan **97** F4 also spelt Shamgong
Zhen'an China **87** D1 also known as Yongle
Zhenba China **87** C1
Zheng'an China **87** C2 also known as Fengyi
Zhengding China **85** G4
Zhenghe China **87** F3 also known as Xiongshan
Zhengjiakou China see **Gucheng**
Zhengjiatun China see **Shuangliao**
Zhengkou China see **Gucheng**
Zhenglan Qi China see **Dund Hot**
Zhengning China **85** F5 also known as Shanhe
Zhengxiangbai Qi China see **Qagan Nur**
Zhengyang China **87** E1 also known as Zhenyang
Zhengzhou China **87** E1 formerly spelt Chengchow
Zhenhai China **87** G2
Zhenjiang China see **Dantu**
Zhenjiangguan China **86** B1
Zhenlai China **85** I2
Zhenning China **86** C3
Zhenping China **87** D2
Zhenwudong China see **Ansai**
Zhenxi China **85** I2
Zhenxiong China **86** C3 also known as Wufeng
Zhenyang China see **Zhengyang**
Zhenyuan Gansu China **85** E5
Zhenyuan Guizhou China **87** D3 also known as Wuyang
Zhenyuan Yunnan China **86** B4 also known as Enle
Zhenziling China **87** D2
Zherdevka Rus. Fed. **41** G6 formerly known as Chibizovka
Zherdevo Rus. Fed. **43** R8
Zherong China **87** F3 also known as Shuangcheng
Zheshart Rus. Fed. **40** I3
Zhestylevo Rus. Fed. **43** S5
Zhetibay Kazakh. see **Zhetybay**
Zhetikara Kazakh. see **Zhitikara**
Zhetisay Kazakh. see **Zhetysay**
Zhetybay Kazakh. **102** C4 also spelt Zhetibay
Zhety-Kol', Ozero l. Rus. Fed. **103** E2
Zhetysay Kazakh. **103** G4 also spelt Zhetisay; formerly spelt Dzhetysay
Zhêxam China **89** D6
Zhexi Shuiku resr China **87** D2
Zhezdy Kazakh. **103** F2 formerly known as Marganets; formerly spelt Dzhezdy
Zhezkazgan Kazakh. **103** F3 also spelt Zhezqazghan; formerly spelt Dzhezkazgan
Zhezqazghan Kazakh. see **Zhezkazgan**
Zhicheng China see **Changxing**
Zhichitsy Rus. Fed. **43** M6
Zhidan China **85** F4 also known as Bao'an
Zhidoi China **97** G2 also known as Gyaijêpozhanggê
Zhigansk Rus. Fed. **39** M3
Zhigung China **89** E6
Zhijiang China **87** D3
Zhijin China **86** C3
Zhilevo Rus. Fed. **43** T7
Zhilino Rus. Fed. **43** R8
Zhilyanka Kazakh. see **Kargalinskoye**
Zhi Qu r. China see **Yangtze**
Zhirnovsk Rus. Fed. **41** H6 formerly known as Zhirnovskiy or Zhirnoye
Zhirnovskiy Rus. Fed. see **Zhirnovsk**
Zhirnoye Rus. Fed. see **Zhirnovsk**
Zhiryatino Rus. Fed. **43** O8
Zhitarovo Bulg. see **Vetren**
Zhitikara Kazakh. **103** E1 also spelt Zhetikara; formerly known as Dzhetygara
Zhitkovichi Belarus see **Zhytkavichy**
Zhitkovo Rus. Fed. **43** K1
Zhitkur Rus. Fed. **102** A2
Zhitomir Ukr. see **Zhytomyr**
Zhizdra Rus. Fed. **43** P8
Zhizdra r. Rus. Fed. **43** R7
Zhizhitsa Rus. Fed. **43** M5
Zhizhitskoye, Ozero l. Rus. Fed. **43** M5
Zhlobin Belarus **43** L9
Zhmerinka Ukr. see **Zhmerynka**
Zhmerynka Ukr. **41** D6 also spelt Zhmerinka
Zhob Pak. **101** G4 formerly known as Fort Sandeman
Zhob r. Pak. **101** G3
Zhodzina Belarus **43** J7
Zhokhova, Ostrov i. Rus. Fed. **39** P2
Zholnuskay Kazakh. **88** C1
Zholymbet Kazakh. **103** G2
Zhong'an China see **Fuyuan**
Zhongba China **87** E4
Zhongba China see **Jiangyou**
Zhongcheng China see **Suijiang**
Zhongdian China **86** A3 also known as Zhongxin
Zhongduo China see **Youyang**
Zhongguo country Asia see **China**
Zhongguo Renmin Gongheguo country Asia see **China**
Zhonghe China see **Xiushan**
Zhongmou China **87** E1
Zhongning China **85** E4
Zhongping China see **Huize**
Zhongshan research station Antarctica **223** F2
Zhongshan Guangdong China **87** E4 formerly known as Shiqizhen
Zhongshan Guangxi China **87** D3
Zhongshan China see **Lupanshui**
Zhongsha Qundao sea feature S. China Sea see **Macclesfield Bank**
Zhongshu China see **Luxi**
Zhongshu China see **Luliang**
Zhongtai China see **Lingtai**
Zhongtiao Shan mts China **87** D1
Zhongwei China **84** E4
Zhongxian China **87** D2 also known as Zhongzhou
Zhongxin China **87** E3
Zhongxin China see **Zhongdian**
Zhongxin China see **Huaping**
Zhongxing China see **Siyang**
Zhongxingji China **87** F2
Zhongyang China **85** F4
Zhongyicun China **86** B3
Zhongze China **87** G2
Zhongzhai China **86** C1
Zhongzhou China see **Zhongxian**
Zhosaly Kazakh. see **Dzhusaly**
Zhosaly Kazakh. **103** I2
Zhoujiajing China **84** D4
Zhoujiaping China see **Nanzheng**
Zhoukou China **87** E1
Zhoukou China see **Peng'an**
Zhouning China **87** F3 also known as Shicheng
Zhoushan China **87** G2
Zhoushan Dao i. China **87** G2
Zhoushan Qundao is China **87** G2
Zhouzhi China **87** D1 also known as Erqu
Zhovten' Ukr. **58** L1
Zhovti Vody Ukr. **41** E6 formerly known as Zheltyye Vody
Zhualy Kazakh. **103** E2
Zhuanghe China **85** I4
Zhuanglang China **85** E5 also known as Shuiluocheng
Zhuantobe Kazakh. **103** G3
Zhubgyügoin China **86** A1
Zhucheng China **85** H5
Zhudong Taiwan see **Chutung**
Zhugqu China **86** C1
Zhuhai China **87** E4 formerly known as Chuhai
Zhuji China see **Shangqiu**
Zhuji China **87** G2
Zhujia Chuan r. China **85** F4
Zhujing China see **Jinshan**
Zhukeng China **87** E4
Zhukopa r. Rus. Fed. **43** N5
Zhukovka Rus. Fed. **43** O8
Zhukovo Rus. Fed. **43** R6 formerly known as Ugodskiy Zavod
Zhukovskiy Rus. Fed. **43** T6 formerly known as Stakhanovo
Zhulong r. China **85** G4
Zhumadian China **87** E1
Zhumysker Kazakh. **102** B3
Zhuolu China **85** G3
Zhuoyang China see **Suiping**
Zhuozang r. China **85** G4
Zhuozhou China **85** H4
Zhuozi China **85** G3 also known as Zhuozishan
Zhuozishan China see **Zhuozi**
Zhuravlevka Kazakh. **103** G2
Zhurki Belarus **42** I6
Zhuryn Kazakh. **102** D2 formerly spelt Dzhurun
Zhusandala, Step' plain Kazakh. **103** H3
Zhushan China **87** D1
Zhushan China see **Xuan'en**
Zhuxi China **87** D1
Zhuyang China see **Dazhu**
Zhuzhou Hunan China **87** E3 also known as Lukou
Zhuzhou Hunan China **87** E3
Zhydachiv Ukr. **41** C6
Zhympity Kazakh. **102** C2 formerly known as Dzhambeyty
Zhyngyldy Kazakh. **102** B3 formerly known as Kuybyshevo
Zhytkavichy Belarus **42** I9 also spelt Zhitkovichi
Zhytomyr Ukr. **41** D6 also spelt Zhitomir
Zi r. China **85** H4
Ziama mt. Guinea **124** C4
Ziarat Iran **100** D2
Žiar nad Hronom Slovakia **49** P7
Zibā salt pan Saudi Arabia **109** J7
Zībār Iraq **107** E3
Zibo China **85** H4 formerly known as Zhangdian
Zichang China **85** F4 also known as Wayaobu
Zicheng China see **Zijin**
Zichtauer Berge und Klötzer Forst park Germany **48** I3
Ziddí Tajik. **101** G2
Zidi Pak. **101** F5
Ziębice Poland **49** O5
Ziel, Mount Australia see **Zeil, Mount**
Zielona Góra Poland **49** M4 historically known as Grünberg
Ziemelkursas Augstiene hills Latvia **42** D4
Ziemeris Latvia **42** I4
Ziemupe Latvia **42** C5
Ziesar Germany **49** J3
Zifta Egypt **121** F2
Zigaing Myanmar **78** A3
Zigê Tangco l. China **89** E5
Ziggurat of Ur tourist site Iraq **107** F5
Zīghan Libya **120** D3
Zigon Myanmar **78** A4
Zigong China **86** C2
Ziguey Chad **120** B6
Zigui China **87** D2 also known as Jiandaoyu
Ziguinchor Senegal **124** A3
Žīguri Latvia **42** I4
Zihuatanejo Mex. **185** E5
Zijin China **87** E4 also known as Zicheng
Ziketan China see **Xinghai**
Zikeyevo Rus. Fed. **43** P8
Zikhron Ya'aqov Israel **108** F5
Zilair Rus. Fed. **102** D1
Zilaiskalns Latvia **42** G4
Zile Turkey **106** C2 historically known as Zela
Zilim r. Rus. Fed. **40** K5
Žilina Slovakia **49** P6
Zillah Libya **120** C2
Zillertaler Alpen mts Austria **48** I8
Zilupe Latvia **42** J5
Zima Rus. Fed. **80** G2
Zimapán Mex. **185** F4
Zimatlán Mex. **185** F5
Zimba Zambia **127** E9
▶**Zimbabwe** country Africa **131** F3 formerly known as Rhodesia or Southern Rhodesia
africa [countries] ▶▶ 114–117
Zimbabwe tourist site Zimbabwe see **Great Zimbabwe National Monument**
Zīmkān, Rūdkhāneh-ye r. Iran **100** A3
Zimmerbude Rus. Fed. see **Svetlyy**
Zimmi Sierra Leone **124** C5
Zimnicea Romania **58** G5
Zimniy Bereg coastal area Rus. Fed. **40** F2
Zimovniki Rus. Fed. **41** G7
Ẓin watercourse Israel **108** G6
Zinave, Parque Nacional de nat. park Moz. **131** G4
Zinder Niger **125** H3
Zinder dept Niger **125** H3
Zindo China **86** B2 formerly known as Jimda
Zing Nigeria **125** H4
Zinga Mulike Tanz. **129** C7
Ziniaré Burkina **125** E3
Zinihu China **85** E4
Zinjibār Yemen **105** D5
Zinkwazi Beach S. Africa **133** P6
Zinovo Rus. Fed. **43** V5
Zinoyevsk Ukr. see **Kirovohrad**
Zinzana Mali **124** D3
Zion U.S.A. **172** F8
Zion National Park U.S.A. **183** K4
Ziqudukou China **97** G2
Zīrab Iran **100** C2
Zirbitzkogel mt. Austria **49** L8
Zirc Hungary **49** O8
Žirje i. Croatia **56** H5
Zirkel, Mount U.S.A. **180** F4
Zirkūh i. U.A.E. **105** F2
Ziro India **97** G4
Zi Shui r. China **87** E2
Zistersdorf Austria **49** N7
Zitácuaro Mex. **185** E5
Zitava r. Slovakia **49** P8
Žitište Vojvodina, Srbija Yugo. **58** B3
Zitiua r. Brazil **202** C2
Zito China see **Lhorong**
Zitong China **86** C2 also known as Wenchang

Z index

Žitorsđa *Srbija* Yugo. **58** C5
Zittau Germany **49** L5
Živinice Bos.-Herz. **56** K4
Ziway Häyk' *l.* Eth. **128** C2
Zixi China **87** F3
also known as Hecheng
Zixing China **87** E3
Ziya *r.* China **85** H4
Ziyanchurino Rus. Fed. **102** D2
Ziyang China *see* **Wuyuan**
Ziyang *Shaanxi* China **87** D1
Ziyang *Sichuan* China **86** C2
Ziyaret Dağı *hill* Turkey **108** F1
Ziyuan China **87** D3
also known as Dahe
Ziyun China **86** C3
also known as Songshan
Ziz, Oued *watercourse* Morocco **122** D3
Zizhong China **86** C2
also known as Chonglong
Zizhou China **85** F4
also known as Shuanghuyu
Zlatar *mts* Yugo. **58** A5
Zlaté Moravce Slovakia **49** P7
Zlaten Rog Bulg. **58** D4
Zlatibor *mts* Yugo. **58** A5
Zlatica *r.* Yugo. **58** B3
Zlatna Romania **58** E2
Zlatni Pyasŭtsi *nat. park* Bulg. **58** J5
Zlatograd Bulg. **58** G7
Zlatoust Rus. Fed. **38** F4
Zlatoustovsk Rus. Fed. **82** D1
Zlatý Stôl *mt.* Slovakia **49** R7
Zlín Czech Rep. **49** O6
formerly known as Gottwaldow
Zlīţan Libya **120** B1
Złocieniec Poland **49** N2
Złoczew Poland **49** P4
Złotoryja Poland **49** M4
Złotów Poland **49** O2
Zlynka Rus. Fed. **43** M9
Zmeinogorsk Rus. Fed. **88** C1
Żmigród Poland **49** N4
Zmiyev Ukr. *see* **Zmiyiv**
Zmiyevka Rus. Fed. **43** R9
Zmiyiv Ukr. **41** F6
also spelt Zmiyev; *formerly known as* Gotval'd
Znamenka Kazakh. **103** I2
Znamenka *Altayskiy Kray* Rus. Fed. **103** I1
Znamenka *Orlovskaya Oblast'* Rus. Fed. **43** Q9
Znamenka *Smolenskaya Oblast'* Rus. Fed. **43** P7
Znamenka Ukr. *see* **Znam"yanka**
Znamenskoye *Lipetskaya Oblast'* Rus. Fed. **43** U8
Znamenskoye *Orlovskaya Oblast'* Rus. Fed. **43** Q8
Znam"yanka Ukr. **41** E6
also spelt Znamenka
Żnin Poland **49** O3
Znobivka *r.* Ukr. **43** O9
Znob Novhorods'ke Ukr. **43** O9
Znojmo Czech Rep. **49** N7
Zoar S. Africa **132** F10
Zóbuè Moz. **131** G2
Zogainrawar China *see* **Huashixia**
Zogang China **86** A2
also known as Wangda
Zogqên China **86** A1
Zografos Greece **59** E11
Zohreh *r.* Iran **100** B4
Zoigê China **86** B1
Zoir Uzbek. *see* **Zair**
Zoissa Tanz. **129** C6
Zoji La *pass* Jammu and Kashmir **96** B2
Zola S. Africa **133** K9
Zolochev Ukr. *see* **Zolochiv**
Zolochev Ukr. *see* **Zolochiv**
Zolochiv *Kharkivs'ka Oblast'* Ukr. **41** E6
also spelt Zolochev
Zolochiv *L'vivs'ka Oblast'* Ukr. **41** C6
also spelt Zolochev
Zolotaya Gora Rus. Fed. **82** B1
Zolotinka Rus. Fed. **81** K1
Zolotonosha Ukr. **41** E6
Zolotukhino Rus. Fed. **43** R9
Zomandao *r.* Madag. **131** [inset] J4

▶**Zomba** Malawi **129** B8
Former capital of Malawi.

Zombor *Vojvodina, Srbija* Yugo. *see* **Sombor**
Zomin Uzbek. *see* **Zaamin**
Zongga China *see* **Gyirong**
Zongo Dem. Rep. Congo **126** C3
Zonguldak Turkey **106** B2
Zongyang China **87** F2
Zonūż Iran **100** A2
Zoo Baba *well* Niger **125** I2
Zoppo, Portella dello *pass Sicilia* Italy **57** G11
Zorgho Burkina **125** E3
also spelt Zorgo
Zorgo Burkina *see* **Zorgho**
Zorita Spain **54** F5
Zorleni Romania **58** I2
Zorlenţu Mare Romania **58** C3
Zorn *r.* France **51** O4
Zornitsa Bulg. **58** H6
Zorritos Peru **198** A5
Żory Poland **49** P5
Zorzor Liberia **124** C5
Zossen Germany **49** K3
Zouan-Hounien Côte d'Ivoire **124** C5
Zouar Chad **120** C4
Zoucheng China **85** H5
formerly known as Zouxian
Zouérat Mauritania **122** B5
Zouina *well* Mauritania **124** D2
Zoulang Nanshan *mts* China **84** C4
Zouping China **85** H4
Zourvas, Akra *pt* Greece **59** E11
Zoushi China **87** D2
Zouxian China *see* **Zoucheng**
Zovka Rus. Fed. **43** J3
Zrenjanin *Vojvodina, Srbija* Yugo. **58** B3
also known as Nagybecskerek
Zrmanja *r.* Croatia **56** H4
Zu Afgh. **101** G2
Zuata *r.* Venez. **199** E3
Zubālah, Wādī *watercourse* Saudi Arabia **109** O8
Zubayr, Jazā'ir az *i.* Yemen **104** C5
Zubia Spain **55** H7
Zubkovo Rus. Fed. **43** R8
Zubova Polyana Rus. Fed. **41** G5
Zubovo Rus. Fed. **43** R1
Zubtsov Rus. Fed. **43** P5
Zuckerhütl *mt.* Austria **48** I9
Zuénoula Côte d'Ivoire **124** D5
Zuera Spain **55** K3
Ẓufār *admin. reg.* Oman **105** F4
also spelt Dhofar
Zug Switz. **51** O5
Zugdidi Georgia **107** E2
Zuger See *l.* Switz. **51** O5
Zughaytūn *r.* Iraq **109** P3
Zugm, Birket el *salt l.* Egypt **108** B7
Zugu Nigeria **125** G4
Zuider Zee *l.* Neth. *see* **IJsselmeer**
Zuid-Willemsvaart *canal* Neth. **51** L1
Zuitai China *see* **Kangxian**
Zuitaizi China *see* **Kangxian**
Zuitou China *see* **Taibai**
Zújar *r.* Spain **54** F5
Żukowo Poland **49** P1
Zulia *state* Venez. **198** D2
Zülpich Germany **48** D5
Zumarraga Spain **55** I1
Zumba Ecuador **198** B6
Zumbo Moz. **131** F2
Zumbro *r.* U.S.A. **174** A2
Zumbrota U.S.A. **174** A2
Zummār Iraq **109** N1
Zumpango Mex. **185** F5
Zumpango del Río Mex. **185** F5
Zungeru Nigeria **125** G4
Zunhua China **85** H3
Zuni U.S.A. **181** E6
Zuni *watercourse* U.S.A. **183** O7
Zuni Mountains U.S.A. **181** E6
Zun-Torey, Ozero *l.* Rus. Fed. **85** G1
Zunyi *Guizhou* China **86** C3
also known as Nanbai
Zunyi *Guizhou* China **86** C3
Zuo Jiang *r.* China/Vietnam **87** D4
Zuoquan China **85** G4
Zuoyun China **85** G4
Županja Croatia **56** K3
Zuqāq *i.* Saudi Arabia **104** C4
Žur *Kosovo, Srbija* Yugo. **58** B6
Zūrābād *Khorāsan* Iran **101** E3
Zürich Switz. **51** O5
Zürichsee *l.* Switz. **51** O5
Zurmat *reg.* Afgh. **101** G3
Zŭrnevo Bulg. **58** I5
Żuromin Poland **49** Q2
Zuru Nigeria **125** G4
Zurzuna Turkey *see* **Çıldır**
Zusha *r.* Rus. Fed. **43** R8
Zusmarshausen Germany **48** H7
Zutphen Neth. **48** D3
Zuurberg National Park S. Africa **133** J10
Žuvinto rezervatas *nature res.* Lith. **42** E7
Zuwārah Libya **120** B1
Zuyevka Rus. Fed. **40** I4
Zuytdorp Nature Reserve Australia **151** A5
Zvečan *Kosovo, Srbija* Yugo. **58** B6
Zvejniekciems Latvia **42** F4
Zvenigorod Rus. Fed. **43** R6
Zvenigorodka Ukr. *see* **Zvenyhorodka**
Zvenyhorodka Ukr. **41** D6
also spelt Zvenigorodka
Zverino Bulg. **58** E5
Zvezdë Albania **58** B8
Zvijezda *mts* Bos.-Herz. **56** K4
Zvishavane Zimbabwe **131** F4
formerly spelt Shabani
Zvolen Slovakia **49** Q7
Zvornik Bos.-Herz. **56** L4
Zwarkop S. Africa **132** F7
Zwedru Liberia **124** C5
Zweibrücken Germany **48** E6
Zweletemba S. Africa **132** D10
Zwelitsha S. Africa **133** L9
Zwettl Austria **49** M7
Zwickau Germany **49** J5
Zwierzyniec Poland **49** T5
Zwiesel Germany **49** K6
Zwingli S. Africa **133** K1
Zwoleń Poland **49** S4
Zwolle Neth. **48** D3
Zyal'ki Belarus **43** J6
Żychlin Poland **49** Q3
Zyembin Belarus **43** J7
Żyrardów Poland **49** R3
Zyryan Kazakh. *see* **Zyryanovsk**
Zyryanka Rus. Fed. **39** P3
Zyryanovo Rus. Fed. **39** I3
Zyryanovsk Kazakh. **88** D1
also known as Zyryan
Żywiec Poland **49** Q6

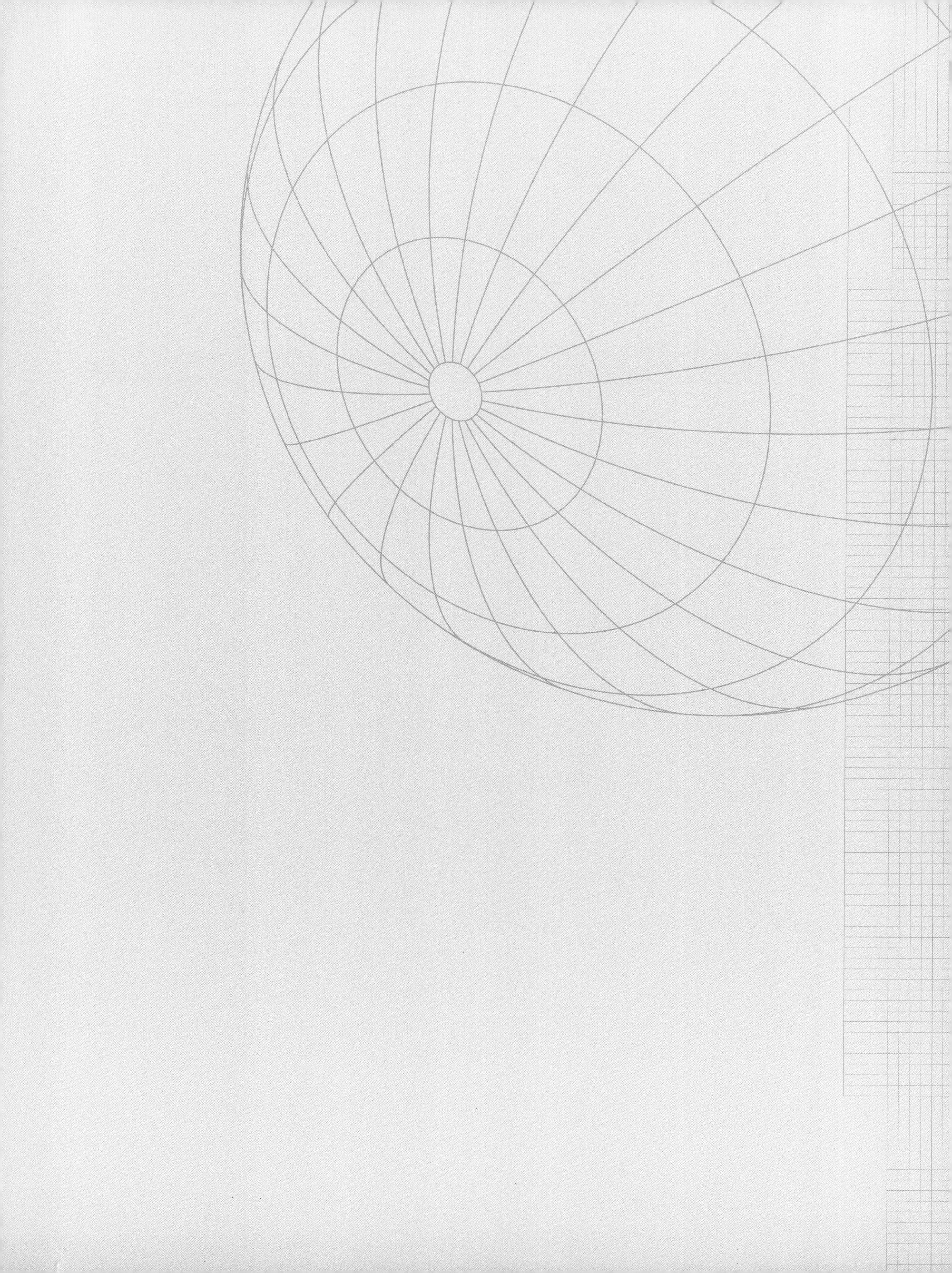

acknowledgements

MAPS AND DATA

General

Maps designed and created by HarperCollins Cartographic, Glasgow, UK

Design: One O'Clock Gun Design Consultants Ltd, Edinburgh, UK

Continental perspective views (pp30–31, 62–63, 112–113, 136–137, 156–157, 190–191) and globes (pp 14–15, 26–27, 214): Alan Collinson Design, Llandudno, UK

The publishers would like to thank all national survey departments, road, rail and national park authorities, statistical offices and national place name committees throughout the world for their valuable assistance, and in particular the following:

British Antarctic Survey, Cambridge, UK

Bureau of Rural Sciences, Barton, ACT, Australia, a scientific agency of the Department of Agriculture, Fisheries and Forestry, Australia

Tony Champion, Professor of Population Geography, University of Newcastle upon Tyne, UK

Mr P J M Geelan, London, UK

International Boundary Research Unit, University of Durham, UK

The Meteorological Office, Bracknell, Berkshire, UK

Permanent Committee on Geographical Names, London, UK

Data

Antarctica (pp222–223): Antarctic Digital Database (versions 1 and 2), © Scientific Committee on Antarctic Research (SCAR), Cambridge, UK (1993, 1998)

Bathymetric data: The GEBCO Digital Atlas published by the British Oceanographic Data Centre on behalf of IOC and IHO, 1994

Earthquakes data (pp14–15, 71): United States Geological Survey (USGS) National Earthquakes Information Center, Denver, USA

Coral reefs data (p141): UNEP World Conservation Monitoring Centre (UNEP-WCMC), Cambridge, UK. 'Reefs at Risk', 1998 Washington, DC, USA from World Resources Institute (WRI), the International Center for Living Aquatic Resources Management (ICLARM) and UNEP-WCMC

PHOTOGRAPHS AND IMAGES

page	image number	credit
3		NASA/Science Photo Library
6		NASA/Science Photo Library
7		NASA
8–9	1	NASA
	2	NASA/Science Photo Library
10–11	1	CNES, 1996 Distribution Spot Image/Science Photo Library
	2	US Geological Survey/Science Photo Library
	3	CNES, 1991 Distribution Spot Image/Science Photo Library
	4	CNES, 1986 Distribution Spot Image/Science Photo Library
12–13	1	NASA
	2	NASA/Science Photo Library
	3	NASA
	4	ImageState
	5	Bernhard Edmater/Science Photo Library
	6	Earth Science Corporation/Science Photo Library
	7	CNES, 1996 Distribution Spot Image/Science Photo Library
	8	Digital image © 1996 CORBIS; Original image courtesy of NASA/CORBIS
14–15	1	Axiom Photographic Agency Ltd
	2	David Parker/Science Photo Library
	3	Chris Johns/NGS Image Collection
16–17	Fig. 1	Courtesy of NASA/JPL/Caltech
	Fig. 2	Courtesy of NASA/JPL/Caltech
	Fig. 3	Courtesy of NASA/JPL/Caltech
	Fig. 4	NRSC Ltd/Science Photo Library
	Fig. 9	NASA/Goddard Space Flight Center
	Fig. 10	Reproduced by permission of The Met Office, Bracknell, Berkshire
	Fig. 11	Reproduced by permission of The Met Office, Bracknell, Berkshire
18–19	1	Francois Suchel/Still Pictures
	2	Earth Satellite Corporation/Science Photo Library
	3	NRSC/Still Pictures
	4	M & C Denis-Huot/Still Pictures
	5	Pictor International - London
	6	Dick Ross/Still Pictures
	7	ImageState
	8	Klaus Andrews/Still Pictures
20–21	1	NASA/Science Photo Library
	2	Earth Satellite Corporation/Science Photo Library
	3	Daniel Dancer/Still Pictures
	4 left	NASA - Goddard Space Flight Center Scientific Visualization Studio
	4 right	NASA - Goddard Space Flight Center Scientific Visualization Studio
	5 left	NPA Group www.satmaps.com
	5 right	NPA Group www.satmaps.com
22–23	1	David Reed/Panos pictures
	2	Cities Revealed ® aerial photography © The GeoInformation ® Group, 1998
24–25	1	Earth Satellite Corporation/Science Photo Library
	2	Spaceimaging.com
	3	NRSC/Still Pictures
	4	NASA
26–27	1	NRSC/Still Pictures
	Fig. 1	TeleGeography, Inc, Washington D.C., USA www.telegeography.com
	Fig. 2	TeleGeography, Inc, Washington D.C., USA www.telegeography.com
28		© Marc Garanger/CORBIS
29		NASA
30–31	1	Digital image © 1996 CORBIS; Original image courtesy of NASA/CORBIS
	2	NASA
	3	NASA
32–33	1	P. Tatlow/Panos Pictures
	2	CNES, 1993 Distribution Spot Image/Science Photo Library
	3	CNES, 1991 Distribution Spot Image/Science Photo Library
34–35	1	Wim Van Cappellen/Still Pictures
	2	NASA
	3	Andrew Tatlow/Panos Pictures

page	image number	credit
36–37	1	Geoslides Photography
	2	Pictor International - London
	3	CNES, 1992 Distribution Spot Image/Science Photo Library
	4	ESA, Eurimage/Science Photo Library
	5	Dick Ross/Still Pictures
	6	NRSC/Science Photo Library
	7	Cities Revealed ® aerial photography © The GeoInformation ® Group, 1999
60		Pictures Colour Library Ltd
61		NASA
62–63	1	ImageState
	2	CNES, 1992 Distribution Spot Image/Science Photo Library
	3	CNES, 1987 Distribution Spot Image/Science Photo Library
64–65	1	Digital image © 1996 CORBIS; Original image courtesy of NASA/CORBIS
	2	Marc Schlossman/Panos pictures
	3	Georg Gerster/NGS Image Collection
66–67	1	NASA
	2	© Hanan Isachar/CORBIS
	3	Pictor International - London
68–69	1 top	© Wolfgang Kaehler/CORBIS
	1 middle	© Keren Su/CORBIS
	1 bottom	DERA/Still Pictures
	2 top	NASA
	2 bottom	NASA
	3 top	Science Photo Library
	3 bottom	CNES, 1987 Distribution Spot Image/Science Photo Library
70–71	1	NOAA
	2	NASA
	3	Shehzad Noorani/Still Pictures
	4	Digital image © 1996 CORBIS; Original image courtesy of NASA/CORBIS
	5	NASA
110		Pictures Colour Library Ltd
111		NASA
112–113	1	CNES, 1988 Distribution Spot Image/Science Photo Library
	2	© CORBIS
	3	NASA/JPL/Caltech
114–115	1	Peter Hering
	2	Libe Taylor/Panos pictures
116–117	1	NASA
	2	NASA
	3	Christian Aid/Glynn Griffiths/Still Pictures
	4	Mark Edwards/Still Pictures
	5 left	CNES, 1998 Distribution Spot Image/Science Photo Library
	5 right	CNES, 2001 Distribution Spot Image/Science Photo Library
118–119	1	Paul Springett/Still Pictures
	2	CNES, 1994 Distribution Spot Image/Science Photo Library
	3	Alan Collinson Design
	4	Pierre Gleizes/Still Pictures
	5	Voltchev-Unep/Still Pictures
	6	Spaceimaging.com
134		Pictures Colour Library Ltd
135		NASA
136–137	1	Pictor International - London
	2	CNES, 1986 Distribution Spot Image/Science Photo Library
	3	Mike Schroder/Still Pictures
138–139	1	The aerial photograph on page 138 is Copyright © Commonwealth of Australia, AUSLIG, Australia's national mapping Agency. All rights reserved. Reproduced by permission of the General Manager, Autralian Surveying and Land Information Group, Department of Industry, Science and Resources, Canberra, ACT.
	2	eMAP Ltd
	3	eMAP Ltd
140–141	1 left	Pictor International - London
	1 right	NASA/Science Photo Library
	2	Bill van Aken © CSIRO Land and Water
	3 left	CNES, Distribution Spot Image/Science Photo Library
	3 right	Gerard & Margi Moss/Still Pictures
	Fig. 1	Bureau of Rural Sciences, Australia

page	image number	credit
142–143	1	NASA
	2	NASA
	3	ImageState
	4	Institute of Geological & Nuclear Sciences, New Zealand
	5	Spaceimaging.com
	6	NASA
	7	Image provided by ORBIMAGE © Orbital Imaging Corporation and processing by NASA Goddard Space Flight Center.
154		Pictures Colour Library Ltd
155		NASA
156–157	1	© Owen Franken/CORBIS
	2	© Lowell Georgia/CORBIS
	3	NASA
158–159	1	Gregor Turk
	2	NASA/Marshall Space Flight Center
	3	NASA
160–161	1	Infoterra Ltd
	2	© Roger Ressmeyer/CORBIS
	3	CNES, 1996 Distribution Spot Image/Science Photo Library
	4	NASA/Goddard Space Flight Center/Science Photo Library
	4 inset	NASA
162–163	1	NRSC/Still Pictures
	2	NASA
	3	Alex S. Maclean/Still Pictures
	4	NASA
	5	© David Muench/CORBIS
	6	Bernhard Edmaier/Science Photo Library
188		Pictures Colour Library Ltd
189		NASA
190–191	1	NASA
	2	© Yann Arthus-Bertrand/CORBIS
	3	NASA
192–193	1	Earth Satellite Corporation/Science Photo Library
	2	CNES, 1995 Distribution Spot Image/Science Photo Library
	3	NASA
194–195	1	Ron Giling/Still Pictures
	2	Jeremy Horner/Panos pictures
	3	NASA
	4	CNES, 1988 Distribution Spot Image/Science Photo Library
	5	Alan Collinson Design
	6	CNES, 1986 Distribution Spot Image/Science Photo Library
	7	Jacques Jangoux/Science Photo Library
	8	Digital image © 1996 CORBIS; Original image courtesy of NASA/CORBIS
	9	NASA
196–197	1	NASA/Science Photo Library
	2	Mark Edwards/Still Pictures
	3 top right	NASA/Goddard Space Flight Center/Science Photo Library
	3 left	Michael Nichols/NGS Image Collection
	3 bottom right	NASA/Goddard Space Flight Center/Science Photo Library
208		Pictures Colour Library Ltd
209		NASA
210–211	1	Alan Collinson Design
	2	WHF Smith, US National Oceanic and Atmospheric Administration (NOAA), USA
	Fig. 2	NASA/JPL
212–213	1	NASA
	2	Data provided by the EOS Distributed Active Archive Center (DAAC) procesed at the National Snow and Ice Data Center, University of Colorado, Boulder, CO.
	3	NASA
	4	Courtesy of the David Vaughan/BEDMAP Consortium
	5	RADARSAT data Canadian Space Agency/Agence Spatiale Canadienne 1997. Received by the Canada Centre for Remote Sensing. Processed and distributed by RADARSAT International.
214–215	1	B&C Alexander
	2	Data provided by the EOS Distributed Active Archive Center (DAAC) procesed at the National Snow and Ice Data Center, University of Colorado, Boulder, CO.
	3	Alan Collinson Design
	4 and 5	B&C Alexander
	6	NASA